2011 Standard Catalog of®
WORLD COINS
2001-Date

George Cuhaj
Editor - New Issues

Thomas Michael
Market Analyst

Harry Miller
U.S. Market Analyst

Merna Dudley
Coordinating Editor

Deborah McCue
Database Specialist

Kay Sanders
Editorial Assistant

Special Contributors
Melvyn Kassenoff
Michel Labourdette
Ole Sjoeland
Wakim Wakim

Bullion Value (VB) Market Valuations

Valuations for all platinum, gold, palladium and silver coins of the more common, basically bullion types, or those possessing only modest numismatic premiums are presented in this edition based on the market ranges of:

$1,450 - $1,650 per ounce for **platinum** $1100 - $1250 per ounce for **gold**

$375 - $475 per ounce for **palladium** $17.50 - $20.00 per ounce for **silver**

Published by

700 East State Street • Iola, WI 54990-0001
715-445-2214 • 888-457-2873
www.krausebooks.com

Our toll-free number to place an order is (800) 258-0929.

ISSN 1935-4339
ISBN-13: 978-1-4402-1160-7
ISBN-10: 1-4402-1160-4

Designed by: Stacy Bloch
Edited by: Debbie Bradley

Printed in the United States of America

ACKNOWLEDGMENTS

Many individuals have contributed countless changes, which have been incorporated into the current edition. While all may not be acknowledged, special appreciation is extended to the following who have exhibited a special enthusiasm for this edition.

David Addey
Esko Ahlroth
James T. Anderson
Raul Aries
Adrian Ataman
Antonio Alessandrini
Oksana Bandrivska
Yuri Barshay
Albert Beck
Anton Belcev
Jan Bendix
Richard Benson
Allen G. Berman
Sharon Blocker
Joseph Boling
K.N. Boon
Al Boulanger
Mahdi Bseiso
Chris Budesa
John T. Bucek
Doru Calin
Ignacio Calvo
Raul Chirila
Michael Hans Lun Chou
Luis V. Costa
Raymond E. Czahor
Howard A. Daniel III
Konstantinos Dellios
Krassy Dimitrov
Yossi Dotan
James R. Douglas

Dr. Jan M. Dyroff
Stephen Eccles
Andrzej Fischer
Thomas Fitzgerald
Eugene Freeman
Arthur Friedburg
Tom Galway
David R. Gotkin
Marcel Häberling
Edward Hackney
J. Halfpenny
Liliana N. Hanganu
Flemming Lyngbeck Hansen
David Harrison
Martin Rodney Hayter
Istvan Hegedus
Frans Hellendall
Serge Huard
Armen Hovsepian
Nelva G. Icaza
Ton Jacobs
A.K. Jain
Hector Carlos Janson
Alex Kaglyan
Melvyn Kassenoff
Craig Keplinger
Rob Looy
Aditya Kulkarni
Michel Labourdette
Samson Kin Chiu Lai
Alex Lazarovici

Rudi Lotter
Ma Tak Wo
Miguel Angel Pratt Mayans
Phil McLoughlin
Dimitar Mihov
Juozas Minikevicius
Andy Mirski
Robert Mish
Ing. Benjamin M. Mizrachi R.
Dr. Richard Montrey
Paul Montz
Edward Moschetti
Arkady Nakhimovsky
Michael G. Nielsen
Bill Nichols
Gus Pappas
Janusz Parchimowicz
Dick Parker
Frank Passic
Martin Peeters
Marc Pelletier
Kirsten F. Petersen
Andreas Pitsillides
Gastone Polacco
Elena Pop
Martin Purdy
Luis R. Ponte Puigbo
Yahya Qureshi
Mircea Raicopol
Dr. Dennis G. Rainey
Ivan Rakitin

Ilan Rinetzky
William M. Rosenblum
Egon Conti Rossini
Pabitra K. Saha
Remy Said
Leon Saryan
Erwin Schäffer
Jacco Scheper
Gerhard Schön
George Schumacher
Dr. Wolfgang Schuster
Alexander Shapiro
Ladislav Sin
Ole Sjoelund
Benjamin Swagerty
Steven Tan
Mehmet Tolga Taner
Anthony Tumonis
Erik J. Van Loon
Carmen Viciedo
Wakim Wakim
Paul Welz
Stewart Westdal
J. Brix Westergaard
J. Hugh Witherow
Ishagh Yousefzadeh
Joseph Zaffern

AUCTION HOUSES

Dix-Noonan-Webb
Heritage World Coin Auctions
Hess-Divo Ltd.
Gerhard Hirsch

Thomas Høiland Møntauktion
Fritz Rudolf Künker
Leu Numismatik AG
MPO Auctions

Münzenhandlung Harald Möller, GmbH
Noble Numismatics, Pty. Ltd.
Ponterio & Associates

Stack's
UBS, AG
World Wide Coins of California

WORLD MINTS, CENTRAL BANKS AND DISTRIBUTORS

Austrian Mint
Banco de Mexico
Banque Centrale Du Luxembourg
Black Mountain Coins
Casa de la Moneda de Cuba
Central Bank of D.P.R. Korea - Kumbyol Trading Corp.
Central Bank of the Russian Federation
CIT
Czech National Bank
Educational Coin Company
Faude & Huguenin
Global Coins & Medals Ltd. - Official Sales Company of the Bulgarian Mint

Imprensa Nacional - Casa da Moeda, S.A.
Israel Coins & Medals Corp.
Istituto Poligrafico e Zecca dello Stato I.p.A.
Jablonex Group - Division of Czech Mint
Japan Mint
Kazakhstan Mint
KOMSCO - South Korea
Latvijas Banka
Lietuvos Bankas
Lithuanian Mint
Magyar Penzvero Zrt.
MDM
Mennica Polska
Mincovna Kremnica

Mint of Finland, Ltd.
Mint of Norway
Monnaie de Paris
Moscow Mint
National Bank of the Republic of Belarus
National Bank of Ukraine
New Zealand Mint
New Zealnad Post
Numiscom
Numistrade Gmbh & Co. kg.
Omni Trading B.V.
Perth Mint
Pobjoy Mint
Real Casa de la Moneda - Spain
Royal Mint
Royal Australian Mint

Royal Belgian Mint
Royal Canadian Mint
Royal Dutch Mint
Royal Thai Mint
Servei D'Emissions Principat D'Andorra
Singapore Mint
South African Mint
Staatliche Munze Berlin
Staatliche Munze Baden-Wurttemberg
Talisman Coins
Thailand Treasury Department
Ufficio Filatelico e Numismatico - Vatican
United States Mint

HOW TO USE THIS CATALOG

This catalog is designed to serve the needs of both the novice and advanced collectors. It is generally arranged so that persons with no more than a basic knowledge of world history and a casual acquaintance with coin collecting can consult it with confidence and ease. The following explanations summarize the general practices used in preparing this catalog's listings.

ARRANGEMENT

Countries are arranged alphabetically. Political changes within a country are arranged chronologically. In countries where Rulers are the single most significant political entity, a chronological arrangement by Ruler has been employed. Distinctive sub-geographic regions are listed alphabetically following the country's main listings.

Diverse coinage types relating to fabrication methods, revaluations, denomination systems, non-circulating categories and such have been identified, separated and arranged in logical fashion. Chronological arrangement is employed for most circulating coinage. Monetary reforms will flow in order of their institution. Non-circulating types such as Essais, Pi
eforts, Patterns, Trial Strikes, Mint and Proof sets will follow the main listings.

Within a coinage type coins will be listed by denomination, from smallest to largest. Numbered types within a denomination will be ordered by their first date of issue.

IDENTIFICATION

The most important step in the identification of a coin is the determination of the nation of origin. This is generally easily accomplished where English-speaking lands are concerned, however, use of the country index is sometimes required.

The coins of many countries beyond the English-language realm, such as those of French, Italian or Spanish heritage, are also quite easy to identify through reference to their legends, which appear in the national languages based on Western alphabets. In many instances the name is spelled exactly the same in English as in the national language, such as France; while in other cases it varies only slightly, like Italia for Italy, Belgique or Belgie for Belgium, Brasil for Brazil and Danmark for Denmark.

This is not always the case, however, as in Norge for Norway, Espana for Spain, Sverige for Sweden and Helvetia for Switzerland. Coins bearing Cyrillic lettering are attributable to Bulgaria, Russia, the Slavic states and Mongolia; the Greek script peculiar to Greece, Crete and the Ionian Islands; the Amharic characters of Ethiopia; or Hebrew in the case of Israel.

The toughra monogram, occurs on some of the coins of Afghanistan, Egypt, Sudan, Pakistan, and Turkey. A predominant design feature on the coins of Nepal is the trident; while neighboring Tibet features a lotus blossom or lion on many of their issues.

DATING

Coin dating is the final basic attribution consideration. Here, the problem can be more difficult because the reading of a coin date is subject not only to the vagaries of numeric styling, but to calendar variations caused by the observance of various religious eras or regal periods from country to country, or even within a country. Here again, with the exception of the sphere from North Africa through the Orient, it will be found that most countries rely on Western date numerals and Christian (AD) era reckoning, although in a few instances, coin dating has been tied to the year of a reign or government. The Vatican, for example dates its coinage according to the year of reign of the current pope, in addition to the Christian-era date.

Countries in the Arabic sphere generally date their coins to the Muslim era (AH).

The following table indicates the year dating for the various eras, which correspond to 2009 in Christian calendar reckoning, but it must be remembered that there are overlaps between the eras in some instances.

Christian era (AD)	-2010
Muslim era (AH)	-AH1431
Solar year (SH)	-SH1388
Monarchic Solar era (MS)	-MS2569
Vikrama Samvat (VS)	-VS2067
Saka era (SE)	-SE1932
Buddhist era (BE)	-BE2553
Bangkok era (RS)	-RS229
Chula-Sakarat era (CS)	-CS1372
Ethiopian era (EE)	-EE2003
Korean era	-4343
Javanese Aji Saka era (AS)	-AS1943
Fasli era (FE)	-FE1420
Jewish era (JE)	-JE5770

More detailed guides to less prevalent coin dating systems, which are strictly local in nature, are presented with the appropriate listings.

Some coins carry dates according to both locally observed and Christian eras. This is particularly true in the Arabic world, where the Hejira date may be indicated in Arabic numerals and the Christian date in Western numerals, or both dates in either form.

HEJIRA DATE CONVERSION CHART

HEJIRA (Hijira, Hegira), the name of the Muslim era (A.H. = Anno Hegirae) dates back to the Christian year 622 when Mohammed "fled" from Mecca, escaping to Medina to avoid persecution from the Koreish tribemen. Based on a lunar year the Muslim year is 11 days shorter.

*=Leap Year (Christian Calendar)

The date actually carried on a given coin is generally cataloged here in the first column (Date) to the right of the catalog number. If this date is by a non-Christian dating system, such as 'AH' (Muslim), the Christian equivalent date will appear in parentheses(), for example AH1336(1917). Dates listed alone in the date column which do not actually appear on a given coin, or dates which are known, but do not appear on the coin, are generally enclosed by parentheses with 'ND' at the left, for example ND(2001).

Timing differentials between some era of reckoning, particularly the 354-day Mohammedan and 365-day Christian years, cause situations whereby coins which carry dates for both eras exist bearing two year dates from one calendar combined with a single date from another.

Countermarked Coinage is presented with both 'Countermark Date' and 'Host Coin' date for each type. Actual date representation follows the rules outlined above.

DENOMINATIONS

The second basic consideration to be met in the attribution of a coin is the determination of denomination. Since denominations are usually expressed in numeric rather than word form on a coin, this is usually quite easily accomplished on coins from nations which use Western numerals, except in those instances where issues are devoid of any mention of face value, and denomination must be attributed by size, metallic composition or weight. Coins listed in this volume are generally illustrated in actual size.

The sphere of countries stretching from North Africa through the Orient, on which numeric symbols generally unfamiliar to Westerners are employed, often provide the collector with a much greater challenge. This is particularly true on nearly all pre-20th Century issues. On some of the more modern issues and increasingly so as the years progress, Western-style numerals usually presented in combination with the local numeric system are becoming more commonplace on these coins.

The included table of Standard International Numeral Systems presents charts of the basic numeric designations found on coins of non-Western origin. Although denomination numerals are generally prominently displayed on coins, it must be remembered that these are general representations of characters, which individual coin engravers may have rendered in widely varying styles. Where numeric or script denominations designation forms peculiar to a given coin or country apply, such as the script used on some Persian (Iranian) issues. They are so indicated or illustrated in conjunction with the appropriate listings.

MINTAGES

Quantities minted of each date are indicated where that information is available, generally stated in millions or rounded off to the nearest 10,000 pieces when more exact figures are not available. On quantities of a few thousand or less, actual mintages are generally indicated. For combined mintage figures the abbreviation "Inc. Above" means Included Above, while "Inc. Below" means Included Below. "Est." beside a mintage figure indicates the number given is an estimate or mintage limit.

METALS

Each numbered type listing will contain a description of the coins metallic content. The traditional coinage metals and their symbolic chemical abbreviations sometimes used in this catalog are:

Platinum - (PT)	Copper - (Cu)
Gold - (Au)	Brass -
Silver - (Ag)	Copper-nickel- (CN)
Billion -	Lead - (Pb)
Nickel - (Ni)	Steel -
Zinc - (Zn)	Tin - (Sn)
Bronze - (Ae)	Aluminum - (Al)

Modern commemorative coins have employed still more unusual methods such as bimetallic coins, color applications and precious metal or gem inlays.

PRECIOUS METAL WEIGHTS

Listings of weight, fineness and actual silver (ASW), gold (AGW), platinum or palladium (APW) content of most machine-struck silver, gold, platinum and palladium coins are provided in this edition. This information will be found incorporated in each separate type listing, along with other data related to the coin.

The ASW, AGW or APW figure can be multiplied by the spot price of each precious metal to determine the current intrinsic value of any coin accompanied by these designations.

As the silver and gold bullion markets have advanced and declined sharply over the years, the fineness and total precious metal content of coins has become especially significant where bullion coins - issues which trade on the basis of their intrinsic metallic content rather than numismatic value - are concerned. In many instances, such issues have become worth more in bullion form than their nominal collector values or denominations indicate.

BULLION VALUE

The simplest method for determining the bullion value of a precious metal coin is to multiply the actual precious metal weight by the current spot price for that

AH Hejira	AD Christian Date	AH Hejira	AD Christian Date
1420	1999, April 17	1436	2014, October 25
1421	2000, April 6*	1437	2015, October 15*
1422	2001, March 26	1438	2016, October 3
1423	2002, March 15	1439	2017, September 22
1424	2003, March 5	1440	2018, September 12
1425	2004, February 22*	1441	2019, September 11*
1426	2005, February 10	1442	2020, August 20
1427	2006, January 31	1443	2021, August 10
1428	2007, January 20	1444	2022, July 30
1429	2008, January 10*	1445	2023, July 19*
1430	2008, December 29	1446	2024, July 8
1431	2009, December 18	1447	2025, June 27
1432	2010, December 8	1448	2026, June 17
1433	2011, November 27*	1449	2027, June 6*
1434	2012, November 15	1450	2028, May 25
1435	2013, November 5		

metal. A silver coin with a .6822 actual silver weight (ASW) would have an intrinsic value of $8.70 when the spot price of silver is $12.75. If the spot price of silver rose to $17.95 that same coins intrinsic value would rise to $12.25.

PHOTOGRAPHS

To assist the reader in coin identification, every effort has been made to present actual size photographs of every coinage type listed. Obverse and reverse are illustrated, except when a change in design is restricted to one side, and the coin has a diameter of 39mm or larger, in which case only the side required for identification of the type is generally illustrated. All coins up to 60mm are illustrated actual size, to the nearest 1/2mm up to 25mm, and to the nearest 1mm thereafter. Coins larger than 60mm diameter are illustrated in reduced size, with the actual size noted in the descriptive text block. Where slight change in size is important to coin type identification, actual millimeter measurements are stated.

VALUATIONS

Values quoted in this catalog represent the current market and are compiled from recommendations provided and verified through various source documents and specialized consultants. It should be stressed, however, that this book is intended to serve only as an aid for evaluating coins, actual market conditions are constantly changing and additional influences, such as particularly strong local demand for certain coin series, fluctuation of international exchange rates, changes in spot price of precious metals and worldwide collection patterns must also be considered. Publication of this catalog is not intended as a solicitation by the publisher, editors or contributors to buy or sell the coins listed at the prices indicated.

All valuations are stated in U.S. dollars, based on careful assessment of the varied international collector market. Valuations for coins priced below $100.00 are generally stated in full amounts - i.e. 37.50 or 95.00 - while valuations at or above that figure are rounded off in even dollars - i.e. $125.00 is expressed 125. A comma is added to indicate thousands of dollars in value.

For the convenience of overseas collectors and for U.S. collectors doing business with overseas dealers, the base exchange rate for the national currencies of approximately 180 countries is presented in the Foreign Exchange Table.

It should be noted that when particularly select uncirculated or proof-like examples of uncirculated coins become available they can be expected to command proportionately high premiums. Such examples in reference to choice Germanic Thalers are referred to as "erst schlage" or first strikes.

NEW ISSUES

All newly released coins dated up to the year 2006 that have been physically observed by our staff or identified by reliable sources and have been confirmed by press time have been incorporated in this edition. Exceptions exist in some countries where current date coin production lags far behind or information on current issues is less accessible.

SETS

Listings in this catalog for specimen, proof and mint sets are for official, government-produced sets. In many instances privately packaged sets also exist.

Mint Sets/Fleur de Coin Sets: Specially prepared by worldwide mints to provide banks, collectors and government dignitaries with examples of current coin-

age. Usually subjected to rigorous inspection to insure that top quality specimens of selected business strikes are provided.

Specimen Sets: Forerunners of today's proof sets. In most cases the coins were specially struck, perhaps even double struck, to produce a very soft or matte finish on the effigies and fields, along with high, sharp, "wire" rims. The finish is rather dull to the naked eye.

The original purpose of these sets was to provide VIPs, monarchs and mintmasters around the world with samples of the highest quality workmanship of a particular mint. These were usually housed in elaborate velvet-lined leather and metal cases.

Proof-like Sets: Proof-like Sets are relatively new to the field of numismatics. During the mid 1950s the Royal Canadian Mint furnished the hobby with specially selected early business strike coins that exhibited some qualities similar to proof coinage. However, the "proof-like" fields are generally flawed and the edges are rounded. These pieces are not double struck. These are commonly encountered in cardboard holders, later in soft plastic or pliofilm packaging. Of late, the Royal Canadian Mint packages such sets in rigid plastic cases.

Many worldwide officially issued proof sets would in reality fall into this category upon careful examination of the quality of the coin's finish.

Another term encountered in this category is "Special Select," used to describe the crowns of the Union of South Africa and 100-schilling coins produced for collectors in the late 1970s by the Austrian Mint.

Proof Sets: This is undoubtedly among the most misused terms in the hobby, not only by collectors and dealers, but also by many of the world mints.

A true proof set must be at least double-struck on specially prepared polished planchets and struck using dies (often themselves polished) of the highest quality.

Modern-day proof quality consists of frosted effigies surrounded by absolute mirror-like fields.

Listings for proof sets in this catalog are for officially issued proof sets so designated by the issuing authority, and may or may not possess what are considered modern proof quality standards.

It is necessary for collectors to acquire the knowledge to allow them to differentiate true proof sets from would-be proof sets and proof-like sets which may be encountered.

CONDITIONS/GRADING

Wherever possible, coin valuations are given in four or five grades of preservation. For modern commemoratives, which do not circulate, only uncirculated values are usually sufficient. Proof issues are indicated by the word "Proof" next to the date, with valuation proceeded by the word "value" following the mintage. For very recent circulating coins and coins of limited value, one, two or three grade values are presented.

There are almost no grading guides for world coins. What follows is an attempt to help bridge that gap until a detailed, illustrated guide becomes available.

In grading world coins, there are two elements to look for: 1) Overall wear, and 2) loss of design details, such as strands of hair, feathers on eagles, designs on coats of arms, etc.

The age, rarity or type of a coin should not be a consideration in grading.

Grade each coin by the weaker of the two sides. This method appears to give results most nearly consistent with conservative American Numismatic Association standards for U.S. coins. Split grades, i.e., F/VF for obverse and reverse, respectively, are normally no more than one grade apart. If the two sides are more than one grade apart, the series of coins probably wears differently on each side and should then be graded by the weaker side alone.

Grade by the amount of overall wear and loss of design detail evident on each side of the coin. On coins with a moderately small design element, which is prone to early wear, grade by that design alone. For example, the 5-ore (KM#554) of Sweden has a crown above the monogram on which the beads on the arches show wear most clearly. So, grade by the crown alone.

For **Brilliant Uncirculated** (BU) grades there will be no visible signs of wear or handling, even under a 30-power microscope. Full mint luster will be present. Ideally no bags marks will be evident.

For **Uncirculated** (Unc. or MS-60) grades there will be no visible signs of wear or handling, even under a 30-power microscope. Bag marks may be present.

For **Almost Uncirculated** (AU or AU-50), all detail will be visible. There will be wear only on the highest point of the coin. There will often be half or more of the original mint luster present.

On the **Extremely Fine** (EF or XF or XF-40) coin, there will be about 95% of the original detail visible. Or, on a coin with a design with no inner detail to wear down, there will be a light wear over nearly all the coin. If a small design is used as the grading area, about 90% of the original detail will be visible. This latter rule stems from the logic that a smaller amount of detail needs to be present because a small area is being used to grade the whole coin.

The **Very Fine** (VF or VF-20) coin will have about 75% of the original detail visible. Or, on a coin with no inner detail, there will be moderate wear over the entire coin. Corners of letters and numbers may be weak. A small grading area will have about 66% of the original detail.

For **Fine** (F or F-12), there will be about 50% of the original detail visible. Or, on a coin with no inner detail, there will be fairly heavy wear over all of the coin. Sides of letters will be weak. A typically uncleaned coin will often appear as dirty or dull. A small grading area will have just under 50% of the original detail.

On the **Very Good** (VG or VG-8) coin, there will be about 25% of the original detail visible. There will be heavy wear on all of the coin.

The **Good** (G or G-4) coin's design will be clearly outlined but with substantial wear. Some of the larger detail may be visible. The rim may have a few weak spots of wear.

On the **About Good** (AG) coin, there will typically be only a silhouette of a large design. The rim will be worn down into the letters if any.

Strong or weak strikes, partially weak strikes, damage, corrosion, attractive or unattractive toning, dipping or cleaning should be described along with the above grades. These factors affect the quality of the coin just as do wear and loss of detail, but are easier to describe.

Coin Alignment   Medal Alignment
COIN vs MEDAL ALIGNMENT

Some coins are struck with obverse and reverse aligned at a rotation of 180 degrees from each other. When a coin is held for vertical viewing with the obverse design aligned upright and the index finger and thumb at the top and bottom, upon rotation from left to right for viewing the reverse, the latter will be upside down. Such alignment is called "coin rotation." Other coins are struck with the obverse and reverse designs mated on an alignment of zero or 360 degrees. If such an example is held and rotated as described, the reverse will appear upright. This is the alignment, which is generally observed in the striking of medals, and for that reason coins produced in this manner are considered struck in "medal rotation". In some instances, often through error, certain coin issues have been struck to both alignment standards, creating interesting collectible varieties, which will be found noted in some listings. In addition, some countries are now producing coins with other designated obverse to reverse alignments which are considered standard for this type.

COUNTRY INDEX

CONTRIBUTING TO THE CATALOG

SENDING SCANNED IMAGES

- Scan images with a resolution of 300 dpi
- Set size at 100%
- Scan in true 4-color
- Save images as 'jpeg'
- Specify the country, denomination and diameter of coin
- Send images to the editor at **George.Cuhaj@fwmedia.com**

OFFERING DATA CORRECTIONS

- Refer to coins by country and catalog number
- Be as clear and specific as possible
- Send your comments to the editor at **George.Cuhaj@fwmedia.com**

SUGGESTING VALUE CHANGES

- Reference the coins country and catalog number
- Specify date and grade
- Explain your sources
- Send your suggestions to the market analyst at **Tom.Michael@fwmedia.com**

FOREIGN EXCHANGE TABLE

The latest foreign exchange rates below apply to trade with banks in the country of origin. The left column shows the number of units per U.S. dollar at the official rate. The right column shows the number of units per dollar at the free market rate.

COUNTRY	Official #/$	Market #/$
Afghanistan (New Afghani)	47	–
Albania (Lek)	101	–
Algeria (Dinar)	74	–
Andorra uses Euro	.733	–
Angola (Readjust Kwanza)	.90	–
Anguilla uses E.C. Dollar	2.7	–
Antigua uses E.C. Dollar	2.7	–
Argentina (Peso)	3.8	–
Armenia (Dram)	378	–
Aruba (Florin)	1.79	–
Australia (Dollar)	1.15	–
Austria (Euro)	.733	–
Azerbaijan (New Manat)	.805	–
Bahamas (Dollar)	1.0	–
Bahrain Is. (Dinar)	.377	–
Bangladesh (Taka)	69	–
Barbados (Dollar)	2.0	–
Belarus (Ruble)	2,899	–
Belgium (Euro)	.733	–
Belize (Dollar)	1.95	–
Benin uses CFA Franc West	470	–
Bermuda (Dollar)	1.0	–
Bhutan (Ngultrum)	47	–
Bolivia (Boliviano)	7.02	–
Bosnia-Herzegovina (Conv. marka)	1.43	–
Botswana (Pula)	6.90	–
British Virgin Islands uses U.S. Dollar	1.0	–
Brazil (Real)	1.88	–
Brunei (Dollar)	1.42	–
Bulgaria (Lev)	1.43	–
Burkina Faso uses CFA Franc West	470	–
Burma (Kyat)	6.51	1,250
Burundi (Franc)	1,230	–
Cambodia (Riel)	4,184	–
Cameroon uses CFA Franc Central	470	–
Canada (Dollar)	1.07	–
Cape Verde (Escudo)	74	–
Cayman Islands (Dollar)	0.82	–
Central African Rep.	470	–
CFA Franc Central	470	–
CFA Franc West	470	–
CFP Franc	87	–
Chad uses CFA Franc Central	470	–
Chile (Peso)	539	–
China, P.R. (Renminbi Yuan)	6.83	–
Colombia (Peso)	2,008	–
Comoros (Franc)	360	–
Congo uses CFA Franc Central	470	–
Congo-Dem.Rep. (Congolese Franc)	913	–
Cook Islands (Dollar)	1.46	–
Costa Rica (Colon)	553	–
Croatia (Kuna)	5.35	–
Cuba (Peso)	1.00	27.00
Cyprus (Euro)	.403	–
Czech Republic (Koruna)	19.0	–
Denmark (Danish Krone)	5.4	–
Djibouti (Franc)	178	–
Dominica uses E.C. Dollar	2.7	–
Dominican Republic (Peso)	36	–
East Caribbean (Dollar)	2.7	–
Ecuador (U.S. Dollar)	1.00	–
Egypt (Pound)	5.47	–
El Salvador (U.S. Dollar)	1.00	–
Equatorial Guinea uses CFA Franc Central	470	–
Eritrea (Nafka)	15	–
Estonia (Kroon)	11.4	–
Ethiopia (Birr)	11.4	–
Euro	.733	–
Falkland Is. (Pound)	.641	–
Faroe Islands (Krona)	5.4	–
Fiji Islands (Dollar)	1.97	–
Finland (Euro)	.733	–
France (Euro)	.733	–
French Polynesia uses CFP Franc	87	–
Gabon (CFA Franc)	470	–
Gambia (Dalasi)	27	–
Georgia (Lari)	1.72	–
Germany (Euro)	.733	–
Ghana (New Cedi)	1.44	–
Gibraltar (Pound)	.641	–
Greece (Euro)	.733	–
Greenland uses Danish Krone	5.4	–
Grenada uses E.C. Dollar	2.7	–
Guatemala (Quetzal)	8.2	–
Guernsey uses Sterling Pound	.641	–
Guinea Bissau (CFA Franc)	470	–
Guinea Conakry (Franc)	5,025	–
Guyana (Dollar)	205	–
Haiti (Gourde)	40	–
Honduras (Lempira)	19	–
Hong Kong (Dollar)	7.77	–
Hungary (Forint)	201	–
Iceland (Krona)	129	–
India (Rupee)	47	–
Indonesia (Rupiah)	9,410	–
Iran (Rial)	9,899	–
Iraq (Dinar)	1,169	–
Ireland (Euro)	.733	–
Isle of Man uses Sterling Pound	.641	–
Israel (New Sheqalim)	3.75	–
Italy (Euro)	.733	–
Ivory Coast uses CFA Franc West	470	–
Jamaica (Dollar)	90	–
Japan (Yen)	89	–
Jersey uses Sterling Pound	.641	–
Jordan (Dinar)	.708	–
Kazakhstan (Tenge)	148	–
Kenya (Shilling)	77	–
Kiribati uses Australian Dollar	1.15	–
Korea-PDR (Won)	2.2	143
Korea-Rep. (Won)	1,169	–
Kuwait (Dinar)	.289	–
Kyrgyzstan (Som)	44	–
Laos (Kip)	8,492	–
Latvia (Lats)	.518	–
Lebanon (Pound)	1,501	–
Lesotho (Maloti)	7.78	–
Liberia (Dollar)	72	–
Libya (Dinar)	1.24	–
Liechtenstein uses Swiss Franc	1.08	–
Lithuania (Litas)	2.52	–
Luxembourg (Euro)	.733	–
Macao (Pataca)	8.0	–
Macedonia (New Denar)	45	–
Madagascar (Franc)	2,165	–
Malawi (Kwacha)	151	–
Malaysia (Ringgit)	3.44	–
Maldives (Rufiya)	12.8	–
Mali uses CFA Franc West	470	–
Malta (Euro)	.733	–
Marshall Islands uses U.S.Dollar	1.00	–
Mauritania (Ouguiya)	262	–
Mauritius (Rupee)	30	–
Mexico (Peso)	13.2	–
Moldova (Leu)	12.8	–
Monaco uses Euro	.733	–
Mongolia (Tugrik)	1,452	–
Montenegro uses Euro	.733	–
Montserrat uses E.C. Dollar	2.7	–
Morocco (Dirham)	8.2	–
Mozambique (New Metical)	31	–
Namibia (Rand)	7.78	–
Nauru uses Australian Dollar	1.15	–
Nepal (Rupee)	75	–
Netherlands (Euro)	.733	–
Netherlands Antilles (Gulden)	1.79	–
New Caledonia uses CFP Franc	87	–
New Zealand (Dollar)	1.46	–
Nicaragua (Cordoba Oro)	21	–
Niger uses CFA Franc West	470	–
Nigeria (Naira)	152	–
Northern Ireland uses Sterling Pound	.641	–
Norway (Krone)	5.99	–
Oman (Rial)	.385	–
Pakistan (Rupee)	85	–
Palau uses U.S.Dollar	1.00	–
Panama (Balboa) uses U.S.Dollar	1.00	–
Papua New Guinea (Kina)	2.65	–
Paraguay (Guarani)	4,685	–
Peru (Nuevo Sol)	2.9	–
Philippines (Peso)	47	–
Poland (Zloty)	2.99	–
Portugal (Euro)	.733	–
Qatar (Riyal)	3.64	–
Romania (New Leu)	3.0	–
Russia (Ruble)	30	–
Rwanda (Franc)	573	–
St. Helena (Pound)	.641	–
St. Kitts uses E.C. Dollar	2.7	–
St. Lucia uses E.C. Dollar	2.7	–
St. Vincent uses E.C. Dollar	2.7	–
San Marino uses Euro	.733	–
Sao Tome e Principe (Dobra)	17,826	–
Saudi Arabia (Riyal)	3.75	–
Scotland uses Sterling Pound	.641	–
Senegal uses CFA Franc West	470	–
Serbia (Dinar)	72	–
Seychelles (Rupee)	11	–
Sierra Leone (Leone)	3,895	–
Singapore (Dollar)	1.42	–
Slovakia (Sk. Koruna)	22	–
Slovenia (Euro)	.733	–
Solomon Islands (Dollar)	7.9	–
Somalia (Shilling)	1,496	–
Somaliland (Somali Shilling)	1,450	4,000
South Africa (Rand)	7.78	–
Spain (Euro)	.733	–
Sri Lanka (Rupee)	115	–
Sudan (Pound)	2.32	–
Surinam (Dollar)	2.75	–
Swaziland (Lilangeni)	7.78	–
Sweden (Krona)	7.4	–
Switzerland (Franc)	1.08	–
Syria (Pound)	46	–
Taiwan (NT Dollar)	32	–
Tajikistan (Somoni)	4.37	–
Tanzania (Shilling)	1,345	–
Thailand (Baht)	33	–
Togo uses CFA Franc West	470	–
Tonga (Pa'anga)	1.94	–
Transdniestra (Ruble)	–	–
Trinidad & Tobago (Dollar)	6.34	–
Tunisia (Dinar)	1.38	–
Turkey (New Lira)	1.53	–
Turkmenistan (Manat)	14,250	–
Turks & Caicos uses U.S. Dollar	1.00	–
Tuvalu uses Australian Dollar	1.15	–
Uganda (Shilling)	1,975	–
Ukraine (Hryvnia)	8.0	–
United Arab Emirates (Dirham)	3.67	–
United Kingdom (Sterling Pound)	.641	–
Uruguay (Peso Uruguayo)	20	–
Uzbekistan (Sum)	1,527	–
Vanuatu (Vatu)	102	–
Vatican City uses Euro	.733	–
Venezuela (New Bolivar)	4.30	5.7
Vietnam (Dong)	18,469	–
Western Samoa (Tala)	2.51	–
Yemen (Rial)	212	–
Zambia (Kwacha)	4,660	–
Zimbabwe (Dollar)	–	–

 **Pobjoy Mint**

Welcome to Pobjoy Mint for Collectors and Commemorative Issues
Over 300 Years of Tradition

| Home | Shop | Governments | About Us | Trade | News | Contact | Custom Minting | Top Ten | Coin Types |

Official Minters to Foreign Governments - Custom Minters to the World

Winner of 13 COIN OF THE YEAR AWARDS

Featured Products

Coins, Regalia, Objects D'art and Custom Minting

Andorra	Macau
Ascension Island	Madeira
Bahrain	Maldive Islands
Bhutan	Mauritius
Bolivia	Nigeria
Bosnia & Herzegovina	Niue
	Oman
British Antarctic Territory	Peru
British Indian Ocean Territory	Philippines
British Virgin Islands	Pitcairn Islands
Burundi	Senegal
Cook Islands	Sierra Leone
Dubai	Solomon Islands
Eritrea	Somaliland
Ethiopia	South Georgia & the South Sandwich Islands
Falkland Islands	Spain
Gibraltar	Tajikistan
Hong Kong	Tokelau
Isle of Man	Tonga
Jamaica	Tristan da Cunha
Kenya	Uganda
Kuwait	Uzbekistan
Kyrghystan	Vanuatu
Liberia	Western Samoa

Pobjoy, more than a name, a guarantee!

Silver and Crystal Lioness

BORN FREE

2010 Abyssinian Cat Coin

High Relief Silver Angel

Elgin Marbles Bronze Coin

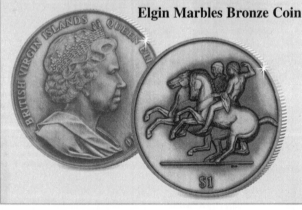

175th Anniversary of Hans Christian Andersen's First Book of Fairy Tales

Head Office: Millennia House, Kingswood Park, Bonsor Drive,
Kingswood, Surrey, KT20 6AY, U.K.
TEL: (+44) 1737 818181   FAX: (+44) 1737 818199
Internet: www.pobjoy.com   Email: mint@pobjoy.com

USA Branch: P.O. Box 109,
Rosemount, MN 55068 USA
Tel: Toll Free 1-877-4 POBJOY (1-877-476 2569)
Fax: (651) 322 5527   Email: usasales@pobjoy.com

AFGHANISTAN

The Islamic State of Afghanistan, which occupies a mountainous region of Southwest Asia, has an area of 251,825 sq. mi. (652,090 sq. km.) and a population of 25.59 million. Presently, about a fifth of the total population lives in exile as refugees, (mostly in Pakistan). Capital: Kabul. It is bordered by Iran, Pakistan, Turkmenistan, Uzbekistan, Tajikistan, and China's Sinkiang Province. Agriculture and herding are the principal industries; textile mills and cement factories add to the industrial sector. Cotton, wool, fruits, nuts, oil, sheepskin coats and hand-woven carpets are normally exported but foreign trade has been interrupted since 1979.

ISLAMIC STATE
SH1373-1381 / 1994-2002AD
DECIMAL COINAGE

100 Pul = 1 Afghani; 20 Afghani = 1 Amani

KM# 1048   500 AFGHANIS
15.0000 g., Silver, 35.08 mm. **Subject:** 100th Anniversary Death of Giuseppe Verdi **Obv:** National arms **Rev:** Bust of Verdi 3/4 left, music score below **Edge:** Plain

Date	Mintage	F	VF	XF	Unc	BU
SH1380(2001) Proof	—	Value: 35.00				

STANDARD COINAGE

KM# 1043   500 AFGHANIS
19.8700 g., 0.9990 Silver 0.6382 oz. ASW, 37.9 mm. **Subject:** World Championship of Soccer - 2006 - Germany **Obv:** State Emblem **Rev:** Soccer ball on German map **Edge:** Reeded

Date	Mintage	F	VF	XF	Unc	BU
2001 Proof	—	Value: 40.00				

REPUBLIC
SH1381- / 2002- AD
DECIMAL COINAGE

100 Pul = 1 Afghani; 20 Afghani = 1 Amani

KM# 1044   AFGHANI
3.2800 g., Copper Plated Steel, 20 mm. **Obv:** Value, legend above, legend and date below **Rev:** Mosque with flags in wreath

Date	Mintage	F	VF	XF	Unc	BU
SH1383(2004)	—	—	—	—	1.50	2.00
SH1384(2005)	—	—	—	—	1.50	2.00

KM# 1045   2 AFGHANIS
4.1000 g., Stainless Steel, 22 mm. **Obv:** Value, legend above, legend and date below **Rev:** Mosque with flags in wreath

Date	Mintage	F	VF	XF	Unc	BU
SH1383(2004)	—	—	—	—	2.00	2.50
SH1384(2005)	—	—	—	—	2.00	2.50

KM# 1046   5 AFGHANIS
5.0800 g., Brass, 24 mm. **Obv:** Value, legend above, legend and date below **Rev:** Mosque with flags in wreath

Date	Mintage	F	VF	XF	Unc	BU
SH1383(2004)	—	—	—	—	2.50	3.00
SH1384(2005)	—	—	—	—	2.50	3.00

ALBANIA

The Republic of Albania, a Balkan republic bounded by Macedonia, Greece, Montenegro, and the Adriatic Sea, has an area of 11,100 sq. mi. (28,748 sq. km.) and a population of 3.49 million. Capital: Tirane. The country is predominantly agricultural, although recent progress has been made in the manufacturing and mining sectors. Petroleum, chrome, iron, copper, cotton textiles, tobacco and wood products are exported.

MINT MARKS
L – London
R - Rome
V – Vienna

MONETARY SYSTEM
100 Qindar Leku = 1 Lek
100 Qindar Ari = 1 Frang Ar = 5 Lek

REPUBLIC
STANDARD COINAGE

KM# 93   10 LEKE
3.5400 g., Aluminum-Nickel-Bronze, 21.34 mm. **Subject:** 85th Anniversary Tirana as capital **Obv:** Archaic tomb **Obv. Legend:** SHQIPERI • ALBANIA **Rev:** Outlined bird above value **Edge:** Reeded

Date	Mintage	F	VF	XF	Unc	BU
2005	—	—	—	—	2.00	3.00

KM# 94   10 LEKE
3.6600 g., Aluminum-Nickel-Bronze, 21.40 mm. **Subject:** Culture **Obv:** Ornate vest **Obv. Legend:** SHQIPERI • ALBANIA **Rev:** Ornate value **Rev. Legend:** OBJEKTE TE TRASHEGIMISE KULTURORE **Edge:** Reeded

Date	Mintage	F	VF	XF	Unc	BU
2005	—	—	—	—	2.00	3.00

KM# 87   20 LEKE
8.5400 g., Brass, 26.1 mm. **Subject:** Prehistoric art **Obv:** Horseman **Rev:** Ancient coin design with Apollo portrait **Edge:** Reeded

Date	Mintage	F	VF	XF	Unc	BU
2002	—	—	—	—	3.00	4.00

KM# 81   50 LEKE
7.5000 g., Copper-Nickel, 28 mm. **Subject:** Michaelangelo's "David" **Obv:** Towered building **Rev:** Statue's head and denomination **Edge:** Plain

Date	Mintage	F	VF	XF	Unc	BU
2001	1,000	—	—	—	6.50	8.00

KM# 88   50 LEKE
11.9200 g., Brass, 28.1 mm. **Obv:** Value within circle **Rev:** Bust facing, dates below **Edge:** Reeded

Date	Mintage	F	VF	XF	Unc	BU
2002	—	—	—	—	3.00	4.00

KM# 89   50 LEKE
11.8400 g., Brass, 28 mm. **Obv:** Bust 3/4 facing, dates below, circle surrounds **Rev:** Value within box within circle **Edge:** Plain

Date	Mintage	F	VF	XF	Unc	BU
2003	—	—	—	—	3.00	4.00

KM# 86   50 LEKE
5.4600 g., Copper-Nickel, 24.2 mm. **Obv:** Value and legend **Rev:** Ancient Illyrian helmet **Edge:** Reeded

Date	Mintage	F	VF	XF	Unc	BU
2003 (2004)	200,000	—	—	—	6.00	7.50

KM# 90   50 LEKE
5.5000 g., Copper-Nickel, 24.2 mm. **Obv:** Wheel design **Rev:** Ancient bust above value within circle **Edge:** Reeded

Date	Mintage	F	VF	XF	Unc	BU
2004	—	—	—	—	3.00	4.00

KM# 91   50 LEKE
5.5000 g., Copper-Nickel, 24.2 mm. **Obv:** Soldier within circle **Rev:** Value within circle **Edge:** Reeded

Date	Mintage	F	VF	XF	Unc	BU
2004	—	—	—	—	3.00	4.00

KM# 82   100 LEKE
15.7000 g., 0.9250 Silver 0.4669 oz. ASW, 32.65 mm. **Subject:** Michaelangelo's "David" **Obv:** Arch of Triumph **Rev:** Statue's upper half and denomination **Edge:** Plain

Date	Mintage	F	VF	XF	Unc	BU
2001	1,000	—	—	—	32.00	35.00

KM# 84   100 LEKE
15.0000 g., 0.9250 Silver 0.4461 oz. ASW, 32 mm. **Subject:**
Albanian-European Integration **Obv:** Dove in flight, stars encircle
Rev: European and Albanian maps, stars encircle **Edge:** Plain

Date	Mintage	F	VF	XF	Unc	BU
2001	1,000	—	—	—	27.50	30.00

KM# 92   100 LEKE
15.7000 g., 0.9250 Silver 0.4669 oz. ASW **Subject:** 90th
Anniversary - Ismail Qemali as President of National Assembly
Obv: Crossed rifle and pistol on manuscript, quill pen **Obv.
Legend:** SHQIPERI - ALBANIA **Rev:** Bust of Qemali 3/4 right

Date	Mintage	F	VF	XF	Unc	BU
2002 Proof	—	Value: 50.00				

KM# 83   200 LEKE
7.6500 g., 0.9000 Gold 0.2213 oz. AGW, 25.45 mm.
Subject: Michaelangelo's "David" **Obv:** City plaza **Rev:** Statue
of "David" and denomination **Edge:** Plain

Date	Mintage	F	VF	XF	Unc	BU
2001	500	—	—	—	275	300

KM# 85   200 LEKE
15.0000 g., 0.9250 Silver 0.4461 oz. ASW, 32 mm.
Subject: Albanian-European Integration **Obv:** Dove in flight
within inner circle, stars encircle **Rev:** Adult and infant hand within
inner circle, stars encircle **Edge:** Plain

Date	Mintage	F	VF	XF	Unc	BU
2001	1,000	—	—	—	37.50	40.00

MINT SETS

KM#	Date	Mintage	Identification	Issue Price	Mkt Val
MS3	2002-03 (4)	—	KM86, 89 (2003), 87, 88 (2002)	—	22.50

ALDERNEY

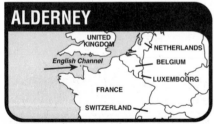

Alderney, the northernmost and third largest of the Channel
Islands, separated from the coast of France by the dangerous 8-
mile-wide tidal channel, has an area of 3 sq. mi. (8 km.) and a population of 1,686. It is a dependency of the British island of Guernsey, to the southwest. Capital: St. Anne. Principal industries are
agriculture and raising cattle.

The Channel Islands have never been subject to the British
Parliament and are self-governing units under the direct rule of the
Crown acting through the Privy Council. Alderney is one of the
nine Channel Islands, the only part of the Duchy of Normandy still
belonging to the British Crown, and has been a British possession
since the Norman Conquest of 1066. Legislation was only
recently introduced for the issue of its own coinage, a right it now
shares with Jersey and Guernsey.

RULER
British

MONETARY SYSTEM
100 Pence = 1 Pound Sterling

DEPENDENCY

STANDARD COINAGE

KM# 75   50 PENCE
8.0000 g., 0.9250 Silver 0.2379 oz. ASW **Ruler:** Elizabeth II
Subject: 50th Anniversary of Coronation **Obv:** Crowned head
right **Rev:** Royal coach **Edge:** Plain **Shape:** 7-sided

Date	Mintage	F	VF	XF	Unc	BU
2003 Proof	—	Value: 20.00				

KM# 76   50 PENCE
8.0000 g., 0.9250 Silver 0.2379 oz. ASW **Ruler:** Elizabeth II
Subject: 50th Anniversary of Coronation **Obv:** Crowned head
right **Rev:** St. Edward's crown **Edge:** Plain **Shape:** 7-sided

Date	Mintage	F	VF	XF	Unc	BU
2003 Proof	—	Value: 20.00				

KM# 77   50 PENCE
8.0000 g., 0.9250 Silver 0.2379 oz. ASW **Ruler:** Elizabeth II
Subject: 50th Anniversay of Coronation **Obv:** Crowned head
right **Rev:** Elizabeth II horseback **Edge:** Plain **Shape:** 7-sided

Date	Mintage	F	VF	XF	Unc	BU
2003 Proof	—	Value: 20.00				

KM# 78   50 PENCE
8.0000 g., 0.9250 Silver 0.2379 oz. ASW **Ruler:** Elizabeth II
Subject: 50th Anniversary of Coronation **Obv:** Crowned head right
Rev: Elizabeth II seated on throne **Edge:** Plain **Shape:** 7-sided

Date	Mintage	F	VF	XF	Unc	BU
2003 Proof	—	Value: 20.00				

KM# 73   POUND
9.5000 g., 0.9250 Silver 0.2825 oz. ASW **Ruler:** Elizabeth II
Subject: Queen's 75th Birthday **Obv:** Crowned head right

Date	Mintage	F	VF	XF	Unc	BU
2001 Proof	—	Value: 20.00				

KM# 84   POUND
1.2400 g., 0.9990 Gold 0.0398 oz. AGW, 13.92 mm.
Ruler: Elizabeth II **Subject:** Mini Cooper 50th Anniversary
Rev: Mini Cooper on tiled floor **Rev. Designer:** David Cornell

Date	Mintage	F	VF	XF	Unc	BU
2009 Proof	5,000	Value: 100				

KM# 59   5 POUNDS
28.2800 g., 0.9250 Silver 0.8410 oz. ASW, 38.6 mm.
Ruler: Elizabeth II **Subject:** Queen's 75th Birthday **Obv:** Queens
portrait right **Obv. Designer:** Raphael Maklouf **Rev:** Queen in
casual dress surrounded by rose, thistle, daffodil and pimper
nickel **Rev. Designer:** David Cornell

Date	Mintage	F	VF	XF	Unc	BU
2001 Proof	—	Value: 50.00				

KM# 60   5 POUNDS
28.2800 g., Copper-Nickel, 38.6 mm. **Ruler:** Elizabeth II
Subject: Queen's 75th Birrthday **Obv:** Queens portrait right
Obv. Designer: Raphael Maklouf **Rev:** Queen in casual dress
surrounded by rose, thistle, daffodil and primper nickel
Rev. Designer: David Cornell

Date	Mintage	F	VF	XF	Unc	BU
2001	—	—	—	—	13.50	15.00

KM# 24   5 POUNDS
28.2800 g., 0.9250 Copper-Nickel 0.8410 oz., 38.6 mm.
Ruler: Elizabeth II **Subject:** Queen Elizabeth II - 50 Years of
Reigh **Obv:** Queen's head right **Rev:** Sword hilt and denomination
with royal arms background **Rev. Designer:** Marcel Canioni
Edge: Reeded

Date	Mintage	F	VF	XF	Unc	BU
2002 Proof	15,000	Value: 50.00				

KM# 24a   5 POUNDS
28.2800 g., 0.9250 Silver 0.8410 oz. ASW, 38.6 mm.
Ruler: Elizabeth II **Subject:** Queen Elizabeth II - 50 Years of
Reign **Obv:** Queen's head right **Rev:** Sword hilt and denomination
with royal arms background **Rev. Designer:** Marcel Canioni
Edge: Reeded

Date	Mintage	F	VF	XF	Unc	BU
2002 Proof	15,000	Value: 40.00				

KM# 25   5 POUNDS
28.2800 g., 0.9250 Silver 0.8410 oz. ASW, 38.6 mm. **Ruler:**
Elizabeth II **Subject:** Queen's Golden Jubilee **Obv:** Queens
portrait **Rev:** Honor guard and trumpets **Rev. Designer:** Robert
Lowe **Edge:** Reeded

Date	Mintage	F	VF	XF	Unc	BU
2002 Proof	15,000	Value: 45.00				

KM# 27   5 POUNDS
28.2800 g., Copper-Nickel, 38.6 mm. **Ruler:** Elizabeth II
Subject: 5th Anniversary Death of Princess Diana **Obv:** Crowned
head right **Rev:** Diana accepting flowers from girl **Edge:** Reeded

Date	Mintage	F	VF	XF	Unc	BU
2002	—	—	—	—	13.50	15.00

KM# 27a   5 POUNDS
28.2800 g., 0.9250 Silver 0.8410 oz. ASW, 38.6 mm.
Ruler: Elizabeth II **Subject:** 5th Anniversary Death of Princess
Diana **Obv:** Crowned head right **Rev:** Diana accepting flowers
from girl **Edge:** Reeded

Date	Mintage	F	VF	XF	Unc	BU
2002 Proof	20,000	Value: 45.00				

KM# 27b   5 POUNDS
39.9400 g., 0.9167 Gold 1.1771 oz. AGW, 38.6 mm.
Ruler: Elizabeth II **Subject:** 5th Anniversary Death of Princess
Diana **Obv:** Crowned head right **Rev:** Diana accepting flowers
from girl **Edge:** Reeded

Date	Mintage	F	VF	XF	Unc	BU
2002 Proof	100	Value: 1,500				

KM# 29   5 POUNDS
28.2800 g., Copper-Nickel, 38.6 mm. **Ruler:** Elizabeth II
Subject: 150th Anniversary Death of the Duke of Wellington
Obv: Queens portrait **Rev:** Coat of arms, castle and portrait
Rev. Designer: Willem Vis **Edge:** Reeded

Date	Mintage	F	VF	XF	Unc	BU
2002	—	—	—	—	13.50	15.00

KM# 29a   5 POUNDS
28.2800 g., 0.9250 Silver 0.8410 oz. ASW, 38.6 mm.
Ruler: Elizabeth II **Subject:** 150th Anniversary Death of the Duke
of Wellington **Obv:** Queens portrait **Rev:** Multicolor coat of arms,
portrait and castle **Rev. Designer:** Willem Vis **Edge:** Reeded

Date	Mintage	VG	F	VF	XF	Unc
2002 Proof	15,000	Value: 55.00				

KM# 29b   5 POUNDS
39.9400 g., 0.9167 Gold 1.1771 oz. AGW, 38.6 mm.
Ruler: Elizabeth II **Subject:** 150th Anniversary Death of the Duke
of Wellington **Obv:** Queens portrait **Rev:** Coat of arms, castle
and portrait **Rev. Designer:** Willem Vis **Edge:** Reeded

Date	Mintage	VG	F	VF	XF	Unc
2002 Proof	200	Value: 1,450				

KM# 31 5 POUNDS
28.2800 g., Copper-Nickel, 38.6 mm. **Ruler:** Elizabeth II
Subject: Prince William **Obv:** Queens portrait **Obv. Designer:**
Raphael Maklouf **Rev:** Portrait with open shirt collar **Edge:** Reeded

Date	Mintage	F	VF	XF	Unc	BU
2003	—	—	—	—	16.50	18.00

KM# 44 5 POUNDS
28.2800 g., Copper-Nickel, 38.6 mm. **Ruler:** Elizabeth II
Obv: Queens portrait **Rev:** HMS Mary Rose **Rev. Designer:**
Willem Vis **Edge:** Reeded

Date	Mintage	F	VF	XF	Unc	BU
2003	—	—	—	—	12.00	13.50

KM# 44a 5 POUNDS
28.2800 g., 0.9250 Silver 0.8410 oz. ASW, 38.6 mm. **Ruler:**
Elizabeth II **Obv:** Queens portrait **Rev:** HMS Mary Rose below
multicolor flag **Rev. Designer:** Willem Vis **Edge:** Reeded

Date	Mintage	F	VF	XF	Unc	BU
2003 Proof	15,000	Value: 60.00				

KM# 45 5 POUNDS
28.2800 g., Copper-Nickel, 38.6 mm. **Ruler:** Elizabeth II
Obv: Queens portrait **Rev:** Alfred the Great on ship
Rev. Designer: Willem Vis **Edge:** Reeded

Date	Mintage	F	VF	XF	Unc	BU
2003	—	—	—	—	12.00	13.50

KM# 45a 5 POUNDS
28.2800 g., 0.9250 Silver 0.8410 oz. ASW, 38.6 mm. **Ruler:**
Elizabeth II **Obv:** Queens portrait **Rev:** Alfred the Great on ship
below multicolor flag **Rev. Designer:** Willem Vis **Edge:** Reeded

Date	Mintage	F	VF	XF	Unc	BU
2003 Proof	15,000	Value: 60.00				

KM# 45b 5 POUNDS
39.9400 g., 0.9167 Gold 1.1771 oz. AGW, 38.6 mm. **Ruler:**
Elizabeth II **Obv:** Queens portrait **Rev:** Alfred the Great on ship
Rev. Designer: Willem Vis **Edge:** Reeded

Date	Mintage	F	VF	XF	Unc	BU
2003 Proof	500	Value: 1,450				

KM# 31a 5 POUNDS
28.2800 g., 0.9250 Silver 0.8410 oz. ASW, 38.6 mm.
Ruler: Elizabeth II **Subject:** Prince William **Obv:** Queens portrait
Obv. Designer: Raphael Maklouf **Rev:** Portrait with open shirt
collar **Edge:** Reeded

Date	Mintage	F	VF	XF	Unc	BU
2003 Proof	—	Value: 47.50				

KM# 31b 5 POUNDS
39.9400 g., 0.9166 Gold 1.1770 oz. AGW, 38.6 mm.
Ruler: Elizabeth II **Subject:** Prince William **Obv:** Queens portrait
Obv. Designer: Raphael Maklouf **Rev:** Portrait with open shirt
collar **Edge:** Reeded

Date	Mintage	F	VF	XF	Unc	BU
2003 Proof	200	Value: 1,450				

KM# 35a 5 POUNDS
28.5500 g., 0.9250 Silver 0.8490 oz. ASW, 38.61 mm.
Ruler: Elizabeth II **Subject:** Last Flight of the Concorde, October
24, 2003 **Obv:** Crowned bust right **Obv. Legend:** ELIZABETH II
- ALDERNEY **Obv. Designer:** Raphael Maklouf **Rev:** Concorde
in flight **Rev. Legend:** CONCORDE 1969 - 2003 **Rev. Designer:**
Emma Noble **Edge:** Reeded

Date	Mintage	F	VF	XF	Unc	BU
2003 Proof	5,000	Value: 50.00				

KM# 35 5 POUNDS
Copper-Nickel, 38.61 mm. **Ruler:** Elizabeth II **Subject:** Last
Flight of the Concorde, October 24, 2003 **Obv:** Crowned bust
right **Obv. Legend:** ELIZABETH II - ALDERNEY **Obv. Designer:**
Raphael Maklouf **Rev:** Concorde in flight **Rev. Legend:**
CONCORDE 1969 - 2003 **Rev. Designer:** Emma Noble
Edge: Reeded

Date	Mintage	F	VF	XF	Unc	BU
2003	5,000	—	—	—	12.00	15.50

KM# 35b 5 POUNDS
39.9400 g., 0.9166 Gold 1.1770 oz. AGW, 38.6 mm.
Ruler: Elizabeth II **Obv:** Queens portrait **Rev:** Concorde in flight,
October 24, 2003 **Rev. Designer:** Emma Noble **Edge:** Reeded

Date	Mintage	F	VF	XF	Unc	BU
2003 Proof	500	Value: 1,450				

KM# 38 5 POUNDS
28.2800 g., Copper-Nickel, 38.6 mm. **Ruler:** Elizabeth II
Obv: Queens portrait **Rev:** Battleship and transports, HMS
Belfast **Rev. Designer:** Mike Guilfoyle **Edge:** Reeded
Note: D-Day

Date	Mintage	F	VF	XF	Unc	BU
2004	—	—	—	—	15.00	17.50

KM# 38a 5 POUNDS
28.2800 g., 0.9250 Silver 0.8410 oz. ASW, 38.6 mm.
Ruler: Elizabeth II **Obv:** Queens portrait **Rev:** Battleship and
transports **Rev. Designer:** Mike Guilfoyle

Date	Mintage	F	VF	XF	Unc	BU
2004 Proof	10,000	Value: 85.00				

KM# 38b 5 POUNDS
39.9400 g., 0.9167 Gold 1.1771 oz. AGW, 38.6 mm.
Ruler: Elizabeth II **Obv:** Queens portrait **Rev:** Battleship and
transports **Rev. Designer:** Mike Guilfoyle

Date	Mintage	F	VF	XF	Unc	BU
2004 Proof	500	Value: 1,450				

KM# 42 5 POUNDS
28.2800 g., Copper-Nickel, 38.6 mm. **Ruler:** Elizabeth II **Obv:**
Crowned head right **Rev:** Florence Nightingale **Edge:** Reeded

Date	Mintage	F	VF	XF	Unc	BU
2004	—	—	—	—	18.00	20.00

KM# 42a 5 POUNDS
28.2800 g., 0.9250 Silver 0.8410 oz. ASW, 38.6 mm.
Ruler: Elizabeth II **Obv:** Queens portrait **Rev:** Florence
Nightingale **Edge:** Reeded

Date	Mintage	F	VF	XF	Unc	BU
2004 Proof	25,000	Value: 70.00				

KM# 43 5 POUNDS
28.2800 g., Copper-Nickel, 38.6 mm. **Ruler:** Elizabeth II
Subject: 150th Anniversary of the Crimean War **Obv:** Crowned
head right **Rev:** Florence Nightingale head above the Battle of
Inkerman scene with one multicolor soldier **Edge:** Reeded

Date	Mintage	F	VF	XF	Unc	BU
2004 plain	—	—	—	—	25.00	27.50
2004 partial color	—	—	—	—	25.00	27.50

KM# 43a 5 POUNDS
28.2800 g., 0.9250 Silver 0.8410 oz. ASW, 38.6 mm.
Ruler: Elizabeth II **Subject:** 150th Anniversary Crimean War
Obv: Crowned head right **Rev:** Florence Nightingale head above
Battle of Inkerman scene with one multicolor soldier
Edge: Reeded

Date	Mintage	F	VF	XF	Unc	BU
2004 Proof	10,000	Value: 85.00				

KM# 43b 5 POUNDS
39.9400 g., 0.9166 Gold 1.1770 oz. AGW, 38.6 mm. **Ruler:**
Elizabeth II **Subject:** 150th Anniversary Crimean War **Obv:**
Crowned head right **Rev:** Florence Nightingale head above Battle
of Inkerman scene with one multicolor soldier **Edge:** Reeded

Date	Mintage	F	VF	XF	Unc	BU
2004 Proof	500	Value: 1,450				

KM# 47 5 POUNDS
28.2800 g., Copper-Nickel, 38.6 mm. **Ruler:** Elizabeth II
Obv: Queens portrait **Rev:** Locomotive, The Rocket
Rev. Designer: Robert Lowe **Edge:** Reeded

Date	Mintage	F	VF	XF	Unc	BU
2004	—	—	—	—	16.00	18.50

KM# 47a 5 POUNDS
28.2800 g., 0.9250 Silver 0.8410 oz. ASW, 38.6 mm.
Ruler: Elizabeth II **Obv:** Queens portrait **Rev:** Locomotive, The
Rocket **Rev. Designer:** Robert Lowe **Edge:** Reeded

Date	Mintage	F	VF	XF	Unc	BU
2004 Proof	20,000	Value: 60.00				

KM# 47b 5 POUNDS
39.9400 g., 0.9167 Gold 1.1771 oz. AGW, 38.6 mm.
Ruler: Elizabeth II **Obv:** Queens portrait **Rev:** Locomotive, The
Rocket **Rev. Designer:** Robert Lowe **Edge:** Reeded

Date	Mintage	F	VF	XF	Unc	BU
2004 Proof	500	Value: 1,450				

KM# 48 5 POUNDS
28.2800 g., Copper-Nickel, 38.6 mm. **Ruler:** Elizabeth II
Obv: Queens portrait **Rev:** Locomotive, The Royal Scot
Rev. Designer: Robert Lowe **Edge:** Reeded

Date	Mintage	F	VF	XF	Unc	BU
2004	—	—	—	—	16.00	18.50

KM# 48a 5 POUNDS
28.2800 g., 0.9250 Silver 0.8410 oz. ASW, 38.6 mm.
Ruler: Elizabeth II **Obv:** Queens portrait **Rev:** Locomotive, The
Royal Scot **Rev. Designer:** Robert Lowe **Edge:** Reeded

Date	Mintage	F	VF	XF	Unc	BU
2004 Proof	10,000	Value: 60.00				

KM# 49 5 POUNDS
28.2800 g., Copper-Nickel, 38.6 mm. **Ruler:** Elizabeth II
Obv: Queens portrait **Rev:** Locomotive, The Merchant Navy
21C1 **Edge:** Reeded

Date	Mintage	F	VF	XF	Unc	BU
2004	—	—	—	—	16.00	18.50

KM# 49a 5 POUNDS
28.2800 g., 0.9250 Silver 0.8410 oz. ASW, 38.6 mm.
Ruler: Elizabeth II **Obv:** Queens portrait **Rev:** Locomotive, The
Merchant Navy 21C1 **Rev. Designer:** Robert Lowe
Edge: Reeded

Date	Mintage	F	VF	XF	Unc	BU
2004 Proof	10,000	Value: 60.00				

KM# 53a 5 POUNDS
28.2800 g., 0.9250 Silver 0.8410 oz. ASW, 38.6 mm.
Ruler: Elizabeth II **Subject:** End of WWII **Obv:** Elizabeth II by
Maklouf **Rev:** Flag waving crowd **Edge:** Reeded

Date	Mintage	F	VF	XF	Unc	BU
2005 Proof	5,000	Value: 85.00				

KM# 79 5 POUNDS
Copper-Nickel **Ruler:** Elizabeth II **Subject:** 200th Anniversary
Battle of Trafalgar **Obv:** Crowned head right

Date	Mintage	F	VF	XF	Unc	BU
2005	—	—	—	—	16.00	18.50

KM# 83 5 POUNDS
28.4300 g., Silver, 38 mm. **Ruler:** Elizabeth II **Subject:** History
of the Royal Navy **Obv:** Heraldic shield **Rev:** Admiral John
Woodward, partially colored

Date	Mintage	F	VF	XF	Unc	BU
2005 Proof	—	Value: 40.00				

KM# 79a 5 POUNDS

28.2800 g., 0.9250 Silver 0.8410 oz. ASW **Ruler:** Elizabeth II **Subject:** 200th Anniversary Battle of Trafalgar **Obv:** Crowned head right

Date	Mintage	F	VF	XF	Unc	BU
2005 Proof	—	Value: 60.00				

KM# 53b 5 POUNDS

39.9400 g., 0.9167 Gold 1.1771 oz. AGW, 38.6 mm. **Ruler:** Elizabeth II **Subject:** End of WWII **Obv:** Elizabeth II by Maklouf **Rev:** Flag waving crowd **Edge:** Reeded

Date	Mintage	F	VF	XF	Unc	BU
2005 Proof	150	Value: 1,500				

KM# 54a 5 POUNDS

39.9400 g., 0.9167 Gold 1.1771 oz. AGW, 38.6 mm. **Ruler:** Elizabeth II **Subject:** WWII Liberation **Obv:** Elizabeth II by Maklouf **Rev:** Churchill flashing the "V" sign **Edge:** Reeded

Date	Mintage	F	VF	XF	Unc	BU
2005 Proof	150	Value: 1,500				

KM# 66 5 POUNDS

28.2800 g., Copper-Nickel, 38.6 mm. **Ruler:** Elizabeth II **Subject:** Viscount Samuel Hood on his flagship after the Battle of Saints Passage in 1782 **Obv:** Queens portrait **Rev. Designer:** Willem Vis

Date	Mintage	F	VF	XF	Unc	BU
2005	—	—	—	—	13.50	15.00

KM# 66a 5 POUNDS

28.2800 g., 0.9250 Silver 0.8410 oz. ASW, 38.6 mm. **Ruler:** Elizabeth II **Subject:** Viscount Samuel Hood on his flagship after the Battle of Saints Passage in 1782 **Obv:** Queens portrait **Rev. Designer:** Willem Vis **Note:** Ensign is colored.

Date	Mintage	F	VF	XF	Unc	BU
2005 Proof	—	Value: 50.00				

KM# 68 5 POUNDS

28.2800 g., Copper-Nickel, 38.6 mm. **Ruler:** Elizabeth II **Obv:** Crowned head right **Rev:** HMS Revenge fighting at Azores, 1591 **Rev. Designer:** Willem Vis

Date	Mintage	F	VF	XF	Unc	BU
2005	—	—	—	—	12.00	14.00

KM# 68a 5 POUNDS

28.2800 g., 0.9250 Silver 0.8410 oz. ASW, 38.6 mm. **Ruler:** Elizabeth II **Obv:** Crowned head right **Rev:** HMS Revenge fighting at Azores, 1591 **Rev. Designer:** Willem Vis **Note:** Ensign is colorized.

Date	Mintage	F	VF	XF	Unc	BU
2005 Proof	—	Value: 60.00				

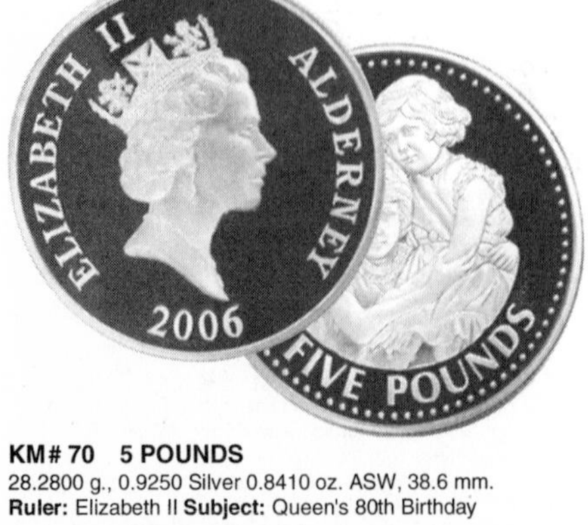

KM# 70 5 POUNDS

28.2800 g., 0.9250 Silver 0.8410 oz. ASW, 38.6 mm. **Ruler:** Elizabeth II **Subject:** Queen's 80th Birthday **Obv:** Crowned bust right - gilt **Obv. Legend:** ELIZABETH II - ALDERNARY **Rev:** 1/2 length figures of Queen mother and daughter hugging, facing

Date	Mintage	F	VF	XF	Unc	BU
2006 Proof	—	Value: 40.00				

KM# 85 5 POUNDS

28.2800 g., Copper-Nickel, 38.61 mm. **Ruler:** Elizabeth II **Subject:** Mini Cooper 50th Anniversary **Rev:** 1959 Mini Cooper on tiled floor **Rev. Designer:** David Cornell

Date	Mintage	F	VF	XF	Unc	BU
2009	50,000	—	—	—	—	17.50

KM# 86 5 POUNDS

28.2800 g., 0.9250 Silver 0.8410 oz. ASW, 38.61 mm. **Ruler:** Elizabeth II **Subject:** Mini Cooper, 50th Anniversary **Rev:** 1959 Mini Cooper multicolor British flag on roof **Rev. Designer:** David Cornell

Date	Mintage	F	VF	XF	Unc	BU
2009 Proof	—	Value: 75.00				

KM# 87 5 POUNDS

28.2800 g., 0.9250 Silver 0.8410 oz. ASW, 38.61 mm. **Ruler:** Elizabeth II **Subject:** Mini Cooper, 50th Anniversary **Rev:** Mini Cooper, red and pink flowers **Rev. Designer:** David Cornell

Date	Mintage	F	VF	XF	Unc	BU
2009 Proof	2,000	Value: 75.00				

KM# 88 5 POUNDS

28.2800 g., 0.9250 Silver 0.8410 oz. ASW, 38.61 mm. **Ruler:** Elizabeth II **Subject:** Mini Cooper, 50th Anniversary **Rev:** Mini Cooper, 4 views **Rev. Designer:** Kerry Jones

Date	Mintage	F	VF	XF	Unc	BU
2009 Proof	2,000	Value: 75.00				

KM# 89 5 POUNDS

28.2800 g., 0.9250 Silver 0.8410 oz. ASW, 38.61 mm. **Ruler:** Elizabeth II **Subject:** Mini Cooper, 50th Anniversary **Rev:** Rally Minis **Rev. Designer:** Kerry Jones and David Cornell

Date	Mintage	F	VF	XF	Unc	BU
2009 Proof	2,000	Value: 75.00				

KM# 36 10 POUNDS

155.5170 g., 0.9250 Silver 4.6248 oz. ASW, 65.06 mm. **Ruler:** Elizabeth II **Subject:** Last Flight of the Concorde **Obv:** Crowned bust right **Obv. Legend:** ELIIZABETH II - ALDERNEY **Obv. Designer:** Raphael Maklouf **Rev:** Concorde in flight **Rev. Legend:** CONCORDE 1969 - 2003 **Rev. Designer:** Emma Noble **Edge:** Reeded **Note:** Illustration reduced.

Date	Mintage	F	VF	XF	Unc	BU
2003 Proof	1,969	Value: 200				

KM# 55 10 POUNDS

155.5100 g., 0.9250 Silver 4.6246 oz. ASW, 65 mm. **Ruler:** Elizabeth II **Subject:** WWII Liberation **Obv:** Elizabeth II by Maklouf sign **Rev:** Churchill flashing the "V" **Edge:** Reeded

Date	Mintage	F	VF	XF	Unc	BU
2005 Proof	1,945	Value: 350				

KM# 82 10 POUNDS

155.5170 g., Silver, 65.03 mm. **Ruler:** Elizabeth II **Obv:** Crowned bust right **Obv. Legend:** ELIZABETH II - ALDERNEY **Obv. Designer:** Raphael Maklouf **Rev:** Four small gilt coinage busts in ornate quadralobe **Rev. Legend:** + HER MAJESTY QUEEN ELIZABETH II + EIGHTIETH BIRTHDAY + **Rev. Designer:** Michael Guilfoyle **Edge:** Reeded, gilt **Note:** Illustration reduced

Date	Mintage	F	VF	XF	Unc	BU
2006 Proof	1,926	Value: 200				

KM# 61 25 POUNDS

7.9800 g., 0.9167 Gold 0.2352 oz. AGW, 22 mm. **Ruler:** Elizabeth II **Subject:** Queen's 75th Birthday **Obv:** Queens portrait right **Obv. Designer:** Raphael Maklouf **Rev:** Queen in casual dress surrounded by rose, thistle, daffodil and pimpernel **Rev. Designer:** David Cornell

Date	Mintage	F	VF	XF	Unc	BU
2001 Proof	—	Value: 325				

KM# 74 25 POUNDS

7.9800 g., 0.9166 Gold 0.2352 oz. AGW **Ruler:** Elizabeth II **Subject:** Queen Elizabet II - Golden Jubilee of Reign **Obv:** Crowned head right **Rev:** Honor guard and trumpets

Date	Mintage	F	VF	XF	Unc	BU
2002 Proof	—	Value: 325				

KM# 28 25 POUNDS

7.9800 g., 0.9167 Gold 0.2352 oz. AGW, 22.05 mm. **Ruler:** Elizabeth II **Subject:** 5th Anniversary Death of Princess Diana **Obv:** Queens portrait **Rev:** Diana's cameo portrait above denomination **Rev. Designer:** Avril Vaughan **Edge:** Reeded

Date	Mintage	VG	F	VF	XF	Unc
2002 Proof	2,500	Value: 300				

KM# 30 25 POUNDS

7.9800 g., 0.9166 Gold 0.2352 oz. AGW, 22 mm. **Ruler:** Elizabeth II **Subject:** 150th Anniversary Death of the Duke of Wellington **Obv:** Queens portrait **Rev:** Coat of arms, castle and portrait **Rev. Designer:** Willem Vis **Edge:** Reeded

Date	Mintage	VG	F	VF	XF	Unc
2002 Proof	2,500	Value: 314				

KM# 58 25 POUNDS

7.9800 g., 0.9166 Gold 0.2352 oz. AGW, 22 mm. **Ruler:** Elizabeth II **Subject:** Queen Elizabeth II - Golden Jubilee of Reign **Obv:** Crowned head right **Rev:** Sword hilt and denomination with royal arms in background

Date	Mintage	F	VF	XF	Unc	BU
2002 Proof	2,500	Value: 315				

KM# 32 25 POUNDS

7.9800 g., 0.9166 Gold 0.2352 oz. AGW, 22 mm. **Ruler:** Elizabeth II **Subject:** Prince William **Obv:** Queens portrait **Rev:** Portrait with open shirt collar **Edge:** Reeded

Date	Mintage	F	VF	XF	Unc	BU
2003 Proof	1,500	Value: 345				

KM# 46 25 POUNDS

7.9800 g., 0.9167 Gold 0.2352 oz. AGW, 22 mm. **Ruler:** Elizabeth II **Obv:** Queens portrait **Rev:** HMS Mary Rose **Rev. Designer:** Willem Vis **Edge:** Reeded

Date	Mintage	F	VF	XF	Unc	BU
2003 Proof	2,500	Value: 365				

KM# 39 25 POUNDS

7.9800 g., 0.9167 Gold 0.2352 oz. AGW, 22 mm. **Ruler:** Elizabeth II **Subject:** D-Day **Obv:** Queens portrait **Rev:** Battleship and transports **Edge:** Reeded

Date	Mintage	F	VF	XF	Unc	BU
2004 Proof	500	Value: 345				

KM# 50 25 POUNDS

7.9800 g., 0.9167 Gold 0.2352 oz. AGW, 22 mm. **Ruler:** Elizabeth II **Obv:** Queens portrait **Rev:** Locomotive, The Rocket **Rev. Designer:** Robert Lowe **Edge:** Reeded

Date	Mintage	F	VF	XF	Unc	BU
2004 Proof	2,500	Value: 365				

KM# 51 25 POUNDS

7.9800 g., 0.9167 Gold 0.2352 oz. AGW, 22 mm. **Ruler:** Elizabeth II **Obv:** Queens portrait **Rev:** Locomotive, The Merchant Navy 21C1 **Rev. Designer:** Robert Lowe **Edge:** Reeded

Date	Mintage	F	VF	XF	Unc	BU
2004 Proof	1,500	Value: 365				

KM# 67 25 POUNDS

7.9800 g., 0.9167 Gold 0.2352 oz. AGW, 22 mm. **Ruler:** Elizabeth II **Subject:** Viscount Samuel Hood on his flagship after the Battle of Saints Passage in 1782 **Obv:** Queens portrait **Rev. Designer:** Willem Vis

Date	Mintage	F	VF	XF	Unc	BU
2005 Proof	—	Value: 315				

KM# 69 25 POUNDS

7.9800 g., 0.9167 Gold 0.2352 oz. AGW, 22 mm. **Ruler:** Elizabeth II **Obv:** Queens portrait right **Rev:** HMS Revenge fighting at Azores, 1591 **Rev. Designer:** Willem Vis

Date	Mintage	F	VF	XF	Unc	BU
2005 Proof	—	Value: 365				

KM# 62 50 POUNDS

1000.0000 g., 0.9250 Silver 29.738 oz. ASW, 100 mm. **Ruler:** Elizabeth II **Subject:** 50th Anniversary of Coronation **Obv:** Queens portrait right **Rev:** State coach in which the Queen travelled to and from her coronation

Date	Mintage	F	VF	XF	Unc	BU
2003 Proof	—	Value: 1,000				

KM# 33 50 POUNDS

1000.0000 g., 0.9250 Silver 29.738 oz. ASW, 100 mm. **Ruler:** Elizabeth II **Subject:** Prince William **Obv:** Queens portrait **Rev:** Portrait with open shirt collar **Edge:** Reeded

Date	Mintage	F	VF	XF	Unc	BU
2003 Proof	500	Value: 995				

KM# 63 50 POUNDS

1000.0000 g., 0.9250 Silver 29.738 oz. ASW, 100 mm. **Ruler:** Elizabeth II **Subject:** 50th Anniversary of Coronation **Obv:** Queens portrait right **Rev:** St. Edward's crown, royal scepter, orb of England

Date	Mintage	F	VF	XF	Unc	BU
2003 Proof	—	Value: 1,000				

KM# 64 50 POUNDS

1000.0000 g., 0.9250 Silver 29.738 oz. ASW, 100 mm. **Ruler:** Elizabeth II **Subject:** 50th Anniversary of Coronation **Obv:** Queens portrait right **Rev:** Queen on horseback dressed in the ceremonial uniform of the Colonel in Chief of the Household Brigade

Date	Mintage	F	VF	XF	Unc	BU
2003 Proof	—	Value: 1,000				

KM# 65 50 POUNDS

1000.0000 g., 0.9250 Silver 29.738 oz. ASW, 100 mm. **Ruler:** Elizabeth II **Subject:** 50th Anniversary of Coronation **Obv:** Queens portrait right **Rev:** The Queen crowned, seated, holding the orb and scepter

Date	Mintage	F	VF	XF	Unc	BU
2003 Proof	—	Value: 1,000				

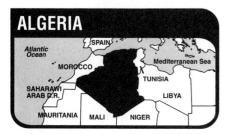

KM# 40 50 POUNDS
1000.0000 g., 0.9250 Silver 29.738 oz. ASW, 100 mm.
Ruler: Elizabeth II **Subject:** D-Day **Obv:** Queens portrait
Rev: US and British troops wading ashore **Rev. Designer:** Matthew Bonaccorsi **Edge:** Reeded

Date	Mintage	F	VF	XF	Unc	BU
2004 Proof	600	Value: 1,200				

KM# 80 50 POUNDS
1000.0000 g., 0.9250 Silver 29.738 oz. ASW **Ruler:** Elizabeth II
Subject: 200th Anniversary Battle of Trafalgar **Obv:** Crowned head right

Date	Mintage	F	VF	XF	Unc	BU
2005 Proof	—	Value: 1,200				

KM# 34 100 POUNDS
1000.0000 g., 0.9166 Gold 29.468 oz. AGW, 100 mm.
Ruler: Elizabeth II **Subject:** Prince William **Obv:** Queens portrait
Rev: Portrait with open shirt collar **Edge:** Reeded

Date	Mintage	F	VF	XF	Unc	BU
2003 Proof	—	Value: 37,500				

KM# 81 100 POUNDS
1000.0000 g., 0.9166 Gold 29.468 oz. AGW **Ruler:** Elizabeth II
Subject: 200th Anniversary Battle of Trafalgar **Obv:** Crowned head right

Date	Mintage	F	VF	XF	Unc	BU
2005 Proof	—	Value: 37,500				

KM# 37 1000 POUNDS
1090.8600 g., 0.9166 Gold 32.145 oz. AGW, 100 mm.
Ruler: Elizabeth II **Subject:** Last Flight of the Concorde
Obv: Queens portrait **Rev:** Concorde in flight **Edge:** Reeded

Date	Mintage	F	VF	XF	Unc	BU
2003 Proof	34	Value: 41,500				

KM# 41 1000 POUNDS
1000.0000 g., 0.9167 Gold 29.471 oz. AGW, 100 mm.
Ruler: Elizabeth II **Subject:** D-Day **Obv:** Queens portrait
Rev: US and British troops wading ashore **Rev. Designer:** Matthew Bonaccorsi **Edge:** Reeded

Date	Mintage	F	VF	XF	Unc	BU
2004 Proof	60	Value: 37,500				

MINT SETS

KM#	Date	Mintage	Identification	Issue Price	Mkt Val
MS1	2004 (1)	—	Alderney KM#43, Guernsey KM#155, Jersey KM#126, 150th Anniversary of the Crimean War	—	80.00

ALGERIA

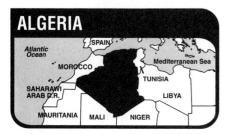

The Democratic and Popular Republic of Algeria, a North African country fronting on the Mediterranean Sea between Tunisia and Morocco, has an area of 919,595 sq. mi. (2,381,740 sq. km.) and a population of 31.6 million. Capital: Algiers (Alger). Most of the country's working population is engaged in agriculture although a recent industrial diversification, financed by oil revenues, is making steady progress. Wines, fruits, iron and zinc ores, phosphates, tobacco products, liquified natural gas, and petroleum are exported.

MONETARY SYSTEMS
100 Centimes = 1 Franc

REPUBLIC

MONETARY SYSTEM
100 Centimes = 1 Dinar

STANDARD COINAGE

KM# 127 1/4 DINAR
1.1400 g., Aluminum, 16.53 mm. **Subject:** Fennec Fox
Obv: Value in small circle **Rev:** Head facing

Date	Mintage	F	VF	XF	Unc	BU
2003-AH1423	—	—	1.50	3.00	4.50	5.50

KM# 129 DINAR
4.2400 g., Steel, 20.48 mm. **Obv:** Value on silhouette of country, within circle **Rev:** African buffalo's head 3/4 left, ancient drawings above **Edge:** Plain

Date	Mintage	F	VF	XF	Unc	BU
AH1422-2002	—	—	1.00	2.00	3.50	5.50
AH1423-2002	—	—	1.00	2.00	3.50	5.50
AH1423-2003	—	—	1.00	2.00	3.50	5.50
AH1424-2003	—	—	1.00	2.00	3.50	5.50
AH1424-2004	—	—	1.00	2.00	3.50	5.50
AH1426-2005	—	—	1.00	2.00	3.50	5.50
AH1427-2006	—	—	1.00	2.00	3.50	5.50
AH1428-2007	—	—	1.00	2.00	3.50	5.50

KM# 130 2 DINARS
5.1300 g., Steel, 22.5 mm. **Obv:** Value on silhouette of country **Rev:** Dromedary camel's head right **Edge:** Plain

Date	Mintage	F	VF	XF	Unc	BU
AH1422-2002	—	—	1.00	2.00	4.00	6.00
AH1423-2002	—	—	1.00	2.00	4.00	6.00
AH1424-2003	—	—	1.00	2.00	4.00	6.00
AH1424-2004	—	—	1.00	2.00	4.00	6.00
AH1426-2005	—	—	1.00	2.00	4.00	6.00
AH1427-2006	—	—	1.00	2.00	4.00	6.00
AH1428-2007	—	—	1.00	2.00	4.00	6.00

KM# 123 5 DINARS
6.2000 g., Steel, 24.43 mm. **Obv:** Denomination within circle
Rev: Forepart of African elephant right **Edge:** Plain

Date	Mintage	F	VF	XF	Unc	BU
AH1422-2003	—	—	1.50	3.50	6.50	9.50
AH1423-2003	—	—	1.50	3.50	6.50	9.50
AH1424-2003	—	—	1.00	3.00	5.50	8.00
AH1424-2004	—	—	1.50	3.50	6.50	9.50
AH1426-2005	—	—	1.00	3.00	5.50	8.00
AH1426-2006	—	—	1.00	3.50	6.50	9.50
AH1427-2006	—	—	1.00	3.00	5.50	8.00
AH1428-2007	—	—	1.00	3.00	5.50	8.00

KM# 124 10 DINARS
4.9500 g., Bi-Metallic Aluminum center in Steel ring, 26.5 mm.
Obv: Denomination **Rev:** Barbary falcon's head right **Edge:** Plain

Date	Mintage	F	VF	XF	Unc	BU
AH1422-2002	—	—	1.75	4.00	9.00	—
AH1423-2002	—	—	1.75	4.00	9.00	—
AH1424-2003	—	—	1.75	4.00	9.00	—
AH1425-2004	—	—	1.75	4.00	9.00	—
AH1427-2006	—	—	1.75	4.00	9.00	—

KM# 125 20 DINARS
8.6200 g., Bi-Metallic Brass center in Steel ring, 27.5 mm.
Subject: Lion **Obv:** Denomination **Rev:** Head left

Date	Mintage	F	VF	XF	Unc	BU
AH1424-2004	—	—	3.00	6.00	12.00	—
AH1426-2005	—	—	3.00	6.00	12.00	—
AH1428-2007	—	—	—	6.00	12.00	—

KM# 126 50 DINARS
9.2700 g., Bi-Metallic Steel center in Brass ring, 28.5 mm.
Obv: Denomination **Rev:** Dama gazelle with head left

Date	Mintage	F	VF	XF	Unc	BU
AH1424-2003	—	—	4.00	8.00	16.50	—
AH1425-2004	—	—	4.00	8.00	16.50	—

KM# 138 50 DINARS
Bi-Metallic Stainless Steel center in Aluminum-Nickel-Bronze ring
Subject: 50th Anniversary of Liberation **Obv:** Large value
Rev: Stylized flag and two revolutionaries

Date	Mintage	F	VF	XF	Unc	BU
2004	3,000,000	—	—	5.00	12.50	15.00

KM# 132 100 DINARS
11.0000 g., Bi-Metallic Aluminum-Bronze center in Stainless Steel ring, 29.5 mm. **Obv:** Denomination stylized with reverse design **Rev:** Horse head right

Date	Mintage	F	VF	XF	Unc	BU
AH1422-2002	—	—	5.00	10.00	20.00	24.00
AH1423-2002	—	—	5.00	10.00	20.00	24.00
AH1423-2003	—	—	5.00	10.00	20.00	24.00
AH1425-2004	—	—	5.00	10.00	20.00	24.00

KM# 137 100 DINARS
11.0000 g., Bi-Metallic Brass center in Stainless Steel ring, 29.5 mm. **Subject:** 40th Anniversary of Independence
Obv: Stylized value using palm tree in doorway and two coins depicting horses' heads **Rev:** Number 40 and stylized face
Edge: Reeded

Date	Mintage	F	VF	XF	Unc	BU
AH1422-2002	—	—	—	—	25.00	28.00

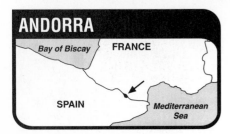

ANDORRA

Bay of Biscay — FRANCE

SPAIN — *Mediterranean Sea*

Principality of Andorra (Principat d'Andorra), situated on the southern slopes of the Pyrenees Mountains between France and Spain, has an area of 181 sq. mi. (453 sq. km.) and a population of 80,000. Capital: Andorra la Vella. Tourism is the chief source of income. Timber, cattle and derivatives, and furniture are exported.

RULER
Joan D.M. Bisbe D'Urgell I

MONETARY SYSTEM
100 Centims = 1 Diner
NOTE: The Diners have been struck for collectors while the Euro is used in everyday commerce.

MINT MARK
Crowned M = Madrid

PRINCIPALITY

DECIMAL COINAGE

KM# 176 CENTIM
2.1000 g., Aluminum, 27 mm. **Subject:** Charlemagne **Obv:** National arms, date below **Rev:** Crowned head facing, denomination below **Edge:** Plain

Date	Mintage	F	VF	XF	Unc	BU
2002	—	—	—	—	1.50	2.00

KM# 177 CENTIM
2.1300 g., Aluminum, 27 mm. **Subject:** Isard **Obv:** National arms, date below **Rev:** Chamois left facing, denomination at right **Edge:** Plain

Date	Mintage	F	VF	XF	Unc	BU
2002	—	—	—	—	1.50	2.00

KM# 178 CENTIM
2.1400 g., Aluminum, 27 mm. **Subject:** Agnus Dei **Obv:** National arms **Rev:** Lamb of God **Edge:** Plain

Date	Mintage	F	VF	XF	Unc	BU
2002	—	—	—	—	1.00	1.50

KM# 198 CENTIM
Aluminum-Magnesium, 27 mm. **Obv:** National arms **Rev:** A piece of the wall paintings belonging to the 12th century Romanesque church of St. Marti de la Cortinado

Date	Mintage	F	VF	XF	Unc	BU
2003	—	—	—	—	1.25	1.75

KM# 200 CENTIM
Aluminum-Magnesium, 27 mm. **Obv:** National arms **Rev:** Image of the 12th century Romanesque church of St. Miquel d'Engolasters with its bell tower, the Romanesque apse, the small portico and the large Lombard windows

Date	Mintage	F	VF	XF	Unc	BU
2003	—	—	—	—	1.25	1.75

KM# 199 CENTIM
Aluminum-Magnesium, 27 mm. **Obv:** National arms **Rev:** Pont de la Margineda, reproduction of the bridge

Date	Mintage	F	VF	XF	Unc	BU
2003	—	—	—	—	1.25	1.75

KM# 229 CENTIM
Aluminum **Obv:** Crowned arms **Rev:** Santa Coloma

Date	Mintage	F	VF	XF	Unc	BU
2004	—	—	—	—	0.90	1.20

KM# 230 CENTIM
Aluminum **Obv:** Crowned arms **Rev:** Sant Martí de la Cortinada

Date	Mintage	F	VF	XF	Unc	BU
2004	—	—	—	—	0.90	1.20

KM# 231 CENTIM
Aluminum **Obv:** Crowned arms **Rev:** Altar at Santa Coloma

Date	Mintage	F	VF	XF	Unc	BU
2004	—	—	—	—	0.90	1.20

KM# 236 CENTIM
Aluminum-Bronze **Subject:** Death of Pope John-Paul II **Obv:** National arms

Date	Mintage	F	VF	XF	Unc	BU
2005	—	—	—	0.30	0.80	1.20

KM# 245 CENTIM
Aluminum-Bronze **Obv:** National arms **Rev:** Findern flower - "Poet's Daffodil"

Date	Mintage	F	VF	XF	Unc	BU
2005	—	—	—	0.30	0.80	1.20

KM# 179 2 CENTIMS
Brass, 18 mm. **Subject:** Grandalla **Obv:** National arms **Rev:** Edelweiss flower **Edge:** Plain

Date	Mintage	F	VF	XF	Unc	BU
2002	—	—	—	—	1.50	2.00

KM# 201 2 CENTIMS
Copper-Zinc-Nickel, 18.15 mm. **Obv:** National arms **Rev:** Clavell Deltoide, a flower found in Andorra

Date	Mintage	F	VF	XF	Unc	BU
2003	—	—	—	—	1.75	2.50

KM# 232 2 CENTIMS
Brass **Obv:** Crowned arms **Rev:** West Gothic robe

Date	Mintage	F	VF	XF	Unc	BU
2004	—	—	—	—	1.20	1.60

KM# 237 2 CENTIMS
Aluminum-Bronze **Subject:** Death of Pope John-Paul II **Obv:** National arms

Date	Mintage	F	VF	XF	Unc	BU
2005	—	—	—	0.50	1.20	1.60

KM# 246 2 CENTIMS
Aluminum-Bronze **Obv:** National arms **Rev:** Pyrenean Chamois

Date	Mintage	F	VF	XF	Unc	BU
2005	—	—	—	0.50	1.20	1.60

KM# 180 5 CENTIMS
Brass, 21.8 mm. **Subject:** Squirrel **Obv:** National arms **Rev:** Red Squirrel on tree stump **Edge:** Plain

Date	Mintage	F	VF	XF	Unc	BU
2002	—	—	—	—	2.00	2.50

KM# 181 5 CENTIMS
Brass, 21.8 mm. **Subject:** Gall Fer **Obv:** National arms **Rev:** Male Eurasian Capercaillie (grouse) displaying plumage **Edge:** Plain

Date	Mintage	F	VF	XF	Unc	BU
2002	—	—	—	—	2.00	2.50

KM# 203 5 CENTIMS
Copper-Zinc, 21.8 mm. **Obv:** National arms **Rev:** Wall painting from the 11th century church of Sant Serni de Nagol showing an eagle

Date	Mintage	F	VF	XF	Unc	BU
2003	—	—	—	—	2.25	2.75

KM# 202 5 CENTIMS
Copper-Zinc, 21.8 mm. **Obv:** National arms **Rev:** The cross of Seven Arms, traditional Gothic cross

Date	Mintage	F	VF	XF	Unc	BU
2003	—	—	—	—	2.25	2.75

KM# 233 5 CENTIMS
Brass **Obv:** Crowned arms **Rev:** Gothic cross

Date	Mintage	F	VF	XF	Unc	BU
2004	—	—	—	—	1.80	2.40

KM# 234 5 CENTIMS
Brass **Obv:** Crowned arms **Rev:** Lady of Canolic

Date	Mintage	F	VF	XF	Unc	BU
2004	—	—	—	—	1.80	2.40

KM# 238 5 CENTIMS
Aluminum-Bronze **Subject:** Death of Pope John-Paul II **Obv:** National arms

Date	Mintage	F	VF	XF	Unc	BU
2005	—	—	—	0.70	1.80	2.40

KM# 247 5 CENTIMS
Aluminum-Bronze **Obv:** National arms **Rev:** Wall painting from Santa Coloma church

Date	Mintage	F	VF	XF	Unc	BU
2005	—	—	—	0.70	1.80	2.40

KM# 182 10 CENTIMS
Brass **Subject:** St. Joan de Caselles **Obv:** National arms **Rev:** Tower and building **Edge:** Plain

Date	Mintage	F	VF	XF	Unc	BU
2002	—	—	—	—	3.00	4.00

KM# 204 10 CENTIMS
Nickel Plated Steel, 27.8 mm. **Obv:** National arms **Rev:** 12th century wood carving image from Our Lady of Meritxell

Date	Mintage	F	VF	XF	Unc	BU
2003	—	—	—	—	3.50	4.50

KM# 235 10 CENTIMS
Nickel Plated Steel **Obv:** Crowned arms **Rev:** Casa de la Vall

Date	Mintage	F	VF	XF	Unc	BU
2004	—	—	—	—	3.00	4.00

KM# 239 10 CENTIMS
Copper-Nickel **Subject:** Death of Pope John-Paul II **Obv:** National arms

Date	Mintage	F	VF	XF	Unc	BU
2005	—	—	—	1.00	2.40	3.20

KM# 248 10 CENTIMS
Copper-Nickel **Obv:** National arms **Rev:** Sant Vincenc Denclar church

Date	Mintage	F	VF	XF	Unc	BU
2005	—	—	—	1.00	2.40	3.20

KM# 240 25 CENTIMS
Copper-Nickel **Subject:** Death of Pope John-Paul II **Obv:** National arms

Date	Mintage	F	VF	XF	Unc	BU
2005	—	—	—	1.20	3.00	4.00

KM# 249 25 CENTIMS
Copper-Nickel **Obv:** National arms **Rev:** Our Lady of Meritxell sanctuary

Date	Mintage	F	VF	XF	Unc	BU
2005	—	—	—	1.20	3.00	4.00

KM# 241 50 CENTIMS
Copper-Nickel **Subject:** Death of Pope John-Paul II **Obv:** National arms

Date	Mintage	F	VF	XF	Unc	BU
2005	—	—	—	2.70	3.60	4.80

KM# 242 DINER
Bi-Metallic Aluminum-Nickel-Bronze center in Copper-Nickel ring **Subject:** Death of Pope John-Paul II **Obv:** National arms

Date	Mintage	F	VF	XF	Unc	BU
2005	—	—	—	1.60	4.00	6.00

KM# 251 DINER
Bi-Metallic Aluminum-Nickel-Bronze center in Copper-Nickel ring **Obv:** National arms **Rev:** Our Lady of Meritxell

Date	Mintage	F	VF	XF	Unc	BU
2005	—	—	—	1.80	4.50	6.00

KM# 243 2 DINERS
Bi-Metallic Copper-Nickel center in Aluminum-Nickel-Bronze ring **Subject:** Death of Pope John-Paul II **Obv:** National arms

Date	Mintage	F	VF	XF	Unc	BU
2005	—	—	—	2.40	6.00	8.00

KM# 252 2 DINERS
Bi-Metallic Copper-Nickel center in Aluminum-Nickel-Bronze ring **Obv:** National arms **Rev:** Signing of the Umpirage between the Bishop of Urgell and Count of Foix

Date	Mintage	F	VF	XF	Unc	BU
2005	—	—	—	2.40	6.00	8.00

KM# 193 5 DINERS
1.2400 g., 0.9990 Gold 0.0398 oz. AGW, 13.92 mm. **Obv:** National arms **Rev:** The Escorial Palace in Madrid **Edge:** Reeded

Date	Mintage	F	VF	XF	Unc	BU
2004 Proof	3,000	Value: 65.00				

KM# 194 5 DINERS
1.2400 g., 0.9990 Gold 0.0398 oz. AGW, 13.92 mm.
Obv: National arms **Rev:** Eiffel Tower **Edge:** Reeded

Date	Mintage	F	VF	XF	Unc	BU
2004 Proof	3,000	Value: 65.00				

KM# 195 5 DINERS
1.2400 g., 0.9990 Gold 0.0398 oz. AGW, 13.92 mm. **Obv:**
National arms **Rev:** Atomic model monument **Edge:** Reeded

Date	Mintage	F	VF	XF	Unc	BU
2004 Proof	3,000	Value: 65.00				

KM# 196 5 DINERS
1.2400 g., 0.9990 Gold 0.0398 oz. AGW, 13.92 mm. **Subject:**
Andorran membership in the United Nations **Obv:** National arms
Rev: Seated woman, world globe and UN logo **Edge:** Reeded

Date	Mintage	F	VF	XF	Unc	BU
2004 Proof	3,000	Value: 75.00				

KM# 172 10 DINERS
31.4700 g., 0.9250 Silver 0.9359 oz. ASW, 38.6 mm. **Subject:**
Europa **Obv:** National arms **Rev:** Europa in chariot **Edge:** Reeded

Date	Mintage	F	VF	XF	Unc	BU
2001 Proof	15,000	Value: 40.00				

KM# 173 10 DINERS
31.4700 g., 0.9250 Silver 0.9359 oz. ASW, 38.6 mm.
Subject: Concordia Europea **Obv:** National arms **Rev:** Two
crowned women holding hands **Edge:** Reeded

Date	Mintage	F	VF	XF	Unc	BU
2001 Proof	15,000	Value: 40.00				

KM# 175 10 DINERS
31.4700 g., 0.9250 Silver 0.9359 oz. ASW, 38.6 mm. **Subject:**
Olympics **Obv:** National arms **Rev:** Snowboarder **Edge:** Reeded

Date	Mintage	F	VF	XF	Unc	BU
2002 Proof	15,000	Value: 40.00				

KM# 183 10 DINERS
31.4700 g., 0.9250 Silver 0.9359 oz. ASW, 38.6 mm. **Subject:**
Mouflon **Obv:** National arms **Rev:** Mouflon ram **Edge:** Reeded

Date	Mintage	F	VF	XF	Unc	BU
2002 Proof	15,000	Value: 50.00				

KM# 188 10 DINERS
31.1035 g., 0.9250 Silver 0.9250 oz. ASW, 38.6 mm.
Obv: National arms **Rev:** Pope with doves **Edge:** Reeded

Date	Mintage	F	VF	XF	Unc	BU
2004 Proof	9,999	Value: 40.00				

KM# 189 10 DINERS
31.1035 g., 0.9250 Silver 0.9250 oz. ASW, 38.6 mm. **Obv:** National
arms **Rev:** Pope holding staff with 2 hands **Edge:** Reeded

Date	Mintage	F	VF	XF	Unc	BU
2004 Proof	9,999	Value: 40.00				

KM# 190 10 DINERS
31.1035 g., 0.9250 Silver 0.9250 oz. ASW, 38.6 mm. **Obv:**
National arms **Rev:** Pope raising a chalice **Edge:** Reeded

Date	Mintage	F	VF	XF	Unc	BU
2004 Proof	9,999	Value: 40.00				

KM# 191 10 DINERS
31.1035 g., 0.9250 Silver 0.9250 oz. ASW, 38.6 mm.
Obv: National arms **Rev:** Pope with hammer **Edge:** Reeded

Date	Mintage	F	VF	XF	Unc	BU
2004 Proof	9,999	Value: 40.00				

KM# 192 10 DINERS
31.1035 g., 0.9250 Silver 0.9250 oz. ASW, 38.6 mm. **Obv:**
National arms **Rev:** Gold-plated Pope writing **Edge:** Reeded

Date	Mintage	F	VF	XF	Unc	BU
2004 Proof	9,999	Value: 40.00				

KM# 205 10 DINERS
31.1000 g., 0.9250 Silver 0.9249 oz. ASW, 38.6 mm.
Obv. Designer: National arms **Rev:** Gold plated Pope John Paul
II wearing mitre and holding crucifix staff **Edge:** Reeded

Date	Mintage	F	VF	XF	Unc	BU
2005 Proof	9,999	Value: 40.00				

KM# 206 10 DINERS
31.1000 g., 0.9250 Silver 0.9249 oz. ASW, 38.6 mm.
Obv: National arms **Rev:** Pope John Paul II with the Holy Virgin
in background **Edge:** Reeded

Date	Mintage	F	VF	XF	Unc	BU
2005 Proof	9,999	Value: 40.00				

KM# 207 10 DINERS
31.1000 g., 0.9250 Silver 0.9249 oz. ASW, 38.6 mm.
Obv: National arms **Rev:** Pope John Paul II in prayer with crucifix
at right **Edge:** Reeded

Date	Mintage	F	VF	XF	Unc	BU
2005 Proof	9,999	Value: 40.00				

KM# 208 10 DINERS
31.1000 g., 0.9250 Silver 0.9249 oz. ASW, 38.6 mm.
Obv: National arms **Rev:** Pope John Paul II blessing Vatican
crowd **Edge:** Reeded

Date	Mintage	F	VF	XF	Unc	BU
2005 Proof	9,999	Value: 40.00				

KM# 209 10 DINERS
31.1000 g., 0.9250 Silver 0.9249 oz. ASW, 38.6 mm.
Obv: National arms **Rev:** Pope John Paul II and Mother Teresa
Edge: Reeded

Date	Mintage	F	VF	XF	Unc	BU
2005 Proof	9,999	Value: 40.00				

KM# 210 10 DINERS

31.1000 g., 0.9250 Silver 0.9249 oz. ASW, 38.6 mm. **Obv:** National arms **Rev:** Bearded man above Vatican City **Edge:** Reeded

Date	Mintage	F	VF	XF	Unc	BU
2005 Proof	9,999	Value: 40.00				

KM# 211 10 DINERS

31.1000 g., 0.9250 Silver 0.9249 oz. ASW, 38.6 mm. **Obv:** National arms **Rev:** Sad woman above Fatima **Edge:** Reeded

Date	Mintage	F	VF	XF	Unc	BU
2005 Proof	9,999	Value: 40.00				

KM# 212 10 DINERS

31.1000 g., 0.9250 Silver 0.9249 oz. ASW, 38.6 mm. **Obv:** National arms **Rev:** Radiant woman above Guadalupe Cathedral **Edge:** Reeded

Date	Mintage	F	VF	XF	Unc	BU
2005 Proof	9,999	Value: 40.00				

KM# 213 10 DINERS

31.1000 g., 0.9250 Silver 0.9249 oz. ASW, 38.6 mm. **Obv:** National arms **Rev:** Sea shell above Santiago De Compostel-la Cathedral **Edge:** Reeded

Date	Mintage	F	VF	XF	Unc	BU
2005 Proof	9,999	Value: 40.00				

KM# 214 10 DINERS

31.1000 g., 0.9250 Silver 0.9249 oz. ASW, 38.6 mm. **Obv:** National arms **Rev:** Dead man's face with Church of the Holy Sepulchre in the background **Edge:** Reeded

Date	Mintage	F	VF	XF	Unc	BU
2005 Proof	9,999	Value: 40.00				

KM# 215 10 DINERS

28.8000 g., 0.9250 Silver 0.8565 oz. ASW, 38.6 mm. **Obv:** National arms **Rev:** 2006 Olympics freestyle skier **Edge:** Reeded

Date	Mintage	F	VF	XF	Unc	BU
2005 Proof	15,000	Value: 35.00				

KM# 217 10 DINERS

3.1100 g., 0.9999 Gold 0.1000 oz. AGW, 20 mm. **Obv:** National arms **Rev:** Jesus carrying the cross **Edge:** Reeded

Date	Mintage	F	VF	XF	Unc	BU
2006 Proof	9,999	Value: 135				

KM# 218 10 DINERS

31.1035 g., 0.9250 Silver 0.9250 oz. ASW, 38.6 mm. **Obv:** National arms **Rev:** Birth of Jesus **Edge:** Reeded

Date	Mintage	F	VF	XF	Unc	BU
2006 Proof	9,999	Value: 40.00				

KM# 219 10 DINERS

31.1035 g., 0.9250 Silver 0.9250 oz. ASW, 38.6 mm. **Obv:** National arms **Rev:** The Last Supper **Edge:** Reeded

Date	Mintage	F	VF	XF	Unc	BU
2006 Proof	9,999	Value: 40.00				

KM# 244 10 DINERS

28.2800 g., 0.9250 Silver 0.8410 oz. ASW **Obv:** Mona lisa, national arms at lower left, multicolor **Rev:** Head of Leonardo daVinci at lower left, study of man in background, multicolor **Edge:** Plain **Shape:** Rectangular, 28 x 40 mm

Date	Mintage	F	VF	XF	Unc	BU
2008	15,000	—	—	—	—	60.00

KM# 174 25 DINERS

12.4414 g., 0.9990 Gold 0.3996 oz. AGW, 26 mm. **Subject:** Christmas **Obv:** National arms **Rev:** Nativity scene **Edge:** Reeded

Date	Mintage	F	VF	XF	Unc	BU
2001 Proof	3,000	Value: 560				

KM# 184 25 DINERS

10.0000 g., 0.9999 Gold 0.3215 oz. AGW, 26 mm. **Subject:** Christmas **Obv:** National arms **Rev:** Standing Christ child **Edge:** Reeded

Date	Mintage	F	VF	XF	Unc	BU
2002 Proof	2,000	Value: 525				

KM# 185 25 DINERS

7.7759 g., 0.9990 Gold 0.2497 oz. AGW, 26 mm. **Subject:** Christmas **Obv:** National arms **Rev:** Madonna-like mother and child **Edge:** Reeded

Date	Mintage	F	VF	XF	Unc	BU
2003 Proof	3,000	Value: 335				

KM# 197 25 DINERS

8.0000 g., 0.9990 Gold 0.2569 oz. AGW, 26 mm. **Subject:** Christmas **Obv:** National arms **Rev:** Nativity scene **Edge:** Reeded

Date	Mintage	F	VF	XF	Unc	BU
2004 Proof	5,000	Value: 350				

KM# 216 25 DINERS

6.0000 g., 0.9999 Gold 0.1929 oz. AGW, 26 mm. **Obv:** National arms **Rev:** St. Joseph holding infant Jesus **Edge:** Reeded

Date	Mintage	F	VF	XF	Unc	BU
2005 Proof	9,999	Value: 260				

KM# 186 50 DINERS

159.5000 g., 0.9990 Bi-Metallic .999 Silver 155.5g coin with .999 Gold 4g, 20x50mm insert 5.1227 oz., 65 mm. **Subject:** 10th

Anniversary of Constitution **Obv:** National arms **Rev:** Seated allegorical woman holding scrolled constitution **Edge:** Reeded

Date	Mintage	F	VF	XF	Unc	BU
2003	3,000	—	—	—	275	325

ARGENTINA

The Argentine Republic, located in southern South America, has an area of 1,073,518 sq. mi. (3,761,274 sq. km.) and an estimated population of 37.03 million. Capital: Buenos Aires. Its varied topography ranges from the subtropical lowlands of the north to the towering Andean Mountains in the west and the wind-swept Patagonian steppe in the south. The rolling, fertile pampas of central Argentina are ideal for agriculture and grazing, and support most of the republic's population. Meatpacking, flour milling, textiles, sugar refining and dairy products are the principal industries. Oil is found in Patagonia, but most mineral requirements must be imported.

Internal conflict through the first half century of Argentine independence resulted in a provisional national coinage, chiefly of crown-sized silver. Provincial issues mainly of minor denominations supplemented this.

REPUBLIC

REFORM COINAGE

1992; 100 Centavos = 1 Peso

KM# 109a.2 5 CENTAVOS

Copper-Nickel **Obv:** Radiant sunface. Bold lettering **Note:** Prev. KM#84a.2.

Date	Mintage	F	VF	XF	Unc	BU
2004	30,000,000	—	—	—	0.45	0.60
2005	76,000,000	—	—	—	0.45	0.60
2006	23,800,000	—	—	—	0.45	0.60
2007	183,000,000	—	—	—	0.45	0.60
2008	114,000,000	—	—	—	0.45	0.60
2009	—	—	—	—	0.45	0.60

KM# 109 5 CENTAVOS

Brass **Obv:** Radiant sunface **Rev:** Large value, date below **Note:** Prev. KM#84.

Date	Mintage	F	VF	XF	Unc	BU
2005	—	—	—	—	0.45	0.60

KM# 107 10 CENTAVOS

2.3000 g., Aluminum-Bronze, 18.3 mm. **Obv:** Argentine arms **Rev:** Value, date below **Edge:** Reeded **Note:** Prev. KM#82.

Date	Mintage	F	VF	XF	Unc	BU
2004	190,000,000	—	—	—	0.65	0.85
2005	114,400,000	—	—	—	0.65	0.85
2006	99,600,000	—	—	—	0.65	0.85
2007	204,000,000	—	—	—	0.65	0.85
2008	317,000,000	—	—	—	0.65	0.85
2009	—	—	—	—	0.65	0.85

KM# 110a 25 CENTAVOS
6.1000 g., Copper-Nickel, 24.3 mm. **Obv:** Towered building, bold lettering **Note:** Prev. KM#85a.

Date	Mintage	F	VF	XF	Unc	BU
2009	—	—	—	—	1.25	1.50

KM# 111.2 50 CENTAVOS
Copper-Nickel **Obv:** Tucuman Province Capital Building; bold lettering. **Note:** Prev. KM#86.2.

Date	Mintage	F	VF	XF	Unc	BU
2009	—	—	—	—	1.75	2.00

KM# 132.1 PESO
6.4000 g., Bi-Metallic Brass center in Copper-Nickel ring, 23 mm. **Subject:** General Urquiza **Obv:** Stylized portrait facing **Rev:** Church tower and denomination **Edge:** Reeded

Date	Mintage	F	VF	XF	Unc	BU
2001	995,000	—	—	—	3.75	4.50

KM# 132.2 PESO
6.3500 g., Bi-Metallic Copper-Aluminum-Nickel center in Copper-Nickel ring, 23 mm. **Subject:** General Urquiza **Obv:** Stylized portrait facing **Rev:** Church tower and denomination **Edge:** Plain

Date	Mintage	F	VF	XF	Unc	BU
2001	5,000	—	—	—	7.50	8.00

KM# 141 PESO
24.8100 g., 0.9000 Silver 0.7179 oz. ASW, 36.9 mm. **Obv:** Maria Eva Duarte de Peron **Rev:** "EVITA" audience **Edge:** Reeded

Date	Mintage	F	VF	XF	Unc	BU
ND (2004) Proof	5,000	Value: 40.00				

KM# 140 PESO
25.0000 g., 0.9000 Silver 0.7234 oz. ASW, 37 mm. **Subject:** 70th Anniversary of Central Bank **Obv:** Bank building **Rev:** Liberty head in wreath **Edge:** Reeded

Date	Mintage	F	VF	XF	Unc	BU
2005 Proof	2,000	Value: 50.00				

KM# 155 PESO
25.0000 g., 0.9000 Silver 0.7234 oz. ASW, 37 mm. **Subject:** Jorge Luis Borges **Obv:** Stylized bust facing **Rev:** Man walking at street corner

Date	Mintage	F	VF	XF	Unc	BU
2006A	—	—	—	—	—	40.00

KM# 112.1 PESO
6.4000 g., Bi-Metallic Brass center in Copper-Nickel ring, 23 mm. **Obv:** Argentine arms in circle **Rev:** Design of first Argentine coin in center **Edge:** Plain **Note:** Prev. KM#87.1.

Date	Mintage	F	VF	XF	Unc	BU
2006	30,000,000	—	—	0.50	1.20	1.60
2007	33,000,000	—	—	0.50	1.20	1.60
2008	89,600,000	—	—	0.50	1.20	1.60
2009	—	—	—	0.50	1.20	1.60

KM# 153 PESO
25.0000 g., 0.9000 Silver 0.7234 oz. ASW, 37 mm. **Subject:** 25th Anniversary Malvinas Islands Occupation - Heroes **Obv:** Soldier's bust facing **Obv. Legend:** REPUBLICA ARGENTINA -1982 - 2007 - LA NACIÓN A SUS HÉROES **Rev:** Outlined map of islands **Rev. Legend:** MALVINAS ARGENTINAS **Rev. Inscription:** 2 DE APRIL / 1982 **Edge:** Reeded

Date	Mintage	F	VF	XF	Unc	BU
2007 Proof	3,000	Value: 75.00				

KM# 135.1 2 PESOS
10.4400 g., Copper-Nickel, 30.2 mm. **Subject:** Eva Peron **Obv:** Head left **Rev:** Stylized crowd scene, value **Rev. Inscription:** EVITA **Edge:** Reeded

Date	Mintage	F	VF	XF	Unc	BU
2002	1,995,000	—	—	0.85	1.85	2.50

KM# 135.2 2 PESOS
10.4400 g., Copper-Nickel, 30 mm. **Subject:** Eva Peron **Obv:** Head left **Rev:** Stylized crowd scene, value **Rev. Inscription:** EVITA **Edge:** Plain

Date	Mintage	F	VF	XF	Unc	BU
2002	5,000	—	—	—	6.00	8.00

KM# 144.1 2 PESOS
10.4700 g., Copper-Nickel, 30.35 mm. **Subject:** 25th Anniversary Malvinas Islands Occupation - Heroes **Obv:** Soldier's bust facing **Obv. Legend:** REPUBLICA ARGENTINA - 1982 - 2007 - LA NACIÓN A SUS HÉROES **Rev:** Outlined map of islands **Rev. Legend:** MALVINAS ARGENTINAS **Rev. Inscription:** 2 DE APRIL / 1982 **Edge:** Reeded

Date	Mintage	F	VF	XF	Unc	BU
2007	1,995,000	—	—	0.85	1.85	2.50

KM# 144.2 2 PESOS
10.4700 g., Copper-Nickel, 30.35 mm. **Subject:** 25th Anniversary Malvinas Islands Occupation - Heroes **Obv:** Soldier's bust facing **Obv. Legend:** REPUBLICA ARGENTINA - 1982 - 2007 - LA NACIÓN A SUS HÉROES **Rev:** Outlined map of islands **Rev. Legend:** MALVINAS ARGENTINAS **Rev. Inscription:** 2 DE APRIL / 1982 **Edge:** Plain

Date	Mintage	F	VF	XF	Unc	BU
2007	5,000	—	—	—	—	9.00

KM# 145 2 PESOS
Copper-Nickel, 30.35 mm. **Subject:** 100th Anniversary First Oil Well **Obv:** First oil well **Obv. Legend:** REPÚBLICA ARGENTINA - DESCUBRIMIENTO DEL PETRÓLEO **Rev:** Modern pump **Rev. Inscription:** CHUBUT **Edge:** Reeded

Date	Mintage	F	VF	XF	Unc	BU
2007	995,000	—	—	—	6.00	8.00

KM# 133 5 PESOS
8.0640 g., 0.9000 Gold 0.2333 oz. AGW, 22 mm. **Subject:** Gral. Justo Jose de Urquiza **Obv:** Stylized portrait facing **Rev:** Church tower and denomination **Edge:** Reeded

Date	Mintage	F	VF	XF	Unc	BU
2001 Proof	1,000	Value: 300				

KM# 149 5 PESOS
8.0640 g., 0.9000 Gold 0.2333 oz. AGW **Subject:** 100th Anniverary City of Comodoro Rivadavia

Date	Mintage	F	VF	XF	Unc	BU
2001 Proof	750	Value: 325				

KM# 143 5 PESOS
27.0000 g., 0.9250 Silver 0.8029 oz. ASW, 40 mm. **Subject:** FIFA - XVIII World Championship Football - Germany 2006 **Obv:** Football at right on grass, chaff in backgound **Obv. Legend:** REPÚBLICA ARGENTINA **Rev:** Logo **Rev. Legend:** COPA MUNDIAL DE LA FIFA **Rev. Inscription:** ALEMANIA **Edge:** Reeded

Date	Mintage	F	VF	XF	Unc	BU
2003 Proof	50,000	Value: 50.00				

KM# 146   5 PESOS
27.0000 g., 0.9250 Silver 0.8029 oz. ASW **Subject:** FIFA - XVIII
World Footbal Championship - Germany 2006 **Obv. Legend:**
REPÚBLICA ARGENTINA **Rev:** Logo **Edge:** Reeded

Date	Mintage	F	VF	XF	Unc	BU
2004 Proof	50,000	Value: 50.00				

KM# 142   5 PESOS
8.0640 g., 0.9000 Gold 0.2333 oz. AGW, 22 mm. **Obv:** Maria
Eva Duarte de Peron **Rev:** "EVITA" and audience

Date	Mintage	F	VF	XF	Unc	BU
ND (2004) Proof	1,000	Value: 315				

KM# 150   5 PESOS
27.0000 g., 0.9250 Silver 0.8029 oz. ASW **Subject:** FIFA - XVIII
World Championship Football - Germany 2006 **Obv:** Forward
player **Rev:** Logo

Date	Mintage	F	VF	XF	Unc	BU
2005 Proof	—	Value: 65.00				

KM# 154   5 PESOS
8.0640 g., 0.9000 Gold 0.2333 oz. AGW, 22 mm. **Subject:** 25th
Anniversary Malvinas Islands Occupation - Heroes **Obv:**
Soldier's bust facing **Obv. Legend:** REPUBLICA ARGENTINA
- 1982 - 2007 - LA NACIÓN A SUS HÉROES **Rev:** Outlined map
of islands **Rev. Legend:** MALVINAS ISLANDS **Rev. Inscription:**
2 DE APRIL / 1982 **Edge:** Reeded

Date	Mintage	F	VF	XF	Unc	BU
2007 Proof	1,000	Value: 400				

KM# 147   10 PESOS
6.7500 g., 0.9990 Gold 0.2168 oz. AGW **Subject:** FIFA - XVIII
World Footbal Championship - Germany 2006 **Obv. Legend:**
REPÚBLICA ARGENTINA **Edge:** Reeded

Date	Mintage	F	VF	XF	Unc	BU
2004 Proof	25,000	Value: 350				

KM# 151   10 PESOS
6.7500 g., 0.9990 Gold 0.2168 oz. AGW **Subject:** FIFA - XVIII
World Championship Football - Germany 2006 **Obv:** Forward
player **Rev:** Logo

Date	Mintage	F	VF	XF	Unc	BU
2005 Proof	—	Value: 350				

KM# 138   25 PESOS
27.0000 g., 0.9250 Silver 0.8029 oz. ASW, 40 mm. **Subject:**
IBERO-AMERICA Series **Obv:** Coats of arms **Rev:** Tall ship
"Presidente Sarmiento" **Edge:** Reeded

Date	Mintage	F	VF	XF	Unc	BU
2002 Proof	—	Value: 55.00				

KM# 139   25 PESOS
27.0000 g., 0.9250 Silver 0.8029 oz. ASW, 40 mm. **Subject:**
Ibero-America **Obv:** National arms in circle of arms **Rev:** Colon
Theater building **Edge:** Reeded

Date	Mintage	F	VF	XF	Unc	BU
2005 Proof	15,500	Value: 50.00				

PROOF SETS

KM#	Date	Mintage Identification	Issue Price	Mkt Val
PS6	2007 (2)	300 KM#153, 154	475	475

ARMENIA

The Republic of Armenia, formerly Armenian S.S.R., is bordered to the north by Georgia, the east by Azerbaijan and the
south and west by Turkey and Iran. It has an area of 11,506 sq.
mi. (29,800 sq. km) and an estimated population of 3.66 million.
Capital: Yerevan. Agriculture including cotton, vineyards and
orchards, hydroelectricity, chemicals - primarily synthetic rubber
and fertilizers, vast mineral deposits of copper, zinc and aluminum, and production of steel and paper are major industries.

Fighting between Christians in Armenia and Muslim forces of
Azerbaijan escalated in 1992 and continued through early 1994.
Each country claimed the Nagorno-Karabakh, an Armenian ethnic enclave, in Azerbaijan. A temporary cease-fire was
announced in May 1994.

MONETARY SYSTEM
100 Luma = 1 Dram

MINT NAME
Revan, (Erevan, now Yerevan)

REPUBLIC
STANDARD COINAGE

KM# 112   10 DRAM
1.3000 g., Aluminum, 20 mm. **Obv:** National arms **Rev:** Value
Edge: Reeded

Date	Mintage	F	VF	XF	Unc	BU
2004	—	—	—	—	1.00	1.50

KM# 93   20 DRAM
2.8000 g., Copper Plated Steel, 20.5 mm. **Obv:** National arms
Rev: Denomination **Edge:** Plain

Date	Mintage	F	VF	XF	Unc	BU
2003	—	—	—	—	1.00	1.50

KM# 94   50 DRAM
3.4500 g., Brass Plated Steel, 21.5 mm. **Obv:** National arms
Rev: Value **Edge:** Reeded

Date	Mintage	F	VF	XF	Unc	BU
2003	—	—	—	—	1.25	1.50

KM# 86   100 DRAM
31.1000 g., 0.9990 Silver 0.9988 oz. ASW, 38 mm.
Obv: National arms **Rev:** Bust of General Garegin Nzhdeh facing
at right **Edge:** Plain **Edge Lettering:** Serial number

Date	Mintage	F	VF	XF	Unc	BU
2001 Proof	170	Value: 1,000				

KM# 86a   100 DRAM
31.1000 g., 0.9990 Silver Gilt 0.9988 oz. ASW, 38 mm.
Obv: National arms **Obv. Inscription:** Bust of General Garegin
Nzhdeh facing at right **Edge:** Plain **Edge Lettering:** Serial number

Date	Mintage	F	VF	XF	Unc	BU
2001 Proof	30	Value: 3,000				

KM# 87   100 DRAM
31.0400 g., 0.9990 Silver 0.9969 oz. ASW, 38 mm.
Subject: Armenian Membership in the Council of Europe joined
January 1, 2001 **Obv:** National arms **Rev:** Spiral design with star
circle **Edge:** Plain **Edge Lettering:** Serial number

Date	Mintage	F	VF	XF	Unc	BU
2001 Proof	200	Value: 300				

KM# 98 100 DRAM
31.1000 g., 0.9250 Silver 0.9249 oz. ASW, 40 mm. **Obv:** National arms **Rev:** Aram Khachatryan, Birth Centennial **Edge:** Reeded

Date	Mintage	F	VF	XF	Unc	BU
2002	300	—	—	—	65.00	100

KM# 99 100 DRAM
31.1000 g., 0.9250 Silver 0.9249 oz. ASW, 40 mm. **Obv:** The Book of Sadness **Rev:** Saint Grigor Narekatsi with book and quill millenium of his poem "The Book of Sadness" **Edge:** Reeded

Date	Mintage	F	VF	XF	Unc	BU
2002 Proof	500	Value: 100				

KM# 110 100 DRAM
33.9200 g., 0.9250 Silver 1.0087 oz. ASW, 39 mm. **Subject:** 110th Anniversary of State Banking in Armenia and 10th Year of National Currency October 7 1893 - November 22, 1993 **Obv:** Building above value **Rev:** State Bank emblem **Edge:** Reeded

Date	Mintage	F	VF	XF	Unc	BU
2003 Proof	300	Value: 200				

KM# 95 100 DRAM
4.0000 g., Nickel Plated Steel, 22.5 mm. **Obv:** National arms **Rev:** Value **Edge:** Reeded

Date	Mintage	F	VF	XF	Unc	BU
2003	—	—	—	—	1.50	2.00

KM# 111 100 DRAM
28.2800 g., 0.9250 Silver 0.8410 oz. ASW, 38.6 mm. **Subject:** FIFA World Cup Soccer Games - Germany **Obv:** National arms **Rev:** Three soccer players

Date	Mintage	F	VF	XF	Unc	BU
2004 Proof	300	Value: 150				

KM# 113 100 DRAM
31.1000 g., 0.9990 Silver 0.9988 oz. ASW, 38 mm. **Subject:** Gandzasar Monastery **Obv:** Monastery **Rev:** Folk art crucifix and denomination

Date	Mintage	F	VF	XF	Unc	BU
2004 Proof	500	Value: 100				

KM# 115 100 DRAM
31.1000 g., 0.9250 Silver 0.9249 oz. ASW, 40 mm. **Subject:** Anania Shirakatsi 1400 Anniversary, Scientist **Obv:** Profile of Shirakatsi, deep in thought **Rev:** Planets and stars, denomination

Date	Mintage	F	VF	XF	Unc	BU
2005 Proof	500	Value: 100				

KM# 123 100 DRAM
31.1000 g., 0.9250 Silver 0.9249 oz. ASW, 40.00 mm. **Subject:** Creation of the Armenian alphabet **Obv:** National arms **Rev:** King Vramshapuh standing at left, alphabet at right

Date	Mintage	F	VF	XF	Unc	BU
2005 Proof	500	Value: 150				

KM# 124 100 DRAM
31.1000 g., 0.9250 Silver 0.9249 oz. ASW, 40.00 mm. **Subject:** Creation of the Armenian alphabet **Obv:** National arms **Rev:** Sahak Partev standing at left, alphabet at right

Date	Mintage	F	VF	XF	Unc	BU
2005 Proof	500	Value: 150				

KM# 125 100 DRAM
31.1000 g., 0.9250 Silver 0.9249 oz. ASW, 40.00 mm. **Subject:** 100th Anniversary - Birth of Artem Mikoyan - Inventor of MIG Jet **Obv:** Three jet airplanes **Rev:** Bust of Mikoyan 3/4 left

Date	Mintage	F	VF	XF	Unc	BU
2005 Proof	500	Value: 125				

KM# 127 100 DRAM
28.2800 g., 0.9250 Silver 0.8410 oz. ASW, 38.61 mm. **Subject:** International Polar Year **Obv:** National arms **Obv. Legend:** REPUBLIC OF ARMENIA **Rev:** Bust of Fridtjof Nansen right at left, ship stuck in ice at lower right, multicolor emblem above

Date	Mintage	F	VF	XF	Unc	BU
2006 Proof	10,000	Value: 100				

KM# 129 100 DRAM
28.2800 g., 0.9250 Silver 0.8410 oz. ASW **Subject:** Hovhannes Aivazovsky **Obv:** National arms at lower left, sailing ship listing at center right multicolor **Rev:** Bust of Aivazovsky 3/4 left at lower left, sailing ships at center right **Shape:** Rectangular, 40 x 28 mm

Date	Mintage	F	VF	XF	Unc	BU
2006 Proof	5,000	Value: 700				

KM# 119 100 DRAM
28.3500 g., 0.9250 Silver 0.8431 oz. ASW, 38.5 mm. **Obv:** National arms **Rev:** Brown bear and two red lines **Edge:** Plain

Date	Mintage	F	VF	XF	Unc	BU
2006 Proof	3,000	Value: 185				

KM# 120 100 DRAM
28.3500 g., 0.9250 Silver 0.8431 oz. ASW, 38.5 mm. **Obv:** National arms **Rev:** Long-eared Hedgehog and two red lines **Edge:** Plain

Date	Mintage	F	VF	XF	Unc	BU
2006 Proof	3,000	Value: 185				

KM# 121 100 DRAM
28.2800 g., 0.9250 Silver 0.8410 oz. ASW, 38.6 mm. **Obv:** National arms, date and value **Rev:** Caucasian Forest Cat **Edge:** Plain

Date	Mintage	F	VF	XF	Unc	BU
2006 Proof	3,000	Value: 100				

KM# 122 100 DRAM
28.2800 g., 0.9250 Silver 0.8410 oz. ASW, 38.6 mm. **Obv:** National arms, date and value **Rev:** Armenian Tortoise **Edge:** Plain

Date	Mintage	F	VF	XF	Unc	BU
2006 Proof	3,000	Value: 135				

KM# 135 100 DRAM
28.2400 g., 0.9250 Silver 0.8398 oz. ASW, 38.53 mm. **Subject:** Caucasian Leopard **Obv:** National arms **Obv. Legend:** REPUBLIC OF ARMENIA **Rev:** Leopard walking left **Edge:** Plain

Date	Mintage	F	VF	XF	Unc	BU
2007 Proof	3,000	Value: 110				

KM# 136 100 DRAM
28.2400 g., 0.9250 Silver 0.8398 oz. ASW, 38.5 mm. **Subject:** Northern Shoveler duck **Obv:** National arms **Obv. Legend:** REPUBLIC OF ARMENIA **Rev:** Duck standing left **Edge:** Plain

Date	Mintage	F	VF	XF	Unc	BU
2007 Proof	3,000	Value: 85.00				

KM# 141   100 DRAM
28.2800 g., 0.9250 Silver Zircon crystal attached. 0.8410 oz.
ASW, 38.5 mm. **Series:** Signs of the Zodiac **Obv:** National arms
within ring of signs of the Zodiac **Obv. Legend:** REPUBLIC OF
ARMENIA **Obv. Designer:** Ursula Valenazh **Rev:** Capricorn with
jeweled star at left, multicolor **Edge:** Plain

Date	Mintage	F	VF	XF	Unc	BU
2007 Proof	12,000	Value: 85.00				

KM# 153   100 DRAM
28.2800 g., 0.9250 Silver 0.8410 oz. ASW, 38.6 mm.
Obv: National arms **Obv. Legend:** REPUBLIC OF ARMENIA
Rev: Lake Sevan Salmon

Date	Mintage	F	VF	XF	Unc	BU
2007 Proof	3,000	Value: 100				

KM# 154   100 DRAM
28.2800 g., 0.9250 Silver 0.8410 oz. ASW, 38.6 mm.
Obv: National arms **Obv. Legend:** REPUBLIC OF ARMENIA
Rev: Armenian viper

Date	Mintage	F	VF	XF	Unc	BU
2007 Proof	3,000	Value: 85.00				

KM# 157   100 DRAM
28.2800 g., 0.9250 Silver 0.8410 oz. ASW, 38.6 mm.
Subject: Aquarius

Date	Mintage	F	VF	XF	Unc	BU
2007 Proof	—	Value: 100				

KM# 158   100 DRAM
28.2800 g., 0.9250 Silver 0.8410 oz. ASW, 38.6 mm.
Subject: Pisces

Date	Mintage	F	VF	XF	Unc	BU
2007 Proof	—	—				—

KM# 155   100 DRAM
28.2800 g., 0.9250 Silver 0.8410 oz. ASW, 39 mm.
Subject: National Arms **Obv:** Roussana and Andrzej
Nowakowscy **Rev:** Caucasian owl on branch, (Aegolius
Funereus Caucasious) red arcs at top and bottom

Date	Mintage	F	VF	XF	Unc	BU
2008 Proof	3,000	Value: 75.00				

KM# 159   100 DRAM
28.2800 g., 0.9250 Silver 0.8410 oz. ASW, 38.6 mm.
Subject: Aries

Date	Mintage	F	VF	XF	Unc	BU
2008 Proof	—	Value: 100				

KM# 160   100 DRAM
28.2800 g., 0.9250 Silver 0.8410 oz. ASW, 38.6 mm.
Subject: Taurus

Date	Mintage	F	VF	XF	Unc	BU
2008 Proof	—	Value: 100				

KM# 161   100 DRAM
28.2800 g., 0.9250 Silver 0.8410 oz. ASW, 38.6 mm.
Subject: Gemini

Date	Mintage	F	VF	XF	Unc	BU
2008 Proof	—	Value: 100				

KM# 162   100 DRAM
28.2800 g., 0.9250 Silver 0.8410 oz. ASW **Subject:** Cancer

Date	Mintage	F	VF	XF	Unc	BU
2008 Proof	—	Value: 100				

KM# 163   100 DRAM
28.2800 g., 0.9250 Silver 0.8410 oz. ASW, 38.6 mm. **Subject:** Leo

Date	Mintage	F	VF	XF	Unc	BU
2008 Proof	—	Value: 100				

KM# 164   100 DRAM
, 38.6 mm. **Subject:** Virgo

Date	Mintage	F	VF	XF	Unc	BU
2008 Proof	—	Value: 100				

KM# 165   100 DRAM
28.2800 g., 0.9250 Silver 0.8410 oz. ASW, 38.6 mm.
Subject: Libra

Date	Mintage	F	VF	XF	Unc	BU
2008 Proof	—	Value: 100				

KM# 167   100 DRAM
28.2800 g., 0.9250 Silver 0.8410 oz. ASW, 38.6 mm.
Subject: Bezoar

Date	Mintage	F	VF	XF	Unc	BU
2008 Proof	—	Value: 100				

KM# 172   100 DRAM
28.2800 g., 0.9250 Silver 0.8410 oz. ASW, 38.6 mm.
Subject: Scorpio

Date	Mintage	F	VF	XF	Unc	BU
2008 Proof	—	Value: 100				

KM# 174   100 DRAM
28.2800 g., 0.9250 Silver 0.8410 oz. ASW, 38.6 mm.
Subject: Sagittarus

Date	Mintage	F	VF	XF	Unc	BU
2008 Proof	—	Value: 100				

KM# 177   100 DRAM
28.2800 g., 0.9250 Silver 0.8410 oz. ASW, 38.6 mm.
Subject: Armenian Moufflon

Date	Mintage	F	VF	XF	Unc	BU
2008 Proof	—	Value: 75.00				

KM# 178   100 DRAM
28.2800 g., 0.9250 Silver 0.8410 oz. ASW, 38.6 mm.
Subject: Toad Agama

Date	Mintage	F	VF	XF	Unc	BU
2008 Proof	—	Value: 75.00				

KM# 182   100 DRAM
28.2800 g., 0.9250 Silver 0.8410 oz. ASW, 38.6 mm. **Subject:** Pele

Date	Mintage	F	VF	XF	Unc	BU
2008 Proof	—	Value: 50.00				

KM# 183   100 DRAM
28.2800 g., 0.9250 Silver 0.8410 oz. ASW, 38.6 mm.
Subject: Eusebio

Date	Mintage	F	VF	XF	Unc	BU
2008 Proof	—	Value: 50.00				

KM# 184   100 DRAM
28.2800 g., 0.9250 Silver 0.8410 oz. ASW, 38.6 mm.
Subject: Lev Jashin

Date	Mintage	F	VF	XF	Unc	BU
2008 Proof	—	Value: 50.00				

KM# 187   100 DRAM
28.2800 g., 0.9250 Silver 0.8410 oz. ASW, 38.6 mm.
Subject: Franz Beckenbauer

Date	Mintage	F	VF	XF	Unc	BU
2008 Proof	—	Value: 50.00				

KM# 156   100 DRAM
28.2800 g., 0.9250 Silver 0.8410 oz. ASW, 38.6 mm.
Subject: Zbigniew Boniek **Rev:** Portrait facing, multicolor flag

Date	Mintage	F	VF	XF	Unc	BU
2009 Proof	50,000	Value: 85.00				

KM# 96   200 DRAM
4.5000 g., Brass, 24 mm. **Obv:** National arms **Rev:** Value
Edge: Reeded

Date	Mintage	F	VF	XF	Unc	BU
2003	—	—	—	—	3.00	4.00

KM# 106   500 DRAM
155.5000 g., 0.9250 Silver 4.6243 oz. ASW, 63 mm.
Subject: 10th Anniversary of Independence **Obv:** National arms
Rev: Tower with flag, logo at right 9-21-91

Date	Mintage	F	VF	XF	Unc	BU
2001 Proof	200	Value: 400				

KM# 97   500 DRAM
5.0000 g., Bi-Metallic Copper-Nickel center in a Brass ring, 22 mm.
Obv: National arms **Rev:** Value **Edge:** Segmented reeding

Date	Mintage	F	VF	XF	Unc	BU
2003	—	—	—	—	6.00	8.00

KM# 109   1000 DRAM
15.5500 g., 0.5850 Gold 0.2925 oz. AGW, 26 mm.
Obv: National arms on ancient coin design **Rev:** Tigran the Great
ancient coin portrait

Date	Mintage	F	VF	XF	Unc	BU
2003	500	—	—	—	785	1,200

KM# 128   1000 DRAM
33.6000 g., 0.9250 Silver 0.9992 oz. ASW, 38 mm.
Subject: 100th Anniversary Birth of Marshal Babajanian
Obv: National arms **Rev:** Bust of Babajanian 3/4 right

Date	Mintage	F	VF	XF	Unc	BU
2006 Proof	500	Value: 150				

KM# 133   1000 DRAM
33.6000 g., 0.9250 Silver 0.9992 oz. ASW, 40 mm.
Series: Armenian grapes **Obv:** National arms **Rev:** Large bunch
of grapes at left

Date	Mintage	F	VF	XF	Unc	BU
2007 Proof	5,000	Value: 150				

KM# 169   1000 DRAM
33.6000 g., 0.9250 Silver 0.9992 oz. ASW, 40 mm.
Subject: Viktor Ambartsumian, 100th Anniversary of birth

Date	Mintage	F	VF	XF	Unc	BU
2008 Proof	—	Value: 100				

KM# 171   1000 DRAM
33.6000 g., 0.9250 Silver 0.9992 oz. ASW, 40 mm. **Subject:** A.
Spendiaryan Theater of Ballet and Opera, 75th Anniversary

Date	Mintage	F	VF	XF	Unc	BU
2008 Proof	—	Value: 100				

KM# 192   1000 DRAM
33.6000 g., 0.9250 Silver 0.9992 oz. ASW, 40 mm.
Subject: Mkhitar Gosh - The Codex

Date	Mintage	F	VF	XF	Unc	BU
2009 Proof	—	Value: 50.00				

KM# 193   1000 DRAM
31.1000 g., 0.9990 Silver 0.9988 oz. ASW, 38 mm. **Subject:**
Gladzor University, 750th Anniversary

Date	Mintage	F	VF	XF	Unc	BU
2009 Proof	—	Value: 50.00				

KM# 134   1957 DRAM
33.6000 g., 0.9250 Silver 0.9992 oz. ASW, 40 mm. **Subject:**
50th Anniversay of Matenadaran **Obv:** Small national arms at
center surrounded by intricate pattern **Rev:** Building at left center

Date	Mintage	F	VF	XF	Unc	BU
2007 Proof	500	Value: 125				

KM# 117   5000 DRAM
31.1000 g., 0.9250 Silver 0.9249 oz. ASW, 38 mm.
Subject: Armenian Armed Forces **Obv:** Order of the Combat
Cross of the Second Degree and the Emblem of the Ministry of
Defense of the Republic of Armenia **Obv. Designer:** H.
Samuelian **Rev:** Arms, date and denomination **Shape:** Octagonal

Date	Mintage	F	VF	XF	Unc	BU
2005 Proof	500	Value: 130				

KM# 126 5000 DRAM
168.1000 g., 0.9250 Silver 4.9990 oz. ASW, 63 mm. **Subject:** 15th Anniversary of Independence **Obv:** National arms **Rev:** Building at center left, multicolor emblem above, mountains in background

Date	Mintage	F	VF	XF	Unc	BU
2006 Proof	300	Value: 400				

KM# 139 5000 DRAM
4.3000 g., 0.9000 Gold 0.1244 oz. AGW, 18 mm. **Subject:** Haik Nahapet **Obv:** Small national arms at upper left, Orion constellation at right **Rev:** 3/4 length classical Archer right

Date	Mintage	F	VF	XF	Unc	BU
2007 Proof	3,000	Value: 400				

KM# 179 5000 DRAM
168.1000 g., 0.9250 Silver partially gold plated 4.9990 oz. ASW, 63 mm. **Subject:** National Currency, 15th Anniversary

Date	Mintage	F	VF	XF	Unc	BU
2008 Proof	—	Value: 150				

KM# 195 5000 DRAM
4.3000 g., 0.9000 Gold 0.1244 oz. AGW, 18 mm. **Subject:** St. Sargis the Commander

Date	Mintage	F	VF	XF	Unc	BU
2009 Proof	—	Value: 175				

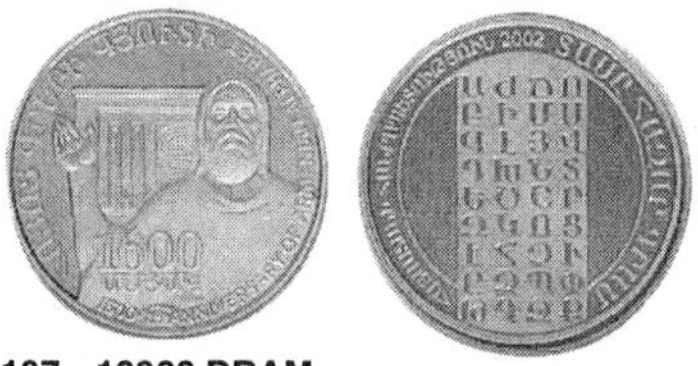

KM# 107 10000 DRAM
8.6000 g., 0.9990 Gold 0.2762 oz. AGW, 22 mm. **Obv:** Mesrop Mashtots, creator of the Armenian alphabet **Rev:** Armenian alphabet

Date	Mintage	F	VF	XF	Unc	BU
2002 Proof	1,000	Value: 400				

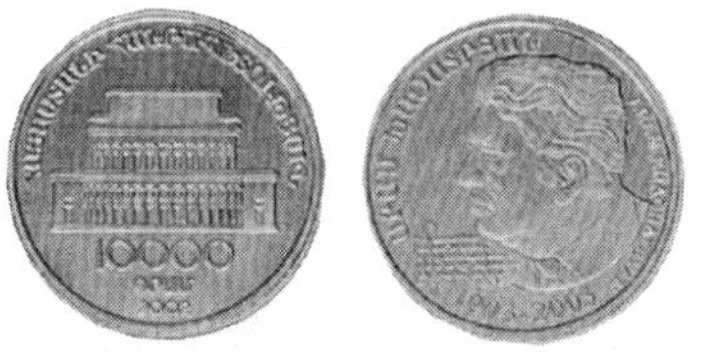

KM# 108 10000 DRAM
8.6000 g., 0.9990 Gold 0.2762 oz. AGW, 22 mm. **Obv:** Building above value **Rev:** Aram Khachatryan left birth centennial

Date	Mintage	F	VF	XF	Unc	BU
2002 Proof	500	Value: 400				

KM# 114 10000 DRAM
8.6000 g., 0.9990 Gold 0.2762 oz. AGW, 22 mm.
Subject: Arshile Gorky birth April 15, 1904 **Obv:** Bust of Gorky **Rev:** Denomination

Date	Mintage	F	VF	XF	Unc	BU
2004 Proof	1,000	Value: 400				

KM# 116 10000 DRAM
8.6000 g., 0.9990 Gold 0.2762 oz. AGW, 22 mm.
Subject: Martiros Saryan 125th Anniversary of Birth **Obv:** Bust of Saryan **Rev:** Landscape, denomination

Date	Mintage	F	VF	XF	Unc	BU
2005 Proof	1,000	Value: 400				

KM# 130 10000 DRAM
8.6000 g., 0.9990 Gold 0.2762 oz. AGW, 22 mm.
Subject: Komitas Vardapet **Obv:** Musical notations and score **Rev:** Bust of Vardapet 3/4 right

Date	Mintage	F	VF	XF	Unc	BU
2006 Proof	1,000	Value: 500				

KM# 131 10000 DRAM
8.6000 g., 0.9000 Gold 0.2488 oz. AGW, 22 mm. **Subject:** 37th Chess Olympiad **Obv:** Chess piece at right **Rev:** National arms within 6 chess pieces in circle

Date	Mintage	F	VF	XF	Unc	BU
2006 Proof	1,000	Value: 450				

KM# 132 10000 DRAM
8.6000 g., 0.9000 Gold 0.2488 oz. AGW, 22 mm. **Subject:** Hakob Gurjian **Obv:** Seated female sculpture **Rev:** Head 3/4 right

Date	Mintage	F	VF	XF	Unc	BU
2006 Proof	1,000	Value: 500				

KM# 137 10000 DRAM
8.6000 g., 0.9000 Gold 0.2488 oz. AGW, 22 mm. **Subject:** Jean Carzou **Obv:** National arms with stylized view of shopping bourse **Rev:** Bust of Carzou 3/4 right at laft center

Date	Mintage	F	VF	XF	Unc	BU
2007 Proof	1,000	Value: 500				

KM# 138 10000 DRAM
8.6000 g., 0.9000 Gold 0.2488 oz. AGW, 22 mm. **Subject:** 15th Anniversary of Armenian Army **Obv:** National arms **Rev:** Military badge

Date	Mintage	F	VF	XF	Unc	BU
2007 Proof	1,000	Value: 500				

KM# 140 10000 DRAM
8.6000 g., 0.9000 Gold 0.2488 oz. AGW, 22 mm. **Subject:** 15th Anniversary Liberation of Shusi **Obv:** Bird with wings outspread above two shields **Rev:** Swirl in background

Date	Mintage	F	VF	XF	Unc	BU
2007 Proof	1,000	Value: 500				

KM# 175 10000 DRAM
28.2800 g., 0.9250 Gold 0.8410 oz. AGW, 22 mm.
Subject: Sagittarus

Date	Mintage	F	VF	XF	Unc	BU
2008 Proof	—	Value: 100				

KM# 166 10000 DRAM
8.6000 g., 0.9000 Gold 0.2488 oz. AGW, 22 mm. **Subject:** Libra

Date	Mintage	F	VF	XF	Unc	BU
2008 Proof	—	Value: 325				

KM# 168 10000 DRAM
8.6000 g., 0.9000 Gold 0.2488 oz. AGW, 22 mm.
Subject: Court, 10th Anniversary

Date	Mintage	F	VF	XF	Unc	BU
2008 Proof	—	Value: 325				

KM# 170 10000 DRAM
8.6000 g., 0.9000 Gold 0.2488 oz. AGW, 22 mm.
Subject: William Saroyan, 100th Anniversary of birth

Date	Mintage	F	VF	XF	Unc	BU
2008 Proof	—	Value: 325				

KM# 173 10000 DRAM
8.6000 g., 0.9000 Gold 0.2488 oz. AGW, 22 mm. **Subject:** Scorpio

Date	Mintage	F	VF	XF	Unc	BU
2008 Proof	—	Value: 325				

KM# 176 10000 DRAM
8.6000 g., 0.9000 Gold 0.2488 oz. AGW, 22 mm.
Subject: Capricorn

Date	Mintage	F	VF	XF	Unc	BU
2008 Proof	—	Value: 325				

KM# 180 10000 DRAM
8.6000 g., 0.9000 Gold 0.2488 oz. AGW, 22 mm.
Subject: Aquarius

Date	Mintage	F	VF	XF	Unc	BU
2008 Proof	—	Value: 325				

KM# 181 10000 DRAM
8.6000 g., 0.9000 Gold 0.2488 oz. AGW, 22 mm. **Subject:** Pisces

Date	Mintage	F	VF	XF	Unc	BU
2008 Proof	—	Value: 325				

KM# 185 10000 DRAM
8.6000 g., 0.9000 Gold 0.2488 oz. AGW, 22 mm. **Subject:** Aries

Date	Mintage	F	VF	XF	Unc	BU
2008 Proof	—	Value: 325				

KM# 186 10000 DRAM
8.6000 g., 0.9000 Gold 0.2488 oz. AGW, 22 mm.
Subject: Taurus

Date	Mintage	F	VF	XF	Unc	BU
2008 Proof	—	Value: 325				

KM# 188 10000 DRAM
8.6000 g., 0.9000 Gold 0.2488 oz. AGW, 22 mm.
Subject: Gemini

Date	Mintage	F	VF	XF	Unc	BU
2008 Proof	—	Value: 325				

KM# 189 10000 DRAM
8.6000 g., 0.9000 Gold 0.2488 oz. AGW, 22 mm.
Subject: Cancer

Date	Mintage	F	VF	XF	Unc	BU
2008 Proof	—	Value: 325				

KM# 190 10000 DRAM
8.6000 g., 0.9000 Gold 0.2488 oz. AGW, 22 mm. **Subject:** Leo

Date	Mintage	F	VF	XF	Unc	BU
2008 Proof	—	Value: 325				

KM# 191 10000 DRAM
8.6000 g., 0.9000 Gold 0.2488 oz. AGW, 22 mm. **Subject:** Virgo

Date	Mintage	F	VF	XF	Unc	BU
2009 Proof	—	Value: 325				

KM# 194 10000 DRAM
8.6000 g., 0.9000 Gold 0.2488 oz. AGW, 22 mm.
Subject: Khachatour Aboryan, 200th Anniversary of birth

Date	Mintage	F	VF	XF	Unc	BU
2009 Proof	—	Value: 325				

KM# 118 50000 DRAM
8.6000 g., 0.9990 Gold 0.2762 oz. AGW, 22 mm.
Subject: Armenian Armed Forces **Obv:** Order of the Combat Cross of the Second Degree and the Emblem of the Ministry of Defense of the Republic of Armenia **Obv. Designer:** H. Samuelian **Rev:** Arms, date and denomination

Date	Mintage	F	VF	XF	Unc	BU
2005 Proof	1,000	Value: 400				

ARUBA

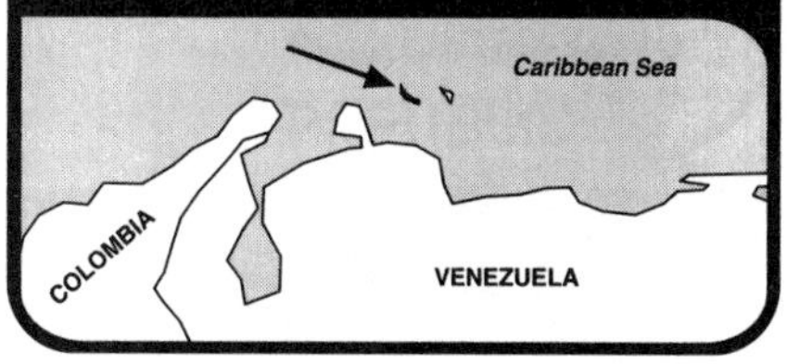

The second largest island of the Netherlands Antilles, Aruba is situated near the Venezuelan coast. The island has an area of 74-1/2 sq. mi. (193 sq. km.) and a population of 65,974. Capital: Oranjestad, named after the Dutch royal family. Aruba was important in the processing and transportation of petroleum products in the first part of the twentieth century, but today the chief industry is tourism.

For earlier issues see Curacao and the Netherlands Antilles.

RULER
Dutch

MINT MARKS
(u) Utrecht - Privy marks only
Wine tendril with grapes, 2001-
Wine tendril with grapes plus star, 2002-
Sails of a clipper, 2003-

MONETARY SYSTEM
100 Cents = 1 Florin

DUTCH STATE
"Status Aparte"

DECIMAL COINAGE

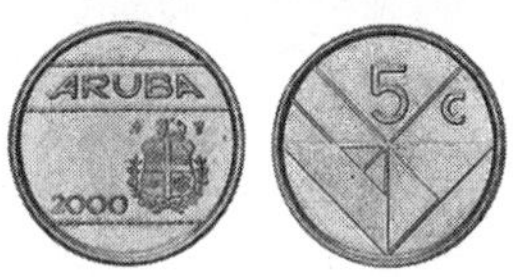

KM# 1 5 CENTS
2.0000 g., Nickel Bonded Steel, 16 mm. **Ruler:** Beatrix **Obv:** National arms **Rev:** Geometric design with value **Edge:** Plain

Date	Mintage	F	VF	XF	Unc	BU
2001(u)	946,900	—	—	—	0.30	0.60
2002(u)	1,006,000	—	—	—	0.20	0.50
2003(u)	1,104,100	—	—	—	0.20	0.50
2004(u)	502,500	—	—	0.20	0.50	1.00
2005(u)	602,500	—	—	—	0.20	0.50
2006(u)	602,000	—	—	—	0.20	0.50
2007(u)	1,152,000	—	—	—	0.20	0.50
2008(u)	1,152,000	—	—	—	0.20	0.50
2009(u)	—	—	—	—	0.20	0.50
2010(u)	—	—	—	—	0.20	0.50

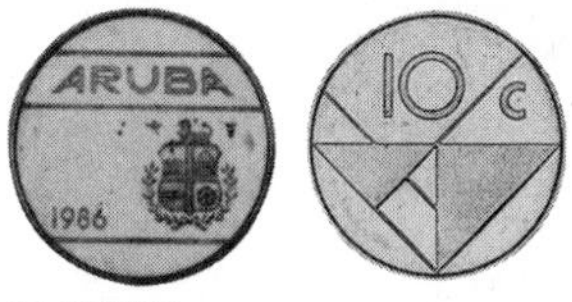

KM# 2 10 CENTS
3.0000 g., Nickel Bonded Steel, 17.9 mm. **Ruler:** Beatrix **Obv:** National arms **Rev:** Geometric design with value **Edge:** Reeded

Date	Mintage	F	VF	XF	Unc	BU
2001(u)	1,006,900	—	—	—	0.30	0.50
2002(u)	1,006,000	—	—	—	0.30	0.50
2003(u)	1,004,000	—	—	—	0.30	0.50
2004(u)	402,500	—	0.20	0.35	0.60	0.75
2005(u)	402,500	—	—	—	0.30	0.50
2006(u)	452,500	—	—	—	0.30	0.50
2007(u)	1,102,000	—	—	—	0.30	0.50
2008(u)	1,442,000	—	—	—	0.30	0.50
2009(u)	—	—	—	—	0.30	0.50
2009(u)	—	—	—	—	0.30	0.50
2010(u)	—	—	—	—	0.30	0.50

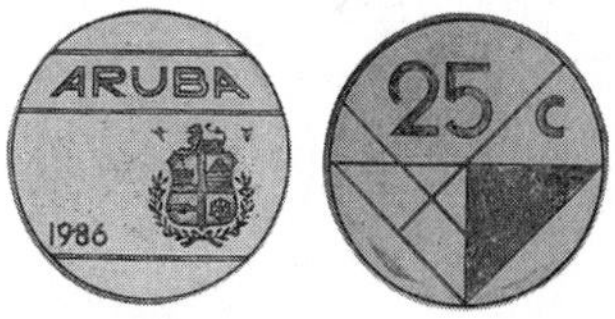

KM# 3 25 CENTS
3.5000 g., Nickel Bonded Steel, 20 mm. **Ruler:** Beatrix **Obv:** National arms **Rev:** Geometric design with value **Edge:** Plain

Date	Mintage	F	VF	XF	Unc	BU
2001(u)	716,900	—	—	—	0.35	0.80
2002(u)	806,000	—	—	—	0.35	0.80
2003(u)	804,000	—	—	—	0.35	0.80
2004(u)	362,500	—	—	—	0.40	0.80
2005(u)	302,500	—	—	—	0.40	0.80
2006(u)	302,000	—	—	—	0.40	0.80
2007(u)	202,000	—	—	—	0.50	1.00
2008(u)	202,000	—	—	—	0.50	1.00
2009(u)	—	—	—	—	0.50	1.00

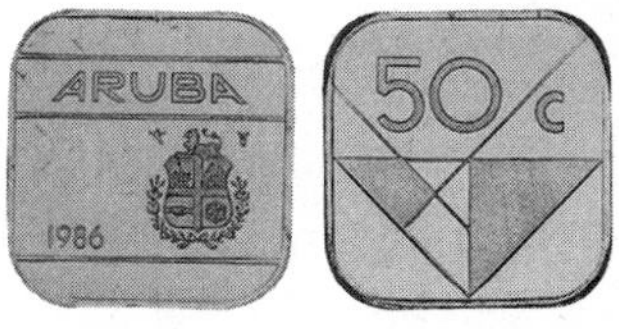

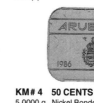

KM# 4 50 CENTS
5.0000 g., Nickel Bonded Steel, 20 mm. **Ruler:** Beatrix **Obv:** National arms **Rev:** Geometric design with value **Edge:** Plain **Shape:** 4-sided

Date	Mintage	F	VF	XF	Unc	BU
2001(u)	506,900	—	—	0.30	0.65	0.80
2002(u)	306,000	—	—	0.30	0.65	0.80
2003(u)	279,000	—	—	0.40	0.80	1.00
2004(u)	402,500	—	—	0.50	0.85	1.10
2005(u)	102,500	—	—	0.35	0.65	0.85

Date	Mintage	F	VF	XF	Unc	BU
2006(u)	102,500	—	—	0.35	0.65	0.85
2007(u)	32,000	—	—	0.60	1.20	1.50
2008(u)	302,000	—	—	0.60	1.20	1.50
2009(u)	—	—	—	0.60	1.20	1.50
2010(u)	—	—	—	0.60	1.20	1.50

KM# 5 FLORIN
8.4300 g., Nickel Bonded Steel, 26 mm. **Ruler:** Beatrix
Obv: Head left **Rev:** National arms **Edge:** Lettered
Edge Lettering: GOD * ZiJ * MET * ONS

Date	Mintage	F	VF	XF	Unc	BU
2001(u)	406,900	—	—	0.65	1.25	2.25
2002(u)	206,000	—	—	0.75	1.30	2.50
2003(u)	179,000	—	—	0.80	1.50	3.00
2004(u)	410,000	—	—	0.70	1.35	2.35
2005(u)	352,500	—	—	0.70	1.35	2.35
2006(u)	402,000	—	—	0.70	1.35	2.35
2007(u)	502,000	—	—	0.70	1.35	2.35
2008(u)	289,000	—	—	0.70	1.35	2.35
2009(u)	—	—	—	0.70	1.35	2.35
2010(u)	—	—	—	0.70	1.35	2.35

KM# 6 2-1/2 FLORIN
10.3000 g., Nickel Bonded Steel, 30 mm. **Ruler:** Beatrix
Obv: Head left **Rev:** National arms **Edge:** Lettered
Edge Lettering: GOD * ZiJ * MET * ONS

Date	Mintage	F	VF	XF	Unc	BU
2001(u) In sets only	6,900	—	—	—	3.50	5.00
2002(u) In sets only	6,000	—	—	—	3.50	5.00
2003(u) In sets only	4,000	—	—	—	3.50	5.00
2004(u) In sets only	2,500	—	—	—	3.50	5.00
2005(u) In sets only	2,500	—	—	—	3.50	5.00
2006(u) In sets only	2,000	—	—	—	3.50	5.00
2007(u) In sets only	2,000	—	—	—	3.50	5.00
2008(u) In sets only	2,000	—	—	—	3.50	5.00
2009(u) In sets only	2,000	—	—	—	3.50	5.00
2010(u) In sets only	—	—	—	—	3.50	5.00

KM# 12 5 FLORIN
8.6400 g., Nickel Bonded Steel, 26 mm. **Ruler:** Beatrix
Obv: Head left **Rev:** National arms **Edge:** Plain **Shape:** Square

Date	Mintage	F	VF	XF	Unc	BU
2001(u) In sets only	6,900	—	—	—	6.00	7.50
2002(u) In sets only	6,000	—	—	—	6.00	7.50
2003(u) In sets only	4,000	—	—	—	6.00	7.50
2004(u) In sets only	2,500	—	—	—	7.00	8.50
2005(u) In sets only	2,500	—	—	—	7.00	8.50

KM# 25 5 FLORIN
11.9000 g., 0.9250 Silver 0.3539 oz. ASW, 29 mm.
Ruler: Beatrix **Subject:** 50th Anniversary Charter for the
Kingdom of the Netherlands including Netherlands Antilles
Obv: Head left **Rev:** Royal seal **Rev. Designer:** E. Fingal
Edge: Lettered **Edge Lettering:** GOD ZIJ MET ONS

Date	Mintage	F	VF	XF	Unc	BU
2004(u) Proof	4,000	Value: 38.00				

KM# 34 5 FLORIN
11.9000 g., 0.9250 Silver 0.3539 oz. ASW, 29 mm.
Ruler: Beatrix **Subject:** Queen's Silver Jubilee **Obv:** Head left
Rev: Flag **Rev. Designer:** F.L. Croes **Edge:** lettered
Edge Lettering: GOD Z'J MET ONS

Date	Mintage	F	VF	XF	Unc	BU
2005(u) Proof	4,000	Value: 32.50				

KM# 38 5 FLORIN
8.4000 g., Nickel Bonded Steel, 22.5 mm. **Ruler:** Beatrix
Obv: Queen **Rev:** Value and arms **Edge:** Reeded and lettered
Edge Lettering: GOD Z'J MET ONS **Shape:** Round

Date	Mintage	F	VF	XF	Unc	BU
2005(u)	827,500	—	—	—	5.50	7.00
2006(u)	102,000	—	—	—	5.50	8.00
2007(u)	52,000	—	—	—	5.50	8.00
2008(u)	22,000	—	—	—	5.50	7.00
2009(u)	—	—	—	—	5.50	7.00
2010(u)	—	—	—	—	5.50	7.00

KM# 41 5 FLORIN
Silver **Ruler:** Beatrix **Obv:** Head left **Rev:** Two dolphins bounding out of the water

Date	Mintage	F	VF	XF	Unc	BU
2007 Proof	—	Value: 35.00				

KM# 38a 5 FLORIN
Aluminum-Bronze **Ruler:** Beatrix **Obv:** Queen **Rev:** Value and arms **Shape:** Round

Date	Mintage	F	VF	XF	Unc	BU
2008(u)	—	—	—	—	5.50	7.00

KM# 42 5 FLORIN
Silver **Ruler:** Beatrix **Subject:** Fiesta de San Juan **Rev:** Phoenix rising from flames and dancers

Date	Mintage	F	VF	XF	Unc	BU
2008 Proof	—	Value: 50.00				

KM# 43 5 FLORIN
Silver **Ruler:** Beatrix **Subject:** Dante at New Year's **Obv:** Head left **Rev:** Dance at New Year's

Date	Mintage	F	VF	XF	Unc	BU
2009 Proof	—	Value: 50.00				

KM# 20 10 FLORIN
25.0000 g., 0.9250 Silver 0.7435 oz. ASW, 38 mm.
Ruler: Beatrix **Subject:** Green Sea Turtles **Obv:** Head left **Rev:** Seven sea turtles **Edge:** Plain **Designer:** E. Fingal

Date	Mintage	F	VF	XF	Unc	BU
2001(u) Prooflike	2,000	—	—	—	—	60.00

KM# 24 10 FLORIN
17.8000 g., 0.9250 Silver 0.5293 oz. ASW, 33 mm.
Ruler: Beatrix **Subject:** Crown Prince's Wedding **Obv:** Head left
Rev: Conjoined busts of prince and princess Maxima, right
Edge Lettering: GOD ZIJ MET ONS **Designer:** G. Colley

Date	Mintage	F	VF	XF	Unc	BU
ND(2002)(u) Prooflike	5,000	—	—	—	—	40.00

KM# 27 10 FLORIN
25.0000 g., 0.9250 Silver 0.7435 oz. ASW, 38 mm.
Ruler: Beatrix **Obv:** Head left **Obv. Designer:** E. Fingal
Rev: Sea shell **Edge:** Plain

Date	Mintage	F	VF	XF	Unc	BU
2003(u) Proof	2,000	Value: 50.00				

KM# 28 10 FLORIN
25.0000 g., 0.9250 Silver 0.7435 oz. ASW, 38 mm.
Ruler: Beatrix **Obv:** Head left **Obv. Designer:** E. Fingal
Rev: Snake **Edge:** Plain

Date	Mintage	F	VF	XF	Unc	BU
2003(u) Proof	2,000	Value: 50.00				

KM# 29 10 FLORIN
25.0000 g., 0.9250 Silver 0.7435 oz. ASW, 38 mm. **Ruler:** Beatrix
Obv: Head left **Obv. Designer:** E. Fingal **Rev:** Owl **Edge:** Plain

Date	Mintage	F	VF	XF	Unc	BU
2003(u) Proof	1,000	Value: 65.00				

KM# 30 10 FLORIN
25.0000 g., 0.9250 Silver 0.7435 oz. ASW, 38 mm. **Ruler:** Beatrix
Obv: Head left **Obv. Designer:** E. Fingal **Rev:** Frog **Edge:** Plain

Date	Mintage	F	VF	XF	Unc	BU
2004(u) Proof	1,000	Value: 65.00				

KM# 31 10 FLORIN
25.0000 g., 0.9250 Silver 0.7435 oz. ASW, 38 mm. **Ruler:** Beatrix
Obv: Head left **Obv. Designer:** E. Fingal **Rev:** Fish **Edge:** Plain

Date	Mintage	F	VF	XF	Unc	BU
2004(u) Proof	1,000	Value: 65.00				

KM# 33 10 FLORIN
1.2442 g., 0.9990 Gold 0.0400 oz. AGW, 13.9 mm.
Ruler: Beatrix **Subject:** Death of Juliana **Obv:** Head left
Obv. Designer: E. Fingal **Rev:** Juliana in center **Edge:** Reeded

Date	Mintage	F	VF	XF	Unc	BU
ND (2004)(u) Proof	10,000	Value: 65.00				

KM# 26 10 FLORIN
6.7200 g., 0.9000 Gold 0.1944 oz. AGW, 22.5 mm.
Ruler: Beatrix **Subject:** 50th Anniversary of Autonomy **Obv:** Head left **Rev:** Royal seal **Edge:** Reeded **Designer:** E. Fingal

Date	Mintage	F	VF	XF	Unc	BU
2004(u) Proof	1,000	Value: 250				

KM# 35 10 FLORIN
6.7200 g., 0.9000 Gold 0.1944 oz. AGW, 22.5 mm.
Ruler: Beatrix **Subject:** Queen's Silver Jubilee **Obv:** Head left
Rev: Flag **Edge:** Reeded **Designer:** F.L. Croes

Date	Mintage	F	VF	XF	Unc	BU
2005(u) Proof	1,500	Value: 240				

KM# 36 10 FLORIN
25.0000 g., 0.9250 Silver 0.7435 oz. ASW, 38 mm.
Ruler: Beatrix **Subject:** Status Aparte **Obv:** Queen's portrait
Rev: Queen standing next to value and country name
Edge Lettering: DIOS TA CU NOS

Date	Mintage	F	VF	XF	Unc	BU
2006(u) Proof	2,000	Value: 35.00				

KM# 39 10 FLORIN
25.0000 g., 0.9250 Silver 0.7435 oz. ASW **Ruler:** Beatrix
Subject: Status Aparte 20th Anniversary - Flag 30th Anniversary
Obv: Female standing at right

Date	Mintage	F	VF	XF	Unc	BU
2006 Proof	—	Value: 50.00				

KM# 44 10 FLORIN
0.9000 Gold **Ruler:** Beatrix **Subject:** Carnival **Obv:** Head left
Rev: Costume headdress

Date	Mintage	F	VF	XF	Unc	BU
2009 Proof	—	Value: 75.00				

KM# 22 25 FLORIN
25.0000 g., 0.9250 Silver 0.7435 oz. ASW, 38 mm.
Ruler: Beatrix **Subject:** 15th Anniversary of Autonomy **Obv:**
Head left **Rev:** National arms and inscription **Edge:** Plain

Date	Mintage	F	VF	XF	Unc	BU
2001(u) Proof	3,000	Value: 45.00				

KM# 40 25 FLORIN
6.7200 g., 0.9000 Gold 0.1944 oz. AGW. **Ruler:** Beatrix
Subject: Status Aparte, 20th Anniversary - Flag 30th Anniversary
Obv: Female standing at right

Date	Mintage	F	VF	XF	Unc	BU
2006 Proof	—	Value: 275				

KM# 37 25 FLORIN
6.7200 g., 0.9000 Gold 0.1944 oz. AGW, 22.5 mm.
Ruler: Beatrix **Obv:** Queen's portrait **Rev:** Queen standing next to value and country name **Edge:** Reeded **Note:** Status Aparte

Date	Mintage	F	VF	XF	Unc	BU
2006(u) Proof	1,500	Value: 240				

KM# 23 100 FLORIN
6.7200 g., Gold, 22.5 mm. **Ruler:** Beatrix **Subject:**
Independence **Obv:** Arms, treaty name, dates **Rev:** Head left
Edge: Grained

Date	Mintage	F	VF	XF	Unc	BU
2001(u) Proof	1,000	Value: 275				

MINT SETS

KM#	Date	Mintage	Identification	Issue Price	Mkt Val
MS18	2001 (7)	—	KM#1-6, 12, with medal	15.00	20.00
MS19	2001 (7)	6,900	KM#1-6, 12	13.25	20.00
MS20	2002 (6)	6,000	KM# 1-6, 12	15.00	20.00
MS21	2003 (7)	4,000	KM# 1-6, 12	15.00	20.00
MS22	2004 (7)	2,500	KM# 1-6, 12	15.00	22.50
MS23	2005 (7)	2,500	KM# 1-6, 12	15.00	22.50
XMS1	2005 (8)	10,000	X#Pn1-Pn8	—	30.00
MS24	2006 (7)	2,000	KM# 1-6, 38	15.00	20.00
MS25	2007 (7)	2,500	KM#1-6, 38	20.00	20.00
MS26	2008 (7)	2,000	KM#1-6, 38	26.00	20.00
MS27	2009 (7)	2,000	KM#1-6, 38	26.00	20.00

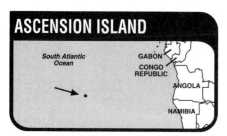

ASCENSION ISLAND

An island of volcanic origin, Ascension Island lies in the South Atlantic, 700 miles (1,100 km.) northwest of St. Helena. It has an area of 34 sq. mi. (88 sq. km.) on an island 9 miles (14 km.) long and 6 miles (10 km.) wide. Approximate population: 1,146. Although having little vegetation and scant rainfall, the island has a very healthy climate. The island is the nesting place for a large number of sea turtles and sooty terns. Phosphates and guano are the chief natural sources of income. Ascension is a dependency of the British Colony of St. Helena.

RULER
British

MINT MARKS
PM - Pobjoy Mint

BRITISH ADMINISTRATION
STANDARD COINAGE

KM# 13 50 PENCE
28.6300 g., Copper-Nickel, 38.6 mm. **Subject:** 75th Birthday of Queen Elizabeth **Obv:** Crowned bust right, denomination below
Obv. Designer: Raphael Maklouf **Rev:** Crowned monogram above flowers within circle, date below **Edge:** Reeded

Date	Mintage	F	VF	XF	Unc	BU
2001	—	—	—	—	8.00	9.50

KM# 13a 50 PENCE
28.2800 g., 0.9250 Silver 0.8410 oz. ASW, 38.6 mm.
Subject: Queen Elizabeth II's 75th Birthday **Obv:** Crowned bust right, denomination below **Obv. Designer:** Raphael Maklouf
Rev: Crowned monogram above roses within circle, date below
Edge: Reeded

Date	Mintage	F	VF	XF	Unc	BU
2001 Proof	10,000	Value: 40.00				

KM# 13b 50 PENCE
47.5400 g., 0.9166 Gold 1.4009 oz. AGW, 38.6 mm.
Subject: Queen Elizabeth II's 75th Birthday **Obv:** Crowned bust right, denomination below **Obv. Designer:** Raphael Maklouf
Rev: Crowned monogram above roses within circle, date below
Edge: Reeded

Date	Mintage	F	VF	XF	Unc	BU
2001 Proof	75	Value: 1,750				

KM# 14 50 PENCE
28.6300 g., Copper-Nickel, 38.6 mm. **Subject:** Centennial - Queen Victoria's Death **Obv:** Crowned bust right, denomination below **Obv. Designer:** Raphael Maklouf **Rev:** Crowned bust left, three dates **Edge:** Reeded

Date	Mintage	F	VF	XF	Unc	BU
2001	—	—	—	—	8.00	9.50

KM# 14a 50 PENCE
28.2800 g., 0.9250 Silver 0.8410 oz. ASW, 38.6 mm.
Subject: Centennial of Queen Victoria's Death **Obv:** Crowned bust right, denomination below **Obv. Designer:** Raphael Maklouf
Rev: Crowned bust left, three dates **Edge:** Reeded

Date	Mintage	F	VF	XF	Unc	BU
2001 Proof	10,000	Value: 40.00				

KM# 14b 50 PENCE
47.5400 g., 0.9166 Gold 1.4009 oz. AGW, 38.6 mm.
Subject: Centennial of Queen Victoria's Death **Obv:** Crowned bust right, denomination below **Obv. Designer:** Raphael Maklouf
Rev: Crowned bust left, three dates **Edge:** Reeded

Date	Mintage	F	VF	XF	Unc	BU
2001 Proof	100	Value: 1,750				

KM# 15 50 PENCE
28.3500 g., Copper-Nickel, 38.6 mm. **Subject:** Queen's Golden Jubilee **Obv:** Crowned bust right, denomination below
Obv. Designer: Raphael Maklouf **Rev:** Westminster Abbey, monogram at left, circle surrounds, two dates below
Edge: Reeded

Date	Mintage	F	VF	XF	Unc	BU
ND(2002)	—	—	—	—	8.00	9.50

KM# 15a 50 PENCE
28.2800 g., 0.9250 Silver 0.8410 oz. ASW, 38.6 mm.
Subject: Queen Elizabeth II's Golden Jubilee **Obv:** Gold plated crowned bust right, denomination below **Obv. Designer:**
Raphael Maklouf **Rev:** Monogram and Westminster Abbey within circle, dates below **Edge:** Reeded

Date	Mintage	F	VF	XF	Unc	BU
ND(2002) Proof	10,000	Value: 40.00				

KM# 18 50 PENCE
28.2800 g., Copper-Nickel, 38.6 mm. **Subject:** Death of Queen Mother **Obv:** Crowned bust right, denomination below
Obv. Designer: Raphael Maklouf **Rev:** Queen Mother bust right, between her life dates **Edge:** Reeded

Date	Mintage	F	VF	XF	Unc	BU
ND(2002)	—	—	—	—	10.00	12.00

KM# 18a 50 PENCE
28.2800 g., 0.9250 Silver 0.8410 oz. ASW, 38.6 mm.
Subject: Death of Queen Mother **Obv:** Crowned bust right, denomination below **Rev:** Queen Mother bust right, between her life dates **Edge:** Reeded

Date	Mintage	F	VF	XF	Unc	BU
ND(2002) Proof	10,000	Value: 35.00				

KM# 16 50 PENCE
28.3600 g., Copper-Nickel, 38.6 mm. **Subject:** Coronation Jubilee **Obv:** Crowned bust right, denomination below
Obv. Designer: Raphael Maklouf **Rev:** Crown, two sceptres and the ampula **Edge:** Reeded

Date	Mintage	F	VF	XF	Unc	BU
ND (2003) Prooflike	—	—	—	—	10.00	12.00

KM# 16a 50 PENCE
28.2800 g., 0.9250 Silver 0.8410 oz. ASW, 38.6 mm. **Subject:** Queen Elizabeth II's - 50th Anniversary of Coronation **Obv:** Crowned bust right, denomination below **Obv. Designer:** Raphael Maklouf **Rev:** Crown, two sceptres and the ampula **Edge:** Reeded

Date	Mintage	F	VF	XF	Unc	BU
ND(2003) Proof	5,000	Value: 50.00				

KM# 16b 50 PENCE
39.9400 g., 0.9166 Gold 1.1770 oz. AGW, 38.6 mm. **Subject:** Queen Elizabeth II's - 50th Anniversary of Coronation **Obv:** Crowned bust right, denomination below **Obv. Designer:** Raphael Maklouf **Rev:** Crown, two sceptres and the ampula **Edge:** Reeded

Date	Mintage	F	VF	XF	Unc	BU
ND(2003) Proof	50	Value: 1,500				

KM# 17 50 PENCE
28.2800 g., Copper-Nickel, 38.6 mm. **Subject:** Queen Elizabeth II's - 50th Anniversary of Coronation **Obv:** Crowned head right, denomination below **Obv. Designer:** Raphael Maklouf **Rev:** Crowned monogram **Edge:** Reeded

Date	Mintage	F	VF	XF	Unc	BU
ND(2003)	—	—	—	—	10.00	12.00

KM# 17a 50 PENCE
28.2800 g., 0.9250 Silver 0.8410 oz. ASW, 38.6 mm. **Subject:** Queen Elizabeth II's- 50th Anniversary of Coronation **Obv:** Crowned head right, denomination below **Obv. Designer:** Raphael Maklouf **Rev:** Crowned monogram **Edge:** Reeded

Date	Mintage	F	VF	XF	Unc	BU
ND(2003) Proof	5,000	Value: 50.00				

KM# 17b 50 PENCE
39.9400 g., 0.9166 Gold 1.1770 oz. AGW, 38.6 mm. **Subject:** Queen Elizabeth II's- 50th Anniversary of Coronation **Obv:** Crowned bust right, denomination below **Obv. Designer:** Raphael Maklouf **Rev:** Crowned monogram **Edge:** Reeded

Date	Mintage	F	VF	XF	Unc	BU
ND(2003) Proof	50	Value: 1,500				

AUSTRALIA

The Commonwealth of Australia, the smallest continent in the world, is located south of Indonesia between the Indian and Pacific oceans. It has an area of 2,967,893 sq. mi. (7,686,850 sq. km.) and an estimated population of 18.84 million. Capital: Canberra. Due to its early and sustained isolation, Australia is the habitat of such curious and unique fauna as the kangaroo, koala, platypus, wombat, echidna and frilled-necked lizard. The con-

tinent possesses extensive mineral deposits, the most important of which are iron ore, coal, gold, silver, nickel, uranium, lead and zinc. Raising livestock, mining and manufacturing are the principal industries. Chief exports are wool, meat, wheat, iron ore, coal and nonferrous metals.

Australia is a founding member of the Commonwealth of Nations. Elizabeth II is the Head of State as Queen of Australia; the Prime Minister is Head of Government.

NOTE: Home market grading of Australian coinage is generally stricter than USA practiced standards. The pricing in this catalog reflects strict home market grading standard.

RULER
British until 1942

MONETARY SYSTEM
100 Cents = 1 Dollar

COMMONWEALTH OF AUSTRALIA

MINT MARKS
M – Melbourne
P – Perth
S – Sydney
(sy) - Sydney

DECIMAL COINAGE

KM# 767 CENT
2.5900 g., Bronze, 17.53 mm. **Ruler:** Elizabeth II **Obv:** Head with tiara right **Obv. Designer:** Ian Rank-Broadley **Rev:** Feather-tailed glider **Rev. Designer:** Stuart Devlin **Edge:** Plain

Date	Mintage	F	VF	XF	Unc	BU
2006B In sets only	—	—	—	—	2.25	3.00
2006B Proof	—	—	Value: 5.00			

KM# 62a CENT
2.5900 g., 0.9990 Silver 0.0832 oz. ASW, 17.53 mm. **Ruler:** Elizabeth II **Obv:** Young bust right **Rev:** Feather-tailed glider **Rev. Designer:** Stuart Devlin **Edge:** Plain

Date	Mintage	F	VF	XF	Unc	BU
2006 Proof	6,500	Value: 15.00				

KM# 767b CENT
5.6100 g., 0.9990 Gold 0.1802 oz. AGW, 17.53 mm. **Ruler:** Elizabeth II **Obv:** Head with tiara right **Obv. Designer:** Ian Rank-Broadley **Rev:** Feather-tailed glider **Rev. Designer:** Stuart Devlin **Edge:** Plain

Date	Mintage	F	VF	XF	Unc	BU
2006 Proof	300	Value: 600				

KM# 1249 CENT
2.4300 g., 0.9990 Silver 0.0780 oz. ASW, 17.6 mm. **Ruler:** Elizabeth II **Subject:** 1966 Decimal Pattern **Obv:** Head right **Obv. Designer:** Ian Rank-Broadley **Rev:** Waratah, flower of New South Wales **Rev. Designer:** Andor Meszaros

Date	Mintage	F	VF	XF	Unc	BU
2009P Proof	7,500	Value: 15.00				

KM# 768 2 CENTS
5.1800 g., Bronze, 21.59 mm. **Ruler:** Elizabeth II **Obv:** Head with tiara right **Obv. Designer:** Ian Rank-Broadley **Rev:** Frill-necked Lizard

Date	Mintage	F	VF	XF	Unc	BU
2006B	—	—	—	—	2.25	3.00
2006B Proof	—	—	Value: 5.00			

KM# 63a 2 CENTS
5.1800 g., 0.9990 Silver 0.1664 oz. ASW, 21.59 mm. **Ruler:** Elizabeth II **Obv:** Young bust right **Obv. Designer:** Arnold

Machin **Rev:** Frill-necked Lizard **Rev. Designer:** Stuart Devlin **Edge:** Plain

Date	Mintage	F	VF	XF	Unc	BU
2006 Proof	6,500	Value: 15.00				

KM# 768b 2 CENTS
11.3100 g., 0.9990 Gold 0.3632 oz. AGW, 21.59 mm. **Ruler:** Elizabeth II **Obv:** Head with tiara right **Obv. Designer:** Ian Rank-Broadley **Rev:** Frill-necked Lizard **Rev. Designer:** Stuart Devlin **Edge:** Plain

Date	Mintage	F	VF	XF	Unc	BU
2006 Proof	300	Value: 600				

KM# 1250 2 CENTS
5.5300 g., 0.9990 Silver 0.1776 oz. ASW, 21.6 mm. **Ruler:** Elizabeth II **Subject:** 1966 Decimal Pattern **Obv:** Head right **Obv. Designer:** Ian Rank-Broadley **Rev:** Wattle, national flower **Rev. Designer:** Andor Meszaros

Date	Mintage	F	VF	XF	Unc	BU
2009P Proof	7,500	Value: 20.00				

KM# 401 5 CENTS
2.8300 g., Copper-Nickel, 19.4 mm. **Ruler:** Elizabeth II **Obv:** Head with tiara right **Obv. Designer:** Ian Rank-Broadley **Rev:** Echidna **Rev. Designer:** Stuart Devlin **Edge:** Reeded

Date	Mintage	F	VF	XF	Unc	BU
2001	174,579,000	—	—	—	—	0.20
	Note: Large obverse head, IRB spaced					
2001	Inc. above	—	—	—	—	0.20
	Note: Smaller obverse head, RB joined					
2001 Proof	59,569	Value: 3.00				
2002	148,812,000	—	—	—	—	0.20
2002 Proof	39,514	Value: 2.50				
2003	113,470,000	—	—	—	—	0.20
2003 Proof	39,090	Value: 2.00				
2004	147,658,000	—	—	—	—	0.20
	Note: Normal sized SD					
2004	Inc. above	—	—	—	—	0.20
	Note: Smaller SD					
2004 Proof	50,000	Value: 2.50				
2005	194,300,000	—	—	—	—	0.20
	Note: Normal sized SD					
2005	Inc. above	—	—	—	—	0.20
	Note: Smaller SD					
2005 Proof	33,520	Value: 2.50				
2006	—	—	—	—	—	0.20
2006 Proof	—	Value: 2.50				
2007	—	—	—	—	—	0.20
2007 Proof	—	Value: 2.00				
2008	—	—	—	—	—	0.20
2008 Proof	—	Value: 2.00				
2009	—	—	—	—	—	0.20
2009 Proof	—	Value: 2.00				

KM# 401a 5 CENTS
6.0300 g., 0.9990 Gold 0.1937 oz. AGW, 19.41 mm. **Ruler:** Elizabeth II **Subject:** Federation Centennial **Obv:** Head with tiara right **Obv. Designer:** Ian Rank-Broadley **Rev:** Echidna **Rev. Designer:** Stuart Devlin

Date	Mintage	F	VF	XF	Unc	BU
2001B Proof	650	Value: 600				
2005B Proof	650	Value: 350				
2006B Proof	300	Value: 600				

KM# 401b 5 CENTS
3.2400 g., 0.9990 Silver 0.1042 oz. ASW, 19.41 mm. **Ruler:** Elizabeth II **Obv:** Head with tiara right **Obv. Designer:** Ian Rank-Broadley **Rev:** Echidna **Rev. Designer:** Stuart Devlin **Edge:** Reeded

Date	Mintage	F	VF	XF	Unc	BU
2003B Proof	6,500	Value: 20.00				
2004B Proof	6,500	Value: 15.00				
2005B Proof	6,500	Value: 15.00				
2006B Proof	—	Value: 15.00				
2007B Proof	—	Value: 15.00				
2008B Proof	—	Value: 15.00				
2009B Proof	—	Value: 15.00				

KM# 64a 5 CENTS
3.2400 g., 0.9990 Silver 0.1041 oz. ASW, 19.41 mm. **Ruler:** Elizabeth II **Obv:** Young bust right **Obv. Designer:** Arnold Machin **Rev:** Echidna **Rev. Designer:** Stuart Devlin **Edge:** Reeded

Date	Mintage	F	VF	XF	Unc	BU
2006 Proof	6,500	Value: 15.00				

KM# 1251 5 CENTS
2.7400 g., 0.9990 Silver 0.0880 oz. ASW, 19.6 mm. **Ruler:** Elizabeth II **Subject:** 1966 Decimal Pattern **Obv:** Head right **Obv. Designer:** Ian Rank-Broadley **Rev:** Platypus and yabbie **Rev. Designer:** Andor Meszaros

Date	Mintage	F	VF	XF	Unc	BU
2009P Proof	7,500	Value: 30.00				

KM# 402   10 CENTS
5.6600 g., Copper-Nickel, 23.6 mm.   **Ruler:** Elizabeth II
Obv: Head with tiara right **Obv. Designer:** Ian Rank-Broadley
Rev: Lyrebird **Rev. Designer:** Stuart Devlin **Edge:** Reeded

Date	Mintage	F	VF	XF	Unc	BU
2001	109,357,000	—	—	—	—	0.50
Note: Large obverse head, IRB spaced						
2001	Inc. above	—	—	—	—	0.50
Note: Smaller obverse head, RB joined						
2001 Proof	59,569	Value: 3.00				
2002	70,329,000	—	—	—	—	0.50
2002 Proof	39,514	Value: 3.00				
2003	53,635,000	—	—	—	—	0.50
2003 Proof	39,090	Value: 3.00				
2004	147,658,000	—	—	—	—	0.50
2004 Proof	50,000	Value: 3.00				
2005	—	—	—	—	—	0.50
2005 Proof	33,520	Value: 3.00				
2006	—	—	—	—	—	0.50
2006 Proof	—	Value: 3.00				
2007	—	—	—	—	—	0.50
2007 Proof	—	Value: 3.00				
2008	—	—	—	—	—	0.50
2008 Proof	—	Value: 3.00				
2009	—	—	—	—	—	0.50
2009 Proof	—	Value: 3.00				

KM# 402a   10 CENTS
12.1400 g., 0.9999 Gold 0.3903 oz. AGW, 23.6 mm.
Ruler: Elizabeth II **Subject:** Federation Centennial **Obv:** Head
with tiara right **Obv. Designer:** Ian Rank-Broadley **Rev:** Lyrebird
Rev. Designer: Stuart Devlin **Edge:** Reeded

Date	Mintage	F	VF	XF	Unc	BU
2001B Proof	650	Value: 650				
2005B Proof	650	Value: 500				
2006B Proof	300	Value: 650				

KM# 402b   10 CENTS
6.5700 g., 0.9999 Silver 0.2112 oz. ASW, 23.6 mm.
Ruler: Elizabeth II **Obv:** Head with tiara right **Obv. Designer:**
Ian Rank-Broadley **Rev:** Lyrebird **Rev. Designer:** Stuart Devlin
Edge: Reeded

Date	Mintage	F	VF	XF	Unc	BU
2003B Proof	6,500	Value: 20.00				
2004B Proof	6,500	Value: 15.00				
2005B Proof	6,500	Value: 15.00				
2006B Proof	—	Value: 15.00				
2007B Proof	—	Value: 15.00				
2008B Proof	—	Value: 15.00				
2009B Proof	—	Value: 15.00				

KM# 65a   10 CENTS
6.5700 g., 0.9990 Silver 0.2110 oz. ASW, 23.6 mm.
Ruler: Elizabeth II **Obv:** Young bust right **Obv. Designer:** Arnold
Machin **Rev:** Superb Lyrebird **Rev. Designer:** Stuart Devlin
Edge: Reeded

Date	Mintage	F	VF	XF	Unc	BU
2006 Proof	6,500	Value: 15.00				

KM# 1252   10 CENTS
6.0700 g., 0.9990 Silver 0.1950 oz. ASW, 23.6 mm.
Ruler: Elizabeth II **Subject:** 1966 Decimal Pattern **Obv:** Head
right **Obv. Designer:** Ian Rank-Broadley **Rev:** Kookaburra eating
snake **Rev. Designer:** Andor Meszaros

Date	Mintage	F	VF	XF	Unc	BU
2009P Proof	7,500	Value: 45.00				

KM# 403   20 CENTS
11.3000 g., Copper-Nickel, 28.5 mm.   **Ruler:** Elizabeth II
Obv: Head with tiara right **Obv. Designer:** Ian Rank-Broadley
Rev: Duckbill Platypus **Rev. Designer:** Stuart Devlin
Edge: Reeded

Date	Mintage	F	VF	XF	Unc	BU
2001	81,967,000	—	—	—	—	0.80
Note: IRB spaced						
2001	Inc. above	—	—	—	—	0.80
Note: RB joined						
2001	Inc. above	—	—	—	—	0.80
Note: IRB joined						
2001 Proof	59,569	Value: 10.00				
2002	27,244,000	—	—	—	—	0.80
2002 Proof	39,514	Value: 6.00				
2004	74,609,000	—	—	—	—	0.80
Note: Small obverse head, flat top A						
2004	Est. 400,000	—	—	—	4.00	7.00
Note: Large obverse head, pointed A						
2004 Proof	50,000	Value: 6.00				
Note: Large obverse head, pointed top A						
2004 Proof	Inc. above	Value: 6.00				
Note: Small obverse head, flat top A						
2005	1,600,000	—	—	—	5.00	7.50
2005 Proof	—	Value: 6.00				
2006	—	—	—	—	—	0.80
2006 Proof	—	Value: 6.00				
2007	—	—	—	—	—	0.80
2007 Proof	—	Value: 6.00				
2008	—	—	—	—	—	0.80
2008 Proof	—	Value: 6.00				
2009	—	—	—	—	—	0.80
2009 Proof	—	Value: 6.00				

KM# 532   20 CENTS
11.3100 g., Copper-Nickel, 28.52 mm.   **Ruler:** Elizabeth II **Subject:**
Centenary of Federation - Norfolk Island **Obv:** Head with tiara right
Obv. Designer: Ian Rank-Broadley **Rev:** Norfolk Pine over map of
island **Rev. Designer:** Megan Cummings **Edge:** Reeded

Date	Mintage	F	VF	XF	Unc	BU
2001B	2,000,000	—	—	—	3.50	5.00
2001B Proof	—	Value: 10.00				

KM# 550   20 CENTS
11.3000 g., Copper-Nickel, 28.5 mm.   **Ruler:** Elizabeth II
Series: Centenary of Federation - New South Wales **Obv:** Head
with tiara right **Obv. Designer:** Ian Rank-Broadley **Rev:** Waratah
on state map **Rev. Designer:** Joseph Neve **Edge:** Reeded

Date	Mintage	F	VF	XF	Unc	BU
2001	2,000,000	—	—	—	3.50	5.00
2001 Proof	—	Value: 10.00				

KM# 552   20 CENTS
11.3000 g., Copper-Nickel, 28.5 mm.   **Ruler:** Elizabeth II **Series:**
Centenary of Federation - Australian Capital Territory **Obv:** Head
with tiara right **Obv. Designer:** Ian Rank-Broadley **Rev:**
Parliament House, map, flowers **Rev. Designer:** Stacy Jo-Ann
Paine **Edge:** Reeded **Note:** Prev. KM#551.

Date	Mintage	F	VF	XF	Unc	BU
2001	2,000,000	—	—	—	3.50	5.00
2001 Proof	—	Value: 10.00				

KM# 554   20 CENTS
11.3000 g., Copper-Nickel, 28.5 mm.   **Ruler:** Elizabeth II
Series: Centenary of Federation - Queensland **Obv:** Head with
tiara right **Obv. Designer:** Ian Rank-Broadley **Rev:** Jennifer Gray
Edge: Reeded

Date	Mintage	F	VF	XF	Unc	BU
2001	2,320,000	—	—	—	3.50	5.00
2001 Proof	—	Value: 10.00				

KM# 556   20 CENTS
11.3000 g., Copper-Nickel, 28.5 mm.   **Ruler:** Elizabeth II
Series: Centenary of Federation - Victoria **Obv:** Head with tiara
right **Obv. Designer:** Ian Rank-Broadley **Rev:** Capital building
Rev. Designer: Ryan Ladd & Mark Kennedy **Edge:** Reeded

Date	Mintage	F	VF	XF	Unc	BU
2001	2,000,000	—	—	—	3.50	5.00
2001 Proof	—	Value: 10.00				

KM# 558   20 CENTS
11.3000 g., Copper-Nickel, 28.5 mm.   **Ruler:** Elizabeth II **Series:**
Centenary of Federation - Northern Territory **Obv:** Head with tiara
right **Obv. Designer:** Ian Rank-Broadley **Rev:** Two brolga cranes
in ritual dance **Rev. Designer:** Lisa Brett **Edge:** Reeded

Date	Mintage	F	VF	XF	Unc	BU
2001	2,100,000	—	—	—	3.50	5.00
2001 Proof	—	Value: 10.00				

KM# 560   20 CENTS
11.3000 g., Copper-Nickel, 28.5 mm.   **Ruler:** Elizabeth II
Series: Centenary of Federation - South Australia **Obv:** Head
with tiara right **Obv. Designer:** Ian Rank-Broadley **Rev:** Sturt's
Desert Pea, landscape and southern cross **Rev. Designer:** Lisa
Murphy **Edge:** Reeded

Date	Mintage	F	VF	XF	Unc	BU
2001	2,320,000	—	—	—	3.50	5.00
2001 Proof	—	Value: 10.00				

KM# 562   20 CENTS
11.3000 g., Copper-Nickel, 28.5 mm.   **Ruler:** Elizabeth II
Series: Centenary of Federation - Western Australia **Obv:** Head
with tiara right **Obv. Designer:** Ian Rank-Broadley **Rev:** Rabbit-
eared Bandicoot (bilby), plant and map **Rev. Designer:** Janice
Ng **Edge:** Reeded

Date	Mintage	F	VF	XF	Unc	BU
2001	2,000,000	—	—	—	3.50	5.50
2001 Proof	—	Value: 10.00				

KM# 564 20 CENTS
11.3000 g., Copper-Nickel, 28.5 mm. **Ruler:** Elizabeth II **Series:** Centenary of Federation - Tasmania **Obv:** Head with tiara right **Obv. Designer:** Ian Rank-Broadley **Rev:** Tasmanian Tiger on map **Rev. Designer:** Abbey MacDonald **Edge:** Reeded

Date	Mintage	F	VF	XF	Unc	BU
2001	2,000,000	—	—	—	3.50	5.50
2001 Proof	—	Value: 10.00				

KM# 589 20 CENTS
11.3000 g., Copper-Nickel, 28.5 mm. **Ruler:** Elizabeth II **Subject:** Sir Donald Bradman **Obv:** Head with tiara right **Obv. Designer:** Ian Rank-Broadley **Rev:** Sir Donald Bradman **Rev. Designer:** Vladimir Gottwald **Edge:** Reeded

Date	Mintage	F	VF	XF	Unc	BU
2001B	10,000,000	—	—	—	1.50	3.00

KM# 819 20 CENTS
24.3600 g., 0.9990 Gold 0.7824 oz. AGW, 28.52 mm. **Ruler:** Elizabeth II **Obv:** Head with tiara right **Obv. Designer:** Ian Rank-Broadley **Rev:** Platypus with Federation Star **Rev. Designer:** Stuart Devlin **Edge:** Reeded

Date	Mintage	F	VF	XF	Unc	BU
2001 Proof	650	Value: 975				

KM# 403a 20 CENTS
13.3600 g., 0.9999 Silver 0.4295 oz. ASW, 28.52 mm. **Ruler:** Elizabeth II **Obv:** Head with tiara right **Obv. Designer:** Ian Rank-Broadley **Rev:** Platypus **Rev. Designer:** Stuart Devlin **Edge:** Reeded

Date	Mintage	F	VF	XF	Unc	BU
2003B Proof	6,500	Value: 20.00				
2004B Proof	6,500	Value: 15.00				
2006B Proof	6,500	Value: 15.00				
2007B Proof	—	Value: 15.00				
2008B Proof	—	Value: 15.00				
2009B Proof	—	Value: 15.00				

KM# 688 20 CENTS
11.3000 g., Copper-Nickel, 28.52 mm. **Ruler:** Elizabeth II **Obv:** Head with tiara right **Obv. Designer:** Ian Rank-Broadley **Rev:** Group of Australian Volunteers **Rev. Designer:** Sir Vladimir Gottwald **Edge:** Reeded

Date	Mintage	F	VF	XF	Unc	BU
2003B	7,600,000	—	—	—	1.50	2.50
2003B Proof	—	Value: 4.00				

KM# 688a 20 CENTS
11.3000 g., 0.9990 Silver 0.3629 oz. ASW, 28.52 mm. **Ruler:** Elizabeth II **Obv:** Head right **Rev:** Group of Australian Volunteers **Edge:** Reeded

Date	Mintage	F	VF	XF	Unc	BU
2003B Proof	6,500	Value: 25.00				

KM# 688b 20 CENTS
24.3600 g., 0.9990 Gold 0.7824 oz. AGW, 28.52 mm. **Ruler:** Elizabeth II **Obv:** Head with tiara right **Obv. Designer:** Ian Rank-Broadley **Rev:** Group of Australian Volunteers **Rev. Designer:** Vladimir Gottwald **Edge:** Reeded

Date	Mintage	F	VF	XF	Unc	BU
2003B Proof	650	Value: 975				

KM# 745 20 CENTS
11.3000 g., Copper-Nickel, 28.52 mm. **Ruler:** Elizabeth II **Obv:** Head right **Obv. Designer:** Ian Rank-Broadley **Rev:** Soldier with wife and child **Rev. Designer:** Vladimir Gottwald **Edge:** Reeded

Date	Mintage	F	VF	XF	Unc	BU
2005B	33,500,000	—	—	—	1.50	2.00
2005B Proof	—	Value: 6.00				

KM# 745a 20 CENTS
13.3600 g., 0.9990 Silver 0.4291 oz. ASW, 28.52 mm. **Ruler:** Elizabeth II **Obv:** Head right **Rev:** Soldier with wife and child **Edge:** Reeded

Date	Mintage	F	VF	XF	Unc	BU
2005B Proof	6,500	Value: 15.00				

KM# 745b 20 CENTS
24.3600 g., 0.9999 Gold 0.7831 oz. AGW, 28.52 mm. **Ruler:** Elizabeth II **Obv:** Head right **Rev:** Soldier with wife and child **Edge:** Reeded

Date	Mintage	F	VF	XF	Unc	BU
2005B Proof	650	Value: 975				

KM# 66a 20 CENTS
13.3600 g., 0.9990 Silver 0.4291 oz. ASW, 28.52 mm. **Ruler:** Elizabeth II **Obv:** Young bust right **Obv. Designer:** Arnold Machin **Rev:** Platypus **Rev. Designer:** Stuart Devlin **Edge:** Reeded

Date	Mintage	F	VF	XF	Unc	BU
2006 Proof	6,500	Value: 15.00				

KM# 403b 20 CENTS
24.5600 g., 0.9999 Gold 0.7895 oz. AGW, 28.52 mm. **Ruler:** Elizabeth II **Subject:** Federation Centennial **Obv:** Head with tiara right **Obv. Designer:** Ian Rank-Broadley **Rev:** Duckbill Platyus **Rev. Designer:** Stuart Devlin **Edge:** Reeded

Date	Mintage	F	VF	XF	Unc	BU
2006B Proof	300	Value: 1,000				

KM# 820 20 CENTS
11.3100 g., Copper-Nickel, 28.52 mm. **Ruler:** Elizabeth II **Subject:** Year of the Surf Lifesaver **Obv:** Head with tiara right **Obv. Designer:** Ian Rank-Broadley **Rev:** Lifesaver working line **Rev. Designer:** Vladimir Gottwald **Edge:** Reeded

Date	Mintage	F	VF	XF	Unc	BU
2007	—	—	—	—	3.50	6.00
2007 Proof	—	Value: 10.00				

KM# 1043 20 CENTS
15.5500 g., Copper-Nickel, 28.52 mm. **Ruler:** Elizabeth II **Subject:** Year of the surfer lifesaver **Rev:** Female within rope line

Date	Mintage	F	VF	XF	Unc	BU
2007B	—	—	—	—	4.00	6.00

KM# 1043a 20 CENTS
13.3600 g., 0.9990 Silver 0.4291 oz. ASW, 28.52 mm. **Ruler:** Elizabeth II **Subject:** Year of the surfer lifesaver **Rev:** Female with rope line

Date	Mintage	F	VF	XF	Unc	BU
2007B Proof	—	Value: 20.00				

KM# 1058 20 CENTS
11.3000 g., Copper-Nickel, 28.52 mm. **Ruler:** Elizabeth II **Subject:** Planet earth **Rev:** Map of Australia with water and rocks around **Rev. Designer:** V. Gottwald

Date	Mintage	F	VF	XF	Unc	BU
2008 Unc	—	—	—	—	4.00	6.00
2008 Proof	—	Value: 20.00				

KM# 1075 20 CENTS
15.5500 g., Copper-Nickel, 28.52 mm. **Ruler:** Elizabeth II **Subject:** Year of Astronomy **Rev:** Star gazers

Date	Mintage	F	VF	XF	Unc	BU
2009 Unc	—	—	—	—	4.00	6.00
2009 Proof	—	Value: 20.00				

KM# 1088 20 CENTS
15.5500 g., Copper-Nickel, 28.52 mm. **Ruler:** Elizabeth II **Rev:** Poppy

Date	Mintage	F	VF	XF	Unc	BU
2009	—	—	—	—	4.00	6.00

KM# 1253 20 CENTS
12.8600 g., 0.9990 Silver 0.4130 oz. ASW, 28.6 mm. **Ruler:** Elizabeth II **Subject:** 1966 Decimal Pattern **Obv:** Head right **Obv. Designer:** Ian Rank-Broadley **Rev:** Black swan in flight **Rev. Designer:** Andor Meszaros

Date	Mintage	F	VF	XF	Unc	BU
2009P Proof	10,000	Value: 65.00				

KM# 599 25 CENTS
7.7750 g., 0.9990 Silver 0.2497 oz. ASW, 24.8 mm. **Ruler:** Elizabeth II **Obv:** Head with tiara right **Obv. Designer:** Ian Rank-Broadley **Rev:** Parliament House **Edge:** Plain **Shape:** 7-pointed star **Note:** "The Dump" portion of the "Holey Dollar" KM#598.

Date	Mintage	F	VF	XF	Unc	BU
2001 Prooflike	30,000	—	—	—	—	17.50

KM# 1010 25 CENTS
0.9990 Silver Gilt, 17.8 mm. **Ruler:** Elizabeth II **Obv:** Bust with tiara right **Obv. Legend:** ELIZABETH II - AUSTRALIA **Obv. Designer:** Ian Rank-Broadley **Rev:** 4 Chinese characters **Rev. Legend:** LUNAR NEW YEAR - GOOD FORTUNE & PROSPERITY

Date	Mintage	F	VF	XF	Unc	BU
2007 Proof	8,888	Value: 35.00				

KM# 491.1 50 CENTS
15.7000 g., Copper-Nickel, 32 mm. **Ruler:** Elizabeth II **Subject:** Centenary of Federation, 1901-2001 **Obv:** Head with tiara right **Obv. Designer:** Ian Rank-Broadley **Rev:** Commonwealth coat of arms **Edge:** Plain **Shape:** 12-sided **Note:** Prev. KM#491.

Date	Mintage	F	VF	XF	Unc	BU
2001B	43,149,600	—	—	—	2.00	3.00
2001B Proof	—	Value: 5.00				

KM# 491.1a 50 CENTS
33.8800 g., 0.9999 Gold 1.0891 oz. AGW, 31.51 mm. **Ruler:** Elizabeth II **Subject:** Federation Centennial **Obv:** Elizabeth II **Obv. Designer:** Ian Rank-Broadley **Rev:** Commonwealth arms above value

Date	Mintage	F	VF	XF	Unc	BU
2001B Proof	650	Value: 1,400				

KM# 491.2 50 CENTS
15.5500 g., Copper-Nickel, 31.51 mm. **Ruler:** Elizabeth II **Subject:** Federation Centennial **Obv:** Elizabeth II right **Obv. Designer:** Ian Rank-Broadley **Rev:** Multicolor arms above value **Edge:** Plain **Shape:** 12-sided

Date	Mintage	F	VF	XF	Unc	BU
2001B Proof	60,000	Value: 20.00				

KM# 491.2a   50 CENTS
Copper-Nickel, 31.5 mm.   **Ruler:** Elizabeth II **Subject:**
Centenary of Federation, 1901-2001 **Obv:** Head with tiara right
Obv. Designer: Ian Rank-Broadley **Rev:** Multicolored
Commonwealth coat of arms **Edge:** Plain **Shape:** 12-sided
Note: Prev. KM#491a.

Date	Mintage	F	VF	XF	Unc	BU
2001B Proof	—	Value: 27.50				

KM# 533   50 CENTS
15.6000 g., Copper-Nickel, 31.51 mm.   **Ruler:** Elizabeth II
Subject: Centennial - Norfolk Island Federation **Obv:** Head with
tiara right **Obv. Designer:** Ian Rank-Broadley **Rev:** Norfolk Island
coat of arms **Edge:** Plain **Shape:** 12-sided

Date	Mintage	F	VF	XF	Unc	BU
2001B	2,000,000	—	—	—	3.50	5.00
2001B Proof	—	Value: 12.50				

KM# 535   50 CENTS
16.8860 g., 0.9990 Silver 0.5423 oz. ASW, 32.1 mm.
Ruler: Elizabeth II **Subject:** Year of the Snake **Obv:** Head right
Obv. Designer: Ian Rank-Broadley **Rev:** Snake with eggs
Edge: Plain

Date	Mintage	F	VF	XF	Unc	BU
2001	500,000	—	—	—	—	12.50
2001P Proof	5,000	Value: 30.00				

KM# 551   50 CENTS
15.5500 g., Copper-Nickel, 31.5 mm.   **Ruler:** Elizabeth II
Series: Centenary of Federation - New South Wales **Obv:** Head
with tiara right **Obv. Designer:** Ian Rank-Broadley **Rev:** New
South Wales state arms **Edge:** Plain **Shape:** 12-sided

Date	Mintage	F	VF	XF	Unc	BU
2001	3,000,000	—	—	—	3.50	5.00
2001 Proof	—	Value: 12.50				

KM# 553   50 CENTS
15.5500 g., Copper-Nickel, 31.5 mm.   **Ruler:** Elizabeth II
Series: Centenary of Federation - Australian Capital Territory
Obv: Head right **Obv. Designer:** Ian Rank-Broadley
Rev: Australian Capital Territory arms **Edge:** Plain
Shape: 12-sided

Date	Mintage	F	VF	XF	Unc	BU
2001	2,000,000	—	—	—	3.50	5.00
2001 Proof	—	Value: 12.50				

KM# 555   50 CENTS
15.5500 g., Copper-Nickel, 31.5 mm.   **Ruler:** Elizabeth II
Series: Centenary of Federation - Queensland **Obv:** Head with
tiara right **Obv. Designer:** Ian Rank-Broadley **Rev:** Queensland
state arms **Edge:** Plain **Shape:** 12-sided

Date	Mintage	F	VF	XF	Unc	BU
2001	2,300,000	—	—	—	3.50	5.00
2001 Proof	—	Value: 12.50				

KM# 557   50 CENTS
15.5500 g., Copper-Nickel, 31.5 mm.   **Ruler:** Elizabeth II
Series: Centenary of Federation - Victoria **Obv:** Head with tiara
right **Obv. Designer:** Ian Rank-Broadley **Rev:** Victoria state arms
Edge: Plain **Shape:** 12-sided

Date	Mintage	F	VF	XF	Unc	BU
2001	2,800,000	—	—	—	3.50	5.00
2001 Proof	—	Value: 12.50				

KM# 559   50 CENTS
15.5500 g., Copper-Nickel, 31.5 mm.   **Ruler:** Elizabeth II
Series: Centenary of Federation - Northern Territory **Obv:** Head
with tiara right **Obv. Designer:** Ian Rank-Broadley **Rev:** Northern
Territory state arms **Edge:** Plain **Shape:** 12-sided

Date	Mintage	F	VF	XF	Unc	BU
2001	2,100,000	—	—	—	3.50	5.00
2001 Proof	—	Value: 12.50				

KM# 561   50 CENTS
15.5500 g., Copper-Nickel, 31.5 mm.   **Ruler:** Elizabeth II
Series: Centenary of Federation - South Australia **Obv:** Head
with tiara right **Obv. Designer:** Ian Rank-Broadley **Rev:** South
Australia state arms **Edge:** Plain **Shape:** 12-sided

Date	Mintage	F	VF	XF	Unc	BU
2001	2,400,000	—	—	—	3.50	5.00
2001 Proof	—	Value: 12.50				

KM# 563   50 CENTS
15.5500 g., Copper-Nickel, 31.5 mm.   **Ruler:** Elizabeth II
Series: Centenary of Federation - Western Australia **Obv:** Head
with tiara right **Obv. Designer:** Ian Rank-Broadley **Rev:** Western
Australia state arms **Edge:** Plain **Shape:** 12-sided

Date	Mintage	F	VF	XF	Unc	BU
2001	2,400,000	—	—	—	3.50	5.00
2001 Proof	—	Value: 12.50				

KM# 565   50 CENTS
15.5500 g., Copper-Nickel, 31.5 mm.   **Ruler:** Elizabeth II
Series: Centenary of Federation - Tasmania **Obv:** Head with
tiara right **Obv. Designer:** Ian Rank-Broadley **Rev:** Tasmania
state arms **Edge:** Plain **Shape:** 12-sided

Date	Mintage	F	VF	XF	Unc	BU
2001	2,200,000	—	—	—	3.50	5.00
2001 Proof	—	Value: 12.50				

KM# 602   50 CENTS
15.5500 g., Copper-Nickel, 31.5 mm.   **Ruler:** Elizabeth II
Subject: The Outback Region **Obv:** Head right **Obv. Designer:**
Ian Rank-Broadley **Rev:** Windmill **Rev. Designer:** Wojciech
Pietranik **Edge:** Plain **Shape:** 12-sided

Date	Mintage	F	VF	XF	Unc	BU
2002B	11,507,000	—	—	—	3.00	4.50
2002B Proof	39,000	Value: 10.00				

KM# 645   50 CENTS
15.5500 g., Copper-Nickel, 31.51 mm.   **Ruler:** Elizabeth II
Subject: Queen's 50th Anniversary of Accession **Obv:** Head right
Rev: Crown and star **Rev. Designer:** Peter Soobik & Wojciech
Pietranik **Shape:** 12-sided

Date	Mintage	F	VF	XF	Unc	BU
2002B	32,102	—	—	—	40.00	60.00
Note: Issued only in PNC cover						

KM# 645a   50 CENTS
18.2400 g., 0.9990 Silver 0.5858 oz. ASW, 31.51 mm.
Ruler: Elizabeth II **Subject:** Queen's 50th Anniversary of
Accession **Obv:** Head right **Rev:** Crown and star **Rev. Designer:**
Peter Soobik & Wojciech Pietranik **Shape:** 12-sided

Date	Mintage	F	VF	XF	Unc	BU
2002B Proof	13,500	Value: 45.00				

KM# 404a   50 CENTS
18.2400 g., 0.9999 Silver 0.5863 oz. ASW, 31.51 mm.
Ruler: Elizabeth II **Obv:** Head with tiara right **Obv. Designer:**
Ian Rank-Broadley **Rev:** Arms **Rev. Designer:** Stuart Devlin
Edge: Plain **Shape:** 12-sided

Date	Mintage	F	VF	XF	Unc	BU
2003B Proof	—	Value: 16.50				
2004B Proof	6,500	Value: 16.50				

Date	Mintage	F	VF	XF	Unc	BU
2005B Proof	—	Value: 16.50				
2006B Proof	—	Value: 16.50				
2007B Proof	—	Value: 16.50				
2008B Proof	—	Value: 16.50				
2009B Proof	—	Value: 16.50				

KM# 689 50 CENTS

15.5500 g., Copper-Nickel, 31.5 mm. **Ruler:** Elizabeth II **Obv:** Head right **Obv. Designer:** Ian Rank-Broadley **Rev:** Value within circle of volunteer activities **Rev. Designer:** Vladimir Gottwald **Edge:** Plain **Shape:** 12-sided

Date	Mintage	F	VF	XF	Unc	BU
2003B	13,927,000	—	—	—	3.00	4.50
2003B Proof	—	Value: 7.50				

KM# 689a 50 CENTS

15.5500 g., 0.9990 Silver 0.4994 oz. ASW, 31.5 mm. **Ruler:** Elizabeth II **Obv:** Head right **Rev:** Value within circle of volunteer activities

Date	Mintage	F	VF	XF	Unc	BU
2003B Proof	6,500	Value: 35.00				

KM# 799 50 CENTS

14.0900 g., Aluminum-Bronze, 31.51 mm. **Ruler:** Elizabeth II **Subject:** 50th Anniversary of the Coronation of Elizabeth II **Obv:** Head with tiara right **Obv. Designer:** Ian Rank-Broadley **Rev:** Crown, Federation star, dates **Rev. Designer:** Peter Soobik & Wojciech Pietranik **Edge:** Plain **Shape:** 12-sided

Date	Mintage	F	VF	XF	Unc	BU
2003	65,003	—	—	—	15.00	17.50

KM# 799a 50 CENTS

18.2400 g., 0.9990 Silver 0.5858 oz. ASW, 31.51 mm. **Ruler:** Elizabeth II **Subject:** 50th Anniversary of the Coronation of Elizabeth II **Obv:** Head with tiara right **Obv. Designer:** Ian Rank-Broadley **Rev:** Crown, Federation star, dates **Rev. Designer:** Peter Soobik & Wojciech Pietranik **Edge:** Plain **Shape:** 12-sided

Date	Mintage	F	VF	XF	Unc	BU
2003 Proof	6,967	Value: 35.00				

KM# 404 50 CENTS

15.6000 g., Copper-Nickel, 32 mm. **Ruler:** Elizabeth II **Obv:** Head with tiara right **Obv. Designer:** Ian Rank-Broadley **Rev:** Australian coat of arms with kangaroo and emu supporters **Rev. Designer:** Stuart Devlin **Edge:** Plain **Shape:** 12-sided

Date	Mintage	F	VF	XF	Unc	BU
2004	17,918,000	—	—	—	2.00	3.00
2004 Proof	—	Value: 10.00				
2005	30,000	—	—	—	25.00	40.00
Note: Issued as part of a PNC only						
2005 Proof	—	Value: 10.00				
2006	—	—	—	—	1.00	1.50
2006 Proof	—	Value: 10.00				
2007	—	—	—	—	1.00	1.50
2007 Proof	—	Value: 10.00				
2008	—	—	—	—	1.00	1.50
2008 Proof	—	Value: 10.00				
2009	—	—	—	—	1.00	1.50
2009 Proof	—	Value: 10.00				

KM# 694 50 CENTS

15.7200 g., Copper-Nickel, 32 mm. **Ruler:** Elizabeth II **Obv:** Head with tiara right **Obv. Designer:** Ian Rank-Broadley **Rev:** Koala, Lorikeet (bird) and a Wombat **Rev. Designer:** John Serranno & Vladimir Gottwald **Edge:** Plain **Shape:** 12-sided

Date	Mintage	F	VF	XF	Unc	BU
2004B	10,577,000	—	—	—	3.00	5.00

KM# 694a 50 CENTS

18.2400 g., 0.9990 Silver 0.5858 oz. ASW, 31.5 mm. **Ruler:** Elizabeth II **Obv:** Head with tiara right **Rev:** Wombat, lorikeet and koala **Rev. Designer:** John Serranno & Vladimir Gottwald **Edge:** Plain **Shape:** 12-sided

Date	Mintage	F	VF	XF	Unc	BU
2004B Proof	8,203	Value: 45.00				

KM# 746 50 CENTS

15.5500 g., Copper-Nickel, 31.51 mm. **Ruler:** Elizabeth II **Obv:** Head with tiara right **Obv. Designer:** Ian Rank-Broadley **Rev:** Military cemetery scene **Rev. Designer:** Wojciech Pietranik **Edge:** Plain **Shape:** 12-sided

Date	Mintage	F	VF	XF	Unc	BU
2005B	11,033,000	—	—	—	2.50	3.50
2005B Proof	—	Value: 10.00				

KM# 746a 50 CENTS

18.2400 g., 0.9990 Silver 0.5858 oz. ASW, 31.51 mm. **Ruler:** Elizabeth II **Obv:** Head with tiara right **Obv. Designer:** Ian Rank-Broadley **Rev:** Military cemetery scene **Rev. Designer:** Wojciech Pietranik **Edge:** Plain **Shape:** 12-sided

Date	Mintage	F	VF	XF	Unc	BU
2005B Proof	6,500	Value: 28.00				

KM# 746b 50 CENTS

33.6300 g., 0.9999 Gold 1.0811 oz. AGW, 31.51 mm. **Ruler:** Elizabeth II **Obv:** Head with tiara right **Obv. Designer:** Ian Rank-Broadley **Rev:** Military cemetery scene **Rev. Designer:** Wojciech Pietranik **Edge:** Plain **Shape:** 12-sided

Date	Mintage	F	VF	XF	Unc	BU
2005B Proof	650	Value: 1,350				

KM# 769 50 CENTS

Copper-Nickel **Ruler:** Elizabeth II **Subject:** Commonweath Games, Secondary School Design Competition **Obv:** Head with tiara right **Obv. Designer:** Ian Rank-Broadley **Rev:** Athletes **Rev. Designer:** Kelly Just

Date	Mintage	F	VF	XF	Unc	BU
2005	20,500,000	—	—	—	2.50	3.50
2005 Proof	5,402	Value: 35.00				

KM# 774 50 CENTS

15.5500 g., Copper-Nickel, 31.50 mm. **Ruler:** Elizabeth II **Subject:** Gymnastics **Obv:** Head with tiara right **Obv. Legend:** ELIZABETH II - AUSTRALIA **Obv. Designer:** Ian Rank-Broadley **Rev:** Gymnast standing with right leg up, Melbourne 2006 logo at left **Rev. Legend:** XVIII COMMONWEALTH GAMES **Rev. Designer:** Wojciech Pietranik **Edge:** Plain **Shape:** 12-sided

Date	Mintage	F	VF	XF	Unc	BU
2006	3,000	—	—	—	8.50	10.00

KM# 67a 50 CENTS

18.2400 g., 0.9990 Silver 0.5858 oz. ASW, 31.51 mm. **Ruler:** Elizabeth II **Obv:** Young bust right **Obv. Designer:** Arnold Machin **Rev:** Australian coat of arms **Rev. Designer:** Stuart Devlin **Edge:** Reeded

Date	Mintage	F	VF	XF	Unc	BU
2006 Proof	6,500	Value: 50.00				

KM# 770 50 CENTS

15.5500 g., Copper-Nickel, 31.50 mm. **Ruler:** Elizabeth II **Subject:** Basketball **Obv:** Head with tiara right **Obv. Legend:** ELIZABETH II - AUSTRALIA **Obv. Designer:** Ian Rank-Broadley **Rev:** Basketball player shooting basket, Melbourne 2006 logo at left **Rev. Legend:** XVIII COMMONWEALTH GAMES **Rev. Designer:** Wojciech Pietranik **Shape:** 12-sided

Date	Mintage	F	VF	XF	Unc	BU
2006	5,002	—	—	—	8.50	10.00

KM# 771 50 CENTS

15.5500 g., Copper-Nickel, 31.50 mm. **Ruler:** Elizabeth II **Subject:** Hockey **Obv:** Head with tiara right **Obv. Legend:** ELIZABETH II - AUSTRALIA **Obv. Designer:** Ian Rank-Broadley **Rev:** Hockey player hitting puck, Melboune 2006 logo at upper left **Rev. Legend:** XVIII COMMONWEALTH GAMES **Rev. Designer:** Wojciech Pietranik **Shape:** 12-sided

Date	Mintage	F	VF	XF	Unc	BU
2006	4,082	—	—	—	8.50	10.00

KM# 772 50 CENTS

15.5500 g., Copper-Nickel, 31.50 mm. **Ruler:** Elizabeth II **Subject:** Shooting **Obv:** Head with tiara right **Obv. Legend:** ELIZABETH II - AUSTRALIA **Obv. Designer:** Ian Rank-Broadley **Rev:** Shooter, Melbourne 2006 logo at upper right **Rev. Legend:** XVIII COMMONWEALTH GAMES **Rev. Designer:** Wojciech Pietranik **Shape:** 12-sided

Date	Mintage	F	VF	XF	Unc	BU
2006	4,302	—	—	—	8.50	10.00

KM# 773 50 CENTS

15.5500 g., Copper-Nickel, 31.50 mm. **Ruler:** Elizabeth II **Subject:** Weightlifting **Obv:** Head with tiara right **Obv. Legend:** ELIZABETH II - AUSTRALIA **Obv. Designer:** Ian Rank-Broadley **Rev:** Weightlifter holding barbells above head, Melbourne 2006 logo at left **Rev. Legend:** XVIII COMMONWEALTH GAMES **Rev. Designer:** Wojciech Pietranik **Shape:** 12-sided

Date	Mintage	F	VF	XF	Unc	BU
2006	4,402	—	—	—	8.50	10.00

KM# 775 50 CENTS

15.5500 g., Copper-Nickel, 31.50 mm. **Ruler:** Elizabeth II **Subject:** Rugby 7's **Obv:** Head with tiara right **Obv. Legend:** ELIZABETH II - AUSTRALIA **Obv. Designer:** Ian Rank-Broadley **Rev:** Rugby player running right, Melbourne 2006 logo at upper left **Rev. Legend:** XVIII COMMONWEALTH GAMES **Rev. Designer:** Wojciech Pietranik **Shape:** 12-sided

Date	Mintage	F	VF	XF	Unc	BU
2006	2,992	—	—	—	8.50	10.00

KM# 776 50 CENTS

15.5500 g., Copper-Nickel, 31.50 mm. **Ruler:** Elizabeth II **Subject:** Cycling **Obv:** Head with tiara right **Obv. Legend:** ELIZABETH II - AUSTRALIA **Obv. Designer:** Ian Rank-Broadley **Rev:** Cyclist heading right, Melbourne 2006 logo at upper right **Rev. Legend:** XVIII COMMONWEALTH GAMES **Rev. Designer:** Wojciech Pietranik **Shape:** 12-sided

Date	Mintage	F	VF	XF	Unc	BU
2006	—	—	—	—	8.50	10.00

KM# 777 50 CENTS

15.5500 g., Copper-Nickel, 31.50 mm. **Ruler:** Elizabeth II **Subject:** Athletics **Obv:** Head with tiara right **Obv. Legend:** ELIZABETH II - AUSTRALIA **Obv. Designer:** Ian Rank-Broadley **Rev:** Runner right, Melbourne 2006 logo at lower right **Rev. Legend:** XVIII COMMONWEALTH GAMES **Rev. Designer:** Wojciech Pietranik **Shape:** 12-sided

Date	Mintage	F	VF	XF	Unc	BU
2006	—	—	—	—	8.50	10.00

KM# 778 50 CENTS

15.5500 g., Copper-Nickel, 31.50 mm. **Ruler:** Elizabeth II **Subject:** Triathlon **Obv:** Head with tiara right **Obv. Legend:** ELIZABETH II - AUSRALIA **Obv. Designer:** Ian Rank-Broadley **Rev:** Bicycle, runner, Melbourne 2006 logo below **Rev. Legend:** XVIII COMMONWEALTH GAMES **Rev. Designer:** Wojciech Pietranik **Shape:** 12-sided

Date	Mintage	F	VF	XF	Unc	BU
2006	—	—	—	—	8.50	10.00

KM# 779 50 CENTS

15.5500 g., Copper-Nickel, 31.50 mm. **Ruler:** Elizabeth II **Subject:** Netball **Obv:** Head with tiara right **Obv. Legend:** ELIZABETH II - AUSTRALIA **Obv. Designer:** Ian Rank-Broadley **Rev:** Player shooting basket, Melbourne 2006 logo at upper left **Rev. Legend:** XVIII COMMONWEALTH GAMES **Rev. Designer:** Wojciech Pietranik **Shape:** 12-sided

Date	Mintage	F	VF	XF	Unc	BU
2006	—	—	—	—	8.50	10.00

KM# 780 50 CENTS

15.5500 g., Copper-Nickel, 31.50 mm. **Ruler:** Elizabeth II **Subject:** Table tennis **Obv:** Head with tiara right **Obv. Legend:** ELIZABETH II - AUSTRALIA **Obv. Designer:** Ian Rank-Broadley **Rev:** Player hitting ball, Melbourne 2006 logo below **Rev. Legend:** XVIII COMMONWEALTH GAMES **Rev. Designer:** Wojciech Pietranik **Shape:** 12-sided

Date	Mintage	F	VF	XF	Unc	BU
2006	—	—	—	—	8.50	10.00

KM# 781 50 CENTS

15.5500 g., Copper-Nickel, 31.50 mm. **Ruler:** Elizabeth II
Subject: Aquatics **Obv:** Head with tiara right **Obv. Legend:**
ELIZABETH II - AUSTRALIA **Obv. Designer:** Ian Rank-Broadley
Rev: Swimmer, Melbourne 2006 logo **Rev. Legend:** XVIII
COMMONWEALTH GAMES **Rev. Designer:** Wojciech Pietranik
Shape: 12-sided

Date	Mintage	F	VF	XF	Unc	BU
2006	—			—	8.50	10.00

KM# 801 50 CENTS

15.5500 g., Copper-Nickel, 31.51 mm. **Ruler:** Elizabeth II
Subject: 80th Birthday of Queen Elizabeth II **Obv:** Head with
tiara right **Obv. Designer:** Ian Rank-Broadley **Rev:** Royal Cipher
Rev. Designer: Stuart Devlin **Shape:** 12-sided

Date	Mintage	F	VF	XF	Unc	BU
2006	—			—	5.00	8.50

KM# 801a 50 CENTS

18.2400 g., 0.9990 Silver partially gilt 0.5858 oz. ASW,
31.51 mm. **Ruler:** Elizabeth II **Subject:** 80th Birthday of Queen
Elizabeth II **Obv:** Head with tiara right **Obv. Designer:** Ian Rank-
Broadley **Rev:** Crowned Royal Cipher on large 80, border of
alternating British and Australian flags **Rev. Designer:** Stuart
Devlin **Shape:** 12-sided

Date	Mintage	F	VF	XF	Unc	BU
2006 Proof	7,500	Value: 50.00				

KM# 802 50 CENTS

15.5500 g., Copper-Nickel, 31.51 mm. **Ruler:** Elizabeth II
Subject: Visit of Queen Elizabeth II **Obv:** Head with tiara right
Obv. Designer: Ian Rank-Broadley **Rev:** Australian map and
world globe **Rev. Designer:** Stuart Devlin **Shape:** 12-sided

Date	Mintage	F	VF	XF	Unc	BU
2006	—			—	5.00	8.50

KM# 802a 50 CENTS

18.2400 g., 0.9990 Silver partially gilt 0.5858 oz. ASW,
31.51 mm. **Ruler:** Elizabeth II **Subject:** Visit of Queen Elizabeth
II **Obv:** Head with tiara right **Obv. Designer:** Ian Rank-Broadley
Rev: Australian map and world globe **Rev. Designer:** Stuart
Devlin **Shape:** 12-sided

Date	Mintage	F	VF	XF	Unc	BU
2006 Proof	7,500	Value: 50.00				

KM# 821 50 CENTS

13.2800 g., 0.8000 Silver 0.3416 oz. ASW, 31.51 mm.
Ruler: Elizabeth II **Obv:** Head with tiara right **Obv. Designer:**
Ian Rank-Broadley **Rev:** Australian coat of arms **Rev. Designer:**
Stuart Devlin **Edge:** Reeded

Date	Mintage	F	VF	XF	Unc	BU
2006 Proof	—	Value: 50.00				

KM# 821a 50 CENTS

25.3000 g., 0.9990 Gold 0.8126 oz. AGW, 31.51 mm.
Ruler: Elizabeth II **Obv:** Head with tiara right **Obv. Designer:**
Ian Rank-Broadley **Rev:** Australian coat of arms **Rev. Designer:**
Stuart Devlin **Edge:** Reeded

Date	Mintage	F	VF	XF	Unc	BU
2006 Proof	300	Value: 1,000				

KM# 1001 50 CENTS

15.5500 g., Copper-Nickel, 31.50 mm. **Ruler:** Elizabeth II
Subject: Badminton **Obv:** Head with tiara right **Obv. Legend:**
ELIZABETH II - AUSTRALIA **Obv. Designer:** Ian Rank-Broadley
Rev: Player, Melbourne 2006 logo **Rev. Legend:** XVIII
COMMONWEALTH GAMES **Rev. Designer:** Wojciech Pietranik
Edge: Plain **Shape:** 12-sided

Date	Mintage	F	VF	XF	Unc	BU
2006	—			—	2.50	4.50

KM# 1002 50 CENTS

15.5500 g., Copper-Nickel, 31.50 mm. **Ruler:** Elizabeth II
Subject: Lawn bowling **Obv:** Head with tiara right **Obv. Legend:**
ELIZABETH II - AUSTRALIA **Obv. Designer:** Ian Rank-Broadley
Rev: Bowler, Melbourne 2006 **Rev. Legend:** XVIII
COMMONWEALTH GAMES **Rev. Designer:** Wojciech Pietranik
Edge: Plain **Shape:** 12-sided

Date	Mintage	F	VF	XF	Unc	BU
2006	—			—	2.50	4.50

KM# 1003 50 CENTS

15.5500 g., Copper-Nickel, 31.50 mm. **Ruler:** Elizabeth II
Subject: Boxing **Obv:** Head with tiarra right **Obv. Legend:**
ELIZABETH II - AUSTRALIA **Obv. Designer:** Ian Rank-Broadley
Rev: Boxer, Melbourne 2006 logo **Rev. Legend:** XVIII
COMMONWEALTH GAMES **Rev. Designer:** Wojciech Pietranik
Edge: Plain **Shape:** 12-sided

Date	Mintage	F	VF	XF	Unc	BU
2006	—			—	2.50	4.50

KM# 1004 50 CENTS

Aluminum-Bronze, 30 mm. **Ruler:** Elizabeth II **Obv:** Head with
tiara right **Obv. Legend:** ELIZABETH II - AUSTRALIA
Obv. Designer: Ian Rank-Broadley **Rev:** Everage head facing,
multicolor **Rev. Legend:** DAME EDNA EVERAGE - 50TH
ANNIVERSARY

Date	Mintage	F	VF	XF	Unc	BU
ND(2006)P	—			—	2.50	4.50

KM# 1041 50 CENTS

15.5500 g., Copper-Nickel, 31.5 mm. **Ruler:** Elizabeth II
Subject: Elizabeth and Philip Wedding Anniversary **Rev:** Profile
portraits and diamond at center of circle of trumpets
Rev. Designer: Stuart Devlin

Date	Mintage	F	VF	XF	Unc	BU
2007B	—			—	5.00	7.00

KM# 1049 50 CENTS

15.5500 g., Copper-Nickel, 31.51 mm. **Ruler:** Elizabeth II
Subject: Scouting Centennial in Australia **Rev:** Australian Scout
Emblem **Rev. Designer:** C. Goodall

Date	Mintage	F	VF	XF	Unc	BU
2008	—			—	4.00	5.00

KM# 1062 50 CENTS

31.5100 g., Copper-Nickel, 31.51 mm. **Ruler:** Elizabeth II
Subject: 25th Anniversary Australia's Win of the America's Cup
Rev: Yacht Australia II

Date	Mintage	F	VF	XF	Unc	BU
2008	—			—	7.50	8.00

KM# 1100 50 CENTS

15.5500 g., 0.9990 Silver 0.4994 oz. ASW, 36.6 mm.
Ruler: Elizabeth II **Subject:** Great Barrier Reef **Obv:** Head right
Obv. Designer: Ian rank-Broadley **Rev:** Lion fish, multicolor
Edge: reeded

Date	Mintage	F	VF	XF	Unc	BU
2009(p) Proof	Est. 10,000	Value: 50.00				

KM# 1101 50 CENTS

15.5500 g., 0.9990 Silver 0.4994 oz. ASW, 36.6 mm.
Ruler: Elizabeth II **Subject:** Great Barrier Reef **Obv:** Head right
Obv. Designer: Ian Rank-Broadley **Rev:** Leafy Sea Dragon,
multicolor **Edge:** Reeded

Date	Mintage	F	VF	XF	Unc	BU
2009(p) Proof	Est. 10,000	Value: 50.00				

KM# 1254 55 CENTS

15.5500 g., 0.9990 Silver 0.4994 oz. ASW, 26x38 mm. **Ruler:**
Elizabeth II **Subject:** Postal Service, 200th Anniversary **Obv:**
Head right **Obv. Designer:** Ian Rank-Broadley **Rev:** Early post
box **Edge:** Irregular as with a stamp **Shape:** Vertical rectangle

Date	Mintage	F	VF	XF	Unc	BU
2009P Proof	8,700	Value: 90.00				

KM# 1255 55 CENTS

15.5500 g., 0.9990 Silver 0.4994 oz. ASW, 26x38 mm.
Ruler: Elizabeth II **Subject:** Postal Service, 200th Anniversary
Obv: Head right **Obv. Designer:** Ian Rank-Broadley **Rev:** Home
delivery **Edge:** Irregular as with a stamp **Shape:** Vertical
rectangle

Date	Mintage	F	VF	XF	Unc	BU
2009P Proof	8,700	Value: 90.00				

KM# 489 DOLLAR

9.0000 g., Aluminum-Bronze, 25 mm. **Ruler:** Elizabeth II
Obv: Head with tiara right **Obv. Designer:** Ian Rank-Broadley
Rev: Circle of 5 kangaroos **Rev. Designer:** Stuart Devlin **Edge:**
Reeded and plain sections

Date	Mintage	F	VF	XF	Unc	BU
2001B Proof	1,001,000	Value: 45.00				
2004B	9,565,000	—		—	3.50	5.00
2004B	50,000	—		—	65.00	
2005B	5,792,000	—		—	3.50	5.00
2005B Proof	33,520	Value: 75.00				
2006B	—					5.00
2006B Proof	—	Value: 45.00				
2006B Special Proof 25-35 pieces	—	Value: 3,500				
2007B	—					5.00
2007B Proof	—	Value: 45.00				
2008B	—					5.00
2008B Proof	—	Value: 45.00				
2009B	—					5.00
2009B Proof	—	Value: 45.00				

KM# 588   DOLLAR
9.0000 g., Aluminum-Bronze, 25 mm.   **Ruler:** Elizabeth II
Subject: 90th Anniversary Royal Australian Navy **Obv:** Head with
tiara right **Obv. Designer:** Ian Rank-Broadley **Rev:** Navy crest
Rev. Designer: Vladimir Gottwald **Edge:** Segmented reeding

Date	Mintage	F	VF	XF	Unc	BU
2001	62,429	—	—	—	15.00	20.00

KM# 530   DOLLAR
9.0000 g., Aluminum-Bronze, 25 mm.   **Ruler:** Elizabeth II
Subject: Army Centennial **Obv:** Head with tiara right
Obv. Designer: Ian Rank-Broadley **Rev:** Army crest
Rev. Designer: Vladimir Gottwald **Edge:** Segmented reeding

Date	Mintage	F	VF	XF	Unc	BU
2001C	125,186	—	—	—	6.00	10.00
Note: Large head, IRB spaced						
2001C	Inc. above	—	—	—	6.00	10.00
Note: Small head, IRB joined						
2001S	38,095	—	—	—	10.00	15.00

KM# 530a   DOLLAR
11.6600 g., 0.9990 Silver 0.3745 oz. ASW, 24.9 mm.
Ruler: Elizabeth II **Subject:** Army Centennial **Obv:** Head with
tiara right **Obv. Designer:** Ian Rank-Broadley **Rev:** Army crest
Rev. Designer: Vladimir Gottwald **Edge:** Segmented reeding

Date	Mintage	F	VF	XF	Unc	BU
2001 Proof	17,839	Value: 40.00				

KM# 531   DOLLAR
9.0000 g., Aluminum-Bronze, 25 mm.   **Ruler:** Elizabeth II
Subject: 80th Anniversary Royal Australian Air Force **Obv:** Head
with tiara right **Obv. Designer:** Ian Rank-Broadley **Rev:** Air Force
crest **Rev. Designer:** Vladimir Gottwald **Edge:** Reeded and plain
sections

Date	Mintage	F	VF	XF	Unc	BU
2001B	99,281	—	—	—	6.00	10.00
Note: IRB spaced						
2001B	Inc. above	—	—	—	6.00	10.00
Note: IRB joined						

KM# 534.1   DOLLAR
9.0000 g., Aluminum-Bronze, 25 mm.   **Ruler:** Elizabeth II
Subject: Australian Centenary of Federation - Norfolk Island
Obv: Head with tiara right **Obv. Designer:** Ian Rank-Broadley
Rev: Stylized ribbon map of Australia with star **Rev. Designer:**
Wojciech Pietranik **Edge:** Plain and reeded sections
Note: Reverse design raised above field. Prev. KM#534.

Date	Mintage	F	VF	XF	Unc	BU
2001B	6,781,200	—	—	—	2.50	3.50
Note: IRB joined						
2001B	Inc. above	—	—	—	5.00	10.00
Note: IRB spaced						
2001B Proof	—	Value: 5.00				

KM# 534.1a   DOLLAR
21.7000 g., 0.9999 Gold 0.6976 oz. AGW, 25 mm.
Ruler: Elizabeth II **Subject:** Federation Centennial
Obv: Elizabeth II **Rev:** Federation logo

Date	Mintage	F	VF	XF	Unc	BU
2001B Proof	650	Value: 1,130				

KM# 534.2   DOLLAR
9.0000 g., Aluminum-Bronze, 25 mm.   **Ruler:** Elizabeth II
Subject: Australian Centenary of Federation - Norfolk Island
Obv: Head with tiara right **Obv. Designer:** Ian Rank-Broadley
Rev: Multicolor ribbon design of Australia with star, printed on
the surface. **Rev. Designer:** Wojciech Pietranik
Edge: Segmented reeding

Date	Mintage	F	VF	XF	Unc	BU
2001 Proof	—	Value: 12.50				

KM# 594   DOLLAR
31.1035 g., 0.9990 Silver partially gilt 0.9990 oz. ASW, 40 mm.
Ruler: Elizabeth II **Subject:** Millennium **Obv:** Head with tiara right
Obv. Designer: Ian Rank-Broadley **Rev:** Gold inset Sun on
multicolor Earth above Egyptian obelisk **Edge:** Reeded

Date	Mintage	F	VF	XF	Unc	BU
2001 Prooflike	30,000	—	—	—	15.00	20.00

KM# 598   DOLLAR
31.1000 g., 0.9990 Silver 0.9988 oz. ASW, 40.4 mm.
Ruler: Elizabeth II **Subject:** Centenary of Federation "Holey
Dollar" **Obv:** Legend around star-shaped center hole **Rev:** Seven
coats of arms around star-shaped hole **Edge:** Reeded

Date	Mintage	F	VF	XF	Unc	BU
ND(2001) Prooflike	30,000	—	—	—	28.00	32.00

KM# 682   DOLLAR
9.0000 g., Aluminum-Bronze, 25 mm.   **Ruler:** Elizabeth II
Subject: International Year of Volunteers **Obv. Designer:** Ian
Rank-Broadley **Rev:** Volunteers in wreath **Rev. Designer:**
Wojciech Pietranik **Edge:** Segmented reeding

Date	Mintage	F	VF	XF	Unc	BU
2001B	6,000,000	—	—	—	3.00	4.50

KM# 600.1   DOLLAR
9.0000 g., Aluminum-Bronze, 25 mm.   **Ruler:** Elizabeth II
Subject: Year of the Outback **Obv:** Head with tiara right
Obv. Designer: Ian Rank-Broadley **Rev:** Stylized map of
Australia **Rev. Designer:** Wojciech Pietranik **Edge:** Segmented
reeding **Note:** Prev. KM#600.

Date	Mintage	F	VF	XF	Unc	BU
2002	34,074,000	—	—	—	2.50	3.50
2002 Proof	—	Value: 4.00				
2002B	32,698	—	—	—	4.50	6.50
2002C	68,447	—	—	—	3.50	5.00
2002M	31,694	—	—	—	2.50	3.00
2002S	36,931	—	—	—	4.00	6.00

KM# 600.1a   DOLLAR
11.6600 g., 0.9900 Silver 0.3711 oz. ASW, 25 mm.
Ruler: Elizabeth II **Subject:** Year of the Outback **Obv:** Head with
tiara right **Obv. Designer:** Ian Rank-Broadley **Rev:** Stylized map
of Australia **Rev. Designer:** Elizabeth Robinson and Wojciech
Pietranik **Edge:** Segmented reeding

Date	Mintage	F	VF	XF	Unc	BU
2002B Proof	12,500	Value: 40.00				

KM# 600.2   DOLLAR
9.0000 g., Aluminum-Bronze, 25 mm.   **Ruler:** Elizabeth II **Subject:**
Year of the Outback **Obv:** Head with tiara right **Obv. Designer:** Ian
Rank-Broadley **Rev:** Multicolor stylized map of Australia **Rev.
Designer:** Wojciech Pietranik **Edge:** Segmented reeding

Date	Mintage	F	VF	XF	Unc	BU
2002B Proof	39,514	Value: 15.00				

KM# 632   DOLLAR
31.1035 g., 0.9990 Silver 0.9990 oz. ASW, 40 mm. **Ruler:**
Elizabeth II **Subject:** Queen's Golden Jubilee **Obv:** Head right **Rev:**
Queen on horse with multicolor flag background **Edge:** Reeded

Date	Mintage	F	VF	XF	Unc	BU
2002P Proof	40,000	Value: 35.00				

KM# 660   DOLLAR
31.1035 g., 0.9990 Silver partially gilt 0.9990 oz. ASW, 40 mm.
Ruler: Elizabeth II **Subject:** Melbourne Mint **Obv:** Head with tiara
right **Obv. Designer:** Ian Rank-Broadley **Rev:** Mint entrance
between two gold foil inserts replicating gold sovereign reverse
designs **Edge:** Reeded

Date	Mintage	F	VF	XF	Unc	BU
2002B Proof	13,328	Value: 37.50				

KM# 489a   DOLLAR
11.6600 g., 0.9990 Silver 0.3745 oz. ASW, 25 mm.
Ruler: Elizabeth II **Obv:** Head with tiara right **Obv. Designer:**
Ian Rank-Broadley **Rev:** Kangaroos **Rev. Designer:** Stuart
Devlin **Edge:** Segmented reeding

Date	Mintage	F	VF	XF	Unc	BU
2003B Proof	—	Value: 30.00				
2004B Proof	6,500	Value: 30.00				

Date	Mintage	F	VF	XF	Unc	BU
2005B Proof	—	Value: 30.00				
2006B Proof	—	Value: 30.00				
2007B Proof	—	Value: 30.00				
2008B Proof	—	Value: 30.00				
2009B Proof	—	Value: 30.00				

KM# 823 DOLLAR
31.1035 g., 0.9990 Silver 0.9990 oz. ASW, 40 mm.
Ruler: Elizabeth II **Subject:** 50th Anniversary Coronation
Elizabeth II **Obv:** Head with tiara right **Obv. Designer:** Ian Rank-Broadley **Rev:** Crown in lettered garland **Note:** Colored design.

Date	Mintage	F	VF	XF	Unc	BU
2003P Proof	40,400	Value: 35.00				

KM# 663 DOLLAR
9.0000 g., Aluminum-Bronze, 25 mm. **Ruler:** Elizabeth II
Subject: 50th Anniversary of the end of Korean War **Obv:** Head with tiara right **Obv. Designer:** Ian Rank-Broadley **Rev:** Dove of Peace **Rev. Designer:** Vladimir Gottwald **Edge:** Segmented reeding

Date	Mintage	F	VF	XF	Unc	BU
2003B	34,949	—	—	—	3.50	5.00
2003C	93,572	—	—	—	2.50	3.50
2003M	36,142	—	—	—	3.50	5.00
2003S	36,091	—	—	—	3.50	5.00

KM# 663a DOLLAR
11.6600 g., 0.9990 Silver 0.3745 oz. ASW, 25 mm.
Ruler: Elizabeth II **Subject:** Korean War **Obv:** Queens head right **Obv. Designer:** Ian Rank-Broadley **Rev:** Dove of Peace **Rev. Designer:** Vladimir Gottwald **Edge:** Segmented reeding

Date	Mintage	F	VF	XF	Unc	BU
2003B	15,000	Value: 20.00				

KM# 685 DOLLAR
31.1035 g., 0.9990 Silver 0.9990 oz. ASW, 40.6 mm. **Obv:**
Ruler: Elizabeth II **Subject:** 21st Birthday of William **Obv:** Head right **Rev:** Multicolor Prince William **Edge:** Segmented reeding

Date	Mintage	F	VF	XF	Unc	BU
ND(2003)P Proof	12,500	Value: 28.00				

KM# 690 DOLLAR
9.0000 g., Aluminum-Bronze, 25 mm. **Ruler:** Elizabeth II
Obv: Queens head right **Rev:** Australia Volunteers logo
Edge: Segmented reeding

Date	Mintage	F	VF	XF	Unc	BU
2003B	4,149,000	—	—	—	3.50	4.50

KM# 690.1 DOLLAR
9.0000 g., Aluminum-Bronze, 25 mm. **Ruler:** Elizabeth II
Subject: Australia's Volunteers **Obv:** Elizabeth II **Rev:** Multicolor Australia's Volunteers logo **Edge:** Segmented reeding

Date	Mintage	F	VF	XF	Unc	BU
2003B Proof	39,090	Value: 15.00				

KM# 754 DOLLAR
9.0000 g., Aluminum-Bronze, 25 mm. **Ruler:** Elizabeth II
Subject: Womens Suffrage **Obv:** Queens head right
Obv. Designer: Ian Rank-Broadley **Rev:** Suffragette talking to Britannia **Rev. Designer:** Vladimir Gottwald **Edge:** Segmented reeding

Date	Mintage	F	VF	XF	Unc	BU
2003B	10,007,000	—	—	—	3.00	4.00

KM# 763 DOLLAR
13.3600 g., 0.9990 Silver 0.4291 oz. ASW, 28.5 mm.
Ruler: Elizabeth II **Series:** Masterpieces in Silver - Port Phillip Patterns **Obv:** 1/4 Ounce design **Rev:** Kangaroo design
Edge: Reeded

Date	Mintage	F	VF	XF	Unc	BU
2003B Proof	10,000	Value: 9.50				

KM# 803 DOLLAR
9.0000 g., Aluminum-Bronze, 25 mm. **Ruler:** Elizabeth II
Subject: Vietnam War Veterans 1962-1973 **Obv:** Head with tiara right **Obv. Designer:** Ian Rank-Broadley **Rev:** Australian Vietnam Forces National Memorial **Rev. Designer:** Wojciech Pietranik

Date	Mintage	F	VF	XF	Unc	BU
2003	—	—	—	—	3.50	5.00

KM# 822 DOLLAR
54.3000 g., 0.9990 Silver 1.7440 oz. ASW, 50 mm.
Ruler: Elizabeth II **Obv:** Superimposed head above replica of Holey Dollar **Obv. Designer:** Ian Rank-Broadley **Rev:** Replica of Holey Dollar **Edge:** Reeded **Note:** Holey Dollar replica is embedded in silver collar and comes with replica Dump also in 0.999 silver.

Date	Mintage	F	VF	XF	Unc	BU
2003 Proof	14,204	Value: 85.00				

KM# 824 DOLLAR
31.1035 g., 0.9990 Silver 0.9990 oz. ASW, 40 mm.
Ruler: Elizabeth II **Subject:** Golden Pipeline **Obv:** Head with tiara right **Obv. Designer:** Ian Rank-Broadley **Rev:** Charles Yelverton O'Connor, innovative engineer, multicolor

Date	Mintage	F	VF	XF	Unc	BU
2003P Proof	5,000	Value: 90.00				

KM# 690a DOLLAR
9.0000 g., 0.9990 Silver 0.2891 oz. ASW, 25 mm. **Ruler:**
Elizabeth II **Obv:** Queens head right **Rev:** Australia Volunteers logo

Date	Mintage	F	VF	XF	Unc	BU
2003B Proof	6,500	Value: 20.00				

KM# 725 DOLLAR
56.2300 g., 0.9990 Bi-Metallic Copper center in Silver ring 1.8060 oz., 50 mm. **Ruler:** Elizabeth II **Subject:** The Last Penny
Obv: 1964 dated penny obverse **Rev:** 1964 date penny reverse
Edge: Reeded

Date	Mintage	F	VF	XF	Unc	BU
2004B Proof	16,437	Value: 55.00				

KM# 726 DOLLAR
9.0000 g., Aluminum-Bronze, 25 mm. **Ruler:** Elizabeth II
Subject: Eureka Stockade 1854-2004 **Obv:** Head with tiara right **Obv. Designer:** Ian Rank-Broadley **Rev:** Stockade and stylized soldiers **Rev. Designer:** Wojciech Pietranik **Edge:** Segmented reeding

Date	Mintage	F	VF	XF	Unc	BU
2004	—	—	—	—	20.00	50.00
2004B	33,835	—	—	—	3.50	5.00
2004C	70,913	—	—	—	2.50	3.50
2004 E	95,948	—	—	—	2.50	3.50
2004S	45,098	—	—	—	3.50	5.00
2004M	37,526	—	—	—	3.50	5.00
2004 3 known	—	—	—	—	—	1,000

KM# 726a DOLLAR
11.6600 g., 0.9990 Silver 0.3745 oz. ASW, 25 mm.
Ruler: Elizabeth II **Subject:** Eureka Stockade **Obv:** Head with tiara right **Obv. Designer:** Ian Rank-Broadley **Rev:** Stockade and stylized soldiers **Rev. Designer:** Wojciech Pietranik
Edge: Segmented reeding

Date	Mintage	F	VF	XF	Unc	BU
2004B Proof	17,697	Value: 38.00				

KM# 733 DOLLAR
9.0000 g., Aluminum-Bronze, 25 mm. **Ruler:** Elizabeth II
Obv: Head with tiara right **Obv. Designer:** Ian Rank-Broadley
Rev: Multicolor holographic five kangaroos design
Rev. Designer: Stuart Devlin **Edge:** Segmented reeding

Date	Mintage	F	VF	XF	Unc	BU
2004B Proof	—	Value: 15.00				

KM# 733.1 DOLLAR
9.0000 g., Aluminum-Bronze, 25 mm. **Ruler:** Elizabeth II
Rev: Five kangaroos **Edge:** Segmented reeding

Date	Mintage	F	VF	XF	Unc	BU
2004B	—	—	—	—	—	4.50

KM# 733.1a DOLLAR
11.6600 g., 0.9999 Silver 0.3748 oz. ASW, 25 mm.
Ruler: Elizabeth II

Date	Mintage	F	VF	XF	Unc	BU
2004B Proof	6,500	Value: 25.00				

KM# 734 DOLLAR
31.1035 g., 0.9990 Silver 0.9990 oz. ASW, 40 mm.
Ruler: Elizabeth II **Subject:** First Moon Walk **Obv:** Head with tiara right **Rev:** Multicolor rocket in flight **Edge:** Reeded

Date	Mintage	F	VF	XF	Unc	BU
2004P Proof	40,000	Value: 28.00				

KM# 735 DOLLAR
31.1035 g., 0.9990 Silver 0.9990 oz. ASW, 40 mm.
Ruler: Elizabeth II **Subject:** First Moon Walk **Obv:** Head with tiara right **Rev:** Multicolor scene of astronauts planting flag on moon **Edge:** Reeded

Date	Mintage	F	VF	XF	Unc	BU
2004P Proof	40,000	Value: 28.00				

KM# 736 DOLLAR
31.1035 g., 0.9990 Silver 0.9990 oz. ASW, 40 mm.
Ruler: Elizabeth II **Subject:** First Moon Walk **Obv:** Head with tiara right **Rev:** Multicolor close up of astronaut on moon **Edge:** Reeded

Date	Mintage	F	VF	XF	Unc	BU
2004P Proof	40,000	Value: 28.00				

KM# 738 DOLLAR
31.1035 g., 0.9990 Silver partially gilt 0.9990 oz. ASW, 40 mm.
Ruler: Elizabeth II **Subject:** 50th Anniversary of Royal Visit **Obv:** Queens head right **Rev:** Gilt lion and kangaroo
Rev. Designer: Leslie Bowles **Edge:** Reeded

Date	Mintage	F	VF	XF	Unc	BU
ND (2004) Proof	12,500	Value: 32.00				

KM# 740 DOLLAR
24.3750 g., 0.9990 Silver Encapsulated gold nuggets in center 0.7829 oz. ASW, 40.6 mm. **Ruler:** Elizabeth II **Obv:** Crowned head right **Obv. Designer:** Ian Rank-Broadley **Rev:** Eureka Stockade leader, miners and flag **Rev. Designer:** Wojciech Pietranik **Edge:** Reeded

Date	Mintage	F	VF	XF	Unc	BU
2004 Proof	12,500	Value: 50.00				

KM# 747 DOLLAR
9.0000 g., Aluminum-Bronze, 25 mm. **Ruler:** Elizabeth II
Subject: 60th Anniversary World War II **Obv:** Head with tiara right **Obv. Designer:** Ian Rank-Broadley **Rev:** Rejoicing serviceman **Rev. Designer:** Wojciech Pietranik
Edge: Segmented reeding

Date	Mintage	F	VF	XF	Unc	BU
2005B	10,607,000	—	—	—	2.00	3.00
2005B Proof		Value: 35.00				

KM# 747a DOLLAR
11.6600 g., 0.9990 Silver 0.3745 oz. ASW, 25 mm.
Ruler: Elizabeth II **Obv:** Queens head right **Rev:** Rejoicing servicemen **Edge:** Segmented reeding

Date	Mintage	F	VF	XF	Unc	BU
2005B Proof	6,500	Value: 42.00				

KM# 747b DOLLAR
21.5200 g., 0.9999 Gold 0.6918 oz. AGW, 25 mm.
Ruler: Elizabeth II **Obv:** Queens head right **Rev:** Rejoicing servicemen **Edge:** Segmented reeding

Date	Mintage	F	VF	XF	Unc	BU
2005B Proof	629	Value: 875				

KM# 748 DOLLAR
9.0000 g., Aluminum-Bronze, 25 mm. **Ruler:** Elizabeth II
Subject: 90th Anniversary Gallipoli Landing 1915-2005
Obv: Head with tiara right **Obv. Designer:** Ian Rank-Broadley
Rev: Bugler silhouette **Rev. Designer:** Vladimir Gottwald
Edge: Segmented reeding

Date	Mintage	F	VF	XF	Unc	BU
2005	15,000	—	—	—	25.00	30.00
2005B	36,108	—	—	—	3.50	5.00
2005C	76,173	—	—	—	2.50	3.50
2005G	35,452	—	—	—	20.00	30.00
2005M		—	—	—	2.50	3.50
2005S	39,569	—	—	—	3.50	5.00

KM# 748a DOLLAR
11.6600 g., 0.9990 Silver 0.3745 oz. ASW, 25 mm.
Ruler: Elizabeth II **Obv:** Queens head right
Rev: Bugler silhouette **Edge:** Segmented reeding

Date	Mintage	F	VF	XF	Unc	BU
2005B Proof	17,749	Value: 45.00				
2005B Proof, 2 known		Value: 1,500				

KM# 749 DOLLAR
31.6000 g., 0.9990 Silver 1.0149 oz. ASW, 40 mm.
Ruler: Elizabeth II **Obv:** Head with tiara right **Obv. Designer:** Ian Rank-Broadley **Rev:** Kangaroo bounding under Southern Cross and above Federation Star **Rev. Designer:** Wojciech Pietranik **Edge:** Reeded

Date	Mintage	F	VF	XF	Unc	BU
2005	—	—	—	—	20.00	22.50
2005 Proof	12,500	Value: 32.00				

KM# 749a DOLLAR
31.1035 g., 0.9990 Silver Partially Gold Plated 0.9990 oz. ASW, 40 mm. **Ruler:** Elizabeth II **Obv:** Head with tiara right
Obv. Designer: Ian Rank-Broadley **Rev:** Kangaroo bounding under Southern Cross and above Federation Star
Rev. Designer: Wojciech Pietranik **Edge:** Reeded

Date	Mintage	F	VF	XF	Unc	BU
2005B Proof	12,500	Value: 35.00				

KM# 825 DOLLAR
56.4500 g., 0.9990 Silver partially gilt 1.8130 oz. ASW, 50 mm.
Ruler: Elizabeth II **Obv:** Small head with tiara right superimposed above replica of Sydney Mint Sovereign **Obv. Designer:** Ian Rank-Broadley **Rev:** Replica of Sydney Mint Sovereign **Edge:** Reeded

Date	Mintage	F	VF	XF	Unc	BU
2005 Proof	11,845	Value: 80.00				

KM# 830 DOLLAR
31.6000 g., 0.9990 Silver 1.0149 oz. ASW, 40 mm.
Ruler: Elizabeth II **Subject:** Centenary Australian Tennis Open 1905-2005 **Obv:** Head with tiara right **Obv. Designer:** Ian Rank-Broadley **Rev:** Tennis players

Date	Mintage	F	VF	XF	Unc	BU
2005 Proof	10,000	—	—	—	—	40.00

KM# 831 DOLLAR
31.6000 g., 0.9990 Silver 1.0149 oz. ASW, 40 mm.
Ruler: Elizabeth II **Subject:** Centenary Australian PGA Gold Open 1905-2005 **Obv:** Head with tiara right **Obv. Designer:** Ian Rank-Broadley **Rev:** Golfer

Date	Mintage	F	VF	XF	Unc	BU
2005 Proof	7,500	Value: 40.00				

KM# 832 DOLLAR
31.6000 g., 0.9990 Silver 1.0149 oz. ASW, 40 mm.
Ruler: Elizabeth II **Subject:** Centenary Rotary 1905-2005
Obv: Head with tiara right **Obv. Designer:** Ian Rank-Broadley
Rev: Rotary International Logo

Date	Mintage	F	VF	XF	Unc	BU
2005 Proof	10,000	Value: 40.00				

KM# 833 DOLLAR
31.1035 g., 0.9990 Silver 0.9990 oz. ASW, 40 mm.
Ruler: Elizabeth II **Subject:** 90th Anniversary Gallipoli Landings **Obv:** Head with tiara right **Obv. Designer:** Ian Rank-Broadley **Rev:** Multicolor Australian and New Zealand soldiers beneath Australian flag

Date	Mintage	F	VF	XF	Unc	BU
2005 Proof	15,000	Value: 85.00				

KM# 834 DOLLAR
31.1035 g., 0.9990 Silver 0.9990 oz. ASW, 40 mm.
Ruler: Elizabeth II **Subject:** 50th Anniversary Cocos Keeling Islands **Obv:** Head with tiara right **Obv. Designer:** Ian Rank-Broadley **Rev:** Booby on island

Date	Mintage	F	VF	XF	Unc	BU
2005 Proof	7,500	Value: 25.00				

KM# 835 DOLLAR
Aluminum-Bronze, 38.74 mm. **Ruler:** Elizabeth II
Subject: Living Icons of Australia and New Zealand **Obv:** Head with tiara right **Obv. Designer:** Ian Rank-Broadley **Rev:** Indigenous image of kangaroo **Rev. Designer:** Charmaine Cole

Date	Mintage	F	VF	XF	Unc	BU
2005	20,000	—	—	—	15.00	20.00

KM# 836 DOLLAR
31.1035 g., 0.9990 Silver 0.9990 oz. ASW, 40 mm.
Ruler: Elizabeth II **Subject:** 21st Birthday Prince Harry of Wales **Obv:** Head with tiara right **Obv. Designer:** Ian Rank-Broadley **Rev:** Prince Harry

Date	Mintage	F	VF	XF	Unc	BU
2005 Proof	12,500	Value: 25.00				

KM# 77a DOLLAR
11.6600 g., 0.9990 Silver 0.3745 oz. ASW, 25 mm.
Ruler: Elizabeth II **Obv:** Young bust right **Obv. Designer:** Arnold Machin **Rev:** Kangaroos **Rev. Designer:** Stuart Devlin **Edge:** Segmented reeding

Date	Mintage	F	VF	XF	Unc	BU
2006 Proof	6,500	Value: 30.00				

KM# 489b DOLLAR
21.5200 g., 0.9990 Gold 0.6912 oz. AGW, 25 mm.
Ruler: Elizabeth II **Obv:** Head with tiara right **Obv. Designer:** Ian Rank-Broadley **Rev:** Kangaroos **Rev. Designer:** Stuart Devlin **Edge:** Segmented reeding

Date	Mintage	F	VF	XF	Unc	BU
2006 Proof	300	Value: 875				

KM# 804 DOLLAR
9.0000 g., Aluminum-Bronze, 25 mm. **Ruler:** Elizabeth II **Subject:** XXIII Commonwealth Games **Obv:** Head with tiara right

Date	Mintage	F	VF	XF	Unc	BU
2006	—	—	—	—	3.50	5.00

KM# 805 DOLLAR
9.0000 g., Aluminum-Bronze, 25 mm. **Ruler:** Elizabeth II **Subject:** 50 Years of Television **Obv:** Head with tiara right **Obv. Designer:** Ian Rank-Broadley **Rev:** TV mast and camera **Rev. Designer:** Vladimir Gottwald **Edge:** Segmented reeding

Date	Mintage	F	VF	XF	Unc	BU
2006C	135,221	—	—	—	2.50	3.50
2006 TV	46,370	—	—	—	7.50	10.00
2006S	48,490	—	—	—	2.50	3.50
2006B	53,739	—	—	—	3.50	5.50
2006M	47,836	—	—	—	3.50	5.50
2006 4 known	—	—	—	—	—	1,000

KM# 805a DOLLAR
11.6600 g., 0.9990 Silver 0.3745 oz. ASW, 25 mm.
Ruler: Elizabeth II **Subject:** 50 Years of Television **Obv:** Head with tiara right **Obv. Designer:** Ian Rank-Broadley **Rev:** TV mast and camera **Rev. Designer:** Vladimir Gottwald **Edge:** Segmented reeding

Date	Mintage	F	VF	XF	Unc	BU
2006 Proof	10,790	Value: 25.00				
2006A Proof	3,859	Value: 35.00				

KM# 806 DOLLAR
9.0000 g., Aluminum-Bronze Issued in folder., 25 mm.
Ruler: Elizabeth II **Series:** Colored Oceans **Obv:** Head with tiara right **Obv. Designer:** Ian Rank-Broadley **Rev:** Multicolor jumping Bottlenose dolphins **Rev. Designer:** T. Dean **Edge:** Segmented reeding

Date	Mintage	F	VF	XF	Unc	BU
2006	29,310	—	—	—	—	15.00

KM# 807 DOLLAR
9.0000 g., Aluminum-Bronze, 25 mm. **Ruler:** Elizabeth II **Series:** Colored Oceans **Obv:** Head with tiara right **Obv. Designer:** Ian Rank-Broadley **Rev:** Multicolor clown fish **Rev. Designer:** T. Dean **Edge:** Segmented reeding **Note:** Issued in folder.

Date	Mintage	F	VF	XF	Unc	BU
2006	29,310	—	—	—	—	15.00

KM# 826 DOLLAR
60.5000 g., 0.9990 Silver 1.9431 oz. ASW, 50 mm.
Ruler: Elizabeth II **Obv:** Replica of 1758 Mexico City Mint 8 Reales **Obv. Legend:** ELIZABETH II (small head right) AUSTRALIA **Rev:** Replica of 1758 Mexico City Mint 8 Reales **Rev. Legend:** PILLAR DOLLAR **Edge:** Reeded

Date	Mintage	F	VF	XF	Unc	BU
2006	9,846	—	—	—	80.00	—

KM# 839 DOLLAR
31.1035 g., 0.9990 Silver 0.9990 oz. ASW **Ruler:** Elizabeth II **Subject:** Tercentenary of first European Landing on Australian Mainland **Obv:** Head with tiara right **Obv. Designer:** Ian Rank-Broadley **Rev:** Dutch yacht Duyfken in sail, Janzoons map of Cape York

Date	Mintage	F	VF	XF	Unc	BU
2006 Proof	10,000	Value: 40.00				

KM# 840 DOLLAR
31.1035 g., 0.9990 Silver 0.9990 oz. ASW, 40 mm.
Ruler: Elizabeth II **Subject:** Antarctic Territory **Obv:** Head with tiara right **Obv. Designer:** Ian Rank-Broadley **Rev:** Edgeworth David Base

Date	Mintage	F	VF	XF	Unc	BU
2006 Proof	7,500	Value: 25.00				

KM# 841 DOLLAR
31.1035 g., 0.9990 Silver Colorized lenticular display. 0.9990 oz. ASW **Ruler:** Elizabeth II **Subject:** 50 Years of Television in Australia 1956-2006 **Obv:** Head with tiara right **Obv. Designer:** Ian Rank-Broadley **Rev:** Historic TV images **Shape:** Square with rounded corners

Date	Mintage	F	VF	XF	Unc	BU
2006 Proof	12,500	Value: 45.00				

KM# 842 DOLLAR
31.1035 g., 0.9990 Silver 0.9990 oz. ASW, 40 mm.
Ruler: Elizabeth II **Subject:** 40th Anniversary of Demise of Pre-Decimal Coins **Obv:** Head with tiara right above transparent locket containing small replicas of pre-decimal currency **Obv. Designer:** Ian Rank-Broadley **Rev:** Rim legend about locket

Date	Mintage	F	VF	XF	Unc	BU
2006P Proof	7,500	Value: 100				

KM# 843 DOLLAR
31.1035 g., 0.9990 Silver 0.9990 oz. ASW, 40 mm.
Ruler: Elizabeth II **Subject:** 80th Birthday of Queen Elizabeth II **Obv:** Head with tiara right **Obv. Designer:** Ian Rank-Broadley **Rev:** Queen Elizabeth II

Date	Mintage	F	VF	XF	Unc	BU
2006P Proof	12,500	Value: 25.00				

KM# 844 DOLLAR
31.1035 g., 0.9990 Silver 0.9990 oz. ASW, 40 mm.
Ruler: Elizabeth II **Subject:** Figures of Note **Obv:** Head with tiara right **Obv. Designer:** Ian Rank-Broadley **Rev:** Queen Elizabeth as portrayed on Australia 1 dollar banknote

Date	Mintage	F	VF	XF	Unc	BU
2006P Proof	1,000	Value: 40.00				

KM# 845 DOLLAR
31.1035 g., 0.9990 Silver 0.9990 oz. ASW, 40 mm.
Ruler: Elizabeth II **Subject:** Figures of Note **Obv:** Head with tiara right **Obv. Designer:** Ian Rank-Broadley **Rev:** MacArthur and Farrer as portrayed on Australia 2 dollar banknote

Date	Mintage	F	VF	XF	Unc	BU
2006P Proof	1,000	Value: 40.00				

KM# 846 DOLLAR
31.1035 g., 0.9990 Silver 0.9990 oz. ASW, 40 mm.
Ruler: Elizabeth II **Subject:** Figures of Note **Obv:** Head with tiara right **Obv. Designer:** Ian Rank-Broadley **Rev:** Banks and Chisholm as portrayed on Australia 5 dollar banknote

Date	Mintage	F	VF	XF	Unc	BU
2006P Proof	1,000	Value: 40.00				

KM# 847 DOLLAR
31.1035 g., 0.9990 Silver 0.9990 oz. ASW, 40 mm.
Ruler: Elizabeth II **Subject:** Figures of Note **Obv:** Head with tiara right **Obv. Designer:** Ian Rank-Broadley **Rev:** Greenway and Lawson as portrayed on Australia 10 dollar banknote

Date	Mintage	F	VF	XF	Unc	BU
2006P Proof	1,000	Value: 40.00				

KM# 848 DOLLAR
31.1035 g., 0.9990 Silver 0.9990 oz. ASW, 40 mm.
Ruler: Elizabeth II **Subject:** Figures of Note **Obv:** Head with tiara right **Obv. Designer:** Ian Rank-Broadley **Rev:** Kingsford-Smith and Hargrave as portrayed on Australia 20 dollar banknote

Date	Mintage	F	VF	XF	Unc	BU
2006P Proof	1,000	Value: 40.00				

KM# 849 DOLLAR
31.1035 g., 0.9990 Silver 0.9990 oz. ASW, 40 mm.
Ruler: Elizabeth II **Subject:** 50th Anniversary of Dame Edna Everage **Obv:** Head with tiara right **Obv. Designer:** Ian Rank-Broadley **Rev:** Dame Edna

Date	Mintage	F	VF	XF	Unc	BU
2006P Proof	6,500	Value: 22.50				

KM# 1005 DOLLAR
31.1030 g., 0.9990 Silver 0.9989 oz. ASW, 40 mm.
Ruler: Elizabeth II **Obv:** Head with tiara right **Obv. Legend:** ELIZABETH II - AUSTRALIA **Obv. Designer:** Ian Rank-Broadley **Rev:** Everage head facing, multicolor **Rev. Legend:** DAME EDNA EVERAGE - 50TH ANNIVERSARY

Date	Mintage	F	VF	XF	Unc	BU
ND(2006)P Proof	6,500	Value: 25.00				

KM# 808 DOLLAR
9.0000 g., Aluminum-Bronze, 25 mm. **Ruler:** Elizabeth II **Subject:** Ashes Cricket Series 1882-2007 **Obv:** Head with tiara right **Obv. Designer:** Ian Rank-Broadley **Rev:** Urn with supporters **Rev. Designer:** Vladimir Gottwald **Edge:** Segmented reeding

Date	Mintage	F	VF	XF	Unc	BU
2007	—	—	—	—	3.00	4.00

KM# 809 DOLLAR
9.0000 g., Aluminum-Bronze, 25 mm. **Ruler:** Elizabeth II **Subject:** Year of the Pig **Obv:** Head with tiara right **Obv. Designer:** Ian Rank-Broadley **Rev:** Pig **Rev. Designer:** Vladimir Gottwald **Edge:** Segmented reeding

Date	Mintage	F	VF	XF	Unc	BU
2007	—	—	—	—	3.00	4.00

KM# 809a DOLLAR
11.6600 g., 0.9990 Silver 0.3745 oz. ASW, 25 mm.
Ruler: Elizabeth II **Subject:** Year of the Pig **Obv:** Head with tiara right **Obv. Designer:** Ian Rank-Broadley **Rev:** Pig **Rev. Designer:** Vladimir Gottwald **Edge:** Segmented reeding

Date	Mintage	F	VF	XF	Unc	BU
2007 Proof	—	Value: 25.00				

KM# 828 DOLLAR
9.0000 g., Aluminum-Bronze, 25 mm. **Ruler:** Elizabeth II **Subject:** Year of the Surf Lifesaver **Obv:** Head with tiara right **Obv. Designer:** Ian Rank-Broadley **Rev:** Lifesavers with rescued person **Rev. Designer:** Vladimir Gottwald **Edge:** Segmented reeding

Date	Mintage	F	VF	XF	Unc	BU
2007 Proof	—	Value: 20.00				

KM# 829 DOLLAR
9.0000 g., Aluminum-Bronze, 25 mm. **Ruler:** Elizabeth II **Subject:** Norman Lindsay and his Magic Pudding **Obv:** Head with tiara right **Obv. Designer:** Ian Rank-Broadley **Rev:** Lindsay and Pudding characters **Rev. Designer:** Vladimir Gottwald **Edge:** Segmented reeding

Date	Mintage	F	VF	XF	Unc	BU
2007	—	—	—	—	—	17.50

KM# 850 DOLLAR
27.2200 g., Copper-Nickel, 38.74 mm. **Ruler:** Elizabeth II **Obv:** Head with tiara right **Obv. Designer:** Ian Rank-Broadley **Rev:** Kangaroo mother and joey **Rev. Designer:** Rolf Harris **Edge:** Reeded

Date	Mintage	F	VF	XF	Unc	BU
2007	—	—	—	—	12.50	15.00

KM# 1009 DOLLAR
31.1030 g., 0.9990 Silver 0.9989 oz. ASW, 40 mm.
Ruler: Elizabeth II **Subject:** 75th Anniversary Death of Phar Lap **Obv:** Head with tiara right **Obv. Legend:** ELIZABETH II - AUSTRALIA **Rev:** Horse and rider racing right

Date	Mintage	F	VF	XF	Unc	BU
ND(2007)P Proof	7,500	Value: 67.50				

KM# 1011 DOLLAR
0.9990 Silver, 40 mm. **Ruler:** Elizabeth II **Obv:** Crowned bust right at top **Obv. Legend:** ELIZABETH II - AUSTRALIA **Rev:** 12 Lunar figures

Date	Mintage	F	VF	XF	Unc	BU
2007 Proof	8,888	Value: 50.00				

KM# 1012 DOLLAR
31.1030 g., 0.9990 Silver 0.9989 oz. ASW, 40 mm.
Ruler: Elizabeth II **Obv:** Bust with tiara right **Obv. Legend:** ELIZABETH II - AUSTRALIA **Obv. Designer:** Ian Rank-Broadley **Rev:** Bridge, multicolor fireworks above **Rev. Legend:** 75th ANNIVERSARY - SYDNEY HARBOUR BRIDGE **Rev. Designer:** Vladimir Gottwald

Date	Mintage	F	VF	XF	Unc	BU
ND(2007)P Proof	10,000	Value: 67.50				

KM# 1016 DOLLAR
11.6600 g., 0.9990 Silver 0.3745 oz. ASW, 25 mm. **Ruler:** Elizabeth II **Subject:** 75th Anniversary **Obv:** Head with tiara right **Obv. Legend:** ELIZABETH II _ AUSTRALIA **Obv. Designer:** Ian

Rank-Broadley **Rev:** Three men standing at bridge joint **Rev.**
Legend: SYDNEY HARBOUR BRIDGE **Edge:** Segmented reeding

Date	Mintage	F	VF	XF	Unc	BU
2007B Proof	12,500	Value: 30.00				

KM# 1024 DOLLAR
9.0000 g., Aluminum-Bronze, 25 mm. **Ruler:** Elizabeth II
Series: Colored Oceans **Obv:** Head with tiara right **Obv. Designer:**
Ian Rank-Broadley **Rev:** Biscuit Star - multicolor **Rev. Designer:**
T. Dean **Edge:** Segmented reeding **Note:** Issued in folder.

Date	Mintage	F	VF	XF	Unc	BU
2007	—	—	—	—	—	15.00

KM# 1025 DOLLAR
9.0000 g., Aluminum-Bronze, 25 mm. **Ruler:** Elizabeth II
Series: Colored Oceans **Obv:** Head with tiara right
Obv. Designer: Ian Rank-Broadley **Rev:** Longfin Banner fish -
multicolor **Rev. Designer:** T. Dean **Edge:** Segmented reeding

Date	Mintage	F	VF	XF	Unc	BU
2007	—	—	—	—	—	15.00

KM# 1026 DOLLAR
9.0000 g., Aluminum-Bronze, 25 mm. **Ruler:** Elizabeth II
Series: Colored Oceans **Obv:** Head with tiara right **Obv. Designer:**
Ian Rank-Broadley **Rev:** White Shark - multicolor **Rev. Designer:**
T. Dean **Edge:** Segmented reeding **Note:** Issued in folder.

Date	Mintage	F	VF	XF	Unc	BU
2007	—	—	—	—	—	15.00

KM# 1027 DOLLAR
9.0000 g., Aluminum-Bronze, 25 mm. **Ruler:** Elizabeth II
Series: Colored Oceans **Obv:** Head with tiara right
Obv. Designer: Ian Rank-Broadley **Rev:** Big Belly seahorse
Edge: Segmented reeding

Date	Mintage	F	VF	XF	Unc	BU
2007	—	—	—	—	—	15.00

KM# 1040 DOLLAR
9.0000 g., Aluminum-Bronze, 25 mm. **Ruler:** Elizabeth II
Subject: APEC **Rev:** Multiple stars

Date	Mintage	F	VF	XF	Unc	BU
2007B Unc	—	—	—	—	2.50	3.00

KM# 1042 DOLLAR
9.0000 g., Aluminum-Brass, 25 mm. **Ruler:** Elizabeth II
Subject: Peacekeepers, 60th Anniversary **Rev:** Hand holding
globe within wreath, dove above

Date	Mintage	F	VF	XF	Unc	BU
2007B	—	—	—	—	—	15.00

KM# 1044 DOLLAR
9.0000 g., Aluminum-Bronze, 25 mm. **Ruler:** Elizabeth II
Subject: Year of the surfer lifesaver **Rev:** Three men saving fourth

Date	Mintage	F	VF	XF	Unc	BU
2007B	—	—	—	—	3.00	5.00

KM# 1044a DOLLAR
11.6600 g., 0.9990 Silver 0.3745 oz. ASW, 25 mm.
Ruler: Elizabeth II **Subject:** Year of the surfer lifesaver
Rev: Three men saving fourth

Date	Mintage	F	VF	XF	Unc	BU
2007B	—	Value: 30.00				

KM# 1047 DOLLAR
9.0000 g., Aluminum-Brass, 25 mm. **Ruler:** Elizabeth II
Rev: First coat of arms

Date	Mintage	F	VF	XF	Unc	BU
2008B	—	—	—	—	2.50	3.00
2008M	—	—	—	—	2.50	3.00
2008C	—	—	—	—	2.50	3.00
2008S	—	—	—	—	2.50	3.00

KM# 1063 DOLLAR
9.0000 g., Aluminum-Brass, 25 mm. **Ruler:** Elizabeth II
Subject: Saint Sister Mary Mackillop **Rev:** Nun and three children
Rev. Designer: V. Gottwald

Date	Mintage	F	VF	XF	Unc	BU
2008	—	—	—	—	12.00	13.00

KM# 1060 DOLLAR
9.0000 g., Aluminum-Brass, 25 mm. **Ruler:** Elizabeth II
Subject: Norman Lindsay **Rev:** Portrait and four characters to
left **Rev. Designer:** V. Gottwald

Date	Mintage	F	VF	XF	Unc	BU
2008 Unc	—	—	—	—	14.00	15.00

KM# 1047a DOLLAR
11.6000 g., 0.9990 Silver 0.3726 oz. ASW, 25 mm.
Ruler: Elizabeth II **Rev:** First coat of arms

Date	Mintage	F	VF	XF	Unc	BU
2008C Proof	12,500	Value: 40.00				

KM# 1052 DOLLAR
9.0000 g., Aluminum-Brass, 25 mm. **Ruler:** Elizabeth II
Subject: Rugby League Centennial **Rev:** Rugby Anniversary
Logo **Rev. Designer:** V. Gottwald

Date	Mintage	F	VF	XF	Unc	BU
2008	—	—	—	—	13.00	14.00

KM# 1056 DOLLAR
9.0000 g., Aluminum-Brass, 25 mm. **Ruler:** Elizabeth II
Subject: Year of the Rat **Rev. Designer:** V. Gottwald

Date	Mintage	F	VF	XF	Unc	BU
2008	—	—	—	—	13.00	14.00

KM# 1056a DOLLAR
11.6600 g., 0.9990 Silver 0.3745 oz. ASW, 25 mm.
Ruler: Elizabeth II **Subject:** Year of the Rat

Date	Mintage	F	VF	XF	Unc	BU
2008 Proof	10,000	Value: 40.00				

KM# 1059 DOLLAR
9.0000 g., Aluminum-Bronze, 25 mm. **Ruler:** Elizabeth II
Subject: Planet earth **Rev:** Four hands and elements
Rev. Designer: V. Gottwald

Date	Mintage	F	VF	XF	Unc	BU
2008 Unc	—	—	—	—	12.00	14.00
2008 Proof	—	Value: 20.00				

KM# 1061 DOLLAR
27.2200 g., Copper-Nickel, 38.74 mm. **Ruler:** Elizabeth II
Rev: Kangaroo holding football **Rev. Designer:** Reg Mombassa

Date	Mintage	F	VF	XF	Unc	BU
2008 Unc	—	—	—	—	—	25.00

KM# 1061a DOLLAR
31.1050 g., 0.9990 Silver 0.9990 oz. ASW, 40 mm.
Ruler: Elizabeth II **Rev:** Kangaroo holding football
Rev. Designer: Reg Mombassa

Date	Mintage	F	VF	XF	Unc	BU
2008 Unc	20,000	—	—	—	—	50.00
2008 Proof	20,000	Value: 65.00				

KM# 1061b DOLLAR
31.1050 g., 0.9990 Silver 0.9990 oz. ASW, 40 mm.
Ruler: Elizabeth II **Rev:** Kangaroo holding football
Rev. Designer: Reg Mombassa

Date	Mintage	F	VF	XF	Unc	BU
2008 Proof	12,500	Value: 95.00				

KM# 1064 DOLLAR
9.0000 g., Aluminum-Brass, 25 mm. **Ruler:** Elizabeth II
Subject: Centennial of Quarantine **Rev:** Beagle and suitcase like
map of Australia **Rev. Designer:** W. Pietranik

Date	Mintage	F	VF	XF	Unc	BU
2008	—	—	—	—	12.00	13.00

KM# 1068 DOLLAR
9.0000 g., Aluminum-Brass, 25 mm. **Ruler:** Elizabeth II
Rev: Multicolor Echidna **Rev. Designer:** S. Foster

Date	Mintage	F	VF	XF	Unc	BU
2008	—	—	—	—	—	7.00

KM# 1069 DOLLAR
9.0000 g., Aluminum-Brass, 25 mm. **Ruler:** Elizabeth II
Rev: Multicolor Rock Wallaby **Rev. Designer:** S. Foster

Date	Mintage	F	VF	XF	Unc	BU
2008	—	—	—	—	—	7.00

KM# 1070 DOLLAR
9.0000 g., Aluminum-Brass, 25 mm. **Ruler:** Elizabeth II
Rev: Multicolor Koala **Rev. Designer:** S. Foster

Date	Mintage	F	VF	XF	Unc	BU
2008	—	—	—	—	—	7.00

KM# 1071 DOLLAR
9.0000 g., Aluminum-Brass, 25 mm. **Ruler:** Elizabeth II
Rev: Multicolor Wombat **Rev. Designer:** S. Foster

Date	Mintage	F	VF	XF	Unc	BU
2008	—	—	—	—	—	7.00

KM# 1090 DOLLAR
13.5000 g., Aluminum-Bronze, 29.5 mm. **Ruler:** Elizabeth II
Subject: Ghost Bat **Obv:** Head right **Rev:** Ghost bat against night
sky **Edge:** Reeded

Date	Mintage	F	VF	XF	Unc	BU
2008	—	—	—	—	10.00	12.00

KM# 1091 DOLLAR
31.1350 g., 0.9990 Silver 100000 oz. ASW, 40.6 mm.
Ruler: Elizabeth II **Subject:** UNESCO Heritage site - Kakadu
national Park **Rev:** Saltwater Crocodile and multicolor swamp

Date	Mintage	F	VF	XF	Unc	BU
2008P Proof	7,500	Value: 70.00				

KM# 1168 DOLLAR
Aluminum-Bronze, 31 mm. **Ruler:** Elizabeth II **Obv:** Head right
Obv. Designer: Ian Rank-Broadley **Rev:** Common wombat

Date	Mintage	F	VF	XF	Unc	BU
2008P	—	—	—	—	—	10.00

KM# 1169 DOLLAR
Aluminum-Bronze, 31 mm. **Ruler:** Elizabeth II **Obv:** Head right **Obv. Designer:** Ian Rank-Broadley **Rev:** Echidna

Date	Mintage	F	VF	XF	Unc	BU
2008P	—	—	—	—	—	10.00

KM# 1170 DOLLAR
Aluminum-Bronze, 31 mm. **Ruler:** Elizabeth II **Obv:** Head right **Obv. Designer:** Ian Rank-Broadley **Rev:** Frilled neck lizard

Date	Mintage	F	VF	XF	Unc	BU
2008P	—	—	—	—	—	10.00

KM# 1171 DOLLAR
Aluminum-Bronze, 31 mm. **Ruler:** Elizabeth II **Obv:** Head right **Obv. Designer:** Ian Rank-Broadley **Rev:** Grey Kangaroo

Date	Mintage	F	VF	XF	Unc	BU
2008P	—	—	—	—	—	10.00

KM# 1172 DOLLAR
Aluminum-Bronze, 31 mm. **Ruler:** Elizabeth II **Obv:** Head right **Obv. Designer:** Ian Rank-Broadley **Rev:** Splendid wren

Date	Mintage	F	VF	XF	Unc	BU
2008P	—	—	—	—	—	10.00

KM# 1173 DOLLAR
Aluminum-Bronze, 31 mm. **Ruler:** Elizabeth II **Obv:** Head right **Obv. Designer:** Ian Rank-Broadley **Rev:** Palm cockatoo

Date	Mintage	F	VF	XF	Unc	BU
2008P	—	—	—	—	—	10.00

KM# 1174 DOLLAR
Aluminum-Bronze, 31 mm. **Ruler:** Elizabeth II **Obv:** Head right **Obv. Designer:** Ian Rank-Broadley **Rev:** Wedge tailed eagle

Date	Mintage	F	VF	XF	Unc	BU
2008P	—	—	—	—	—	10.00

KM# 1175 DOLLAR
Aluminum-Bronze, 31 mm. **Ruler:** Elizabeth II **Obv:** Head right **Obv. Designer:** Ian Rank-Broadley **Rev:** Whale shark

Date	Mintage	F	VF	XF	Unc	BU
2008P	—	—	—	—	—	10.00

KM# 1176 DOLLAR
Aluminum-Bronze, 31 mm. **Ruler:** Elizabeth II **Obv:** Head right **Obv. Designer:** Ian Rank-Broadley **Rev:** Green turtle

Date	Mintage	F	VF	XF	Unc	BU
2008P	—	—	—	—	—	10.00

KM# 1177 DOLLAR
Aluminum-Bronze, 31 mm. **Ruler:** Elizabeth II **Obv:** Head right **Obv. Designer:** Ian Rank-Broadley **Rev:** Platypus

Date	Mintage	F	VF	XF	Unc	BU
2008P	—	—	—	—	—	10.00

KM# 1178 DOLLAR
Aluminum-Bronze, 31 mm. **Ruler:** Elizabeth II **Obv:** Head right **Obv. Designer:** Ian Rank-Broadley **Rev:** Australian sea lion

Date	Mintage	F	VF	XF	Unc	BU
2008P	—	—	—	—	—	10.00

KM# 1179 DOLLAR
31.1050 g., 0.9990 Silver 0.9990 oz. ASW, 40.6 mm. **Ruler:** Elizabeth II **Subject:** End of WWI, 90th Anniversary **Obv:** Head right **Obv. Designer:** Ian Rank-Broadley **Rev:** Silouette of Bugler, multicolor poppies below

Date	Mintage	F	VF	XF	Unc	BU
2008P Proof	12,500	Value: 90.00				

KM# 1111 DOLLAR
31.1050 g., 0.9990 Silver 0.9990 oz. ASW, 40.6 mm. **Ruler:** Elizabeth II **Rev:** Kola seated left on branch, shimmer background **Rev. Designer:** Darryl Bellotti

Date	Mintage	F	VF	XF	Unc	BU
2009P	—	—	—	—	—	30.00

KM# 1092 DOLLAR
13.3000 g., Aluminum-Bronze, 30.6 mm. **Ruler:** Elizabeth II **Subject:** Celebrate Australia - Western Australia **Rev:** Kangaroo and multicolor Perth city view

Date	Mintage	F	VF	XF	Unc	BU
2009	—	—	—	—	—	13.00

KM# 1099 DOLLAR
13.3000 g., Aluminum-Bronze, 30.6 mm. **Ruler:** Elizabeth II **Subject:** Celebrate Australia - Capital Territoty, Canberra **Rev:** Cockatoo and multicolor design

Date	Mintage	F	VF	XF	Unc	BU
2009P	—	—	—	—	—	13.00

KM# 1102 DOLLAR
31.1050 g., 0.9990 Silver 0.9990 oz. ASW **Ruler:** Elizabeth II **Subject:** Great Barrier Reef **Rev:** Sea Turtle, multicolor

Date	Mintage	F	VF	XF	Unc	BU
2009 Proof	—	Value: 70.00				

KM# 1076 DOLLAR
9.0000 g., Aluminum-Brass, 25 mm. **Ruler:** Elizabeth II **Subject:** Year of Astronomy **Rev:** Parkes Telescope **Rev. Designer:** Caitlin Goodall

Date	Mintage	F	VF	XF	Unc	BU
2009 Unc	—	—	—	—	12.00	14.00
2009 Proof	—	Value: 25.00				

KM# 1077 DOLLAR
9.0000 g., Aluminum-Brass, 25 mm. **Ruler:** Elizabeth II **Subject:** Dorothy Wall **Rev:** Portrait and four characters to right **Rev. Designer:** C. Goodall

Date	Mintage	F	VF	XF	Unc	BU
2009	—	—	—	—	—	10.00

KM# 1078 DOLLAR
9.0000 g., Aluminum-Brass, 25 mm. **Ruler:** Elizabeth II **Subject:** Year of the Ox **Rev:** V. Gottwald

Date	Mintage	F	VF	XF	Unc	BU
2009	—	—	—	—	12.00	13.00

KM# 1078a DOLLAR
11.6600 g., 0.9990 Silver 0.3745 oz. ASW, 25 mm. **Ruler:** Elizabeth II **Subject:** Year of the Ox **Rev. Designer:** V. Gottwald

Date	Mintage	F	VF	XF	Unc	BU
2009 Proof	10,000	Value: 45.00				

KM# 1082 DOLLAR
27.2200 g., Copper-Nickel, 38.74 mm. **Ruler:** Elizabeth II **Rev:** Kangaroo **Rev. Designer:** K. Done

Date	Mintage	F	VF	XF	Unc	BU
2009	—	—	—	—	—	25.00

KM# 1083 DOLLAR
31.1050 g., 0.9990 Silver 0.9990 oz. ASW, 40 mm. **Ruler:** Elizabeth II **Rev:** Kangaroo **Rev. Designer:** K. Done

Date	Mintage	F	VF	XF	Unc	BU
2009 Unc	20,000	—	—	—	—	50.00
2009 Proof	20,000	Value: 65.00				

KM# 1083a DOLLAR
31.1050 g., 0.9990 Silver Partially gilt 0.9990 oz. ASW, 40 mm. **Ruler:** Elizabeth II **Rev:** Kangaroo **Rev. Designer:** K. Done

Date	Mintage	F	VF	XF	Unc	BU
2009 Unc	—	—	—	—	—	90.00

KM# 1087 DOLLAR
9.0000 g., Aluminum-Brass, 25 mm. **Ruler:** Elizabeth II **Subject:** Citizenship **Obv:** Head right **Rev:** Portraits around globe

Date	Mintage	F	VF	XF	Unc	BU
2009 Proof	—	Value: 28.00				

KM# 1087a DOLLAR
11.9000 g., 0.9990 Silver 0.3822 oz. ASW, 25 mm. **Ruler:** Elizabeth II **Subject:** Citizenship, 60th Anniversary

Date	Mintage	F	VF	XF	Unc	BU
2009 Proof	—	Value: 40.00				

KM# 1093 DOLLAR
13.3000 g., Aluminum-Bronze, 30.6 mm. **Ruler:** Elizabeth II **Series:** Celebrate Australia - Victoria **Rev:** Little Penguin and melticolor Melbourne city view

Date	Mintage	F	VF	XF	Unc	BU
2009	—	—	—	—	—	13.00

KM# 1094 DOLLAR
13.3000 g., Aluminum-Bronze, 30.6 mm. **Ruler:** Elizabeth II **Subject:** Celebrate Australia - Tasmania **Rev:** Tasmanian Devil and multicolor Cradle Mountain National Park

Date	Mintage	F	VF	XF	Unc	BU
2009P	—	—	—	—	—	13.00

KM# 1095 DOLLAR
13.3000 g., Aluminum-Bronze, 30.6 mm. **Ruler:** Elizabeth II **Subject:** Celebrate Australia - South Australia **Rev:** Wombat and multicolor Cathedral

Date	Mintage	F	VF	XF	Unc	BU
2009P	—	—	—	—	—	13.00

KM# 1096 DOLLAR
13.3000 g., Aluminum-Bronze, 30.6 mm. **Ruler:** Elizabeth II **Subject:** Celebrate Australia - Queensland **Rev:** Sea Turtle with multicolor skyline of Brisbane

Date	Mintage	F	VF	XF	Unc	BU
2009P	—	—	—	—	—	13.00

KM# 1097 DOLLAR
13.3000 g., Aluminum-Bronze, 30.6 mm. **Ruler:** Elizabeth II **Subject:** Celebrate Australia - Northern Territoty **Rev:** Saltwater Crocodile and multicolor Kakadu National Park

Date	Mintage	F	VF	XF	Unc	BU
2009P	—	—	—	—	—	13.00

KM# 1098 DOLLAR
13.3000 g., Aluminum-Bronze, 30.6 mm. **Ruler:** Elizabeth II **Subject:** Celebrate Australia - New South Wales **Rev:** Koala, multicolor Sydney Opera House and Harbor Bridge

Date	Mintage	F	VF	XF	Unc	BU
2009P	—	—	—	—	—	13.00

KM# 1103 DOLLAR
31.1050 g., 0.9990 Silver 0.9990 oz. ASW, 27x47 mm. **Ruler:** Elizabeth II **Rev:** Turtle Dreaming **Rev. Designer:** Darryl Bellotti **Shape:** Rectangle

Date	Mintage	F	VF	XF	Unc	BU
2009 Proof	—	Value: 55.00				

KM# 1107 DOLLAR
31.1050 g., 0.9999 Silver 0.9999 oz. ASW, 27x47 mm. **Ruler:** Elizabeth II **Rev:** Kangaroo Dreaming **Rev. Designer:** Darryl Bellotti **Shape:** vertical rectangle

Date	Mintage	F	VF	XF	Unc	BU
2009 Proof	—	Value: 55.00				

KM# 1111a DOLLAR
31.1050 g., 0.9999 Silver partially gilt 0.9999 oz. ASW, 40.6 mm. **Ruler:** Elizabeth II **Rev:** Kola seated left on branch **Rev. Designer:** Darryl Bellotti

Date	Mintage	F	VF	XF	Unc	BU
2009P Proof	10,000	Value: 60.00				

KM# 1211 DOLLAR
31.1050 g., 0.9990 Silver 0.9990 oz. ASW, 40.6 mm. **Ruler:** Elizabeth II **Subject:** Antartic Territory **Obv:** Head right **Obv. Designer:** Ian Rank-Broadley **Rev:** Douglas Mawson, one of two men standing on magnetic South Pole

Date	Mintage	F	VF	XF	Unc	BU
2009P Proof	7,500	Value: 85.00				

KM# 1245 DOLLAR
31.1050 g., 0.9990 Silver 0.9990 oz. ASW **Ruler:** Elizabeth II **Subject:** 2010 FIFA World Cup, South Africa **Obv:** Head right **Obv. Designer:** Ian Rank-Broadley **Rev:** Soccer player and kangaroo in background

Date	Mintage	F	VF	XF	Unc	BU
2009P Proof	15,000	Value: 100				

KM# 1248 DOLLAR
31.1050 g., 0.9990 Silver 0.9990 oz. ASW, 40.6 mm. **Ruler:** Elizabeth II **Subject:** World Masters Games **Obv:** Head right **Obv. Designer:** Ian Rank-Broadley **Rev:** Sydney Harbor Bridge, multicolor

Date	Mintage	F	VF	XF	Unc	BU
2009P Proof	5,000	Value: 100				

KM# 1256 DOLLAR
Aluminum-Bronze, 31 mm. **Ruler:** Elizabeth II **Subject:** Space Topics - Telescope **Obv:** Head right **Obv. Designer:** Ian Rank-Broadley **Rev:** Galileo Galilei and telescope

Date	Mintage	F	VF	XF	Unc	BU
2009P	—	—	—	—	—	10.00

KM# 1257 DOLLAR
Aluminum-Bronze, 31 mm. **Ruler:** Elizabeth II **Subject:** Space Topics - Craters **Obv:** Head right **Obv. Designer:** Ian Rank-Broadley **Rev:** Moon crater Daedalus

Date	Mintage	F	VF	XF	Unc	BU
2009P	—	—	—	—	—	10.00

KM# 1258 DOLLAR
Aluminum-Bronze, 31 mm. **Ruler:** Elizabeth II **Subject:** Space Topics - Moon Exploration **Obv:** Head right **Obv. Designer:** Ian Rank-Broadley **Rev:** Apollo astronaut on moon walk

Date	Mintage	F	VF	XF	Unc	BU
2009P Proof	—	—	—	—	—	10.00

KM# 1259 DOLLAR
Aluminum-Bronze, 31 mm. **Ruler:** Elizabeth II **Subject:** Space Topics - Observatories **Obv:** Head right **Obv. Designer:** Ian Rank-Broadley **Rev:** Parkes Observatory, New South Wales

Date	Mintage	F	VF	XF	Unc	BU
2009P	—	—	—	—	—	10.00

KM# 1260 DOLLAR
Aluminum-Bronze, 31 mm. **Ruler:** Elizabeth II **Subject:** Space Topics - Rockets **Obv:** Head right **Obv. Designer:** Ian Rank-Broadley **Rev:** Saturn V rocket on launch pad

Date	Mintage	F	VF	XF	Unc	BU
2009P	—	—	—	—	—	10.00

KM# 1261 DOLLAR
Aluminum-Bronze, 31 mm. **Ruler:** Elizabeth II **Subject:** Space Topics - Rovers **Obv:** Head right **Obv. Designer:** Ian Rank-Broadley **Rev:** Mars rover - Spirit and Opportunity

Date	Mintage	F	VF	XF	Unc	BU
2009P	—	—	—	—	—	10.00

KM# 1262 DOLLAR
Aluminum-Bronze, 31 mm. **Ruler:** Elizabeth II **Subject:** Space Topics - Shuttle **Obv:** Head right **Obv. Designer:** Ian Rank-Broadley **Rev:** SHuttle Discovery adn Space Exploration

Date	Mintage	F	VF	XF	Unc	BU
2009P	—	—	—	—	—	10.00

KM# 1263 DOLLAR
Aluminum-Bronze, 31 mm. **Ruler:** Elizabeth II **Subject:** Space Topics - Probes **Obv:** Head right **Obv. Designer:** Ian Rank-Broadley **Rev:** Deep Space Probes - Pioneer 11 and 11

Date	Mintage	F	VF	XF	Unc	BU
2009P	—	—	—	—	—	10.00

KM# 1264 DOLLAR
Aluminum-Bronze, 31 mm. **Ruler:** Elizabeth II **Subject:** Space Topics - Space Telescope **Obv:** Head right **Obv. Designer:** Ian Rank-Broadley **Rev:** Hubble Space Telescope

Date	Mintage	F	VF	XF	Unc	BU
2009P	—	—	—	—	—	10.00

KM# 1265 DOLLAR
Aluminum-Bronze, 27x48 mm. **Ruler:** Elizabeth II **Subject:** Chinese Mythological Character - Wealth **Obv:** Head right **Obv. Designer:** Ian Rank-Broadley **Rev:** Man standing, multicolor **Shape:** Vertical rectangle

Date	Mintage	F	VF	XF	Unc	BU
2009P	—	—	—	—	—	65.00

KM# 1266 DOLLAR
31.1050 g., 0.9990 Silver 0.9990 oz. ASW, 27x48 mm. **Ruler:** Elizabeth II **Subject:** Chinese Mythological Character - Longevity **Obv:** Head right **Obv. Designer:** Ian Rank-Broadley **Rev:** Man standing with staff, multicolor **Edge Lettering:** Vertical rectangle

Date	Mintage	F	VF	XF	Unc	BU
2009P	—	—	—	—	—	65.00

KM# 1267 DOLLAR
31.1050 g., 0.9990 Silver 0.9990 oz. ASW, 27x48 mm.
Ruler: Elizabeth II **Subject:** Chinese Mythological Character - Success **Obv:** Head right **Obv. Designer:** Ian rank-Broadley **Rev:** Man standing with deer, multicolor **Shape:** Vertical rectangle

Date	Mintage	F	VF	XF	Unc	BU
2009P	—	—	—	—	—	65.00

KM# 1268 DOLLAR
31.1050 g., 0.9990 Silver 0.9990 oz. ASW, 27x48 mm.
Ruler: Elizabeth II **Subject:** Chinese Mythological Character - Fortune **Obv:** Head right **Obv. Designer:** Ian Rank-Broadley **Rev:** Man standing with scroll, multicolor **Shape:** Vertical rectangle

Date	Mintage	F	VF	XF	Unc	BU
2009P	—	—	—	—	—	65.00

KM# 1324 DOLLAR
31.1050 g., 0.9990 Silver 0.9990 oz. ASW, 41 mm.
Ruler: Elizabeth II **Subject:** Lachen Macquarie, Governor of New South Wales **Obv:** Head right **Obv. Designer:** Ian Rank-Broadley **Rev:** Macquarie, Sydney's "Rum" Hospital, Holey Dollar

Date	Mintage	F	VF	XF	Unc	BU
2010P Proof	7,500	Value: 90.00				

KM# 1325 DOLLAR
31.1050 g., 0.9990 Silver 0.9990 oz. ASW, 41 mm.
Ruler: Elizabeth II **Subject:** 2010 Australian Olympic Team **Obv:** Head right **Obv. Designer:** Ian Rank-Broadley **Rev:** Downhill skier, multicolor Australian flag

Date	Mintage	F	VF	XF	Unc	BU
2010P Proof	5,000	Value: 100				

KM# 1326 DOLLAR
31.1050 g., 0.9990 Silver 0.9990 oz. ASW, 41 mm.
Ruler: Elizabeth II **Subject:** Century of Flight in Australia **Obv:** Head right **Obv. Designer:** Ian Rank-Broadley **Rev:** Bi-plane, multicolor

Date	Mintage	F	VF	XF	Unc	BU
2010P Proof	7,500	Value: 90.00				

KM# 406 2 DOLLARS
6.6000 g., Aluminum-Bronze, 20.42 mm. **Ruler:** Elizabeth II **Obv:** Head right **Obv. Designer:** Ian Rank-Broadley **Rev:** Aboriginal Elder at left, stars above at right **Rev. Designer:** Horst Hahne **Edge:** Reeded, smooth alternating edge

Date	Mintage	F	VF	XF	Unc	BU
2001	3,565,000	—	—	—	4.00	6.00
Note: Large obverse head, IRB spaced						
2001	Inc. above	—	—	—	—	—
Note: Smaller obverse head, IRB joined						
2001 Proof	59,569	Value: 8.00				
2002	29,689,000	—	—	—	4.00	6.00
2002 Proof	39,514	Value: 8.00				
2003	13,656,000	—	—	—	4.00	6.00
2003 Proof	39,090	Value: 8.00				
2004	20,084,000	—	—	—	3.50	5.00
2004 Proof	50,000	Value: 7.00				
2005	—	—	—	—	3.50	5.00
2005 Proof	33,520	Value: 7.00				
2006	—	—	—	—	3.50	5.00
2006 Proof	—	Value: 7.00				
2007	—	—	—	—	3.00	4.50
2007 Proof	—	Value: 6.00				
2008	—	—	—	—	3.00	4.50
2008 Proof	—	Value: 6.00				
2009	—	—	—	—	3.00	4.50
2009 Proof	—	Value: 6.00				

KM# 406a 2 DOLLARS
15.8800 g., 0.9999 Gold 0.5105 oz. AGW, 20.5 mm.
Ruler: Elizabeth II **Subject:** Federation Centennial **Obv:** Head with tiara right **Obv. Designer:** Ian Rank-Broadley **Rev:** Aboriginal elder **Rev. Designer:** Horst Hahne **Edge:** Segmented reeding

Date	Mintage	F	VF	XF	Unc	BU
2001B Proof	350	Value: 675				
2005B Proof	650	Value: 650				
2006B Proof	300	Value: 700				

KM# 406b 2 DOLLARS
8.5500 g., 0.9999 Silver 0.2748 oz. ASW, 20.5 mm.
Ruler: Elizabeth II **Obv:** Head with tiara right **Obv. Designer:** Ian Rank-Broadley **Rev:** Aboriginal elder **Rev. Designer:** Horst Hahne **Edge:** Segmented reeding

Date	Mintage	F	VF	XF	Unc	BU
2003B Proof	6,500	Value: 20.00				
2004B Proof	6,500	Value: 20.00				
2005B Proof	6,500	Value: 20.00				

KM# 764 2 DOLLARS
18.2200 g., 0.9990 Silver 0.5852 oz. ASW, 32.5 mm.
Ruler: Elizabeth II **Series:** Masterpieces in Silver - Port Phillip Patterns **Obv:** 1/2 Ounce design **Rev:** Kangaroo design **Edge:** Reeded

Date	Mintage	F	VF	XF	Unc	BU
2003B Proof	10,000	Value: 15.00				

KM# 755 2 DOLLARS
62.2700 g., 0.9990 Silver 1.9999 oz. ASW, 50.3 mm.
Ruler: Elizabeth II **Series:** Australian Peacekeepers **Obv:** Queens head right **Rev:** Australian army and color insignia **Edge:** Reeded

Date	Mintage	F	VF	XF	Unc	BU
2005P Proof	2,500	Value: 65.00				

KM# 756 2 DOLLARS
62.2700 g., 0.9990 Silver 1.9999 oz. ASW, 50.3 mm.
Ruler: Elizabeth II **Series:** Australian Peacekeepers **Obv:** Queens head right **Rev:** Australian Navy and color insignia **Edge:** Reeded

Date	Mintage	F	VF	XF	Unc	BU
2005P Proof	2,500	Value: 65.00				

KM# 757 2 DOLLARS
62.2700 g., 0.9990 Silver 1.9999 oz. ASW, 50.3 mm.
Ruler: Elizabeth II **Subject:** Australian Peacekeepers Set **Obv:** Queens head right **Rev:** Australian Airforce and color insignia **Edge:** Reeded

Date	Mintage	F	VF	XF	Unc	BU
2005P Proof	2,500	Value: 65.00				

KM# 758 2 DOLLARS
62.2700 g., 0.9990 Silver 1.9999 oz. ASW, 50.3 mm.
Ruler: Elizabeth II **Series:** Australian Peacekeepers **Obv:** Queens head right **Rev:** Australian Federal Police and color insignia **Edge:** Reeded

Date	Mintage	F	VF	XF	Unc	BU
2005P Proof	2,500	Value: 65.00				

KM# 759 2 DOLLARS
62.2700 g., 0.9990 Silver 1.9999 oz. ASW, 50.3 mm.
Ruler: Elizabeth II **Series:** Australian Peacekeepers **Obv:** Queens head right **Rev:** Australian Agency for International Development and color insignia **Edge:** Reeded

Date	Mintage	F	VF	XF	Unc	BU
2005P Proof	2,500	Value: 65.00				

KM# 852 2 DOLLARS
8.8500 g., 0.9990 Silver 0.2842 oz. ASW, 20.5 mm.
Ruler: Elizabeth II **Obv:** Young bust right **Obv. Designer:** Arnold Machin **Rev:** Aboriginal elder **Rev. Designer:** Horst Hahn **Edge:** Segmented reeding

Date	Mintage	F	VF	XF	Unc	BU
2006 Proof	6,500	Value: 20.00				

KM# 853 2 DOLLARS
1.2441 g., 0.9990 Gold 0.0400 oz. AGW **Ruler:** Elizabeth II **Obv:** Head with tiara right **Obv. Designer:** Ian Rank-Broadley **Rev:** FIFA World Cup

Date	Mintage	F	VF	XF	Unc	BU
2006P Proof	50,000	Value: 55.00				

KM# 1246 2 DOLLARS
0.5000 g., 0.9990 Gold 0.0161 oz. AGW, 12 mm.
Ruler: Elizabeth II **Subject:** 2010 FIFA World Cup, South Africa **Obv:** Head right **Obv. Designer:** Ian Rank-Broadley **Rev:** Dream kangaroo and soccer ball

Date	Mintage	F	VF	XF	Unc	BU
2009P Proof	7,500	Value: 80.00				

KM# 591 5 DOLLARS
36.3100 g., 0.9990 Silver 1.1662 oz. ASW, 38.74 mm.
Ruler: Elizabeth II **Subject:** Centennial of Federation Series Finale **Obv:** Queens head right **Rev:** Multicolor dual hologram: map and rotunda **Edge:** Reeded

Date	Mintage	F	VF	XF	Unc	BU
2001B Proof	—	Value: 35.00				

KM# 592 5 DOLLARS
36.3100 g., 0.9990 Silver 1.1662 oz. ASW, 38.74 mm.
Ruler: Elizabeth II **Subject:** Barton and Reid **Obv:** Queens head right **Rev:** Portraits of Dame Flora Reid and Lady Jean Barton **Edge:** Reeded

Date	Mintage	F	VF	XF	Unc	BU
2001B Proof	5,000	Value: 50.00				

KM# 637 5 DOLLARS
36.3100 g., 0.9990 Silver 1.1662 oz. ASW, 38.74 mm.
Ruler: Elizabeth II **Subject:** Kingston, Barton and Deakin **Obv:** Queens head right **Rev:** Three rectangular portraits and value **Edge:** Reeded

Date	Mintage	F	VF	XF	Unc	BU
2001B Proof	5,000	Value: 50.00				

KM# 638 5 DOLLARS
36.3100 g., 0.9990 Silver 1.1662 oz. ASW, 38.74 mm.
Ruler: Elizabeth II **Subject:** Clark, Parkes and Griffith **Obv:** Queens head right **Rev:** Three rectangular portraits and value **Edge:** Reeded

Date	Mintage	F	VF	XF	Unc	BU
2001B Proof	5,000	Value: 50.00				

KM# 639 5 DOLLARS
36.3100 g., 0.9990 Silver 1.1662 oz. ASW, 38.74 mm.
Ruler: Elizabeth II **Subject:** Spence, Nicholls and Anderson **Obv:** Queens head right **Rev:** Three circular portraits and value **Edge:** Reeded

Date	Mintage	F	VF	XF	Unc	BU
2001B Proof	5,000	Value: 50.00				

KM# 640 5 DOLLARS
36.3100 g., 0.9990 Silver 1.1662 oz. ASW, 38.74 mm.
Ruler: Elizabeth II **Subject:** Reid, Forrest and Quick **Obv:** Queens head right **Rev:** Three rectangular portraits and value **Edge:** Reeded

Date	Mintage	F	VF	XF	Unc	BU
2001B Proof	5,000	Value: 50.00				

KM# 641 5 DOLLARS
36.3100 g., 0.9990 Silver 1.1662 oz. ASW, 38.74 mm.
Ruler: Elizabeth II **Subject:** Bathurst Ladies Organizing Committee **Obv:** Queens head right **Rev:** Circular design with names above value **Edge:** Reeded

Date	Mintage	F	VF	XF	Unc	BU
2001B Proof	5,000	Value: 50.00				

KM# 662 5 DOLLARS
36.3100 g., 0.9990 Silver 1.1662 oz. ASW, 38.74 mm.
Ruler: Elizabeth II **Subject:** Year of the Outback **Obv:** Queens head right **Rev:** Multicolor holographic landscape **Edge:** Reeded

Date	Mintage	F	VF	XF	Unc	BU
2002B Proof	15,000	Value: 100				

KM# 761 5 DOLLARS
36.3100 g., 0.9990 Silver 1.1662 oz. ASW **Ruler:** Elizabeth II **Obv:** Queens head right **Rev:** Sir Donald Bradman

Date	Mintage	F	VF	XF	Unc	BU
2001 Proof	—	Value: 35.00				

KM# 762   5 DOLLARS
20.0000 g., Aluminum-Bronze, 38.74 mm. **Ruler:** Elizabeth II
Obv: Queens head right **Rev:** Sir Donald Bradman

Date	Mintage	F	VF	XF	Unc	BU
2001	—	—	—	—	8.50	9.50

KM# 601   5 DOLLARS
10.5200 g., Bi-Metallic Aluminumn-Bronze center in Stainless
Steel ring, 27.8 mm. **Ruler:** Elizabeth II **Subject:** Battle of Sunda
Strait **Obv:** Head with tiara right **Obv. Designer:** Ian Rank-
Broadley **Rev:** Ships bell from the "USS Houston", denomination
below **Rev. Designer:** Vladimir Gottwald **Shape:** 24-sided
Note: Demagnetized.

Date	Mintage	F	VF	XF	Unc	BU
2002B	—	—	—	—	7.50	9.50

KM# 647   5 DOLLARS
28.0000 g., Aluminum-Bronze, 38.74 mm. **Ruler:** Elizabeth II
Subject: Battle of Sunda Strait **Obv:** Queens head right
Rev: Two ships; USS Houston and HMS Perth **Edge:** Reeded

Date	Mintage	F	VF	XF	Unc	BU
2002B Proof	15,000		Value: 25.00			

KM# 650   5 DOLLARS
20.0000 g., Aluminum-Bronze, 38.74 mm. **Ruler:** Elizabeth II
Subject: Commonwealth Games **Obv:** Head with tiara right,
denomination below **Obv. Designer:** Ian Rank-Broadley **Rev:** Eight
arms, each represents an event at the games **Edge:** Reeded

Date	Mintage	F	VF	XF	Unc	BU
2002B	11,145	—	—	—	8.50	9.50

KM# 651   5 DOLLARS
20.0000 g., Aluminum-Bronze, 38.74 mm. **Ruler:** Elizabeth II
Subject: Commonwealth Games **Obv:** Head with tiara right,
denomination below **Rev:** Blue games logo; star above stylized
kangaroo and torch **Edge:** Reeded

Date	Mintage	F	VF	XF	Unc	BU
2002B	11,145	—	—	—	8.50	9.50

KM# 652   5 DOLLARS
36.3100 g., 0.9990 Silver 1.1662 oz. ASW, 38.74 mm.
Ruler: Elizabeth II **Subject:** Commonwealth Games **Obv:** Head
with tiara right, denomination below **Obv. Designer:** Ian Rank-
Broadley **Rev:** Victorious athletes **Edge:** Reeded

Date	Mintage	F	VF	XF	Unc	BU
2002B Proof	7,581		Value: 37.50			

KM# 653   5 DOLLARS
36.3100 g., 0.9990 Silver 1.1662 oz. ASW, 38.74 mm.
Ruler: Elizabeth II **Obv:** Queens head right **Rev:** Dutch sailing
ship, The Duyfken **Edge:** Reeded

Date	Mintage	F	VF	XF	Unc	BU
2002B Proof	9,096		Value: 35.00			

KM# 654   5 DOLLARS
36.3100 g., 0.9990 Silver 1.1662 oz. ASW, 38.74 mm.
Ruler: Elizabeth II **Obv:** Queens head right **Rev:** HMS
Endeavour sailing ship **Edge:** Reeded

Date	Mintage	F	VF	XF	Unc	BU
2002B Proof	9,096		Value: 35.00			

KM# 655   5 DOLLARS
36.3100 g., 0.9990 Silver 1.1662 oz. ASW, 38.74 mm.
Ruler: Elizabeth II **Obv:** Queens head right **Rev:** HMS Sirius
sailing ship **Edge:** Reeded

Date	Mintage	F	VF	XF	Unc	BU
2002B Proof	9,096		Value: 35.00			

KM# 656   5 DOLLARS
36.3100 g., 0.9990 Silver 1.1662 oz. ASW, 38.74 mm.
Ruler: Elizabeth II **Obv:** Queens head right **Rev:** HMS
Investigator sailing ship **Edge:** Reeded

Date	Mintage	F	VF	XF	Unc	BU
2002B Proof	9,096		Value: 35.00			

KM# 649   5 DOLLARS
20.0000 g., Aluminum-Bronze, 38.74 mm. **Ruler:** Elizabeth II
Subject: Commonwealth Games **Obv:** Head with tiara right,
denomination below **Obv. Designer:** Ian Rank-Broadley
Rev: Eight arms, each represents an event of the games
Edge: Reeded

Date	Mintage	F	VF	XF	Unc	BU
2002B	11,145	—	—	—	8.50	9.50

KM# 659   5 DOLLARS
31.1035 g., 0.9990 Silver 0.9990 oz. ASW, 40 mm.
Ruler: Elizabeth II **Subject:** Queen Mother **Obv:** Queens head
right **Rev:** Queen Mother circa 1927 within wreath of roses
Rev. Designer: Stuart Devlin **Edge:** Reeded

Date	Mintage	F	VF	XF	Unc	BU
2002B Proof	30,000		Value: 25.00			

KM# 765   5 DOLLARS
36.3100 g., 0.9990 Silver 1.1662 oz. ASW, 38.7 mm.
Ruler: Elizabeth II **Series:** Masterpieces in Silver - Port Phillip
Patterns **Obv:** 1 Ounce design **Rev:** Kangaroo design
Edge: Reeded

Date	Mintage	F	VF	XF	Unc	BU
2003B Proof	10,000		Value: 35.00			

KM# 810   5 DOLLARS
36.3100 g., 0.9950 Silver partially gilt 1.1615 oz. ASW, 40 mm.
Ruler: Elizabeth II **Subject:** Rugby World Cup **Obv:** Head with tiara right **Obv. Designer:** Ian Rank-Broadley **Rev:** Rugby World Cup and official logos **Edge:** Reeded

Date	Mintage	F	VF	XF	Unc	BU
2003 Proof	20,501		Value: 85.00			

KM# 854   5 DOLLARS
20.0000 g., Aluminum-Bronze, 38.74 mm. **Ruler:** Elizabeth II **Subject:** Rugby World Cup **Obv:** Head with tiara right **Obv. Designer:** Ian Rank-Broadley **Rev:** Player kicking ball at posts, Official logo **Edge:** Reeded

Date	Mintage	F	VF	XF	Unc	BU
2003	43,802	—	—	—	15.00	16.50

KM# 1017   5 DOLLARS
36.2100 g., 0.9990 Silver 1.1630 oz. ASW, 38.7 mm.
Ruler: Elizabeth II **Obv:** Head with tiara right **Obv. Legend:** ELIZABETH II - AUSTRALIA **Rev:** Faces in oval hologram in ornate frame **Rev. Legend:** AUSTRALIA'S VOLUNTEERS - MAKING A DIFFERENCE **Edge:** Reeded

Date	Mintage	F	VF	XF	Unc	BU
2003B Proof	15,000		Value: 40.00			

KM# 727   5 DOLLARS
36.3100 g., 0.9990 Silver 1.1662 oz. ASW, 38.74 mm.
Ruler: Elizabeth II **Subject:** Olympics **Obv:** Queens head right **Rev:** Parthenon, Sydney Opera House and shield with multicolor flag and rings **Edge:** Reeded

Date	Mintage	F	VF	XF	Unc	BU
2004B Proof	17,500		Value: 35.00			

KM# 728   5 DOLLARS
36.3100 g., 0.9990 Silver 1.1662 oz. ASW, 38.74 mm.
Ruler: Elizabeth II **Subject:** Tasmania **Obv:** Queens head right **Rev:** Ship on island map **Edge:** Reeded

Date	Mintage	F	VF	XF	Unc	BU
2004B Proof	7,500		Value: 35.00			

KM# 728a   5 DOLLARS
20.0000 g., Aluminum-Bronze, 38.74 mm. **Ruler:** Elizabeth II **Subject:** Tasmanian Bicentennial **Obv:** Head with tiara right **Obv. Designer:** Ian Rank-Broadley **Rev:** Ship, map, state flower **Edge:** Reeded

Date	Mintage	F	VF	XF	Unc	BU
2004	18,561	—	—	—	12.00	14.00
2004H	2,841	—	—	—	17.50	20.00

KM# 729   5 DOLLARS
31.1035 g., 0.9990 Silver 0.9990 oz. ASW, 40 mm.
Ruler: Elizabeth II **Subject:** Adelaide to Darwin Railroad **Obv:** Queens head right **Rev:** Train, tracks and outline map **Edge:** Reeded

Date	Mintage	F	VF	XF	Unc	BU
2004B Proof	12,500		Value: 32.00			

KM# 730   5 DOLLARS
31.1035 g., 0.9990 Silver 0.9990 oz. ASW, 40 mm.
Ruler: Elizabeth II **Subject:** 150 Years of Australian Steam Railways **Obv:** Queens head right **Rev:** Old steam train **Edge:** Reeded

Date	Mintage	F	VF	XF	Unc	BU
2004B Proof	15,000		Value: 30.00			

KM# 811   5 DOLLARS
Aluminum-Bronze, 38.74 mm. **Ruler:** Elizabeth II **Subject:** Bicentenary of Tasmania **Obv:** Head with tiara right

Date	Mintage	F	VF	XF	Unc	BU
2004	—	—	—	—	12.00	14.00

KM# 812   5 DOLLARS
Aluminum-Bronze, 38.74 mm. **Ruler:** Elizabeth II **Subject:** Olympic Games 2000-2004 **Obv:** Head with tiara right

Date	Mintage	F	VF	XF	Unc	BU
2004	—	—	—	—	15.00	16.50

KM# 855   5 DOLLARS
27.2500 g., Copper-Nickel partially gilt, 38.74 mm.
Ruler: Elizabeth II **Subject:** Australia's Own Game **Obv:** Head with tiara right **Obv. Designer:** Ian Rank-Broadley **Rev:** Cup and logos **Edge:** Reeded

Date	Mintage	F	VF	XF	Unc	BU
2004	16,163	—	—	—	—	14.00

KM# 856   5 DOLLARS
20.0000 g., Aluminum-Bronze, 38.74 mm. **Ruler:** Elizabeth II **Subject:** Olympic Games - Sydney To Athens **Obv:** Head with tiara right **Obv. Designer:** Ian Rank-Broadley **Rev:** Silhouettes ancient Greek athlete and Aboriginal **Edge:** Reeded

Date	Mintage	F	VF	XF	Unc	BU
2004	24,376	—	—	—	15.00	16.50

KM# 750   5 DOLLARS
20.0000 g., Aluminum-Brass, 38.74 mm. **Ruler:** Elizabeth II **Obv:** Queens head right **Rev:** Tennis player **Edge:** Reeded

Date	Mintage	F	VF	XF	Unc	BU
2005B					7.50	8.50

KM# 859   5 DOLLARS
36.3100 g., 0.9990 Silver 1.1662 oz. ASW, 38.74 mm.
Ruler: Elizabeth II **Subject:** 150 Year of State Government **Obv:** Head with tiara right **Obv. Designer:** Ian Rank-Broadley **Rev:** Outline map of State of Victoria **Rev. Designer:** Wojciech Pietranik **Edge:** Reeded

Date	Mintage	F	VF	XF	Unc	BU
2006 Proof	12,500		Value: 85.00			

KM# 782   5 DOLLARS
36.3100 g., 0.9999 Silver 1.1672 oz. ASW, 38.74 mm.
Ruler: Elizabeth II **Subject:** XVIII Commonwealth Games City of Sport **Obv:** Head with tiara right, denomination below **Obv. Designer:** Ian Rank-Broadley **Rev:** City skyline alongside river

Date	Mintage	F	VF	XF	Unc	BU
2006 Proof	10,000		Value: 50.00			

KM# 783   5 DOLLARS
20.0000 g., Aluminum-Bronze, 38.74 mm. **Ruler:** Elizabeth II **Subject:** XVIII Commonwealth Games, Commonwealth of Nations **Obv:** Head with tiara right, denomination below **Obv. Designer:** Ian Rank-Broadley **Rev:** Games logo and crown surrounded by stylized athletes **Rev. Designer:** Wojciech Pietranik **Edge:** Reeded

Date	Mintage	F	VF	XF	Unc	BU
2006	—	—	—	—	15.00	16.50

KM# 786   5 DOLLARS
20.0000 g., Aluminum-Bronze, 38.74 mm. **Ruler:** Elizabeth II **Subject:** XVIII Commonwealth Games Queen's Baton Relay **Obv:** Head with tiara right **Obv. Designer:** Ian Rank-Broadley **Rev:** Stylized baton running **Rev. Designer:** Peter Soobik **Edge:** Reeded

Date	Mintage	F	VF	XF	Unc	BU
2006	20,488	—	—	—	15.00	16.50

KM# 786a   5 DOLLARS
36.3100 g., 0.9990 Silver 1.1662 oz. ASW, 38.74 mm.
Ruler: Elizabeth II **Subject:** XVIII Commonwealth Games Queen's Baton Relay **Obv:** Head with tiara right **Obv. Designer:** Ian Rank-Broadley **Rev:** Stylized baton running **Rev. Designer:** Peter Soobik **Edge:** Reeded

Date	Mintage	F	VF	XF	Unc	BU
2006 Proof	9,100		Value: 75.00			

KM# 787   5 DOLLARS
36.3100 g., 0.9990 Silver 1.1662 oz. ASW, 38.74 mm.
Ruler: Elizabeth II **Subject:** Masterpieces in Silver: Australia's Artists **Obv:** Head with tiara right **Obv. Designer:** Ian Rank-Broadley **Rev:** Sidney Nolan: Burke & Wills **Rev. Designer:** Vladimir Gottwald

Date	Mintage	F	VF	XF	Unc	BU
2006 Proof	10,000		Value: 60.00			

KM# 788 5 DOLLARS

Silver **Ruler:** Elizabeth II **Subject:** Masters in Art - Siding

Date	Mintage	F	VF	XF	Unc	BU
2006 Proof	10,000	Value: 55.00				

KM# 789 5 DOLLARS

36.3100 g., 0.9990 Silver 1.1662 oz. ASW, 38.74 mm.
Ruler: Elizabeth II **Subject:** Masterpieces in Silver: Australia's Artists **Obv:** Head with tiara right **Obv. Designer:** Ian Rank-Broadley **Rev:** Brett Whitley: Self Portrait in the Studio **Rev. Designer:** Vladimir Gottwald

Date	Mintage	F	VF	XF	Unc	BU
2006 Proof	10,000	Value: 60.00				

KM# 790 5 DOLLARS

36.3100 g., 0.9990 Silver 1.1662 oz. ASW, 38.74 mm.
Ruler: Elizabeth II **Subject:** Masterpieces in Silver: Australia's Artists **Obv:** Head with tiara right **Obv. Designer:** Ian Rank-Broadley **Rev:** Russell Drysdale: The Drover's Wife **Rev. Designer:** Vladimir Gottwald

Date	Mintage	F	VF	XF	Unc	BU
2006 Proof	10,000	Value: 60.00				

KM# 813 5 DOLLARS

20.0000 g., Aluminum-Bronze, 38.74 mm. **Ruler:** Elizabeth II
Subject: Voyage of Discovery 1606 **Obv:** Head with tiara right
Obv. Designer: Ian Rank-Broadley **Rev:** Dutch yacht Duyfken
Rev. Designer: Wojciech Pietranik **Edge:** Reeded
Note: Mintmark: G.

Date	Mintage	F	VF	XF	Unc	BU
2006	—	—	—	—	15.00	16.50

KM# 813a 5 DOLLARS

36.3100 g., 0.9990 Silver 1.1662 oz. ASW, 38.74 mm.
Ruler: Elizabeth II **Subject:** Voyage of Discovery 1606
Obv: Head with tiara right **Obv. Designer:** Ian Rank-Broadley
Rev: Dutch yacht Duyfken **Rev. Designer:** Wojciech Pietranik
Edge: Reeded **Note:** Mintmark: Tulip.

Date	Mintage	F	VF	XF	Unc	BU
2006P Proof	8,500	Value: 125				

KM# 815a 5 DOLLARS

1.2441 g., 0.9990 Gold 0.0400 oz. AGW **Ruler:** Elizabeth II
Obv: Head with tiara right **Obv. Designer:** Ian Rank-Broadley
Rev: Sydney Opera House

Date	Mintage	F	VF	XF	Unc	BU
2006P Proof	—	Value: 85.00				

KM# 857 5 DOLLARS

36.3100 g., 0.9999 Silver 1.1672 oz. ASW, 38.74 mm.
Ruler: Elizabeth II **Subject:** 150 Year of State Government
Obv: Head with tiara right **Obv. Designer:** Ian Rank-Broadley
Rev: Outline map of State of New South Wales
Rev. Designer: Wojciech Pietranik **Edge:** Reeded

Date	Mintage	F	VF	XF	Unc	BU
2006 Proof	12,500	Value: 85.00				

KM# 858 5 DOLLARS

36.3100 g., 0.9990 Silver 1.1662 oz. ASW, 38.74 mm.
Ruler: Elizabeth II **Subject:** 150 Year of State Government
Obv: Head with tiara right **Obv. Designer:** Ian Rank-Broadley
Rev: Outline map of State of Tasmania **Rev. Designer:** Wojciech Pietranik **Edge:** Reeded

Date	Mintage	F	VF	XF	Unc	BU
2006 Proof	12,500	Value: 85.00				

KM# 860 5 DOLLARS

36.3100 g., 0.9990 Silver 1.1662 oz. ASW, 38.74 mm.
Ruler: Elizabeth II **Subject:** Masterpieces in Silver: Australia's Artists **Obv:** Head with tiara right **Obv. Designer:** Ian Rank-Broadley **Rev:** Jeffrey Smart: Keswick Siding **Rev. Designer:** Vladimir Gottwald

Date	Mintage	F	VF	XF	Unc	BU
2006 Proof	10,000	Value: 60.00				

KM# 1014 5 DOLLARS

1.2441 g., 0.9999 Gold 0.0400 oz. AGW, 19 mm.
Ruler: Elizabeth II **Obv:** Bust with tiara right **Obv. Legend:**
ELIZABETH II - AUSTRALIA **Obv. Designer:** Ian Rank-Broadley
Rev: Sydney Opera House

Date	Mintage	F	VF	XF	Unc	BU
2006P Proof	100,000	Value: 60.00				

KM# 1116 5 DOLLARS

1.2400 g., 0.9990 Gold 0.0398 oz. AGW, 14 mm.
Ruler: Elizabeth II **Obv:** Head right **Obv. Designer:** Ian Rank-Broadley **Rev:** Opera house

Date	Mintage	F	VF	XF	Unc	BU
2006P Proof	100,000	Value: 100				

KM# 861 5 DOLLARS

36.3100 g., 0.9990 Silver 1.1662 oz. ASW, 8.74 mm.
Ruler: Elizabeth II **Subject:** Masterpieces in Silver: Australia's Artists **Obv:** Head with tiara right **Obv. Designer:** Ian Rank-Broadley **Rev:** Grace Cossington-Smith: Curve of the Bridge
Rev. Designer: Vladimir Gottwald

Date	Mintage	F	VF	XF	Unc	BU
2007 Proof	10,000	Value: 50.00				

KM# 862 5 DOLLARS

36.3100 g., 0.9990 Silver 1.1662 oz. ASW, 38.74 mm.
Ruler: Elizabeth II **Subject:** Masterpieces in Silver: Australia's Artists **Obv:** Head with tiara right **Obv. Designer:** Ian Rank-Broadley **Rev:** Clifford Possum Tjpaltjarri: Yuelamu Honey Ant Dreaming **Rev. Designer:** Vladimir Gottwald

Date	Mintage	F	VF	XF	Unc	BU
2007 Proof	10,000	Value: 50.00				

KM# 863 5 DOLLARS

36.3100 g., 0.9990 Silver 1.1662 oz. ASW, 38.74 mm.
Ruler: Elizabeth II **Subject:** Masterpieces in Silver: Australia's Artists **Obv:** Head with tiara right **Obv. Designer:** Ian Rank-Broadley **Rev:** William Dobell: Margaret Olley **Rev. Designer:** Vladimir Gottwald

Date	Mintage	F	VF	XF	Unc	BU
2007 Proof	10,000	Value: 50.00				

KM# 864 5 DOLLARS

36.3100 g., 0.9990 Silver 1.1662 oz. ASW, 38.74 mm.
Ruler: Elizabeth II **Subject:** Masterpieces in Silver: Australia's Artists **Obv:** Ian Rank-Broadley **Rev:** Margaret Preston: Implement Blue **Rev. Designer:** Vladimir Gottwald

Date	Mintage	F	VF	XF	Unc	BU
2007 Proof	10,000	Value: 50.00				

KM# 865 5 DOLLARS

36.3100 g., 0.9990 Silver 1.1662 oz. ASW, 38.74 mm.
Ruler: Elizabeth II **Subject:** Ashes Cricket Series 1882-2007
Obv: Head with tiara right **Obv. Designer:** Ian Rank-Broadley
Rev: Urn with supporters **Rev. Designer:** Vladimir Gottwald
Edge: Reeded

Date	Mintage	F	VF	XF	Unc	BU
2007 Proof	12,500	Value: 45.00				

KM# 1013 5 DOLLARS

36.3100 g., 0.9990 Silver 1.1662 oz. ASW, 38.74 mm.
Ruler: Elizabeth II **Subject:** Sydney Harbour Bridge, 75th Anniversary **Obv:** Bust with tiara right **Obv. Legend:** ELIZABETH II - AUSTRALIA **Obv. Designer:** Ian Rank-Broadley **Rev:** Bridge **Rev. Inscription:** SYDNEY / HARBOUR / BRIDGE

Date	Mintage	F	VF	XF	Unc	BU
2007 Proof	12,500	Value: 50.00				

KM# 1045 5 DOLLARS

36.3100 g., 0.9990 Silver 1.1662 oz. ASW, 38.74 mm.
Ruler: Elizabeth II **Subject:** Year of the surfer lifesaver **Rev:** Row boat in rough seas

Date	Mintage	F	VF	XF	Unc	BU
2007B Proof	12,500	Value: 65.00				

KM# 1046 5 DOLLARS

36.3100 g., 0.9990 Silver 1.1662 oz. ASW, 38.74 mm. **Ruler:** Elizabeth II **Subject:** South Australia State Government **Rev:** Australia map and state enlarged **Rev. Designer:** W. Pietranik

Date	Mintage	F	VF	XF	Unc	BU
2007B Proof	12,500	Value: 65.00				

KM# 1117 5 DOLLARS

1.2400 g., 0.9990 Gold 0.0398 oz. AGW, 14 mm.
Ruler: Elizabeth II **Subject:** Sydney Harbor Bridge **Obv:** Head right **Obv. Designer:** Ian Rank-Broadley **Rev:** Bridge view

Date	Mintage	F	VF	XF	Unc	BU
2007P Proof	100,000	Value: 100				

KM# 1050 5 DOLLARS

31.1050 g., 0.9990 Silver 0.9990 oz. ASW, 38.74 mm.
Ruler: Elizabeth II **Subject:** Scouting Centennial in Australia
Rev: Scout sign and map **Rev. Designer:** C. Goodall

Date	Mintage	F	VF	XF	Unc	BU
2008 Proof	5,000	Value: 65.00				

KM# 1053 5 DOLLARS

36.3100 g., 0.9990 Silver 1.1662 oz. ASW, 38.74 mm.
Ruler: Elizabeth II **Subject:** Rugby League **Rev:** Two players

Date	Mintage	F	VF	XF	Unc	BU
2008 Proof	10,000	Value: 65.00				

KM# 1055   5 DOLLARS
3.1050 g., 0.9990 Silver 0.0997 oz. ASW, 38.74 mm.
Ruler: Elizabeth II **Rev:** Antarctic skua in flight over map

Date	Mintage	F	VF	XF	Unc	BU
2008 Proof	12,500	Value: 65.00				

KM# 1065   5 DOLLARS
36.3100 g., 0.9990 Silver 1.1662 oz. ASW, 38.74 mm.
Ruler: Elizabeth II **Subject:** 30th Anniversary - Northern
Territorial Government **Rev:** Territory map and Australia map
Rev. Designer: W. Pietranik

Date	Mintage	F	VF	XF	Unc	BU
2008 Proof	12,500	Value: 65.00				

KM# 1066   5 DOLLARS
1.1500 g., 0.9990 Gold 0.0369 oz. AGW, 14 mm.
Ruler: Elizabeth II **Rev:** Kisp Koala

Date	Mintage	F	VF	XF	Unc	BU
2008 Proof	10,000	Value: 100				

KM# 1067   5 DOLLARS
1.1500 g., 0.9990 Gold 0.0369 oz. AGW, 14 mm.
Ruler: Elizabeth II **Rev:** Binny Bilby

Date	Mintage	F	VF	XF	Unc	BU
2008 Proof	10,000	Value: 100				

KM# 1072   5 DOLLARS
36.3100 g., 0.9990 Silver 1.1662 oz. ASW, 38.74 mm.
Ruler: Elizabeth II **Rev:** Avro 504K Airplane

Date	Mintage	F	VF	XF	Unc	BU
2008 Proof	10,000	Value: 65.00				

KM# 1073   5 DOLLARS
36.3100 g., 0.9990 Silver 1.1662 oz. ASW, 38.74 mm.
Ruler: Elizabeth II **Rev:** Airbus A380 Airplane

Date	Mintage	F	VF	XF	Unc	BU
2008 Proof	10,000	Value: 65.00				

KM# 1080   5 DOLLARS
36.3100 g., 0.9990 Silver 1.1662 oz. ASW, 38.74 mm.
Ruler: Elizabeth II **Rev:** Three arctic explorers on map
Rev. Designer: W. Pietranik

Date	Mintage	F	VF	XF	Unc	BU
2009 Proof	12,500	Value: 65.00				

KM# 1081   5 DOLLARS
36.3100 g., 0.9990 Silver 1.1662 oz. ASW, 38.74 mm.
Ruler: Elizabeth II **Subject:** Aurora Australis **Obv:** Head right
Rev: Sailing ship in Antartic ice in hologram **Rev. Designer:** W.
Pietranik

Date	Mintage	F	VF	XF	Unc	BU
2009 Proof	12,500	Value: 50.00				

KM# 1084   5 DOLLARS
38.7400 g., Aluminum-Brass, 38.74 mm.   **Ruler:** Elizabeth II
Subject: Don Bradman 100th Anniversary of Birth **Rev:** Player
with bat **Rev. Designer:** V. Gottwald

Date	Mintage	F	VF	XF	Unc	BU
2009 Unc	—	—	—	—	—	10.00

KM# 1085   5 DOLLARS
1.2000 g., 0.9990 Gold 0.0385 oz. AGW, 14 mm.
Ruler: Elizabeth II **Obv:** Head right **Rev:** Lilly Pilly full-neck lizard

Date	Mintage	F	VF	XF	Unc	BU
2009 Proof	10,000	Value: 65.00				

KM# 1086   5 DOLLARS
1.2000 g., 0.9990 Gold 0.0385 oz. AGW, 14 mm.
Ruler: Elizabeth II **Obv:** Head right **Rev:** Petey Platypus

Date	Mintage	F	VF	XF	Unc	BU
2009 Proof	10,000	Value: 65.00				

KM# 1113   5 DOLLARS
1.2440 g., 0.9999 Gold 0.0400 oz. AGW, 14.1 mm.
Ruler: Elizabeth II **Rev:** Kola seated left on branch
Rev. Designer: Darryl Bellotti

Date	Mintage	F	VF	XF	Unc	BU
2009P Proof	15,000	Value: 100				

KM# 1269   8 DOLLARS
5.0000 g., 0.9990 Gold 0.1606 oz. AGW, 14x23 mm.
Ruler: Elizabeth II **Subject:** Chinese Mythological Character
Obv: Head right **Obv. Designer:** Ian Rank-Broadley **Rev:** Man
standing, multicolor **Shape:** Vertical rectangle

Date	Mintage	F	VF	XF	Unc	BU
2009P	—	—	—	—	—	430

KM# 1270   8 DOLLARS
5.0000 g., 0.9990 Gold 0.1606 oz. AGW, 14x23 mm.
Ruler: Elizabeth II **Subject:** Chinese Mythological Character -
Longevity **Obv:** Head right **Obv. Designer:** Ian Rank-Broadley
Rev: Nam standing with staff, multicolor **Shape:** Vertical
rectangle

Date	Mintage	F	VF	XF	Unc	BU
2009P	—	—	—	—	—	430

KM# 1271   8 DOLLARS
5.0000 g., 0.9990 Gold 0.1606 oz. AGW, 14x23 mm.   **Ruler:**
Elizabeth II **Subject:** Chinese Mythological Character - Success
Obv: Hand right **Obv. Designer:** Ian Rank-Broadley **Rev:** Man
standing with deer, multicolor **Shape:** Vertical rectangle

Date	Mintage	F	VF	XF	Unc	BU
2009P	—	—	—	—	—	430

KM# 1272   8 DOLLARS
5.0000 g., 0.9990 Gold 0.1606 oz. AGW, 14x23 mm.
Ruler: Elizabeth II **Subject:** Mythological Chinese Character -
Fortune **Obv:** Head right **Obv. Designer:** Ian Rank-Broadley
Rev: Man standing with scroll, multicolor **Shape:** Vertical
rectangle

Date	Mintage	F	VF	XF	Unc	BU
2009P	—	—	—	—	—	430

KM# 1273   8 DOLLARS
10.0000 g., 0.9990 Gold 0.3212 oz. AGW, 15x25 mm.
Ruler: Elizabeth II **Subject:** Mythological Chinese Character -
Wealth **Obv:** Head right **Obv. Designer:** Ian Rank-Broadley
Rev: Man standing **Shape:** Vertical rectangle

Date	Mintage	F	VF	XF	Unc	BU
2009P	—	—	—	—	—	800

KM# 593   10 DOLLARS
33.3100 g., Bi-Metallic Gold plated .999 Silver center in Copper
ring, 38.74 mm.   **Ruler:** Elizabeth II **Subject:** "The Future"
Obv: Queens portrait **Rev:** Tree, map and denomination **Rev.
Designer:** Peter Soobik and Wojciech Pietrainik **Edge:** Reeded

Date	Mintage	F	VF	XF	Unc	BU
2001B Proof	20,000	Value: 45.00				

KM# 661   10 DOLLARS
60.5000 g., 0.9990 Silver 1.9431 oz. ASW, 50 mm.
Ruler: Elizabeth II **Subject:** The Adelaide Pound **Obv:** Queens
portrait above gold plated coin design **Rev:** Legend around gold
plated coin design **Edge:** Reeded

Date	Mintage	F	VF	XF	Unc	BU
2002B Proof	10,000	Value: 65.00				

KM# 751   10 DOLLARS
60.5000 g., 0.9990 Silver Partially gilt 1.9431 oz. ASW, 50 mm.
Ruler: Elizabeth II **Subject:** 150th Anniversary - Sydney Mint
Obv: Head with tiara right above gilt above of Sovereign Pattern of
Queen Victoria facing left **Obv. Designer:** Ian Rank-Broadley
Rev: Gilt reverse of Sovereign Pattern **Rev. Designer:** Vladimir
Gottwald **Edge:** Reeded

Date	Mintage	F	VF	XF	Unc	BU
2003B Proof	10,000	Value: 85.00				
ND(2005)B Proof	10,000	Value: 55.00				

KM# 766   10 DOLLARS
36.3100 g., 0.9990 Silver 1.1662 oz. ASW, 38.7 mm.   **Ruler:**
Elizabeth II **Series:** Masterpieces in Silver - Port Phillip Patterns
Obv: Queens head right **Rev:** Kangaroo design **Edge:** Reeded

Date	Mintage	F	VF	XF	Unc	BU
2003B Proof	10,000	Value: 70.00				

KM# 866   10 DOLLARS
7.7508 g., 0.9990 Gold 0.2489 oz. AGW   **Ruler:** Elizabeth II
Subject: 90th Anniversary Gallipoli Landings **Obv:** Head with
tiara right **Obv. Designer:** Ian Rank-Broadley **Rev:** Australian
slouch hat on inverted rifle before memorial

Date	Mintage	F	VF	XF	Unc	BU
2005 Proof	1,000	Value: 750				

KM# 869   10 DOLLARS
7.7759 g., 0.9990 Gold 0.2497 oz. AGW, 17.53 mm.
Ruler: Elizabeth II **Subject:** FIFA World Cup **Obv:** Head with
tiara right **Obv. Designer:** Ian Rank-Broadley **Rev:** Kangaroo
and players on football

Date	Mintage	F	VF	XF	Unc	BU
2006P Proof	25,000	Value: 325				

KM# 867   10 DOLLARS
3.1103 g., 0.9990 Gold 0.0999 oz. AGW   **Ruler:** Elizabeth II
Subject: Ashes Cricket Series 1882-2007 **Obv:** Head with tiara
right **Obv. Designer:** Ian Rank-Broadley **Rev:** Urn and
supporters **Rev. Designer:** Vladimir Gottwald **Edge:** Reeded

Date	Mintage	F	VF	XF	Unc	BU
2007 Proof	—	Value: 125				

KM# 1000   10 DOLLARS
3.1103 g., 0.9990 Gold 0.0999 oz. AGW, 17.53 mm.
Ruler: Elizabeth II **Subject:** Year of the Pig **Obv:** Head with tiara
right **Obv. Designer:** Ian Rank-Broadley **Rev:** Mother kangaroo
with joey **Rev. Designer:** Rolf Harris **Edge:** Reeded

Date	Mintage	F	VF	XF	Unc	BU
2007 Proof	—	Value: 135				

KM# 1057   10 DOLLARS
3.1100 g., 0.9990 Gold 0.0999 oz. AGW, 17.53 mm.
Ruler: Elizabeth II **Subject:** Year of the Rat

Date	Mintage	F	VF	XF	Unc	BU
2008 Proof	2,500	Value: 200				

KM# 1051 10 DOLLARS
3.1000 g., 0.9990 Gold 0.0996 oz. AGW, 17.5 mm.
Ruler: Elizabeth II **Subject:** Scouting Centennial in Australia
Rev: Shadow linear portrait of Baden-Powell **Rev. Designer:** C. Goodall

Date	Mintage	F	VF	XF	Unc	BU
2008 Proof	1,500	Value: 325				

KM# 1054 10 DOLLARS
3.1100 g., 0.9990 Gold 0.0999 oz. AGW, 17.53 mm.
Ruler: Elizabeth II **Subject:** Rugby League

Date	Mintage	F	VF	XF	Unc	BU
2008 Proof	3,000	Value: 225				

KM# 1079 10 DOLLARS
3.1100 g., 0.9990 Gold 0.0999 oz. AGW, 17.53 mm.
Ruler: Elizabeth II **Subject:** Year of the Ox

Date	Mintage	F	VF	XF	Unc	BU
2009 Proof	2,500	Value: 245				

KM# 1104 15 DOLLARS
2.5000 g., 0.9999 Gold 0.0804 oz. AGW, 13x22 mm.
Ruler: Elizabeth II **Rev:** Turtle Dreaming **Rev. Designer:** Darryl Bellotti **Shape:** Rectangle

Date	Mintage	F	VF	XF	Unc	BU
2009 Proof	—	Value: 175				

KM# 1108 15 DOLLARS
2.5000 g., 0.9999 Gold 0.0804 oz. AGW, 13x22 mm.
Ruler: Elizabeth II **Rev:** Kangaroo Dreaming
Rev. Designer: Darryl Bellotti **Shape:** Vertical rectangle

Date	Mintage	Good	VG	F	VF	XF
2009 Proof	—	Value: 175				

KM# 1114 15 DOLLARS
3.1080 g., 0.9999 Gold 0.0999 oz. AGW, 16.1 mm.
Ruler: Elizabeth II **Rev:** Koala seated left on tree branch
Rev. Designer: Darryl Bellotti

Date	Mintage	F	VF	XF	Unc	BU
2009P Proof	5,000	Value: 200				

KM# 595 20 DOLLARS
14.0300 g., Bi-Metallic .999 4.5287 Silver center in .9999 9.499 Gold ring, 32.1 mm. **Ruler:** Elizabeth II **Subject:** Gregorian Millennium **Obv:** Head with tiara right **Obv. Designer:** Ian Rank-Broadley **Rev:** Chronograph watch face with observatory in center and three depictions of the Earth's rotation **Edge:** Reeded

Date	Mintage	F	VF	XF	Unc	BU
2001 Prooflike	7,500	—	—	—	—	350

KM# 597 20 DOLLARS
19.6300 g., Bi-Metallic .9999 8.8645 Gold center in .9999 10.7618 Silver ring, 32.1 mm. **Ruler:** Elizabeth II **Subject:** Centenary of Federation **Obv:** Head with tiara right within star design **Obv. Designer:** Ian Rank-Broadley **Rev:** National arms on a flowery background **Edge:** Reeded

Date	Mintage	F	VF	XF	Unc	BU
ND(2001) Prooflike	7,500	—	—	—	—	425

KM# 760 20 DOLLARS
Bi-Metallic Gold center in Silver ring **Ruler:** Elizabeth II **Rev:** Sir Donald Bradman portrait

Date	Mintage	F	VF	XF	Unc	BU
2001 Proof	—	Value: 375				

KM# 634 20 DOLLARS
18.3510 g., Bi-Metallic .999 Silver, 4.6655g, breast star shaped center in a .9999 Gold ,13.6855g outer ring, 32.1 mm. **Ruler:** Elizabeth II **Subject:** Queen's Golden Jubilee **Obv:** Queens head right **Rev:** Queen before Buckingham Palace **Edge:** Reeded

Date	Mintage	F	VF	XF	Unc	BU
2002P Proof	7,500	Value: 450				

KM# 687 20 DOLLARS
13.4056 g., Bi-Metallic .999 Gold 8.3979g Center in a .999 Silver 5.0077g Ring, 32 mm. **Ruler:** Elizabeth II **Subject:** Golden Jubilee of Coronation **Obv:** Head with tiara right **Obv. Designer:** Ian Rank-Broadley **Rev:** Four different coinage portraits of Queen Elizabeth II **Rev. Designer:** Mary Gillick, Arnold Machin, Raphael Maklouf and Ian Rank-Broadley **Edge:** Reeded

Date	Mintage	F	VF	XF	Unc	BU
2003P Proof	7,500	Value: 600				

KM# 1105 20 DOLLARS
5.0000 g., 0.9999 Gold 0.1607 oz. AGW, 14x23.2 mm.
Ruler: Elizabeth II **Rev:** Turtle Dreaming **Rev. Designer:** Darryl Bellotti **Shape:** Rectangle

Date	Mintage	F	VF	XF	Unc	BU
2009 Proof	—	Value: 325				

KM# 1109 20 DOLLARS
5.0000 g., 0.9999 Gold 0.1607 oz. AGW, 14x23.2 mm.
Ruler: Elizabeth II **Rev:** Kangaroo Dreaming **Rev. Designer:** Darryl Bellotti **Shape:** Vertical Rectangle

Date	Mintage	F	VF	XF	Unc	BU
2009 Proof	—	Value: 325				

KM# 868 25 DOLLARS
7.9881 g., 0.9167 Gold 0.2354 oz. AGW **Ruler:** Elizabeth II **Subject:** 150th Anniversary First Australian Sovereign **Obv:** Head with tiara right **Obv. Designer:** Ian Rank-Broadley

Date	Mintage	F	VF	XF	Unc	BU
2005 Proof	7,500	Value: 300				

KM# 1180 25 DOLLARS
7.7700 g., 0.9990 Gold 0.2496 oz. AGW, 20 mm.
Ruler: Elizabeth II **Subject:** End of WWI, 90th Anniversary **Obv:** Head right **Rev:** Field cross, multicolor poppies **Rev. Legend:** Ian Rank-Broadley

Date	Mintage	F	VF	XF	Unc	BU
2008P Proof	1,918	Value: 650				

KM# 1106 25 DOLLARS
10.0000 g., 0.9999 Gold 0.3215 oz. AGW, 15.4x25.4 mm.
Ruler: Elizabeth II **Rev:** Turtle Dreaming **Rev. Designer:** Darryk Bellotti **Shape:** Rectangle

Date	Mintage	F	VF	XF	Unc	BU
2009 Proof	—	Value: 600				

KM# 1110 25 DOLLARS
10.0000 g., 0.9999 Gold 0.3215 oz. AGW, 15.4x25.4 mm.
Ruler: Elizabeth II **Rev:** Kangaroo dreaming **Rev. Designer:** Darryl Bellotti **Shape:** Vertical rectangle

Date	Mintage	F	VF	XF	Unc	BU
2009 Proof	—	Value: 600				

KM# 1244 25 DOLLARS
0.9170 Gold **Ruler:** Elizabeth II **Subject:** Sovereign **Obv:** Head right **Obv. Designer:** Ian Rank-Broadley **Rev:** National arms

Date	Mintage	F	VF	XF	Unc	BU
2009 Proof	2,500	Value: 650				

KM# 1247 25 DOLLARS
7.7700 g., 0.9990 Gold 0.2496 oz. AGW, 21 mm.
Ruler: Elizabeth II **Subject:** 2010 FIFA World Cup, South Africa **Obv:** Head right **Obv. Designer:** Ian Rank-Broadley **Rev:** Soccer player and kangaroo

Date	Mintage	F	VF	XF	Unc	BU
2009 Proof	7,500	Value: 750				

KM# 1274 25 DOLLARS
10.0000 g., 0.9990 Gold 0.3212 oz. AGW, 15x25 mm. **Ruler:** Elizabeth II **Subject:** Mythological Chinese Character - Longivity **Obv:** Head right **Obv. Designer:** Ian rank-Broadley **Rev:** Man standing with staff **Shape:** Vertical rectangle

Date	Mintage	F	VF	XF	Unc	BU
2009P					—	800

KM# 1275 25 DOLLARS
10.0000 g., 0.9990 Gold 0.3212 oz. AGW, 15x25 mm.
Ruler: Elizabeth II **Subject:** Mythological Chinese Character - Success **Obv:** Head right **Obv. Designer:** Ian Rank-Broadley **Rev:** Man standing with deer **Shape:** Vertical rectangle

Date	Mintage	F	VF	XF	Unc	BU
2009P	—	—	—	—	—	800

KM# 1276 25 DOLLARS
10.0000 g., 0.9990 Gold 0.3212 oz. AGW, 15x25 mm.
Ruler: Elizabeth II **Subject:** Mythological Chinese Character - Fortune **Obv:** Head right **Obv. Designer:** Ian Rank-Broadley **Rev:** Man standing with scroll **Shape:** Vertical rectangle

Date	Mintage	F	VF	XF	Unc	BU
2009P	—	—	—	—	—	800

KM# 784 30 DOLLARS
1000.0000 g., 0.9990 Silver 32.117 oz. ASW **Ruler:** Elizabeth II **Subject:** Commonwealth Games **Obv:** Head with tiara right **Rev:** Two figures within circle of all the sports

Date	Mintage	F	VF	XF	Unc	BU
2006 Proof	500	Value: 650				

KM# 1112 30 DOLLARS
1000.0000 g., 0.9999 Silver 32.146 oz. ASW, 101 mm.
Ruler: Elizabeth II **Rev:** Kola seated left on branch
Rev. Designer: Darryl Bellotti

Date	Mintage	F	VF	XF	Unc	BU
2009P Prooflike	—	—	—	—	—	700

KM# 648 50 DOLLARS
36.5100 g., Tri-Metallic .9999 Gold 7.8g, 13.1 mm center in .999 Silver 13.39g, 26.85mm inner ring within a copper 15.32g, 3, 38.74 mm. **Ruler:** Elizabeth II **Subject:** Commonwealth Games **Obv:** Head with tiara right **Obv. Designer:** Ian Rank-Broadley **Rev:** Victorious athletes within inscriptions and runners **Edge:** Reeded

Date	Mintage	F	VF	XF	Unc	BU
2002B Proof	5,000	Value: 550				

KM# 724 50 DOLLARS
36.5100 g., Tri-Metallic .999 Gold 7.8g center in .999 Silver 13.39g ring within .999 Copper 15.32g outer ring, 38.74 mm. **Ruler:** Elizabeth II **Subject:** Olympics - Sydney to Athens **Obv:** Head with tiara right, denomination below **Obv. Designer:** Ian Rank-Broadley **Rev:** Crossed olive and wattle branches about Australian flag and Olympic ring logo **Rev. Designer:** Wojciech Pietranik **Edge:** Reeded

Date	Mintage	F	VF	XF	Unc	BU
2004B Proof	2,500	Value: 575				

KM# 785 50 DOLLARS
Tri-Metallic Gold center within Silver ring within Copper outer ring, 38.74 mm. **Ruler:** Elizabeth II **Subject:** Melbourne Commonwealth Games **Obv:** Head with tiara right, denomination below **Obv. Designer:** Ian Rank-Broadley **Rev:** Two stylized athletes on central plug surrounded by Games legend and circle of athletes **Rev. Designer:** Wojciech Pietranik

Date	Mintage	F	VF	XF	Unc	BU
2006 Proof	5,000	Value: 500				

KM# 643 100 DOLLARS
10.3678 g., 0.9999 Gold 0.3333 oz. AGW, 25 mm. **Ruler:** Elizabeth II **Subject:** Golden Wattle Flower **Obv:** Queens head right **Rev:** Flower and denomination **Edge:** Reeded

Date	Mintage	F	VF	XF	Unc	BU
2001B	3,000	—	—	—	425	440
2001B Proof	2,500	Value: 460				

KM# 635 100 DOLLARS
31.1035 g., 0.9999 Gold 0.9999 oz. AGW, 32.1 mm. **Ruler:** Elizabeth II **Subject:** Gold Panning **Obv:** Queens head right **Rev:** Two prospectors dry panning for gold with color highlighted pans and dust **Edge:** Reeded

Date	Mintage	F	VF	XF	Unc	BU
2002P Proof	1,500	Value: 1,250				

KM# 636 100 DOLLARS
31.1035 g., 0.9995 Platinum 0.9995 oz. APW, 32.1 mm. **Ruler:** Elizabeth II **Subject:** Multiculturalism **Obv:** Head with tiara right **Obv. Designer:** Ian Rank-Broadley **Rev:** Six racially diverse portraits against a blue background **Edge:** Reeded

Date	Mintage	F	VF	XF	Unc	BU
2002 Proof	1,000	Value: 1,650				

KM# 646 100 DOLLARS
31.4000 g., 0.9999 Gold 1.0094 oz. AGW, 34.1 mm. **Ruler:** Elizabeth II **Subject:** Queen's 50th Anniversary of Accession **Obv:** Queens head right **Rev:** Silhouette of George VI, Queen's portrait and denomination **Rev. Designer:** Peter Soobik **Edge:** Reeded

Date	Mintage	F	VF	XF	Unc	BU
2002B Proof	2,002	Value: 1,250				

KM# 657 100 DOLLARS
10.3678 g., 0.9999 Gold 0.3333 oz. AGW, 25 mm. **Ruler:** Elizabeth II **Obv:** Queens head right **Rev:** Sturt's Desert Rose **Rev. Designer:** Horst Hahne **Edge:** Reeded

Date	Mintage	F	VF	XF	Unc	BU
2002B	3,000	—	—	—	425	440
2002B Proof	2,500	Value: 460				

KM# 800 100 DOLLARS
31.1036 g., 0.9990 Gold 0.9990 oz. AGW, 34 mm. **Ruler:** Elizabeth II **Subject:** 50th Anniversary of the Coronation of Elizabeth II **Obv:** Head with tiara right **Rev:** Young portrait of Queen Elizabeth facing left, royal cipher, crown **Rev. Designer:** Peter Soobik **Edge:** Plain

Date	Mintage	F	VF	XF	Unc	BU
2003 Proof	660	Value: 1,300				

KM# 870 100 DOLLARS
10.3670 g., 0.9990 Gold 0.3330 oz. AGW, 25 mm. **Ruler:** Elizabeth II **Subject:** State Floral Emblems **Obv:** Head with tiara right **Obv. Designer:** Ian Rank-Broadley **Rev:** Royal Blue Bell flowers **Rev. Designer:** Horst Hahne **Edge:** Reeded

Date	Mintage	F	VF	XF	Unc	BU
2003 Proof	1,383	Value: 445				

KM# 741 100 DOLLARS
31.1035 g., 0.9999 Gold 0.9999 oz. AGW, 32 mm. **Ruler:** Elizabeth II **Subject:** Eureka Stockade **Obv:** Head with tiara right, denomination below **Obv. Designer:** Ian Rank-Broadley **Rev:** Eureka Stockade leader Peter Lalor and blue flag, colored image **Edge:** Reeded

Date	Mintage	F	VF	XF	Unc	BU
2004	1,500	—	—	—	1,250	
2004P Proof	1,500	Value: 1,300				

KM# 742 100 DOLLARS
31.1035 g., 0.9995 Platinum 0.9995 oz. APW, 32.1 mm. **Ruler:** Elizabeth II **Obv:** Head with tiara right, denomination below **Obv. Designer:** Ian Rank-Broadley **Rev:** Sports: Australian sportsmen and women, colored image **Edge:** Reeded

Date	Mintage	F	VF	XF	Unc	BU
2004P Proof	1,000	Value: 1,700				

KM# 797 100 DOLLARS
31.1070 g., 0.9990 Gold 0.9991 oz. AGW, 25.1 mm. **Ruler:** Elizabeth II **Subject:** 60th Anniversary of end of World War II **Obv:** Head with tiara right **Obv. Designer:** Ian Rank-Broadley **Rev:** Latent news real photographic images of a dancing man celebrating the end of WWII

Date	Mintage	F	VF	XF	Unc	BU
2005P Proof	750	Value: 1,300				

KM# 1243 100 DOLLARS
31.1050 g., 0.9990 Gold 0.9990 oz. AGW, 36 mm. **Ruler:** Elizabeth II **Subject:** Treasures of Australia **Obv:** Head right **Obv. Designer:** Ian Rank-Broadley **Rev:** Mountains **Note:** Insert container with 1 carat of diamonds.

Date	Mintage	F	VF	XF	Unc	BU
2009P Proof	1,000	Value: 2,100				

KM# 644 150 DOLLARS
15.5517 g., 0.9999 Gold 0.4999 oz. AGW, 30 mm. **Ruler:** Elizabeth II **Obv:** Queens head right **Rev:** Golden Wattle Flower, value **Edge:** Reeded

Date	Mintage	F	VF	XF	Unc	BU
2001B Proof	1,500	Value: 625				

KM# 658 150 DOLLARS
15.5517 g., 0.9999 Gold 0.4999 oz. AGW, 30 mm. **Ruler:** Elizabeth II **Subject:** Sturt's Desert Rose Flower **Obv:** Queens head right **Rev:** Flowers **Rev. Designer:** Horst Hahne **Edge:** Reeded

Date	Mintage	F	VF	XF	Unc	BU
2002B Proof	1,500	Value: 625				

KM# 872 150 DOLLARS
15.5510 g., 0.9990 Gold 0.4995 oz. AGW, 30 mm. **Ruler:** Elizabeth II **Subject:** State Floral Emblems **Obv:** Head

with tiara right **Obv. Designer:** Ian Rank-Broadley **Rev:** Royal Blue Bell flowers **Rev. Designer:** Horst Hahne **Edge:** Reeded

Date	Mintage	F	VF	XF	Unc	BU
2003	1,105	Value: 625				

KM# 874 150 DOLLARS
15.5510 g., 0.9990 Gold 0.4995 oz. AGW, 30 mm. **Ruler:** Elizabeth II **Subject:** Rare Australian Birds **Obv:** Head with tiara right **Obv. Designer:** Ian Rank-Broadley **Rev:** Red-tailed Black Cockatoo **Rev. Designer:** Wojciech Pietranik **Edge:** Reeded

Date	Mintage	F	VF	XF	Unc	BU
2003 Proof	2,500	Value: 625				

KM# 731 150 DOLLARS
10.3678 g., 0.9990 Gold 0.3330 oz. AGW, 25 mm. **Ruler:** Elizabeth II **Obv:** Queens head right **Rev:** Cassowary bird **Edge:** Reeded

Date	Mintage	F	VF	XF	Unc	BU
2004B Proof	2,500	Value: 425				

KM# 752 150 DOLLARS
10.3678 g., 0.9990 Gold 0.3330 oz. AGW, 25 mm. **Ruler:** Elizabeth II **Obv:** Queens head right **Rev:** Malleefowl bird **Edge:** Reeded

Date	Mintage	F	VF	XF	Unc	BU
2005B Proof	2,500	Value: 445				

KM# 873 150 DOLLARS
10.3670 g., 0.9990 Gold 0.3330 oz. AGW, 25 mm. **Ruler:** Elizabeth II **Subject:** Rare Australian Birds **Obv:** Head with tiara right **Obv. Designer:** Ian Rank-Broadley **Rev:** Red-tailed Black Cockatoo **Rev. Designer:** Wojciech Pietranik **Edge:** Reeded

Date	Mintage	F	VF	XF	Unc	BU
2006	2,500	Value: 485				

KM# 732 200 DOLLARS
15.5518 g., 0.9990 Gold 0.4995 oz. AGW, 30 mm. **Ruler:** Elizabeth II **Obv:** Queens head right **Rev:** Cassowary bird **Edge:** Reeded

Date	Mintage	F	VF	XF	Unc	BU
2004B Proof	2,500	Value: 625				

KM# 753 200 DOLLARS
15.5518 g., 0.9999 Gold 0.4999 oz. AGW, 30 mm. **Ruler:** Elizabeth II **Obv:** Queens head right **Rev:** Malleefowl bird **Edge:** Reeded

Date	Mintage	F	VF	XF	Unc	BU
2005B Proof	2,500	Value: 625				

BULLION - KANGAROO

KM# 590 DOLLAR
31.1035 g., 0.9990 Silver 0.9990 oz. ASW, 40 mm. **Ruler:** Elizabeth II **Obv:** Queens portrait **Rev:** Aboriginal kangaroo design with dots **Rev. Designer:** Jeanette Timbery **Edge:** Reeded

Date	Mintage	F	VF	XF	Unc	BU
2001B Frosted Unc	—	—	—	—	—	20.00
2001B Proof	—	Value: 25.00				

KM# 642 DOLLAR
31.1035 g., 0.9990 Silver 0.9990 oz. ASW, 40 mm. **Ruler:**
Elizabeth II **Obv:** Head with tiara right, denomination below **Rev:**
Aboriginal style kangaroo with wavy line background **Edge:** Reeded

Date	Mintage	F	VF	XF	Unc	BU
2002B	—	—	—	—	24.00	26.00
2002B Proof	—	Value: 35.00				

KM# 798 DOLLAR
31.1035 g., 0.9990 Silver 0.9990 oz. ASW, 40 mm.
Ruler: Elizabeth II **Obv:** Head with tiara right **Obv. Designer:**
Ian Rank-Broadley **Rev:** Aboriginal style kangaroo design
Rev. Designer: Wojcieck Pietranik **Edge:** Reeded

Date	Mintage	F	VF	XF	Unc	BU
2003	35,230	—	—	—	—	30.00
2003 Proof	20,400	Value: 35.00				

KM# 798a DOLLAR
31.1035 g., 0.9990 Silver partially gilt 0.9990 oz. ASW, 40 mm.
Ruler: Elizabeth II **Obv:** Head with tiara right **Obv. Designer:**
Ian Rank-Broadley **Rev:** Aboriginal style kangaroo design
Rev. Designer: Wojcieck Pietanik **Edge:** Reeded

Date	Mintage	F	VF	XF	Unc	BU
2003	7,450	—	—	—	—	125

KM# 723 DOLLAR
31.1035 g., 0.9990 Silver 0.9990 oz. ASW, 40 mm.
Ruler: Elizabeth II **Obv:** Head with tiara right, denomination
below **Rev:** Kangaroo with semi-circle background
Edge: Reeded

Date	Mintage	F	VF	XF	Unc	BU
2004B Frosted Unc	—	—	—	—	—	22.00
2004B Proof	12,500	Value: 40.00				

KM# 723a DOLLAR
31.1035 g., 0.9990 Silver partially gilt 0.9990 oz. ASW, 40 mm.
Ruler: Elizabeth II **Obv:** Head with tiara right, denomination below
Rev: Kangaroo with semi-circle background **Edge:** Reeded

Date	Mintage	F	VF	XF	Unc	BU
2004B Frosted Unc	—	—	—	—	—	60.00

KM# 838 DOLLAR
31.1035 g., 0.9990 Silver 0.9990 oz. ASW, 40 mm.
Ruler: Elizabeth II **Subject:** Australain-Japan Year of Exchange
Obv: Head with tiara right **Obv. Designer:** Ian Rank-Broadley
Rev: Kangaroo leaping with kangaroo rim decoration

Date	Mintage	F	VF	XF	Unc	BU
2006 Proof	5,000	Value: 22.00				

KM# 837 DOLLAR
31.6000 g., 0.9990 Silver 1.0149 oz. ASW, 40 mm.
Ruler: Elizabeth II **Obv:** Head with tiara right **Obv. Designer:**
Ian Rank-Broadley **Rev:** Kangaroo bounding under Australian
sun **Rev. Designer:** Wojcieck Pietranik **Edge:** Reeded

Date	Mintage	F	VF	XF	Unc	BU
2006	—	—	—	—	—	30.00
2006 Proof	12,500	Value: 35.00				

KM# 837a DOLLAR
31.6000 g., 0.9990 Silver partially gilt 1.0149 oz. ASW, 40 mm.
Ruler: Elizabeth II **Obv:** Head with tiara right **Obv. Designer:**
Ian Rank-Broadley **Rev:** Kangaroo bounding under Australian
sun **Rev. Designer:** Wojcieck Pietranik **Edge:** Reeded

Date	Mintage	F	VF	XF	Unc	BU
2006	7,500	—	—	—	—	50.00

KM# 851 DOLLAR
31.6000 g., 0.9990 Silver 1.0149 oz. ASW, 40 mm.
Ruler: Elizabeth II **Obv:** Head with tiara right **Obv. Designer:**
Ian Rank-Broadley **Rev:** Kangaroo mother and joey
Rev. Designer: Rolf Harris **Edge:** Reeded

Date	Mintage	F	VF	XF	Unc	BU
2007	15,000	—	—	—	—	40.00
2007 Proof	12,500	Value: 35.00				

KM# 893 5 DOLLARS
1.5710 g., 0.9990 Gold 0.0505 oz. AGW **Ruler:** Elizabeth II
Obv: Head with tiara right **Obv. Designer:** Ian Rank-Broadley
Rev: Two kangaroos on map of Australia

Date	Mintage	F	VF	XF	Unc	BU
2001	10,000	—	—	—	65.00	70.00

KM# 894 15 DOLLARS
3.1101 g., 0.9990 Gold 0.0999 oz. AGW **Ruler:** Elizabeth II
Obv: Head with tiara right **Obv. Designer:** Ian Rank-Broadley
Rev: Two kangaroos on map of Australia

Date	Mintage	F	VF	XF	Unc	BU
2001	800	—	—	—	—	125

KM# 897 15 DOLLARS
3.1101 g., 0.9990 Gold 0.0999 oz. AGW **Ruler:** Elizabeth II
Obv: Head with tiara right **Obv. Designer:** Ian Rank-Broadley
Rev: Kangaroo browsing

Date	Mintage	F	VF	XF	Unc	BU
2002	800	—	—	—	—	125

KM# 902 15 DOLLARS
3.1101 g., 0.9990 Gold 0.0999 oz. AGW **Ruler:** Elizabeth II
Obv: Head with tiara right **Obv. Designer:** Ian Rank-Broadley
Rev: Two kangaroos hopping

Date	Mintage	F	VF	XF	Unc	BU
2003	500	—	—	—	—	135

KM# 907 15 DOLLARS
3.1101 g., 0.9990 Gold 0.0999 oz. AGW **Ruler:** Elizabeth II
Obv: Head with tiara right **Obv. Designer:** Ian Rank-Broadley
Rev: Crouching kangaroos facing left, Grass tree plant at right

Date	Mintage	F	VF	XF	Unc	BU
2004	500	—	—	—	—	135

KM# 911 15 DOLLARS
3.1101 g., 0.9990 Gold 0.0999 oz. AGW **Ruler:** Elizabeth II
Obv: Head with tiara right **Obv. Designer:** Ian Rank-Broadley
Rev: Kangaroo in bush

Date	Mintage	F	VF	XF	Unc	BU
2005	500	—	—	—	—	135

KM# 895 25 DOLLARS
7.7508 g., 0.9990 Gold 0.2489 oz. AGW **Ruler:** Elizabeth II
Obv: Head with tiara right **Obv. Designer:** Ian Rank-Broadley
Rev: Two kangaroos on map of Australia

Date	Mintage	F	VF	XF	Unc	BU
2001	500	—	—	—	—	325

KM# 898 25 DOLLARS
7.7508 g., 0.9990 Gold 0.2489 oz. AGW **Ruler:** Elizabeth II
Obv: Head with tiara right **Obv. Designer:** Ian Rank-Broadley
Rev: Kangaroo browsing

Date	Mintage	F	VF	XF	Unc	BU
2002	500	—	—	—	—	325

KM# 903 25 DOLLARS
7.7508 g., 0.9990 Gold 0.2489 oz. AGW **Ruler:** Elizabeth II
Obv: Head with tiara right **Obv. Designer:** Ian Rank-Broadley
Rev: Two kangaroos hopping

Date	Mintage	F	VF	XF	Unc	BU
2003	250	—	—	—	—	325

KM# 908 25 DOLLARS
7.7508 g., 0.9990 Gold 0.2489 oz. AGW **Ruler:** Elizabeth II
Obv: Head with tiara right **Obv. Designer:** Ian Rank-Broadley
Rev: Crouching kangaroos facing left, Grass tree plant at right

Date	Mintage	F	VF	XF	Unc	BU
2004	250	—	—	—	—	325

KM# 912 25 DOLLARS
7.7508 g., 0.9990 Gold 0.2489 oz. AGW **Ruler:** Elizabeth II
Obv: Head with tiara right **Obv. Designer:** Ian Rank-Broadley
Rev: Kangaroo in bush

Date	Mintage	F	VF	XF	Unc	BU
2005	250	—	—	—	—	325

KM# 692 50 DOLLARS
15.5017 g., 0.9999 Gold 0.4983 oz. AGW, 25.1 mm. **Ruler:**
Elizabeth II **Subject:** Tribute to Liberty **Obv:** Head with tiara right,
denomination below **Obv. Designer:** Ian Rank-Broadley **Rev:** Two
kangaroos on map above silver Liberty Bell insert **Edge:** Reeded

Date	Mintage	F	VF	XF	Unc	BU
2001	650	—	—	—	625	—
2002	1,498	—	—	—	625	—
2002 Proof	—	Value: 650				

KM# 899 50 DOLLARS
15.5017 g., 0.9990 Gold 0.4979 oz. AGW **Ruler:** Elizabeth II
Obv: Head with tiara right **Obv. Designer:** Ian Rank-Broadley
Rev: Kangaroo browsing

Date	Mintage	F	VF	XF	Unc	BU
2002	650	—	—	—	635	—

KM# 904 50 DOLLARS
15.5017 g., 0.9990 Gold 0.4979 oz. AGW **Ruler:** Elizabeth II
Obv: Head with tiara right **Obv. Designer:** Ian Rank-Broadley
Rev: Two kangaroos hopping

Date	Mintage	F	VF	XF	Unc	BU
2003	500	—	—	—	635	—

KM# 909 50 DOLLARS
15.5017 g., 0.9990 Gold 0.4979 oz. AGW **Ruler:** Elizabeth II
Obv: Head with tiara right **Obv. Designer:** Ian Rank-Broadley
Rev: Crouching kangaroos facing left, Grass tree plant at right

Date	Mintage	F	VF	XF	Unc	BU
2004	500	—	—	—	635	—

Note: In sets only

KM# 913 50 DOLLARS
15.5017 g., 0.9990 Gold 0.4979 oz. AGW **Ruler:** Elizabeth II
Obv: Head with tiara right **Obv. Designer:** Ian Rank-Broadley
Rev: Kangaroo in bush

Date	Mintage	F	VF	XF	Unc	BU
2005	500	—	—	—	635	—

KM# 693 100 DOLLARS
31.1035 g., 0.9999 Gold 0.9999 oz. AGW, 32.1 mm.
Ruler: Elizabeth II **Subject:** Tribute to Liberty **Obv:** Head with
tiara right, denomination below **Obv. Designer:** Ian Rank-
Broadley **Rev:** Two kangaroos on map above silver Liberty Bell
insert, colored image **Edge:** Reeded

Date	Mintage	F	VF	XF	Unc	BU
2001	1,498	—	—	—	1,275	—
2002	—	—	—	—	—	1,275

KM# 900 100 DOLLARS
31.1035 g., 0.9999 Gold 0.9999 oz. AGW **Ruler:** Elizabeth II
Obv: Head with tiara right **Obv. Designer:** Ian Rank-Broadley
Rev: Prospectors dry-blowing gold dust, colored image

Date	Mintage	F	VF	XF	Unc	BU
2002	1,500	—	—	—	1,275	—

KM# 906 100 DOLLARS
31.1035 g., 0.9990 Gold 0.9990 oz. AGW **Ruler:** Elizabeth II
Obv: Head with tiara right **Obv. Designer:** Ian Rank-Broadley
Rev: Prospectors camp, colored image

Date	Mintage	F	VF	XF	Unc	BU
2003	1,500	—	—	—	1,275	—

KM# 915 100 DOLLARS
31.1035 g., 0.9990 Gold 0.9990 oz. AGW **Ruler:** Elizabeth II
Subject: Welcome Stranger Nugget **Obv:** Head with tiara right
Obv. Designer: Ian Rank-Broadley **Rev:** Welcome Stranger
Nugget surrounded by Outback setting, colored image

Date	Mintage	F	VF	XF	Unc	BU
2005	1,500	—	—	—	—	1,275

KM# 896 200 DOLLARS
62.2140 g., 0.9990 Gold 1.9981 oz. AGW **Ruler:** Elizabeth II
Obv: Head with tiara right **Obv. Designer:** Ian Rank-Broadley
Rev: Two kangaroos on map of Australia

Date	Mintage	F	VF	XF	Unc	BU
2001	300	—	—	—	2,500	—

KM# 901 200 DOLLARS
62.2140 g., 0.9990 Gold 1.9981 oz. AGW **Ruler:** Elizabeth II
Obv: Head with tiara right **Obv. Designer:** Ian Rank-Broadley
Rev: Kangaroo browsing

Date	Mintage	F	VF	XF	Unc	BU
2002	300	—	—	—	2,500	—

KM# 905 200 DOLLARS
62.2140 g., 0.9990 Gold 1.9981 oz. AGW **Ruler:** Elizabeth II
Obv: Head with tiara right **Obv. Designer:** Ian Rank-Broadley
Rev: Two kangaroos hopping

Date	Mintage	F	VF	XF	Unc	BU
2003	200	—	—	—	2,500	—

KM# 910 200 DOLLARS
62.2140 g., 0.9990 Gold 1.9981 oz. AGW **Ruler:** Elizabeth II
Obv: Head with tiara right **Obv. Designer:** Ian Rank-Broadley
Rev: Crouching kangaroos facing left, Grass tree plant at right

Date	Mintage	F	VF	XF	Unc	BU
2004	200	—	—	—	2,500	—

KM# 914 200 DOLLARS
62.2140 g., 0.9990 Gold 1.9981 oz. AGW **Ruler:** Elizabeth II
Obv: Head with tiara right **Obv. Designer:** Ian Rank-Broadley
Rev: Kangaroo in bush

Date	Mintage	F	VF	XF	Unc	BU
2005	200	—	—	—	2,500	—

BULLION - KOOKABURRA

KM# 875 50 CENTS
15.5500 g., 0.9990 Silver 0.4994 oz. ASW, 38.74 mm. **Ruler:**
Elizabeth II **Obv:** Head with tiara right **Obv.** Ian Rank-
Broadley **Rev:** Kookaburra on branch, tail above, two leaves
Edge: Reeded **Shape:** Square with rounded corners **Note:**
Lenticular technology makes kookaburra appear to move.

Date	Mintage	F	VF	XF	Unc	BU
2002P Proof	75,350	Value: 35.00				

KM# 684 50 CENTS
15.5500 g., 0.9990 Silver 0.4994 oz. ASW, 32.1 mm. **Ruler:**
Elizabeth II **Obv:** Head with tiara right, denomination below **Obv.**
Designer: Ian Rank-Broadley **Rev:** Two Kookaburras, one in
flight **Edge:** Reeded **Shape:** Square with rounded corners

Date	Mintage	F	VF	XF	Unc	BU
2003P Proof	75,350	Value: 30.00				

KM# 876 50 CENTS
15.5500 g., 0.9990 Silver 0.4994 oz. ASW, 38.74 mm. **Ruler:**
Elizabeth II **Obv:** Head with tiara right **Obv. Designer:** Ian Rank-
Broadley **Rev:** Kookaburra perched on branch, tail below, four
leaves **Edge:** Reeded **Shape:** Square with rounded corners

Date	Mintage	F	VF	XF	Unc	BU
2004P Proof	30,350	Value: 30.00				

KM# 877 50 CENTS
15.5500 g., 0.9990 Silver 0.4994 oz. ASW, 38.74 mm.
Ruler: Elizabeth II **Obv:** Head with tiara right **Obv. Designer:**
Ian Rank-Broadley **Rev:** Two kookaburras on branch, one
laughing **Edge:** Reeded **Shape:** Squar with rounded corners

Date	Mintage	F	VF	XF	Unc	BU
2005P Proof	30,350	Value: 30.00				

KM# 691.1 DOLLAR
31.1035 g., 0.9990 Silver 0.9990 oz. ASW, 40 mm.
Ruler: Elizabeth II **Obv:** Head with tiara right, denomination
below **Obv. Designer:** Ian Rank-Broadley **Rev:** Kookaburra
flying over map of Australia **Edge:** Reeded

Date	Mintage	F	VF	XF	Unc	BU
2001P Proof	5,000	Value: 30.00				
2002	—	—	—	—	22.50	25.00

KM# 479 DOLLAR
31.9700 g., 0.9990 Silver 1.0268 oz. ASW **Ruler:** Elizabeth II **Obv:**
Head with tiara right, denomination below **Obv. Designer:** Ian
Rank-Broadley **Rev:** Two Kookaburras back to back on branch

Date	Mintage	F	VF	XF	Unc	BU
2001	—	—	—	—	20.00	
2001	10,000	—	—	—	35.00	
Note: Federation star privy mark						
2001	50,000	—	—	—	25.00	
Note: Santa Claus privy mark						
2001	1,000	—	—	—	120	
Note: Love token personal message						
2001	75,000	—	—	—	32.00	
Note: New York State Quarter privy mark						
2001	75,000	—	—	—	32.00	
Note: North Carolina State Quarter privy mark						
2001	75,000	—	—	—	32.00	
Note: Rhode Island State Quarter privy mark						
2001	75,000	—	—	—	32.00	
Note: Vermont State Quarter privy mark						
2001	75,000	—	—	—	32.00	
Note: Kentucky State Quarter privy mark						

KM# 625 DOLLAR
31.1035 g., 0.9990 Silver 0.9990 oz. ASW, 40.4 mm.
Ruler: Elizabeth II **Subject:** U.S. State Quarter

Date	Mintage	F	VF	XF	Unc	BU
2002	75,000	—	—	—	32.00	
Note: Tennessee State Quarter privy mark						
2002	75,000	—	—	—	32.00	
Note: Ohio State Quarter privy mark						
2002	75,000	—	—	—	32.00	
Note: Louisiana State Quarter privy mark						
2002	75,000	—	—	—	32.00	
Note: Indiana State Quarter privy mark						
2002	75,000	—	—	—	32.00	
Note: Mississippi State Quarter privy mark						

KM# 666 DOLLAR
31.6200 g., 0.9990 Silver 1.0155 oz. ASW, 40.3 mm.
Ruler: Elizabeth II **Obv:** Head with tiara right, denomination
below **Obv. Designer:** Ian Rank-Broadley **Rev:** Kookaburra
perched on branch **Edge:** Reeded

Date	Mintage	F	VF	XF	Unc	BU
2002	5,000	Value: 25.00				

KM# 691.2 DOLLAR
31.6200 g., 0.9990 Silver 1.0155 oz. ASW, 40.5 mm.
Ruler: Elizabeth II **Obv:** Head with tiara right, denomination
below **Obv. Designer:** Ian Rank-Broadley **Rev:** Multicolor US
flag above a kookaburra flying over Australia **Edge:** Reeded

Date	Mintage	F	VF	XF	Unc	BU
2002	18,500	—	—	—	25.00	30.00

KM# 683 DOLLAR
31.1035 g., 0.9990 Silver 0.9990 oz. ASW, 40 mm.
Ruler: Elizabeth II **Obv:** Head with tiara right, denomination
below **Obv. Designer:** Ian Rank-Broadley **Rev:** Two
kookaburras, one in flight **Edge:** Reeded **Note:** Gilded.

Date	Mintage	F	VF	XF	Unc	BU
2003P Proof	5,000	Value: 25.00				
2004	10,000	—	—	—	—	25.00
2004 Proof	15,000	Value: 35.00				

KM# 883 DOLLAR
31.5600 g., 0.9990 Silver 1.0136 oz. ASW, 40.5 mm.
Ruler: Elizabeth II **Obv:** Head with tiara right **Obv. Designer:**
Ian Rank-Broadley **Rev:** Kookaburra perched on branch with four
leaves **Edge:** Reeded

Date	Mintage	F	VF	XF	Unc	BU
2004P Proof	5,000	Value: 25.00				
2005	5,000	—	—	—	32.00	—
Note: Gemini privy mark						
2005	5,000	—	—	—	32.00	—
Note: Aquarius privy mark						
2005	5,000	—	—	—	32.00	—
Note: Pisces privy mark						
2005	5,000	—	—	—	32.00	—
Note: Aries privy mark						
2005	5,000	—	—	—	32.00	—
Note: Taurus privy mark						
2005	5,000	—	—	—	32.00	—
Note: Cancer privy mark						
2005	5,000	—	—	—	32.00	—
Note: Leo privy mark						
2005	5,000	—	—	—	32.00	—
Note: Virgo privy mark						
2005	5,000	—	—	—	32.00	—
Note: Libra privy mark						
2005	5,000	—	—	—	32.00	—
Note: Scorpio privy mark						
2005	5,000	—	—	—	32.00	—
Note: Sagittarius privy mark						
2005	5,000	—	—	—	32.00	—
Note: Capricorn privy mark						

KM# 883a DOLLAR
31.1035 g., 0.9990 Silver 0.9990 oz. ASW, 40 mm.
Ruler: Elizabeth II **Obv:** Head with tiara right **Obv. Designer:**
Ian Rank-Broadley **Rev:** Kookaburra purched on branch with four
leaves **Note:** Gilded.

Date	Mintage	F	VF	XF	Unc	BU
2004	10,000	—	—	—	50.00	—

KM# 720 DOLLAR
1.0350 g., 0.9990 Silver 0.0332 oz. ASW **Ruler:** Elizabeth II
Obv: Head with tiara right, denomination below **Rev:** Kookabarra

Date	Mintage	F	VF	XF	Unc	BU
2005	—	—	—	—	22.00	25.00

KM# 886 DOLLAR
31.5600 g., 0.9990 Silver 1.0136 oz. ASW, 40.5 mm.
Ruler: Elizabeth II **Obv:** Head with tiara right **Obv. Designer:**
Ian Rank-Broadley **Rev:** Two kookaburras on branch, one
laughing **Edge:** Reeded

Date	Mintage	F	VF	XF	Unc	BU
2005P Proof	5,000	Value: 30.00				

KM# 889 DOLLAR
31.5600 g., 0.9990 Silver 1.0136 oz. ASW, 40.5 mm.
Ruler: Elizabeth II **Obv:** Head with tiara right **Obv. Designer:**
Ian Rank-Broadley **Rev:** Kookaburras on branch, no leaves

Date	Mintage	F	VF	XF	Unc	BU
2007	300,000	—	—	—	25.00	28.00

KM# 1277 DOLLAR
31.1050 g., 0.9990 Silver 0.9990 oz. ASW, 40 mm.
Ruler: Elizabeth II **Subject:** Kookaburra 20th Anniversary
Obv: Head right **Obv. Designer:** Ian Rank-Broadley
Rev: Kookaburra standing right

Date	Mintage	F	VF	XF	Unc	BU
2009 P20 Proof	10,000	Value: 45.00				

KM# 1278 DOLLAR
31.1050 g., 0.9990 Silver 0.9990 oz. ASW, 40 mm.
Ruler: Elizabeth II **Subject:** Kookaburra 20th Anniversary
Obv: Head right **Obv. Designer:** Ian Rank-Broadley
Rev: Kookaburra on branch, head right

Date	Mintage	F	VF	XF	Unc	BU
2009 P20 Proof	10,000	Value: 45.00				

KM# 1279 DOLLAR
31.1050 g., 0.9990 Silver 0.9990 oz. ASW, 40 mm.
Ruler: Elizabeth II **Subject:** Kookaburra 20th Anniversary **Obv:** Head right **Obv. Designer:** Ian Rank-Broadley **Rev:** Kookaburra on branch left, head upwards

Date	Mintage	F	VF	XF	Unc	BU
2009 P20 Proof	10,000	Value: 45.00				

KM# 1280 DOLLAR
31.1050 g., 0.9990 Silver 0.9990 oz. ASW, 40 mm.
Ruler: Elizabeth II **Subject:** Kookaburra 20th Anniversary **Obv:** Head right **Obv. Designer:** Ian Rank-Broadley **Rev:** Kookaburra feeding young in nest at right

Date	Mintage	F	VF	XF	Unc	BU
2009 P20 Proof	10,000	Value: 45.00				

KM# 1281 DOLLAR
31.1050 g., 0.9990 Silver 0.9990 oz. ASW, 40 mm.
Ruler: Elizabeth II **Subject:** Kookaburra 20th Anniversary **Obv:** Head right **Obv. Designer:** Ian Rank-Broadley **Rev:** Kookaburra pair on branch

Date	Mintage	F	VF	XF	Unc	BU
2009 P20 Proof	10,000	Value: 45.00				

KM# 1282 DOLLAR
31.1050 g., 0.9990 Silver 0.9990 oz. ASW, 40 mm.
Ruler: Elizabeth II **Obv:** Head right **Obv. Designer:** Ian Rank-Broadley **Rev:** Kookaburra on branch, head left

Date	Mintage	F	VF	XF	Unc	BU
2009 P20 Proof	10,000	Value: 45.00				

KM# 1283 DOLLAR
31.1050 g., 0.9990 Silver 0.9990 oz. ASW, 40 mm.
Ruler: Elizabeth II **Subject:** Kookaburra 20th Anniversary **Obv:** Head right **Obv. Designer:** Ian rank-Broadley **Rev:** Kookaburra in flight right

Date	Mintage	F	VF	XF	Unc	BU
2009 P20 Proof	10,000	Value: 45.00				

KM# 1284 DOLLAR
31.1050 g., 0.9990 Silver 0.9990 oz. ASW, 40 mm.
Ruler: Elizabeth II **Subject:** Kookaburra 20th Anniversary **Obv:** Head right **Obv. Designer:** Ian rank-Broadley **Rev:** Kookaburra by nest at left

Date	Mintage	F	VF	XF	Unc	BU
2009 P20 Proof	10,000	Value: 45.00				

KM# 1285 DOLLAR
31.1050 g., 0.9990 Silver 0.9990 oz. ASW, 40 mm.
Ruler: Elizabeth II **Subject:** Kookaburra 20th Anniversary **Obv:** Head right **Obv. Designer:** Ian rank-Broadley **Rev:** Kookaburra on fence post

Date	Mintage	F	VF	XF	Unc	BU
2009 P20 Proof	10,000	Value: 45.00				

KM# 1286 DOLLAR
31.1050 g., 0.9990 Silver 0.9990 oz. ASW, 40 mm.
Ruler: Elizabeth II **Subject:** Kookaburra 20th Anniversary **Obv:** Head right **Obv. Designer:** Ian rank-Broadley **Rev:** Kookaburra pair on branch left

Date	Mintage	F	VF	XF	Unc	BU
2009 P20 Proof	10,000	Value: 45.00				

KM# 1287 DOLLAR
31.1050 g., 0.9990 Silver 0.9990 oz. ASW, 40 mm.
Ruler: Elizabeth II **Subject:** Kookaburra 20th Anniversary **Obv:** Head right **Obv. Designer:** Ian Rank-Broadley **Rev:** Kookaburra on leafy branch left

Date	Mintage	F	VF	XF	Unc	BU
2009 P20 Proof	10,000	Value: 45.00				

KM# 1288 DOLLAR
31.1050 g., 0.9990 Silver 0.9990 oz. ASW, 40 mm.
Ruler: Elizabeth II **Subject:** Kookaburra 20th Anniversary **Obv:** Head right **Obv. Designer:** Ian Rank-Broadley **Rev:** Kookaburra pair on branch, beaks upwards

Date	Mintage	F	VF	XF	Unc	BU
2009 P20 Proof	10,000	Value: 45.00				

KM# 1289 DOLLAR
31.1050 g., 0.9990 Silver 0.9990 oz. ASW, 40 mm.
Ruler: Elizabeth II **Subject:** Kookaburra 20th Anniversary **Obv:** Head right **Obv. Designer:** Ian rank-Broadley **Rev:** Kookaburra in flight on map of Australia

Date	Mintage	F	VF	XF	Unc	BU
2009 P20 Proof	10,000	Value: 45.00				

KM# 1290 DOLLAR
31.1050 g., 0.9990 Silver 0.9990 oz. ASW, 40 mm.
Ruler: Elizabeth II **Subject:** Kookaburra 20th Anniversary **Obv:** Head right **Obv. Designer:** Ian Rank-Broadley **Rev:** Kookaburra on branch right

Date	Mintage	F	VF	XF	Unc	BU
2009 P20 Proof	10,000	Value: 45.00				

KM# 1291 DOLLAR
31.1050 g., 0.9990 Silver 0.9990 oz. ASW, 40 mm.
Ruler: Elizabeth II **Subject:** Kookaburra 20th Anniversary **Obv:** Head right **Obv. Designer:** Ian rank-Broadley **Rev:** Kookaburra, one in flight, one on branch

Date	Mintage	F	VF	XF	Unc	BU
2009 P20 Proof	10,000	Value: 45.00				

KM# 1292 DOLLAR
31.1050 g., 0.9990 Silver 0.9990 oz. ASW, 40 mm.
Ruler: Elizabeth II **Subject:** Kookaburra 20th Anniversary **Obv:** Head right **Obv. Designer:** Ian Rank-Broadley **Rev:** Kookaburra on branch, head right

Date	Mintage	F	VF	XF	Unc	BU
2009 P20 Proof	10,000	Value: 45.00				

KM# 1293 DOLLAR
31.1050 g., 0.9990 Silver 0.9990 oz. ASW, 40 mm.
Ruler: Elizabeth II **Subject:** Kookaburra 20th Anniversary **Obv:** Head right **Obv. Designer:** Ian Rank-Broadley **Rev:** Kookaburra pair on branch left

Date	Mintage	F	VF	XF	Unc	BU
2009 P20 Proof	10,000	Value: 45.00				

KM# 1294 DOLLAR
31.1050 g., 0.9990 Silver 0.9990 oz. ASW, 40 mm.
Ruler: Elizabeth II **Subject:** Kookaburra 20th Anniversary **Obv:** Head right **Obv. Designer:** Ian Rank-Broadley **Rev:** Kookaburra on branch left

Date	Mintage	F	VF	XF	Unc	BU
2009 P20 Proof	10,000	Value: 45.00				

KM# 1295 DOLLAR
31.1050 g., 0.9990 Silver 0.9990 oz. ASW, 40 mm.
Ruler: Elizabeth II **Subject:** Kookaburra 20th Anniversary **Obv:** Head right **Obv. Designer:** Ian Rank-Broadley **Rev:** Kookaburra admiring spider web

Date	Mintage	F	VF	XF	Unc	BU
2009 P20 Proof	10,000	Value: 45.00				

KM# 1296 DOLLAR
31.1050 g., 0.9990 Silver 0.9990 oz. ASW, 40 mm.
Ruler: Elizabeth II **Subject:** Kookaburra 20th Anniversary **Obv:** Head right **Obv. Designer:** Ian Rank-Broadley **Rev:** Kookaburra on branch, sunburst in background

Date	Mintage	F	VF	XF	Unc	BU
2009 P20 Proof	10,000	Value: 45.00				

KM# 678 2 DOLLARS
62.2070 g., 0.9990 Silver 1.9979 oz. ASW, 40 mm.
Ruler: Elizabeth II **Obv:** Head with tiara right, denomination below **Obv. Designer:** Ian Rank-Broadley **Rev:** Kookaburra flying over Australian map **Edge:** Reeded

Date	Mintage	F	VF	XF	Unc	BU
2001P Proof	5,000	Value: 60.00				
2002	1,500	—	—	—	45.00	—
Note: 1661 Spanish cob privy mark						
2002	1,500	—	—	—	45.00	—
Note: 1771 Spanish pillar dllar privy mark						
2002	1,500	—	—	—	45.00	—
Note: 1881 Gold sovereign privy mark						
2002	1,500	—	—	—	45.00	—
Note: 1991 Gld Australian nugget privy mark						

KM# 623.1 2 DOLLARS
62.8500 g., 0.9990 Silver 2.0186 oz. ASW, 50 mm.
Ruler: Elizabeth II **Obv:** Head with tiara right, denomination below **Rev:** Two Kookaburras back to back **Edge:** Reeded

Date	Mintage	F	VF	XF	Unc	BU
2001	—	—	—	—	50.00	55.00

KM# 623.2 2 DOLLARS
62.2070 g., 0.9990 Silver 1.9979 oz. ASW **Ruler:** Elizabeth II **Subject:** USA State Quarters - 2001 **Obv:** Head with tiara right, denomination below **Rev:** Two kookaburras on branch with five state quarter designs added **Edge:** Reeded and plain sections **Note:** Prev. KM#623

Date	Mintage	F	VF	XF	Unc	BU
2001	10,000	—	—	—	145	160

KM# 879 2 DOLLARS
62.8500 g., 0.9990 Silver 2.0186 oz. ASW, 40 mm.
Ruler: Elizabeth II **Obv:** Head with tiara right **Obv. Designer:** Ian Rank-Broadley **Rev:** Kookaburra on branch plus two leaves **Edge:** Reeded

Date	Mintage	F	VF	XF	Unc	BU
2002P Proof	5,000	Value: 60.00				
2003	1,000	—	—	—	100	—
Note: Boer War privy mark						
2003	1,000	—	—	—	100	—
Note: World War I privy mark						
2003	1,000	—	—	—	100	—
Note: World War II privy mark						
2003	1,000	—	—	—	100	—
Note: Korean War privy mark						
2003	1,000	—	—	—	100	—
Note: Vietnam War privy mark						

KM# 881 2 DOLLARS
62.2070 g., 0.9990 Silver 1.9979 oz. ASW, 50 mm. **Ruler:** Elizabeth II **Obv:** Head with tiara right **Obv. Designer:** Ian Rank-Broadley **Rev:** Two kookaburras, one in flight **Edge:** Reeded

Date	Mintage	F	VF	XF	Unc	BU
2003P Proof	800	Value: 60.00				

KM# 884 2 DOLLARS
62.2070 g., 0.9990 Silver 1.9979 oz. ASW, 50 mm.
Ruler: Elizabeth II **Obv:** Head with tiara right **Obv. Designer:** Ian Rank-Broadley **Rev:** Kookaburra perched on branch with four leaves **Edge:** Reeded

Date	Mintage	F	VF	XF	Unc	BU
2004P Proof	800	Value: 60.00				

KM# 887 2 DOLLARS
62.2070 g., 0.9990 Silver 1.9979 oz. ASW, 50 mm.
Ruler: Elizabeth II **Obv:** Head with tiara right **Obv. Designer:** Ian Rank-Broadley **Rev:** Two kookaburras on branch, one laughing **Edge:** Reeded

Date	Mintage	F	VF	XF	Unc	BU
2005P Proof	800	Value: 60.00				

KM# 890 2 DOLLARS
62.2070 g., 0.9990 Silver 1.9979 oz. ASW, 50 mm.
Ruler: Elizabeth II **Obv:** Head with tiara right **Obv. Designer:** Ian Rank-Broadley **Rev:** Kookaburra on branch, no leaves

Date	Mintage	F	VF	XF	Unc	BU
2007	—	—	—	—	50.00	—

KM# 1297 5 DOLLARS
1.5500 g., 0.9990 Gold 0.0498 oz. AGW, 14 mm.
Ruler: Elizabeth II **Subject:** Kookaburra 20th Anniversary **Obv:** Head right **Obv. Designer:** Ian Rank-Broadley **Rev:** Kookaburra standing on stump right

Date	Mintage	F	VF	XF	Unc	BU
2009 P20 Proof	2,009	Value: 120				

KM# 1298 5 DOLLARS
1.5500 g., 0.9990 Gold 0.0498 oz. AGW, 14 mm.
Ruler: Elizabeth II **Subject:** Kookaburra 20th Anniversary **Obv:** Head right **Obv. Designer:** Ian rank-Broadley **Rev:** Kookaburra on branch, head right

Date	Mintage	F	VF	XF	Unc	BU
2009 P20 Proof	2,009	Value: 120				

KM# 1299 5 DOLLARS
1.5500 g., 0.9990 Gold 0.0498 oz. AGW, 14 mm.
Ruler: Elizabeth II **Subject:** Kookaburra 20th Anniversary **Obv:** Head right **Obv. Designer:** Ian Rank-Broadley **Rev:** Kookaburra on branch left

Date	Mintage	F	VF	XF	Unc	BU
2009 P20 Proof	2,009	Value: 120				

KM# 1300 5 DOLLARS
1.5500 g., 0.9990 Gold 0.0498 oz. AGW, 14 mm.
Ruler: Elizabeth II **Subject:** Kookaburra 20th Anniversary **Obv:** Head right **Obv. Designer:** Ian Rank-Broadley **Rev:** Kookaburra on branch feeding young at right

Date	Mintage	F	VF	XF	Unc	BU
2009 P20 Proof	2,009	Value: 120				

KM# 1301 5 DOLLARS
1.5500 g., 0.9990 Gold 0.0498 oz. AGW, 14 mm.
Ruler: Elizabeth II **Subject:** Kookaburra 20th Anniversary **Obv:** Head right **Obv. Designer:** Ian Rank-Broadley **Rev:** Kookaburra pair on branch, heads oposite

Date	Mintage	F	VF	XF	Unc	BU
2009 P20 Proof	2,009	Value: 120				

KM# 1302 5 DOLLARS
1.5500 g., 0.9990 Gold 0.0498 oz. AGW, 14 mm.
Ruler: Elizabeth II **Subject:** Kookaburra 20th Anniversary **Obv:** Head right **Obv. Designer:** Ian Rank-Broadley **Rev:** Kookaburra on branch, head left

Date	Mintage	F	VF	XF	Unc	BU
2009 P20 Proof	2,009	Value: 120				

KM# 1303 5 DOLLARS
1.5500 g., 0.9990 Gold 0.0498 oz. AGW, 14 mm.
Ruler: Elizabeth II **Subject:** Kookaburra 20th Anniversary **Obv:** Head right **Obv. Designer:** Ian Rank-Broadley **Rev:** Kookaburra in flight right

Date	Mintage	F	VF	XF	Unc	BU
2009 P20 Proof	2,009	Value: 120				

KM# 1304 5 DOLLARS
1.5500 g., 0.9990 Gold 0.0498 oz. AGW, 14 mm.
Ruler: Elizabeth II **Subject:** Kookaburra 20th Anniversary **Obv:** Head right **Obv. Designer:** Ian Rank-Broadley **Rev:** Kookaburra at nest left, head right

Date	Mintage	F	VF	XF	Unc	BU
2009 P20 Proof	2,009	Value: 120				

KM# 1305 5 DOLLARS
1.5500 g., 0.9990 Gold 0.0498 oz. AGW, 14 mm.
Ruler: Elizabeth II **Subject:** Kookaburra 20th Anniversary **Obv:** Head right **Obv. Designer:** Ian Rank-Broadley **Rev:** Kookaburra on fence post

Date	Mintage	F	VF	XF	Unc	BU
2009 P20 Proof	2,009	Value: 120				

KM# 1306 5 DOLLARS
1.5500 g., 0.9990 Gold 0.0498 oz. AGW, 14 mm. **Ruler:** Elizabeth II **Subject:** Kookaburra 20th Anniversary **Obv:** Head right **Obv. Designer:** Ian Rank-Broadley **Rev:** Kookaburra pair left

Date	Mintage	F	VF	XF	Unc	BU
2009 P20 Proof	2,009	Value: 120				

KM# 1307 5 DOLLARS
1.5500 g., 0.9990 Gold 0.0498 oz. AGW, 14 mm.
Ruler: Elizabeth II **Subject:** Kookaburra 20th Anniversary
Obv: Head right **Obv. Designer:** Ian Rank-Broadley
Rev: Kookaburra left on leafy branch

Date	Mintage	F	VF	XF	Unc	BU
2009 P20 Proof	2,009	Value: 120				

KM# 1308 5 DOLLARS
1.5500 g., 0.9990 Gold 0.0498 oz. AGW, 14 mm.
Ruler: Elizabeth II **Subject:** Kookaburra 20th Anniversary
Obv: Head right **Obv. Designer:** Ian Rank-Broadley
Rev: Kookaburra pair facing oposite

Date	Mintage	F	VF	XF	Unc	BU
2009 P20 Proof	2,009	Value: 120				

KM# 1309 5 DOLLARS
1.5500 g., 0.9990 Gold 0.0498 oz. AGW, 14 mm.
Ruler: Elizabeth II **Subject:** Kookaburra 20th Anniversary
Obv: Head right **Obv. Designer:** Ian Rank-Broadley
Rev: Kookaburra in flight on map of Australia

Date	Mintage	F	VF	XF	Unc	BU
2009 P20 Proof	2,009	Value: 120				

KM# 1310 5 DOLLARS
1.5500 g., 0.9990 Gold 0.0498 oz. AGW, 14 mm.
Ruler: Elizabeth II **Subject:** Kookaburra 20th Anniversary
Obv: Head right **Obv. Designer:** Ian Rank-Broadley
Rev: Kookaburra on branch right

Date	Mintage	F	VF	XF	Unc	BU
2009 P20 Proof	2,009	Value: 120				

KM# 1311 5 DOLLARS
1.5500 g., 0.9990 Gold 0.0498 oz. AGW, 14 mm.
Ruler: Elizabeth II **Subject:** Kookaburra 20th Anniversary
Obv: Head right **Obv. Designer:** Ian Rank-Broadley
Rev: Kookaburras, one in flight, one on branch

Date	Mintage	F	VF	XF	Unc	BU
2009 P20 Proof	2,009	Value: 120				

KM# 1312 5 DOLLARS
1.5500 g., 0.9990 Gold 0.0498 oz. AGW, 14 mm.
Ruler: Elizabeth II **Subject:** Kookaburra 20th Anniversary
Obv: Head right **Obv. Designer:** Ian Rank-Broadley
Rev: Kookaburra on branch, head right

Date	Mintage	F	VF	XF	Unc	BU
2009 P20 Proof	2,009	Value: 120				

KM# 1313 5 DOLLARS
1.5500 g., 0.9990 Gold 0.0498 oz. AGW, 14 mm.
Ruler: Elizabeth II **Subject:** Kookaburra 20th Anniversary
Obv: Head right **Obv. Designer:** Ian Rank-Broadley
Rev: Kookaburra pair on branch, one with head upward

Date	Mintage	F	VF	XF	Unc	BU
2009 P20 Proof	2,009	Value: 120				

KM# 1314 5 DOLLARS
1.5500 g., 0.9990 Gold 0.0498 oz. AGW, 14 mm.
Ruler: Elizabeth II **Subject:** Kookaburra 20th Anniversary
Obv: Head right **Obv. Designer:** Ian Rank-Broadley
Rev: Kookaburra on branch left

Date	Mintage	F	VF	XF	Unc	BU
2009 P20 Proof	2,009	Value: 120				

KM# 1315 5 DOLLARS
1.5500 g., 0.9990 Gold 0.0498 oz. AGW, 14 mm.
Ruler: Elizabeth II **Subject:** Kookaburra 20th Anniversary
Obv: Head right **Obv. Designer:** Ian Rank-Broadley
Rev: Kookaburra on branch admiring spider web

Date	Mintage	F	VF	XF	Unc	BU
2009 P20 Proof	2,009	Value: 120				

KM# 1316 5 DOLLARS
1.5500 g., 0.9990 Gold 0.0498 oz. AGW, 14 mm.
Ruler: Elizabeth II **Subject:** Kookaburra 20th Anniversary
Obv: Head right **Obv. Designer:** Ian Rank-Broadley
Rev: Kookaburra on branch, sunburst in background

Date	Mintage	F	VF	XF	Unc	BU
2009 P20 Proof	2,009	Value: 120				

KM# 596 10 DOLLARS
311.0350 g., 0.9990 Silver 9.9896 oz. ASW, 75.5 mm.
Ruler: Elizabeth II **Subject:** Calendar Evolution **Obv:** Head with tiara right, denomination below **Obv. Designer:** Ian Rank-Broadley **Rev:** Multicolor solar system in center, zodiac symbols in outer circle **Edge:** Segmented reeding **Note:** Illustration reduced.

Date	Mintage	F	VF	XF	Unc	BU
ND(2001) Proof	15,000	Value: 250				

KM# 603 10 DOLLARS
311.0350 g., 0.9990 Silver 9.9896 oz. ASW, 74.9 mm.
Ruler: Elizabeth II **Subject:** Kookaburra **Obv:** Head with tiara right, denomination below **Obv. Designer:** Ian Rank-Broadley **Rev:** Flying bird over map **Edge:** Reeded

Date	Mintage	F	VF	XF	Unc	BU
2002 Proof	—	Value: 225				

KM# 633 10 DOLLARS
311.0350 g., 0.9990 Silver 9.9896 oz. ASW, 75.5 mm.
Ruler: Elizabeth II **Subject:** Evolution of Time **Obv:** Queens portrait right **Rev:** Various time keeping devices **Edge:** Segmented reeding

Date	Mintage	F	VF	XF	Unc	BU
2002P Proof	1,500	Value: 275				

KM# 686 10 DOLLARS
311.0000 g., 0.9990 Silver 9.9885 oz. ASW, 75.5 mm.
Ruler: Elizabeth II **Obv:** Queens head right **Rev:** Alphabet Evolution design **Edge:** Reeded

Date	Mintage	F	VF	XF	Unc	BU
2003P Proof	1,500	Value: 285				

KM# 739 10 DOLLARS
311.0350 g., 0.9990 Silver 9.9896 oz. ASW, 75.5 mm.
Ruler: Elizabeth II **Subject:** Evolution of Numbers **Obv:** Queens head right **Rev:** Numbers, symbols, abacus and calculator **Edge:** Reeded

Date	Mintage	F	VF	XF	Unc	BU
2004 Proof	1,500	Value: 275				

KM# 744 10 DOLLARS
311.3460 g., 0.9990 Silver 9.9996 oz. ASW, 75.5 mm.
Ruler: Elizabeth II **Obv:** Queens head right **Rev:** Multicolor symbolic design **Edge:** Reeded

Date	Mintage	F	VF	XF	Unc	BU
2005 Proof	1,500	Value: 275				

KM# 891 10 DOLLARS
311.0350 g., 0.9990 Silver 9.9896 oz. ASW, 74.9 mm.
Ruler: Elizabeth II **Obv:** Head with tiara right **Obv. Designer:** Ian Rank-Broadley **Rev:** Kookaburra on branch, no leaves

Date	Mintage	F	VF	XF	Unc	BU
2007	—	—			225	—

KM# 630 20 DOLLARS
62.2070 g., 0.9990 Silver 1.9979 oz. ASW **Ruler:** Elizabeth II **Subject:** USA State Quarters - 2002 **Obv:** Head with tiara right, denomination below **Rev:** Kookaburra on branch with five state quarter designs added below **Edge:** Reeded and plain sections

Date	Mintage	F	VF	XF	Unc	BU
2002	10,000	—	—	—	52.00	55.00

KM# 680 30 DOLLARS
1002.5020 g., 0.9990 Silver 32.197 oz. ASW, 101 mm.
Ruler: Elizabeth II **Obv:** Head with tiara right, denomination below **Obv. Designer:** Ian Rank-Broadley **Rev:** Kookaburra in flight above Australian map **Edge:** Segmented reeding

Date	Mintage	F	VF	XF	Unc	BU
2001P Proof	350	Value: 650				
2002	—	—				675

KM# 624 30 DOLLARS
1002.5020 g., 0.9990 Silver 32.197 oz. ASW **Ruler:** Elizabeth II **Subject:** USA State Quarters - 2001 **Obv:** Head with tiara right, denomination below **Rev:** Two kookaburras on branch with five state quarter designs added below **Edge:** Reeded and plain sections

Date	Mintage	F	VF	XF	Unc	BU
2001	1,000	—	—	—	—	650

KM# 631 30 DOLLARS
1002.5020 g., 0.9990 Silver 32.197 oz. ASW **Ruler:** Elizabeth II **Subject:** USA State Quarters - 2002 **Obv:** Head with tiara right, denomination below **Rev:** Kookaburra on branch with five state quarter designs added in gold **Edge:** Reeded and plain sections

Date	Mintage	F	VF	XF	Unc	BU
2002	1,000	—	—	—	—	650

KM# 880 30 DOLLARS
1002.5020 g., 0.9990 Silver 32.197 oz. ASW, 101 mm. **Ruler:** Elizabeth II **Obv:** Head with tiara right **Obv. Designer:** Ian Rank-Broadley **Rev:** Kookaburra standing on branch **Edge:** Reeded

Date	Mintage	F	VF	XF	Unc	BU
2002P Proof	350	Value: 675				

KM# 882 30 DOLLARS
1002.5020 g., 0.9990 Silver 32.197 oz. ASW, 101 mm. **Ruler:** Elizabeth II **Obv:** Head with tiara right **Obv. Designer:** Ian Rank-Broadley **Rev:** Two kookaburras, one in flight **Edge:** Reeded

Date	Mintage	F	VF	XF	Unc	BU
2003P Proof	350	Value: 675				

KM# 1279 DOLLAR
31.1050 g., 0.9990 Silver 0.9990 oz. ASW, 40 mm.
Ruler: Elizabeth II **Subject:** Kookaburra 20th Anniversary
Obv: Head right **Obv. Designer:** Ian Rank-Broadley
Rev: Kookaburra on branch left, head upwards

Date	Mintage	F	VF	XF	Unc	BU
2009 P20 Proof	10,000	Value: 45.00				

KM# 1280 DOLLAR
31.1050 g., 0.9990 Silver 0.9990 oz. ASW, 40 mm.
Ruler: Elizabeth II **Subject:** Kookaburra 20th Anniversary
Obv: Head right **Obv. Designer:** Ian Rank-Broadley
Rev: Kookaburra feeding young in nest at right

Date	Mintage	F	VF	XF	Unc	BU
2009 P20 Proof	10,000	Value: 45.00				

KM# 1281 DOLLAR
31.1050 g., 0.9990 Silver 0.9990 oz. ASW, 40 mm.
Ruler: Elizabeth II **Subject:** Kookaburra 20th Anniversary
Obv: Head right **Obv. Designer:** Ian Rank-Broadley
Rev: Kookaburra pair on branch

Date	Mintage	F	VF	XF	Unc	BU
2009 P20 Proof	10,000	Value: 45.00				

KM# 1282 DOLLAR
31.1050 g., 0.9990 Silver 0.9990 oz. ASW, 40 mm.
Ruler: Elizabeth II **Obv:** Head right **Obv. Designer:** Ian Rank-Broadley **Rev:** Kookaburra on branch, head left

Date	Mintage	F	VF	XF	Unc	BU
2009 P20 Proof	10,000	Value: 45.00				

KM# 1283 DOLLAR
31.1050 g., 0.9990 Silver 0.9990 oz. ASW, 40 mm.
Ruler: Elizabeth II **Subject:** Kookaburra 20th Anniversary
Obv: Head right **Obv. Designer:** Ian rank-Broadley
Rev: Kookaburra in flight right

Date	Mintage	F	VF	XF	Unc	BU
2009 P20 Proof	10,000	Value: 45.00				

KM# 1284 DOLLAR
31.1050 g., 0.9990 Silver 0.9990 oz. ASW, 40 mm.
Ruler: Elizabeth II **Subject:** Kookaburra 20th Anniversary
Obv: Head right **Obv. Designer:** Ian rank-Broadley
Rev: Kookaburra by nest at left

Date	Mintage	F	VF	XF	Unc	BU
2009 P20 Proof	10,000	Value: 45.00				

KM# 1285 DOLLAR
31.1050 g., 0.9990 Silver 0.9990 oz. ASW, 40 mm.
Ruler: Elizabeth II **Subject:** Kookaburra 20th Anniversary
Obv: Head right **Obv. Designer:** Ian rank-Broadley
Rev: Kookaburra on fence post

Date	Mintage	F	VF	XF	Unc	BU
2009 P20 Proof	10,000	Value: 45.00				

KM# 1286 DOLLAR
31.1050 g., 0.9990 Silver 0.9990 oz. ASW, 40 mm.
Ruler: Elizabeth II **Subject:** Kookaburra 20th Anniversary
Obv: Head right **Obv. Designer:** Ian rank-Broadley
Rev: Kookaburra pair on branch left

Date	Mintage	F	VF	XF	Unc	BU
2009 P20 Proof	10,000	Value: 45.00				

KM# 1287 DOLLAR
31.1050 g., 0.9990 Silver 0.9990 oz. ASW, 40 mm.
Ruler: Elizabeth II **Subject:** Kookaburra 20th Anniversary
Obv: Head right **Obv. Designer:** Ian Rank-Broadley
Rev: Kookaburra on leafy branch left

Date	Mintage	F	VF	XF	Unc	BU
2009 P20 Proof	10,000	Value: 45.00				

KM# 1288 DOLLAR
31.1050 g., 0.9990 Silver 0.9990 oz. ASW, 40 mm.
Ruler: Elizabeth II **Subject:** Kookaburra 20th Anniversary
Obv: Head right **Obv. Designer:** Ian Rank-Broadley
Rev: Kookaburra pair on branch, beaks upwards

Date	Mintage	F	VF	XF	Unc	BU
2009 P20 Proof	10,000	Value: 45.00				

KM# 1289 DOLLAR
31.1050 g., 0.9990 Silver 0.9990 oz. ASW, 40 mm.
Ruler: Elizabeth II **Subject:** Kookaburra 20th Anniversary
Obv: Head right **Obv. Designer:** Ian rank-Broadley
Rev: Kookaburra in flight on map of Australia

Date	Mintage	F	VF	XF	Unc	BU
2009 P20 Proof	10,000	Value: 45.00				

KM# 1290 DOLLAR
31.1050 g., 0.9990 Silver 0.9990 oz. ASW, 40 mm.
Ruler: Elizabeth II **Subject:** Kookaburra 20th Anniversary
Obv: Head right **Obv. Designer:** Ian Rank-Broadley
Rev: Kookaburra on branch right

Date	Mintage	F	VF	XF	Unc	BU
2009 P20 Proof	10,000	Value: 45.00				

KM# 1291 DOLLAR
31.1050 g., 0.9990 Silver 0.9990 oz. ASW, 40 mm.
Ruler: Elizabeth II **Subject:** Kookaburra 20th Anniversary
Obv: Head right **Obv. Designer:** Ian rank-Broadley
Rev: Kookaburra, one in flight, one on branch

Date	Mintage	F	VF	XF	Unc	BU
2009 P20 Proof	10,000	Value: 45.00				

KM# 1292 DOLLAR
31.1050 g., 0.9990 Silver 0.9990 oz. ASW, 40 mm.
Ruler: Elizabeth II **Subject:** Kookaburra 20th Anniversary
Obv: Head right **Obv. Designer:** Ian Rank-Broadley
Rev: Kookaburra on branch, head right

Date	Mintage	F	VF	XF	Unc	BU
2009 P20 Proof	10,000	Value: 45.00				

KM# 1293 DOLLAR
31.1050 g., 0.9990 Silver 0.9990 oz. ASW, 40 mm.
Ruler: Elizabeth II **Subject:** Kookaburra 20th Anniversary
Obv: Head right **Obv. Designer:** Ian Rank-Broadley
Rev: Kookaburra pair on branch left

Date	Mintage	F	VF	XF	Unc	BU
2009 P20 Proof	10,000	Value: 45.00				

KM# 1294 DOLLAR
31.1050 g., 0.9990 Silver 0.9990 oz. ASW, 40 mm.
Ruler: Elizabeth II **Subject:** Kookaburra 20th Anniversary
Obv: Head right **Obv. Designer:** Ian Rank-Broadley
Rev: Kookaburra on branch left

Date	Mintage	F	VF	XF	Unc	BU
2009 P20 Proof	10,000	Value: 45.00				

KM# 1295 DOLLAR
31.1050 g., 0.9990 Silver 0.9990 oz. ASW, 40 mm.
Ruler: Elizabeth II **Subject:** Kookaburra 20th Anniversary
Obv: Head right **Obv. Designer:** Ian Rank-Broadley
Rev: Kookaburra admiring spider web

Date	Mintage	F	VF	XF	Unc	BU
2009 P20 Proof	10,000	Value: 45.00				

KM# 1296 DOLLAR
31.1050 g., 0.9990 Silver 0.9990 oz. ASW, 40 mm.
Ruler: Elizabeth II **Subject:** Kookaburra 20th Anniversary
Obv: Head right **Obv. Designer:** Ian Rank-Broadley
Rev: Kookaburra on branch, sunburst in background

Date	Mintage	F	VF	XF	Unc	BU
2009 P20 Proof	10,000	Value: 45.00				

KM# 678 2 DOLLARS
62.2070 g., 0.9990 Silver 1.9979 oz. ASW, 40 mm.
Ruler: Elizabeth II **Obv:** Head with tiara right, denomination below **Obv. Designer:** Ian Rank-Broadley **Rev:** Kookaburra flying over Australian map **Edge:** Reeded

Date	Mintage	F	VF	XF	Unc	BU
2001P Proof	5,000	Value: 60.00				
2002	1,500	—	—	—	45.00	—
Note: 1661 Spanish cob privy mark						
2002	1,500	—	—	—	45.00	—
Note: 1771 Spanish pillar dllar privy mark						
2002	1,500	—	—	—	45.00	—
Note: 1881 Gold sovereign privy mark						
2002	1,500	—	—	—	45.00	—
Note: 1991 Gld Australian nugget privy mark						

KM# 623.1 2 DOLLARS
62.8500 g., 0.9990 Silver 2.0186 oz. ASW, 50 mm.
Ruler: Elizabeth II **Obv:** Head with tiara right, denomination below **Rev:** Two Kookaburras back to back **Edge:** Reeded

Date	Mintage	F	VF	XF	Unc	BU
2001	—	—	—	—	50.00	55.00

KM# 623.2 2 DOLLARS
62.2070 g., 0.9990 Silver 1.9979 oz. ASW **Ruler:** Elizabeth II **Subject:** USA State Quarters - 2001 **Obv:** Head with tiara right, denomination below **Rev:** Two kookaburras on branch with five state quarter designs added **Edge:** Reeded and plain sections **Note:** Prev. KM#623

Date	Mintage	F	VF	XF	Unc	BU
2001	10,000	—	—	—	145	160

KM# 879 2 DOLLARS
62.8500 g., 0.9990 Silver 2.0186 oz. ASW, 40 mm.
Ruler: Elizabeth II **Obv:** Head with tiara right **Obv. Designer:** Ian Rank-Broadley **Rev:** Kookaburra on branch plus two leaves **Edge:** Reeded

Date	Mintage	F	VF	XF	Unc	BU
2002P Proof	5,000	Value: 60.00				
2003	1,000	—	—	—	100	—
Note: Boer War privy mark						
2003	1,000	—	—	—	100	—
Note: World War I privy mark						
2003	1,000	—	—	—	100	—
Note: World War II privy mark						
2003	1,000	—	—	—	100	—
Note: Korean War privy mark						
2003	1,000	—	—	—	100	—
Note: Vietnam War privy mark						

KM# 881 2 DOLLARS
62.2070 g., 0.9990 Silver 1.9979 oz. ASW, 50 mm. **Ruler:** Elizabeth II **Obv:** Head with tiara right **Obv. Designer:** Ian Rank-Broadley **Rev:** Two kookaburras, one in flight **Edge:** Reeded

Date	Mintage	F	VF	XF	Unc	BU
2003P Proof	800	Value: 60.00				

KM# 884 2 DOLLARS
62.2070 g., 0.9990 Silver 1.9979 oz. ASW, 50 mm.
Ruler: Elizabeth II **Obv:** Head with tiara right **Obv. Designer:** Ian Rank-Broadley **Rev:** Kookaburra perched on branch with four leaves **Edge:** Reeded

Date	Mintage	F	VF	XF	Unc	BU
2004P Proof	800	Value: 60.00				

KM# 887 2 DOLLARS
62.2070 g., 0.9990 Silver 1.9979 oz. ASW, 50 mm.
Ruler: Elizabeth II **Obv:** Head with tiara right **Obv. Designer:** Ian Rank-Broadley **Rev:** Two kookaburras on branch, one laughing **Edge:** Reeded

Date	Mintage	F	VF	XF	Unc	BU
2005P Proof	800	Value: 60.00				

KM# 890 2 DOLLARS
62.2070 g., 0.9990 Silver 1.9979 oz. ASW, 50 mm.
Ruler: Elizabeth II **Obv:** Head with tiara right **Obv. Designer:** Ian Rank-Broadley **Rev:** Kookaburra on branch, no leaves

Date	Mintage	F	VF	XF	Unc	BU
2007	—	—	—	—	50.00	—

KM# 1297 5 DOLLARS
1.5500 g., 0.9990 Gold 0.0498 oz. AGW, 14 mm.
Ruler: Elizabeth II **Subject:** Kookaburra 20th Anniversary
Obv: Head right **Obv. Designer:** Ian Rank-Broadley
Rev: Kookaburra standing on stump right

Date	Mintage	F	VF	XF	Unc	BU
2009 P20 Proof	2,009	Value: 120				

KM# 1298 5 DOLLARS
1.5500 g., 0.9990 Gold 0.0498 oz. AGW, 14 mm.
Ruler: Elizabeth II **Subject:** Kookaburra 20th Anniversary
Obv: Head right **Obv. Designer:** Ian rank-Broadley
Rev: Kookaburra on branch, head right

Date	Mintage	F	VF	XF	Unc	BU
2009 P20 Proof	2,009	Value: 120				

KM# 1299 5 DOLLARS
1.5500 g., 0.9990 Gold 0.0498 oz. AGW, 14 mm.
Ruler: Elizabeth II **Subject:** Kookaburra 20th Anniversary
Obv: Head right **Obv. Designer:** Ian Rank-Broadley
Rev: Kookaburra on branch left

Date	Mintage	F	VF	XF	Unc	BU
2009 P20 Proof	2,009	Value: 120				

KM# 1300 5 DOLLARS
1.5500 g., 0.9990 Gold 0.0498 oz. AGW, 14 mm.
Ruler: Elizabeth II **Subject:** Kookaburra 20th Anniversary
Obv: Head right **Obv. Designer:** Ian Rank-Broadley
Rev: Kookaburra on branch feeding young at right

Date	Mintage	F	VF	XF	Unc	BU
2009 P20 Proof	2,009	Value: 120				

KM# 1301 5 DOLLARS
1.5500 g., 0.9990 Gold 0.0498 oz. AGW, 14 mm.
Ruler: Elizabeth II **Subject:** Kookaburra 20th Anniversary
Obv: Head right **Obv. Designer:** Ian Rank-Broadley
Rev: Kookaburra pair on branch, heads oposite

Date	Mintage	F	VF	XF	Unc	BU
2009 P20 Proof	2,009	Value: 120				

KM# 1302 5 DOLLARS
1.5500 g., 0.9990 Gold 0.0498 oz. AGW, 14 mm.
Ruler: Elizabeth II **Subject:** Kookaburra 20th Anniversary
Obv: Head right **Obv. Designer:** Ian Rank-Broadley
Rev: Kookaburra on branch, head left

Date	Mintage	F	VF	XF	Unc	BU
2009 P20 Proof	2,009	Value: 120				

KM# 1303 5 DOLLARS
1.5500 g., 0.9990 Gold 0.0498 oz. AGW, 14 mm.
Ruler: Elizabeth II **Subject:** Kookaburra 20th Anniversary
Obv: Head right **Obv. Designer:** Ian Rank-Broadley
Rev: Kookaburra in flight right

Date	Mintage	F	VF	XF	Unc	BU
2009 P20 Proof	2,009	Value: 120				

KM# 1304 5 DOLLARS
1.5500 g., 0.9990 Gold 0.0498 oz. AGW, 14 mm.
Ruler: Elizabeth II **Subject:** Kookaburra 20th Anniversary
Obv: Head right **Obv. Designer:** Ian Rank-Broadley
Rev: Kookaburra at nest left, head right

Date	Mintage	F	VF	XF	Unc	BU
2009 P20 Proof	2,009	Value: 120				

KM# 1305 5 DOLLARS
1.5500 g., 0.9990 Gold 0.0498 oz. AGW, 14 mm.
Ruler: Elizabeth II **Subject:** Kookaburra 20th Anniversary
Obv: Head right **Obv. Designer:** Ian Rank-Broadley
Rev: Kookaburra on fence post

Date	Mintage	F	VF	XF	Unc	BU
2009 P20 Proof	2,009	Value: 120				

KM# 1306 5 DOLLARS
1.5500 g., 0.9990 Gold 0.0498 oz. AGW, 14 mm. **Ruler:** Elizabeth II **Subject:** Kookaburra 20th Anniversary **Obv:** Head right **Obv. Designer:** Ian Rank-Broadley **Rev:** Kookaburra pair left

Date	Mintage	F	VF	XF	Unc	BU
2009 P20 Proof	2,009	Value: 120				

KM# 1307 5 DOLLARS
1.5500 g., 0.9990 Gold 0.0498 oz. AGW, 14 mm.
Ruler: Elizabeth II **Subject:** Kookaburra 20th Anniversary
Obv: Head right **Obv. Designer:** Ian Rank-Broadley
Rev: Kookaburra left on leafy branch

Date	Mintage	F	VF	XF	Unc	BU
2009 P20 Proof	2,009	Value: 120				

KM# 1308 5 DOLLARS
1.5500 g., 0.9990 Gold 0.0498 oz. AGW, 14 mm.
Ruler: Elizabeth II **Subject:** Kookaburra 20th Anniversary
Obv: Head right **Obv. Designer:** Ian Rank-Broadley
Rev: Kookaburra pair facing opposite

Date	Mintage	F	VF	XF	Unc	BU
2009 P20 Proof	2,009	Value: 120				

KM# 1309 5 DOLLARS
1.5500 g., 0.9990 Gold 0.0498 oz. AGW, 14 mm.
Ruler: Elizabeth II **Subject:** Kookaburra 20th Anniversary
Obv: Head right **Obv. Designer:** Ian Rank-Broadley
Rev: Kookaburra in flight on map of Australia

Date	Mintage	F	VF	XF	Unc	BU
2009 P20 Proof	2,009	Value: 120				

KM# 1310 5 DOLLARS
1.5500 g., 0.9990 Gold 0.0498 oz. AGW, 14 mm.
Ruler: Elizabeth II **Subject:** Kookaburra 20th Anniversary
Obv: Head right **Obv. Designer:** Ian Rank-Broadley
Rev: Kookaburra on branch right

Date	Mintage	F	VF	XF	Unc	BU
2009 P20 Proof	2,009	Value: 120				

KM# 1311 5 DOLLARS
1.5500 g., 0.9990 Gold 0.0498 oz. AGW, 14 mm.
Ruler: Elizabeth II **Subject:** Kookaburra 20th Anniversary
Obv: Head right **Obv. Designer:** Ian Rank-Broadley
Rev: Kookaburras, one in flight, one on branch

Date	Mintage	F	VF	XF	Unc	BU
2009 P20 Proof	2,009	Value: 120				

KM# 1312 5 DOLLARS
1.5500 g., 0.9990 Gold 0.0498 oz. AGW, 14 mm.
Ruler: Elizabeth II **Subject:** Kookaburra 20th Anniversary
Obv: Head right **Obv. Designer:** Ian Rank-Broadley
Rev: Kookaburra on branch, head right

Date	Mintage	F	VF	XF	Unc	BU
2009 P20 Proof	2,009	Value: 120				

KM# 1313 5 DOLLARS
1.5500 g., 0.9990 Gold 0.0498 oz. AGW, 14 mm.
Ruler: Elizabeth II **Subject:** Kookaburra 20th Anniversary
Obv: Head right **Obv. Designer:** Ian Rank-Broadley
Rev: Kookaburra pair on branch, one with head upward

Date	Mintage	F	VF	XF	Unc	BU
2009 P20 Proof	2,009	Value: 120				

KM# 1314 5 DOLLARS
1.5500 g., 0.9990 Gold 0.0498 oz. AGW, 14 mm.
Ruler: Elizabeth II **Subject:** Kookaburra 20th Anniversary
Obv: Head right **Obv. Designer:** Ian Rank-Broadley
Rev: Kookaburra on branch left

Date	Mintage	F	VF	XF	Unc	BU
2009 P20 Proof	2,009	Value: 120				

KM# 1315 5 DOLLARS
1.5500 g., 0.9990 Gold 0.0498 oz. AGW, 14 mm.
Ruler: Elizabeth II **Subject:** Kookaburra 20th Anniversary
Obv: Head right **Obv. Designer:** Ian Rank-Broadley
Rev: Kookaburra on branch admiring spider web

Date	Mintage	F	VF	XF	Unc	BU
2009 P20 Proof	2,009	Value: 120				

KM# 1316 5 DOLLARS
1.5500 g., 0.9990 Gold 0.0498 oz. AGW, 14 mm.
Ruler: Elizabeth II **Subject:** Kookaburra 20th Anniversary
Obv: Head right **Obv. Designer:** Ian Rank-Broadley
Rev: Kookaburra on branch, sunburst in background

Date	Mintage	F	VF	XF	Unc	BU
2009 P20 Proof	2,009	Value: 120				

KM# 596 10 DOLLARS
311.0350 g., 0.9990 Silver 9.9896 oz. ASW, 75.5 mm.
Ruler: Elizabeth II **Subject:** Calendar Evolution **Obv:** Head with tiara right, denomination below **Obv. Designer:** Ian Rank-Broadley **Rev:** Multicolor solar system in center, zodiac symbols in outer circle **Edge:** Segmented reeding **Note:** Illustration reduced.

Date	Mintage	F	VF	XF	Unc	BU
ND(2001) Proof	15,000	Value: 250				

KM# 603 10 DOLLARS
311.0350 g., 0.9990 Silver 9.9896 oz. ASW, 74.9 mm.
Ruler: Elizabeth II **Subject:** Kookaburra **Obv:** Head with tiara right, denomination below **Obv. Designer:** Ian Rank-Broadley **Rev:** Flying bird over map **Edge:** Reeded

Date	Mintage	F	VF	XF	Unc	BU
2002 Proof	—	Value: 225				

KM# 633 10 DOLLARS
311.0350 g., 0.9990 Silver 9.9896 oz. ASW, 75.5 mm.
Ruler: Elizabeth II **Subject:** Evolution of Time **Obv:** Queens portrait right **Rev:** Various time keeping devices **Edge:** Segmented reeding

Date	Mintage	F	VF	XF	Unc	BU
2002P Proof	1,500	Value: 275				

KM# 686 10 DOLLARS
311.0000 g., 0.9990 Silver 9.9885 oz. ASW, 75.5 mm.
Ruler: Elizabeth II **Obv:** Queens head right **Rev:** Alphabet Evolution design **Edge:** Reeded

Date	Mintage	F	VF	XF	Unc	BU
2003P Proof	1,500	Value: 285				

KM# 739 10 DOLLARS
311.0350 g., 0.9990 Silver 9.9896 oz. ASW, 75.5 mm.
Ruler: Elizabeth II **Subject:** Evolution of Numbers **Obv:** Queens head right **Rev:** Numbers, symbols, abacus and calculator **Edge:** Reeded

Date	Mintage	F	VF	XF	Unc	BU
2004 Proof	1,500	Value: 275				

KM# 744 10 DOLLARS
311.3460 g., 0.9990 Silver 9.9996 oz. ASW, 75.5 mm.
Ruler: Elizabeth II **Obv:** Queens head right **Rev:** Multicolor symbolic design **Edge:** Reeded

Date	Mintage	F	VF	XF	Unc	BU
2005 Proof	1,500	Value: 275				

KM# 891 10 DOLLARS
311.0350 g., 0.9990 Silver 9.9896 oz. ASW, 74.9 mm.
Ruler: Elizabeth II **Obv:** Head with tiara right **Obv. Designer:** Ian Rank-Broadley **Rev:** Kookaburra on branch, no leaves

Date	Mintage	F	VF	XF	Unc	BU
2007	—	—	—	—	225	—

KM# 630 20 DOLLARS
62.2070 g., 0.9990 Silver 1.9979 oz. ASW **Ruler:** Elizabeth II **Subject:** USA State Quarters - 2002 **Obv:** Head with tiara right, denomination below **Rev:** Kookaburra on branch with five state quarter designs added below **Edge:** Reeded and plain sections

Date	Mintage	F	VF	XF	Unc	BU
2002	10,000	—	—	52.00	55.00	

KM# 680 30 DOLLARS
1002.5020 g., 0.9990 Silver 32.197 oz. ASW, 101 mm.
Ruler: Elizabeth II **Obv:** Head with tiara right, denomination below **Obv. Designer:** Ian Rank-Broadley **Rev:** Kookaburra in flight above Australian map **Edge:** Segmented reeding

Date	Mintage	F	VF	XF	Unc	BU
2001P Proof	350	Value: 650				
2002	—	—	—	—	675	

KM# 624 30 DOLLARS
1002.5020 g., 0.9990 Silver 32.197 oz. ASW **Ruler:** Elizabeth II **Subject:** USA State Quarters - 2001 **Obv:** Head with tiara right, denomination below **Rev:** Two kookaburras on branch with five state quarter designs added below **Edge:** Reeded and plain sections

Date	Mintage	F	VF	XF	Unc	BU
2001	1,000	—	—	—	650	

KM# 631 30 DOLLARS
1002.5020 g., 0.9990 Silver 32.197 oz. ASW **Ruler:** Elizabeth II **Subject:** USA State Quarters - 2002 **Obv:** Head with tiara right, denomination below **Rev:** Kookaburra on branch with five state quarter designs added in gold **Edge:** Reeded and plain sections

Date	Mintage	F	VF	XF	Unc	BU
2002	1,000	—	—	—	650	

KM# 880 30 DOLLARS
1002.5020 g., 0.9990 Silver 32.197 oz. ASW, 101 mm. **Ruler:** Elizabeth II **Obv:** Head with tiara right **Obv. Designer:** Ian Rank-Broadley **Rev:** Kookaburra standing on branch **Edge:** Reeded

Date	Mintage	F	VF	XF	Unc	BU
2002P Proof	350	Value: 675				

KM# 882 30 DOLLARS
1002.5020 g., 0.9990 Silver 32.197 oz. ASW, 101 mm. **Ruler:** Elizabeth II **Obv:** Head with tiara right **Obv. Designer:** Ian Rank-Broadley **Rev:** Two kookaburras, one in flight **Edge:** Reeded

Date	Mintage	F	VF	XF	Unc	BU
2003P Proof	350	Value: 675				

KM# 885 30 DOLLARS
1002.5020 g., 0.9990 Silver 32.197 oz. ASW, 101 mm.
Ruler: Elizabeth II **Obv:** Head with tiara right **Obv. Designer:** Ian Rank-Broadley **Rev:** Kookaburra perched on branch with four leaves **Edge:** Reeded

Date	Mintage	F	VF	XF	Unc	BU
2004P Proof	350	Value: 675				

KM# 888 30 DOLLARS
1002.5020 g., 0.9990 Silver 32.197 oz. ASW, 101 mm. **Ruler:** Elizabeth II **Obv:** Head with tiara right **Obv. Designer:** Ian Rank-Broadley **Rev:** Two kookaburras on branch, one laughing **Edge:** Reeded

Date	Mintage	F	VF	XF	Unc	BU
2005P Proof	800	Value: 675				

KM# 892 30 DOLLARS
1002.5020 g., 0.9990 Silver 32.197 oz. ASW, 101 mm.
Ruler: Elizabeth II **Obv:** Head with tiara right **Obv. Designer:** Ian Rank-Broadley **Rev:** Kookaburras on branch, no leaves

Date	Mintage	F	VF	XF	Unc	BU
2007	—	—	—	—	650	—

KM# 1115 30 DOLLARS
1000.0000 g., 0.9990 Silver 32.117 oz. ASW, 101 mm.
Ruler: Elizabeth II **Rev:** Kookaburra on branch, sunburst background **Rev. Designer:** Darryl Bettolli

Date	Mintage	F	VF	XF	Unc	BU
2009P Proof	—	Value: 700				

KM# 878 200 DOLLARS
31.6000 g., 0.9990 Silver 1.0149 oz. ASW, 40 mm.
Ruler: Elizabeth II **Obv:** Head with tiara right with denomination **Obv. Designer:** Ian Rank-Broadley **Rev:** Kookaburra in flight over map of Australia **Note:** Mule.

Date	Mintage	F	VF	XF	Unc	BU
ND(2001) Proof	Est. 20	Value: 2,500				

BULLION - KOALA

KM# 916 5 DOLLARS
1.5710 g., 0.9990 Platinum 0.0505 oz. APW **Ruler:** Elizabeth II **Obv:** Head with tiara right **Obv. Designer:** Ian Rank-Broadley **Rev:** Two koalas on branch

Date	Mintage	F	VF	XF	Unc	BU
2001 Proof	5,000	Value: 90.00				

KM# 917 15 DOLLARS
3.1101 g., 0.9990 Platinum 0.0999 oz. APW **Ruler:** Elizabeth II **Obv:** Head with tiara right **Obv. Designer:** Ian Rank-Broadley **Rev:** Two koalas on a branch

Date	Mintage	F	VF	XF	Unc	BU
2001 Proof	650	Value: 180				

KM# 922 15 DOLLARS
3.1101 g., 0.9990 Platinum 0.0999 oz. APW **Ruler:** Elizabeth II **Obv:** Head with tiara right **Obv. Designer:** Ian Rank-Broadley **Rev:** Koala up a gum tree

Date	Mintage	F	VF	XF	Unc	BU
2002 Proof	650	Value: 180				

KM# 926 15 DOLLARS
3.1101 g., 0.9990 Platinum 0.0999 oz. APW **Ruler:** Elizabeth II **Obv:** Head with tiara right **Obv. Designer:** Ian Rank-Broadley **Rev:** Mother and baby koala

Date	Mintage	F	VF	XF	Unc	BU
2003 Proof	500	Value: 180				

KM# 931 15 DOLLARS
3.1101 g., 0.9990 Platinum 0.0999 oz. APW **Ruler:** Elizabeth II **Obv:** Head with tiara right **Obv. Designer:** Ian Rank-Broadley **Rev:** Single koala on branch

Date	Mintage	F	VF	XF	Unc	BU
2004 Proof	500	Value: 180				

KM# 935 15 DOLLARS
3.1101 g., 0.9990 Platinum 0.0999 oz. APW **Ruler:** Elizabeth II **Obv:** Head with tiara right **Obv. Designer:** Ian Rank-Broadley **Rev:** Single koala with gum leaves

Date	Mintage	F	VF	XF	Unc	BU
2005 Proof	500	Value: 180				

KM# 918 25 DOLLARS
7.7508 g., 0.9990 Platinum 0.2489 oz. APW **Ruler:** Elizabeth II **Obv:** Head with tiara right **Obv. Designer:** Ian Rank-Broadley **Rev:** Two koalas on a branch

Date	Mintage	F	VF	XF	Unc	BU
2001 Proof	275	Value: 475				

KM# 923 25 DOLLARS
7.7508 g., 0.9990 Platinum 0.2489 oz. APW **Ruler:** Elizabeth II **Obv:** Head with tiara right **Obv. Designer:** Ian Rank-Broadley **Rev:** Koala up a gum tree

Date	Mintage	F	VF	XF	Unc	BU
2002 Proof	275	Value: 475				

KM# 927 25 DOLLARS
7.7508 g., 0.9990 Platinum 0.2489 oz. APW **Ruler:** Elizabeth II **Obv:** Head with tiara right **Obv. Designer:** Ian Rank-Broadley **Rev:** Mother and baby koala

Date	Mintage	F	VF	XF	Unc	BU
2003 Proof	200	Value: 475				

KM# 932 25 DOLLARS
7.7508 g., 0.9990 Platinum 0.2489 oz. APW **Ruler:** Elizabeth II **Obv:** Head with tiara right **Obv. Designer:** Ian Rank-Broadley **Rev:** Single koala on branch

Date	Mintage	F	VF	XF	Unc	BU
2004 Proof	200	Value: 475				

KM# 936 25 DOLLARS
7.7508 g., 0.9990 Platinum 0.2489 oz. APW **Ruler:** Elizabeth II **Obv:** Head with tiara right **Obv. Designer:** Ian Rank-Broadley **Rev:** Single koala with gum leaves

Date	Mintage	F	VF	XF	Unc	BU
2005 Proof	200	Value: 450				

KM# 919 50 DOLLARS
15.5017 g., 0.9990 Platinum 0.4979 oz. APW **Ruler:** Elizabeth II **Obv:** Head with tiara right **Obv. Designer:** Ian Rank-Broadley **Rev:** Two koalas on a branch

Date	Mintage	F	VF	XF	Unc	BU
2001 Proof	350	Value: 850				

KM# 924 50 DOLLARS
15.5017 g., 0.9990 Platinum 0.4979 oz. APW **Ruler:** Elizabeth II **Obv:** Head with tiara right **Obv. Designer:** Ian Rank-Broadley **Rev:** Koala up a gum tree

Date	Mintage	F	VF	XF	Unc	BU
2002 Proof	350	Value: 850				

KM# 928 50 DOLLARS
15.5017 g., 0.9990 Platinum 0.4979 oz. APW **Ruler:** Elizabeth II **Obv:** Head with tiara right **Obv. Designer:** Ian Rank-Broadley **Rev:** Mother and baby koala

Date	Mintage	F	VF	XF	Unc	BU
2003 Proof	350	Value: 850				

KM# 933 50 DOLLARS
15.5017 g., 0.9990 Platinum 0.4979 oz. APW **Ruler:** Elizabeth II **Obv:** Head with tiara right **Obv. Designer:** Ian Rank-Broadley **Rev:** Single koala on branch

Date	Mintage	F	VF	XF	Unc	BU
2004 Proof	350	Value: 850				

KM# 937 50 DOLLARS
15.5017 g., 0.9990 Platinum 0.4979 oz. APW **Ruler:** Elizabeth II **Obv:** Head with tiara right **Obv. Designer:** Ian Rank-Broadley **Rev:** Single koala with gum leaves

Date	Mintage	F	VF	XF	Unc	BU
2005 Proof	350	Value: 850				

KM# 921 100 DOLLARS
31.1035 g., 0.9990 Platinum 0.9990 oz. APW **Ruler:** Elizabeth II **Obv:** Head with tiara right **Obv. Designer:** Ian Rank-Broadley **Rev:** Federation: Sir Henry Parkes, flag, parliament house, colored image **Note:** Colored image.

Date	Mintage	F	VF	XF	Unc	BU
2001 Proof	1,000	Value: 1,700				

KM# 930 100 DOLLARS
31.1035 g., 0.9990 Platinum 0.9990 oz. APW **Ruler:** Elizabeth II **Obv:** Head with tiara right **Obv. Designer:** Ian Rank-Broadley **Rev:** The Arts: Dancers, paint brushes, opera house, colored image

Date	Mintage	F	VF	XF	Unc	BU
2003 Proof	1,000	Value: 1,700				

KM# 939 100 DOLLARS
31.1035 g., 0.9990 Platinum 0.9990 oz. APW **Ruler:** Elizabeth II **Obv:** Head with tiara right **Obv. Designer:** Ian Rank-Broadley **Rev:** Two workers and machine, colored image

Date	Mintage	F	VF	XF	Unc	BU
2005 Proof	1,000	Value: 1,700				

KM# 920 200 DOLLARS
62.2140 g., 0.9990 Platinum 1.9981 oz. APW **Ruler:** Elizabeth II **Obv:** Head with tiara right **Obv. Designer:** Ian Rank-Broadley **Rev:** Two koalas sitting on branch

Date	Mintage	F	VF	XF	Unc	BU
2001	250	Value: 3,300				

KM# 925 200 DOLLARS
62.2140 g., 0.9990 Platinum 1.9981 oz. APW **Ruler:** Elizabeth II **Obv:** Head with tiara right **Obv. Designer:** Ian Rank-Broadley **Rev:** Koala up a gum tree

Date	Mintage	F	VF	XF	Unc	BU
2002 Proof	250	Value: 3,300				

KM# 929 200 DOLLARS
62.2140 g., 0.9990 Platinum 1.9981 oz. APW **Ruler:** Elizabeth II **Obv:** Head with tiara right **Obv. Designer:** Ian Rank-Broadley **Rev:** Mother and baby koala

Date	Mintage	F	VF	XF	Unc	BU
2003 Proof	200	Value: 3,300				

KM# 934 200 DOLLARS
62.2140 g., 0.9990 Platinum 1.9981 oz. APW **Ruler:** Elizabeth II **Obv:** Head with tiara right **Obv. Designer:** Ian Rank-Broadley **Rev:** Single koala on branch

Date	Mintage	F	VF	XF	Unc	BU
2004 Proof	200	Value: 3,300				

KM# 938 200 DOLLARS
62.2140 g., 0.9990 Platinum 1.9981 oz. APW **Ruler:** Elizabeth II **Obv:** Head with tiara right **Obv. Designer:** Ian Rank-Broadley **Rev:** Single koala with gum leaves

Date	Mintage	F	VF	XF	Unc	BU
2005 Proof	200	Value: 3,300				

BULLION - DISCOVER AUSTRALIA

KM# 737 DOLLAR
31.1035 g., 0.9990 Silver 0.9990 oz. ASW, 40 mm. **Ruler:** Elizabeth II **Obv:** Head with tiara right **Rev:** Multicolor Antarctic view of Mawson Station and penguins **Edge:** Reeded

Date	Mintage	F	VF	XF	Unc	BU
2004P Proof	7,500	Value: 35.00				

KM# 1015 DOLLAR
31.6000 g., 0.9990 Silver 1.0149 oz. ASW, 40.5 mm.
Ruler: Elizabeth II **Subject:** 50th Anniversary Australian Territory **Obv:** Head with tiara right **Obv. Legend:** ELIZABETH II • AUSTRALIA **Obv. Designer:** Ian Rank-Broadley **Rev:** Red-footed Booby perched on a branch, multicolor **Rev. Legend:** COCOS (KEELING) ISLANDS **Edge:** Reeded

Date	Mintage	F	VF	XF	Unc	BU
2005P Proof	7,500	Value: 60.00				

KM# 1018 DOLLAR
31.7500 g., 0.9990 Silver 1.0197 oz. ASW, 40.5 mm.
Ruler: Elizabeth II **Obv:** Head with tiara right **Obv. Legend:** ELIZABETH II - AUSTRALIA **Obv. Designer:** Ian Rank-Broadley **Rev:** Leopard seal with pup on ice, multicolor **Rev. Legend:** Australian Antarctic Territory **Edge:** Reeded

Date	Mintage	F	VF	XF	Unc	BU
2005P Proof	7,500	Value: 50.00				

KM# 1019 DOLLAR
31.3000 g., 0.9990 Silver 1.0053 oz. ASW, 40.5 mm.
Ruler: Elizabeth II **Subject:** 20th Anniversary of base **Obv:** Head with tiara right **Obv. Legend:** ELIZABETH II - AUSTRALIA **Obv. Designer:** Ian Rank-Broadley **Rev:** Plane above Albatross and chick on ice, multicolor **Rev. Legend:** Australian Antarctic Territory - EDGEWORTH DAVID BASE **Edge:** Reeded

Date	Mintage	F	VF	XF	Unc	BU
ND(2006)P Proof	7,500	Value: 50.00				

KM# 940 DOLLAR

31.1035 g., 0.9990 Silver 0.9990 oz. ASW **Ruler:** Elizabeth II **Subject:** Australian Landmarks **Obv:** Head with tiara right **Obv. Designer:** Ian Rank-Broadley **Rev:** Melbourne

Date	Mintage	F	VF	XF	Unc	BU
2006 Proof	7,500	Value: 35.00				

KM# 941 DOLLAR

31.1035 g., 0.9990 Silver 0.9990 oz. ASW **Ruler:** Elizabeth II **Subject:** Australian Landmarks **Obv:** Head with tiara right **Obv. Designer:** Ian Rank-Broadley **Rev:** Uluru

Date	Mintage	F	VF	XF	Unc	BU
2006 Proof	7,500	Value: 35.00				

KM# 942 DOLLAR

31.1035 g., 0.9990 Silver 0.9990 oz. ASW **Ruler:** Elizabeth II **Subject:** Australian Landmarks **Obv:** Head with tiara right **Obv. Designer:** Ian Rank-Broadley **Rev:** Canberra

Date	Mintage	F	VF	XF	Unc	BU
2006 Proof	7,500	Value: 35.00				

KM# 943 DOLLAR

31.1035 g., 0.9990 Silver 0.9990 oz. ASW **Ruler:** Elizabeth II **Subject:** Australian Landmarks **Obv:** Head with tiara right **Obv. Designer:** Ian Rank-Broadley **Rev:** Perth

Date	Mintage	F	VF	XF	Unc	BU
2006 Proof	7,500	Value: 35.00				

KM# 944 DOLLAR

31.1035 g., 0.9990 Silver 0.9990 oz. ASW **Ruler:** Elizabeth II **Subject:** Australian Landmarks **Obv:** Head with tiara right **Obv. Designer:** Ian Rank-Broadley **Rev:** Great Barrier Reef

Date	Mintage	F	VF	XF	Unc	BU
2006 Proof	7,500	Value: 35.00				

KM# 1008 DOLLAR

31.1030 g., 0.9990 Silver 0.9989 oz. ASW, 40.5 mm. **Ruler:** Elizabeth II **Subject:** Quadricentennial **Obv:** Head with tiara right **Obv. Legend:** ELIZABETH II - AUSTRALIA **Obv. Designer:** Ian Rank-Broadley **Rev:** Sailing ship at left, early map at right **Rev. Legend:** Australia on the Map

Date	Mintage	F	VF	XF	Unc	BU
ND(2006)	—	—	—	—	—	30.00

KM# 945 DOLLAR

31.1035 g., 0.9990 Silver 0.9990 oz. ASW **Ruler:** Elizabeth II **Subject:** Australian Landmarks **Obv:** Head with tiara right **Obv. Designer:** Ian Rank-Broadley **Rev:** Gold Coast

Date	Mintage	F	VF	XF	Unc	BU
2007 Proof	7,500	Value: 35.00				

KM# 946 DOLLAR

31.1035 g., 0.9990 Silver 0.9990 oz. ASW **Ruler:** Elizabeth II **Subject:** Australian Landmarks **Obv:** Head with tiara right **Obv. Designer:** Ian Rank-Broadley **Rev:** Phillip Island

Date	Mintage	F	VF	XF	Unc	BU
2007 Proof	7,500	Value: 35.00				

KM# 947 DOLLAR

31.1035 g., 0.9990 Silver 0.9990 oz. ASW **Ruler:** Elizabeth II **Subject:** Australian Landmarks **Obv:** Head with tiara right **Obv. Designer:** Ian Rank-Broadley **Rev:** Port Arthur

Date	Mintage	F	VF	XF	Unc	BU
2007 Proof	7,500	Value: 35.00				

KM# 948 DOLLAR

31.1035 g., 0.9990 Silver 0.9990 oz. ASW **Ruler:** Elizabeth II **Subject:** Australian Landmarks **Obv:** Head with tiara right **Obv. Designer:** Ian Rank-Broadley **Rev:** Adelaide

Date	Mintage	F	VF	XF	Unc	BU
2007 Proof	7,500	Value: 35.00				

KM# 949 DOLLAR

31.1035 g., 0.9990 Silver 0.9990 oz. ASW **Ruler:** Elizabeth II **Subject:** Australian Landmarks **Obv:** Head with tiara right **Obv. Designer:** Ian Rank-Broadley **Rev:** Sydney

Date	Mintage	F	VF	XF	Unc	BU
2007	7,500	Value: 35.00				

KM# 1020 DOLLAR

31.4800 g., 0.9990 Silver 1.0111 oz. ASW, 40.5 mm. **Ruler:** Elizabeth II **Subject:** 50th Anniversary of Station **Obv:** Head with tiara right **Obv. Legend:** ELIZABETH II - AUSTRALIA **Obv. Designer:** Ian Rank-Broadley **Rev:** Ship "Kista Dan", multicolor **Rev. Legend:** Australian Antarctic Territory - DAVIS STATION **Edge:** Reeded

Date	Mintage	F	VF	XF	Unc	BU
ND(2007)P Proof	7,500	Value: 50.00				

KM# 1021 DOLLAR

31.6000 g., Silver, 40.47 mm. **Ruler:** Elizabeth II **Series:** Discover Australia **Obv:** Head with tiara right **Rev:** Sydney opera and bridge, sky multicolor **Edge:** Reeded

Date	Mintage	F	VF	XF	Unc	BU
2007P Proof	—	Value: 60.00				

KM# 1181 DOLLAR

31.1050 g., 0.9990 Silver 0.9990 oz. ASW **Ruler:** Elizabeth II **Subject:** Darwin **Obv:** Head right **Obv. Designer:** Ian Rank-Broadley **Rev:** Harbor, multicolor **Rev. Legend:** DISCOVER AUSTRALIA

Date	Mintage	F	VF	XF	Unc	BU
2008P Proof	7,500	Value: 80.00				

KM# 1182 DOLLAR

31.1050 g., 0.9990 Silver 0.9990 oz. ASW **Ruler:** Elizabeth II **Subject:** Kakadl **Obv:** Head right **Obv. Designer:** Ian Rank-Broadley **Rev:** Crocodile and multicolor **Rev. Legend:** DISCOVER AUSTRALIA

Date	Mintage	F	VF	XF	Unc	BU
2008P Proof	7,500	Value: 80.00				

KM# 1183 DOLLAR

31.1050 g., 0.9990 Silver 0.9990 oz. ASW **Ruler:** Elizabeth II **Subject:** Brisbane **Obv:** Head right **Obv. Designer:** Ian Rank-Broadley **Rev:** Bridge and view **Rev. Legend:** DISCOVER AUSTRALIA

Date	Mintage	F	VF	XF	Unc	BU
2008P Proof	7,500	Value: 80.00				

KM# 1184 DOLLAR

31.1050 g., 0.9990 Silver 0.9990 oz. ASW **Ruler:** Elizabeth II **Subject:** Broome **Obv:** Head right **Obv. Designer:** Ian Rank-Broadley **Rev:** Seascape, pearls and multicolor **Rev. Legend:** DISCOVER AUSTRALIA

Date	Mintage	F	VF	XF	Unc	BU
2008P Proof	7,500	Value: 80.00				

KM# 1185 DOLLAR

31.1050 g., 0.9990 Silver 0.9990 oz. ASW **Ruler:** Elizabeth II **Subject:** Sydney **Obv:** Head right **Obv. Designer:** Ian Rank-Broadley **Rev:** Opera House, Harbor Bridge and multicolor **Rev. Legend:** DISCOVER AUSTRALIA

Date	Mintage	F	VF	XF	Unc	BU
2008P Proof	7,500	Value: 80.00				

KM# 1188 DOLLAR

1.2400 g., 0.9990 Gold 0.0398 oz. AGW, 14 mm. **Ruler:** Elizabeth II **Obv:** Head right **Obv. Designer:** Ian Rank-Broadley **Rev:** Brolga **Rev. Legend:** DISCOVER AUSTRALIA

Date	Mintage	F	VF	XF	Unc	BU
2008P Proof	25,000	Value: 100				

KM# 1212 DOLLAR

31.1050 g., 0.9990 Silver 0.9990 oz. ASW, 40.6 mm. **Ruler:** Elizabeth II **Obv:** Head right **Obv. Designer:** Ian Rank-Broadley **Rev:** Dreaming Kangaroo, multicolor **Rev. Legend:** DISCOVER AUSTRALIA **Rev. Designer:** Darryl Bellotti

Date	Mintage	F	VF	XF	Unc	BU
2009P Proof	10,000	Value: 90.00				

KM# 1213 DOLLAR

31.1050 g., 0.9990 Silver 0.9990 oz. ASW **Ruler:** Elizabeth II **Obv:** Head right **Obv. Designer:** Ian Rank-Broadley **Rev:** Dreaming dolphin, multicolor **Rev. Legend:** DISCOVER AUSTRALIA **Rev. Designer:** Darryl Bellotti **Shape:** 40.6

Date	Mintage	F	VF	XF	Unc	BU
2009P Proof	10,000	Value: 90.00				

KM# 1214 DOLLAR

31.1050 g., 0.9990 Silver 0.9990 oz. ASW, 40.6 mm. **Ruler:** Elizabeth II **Obv:** Head right **Obv. Designer:** Ian Rank-Broadley **Rev:** Dreaming king brown snake, multicolor **Rev. Legend:** DISCOVER AUSTRALIA **Rev. Designer:** Darryl Bellotti

Date	Mintage	F	VF	XF	Unc	BU
2009P Proof	10,000	Value: 90.00				

KM# 1215 DOLLAR

31.1050 g., 0.9990 Silver 0.9990 oz. ASW, 40.6 mm. **Ruler:** Elizabeth II **Obv:** Head right **Obv. Designer:** Ian Rank-Broadley **Rev:** Dreaming brolga, multicolor **Rev. Designer:** Darryl Berllotti

Date	Mintage	F	VF	XF	Unc	BU
2009P Proof	10,000	Value: 90.00				

KM# 1216 DOLLAR

31.1050 g., 0.9990 Silver 0.9990 oz. ASW, 40.6 mm. **Ruler:** Elizabeth II **Obv:** Head right **Obv. Designer:** Ian Rank-Broadley **Rev:** Dreaming Echidna, multicolor **Rev. Designer:** Darryl Berllotti

Date	Mintage	F	VF	XF	Unc	BU
2009P Proof	10,000	Value: 90.00				

KM# 1218 DOLLAR

1.2500 g., 0.9990 Gold 0.0401 oz. AGW, 14 mm. **Ruler:** Elizabeth II **Obv:** Head right **Obv. Designer:** Ian Rank-Broadley **Rev:** Dreaming dolphin **Rev. Designer:** Darryl Berttolli

Date	Mintage	F	VF	XF	Unc	BU
2009P Proof	25,000	Value: 125				

KM# 1222 DOLLAR

3.1100 g., 0.9990 Gold 0.0999 oz. AGW, 16 mm. **Ruler:** Elizabeth II **Obv:** Head right **Obv. Designer:** Ian Rank-Broadley **Rev:** Dreaming kangaroo **Rev. Designer:** Darryl Berttolli

Date	Mintage	F	VF	XF	Unc	BU
2009P Proof	2,500	Value: 175				

KM# 1242 DOLLAR

31.1050 g., 0.9990 Silver 0.9990 oz. ASW, 40.6 mm. **Ruler:** Elizabeth II **Subject:** Treasures of Australia **Obv:** Head right **Obv. Designer:** Ian Rank-Broadley **Rev:** Mountains **Note:** Insert container with 1 carat of diamonds.

Date	Mintage	F	VF	XF	Unc	BU
2009P Proof	7,500	Value: 110				

KM# 950 5 DOLLARS

1.2441 g., 0.9990 Gold 0.0400 oz. AGW **Ruler:** Elizabeth II **Subject:** Australian Fauna **Obv:** Head with tiara right **Obv. Designer:** Ian Rank-Broadley **Rev:** Saltwater Crocodile

Date	Mintage	F	VF	XF	Unc	BU
2006 Proof	25,000	Value: 75.00				

KM# 953 5 DOLLARS

1.2441 g., 0.9990 Gold 0.0400 oz. AGW **Ruler:** Elizabeth II **Subject:** Australian Fauna **Obv:** Head with tiara right **Obv. Designer:** Ian Rank-Broadley **Rev:** Grey kangaroo

Date	Mintage	F	VF	XF	Unc	BU
2006 Proof	25,000	Value: 75.00				

KM# 956 5 DOLLARS

1.2441 g., 0.9990 Gold 0.0400 oz. AGW **Ruler:** Elizabeth II **Subject:** Australian Fauna **Obv:** Head with tiara right **Obv. Designer:** Ian Rank-Broadley **Rev:** Emu

Date	Mintage	F	VF	XF	Unc	BU
2006 Proof	25,000	Value: 75.00				

KM# 959 5 DOLLARS

1.2441 g., 0.9990 Gold 0.0400 oz. AGW **Ruler:** Elizabeth II **Subject:** Australian Fauna **Obv:** Head with tiara right **Obv. Designer:** Ian Rank-Broadley **Rev:** Koala

Date	Mintage	F	VF	XF	Unc	BU
2006 Proof	25,000	Value: 75.00				

KM# 962 5 DOLLARS

1.2441 g., 0.9990 Gold 0.0400 oz. AGW **Ruler:** Elizabeth II **Subject:** Australian Fauna **Obv:** Head with tiara right **Obv. Designer:** Ian Rank-Broadley **Rev:** Kookaburra

Date	Mintage	F	VF	XF	Unc	BU
2006 Proof	25,000	Value: 75.00				

KM# 965 5 DOLLARS

1.2441 g., 0.9990 Gold 0.0400 oz. AGW **Ruler:** Elizabeth II **Subject:** Australian Fauna **Obv:** Head with tiara right **Obv. Designer:** Ian Rank-Broadley **Rev:** Echidna

Date	Mintage	F	VF	XF	Unc	BU
2007 Proof	25,000	Value: 75.00				

KM# 968 5 DOLLARS

1.2441 g., 0.9990 Gold 0.0400 oz. AGW **Ruler:** Elizabeth II **Subject:** Australian Fauna **Obv:** Head with tiara right **Obv. Designer:** Ian Rank-Broadley **Rev:** Common Wombat

Date	Mintage	F	VF	XF	Unc	BU
2007 Proof	25,000	Value: 75.00				

KM# 971 5 DOLLARS

1.2441 g., 0.9990 Gold 0.0400 oz. AGW **Ruler:** Elizabeth II **Subject:** Australian Fauna **Obv:** Head with tiara right **Obv. Designer:** Ian Rank-Broadley **Rev:** Tasmanian Devil

Date	Mintage	F	VF	XF	Unc	BU
2007 Proof	25,000	Value: 75.00				

KM# 974 5 DOLLARS

1.2441 g., 0.9990 Gold 0.0400 oz. AGW **Ruler:** Elizabeth II **Subject:** Australian Fauna **Obv:** Head with tiara right **Obv. Designer:** Ian Rank-Broadley **Rev:** Great White Shark

Date	Mintage	F	VF	XF	Unc	BU
2007 Proof	25,000	Value: 75.00				

KM# 977 5 DOLLARS

1.2441 g., 0.9990 Gold 0.0400 oz. AGW **Ruler:** Elizabeth II **Subject:** Australian Fauna **Obv:** Head with tiara right **Obv. Designer:** Ian Rank-Broadley **Rev:** Platypus

Date	Mintage	F	VF	XF	Unc	BU
2007 Proof	25,000	Value: 75.00				

KM# 1217 5 DOLLARS

1.2500 g., 0.9990 Gold 0.0401 oz. AGW, 14 mm. **Ruler:** Elizabeth II **Obv:** Head right **Obv. Designer:** Ian Rank-Broadley **Rev:** Dreaming kangaroo **Rev. Designer:** Darryl Berllotti

Date	Mintage	F	VF	XF	Unc	BU
2009P Proof	25,000	Value: 125				

KM# 1219 5 DOLLARS
1.2500 g., 0.9990 Gold 0.0401 oz. AGW, 14 mm. **Ruler:** Elizabeth II **Obv:** Head right **Obv. Designer:** Ian Rank-Broadley **Rev:** Dreaming king brown snake **Rev. Designer:** Darryl Berttolli

Date	Mintage	F	VF	XF	Unc	BU
2009P Proof	25,000	Value: 125				

KM# 1220 5 DOLLARS
1.2500 g., 0.9990 Gold 0.0401 oz. AGW, 14 mm. **Ruler:** Elizabeth II **Obv:** Head right **Obv. Designer:** Ian Rank-Broadley **Rev:** Dreaming brolga **Rev. Designer:** Darryl Berttolli

Date	Mintage	F	VF	XF	Unc	BU
2009P Proof	25,000	Value: 125				

KM# 1221 5 DOLLARS
1.2500 g., 0.9990 Gold 0.0401 oz. AGW, 14 mm. **Ruler:** Elizabeth II **Obv:** Head right **Obv. Designer:** Ian Rank-Broadley **Rev:** Dreaming Echidna **Rev. Designer:** Darryl Berttolli

Date	Mintage	F	VF	XF	Unc	BU
2009P Proof	25,000	Value: 125				

KM# 1224 5 DOLLARS
3.1100 g., 0.9990 Gold 0.0999 oz. AGW, 16 mm. **Ruler:** Elizabeth II **Obv:** Head right **Obv. Designer:** Ian Rank-Broadley **Rev:** Dreaming brown snake **Rev. Designer:** Darryl Berttolli

Date	Mintage	F	VF	XF	Unc	BU
2009P Proof	2,500	Value: 175				

KM# 1118 10 DOLLARS
1.2400 g., 0.9990 Gold 0.0398 oz. AGW, 14 mm. **Ruler:** Elizabeth II **Obv:** Bust right **Obv. Designer:** Ian-Rank-Broadley **Rev:** Saltwater crocodile **Rev. Legend:** Discover Australia

Date	Mintage	F	VF	XF	Unc	BU
2006P Proof	25,000	Value: 100				

KM# 1119 10 DOLLARS
1.2400 g., 0.9990 Gold 0.0398 oz. AGW, 14 mm. **Ruler:** Elizabeth II **Obv:** Head right **Obv. Designer:** Ian Rank-Broadley **Rev:** Grey Kangaroo **Rev. Legend:** DISCOVER AUSTRALIA

Date	Mintage	F	VF	XF	Unc	BU
2006P Proof	25,000	Value: 100				

KM# 1120 10 DOLLARS
1.2400 g., 0.9990 Gold 0.0398 oz. AGW, 14 mm. **Ruler:** Elizabeth II **Obv:** Head right **Obv. Designer:** Ian Rank-Broadley **Rev:** Emu **Rev. Legend:** DISCOVER AUSTRALIA

Date	Mintage	F	VF	XF	Unc	BU
2006P Proof	25,000	Value: 100				

KM# 1121 10 DOLLARS
1.2400 g., 0.9990 Gold 0.0398 oz. AGW, 14 mm. **Ruler:** Elizabeth II **Obv:** Head right **Obv. Designer:** Ian Rank-Broadley **Rev:** Koala **Rev. Legend:** DISCOVER AUSTRALIA

Date	Mintage	F	VF	XF	Unc	BU
2006P Proof	25,000	Value: 100				

KM# 1122 10 DOLLARS
1.2400 g., 0.9990 Gold 0.0398 oz. AGW, 14 mm. **Ruler:** Elizabeth II **Obv:** Head right **Obv. Designer:** Ian Rank-Broadley **Rev:** Kookaburra **Rev. Legend:** DISCOVER AUSTRALIA

Date	Mintage	F	VF	XF	Unc	BU
2006P Proof	25,000	Value: 100				

KM# 1133 10 DOLLARS
3.1000 g., 0.9990 Platinum 0.0996 oz. APW, 16 mm. **Ruler:** Elizabeth II **Obv:** Head right **Obv. Designer:** Ian rank-Broadley **Rev:** Cooktown orchid, multicolor **Rev. Legend:** DISCOVER AUSTRALIA

Date	Mintage	F	VF	XF	Unc	BU
2006P Proof	2,500	Value: 325				

KM# 1134 10 DOLLARS
3.1000 g., 0.9990 Platinum 0.0996 oz. APW, 16 mm. **Ruler:** Elizabeth II **Obv:** Head right **Obv. Designer:** Ian Rank-Broadley **Rev:** Sturt's Desert Rose, multicolor **Rev. Legend:** DISCOVER AUSTRALIA

Date	Mintage	F	VF	XF	Unc	BU
2006P Proof	2,500	Value: 325				

KM# 1135 10 DOLLARS
3.1000 g., 0.9990 Platinum 0.0996 oz. APW, 16 mm. **Ruler:** Elizabeth II **Obv:** Head right **Obv. Designer:** Ian Rank-Broadley **Rev:** Royal Bluebell, multicolor **Rev. Legend:** DISCOVER AUSTRALIA

Date	Mintage	F	VF	XF	Unc	BU
2006P Proof	2,500	Value: 325				

KM# 1136 10 DOLLARS
3.1000 g., 0.9990 Platinum 0.0996 oz. APW, 16 mm. **Ruler:** Elizabeth II **Obv:** Head right **Obv. Designer:** Ian Rank-Broadley **Rev:** Red and green kangaroo paw, multicolor **Rev. Legend:** DISCOVER AUSTRALIA

Date	Mintage	F	VF	XF	Unc	BU
2006P Proof	2,500	Value: 325				

KM# 1137 10 DOLLARS
3.1000 g., 0.9990 Platinum 0.0996 oz. APW, 16 mm. **Ruler:** Elizabeth II **Obv:** Head right **Obv. Designer:** Ian Rank-Broadley **Rev:** Common pink heath, multicolor **Rev. Legend:** DISCOVER AUSTRALIA

Date	Mintage	F	VF	XF	Unc	BU
2006P Proof	2,500	Value: 325				

KM# 1143 10 DOLLARS
1.2400 g., 0.9990 Gold 0.0398 oz. AGW, 14 mm. **Ruler:** Elizabeth II **Obv:** Head right **Obv. Designer:** Ian Rank-Broadley **Rev:** Echidna **Rev. Legend:** DISCOVER AUSTRALIA

Date	Mintage	F	VF	XF	Unc	BU
2007P Proof	25,000	Value: 100				

KM# 1144 10 DOLLARS
1.2400 g., 0.9990 Gold 0.0398 oz. AGW, 14 mm. **Ruler:** Elizabeth II **Obv:** Head right **Obv. Designer:** Ian rank-Broadley **Rev:** Common wombat **Rev. Legend:** DISCOVER AUSTRALIA

Date	Mintage	F	VF	XF	Unc	BU
2007P Proof	25,000	Value: 100				

KM# 1145 10 DOLLARS
1.2400 g., 0.9990 Gold 0.0398 oz. AGW, 14 mm. **Ruler:** Elizabeth II **Obv:** Head right **Obv. Designer:** Ian Rank-Broadley **Rev:** Tasmanian devil **Rev. Legend:** DISCOVER AUSTRALIA

Date	Mintage	F	VF	XF	Unc	BU
2007P Proof	25,000	Value: 100				

KM# 1146 10 DOLLARS
1.2400 g., 0.9990 Gold 0.0398 oz. AGW, 14 mm. **Ruler:** Elizabeth II **Obv:** Head right **Obv. Designer:** Ian rank-Broadley **Rev:** Great white shark **Rev. Legend:** DISCOVER AUSTRALIA

Date	Mintage	F	VF	XF	Unc	BU
2007P Proof	25,000	Value: 100				

KM# 1147 10 DOLLARS
1.2400 g., 0.9990 Gold 0.0398 oz. AGW, 14 mm. **Ruler:** Elizabeth II **Obv:** Head right **Obv. Designer:** Ian Rank-Broadley **Rev:** Platypus **Rev. Legend:** DISCOVER AUSTRALIA

Date	Mintage	F	VF	XF	Unc	BU
2007P Proof	25,000	Value: 100				

KM# 1159 10 DOLLARS
3.1000 g., 0.9990 Platinum 0.0996 oz. APW, 16 mm. **Ruler:** Elizabeth II **Obv:** Head right **Obv. Designer:** Ian Rank-Broadley **Rev:** Sturt's desert pea, multicolor **Rev. Legend:** DISCOVER AUSTRALIA

Date	Mintage	F	VF	XF	Unc	BU
2007P Proof	2,500	Value: 325				

KM# 1160 10 DOLLARS
3.1000 g., 0.9990 Platinum 0.0996 oz. APW, 16 mm. **Ruler:** Elizabeth II **Obv:** Head right **Obv. Designer:** Ian rank-Broadley **Rev:** Tasmanian bluegum, multicolor **Rev. Legend:** DISCOVER AUSTRALIA

Date	Mintage	F	VF	XF	Unc	BU
2007P Proof	2,500	Value: 325				

KM# 1161 10 DOLLARS
3.1000 g., 0.9990 Platinum 0.0996 oz. APW, 16 mm. **Ruler:** Elizabeth II **Obv:** Head right **Obv. Designer:** Ian Rank-Broadley **Rev:** Waratah, multicolor **Rev. Legend:** DISCOVER AUSTRALIA

Date	Mintage	F	VF	XF	Unc	BU
2007P Proof	2,500	Value: 325				

KM# 1162 10 DOLLARS
3.1000 g., 0.9990 Platinum 0.0996 oz. APW, 16 mm. **Ruler:** Elizabeth II **Obv:** Head right **Obv. Designer:** Ian Rank-Broadley **Rev:** Golden wattle, multicolor **Rev. Legend:** DISCOVER AUSTRALIA

Date	Mintage	F	VF	XF	Unc	BU
2007P Proof	2,500	Value: 325				

KM# 1186 10 DOLLARS
1.2400 g., 0.9990 Gold 0.0398 oz. AGW, 14 mm. **Ruler:** Elizabeth II **Obv:** Head right **Obv. Designer:** Ian Rank-Broadley **Rev:** Dolphin **Rev. Legend:** DISCOVER AUSTRALIA

Date	Mintage	F	VF	XF	Unc	BU
2008P Proof	25,000	Value: 100				

KM# 1187 10 DOLLARS
1.2400 g., 0.9990 Gold 0.0398 oz. AGW, 14 mm. **Ruler:** Elizabeth II **Obv:** Head right **Obv. Designer:** Ian Rank-Broadley **Rev:** King brown snake **Rev. Legend:** DISCOVER AUSTRALIA

Date	Mintage	F	VF	XF	Unc	BU
2008P Proof	25,000	Value: 100				

KM# 1189 10 DOLLARS
1.2400 g., 0.9990 Gold 0.0398 oz. AGW, 14 mm. **Ruler:** Elizabeth II **Obv:** Head right **Obv. Designer:** Ian Rank-Broadley **Rev:** Dingo **Rev. Legend:** DISCOVER AUSTRALIA

Date	Mintage	F	VF	XF	Unc	BU
2008P Proof	25,000	Value: 100				

KM# 1190 10 DOLLARS
1.2400 g., 0.9990 Gold 0.0398 oz. AGW, 14 mm. **Ruler:** Elizabeth II **Obv:** Head right **Obv. Designer:** Ian Rank-Broadley **Rev:** Frilled neck lizard **Rev. Legend:** DISCOVER AUSTRALIA

Date	Mintage	F	VF	XF	Unc	BU
2008P Proof	25,000	Value: 100				

KM# 1201 10 DOLLARS
3.1000 g., 0.9990 Platinum 0.0996 oz. APW, 16 mm. **Ruler:** Elizabeth II **Obv:** Head right **Obv. Designer:** Ian Rank-Broadley **Rev:** Black anther fax lilly, multicolor **Rev. Legend:** DISCOVER AUSTRALIA

Date	Mintage	F	VF	XF	Unc	BU
2008P Proof	2,500	Value: 325				

KM# 1202 10 DOLLARS
3.1000 g., 0.9990 Platinum 0.0996 oz. APW, 16 mm. **Ruler:** Elizabeth II **Obv:** Head right **Obv. Designer:** Ian Rank-Broadley **Rev:** Native frangipani, multicolor **Rev. Legend:** DISCOVER AUSTRALIA

Date	Mintage	F	VF	XF	Unc	BU
2008P Proof	2,500	Value: 325				

KM# 1203 10 DOLLARS
3.1000 g., 0.9990 Platinum 0.0996 oz. APW, 16 mm. **Ruler:** Elizabeth II **Obv:** Head right **Obv. Designer:** DISCOVER AUSTRALIA **Rev:** Geraldton wax, multicolor **Rev. Designer:** Ian Rank-Broadley

Date	Mintage	F	VF	XF	Unc	BU
2008P Proof	2,500	Value: 325				

KM# 1204 10 DOLLARS
3.1000 g., 0.9990 Platinum 0.0996 oz. APW, 16 mm. **Ruler:** Elizabeth II **Obv:** Head right **Obv. Designer:** Ian Rank-Broadley **Rev:** Red flowered kurrajong, multicolor **Rev. Legend:** DISCOVER AUSTRALIA

Date	Mintage	F	VF	XF	Unc	BU
2008P Proof	2,500	Value: 325				

KM# 1205 10 DOLLARS
3.1000 g., 0.9990 Platinum 0.0996 oz. APW, 16 mm. **Ruler:** Elizabeth II **Obv:** Head right **Obv. Designer:** Ian Rank-Broadley **Rev:** Small leaf lilly pilly, multicolor **Rev. Legend:** DISCOVER AUSTRALIA

Date	Mintage	F	VF	XF	Unc	BU
2008P Proof	2,500	Value: 325				

KM# 1206 10 DOLLARS
15.5500 g., 0.9990 Gold 0.4994 oz. AGW, 26 mm. **Ruler:** Elizabeth II **Obv:** Head right **Obv. Designer:** Ian Rank-Broadley **Rev:** Black anther flax lilly, multicolor **Rev. Legend:** DISCOVER AUSTRALIA

Date	Mintage	F	VF	XF	Unc	BU
2008P Proof	1,000	Value: 1,500				

KM# 980 15 DOLLARS
3.1101 g., 0.9990 Platinum 0.0999 oz. APW **Ruler:** Elizabeth II **Subject:** Australian Flora **Obv:** Head with tiara right **Obv. Designer:** Ian Rank-Broadley **Rev:** Cooktown Orchid

Date	Mintage	F	VF	XF	Unc	BU
2006 Proof	2,500	Value: 195				

KM# 982 15 DOLLARS
3.1101 g., 0.9990 Platinum 0.0999 oz. APW **Ruler:** Elizabeth II **Subject:** Australian Flora **Obv:** Head with tiara right **Obv. Designer:** Ian Rank-Broadley **Rev:** Sturt's Desert Rose

Date	Mintage	F	VF	XF	Unc	BU
2006 Proof	2,500	Value: 195				

KM# 984 15 DOLLARS
3.1101 g., 0.9990 Platinum 0.0999 oz. APW **Ruler:** Elizabeth II **Subject:** Australian Flora **Obv:** Head with tiara right **Obv. Designer:** Ian Rank-Broadley **Rev:** Royal Bluebell

Date	Mintage	F	VF	XF	Unc	BU
2006 Proof	2,500	Value: 195				

KM# 986 15 DOLLARS
3.1101 g., 0.9990 Platinum 0.0999 oz. APW **Ruler:** Elizabeth II **Subject:** Australian Flora **Obv:** Head with tiara right **Obv. Designer:** Ian Rank-Broadley **Rev:** Kangaroo Paw

Date	Mintage	F	VF	XF	Unc	BU
2006 Proof	2,500	Value: 195				

KM# 988 15 DOLLARS
3.1101 g., 0.9990 Platinum 0.0999 oz. APW **Ruler:** Elizabeth II **Subject:** Australian Flora **Obv:** Head with tiara right **Obv. Designer:** Ian Rank-Broadley **Rev:** Common Pink Heath

Date	Mintage	F	VF	XF	Unc	BU
2006 Proof	2,500	Value: 195				

KM# 951 15 DOLLARS
3.1101 g., 0.9990 Gold 0.0999 oz. AGW **Ruler:** Elizabeth II **Subject:** Australian Fauna **Obv:** Head with tiara right **Obv. Designer:** Ian Rank-Broadley **Rev:** Saltwater Crocodile

Date	Mintage	F	VF	XF	Unc	BU
2006 Proof	2,500	Value: 145				

KM# 954 15 DOLLARS
3.1101 g., 0.9990 Gold 0.0999 oz. AGW **Ruler:** Elizabeth II **Subject:** Australian Fauna **Obv:** Head with tiara right **Obv. Designer:** Ian Rank-Broadley **Rev:** Grey kangaroo

Date	Mintage	F	VF	XF	Unc	BU
2006 Proof	2,500	Value: 145				

KM# 957 15 DOLLARS
3.1101 g., 0.9990 Gold 0.0999 oz. AGW **Ruler:** Elizabeth II **Subject:** Australian Fauna **Obv:** Head with tiara right **Obv. Designer:** Ian Rank-Broadley **Rev:** Emu

Date	Mintage	F	VF	XF	Unc	BU
2006 Proof	2,500	Value: 145				

KM# 960 15 DOLLARS
3.1101 g., 0.9990 Gold 0.0999 oz. AGW **Ruler:** Elizabeth II **Subject:** Australian Fauna **Obv:** Head with tiara right **Obv. Designer:** Ian Rank-Broadley **Rev:** Koala

Date	Mintage	F	VF	XF	Unc	BU
2006 Proof	2,500	Value: 145				

KM# 963 15 DOLLARS
3.1101 g., 0.9990 Gold 0.0999 oz. AGW **Ruler:** Elizabeth II **Subject:** Australian Fauna **Obv:** Head with tiara right **Obv. Designer:** Ian Rank-Broadley **Rev:** Kookaburra

Date	Mintage	F	VF	XF	Unc	BU
2006 Proof	2,500	Value: 145				

KM# 966 15 DOLLARS
3.1101 g., 0.9990 Gold 0.0999 oz. AGW **Ruler:** Elizabeth II **Subject:** Australian Fauna **Obv:** Head with tiara right **Obv. Designer:** Ian Rank-Broadley **Rev:** Echidna

Date	Mintage	F	VF	XF	Unc	BU
2007 Proof	2,500	Value: 145				

KM# 969 15 DOLLARS
3.1101 g., 0.9990 Gold 0.0999 oz. AGW **Ruler:** Elizabeth II **Subject:** Australian Fauna **Obv:** Head with tiara right **Obv. Designer:** Ian Rank-Broadley **Rev:** Common Wombat

Date	Mintage	F	VF	XF	Unc	BU
2007 Proof	2,500	Value: 145				

KM# 972 15 DOLLARS
3.1101 g., 0.9990 Gold 0.0999 oz. AGW **Ruler:** Elizabeth II **Subject:** Australian Fauna **Obv:** Head with tiara right **Obv. Designer:** Ian Rank-Broadley **Rev:** Tasmanian Devil

Date	Mintage	F	VF	XF	Unc	BU
2007 Proof	2,500	Value: 145				

KM# 975 15 DOLLARS
3.1101 g., 0.9990 Gold 0.0999 oz. AGW **Ruler:** Elizabeth II **Subject:** Australian Fauna **Obv:** Head with tiara right **Obv. Designer:** Ian Rank-Broadley **Rev:** Great White Shark

Date	Mintage	F	VF	XF	Unc	BU
2007 Proof	2,500	Value: 145				

KM# 978 15 DOLLARS
3.1101 g., 0.9990 Gold 0.0999 oz. AGW **Ruler:** Elizabeth II **Subject:** Australian Fauna **Obv:** Head with tiara right **Obv. Designer:** Ian Rank-Broadley **Rev:** Platypus

Date	Mintage	F	VF	XF	Unc	BU
2007 Proof	2,500	Value: 145				

KM# 990 15 DOLLARS
3.1101 g., 0.9990 Platinum 0.0999 oz. APW **Ruler:** Elizabeth II **Subject:** Australian Flora **Obv:** Head with tiara right **Obv. Designer:** Ian Rank-Broadley **Rev:** Anemone Buttercup

Date	Mintage	F	VF	XF	Unc	BU
2007 Proof	2,500	Value: 195				

KM# 992 15 DOLLARS
3.1101 g., 0.9990 Platinum 0.0999 oz. APW **Ruler:** Elizabeth II **Subject:** Australian Flora **Obv:** Head with tiara right **Obv. Designer:** Ian Rank-Broadley **Rev:** Sturt's Desert Pea

Date	Mintage	F	VF	XF	Unc	BU
2007 Proof	2,500	Value: 195				

KM# 994 15 DOLLARS
3.1101 g., 0.9990 Platinum 0.0999 oz. APW **Ruler:** Elizabeth II **Subject:** Australian Flora **Obv:** Head with tiara right **Obv. Designer:** Ian Rank-Broadley **Rev:** Tasmanian Bluegum

Date	Mintage	F	VF	XF	Unc	BU
2007 Proof	2,500	Value: 195				

KM# 996 15 DOLLARS
3.1101 g., 0.9990 Platinum 0.0999 oz. APW **Ruler:** Elizabeth II **Subject:** Australian Flora **Obv:** Head with tiara right **Obv. Designer:** Ian Rank-Broadley **Rev:** Waratah

Date	Mintage	F	VF	XF	Unc	BU
2007 Proof	2,500	Value: 195				

KM# 998 15 DOLLARS
3.1101 g., 0.9990 Platinum 0.0999 oz. APW **Ruler:** Elizabeth II **Subject:** Australian Flora **Obv:** Head with tiara right **Obv. Designer:** Ian Rank-Broadley **Rev:** Golden Wattle

Date	Mintage	F	VF	XF	Unc	BU
2007 Proof	2,500	Value: 195				

KM# 1223 15 DOLLARS
3.1100 g., 0.9990 Gold 0.0999 oz. AGW, 16 mm. **Ruler:** Elizabeth II **Obv:** Head right **Obv. Designer:** Ian Rank-Broadley **Rev:** Dreaming dolphin **Rev. Designer:** Darryl Berttolli

Date	Mintage	F	VF	XF	Unc	BU
2009P Proof	2,500	Value: 175				

KM# 1225 15 DOLLARS
3.1100 g., 0.9990 Gold 0.0999 oz. AGW, 16 mm. **Ruler:** Elizabeth II **Obv:** Head right **Obv. Designer:** Ian Rank-Broadley **Rev:** Dreaming brolga **Rev. Designer:** Darryl Berttolli

Date	Mintage	F	VF	XF	Unc	BU
2009P Proof	2,500	Value: 175				

KM# 1226 15 DOLLARS
3.1100 g., 0.9990 Gold 0.0999 oz. AGW, 16 mm. **Ruler:** Elizabeth II **Obv:** Head right **Obv. Designer:** Ian Rank-Broadley **Rev:** Dreaming echidna **Rev. Designer:** Darryl Berttolli

Date	Mintage	F	VF	XF	Unc	BU
2009P Proof	2,500	Value: 175				

KM# 1228 15 DOLLARS
15.5500 g., 0.9990 Gold 0.4994 oz. AGW, 25 mm. **Ruler:** Elizabeth II **Obv:** Head right **Obv. Designer:** Ian Rank-Broadley **Rev:** Dreaming dolphin **Rev. Designer:** Darryl Berttolli

Date	Mintage	F	VF	XF	Unc	BU
2009P Proof	1,000	Value: 1,100				

KM# 1232 15 DOLLARS
3.1100 g., 0.9990 Platinum 0.0999 oz. APW, 16 mm. **Ruler:** Elizabeth II **Obv:** Head right **Obv. Designer:** Ian Rank-Broadley **Rev:** Dreaming kangaroo, multicolor **Rev. Designer:** Darryl Berttolli

Date	Mintage	F	VF	XF	Unc	BU
2009P Proof	2,500	Value: 400				

KM# 1233 15 DOLLARS
3.1100 g., 0.9990 Platinum 0.0999 oz. APW, 16 mm. **Ruler:** Elizabeth II **Obv:** Head right **Obv. Designer:** Ian Rank-Broadley **Rev:** Dreaming dolphin, multicolor **Rev. Designer:** Darryl Berttolli

Date	Mintage	F	VF	XF	Unc	BU
2009P Proof	2,500	Value: 400				

KM# 1234 15 DOLLARS
3.1100 g., 0.9990 Platinum 0.0999 oz. APW, 16 mm. **Ruler:** Elizabeth II **Obv:** Head right **Obv. Designer:** Ian Rank-Broadley **Rev:** Dreaming king brown snake, multicolor **Rev. Designer:** Darryl Berttolli

Date	Mintage	F	VF	XF	Unc	BU
2009P Proof	2,500	Value: 400				

KM# 1235 15 DOLLARS
3.1100 g., 0.9990 Platinum 0.0999 oz. APW, 16 mm. **Ruler:** Elizabeth II **Obv:** Head right **Obv. Designer:** Ian Rank-Broadley **Rev:** Dreaming brolga **Rev. Designer:** Darryl Berttolli

Date	Mintage	F	VF	XF	Unc	BU
2009P Proof	2,500	Value: 400				

KM# 1236 15 DOLLARS
3.1100 g., 0.9990 Platinum 0.0999 oz. APW, 16 mm. **Ruler:** Elizabeth II **Obv:** Head right **Obv. Designer:** Ian Rank-Broadley **Rev:** Dreaming echidna, multicolor **Rev. Designer:** Darryl Berttolli

Date	Mintage	F	VF	XF	Unc	BU
2009P Proof	2,500	Value: 400				

KM# 1127 25 DOLLARS
3.1000 g., 0.9990 Gold 0.0996 oz. AGW, 15.5 mm. **Ruler:** Elizabeth II **Obv:** Head right **Obv. Designer:** Ian Rank-Broadley **Rev:** Kookaburra **Rev. Legend:** DISCOVER AUSTRALIA

Date	Mintage	F	VF	XF	Unc	BU
2006P Proof	2,500	Value: 185				

KM# 1123 25 DOLLARS
3.1000 g., 0.9990 Gold 0.0996 oz. AGW, 15.5 mm. **Ruler:** Elizabeth II **Obv:** Head right **Obv. Designer:** Ian Rank-Broadley **Rev:** Saltwater crocodile **Rev. Legend:** DISCOVER AUSTRALIA

Date	Mintage	F	VF	XF	Unc	BU
2006P Proof	2,500	Value: 185				

KM# 1124 25 DOLLARS
3.1000 g., 0.9990 Gold 0.0996 oz. AGW, 15.5 mm. **Ruler:** Elizabeth II **Obv:** Head right **Obv. Designer:** Ian Rank-Broadley **Rev:** Grey Kangaroo **Rev. Legend:** DISCOVER AUSTRALIA

Date	Mintage	F	VF	XF	Unc	BU
2006P Proof	2,500	Value: 185				

KM# 1125 25 DOLLARS
3.1000 g., 0.9990 Gold 0.0996 oz. AGW, 15.5 mm. **Ruler:** Elizabeth II **Obv:** Head right **Obv. Designer:** Ian Rank-Broadley **Rev:** Emu **Rev. Legend:** DISCOVER AUSTRALIA

Date	Mintage	F	VF	XF	Unc	BU
2006P Proof	2,500	Value: 185				

KM# 1126 25 DOLLARS
3.1000 g., 0.9990 Gold 0.0996 oz. AGW, 15.5 mm. **Ruler:** Elizabeth II **Obv:** Head right **Obv. Designer:** Ian Rank-Broadley **Rev:** Koala **Rev. Legend:** DISCOVER AUSTRALIA

Date	Mintage	F	VF	XF	Unc	BU
2006P Proof	2,500	Value: 185				

KM# 1148 25 DOLLARS
3.1000 g., 0.9990 Gold 0.0996 oz. AGW, 15.5 mm. **Ruler:** Elizabeth II **Obv:** Head right **Obv. Designer:** Ian Rank-Broadley **Rev:** Echinda **Rev. Legend:** DISCOVER AUSTRALIA

Date	Mintage	F	VF	XF	Unc	BU
2007P Proof	2,500	Value: 185				

KM# 1149 25 DOLLARS
3.1000 g., 0.9990 Gold 0.0996 oz. AGW, 15.5 mm. **Ruler:** Elizabeth II **Obv:** Head right **Obv. Designer:** Ian Rank-Broadley **Rev:** Common wombat **Rev. Legend:** DISCOVER AUSTRALIA

Date	Mintage	F	VF	XF	Unc	BU
2007P Proof	2,500	Value: 185				

KM# 1150 25 DOLLARS
3.1000 g., 0.9990 Gold 0.0996 oz. AGW, 15.5 mm. **Ruler:** Elizabeth II **Obv:** Head right **Obv. Designer:** Ian Rank-Braodley **Rev:** Tasmanian Devil **Rev. Legend:** DISCOVER AUSTRALIA

Date	Mintage	F	VF	XF	Unc	BU
2007P Proof	2,500	Value: 185				

KM# 1151 25 DOLLARS
3.1000 g., 0.9990 Gold 0.0996 oz. AGW, 15.5 mm. **Ruler:** Elizabeth II **Obv:** Head right **Obv. Designer:** Ian Rank-Broadley **Rev:** Great white shark **Rev. Legend:** DISCOVER AUSTRALIA

Date	Mintage	F	VF	XF	Unc	BU
2007P Proof	2,500	Value: 185				

KM# 1152 25 DOLLARS
3.1000 g., 0.9990 Gold 0.0996 oz. AGW, 15.5 mm. **Ruler:** Elizabeth II **Obv:** Head right **Obv. Designer:** Ian Rank-Broadley **Rev:** Platypus **Rev. Legend:** DISCOVER AUSTRALIA

Date	Mintage	F	VF	XF	Unc	BU
2007P Proof	2,500	Value: 185				

KM# 1158 25 DOLLARS
3.1000 g., 0.9990 Platinum 0.0996 oz. APW, 16 mm. **Ruler:** Elizabeth II **Obv:** Head right **Obv. Designer:** Ian Rank-Broadley **Rev:** Anemone buttercup, multicolor **Rev. Legend:** DISCOVER AUSTRALIA

Date	Mintage	F	VF	XF	Unc	BU
2007P Proof	2,500	Value: 325				

KM# 1191 25 DOLLARS
3.1000 g., 0.9990 Gold 0.0996 oz. AGW, 15.5 mm. **Ruler:** Elizabeth II **Obv:** Head right **Obv. Designer:** Ian Rank-Broadley **Rev:** Dolphin **Rev. Legend:** DISCOVER AUSTRALIA

Date	Mintage	F	VF	XF	Unc	BU
2008P Proof	2,500	Value: 185				

KM# 1192 25 DOLLARS
3.1000 g., 0.9990 Gold 0.0996 oz. AGW, 15.5 mm. **Ruler:** Elizabeth II **Obv:** Head right **Obv. Designer:** Ian Rank-Broadley **Rev:** King brown snake **Rev. Legend:** DISCOVER AUSTRALIA

Date	Mintage	F	VF	XF	Unc	BU
2008P Proof	2,500	Value: 185				

KM# 1193 25 DOLLARS
3.1000 g., 0.9990 Gold 0.0996 oz. AGW, 15.5 mm. **Ruler:** Elizabeth II **Obv:** Head right **Obv. Designer:** Ian Rank-Broadley **Rev:** Brolga **Rev. Legend:** DISCOVER AUSTRALIA

Date	Mintage	F	VF	XF	Unc	BU
2008P Proof	2,500	Value: 185				

KM# 1194 25 DOLLARS
3.1000 g., 0.9990 Gold 0.0996 oz. AGW, 15.5 mm. **Ruler:** Elizabeth II **Obv:** Head right **Obv. Designer:** Ian Rank-Broadley **Rev:** Dingo **Rev. Legend:** DISCOVER AUSTRALIA

Date	Mintage	F	VF	XF	Unc	BU
2008P Proof	2,500	Value: 185				

KM# 1195 25 DOLLARS
3.1000 g., 0.9990 Gold 0.0996 oz. AGW, 15.5 mm. **Ruler:** Elizabeth II **Obv:** Head right **Obv. Designer:** Ian Rank-Broadley **Rev:** Frilled neck lizard **Rev. Legend:** DISCOVER AUSTRALIA

Date	Mintage	F	VF	XF	Unc	BU
2008P Proof	2,500	Value: 185				

KM# 952 50 DOLLARS
15.5017 g., 0.9990 Gold 0.4979 oz. AGW **Ruler:** Elizabeth II **Subject:** Australian Fauna **Obv:** Head with tiara right **Obv. Designer:** Ian Rank-Broadley **Rev:** Saltwater Crocodile

Date	Mintage	F	VF	XF	Unc	BU
2006 Proof	1,000	Value: 650				

KM# 955 50 DOLLARS
15.5017 g., 0.9990 Gold 0.4979 oz. AGW **Ruler:** Elizabeth II **Subject:** Australian Fauna **Obv:** Head with tiara right **Obv. Designer:** Ian Rank-Broadley **Rev:** Grey kangaroo

Date	Mintage	F	VF	XF	Unc	BU
2006 Proof	1,000	Value: 650				

KM# 958 50 DOLLARS
15.5017 g., 0.9990 Gold 0.4979 oz. AGW **Ruler:** Elizabeth II **Subject:** Australian Fauna **Obv:** Head with tiara right **Obv. Designer:** Ian Rank-Broadley **Rev:** Emu

Date	Mintage	F	VF	XF	Unc	BU
2006 Proof	1,000	Value: 650				

KM# 961 50 DOLLARS
15.5017 g., 0.9990 Gold 0.4979 oz. AGW **Ruler:** Elizabeth II **Subject:** Australian Fauna **Obv:** Head with tiara right **Obv. Designer:** Ian Rank-Broadley **Rev:** Koala

Date	Mintage	F	VF	XF	Unc	BU
2006 Proof	1,000	Value: 650				

KM# 964 50 DOLLARS
15.5017 g., 0.9990 Gold 0.4979 oz. AGW **Ruler:** Elizabeth II **Subject:** Australian Fauna **Obv:** Head with tiara right **Obv. Designer:** Ian Rank-Broadley **Rev:** Kookaburra

Date	Mintage	F	VF	XF	Unc	BU
2006 Proof	1,000	Value: 650				

KM# 981 50 DOLLARS
15.5017 g., 0.9990 Platinum 0.4979 oz. APW **Ruler:** Elizabeth II **Subject:** Australian Flora **Obv:** Head with tiara right **Obv. Designer:** Ian Rank-Broadley **Rev:** Cooktown Orchid

Date	Mintage	F	VF	XF	Unc	BU
2006 Proof	1,000	Value: 975				

KM# 983 50 DOLLARS
15.5017 g., 0.9990 Gold 0.4979 oz. AGW **Ruler:** Elizabeth II **Subject:** Australian Flora **Obv:** Head with tiara right **Obv. Designer:** Ian Rank-Broadley **Rev:** Sturt's Desert Rose

Date	Mintage	F	VF	XF	Unc	BU
2006 Proof	1,000	Value: 975				

KM# 985 50 DOLLARS
15.5017 g., 0.9990 Platinum 0.4979 oz. APW **Ruler:** Elizabeth II **Subject:** Australian Flora **Obv:** Head with tiara right **Obv. Designer:** Ian Rank-Broadley **Rev:** Royal Bluebell

Date	Mintage	F	VF	XF	Unc	BU
2006 Proof	1,000	Value: 975				

KM# 987 50 DOLLARS
15.5017 g., 0.9990 Platinum 0.4979 oz. APW **Ruler:** Elizabeth II **Subject:** Australian Flora **Obv:** Head with tiara right **Obv. Designer:** Ian Rank-Broadley **Rev:** Kangaroo Paw

Date	Mintage	F	VF	XF	Unc	BU
2006 Proof	1,000	Value: 975				

KM# 989 50 DOLLARS
15.5017 g., 0.9990 Platinum 0.4979 oz. APW **Ruler:** Elizabeth II **Subject:** Australian Flora **Obv:** Head with tiara right **Obv. Designer:** Ian Rank-Broadley **Rev:** Common Pink Heath

Date	Mintage	F	VF	XF	Unc	BU
2006 Proof	1,000	Value: 975				

KM# 1128 50 DOLLARS
15.5500 g., 0.9990 Gold 0.4994 oz. AGW, 25 mm. **Ruler:** Elizabeth II **Obv:** Head right **Obv. Designer:** Ian Rank-Broadley **Rev:** Saltwater crocodile **Rev. Legend:** DISCOVER AUSTRALIA

Date	Mintage	F	VF	XF	Unc	BU
2006P Proof	1,000	Value: 800				

KM# 1129 50 DOLLARS
15.5500 g., 0.9990 Gold 0.4994 oz. AGW, 25 mm. **Ruler:** Elizabeth II **Obv:** Head right **Obv. Designer:** Ian Rank-Broadley **Rev:** Krey Kangaroo **Rev. Legend:** DISCOVER AUSTRALIA

Date	Mintage	F	VF	XF	Unc	BU
2006P Proof	1,000	Value: 800				

KM# 1130 50 DOLLARS
15.5500 g., 0.9990 Gold 0.4994 oz. AGW, 25 mm. **Ruler:** Elizabeth II **Obv:** Head right **Obv. Designer:** Ian Rank-Broadley **Rev:** Emu **Rev. Legend:** DISCOVER AUSTRALIA

Date	Mintage	F	VF	XF	Unc	BU
2006P Proof	1,000	Value: 800				

KM# 1131 50 DOLLARS
15.5500 g., 0.9990 Gold 0.4994 oz. AGW, 25 mm. **Ruler:** Elizabeth II **Obv:** Head right **Obv. Designer:** Ian Rank-Broadley **Rev:** Koala **Rev. Legend:** DISCOVER AUSTRALIA

Date	Mintage	F	VF	XF	Unc	BU
2006P Proof	1,000	Value: 800				

KM# 1132 50 DOLLARS
15.5500 g., 0.9990 Gold 0.4994 oz. AGW, 25 mm. **Ruler:** Elizabeth II **Obv:** Head right **Obv. Designer:** Ian Rank-Broadley **Rev:** Kookaburra **Rev. Legend:** DISCOVER AUSTRALIA

Date	Mintage	F	VF	XF	Unc	BU
2006P Proof	1,000	Value: 800				

KM# 1138 50 DOLLARS
15.5500 g., 0.9990 Platinum 0.4994 oz. APW, 26 mm. **Ruler:** Elizabeth II **Obv:** Head right **Obv. Designer:** Ian Rank-Broadley **Rev:** Cooktown orchid, multicolor **Rev. Legend:** DISCOVER AUSTRALIA

Date	Mintage	F	VF	XF	Unc	BU
2006P Proof	1,000	Value: 1,500				

KM# 1139 50 DOLLARS
15.5500 g., 0.9990 Platinum 0.4994 oz. APW, 26 mm.
Ruler: Elizabeth II **Obv:** Head right **Obv. Designer:** Ian rank-Broadley **Rev:** Sturt's desert rose, multicolor **Rev. Legend:** DISCOVER AUSTRALIA

Date	Mintage	F	VF	XF	Unc	BU
2006P Proof	1,000	Value: 1,500				

KM# 1140 50 DOLLARS
15.5500 g., 0.9990 Platinum 0.4994 oz. APW **Ruler:** Elizabeth II **Obv:** Head right **Obv. Designer:** Ian Rank-Broadley **Rev:** Royal bluebell, multicolor **Rev. Legend:** DISCOVER AUSTRALIA **Shape:** 26

Date	Mintage	F	VF	XF	Unc	BU
2006P Proof	1,000	Value: 1,500				

KM# 1141 50 DOLLARS
15.5500 g., 0.9990 Platinum 0.4994 oz. APW, 26 mm.
Ruler: Elizabeth II **Obv:** Head right **Obv. Designer:** Ian Rank-Broadley **Rev:** Red and green kangaroo paw, multicolor **Rev. Legend:** DISCOVER AUSTRALIA

Date	Mintage	F	VF	XF	Unc	BU
2006P Proof	1,000	Value: 1,500				

KM# 1142 50 DOLLARS
15.5500 g., 0.9990 Platinum 0.4994 oz. APW, 26 mm.
Ruler: Elizabeth II **Obv:** Head right **Obv. Designer:** Ian Rank-Broadley **Rev:** Common pink heath, multicolor **Rev. Legend:** DISCOVER AUSTRALIA

Date	Mintage	F	VF	XF	Unc	BU
2006P Proof	1,000	Value: 1,500				

KM# 991 50 DOLLARS
15.5017 g., 0.9990 Platinum 0.4979 oz. APW **Ruler:** Elizabeth II **Subject:** Australian Flora **Obv:** Head with tiara right **Obv. Designer:** Ian Rank-Broadley **Rev:** Anemone Buttercup

Date	Mintage	F	VF	XF	Unc	BU
2007 Proof	1,000	Value: 975				

KM# 993 50 DOLLARS
15.5017 g., 0.9990 Platinum 0.4979 oz. APW **Ruler:** Elizabeth II **Subject:** Australian Flora **Obv:** Head with tiara right **Obv. Designer:** Ian Rank-Broadley **Rev:** Sturt's Desert Pea

Date	Mintage	F	VF	XF	Unc	BU
2007 Proof	1,000	Value: 975				

KM# 995 50 DOLLARS
15.5017 g., 0.9990 Platinum 0.4979 oz. APW **Ruler:** Elizabeth II **Subject:** Australian Flora **Obv:** Head with tiara right **Obv. Designer:** Ian Rank-Broadley **Rev:** Tasmanian Bluegum

Date	Mintage	F	VF	XF	Unc	BU
2007 Proof	1,000	Value: 975				

KM# 997 50 DOLLARS
15.5017 g., 0.9990 Platinum 0.4979 oz. APW **Ruler:** Elizabeth II **Subject:** Australian Flora **Obv:** Head with tiara right **Obv. Designer:** Ian Rank-Broadley **Rev:** Waratah

Date	Mintage	F	VF	XF	Unc	BU
2007 Proof	1,000	Value: 975				

KM# 999 50 DOLLARS
15.5017 g., 0.9990 Platinum 0.4979 oz. APW **Ruler:** Elizabeth II **Subject:** Australian Flora **Obv:** Head with tiara right **Obv. Designer:** Ian Rank-Broadley **Rev:** Golden Wattle

Date	Mintage	F	VF	XF	Unc	BU
2007 Proof	1,000	Value: 975				

KM# 967 50 DOLLARS
15.5017 g., 0.9990 Gold 0.4979 oz. AGW **Ruler:** Elizabeth II **Subject:** Australian Fauna **Obv:** Head with tiara right **Obv. Designer:** Ian Rank-Broadley **Rev:** Echidna

Date	Mintage	F	VF	XF	Unc	BU
2007 Proof	1,000	Value: 650				

KM# 970 50 DOLLARS
15.5017 g., 0.9990 Gold 0.4979 oz. AGW **Ruler:** Elizabeth II **Subject:** Australian Fauna **Obv:** Head with tiara right **Obv. Designer:** Ian Rank-Broadley **Rev:** Common Wombat

Date	Mintage	F	VF	XF	Unc	BU
2007 Proof	1,000	Value: 650				

KM# 973 50 DOLLARS
15.5017 g., 0.9990 Gold 0.4979 oz. AGW **Ruler:** Elizabeth II **Subject:** Australian Fauna **Obv:** Head with tiara right **Obv. Designer:** Ian Rank-Broadley **Rev:** Tasmanian Devil

Date	Mintage	F	VF	XF	Unc	BU
2007 Proof	1,000	Value: 650				

KM# 976 50 DOLLARS
15.5017 g., 0.9990 Gold 0.4979 oz. AGW **Ruler:** Elizabeth II **Subject:** Australian Fauna **Obv:** Head with tiara right **Obv. Designer:** Ian Rank-Broadley **Rev:** Great White Shark

Date	Mintage	F	VF	XF	Unc	BU
2007 Proof	1,000	Value: 650				

KM# 979 50 DOLLARS
15.5017 g., 0.9990 Gold 0.4979 oz. AGW **Ruler:** Elizabeth II **Subject:** Australian Fauna **Obv:** Head with tiara right **Obv. Designer:** Ian Rank-Broadley **Rev:** Platypus

Date	Mintage	F	VF	XF	Unc	BU
2007 Proof	1,000	Value: 650				

KM# 1153 50 DOLLARS
15.5500 g., 0.9990 Gold 0.4994 oz. AGW, 25 mm. **Ruler:** Elizabeth II **Obv:** Head right **Obv. Designer:** Ian Rank-Broadley **Rev:** Echinda **Rev. Legend:** DISCOVER AUSTRALIA

Date	Mintage	F	VF	XF	Unc	BU
2007P Proof	1,000	Value: 800				

KM# 1154 50 DOLLARS
15.5500 g., 0.9990 Gold 0.4994 oz. AGW, 25 mm. **Ruler:** Elizabeth II **Obv:** Head right **Obv. Designer:** Ian rank-Broadley **Rev:** Common wombat **Rev. Legend:** DISCOVER AUSTRALIA

Date	Mintage	F	VF	XF	Unc	BU
2007P Proof	1,000	Value: 800				

KM# 1155 50 DOLLARS
15.5500 g., 0.9990 Gold 0.4994 oz. AGW, 25 mm.
Ruler: Elizabeth II **Obv:** Head right **Obv. Designer:** Ian rank-Broadley **Rev:** Tasmanian devil **Rev. Legend:** DISCOVER AUSTRALIA

Date	Mintage	F	VF	XF	Unc	BU
2007P Proof	1,000	Value: 800				

KM# 1156 50 DOLLARS
15.5500 g., 0.9990 Gold 0.4994 oz. AGW, 25 mm. **Ruler:** Elizabeth II **Obv:** Head right **Obv. Designer:** Ian Rank-Broadley **Rev:** Great white shark **Rev. Legend:** DISCOVER AUSTRALIA

Date	Mintage	F	VF	XF	Unc	BU
2007P Proof	1,000	Value: 800				

KM# 1157 50 DOLLARS
15.5500 g., 0.9990 Gold 0.4994 oz. AGW, 25 mm.
Ruler: Elizabeth II **Obv:** Head right **Obv. Designer:** Ian rank-Broadley **Rev:** Platypus **Rev. Legend:** DISCOVER AUSTRALIA

Date	Mintage	F	VF	XF	Unc	BU
2007P Proof	1,000	Value: 800				

KM# 1163 50 DOLLARS
15.5500 g., 0.9990 Platinum 0.4994 oz. APW, 26 mm.
Ruler: Elizabeth II **Obv:** Head right **Obv. Designer:** Ian Rank-Broadley **Rev:** Anemone buttercup, multicolor **Rev. Legend:** DISCOVER AUSTRALIA

Date	Mintage	F	VF	XF	Unc	BU
2007P Proof	1,000	Value: 1,500				

KM# 1164 50 DOLLARS
15.5500 g., 0.9990 Platinum 0.4994 oz. APW, 26 mm.
Ruler: Elizabeth II **Obv:** Head right **Obv. Designer:** Ian Rank-Broadley **Rev:** Sturt's desert pea, multicolor **Rev. Legend:** DISCOVER AUSTRALIA

Date	Mintage	F	VF	XF	Unc	BU
2007P Proof	1,000	Value: 1,500				

KM# 1165 50 DOLLARS
15.5500 g., 0.9990 Platinum 0.4994 oz. APW, 26 mm.
Ruler: Elizabeth II **Obv:** Head right **Obv. Designer:** Ian Rank-Broadley **Rev:** Tasmanian bluegum, multicolor **Rev. Legend:** DISCOVER AUSTRALIA

Date	Mintage	F	VF	XF	Unc	BU
2007P Proof	1,000	Value: 1,500				

KM# 1166 50 DOLLARS
15.5500 g., 0.9990 Platinum 0.4994 oz. APW, 26 mm.
Ruler: Elizabeth II **Obv:** Head right **Obv. Designer:** Ian Rank-Broadley **Rev:** Waratah, multicolor **Rev. Legend:** DISCOVER AUSTRALIA

Date	Mintage	F	VF	XF	Unc	BU
2007P Proof	1,000	Value: 1,500				

KM# 1167 50 DOLLARS
15.5500 g., 0.9990 Platinum 0.4994 oz. APW, 26 mm.
Ruler: Elizabeth II **Obv:** Head right **Obv. Designer:** Ian Rank-Broadley **Rev:** Golden wattle, multicolor **Rev. Legend:** DISCOVER AUSTRALIA

Date	Mintage	F	VF	XF	Unc	BU
2007P Proof	1,000	Value: 1,500				

KM# 1207 50 DOLLARS
15.5500 g., 0.9990 Platinum 0.4994 oz. APW, 26 mm.
Ruler: Elizabeth II **Obv:** Head right **Obv. Designer:** Ian Rank-Broadley **Rev:** Native fragipan, multicolor **Rev. Legend:** DISCOVER AUSTRALIA

Date	Mintage	F	VF	XF	Unc	BU
2008P Proof	1,000	Value: 1,500				

KM# 1196 50 DOLLARS
15.5500 g., 0.9990 Gold 0.4994 oz. AGW, 25 mm. **Ruler:** Elizabeth II **Obv:** Head right **Obv. Designer:** Ian Rank-Broadley **Rev:** Dolphin **Rev. Legend:** DISCOVER AUSTRALIA

Date	Mintage	F	VF	XF	Unc	BU
2008P Proof	1,000	Value: 800				

KM# 1197 50 DOLLARS
15.5500 g., 0.9990 Gold 0.4994 oz. AGW, 25 mm. **Ruler:** Elizabeth II **Obv:** Head right **Obv. Designer:** Ian Rank-Broadley **Rev:** King brown snake **Rev. Legend:** DISCOVER AUSTRALIA

Date	Mintage	F	VF	XF	Unc	BU
2008P Proof	1,000	Value: 800				

KM# 1198 50 DOLLARS
15.5500 g., 0.9990 Gold 0.4994 oz. AGW, 25 mm. **Ruler:** Elizabeth II **Obv:** Head right **Obv. Designer:** Ian Rank-Broadley **Rev:** Brogla **Rev. Legend:** DISCOVER AUSTRALIA

Date	Mintage	F	VF	XF	Unc	BU
2008P Proof	1,000	Value: 800				

KM# 1199 50 DOLLARS
15.5500 g., 0.9990 Gold 0.4994 oz. AGW, 25 mm. **Ruler:** Elizabeth II **Obv:** Head right **Obv. Designer:** Ian Rank-Broadley **Rev:** Dingo **Rev. Legend:** DISCOVER AUSTRALIA

Date	Mintage	F	VF	XF	Unc	BU
2008P Proof	1,000	Value: 800				

KM# 1200 50 DOLLARS
15.5500 g., 0.9990 Gold 0.4994 oz. AGW, 25 mm. **Ruler:** Elizabeth II **Obv:** Head right **Obv. Designer:** Ian Rank-Broadley **Rev:** Frilled neck lizard **Rev. Legend:** DISCOVER AUSTRALIA

Date	Mintage	F	VF	XF	Unc	BU
2008P Proof	1,000	Value: 800				

KM# 1208 50 DOLLARS
15.5500 g., 0.9990 Platinum 0.4994 oz. APW, 26 mm. **Ruler:** Elizabeth II **Obv:** Head right **Obv. Designer:** Ian Rank-Broadley **Rev:** Geraldton wax, multicolor **Rev. Legend:** DISCOVER AUSTRALIA

Date	Mintage	F	VF	XF	Unc	BU
2008P Proof	1,000	Value: 1,500				

KM# 1209 50 DOLLARS
15.5500 g., 0.9990 Platinum 0.4994 oz. APW, 26 mm.
Ruler: Elizabeth II **Obv:** Head right **Obv. Designer:** Ian Rank-Broadley **Rev:** Red flowered kurrajong, multicolor **Rev. Legend:** DISCOVER AUSTRALIA

Date	Mintage	F	VF	XF	Unc	BU
2008P Proof	1,000	Value: 1,500				

KM# 1210 50 DOLLARS
15.5500 g., 0.9990 Platinum 0.4994 oz. APW **Ruler:** Elizabeth II **Obv:** Head right **Obv. Designer:** Ian Rank-Broadley **Rev:** Small leaf lilly pilly, multicolor **Rev. Legend:** DISCOVER AUSTRALIA

Date	Mintage	F	VF	XF	Unc	BU
2008P Proof	1,500	Value: 1,500				

KM# 1229 50 DOLLARS
15.5500 g., 0.9990 Gold 0.4994 oz. AGW, 25 mm. **Ruler:** Elizabeth II **Obv:** Head right **Obv. Designer:** Ian Rank-Broadley **Rev:** Dreaming king brown snake **Rev. Designer:** Darryl Berttolli

Date	Mintage	F	VF	XF	Unc	BU
2009P Proof	1,000	Value: 1,100				

KM# 1227 50 DOLLARS
15.5500 g., 0.9990 Gold 0.4994 oz. AGW, 25 mm. **Ruler:** Elizabeth II **Obv:** Head right **Obv. Designer:** Ian Rank-Broadley **Rev:** Dreaming kangaroo **Rev. Designer:** Darryl Berttolli

Date	Mintage	F	VF	XF	Unc	BU
2009P Proof	1,000	Value: 1,100				

KM# 1230 50 DOLLARS
15.5500 g., 0.9990 Gold 0.4994 oz. AGW, 25 mm. **Ruler:** Elizabeth II **Obv:** Head right **Obv. Designer:** Ian Rank-Broadley **Rev:** Dreaming brolga **Rev. Designer:** Darryl Berttolli

Date	Mintage	F	VF	XF	Unc	BU
2009P Proof	1,000	Value: 1,100				

KM# 1231 50 DOLLARS
15.5500 g., 0.9990 Gold 0.4994 oz. AGW, 25 mm.
Ruler: Elizabeth II **Obv:** Head right **Obv. Designer:** Ian Rank-Broadley **Rev:** Dreaming echidna **Rev. Designer:** Darryl Berttolli

Date	Mintage	F	VF	XF	Unc	BU
2009P Proof	1,000	Value: 1,100				

KM# 1237 50 DOLLARS
15.5500 g., 0.9990 Platinum 0.4994 oz. APW, 25 mm.
Ruler: Elizabeth II **Obv:** Head right **Obv. Designer:** Ian Rank-Broadley **Rev:** Dreaming kangaroo, multicolor **Rev. Designer:** Darryl Berttolli

Date	Mintage	F	VF	XF	Unc	BU
2009P Proof	1,000	Value: 1,500				

KM# 1238 50 DOLLARS
15.5500 g., 0.9990 Platinum 0.4994 oz. APW, 25 mm. **Ruler:** Elizabeth II **Obv:** Head right **Obv. Designer:** Ian Rank-Broadley **Rev:** Dreaming dolphin, multicolor **Rev. Designer:** Darryl Berttolli

Date	Mintage	F	VF	XF	Unc	BU
2009P Proof	1,000	Value: 1,500				

KM# 1239 50 DOLLARS
15.5500 g., 0.9990 Platinum 0.4994 oz. APW, 25 mm.
Ruler: Elizabeth II **Obv:** Head right **Obv. Designer:** Ian Rank-Broadley **Rev:** Dreaming king brown snake, multicolor **Rev. Designer:** Darryl Berttolli

Date	Mintage	F	VF	XF	Unc	BU
2009P Proof	1,000	Value: 1,500				

KM# 1240 50 DOLLARS
15.5500 g., 0.9990 Platinum 0.4994 oz. APW, 25 mm. **Ruler:** Elizabeth II **Obv:** Head right **Obv. Designer:** Ian Rank-Broadley **Rev:** Dreaming brolga, multicolor **Rev. Designer:** Darryl Berttolli

Date	Mintage	F	VF	XF	Unc	BU
2009P Proof	1,000	Value: 1,500				

KM# 1241 50 DOLLARS
15.5500 g., 0.9990 Platinum 0.4994 oz. APW, 25 mm. **Ruler:** Elizabeth II **Obv:** Head right **Obv. Designer:** Ian Rank-Broadley **Rev:** Dreaming echidna, multicolor **Rev. Designer:** Darryl Berttolli

Date	Mintage	F	VF	XF	Unc	BU
2009P Proof	1,000	Value: 1,500				

BULLION - LUNAR YEAR

KM# 579 50 CENTS
15.5518 g., 0.9990 Silver 0.4995 oz. ASW, 32.1 mm.
Ruler: Elizabeth II **Subject:** Year of the Horse **Obv:** Head with tiara right, denomination below **Obv. Designer:** Ian Rank-Broadley **Rev:** Horse running left **Edge:** Reeded

Date	Mintage	F	VF	XF	Unc	BU
2002P Proof	5,000	Value: 35.00				

KM# 664 50 CENTS
16.4000 g., 0.9990 Silver 0.5267 oz. ASW, 31.9 mm.
Ruler: Elizabeth II **Subject:** Year of the Goat **Obv:** Head with tiara right, denomination below **Obv. Designer:** Ian Rank-Broadley **Rev:** Two goats **Edge:** Reeded

Date	Mintage	F	VF	XF	Unc	BU
2003	—	—	—	—	15.00	20.00
2003 Proof	—	Value: 35.00				

KM# 673 50 CENTS
15.5518 g., 0.9990 Silver 0.4995 oz. ASW, 32.1 mm.
Ruler: Elizabeth II **Subject:** Year of the Monkey **Obv:** Head with tiara right, denomination below **Rev:** Monkey sitting on branch **Edge:** Reeded

Date	Mintage	F	VF	XF	Unc	BU
2004 Proof	11,000	Value: 35.00				

KM# 791 50 CENTS
15.5680 g., 0.9990 Silver 0.5000 oz. ASW, 32.1 mm.
Ruler: Elizabeth II **Subject:** Year of the Rooster **Obv:** Elizabeth II **Rev:** Standing Rooster looking backwards **Edge:** Reeded

Date	Mintage	F	VF	XF	Unc	BU
2005P Proof	6,000	Value: 50.00				

KM# 814 50 CENTS
15.5500 g., 0.9990 Silver 0.4994 oz. ASW **Ruler:** Elizabeth II **Subject:** Bullion Lunar Year - Rooster **Obv:** Head with tiara right

Date	Mintage	F	VF	XF	Unc	BU
2005	—	—	—	—	—	15.00

KM# 536 DOLLAR
31.1035 g., 0.9990 Silver 0.9990 oz. ASW, 40.6 mm.
Ruler: Elizabeth II **Subject:** Year of the Snake **Obv:** Head with tiara right, denomination below **Obv. Designer:** Ian Rank-Broadley **Rev:** Snake with eggs **Edge:** Reeded

Date	Mintage	F	VF	XF	Unc	BU
2001	300,000	—	—	—	25.00	30.00
2001P Proof	2,500	Value: 45.00				

KM# 536a DOLLAR
31.6350 g., 0.9990 Silver partially gilt 1.0160 oz. ASW, 40.6 mm.
Ruler: Elizabeth II **Subject:** Year of the Snake **Obv:** Head with tiara right, denomination below **Rev:** Gold-plated snake **Edge:** Reeded

Date	Mintage	F	VF	XF	Unc	BU
2001	50,000	—	—	—	45.00	50.00

KM# 580 DOLLAR
31.1035 g., 0.9990 Silver 0.9990 oz. ASW, 40.6 mm.
Ruler: Elizabeth II **Subject:** Year of the Horse **Obv:** Head with tiara right, denomination below **Obv. Designer:** Ian Rank-Broadley **Rev:** Horse running left **Edge:** Reeded

Date	Mintage	F	VF	XF	Unc	BU
2002P	—	—	—	—	25.00	30.00
2002P Proof	2,500	Value: 45.00				

KM# 580a DOLLAR
31.6350 g., 0.9990 Silver partially gilt 1.0160 oz. ASW, 40.6 mm.
Ruler: Elizabeth II **Obv:** Head with tiara right **Rev:** Gold-plated horse **Edge:** Reeded

Date	Mintage	F	VF	XF	Unc	BU
2002	50,000	—	—	—	25.00	30.00

KM# 665 DOLLAR
31.6200 g., 0.9990 Silver 1.0155 oz. ASW, 40.3 mm.
Ruler: Elizabeth II **Subject:** Year of the Goat **Obv:** Head with tiara right, denomination below **Obv. Designer:** Ian Rank-Broadley **Rev:** Two goats **Edge:** Reeded

Date	Mintage	F	VF	XF	Unc	BU
2003	—	—	—	—	22.50	25.00
2003 Proof	—	Value: 35.00				

KM# 665a DOLLAR
31.6350 g., 0.9990 Silver partially gilt 1.0160 oz. ASW, 40.6 mm.
Ruler: Elizabeth II **Subject:** Year of the Goat **Obv:** Head with tiara right, denomination below **Rev:** Gold-plated goat **Edge:** Reeded

Date	Mintage	F	VF	XF	Unc	BU
2003	50,000	—	—	—	50.00	55.00

KM# 674a DOLLAR
31.6350 g., 0.9990 Silver partially gilt 1.0160 oz. ASW, 40.6 mm.
Ruler: Elizabeth II **Subject:** Year of the Monkey **Obv:** Head with tiara right, denomination below **Rev:** Gold-plated Monkey **Edge:** Reeded

Date	Mintage	F	VF	XF	Unc	BU
2004	50,000	—	—	—	50.00	55.00

KM# 674 DOLLAR
31.1035 g., 0.9990 Silver 0.9990 oz. ASW, 40.6 mm. **Ruler:** Elizabeth II **Subject:** Year of the Monkey **Obv:** Head with tiara right, denomination below **Rev:** Monkey sitting on branch **Edge:** Reeded

Date	Mintage	F	VF	XF	Unc	BU
2004	—	—	—	—	22.50	25.00
2004 Proof	8,500	Value: 35.00				

KM# 695 DOLLAR
31.6350 g., 0.9990 Silver 1.0160 oz. ASW, 40.5 mm.
Ruler: Elizabeth II **Subject:** Year of the Rooster **Obv:** Head with tiara right, denomination below **Rev:** Rooster **Edge:** Reeded

Date	Mintage	F	VF	XF	Unc	BU
2005 Proof	—	Value: 70.00				

KM# 695a DOLLAR
31.6350 g., 0.9990 Silver 1.0160 oz. ASW, 40.5 mm. **Ruler:** Elizabeth II **Subject:** Year of the Rooster **Obv:** Head with tiara right, denomination below **Rev:** Gold-plated Rooster **Edge:** Reeded

Date	Mintage	F	VF	XF	Unc	BU
2005 Polished fields	47,200	—	—	—	45.00	50.00
2005 Matte fields	2,800	—	—	—	175	185

KM# 792 DOLLAR
31.1035 g., 0.9990 Silver 0.9990 oz. ASW, 40.6 mm.
Ruler: Elizabeth II **Subject:** Year of the Rooster **Obv:** Elizabeth II **Rev:** Standing Rooster looking backwards **Edge:** Reeded

Date	Mintage	F	VF	XF	Unc	BU
2005P Proof	3,500	Value: 37.50				

KM# 1317 DOLLAR
31.1050 g., 0.9990 Silver 0.9990 oz. ASW, 46 mm.
Ruler: Elizabeth II **Subject:** Year of the Tiger **Obv:** Head right **Obv. Designer:** Ian Rank-Broadley **Rev:** Tiger seated left

Date	Mintage	F	VF	XF	Unc	BU
2010P	—	—	—	—	—	40.00
2010P Proof	1,000	Value: 75.00				

KM# 1317a DOLLAR
31.1050 g., 0.9990 Silver 0.9990 oz. ASW, 46 mm.
Ruler: Elizabeth II **Subject:** Year of the Tiger **Obv:** Head right **Obv. Designer:** Ian Rank-Broadley **Rev:** Tiger seated left, partially gilt

Date	Mintage	F	VF	XF	Unc	BU
2010P Proof	50,000	Value: 80.00				

KM# 1318 DOLLAR
31.1050 g., 0.9990 Silver 0.9990 oz. ASW, 46 mm.
Ruler: Elizabeth II **Subject:** Year of the Tiger **Obv:** Head right **Obv. Designer:** Ian Rank-Broadley **Rev:** Tiger seated left, multicolor

Date	Mintage	F	VF	XF	Unc	BU
2010P Proof	170,000	Value: 75.00				

KM# 537 2 DOLLARS
62.2070 g., 0.9990 Silver 1.9979 oz. ASW, 50.3 mm.
Ruler: Elizabeth II **Subject:** Year of the Snake **Obv:** Head with tiara right, denomination below **Rev:** Snake with eggs **Edge:** Segmented reeding

Date	Mintage	F	VF	XF	Unc	BU
2001	—	—	—	—	55.00	60.00
2001P Proof	1,000	Value: 100				

KM# 581 2 DOLLARS
62.2070 g., 0.9990 Silver 1.9979 oz. ASW, 50 mm. **Ruler:** Elizabeth II **Subject:** Year of the Horse **Obv:** Head with tiara right, denomination below **Rev:** Horse running left **Edge:** Reeded

Date	Mintage	F	VF	XF	Unc	BU
2002	—	—	—	—	55.00	60.00
2002P Proof	1,000	Value: 100				

KM# 679 2 DOLLARS
62.8500 g., 0.9990 Silver 2.0186 oz. ASW, 50 mm. **Ruler:** Elizabeth II **Subject:** Year of the Goat **Obv:** Head with tiara right, denomination below **Rev:** Two goats **Edge:** Reeded

Date	Mintage	F	VF	XF	Unc	BU
2003	—	—	—	—	55.00	60.00

KM# 675 2 DOLLARS
62.2070 g., 0.9990 Silver 1.9979 oz. ASW, 50 mm. **Ruler:** Elizabeth II **Subject:** Year of the Monkey **Obv:** Head with tiara right, denomination below **Rev:** Monkey sitting on branch **Edge:** Reeded

Date	Mintage	F	VF	XF	Unc	BU
2004	—	—	—	—	55.00	60.00
2004 Proof	7,000	Value: 90.00				

KM# 793 2 DOLLARS
62.2700 g., 0.9990 Silver 1.9999 oz. ASW, 50.3 mm.
Ruler: Elizabeth II **Subject:** Year of the Rooster **Obv:** Elizabeth II **Rev:** Standing Rooster looking backwards **Edge:** Reeded

Date	Mintage	F	VF	XF	Unc	BU
2005P Proof	2,000	Value: 140				

KM# 1320 2 DOLLARS
62.2100 g., 0.9990 Silver 1.9980 oz. ASW, 46 mm.
Ruler: Elizabeth II **Subject:** Year of the Tiger **Obv:** Head right **Obv. Designer:** Ian Rank-Broadley **Rev:** Tiger seated left

Date	Mintage	F	VF	XF	Unc	BU
2010P Proof	1,000	Value: 150				

KM# 538 5 DOLLARS
1.5710 g., 0.9990 Gold 0.0505 oz. AGW, 14.1 mm.
Ruler: Elizabeth II **Subject:** Year of the Snake **Obv:** Head with tiara right, denomination below **Rev:** Snake in tree **Edge:** Reeded

Date	Mintage	F	VF	XF	Unc	BU
2001	100,000	—	—	—	—	70.00
2001P Proof	100,000	Value: 75.00				

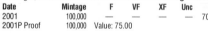

KM# 582 5 DOLLARS
1.5552 g., 0.9990 Gold 0.0499 oz. AGW, 14.1 mm. **Ruler:** Elizabeth II **Subject:** Year of the Horse **Obv:** Head with tiara right, denomination below **Rev:** Horse galloping left **Edge:** Reeded

Date	Mintage	F	VF	XF	Unc	BU
2002P	100,000	—	—	—	—	70.00

KM# 668 5 DOLLARS
1.5710 g., 0.9999 Gold 0.0505 oz. AGW, 14.1 mm.
Ruler: Elizabeth II **Subject:** Year of the Monkey **Obv:** Head with tiara right, denomination below **Obv. Designer:** Ian Rank-Broadley **Rev:** Monkey **Edge:** Reeded

Date	Mintage	F	VF	XF	Unc	BU
2004P Proof	100,000	Value: 70.00				

KM# 1022.1 5 DOLLARS
1.5700 g., 0.9999 Gold 0.0505 oz. AGW, 13.93 mm. **Ruler:** Elizabeth II **Obv:** Head with tiara right **Rev:** Rooster standing right **Edge:** Reeded **Note:** Polished images with matte fields.

Date	Mintage	F	VF	XF	Unc	BU
2005 Proof	28,000	Value: 85.00				

KM# 1022.2 5 DOLLARS
1.5700 g., 0.9999 Gold 0.0505 oz. AGW, 13.93 mm. **Ruler:** Elizabeth II **Subject:** Year of the Rooster **Obv:** Head with tiara right **Rev:** Rooster standing right multicolor **Edge:** Reeded

Date	Mintage	F	VF	XF	Unc	BU
2005 Proof	1,000	Value: 90.00				

KM# 743 8 DOLLARS
155.5175 g., 0.9990 Silver 4.9948 oz. ASW, 65 mm. **Ruler:** Elizabeth II **Subject:** Year of the Monkey **Obv:** Head with tiara right, denomination below **Rev:** Gold-plated seated monkey and multicolored ornamentation **Edge:** Reeded

Date	Mintage	F	VF	XF	Unc	BU
2004	6,000	—	—	—	—	200

KM# 1023 8 DOLLARS
155.5150 g., 0.9990 Silver Gilt 4.9947 oz. ASW **Ruler:** Elizabeth II **Subject:** Year of the Rooster **Obv:** Head with tiara right **Rev:** Rooster standing left multicolor **Edge:** Reeded

Date	Mintage	F	VF	XF	Unc	BU
2005 Proof	10,000	Value: 300				

KM# 539 10 DOLLARS
311.0350 g., 0.9990 Silver 9.9896 oz. ASW, 75.5 mm. **Ruler:** Elizabeth II **Subject:** Year of the Snake **Obv:** Head with tiara right, denomination below **Rev:** Snake with eggs **Edge:** Segmented reeding

Date	Mintage	F	VF	XF	Unc	BU
2001	—	—	—	—	220	240
2001P Proof	250	Value: 300				

KM# 583 10 DOLLARS
311.0350 g., 0.9990 Silver 9.9896 oz. ASW, 75.5 mm. **Ruler:** Elizabeth II **Subject:** Year of the Horse **Obv:** Head with tiara right, denomination below **Rev:** Horse running left **Edge:** Segmented reeding

Date	Mintage	F	VF	XF	Unc	BU
2002	—	—	—	—	220	240
2002P Proof	500	Value: 285				

KM# 710 10 DOLLARS
311.0350 g., 0.9990 Silver 9.9896 oz. ASW **Ruler:** Elizabeth II **Subject:** Year of the Goat **Obv:** Head with tiara right, denomination below **Rev:** Goat

Date	Mintage	F	VF	XF	Unc	BU
2003	—	—	—	—	220	240
2003 Proof	—	Value: 285				

KM# 676 10 DOLLARS
311.0350 g., 0.9990 Silver 9.9896 oz. ASW, 75.5 mm. **Ruler:** Elizabeth II **Subject:** Year of the Monkey **Obv:** Head with tiara right, denomination below **Rev:** Monkey sitting on branch **Edge:** Segmented reeding

Date	Mintage	F	VF	XF	Unc	BU
2004	—	—	—	—	220	240
2004 Proof	5,000	Value: 275				

KM# 696 10 DOLLARS
311.0350 g., 0.9990 Silver 9.9896 oz. ASW **Ruler:** Elizabeth II **Subject:** Year of the Rooster **Obv:** Head with tiara right, denomination below **Rev:** Rooster

Date	Mintage	F	VF	XF	Unc	BU
2005	—	—	—	—	220	240
2005 Proof	—	Value: 285				

KM# 1321 10 DOLLARS
3.1100 g., 0.9990 Gold 0.0999 oz. AGW, 19 mm. **Ruler:** Elizabeth II **Subject:** Year of the Tiger **Obv:** Head right **Obv. Designer:** Ian Rank-Broadley **Rev:** Tiger head facing

Date	Mintage	F	VF	XF	Unc	BU
2010P Proof	8,000	Value: 260				

KM# 540 15 DOLLARS
3.1103 g., 0.9990 Gold 0.0999 oz. AGW, 16.1 mm. **Ruler:** Elizabeth II **Subject:** Year of the Snake **Obv:** Head with tiara right, denomination below **Rev:** Snake in tree **Edge:** Reeded

Date	Mintage	F	VF	XF	Unc	BU
2001	80,000	—	—	—	—	135
2001P Proof	7,000	Value: 150				

KM# 584 15 DOLLARS
3.1103 g., 0.9990 Gold 0.0999 oz. AGW, 16.1 mm. **Ruler:** Elizabeth II **Subject:** Year of the Horse **Obv:** Head with tiara right, denomination below **Rev:** Horse galloping half left **Edge:** Reeded

Date	Mintage	F	VF	XF	Unc	BU
2002P	—	—	—	—	—	135
2002P Proof	7,000	Value: 150				

KM# 711 15 DOLLARS
3.1100 g., 0.9999 Gold 0.1000 oz. AGW **Ruler:** Elizabeth II **Subject:** Year of the Goat **Obv:** Head with tiara right, denomination below **Rev:** Goat

Date	Mintage	F	VF	XF	Unc	BU
2003	—	—	—	—	—	135
2003 Proof	—	Value: 150				

KM# 669 15 DOLLARS
3.1103 g., 0.9999 Gold 0.1000 oz. AGW, 16.1 mm. **Ruler:** Elizabeth II **Subject:** Year of the Monkey **Obv:** Head with tiara right, denomination below **Rev:** Monkey **Edge:** Reeded

Date	Mintage	F	VF	XF	Unc	BU
2004P	—	—	—	—	—	135
2004P Proof	80,000	Value: 150				

KM# 794 15 DOLLARS
3.1103 g., 0.9999 Gold 0.1000 oz. AGW, 16.1 mm. **Ruler:** Elizabeth II **Subject:** Year of the Rooster **Obv:** Elizabeth II **Rev:** Standing Rooster right **Edge:** Reeded

Date	Mintage	F	VF	XF	Unc	BU
2005P Proof	7,000	Value: 150				

KM# 794a 15 DOLLARS
31.1030 g., 0.7500 Gold 0.7500 oz. AGW **Ruler:** Elizabeth II **Subject:** Year of the Rooster **Obv:** Head with tiara right **Rev:** Rooster standing right **Edge:** Reeded

Date	Mintage	F	VF	XF	Unc	BU
2005P Proof	15,000	Value: 975				

KM# 541 25 DOLLARS
7.7508 g., 0.9990 Gold 0.2489 oz. AGW, 20.1 mm. **Ruler:** Elizabeth II **Subject:** Year of the Snake **Obv:** Head with tiara right, denomination below **Rev:** Snake in tree **Edge:** Reeded

Date	Mintage	F	VF	XF	Unc	BU
2001	60,000	—	—	—	—	325
2001P Proof	7,000	Value: 350				

KM# 585 25 DOLLARS
7.7759 g., 0.9990 Gold 0.2497 oz. AGW, 20.1 mm. **Ruler:** Elizabeth II **Subject:** Year of the Horse **Obv:** Head with tiara right, denomination below **Rev:** Horse galloping half left **Edge:** Reeded

Date	Mintage	F	VF	XF	Unc	BU
2002P	—	—	—	—	—	325
2002P Proof	7,000	Value: 350				

KM# 712 25 DOLLARS
7.7500 g., 0.9999 Gold 0.2491 oz. AGW **Ruler:** Elizabeth II **Subject:** Year of the Goat **Obv:** Head with tiara right, denomination below **Rev:** Goat

Date	Mintage	F	VF	XF	Unc	BU
2003	—	—	—	—	—	325
2003 Proof	—	Value: 350				

KM# 670 25 DOLLARS
7.7508 g., 0.9999 Gold 0.2492 oz. AGW, 20.1 mm. **Ruler:** Elizabeth II **Subject:** Year of the Monkey **Obv:** Head with tiara right, denomination below **Rev:** Monkey **Edge:** Reeded

Date	Mintage	F	VF	XF	Unc	BU
2004P	—	—	—	—	—	325
2004P Proof	60,000	Value: 350				

KM# 795 25 DOLLARS
7.7759 g., 0.9999 Gold 0.2500 oz. AGW, 20.1 mm. **Ruler:** Elizabeth II **Subject:** Year of the Rooster **Obv:** Elizabeth II **Rev:** Standing Rooster right **Edge:** Reeded

Date	Mintage	F	VF	XF	Unc	BU
2005P Proof	7,000	Value: 350				

KM# 1322 25 DOLLARS
7.7700 g., 0.9990 Gold 0.2496 oz. AGW, 22 mm. **Ruler:** Elizabeth II **Subject:** Year of the Tiger **Obv:** Head right **Obv. Designer:** Ian Rank-Broadley **Rev:** Tiger head facing

Date	Mintage	F	VF	XF	Unc	BU
2010P Proof	8,000	Value: 650				

KM# 542 30 DOLLARS
1002.5020 g., 0.9990 Silver 32.197 oz. ASW, 101 mm. **Ruler:** Elizabeth II **Subject:** Year of the Snake **Obv:** Head with tiara right, denomination below **Rev:** Snake with eggs **Edge:** Segmented reeding

Date	Mintage	F	VF	XF	Unc	BU
2001	—	—	—	—	—	675
2001P Proof	250	Value: 700				

KM# 586 30 DOLLARS
1002.5020 g., 0.9990 Silver 32.197 oz. ASW, 101 mm. **Ruler:** Elizabeth II **Subject:** Year of the Horse **Obv:** Head with tiara right, denomination below **Rev:** Horse running left **Edge:** Segmented reeding **Note:** Illustration reduced.

Date	Mintage	F	VF	XF	Unc	BU
2002	—	—	—	—	—	675
2002P Proof	250	Value: 700				

KM# 681 30 DOLLARS
1000.0000 g., 0.9990 Silver 32.117 oz. ASW, 101 mm. **Ruler:** Elizabeth II **Subject:** Year of the Goat **Obv:** Head with tiara right, denomination below **Rev:** Nanny goat and kid **Edge:** Segmented reeding

Date	Mintage	F	VF	XF	Unc	BU
2003	—	—	—	—	—	675
2003P Proof	—	Value: 700				

KM# 677.1 30 DOLLARS
1000.0000 g., 0.9990 Silver 32.117 oz. ASW, 101 mm. **Ruler:** Elizabeth II **Subject:** Year of the Monkey **Obv:** Head with tiara right, denomination below **Rev:** Monkey sitting on branch **Edge:** Segmented reeding

Date	Mintage	F	VF	XF	Unc	BU
2004	—	—	—	—	—	525
2004 Proof	5,250	Value: 585				

KM# 677.2 30 DOLLARS
1000.0000 g., 0.9990 Silver 32.117 oz. ASW, 101 mm. **Ruler:** Elizabeth II **Subject:** Year of the Monkey **Obv:** Head with tiara right, denomination below **Obv. Designer:** Ian Rank-Broadley **Rev:** Multicolor ornamentation and Monkey with diamond chip eyes sitting on branch **Edge:** Segmented reeding **Note:** Illustration reduced.

Date	Mintage	F	VF	XF	Unc	BU
2004 Proof	5,000	Value: 700				

KM# 697 30 DOLLARS
1000.0000 g., 0.9990 Silver 32.117 oz. ASW **Ruler:** Elizabeth II **Subject:** Year of the Rooster **Obv:** Head with tiara right, denomination below **Rev:** Rooster

Date	Mintage	F	VF	XF	Unc	BU
2005	—	—	—	—	—	675
2005 Proof	—	Value: 700				

Column 1

KM# 1319 30 DOLLARS
1000.0000 g., 0.9990 Silver 32.117 oz. ASW, 100.6 mm.
Ruler: Elizabeth II **Subject:** Year of the Tiger **Obv:** Head right
Obv. Designer: Ian Rank-Broadley **Rev:** Tiger seated left

Date	Mintage	F	VF	XF	Unc	BU
2010P Proof	5,000	Value: 1,600				

KM# 671 50 DOLLARS
15.5940 g., 0.9999 Gold 0.5013 oz. AGW, 25.1 mm.
Ruler: Elizabeth II **Subject:** Year of the Monkey **Obv:** Head with tiara right, denomination below **Rev:** Monkey **Edge:** Reeded

Date	Mintage	F	VF	XF	Unc	BU
2004P Proof	40,000	Value: 650				

KM# 543 100 DOLLARS
31.1035 g., 0.9990 Gold 0.9990 oz. AGW, 32.1 mm.
Ruler: Elizabeth II **Subject:** Year of the Snake **Obv:** Head with tiara right, denomination below **Obv. Designer:** Ian Rank-Broadley **Rev:** Snake in tree **Edge:** Reeded

Date	Mintage	F	VF	XF	Unc	BU
2001	30,000	—	—	—	—	1,250
2001P Proof	—	Value: 1,300				

KM# 587 100 DOLLARS
31.1035 g., 0.9990 Gold 0.9990 oz. AGW, 32.1 mm.
Ruler: Elizabeth II **Subject:** Year of the Horse **Obv:** Head with tiara right, denomination below **Rev:** Horse running left
Edge: Reeded

Date	Mintage	F	VF	XF	Unc	BU
2002	—	—	—	—	—	1,250
2002P Proof	—	Value: 1,300				

KM# 713 100 DOLLARS
31.1035 g., 0.9999 Gold 0.9999 oz. AGW, 32.1 mm.
Ruler: Elizabeth II **Subject:** Year of the Goat **Obv:** Head with tiara right, denomination below **Rev:** Goat

Date	Mintage	F	VF	XF	Unc	BU
2003	—	—	—	—	—	1,250
2003 Proof	—	Value: 1,300				

KM# 672 100 DOLLARS
31.1035 g., 0.9999 Gold 0.9999 oz. AGW, 32.1 mm. **Ruler:** Elizabeth II **Subject:** Year of the Monkey **Obv:** Head with tiara right, denomination below **Rev:** Monkey **Edge:** Reeded

Date	Mintage	F	VF	XF	Unc	BU
2004	30,000	—	—	—	—	1,250
2004P Proof	—	Value: 1,300				

KM# 796 100 DOLLARS
31.1035 g., 0.9999 Gold 0.9999 oz. AGW, 32.1 mm.
Ruler: Elizabeth II **Subject:** Year of the Rooster **Obv:** Elizabeth II **Rev:** Standing Rooster right **Edge:** Reeded

Date	Mintage	F	VF	XF	Unc	BU
2005P Proof	3,000	Value: 1,300				

KM# 1323 100 DOLLARS
31.1050 g., 0.9990 Gold 0.9990 oz. AGW, 40 mm.
Ruler: Elizabeth II **Subject:** Year of the Tiger **Obv:** Head right **Obv. Designer:** Ian Rank-Broadley **Rev:** Tiger head facing

Date	Mintage	F	VF	XF	Unc	BU
2010P Proof	6,000	Value: 2,430				

KM# 704 200 DOLLARS
62.2140 g., 0.9999 Gold 1.9999 oz. AGW **Ruler:** Elizabeth II **Subject:** Year of the Snake **Obv:** Head with tiara right, denomination below **Rev:** Snake

Date	Mintage	F	VF	XF	Unc	BU
2001 Proof	—	Value: 2,750				

KM# 707 200 DOLLARS
62.2140 g., 0.9999 Gold 1.9999 oz. AGW **Ruler:** Elizabeth II **Subject:** Year of the Horse **Rev:** Horse

Date	Mintage	F	VF	XF	Unc	BU
2002 Proof	—	Value: 2,750				

KM# 714 200 DOLLARS
62.2140 g., 0.9999 Gold 1.9999 oz. AGW **Ruler:** Elizabeth II **Subject:** Year of the Goat **Obv:** Head with tiara right **Rev:** Goat

Date	Mintage	F	VF	XF	Unc	BU
2003 Proof	—	Value: 2,750				

Column 2

KM# 717 200 DOLLARS
62.2100 g., 0.9999 Gold 1.9998 oz. AGW **Ruler:** Elizabeth II **Subject:** Year of the Monkey **Obv:** Head with tiara right **Rev:** Monkey

Date	Mintage	F	VF	XF	Unc	BU
2004 Proof	—	Value: 2,750				

KM# 698 200 DOLLARS
62.2100 g., 0.9999 Gold 1.9998 oz. AGW **Ruler:** Elizabeth II **Subject:** Year of the Rooster **Obv:** Head with tiara right **Rev:** Rooster

Date	Mintage	F	VF	XF	Unc	BU
2005 Proof	—	Value: 2,750				

KM# 1006 300 DOLLARS
10000.0000 g., 0.9990 Silver 321.17 oz. ASW **Ruler:** Elizabeth II **Series:** Lunar year **Subject:** Year of the Dog **Obv:** Head with tiara right **Obv. Legend:** ELIZABETH II - AUSTRALIA **Obv. Designer:** Ian Rank-Broadley **Rev:** Dog sitting, facing right

Date	Mintage	F	VF	XF	Unc	BU
2006	—	—	—	—	—	6,500

KM# 705 1000 DOLLARS
311.0480 g., 0.9999 Gold 9.9990 oz. AGW **Ruler:** Elizabeth II **Subject:** Year of the Snake **Obv:** Head with tiara right, denomination below **Rev:** Snake

Date	Mintage	F	VF	XF	Unc	BU
2001	—	—	—	—	—	12,500

KM# 708 1000 DOLLARS
311.0480 g., 0.9999 Gold 9.9990 oz. AGW **Ruler:** Elizabeth II **Subject:** Year of the Horse **Obv:** Head with tiara right **Rev:** Horse

Date	Mintage	F	VF	XF	Unc	BU
2002	—	—	—	—	—	12.00

KM# 715 1000 DOLLARS
311.0480 g., 0.9999 Gold 9.9990 oz. AGW **Ruler:** Elizabeth II **Subject:** Year of the Goat **Obv:** Head with tiara right, denomination below **Rev:** Goat

Date	Mintage	F	VF	XF	Unc	BU
2003	—	—	—	—	—	12.00

KM# 718 1000 DOLLARS
311.0480 g., 0.9999 Gold 9.9990 oz. AGW **Ruler:** Elizabeth II **Subject:** Year of the Monkey **Obv:** Head with tiara right, denomination below **Rev:** Monkey

Date	Mintage	F	VF	XF	Unc	BU
2004	—	—	—	—	—	12.00

KM# 699 1000 DOLLARS
311.0480 g., 0.9999 Gold 9.9990 oz. AGW **Ruler:** Elizabeth II **Subject:** Year of the Rooster **Obv:** Head with tiara right, denomination below **Rev:** Rooster

Date	Mintage	F	VF	XF	Unc	BU
2005	—	—	—	—	—	12.00

KM# 706 3000 DOLLARS
1000.0000 g., 0.9999 Gold 32.146 oz. AGW **Ruler:** Elizabeth II **Subject:** Year of the Snake **Obv:** Head with tiara right, denomination below **Rev:** Snake

Date	Mintage	F	VF	XF	Unc	BU
2001	—	—	—	—	BV+3%	—

KM# 709 3000 DOLLARS
1000.0000 g., 0.9999 Gold 32.146 oz. AGW **Ruler:** Elizabeth II **Subject:** Year of the Horse **Obv:** Head with tiara right, denomination below **Rev:** Horse

Date	Mintage	F	VF	XF	Unc	BU
2002	—	—	—	—	BV+3%	—

KM# 716 3000 DOLLARS
1000.0000 g., 0.9999 Gold 32.146 oz. AGW **Ruler:** Elizabeth II **Subject:** Year of the Goat **Obv:** Head with tiara right, denomination below **Rev:** Goat

Date	Mintage	F	VF	XF	Unc	BU
2003	—	—	—	—	BV+3%	—

KM# 719 3000 DOLLARS
1000.0000 g., 0.9999 Gold 32.146 oz. AGW **Ruler:** Elizabeth II **Subject:** Year of the Monkey **Obv:** Head with tiara right, denomination below **Rev:** Monkey

Date	Mintage	F	VF	XF	Unc	BU
2004	—	—	—	—	BV+3%	—

KM# 700 3000 DOLLARS
1000.0000 g., 0.9999 Gold 32.146 oz. AGW **Ruler:** Elizabeth II **Subject:** Year of the Rooster **Obv:** Head with tiara right, denomination below **Rev:** Rooster

Date	Mintage	F	VF	XF	Unc	BU
2005	—	—	—	—	BV+3%	—

KM# 1007 30000 DOLLARS
10000.0000 g., 0.9999 Gold 321.46 oz. AGW, 40.5 mm.
Ruler: Elizabeth II **Series:** Lunar year **Subject:** Year of the Dog **Obv:** Head with tiara right **Obv. Legend:** ELIZABETH II - AUSTRALIA **Obv. Designer:** Ian Rank-Broadley **Rev:** Dog standing left

Date	Mintage	F	VF	XF	Unc	BU
2006	—	—	—	—	BV+3%	—

BABY MINT SETS

KM#	Date	Mintage Identification	Issue Price	Mkt Val
BMS9	2001 (6)	32,494 KM#401-403, 406, 491.1, 534.1 plus bronze medal	—	110
BMS10	2002 (6)	32,479 KM#401-403, 406, 600.1, 602 plus bronze medal	—	47.50
BMS11	2003 (6)	37,748 KM#401-402, 406, 688-690 plus bronze medal	—	40.00
BMS12	2004 (6)	31,000 KM#401-404, 406, 733.1 plus bronze medal	—	40.00

Column 3

KM#	Date	Mintage Identification	Issue Price	Mkt Val
BMS13	2005 (6)	34,748 KM#401-402, 406, 745-747 plus bronze medal	24.00	25.00
BMS14	2006 (6)	— KM#401-404, 406, 489 plus bronze medal	24.00	25.00

BABY PROOF SETS

KM#	Date	Mintage Identification	Issue Price	Mkt Val
BPS7	2001 (6)	15,011 KM#401-403, 406, 491.1, 534.1 plus silver medal	—	165
BPS8	2002 (6)	13,996 KM#401, 403, 406, 600.2, 602 plus silver medal	—	153
BPS9	2003 (6)	14,799 KM#401-402, 406, 688-689, 690.1 plus silver medal	—	125
BPS10	2004 (6)	13,996 KM#401-404, 406, 733 plus silver medal	—	110
BPS11	2005 (6)	— KM#401-402, 406, 745-747 plus silver medal	—	95.00
BPS12	2006 (6)	— KM#401-404, 406, 489 plus silver medal	—	95.00

MINT SETS

KM#	Date	Mintage Identification	Issue Price	Mkt Val
MS49	2001 (6)	— KM#401-403, 406, 491.1, 534.1	—	50.00
MS39	2001 (3)	— KM532-533, 534.1	7.80	15.00
MS48	2001 (20)	— KM532-533, 534.1, 491.1, 550-565	43.68	100
MS40	2001 (3)	— KM534.1, 550-551	7.80	15.00
MS41	2001 (3)	— KM534.1, 552-553	7.80	15.00
MS42	2001 (3)	— KM534.1, 554-555	7.80	15.00
MS43	2001 (3)	— KM534.1, 556-557	7.80	15.00
MS44	2001 (3)	— KM534.1, 558-559	7.80	15.00
MS45	2001 (3)	— KM534.1, 560, 561	7.80	15.00
MS46	2001 (3)	— KM534.1, 562-563	7.80	15.00
MS47	2001 (3)	— KM534.1, 564, 565	7.80	15.00
MS51	2002 (3)	— KM#691.2, 692, 693	—	2,000
MS50	2002 (6)	— KM#401-403, 406, 600.1, 602	—	32.50
MS52	2003 (5)	— KM401, 402, 406, 689, 690	—	25.00
MS53	2004 (6)	— KM401-404, 406, 733.1	—	25.00
MS54	2005 (6)	— KM#401, 402, 406, 745-747	—	20.00
MS55	2006 (8)	— KM#401-404, 406, 489, 767-768 40 Years of Decimal Currency	18.50	22.50
MS56	2006 (15)	— KM#770-781, 1001-1003	80.00	140

PROOF SETS

KM#	Date	Mintage Identification	Issue Price	Mkt Val
PS107	2001 (3)	— KM532, 533, 534.2	21.00	35.00
PS108	2001 (3)	— KM534.2, 550, 551	21.00	35.00
PS109	2001 (3)	— KM534.2, 552, 553	21.00	35.00
PS110	2001 (3)	— KM534.2, 554, 555	21.00	35.00
PS111	2001 (3)	— KM534.2, 556, 557	21.00	35.00
PS112	2001 (3)	— KM534.2, 558-559	21.00	35.00
PS113	2001 (3)	— KM534.2, 560-561	21.00	35.00
PS114	2001 (3)	— KM534.2, 562-563	21.00	35.00
PS115	2001 (3)	— KM534.2, 564, 565	21.00	35.00
PS116	2001 (20)	— KM491.2, 532-533, 534.2, 549.2, 550-565	120	250
PS117	2001 (6)	— KM#401-403, 406, 491.1, 534.1	—	145
PS118	2001 (6)	650 Federation Centennial Set	—	6,000
PS119	2002 (6)	39,513 KM#401-403, 406, 600.2, 602	—	95.00
PS120	2006 (6)	39,090 KM#401-402, 406, 688-689, 690.1	—	70.00
PS121	2003 (6)	6,500 KM#401b, 402b, 406b, 688a, 689a, 690a	—	275
PS122	2003 (4)	10,000 KM763-766	118	128
PS123	2004 (6)	50,000 KM#401-404, 406, 733	—	78.00
PS124	2004 (6)	6,500 KM#401b, 402b, 403b, 404a, 406b, 733.1a	—	200
PS125	2005 (6)	— KM#401, 402, 406, 745-747	—	70.00
PS126	2005 (6)	6,500 KM#401b, 402b, 406b, 745a, 746a, 747a	—	200
PS127	2005 (6)	650 KM#401a, 402a, 406a, 745b, 746b, 747b	—	5,850
PS128	2006 (8)	— KM#401-404, 406, 489, 767-768	62.50	90.00
PS129	2006 (8)	6,500 KM#62a, 63a, 64a, 65a, 66a, 77a, 852	180	185

WEDDING SPECIMEN SETS

KM#	Date	Mintage Identification	Issue Price	Mkt Val
WSS1	2002 (6)	3,322 KM#401-403, 406, 600.1, 602 Plaque	—	97.50
WSS2	2003 (6)	3,249 KM#401-402, 406, 688-690 Plaque	—	55.00
WSS3	2004 (6)	4,000 KM#401-404, 406, 733.1 Plaque	—	58.50
WSS4	2005 (6)	— KM#401-402, 406, 745-747 Plaque	60.00	60.00
WSS5	2006 (8)	— KM#401-404, 406, 489, 767-768 Plaque	60.00	60.00

AUSTRIA

The Republic of Austria, a parliamentary democracy located in mountainous central Europe, has an area of 32,374 sq. mi. (83,850 sq. km.) and a population of 8.08 million. Capital: Wien (Vienna). Austria is primarily an industrial country. Machinery, iron, steel, textiles, yarns and timber are exported.

REPUBLIC

POST WWII DECIMAL COINAGE
100 Groschen - 1 Schilling

KM# 2878   10 GROSCHEN
1.1000 g., Aluminum, 20 mm. **Obv:** Small Imperial Eagle with Austrian shield on breast, at top between numbers, scalloped rim, stylized inscription below **Rev:** Large value above date, scalloped rim **Edge:** Plain **Designer:** Hans Köttenstorfer

Date	Mintage	F	VF	XF	Unc	BU
2001	—	—	—	—	0.45	—
2001 Special Unc	75,000	—	—	—	—	1.50

KM# 2885   50 GROSCHEN
3.0000 g., Aluminum-Bronze, 19.4 mm. **Obv:** Austrian shield **Obv. Designer:** Hans Köttenstorfer **Rev:** Large value above date **Rev. Designer:** Ferdinand Welz **Edge:** Reeded

Date	Mintage	F	VF	XF	Unc	BU
2001	—	—	—	—	0.45	—
2001 Special Unc	75,000	—	—	—	—	2.00

KM# 2886   SCHILLING
4.2000 g., Aluminum-Bronze, 22.5 mm. **Obv:** Large value above date **Obv. Designer:** Edwin Grienauer **Rev:** Edelweiss flower **Rev. Designer:** Ferdinand Welz **Edge:** Plain

Date	Mintage	F	VF	XF	Unc	BU
2001 Special Unc	75,000	—	—	—	—	2.00

KM# 2889a   5 SCHILLING
4.8000 g., Copper-Nickel, 23.5 mm. **Obv:** Lippizaner stallion with rider, rearing left **Obv. Designer:** Hans Köttenstorfer **Rev:** Austrian shield divides date, value above, sprays below **Rev. Designer:** Josef Köblinger **Edge:** Plain

Date	Mintage	F	VF	XF	Unc	BU
2001 Special Unc	75,000	—	—	—	—	2.50

KM# 2918   10 SCHILLING
6.2000 g., Copper-Nickel Plated Nickel, 26 mm. **Obv:** Imperial Eagle with Austrian shield on breast, holding hammer and sickle **Obv. Designer:** Kurt Bodlak **Rev:** Woman of Wachau left, value and date right of hat **Rev. Designer:** Ferdinand Welz

Date	Mintage	F	VF	XF	Unc	BU
2001 Special Unc	75,000	—	—	—	—	2.50

KM# 3075   20 SCHILLING
8.0000 g., Copper-Aluminum-Nickel, 27.7 mm. **Subject:** Johann Nepomuk Nestroy **Obv:** Denomination within square **Rev:** Bust half left **Edge:** 19 incuse dots **Designer:** Herbert Wähner

Date	Mintage	F	VF	XF	Unc	BU
2001	225,000	—	—	—	4.50	—
2001 Special Unc	75,000	—	—	—	—	10.00

KM# 3076   50 SCHILLING
8.1500 g., Bi-Metallic Copper-Nickel clad Nickel center in Aluminum-Bronze ring, 26.5 mm. **Subject:** The Schilling Era **Obv:** Denomination and shields **Rev:** Four old coin designs **Edge:** Plain

Date	Mintage	F	VF	XF	Unc	BU
2001	600,000	—	—	—	7.50	—
2001 Special Unc.	100,000	—	—	—	—	9.50

KM# 3073   100 SCHILLING
13.7000 g., Bi-Metallic Titanium center in silver ring., 34 mm. **Subject:** Transportation **Obv:** Automobile engine **Obv. Designer:** Thomas Pesendorfer **Rev:** Car, train, truck, and plane **Rev. Designer:** Andreas Zanaschka **Edge:** Plain

Date	Mintage	F	VF	XF	Unc	BU
2001 Proof	50,000	Value: 40.00				

KM# 3077   100 SCHILLING
20.0000 g., 0.9000 Silver 0.5787 oz. ASW, 34 mm. **Subject:** Charlemagne **Obv:** Holy Roman Emperor's crown above denomination **Obv. Designer:** Thomas Pesendorfer **Rev:** Bust 3/4 facing with scepter, two shields at right **Rev. Designer:** Herbert Wähner **Edge:** Reeded

Date	Mintage	F	VF	XF	Unc	BU
2001 Proof	50,000	Value: 40.00				

KM# 3079   100 SCHILLING
20.0000 g., 0.9000 Silver 0.5787 oz. ASW, 34 mm. **Subject:** Duke Rudolf IV **Obv:** University teaching scene **Obv. Designer:** Thomas Pesendorfer **Rev:** Bust on right looking left, St. Stephen's Cathedral at left **Rev. Designer:** Herbert Wähner **Edge:** Reeded

Date	Mintage	F	VF	XF	Unc	BU
2001 Proof	50,000	Value: 40.00				

KM# 3074   500 SCHILLING
10.1400 g., 0.9860 Gold 0.3214 oz. AGW, 22 mm. **Subject:** 2000 Years of Christianity - Bible and symbols of the saints: Matthew, Luke, Mark, and John **Rev:** St. Paul reading from a scroll to two listeners **Designer:** Thomas Pesendorfer

Date	Mintage	F	VF	XF	Unc	BU
2001 Proof	50,000	Value: 400				

KM# 3078   500 SCHILLING
24.0000 g., 0.9250 Silver 0.7137 oz. ASW, 37 mm. **Subject:** Kufstein Castle **Obv:** Castle view above denomination **Rev:** Emperor Maximilian being shown one of his new cannons **Edge:** Plain with engraved lettering **Designer:** Thomas Pesendorfer

Date	Mintage	F	VF	XF	Unc	BU
2001	50,000	—	—	—	45.00	—
2001 Special Unc.	15,000	—	—	—	—	50.00
2001 Proof	30,000	Value: 60.00				

KM# 3080   500 SCHILLING
24.0000 g., 0.9250 Silver 0.7137 oz. ASW, 37 mm. **Subject:** Schattenburg Castle **Obv:** Castle view **Obv. Designer:** Thomas Pesendorfer **Rev:** Two medieval armourers at work **Rev. Designer:** Helmut Andexlinger **Edge:** Plain with engraved lettering

Date	Mintage	F	VF	XF	Unc	BU
2001	37,000	—	—	—	42.00	—
2001 Special Unc	15,000	—	—	—	—	50.00
2001 Proof	43,000	Value: 60.00				

KM# 3081 1000 SCHILLING
16.2200 g., 0.9860 Gold 0.5142 oz. AGW, 30 mm.
Subject: Austrian National Library **Obv:** Archduke Maximilian as
a student **Obv. Designer:** Thomas Pesendorfer **Rev:** Library
interior view **Rev. Designer:** Herbert Wähner **Edge:** Reeded

Date	Mintage	F	VF	XF	Unc	BU
2001	30,000	—	—	—	—	650

BULLION COINAGE
Philharmonic Issues

KM# 3004 200 SCHILLING
3.1100 g., 0.9999 Gold 0.1000 oz. AGW, 16 mm. **Series:** Vienna
Philharmonic Orchestra **Obv:** The Golden Hall organ **Rev:** Wind
and string instruments **Designer:** Thomas Pesendorfer

Date	Mintage	F	VF	XF	Unc	BU
2001	26,400	—	—	—	—BV+13%	—

KM# 2989 500 SCHILLING
7.7760 g., 0.9999 Gold 0.2500 oz. AGW, 22 mm. **Series:** Vienna
Philharmonic Orchestra **Obv:** The Golden Hall organ **Rev:** Wind
and string instruments **Designer:** Thomas Pesendorfer

Date	Mintage	F	VF	XF	Unc	BU
2001	25,800	—	—	—	—BV+10%	—

KM# 3031 1000 SCHILLING
15.5500 g., 0.9999 Gold 0.4999 oz. AGW, 28 mm. **Series:** Vienna
Philharmonic Orchestra **Obv:** The Golden Hall organ **Rev:** Wind
and string instruments **Designer:** Thomas Pesendorfer

Date	Mintage	F	VF	XF	Unc	BU
2001	26,800	—	—	—	— BV+8%	—

KM# 2990 2000 SCHILLING
31.1035 g., 0.9999 Gold 0.9999 oz. AGW, 37 mm. **Series:** Vienna
Philharmonic Orchestra **Obv:** The Golden Hall organ **Rev:** Wind
and string instruments **Designer:** Thomas Pesendorfer

Date	Mintage	F	VF	XF	Unc	BU
2001	54,700	—	—	—	BV+4%	—

EURO COINAGE
European Union Issues

KM# 3082 EURO CENT
2.3000 g., Copper Plated Steel, 16.3 mm. **Obv:** Gentian flower
Obv. Legend: EIN EURO CENT **Obv. Designer:** Josef Kaiser
Rev: Denomination and globe **Rev. Designer:** Luc Luycx
Edge: Plain

Date	Mintage	F	VF	XF	Unc	BU
2002	378,400,000	—	—	—	0.35	—
2002 Special Unc	100,000	—	—	—	—	0.50
2002 Proof	10,000	Value: 15.00				
2003	10,800,000	—	—	—	0.35	—
2003 Special Unc	125,000	—	—	—	—	0.50

Date	Mintage	F	VF	XF	Unc	BU
2003 Proof	25,000	Value: 3.00				
2004	115,000,000	—	—	—	0.35	—
2004 Special Unc	100,000	—	—	—	—	0.50
2004 Proof	20,000	Value: 3.00				
2005	122,900,000	—	—	—	0.35	—
2005 Special Unc	100,000	—	—	—	—	0.50
2005 Proof	20,000	Value: 4.00				
2006	48,300,000	—	—	—	0.35	—
2006 Special Unc	100,000	—	—	—	—	0.50
2006 Proof	20,000	Value: 4.00				
2007	111,900,000	—	—	—	0.35	—
2007 Special Unc	75,000	—	—	—	—	0.50
2007 Proof	20,000	Value: 4.00				
2008	50,900,000	—	—	—	0.35	—
2008	50,000	—	—	—	—	0.50
2008 Proof	15,000	Value: 4.00				
2009	—	—	—	—	0.35	—
2009 Special Unc	75,000	—	—	—	—	0.50
2009 Proof	15,000	Value: 4.00				

KM# 3083 2 EURO CENT
3.1000 g., Copper Plated Steel, 18.8 mm. **Obv:** Edelweiss flower
in inner circle, stars in outer circle **Obv. Legend:** ZWEI EURO
CENT **Obv. Designer:** Josef Kaiser **Rev:** Denomination and
globe **Rev. Designer:** Luc Luycx **Edge:** Plain

Date	Mintage	F	VF	XF	Unc	BU
2002	364,400,000	—	—	—	0.50	—
2002 Special Unc	100,000	—	—	—	—	0.65
2002 Proof	10,000	Value: 20.00				
2003	118,500,000	—	—	—	0.50	—
2003 Special Unc	125,000	—	—	—	—	0.65
2003 Proof	25,000	Value: 5.00				
2004	156,400,000	—	—	—	0.50	—
2004 Special Unc	100,000	—	—	—	—	0.65
2004 Proof	20,000	Value: 5.00				
2005	113,000,000	—	—	—	0.50	—
2005 Special Unc	100,000	—	—	—	—	0.65
2005 Proof	20,000	Value: 6.00				
2006	39,800,000	—	—	—	0.35	—
2006 Special Unc	100,000	—	—	—	—	0.65
2006 Proof	20,000	Value: 6.00				
2007	72,200,000	—	—	—	0.35	—
2007 Special Unc	75,000	—	—	—	—	0.65
2007 Proof	20,000	Value: 6.00				
2008	125,100,000	—	—	—	0.35	—
2008 Proof	50,000	—	—	—	—	0.65
2008 Proof	15,000	Value: 6.00				
2009	—	—	—	—	0.35	—
2009 Special Unc	75,000	—	—	—	—	0.65
2009 Proof	15,000	Value: 6.00				

KM# 3084 5 EURO CENT
3.9000 g., Copper Plated Steel, 21.3 mm. **Obv:** Alpine prim rose
flower in inner ring, stars in outer ring **Obv. Legend:** FUNF EURO
CENT **Obv. Designer:** Josef Kaiser **Rev:** Denomination and
globe **Rev. Designer:** Luc Luycx **Edge:** Plain

Date	Mintage	F	VF	XF	Unc	BU
2002	217,000,000	—	—	—	0.75	—
2002 Special Unc	100,000	—	—	—	—	1.00
2002 Proof	10,000	Value: 30.00				
2003	108,500,000	—	—	—	0.75	—
2003 Special Unc	125,000	—	—	—	—	1.00
2003 Proof	25,000	Value: 8.50				
2004	89,300,000	—	—	—	0.75	—
2004 Special Unc	100,000	—	—	—	—	1.00
2004 Proof	20,000	Value: 9.00				
2005	66,100,000	—	—	—	0.75	—
2005 Special Unc	100,000	—	—	—	—	1.00
2005 Proof	20,000	Value: 10.00				
2006	5,600,000	—	—	—	0.75	—
2006 Special Unc	100,000	—	—	—	—	1.00
2006 Proof	20,000	Value: 10.00				
2007	52,700,000	—	—	—	0.75	—
2007 Special Unc	75,000	—	—	—	—	1.00
2007 Proof	20,000	Value: 10.00				
2008	96,700,000	—	—	—	0.75	—
2008 Special Unc	50,000	—	—	—	—	1.00
2008	15,000	Value: 10.00				
2009	—	—	—	—	0.75	—
2009 Special Unc	75,000	—	—	—	—	1.00
2009 Proof	15,000	Value: 10.00				

KM# 3085 10 EURO CENT
4.1000 g., Brass, 19.7 mm. **Obv:** St. Stephen's Cathedral spires
Obv. Designer: Josef Kaiser **Rev:** Relief map of European Union
at left, denomination at center right **Rev. Designer:** Luc Luycx
Edge: Reeded

Date	Mintage	F	VF	XF	Unc	BU
2002	44,160,000	—	—	—	0.75	—
2002 Special Unc	100,000	—	—	—	—	1.00
2002 Proof	10,000	Value: 45.00				
2003 Special Unc	125,000	—	—	—	—	2.50
2003 Proof	25,000	Value: 8.50				
2004	5,200,000	—	—	—	0.80	—
2004 Special Unc	100,000	—	—	—	—	1.00
2004 Proof	20,000	Value: 9.00				
2005	5,200,000	—	—	—	0.80	—
2005 Special Unc	100,000	—	—	—	—	1.00
2005 Proof	20,000	Value: 10.00				
2006	40,000,000	—	—	—	0.75	—
2006 Special Unc	100,000	—	—	—	—	1.00
2006 Proof	20,000	Value: 10.00				
2007	81,300,000	—	—	—	0.75	—
2007 Special Unc	75,000	—	—	—	—	1.00
2007 Proof	20,000	Value: 10.00				

KM# 3139 10 EURO CENT
4.0000 g., Brass, 19.8 mm. **Obv:** St. Stephen's Cathedral spires
Obv. Designer: Josef Kaiser **Rev:** Relief Map of Western
Europe, stars, lines and value **Rev. Designer:** Luc Luycx
Edge: Reeded

Date	Mintage	F	VF	XF	Unc	BU
2008	—	—	—	—	—	0.75
2008 Proof	15,000	Value: 10.00				
2009	—	—	—	—	—	0.75
2009 Proof	—	Value: 10.00				

KM# 3086 20 EURO CENT
5.7200 g., Brass, 22.2 mm. **Obv:** Belvedere Palace gate
Obv. Designer: Josef Kaiser **Rev:** Relief map of European Union
at left, denomination at center right **Rev. Designer:** Luc Luycx
Edge: Notched

Date	Mintage	F	VF	XF	Unc	BU
2002	20,340,000	—	—	—	1.00	—
2002 Special Unc	100,000	—	—	—	—	1.25
2002 Proof	10,000	Value: 60.00				
2003	50,900,000	—	—	—	1.00	—
2003 Special Unc	125,000	—	—	—	—	1.25
2003 Proof	25,000	Value: 10.00				
2004	54,800,000	—	—	—	1.00	—
2004 Special Unc	100,000	—	—	—	—	1.25
2004 Proof	20,000	Value: 11.50				
2005	4,100,000	—	—	—	1.10	—
2005 Special Unc	100,000	—	—	—	—	1.25
2005 Proof	20,000	Value: 12.50				
2006	8,200,000	—	—	—	1.00	—
2006 Special Unc	100,000	—	—	—	—	1.25
2006 Proof	20,000	Value: 12.50				
2007	45,000,000	—	—	—	1.00	—
2007 Special Unc	75,000	—	—	—	—	1.25
2007 Proof	20,000	Value: 12.50				

KM# 3140 20 EURO CENT
5.7000 g., Brass, 22.3 mm. **Obv:** Belvedere Palace gate
Obv. Designer: Josef Kaiser **Rev:** Expanded relief map of
European Union at left, denomination at center right
Rev. Designer: Luc Luycx **Edge:** Notched

Date	Mintage	F	VF	XF	Unc	BU
2008	45,300,000	—	—	—	1.00	—
2008 Special Unc.	—	—	—	—	—	1.50
2008 Proof	15,000	Value: 12.50				
2009	—	—	—	—	1.00	—
2009 Special Unc.	—	—	—	—	—	1.50
2009 Proof	15,000	Value: 12.50				

KM# 3087 50 EURO CENT

7.8000 g., Brass, 24.3 mm. **Obv:** Secession building in Vienna **Obv. Designer:** Josef Kaiser **Rev:** Relief map of European Union at left, denomination at center right **Rev. Designer:** Luc Luycx **Edge:** Reeded

Date	Mintage	F	VF	XF	Unc	BU
2002	16,910,000	—	—	—	1.25	—
2002 Special Unc	100,000	—	—	—	—	1.50
2002 Proof	10,000	Value: 75.00				
2003	9,100,000	—	—	—	1.25	—
2003 Special Unc	125,000	—	—	—	—	1.50
2003 Proof	25,000	Value: 12.50				
2004	3,100,000	—	—	—	1.25	—
2004 Special Unc	100,000	—	—	—	—	1.50
2004 Proof	20,000	Value: 13.50				
2005	3,100,000	—	—	—	1.25	—
2005 Special Unc	100,000	—	—	—	—	1.50
2005 Proof	20,000	Value: 15.00				
2006	3,200,000	—	—	—	1.25	—
2006 Special Unc	100,000	—	—	—	—	1.50
2006 Proof	20,000	Value: 15.00				
2007	300,000	—	—	—	1.25	—
2007 Special Unc	75,000	—	—	—	—	1.50
2007 Proof	20,000	Value: 15.00				

KM# 3141 50 EURO CENT

7.8000 g., Brass, 24.3 mm. **Obv:** Secession building in Vienna **Obv. Designer:** Josef Kaiser **Rev:** Expanded relief map of European Union at left, denomination at right **Rev. Designer:** Luc Luycx **Edge:** Reeded

Date	Mintage	F	VF	XF	Unc	BU
2008	3,000,000	—	—	—	1.25	—
2008 Special Unc	50,000	—	—	—	—	1.50
2008 Proof	15,000	Value: 15.00				
2009		—	—	—	1.25	—
2009 Special Unc	75,000	—	—	—	—	1.50
2009 Proof	15,000	Value: 15.00				

KM# 3088 EURO

7.5000 g., Bi-Metallic Copper-Nickel center in Brass ring, 23.2 mm. **Obv:** Bust of Mozart right within inner circle, stars in outer circle **Obv. Designer:** Josef Kaiser **Rev:** Value at left, relief map of European Union at right **Rev. Designer:** Luc Luycx **Edge:** Reeded and plain sections

Date	Mintage	F	VF	XF	Unc	BU
2002	223,500,000	—	—	—	2.50	—
2002 Special Unc	100,000	—	—	—	—	2.75
2002 Proof	10,000	Value: 100				
2003 Special Unc	125,000	—	—	—	—	5.00
2003 Proof	25,000	Value: 16.50				
2004	2,600,000	—	—	—	2.50	—
2004 Special Unc	100,000	—	—	—	—	2.75
2004 Proof	20,000	Value: 17.50				
2005	2,600,000	—	—	—	2.50	—
2005 Special Unc	100,000	—	—	—	—	2.75
2005 Proof	20,000	Value: 18.50				
2006	7,700,000	—	—	—	2.50	—
2006 Special Unc	100,000	—	—	—	—	2.75
2006 Proof	20,000	Value: 18.50				
2007	41,100,000	—	—	—	2.50	—
2007 Special Unc	75,000	—	—	—	—	2.75
2007 Proof	20,000	Value: 18.50				

KM# 3142 EURO

7.5000 g., Bi-Metallic Copper-Nickel center in Brass ring, 23.2 mm. **Obv:** Bust of Mozart right within inner circle, stars in outer circle **Obv. Designer:** Josef Kaiser **Rev:** Value at left, expanded relief map of European Union at right **Rev. Designer:** Luc Luycx **Edge:** Reeded and plain sections

Date	Mintage	F	VF	XF	Unc	BU
2008	65,500,000	—	—	—	2.00	—
2008 Special Unc		—	—	—	—	2.75
2008 Proof	15,000	Value: 15.00				
2009		—	—	—	2.00	—
2009 Special Unc		—	—	—	—	2.75
2009 Proof		Value: 15.00				

KM# 3089 2 EURO

8.5000 g., Bi-Metallic Brass center in Copper-Nickel ring, 25.75 mm. **Obv:** Bust of Bertha von Suttner, Novelist and winner of 1905 Peace Prize, facing left within inner circle, stars in outer circle **Obv. Designer:** Joaef Kaiser **Rev:** Value at left, relief map of European Union at right **Rev. Designer:** Luc Luycx **Edge:** Reeded and lettered: 2 EURO (star) (star) (star) (star)

Date	Mintage	F	VF	XF	Unc	BU
2002	196,400,000	—	—	—	3.75	—
2002 Special Unc	100,000	—	—	—	—	4.00
2002 Proof	10,000	Value: 125				
2003	4,700,000	—	—	—	3.75	—
2003 Special Unc	125,000	—	—	—	—	4.00
2003 Proof	25,000	Value: 25.00				
2004	2,500,000	—	—	—	3.75	—
2004 Special Unc	100,000	—	—	—	—	4.00
2004 Proof	20,000	Value: 27.50				
2006	2,300,000	—	—	—	3.75	—
2006 Special Unc	100,000	—	—	—	—	4.00
2006 Proof	20,000	Value: 27.50				
2008		—	—	—	3.75	—
2008 Proof		Value: 27.50				

KM# 3124 2 EURO

8.5200 g., Bi-Metallic Brass center in Copper-Nickel ring, 25.7 mm. **Subject:** 50th Anniversary of the State Treaty **Obv:** Treaty seals and signatures **Rev:** Denomination and map **Edge:** Reeding over lettering **Edge Lettering:** "2 EURO" and 3 stars repeated four times

Date	Mintage	F	VF	XF	Unc	BU
2005	6,880,000	—	—	—	5.00	—
2005 Special Unc	100,000	—	—	—	—	6.00
2005 Proof	20,000	Value: 27.50				

KM# 3150 2 EURO

8.5200 g., Bi-Metallic Brass center in Copper-Nickel ring **Subject:** 50th Anniversary - Treaty of Rome

Date	Mintage	F	VF	XF	Unc	BU
2007	8,900,000	—	—	—	4.00	5.00
2007 Proof	20,000	Value: 27.50				

KM# 3143 2 EURO

8.5000 g., Bi-Metallic Brass center in Copper-Nickel ring, 25.8 mm. **Obv:** Bust of Bertha von Suttner, Novelist and winner of 1905 Peace Prize, at right facing left in inner circle, stars in outer circle **Obv. Designer:** Josef Kaiser **Rev:** Value at left, expanded relief map of European Union at right **Rev. Designer:** Luc Luycx **Edge:** Reeded and lettered: 2 EURO ★ ★ ★

Date	Mintage	F	VF	XF	Unc	BU
2008	2,600,000	—	—	—	5.00	—
2008 Special Unc	50,000	—	—	—	—	6.00
2008 Proof	15,000	Value: 25.00				
2009		—	—	—	5.00	6.00
2009 Proof		Value: 25.00				

KM# 3175 2 EURO

8.5000 g., Bi-Metallic Copper-nickel center in brass ring, 25.75 mm. **Subject:** 10th Anniversary - European Monetary Union

Date	Mintage	F	VF	XF	Unc	BU
2009	4,910,000	—	—	—	7.50	—
2009 Special Unc	15,000	—	—	—	—	—
2009 Proof		Value: 25.00				

KM# 3091 5 EURO

10.0000 g., 0.8000 Silver 0.2572 oz. ASW, 28.5 mm. **Subject:** Schoenbrunn Zoo **Obv:** Denomination within sun design at center, provincial arms surround **Rev:** Building and animals **Edge:** Plain **Shape:** 9-sided

Date	Mintage	F	VF	XF	Unc	BU
ND(2002)	500,000	—	—	—	12.50	—
ND(2002) Special Unc	100,000	—	—	—	—	22.50

KM# 3105 5 EURO

10.0000 g., 0.8000 Silver 0.2572 oz. ASW, 28.5 mm. **Subject:** Water Power **Obv:** Denomination within sun design at center, provincial arms surround **Rev:** Dam with turbine, electric power plant and fish **Edge:** Plain **Shape:** 9-sided

Date	Mintage	F	VF	XF	Unc	BU
2003	500,000	—	—	—	10.00	—
2003 Special Unc	100,000	—	—	—	—	15.00

KM# 3122 5 EURO

10.0000 g., 0.8000 Silver 0.2572 oz. ASW, 28.5 mm. **Subject:** Enlargement of the European Union **Obv:** Denomination within sun design at center, provincial arms surround **Rev:** Map of Europe above country names **Edge:** Plain **Shape:** 9-sided

Date	Mintage	F	VF	XF	Unc	BU
2004	275,000	—	—	—	9.50	—
2004 Special select	125,000	—	—	—	—	12.50

KM# 3113 5 EURO

8.0000 g., 0.8000 Silver 0.2058 oz. ASW, 28.5 mm. **Obv:** Denomination within sun design at center, provincial arms surround **Rev:** Soccer player scoring a goal **Edge:** Plain **Shape:** 9-sided **Note:** Centennial of Austrian Soccer

Date	Mintage	F	VF	XF	Unc	BU
2004	600,000	—	—	—	9.50	—
2004 Special Unc	100,000	—	—	—	—	12.50

KM# 3117   5 EURO
10.0000 g., 0.8000 Silver 0.2572 oz. ASW, 28.5 mm.
Subject: Centennial of sport Skiing **Obv:** Denomination within sun design at center, provincial arms surround **Rev:** Skier within snowflake design **Edge:** Plain **Shape:** 9-sided

Date	Mintage	F	VF	XF	Unc	BU
2005	500,000	—	—	—	9.50	—
2005 Special Unc	100,000	—	—	—	—	14.50

KM# 3120   5 EURO
10.0000 g., 0.8000 Silver 0.2572 oz. ASW, 28.5 mm.
Subject: 10th Anniversary of Austrian E U Membership **Obv:** Denomination within sun design at center, provincial arms surround **Rev:** Carinthian Gate Theater and Beethoven cameo portrait **Edge:** Plain **Shape:** 9-sided

Date	Mintage	F	VF	XF	Unc	BU
2005	275,000	—	—	—	12.50	—
2005 Special Unc	125,000	—	—	—	—	14.50

KM# 3131   5 EURO
10.0000 g., 0.8000 Silver 0.2572 oz. ASW, 28.5 mm.
Subject: Mozart **Obv:** Denomination within sun design at center, provincial arms surround **Rev:** Mozart and the Salzburg Cathedral **Edge:** Plain **Shape:** Nine sided

Date	Mintage	F	VF	XF	Unc	BU
2006	375,000	—	—	—	15.00	—
2006 Special Unc	125,000	—	—	—	—	17.50

KM# 3132   5 EURO
10.0000 g., 0.8000 Silver 0.2572 oz. ASW, 28.5 mm.
Subject: Austrian Presidency of the EU **Obv:** Value in circle of arms **Rev:** Vienna Hofburg and Josefsplatz view **Edge:** Plain **Shape:** Nine sided

Date	Mintage	F	VF	XF	Unc	BU
2006	250,000	—	—	—	12.50	—
2006 Special Unc	100,000	—	—	—	—	14.50

KM# 3144   5 EURO
10.0000 g., 0.8000 Silver 0.2572 oz. ASW, 28.5 mm.
Subject: Universal Male Suffrage Centennial **Obv:** Value in circle of shields **Rev:** Cameo portraits of Franz Joseph and von Beck on Reichsrat scene **Edge:** Plain **Shape:** 9-sided

Date	Mintage	F	VF	XF	Unc	BU
2007	150,000	—	—	—	13.00	—
2007 Special Unc	100,000	—	—	—	—	15.00

KM# 3145   5 EURO
10.0000 g., 0.8000 Silver 0.2572 oz. ASW, 28.5 mm.
Obv: Value in circle of shields **Rev:** Mariazell church **Edge:** Plain. **Shape:** 9-sided

Date	Mintage	F	VF	XF	Unc	BU
2007	450,000	—	—	—	12.50	—
2007 Special Unc	100,000	—	—	—	—	15.00

KM# 3156   5 EURO
0.8000 Silver, 28.5 mm.   **Subject:** Herbert Von Karajan, 100th Birth Anniversary **Obv:** Value and nine provincial shields **Rev:** Bust and notes of Beethoven's Ninth Symphony **Shape:** 9-sided

Date	Mintage	F	VF	XF	Unc	BU
2008	150,000	—	—	—	17.00	—
2008 Special Unc	100,000	—	—	—	—	17.50

KM# 3163   5 EURO
10.0000 g., 0.8000 Silver 0.2572 oz. ASW, 28.5 mm.
Obv: Value within center of nine shields **Rev:** Two soccer players **Shape:** 9-sided

Date	Mintage	F	VF	XF	Unc	BU
2008	225,000	—	—	—	9.50	—
2008 Special Unc	100,000	—	—	—	—	12.50

KM# 3164   5 EURO
10.0000 g., 0.8000 Silver 0.2572 oz. ASW, 28.5 mm.
Obv: Value within center of nine shields **Rev:** One soccer player **Shape:** 9-sided

Date	Mintage	F	VF	XF	Unc	BU
2008	225,000	—	—	—	9.50	—
2008 Special Unc	100,000	—	—	—	—	12.50

KM# 3170   5 EURO
10.0000 g., 0.8000 Silver 0.2572 oz. ASW, 28.5 mm.
Subject: Joseph Haydn, 200th Anniversary of Death **Obv:** Value at center of nine shields **Rev:** Bust facing right at left, pair of violins at right **Shape:** 7-sided

Date	Mintage	F	VF	XF	Unc	BU
2009	100,000	—	—	—	15.00	—

KM# 3177   5 EURO
10.0000 g., 0.8000 Silver 0.2572 oz. ASW, 28.5 mm.
Subject: Tyrolean Resistance Fighters, 1809

Date	Mintage	F	VF	XF	Unc	BU
2009	250,000	—	—	—	20.00	—
2009 Special Unc	100,000	—	—	—	—	35.00

KM# 3096   10 EURO
17.3000 g., 0.9250 Silver 0.5145 oz. ASW, 32 mm.
Subject: Ambras Palace **Obv:** Palace, denomination below **Rev:** Three strolling musicians **Edge:** Reeded

Date	Mintage	F	VF	XF	Unc	BU
2002	130,000	—	—	—	17.00	—
2002 Special Unc	20,000	—	—	—	—	30.00
2002 Proof	50,000	Value: 40.00				

KM# 3099   10 EURO
17.3000 g., 0.9250 Silver 0.5145 oz. ASW, 32 mm.
Subject: Eggenberg Palace and Johannes Kepler **Obv:** Palace, denomination below **Rev:** Half figure seated with tools **Edge:** Reeded

Date	Mintage	F	VF	XF	Unc	BU
2002	130,000	—	—	—	17.50	—
2002 Special Unc	20,000	—	—	—	—	30.00
2002 Proof	50,000	Value: 32.50				

KM# 3103   10 EURO
17.3000 g., 0.9250 Silver 0.5145 oz. ASW, 32 mm.
Subject: Castle of Schloss Hof **Obv:** Baroque fountain and palace, denomination below **Rev:** Two gardeners at work **Edge:** Reeded

Date	Mintage	F	VF	XF	Unc	BU
2003	130,000	—	—	—	17.50	—
2003 Special Unc	20,000	—	—	—	—	30.00
2003 Proof	50,000	Value: 32.50				

KM# 3106   10 EURO
17.3000 g., 0.9250 Silver 0.5145 oz. ASW, 32 mm.
Subject: Schoenbrunn Palace **Obv:** Fountain with palace background, denomination below **Rev:** Palmenhaus greenhouse **Edge:** Reeded

Date	Mintage	F	VF	XF	Unc	BU
2003	100,000	—	—	—	17.50	—
2003 Special Unc	40,000	—	—	—	—	27.50
2003 Proof	60,000	Value: 30.00				

KM# 3111 10 EURO
17.2973 g., 0.9250 Silver 0.5144 oz. ASW, 32 mm.
Obv: Hellbrunn Castle, denomination below **Rev:** Archbishop Marcus Sitticus and Hellbrunn's "Roman Theatre" **Edge:** Reeded

Date	Mintage	F	VF	XF	Unc	BU
2004	130,000	—	—	—	17.00	—
2004 Special Unc	40,000	—	—	—	—	25.00
2004 Proof	60,000	Value: 30.00				

KM# 3115 10 EURO
17.2973 g., 0.9250 Silver 0.5144 oz. ASW, 32 mm.
Obv: Artstetten Castle, denomination below portraits of Franz Ferdinand and Sophie **Edge:** Reeded

Date	Mintage	F	VF	XF	Unc	BU
2004	130,000	—	—	—	17.00	—
2004 Special Unc	40,000	—	—	—	—	25.00
2004 Proof	60,000	Value: 30.00				

KM# 3121 10 EURO
17.3000 g., 0.9250 Silver 0.5145 oz. ASW, 32 mm.
Subject: 60th Anniversary of the Second Republic **Obv:** Statue of Athena, nine provincial shields and denomination at right **Rev:** Parliament building above broken chain, crowd below

Date	Mintage	F	VF	XF	Unc	BU
2005	130,000	—	—	—	17.00	—
2005 Special Unc	40,000	—	—	—	—	25.00
2005 Proof	60,000	Value: 35.00				

KM# 3125 10 EURO
17.3000 g., 0.9250 Silver 0.5145 oz. ASW, 32 mm.
Subject: Reopening of the Burg Theater and Opera **Obv:** Two large buildings, denomination at left **Rev:** Comedy and Tragedy Masks **Edge:** Reeded

Date	Mintage	F	VF	XF	Unc	BU
2005	130,000	—	—	—	17.00	—
2005 Proof	60,000	Value: 35.00				
2005 Special Unc	40,000	—	—	—	—	25.00

KM# 3129 10 EURO
17.2973 g., 0.9250 Silver 0.5144 oz. ASW, 32 mm.
Subject: Nonnenberg Abbey **Obv:** Abbey view, denomination below **Rev:** Statue of St. Erentrudis **Edge:** Reeded

Date	Mintage	F	VF	XF	Unc	BU
2006	130,000	—	—	—	17.00	—
2006 Special Unc	40,000	—	—	—	—	25.00
2006 Proof	60,000	Value: 35.00				

KM# 3137 10 EURO
17.3000 g., 0.9250 Silver 0.5145 oz. ASW, 32 mm. **Obv:** Gottweig Abby above value **Rev:** Charles VI and staircase **Edge:** Reeded

Date	Mintage	F	VF	XF	Unc	BU
2006	130,000	—	—	—	17.00	—
2006 Special Unc	40,000	—	—	—	—	30.00
2006 Proof	60,000	Value: 40.00				

KM# 3146 10 EURO
17.3000 g., 0.9250 Silver 0.5145 oz. ASW, 32 mm. **Obv:** Melk Abbey view **Rev:** Inner view of the Melk Abbey dome **Edge:** Reeded

Date	Mintage	F	VF	XF	Unc	BU
2007	130,000	—	—	—	17.00	—
2007 Special Unc	40,000	—	—	—	—	25.00
2007 Proof	60,000	Value: 35.00				

KM# 3148 10 EURO
17.3000 g., 0.9250 Silver 0.5145 oz. ASW, 32 mm. **Obv:** St. Paul's Abbey complex **Obv. Legend:** ST. PAUL IM LAVANTTAL **Obv. Inscription:** REPUBLIK / ÖSTERREICH **Rev:** Entrance facade

Date	Mintage	F	VF	XF	Unc	BU
2007	130,000	—	—	—	17.00	—
2007 Special Unc	60,000	—	—	—	—	25.00
2007 Proof	40,000	Value: 35.00				

KM# 3157 10 EURO
17.3000 g., 0.9250 Silver 0.5145 oz. ASW, 32 mm. **Subject:** Abby of Klosterneuburg **Obv:** Aerial exterior view of church complex **Rev:** Cloister

Date	Mintage	F	VF	XF	Unc	BU
2008	130,000	—	—	—	17.00	—
2008 Special Unc	40,000	—	—	—	—	25.00
2008 Proof	60,000	Value: 45.00				

KM# 3162 10 EURO
17.3000 g., 0.9250 Silver 0.5145 oz. ASW, 32 mm.
Subject: Seckau Abbey **Obv:** Exterior of abby, value, date and inscriptions "BENEDIKTINERABTEI SECKAU" and "REPUBLIK OESTERREICH" **Rev:** Interior of abbey

Date	Mintage	F	VF	XF	Unc	BU
2008	130,000	—	—	—	17.00	—
2008 Special Unc	40,000	—	—	—	—	25.00
2008 Proof	60,000	Value: 45.00				

KM# 3176 10 EURO
17.3000 g., 0.9250 Silver 0.5145 oz. ASW, 32 mm.
Series: Tales and Legends **Subject:** Basilisk of Vienna

Date	Mintage	F	VF	XF	Unc	BU
2009	130,000	—	—	—	17.00	—
2009 Special Unc	30,000	—	—	—	—	25.00
2009 Proof	40,000	Value: 40.00				

KM# 3180 10 EURO
17.3000 g., 0.9250 Silver 0.5145 oz. ASW, 32 mm.
Series: Tales and Legends **Subject:** Richard the Lionheart in Dürnstein

Date	Mintage	F	VF	XF	Unc	BU
2009	130,000	—	—	—	20.00	—
2009 Special Unc	30,000	—	—	—	—	25.00
2009 Proof	40,000	Value: 45.00				

KM# 3097 20 EURO
20.0000 g., 0.9000 Silver 0.5787 oz. ASW, 34 mm.
Subject: Ferdinand I - Renaissance **Obv:** Hofburg Palace "Swiss Gate" with two guards, denomination below **Rev:** Bust looking left, coat of arms at left, dates at right **Edge:** Reeded

Date	Mintage	F	VF	XF	Unc	BU
2002 Proof	50,000	Value: 37.50				

KM# 3098 20 EURO
20.0000 g., 0.9000 Silver 0.5787 oz. ASW, 34 mm.
Subject: Prince Eugen - Baroque Period **Obv:** Baroque staircase with statues, denomination below **Rev:** Uniformed bust 1/4 left and dates at right, flags above cannons at left **Edge:** Reeded

Date	Mintage	F	VF	XF	Unc	BU
2002 Proof	50,000	Value: 42.00				

KM# 3104   20 EURO
20.0000 g., 0.9000 Silver 0.5787 oz. ASW, 34 mm. **Subject:** Prince Metternich **Obv:** Early steam locomotive, denomination below **Rev:** Portrait with map background **Edge:** Reeded

Date	Mintage	F	VF	XF	Unc	BU
2003 Proof	50,000	Value: 45.00				

KM# 3107   20 EURO
20.0000 g., 0.9000 Silver 0.5787 oz. ASW, 34 mm. **Obv:** Republic of Austria arms, denomination below **Rev:** Four men in a jeep **Edge:** Reeded **Note:** Post War Austrian Reconstruction

Date	Mintage	F	VF	XF	Unc	BU
2003 Proof	50,000	Value: 50.00				

KM# 3112   20 EURO
20.0000 g., 0.9000 Silver 0.5787 oz. ASW, 34 mm. **Obv:** S.M.S Novara under sail in Chinese waters, denomination below **Rev:** Standing figures behind table with globe and microscope **Edge:** Reeded **Note:** First Global Circumnavigation by an Austrian ship.

Date	Mintage	F	VF	XF	Unc	BU
2004 Proof	50,000	Value: 50.00				

KM# 3114   20 EURO
20.0000 g., 0.9000 Silver 0.5787 oz. ASW, 34 mm. **Obv:** SMS Erzherzog Ferdinand Max sailing to the Battle of Lissa, denomination below **Rev:** Sailors at the wheel with Admiral Tegetthof in background **Edge:** Reeded

Date	Mintage	F	VF	XF	Unc	BU
2004 Proof	50,000	Value: 52.50				

KM# 3126   20 EURO
20.0000 g., 0.9000 Silver 0.5787 oz. ASW, 34 mm. **Obv:** Ship, "Admiral Tegetthoff" in arctic waters, denomination below **Rev:** Expedition leaders, von Payer and Weyprecht with their icebound ship behind them **Edge:** Reeded

Date	Mintage	F	VF	XF	Unc	BU
2005 Proof	50,000	Value: 50.00				

KM# 3127   20 EURO
20.0000 g., 0.9000 Silver 0.5787 oz. ASW, 34 mm. **Obv:** SMS St. George sailing past the Statue of Liberty, denomination below **Rev:** Shipyard at Pola, boat on water **Edge:** Reeded

Date	Mintage	F	VF	XF	Unc	BU
2005 Proof	50,000	Value: 50.00				

KM# 3133   20 EURO
20.0000 g., 0.9000 Silver 0.5787 oz. ASW, 34 mm. **Subject:** Austrian Merchant Marine **Obv:** Two passing steam ships **Rev:** 19th Century Triest harbor view **Edge:** Reeded

Date	Mintage	F	VF	XF	Unc	BU
2006 Proof	50,000	Value: 50.00				

KM# 3134   20 EURO
20.0000 g., 0.9000 Silver 0.5787 oz. ASW, 34 mm. **Obv:** SMS Viribus Unitis, flag ship of the Austrian fleet, and other ships steaming left **Rev:** SMS Viribus Unitis, submarine conning tower and seaplane **Edge:** Reeded

Date	Mintage	F	VF	XF	Unc	BU
2006 Proof	50,000	Value: 50.00				

KM# 3149   20 EURO
20.0000 g., 0.9000 Silver 0.5787 oz. ASW, 34 mm. **Series:** Austrian Railways **Obv:** Steam locomotive 1837 with passenger wagons **Obv. Legend:** REPUBLIK ØSTERREICH **Obv. Inscription:** DAMPFLOKOMOTIVE / AUSTRIA / 1837 **Rev:** People waving at passenger train crossing a trestle **Rev. Legend:** KAISER - FERDINANDS - NORDBAHN **Edge:** Reeded

Date	Mintage	F	VF	XF	Unc	BU
2007 Proof	50,000	Value: 50.00				

KM# 3151   20 EURO
20.0000 g., 0.9000 Silver 0.5787 oz. ASW, 34 mm. **Series:** Austrian Railways **Obv:** Steam locomotive 1848 standing still, viaduct in background **Obv. Legend:** REPUBLIK ØSTERREICH **Obv. Inscription:** DAMPF- / LOKOMOTIVE / STEINBRØCK / 1848 **Rev:** Steam train traveling right through city **Rev. Legend:** K.K. SØDBAHN WIEN - TRIEST **Edge:** Reeded

Date	Mintage	F	VF	XF	Unc	BU
2007 Proof	50,000	Value: 50.00				

KM# 3154   20 EURO
20.0000 g., 0.9000 Silver 0.5787 oz. ASW, 34 mm. **Subject:** Southern Railways **Obv:** Steam Locomotive on iron railway bridge **Obv. Inscription:** KOK kkStB 306 **Rev:** Statue of Empress Elizabeth and train platform in Vienna's West Railway station **Rev. Inscription:** KAISERIN-/ ELIZABETH-/ WESTBAHN **Edge:** Reeded

Date	Mintage	F	VF	XF	Unc	BU
2008 Proof	50,000	Value: 70.00				

KM# 3161   20 EURO
20.0000 g., 0.9000 Silver 0.5787 oz. ASW **Subject:** Imperal - Royal State Railway **Obv:** Locomotive steaming left **Obv. Legend:** Nordbahnhof/Wein **Rev:** Female on platform **Shape:** 34

Date	Mintage	F	VF	XF	Unc	BU
2008 Proof	50,000	Value: 70.00				

KM# 3178 20 EURO
20.0000 g., 0.9000 Silver 0.5787 oz. ASW, 34 mm. **Subject:** The Electric Railway **Obv:** Locomotive model 1189, the Crocodile **Obv. Designer:** Thomas Pesendorfer **Rev:** Train on the Trisanna Bridge, Wiesburg Castle in background **Rev. Designer:** Herbert Wahner

Date	Mintage	F	VF	XF	Unc	BU
2009 Proof	50,000	Value: 50.00				

KM# 3179 20 EURO
20.0000 g., 0.9000 Silver 0.5787 oz. ASW, 34 mm. **Subject:** Railways of the Future **Obv:** Railjet highspeed OBB train **Obv. Designer:** Helmut Andexlinger **Rev:** Electric locomotive of the 1063 class in freight yard **Rev. Designer:** Thomas Pesendorfer

Date	Mintage	F	VF	XF	Unc	BU
2009 Proof	50,000				50.00	—

KM# 3101 25 EURO
17.1500 g., Bi-Metallic 7.15g pure Niobium (Columbium) blue color center in a 9 g., .900 Silver ring, 34 mm. **Subject:** City of Hall in Tyrol **Obv:** Satellite mapping the city from outer space **Rev:** Depiction of the die face used to strike the 1486 guldiner coin **Edge:** Plain

Date	Mintage	F	VF	XF	Unc	BU
2003 Special Unc	50,000	—	—	—	—	125

KM# 3109 25 EURO
17.1500 g., Bi-Metallic Niobium center (7.15) in .900 SILVER 10g, ring, 34 mm. **Subject:** Semmering Alpine Railway **Obv:** Modern and antique locomotives **Rev:** Steam train **Edge:** Plain

Date	Mintage	F	VF	XF	Unc	BU
2004 Special Unc	50,000	—	—	—	—	100

KM# 3119 25 EURO
16.1500 g., Bi-Metallic Purple color pure Niobium 7.15g center in .900 Silver 9g, ring, 34 mm. **Subject:** 50 Years Austrian Television **Obv:** The original test pattern of the 1950's **Rev:** World globe behind "rabbit ear" antenna. Television developmental milestones from 7-1 oclock **Edge:** Plain

Date	Mintage	F	VF	XF	Unc	BU
2005 Special Unc	65,000	—	—	—	—	60.00

KM# 3135 25 EURO
17.5000 g., Bi-Metallic Niobium 7.15g center in .900 Silver 10g ring, 34 mm. **Subject:** European Satellite Navigation **Obv:** Austrian Mint's global location inscribed on a compass face **Rev:** Satellites in orbit around the world globe **Edge:** Plain

Date	Mintage	F	VF	XF	Unc	BU
2006 Special Unc	65,000	—	—	—	—	60.00

KM# 3147 25 EURO
16.5000 g., Bi-Metallic 6.5g Niobium center in .900 Silver 10g ring, 34 mm. **Subject:** Austrian Aviation **Obv:** Interior view of modern cockpit **Rev:** Taube airplane flying above glider and pilot **Edge:** Plain

Date	Mintage	F	VF	XF	Unc	BU
2007 Special Unc	65,000	—	—	—	—	60.00

KM# 3158 25 EURO
16.5000 g., Bi-Metallic Niobium center in silver ring, 34 mm. **Subject:** 150th Anniversary of Birth - Carl Baron Auer von Welsbach, **Obv:** Lighting gas lamp before Vienna City Wall **Obv. Designer:** Herbert Waehner **Rev:** Head of Welsbach, development of light bulbs

Date	Mintage	F	VF	XF	Unc	BU
2008 Special Unc	65,000	—	—	—	—	75.00

KM# 3174 25 EURO
16.5000 g., Bi-Metallic Niobium center in silver ring, 34 mm. **Subject:** Year of Astronomy **Obv:** Galileo head and instruments **Rev:** Space Exploration Satelite

Date	Mintage	F	VF	XF	Unc	BU
2009 Special Unc	65,000	—	—	—	—	75.00

KM# 3090 50 EURO
10.1400 g., 0.9860 Gold 0.3214 oz. AGW, 22 mm. **Subject:** Saints Benedict and Scholastica **Obv:** St. Benedict and his sister St. Scholastica **Rev:** Monk copying a manuscript **Edge:** Reeded

Date	Mintage	F	VF	XF	Unc	BU
2002 Proof	50,000	Value: 420				

KM# 3102 50 EURO
10.1420 g., 0.9860 Gold 0.3215 oz. AGW, 22 mm. **Subject:** Christian Charity **Obv:** Nursing Sister with hospital patient **Rev:** The Good Samaritan **Edge:** Reeded

Date	Mintage	F	VF	XF	Unc	BU
2003 Proof	50,000	Value: 425				

KM# 3110 50 EURO
10.1420 g., 0.9860 Gold 0.3215 oz. AGW, 22 mm. **Subject:** Great Composers - Joseph Haydn (1732-1809) **Obv:** Esterhazy Palace **Rev:** Bust 3/4 right

Date	Mintage	F	VF	XF	Unc	BU
2004 Proof	50,000	Value: 425				

KM# 3118 50 EURO
10.1420 g., 0.9860 Gold 0.3215 oz. AGW, 22 mm. **Subject:** Great Composers - Ludwig Van Beethoven (1770-1827) **Obv:** Lobkowitz Palace above value and document **Rev:** Bust 3/4 facing, dates at left

Date	Mintage	F	VF	XF	Unc	BU
2005 Proof	50,000	Value: 420				

KM# 3130 50 EURO
10.1420 g., 0.9860 Gold 0.3215 oz. AGW, 22 mm. **Subject:** Great Composers - Mozart **Obv:** Mozart's birthplace, denomination below **Rev:** Leopold and Wolfgang Mozart

Date	Mintage	F	VF	XF	Unc	BU
2006 Proof	50,000	Value: 425				

KM# 3138 50 EURO
10.1400 g., 0.9860 Gold 0.3214 oz. AGW, 22 mm. **Obv:** Gerard Van Swieten holding book and facing left **Rev:** Akademie der Wissenschaften building

Date	Mintage	F	VF	XF	Unc	BU
2007 Proof	50,000	Value: 420				

KM# 3153 50 EURO
10.1400 g., 0.9860 Gold 0.3214 oz. AGW, 22 mm. **Subject:** Ignaz Philipp Sammelweis - Personal Hygiene **Obv:** Bust of Sammelweis 3/4 right, staff of Aesculapius at lower right **Obv. Legend:** REPUBLIK ÖSTERREICH **Rev:** Vienna General Hospital, Sammelweis helping patient wash at lower right **Rev. Legend:** ALLGEMEINES KRANKENHAUS WEIN

Date	Mintage	F	VF	XF	Unc	BU
2008 Proof	50,000	Value: 435				

KM# 3171 50 EURO
10.1400 g., 0.9860 Gold 0.3214 oz. AGW **Subject:** Theodor Billroth **Obv:** Bust and Aesculapius staff **Rev:** Operation scene

Date	Mintage	F	VF	XF	Unc	BU
2009 Proof	50,000	Value: 450				

KM# 3100 100 EURO
16.2272 g., 0.9860 Gold 0.5144 oz. AGW, 30 mm. **Subject:** Raphael Donner **Obv:** Portrait in front of building **Rev:** Providentia Fountain **Edge:** Reeded

Date	Mintage	F	VF	XF	Unc	BU
2002 Proof	30,000	Value: 650				

KM# 3108   100 EURO
16.2272 g., 0.9860 Gold 0.5144 oz. AGW, 30 mm. **Obv:** Gustav Klimt standing **Rev:** Klimt's painting "The Kiss" **Edge:** Reeded

Date	Mintage	F	VF	XF	Unc	BU
2003 Proof	30,000	Value: 650				

KM# 3116   100 EURO
16.2272 g., 0.9860 Gold 0.5144 oz. AGW, 30 mm.
Obv: Secession Exhibit Hall in Vienna **Rev:** Knight in armor, "strength" with two women, "ambition and sympathy"

Date	Mintage	F	VF	XF	Unc	BU
2004 Proof	30,000	Value: 650				

KM# 3128   100 EURO
16.2272 g., 0.9860 Gold 0.5144 oz. AGW, 30 mm. **Subject:** St. Leopold's Church at Steinhof **Obv:** Domed church building, denomination below **Rev:** Two angels flank stained glass portrait

Date	Mintage	F	VF	XF	Unc	BU
2005 Proof	30,000	Value: 650				

KM# 3136   100 EURO
16.2272 g., 0.9860 Gold 0.5144 oz. AGW, 30 mm.
Subject: Vienna's River Gate Park **Obv:** Bridge over river scene **Rev:** One of two "sculpted ladies" flanking the park entrance

Date	Mintage	F	VF	XF	Unc	BU
2006 Proof	30,000	Value: 650				

KM# 3155   100 EURO
15.2270 g., 0.9860 Gold 0.4827 oz. AGW, 30 mm. **Obv:** Building at Linke Wienzeile Nr 38 by architect Otto Koloman Wagner **Rev:** Ornate elevator and stairwell

Date	Mintage	F	VF	XF	Unc	BU
2007 Proof	30,000	Value: 650				

KM# 3160   100 EURO
16.2270 g., 0.9860 Gold 0.5144 oz. AGW, 30 mm. **Obv:** Crown of the Holy Roman Emperor set upon coronation robe **Rev:** Otto I seated facing and old St. Peter's Bastilica, Rome

Date	Mintage	F	VF	XF	Unc	BU
2008 Proof	30,000	Value: 650				

KM# 3181   100 EURO
16.2270 g., 0.9860 Gold 0.5144 oz. AGW, 30 mm.
Series: Crowns of the Habsburgs **Subject:** Archducal crown of Austria **Obv:** Crown resting on pillow **Rev:** Procession of the crown, orb and sceptre, Plague memorial column in background

Date	Mintage	F	VF	XF	Unc	BU
2009 Proof	30,000	Value: 650				

EURO BULLION COINAGE
Philharmonic Issues

KM# 3159   1-1/2 EURO
31.1030 g., 0.9990 Silver 0.9989 oz. ASW, 37 mm. **Obv:** Golden Concert Hall **Rev:** Bouquet of Instruments **Edge:** Plain

Date	Mintage	F	VF	XF	Unc	BU
2008	—	—	—	—	—	22.50
2009	—	—	—	—	—	22.50

KM# 3092   10 EURO
3.1210 g., 0.9999 Gold 0.1003 oz. AGW, 16 mm.
Subject: Vienna Philharmonic **Obv:** The Golden Hall organ **Rev:** Musical instruments **Edge:** Segmented reeding

Date	Mintage	F	VF	XF	Unc	BU
2002	75,789	—	—	—	—	BV+13%
2003	59,654	—	—	—	—	BV+13%
2004	67,994	—	—	—	—	BV+13%
2005	62,071	—	—	—	—	BV+13%
2006	39,892	—	—	—	—	BV+13%
2007	76,325	—	—	—	—	BV+13%
2008	176,700	—	—	—	—	BV+13%
2009	—	—	—	—	—	BV+13%

KM# 3093   25 EURO
7.7760 g., 0.9999 Gold 0.2500 oz. AGW, 22 mm. **Subject:** Vienna Philharmonic **Obv:** The Golden Hall organ **Rev:** Musical instruments **Edge:** Segmented reeding

Date	Mintage	F	VF	XF	Unc	BU
2002	40,807	—	—	—	—	BV+10%
2003	34,619	—	—	—	—	BV+10%
2004	32,449	—	—	—	—	BV+10%
2005	32,817	—	—	—	—	BV+10%
2006	29,609	—	—	—	—	BV+10%
2007	34,631	—	—	—	—	BV+10%
2008	97,100	—	—	—	—	BV+10%
2009	—	—	—	—	—	BV+10%

KM# 3094   50 EURO
15.5520 g., 0.9999 Gold 0.4999 oz. AGW, 28 mm.
Subject: Vienna Philharmonic **Obv:** The Golden Hall organ **Rev:** Musical instruments **Edge:** Segmented reeding

Date	Mintage	F	VF	XF	Unc	BU
2002	40,922	—	—	—	—	BV+8%
2003	26,848	—	—	—	—	BV+8%
2004	24,269	—	—	—	—	BV+8%
2005	21,049	—	—	—	—	BV+8%
2006	20,085	—	—	—	—	BV+8%
2007	25,091	—	—	—	—	BV+8%
2008	73,800	—	—	—	—	BV+8%
2009	—	—	—	—	—	BV+8%

KM# 3095   100 EURO
31.1035 g., 0.9999 Gold 0.9999 oz. AGW, 37 mm.
Subject: Vienna Philharmonic **Obv:** The Golden Hall organ **Rev:** Musical instruments **Edge:** Segmented reeding

Date	Mintage	F	VF	XF	Unc	BU
2002	164,105	—	—	—	—	BV+4%
2003	179,881	—	—	—	—	BV+4%
2004	176,319	—	—	—	—	BV+4%
2005	158,564	—	—	—	—	BV+4%
2006	82,174	—	—	—	—	BV+4%
2007	108,675	—	—	—	—	BV+4%
2008	715,800	—	—	—	—	BV+4%
2009	—	—	—	—	—	BV+4%

KM# 3123   100000 EURO
31103.5000 g., 0.9999 Gold 999.85 oz. AGW **Obv:** The Golden Hall organ **Rev:** Musical instruments **Edge:** Reeded

Date	Mintage	F	VF	XF	Unc	BU
2004	15	BV+3%				

MINT SETS

KM#	Date	Mintage	Identification	Issue Price	Mkt Val
MS10	2001 (6)	75,000	KM#2878, 2885, 2886, 2889a, 2918, 3075	25.00	25.00
MS11	2002 (8)	100,000	KM#3082-3089	22.50	25.00
MS12	2003 (8)	125,000	KM#3082-3089	22.50	25.00
MS13	2004 (8)	100,000	KM#3082-3089	—	25.00
MS14	2005 (8)	100,000	KM#3082-3088, 3124	—	25.00
MS15	2006	100,000	KM#3082-3089	—	35.00
MS16	2007 (8)	75,000	KM#3082-3088, 3152	—	—
MS17	2008 (8)	50,000	KM#3082-3084, 3089, 3139-3142	—	25.00
MS18	2009 (8)	75,000	KM#3082-3084, 3139-3142, 3175	—	25.00

PROOF SETS

KM#	Date	Mintage	Identification	Issue Price	Mkt Val
PS63	2002 (8)	10,000	KM#3082-3089	85.00	475
PS64	2003 (8)	25,000	KM#3082-3089	85.00	95.00
PS65	2004 (8)	20,000	KM#3082-3089	—	100
PS66	2005 (8)	20,000	KM#3082-3088, 3124	—	105
PS67	2006 (8)	20,000	KM#3082-3089	—	110
PS68	2007 (8)	20,000	KM#3082-3088, 3150	—	110
PS69	2008 (8)	15,000	KM#3082-3084, 3089, 3139-3142	—	120
PS70	2009 (8)	15,000	KM#3082-3084, 3139-3142, 3175	—	120

AZERBAIJAN

The Republic of Azerbaijan (formerly Azerbaijan S.S.R.) includes the Nakhichevan Autonomous Republic. Situated in the eastern area of Transcaucasia, it is bordered in the west by Armenia, in the north by Georgia and Dagestan, to the east by the Caspian Sea and to the south by Iran. It has an area of 33,430 sq. mi. (86,600 sq. km.) and a population of 7.8 million. Capital: Baku. The area is rich in mineral deposits of aluminum, copper, iron, lead, salt and zinc, with oil as its leading industry. Agriculture and livestock follow in importance.

MONETARY SYSTEM
100 Qapik = 1 Manat

REPUBLIC
DECIMAL COINAGE

KM# 39   QAPIK
2.7000 g., Copper Plated Steel, 16.2 mm. **Obv:** Map above value **Rev:** Value and musical instruments **Edge:** Plain
Designer: Robert Kalina

Date	Mintage	F	VF	XF	Unc	BU
ND (2006)	—	—	—	—	—	2.00

KM# 40   3 QAPIK
3.4000 g., Copper Plated Steel, 18 mm.   **Obv:** Map above value **Rev:** Value above books **Edge:** Grooved **Designer:** Robert Kalina

Date	Mintage	F	VF	XF	Unc	BU
ND (2006)	—					2.50

KM# 41   5 QAPIK
4.7200 g., Copper Plated Steel, 19.8 mm.   **Obv:** Map above value **Rev:** The Maiden Tower, Baku, above value **Edge:** Reeded **Designer:** Robert Kalina

Date	Mintage	F	VF	XF	Unc	BU
ND (2006)	—					2.75

KM# 42   10 QAPIK
5.1000 g., Copper Plated Steel, 22.2 mm.   **Obv:** Map above value **Rev:** Value and Military Helmet, Symbolic of desire to regain Nagorno-Karabakh **Edge:** Notched **Designer:** Robert Kalina

Date	Mintage	F	VF	XF	Unc	BU
ND (2006)	—					3.00

KM# 43   20 QAPIK
6.5000 g., Brass Plated Steel, 24.3 mm.   **Obv:** Map above value **Rev:** Value and spiral staircase **Edge:** Segmented reeding **Designer:** Robert Kalina

Date	Mintage	F	VF	XF	Unc	BU
ND (2006)	—					4.00

KM# 44   50 QAPIK
7.4200 g., Bi-Metallic Brass plated Steel center in Stainless Steel ring, 25.4 mm.   **Obv:** Map above value **Rev:** Two oil wells **Edge:** Reeding over lettering **Designer:** Robert Kalina

Date	Mintage	F	VF	XF	Unc	BU
ND (2006)	—					5.00

KM# 37   50 MANAT
28.3400 g., 0.9250 Silver 0.8428 oz. ASW, 38.6 mm. **Subject:** Heydær Æliyev **Obv:** National map **Rev:** Bust 3/4 right **Edge:** Reeded

Date	Mintage	F	VF	XF	Unc	BU
2004 Proof	2,000	Value: 75.00				

KM# 46   100 MANAT
39.9400 g., 0.9167 Gold 1.1771 oz. AGW   **Subject:** Heydær Æliyev **Obv:** National map **Rev:** Bust 3/4 right **Edge:** Reeded

Date	Mintage	F	VF	XF	Unc	BU
2004 Proof	1,000	Value: 1,650				

KM# 47   500 MANAT
50.0000 g., 0.9990 Platinum 1.6059 oz. APW   **Subject:** Heydær Æliyev **Obv:** National map **Rev:** Bust 3/4 right **Edge:** Reeded

Date	Mintage	F	VF	XF	Unc	BU
2004 Proof	100	Value: 3,500				

BAHAMAS

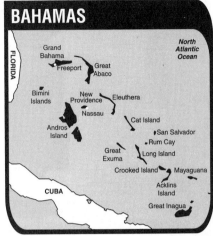

The Commonwealth of the Bahamas is an archipelago of about 3,000 islands, cays and rocks located in the Atlantic Ocean east of Florida and north of Cuba. The total land area of the 800 mile (1,287 km.) long chain of islands is 5,382 sq. mi. (13,935 sq. km.). They have a population of 302,000. Capital: Nassau. The Bahamas import most of their food and manufactured products and export cement, refined oil, pulpwood and lobsters. Tourism is the principal industry. The Bahamas is a member of the Commonwealth of Nations. Elizabeth II is Head of State as Queen of The Bahamas.

The coinage of Great Britain was legal tender in the Bahamas from 1825 to the issuing of a definitive coinage in 1966.

RULER
British

COMMONWEALTH

DECIMAL COINAGE
100 Cents = 1 Dollar

KM# 59a   CENT
2.5000 g., Copper Plated Zinc, 19.05 mm.   **Ruler:** Elizabeth II **Obv:** National arms above date **Obv. Legend:** COMMONWEALTH OF THE BAHAMAS **Rev:** Starfish, value at top **Edge:** Plain

Date	Mintage	F	VF	XF	Unc	BU
2000	—		—	0.10	0.25	0.75
2001	—		—	0.10	0.25	0.75
2004	—		—	0.10	0.25	0.75
2006	—		—	0.10	0.25	0.75
2007	—		—	0.10	0.25	0.75

KM# 60   5 CENTS
3.9400 g., Copper-Nickel, 21 mm.   **Ruler:** Elizabeth II **Obv:** National arms above date **Obv. Legend:** COMMONWEALTH OF THE BAHAMAS **Rev:** Pineapple above garland divides value at top **Rev. Designer:** Arnold Machin **Edge:** Smooth

Date	Mintage	F	VF	XF	Unc	BU
2004	—		—	0.10	0.25	0.75
2005	—		—	0.10	0.25	0.75

KM# 61   10 CENTS
5.5400 g., Copper-Nickel, 23 mm.   **Ruler:** Elizabeth II **Obv:** National arms, date below, within beaded circle **Rev:** Arnold Machin **Edge:** Smooth **Shape:** Scalloped

Date	Mintage	F	VF	XF	Unc	BU
2005	—		—	0.25	0.60	0.80
2007	—		—	0.25	0.60	0.80

KM# 63.2   25 CENTS
5.7000 g., Copper-Nickel, 24 mm.   **Ruler:** Elizabeth II **Edge:** Reeded

Date	Mintage	F	VF	XF	Unc	BU
2005	—		—	0.30	0.50	1.50

BAHRAIN

The Kingdom of Bahrain, a group of islands in the Persian Gulf off Saudi Arabia, has an area of 268 sq. mi. (622 sq. km.) and a population of 618,000. Capital: Manama. Prior to the depression of the 1930's, the economy was based on pearl fishing. Petroleum and aluminum industries and transit trade are the vital factors in the economy today.

The coinage of the Kingdom of Bahrain was struck at the Royal Mint, London, England.

RULERS

Al Khalifa Dynasty
Hamed Bin Isa, 1999-

TITLES

دولة البحرين

State of Bahrain

مملكة البحرين

Kingdom of Bahrain

KINGDOM
STANDARD COINAGE

KM# 30   5 FILS
2.5000 g., Brass, 18.97 mm.   **Ruler:** Hamed Bin Isa **Obv:** Palm tree **Obv. Legend:** KINGDOM OF BAHRAIN **Rev:** Denomination in chain link border **Edge:** Plain

Date	Mintage	F	VF	XF	Unc	BU
AH1426-2005	—				0.50	0.75

KM# 28   10 FILS
3.3500 g., Brass, 21 mm.   **Ruler:** Hamed Bin Isa **Obv:** Palm tree **Obv. Legend:** KINGDOM OF BAHRAIN **Rev:** Denomination in chain link border **Edge:** Plain

Date	Mintage	F	VF	XF	Unc	BU
AH1423-2002	—	—	—	0.30	0.75	1.00
AH1424-2004	—	—	—	0.30	0.75	1.00
AH1426-2005	—	—	—	0.30	0.75	1.00
AH1428-2007	—	—	—	0.30	0.75	1.00

KM# 24   25 FILS
3.5300 g., Copper-Nickel, 19.8 mm. **Ruler:** Hamed Bin Isa
Obv: Ancient painting **Obv. Legend:** KINGDOM OF BAHRAIN
Rev: Denomination in chain link border **Edge:** Reeded

Date	Mintage	F	VF	XF	Unc	BU
AH1423-2002	—	—	—	0.45	1.10	1.50
AH1426-2005	—	—	—	0.45	1.10	1.50
AH1428-2007	—	—	—	0.45	1.10	1.50

KM# 25   50 FILS
4.4700 g., Copper-Nickel, 21.8 mm. **Ruler:** Hamed Bin Isa
Subject: Kingdom **Obv:** Stylized sailboats **Obv. Legend:**
KINGDOM OF BAHRAIN **Rev:** Denomination in chain link border
Edge: Reeded

Date	Mintage	F	VF	XF	Unc	BU
AH1423-2002	—	—	—	0.60	1.50	2.00
AH1426-2005	—	—	—	0.60	1.50	2.00
AH1428-2007	—	—	—	0.60	1.50	2.00

KM# 20   100 FILS
5.9600 g., Bi-Metallic Copper-Nickel center in Brass ring, 24 mm.
Obv: Coat of arms within circle, dates at either side **Obv. Legend:**
STATE OF BAHRAIN **Rev:** Numeric denomination back of boxed
denomination within circle, chain surrounds **Edge:** Reeded

Date	Mintage	F	VF	XF	Unc	BU
AH1420-2001	—	—	—	—	3.50	4.00
AH1422-2001	—	—	—	—	3.50	4.00

KM# 26   100 FILS
5.9500 g., Bi-Metallic Copper-Nickel center in Brass ring,
23.9 mm. **Ruler:** Hamed Bin Isa **Subject:** Kingdom
Obv: National arms **Obv. Legend:** KINGDOM OF BAHRAIN
Rev: Denomination in chain link border **Edge:** Reeded

Date	Mintage	F	VF	XF	Unc	BU
AH1423-2002	—	—	—	0.90	2.25	3.00
AH1426-2005	—	—	—	0.90	2.25	3.00
AH1427-2006	—	—	—	0.90	2.25	3.00
AH1428-2007	—	—	—	0.90	2.25	3.00
AH1429-2008	—	—	—	0.90	2.25	3.00

KM# 29   100 FILS
5.9500 g., Bi-Metallic Copper-Nickel center in Brass ring,
23.9 mm. **Subject:** 1st Bahrain Grand Prix **Obv:** Maze design
within circle **Rev:** Numeric denomination back of boxed
denomination within circle, chain surrounds **Edge:** Reeded

Date	Mintage	F	VF	XF	Unc	BU
AH1425-2004	30,000	—	—	—	12.50	15.00

KM# 22   500 FILS
Bi-Metallic Brass center in Copper-Nickel ring, 27 mm.
Ruler: Hamed Bin Isa **Obv:** Monument and inscription
Obv. Inscription: STATE OF BAHRAIN **Rev:** Denomination
Edge: Reeded **Note:** Total weight: 9.05 grams.

Date	Mintage	F	VF	XF	Unc	BU
2001	—	—	—	—	6.00	7.50

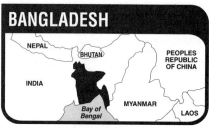

KM# 27   500 FILS
9.0500 g., Bi-Metallic Brass center Copper-Nickel ring, 27 mm.
Subject: Kingdom **Obv:** Monument and inscription **Obv. Legend:**
KINGDOM OF BAHRAIN **Rev:** Denomination **Edge:** Reeded

Date	Mintage	F	VF	XF	Unc	BU
2002	—	—	—	—	6.50	8.00

BANGLADESH

The Peoples Republic of Bangladesh (formerly East Pakistan), a parliamentary democracy located on the Bay of Bengal
bordered by India and Burma, has an area of 55,598 sq. mi.
(143,998 sq. km.) and a population of 128.1 million. Capital:
Dhaka. The economy is predominantly agricultural. Jute products, jute and tea are exported.

Bangladesh is a member of the Commonwealth of Nations.
The president is the Head of State and the Government.

MONETARY SYSTEM
100 Poisha = 1 Taka

DATING
Christian era using Bengali numerals.

PEOPLES REPUBLIC

STANDARD COINAGE

KM# 24   50 POISHA
2.6000 g., Stainless Steel, 19.3 mm. **Obv:** National emblem,
Shapla (water lily) within wreath above water **Rev:** Fish, chicken
and produce within inner circle **Edge:** Plain **Shape:** Octagonal

Date	Mintage	F	VF	XF	Unc	BU
2001	—	—	—	—	1.50	2.50

KM# 9c   TAKA
4.2500 g., Stainless Steel, 24.91 mm. **Obv:** National emblem,
Shapla (water lily) within wreath above water in octagonal frame
Rev: Stylized family, value at right within octagonal frame
Edge: Reeded **Note:** Prev. KM# 9.5.

Date	Mintage	F	VF	XF	Unc	BU
2001	—	—	—	0.80	2.00	3.00
2002	—	—	—	0.80	2.00	3.00
2003	—	—	—	0.80	2.00	3.00
2007	—	—	—	0.80	2.00	3.00

KM# 9b   TAKA
4.0000 g., Brass, 25 mm. **Obv:** National emblem, Shapla (water
lily) **Rev:** Stylized family, value at right **Edge:** Reeded **Note:** Prev.
KM# 9.3.

Date	Mintage	F	VF	XF	Unc	BU
2003	—	—	0.20	0.55	1.20	1.60

KM# 25   2 TAKA
7.0000 g., Stainless Steel, 26.03 mm. **Obv:** State emblem and
"TWO 2 TAKA" within beaded border **Rev:** Two children reading
and legend within beaded border **Edge:** Plain

Date	Mintage	F	VF	XF	Unc	BU
2004	—	—	—	1.20	3.00	4.00

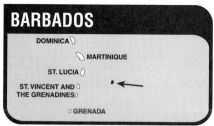

KM# 26   5 TAKA
8.1700 g., Steel, 26.8 mm. **Obv:** National emblem, Shapla
(water lily) within wreath above water **Rev:** Bridge, date and
denomination below **Note:** Prev. KM#18.3.

Date	Mintage	F	VF	XF	Unc	BU
2006	—	—	—	1.00	2.50	3.50

BARBADOS

Barbados, a Constitutional Monarchy within the Commonwealth of Nations, is located in the Windward Islands of the West
Indies east of St. Vincent. The coral island has an area of 166 sq.
mi. (430 sq. km.) and a population of 269,000. Capital: Bridge-
town. The economy is based on sugar and tourism. Sugar, petroleum products, molasses, and rum are exported.

MONETARY SYSTEM
100 Cents = 1 Dollar

COMMONWEALTH

DECIMAL COINAGE

KM# 10a   CENT
2.5000 g., Copper Plated Zinc, 19 mm. **Obv:** National arms
Rev: Broken trident above value **Rev. Designer:** Philip Nathan
Edge: Plain

Date	Mintage	F	VF	XF	Unc	BU
2001	—	—	—	0.10	0.25	0.75
2004	—	—	—	0.10	0.25	0.75

KM# 11   5 CENTS
3.8000 g., Brass, 20.98 mm. **Obv:** National arms **Rev:** South
Point Lighthouse **Rev. Designer:** Philip Nathan **Edge:** Plain

Date	Mintage	F	VF	XF	Unc	BU
2001	—	—	—	0.10	0.25	0.75
2004	—	—	—	0.10	0.25	0.75
2006	—	—	—	0.10	0.25	0.75

KM# 12 10 CENTS
2.2900 g., Copper-Nickel, 17.74 mm. **Obv:** National arms
Rev: Laughing Gull left **Rev. Designer:** Philip Nathan
Edge: Reeded

Date	Mintage	F	VF	XF	Unc	BU
2001	—	—	0.10	0.15	0.50	1.50
2003	—	—	0.10	0.15	0.50	1.50
2005	—	—	0.10	0.15	0.50	1.50

KM# 13 25 CENTS
5.6700 g., Copper-Nickel, 23.6 mm. **Obv:** National arms
Rev: Morgan Lewis Sugar Mill **Edge:** Reeded **Designer:** Philip
Nathan

Date	Mintage	F	VF	XF	Unc	BU
2001	—	—	—	0.30	0.60	1.60
2004	—	—	0.15	0.30	0.60	1.60

KM# 69 5 DOLLARS
28.2700 g., 0.9250 Silver 0.8407 oz. ASW, 38.6 mm.
Subject: UNICEF **Obv:** National arms divide date, denomination
below **Rev:** Three boys playing cricket **Edge:** Reeded

Date	Mintage	F	VF	XF	Unc	BU
2001 Proof	—	Value: 42.50				

BELARUS

Belarus (Byelorussia, Belorussia, or White Russia- formerly
the Belorussian S.S.R.) is situated along the western Dvina and
Dnieper Rivers, bounded in the west by Poland, to the north by
Latvia and Lithuania, to the east by Russia and the south by the
Ukraine. It has an area of 80,154 sq. mi. (207,600 sq. km.) and
a population of 4.8 million. Capital: Minsk. Chief products: peat,
salt, and agricultural products including flax, fodder and grasses
for cattle breeding and dairy products.

MONETARY SYSTEM
100 Kapeek = 1 Rouble

REPUBLIC

STANDARD COINAGE

KM# 110 ROUBLE
Copper-Nickel, 32 mm. **Subject:** 900th Anniversary of
Euphrasinta **Obv:** National arms **Rev:** Euphrasinta of Polatsk
Designer: S.P. Zaskevitch

Date	Mintage	F	VF	XF	Unc	BU
2001	Est. 2,000	—	—	—	50.00	

KM# 112 ROUBLE
Copper-Nickel, 32 mm. **Subject:** Tower of Kamyantes
Obv: National arms **Rev:** Kamyanets Tower, seal **Designer:** S.P.
Zaskevich

Date	Mintage	F	VF	XF	Unc	BU
2001	2,000	—	—	—	40.00	

KM# 47 ROUBLE
13.1400 g., Copper-Nickel, 31.9 mm. **Obv:** National arms
Rev: European Bison **Edge:** Reeded **Designer:** S.P. Zaskevich

Date	Mintage	F	VF	XF	Unc	BU
2001 Proof	5,000	Value: 40.00				

KM# 50 ROUBLE
13.1500 g., Copper-Nickel, 28.7 mm. **Subject:** 2002 Winter
Olympics **Obv:** National arms **Rev:** Two freestyle skiers
Edge: Reeded **Designer:** S.P. Zaskevich

Date	Mintage	F	VF	XF	Unc	BU
2001 Prooflike	2,000	—	—	—	35.00	

KM# 69 ROUBLE
Copper-Nickel, 33 mm. **Subject:** 80th Anniversary of the
Savings Bank **Obv:** Folk art design **Obv. Designer:** S.P.
Zaskevich **Rev. Designer:** V. Titor

Date	Mintage	F	VF	XF	Unc	BU
2002 Prooflike	10,000	—	—	—	15.00	

KM# 105 ROUBLE
Copper-Nickel, 31.9 mm. **Subject:** Pointer Yanka Kupala 188-1942

Date	Mintage	F	VF	XF	Unc	BU
2002 Proof	2,000	Value: 35.00				

KM# 106 ROUBLE
Copper-Nickel, 31.9 mm. **Subject:** Jakub Kalas 1881-1956

Date	Mintage	F	VF	XF	Unc	BU
2002 Proof	2,000	Value: 35.00				

KM# 44 ROUBLE
13.1400 g., Copper-Nickel, 31.9 mm. **Obv:** National arms
Rev: Eurasian Beaver and young **Edge:** Reeded **Designer:** S.P.
Zaskevich

Date	Mintage	F	VF	XF	Unc	BU
2002 Proof	5,000	Value: 25.00				

KM# 114 ROUBLE
Copper-Nickel, 32 mm. **Subject:** 200th Birthday of Ignatius
Dameika **Obv:** National arms **Rev:** Ignatius Dameika, hammer
Rev. Designer: S.P. Zaskevich

Date	Mintage	F	VF	XF	Unc	BU
2002 Prooflike	2,000	—	—	—	40.00	

KM# 116 ROUBLE
33.0000 Copper-Nickel, 33 mm. **Subject:** 120th Birthday of
Yanka Kupala **Obv:** National arms **Rev:** Yanka Kupala, 1882-
1942 **Rev. Designer:** S.P. Zaskevich

Date	Mintage	F	VF	XF	Unc	BU
2002 Prooflike	2,000	—	—	—	40.00	

KM# 118 ROUBLE
Copper-Nickel, 33 mm. **Subject:** 120th Birthday of Yakub Kolas
Obv: National arms **Rev:** Yukab Kolas, 1882-1956
Rev. Designer: S.P. Zaskevich

Date	Mintage	F	VF	XF	Unc	BU
2002	2,000	—	—	—	40.00	—

KM# 61 ROUBLE
12.5000 g., Copper-Nickel, 32 mm. **Obv:** National arms
Rev: Wrestlers **Edge:** Reeded **Designer:** S.P. Zaskevich

Date	Mintage	F	VF	XF	Unc	BU
2003 Proof	5,000	Value: 10.00				

KM# 54 ROUBLE
13.1200 g., Copper-Nickel, 31.9 mm. **Obv:** National arms
Rev: Mute swans on water with reflections **Edge:** Reeded
Designer: S.P. Zaskevich

Date	Mintage	F	VF	XF	Unc	BU
2003 Proof	5,000	Value: 30.00				

KM# 55 ROUBLE
13.1000 g., Copper-Nickel, 31.9 mm. **Obv:** State arms **Rev:**
Herring Gull in flight **Edge:** Reeded **Designer:** S.P. Zaskevich

Date	Mintage	F	VF	XF	Unc	BU
2003 Proof	5,000	Value: 25.00				

KM# 56 ROUBLE
13.1000 g., Copper-Nickel, 32 mm. **Obv:** National arms
Rev: Church of the Savior and Transfiguration **Edge:** Reeded
Designer: S.P. Zaskevich

Date	Mintage	F	VF	XF	Unc	BU
2003	2,000	—	—	—	35.00	—

KM# 60 ROUBLE
13.1000 g., Copper-Nickel, 31.9 mm. **Obv:** National arms **Rev:**
Two Common Cranes **Edge:** Reeded **Designer:** S.P. Zaskevich

Date	Mintage	F	VF	XF	Unc	BU
2004 Proof	5,000	Value: 25.00				

KM# 75   ROUBLE
15.9200 g., Copper-Nickel Antiqued Finish, 33 mm.
Subject: "Kupalle" **Obv:** Folk art cross design **Rev:** Flower above ferns **Edge:** Reeded **Designer:** S.P. Zaskevich

Date	Mintage	F	VF	XF	Unc	BU
2004	5,000	—	—	—	40.00	—

KM# 76   ROUBLE
15.9200 g., Copper-Nickel, 33 mm.   **Subject:** "Kalyady"
Obv: Folk art cross design **Rev:** Stylized sun flower
Edge: Reeded **Designer:** S.P. Zaskevich

Date	Mintage	F	VF	XF	Unc	BU
2004	5,000	—	—	—	35.00	—

KM# 78   ROUBLE
15.9000 g., Copper-Nickel, 33 mm.   **Obv:** National arms
Rev: Radziwill's Castle in Neswizh **Edge:** Reeded
Designer: S.P. Zaskevich

Date	Mintage	F	VF	XF	Unc	BU
2004 Prooflike	2,000	—	—	—	—	35.00

KM# 80   ROUBLE
15.9000 g., Copper-Nickel, 33 mm.   **Subject:** Defenders of Brest
Obv: Soviet Patriotic War Order **Rev:** "Courage" monument
Edge: Reeded **Designer:** S.P. Zaskevich

Date	Mintage	F	VF	XF	Unc	BU
2004	5,000	—	—	—	25.00	—

KM# 85   ROUBLE
Copper-Nickel, 33 mm.   **Subject:** Soviet Warriors - Liberators
Obv: Order of the Patriotric War **Obv. Designer:** S.P. Zaskevich
Rev: Partisans with blown up railway track **Rev. Designer:** E.N. Vishnyakova

Date	Mintage	F	VF	XF	Unc	BU
2004	3,000	—	—	—	25.00	—

KM# 83   ROUBLE
Copper-Nickel, 33 mm.   **Subject:** Memory of Facist Victims **Obv:** National arms **Obv. Designer:** S.P. Zaskevich **Rev:** Man holding dead **Rev. Designer:** E.N. Vishnyakova

Date	Mintage	F	VF	XF	Unc	BU
2004	3,000	—	—	—	25.00	—

KM# 62   ROUBLE
Copper-Nickel, 31.9 mm.   **Subject:** Sculling **Obv:** National arms
Obv. Designer: S.P. Zaskevich **Rev:** Two rowers against a background of stylized oars **Rev. Designer:** S.V. Nekrasova

Date	Mintage	F	VF	XF	Unc	BU
2004	3,000	—	—	—	15.00	—

KM# 81   ROUBLE
Copper-Nickel, 33 mm.   **Subject:** 60th Anniversary of Victory
Obv: Order of the Victory **Rev:** Star and arrows
Rev. Designer: S.V. Necrasova

Date	Mintage	F	VF	XF	Unc	BU
2005	2,000	—	—	—	25.00	—

KM# 127   ROUBLE
Copper-Nickel, 32 mm.   **Subject:** 1000th Anniversary of Vaukavysk **Obv:** National arms **Rev:** National arms of Vaukavysk **Rev. Designer:** S.P. Zaskevitch

Date	Mintage	F	VF	XF	Unc	BU
2005	2,000	—	—	—	40.00	—

KM# 130   ROUBLE
Copper-Nickel, 32 mm.   **Subject:** Jesnit Roman Catholic Church
Obv: National arms **Rev:** Jesnit Roman Catholic Church in Neswizh **Designer:** S.P. Zaskevich

Date	Mintage	F	VF	XF	Unc	BU
2005	2,000	—	—	—	40.00	—

KM# 104   ROUBLE
Copper-Nickel, 33 mm.   **Subject:** Easter Egg **Obv:** National arms and solar symbol **Rev:** Easter egg with an inserted lilac colored crystal **Designer:** S.P. Zaskevich

Date	Mintage	F	VF	XF	Unc	BU
2005	5,000	—	—	—	35.00	—

KM# 107   ROUBLE
Copper-Nickel, 31.9 mm.   **Subject:** Bagach - Candle in Basket
Obv: National arms and solar symbol **Rev:** Basket of grain, candle, ear, table, tablecloth

Date	Mintage	F	VF	XF	Unc	BU
2005	5,000	—	—	—	35.00	—

KM# 132   ROUBLE
Copper-Nickel, 33 mm.   **Subject:** Usyaslau of Polatsk
Obv: Cathedral of St. Sophia **Rev:** Usyaslau of Polatsk, wolf on a solar disk

Date	Mintage	F	VF	XF	Unc	BU
2005 Proof	5,000	Value: 15.00				

KM# 134   ROUBLE
Copper-Nickel, 33 mm.   **Subject:** Tennis **Obv:** National arms
Rev: Tennis player against racket background
Rev. Designer: S.V. Necrasova

Date	Mintage	F	VF	XF	Unc	BU
2005	5,000	—	—	—	12.00	—

KM# 97   ROUBLE
14.5000 g., Copper-Nickel, 33 mm.   **Subject:** Almany Bogs
Obv: Blooming plant on frosted design **Rev:** Great Grey Owl
Edge: Lettered **Designer:** S.V. Nekrasova

Date	Mintage	F	VF	XF	Unc	BU
2005 Proof	5,000	Value: 25.00				

KM# 135   ROUBLE
Copper-Nickel, 32 mm.   **Subject:** Vtaselle Wedding
Obv: National arms, birds, shamrock **Rev:** Loaf of bread, wedding rings, diadem of flowers, background of honeycomb

Date	Mintage	F	VF	XF	Unc	BU
2006	5,000	—	—	—	12.00	—

KM# 138   ROUBLE
Copper-Nickel, 33 mm.   **Subject:** Sophia of Galshany 600th Anniversary **Obv:** Castle of Galshany **Rev:** National arms and Sophia of Galshany **Designer:** S.P. Zaskevich

Date	Mintage	F	VF	XF	Unc	BU
2006	5,000	—	—	—	20.00	—

KM# 140   ROUBLE
Copper-Nickel, 33 mm.   **Subject:** Syomukha **Obv:** National arms, solar symbol **Rev:** Chalice, Chaplet of birch, maple, rowan sweet flag leaves **Designer:** S.P. Zaskevich

Date	Mintage	F	VF	XF	Unc	BU
2006	5,000	—	—	—	25.00	—

KM# 146   ROUBLE
Copper-Nickel, 33 mm.   **Subject:** Chyrvomy Bar **Obv:** National arms, blooming plant **Rev:** European Mink **Designer:** S.V. Nekrasova

Date	Mintage	F	VF	XF	Unc	BU
2006 Proof	5,000	Value: 15.00				

KM# 150   ROUBLE
16.0000 g., Copper-Nickel, 33 mm.   **Subject:** Holidays and Ceremonies **Obv:** Small arms above quilted star design
Rev: Food, bowl with spoon - Maslenica

Date	Mintage	F	VF	XF	Unc	BU
2007 Antique finish	5,000	—	—	—	—	35.00

KM# 151   ROUBLE
13.2400 g., Copper-Nickel, 31.86 mm.   **Obv:** Thrush Nightingale in hands in oval **Obv. Legend:** РЭСПУБЛІКА БЕЛАРУСЬ **Rev:** Thrush Nightingale perched on branch in oval **Edge:** Reeded

Date	Mintage	F	VF	XF	Unc	BU
2007 Proof	5,000	Value: 12.00				

KM# 64   10 ROUBLES
16.8200 g., 0.9250 Silver 0.5002 oz. ASW, 32.9 mm.
Obv: National arms **Rev:** Jakub Kolas (1882-1956)
Edge: Reeded **Designer:** S.P. Zaskevich

Date	Mintage	F	VF	XF	Unc	BU
2002 Proof	1,000	Value: 150				

KM# 117   10 ROUBLES
15.5500 g., 0.9250 Silver 0.4624 oz. ASW, 33 mm.
Subject: 120th Birthday of Yanka Kupala **Obv:** National arms
Rev: Yanka Kupala, 1882-1942 **Rev. Designer:** S.P. Zaskevich

Date	Mintage	F	VF	XF	Unc	BU
2002 Proof	1,000	Value: 150				

KM# 129   10 ROUBLES
1.2400 g., 0.9990 Gold 0.0398 oz. AGW, 13.92 mm.
Subject: Belarussian Ballet **Obv:** National arms
Obv. Designer: S.P. Zaskevich **Rev:** Dancing ballerina
Rev. Designer: Michael Schulze

Date	Mintage	F	VF	XF	Unc	BU
2005	25,000	—	—	—	50.00	—

KM# 156   10 ROUBLES
16.8100 g., 0.9250 Silver 0.4999 oz. ASW, 32 mm.   **Subject:** Alena Aladana **Rev:** 1/2 length figure facing, picture in background

Date	Mintage	F	VF	XF	Unc	BU
2007 Proof	4,000	Value: 40.00				

KM# 157   10 ROUBLES
16.8100 g., 0.9250 Silver 0.4999 oz. ASW, 32 mm.
Subject: Thrush Nightingale **Rev:** Bird standing right on branch

Date	Mintage	F	VF	XF	Unc	BU
2007 Proof	5,000	Value: 40.00				

KM# 172   10 ROUBLES
16.8100 g., 0.9250 Silver 0.4999 oz. ASW, 32 mm.
Subject: Zair Azgur **Rev:** Profile right

Date	Mintage	F	VF	XF	Unc	BU
2008 Proof	3,000	Value: 40.00				

KM# 173   10 ROUBLES
16.8100 g., 0.9250 Silver 0.4999 oz. ASW, 32 mm.   **Subject:** Great White Egret **Rev:** Bird standing left

Date	Mintage	F	VF	XF	Unc	BU
2008 Proof	5,000	Value: 40.00				

KM# 174   10 ROUBLES
16.8100 g., 0.9250 Silver 0.4999 oz. ASW, 32 mm.   **Subject:** Vincent Dunin **Rev:** Bust facing

Date	Mintage	F	VF	XF	Unc	BU
2008 Proof	3,000	Value: 40.00				

KM# 175 10 ROUBLES
16.8100 g., 0.9250 Silver 0.4999 oz. ASW, 32 mm. **Subject:** St. Euphrosyne of Polotsk **Rev:** Half-length figure facing within frame

Date	Mintage	F	VF	XF	Unc	BU
2008 Proof	5,000	Value: 40.00				

KM# 176 10 ROUBLES
16.8100 g., 0.9250 Silver 0.4999 oz. ASW, 32 mm. **Subject:** St. Steraphin of Sarov **Rev:** Half-length figure standing within frame

Date	Mintage	F	VF	XF	Unc	BU
2008 Proof	5,000	Value: 40.00				

KM# 177 10 ROUBLES
16.8100 g., 0.9250 Silver 0.4999 oz. ASW, 32 mm. **Subject:** St. Sergii of Radonezh **Rev:** Half-length figure standing within frame

Date	Mintage	F	VF	XF	Unc	BU
2008 Proof	5,000	Value: 40.00				

KM# 178 10 ROUBLES
16.8100 g., 0.9250 Silver 0.4999 oz. ASW, 32 mm. **Subject:** St. Nicholas **Rev:** Half-length figure standing within frame

Date	Mintage	F	VF	XF	Unc	BU
2008 Proof	5,000	Value: 40.00				

KM# 179 10 ROUBLES
16.8100 g., 0.9250 Silver 0.4999 oz. ASW, 32 mm. **Subject:** St. Panteleimon **Rev:** Half-length figure standing within frame

Date	Mintage	F	VF	XF	Unc	BU
2008 Proof	5,000	Value: 40.00				

KM# 194 10 ROUBLES
16.8100 g., 0.9250 Silver 0.4999 oz. ASW, 32 mm. **Subject:** Academy of Science, 80th Anniversary **Rev:** Building

Date	Mintage	F	VF	XF	Unc	BU
2009 Proof	3,000	Value: 40.00				

KM# 195 10 ROUBLES
16.8100 g., 0.9250 Silver 0.4999 oz. ASW, 32 mm. **Subject:** Greylag goose **Rev:** Goose swimming left

Date	Mintage	F	VF	XF	Unc	BU
2009 Proof	5,000	Value: 32.00				

KM# 111 20 ROUBLES
31.1000 g., 0.9250 Silver 0.9249 oz. ASW, 38.61 mm. **Subject:** 900th Anniversary of Euphrasinta **Rev:** Euphrasinta of Polatsk, gold cross **Designer:** S.P. Zaskevitch

Date	Mintage	F	VF	XF	Unc	BU
2001 Proof	Est. 2,000	Value: 350				

KM# 113 20 ROUBLES
31.1000 g., 0.9250 Silver 0.9249 oz. ASW, 38.61 mm. **Subject:** Tower of Kamyantes **Obv:** National arms **Rev:** Kamyanets Tower, seal **Designer:** S.P. Zaskevich

Date	Mintage	F	VF	XF	Unc	BU
2001 Proof	2,000	Value: 100				

KM# 46 20 ROUBLES
33.7300 g., 0.9250 Silver 1.0031 oz. ASW, 38.6 mm. **Subject:** Wildlife **Obv:** National arms **Rev:** European Bison **Edge:** Reeded **Designer:** S.P. Zaskevich

Date	Mintage	F	VF	XF	Unc	BU
2001 Proof	2,000	Value: 650				

KM# 49 20 ROUBLES
28.3200 g., 0.9250 Silver 0.8422 oz. ASW, 38.6 mm. **Subject:** 2002 Winter Olympics **Obv:** National arms **Rev:** Marksman aiming at bullseye **Edge:** Reeded **Designer:** S.P. Zaskevich

Date	Mintage	F	VF	XF	Unc	BU
2001 Proof	15,000	Value: 45.00				

KM# 51 20 ROUBLES
33.6500 g., 0.9250 Silver 1.0007 oz. ASW, 38.6 mm. **Subject:** 2002 Winter Olympics **Obv:** National arms **Rev:** Two freestyle skiers **Edge:** Reeded **Designer:** S.P. Zaskevich

Date	Mintage	F	VF	XF	Unc	BU
2001 Proof	2,000	Value: 60.00				

KM# 45 20 ROUBLES
33.7300 g., 0.9250 Silver 1.0031 oz. ASW, 38.8 mm. **Obv:** National arms **Rev:** European Beaver and young **Edge:** Reeded **Designer:** S.P. Zaskevich

Date	Mintage	F	VF	XF	Unc	BU
2002 Proof	2,000	Value: 200				

KM# 115 20 ROUBLES
31.1000 g., 0.9250 Silver 0.9249 oz. ASW, 38.61 mm. **Subject:** 200th Birthday of Ignatius Dameika **Obv:** National arms **Rev:** Ignatius Dameika, hammer and inset with a dameikit stone **Rev. Designer:** S.P. Zaskevich

Date	Mintage	F	VF	XF	Unc	BU
2002 Proof	1,000	Value: 350				

KM# 119 20 ROUBLES
31.1000 g., 0.9250 Silver 0.9249 oz. ASW, 38.61 mm. **Subject:** 2006 World Cup Football **Obv:** National arms **Rev:** Stylized 2006, football **Designer:** S.P. Zaskevich

Date	Mintage	F	VF	XF	Unc	BU
2002 Proof	Est. 25,000	Value: 45.00				

KM# 59 20 ROUBLES
28.6300 g., 0.9250 Silver 0.8514 oz. ASW, 38.6 mm. **Obv:** National arms **Obv. Designer:** S.P. Zaskevich **Rev:** Brown Bear with two cubs **Rev. Designer:** Waldemar Vronski **Edge:** Reeded

Date	Mintage	F	VF	XF	Unc	BU
2002 Proof	5,000	Value: 120				

KM# 70 20 ROUBLES
33.8500 g., 0.9250 Silver 1.0066 oz. ASW, 38.61 mm. **Obv:** National arms **Obv. Designer:** S.P. Zaskevich **Rev:** 80th Anniversary - National Savings Bank **Rev. Designer:** V. Titov **Edge:** Reeded

Date	Mintage	F	VF	XF	Unc	BU
2002 Proof	1,000	Value: 225				

KM# 120 20 ROUBLES
31.1000 g., 0.9250 Silver 0.9249 oz. ASW, 38.61 mm. **Subject:** Freestyle Wrestling **Obv:** National arms **Rev:** Two wrestlers **Designer:** S.P. Zaskevich

Date	Mintage	F	VF	XF	Unc	BU
2003 Proof	3,000	Value: 50.00				

KM# 122 20 ROUBLES
31.1000 g., 0.9250 Silver 0.9249 oz. ASW, 38.61 mm. **Subject:** Herring Gull **Obv:** National arms **Rev:** Herring gull in flight **Designer:** S.P. Zaskevitch

Date	Mintage	F	VF	XF	Unc	BU
2003 Proof	2,000	Value: 150				

KM# 53 20 ROUBLES
33.8400 g., 0.9250 Silver 1.0063 oz. ASW, 38.5 mm. **Obv:** State arms **Rev:** Two Mute swans on water with reflections **Edge:** Reeded **Designer:** S.P. Zaskevich

Date	Mintage	F	VF	XF	Unc	BU
2003 Proof	2,000	Value: 200				

KM# 57   20 ROUBLES
31.1000 g., 0.9250 Silver 0.9249 oz. ASW, 38.6 mm.
Obv: National arms **Rev:** Church of the Savior and
Transfiguration **Edge:** Reeded **Designer:** S.P. Zaskevich

Date	Mintage	F	VF	XF	Unc	BU
2003 Proof	100	Value: 100				

KM# 149   20 ROUBLES
26.1600 g., 0.9250 Silver 0.7780 oz. ASW, 38.61 mm.
Subject: 2004 Olympic Games **Obv:** National arms **Rev:** Female
shot-putter **Designer:** S.P. Zaskevich

Date	Mintage	F	VF	XF	Unc	BU
2003 Proof	25,000	Value: 30.00				

KM# 91   20 ROUBLES
31.1000 g., 0.9250 Silver 0.9249 oz. ASW, 38.61 mm.
Subject: Trade Union Movement Centennial **Obv:** National arms
Obv. Designer: S.P. Zaskevich **Rev. Designer:** G.A. Maximor

Date	Mintage	F	VF	XF	Unc	BU
2004 Proof	1,500	Value: 200				

KM# 86   20 ROUBLES
31.1000 g., 0.9250 Silver 0.9249 oz. ASW, 38.61 mm.
Subject: Soviet Warriors - Liberators **Obv:** Multicolored Order of
the Patriotic War **Obv. Designer:** S.P. Zaskevich **Rev:** Partisans
with blown up railway track **Rev. Designer:** E.N. Vishnyakova

Date	Mintage	F	VF	XF	Unc	BU
2004	2,000	—	—	—	100	—

KM# 84   20 ROUBLES
31.1000 g., 0.9250 Silver 0.9249 oz. ASW, 38.61 mm.
Subject: Memory of Facist Victims **Obv:** Multicolored Order of
the Patriotic War **Obv. Designer:** S.P. Zaskevich **Rev:** Man
holding dead **Rev. Designer:** E.N. Vishnyakova

Date	Mintage	F	VF	XF	Unc	BU
2004	2,000	—	—	—	100	—

KM# 124   20 ROUBLES
31.1000 g., 0.9250 Silver 0.9249 oz. ASW, 38.61 mm.
Subject: Sculling **Obv:** National arms **Obv. Designer:** S.P.
Zaskevich **Rev:** Two rowers against a background of stylized
oars **Rev. Designer:** S.V. Nekrasova

Date	Mintage	F	VF	XF	Unc	BU
2004	3,000	—	—	—	50.00	—

KM# 73   20 ROUBLES
31.1000 g., 0.9250 Silver 0.9249 oz. ASW, 38.6 mm.
Obv: National arms **Rev:** 2 common cranes **Edge:** Reeded

Date	Mintage	F	VF	XF	Unc	BU
2004 Proof	2,000	Value: 150				

KM# 77   20 ROUBLES
31.1000 g., 0.9250 Silver 0.9249 oz. ASW, 38.6 mm.
Subject: "Kalyady" **Obv:** Folk art cross design **Rev:** Stylized
sunflower with inset blue synthetic crystal **Edge:** Reeded
Designer: S.P. Zaskevich

Date	Mintage	F	VF	XF	Unc	BU
2004 Antique finish	5,000	—	—	—	350	—

KM# 79   20 ROUBLES
31.1000 g., 0.9250 Silver 0.9249 oz. ASW, 38.6 mm.
Obv: National arms **Rev:** Radziwill's Castle in Neswizh
Edge: Reeded **Designer:** S.P. Zaskevich

Date	Mintage	F	VF	XF	Unc	BU
2004 Proof	2,000	Value: 100				

KM# 82   20 ROUBLES
28.7200 g., 0.9250 Silver 0.8541 oz. ASW, 38.6 mm.
Subject: WW II Victory **Obv:** Multicolor Soviet Order of Victory
Rev: Soviet soldiers raising their flag in the Reichstag in Berlin
Rev. Designer: S.V. Necrasova **Edge:** Reeded

Date	Mintage	F	VF	XF	Unc	BU
2005 Proof	12,000	Value: 50.00				

KM# 92   20 ROUBLES
28.6300 g., 0.9250 Silver 0.8514 oz. ASW, 38.6 mm. **Obv:** Two
children sitting on crescent moon **Rev:** Symon the Musician and
inset orange color glass crystal **Edge:** Plain **Designer:** S.V.
Necrasova

Date	Mintage	F	VF	XF	Unc	BU
2005 Antique finish	20,000	—	—	—	50.00	—

KM# 93   20 ROUBLES
28.6300 g., 0.9250 Silver 0.8514 oz. ASW, 38.6 mm.
Subject: Kalyady's star **Obv:** Two children sitting on a crescent
moon **Rev:** Snow Queen; Blue glass crystal inset on forehead,
flower **Edge:** Plain **Designer:** S.V. Necrasova

Date	Mintage	F	VF	XF	Unc	BU
2005 Antique finish	20,000	—	—	—	50.00	—

KM# 94   20 ROUBLES
28.6300 g., 0.9250 Silver 0.8514 oz. ASW, 38.6 mm. **Obv:** Two
children sitting on a crescent moon **Rev:** White glass crystal inset
above landscape with fox, the Little Prince **Edge:** Plain
Designer: S.V. Necrasova

Date	Mintage	F	VF	XF	Unc	BU
2005 Antique finish	20,000	—	—	—	50.00	—

KM# 95   20 ROUBLES
28.6300 g., 0.9250 Silver 0.8514 oz. ASW, 38.61 mm.
Obv: Two children sitting on a crescent moon **Rev:** The Stone
Flower, Yellow glass crystal inset in flower design, heads flank
Edge: Plain **Designer:** S.V. Necrasova

Date	Mintage	F	VF	XF	Unc	BU
2005 Antique finish	20,000	—	—	—	50.00	—

KM# 71   20 ROUBLES
31.1000 g., 0.9250 Silver 0.9249 oz. ASW, 38.6 mm. **Subject:**
"Kupalle" **Obv:** Folk art design **Rev:** Fern flower with inset red
synthetic crystal **Edge:** Reeded **Designer:** S.P. Zaskevich

Date	Mintage	F	VF	XF	Unc	BU
2004 Antique finish	3,000	—	—	—	600	—

KM# 72   20 ROUBLES
31.1000 g., 0.9250 Silver 0.9249 oz. ASW, 38.6 mm.
Subject: Defense of Brest **Obv:** Multicolor Soviet Order of the
Patriotic War **Rev:** "Courage" monument **Edge:** Reeded
Designer: S.P. Zaskevich

Date	Mintage	F	VF	XF	Unc	BU
2004 Proof	3,000	Value: 100				

KM# 96   20 ROUBLES

33.6600 g., 0.9250 Silver 1.0010 oz. ASW, 38.6 mm. **Obv:** Small national arms above quilted star design **Rev:** Yellow glass crystal inset in candle flame above basket **Edge:** Reeded **Designer:** S.P. Zaskevich

Date	Mintage	F	VF	XF	Unc	BU
2005 Antique finish	5,000	—	—	—	170	—

KM# 98   20 ROUBLES

33.6300 g., 0.9250 Silver 1.0000 oz. ASW, 38.6 mm.   **Subject:** Almany Bogs **Obv:** Blooming plant on frosted design **Rev:** Great Grey Owl in flight **Edge:** Reeded **Designer:** S.V. Nekrasova

Date	Mintage	F	VF	XF	Unc	BU
2005 Proof	5,000	Value: 50.00				

KM# 99   20 ROUBLES

31.1000 g., 0.9250 Silver 0.9249 oz. ASW, 38.6 mm. **Series:** Easter Egg **Obv:** Quilted cross design **Rev:** Decorated Easter egg with inset pink glass crystal

Date	Mintage	F	VF	XF	Unc	BU
2005 Oxidized finish	5,000	—	—	—	250	—

KM# 100   20 ROUBLES

33.6200 g., 0.9250 Silver 0.9998 oz. ASW, 38.6 mm. **Obv:** Large church **Rev:** Usyaslau of Polatsk

Date	Mintage	F	VF	XF	Unc	BU
2005 Proof	5,000	Value: 50.00				

KM# 102   20 ROUBLES

33.9400 g., 0.9250 Silver 1.0093 oz. ASW, 39 mm. **Obv:** National arms **Rev:** Female tennis player

Date	Mintage	F	VF	XF	Unc	BU
2005 Proof	7,000	Value: 50.00				

KM# 128   20 ROUBLES

31.1000 g., 0.9250 Silver 0.9249 oz. ASW, 38.61 mm. **Subject:** 1000th Anniversary of Vaukavysk **Obv:** National arms **Rev:** National arms of Vaukavysk **Rev. Designer:** S.P. Zaskevitch

Date	Mintage	F	VF	XF	Unc	BU
2005 Proof	2,000	Value: 100				

KM# 131   20 ROUBLES

31.1000 g., 0.9250 Silver 0.9249 oz. ASW, 38.61 mm. **Subject:** Jesnit Roman Catholic Church **Obv:** National arms **Rev:** Jesnit Roman Catholic Church in Niasvizh **Designer:** S.P. Zaskevich

Date	Mintage	F	VF	XF	Unc	BU
2005 Proof	2,000	Value: 100				

KM# 133   20 ROUBLES

26.1600 g., 0.9250 Silver 0.7780 oz. ASW, 38.61 mm. **Subject:** 2006 Olympic Games **Obv:** National arms **Obv. Designer:** S.P. Zaskevich **Rev:** Two hockey players **Rev. Designer:** S.V. Necrasova and Ruth Oswald Koppers

Date	Mintage	F	VF	XF	Unc	BU
2005	15,000	—	—	—	20.00	—

KM# 101   20 ROUBLES

25.0000 g., 0.9250 Silver 0.7435 oz. ASW, 38.6 mm. **Subject:** 2006 FIFA World Cup Germany **Obv:** National arms **Rev:** Multicolor Europe, Asia and African maps on soccer ball **Rev. Designer:** S.V. Nekrasova **Note:** 2006 World Cup Soccer

Date	Mintage	F	VF	XF	Unc	BU
2005 Proof	50,000	Value: 50.00				

KM# 148   20 ROUBLES

28.2800 g., 0.9250 Silver 0.8410 oz. ASW, 38.5 mm. **Subject:** Twelve Months **Obv:** Two children sitting on a crescent moon **Rev:** Campfire with inset amber in a circle of produce **Edge:** Plain **Note:** Antiqued finish. Prev. duplicate of KM #137.

Date	Mintage	F	VF	XF	Unc	BU
2006	20,000	—	—	—	50.00	—

KM# 136   20 ROUBLES

33.6300 g., 0.9250 Silver 1.0000 oz. ASW, 38.61 mm. **Subject:** Vtaselle Wedding **Obv:** National arms, birds, shamrock **Rev:** Loaf of bread, golden wedding rings, diadem of flowers, background of honeycomb

Date	Mintage	F	VF	XF	Unc	BU
2006	25,000	—	—	—	70.00	—

KM# 139   20 ROUBLES

33.6200 g., 0.9250 Silver 0.9998 oz. ASW, 38.61 mm. **Subject:** Sophia of Galshany 600th Anniversary **Obv:** Castle of Galshany **Rev:** National arms and Sophia of Galshany **Designer:** S.P. Zaskevich

Date	Mintage	F	VF	XF	Unc	BU
2006 Proof	5,000	Value: 50.00				

KM# 141   20 ROUBLES

33.6200 g., 0.9250 Silver 0.9998 oz. ASW, 38.61 mm. **Subject:** Syomukha **Obv:** National arms, solar symbol **Rev:** Chalice, Chaplet of birch, maple, rowan, sweet flag leaves inserted in green crystal **Designer:** S.P. Zaskevich

Date	Mintage	F	VF	XF	Unc	BU
2006	5,000	—	—	—	150	—

KM# 147   20 ROUBLES

33.6300 g., 0.9250 Silver 1.0000 oz. ASW, 38.61 mm. **Subject:** Chyrvomy Bar **Obv:** National arms, blooming plant **Rev:** European Mink **Designer:** S.V. Nekrasova

Date	Mintage	F	VF	XF	Unc	BU
2006 Proof	5,000	Value: 50.00				

KM# 155   20 ROUBLES

33.6200 g., 0.9250 Silver 0.9998 oz. ASW, 36x36 mm. **Subject:** Struve Geodetric Arc **Rev:** Map of Eastern Europe **Shape:** Square

Date	Mintage	F	VF	XF	Unc	BU
2006 Proof	5,000	Value: 50.00				

KM# 166   20 ROUBLES

33.6200 g., 0.9250 Silver 0.9998 oz. ASW, 38.61 mm. **Subject:** Legend of the Stork **Rev:** Stylized bird

Date	Mintage	F	VF	XF	Unc	BU
2007 Proof	5,000	Value: 50.00				

KM# 158   20 ROUBLES

33.6200 g., 0.9250 Silver 0.9998 oz. ASW, 38.61 mm. **Subject:** Belarus - China diplomatic relations **Rev:** Double arches with country scene

Date	Mintage	F	VF	XF	Unc	BU
2007 Proof	2,000	Value: 100				

KM# 159   20 ROUBLES

33.6200 g., 0.9250 Silver 0.9998 oz. ASW, 38.61 mm. **Subject:** Maslenitsea **Rev:** Pancake and syrup

Date	Mintage	F	VF	XF	Unc	BU
2007 Proof	5,000	Value: 130				

KM# 160   20 ROUBLES

33.6300 g., 0.9250 Silver 1.0000 oz. ASW, 38.61 mm. **Subject:** Napoleon Orda **Rev:** Bust facing, record and musical notes in background

Date	Mintage	F	VF	XF	Unc	BU
2007 Proof	5,000	Value: 45.00				

KM# 161   20 ROUBLES

28.2800 g., 0.9250 Silver 0.8410 oz. ASW, 38.61 mm. **Subject:** Alice in Wonderland **Rev:** Alice and the March Hare

Date	Mintage	F	VF	XF	Unc	BU
2007 Matte Proof	20,000	Value: 50.00				

KM# 162   20 ROUBLES

28.2800 g., 0.9250 Silver 0.8410 oz. ASW, 38.61 mm. **Subject:** Alice Through the Looking Glass **Rev:** Alice and chess board

Date	Mintage	F	VF	XF	Unc	BU
2007 Matte Proof	20,000	Value: 50.00				

KM# 163   20 ROUBLES
31.1050 g., 0.9990 Silver 0.9990 oz. ASW, 40 mm.
Subject: Belarusian Ballet **Rev:** Ballerina and mirror view

Date	Mintage	F	VF	XF	Unc	BU
2007 Proof	10,000	Value: 50.00				

KM# 164   20 ROUBLES
31.1000 g., 0.9250 Silver 0.9249 oz. ASW, 38.61 mm.
Subject: International Polar Year **Rev:** Antartic and two penguins

Date	Mintage	F	VF	XF	Unc	BU
2007 Proof	10,000	Value: 45.00				

KM# 165   20 ROUBLES
33.6200 g., 0.9250 Silver 0.9998 oz. ASW, 38.61 mm.
Subject: Bleb of Mensk **Rev:** Knight seated left

Date	Mintage	F	VF	XF	Unc	BU
2007 Proof	5,000	Value: 50.00				

KM# 167   20 ROUBLES
31.1050 g., 0.9990 Silver 0.9990 oz. ASW, 38.61 mm.
Subject: Wolf - Canis Lupus **Rev:** Wolf head facing

Date	Mintage	F	VF	XF	Unc	BU
2007 Proof	7,000	Value: 60.00				

KM# 168   20 ROUBLES
31.1050 g., 0.9990 Silver 0.9990 oz. ASW, 38.61 mm.
Subject: Wolf - Canis Lupis **Rev:** Wolf standing on rock ledge, second wolf's head facing

Date	Mintage	F	VF	XF	Unc	BU
2007 Proof	7,000	Value: 60.00				

KM# 169   20 ROUBLES
33.6300 g., 0.9250 Silver 1.0000 oz. ASW, 38.61 mm.
Subject: Dniepra - Sozhsky **Rev:** Sturgon fish

Date	Mintage	F	VF	XF	Unc	BU
2007 Proof	5,000	Value: 50.00				

KM# 180   20 ROUBLES
33.6300 g., 0.9250 Silver 1.0000 oz. ASW, 38.61 mm.
Subject: Minsk **Rev:** Old and new city views

Date	Mintage	F	VF	XF	Unc	BU
2008 Proof	7,000	Value: 50.00				

KM# 181   20 ROUBLES
33.6300 g., 0.9250 Silver 1.0000 oz. ASW, 38.61 mm.
Subject: Financial system, 90th Anniversary **Rev:** Shield

Date	Mintage	F	VF	XF	Unc	BU
2008 Proof	3,000	Value: 60.00				

KM# 182   20 ROUBLES
33.6300 g., 0.9250 Silver 1.0000 oz. ASW, 38.61 mm.
Subject: Lipichanskaya Pushcha **Rev:** Bird seated on branch

Date	Mintage	F	VF	XF	Unc	BU
2008 Proof	5,000	Value: 50.00				

KM# 183   20 ROUBLES
33.6200 g., 0.9250 Silver 0.9998 oz. ASW, 38.61 mm.
Subject: Dzyady **Rev:** Two angels above table

Date	Mintage	F	VF	XF	Unc	BU
2008 Matte Proof	—	Value: 90.00				

KM# 184   20 ROUBLES
33.6200 g., 0.9250 Silver 0.9998 oz. ASW, 38.61 mm.
Subject: David of Garadzen **Rev:** Half-length figure of knight

Date	Mintage	F	VF	XF	Unc	BU
2008 Proof	5,000	Value: 50.00				

KM# 185   20 ROUBLES
31.1050 g., 0.9990 Silver 0.9990 oz. ASW, 40 mm. **Rev:** Figure skater

Date	Mintage	F	VF	XF	Unc	BU
2008 Proof	10,000	Value: 50.00				

KM# 186   20 ROUBLES
31.1050 g., 0.9990 Silver 0.9990 oz. ASW, 38.61 mm.
Subject: Lynx **Rev:** Lynx head facing

Date	Mintage	F	VF	XF	Unc	BU
2008 Proof	8,000	Value: 60.00				

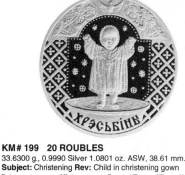

KM# 187 20 ROUBLES
31.1050 g., 0.9990 Silver 0.9990 oz. ASW, 38.61 mm.
Subject: Lynx **Rev:** Lynx mom and cub

Date	Mintage	F	VF	XF	Unc	BU
2008 Proof	8,000			Value: 60.00		

KM# 191 20 ROUBLES
28.2800 g., 0.9250 Silver 0.8410 oz. ASW, 38.61 mm.
Subject: Sedov **Obv:** Compass star, multicolor **Rev:** Sailing ship

Date	Mintage	F	VF	XF	Unc	BU
2008 Proof	25,000			Value: 50.00		

KM# 199 20 ROUBLES
33.6300 g., 0.9990 Silver 1.0801 oz. ASW, 38.61 mm.
Subject: Christening **Rev:** Child in christening gown

Date	Mintage	F	VF	XF	Unc	BU
2009 Proof	5,000			Value: 80.00		

KM# 188 20 ROUBLES
33.6200 g., 0.9250 Silver 0.9998 oz. ASW, 38.61 mm.
Subject: Cockoo Legend **Rev:** Stylized Cockoo

Date	Mintage	F	VF	XF	Unc	BU
2008 Proof	5,000			Value: 50.00		

KM# 196 20 ROUBLES
33.6300 g., 0.9250 Silver 1.0000 oz. ASW, 38.61 mm.
Subject: 65th Anniversary of Liberation **Rev:** Child looking upward to freeded birds

Date	Mintage	F	VF	XF	Unc	BU
2009 Proof	4,000			Value: 50.00		

KM# 200 20 ROUBLES
28.2800 g., 0.9250 Silver 0.8410 oz. ASW, 38.61 mm.
Subject: Dar Pomorza **Rev:** Sail training vessel

Date	Mintage	F	VF	XF	Unc	BU
2009 Proof	25,000			Value: 50.00		

KM# 189 20 ROUBLES
28.2800 g., 0.9250 Silver 0.8410 oz. ASW, 38.61 mm.
Subject: Turandot **Rev:** Female opera character

Date	Mintage	F	VF	XF	Unc	BU
2008 Matte Proof	—			Value: 50.00		

KM# 197 20 ROUBLES
28.2800 g., 0.9250 Silver 0.8410 oz. ASW, 40x28 mm.
Subject: Llya Repin **Rev:** Bust and house, artist's palet in corner **Shape:** Rectangle

Date	Mintage	F	VF	XF	Unc	BU
2009 Proof	1,500			Value: 50.00		

KM# 201 20 ROUBLES
33.6300 g., 0.9250 Silver 1.0000 oz. ASW, 38.61 mm.
Subject: White stork **Rev:** Bird and nest

Date	Mintage	F	VF	XF	Unc	BU
2009 Proof	7,000			Value: 50.00		

KM# 190 20 ROUBLES
38.6100 g., 0.9250 Silver 1.1482 oz. ASW, 38.61 mm.
Subject: House Warming **Rev:** Plated key within fouse facade

Date	Mintage	F	VF	XF	Unc	BU
2008 Proof	25,000			Value: 50.00		

KM# 198 20 ROUBLES
28.2800 g., 0.9250 Silver 0.8410 oz. ASW, 38.61 mm.
Subject: Sapsy **Rev:** Bee honey comb, apple tree, grain

Date	Mintage	F	VF	XF	Unc	BU
2009 Proof	5,000			Value: 80.00		

KM# 202 20 ROUBLES
33.6300 g., 0.9250 Silver 1.0000 oz. ASW, 38.61 mm.
Subject: Belavezhskaya Pushcha **Rev:** Range animals

Date	Mintage	F	VF	XF	Unc	BU
2009 Proof	8,000			Value: 50.00		

KM# 203   20 ROUBLES
28.2800 g., 0.9250 Silver 0.8410 oz. ASW, 38.61 mm.
Series: Zodiac - Pisces **Rev:** Two fish

Date	Mintage	F	VF	XF	Unc	BU
2009 Matte Proof	25,000	Value: 50.00				

KM# 204   20 ROUBLES
28.2800 g., 0.9250 Silver 0.8410 oz. ASW, 38.61 mm.
Subject: Zodiac - Aries **Rev:** Ram

Date	Mintage	F	VF	XF	Unc	BU
2009 Matte Proof	25,000	Value: 50.00				

KM# 205   20 ROUBLES
28.2800 g., 0.9250 Silver 0.8410 oz. ASW, 38.61 mm.
Subject: Zodiac - Taurus **Rev:** Bull

Date	Mintage	F	VF	XF	Unc	BU
2009 Matte Proof	25,000	Value: 50.00				

KM# 206   20 ROUBLES
28.2800 g., 0.9250 Silver 0.8410 oz. ASW, 38.61 mm.
Subject: Zodiac - Gemini **Rev:** Twins

Date	Mintage	F	VF	XF	Unc	BU
2009 Matte Proof	25,000	Value: 50.00				

KM# 207   20 ROUBLES
28.2800 g., 0.9250 Silver 0.8410 oz. ASW, 38.61 mm.
Subject: Zodiac - Cancer **Rev:** Crab

Date	Mintage	F	VF	XF	Unc	BU
2009 Matte Proof	25,000	Value: 50.00				

KM# 208   20 ROUBLES
28.2800 g., 0.9250 Silver 0.8410 oz. ASW, 38.61 mm.
Subject: Zodiac - Leo **Rev:** Lion

Date	Mintage	F	VF	XF	Unc	BU
2009 Matte Proof	25,000	Value: 50.00				

KM# 209   20 ROUBLES
28.2800 g., 0.9250 Silver 0.8410 oz. ASW, 38.61 mm.
Subject: Zodiac - Virgo **Rev:** Little girl

Date	Mintage	F	VF	XF	Unc	BU
2009 Matte Proof	25,000	Value: 50.00				

KM# 210   20 ROUBLES
28.2800 g., 0.9250 Silver 0.8410 oz. ASW, 38.61 mm.
Subject: Zodiac - Libra **Rev:** Balance scales

Date	Mintage	F	VF	XF	Unc	BU
2009 Matte Proof	25,000	Value: 50.00				

KM# 211   20 ROUBLES
28.2800 g., 0.9250 Silver 0.8410 oz. ASW, 38.61 mm.
Obv. Designer: Zodiac - Scorpio **Rev:** Scorpion

Date	Mintage	F	VF	XF	Unc	BU
2009 Matte Proof	25,000	Value: 50.00				

KM# 121   50 ROUBLES
4.4500 g., 0.9990 Gold 0.1429 oz. AGW, 25 mm. **Subject:** Fox
Obv: National arms **Obv. Designer:** S.P. Zaskevich **Rev:** Red
fox with inset diamond eyes **Rev. Designer:** Waldemar Wronski

Date	Mintage	F	VF	XF	Unc	BU
2002	Est. 2,000	—	—	—	1,000	—

KM# 126   50 ROUBLES
62.2000 g., 0.9250 Silver 1.8497 oz. ASW, 50 mm. **Subject:** 60th
Anniversary of Victory **Obv:** Order of the Victory, multicolored
Rev: Stars and arrows **Rev. Designer:** S.V. Necrasova

Date	Mintage	F	VF	XF	Unc	BU
2005	2,000	—	—	—	—	—
2005 Proof	—	Value: 220				

KM# 142   50 ROUBLES
7.7800 g., 0.9990 Gold 0.2499 oz. AGW, 25 mm. **Subject:**
Peregrine Falcon **Obv:** National arms **Obv. Designer:** S.P.
Zaskevich **Rev:** Peregrine falcon with inset diamond eye
Rev. Designer: S.V. Nekrasova

Date	Mintage	F	VF	XF	Unc	BU
2006	2,000	—	—	750	1,000	—

KM# 143   50 ROUBLES
7.2000 g., 0.9000 Gold 0.2083 oz. AGW, 21 mm. **Subject:** Bison
Obv: National arms **Rev:** European Bison **Designer:** S.P.
Zaskevich

Date	Mintage	F	VF	XF	Unc	BU
2006	3,000	—	—	—	400	—

KM# 144   50 ROUBLES
7.2000 g., 0.9000 Gold 0.2083 oz. AGW, 21 mm.
Subject: Beaver **Obv:** National arms **Rev:** Family of Eurasian
beavers **Designer:** S.P. Zaskovich

Date	Mintage	F	VF	XF	Unc	BU
2006	3,000	—	—	—	370	—

KM# 145   50 ROUBLES
7.2000 g., 0.9000 Gold 0.2083 oz. AGW, 21 mm. **Subject:** Mute
Swan **Obv:** National arms **Rev:** Pair of mute swans
Designer: S.P. Zaskevich

Date	Mintage	F	VF	XF	Unc	BU
2006	3,000	—	—	—	370	—

KM# 123   50 ROUBLES
7.2000 g., 0.9000 Silver 0.2083 oz. ASW, 21 mm.
Subject: Herring Gull **Obv:** National arms **Rev:** Herring gull in
flight **Designer:** S.P. Zaskevitch

Date	Mintage	F	VF	XF	Unc	BU
2006	3,000	—	—	—	350	—

KM# 125   50 ROUBLES
7.2000 g., 0.9000 Gold 0.2083 oz. AGW, 21 mm. **Obv:** National
arms **Rev:** Pair of common cranes **Designer:** S.P. Zaskevich

Date	Mintage	F	VF	XF	Unc	BU
2006	3,000	—	—	—	350	—

KM# 58   100 ROUBLES
155.5000 g., 0.9250 Silver 4.6243 oz. ASW, 64 mm.
Obv: Theater building **Rev:** Two ballet dancers **Edge:** Reeded
Designer: S.P. Zaskevich **Note:** Illustration reduced.

Date	Mintage	F	VF	XF	Unc	BU
2003 Proof	1,000	Value: 750				

KM# 192 100 ROUBLES
155.5000 g., 0.9990 Silver 4.9942 oz. ASW, 65 mm.
Subject: Figure skating **Rev:** Pair of Skates and snowflakes
Note: Illustration reduced.

Date	Mintage	F	VF	XF	Unc	BU
2008 Proof	500	Value: 450				

KM# 193 100 ROUBLES
155.5000 g., 0.9990 Silver 4.9942 oz. ASW, 65 mm.
Subject: White Stork legend **Rev:** Stylized stork

Date	Mintage	F	VF	XF	Unc	BU
2008 Proof	500	Value: 150				

KM# 103 200 ROUBLES
31.1000 g., 0.9990 Gold 0.9988 oz. AGW, 40 mm.
Obv: National arms **Obv. Designer:** S.P. Zaskevich **Rev:**
Belarussian ballerina **Rev. Designer:** Michael Schulze

Date	Mintage	F	VF	XF	Unc	BU
2005 Proof	1,500	Value: 1,650				

KM# 74 1000 ROUBLES
1000.0000 g., 0.9990 Silver 32.117 oz. ASW, 100 mm.
Subject: 2004 Olympics **Obv:** National arms **Rev:** Ancient
charioteer **Rev. Designer:** Waldemar Wronski **Note:** Illustration
reduced.

Date	Mintage	F	VF	XF	Unc	BU
2004 Proof	650	Value: 1,500				

KM# 170 1000 ROUBLES
1000.0000 g., 0.9250 Silver 29.738 oz. ASW, 100 mm.
Subject: Belarusian Ballet **Rev:** Ballerina and mirror image
Note: Illustration reduced.

Date	Mintage	F	VF	XF	Unc	BU
2007 Proof	300	Value: 1,000				

KM# 171 1000 ROUBLES
1083.8000 g., 0.9250 Silver partially gilt 32.230 oz. ASW,
100 mm. **Subject:** Cross of St. Euphrosyne of Polotsk
Rev: Gold plated pectorial cross **Note:** Illustration reduced.

Date	Mintage	F	VF	XF	Unc	BU
2007 Proof	2,000	Value: 1,000				

BELGIUM

The Kingdom of Belgium, a constitutional monarchy in northwest Europe, has an area of 11,780 sq. mi. (30,519 sq. km.) and
a population of 10.1 million, chiefly Dutch-speaking Flemish and
French-speaking Walloons. Capital: Brussels. Agriculture, dairy
farming, and the processing of raw materials for re-export are the
principal industries. Beurs voor Diamant in Antwerp is the world's
largest diamond trading center. Iron and steel, machinery motor
vehicles, chemicals, textile yarns and fabrics comprise the principal exports.

RULER
Albert II, 1993-

MINT MARK
Angel head - Brussels

MINTMASTERS' INITIALS & PRIVY MARKS
(b) - bird - Vogelier
Lamb head – Lambret
   NOTE: Beginning in 1987, the letters "qp" appear on the
coins - (quality proof)

MONETARY SYSTEM
100 Centimes = 1 Franc
1 Euro = 100 Cents

LEGENDS
   Belgian coins are usually inscribed either in Dutch, French
or both. However some modern coins are being inscribed in Latin
or German. The language used is best told by noting the spelling
of the name of the country.
(Fr) French: BELGIQUE or BELGES
(Du) Dutch: BELGIE or BELGEN
(La) Latin: BELGICA
(Ge) German: BELGIEN

KINGDOM
DECIMAL COINAGE

KM# 148.1 50 CENTIMES
2.7000 g., Bronze, 19 mm. **Ruler:** Baudouin I **Obv:** Crowned
denomination divides date, legend in French **Obv. Legend:**
BELGIQUE **Rev:** Helmeted mine worker, miner's lamp at right
large head, tip of neck 1/2 mm from rim **Edge:** Plain **Designer:** Rau

Date	Mintage	F	VF	XF	Unc	BU
2001	60,000	—	—	—	2.00	—
Note: In sets only						
2001 Proof	5,000	Value: 25.00				
Note: Medal alignment						

KM# 149.1 50 CENTIMES
2.7500 g., Bronze, 19 mm. **Ruler:** Baudouin I **Obv:** Crowned
denomination divides date, legend in Dutch **Obv. Legend:** BELGIE
Rev: Helmeted mine worker left, miner's lamp at right, large head
Edge: Plain **Designer:** Rau

Date	Mintage	F	VF	XF	Unc	BU
2001	60,000	—	—	—	3.00	—
Note: In sets only						
2001 Proof	5,000	Value: 25.00				
Note: Medal alignment						
2007	60,000	—	—	—	2.00	—
Note: In sets only						

KM# 148.2 50 CENTIMES
2.7500 g., Bronze, 19 mm. **Ruler:** Baudouin I **Obv:** Crowned
denomination divides date, legend in French **Obv. Legend:**
BELGIQUE **Rev:** Helmeted mine worker, left, miner's lamp at right
large head, tip of neck 1/2 mm from rim **Edge:** Plain **Designer:** Rau
Note: Medal alignment.

Date	Mintage	F	VF	XF	Unc	BU
2001 Proof	—	Value: 30.00				
Note: In sets only						

KM# 149.2 50 CENTIMES
2.7500 g., Bronze, 19 mm. **Ruler:** Baudouin I **Obv:** Crowned
denomination divides date, legend in French **Obv. Legend:**
BELGIQUE **Rev:** Helmeted mine worker, left, miner's lamp at
right large head, tip of neck 1/2 mm from rim **Edge:** Plain
Designer: Rau **Note:** Medal alignment.

Date	Mintage	F	VF	XF	Unc	BU
2001 Proof	—	Value: 30.00				
Note: In sets only						

KM# 188 FRANC
2.7500 g., Nickel Plated Iron, 18 mm. **Ruler:** Albert II **Obv:** Head
left, outline around back of head **Rev:** Vertical line divides date
and large denomination, legend in Dutch **Rev. Legend:** BELGIE
Edge: Plain

Date	Mintage	F	VF	XF	Unc	BU
2001	60,000	—	—	—	3.00	—
Note: In sets only						
2001 Proof	5,000	Value: 25.00				
Note: Medal alignment; in sets only						

KM# 187 FRANC
2.7500 g., Nickel Plated Iron, 18 mm. **Ruler:** Albert II **Obv:** Head
left, outline around back of head **Rev:** Vertical line divides date
and large denomination, legend in French **Rev. Legend:**
BELGIQUE **Note:** Mint mark - Angel Head. Unknown
mintmaster's privy mark - scales.

Date	Mintage	F	VF	XF	Unc	BU
2001	60,000	—	—	—	3.00	—
Note: In sets only						
2001 Proof	5,000	Value: 25.00				
Note: Medal alignment; in sets only						

KM# 189 5 FRANCS (5 Frank)

5.5000 g., Aluminum-Bronze, 24 mm. **Ruler:** Albert II **Obv:** Head left, outline around back of head **Rev:** Vertical line divides date and denomination, legend in French **Rev. Legend:** BELGIQUE **Note:** Mint mark - Angel head. Mintmaster R. Coenen's privy mark - Scale.

Date	Mintage	F	VF	XF	Unc	BU
2001	60,000	—	—	—	4.00	—
Note: In sets only						
2001 Proof	5,000	Value: 25.00				
Note: Medal alignment; in sets only						

KM# 190 5 FRANCS (5 Frank)

5.5000 g., Aluminum-Bronze, 24 mm. **Ruler:** Albert II **Obv:** Head left, outline around back of head **Rev:** Vertical line divides date and large denomination, legend in Dutch **Rev. Legend:** BELGIE **Note:** Mint mark - Angel head. Mintmaster R. Coenen's privy mark - Scale.

Date	Mintage	F	VF	XF	Unc	BU
2001	60,000	—	—	—	4.00	—
Note: In sets only						
2001 Proof	5,000	Value: 25.00				
Note: Medal alignment, in sets only						

KM# 191 20 FRANCS (20 Frank)

8.5000 g., Nickel-Bronze, 25.65 mm. **Ruler:** Albert II **Obv:** Head left, outline around back of head **Rev:** Vertical line divides date and large denomination, legend in French **Rev. Legend:** BELGIQUE **Note:** Mint mark - Angel head. Mintmaster R. Coenen's privy mark - Scale.

Date	Mintage	F	VF	XF	Unc	BU
2001	60,000	—	—	—	4.00	—
Note: In sets only						
2001 Proof	5,000	Value: 25.00				
Note: Medal alignment; in sets only						

KM# 192 20 FRANCS (20 Frank)

8.5000 g., Nickel-Bronze, 25.7 mm. **Ruler:** Albert II **Obv:** Head left, outline around back of head **Rev:** Vertical line divides date and large denomination, legend in Dutch **Rev. Legend:** BELGIE **Note:** Mint mark - Angel head. Mintmaster R. Coenen's privy mark - Scale.

Date	Mintage	F	VF	XF	Unc	BU
2001	60,000	—	—	—	5.00	—
Note: In sets only						
2001 Proof	5,000	Value: 25.00				
Note: Medal alignment; in sets only						

KM# 193 50 FRANCS (50 Frank)

7.0000 g., Nickel, 22.7 mm. **Ruler:** Albert II **Obv:** Head left, outline around back of head **Rev:** Vertical line divides large denomination and date, legend in French **Rev. Legend:** BELGIQUE **Note:** Mint mark - Angel head. Mintmaster R. Coenen's privy mark - Scale.

Date	Mintage	F	VF	XF	Unc	BU
2001	60,000	—	—	—	8.00	—
Note: In sets only						
2001 Proof	5,000	Value: 25.00				
Note: Medal alignment; in sets only						

KM# 194 50 FRANCS (50 Frank)

7.0000 g., Nickel, 22.75 mm. **Ruler:** Albert II **Obv:** Head left, outline around back of head **Rev:** Vertical line divides large denomination and date, legend in Dutch **Rev. Legend:** BELGIE **Note:** Mint mark - Angel head. Mintmaster R. Coenen's privy mark - Scale.

Date	Mintage	F	VF	XF	Unc	BU
2001	60,000	—	—	—	8.00	—
Note: In sets only						
2001 Proof	5,000	Value: 25.00				
Note: Medal alignment; in sets only						

KM# 222 500 FRANCS (500 Frank)

22.8500 g., 0.9250 Silver 0.6795 oz. ASW, 37 mm. **Ruler:** Albert II **Subject:** Europe: Europa and the Bull **Obv:** Map and denomination **Rev:** Europa sitting on a bull **Edge:** Plain

Date	Mintage	F	VF	XF	Unc	BU
2001 (qp) Proof	40,000	Value: 50.00				

KM# 223 5000 FRANCS

15.5500 g., 0.9990 Gold 0.4994 oz. AGW, 29 mm. **Ruler:** Albert II **Subject:** Europe: Europa and the Bull **Obv:** Map and denomination **Rev:** Europa sitting on a bull **Edge:** Plain

Date	Mintage	F	VF	XF	Unc	BU
2001 (qp) Proof	2,000	Value: 750				

EURO COINAGE

European Union Issues

KM# 259 12 1/2 EURO

1.2500 g., 0.9990 Gold 0.0401 oz. AGW, 14 mm. **Ruler:** Albert II **Subject:** Sace-Coburg-Gotha, 175th Anniversary **Obv:** Lion and tablet with constitution **Rev:** Head of Leopold I left

Date	Mintage	F	VF	XF	Unc	BU
2006 Proof	15,000	Value: 75.00				

KM# 224 EURO CENT

2.2700 g., Copper Plated Steel, 16.2 mm. **Ruler:** Albert II **Obv:** Head left within inner circle, stars 3/4 surround, date below **Obv. Designer:** Jan Alfons Keustermans **Rev:** Denomination and globe **Rev. Designer:** Luc Luycx **Edge:** Plain

Date	Mintage	F	VF	XF	Unc	BU
2001	99,840,000	—	—	0.30	0.75	1.00
2001 Proof	15,000	Value: 12.00				
2002 In sets only	140,000	—	—	—	18.50	22.50
2002 Proof	15,000	Value: 15.00				
2003	10,135,000	—	—	0.25	0.60	0.80
2003 Proof	15,000	Value: 12.00				
2004	180,000,000	—	—	0.25	0.60	0.80
2004 Proof	—	Value: 12.00				
2005 In sets only	—	—	—	—	—	18.50
2005 Proof	3,000	Value: 12.00				
2006	15,000,000	—	—	0.25	0.60	0.80
2006 Proof	—	Value: 12.00				
2007	60,000,000	—	—	0.25	0.60	0.80
2007 Proof	—	Value: 12.00				

KM# 274 EURO CENT

2.2700 g., Copper Plated Steel, 16.2 mm. **Ruler:** Albert II **Obv:** Head of Albert II left, crowned monogram at right, date below

Date	Mintage	F	VF	XF	Unc	BU
2008 (os)	50,000,000	—	—	—	0.35	0.75
2008 (os) Proof	—	Value: 12.00				
2009 (os)	—	—	—	—	0.35	0.75
2009 (os) Proof	—	Value: 12.00				
2010 (of)	—	—	—	—	0.35	0.75
2010 (of) Proof	—	Value: 12.00				

KM# 225 2 EURO CENT

3.0300 g., Copper Plated Steel, 18.7 mm. **Ruler:** Albert II **Obv:** Head left within circle, stars 3/4 surround, date below **Obv. Designer:** Jan Alfons Keustermans **Rev:** Denomination and globe **Rev. Designer:** Luc Luycx **Edge:** Grooved

Date	Mintage	F	VF	XF	Unc	BU
2001 In sets only	40,000	—	—	—	—	9.00
Note: Only available in sets at present, circulation strikes not yet released						
2001 Proof	15,000	Value: 15.00				
2002 In sets only	140,000	—	—	—	—	6.50
2002 Proof	15,000	Value: 12.00				
2003	40,135,000	—	—	0.30	0.75	1.00
2003 Proof	15,000	Value: 12.00				
2004	140,000,000	—	—	0.30	0.75	1.00
2004 Proof	15,000	Value: 12.00				
2005 In sets only	—	—	—	—	—	1.00
2005 Proof	—	Value: 12.00				
2006	30,000,000	—	—	0.30	0.75	1.00
2006 Proof	—	Value: 12.00				
2007	70,000,000	—	—	0.30	0.75	1.00
2007 Proof	—	Value: 12.00				

KM# 275 2 EURO CENT

3.0300 g., Copper Plated Steel, 18.7 mm. **Ruler:** Albert II **Obv:** Head of Albert II left, crowned monogram at right, date below

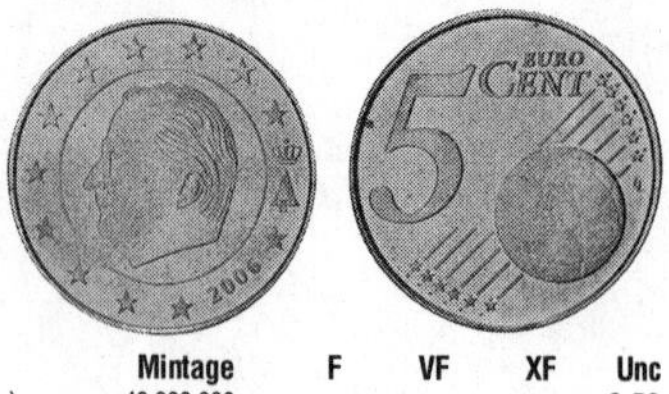

Date	Mintage	F	VF	XF	Unc	BU
2008 (os)	40,000,000	—	—	—	0.50	1.00
2008 (os) Proof	—	Value: 12.00				
2009 (os)	—	—	—	—	0.50	1.00
2009 (os) Proof	—	Value: 12.00				
2010 (of)	—	—	—	—	0.50	1.00
2010 (of) Proof	—	Value: 12.00				

KM# 226 5 EURO CENT

3.8600 g., Copper Plated Steel, 21.2 mm. **Ruler:** Albert II **Obv:** Head left within circle, stars 3/4 surround, date below **Obv. Designer:** Jan Alfons Keustermans **Rev:** Denomination and globe **Rev. Designer:** Luc Luycx **Edge:** Plain

Date	Mintage	F	VF	XF	Unc	BU
2001 In sets only	40,000	—	—	—	—	12.50
2001 Proof	15,000	Value: 15.00				
2002 In sets only	140,000	—	—	—	—	8.00
2002 Proof	15,000	Value: 15.00				
2003	30,135,000	—	—	0.30	0.80	1.20
2003 Proof	15,000	Value: 12.00				
2004	75,000,000	—	—	0.30	0.80	1.20
2004 Proof	—	Value: 12.00				
2005	110,000,000	—	—	0.30	0.80	1.20
2005 Proof	3,000	Value: 12.00				
2006	35,000,000	—	—	0.30	0.80	1.20
2006 Proof	—	Value: 12.00				
2007 In sets only	—	—	—	—	—	8.00
2007 Proof	—	Value: 12.00				

KM# 276 5 EURO CENT

3.8600 g., Copper Plated Steel **Ruler:** Albert II **Obv:** Head of Albert II left, crowned monogram right, date below **Shape:** 21.2

Date	Mintage	F	VF	XF	Unc	BU
2008 (os)	—	—	—	—	—	6.50
2008 (os) Proof	—	Value: 12.00				
2009 (os)	—	—	—	—	0.50	1.00
2009 (os) Proof	—	Value: 12.00				
2010 (of)	—	—	—	—	0.50	1.00
2010 (of) Proof	—	Value: 12.00				

KM# 227 10 EURO CENT

4.0700 g., Brass, 19.7 mm. **Ruler:** Albert II **Obv:** Head left within inner circle, stars 3/4 surround, date below **Obv. Designer:** Jan Alfons Keustermans **Rev:** Denomination and map **Rev. Designer:** Luc Luycx **Edge:** Reeded

Date	Mintage	F	VF	XF	Unc	BU
2001	145,790,000	—	—	—	0.75	1.25
2001 Proof	15,000	Value: 12.00				
2002 In sets only	140,000	—	—	—	6.00	8.00
2002 Proof	15,000	Value: 15.00				
2003 In sets only	135,000	—	—	—	6.00	8.00
2003 Proof	15,000	Value: 15.00				
2004	20,000,000	—	—	—	1.00	1.50
2004 Proof	—	Value: 12.00				
2005	10,000,000	—	—	—	1.00	1.50
2005 Proof	3,000	Value: 12.00				
2006 In sets only	—	—	—	—	1.00	1.50
2006 Proof	—	Value: 12.00				

KM# 242 10 EURO CENT

4.0700 g., Brass, 19.7 mm. **Ruler:** Albert II **Obv:** King's portrait **Obv. Designer:** Jan Alfons Keustermans **Rev:** Relief Map of Western Europe, stars, lines and value **Rev. Designer:** Luc Luycx **Edge:** Reeded

Date	Mintage	F	VF	XF	Unc	BU
2007	—	—	—	—	1.00	1.50
2007 Proof	—	—	—	—	—	—

KM# 277 10 EURO CENT

4.0700 g., Brass, 19.7 mm. **Ruler:** Albert II **Obv:** Head of Albert II left, crowned monogram right, date below

Date	Mintage	F	VF	XF	Unc	BU
2008 (os)	—	—	—	—	—	12.50
2008 (os) Proof	—	Value: 12.00				
2009 (os)	—	—	—	—	0.50	1.00
2009 (os) Proof	—	Value: 12.00				
2010 (of)	—	—	—	—	0.50	1.00
2010 (of) Proof	—	Value: 12.00				

KM# 228 20 EURO CENT
5.7300 g., Brass, 22.1 mm. **Ruler:** Albert II **Obv:** Head left within circle, stars 3/4 surround, date below **Obv. Designer:** Jan Alfons Keustermans **Rev:** Denomination and map **Rev. Designer:** Luc Luycx **Edge:** Notched

Date	Mintage	F	VF	XF	Unc	BU
2001 In sets only	40,000	—	—	—	10.00	12.50
Note: Only available in sets at present, circulation strikes not yet released						
2001 Proof	15,000	Value: 15.00				
2002	104,140,000	—	—	—	1.00	1.50
2002 Proof	15,000	Value: 12.00				
2003	30,135,000	—	—	—	1.25	1.75
2003 Proof	15,000	Value: 12.00				
2004	109,550,000	—	—	—	1.25	1.75
2004 Proof	—	Value: 12.00				
2005	10,000,000	—	—	—	1.25	1.75
2005 Proof	3,000	Value: 12.00				
2006	40,000,000	—	—	—	1.25	1.75
2006 Proof	—	Value: 12.00				

KM# 254 20 EURO CENT
22.8500 g., 0.9990 Silver 0.7339 oz. ASW, 37 mm. **Ruler:** Albert II **Subject:** FIFA World Cup in Germany **Obv:** Albert II head left **Rev:** Soccer player with ball

Date	Mintage	F	VF	XF	Unc	BU
2005 Proof	25,000	Value: 65.00				

KM# 243 20 EURO CENT
5.7300 g., Brass, 22.1 mm. **Ruler:** Albert II **Obv:** King's portrait **Obv. Designer:** Jan Alfons Keustermans **Rev:** Relief Map of Western Europe, stars, lines and value **Rev. Designer:** Luc Luycx **Edge:** Notched

Date	Mintage	F	VF	XF	Unc	BU
2007	—	—	—	—	1.25	1.75
2007 Proof	—	Value: 12.00				

KM# 278 20 EURO CENT
5.7300 g., Brass, 22.1 mm. **Ruler:** Albert II **Obv:** Head of Albert II left, crowned monogram right, date below

Date	Mintage	F	VF	XF	Unc	BU
2008 (os)	—	—	—	—	—	12.50
2008 (os) Proof	—	Value: 12.00				
2009 (os)	—	—	—	—	1.00	2.00
2009 (os) Proof	—	Value: 12.00				
2010 (of)	—	—	—	—	1.00	2.00
2010 (of) Proof	—	Value: 12.00				

KM# 229 50 EURO CENT
7.8100 g., Brass, 24.2 mm. **Ruler:** Albert II **Obv:** Head left within circle, stars 3/4 surround, date below **Obv. Designer:** Jan Alfons Keustermans **Rev:** Denomination and map **Rev. Designer:** Luc Luycx **Edge:** Reeded

Date	Mintage	F	VF	XF	Unc	BU
2001 In sets only	40,000	—	—	—	10.00	12.50
2001 Proof	15,000	Value: 15.00				
2002	50,040,000	—	—	—	1.00	1.50
2002 Proof	15,000	Value: 12.00				
2003 In sets only	135,000	—	—	—	—	12.50
2003 Proof	15,000	Value: 12.00				
2004	8,000,000	—	—	—	1.25	1.75
2004 Proof	—	Value: 12.00				
2005 In sets only	—	—	—	—	—	12.50
2005 Proof	3,000	Value: 12.00				
2006 In sets only	—	—	—	—	—	12.50
2006 Proof	—	Value: 12.00				

KM# 244 50 EURO CENT
7.8100 g., Brass, 24.2 mm. **Ruler:** Albert II **Obv:** King's portrait **Obv. Designer:** Jan Alfons Keustermans **Rev:** Relief Map of Western Europe, stars, lines and value **Rev. Designer:** Luc Luycx **Edge:** Reeded

Date	Mintage	F	VF	XF	Unc	BU
2007	—	—	—	—	1.25	1.75
2007 Proof	—	Value: 12.00				

KM# 279 50 EURO CENT
7.8100 g., Brass, 24.4 mm. **Ruler:** Albert II **Obv:** Head of Albert II left, crowned monogram right date below

Date	Mintage	F	VF	XF	Unc	BU
2008 (os)	—	—	—	—	—	12.00
2008 (os) Proof	—	Value: 12.00				
2009 (os)	—	—	—	—	2.00	3.00
2009 (os) Proof	—	Value: 12.00				
2010 (of)	—	—	—	—	2.00	3.00
2010 (of) Proof	—	Value: 12.00				

KM# 230 EURO
7.5700 g., Bi-Metallic Copper-Nickel center in Brass ring, 23.2 mm. **Ruler:** Albert II **Obv:** Head left within circle, stars 3/4 surround, date below **Obv. Designer:** Jan Alfons Keustermans **Rev:** Denomination and map **Rev. Designer:** Luc Luycx **Edge:** Reeded and plain sections

Date	Mintage	F	VF	XF	Unc	BU
2001 In sets only	40,000	—	—	—	—	15.00
Note: Only available in sets at present, circulation strikes not yet released						
2001 Proof	15,000	Value: 18.00				
2002	90,640,000	—	—	—	3.00	5.00
Note: Only a fraction of the mintage released at present						
2002 Proof	15,000	Value: 15.00				
2003	6,000,000	—	—	—	3.00	5.00
2003 Proof	15,000	Value: 15.00				
2004	15,000,000	—	—	—	3.00	5.00
2004 Proof	—	Value: 15.00				
2005 In sets only	—	—	—	—	—	15.00
2005 Proof	3,000	Value: 15.00				
2006 In sets only	—	—	—	—	—	15.00
2006 Proof	—	Value: 15.00				

KM# 245 EURO
7.5000 g., Bi-Metallic Copper-Nickel center in Brass ring, 23.2 mm. **Ruler:** Albert II **Obv:** King's portrait **Obv. Designer:** Jan Alfons Keustermans **Rev:** Relief Map of Western Europe, stars, lines and value **Rev. Designer:** Luc Luycx **Edge:** Reeded and plain sections

Date	Mintage	F	VF	XF	Unc	BU
2007	—	—	—	—	3.00	5.00
2007 Proof	—	Value: 15.00				

KM# 280 EURO
7.5000 g., Bi-Metallic Copper-nickel center in brass ring, 23.2 mm. **Ruler:** Albert II **Obv:** Head of Albert II right

Date	Mintage	F	VF	XF	Unc	BU
2008 (os)	—	—	—	—	—	12.50
2008 (os) Proof	—	Value: 12.50				
2009 (os)	—	—	—	—	2.00	3.00
2009 (os) Proof	—	Value: 12.50				
2010 (of)	—	—	—	—	2.00	3.00
2010 (of) Proof	—	Value: 12.50				

KM# 231 2 EURO
8.5200 g., Bi-Metallic Brass center in Copper-Nickel ring, 25.7 mm. **Ruler:** Albert II **Obv:** Head left within circle, stars 3/4 surround, date below **Obv. Designer:** Jan Alfons Keustermans **Rev:** Denomination and map **Rev. Designer:** Luc Luycx **Edge:** Reeded with 2's and stars

Date	Mintage	F	VF	XF	Unc	BU
2001 In sets only	40,000	—	—	—	12.50	15.00
Note: Only available in sets at present, circulation strikes not yet released						
2001 Proof	15,000	Value: 20.00				
2002	50,140,000	—	—	—	3.75	6.00
2002 Proof	15,000	Value: 18.00				
2003	30,135,000	—	—	—	3.75	6.00
2003 Proof	15,000	Value: 18.00				
2004	65,500,000	—	—	—	3.75	6.00
2004 Proof	—	Value: 18.00				
2005	10,500,000	—	—	—	3.75	6.00
2005 Proof	3,000	Value: 18.00				
2006	20,000,000	—	—	—	3.75	6.00
2006 Proof	—	Value: 18.00				

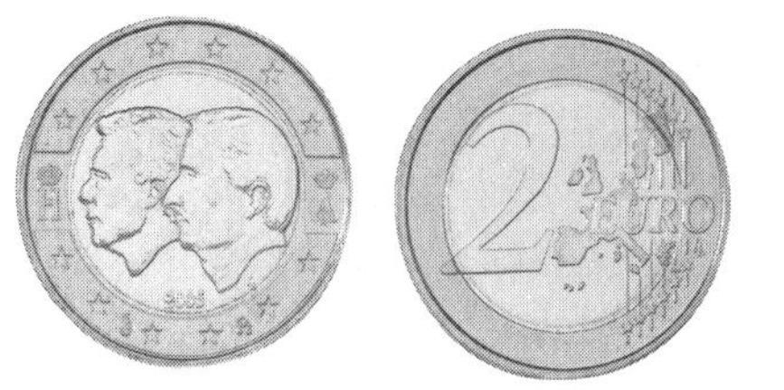

KM# 240 2 EURO
8.5200 g., Bi-Metallic Brass center in Copper-Nickel ring, 25.7 mm. **Ruler:** Albert II **Subject:** Schengen Agreement **Obv:** Albert II of Belgium and Henri of Luxembourg **Rev:** Value and map **Edge:** Reeding over stars

Date	Mintage	F	VF	XF	Unc	BU
2005	5,977,000	—	—	—	5.00	7.50
2005 Prooflike	20,000	—	—	—	—	20.00
2005 Proof	3,000	Value: 25.00				

KM# 241 2 EURO
8.5200 g., Bi-Metallic Brass center in Copper-Nickel ring, 25.7 mm. **Ruler:** Albert II **Obv:** Atomic model **Rev:** Value and map **Edge:** Reeding over stars and 2's

Date	Mintage	F	VF	XF	Unc	BU
2006	4,977,000	—	—	—	4.00	6.00
2006 Prooflike	20,000	—	—	—	—	25.00
2006 Proof	3,000	Value: 100				

KM# 246 2 EURO
8.5200 g., Bi-Metallic Brass center in Copper-Nickel ring, 25.7 mm. **Ruler:** Albert II **Obv:** King's portrait **Obv. Designer:** Jan Alfons Keustermans **Rev:** Relief Map of Western Europe, stars, lines and value **Rev. Designer:** Luc Luycx **Edge:** Reeded with 2's and stars

Date	Mintage	F	VF	XF	Unc	BU
2007	—	—	—	—	3.75	6.00

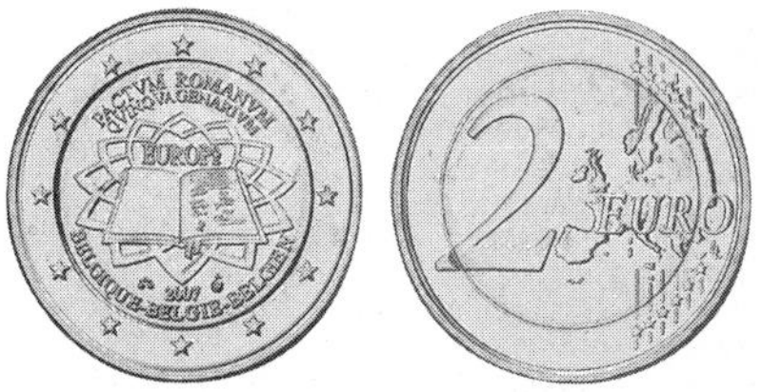

KM# 247 2 EURO
8.4500 g., Bi-Metallic Brass center in Copper-Nickel ring, 25.7 mm. **Ruler:** Albert II **Subject:** 50th Anniversary Treaty of Rome **Obv:** Open treaty book **Rev:** Large value at left, modified outline of Europe at right **Edge:** Reeded with stars and 2's

Date	Mintage	F	VF	XF	Unc	BU
2007	4,960,000	—	—	—	—	9.00
2007 Prooflike	35,000	—	—	—	—	25.00
2007 Proof	10,000	Value: 75.00				

KM# 248 2 EURO
8.5000 g., Bi-Metallic Bronze center in Copper-Nickel ring, 25.7 mm. **Ruler:** Albert II **Subject:** Universal Declaration of Human Rights **Obv:** Book in bow **Rev:** Large value "2" at left, modified map of Europe at right **Edge:** Reeded with incuse stars

Date	Mintage	F	VF	XF	Unc	BU
2008	—	—	—	—	—	6.00

KM# 281 2 EURO
8.5000 g., Bi-Metallic Brass center in Copper-Nickel ring, 25.7 mm. **Ruler:** Albert II **Obv:** Head of Albert II left, crowned monogram right, date below

Date	Mintage	F	VF	XF	Unc	BU
2008 (os)	—	—	—	—	—	12.50
2008 (os) Proof	—	Value: 12.50				
2009 (os)	—	—	—	—	2.00	3.00
2009 (os) Proof	—	Value: 12.50				
2010 (of)	—	—	—	—	2.00	3.00
2010 (of) Proof	—	Value: 12.50				

KM# 282 2 EURO
8.5000 g., Bi-Metallic Brass center in copper-nickel ring, 25.7 mm. **Ruler:** Albert II **Obv:** Stick figure and E symbol

Date	Mintage	F	VF	XF	Unc	BU
2009	—	—	—	—	15.00	—
2009	—	—	—	—	—	20.00
2009 Proof	—	Value: 70.00				

KM# 288 2 EURO
Bi-Metallic **Ruler:** Albert II **Subject:** Louis Braille, 200th Anniversary of birth

Date	Mintage	F	VF	XF	Unc	BU
2009	—	—	—	—	—	5.00

KM# 270 5 EURO
14.6000 g., 0.9250 Silver 0.4342 oz. ASW, 30 mm. **Ruler:** Albert II **Subject:** Smurfs - 50th Anniversary **Obv:** Map of Western Europe **Rev:** Smurf

Date	Mintage	F	VF	XF	Unc	BU
2008 Proof	25,000	Value: 50.00				

KM# 270a 5 EURO
14.6000 g., 0.9250 Silver 0.4342 oz. ASW, 30 mm. **Ruler:** Albert II **Subject:** Smurf - 50th Anniversary **Obv:** Map of Western Europe **Rev:** Multicolor 50 and Smurf

Date	Mintage	F	VF	XF	Unc	BU
2008 Proof	—	Value: 75.00				

KM# 233 10 EURO
18.9300 g., 0.9250 Silver 0.5629 oz. ASW, 32.9 mm.
Ruler: Albert II **Subject:** Belgian Railway System **Obv:** Value, head at right transposed on map **Rev:** Train exiting tunnel **Edge:** Reeded

Date	Mintage	F	VF	XF	Unc	BU
ND (2002) Proof	50,000	Value: 50.00				

KM# 235 10 EURO
18.9300 g., 0.9250 Silver 0.5629 oz. ASW, 32.9 mm.
Ruler: Albert II **Subject:** "Simenon" **Edge:** Reeded

Date	Mintage	F	VF	XF	Unc	BU
2003 Proof	50,000	Value: 40.00				

KM# 236 10 EURO
18.9300 g., 0.9250 Silver 0.5629 oz. ASW, 32.9 mm.
Ruler: Albert II **Subject:** "Tintin" **Edge:** Reeded

Date	Mintage	F	VF	XF	Unc	BU
2004 Proof	50,000	Value: 85.00				

KM# 234 10 EURO
18.7500 g., 0.9250 Silver 0.5576 oz. ASW, 33 mm.
Ruler: Albert II **Obv:** Value **Rev:** Western Europe map and Goddess Europa riding a bull **Edge:** Reeded

Date	Mintage	F	VF	XF	Unc	BU
2004 Proof	50,000	Value: 40.00				

KM# 252 10 EURO
18.7500 g., 0.9250 Silver 0.5576 oz. ASW, 33 mm.
Ruler: Albert II **Subject:** 60th Anniversary of Liberation **Obv:** Map of Western Europe and stars **Rev:** Phoenix

Date	Mintage	F	VF	XF	Unc	BU
2005 Proof	50,000	Value: 50.00				

KM# 251 10 EURO
18.7500 g., 0.9250 Silver 0.5576 oz. ASW, 33 mm. **Ruler:** Albert II **Subject:** Netherland-Belgium Soccer, 75th Anniversary **Obv:** Map of Western Europe and stars **Rev:** Soccer Player

Date	Mintage	F	VF	XF	Unc	BU
2005 Proof	50,000	Value: 45.00				

KM# 255 10 EURO
18.7500 g., 0.9250 Silver 0.5576 oz. ASW, 33 mm.
Ruler: Albert II **Subject:** Justus Lipsius, 400th Anniversary of Death **Obv:** Map of Western Europe and stars **Rev:** Half length figure of Justus Lipsius

Date	Mintage	F	VF	XF	Unc	BU
2006 Proof	50,000	Value: 45.00				

KM# 257 10 EURO
18.7500 g., 0.9250 Silver 0.5576 oz. ASW, 33 mm.
Ruler: Albert II **Subject:** 50th Anniversary - Mine Accident in Marcinelle **Obv:** Map of Western Europe and stars **Rev:** Male head and industrial mine scene

Date	Mintage	F	VF	XF	Unc	BU
2006 Proof	50,000	Value: 45.00				

KM# 257a 10 EURO
18.7500 g., 0.9250 Silver 0.5576 oz. ASW, 33 mm.
Ruler: Albert II **Subject:** 50th Anniversary, Mine Accident in Marcinelle **Obv:** Map of Western Europe and stars
Rev: Multicolor male head and industrial mine scene

Date	Mintage	F	VF	XF	Unc	BU
2006 Proof	2,000	Value: 75.00				

KM# 260 10 EURO
18.7500 g., 0.9250 Silver 0.5576 oz. ASW, 33 mm.
Ruler: Albert II **Subject:** Treaty of Rome, 50th Anniversary **Obv:** Map of Western Europe **Rev:** Document & feather pen

Date	Mintage	F	VF	XF	Unc	BU
2007 Proof	40,000	Value: 45.00				

KM# 263 10 EURO
18.7500 g., 0.9250 Silver 0.5576 oz. ASW, 33 mm.
Ruler: Albert II **Subject:** International Polar Year **Obv:** Map of Western Europe **Rev:** Wind farm and polar sation

Date	Mintage	F	VF	XF	Unc	BU
2007 Proof	40,000	Value: 50.00				

KM# 266 10 EURO
18.7500 g., 33.0000 Silver 19.892 oz. ASW, 33 mm.
Ruler: Albert II **Subject:** 100th Anniversary Maurice Maeterlinck **Obv:** Map of Western Europe **Rev:** Gateway and done in blue

Date	Mintage	F	VF	XF	Unc	BU
2008 Proof	20,000	Value: 75.00				

KM# 268 10 EURO
18.7500 g., 0.9250 Silver 0.5576 oz. ASW, 33 mm.
Ruler: Albert II **Subject:** Beijing Olympics **Obv:** Map of Western Europe **Rev:** Sport Events, logo and torch

Date	Mintage	F	VF	XF	Unc	BU
2008 Proof	20,000	Value: 50.00				

KM# 284 10 EURO
10.9300 g., 0.9250 Silver 0.3250 oz. ASW **Ruler:** Albert II
Subject: 75th Birthday of the King **Obv:** Head at left, laurel sprigs

Date	Mintage	F	VF	XF	Unc	BU
2009	—	—	—	—	—	50.00

KM# 285 10 EURO
18.9300 g., 0.9250 Silver 0.5629 oz. ASW **Ruler:** Albert II
Subject: Erasmus

Date	Mintage	F	VF	XF	Unc	BU
2009	—	—	—	—	—	50.00

KM# 265 12 1/2 EURO
1.2500 g., 0.9990 Gold 0.0401 oz. AGW, 14 mm. **Subject:** 175th Anniversary Saxe Coburg Gotha **Obv:** Lion and tablet
Rev: Leopole II head left

Date	Mintage	F	VF	XF	Unc	BU
2007 Proof	15,000	Value: 75.00				

KM# 271 12 1/2 EURO
1.2500 g., 0.9990 Gold 0.0401 oz. AGW, 14 mm. **Subject:** 175th Anniversary - Saxe Coburg Gotha **Obv:** Lion and tablet
Rev: Albert I bust right

Date	Mintage	F	VF	XF	Unc	BU
2008 Proof	15,000	Value: 75.00				

KM# 262 20 EURO
22.8500 g., 0.9250 Silver 0.6795 oz. ASW, 37 mm.
Ruler: Albert II **Subject:** Georges Remi, 100th Anniversary of Birth **Obv:** Map of Western Europe and stars **Rev:** Profile of Georges Renir and his character Tin Tin right

Date	Mintage	F	VF	XF	Unc	BU
2007 Proof	50,000	Value: 75.00				

KM# 287 20 EURO
22.8500 g., 0.9500 Silver 0.6979 oz. ASW, 37 mm.
Ruler: Albert II **Obv:** Value and map of Euro countries
Rev: Fr. Damien and churches in Tremblo and Molokai, date of canionization below

Date	Mintage	F	VF	XF	Unc	BU
2009 Proof	15,000	Value: 75.00				

KM# 269 25 EURO
3.1100 g., 0.9990 Gold 0.0999 oz. AGW, 18 mm. **Ruler:** Albert II
Subject: Beijing Olympics **Obv:** Map of Western Europe
Rev: Sport Events, logo, torch

Date	Mintage	F	VF	XF	Unc	BU
2008 Proof	5,000	Value: 200				

KM# 250 50 EURO
6.2200 g., Gold, 21 mm. **Ruler:** Albert II **Subject:** Albert II, 70th Birthday **Obv:** Map of Western Durope and stars **Rev:** Portrait of Albert II

Date	Mintage	F	VF	XF	Unc	BU
2004 Proof	10,000	Value: 225				

KM# 256 50 EURO
6.2200 g., 0.9990 Gold 0.1998 oz. AGW, 21 mm. **Ruler:** Albert II
Subject: Justus Lipsius, 400th Anniversary of Death **Obv:** Map of Western Europe and stars **Rev:** Half-length figure of Justus Lipius right

Date	Mintage	F	VF	XF	Unc	BU
2006 Proof	2,500	Value: 315				

KM# 261 50 EURO
6.2200 g., 0.9990 Gold 0.1998 oz. AGW, 21 mm. **Ruler:** Albert II
Subject: Treaty of Rome, 50th Anniversary **Obv:** Map of Western Europe **Rev:** Document and feather pen

Date	Mintage	F	VF	XF	Unc	BU
2007 Proof	2,500	Value: 315				

KM# 267 50 EURO
6.2200 g., 0.9990 Gold 0.1998 oz. AGW, 21 mm. **Ruler:** Albert II
Subject: 100th Anniversary Maurice Maeterlinck **Obv:** Map of Western Europe **Rev:** Gate and dove

Date	Mintage	F	VF	XF	Unc	BU
2008 Proof	2,500	Value: 400				

KM# 286 50 EURO
8.4500 g., 0.9990 Gold 0.2714 oz. AGW **Ruler:** Albert II
Subject: Erasmus

Date	Mintage	F	VF	XF	Unc	BU
2009	—	—	—	—	—	350

KM# 237 100 EURO
15.5500 g., 0.9990 Gold 0.4994 oz. AGW, 29 mm.
Ruler: Albert II **Subject:** Founding Fathers

Date	Mintage	F	VF	XF	Unc	BU
2002 Proof	5,000	Value: 650				

KM# 238 100 EURO
15.5500 g., 0.9990 Gold 0.4994 oz. AGW, 29 mm.
Ruler: Albert II **Subject:** 10th Anniversary of Reign

Date	Mintage	F	VF	XF	Unc	BU
2003 Proof	5,000	Value: 550				

KM# 239 100 EURO
15.5500 g., 0.9990 Gold 0.4994 oz. AGW, 29 mm.
Ruler: Albert II **Subject:** Franc Germinal

Date	Mintage	F	VF	XF	Unc	BU
2004 Proof	5,000	Value: 550				

KM# 253 100 EURO
15.5500 g., 0.9990 Gold 0.4994 oz. AGW, 29 mm.
Ruler: Albert II **Subject:** 175th Anniversary of Liberty **Obv:** Albert II head left **Rev:** Scene of the 1830 Revolution

Date	Mintage	F	VF	XF	Unc	BU
2005 Proof	5,000	Value: 550				

KM# 258 100 EURO
15.5500 g., 0.9990 Gold 0.4994 oz. AGW, 29 mm.
Ruler: Albert II **Subject:** Saxe-Coburg-Gotha, 175th Anniversary **Obv:** Map of Western Europe and stars **Rev:** Church in Laeken, Kings monogram around

Date	Mintage	F	VF	XF	Unc	BU
2006 Proof	5,000	Value: 550				

KM# 264 100 EURO
15.5500 g., 0.9990 Gold 0.4994 oz. AGW, 29 mm.
Ruler: Albert II **Subject:** Belgian Coins 175th Anniversary
Obv: Map of Western Europe **Rev:** Screw press, coin designs

Date	Mintage	F	VF	XF	Unc	BU
2007 Proof	5,000	Value: 700				

KM# 272 100 EURO
15.5500 g., 0.9990 Gold 0.4994 oz. AGW, 29 mm.
Ruler: Albert II **Subject:** 50th Anniversary: Brussels Exposition
Obv: Map of Western Europe

Date	Mintage	F	VF	XF	Unc	BU
2008 Proof	5,000	Value: 700				

KM# 283 100 EURO
15.5500 g., 0.9990 Gold 0.4994 oz. AGW **Ruler:** Albert II
Subject: Royal Wedding Anniversary **Obv:** Conjoined leads at right

Date	Mintage	F	VF	XF	Unc	BU
2009 Proof	—	Value: 700				

MINT SETS

KM#	Date	Mintage	Identification	Issue Price	Mkt Val
MS14	2001 (10)	60,000	KM#148.1, 149.1, 187-194	15.00	45.00

PROOF SETS

KM#	Date	Mintage	Identification	Issue Price	Mkt Val
PS10	2001 (8)	15,000	KM#224-231	80.00	125
PS11	2002 (8)	15,000	KM#224-231	80.00	115
PS12	2003 (8)	15,000	KM#224-231	80.00	110
PS13	2004 (8)	15,000	KM#224-231	80.00	105

BELIZE (British Honduras)

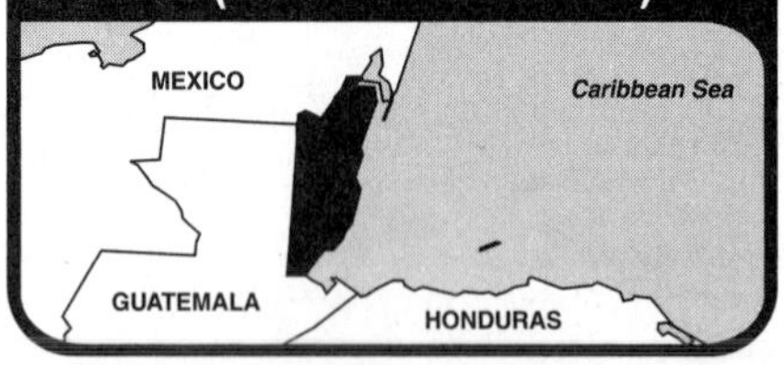

Belize, formerly British Honduras, but now a Constitutional Monarchy within the Commonwealth of Nations, is situated in Central America south of Mexico and east and north of Guatemala, with an area of 8,867 sq. mi. (22,960 sq. km.) and a population of *242,000. Capital: Belmopan. Tourism now augments Belize's economy, in addition to sugar, citrus fruits, chicle and hardwoods, which are exported.

MONETARY SYSTEM
100 Cents = 1 Dollar

COMMONWEALTH

DECIMAL COINAGE

KM# 33a CENT
0.8000 g., Aluminum, 19.5 mm. **Obv:** Bust of Queen Elizabeth right **Rev:** Denomination within circle **Edge:** Smooth, scalloped

Date	Mintage	F	VF	XF	Unc	BU
2002	—	—	—	0.10	0.15	0.45
2005	—	—	—	0.10	0.15	0.45
2007	—	—	—	0.10	0.15	0.45

KM# 34a 5 CENTS
1.0400 g., Aluminum, 20.2 mm. **Obv:** Bust of Queen Elizabeth II right **Obv. Designer:** Cecil Thomas **Rev:** Denomination within circle **Edge:** Plain

Date	Mintage	F	VF	XF	Unc	BU
2002	—	—	—	0.10	0.20	0.45
2003	—	—	—	0.10	0.20	0.45
2006	—	—	—	0.10	0.20	0.45

KM# 115 5 CENTS
1.0500 g., Aluminum, 20.2 mm.

Date	Mintage	F	VF	XF	Unc	BU
2002	—	—	—	0.10	0.20	0.40

KM# 36 25 CENTS
5.7200 g., Copper-Nickel, 23.6 mm. **Obv:** Crowned bust of Queen Elizabeth II right **Obv. Designer:** Cecil Thomas **Rev:** Denomination within circle, date below **Edge:** Reeded

Date	Mintage	F	VF	XF	Unc	BU
2003	—	—	0.20	0.35	0.75	1.50
2007	—	—	0.20	0.35	0.75	1.50

KM# 134 DOLLAR
30.9400 g., 0.9990 Silver 0.9937 oz. ASW, 39.9 mm. **Subject:** Mayan King **Obv:** National arms **Rev:** Mayan portrait in ornate headdress **Edge:** Reeded

Date	Mintage	F	VF	XF	Unc	BU
2002	—	—	—	—	35.00	37.50

KM# 99 DOLLAR
8.9000 g., Nickel-Brass, 27 mm. **Obv:** Crowned bust of Queen Elizabeth II right **Obv. Designer:** Raphael Maklouf **Rev:** Columbus' three ships, denomination above, date below **Rev. Designer:** Robert Elderton **Edge:** Alternating reeded and plain **Shape:** 10-sided

Date	Mintage	F	VF	XF	Unc	BU
2003	—	—	—	—	2.25	3.00
2007	—	—	—	—	2.25	3.00

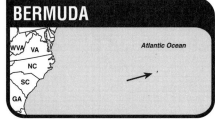

BERMUDA

The Parliamentary British Colony of Bermuda, situated in the western Atlantic Ocean 660 miles (1,062 km.) east of North Carolina, has an area of 20.6 sq. mi. (53 sq. km.) and a population of 61,600. Capital: Hamilton. Concentrated essences, beauty preparations, and cut flowers are exported. Most Bermudians derive their livelihood from tourism. The British monarch is the head of state and is represented by a governor. U.S. Currency circulates in common with the Eastern Caribbean Dollar.

RULER
British

BRITISH COLONY
DECIMAL COINAGE

100 Cents = 1 Dollar

KM# 107 CENT
Copper Plated Zinc, 19 mm. **Ruler:** Elizabeth II **Obv:** Head with tiara right **Obv. Designer:** Ian Rank-Broadley **Rev:** Wild boar left **Rev. Designer:** Michael Rizzello **Edge:** Smooth

Date	Mintage	F	VF	XF	Unc	BU
2001	1,600,000	—	—	—	0.50	0.75
2002	1,120,000	—	—	—	0.50	0.75
2003	800,000	—	—	—	0.50	0.75
2004	1,600,000	—	—	—	0.25	0.50
2005	3,200,000	—	—	—	0.25	0.50
2006	800,000	—	—	—	0.25	0.50
2008	2,400,000	—	—	—	0.25	0.50
2009	400,000	—	—	—	0.25	0.50

KM# 108 5 CENTS
5.0600 g., Copper-Nickel, 21 mm. **Ruler:** Elizabeth II **Obv:** Head with tiara right **Obv. Designer:** Ian Rank-Broadley **Rev:** Queen angel fish left **Rev. Designer:** Michael Rizzello **Edge:** Smooth

Date	Mintage	F	VF	XF	Unc	BU
2001	1,000,000	—	—	—	0.75	1.00
2002	700,000	—	—	—	0.75	1.00
2003	700,000	—	—	—	0.75	1.00
2004	700,000	—	—	—	0.75	1.00
2005	600,000	—	—	—	0.75	1.00
2008	500,000	—	—	—	0.75	1.00
2009	1,500,000	—	—	—	0.50	0.75

KM# 109 10 CENTS
2.5000 g., Copper-Nickel, 17.8 mm. **Ruler:** Elizabeth II **Obv:** Head with tiara right **Obv. Designer:** Ian Rank-Broadley **Rev:** Bermuda lily **Rev. Designer:** Michael Rizzello **Edge:** Reeded

Date	Mintage	F	VF	XF	Unc	BU
2001	1,400,000	—	—	—	0.85	1.00
2002	800,000	—	—	—	0.85	1.00
2003	600,000	—	—	—	0.85	1.00
2004	800,000	—	—	—	0.85	1.00
2005	800,000	—	—	—	0.85	1.00
2008	2,000,000	—	—	—	0.50	0.75
2009	2,000,000	—	—	—	0.50	0.75

KM# 110 25 CENTS
Copper-Nickel, 24 mm. **Ruler:** Elizabeth II **Obv:** Head with tiara right **Obv. Designer:** Ian Rank-Broadley **Rev:** Yellow-billed tropical bird right **Rev. Designer:** Michael Rizzello **Edge:** Reeded

Date	Mintage	F	VF	XF	Unc	BU
2001	800,000	—	—	—	1.50	2.00
2002	800,000	—	—	—	1.50	2.00
2003	800,000	—	—	—	1.50	2.00
2004	800,000	—	—	—	1.50	2.00
2005	1,440,000	—	—	—	1.50	2.00
2006	320,000	—	—	—	1.50	2.00
2008	1,200,000	—	—	—	1.00	1.50
2009	200,000	—	—	—	1.00	1.50

KM# 111 DOLLAR
Nickel-Brass, 26 mm. **Ruler:** Elizabeth II **Obv:** Head with tiara right **Obv. Designer:** Rank-Broadley **Rev:** Sailboat **Rev. Designer:** Eldron Trimingham III

Date	Mintage	F	VF	XF	Unc	BU
2001	12,000	—	—	—	3.00	3.50
2002	12,000	—	—	—	3.00	3.50
2003	12,000	—	—	—	3.00	3.50
2004	12,000	—	—	—	3.00	3.50
2005	240,000	—	—	—	2.00	3.00
2008	300,000	—	—	—	2.00	3.00
2009	600,000	—	—	—	2.00	3.00

KM# 139 DOLLAR
28.2800 g., Copper-Nickel, 38.6 mm. **Obv:** Head with tiara right **Obv. Designer:** Ian Rank-Broadley **Rev:** 4 Gombey dancers **Rev. Designer:** Robert Elderton **Edge:** Reeded

Date	Mintage	F	VF	XF	Unc	BU
2001	—	—	—	—	10.00	12.00

KM# 124 DOLLAR
28.4100 g., Copper-Nickel, 38.5 mm. **Ruler:** Elizabeth II **Subject:** Queen's Golden Jubilee **Obv:** Head with tiara right **Obv. Designer:** Ian Rank-Broadley **Rev:** Stylized trumpeters above monogram and date **Edge:** Reeded

Date	Mintage	F	VF	XF	Unc	BU
2002	—	—	—	—	10.00	12.00

KM# 380 2 DOLLARS
31.6040 g., 0.9990 Silver 1.0150 oz. ASW, 38.61 mm. **Ruler:** Elizabeth II **Subject:** Bermuca Hawksbill Turtle **Obv:** Bust right **Rev:** Turtle **Rev. Legend:** BERMUDA HAWKSBILL TURTLE / TWO DOLLARS

Date	Mintage	F	VF	XF	Unc	BU
2008 Proof	2,500	Value: 50.00				

KM# 157 3 DOLLARS
33.6300 g., 0.9250 Silver 1.0000 oz. ASW, 35 mm. **Subject:** Shipwrecks Series **Obv:** Elizabeth II **Rev:** Gold plated image of the Hunter Galley **Edge:** Plain

Date	Mintage	F	VF	XF	Unc	BU
2006 Proof	15,000	Value: 90.00				

KM# 158　3 DOLLARS

33.6300 g., 0.9250 Silver 1.0000 oz. ASW, 35 mm.
Subject: Shipwrecks Series **Obv:** Elizabeth II **Rev:** Gold plated image of the North Carolina **Edge:** Plain

Date	Mintage	F	VF	XF	Unc	BU
2006 Proof	15,000	Value: 90.00				

KM# 159　3 DOLLARS

33.6300 g., 0.9250 Silver 1.0000 oz. ASW, 35 mm.
Subject: Shipwrecks Series **Obv:** Elizabeth II **Rev:** Gold plated image of the Pollockshields **Edge:** Plain

Date	Mintage	F	VF	XF	Unc	BU
2006 Proof	15,000	Value: 90.00				

KM# 140　3 DOLLARS

33.6300 g., 0.9250 Silver 1.0000 oz. ASW, 35 mm.
Subject: Shipwreck Series **Obv:** Elizabeth II **Rev:** The Mary Celestia gold plated image **Edge:** Plain **Shape:** Triangular

Date	Mintage	F	VF	XF	Unc	BU
2006 Proof	15,000	Value: 90.00				

KM# 141　3 DOLLARS

1.5550 g., 0.9990 Gold 0.0499 oz. AGW, 15 mm.
Subject: Shipwreck Series **Obv:** Elizabeth II **Rev:** The Mary Celestia **Edge:** Plain **Shape:** Triangular

Date	Mintage	F	VF	XF	Unc	BU
2006 Proof	15,000	Value: 100				

KM# 148　3 DOLLARS

33.6300 g., 0.9250 Silver 1.0000 oz. ASW, 35 mm.
Subject: Shipwreck Series **Obv:** Elizabeth II **Rev:** The Constellation in gold plated image **Edge:** Plain **Shape:** Triangular

Date	Mintage	F	VF	XF	Unc	BU
2006 Proof	15,000	Value: 90.00				

KM# 149　3 DOLLARS

1.5550 g., 0.9990 Gold 0.0499 oz. AGW, 15 mm.
Subject: Shipwreck Series **Obv:** Elizabeth II **Rev:** The Constellation **Edge:** Plain **Shape:** Triangular

Date	Mintage	F	VF	XF	Unc	BU
2006 Proof	15,000	Value: 100				

KM# 156　3 DOLLARS

33.6300 g., 0.9250 Silver 1.0000 oz. ASW, 35 mm.
Subject: Shipwrecks Series **Obv:** Elizabeth II **Rev:** Gold plated image of the Sea Venture **Edge:** Plain

Date	Mintage	F	VF	XF	Unc	BU
2007 Proof	15,000	Value: 90.00				

KM# 164　3 DOLLARS

34.2600 g., 0.9250 Silver 1.0188 oz. ASW, 35 mm. **Ruler:** Elizabeth II **Series:** Bermuda Shipwrecks **Obv:** Head with tiara right, gilt **Obv. Designer:** Ian Rank-Broadley **Rev:** Dutchman sailing ship "Manilla", gilt, 1739 **Edge:** Plain, gilt **Shape:** Triangular

Date	Mintage	F	VF	XF	Unc	BU
2007 Proof	15,000	Value: 82.50				

KM# 165　3 DOLLARS

33.6300 g., 0.9250 Silver 1.0000 oz. ASW, 35 mm.
Ruler: Elizabeth II **Series:** Bermuda Shipwrecks **Obv:** Head with tiara right, gilt **Obv. Designer:** Ian Rank-Broadley **Rev:** 16th century Spanish sailing ship "Santa Lucia", gilt, 1584 **Edge:** Plain, gilt **Shape:** Triangular

Date	Mintage	F	VF	XF	Unc	BU
2007 Proof	15,000	Value: 82.50				

KM# 166　3 DOLLARS

33.6300 g., 0.9250 Silver 1.0000 oz. ASW **Ruler:** Elizabeth II **Series:** Bermuda Shipwrecks **Obv:** Head with tiara right, gilt **Obv. Designer:** Ian Rank-Broadley **Rev:** Spanish luxury steamship "Cristobal Colon", gilt, 1936 **Edge:** Plain

Date	Mintage	F	VF	XF	Unc	BU
2007 Proof	15,000	Value: 82.50				

KM# 167　3 DOLLARS

33.6300 g., 0.9250 Silver 1.0000 oz. ASW, 35 mm.
Ruler: Elizabeth II **Series:** Bermuda Shipwrecks **Obv:** Head with tiara right, gilt **Obv. Designer:** Ian Rank-Broadley **Rev:** English iron hulled steamer with sails "Kate", gilt, 1878 **Edge:** Plain **Shape:** Triangular

Date	Mintage	F	VF	XF	Unc	BU
2007 Proof	15,000	Value: 82.50				

KM# 168　3 DOLLARS

33.6300 g., 0.9250 Silver 1.0000 oz. ASW, 35 mm.
Ruler: Elizabeth II **Series:** Bermuda Shipwrecks **Obv:** Head with tiara right, gilt **Obv. Designer:** Ian Rank-Broadley **Rev:** 16th century Spanish sailing ship "San Pedro", gilt, 1596 **Edge:** Plain, gilt **Shape:** Triangular

Date	Mintage	F	VF	XF	Unc	BU
2007 Proof	15,000	Value: 82.50				

KM# 169　3 DOLLARS

33.6300 g., 0.9250 Silver 1.0000 oz. ASW, 35 mm. **Ruler:** Elizabeth II **Series:** Bermuda Shipwrecks **Obv:** Head with tiara right, gilt **Obv. Designer:** Ian Rank-Broadley **Rev:** American luxury yacht "Col. William G. Ball", gilt, 1943 **Edge:** Plain, gilt **Shape:** Triangular

Date	Mintage	F	VF	XF	Unc	BU
2007 Proof	15,000	Value: 82.50				

KM# 381　4 DOLLARS

34.0000 g., 0.9250 Silver 1.0111 oz. ASW, 40 mm.
Ruler: Elizabeth II **Obv:** Bust right **Obv. Legend:** Elizabeth II, Value, BERMUDA **Rev:** Sea venture sailing ship **Rev. Legend:** 1609-2009 400th ANNIVERSARY OF THE SETTLEMENT OF BERMUDA **Shape:** Square

Date	Mintage	F	VF	XF	Unc	BU
ND(2009) Proof	2,000	Value: 50.00				

KM# 120　5 DOLLARS

28.2800 g., 0.9250 Silver 0.8410 oz. ASW, 38.6 mm.
Subject: Gombey Dancers **Obv:** Head with tiara right **Obv. Designer:** Ian Rank-Broadley **Rev:** Multicolor costumed dancers **Edge:** Reeded

Date	Mintage	F	VF	XF	Unc	BU
2001 Proof	3,500	Value: 50.00				

KM# 161 5 DOLLARS
28.2800 g., 0.9250 Silver 0.8410 oz. ASW, 38.6 mm.
Ruler: Elizabeth II **Obv:** Bust with tiara right **Rev:** Statehouse facade, St. George's **Edge:** Reeded

Date	Mintage	F	VF	XF	Unc	BU
2001 Proof	3,500	Value: 45.00				

KM# 129 5 DOLLARS
28.2800 g., 0.9250 Silver 0.8410 oz. ASW, 38.6 mm.
Subject: Queen's Jubilee **Obv:** Gold-plated head with tiara right, denomination below **Rev:** Trumpeters, monogram and date below **Edge:** Reeded

Date	Mintage	F	VF	XF	Unc	BU
2002 Proof	20,000	Value: 40.00				

KM# 162 5 DOLLARS
28.2800 g., 0.9250 Silver 0.8410 oz. ASW, 38.61 mm.
Ruler: Elizabeth II **Subject:** 100th Anniversary Cup Match - Cricket **Obv:** Head with tiara right **Rev:** Two players with caps and teams shields below multicolor **Edge:** Reeded

Date	Mintage	F	VF	XF	Unc	BU
2002 Proof	3,500	Value: 45.00				

KM# 171 5 DOLLARS
28.2800 g., 0.9250 Silver 0.8410 oz. ASW, 38.5 mm.
Ruler: Elizabeth II **Subject:** Queen's Golden Jubilee **Obv:** Head with tiara right **Obv. Designer:** Ian Rank-Broadley **Rev:** Stylized trumpeters above monogram and date **Edge:** Reeded

Date	Mintage	F	VF	XF	Unc	BU
2002 Proof	3,500	Value: 50.00				

KM# 170 5 DOLLARS
28.2800 g., 0.9250 Silver 0.8410 oz. ASW, 38.61 mm.
Ruler: Elizabeth II **Subject:** 100th Anniversary Fitted Dinghy Racing **Obv:** Head with tiara right **Rev:** Two dinghies, multicolor sails **Edge:** Reeded

Date	Mintage	F	VF	XF	Unc	BU
ND(2003) Proof	3,500	Value: 50.00				

KM# 128 5 DOLLARS
28.2800 g., 0.9250 Silver 0.8410 oz. ASW, 38.6 mm. **Obv:** Head with tiara right **Rev:** 2 fitted racing dinghys with multicolor sails **Edge:** Reeded

Date	Mintage	F	VF	XF	Unc	BU
ND (2003) Proof	3,500	Value: 60.00				

KM# 130 5 DOLLARS
28.2800 g., 0.9250 Silver 0.8410 oz. ASW, 38.6 mm.
Subject: Queen's Jubilee **Obv:** Gold-plated head with tiara right **Rev:** Royal visit scene **Edge:** Reeded

Date	Mintage	F	VF	XF	Unc	BU
2003 Proof	20,000	Value: 40.00				

KM# 131 5 DOLLARS
28.2800 g., 0.9250 Silver 0.8410 oz. ASW, 38.6 mm. **Obv:** Head with tiara right **Rev:** Bermudan stone quarrying scene **Edge:** Reeded

Date	Mintage	F	VF	XF	Unc	BU
2004 Proof	3,500	Value: 60.00				

KM# 160 5 DOLLARS
14.5000 g., 0.9250 Silver 0.4312 oz. ASW, 30.89 mm.
Ruler: Elizabeth II **Subject:** Bermuda Quincentennial **Obv:** Head with tiara right, gilt **Rev:** Caravel type sailing ship in partially gold plated compass face and rim **Edge:** Plain, gilt **Shape:** Pentagonal

Date	Mintage	F	VF	XF	Unc	BU
2005 Proof	2,500	Value: 40.00				

KM# 160a 5 DOLLARS
, 30.89 mm. **Ruler:** Elizabeth II **Obv:** Queen Elizabeth II **Rev:** Caravel type sailing ship in compass face **Edge:** Plain **Shape:** Pentagonal **Note:** Bermuda Quincentennial

Date	Mintage	F	VF	XF	Unc	BU
2005 Proof	3,000	Value: 500				

KM# 142 9 DOLLARS
155.5200 g., 0.9990 Silver 4.9949 oz. ASW, 65 mm.
Subject: Shipwreck Series **Obv:** Elizabeth II **Rev:** The Mary Celestia **Edge:** Plain **Shape:** Triangular

Date	Mintage	F	VF	XF	Unc	BU
2007 Proof	1,000	Value: 200				

KM# 150 9 DOLLARS
155.5200 g., 0.9990 Silver 4.9949 oz. ASW, 65 mm.
Subject: Shipwreck Series **Obv:** Elizabeth II **Rev:** The Constellation **Edge:** Plain **Shape:** Triangular

Date	Mintage	F	VF	XF	Unc	BU
2007 Proof	1,000	Value: 200				

KM# 143 30 DOLLARS
31.4890 g., 0.9990 Gold 1.0113 oz. AGW, 35 mm.
Subject: Shipwreck Series **Obv:** Elizabeth II **Rev:** The Mary Celestia **Edge:** Plain **Shape:** Triangular

Date	Mintage	F	VF	XF	Unc	BU
2006 Proof	750	Value: 985				

KM# 151 30 DOLLARS
31.4890 g., 0.9990 Gold 1.0113 oz. AGW, 35 mm.
Subject: Shipwreck Series **Obv:** Elizabeth II **Rev:** The Constellation **Edge:** Plain **Shape:** Triangular

Date	Mintage	F	VF	XF	Unc	BU
2006 Proof	750	Value: 985				

KM# 144 60 DOLLARS
1000.0000 g., 0.9990 Silver 32.117 oz. ASW, 100 mm.
Subject: Shipwreck Series **Obv:** Elizabeth II **Rev:** The Mary Celestia **Edge:** Plain

Date	Mintage	F	VF	XF	Unc	BU
2007 Proof	300	Value: 600				

KM# 152 60 DOLLARS
1000.0000 g., 0.9990 Silver 32.117 oz. ASW, 100 mm.
Subject: Shipwreck Series **Obv:** Elizabeth II **Rev:** The Constellation **Edge:** Plain **Shape:** Triangular

Date	Mintage	F	VF	XF	Unc	BU
2007 Proof	300	Value: 600				

KM# 145 90 DOLLARS
155.5200 g., 0.9990 Gold 4.9949 oz. AGW, 65 mm.
Subject: Shipwreck Series **Obv:** Elizabeth II **Rev:** The Mary Celestia **Edge:** Plain **Shape:** Triangular

Date	Mintage	F	VF	XF	Unc	BU
2006 Proof	90	Value: 5,000				

KM# 153 90 DOLLARS
155.5200 g., 0.9990 Gold 4.9949 oz. AGW, 65 mm.
Subject: Shipwreck Series **Obv:** Elizabeth II **Rev:** The Constellation **Edge:** Plain **Shape:** Triangular

Date	Mintage	F	VF	XF	Unc	BU
2006 Proof	90	Value: 5,000				

KM# 146 300 DOLLARS
155.5200 g., 0.9995 Platinum 4.9974 oz. APW, 65 mm.
Subject: Shipwrecks Series **Obv:** Elizabeth II **Rev:** The Mary Celestia **Edge:** Plain **Shape:** Triangular

Date	Mintage	F	VF	XF	Unc	BU
2006 Proof	60	Value: 6,650				

KM# 154 300 DOLLARS
155.5200 g., 0.9995 Platinum 4.9974 oz. APW, 65 mm.
Subject: Shipwreck Series **Obv:** Elizabeth II **Rev:** The Constellation **Edge:** Plain **Shape:** Triangular

Date	Mintage	F	VF	XF	Unc	BU
2006 Proof	60	Value: 8,000				

KM# 147 600 DOLLARS
1096.0000 g., 0.9180 Gold 32.346 oz. AGW, 100 mm.
Subject: Shipwreck Series **Obv:** Elizabeth II **Rev:** The Mary Celestia **Edge:** Plain **Shape:** Triangular

Date	Mintage	F	VF	XF	Unc	BU
2007 Proof	300	Value: 32,500				

KM# 155 600 DOLLARS
1096.0000 g., 0.9180 Gold 32.346 oz. AGW, 100 mm.
Subject: Shipwreck Series **Obv:** Elizabeth II **Rev:** The Constellation **Edge:** Plain **Shape:** Triangular

Date	Mintage	F	VF	XF	Unc	BU
2007 Proof	300	Value: 32,500				

PIEFORTS

KM#	Date	Mintage	Identification	Mkt Val
P3	2005	250	5 Dollars. 0.9250 Silver. 29.0000 g. 30.89 mm. Gold plated bust and rim. Caravel type sailing ship in partially gold plated compass face and rim. Plain, gold plated edge.	—

MINT SETS

KM#	Date	Mintage	Identification	Issue Price	Mkt Val
MS8	2004 (5)	2,300	KM#107-111.	—	10.00

BHUTAN

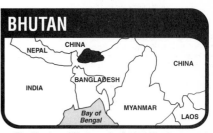

The Kingdom of Bhutan, a landlocked Himalayan country bordered by Tibet and India, has an area of 18,150 sq. mi. (47,000 sq. km.) and a population of *2.03 million. Capital: Thimphu. Virtually the entire population is engaged in agricultural and pastoral activities. Rice, wheat, barley, and yak butter are produced in sufficient quantity to make the country self-sufficient in food. The economy of Bhutan is primitive and many transactions are conducted on a barter basis.

RULER
Jigme Singye Wangchuck, 1972-2006
King Jigme Khesar Namgyel Wangchuck, 2006-

KINGDOM

REFORM COINAGE

Commencing 1974; 100 Chetrums (Paisa) = 1 Ngultrum (Rupee); 100 Ngultrums = 1 Sertum

KM# 105 5 CHETRUMS
3.8600 g., Brass, 21.9 mm. **Obv:** Monkey right, date below **Rev:** Effigy of the old "Ma-tam", value below **Edge:** Plain

Date	Mintage	F	VF	XF	Unc	BU
2003	—	—	—	—	0.25	0.50

KM# 116 NGULTRUM
8.1000 g., Nickel Plated Steel **Ruler:** Jigme Khesar Namgyel Wangchuck

Date	Mintage	F	VF	XF	Unc	BU
2008	—	—	—	—	3.00	4.00

KM# 115 100 NGULTRUMS
20.2000 g., Silver, 38 mm. **Ruler:** Jigme Khesar Namgyel Wangchuck **Subject:** Coronation **Obv:** Portrait left **Rev:** Seal

Date	Mintage	F	VF	XF	Unc	BU
2008 Proof	—	Value: 50.00				

BOLIVIA

The Republic of Bolivia, a landlocked country in west central South America, has an area of 424,165 sq. mi. (1,098,580 sq. km.) and a population of *8.33 million. Its capitals are: La Paz (administrative) and Sucre (constitutional). Principal exports are tin, zinc, antimony, tungsten, petroleum, natural gas, cotton and coffee.

MINT MARKS
A - Paris
(a) - Paris, privy marks only
CHI - Valcambia
H - Heaton
KN - Kings' Norton

REPUBLIC
REFORM COINAGE
1987-; 1,000,000 Peso Bolivianos = 1 Boliviano;
100 Centavos = 1 Boliviano

KM# 213   10 CENTAVOS
Copper Clad Steel

Date	Mintage	F	VF	XF	Unc	BU
2001	—				0.50	1.00

KM# 202   10 CENTAVOS
Stainless Steel **Obv:** National arms, star below **Rev:** Denomination within circle, date below

Date	Mintage	F	VF	XF	Unc	BU
2006	—			0.20	0.50	0.70

KM# 202a   10 CENTAVOS
2.2300 g., Copper Clad Steel, 18.94 mm. **Obv:** National arms **Obv. Legend:** REPUBLICA DE BOLIVIA **Rev. Legend:** LA UNION ES LA FUERZA **Edge:** Plain

Date	Mintage	F	VF	XF	Unc	BU
2006	—			0.20	0.50	0.65

KM# 203   20 CENTAVOS
3.3000 g., Stainless Steel, 22 mm. **Obv:** National arms, star below **Obv. Legend:** REPUBLICA DE BOLIVIA **Rev:** Denomination within circle, date below **Rev. Legend:** LA UNION ES LA FUERZA **Edge:** Plain

Date	Mintage	F	VF	XF	Unc	BU
2001	—			0.25	0.60	0.80
2006	—			0.25	0.60	0.80

KM# 204   50 CENTAVOS
3.8000 g., Stainless Steel, 24 mm. **Obv:** National arms, star below **Obv. Legend:** REPUBLICA DE BOLIVIA **Rev:** Denomination within circle, date below **Rev. Legend:** LA UNION ES LA FUERTZA **Edge:** Plain

Date	Mintage	F	VF	XF	Unc	BU
2001	—			0.30	0.75	1.00
2006	—			0.30	0.75	1.00

KM# 205   BOLIVIANO
5.0800 g., Stainless Steel, 26.92 mm. **Obv:** National arms, star below **Obv. Legend:** REPUBLICA DE BOLIVIA **Rev:** Denomination within circle, date below sprays **Rev. Legend:** LA UNION ES LA FUERZA **Edge:** Plain

Date	Mintage	F	VF	XF	Unc	BU
2004	—			0.35	0.90	1.20

KM# 212   5 BOLIVIANOS
5.0000 g., Bi-Metallic Bronze clad Steel center in Stainless Steel ring, 23 mm. **Obv:** National arms **Obv. Legend:** REPUBLICA DE BOLIVIA **Rev:** Denomination **Rev. Legend:** LA UNION ES LA FUERZA **Edge:** Reeded

Date	Mintage	F	VF	XF	Unc	BU
2001	—			0.90	2.25	3.00
2004	—			0.90	2.25	3.00

BOSNIA - HERZEGOVINA

The Republic of Bosnia and Herzegovina borders Croatia to the north and west, Serbia to the east and Montenegro in the southeast with only 12.4 mi. of coastline. The total land area is 19,735 sq. mi. (51,129 sq. km.). They have a population of *4.34 million. Capital: Sarajevo. Electricity, mining and agriculture are leading industries.

MONETARY SYSTEM
1 Convertible Marka = 100 Convertible Feniga = 1 Deutschemark 1998-
NOTE: German Euros circulate freely.

REPUBLIC
REFORM COINAGE
1998-

KM# 121   5 FENIGA
2.6600 g., Steel, 18 mm. **Obv:** Denomination on map **Rev:** Triangle and stars **Edge:** Reeded

Date	Mintage	F	VF	XF	Unc	BU
2005	—				1.00	1.25

KM# 115   10 FENINGA
3.9000 g., Copper Plated Steel, 20 mm. **Obv:** Denomination on map within circle **Rev:** Triangle and stars, date at left, within circle **Edge:** Plain

Date	Mintage	F	VF	XF	Unc	BU
2004	—				0.50	0.75

KM# 116   20 FENINGA
4.5000 g., Copper Plated Steel, 22 mm. **Obv:** Denomination on map within circle **Rev:** Triangle and stars, date at left, within circle

Date	Mintage	F	VF	XF	Unc	BU
2004	—				1.00	1.25

KM# 117   50 FENINGA
5.1500 g., Copper Plated Steel, 24.5 mm. **Obv:** Denomination on map within circle **Rev:** Triangle and stars, date at left, within circle

Date	Mintage	F	VF	XF	Unc	BU
2007	—					3.00

KM# 118   KONVERTIBLE MARKA
4.9000 g., Nickel Plated Steel, 24 mm. **Obv:** Denomination **Rev:** Coat of arms above date **Edge:** Reeded and plain sections

Date	Mintage	F	VF	XF	Unc	BU
2002	—				5.50	6.00
2003	—				5.50	6.00
2006	—				4.00	5.00

KM# 119   2 KONVERTIBLE MARKA
6.9000 g., Bi-Metallic Copper-Nickel center in Nickel-Brass ring, 25.75 mm. **Obv:** Denomination within circle **Rev:** Dove of peace, date at right, within circle **Edge:** Reeded and plain sections

Date	Mintage	F	VF	XF	Unc	BU
2002	—				13.50	15.00
2003	—				13.50	15.00

KM# 120   5 KONVERTIBLE MARKA
10.3500 g., Bi-Metallic Brass center in Copper-nickel ring, 30 mm. **Obv:** Denomination within circle **Rev:** Dove of Peace in flight **Edge:** Reeded

Date	Mintage	F	VF	XF	Unc	BU
2005	—				17.50	20.00

BOTSWANA

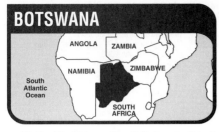

The Republic of Botswana (formerly Bechuanaland), located in south central Africa between Namibia and Zimbabwe, has an area of 224,607 sq. mi. (600,370 sq. km.) and a population of *1.62 million. Capital: Gaborone. Botswana is a member of a Customs Union with South Africa, Lesotho, and Swaziland. The economy is primarily pastoral with a rapidly developing mining industry, of which diamonds, copper and nickel are the chief elements. Meat products and diamonds comprise 85 percent of the exports.

Botswana is a member of the Commonwealth of Nations. The president is Chief of State and Head of government.

MINT MARK
B - Berne

MONETARY SYSTEM
100 Cents = 1 Thebe

REPUBLIC

REFORM COINAGE
100 Thebe = 1 Pula

KM# 26 5 THEBE
2.4100 g., Bronze Clad Steel, 16.9 mm. **Obv:** National arms **Rev:** Toko bird **Rev. Designer:** Mike Hibbit **Edge:** Plain **Shape:** 7-sided

Date	Mintage	F	VF	XF	Unc	BU
2007	—	—	0.15	0.25	0.50	1.00

KM# 27 10 THEBE
Nickel Clad Steel **Obv:** National arms, date below **Rev:** South African Oryx right, denomination above **Rev. Designer:** Mike Hibbit

Date	Mintage	F	VF	XF	Unc	BU
2002	—	—	0.20	0.30	0.75	1.25

KM# 28 25 THEBE
3.5000 g., Nickel Clad Steel **Obv:** National arms with supporters, date below **Rev:** Zebu bull, left, denomination above **Rev. Designer:** Mike Hibbit **Shape:** 7-sided

Date	Mintage	F	VF	XF	Unc	BU
2007	—	—	0.30	0.60	1.50	2.00

KM# 29 50 THEBE
4.8200 g., Nickel Clad Steel, 21.5 mm. **Obv:** National arms with supporters, date below **Rev:** African Fish Eagle left, denomination above **Rev. Designer:** Mike Hibbit

Date	Mintage	F	VF	XF	Unc	BU
2001	—	—	0.50	1.00	2.00	2.50

KM# 24 PULA
8.7000 g., Nickel-Brass, 23.5 mm. **Obv:** National arms with supporters, date below **Rev:** Zebra left, denomination above **Rev. Designer:** Mike Hibbit **Shape:** 7-sided

Date	Mintage	F	VF	XF	Unc	BU
2007	—	—	1.00	1.75	3.50	6.00

KM# 25a 2 PULA
Brass **Subject:** Wildlife **Obv:** National arms with supporters, date below **Rev:** Rhinoceros, left, denomination above **Shape:** 7-sided

Date	Mintage	F	VF	XF	Unc	BU
2004	—	—	—	—	2.75	3.50

KM# 30 5 PULA
6.2000 g., Bi-Metallic Copper-Nickel center in Brass ring, 23.4 mm. **Obv:** National arms with supporters, date below, within circle **Rev:** Mophane worm on a mophane leaf, denomination below, within circle **Edge:** Reeded

Date	Mintage	F	VF	XF	Unc	BU
2007	—	—	—	—	6.50	10.00

BRAZIL

The Federative Republic of Brazil, which comprises half the continent of South America and is the only Latin American country deriving its culture and language from Portugal, has an area of 3,286,488 sq. mi. (8,511,965 sq. km.) and a population of *169.2 million. Capital: Brasilia. The economy of Brazil is as varied and complex as any in the developing world. Agriculture is a mainstay of the economy, while only 4 percent of the area is under cultivation. Known mineral resources are almost unlimited in variety and size of reserves. A large, relatively sophisticated industry ranges from basic steel and chemical production to finished consumer goods. Coffee, cotton, iron ore and cocoa are the chief exports.

MINT MARKS
(a) - Paris, privy marks only
B - Bahia

REPUBLIC

REFORM COINAGE
1994-present

2750 Cruzeiros Reais = 1 Real; 100 Centavos = 1 Real

KM# 647 CENTAVO
2.4300 g., Copper Plated Steel, 17 mm. **Obv:** Cabral bust at right **Rev:** Denomination on linear design at left, 3/4 globe with sash on right, date below **Edge:** Plain

Date	Mintage	F	VF	XF	Unc	BU
2001	242,924,000	—	—	—	0.10	0.20
2002	161,824,000	—	—	—	0.10	0.20
2003	250,000,000	—	—	—	0.10	0.20
2004	167,232,000	—	—	—	0.10	0.20

KM# 648 5 CENTAVOS
4.2000 g., Copper Plated Steel, 22 mm. **Obv:** Tiradente bust at right, dove at left **Rev:** Denomination on linear design at left, 3/4 globe with sash on right, date below **Edge:** Plain

Date	Mintage	F	VF	XF	Unc	BU
2001	175,940,000	—	—	—	0.45	0.65
2002	153,088,000	—	—	—	0.45	0.65
2003	260,000,000	—	—	—	0.45	0.65
2004	262,656,000	—	—	—	0.45	0.65
2005	230,144,000	—	—	—	0.45	0.65
2006	255,488,000	—	—	—	0.45	0.65
2007	242,432,000	—	—	—	0.45	0.65
2008	28,672,000	—	—	—	0.45	0.65

KM# 649.2 10 CENTAVOS
4.8000 g., Brass Plated Steel, 20 mm. **Obv:** Bust of Pedro at right, horseman with sword in right hand at left **Rev:** Denomination on linear design at left, 3/4 globe with sash on right, date below **Edge:** Reeded

Date	Mintage	F	VF	XF	Unc	BU
2001	134,701,000	—	—	—	0.60	0.80
2002	172,032,000	—	—	—	0.60	0.80
2003	252,666,000	—	—	—	0.60	0.80
2004	348,480,000	—	—	—	0.60	0.80
2005	362,112,000	—	—	—	0.60	0.80
2006	265,728,000	—	—	—	0.60	0.80
2007	316,800,000	—	—	—	0.60	0.80

KM# 649.3 10 CENTAVOS
4.8000 g., Brass Plated Steel, 20.2 mm. **Obv:** Pedro I and horseman **Rev:** Value **Edge:** Reeded

Date	Mintage	F	VF	XF	Unc	BU
2006	265,728,000	—	—	—	0.50	0.75
2007	316,800,000	—	—	—	0.50	0.75
2008	270,144,000	—	—	—	0.50	0.75

KM# 650 25 CENTAVOS
7.5500 g., Brass Plated Steel, 25 mm. **Obv:** Deodoro bust at right, national arms at left **Rev:** Denomination on linear design at left, 3/4 globe with sash on right, date below **Edge:** Reeded

Date	Mintage	F	VF	XF	Unc	BU
2001	92,642,000	—	—	—	0.75	1.00
2002	100,096,000	—	—	—	0.75	1.00
2003	147,200,000	—	—	—	0.75	1.00
2004	160,000,000	—	—	—	0.75	1.00
2005	100,096,000	—	—	—	0.75	1.00
2006	110,720,000	—	—	—	0.75	1.00
2007	118,784,000	—	—	—	0.75	1.00
2008	150,016,000	—	—	—	0.75	1.00

KM# 651 50 CENTAVOS
9.2500 g., Copper-Nickel, 23 mm. **Obv:** Rio Branco bust at right, map at left **Rev:** Denomination on linear design at left, 3/4 globe with sash on right, date below **Edge Lettering:** BRASIL ORDEM E PROGRESSO

Date	Mintage	F	VF	XF	Unc	BU
2001	14,735,000	—	—	—	1.50	1.75

KM# 651a 50 CENTAVOS
8.0000 g., Stainless Steel, 23 mm. **Obv:** Rio Branco bust at right, map at left **Rev:** Denomination on linear design at left, 3/4 globe with sash on right, date below

Date	Mintage	F	VF	XF	Unc	BU
2002	189,952,000	—	—	—	1.25	1.50
2003	143,696,000	—	—	—	1.25	1.50
2005	122,416,000	—	—	—	1.25	1.50
2006	39,948,000	—	—	—	1.25	1.50
2007	130,032,000	—	—	—	1.25	1.50
2008	290,080,000	—	—	—	1.25	1.50

KM# 652a REAL
7.0000 g., Bi-Metallic Stainless Steel center in Brass Plated Steel ring, 27 mm. **Obv:** Allegorical portrait **Rev:** Denomination on linear design at left, 3/4 globe with sash on right, date below **Edge:** Segmented reeding

Date	Mintage	F	VF	XF	Unc	BU
2002	54,192,000	—	—	—	3.50	4.50
2003	100,000,000	—	—	—	3.50	4.50
2004	150,016,000	—	—	—	3.50	4.50
2005	43,776,000	—	—	—	3.50	4.50
2006	179,968,000	—	—	—	3.50	4.50
2007	275,712,000	—	—	—	3.50	4.50
2008	400,000,000	—	—	—	3.50	4.50

KM# 656 REAL
7.0000 g., Bi-Metallic Stainless Steel center in Brass Plated Steel ring, 27 mm. **Subject:** Centennial of Juscelino Kubitschek, president **Obv:** Head left **Obv. Designer:** Alzira Duim **Rev:** Denomination on linear design at left, 3/4 globe with sash on right, date below **Edge:** Segmented reeding

Date	Mintage	F	VF	XF	Unc	BU
2002	50,000,000	—	—	—	3.50	4.50

KM# 668 REAL
7.0000 g., Bi-Metallic Stainless Steel center in Brass plated Stainless Steel ring, 27 mm. **Subject:** 40th Anniversary of Central Bank **Obv:** Monument **Rev:** Value on flag **Edge:** Segmented reeding

Date	Mintage	F	VF	XF	Unc	BU
2005	40,000,000	—	—	—	5.00	6.50

KM# 657 2 REAIS
28.0000 g., 0.9990 Silver 0.8993 oz. ASW, 40 mm. **Subject:** Centennial - Carlos Drummond de Andrade **Obv:** Denomination and writer **Rev:** Stylized portrait **Edge:** Reeded

Date	Mintage	F	VF	XF	Unc	BU
ND(2002) Proof	6,999	Value: 60.00				

KM# 658 2 REAIS
28.0000 g., 0.9990 Silver 0.8993 oz. ASW, 40 mm. **Subject:** Centennial - Juscelino Kubitschek **Obv:** Bust facing in upper right, initials at left **Rev:** Denomination **Edge:** Reeded

Date	Mintage	F	VF	XF	Unc	BU
2002 Proof	12,999	Value: 55.00				

KM# 663 2 REAIS
27.0000 g., 0.9250 Silver 0.8029 oz. ASW, 40 mm. **Obv:** Value and piano player **Rev:** Ary Barroso singing **Edge:** Reeded

Date	Mintage	F	VF	XF	Unc	BU
2003 Proof	7,000	Value: 45.00				

KM# 665 2 REAIS
27.0000 g., 0.9250 Silver 0.8029 oz. ASW, 40 mm. **Subject:** Centennial - Portinari **Obv:** Starving family scene, value and country name **Rev:** Portinari's portrait, stars in squares design **Edge:** Reeded

Date	Mintage	F	VF	XF	Unc	BU
ND(2003) Proof	2,000	Value: 50.00				

KM# 666 2 REAIS
27.0000 g., 0.9250 Silver 0.8029 oz. ASW, 40 mm. **Subject:** FIFA Centennial **Obv:** Soccer ball and value **Rev:** Center part of a Brazilian flag and stars **Edge:** Reeded

Date	Mintage	F	VF	XF	Unc	BU
2004 Proof	12,166	Value: 55.00				

KM# 671 2 REAIS
27.0000 g., Silver, 40 mm. **Subject:** Centennial of Flight 14 bis **Obv:** Image of 14 Bis **Rev:** Image and signature of Santos Dumont and value

Date	Mintage	F	VF	XF	Unc	BU
2006 Proof	4,000	Value: 45.00				

KM# 672 2 REAIS
10.1700 g., Copper-Nickel, 30 mm. **Subject:** Pan-American Games XV **Obv:** Official logo of Pan-American Games XV **Rev:** Image of running athlete, XV Jogos Pan-Americanos, value, Brasil and date.

Date	Mintage	F	VF	XF	Unc	BU
2007 Proof	10,000	Value: 30.00				

KM# 661 5 REAIS
28.0000 g., 0.9990 Silver 0.8993 oz. ASW, 40 mm. **Obv:** Soccer player and Brazilian flag **Rev:** Soccer ball and value **Edge:** Reeded

Date	Mintage	F	VF	XF	Unc	BU
2002 Proof	10,149	Value: 45.00				

KM# 673 5 REAIS
27.0000 g., Silver, 40 mm. **Subject:** Pan-American Games XV **Obv:** Official logo of Pan-American Games XV **Rev:** Sugar Loaf, lines of Copacabana sidewalk, "XV Jogos Pan-Americanos", value, Brasil and date.

Date	Mintage	F	VF	XF	Unc	BU
2007 Proof	4,000	Value: 45.00				

KM# 659 20 REAIS
8.0000 g., 0.9000 Gold 0.2315 oz. AGW, 22 mm. **Obv:** Juscelino Kubitschek de Oliveira's portrait **Rev:** Value **Edge:** Reeded

Date	Mintage	F	VF	XF	Unc	BU
2002 Proof	2,499	Value: 245				

KM# 660 20 REAIS
8.0000 g., 0.9000 Gold 0.2315 oz. AGW, 22 mm. **Obv:** Carlos Drummond de Andrade portrait and value **Rev:** Andrade caricature, name and dates **Edge:** Reeded

Date	Mintage	F	VF	XF	Unc	BU
ND(2002) Proof	2,499	Value: 300				

KM# 662 20 REAIS
8.0000 g., 0.9000 Gold 0.2315 oz. AGW, 22 mm. **Obv:** Soccer player **Rev:** Value, inscription and shooting stars **Edge:** Reeded

Date	Mintage	F	VF	XF	Unc	BU
2002	2,499	Value: 300				

KM# 664 20 REAIS
8.0000 g., 0.9000 Gold 0.2315 oz. AGW, 22 mm. **Subject:** Centennial - Ary Barroso **Obv:** Piano keyboard and music above value **Rev:** Caricature of Ary Barroso **Edge:** Reeded

Date	Mintage	F	VF	XF	Unc	BU
2003 Proof	2,500	Value: 300				

BRITISH ANTARCTIC TERRITORY

BRITISH TERRITORY

DECIMAL COINAGE

KM# 1 2 POUNDS
Copper-Nickel, 38.6 mm. **Ruler:** Elizabeth II **Subject:** 200th Anniversary of the Granting of Letters Patent **Obv:** Elizabeth II bust facing right **Rev:** Arms with denomination below **Rev. Legend:** 1908 . CENTENARY OF GRANTING OF LETTERS PATENT . 2008

Date	Mintage	F	VF	XF	Unc	BU
2008	—	—	—	—	17.50	20.00

KM# 5 2 POUNDS
28.2800 g., Copper-Nickel **Ruler:** Elizabeth II **Obv:** Bust right **Rev:** Whale and other Antarctic wildlife **Shape:** 38.6

Date	Mintage	F	VF	XF	Unc	BU
2009	50,000	—	—	—	—	15.00

KM# 5a 2 POUNDS
28.2800 g., 0.9250 Silver 0.8410 oz. ASW, 38.6 mm. **Ruler:** Elizabeth II **Obv:** Bust right **Rev:** Whale and other Antarctic wildlife

Date	Mintage	F	VF	XF	Unc	BU
2009 Proof	10,000	Value: 35.00				

BRITISH VIRGIN ISLANDS

The Colony of the Virgin Islands, a British colony situated in the Caribbean Sea northeast of Puerto Rico and west of the Leeward Islands, has an area of 59 sq. mi. (155 sq. km.) and a population of 13,000. Capital: Road Town. The principal islands of the 36-island group are Tortola, Virgin Gorda, Anegada, and Jost Van Dyke. The chief industries are fishing and stock raising. Fish, livestock and bananas are exported. U.S. currency and Sterling circulate in common with the East Caribbean Dollar.

BRITISH COLONY
STANDARD COINAGE

KM# 196 DOLLAR
28.2800 g., Copper-Nickel, 38.6 mm. **Subject:** Queen's Golden Jubilee **Obv:** Queen's bust right **Obv. Designer:** Ian Rank-Broadley **Rev:** Carnival dancers **Edge:** Reeded

Date	Mintage	F	VF	XF	Unc	BU
2002	—	—	—	—	7.50	9.50

KM# 180 DOLLAR
28.2800 g., Copper-Nickel, 25.7 mm. **Subject:** Sir Francis Drake **Obv:** Queen's bust right **Obv. Designer:** Ian Rank-Broadley **Rev:** Ship, portrait and map **Edge:** Reeded

Date	Mintage	F	VF	XF	Unc	BU
2002	—	—	—	—	7.50	9.50

KM# 183 DOLLAR
28.2800 g., Copper-Nickel, 38.6 mm. **Subject:** Sir Walter Raleigh **Obv:** Queen's bust right **Obv. Designer:** Ian Rank-Broadley **Rev:** Ship, portrait and map **Edge:** Reeded

Date	Mintage	F	VF	XF	Unc	BU
2002	—	—	—	—	7.50	9.50

KM# 187 DOLLAR
28.2800 g., Copper-Nickel, 38.6 mm. **Subject:** Queen's Golden Jubilee **Obv:** Queen's bust right **Obv. Designer:** Ian Rank-Broadley **Rev:** Queen on horse **Edge:** Reeded

Date	Mintage	F	VF	XF	Unc	BU
2002	—	—	—	—	7.50	9.50

KM# 190 DOLLAR
28.2800 g., Copper-Nickel, 38.6 mm. **Subject:** Queen's Golden Jubilee **Obv:** Queen's bust right **Obv. Designer:** Ian Rank-Broadley **Rev:** Queen on throne **Edge:** Reeded

Date	Mintage	F	VF	XF	Unc	BU
2002	—	—	—	—	7.50	9.50

KM# 193 DOLLAR
28.2800 g., Copper-Nickel, 38.6 mm. **Subject:** Queen's Golden Jubilee **Obv:** Queen's bust right **Obv. Designer:** Ian Rank-Broadley **Rev:** Queen with President Ronald Reagan and First Lady Nancy Reagan **Edge:** Reeded

Date	Mintage	F	VF	XF	Unc	BU
2002	—	—	—	—	7.50	9.50

KM# 199 DOLLAR
28.2800 g., Copper-Nickel, 38.6 mm. **Subject:** Teddy Bear Centennial **Obv:** Queen's bust right **Obv. Designer:** Ian Rank-Broadley **Rev:** Teddy bear **Edge:** Reeded

Date	Mintage	F	VF	XF	Unc	BU
2002	—	—	—	—	8.50	15.00

KM# 204 DOLLAR
28.2800 g., Copper-Nickel, 38.6 mm. **Subject:** Princess Diana **Obv:** Queen's bust right **Obv. Designer:** Ian Rank-Broadley **Rev:** Diana's portrait **Edge:** Reeded

Date	Mintage	F	VF	XF	Unc	BU
2002	—	—	—	—	7.50	9.50

KM# 207 DOLLAR
28.2800 g., Copper-Nickel, 38.6 mm. **Subject:** September 11, 2001 **Obv:** Queen's bust right **Obv. Designer:** Ian Rank-Broadley **Rev:** World Trade Center twin towers **Edge:** Reeded

Date	Mintage	F	VF	XF	Unc	BU
2002	—	—	—	—	12.00	13.50

KM# 210 DOLLAR
28.2800 g., Copper-Nickel, 38.6 mm. **Subject:** September 11, 2001 **Obv:** Queen's bust right **Obv. Designer:** Ian Rank-Broadley **Rev:** Statue of Liberty **Edge:** Reeded

Date	Mintage	F	VF	XF	Unc	BU
2002	—	—	—	—	12.00	13.50

KM# 213 DOLLAR
28.2800 g., Copper-Nickel, 38.6 mm. **Subject:** Queen Mother **Obv:** Queen's bust right **Obv. Designer:** Ian Rank-Broadley **Rev:** Queen Mother and a young Prince Charles **Edge:** Reeded

Date	Mintage	F	VF	XF	Unc	BU
2002PM	—	—	—	—	10.00	12.00

KM# 216 DOLLAR
28.2800 g., Copper-Nickel, 38.6 mm. **Subject:** Queen Mother **Obv:** Queen's bust right **Obv. Designer:** Ian Rank-Broadley **Rev:** Queen Mother with four grandchildren **Edge:** Reeded

Date	Mintage	F	VF	XF	Unc	BU
2002PM	—	—	—	—	10.00	12.00

KM# 219 DOLLAR
28.2800 g., Copper-Nickel, 38.6 mm. **Subject:** Queen Mother Series **Obv:** Queen's bust right **Obv. Designer:** Ian Rank-Broadley **Rev:** Queen Mother with uniformed Prince Charles **Edge:** Reeded

Date	Mintage	F	VF	XF	Unc	BU
2002PM	—	—	—	—	10.00	12.00

KM# 222 DOLLAR
28.2800 g., Copper-Nickel, 38.6 mm. **Subject:** Queen Mother Series **Obv:** Queen's bust right **Obv. Designer:** Ian Rank-Broadley **Rev:** Queen Mother's coffin **Edge:** Reeded

Date	Mintage	F	VF	XF	Unc	BU
2002PM	—	—	—	—	10.00	12.00

KM# 225 DOLLAR
28.4400 g., Copper-Nickel, 38.6 mm. **Subject:** Kennedy Assassination **Obv:** Queen's bust right **Obv. Designer:** Ian Rank-Broadley **Rev:** President Kennedy's portrait left **Edge:** Reeded

Date	Mintage	F	VF	XF	Unc	BU
2003	—	—	—	—	10.00	12.00

KM# 229 DOLLAR
28.2800 g., Copper-Nickel, 38.6 mm. **Subject:** Powered Flight Centennial **Obv:** Queen's bust right **Obv. Designer:** Ian Rank-Broadley **Rev:** Three historic airplanes and rocket **Edge:** Reeded

Date	Mintage	F	VF	XF	Unc	BU
2003	—	—	—	—	10.00	12.00

KM# 232 DOLLAR
28.2800 g., Copper-Nickel, 38.6 mm. **Obv:** Queen's bust right **Obv. Designer:** Ian Rank-Broadley **Rev:** Henry VIII and Elizabeth I **Edge:** Reeded

Date	Mintage	F	VF	XF	Unc	BU
2003	—	—	—	—	10.00	12.00

KM# 235 DOLLAR
28.2800 g., Copper-Nickel, 38.6 mm. **Obv:** Queen's bust right **Obv. Designer:** Ian Rank-Broadley **Rev:** Matthew Parker, Archbishop of Canterbury **Edge:** Reeded

Date	Mintage	F	VF	XF	Unc	BU
2003	—	—	—	—	10.00	12.00

KM# 238 DOLLAR
28.2800 g., Copper-Nickel, 38.6 mm. **Obv:** Queen's bust right **Obv. Designer:** Ian Rank-Broadley **Rev:** Sir Francis Drake and ships **Edge:** Reeded

Date	Mintage	F	VF	XF	Unc	BU
2003	—	—	—	—	10.00	12.00

KM# 241 DOLLAR
28.2800 g., Copper-Nickel, 38.6 mm. **Obv:** Queen's bust right **Obv. Designer:** Ian Rank-Broadley **Rev:** Sir Walter Raleigh **Edge:** Reeded

Date	Mintage	F	VF	XF	Unc	BU
2003	—	—	—	—	10.00	12.00

KM# 244 DOLLAR
28.2800 g., Copper-Nickel, 38.6 mm. **Obv:** Queen's bust right **Obv. Designer:** Ian Rank-Broadley **Rev:** Sir William Shakespeare **Edge:** Reeded

Date	Mintage	F	VF	XF	Unc	BU
2003	—	—	—	—	10.00	12.00

KM# 247 DOLLAR
28.2800 g., Copper-Nickel, 38.6 mm. **Obv:** Queen's bust right **Obv. Designer:** Ian Rank-Broadley **Rev:** Elizabeth I above her funeral procession **Edge:** Reeded

Date	Mintage	F	VF	XF	Unc	BU
2003	—	—	—	—	10.00	12.00

KM# 250 DOLLAR
28.2800 g., Copper-Nickel, 38.6 mm. **Subject:** Olympics **Obv:** Queen's bust right **Obv. Designer:** Ian Rank-Broadley **Rev:** Ancient bust, runners and coin **Edge:** Reeded

Date	Mintage	F	VF	XF	Unc	BU
2003	—	—	—	—	10.00	12.00

KM# 253 DOLLAR
28.2800 g., Copper-Nickel, 38.6 mm. **Subject:** Olympics **Obv:** Queen's bust right **Obv. Designer:** Ian Rank-Broadley **Rev:** Ancient bust, charioteer and coin **Edge:** Reeded

Date	Mintage	F	VF	XF	Unc	BU
2003	—	—	—	—	10.00	12.00

KM# 303 DOLLAR
28.2800 g., Copper-Nickel, 38.6 mm. **Subject:** 2004 Athens Olympics **Obv:** Queen's bust right **Obv. Designer:** Ian Rank-Broadley **Rev:** Ancient athlete's bust right, runners at lower right, ancient coin with owl at upper right coin **Edge:** Reeded

Date	Mintage	F	VF	XF	Unc	BU
2003	—	—	—	—	10.00	12.00

KM# 306 DOLLAR
28.2800 g., Copper-Nickel, 38.6 mm. **Subject:** 2004 Athens Olympics **Obv:** Queen's bust right **Obv. Designer:** Ian Rank-Broadley **Rev:** Ancient athlete bust left, chariot race at lower left, ancient coin at upper left **Edge:** Reeded

Date	Mintage	F	VF	XF	Unc	BU
2003	—	—	—	—	10.00	12.00

KM# 310 DOLLAR

28.2800 g., Copper-Nickel, 38.6 mm. **Subject:** Queen Elizabeth's Golden Coronation Jubilee **Obv:** Elizabeth II **Rev:** Cameo portraits above the ship "Gothic" **Edge:** Reeded

Date	Mintage	F	VF	XF	Unc	BU
2003					7.50	9.50

KM# 319 DOLLAR

28.2800 g., Copper-Nickel **Subject:** 50th Anniversary of Coronation **Rev:** Queen riding in automobile

Date	Mintage	F	VF	XF	Unc	BU
2003	—	—	—	—	10.00	15.00

KM# 320 DOLLAR

28.2800 g., Copper-Nickel **Subject:** Golden Jubilee of Coronation **Rev:** Sir. Edmond Hillary on Mt. Everest, Queen II above mountain climbers

Date	Mintage	F	VF	XF	Unc	BU
2003	—	—	—	—	10.00	15.00

KM# 321 DOLLAR

28.2800 g., Copper-Nickel **Rev:** Queen presenting Ascot Horse Racing prize

Date	Mintage	F	VF	XF	Unc	BU
2003	—	—	—	—	10.00	12.00

KM# 265 DOLLAR

28.2800 g., Copper-Nickel, 38.6 mm. **Obv:** Queen's bust right **Obv. Designer:** Ian Rank-Broadley **Rev:** Sir Francis Drake, ship and map **Edge:** Reeded

Date	Mintage	F	VF	XF	Unc	BU
2004	—	—	—	—	10.00	12.00

KM# 267.1 DOLLAR

28.2800 g., Copper-Nickel, 38.6 mm. **Obv:** Queen's bust right **Obv. Designer:** Ian Rank-Broadley **Rev:** Peter Rabbit **Edge:** Reeded

Date	Mintage	F	VF	XF	Unc	BU
2004	—	—	—	—	15.00	17.00

KM# 267.2 DOLLAR

28.2800 g., Copper-Nickel, 38.6 mm. **Obv:** Queen's bust right **Obv. Designer:** Ian Rank-Broadley **Rev:** Multicolor Peter Rabbit **Edge:** Reeded

Date	Mintage	F	VF	XF	Unc	BU
2004	—	—	—	—	20.00	22.00

KM# 268 DOLLAR

3.1100 g., 0.9990 Silver 0.0999 oz. ASW, 18 mm. **Obv:** Queen's bust right **Obv. Designer:** Ian Rank-Broadley **Rev:** Peter Rabbit **Edge:** Reeded

Date	Mintage	F	VF	XF	Unc	BU
2004 Proof	10,000	Value: 25.00				

KM# 281 DOLLAR

28.2800 g., Copper-Nickel, 38.6 mm. **Obv:** Queen's bust right **Obv. Designer:** Ian Rank-Broadley **Rev:** Sailor above two D-Day landing craft **Edge:** Reeded

Date	Mintage	F	VF	XF	Unc	BU
2004	—	—	—	—	10.00	12.00

KM# 286 DOLLAR

28.2800 g., Copper-Nickel, 38.6 mm. **Obv:** Queen's bust right **Obv. Designer:** Ian Rank-Broadley **Rev:** Dolphin **Edge:** Reeded

Date	Mintage	F	VF	XF	Unc	BU
2004	—	—	—	—	10.00	14.00

KM# 297 DOLLAR

28.2800 g., Copper-Nickel, 38.6 mm. **Obv:** Queen's bust right **Obv. Designer:** Ian Rank-Broadley **Rev:** Soldier above tank and jeeps **Edge:** Reeded

Date	Mintage	F	VF	XF	Unc	BU
2004	—	—	—	—	10.00	12.00

KM# 300 DOLLAR

28.2800 g., Copper-Nickel, 38.6 mm. **Obv:** Queen's bust right **Obv. Designer:** Ian Rank-Broadley **Rev:** Pilot and planes above D-Day landing **Edge:** Reeded

Date	Mintage	F	VF	XF	Unc	BU
2004	—	—	—	—	10.00	12.00

KM# 330 DOLLAR

Copper-Nickel **Ruler:** Elizabeth II **Rev:** Battle of Britain

Date	Mintage	F	VF	XF	Unc	BU
2005	—	—	—	—	15.00	17.00

KM# 331 DOLLAR

Copper-Nickel **Ruler:** Elizabeth II **Rev:** Battle of Berlin

Date	Mintage	F	VF	XF	Unc	BU
2005	—	—	—	—	15.00	17.00

KM# 312 DOLLAR

28.2800 g., Copper-Nickel, 38.6 mm. **Obv:** Bust of Queen Elizabeth II right **Rev:** Mother and baby dolphins **Edge:** Reeded

Date	Mintage	F	VF	XF	Unc	BU
2005	—	—	—	—	10.00	14.00

KM# 322 DOLLAR

28.2800 g., Copper-Nickel **Rev:** VJ Day, McArthur and U.S.S. Missiouri Battleship

Date	Mintage	F	VF	XF	Unc	BU
2005	—	—	—	—	10.00	12.00

KM# 323 DOLLAR

28.2800 g., Copper-Nickel **Rev:** Warships near Arlantic coast, West Indies islands

Date	Mintage	F	VF	XF	Unc	BU
2005	—	—	—	—	10.00	12.00

KM# 324 DOLLAR

28.2800 g., Copper-Nickel **Rev:** Death of Nelson

Date	Mintage	F	VF	XF	Unc	BU
2005	—	—	—	—	10.00	12.00

KM# 325 DOLLAR

28.2800 g., Copper-Nickel **Rev:** Nelson and Order Star above ships

Date	Mintage	F	VF	XF	Unc	BU
2005	—	—	—	—	10.00	12.00

KM# 326 DOLLAR

28.2800 g., Copper-Nickel **Rev:** Nelson and Napoleon

Date	Mintage	F	VF	XF	Unc	BU
2005	—	—	—	—	10.00	12.00

KM# 327 DOLLAR

28.2800 g., Copper-Nickel **Rev:** Nelson's Column, statue and ships

Date	Mintage	F	VF	XF	Unc	BU
2005	—	—	—	—	10.00	12.00

KM# 328 DOLLAR

28.2800 g., Copper-Nickel **Rev:** V.E. Day, Montgomery and Eisenhower

Date	Mintage	F	VF	XF	Unc	BU
2005	—	—	—	—	10.00	12.00

KM# 329 DOLLAR

Copper-Nickel **Rev:** Two dolphins

Date	Mintage	F	VF	XF	Unc	BU
2006	—	—	—	—	10.00	12.00

KM# 349 DOLLAR

28.2800 g., Copper-Nickel, 38.60 mm. **Ruler:** Elizabeth II **Subject:** 5th Anniversary Attack on Twin Towers, New York City **Obv:** Crowned bust right **Obv. Legend:** BRITISH VIRGIN ISLANDS - QUEEN ELIZABETH II **Rev:** Twin Towers in sprays, remembrance ribbon privy mark at upper right **Rev. Inscription:** LEST WE FORGET **Edge:** Reeded

Date	Mintage	F	VF	XF	Unc	BU
2006	—	—	—	—	15.00	17.00

KM# 332 DOLLAR

28.2800 g., Copper-Nickel, 38.60 mm. **Ruler:** Elizabeth II **Subject:** 400th Anniversary Founding of Jamestown **Obv:** Bust with tiara right **Obv. Legend:** BRITISH VIRGIN ISLANDS - QUEEN ELIZABETH II **Rev:** British lion laying, American Eagle perched on sprays **Rev. Legend:** UNITED IN FRIENDSHIP **Edge:** Reeded

Date	Mintage	F	VF	XF	Unc	BU
2007	—	—	—	—	16.50	18.50

KM# 370 DOLLAR

28.2800 g., Copper-Nickel, 38.6 mm. **Ruler:** Elizabeth II **Obv:** Bust right **Rev:** Two soccer players and leopard

Date	Mintage	F	VF	XF	Unc	BU
2009	—	—	—	—	—	15.00

KM# 373 DOLLAR

28.2800 g., Copper-Nickel, 38.6 mm. **Ruler:** Elizabeth II **Obv:** Bust right **Rev:** Queen Elizabeth I aboard ship

Date	Mintage	F	VF	XF	Unc	BU
2009	—	—	—	—	—	15.00

KM# 375 DOLLAR

28.2800 g., Copper-Nickel, 38.6 mm. **Ruler:** Elizabeth II **Obv:** Bust right **Rev:** Elizabeth I between two columns

Date	Mintage	F	VF	XF	Unc	BU
2009	—	—	—	—	—	15.00

KM# 278 2 DOLLARS

58.0000 g., Bronze, 50 mm. **Obv:** Queen's bust right **Obv. Designer:** Ian Rank-Broadley **Rev:** 1896 Olympic medal design **Edge:** Reeded

Date	Mintage	F	VF	XF	Unc	BU
2004 Proof	3,500	Value: 20.00				

KM# 269.1 2.50 DOLLARS

7.7758 g., 0.9990 Silver 0.2497 oz. ASW, 26 mm. **Obv:** Queen's bust right **Obv. Designer:** Ian Rank-Broadley **Rev:** Peter Rabbit **Edge:** Reeded

Date	Mintage	F	VF	XF	Unc	BU
2004 Proof	—	Value: 15.00				

KM# 269.2 2.50 DOLLARS

7.7758 g., 0.9990 Silver 0.2497 oz. ASW, 26 mm. **Obv:** Queen's bust right **Obv. Designer:** Ian Rank-Broadley **Rev:** Multicolor Peter Rabbit **Edge:** Reeded

Date	Mintage	F	VF	XF	Unc	BU
2004 Proof	7,500	Value: 25.00				

KM# 284 5 DOLLARS

10.0000 g., 0.9900 Titanium 0.3183 oz., 36.1 mm. **Obv:** Queen's bust right **Obv. Designer:** Ian Rank-Broadley **Rev:** British Guiana stamp design **Edge:** Reeded

Date	Mintage	F	VF	XF	Unc	BU
2004 Proof	7,500	Value: 70.00				

KM# 340 5 DOLLARS

0.9999 Bi-Metallic Silver center in Gold ring. **Ruler:** Elizabeth II **Obv:** Conjoined busts with Philip right, within gold ring **Obv. Legend:** BRITISH VIRGIN ISLANDS — QUEEN ELIZABETH II **Rev:** Conjoined busts of Princess Elizabeth and Prince Philip right within gold ring **Rev. Legend:** WITH THIS RING, I THEE WED **Edge:** Reeded

Date	Mintage	F	VF	XF	Unc	BU
2007 Proof	—	Value: 450				

KM# 181 10 DOLLARS

28.2800 g., 0.9250 Silver 0.8410 oz. ASW, 38.6 mm. **Subject:** Sir Francis Drake **Obv:** Queen's bust right **Obv. Designer:** Ian Rank-Broadley **Rev:** Ship, portrait and map **Edge:** Reeded

Date	Mintage	F	VF	XF	Unc	BU
2002 Proof	—	Value: 40.00				

KM# 184 10 DOLLARS

28.2800 g., 0.9250 Silver 0.8410 oz. ASW, 38.6 mm. **Subject:** Sir Walter Raleigh **Obv:** Queen's bust right **Obv. Designer:** Ian Rank-Broadley **Rev:** Ship, portrait and map **Edge:** Reeded

Date	Mintage	F	VF	XF	Unc	BU
2002 Proof	—	Value: 40.00				

KM# 188 10 DOLLARS

28.2800 g., 0.9250 Gold Clad Silver 0.8410 oz., 38.6 mm. **Subject:** Queen's Golden Jubilee **Obv:** Queen's bust right **Obv. Designer:** Ian Rank-Broadley **Rev:** Queen on horse trotting left **Edge:** Reeded

Date	Mintage	F	VF	XF	Unc	BU
2002 Proof	10,000	Value: 42.50				

KM# 191 10 DOLLARS

28.2800 g., 0.9250 Gold Clad Silver 0.8410 oz., 38.6 mm. **Subject:** Queen's Golden Jubilee **Obv:** Queen's bust right **Obv. Designer:** Ian Rank-Broadley **Rev:** 3/4-length Queen seated on throne **Edge:** Reeded

Date	Mintage	F	VF	XF	Unc	BU
2002 Proof	10,000	Value: 45.00				

KM# 194 10 DOLLARS

28.2800 g., 0.9250 Gold Clad Silver 0.8410 oz., 38.6 mm. **Subject:** Queen's Golden Jubilee **Obv:** Queen's bust right **Obv. Designer:** Ian Rank-Broadley **Rev:** Queen with President Ronald Reagan and First Lady Nancy Reagan **Edge:** Reeded

Date	Mintage	F	VF	XF	Unc	BU
2002 Proof	10,000	Value: 45.00				

KM# 197   10 DOLLARS
28.2800 g., 0.9250 Gold Clad Silver 0.8410 oz., 38.6 mm.
Subject: Queen's Golden Jubilee **Obv:** Queen's bust right
Obv. Designer: Ian Rank-Broadley **Rev:** Carnival dancers
Edge: Reeded

Date	Mintage	F	VF	XF	Unc	BU
2002 Proof	10,000	Value: 45.00				

KM# 200   10 DOLLARS
28.2800 g., 0.9250 Silver 0.8410 oz. ASW, 38.6 mm.
Subject: Teddy Bear Centennial **Obv:** Queen's bust right
Obv. Designer: Ian Rank-Broadley **Rev:** Teddy bear
Edge: Reeded

Date	Mintage	F	VF	XF	Unc	BU
2002 Proof	10,000	Value: 40.00				

KM# 205   10 DOLLARS
28.2800 g., 0.9250 Silver 0.8410 oz. ASW, 38.6 mm.
Subject: Princess Diana **Obv:** Queen's bust right
Obv. Designer: Ian Rank-Broadley **Rev:** Diana's portrait
Edge: Reeded

Date	Mintage	F	VF	XF	Unc	BU
2002 Proof	10,000	Value: 40.00				

KM# 208.1   10 DOLLARS
28.2800 g., 0.9250 Silver 0.8410 oz. ASW, 38.6 mm.
Subject: September 11, 2001 **Obv:** Queen's bust right
Obv. Designer: Ian Rank-Broadley **Rev:** World Trade Center
twin towers **Edge:** Reeded

Date	Mintage	F	VF	XF	Unc	BU
2002 Proof	10,000	Value: 40.00				

KM# 208.2   10 DOLLARS
28.2800 g., 0.9250 Silver 0.8410 oz. ASW, 38.6 mm.
Subject: September 11, 2001 **Obv:** Queen's bust right
Obv. Designer: Ian Rank-Broadley **Rev:** Holographic multicolor
World Trade Center twin towers **Edge:** Reeded

Date	Mintage	F	VF	XF	Unc	BU
2002 Proof	10,000	Value: 45.00				

KM# 211   10 DOLLARS
28.2800 g., 0.9250 Silver 0.8410 oz. ASW, 38.6 mm.
Subject: September 11, 2001 **Obv:** Queen's bust right
Obv. Designer: Ian Rank-Broadley **Rev:** Statue of Liberty
Edge: Reeded

Date	Mintage	F	VF	XF	Unc	BU
2002 Proof	10,000	Value: 40.00				

KM# 214   10 DOLLARS
28.2800 g., 0.9250 Silver 0.8410 oz. ASW, 38.6 mm.
Subject: Queen Mother **Obv:** Queen's bust right **Obv. Designer:**
Ian Rank-Broadley **Rev:** Queen Mother with young Prince
Charles **Edge:** Reeded

Date	Mintage	F	VF	XF	Unc	BU
2002PM Proof	10,000	Value: 40.00				

KM# 217   10 DOLLARS
28.2800 g., 0.9250 Silver 0.8410 oz. ASW, 38.6 mm.
Subject: Queen Mother Series **Obv:** Queen's bust right
Obv. Designer: Ian Rank-Broadley **Rev:** Queen Mother with four
grandchildren **Edge:** Reeded

Date	Mintage	F	VF	XF	Unc	BU
2002PM Proof	10,000	Value: 40.00				

KM# 220   10 DOLLARS
28.2800 g., 0.9250 Silver 0.8410 oz. ASW, 38.6 mm.
Subject: Queen Mother Series **Obv:** Queen's bust right
Obv. Designer: Ian Rank-Broadley **Rev:** Queen Mother with
uniformed Prince Charles **Edge:** Reeded

Date	Mintage	F	VF	XF	Unc	BU
2002PM Proof	10,000	Value: 40.00				

KM# 223   10 DOLLARS
28.2800 g., 0.9250 Silver 0.8410 oz. ASW, 38.6 mm.
Subject: Queen Mother Series **Obv:** Queen's bust right
Obv. Designer: Ian Rank-Broadley **Rev:** Queen Mother's coffin
Edge: Reeded

Date	Mintage	F	VF	XF	Unc	BU
2002PM Proof	10,000	Value: 40.00				

KM# 226   10 DOLLARS
28.2800 g., 0.9250 Silver 0.8410 oz. ASW, 38.6 mm.
Subject: Kennedy Assassination **Obv:** Queen's bust right
Obv. Designer: Ian Rank-Broadley **Rev:** President Kennedy's
head left **Edge:** Reeded

Date	Mintage	F	VF	XF	Unc	BU
2003 Proof	10,000	Value: 40.00				

KM# 230   10 DOLLARS
28.2800 g., 0.9250 Silver 0.8410 oz. ASW, 38.6 mm.
Subject: Powered Flight Centennial **Obv:** Queen's bust right
Obv. Designer: Ian Rank-Broadley **Rev:** Three historic airplanes
and rocket **Edge:** Reeded

Date	Mintage	F	VF	XF	Unc	BU
2003 Proof	10,000	Value: 45.00				

KM# 233   10 DOLLARS
28.2800 g., 0.9250 Silver 0.8410 oz. ASW, 38.6 mm.
Obv: Queen's bust right **Obv. Designer:** Ian Rank-Broadley
Rev: Henry VIII and Elizabeth I **Edge:** Reeded

Date	Mintage	F	VF	XF	Unc	BU
2003 Proof	10,000	Value: 40.00				

KM# 236 10 DOLLARS
28.2800 g., 0.9250 Silver 0.8410 oz. ASW, 38.6 mm.
Obv: Queen's bust right **Obv. Designer:** Ian Rank-Broadley
Rev: Matthew Parker, Archbishop of Canterbury **Edge:** Reeded

Date	Mintage	F	VF	XF	Unc	BU
2003 Proof	10,000	Value: 40.00				

KM# 239 10 DOLLARS
28.2800 g., 0.9250 Silver 0.8410 oz. ASW, 38.6 mm.
Obv: Queen's bust right **Obv. Designer:** Ian Rank-Broadley
Rev: Sir Francis Drake and ships **Edge:** Reeded

Date	Mintage	F	VF	XF	Unc	BU
2003 Proof	10,000	Value: 40.00				

KM# 242 10 DOLLARS
28.2800 g., 0.9250 Silver 0.8410 oz. ASW, 38.6 mm.
Obv: Queen's bust right **Obv. Designer:** Ian Rank-Broadley
Rev: Sir Walter Raleigh **Edge:** Reeded

Date	Mintage	F	VF	XF	Unc	BU
2003 Proof	10,000	Value: 40.00				

KM# 245 10 DOLLARS
28.2800 g., 0.9250 Silver 0.8410 oz. ASW, 38.6 mm.
Obv: Queen's bust right **Obv. Designer:** Ian Rank-Broadley
Rev: Sir William Shakespeare **Edge:** Reeded

Date	Mintage	F	VF	XF	Unc	BU
2003 Proof	10,000	Value: 40.00				

KM# 248 10 DOLLARS
28.2800 g., 0.9250 Silver 0.8410 oz. ASW, 38.6 mm.
Obv: Queen's bust right **Obv. Designer:** Ian Rank-Broadley
Rev: Elizabeth I above her funeral procession **Edge:** Reeded

Date	Mintage	F	VF	XF	Unc	BU
2003 Proof	10,000	Value: 40.00				

KM# 251 10 DOLLARS
28.2800 g., 0.9250 Silver 0.8410 oz. ASW, 38.6 mm. **Subject:**
Olympics **Obv:** Queen's bust right **Obv. Designer:** Ian Rank-
Broadley **Rev:** Ancient bust, runners and coin **Edge:** Reeded

Date	Mintage	F	VF	XF	Unc	BU
2003 Proof	10,000	Value: 40.00				

KM# 254 10 DOLLARS
28.2800 g., 0.9250 Silver 0.8410 oz. ASW, 38.6 mm. **Subject:**
Olympics **Obv:** Queen's bust right **Obv. Designer:** Ian Rank-
Broadley **Rev:** Ancient bust, charioteer and coin **Edge:** Reeded

Date	Mintage	F	VF	XF	Unc	BU
2003 Proof	10,000	Value: 40.00				

KM# 311 10 DOLLARS
28.3000 g., 0.9250 Gold Clad Silver 0.8416 oz., 38.6 mm.
Subject: Queen Elizabeth's Golden Coronation Jubilee
Obv: Elizabeth II **Rev:** Cameo portrait above ship "Gothic"
Edge: Reeded

Date	Mintage	F	VF	XF	Unc	BU
2003 Proof	—	Value: 50.00				

KM# 266 10 DOLLARS
28.2800 g., 0.9250 Silver 0.8410 oz. ASW, 38.6 mm.
Obv: Queen's bust right **Obv. Designer:** Ian Rank-Broadley
Rev: Sir Francis Drake, ship and map **Edge:** Reeded

Date	Mintage	F	VF	XF	Unc	BU
2004 Proof	10,000	Value: 45.00				

KM# 270.1 10 DOLLARS
28.2800 g., 0.9250 Silver 0.8410 oz. ASW, 38.6 mm.
Obv: Queen's bust right **Obv. Designer:** Ian Rank-Broadley
Rev: Peter Rabbit **Edge:** Reeded

Date	Mintage	F	VF	XF	Unc	BU
2004 Proof	5,000	Value: 47.50				

KM# 270.2 10 DOLLARS
28.2800 g., 0.9250 Silver 0.8410 oz. ASW, 38.6 mm.
Obv: Queen's bust right **Obv. Designer:** Ian Rank-Broadley
Rev: Multicolor Peter Rabbit **Edge:** Reeded

Date	Mintage	F	VF	XF	Unc	BU
2004 Proof	—	Value: 65.00				

KM# 274 10 DOLLARS
1.2440 g., 0.9999 Gold 0.0400 oz. AGW, 14 mm. **Obv:** Queen's
bust right **Obv. Designer:** Ian Rank-Broadley **Rev:** Hernando
Pizarro **Edge:** Reeded

Date	Mintage	F	VF	XF	Unc	BU
2004 Proof	350	Value: 75.00				

KM# 282 10 DOLLARS
28.2800 g., 0.9250 Silver 0.8410 oz. ASW, 38.6 mm.
Obv: Queen's bust right **Obv. Designer:** Ian Rank-Broadley
Rev: Sailor above two D-Day landing craft **Edge:** Reeded

Date	Mintage	F	VF	XF	Unc	BU
2004 Proof	10,000	Value: 50.00				

KM# 287 10 DOLLARS
31.1035 g., 0.9990 Silver 0.9990 oz. ASW, 38.6 mm.
Obv: Queen's bust right **Obv. Designer:** Ian Rank-Broadley
Rev: Dolphin **Edge:** Reeded

Date	Mintage	F	VF	XF	Unc	BU
2004 Proof	10,000	Value: 50.00				

KM# 288 10 DOLLARS
1.2440 g., 0.9999 Gold 0.0400 oz. AGW, 14 mm. **Obv:** Queen's
bust right **Obv. Designer:** Ian Rank-Broadley **Rev:** Dolphin
Edge: Reeded

Date	Mintage	F	VF	XF	Unc	BU
2004 Proof	10,000	Value: 55.00				

KM# 298 10 DOLLARS
28.2800 g., 0.9250 Silver 0.8410 oz. ASW, 38.6 mm.
Obv: Queen's bust right **Obv. Designer:** Ian Rank-Broadley
Rev: Soldier above tank and jeeps **Edge:** Reeded

Date	Mintage	F	VF	XF	Unc	BU
2004 Proof	10,000	Value: 50.00				

KM# 301 10 DOLLARS
28.2800 g., 0.9250 Silver 0.8410 oz. ASW, 38.6 mm.
Obv: Queen's bust right **Obv. Designer:** Ian Rank-Broadley
Rev: Pilot and planes above D-Day landing **Edge:** Reeded

Date	Mintage	F	VF	XF	Unc	BU
2004 Proof	10,000	Value: 50.00				

KM# 304 10 DOLLARS
28.2800 g., 0.9250 Silver 0.8410 oz. ASW, 38.6 mm.
Obv: Queen's bust right **Obv. Designer:** Ian Rank-Broadley
Rev: Ancient Olympic bust, runners and owl coin **Edge:** Reeded

Date	Mintage	F	VF	XF	Unc	BU
2004 Proof	10,000	Value: 50.00				

KM# 307 10 DOLLARS
28.2800 g., 0.9250 Silver 0.8410 oz. ASW, 38.6 mm.
Obv: Queen's bust right **Obv. Designer:** Ian Rank-Broadley
Rev: Ancient Olympic bust, charioteer and Zeus coin
Edge: Reeded

Date	Mintage	F	VF	XF	Unc	BU
2004 Proof	10,000	Value: 50.00				

KM# 313 10 DOLLARS
31.1030 g., 0.9990 Silver 0.9989 oz. ASW, 38.6 mm. **Obv:** Bust
of Queen Elizabeth II right **Rev:** Mother and baby dolphins
Edge: Reeded

Date	Mintage	F	VF	XF	Unc	BU
2005 Proof	10,000	Value: 50.00				

KM# 314 10 DOLLARS
1.2440 g., 0.9999 Gold 0.0400 oz. AGW, 13.92 mm. **Obv:** Bust
of Queen Elizabeth II right **Rev:** Mother and baby dolphins
Edge: Reeded

Date	Mintage	F	VF	XF	Unc	BU
2005 Proof	10,000	Value: 50.00				

KM# 350 10 DOLLARS
28.2800 g., 0.9250 Silver 0.8410 oz. ASW, 38.60 mm.
Ruler: Elizabeth II **Subject:** 5th Anniversary - Attack on Twin
Towers, New York City **Obv:** Crowned bust right **Obv. Legend:**
BRITISH VIRGIN ISLANDS - QUEEN ELIZABETH II **Rev:** Twin
Towers in sprays, remembrance ribbon privy mark at upper right
Rev. Inscription: LEST WE FORGET **Edge:** Reeded

Date	Mintage	F	VF	XF	Unc	BU
2006 Proof	10,000	Value: 77.50				

KM# 333 10 DOLLARS
28.2800 g., 0.9167 Silver ASW 0.8335 0.8334 oz. ASW,
38.60 mm. **Ruler:** Elizabeth II **Subject:** 400th Anniversary
Founding of Jamestown **Obv:** Bust with tiara **Obv. Legend:**
BRITISH VIRGIN ISLANDS - QUEEN ELIZABETH II **Rev:** British
lion laying, American Eagle perched on sprays **Rev. Legend:**
UNITED IN FRIENDSHIP **Edge:** Reeded

Date	Mintage	F	VF	XF	Unc	BU
2007 Proof	25,000	Value: 75.00				

KM# 334 10 DOLLARS
1.2444 g., 0.9999 Gold AGW 0.0400 0.0400 oz. AGW,
13.92 mm. **Ruler:** Elizabeth II **Subject:** 400th Anniversary
Founding of Jamestown **Obv:** Bust with tiara right **Obv. Legend:**
BRITISH VIRGIN ISLANDS - QUEEN ELIZABETH II **Rev:** British
lion laying, American Eagle perched on sprays **Rev. Legend:**
UNITED IN FRIENDSHIP **Edge:** Reeded

Date	Mintage	F	VF	XF	Unc	BU
2007 Proof	20,000	Value: 75.00				

KM# 339 10 DOLLARS
Copper-Nickel **Ruler:** Elizabeth II **Subject:** 10th Anniversary
Death of Princess Diana **Obv:** Bust with tiara right **Obv. Legend:**
BRITISH VIRGIN ISLANDS - QUEEN ELIZABETH II **Rev:** Mother
Teresa at left, Princess Diana at right **Rev. Legend:** MOTHER
TERESA • IN LOVING MEMORY • PRINCESS DIANA
Edge: Reeded

Date	Mintage	F	VF	XF	Unc	BU
2007	—	—	—	—	18.50	

KM# 339a 10 DOLLARS
0.9167 Silver **Ruler:** Elizabeth II **Subject:** 10th Anniversary - Death of Princess Diana **Obv:** Bust with tiara right **Obv. Legend:** BRITISH VIRGIN ISLANDS - QUEEN ELIZABETH II **Rev:** Mother Teresa at left, Princess Diana at right **Rev. Legend:** MOTHER TERESA • IN LOVING MEMORY • PRINCESS DIANA **Edge:** Reeded

Date	Mintage	F	VF	XF	Unc	BU
2007 Proof	—	Value: 75.00				

KM# 341 10 DOLLARS
Copper-Nickel **Ruler:** Elizabeth II **Subject:** Diamond Wedding Anniversary **Obv:** Conjoined busts with Philip right **Obv. Legend:** BRITISH VIRGIN ISLANDS — QUEEN ELIZABETH II **Rev:** Bride to be and King George VI standing facing **Rev. Legend:** Diamond Wedding of H.M. Queen Elizabeth II & H.R.H. Prince Philip **Rev. Inscription:** THE GIVING AWAY **Edge:** Reeded

Date	Mintage	F	VF	XF	Unc	BU
2007	—	—	—	—	16.50	18.50

KM# 341A 10 DOLLARS
0.9167 Silver **Ruler:** Elizabeth II **Subject:** Diamond Wedding Anniversary **Obv:** Conjoined busts with Philip right **Obv. Legend:** BRITISH VIRGIN ISLANDS — QUEEN ELIZABETH II **Rev:** Bride to be and King George VI standing facing **Rev. Legend:** Diamond Wedding of H.M. Queen Elizabeth II & H.R.H. Prince Philip **Rev. Inscription:** THE GIVING AWAY **Edge:** Reeded

Date	Mintage	F	VF	XF	Unc	BU
2007 Proof	—	Value: 75.00				

KM# 342 10 DOLLARS
Copper-Nickel **Ruler:** Elizabeth II **Subject:** Diamond Wedding Anniversary **Obv:** Conjoined busts with Philip right **Obv. Legend:** BRITISH VIRGIN ISLANDS — QUEEN ELIZABETH II **Rev. Legend:** Diamond Wedding of H.M. Queen Elizabeth II & H.R.H. Prince Philip **Rev. Inscription:** THE GLASS COACH **Edge:** Reeded

Date	Mintage	F	VF	XF	Unc	BU
2007	—	—	—	—	16.50	18.50

KM# 342a 10 DOLLARS
0.9167 Silver **Ruler:** Elizabeth II **Subject:** Diamond Wedding Anniversary **Obv:** Conjoined busts with Philip right **Obv. Legend:** BRITISH VIRGIN ISLANDS — QUEEN ELIZABETH II **Rev. Legend:** Diamond Wedding of H.M. Queen Elizabeth II & H.R.H. Prince Philip **Rev. Inscription:** THE GLASS COACH **Edge:** Reeded

Date	Mintage	F	VF	XF	Unc	BU
2007 Proof	—	Value: 75.00				

KM# 343 10 DOLLARS
Copper-Nickel **Ruler:** Elizabeth II **Subject:** Diamond Wedding Anniversary **Obv:** Conjoined busts with Philip right **Obv. Legend:** BRITISH VIRGIN ISLANDS — QUEEN ELIZABETH II **Rev. Legend:** Diamond Wedding of H.M. Queen Elizabeth II & H.R.H. Prince Philip **Rev. Inscription:** THE HONEYMOON **Edge:** Reeded

Date	Mintage	F	VF	XF	Unc	BU
2007	—	—	—	—	16.50	18.50

KM# 343a 10 DOLLARS
0.9167 Silver **Ruler:** Elizabeth II **Subject:** Diamond Wedding Anniversary **Obv:** Conjoined busts with Philip right **Obv. Legend:** BRITISH VIRGIN ISLANDS — QUEEN ELIZABETH II **Rev. Legend:** Diamond Wedding of H.M. Queen Elizabeth II & H.R.H. Prince Philip **Rev. Inscription:** THE HONEYMOON **Edge:** Reeded

Date	Mintage	F	VF	XF	Unc	BU
2007 Proof	—	Value: 75.00				

KM# 344 10 DOLLARS
Copper-Nickel **Ruler:** Elizabeth II **Subject:** Diamond Wedding Anniversary **Obv:** Conjoined busts with Philip right **Obv. Legend:** BRITISH VIRGIN ISLANDS — QUEEN ELIZABETH II **Rev. Legend:** Diamond Wedding of H.M. Queen Elizabeth II & H.R.H. Prince Philip **Rev. Inscription:** THE WEDDING PROGRAM **Edge:** Reeded

Date	Mintage	F	VF	XF	Unc	BU
2007	—	—	—	—	16.50	18.50

KM# 344a 10 DOLLARS
0.9167 Silver **Ruler:** Elizabeth II **Subject:** Diamond Wedding Anniversary **Obv:** Conjoined busts with Philip right **Obv. Legend:** BRITISH VIRGIN ISLANDS ? QUEEN ELIZABETH II **Rev. Legend:** Diamond Wedding of H.M. Queen Elizabeth II & H.R.H. Prince Philip **Rev. Inscription:** THE WEDDING PROGRAM **Edge:** Reeded

Date	Mintage	F	VF	XF	Unc	BU
2007	—	Value: 75.00				

KM# 371 10 DOLLARS
28.2800 g., 0.9250 Silver 0.8410 oz. ASW, 38.6 mm. **Ruler:** Elizabeth II **Obv:** Bust right **Rev:** Two soccer players and leopard

Date	Mintage	F	VF	XF	Unc	BU
2009 Proof	10,000	Value: 35.00				

KM# 372 10 DOLLARS
1.2400 g., 0.9990 Gold 0.0398 oz. AGW, 13.92 mm. **Ruler:** Elizabeth II **Obv:** Bust right **Rev:** Henry VIII facing

Date	Mintage	F	VF	XF	Unc	BU
2009PM Proof	5,000	Value: 80.00				

KM# 374 10 DOLLARS
28.2800 g., 0.9250 Silver 0.8410 oz. ASW, 38.6 mm. **Ruler:** Elizabeth II **Obv:** Bust right **Rev:** Elizabeth I aboard ship

Date	Mintage	F	VF	XF	Unc	BU
2009 Proof	10,000	Value: 35.00				

KM# 376 10 DOLLARS
28.2800 g., 0.9250 Silver 0.8410 oz. ASW, 38.6 mm. **Ruler:** Elizabeth II **Obv:** Bust right **Rev:** Elizabeth I between two columns

Date	Mintage	F	VF	XF	Unc	BU
2009 Proof	10,000	Value: 35.00				

KM# 201 20 DOLLARS
1.2441 g., 0.9999 Gold 0.0400 oz. AGW, 13.92 mm. **Subject:** Teddy Bear Centennial **Obv:** Queen's bust right **Obv. Designer:** Ian Rank-Broadley **Rev:** Teddy bear **Edge:** Reeded

Date	Mintage	F	VF	XF	Unc	BU
2002 Proof	10,000	Value: 45.00				

KM# 227 20 DOLLARS
1.2400 g., 0.9999 Gold 0.0399 oz. AGW, 13.92 mm. **Subject:** Kennedy Assassination **Obv:** Queen's bust right **Obv. Designer:** Ian Rank-Broadley **Rev:** President Kennedy's portrait **Edge:** Reeded

Date	Mintage	F	VF	XF	Unc	BU
2003 Proof	10,000	Value: 45.00				

KM# 279a 20 DOLLARS
63.5900 g., 0.9990 Silver Gilt 2.0423 oz. ASW, 49.93 mm. **Ruler:** Elizabeth II **Subject:** XXVII Olympic Games **Obv:** Bust with tiara right **Rev:** 1896 Olympic medal design **Edge:** Reeded

Date	Mintage	F	VF	XF	Unc	BU
2004PM Proof	—	Value: 100				

KM# 271 20 DOLLARS
1.2440 g., 0.9999 Gold 0.0400 oz. AGW, 14 mm. **Obv:** Queen's bust right **Obv. Designer:** Ian Rank-Broadley **Rev:** Peter Rabbit **Edge:** Reeded

Date	Mintage	F	VF	XF	Unc	BU
2004 Proof	5,000	Value: 50.00				

KM# 279 20 DOLLARS
58.0000 g., 0.9990 Silver 1.8628 oz. ASW, 50 mm. **Subject:** XXVIII Olympic Games **Obv:** Bust with tiara right **Obv. Designer:** Ian Rank-Broadley **Rev:** 1896 Olympic medal design **Edge:** Reeded

Date	Mintage	F	VF	XF	Unc	BU
2004PM Proof	2,004	Value: 75.00				

KM# 345 20 DOLLARS
3.9600 g., 0.7500 Gold 0.0955 oz. AGW, 21.78 mm. **Ruler:** Elizabeth II **Subject:** 500th Anniversary - Death of Columbus **Obv:** Crowned bust right **Obv. Legend:** BRITISH VIRGIN ISLANDS - QUEEN ELIZABETH II **Rev:** Bust of Columbus facing 3/4 left at right, outlined map of the Americas at left **Rev. Legend:** 1451 - CHRISTOPHER COLUMBUS - 1506 **Edge:** Reeded **Note:** Struck in white gold.

Date	Mintage	F	VF	XF	Unc	BU
2006 Proof	1,506	Value: 115				

KM# 346 20 DOLLARS
4.0200 g., 0.7500 Gold 0.0969 oz. AGW, 21.78 mm. **Ruler:** Elizabeth II **Subject:** 500th Anniversary - Death of Columbus **Obv:** Crowned bust right **Obv. Legend:** BRITISH VIRGIN ISLANDS - QUEEN ELIZABETH II **Rev:** Sailing ship "Santa Maria" **Rev. Legend:** 1451 - CHRISTOPHER COLUMBUS - 1506 **Edge:** Reeded **Note:** Struck in rose gold.

Date	Mintage	F	VF	XF	Unc	BU
2006 Proof	1,506	Value: 120				

KM# 347 20 DOLLARS
3.9900 g., 0.7500 Gold 0.0962 oz. AGW, 21.78 mm. **Ruler:** Elizabeth II **Subject:** 500th Anniversary - Death of Columbus **Obv:** Crowned bust right **Obv. Legend:** BRITISH VIRGIN ISLANDS - QUEEN ELIZABETH II **Rev:** Sailing ships "Niña" and "Pinta" **Rev. Legend:** 1451 - CHRISTOPHER COLUMBUS - 1506 **Edge:** Reeded **Note:** Struck in yellow gold

Date	Mintage	F	VF	XF	Unc	BU
2006 Proof	1,506	Value: 115				

KM# 379 30 DOLLARS
155.5000 g., 0.9990 Silver 4.9942 oz. ASW **Ruler:** Elizabeth II **Subject:** Nelson's victory at Trafalgar **Rev:** Two ships

Date	Mintage	F	VF	XF	Unc	BU
2008 Proof	—	Value: 250				

KM# 275 25 DOLLARS
3.1100 g., 0.9999 Gold 0.1000 oz. AGW, 18 mm. **Obv:** Queen's bust right **Obv. Designer:** Ian Rank-Broadley **Rev:** Hernando Pizarro portrait and life events pictorial **Edge:** Reeded

Date	Mintage	F	VF	XF	Unc	BU
2004 Proof	350	Value: 135				

KM# 289 25 DOLLARS
3.1100 g., 0.9999 Gold 0.1000 oz. AGW, 18 mm. **Obv:** Queen's bust right **Obv. Designer:** Ian Rank-Broadley **Rev:** Dolphin **Edge:** Reeded

Date	Mintage	F	VF	XF	Unc	BU
2004 Proof	6,000	Value: 125				

KM# 315 25 DOLLARS
3.1100 g., 0.9999 Gold 0.1000 oz. AGW, 18 mm. **Obv:** Bust of Queen Elizabeth II right **Rev:** Mother and baby dolphins **Edge:** Reeded

Date	Mintage	F	VF	XF	Unc	BU
2005 Proof	6,000	Value: 125				

KM# 335 25 DOLLARS
3.1120 g., 0.9999 Gold AGW 0.1004 0.1000 oz. AGW, 17.95 mm. **Ruler:** Elizabeth II **Subject:** 400th Anniversary Founding of Jamestown **Obv:** Bust with tiara right **Obv. Legend:** BRITISH VIRGIN ISLANDS - QUEEN ELIZABETH II **Rev:** British lion laying, American Eagle perched on sprays **Rev. Legend:** UNITED IN FRIENDSHIP **Edge:** Reeded

Date	Mintage	VG	F	VF	XF	Unc
2007 Proof	7,500	Value: 120				

KM# 202 50 DOLLARS
3.1104 g., 0.9999 Gold 0.1000 oz. AGW, 17.95 mm. **Subject:** Teddy Bear Centennial **Obv:** Queen's bust right **Obv. Designer:** Ian Rank-Broadley **Rev:** Teddy bear **Edge:** Reeded

Date	Mintage	F	VF	XF	Unc	BU
2002 Proof	7,000	Value: 120				

KM# 272 50 DOLLARS
3.1100 g., 0.9999 Gold 0.1000 oz. AGW, 18 mm. **Obv:** Queen's bust right **Obv. Designer:** Ian Rank-Broadley **Rev:** Peter Rabbit **Edge:** Reeded

Date	Mintage	F	VF	XF	Unc	BU
2004 Proof	3,000	Value: 120				

KM# 276 50 DOLLARS
6.2200 g., 0.9999 Gold 0.1999 oz. AGW, 22 mm. **Obv:** Queen's bust right **Obv. Designer:** Ian Rank-Broadley **Rev:** Treasure ship with blue color sail **Edge:** Reeded

Date	Mintage	F	VF	XF	Unc	BU
2004 Proof	350	Value: 245				

KM# 290 50 DOLLARS
6.2200 g., 0.9999 Gold 0.1999 oz. AGW, 22 mm. **Obv:** Queen's bust right **Obv. Designer:** Ian Rank-Broadley **Rev:** Dolphin **Edge:** Reeded

Date	Mintage	F	VF	XF	Unc	BU
2004 Proof	3,500	Value: 235				

KM# 316 50 DOLLARS
6.2200 g., 0.9999 Gold 0.1999 oz. AGW, 22 mm. **Obv:** Bust of Queen Elizabeth II right **Rev:** Mother and baby dolphins **Edge:** Reeded

Date	Mintage	F	VF	XF	Unc	BU
2005	3,500	Value: 250				

KM# 351 50 DOLLARS
6.2200 g., 0.9999 Gold 0.1999 oz. AGW, 22.00 mm.
Ruler: Elizabeth II **Subject:** 5th Anniversary - Attack on Twin Towers, New York City **Obv:** Crowned bust right **Obv. Legend:** BRISH VIRGIN ISLANDS - QUEEN ELIZABETH II **Rev:** Twin Towers in sprays, remembrance ribbon privy mark at upper right **Rev. Inscription:** LEST WE FORGET **Edge:** Reeded

Date	Mintage	F	VF	XF	Unc	BU
2006 Proof	2,000	Value: 335				

KM# 336 50 DOLLARS
6.2230 g., 0.9999 Gold AGW 0.1999 0.2000 oz. AGW, 22.00 mm. **Ruler:** Elizabeth II **Subject:** 400th Anniversary Founding of Jamestown **Obv:** Bust with tiara right **Obv. Legend:** BRITISH VIRGIN ISLANDS - QUEEN ELIZABETH II **Rev:** British lion laying, American Eagle perched on sprays **Rev. Legend:** UNITED IN FRIENDSHIP **Edge:** Reeded

Date	Mintage	F	VF	XF	Unc	BU
2007 Proof	5,000	Value: 225				

KM# 377 50 DOLLARS
6.2200 g., 0.9990 Gold 0.1998 oz. AGW, 22 mm.
Ruler: Elizabeth II **Obv:** Bust right **Rev:** Elizabeth II aboard ship with 1mm pearl

Date	Mintage	F	VF	XF	Unc	BU
2009 Proof	750	Value: 275				

KM# 378 50 DOLLARS
6.2200 g., 0.9990 Gold 0.1998 oz. AGW, 22 mm.
Ruler: Elizabeth II **Obv:** Bust right **Rev:** Elizabeth II between two columns, .01ct ruby insert

Date	Mintage	F	VF	XF	Unc	BU
2009 Proof	750	Value: 275				

KM# 285 75 DOLLARS
11.0000 g., Bi-Metallic .990 Titanium 2g center in .9999 Gold 9g ring, 36.5 mm. **Obv:** Queen's bust right **Obv. Designer:** Ian Rank-Broadley **Rev:** British Guiana stamp design **Edge:** Reeded

Date	Mintage	F	VF	XF	Unc	BU
2004 Proof	2,500	Value: 350				

KM# 182 100 DOLLARS
6.2200 g., 0.9990 Gold 0.1998 oz. AGW, 22 mm. **Subject:** Sir Francis Drake **Obv:** Queen's bust right **Obv. Designer:** Ian Rank-Broadley **Rev:** Ship, portrait and map **Edge:** Reeded

Date	Mintage	F	VF	XF	Unc	BU
2002 Proof	5,000	Value: 225				

KM# 185 100 DOLLARS
6.2200 g., 0.9990 Gold 0.1998 oz. AGW, 22 mm. **Subject:** Sir Walter Raleigh **Obv:** Queen's bust right **Obv. Designer:** Ian Rank-Broadley **Rev:** Ship, portrait and map **Edge:** Reeded

Date	Mintage	F	VF	XF	Unc	BU
2002 Proof	5,000	Value: 225				

KM# 189 100 DOLLARS
6.2208 g., 0.9999 Gold 0.2000 oz. AGW, 22 mm.
Subject: Queen's Golden Jubilee **Obv:** Queen's bust right **Obv. Designer:** Ian Rank-Broadley **Rev:** Queen on horse **Edge:** Reeded

Date	Mintage	F	VF	XF	Unc	BU
2002 Proof	2,002	Value: 240				

KM# 192 100 DOLLARS
6.2208 g., 0.9999 Gold 0.2000 oz. AGW, 22 mm.
Subject: Queen's Golden Jubilee **Obv:** Queen's bust right **Obv. Designer:** Ian Rank-Broadley **Rev:** Queen on throne **Edge:** Reeded

Date	Mintage	F	VF	XF	Unc	BU
2002 Proof	2,002	Value: 240				

KM# 195 100 DOLLARS
6.2208 g., 0.9999 Gold 0.2000 oz. AGW, 22 mm.
Subject: Queen's Golden Jubilee **Obv:** Queen's bust right **Obv. Designer:** Ian Rank-Broadley **Rev:** Queen with President Ronald Reagan and Mrs. Nancy Reagan **Edge:** Reeded

Date	Mintage	F	VF	XF	Unc	BU
2002 Proof	2,002	Value: 240				

KM# 198 100 DOLLARS
6.2208 g., 0.9999 Gold 0.2000 oz. AGW, 22 mm.
Subject: Queen's Golden Jubilee **Obv:** Queen's bust right **Obv. Designer:** Ian Rank-Broadley **Rev:** Carnival dancers **Edge:** Reeded

Date	Mintage	F	VF	XF	Unc	BU
2002 Proof	2,002	Value: 240				

KM# 203 100 DOLLARS
6.2200 g., 0.9999 Gold 0.1999 oz. AGW, 22 mm.
Subject: Teddy Bear Centennial **Obv:** Queen's bust right **Obv. Designer:** Ian Rank-Broadley **Rev:** Teddy bea r **Edge:** Reeded

Date	Mintage	F	VF	XF	Unc	BU
2002 Proof	5,000	Value: 225				

KM# 206 100 DOLLARS
6.2200 g., 0.9999 Gold 0.1999 oz. AGW, 22 mm.
Subject: Princess Diana **Obv:** Queen's bust right **Obv. Designer:** Ian Rank-Broadley **Rev:** Diana's portrait **Edge:** Reeded

Date	Mintage	F	VF	XF	Unc	BU
2002 Proof	5,000	Value: 225				

KM# 209.1 100 DOLLARS
6.2200 g., 0.9999 Gold 0.1999 oz. AGW, 22 mm.
Subject: September 11, 2001 **Obv:** Queen's bust right **Obv. Designer:** Ian Rank-Broadley **Rev:** World Trade Center twin towers **Edge:** Reeded

Date	Mintage	F	VF	XF	Unc	BU
2002 Proof	5,000	Value: 225				

KM# 209.2 100 DOLLARS
6.2200 g., 0.9999 Gold 0.1999 oz. AGW, 22 mm.
Subject: September 11, 2001 **Obv:** Queen's bust right **Obv. Designer:** Ian Rank-Broadley **Rev:** Holographic multicolor World Trade Center twin towers **Edge:** Reeded

Date	Mintage	F	VF	XF	Unc	BU
2002 Proof	5,000	Value: 225				

KM# 212 100 DOLLARS
6.2200 g., 0.9999 Gold 0.1999 oz. AGW, 22 mm.
Subject: September 11, 2001 **Obv:** Queen's bust right **Obv. Designer:** Ian Rank-Broadley **Rev:** Statue of Liberty **Edge:** Reeded

Date	Mintage	F	VF	XF	Unc	BU
2002 Proof	5,000	Value: 225				

KM# 215 100 DOLLARS
6.2200 g., 0.9999 Gold 0.1999 oz. AGW, 22 mm.
Subject: Queen Mother Series **Obv:** Queen's bust right **Obv. Designer:** Ian Rank-Broadley **Rev:** Queen Mother with young Prince Charles **Edge:** Reeded

Date	Mintage	F	VF	XF	Unc	BU
2002PM Proof	5,000	Value: 225				

KM# 218 100 DOLLARS
6.2200 g., 0.9999 Gold 0.1999 oz. AGW, 22 mm.
Subject: Queen Mother Series **Obv:** Queen's bust right **Obv. Designer:** Ian Rank-Broadley **Rev:** Queen Mother with four grandchildren **Edge:** Reeded

Date	Mintage	F	VF	XF	Unc	BU
2002PM Proof	5,000	Value: 225				

KM# 221 100 DOLLARS
6.2200 g., 0.9999 Gold 0.1999 oz. AGW, 22 mm.
Subject: Queen Mother Series **Obv:** Queen's bust right **Obv. Designer:** Ian Rank-Broadley **Rev:** Queen Mother with uniformed Prince Charles **Edge:** Reeded

Date	Mintage	F	VF	XF	Unc	BU
2002PM Proof	5,000	Value: 225				

KM# 224 100 DOLLARS
6.2200 g., 0.9999 Gold 0.1999 oz. AGW, 22 mm.
Subject: Queen Mother Series **Obv:** Queen's bust right **Obv. Designer:** Ian Rank-Broadley **Rev:** Queen Mother's coffin **Edge:** Reeded

Date	Mintage	F	VF	XF	Unc	BU
2002PM Proof	5,000	Value: 225				

KM# 228 100 DOLLARS
6.2200 g., 0.9999 Gold 0.1999 oz. AGW, 22 mm.
Subject: Kennedy Assassination **Obv:** Queen's bust right **Obv. Designer:** Ian Rank-Broadley **Rev:** President Kennedy's portrait **Edge:** Reeded

Date	Mintage	F	VF	XF	Unc	BU
2003 Proof	5,000	Value: 225				

KM# 231 100 DOLLARS
15.5500 g., 0.9999 Gold 0.4999 oz. AGW, 30 mm.
Subject: Powered Flight Centennial **Obv:** Queen's bust right **Obv. Designer:** Ian Rank-Broadley **Rev:** Three historic airplanes and rocket **Edge:** Reeded

Date	Mintage	F	VF	XF	Unc	BU
2003 Proof	—	Value: 600				

KM# 234 100 DOLLARS
6.2200 g., 0.9999 Gold 0.1999 oz. AGW, 22 mm. **Obv:** Queen's bust right **Obv. Designer:** Ian Rank-Broadley **Rev:** Henry VIII and Elizabeth I **Edge:** Reeded

Date	Mintage	F	VF	XF	Unc	BU
2003 Proof	5,000	Value: 225				

KM# 237 100 DOLLARS
6.2200 g., 0.9999 Gold 0.1999 oz. AGW, 22 mm. **Obv:** Queen's bust right **Obv. Designer:** Ian Rank-Broadley **Rev:** Matthew Parker, Archbishop of Canterbury **Edge:** Reeded

Date	Mintage	F	VF	XF	Unc	BU
2003 Proof	5,000	Value: 225				

KM# 240 100 DOLLARS
6.2200 g., 0.9999 Gold 0.1999 oz. AGW, 22 mm. **Obv:** Queen's bust right **Obv. Designer:** Ian Rank-Broadley **Rev:** Sir Francis Drake and ships **Edge:** Reeded

Date	Mintage	F	VF	XF	Unc	BU
2003 Proof	5,000	Value: 225				

KM# 243 100 DOLLARS
6.2200 g., 0.9999 Gold 0.1999 oz. AGW, 22 mm. **Obv:** Queen's bust right **Obv. Designer:** Ian Rank-Broadley **Rev:** Sir Walter Raleigh **Edge:** Reeded

Date	Mintage	F	VF	XF	Unc	BU
2003 Proof	5,000	Value: 225				

KM# 246 100 DOLLARS
6.2200 g., 0.9999 Gold 0.1999 oz. AGW, 22 mm. **Obv:** Queen's bust right **Obv. Designer:** Ian Rank-Broadley **Rev:** Sir William Shakespeare **Edge:** Reeded

Date	Mintage	F	VF	XF	Unc	BU
2003 Proof	5,000	Value: 225				

KM# 249 100 DOLLARS
6.2200 g., 0.9999 Gold 0.1999 oz. AGW, 22 mm. **Obv:** Queen's bust right **Obv. Designer:** Ian Rank-Broadley **Rev:** Elizabeth I above her funeral procession **Edge:** Reeded

Date	Mintage	F	VF	XF	Unc	BU
2003 Proof	5,000	Value: 225				

KM# 252 100 DOLLARS
6.2200 g., 0.9999 Gold 0.1999 oz. AGW, 22 mm.
Subject: Olympics **Obv:** Queen's bust right **Obv. Designer:** Ian Rank-Broadley **Rev:** Ancient bust, runners and coin **Edge:** Reeded

Date	Mintage	F	VF	XF	Unc	BU
2003 Proof	5,000	Value: 225				

KM# 255 100 DOLLARS
6.2200 g., 0.9999 Gold 0.1999 oz. AGW, 22 mm.
Subject: Olympics **Obv:** Queen's bust right **Obv. Designer:** Ian Rank-Broadley **Rev:** Ancient bust, charioteer and coin **Edge:** Reeded

Date	Mintage	F	VF	XF	Unc	BU
2003 Proof	5,000	Value: 225				

KM# 273.1 100 DOLLARS
6.2200 g., 0.9999 Gold 0.1999 oz. AGW, 22 mm. **Obv:** Queen's bust right **Obv. Designer:** Ian Rank-Broadley **Rev:** Peter Rabbit **Edge:** Reeded

Date	Mintage	F	VF	XF	Unc	BU
2004 Proof	2,000	Value: 245				

KM# 273.2 100 DOLLARS
6.2200 g., 0.9999 Gold 0.1999 oz. AGW, 22 mm. **Obv:** Queen's bust right **Obv. Designer:** Ian Rank-Broadley **Rev:** Multicolor Peter Rabbit **Edge:** Reeded

Date	Mintage	F	VF	XF	Unc	BU
2004 Proof	—	Value: 250				

KM# 283 100 DOLLARS
6.2200 g., 0.9999 Gold 0.1999 oz. AGW, 22 mm. **Obv:** Queen's bust right **Obv. Designer:** Ian Rank-Broadley **Rev:** Sailor above two D-Day landing craft **Edge:** Reeded

Date	Mintage	F	VF	XF	Unc	BU
2004 Proof	5,000	Value: 225				

KM# 299 100 DOLLARS
6.2200 g., 0.9999 Gold 0.1999 oz. AGW, 22 mm. **Obv:** Queen's bust right **Obv. Designer:** Ian Rank-Broadley **Rev:** Soldier above tank and jeeps **Edge:** Reeded

Date	Mintage	F	VF	XF	Unc	BU
2004 Proof	5,000	Value: 225				

KM# 302 100 DOLLARS
6.2200 g., 0.9999 Gold 0.1999 oz. AGW, 22 mm. **Obv:** Queen's bust right **Obv. Designer:** Ian Rank-Broadley **Rev:** Pilot and planes above D-Day landing **Edge:** Reeded

Date	Mintage	F	VF	XF	Unc	BU
2004 Proof	5,000	Value: 225				

KM# 305 100 DOLLARS
6.2200 g., 0.9999 Gold 0.1999 oz. AGW, 22 mm. **Obv:** Queen's bust right **Obv. Designer:** Ian Rank-Broadley **Rev:** Ancient Olympic bust, runners and owl coin **Edge:** Reeded

Date	Mintage	F	VF	XF	Unc	BU
2004 Proof	5,000	Value: 225				

KM# 308 100 DOLLARS
6.2200 g., 0.9999 Gold 0.1999 oz. AGW, 22 mm. **Obv:** Queen's bust right **Obv. Designer:** Ian Rank-Broadley **Rev:** Ancient Olympic bust, charioteer and Zeus coin **Edge:** Reeded

Date	Mintage	F	VF	XF	Unc	BU
2004 Proof	5,000	Value: 225				

KM# 317 125 DOLLARS
15.5510 g., 0.9999 Gold 0.4999 oz. AGW, 30 mm. **Obv:** Bust of Queen Elizabeth II right **Rev:** Mother and baby dolphins **Edge:** Reeded

Date	Mintage	F	VF	XF	Unc	BU
2005	1,500	Value: 650				

KM# 337 125 DOLLARS
15.5590 g., 0.9999 Gold AGW 0.5000 0.5002 oz. AGW, 30.00 mm. **Ruler:** Elizabeth II **Subject:** 400th Anniversary Founding of Jamestown **Obv:** Bust with tiara right **Obv. Legend:** BRITISH VIRGIN ISLANDS - QUEEN ELIZABETH II **Rev:** British lion laying, American Eagle perched on sprays **Rev. Legend:** UNITED IN FRIENDSHIP **Edge:** Reeded

Date	Mintage	F	VF	XF	Unc	BU
2007 Proof	3,000	Value: 600				

KM# 309 250 DOLLARS
15.5517 g., 0.9990 Gold 0.4995 oz. AGW, 30 mm. **Obv:** Queen's bust right **Obv. Designer:** Ian Rank-Broadley **Rev:** Statue of Liberty and the date "11 Sept. 2001" **Edge:** Reeded

Date	Mintage	F	VF	XF	Unc	BU
2002	250	Value: 700				

KM# 280 250 DOLLARS
58.0000 g., 0.5000 Gold 0.9323 oz. AGW, 50 mm. **Obv:** Queen's bust right **Obv. Designer:** Ian Rank-Broadley **Rev:** 1896 Olympic medal design **Edge:** Reeded

Date	Mintage	F	VF	XF	Unc	BU
2004 Proof	1,000	Value: 1,100				

KM# 318 250 DOLLARS
31.1030 g., 0.9999 Gold 0.9998 oz. AGW, 32.7 mm. **Obv:** Bust of Queen Elizabeth II right **Rev:** Mother and baby dolphins **Edge:** Reeded

Date	Mintage	F	VF	XF	Unc	BU
2005 Proof	750	Value: 1,200				

KM# 338 250 DOLLARS
31.1030 g., 0.9999 Gold AGW 0.9999 0.9998 oz. AGW,
32.70 mm. **Ruler:** Elizabeth II **Subject:** 400th Anniversary
Founding of Jamestown **Obv:** Bust with tiara right **Obv. Legend:**
BRITISH VIRGIN ISLANDS - QUEEN ELIZABETH II **Rev:** British
lion laying, American eagle perched on sprays **Rev. Legend:**
UNITED IN FRIENDSHIP **Edge:** Reeded

Date	Mintage	F	VF	XF	Unc	BU
2007 Proof	1,000	Value: 1,150				

KM# 277 500 DOLLARS
160.7562 g., 0.9990 Gold 5.1630 oz. AGW, 150 mm.
Obv: Queen's bust right **Obv. Designer:** Ian Rank-Broadley
Rev: Gold-plated portrait of Hernando Pizarro, small inset
emerald above Pizarro's life events pictoral **Edge:** Reeded
Note: Photo reduced.

Date	Mintage	F	VF	XF	Unc	BU
2004 Proof	500	Value: 5,750				

KM# 348 500 DOLLARS
160.7562 g., 0.9990 Gold 5.1630 oz. AGW, 150.00 mm.
Ruler: Elizabeth II **Subject:** 500th Anniversary - Death of
Columbus **Obv:** Crowned bust right **Obv. Legend:** BRITISH
VIRGIN ISLANDS - QUEEN ELIZABETH II **Rev:** Ship in
background at left, Columbus standing at right with right arm
outstreched looking right, compass below. **Rev. Legend:** 1451 -
DISCOVERER OF AMERICA - CHRISTOPHER COLUMBUS -
1506 **Edge:** Reeded

Date	Mintage	F	VF	XF	Unc	BU
2006 Proof	1,506	Value: 5,500				

MINT SETS

KM#	Date	Mintage Identification	Issue Price	Mkt Val
MS12	2007 (4)	— KM# 341 - 344	65.00	70.00

PROOF SETS

KM#	Date	Mintage Identification	Issue Price	Mkt Val
PS20	2007 (4)	— KM# 341a - 344a	300	300

BRUNEI

Negara Brunei Darussalam (State of Brunei), an independent sultanate on the northwest coast of the island of Borneo, has
an area of 2,226 sq. mi. (5,765 sq. km.) and a population of
*326,000. Capital: Bandar Seri Begawan. Crude oil and rubber
are exported. Brunei is a member of the Commonwealth of
Nations. The Sultan is the Head of State.

RULERS
Sultan Hassanal Bolkiah, 1967-

SULTANATE

DECIMAL COINAGE
100 Sen = 1 Dollar (Ringgit)

KM# 34 SEN
1.7500 g., Copper Clad Steel, 17.74 mm. **Ruler:** Sultan
Hassanal Bolkiah **Obv:** Uniformed bust facing **Rev:** Native
design denomination below, date at right **Edge:** Plain

Date	Mintage	F	VF	XF	Unc	BU
2001	576,000	—	—	0.15	0.40	0.50
2002	804,900	—	—	0.15	0.40	0.50
2005	—	—	—	0.15	0.40	0.50

KM# 35 5 SEN
1.2500 g., Copper-Nickel, 16.19 mm. **Ruler:** Sultan Hassanal
Bolkiah **Obv:** Uniformed bust facing **Rev:** Native design,
denomination below, date at right **Edge:** Reeded

Date	Mintage	F	VF	XF	Unc	BU
2001	808,000	—	—	0.20	0.50	0.75
2002	1,418,178	—	—	0.20	0.50	0.75
2005	—	—	—	0.20	0.50	0.75

KM# 36 10 SEN
2.8200 g., Copper-Nickel, 19.41 mm. **Ruler:** Sultan Hassanal
Bolkiah **Obv:** Uniformed bust facing **Rev:** Native design,
denomination below, date at right **Edge:** Reeded

Date	Mintage	F	VF	XF	Unc	BU
2001	164,000	—	—	0.30	0.75	1.00
2002	476,452	—	—	0.30	0.75	1.00
2005	—	—	—	0.30	0.75	1.00

KM# 37 20 SEN
5.6700 g., Copper-Nickel, 23.62 mm. **Ruler:** Sultan Hassanal
Bolkiah **Obv:** Uniformed bust facing **Rev:** Native design,
denomination below, date at right **Edge:** Reeded

Date	Mintage	F	VF	XF	Unc	BU
2001	270,647	—	—	0.45	1.10	1.50
2002	597,272	—	—	0.45	1.10	1.50
2004	—	—	—	0.45	1.10	1.50

KM# 38 50 SEN
9.3000 g., Copper-Nickel, 27.75 mm. **Ruler:** Sultan Hassanal
Bolkiah **Obv:** Uniformed bust facing **Rev:** National arms within
circle, denomination below, date at right **Edge:** Reeded and
security edge

Date	Mintage	F	VF	XF	Unc	BU
2001	50,000	—	—	1.00	2.50	3.00
2002	1,325	—	—	1.40	3.50	5.00
2005	—	—	—	0.75	1.80	2.50

KM# 80 2 DOLLARS
31.1000 g., Copper-Nickel, 40.7 mm. **Ruler:** Sultan Hassanal
Bolkiah **Subject:** 20th Anniversary of Independence **Obv:** Bust
3/4 left, facing **Obv. Legend:** SULTAN HAJI HASSANAL
BOLKIAH **Rev:** National arms **Rev. Legend:** NEGERI BRUNEI
DARUSSALAM

Date	Mintage	F	VF	XF	Unc	BU
2004 Proof	4,000	Value: 65.00				

KM# 86 2 DOLLARS
31.1000 g., Copper-Nickel, 40.7 mm. **Ruler:** Sultan Hassanal
Bolkiah **Subject:** 60th Birthday **Obv:** Bust 3/4 left, facing
Obv. Legend: SULTAN HAJI HASSANAL BOLKIAH
Rev: Multicolor 1/2 length figure in civilian clothes, facing

Date	Mintage	F	VF	XF	Unc	BU
2006 Proof	200	Value: 120				

KM# 77 3 DOLLARS
24.0000 g., Copper-Nickel, 40 mm. **Ruler:** Sultan Hassanal
Bolkiah **Obv:** Uniformed bust facing **Obv. Legend:** SULTAN
HAJI HASSANAL BOLKIAH **Rev:** Logo at center
Rev. Legend: COMMONWEALTH FINANCE MINISTERS
MEETING **Edge:** Reeded

Date	Mintage	F	VF	XF	Unc	BU
2003 Proof	4,000	Value: 40.00				

KM# 83 3 DOLLARS
31.1000 g., Copper-Nickel, 40.7 mm. **Ruler:** Sultan Hassanal
Bolkiah **Subject:** Royal Wedding **Obv:** Multicolor portraits of
Royal couple

Date	Mintage	F	VF	XF	Unc	BU
2004 Proof	5,000	Value: 50.00				

KM# 81 20 DOLLARS
31.1000 g., 0.9990 Silver 0.9988 oz. ASW, 40.7 mm.
Ruler: Sultan Hassanal Bolkiah **Subject:** 20th Anniversary of
Independence **Obv:** Bust 3/4 left, facing **Obv. Legend:** SULTAN
HAJI HASSANAL BOLKIAH **Rev:** National arms
Rev. Legend: NEGARI BRUNEI DARUSSALAM

Date	Mintage	F	VF	XF	Unc	BU
2004 Proof	1,000	Value: 120				

KM# 87 20 DOLLARS
31.1000 g., 0.9990 Silver 0.9988 oz. ASW, 40.7 mm. **Ruler:**
Sultan Hassanal Bolkiah **Subject:** 60th Birthday **Obv:** Bust 3/4
left, facing **Obv. Legend:** SULTAN HAJI HASSANAL BOLKIAH
Rev: Multicolor 1/2-length figure in civilian clothes, facing

Date	Mintage	F	VF	XF	Unc	BU
2006 Proof	200	Value: 275				

KM# 78 30 DOLLARS
62.2000 g., 0.9990 Silver 1.9977 oz. ASW **Ruler:** Sultan
Hassanal Bolkiah **Subject:** Commonwealth Finance Ministers'
Meeting **Obv:** Logo at upper left, multicolor bust of Sultan 3/4 left,
facing at right **Obv. Legend:** SULTAN HAJI HASSANAL BOLIAH
Rev: World map at left - center, national arms at upper right
Shape: Rectangular, 65 x 31 mm

Date	Mintage	F	VF	XF	Unc	BU
2003 Proof	200	Value: 210				

KM# 84 30 DOLLARS
31.1000 g., 0.9990 Silver 0.9988 oz. ASW, 40.7 mm. **Ruler:**
Sultan Hassanal Bolkiah **Subject:** Royal Wedding **Obv:**
Multicolor portraits of Royal couple

Date	Mintage	F	VF	XF	Unc	BU
2004 Proof	1,000	Value: 180				

KM# 82 200 DOLLARS
31.1000 g., 0.9999 Gold 0.9997 oz. AGW, 32.1 mm. **Ruler:**
Sultan Hassanal Bolkiah **Subject:** 20th Anniversary of
Independence **Obv:** Bust 3/4 left, facing **Obv. Legend:** SULTAN
HAJI HASSANAL BOLKIAH **Rev:** National arms **Rev. Legend:**
NEGARI BRUNEI DARUSSALAM

Date	Mintage	F	VF	XF	Unc	BU
2004 Proof	200	Value: 1,200				

KM# 85 200 DOLLARS
31.1000 g., 0.9999 Gold 0.9997 oz. AGW, 32 mm. **Ruler:**
Sultan Hassanal Bolkiah **Subject:** Royal Wedding **Obv:**
Multicolor portraits of Royal couple

Date	Mintage	F	VF	XF	Unc	BU
2004 Proof	200	Value: 1,200				

KM# 88 200 DOLLARS
31.1000 g., 0.9999 Gold 0.9997 oz. AGW, 32.1 mm. **Ruler:**
Sultan Hassanal Bolkiah **Subject:** 60th Birthday **Obv:** Bust 3/4
left, facing **Obv. Legend:** SULTAN HAJI HASSANAL BOLKIAH
Rev: Multicolor 1/2-length figure in civilian clothes, facing

Date	Mintage	F	VF	XF	Unc	BU
2006 Proof	200	Value: 1,800				

PROOF SETS

KM#	Date	Mintage Identification	Issue Price	Mkt Val
PS20	2003 (2)	500 KM#77-78	—	250
PS21	2004 (3)	200 KM#80-82	—	1,400
PS22	2004 (3)	200 KM#83-85	—	1,425
PS23	2006 (3)	200 KM#86-88	—	2,200

BULGARIA

The Republic of Bulgaria, formerly the Peoples Republic of Bulgaria, a Balkan country on the Black Sea in southeastern Europe, has an area of 42,855 sq. mi. (110,910 sq. km.) and a population of *8.31 million. Capital: Sofia. Agriculture remains a key component of the economy but industrialization, particularly heavy industry, has been emphasized since the late 1940s. Machinery, tobacco and cigarettes, wines and spirits, clothing and metals are the chief exports. Bulgaria joined the European Union in January 2007.

MONETARY SYSTEM
100 Stotinki = 1 Lev

REPUBLIC

REFORM COINAGE

KM# 237   STOTINKA
1.8000 g., Brass, 16 mm. **Obv:** Madara horseman right, animal below **Rev:** Denomination above date **Edge:** Plain

Date	Mintage	F	VF	XF	Unc	BU
2002 Proof	10,000	Value: 1.00				

KM# 237a   STOTINKA
1.8000 g., Brass Plated Steel, 16 mm. **Obv:** Madara horseman right **Rev:** Denomination above date

Date	Mintage	F	VF	XF	Unc	BU
2002 Proof	10,000	Value: 1.00				

KM# 238   2 STOTINKI
2.5000 g., Brass, 18 mm. **Obv:** Madara horseman right, animal below **Rev:** Denomination above date **Edge:** Plain

Date	Mintage	F	VF	XF	Unc	BU
2002 Proof	10,000	Value: 1.50				

KM# 238a   2 STOTINKI
2.5000 g., Brass Plated Steel, 18 mm. **Obv:** Madara horseman right **Rev:** Denomination above date

Date	Mintage	F	VF	XF	Unc	BU
2002 Proof	10,000	Value: 1.50				

KM# 239a   5 STOTINKI
3.5000 g., Brass Plated Steel, 20 mm. **Obv:** Madara horseman right **Rev:** Denomination above date

Date	Mintage	F	VF	XF	Unc	BU
2002 Proof	10,000	Value: 2.00				

KM# 239   5 STOTINKI
3.5000 g., Brass, 20 mm. **Obv:** Madara horseman right, animal below **Rev:** Denomination above date **Edge:** Plain **Note:** Prev. KM#A239.

Date	Mintage	F	VF	XF	Unc	BU
2002 Proof	10,000	Value: 2.00				

KM# 240   10 STOTINKI
Copper-Nickel, 18.5 mm. **Obv:** Madara horseman right, animal below **Rev:** Denomination above date **Edge:** Reeded

Date	Mintage	F	VF	XF	Unc	BU
2002 Proof	10,000	Value: 2.50				

KM# 241   20 STOTINKI
Copper-Nickel, 20.5 mm. **Obv:** Madara horseman right, animal below **Rev:** Denomination above date **Edge:** Reeded

Date	Mintage	F	VF	XF	Unc	BU
2002 Proof	10,000	Value: 3.00				

KM# 242   50 STOTINKI
Copper-Nickel, 22.5 mm. **Obv:** Madara horseman right, animal below **Rev:** Denomination above date **Edge:** Reeded

Date	Mintage	F	VF	XF	Unc	BU
2002 Proof	10,000	Value: 5.00				

KM# 272   50 STOTINKI
Copper-Nickel, 22.5 mm. **Obv:** Stylized Bulgarian arms, lion left, NATO - 2004 under lion **Rev:** Denomination above date **Edge:** Reeded

Date	Mintage	F	VF	XF	Unc	BU
2004	—	—	—	—	2.00	3.00

KM# 282   50 STOTINKI
5.0300 g., Copper-Nickel, 22.6 mm. **Obv:** European Union seated woman allegory **Rev:** Value above date **Edge:** Reeded **Note:** Prev. KM#274.

Date	Mintage	F	VF	XF	Unc	BU
2005	—	—	—	—	1.25	1.75

KM# 291   50 STOTINKI
5.0000 g., Copper-Zinc-Nickel, 22.5 mm. **Obv:** Value **Rev:** Pillar behind open book **Edge:** Reeded **Note:** Prev. KM#276.

Date	Mintage	F	VF	XF	Unc	BU
2007	500,000	—	—	—	—	1.50

KM# 254   LEV
7.0300 g., Bi-Metallic Copper-Nickel center in Brass ring, 24.3 mm. **Obv:** St. Ivan of Rila **Rev:** Denomination **Edge:** Reeded and plain sections

Date	Mintage	F	VF	XF	Unc	BU
2002	24,842,000	—	—	—	3.00	4.00
2002 Proof	10,000	Value: 10.00				

KM# 257   LEV
15.5500 g., 0.9990 Gold 0.4994 oz. AGW **Obv:** St. Ivan of Rila **Rev:** Large number one **Edge:** Plain

Date	Mintage	F	VF	XF	Unc	BU
2002 Proof	2,000	Value: 550				

KM# 290   1.95583 LEVA
20.0000 g., 0.9990 Silver Partially gold plated 0.6423 oz. ASW, 40 mm. **Subject:** Bulgaria in the EU **Obv:** National Arms **Rev:** Column and open window design **Rev. Designer:** Bogomil Nikolov and Elena Dimitrova

Date	Mintage	F	VF	XF	Unc	BU
2007 Proof	14,000	Value: 40.00				

KM# 304   2 LEVA
16.4000 g., 0.9990 Copper 0.5267 oz., 34.2 mm. **Subject:** Dechko, Uzunov 110th Anniversary of Birth **Obv:** National arms **Rev:** Petar Stoikov

Date	Mintage	F	VF	XF	Unc	BU
2009 Proof	8,000	Value: 15.00				

KM# 258   5 LEVA
1.2400 g., 0.9990 Gold 0.0398 oz. AGW **Obv:** Denomination **Rev:** Olympic archer **Edge:** Plain

Date	Mintage	F	VF	XF	Unc	BU
2002 Proof	12,000	Value: 47.50				

KM# 259   5 LEVA
1.2400 g., 0.9990 Gold 0.0398 oz. AGW **Obv:** Denomination **Rev:** Olympic cyclist **Edge:** Plain

Date	Mintage	F	VF	XF	Unc	BU
2002 Proof	12,000	Value: 47.50				

KM# 260   5 LEVA
1.2400 g., 0.9990 Gold 0.0398 oz. AGW **Obv:** Denomination **Rev:** Olympic fencing **Edge:** Plain

Date	Mintage	F	VF	XF	Unc	BU
2002 Proof	12,000	Value: 47.50				

KM# 261   5 LEVA
1.2400 g., 0.9990 Gold 0.0398 oz. AGW **Obv:** Denomination **Rev:** Olympic wrestling **Edge:** Plain

Date	Mintage	F	VF	XF	Unc	BU
2002 Proof	12,000	Value: 47.50				

KM# 262   5 LEVA
1.2400 g., 0.9990 Gold 0.0398 oz. AGW, 14 mm. **Obv:** Denomination **Rev:** Olympic gymnastics **Edge:** Plain

Date	Mintage	F	VF	XF	Unc	BU
2002 Proof	12,000	Value: 47.50				

KM# 263   5 LEVA
1.2400 g., 0.9990 Gold 0.0398 oz. AGW, 14 mm. **Obv:** Denomination **Rev:** Olympics founder Pierre du Coubertin **Edge:** Plain

Date	Mintage	F	VF	XF	Unc	BU
2002 Proof	17,000	Value: 47.50				

KM# 264   5 LEVA
1.2400 g., 0.9990 Gold 0.0398 oz. AGW, 14 mm. **Obv:** Denomination **Rev:** Olympic running **Edge:** Plain

Date	Mintage	F	VF	XF	Unc	BU
2002 Proof	12,000	Value: 47.50				

KM# 265   5 LEVA
1.2400 g., 0.9990 Gold 0.0398 oz. AGW, 14 mm. **Obv:** Denomination **Rev:** Olympic swimming **Edge:** Plain

Date	Mintage	F	VF	XF	Unc	BU
2002 Proof	12,000	Value: 47.50				

KM# 266   5 LEVA
1.2400 g., 0.9990 Gold 0.0398 oz. AGW, 14 mm. **Obv:** Denomination **Rev:** Olympic tennis **Edge:** Plain

Date	Mintage	F	VF	XF	Unc	BU
2002 Proof	12,000	Value: 47.50				

KM# 267   5 LEVA
1.2400 g., 0.9990 Gold 0.0398 oz. AGW, 14 mm. **Obv:** Denomination **Rev:** Olympic weight lifting **Edge:** Plain

Date	Mintage	F	VF	XF	Unc	BU
2002 Proof	12,000	Value: 47.50				

KM# 274   5 LEVA
15.0000 g., Copper-Nickel, 34.2 mm. **Subject:** Sourvakari **Obv:** National arms **Rev:** Multicolor children in winter clothes **Rev. Designer:** Stephan Nenov

Date	Mintage	F	VF	XF	Unc	BU
2002 Proof	5,000	Value: 15.00				

KM# 276 5 LEVA
15.0000 g., Copper-Nickel, 34.2 mm. **Obv:** National arms, date and denomination below **Rev:** Multicolor child on rocking horse **Edge:** Plain **Note:** Prev. KM#275.

Date	Mintage	F	VF	XF	Unc	BU
2003 Proof	10,000	Value: 35.00				

KM# 268 5 LEVA
28.2800 g., 0.9250 Silver 0.8410 oz. ASW, 38.5 mm. **Obv:** Denomination **Rev:** FIFA Soccer trophy cup **Edge:** reeded

Date	Mintage	F	VF	XF	Unc	BU
2003 Proof	50,000	Value: 37.50				

KM# 277 5 LEVA
15.0000 g., Copper-Nickel, 34.2 mm. **Subject:** Palm Sunday **Obv:** National Arms **Rev:** Bogomil Nikolov and Elena Dimitrova

Date	Mintage	F	VF	XF	Unc	BU
2004 Proof	10,000	Value: 15.00				

KM# 279 5 LEVA
15.0000 g., Copper-Nickel, 34.2 mm. **Subject:** Baba Marta **Obv:** National Arms **Rev:** Multicolor flora and butterfly **Rev. Designer:** Vanya Dimitrova

Date	Mintage	F	VF	XF	Unc	BU
2005 Proof	10,000	Value: 15.00				

KM# 284 5 LEVA
23.3000 g., 0.5000 Silver 0.3745 oz. ASW, 38.6 mm. **Subject:** Bulgaria Crafts - winemaking **Obv:** National Arms **Rev:** Multicolor grapes - wine caraffe **Rev. Designer:** Ivan Todorov and Plamen Dzhermanov

Date	Mintage	F	VF	XF	Unc	BU
2006 Proof	10,000	Value: 30.00				

KM# 296 5 LEVA
23.3000 g., 0.5000 Silver 0.3745 oz. ASW, 38.6 mm. **Subject:** Bulgarian Crafts - Carpet Weaving **Obv:** National Arms **Rev:** Ivan Todorov and Plamen Dzhermanov

Date	Mintage	F	VF	XF	Unc	BU
2007 Proof	7,000	Value: 30.00				

KM# 305 5 LEVA
23.3000 g., 0.9990 Silver 0.7483 oz. ASW, 38.6 mm. **Subject:** Bulgarian National Bank, 130th Anniversary **Obv:** Bank emblem **Obv. Designer:** Razvigor Kolev and Borislav Kyossev **Rev:** Multicolor lion mozaic, fragment of stained glass

Date	Mintage	F	VF	XF	Unc	BU
2009 Proof	4,000	Value: 45.00				

KM# 306 5 LEVA
0.5000 Silver **Subject:** Traditional Bulgarian Crafts - Pottery

Date	Mintage	F	VF	XF	Unc	BU
2009	—	—	—	—	—	35.00

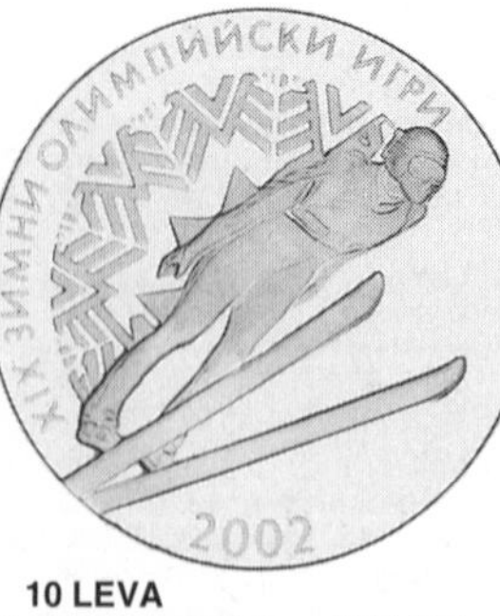

KM# 247 10 LEVA
23.3300 g., 0.9250 Silver 0.6938 oz. ASW, 38.5 mm. **Subject:** Olympics **Obv:** National arms, date and denomination below **Rev:** Ski jumper **Edge:** Plain with serial number

Date	Mintage	F	VF	XF	Unc	BU
2001 Proof	25,000	Value: 45.00				

KM# 246 10 LEVA
23.6000 g., 0.9250 Silver 0.7018 oz. ASW, 38.5 mm. **Subject:** Higher Education **Obv:** National arms, date and denomination below **Rev:** Graduate before building **Edge:** Plain

Date	Mintage	F	VF	XF	Unc	BU
2001 Proof	10,000	Value: 45.00				

KM# 275 10 LEVA
23.3000 g., 0.9250 Silver 0.6929 oz. ASW, 38.6 mm. **Obv:** National arms **Rev:** Head and Star of David **Rev. Designer:** Peter Stoikov

Date	Mintage	F	VF	XF	Unc	BU
2003 Proof	2,000	Value: 40.00				

KM# 270 10 LEVA
23.3300 g., 0.9990 Silver 0.7493 oz. ASW, 38.6 mm. **Subject:** National Theater Centennial **Edge:** Plain

Date	Mintage	F	VF	XF	Unc	BU
2004 Proof	5,000	Value: 50.00				

KM# 273 10 LEVA
23.2000 g., 0.9250 Silver 0.6899 oz. ASW, 38.5 mm. **Obv:** National arms, date and denomination below **Rev:** St. Nikolay Mirlikiisky Chudofvorez with gold plated crosses and halo **Edge:** Plain

Date	Mintage	F	VF	XF	Unc	BU
2004 Proof	10,000	Value: 45.00				

KM# 280 10 LEVA
23.3000 g., 0.9250 Silver 0.6929 oz. ASW, 38.6 mm. **Subject:** XX Olympic Games - Turino, Italy **Obv:** National Arms **Rev:** Short track speedskater **Rev. Designer:** Plamen Chernev

Date	Mintage	F	VF	XF	Unc	BU
2005 Proof	4,000	Value: 40.00				

KM# 283 10 LEVA
20.0000 g., 0.9990 Silver Partially gold plated 0.6423 oz. ASW, 40 mm. **Obv:** National Arms **Rev:** Ancient sculpture

Date	Mintage	F	VF	XF	Unc	BU
2005 Proof	10,000	Value: 40.00				

KM# 285 10 LEVA
23.3000 g., 0.9250 Silver 0.6929 oz. ASW, 38.6 mm. **Subject:** National Parks: Black Sea Coast **Obv:** National Arms **Rev:** Map and three circular motifs **Rev. Designer:** Eugenia Isankoa and Plamen Chernev

Date	Mintage	F	VF	XF	Unc	BU
2006 Proof	7,000	Value: 40.00				

KM# 286 10 LEVA
20.0000 g., 0.9990 Silver 0.6423 oz. ASW, 40 mm. **Subject:** Treasures of Bulgaria - Letnitsa **Obv:** National Arms **Rev:** Horseman statue **Rev. Designer:** Eugenie Evtimov

Date	Mintage	F	VF	XF	Unc	BU
2006 Proof	10,000	Value: 40.00				

KM# 295 10 LEVA
23.3000 g., 9.2500 Silver 6.9290 oz. ASW, 38.6 mm. **Subject:** National Parks - Pirin Mountain **Obv:** National Arms **Rev:** Vanya Dimitrova

Date	Mintage	F	VF	XF	Unc	BU
2007 Proof	6,000	Value: 40.00				

KM# 297 10 LEVA
20.0000 g., 0.9990 Silver Partially gold plated 0.6423 oz. ASW, 40 mm. **Subject:** Treasures of Bulgaria - Pegasus from Vayovo **Obv:** National Arms **Rev:** Pegasus forepart **Rev. Designer:** Razvigor Klov, Borislav Kyossev and Krassimis Angelov

Date	Mintage	F	VF	XF	Unc	BU
2007 Proof	10,000	Value: 40.00				

KM# 292 10 LEVA
31.1000 g., 0.9990 Silver 0.9988 oz. ASW, 40 mm. **Subject:** Boris Christov **Obv:** National arms **Obv. Legend:** БЪЛГАРСКА НАРОДНА БАНКА **Rev:** Early regal 1/2 length male figure facing holding orb **Rev. Legend:** ИМЕНИТИ БЪГАРСКИ ГЛАСОВЕ **Note:** Prev. KM#277.

Date	Mintage	F	VF	XF	Unc	BU
2007 Proof	10,000	Value: 45.00				

KM# 298 10 LEVA
23.3000 g., 0.9250 Silver 0.6929 oz. ASW, 38.6 mm. **Subject:** Bulgarian Liberation, 130th Anniversary **Obv:** National Arms **Rev:** Two figures in 19th century coats

Date	Mintage	F	VF	XF	Unc	BU
2008 Proof	10,000	Value: 40.00				

KM# 299 10 LEVA
23.3000 g., 0.9250 Silver 0.6929 oz. ASW, 38.6 mm. **Subject:** Shooting sports **Obv:** National Arms **Rev:** Target, bowhunter, rifleman **Rev. Designer:** Todor Todorov and Yana Vassileva

Date	Mintage	F	VF	XF	Unc	BU
2008 Proof	5,000	Value: 40.00				

KM# 300 10 LEVA
20.0000 g., 0.9990 Silver Partially gold plated 0.6423 oz. ASW, 40 mm. **Subject:** Treasures of Bulgaria - Sevt III **Obv:** Statue head of King Sevt III **Rev:** Elena Todorova and Todor Todorav

Date	Mintage	F	VF	XF	Unc	BU
2008 Proof	8,000	Value: 40.00				

KM# 301 10 LEVA
23.3000 g., 0.9250 Silver 0.6929 oz. ASW, 38.6 mm. **Subject:** Bulgarian Independence - 100th Anniversary **Rev:** Crowned shield **Rev. Designer:** Ivan Todorov

Date	Mintage	F	VF	XF	Unc	BU
2008 Proof	5,000	Value: 40.00				

KM# 302 10 LEVA
31.1000 g., 0.9990 Silver Partially gold plated 0.9988 oz. ASW, 40 mm. **Subject:** Great Bulgarian Voices: Nikolay Gyaurov **Obv:** National arms **Rev:** Elena Todorov and Todor Todorov

Date	Mintage	F	VF	XF	Unc	BU
2008 Proof	6,000	Value: 50.00				

KM# 269 20 LEVA
1.5500 g., 0.9990 Gold 0.0498 oz. AGW, 16 mm. **Obv:** Denomination **Rev:** Mother of God **Edge:** Plain

Date	Mintage	F	VF	XF	Unc	BU
2003 Proof	20,000	Value: 55.00				

KM# 287 20 LEVA
1.5500 g., 0.9990 Gold 0.0498 oz. AGW, 13.9 mm. **Subject:** Iconography St John the Baptist **Obv:** National Arms **Rev:** Saint facing **Rev. Designer:** Rada Dimitroua

Date	Mintage	F	VF	XF	Unc	BU
2006 Proof	12,000	Value: 60.00				

KM# 294 20 LEVA
1.5500 g., 0.9990 Gold 0.0498 oz. AGW, 13.9 mm. **Subject:** Iconography - St. George the Victorious **Rev:** St. George slaying dragon **Rev. Designer:** Plamen Chernev

Date	Mintage	F	VF	XF	Unc	BU
2007 Proof	8,000	Value: 60.00				

KM# 303 20 LEVA
1.5500 g., 0.9990 Gold 0.0498 oz. AGW, 13.9 mm. **Subject:** Tsar Boris I, the Baptist **Obv:** Half length figure facing **Rev:** Krassimir Angelov, Borislav Kyossev, Razvigov Kolev

Date	Mintage	F	VF	XF	Unc	BU
2008 Proof	8,000	Value: 60.00				

KM# 293 100 LEVA
8.6400 g., 0.9990 Gold 0.2775 oz. AGW **Subject:** Iconography - St. George the Victorious **Obv:** National Arms **Rev:** Plamen Chernev

Date	Mintage	F	VF	XF	Unc	BU
2007 Proof	1,500	Value: 350				

KM# 307 100 LEVA
0.9990 Gold **Subject:** Bulgarian Iconography - St. Dimitar the Wonder Worker

Date	Mintage	F	VF	XF	Unc	BU
2009	—	—	—	—	—	125

KM# 271 125 LEVA
7.7800 g., 0.9990 Gold 0.2499 oz. AGW, 21 mm. **Subject:** Bulgarian National Bank 125th Anniversary

Date	Mintage	F	VF	XF	Unc	BU
2004 Proof	3,000	Value: 300				

PIEFORTS

KM#	Date	Mintage	Identification	Mkt Val
P4	2004	5,000	10 Leva. 0.9990 Silver. 46.6600 g. 100 Years - National Theatre, 38.61mm.	75.00

PROOF SETS

KM#	Date	Mintage	Identification	Issue Price	Mkt Val
PS8	2002 (7)	10,000	KM#237-242, 254	—	25.00

CAMBODIA

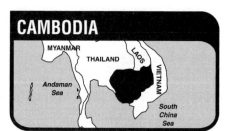

The State of Cambodia, formerly Democratic Kampuchea and the Khmer Republic, a land of paddy fields and forest-clad hills located on the Indo-Chinese peninsula, fronting on the Gulf of Thailand, has an area of 70,238 sq. mi. (181,040 sq. km.) and a population of *11.21 million. Capital: Phnom Penh. Agriculture is the basis of the economy, with rice the chief crop. Native industries include cattle breeding, weaving and rice milling. Rubber, cattle, corn, and timber are exported.

RULERS
Kings of Cambodia
Norodom Sihanouk, 1991-1993
Chairman, Supreme National Council
King, 1993-

KINGDOM
1993 -
DECIMAL COINAGE

KM# 98 500 RIELS
19.9200 g., Brass, 38.7 mm. **Subject:** Angkor Wat
Obv: Armless statue of Jayavarman VII **Rev:** View of Angkor Wat
in center **Edge:** Reeded

Date	Mintage	F	VF	XF	Unc	BU
2001	28,000	—	—	—	7.50	10.00

KM# 99 3000 RIELS
1.2441 g., 0.9999 Gold 0.0400 oz. AGW, 13.92 mm.
Subject: Angkor Wat **Obv:** Armless statue of Jayavarman VII
Rev: View of Angkor Wat in center **Edge:** Reeded

Date	Mintage	F	VF	XF	Unc	BU
2001	28,000	—	—	—	70.00	80.00

KM# 100 3000 RIELS
20.0000 g., 0.9250 Silver 0.5948 oz. ASW, 38.7 mm.
Subject: Buddha **Obv:** Armless statue of Jayavarman VII
Rev: Radiant Buddha next to a carved Buddha face
Edge: Reeded

Date	Mintage	F	VF	XF	Unc	BU
2001 Proof	10,000	Value: 55.00				

KM# 101 3000 RIELS
20.0000 g., 0.9250 Silver 0.5948 oz. ASW, 38.7 mm.
Subject: Apsara Dance **Obv:** Armless statue of Jayavarman VII
Rev: Dancer next to multicolor carpet pattern **Edge:** Reeded

Date	Mintage	F	VF	XF	Unc	BU
2001 Proof	10,000	Value: 60.00				

KM# 103 3000 RIELS
20.0000 g., 0.9990 Silver 0.6423 oz. ASW, 38.7 mm. **Obv:** King
Jayavarman VII (1162-1201) **Rev:** Multicolor Tutankhamen's
mask **Edge:** Reeded

Date	Mintage	F	VF	XF	Unc	BU
2004 Proof	9,100	Value: 65.00				

KM# 104 3000 RIELS
1.2440 g., 0.9990 Gold 0.0400 oz. AGW, 13.92 mm. **Obv:** King
Jayavarman VII (1162-1201) **Rev:** Sphinx and pyramid
Edge: Reeded

Date	Mintage	F	VF	XF	Unc	BU
2004 Proof	27,900	Value: 95.00				

KM# 124 3000 RIELS
1.2400 g., 0.9990 Gold 0.0398 oz. AGW, 13.92 mm.
Rev: Pyramids

Date	Mintage	F	VF	XF	Unc	BU
2004	—	—	—	—	—	80.00

KM# 126 3000 RIELS
1.2200 g., 0.9990 Gold 0.0392 oz. AGW, 13.92 mm. **Rev:** Taj
Mahal

Date	Mintage	F	VF	XF	Unc	BU
2005	—	—	—	—	—	80.00

KM# 127 3000 RIELS
31.1050 g., Silver, 38.7 mm. **Rev:** Indian Dancer, multicolor

Date	Mintage	F	VF	XF	Unc	BU
2005	—	Value: 65.00				

KM# 129 3000 RIELS
1.2200 g., 0.9990 Gold 0.0392 oz. AGW, 13.92 mm.
Rev: Colesum in Rome

Date	Mintage	F	VF	XF	Unc	BU
2006	—	—	—	—	—	80.00

KM# 130 3000 RIELS
Silver, 38.7 mm. **Rev:** Roman soldier, multicolor

Date	Mintage	F	VF	XF	Unc	BU
2006 Proof	—	Value: 80.00				

KM# 110 3000 RIELS
31.1050 g., 0.9990 Silver 0.9990 oz. ASW, 40.7 mm.
Subject: Year of the Dog **Rev:** Multicolor St. Bernard

Date	Mintage	F	VF	XF	Unc	BU
2006 Prooflike	4,000	—	—	—	—	80.00

KM# 111 3000 RIELS
31.1050 g., 0.9990 Silver 0.9990 oz. ASW, 40.7 mm.
Subject: Year of the Dog **Rev:** Multicolor Bloodhound

Date	Mintage	F	VF	XF	Unc	BU
2006 Prooflike	4,000	—	—	—	—	80.00

KM# 112 3000 RIELS
31.1050 g., 0.9990 Silver 0.9990 oz. ASW, 40.7 mm.
Subject: Year of the Dog **Rev:** Multicolor Siberian Huskey

Date	Mintage	F	VF	XF	Unc	BU
2006 Prooflike	4,000	—	—	—	—	80.00

KM# 113 3000 RIELS
31.1050 g., 0.9990 Silver 0.9990 oz. ASW, 40.7 mm.
Subject: Year of the Dog **Rev:** Multicolor Shar Pei

Date	Mintage	F	VF	XF	Unc	BU
2006 Prooflike	4,000	—	—	—	—	80.00

KM# 114 3000 RIELS
31.1050 g., 0.9990 Silver 0.9990 oz. ASW, 40.7 mm.
Subject: Year of the Dog **Rev:** Multicolor Borzaya

Date	Mintage	F	VF	XF	Unc	BU
2006 Prooflike	51,000	—	—	—	—	80.00

KM# 115 3000 RIELS
31.1050 g., 0.9990 Silver 0.9990 oz. ASW, 40.7 mm.
Subject: Year of the Dog **Rev:** Multicolor Labrador

Date	Mintage	F	VF	XF	Unc	BU
2006 Prooflike	51,000	—	—	—	—	80.00

KM# 116 3000 RIELS
31.1050 g., 0.9990 Silver 0.9990 oz. ASW, 40.7 mm.
Subject: Year of the Dog **Rev:** Multicolor Russian Spaniel

Date	Mintage	F	VF	XF	Unc	BU
2006 Prooflike	51,000	—	—	—	—	80.00

KM# 117 3000 RIELS
31.1050 g., 0.9990 Silver 0.9990 oz. ASW, 40.7 mm.
Subject: Year of the Dog **Rev:** Multiocolor Newfoundland

Date	Mintage	F	VF	XF	Unc	BU
2006 Prooflike	51,000	—	—	—	—	80.00

KM# 132 3000 RIELS
1.2200 g., 0.9990 Gold 0.0392 oz. AGW, 13.92 mm.
Rev: Borobudur Temple, Indonesia

Date	Mintage	F	VF	XF	Unc	BU
2007	—	—	—	—	—	80.00

KM# 133 3000 RIELS
Silver, 38.7 mm. **Rev:** Legomo dancer, multicolor

Date	Mintage	F	VF	XF	Unc	BU
2007 Proof	—	Value: 80.00				

KM# 118 3000 RIELS
31.1050 g., 0.9990 Silver 0.9990 oz. ASW, 40.7 mm.
Subject: Year of the Pig **Rev:** Multicolor pig

Date	Mintage	F	VF	XF	Unc	BU
2007 Prooflike	—	—	—	—	—	80.00

KM# 121 3000 RIELS
1.2400 g., 0.9990 Gold 0.0398 oz. AGW, 13.9 mm.
Subject: Statue torso **Rev:** Shwe Dragon Pagoda, Mynamar

Date	Mintage	F	VF	XF	Unc	BU
2008 Proof	—	Value: 50.00				

KM# 123 3000 RIELS
31.1035 g., 0.9990 Silver 0.9990 oz. ASW, 40.7 mm.
Obv: Statue torso **Rev:** Multicolor Padaung

Date	Mintage	F	VF	XF	Unc	BU
2009 Proof	—	Value: 75.00				

KM# 102 10000 RIELS
31.1035 g., 0.9990 Bi-Metallic Gold center in silver ring. 0.9990 oz., 40.7 mm. **Subject:** Angkor Wat **Obv:** Armless statue of Jayavarman **Rev:** Multicolor holographic view of Angkor Wat in center **Edge:** Reeded

Date	Mintage	F	VF	XF	Unc	BU
2001 Proof	3,000	Value: 325				

KM# 125 10000 RIELS
31.1050 g., 0.9990 Silver 0.9990 oz. ASW, 40.7 mm. **Rev:** Great Wall of China, holographic insert

Date	Mintage	F	VF	XF	Unc	BU
2003 Proof	—	Value: 300				

KM# 105 10000 RIELS
31.1035 g., 0.9990 Silver 0.9990 oz. ASW, 40.7 mm. **Obv:** King Jayavarman VII (1162-1201) **Rev:** Sphinx and pyramid on holographic gold insert **Edge:** Reeded

Date	Mintage	F	VF	XF	Unc	BU
2004 Proof	2,100	Value: 300				

KM# 119 10000 RIELS
31.1050 g., 0.9990 Silver 0.9990 oz. ASW, 38.7 mm. **Subject:** Zheng He 600th Anniversary **Rev:** Sailing ship with latent image

Date	Mintage	F	VF	XF	Unc	BU
2005 Proof	200	Value: 75.00				

KM# 120 10000 RIELS
31.1050 g., 0.9990 Silver 0.9990 oz. ASW, 38.7 mm. **Subject:** Zheng He 600th Anniversary **Rev:** Multicolor figure standing

Date	Mintage	F	VF	XF	Unc	BU
2005 Proof	200	Value: 75.00				

KM# 128 10000 RIELS
31.1050 g., 0.9990 Silver 0.9990 oz. ASW, 40.7 mm. **Rev:** Taj Mahal in multicolor hologram at center

Date	Mintage	F	VF	XF	Unc	BU
2005 Proof	—	Value: 300				

KM# 131 10000 RIELS
Silver, 40.7 mm. **Rev:** Colesum in multicolor hologram

Date	Mintage	F	VF	XF	Unc	BU
2006 Proof	—	Value: 300				

KM# 134 10000 RIELS
31.1050 g., Silver, 40.7 mm. **Rev:** Boraburdur temple, Indonesia

Date	Mintage	F	VF	XF	Unc	BU
2007	—	—	—	—	—	300

KM# 122 10000 RIELS
31.1035 g., 0.9990 Silver 0.9990 oz. ASW, 40.7 mm. **Obv:** Statue torso **Rev:** Hologram of Shwe Dragon Pagoda, Mynamar

Date	Mintage	F	VF	XF	Unc	BU
2009 Proof	—	Value: 75.00				

CANADA

Canada is located to the north of the United States, and spans the full breadth of the northern portion of North America from Atlantic to Pacific oceans, except for the State of Alaska. It has a total area of 3,850,000 sq. mi. (9,971,550 sq. km.) and a population of 30.29 million. Capital: Ottawa.

Canada is a member of the Commonwealth of Nations. Elizabeth II is Head of State as Queen of Canada.

RULER
British 1763-

MONETARY SYSTEM
1 Dollar = 100 Cents

CONFEDERATION

CIRCULATION COINAGE

KM# 289 CENT
Comp.: Copper Plated Steel **Ruler:** Elizabeth II **Obv.:** Crowned head right **Obv. Des.:** Dora dePédery-Hunt **Rev.:** Maple twig design **Rev. Des.:** George E. Kruger-Gray **Edge:** Round and plain **Size:** 19.1 mm.

Date	Mintage	MS-63	Proof
2001	919,358,000	0.30	—
2001P Proof	—	—	5.00
2003	92,219,775	0.30	—
2003P Proof	—	—	5.00
2003P	235,936,799	1.50	—

KM# 445 CENT
Comp.: Copper Plated Steel **Ruler:** Elizabeth II **Subject:** Elizabeth II Golden Jubilee **Obv.:** Crowned head right, Jubilee commemorative dates 1952-2002 **Obv. Des.:** Dora dePédery-Hunt **Rev.:** Denomination above maple leaves **Rev. Des.:** George E. Kruger-Gray **Edge:** Plain **Size:** 19.1 mm.

Date	Mintage	MS-63	Proof
ND(2002)	716,366,000	0.75	—
ND(2002)P	114,212,000	1.00	—
ND(2002)P Proof	32,642	—	5.00

KM# 445a CENT
Comp.: 0.9250 Silver **Ruler:** Elizabeth II **Subject:** Elizabeth II Golden Jubilee **Obv.:** Crowned head right, Jubilee commemorative dates 1952-2002 **Obv. Des.:** Dora dePédery-Hunt **Rev.:** Denomination above maple leaves **Rev. Des.:** George E. Kruger-Gray

Date	Mintage	MS-63	Proof
ND(2002)	21,537	—	3.00

Note: In sets only

KM# 490 CENT
Weight: 2.3500 g. **Comp.:** Copper Plated Zinc **Ruler:** Elizabeth II **Obv.:** New effigy of Queen Elizabeth II right **Obv. Des.:** Susanna Blunt **Rev.:** Two maple leaves **Edge:** Plain **Size:** 19.1 mm.

Date	Mintage	MS-63	Proof
2003	56,877,144	0.25	—
2004	653,317,000	0.25	—
2004 Proof	—	—	2.50
2005	759,658,000	0.25	—
2005 Proof	—	—	2.50
2006	886,275,000	0.25	—
2006 Proof	—	—	2.50

KM# 490a CENT
Weight: 2.2500 g. **Comp.:** Copper Plated Steel **Ruler:** Elizabeth II **Obv.:** Bust right **Obv. Des.:** Susanna Blunt **Rev.:** Two maple leaves **Rev. Des.:** G. E. Kruger-Gray **Size:** 19.5 mm.

Date	Mintage	MS-63	Proof
2003P	591,257,000	0.25	—
2003 WP	Inc. above	0.25	—
2004P	134,906,000	0.25	—
2005P	30,525,000	0.25	—
2006P	137,733,000	0.25	—
2006(ml)	Inc. above	0.25	—
2007(ml)	938,270,000	0.25	—
2007(ml) Proof	—	—	2.50
2008(ml)	—	0.25	—
2008(ml) Proof	—	—	2.50
2009(ml)	—	0.25	—
2009(ml) Proof	—	—	2.50

KM# 468 CENT
Comp.: Copper **Ruler:** Elizabeth II **Subject:** 50th Anniversary of the Coronation of Elizabeth II **Obv.:** 1953 effigy of the Queen, Jubilee commemorative dates 1952-2002 **Obv. Des.:** Mary Gillick

Date	Mintage	MS-63	Proof
ND(2002) Proof	—	—	2.50

KM# 490b CENT
Comp.: Copper Plated Zinc **Ruler:** Elizabeth II **Obv.:** Head right **Rev.:** Maple leaf, selectively gold plated **Note:** Bound into Annual Report.

Date	Mintage	MS-63	Proof
2004 Proof	7,746		

KM# 410 3 CENTS
Weight: 3.1100 g. **Comp.:** 0.9250 Silver Gilt 0.0925 oz. ASW **Ruler:** Elizabeth II **Subject:** 1st Canadian Postage Stamp **Obv.:** Crowned head right **Obv. Des.:** Dora dePédery-Hunt **Rev.:** Partial stamp design **Rev. Des.:** Sandford Fleming **Edge:** Plain **Size:** 21.3 mm.

Date	Mintage	MS-63	Proof
2001 Proof	59,573	—	12.50

KM# 182 5 CENTS
Weight: 4.6000 g. **Comp.:** Copper-Nickel **Ruler:** Elizabeth II **Obv.:** Crowned head right **Obv. Des.:** Dora dePedery-Hunt **Rev.:** Beaver on rock divides dates and denomination **Rev. Des.:** George E. Kruger-Gray **Edge:** Plain **Size:** 19.55 mm.

Date	Mintage	MS-63	Proof
2001	30,035,000	12.50	—
2001P Proof	—	—	10.00
2003	—	0.30	—

KM# 182b 5 CENTS
Weight: 3.9000 g. **Comp.:** Nickel Plated Steel **Ruler:** Elizabeth II **Obv.:** Crowned head right **Obv. Des.:** Dora dePedery-Hunt **Rev.:** Beaver on rock divides date and denomination **Rev. Des.:** George E. Kruger-Gray **Edge:** Plain **Size:** 21.2 mm.

Date	Mintage	MS-63	Proof
2001 P	136,650,000	0.35	—
2003 P	32,986,921	0.35	—

KM# 182a 5 CENTS **Weight:** 5.3500 g. **Comp.:** 0.9250 Silver 0.1591 oz. ASW **Ruler:** Elizabeth II **Obv.:** Crowned head right **Obv. Des.:** Dora dePedery-Hunt **Rev.:** Beaver on rock divides date and denomination **Rev. Des.:** George E. Kruger-Gray **Size:** 21.2 mm.

Date	Mintage	MS-63	Proof
2001 Proof	—	—	5.00
2003 Proof	—	—	5.00

KM# 413 5 CENTS **Weight:** 5.3500 g. **Comp.:** 0.9250 Silver 0.1591 oz. ASW **Ruler:** Elizabeth II **Subject:** Royal Military College **Obv.:** Crowned head right **Rev. Des.:** Marching cadets and arch **Rev. Des.:** Gerald T. Locklin **Edge:** Plain **Size:** 21.2 mm.

Date	Mintage	MS-63	Proof
2001 Proof	25,834	—	7.00

KM# 446 5 CENTS **Comp.:** Nickel Plated Steel **Ruler:** Elizabeth II **Subject:** Elizabeth II Golden Jubilee **Obv.:** Crowned head right, Jubilee commemorative dates 1952-2002 **Obv. Des.:** Dora dePedery-Hunt **Rev. Des.:** George E. Kruger-Gray **Size:** 21.2 mm. **Note:** Magnetic.

Date	Mintage	MS-63	Proof
ND(2002)P	135,960,000	0.45	—
ND(2002)P Proof	32,642	—	10.00

KM# 446a 5 CENTS **Comp.:** 0.9250 Silver **Ruler:** Elizabeth II **Subject:** Elizabeth II Golden Jubilee **Obv.:** Queen, Jubilee commemorative dates 1952-2002 **Size:** 21.2 mm.

Date	Mintage	MS-63	Proof
ND(2002) Proof	21,573	—	11.50

KM# 453 5 CENTS **Comp.:** 0.9250 Silver **Ruler:** Elizabeth II **Subject:** Vimy Ridge - WWI **Obv.:** Crowned head right **Rev.:** Vimy Ridge Memorial, allegorical figure and dates 1917-2002 **Rev. Des.:** S. A. Allward **Size:** 21.2 mm.

Date	Mintage	MS-63	Proof
ND(2002) Proof	22,646	—	11.50

KM# 491 5 CENTS **Weight:** 3.9300 g. **Comp.:** Nickel Plated Steel **Ruler:** Elizabeth II **Obv.:** Bare head right **Obv. Des.:** Susanna Blunt **Rev.:** Beaver divides date and denomination **Rev. Des.:** George E. Kruger-Gray **Size:** 21.2 mm. **Note:** Magnetic.

Date	Mintage	MS-63	Proof
2003P	61,392,180	0.45	—
2004P	132,097,000	0.45	—
2004P Proof	—	—	2.50
2005P	89,664,000	0.45	—
2005P Proof	—	—	2.50
2006P	139,308,000	0.50	—
2006P Proof	—	—	2.50
2006(ml)	221,472,000	0.45	—
2006(ml) Proof	—	—	2.50
2007(ml)	—	0.45	—
2007(ml) Proof	—	—	2.50
2008(ml)	—	0.45	—
2008(ml) Proof	—	—	2.50
2009(ml)	—	0.45	—
2009(ml) Proof	—	—	2.50

KM# 469 5 CENTS **Comp.:** 0.9250 Silver **Ruler:** Elizabeth II **Subject:** 50th Anniversary of the Coronation of Elizabeth II **Obv.:** Crowned head right, Jubilee commemorative dates 1953-2003 **Obv. Des.:** Mary Gillick **Size:** 21.2 mm.

Date	Mintage	MS-63	Proof
ND(2003) Proof	21,573	—	11.50

KM# 491a 5 CENTS **Weight:** 5.3500 g. **Comp.:** 0.9250 Silver 0.1591 oz. ASW **Ruler:** Elizabeth II **Obv.:** Crowned head right **Obv. Des.:** Susanna Blunt **Rev.:** Beaver divides date and denomination **Edge:** Plain **Size:** 21.1 mm.

Date	Mintage	MS-63	Proof
2004 Proof	—	—	3.50

KM# 506 5 CENTS **Weight:** 5.3500 g. **Comp.:** 0.9250 Silver 0.1591 oz. ASW **Ruler:** Elizabeth II **Obv.:** Bare head right **Rev.:** "Victory " design of the KM-40 reverse **Edge:** Plain **Shape:** 12-sided **Size:** 21.3 mm.

Date	Mintage	MS-63	Proof
ND(2004) Proof	20,019	—	15.00

KM# 627 5 CENTS **Weight:** 3.9000 g. **Comp.:** Nickel **Ruler:** Elizabeth II **Subject:** 60th Anniversary, Victory in Europe 1945-2005 **Obv.:** Head right **Rev.:** Large V **Edge:** Plain **Size:** 21.18 mm.

Date	Mintage	MS-63	Proof
ND2005P	59,269,192	4.50	—

KM# 758 5 CENTS **Weight:** 5.3000 g. **Comp.:** 0.9250 Silver 0.1576 oz. ASW **Ruler:** Elizabeth II **Obv.:** George VI head left **Rev.:** Torch and large V

Date	Mintage	MS-63	Proof
ND(1945-2005)	42,792	—	35.00

KM# 758a 5 CENTS **Weight:** 5.3000 g. **Comp.:** 0.9250 Silver selectively gold plated 0.1576 oz. ASW **Ruler:** Elizabeth II **Obv.:** George VI head left **Rev.:** Torch and large V **Note:** Bound into Annual Report

Date	Mintage	MS-63	Proof
ND(1945-2005) Proof	6,065	—	40.00

KM# 491b 5 CENTS **Comp.:** Copper-Nickel **Ruler:** Elizabeth II **Obv.:** Bust right **Rev.:** Beaver

Date	Mintage	MS-63	Proof
2006	43,008,000	5.00	—

KM# 412a 10 CENTS **Weight:** 2.4000 g. **Comp.:** 0.9250 Silver 0.0714 oz. ASW **Ruler:** Elizabeth II **Subject:** Year of the Volunteer **Obv.:** Crowned head right **Rev.:** 3 portraits left above banner, radiant sun below **Edge:** Reeded **Size:** 18 mm.

Date	Mintage	MS-63	Proof
2001P Proof	40,634	—	9.00

KM# 183b 10 CENTS **Comp.:** Nickel Plated Steel **Ruler:** Elizabeth II **Obv.:** Crowned head right **Obv. Des.:** Dora dePedery-Hunt **Rev.:** Bluenose sailing left, date at right, denomination below **Rev. Des.:** Emanuel Hahn **Edge:** Reeded **Size:** 18.03 mm.

Date	Mintage	MS-63	Proof
2001 P	266,000,000	0.45	—
2003 P	162,398,000	0.20	—

KM# 183a 10 CENTS **Weight:** 2.4000 g. **Comp.:** 0.9250 Silver 0.0714 oz. ASW **Ruler:** Elizabeth II **Obv.:** Crowned head right **Rev.:** Bluenose sailing left, date at right, denomination below **Size:** 18.03 mm.

Date	Mintage	MS-63	Proof
2001 Proof	—	—	5.00
2002 Proof	—	—	7.50
2003 Proof	—	—	7.50

KM# 412 10 CENTS **Weight:** 1.7700 g. **Comp.:** Nickel Plated Steel **Ruler:** Elizabeth II **Subject:** Year of the Volunteer **Obv.:** Crowned head right **Rev.:** Three portraits left and radiant sun **Edge:** Reeded **Size:** 18 mm.

Date	Mintage	MS-63	Proof
2001P	224,714,000	4.50	—

KM# 447 10 CENTS **Weight:** 1.7700 g. **Comp.:** Nickel Plated Steel **Ruler:** Elizabeth II **Subject:** Elizabeth II Golden Jubilee **Obv.:** Crowned head right, Jubilee commemorative dates 1952-2002 **Size:** 18 mm.

Date	Mintage	MS-63	Proof
ND(2002)P	252,563,000	1.00	—
ND(2002) Proof	32,642	—	2.50

KM# 447a 10 CENTS **Comp.:** 0.9250 Silver **Ruler:** Elizabeth II **Subject:** Elizabeth II Golden Jubilee **Obv.:** Crowned head right, Jubilee commemorative dates 1952-2002 **Size:** 18 mm.

Date	Mintage	MS-63	Proof
ND(2002) Proof	21,537	—	12.50

KM# 492 10 CENTS **Weight:** 1.7700 g. **Comp.:** Nickel Plated Steel **Ruler:** Elizabeth II **Obv.:** Head right **Obv. Des.:** Susanna Blunt **Rev.:** Bluenose sailing left **Size:** 18 mm.

Date	Mintage	MS-63	Proof
2003P	—	1.25	—
2004	211,924,000	0.60	—
2004P Proof	—	—	2.50
2005P	212,175,000	0.60	—
2005P Proof	—	—	2.50
2006P	312,122,000	0.60	—
2006P Proof	—	—	2.50

Date	Mintage	MS-63	Proof
2007(ml) Straight 7	304,110,000	0.60	—
2007(ml) Curved 7	Inc. above	0.60	—
2007(ml) Proof	—	—	2.50
2008(ml)	—	0.60	—
2008(ml) Proof	—	—	2.50
2009(ml)	—	0.60	—
2009(ml) Proof	—	—	2.50

KM# 470 10 CENTS **Weight:** 2.3200 g. **Comp.:** 0.9250 Silver 0.0690 oz. ASW **Ruler:** Elizabeth II **Subject:** 50th Anniversary of the Coronation of Elizabeth II **Obv.:** Head right **Rev.:** Bluenose sailing left

Date	Mintage	MS-63	Proof
ND(2003) Proof	21,537	—	12.00

KM# 492a 10 CENTS **Weight:** 2.4000 g. **Comp.:** 0.9250 Silver 0.0714 oz. ASW **Ruler:** Elizabeth II **Obv.:** Bare head right **Obv. Des.:** Susanna Blunt **Rev.:** Sailboat **Edge:** Reeded **Size:** 18 mm.

Date	Mintage	MS-63	Proof
2004 Proof	—	—	5.00

KM# 524 10 CENTS **Weight:** 2.4000 g. **Comp.:** 0.9250 Silver 0.0714 oz. ASW **Ruler:** Elizabeth II **Subject:** Golf, Championship of Canada, Centennial. **Obv.:** Head right **Size:** 18 mm.

Date	Mintage	MS-63	Proof
2004	39,486	12.50	—

KM# 184 25 CENTS **Weight:** 5.0700 g. **Comp.:** Nickel **Ruler:** Elizabeth II **Obv.:** Crowned head right **Obv. Des.:** Dora dePedery-Hunt **Rev.:** Caribou left, denomination above, date at right **Rev. Des.:** Emanuel Hahn **Size:** 23.88 mm.

Date	Mintage	MS-63	Proof
2001	8,415,000	5.00	—
2001 Proof	—	—	7.50

KM# 184b 25 CENTS **Weight:** 4.4000 g. **Comp.:** Nickel Plated Steel **Ruler:** Elizabeth II **Obv.:** Crowned head right **Rev.:** Caribou left, denomination above, date at right **Size:** 23.88 mm.

Date	Mintage	MS-63	Proof
2001 P	55,773,000	0.95	—
2001 P Proof	—	—	5.00
2002 P	156,105,000	2.50	—
2002 P Proof	—	—	5.00
2003 P	87,647,000	2.50	—
2003 P Proof	—	—	5.00

KM# 184a 25 CENTS **Weight:** 5.9000 g. **Comp.:** 0.9250 Silver 0.1755 oz. ASW **Ruler:** Elizabeth II **Obv.:** Crowned head right **Rev.:** Caribou left, denomination above, date at right **Size:** 23.88 mm.

Date	Mintage	MS-63	Proof
2001 Proof	—	—	6.50
2003 Proof	—	—	6.50

KM# 419 25 CENTS **Weight:** 4.4000 g. **Comp.:** Nickel Plated Steel **Ruler:** Elizabeth II **Subject:** Canada Day **Obv.:** Crowned head right **Rev.:** Maple leaf at center, children holding hands below **Rev. Des.:** Silke Ware **Edge:** Reeded **Size:** 23.9 mm.

Date	Mintage	MS-63	Proof
2001	96,352	7.00	—

KM# 448 25 CENTS **Weight:** 4.4000 g. **Comp.:** Nickel Plated Steel **Ruler:** Elizabeth II **Subject:** Elizabeth II Golden Jubilee **Obv.:** Crowned head right **Rev.:** Caribou left **Size:** 23.9 mm.

Date	Mintage	MS-63	Proof
ND(2002)P	152,485,000	2.00	—
ND(2002)P Proof	32,642	—	6.00

KM# 448a 25 CENTS **Comp.:** 0.9250 Silver **Ruler:** Elizabeth II **Subject:** Elizabeth II Golden Jubilee **Obv.:** Crowned head right, Jubilee commemorative dates 1952-2002 **Size:** 23.9 mm.

Date	Mintage	MS-63	Proof
ND(2002) Proof	100,000	—	12.50

KM# 451 25 CENTS **Weight:** 4.4000 g. **Comp.:** Nickel Plated Steel **Ruler:** Elizabeth II **Rev.:** Small Human figures supporting large maple leaf **Size:** 23.9 mm.

Date	Mintage	MS-63	Proof
ND(1952-2002)P	30,627,000	5.00	—

KM# 451a 25 CENTS **Weight:** 4.4000 g. **Comp.:** Nickel Plated Steel **Ruler:** Elizabeth II **Subject:** Canada Day **Obv.:** Crowned head right **Rev.:** Human figures supporting large red maple leaf **Edge:** Reeded **Size:** 23.9 mm.

Date	Mintage	MS-63	Proof
ND(1952-2002)P	49,903	6.00	—

KM# 471 25 CENTS **Weight:** 5.9000 g. **Comp.:** 0.9250 Silver 0.1755 oz. ASW **Ruler:** Elizabeth II **Subject:** 50th Anniversary of the Coronation of Elizabeth II **Obv.:** 1953 effigy of the Queen, Jubilee commemorative dates 1952-2002 **Obv. Des.:** Mary Gillick **Size:** 23.9 mm.

Date	Mintage	MS-63	Proof
ND(2002) Proof	21,537	—	12.50

KM# 493 25 CENTS **Weight:** 4.4500 g. **Comp.:** Nickel Plated Steel **Ruler:** Elizabeth II **Obv.:** Bare head right **Obv. Des.:** Susanna Blunt **Size:** 23.9 mm.

Date	Mintage	MS-63	Proof
2003P	66,861,633	2.00	—
2003P W	—	—	—
2004P	177,466,000	2.50	—
2004P Proof	—	—	5.00
2005P	206,346,000	2.50	—
2005P Proof	—	—	5.00
2006P	423,189,000	2.50	—
2006P Proof	—	—	5.00
2007(ml)	274,763,000	2.50	—
2007(ml) Proof	—	—	5.00
2008(ml)	—	2.50	—
2008(ml) Proof	—	—	5.00
2009(ml)	—	2.50	—
2009(ml) Proof	—	—	5.00

KM# 474 25 CENTS **Weight:** 4.4000 g. **Comp.:** 0.9250 Silver 0.1308 oz. ASW **Ruler:** Elizabeth II **Subject:** Canada Day **Obv.:** Queens head right **Rev.:** Polar bear and red colored maple leaves **Size:** 23.9 mm.

Date	Mintage	MS-63	Proof
2003 Proof	—	—	12.00

KM# 493a 25 CENTS **Weight:** 5.9000 g. **Comp.:** 0.9250 Silver 0.1755 oz. ASW **Ruler:** Elizabeth II **Obv.:** Bare head right **Obv. Des.:** Suanne Blunt **Rev.:** Caribou **Edge:** Reeded **Size:** 23.9 mm.

Date	Mintage	MS-63	Proof
2004 Proof	—	—	6.50

KM# 510 25 CENTS **Weight:** 4.4000 g. **Comp.:** Nickel Plated Steel **Ruler:** Elizabeth II **Obv.:** Bare head right **Rev.:** Red Poppy in center of maple leaf **Edge:** Reeded **Size:** 23.9 mm.

Date	Mintage	MS-63	Proof
2004	28,500,000	5.00	—

KM# 510a 25 CENTS **Weight:** 5.9000 g. **Comp.:** 0.9250 Silver 0.1755 oz. ASW **Ruler:** Elizabeth II **Obv.:** Bare head right **Rev.:** Poppy at center of maple leaf, selectively gold plated **Edge:** Reeded **Size:** 23.9 mm. **Note:** Housed in Annual Report.

Date	Mintage	MS-63	Proof
2004 Proof	12,677	—	20.00

KM# 525 25 CENTS **Weight:** 4.4000 g. **Comp.:** Nickel Plated Steel **Ruler:** Elizabeth II **Obv.:** Bare head right **Rev.:** Maple leaf, colorized **Size:** 23.9 mm.

Date	Mintage	MS-63	Proof
2004	16,028	8.00	—

KM# 628 25 CENTS **Weight:** 4.4600 g. **Comp.:** Nickel Plated Steel **Ruler:** Elizabeth II **Subject:** First Settlement, Ile Ste Croix 1604-2004 **Obv.:** Bare head right **Rev.:** Sailing ship Bonne-Renommee **Size:** 23.9 mm.

Date	Mintage	MS-63	Proof
ND2004P	15,400,000	5.00	—

KM# 698 25 CENTS **Weight:** 4.4000 g. **Comp.:** Nickel Plated Steel **Ruler:** Elizabeth II **Rev.:** Santa, colorized

Date	Mintage	MS-63	Proof
2004	62,777	5.00	—

KM# 699 25 CENTS **Weight:** 4.4000 g. **Comp.:** Nickel Plated Steel **Ruler:** Elizabeth II **Series:** Canada Day **Rev.:** Moose head, humorous **Size:** 23.9 mm.

Date	Mintage	MS-63	Proof
2004	44,752	5.00	—

KM# 529 25 CENTS **Weight:** 4.4300 g. **Comp.:** Nickel Plated Steel **Ruler:** Elizabeth II **Subject:** WWII, 60th Anniversary **Obv.:** Head right **Rev.:** Three soldiers and flag **Size:** 23.9 mm.

Date	Mintage	MS-63	Proof
2005	3,500	20.00	—

KM# 530 25 CENTS **Weight:** 4.4300 g. **Comp.:** Nickel Plated Steel **Ruler:** Elizabeth II **Subject:** Alberta **Obv.:** Head right **Size:** 23.9 mm.

Date	Mintage	MS-63	Proof
2005P	20,640,000	7.00	—

KM# 531 25 CENTS **Weight:** 4.4300 g. **Comp.:** Nickel Plated Steel **Ruler:** Elizabeth II **Subject:** Canada Day **Obv.:** Head right **Rev.:** Beaver, colorized **Size:** 23.9 mm.

Date	Mintage	MS-63	Proof
2005P	58,370	8.50	—

KM# 532 25 CENTS **Weight:** 4.4300 g. **Comp.:** Nickel Plated Steel **Ruler:** Elizabeth II **Subject:** Saskatchewan **Obv.:** Head right **Size:** 23.9 mm.

Date	Mintage	MS-63	Proof
2005P	19,290,000	7.00	—

KM# 533 25 CENTS **Weight:** 4.4300 g. **Comp.:** Nickel Plated Steel **Ruler:** Elizabeth II **Obv.:** Head right **Rev.:** Stuffed bear in Christmas stocking, colorized **Size:** 23.9 mm.

Date	Mintage	MS-63	Proof
2005P	72,831	10.00	—

KM# 535 25 CENTS **Weight:** 4.4300 g. **Comp.:** Nickel Plated Steel **Ruler:** Elizabeth II **Subject:** Year of the Veteran **Obv.:** Head right **Rev.:** Conjoined busts of young and veteran left **Edge:** Reeded **Size:** 23.9 mm.

Date	Mintage	MS-63	Proof
2005P	29,390,000	7.00	—

KM# 576 25 CENTS **Weight:** 4.4300 g. **Comp.:** Nickel Plated Steel **Ruler:** Elizabeth II **Subject:** Quebec Winter Carnival **Obv.:** Head right **Rev.:** Snowman, colorized **Size:** 23.9 mm.

Date	Mintage	MS-63	Proof
2006	8,200	10.00	—

KM# 534 25 CENTS **Weight:** 4.4300 g. **Comp.:** Nickel Plated Steel **Ruler:** Elizabeth II **Subject:** Toronto Maple Leafs **Obv.:** Head right **Rev.:** Colorized team logo **Size:** 23.9 mm.

Date	Mintage	MS-63	Proof
2006P	—	12.50	—

KM# 575 25 CENTS **Weight:** 4.4300 g. **Comp.:** Nickel Plated Steel **Ruler:** Elizabeth II **Subject:** Montreal Canadiens **Obv.:** Head right **Rev.:** Colorized logo **Size:** 23.9 mm.

Date	Mintage	MS-63	Proof
2006P	—	12.50	—

KM# 629 25 CENTS **Weight:** 4.4300 g. **Comp.:** Nickel Plated Steel **Ruler:** Elizabeth II **Obv.:** Head right **Rev.:** Medal of Bravery **Edge:** Reeded **Size:** 23.9 mm.

Date	Mintage	MS-63	Proof
2006(ml)	20,040,000	2.50	—

KM# 632 25 CENTS **Weight:** 12.6100 g. **Comp.:** Nickel Plated Steel **Ruler:** Elizabeth II **Subject:** Queen Elizabeth II 80th Birthday **Rev.:** Crown, colorized **Size:** 35 mm.

Date	Mintage	MS-63	Proof
2006 Specimen	24,977	—	25.00

KM# 633 25 CENTS **Weight:** 4.4300 g. **Comp.:** Nickel Plated Steel **Ruler:** Elizabeth II **Subject:** Canada Day **Obv.:** Crowned head right **Rev.:** Boy marching with flag, colorized **Size:** 23.9 mm.

Date	Mintage	MS-63	Proof
2006P	29,760	6.00	—

KM# 634 25 CENTS **Weight:** 4.4300 g. **Comp.:** Nickel Plated Steel **Ruler:** Elizabeth II **Subject:** Breast Cancer **Rev.:** Four ribbons, all colorized **Note:** Sold housed in a bookmark.

Date	Mintage	MS-63	Proof
2006P	40,911	10.00	—

KM# 635 25 CENTS **Weight:** 4.4300 g. **Comp.:** Nickel Plated Steel **Ruler:** Elizabeth II **Subject:** Breast Cancer **Rev.:** Colorized pink ribbon applique in center.

Date	Mintage	MS-63	Proof
2006P	29,798,000	1.50	—

KM# 636 25 CENTS **Weight:** 4.4000 g. **Comp.:** Nickel Plated Steel **Ruler:** Elizabeth II **Obv.:** Head right **Obv. Des.:** Susana Blunt **Rev.:** Medal of Bravery design (Maple leaf within wreath)

Date	Mintage	MS-63	Proof
2006	20,045,111	7.00	—

KM# 637 25 CENTS **Weight:** 4.4300 g. **Comp.:** Nickel Plated Steel **Ruler:** Elizabeth II **Subject:** Wedding **Rev.:** Colorized bouquet of flowers

Date	Mintage	MS-63	Proof
2007(ml)	10,318	5.00	—

KM# 642 25 CENTS **Weight:** 4.4300 g. **Comp.:** Nickel Plated Steel **Ruler:** Elizabeth II **Subject:** Ottawa Senators **Obv.:** Head right **Rev.:** Logo

Date	Mintage	MS-63	Proof
2006P	—	12.50	—

KM# 644 25 CENTS **Weight:** 4.4300 g. **Comp.:** Nickel Plated Steel **Ruler:** Elizabeth II **Subject:** Calgary Flames **Obv.:** Head right **Rev.:** Logo

Date	Mintage	MS-63	Proof
2007(ml)	832	12.50	—

KM# 645 25 CENTS **Weight:** 4.4300 g. **Comp.:** Nickel Plated Steel **Ruler:** Elizabeth II **Subject:** Edmonton Oilers **Obv.:** Head right **Rev.:** Logo

Date	Mintage	MS-63	Proof
2007(ml)	2,213	12.50	—

KM# 647 25 CENTS **Weight:** 4.4300 g. **Comp.:** Nickel Plated Steel **Ruler:** Elizabeth II **Subject:** Santa and Rudolph **Rev.:** Colorized Santa in sled, lead by Rudolph

Date	Mintage	MS-63	Proof
2006P	99,258	5.00	—

KM# 711 25 CENTS **Weight:** 12.6100 g. **Comp.:** Nickel Plated Steel **Ruler:** Elizabeth II **Subject:** 60th Wedding Anniversary **Obv.:** Bust right **Rev.:** Carriage, multicolor **Size:** 35 mm.

Date	Mintage	MS-63	Proof
ND(2007)	16,264	19.50	—

KM# 638 25 CENTS **Weight:** 4.4300 g. **Comp.:** Nickel Plated Steel **Ruler:** Elizabeth II **Subject:** Birthday **Rev.:** Colorized baloons

Date	Mintage	MS-63	Proof
2007(ml)	24,531	5.00	—

KM# 639 25 CENTS **Weight:** 4.4300 g. **Comp.:** Nickel Plated Steel **Ruler:** Elizabeth II **Subject:** Baby birth **Rev.:** Colorized baby rattle **Edge:** Reeded

Date	Mintage	MS-63	Proof
2007(ml)	29,964	5.00	—

KM# 640 25 CENTS **Weight:** 4.4300 g. **Comp.:** Nickel Plated Steel **Ruler:** Elizabeth II **Subject:** Oh Canada **Obv.:** Head right **Rev.:** Maple leaf, colorized

Date	Mintage	MS-63	Proof
2006(ml)	23,582	8.50	—

KM# 641 25 CENTS **Weight:** 4.4300 g. **Comp.:** Nickel Plated Steel **Ruler:** Elizabeth II **Subject:** Congratulations **Obv.:** Head right **Rev.:** Fireworks, colorized

Date	Mintage	MS-63	Proof
2006(ml)	8,910	8.00	—

KM# 643 25 CENTS **Weight:** 4.4300 g. **Comp.:** Nickel Plated Steel **Ruler:** Elizabeth II **Subject:** Vancouver Canucks **Obv.:** Head right **Rev.:** Logo

Date	Mintage	MS-63	Proof
2007(ml)	1,264	12.50	—

KM# 682 25 CENTS **Weight:** 4.4300 g. **Comp.:** Nickel Plated Steel **Ruler:** Elizabeth II **Subject:** Curling **Obv.:** Head right

Date	Mintage	MS-63	Proof
2007	22,400,000	7.50	—

KM# 683 25 CENTS **Weight:** 4.4300 g. **Comp.:** Nickel Plated Steel **Ruler:** Elizabeth II **Subject:** Ice Hockey **Obv.:** Head right

Date	Mintage	MS-63	Proof
2007	22,400,000	7.50	—

KM# 684 25 CENTS **Weight:** 4.4300 g. **Comp.:** Nickel Plated Steel **Ruler:** Elizabeth II **Subject:** Paraolympic Winter Games **Obv.:** Head right **Rev.:** Wheelchair curling

Date	Mintage	MS-63	Proof
2007	22,400,000	7.50	—

KM# 685 25 CENTS **Weight:** 4.4300 g. **Comp.:** Nickel Plated Steel **Ruler:** Elizabeth II **Subject:** Biathlon **Obv.:** Head right

Date	Mintage	MS-63	Proof
2007	22,400,000	7.50	—

KM# 686 25 CENTS **Weight:** 4.4300 g. **Comp.:** Nickel Plated Steel **Ruler:** Elizabeth II **Subject:** Alpine Skiing **Obv.:** Head right

Date	Mintage	MS-63	Proof
2007	22,400,000	7.50	—

KM# 695 25 CENTS **Weight:** 4.4300 g. **Comp.:** Nickel Plated Steel **Ruler:** Elizabeth II **Rev.:** Curling **Note:** Mule obverse 2008, reverse 2007

Date	Mintage	MS-63	Proof
2007 Proof	—	—	20.00

KM# 696 25 CENTS **Weight:** 4.4300 g. **Comp.:** Nickel Plated Steel **Ruler:** Elizabeth II **Rev.:** Ice Hockey **Note:** Mule obverse 2008, reverse 2007

Date	Mintage	MS-63	Proof
2007 Proof	—	—	20.00

KM# 697 25 CENTS **Weight:** 4.4300 g. **Comp.:** Nickel Plated Steel **Ruler:** Elizabeth II **Rev.:** Wheelchair curling **Note:** Mule obverse 2008, reverse 2007

Date	Mintage	MS-63	Proof
2007 Proof	—	—	20.00

KM# 701 25 CENTS **Weight:** 4.4300 g. **Comp.:** Nickel Plated Steel **Ruler:** Elizabeth II **Subject:** Birthday **Rev.:** Party hat, multicolor

Date	Mintage	MS-63	Proof
2007	—	8.00	—

KM# 702 25 CENTS **Weight:** 4.4300 g. **Comp.:** Nickel Plated Steel **Ruler:** Elizabeth II **Subject:** Congratulations **Rev.:** Trophy, multicolor

Date	Mintage	MS-63	Proof
2007	—	8.00	—

KM# 703 25 CENTS **Weight:** 4.4300 g. **Comp.:** Nickel Plated Steel **Ruler:** Elizabeth II **Subject:** Wedding **Rev.:** Cake, multicolor

Date	Mintage	MS-63	Proof
2007	—	8.00	—

KM# 704 25 CENTS **Weight:** 4.4300 g. **Comp.:** Nickel Plated Steel **Ruler:** Elizabeth II **Subject:** Canada Day **Rev.:** Mountie, colorized

Date	Mintage	MS-63	Proof
2007(ml)	27,743	8.00	—

KM# 705 25 CENTS **Weight:** 4.4300 g. **Comp.:** Nickel Plated Steel **Ruler:** Elizabeth II **Subject:** Christmas **Rev.:** Multicolor tree

Date	Mintage	MS-63	Proof
2007	—	8.00	—

KM# 706 25 CENTS **Weight:** 12.6100 g. **Comp.:** Nickel Plated Steel **Ruler:** Elizabeth II **Subject:** Red-breasted Nuthatch **Obv.:** Head right **Obv. Leg.:** ELIZABETH II - D • G • REGINA **Obv. Des.:** Susanna Blunt **Rev.:** Nuthatch perched on pine branch multicolor **Rev. Leg.:** CANADA **Rev. Des.:** Arnold Nogy **Edge:** Plain **Size:** 35.0 mm.

Date	Mintage	MS-63	Proof
2007(ml) Specimen	10,581	25.00	—

KM# 707 25 CENTS **Weight:** 12.6100 g. **Comp.:** Nickel Plated Steel **Ruler:** Elizabeth II **Obv.:** Elizabeth II **Rev.:** Multicolor Ruby-throated Hummingbird and flower **Edge:** Plain **Size:** 35 mm.

Date	Mintage	MS-63	Proof
2007 Specimen	16,256	—	25.00

KM# 708 25 CENTS **Weight:** 5.9000 g. **Comp.:** 0.9250 Silver 0.1755 oz. ASW **Ruler:** Elizabeth II **Subject:** Queen's 60th Wedding Anniversary **Rev.:** Royal carriage

Date	Mintage	MS-63	Proof
2007 Specimen	16,264	—	24.00

KM# 713 25 CENTS **Weight:** 4.4000 g. **Comp.:** Nickel Plated Steel **Ruler:** Elizabeth II **Rev.:** Toronto Maple Leaf logo, colorized

Date	Mintage	MS-63	Proof
2007(ml)	—	5.00	—

KM# 714 25 CENTS **Weight:** 4.4000 g. **Comp.:** Nickel Plated Steel **Ruler:** Elizabeth II **Rev.:** Ottawa Senators logo, colorized

Date	Mintage	MS-63	Proof
2007(ml)	—	5.00	—

KM# 723 25 CENTS **Weight:** 4.4000 g. **Comp.:** Nickel Plated Steel **Ruler:** Elizabeth II **Rev.:** Montreal Canadians logo, colorized

Date	Mintage	MS-63	Proof
2007(ml)	—	5.00	—

KM# 693 25 CENTS **Weight:** 4.4300 g. **Comp.:** Nickel Plated Steel **Ruler:** Elizabeth II **Rev.:** Alpine skiing **Note:** Mule obverse of 2008 quarter, reverse 2007

Date	Mintage	MS-63	Proof
2008	—	8.00	—

KM# 694 25 CENTS **Weight:** 4.4300 g. **Comp.:** Nickel Plated Steel **Ruler:** Elizabeth II **Rev.:** Biathlon **Note:** Mule obverse of 2008, reverse 2007

Date	Mintage	MS-63	Proof
2008	—	8.00	—

KM# 760 25 CENTS **Weight:** 4.4300 g. **Comp.:** Nickel Plated Steel **Ruler:** Elizabeth II **Subject:** Baby **Rev.:** Multicolor blue teddy bear

Date	Mintage	MS-63	Proof
2008	—	8.00	—

KM# 761 25 CENTS **Weight:** 4.4300 g. **Comp.:** Nickel Plated Steel **Ruler:** Elizabeth II **Subject:** Birthday **Rev.:** Multicolor party hat

Date	Mintage	MS-63	Proof
2008	—	8.00	—

KM# 762 25 CENTS **Weight:** 4.4300 g. **Comp.:** Nickel Plated Steel **Ruler:** Elizabeth II **Subject:** Congratulations **Rev.:** Multicolor trophy

Date	Mintage	MS-63	Proof
2008	—	8.00	—

KM# 763 25 CENTS **Weight:** 4.4300 g. **Comp.:** Nickel Plated Steel **Ruler:** Elizabeth II **Subject:** Wedding **Rev.:** Multicolor wedding cake

Date	Mintage	MS-63	Proof
2008	—	8.00	—

KM# 764 25 CENTS **Weight:** 4.4300 g. **Comp.:** Nickel Plated Steel **Ruler:** Elizabeth II **Subject:** Santa Claus **Rev.:** Multicolor Santa

Date	Mintage	MS-63	Proof
2008	—	8.00	—

KM# 765 25 CENTS **Weight:** 4.4300 g. **Comp.:** Nickel Plated Steel **Ruler:** Elizabeth II **Subject:** Vancouver Olympics **Rev.:** Freestyle skiing **Size:** 23.9 mm.

Date	Mintage	MS-63	Proof
2008	—	2.00	—

KM# 766 25 CENTS **Weight:** 4.4300 g. **Comp.:** Nickel Plated Steel **Ruler:** Elizabeth II **Subject:** Vancouver Olympics **Rev.:** Figure skating

Date	Mintage	MS-63	Proof
2008	—	2.00	—

KM# 768 25 CENTS **Weight:** 4.4300 g. **Comp.:** Nickel Plated Steel **Ruler:** Elizabeth II **Subject:** Vancouver Olympics **Rev.:** Snow boarding

Date	Mintage	MS-63	Proof
2008	—	2.00	—

KM# 769 25 CENTS **Weight:** 4.4300 g. **Comp.:** Nickel Plated Steel **Ruler:** Elizabeth II **Subject:** Vancouver Olympics **Rev.:** Olympic mascot - Miga

Date	Mintage	MS-63	Proof
2008	—	3.00	—

KM# 770 25 CENTS **Weight:** 4.4300 g. **Comp.:** Nickel Plated Steel **Ruler:** Elizabeth II **Subject:** Vancouver Olympics **Rev.:** Olympic mascott - Quatchi

Date	Mintage	MS-63	Proof
2008	—	3.00	—

KM# 771 25 CENTS **Weight:** 4.4300 g. **Comp.:** Nickel Plated Steel **Ruler:** Elizabeth II **Subject:** Vancouver Olympics **Rev.:** Olympic mascott - Sumi

Date	Mintage	MS-63	Proof
2008	—	3.00	—

KM# 772 25 CENTS **Weight:** 4.4300 g. **Comp.:** Nickel Plated Steel **Ruler:** Elizabeth II **Subject:** Oh Canada **Rev.:** Multicolor red flag

Date	Mintage	MS-63	Proof
2008	—	3.00	—

KM# 773 25 CENTS **Weight:** 12.6000 g. **Comp.:** Nickel Plated Steel **Ruler:** Elizabeth II **Obv.:** Bust right **Obv. Des.:** Susanna Blunt **Rev.:** Downy Woodpecker in tree, multicolor **Rev. Des.:** Arnold Nogy **Edge:** Plain **Size:** 35 mm. **Note:** Prev. KM#717.

Date	Mintage	MS-63	Proof
2008(ml)	25,000	24.00	—

KM# 774 25 CENTS **Weight:** 12.6100 g. **Comp.:** Nickel Plated Steel **Ruler:** Elizabeth II **Obv.:** Bust right **Obv. Des.:** Susanna Blunt **Rev.:** Northern Cardinal perched on branch - multicolor **Rev. Des.:** Arnold Nogy **Edge:** Plain **Size:** 35 mm. **Note:** Prev. KM#718.

Date	Mintage	MS-63	Proof
2008(ml)	25,000	25.00	—

KM# 775 25 CENTS **Weight:** 4.4300 g. **Comp.:** Nickel Plated Steel **Ruler:** Elizabeth II **Subject:** End of WWI, 90th Anniversary **Rev.:** Multicolor poppy

Date	Mintage	MS-63	Proof
2008	—	8.00	—

KM# 776 25 CENTS **Weight:** 12.6000 g. **Comp.:** Nickel Plated Steel **Ruler:** Elizabeth II **Subject:** Anne of Green Gables **Rev.:** Image of young girl, multicolor **Rev. Des.:** Ben Stahl **Size:** 35 mm.

Date	Mintage	MS-63	Proof
2008	25,000	17.50	—

KM# 886 25 CENTS **Weight:** 12.5000 g. **Comp.:** Nickel Plated Steel **Ruler:** Elizabeth II **Subject:** Notre-Dame-Du-Saguenay **Obv.:** Bust right **Obv. Leg.:** Elizabeth II DG Regina **Obv. Des.:** Susanna Blunt **Rev.:** Color photo of fjord and statue **Rev. Leg.:** Canada 25 cents **Size:** 35 mm.

Date	Mintage	MS-63	Proof
2009 Specimen	—	25.00	—

KM# 885 25 CENTS **Weight:** 4.4000 g. **Comp.:** Nickel Plated Steel **Ruler:** Elizabeth II **Subject:** Canada Day **Rev.:** Animals in boat with flag **Rev. Leg.:** Canada 25 cents **Size:** 35 mm.

Date	Mintage	MS-63	Proof
2009	—	6.00	—

KM# 915 25 CENTS **Weight:** 4.4300 g. **Comp.:** Nickel Plated Steel **Ruler:** Elizabeth II **Subject:** Surprise birthday **Obv.:** Bust right **Obv. Des.:** Susanna Blunt **Rev.:** Colorized **Size:** 23.9 mm.

Date	Mintage	MS-63	Proof
2009	—	18.50	—

KM# 916   25 CENTS   Weight: 4.4300 g. **Comp.:** Nickel
Plated Steel **Ruler:** Elizabeth II **Subject:** Share the excitement
Obv.: Bust right **Obv. Des.:** Susanna Blunt **Rev.:** Colorized
Size: 23.9 mm.

Date	Mintage	MS-63	Proof
2009	—	18.50	—

KM# 917   25 CENTS   Weight: 4.4300 g. **Comp.:** Nickel
Plated Steel **Ruler:** Elizabeth II **Subject:** Share the love
Obv.: Bust right **Obv. Des.:** Susanna Blunt **Rev.:** Colorized
Size: 23.9 mm.

Date	Mintage	MS-63	Proof
2009	—	18.50	—

KM# 918   25 CENTS   Weight: 4.4300 g. **Comp.:** Nickel
Plated Steel **Ruler:** Elizabeth II **Subject:** Thank you **Obv.:** Bust
right **Obv. Des.:** Susanna Blunt **Rev.:** Colorized **Size:** 23.9 mm.

Date	Mintage	MS-63	Proof
2009	—	18.50	—

KM# 840   25 CENTS   Weight: 4.4300 g. **Comp.:** Nickel
Plated Steel **Ruler:** Elizabeth II **Subject:** Edmonton Olympics
Rev.: Cross Country Skiing **Size:** 23.9 mm.

Date	Mintage	MS-63	Proof
2009	—	3.00	—

KM# 841   25 CENTS   Weight: 4.4300 g. **Comp.:** Nickel
Plated Steel **Ruler:** Elizabeth II **Subject:** Vancouver Olympics
Rev.: Bobleigh

Date	Mintage	MS-63	Proof
2009	—	3.00	—

KM# 842   25 CENTS   Weight: 4.4300 g. **Comp.:** Nickel
Plated Steel **Ruler:** Elizabeth II **Subject:** Edmonton Olympics
Rev.: Speed skating **Size:** 23.9 mm.

Date	Mintage	MS-63	Proof
2009	—	3.00	—

KM# 880   25 CENTS   Weight: 4.4000 g. **Comp.:** Nickel
Plated Steel **Ruler:** Elizabeth II **Subject:** Miga Mascot Vancouver
Olympics **Rev.:** Mica Mascot - color **Rev. Leg.:** Vancouver 2010
25 cents **Size:** 23.88 mm.

Date	Mintage	MS-63	Proof
2010	—	3.00	—

KM# 881   25 CENTS   Weight: 4.4000 g. **Comp.:** Nickel
Plated Steel **Ruler:** Elizabeth II **Subject:** Quatchi Mascot -
Vancouver Olympics **Obv.:** Bust right **Rev.:** Quatchi Mascot color
Rev. Leg.: Vancouver 2010 25 cents **Size:** 23.88 mm.

Date	Mintage	MS-63	Proof
2010	—	3.00	—

KM# 882   25 CENTS   Weight: 4.4000 g. **Comp.:** Nickel
Plated Steel **Ruler:** Elizabeth II **Subject:** Sumi Mascot
Rev.: Sumi Mascot color **Rev. Leg.:** Vancouver 2010 25 cents
Size: 23.88 mm.

Date	Mintage	MS-63	Proof
2010	—	3.00	—

KM# 290   50 CENTS   Weight: 6.9000 g. **Comp.:** Nickel
Ruler: Elizabeth II **Obv.:** Crowned head right **Obv. Des.:** Dora
dePedery-Hunt **Rev.:** Redesigned arms **Rev. Des.:** Cathy
Bursey-Sabourin **Size:** 27.13 mm.

Date	Mintage	MS-63	Proof
2001P	—	1.50	—
2001P Proof	—	—	5.00
2003P	—	1.50	—
2003P Proof	—	—	5.00

KM# 290b   50 CENTS   Weight: 6.9000 g. **Comp.:** Nickel
Plated Steel **Ruler:** Elizabeth II **Obv.:** Crowned head right
Obv. Des.: Dora dePedery-Hunt **Rev.:** Redesigned arms
Rev. Des.: Cathy Bursey-Sabourin **Size:** 27.13 mm.

Date	Mintage	MS-63	Proof
2001 P	389,000	1.50	—
2003 P	—	5.00	—

KM# 290a   50 CENTS   Weight: 11.6380 g.
Comp.: 0.9250 Silver 0.3461 oz. ASW **Ruler:** Elizabeth II
Obv.: Crowned head right **Obv. Des.:** Dora dePedery-Hunt
Rev.: Redesigned arms **Rev. Des.:** Cathy Bursey-Sabourin
Size: 27.13 mm.

Date	Mintage	MS-63	Proof
2001 Proof	—	—	10.00
2003 Proof	—	—	10.00

KM# 420   50 CENTS   Weight: 9.3000 g. **Comp.:** 0.9250
Silver 0.2766 oz. ASW **Ruler:** Elizabeth II **Series:** Festivals -
Quebec **Obv.:** Crowned head right **Rev.:** Snowman and Chateau
Frontenac **Rev. Des.:** Sylvie Daigneault **Edge:** Reeded
Size: 27.13 mm.

Date	Mintage	MS-63	Proof
2001 Proof	58,123	—	8.50

KM# 421   50 CENTS   Weight: 9.3000 g. **Comp.:** 0.9250
Silver 0.2766 oz. ASW **Ruler:** Elizabeth II **Series:** Festivals -
Nunavut **Obv.:** Crowned head right **Rev.:** Dancer, dog sled and
snowmobiles **Rev. Des.:** John Mardon **Edge:** Reeded
Size: 27.13 mm.

Date	Mintage	MS-63	Proof
2001 Proof	58,123	—	8.50

KM# 422   50 CENTS   Weight: 9.3000 g. **Comp.:** 0.9250
Silver 0.2766 oz. ASW **Ruler:** Elizabeth II **Series:** Festivals -
Newfoundland **Obv.:** Crowned head right **Rev.:** Sailor and
musical people **Rev. Des.:** David Craig **Edge:** Reeded
Size: 27.13 mm.

Date	Mintage	MS-63	Proof
2001 Proof	58,123	—	8.50

KM# 423   50 CENTS   Weight: 9.3000 g. **Comp.:** 0.9250
Silver 0.2766 oz. ASW **Ruler:** Elizabeth II **Series:** Festivals -
Prince Edward Island **Obv.:** Crowned head right **Rev.:** Family,
juggler and building **Rev. Des.:** Brenda Whiteway **Edge:** Reeded
Size: 27.13 mm.

Date	Mintage	MS-63	Proof
2001 Proof	58,123	—	8.50

KM# 424   50 CENTS   Weight: 9.3000 g. **Comp.:** 0.9250
Silver 0.2766 oz. ASW **Ruler:** Elizabeth II **Series:** Folklore - The
Sled **Obv.:** Crowned head right **Rev.:** Family scene
Rev. Des.: Valentina Hotz-Entin **Edge:** Reeded **Size:** 27.13 mm.

Date	Mintage	MS-63	Proof
2001 Proof	28,979	—	9.00

KM# 425   50 CENTS   Weight: 9.3000 g. **Comp.:** 0.9250
Silver 0.2766 oz. ASW **Ruler:** Elizabeth II **Series:** Folklore - The
Maiden's Cave **Obv.:** Crowned head right **Rev.:** Woman shouting
Rev. Des.: Peter Kiss **Edge:** Reeded **Size:** 27.13 mm.

Date	Mintage	MS-63	Proof
2001 Proof	28,979	—	9.00

KM# 426   50 CENTS   Weight: 9.3000 g. **Comp.:** 0.9250
Silver 0.2766 oz. ASW **Ruler:** Elizabeth II **Series:** Folklore - The
Small Jumpers **Obv.:** Crowned head right **Rev.:** Jumping children
on seashore **Rev. Des.:** Miynki Tanobe **Edge:** Reeded
Size: 27.13 mm.

Date	Mintage	MS-63	Proof
2001 Proof	28,979	—	9.00

KM# 509   50 CENTS   Weight: 6.9000 g. **Comp.:** Nickel
Plated Steel **Ruler:** Elizabeth II **Obv.:** Crowned head right
Rev.: National arms **Edge:** Reeded **Size:** 27.13 mm.

Date	Mintage	MS-63	Proof
ND(2001) P	—	1.50	—

KM# 444   50 CENTS   Weight: 6.9000 g. **Comp.:** Nickel
Plated Steel **Ruler:** Elizabeth II **Subject:** Queen's Golden Jubilee
Obv.: Coronation crowned head right and monogram
Rev.: Canadian arms **Rev. Des.:** Bursey Sabourin **Edge:**
Reeded **Size:** 27.13 mm.

Date	Mintage	MS-63	Proof
ND(2002)P	14,440,000	2.50	—

KM# 444a   50 CENTS   Weight: 9.3000 g. **Comp.:** 0.9250
Silver 0.2766 oz. ASW **Ruler:** Elizabeth II **Subject:** Elizabeth II
Golden Jubilee **Obv.:** Crowned head right, Jubilee
commemorative dates 1952-2002 **Size:** 27.13 mm.

Date	Mintage	MS-63	Proof
ND(2002) Proof	100,000	—	17.50

KM# 444b   50 CENTS   Weight: 9.3000 g. **Comp.:** 0.9250
Silver Gilt 0.2766 oz. ASW **Ruler:** Elizabeth II **Subject:** Queen's
Golden Jubilee **Obv.:** Crowned head right and monogram
Rev.: Canadian arms **Edge:** Reeded **Size:** 27.13 mm.
Note: Special 24 karat gold plated issue of KM#444.

Date	Mintage	MS-63	Proof
ND(2002) Proof	32,642	—	35.00

KM# 454   50 CENTS   Weight: 9.3000 g. **Comp.:** 0.9250
Silver 0.2766 oz. ASW **Ruler:** Elizabeth II **Subject:** Nova Scotia
Annapolis Valley Apple Blossom Festival **Obv.:** Crowned head
right **Rev. Des.:** Bonnie Ross **Size:** 27.13 mm.

Date	Mintage	MS-63	Proof
2002 Proof	59,998	—	8.50

KM# 455   50 CENTS   Weight: 9.3000 g. **Comp.:** 0.9250
Silver 0.2766 oz. ASW **Ruler:** Elizabeth II **Subject:** Stratford
Festival **Obv.:** Crowned head right **Rev.:** Couple with building in
background **Rev. Des.:** Laurie McGaw **Size:** 27.13 mm.

Date	Mintage	MS-63	Proof
2002 Proof	59,998	—	8.50

KM# 456 50 CENTS **Weight:** 9.3000 g. **Comp.:** 0.9250 Silver 0.2766 oz. ASW **Ruler:** Elizabeth II **Subject:** Folklorama **Obv.:** Crowned head right **Rev. Des.:** William Woodruff **Size:** 27.13 mm.

Date	Mintage	MS-63	Proof
2002 Proof	59,998	—	8.50

KM# 457 50 CENTS **Weight:** 9.3000 g. **Comp.:** 0.9250 Silver 0.2766 oz. ASW **Ruler:** Elizabeth II **Subject:** Calgary Stampede **Obv.:** Crowned head right **Rev. Des.:** Stan Witten **Size:** 27.13 mm.

Date	Mintage	MS-63	Proof
2002 Proof	59,998	—	8.50

KM# 458 50 CENTS **Weight:** 9.3000 g. **Comp.:** 0.9250 Silver 0.2766 oz. ASW **Ruler:** Elizabeth II **Subject:** Squamish Days Logger Sports **Obv.:** Crowned head right **Rev. Des.:** Jose Osio **Size:** 27.13 mm.

Date	Mintage	MS-63	Proof
2002 Proof	59,998	—	8.50

KM# 459 50 CENTS **Weight:** 9.3000 g. **Comp.:** 0.9250 Silver 0.2766 oz. ASW **Ruler:** Elizabeth II **Series:** Folklore and Legends **Obv.:** Crowned head right **Rev.:** The Shoemaker in Heaven **Rev. Des.:** Francine Gravel **Size:** 27.13 mm.

Date	Mintage	MS-63	Proof
2002 Proof	19,267	—	9.50

KM# 460 50 CENTS **Weight:** 9.3000 g. **Comp.:** 0.9250 Silver 0.2766 oz. ASW **Ruler:** Elizabeth II **Series:** Folklore and Legends **Subject:** The Ghost Ship **Obv.:** Crowned head right **Rev. Des.:** Colette Boivin **Size:** 27.13 mm.

Date	Mintage	MS-63	Proof
2002 Proof	19,267	—	9.50

KM# 461 50 CENTS **Weight:** 9.3000 g. **Comp.:** 0.9250 Silver 0.2766 oz. ASW **Ruler:** Elizabeth II **Series:** Folklore and Legends **Subject:** The Pig That Wouldn't Get Over the Stile **Obv.:** Crowned head right **Rev. Des.:** Laura Jolicoeur **Size:** 27.13 mm.

Date	Mintage	MS-63	Proof
2002 Proof	19,267	—	9.50

KM# 494 50 CENTS **Weight:** 6.9000 g. **Comp.:** Nickel Plated Steel **Ruler:** Elizabeth II **Obv.:** Crowned head right **Obv. Des.:** Susanna Blunt **Rev. Des.:** Cathy Bursey-Sabourin **Size:** 27.13 mm.

Date	Mintage	MS-63	Proof
2003P W	—	5.00	—
2003P W Proof	—	—	7.50
2004P	—	5.00	—
2004P Proof	—	—	7.50
2005P	—	1.50	—
2005P Proof	—	—	5.00
2006P	—	1.50	—
2006P Proof	—	—	5.00
2007(ml)	—	1.50	—
2007(ml) Proof	—	—	5.00
2008(ml)	—	1.50	—
2008(ml) Proof	—	—	5.00
2009(ml)	—	1.50	—
2009(ml) Proof	—	—	5.00

KM# 472 50 CENTS **Weight:** 11.6200 g. **Comp.:** 0.9250 Silver 0.3456 oz. ASW **Ruler:** Elizabeth II **Subject:** 50th Anniversary of the Coronation of Elizabeth II **Obv.:** Crowned head right, Jubilee commemorative dates 1952-2002 **Obv. Des.:** Mary Gillick **Size:** 27.13 mm.

Date	Mintage	MS-63	Proof
ND(2003) Proof	30,000	—	15.00

KM# 475 50 CENTS **Comp.:** 0.9250 Silver **Ruler:** Elizabeth II **Obv.:** Crowned head right **Obv. Des.:** Dora dePédery-Hunt **Rev.:** Golden daffodil **Rev. Des.:** Christie Paquet, Stan Witten **Size:** 27.13 mm.

Date	Mintage	MS-63	Proof
2003 Proof	36,293	—	25.00

KM# 476 50 CENTS **Weight:** 9.3000 g. **Comp.:** 0.9250 Silver 0.2766 oz. ASW **Ruler:** Elizabeth II **Subject:** Yukon International Storytelling Festival **Obv.:** Crowned head right **Obv. Des.:** Dora dePédery-Hunt **Rev. Des.:** Ken Anderson, Jose Oslo **Size:** 27.13 mm.

Date	Mintage	MS-63	Proof
2003 Proof	—	—	11.00

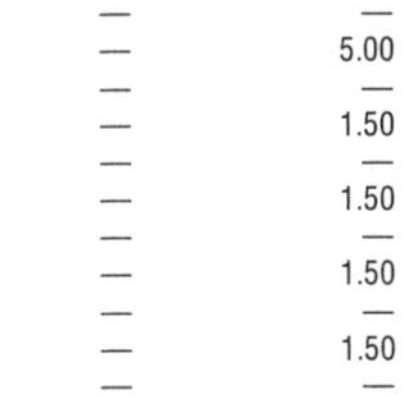

KM# 477 50 CENTS **Weight:** 9.3000 g. **Comp.:** 0.9250 Silver 0.2766 oz. ASW **Ruler:** Elizabeth II **Subject:** Festival Acadien de Caraquet **Obv.:** Crowned head right **Obv. Des.:** Dora dePédery-Hunt **Rev.:** Sailboat and couple **Rev. Des.:** Susan Taylor, Hudson Design Group **Size:** 27.13 mm.

Date	Mintage	MS-63	Proof
2003 Proof	—	—	11.00

KM# 478 50 CENTS **Weight:** 9.3000 g. **Comp.:** 0.9250 Silver 0.2766 oz. ASW **Ruler:** Elizabeth II **Subject:** Back to Batoche **Obv.:** Crowned head right **Obv. Des.:** Dora dePédery-Hunt **Rev. Des.:** David Hannan, Stan Witten **Size:** 27.13 mm.

Date	Mintage	MS-63	Proof
2003 Proof	—	—	11.00

KM# 479 50 CENTS **Weight:** 9.3000 g. **Comp.:** 0.9250 Silver 0.2766 oz. ASW **Ruler:** Elizabeth II **Subject:** Great Northern Arts Festival **Obv.:** Crowned head right **Obv. Des.:** Dora dePédery-Hunt **Rev. Des.:** Dawn Oman, Susan Taylor **Size:** 27.13 mm.

Date	Mintage	MS-63	Proof
2003 Proof	—	—	11.00

KM# 494a 50 CENTS **Weight:** 9.3000 g. **Comp.:** 0.9250 Silver 0.2766 oz. ASW **Ruler:** Elizabeth II **Obv.:** Crowned head right **Obv. Des.:** Susanna Blunt **Rev.:** Canadian coat of arms **Edge:** Reeded **Size:** 27.13 mm.

Date	Mintage	MS-63	Proof
2004 Proof	—	—	7.50

KM# 526 50 CENTS **Weight:** 1.2700 g. **Comp.:** 0.9999 Gold 0.0408 oz. AGW **Ruler:** Elizabeth II **Subject:** Moose **Obv.:** Head right **Rev.:** Moose head facing right **Size:** 14 mm.

Date	Mintage	MS-63	Proof
2004 Proof	—	—	85.00

KM# 606 50 CENTS **Weight:** 9.3000 g. **Comp.:** 0.9250 Silver 0.2766 oz. ASW **Ruler:** Elizabeth II **Obv.:** Head right **Obv. Des.:** Susanna Blunt **Rev.:** Clouded Sulphur Butterfly, hologram **Rev. Des.:** Susan Taylor **Size:** 27.13 mm.

Date	Mintage	MS-63	Proof
2004 Proof	15,281	—	30.00

KM# 712 50 CENTS **Weight:** 9.3000 g. **Comp.:** 0.9250 Silver 0.2766 oz. ASW **Ruler:** Elizabeth II **Rev.:** Hologram of Tiger Swallowtail Butterfly **Size:** 27.13 mm.

Date	Mintage	MS-63	Proof
2004 Proof	20,462	—	30.00

KM# 536 50 CENTS **Weight:** 9.3000 g. **Comp.:** 0.9250 Silver with partial gold plating 0.2766 oz. ASW **Ruler:** Elizabeth II **Subject:** Golden rose **Obv.:** Head right **Obv. Des.:** Susanna Blunt **Rev. Des.:** Christie Paquet **Size:** 27.13 mm.

Date	Mintage	MS-63	Proof
2005 Proof	17,418	—	19.00

KM# 537 50 CENTS **Weight:** 9.3000 g. **Comp.:** 0.9250 Silver 0.2766 oz. ASW **Ruler:** Elizabeth II **Subject:** Great Spangled Fritillary butterfly, hologram **Obv.:** Head right **Obv. Des.:** Susanna Blunt **Rev. Des.:** Jianping Yan **Size:** 27.13 mm.

Date	Mintage	MS-63	Proof
2005 Proof	20,000	—	35.00

KM# 538 50 CENTS **Weight:** 9.3000 g. **Comp.:** 0.9250 Silver 0.2766 oz. ASW **Ruler:** Elizabeth II **Subject:** Toronto Maple Leafs **Obv.:** Head right **Obv. Des.:** Susanna Blunt **Rev.:** Darryl Sittler **Size:** 27.13 mm.

Date	Mintage	MS-63	Proof
2005 Specimen	25,000	—	16.00

KM# 539 50 CENTS **Weight:** 9.3000 g. **Comp.:** 0.9250 Silver 0.2766 oz. ASW **Ruler:** Elizabeth II **Subject:** Toronto Maple Leafs **Obv.:** Head right **Obv. Des.:** Susanna Blunt **Rev.:** Dave Keon **Size:** 27.13 mm.

Date	Mintage	MS-63	Proof
2005 Specimen	25,000	—	16.00

KM# 540 50 CENTS **Weight:** 9.3000 g. **Comp.:** 0.9250 Silver 0.2766 oz. ASW **Ruler:** Elizabeth II **Subject:** Toronto Maple Leafs **Obv.:** Head right **Obv. Des.:** Susanna Blunt **Rev.:** Jonny Bover **Size:** 27.13 mm.

Date	Mintage	MS-63	Proof
2005 Specimen	25,000	—	16.00

KM# 541 50 CENTS **Weight:** 9.3000 g. **Comp.:** 0.9250 Silver 0.2766 oz. ASW **Ruler:** Elizabeth II **Subject:** Toronto Maple Leafs **Obv.:** Head right **Obv. Des.:** Susanna Blunt **Rev.:** Tim Horton **Size:** 27.13 mm.

Date	Mintage	MS-63	Proof
2005 Specimen	25,000	—	16.00

KM# 542 50 CENTS **Weight:** 1.2700 g. **Comp.:** 0.9999 Gold 0.0408 oz. AGW **Ruler:** Elizabeth II **Subject:** Voyageurs **Obv.:** Head right

Date	Mintage	MS-63	Proof
2005 Proof	—	—	65.00

KM# 543 50 CENTS **Comp.:** Silver **Ruler:** Elizabeth II **Subject:** WWII - Battle of Britain **Obv.:** Head right **Rev.:** Fighter plane in sky

Date	Mintage	MS-63	Proof
2005 Specimen	20,000	—	22.50

KM# 544 50 CENTS **Weight:** 9.3000 g. **Comp.:** 0.9250 Silver 0.2766 oz. ASW **Ruler:** Elizabeth II **Subject:** WWII - Battle of Scheldt **Obv.:** Head right **Obv. Des.:** Susanna Blunt **Rev.:** Four soldiers walking down road **Rev. Des.:** Peter Mossman **Size:** 27.13 mm.

Date	Mintage	MS-63	Proof
2005 Specimen	20,000	—	19.00

KM# 545 50 CENTS **Weight:** 9.3000 g. **Comp.:** 0.9250 Silver 0.2766 oz. ASW **Ruler:** Elizabeth II **Subject:** WWII - Battle of the Atlantic **Obv.:** Head right **Obv. Des.:** Susanna Blunt **Rev.:** Merchant ship sinking **Rev. Des.:** Peter Mossman **Size:** 27.13 mm.

Date	Mintage	MS-63	Proof
2005 Specimen	20,000	—	19.00

KM# 546 50 CENTS **Weight:** 9.3000 g. **Comp.:** 0.9250 Silver 0.2766 oz. ASW **Ruler:** Elizabeth II **Subject:** WWII - Conquest of Sicily **Obv.:** Head right **Obv. Des.:** Susanna Blunt **Rev.:** Tank among town ruins **Rev. Des.:** Peter Mossman **Size:** 27.13 mm.

Date	Mintage	MS-63	Proof
2005 Specimen	20,000	—	19.00

KM# 547 50 CENTS **Weight:** 9.3000 g. **Comp.:** 0.9250 Silver 0.2766 oz. ASW **Ruler:** Elizabeth II **Subject:** WWII - Liberation of the Netherlands **Obv.:** Head right **Obv. Des.:** Susanna Blunt **Rev.:** Soldiers in parade, one holding flag **Rev. Des.:** Peter Mossman **Size:** 27.13 mm.

Date	Mintage	MS-63	Proof
2005 Specimen	20,000	—	19.00

KM# 548 50 CENTS **Weight:** 9.3000 g. **Comp.:** 0.9250 Silver 0.2766 oz. ASW **Ruler:** Elizabeth II **Subject:** WWII - Raid of Dieppe **Obv.:** Head right **Obv. Des.:** Susanna Blunt **Rev.:** Three soldiers exiting landing craft **Rev. Des.:** Peter Mossman **Size:** 27.13 mm.

Date	Mintage	MS-63	Proof
2005 Specimen	20,000	—	19.00

KM# 577 50 CENTS **Weight:** 9.3000 g. **Comp.:** 0.9250 Silver 0.2766 oz. ASW **Ruler:** Elizabeth II **Subject:** Montreal Canadiens **Obv.:** Head right **Obv. Des.:** Susanna Blunt **Rev.:** Guy LaFleur **Size:** 27.13 mm.

Date	Mintage	MS-63	Proof
2005 Specimen	25,000	—	17.50

KM# 578 50 CENTS **Weight:** 9.3000 g. **Comp.:** 0.9250 Silver 0.2766 oz. ASW **Ruler:** Elizabeth II **Subject:** Montreal Canadiens **Obv.:** Head right **Obv. Des.:** Susanna Blunt **Rev.:** Jaque Plante **Size:** 27.13 mm.

Date	Mintage	MS-63	Proof
2005 Specimen	25,000	—	17.50

KM# 579 50 CENTS **Weight:** 9.3000 g. **Comp.:** 0.9250 Silver 0.2766 oz. ASW **Ruler:** Elizabeth II **Subject:** Montreal Canadiens **Obv.:** Head right **Obv. Des.:** Susanna Blunt **Rev.:** Jean Beliveau **Size:** 27.13 mm.

Date	Mintage	MS-63	Proof
2005 Specimen	25,000	—	17.50

KM# 580 50 CENTS **Weight:** 9.3000 g. **Comp.:** 0.9250 Silver 0.2766 oz. ASW **Ruler:** Elizabeth II **Subject:** Montreal Canadiens **Obv.:** Head right **Obv. Des.:** Susanna Blunt **Rev.:** Maurice Richard **Size:** 27.13 mm.

Date	Mintage	MS-63	Proof
2005 Specimen	25,000	—	17.50

KM# 599 50 CENTS **Weight:** 9.3000 g. **Comp.:** 0.9250 Silver 0.2766 oz. ASW **Ruler:** Elizabeth II **Subject:** Monarch Butterfly, colorized **Obv.:** Head right **Obv. Des.:** Susanna Blunt **Rev. Des.:** Susan Taylor **Size:** 27.13 mm.

Date	Mintage	MS-63	Proof
2005 Proof	20,000	—	35.00

KM# 648 50 CENTS **Weight:** 9.3000 g. **Comp.:** 0.9250 Silver With Partial Gold Plating 0.2766 oz. ASW **Ruler:** Elizabeth II **Subject:** Golden Daisy **Obv.:** Head right

Date	Mintage	MS-63	Proof
2006	18,190	22.00	—

KM# 649 50 CENTS **Weight:** 9.3000 g. **Comp.:** 0.9250 Silver 0.2766 oz. ASW **Ruler:** Elizabeth II **Subject:** Short tailed swallotail **Obv.:** Head right **Rev.:** Colorized butterfly

Date	Mintage	MS-63	Proof
2006	20,000	25.00	—

KM# 650 50 CENTS **Weight:** 9.3000 g. **Comp.:** 0.9250 Silver 0.2766 oz. ASW **Ruler:** Elizabeth II **Subject:** Butterfly hologram **Obv.:** Head right **Rev.:** Silvery blue hologram

Date	Mintage	MS-63	Proof
2006	16,000	25.00	—

KM# 651 50 CENTS **Weight:** 9.3000 g. **Comp.:** 0.9250 Silver 0.2766 oz. ASW **Ruler:** Elizabeth II **Subject:** Cowboy **Obv.:** Head right

Date	Mintage	MS-63	Proof
2006	—	17.50	—

KM# 716 50 CENTS Weight: 9.3000 g. **Comp.:**
Silver 0.2766 oz. ASW **Ruler:** Elizabeth II **Rev.:** Multicolor
holiday ornaments

Date	Mintage	MS-63	Proof
2006	16,989	17.50	

KM# 717 50 CENTS Weight: 1.2400 g. **Comp.:** 0.9990
Gold 0.0398 oz. AGW **Ruler:** Elizabeth II **Rev.:** Wolf

Date	Mintage	MS-63	Proof
2006	—		60.00

KM# 715 50 CENTS Weight: 9.3000 g. **Comp.:** 0.9250
Silver with partial gold plating 0.2766 oz. ASW **Ruler:** Elizabeth
II **Rev.:** Forget-me-not flower **Size:** 27.12 mm.

Date	Mintage	MS-63	Proof
2007 Proof	22,882	—	29.00

KM# 777 50 CENTS Weight: 7.7700 g. **Comp.:** Gold
Ruler: Elizabeth II **Subject:** DeHavilland beaver

Date	Mintage	MS-63	Proof
2008	20,000	320	

KM# 778 50 CENTS Weight: 20.0000 g. **Comp.:** 0.9250
Silver colorized green 0.5948 oz. ASW **Ruler:** Elizabeth II
Subject: Milk delivery **Obv.:** Bust right **Rev.:** Cow head and milk
can **Shape:** Triangle **Size:** 34.06 mm.

Date	Mintage	MS-63	Proof
2008 Proof	25,000	—	35.00

KM# 779 50 CENTS Weight: 9.3000 g. **Comp.:** 0.9250
Silver 0.2766 oz. ASW **Ruler:** Elizabeth II **Rev.:** Multicolor
snowman

Date	Mintage	MS-63	Proof
2008	—	17.50	

KM# 780 50 CENTS Weight: 9.3000 g. **Comp.:** 9.2500
Silver 2.7657 oz. ASW **Ruler:** Elizabeth II **Subject:** Ottawa Mint
Centennial 1908-2008

Date	Mintage	MS-63	Proof
2008	—	20.00	

KM# 857 50 CENTS Weight: 6.9000 g. **Comp.:** Nickel
Plated Steel **Ruler:** Elizabeth II **Rev.:** Calgary Flames lenticular
old and new logos **Size:** 35 mm.

Date	Mintage	MS-63	Proof
2009	—	25.00	

KM# 858 50 CENTS Weight: 6.9000 g. **Comp.:** Nickel
Plated Steel **Ruler:** Elizabeth II **Rev.:** Edmonton Oilers lenticular
old and new logos **Size:** 35 mm.

Date	Mintage	MS-63	Proof
2009	—	25.00	

KM# 859 50 CENTS Weight: 35.0000 g. **Comp.:** Nickel
Plated Steel **Ruler:** Elizabeth II **Rev.:** Montreal Canadiens
lenticular old and new logo **Size:** 35 mm.

Date	Mintage	MS-63	Proof
2009	—	25.00	

KM# 845 50 CENTS Weight: 9.3000 g. **Comp.:** 0.9250
Silver 0.2766 oz. ASW **Ruler:** Elizabeth II **Rev.:** Calgary Flames
lenticular design, old and new logos **Size:** 27.13 mm.

Date	Mintage	MS-63	Proof
2009	—	15.00	

KM# 846 50 CENTS Weight: 9.3000 g. **Comp.:** 0.9250
Silver 0.2766 oz. ASW **Ruler:** Elizabeth II **Rev.:** Edmonton
Oiler's lenticular design, old and new logos **Size:** 27.13 mm.

Date	Mintage	MS-63	Proof
2009	—	15.00	

KM# 847 50 CENTS Weight: 9.3000 g. **Comp.:** 0.9250
Silver 0.2766 oz. ASW **Ruler:** Elizabeth II **Rev.:** Montreal
Canadians lenticular design, old and new logos **Size:** 27.13 mm.

Date	Mintage	MS-63	Proof
2009	—	15.00	

KM# 848 50 CENTS Weight: 9.3000 g. **Comp.:** 0.9250
Silver 0.2766 oz. ASW **Ruler:** Elizabeth II **Rev.:** Ottawa Senators
lenticular design, old and new logos **Size:** 27.13 mm.

Date	Mintage	MS-63	Proof
2009	—	15.00	

KM# 849 50 CENTS Weight: 9.3000 g. **Comp.:** 0.9250
Silver 0.2766 oz. ASW **Ruler:** Elizabeth II **Rev.:** Toronto Maple
Leafs lenticular design, old and new logos **Size:** 27.13 mm.

Date	Mintage	MS-63	Proof
2009	—	15.00	

KM# 850 50 CENTS Weight: 9.3000 g. **Comp.:** 0.9250
Silver 0.2766 oz. ASW **Ruler:** Elizabeth II **Rev.:** Vancouver
Canucks lenticular design, old and new logos **Size:** 27.13 mm.

Date	Mintage	MS-63	Proof
2009	—	15.00	

KM# 860 50 CENTS Weight: 6.9000 g. **Comp.:** Nickel
Plated Steel **Ruler:** Elizabeth II **Rev.:** Ottawa Senators lenticular
old and new logos **Size:** 35 mm.

Date	Mintage	MS-63	Proof
2009	—	25.00	

KM# 861 50 CENTS Weight: 6.9000 g. **Comp.:** Nickel
Plated Steel **Ruler:** Elizabeth II **Rev.:** Toronto Maple Leafs
lenticular old and new logos **Size:** 35 mm.

Date	Mintage	MS-63	Proof
2009	—	25.00	

KM# 862 50 CENTS Weight: 6.9000 g. **Comp.:** Nickel
Plated Steel **Ruler:** Elizabeth II **Rev.:** Vancouver Canucks
lenticular old and new logos **Size:** 35 mm.

Date	Mintage	MS-63	Proof
2009	—	25.00	

KM# 887 50 CENTS Weight: 19.1000 g. **Comp.:**
Copper-Nickel **Ruler:** Elizabeth II **Subject:** Six-string national
guitar **Obv.:** Bust right **Obv. Leg.:** Elizabeth II DG Regina
Obv. Des.: Susanna Blunt **Rev.:** Hologram with 6 "strings"
Rev. Leg.: 50 cents Canada **Shape:** Triangle **Size:** 34.06 mm.

Date	Mintage	MS-63	Proof
2009 Proof	30,000		50.00

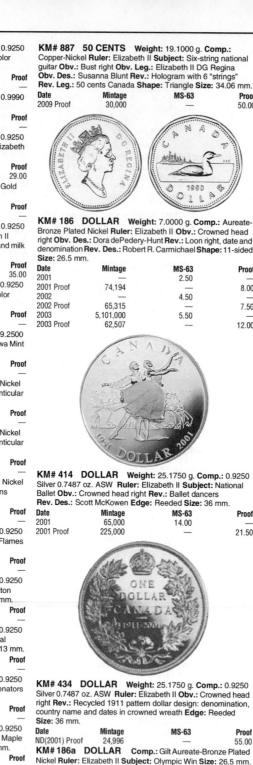

KM# 186 DOLLAR Weight: 7.0000 g. **Comp.:** Aureate-
Bronze Plated Nickel **Ruler:** Elizabeth II **Obv.:** Crowned head
right **Obv. Des.:** Dora dePedery-Hunt **Rev.:** Loon right, date and
denomination **Rev. Des.:** Robert R. Carmichael **Shape:** 11-sided
Size: 26.5 mm.

Date	Mintage	MS-63	Proof
2001	—	2.50	
2001 Proof	74,194	—	8.00
2002	—	4.50	
2002 Proof	65,315	—	7.50
2003	5,101,000	5.50	
2003 Proof	62,507	—	12.00

KM# 414 DOLLAR Weight: 25.1750 g. **Comp.:** 0.9250
Silver 0.7487 oz. ASW **Ruler:** Elizabeth II **Subject:** National
Ballet **Obv.:** Crowned head right **Rev.:** Ballet dancers
Rev. Des.: Scott McKowen **Edge:** Reeded **Size:** 36 mm.

Date	Mintage	MS-63	Proof
2001	65,000	14.00	
2001 Proof	225,000	—	21.50

KM# 434 DOLLAR Weight: 25.1750 g. **Comp.:** 0.9250
Silver 0.7487 oz. ASW **Ruler:** Elizabeth II **Obv.:** Crowned head
right **Rev.:** Recycled 1911 pattern dollar design: denomination,
country name and dates in crowned wreath **Edge:** Reeded
Size: 36 mm.

Date	Mintage	MS-63	Proof
ND(2001) Proof	24,996	—	55.00

KM# 186a DOLLAR **Comp.:** Gilt Aureate-Bronze Plated
Nickel **Ruler:** Elizabeth II **Subject:** Olympic Win **Size:** 26.5 mm.

Date	Mintage	MS-63	Proof
2002 Proof	—	—	40.00

KM# 443 DOLLAR Weight: 25.1750 g. **Comp.:** 0.9250
Silver 0.7487 oz. ASW **Ruler:** Elizabeth II **Subject:** Queen's Golden
Jubilee **Obv.:** Crowned head right, with anniversary date at left
Obv. Des.: Dora dePédery-Hunt **Rev.:** Queen in her coach and a
view of the coach, denomination below **Edge:** Reeded **Size:** 36 mm.

Date	Mintage	MS-63	Proof
ND(2002)	65,140	21.00	
ND(2002) Proof	29,688	—	40.00

KM# 443a DOLLAR Weight: 25.1800 g. **Comp.:** 0.9250
Silver Gilt 0.7488 oz. ASW **Ruler:** Elizabeth II **Subject:** Queen's
Golden Jubilee **Obv.:** Crowned head right with anniversary date
Rev.: Queen in her coach and a view of the coach **Edge:** Reeded
Size: 36 mm. **Note:** Special 24 karat gold plated issue of KM#443.

Date	Mintage	MS-63	Proof
ND(2002) Proof	32,642	—	45.00

KM# 462 DOLLAR Weight: 7.0000 g. **Comp.:** Aureate-
Bronze Plated Nickel **Ruler:** Elizabeth II **Subject:** Commemorative
dates 1952-2002 **Obv. Des.:** Dora dePédery-Hunt **Rev.:** Family
of Loons

Date	Mintage	MS-63	Proof
ND(2002) Specimen	67,672	—	

KM# 467 DOLLAR Weight: 7.0000 g. **Comp.:** Aureate-
Bronze Plated Nickel **Ruler:** Elizabeth II **Subject:** Elizabeth II
Golden Jubilee **Obv.:** Crowned head right, Jubilee
commemorative dates 1952-2002 **Obv. Des.:** Dora dePédery-
Hunt

Date	Mintage	MS-63	Proof
ND(2002)	2,302,000	2.50	—
ND(2002) Proof	—	—	8.00

KM# 467a DOLLAR **Comp.:** Gold **Ruler:** Elizabeth II
Subject: 50th Anniversary, Accession to the Throne **Obv.:**
Crowned head right **Note:** Sold on the internet.

Date	Mintage	MS-63	Proof
ND(2002)	1	—	55,500

KM# 503 DOLLAR Weight: 25.1750 g. **Comp.:** 0.9250
Silver 0.7487 oz. ASW **Ruler:** Elizabeth II **Subject:** Queen
Mother **Obv.:** Crowned head right **Obv. Des.:** Dora de Pedery-
Hunt **Rev.:** Queen Mother facing **Size:** 36 mm.

Date	Mintage	MS-63	Proof
2002 Proof	9,994	—	250

KM# 495 DOLLAR Weight: 7.0000 g. **Comp.:** Aureate-
Bronze Plated Nickel **Ruler:** Elizabeth II **Obv.:** Bare head right
Obv. Des.: Susanna Blunt **Rev. Des.:** Robert R. Carmichael
Size: 26.5 mm.

Date	Mintage	MS-63	Proof
2003	5,102,000	5.50	
2003 Proof	—	—	7.50
2003W	—	7.50	
2004	3,409,000	1.75	
2004 Proof	—	—	12.00
2005	—	3.00	
2005 Proof	—	—	7.50
2006	—	3.00	
2006 Proof	—	—	7.50
2006(ml)	—	3.00	
2006(ml) Proof	—	—	7.50
2007(ml)	—	3.00	
2007(ml) Proof	—	—	7.50
2008(ml)	—	3.00	
2008(ml) Proof	—	—	7.50
2009(ml)	—	3.00	
2009(ml) Proof	—	—	7.50

KM# 450 DOLLAR Weight: 25.1750 g. **Comp.:** 0.9999
Silver Gilt 0.8093 oz. ASW **Ruler:** Elizabeth II **Subject:** Cobalt
Mining Centennial **Obv.:** Queens portrait right **Obv. Des.:** Dora
dePédery-Hunt **Rev.:** Mine tower and fox **Edge:** Reeded **Size:**
36 mm.

Date	Mintage	MS-63	Proof
ND(2003)	51,130	20.00	—
ND(2003) Proof	88,536	—	28.00

KM# 473 DOLLAR Weight: 25.1750 g. **Comp.:** 0.9999
Silver 0.8093 oz. ASW **Ruler:** Elizabeth II **Subject:** 50th
Anniversary of the Coronation of Elizabeth II **Obv.:** 1953 effigy
of the Queen, Jubilee Commemorative dates 1953-2003
Obv. Des.: Mary Gillick **Rev.:** Voyageur, date and denomination
below

Date	Mintage	MS-63	Proof
ND(2003) Proof	29,586	—	35.00

KM# 473a DOLLAR **Comp.:** Gold **Ruler:** Elizabeth II
Subject: 50th Anniversary of Coronation **Obv. Des.:** Mary Gilick
Rev.: Voyageur **Note:** Sold on the internet.

Date	Mintage	MS-63	Proof
2003	1	—	62,750

KM# 480 DOLLAR Weight: 25.1750 g. **Comp.:** 0.9999
Silver 0.8093 oz. ASW **Ruler:** Elizabeth II **Subject:** Coronation
of Queen Elizabeth II **Obv.:** Head right **Rev.:** Voyaguers
Rev. Des.: Emanuel Hahn

Date	Mintage	MS-63	Proof
ND2003 Proof	21,400	—	38.00

KM# 507 DOLLAR **Weight:** 7.0000 g. **Comp.:** Aureate-Bronze Plated Nickel **Ruler:** Elizabeth II **Obv.:** Bare head right, date below **Obv. Des.:** Susanna Blunt **Rev.:** Loon **Edge:** Plain **Shape:** 11-sided **Size:** 26.5 mm.

Date	Mintage	MS-63	Proof
2004 Proof	12,550	—	12.50

KM# 512 DOLLAR **Weight:** 25.1750 g. **Comp.:** 0.9999 Silver 0.8093 oz. ASW **Ruler:** Elizabeth II **Subject:** First French Settlement in America **Obv.:** Crowned head right **Rev.:** Sailing ship **Edge:** Reeded **Size:** 36 mm.

Date	Mintage	MS-63	Proof
2004	42,582	21.00	—
2004 Fleur-dis-lis	8,315	50.00	—
2004 Proof	106,974	—	35.00

KM# 513 DOLLAR **Weight:** 7.0000 g. **Comp.:** Aureate-Bronze Plated Nickel **Ruler:** Elizabeth II **Subject:** Olympics **Obv.:** Bare head right **Rev.:** Maple leaf, Olympic flame and rings above loon **Edge:** Plain **Shape:** 11-sided **Size:** 26.5 mm.

Date	Mintage	MS-63	Proof
2004	6,526,000	8.00	—

KM# 513a DOLLAR **Weight:** 9.3100 g. **Comp.:** 0.9250 Silver 0.2769 oz. ASW **Ruler:** Elizabeth II **Subject:** Olympics **Obv.:** Bare head right **Rev.:** Multicolor maple leaf, Olympic flame and rings above loon **Edge:** Plain **Shape:** 11-sided **Size:** 26.5 mm.

Date	Mintage	MS-63	Proof
2004 Proof	19,994	—	50.00

KM# 718 DOLLAR **Weight:** 0.5000 g. **Comp.:** 0.9990 Silver 0.0161 oz. ASW **Ruler:** Elizabeth II **Obv.:** Bust right **Rev.:** Grey Wolf standing with moon in background **Rev. Des.:** William Woodruff **Edge:** Reeded **Size:** 32 mm.

Date	Mintage	MS-63	Proof
2005	106,800	40.00	—
2006 WW	—	40.00	—
2007	—	40.00	—

KM# 549 DOLLAR **Weight:** 25.1750 g. **Comp.:** 0.9250 Silver 0.7487 oz. ASW **Ruler:** Elizabeth II **Subject:** 40th Anniversary of National Flag **Obv.:** Head right **Obv. Des.:** Susanna Blunt **Rev. Des.:** William Woodruff

Date	Mintage	MS-63	Proof
2005	50,948	23.00	—
2005 Proof	95,431	—	35.00

KM# 549a DOLLAR **Weight:** 7.0000 g. **Comp.:** 0.9250 Silver partially gilt 0.2082 oz. ASW **Ruler:** Elizabeth II **Subject:** 40th Anniversary of National Flag **Obv.:** Head right

Date	Mintage	MS-63	Proof
2005	62,483	65.00	—

KM# 549b DOLLAR **Weight:** 25.1800 g. **Comp.:** 0.9250 Silver 0.7488 oz. ASW **Ruler:** Elizabeth II **Subject:** 40th Anniversary National Flag **Rev.:** National flag, colorized **Size:** 36.07 mm.

Date	Mintage	MS-63	Proof
ND(1965-2005)	4,898	—	—

KM# 552 DOLLAR **Weight:** 7.0000 g. **Comp.:** Aureate-Bronze Plated Nickel **Ruler:** Elizabeth II **Subject:** Terry Fox **Obv.:** Head right

Date	Mintage	MS-63	Proof
2005	1,290,900	3.50	—

KM# 553 DOLLAR **Weight:** 7.0000 g. **Comp.:** Aureate-Bronze Plated Nickel **Ruler:** Elizabeth II **Subject:** Tuffed Puffin **Obv.:** Head right **Obv. Des.:** Susanna Blunt

Date	Mintage	MS-63	Proof
2005 Specimen	40,000	—	30.00

KM# 581 DOLLAR **Weight:** 7.0000 g. **Comp.:** 0.9250 Silver 0.2082 oz. ASW **Ruler:** Elizabeth II **Subject:** Lullabies Loonie **Obv.:** Head right **Obv. Des.:** Susanna Blunt **Rev.:** Loon and moon, teddy bear in stars

Date	Mintage	MS-63	Proof
2006	18,103	4.50	—

KM# 582 DOLLAR **Weight:** 7.0000 g. **Comp.:** Aureate-Bronze Plated Nickel **Ruler:** Elizabeth II **Subject:** Snowy owl **Obv.:** Head right **Obv. Des.:** Susanna Blunt **Rev.:** Snowy owl with year above

Date	Mintage	MS-63	Proof
2006 Specimen	40,000	—	30.00

KM# 583 DOLLAR **Weight:** 25.1750 g. **Comp.:** 0.9250 Silver 0.7487 oz. ASW **Ruler:** Elizabeth II **Subject:** Victoria Cross **Obv.:** Head right

Date	Mintage	MS-63	Proof
2006	27,254	24.00	—
2006 Proof	54,835	—	35.00

KM# 583a DOLLAR **Weight:** 25.1750 g. **Comp.:** 0.9250 Silver with partial gold plating 0.7487 oz. ASW **Ruler:** Elizabeth II **Subject:** Victoria Cross **Obv.:** Head right

Date	Mintage	MS-63	Proof
2006 Proof	—	—	60.00

KM# 630 DOLLAR **Weight:** 7.0000 g. **Comp.:** 0.9250 Silver with multicolor enamel 0.2082 oz. ASW **Ruler:** Elizabeth II **Subject:** Olympic Games **Obv.:** Crowned head right **Rev.:** Loon in flight, colored olympic logo above

Date	Mintage	MS-63	Proof
2006	19,956	30.00	—

KM# 653 DOLLAR **Weight:** 25.1750 g. **Comp.:** 0.9250 Silver 0.7487 oz. ASW **Ruler:** Elizabeth II **Subject:** Thayendanegea **Obv.:** Head right **Rev.:** Bust **Size:** 36.07 mm.

Date	Mintage	MS-63	Proof
2006(ml)	16,378	30.00	—
2006(ml) Proof	65,000	—	40.00

KM# 653a DOLLAR **Weight:** 25.1750 g. **Comp.:** 0.9250 Silver 0.7487 oz. ASW **Ruler:** Elizabeth II **Subject:** Thayendanega **Obv.:** Bust right **Rev.:** Bust, partially gilt **Size:** 36.07 mm.

Date	Mintage	MS-63	P/L	Proof
2006	60,000	—	—	50.00

KM# 654 DOLLAR **Weight:** 7.0000 g. **Comp.:** 0.9250 Silver 0.2082 oz. ASW **Ruler:** Elizabeth II **Obv.:** Head right **Rev.:** Snowflake, colorized **Note:** Sold in a CD package.

Date	Mintage	MS-63	Proof
2006(ml)	34,014	30.00	—

KM# 655 DOLLAR **Weight:** 7.0000 g. **Comp.:** 0.9250 Silver 0.2082 oz. ASW **Ruler:** Elizabeth II **Subject:** Baby Rattle **Obv.:** Head right **Rev.:** Baby rattle

Date	Mintage	MS-63	Proof
2006	3,207	20.00	—

KM# 656 DOLLAR **Weight:** 28.1750 g. **Comp.:** 0.9250 Silver 0.8379 oz. ASW **Ruler:** Elizabeth II **Subject:** Medal of Bravery **Obv.:** Head right

Date	Mintage	MS-63	Proof
2006	7,846	20.00	—

KM# 656a DOLLAR **Weight:** 28.1750 g. **Comp.:** 0.9250 Silver with multicolor enamel 0.8379 oz. ASW **Ruler:** Elizabeth II **Subject:** Medal of Bravery **Obv.:** Head right **Rev.:** Maple leaf within wreath. Colorized.

Date	Mintage	MS-63	Proof
2006	4,951	35.00	—

KM# 687 DOLLAR **Weight:** 28.1750 g. **Comp.:** 0.9250 Silver with partial gold plating 0.8379 oz. ASW **Ruler:** Elizabeth II **Subject:** Joseph Brant **Obv.:** Head right

Date	Mintage	MS-63	Proof
2007	—	20.00	—

KM# 688 DOLLAR **Weight:** 7.0000 g. **Comp.:** Aureate-Bronze Plated Nickel **Ruler:** Elizabeth II **Subject:** Trumpeter Swan **Obv.:** Head right **Rev.:** Loon

Date	Mintage	MS-63	Proof
2007(ml)	40,000	20.00	—

KM# 720 DOLLAR **Weight:** 25.1800 g. **Comp.:** 0.9250 Silver 0.7488 oz. ASW **Ruler:** Elizabeth II **Obv.:** Bust right **Rev.:** Thayendanega multicolor **Size:** 36.07 mm.

Date	Mintage	MS-63	Proof
2007	4,760	20.00	—

KM# 720a DOLLAR **Weight:** 2.0000 g. **Comp.:** 0.9250 Silver 0.0595 oz. ASW **Ruler:** Elizabeth II **Subject:** Thayendanega **Rev.:** Partially gold plated **Size:** 36.07 mm.

Date	Mintage	MS-63	Proof
2007 Proof	60,000	—	70.00

KM# 655a DOLLAR **Weight:** 7.0000 g. **Comp.:** 0.9250 Silver 0.2082 oz. ASW **Ruler:** Elizabeth II **Obv.:** Bust right **Rev.:** Baby Rattle, partially gilt

Date	Mintage	MS-63	Proof
2007	1,911	15.00	—

KM# 700 DOLLAR **Weight:** 7.0000 g. **Comp.:** 0.9250 Silver 0.2082 oz. ASW **Ruler:** Elizabeth II **Rev.:** Alphabet Letter Blocks

Date	Mintage	MS-63	Proof
2007	3,229	—	25.00

KM# 719 DOLLAR **Weight:** 25.1800 g. **Comp.:** 0.9250 Silver 0.7488 oz. ASW **Ruler:** Elizabeth II **Subject:** Celebration of the Arts **Rev.:** Book, TV set, musical instruments, film montage **Rev. Des.:** Friedrich Peter **Edge:** Reeded **Size:** 36.07 mm.

Date	Mintage	MS-63	Proof
2007	6,466	—	50.00

KM# A727 DOLLAR **Weight:** 7.0000 g. **Comp.:** Nickel-Bronze **Ruler:** Elizabeth II **Subject:** Vancouver Olympic Games **Rev.:** Loon splashing in water, Olympics logo at right **Size:** 26.5 mm.

Date	Mintage	MS-63	Proof
2007(ml)	—	3.00	—

KM# 721 DOLLAR **Weight:** 7.0000 g. **Comp.:** Nickel-Bronze **Ruler:** Elizabeth II **Obv.:** Bust right **Rev.:** Calgary flames, multicolor in circle **Size:** 26.5 mm.

Date	Mintage	MS-63	Proof
2008	—	25.00	—

KM# 722 DOLLAR **Weight:** 7.0000 g. **Comp.:** Nickel-Bronze **Ruler:** Elizabeth II **Obv.:** Bust **Rev.:** Edmonton Oilers logo, multicolor in logo **Size:** 26.5 mm.

Date	Mintage	MS-63	Proof
2008	—	25.00	—

KM# 723A DOLLAR **Weight:** 7.0000 g. **Comp.:** Nickel-Bronze **Ruler:** Elizabeth II **Obv.:** Bust right **Rev.:** Montreal Canadians, multicolor logo in circle **Size:** 26.5 mm.

Date	Mintage	MS-63	Proof
2008	—	25.00	—

KM# 724 DOLLAR **Weight:** 7.0000 g. **Comp.:** Nickel **Ruler:** Elizabeth II **Rev.:** Ottowa Senators, multicolor logo in circle **Size:** 26.5 mm.

Date	Mintage	MS-63	Proof
2008	—	25.00	—

KM# 725 DOLLAR **Weight:** 7.0000 g. **Comp.:** Nickel-Bronze **Ruler:** Elizabeth II **Obv.:** Bust right **Rev.:** Toronto Maple Leafs, multicolor logo in circle **Size:** 26.5 mm.

Date	Mintage	MS-63	Proof
2008	—	25.00	—

KM# 726 DOLLAR **Weight:** 7.0000 g. **Comp.:** Nickel-Bronze **Ruler:** Elizabeth II **Obv.:** Bust left **Rev.:** Vancouver Canucks, logo in center **Size:** 26.5 mm.

Date	Mintage	MS-63	Proof
2008	—	25.00	—

KM# 781 DOLLAR **Weight:** 25.1800 g. **Comp.:** 0.9250 Silver 0.7488 oz. ASW **Ruler:** Elizabeth II **Subject:** Ottawa Mint Centennial 1908-2008 **Rev.:** Maple leaf transforming into a common loon **Rev. Des.:** Jason Bowman **Size:** 36.07 mm.

Date	Mintage	MS-63	Proof
2008 Proof	25,000	—	50.00

KM# 784 DOLLAR **Weight:** 7.0000 g. **Comp.:** Nickel-Bronze **Ruler:** Elizabeth II **Rev.:** Common elder **Size:** 26.5 mm.

Date	Mintage	MS-63	Proof
2008 Specimen	40,000	—	50.00

KM# 785 DOLLAR **Weight:** 25.1800 g. **Comp.:** 0.9250 Silver 0.7488 oz. ASW **Ruler:** Elizabeth II **Subject:** Founding of Quebec 400th Anniversary **Rev.:** Samuel de Champlain, ship and town view **Rev. Des.:** Susanne Duranceau **Size:** 36.07 mm.

Date	Mintage	MS-63	Proof
2008 Proof	65,000	—	30.00

KM# 785a DOLLAR **Weight:** 25.1800 g. **Comp.:** 0.9250 Silver 0.7488 oz. ASW **Ruler:** Elizabeth II **Subject:** Founding of Quebec 400th Anniversary **Rev.:** Samuel de Champlain selectively gold plated, ship, town view **Rev. Des.:** Susanne Duranceau **Size:** 36.07 mm.

Date	Mintage	MS-63	Proof
2008	—	27.00	—

KM# 787a DOLLAR **Weight:** 7.0000 g. **Comp.:** 0.9250 Silver 0.2082 oz. ASW **Ruler:** Elizabeth II **Rev.:** Loon splashing with Olympic logo and maple leaf in color above **Rev. Des.:** Steve Hepurn **Size:** 26.5 mm.

Date	Mintage	MS-63	Proof
2008 Proof	—	—	25.00

KM# 787 DOLLAR Weight: 7.0000 g. Comp.: Nickel-Brass Ruler: Elizabeth II Subject: Lucky Loonie Rev.: Loon splashing and Olympic logo at right Rev. Des.: Steve Hepurn Size: 26.5 mm.

Date	Mintage	MS-63	Proof
2008	—	20.00	

KM# 790 DOLLAR Comp.: 0.9990 Silver Ruler: Elizabeth II Rev.: Calgary Flames

Date	Mintage	MS-63	Proof
2008	—	25.00	—

KM# 791 DOLLAR Comp.: 0.9990 Silver Ruler: Elizabeth II Rev.: Edmonton Oilers

Date	Mintage	MS-63	Proof
2008	—	25.00	—

KM# 792 DOLLAR Comp.: 0.9990 Silver Ruler: Elizabeth II Rev.: Montreal Canadians

Date	Mintage	MS-63	Proof
2008	—	25.00	—

KM# 793 DOLLAR Comp.: 0.9990 Silver Ruler: Elizabeth II Rev.: Ottawa Senators

Date	Mintage	MS-63	Proof
2008	—	25.00	—

KM# 794 DOLLAR Comp.: 0.9990 Silver Ruler: Elizabeth II Rev.: Toronto Maple Leafs

Date	Mintage	MS-63	Proof
2008	—	25.00	—

KM# 795 DOLLAR Comp.: 0.9990 Silver Ruler: Elizabeth II Rev.: Vancouver Canucks

Date	Mintage	MS-63	Proof
2008	—	25.00	—

KM# 889 DOLLAR Weight: 25.1800 g. Comp.: 0.9250 Silver 0.7488 oz. ASW Ruler: Elizabeth II Subject: 100th Anniversary of flight in Canada Obv.: Bust right Obv. Leg.: Elizabeth II DG Regina Obv. Des.: Susanna Blunt Rev.: Silhouette with arms spread, 3 planes, plane cutout Rev. Leg.: Canada Dollar 1909-2009 Rev. Des.: Jason Bouwman Size: 36.07 mm.

Date	Mintage	MS-63	Proof
2009	50,000	35.00	—
2009 Proof	50,000		55.00

KM# 914 DOLLAR Weight: 7.0000 g. Comp.: Aureate-Bronze Plated Nickel Ruler: Elizabeth II Obv. Des.: Susanna Blunt Rev.: Blue heron in flight Size: 26.5 mm.

Date	Mintage	MS-63	Proof
2009 Specimen	40,000	50.00	—

KM# 921 DOLLAR Weight: 25.1700 g. Comp.: 0.9250 Silver 0.7485 oz. ASW Ruler: Elizabeth II Subject: Montreal Canadians 100th Anniversary Obv.: Bust right Obv. Des.: Susanna Blunt Rev.: Montral Canadians logo partially gilt Size: 36.07 mm.

Date	Mintage	MS-63	Proof
2009 Proof	1,500	—	150

KM# 851 DOLLAR Weight: 33.6500 g. Comp.: Nickel Ruler: Elizabeth II Rev.: Calgary Flames Jersey Size: 26.5 mm.

Date	Mintage	MS-63	Proof
2009	—	25.00	—

KM# 852 DOLLAR Weight: 33.6500 g. Comp.: 0.9990 Nickel 1.0807 oz. Ruler: Elizabeth II Rev.: Edmonton Oilers Jersey Size: 26.5 mm.

Date	Mintage	MS-63	Proof
2009	—	25.00	—

KM# 853 DOLLAR Weight: 33.6500 g. Comp.: Nickel Ruler: Elizabeth II Rev.: Montreal Canadians Jersey Size: 26.5 mm.

Date	Mintage	MS-63	Proof
2009	—	25.00	—

KM# 854 DOLLAR Weight: 33.6500 g. Comp.: Nickel Ruler: Elizabeth II Rev.: Ottawa Senators Jersey Size: 26.5 mm.

Date	Mintage	MS-63	Proof
2009	—	25.00	—

KM# 855 DOLLAR Weight: 33.6500 g. Comp.: Nickel Ruler: Elizabeth II Rev.: Toronto Maple Leafs Jersey Size: 26.5 mm.

Date	Mintage	MS-63	Proof
2009	—	25.00	—

KM# 856 DOLLAR Weight: 33.6500 g. Comp.: 0.9990 Nickel 1.0807 oz. Ruler: Elizabeth II Rev.: Vancouver Canucks Jersey Size: 26.5 mm.

Date	Mintage	MS-63	Proof
2009	—	25.00	—

KM# 889a DOLLAR Weight: 25.1800 g. Comp.: 0.9250 Silver partially gilt. 0.7488 oz. ASW Ruler: Elizabeth II Obv.: Bust right Rev.: Silouette with arms spread, 3 planes, plane shadow partially gilt Size: 36.07 mm.

Date	Mintage	MS-63	Proof
2009(ml) Proof	—	—	50.00

KM# 883 DOLLAR Weight: 7.0000 g. Comp.: Bronze-Nickel Ruler: Elizabeth II Subject: Lucky Loonie Obv.: Bust right Obv. Leg.: Elizabeth II DG Regina Rev.: Canadian Olympic Team logo Rev. Leg.: Canada Dollar Size: 26.5 mm.

Date	Mintage	MS-63	Proof
2010	12,000		—

KM# 883a DOLLAR Weight: 7.0000 g. Comp.: 0.9250 Silver 0.2082 oz. ASW Ruler: Elizabeth II Subject: Lucky Loonie Obv.: Bust right Obv. Leg.: Elizabeth II DG Regina Rev.: Canadian Olympic Team logo in color Rev. Leg.: Vancouver 2010 Canada Dollar Shape: 11-sided Size: 26.5 mm.

Date	Mintage	MS-63	Proof
2010 Proof	4,000		—

KM# 727 DOLLAR Weight: 7.0000 g. Comp.: Aureate Bonded Bronze Ruler: Elizabeth II Rev.: Vancouver Olympics "stone man" logo Shape: 11-sided Size: 26.5 mm.

Date	Mintage	MS-63	Proof
2010	—	5.00	—

Note: Issued in 2007.

KM# 652 DOLLAR (Louis) Weight: 1.5000 g. Comp.: 0.9990 Gold 0.0482 oz. AGW Ruler: Elizabeth II Subject: Gold Louis Obv.: Bust right Obv. Des.: Susanna Blunt Rev.: Crowned double L monogram within wreath Size: 14.1 mm.

Date	Mintage	MS-63	Proof
2006 Proof	5,648	—	100

KM# 756 DOLLAR (Louis) Weight: 1.5550 g. Comp.: 0.9990 Gold 0.0499 oz. AGW Ruler: Elizabeth II Obv.: Bust right Obv. Des.: Susanna Blunt Rev.: Crown above two oval shields Size: 14.1 mm.

Date	Mintage	MS-63	Proof
2007 Proof	3,457	—	100

KM# 834 DOLLAR (Louis) Weight: 1.5550 g. Comp.: 0.9990 Gold 0.0499 oz. AGW Ruler: Elizabeth II Obv.: Bust right Obv. Des.: Susanna Blunt Size: 14 mm.

Date	Mintage	MS-63	Proof
2008 Proof	—	—	125

KM# 270c 2 DOLLARS Weight: 8.8300 g. Comp.: 0.9250 Silver gold plated center 0.2626 oz. ASW Ruler: Elizabeth II Obv.: Crowned head right within circle, date below Rev.: Polar bear right within circle, denomination below Size: 28 mm. Note: 1.9mm thick.

Date	Mintage	MS-63	Proof
2001 Proof	—	—	12.00

KM# 270 2 DOLLARS Weight: 7.3000 g. Comp.: Bi-Metallic Aluminumn-Bronze center in Nickel ring Ruler: Elizabeth II Obv.: Crowned head right within circle, date below Obv. Des.: Dora dePedery-Hunt Rev.: Polar bear right within circle, denomination below Rev. Des.: Brent Townsend Size: 28 mm.

Date	Mintage	MS-63	P/L	Proof
2001	27,008,000	5.00	—	—
2001 Proof	74,944	—	—	12.50
2002	11,910,000	5.00	—	—
2002 Proof	65,315	—	—	12.50
2003	7,123,697	5.00	—	—
2003 Proof	62,007	—	—	12.50

KM# 449 2 DOLLARS Weight: 7.3000 g. Comp.: Bi-Metallic Aluminum-Bronze center in Nickel ring Ruler: Elizabeth II Subject: Elizabeth II Golden Jubilee Obv.: Crowned head right, jubilee commemorative dates 1952-2002

Date	Mintage	MS-63	Proof
ND(2002)	27,020,000	4.00	

KM# 449a 2 DOLLARS Weight: 8.8300 g. Comp.: 0.9250 Silver gold plated center 0.2626 oz. ASW Ruler: Elizabeth II Subject: Elizabeth II Golden Jubilee Obv.: Crowned head right, jubilee commemorative dates 1952-2002

Date	Mintage	MS-63	Proof
ND(2002) Proof	100,000	—	14.00

KM# 496 2 DOLLARS Weight: 7.3000 g. Comp.: Bi-Metallic Aluminum-Bronze center in Nickel ring Ruler: Elizabeth II Obv.: Head right Obv. Des.: Susanna Blunt Rev. Des.: Brent Townsend

Date	Mintage	MS-63	Proof
2003	4,120,104	5.00	—
2003W	71,142	25.00	—
2004	12,907,000	5.00	—
2004 Proof	—	—	12.50
2005	38,318,000	5.00	—
2005 Proof	—	—	12.50
2006(ml)	25,274,000	5.00	—
2006(ml) Proof	—	—	12.50
2007(ml)	—	5.00	—
2007(ml) Proof	—	—	12.50
2008(ml)	—	5.00	—
2008(ml) Proof	—	—	12.50
2009(ml) Proof	—	—	12.50

KM# 270d 2 DOLLARS Weight: 8.8300 g. Comp.: 0.9250 Silver gold plated center 0.2626 oz. ASW Ruler: Elizabeth II Subject: 100th Anniversary of the Cobalt Silver Strike Obv.: Crowned head right, within circle, date below Rev.: Polar bear right, within circle, denomination below

Date	Mintage	MS-63	Proof
2003 Proof	100,000	—	25.00

KM# 835 2 DOLLARS Weight: 8.8000 g. Comp.: 0.9250 Silver 0.2617 oz. ASW Ruler: Elizabeth II Rev.: Proud Polar Bear advancing right Size: 27.95 mm.

Date	Mintage	MS-63	Proof
2004 Proof	12,607	—	40.00

KM# 496a 2 DOLLARS Weight: 10.8414 g. Comp.: 0.9250 Bi-Metallic Gold plated Silver center in Silver ring 0.3224 oz. Ruler: Elizabeth II Obv.: Head right Obv. Des.: Suanne Blunt Rev.: Polar Bear Edge: Segmented reeding Size: 28 mm.

Date	Mintage	MS-63	Proof
2004 Proof	—	—	25.00

KM# 836 2 DOLLARS Comp.: Bi-Metallic Ruler: Elizabeth II Subject: 10th Anniversary, 2 dollar coin Rev.: "Churchill" Polar Bear, northern lights

Date	Mintage	MS-63	Proof
ND(1996-2006)(ml)	—	7.50	

KM# 837 2 DOLLARS Comp.: Bi-Metallic Ruler: Elizabeth II Obv.: Bust left, date at top Rev.: Polar Bear advancing right

Date	Mintage	MS-63	Proof
2006(ml)	—	7.50	
2007(ml)	38,957,000	7.50	

KM# 631 2 DOLLARS Comp.: Bi-Metallic Ruler: Elizabeth II Subject: 10th Anniversary of $2 coin Obv.: Crowned head right

Date	Mintage	MS-63	Proof
ND(2006)(ml)	5,005,000	25.00	—
ND(2006)(ml) Proof	—	—	40.00

KM# 631a 2 DOLLARS Comp.: Bi-Metallic 22 Kt Gold ring around 4.1 Kt. Gold core Ruler: Elizabeth II Subject: 10th Anniversary of $2 coin Obv.: Crowned head right Rev.: Polar bear

Date	Mintage	MS-63	Proof
ND(2006) Proof	2,068	—	400

KM# 796 2 DOLLARS Weight: 8.8300 g. Comp.: 0.9250 Silver 0.2626 oz. ASW Ruler: Elizabeth II Rev.: Bear, gold plated center Size: 28.07 mm.

Date	Mintage	MS-63	Proof
2008	—	25.00	—

KM# 657 3 DOLLARS Comp.: 0.9250 Silver Gilt Ruler: Elizabeth II Rev.: Beaver within wreath Shape: Square Size: 27x27 mm.

Date	Mintage	MS-63	Proof
2006 Proof	19,963	—	200

KM# 728 4 DOLLARS Weight: 15.8700 g. Comp.: 0.9250 Silver 0.4719 oz. ASW Ruler: Elizabeth II Subject: Dinosaur fossil Obv.: Bust right Rev.: Parasaurolophus, selective enameling Size: 34 mm.

Date	Mintage	MS-63	Proof
2007	13,010	50.00	—

KM# 797 4 DOLLARS Weight: 15.8700 g.
Comp.: 0.9990 Silver 0.5097 oz. ASW **Ruler:** Elizabeth II
Subject: Dinosaur fossil **Obv.:** Bust right **Rev.:** Triceratops,
enameled **Rev. Des.:** Kerri Burnett **Size:** 34 mm.

Date	Mintage	MS-63	Proof
2008	20,000	25.00	—

KM# 890 4 DOLLARS Weight: 15.8700 g.
Comp.: 0.9990 Silver 0.5097 oz. ASW **Ruler:** Elizabeth II
Subject: Tyrannosaurus Rex **Obv.:** Bust right **Obv. Leg.:**
Elizabeth II DG Regina **Obv. Des.:** Susanna Blunt **Rev.:** T-Rex
skeleton in selective aging **Rev. Leg.:** Canada 4 Dollars
Rev. Des.: Kerri Burnette **Size:** 34 mm.

Date	Mintage	MS-63	Proof
2009 Proof	20,000	25.00	—

KM# 435 5 DOLLARS Weight: 16.8600 g.
Comp.: 0.9250 Silver 0.5014 oz. ASW **Ruler:** Elizabeth II
Subject: Guglielmo Marconi **Obv.:** Crowned head right
Rev.: Gold-plated cameo portrait of Marconi **Rev. Des.:** Cosme
Saffioti **Edge:** Reeded **Size:** 28.4 mm. **Note:** Only issued in two
coin set with British 2 pounds KM#1014a.

Date	Mintage	MS-63	Proof
ND(2001) Proof	15,011	—	22.00

KM# 519 5 DOLLARS Weight: 8.3600 g. **Comp.:**
0.9000 Gold 0.2419 oz. AGW **Ruler:** Elizabeth II **Obv.:** Crowned
head right **Rev.:** National arms **Edge:** Reeded **Size:** 21.6 mm.

Date	Mintage	MS-63	Proof
ND (2002) Proof	2,002	—	325

KM# 518 5 DOLLARS Weight: 31.1200 g. **Comp.:**
0.9999 Silver 1.0004 oz. ASW **Ruler:** Elizabeth II **Subject:**
F.I.F.A. World Cup Soccer, Germany 2006 **Obv.:** Crowned head
right, denomination **Rev.:** Goalie on knees **Edge:** Reeded
Size: 38 mm.

Date	Mintage	MS-63	Proof
2003 Proof	21,542	—	29.00

KM# 514 5 DOLLARS Weight: 31.1200 g.
Comp.: 0.9999 Silver 1.0004 oz. ASW **Ruler:** Elizabeth II
Obv.: Crowned head right **Rev.:** Moose **Edge:** Reeded
Size: 38 mm.

Date	Mintage	MS-63	Proof
2004 Proof	12,822	—	125

KM# 527 5 DOLLARS Weight: 31.1200 g. **Comp.:**
0.9999 Silver 1.0004 oz. ASW **Ruler:** Elizabeth II **Subject:** Golf,
Championship of Canada, Centennial **Obv.:** Head right

Date	Mintage	MS-63	Proof
2004 Proof	18,750	—	25.00

KM# 554 5 DOLLARS Weight: 31.1200 g.
Comp.: 0.9999 Silver 1.0004 oz. ASW **Ruler:** Elizabeth II
Subject: Alberta **Obv. Des.:** Head right **Rev. Des.:** Michelle
Grant

Date	Mintage	MS-63	Proof
2005 Proof	20,000	—	35.00

KM# 555 5 DOLLARS Weight: 31.1200 g.
Comp.: 0.9999 Silver 1.0004 oz. ASW **Ruler:** Elizabeth II
Subject: Saskatchewan **Obv.:** Head right **Obv. Des.:** Susanna
Blunt **Rev. Des.:** Paulett Sapergia

Date	Mintage	MS-63	Proof
2005 Proof	20,000	—	35.00

KM# 556.1 5 DOLLARS Weight: 31.1200 g.
Comp.: 0.9990 Silver 0.9995 oz. ASW **Ruler:** Elizabeth II
Subject: 60th Anniversay Victory WWII - Veterans **Obv.:** Bust
right **Rev.:** Large V and heads of sailor, soldier and aviator on
large maple leaf **Edge:** Reeded **Size:** 38.02 mm.

Date	Mintage	MS-63	Proof
2005	25,000	30.00	—

KM# 556.2 5 DOLLARS Weight: 31.1200 g.
Comp.: 0.9999 Silver 1.0004 oz. ASW **Ruler:** Elizabeth II
Subject: 60th Anniversary Victory WW II - Veterans **Obv.:** Bust
right **Rev.:** Large V and heads of sailor, soldier and aviator on
maple leaf with small maple leaf added at left and right
Edge: Reeded **Size:** 38.02 mm.

Date	Mintage	MS-63	Proof
2005	10,000	100	—

KM# 557 5 DOLLARS Weight: 31.1200 g.
Comp.: 0.9999 Silver 1.0004 oz. ASW **Ruler:** Elizabeth II
Subject: Walrus and calf **Obv.:** Head right **Obv. Des.:** Susanna
Blunt **Rev.:** Two walrusus and calf **Rev. Des.:** Pierre Leduc
Size: 36 mm.

Date	Mintage	MS-63	Proof
2005 Proof	5,519	—	35.00

KM# 558 5 DOLLARS Weight: 31.1200 g.
Comp.: 0.9999 Silver 1.0004 oz. ASW **Ruler:** Elizabeth II
Subject: White tailed deer **Obv.:** Head right **Obv. Des.:** Susanna
Blunt **Rev.:** Two deer standing **Rev. Des.:** Xerxes Irani
Size: 36 mm.

Date	Mintage	MS-63	Proof
2005 Proof	6,439	—	35.00

KM# 585 5 DOLLARS Weight: 31.1200 g.
Comp.: 0.9999 Silver 1.0004 oz. ASW **Ruler:** Elizabeth II
Obv.: Head right **Obv. Des.:** Susanna Blunt **Rev.:** Peregrine
Falcon feeding young ones **Rev. Des.:** Dwayne Harty
Size: 36 mm.

Date	Mintage	MS-63	Proof
2006 Proof	6,145	—	40.00

KM# 586 5 DOLLARS Weight: 31.1200 g.
Comp.: 0.9999 Silver 1.0004 oz. ASW **Ruler:** Elizabeth II
Subject: Sable Island horses **Obv.:** Head right **Obv. Des.:**
Susanna Blunt **Rev.:** Horse and foal standing **Rev. Des.:** Christie
Paquet **Size:** 36 mm.

Date	Mintage	MS-63	Proof
2006 Proof	7,589	—	40.00

KM# 658 5 DOLLARS Weight: 31.1200 g.
Comp.: 0.9999 Silver 1.0004 oz. ASW **Ruler:** Elizabeth II
Subject: Breast Cancer Awareness **Rev.:** Colorized pink ribbon
Size: 36.07 mm.

Date	Mintage	MS-63	Proof
2006 Proof	11,048	—	50.00

KM# 659 5 DOLLARS Weight: 31.1200 g.
Comp.: 0.9999 Silver 1.0004 oz. ASW **Ruler:** Elizabeth II
Subject: C.A.F. Snowbirds Acrobatic Jet Flying Team
Rev.: Image of fighter jets and piolt

Date	Mintage	MS-63	Proof
2006 Proof	7,896	—	50.00

KM# A799 5 DOLLARS Weight: 25.1750 g.
Comp.: 0.9959 Silver 0.8060 oz. ASW **Ruler:** Elizabeth II
Subject: Breast Cancer Awareness **Rev.:** Pink ribbon and groups
of people **Size:** 36.07 mm.

Date	Mintage	MS-63	Proof
2006 Proof	11,048	—	60.00

KM# 799 5 DOLLARS Weight: 31.1050 g.
Comp.: 0.9990 Silver 0.9990 oz. ASW **Ruler:** Elizabeth II
Subject: Breast Cancer Awareness **Rev.:** Multicolor, green
maple leaf and pink ribbon **Size:** 38 mm.

Date	Mintage	MS-63	Proof
2008	—	85.00	—

KM# 863 5 DOLLARS Weight: 31.1030 g.
Comp.: 0.9990 Silver 0.9989 oz. ASW **Ruler:** Elizabeth II
Subject: Edmonton Olympics **Rev.:** Thunderbird **Size:** 38 mm.

Date	Mintage	MS-63	Proof
2009 Proof	—	—	50.00

KM# 515 8 DOLLARS Weight: 28.8000 g.
Comp.: 0.9250 Silver 0.8565 oz. ASW **Ruler:** Elizabeth II
Obv.: Head right **Obv. Des.:** Susanna Blunt **Rev.:** Grizzly bear
walking left **Edge:** Reeded **Size:** 39 mm.

Date	Mintage	MS-63	Proof
2004 Proof	12,942	—	60.00

KM# 597 8 DOLLARS Weight: 32.1500 g.
Comp.: 0.9999 Silver 1.0335 oz. ASW **Ruler:** Elizabeth II
Subject: Canadian Pacific Railway, 120th Anniversary
Obv.: Head right **Obv. Des.:** Susanna Blunt **Rev.:** Railway bridge

Date	Mintage	MS-63	Proof
2005 Proof	9,892	—	45.00

KM# 598 8 DOLLARS Weight: 32.1500 g.
Comp.: 0.9999 Silver 1.0335 oz. ASW **Ruler:** Elizabeth II
Subject: Canadian Pacific Railway, 120th Anniversary
Obv.: Head right **Rev.:** Railway memorial to the Chinese workers

Date	Mintage	MS-63	Proof
2005 Proof	9,892	—	45.00

KM# 730 8 DOLLARS Weight: 25.1800 g.
Comp.: 0.9999 Silver 0.8094 oz. ASW **Ruler:** Elizabeth II
Obv.: Queens's head at top in circle, three Chinese characters
Rev.: Dragon and other creatures **Size:** 36.1 mm.

Date	Mintage	MS-63	Proof
2007 Proof	19,954	—	55.00

KM# 520 10 DOLLARS Weight: 16.7200 g. **Comp.:**
0.9000 Gold 0.4838 oz. AGW **Ruler:** Elizabeth II **Obv.:** Crowned
head right **Rev.:** National arms **Edge:** Reeded **Size:** 26.92 mm.

Date	Mintage	MS-63	Proof
ND (2002) Proof	2,002	—	650

KM# 559 10 DOLLARS Weight: 25.1750 g.
Comp.: 0.9999 Silver 0.8093 oz. ASW **Ruler:** Elizabeth II
Subject: Pope John Paul II **Obv.:** Head right

Date	Mintage	MS-63	Proof
2005 Proof	24,716	—	35.00

KM# 757 10 DOLLARS Weight: 25.1750 g.
0.9999 Silver 0.8093 oz. ASW **Ruler:** Elizabeth II **Subject:** Year
of the Veteran **Rev.:** Profile left of young and old veteran

Date	Mintage	MS-63	Proof
2005 Proof	6,549	—	45.00

KM# 661 10 DOLLARS Weight: 25.1750 g.
Comp.: 0.9999 Silver 0.8093 oz. ASW **Ruler:** Elizabeth II
Subject: National Historic Sites **Obv.:** Head right **Rev.:** Fortress
of Louisbourg

Date	Mintage	MS-63	Proof
2006 Proof	5,544	—	35.00

KM# 415 15 DOLLARS **Weight:** 33.6300 g.
Comp.: 0.9250 Silver with gold insert 1.0000 oz. ASW
Ruler: Elizabeth II **Subject:** Year of the Snake **Obv.:** Crowned
head right **Rev.:** Snake within circle of lunar calendar signs
Rev. Des.: Harvey Chain **Edge:** Reeded **Size:** 40 mm.

Date	Mintage	MS-63	Proof
2001 Proof	60,754	—	45.00

KM# 463 15 DOLLARS **Weight:** 33.6300 g.
Comp.: 0.9250 Silver 24-Karat Gold-plated central Cameo
1.0000 oz. ASW **Ruler:** Elizabeth II **Subject:** Year of the Horse
Obv.: Crowned head right **Obv. Des.:** Dora dePédery-Hunt
Rev.: Horse in center with Chinese Lunar calendar around
Rev. Des.: Harvey Chain

Date	Mintage	MS-63	Proof
2002 Proof	59,395	—	65.00

KM# 481 15 DOLLARS **Weight:** 33.6300 g.
Comp.: 0.9250 Silver 1.0000 oz. ASW **Ruler:** Elizabeth II
Subject: Year of the Sheep **Obv.:** Crowned head right
Rev.: Sheep in center with Chinese Lunar calendar around
Rev. Des.: Harvey Chain **Size:** 40 mm.

Date	Mintage	MS-63	Proof
2003 Proof	53,714	—	60.00

KM# 610 15 DOLLARS **Weight:** 33.6300 g.
Comp.: 0.9250 Silver Gold octagon applique in center 1.0000 oz.
ASW **Ruler:** Elizabeth II **Subject:** Year of the Monkey
Obv.: Crowned head right **Rev.:** Monkey in center with Chinese
Lunar calendar around

Date	Mintage	MS-63	Proof
2004 Proof	46,175	—	150

KM# 560 15 DOLLARS **Weight:** 33.6300 g.
Comp.: 0.9250 Silver Gold applique 1.0000 oz. ASW **Ruler:**
Elizabeth II **Subject:** Year of the Rooster **Obv.:** Crowned head
right **Rev.:** Rooster in center with Chinese Lunar calendar around

Date	Mintage	MS-63	Proof
2005 Proof	44,690	—	75.00

KM# 587 15 DOLLARS **Weight:** 33.6300 g.
Comp.: 0.9250 Silver Gold applique 1.0000 oz. ASW **Ruler:**
Elizabeth II **Subject:** Year of the Dog **Obv.:** Crowned head left
Rev.: Dog in center with Chinese Lunar calendar around

Date	Mintage	MS-63	Proof
2006 Proof	41,617	—	65.00

KM# 662 15 DOLLARS **Weight:** 33.6300 g. **Comp.:**
0.9250 Silver Gold applique 1.0000 oz. ASW **Ruler:** Elizabeth II
Subject: Year of the Pig **Obv.:** Crowned head right **Rev.:** Pig in
center with Chinese Lunar calendar around

Date	Mintage	MS-63	Proof
2006 Proof	48,888	—	80.00

KM# 732 15 DOLLARS **Weight:** 34.0000 g. **Comp.:**
0.9250 Silver gold inlay 1.0111 oz. ASW **Ruler:** Elizabeth II
Subject: Year of Pig **Rev.:** Octagonal gold insert **Size:** 40 mm.

Date	Mintage	MS-63	Proof
2007 Proof	48,888	—	80.00

KM# 801 15 DOLLARS **Weight:** 34.0000 g. **Comp.:**
0.9250 Silver 1.0111 oz. ASW **Ruler:** Elizabeth II **Subject:** Year
of the Rat **Rev.:** Rat, gold octagonal insert at center **Size:** 40 mm.

Date	Mintage	MS-63	Proof
2008 Proof	—	—	75.00

KM# 803 15 DOLLARS **Weight:** 30.0000 g. **Comp.:**
0.9250 Silver 0.8921 oz. ASW **Ruler:** Elizabeth II **Rev.:** Queen
Victoria's coinage portrait **Size:** 36.15 mm.

Date	Mintage	MS-63	Proof
2008	10,000	100	—

KM# 804 15 DOLLARS **Weight:** 30.0000 g. **Comp.:**
0.9250 Silver 0.8921 oz. ASW **Ruler:** Elizabeth II **Rev.:** Edward
VII coinage portrait **Rev. Des.:** G. W. DeSaulles **Size:** 36.15 mm.

Date	Mintage	MS-63	Proof
2008	10,000	100	—

KM# 805 15 DOLLARS **Weight:** 20.0000 g. **Comp.:**
0.9250 Silver 0.5948 oz. ASW **Ruler:** Elizabeth II **Rev.:** George
V coinage portrait **Size:** 36.15 mm.

Date	Mintage	MS-63	Proof
2008	10,000	100	—

KM# 806 15 DOLLARS **Weight:** 31.5600 g. **Comp.:**
0.9250 Silver 0.9385 oz. ASW **Ruler:** Elizabeth II **Rev.:** Queen
of Spades, multicolor playing card **Size:** 49.8 x 28.6 mm.

Date	Mintage	MS-63	Proof
2008	25,000	90.00	—

KM# 807 15 DOLLARS **Weight:** 31.5600 g. **Comp.:**
0.9250 Silver 0.9385 oz. ASW **Ruler:** Elizabeth II **Rev.:** Jack of
Hearts, multicolor playing card **Size:** 49.8 x 28.6 mm.

Date	Mintage	MS-63	Proof
2008	25,000	90.00	—

KM# 919 15 DOLLARS **Weight:** 31.5600 g. **Comp.:**
0.9250 Silver 0.9385 oz. ASW **Ruler:** Elizabeth II **Obv.:** Bust
right **Obv. Des.:** Susanna Blunt **Rev.:** Ten of spades, multicolor
Shape: rectangle **Size:** 49.8 x 28.6 mm.

Date	Mintage	MS-63	Proof
2009 Proof	25,000	—	100

KM# 920 15 DOLLARS **Weight:** 31.5600 g. **Comp.:**
0.9250 Silver 0.9385 oz. ASW **Ruler:** Elizabeth II **Obv.:** Bust
right **Obv. Des.:** Susanna Blunt **Rev.:** King of hearts, multicolor
Shape: Rectangle **Size:** 49.8 x 28.6 mm.

Date	Mintage	MS-63	Proof
2009 Proof	25,000	—	100

KM# 866 15 DOLLARS **Weight:** 34.0000 g.
Comp.: 0.9250 Silver 1.0111 oz. ASW **Ruler:** Elizabeth II
Subject: Year of the Ox **Rev.:** Ox, octagon gold insert
Size: 40 mm.

Date	Mintage	MS-63	Proof
2009 Proof	—	—	80.00

KM# 922 15 DOLLARS **Weight:** 30.0000 g.
Comp.: 0.9250 Silver 0.8921 oz. ASW **Ruler:** Elizabeth II
Obv.: Bust right **Obv. Des.:** Susanna Blunt **Rev.:** Pages portrait
of George VI **Size:** 36.15 mm.

Date	Mintage	MS-63	P/L	Proof
2009(ml) Prooflike	10,000	—	100.00	—

KM# 923 15 DOLLARS **Weight:** 30.0000 g.
Comp.: 0.9250 Silver 0.8921 oz. ASW **Ruler:** Elizabeth II
Obv.: Bust right **Obv. Des.:** Susanna Blunt **Rev.:** Glick portrait
of Queen Elizabeth II **Size:** 36.15 mm.

Date	Mintage	MS-63	Proof
2009(ml) Prooflike	10,000	—	—

KM# 411 20 DOLLARS **Weight:** 31.1035 g.
Comp.: 0.9250 Silver 0.9250 oz. ASW **Ruler:** Elizabeth II
Subject: Transportation - Steam Locomotive **Obv.:** Crowned
head right **Obv. Des.:** Dora dePédery-Hunt **Rev.:** First Canadian
Steel Steam Locomotive and cameo hologram **Rev. Des.:** Don
Curely **Edge:** Reeded and plain sections **Size:** 38 mm.

Date	Mintage	MS-63	Proof
2001 Proof	15,000	—	35.00

KM# 427 20 DOLLARS **Weight:** 31.1030 g.
Comp.: 0.9250 Silver 0.9249 oz. ASW **Ruler:** Elizabeth II
Series: Transportation - The Marco Polo **Obv.:** Crowned head
right **Rev.:** Sailship with hologram cameo **Rev. Des.:** J. Franklin
Wright **Edge:** Reeded and plain sections **Size:** 38 mm.

Date	Mintage	MS-63	Proof
2001 Proof	15,000	—	35.00

KM# 428 20 DOLLARS **Weight:** 31.1030 g.
Comp.: 0.9250 Silver 0.9249 oz. ASW **Ruler:** Elizabeth II
Series: Transportation - Russell Touring Car **Obv.:** Crowned
head right **Rev.:** Russell touring car with hologram cameo
Rev. Des.: John Mardon **Edge:** Reeded and plain sections
Size: 38 mm.

Date	Mintage	MS-63	Proof
2001 Proof	15,000	—	35.00

KM# 464 20 DOLLARS **Weight:** 31.1030 g.
Comp.: 0.9250 Silver 0.9249 oz. ASW **Ruler:** Elizabeth II
Obv.: Crowned head right **Obv. Des.:** Dora dePédery-Hunt
Rev.: Gray-Dort Model 25-SM with cameo hologram
Rev. Des.: John Mardon

Date	Mintage	MS-63	Proof
2002 Proof	15,000	—	40.00

KM# 465 20 DOLLARS **Weight:** 31.1030 g.
Comp.: 0.9250 Silver 0.9249 oz. ASW **Ruler:** Elizabeth II
Obv.: Crowned head right **Obv. Des.:** Dora dePédery-Hunt
Rev.: Sailing ship William D. Lawrence **Rev. Des.:** Bonnie Ross

Date	Mintage	MS-63	Proof
2002 Proof	15,000	—	40.00

KM# 523 20 DOLLARS **Weight:** 31.3900 g.
Comp.: 0.9990 Silver 1.0082 oz. ASW **Ruler:** Elizabeth II
Subject: Canadian Rockies, colorized **Obv.:** Crowned head right
Obv. Des.: Dora dePédery-Hunt **Rev.:** Canadian Rockies

Date	Mintage	MS-63	Proof
2003 Proof	29,967	—	50.00

KM# 483 20 DOLLARS **Weight:** 31.1030 g.
Comp.: 0.9250 Silver with selective gold plating 0.9249 oz. ASW
Ruler: Elizabeth II **Subject:** The HMCS Bras d'or (FHE-400)
Obv.: Crowned head right **Obv. Des.:** Dora dePédery-Hunt
Rev.: Ship in water **Rev. Des.:** Donald Curley, Stan Witten

Date	Mintage	MS-63	Proof
2003 Proof	15,000	—	40.00

KM# 482 20 DOLLARS **Weight:** 31.3900 g. **Comp.:** 0.9999 Silver 1.0091 oz. ASW **Ruler:** Elizabeth II **Obv.:** Crowned head right **Obv. Des.:** Dora dePédery-Hunt **Rev.:** Niagara Falls hologram **Rev. Des.:** Gary Corcoran

Date	Mintage	MS-63	Proof
2003 Proof	29,967	—	65.00

KM# 484 20 DOLLARS **Weight:** 31.1030 g. **Comp.:** 0.9250 Silver with selective gold plating 0.9249 oz. ASW **Ruler:** Elizabeth II **Subject:** Canadian National FA-1 diesel-electric locomotive **Obv.:** Crowned head right **Obv. Des.:** Dora dePédery-Hunt **Rev. Des.:** John Mardon, William Woodruff

Date	Mintage	MS-63	Proof
2003 Proof	15,000	—	40.00

KM# 485 20 DOLLARS **Weight:** 31.1030 g. **Comp.:** 0.9250 Silver with selective gold plating 0.9249 oz. ASW **Ruler:** Elizabeth II **Obv.:** Crowned head right **Obv. Des.:** Dora dePédery-Hunt **Rev.:** The Bricklin SV-1 **Rev. Des.:** Brian Hughes, José Oslo

Date	Mintage	MS-63	Proof
2003 Proof	15,000	—	45.00

KM# 611 20 DOLLARS **Weight:** 31.3900 g. **Comp.:** 0.9999 Silver 1.0091 oz. ASW **Ruler:** Elizabeth II **Obv.:** Head right **Obv. Des.:** Susanna Blunt **Rev.:** Iceberg, hologram

Date	Mintage	MS-63	Proof
2004 Proof	24,879	—	45.00

KM# 838 20 DOLLARS **Weight:** 31.3900 g. **Comp.:** 0.9999 Silver selectively gold plated 1.0091 oz. ASW **Ruler:** Elizabeth II **Rev.:** Hopewell Rocks

Date	Mintage	MS-63	Proof
2004 Proof	16,918	—	45.00

KM# 561 20 DOLLARS **Weight:** 31.3900 g. **Comp.:** 0.9999 Silver 1.0091 oz. ASW **Ruler:** Elizabeth II **Subject:** Three-masted sailing ship, hologram **Obv.:** Head right **Obv. Des.:** Susanna Blunt **Rev. Des.:** Bonnie Ross

Date	Mintage	MS-63	Proof
2005 Proof	18,276	—	55.00

KM# 562 20 DOLLARS **Weight:** 31.3900 g. **Comp.:** 0.9999 Silver 1.0091 oz. ASW **Ruler:** Elizabeth II **Subject:** Northwest Territories Diamonds **Obv.:** Head right **Obv. Des.:** Susanna Blunt **Rev.:** Multicolor diamond hologram on landscape **Rev. Des.:** José Oslo **Edge:** Reeded **Size:** 38 mm.

Date	Mintage	MS-63	Proof
2005 Proof	35,000	—	45.00

KM# 563 20 DOLLARS **Weight:** 31.3900 g. **Comp.:** 0.9999 Silver 1.0091 oz. ASW **Ruler:** Elizabeth II **Subject:** Mingan Archepelago **Obv.:** Head right **Obv. Des.:** Susanna Blunt **Rev.:** Cliffs with whale tail out of water **Rev. Des.:** Pierre Leduc

Date	Mintage	MS-63	Proof
2005 Proof	—	—	45.00

KM# 564 20 DOLLARS **Weight:** 31.3900 g. **Comp.:** 0.9999 Silver 1.0091 oz. ASW **Ruler:** Elizabeth II **Subject:** Rainforests of the Pacific Northwest **Obv.:** Head right **Rev.:** Open winged bird

Date	Mintage	MS-63	Proof
2005 Proof	—	—	45.00

KM# 565 20 DOLLARS **Weight:** 31.3900 g. **Comp.:** 0.9999 Silver 1.0091 oz. ASW **Ruler:** Elizabeth II **Subject:** Toronto Island National Park **Obv.:** Head right **Rev.:** Toronto Island Lighthouse

Date	Mintage	MS-63	Proof
2005 Proof	—	—	45.00

KM# 588 20 DOLLARS **Weight:** 31.3900 g. **Comp.:** 0.9999 Silver 1.0091 oz. ASW **Ruler:** Elizabeth II **Subject:** Georgian Bay National Park **Obv.:** Head right **Rev.:** Canoe and small trees on island

Date	Mintage	MS-63	Proof
2006 Proof	—	—	60.00

KM# 589 20 DOLLARS **Weight:** 31.1000 g. **Comp.:** 0.9999 Silver 0.9997 oz. ASW **Ruler:** Elizabeth II **Subject:** Notre Dame Basilica, Montreal, as a hologram **Obv.:** Head right

Date	Mintage	MS-63	Proof
2006 Proof	15,000	—	50.00

KM# 663 20 DOLLARS **Weight:** 31.3900 g. **Comp.:** 0.9999 Silver 1.0091 oz. ASW **Ruler:** Elizabeth II **Subject:** Nahanni National Park **Obv.:** Head right **Rev.:** Bear walking along sream, cliff in background

Date	Mintage	MS-63	Proof
2006 Proof	—	—	60.00

KM# 664 20 DOLLARS **Weight:** 31.3900 g. **Comp.:** 0.9999 Silver 1.0091 oz. ASW **Ruler:** Elizabeth II **Subject:** Jasper National Park **Obv.:** Head right **Rev.:** Cowboy on horseback in majestic scene

Date	Mintage	MS-63	Proof
2006 Proof	—	—	60.00

KM# 665 20 DOLLARS **Weight:** 31.1000 g. **Comp.:** 0.9999 Silver 0.9997 oz. ASW **Ruler:** Elizabeth II **Subject:** CN Tower, Toronto **Obv.:** Head right **Rev.:** Holographic rendering of CN Tower

Date	Mintage	MS-63	Proof
2006 Proof	15,000	—	60.00

KM# 666 20 DOLLARS **Weight:** 31.1000 g. **Comp.:** 0.9999 Silver 0.9997 oz. ASW **Ruler:** Elizabeth II **Subject:** Pengrowth (Calgary Saddledome) **Obv.:** Head right **Rev.:** Holographic view of Saddledome

Date	Mintage	MS-63	Proof
2006 Proof	15,000	—	55.00

KM# 667 20 DOLLARS **Weight:** 31.3900 g. **Comp.:** 0.9999 Silver 1.0091 oz. ASW **Ruler:** Elizabeth II **Subject:** Tall Ship **Obv.:** Head right **Rev.:** Ketch and holographic image

Date	Mintage	MS-63	Proof
2006 Proof	10,299	—	60.00

KM# 734 20 DOLLARS **Weight:** 31.1000 g. **Comp.:** 0.9990 Silver 0.9988 oz. ASW **Ruler:** Elizabeth II **Rev.:** Holiday sleigh ride **Size:** 38 mm.

Date	Mintage	MS-63	Proof
2007 Proof	6,041	—	50.00

KM# 735 20 DOLLARS **Weight:** 31.1000 g. **Comp.:** 0.9990 Silver 0.9988 oz. ASW **Ruler:** Elizabeth II **Rev.:** Snowflake, blue crystal

Date	Mintage	MS-63	Proof
2007 Proof	1,433	—	175

KM# 737 20 DOLLARS **Weight:** 31.1000 g. **Comp.:** 0.9990 Silver 0.9988 oz. ASW **Ruler:** Elizabeth II **Subject:** International Polar Year **Size:** 38 mm.

Date	Mintage	MS-63	Proof
2007 Proof	8,352	—	50.00

KM# 737a 20 DOLLARS **Weight:** 31.1000 g. **Comp.:** 0.9990 Silver 0.9988 oz. ASW **Ruler:** Elizabeth II **Subject:** International Polar Year **Rev.:** Blue plasma coating **Size:** 38 mm.

Date	Mintage	MS-63	Proof
2007 Proof	3,005	—	150

KM# 738 20 DOLLARS **Weight:** 31.3900 g. **Comp.:** 0.9999 Silver 1.0091 oz. ASW **Ruler:** Elizabeth II **Subject:** Tall ships **Rev.:** Brigantine in harbor, hologram **Size:** 38 mm.

Date	Mintage	MS-63	Proof
2007 Proof	16,000	—	60.00

KM# 839 20 DOLLARS **Weight:** 31.3900 g. **Comp.:** 0.9999 Silver 1.0091 oz. ASW **Ruler:** Elizabeth II **Rev.:** Northern lights in hologram

Date	Mintage	MS-63	Proof
2007	—	35.00	—

KM# 808 20 DOLLARS **Weight:** 31.5000 g. **Comp.:** 0.9250 Silver 0.9368 oz. ASW **Ruler:** Elizabeth II **Subject:** Agriculture trade **Size:** 40 mm.

Date	Mintage	MS-63	Proof
2008 Proof	10,000	—	50.00

KM# 809 20 DOLLARS **Weight:** 31.1050 g. **Comp.:** 0.9990 Silver 0.9990 oz. ASW **Ruler:** Elizabeth II **Rev.:** Royal Hudson Steam locomotive **Size:** 38 mm.

Date	Mintage	MS-63	Proof
2008 Proof	—	—	50.00

KM# 810 20 DOLLARS **Weight:** 31.3900 g. **Comp.:** 0.9990 Silver 1.0082 oz. ASW **Ruler:** Elizabeth II **Rev.:** Green leaf and crystal raindrop **Rev. Des.:** Stanley Witten **Size:** 38 mm.

Date	Mintage	MS-63	Proof
2008 Proof	—	—	65.00

KM# 811 20 DOLLARS **Weight:** 31.1050 g. **Comp.:** 0.9990 Silver 0.9990 oz. ASW **Ruler:** Elizabeth II **Rev.:** Snowflake, amethyst crystal

Date	Mintage	MS-63	Proof
2008 Proof	—	—	90.00

KM# 813 20 DOLLARS **Weight:** 31.1050 g. **Comp.:** 0.9990 Silver 0.9990 oz. ASW **Ruler:** Elizabeth II **Rev.:** Carolers around tree **Size:** 38 mm.

Date	Mintage	MS-63	Proof
2008	—	50.00	—

KM# 872 20 DOLLARS **Weight:** 31.1050 g. **Comp.:** 0.9990 Silver 0.9990 oz. ASW **Ruler:** Elizabeth II **Rev.:** Snowflake, sapphire crystal **Size:** 38 mm.

Date	Mintage	MS-63	Proof
2008 Proof	—	—	85.00

KM# 893 20 DOLLARS **Weight:** 31.3900 g. **Comp.:** 0.9990 Silver 1.0082 oz. ASW **Ruler:** Elizabeth II **Subject:** Coal mining trade **Obv.:** Bust right **Obv. Leg.:** Elizabeth II DG Regina **Obv. Des.:** Susanna Blunt **Rev.:** Miner pushing cart with coal **Rev. Leg.:** Canada 20 Dollars **Rev. Des.:** John Marder **Size:** 38 mm.

Date	Mintage	MS-63	Proof
2009 Proof	10,000	—	—

KM# 891 20 DOLLARS **Weight:** 31.3900 g. **Comp.:** 0.9990 Silver 1.0082 oz. ASW **Ruler:** Elizabeth II **Subject:** Great Canadian Locomotives - Jubilee **Obv.:** Bust right **Obv. Leg.:** Elizabeth II DG Regina **Obv. Des.:** Susanna Blunt **Rev.:** Jubilee locomotive side view **Rev. Leg.:** Canada 20 Dollars **Edge Lettering:** Jubilee **Size:** 38 mm.

Date	Mintage	MS-63	Proof
2009 Proof	10,000	—	—

KM# 892 20 DOLLARS **Weight:** 31.3900 g. **Comp.:** 0.9990 Silver 1.0082 oz. ASW **Ruler:** Elizabeth II **Subject:** Crystal raindrop **Obv.:** Bust right **Obv. Leg.:** Elizabeth II DG Regina **Obv. Des.:** Susanna Blunt **Rev.:** Colored maple leaves with crystal raindrop **Rev. Leg.:** Canada 20 Dollars **Rev. Des.:** Celia Godkin **Size:** 38 mm.

Date	Mintage	MS-63	Proof
2009 Proof	10,000	—	—

KM# 871 20 DOLLARS **Weight:** 27.7800 g. **Comp.:** 0.9250 Silver 0.8261 oz. ASW **Ruler:** Elizabeth II **Rev.:** Edmonton Oilers goalie mask, multicolor on goal net **Size:** 40 mm.

Date	Mintage	MS-63	Proof
2009	10,000	35.00	—

KM# 870 20 DOLLARS **Weight:** 27.7800 g. **Comp.:** 0.9250 Silver 0.8261 oz. ASW **Ruler:** Elizabeth II **Rev.:** Calgary Flames goalie mask multicolor on goal net **Size:** 40 mm.

Date	Mintage	MS-63	Proof
2009	10,000	35.00	—

KM# 872A 20 DOLLARS **Weight:** 27.7800 g. **Comp.:** 0.9250 Silver 0.8261 oz. ASW **Ruler:** Elizabeth II **Rev.:** Montreal Canadians goalie mask multicolor **Size:** 40 mm.

Date	Mintage	MS-63	Proof
2009	10,000	25.00	—

KM# 873 20 DOLLARS **Weight:** 27.7800 g. **Comp.:** 0.9250 Silver 0.8261 oz. ASW **Ruler:** Elizabeth II **Rev.:** Ottawa Senators goalie mask on goal net **Size:** 40 mm.

Date	Mintage	MS-63	Proof
2009	10,000	25.00	—

KM# 874 20 DOLLARS **Weight:** 27.7800 g . **Comp.:** 0.9250 Silver 0.8261 oz. ASW **Ruler:** Elizabeth II **Rev.:** Toronto Maple Leafs goalie mask, multicolor on goal net **Size:** 40 mm.

Date	Mintage	MS-63	Proof
2009	10,000	25.00	—

KM# 875 20 DOLLARS **Weight:** 27.7800 g. **Comp.:** 0.9250 Silver 0.8261 oz. ASW **Ruler:** Elizabeth II **Rev.:** Vancouver Canucks goalie mask, multicolor on goal net **Size:** 40 mm.

Date	Mintage	MS-63	Proof
2009	10,000	25.00	—

KM# 876 20 DOLLARS **Weight:** 31.5000 g. **Comp.:** 0.9250 Silver 0.9368 oz. ASW **Ruler:** Elizabeth II **Rev.:** Summer moon mask **Size:** 40 mm.

Date	Mintage	MS-63	Proof
2009 Proof	—	—	75.00

KM# 742 25 DOLLARS Weight: 27.7800 g. Comp.:
0.9250 Silver 0.8261 oz. ASW Ruler: Elizabeth II Subject:
Vancouver Olympics Rev.: Alpine skiing, hologram Size: 40 mm.

Date	Mintage	MS-63	Proof
2007 Proof	45,000		50.00

KM# 743 25 DOLLARS Weight: 27.7800 g.
Comp.: 0.9250 Silver 0.8261 oz. ASW Ruler: Elizabeth II
Subject: Vancouver Olympics Rev.: Athletics pride hologram
Size: 40 mm.

Date	Mintage	MS-63	Proof
2007 Proof	45,000		50.00

KM# 744 25 DOLLARS Weight: 27.7500 g. Comp.:
0.9250 Silver 0.8252 oz. ASW Ruler: Elizabeth II Subject:
Vancouver Olympics Rev.: Biathleon hologram Size: 40 mm.

Date	Mintage	MS-63	Proof
2007 Proof	54,000		50.00

KM# 745 25 DOLLARS Weight: 27.7800 g.
Comp.: 0.9250 Silver 0.8261 oz. ASW Ruler: Elizabeth II
Subject: Vancouver Olympics Rev.: Curling hologram
Size: 40 mm.

Date	Mintage	MS-63	Proof
2007 Proof	—		50.00

KM# 746 25 DOLLARS Weight: 27.7800 g.
Comp.: 0.9250 Silver 0.8261 oz. ASW Ruler: Elizabeth II
Subject: Vancouver Olympics Rev.: Hockey, hologram
Size: 40 mm.

Date	Mintage	MS-63	Proof
2007 Proof	45,000		50.00

KM# 814 25 DOLLARS Weight: 27.7800 g.
Comp.: 0.9250 Silver 0.8261 oz. ASW Ruler: Elizabeth II
Subject: Vancouver Olympics Rev.: Bobsleigh, hologram
Size: 40 mm.

Date	Mintage	MS-63	Proof
2008 Proof	45,000		50.00

KM# 815 25 DOLLARS Weight: 27.7800 g.
Comp.: 0.9250 Silver 0.8261 oz. ASW Ruler: Elizabeth II
Subject: Vancouver Olympics Rev.: Figure skating, hologram
Size: 40 mm.

Date	Mintage	MS-63	Proof
2008 Proof	45,000		50.00

KM# 816 25 DOLLARS Weight: 27.7800 g.
Comp.: 0.9250 Silver 0.8261 oz. ASW Ruler: Elizabeth II
Subject: Vancouver Olympics Rev.: Freestyle skating, hologram
Size: 40 mm.

Date	Mintage	MS-63	Proof
2008 Proof	45,000		50.00

KM# 817 25 DOLLARS Weight: 27.7800 g.
Comp.: 0.9250 Silver 0.8261 oz. ASW Ruler: Elizabeth II
Subject: Vancouver Olympics Rev.: Snowboarding, hologram
Size: 40 mm.

Date	Mintage	MS-63	Proof
2008 Proof	45,000		50.00

KM# 818 25 DOLLARS Weight: 27.7800 g.
Comp.: 0.9250 Silver 0.8261 oz. ASW Ruler: Elizabeth II
Subject: Vancouver Olympics Rev.: Home of the 2010 Olympics
Size: 40 mm.

Date	Mintage	MS-63	Proof
2008 Proof	45,000		50.00

KM# 903 25 DOLLARS Weight: 27.7800 g.
Comp.: 0.9250 Silver 0.8261 oz. ASW Ruler: Elizabeth II
Subject: 2010 Vancouver Olympics Obv.: Bust right
Obv. Des.: Susanna Blunt Rev.: Cross Country Skiing and
hologram at left Size: 40 mm.

Date	Mintage	MS-63	Proof
2009 Proof	45,000		50.00

KM# 904 25 DOLLARS Weight: 27.7800 g.
Comp.: 0.9250 Silver 0.8261 oz. ASW Ruler: Elizabeth II
Subject: 2010 Vancouver Olympics Obv.: Bust right
Obv. Des.: Susanna Blunt Rev.: Olympians holding torch,
hologram at left Size: 40 mm.

Date	Mintage	MS-63	Proof
2009 Proof	45,000	—	50.00

KM# 905 25 DOLLARS Weight: 27.7800 g.
Comp.: 0.9250 Silver 0.8261 oz. ASW Ruler: Elizabeth II
Subject: 2010 Vancouver Olympics Obv.: Bust right Obv. Des.:
Susanna Blunt Rev.: Sled, hologram at left Size: 40 mm.

Date	Mintage	MS-63	Proof
2009 Proof	45,000	—	50.00

KM# 906 25 DOLLARS Weight: 27.7800 g.
Comp.: 0.9250 Silver 0.8261 oz. ASW Ruler: Elizabeth II
Subject: 2010 Vancouver Olympics Obv.: Bust right Obv. Des.:
Susanna Blunt Rev.: Ski Jumper, hologram at left Size: 40 mm.

Date	Mintage	MS-63	Proof
2009 Proof	45,000	—	50.00

KM# 907 25 DOLLARS Weight: 27.7800 g.
Comp.: 0.9250 Silver 0.8261 oz. ASW Ruler: Elizabeth II
Subject: 2010 Vancouver Olympics Obv.: Bust right
Obv. Des.: Susanna Blunt Rev.: Speed Skaters, hologram at left
Size: 40 mm.

Date	Mintage	MS-63	Proof
2009 Proof	45,000		50.00

KM# 590 30 DOLLARS Weight: 31.5000 g.
Comp.: 0.9250 Silver 0.9368 oz. ASW Ruler: Elizabeth II
Subject: Pacific Northwest Wood Carvings Obv.: Head right
Rev.: Welcome figure totem pole

Date	Mintage	MS-63	Proof
2006 Proof	9,904		55.00

KM# 668 30 DOLLARS Weight: 31.5000 g.
Comp.: 0.9250 Silver 0.9368 oz. ASW Ruler: Elizabeth II
Subject: Canadarm and Col. C. Hadfield Obv.: Head right
Rev.: Hologram of Canadarm

Date	Mintage	MS-63	Proof
2006 Proof	9,357	—	60.00

KM# 669 30 DOLLARS Weight: 31.5000 g.
Comp.: 0.9250 Silver 0.9368 oz. ASW Ruler: Elizabeth II
Subject: National War Memorial Obv.: Head right Rev.: Statue
of three soldiers

Date	Mintage	MS-63	Proof
2006 Proof	8,876	—	80.00

KM# 670 30 DOLLARS Weight: 31.5000 g.
Comp.: 0.9250 Silver 0.9368 oz. ASW Ruler: Elizabeth II
Subject: Beaumont Hamel Newfoundland Obv.: Head right
Rev.: Caribou statue on rock outcrop

Date	Mintage	MS-63	Proof
2006 Proof	15,325	—	75.00

KM# 671 30 DOLLARS Weight: 31.5000 g.
Comp.: 0.9250 Silver 0.9368 oz. ASW Ruler: Elizabeth II
Subject: Dog Sled Team Obv.: Head right Rev.: Colorized

Date	Mintage	MS-63	Proof
2006 Proof	7,384	—	80.00

KM# 739 30 DOLLARS Weight: 31.5000 g.
Comp.: 0.9250 Silver 0.9368 oz. ASW Ruler: Elizabeth II
Rev.: Niagra Falls panoramic hologram Size: 40 mm.

Date	Mintage	MS-63	Proof
2007 Proof	5,181	—	50.00

KM# 741 30 DOLLARS Weight: 31.5000 g.
Comp.: 0.9250 Silver 0.9368 oz. ASW Ruler: Elizabeth II
Rev.: War Memorial, Vimy Ridge Size: 40 mm.

Date	Mintage	MS-63	Proof
2007 Proof	5,190	—	75.00

KM# 819 30 DOLLARS Weight: 31.5000 g.
Comp.: 0.9250 Silver 0.9368 oz. ASW Ruler: Elizabeth II
Rev.: IMAX Size: 40 mm.

Date	Mintage	MS-63	Proof
2008 Proof	—		70.00

KM# 895 30 DOLLARS Weight: 33.7500 g.
Comp.: 0.9250 Silver 1.0037 oz. ASW Ruler: Elizabeth II
Subject: International year of astronomy Obv.: Bust right
Obv. Leg.: Elizabeth II 30 Dollars DG Regina Obv. Des.:
Susanna Blunt Rev.: Observatory with planets and colored sky
Rev. Leg.: Canada Rev. Des.: Colin Mayne Size: 40 mm.

Date	Mintage	MS-63	Proof
2009 Proof	10,000		75.00

KM# 566 50 DOLLARS Weight: 12.0000 g. Comp.:
0.5833 Gold 0.2250 oz. AGW Ruler: Elizabeth II Subject: WWII
Obv.: Head right Rev.: Large V and three portraits Size: 27 mm.

Date	Mintage	MS-63	Proof
2005 Specimen	4,000	—	300

KM# 672 50 DOLLARS Weight: 31.1600 g.
Comp.: 0.9995 Palladium 1.0013 oz. **Ruler:** Elizabeth II
Subject: Constellation Spring **Rev.:** Large Bear at top

Date	Mintage	MS-63	Proof
2006 Proof	297	—	1,200

KM# 673 50 DOLLARS Weight: 31.1600 g.
Comp.: 0.9995 Palladium 1.0013 oz. **Ruler:** Elizabeth II
Subject: Constellation Summer **Rev.:** Large Bear at left.

Date	Mintage	MS-63	Proof
2006 Proof	296	—	1,200

KM# 674 50 DOLLARS Weight: 31.1600 g.
Comp.: 0.9995 Palladium 1.0013 oz. **Ruler:** Elizabeth II
Subject: Constellation Autumn **Rev.:** Large Bear towards bottom

Date	Mintage	MS-63	Proof
2006 Proof	296	—	1,200

KM# 675 50 DOLLARS Weight: 31.1600 g.
Comp.: 0.9995 Palladium 1.0013 oz. **Ruler:** Elizabeth II
Subject: Constellation Winter **Rev.:** Large Bear towards right.

Date	Mintage	MS-63	Proof
2006 Proof	293	—	1,200

KM# 709 50 DOLLARS Weight: 155.5000 g.
Comp.: 0.9999 Silver 4.9987 oz. ASW **Ruler:** Elizabeth II
Subject: Queen's 60th Wedding Anniversary **Rev.:** Coat of Arms
and Mascots of Elizabeth and Philip

Date	Mintage	MS-63	Proof
2007	4,000	300	—

KM# 783 50 DOLLARS Weight: 156.7700 g.
Comp.: 0.9990 Silver 5.0350 oz. ASW **Ruler:** Elizabeth II
Subject: Ottawa Mint Centennial 1908-2008 **Rev.:** Mint building
facade **Size:** 65 mm.

Date	Mintage	MS-63	Proof
2008	4,000	400	—

KM# 896 50 DOLLARS Weight: 156.7700 g. **Comp.:**
0.9990 Silver 5.0350 oz. ASW **Ruler:** Elizabeth II **Subject:** 150
Anniversary of the start of construction of the parliament buildings
Obv.: Bust right **Obv. Leg.:** Elizabeth II Canada DG Regina
Obv. Des.: Susanna Blunt **Rev.:** Incomplete west block, original
architecture **Rev. Leg.:** 50 Dollars 1859-2009 **Size:** 65.25 mm.

Date	Mintage	MS-63	Proof
2009 Proof	2,000	—	200

KM# 567 75 DOLLARS Weight: 31.4400 g.
Comp.: 0.4166 Gold 0.4211 oz. AGW **Ruler:** Elizabeth II
Subject: Pope John Paul II **Obv.:** Head right **Rev.:** Pope giving
blessing

Date	Mintage	MS-63	Proof
2005 Proof	1,870	—	550

KM# 747 75 DOLLARS Weight: 12.0000 g.
Comp.: 0.5830 Gold 0.2249 oz. AGW **Ruler:** Elizabeth II
Subject: Vancouver Olympics **Rev.:** Athletics Pride, multicolor
flag **Size:** 27 mm.

Date	Mintage	MS-63	Proof
2007 Proof	8,000	—	300

KM# 748 75 DOLLARS Weight: 12.0000 g.
Comp.: 0.5830 Gold 0.2249 oz. AGW **Ruler:** Elizabeth II
Obv.: Bust right **Obv. Des.:** SUsanna Blunt **Rev.:** Canada geese
in flight left, multicolor **Size:** 27 mm.

Date	Mintage	MS-63	Proof
2007 Proof	8,000	—	300

KM# 749 75 DOLLARS Weight: 12.0000 g.
Comp.: 0.5830 Gold 0.2249 oz. AGW **Ruler:** Elizabeth II
Rev.: Mountie, multicolor **Size:** 27 mm.

Date	Mintage	MS-63	Proof
2007 Proof	8,000	—	300

KM# 821 75 DOLLARS Weight: 12.0000 g.
Comp.: 0.5830 Gold 0.2249 oz. AGW **Ruler:** Elizabeth II
Subject: Host Nations of the 2010 Olympics **Obv.:** Bust right
Rev.: Four masks **Size:** 27 mm.

Date	Mintage	MS-63	Proof
2008 Proof	8,000	—	300

KM# 822 75 DOLLARS Weight: 12.0000 g.
Comp.: 0.5830 Gold 0.2249 oz. AGW **Ruler:** Elizabeth II
Rev.: Four Host Nations emblem, colored **Rev. Des.:** Jody
Broomfield **Size:** 27 mm.

Date	Mintage	MS-63	Proof
2008 Proof	—	—	300

KM# 908 75 DOLLARS Weight: 12.0000 g.
Comp.: 0.5830 Gold 0.2249 oz. AGW **Ruler:** Elizabeth II
Subject: 2010 Vancouver Olympics **Obv.:** Bust right
Obv. Des.: Susana Blunt **Rev.:** Multicolor moose **Size:** 27 mm.

Date	Mintage	MS-63	Proof
2009 Proof	800	—	300

KM# 909 75 DOLLARS Weight: 12.0000 g.
Comp.: 0.5830 Gold 0.2249 oz. AGW **Ruler:** Elizabeth II
Subject: 2010 Vancouver Olympics **Obv.:** Bust right **Obv. Des.:**
Susanna Blunt **Rev.:** Multicolor athletics and torch **Size:** 27 mm.

Date	Mintage	MS-63	Proof
2009 Proof	800	—	300

KM# 910 75 DOLLARS Weight: 12.0000 g.
Comp.: 0.5830 Gold 0.2249 oz. AGW **Ruler:** Elizabeth II
Subject: 2010 Vancouver Olympics **Obv.:** Bust right
Obv. Des.: Susanna Blunt **Rev.:** Wolf, multicolor **Size:** 27 mm.

Date	Mintage	MS-63	Proof
2009 Proof	800	—	300

KM# 416 100 DOLLARS Weight: 13.3375 g.
Comp.: 0.5830 Gold alloyed with 5.5579 g of .999 Silver, .1787
oz ASW 0.2500 oz. AGW **Ruler:** Elizabeth II **Subject:** Library of
Parliament **Obv.:** Crowned head right **Obv. Des.:** Dora
dePedery-Hunt **Rev.:** Statue in domed building
Rev. Des.: Robert R. Carmichael **Edge:** Reeded **Size:** 27 mm.

Date	Mintage	MS-63	Proof
2001 Proof	8,080	—	320

KM# 452 100 DOLLARS Weight: 13.3375 g.
Comp.: 0.5830 Gold 0.2500 oz. AGW **Ruler:** Elizabeth II
Subject: Discovery of Oil in Alberta **Obv.:** Crowned head right
Rev.: Oil well with black oil spill on ground **Rev. Des.:** John
Marden **Edge:** Reeded **Size:** 27 mm.

Date	Mintage	MS-63	Proof
2002 Proof	9,994	—	325

KM# 486 100 DOLLARS Weight: 13.3375 g. **Comp.:**
0.5830 Gold 0.2500 oz. AGW **Ruler:** Elizabeth II **Subject:** 100th
Anniversary of the Discovery of Marquis Wheat **Obv.:** Head right

Date	Mintage	MS-63	Proof
2003 Proof	9,993	—	325

KM# 528 100 DOLLARS Weight: 12.0000 g. **Comp.:**
0.5830 Gold 0.2249 oz. AGW **Ruler:** Elizabeth II **Subject:** St.
Lawrence Seaway, 50th Anniversary **Obv.:** Head right

Date	Mintage	MS-63	Proof
2004 Proof	7,454	—	300

KM# 616 100 DOLLARS Weight: 12.0000 g.
Comp.: 0.5833 Gold 0.2250 oz. AGW **Ruler:** Elizabeth II
Subject: Supreme Court **Obv.:** Head right **Rev.:** Draped figure
with sword

Date	Mintage	MS-63	Proof
2005 Proof	5,092	—	300

KM# 591 100 DOLLARS Weight: 12.0000 g.
Comp.: 0.5833 Gold 0.2250 oz. AGW **Ruler:** Elizabeth II
Subject: 75th Anniversary, Hockey Classic between Royal
Military College and U.S. Military Academy **Obv.:** Head right

Date	Mintage	MS-63	Proof
2006 Proof	5,439	—	300

KM# 593 100 DOLLARS Weight: 12.0000 g.
Comp.: 0.5833 Gold 0.2250 oz. AGW **Ruler:** Elizabeth II
Subject: 130th Anniversary, Supreme Court **Obv.:** Head right

Date	Mintage	MS-63	Proof
2006 Proof	5,092	—	420

KM# 689 100 DOLLARS Weight: 12.0000 g.
Comp.: 0.5833 Gold 0.2250 oz. AGW **Ruler:** Elizabeth II
Subject: 140th Anniversary Dominion **Obv.:** Head right
Size: 27 mm.

Date	Mintage	MS-63	Proof
2007 Proof	4,453	—	300

KM# 823 100 DOLLARS Weight: 12.0000 g.
Comp.: 0.5830 Gold 0.2249 oz. AGW **Ruler:** Elizabeth II
Rev.: Fraser River **Size:** 27 mm.

Date	Mintage	MS-63	Proof
2008 Proof	5,000	—	350

KM# 898   100 DOLLARS   Weight: 12.0000 g.
Comp.: 0.5830 Gold 0.2249 oz. AGW **Ruler:** Elizabeth II
Subject: 10th Anniversary of Nunavut **Obv.:** Bust right
Obv. Leg.: Elizabeth II DG Regina **Obv. Des.:** Susanna Blunt
Rev.: Inuit dancer with 3 faces behind **Rev. Leg.:** Canada 100
Dollars 1999-2009 **Size:** 27 mm.

Date	Mintage	MS-63	Proof
2009 Proof	5,000	—	500

KM# 417   150 DOLLARS   Weight: 13.6100 g.
Comp.: 0.7500 Gold 0.3282 oz. AGW **Ruler:** Elizabeth II
Subject: Year of the Snake **Obv.:** Crowned head right
Obv. Des.: Dora dePedery-Hunt **Rev.:** Multicolor snake
hologram **Edge:** Reeded **Size:** 28 mm.

Date	Mintage	MS-63	Proof
2001 Proof	6,571	—	425

KM# 604   150 DOLLARS   Weight: 13.6100 g.
Comp.: 0.7500 Gold 0.3282 oz. AGW **Ruler:** Elizabeth II
Obv.: Head right **Rev.:** Stylized horse left

Date	Mintage	MS-63	Proof
2002 Proof	6,843	—	425

KM# 487   150 DOLLARS   Weight: 13.6100 g.
Comp.: 0.7500 Gold 0.3282 oz. AGW **Ruler:** Elizabeth II
Subject: Year of the Ram **Obv.:** Crowned head right
Rev.: Stylized ram left **Rev. Des.:** Harvey Chan

Date	Mintage	MS-63	Proof
2003 Proof	3,927	—	425

KM# 614   150 DOLLARS   Weight: 13.6100 g.
Comp.: 0.7500 Gold 0.3282 oz. AGW **Ruler:** Elizabeth II
Obv.: Head right **Rev.:** Year of the Monkey, hologram

Date	Mintage	MS-63	Proof
2004 Proof	3,392	—	425

KM# 568   150 DOLLARS   Weight: 13.6100 g.
Comp.: 0.7500 Gold 0.3282 oz. AGW **Ruler:** Elizabeth II
Subject: Year of the Rooster **Obv.:** Head right **Rev.:** Rooster left

Date	Mintage	MS-63	Proof
2005 Proof	3,731	—	425

KM# 592   150 DOLLARS   Weight: 13.6100 g. **Comp.:**
0.7500 Gold 0.3282 oz. AGW **Ruler:** Elizabeth II **Subject:** Year
of the Dog, hologram **Obv.:** Head right **Rev.:** Stylized dog left

Date	Mintage	MS-63	Proof
2006 Proof	2,604	—	425

KM# 733   150 DOLLARS   Weight: 11.8400 g.
Comp.: 0.7500 Gold 0.2855 oz. AGW **Ruler:** Elizabeth II
Subject: Year of the Pig **Obv.:** Head right **Rev.:** Pig in center
with Chinese lunar calendar around, hologram **Size:** 28 mm.

Date	Mintage	MS-63	Proof
2007 Proof	4,888	—	450

KM# 802   150 DOLLARS   Weight: 11.8400 g.
Comp.: 0.7500 Gold 0.2855 oz. AGW **Ruler:** Elizabeth II
Subject: Year of the Rat **Rev.:** Rat, hologram **Size:** 28 mm.

Date	Mintage	MS-63	Proof
2008 Proof	4,888	—	450

KM# 899   150 DOLLARS   Weight: 10.4000 g.
Comp.: 0.9990 Gold 0.3340 oz. AGW **Ruler:** Elizabeth II
Subject: Blessings of wealth **Obv.:** Bust right **Obv. Leg.:**
Elizabeth II, DG Regina, Fine Gold 99999 or PUR
Obv. Des.: Susanna Blunt **Rev.:** Three goldfish surround peony,
clouds **Rev. Leg.:** Canada 150 Dollars (Chinese symbols of good
fortune) **Rev. Des.:** Harvey Chan **Edge:** Scalloped
Size: 22.5 mm.

Date	Mintage	MS-63	Proof
2009 Proof	50,000	—	650

KM# 867   150 DOLLARS   Weight: 11.8400 g.
Comp.: 0.7500 Gold 0.2855 oz. AGW **Ruler:** Elizabeth II
Subject: Year of the Ox **Rev.:** Ox, hologram **Size:** 28 mm.

Date	Mintage	MS-63	Proof
2009 Proof	—	—	450

KM# 418   200 DOLLARS   Weight: 17.1350 g.
Comp.: 0.9166 Gold 0.5049 oz. AGW **Ruler:** Elizabeth II
Subject: Cornelius D. Krieghoff's "The Habitant farm"
Obv.: Queens head right **Edge:** Reeded **Size:** 29 mm.

Date	Mintage	MS-63	Proof
2001 Proof	5,406	—	675

KM# 466   200 DOLLARS   Weight: 17.1350 g.
Comp.: 0.9166 Gold 0.5049 oz. AGW **Ruler:** Elizabeth II
Subject: Thomas Thompson "The Jack Pine" (1916-17)
Obv.: Crowned head right **Size:** 29 mm.

Date	Mintage	MS-63	Proof
2002 Proof	5,264	—	675

KM# 488   200 DOLLARS   Weight: 17.1350 g.
Comp.: 0.9166 Gold 0.5049 oz. AGW **Ruler:** Elizabeth II
Subject: Fitzgerald's "Houses" (1929) **Obv.:** Crowned head right
Rev.: House with trees

Date	Mintage	MS-63	Proof
2003 Proof	4,118	—	675

KM# 516   200 DOLLARS   Weight: 16.0000 g.
Comp.: 0.9166 Gold 0.4715 oz. AGW **Ruler:** Elizabeth II
Subject: "Fragments" **Obv.:** Crowned head right
Rev.: Fragmented face **Edge:** Reeded **Size:** 29 mm.

Date	Mintage	MS-63	Proof
2004 Proof	3,917	—	625

KM# 569   200 DOLLARS   Weight: 16.0000 g.
Comp.: 0.9166 Gold 0.4715 oz. AGW **Ruler:** Elizabeth II
Subject: Fur traders **Obv.:** Head right **Rev.:** Men in canoe riding
wave

Date	Mintage	MS-63	Proof
2005 Proof	3,669	—	625

KM# 594   200 DOLLARS   Weight: 16.0000 g.
Comp.: 0.9166 Gold 0.4715 oz. AGW **Ruler:** Elizabeth II
Subject: Timber trade **Obv.:** Head right **Rev.:** Lumberjacks
felling tree

Date	Mintage	MS-63	Proof
2006 Proof	3,185	—	625

KM# 691   200 DOLLARS   Weight: 16.0000 g.
Comp.: 0.9166 Gold 0.4715 oz. AGW **Ruler:** Elizabeth II
Subject: Fishing Trade **Obv.:** Head right

Date	Mintage	MS-63	Proof
2007 Proof	4,000	—	625

KM# 750   200 DOLLARS   Weight: 31.1500 g.
Comp.: 1.0000 Gold 1.0014 oz. AGW **Ruler:** Elizabeth II
Rev.: Three maple leaves **Size:** 30 mm.

Date	Mintage	MS-63	Proof
2007 Proof	500	—	1,275

KM# 824   200 DOLLARS   Weight: 16.0000 g.
Comp.: 0.9170 Gold 0.4717 oz. AGW **Ruler:** Elizabeth II
Subject: Commerce **Rev.:** Horse drawn plow **Size:** 29 mm.

Date	Mintage	MS-63	Proof
2008 Proof	4,000	—	625

KM# 894   200 DOLLARS   Weight: 16.0000 g.
Comp.: 0.9160 Gold 0.4712 oz. AGW **Ruler:** Elizabeth II
Subject: Coal mining trade **Obv.:** Bust right **Obv. Leg.:** Elizabeth
II DG Regina **Obv. Des.:** Susanna Blunt **Rev.:** Miner pushing
cart with black coal **Rev. Leg.:** Canada 200 Dollars
Rev. Des.: John Marder **Size:** 29 mm.

Date	Mintage	MS-63	Proof
2009 Proof	4,000	—	750

KM# 677   250 DOLLARS   Weight: 45.0000 g.
Comp.: 0.5833 Gold 0.8439 oz. AGW **Ruler:** Elizabeth II
Subject: Dog Sled Team

Date	Mintage	MS-63	Proof
2006 Proof	953	—	1,100

KM# 751   250 DOLLARS   Weight: 1000.0000 g.
Comp.: 0.9999 Silver 32.146 oz. ASW **Ruler:** Elizabeth II
Subject: Vancouver Olympics, 2010 **Rev.:** Early Canada motif
Size: 101.6 mm. **Note:** Illustration reduced.

Date	Mintage	MS-63	Proof
2007 Proof	2,500	—	1,250

KM# 833   250 DOLLARS   Weight: 1000.0000 g.
Comp.: 0.9990 Silver 32.117 oz. ASW **Ruler:** Elizabeth II
Subject: Vancouver Olympics 2010 **Rev.:** Towards
confederation **Size:** 101.6 mm. **Note:** Illustration reduced.

Date	Mintage	MS-63	Proof
2008 Proof	2,500	—	1,200

KM# 913   250 DOLLARS   Weight: 1000.0000 g.
Comp.: 0.9999 Silver 32.146 oz. ASW **Ruler:** Elizabeth II
Obv.: Bust right **Obv. Des.:** Susanna Blunt **Rev.:** Mask with fish
- Surviving the flood **Note:** Illustration reduced.

Date	Mintage	MS-63	Proof
2009 Proof	—	—	5,000

KM# 878   250 DOLLARS   Weight: 1000.0000 g.
Comp.: 0.9990 Silver 32.117 oz. ASW **Ruler:** Elizabeth II
Subject: Vancouver Olympics, 2010 **Rev.:** Surviving the flood
Size: 101.6 mm. **Note:** Illustration reduced.

Date	Mintage	MS-63	Proof
2009 Proof	2,500	—	1,200

KM# 501   300 DOLLARS   Weight: 60.0000 g.
Comp.: 0.5833 Gold 1.1252 oz. AGW **Ruler:** Elizabeth II
Obv.: Triple cameo portraits of Queen Elizabeth II by Gillick,
Machin and de Pedery-Hunt, each in 14K gold, rose in center
Rev.: Dates "1952-2002" and denomination in legend, rose in
center **Size:** 50 mm. **Note:** Housed in anodized gold-colored
aluminum box with cherrywood stained siding

Date	Mintage	MS-63	Proof
ND(2002) Proof	999	—	1,500

KM# 517   300 DOLLARS   Weight: 60.0000 g.
Comp.: 0.5833 Gold 1.1252 oz. AGW **Ruler:** Elizabeth II
Obv.: Four coinage portraits of Elizabeth II **Rev.:** Canadian arms
above value **Edge:** Plain **Size:** 50 mm.

Date	Mintage	MS-63	Proof
2004 Proof	998	—	1,500

KM# 570.1 300 DOLLARS Weight: 60.0000 g.
Comp.: 0.5833 Gold 1.1252 oz. AGW Ruler: Elizabeth II
Subject: Standard Time - 4 AM Pacific Obv.: Head right
Rev.: Roman numeral clock with world inside

Date	Mintage	MS-63	Proof
2005 Proof	200	—	1,500

KM# 596 300 DOLLARS Weight: 60.0000 g.
Comp.: 0.5833 Gold 1.1252 oz. AGW Ruler: Elizabeth II
Subject: Shinplaster Obv.: Head right Rev.: Britannia bust, spear over shoulder

Date	Mintage	MS-63	Proof
2005 Proof	994	—	1,500

KM# 600 300 DOLLARS Weight: 60.0000 g.
Comp.: 0.5833 Gold 1.1252 oz. AGW Ruler: Elizabeth II
Subject: Welcome Figure Totem Pole Obv.: Head right
Rev.: Men with totem pole

Date	Mintage	MS-63	Proof
2005 Proof	947	—	1,500

KM# 570.2 300 DOLLARS Weight: 60.0000 g.
Comp.: 0.5830 Gold 1.1246 oz. AGW Ruler: Elizabeth II
Subject: Standard Time - Mountian 5 AM Obv.: Head right
Rev.: Roman numeral clock with world inside.

Date	Mintage	MS-63	Proof
2005 Proof	200	—	1,500

KM# 570.3 300 DOLLARS Weight: 60.0000 g.
Comp.: 0.5830 Gold 1.1246 oz. AGW Ruler: Elizabeth II
Subject: Standard Time - Central 6 PM Obv.: Head right
Rev.: Roman numeral clock with world inside

Date	Mintage	MS-63	Proof
2005 Proof	200	—	1,500

KM# 570.4 300 DOLLARS Weight: 60.0000 g.
Comp.: 0.5830 Gold 1.1246 oz. AGW Ruler: Elizabeth II
Subject: Standard Time - Eastern 7 AM Obv.: Head right
Rev.: Roman numeral clock with world inside

Date	Mintage	MS-63	Proof
2005 Proof	200	—	1,500

KM# 570.5 300 DOLLARS Weight: 60.0000 g.
Comp.: 0.5830 Gold 1.1246 oz. AGW Ruler: Elizabeth II
Subject: Standard Time - Atlantic 8 AM Obv.: Head right
Rev.: Roman numeral clock with world inside

Date	Mintage	MS-63	Proof
2005 Proof	200	—	1,500

KM# 570.6 300 DOLLARS Weight: 60.0000 g.
Comp.: 0.5830 Gold 1.1246 oz. AGW Ruler: Elizabeth II
Subject: Standard Time - Newfoundland 8:30 Obv.: Head right
Rev.: Roman numeral clock with world inside

Date	Mintage	MS-63	Proof
2005 Proof	200	—	1,500

KM# 595 300 DOLLARS Weight: 60.0000 g.
Comp.: 0.5833 Gold 1.1252 oz. AGW Ruler: Elizabeth II
Subject: Shinplaster Obv.: Head right Rev.: Seated Britannia with shield

Date	Mintage	MS-63	Proof
2006 Proof	940	—	1,500

KM# 678 300 DOLLARS Weight: 45.0000 g.
Comp.: 0.5833 Gold 0.8439 oz. AGW Ruler: Elizabeth II
Subject: Canadam and Col. C. Hadfield Rev.: Hologram of Canadarm

Date	Mintage	MS-63	Proof
2006 Proof	581	—	1,100

KM# 679 300 DOLLARS Weight: 60.0000 g.
Comp.: 0.5833 Gold 1.1252 oz. AGW Ruler: Elizabeth II
Subject: Queen Elizabeth's 80th Birthday Rev.: State Crown, colorized

Date	Mintage	MS-63	Proof
2006 Proof	996	—	1,500

KM# 680 300 DOLLARS Weight: 60.0000 g.
Comp.: 0.5833 Gold 1.1252 oz. AGW Ruler: Elizabeth II
Subject: Crystal Snowflake

Date	Mintage	MS-63	Proof
2006 Proof	998	—	1,500

KM# 692 300 DOLLARS Weight: 60.0000 g.
Comp.: 0.5833 Gold 1.1252 oz. AGW Ruler: Elizabeth II
Subject: Shinplaster Rev.: 1923 25 cent bank note

Date	Mintage	MS-63	Proof
2007 Proof	778	—	1,500

KM# 740 300 DOLLARS Weight: 45.0000 g.
Comp.: 0.5830 Gold 0.8434 oz. AGW Ruler: Elizabeth II
Rev.: Canadian Rockies panoramic hologram Size: 40 mm.

Date	Mintage	MS-63	Proof
2007 Proof	511	—	1,100

KM# 752 300 DOLLARS Weight: 60.0000 g.
Comp.: 0.5830 Gold 1.1246 oz. AGW Ruler: Elizabeth II
Subject: Vancouver Olympics Rev.: Olympic ideals, classic figures and torch Size: 50 mm.

Date	Mintage	MS-63	Proof
2007 Proof	2,500	—	1,500

KM# 825 300 DOLLARS Weight: 45.0000 g.
Comp.: 0.5830 Gold 0.8434 oz. AGW Ruler: Elizabeth II
Rev.: Alberta Coat of Arms Size: 40 mm.

Date	Mintage	MS-63	Proof
2008 Proof	—	—	1,100

KM# 826 300 DOLLARS Weight: 45.0000 g.
Comp.: 0.5830 Gold 0.8434 oz. AGW Ruler: Elizabeth II
Rev.: Newfoundland and Labrador Coat of Arms Size: 40 mm.

Date	Mintage	MS-63	Proof
2008 Proof	1,000	—	1,250

KM# 827 300 DOLLARS Weight: 45.0000 g.
Comp.: 0.5830 Gold 0.8434 oz. AGW Ruler: Elizabeth II
Subject: Canadian achievements Rev.: IMAX Size: 40 mm.

Date	Mintage	MS-63	Proof
2008 Proof	—	—	1,100

KM# 828 300 DOLLARS Weight: 45.0000 g.
Comp.: 0.5830 Gold 0.8434 oz. AGW Ruler: Elizabeth II
Rev.: Four seasons moon mask Size: 40 mm.

Date	Mintage	MS-63	Proof
2008 Proof	1,200	—	1,100

KM# 829 300 DOLLARS Weight: 60.0000 g.
Comp.: 0.5830 Gold 1.1246 oz. AGW Ruler: Elizabeth II
Rev.: Cedar Summer Moon mask carved by Judy Broomfield Size: 50 mm.

Date	Mintage	MS-63	Proof
2008 Proof	—	—	1,100

KM# 830 300 DOLLARS Weight: 60.0000 g.
Comp.: 0.5830 Gold 1.1246 oz. AGW Ruler: Elizabeth II
Subject: Vancouver Olympics Rev.: Olympic competition, athletics and torch Size: 50 mm.

Date	Mintage	MS-63	Proof
2008 Proof	—	—	1,500

KM# 900 300 DOLLARS Weight: 60.0000 g.
Comp.: 0.5830 Gold 1.1246 oz. AGW Ruler: Elizabeth II
Subject: Yukon Coat of Arms Obv.: Bust right Obv. Leg.: Elizabeth II DG Regina Obv. Des.: Susanna Blunt Rev.: Yukon Coat of Arms Rev. Leg.: Canada 300 Dollars Size: 50 mm.

Date	Mintage	MS-63	Proof
2009 Proof	1,000	—	1,650

KM# 911 300 DOLLARS Weight: 60.0000 g.
Comp.: 0.5830 Gold 1.1246 oz. AGW Ruler: Elizabeth II
Subject: 2010 Vancouver Olympics Obv.: Bust right
Obv. Des.: Susanna Blunt Rev.: Athletics with torch - Olympic firendship Size: 50 mm.

Date	Mintage	MS-63	Proof
2009 Proof	—	—	1,500

KM# 877 300 DOLLARS Weight: 45.0000 g.
Comp.: 0.5830 Gold 0.8434 oz. AGW Ruler: Elizabeth II
Rev.: Summer moon mask, enameled Size: 40 mm.

Date	Mintage	MS-63	Proof
2009 Proof	—	—	1,100

KM# 433 350 DOLLARS Weight: 38.0500 g.
Comp.: 0.9999 Gold 1.2232 oz. AGW Ruler: Elizabeth II
Subject: The Mayflower Flower Obv.: Crowned head right
Rev.: Two flowers Rev. Des.: Bonnie Ross Edge: Reeded
Size: 34 mm.

Date	Mintage	MS-63	Proof
2001 Proof	1,988	—	1,600

KM# 502 350 DOLLARS Weight: 38.0500 g.
Comp.: 0.9999 Gold 1.2232 oz. AGW Ruler: Elizabeth II
Subject: The Wild Rose Obv.: Crowned head right
Obv. Des.: Dora de Pedery-Hunt Rev.: Wild rose plant
Rev. Des.: Dr. Andreas Kare Hellum Size: 34 mm.

Date	Mintage	MS-63	Proof
2002 Proof	2,001	—	1,600

KM# 504 350 DOLLARS Weight: 38.0500 g.
Comp.: 0.9999 Gold 1.2232 oz. AGW Ruler: Elizabeth II
Subject: The White Trillium Obv.: Crowned head right
Obv. Des.: Dora de Pedery-Hunt Rev.: White Trillium
Size: 34 mm.

Date	Mintage	MS-63	Proof
2003 Proof	1,865	—	1,600

KM# 601 350 DOLLARS Weight: 38.0500 g. Comp.:
0.9999 Gold 1.2232 oz. AGW Ruler: Elizabeth II Subject:
Western Red Lilly Obv.: Head right Rev.: Western Red Lilies

Date	Mintage	MS-63	Proof
2005 Proof	1,634	—	1,600

KM# 626 350 DOLLARS Weight: 38.0500 g. Comp.:
0.9999 Gold 1.2232 oz. AGW Ruler: Elizabeth II Subject: Iris
Vericolor Obv.: Crowned head right Rev.: Iris Size: 34 mm.

Date	Mintage	MS-63	Proof
2006 Proof	1,995	—	1,600

KM# 754 350 DOLLARS Weight: 35.0000 g.
Comp.: 0.9999 Gold 1.1251 oz. AGW Ruler: Elizabeth II
Rev.: Purple violet Size: 34 mm.

Date	Mintage	MS-63	Proof
2007 Proof	1,171	—	1,500

KM# 832 350 DOLLARS Weight: 35.0000 g.
Comp.: 0.9999 Gold 1.1251 oz. AGW Ruler: Elizabeth II
Rev.: Purple saxifrage Size: 34 mm.

Date	Mintage	MS-63	Proof
2008 Proof	1,400	—	1,500

KM# 901 350 DOLLARS Weight: 35.0000 g.
Comp.: 0.9990 Gold 1.1241 oz. AGW Ruler: Elizabeth II
Subject: Pitcher plant Obv.: Bust right Obv. Leg.: Elizabeth II
Canada DG Regina Fine Gold 350 Dollars or PUR 99999
Obv. Des.: Susana Blunt Rev.: Cluster of pitcher flowers
Rev. Leg.: Julie Wilson Size: 34 mm.

Date	Mintage	MS-63	Proof
2009 Proof	1,400	—	2,000

KM# 710 500 DOLLARS Weight: 155.5000 g.
Comp.: 0.9999 Gold 4.9987 oz. AGW Ruler: Elizabeth II
Subject: Queen's 60th Wedding Rev.: Coat of Arms and Mascots of Elizabeth and Philip Size: 60 mm.

Date	Mintage	MS-63	Proof
2007	198	8,500	—

KM# 782   500 DOLLARS   **Weight:** 155.7600 g.
Comp.: 0.9990 Gold 5.0026 oz. AGW **Ruler:** Elizabeth II
Subject: Ottawa Mint Centennial 1908-2008 **Rev.:** Mint building
facade **Size:** 60 mm.

Date	Mintage	MS-63	Proof
2008	250	8,500	—

KM# 897   500 DOLLARS   **Weight:** 156.0500 g.
Comp.: 0.9990 Gold 5.0119 oz. AGW **Ruler:** Elizabeth II
Subject: 150th Anniversary of the start of construction of the
Parliament Buildings **Obv.:** Bust right **Rev.:** Incomplete west
block, original architecture **Rev. Leg.:** 500 Dollars 1859-2009
Size: 60.15 mm.

Date	Mintage	MS-63	Proof
2009 Proof	200	—	9,500

KM# 902   2500 DOLLARS   **Weight:** 1000.0000 g.
Comp.: 0.9990 Silver 32.117 oz. ASW **Ruler:** Elizabeth II
Series: History and Culture Collection **Subject:** Modern Canada
Obv.: Bust right **Obv. Leg.:** Vancouver 2010, 2500 Dollars,
Elizabeth II **Obv. Des.:** Susanna Blunt **Rev.:** Canadian
landscape with modern elements **Size:** 101.6 mm.

Date	Mintage	MS-63	Proof
2009 Proof	2,500	—	750

KM# 902a   2500 DOLLARS   **Weight:** 1000.0000 g.
Comp.: 0.9990 Silver 32.117 oz. AGW **Ruler:** Elizabeth II
Series: History and Culture Collection **Subject:** Modern Canada
Obv.: Bust right **Obv. Leg.:** Vancouver 2010, 2500 Dollars,
Elizabeth II **Obv. Des.:** Susana Blunt **Rev.:** Canadian landscape
with modern elements **Size:** 101.6 mm.

Date	Mintage	MS-63	Proof
2009 Proof	50	—	45,000

KM# 912   2500 DOLLARS   **Weight:** 1000.0000 g.
Comp.: 0.9999 Gold 32.146 oz. AGW **Ruler:** Elizabeth II
Obv.: Bust right **Obv. Des.:** Susanna Blunt **Rev.:** Mask with fish
- Surviving the flood **Size:** 101 mm. **Note:** Illustration reduced.

Date	Mintage	MS-63	Proof
2009 Proof	—	—	46,000

SILVER BULLION COINAGE

KM# 617   DOLLAR   **Weight:** 1.5550 g. **Comp.:** 0.9999
Silver 0.0500 oz. ASW **Ruler:** Elizabeth II **Obv.:** Crowned head
right **Rev.:** Holographic Maple leaf **Edge:** Reeded **Size:** 16 mm.

Date	Mintage	MS-63	Proof
2003 Proof	—	—	4.50

KM# 621   DOLLAR   **Weight:** 1.5550 g. **Comp.:** 0.9999
Silver 0.0500 oz. ASW **Ruler:** Elizabeth II **Obv.:** Crowned head
right **Rev.:** Maple leaf **Edge:** Reeded **Size:** 17 mm.

Date	Mintage	MS-63	Proof
2004 Mint logo privy mark Proof	13,859	—	4.50

KM# 618   2 DOLLARS   **Weight:** 3.1100 g.
Comp.: 0.9999 Silver 0.1000 oz. ASW **Ruler:** Elizabeth II
Obv.: Crowned head right **Rev.:** Holographic Maple leaf
Edge: Reeded **Size:** 20.1 mm.

Date	Mintage	MS-63	Proof
2003 Proof	—	—	7.50

KM# 622   2 DOLLARS   **Weight:** 3.1100 g.
Comp.: 0.9999 Silver 0.1000 oz. ASW **Ruler:** Elizabeth II
Obv.: Crowned head right **Rev.:** Maple leaf **Edge:** Reeded
Size: 21 mm.

Date	Mintage	MS-63	Proof
2004 Mint logo privy mark Proof	13,859	—	7.50

KM# 571   2 DOLLARS   **Weight:** 3.1050 g.
Comp.: 0.9999 Silver 0.0998 oz. ASW **Ruler:** Elizabeth II
Obv.: Head right **Rev.:** Lynx

Date	Mintage	MS-63	Proof
2005 Proof	—	—	7.50

KM# 619   3 DOLLARS   **Weight:** 7.7760 g.
Comp.: 0.9999 Silver 0.2500 oz. ASW **Ruler:** Elizabeth II
Obv.: Crowned head right **Rev.:** Holographic Maple leaf
Edge: Reeded **Size:** 26.9 mm.

Date	Mintage	MS-63	Proof
2003 Proof	—	—	15.00

KM# 623   3 DOLLARS   **Weight:** 7.7760 g.
Comp.: 0.9999 Silver 0.2500 oz. ASW **Ruler:** Elizabeth II
Obv.: Crowned head right **Rev.:** Maple leaf **Edge:** Reeded
Size: 27 mm.

Date	Mintage	MS-63	Proof
2004 Mint logo privy mark Proof	13,859	—	12.50

KM# 572   3 DOLLARS   **Weight:** 7.7760 g.
Comp.: 0.9999 Silver 0.2500 oz. ASW **Ruler:** Elizabeth II
Obv.: Head right **Rev.:** Lynx

Date	Mintage	MS-63	Proof
2005 Proof	—	—	12.50

KM# 620   4 DOLLARS   **Weight:** 15.5500 g.
Comp.: 0.9999 Silver 0.4999 oz. ASW **Ruler:** Elizabeth II
Obv.: Crowned head right **Rev.:** Holographic Maple leaf
Edge: Reeded **Size:** 33.9 mm.

Date	Mintage	MS-63	Proof
2003 Proof	—	—	30.00

KM# 624   4 DOLLARS   **Weight:** 15.5500 g.
Comp.: 0.9999 Silver 0.4999 oz. ASW **Ruler:** Elizabeth II
Obv.: Crowned head right **Rev.:** Maple leaf **Edge:** Reeded
Size: 34 mm.

Date	Mintage	MS-63	Proof
2004 Mint logo privy mark Proof	13,859	—	25.00

KM# 573   4 DOLLARS   **Weight:** 15.5500 g.
Comp.: 0.9999 Silver 0.4999 oz. ASW **Ruler:** Elizabeth II
Obv.: Head right **Rev.:** Lynx

Date	Mintage	MS-63	Proof
2005 Proof	—	—	22.50

KM# 437   5 DOLLARS   **Weight:** 31.1035 g.
Comp.: 0.9999 Silver 0.9999 oz. ASW **Ruler:** Elizabeth II
Obv.: Crowned head right, date and denomination below
Rev.: Radiant maple leaf hologram **Edge:** Reeded **Size:** 38 mm.

Date	Mintage	MS-63	Proof
2001 Good fortune privy mark	29,906	75.00	—

KM# 187   5 DOLLARS   **Weight:** 31.1000 g.
Comp.: 0.9999 Silver 0.9997 oz. ASW **Ruler:** Elizabeth II
Obv.: Crowned head right, date and denomination below
Obv. Des.: Dora de Pedery-Hunt **Rev.:** Maple leaf flanked
by 9999

Date	Mintage	MS-63	Proof
2001	398,563	20.00	—
2001 Snake privy mark	25,000	25.00	
2002	576,196	20.00	—
2002 Horse privy mark	25,000	25.00	
2003	—	20.00	—
2003 Sheep privy mark	25,000	22.00	

KM# 436   5 DOLLARS   **Weight:** 31.1035 g. **Comp.:**
0.9999 Silver 0.9999 oz. ASW **Ruler:** Elizabeth II **Obv.:** Crowned
head right, date and denomination below **Rev.:** Three maple
leaves in autumn colors, 9999 flanks **Rev. Des.:** Debbie Adams
Edge: Reeded **Size:** 38 mm.

Date	Mintage	MS-63	Proof
2001 Proof	49,709	—	32.50

KM# 505   5 DOLLARS   **Weight:** 31.1035 g.
Comp.: 0.9999 Silver 0.9999 oz. ASW **Ruler:** Elizabeth II
Obv.: Crowned head right, date and denomination below
Rev.: Two maple leaves in spring color (green) **Edge:** Reeded
Size: 38 mm.

Date	Mintage	MS-63	Proof
2002	29,509	35.00	—

KM# 603 5 DOLLARS Weight: 31.1050 g.
Comp.: 0.9999 Silver 0.9999 oz. ASW **Ruler:** Elizabeth II
Obv.: Head right **Rev.:** Loon splashing in the water, hologram

Date	Mintage	MS-63	Proof
2002 Satin Proof	30,000	—	45.00

KM# 521 5 DOLLARS Weight: 31.1035 g.
Comp.: 0.9999 Silver 0.9999 oz. ASW **Ruler:** Elizabeth II
Obv.: Head right **Rev.:** Maple leaf, summer colors
Rev. Des.: Stan Witten

Date	Mintage	MS-63	Proof
2003	29,416	30.00	—

KM# 607 5 DOLLARS Weight: 31.1200 g.
Comp.: 0.9999 Silver 1.0004 oz. ASW **Ruler:** Elizabeth II
Obv.: Head right **Rev.:** Maple leaf, winter colors

Date	Mintage	MS-63	Proof
2004	—	—	35.00

KM# 625 5 DOLLARS Weight: 31.1035 g.
Comp.: 0.9999 Silver 0.9999 oz. ASW **Ruler:** Elizabeth II
Obv.: Bust right **Obv. Des.:** Susanna Blunt **Rev.:** Maple leaf
Edge: Reeded **Size:** 38 mm.

Date	Mintage	MS-63	Proof
2004 Mint logo privy mark Specimen	13,859	—	35.00
2004 Monkey privy mark Specimen	25,000	—	35.00
2004 D-Day privy mark Specimen	11,698	—	35.00
2004 Desjardins privy mark	15,000	35.00	—
2004 Capricorn privy Mark Reverse proof	5,000	—	35.00
2004 Aquarius privy mark Reverse proof	5,000	—	35.00
2004 Pisces privy mark Reverse proof	5,000	—	35.00
2004 Aries privy mark Reverse proof	5,000	—	35.00
2004 Taurus privy mark Reverse proof	5,000	—	35.00
2004 Gemini privy mark Reverse proof	5,000	—	35.00
2004 Cancer privy mark Reverse proof	5,000	—	35.00
2004 Leo privy mark Reverse proof	5,000	—	35.00
2004 Virgo privy mark Reverse proof	5,000	—	35.00
2004 Libra privy mark Reverse proof	5,000	—	35.00
2004 Scorpio privy mark Reverse proof	5,000	—	35.00
2004 Sagittarius privy mark Reverse proof	5,000	—	35.00

KM# 508 5 DOLLARS Weight: 31.1035 g.
Comp.: 0.9999 Silver 0.9999 oz. ASW **Ruler:** Elizabeth II
Obv.: Crowned head right, date and denomination below
Obv. Des.: Dora de Pedery-Hunt **Rev.:** Holographic Maple leaf flanked by 9999 **Edge:** Reeded **Size:** 38 mm.

Date	Mintage	MS-63	Proof
2003 Proof	—	—	35.00

KM# 522 5 DOLLARS Weight: 31.1050 g.
Comp.: 0.9999 Silver 0.9999 oz. ASW **Ruler:** Elizabeth II
Obv.: Head right **Rev.:** Maple leaf, winter color **Rev. Des.:** Stan Witten

Date	Mintage	MS-63	Proof
2004	26,763	32.50	—

KM# 574 5 DOLLARS Weight: 1.1035 g.
Comp.: 0.9999 Silver 0.0355 oz. ASW **Ruler:** Elizabeth II
Obv.: Head right **Rev.:** Lynx

Date	Mintage	MS-63	Proof
2005 Proof	—	—	35.00

KM# 550 5 DOLLARS Weight: 31.1035 g.
Comp.: 0.9999 Silver 0.9999 oz. ASW **Ruler:** Elizabeth II
Obv.: Head right **Rev.:** Big Leaf Maple, colorized **Rev. Des.:** Stan Witten

Date	Mintage	MS-63	Proof
2005	21,233	30.00	—

KM# 660 5 DOLLARS Weight: 31.1035 g.
Comp.: 0.9990 Silver 0.9990 oz. ASW **Ruler:** Elizabeth II
Obv.: Bust right **Obv. Des.:** Susanna Blunt **Rev.:** Silver maple, colorized **Rev. Des.:** Stan Witten

Date	Mintage	MS-63	Proof
2006	14,157	35.00	—

KM# 729 5 DOLLARS Weight: 31.1050 g.
Comp.: 0.9990 Silver 0.9990 oz. ASW **Ruler:** Elizabeth II
Obv.: Bust right **Rev.:** Maple leaf orange multicolor **Size:** 38 mm.

Date	Mintage	MS-63	Proof
2007 Proof	—	—	45.00

KM# 925 5 DOLLARS Weight: 31.1050 g.
Comp.: 0.9990 Silver 0.9990 oz. ASW **Ruler:** Elizabeth II
Obv.: Bust right **Obv. Des.:** Susanna Blunt **Rev.:** Sugar maple, colorized **Rev. Des.:** Stan Witten

Date	Mintage	MS-63	Proof
2007	11,495	35.00	—

KM# 800 5 DOLLARS Weight: 31.1050 g.
Comp.: 0.9990 Silver 0.9990 oz. ASW **Ruler:** Elizabeth II
Subject: Vancouver Olympics **Obv.:** Bust right **Obv. Des.:** Susanna Blunt **Rev.:** Maple leaf, Olympic logo at left **Size:** 38 mm.

Date	Mintage	MS-63	Proof
2008	—	28.00	—
2009	—	28.00	—
2010	—	28.00	—

KM# 798 5 DOLLARS Weight: 31.1050 g.
Comp.: 0.9990 Silver 0.9990 oz. ASW **Ruler:** Elizabeth II
Subject: Maple Leaf 20th Anniversary **Rev.:** Maple Leaf, selective gold plating **Size:** 38 mm.

Date	Mintage	MS-63	Proof
2008 Proof	10,000	—	28.00

KM# 731 8 DOLLARS Comp.: 0.9990 Silver
Ruler: Elizabeth II **Rev.:** Maple leaf, long life hologram

Date	Mintage	MS-63	Proof
2007	—	35.00	—

KM# 676 250 DOLLARS Weight: 1000.0000 g.
Comp.: 0.9999 Silver 32.146 oz. ASW **Ruler:** Elizabeth II
Subject: Kilo

Date	Mintage	MS-63	Proof
2006	—	650	—

GOLD BULLION COINAGE

KM# 888 50 CENTS Weight: 1.2700 g. **Comp.:** 0.9990 Gold 0.0408 oz. AGW **Ruler:** Elizabeth II **Subject:** Red maple **Obv.:** Bust right **Obv. Leg.:** Elizabeth II 50 cents **Obv. Des.:** Susanna Blunt **Rev.:** Two maple leaves **Rev. Leg.:** Canada, Fine gold 1/25 oz or PUR 9999 **Size:** 13.92 mm.

Date	Mintage	MS-63	Proof
2009 Proof	150,000	—	60.00

KM# 438 DOLLAR Weight: 1.5810 g. **Comp.:** 0.9990 Gold 0.0508 oz. AGW **Ruler:** Elizabeth II **Subject:** Holographic Maple Leaves **Obv.:** Crowned head right **Rev.:** Three maple leaves multicolor hologram **Edge:** Reeded. **Size:** 14.1 mm.

Date	Mintage	MS-63	Proof
2001 in sets only	600	75.00	—

KM# 439 5 DOLLARS Weight: 3.1310 g. **Comp.:** 0.9999 Gold 0.1006 oz. AGW **Ruler:** Elizabeth II **Subject:** Holographic Maple Leaves **Obv.:** Crowned head right **Rev.:** Three maple leaves multicolor hologram **Edge:** Reeded **Size:** 16 mm.

Date	Mintage	MS-63	Proof
2001	600	150	—

KM# 440 10 DOLLARS Weight: 7.7970 g.
Comp.: 0.9999 Gold 0.2506 oz. AGW **Ruler:** Elizabeth II
Subject: Holographic Maples Leaves **Obv.:** Crowned head right **Rev.:** Three maple leaves multicolor hologram **Edge:** Reeded **Size:** 20 mm.

Date	Mintage	MS-63	Proof
2001	15,000	325	—

KM# 441 20 DOLLARS Weight: 15.5840 g.
Comp.: 0.9999 Gold 0.5010 oz. AGW **Ruler:** Elizabeth II
Subject: Holographic Maples Leaves **Obv.:** Crowned head right **Rev.:** Three maple leaves multicolor hologram **Edge:** Reeded **Size:** 25 mm.

Date	Mintage	MS-63	Proof
2001	600	675	—

KM# 442 50 DOLLARS Weight: 31.1500 g.
Comp.: 0.9999 Gold 1.0014 oz. AGW **Ruler:** Elizabeth II
Subject: Holographic Maples Leaves **Obv.:** Crowned head right **Rev.:** Three maple leaves multicolor hologram **Edge:** Reeded **Size:** 30 mm.

Date	Mintage	MS-63	Proof
2001	600	1,350	—

KM# 681 2500 DOLLARS Weight: 1000.0000 g.
Comp.: 0.9999 Gold 32.146 oz. AGW **Ruler:** Elizabeth II
Subject: Kilo **Rev.:** Common Characters, Early Canada
Size: 101.6 mm. **Note:** Illustration reduced.

Date	Mintage	MS-63	Proof
2007	20	42,500	—

KM# 755 1000000 DOLLARS Weight: 100000.0000 g.
Comp.: 0.9999 Gold 3214.6 oz. AGW **Ruler:** Elizabeth II
Rev.: Maple leaf **Note:** Cast

Date	Mintage	MS-63	Proof
2007	10	4,250,000	—

PLATINUM BULLION COINAGE

KM# 429 30 DOLLARS Weight: 3.1100 g.
Comp.: 0.9995 Platinum 0.0999 oz. APW **Ruler:** Elizabeth II
Obv.: Crowned head right **Rev.:** Harlequin duck's head
Rev. Des.: Cosme Saffioti and Susan Taylor **Edge:** Reeded
Size: 16 mm.

Date	Mintage	MS-63	Proof
2001 Proof	448	—	175

KM# 430 75 DOLLARS Weight: 7.7760 g.
Comp.: 0.9995 Platinum 0.2499 oz. APW **Ruler:** Elizabeth II
Obv.: Crowned head right **Rev.:** Harlequin duck in flight
Rev. Des.: Cosme Saffioti and Susan Taylor **Edge:** Reeded
Size: 20 mm.

Date	Mintage	MS-63	Proof
2001 Proof	448	—	500

KM# 431 150 DOLLARS Weight: 15.5500 g.
Comp.: 0.9995 Platinum 0.4997 oz. APW **Ruler:** Elizabeth II
Obv.: Crowned head right **Rev.:** Two harlequin ducks **Rev. Des.:** Cosme Saffioti and Susan Taylor **Edge:** Reeded **Size:** 25 mm.

Date	Mintage	MS-63	Proof
2001 Proof	448	—	900

KM# 432 300 DOLLARS Weight: 31.1035 g.
Comp.: 0.9995 Platinum 0.9995 oz. APW **Ruler:** Elizabeth II
Obv.: Crowned head right **Rev.:** Two standing harlequin ducks
Rev. Des.: Cosme Saffioti and Susan Taylor **Edge:** Reeded
Size: 30 mm.

Date	Mintage	MS-63	Proof
2001 Proof	448	—	1,800

KM# 753 300 DOLLARS Weight: 31.1050 g.
Comp.: 0.9999 Platinum 0.9999 oz. APW **Ruler:** Elizabeth II
Rev.: Wooly mammoth **Size:** 50 mm.

Date	Mintage	MS-63	Proof
2007 Proof	—	—	1,700

KM# 831 300 DOLLARS Weight: 31.1050 g.
Comp.: 0.9990 Platinum 0.9990 oz. APW **Ruler:** Elizabeth II
Rev.: Scimitar cat

Date	Mintage	MS-63	Proof
2008 Proof	—	—	1,700

MINT SETS

KM	Date	Mintage	Identification	Issue Price	Mkt Val
MS8	2001	600	KM438-442	1,996	2,600
MS9	2002	135,000	Double-dated 1952-2002, KM#444-449, 467	11.75	16.00
MS10	2002	—	KM#444-449, 467, Oh! Canada! 135th Birthday Gift set.	17.00	16.00
MS11	2002	—	KM#444-449, 467, Tiny Treasures Uncirculated Gift Set	17.00	16.00
MS12	2003	135,000	KM#289, 182b, 183b, 184b, 290, 186, 270	12.00	16.00
MS13	2003	75,000	KM490-496	13.25	20.00

KM	Date	Mintage	Identification	Issue Price	Mkt Val
MS14	2003	—	KM289, 182-184, 290, 186, 270, Oh! Canada!	17.75	16.00
MS15	2003	—	KM289, 182-184, 290, 186, 270, Tiny Treasures Uncirculated Gift Set	17.75	16.00

PROOF SETS

KM	Date	Mintage	Identification	Issue Price	Mkt Val
PS51	2001	—	KM429, 430, 431, 432	—	3,400
PS52	2002	100,000	KM#443, 444a,445,446a-449a, 467	60.00	125
PS54	2002	—	KM#519, 520	750	1,000
PS53	2002	—	KM#459-461	57.50	35.00
PS56	2003	30,000	KM#468-473	75.00	95.00
PS55	2003	100,000	KM#182a,183a,184a, 186, 270d, 289, 290a, 450	62.50	105
PS57	2004	—	KM#490, 491a-494a, 495, 496a, 512	—	105
PS58	2004	25,000	KM#621-625	—	100

SPECIMEN SETS (SS)

KM	Date	Mintage	Identification	Issue Price	Mkt Val
SS90	2002	75,000	KM#444-449,462	30.00	50.00
SS91	2003	75,000	KM#(uncertain), 270, 289, 290	30.00	50.00

CAPE VERDE

The Republic of Cape Verde, Africa's smallest republic, is located in the Atlantic Ocean, about 370 miles (595 km.) west of Dakar, Senegal, off the coast of Africa. The 14-island republic has an area of 1,557 sq. mi. (4,033 sq. km.) and a population of 435,983. Capital: Praia. The refueling of ships and aircraft is the chief economic function of the country. Fishing is important and agriculture is widely practiced, but the Cape Verdes are not self-sufficient in food. Fish products, salt, bananas, and shellfish are exported.

After 500 years of Portuguese rule, the Cape Verdes became independent on July 5, 1975. At the first general election, all seats of the new national assembly were won by the Party for the Independence of Guinea-Bissau and Cape Verde (PAIGC). The PAIGC linked the two former colonies into one state. Antonio Mascarenhas Monteiro won the first free presidential election in 1991.

MONETARY SYSTEM
100 Centavos = 1 Escudo

REPUBLIC

DECIMAL COINAGE

KM# 46   25 ESCUDOS
15.5517 g., 0.9990 Silver 0.4995 oz. ASW, 30.4 mm.
Obv: Value above national arms **Rev:** Jesus **Edge:** Plain

Date	Mintage	F	VF	XF	Unc	BU
2006 Proof	—	Value: 40.00				

KM# 47   50 ESCUDOS
1.5550 g., 0.9990 Gold 0.0499 oz. AGW, 16 mm. **Obv:** Value above national arms **Rev:** Jesus **Edge:** Plain

Date	Mintage	F	VF	XF	Unc	BU
2006 Proof	—	Value: 70.00				

KM# 48   50 ESCUDOS
25.1600 g., 0.9250 Silver 0.7482 oz. ASW, 38.8 mm.
Subject: 500th Anniversary Death of Christopher Columbus
Obv: National arms **Obv. Legend:** CABO VERDE **Rev:** Sailing ship *Santa Maria* **Rev. Legend:** A SANTA MARIA DE CHRIST?V?O COLOMBO **Edge:** Reeded

Date	Mintage	F	VF	XF	Unc	BU
2006 Proof	—	Value: 55.00				

KM# 49   50 ESCUDOS
25.0000 g., 0.9250 Silver 0.7435 oz. ASW, 38.6 mm.
Subject: Appearance in Grotto **Obv:** National arms **Obv. Legend:** CABO VERDE **Rev:** Maria standing facing 3/4 left at right **Rev. Legend:** AVE MARIA - LOURDES **Edge:** Reeded

Date	Mintage	F	VF	XF	Unc	BU
2006 Proof	—	Value: 65.00				

KM# 50   50 ESCUDOS
25.2000 g., 0.9250 Silver 0.7494 oz. ASW **Obv:** National arms **Rev:** Red Kite bird

Date	Mintage	F	VF	XF	Unc	BU
2006 Proof	—	Value: 65.00				

KM# 45   200 ESCUDOS
7.8000 g., Copper-Nickel, 29.5 mm. **Subject:** 30th Anniversary of Independence **Obv:** National arms in number 2 of 200 **Rev:** Symbolic education design **Edge:** Reeded **Shape:** Round

Date	Mintage	F	VF	XF	Unc	BU
2005	—				8.50	10.00

KM# 45a   200 ESCUDOS
18.2800 g., 0.9250 Silver 0.5436 oz. ASW **Subject:** 30th Anniversary of Independence **Obv:** National arms in number 2 of 200 **Rev:** Symbolic education design **Edge:** Reeded **Shape:** Round

Date	Mintage	F	VF	XF	Unc	BU
2005 Proof	—	Value: 70.00				

CAYMAN ISLANDS

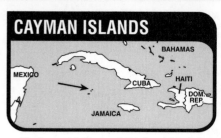

The Cayman Islands are a British Crown Colony situated about 180 miles (280 km) northwest of Jamaica. It consists of three islands: Grand Cayman, Little Cayman, and Cayman Brac. The islands have an area of 102 sq. mi. (259 sq. km.) and a population of 33,200. Capital: George Town. Seafaring, commerce, banking, and tourism are the principal industries. Rope, turtle shells, and sharkskins are exported.

RULER
British

MINT MARKS
CHI - Valcambi

MONETARY SYSTEM
100 Cents = 1 Dollar

BRITISH COLONY

DECIMAL COINAGE

KM# 131   CENT
2.5300 g., Bronze Plated Steel, 17 mm. **Ruler:** Elizabeth II
Obv: Crowned head right **Rev:** Grand Caiman thrush
Rev. Designer: Stuart Devlin

Date	Mintage	F	VF	XF	Unc	BU
2002	—	—	—	0.20	0.50	1.00
2005	—	—	—	0.20	0.50	1.00

KM# 132   5 CENTS
2.0000 g., Nickel Clad Steel, 18 mm. **Ruler:** Elizabeth II
Obv: Crowned head right **Rev:** Pink-spotted shrimp
Rev. Designer: Stuart Devlin **Edge:** Plain

Date	Mintage	F	VF	XF	Unc	BU
2002	—	—	—	0.20	0.50	1.00
2005	—	—	—	0.20	0.50	1.00

KM# 133   10 CENTS
3.4300 g., Nickel Clad Steel, 21 mm. **Ruler:** Elizabeth II
Obv: Head with tiara right **Rev:** Green turtle surfacing
Rev. Designer: Stuart Devlin **Edge:** Reeded

Date	Mintage	F	VF	XF	Unc	BU
2002	—		0.25	0.40	1.00	1.25
2005	—		0.25	0.40	1.00	1.25

KM# 134   25 CENTS
5.0400 g., Nickel Clad Steel, 24.2 mm. **Ruler:** Elizabeth II
Obv: Head with tiara right **Rev:** Schooner sailing right
Rev. Designer: Stuart Devlin **Edge:** Reeded

Date	Mintage	F	VF	XF	Unc	BU
2002	—	—	—	0.75	1.50	1.75
2005	—	—	—	0.75	1.50	1.75

KM# 136 2 DOLLARS
28.3400 g., 0.9250 Silver 0.8428 oz. ASW, 38.6 mm.
Ruler: Elizabeth II **Obv:** Gold plated Queen Elizabeth II
Rev: British crown and value **Edge:** Reeded

Date	Mintage	F	VF	XF	Unc	BU
2002 Proof	—	Value: 35.00				

KM# 135 2 DOLLARS
28.2800 g., 0.9250 Silver 0.8410 oz. ASW, 38.6 mm.
Ruler: Elizabeth II **Subject:** 500th Anniversary - Christopher
Columbus First Recorded Sighting of the Cayman Islands
Obv: Crowned head right **Rev:** Quincentennial Celebrations
Logo in color

Date	Mintage	F	VF	XF	Unc	BU
2003 Proof	1,500	Value: 75.00				

KM# 138 2 DOLLARS
28.2800 g., 0.9250 Silver 0.8410 oz. ASW, 38.61 mm.
Ruler: Elizabeth II **Subject:** Royal Horticulture Society
Obv: Head right, gilt portrait **Rev:** RHS Tent adn flowers

Date	Mintage	F	VF	XF	Unc	BU
2003 Proof	—	Value: 35.00				

KM# 137 5 DOLLARS
0.9250 Silver **Ruler:** Elizabeth II **Subject:** Elizabeth II's 80th
Birthday **Obv:** Crowned head right - gilt **Obv. Legend:** CAYMAN
ISLANDS - ELIZABETH II **Obv. Designer:** Ian Rank-Broadley
Rev: Queen crowning Charles as Prince of Wales

Date	Mintage	F	VF	XF	Unc	BU
2006 Proof	—	Value: 40.00				

KM# 141 5 DOLLARS
28.2800 g., 0.9250 Silver 0.8410 oz. ASW, 38.6 mm. **Ruler:**
Elizabeth II **Subject:** Constitutional Government, 50th
Anniversary **Obv:** Bust right **Rev:** Coat of arms

Date	Mintage	F	VF	XF	Unc	BU
2009 Proof	300	Value: 75.00				

KM# 139 10 DOLLARS
28.2800 g., 0.9250 Silver 0.8410 oz. ASW, 38.61 mm. **Ruler:**
Elizabeth II **Subject:** Cayman Islands Monetary Authority, 10th
Anniversary **Obv:** Bust right **Rev:** Island's coat of arms

Date	Mintage	F	VF	XF	Unc	BU
2007 Proof	200	Value: 110				

KM# 140 10 DOLLARS
7.9800 g., 0.9167 Gold 0.2352 oz. AGW **Ruler:** Elizabeth II
Subject: Cayman Islands Monetary Authority, 10th Anniversary
Obv: Bust right **Rev:** Island's coat of arms

Date	Mintage	F	VF	XF	Unc	BU
2007 Proof	75	Value: 340				

KM# 142 10 DOLLARS
7.0000 g., 0.9167 Gold 0.2063 oz. AGW **Ruler:** Elizabeth II
Subject: Constitutional Government, 50th Anniversary **Obv:**
Bust right **Rev:** Coat of Arms

Date	Mintage	F	VF	XF	Unc	BU
2009 Proof	125	Value: 375				

CENTRAL AFRICAN STATES

The Central African States, a monetary union comprised of
Equatorial Guinea (a former Spanish possession), the former
French possessions and now independent states of the Republic
of Congo (Brazzaville), Gabon, Central African Republic, Chad and
Cameroon, issues a common currency for the member states from
a common central bank. The monetary unit, the African Financial
Community franc, is tied to and supported by the French franc.

In 1960, an attempt was made to form a union of the newly
independent republics of Chad, Congo, Central Africa and
Gabon. The proposal was discarded when Chad refused to
become a constituent member. The four countries then linked
into an Equatorial Customs Unit, to which Cameroon became an
associate member in 1961. A more extensive cooperation of the
five republics, identified as the Central African Customs and Economic Union, was entered into force at the beginning of 1966.

In 1974 the Central Bank of the Equatorial African States,
which had issued coins and paper currency in its own name and
with the names of the constituent member nations, changed its
name to the Bank of the Central African States. Equatorial
Guinea converted to the CFA currency system issuing its first 100
Franc in 1985.

For earlier coinage see French Equatorial Africa.

MONETARY UNION

STANDARD COINAGE

KM# 16 FRANC
1.6100 g., Stainless Steel, 14.9 mm. **Obv:** Value above produce
Rev: Value **Edge:** Plain

Date	Mintage	F	VF	XF	Unc	BU
2006(a)	—	—	—	—	0.15	0.25

KM# 17 2 FRANCS
2.4300 g., Stainless Steel, 17.9 mm. **Obv:** Value above produce
Rev: Value **Edge:** Plain

Date	Mintage	F	VF	XF	Unc	BU
2006(a)	—	—	—	—	0.25	0.35

KM# 7 5 FRANCS
3.0000 g., Aluminum-Bronze, 20 mm. **Obv:** Three giant eland
left, date below **Obv. Designer:** G.B.L. Bazor **Rev:** Denomination
within wreath

Date	Mintage	F	VF	XF	Unc	BU
2003	—	0.15	0.30	0.60	1.25	—

KM# 18 5 FRANCS
2.4100 g., Brass, 15.9 mm. **Obv:** Value above produce
Rev: Value **Edge:** Reeded

Date	Mintage	F	VF	XF	Unc	BU
2006(a)	—	—	—	—	0.50	0.65

KM# 9 10 FRANCS
4.0000 g., Aluminum-Bronze, 23 mm. **Obv:** Three giant eland
left, date below **Obv. Designer:** G.B.L. Bazor **Rev:** Denomination
within wreath

Date	Mintage	F	VF	XF	Unc	BU
2003(a)	—	0.20	0.35	0.75	1.50	—

KM# 19 10 FRANCS
3.0000 g., Brass, 17.9 mm. **Obv:** Value above produce
Rev: Value **Edge:** Reeded

Date	Mintage	F	VF	XF	Unc	BU
2006(a)	—	—	—	—	0.75	1.00

KM# 10 25 FRANCS
8.0000 g., Aluminum-Bronze, 27.2 mm. **Obv:** Three giant eland
left, date below **Obv. Designer:** G.B.L. Bazor **Rev:** Denomination
within wreath

Date	Mintage	F	VF	XF	Unc	BU
2003(a)	—	0.25	0.50	1.00	2.00	—

KM# 20 25 FRANCS
4.2000 g., Brass, 22.7 mm. **Obv:** Value above produce
Rev: Value **Edge:** Reeded

Date	Mintage	F	VF	XF	Unc	BU
2006(a)	—	—	—	—	1.00	1.25

KM# 11 50 FRANCS
4.7000 g., Nickel, 21.5 mm. **Obv:** Three giant eland left, date
below **Obv. Designer:** G.B.L. Bazor **Rev:** Denomination within
flower design **Note:** Starting in 1996 an extra flora item was added
where the mintmark was formerly located.

Date	Mintage	F	VF	XF	Unc	BU
2003(a) Cocoa bean	—	0.75	1.50	3.50	6.00	—

KM# 21 50 FRANCS
4.9000 g., Stainless Steel, 22 mm. **Obv:** Value above produce
Rev: Value **Edge:** Reeded

Date	Mintage	F	VF	XF	Unc	BU
2006(a)	—	—	—	—	1.25	1.50

KM# 15 100 FRANCS
6.0000 g., Bi-Metallic Stainless Steel center in Brass ring,
23.9 mm. **Obv:** Denomination above initials within beaded circle
Rev: Value above produce **Edge:** Reeded

Date	Mintage	F	VF	XF	Unc	BU
2006(a)	—	—	—	—	5.00	6.50

KM# 22 500 FRANCS
8.1000 g., Copper-Nickel, 26 mm. **Obv:** Value above produce
Rev: Value **Edge:** Segmented reeding and lettering

Date	Mintage	F	VF	XF	Unc	BU
2006(a)	—	—	—	—	8.00	10.00

CHAD

The Republic of Chad, a landlocked country of central Africa, is the largest country of former French Equatorial Africa. It has an area of 495,755 sq. mi. (1,284,000 sq. km.) and a population of *7.27 million. Capital: N'Djamena. An expanding livestock industry produces camels, cattle and sheep. Cotton (the chief product), ivory and palm oil are important exports.

NOTE: For earlier and related coinage see French Equatorial Africa and the Equatorial African States. For later coinage see Central African States.

MINT MARKS
(a) - Paris, privy marks only
(b) = Brussels
NI - Numismatic Italiana, Arezzo, Italy

REPUBLIC

DECIMAL COINAGE

KM# 30   500 FRANCS
Silver, 31 mm.   **Obv:** Native portrait within circle **Rev:** Rhino mom and baby

Date	Mintage	F	VF	XF	Unc	BU
2001 Proof	—	Value: 30.00				

KM# 20   1000 FRANCS
15.0000 g., 0.9990 Silver 0.4818 oz. ASW, 35 mm.   **Obv:** Native portrait within circle, denomination below **Rev:** Ancient Arabic war ship **Edge:** Plain

Date	Mintage	F	VF	XF	Unc	BU
2001 Proof	—	Value: 40.00				

KM# 21   1000 FRANCS
25.1000 g., 0.9990 Silver 0.8061 oz. ASW, 40 mm.   **Obv:** Native portrait within circle, denomination below **Rev:** Soccer player and stadium **Edge:** Reeded

Date	Mintage	F	VF	XF	Unc	BU
2001 Proof	—	Value: 40.00				

KM# 29   1000 FRANCS
15.0000 g., 0.9990 Silver 0.4818 oz. ASW, 36 mm.   **Obv:** Native portrait within circle **Rev:** Multicolor orang-outan

Date	Mintage	F	VF	XF	Unc	BU
2001 Proof	—	Value: 35.00				

KM# 22   1000 FRANCS
20.0000 g., 0.9990 Silver 0.6423 oz. ASW, 40 mm.   **Obv:** Native portrait within circle, denomination below **Rev:** Horizontal soccer player above stadium **Edge:** Reeded

Date	Mintage	F	VF	XF	Unc	BU
2002 Proof	5,000	Value: 40.00				

KM# 23   1000 FRANCS
20.1500 g., 0.9990 Silver 0.6472 oz. ASW, 40 mm.   **Obv:** Native portrait within circle, denomination below **Rev:** Soccer player and Arch of Triumph **Edge:** Reeded

Date	Mintage	F	VF	XF	Unc	BU
2002 Proof	—	Value: 40.00				

CHILE

The Republic of Chile, a ribbon-like country on the Pacific coast of southern South America, has an area of 292,135 sq. mi. (756,950 sq. km.) and a population of *15.21 million. Capital: Santiago. Historically, the economic base of Chile has been the rich mineral deposits of its northern provinces. Copper has accounted for more than 75 percent of Chile's export earnings in recent years. Other important mineral exports are iron ore, iodine and nitrate of soda. Fresh fruits and vegetables, as well as wine are increasingly significant in inter-hemispheric trade.

MINT MARK
So – Santiago
(ml) – Maple leaf – Royal Canadian Mint (RCM)

REPUBLIC

REFORM COINAGE
100 Centavos = 1 Peso; 1000 Old Escudos = 1 Peso

KM# 231   PESO
0.7000 g., Aluminum, 16.32 mm.   **Obv:** Gen. Bernardo O'Higgins bust right **Obv. Legend:** REPUBLICA - DE CHILE **Rev:** Denomination above date within wreath **Edge:** Plain **Shape:** 8-sided **Note:** Varieties exist.

Date	Mintage	F	VF	XF	Unc	BU
2001So Narrow date	—	—	—	—	0.10	0.20
2002So Narrow date	—	—	—	—	0.10	0.20
2003So Narrow date	—	—	—	—	0.10	0.20
2004So Narrow date	—	—	—	—	0.10	0.20
2005So Narrow date	—	—	—	—	0.10	0.20
2006So Narrow date	—	—	—	—	0.10	0.20

KM# 232   5 PESOS
2.1600 g., Aluminum-Bronze, 16.43 mm.   **Obv:** Gen. Bernardo O'Higgins bust right **Obv. Legend:** REPUBLICA - DE CHILE **Rev:** Denomination above date within wreath **Edge:** Plain **Shape:** 8-sided **Note:** Varieties exist.

Date	Mintage	F	VF	XF	Unc	BU
2001So Narrow date	—	—	—	0.10	0.35	0.60
2001So (sa) Wide date	—	—	—	0.15	0.50	0.75
Note: Without name of sculptor						
2002So Narrow date	—	—	—	0.15	0.50	0.75
2002So Wide date	—	—	—	0.10	0.35	0.60
2003So	—	—	—	0.10	0.35	0.60
2004So	—	—	—	0.10	0.35	0.60
2005So	—	—	—	0.10	0.35	0.60
2006So	—	—	—	0.10	0.35	0.60

KM# 228.2   10 PESOS
3.5500 g., Nickel-Brass, 20.92 mm.   **Obv:** Bust of Gen. Bernardo O'Higgins right **Obv. Legend:** REPUBLICA - DE CHILE **Rev:** Denomination above date within sprays **Edge:** Reeded **Note:** All 9's are curl tail 9's except for the 1999 date, these are straight tail 9's. Normal rim.

Date	Mintage	F	VF	XF	Unc	BU
2001So	—	—	0.10	0.20	0.50	0.65
2002So	—	—	0.10	0.20	0.50	0.65
2003So	—	—	0.10	0.20	0.50	0.65
2004So	—	—	0.10	0.20	0.50	0.65
2005So	—	—	0.10	0.20	0.50	0.65
2006So	—	—	0.10	0.20	0.50	0.65
2007	—	—	0.10	0.20	0.50	0.65
Note: Struck in Canada						
2008So	—	—	0.10	0.20	0.50	0.65

KM# 240   20 PESOS
Aluminum-Brass   **Subject:** Chile - 200th Anniversary

Date	Mintage	F	VF	XF	Unc	BU
2010	—	—	—	—	0.75	1.00

KM# 219.2   50 PESOS
7.0500 g., Aluminum-Bronze, 25.40 mm.   **Obv:** Bust of Gen. Bernardo O'Higgins right **Obv. Legend:** REPUBLICA - DE CHILE **Rev:** Denomination above date within sprays **Edge:** Ornamented **Shape:** 10-sided **Note:** Narrow date.

Date	Mintage	F	VF	XF	Unc	BU
2001So	—	—	0.25	0.50	1.25	1.50
2002So	—	—	0.25	0.50	1.25	1.50
2005So	—	—	0.25	0.50	1.00	1.25
2006So	—	—	0.25	0.50	1.00	1.25
2007	—	—	0.25	0.50	1.00	1.25
Note: Struck in Canada						

KM# 236   100 PESOS
7.5800 g., Bi-Metallic Copper-nickel center in Brass ring, 23.43 mm.   **Subject:** Native people **Obv:** Bust of native Mapuche girl facing **Obv. Legend:** REPUBLICA DE CHILE - PUEBLOS ORIGINARIOS **Rev:** National arms above denomination **Edge:** Segmented reeding, 3 reeded & 3 plain regmenti

Date	Mintage	F	VF	XF	Unc	BU
2001So	—	—	0.35	0.90	2.25	3.00
2003So	—	—	0.35	0.90	2.25	3.00

Date	Mintage	F	VF	XF	Unc	BU
2004So	—	—	0.35	0.90	2.25	3.00
2005So	—	—	0.35	0.90	2.25	3.00
2006So	—	—	0.35	0.90	2.25	3.00
2008So	—	—	0.35	0.90	2.25	3.00

KM# 241 200 PESOS
Aluminum-Bronze **Subject:** Chile - 200th Anniversary

Date	Mintage	F	VF	XF	Unc	BU
2010	—	—	—	—	1.50	2.00

KM# 235 500 PESOS
6.6000 g., Bi-Metallic Aluminum-Bronze center in Copper-Nickel ring, 26 mm. **Subject:** Cardinal Raul Silva Henriquez **Obv:** Bust of cardinal within inner ring facing left **Rev:** Denomination above date within wreath **Edge:** Reeded

Date	Mintage	F	VF	XF	Unc	BU
2001So	—	—	—	—	6.00	6.50
2002So 4.1mm date	—	—	—	—	6.00	6.50
2002So 5.2mm date	—	—	—	—	6.00	6.50
2003So	—	—	—	—	6.00	6.50

CHINA / Peoples Republic

The Peoples Republic of China, located in eastern Asia, has an area of 3,696,100 sq. mi. (9,596,960 sq. km.) (including Manchuria and Tibet) and a population of *1.20 billion. Capital: Peking (Beijing). The economy is based on agriculture, mining, and manufacturing. Textiles, clothing, metal ores, tea and rice are exported.

MONETARY SYSTEM
10 Fen (Cents) = 1 Jiao
10 Jiao = 1 Renminbi Yuan

MINT MARKS
(b) - Beijing (Peking)
(s) - Shanghai
(y) - Shenyang (Mukden)

OBVERSE LEGENDS

ZHONGHUA RENMIN GONGHEGUO (Peoples Republic of China)

ZHONGGUO RENMIN YINHANG (Peoples Bank of China

PEOPLES REPUBLIC
STANDARD COINAGE

KM# 1 FEN
0.7000 g., Aluminum, 18 mm. **Obv:** National emblem **Rev:** Value in sprays, date below **Edge:** Reeded **Note:** Prev. Y#1.

Date	Mintage	F	VF	XF	Unc	BU
2005	—	—	—	0.10	0.15	0.25
2007	—	—	—	0.10	0.15	0.25

KM# 1210 JIAO
1.1200 g., Aluminum, 19 mm. **Obv:** Denomination, date below **Rev:** Orchid **Rev. Legend:** ZHONGGUA RENMIN YINHANG **Edge:** Plain **Note:** Prev. Y#1068.

Date	Mintage	F	VF	XF	Unc	BU
2001	—	—	—	—	0.50	0.75
2002	—	—	—	—	0.50	0.75
2003	—	—	—	—	0.50	0.75

KM# 1210a JIAO
Copper-Nickel, 19 mm. **Obv:** Denomination, date below **Note:** Prev. Y#1068a.

Date	Mintage	F	VF	XF	Unc	BU
2005	—	—	—	—	0.50	0.75

KM# 1210b JIAO
3.2200 g., Steel, 19.03 mm. **Obv:** Value, date below **Rev:** Orchid **Rev. Legend:** ZHONGGUA RENMIN YINHANG **Edge:** Plain **Note:** Prev. Y#1068b.

Date	Mintage	F	VF	XF	Unc	BU
2005	—	—	—	—	—	0.25
2006	—	—	—	—	—	0.25
2007	—	—	—	—	—	0.25
2008	—	—	—	—	—	0.25

KM# 336 5 JIAO
3.8300 g., Brass, 20.5 mm. **Obv:** National emblem, date below **Rev:** Denomination above flowers **Edge:** Segmented reeding **Note:** Prev. Y#329.

Date	Mintage	F	VF	XF	Unc	BU
2001	—	—	—	—	1.00	1.25

KM# 1411 5 JIAO
3.8000 g., Brass, 20.5 mm. **Obv:** Denomination **Rev:** Flower **Rev. Legend:** ZHONGGUA RENMIN YINHANG **Edge:** Reeded and plain sections **Note:** Prev. Y#1106.

Date	Mintage	F	VF	XF	Unc	BU
2002	—	—	—	—	1.50	1.75
2003	—	—	—	—	1.50	1.75
2004	—	—	—	—	1.50	1.75
2005	—	—	—	—	1.50	1.75
2006	—	—	—	—	1.50	1.75
2007	—	—	—	—	1.50	1.75
2008	—	—	—	—	1.50	1.75

KM# 1212 YUAN
6.1000 g., Nickel Plated Steel, 24.9 mm. **Obv:** Denomination, date below **Rev:** Chrysanthemum **Rev. Legend:** ZHONGGUA RENMIN YINHANG **Edge:** "RMB" three times **Note:** Prev. Y#1069.

Date	Mintage	F	VF	XF	Unc	BU
2001	—	—	—	—	2.00	2.50
2002	—	—	—	—	2.00	2.50
2003	—	—	—	—	2.00	2.50
2004	—	—	—	—	2.00	2.50
2005	—	—	—	—	2.00	2.50
2006	—	—	—	—	2.00	2.50
2007	—	—	—	—	2.00	2.50
2008	—	—	—	—	2.00	2.50

KM# 1465 YUAN
6.8500 g., Brass, 25 mm. **Obv:** Value **Rev:** Celebrating child and ram **Edge:** Lettered **Edge Lettering:** "RMB" three times **Note:** Prev. Y#1125.

Date	Mintage	F	VF	XF	Unc	BU
2003	—	—	—	—	5.00	6.00

KM# 1521 YUAN
Nickel Clad Steel **Obv:** Denomination **Rev:** Celebrating Child **Note:** Prev. Y#1247.

Date	Mintage	F	VF	XF	Unc	BU
2004	—	—	—	—	2.50	3.00

KM# 1522 YUAN
Nickel Clad Steel **Obv:** Palace **Rev:** Deng Xiao Ping 1904-2004 **Note:** Prev. Y#1248.

Date	Mintage	F	VF	XF	Unc	BU
2004	—	—	—	—	3.50	4.00

KM# 1523 YUAN
Nickel Clad Steel **Subject:** 50th Year of Peoples Congress **Obv:** Congress building **Note:** Prev. Y#1249.

Date	Mintage	F	VF	XF	Unc	BU
2004	—	—	—	—	3.50	4.00

KM# 1575 YUAN
Nickel Clad Steel **Subject:** Year of the Rooster **Obv:** Denomination **Rev:** Celebrating Child **Note:** Prev. Y#1250.

Date	Mintage	F	VF	XF	Unc	BU
2005	—	—	—	—	3.00	3.50

KM# 1574 YUAN
5.9600 g., Nickel Clad Steel, 25 mm. **Obv:** Building **Rev:** Bust of Chenyun **Edge:** Lettered **Note:** Prev. Y#1208.

Date	Mintage	F	VF	XF	Unc	BU
2005	—	—	—	—	3.50	4.00

KM# 1650 YUAN
Nickel Clad Steel **Subject:** Year of the Dog **Obv:** Denomination **Rev:** Celebrating Child **Note:** Prev. Y#1251.

Date	Mintage	F	VF	XF	Unc	BU
2006	—	—	—	—	7.00	8.00

KM# 1775 YUAN
6.7500 g., Brass, 25 mm. **Subject:** 29th Olympics **Obv:** Stylized Olympics logo **Rev:** Cartoon swimmer **Edge:** Reeded **Note:** Prev. Y#1256.

Date	Mintage	F	VF	XF	Unc	BU
2008 (2006)(y)	—	—	—	—	5.00	6.00

KM# 1776 YUAN
6.7500 g., Brass, 25 mm. **Subject:** 29th Olympics **Obv:** Stylized Olympics logo **Rev:** Cartoon Weight Lifter **Edge:** Reeded **Note:** Prev. Y#1257.

Date	Mintage	F	VF	XF	Unc	BU
2008 (2006)	—	—	—	—	5.00	6.00

KM# 1810 YUAN
Brass, 25 mm. **Obv:** Beijing olympic logo **Rev:** Character with soccer ball

Date	Mintage	F	VF	XF	Unc	BU
2008	—	—	—	—	2.50	3.00

KM# 1811   YUAN
Brass, 25 mm. **Obv:** Beijing Olympic logo **Rev:** Character fencing

Date	Mintage	F	VF	XF	Unc	BU
2008	—	—	—	—	2.50	3.00

KM# 1812   YUAN
Brass, 25 mm. **Obv:** Beijing Olympic logo **Rev:** Character on horseback

Date	Mintage	F	VF	XF	Unc	BU
2008	—	—	—	—	2.50	3.00

KM# 1813   YUAN
Brass, 25 mm. **Obv:** Large value **Rev:** Boy with rat pattern chinese knot & cluster of fireworks

Date	Mintage	F	VF	XF	Unc	BU
2008	10,000,000	—	—	—	2.50	3.00

KM# 1364   5 YUAN
12.8000 g., Brass, 30 mm. **Subject:** Revolution: 90th Anniversary **Obv:** National emblem **Rev:** Battle scene **Edge:** Reeded **Note:** Prev. Y#1109.

Date	Mintage	F	VF	XF	Unc	BU
2001	—	—	—	—	7.50	8.50

KM# 1363   5 YUAN
12.8000 g., Brass, 30 mm. **Subject:** 50th Anniversary - Chinese Occupation of Tibet **Obv:** National emblem **Rev:** Potala Palace, value and two dancers **Edge:** Reeded **Note:** Prev. Y#1126.

Date	Mintage	F	VF	XF	Unc	BU
2001(y)	10,000,000	—	—	—	8.00	—

KM# 1412   5 YUAN
12.8000 g., Brass, 30 mm. **Subject:** The Great Wall **Obv:** State arms, icroscopic inscription repeated four times on the inner raised rim **Obv. Inscription:** SHI JIE WEN HUA YI CHAN **Rev:** Two views of the Great Wall **Edge:** Reeded **Note:** Prev. Y#1107.

Date	Mintage	F	VF	XF	Unc	BU
2002	—	—	—	—	7.00	8.00

KM# 1413   5 YUAN
12.8000 g., Brass, 30 mm. **Subject:** Terra Cotta Army **Obv:** State arms and the microscopic inscription repeated four times on the raised inner rim. **Obv. Inscription:** SHI JIE WEN HUA YI CHAN **Rev:** Terra Cotta Soldier close-up with many more in background **Edge:** Reeded **Note:** Prev. Y#1108.

Date	Mintage	F	VF	XF	Unc	BU
2002	—	—	—	—	7.00	8.00

KM# 1463   5 YUAN
12.8000 g., Brass, 30 mm. **Subject:** Chaotian Temple in Beijing **Obv:** State emblem **Rev:** Buildings **Edge:** Reeded **Note:** Prev. Y#1230.

Date	Mintage	F	VF	XF	Unc	BU
2003	10,000,000	—	—	—	7.00	8.00

KM# 1464   5 YUAN
Brass, 30 mm. **Obv:** National emblem **Rev:** Imperial Palace **Note:** Prev. Y#1252.

Date	Mintage	F	VF	XF	Unc	BU
2003	—	—	—	—	7.00	8.00

KM# 1461   5 YUAN
12.8000 g., Brass, 30 mm. **Obv:** National emblem **Rev:** Chaotian Temple in Beigang Taiwan **Edge:** Reeded **Note:** Prev. Y#1127.

Date	Mintage	F	VF	XF	Unc	BU
2003	10,000,000	—	—	—	7.00	8.00

KM# 1462   5 YUAN
12.8000 g., Brass, 30 mm. **Obv:** National emblem **Rev:** Chikan Tower on Treasure Island Taiwan **Edge:** Reeded **Note:** Prev. Y#1128.

Date	Mintage	F	VF	XF	Unc	BU
2003(y)	10,000,000	—	—	—	7.00	8.00

KM# 1526   5 YUAN
12.7000 g., Brass, 30 mm. **Obv:** National emblem **Rev:** Peking Man bust and discovery site view **Edge:** Reeded **Note:** Prev. Y#1201.

Date	Mintage	F	VF	XF	Unc	BU
2004	6,000,000	—	—	—	6.00	7.00

KM# 1527   5 YUAN
12.7000 g., Brass, 30 mm. **Obv:** National emblem **Rev:** Pavillion and bridge **Edge:** Reeded **Note:** Prev. Y#1202.

Date	Mintage	F	VF	XF	Unc	BU
2004	6,000,000	—	—	—	6.00	7.00

KM# 1524   5 YUAN
Brass, 30 mm. **Obv:** National emblem **Rev:** Island scene **Note:** Prev. Y#1253.

Date	Mintage	F	VF	XF	Unc	BU
2004	—	—	—	—	6.00	7.00

KM# 1525   5 YUAN
Brass, 30 mm. **Obv:** National emblem **Rev:** Lighthouse **Note:** Prev. Y#1254.

Date	Mintage	F	VF	XF	Unc	BU
2004	—	—	—	—	6.00	7.00

KM# 1577   5 YUAN
12.8000 g., Brass, 30 mm. **Subject:** "Taiwan" **Obv:** State emblem **Rev:** Tower and terrace **Edge:** Reeded **Note:** Prev. Y#1231.

Date	Mintage	F	VF	XF	Unc	BU
2005	—	—	—	—	6.00	7.00

KM# 1576   5 YUAN
12.9200 g., Brass, 30 mm. **Obv:** National emblem **Rev:** Lijiang building **Edge:** Reeded **Note:** Prev. Y#1209.

Date	Mintage	F	VF	XF	Unc	BU
2005	—	—	—	—	6.00	7.00

KM# 1578   5 YUAN
12.9200 g., Brass, 30 mm. **Obv:** National emblem **Rev:** Green City Hall **Edge:** Reeded **Note:** Prev. Y#1210.

Date	Mintage	F	VF	XF	Unc	BU
2005	—	—	—	—	6.00	7.00

KM# 1068   5 YUAN
22.0000 g., 0.9000 Silver 0.6366 oz. ASW, 36 mm. **Obv:** Great Wall **Rev:** Gymnast, denomination at right **Edge:** Reeded **Note:** Prev. Y#1189.

Date	Mintage	F	VF	XF	Unc	BU
2005(y)	—	—	—	—	22.50	25.00

KM# 1731   5 YUAN
Brass, 30 mm. **Obv:** State emblem **Rev:** Large statue head

Date	Mintage	F	VF	XF	Unc	BU
2006 Proof	10,000,000	Value: 3.00				

KM# 1400   10 YUAN
31.1035 g., 0.9990 Silver 0.9990 oz. ASW, 40 mm. **Subject:** Bejing opera **Rev:** Two multicolor actors, one with tassles

Date	Mintage	F	VF	XF	Unc	BU
2001 Proof	38,000	Value: 60.00				

KM# 1395   10 YUAN
31.1035 g., 0.9990 Silver 0.9990 oz. ASW, 40 mm. **Subject:** 2008 Olympics Beijing bid **Obv:** Gold-plated "V" design **Rev:** Radiant Temple of Heaven **Edge:** Reeded **Note:** Prev. Y#1103.

Date	Mintage	F	VF	XF	Unc	BU
2001 Proof	60,000	Value: 50.00				

KM# 1384 10 YUAN
31.1035 g., 0.9990 Silver 0.9990 oz. ASW **Series:** Folk fairy tails **Rev:** Heroic figure putting ax to mountains

Date	Mintage	F	VF	XF	Unc	BU
2001 Proof	30,000	Value: 60.00				

KM# 1385 10 YUAN
31.1035 g., 0.9990 Silver 0.9990 oz. ASW, 40 mm. **Series:** Folk fairy tails **Rev:** Multicolor angelic figure

Date	Mintage	F	VF	XF	Unc	BU
2001 Proof	30,000	Value: 60.00				

KM# 1396 10 YUAN
31.1035 g., 0.9990 Silver 0.9990 oz. ASW, 40 mm. **Series:** Folk customs **Subject:** Mid autumn festival **Rev:** Flora and sun

Date	Mintage	F	VF	XF	Unc	BU
2001 Proof	40,000	Value: 60.00				

KM# 1397 10 YUAN
31.1035 g., 0.9990 Silver 0.9990 oz. ASW, 32 mm. **Subject:** Bejing International Coin Expo **Obv:** Globe hemisphere view **Rev:** Bejing city view

Date	Mintage	F	VF	XF	Unc	BU
2001 Proof	40,000	Value: 60.00				

KM# 1398 10 YUAN
31.1035 g., 0.9990 Silver 0.9990 oz. ASW, 40 mm. **Subject:** Bejing opera **Rev:** Two multicolor actors, one with hankie

Date	Mintage	F	VF	XF	Unc	BU
2001 Proof	38,000	Value: 60.00				

KM# 1399 10 YUAN
31.1035 g., 0.9990 Silver 0.9990 oz. ASW, 40 mm. **Subject:** Bejing opera **Rev:** Two actors, one with blue ribbon

Date	Mintage	F	VF	XF	Unc	BU
2001 Proof	38,000	Value: 60.00				

KM# 1401 10 YUAN
31.1035 g., 0.9990 Silver 0.9990 oz. ASW, 40 mm. **Subject:** Bejing opera **Rev:** Two multicolor actors, white or black beard

Date	Mintage	F	VF	XF	Unc	BU
2001 Proof	38,000	Value: 60.00				

KM# 1428 10 YUAN
31.1035 g., 0.9990 Silver 0.9990 oz. ASW, 40 mm. **Series:** Folk fiary tails **Rev:** Multicolor male figure seated

Date	Mintage	F	VF	XF	Unc	BU
2002 Proof	30,000	Value: 60.00				

KM# 1455 10 YUAN
31.1035 g., 0.9990 Silver 0.9990 oz. ASW, 40 mm. **Subject:** Shanghai World Expo of 2010 **Obv:** Flower design with inset pearl **Rev:** 2010 Logo incorporating a tower **Edge:** Reeded **Note:** Prev. Y#1233.

Date	Mintage	F	VF	XF	Unc	BU
2002 Proof	50,000	Value: 50.00				

KM# 1429 10 YUAN
31.1035 g., 0.9990 Silver Colorized 0.9990 oz. ASW, 40 mm. **Series:** Folk fairy tails **Rev:** Male figure brandishing sword

Date	Mintage	F	VF	XF	Unc	BU
2002 Proof	30,000	Value: 60.00				

KM# 1438 10 YUAN
31.1035 g., 0.9990 Silver 0.9990 oz. ASW, 40 mm. **Series:** Folk customs **Rev:** Dragon boat

Date	Mintage	F	VF	XF	Unc	BU
2002 Proof	40,000	Value: 60.00				

KM# 1441 10 YUAN
31.1035 g., 0.9990 Silver Colorized 0.9990 oz. ASW, 40 mm. **Series:** Classic literature **Rev:** Black and red dressed women seated **Shape:** Hexagon

Date	Mintage	F	VF	XF	Unc	BU
2002 Proof	38,000	Value: 50.00				

KM# 1442 10 YUAN
31.1035 g., 0.9990 Silver 0.9990 oz. ASW, 40 mm. **Series:** Classic literature **Rev:** Multicolor white dressed woman standing **Shape:** Hexagon

Date	Mintage	F	VF	XF	Unc	BU
2002 Proof	38,000	Value: 50.00				

KM# 1443 10 YUAN
31.1035 g., 0.9990 Silver 0.9990 oz. ASW, 40 mm. **Series:** Classic literature **Rev:** Multicolor yellow dressed woman walking left **Shape:** Hexagon

Date	Mintage	F	VF	XF	Unc	BU
2002 Proof	38,000	Value: 50.00				

KM# 1444 10 YUAN
31.1035 g., 0.9990 Silver 0.9990 oz. ASW, 40 mm. **Series:** Classic literature **Obv:** Multicolor purple dressed woman **Shape:** Hexagon

Date	Mintage	F	VF	XF	Unc	BU

KM# 1447 10 YUAN
31.1035 g., 0.9990 Silver 0.9990 oz. ASW, 40 mm. **Subject:** Bejing Coin and Stamp Fair **Obv:** Hemisphere map **Rev:** Highway design

Date	Mintage	F	VF	XF	Unc	BU
2002 Proof	40,000	Value: 50.00				

KM# 1448 10 YUAN
31.1035 g., 0.9990 Silver 0.9990 oz. ASW, 40 mm. **Subject:** Table tennis, 50th anniversary **Rev:** Trophies, flag

Date	Mintage	F	VF	XF	Unc	BU
2002 Proof	50,000	Value: 50.00				

KM# 1449 10 YUAN
31.1035 g., 0.9990 Silver 0.9990 oz. ASW **Series:** Bejing opera **Rev:** Two multicolor charaters, one seated **Shape:** 40

Date	Mintage	F	VF	XF	Unc	BU
2002 Proof	38,000	Value: 50.00				

KM# 1450 10 YUAN
31.1035 g., 0.9990 Silver 0.9990 oz. ASW, 40 mm. **Series:** Bejing opera **Rev:** Two multicolor characters, white and green

Date	Mintage	F	VF	XF	Unc	BU
2002 Proof	38,000	Value: 50.00				

KM# 1451 10 YUAN
31.1035 g., 0.9990 Silver 0.9990 oz. ASW, 40 mm. **Series:** Bejing opera **Rev:** Bearded character, black

Date	Mintage	F	VF	XF	Unc	BU
2002 Proof	38,000	Value: 50.00				

KM# 1452 10 YUAN
31.1035 g., 0.9990 Silver 0.9990 oz. ASW, 40 mm. **Series:** Bejing opera **Rev:** Multicolor bearded charcter, red

Date	Mintage	F	VF	XF	Unc	BU
2002 Proof	38,000	Value: 50.00				

KM# A1455 10 YUAN
31.1035 g., 0.9990 Silver 0.9990 oz. ASW, 40 mm. **Subject:** World Expo 2010 **Rev:** Tower

Date	Mintage	F	VF	XF	Unc	BU
2002 Proof	50,000	Value: 50.00				

KM# 1507 10 YUAN
31.1035 g., 0.9990 Silver 0.9990 oz. ASW, 40 mm. **Obv:** Stylized forest **Rev:** Cyclists in forest **Edge:** Reeded **Note:** Prev. Y#1132.

Date	Mintage	F	VF	XF	Unc	BU
2003 Proof	30,000	Value: 50.00				

KM# 1508 10 YUAN
31.1035 g., 0.9990 Silver 0.9990 oz. ASW, 40 mm. **Obv:** Stylized forest **Rev:** Birds flying over forest **Edge:** Reeded **Note:** Prev. Y#1133.

Date	Mintage	F	VF	XF	Unc	BU
2003(y) Proof	30,000	Value: 50.00				

KM# 1510 10 YUAN
31.1035 g., 0.9990 Silver 0.9990 oz. ASW, 40 mm. **Obv:** Solar system design **Rev:** Multicolor Chinese Astronaut **Edge:** Reeded **Note:** Prev. Y#1134.

Date	Mintage	F	VF	XF	Unc	BU
2003(y) Proof	60,000	Value: 60.00				

KM# 1487 10 YUAN
31.1035 g., 0.9990 Silver 0.9990 oz. ASW, 40 mm. **Rev:** Two Koi

Date	Mintage	F	VF	XF	Unc	BU
2003 Proof	100,000	Value: 60.00				

KM# 1489 10 YUAN
31.1035 g., 0.9990 Silver 0.9990 oz. ASW, 40 mm. **Subject:** Arbor Day **Rev:** Trees with bike riders

Date	Mintage	F	VF	XF	Unc	BU
2003 Proof	30,000	Value: 60.00				

KM# 1490 10 YUAN
31.1035 g., 0.9990 Silver 0.9990 oz. ASW, 40 mm. **Subject:** Arbor Day **Rev:** Close-up of leaves, birds in flight

Date	Mintage	F	VF	XF	Unc	BU
2003 Proof	30,000	Value: 60.00				

KM# 1491 10 YUAN
31.1035 g., 0.9990 Silver 0.9990 oz. ASW, 40 mm. **Series:** Fairy tails **Rev:** Multicolor blue female

Date	Mintage	F	VF	XF	Unc	BU
2003 Proof	30,000	Value: 60.00				

KM# 1492 10 YUAN
31.1035 g., 0.9990 Silver 0.9990 oz. ASW, 40 mm. **Subject:** Fairy tails **Rev:** Multicolor red bloused girl

Date	Mintage	F	VF	XF	Unc	BU
2003 Proof	30,000	Value: 60.00				

KM# 1496 10 YUAN
31.1035 g., 0.9990 Silver 0.9990 oz. ASW, 40 mm. **Series:** Class literature **Rev:** Multicolor purple cloaked man and monkey

Date	Mintage	F	VF	XF	Unc	BU
2003 Proof	38,000	Value: 60.00				

KM# 1497 10 YUAN
31.1035 g., 0.9990 Silver 0.9990 oz. ASW, 40 mm. **Series:** Classic literature **Rev:** Two multicolor men fighting in clouds

Date	Mintage	F	VF	XF	Unc	BU
2003 Proof	38,000	Value: 60.00				

KM# 1498 10 YUAN
31.1035 g., 0.9990 Silver 0.9990 oz. ASW, 40 mm. **Rev:** Multicolor female standing, black dress **Shape:** Hexagon

Date	Mintage	F	VF	XF	Unc	BU
2003 Proof	38,000	Value: 60.00				

KM# 1499 10 YUAN
31.1035 g., 0.9990 Silver 0.9990 oz. ASW, 40 mm. **Series:** Class Literature **Rev:** Multicolor female kneeling **Shape:** Hexagon

Date	Mintage	F	VF	XF	Unc	BU
2003 Proof	38,000	Value: 60.00				

KM# 1500 10 YUAN
31.1035 g., 0.9990 Silver 0.9990 oz. ASW, 40 mm. **Series:** Class literature **Rev:** Multicolor female walking, rose dress **Shape:** Hexagon

Date	Mintage	F	VF	XF	Unc	BU
2003 Proof	—	Value: 60.00				

KM# 1501 10 YUAN
31.1035 g., 0.9990 Silver 0.9990 oz. ASW, 40 mm. **Series:** Class literature **Rev:** Multicolor female kneeling, red dress **Shape:** Hexagon

Date	Mintage	F	VF	XF	Unc	BU
2003 Proof	—	Value: 60.00				

KM# 1559 10 YUAN
31.1035 g., 0.9990 Silver 0.9990 oz. ASW, 40 mm. **Obv:** Monkey King leading the Master over bridge **Rev:** Multicolor Monkey King fighting the "Ox Fiend" **Edge:** Reeded **Note:** Prev. Y#1214.

Date	Mintage	F	VF	XF	Unc	BU
2004 Proof	38,000	Value: 55.00				

KM# 1558 10 YUAN
31.1035 g., 0.9990 Silver 0.9990 oz. ASW, 40 mm.
Obv: Monkey King leading the Master over bridge **Rev:** Multicolor Pig carrying Monkey King piggy-back style **Edge:** Reeded **Note:** Prev. Y#1215.

Date	Mintage	F	VF	XF	Unc	BU
2004 Proof	38,000	Value: 55.00				

KM# 1566 10 YUAN
31.1035 g., 0.9990 Silver 0.9990 oz. ASW, 40 mm.
Obv: Guangan Exposition Hall **Rev:** Deng Xiaoping and value **Edge:** Reeded **Note:** Prev. Y#1240.

Date	Mintage	F	VF	XF	Unc	BU
2004 Proof	80,000	Value: 60.00				

KM# 1570 10 YUAN
31.1035 g., 0.9990 Silver 0.9990 oz. ASW, 40 mm. **Obv:** National arms above People's Congress Hall and ornamental column **Rev:** Multicolor hologram depicting the hall's overhead lighting **Edge:** Reeded **Note:** Prev. KM#1212.

Date	Mintage	F	VF	XF	Unc	BU
2004 Proof	50,000	Value: 65.00				

KM# 1539 10 YUAN
31.1035 g., 0.9990 Silver 0.9990 oz. ASW, 40 mm.
Subject: 20th Anniversary / Bank of China Industrial and Commercial **Rev:** Panda walking with cub

Date	Mintage	F	VF	XF	Unc	BU
2004 Proof	120,000	Value: 60.00				

KM# 1541 10 YUAN
31.1035 g., 0.9990 Silver 0.9990 oz. ASW, 40 mm. **Subject:** 50th Anniversary China Construction Bank **Rev:** Panda walking with cub

Date	Mintage	F	VF	XF	Unc	BU
2004 Proof	170,000	Value: 60.00				

KM# 1543 10 YUAN
31.1035 g., 0.9990 Silver 0.9990 oz. ASW, 40 mm.
Subject: Bejing International Coin Expo **Rev:** Panda walking with cub, gold plated center

Date	Mintage	F	VF	XF	Unc	BU
2004 Proof	30,000	Value: 60.00				

KM# A1557 10 YUAN
31.1035 g., 0.9990 Silver Colorized 0.9990 oz. ASW, 40 mm.
Subject: 100th Anniversary Red Cross **Obv:** Red Cross within wreath **Rev:** Dove **Note:** Colorized

Date	Mintage	F	VF	XF	Unc	BU
2004 Proof	60,000	Value: 60.00				

KM# 1580 10 YUAN
31.1035 g., 0.9990 Silver 0.9990 oz. ASW, 40 mm.
Subject: 600th Anniversary of Zheng He's voyage **Obv:** Multicolor stylized sailboat on water **Rev:** Ancient Chinese navigational instruments **Edge:** Reeded **Note:** Prev. Y#1239.

Date	Mintage	F	VF	XF	Unc	BU
2005(y) Proof	—	Value: 50.00				

KM# 1592 10 YUAN
31.1050 g., 0.9990 Silver 0.9990 oz. ASW, 40 mm. **Obv:** Temple of Heaven **Rev:** Panda cub and mom seated in bamboo **Note:** Gilt rim

Date	Mintage	F	VF	XF	Unc	BU
2005 Proof	30,000	Value: 50.00				

KM# 1601 10 YUAN
31.1050 g., 0.9990 Silver 0.9990 oz. ASW, 40 mm. **Subject:** Foundation of Industrial & Commercial Bank **Obv:** Temple of Heaven, gilt rim **Rev:** Panda cub and mom seated in bamboo

Date	Mintage	F	VF	XF	Unc	BU
2005 Proof	100,000	Value: 50.00				

KM# 1603 10 YUAN
31.1050 g., 0.9990 Silver 0.9990 oz. ASW, 40 mm. **Subject:** 100th Anniversary of Bank of Shanghai **Obv:** Temple of Heaven **Rev:** Panda cub and mom seated in bamboo

Date	Mintage	F	VF	XF	Unc	BU
2005 Proof	50,000	Value: 50.00				

KM# 1618 10 YUAN
31.1050 g., 0.9990 Silver 0.9990 oz. ASW, 40 mm. **Subject:** 2006 World Cup - Germany **Obv:** Multicolor logo **Rev:** Classical soccer player and goal net **Note:** Prev - Y1255, KM1670

Date	Mintage	F	VF	XF	Unc	BU
2005 Proof	50,000	Value: 60.00				

KM# 1626 10 YUAN
31.1050 g., 0.9990 Silver 0.9990 oz. ASW, 40 mm.
Subject: 600th Anniversary - Zheng He's Voyages
Obv: Multicolor logo **Rev:** Nautical invention

Date	Mintage	F	VF	XF	Unc	BU
2005 Proof	60,000	Value: 55.00				

KM# 1628 10 YUAN
31.1050 g., 0.9990 Silver 0.9990 oz. ASW, 40 mm.
Subject: Chen Yun Birth Centennial **Obv:** House **Rev:** Half-length figure facing

Date	Mintage	F	VF	XF	Unc	BU
2005 Proof	15,000	Value: 70.00				

KM# 1629 10 YUAN
31.1050 g., 0.9990 Silver 0.9990 oz. ASW, 40 mm.
Subject: Chen Yun Birth Centennial **Obv:** House **Rev:** Figure seated in chair, arm outstretched

Date	Mintage	F	VF	XF	Unc	BU
2005 Proof	15,000	Value: 70.00				

KM# 1631 10 YUAN
31.1050 g., 0.9990 Silver 0.9990 oz. ASW, 40 mm.
Subject: 60th Anniversary of Victory - War of Resistance
Obv: Monument **Rev:** People celebrating

Date	Mintage	F	VF	XF	Unc	BU
2005 Proof	30,000	Value: 70.00				

KM# 1636 10 YUAN
31.1050 g., 0.9990 Silver 0.9990 oz. ASW, 40 mm.
Series: Classical Literature **Obv:** Horseman on arch bridge **Rev:** Multicolor monkey and female

Date	Mintage	F	VF	XF	Unc	BU
2005 Proof	38,000	Value: 65.00				

KM# 1637 10 YUAN
31.1050 g., 0.9990 Silver 0.9990 oz. ASW, 40 mm.
Series: Classical Literature **Obv:** Horseman on arch bridge **Rev:** Multicolor man slaying spider on web

Date	Mintage	F	VF	XF	Unc	BU
2005 Proof	38,000	Value: 65.00				

KM# 1639 10 YUAN
31.1050 g., 0.9990 Silver 0.9990 oz. ASW, 40 mm.
Subject: Chinese Movie Centennial **Obv:** Winged column **Rev:** Old time movie camera

Date	Mintage	F	VF	XF	Unc	BU
2005 Proof	60,000	Value: 55.00				

KM# 1686 10 YUAN
31.1035 g., 0.9990 Silver 0.9990 oz. ASW **Obv:** Qing Yuan Gate of the China Great Wall **Rev:** 2 dogs at play **Shape:** Fan-like **Note:** Prev. Y#1219; KM#1651.

Date	Mintage	F	VF	XF	Unc	BU
2006 Proof	66,000	Value: 65.00				

KM# 1687 10 YUAN
31.1035 g., 0.9990 Silver 0.9990 oz. ASW, 40 mm. **Obv:** Belt-hook in dog shape from Chinese ancient bronze ware and a decorative design of dog tail-shaped plant leaves **Rev:** 2 dogs at play **Note:** Prev. Y#1221; KM#1653.

Date	Mintage	F	VF	XF	Unc	BU
2006 Proof	100,000	Value: 50.00				

KM# 1685 10 YUAN
31.1035 g., 0.9990 Silver 0.9990 oz. ASW, 40 mm. **Obv:** Dog-shaped belt-hook depicted from ancient Chinese bronze ware and a decorative design of dog tail-shaped plant leaves **Rev:** 2 smart dogs **Shape:** Scalloped **Note:** Prev. Y#1223; KM#1655.

Date	Mintage	F	VF	XF	Unc	BU
2006 Proof	60,000	Value: 55.00				

KM# 1670 10 YUAN
31.1035 g., 0.9990 Silver 0.9990 oz. ASW **Subject:** World Cup Soccer **Obv:** Colorized logo **Rev:** Classically dressed athlete scoring goal **Note:** Prev. Y#1255.

Date	Mintage	F	VF	XF	Unc	BU
2006 Proof	—	Value: 65.00				

KM# 1666 10 YUAN
31.1050 g., 0.9990 Silver 0.9990 oz. ASW, 40 mm. **Obv:** Temple of Heaven **Rev:** Two panda seated with bamboo

Date	Mintage	F	VF	XF	Unc	BU
2006 Proof	50,000	Value: 50.00				

KM# 1668 10 YUAN
0.9990 Silver, 40 mm. **Subject:** 10th Anniversary of China Minsheng Banking Corp **Obv:** Temple of Heaven **Rev:** Two pandas seated with bamboo

Date	Mintage	F	VF	XF	Unc	BU
2006 Proof	70,000	Value: 55.00				

KM# A1670 10 YUAN
31.1050 g., 0.9990 Silver 0.9990 oz. ASW, 40 mm.
Subject: Shengang Horticultural Expo **Obv:** Temple of Heaven **Rev:** Two pandas seated with bamboo

Date	Mintage	F	VF	XF	Unc	BU
2006 Proof	30,000	Value: 50.00				

KM# 1675 10 YUAN
31.1050 g., 0.9990 Silver 0.9990 oz. ASW, 40 mm.
Subject: 10th Anniversary Jinan City Commercial Bank **Obv:** Temple of Heaven **Rev:** Two pandas seated with bamboo

Date	Mintage	F	VF	XF	Unc	BU
2006 Proof	20,000	Value: 50.00				

KM# 1676 10 YUAN
31.1050 g., 0.9990 Silver 0.9990 oz. ASW, 40 mm. **Subject:** Beijing International Stamp and Coin Expo **Obv:** Temple of Heaven, gold plated outer ring **Rev:** Two pandas seated with bamboo

Date	Mintage	F	VF	XF	Unc	BU
2006 Proof	20,000	Value: 60.00				

KM# 1690 10 YUAN
31.1050 g., 0.9990 Silver 0.9990 oz. ASW, 40 mm.
Subject: Yvelv Academy **Obv:** Front door of Academy
Rev: Exterior view

Date	Mintage	F	VF	XF	Unc	BU
2006 Proof	40,000	Value: 55.00				

KM# 1691 10 YUAN
31.1050 g., 0.9990 Silver 0.9990 oz. ASW, 40 mm.
Subject: Qinghai - Tibet Railway Opening **Obv:** Lhasa Railway Station with mountains in background **Rev:** Yvante Bridge over the Yangtse River and tibetan antelope and yak

Date	Mintage	F	VF	XF	Unc	BU
2006 Proof	36,000	Value: 75.00				

KM# 1693 10 YUAN
31.1050 g., 0.9990 Silver 0.9990 oz. ASW, 40 mm. **Obv:** Map of marches and hammer and cycle **Rev:** Group of marches in snow

Date	Mintage	F	VF	XF	Unc	BU
2006 Proof	25,000	Value: 55.00				

KM# 1729 10 YUAN
31.1050 g., 0.9990 Silver 0.9990 oz. ASW, 40 mm.
Subject: 60th Anniversary - Foundry of Mongolia Autonomous Region **Obv:** Wheel of Mongolian Lele Cart **Rev:** Grassland view of Mongolia, huts and horsemen

Date	Mintage	F	VF	XF	Unc	BU
2007 Proof	20,000	Value: 55.00				

KM# 1703 10 YUAN
31.1050 g., 0.9990 Silver 0.9990 oz. ASW, 40 mm.
Subject: 2007 Summer Olympics **Obv:** Beijing Olympics logo **Rev:** Two children playing leapfrog, multicolor **Note:** Issued in 2006

Date	Mintage	F	VF	XF	Unc	BU
2008 Proof	16,000	Value: 65.00				

KM# 1702 10 YUAN
31.1050 g., 0.9990 Silver 0.9990 oz. ASW **Subject:** 2007 Summer Olympics **Obv:** Beijing Olympic logo **Rev:** Child with kite, multicolor design **Shape:** 40 **Note:** Issued in 2006

Date	Mintage	F	VF	XF	Unc	BU
2008 Proof	160,000	Value: 45.00				

KM# 1704 10 YUAN
31.1050 g., 0.9990 Silver 0.9990 oz. ASW, 40 mm.
Subject: 2007 Summer Olympics **Obv:** Beijing Olympics logo **Rev:** Child rolling ring with stick, multicolor **Note:** Issued in 2006

Date	Mintage	F	VF	XF	Unc	BU
2008 Proof	160,000	Value: 55.00				

KM# 1705 10 YUAN
31.1050 g., 0.9990 Silver 0.9990 oz. ASW, 40 mm.
Subject: 2007 Summer Olympics **Obv:** Beijing Olympic's logo **Rev:** Young girl dancing, multicolor **Note:** Issued in 2006

Date	Mintage	F	VF	XF	Unc	BU
2008 Proof	160,000	Value: 55.00				

KM# 1825 10 YUAN
31.1050 g., 0.9990 Silver 0.9990 oz. ASW, 40 mm.
Subject: Bank of Communications, Centennial

Date	Mintage	F	VF	XF	Unc	BU
2008 Proof	—	Value: 55.00				

KM# 1843 10 YUAN
31.1050 g., 0.9990 Silver 0.9990 oz. ASW, 40 mm.
Subject: Beijing Olympics **Rev:** Multicolor mask, stall tea scene

Date	Mintage	F	VF	XF	Unc	BU
2008 Proof	160,000	Value: 55.00				

KM# 1844 10 YUAN
31.1050 g., 0.9990 Silver 0.9990 oz. ASW, 40 mm.
Subject: Beijing Olympics **Rev:** Multicolor mask, lion dancer

Date	Mintage	F	VF	XF	Unc	BU
2008 Proof	160,000	Value: 55.00				

KM# 1845 10 YUAN
31.1050 g., 0.9990 Silver 0.9990 oz. ASW, 40 mm.
Subject: Beijing Olympics **Rev:** Multicolor mask, Yangtze dancer

Date	Mintage	F	VF	XF	Unc	BU
2008 Proof	160,000	Value: 55.00				

KM# 1846 10 YUAN
31.1050 g., 0.9990 Silver 0.9990 oz. ASW, 40 mm.
Subject: Beijing Olympics **Rev:** Multicolor mask, Beijing Opera

Date	Mintage	F	VF	XF	Unc	BU
2008 Proof	160,000	Value: 45.00				

KM# 1852 10 YUAN
31.1050 g., 0.9990 Silver 0.9990 oz. ASW, 40 mm.
Subject: Hainan Special Economic Zone

Date	Mintage	F	VF	XF	Unc	BU
2008 Proof	20,000	Value: 60.00				

KM# 1854 10 YUAN
31.1050 g., 0.9990 Silver 0.9990 oz. ASW, 40 mm.
Subject: Para Olympics

Date	Mintage	F	VF	XF	Unc	BU
2008 Proof	30,000	Value: 65.00				

KM# 1856 10 YUAN
31.1050 g., 0.9990 Silver 0.9990 oz. ASW, 40 mm.
Subject: Ningxia Hui Autonomous Region

Date	Mintage	F	VF	XF	Unc	BU
2008 Proof	20,000	Value: 70.00				

KM# 1858 10 YUAN
31.1050 g., 0.9990 Silver 0.9990 oz. ASW, 40 mm.
Subject: Beijing Coin and Stamp Expo

Date	Mintage	F	VF	XF	Unc	BU
2008 Proof	30,000	Value: 50.00				

KM# 1859 10 YUAN
31.1050 g., 0.9990 Silver 0.9990 oz. ASW, 40 mm.
Subject: Guangxi Zhuang Autonomous Region

Date	Mintage	F	VF	XF	Unc	BU
2008 Proof	20,000	Value: 60.00				

KM# 1907 10 YUAN
31.1050 g., 0.9990 Silver 0.9990 oz. ASW, 40 mm.
Subject: Shanghai Expo

Date	Mintage	F	VF	XF	Unc	BU
2009 Proof	—	Value: 40.00				

KM# 1891 10 YUAN
31.1050 g., 0.9990 Silver 0.9990 oz. ASW, 40 mm.
Subject: Precious Metal Commemoratives, 30th Anniversary

Date	Mintage	F	VF	XF	Unc	BU
2009	300,000	—	—	—	—	40.00

KM# 1892 10 YUAN
31.1050 g., 0.9990 Silver 0.9990 oz. ASW, 40 mm.
Subject: Beijing International Coin & Stamp Show

Date	Mintage	F	VF	XF	Unc	BU
2009	30,000	—	—	—	—	50.00

KM# 1896 10 YUAN
31.1050 g., 0.9990 Silver 0.9990 oz. ASW, 40 mm.
Subject: P.R.C. 60th Anniversary

Date	Mintage	F	VF	XF	Unc	BU
2009 Proof	100,000	Value: 50.00				

KM# 1898 10 YUAN
31.1050 g., 0.9990 Silver 0.9990 oz. ASW, 40 mm.
Subject: P.R.C. 60th Anniversary **Rev:** Multicolor

Date	Mintage	F	VF	XF	Unc	BU
2009 Proof	100,000	Value: 55.00				

KM# 1902 10 YUAN
31.1050 g., 0.9990 Silver 0.9990 oz. ASW, 40 mm.
Subject: Outlaws of the Marsh, series 1 **Rev:** Multicolor

Date	Mintage	F	VF	XF	Unc	BU
2009 Proof	60,000	Value: 50.00				

KM# 1903 10 YUAN
31.1050 g., 0.9990 Silver 0.9990 oz. ASW, 40 mm.
Subject: Outlaws of the Marsh, series 1 **Rev:** Multicolor

Date	Mintage	F	VF	XF	Unc	BU
2009 Proof	60,000	Value: 50.00				

KM# 1905 10 YUAN
31.1050 g., 0.9990 Silver 0.9990 oz. ASW, 40 mm.
Subject: 16th Asian Games

Date	Mintage	F	VF	XF	Unc	BU
2009 Proof	60,000	Value: 40.00				

KM# 1908 10 YUAN
31.1050 g., 0.9990 Silver 0.9990 oz. ASW, 40 mm.
Subject: Shanghai Expo

Date	Mintage	F	VF	XF	Unc	BU
2009 Proof	—	Value: 40.00				

KM# 1910 10 YUAN
31.1050 g., 0.9990 Silver 0.9990 oz. ASW, 40 mm.
Subject: China Agricultural Bank

Date	Mintage	F	VF	XF	Unc	BU
2009	100,000	—	—	—	—	40.00

KM# 1939 10 YUAN
31.1050 g., 0.9990 Silver 0.9990 oz. ASW, 40 mm.
Series: Outlaws of the Marsh, series 2 **Rev:** Multicolor

Date	Mintage	F	VF	XF	Unc	BU
2010 Proof	70,000	Value: 50.00				

KM# 1940 10 YUAN
31.1050 g., 0.9990 Silver 0.9990 oz. ASW, 40 mm.
Series: Outlaws of the Marsh, series 2 **Rev:** Multicolor

Date	Mintage	F	VF	XF	Unc	BU
2010 Proof	70,000	Value: 50.00				

KM# 1942 10 YUAN
10.3600 g., 0.9990 Gold 0.3327 oz. AGW **Subject:** Shanghai World Expo, 2010

Date	Mintage	F	VF	XF	Unc	BU
2010 Proof	60,000	Value: 450				

KM# 1943 10 YUAN
31.1050 g., 0.9990 Silver 0.9990 oz. ASW, 40 mm.
Subject: Shanghai World Expo, 2010

Date	Mintage	F	VF	XF	Unc	BU
2010 Proof	80,000	Value: 50.00				

KM# 1944 10 YUAN
31.1050 g., 0.9990 Silver 0.9990 oz. ASW, 40 mm.
Subject: Shanghai World Expo, 2010

Date	Mintage	F	VF	XF	Unc	BU
2010 Proof	80,000	Value: 50.00				

KM# 1946 10 YUAN
31.1050 g., 0.9990 Silver 0.9990 oz. ASW, 40 mm.
Subject: Wudang Mountain

Date	Mintage	F	VF	XF	Unc	BU
2010 Proof	60,000	Value: 50.00				

KM# 1953 10 YUAN
31.1050 g., 0.9990 Silver 0.9990 oz. ASW **Subject:** Shenzhen Economic Zone

Date	Mintage	F	VF	XF	Unc	BU
2010 Proof	30,000	Value: 40.00				

KM# 1955 10 YUAN
31.1050 g., 0.9990 Silver 0.9990 oz. ASW, 40 mm.
Subject: 16th Asian Games

Date	Mintage	F	VF	XF	Unc	BU
2010 Proof	60,000	Value: 40.00				

KM# 1957 10 YUAN
31.1050 g., 0.9990 Silver 0.9990 oz. ASW, 40 mm.
Subject: Bejing Opera, series 1 **Rev:** Multicolor face mask

Date	Mintage	F	VF	XF	Unc	BU
2010 Proof	50,000	Value: 40.00				

KM# 1958 10 YUAN
31.1050 g., 0.9990 Silver 0.9990 oz. ASW, 40 mm.
Subject: Bejing Opera, series 1 **Rev:** Multicolor face mask

Date	Mintage	F	VF	XF	Unc	BU
2010 Proof	50,000	Value: 40.00				

KM# 1959 10 YUAN
31.1050 g., 0.9990 Silver 0.9990 oz. ASW, 40 mm.
Subject: Bejing Stamp & Coin Expo

Date	Mintage	F	VF	XF	Unc	BU
2010 Proof	30,000	Value: 40.00				

KM# 1388 20 YUAN
62.2070 g., 0.9990 Silver 1.9979 oz. ASW, 40 mm.
Subject: Mogao Grottos **Obv:** 8-story building **Rev:** Buddha-like statue **Edge:** Reeded **Note:** Prev. Y#1082.

Date	Mintage	F	VF	XF	Unc	BU
2001 Proof	30,000	Value: 100				

KM# 1432 20 YUAN
62.2070 g., 0.9990 Silver 1.9979 oz. ASW, 40 mm.
Rev: Buddha-like statue

Date	Mintage	F	VF	XF	Unc	BU
2002 Proof	30,000	Value: 100				

KM# 1563 20 YUAN
31.1035 g., 0.9990 Silver 0.9990 oz. ASW, 40 mm.
Series: Maijishan grotto art **Rev:** Two figures standing

Date	Mintage	F	VF	XF	Unc	BU
2004 Proof	20,000	Value: 60.00				

KM# 1390 50 YUAN
155.5175 g., 0.9990 Silver 4.9948 oz. ASW, 70 mm.
Subject: Mogao Grottoes **Obv:** Eight story building **Rev:** Four musicians **Edge:** Reeded. **Note:** Prev. Y#1083.

Date	Mintage	F	VF	XF	Unc	BU
2001 Proof	8,000	Value: 200				

KM# 1389 50 YUAN
3.1104 g., 0.9990 Gold 0.0999 oz. AGW **Subject:** Mogao Grottoes **Obv:** Eight story building **Rev:** Buddha-like statue **Edge:** Reeded. **Note:** Prev. Y#1084.

Date	Mintage	F	VF	XF	Unc	BU
2001 Proof	50,000	Value: 160				

KM# 1394 50 YUAN
155.5175 g., 0.9990 Silver 4.9948 oz. ASW, 90 x 40 mm.
Subject: Han Xizai's Dinner Party **Obv:** Tang dynasty buildings **Rev:** Multicolor "Five Dynasties" painting **Edge:** Plain **Shape:** Rectangular **Note:** Prev. Y#1104.

Date	Mintage	F	VF	XF	Unc	BU
2001 Proof	18,800	Value: 175				

KM# 1386 50 YUAN
155.5175 g., 0.9990 Silver 4.9948 oz. ASW, 90 x 40 mm.
Series: Folk fairy tails **Rev:** Seven multicolor figures on beach **Shape:** Rectangle

Date	Mintage	F	VF	XF	Unc	BU
2001 Proof	10,000	Value: 200				

KM# 1402 50 YUAN
155.5190 g., 0.9990 Silver 4.9948 oz. ASW, 90 x 50 mm.
Subject: Bejing opera **Rev:** Four multicolor actors **Shape:** Rectangle

Date	Mintage	F	VF	XF	Unc	BU
2001 Proof	11,800	Value: 200				

KM# 1433 50 YUAN
155.5190 g., 0.9990 Silver 4.9948 oz. ASW, 70 mm.
Series: Long men grottoes **Rev:** Two figures

Date	Mintage	F	VF	XF	Unc	BU
2002 Proof	8,000	Value: 200				

KM# 1445 50 YUAN
155.5190 g., 0.9990 Silver 4.9948 oz. ASW, 65 x 26 mm.
Series: Classic literature **Rev:** Multicolor crowd of women **Shape:** Fan-like

Date	Mintage	F	VF	XF	Unc	BU
2002 Proof	11,800	Value: 200				

KM# 1430 50 YUAN
155.7900 g., 0.9990 Silver 5.0035 oz. ASW, 90 x 40 mm.
Series: Folk fairy tails **Rev:** Multicolor female with red ribbon **Shape:** Rectangle

Date	Mintage	F	VF	XF	Unc	BU
2002 Proof	—	Value: 300				

KM# 1437 50 YUAN
3.1100 g., 0.9990 Gold 0.0999 oz. AGW, 18 mm. **Subject:** Kuan yin **Rev. Designer:** Female holding child, hologram

Date	Mintage	F	VF	XF	Unc	BU
2002 Proof	33,000	Value: 160				

KM# 1453 50 YUAN
155.5190 g., 0.9990 Silver 4.9948 oz. ASW, 90 x 40 mm.
Series: Bejing opera **Rev:** Three multicolor characters one with spikes in costume **Shape:** Rectangle

Date	Mintage	F	VF	XF	Unc	BU
2002 Proof	11,800	Value: 200				

KM# 1493 50 YUAN
155.3500 g., 0.9990 Silver 4.9894 oz. ASW, 90 x 40 mm.
Series: Fairy tails **Rev:** Multicolor man with two boys in buckets, jenole in flight at left **Shape:** Rectangle

Date	Mintage	F	VF	XF	Unc	BU
2003 Proof	10,000	Value: 250				

KM# 1512 50 YUAN
3.1104 g., 0.9990 Gold 0.0999 oz. AGW, 18 mm. **Obv:** Putuo Mountain Pilgrimage Gate **Rev:** Seated Kuanyin with holographic background **Edge:** Reeded **Note:** Prev. Y#1234.

Date	Mintage	F	VF	XF	Unc	BU
2003 Proof	33,000	Value: 160				

KM# 1502 50 YUAN
155.5000 g., 0.9990 Silver 4.9942 oz. ASW, 80 x 50 mm.
Series: Class literature **Rev:** Multicolor man lying on couch **Shape:** Rectangle

Date	Mintage	F	VF	XF	Unc	BU
2003 Proof	10,000	Value: 250				

KM# 1503 50 YUAN
155.1500 g., 0.9990 Silver 4.9830 oz. ASW, 65 x 125 mm. **Series:** Class literature **Rev:** Six people **Shape:** Arc **Note:** Colorized

Date	Mintage	F	VF	XF	Unc	BU
2003 Proof	11,800	Value: 250				

KM# 1572 50 YUAN
3.1100 g., 0.9990 Gold 0.0999 oz. AGW, 18 mm. **Obv:** Putuo Mountain Pilgrimage Gate **Rev:** Kuanyin and value **Edge:** Reeded **Note:** Prev. Y#1237.

Date	Mintage	F	VF	XF	Unc	BU
2004 Proof	33,000	Value: 160				

KM# 1560 50 YUAN
155.5175 g., 0.9990 Silver 4.9948 oz. ASW, 80x50 mm.
Obv: Monkey King leading the Master over bridge **Rev:** Multicolor Monkey King fighting the Pig Demon of Bones **Edge:** Plain **Shape:** Rectangle **Note:** Prev. Y#1216.

Date	Mintage	F	VF	XF	Unc	BU
2004 Proof	10,000	Value: 300				

KM# 1635 50 YUAN
155.0000 g., 0.9990 Silver 4.9782 oz. ASW, 80 x 50 mm.
Series: Classical Literature **Obv:** Horseman on arch bridge **Rev:** Multicolor femal and lion **Shape:** Rectangle

Date	Mintage	F	VF	XF	Unc	BU
2005 Proof	10,000	Value: 250				

KM# 1681 50 YUAN
3.1103 g., 0.9990 Gold 0.0999 oz. AGW, 18 mm. **Obv:** Dog-shaped belt-hook , an ancient Chinese bronze ware, decorative disign of dog tail-shaped plant leaves **Rev:** 2 dogs at play **Note:** Prev. Y#1222; KM#1654.

Date	Mintage	F	VF	XF	Unc	BU
2006 Proof	30,000	Value: 145				

KM# 1683 50 YUAN
0.9990 Silver, 60 x 50 mm. **Subject:** Year of the dog **Obv:** Classical dog **Rev:** Two dogs **Shape:** Rectangle

Date	Mintage	F	VF	XF	Unc	BU
2006 Proof	1,888	Value: 250				

KM# 1901 50 YUAN
155.5000 g., 0.9990 Silver 4.9942 oz. ASW, 80x50 mm.
Subject: Outlaws of the Marsh, series 1 **Rev:** Multicolor **Shape:** Rectangle

Date	Mintage	F	VF	XF	Unc	BU
2009 Proof	10,000	Value: 150				

KM# 1938 50 YUAN
155.5000 g., 0.9990 Silver 4.9942 oz. ASW **Subject:** Outlasws of the Marsh, series 2 **Rev:** Multicolor **Shape:** Regtangle

Date	Mintage	F	VF	XF	Unc	BU
2010 Proof	12,000	Value: 125				

KM# 1951 50 YUAN
62.1000 g., 0.9990 Silver 1.9945 oz. ASW **Subject:** Yungang Grotto Art

Date	Mintage	F	VF	XF	Unc	BU
2010 Proof	20,000	Value: 80.00				

KM# 1514 100 YUAN
3.1013 g., 0.9990 Platinum 0.0996 oz. APW, 18 mm.
Series: Guan Yi

Date	Mintage	F	VF	XF	Unc	BU
2003 Proof	33,000	Value: 200				

KM# 1534 100 YUAN
15.5500 g., 0.9990 Palladium 0.4994 oz., 27 mm. **Obv:** Temple of Heaven **Rev:** Panda mother and cub, "kissing pandas" **Edge:** Reeded **Note:** Prev. Y#1211.

Date	Mintage	F	VF	XF	Unc	BU
2004 Proof	8,000	Value: 450				

KM# 1573 100 YUAN
3.1100 g., 0.9995 Platinum 0.0999 oz. APW, 18 mm.
Obv: Putuo Mountain Pilgrimage Gate **Rev:** Kuanyin and value **Edge:** Reeded **Note:** Prev. Y#1238.

Date	Mintage	F	VF	XF	Unc	BU
2004 Proof	33,000	Value: 200				

KM# 1540 100 YUAN
7.8500 g., 0.9990 Gold 0.2521 oz. AGW, 22 mm. **Subject:** 20th Anniversary / Bank of China Industrial and Commercial
Rev: Panda walking with cub

Date	Mintage	F	VF	XF	Unc	BU
2004 Proof	50,000	Value: 315				

KM# 1542 100 YUAN
7.8400 g., 0.9990 Gold 0.2518 oz. AGW, 22 mm. **Subject:** 50th Anniversary China Construction Bank **Rev:** Panda walking with cub

Date	Mintage	F	VF	XF	Unc	BU
2004 Proof	60,000	Value: 315				

KM# 1600 100 YUAN
7.7700 g., 0.9990 Gold 0.2496 oz. AGW, 22 mm. **Subject:** Foundation of Industrial & Commercial Bank **Obv:** Temple of Heaven **Rev:** Panda cub and mom seated in bamboo

Date	Mintage	F	VF	XF	Unc	BU
2005 Proof	40,000	Value: 315				

KM# 1602 100 YUAN
7.7700 g., 0.9990 Gold 0.2496 oz. AGW, 22 mm. **Subject:** 100th Anniversary of Bank of Shanghai **Obv:** Temple of Heaven
Rev: Panda cub and mom seated in bamboo

Date	Mintage	F	VF	XF	Unc	BU
2005 Proof	40,000	Value: 315				

KM# 1616 100 YUAN
7.7000 g., 0.9990 Gold 0.2473 oz. AGW, 22 mm. **Subject:** 2006 World Cup - Germany **Obv:** Multicolor logo **Rev:** Temple of Heaven and soccer ball

Date	Mintage	F	VF	XF	Unc	BU
2005 Proof	10,000	Value: 350				

KM# A979 100 YUAN
8.5000 g., 0.9990 Gold 0.2730 oz. AGW, 22 mm. **Subject:** 10th Anniversary Bank of Beijing **Obv:** Temple of Heaven **Rev:** Two pandas

Date	Mintage	F	VF	XF	Unc	BU
2006	100	—	—	—	—	400

KM# A980 100 YUAN
8.5000 g., 0.9990 Gold 0.2730 oz. AGW, 22 mm. **Subject:** 10th Anniversary China Minsheng Banking Corp. **Obv:** Temple of Heaven **Rev:** Two Panda munching on bamboo

Date	Mintage	F	VF	XF	Unc	BU
2006	100	—	—	—	—	400

KM# 1665 100 YUAN
7.7700 g., 0.9990 Gold 0.2496 oz. AGW, 22 mm. **Subject:** 10th Anniversary Bank of Beijing **Obv:** Temple of Heaven **Rev:** Two pandas seated with bamboo

Date	Mintage	F	VF	XF	Unc	BU
2006 Proof	150,000	Value: 315				

KM# 1667 100 YUAN
7.7700 g., 0.9990 Silver 0.2496 oz. ASW, 22 mm. **Subject:** 10th Anniversary - China Minsheng Banking Corp **Obv:** Temple of Heaven **Rev:** Two pandas seated with bamboo

Date	Mintage	F	VF	XF	Unc	BU
2006 Proof	20,000	Value: 315				

KM# 1669 100 YUAN
7.7700 g., 0.9990 Gold 0.2496 oz. AGW, 22 mm.
Subject: Shenyang Horticultural Expo **Obv:** Temple of Heaven
Rev: Two pandas seated with bamboo

Date	Mintage	F	VF	XF	Unc	BU
2006 Proof	10,000	Value: 350				

KM# A1690 100 YUAN
7.7700 g., 0.9990 Gold 0.2496 oz. AGW, 22 mm.
Subject: Qinghai - Tibet Railway Opening **Obv:** Map of railway route and track layer **Rev:** Kun Lun Tunnel Portal

Date	Mintage	F	VF	XF	Unc	BU
2006 Proof	16,000	Value: 350				

KM# 1730 100 YUAN
7.7700 g., 0.9990 Gold 0.2496 oz. AGW, 22 mm. **Subject:** 60th Anniversary - Foundry of Mongolia Autonomous Region
Obv: Wheel of Mongolian Lele Cart **Rev:** Female Mongolian in posture of welcome

Date	Mintage	F	VF	XF	Unc	BU
2007 Proof	10,000	Value: 350				

KM# 1824 100 YUAN
7.7700 g., 0.9990 Gold 0.2496 oz. AGW, 23 mm. **Subject:** Bank of Communications, Centennial **Rev:** Panda

Date	Mintage	F	VF	XF	Unc	BU
2008 Proof	10,000	Value: 315				

KM# 1853 100 YUAN
7.7700 g., 0.9990 Gold 0.2496 oz. AGW **Subject:** Hainan Special Economic Zone

Date	Mintage	F	VF	XF	Unc	BU
2008 Proof	10,000	Value: 325				

KM# 1857 100 YUAN
7.7700 g., 0.9990 Gold 0.2496 oz. AGW **Subject:** Ningxia Hui Autonomous Region

Date	Mintage	F	VF	XF	Unc	BU
2008 Proof	10,000	Value: 325				

KM# 1860 100 YUAN
7.7700 g., 0.9990 Gold 0.2496 oz. AGW **Subject:** Guangzi Zhuang Autonomous Region

Date	Mintage	F	VF	XF	Unc	BU
2008 Proof	10,000	Value: 325				

KM# 1890 100 YUAN
7.7700 g., 0.9990 Gold 0.2496 oz. AGW **Subject:** Precious Metal Commemoratives, 30th Anniversary

Date	Mintage	F	VF	XF	Unc	BU
2009	10,000	—	—	—	—	300

KM# 1895 100 YUAN
7.7700 g., 0.9990 Gold 0.2496 oz. AGW, 22 mm.
Subject: P.R.C. 60th Anniversary

Date	Mintage	F	VF	XF	Unc	BU
2009 Proof	100,000	Value: 350				

KM# 1904 100 YUAN
7.7700 g., 0.9990 Gold 0.2496 oz. AGW, 22 mm. **Subject:** 16th Asian Games

Date	Mintage	F	VF	XF	Unc	BU
2009 Proof	30,000	Value: 350				

KM# 1909 100 YUAN
7.7700 g., 0.9990 Gold 0.2496 oz. AGW, 22 mm.
Subject: China Agricultural Bank

Date	Mintage	F	VF	XF	Unc	BU
2009	100,000	—	—	—	—	350

KM# 1945 100 YUAN
7.7700 g., 0.9990 Gold 0.2496 oz. AGW **Subject:** Wudang Mountain

Date	Mintage	F	VF	XF	Unc	BU
2010 Proof	30,000	Value: 350				

KM# 1952 100 YUAN
7.7700 g., 0.9990 Gold 0.2496 oz. AGW **Subject:** Shenzhen Economic Zone

Date	Mintage	F	VF	XF	Unc	BU
2010 Proof	20,000	Value: 350				

KM# 1954 100 YUAN
7.7700 g., 0.9990 Gold 0.2496 oz. AGW **Subject:** 16th Asian Games

Date	Mintage	F	VF	XF	Unc	BU
2010 Proof	30,000	Value: 350				

KM# 1956 100 YUAN
7.7700 g., 0.9990 Gold 0.2496 oz. AGW **Subject:** Bejing Opera, series 1 **Rev:** Multicolor

Date	Mintage	F	VF	XF	Unc	BU
2010 Proof	30,000	Value: 350				

KM# 1488 150 YUAN
10.0500 g., 0.9990 Gold 0.3228 oz. AGW, 23 mm. **Subject:** Spring festival **Obv:** Tree with berries **Rev:** Two Koi in ribbon sea

Date	Mintage	F	VF	XF	Unc	BU
2003 Proof	50,000	Value: 385				

KM# 1511 150 YUAN
10.1300 g., 0.9990 Gold 0.3253 oz. AGW, 23 mm.
Subject: Space flight **Rev:** Multicolor astronaut and ship

Date	Mintage	F	VF	XF	Unc	BU
2003 Proof	30,000	Value: 400				

KM# 1556 150 YUAN
10.5000 g., 0.9990 Gold 0.3372 oz. AGW, 23 mm. **Series:** Folk customs **Subject:** Lantern Festival **Rev:** Boy holding lantern **Note:** Colorized

Date	Mintage	F	VF	XF	Unc	BU
2004 Proof	20,000	Value: 400				

KM# 1638 150 YUAN
10.0500 g., 0.9990 Gold 0.3228 oz. AGW, 23 mm.
Subject: Chinese Movie Centennial **Obv:** Winged column
Rev: Movie clipboard

Date	Mintage	F	VF	XF	Unc	BU
2005 Proof	20,000	Value: 400				

KM# 1848 150 YUAN
10.1000 g., 0.9990 Gold 0.3244 oz. AGW, 23 mm.
Subject: Beijing Olympics **Obv:** Beijing Olympics **Rev:** Classical soccer player

Date	Mintage	F	VF	XF	Unc	BU
2008 Proof	60,000	Value: 385				

KM# 1847 150 YUAN
10.1000 g., 0.9990 Gold 0.3244 oz. AGW, 23 mm.
Subject: Beijing Olympics **Rev:** Classical wrestlers

Date	Mintage	F	VF	XF	Unc	BU
2008 Proof	60,000	Value: 385				

KM# 1700 150 YUAN
10.0500 g., 0.9990 Gold 0.3228 oz. AGW, 23 mm.
Subject: 29th Summer Olympics **Obv:** Beijing Olympic logo
Rev: Ancient horsemaid and new logo **Note:** Issued in 2006

Date	Mintage	F	VF	XF	Unc	BU
2008 Proof	60,000	Value: 385				

KM# 1701 150 YUAN
10.0500 g., 0.9990 Gold 0.3228 oz. AGW, 23 mm.
Subject: 29th Summer Olympics **Obv:** Beijing Olympic logo
Rev: Ancient archer and new logo **Note:** Issued in 2006

Date	Mintage	F	VF	XF	Unc	BU
2008 Proof	60,000	Value: 385				

KM# 1855 150 YUAN
10.1000 g., 0.9990 Gold 0.3244 oz. AGW **Subject:** Para Olympics

Date	Mintage	F	VF	XF	Unc	BU
2008 Proof	15,000	Value: 450				

KM# 1900 150 YUAN
10.3600 g., 0.9990 Gold 0.3327 oz. AGW, 23 mm.
Subject: Outlaws of the Marsh, series 1 **Rev:** Multicolor

Date	Mintage	F	VF	XF	Unc	BU
2009 Proof	30,000	Value: 450				

KM# 1906 150 YUAN
10.3500 g., 0.9990 Gold 0.3324 oz. AGW **Subject:** Shanghai Expo

Date	Mintage	F	VF	XF	Unc	BU
2009 Proof	—	Value: 450				

KM# 1937 150 YUAN
10.3500 g., 0.9990 Gold 0.3324 oz. AGW **Subject:** Outlaws of the Marsh, series 2 **Rev:** Multicolor

Date	Mintage	F	VF	XF	Unc	BU
2010 Proof	35,000	Value: 450				

KM# 1941 150 YUAN
155.5500 g., 0.9990 Gold 4.9958 oz. AGW **Subject:** Shanghai World Expo, 2010

Date	Mintage	F	VF	XF	Unc	BU
2010 Proof	1,000	Value: 6,500				

KM# 1403 200 YUAN
15.5520 g., 0.9990 Gold 0.4995 oz. AGW, 27 mm.
Subject: Bejing opera **Rev:** Multicolor ribbon dancer

Date	Mintage	F	VF	XF	Unc	BU
2001 Proof	8,000	Value: 800				

KM# 1391 200 YUAN
15.5518 g., 0.9990 Gold 0.4995 oz. AGW, 27 mm.
Subject: Mogao Grottoes **Obv:** Eight story building **Rev:** Dancing drummer **Edge:** Reeded. **Note:** Prev. Y#1085.

Date	Mintage	F	VF	XF	Unc	BU
2001 Proof	8,800	Value: 750				

KM# 1393 200 YUAN
15.5518 g., 0.9990 Gold 0.4995 oz. AGW, 27 mm.
Subject: 50th Anniversary Chinese Occupation of Tibet
Obv: Five stars **Rev:** Denomination in flower **Edge:** Reeded
Note: Prev. Y#1087.

Date	Mintage	F	VF	XF	Unc	BU
2001 Proof	15,000	Value: 675				

KM# 1387 200 YUAN
15.5519 g., 0.9990 Gold 0.4995 oz. AGW, 27 mm. **Series:** Folk fairy tails **Rev:** Multicolor heroic figure putting ax to clouds

Date	Mintage	F	VF	XF	Unc	BU
2001 Proof	8,800	Value: 750				

KM# 1434 200 YUAN
15.5500 g., 0.9990 Gold 0.4994 oz. AGW, 27 mm.
Subject: Budda **Note:** Prev. Y#1145.

Date	Mintage	F	VF	XF	Unc	BU
2002 Proof	8,800	Value: 750				

KM# 1454 200 YUAN
15.5000 g., 0.9990 Gold 0.4978 oz. AGW **Subject:** Peking Opera **Note:** Prev. Y#1146.

Date	Mintage	F	VF	XF	Unc	BU
2002 Proof	8,000	Value: 750				

KM# 1446 200 YUAN
15.5000 g., 0.9990 Gold 0.4978 oz. AGW **Subject:** Dream of the Red Mansion **Shape:** Octagon **Note:** Prev. Y#1147.

Date	Mintage	F	VF	XF	Unc	BU
2002 Proof	8,000	Value: 800				

KM# 1431 200 YUAN
15.5000 g., 0.9990 Gold 0.4978 oz. AGW **Subject:** Cave man art **Rev:** Multicolor. **Note:** Prev. Y#1148.

Date	Mintage	F	VF	XF	Unc	BU
2002 Proof	8,800	Value: 750				

KM# 1440 200 YUAN
15.5000 g., 0.9990 Gold 0.4978 oz. AGW **Subject:** Ceremonial Mask **Note:** Prev. Y#1149.

Date	Mintage	F	VF	XF	Unc	BU
2002 Proof	5,000	Value: 800				

KM# 1439 200 YUAN
15.5190 g., 0.9990 Gold 0.4984 oz. AGW, 27 mm.
Subject: Sichuan Sanxingdui relics **Obv:** Museum building
Rev: Face mask

Date	Mintage	F	VF	XF	Unc	BU
2002 Proof	8,800	Value: 750				

KM# 1504 200 YUAN
15.5519 g., 0.9999 Gold 0.4999 oz. AGW **Subject:** Pilgrimage to the West **Note:** Prev. Y#1159.

Date	Mintage	F	VF	XF	Unc	BU
2003 Proof	11,800	Value: 675				

KM# 1494 200 YUAN
15.5519 g., 0.9999 Gold 0.4999 oz. AGW **Subject:** Chinese Mythical Folk Tales **Note:** Prev. Y#1160.

Date	Mintage	F	VF	XF	Unc	BU
2003 Proof	8,800	Value: 750				

KM# 1495   200 YUAN
15.5150 g., 0.9990 Gold 0.4983 oz. AGW, 27 mm.
Subject: Finger Sarira of Sakyanmunt **Obv:** Tall tower **Rev:** Flora design

Date	Mintage	F	VF	XF	Unc	BU
2003 Proof	12,000	Value: 675				

KM# 1506   200 YUAN
15.5130 g., 0.9990 Gold 0.4982 oz. AGW, 40 mm.
Series: Classical literature **Rev:** Multicolor blue seated female
Shape: Hexagon

Date	Mintage	F	VF	XF	Unc	BU
2003 Proof	8,000	Value: 750				

KM# 1509   200 YUAN
15.5150 g., 0.9990 Gold 0.4983 oz. AGW, 27 mm.
Series: Wulingyan Scenic Resort

Date	Mintage	F	VF	XF	Unc	BU
2003 Proof	8,000	Value: 675				

KM# 1571   200 YUAN
15.5500 g., 0.9990 Gold 0.4994 oz. AGW, 27 mm.
Obv: National arms above People's Congress Hall and ornamental column **Rev:** Multicolor hologram depicting the hall's overhead lighting **Edge:** Reeded **Note:** Prev. Y#1213.

Date	Mintage	F	VF	XF	Unc	BU
2004 Proof	5,000	Value: 750				

KM# 1561   200 YUAN
15.5500 g., 0.9990 Gold 0.4994 oz. AGW, 27 mm. **Obv:** Monkey King leading the Master over bridge **Rev:** Multicolor Monkey King on one knee meeting the Master **Edge:** Reeded **Note:** Prev. Y#1217.

Date	Mintage	F	VF	XF	Unc	BU
2004 Proof	11,800	Value: 675				

KM# 1567   200 YUAN
15.5518 g., 0.9990 Gold 0.4995 oz. AGW, 27 mm.
Obv: Guangan Exposition Hall **Rev:** Deng Xiaoping and value **Edge:** Reeded **Note:** Prev. Y#1241.

Date	Mintage	F	VF	XF	Unc	BU
2004 Proof	10,000	Value: 675				

KM# 1564   200 YUAN
15.5600 g., 0.9990 Gold 0.4997 oz. AGW, 27 mm.
Series: Maijishan grotto art **Rev:** Buddha statue

Date	Mintage	F	VF	XF	Unc	BU
2004 Proof	8,800	Value: 750				

KM# 1625   200 YUAN
15.5500 g., 0.9990 Gold 0.4994 oz. AGW, 27 mm.
Subject: 600th Anniversary of Zheng He's Voyages
Obv: Multicolor logo **Rev:** Zheng He in linear form

Date	Mintage	F	VF	XF	Unc	BU
2005 Proof	6,000	Value: 675				

KM# 1627   200 YUAN
15.5500 g., 0.9990 Gold 0.4994 oz. AGW, 27 mm. **Subject:** Chen Yun Birth Centennial **Obv:** House **Rev:** Head 3/4 right

Date	Mintage	F	VF	XF	Unc	BU
2005 Proof	5,000	Value: 675				

KM# 1630   200 YUAN
15.5500 g., 0.9990 Gold 0.4994 oz. AGW, 27 mm.
Subject: 60th Anniverasary of Victory - War of Resistance
Obv: Monument **Rev:** Mob of Peoples Army

Date	Mintage	F	VF	XF	Unc	BU
2005 Proof	5,000	Value: 675				

KM# 1633   200 YUAN
15.5500 g., 0.9990 Gold 0.4994 oz. AGW, 27 mm.
Series: Classical Literature **Obv:** Horseman on arch bridge
Rev: Two multicolor women, one with monkey, other with rabbit

Date	Mintage	F	VF	XF	Unc	BU
2005 Proof	11,800	Value: 675				

KM# 1689   200 YUAN
15.5500 g., 0.9990 Gold 0.4994 oz. AGW, 27 mm.
Subject: Yvelv Academy **Obv:** Front door of Academy
Rev: Interior room

Date	Mintage	F	VF	XF	Unc	BU
2006 Proof	7,000	Value: 675				

KM# 1692   200 YUAN
15.5500 g., 0.9990 Gold 0.4994 oz. AGW, 27 mm.
Subject: 70th Anniversary of Long March **Obv:** Route of the marches, hammer and cycle symbol **Rev:** Group of marchers advancing with rifles

Date	Mintage	F	VF	XF	Unc	BU
2006 Proof	10,000	Value: 675				

KM# 1949   200 YUAN
15.5500 g., 0.9990 Gold 0.4994 oz. AGW **Subject:** Yungang Grotto Art

Date	Mintage	F	VF	XF	Unc	BU
2010 Proof	10,000	Value: 700				

KM# 1435   300 YUAN
1000.0000 g., 0.9990 Silver 32.117 oz. ASW, 100 mm.
Series: Long men grottoes **Rev:** Large female statue

Date	Mintage	F	VF	XF	Unc	BU
2002 Proof	8,000	Value: 1,000				

KM# 1513   300 YUAN
1000.0000 g., 0.9990 Silver 32.117 oz. ASW, 100 mm.
Series: Guan Yi

Date	Mintage	F	VF	XF	Unc	BU
2003 Proof	3,800	Value: 3,500				

KM# 1568   300 YUAN
1000.0000 g., 0.9990 Silver 32.117 oz. ASW, 100 mm.
Obv: Guangan Exposition Hall **Rev:** Deng Xiaoping and value
Edge: Reeded **Note:** Prev. Y#1242.

Date	Mintage	F	VF	XF	Unc	BU
2004 Proof	5,000	Value: 750				

KM# A1574   300 YUAN
1000.0000 g., 0.9990 Silver 32.117 oz. ASW, 100 mm.
Series: Kuan Yin **Rev:** Female seated holidng flower

Date	Mintage	F	VF	XF	Unc	BU
2004 Proof	3,800	Value: 750				

KM# 1617   300 YUAN
1000.0000 g., 0.9990 Silver 32.117 oz. ASW, 100 mm.
Subject: 2006 World Cup - Germany **Obv:** Multicolor logo
Rev: World Cup Trophy

Date	Mintage	F	VF	XF	Unc	BU
2005 Proof	3,000	Value: 1,500				

KM# 1634   300 YUAN
1000.0000 g., 0.9990 Silver 32.117 oz. ASW, 100 mm.
Series: Classical Literature **Obv:** Horseman on arch bridge
Rev: Multicolor heavenly buddha

Date	Mintage	F	VF	XF	Unc	BU
2005 Proof	5,000	Value: 1,500				

KM# 1682   300 YUAN
1000.0000 g., 0.9990 Silver 32.117 oz. ASW, 100 mm.
Obv: Dog-shaped belt-hook from ancient Chinese bronze ware, decorative design of dog tail-shaped plant leaves **Rev:** 2 dogs
Note: Prev. Y#1227; KM#1659.

Date	Mintage	F	VF	XF	Unc	BU
2006 Proof	3,800	Value: 750				

KM# 1849   300 YUAN
1000.0000 g., 0.9990 Silver 32.117 oz. ASW, 100 mm.
Subject: Beijing Olympics **Obv:** Multicolor logo **Rev:** Classical tug of war

Date	Mintage	F	VF	XF	Unc	BU
2008 Proof	20,008	Value: 1,500				

KM# 1897   300 YUAN
1000.0000 g., 0.9990 Silver 32.117 oz. ASW, 100 mm.
Subject: P.R.C. 60th Anniversary

Date	Mintage	F	VF	XF	Unc	BU
2009 Proof	6,000	Value: 700				

KM# 1950   300 YUAN
1000.0000 g., 0.9990 Silver 32.117 oz. ASW **Subject:** Yungang Grotto Art

Date	Mintage	F	VF	XF	Unc	BU
2010 Proof	3,800	Value: 700				

KM# 1392   2000 YUAN
155.5175 g., 0.9990 Gold 4.9948 oz. AGW, 60 mm.
Subject: Mogao Grottoes **Obv:** Eight story building **Rev:** Two dancers **Edge:** Reeded **Note:** Prev. #Y1086.

Date	Mintage	F	VF	XF	Unc	BU
2001 Proof	288	Value: 10,000				

KM# 1436   2000 YUAN
155.5175 g., 0.9990 Gold 4.9948 oz. AGW, 60 mm.
Subject: Chinese grottos art - Longmen **Note:** Prev. #Y1151.

Date	Mintage	F	VF	XF	Unc	BU
2002	288	Value: 10,000				

KM# 1505   2000 YUAN
155.5000 g., 0.9990 Gold 4.9942 oz. AGW, 64 x 40 mm.
Series: Class literature **Rev:** Two multicolor monkey kings
Shape: Rectangle

Date	Mintage	F	VF	XF	Unc	BU
2003 Proof	500	Value: 8,000				

KM# 1565   2000 YUAN
155.5175 g., 0.9990 Gold 4.9948 oz. AGW, 60 mm.
Subject: Maijishan Grottos **Obv:** Grotto view **Rev:** Buddha portrait within halo of flying devatas **Edge:** Reeded **Note:** Prev. #Y1206.

Date	Mintage	F	VF	XF	Unc	BU
2004(y) Proof	288	Value: 9,000				

KM# 1562   2000 YUAN
155.5175 g., 0.9990 Gold 4.9948 oz. AGW, 64x40 mm.
Obv: Monkey King leading Master over bridge **Rev:** Multicolor Monkey King fighting the Pig "Demon of Bones" **Edge:** Plain **Shape:** Ingot **Note:** Prev. #Y1218. Illustration reduced.

Date	Mintage	F	VF	XF	Unc	BU
2004 Proof	500	Value: 8,000				

KM# 1569   2000 YUAN
155.5175 g., 0.9990 Gold 4.9948 oz. AGW, 60 mm.
Obv: Guangan Exposition Hall **Rev:** Deng Xiaoping and value
Edge: Reeded **Note:** Prev. #Y1243.

Date	Mintage	F	VF	XF	Unc	BU
2004 Proof	600	Value: 8,000				

KM# 1632   2000 YUAN
155.0000 g., 0.9990 Gold 4.9782 oz. AGW, 64 x 40 mm.
Series: Classic Literature Pilgrimage To The West
Obv: Horseback rider on arch bridge **Rev:** Multicolor court scene
Shape: Rectangle

Date	Mintage	F	VF	XF	Unc	BU
2005 Proof	500	Value: 8,000				

KM# 1850   2000 YUAN
155.5175 g., 0.9990 Gold 4.9958 oz. AGW, 60 mm.
Subject: Beijing Olympics **Obv:** Multicolor logo **Rev:** Four sports

Date	Mintage	F	VF	XF	Unc	BU
2008 Proof	—	Value: 16,500				

KM# 1894   2000 YUAN
155.5000 g., 0.9990 Gold 4.9942 oz. AGW, 60 mm.
Subject: P.R.C. 60th Anniversary

Date	Mintage	F	VF	XF	Unc	BU
2009 Proof	600	Value: 6,500				

KM# 1899   2000 YUAN
155.5000 g., 0.9990 Gold 4.9942 oz. AGW, 64c40 mm.
Subject: Outlaws of the Marsh, series 1 **Rev:** Multicolor
Shape: Rectangle

Date	Mintage	F	VF	XF	Unc	BU
2009 Proof	800	Value: 6,500				

KM# 1936   2000 YUAN
155.5500 g., 0.9990 Gold 4.9958 oz. AGW **Series:** Outlaws of the Marsh, series 2 **Rev:** Multicolor **Shape:** Rectangle

Date	Mintage	F	VF	XF	Unc	BU
2010 Proof	900	Value: 6,500				

KM# 1948   2000 YUAN
155.5000 g., 0.9990 Gold 4.9942 oz. AGW **Subject:** Yungang
Grotto Art

Date	Mintage	F	VF	XF	Unc	BU
2010 Proof	800	Value: 6,500				

KM# 1893   10000 YUAN
1000.0000 g., 0.9990 Gold 32.117 oz. AGW, 90 mm.
Subject: P.R.C. 60th Anniversary

Date	Mintage	F	VF	XF	Unc	BU
2009 Proof	100	Value: 40,250				

KM# 1947   10000 YUAN
1000.0000 g., 0.9990 Gold 32.117 oz. AGW **Subject:** Yungang
Grotto Art

Date	Mintage	F	VF	XF	Unc	BU
2010 Proof	100	Value: 40,500				

KM# 1851   100000 YUAN
10000.0000 g., 0.9990 Gold 321.17 oz. AGW, 180 mm.
Subject: Beijing Olympics **Obv:** Multicolor logo **Rev:** Sports
montage, Temple of Heaven

Date	Mintage	F	VF	XF	Unc	BU
2008 Proof	29	Value: 600,000				

SILVER BULLION COINAGE
Lunar Series

KM# 1613   YUAN
31.1050 g., 0.9990 Silver 0.9990 oz. ASW, 40 mm.
Subject: Year of the rooster **Obv:** Classical rooster **Rev:** Rooster,
hen and chicks **Shape:** Scallop

Date	Mintage	F	VF	XF	Unc	BU
2005 Proof	60,000	Value: 50.00				

KM# 1379   10 YUAN
30.8400 g., 0.9990 Silver 0.9905 oz. ASW, 39.9 mm.
Subject: Year of the Snake **Obv:** Traditional style building
Rev: Snake **Shape:** Scalloped **Note:** Prev. Y#1041.

Date	Mintage	F	VF	XF	Unc	BU
2001 Proof	6,800	Value: 65.00				

KM# 1382   10 YUAN
31.1035 g., 0.9990 Silver 0.9990 oz. ASW **Subject:** Year of the
Snake **Shape:** Fan-like **Note:** Prev. Y#1042.

Date	Mintage	F	VF	XF	Unc	BU
2001	66,000	—	—	—	40.00	45.00

KM# 1375   10 YUAN
31.1035 g., 0.9990 Silver 0.9990 oz. ASW, 40 mm.
Subject: Year of the Snake **Rev:** Multicolor

Date	Mintage	F	VF	XF	Unc	BU
2001 Proof	6,800	Value: 60.00				

KM# 1418.1   10 YUAN
31.1035 g., 0.9990 Silver 0.9990 oz. ASW, 40 mm.
Subject: Year of the Horse **Obv:** Da Zheng Hall **Rev:** Stylized
horse head **Edge:** Reeded **Note:** Prev. Y#1232.

Date	Mintage	F	VF	XF	Unc	BU
2002	50,000	—	—	—	—	55.00

KM# 1418.2   10 YUAN
31.1035 g., 0.9990 Silver Colorized 0.9990 oz. ASW, 40 mm.
Subject: Year of the horse **Rev:** Horse prancing right

Date	Mintage	F	VF	XF	Unc	BU
2002 Proof	10,000	Value: 60.00				

KM# 1423   10 YUAN
31.1035 g., 0.9990 Silver 0.9990 oz. ASW **Subject:** Year of the
horse **Shape:** Fan-like

Date	Mintage	F	VF	XF	Unc	BU
2002 Proof	50,000	Value: 70.00				

KM# 1425   10 YUAN
31.1035 g., 0.9990 Silver 0.9990 oz. ASW, 40 mm.
Subject: Year of the Horse **Shape:** Scalloped

Date	Mintage	F	VF	XF	Unc	BU
2002 Proof	6,800	Value: 75.00				

KM# A1477   10 YUAN
31.1035 g., 0.9990 Silver 0.9990 oz. ASW, 40 mm.
Subject: Year of the Sheep

Date	Mintage	F	VF	XF	Unc	BU
2003 Proof	66,000	Value: 60.00				

KM# 1477   10 YUAN
31.1035 g., 0.9990 Silver 0.9990 oz. ASW, 40 mm.
Subject: Year of the Sheep **Rev:** Multicolor

Date	Mintage	F	VF	XF	Unc	BU
2003 Proof	6,800	Value: 60.00				

KM# 1485   10 YUAN
31.1035 g., 0.9990 Silver 0.9990 oz. ASW, 30 x 85 mm.
Subject: Year of the Sheep **Shape:** Fan-like

Date	Mintage	F	VF	XF	Unc	BU
2003 Proof	66,000	Value: 70.00				

KM# A1545   10 YUAN
31.1035 g., 0.9990 Silver 0.9990 oz. ASW, 40 mm.
Series: Lunar New Year **Subject:** Year of the Monkey
Rev: Multicolor monkey

Date	Mintage	F	VF	XF	Unc	BU
2004 Proof	—	Value: 60.00				

KM# 1545   10 YUAN
31.1035 g., 0.9990 Silver 0.9990 oz. ASW, 40 mm.
Series: Lunar New Year **Subject:** Year of the Monkey

Date	Mintage	F	VF	XF	Unc	BU
2004 Proof	80,000	Value: 60.00				

KM# 1548   10 YUAN
31.1035 g., 0.9990 Silver 0.9990 oz. ASW, 40 mm.
Subject: Lunar New Year **Rev:** Monkey **Shape:** Scalloped

Date	Mintage	F	VF	XF	Unc	BU
2004 Proof	6,800	Value: 75.00				

KM# 1553   10 YUAN
31.1035 g., 0.9990 Silver 0.9990 oz. ASW, 30 x 85 mm.
Series: Lunar New Year **Subject:** Year of the Monkey
Rev: Monkey **Shape:** Fan-like

Date	Mintage	F	VF	XF	Unc	BU
2004 Proof	66,000	Value: 70.00				

KM# 1612   10 YUAN
31.1050 g., 0.9990 Silver 0.9990 oz. ASW, 40 mm. **Subject:**
Year of the rooster **Obv:** Classical rooster **Rev:** Multicolor rooster

Date	Mintage	F	VF	XF	Unc	BU
2005 Proof	100,000	Value: 75.00				

KM# 1614   10 YUAN
31.1050 g., 0.9990 Silver 0.9990 oz. ASW, 40 mm. **Subject:**
Year of the rooster **Obv:** Classical rooster **Rev:** Rooster, hen and
chicks

Date	Mintage	F	VF	XF	Unc	BU
2005 Proof	8,000	Value: 60.00				

KM# 1615   10 YUAN
31.1050 g., 0.9990 Silver 0.9990 oz. ASW, 30 x 85 mm.
Subject: Year of the rooster **Obv:** Temple **Rev:** Rooster, hen
and chicks **Shape:** Fan-like

Date	Mintage	F	VF	XF	Unc	BU
2005 Proof	66,000	Value: 75.00				

KM# 1684   10 YUAN
31.1035 g., 0.9990 Silver 0.9990 oz. ASW, 40 mm. **Obv:** Dog-
shaped belt-hook from ancient Chinese bronze ware, decorative
design of dog tail-shaped plant leaves **Rev:** 2 smart dogs
Note: Prev. Y#1225; 1657.

Date	Mintage	F	VF	XF	Unc	BU
2006	80,000	—	—	—	—	50.00

KM# 1716   10 YUAN
31.1050 g., 0.9990 Silver 0.9990 oz. ASW, 40 mm. **Subject:**
Year of the pig **Obv:** Classical pig **Rev:** Pig walking right

Date	Mintage	F	VF	XF	Unc	BU
2007 Proof	80,000	Value: 55.00				

KM# 1717   10 YUAN
31.1050 g., 0.9990 Silver 0.9990 oz. ASW, 40 mm.
Subject: Year of the pig **Obv:** Classical pig **Rev:** Multicolor sow
and four piglets sucking

Date	Mintage	F	VF	XF	Unc	BU
2007 Proof	100,000	Value: 50.00				

KM# 1718   10 YUAN
31.1050 g., 0.9990 Silver 0.9990 oz. ASW, 85 x 60 mm.
Subject: Year of the pig **Obv:** Temple **Rev:** Sow and four piglets
Shape: Fan-like

Date	Mintage	F	VF	XF	Unc	BU
2007 Proof	66,000	Value: 75.00				

KM# 1719   10 YUAN
31.1050 g., 0.9990 Silver 0.9990 oz. ASW, 40 mm.
Subject: Year of the pig **Obv:** Classical pig **Rev:** Pig walking
right **Shape:** Scalloped

Date	Mintage	F	VF	XF	Unc	BU
2007 Proof	60,000	Value: 55.00				

KM# 1830   10 YUAN
31.1050 g., 0.9990 Silver 0.9990 oz. ASW, 40 mm.
Rev: Multicolor

Date	Mintage	F	VF	XF	Unc	BU
2008 Proof	—	Value: 55.00				

KM# 1831   10 YUAN
31.1050 g., 0.9990 Silver 0.9990 oz. ASW, 40 mm.
Subject: Year of the rat

Date	Mintage	F	VF	XF	Unc	BU
2008 Proof	—	Value: 55.00				

KM# 1832   10 YUAN
31.1050 g., 0.9990 Silver 0.9990 oz. ASW, 40 mm.
Subject: Year of the rat **Shape:** Scallop

Date	Mintage	F	VF	XF	Unc	BU
2008 Proof	—	Value: 55.00				

KM# 1833   10 YUAN
31.1050 g., 0.9990 Silver 0.9990 oz. ASW, 85 x 60 mm.
Subject: Year of the rat **Shape:** Fan-like

Date	Mintage	F	VF	XF	Unc	BU
2008 Proof	—	Value: 75.00				

KM# 1875   10 YUAN
31.1050 g., 0.9990 Silver 0.9990 oz. ASW, 40 mm.
Rev: Multicolor

Date	Mintage	F	VF	XF	Unc	BU
2009 Proof	—	Value: 50.00				

KM# 1876   10 YUAN
31.1050 g., 0.9990 Silver 0.9990 oz. ASW, 40 mm.
Subject: Year of the Ox

Date	Mintage	F	VF	XF	Unc	BU
2009 Proof	100,000	Value: 50.00				

KM# 1877   10 YUAN
31.1050 g., 0.9990 Silver 0.9990 oz. ASW **Subject:** Year of the
Ox

Date	Mintage	F	VF	XF	Unc	BU
2009 Proof	66,000	Value: 55.00				

KM# 1878   10 YUAN
31.1050 g., 0.9990 Silver 0.9990 oz. ASW **Shape:** Fan-like

Date	Mintage	F	VF	XF	Unc	BU
2009 Proof	66,000	Value: 75.00				

KM# 1922   10 YUAN
31.1050 g., 0.9990 Silver 0.9990 oz. ASW **Subject:** Year of the
Tiger **Shape:** Arc

Date	Mintage	F	VF	XF	Unc	BU
2010	66,000	—	—	—	—	40.00

KM# 1923   10 YUAN
31.1050 g., 0.9990 Silver 0.9990 oz. ASW **Subject:** Year of the
Tiger **Shape:** Scalloped

Date	Mintage	F	VF	XF	Unc	BU
2010 Proof	60,000	Value: 40.00				

KM# 1924   10 YUAN
31.1050 g., 0.9990 Silver 0.9990 oz. ASW **Subject:** Year of the
Tiger

Date	Mintage	F	VF	XF	Unc	BU
2010 Proof	100,000	Value: 40.00				

KM# 1925   10 YUAN
31.1050 g., 0.9990 Silver 0.9990 oz. ASW **Subject:** Year of the
Tiger **Rev:** Multicolor

Date	Mintage	F	VF	XF	Unc	BU
2010 Proof	100,000	Value: 50.00				

KM# 1971   10 YUAN
31.1050 g., 0.9990 Silver 0.9990 oz. ASW **Subject:** Year of the
Rabbit

Date	Mintage	F	VF	XF	Unc	BU
2011	66,000	—	—	—	—	40.00

KM# 1972   10 YUAN
31.1050 g., 0.9990 Silver 0.9990 oz. ASW **Subject:** Year of the
Rabbit **Shape:** Scalloped

Date	Mintage	F	VF	XF	Unc	BU
2011 Proof	60,000	Value: 40.00				

KM# 1973   10 YUAN
31.1050 g., 0.9990 Silver 0.9990 oz. ASW, 40 mm.
Subject: Year of the Rabbit

Date	Mintage	F	VF	XF	Unc	BU
2011 Proof	100,000	Value: 40.00				

KM# 1974   10 YUAN
31.1050 g., 0.9990 Silver 0.9990 oz. ASW **Subject:** Year of the
Rabbit **Rev:** Multicolor

Date	Mintage	F	VF	XF	Unc	BU
2011 Proof	100,000	Value: 40.00				

KM# 1377   50 YUAN
155.4400 g., 0.9990 Silver 4.9923 oz. ASW, 80.6 x 50.5 mm.
Subject: Year of the Snake **Obv:** Traditional style building
Rev: Snake **Edge:** Plain **Shape:** Rectangle **Note:** Illustration
reduced. Prev. Y#1040.

Date	Mintage	F	VF	XF	Unc	BU
2001 Proof	1,888	Value: 850				

KM# 1421 50 YUAN
155.5190 g., 0.9990 Silver 4.9948 oz. ASW, 80 x 50 mm. **Subject:** Year of the horse **Rev:** Three horses running left **Shape:** Rectangle

Date	Mintage	F	VF	XF	Unc	BU
2002 Proof	1,888	Value: 850				

KM# 1484 50 YUAN
155.5000 g., 0.9990 Silver 4.9942 oz. ASW, 80 x 50 mm. **Subject:** Year of the Sheep **Shape:** Rectangle

Date	Mintage	F	VF	XF	Unc	BU
2003 Proof	1,888	Value: 850				

KM# 1551 50 YUAN
155.5000 g., 0.9990 Silver 4.9942 oz. ASW, 80 x 50 mm. **Series:** Lunar New Year **Subject:** Year of the Monkey **Rev:** Monkey **Shape:** Rectangle

Date	Mintage	F	VF	XF	Unc	BU
2004 Proof	1,888	Value: 850				

KM# 1611 50 YUAN
155.0000 g., 0.9990 Silver 4.9782 oz. ASW, 80 x 50 mm. **Subject:** Year of the rooster **Obv:** Classical rooster **Rev:** Rooster, hen and chicks **Shape:** Rectangle

Date	Mintage	F	VF	XF	Unc	BU
2005 Proof	1,888	Value: 850				

KM# 1720 50 YUAN
155.5500 g., 0.9990 Silver 4.9958 oz. ASW, 80 x 50 mm. **Subject:** Year of the pig **Obv:** Classical pig **Rev:** Sow and four pigletts **Shape:** Rectangle

Date	Mintage	F	VF	XF	Unc	BU
2007 Proof	1,888	Value: 850				

KM# 1834 50 YUAN
155.5000 g., 0.9990 Silver 4.9942 oz. ASW, 80 x 50 mm. **Subject:** Year of the rat **Shape:** Rectangle

Date	Mintage	F	VF	XF	Unc	BU
2008 Proof	—	Value: 850				

KM# 1879 50 YUAN
Silver **Subject:** Year of the Ox

Date	Mintage	F	VF	XF	Unc	BU
2009 Proof	1,888	Value: 850				

KM# 1920 50 YUAN
155.5000 g., 0.9990 Silver 4.9942 oz. ASW **Subject:** Year of the Tiger **Shape:** Rectangle

Date	Mintage	F	VF	XF	Unc	BU
2010 Proof	1,888	—	—	—	—	125

KM# 1921 50 YUAN
155.5000 g., 0.9990 Silver 4.9942 oz. ASW **Subject:** Year of the Tiger

Date	Mintage	F	VF	XF	Unc	BU
2010 Proof	8,800	Value: 150				

KM# 1969 50 YUAN
155.5000 g., 0.9990 Silver 4.9942 oz. ASW **Subject:** Year of the Rabbit **Shape:** Rectangle

Date	Mintage	F	VF	XF	Unc	BU
2011 Proof	1,888	Value: 125				

KM# 1970 50 YUAN
155.5000 g., 0.9990 Silver 4.9942 oz. ASW **Subject:** Year of the Rabbit **Rev:** Multicolor

Date	Mintage	F	VF	XF	Unc	BU
2011 Proof	8,800	Value: 125				

KM# 1420 300 YUAN
1000.0000 g., 0.9990 Silver 32.117 oz. ASW, 100 mm. **Series:** Lunar **Subject:** Year of the Horse

Date	Mintage	F	VF	XF	Unc	BU
2002 Proof	3,800	Value: 6,500				

KM# 1479 300 YUAN
1000.0000 g., 0.9990 Silver 32.117 oz. ASW, 100 mm. **Subject:** Year of the Sheep

Date	Mintage	F	VF	XF	Unc	BU
2003 Proof	3,800	Value: 7,500				

KM# 1547 300 YUAN
1000.0000 g., 0.9990 Silver 32.117 oz. ASW, 100 mm. **Series:** Lunar New Year **Subject:** Year of the Monkey **Rev:** Monkey

Date	Mintage	F	VF	XF	Unc	BU
2004 Proof	3,800	Value: 9,000				

KM# 1610 300 YUAN
1000.0000 g., 0.9990 Silver 32.117 oz. ASW, 100 mm. **Subject:** Year of the rooster **Obv:** Classical rooster **Rev:** Rooster strutting

Date	Mintage	F	VF	XF	Unc	BU
2005 Proof	3,800	Value: 5,000				

KM# 1725 300 YUAN
1000.0000 g., 0.9990 Silver 32.117 oz. ASW, 100 mm. **Subject:** Year of the pig **Obv:** Classical pig **Rev:** Three pigs

Date	Mintage	F	VF	XF	Unc	BU
2007 Proof	3,800	Value: 5,000				

KM# 1839 300 YUAN
1000.0000 g., 0.9990 Silver 32.117 oz. ASW, 100 mm. **Subject:** Year of the rat

Date	Mintage	F	VF	XF	Unc	BU
2008 Proof	—	Value: 5,000				

KM# 1884 300 YUAN
1000.0000 g., 0.9990 Silver 32.117 oz. ASW **Subject:** Year of the Ox

Date	Mintage	F	VF	XF	Unc	BU
2009 Proof	3,800	Value: 5,000				

KM# 1919 300 YUAN
1000.0000 g., 0.9990 Silver 32.117 oz. ASW **Subject:** Year of the Tiger

Date	Mintage	F	VF	XF	Unc	BU
2010 Proof	3,800	Value: 700				

KM# 1968 300 YUAN
1000.0000 g., 0.9990 Silver 32.117 oz. ASW **Subject:** Year of the Rabbit

Date	Mintage	F	VF	XF	Unc	BU
2011 Proof	1,888	Value: 700				

SILVER BULLION COINAGE

Panda Series

KM# 1740 3 YUAN
7.7700 g., 0.9990 Silver 0.2496 oz. ASW, 25 mm. **Obv:** Temple of Heaven **Rev:** Panda seated with branch

Date	Mintage	F	VF	XF	Unc	BU
2007 Proof	30,000	Value: 10.00				

KM# 1742 3 YUAN
7.7700 g., 0.9990 Silver 0.2496 oz. ASW, 25 mm. **Obv:** Temple of Heaven **Rev:** Panda walking right

Date	Mintage	F	VF	XF	Unc	BU
2007 Proof	30,000	Value: 10.00				

KM# 1744 3 YUAN
7.7700 g., 0.9990 Silver 0.2496 oz. ASW, 25 mm. **Obv:** Temple of Heaven **Rev:** Panda seated with bamboo branch

Date	Mintage	F	VF	XF	Unc	BU
2007 Proof	30,000	Value: 10.00				

KM# 1772 3 YUAN
7.7700 g., 0.9990 Silver 0.2496 oz. ASW, 25 mm. **Obv:** Temple of Heaven **Rev:** Panda seated on rock

Date	Mintage	F	VF	XF	Unc	BU
2007 Proof	30,000	Value: 10.00				

KM# 1780 3 YUAN
7.7700 g., 0.9990 Silver 0.2496 oz. ASW, 25 mm. **Obv:** Temple of Heaven **Rev:** Panda looking forward

Date	Mintage	F	VF	XF	Unc	BU
2007 Proof	30,000	Value: 10.00				

KM# 1746 3 YUAN
7.7700 g., 0.9990 Silver 0.2496 oz. ASW **Obv:** Temple of Heaven **Rev:** Panda hanging from branch

Date	Mintage	F	VF	XF	Unc	BU
2007 Proof	30,000	Value: 10.00				

KM# 1748 3 YUAN
7.7700 g., 0.9990 Silver 0.2496 oz. ASW, 25 mm. **Obv:** Temple of Heaven **Rev:** Panda walking forward

Date	Mintage	F	VF	XF	Unc	BU
2007 Proof	30,000	Value: 10.00				

KM# 1750 3 YUAN
7.7700 g., 0.9990 Silver 0.2496 oz. ASW, 25 mm. **Obv:** Temple of Heaven **Rev:** Panda drinking water

Date	Mintage	F	VF	XF	Unc	BU
2007 Proof	30,000	Value: 10.00				

KM# 1752 3 YUAN
7.7700 g., 0.9990 Silver 0.2496 oz. ASW, 25 mm. **Obv:** Tample of Heaven **Rev:** Panda seated in oval with branch

Date	Mintage	F	VF	XF	Unc	BU
2007 Proof	30,000	Value: 10.00				

KM# 1754 3 YUAN
7.7700 g., 0.9990 Silver 0.2496 oz. ASW, 25 mm. **Obv:** Temple of Heaven **Rev:** Panda seated on geometric background

Date	Mintage	F	VF	XF	Unc	BU
2007 Proof	30,000	Value: 10.00				

KM# 1756 3 YUAN
7.7700 g., 0.9990 Silver 0.2496 oz. ASW, 10 mm. **Obv:** Temple of Heaven **Rev:** Panda on rock

Date	Mintage	F	VF	XF	Unc	BU
2007 Proof	30,000	Value: 10.00				

KM# 1758 3 YUAN
7.7700 g., 0.9990 Silver 0.2496 oz. ASW, 25 mm. **Obv:** Temple of Heaven **Rev:** Panda seated on river bank

Date	Mintage	F	VF	XF	Unc	BU
2007 Proof	30,000	Value: 10.00				

KM# 1760 3 YUAN
7.7700 g., 0.9990 Silver 0.2496 oz. ASW, 25 mm. **Obv:** Temple of Heaven **Rev:** Panda on tree branch

Date	Mintage	F	VF	XF	Unc	BU
2007 Proof	30,000	Value: 10.00				

KM# 1762 3 YUAN
7.7700 g., 0.9990 Silver 0.2496 oz. ASW, 25 mm. **Obv:** Temple of Heaven **Rev:** Panda on rock ledge

Date	Mintage	F	VF	XF	Unc	BU
2007 Proof	30,000	Value: 10.00				

KM# 1764 3 YUAN
7.7700 g., 0.9990 Silver 0.2496 oz. ASW, 25 mm. **Obv:** Temple of Heaven **Rev:** Panda seated munching bamboo

Date	Mintage	F	VF	XF	Unc	BU
2007 Proof	30,000	Value: 10.00				

KM# 1766 3 YUAN
7.7700 g., 0.9990 Silver 0.2496 oz. ASW, 25 mm. **Obv:** Temple of Heaven **Rev:** Panda pulling bamboo

Date	Mintage	F	VF	XF	Unc	BU
2007 Proof	30,000	Value: 10.00				

KM# 1768 3 YUAN
7.7700 g., 0.9990 Silver 0.2496 oz. ASW, 25 mm. **Obv:** Temple of Heaven **Rev:** Panda in tree

Date	Mintage	F	VF	XF	Unc	BU
2007 Proof	30,000	Value: 10.00				

KM# 1770 3 YUAN
7.7700 g., 0.9990 Silver 0.2496 oz. ASW, 25 mm. **Obv:** Temple of Heaven **Rev:** Panda looking over branch

Date	Mintage	F	VF	XF	Unc	BU
2007 Proof	30,000	Value: 10.00				

KM# 1774 3 YUAN
7.7700 g., 0.9990 Silver 0.2496 oz. ASW, 25 mm. **Obv:** Temple of Heaven **Rev:** Panda looking out over rock

Date	Mintage	F	VF	XF	Unc	BU
2007 Proof	30,000	Value: 10.00				

KM# A1776 3 YUAN
7.7700 g., 0.9990 Silver 0.2496 oz. ASW, 25 mm. **Obv:** Temple of Heaven **Rev:** Panda seated on frosted background

Date	Mintage	F	VF	XF	Unc	BU
2007 Proof	30,000	Value: 10.00				

KM# 1778 3 YUAN
7.7700 g., 0.9990 Silver 0.2496 oz. ASW, 25 mm. **Obv:** Temple of Heaven **Rev:** Panda walking amongst bamboo

Date	Mintage	F	VF	XF	Unc	BU
2007 Proof	30,000	Value: 10.00				

KM# 1782 3 YUAN
7.7700 g., 0.9990 Silver 0.2496 oz. ASW, 25 mm. **Obv:** Temple of Heaven **Rev:** Panda and cub walking right

Date	Mintage	F	VF	XF	Unc	BU
2007 Proof	30,000	Value: 10.00				

KM# 1784 3 YUAN
7.7700 g., 0.9990 Silver 0.2496 oz. ASW, 25 mm. **Obv:** Temple of Heaven **Rev:** Panda seated with cub on left

Date	Mintage	F	VF	XF	Unc	BU
2007 Proof	30,000	Value: 10.00				

KM# 1786 3 YUAN
7.7700 g., 0.9990 Silver 0.2496 oz. ASW, 25 mm. **Obv:** Temple of Heaven **Rev:** Panda seated with cub on right

Date	Mintage	F	VF	XF	Unc	BU
2007 Proof	30,000	Value: 10.00				

KM# 1788 3 YUAN
7.7700 g., 0.9990 Silver 0.2496 oz. ASW, 25 mm. **Obv:** Temple of Heaven **Rev:** Panda seated with cub, both munching bamboo

Date	Mintage	F	VF	XF	Unc	BU
2007 Proof	30,000	Value: 10.00				

KM# 1365 10 YUAN
31.1035 g., 0.9990 Silver 0.9990 oz. ASW, 40.1 mm. **Obv:** Temple of Heaven with incuse legend **Rev:** Panda walking left through bamboo **Edge:** Oblique reeding **Note:** Large and small date varieties exist. Prev. Y#1111.

Date	Mintage	F	VF	XF	Unc	BU
2001	250,000	—	—	—	27.50	32.50
2001 D Proof	—	Value: 50.00				
2002 Proof	—	Value: 50.00				

KM# A1365 10 YUAN
31.2300 g., 0.9990 Silver 1.0030 oz. ASW, 40 mm. **Obv:** Temple of Heaven, incuse legend **Rev:** Multicolor panda walking in bamboo **Edge:** Slanted reeding **Note:** Large and small date varieties exist.

Date	Mintage	F	VF	XF	Unc	BU
2002 Proof	—	Value: 60.00				

Note: Privately colored

KM# 1466 10 YUAN

31.1035 g., 0.9990 Silver 0.9990 oz. ASW, 40 mm. **Obv:** Temple of Heaven **Rev:** Panda eating bamboo in a frosted circle **Edge:** Slant reeded **Note:** Prev. Y#1244.

Date	Mintage	F	VF	XF	Unc	BU
2003 Proof	—	Value: 60.00				

KM# 1528 10 YUAN

31.1035 g., 0.9990 Silver 0.9990 oz. ASW, 40 mm. **Obv:** Temple of Heaven **Rev:** Panda nuzzling her cub **Edge:** Slant reeded **Note:** Prev. Y#1245.

Date	Mintage	F	VF	XF	Unc	BU
2004 Proof	—	Value: 60.00				

KM# 1589 10 YUAN

31.1050 g., 0.9990 Silver 0.9990 oz. ASW, 40 mm. **Obv:** Temple of Heaven **Rev:** Panda cub and mom seated in bamboo

Date	Mintage	F	VF	XF	Unc	BU
2005 Proof	60,000	Value: 60.00				

KM# 1664 10 YUAN

31.1050 g., 0.9990 Silver 0.9990 oz. ASW, 40 mm. **Obv:** Temple of Heaven **Rev:** Two pandas seated with bamboo

Date	Mintage	F	VF	XF	Unc	BU
2006 Proof	600,000	Value: 50.00				

KM# 1706 10 YUAN

31.1050 g., 0.9990 Silver 0.9990 oz. ASW, 40 mm. **Obv:** Temple of Heaven **Rev:** Two pandas, one walking, one seated

Date	Mintage	F	VF	XF	Unc	BU
2007 Proof	600,000	Value: 50.00				

KM# 1865 10 YUAN

31.1050 g., 0.9990 Silver 0.9990 oz. ASW, 40 mm. **Obv:** Temple of Heaven **Rev:** Two panda seated

Date	Mintage	F	VF	XF	Unc	BU
2008 Proof	—	Value: 50.00				

KM# 1814 10 YUAN

31.1050 g., 0.9990 Silver 0.9990 oz. ASW, 40 mm. **Rev:** Panda cub pawing mom

Date	Mintage	F	VF	XF	Unc	BU
2008 Proof	—	Value: 50.00				

KM# 1931 10 YUAN

31.1050 g., 0.9990 Silver 0.9990 oz. ASW **Obv:** Temple of Heaven **Rev:** Two pandas, one lying on back

Date	Mintage	F	VF	XF	Unc	BU
2010	800,000	—	—	—	—	50.00

KM# 1468 50 YUAN

151.5000 g., 0.9990 Silver 4.8658 oz. ASW, 80 x 50 mm. **Rev. Designer:** Panda and bamboo **Shape:** Rectangle

Date	Mintage	F	VF	XF	Unc	BU
2003 Proof	1,888	Value: 350				

KM# 1530 50 YUAN

155.5000 g., 0.9990 Silver 4.9942 oz. ASW, 70 mm. **Rev:** Panda walking with cub

Date	Mintage	F	VF	XF	Unc	BU
2004 Proof	10,000	Value: 275				

KM# 1588 50 YUAN

155.0000 g., 0.9990 Silver 4.9782 oz. ASW, 70 mm. **Obv:** Temple of Heaven **Rev:** Panda cub and mom seated in bamboo

Date	Mintage	F	VF	XF	Unc	BU
2005 Proof	10,000	Value: 275				

KM# 1663 50 YUAN

155.5500 g., 0.9990 Silver 4.9958 oz. ASW, 70 mm. **Obv:** Temple of Heaven **Rev:** Two pandas seated with bamboo

Date	Mintage	F	VF	XF	Unc	BU
2006 Proof	10,000	Value: 275				

KM# 1708 50 YUAN

155.5500 g., 0.9990 Silver 4.9958 oz. ASW, 70 mm. **Obv:** Temple of Heaven **Rev:** Two pandas, one walking, one seated

Date	Mintage	F	VF	XF	Unc	BU
2007 Proof	10,000	Value: 275				

KM# 1867 50 YUAN

155.5000 g., 0.9990 Silver 4.9942 oz. ASW

Date	Mintage	F	VF	XF	Unc	BU
2008 Proof	—	Value: 275				

KM# 1816 50 YUAN

155.5000 g., Silver, 70 mm. **Rev:** Panda cub pawing mom

Date	Mintage	F	VF	XF	Unc	BU
2008 Proof	—	Value: 275				

KM# 1935 50 YUAN

155.5500 g., 0.9990 Silver 4.9958 oz. ASW **Obv:** Temple of Heaven **Rev:** Two pandas, one lying on back

Date	Mintage	F	VF	XF	Unc	BU
2010 Proof	10,000	Value: 125				

KM# 1370 300 YUAN

1000.0000 g., 0.9990 Silver 32.117 oz. ASW, 100 mm. **Rev:** Panda walking thru bamboo

Date	Mintage	F	VF	XF	Unc	BU
2001 D Proof	2,000	Value: 1,500				

KM# 1416 300 YUAN

1000.0000 g., 0.9990 Silver 32.117 oz. ASW, 100 mm. **Subject:** Panda Coinage 20th Anniversary **Obv:** Temple of Heaven **Rev:** Two gold inserts with the 1982 and 2002 panda designs on bamboo leaves **Edge:** Plain **Note:** Large and small date varieties exist. Prev. Y#1116.

Date	Mintage	F	VF	XF	Unc	BU
2002 Proof	6,000	Value: 1,000				

KM# 1473 300 YUAN

1000.0000 g., 0.9990 Silver 32.117 oz. ASW **Rev:** Panda and bamboo **Shape:** 100

Date	Mintage	F	VF	XF	Unc	BU
2003 Proof	7,500	Value: 7,500				

KM# 1536 300 YUAN

1000.0000 g., 0.9990 Silver 32.117 oz. ASW, 100 mm. **Rev:** Panda walking with cub

Date	Mintage	F	VF	XF	Unc	BU
2004 Proof	4,000	Value: 9,000				

KM# 1587 300 YUAN

1000.0000 g., 0.9990 Silver 32.117 oz. ASW, 100 mm. **Obv:** Temple of Heaven **Rev:** Panda cub and mom seated in bamboo

Date	Mintage	F	VF	XF	Unc	BU
2005 Proof	4,000	Value: 1,250				

KM# 1662 300 YUAN

1000.0000 g., 0.9990 Silver 32.117 oz. ASW, 100 mm. **Obv:** Temple of Heaven **Rev:** Two pandas seated with bamboo

Date	Mintage	F	VF	XF	Unc	BU
2006 Proof	4,000	Value: 1,250				

KM# 1712 300 YUAN

1000.0000 g., 0.9990 Silver 32.117 oz. ASW, 100 mm. **Obv:** Temple of Heaven **Rev:** Two pandas, one walking, one seated

Date	Mintage	F	VF	XF	Unc	BU
2007 Proof	4,000	Value: 1,250				

KM# 1820 300 YUAN

1000.0000 g., 0.9990 Silver 32.117 oz. ASW, 100 mm. **Rev:** Panda cub pawing mom

Date	Mintage	F	VF	XF	Unc	BU
2008 Proof	—	Value: 4,000				

KM# 1871 300 YUAN

1000.0000 g., 0.9990 Silver 32.117 oz. ASW

Date	Mintage	F	VF	XF	Unc	BU
2008 Proof	—	Value: 4,000				

KM# 1934 300 YUAN

1000.0000 g., 0.9990 Silver 32.117 oz. ASW **Obv:** Temple of Heaven **Rev:** Two pandas, one lying on back

Date	Mintage	F	VF	XF	Unc	BU
2010 Proof	4,000	Value: 700				

GOLD BULLION COINAGE

Panda Series

KM# 1779 15 YUAN

1.2400 g., 0.9990 Gold 0.0398 oz. AGW, 12 mm. **Obv:** Temple of Heaven **Rev:** Panda walking amongst bamboo

Date	Mintage	F	VF	XF	Unc	BU
2007 Proof	18,000	Value: 65.00				

KM# 1741 15 YUAN

1.2400 g., 0.9990 Gold 0.0398 oz. AGW, 12 mm. **Obv:** Temple of Heaven **Rev:** Panda seated with branch

Date	Mintage	F	VF	XF	Unc	BU
2007 Proof	18,000	Value: 65.00				

KM# 1743 15 YUAN

1.2400 g., 0.9990 Gold 0.0398 oz. AGW, 12 mm. **Obv:** Temple of heaven **Rev:** Panda walking right

Date	Mintage	F	VF	XF	Unc	BU
2007 Proof	18,000	Value: 65.00				

KM# 1745 15 YUAN

1.2400 g., 0.9990 Gold 0.0398 oz. AGW, 12 mm. **Obv:** Temple of heaven **Rev:** Panda seated with bamboo branch

Date	Mintage	F	VF	XF	Unc	BU
2007 Proof	18,000	Value: 65.00				

KM# 1747 15 YUAN

1.2400 g., 0.9990 Gold 0.0398 oz. AGW, 12 mm. **Obv:** Temple of Heaven **Rev:** Panda hanging from branch

Date	Mintage	F	VF	XF	Unc	BU
2007 Proof	18,000	Value: 65.00				

KM# 1749 15 YUAN

1.2400 g., 0.9990 Gold 0.0398 oz. AGW, 12 mm. **Obv:** Temple of Heaven **Rev:** Panda walking forward

Date	Mintage	F	VF	XF	Unc	BU
2007 Proof	18,000	Value: 65.00				

KM# 1751 15 YUAN

1.2400 g., 0.9990 Gold 0.0398 oz. AGW, 12 mm. **Obv:** Temple of Heaven **Rev:** Panda drinking water

Date	Mintage	F	VF	XF	Unc	BU
2007 Proof	18,000	Value: 65.00				

KM# 1753 15 YUAN

1.2400 g., 0.9990 Gold 0.0398 oz. AGW, 12 mm. **Obv:** Temple of Heaven **Rev:** Panda seated in oval with branch

Date	Mintage	F	VF	XF	Unc	BU
2007 Proof	18,000	Value: 65.00				

KM# 1755 15 YUAN

1.2400 g., 0.9990 Gold 0.0398 oz. AGW, 12 mm. **Rev:** Panda seated on geometric background

Date	Mintage	F	VF	XF	Unc	BU
2007 Proof	18,000	Value: 65.00				

KM# 1757 15 YUAN

1.2400 g., 0.9990 Gold 0.0398 oz. AGW, 12 mm. **Obv:** Temple of Heaven **Rev:** Panda on rock

Date	Mintage	F	VF	XF	Unc	BU
2007 Proof	18,000	Value: 65.00				

KM# 1759 15 YUAN

1.2400 g., 0.9990 Gold 0.0398 oz. AGW, 12 mm. **Obv:** Temple of Heaven **Rev:** Panda seated on river bank

Date	Mintage	F	VF	XF	Unc	BU
2007 Proof	18,000	Value: 65.00				

KM# 1761 15 YUAN

1.2400 g., 0.9990 Gold 0.0398 oz. AGW, 12 mm. **Obv:** Temple of Heaven **Rev:** Panda on tree branch

Date	Mintage	F	VF	XF	Unc	BU
2007 Proof	18,000	Value: 65.00				

KM# 1763 15 YUAN

1.2400 g., 0.9990 Gold 0.0398 oz. AGW, 12 mm. **Obv:** Temple of Heaven **Rev:** Panda on rock ledge

Date	Mintage	F	VF	XF	Unc	BU
2007 Proof	18,000	Value: 65.00				

KM# 1765 15 YUAN

1.2400 g., 0.9990 Gold 0.0398 oz. AGW, 12 mm. **Obv:** Temple of Heaven **Rev:** Panda seated munching bamboo

Date	Mintage	F	VF	XF	Unc	BU
2007 Proof	18,000	Value: 65.00				

KM# 1767 15 YUAN

1.2400 g., 0.9990 Gold 0.0398 oz. AGW **Obv:** Temple of Heaven **Rev:** Panda pulling bamboo **Shape:** 12

Date	Mintage	F	VF	XF	Unc	BU
2007 Proof	1,800	Value: 65.00				

KM# 1769 15 YUAN

1.2400 g., 0.9990 Gold 0.0398 oz. AGW, 12 mm. **Obv:** Temple of Heaven **Rev:** Panda in tree

Date	Mintage	F	VF	XF	Unc	BU
2007 Proof	18,000	Value: 65.00				

KM# 1771 15 YUAN

1.2400 g., 0.9990 Gold 0.0398 oz. AGW **Obv:** Temple of Heaven **Rev:** Panda looking over branch

Date	Mintage	F	VF	XF	Unc	BU
2007 Proof	18,000	Value: 65.00				

KM# 1773 15 YUAN

1.2400 g., 0.9990 Gold 0.0398 oz. AGW, 12 mm. **Obv:** Temple of Heaven **Rev:** Panda seated on rock

Date	Mintage	F	VF	XF	Unc	BU
2007 Proof	18,000	Value: 65.00				

KM# A1775 15 YUAN
1.2400 g., 0.9990 Gold 0.0398 oz. AGW, 12 mm. **Obv:** Temple of Heaven **Rev:** Panda looking out from rock

Date	Mintage	F	VF	XF	Unc	BU
2007 Proof	18,000	Value: 65.00				

KM# 1777 15 YUAN
1.2400 g., 0.9990 Gold 0.0398 oz. AGW, 12 mm. **Obv:** Temple of Heaven **Rev:** Panda seated on frosted background

Date	Mintage	F	VF	XF	Unc	BU
2007 Proof	18,000	Value: 65.00				

KM# 1781 15 YUAN
1.2400 g., 0.9990 Gold 0.0398 oz. AGW, 12 mm. **Obv:** Temple of Heaven **Rev:** Panda looking forward

Date	Mintage	F	VF	XF	Unc	BU
2007 Proof	18,000	Value: 65.00				

KM# 1783 15 YUAN
1.2400 g., 0.9990 Gold 0.0398 oz. AGW, 12 mm. **Obv:** Temple of Heaven **Rev:** Panda and cub walking right

Date	Mintage	F	VF	XF	Unc	BU
2007 Proof	18,000	Value: 65.00				

KM# 1785 15 YUAN
1.2400 g., 0.9990 Gold 0.0398 oz. AGW, 12 mm. **Obv:** Temple of Heaven **Rev:** Panda seated with cub on left

Date	Mintage	F	VF	XF	Unc	BU
2007 Proof	18,000	Value: 65.00				

KM# 1787 15 YUAN
1.2400 g., 0.9990 Gold 0.0398 oz. AGW, 12 mm. **Obv:** Temple of Heaven **Rev:** Panda seated with cub on right

Date	Mintage	F	VF	XF	Unc	BU
2007 Proof	18,000	Value: 65.00				

KM# 1789 15 YUAN
1.2400 g., 0.9990 Gold 0.0398 oz. AGW, 12 mm. **Obv:** Temple of Heaven **Rev:** Panda seated with cub, both munching bamboo

Date	Mintage	F	VF	XF	Unc	BU
2007 Proof	18,000	Value: 65.00				

KM# 1366 20 YUAN
1.5600 g., 0.9990 Gold 0.0501 oz. AGW, 14.04 mm. **Obv:** Temple of Heaven **Rev:** Panda walking left through bamboo **Edge:** Reeded **Note:** Large and small date varieties exist. Prev. Y#1112.

Date	Mintage	F	VF	XF	Unc	BU
2001	200,000	—	—	—	75.00	95.00
2001 D	Inc. above	—	—	—	75.00	95.00
2002	74,601	—	—	—	75.00	95.00

KM# 1467 20 YUAN
1.5552 g., 0.9999 Gold 0.0500 oz. AGW, 14.5 mm. **Subject:** Panda **Obv:** Temple of Heaven **Rev:** Panda facing, walking through bamboo **Edge:** Reeded **Note:** Large and small date varieties exist. Prev. Y#1154.

Date	Mintage	F	VF	XF	Unc	BU
2003	117,000	—	—	—	—	75.00

KM# 1529 20 YUAN
1.5552 g., 0.9999 Gold 0.0500 oz. AGW **Subject:** Panda **Note:** Large and small date varieties exist. Prev. Y#1172.

Date	Mintage	F	VF	XF	Unc	BU
2004	101,000	—	—	—	—	75.00

KM# 1586 20 YUAN
1.5500 g., 0.9990 Gold 0.0498 oz. AGW, 14 mm. **Obv:** Temple of Heaven **Rev:** Panda cub and mom seated in bamboo

Date	Mintage	F	VF	XF	Unc	BU
2005 Proof	89,500	Value: 85.00				

KM# 1661 20 YUAN
1.5552 g., 0.9990 Gold 0.0499 oz. AGW, 14 mm. **Obv:** Temple of Heaven **Rev:** Two pandas seated with bamboo

Date	Mintage	F	VF	XF	Unc	BU
2006 Proof	62,000	Value: 95.00				

KM# 1707 20 YUAN
1.5552 g., 0.9990 Gold 0.0499 oz. AGW, 14 mm. **Obv:** Temple of Heaven **Rev:** Two pandas, one walking, one seated

Date	Mintage	F	VF	XF	Unc	BU
2007 Proof	200,000	Value: 75.00				

KM# 1815 20 YUAN
1.5552 g., 0.9990 Gold 0.0499 oz. AGW, 14 mm. **Rev:** Panda cut pawing mom

Date	Mintage	F	VF	XF	Unc	BU
2008 Proof	—	Value: 75.00				

KM# 1866 20 YUAN
1.5552 g., 0.9990 Gold 0.0499 oz. AGW

Date	Mintage	F	VF	XF	Unc	BU
2008 Proof	—	Value: 75.00				

KM# 1930 20 YUAN
1.5500 g., 0.9990 Gold 0.0498 oz. AGW **Obv:** Temple of Heaven **Rev:** Two pandas, one lying on back

Date	Mintage	F	VF	XF	Unc	BU
2010	120,000	—	—	—	—	80.00

KM# 1817 30 YUAN
3.1100 g., 0.9990 Gold 0.0999 oz. AGW, 18 mm. **Rev:** Panda cub pawing mom

Date	Mintage	F	VF	XF	Unc	BU
2008 Proof	—	Value: 175				

KM# 1367 50 YUAN
3.1103 g., 0.9990 Gold 0.0999 oz. AGW, 18 mm. **Obv:** Temple of Heaven **Rev:** Panda walking left through bamboo **Edge:** Reeded **Note:** Large and small date varieties exist. Prev. Y#1113.

Date	Mintage	F	VF	XF	Unc	BU
2001	50,000	—	—	—	—	165
2001 D	150,000	—	—	—	—	150

KM# 1457 50 YUAN
3.1103 g., 0.9999 Gold 0.1000 oz. AGW **Subject:** Temple of Heaven **Rev:** Panda walking

Date	Mintage	F	VF	XF	Unc	BU
2002	36,092	—	—	—	—	185

KM# 1469 50 YUAN
3.1103 g., 0.9999 Gold 0.1000 oz. AGW **Subject:** Panda **Note:** Large and small date varieties exist. Prev. Y#1157.

Date	Mintage	F	VF	XF	Unc	BU
2003	47,500	—	—	—	—	175

KM# 1531 50 YUAN
3.1103 g., 0.9999 Gold 0.1000 oz. AGW **Subject:** Panda **Note:** Large and small date varieties exist. Prev. Y#1173.

Date	Mintage	F	VF	XF	Unc	BU
2004	—	—	—	—	—	150

KM# 1585 50 YUAN
3.1100 g., 0.9990 Gold 0.0999 oz. AGW, 18 mm. **Obv:** Temple of Heaven **Rev:** Panda cub and mom seated in bamboo

Date	Mintage	F	VF	XF	Unc	BU
2005	150,000	—	—	—	—	150

KM# 1660 50 YUAN
3.1100 g., 0.9990 Gold 0.0999 oz. AGW, 18 mm. **Obv:** Temple of Heaven **Rev:** Two pandas seated with bamboo

Date	Mintage	F	VF	XF	Unc	BU
2006	150,000	—	—	—	—	150

KM# 1709 50 YUAN
3.1100 g., 0.9990 Gold 0.0999 oz. AGW, 18 mm. **Obv:** Temple of Heaven **Rev:** Two pandas, one walking, one seated

Date	Mintage	F	VF	XF	Unc	BU
2007	150,000	—	—	—	—	150

KM# 1868 50 YUAN
3.1000 g., 0.9990 Gold 0.0996 oz. AGW, 18 mm. **Rev:** Panda cub pawing mom

Date	Mintage	F	VF	XF	Unc	BU
2008	—	—	—	—	—	150

KM# 1929 50 YUAN
3.1100 g., 0.9990 Gold 0.0999 oz. AGW **Obv:** Temple of Heaven **Rev:** Two pandas, one lying on back

Date	Mintage	F	VF	XF	Unc	BU
2010	120,000	—	—	—	—	150

KM# 1368 100 YUAN
7.7759 g., 0.9990 Gold 0.2497 oz. AGW, 22 mm. **Obv:** Temple of Heaven **Rev:** Panda walking left through bamboo **Edge:** Reeded **Note:** Large and small date varieties exist. Prev. Y#1114.

Date	Mintage	F	VF	XF	Unc	BU
2001	85,010	—	—	—	—	325
2001 D	Inc. above	—	—	—	—	325

KM# 1458 100 YUAN
7.7759 g., 0.9999 Gold 0.2500 oz. AGW **Obv:** Temple of Heaven **Rev:** Panda walking

Date	Mintage	F	VF	XF	Unc	BU
2002	19,205	—	—	—	—	350

KM# 1471 100 YUAN
7.7759 g., 0.9999 Gold 0.2500 oz. AGW **Subject:** Panda **Note:** Large and small date varieties exist. Prev. Y#1158.

Date	Mintage	F	VF	XF	Unc	BU
2003	28,000	—	—	—	—	325

KM# 1533 100 YUAN
7.7759 g., 0.9999 Gold 0.2500 oz. AGW **Subject:** Panda **Note:** Large and small date varieties exist. Prev. Y#1174.

Date	Mintage	F	VF	XF	Unc	BU
2004	41,000	—	—	—	—	335

KM# 1584 100 YUAN
7.7700 g., 0.9990 Gold 0.2496 oz. AGW, 22 mm. **Obv:** Temple of Heaven **Rev:** Panda cub and mom seated in bamboo

Date	Mintage	F	VF	XF	Unc	BU
2005	40,000	—	—	—	—	335

KM# 1659 100 YUAN
7.7700 g., 0.9990 Gold 0.2496 oz. AGW, 22 mm. **Obv:** Temple of Heaven **Rev:** Two pandas seated with bamboo

Date	Mintage	F	VF	XF	Unc	BU
2006	28,500	—	—	—	—	345

KM# 1710 100 YUAN
7.7700 g., 0.9990 Gold 0.2496 oz. AGW, 22 mm. **Obv:** Temple of Heaven **Rev:** Two pandas, one walking, one seated

Date	Mintage	F	VF	XF	Unc	BU
2007	60,000	—	—	—	—	335

KM# 1818 100 YUAN
7.7700 g., 0.9990 Gold 0.2496 oz. AGW, 22 mm. **Rev:** Panda cub pawing mom

Date	Mintage	F	VF	XF	Unc	BU
2008	—	—	—	—	—	325

KM# 1928 100 YUAN
7.7700 g., 0.9990 Gold 0.2496 oz. AGW **Obv:** Temple of Heaven **Rev:** Two panda, one lying on back

Date	Mintage	F	VF	XF	Unc	BU
2010	120,000	—	—	—	—	350

KM# 1369 200 YUAN
15.5518 g., 0.9990 Gold 0.4995 oz. AGW, 27 mm. **Obv:** Temple of Heaven **Rev:** Panda in bamboo forest **Edge:** Slanted reeding **Note:** Illustration reduced. Large and small date varieties exist. Prev. Y#1105.

Date	Mintage	F	VF	XF	Unc	BU
2001	33,215	—	—	—	—	675
2001 D	100,000	—	—	—	—	650

KM# 1459 200 YUAN
15.5518 g., 0.9999 Gold 0.4999 oz. AGW **Rev:** Panda

Date	Mintage	F	VF	XF	Unc	BU
2002	28,514	—	—	—	—	675

KM# 1472 200 YUAN
15.5519 g., 0.9999 Gold 0.4999 oz. AGW **Subject:** Panda **Note:** Large and small date varieties exist. Prev. Y#1162.

Date	Mintage	F	VF	XF	Unc	BU
2003	25,000	—	—	—	—	675

KM# 1535 200 YUAN
15.5519 g., 0.9990 Gold 0.4995 oz. AGW **Subject:** Panda **Note:** Large and small date varieties exist. Prev. Y#1175.

Date	Mintage	F	VF	XF	Unc	BU
2004	42,000	—	—	—	—	650

KM# 1583 200 YUAN
15.5518 g., 0.9990 Gold 0.4995 oz. AGW, 27 mm. **Obv:** Temple of Heaven **Rev:** Panda cub and mom seated in bamboo

Date	Mintage	F	VF	XF	Unc	BU
2005	36,410	—	—	—	—	650

KM# 1658 200 YUAN
15.5500 g., 0.9990 Gold 0.4994 oz. AGW, 27 mm. **Obv:** Temple of Heaven **Rev:** Two pandas seated with bamboo

Date	Mintage	F	VF	XF	Unc	BU
2006	25,600	—	—	—	—	675

KM# 1711 200 YUAN
15.5500 g., 0.9990 Gold 0.4994 oz. AGW **Obv:** Temple of Heaven **Rev:** Two pandas, one walking, one seated

Date	Mintage	F	VF	XF	Unc	BU
2007	60,000	—	—	—	—	650

KM# 1870 200 YUAN
15.5000 g., 0.9990 Gold 0.4978 oz. AGW

Date	Mintage	F	VF	XF	Unc	BU
2009	—	—	—	—	—	650

KM# 1927 200 YUAN
15.5500 g., 0.9990 Gold 0.4994 oz. AGW **Obv:** Temple of Heaven **Rev:** Two panda, one lying on back

Date	Mintage	F	VF	XF	Unc	BU
2010	120,000	—	—	—	—	700

KM# 1405 500 YUAN
31.1050 g., 0.9999 Gold 0.9999 oz. AGW **Rev:** Panda

Date	Mintage	F	VF	XF	Unc	BU
2001	41,411	—	—	—	—	BV+15%

KM# 1371 500 YUAN
31.1035 g., 0.9990 Gold 0.9990 oz. AGW, 32 mm. **Obv:** Temple of Heaven **Rev:** Panda walking through bamboo **Edge:** Reeded **Note:** Prev. Y#1088.

Date	Mintage	F	VF	XF	Unc	BU
2001	—	—	—	—	—	BV+15%
2001 D	150,000	—	—	—	—	BV+15%

KM# 1460   500 YUAN
31.1050 g., 0.9999 Gold 0.9999 oz. AGW **Rev:** Panda

Date	Mintage	F	VF	XF	Unc	BU
2002	28,345	—	—	—	—	BV+20%

KM# 1474   500 YUAN
31.1320 g., 0.9999 Gold 1.0008 oz. AGW **Subject:** Panda
Note: Large and small date varieties exist. Prev. Y#1164.

Date	Mintage	F	VF	XF	Unc	BU
2003	36,300	—	—	—	—	BV+15%

KM# 1537   500 YUAN
31.1035 g., 0.9999 Gold 0.9999 oz. AGW **Subject:** Panda
Note: Large and small date varieties exist. Prev. Y#1176.

Date	Mintage	F	VF	XF	Unc	BU
2004	55,000	—	—	—	—	BV+10%

KM# 1582   500 YUAN
31.1050 g., 0.9990 Gold 0.9990 oz. AGW, 32 mm. **Obv:** Temple of Heaven **Rev:** Panda but and mom seated in bamboo

Date	Mintage	F	VF	XF	Unc	BU
2005	50,300	BV+10%				

KM# 1657   500 YUAN
31.1050 g., 0.9990 Gold 0.9990 oz. AGW, 32 mm. **Obv:** Temple of Heaven **Rev:** Two panda's seated with bamboo

Date	Mintage	F	VF	XF	Unc	BU
2006	115,600	BV+10%				

KM# 1713   500 YUAN
31.1050 g., 0.9990 Gold 0.9990 oz. AGW, 32 mm. **Obv:** Temple of Heaven **Rev:** Two pandas, one walking, one seated

Date	Mintage	F	VF	XF	Unc	BU
2007	150,000	BV+10%				

KM# 1821   500 YUAN
31.1050 g., 0.9990 Gold 0.9990 oz. AGW, 32 mm. **Rev:** Panda cub pawing mom

Date	Mintage	F	VF	XF	Unc	BU
2008	—	BV+10%				

KM# 1872   500 YUAN
31.1050 g., 0.9990 Gold 0.9990 oz. AGW

Date	Mintage	F	VF	XF	Unc	BU
2009	—	BV+10%				

KM# 1926   500 YUAN
31.1050 g., 0.9990 Gold 0.9990 oz. AGW **Obv:** Temple of Heaven **Rev:** Two pandas, one lying on back

Date	Mintage	F	VF	XF	Unc	BU
2010	300,000	—	—	—	—	1,300

KM# 1581   2000 YUAN
155.0000 g., 0.9990 Gold 4.9782 oz. AGW, 60 mm. **Obv:** Temple of Heaven **Rev:** Panda cub and mom seated in bamboo

Date	Mintage	F	VF	XF	Unc	BU
2005 Proof	1,000	BV+25%				

KM# 1656   2000 YUAN
155.5500 g., 0.9990 Gold 4.9958 oz. AGW, 60 mm. **Obv:** Temple of Heaven **Rev:** Two pandas seated with bamboo

Date	Mintage	F	VF	XF	Unc	BU
2006 Proof	1,000	BV+25%				

KM# 1714   2000 YUAN
155.5500 g., 0.9990 Gold 4.9958 oz. AGW, 60 mm. **Obv:** Temple of Heaven **Rev:** Two pandas, one walking, one seated

Date	Mintage	F	VF	XF	Unc	BU
2007 Proof	1,000	BV+25%				

KM# 1822   2000 YUAN
155.5000 g., 0.9990 Gold 4.9942 oz. AGW, 60 mm. **Rev:** Panda cub pawing mom

Date	Mintage	F	VF	XF	Unc	BU
2008 Proof	1,000	BV+25%				

KM# 1873   2000 YUAN
155.5000 g., 0.9990 Gold 4.9942 oz. AGW

Date	Mintage	F	VF	XF	Unc	BU
2009 Proof	1,000	BV+25%				

KM# 1914   2000 YUAN
155.5000 g., 0.9990 Gold 4.9942 oz. AGW **Subject:** Year of the Tiger **Rev:** Multicolor

Date	Mintage	F	VF	XF	Unc	BU
2010 Proof	1,800	Value: 6,500				

KM# 1933   2000 YUAN
155.5000 g., 0.9990 Gold 4.9942 oz. AGW **Obv:** Temple of Heaven **Rev:** Two pandas, one lying on back

Date	Mintage	F	VF	XF	Unc	BU
2010 Proof	1,000	Value: 6,750				

KM# 1372   10000 YUAN
1000.0000 g., 0.9990 Gold 32.117 oz. AGW **Subject:** Panda
Note: Large and small date varieties exist. Prev. #Y1138.

Date	Mintage	F	VF	XF	Unc	BU
2001	68	—	—	—	—	BV+35%

KM# A1475   10000 YUAN
1000.0000 g., 0.9999 Gold 32.146 oz. AGW **Subject:** Panda
Note: Large and small date varieties exist. Prev. #Y1165.

Date	Mintage	F	VF	XF	Unc	BU
2002	68	—	—	—	—	BV+35%

KM# 1475   10000 YUAN
1000.0000 g., 0.9990 Gold 32.117 oz. AGW, 100 mm.
Rev: Panda and bamboo

Date	Mintage	F	VF	XF	Unc	BU
2003 Proof	68	BV+35%				

KM# 1538   10000 YUAN
1000.0000 g., 0.9999 Gold 32.146 oz. AGW **Subject:** Panda
Note: Large and small date varieties exist. Prev. #Y1177.

Date	Mintage	F	VF	XF	Unc	BU
2004	68	—	—	—	—	BV+35%

KM# A1580   10000 YUAN
1000.0000 g., 0.9990 Gold 32.117 oz. AGW, 90 mm. **Obv:** Temple of Heaven **Rev:** Panda cut and mom seated in bamboo

Date	Mintage	F	VF	XF	Unc	BU
2005 Proof	100	BV+25%				

KM# 1655   10000 YUAN
1000.0000 g., 0.9990 Gold 32.117 oz. AGW, 90 mm.
Obv: Temple of Heaven **Rev:** Two pandas seated with bamboo

Date	Mintage	F	VF	XF	Unc	BU
2006 Proof	200	BV+20%				

KM# 1715   10000 YUAN
1000.0000 g., 0.9990 Gold 32.117 oz. AGW **Obv:** Temple of Heaven **Rev:** Two pandas, one walking, one seated

Date	Mintage	F	VF	XF	Unc	BU
2007 Proof	200	BV+20%				

KM# 1823   10000 YUAN
1000.0000 g., 0.9990 Gold 32.117 oz. AGW, 90 mm.
Rev: Panda cub pawing mom

Date	Mintage	F	VF	XF	Unc	BU
2008 Proof	200	BV+20%				

KM# 1874   10000 YUAN
1000.0000 g., 0.9990 Gold 32.117 oz. AGW

Date	Mintage	F	VF	XF	Unc	BU
2009 Proof	200	BV+20%				

KM# 1932   10000 YUAN
1000.0000 g., 0.9990 Gold 32.117 oz. AGW **Obv:** Temple of Heaven **Rev:** Two pandas, one lying on back

Date	Mintage	F	VF	XF	Unc	BU
2010 Proof	200	Value: 40,500				

GOLD BULLION COINAGE
Lunar Series

KM# 1967   20 YUAN
3.1100 g., 0.9990 Gold 0.0999 oz. AGW **Subject:** Year of the Rabbit

Date	Mintage	F	VF	XF	Unc	BU
2011 Proof	80,000	Value: 150				

KM# 1374   50 YUAN
3.1103 g., 0.9990 Gold 0.0999 oz. AGW **Subject:** Year of the Snake **Note:** Prev. Y#1141.1; 1043.

Date	Mintage	F	VF	XF	Unc	BU
2001	48,000	—	—	—	—	175

KM# 1376   50 YUAN
3.1105 g., 0.9999 Gold 0.1000 oz. AGW **Subject:** Year of the Snake **Rev:** Multicolor. **Note:** Prev. Y#1141.2.

Date	Mintage	F	VF	XF	Unc	BU
2001	30,000	—	—	—	—	300

KM# 1419.1   50 YUAN
3.1050 g., 0.9999 Gold 0.0998 oz. AGW **Subject:** Year of the Horse **Note:** Prev. Y#1143.1.

Date	Mintage	F	VF	XF	Unc	BU
2002	48,000	—	—	—	—	200

KM# 1419.2   50 YUAN
3.1050 g., 0.9999 Gold 0.0998 oz. AGW **Subject:** Year of the Horse **Rev:** Multicolor. **Note:** Prev. Y#1143.2.

Date	Mintage	F	VF	XF	Unc	BU
2002	30,000	—	—	—	—	350

KM# 1478.1   50 YUAN
3.1103 g., 0.9999 Gold 0.1000 oz. AGW **Subject:** Year of the Goat **Note:** Prev. Y#1155.1.

Date	Mintage	F	VF	XF	Unc	BU
2003	48,000	—	—	—	—	225

KM# 1478.2   50 YUAN
3.1105 g., 0.9999 Gold 0.1000 oz. AGW **Subject:** Year of the Goat **Rev:** Multicolor. **Note:** Prev. Y#1155.2

Date	Mintage	F	VF	XF	Unc	BU
2003	30,000	—	—	—	—	325

KM# 1546.1   50 YUAN
3.1103 g., 0.9999 Gold 0.1000 oz. AGW **Subject:** Year of the Monkey **Note:** Prev. Y#1167.1.

Date	Mintage	F	VF	XF	Unc	BU
2004	48,000	—	—	—	—	225

KM# 1546.2   50 YUAN
3.1103 g., 0.9999 Gold 0.1000 oz. AGW **Subject:** Year of the Monkey **Rev:** Multicolor. **Note:** Prev. Y#1167.2

Date	Mintage	F	VF	XF	Unc	BU
2004	30,000	—	—	—	—	350

KM# 1608   50 YUAN
3.1100 g., Gold, 18 mm. **Subject:** Year of the rooster
Obv: Classical rooster **Rev:** Multicolor rooster

Date	Mintage	F	VF	XF	Unc	BU
2005 Proof	30,000	Value: 300				

KM# 1609   50 YUAN
3.1100 g., 0.9990 Gold 0.0999 oz. AGW, 18 mm. **Subject:** Year of the rooster **Obv:** Classical rooster **Rev:** Rooster, hen and chicks

Date	Mintage	F	VF	XF	Unc	BU
2005 Proof	60,000	Value: 200				

KM# 1680   50 YUAN
3.1103 g., 0.9990 Gold 0.0999 oz. AGW, 18 mm. **Obv:** Dog-shaped belt-hook from ancient Chinese bronze ware, decorative design of dog tail-shaped plant leaves **Rev:** 2 smart dogs **Note:** Prev. Y#1226; KM#1658.

Date	Mintage	F	VF	XF	Unc	BU
2006	60,000	—	—	—	—	150

KM# 1721   50 YUAN
3.1000 g., 0.9990 Gold 0.0996 oz. AGW, 18 mm. **Subject:** Year of the pig **Obv:** Classical pig **Rev:** Pig walking right

Date	Mintage	F	VF	XF	Unc	BU
2007 Proof	—	Value: 150				

KM# 1722   50 YUAN
3.1000 g., 0.9990 Gold 0.0996 oz. AGW, 18 mm. **Subject:** Year of the pig **Obv:** Classical pig **Rev:** Multicolor sow and piglets sucking

Date	Mintage	F	VF	XF	Unc	BU
2007 Proof	30,000	Value: 450				

KM# 1835   50 YUAN
3.1100 g., 0.9990 Gold 0.0999 oz. AGW **Subject:** Year of the rat **Rev:** Multicolor **Shape:** 18

Date	Mintage	F	VF	XF	Unc	BU
2008 Proof	30,000	Value: 300				

KM# 1836   50 YUAN
3.1100 g., 0.9990 Gold 0.0999 oz. AGW, 18 mm. **Subject:** Year of the rat

Date	Mintage	F	VF	XF	Unc	BU
2008 Proof	60,000	Value: 150				

KM# 1880   50 YUAN
3.1100 g., 0.9990 Gold 0.0999 oz. AGW **Subject:** Year of the Ox colorized

Date	Mintage	F	VF	XF	Unc	BU
2009 Proof	30,000	Value: 325				

KM# 1881   50 YUAN
3.1100 g., 0.9990 Gold 0.0999 oz. AGW **Subject:** Year of the Ox

Date	Mintage	F	VF	XF	Unc	BU
2009 Proof	80,000	Value: 150				

KM# 1917   50 YUAN
3.1100 g., 0.9990 Gold 0.0999 oz. AGW **Subject:** Year of the Tiger

Date	Mintage	F	VF	XF	Unc	BU
2010 Proof	80,000	Value: 150				

KM# 1918   50 YUAN
3.1100 g., 0.9990 Gold 0.0999 oz. AGW **Subject:** Year of the Tiger **Rev:** Multicolor

Date	Mintage	F	VF	XF	Unc	BU
2010 Proof	80,000	Value: 150				

KM# 1966   50 YUAN
3.1100 g., 0.9990 Gold 0.0999 oz. AGW **Subject:** Year of the Rabbit

Date	Mintage	F	VF	XF	Unc	BU
2011 Proof	80,000	Value: 150				

KM# 1383   200 YUAN
15.5518 g., 0.9990 Gold 0.4995 oz. AGW **Subject:** Year of the Snake **Rev:** Fan **Note:** Prev. Y#1044.

Date	Mintage	F	VF	XF	Unc	BU
2001	6,600	—	—	—	—	850

KM# 1380   200 YUAN
15.5518 g., 0.9990 Gold 0.4995 oz. AGW **Subject:** Year of the Snake **Shape:** Flower **Note:** Prev. Y#1045.

Date	Mintage	F	VF	XF	Unc	BU
2001 Proof	2,300	Value: 1,000				

KM# 1426   200 YUAN
15.5000 g., 0.9990 Gold 0.4978 oz. AGW **Subject:** Year of the Horse **Shape:** Flower **Note:** Prev. Y#1150.

Date	Mintage	F	VF	XF	Unc	BU
2002	2,300	—	—	—	—	1,200

KM# 1424   200 YUAN
15.5500 g., 0.9990 Gold 0.4994 oz. AGW **Subject:** Year of the Horse **Shape:** Fan

Date	Mintage	F	VF	XF	Unc	BU
2002	6,600	—	—	—	—	900

KM# 1475.1   200 YUAN
15.5517 g., 0.9999 Gold 0.4999 oz. AGW **Subject:** Year of the Goat **Shape:** Fan

Date	Mintage	F	VF	XF	Unc	BU
2003	6,600	—	—	—	—	800

KM# 1481   200 YUAN
15.5519 g., 0.9999 Gold 0.4999 oz. AGW **Subject:** Year of the Goat **Shape:** Flower **Note:** Prev. Y#1161.

Date	Mintage	F	VF	XF	Unc	BU
2003	2,300	—	—	—	—	1,200

KM# 1486   200 YUAN
15.5130 g., 0.9990 Gold 0.4982 oz. AGW, 58 x 30 mm. **Subject:** Year of the sheep **Shape:** Fan

Date	Mintage	F	VF	XF	Unc	BU
2003 Proof	6,600	Value: 1,000				

KM# 1554   200 YUAN
15.5519 g., 0.9999 Gold 0.4999 oz. AGW **Subject:** Year of the Monkey **Shape:** Fan **Note:** Prev. Y#1168.

Date	Mintage	F	VF	XF	Unc	BU
2004	6,600	—	—	—	—	1,000

KM# 1549   200 YUAN
15.5519 g., 0.9999 Gold 0.4999 oz. AGW **Subject:** Year of the Monkey **Shape:** Flower **Note:** Prev. Y#1169.

Date	Mintage	F	VF	XF	Unc	BU
2004	2,300	—	—	—	—	1,200

KM# 1606   200 YUAN
15.5500 g., 0.9990 Gold 0.4994 oz. AGW, 27 mm.
Series: Classical rooster **Subject:** Year of the rooster
Obv: Rooster, hen and chicks **Shape:** Scallops

Date	Mintage	F	VF	XF	Unc	BU
2005 Proof	8,000	Value: 825				

KM# 1607 200 YUAN
15.5500 g., 0.9990 Gold 0.4994 oz. AGW, 58 x 30 mm. **Subject:** Year of the rooster **Obv:** Temple **Rev:** Rooster, hen and chicks **Shape:** Fan

Date	Mintage	F	VF	XF	Unc	BU
2005 Proof	6,600	Value: 800				

KM# 1679 200 YUAN
15.6300 g., Gold **Subject:** Year of the Dog **Obv:** Qing Yuan Gate of the China Great Wall **Rev:** 2 dogs at play **Shape:** 30° Fan **Note:** Prev. Y#1220; KM#1652.

Date	Mintage	F	VF	XF	Unc	BU
2006 Proof	6,600	Value: 925				

KM# 1677 200 YUAN
15.6300 g., Gold, 27 mm. **Subject:** Year of the Dog **Obv:** Dog-shaped belt-hook from ancient Chinese bronze ware, decorative design of dog tail-shaped plant leaves **Rev:** 2 smart dogs **Shape:** Scalloped **Note:** Prev. Y#1224; KM#1656.

Date	Mintage	F	VF	XF	Unc	BU
2006 Proof	8,000	Value: 1,150				

KM# 1723 200 YUAN
15.5000 g., 0.9990 Gold 0.4978 oz. AGW, 58 x 39 mm. **Subject:** Year of the pig **Obv:** Temple **Rev:** Sow and four piglets **Shape:** Fan

Date	Mintage	F	VF	XF	Unc	BU
2007 Proof	6,600	Value: 985				

KM# 1724 200 YUAN
15.5500 g., 0.9990 Gold 0.4994 oz. AGW, 27 mm. **Subject:** Year of the pig **Obv:** Classical pig **Rev:** Pig walking right **Shape:** Flower

Date	Mintage	F	VF	XF	Unc	BU
2007 Proof	8,000	Value: 850				

KM# 1837 200 YUAN
15.5000 g., 0.9990 Gold 0.4978 oz. AGW, 27 mm. **Subject:** Year of the rat **Shape:** Flower

Date	Mintage	F	VF	XF	Unc	BU
2008 Proof	8,000	Value: 850				

KM# 1838 200 YUAN
15.5000 g., 0.9990 Gold 0.4978 oz. AGW, 58 x 39 mm. **Subject:** Year of the rat **Shape:** Fan

Date	Mintage	F	VF	XF	Unc	BU
2008 Proof	6,600	Value: 900				

KM# 1883 200 YUAN
15.5000 g., 0.9990 Gold 0.4978 oz. AGW **Subject:** Year of the Ox **Shape:** Fan

Date	Mintage	F	VF	XF	Unc	BU
2009 Proof	6,600	Value: 900				

KM# 1882 200 YUAN
15.5000 g., 0.9990 Gold 0.4978 oz. AGW **Subject:** Year of the Ox **Shape:** Flower

Date	Mintage	F	VF	XF	Unc	BU
2009 Proof	8,000	Value: 850				

KM# 1915 200 YUAN
15.5500 g., 0.9990 Gold 0.4994 oz. AGW **Subject:** Year of the Tiger **Shape:** Arc

Date	Mintage	F	VF	XF	Unc	BU
2010	6,600	—	—	—	—	700

KM# 1916 200 YUAN
15.5500 g., 0.9990 Gold 0.4994 oz. AGW **Subject:** Year of the Tiger **Shape:** Scalloped

Date	Mintage	F	VF	XF	Unc	BU
2010 Proof	8,000	Value: 700				

KM# 1964 200 YUAN
15.5000 g., 0.9990 Gold 0.4978 oz. AGW **Subject:** Year of the Rabbit **Shape:** Arc

Date	Mintage	F	VF	XF	Unc	BU
2011	6,600	—	—	—	—	700

KM# 1965 200 YUAN
15.5500 g., 0.9990 Gold 0.4994 oz. AGW **Subject:** Year of the Rabbit **Shape:** Scallop

Date	Mintage	F	VF	XF	Unc	BU
2011 Proof	8,000	Value: 700				

KM# 1378 2000 YUAN
155.5175 g., 0.9990 Gold 4.9948 oz. AGW **Subject:** Year of the Snake **Shape:** Rectangle **Note:** Prev. #Y1046.

Date	Mintage	F	VF	XF	Unc	BU
2001 Proof	118	Value: 20,000				

KM# 1422 2000 YUAN
155.5175 g., 0.9999 Gold 4.9993 oz. AGW **Subject:** Year of the Horse **Shape:** Rectangle **Note:** Prev. #Y1152.

Date	Mintage	F	VF	XF	Unc	BU
2002 Proof	118	Value: 20,000				

KM# 1483 2000 YUAN
155.5190 g., 0.9999 Gold 4.9993 oz. AGW **Subject:** Year of the Goat **Note:** Prev. #Y1163.

Date	Mintage	F	VF	XF	Unc	BU
2003 Proof	118	Value: 20,000				

KM# 1552 2000 YUAN
155.1750 g., 0.9999 Gold 4.9883 oz. AGW **Subject:** Year of the Monkey **Note:** Prev. #Y1170.

Date	Mintage	F	VF	XF	Unc	BU
2004 Proof	118	Value: 20,000				

KM# 1605 2000 YUAN
155.0000 g., 0.9990 Gold 4.9782 oz. AGW, 64 x 40 mm. **Subject:** Year of the rooster **Obv:** Classical rooster **Rev:** Rooster, hen and chicks **Shape:** Rectangle

Date	Mintage	F	VF	XF	Unc	BU
2005 Proof	118	Value: 20,000				

KM# 1678 2000 YUAN
155.5500 g., 0.9990 Gold 4.9958 oz. AGW, 64 x 40 mm. **Subject:** Year of the dog **Obv:** Classical dog **Rev:** Two dogs

Date	Mintage	F	VF	XF	Unc	BU
2006 Proof	118	Value: 20,000				

KM# 1726 2000 YUAN
155.5500 g., 0.9990 Gold 4.9958 oz. AGW, 64 x 40 mm. **Subject:** Year of the pig **Obv:** Classical pig **Rev:** Sow and four pigletts **Shape:** Rectangle

Date	Mintage	F	VF	XF	Unc	BU
2007 Proof	118	Value: 20,000				

KM# 1840 2000 YUAN
155.0000 g., 0.9990 Gold 4.9782 oz. AGW, 64 x 40 mm. **Subject:** Year of the rat **Shape:** Rectangle

Date	Mintage	F	VF	XF	Unc	BU
2008 Proof	118	Value: 20,000				

KM# 1885 2000 YUAN
155.5000 g., 0.9990 Gold 4.9942 oz. AGW **Subject:** Year of the Ox

Date	Mintage	F	VF	XF	Unc	BU
2009 Proof	118	Value: 20,000				

KM# 1913 2000 YUAN
155.2000 g., 0.9990 Gold 4.9846 oz. AGW **Subject:** Year of the Tiger **Shape:** Rectangle

Date	Mintage	F	VF	XF	Unc	BU
2010 Proof	118	Value: 6,500				

KM# 1962 2000 YUAN
155.5000 g., 0.9990 Gold 4.9942 oz. AGW **Subject:** Year of the Rabbit

Date	Mintage	F	VF	XF	Unc	BU
2011 Proof	118	Value: 6,500				

KM# 1963 2000 YUAN
155.5000 g., 0.9990 Gold 4.9942 oz. AGW **Subject:** Year of the Rabbit **Rev:** Multicolor

Date	Mintage	F	VF	XF	Unc	BU
2011 Proof	1,800	Value: 6,500				

KM# 1381 10000 YUAN
1000.0000 g., 0.9990 Gold 32.117 oz. AGW **Subject:** Year of the Snake **Shape:** Scalloped **Note:** Prev. #Y1047.

Date	Mintage	F	VF	XF	Unc	BU
2001 Proof	15	Value: 125,000				

KM# 1427 10000 YUAN
1000.0000 g., 0.9999 Gold 32.146 oz. AGW **Subject:** Year of the Horse **Shape:** Scalloped **Note:** Prev. #Y1153.

Date	Mintage	F	VF	XF	Unc	BU
2002 Proof	15	Value: 90,000				

KM# 1482 10000 YUAN
1000.0000 g., 0.9999 Gold 32.146 oz. AGW **Subject:** Year of the Goat **Note:** Prev. #Y1166.

Date	Mintage	F	VF	XF	Unc	BU
2003 Proof	15	Value: 75,000				

KM# 1550 10000 YUAN
1000.0000 g., 0.9999 Gold 32.146 oz. AGW **Subject:** Year of the Monkey **Note:** Prev. #Y1171.

Date	Mintage	F	VF	XF	Unc	BU
2004 Proof	15	Value: 90,000				

KM# 1727 10000 YUAN
1000.0000 g., 0.9990 Gold 32.117 oz. AGW, 100 mm. **Subject:** Year of the pig **Obv:** Classical pig **Rev:** Three pigs **Shape:** Scalloped

Date	Mintage	F	VF	XF	Unc	BU
2007 Proof	118	Value: 70,000				

KM# 1841 10000 YUAN
1000.0000 g., 0.9990 Gold 32.117 oz. AGW, 100 mm. **Subject:** Year of the rat

Date	Mintage	F	VF	XF	Unc	BU
2008 Proof	118	Value: 70,000				

KM# 1912 10000 YUAN
1000.0000 g., 0.9990 Gold 32.117 oz. AGW **Subject:** Year of the Tiger **Shape:** Scalloped

Date	Mintage	F	VF	XF	Unc	BU
2010 Proof	118	Value: 40,250				

KM# 1961 10000 YUAN
1000.0000 g., 0.9990 Gold 32.117 oz. AGW **Subject:** Year of the Rabbit

Date	Mintage	F	VF	XF	Unc	BU
2011 Proof	118	Value: 40,500				

KM# 1728 100000 YUAN
10000.0000 g., 0.9990 Gold 321.17 oz. AGW, 180 mm. **Subject:** Year of the pig **Obv:** Classical pig **Rev:** Sow with four pigletts sucking

Date	Mintage	F	VF	XF	Unc	BU
2007 Proof	18	Value: 500,000				

KM# 1842 100000 YUAN
10000.0000 g., 0.9990 Gold 321.17 oz. AGW, 180 mm.

Date	Mintage	F	VF	XF	Unc	BU
2008 Proof	18	Value: 500,000				

KM# 1886 100000 YUAN
1000.0000 g., 0.9990 Gold 32.117 oz. AGW **Subject:** Year of the Ox

Date	Mintage	F	VF	XF	Unc	BU
2009 Proof	118	Value: 70,000				

KM# 1911 100000 YUAN
10000.0000 g., 0.9990 Gold 321.17 oz. AGW **Subject:** Year of the Tiger

Date	Mintage	F	VF	XF	Unc	BU
2010 Proof	18	Value: 402,500				

KM# 1960 100000 YUAN
10000.0000 g., 0.9990 Gold 321.17 oz. AGW **Subject:** Year of the Rabbit

Date	Mintage	F	VF	XF	Unc	BU
2011 Proof	18	Value: 402,000				

PALLADIUM BULLION COINAGE

Panda Series

KM# A1531 100 YUAN
15.5590 g., 0.9990 Palladium 0.4997 oz., 14 mm. **Rev:** Panda walking with cub

Date	Mintage	F	VF	XF	Unc	BU
2004 Proof	8,000	Value: 350				

KM# 1590 100 YUAN
15.5500 g., 0.9990 Palladium 0.4994 oz., 30 mm. **Obv:** Temple of Heaven **Rev:** Panda cub and mom seated in bamboo

Date	Mintage	F	VF	XF	Unc	BU
2005 Proof	8,000	Value: 400				

PLATINUM BULLION COINAGE

Panda Series

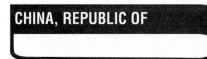

KM# 1470 50 YUAN
1.5500 g., 0.9995 Platinum 0.0498 oz. APW, 14.03 mm. **Obv:** Temple of Heaven, incuse legend **Rev:** Panda standing facing eating bamboo **Edge:** Reeded

Date	Mintage	F	VF	XF	Unc	BU
2003 Proof	50,000	Value: 135				

KM# 1532 50 YUAN
1.4500 g., 0.9995 Platinum 0.0466 oz. APW, 14.02 mm. **Obv:** Temple of Heaven, incuse legend **Rev:** Panda standing facing with cub **Edge:** Reeded

Date	Mintage	F	VF	XF	Unc	BU
2004 Proof	50,000	Value: 135				

KM# 1415 100 YUAN
3.1103 g., 0.9995 Platinum 0.0999 oz. APW, 18 mm. **Subject:** Panda Coinage 20th Anniversary **Obv:** Seated panda design of 1982 **Rev:** Walking panda design of 2002 **Edge:** Reeded **Note:** Prev. Y#1115.

Date	Mintage	F	VF	XF	Unc	BU
2002 Proof	20,000	Value: 250				

KM# 1591 100 YUAN
3.1100 g., Platinum APW, 18 mm. **Obv:** Temple of Heaven **Rev:** Panda cub and mom seated in bamboo

Date	Mintage	F	VF	XF	Unc	BU
2005 Proof	30,000	Value: 185				

CHINA, REPUBLIC OF

TAIWAN

The Republic of China, comprising Taiwan (an island located 90 miles (145 km.) off the southeastern coast of mainland China), the offshore islands of Quemoy and Matsu and nearby islets of the Pescadores chain, has an area of 14,000 sq. mi. (35,980 sq. km.) and a population of 20.2 million. Capital: Taipei. During the past decade, manufacturing has replaced agriculture in importance. Fruits, vegetables, plywood, textile yarns and fabrics and clothing are exported.

The coins of Nationalist China do not carry A.D. dating, but are dated according to the year of the republic, which was established in 1911. However, republican years are added to 1911 to find the western year. Thus republican year 90 plus 1911 equals Gregorian calendar year 2001AD.

REPUBLIC

STANDARD COINAGE

Y# 550 1/2 YUAN
3.0000 g., Bronze, 18 mm. **Obv:** Orchid **Rev:** Value and Chinese symbols **Edge:** Plain

Date	Mintage	F	VF	XF	Unc	BU
90(2001) Proof	—	Value: 10.00				
92(2003)	—	—	0.15	0.30	1.00	1.25
92(2003) Proof	—	Value: 10.00				

Y# 551 YUAN

3.8000 g., Bronze, 19.92 mm. **Obv:** Bust of Chiang Kai-shek left **Rev:** Chinese value in center, 1 below **Edge:** Reeded

Date	Mintage	F	VF	XF	Unc	BU
90(2001) Proof	—	Value: 12.50				
92(2003)	—	—	—	0.15	0.30	0.45
92(2003) Proof	—	Value: 12.50				
95(2006)	—	—	—	0.15	0.30	0.45

Y# 552 5 YUAN

Copper-Nickel **Obv:** Bust of Chiang Kai-shek left **Rev:** Chinese symbols in center, 5 below

Date	Mintage	F	VF	XF	Unc	BU
90(2001) Proof	—	Value: 12.50				
92(2003)	—	—	0.15	0.25	0.50	0.75
92(2003) Proof	—	Value: 12.50				

Y# 553 10 YUAN

7.5000 g., Copper-Nickel, 26 mm. **Obv:** Bust of Chiang Kai-shek left **Rev:** Chinese symbols in center, 10 below

Date	Mintage	F	VF	XF	Unc	BU
90(2001) Proof	—	Value: 15.00				
92(2003)	—	—	0.25	0.45	0.75	1.00
92(2003) Proof	—	Value: 15.00				
95(2006)	—	—	0.25	0.45	0.75	1.00
96(2007)	—	—	0.25	0.45	0.75	1.00
96(2007) Proof	—	Value: 15.00				

Y# 567 10 YUAN

7.4300 g., Copper-Nickel, 26 mm. **Subject:** 90th Anniversary of the Republic **Obv:** Bust of Sun Yat-sen facing **Rev:** Holographic design and denomination **Edge:** Reeded

Date	Mintage	F	VF	XF	Unc	BU
90 (2001)	30,000,000	—	—	—	2.50	3.00

Y# 565 20 YUAN

Bi-Metallic Copper-Nickel center in Brass ring., 26.8 mm. **Obv:** Male portrait **Rev:** Three boats **Edge:** Reeded

Date	Mintage	F	VF	XF	Unc	BU
90 (2001)	—	—	—	—	3.50	4.50
90 (2001) Proof	—	Value: 18.00				
92(2003)	—	—	—	—	3.50	4.50
92(2003) Proof	—	Value: 18.00				

Y# 568 50 YUAN

10.0000 g., Brass, 28 mm. **Obv:** Bust **Rev:** Denomination above latent image denomination **Edge:** Reeding and denomination

Date	Mintage	F	VF	XF	Unc	BU
90-2001 Proof	—	Value: 20.00				
91-2002	—	—	—	—	7.50	10.00
92-2003	—	—	—	—	7.50	10.00
92-2003 Proof	—	Value: 20.00				
95-2006	—	—	—	—	7.50	10.00

Y# 570 50 YUAN

15.5680 g., 0.9990 Silver 0.5000 oz. ASW, 33 mm. **Subject:** World Cup Baseball **Obv:** Player at bat with ball background **Rev:** Mount Jade above denomination **Edge:** Reeded

Date	Mintage	F	VF	XF	Unc	BU
90 (2001)	130,000	—	—	—	25.00	27.50

Y# 569 50 YUAN

15.5680 g., 0.9990 Silver 0.5000 oz. ASW, 33 mm. **Subject:** 90th Anniversary of the Republic **Obv:** Portrait of Sun Yat-sen **Rev:** Latent image above denomination **Edge:** Reeded

Date	Mintage	F	VF	XF	Unc	BU
90(2001)	230,000	—	—	—	25.00	27.50

Y# 571 50 YUAN

31.1035 g., 0.9990 Silver 0.9990 oz. ASW, 38 mm. **Subject:** Third National Expressway **Obv:** Multicolor island map **Rev:** Kao Ping Hsi bridge **Edge:** Reeded

Date	Mintage	F	VF	XF	Unc	BU
Yr 93- 2004	20,000	—	—	—	40.00	45.00

MINT SETS

KM#	Date	Mintage	Identification	Issue Price	Mkt Val
MS9	92(2003) (6)	—	Y550-553, 565, 568 plus C-N Year of the Goat medal	—	20.00

PROOF SETS

KM#	Date	Mintage	Identification	Issue Price	Mkt Val
PS10	90(2001) (6)	210,000	Y#550-553, 565, 568 plus medal	29.40	90.00
PS12	92(2003) (6)	—	Y550-553, 565, 568 plus silver Year of the Goat Medal	—	100

COLOMBIA

The Republic of Colombia, in the northwestern corner of South America, has an area of 440,831 sq. mi. (1,138,910 sq. km.) and a population of *42.3 million. Capital: Bogota. The economy is primarily agricultural with a mild, rich coffee being the chief crop. Colombia has the world's largest platinum deposits and important reserves of coal, iron ore, petroleum and limestone; other precious metals and emeralds are also mined. Coffee, crude oil, bananas, sugar and emeralds are exported.

REPUBLIC

DECIMAL COINAGE

100 Centavos = 1 Peso

KM# 282.2 20 PESOS

3.6000 g., Copper-Aluminum-Nickel, 20.25 mm. **Obv:** Flagged arms, 68 beads circle around the rim **Rev:** Denomination within wreath

Date	Mintage	F	VF	XF	Unc	BU
2003	15,900,000	—	—	—	0.50	0.75

KM# 294 20 PESOS

2.0000 g., Copper-Zinc, 17.23 mm. **Obv:** Head of Simon Bolivar left **Rev:** Value **Edge:** Reeded

Date	Mintage	F	VF	XF	Unc	BU
2004	22,700,000	—	—	—	0.15	0.25
2005	56,100,000	—	—	—	0.15	0.25
2006	63,012,500	—	—	—	0.15	0.25
2007	87,300,000	—	—	—	0.15	0.25
2008	5,850,000	—	—	—	0.20	0.30

KM# 283.2 50 PESOS

4.6000 g., Copper-Nickel-Zinc, 21.8 mm. **Obv:** National arms, date below **Rev:** Denomination within wreath, 72 beads circle around rim **Edge:** Reeded

Date	Mintage	F	VF	XF	Unc	BU
2003	24,000,000	—	—	0.30	0.80	1.20
2004	51,700,000	—	—	0.30	0.80	1.20
2005	47,200,000	—	—	0.30	0.80	1.20
2006	22,000,000	—	—	0.30	0.80	1.20
2007	29,324,000	—	—	0.30	0.80	1.20
2008	67,500,000	—	—	0.30	0.80	1.20

KM# 285.2 100 PESOS

5.3100 g., Copper-Aluminum-Nickel, 23 mm. **Obv:** Flagged arms above date **Rev:** Denomination within wreath, numerals 6mm tall **Edge:** Lettered and segmented reeding **Edge Lettering:** CIEN PESOS (twice) **Note:** Edge varieties exist.

Date	Mintage	F	VF	XF	Unc	BU
2006	59,000,000	—	—	0.60	1.50	2.00
2007	55,000,000	—	—	0.60	1.50	2.00
2008	120,200,000	—	—	0.60	1.50	2.00

KM# 287 200 PESOS

7.0800 g., Copper-Zinc-Nickel, 24.4 mm. **Obv:** Denomination within lined circle, date below **Rev:** Quimbaya artwork **Edge:** Lettered **Edge Lettering:** MOTIVO QUIMBAYA - 200 PESOS

Date	Mintage	F	VF	XF	Unc	BU
2003	26,600,000	—	—	0.60	1.50	2.00
2004	31,200,000	—	—	0.60	1.50	2.00
2005	49,700,000	—	—	0.60	1.50	2.00
2006	75,400,000	—	—	0.60	1.50	2.00
2007	85,000,000	—	—	0.60	1.50	2.00
2008	110,400,000	—	—	0.60	1.50	2.00

KM# 286 500 PESOS
7.4300 g., Bi-Metallic Aluminum-Bronze center in Copper-Nickel ring, 23.58 mm. **Obv:** Guacari tree within circle
Rev: Denomination within circle, date below **Edge:** Segmented reeding

Date	Mintage	F	VF	XF	Unc	BU
2002	38,800,000	—	—	1.20	3.00	4.00
2003	37,900,000	—	—	1.20	3.00	4.00
2004	90,454,000	—	—	1.20	3.00	4.00
2005	97,664,000	—	—	1.20	3.00	4.00
2006	70,700,000	—	—	1.20	3.00	4.00
2007	109,624,000	—	—	1.20	3.00	4.00
2008	132,400,000	—	—	1.20	3.00	4.00

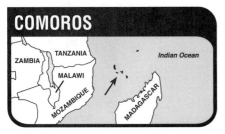

COMOROS

The Federal Islamic Republic of the Comoros, a volcanic archipelago located in the Mozambique Channel of the Indian Ocean 300 miles (483 km.) northwest of Madagascar, has an area of 719 sq. mi. (2,171 sq. km.) and a population of *714,000. Capital: Moroni. The economy of the islands is based on agriculture. There are practically no mineral resources. Vanilla, essence for perfumes, copra, and sisal are exported.

Ancient Phoenician traders were probably the first visitors to the Comoro Islands, but the first detailed knowledge of the area was gathered by Arab sailors. Arab dominion and culture were firmly established when the Portuguese, Dutch, and French arrived in the 16th century. In 1843 a Malagasy ruler ceded the island of Mayotte to France; the other three principal islands of the archipelago-Anjouan, Moheli, and Grand Comore came under French protection in 1886. The islands were joined administratively with Madagascar in 1912. The Comoros became partially autonomous, with the status of a French overseas territory, in 1946, and achieved complete internal autonomy in 1961. On Dec. 31, 1975, after 133 years of French association, the Comoro Islands became the independent Republic of the Comoros.

Mayotte retained the option of determining its future ties and in 1976 voted to remain French. Its present status is that of a French Territorial Collectivity. French currency now circulates there.

TITLES
Daulat Anjazanchiyah

MINT MARKS
- Paris, privy marks only
- Paris, horseshoe privy mark (2001)
A - Paris

MONETARY SYSTEM
100 Centimes = 1 Franc

FEDERAL ISLAMIC REPUBLIC

BANQUE CENTRAL COINAGE

KM# 14a 25 FRANCS
Steel, 20 mm. **Series:** F.A.O. **Obv:** Chickens **Rev:** Denomination above date

Date	Mintage	F	VF	XF	Unc	BU
2001(a) Horseshoe	—	0.20	0.40	0.80	2.00	—

KM# 16a 50 FRANCS
Nickel Plated Steel, 23.9 mm. **Obv:** Crescent and stars above denomination, date below **Rev:** Building with tall tower
Edge: Reeded

Date	Mintage	F	VF	XF	Unc	BU
2001(a)	—	0.25	0.50	1.00	2.50	3.50

KM# 18a 100 FRANCS
Copper-Nickel **Obv:** Crescent and stars above denomination, date below **Rev:** Boat and fish

Date	Mintage	F	VF	XF	Unc	BU
2003(a)	—	—	—	—	3.50	5.00

CONGO REPUBLIC

The Republic of the Congo (formerly the Peoples Republic of the Congo), located on the equator in west-central Africa, has an area of 132,047 sq. mi. (342,000 sq. km.) and a population of *2.98 million. Capital: Brazzaville. Agriculture forestry, mining, and food processing are the principal industries. Timber, industrial diamonds, potash, peanuts, and cocoa beans are exported.

NOTE: For earlier and related coinage see French Equatorial Africa and the Equatorial African States. For later coinage see Central African States.

MINT MARK
(a) - Paris, privy marks only

MONETARY SYSTEM
100 Centimes = 1 Franc

REPUBLIC
Republique du Congo
DECIMAL COINAGE

KM# 47 1000 FRANCS
15.0000 g., 0.9990 Silver 0.4818 oz. ASW, 35 mm. **Obv:** Seated woman with tablet **Rev:** Two soccer players and colosseum
Edge: Plain

Date	Mintage	F	VF	XF	Unc	BU
2001 Proof	—	Value: 40.00				

KM# 48 1000 FRANCS
20.0000 g., 0.9990 Silver 0.6423 oz. ASW, 38 mm. **Obv:** Seated woman with tablet **Rev:** Two soccer players and Mexican pyramid
Edge: Reeded

Date	Mintage	F	VF	XF	Unc	BU
2001 Proof	—	Value: 40.00				

KM# 50 1000 FRANCS
20.2000 g., Silver, 40 mm. **Series:** Endangered Wildlife
Obv: Seated woman with tablet **Obv. Legend:** REPUBLIQUE DU CONGO **Rev:** Gorilla seated with infant **Rev. Legend:** - LE MONDE ANIMAL EN PERIL **Edge:** Reeded

Date	Mintage	F	VF	XF	Unc	BU
2003 Proof	—	Value: 45.00				

KM# 51 1000 FRANCS
15.5000 g., Silver, 35.02 mm. **Obv:** Seated woman with tablet **Obv. Legend:** REPUBLIQUE DU CONGO **Rev:** Head of Michelangelo 3/4 right **Edge:** Plain

Date	Mintage	F	VF	XF	Unc	BU
2005 Proof	—	Value: 35.00				

CONGO DEMOCRATIC REPUBLIC

The Democratic Republic of the Congo (formerly the Republic of Zaire, and earlier the Belgian Congo), located in the south-central part of Africa, has an area of 905,568 sq. mi. (2,345,410 sq. km.) and a population of *47.4 million. Capital: Kinshasa. The mineral-rich country produces copper, tin, diamonds, gold, zinc, cobalt and uranium.

DEMOCRATIC REPUBLIC
REFORM COINAGE

KM# 76 25 CENTIMES
0.8800 g., Aluminum, 19.90 mm. **Obv:** Lion left **Rev:** Mongoose
Edge: Plain

Date	Mintage	F	VF	XF	Unc	BU
2002	—	—	—	—	0.75	1.00

KM# 77 25 CENTIMES
0.8500 g., Aluminum, 20 mm. **Obv:** Lion left **Rev:** Ram right, looking left **Edge:** Plain

Date	Mintage	F	VF	XF	Unc	BU
2002	—	—	—	—	0.75	1.00

KM# 83 25 CENTIMES
1.3000 g., Aluminum, 20 mm. **Obv:** Lion left **Rev:** Wild dog leaping right **Edge:** Plain

Date	Mintage	F	VF	XF	Unc	BU
2002	—	—	—	—	0.75	1.00

KM# 75   50 CENTIMES
2.2000 g., Aluminum, 26.97 mm. **Obv:** Lion left **Rev:** Soccer player right, bumping ball with head **Edge:** Plain

Date	Mintage	F	VF	XF	Unc	BU
2002	—	—	—	—	1.25	1.50

KM# 78   50 CENTIMES
2.1600 g., Aluminum, 27 mm. **Obv:** Lion left **Rev:** Giraffe right, looking left **Edge:** Plain

Date	Mintage	F	VF	XF	Unc	BU
2002	—	—	—	—	1.25	1.50

KM# 79   50 CENTIMES
2.2000 g., Aluminum, 26.92 mm. **Obv:** Lion left **Rev:** Gorilla facing, looking left **Edge:** Plain

Date	Mintage	F	VF	XF	Unc	BU
2002	—	—	—	—	1.00	1.25

KM# 80   50 CENTIMES
2.1600 g., Aluminum, 27 mm. **Obv:** Lion left **Rev:** Butterfly **Edge:** Plain

Date	Mintage	F	VF	XF	Unc	BU
2002	—	—	—	—	1.50	1.75

 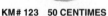

KM# 123   50 CENTIMES
3.9200 g., Stainless Steel, 22.3 mm. **Obv:** Lion left above denomination **Rev:** Verney L. Camereon **Edge:** Plain

Date	Mintage	F	VF	XF	Unc	BU
2002	—	—	—	—	1.00	1.25

KM# 81   FRANC
4.5700 g., Brass, 20.31 mm. **Obv:** Lion left **Rev:** Turtle **Edge:** Plain

Date	Mintage	F	VF	XF	Unc	BU
2002	—	—	—	—	1.25	1.50

KM# 82   FRANC
4.5200 g., Brass, 20.32 mm. **Obv:** Lion left **Rev:** Chicken **Edge:** Plain

Date	Mintage	F	VF	XF	Unc	BU
2002	—	—	—	—	1.50	1.75

KM# 156   FRANC
5.0000 g., Nickel Clad Steel, 24.8 mm. **Subject:** 25th Anniversary - Pope John Paul II's Visit **Obv:** Lion left **Rev:** Pope John Paul II as a priest in 1946 **Edge:** Plain

Date	Mintage	F	VF	XF	Unc	BU
2004	—	—	—	—	2.00	2.50

KM# 157   FRANC
5.0000 g., Nickel Clad Steel, 24.8 mm. **Subject:** 25th Anniversary - Pope John Paul II's Visit **Obv:** Lion left **Rev:** Pope John Paul II as a Cardinal in 1967 **Edge:** Plain

Date	Mintage	F	VF	XF	Unc	BU
2004	—	—	—	—	2.00	2.50

KM# 158   FRANC
5.0000 g., Nickel Clad Steel, 24.8 mm. **Subject:** 25th Anniversary - Pope John Paul II's Visit **Obv:** Lion left **Rev:** Pope John Paul II as newly elected pope in 1978 **Edge:** Plain

Date	Mintage	F	VF	XF	Unc	BU
2004	—	—	—	—	2.00	2.50

KM# 159   FRANC
5.0000 g., Nickel Clad Steel, 24.8 mm. **Subject:** 25th Anniversary - Pope John Paul II's Visit **Obv:** Lion left **Rev:** Pope John Paul II wearing a mitre **Edge:** Plain

Date	Mintage	F	VF	XF	Unc	BU
2004	—	—	—	—	2.00	2.50

KM# 174   FRANC
6.0000 g., Copper-Nickel, 21 mm. **Obv:** Lion left **Rev:** African Golden Cat right **Edge:** Plain

Date	Mintage	F	VF	XF	Unc	BU
2004	5,000	—	—	—	7.25	9.00

KM# 174a   FRANC
8.0000 g., 0.9990 Silver 0.2569 oz. ASW, 21 mm. **Obv:** Lion left **Rev:** African Golden Cat right **Edge:** Plain

Date	Mintage	F	VF	XF	Unc	BU
2004	25	—	—	—	270	300

KM# 56   5 FRANCS
22.4000 g., Copper-Nickel, 39.8 mm. **Series:** Wild Life Protection **Obv:** Lion left **Rev:** Multicolor swallowtail butterfly hologram **Edge:** Reeded **Note:** Prev. KM#79.

Date	Mintage	F	VF	XF	Unc	BU
2002(2001)	20,000	—	—	—	35.00	40.00

KM# 57   5 FRANCS
22.4000 g., Copper-Nickel, 39.8 mm. **Series:** Wild Life Protection **Obv:** Lion left **Rev:** Multicolor dark greenish butterfly hologram **Edge:** Reeded **Note:** Prev. KM#80.

Date	Mintage	F	VF	XF	Unc	BU
2002(2001)	20,000	—	—	—	40.00	—

KM# 58   5 FRANCS
22.4000 g., Copper-Nickel, 39.8 mm. **Series:** Wild Life Protection **Obv:** Lion left **Rev:** Multicolor red and black butterfly hologram **Edge:** Reeded **Note:** Prev. KM#81.

Date	Mintage	F	VF	XF	Unc	BU
2002(2001)	20,000	—	—	—	35.00	40.00

KM# 170   5 FRANCS
24.3000 g., Copper-Nickel, 38.5 mm. **Obv:** Lion left
Rev: Multicolor German 1 mark coin dated 2001 **Edge:** Reeded

Date	Mintage	F	VF	XF	Unc	BU
2002	—	—	—	—	15.00	20.00

KM# 146   5 FRANCS
27.0000 g., Copper-Nickel, 38.6 mm. **Obv:** Lion left
Rev: Multicolor Quetzal bird **Edge:** Reeded

Date	Mintage	F	VF	XF	Unc	BU
2004 Proof	5,000	Value: 45.00				

KM# 147   5 FRANCS
27.0000 g., Copper-Nickel, 38.6 mm. **Obv:** Lion left
Rev: Multicolor Bird of Paradise **Edge:** Reeded

Date	Mintage	F	VF	XF	Unc	BU
2004 Proof	5,000	Value: 45.00				

KM# 148   5 FRANCS
27.0000 g., Copper-Nickel, 38.6 mm. **Obv:** Lion left
Rev: Multicolor Kingfisher bird **Edge:** Reeded

Date	Mintage	F	VF	XF	Unc	BU
2004 Proof	5,000	Value: 45.00				

KM# 164   5 FRANCS
25.4000 g., Copper-Nickel, 38.8 mm. **Subject:** Papal Visit **Obv:**
Lion left **Rev:** Pope John Paul II with staff and mitre **Edge:** Reeded

Date	Mintage	F	VF	XF	Unc	BU
ND (2004) Proof	—	Value: 15.00				

KM# 165   5 FRANCS
49.5000 g., Copper-Nickel, 45.1 mm. **Obv:** Lion left
Rev: Rotating 50 year calender **Edge:** Reeded

Date	Mintage	F	VF	XF	Unc	BU
ND(2004) Matte	—	—	—	—	75.00	—

KM# 128   5 FRANCS
8.0000 g., Iron, 27.26x14.13 mm. **Obv:** Country name, lion and
date in the bowl part of the spoon; value on the handle part
Edge: Reeded **Note:** This is the Spoon part of the Compass and
Spoon set. (The spoon is the compass needle.)

Date	Mintage	F	VF	XF	Unc	BU
2004	5,000	—	—	—	15.00	—

KM# 181   5 FRANCS
25.9200 g., Copper-Nickel, 38.58 mm. **Series:** Wildlife
Protection **Obv:** Lion standing laft **Obv. Legend:** REPUBLIQUE
DENOCRATIQUE DU CONGO **Rev:** Red Perch, multicolor
Edge: Reeded

Date	Mintage	F	VF	XF	Unc	BU
2005	5,000	—	—	—	—	20.00

KM# 182   5 FRANCS
Copper-Nickel Gilt **Obv:** Lion standing left **Rev:** Two cupids
embracing, roses - multicolor **Rev. Legend:** *Endless Love*
Edge: Reeded **Shape:** Heart

Date	Mintage	F	VF	XF	Unc	BU
2005 Proof	5,000	Value: 35.00				

KM# 166   5 FRANCS
2.1600 g., Wood Maple wood, 39.4 mm. **Obv:** Lion, brown ink
Rev: Gorilla, brown ink **Edge:** Plain

Date	Mintage	F	VF	XF	Unc	BU
2005	2,000	—	—	—	20.00	—

KM# 179   5 FRANCS
25.9200 g., Copper-Nickel, 38.58 mm. **Series:** Wildlife
Protection **Obv:** Lion standing left **Obv. Legend:** REPUBLIQUE
DEMOCRATIQUE DU CONGO **Rev:** Butterfly Fish, multicolor
Edge: Reeded

Date	Mintage	F	VF	XF	Unc	BU
2005	5,000	—	—	—	—	20.00

KM# 180   5 FRANCS
25.9200 g., Copper-Nickel, 38.58 mm. **Series:** Wildlife
Protection **Obv:** Lion standing left **Obv. Legend:** REPUBLIQUE
DEMOCRATIQYE DU CONGO **Rev:** African Moony Fish,
multicolor **Edge:** Reeded

Date	Mintage	F	VF	XF	Unc	BU
2005	5,000	—	—	—	—	20.00

KM# 178   5 FRANCS
26.3000 g., Silver Plated Bronze, 38.6 mm. **Obv:** Lion **Rev:**
Multicolor Pope John Paul II wearing a mitre **Edge:** Reeded

Date	Mintage	F	VF	XF	Unc	BU
2007 Proof	—	Value: 30.00				

KM# 72   10 FRANCS
20.0000 g., 0.9250 Silver 0.5948 oz. ASW, 40.1 mm.
Series: Airplanes **Obv:** Lion left **Rev:** Mikoyan-Gurevich Mig 21
fighter flying left **Edge:** Reeded

Date	Mintage	F	VF	XF	Unc	BU
2001 Proof	—	Value: 40.00				

KM# 74   10 FRANCS
31.1035 g., 0.9990 Silver 0.9990 oz. ASW, 40 mm.
Subject: 2004 Olympics **Obv:** Lion left **Rev:** Convex chariot
Edge: Reeded

Date	Mintage	F	VF	XF	Unc	BU
2001 Antique Finish	15,000	—	—	—	37.50	—

KM# 167   10 FRANCS
20.0000 g., 0.9250 Silver 0.5948 oz. ASW, 40.1 mm. **Obv:** Lion left **Rev:** SS Bremen ship at sea **Edge:** Reeded

Date	Mintage	F	VF	XF	Unc	BU
2001 Proof	—	Value: 30.00				

KM# 168   10 FRANCS
20.0000 g., 0.9250 Silver 0.5948 oz. ASW, 40.1 mm. **Obv:** Lion left **Rev:** RMS Queen Elizabeth 2 at sea **Edge:** Reeded

Date	Mintage	F	VF	XF	Unc	BU
2001 Proof	—	Value: 30.00				

KM# 169   10 FRANCS
20.0000 g., 0.9250 Silver 0.5948 oz. ASW, 30 mm. **Obv:** Lion left **Rev:** Sail Ship America **Edge:** Reeded

Date	Mintage	F	VF	XF	Unc	BU
2001 Proof	—	Value: 30.00				

KM# 38   10 FRANCS
31.3000 g., 0.9250 Silver 0.9308 oz. ASW, 27 x 47.1 mm. **Subject:** Illusion **Obv:** Lion left **Rev:** Multicolor couple in flower picture **Edge:** Plain **Shape:** Rectangular **Note:** Prev. KM#61.

Date	Mintage	F	VF	XF	Unc	BU
2001 Proof	—	Value: 50.00				

KM# 59   10 FRANCS
25.9500 g., 0.9250 Silver 0.7717 oz. ASW, 39.9 mm. **Series:** Wild Life Protection **Obv:** Lion left **Rev:** Multicolor swallowtail butterfly hologram **Edge:** Reeded **Note:** Prev. KM#82.

Date	Mintage	F	VF	XF	Unc	BU
2002 (2001) Proof	15,000	Value: 65.00				

KM# 60   10 FRANCS
25.9500 g., 0.9250 Silver 0.7717 oz. ASW, 39.9 mm. **Series:** Wild Life Protection **Obv:** Lion left **Rev:** Multicolor dark greenish butterfly hologram **Edge:** Reeded **Note:** Prev. KM#83.

Date	Mintage	F	VF	XF	Unc	BU
2002 (2001) Proof	15,000	Value: 65.00				

KM# 61   10 FRANCS
25.9500 g., 0.9250 Silver 0.7717 oz. ASW, 39.9 mm. **Series:** Wild Life Protection **Obv:** Lion left **Rev:** Multicolor red and black butterfly hologram **Edge:** Reeded **Note:** Prev. KM#84.

Date	Mintage	F	VF	XF	Unc	BU
2002 (2001) Proof	15,000	Value: 65.00				

KM# 65   10 FRANCS
20.0000 g., 0.9250 Silver 0.5948 oz. ASW, 40.1 mm. **Series:** Airplanes **Obv:** Lion left **Rev:** Vickers Vimy twin engine biplane flying left **Edge:** Reeded **Note:** Prev. KM#88.

Date	Mintage	F	VF	XF	Unc	BU
2001 Proof	—	Value: 40.00				

KM# 66   10 FRANCS
20.0000 g., 0.9250 Silver 0.5948 oz. ASW, 40.1 mm. **Series:** Airplanes **Obv:** Lion left **Rev:** Fokker DR1 triplane flying left **Edge:** Reeded **Note:** Prev. KM#89.

Date	Mintage	F	VF	XF	Unc	BU
2001 Proof	—	Value: 40.00				

KM# 67   10 FRANCS
20.0000 g., 0.9250 Silver 0.5948 oz. ASW, 40.1 mm. **Series:** Airplanes **Obv:** Lion left **Rev:** Lockheed Vega flying left **Edge:** Reeded **Note:** Prev. KM#90.

Date	Mintage	F	VF	XF	Unc	BU
2001 Proof	—	Value: 40.00				

KM# 68   10 FRANCS
20.0000 g., 0.9250 Silver 0.5948 oz. ASW, 40.1 mm. **Series:** Airplanes **Obv:** Lion left **Rev:** Boeing 314 Clipper flying left **Edge:** Reeded **Note:** Prev. KM#91.

Date	Mintage	F	VF	XF	Unc	BU
2001 Proof	—	Value: 40.00				

KM# 69   10 FRANCS
20.0000 g., 0.9250 Silver 0.5948 oz. ASW, 40.1 mm.
Series: Airplanes **Obv:** Lion left **Rev:** Junkers JU-87 Stuka in a dive **Edge:** Reeded **Note:** Prev. KM#92.

Date	Mintage	F	VF	XF	Unc	BU
2001 Proof	—	Value: 40.00				

KM# 70   10 FRANCS
20.0000 g., 0.9250 Silver 0.5948 oz. ASW, 40.1 mm.
Series: Airplanes **Obv:** Lion left **Rev:** B-29 Enola Gay flying left **Edge:** Reeded **Note:** Prev. KM#93.

Date	Mintage	F	VF	XF	Unc	BU
2001 Proof	—	Value: 45.00				

KM# 71   10 FRANCS
20.0000 g., 0.9250 Silver 0.5948 oz. ASW, 40.1 mm.
Series: Airplanes **Obv:** Lion left **Rev:** Bell X-1 rocket plane flying left **Edge:** Reeded **Note:** Prev. KM#94.

Date	Mintage	F	VF	XF	Unc	BU
2001 Proof	—	Value: 40.00				

KM# 175   10 FRANCS
25.8300 g., Silver, 40 mm.   **Obv:** Lion left **Rev:** 3 players **Edge:** Reeded

Date	Mintage	F	VF	XF	Unc	BU
2001	—	—	—	—	50.00	

KM# 91   10 FRANCS
31.1000 g., 0.9990 Silver 0.9988 oz. ASW, 40 mm.
Subject: Olympics **Obv:** Lion left **Rev:** Ancient athlete incuse design **Edge:** Plain **Note:** Design hubs with the design of the 500 sika coin KM-42 of Ghana

Date	Mintage	F	VF	XF	Unc	BU
2002 Antiqued finish	—	—	—	—	37.50	—

KM# 124   10 FRANCS
26.0000 g., 0.9250 Silver 0.7732 oz. ASW, 40 mm.
Subject: Field Marshal Erwin Rommel **Obv:** Lion left above value **Rev:** Rommel, tank and map **Edge:** Reeded

Date	Mintage	F	VF	XF	Unc	BU
2002 Proof	15,000	Value: 42.50				

KM# 125   10 FRANCS
26.0000 g., 0.9250 Silver 0.7732 oz. ASW, 40 mm.
Subject: Field Marshal Erwin Rommel **Obv:** Lion left above value **Rev:** Patton, tank and map **Edge:** Reeded

Date	Mintage	F	VF	XF	Unc	BU
2002 Proof	15,000	Value: 42.50				

KM# 162   10 FRANCS
20.2000 g., 0.9990 Silver 0.6488 oz. ASW, 40 mm.   **Obv:** Lion left **Rev:** Space shuttle and five astronauts **Edge:** Reeded

Date	Mintage	F	VF	XF	Unc	BU
2002 Proof	—	Value: 40.00				

KM# 189   10 FRANCS
26.1500 g., Copper-Nickel, 40.3 mm.   **Series:** Automobiles **Obv:** Lion standing left **Rev:** Rolls Royce **Edge:** Reeded

Date	Mintage	F	VF	XF	Unc	BU
2002 Proof	—	Value: 18.00				

KM# 190   10 FRANCS
26.1500 g., Copper-Nickel, 40.3 mm.   **Series:** Automobiles **Obv:** Lion standing left **Rev:** Peujeot

Date	Mintage	F	VF	XF	Unc	BU
2002 Proof	—	Value: 18.00				

KM# 191   10 FRANCS
26.1500 g., Copper-Nickel, 40.3 mm.   **Series:** Automobiles **Obv:** Lion standing left **Rev:** Opel **Edge:** Reeded

Date	Mintage	F	VF	XF	Unc	BU
2002 Proof	—	Value: 18.00				

KM# 192   10 FRANCS
26.1500 g., Copper-Nickel, 40.3 mm.   **Series:** Automobiles **Obv:** Lion standing left **Rev:** Cadillac

Date	Mintage	F	VF	XF	Unc	BU
2002 Proof	—	Value: 18.00				

KM# 93   10 FRANCS
31.2300 g., 0.9990 Silver 1.0030 oz. ASW, 38.7 mm.   **Obv:** Lion left **Rev:** Bearded portrait of Verney L. Cameroon **Edge:** Reeded

Date	Mintage	F	VF	XF	Unc	BU
2002	—	—	—	—	35.00	40.00

KM# 94   10 FRANCS
26.1500 g., Copper-Nickel, 40.3 mm.   **Subject:** Historic Automobiles **Obv:** Lion left **Rev:** 1908 Berliet car **Edge:** Reeded

Date	Mintage	F	VF	XF	Unc	BU
2002 Proof	—	Value: 18.00				

KM# 95   10 FRANCS
26.1500 g., Copper-Nickel, 40.3 mm.   **Subject:** Historic Automobiles **Obv:** Lion left **Rev:** 1919 Hispano Suiza H6 car right **Edge:** Reeded

Date	Mintage	F	VF	XF	Unc	BU
2002 Proof	—	Value: 18.00				

KM# 96   10 FRANCS
32.0000 g., Silver Plated Copper, 40 mm. **Subject:** World Cup
Soccer **Obv:** Lion left **Rev:** Soccer player and multicolor
American flag **Edge:** Reeded

Date	Mintage	F	VF	XF	Unc	BU
2002 Proof	20,000	Value: 50.00				

KM# 97   10 FRANCS
32.0000 g., Silver Plated Copper, 40 mm. **Subject:** World Cup
Soccer **Obv:** Lion left **Rev:** Two soccer players and multicolor
flag of Ecuador **Edge:** Reeded

Date	Mintage	F	VF	XF	Unc	BU
2002 Proof	20,000	Value: 50.00				

KM# 103   10 FRANCS
19.0000 g., 0.9990 Silver 0.6102 oz. ASW, 40 mm. **Subject:**
Gotha Ursinus G **Obv:** Lion left **Rev:** WWI German bomber flying
left at 8 o'clock **Edge:** Reeded

Date	Mintage	F	VF	XF	Unc	BU
2002 Proof	—	Value: 40.00				

KM# 104   10 FRANCS
19.0000 g., 0.9990 Silver 0.6102 oz. ASW, 40 mm. **Obv:** Lion
left **Rev:** WWII ME 109 German fighter plane flying left
Edge: Reeded

Date	Mintage	F	VF	XF	Unc	BU
2002 Proof	—	Value: 40.00				

KM# 105   10 FRANCS
19.0000 g., 0.9990 Silver 0.6102 oz. ASW, 40 mm. **Obv:** Lion
left **Rev:** Savoia-Marchetti S 55 seaplane flying left
Edge: Reeded

Date	Mintage	F	VF	XF	Unc	BU
2002 Proof	—	Value: 40.00				

KM# 106   10 FRANCS
19.0000 g., 0.9990 Silver 0.6102 oz. ASW, 40 mm. **Obv:** Lion
left **Rev:** B-58 Hustler Delta wing bomber flying left at 8 o'clock
Edge: Reeded

Date	Mintage	F	VF	XF	Unc	BU
2002 Proof	—	Value: 40.00				

KM# 107   10 FRANCS
19.0000 g., 0.9990 Silver 0.6102 oz. ASW, 40 mm. **Obv:** Lion
left **Rev:** CF-105 Arrow jet fighter plane flying right, nose up
Edge: Reeded

Date	Mintage	F	VF	XF	Unc	BU
2002 Proof	—	Value: 40.00				

KM# 108   10 FRANCS
19.0000 g., 0.9990 Silver 0.6102 oz. ASW, 40 mm. **Obv:** Lion
left **Rev:** XB-70 Valkyrie experimental jet bomber flying right
Edge: Reeded

Date	Mintage	F	VF	XF	Unc	BU
2002 Proof	—	Value: 40.00				

KM# 187   10 FRANCS
26.1500 g., Copper-Nickel, 40.3 mm. **Series:** Automobiles
Obv: Lion standing left **Rev:** Buick **Edge:** Reeded

Date	Mintage	F	VF	XF	Unc	BU
2002 Proof	—	Value: 18.00				

KM# 188   10 FRANCS
26.1500 g., Copper-Nickel, 40.3 mm. **Series:** Automobiles
Obv: Lion standing left **Rev:** Land Rover **Edge:** Reeded

Date	Mintage	F	VF	XF	Unc	BU
2002 Proof	—	Value: 18.00				

KM# 193   10 FRANCS
26.1500 g., Copper-Nickel, 40.3 mm. **Series:** Automobiles
Obv: Lion standing left **Rev:** Benz **Shape:** Reeded

Date	Mintage	F	VF	XF	Unc	BU
2002 Proof	—	Value: 18.00				

KM# 194   10 FRANCS
26.1500 g., Copper-Nickel, 40.3 mm. **Series:** Automobiles
Obv: Lion standing left **Rev:** Audi **Edge:** Reeded

Date	Mintage	F	VF	XF	Unc	BU
2002 Proof	—	Value: 18.00				

KM# 195   10 FRANCS
26.1500 g., Copper-Nickel, 40.3 mm. **Series:** Automobiles
Obv: Lion standing left **Rev:** Alfa Romero

Date	Mintage	F	VF	XF	Unc	BU
2002 Proof	—	Value: 18.00				

KM# 196   10 FRANCS
26.1500 g., Copper-Nickel, 40.3 mm. **Series:** Automobiles
Obv: Lion standing left **Rev:** Ford Model 'T' **Edge:** Reeded

Date	Mintage	F	VF	XF	Unc	BU
2002 Proof	—	Value: 18.00				

KM# 163   10 FRANCS
39.1000 g., Acrylic, 49.9 mm. **Obv:** Old World Swallowtail
butterfly above lion and value **Rev:** Rear view of the obverse
Edge: Plain

Date	Mintage	F	VF	XF	Unc	BU
2003	—	—	—	—	75.00	—

KM# 171   10 FRANCS
39.1000 g., Acrylic, 49.9 mm. **Obv:** Gorch Fock sail ship above
lion and value **Rev:** Rear view of the obverse design **Edge:** Plain

Date	Mintage	F	VF	XF	Unc	BU
2003	1,000	—	—	—	75.00	—

KM# 113 10 FRANCS
19.0000 g., 0.9990 Silver 0.6102 oz. ASW, 40 mm. **Obv:** Lion left **Rev:** WWII CA-12 Boomerang fighter plane flying above map at 10 o'clock **Edge:** Reeded

Date	Mintage	F	VF	XF	Unc	BU
2003 Proof	—	Value: 40.00				

KM# 117 10 FRANCS
19.0000 g., 0.9990 Silver 0.6102 oz. ASW, 40 mm. **Obv:** Lion left **Rev:** Panavia Tornado jet fighter-bomber flying left **Edge:** Reeded

Date	Mintage	F	VF	XF	Unc	BU
2003 Proof	—	Value: 40.00				

KM# 109 10 FRANCS
19.0000 g., 0.9990 Silver 0.6102 oz. ASW, 40 mm. **Obv:** Lion left **Rev:** 14 BIS early aircraft in flight **Edge:** Reeded

Date	Mintage	F	VF	XF	Unc	BU
2003 Proof	—	Value: 40.00				

KM# 114 10 FRANCS
19.0000 g., 0.9990 Silver 0.6102 oz. ASW, 40 mm. **Obv:** Lion left **Rev:** B-50A Superfortress bomber flying left **Edge:** Reeded

Date	Mintage	F	VF	XF	Unc	BU
2003 Proof	—	Value: 40.00				

KM# 118 10 FRANCS
19.0000 g., 0.9990 Silver 0.6102 oz. ASW, 40 mm. **Obv:** Lion left **Rev:** Hindustan HF24 jet fighter flying left **Edge:** Reeded

Date	Mintage	F	VF	XF	Unc	BU
2003 Proof	—	Value: 40.00				

KM# 110 10 FRANCS
19.0000 g., 0.9990 Silver 0.6102 oz. ASW, 40 mm. **Obv:** Lion left **Rev:** WWI Sopwith Camel fighter plane flying right **Edge:** Reeded

Date	Mintage	F	VF	XF	Unc	BU
2003 Proof	—	Value: 40.00				

KM# 115 10 FRANCS
19.0000 g., 0.9990 Silver 0.6102 oz. ASW, 40 mm. **Obv:** Lion left **Rev:** WWII Heinkel-178 German jet plane flying left **Edge:** Reeded

Date	Mintage	F	VF	XF	Unc	BU
2003 Proof	—	Value: 40.00				

KM# 119 10 FRANCS
19.0000 g., 0.9990 Silver 0.6102 oz. ASW, 40 mm. **Obv:** Lion left **Rev:** Lockheed F-117 Stealth fighter flying left **Edge:** Reeded

Date	Mintage	F	VF	XF	Unc	BU
2003 Proof	—	Value: 40.00				

KM# 111 10 FRANCS
19.0000 g., 0.9990 Silver 0.6102 oz. ASW, 40 mm. **Obv:** Lion left **Rev:** Curtiss NC-4 early seaplane flying left **Edge:** Reeded

Date	Mintage	F	VF	XF	Unc	BU
2003 Proof	—	Value: 40.00				

KM# 120 10 FRANCS
19.0000 g., 0.9990 Silver 0.6102 oz. ASW, 40 mm. **Obv:** Lion left **Rev:** North American X-15 experimental rocket plane flying right at 1 o'clock **Edge:** Reeded

Date	Mintage	F	VF	XF	Unc	BU
2003 Proof	—	Value: 40.00				

KM# 112 10 FRANCS
19.0000 g., 0.9990 Silver 0.6102 oz. ASW, 40 mm. **Obv:** Lion left **Rev:** Macchi-Castoldi MC-72 seaplane flying left at 8 o'clock **Edge:** Reeded

Date	Mintage	F	VF	XF	Unc	BU
2003 Proof	—	Value: 40.00				

KM# 116 10 FRANCS
19.0000 g., 0.9990 Silver 0.6102 oz. ASW, 40 mm. **Obv:** Lion left **Rev:** Early De Havilland Comet jet liner flying left **Edge:** Reeded

Date	Mintage	F	VF	XF	Unc	BU
2003 Proof	—	Value: 40.00				

KM# 122   10 FRANCS
25.0000 g., 0.9250 Silver 0.7435 oz. ASW, 38.6 mm. **Obv:** Lion
left **Rev:** Multicolor 3D hologram view of Victoria Falls
Edge: Reeded

Date	Mintage	F	VF	XF	Unc	BU
2003 Proof	5,000	Value: 45.00				

KM# 99.1   10 FRANCS
24.9100 g., 0.9250 Silver 0.7408 oz. ASW, 38.6 mm. **Obv:** Lion
left **Rev:** Chameleon **Edge:** Reeded

Date	Mintage	F	VF	XF	Unc	BU
2003 Proof	—	Value: 45.00				

KM# 99.2   10 FRANCS
24.9100 g., 0.9250 Silver 0.7408 oz. ASW, 38.6 mm. **Obv:** Lion
left **Rev:** Multicolor chameleon **Edge:** Reeded

Date	Mintage	F	VF	XF	Unc	BU
2003 Proof	—	Value: 50.00				

KM# 100   10 FRANCS
24.9100 g., 0.9250 Silver 0.7408 oz. ASW, 38.6 mm. **Obv:** Lion
left **Rev:** Striped skunk **Edge:** Reeded

Date	Mintage	F	VF	XF	Unc	BU
2003 Proof	—	Value: 45.00				

KM# 101   10 FRANCS
24.9100 g., 0.9250 Silver 0.7408 oz. ASW, 38.6 mm. **Obv:** Lion
left **Rev:** Porcupine on rock, right **Edge:** Reeded

Date	Mintage	F	VF	XF	Unc	BU
2003 Proof	—	Value: 47.50				

KM# 102   10 FRANCS
24.9100 g., 0.9250 Silver 0.7408 oz. ASW, 38.6 mm. **Obv:** Lion
left **Rev:** Giant Pangolin on rock right **Edge:** Reeded

Date	Mintage	F	VF	XF	Unc	BU
2003 Proof	—	Value: 45.00				

KM# 132   10 FRANCS
25.0000 g., 0.9000 Silver 0.7234 oz. ASW, 40 mm. **Obv:** Lion
left **Rev:** Multicolor dolphin leaping left **Edge:** Reeded

Date	Mintage	F	VF	XF	Unc	BU
2003 Proof	5,000	Value: 50.00				

KM# 133   10 FRANCS
25.0000 g., 0.9000 Silver 0.7234 oz. ASW, 40 mm. **Obv:** Lion
left **Rev:** Multicolor sea turtle left **Edge:** Reeded

Date	Mintage	F	VF	XF	Unc	BU
2003 Proof	5,000	Value: 50.00				

KM# 134   10 FRANCS
25.0000 g., 0.9000 Silver 0.7234 oz. ASW, 40 mm. **Obv:** Lion
left **Rev:** Multicolor killer whale jumping right **Edge:** Reeded

Date	Mintage	F	VF	XF	Unc	BU
2003 Proof	5,000	Value: 50.00				

KM# 135   10 FRANCS
26.0000 g., 0.9990 Silver 0.8350 oz. ASW, 40 mm. **Obv:** Lion
left **Rev:** Pope John Paul II with staff and mitre, waving
Edge: Reeded

Date	Mintage	F	VF	XF	Unc	BU
2003 Proof	—	Value: 50.00				

KM# 141   10 FRANCS
25.0000 g., 0.9250 Silver 0.7435 oz. ASW, 38.6 mm. **Obv:** Lion
left **Rev:** Multicolor Emperor fish swimming left **Edge:** Reeded

Date	Mintage	F	VF	XF	Unc	BU
2004 Proof	5,000	Value: 50.00				

KM# 142   10 FRANCS
25.0000 g., 0.9250 Silver 0.7435 oz. ASW, 38.6 mm. **Obv:** Lion
left **Rev:** Multicolor octopus facing **Edge:** Reeded

Date	Mintage	F	VF	XF	Unc	BU
2004 Proof	5,000	Value: 65.00				

KM# 143 10 FRANCS
25.0000 g., 0.9250 Silver 0.7435 oz. ASW, 38.6 mm. **Obv:** Lion left **Rev:** Formula 1 and GT race cars **Edge:** Reeded

Date	Mintage	F	VF	XF	Unc	BU
2004 Proof	5,000	Value: 45.00				

KM# 145 10 FRANCS
25.0000 g., 0.9250 Silver 0.7435 oz. ASW, 27x47 mm. **Obv:** Lion left **Rev:** Pope with crucifix **Edge:** Plain **Shape:** Rectangular

Date	Mintage	F	VF	XF	Unc	BU
2004 Proof	5,000	Value: 45.00				

KM# 149 10 FRANCS
25.0000 g., 0.9250 Silver 0.7435 oz. ASW, 38.6 mm. **Obv:** Lion left **Rev:** Multicolor Quetzal bird **Edge:** Reeded

Date	Mintage	F	VF	XF	Unc	BU
2004 Proof	5,000	Value: 50.00				

KM# 150 10 FRANCS
25.0000 g., 0.9250 Silver 0.7435 oz. ASW, 38.6 mm. **Obv:** Lion left **Rev:** Multicolor Bird of Paradise on branch left **Edge:** Reeded

Date	Mintage	F	VF	XF	Unc	BU
2004 Proof	5,000	Value: 50.00				

KM# 151 10 FRANCS
25.0000 g., 0.9250 Silver 0.7435 oz. ASW, 38.6 mm. **Obv:** Lion left **Rev:** Multicolor Kingfisher bird left **Edge:** Reeded

Date	Mintage	F	VF	XF	Unc	BU
2004 Proof	5,000	Value: 50.00				

KM# 155 10 FRANCS
Acrylic Clear, 50 mm. **Obv:** Etched nine-masted sailing junk above lion, value and country name **Edge:** Plain

Date	Mintage	F	VF	XF	Unc	BU
2004	2,000	—	—	—	55.00	—

KM# 126 10 FRANCS
25.0000 g., 0.9250 Silver 0.7435 oz. ASW, 38.6 mm. **Obv:** Lion left above value **Rev:** Sundial face with collapsible gnomon **Edge:** Reeded

Date	Mintage	F	VF	XF	Unc	BU
2004 Proof	5,000	Value: 50.00				

KM# 127 10 FRANCS
25.0000 g., 0.9250 Silver 0.7435 oz. ASW, 38.6 mm. **Obv:** Lion left above value **Rev:** Compass face **Edge:** Reeded **Note:** Compass part of the Compass and Spoon set

Date	Mintage	F	VF	XF	Unc	BU
2004 Proof	5,000	Value: 50.00				

KM# 172 10 FRANCS
25.0000 g., Silver, 38.6 mm. **Obv:** Lion left **Rev:** Pope waving half facing at left, cross at upper right, Vatican at lower right

Date	Mintage	F	VF	XF	Unc	BU
2005 Proof	3,000	Value: 50.00				

KM# 179a 10 FRANCS
25.0000 g., 0.9250 Silver 0.7435 oz. ASW, 38.58 mm. **Series:** Wildlife Protection **Obv:** Lion standing left **Obv. Legend:** REPUBLIQUE DEMOCRATIQUE DU CONGO **Rev:** Butterfly Fish, multicolor **Edge:** Reeded

Date	Mintage	F	VF	XF	Unc	BU
2005 Proof	5,000	Value: 45.00				

KM# 180a 10 FRANCS
25.0000 g., 0.9250 Silver 0.7435 oz. ASW, 38.58 mm. **Series:** Wildlife Protection **Obv:** Lion standing left **Obv. Legend:** REPUBLIQUE DEMOCRATIQUE DU CONGO **Rev:** African Moony Fish, multicolor **Edge:** Reeded

Date	Mintage	F	VF	XF	Unc	BU
2005 Proof	5,000	Value: 45.00				

KM# 181a 10 FRANCS
25.0000 g., 0.9250 Silver 0.7435 oz. ASW, 38.58 mm. **Series:** Wildlife Protection **Obv:** Lion standing left **Obv. Legend:** REPUBLIQUE DEMOCRATIQUE DU CONGO **Rev:** Red Perch, multicolor **Edge:** Reeded

Date	Mintage	F	VF	XF	Unc	BU
2005 Proof	5,000	Value: 45.00				

KM# 176 10 FRANCS
32.0000 g., 0.9990 Silver 1.0278 oz. ASW, 40 mm. **Obv:** Lion standing left **Obv. Legend:** REPUBLIQUE DEMOCRATIQUE DU CONGO **Rev:** World Trade Center Twin Towers as they were before 9-11 **Edge:** Reeded

Date	Mintage	F	VF	XF	Unc	BU
2006 Proof	—	Value: 50.00				

KM# 136 20 FRANCS
1.2440 g., 0.9999 Gold 0.0400 oz. AGW, 13.92 mm. **Obv:** Lion left **Rev:** Pope John Paul II with staff and mitre, waving **Edge:** Plain

Date	Mintage	F	VF	XF	Unc	BU
2003 Proof	—	Value: 55.00				

KM# 137 20 FRANCS
1.2440 g., 0.9999 Gold 0.0400 oz. AGW, 13.92 mm. **Obv:** Lion left **Rev:** Skunk **Edge:** Plain

Date	Mintage	F	VF	XF	Unc	BU
2003 Proof	25,000	Value: 55.00				

KM# 138 20 FRANCS
1.2440 g., 0.9999 Gold 0.0400 oz. AGW, 13.92 mm. **Obv:** Lion left **Rev:** Giant anteater right **Edge:** Plain

Date	Mintage	F	VF	XF	Unc	BU
2003 Proof	25,000	Value: 55.00				

KM# 139   20 FRANCS
1.2440 g., 0.9999 Gold 0.0400 oz. AGW, 13.92 mm. **Obv:** Lion left **Rev:** Porcupine right **Edge:** Plain

Date	Mintage	F	VF	XF	Unc	BU
2003 Proof	25,000	Value: 55.00				

KM# 140   20 FRANCS
1.2440 g., 0.9999 Gold 0.0400 oz. AGW, 13.92 mm. **Obv:** Lion left **Rev:** Chameleon **Edge:** Plain

Date	Mintage	F	VF	XF	Unc	BU
2003 Proof	25,000	Value: 55.00				

KM# 184   20 FRANCS
1.2200 g., 0.9999 Gold 0.0392 oz. AGW, 13.74 mm. **Subject:** XXVIII Summer Olympics - Athens **Obv:** Lion standing right **Rev:** Athenian tetradrachm featuring owl perched **Edge:** Reeded

Date	Mintage	F	VF	XF	Unc	BU
2003 Proof	25,000	Value: 55.00				

KM# 186   20 FRANCS
1.2441 g., 0.9999 Gold 0.0400 oz. AGW, 13.92 mm. **Subject:** Christmas **Obv:** Lion standing left **Rev:** Jesus lying in manger

Date	Mintage	F	VF	XF	Unc	BU
ND(2004) Proof	25,000	Value: 50.00				

KM# 144   20 FRANCS
1.2440 g., 0.9999 Gold 0.0400 oz. AGW, 13.92 mm. **Obv:** Lion left **Rev:** Ferrari coat of arms **Edge:** Plain

Date	Mintage	F	VF	XF	Unc	BU
2004 Proof	5,000	Value: 55.00				

KM# 173   20 FRANCS
1.5300 g., 0.9990 Gold 0.0491 oz. AGW, 13.9 mm. **Obv:** Lion left **Rev:** Pope waving at left, cross at upper right, Vatican at lower right

Date	Mintage	F	VF	XF	Unc	BU
2005 Proof	25,000	Value: 60.00				

KM# 185   75 FRANCS
15.5500 g., 0.9999 Gold 0.4999 oz. AGW **Subject:** XXVIII Summer Olympics - Athens **Obv:** Lion standing right **Rev:** Athenian tetradrachm featuring owl perched **Edge:** Reeded

Date	Mintage	F	VF	XF	Unc	BU
2003 Proof	500	Value: 675				

KM# 129   100 FRANCS
31.1000 g., 0.9999 Gold 0.9997 oz. AGW, 40 mm. **Obv:** Lion left **Rev:** Reflective multicolor swallowtail butterfly **Edge:** Reeded

Date	Mintage	F	VF	XF	Unc	BU
2002 Proof	50	Value: 1,275				

KM# 130   100 FRANCS
31.1000 g., 0.9999 Gold 0.9997 oz. AGW, 40 mm. **Obv:** Lion left **Rev:** Reflective multicolor dark greenish butterfly **Edge:** Reeded

Date	Mintage	F	VF	XF	Unc	BU
2002 Proof	50	Value: 1,275				

KM# 131   100 FRANCS
31.1000 g., 0.9999 Gold 0.9997 oz. AGW, 40 mm. **Obv:** Lion left **Rev:** Reflective multicolor red and black butterfly **Edge:** Reeded

Date	Mintage	F	VF	XF	Unc	BU
2002 Proof	50	Value: 1,275				

KM# 152   100 FRANCS
31.1035 g., 0.9999 Gold 0.9999 oz. AGW, 38.6 mm. **Obv:** Lion left **Rev:** Multicolor Quetzal bird **Edge:** Reeded

Date	Mintage	F	VF	XF	Unc	BU
2004 Proof	25	Value: 1,350				

KM# 153   100 FRANCS
31.1035 g., 0.9999 Gold 0.9999 oz. AGW, 38.6 mm. **Obv:** Lion left **Rev:** Multicolor Bird of Paradise left **Edge:** Reeded

Date	Mintage	F	VF	XF	Unc	BU
2004 Proof	25	Value: 1,350				

KM# 154   100 FRANCS
31.1035 g., 0.9999 Gold 0.9999 oz. AGW, 38.6 mm. **Obv:** Lion left **Rev:** Multicolor Kingfisher bird **Edge:** Reeded

Date	Mintage	F	VF	XF	Unc	BU
2004 Proof	25	Value: 1,350				

KM# 179b   100 FRANCS
31.1000 g., 0.9990 Gold 0.9988 oz. AGW, 38.58 mm. **Series:** Wildlife Protection **Obv:** Lion standing left **Obv. Legend:** REPUBLIQUE DEMOCRATIQUE DU CONGO **Rev:** Butterfly Fish, multicolor **Edge:** Reeded

Date	Mintage	F	VF	XF	Unc	BU
2005 Proof	25	Value: 1,350				

KM# 180b   100 FRANCS
31.1000 g., 0.9990 Gold 0.9988 oz. AGW, 38.58 mm. **Series:** Wildlife Protection **Obv:** Lion standing left **Obv. Legend:** REPUBLIQUE DEMOCRATIQUE DU CONGO **Rev:** African Mooney Fish, muticolor **Edge:** Reeded

Date	Mintage	F	VF	XF	Unc	BU
2005 Proof	25	Value: 1,350				

KM# 181b   100 FRANCS
31.1000 g., 0.9990 Gold 0.9988 oz. AGW, 38.58 mm. **Series:** Wildlife Protection **Obv:** Lion standing left **Obv. Legend:** REPUBLIQUE DEMOCRATIQUE DU CONGO **Rev:** Red Perch, multicolor **Edge:** Reeded

Date	Mintage	F	VF	XF	Unc	BU
2005 Proof	25	Value: 1,350				

MINT SETS

KM#	Date	Mintage Identification	Issue Price	Mkt Val
MS2	2004 (4)	— KM#156-159	—	12.50

COOK ISLANDS

Cook Islands, a self-governing dependency of New Zealand consisting of 15 islands, is located in the South Pacific Ocean about 2,000 miles (3,218 km.) northeast of New Zealand. It has an area of 93 sq. mi. (234 sq. km.) and a population of 17,185. Capital: Avarua. The United States claims the islands of Danger, Manahiki, Penrhyn, and Rakahanga atolls. Citrus and canned fruits and juices, copra, clothing, jewelry, and mother-of-pearl shell are exported.

RULER
British

MINT MARK
PM - Pobjoy Mint

MONETARY SYSTEM
100 Cents = 1 Dollar

DEPENDENCY OF NEW ZEALAND
DECIMAL COINAGE

KM# 419   CENT
1.4400 g., Aluminum, 21.9 mm. **Ruler:** Elizabeth II **Obv:** Crowned head right, date below **Rev:** Bust of Capt. James Cook right, denomination below **Edge:** Plain

Date	Mintage	F	VF	XF	Unc	BU
2003	—	—	—	—	1.25	1.50

KM# 420   CENT
1.4400 g., Aluminum, 21.9 mm. **Ruler:** Elizabeth II **Obv:** Crowned head right, date below **Rev:** Collie dog right, denomination below **Edge:** Plain

Date	Mintage	F	VF	XF	Unc	BU
2003	—	—	—	—	0.75	1.00

KM# 421   CENT
1.4400 g., Aluminum, 21.9 mm. **Ruler:** Elizabeth II **Obv:** Crowned head right, date below **Rev:** Pointer dog right, denomination above **Edge:** Plain

Date	Mintage	F	VF	XF	Unc	BU
2003	—	—	—	—	0.75	1.00

KM# 422   CENT
1.4400 g., Aluminum, 21.9 mm. **Ruler:** Elizabeth II **Obv:** Crowned head right, date below **Rev:** Rooster right, denomination above **Edge:** Plain

Date	Mintage	F	VF	XF	Unc	BU
2003	—	—	—	—	0.75	1.00

KM# 423 CENT
1.4400 g., Aluminum, 22 mm. **Ruler:** Elizabeth II **Obv:** Crowned head right, date below **Rev:** Monkey on branch, denomination at left **Edge:** Plain

Date	Mintage	F	VF	XF	Unc	BU
2003	—	—	—	—	0.75	1.00

KM# 396 DOLLAR
24.8828 g., 0.9990 Silver with Acrylic capsule center containing tiny rubies, sapphires and cubic zirconias 0.7992 oz. ASW, 40.6 mm. **Ruler:** Elizabeth II **Subject:** Crown Jewels **Obv:** Crowned head right, legend **Rev:** Crowns and royal regalia **Edge:** Reeded

Date	Mintage	F	VF	XF	Unc	BU
2002 Proof	50,000	Value: 11.50				

KM# 416 DOLLAR
10.7500 g., Copper-Nickel, 28.5 mm. **Ruler:** Elizabeth II **Obv:** Queen's new portrait **Rev:** Tangaroa statue and value **Edge:** Scalloped

Date	Mintage	F	VF	XF	Unc	BU
2003	—	—	—	—	2.50	3.00

KM# 455 DOLLAR
23.9000 g., Copper-Nickel, 38.5 mm. **Ruler:** Elizabeth II **Obv:** Queen Elizabeth II **Rev:** 50th Anniversary - Playboy magazine logo **Edge:** Reeded

Date	Mintage	F	VF	XF	Unc	BU
2003	—	—	—	—	7.00	9.00

KM# 455a DOLLAR
25.2700 g., Copper-Nickel Gilt, 38.3 mm. **Ruler:** Elizabeth II **Obv:** Elizabeth II **Rev:** Playboy magazine's 50th Anniversary logo **Edge:** Reeded

Date	Mintage	F	VF	XF	Unc	BU
2003 Proof	50,000	Value: 20.00				

KM# 455b DOLLAR
25.2700 g., 0.9990 Silver 0.8116 oz. ASW, 38.3 mm. **Ruler:** Elizabeth II **Obv:** Elizabeth II **Rev:** Playboy magazine's 50th Anniversary logo **Edge:** Reeded

Date	Mintage	F	VF	XF	Unc	BU
2003 Proof	—	Value: 40.00				

KM# 455c DOLLAR
25.2700 g., 0.9990 Silver Gilt 0.8116 oz. ASW, 38.3 mm. **Ruler:** Elizabeth II **Obv:** Elizabeth II **Rev:** Playboy magazine's 50th Anniversary logo **Edge:** Reeded

Date	Mintage	F	VF	XF	Unc	BU
2003 Proof	—	Value: 50.00				

KM# 462 DOLLAR
Copper-Nickel, 41 mm. **Ruler:** Elizabeth II **Rev:** Face of 5 Euro Banknote

Date	Mintage	F	VF	XF	Unc	BU
2003	—	—	—	—	7.00	9.00

KM# 463 DOLLAR
Copper-Nickel, 41 mm. **Ruler:** Elizabeth II **Rev:** Face of 10 Euro Banknote

Date	Mintage	F	VF	XF	Unc	BU
2003	—	—	—	—	7.00	9.00

KM# 464 DOLLAR
Copper-Nickel, 41 mm. **Ruler:** Elizabeth II **Rev:** Face of 20 Euro Banknote

Date	Mintage	F	VF	XF	Unc	BU
2003	—	—	—	—	7.00	9.00

KM# 465 DOLLAR
Copper-Nickel, 41 mm. **Ruler:** Elizabeth II **Rev:** Face of 50 Euro Banknote

Date	Mintage	F	VF	XF	Unc	BU
2003	—	—	—	—	7.00	9.00

KM# 466 DOLLAR
Copper-Nickel, 41 mm. **Ruler:** Elizabeth II **Rev:** Face of 100 Euro Banknote

Date	Mintage	F	VF	XF	Unc	BU
2003	—	—	—	—	7.00	9.00

KM# 467 DOLLAR
Copper-Nickel, 41 mm. **Ruler:** Elizabeth II **Rev:** Face of 500 Euro Banknote

Date	Mintage	F	VF	XF	Unc	BU
2003	—	—	—	—	7.00	9.00

KM# 424 DOLLAR
8.5000 g., 0.9990 Silver 0.2730 oz. ASW, 25.1 mm. **Ruler:** Elizabeth II **Subject:** Zodiac Gemstones - Cancer **Obv:** Crowned head above ornamental center **Rev:** Encapsulated emeralds above Crab (Cancer) **Edge:** Reeded

Date	Mintage	F	VF	XF	Unc	BU
ND(2003) Proof	10,000	Value: 25.00				

KM# 424a DOLLAR
8.5000 g., 0.9990 Silver Gilt 0.2730 oz. ASW, 25.1 mm. **Ruler:** Elizabeth II **Obv:** Crowned head above ornamental center **Rev:** Encapsulated emeralds above Crab (cancer)

Date	Mintage	F	VF	XF	Unc	BU
ND(2003) Proof	10,000	Value: 60.00				

KM# 425 DOLLAR
8.5000 g., 0.9990 Silver 0.2730 oz. ASW, 25.1 mm. **Ruler:** Elizabeth II **Subject:** Zodiac Gemstones - Aquarius **Obv:** Crowned head above ornamental center **Rev:** Encapsulated garnets with Aquarius in background **Edge:** Reeded

Date	Mintage	F	VF	XF	Unc	BU
ND(2004) Proof	10,000	Value: 25.00				

KM# 425a DOLLAR
8.5000 g., 0.9990 Silver Gilt 0.2730 oz. ASW, 25.1 mm. **Ruler:** Elizabeth II **Obv:** Crowned head above ornamental center **Rev:** Encapsulated garnets with Aquarius in background

Date	Mintage	F	VF	XF	Unc	BU
ND(2003) Proof	10,000	Value: 60.00				

KM# 426 DOLLAR
8.5000 g., 0.9990 Silver 0.2730 oz. ASW, 25.1 mm. **Ruler:** Elizabeth II **Subject:** Zodiac Gemstones - Aries **Obv:** Crowned head above ornamental center **Rev:** Encapsulated Bloodstones in center with ram at left **Edge:** Reeded

Date	Mintage	F	VF	XF	Unc	BU
ND(2003) Proof	10,000	Value: 25.00				

KM# 426a DOLLAR
8.5000 g., 0.9990 Silver Gilt 0.2730 oz. ASW, 25.1 mm. **Ruler:** Elizabeth II **Obv:** Crowned head above ornamental center **Rev:** Encapsulated Bloodstones in center with ram at left

Date	Mintage	F	VF	XF	Unc	BU
ND(2003) Proof	10,000	Value: 60.00				

KM# 427 DOLLAR
8.5000 g., 0.9990 Silver 0.2730 oz. ASW, 25.1 mm. **Ruler:** Elizabeth II **Subject:** Zodiac Gemstones - Taurus **Obv:** Crowned head above ornamental center **Rev:** Encapsulated Sapphires with bull in background **Edge:** Reeded

Date	Mintage	F	VF	XF	Unc	BU
ND(2003) Proof	10,000	Value: 25.00				

KM# 427a DOLLAR
8.5000 g., 0.9990 Silver Gilt 0.2730 oz. ASW, 25.1 mm. **Ruler:** Elizabeth II **Subject:** Zodiac Gemstones - Taurus **Obv:** Crowned head above ornamental center **Rev:** Encapsulated Sapphires with bull in background **Edge:** Reeded

Date	Mintage	F	VF	XF	Unc	BU
ND(2003) Proof	10,000	Value: 60.00				

KM# 428 DOLLAR
8.5000 g., 0.9990 Silver 0.2730 oz. ASW, 25.1 mm. **Ruler:** Elizabeth II **Obv:** Crowned head above ornamental center **Rev:** Encapsulated Agates between twins **Edge:** Reeded

Date	Mintage	F	VF	XF	Unc	BU
ND(2003) Proof	10,000	Value: 25.00				

KM# 428a DOLLAR
8.5000 g., 0.9990 Silver Gilt 0.2730 oz. ASW, 25.1 mm. **Ruler:** Elizabeth II **Obv:** Crowned head above ornamental center **Rev:** Encapsulated Agates between twins **Edge:** Reeded

Date	Mintage	F	VF	XF	Unc	BU
ND(2003) Proof	10,000	Value: 60.00				

KM# 429 DOLLAR
8.5000 g., 0.9990 Silver 0.2730 oz. ASW, 25.1 mm. **Ruler:** Elizabeth II **Obv:** Crowned head above ornamental center **Rev:** Encapsulated Onyx stones with lion at right **Edge:** Reeded

Date	Mintage	F	VF	XF	Unc	BU
ND(2003) Proof	10,000	Value: 25.00				

KM# 429a DOLLAR
8.5000 g., 0.9990 Silver Gilt 0.2730 oz. ASW, 25.1 mm. **Ruler:** Elizabeth II **Obv:** Crowned head above ornamental center **Rev:** Encapsulated Onyx stones with lion at right **Edge:** Reeded

Date	Mintage	F	VF	XF	Unc	BU
ND(2003) Proof	10,000	Value: 60.00				

KM# 430 DOLLAR
8.5000 g., 0.9990 Silver 0.2730 oz. ASW, 25.1 mm. **Ruler:** Elizabeth II **Subject:** Zodiac Gemstones - Virgo **Obv:** Crowned head above ornamented center **Rev:** Encapsulated Carnelian stones with woman at right **Edge:** Reeded

Date	Mintage	F	VF	XF	Unc	BU
ND(2003) Proof	10,000	Value: 25.00				

KM# 430a DOLLAR
8.5000 g., 0.9990 Silver Gilt 0.2730 oz. ASW, 25.1 mm. **Ruler:** Elizabeth II **Subject:** Zodiac Gemstones - Virgo **Obv:** Crowned head above ornamented center **Rev:** Encapsulated Carnelian stones with Virgo at right **Edge:** Reeded

Date	Mintage	F	VF	XF	Unc	BU
ND(2003) Proof	10,000	Value: 60.00				

KM# 431 DOLLAR
8.5000 g., 0.9990 Silver 0.2730 oz. ASW, 25.1 mm.
Ruler: Elizabeth II **Subject:** Zodiac Gemstones - Libra
Obv: Crowned head above ornamented center **Rev:**
Encapsulated Peridot stones with balance scale **Edge:** Reeded

Date	Mintage	F	VF	XF	Unc	BU
ND(2003) Proof	10,000	Value: 25.00				

KM# 431a DOLLAR
8.5000 g., 0.9990 Silver Gilt 0.2730 oz. ASW, 25.1 mm.
Ruler: Elizabeth II **Subject:** Zodiac Gemstones - Libra **Obv:**
Crowned head above ornamented center **Rev:** Encapsulated
Peridot stones with balance scale **Edge:** Reeded

Date	Mintage	F	VF	XF	Unc	BU
ND(2003) Proof	10,000	Value: 60.00				

KM# 432 DOLLAR
8.5000 g., 0.9990 Silver 0.2730 oz. ASW, 25.1 mm.
Ruler: Elizabeth II **Subject:** Zodiac Gemstones - Scorpio **Obv:**
Crowned head above ornamented center **Rev:** Encapsulated
Aquamarine stones with scorpion at lower right **Edge:** Reeded

Date	Mintage	F	VF	XF	Unc	BU
ND(2003) Proof	10,000	Value: 25.00				

KM# 432a DOLLAR
8.5000 g., 0.9990 Silver Gilt 0.2730 oz. ASW, 25.1 mm.
Ruler: Elizabeth II **Subject:** Zodiac Gemstones - Scorpio **Obv:**
Crowned head above ornamented center **Rev:** Encapsulated
Aquamarine stones with scorpion at lower right **Edge:** Reeded

Date	Mintage	F	VF	XF	Unc	BU
ND(2003) Proof	10,000	Value: 60.00				

KM# 433 DOLLAR
8.5000 g., 0.9990 Silver 0.2730 oz. ASW, 25.1 mm.
Ruler: Elizabeth II **Subject:** Zodiac Gemstones - Sagittarius
Obv: Crowned head above ornamented center
Rev: Encapsulated Topaz stones with centaur at right
Edge: Reeded

Date	Mintage	F	VF	XF	Unc	BU
ND(2003) Proof	10,000	Value: 25.00				

KM# 433a DOLLAR
8.5000 g., 0.9990 Silver Gilt 0.2730 oz. ASW, 25.1 mm.
Ruler: Elizabeth II **Subject:** Zodiac Gemstones - Sagittarius
Obv: Crowned head above ornamented center
Rev: Encapsulated Topaz stones with centaur at right
Edge: Reeded

Date	Mintage	F	VF	XF	Unc	BU
ND(2003) Proof	10,000	Value: 60.00				

KM# 434 DOLLAR
8.5000 g., 0.9990 Silver 0.2730 oz. ASW, 25.1 mm.
Ruler: Elizabeth II **Subject:** Zodiac Gemstones - Capricorn
Obv: Crowned head above ornamental center
Rev: Encapsulated rubies with goat at right **Edge:** Reeded

Date	Mintage	F	VF	XF	Unc	BU
ND(2003) Proof	10,000	Value: 25.00				

KM# 434a DOLLAR
8.5000 g., 0.9990 Silver Gilt 0.2730 oz. ASW, 25.1 mm.
Ruler: Elizabeth II **Subject:** Zodiac Gemstones - Capricorn
Obv: Crowned head above ornamented center
Rev: Encapsulated Rubies with goat at right **Edge:** Reeded

Date	Mintage	F	VF	XF	Unc	BU
ND(2003) Proof	10,000	Value: 60.00				

KM# 435 DOLLAR
8.5000 g., 0.9990 Silver 0.2730 oz. ASW, 25.1 mm.
Ruler: Elizabeth II **Subject:** Zodiac Gemstones - Pices
Obv: Crowned head above ornamented center **Rev:**
Encapsulated Amethyst stones and two fish **Edge:** Reeded

Date	Mintage	F	VF	XF	Unc	BU
ND(2003) Proof	10,000	Value: 25.00				

KM# 435a DOLLAR
8.5000 g., 0.9990 Silver Gilt 0.2730 oz. ASW, 25.1 mm.
Ruler: Elizabeth II **Subject:** Zodiac Gemstones - Pices
Obv: Crowned head above ornamented center **Rev:**
Encapsulated Amethyst stones and 2 fish **Edge:** Reeded

Date	Mintage	F	VF	XF	Unc	BU
ND(2003) Proof	10,000	Value: 60.00				

KM# 438 DOLLAR
31.1035 g., 0.9990 Silver 0.9990 oz. ASW, 40.5 mm. **Ruler:**
Elizabeth II **Obv:** Crowned head right **Rev:** Multicolor Deng
Xiaoping on Chinese map **Edge:** Plain **Shape:** As a map

Date	Mintage	F	VF	XF	Unc	BU
2004	20,000	—	—	—	35.00	40.00

KM# 454 DOLLAR
27.5300 g., 0.9990 Silver Clad Copper-Nickel 0.8842 oz. ASW,
38.6 mm. **Ruler:** Elizabeth II **Subject:** 60th Anniversary - D-
Day Invasion **Obv:** Crowned bust right, new portrait **Rev:**
Invasion scene of soldiers storming the beaches (Sword, Gold, Juno,
Omaha, and Utah) of Normandy

Date	Mintage	F	VF	XF	Unc	BU
2004	—	—	—	—	15.00	18.00

KM# 443 DOLLAR
23.9000 g., Copper-Nickel, 38.5 mm. **Ruler:** Elizabeth II
Subject: Battle of Trafalgar **Obv:** Crowned bust right, new portrait
Rev: HMS Victory and color portrait of Nelson **Edge:** Reeded

Date	Mintage	F	VF	XF	Unc	BU
2005	—	—	—	—	12.00	14.00

KM# 470 DOLLAR
31.1600 g., 0.9990 Silver 1.0008 oz. ASW, 39.02 mm.
Obv: Twin Towers and Statue of Liberty, Queens Head below
Obv. Legend: COOK ISLANDS / WE WILL NEVER FORGET
Rev: Freedom Tower and Statue of Liberty **Rev. Inscription:**
LET / FREEDOM / RING - FREEDOM TOWER **Edge:** Reeded
and plain with lettering **Edge Lettering:** 1 TROY OZ. .999 FINE
SILVER

Date	Mintage	F	VF	XF	Unc	BU
2005 Proof	—	Value: 45.00				
2006 Proof	—	Value: 30.00				

KM# 479 DOLLAR
Copper-Nickel, 38.6 mm. **Ruler:** Elizabeth II **Subject:** Gun ships
of the world **Rev:** HMS Redoutable

Date	Mintage	F	VF	XF	Unc	BU
2006	—	—	—	—	—	25.00

KM# 480 DOLLAR
24.9000 g., Copper-Nickel, 38 mm. **Ruler:** Elizabeth II
Subject: Gunships of the world **Obv:** Crowned bust right
Rev: Ark Royal in color **Edge:** Reeded

Date	Mintage	F	VF	XF	Unc	BU
2006	—	—	—	—	—	25.00

KM# 471 DOLLAR
35.8000 g., 0.9990 Silver 1.1498 oz. ASW **Ruler:** Elizabeth II
Subject: Sputnik 50th Anniversary - 1957-2007 **Obv:** Small bust
divides legend above, center globe with color applique
Rev: Satellite orbiting Earth with color applique
Rev. Legend: SPUTNIK 50th ANNIVERSARY 1957 - 2007
Edge: Plain **Note:** Center piece rotates freely

Date	Mintage	F	VF	XF	Unc	BU
ND2007 Proof	—	Value: 85.00				

KM# 490 DOLLAR
31.1030 g., 0.9990 Silver 0.9989 oz. ASW, 40.6 mm.
Ruler: Elizabeth II **Subject:** Historical Australian Coins
Obv: Head with tiara right **Rev:** 1757 New South Wales Holey
Dollar **Edge:** Reeded

Date	Mintage	F	VF	XF	Unc	BU
2007 Proof	1,500	Value: 125				

KM# 491 DOLLAR
31.1030 g., 0.9990 Silver 0.9989 oz. ASW, 40.6 mm.
Ruler: Elizabeth II **Subject:** Historical Australian Coins
Obv: Head with tiara right **Rev:** Gilt 1857 Sydney Mint Sovereign
Edge: Reeded

Date	Mintage	F	VF	XF	Unc	BU
2007 Proof	1,500	Value: 125				

KM# 492 DOLLAR
31.1030 g., 0.9990 Silver Selective copper plating 0.9989 oz.
ASW, 40.6 mm. **Ruler:** Elizabeth II **Subject:** Historical
Australian Coins **Obv:** Head with tiara right **Rev:** Copper 1937
pattern penny **Edge:** Reeded

Date	Mintage	F	VF	XF	Unc	BU
2007 Proof	1,500	Value: 125				

KM# 493 DOLLAR
31.1030 g., 0.9990 Silver 0.9989 oz. ASW, 40.6 mm.
Ruler: Elizabeth II **Subject:** Historical Australian Coins
Obv: Head with tiara right **Rev:** 1823 MacIntosh and Degraves
Shilling **Edge:** Reeded

Date	Mintage	F	VF	XF	Unc	BU
2008 Proof	1,500	Value: 125				

KM# 494 DOLLAR
31.1030 g., 0.9990 Silver Selective gold plating 0.9989 oz. ASW,
40.6 mm. **Ruler:** Elizabeth II **Subject:** Historic Australian Coins
Obv: Head with tiara right **Rev:** Gilt 1788 George III Spade
Guinea **Edge:** Reeded

Date	Mintage	F	VF	XF	Unc	BU
2008 Proof	1,500	Value: 125				

KM# 495 DOLLAR
31.1030 g., 0.9990 Silver 0.9989 oz. ASW, 40.6 mm.
Ruler: Elizabeth II **Subject:** Historical Australian Coins **Obv:** Head
with tiara right **Rev:** Australian 1910 Florin **Edge:** Reeded

Date	Mintage	F	VF	XF	Unc	BU
2008 Proof	1,500	Value: 125				

KM# 496 DOLLAR
31.1030 g., 0.9990 Silver Selective gold plating 0.9989 oz. ASW,
40.6 mm. **Ruler:** Elizabeth II **Subject:** Historic Australian Coins
Obv: Head with tiara right **Rev:** Gilt 1808-1815 Gold Pagoda
Edge: Reeded

Date	Mintage	F	VF	XF	Unc	BU
2008 Proof	1,500	Value: 125				

KM# 497 DOLLAR
31.1030 g., 0.9990 Silver 0.9989 oz. ASW, 40.6 mm.
Ruler: Elizabeth II **Subject:** Historic Australian Coins **Obv:** Head
with tiara right **Rev:** 1850's Taylor's sixpence pattern
Edge: Reeded

Date	Mintage	F	VF	XF	Unc	BU
2008 Proof	1,500	Value: 125				

KM# 498 DOLLAR
31.1050 g., 0.9990 Silver Selective copper plating 0.9990 oz.
ASW, 40.6 mm. **Ruler:** Elizabeth II **Subject:** Historic Australian
Coins **Obv:** Head with tiara right **Rev:** Copper Australian WWII
Interment Camp Token **Edge:** Reeded

Date	Mintage	F	VF	XF	Unc	BU
2008 Proof	1,500	Value: 125				

KM# 499 DOLLAR
31.1030 g., 0.9990 Silver 0.9989 oz. ASW, 40.6 mm.
Ruler: Elizabeth II **Subject:** Historic Australian Coins **Obv:** Head
with tiara right **Rev:** Australian 1946 Perth Mint Shilling
Edge: Reeded

Date	Mintage	F	VF	XF	Unc	BU
2008 Proof	1,500	Value: 125				

KM# 500 DOLLAR
31.1030 g., 0.9990 Silver 0.9989 oz. ASW, 40.6 mm.
Ruler: Elizabeth II **Subject:** Historic Australian Coins **Obv:** Head
with tiara right **Rev:** Australian 1938 Crown **Edge:** Reeded

Date	Mintage	F	VF	XF	Unc	BU
2008 Proof	1,500	Value: 125				

KM# 501 DOLLAR
31.1030 g., 0.9990 Silver 0.9989 oz. ASW, 40.6 mm.
Ruler: Elizabeth II **Subject:** Historic Australian Coins **Obv:** Head
with tiara right **Rev:** Copper Australian 1930 Penny
Edge: Reeded

Date	Mintage	F	VF	XF	Unc	BU
2008 Proof	1,500	Value: 125				

KM# 502 DOLLAR
31.1030 g., 0.9990 Silver 0.9989 oz. ASW, 40.6 mm.
Ruler: Elizabeth II **Subject:** World War I **Obv:** Head with tiara
right **Rev:** Multicolor image of Australian WWI soldier in Europe
Edge: Reeded

Date	Mintage	F	VF	XF	Unc	BU
2008 Proof	1,918	Value: 100				

KM# 504 DOLLAR
31.1030 g., 0.9990 Silver 0.9989 oz. ASW, 40.6 mm.
Ruler: Elizabeth II **Subject:** WWI **Obv:** Head with tiara right
Rev: Multicolor image of Australian WWI soldier in Mid-East
scene **Edge:** Reeded

Date	Mintage	F	VF	XF	Unc	BU
2008 Proof	1,918	Value: 100				

KM# 506 DOLLAR
31.1030 g., 0.9990 Silver 0.9989 oz. ASW, 40.6 mm.
Ruler: Elizabeth II **Subject:** Captain Cook **Obv:** Head with tiara
right **Rev:** Multicolor image of James Cook within letter C
Edge: Reeded

Date	Mintage	F	VF	XF	Unc	BU
2008 Proof	1,779	Value: 100				

KM# 507 DOLLAR
31.1030 g., 0.9990 Silver 0.9989 oz. ASW, 40.6 mm.
Ruler: Elizabeth II **Subject:** Captain Cook **Obv:** Head with tiara
right **Rev:** Multicolor image of James Cook, Bottany Bay all within
letter O **Edge:** Reeded

Date	Mintage	F	VF	XF	Unc	BU
2008 Proof	1,779	Value: 100				

KM# 508 DOLLAR
31.1030 g., 0.9990 Silver 0.9989 oz. ASW, 40.6 mm.
Ruler: Elizabeth II **Subject:** Captain Cook **Obv:** Head with tiara
right **Rev:** Multicolor image of James Cook, a new world all within
letter O **Edge:** Reeded

Date	Mintage	F	VF	XF	Unc	BU
2008 Proof	1,779	Value: 100				

KM# 509 DOLLAR
31.1030 g., 0.9990 Silver 0.9989 oz. ASW, 40.6 mm.
Ruler: Elizabeth II **Subject:** Captain Cook **Obv:** Head with tiara
right **Rev:** Multicolor image of James Cook, striking the reef, large
letter K in background **Edge:** Reeded

Date	Mintage	F	VF	XF	Unc	BU
2008 Proof	1,779	Value: 100				

KM# 701 DOLLAR

31.1050 g., 0.9990 Silver 0.9990 oz. ASW, 39 mm.
Ruler: Elizabeth II **Subject:** First Man on the Moon, 40th Anniversary **Obv:** Head right at top, multicolor moon in center **Rev:** Rocket, orbiter, moon walk. moon in multicolor at center

Date	Mintage	F	VF	XF	Unc	BU
2009 Proof	25,000	Value: 110				

KM# 702 DOLLAR

31.1050 g., 0.9990 Silver 0.9990 oz. ASW, 33x33 mm.
Ruler: Elizabeth II **Subject:** Cook's Cottage, 75th Anniversary of relocation **Obv:** Head right **Rev:** Cottage and multicolor Captain Cook image **Shape:** Square

Date	Mintage	F	VF	XF	Unc	BU
2009 Proof	5,000	Value: 95.00				

KM# 706 DOLLAR

0.5000 g., 0.9990 Gold 0.0161 oz. AGW, 11 mm.
Ruler: Elizabeth II **Subject:** Pope Benedict XVI visits the Holy Land **Rev:** Dome of the Rock

Date	Mintage	F	VF	XF	Unc	BU
2009 Proof	25,000	Value: 35.00				

KM# 708 DOLLAR

1.0000 g., 0.9990 Gold 0.0321 oz. AGW, 13.9 mm.
Ruler: Elizabeth II **Rev:** Bridge

Date	Mintage	F	VF	XF	Unc	BU
2009 Proof	250	Value: 65.00				

KM# 709 DOLLAR

1.0000 g., 0.9990 Gold 0.0321 oz. AGW, 13.9 mm.
Ruler: Elizabeth II **Rev:** Statue and gardens

Date	Mintage	F	VF	XF	Unc	BU
2009 Proof	250	Value: 65.00				

KM# 710 DOLLAR

1.0000 g., 0.9990 Gold 0.0321 oz. AGW, 13.9 mm.
Ruler: Elizabeth II **Rev:** City Gate tower

Date	Mintage	F	VF	XF	Unc	BU
2009 Proof	250	Value: 65.00				

KM# 711 DOLLAR

1.0000 g., 0.9990 Gold 0.0321 oz. AGW, 13.9 mm. **Ruler:** Elizabeth II **Rev:** Virgin Mary statue and church in background

Date	Mintage	F	VF	XF	Unc	BU
2009 Proof	250	Value: 65.00				

KM# 712 DOLLAR

1.0000 g., 0.9990 Gold 0.0321 oz. AGW, 13.9 mm.
Ruler: Elizabeth II **Rev:** Multiple church spires

Date	Mintage	F	VF	XF	Unc	BU
2009 Proof	250	Value: 65.00				

KM# 713 DOLLAR

1.0000 g., 0.9990 Gold 0.0321 oz. AGW, 13.9 mm.
Ruler: Elizabeth II **Rev:** National Theater

Date	Mintage	F	VF	XF	Unc	BU
2009 Proof	250	Value: 65.00				

KM# 714 DOLLAR

1.0000 g., 0.9990 Gold 0.0321 oz. AGW, 13.9 mm.
Ruler: Elizabeth II **Rev:** Castle

Date	Mintage	F	VF	XF	Unc	BU
2009 Proof	250	Value: 65.00				

KM# 715 DOLLAR

1.0000 g., 0.9990 Gold 0.0321 oz. AGW, 13.9 mm.
Ruler: Elizabeth II **Rev:** Castle on a hill

Date	Mintage	F	VF	XF	Unc	BU
2009 Proof	250	Value: 65.00				

KM# 716 DOLLAR

1.0000 g., 0.9990 Gold 0.0321 oz. AGW, 13.9 mm.
Ruler: Elizabeth II **Rev:** Castle

Date	Mintage	F	VF	XF	Unc	BU
2009 Proof	250	Value: 65.00				

KM# 717 DOLLAR

1.0000 g., 0.9990 Gold 0.0321 oz. AGW, 13.9 mm.
Ruler: Elizabeth II **Rev:** Castle

Date	Mintage	F	VF	XF	Unc	BU
2009 Proof	250	Value: 65.00				

KM# 718 DOLLAR

1.0000 g., 0.9990 Gold 0.0321 oz. AGW, 13.9 mm.
Ruler: Elizabeth II **Rev:** Church

Date	Mintage	F	VF	XF	Unc	BU
2009 Proof	250	Value: 65.00				

KM# 719 DOLLAR

1.0000 g., 0.9990 Gold 0.0321 oz. AGW, 13.9 mm.
Ruler: Elizabeth II **Rev:** Ancient ruins

Date	Mintage	F	VF	XF	Unc	BU
2009 Proof	250	Value: 65.00				

KM# 720 DOLLAR

0.1200 g., 0.9990 Silver 0.0039 oz. ASW, 4 mm.
Ruler: Elizabeth II **Rev:** Fisherman's God statue

Date	Mintage	F	VF	XF	Unc	BU
2010 Prooflike	5,000	—	—	—	—	5.00

KM# 554 2 DOLLARS

31.1050 g., 0.9990 Silver 0.9990 oz. ASW, 40.5 mm.
Ruler: Elizabeth II **Subject:** Asian wildlife **Rev:** Multicolored pheasant-tailed Jacana

Date	Mintage	F	VF	XF	Unc	BU
2001 Proof	3,000	Value: 85.00				

KM# 551 2 DOLLARS

31.1050 g., 0.9990 Silver 0.9990 oz. ASW, 40.5 mm.
Ruler: Elizabeth II **Subject:** Asian wildlife **Rev:** Multicolor Mikado Pheasant

Date	Mintage	F	VF	XF	Unc	BU
2001 Proof	5,000	Value: 85.00				

KM# 552 2 DOLLARS

31.1050 g., 0.9990 Silver 0.9990 oz. ASW, 40.5 mm.
Ruler: Elizabeth II **Subject:** Asian wildlife **Rev:** Multicolor black-faced spoonbill

Date	Mintage	F	VF	XF	Unc	BU
2001 Proof	5,000	Value: 85.00				

KM# 553 2 DOLLARS

31.1050 g., 0.9990 Silver 0.9990 oz. ASW, 40.5 mm. **Ruler:** Elizabeth II **Subject:** Asian wildlife **Rev:** Multicolor Indian Pitta

Date	Mintage	F	VF	XF	Unc	BU
2001 Proof	3,000	Value: 85.00				

KM# 468 2 DOLLARS

Copper-Nickel **Ruler:** Elizabeth II **Rev:** Football championship

Date	Mintage	F	VF	XF	Unc	BU
2002	—	—	—	—	5.00	7.00

KM# 417 2 DOLLARS

7.5500 g., Copper-Nickel, 26 mm. **Ruler:** Elizabeth II **Obv:** Crowned bust right, new portrait **Rev:** Mortar and pestle from Atiu Island **Edge:** Triangular

Date	Mintage	F	VF	XF	Unc	BU
2003	—	—	—	—	3.00	3.50

KM# 536 2 DOLLARS

31.1050 g., 0.9990 Silver 0.9990 oz. ASW, 40.7 mm.
Ruler: Elizabeth II **Subject:** Birds of New Zealand **Rev:** Multicolor tui

Date	Mintage	F	VF	XF	Unc	BU
2005 Prooflike	8,000	—	—	—	—	90.00

KM# 537 2 DOLLARS

31.1050 g., 0.9990 Silver 0.9990 oz. ASW, 40.7 mm.
Subject: Birds of New Zealand **Rev:** Multicolor bell bird

Date	Mintage	F	VF	XF	Unc	BU
2005 Prooflike	8,000	—	—	—	—	90.00

KM# 538 2 DOLLARS

31.1050 g., 0.9990 Silver 0.9990 oz. ASW, 40.7 mm.
Ruler: Elizabeth II **Subject:** Birds of New Zealand **Rev:** Multicolor New Zealand Pigeon

Date	Mintage	F	VF	XF	Unc	BU
2005 Prooflike	8,000	—	—	—	—	90.00

KM# 539 2 DOLLARS

31.1050 g., 0.9990 Silver 0.9990 oz. ASW, 40.7 mm.
Ruler: Elizabeth II **Subject:** Birds of New Zealand **Rev:** Multicolor yellow crowned parakeet

Date	Mintage	F	VF	XF	Unc	BU
2005 Prooflike	8,000	—	—	—	—	90.00

KM# 524 2 DOLLARS

31.1050 g., 0.9990 Silver 0.9990 oz. ASW, 40.7 mm.
Ruler: Elizabeth II **Subject:** Classic Speedsters from the 1930's **Rev:** Multicolor 1935 Auburn 851 Speedster

Date	Mintage	F	VF	XF	Unc	BU
2006 Prooflike	6,000	—	—	—	—	80.00

KM# 525 2 DOLLARS

31.1050 g., 0.9990 Silver 0.9990 oz. ASW, 40.7 mm.
Ruler: Elizabeth II **Subject:** Classic Speedsters from the 1930's **Rev:** Multicolor 1935 Bugatti Type 57SC Atlantic Speedster

Date	Mintage	F	VF	XF	Unc	BU
2006 Prooflike	6,000	—	—	—	—	80.00

KM# 526 2 DOLLARS

31.1050 g., 0.9990 Silver 0.9990 oz. ASW, 40.7 mm.
Ruler: Elizabeth II **Subject:** Speedsters from the 1930's **Rev:** Multicolor 1936 Duesenberg SSJ Speedster

Date	Mintage	F	VF	XF	Unc	BU
2006 Prooflike	—	—	—	—	—	80.00

KM# 527 2 DOLLARS

31.1050 g., 0.9990 Silver 0.9990 oz. ASW, 40.7 mm.
Ruler: Elizabeth II **Subject:** Speedsters from the 1930's **Rev:** Multicolor 1930 Packard 734 Boattail Speedster

Date	Mintage	F	VF	XF	Unc	BU
2006 Prooflike	6,000	—	—	—	—	80.00

KM# 529 2 DOLLARS

31.1050 g., 0.9990 Silver 0.9990 oz. ASW, 40.7 mm.
Ruler: Elizabeth II **Subject:** International Women's Day **Rev:** Multicolor tulips, large 8

Date	Mintage	F	VF	XF	Unc	BU
2007 Prooflike	4,000	—	—	—	—	85.00

KM# 532 2 DOLLARS

31.1050 g., 0.9990 Silver 0.9990 oz. ASW, 40.7 mm.
Ruler: Elizabeth II **Subject:** Sherlock Holmes **Rev:** Multicolor portrait

Date	Mintage	F	VF	XF	Unc	BU
2007 Prooflike	8,000	—	—	—	—	100

KM# 520 2 DOLLARS

31.1050 g., 0.9990 Silver 0.9990 oz. ASW, 40.7 mm.
Ruler: Elizabeth II **Subject:** Racers from the 1930's **Rev:** Multicolor, Hughes H-1 Racer

Date	Mintage	F	VF	XF	Unc	BU
2008 Prooflike	6,000	—	—	—	—	80.00

KM# 510 2 DOLLARS

31.1050 g., 0.9990 Silver 0.9990 oz. ASW, 40.7 mm.
Ruler: Elizabeth II **Subject:** Year of the Rat **Rev:** Multicolor scene of little girl from Russian animated cartoon

Date	Mintage	F	VF	XF	Unc	BU
2008 Prooflike	10,000	—	—	—	—	80.00

KM# 511 2 DOLLARS

31.1050 g., 0.9990 Silver 0.9990 oz. ASW, 40.7 mm.
Ruler: Elizabeth II **Subject:** Year of the Rat **Rev:** Multicolor scene of nutcracker from Russian animated cartoon

Date	Mintage	F	VF	XF	Unc	BU
2008 Prooflike	10,000	—	—	—	—	80.00

KM# 512 2 DOLLARS

39.1050 g., 0.9990 Silver 1.2559 oz. ASW, 40.7 mm.
Ruler: Elizabeth II **Rev:** Multicolor scene of Adventure of Cat Leopold Russian animated cartoon

Date	Mintage	F	VF	XF	Unc	BU
2008 Prooflike	10,000	—	—	—	—	80.00

KM# 513 2 DOLLARS

31.1050 g., 0.9990 Silver 0.9990 oz. ASW, 40.7 mm.
Ruler: Elizabeth II **Subject:** Year of the Rat **Rev:** Multicolor scene of tough toy soldier from Russian animated cartoon

Date	Mintage	F	VF	XF	Unc	BU
2008 Prooflike	10,000	—	—	—	—	80.00

KM# 514 2 DOLLARS

31.1050 g., 0.9990 Silver 0.9990 oz. ASW, 40.7 mm.
Ruler: Elizabeth II **Subject:** Great Motorcycles from the 1930's **Rev:** Multicolor 1930 BSA Sloper

Date	Mintage	F	VF	XF	Unc	BU
2008 Prooflike	6,000	—	—	—	—	80.00

KM# 515 2 DOLLARS

31.1050 g., 0.9990 Silver 0.9990 oz. ASW, 40.7 mm.
Ruler: Elizabeth II **Subject:** Great motorcycles from the 1930's **Rev:** Multicolor 1937 Ariel 1000 Squarefour

Date	Mintage	F	VF	XF	Unc	BU
2008 Prooflike	6,000	—	—	—	—	80.00

KM# 516 2 DOLLARS

31.1050 g., 0.9990 Silver 0.9990 oz. ASW, 40.7 mm.
Ruler: Elizabeth II **Subject:** Great motorcycles from the 1930's **Rev:** Multicolor 1938 12H 8

Date	Mintage	F	VF	XF	Unc	BU
2008 Prooflike	6,000	—	—	—	—	80.00

KM# 517 2 DOLLARS

31.1050 g., 0.9990 Silver 0.9990 oz. ASW, 40.7 mm.
Ruler: Elizabeth II **Subject:** Great motorcycles from the 1930's **Rev:** Multicolor 1931 Matchless Silver Hawk

Date	Mintage	F	VF	XF	Unc	BU
2008 Prooflike	6,000	—	—	—	—	80.00

KM# 518 2 DOLLARS

31.1050 g., 0.9990 Silver 0.9990 oz. ASW, 40.7 mm.
Ruler: Elizabeth II **Subject:** Great motocycles from the 1930's **Rev:** Multicolor 1932 Brough Superior SS100

Date	Mintage	F	VF	XF	Unc	BU
2008 Prooflike	6,000	—	—	—	—	80.00

KM# 519 2 DOLLARS

31.1050 g., 0.9990 Silver 0.9990 oz. ASW, 40.7 mm.
Ruler: Elizabeth II **Subject:** Racers from the 1930's **Rev:** Multicolor Gee Bee

Date	Mintage	F	VF	XF	Unc	BU
2008 Prooflike	6,000	—	—	—	—	80.00

KM# 521 2 DOLLARS

31.1050 g., 0.9990 Silver 0.9990 oz. ASW, 40.7 mm.
Ruler: Elizabeth II **Subject:** Racers from the 1930's **Rev:** Multicolor Laird Turner LTR-14 Meteor

Date	Mintage	F	VF	XF	Unc	BU
2008 Prooflike	6,000	—	—	—	—	80.00

KM# 522 2 DOLLARS

31.1050 g., 0.9990 Silver 0.9990 oz. ASW, 40.7 mm.
Ruler: Elizabeth II **Subject:** Racers from the 1930's **Rev:** Multicolor Spuermarine S.6B Floatplane

Date	Mintage	F	VF	XF	Unc	BU
2008 Prooflike	6,000	—	—	—	—	80.00

KM# 523 2 DOLLARS

31.1050 g., 0.9990 Silver 0.9990 oz. ASW, 40.7 mm.
Ruler: Elizabeth II **Subject:** Racers from the 1930's **Rev:** Multicolor Polikarpov I-16

Date	Mintage	F	VF	XF	Unc	BU
2008 Prooflike	6,000	—	—	—	—	80.00

KM# 528 2 DOLLARS

31.1050 g., 0.9990 Silver 0.9990 oz. ASW, 40.7 mm.
Ruler: Elizabeth II **Subject:** Valentines (Love) **Rev:** Multicolor pair of swans **Rev. Legend:** Love is precious

Date	Mintage	F	VF	XF	Unc	BU
2008 Prooflike	16,000	—	—	—	—	90.00

KM# 530 2 DOLLARS

31.1050 g., 0.9990 Silver 0.9990 oz. ASW, 40.7 mm.
Ruler: Elizabeth II **Subject:** Mikhail Kalasknikov **Rev:** Multicolor portrait in uniform with siver gun

Date	Mintage	F	VF	XF	Unc	BU
2008 Prooflike	20,000	—	—	—	—	100

KM# 531 2 DOLLARS

31.1050 g., 0.9990 Silver 0.9990 oz. ASW, 40.7 mm.
Ruler: Elizabeth II **Subject:** Mikhail Kalashnikov **Rev:** Multicolor red star, soldier and gun

Date	Mintage	F	VF	XF	Unc	BU
2008 Prooflike	20,000	—	—	—	—	100

KM# 533 2 DOLLARS
31.1050 g., 0.9990 Silver 0.9990 oz. ASW, 40.7 mm.
Ruler: Elizabeth II **Subject:** Sherlock Holmes **Rev:** Multicolor scene from Hound of the Baskervilles

Date	Mintage	F	VF	XF	Unc	BU
2008 Prooflike	8,000	—	—	—	—	100

KM# 534 2 DOLLARS
31.1050 g., 0.9990 Silver 0.9990 oz. ASW, 40.7 mm.
Ruler: Elizabeth II **Subject:** Sherlock Holmes **Rev:** Multicolor scehe from the Final Problem

Date	Mintage	F	VF	XF	Unc	BU
2008 Prooflike	8,000	—	—	—	—	100

KM# 535 2 DOLLARS
31.1050 g., 0.9990 Silver 0.9990 oz. ASW, 40.7 mm.
Ruler: Elizabeth II **Subject:** Sherlock Holmes **Rev:** Multicolor scene from the Sign of the Four

Date	Mintage	F	VF	XF	Unc	BU
2008 Prooflike	8,000	—	—	—	—	100

KM# 540 2 DOLLARS
31.1050 g., 0.9990 Silver 0.9990 oz. ASW, 40.7 mm.
Ruler: Elizabeth II **Subject:** Ballet dancers **Rev:** Multicolor Vasley Nijinnsky

Date	Mintage	F	VF	XF	Unc	BU
2008 Prooflike	8,000	—	—	—	—	85.00

KM# 541 2 DOLLARS
31.1050 g., 0.9990 Silver 0.9990 oz. ASW, 40.7 mm.
Ruler: Elizabeth II **Subject:** Ballet Dancers **Rev:** Multicolor Matuilda Kshesinskaya

Date	Mintage	F	VF	XF	Unc	BU
2008 Prooflike	8,000	—	—	—	—	85.00

KM# 542 2 DOLLARS
31.1050 g., 0.9990 Silver 0.9990 oz. ASW, 40.7 mm.
Ruler: Elizabeth II **Subject:** Ballet dancers **Rev:** Multicolor Sergey Lifar

Date	Mintage	F	VF	XF	Unc	BU
2008 Prooflike	8,000	—	—	—	—	85.00

KM# 543 2 DOLLARS
31.1050 g., 0.9990 Silver 0.9990 oz. ASW, 40.7 mm.
Ruler: Elizabeth II **Subject:** Ballet dancers **Rev:** Multicolor Anna Pavlova

Date	Mintage	F	VF	XF	Unc	BU
2008 Prooflike	—	—	—	—	—	85.00

KM# 544 2 DOLLARS
31.1050 g., 0.9990 Silver 0.9990 oz. ASW, 40.7 mm.
Ruler: Elizabeth II **Subject:** White Army **Rev:** Multicolor Anton Denkin

Date	Mintage	F	VF	XF	Unc	BU
2008 Prooflike	6,000	—	—	—	—	85.00

KM# 545 2 DOLLARS
31.1050 g., 0.9990 Silver 0.9990 oz. ASW, 40.7 mm.
Ruler: Elizabeth II **Subject:** White Army **Rev:** Multicolor Pytor Vrangel

Date	Mintage	F	VF	XF	Unc	BU
2008 Prooflike	6,000	—	—	—	—	85.00

KM# 546 2 DOLLARS
31.1050 g., 0.9990 Silver 0.9990 oz. ASW, 40.7 mm.
Ruler: Elizabeth II **Subject:** White Army **Rev:** Multicolor Alexander Kutepov

Date	Mintage	F	VF	XF	Unc	BU
2008 Prooflike	6,000	—	—	—	—	85.00

KM# 547 2 DOLLARS
31.1050 g., 0.9990 Silver 0.9990 oz. ASW, 40.7 mm.
Ruler: Elizabeth II **Subject:** White Army **Rev:** Multicolor Alexander Kolchak

Date	Mintage	F	VF	XF	Unc	BU
2008 Prooflike	6,000	—	—	—	—	85.00

KM# 721 2 DOLLARS
0.1200 g., 0.9990 Gold 0.0039 oz. AGW, 4 mm.
Ruler: Elizabeth II **Rev:** Lady Penrhyn sailing ship

Date	Mintage	F	VF	XF	Unc	BU
2010 Prooflike	5,000	—	—	—	—	10.00

KM# 722 2 DOLLARS
0.1200 g., 0.9950 Platinum 0.0038 oz. APW, 4 mm.
Ruler: Elizabeth II **Rev:** Humpback whale

Date	Mintage	F	VF	XF	Unc	BU
2010 Prooflike	5,000	—	—	—	—	10.00

KM# 418 5 DOLLARS
14.0000 g., Aluminum-Bronze, 31.5 mm. **Ruler:** Elizabeth II **Obv:** Crowned bust right, new portrait **Rev:** Conch shell and value **Shape:** 12-sided

Date	Mintage	F	VF	XF	Unc	BU
2003	—	—	—	—	6.00	8.00

KM# 469 5 DOLLARS
Copper-Nickel, 40 mm. **Obv:** USPS logo, Queens head above **Rev:** 5 cent 1847 Benjamin Franklin stamp

Date	Mintage	F	VF	XF	Unc	BU
2004	—	—	—	—	10.00	12.00

KM# 469a 5 DOLLARS
Silver, 40 mm. **Obv:** USPS logo, Queens head above **Rev:** 5 cent 1847 Benjamin Franklin stamp **Edge:** Reeded

Date	Mintage	F	VF	XF	Unc	BU
2004 Proof	—	Value: 25.00				

KM# 478 5 DOLLARS
Silver Gilt **Ruler:** Elizabeth II **Subject:** Pope Benedict XVI's visit to Valencia, Spain **Obv:** Bust right **Rev:** Valencia Cathedral **Shape:** Cathedral outline **Note:** Jeweled cathedral.

Date	Mintage	F	VF	XF	Unc	BU
2006 Proof	2,500	Value: 60.00				

KM# 560 5 DOLLARS
25.0000 g., 0.9250 Silver partially gilt 0.7435 oz. ASW, 35x31 mm. **Ruler:** Elizabeth II **Subject:** Benedict XVI Annus Secundus **Rev:** Cross in crystals and gilt Papal Arms **Shape:** 6-sided

Date	Mintage	F	VF	XF	Unc	BU
2006 Proof	5,000	Value: 90.00				

KM# 561 5 DOLLARS
25.0000 g., 0.9990 Silver partially gilt 0.8029 oz. ASW, 42x49 mm. **Ruler:** Elizabeth II **Subject:** Benedict XVI visits Germany **Rev:** Cathedral gilt, crystal inserts **Shape:** oval

Date	Mintage	F	VF	XF	Unc	BU
2006 Proof	5,000	Value: 90.00				

KM# 562 5 DOLLARS
25.0000 g., 0.9990 Silver 0.8029 oz. ASW, 35x35 mm. **Ruler:** Elizabeth II **Subject:** Benedict XVI **Rev:** Profile at left, cross in crystal inserts **Shape:** Square

Date	Mintage	F	VF	XF	Unc	BU
2006 Proof	5,000	Value: 90.00				

KM# 563 5 DOLLARS
25.0000 g., 0.9990 Silver partially gilt 0.8029 oz. ASW, 35x38 mm. **Ruler:** Elizabeth II **Subject:** Christmas in St. Peter's Square **Rev:** St. Peter's partially gilt, star crystal insert **Shape:** Triange

Date	Mintage	F	VF	XF	Unc	BU
2006 Proof	5,000	Value: 90.00				

KM# 564 5 DOLLARS
25.0000 g., 0.9990 Silver 0.8029 oz. ASW, 20x44 mm. **Ruler:** Elizabeth II **Subject:** benedict XVI visits Poland **Rev:** Polish icon, partially gilt, crystal insert **Shape:** Candle

Date	Mintage	F	VF	XF	Unc	BU
2006 Proof	564	Value: 90.00				

KM# 565 5 DOLLARS
25.0000 g., 0.9990 Silver partially gilt 0.8029 oz. ASW, 38.6 mm. **Ruler:** Elizabeth II **Rev:** St. Peter's Basilica, partially gilt, crystals as stars

Date	Mintage	F	VF	XF	Unc	BU
2006 Proof	5,000	Value: 90.00				

KM# 566 5 DOLLARS
25.0000 g., 0.9990 Silver partially gilt 0.8029 oz. ASW, 35x35 mm. **Ruler:** Elizabeth II **Subject:** Swiss Guards, 500th Anniversary **Rev:** Four Swiss guards, partially gilt, crystal insert **Shape:** Diamond

Date	Mintage	F	VF	XF	Unc	BU
2006 Proof	5,000	Value: 90.00				

KM# 567 5 DOLLARS
25.0000 g., 0.9990 Silver 0.8029 oz. ASW, 40x25 mm. **Ruler:** Elizabeth II **Subject:** Benedict XVI visits Turkey **Rev:** Pope and Patrarch, partially gilt, crystal insert **Shape:** Rectangle

Date	Mintage	F	VF	XF	Unc	BU
2006 Proof	5,000	Value: 90.00				

KM# 568 5 DOLLARS
25.0000 g., 0.9990 Silver 0.8029 oz. ASW, 40x25 mm. **Ruler:** Elizabeth II **Subject:** Urbi et Orbi message **Rev:** Benedict XVI giving blessing, partially gilt, crystal insert **Shape:** Rectangle

Date	Mintage	F	VF	XF	Unc	BU
2006 Proof	5,000	Value: 90.00				

KM# 569 5 DOLLARS
0.2500 g., 0.9990 Silver partially gilt 0.0080 oz. ASW, 29x42 mm. **Ruler:** Elizabeth II **Subject:** Benedict XVI visits Vallencia **Rev:** Valencia cathedral facade, partially gilt, crystal inserts **Shape:** Irregular

Date	Mintage	F	VF	XF	Unc	BU
2006 Proof	5,000	Value: 75.00				

KM# 570 5 DOLLARS
31.1000 g., 0.9990 Silver 0.9988 oz. ASW, 38.6 mm. **Ruler:** Elizabeth II **Rev:** Statue of Liberty gilt pop-up

Date	Mintage	F	VF	XF	Unc	BU
2006 Proof	5,000	Value: 100				

KM# 571 5 DOLLARS
31.1000 g., 0.9990 Silver 0.9988 oz. ASW, 38.6 mm. **Ruler:** Elizabeth II **Rev:** Ludwig's castle gilt pop-up

Date	Mintage	F	VF	XF	Unc	BU
2006 Proof	5,000	Value: 100				

KM# 572 5 DOLLARS
25.0000 g., 0.9990 Silver partially gilt 0.8029 oz. ASW, 35x35 mm. **Ruler:** Elizabeth II **Subject:** Benedict XVI visits Marianzell **Rev:** Our Lady or Marianzell, partially gilt, crystal inserts **Shape:** Tablet

Date	Mintage	F	VF	XF	Unc	BU
2007 Proof	5,000	Value: 90.00				

KM# 573 5 DOLLARS
25.0000 g., 0.9990 Silver 0.8029 oz. ASW, 35x35 mm. **Ruler:** Elizabeth II **Rev:** St. Francis, tau cross, partially gilt, crystal insert **Shape:** Dove

Date	Mintage	F	VF	XF	Unc	BU
2007 Proof	5,000	Value: 90.00				

KM# 574 5 DOLLARS
25.0000 g., 0.9990 Silver 0.8029 oz. ASW, 31x40 mm. **Ruler:** Elizabeth II **Rev:** Benedict XVI bust left, partially gilt, crystal insert **Shape:** Irregular

Date	Mintage	F	VF	XF	Unc	BU
2007 Proof	5,000	Value: 90.00				

KM# 575 5 DOLLARS
25.0000 g., 0.9990 Silver 0.8029 oz. ASW, 35x45 mm. **Ruler:** Elizabeth II **Subject:** Benedict XVI visits Brazil **Rev:** Christ statue in Rio, partially gilt, crystal insert **Shape:** Diamond

Date	Mintage	F	VF	XF	Unc	BU
2007 Proof	5,000	Value: 90.00				

KM# 576 5 DOLLARS
25.0000 g., 0.9990 Silver 0.8029 oz. ASW, 37 mm. **Ruler:** Elizabeth II **Subject:** Princess Diana, 10th Anniversary of death **Rev:** Bust at left, multicolored rose **Shape:** Heart

Date	Mintage	F	VF	XF	Unc	BU
2007 Proof	1,997	Value: 65.00				

KM# 577 5 DOLLARS
25.0000 g., 0.9990 Silver partially gilt 0.8029 oz. ASW, 39x24 mm. **Ruler:** Elizabeth II **Subject:** Docrine of the Immaculate Conception **Rev:** Virgin Mary and cathedral, partially gilt, crystal insert **Shape:** Rectangle

Date	Mintage	F	VF	XF	Unc	BU
2007 Proof	5,000	Value: 90.00				

KM# 578 5 DOLLARS
25.0000 g., 0.9990 Silver 0.8029 oz. ASW, 31x35 mm. **Ruler:** Elizabeth II **Subject:** Benedict XVI visits Loredo **Rev:** Pope blessing crowd, cathedral, partially gilt, crystal insert **Shape:** 6-sided

Date	Mintage	F	VF	XF	Unc	BU
2007 Proof	5,000	Value: 90.00				

KM# 579 5 DOLLARS
25.0000 g., 0.9990 Silver 0.8029 oz. ASW, 35x35 mm. **Ruler:** Elizabeth II **Subject:** Santo Subito **Rev:** Pope John Paul II, partially gilt, crystal insert **Shape:** Cross

Date	Mintage	F	VF	XF	Unc	BU
2007 Proof	5,000	Value: 100				

KM# 580 5 DOLLARS
25.0000 g., 0.9990 Silver 0.8029 oz. ASW, 30x45 mm. **Ruler:** Elizabeth II **Subject:** Way of the Cross **Rev:** benedict XVI holdign cross, collesum in background, partially gilt, crystal insert **Shape:** Vertical oval

Date	Mintage	F	VF	XF	Unc	BU
2007 Proof	5,000	Value: 90.00				

KM# 581 5 DOLLARS
31.1000 g., 0.9990 Silver 0.9988 oz. ASW, 38.6 mm. **Ruler:** Elizabeth II **Rev:** Parthenon gilt pop-up

Date	Mintage	F	VF	XF	Unc	BU
2007 Proof	5,000	Value: 100				

KM# 583 5 DOLLARS
31.1000 g., 0.9990 Silver 0.9988 oz. ASW, 38.6 mm. **Ruler:** Elizabeth II **Rev:** Rio's Christ statue gilt pop-up

Date	Mintage	F	VF	XF	Unc	BU
2007 Proof	5,000	Value: 100				

KM# 584 5 DOLLARS
31.1000 g., 0.9990 Silver 0.9988 oz. ASW, 38.6 mm. **Ruler:** Elizabeth II **Rev:** Collesum gilt pop-up

Date	Mintage	F	VF	XF	Unc	BU
2007 Proof	5,000	Value: 100				

KM# 586 5 DOLLARS
31.1000 g., 0.9990 Silver 0.9988 oz. ASW, 38.6 mm. **Ruler:** Elizabeth II **Rev:** Eifle Tower gilt pop-up

Date	Mintage	F	VF	XF	Unc	BU
2007 Proof	5,000	Value: 100				

KM# 594 5 DOLLARS
25.0000 g., 0.9990 Silver 0.8029 oz. ASW, 35x35 mm. **Ruler:** Elizabeth II **Subject:** Pope John Paul II Election 30th Anniversary **Rev:** John Paul II coat-of-arms, aprtially gilt, crystal insert **Shape:** Diamond

Date	Mintage	F	VF	XF	Unc	BU
2008 Proof	5,000	Value: 100				

KM# 595 5 DOLLARS
25.0000 g., 0.9990 Silver 0.8029 oz. ASW, 30x45 mm. **Ruler:** Elizabeth II **Subject:** Lourdes, 150th Anniversary **Rev:** Statue of Our Lady of Lourdes, partially gilt, crystal insert **Shape:** Vertical oval

Date	Mintage	F	VF	XF	Unc	BU
2008 Proof	5,000	Value: 110				

KM# 596 5 DOLLARS
25.0000 g., 0.9990 Silver 0.8029 oz. ASW, 30x45 mm. **Ruler:** Elizabeth II **Subject:** Lourdes, 150th Anniversary **Rev:** Our Lady of Lourdes, holigram, partially gilt, crystal insert **Shape:** Vertical oval

Date	Mintage	F	VF	XF	Unc	BU
2008 Proof	5,000	Value: 120				

KM# 597 5 DOLLARS
25.0000 g., 0.9990 Silver 0.8029 oz. ASW, 40x25 mm. **Ruler:** Elizabeth II **Subject:** Benedict XVI Annus Novas **Rev:** Benedict XVI and dove **Shape:** Oval

Date	Mintage	F	VF	XF	Unc	BU
2008 Proof	5,000	Value: 100				

KM# 598 5 DOLLARS
25.0000 g., 0.9990 Silver 0.8029 oz. ASW, 32x41 mm. **Ruler:** Elizabeth II **Rev:** St. Peter's Square, cresch and christmas tree, partially gilt, crystal insert **Shape:** Triangle

Date	Mintage	F	VF	XF	Unc	BU
2008 Proof	5,000	Value: 100				

KM# 599 5 DOLLARS
25.0000 g., 0.9990 Silver 0.8029 oz. ASW, 35x35 mm. **Ruler:** Elizabeth II **Subject:** Crufifixio Domini **Rev:** Benedict XVI before cross, partially gilt, crystal inserts **Shape:** Cross

Date	Mintage	F	VF	XF	Unc	BU
2008 Proof	5,000	Value: 100				

KM# 600 5 DOLLARS
25.0000 g., 0.9990 Silver 0.8029 oz. ASW, 29x42 mm. **Ruler:** Elizabeth II **Subject:** Paulus year **Rev:** Benedict XVI in Basicilica, partially gilt, crystal insert **Shape:** Vertical rectangle

Date	Mintage	F	VF	XF	Unc	BU
2008 Proof	5,000	Value: 100				

KM# 601 5 DOLLARS
25.0000 g., 0.9990 Silver 0.8029 oz. ASW, 40x25 mm. **Ruler:** Elizabeth II **Subject:** Sistine Chapel, 500th Anniversary **Rev:** Adam and god, Sistine Chapel ceiling, partially gilt, crystal insert **Shape:** Rectangle

Date	Mintage	F	VF	XF	Unc	BU
2008 Proof	5,000	Value: 120				

KM# 602 5 DOLLARS
25.0000 g., 0.9990 Silver 0.8029 oz. ASW, 40x42 mm. **Ruler:** Elizabeth II **Rev:** St Martin on horseback, partially gilt, crystal insert **Shape:** 8-sided

Date	Mintage	F	VF	XF	Unc	BU
2008 Proof	5,000	Value: 100				

KM# 603 5 DOLLARS
25.0000 g., 0.9990 Silver 0.8029 oz. ASW, 45x34 mm. **Ruler:** Elizabeth II **Subject:** Benedict XVI visits Sydney **Rev:** Sydney Harbor Bridge and Sydney Opera House, partially gilt, crystal insert **Shape:** Irregular oval

Date	Mintage	F	VF	XF	Unc	BU
2008 Proof	5,000	Value: 100				

KM# 604 5 DOLLARS
25.0000 g., 0.9990 Silver 0.8029 oz. ASW, 35x35 mm. **Ruler:** Elizabeth II **Subject:** Tu Es Peterus **Rev:** Cross Keys, Christ handing keys to kneeling St. Peter. Partially gilt, crystal insert. **Shape:** Square

Date	Mintage	F	VF	XF	Unc	BU
2008 Proof	5,000	Value: 120				

KM# 605 5 DOLLARS
25.0000 g., 0.9990 Silver 0.8029 oz. ASW, 38.6 mm. **Ruler:** Elizabeth II **Rev:** Pope blessing crowd, partially gilt, crystal inserts

Date	Mintage	F	VF	XF	Unc	BU
2008 Proof	5,000	Value: 100				

KM# 606   5 DOLLARS
25.0000 g., 0.9990 Silver 0.8029 oz. ASW, 42x29 mm.
Ruler: Elizabeth II **Subject:** Benedict XVI visits the United States
Rev: Benedict XVI, the White House, Statue of Liberty, UN
Building, partially gilt, crystal inserts **Shape:** Irregular US Map
shape

Date	Mintage	F	VF	XF	Unc	BU
2008 Proof	5,000	Value: 100				

KM# 607   5 DOLLARS
25.0000 g., 0.9990 Silver 0.8029 oz. ASW, 40x42 mm.
Ruler: Elizabeth II **Rev:** St. george slaying dragon, partially gilt,
crystal insert **Shape:** 8-sided

Date	Mintage	F	VF	XF	Unc	BU
2008 Proof	5,000	Value: 100				

KM# 608   5 DOLLARS
31.1050 g., 0.9990 Silver 0.9990 oz. ASW, 38.6 mm.
Ruler: Elizabeth II **Subject:** Conversion of Russia, 1000th
Anniversary **Rev:** Baptism scene **Note:** Exclusive to the Russian
Market.

Date	Mintage	F	VF	XF	Unc	BU
2008 Proof	500	Value: 120				

KM# 609   5 DOLLARS
31.1050 g., 0.9990 Silver 0.9990 oz. ASW, 47x27 mm.
Ruler: Elizabeth II **Subject:** Orthodox Communication
Rev: Patriarch's meeting **Shape:** Rectangle **Note:** Exclusive to
the Russian Market.

Date	Mintage	F	VF	XF	Unc	BU
2008 Proof	500	Value: 120				

KM# 610   5 DOLLARS
25.0000 g., 0.9990 Silver 0.8029 oz. ASW, 30x38 mm.
Ruler: Elizabeth II **Rev:** Icon - Theotokos of Vladimir, wood insert
Shape: Rectangle **Note:** Exclusive to the Russian Market.

Date	Mintage	F	VF	XF	Unc	BU
2008 Proof	2,500	Value: 120				

KM# 611   5 DOLLARS
31.1050 g., 0.9990 Silver 0.9990 oz. ASW, 38.6 mm.
Ruler: Elizabeth II **Subject:** Kiev Churches **Rev:** Church of All
Saints **Note:** Exclusive to the Russian Market.

Date	Mintage	F	VF	XF	Unc	BU
2008 Proof	500	Value: 120				

KM# 612   5 DOLLARS
31.1050 g., 0.9990 Silver 0.9990 oz. ASW, 38.6 mm.
Ruler: Elizabeth II **Subject:** Kiev Churches **Rev:** Dormotion of
Theotokos **Note:** Exclusive to the Russian Market.

Date	Mintage	F	VF	XF	Unc	BU
2008 Proof	500	Value: 120				

KM# 613   5 DOLLARS
31.1050 g., 0.9990 Silver 0.9990 oz. ASW   **Ruler:** Elizabeth II
Subject: Kiev Churches **Rev:** Refractory of Pechersky
Shape: 38.6 **Note:** Exclusive to the Russian Market.

Date	Mintage	F	VF	XF	Unc	BU
2008 Proof	500	Value: 120				

KM# 614   5 DOLLARS
31.1050 g., 0.9990 Silver 0.9990 oz. ASW, 38.6 mm.   **Ruler:**
Elizabeth II **Subject:** Kiev Churches **Rev:** Troitskaya Barbican
Note: Exclusive to the Russian Market.

Date	Mintage	F	VF	XF	Unc	BU
2008 Proof	500	Value: 120				

KM# 615   5 DOLLARS
25.0000 g., 0.9250 Silver 0.7435 oz. ASW, 37 mm.
Ruler: Elizabeth II **Rev:** Cupid and roses **Rev. Legend:** My
Everlasting Love **Shape:** Heart

Date	Mintage	F	VF	XF	Unc	BU
2008 Proof	2,500	Value: 65.00				

KM# 616   5 DOLLARS
25.0000 g., 0.9250 Silver 0.7435 oz. ASW, 38.6 mm.
Ruler: Elizabeth II **Subject:** Endangered Wildlife - Artic
Rev: Polar bear and cubs, crystal inserts

Date	Mintage	F	VF	XF	Unc	BU
2008 Proof	2,500	Value: 70.00				

KM# 617   5 DOLLARS
25.0000 g., 0.9250 Silver 0.7435 oz. ASW, 38.6 mm.
Ruler: Elizabeth II **Subject:** Engangered wildlife - Antartic
Rev: Penguin, crystal insert

Date	Mintage	F	VF	XF	Unc	BU
2008 Proof	2,500	Value: 70.00				

KM# 618   5 DOLLARS
25.0000 g., 0.9250 Silver 0.7435 oz. ASW, 38.6 mm.
Ruler: Elizabeth II **Subject:** Pultusk Meteorite **Rev:** Earth and
Meteorite fragment insert

Date	Mintage	F	VF	XF	Unc	BU
2008 Proof	2,500	Value: 65.00				

KM# 670   5 DOLLARS
141.4000 g., 0.9990 Silver 4.5414 oz. ASW, 65 mm.
Ruler: Elizabeth II **Subject:** Tall Ships **Rev:** Norway's Christian
Raddish

Date	Mintage	F	VF	XF	Unc	BU
2008 Proof	—	Value: 275				

KM# 640   5 DOLLARS
25.0000 g., 0.9990 Silver 0.8029 oz. ASW, 38.6 mm.
Ruler: Elizabeth II **Rev:** Papal Tiara above crossed keys, partially
gilt, crystal inserts

Date	Mintage	F	VF	XF	Unc	BU
2009 Proof	5,000	Value: 120				

KM# 641   5 DOLLARS
25.0000 g., 0.9990 Silver 0.8029 oz. ASW   **Ruler:** Elizabeth II
Subject: Benedict XVI visits Israel **Rev:** Benedict XVI and "Dome
of the Rock", partially gilt, crystal inserts **Shape:** Diamond

Date	Mintage	F	VF	XF	Unc	BU
2009 Proof	5,000	Value: 100				

KM# 642   5 DOLLARS
25.0000 g., 0.9990 Silver 0.8029 oz. ASW   **Ruler:** Elizabeth II
Subject: Benedict XVI visits Africa **Rev:** Bust at left, partially gilt,
crystal inserts **Shape:** Irregular, Africa shape

Date	Mintage	F	VF	XF	Unc	BU
2009 Proof	5,000	Value: 100				

KM# 643   5 DOLLARS
25.0000 g., 0.9990 Silver 0.8029 oz. ASW   **Ruler:** Elizabeth II
Subject: Easter 2009 **Rev:** Statue of the risen Christ, partially
gilt, crystal inserts **Shape:** Fish

Date	Mintage	F	VF	XF	Unc	BU
2009 Proof	5,000	Value: 100				

KM# 644   5 DOLLARS
25.0000 g., 0.9990 Silver 0.8029 oz. ASW, 35 mm.
Ruler: Elizabeth II **Rev:** Star of the Magi, partially gilt, crystal
inserts **Shape:** Star

Date	Mintage	F	VF	XF	Unc	BU
2009 Proof	5,000	Value: 100				

KM# 645   5 DOLLARS
25.0000 g., 0.9990 Silver 0.8029 oz. ASW, 35x35 mm.
Ruler: Elizabeth II **Rev:** Cathedral of Santiago de Composetla,
partially gilt, crystal inserts

Date	Mintage	F	VF	XF	Unc	BU
2009 Proof	5,000	Value: 100				

KM# 646   5 DOLLARS
25.0000 g., 0.9990 Silver 0.8029 oz. ASW, 25x35 mm.
Ruler: Elizabeth II **Rev:** Michangelo's Pieta, partially gilt, crystal
inserts **Shape:** Rectangle

Date	Mintage	F	VF	XF	Unc	BU
2009 Proof	5,000	Value: 100				

KM# 647   5 DOLLARS
25.0000 g., 0.9990 Silver 0.8029 oz. ASW, 30x34 mm.
Ruler: Elizabeth II **Rev:** St. Christopher, partially gilt, crystal
inserts **Shape:** Oval

Date	Mintage	F	VF	XF	Unc	BU
2009 Proof	5,000	Value: 100				

KM# 648   5 DOLLARS
25.0000 g., 0.9990 Silver 0.8029 oz. ASW, 40x25 mm.
Ruler: Elizabeth II **Subject:** Benedict XVI visits the Czech
Republic **Rev:** Benedict XVI in Wenceleses square, partially gilt,
crystal inserts **Shape:** Rectangle

Date	Mintage	F	VF	XF	Unc	BU
2009 Proof	5,000	Value: 100				

KM# 649   5 DOLLARS
25.0000 g., 0.9990 Silver 0.8029 oz. ASW   **Ruler:** Elizabeth II
Rev: Christmas, village scene, partially gilt, crystal inserts
Shape: Diamond

Date	Mintage	F	VF	XF	Unc	BU
2009 Proof	5,000	Value: 100				

KM# 650   5 DOLLARS
31.1050 g., 0.9990 Silver 0.9990 oz. ASW, 38.6 mm.
Ruler: Elizabeth II **Subject:** Kiev Churches **Rev:** Andreevskaya
Church **Note:** Exclusive to the Russian Market.

Date	Mintage	F	VF	XF	Unc	BU
2009 Proof	500	Value: 120				

KM# 651   5 DOLLARS
31.1050 g., 0.9990 Silver 0.9990 oz. ASW, 38.6 mm.
Ruler: Elizabeth II **Subject:** Kiev Churches **Rev:** Kirillovskaya
Church **Note:** Exclusive to the Russian Market.

Date	Mintage	F	VF	XF	Unc	BU
2009 Proof	500	Value: 120				

KM# 652 5 DOLLARS
31.1050 g., 0.9990 Silver 0.9990 oz. ASW, 38.6 mm.
Ruler: Elizabeth II **Subject:** Kiev Chruches **Rev:** Mikailovsky Monastery **Note:** Exclusive to the Russian Market.

Date	Mintage	F	VF	XF	Unc	BU
2009 Proof	500	Value: 120				

KM# 653 5 DOLLARS
31.1050 g., 0.9990 Silver 0.9990 oz. ASW, 38.6 mm.
Ruler: Elizabeth II **Subject:** Kiev Churches **Rev:** Cathedral of St. Sophia **Note:** Exclusive to the Russian Market.

Date	Mintage	F	VF	XF	Unc	BU
2009 Proof	500	Value: 120				

KM# 654 5 DOLLARS
31.1050 g., 0.9990 Silver 0.9990 oz. ASW, 38.61 mm.
Ruler: Elizabeth II **Subject:** Ukraine Landmarks - Bendrological park, Sofiyivka **Rev:** Statue and gardens **Note:** Exclusive to the Russian Market.

Date	Mintage	F	VF	XF	Unc	BU
2009 Proof	500	Value: 100				

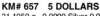

KM# 655 5 DOLLARS
31.1050 g., 0.9990 Silver 0.9990 oz. ASW, 38.61 mm.
Ruler: Elizabeth II **Subject:** Ukraine Landmarks - Holy Dormition Kiev Pechersk Lavra **Rev:** Churches **Note:** Exclusive to the Russian Market.

Date	Mintage	F	VF	XF	Unc	BU
2009 Proof	500	Value: 100				

KM# 656 5 DOLLARS
31.1050 g., 0.9990 Silver 0.9990 oz. ASW, 38.61 mm.
Ruler: Elizabeth II **Subject:** Ukraine Landmarks - Holy Dormition Pochayiv Lavra **Rev:** Buildings **Note:** Exclusive to the Russian Market.

Date	Mintage	F	VF	XF	Unc	BU
2009 Proof	500	Value: 100				

KM# 657 5 DOLLARS
31.1050 g., 0.9990 Silver 0.9990 oz. ASW, 38.61 mm.
Ruler: Elizabeth II **Subject:** Ukraine Landmarks - Holy Dormition Sviatohirsk Lavra **Rev:** Virgin Mary and Church **Note:** Exclusive to the Russian Market.

Date	Mintage	F	VF	XF	Unc	BU
2009 Proof	500	Value: 100				

KM# 658 5 DOLLARS
31.1050 g., 0.9990 Silver 0.9990 oz. ASW, 38.61 mm.
Ruler: Elizabeth II **Subject:** Ukraine Landmarks - Kamyanets National Reserve **Rev:** Fortress **Note:** Exclusive to the Russian Market.

Date	Mintage	F	VF	XF	Unc	BU
2009 Proof	500	Value: 100				

KM# 659 5 DOLLARS
31.1050 g., 0.9990 Silver 0.9990 oz. ASW, 38.6 mm.
Ruler: Elizabeth II **Subject:** Ukraine Landmarks - Khersones Tavrijsky National Reserve **Rev:** Roman ruins **Note:** Exclusive to the Russian Market.

Date	Mintage	F	VF	XF	Unc	BU
2009 Proof	500	Value: 100				

KM# 660 5 DOLLARS
31.1050 g., 0.9990 Silver 0.9990 oz. ASW, 38.6 mm.
Ruler: Elizabeth II **Subject:** Ukraine Landmarks - Khortytsia National Reserve **Rev:** Stone carvings and bridge **Note:** Exclusive to the Russian Market.

Date	Mintage	F	VF	XF	Unc	BU
2009 Proof	500	Value: 100				

KM# 661 5 DOLLARS
31.1050 g., 0.9990 Silver 0.9990 oz. ASW, 38.6 mm.
Ruler: Elizabeth II **Subject:** Ukraine Landmarks - National Theatre of Odessa **Rev:** Opera House **Note:** Exclusive to the Russian Market.

Date	Mintage	F	VF	XF	Unc	BU
2009 Proof	500	Value: 100				

KM# 662 5 DOLLARS
31.1050 g., 0.9990 Silver 0.9990 oz. ASW, 38.6 mm.
Ruler: Elizabeth II **Subject:** Ukraine Landmarks - Olesko Castle **Rev:** Hillside dwelling **Note:** Exclusive to the Russian Market.

Date	Mintage	F	VF	XF	Unc	BU
2009 Proof	500	Value: 100				

KM# 663 5 DOLLARS
31.1050 g., 0.9990 Silver 0.9990 oz. ASW, 38.6 mm.
Ruler: Elizabeth II **Subject:** Ukraine Landmarks - Palanok Castle in Mukachevo **Rev:** Hilltop fortress **Note:** Exclusive to the Russian Market.

Date	Mintage	F	VF	XF	Unc	BU
2009 Proof	500	Value: 100				

KM# 664 5 DOLLARS
31.1050 g., 0.9990 Silver 0.9990 oz. ASW, 38.6 mm.
Ruler: Elizabeth II **Subject:** Ukraine Landmarks - Khotyn Fortress Reserve **Rev:** Road to castle **Note:** Exclusive to the Russian Market.

Date	Mintage	F	VF	XF	Unc	BU
2009 Proof	500	Value: 100				

KM# 665   5 DOLLARS
31.1050 g., 0.9990 Silver 0.9990 oz. ASW, 38.6 mm.
Ruler: Elizabeth II **Subject:** Ukraine Landmarks - Upper Castle of Lutsk **Rev:** Tower **Note:** Exclusive to the Russian Market.

Date	Mintage	F	VF	XF	Unc	BU
2009 Proof	500	Value: 100				

KM# 666   5 DOLLARS
141.4000 g., 0.9990 Silver 4.5414 oz. ASW, 65 mm.
Ruler: Elizabeth II **Subject:** Tall ships **Obv:** Bust right **Rev:** Germany's Preussen, 5-masted square rigger

Date	Mintage	F	VF	XF	Unc	BU
2009 Proof	—	Value: 275				

KM# 667   5 DOLLARS
141.4000 g., 0.9990 Silver 4.5414 oz. ASW, 65 mm.
Ruler: Elizabeth II **Subject:** Tall ships **Rev:** France's France II

Date	Mintage	F	VF	XF	Unc	BU
2009 Proof	—	Value: 275				

KM# 668   5 DOLLARS
141.4000 g., 0.9990 Silver 4.5414 oz. ASW, 65 mm.
Ruler: Elizabeth II **Subject:** Tall Ships **Rev:** America's Thomas W. Lawson, 7-masted schooner

Date	Mintage	F	VF	XF	Unc	BU
2009 Proof	—	Value: 275				

KM# 669   5 DOLLARS
141.4000 g., 0.9990 Silver 4.5414 oz. ASW, 65 mm.
Ruler: Elizabeth II **Subject:** Tall Ships **Rev:** Russia's Sedov, 4-masted barque

Date	Mintage	F	VF	XF	Unc	BU
2009 Proof	—	Value: 275				

KM# 671   5 DOLLARS
141.4000 g., 0.9990 Silver 4.5414 oz. ASW, 65 mm.
Ruler: Elizabeth II **Subject:** Tall Ships **Rev:** Russian 4-masted barque Kruzenshtern

Date	Mintage	F	VF	XF	Unc	BU
2009 Proof	—	Value: 275				

KM# 672   5 DOLLARS
25.0000 g., 0.9250 Silver 0.7435 oz. ASW, 38.6 mm.
Ruler: Elizabeth II **Rev:** HMS Endeavour and James Cook portrait

Date	Mintage	F	VF	XF	Unc	BU
2009 Proof	2,500	Value: 55.00				

KM# 673   5 DOLLARS
25.0000 g., 0.5000 Silver 0.4019 oz. ASW, 38.6 mm.
Ruler: Elizabeth II **Rev:** Ferrari F-2008 Carbon

Date	Mintage	F	VF	XF	Unc	BU
2009 Proof	2,008	Value: 55.00				

KM# 674   5 DOLLARS
20.0000 g., 0.9250 Silver 0.5948 oz. ASW, 38.61 mm.
Ruler: Elizabeth II **Subject:** Endangered Wildlife **Rev:** Giant Anteater

Date	Mintage	F	VF	XF	Unc	BU
2009 Proof	5,000	Value: 50.00				

KM# 675   5 DOLLARS
31.1050 g., 0.9250 Silver 0.9250 oz. ASW, 38.6 mm.
Ruler: Elizabeth II **Series:** International Womens Day **Rev:** Roses and butterfly **Note:** Exclusive to the Russian Market

Date	Mintage	F	VF	XF	Unc	BU
2009 Proof	500	Value: 120				

KM# 676   5 DOLLARS
25.0000 g., 0.9250 Silver 0.7435 oz. ASW, 38.6 mm.
Ruler: Elizabeth II **Rev:** Sir Lancelot

Date	Mintage	F	VF	XF	Unc	BU
2009 Proof	2,500	Value: 55.00				

KM# 677   5 DOLLARS
0.9250 Silver **Ruler:** Elizabeth II **Subject:** Masters of Europe - Vermeer **Rev:** Girl with a pearl earing **Shape:** Vertical rectangle

Date	Mintage	F	VF	XF	Unc	BU
2009 Proof	—	Value: 125				

KM# 678   5 DOLLARS
0.9250 Silver **Ruler:** Elizabeth II **Subject:** Masters of Europe - DaVinci **Rev:** Lady with an ermine **Shape:** Vertical rectangle

Date	Mintage	F	VF	XF	Unc	BU
2009 Proof	—	Value: 145				

KM# 679   5 DOLLARS
0.9250 Silver **Ruler:** Elizabeth II **Subject:** Masters of Europe - Jan Matejko **Rev:** Wernyhora **Shape:** Vertical rectangle

Date	Mintage	F	VF	XF	Unc	BU
2009 Proof	—	Value: 125				

KM# 680   5 DOLLARS
Silver **Ruler:** Elizabeth II **Subject:** 50th Anniversary of Space exploration, 40th Anniversary of Apollo 11 **Obv:** Moon **Rev:** Moonscape and moon rock implant

Date	Mintage	F	VF	XF	Unc	BU
2009 Matte	—	—	—	—	—	150

KM# 681   5 DOLLARS
25.0000 g., 0.9250 Silver copper plated 0.7435 oz. ASW
Ruler: Elizabeth II **Subject:** 400th Anniversary of Mars exploration **Rev:** Mars scape and Mars rock implant

Date	Mintage	F	VF	XF	Unc	BU
2009 Matte	2,500	—	—	—	—	125

KM# 682   5 DOLLARS
25.0000 g., 0.9250 Silver 0.7435 oz. ASW, 38.61 mm.
Ruler: Elizabeth II **Subject:** Year of the Ox **Rev:** Child riding oxen, partially gilt **Note:** Exclusive to the Russian market

Date	Mintage	F	VF	XF	Unc	BU
2009 Proof	1,000	Value: 100				

KM# 683   5 DOLLARS
25.0000 g., 0.9990 Silver 0.8029 oz. ASW **Ruler:** Elizabeth II **Subject:** World of Flowers - Pansey **Rev:** Pansey, multicolor cloisonne

Date	Mintage	F	VF	XF	Unc	BU
2009 Proof	2,500	Value: 55.00				

KM# 684   5 DOLLARS
25.0000 g., 0.9990 Silver 0.8029 oz. ASW, 38.6 mm.
Ruler: Elizabeth II **Subject:** World of flowers - Poppy **Rev:** Poppy, multicolor closinne

Date	Mintage	F	VF	XF	Unc	BU
2009 Proof	2,500	Value: 55.00				

KM# 685   5 DOLLARS
25.0000 g., 0.9250 Silver 0.7435 oz. ASW, 30x43 mm.
Ruler: Elizabeth II **Obv:** Bust right **Rev:** Easter chick, thermal image changing **Shape:** Egg

Date	Mintage	F	VF	XF	Unc	BU
2009 Proof	2,500	Value: 80.00				

KM# 686   5 DOLLARS
25.0000 g., 0.9250 Silver 0.7435 oz. ASW, 35x35 mm.
Ruler: Elizabeth II **Rev:** Season's greetings, rocking horse **Shape:** Square

Date	Mintage	F	VF	XF	Unc	BU
2009 Proof	2,500	Value: 55.00				

KM# 687 5 DOLLARS
25.0000 g., 0.9990 Silver 0.8029 oz. ASW, 30x38 mm.
Ruler: Elizabeth II **Rev:** Kazan Virgin icon **Shape:** Vertical
rectangle **Note:** Exclusive to the Russian market

Date	Mintage	F	VF	XF	Unc	BU
2009 Proof	2,500	Value: 120				

KM# 723 5 DOLLARS
31.1050 g., 0.9990 Silver 0.9990 oz. ASW, 24x47 mm.
Ruler: Elizabeth II **Subject:** War of 1812 **Rev:** Peter Bagraton

Date	Mintage	F	VF	XF	Unc	BU
2010 Antique finish	2,000	—	—	—	—	40.00

KM# 724 5 DOLLARS
31.1050 g., 0.9990 Silver 0.9990 oz. ASW **Ruler:** Elizabeth II
Subject: War of 1812 **Rev:** Mikhail Kutuzov **Shape:** 24x47

Date	Mintage	F	VF	XF	Unc	BU
2010 Antique finish	2,000	—	—	—	—	40.00

KM# 725 5 DOLLARS
31.1050 g., 0.9990 Silver 0.9990 oz. ASW, 27x47 mm.
Ruler: Elizabeth II **Subject:** War of 1812 **Rev:** Bikoly Raevsky

Date	Mintage	F	VF	XF	Unc	BU
2010 Antique finish	2,000	—	—	—	—	40.00

KM# 726 5 DOLLARS
20.0000 g., 0.9990 Silver 0.6423 oz. ASW, 30x43 mm.
Ruler: Elizabeth II **Subject:** Imperial Eggs **Rev:** Blue egg

Date	Mintage	F	VF	XF	Unc	BU
2010 Proof	2,500	Value: 40.00				

KM# 727 5 DOLLARS
20.0000 g., 0.9990 Silver 0.6423 oz. ASW, 30x43 mm.
Ruler: Elizabeth II **Subject:** Imperial Egg **Rev:** Green cloisonne

Date	Mintage	F	VF	XF	Unc	BU
2010 Proof	2,500	Value: 40.00				

KM# 728 5 DOLLARS
20.0000 g., 0.9990 Silver 0.6423 oz. ASW, 30x43 mm.
Ruler: Elizabeth II **Subject:** Imperial Egg **Rev:** Yellow cloisonne
and Bohemian crystals

Date	Mintage	F	VF	XF	Unc	BU
2010 Proof	2,500	Value: 40.00				

KM# 729 5 DOLLARS
25.0000 g., 0.9990 Silver 0.8029 oz. ASW, 38.6 mm.
Ruler: Elizabeth II **Rev:** Martin Luther King, pointing **Note:** Fits
together with KM#730.

Date	Mintage	F	VF	XF	Unc	BU
2010 Antique finish	2,500	—	—	—	—	40.00

KM# 730 5 DOLLARS
25.0000 g., 0.9990 Silver 0.8029 oz. ASW, 38.6 mm.
Ruler: Elizabeth II **Rev:** Barack Obama, pointing **Note:** Fits
together with KM#729.

Date	Mintage	F	VF	XF	Unc	BU
2010 Antique finish	2,500	—	—	—	—	40.00

KM# 731 5 DOLLARS
25.0000 g., 0.9250 Silver 0.7435 oz. ASW, 38.6 mm.
Ruler: Elizabeth II **Subject:** Tender Love **Rev:** Rose in relief
hologram

Date	Mintage	F	VF	XF	Unc	BU
2010 Proof	2,500	Value: 40.00				

KM# 732 5 DOLLARS
25.0000 g., 0.9250 Silver 0.7435 oz. ASW, 30x38 mm.
Ruler: Elizabeth II **Rev:** Holy Trinity icon

Date	Mintage	F	VF	XF	Unc	BU
2010 Proof	2,500	Value: 50.00				

KM# 473 10 DOLLARS
20.1200 g., Silver, 38.62 mm. **Ruler:** Elizabeth II **Subject:** 2004
Summer Olympics - Athens **Obv:** Crowned bust right **Rev:** Male
discus thrower **Edge:** Reeded

Date	Mintage	F	VF	XF	Unc	BU
2001 Proof	—	Value: 35.00				

KM# 549 10 DOLLARS
10.0000 g., 0.9999 Gold 0.3215 oz. AGW, 25 mm.
Ruler: Elizabeth II **Rev:** Multicolored Mikado Pheasant

Date	Mintage	F	VF	XF	Unc	BU
2001 Proof	1,000	Value: 425				

KM# 550 10 DOLLARS
10.0000 g., 0.9999 Gold 0.3215 oz. AGW, 25 mm.
Ruler: Elizabeth II **Rev:** Multicolor black-faced spoonbill

Date	Mintage	F	VF	XF	Unc	BU
2001 Proof	1,000	Value: 425				

KM# 453 10 DOLLARS
186.8300 g., 0.9990 Silver Gilt 6.0005 oz. ASW, 89 mm.
Ruler: Elizabeth II **Obv:** Crowned bust right, unique portrait for
Cook Is. **Rev:** Queen Victoria standing with lion **Rev. Designer:**
W. Wyon **Edge:** Reeded **Note:** Illustration reduced.

Date	Mintage	F	VF	XF	Unc	BU
2003 Proof	198	Value: 350				

KM# 582 10 DOLLARS
31.1000 g., 0.9990 Silver 0.9988 oz. ASW, 38.6 mm.
Ruler: Elizabeth II **Rev:** Chichen Itza gilt pop-up

Date	Mintage	F	VF	XF	Unc	BU
2007 Proof	5,000	Value: 100				

KM# 585 10 DOLLARS
31.1000 g., 0.9990 Silver 0.9988 oz. ASW, 38.6 mm.
Ruler: Elizabeth II **Rev:** Easter Island status gilt pop-up

Date	Mintage	F	VF	XF	Unc	BU
2007 Proof	5,000	Value: 100				

KM# 587 10 DOLLARS
31.1000 g., 0.9990 Silver 0.9988 oz. ASW, 38.6 mm.
Ruler: Elizabeth II **Rev:** Pyrmids gilt pop-up

Date	Mintage	F	VF	XF	Unc	BU
2007 Proof	5,000	Value: 100				

KM# 588 10 DOLLARS
31.1000 g., 0.9990 Silver 0.9988 oz. ASW, 38.6 mm.
Ruler: Elizabeth II **Rev:** Golden Gate Bridge gilt pop-up

Date	Mintage	F	VF	XF	Unc	BU
2007 Proof	5,000	Value: 100				

KM# 589 10 DOLLARS
31.1000 g., 0.9990 Silver 0.9988 oz. ASW, 38.6 mm.
Ruler: Elizabeth II **Rev:** Great Wall of China gilt pop-up

Date	Mintage	F	VF	XF	Unc	BU
2007 Proof	5,000	Value: 100				

KM# 590 10 DOLLARS
31.1000 g., 0.9990 Silver 0.9988 oz. ASW, 38.6 mm.
Ruler: Elizabeth II **Rev:** Sydney Harbor Bridge gilt pop-up

Date	Mintage	F	VF	XF	Unc	BU
2007 Proof	5,000	Value: 100				

KM# 592 10 DOLLARS
31.1000 g., 0.9990 Silver 0.9988 oz. ASW, 38.6 mm.
Ruler: Elizabeth II **Rev:** Petra Treasury gilt pop-up

Date	Mintage	F	VF	XF	Unc	BU
2007 Proof	5,000	Value: 100				

KM# 593 10 DOLLARS
31.1000 g., 0.9990 Silver 0.9988 oz. ASW, 38.6 mm.
Ruler: Elizabeth II **Rev:** Taj mahal gilt pop-up

Date	Mintage	F	VF	XF	Unc	BU
2007 Proof	5,000	Value: 100				

KM# 619   10 DOLLARS
31.1000 g., 0.9990 Silver 0.9988 oz. ASW, 38.6 mm.
Ruler: Elizabeth II **Rev:** Angor Wat temple gilt pop-up

Date	Mintage	F	VF	XF	Unc	BU
2008 Proof	5,000	Value: 100				

KM# 620   10 DOLLARS
31.1000 g., 0.9990 Silver 0.9988 oz. ASW, 38.6 mm.
Ruler: Elizabeth II **Rev:** Ayer's Rock gilt pop-up

Date	Mintage	F	VF	XF	Unc	BU
2008 Proof	5,000	Value: 100				

KM# 621   10 DOLLARS
31.1000 g., 0.9990 Silver 0.9988 oz. ASW, 38.6 mm.   **Ruler:**
Elizabeth II **Rev:** Parliament Buildings and Big Ben pop-up

Date	Mintage	F	VF	XF	Unc	BU
2008 Proof	5,000	Value: 100				

KM# 622   10 DOLLARS
31.1000 g., 0.9990 Silver 0.9988 oz. ASW, 38.6 mm.
Ruler: Elizabeth II **Rev:** Mt. Rushmore figures gilt pop-up

Date	Mintage	F	VF	XF	Unc	BU
2008 Proof	5,000	Value: 100				

KM# 623   10 DOLLARS
31.1000 g., 0.9990 Silver 0.9988 oz. ASW, 38.6 mm.
Ruler: Elizabeth II **Rev:** Sydney Opera House gilt pop-up

Date	Mintage	F	VF	XF	Unc	BU
2008 Proof	5,000	Value: 100				

KM# 624   10 DOLLARS
31.1000 g., 0.9990 Silver 0.9988 oz. ASW, 38.6 mm.
Ruler: Elizabeth II **Rev:** Malaysian Twin Towers gilt pop-up

Date	Mintage	F	VF	XF	Unc	BU
2008 Proof	5,000	Value: 100				

KM# 625   10 DOLLARS
31.1000 g., 0.9990 Silver 0.9988 oz. ASW, 38.6 mm.
Ruler: Elizabeth II **Rev:** Sphinx gilt pop-up

Date	Mintage	F	VF	XF	Unc	BU
2008 Proof	5,000	Value: 100				

KM# 626   10 DOLLARS
31.1000 g., 0.9990 Silver 0.9988 oz. ASW, 38.6 mm.
Ruler: Elizabeth II **Rev:** Stonehedge gilt pop-up

Date	Mintage	F	VF	XF	Unc	BU
2008 Proof	5,000	Value: 100				

KM# 627   10 DOLLARS
62.2050 g., 0.9990 Silver 1.9979 oz. ASW, 50 mm.
Ruler: Elizabeth II **Rev:** Tsar Alexander II, multicolor
Note: Exclusive to the Russian Market.

Date	Mintage	F	VF	XF	Unc	BU
2008 Proof	500	Value: 300				

KM# 628   10 DOLLARS
62.2050 g., 0.9990 Silver 1.9979 oz. ASW   **Ruler:** Elizabeth II
Rev: Tsar Alexi, multicolor **Note:** Exclusive to the Russian
Market.

Date	Mintage	F	VF	XF	Unc	BU
2008 Proof	500	Value: 300				

KM# 629   10 DOLLARS
62.2050 g., 0.9990 Silver 1.9979 oz. ASW, 50 mm.
Ruler: Elizabeth II **Rev:** Tsarina Anna, multicolor

Date	Mintage	F	VF	XF	Unc	BU
2008 Proof	500	Value: 300				

KM# 630   10 DOLLARS
62.2050 g., 0.9990 Silver 1.9979 oz. ASW, 50 mm.
Ruler: Elizabeth II **Rev:** Tsarina Elizabeth, multicolor

Date	Mintage	F	VF	XF	Unc	BU
2008 Proof	500	Value: 300				

KM# 631   10 DOLLARS
62.2050 g., 0.9990 Silver 1.9979 oz. ASW, 50 mm.
Ruler: Elizabeth II **Rev:** Tsar Mikhail, multicolor

Date	Mintage	F	VF	XF	Unc	BU
2008 Proof	500	Value: 300				

KM# 632   10 DOLLARS
62.2050 g., 0.9990 Silver 1.9979 oz. ASW, 50 mm.
Ruler: Elizabeth II **Rev:** Tsar Peter I, multicolor

Date	Mintage	F	VF	XF	Unc	BU
2008 Proof	500	Value: 300				

KM# 633   10 DOLLARS
31.1000 g., 0.9990 Silver 0.9988 oz. ASW, 40 mm.
Ruler: Elizabeth II **Rev:** Nathan Rothschild bust at right, partially
gilt

Date	Mintage	F	VF	XF	Unc	BU
2008 Proof	10,000	Value: 50.00				

KM# 634   10 DOLLARS
31.1050 g., 0.9990 Silver 0.9990 oz. ASW, 40 mm.
Ruler: Elizabeth II **Rev:** Henry ford at left and Model-A car at
right, partially gilt

Date	Mintage	F	VF	XF	Unc	BU
2008 Proof	10,000	Value: 50.00				

KM# 635 10 DOLLARS
31.1000 g., 0.9990 Silver 0.9988 oz. ASW, 40 mm.
Ruler: Elizabeth II **Rev:** John D. Rockefeller Sr., bust right, oil derrick partially gilt.

Date	Mintage	F	VF	XF	Unc	BU
2008 Proof	10,000	Value: 50.00				

KM# 703 10 DOLLARS
1.2400 g., 0.9990 Gold 0.0398 oz. AGW, 13.9 mm.
Ruler: Elizabeth II **Subject:** Nicolaus Copernicus **Rev:** Bust facing and orbit of the planets, crystal insert, partially silver plated

Date	Mintage	F	VF	XF	Unc	BU
2008 Proof	7,500	Value: 65.00				

KM# 704 10 DOLLARS
1.0000 g., 0.9990 Gold 0.0321 oz. AGW, 13.9 mm.
Ruler: Elizabeth II **Subject:** Gorch Fock **Rev:** Sailing vessel right

Date	Mintage	F	VF	XF	Unc	BU
2008 Proof	15,000	Value: 65.00				

KM# 705 10 DOLLARS
62.2100 g., 0.9990 Silver 1.9980 oz. ASW, 50 mm.
Ruler: Elizabeth II **Subject:** Kiev Churches **Rev:** Lavra bell tower

Date	Mintage	F	VF	XF	Unc	BU
2008 Proof	500	—	—	—	—	100

KM# 688 10 DOLLARS
31.1050 g., 0.9990 Silver 0.9990 oz. ASW, 38.6 mm.
Ruler: Elizabeth II **Rev:** Temple at Thebes gilt pop-up

Date	Mintage	F	VF	XF	Unc	BU
2009 Proof	5,000	Value: 100				

KM# 689 10 DOLLARS
31.1050 g., 0.9990 Silver 0.9990 oz. ASW, 38.6 mm.
Ruler: Elizabeth II **Rev:** Arc de Triumph gilt pop-up

Date	Mintage	F	VF	XF	Unc	BU
2009 Proof	5,000	Value: 100				

KM# 690 10 DOLLARS
31.1050 g., 0.9990 Silver 0.9990 oz. ASW, 38.6 mm.
Ruler: Elizabeth II **Rev:** Hagia Sofia gilt pop-up

Date	Mintage	F	VF	XF	Unc	BU
2009 Proof	5,000	Value: 100				

KM# 691 10 DOLLARS
31.1050 g., 0.9990 Silver 0.9990 oz. ASW, 38.6 mm.
Ruler: Elizabeth II **Rev:** Temple of Heaven gilt pop-up

Date	Mintage	F	VF	XF	Unc	BU
2009 Proof	5,000	Value: 100				

KM# 692 10 DOLLARS
31.1050 g., 0.9990 Silver 0.9990 oz. ASW, 38.6 mm.
Ruler: Elizabeth II **Rev:** Brandenberg Gate gilt pop-up

Date	Mintage	F	VF	XF	Unc	BU
2009 Proof	5,000	Value: 100				

KM# 693 10 DOLLARS
31.1050 g., 0.9990 Silver 0.9990 oz. ASW, 38.6 mm.
Ruler: Elizabeth II **Rev:** Ruins of Kaiser Church in Berlin, gilt pop-up

Date	Mintage	F	VF	XF	Unc	BU
2009 Proof	5,000	Value: 100				

KM# 694 10 DOLLARS
31.1050 g., 0.9990 Silver 0.9990 oz. ASW, 38.6 mm.
Ruler: Elizabeth II **Rev:** Statue of Peter I gilt pop-up

Date	Mintage	F	VF	XF	Unc	BU
2009 Proof	5,000	Value: 100				

KM# 695 10 DOLLARS
31.1050 g., 0.9990 Silver 0.9990 oz. ASW, 38.6 mm.
Ruler: Elizabeth II **Rev:** Bridge in Venice, gilt pop-up

Date	Mintage	F	VF	XF	Unc	BU
2009 Proof	5,000	Value: 100				

KM# 696 10 DOLLARS
31.1050 g., 0.9990 Silver 0.9990 oz. ASW, 38.6 mm.
Ruler: Elizabeth II **Rev:** Opera house, gilt pop-up

Date	Mintage	F	VF	XF	Unc	BU
2009 Proof	—	Value: 100				

KM# 591 20 DOLLARS
31.1000 g., 0.9990 Silver 0.9988 oz. ASW, 38.6 mm.
Ruler: Elizabeth II **Rev:** Machu Pichu gilt pop-up

Date	Mintage	F	VF	XF	Unc	BU
2007 Proof	5,000	Value: 100				

KM# 636 20 DOLLARS
93.3000 g., 0.9990 Silver 2.9965 oz. ASW, 55 mm.
Ruler: Elizabeth II **Rev:** Michangelo, Creation of Adam, multicolor with crystal inserts

Date	Mintage	F	VF	XF	Unc	BU
2008 Proof	1,000	Value: 500				

KM# 637 20 DOLLARS
93.3000 g., 0.9990 Silver 2.9965 oz. ASW, 55 mm.
Ruler: Elizabeth II **Rev:** DaVinci, Last Supper, multicolor with crystal inserts

Date	Mintage	F	VF	XF	Unc	BU
2008 Proof	1,000	Value: 600				

KM# 638   20 DOLLARS
93.3000 g., 0.9990 Silver 2.9965 oz. ASW, 55 mm.
Ruler: Elizabeth II **Rev:** Raffaello, School of Athens, multicolor with crystal inserts

Date	Mintage	F	VF	XF	Unc	BU
2008 Proof	1,000	Value: 400				

KM# 700   20 DOLLARS
93.3150 g., 0.9990 Silver 2.9970 oz. ASW, 55 mm.
Ruler: Elizabeth II **Subject:** European Masters - Spitzwig
Rev: The Poor Poet, crystals embedded

Date	Mintage	F	VF	XF	Unc	BU
2009 Proof	—	Value: 500				

KM# 439   30 DOLLARS
10.0000 g., 0.9999 Gold 0.3215 oz. AGW, 16.1 mm.
Ruler: Elizabeth II **Obv:** Crowned head right, date below
Rev: Multicolor Peony flower and denomination **Edge:** Reeded

Date	Mintage	F	VF	XF	Unc	BU
2004	10,000	—	—	—	—	425

KM# 698   20 DOLLARS
93.3150 g., 0.9990 Silver 2.9970 oz. ASW, 55 mm.
Ruler: Elizabeth II **Subject:** European Masters - Rembrandt
Rev: The Night watch, crystals embedded

Date	Mintage	F	VF	XF	Unc	BU
2009 Proof	1,642	Value: 350				

KM# 440   35 DOLLARS
10.0000 g., 0.9999 Gold 0.3215 oz. AGW, 16.1 mm.
Ruler: Elizabeth II **Obv:** Crowned head right, date below
Rev: Multicolor Chinese man beating a tiger and denomination
Edge: Reeded

Date	Mintage	F	VF	XF	Unc	BU
2004	6,000	—	—	—	—	425

KM# 639   20 DOLLARS
93.3000 g., 0.9990 Silver 2.9965 oz. ASW, 55 mm.
Ruler: Elizabeth II **Rev:** Botticelli, Birth of Venus, multicolor with crystal inserts

Date	Mintage	F	VF	XF	Unc	BU
2008 Proof	1,458	Value: 350				

KM# 441   35 DOLLARS
10.0000 g., 0.9999 Gold 0.3215 oz. AGW, 16.1 mm.
Ruler: Elizabeth II **Obv:** Crowned head right, date below
Rev: Multicolor Chinese man riding a horse and denomination
Edge: Reeded

Date	Mintage	F	VF	XF	Unc	BU
2004	10,000	—	—	—	—	425

KM# 699   20 DOLLARS
93.3150 g., 0.9990 Silver 2.9970 oz. ASW, 55 mm.
Ruler: Elizabeth II **Subject:** European Masters - Raffaelo
Rev: Sistine Chapel Madonna, crystals embedded

Date	Mintage	F	VF	XF	Unc	BU
2009 Proof	1,512	Value: 350				

KM# 442   35 DOLLARS
10.0000 g., 0.9999 Gold 0.3215 oz. AGW, 25 x 15 mm.
Ruler: Elizabeth II **Obv:** Crowned head right, date below
Rev: Multicolor "Eight immortals crossing the sea" and denomination **Edge:** Plain **Shape:** Ingot

Date	Mintage	F	VF	XF	Unc	BU
2004	3,000	—	—	—	—	450

KM# 697   20 DOLLARS
93.3150 g., 0.9990 Silver 2.9970 oz. ASW, 55 mm.
Ruler: Elizabeth II **Subject:** European Masters - DaVinci
Rev: Mona Lisa, 12 crystals imbedded

Date	Mintage	F	VF	XF	Unc	BU
2009 Proof	999	Value: 1,300				

KM# 397   100 DOLLARS
23.3276 g., 0.9999 Gold Acrylic capsule center containing tiny diamonds, rubies and sapphires 0.7499 oz. AGW, 32.1 mm.
Ruler: Elizabeth II **Subject:** Crown Jewels **Obv:** Crowned bust right, legend **Rev:** Crowns and royal regalia **Edge:** Reeded

Date	Mintage	F	VF	XF	Unc	BU
2002 Proof	5,000	Value: 950				

KM# 503   100 DOLLARS
31.1030 g., 0.9999 Gold 0.9998 oz. AGW, 40.6 mm.
Ruler: Elizabeth II **Subject:** WWI **Obv:** Head with tiara right
Rev: Multicolor image of Australian WWI soldier in Europe
Edge: Reeded

Date	Mintage	F	VF	XF	Unc	BU
2008 Proof	90	Value: 2,000				

KM# 505   100 DOLLARS
31.1030 g., 0.9999 Gold 0.9998 oz. AGW, 40.6 mm.
Ruler: Elizabeth II **Subject:** WWI **Obv:** Head with tiara right
Rev: Multicolor image of Australian WWI soldier in Mid-East scene **Edge:** Reeded

Date	Mintage	F	VF	XF	Unc	BU
2008 Proof	90	Value: 2,000				

KM# 389   500 DOLLARS
1723.1259 g., 0.9990 Silver 55.342 oz. ASW, 115.2 mm.
Ruler: Elizabeth II **Subject:** Moby Dick **Obv:** Crowned head right
Rev: Whale jumping over a six-man rowboat **Edge:** Plain
Note: Illustration reduced.

Date	Mintage	F	VF	XF	Unc	BU
2001 Proof	—	Value: 1,200				

KM# 548   500 DOLLARS
113.0000 g., 1.0000 Gold 3.6328 oz. AGW, 50 mm.
Ruler: Elizabeth II **Subject:** Jack Nicklaus **Rev:** Portrait facing - two golf poses flanking

Date	Mintage	F	VF	XF	Unc	BU
2006 Proof	113	Value: 4,750				

MAUNDY MONEY
Ceremonial Sterling Pence

KM# 449   PENNY
0.4800 g., 0.9990 Silver 0.0154 oz. ASW, 11.1 mm. **Ruler:** Elizabeth II **Subject:** Maundy **Obv:** Crowned bust right **Rev:** Crowned denomination divides date within wreath **Edge:** Plain

Date	Mintage	F	VF	XF	Unc	BU
2002 Proof	5,000	Value: 8.00				

KM# 450   2 PENCE
0.9400 g., 0.9990 Silver 0.0302 oz. ASW, 13.4 mm.
Ruler: Elizabeth II **Subject:** Maundy **Obv:** Crowned bust right
Rev: Crowned denomination divides date within wreath
Edge: Plain

Date	Mintage	F	VF	XF	Unc	BU
2002 Proof	5,000	Value: 10.00				

KM# 451   3 PENCE
1.4400 g., 0.9990 Silver 0.0462 oz. ASW, 16.1 mm.
Ruler: Elizabeth II **Subject:** Maundy **Obv:** Crowned bust right
Rev: Crowned denomination divides date within wreath
Edge: Plain

Date	Mintage	F	VF	XF	Unc	BU
2002 Proof	5,000	Value: 12.00				

KM# 452   4 PENCE
1.9300 g., 0.9990 Silver 0.0620 oz. ASW, 17.5 mm.
Ruler: Elizabeth II **Subject:** Maundy **Obv:** Crowned bust right
Rev: Crowned denomination divides date within wreath
Edge: Plain

Date	Mintage	F	VF	XF	Unc	BU
2002 Proof	5,000	Value: 15.00				

PROOF SETS

KM#	Date	Mintage	Identification	Issue Price	Mkt Val
PS25	2002 (4)	5,000	KM#449-452 Maundy Set	—	45.00

The Republic of Costa Rica, located in southern Central America between Nicaragua and Panama, has an area of 19,730 sq. mi. (51,100 sq. km.) and a population of 3.4 million. Capital: San Jose. Agriculture predominates; tourism and coffee, bananas, beef and sugar contribute heavily to the country's export earnings.

KEY TO MINT IDENTIFICATION

Key Letter	Mint
(a)	Armant Metalurgica, Santiago, Chile
(g)	Guatemala Mint
(r)	RCM – Royal Canadian Mint
(rm)	Royal Mint, London

REPUBLIC
REFORM COINAGE

KM# 227a.2   5 COLONES
4.0000 g., Brass, 21.6 mm. **Obv:** National arms, date below, large letters in legend, large date, shield is not outlined **Rev:** Denomination above spray, B.C.C.R. below, thin '5' **Edge:** Segmented reeding

Date	Mintage	F	VF	XF	Unc	BU
2001(a)	—	—	—	—	0.65	1.00

KM# 227b   5 COLONES
0.9000 g., Aluminum, 21.4 mm. **Obv:** National arms **Obv. Legend:** REPUBLICA DE COSTA RICA **Rev:** Denomination above sprays, B.C.C.R. **Edge:** Plain

Date	Mintage	F	VF	XF	Unc	BU
2005	—	—	—	—	0.35	0.50
2008	—	—	—	—	0.35	0.50

KM# 228.2   10 COLONES
5.0000 g., Brass, 23.5 mm. **Obv:** National arms, date below, large legend and date, shield not outlined **Rev:** Denomination above spray, B.C.C.R. below, thick '1' **Edge:** Segmented reeding

Date	Mintage	F	VF	XF	Unc	BU
2002(a)	—	—	—	—	1.25	1.50

KM# 228b   10 COLONES
1.1300 g., Aluminum, 22.97 mm. **Obv:** National arms **Obv. Legend:** REPUBLICA DE COSTA RICA **Rev:** Denomination above sprays, B.C.C.R. **Edge:** Plain

Date	Mintage	F	VF	XF	Unc	BU
2005	—	—	—	—	0.50	0.75
2008	—	—	—	—	0.50	0.75

KM# 229a   25 COLONES
7.0000 g., Brass, 25.4 mm. **Obv:** National arms **Obv. Legend:** REPUBLICA DE COSTA RICA **Rev:** Value above sprays, B.C.C.R. below **Edge:** Segmented reeding

Date	Mintage	F	VF	XF	Unc	BU
2001(a)	—	—	—	—	2.50	3.00
2003	—	—	—	—	2.50	3.00
2007	—	—	—	—	2.50	3.00

KM# 229a.1   25 COLONES
7.0000 g., Brass **Obv:** National arms, date below **Rev:** Value above sprays, B.C.C.R. below **Edge:** Plain

Date	Mintage	F	VF	XF	Unc	BU
2005	—	—	—	—	2.50	3.00

KM# 231.1a   50 COLONES
7.9200 g., Aluminum-Bronze, 27.5 mm. **Obv:** National arms, date below **Rev:** Value with spray below **Rev. Legend:** B. C. C. R. **Edge:** Segmented reeding

Date	Mintage	F	VF	XF	Unc	BU
2002	—	—	—	—	3.00	4.00

KM# 231.1b   50 COLONES
Brass Plated Steel, 27.5 mm. **Obv:** National arms above date **Rev:** Value above sprays, B.C.C.R. below

Date	Mintage	F	VF	XF	Unc	BU
2006 reeded edge	—	—	—	—	3.50	5.00
2007 plain edge	—	—	—	—	3.50	5.00

KM# 230a   100 COLONES
Brass, 29.5 mm. **Obv:** National arms, date below, large letters in legend and date, shield outlined **Rev:** Value above spray, B.C.C.R. below **Edge:** Segmented reeding

Date	Mintage	F	VF	XF	Unc	BU
2006(a)	—	—	—	—	4.50	—

KM# 240a   100 COLONES
8.8000 g., Brass Plated Steel, 29.4 mm. **Obv:** National arms above date **Rev:** Value above sprays **Edge:** Reeded

Date	Mintage	F	VF	XF	Unc	BU
2006	—	—	—	—	4.50	6.00
2007	—	—	—	—	4.50	6.00

KM# 239.1   500 COLONES
11.0000 g., Copper-Aluminum-Nickel, 32.9 mm. **Obv:** National arms **Obv. Legend:** REPUBLICA DE COSTA RICA **Rev:** Value above sprays, B.C.C.R. below, thick numerals **Edge:** Segmented reeding

Date	Mintage	F	VF	XF	Unc	BU
2003(a)	—	—	—	2.00	3.00	5.00
2005	—	—	—	2.00	3.00	5.00
2006	—	—	—	2.00	3.00	5.00

KM# 239.2   500 COLONES
Brass, 32.9 mm. **Obv:** National arms, date below **Obv. Legend:** REPUBLICA DE COSTA RICA **Rev:** Denomination above sprays, B.C.C.R. below, thin numerals **Edge:** Segmented reeding

Date	Mintage	F	VF	XF	Unc	BU
2003 Rare	100	—	—	—	—	250

KM# 239.1a   500 COLONES
Brass Plated Steel **Obv:** National arms, date below **Rev:** Value above sprays, B.C.C.R. below **Edge:** Segmented reeding

Date	Mintage	F	VF	XF	Unc	BU
2006	—	—	—	—	—	250
2007	—	—	—	—	—	250

CREEK NATION

POARCH BAND
SOVEREIGN NATION
MILLED COINAGE

KM# 1   DOLLAR
31.1341 g., 0.9990 Silver 0.9999 oz. ASW, 39 mm. **Subject:** Peace **Obv:** Symbol **Obv. Legend:** CREEK NATION OF INDIANS **Rev:** Indian horseback left **Edge:** Reeded

Date	Mintage	VG	F	VF	XF	Unc
2004	20,000	—	—	—	—	20.00
2004 Proof	10,000	Value: 40.00				

KM# 2   DOLLAR
31.1341 g., 0.9990 Silver 0.9999 oz. ASW, 39 mm. **Subject:** 20th Anniversary of Recognition **Obv:** Young sky dancer right, symbol **Obv. Legend:** CREEK NATION OF INDIANS **Rev:** Busts of 5 tribal chiefs, symbol below **Rev. Legend:** SOVEREIGN NATION **Edge:** Reeded

Date	Mintage	VG	F	VF	XF	Unc
ND(2004)	20,000	—	—	—	—	20.00
ND(2004) Proof	10,000	Value: 40.00				

KM# 7   DOLLAR
31.1400 g., 0.9990 Silver 1.0000 oz. ASW, 40.52 mm. **Obv:** Tribal seal **Obv. Legend:** CREEK NATION OF INDIANS **Obv. Designer:** A. Shagin **Rev:** Bust of Chief Menawa 3/4 left **Rev. Legend:** CHIEF MENAWA "THE GREAT WARRIOR" **Edge:** Reeded

Date	Mintage	VG	F	VF	XF	Unc
2005	20,000	—	—	—	—	30.00
2005 Proof	10,000	Value: 50.00				

KM# 8   DOLLAR
31.2700 g., 0.9990 Silver 1.0043 oz. ASW, 40.55 mm. **Obv:** Tribal seal **Obv. Legend:** CREEK NATION OF INDIANS **Obv. Designer:** A. Shagin **Rev:** Tchow-ee-put-o-kaw 3/4 right **Rev. Legend:** TCOW-EE-PUT-O-KAW **Edge:** Reeded

Date	Mintage	VG	F	VF	XF	Unc
2005	20,000	—	—	—	—	30.00
2005 Proof	10,000	Value: 50.00				

KM# 10   DOLLAR
31.1200 g., 0.9990 Silver 0.9995 oz. ASW, 41.61 mm. **Obv:** Dancer left at center right, a tribal seal at lower left **Obv. Legend:** CREEK NATION - OF INDIANS **Obv. Designer:** A. Shagin **Rev:** Warrior horseback 3/4 right **Rev. Legend:** SOVEREIGN NATION **Edge:** Reeded

Date	Mintage	VG	F	VF	XF	Unc
2006	20,000	—	—	—	—	30.00
2006 Proof	10,000	Value: 50.00				

KM# 11 DOLLAR

31.1700 g., 0.9990 Silver 1.0011 oz. ASW, 40.58 mm. **Obv:**
Tribal seal **Obv. Legend:** CREEK NATION OF INDIANS **Obv.**
Designer: A. Shagin **Rev:** Facing busts of Chief Tomochichi and
his son with eagle **Rev. Legend:** CHIEF TOMOCHICHI **Edge:**
Reeded

Date	Mintage	VG	F	VF	XF	Unc
2006	20,000	—	—	—	—	30.00
2006 Proof	10,000	Value: 50.00				

KM# 13 DOLLAR

31.1700 g., 0.9990 Silver 1.0011 oz. ASW, 40.58 mm.
Obv: Sky Dancer **Obv. Legend:** CREEK NATION OF INDIANS
Rev: Warrior on horseback **Rev. Legend:** CHIEF OPOTHLE
YOHOLO **Edge:** Reeded

Date	Mintage	VG	F	VF	XF	Unc
2007 Proof	10,000	Value: 50.00				
2007	—	—	—	—	—	30.00

KM# 4 5 DOLLARS

0.9990 Gold, 22 mm. **Issuer:** Panda America **Subject:** Peace
Obv: Symbol **Obv. Legend:** CREEK NATION OF INDIANS **Rev:**
Indian horseback left **Edge:** Reeded

Date	Mintage	VG	F	VF	XF	Unc
2004 Proof	2,500	Value: 400				

KM# 9 5 DOLLARS

6.1700 g., 0.9990 Gold 0.1982 oz. AGW, 22.18 mm.
Obv: Tribal seal **Obv. Legend:** CREEK NATION OF
INDIANS **Obv. Designer:** A. Shagin **Rev:** Busts of Chief
Hopothle Mico and George Washington 3/4 left
Rev. Legend: CHIEF HOPOTHLE MICO • GEORGE
WASHINGTON **Edge:** Reeded

Date	Mintage	VG	F	VF	XF	Unc
2005 Proof	2,500	Value: 400				

KM# 12 5 DOLLARS

6.1700 g., 0.9990 Gold 0.1982 oz. AGW, 22.2 mm.
Obv: Tribal seal **Obv. Legend:** CREEK NATION OF INDIANS
Obv. Designer: A. Shagin **Rev:** Bust of Chief Stee•Chaco•Me•Co
Rev. Legend: CHIEF STEE • CHACO • ME • CO **Edge:** Reeded

Date	Mintage	VG	F	VF	XF	Unc
2006 Proof	2,500	Value: 400				

KM# 14 5 DOLLARS

6.1700 g., 0.9990 Gold 0.982 oz. AGW, 22.2 mm. **Obv:** Tribal
seal **Obv. Legend:** CREEK NATION OF INDIANS **Rev. Legend:**
CHIEF CALVIN MCGHEE **Edge:** Reeded

Date	Mintage	VG	F	VF	XF	Unc
2007 Proof	2,500	Value: 400				

KM# 5 10 DOLLARS

15.5515 g., 0.9995 Palladium 0.4997 oz., 30 mm.
Subject: 20th Anniversary of Recognition **Obv:** Young sky
dancer right, symbol **Obv. Legend:** CREEK NATION OF
INDIANS **Rev:** Busts of 5 tribal chiefs, symbol below
Rev. Legend: SOVEREIGN NATION **Edge:** Reeded

Date	Mintage	VG	F	VF	XF	Unc
2004 Proof	250	Value: 750				

KM# 6 100 DOLLARS

31.0800 g., 0.9990 Gold 0.9982 oz. AGW, 31.94 mm. **Subject:**
20th Anniversary of Treaty for Autonomy
Obv: Native dancer right at left center, tribal seal at right **Obv.**
Legend: CREEK NATION - OF INDIANS
Obv. Designer: A. Shagin **Rev:** Five portraits left to right, tribal
seal below **Rev. Legend:** • SOVEREIGN NATION • **Edge:**
Reeded

Date	Mintage	VG	F	VF	XF	Unc
ND(2004) Proof	250	Value: 2,000				

CROATIA

The Republic of Croatia, (Hrvatska) bordered on the west by
the Adriatic Sea and the northeast by Hungary, has an area of
21,829 sq. mi. (56,538 sq. km.) and a population of 4.7 million.
Capital: Zagreb.

NOTE: Coin dates starting with 1994 are followed with a
period. Example: 1994.

REPUBLIC

REFORM COINAGE

May 30, 1994 - 1000 Dinara = 1 Kuna; 100 Lipa = 1 Kuna

For the circulating minor coins, the reverse legend
(name of item) is in Croatian for odd dated years and Latin
for even dated years.

KM# 3 LIPA

0.8000 g., Aluminum, 16 mm. **Obv:** Denomination above
crowned arms **Obv. Legend:** REPUBLIKA HRVATSKA
Rev: Ears of corn, date below **Rev. Legend:** KUKURUZ
Edge: Plain **Designer:** Kuzma Kovacic

Date	Mintage	F	VF	XF	Unc	BU
2001.	2,000,000	—	—	0.20	0.50	—
2001. Proof	1,000	Value: 2.50				
2003.	1,500,000	—	—	0.20	0.50	—
2003. Proof	1,000	Value: 2.50				
2005.	—	—	—	0.20	0.50	—
2005. Proof	—	Value: 2.00				
2007. Proof	—	Value: 2.00				

KM# 12 LIPA

0.7000 g., Aluminum, 17 mm. **Obv:** Denomination above
crowned arms **Obv. Legend:** REPUBLIKA HRVATSKA
Rev: Ears of corn, date below **Rev. Legend:** ZEA MAYS
Edge: Plain

Date	Mintage	F	VF	XF	Unc	BU
2002.	3,000,000	—	—	0.40	1.00	—
2002. Proof	1,000	Value: 2.50				
2004.	2,000,000	—	—	0.40	1.00	—
2004. Proof	2,000	Value: 1.50				
2006.	—	—	—	0.40	1.00	—
2006. Proof	—	Value: 1.50				
2008.	—	—	—	0.40	1.00	—
2008. Proof	—	Value: 1.50				

KM# 4 2 LIPE

0.9000 g., Aluminum, 18.97 mm. **Obv:** Denomination above
crowned arms on half braid **Obv. Legend:** REPUBLIKA
HRVATSKA **Rev:** Grapevine, date below **Rev. Legend:** VINOVA
LOZA **Edge:** Plain

Date	Mintage	F	VF	XF	Unc	BU
2001.	2,986,000	—	—	0.40	1.00	—
2001. Proof	1,000	Value: 3.00				
2003.	2,000,000	—	—	0.40	1.00	—
2003. Proof	1,000	Value: 3.00				
2005.	—	—	—	0.40	1.00	—
2005. Proof	—	Value: 3.00				
2007. Proof	—	Value: 3.00				

KM# 14 2 LIPE

0.9200 g., Aluminum, 19 mm. **Obv:** Denomination above
crowned arms on half braid **Obv. Legend:** REPUBLIKA
HRVATSKA **Rev:** Grapevine, date below **Rev. Legend:** VITIS
VINIFERA **Edge:** Plain **Designer:** Kuzma Kovacic

Date	Mintage	F	VF	XF	Unc	BU
2002.	2,000,000	—	—	0.80	2.00	—
2002. Proof	1,000	Value: 3.00				
2004.	2,000,000	—	—	0.80	2.00	—
2004. Proof	2,000	Value: 2.50				
2006.	—	—	—	0.80	2.00	—
2006. Proof	—	Value: 2.50				
2008.	—	—	—	0.80	2.00	—
2008. Proof	—	Value: 2.50				

KM# 5 5 LIPA

2.5400 g., Brass Plated Steel, 17.99 mm. **Obv:** Denomination
above crowned arms **Obv. Legend:** REPUBLIKA HRVATSKA
Rev: Oak leaves, date below **Rev. Legend:** HRAST LUZNJAK
Edge: Plain **Designer:** Kuzma Kovacic

Date	Mintage	F	VF	XF	Unc	BU
2001.	6,598,000	—	—	0.40	1.00	—
2001. Proof	1,000	Value: 4.00				
2003.	13,000,000	—	—	0.40	1.00	—
2003. Proof	2,000	Value: 3.50				
2005.	—	—	—	0.40	1.00	—
2005. Proof	—	Value: 3.50				
2007.	—	—	—	0.40	1.00	—
2007. Proof	—	Value: 3.50				

KM# 15 5 LIPA

2.5000 g., Brass Plated Steel, 18 mm. **Obv:** Denomination
above crowned arms **Obv. Legend:** REPUBLIKA HRVATSKA
Rev: Oak leaves, date below **Rev. Legend:** QUERCUS ROBUR
Edge: Plain **Designer:** Kuzma Kovacic

Date	Mintage	F	VF	XF	Unc	BU
2002.	3,500,000	—	—	0.80	2.00	—
2002. Proof	1,000	Value: 4.00				
2004.	2,000,000	—	—	0.80	2.00	—
2004. Proof	2,000	Value: 3.00				
2006.	—	—	—	0.80	2.00	—
2006. Proof	—	Value: 3.00				
2008	—	—	—	0.80	2.00	—
2008. Proof	—	Value: 3.00				

KM# 6   10 LIPA
3.3200 g., Brass Plated Steel, 20 mm. **Obv:** Denomination above crowned arms **Obv. Legend:** REPUBLIKA HRVATSKA **Rev:** Tobacco plant, date below **Rev. Legend:** DUHAN **Edge:** Plain **Designer:** Kuzma Kovacic

Date	Mintage	F	VF	XF	Unc	BU
2001.	31,500,000	—	—	0.40	1.50	—
2001. Proof	1,000	Value: 5.00				
2003.	12,000,000	—	—	0.40	1.50	—
2003. Proof	1,000	Value: 5.00				
2005.	—	—	—	0.40	1.50	—
2005. Proof	—	Value: 5.00				
2007.	—	—	—	0.40	1.50	—
2007. Proof	—	Value: 5.00				

KM# 16   10 LIPA
3.2500 g., Brass Plated Steel, 20 mm. **Obv:** Denomination above crowned arms on half braid **Obv. Legend:** REPUBLIKA HRVATSKA **Rev:** Tobacco plant, date below **Rev. Legend:** NICOTIANA TABACUM **Edge:** Plain **Designer:** Kuzma Kovacic

Date	Mintage	F	VF	XF	Unc	BU
2002.	2,000,000	—	—	0.80	2.50	—
2002. Proof	1,000	Value: 5.00				
2004.	2,000,000	—	—	0.80	2.50	—
2004. Proof	2,000	Value: 4.50				
2006.	—	—	—	0.80	2.50	—
2006. Proof	—	Value: 4.50				
2008.	—	—	—	0.80	2.50	—
2008. Proof	—	Value: 4.50				

KM# 7   20 LIPA
2.9000 g., Nickel Plated Steel, 18.5 mm. **Obv:** Denomination above crowned arms on half braid **Obv. Legend:** REPUBLIKA HRVATSKA **Rev:** Olive branch, date below **Rev. Legend:** MASLINA **Edge:** Plain **Designer:** Kuzma Kovacic

Date	Mintage	F	VF	XF	Unc	BU
2001.	23,000,000	—	—	0.45	1.50	—
2001. Proof	1,000	Value: 5.00				
2003.	12,500,000	—	—	0.45	1.50	—
2003. Proof	1,000	Value: 5.00				
2005.	—	—	—	0.45	1.50	—
2005. Proof	—	Value: 5.00				
2007.	—	—	—	0.45	1.50	—
2007. Proof	—	Value: 5.00				

KM# 17   20 LIPA
3.0000 g., Nickel Plated Steel, 18.5 mm. **Obv:** Denomination above crowned arms on half braid **Obv. Legend:** REPUBLIKA HRVATSKA **Rev:** Olive branch, date below **Rev. Legend:** OLEA EUROPAEA **Edge:** Plain

Date	Mintage	F	VF	XF	Unc	BU
2002.	2,000,000	—	—	0.80	2.50	—
2002. Proof	1,000	Value: 5.00				
2004.	2,000,000	—	—	0.80	2.50	—
2004. Proof	2,000	Value: 4.50				
2006.	—	—	—	0.80	2.50	—
2006. Proof	—	Value: 4.50				
2008.	—	—	—	0.80	2.50	—
2008. Proof	—	Value: 4.50				

KM# 8   50 LIPA
3.6500 g., Nickel Plated Steel, 20.5 mm. **Obv:** Denomination above crowned arms on half braid **Obv. Legend:** REPUBLIKA HRVATSKA **Rev:** Flowers, date below **Rev. Legend:** VELEBITSKA DEGENIJA **Edge:** Plain **Designer:** Kuzma Kovacic

Date	Mintage	F	VF	XF	Unc	BU
2001.	5,500,000	—	—	0.60	1.50	—
2001. Proof	1,000	Value: 5.50				
2003.	8,000,000	—	—	0.60	1.50	—
2003. Proof	1,000	Value: 5.50				
2005.	—	—	—	0.60	1.50	—
2005. Proof	—	Value: 5.00				
2007. Proof	—	Value: 5.00				

KM# 19   50 LIPA
3.6500 g., Nickel Plated Steel, 20.5 mm. **Obv:** Denomination above crowned arms on half braid **Obv. Legend:** REPUBLIKA HRVATSKA **Rev:** Flowers, date below **Rev. Legend:** DEGENIA VELEBITICA **Edge:** Plain **Designer:** Kuzma Kovacic

Date	Mintage	F	VF	XF	Unc	BU
2002.	2,000,000	—	—	0.80	2.50	—
2002. Proof	1,000	Value: 5.00				
2004.	2,000,000	—	—	0.80	2.50	—
2004. Proof	2,000	Value: 4.50				
2006.	—	—	—	0.80	2.50	—
2006. Proof	—	Value: 4.50				
2008.	—	—	—	0.80	2.50	—
2008. Proof	—	Value: 4.50				

KM# 9.1   KUNA
5.0000 g., Copper-Nickel, 22.5 mm. **Obv:** Marten back of numeral, arms divide branches below **Obv. Legend:** REPUBLIKA HRVATSKA **Rev:** Nightingale left, two dates **Rev. Legend:** SLAVUJ **Edge:** Reeded **Designer:** Kusma Kovacic

Date	Mintage	F	VF	XF	Unc	BU
2001.	1,000,000	—	—	0.75	1.65	2.00
2001. Proof	1,000	Value: 4.50				
2003.	2,000,000	—	—	0.75	1.65	2.00
2003. Proof	1,000	Value: 4.50				
2005.	—	—	—	0.75	1.65	2.00
2005. Proof	—	Value: 4.50				
2007. Proof	—	Value: 4.50				

KM# 9.2   KUNA
4.9300 g., Copper-Nickel, 22.5 mm. **Obv:** Crowned arms flanked by sprays, denomination above on marten **Rev:** Nightingale, left, '1994' above, date below **Edge:** Reeded

Date	Mintage	F	VF	XF	Unc	BU
2001 Proof	—	Value: 4.00				

KM# 20.1   KUNA
5.0000 g., Copper-Nickel, 22.5 mm. **Obv:** Marten back of numeral, arms divide branches below **Rev:** Nightingale left, date below **Rev. Legend:** Error spelling "LUSCINNIA" MEGARHYNCHOS **Designer:** Kuzma Kovacic **Note:** Formerly KM-20

Date	Mintage	F	VF	XF	Unc	BU
2002.	—	—	—	—	—	2.00

KM# 20.2   KUNA
5.0000 g., Copper-Nickel, 22.5 mm. **Obv:** Marten back of numeral, arms divide branches below **Obv. Legend:** REPUBLIKA HRVATSKA **Rev:** Nightingale left, date below **Rev. Legend:** Correct spelling "LUSCINIA" MEGARHYNCHOS **Edge:** Reeded **Designer:** Kuzma Kovacic

Date	Mintage	F	VF	XF	Unc	BU
2002.	1,000,000	—	—	1.00	3.00	—
2002. Proof	1,000	Value: 5.00				
2006.	—	—	—	1.00	3.00	—
2006. Proof	—	Value: 5.00				
2008.	—	—	—	1.00	3.00	—
2008. Proof	—	Value: 5.00				

KM# 79   KUNA
5.0000 g., Copper-Nickel, 22.5 mm. **Subject:** 10th Anniversary of National Currency **Obv:** Crowned arms flanked by sprays, denomination above on marten **Obv. Legend:** REPUBLIKA HRVATSKA **Rev:** Nightingale left, date below **Rev. Legend:** MEGARHYNCHOS **Edge:** Reeded

Date	Mintage	F	VF	XF	Unc	BU
ND(2004)	30,000	—	—	1.00	3.00	—
ND(2004) Proof	2,000	Value: 5.00				

KM# 10   2 KUNE
6.2000 g., Copper-Nickel, 24.5 mm. **Obv:** Marten back of numeral, arms divide branches below **Obv. Legend:** REPUBLIKA HRVATSKA **Rev:** Bluefin tuna right, date below **Rev. Legend:** TUNJ **Edge:** Reeded **Designer:** Kuzma Kovacic

Date	Mintage	F	VF	XF	Unc	BU
2001.	1,250,000	—	—	1.00	2.00	—
2001. Proof	1,000	Value: 6.50				
2003.	7,250,000	—	—	1.00	2.00	—
2003. Proof	1,000	Value: 6.50				
2005.	—	—	—	1.00	2.00	—
2005. Proof	—	Value: 6.50				
2007. Proof	—	Value: 6.50				

KM# 21   2 KUNE
6.3000 g., Copper-Nickel, 24.5 mm. **Obv:** Marten back of numeral, arms divide branches below **Obv. Legend:** REPUBLIKA HRVATSKA **Rev:** Bluefin tuna right, date below **Rev. Legend:** THUNNUS - THYNNUS **Edge:** Reeded **Designer:** Kuzma Kovacic

Date	Mintage	F	VF	XF	Unc	BU
2002.	1,000,000	—	—	1.50	3.00	—
2002. Proof	1,000	Value: 6.00				
2004.	2,000,000	—	—	1.50	3.00	—
2004. Proof	2,000	Value: 5.50				
2006.	—	—	—	1.50	3.00	—
2006. Proof	—	Value: 5.50				
2008.	—	—	—	1.50	3.00	—
2008. Proof	—	Value: 5.50				

KM# 11 5 KUNA

7.5000 g., Copper-Nickel, 26.7 mm. **Obv:** Marten back of numeral, arms divide branches below **Obv. Legend:** REPUBLIKA HRVATSKA **Rev:** Brown bear left, date below **Rev. Legend:** MRKI MEDVJRD **Edge:** Reeded

Date	Mintage	F	VF	XF	Unc	BU
2001.	17,300,000	—	—	1.50	5.00	10.00
2001. Proof	1,000	Value: 9.00				
2003.	1,000,000	—	—	1.50	5.00	10.00
2003. Proof	1,000	Value: 9.00				
2005.	—	—	—	1.50	5.00	10.00
2005. Proof	—	Value: 9.00				
2007. Proof	—	Value: 9.00				

KM# 23 5 KUNA

7.5000 g., Copper-Nickel, 26.5 mm. **Obv:** Marten back of numeral, arms divide branches below **Obv. Legend:** REPUBLIKA HRVATSKA **Rev:** Brown bear left, date below **Rev. Legend:** URSUS ARCTOS **Edge:** Reeded

Date	Mintage	F	VF	XF	Unc	BU
2002.	2,000,000	—	—	2.00	5.00	9.00
2002. Proof	1,000	Value: 9.00				
2004.	2,000,000	—	—	2.00	5.00	9.00
2004. Proof	2,000	Value: 8.00				
2006.	—	—	—	2.00	5.00	9.00
2006. Proof	—	Value: 8.00				
2008.	—	—	—	2.00	5.00	9.00
2008. Proof	—	Value: 8.00				

KM# 66 25 KUNA

Bi-Metallic Brass center in Copper-Nickel ring, 31 mm. **Subject:** 10th Anniversary of International Recognition **Obv:** Denomination in 3-D on outlined marten within circle, arms divide sprays below **Rev:** National map **Edge:** Plain **Shape:** 12-sided

Date	Mintage	F	VF	XF	Unc	BU
ND(2002)	200,000	—	—	—	8.50	—

KM# 78 25 KUNA

12.6500 g., Bi-Metallic, 31 mm. **Subject:** Croatian European Union Candidacy **Obv:** Denomination in 3-D on outlined marten within circle, arms divide sprays below **Rev:** Joined squares within circle of stars **Edge:** Plain **Shape:** 12-sided

Date	Mintage	F	VF	XF	Unc	BU
ND (2004)	30,000	—	—	—	10.00	—
ND (2004) Proof	—	Value: 25.00				

KM# 83 150 KUNA

24.0000 g., 0.9250 Silver 0.7137 oz. ASW, 37 mm. **Subject:** 2006 Winter Olympics - Italy **Obv:** National arms below denomination **Rev:** Slalom skiing

Date	Mintage	F	VF	XF	Unc	BU
ND(2006) Proof	15,000	Value: 40.00				

KM# 84 150 KUNA

24.0000 g., 0.9250 Silver 0.7137 oz. ASW, 37 mm. **Subject:** 2006 World Soccer Championship - Germany **Obv:** National arms below denomination **Rev:** Soccer player

Date	Mintage	F	VF	XF	Unc	BU
ND(2006) Proof	50,000	Value: 30.00				

KM# 85 150 KUNA

24.0000 g., 0.9250 Silver 0.7137 oz. ASW, 37 mm. **Subject:** 2006 World Soccer Championship - Germany **Obv:** National arms above denomination **Rev:** Vignette

Date	Mintage	F	VF	XF	Unc	BU
ND(2006) Proof	10,000	Value: 45.00				

KM# 86 150 KUNA

24.0000 g., 0.9250 Silver 0.7137 oz. ASW, 37 mm. **Subject:** 150th Anniversary - Birth of Nikola Tesla **Obv:** National arms above induction motor and denomination **Rev:** Bust of Tesla

Date	Mintage	F	VF	XF	Unc	BU
ND(2006) Proof	5,000	Value: 50.00				

KM# 87 150 KUNA

24.0000 g., 0.9250 Silver 0.7137 oz. ASW, 37 mm. **Issuer:** Croatian National Bank **Subject:** 2008 Olympic Games - Peoples Republic of China **Obv:** National arms, value in laurel wreath **Rev:** T'ai-ho Tien gate in Beijing, athlete **Edge:** Plain **Edge Lettering:** Ag 925/1000 24 g 37 mm PP HNZ

Date	Mintage	F	VF	XF	Unc	BU
ND(2006) Proof	20,000	Value: 40.00				

KM# 88 150 KUNA

24.0000 g., 0.9250 Silver 0.7137 oz. ASW, 37 mm. **Subject:** Ican Mestrovic **Obv:** Squares and shamrocks **Obv. Designer:** Damir Matauzic **Rev:** Female kneeling with Irish harp

Date	Mintage	F	VF	XF	Unc	BU
2007	4,000	—	—	—	—	45.00

KM# 89 150 KUNA

24.0000 g., 0.9250 Silver 0.7137 oz. ASW, 37 mm. **Subject:** Benedikt Kotruljevic **Obv:** Pile of coins **Obv. Designer:** Damir Matausic **Rev:** Bust right

Date	Mintage	F	VF	XF	Unc	BU
2007	10,000	—	—	—	—	36.00

KM# 90 150 KUNA

24.0000 g., 0.9250 Silver 0.7137 oz. ASW, 37 mm. **Subject:** Historic Ships - Dubrovnik Karaka **Obv:** Sail within compass **Obv. Designer:** Matej Pasalic **Rev:** Ship

Date	Mintage	F	VF	XF	Unc	BU
2007	10,000	—	—	—	—	36.00

KM# 91 1000 KUNA

7.0000 g., 0.9860 Gold 0.2219 oz. AGW, 22 mm. **Subject:** Andrija Monorovicic, 150th Anniversary of Birth **Obv:** Globe bisected showing layers **Obv. Designer:** Stjipan Divkovic **Rev:** Bust facing

Date	Mintage	F	VF	XF	Unc	BU
2007	2,000	—	—	—	—	300

KM# 92 1000 KUNA

7.0000 g., 0.9860 Gold 0.2219 oz. AGW, 22 mm. **Subject:** Marin Drzic **Obv:** Shield flanked by comedy and tragedy masks **Rev:** Half-length figure right

Date	Mintage	F	VF	XF	Unc	BU
2008	2,000	—	—	—	—	300

MINT SETS

KM#	Date	Mintage	Identification	Issue Price	Mkt Val
MS2	2002 (9)	—	KM#12, 14-17, 19, 20.1, 21, 23	—	25.00

PROOF SETS

KM#	Date	Mintage	Identification	Issue Price	Mkt Val
PS32	2001 (9)	—	KM#3-8, 9.2, 10, 11	—	45.00
PS33	2003 (9)	—	KM#3-8, 9.1, 10, 11	—	45.00
PS34	2004 (9)	—	KM#12, 14-17, 19, 21, 23, 79	—	40.00
PS35	2005 (9)	—	KM#3-8, 9.1, 10-11	—	45.00
PS36	2006 (9)	—	KM#12, 14-17, 19, 20.2, 21, 23	—	40.00
PS37	2007 (9)	—	KM#3-8, 9.1, 10-11	—	45.00
PS38	2008 (9)	—	KM#12, 14-17, 19, 20.2, 21, 23	—	40.00

CUBA

The Republic of Cuba, situated at the northern edge of the Caribbean Sea about 90 miles (145 km.) south of Florida, has an area of 42,804 sq. mi. (110,860 sq. km.) and a population of *11.2 million. Capital: Havana. The Cuban economy is based on the cultivation and refining of sugar, which provides 80 percent of export earnings.

MINT MARK
Key - Havana, 1977-

MONETARY SYSTEM
100 Centavos = 1 Peso

SECOND REPUBLIC
DECIMAL COINAGE

KM# 33.3 CENTAVO

0.7500 g., Aluminum, 16.76 mm. **Obv:** Cuban arms within wreath, denomination below **Rev:** Roman denomination within circle of star, date below **Edge:** Plain **Note:** Shield varieties exist.

Date	Mintage	F	VF	XF	Unc	BU
2001	—	—	0.10	0.40	0.80	1.75
2003	—	—	0.10	0.40	0.80	1.75
2004	—	—	0.10	0.40	0.80	1.75
2005	—	—	0.10	0.40	0.80	1.75

KM# 34 5 CENTAVOS

1.5600 g., Aluminum, 21 mm. **Obv:** National arms within wreath, denomination below **Rev:** Roman denomination within circle of star, date below **Note:** Shield varieties exist.

Date	Mintage	F	VF	XF	Unc	BU
2001	6,703,331	—	0.10	0.25	0.75	1.50
2002	14,830,000	—	0.10	0.25	0.75	1.50
	Note: High or low dates exist.					
2003	62,520,000	—	0.10	0.25	0.75	1.50
2004	62,520,000	—	0.10	0.25	0.75	1.50
2006	62,520,000	—	0.10	0.25	0.75	1.50
2007	62,520,000	—	0.10	0.25	0.75	1.50

KM# 35.2 20 CENTAVOS

Aluminum, 24 mm. **Obv:** National arms, revised shield **Rev:** Roman denomination within circle of star

Date	Mintage	F	VF	XF	Unc	BU
2002	—	4.00	7.00	10.00	15.00	
	Note: Large and small dates exist.					
2003	—	4.00	7.00	10.00	15.00	
2005	—	4.00	7.00	10.00	15.00	
2006	—	4.00	7.00	10.00	15.00	

KM# 35.1 20 CENTAVOS

2.0000 g., Aluminum, 24 mm. **Obv:** Cuban arms within wreath, denomination below **Rev:** Roman denomination within circle of star, date below **Note:** Shield varieties exist.

Date	Mintage	F	VF	XF	Unc	BU
2002	25,000,000	—	0.50	1.00	2.00	4.00
2003	11,911,000	—	0.50	1.00	2.00	4.00
2005	—	—	0.50	1.00	2.00	4.00
2006	—	—	0.50	1.00	2.00	4.00
2007	—	—	0.50	1.00	2.00	4.00

KM# 829 PESO

13.0000 g., Copper-Nickel, 32.65 mm. **Obv:** National arms **Rev:** Carpenter bird perched - multicolor **Rev. Legend:** FAUNA CUBANA - PAJERO CARPINTERO **Edge:** Plain

Date	Mintage	F	VF	XF	Unc	BU
2001	—	—	—	—	—	15.00

KM# 834   PESO
Copper-Nickel, 32.65 mm. **Obv:** National arms **Rev:** Butterfly - multicolor **Rev. Legend:** FAUNA CUBANA - PAJERO CARPINTERO

Date	Mintage	F	VF	XF	Unc	BU
2001	—			—		15.00

KM# 347   PESO
5.5000 g., Brass Plated Steel, 24.4 mm. **Subject:** Jose Marti **Obv:** National arms within wreath, denomination below **Rev:** Smaller Bust facing, denomination at left **Rev. Legend:** PATRIA O MUERTE **Note:** Rim varieties exist.

Date	Mintage	F	VF	XF	Unc	BU
2001	—		—	1.00	2.00	4.00
2002	—		—	1.00	2.00	4.00

KM# 830   PESO
13.0000 g., Copper-Nickel, 32.65 mm. **Obv:** National arms **Rev:** Parrot perched - multicolor **Rev. Legend:** FAUNA CUBANA - COTORRA **Edge:** Plain

Date	Mintage	F	VF	XF	Unc	BU
2001	—			—	15.00	

KM# 831   PESO
12.7000 g., Copper-Nickel, 32.5 mm. **Obv:** National arms **Rev:** Pink orchid - multicolor **Rev. Legend:** FLORA CUBANA - ORQUIDEAS **Edge:** Plain

Date	Mintage	F	VF	XF	Unc	BU
2001	—			—	20.00	

KM# 832   PESO
12.7000 g., Copper-Nickel, 32.5 mm. **Obv:** National arms **Rev:** Yellow orchid - multicolor **Rev. Legend:** FLORA CUBANA - ORQUIDEAS **Edge:** Plain

Date	Mintage	F	VF	XF	Unc	BU
2001	—			—	20.00	

KM# 833   PESO
12.7000 g., Copper-Nickel, 32.5 mm. **Obv:** National arms **Rev:** White orchid - multicolor **Rev. Legend:** FLORA CUBANA - ORQUIDEAS **Edge:** Plain

Date	Mintage	F	VF	XF	Unc	BU
2001	—			—	20.00	—

KM# 346a   3 PESOS
8.2000 g., Nickel Clad Steel, 26.3 mm. **Obv:** National arms within wreath, denomination below **Rev:** Head facing, date below **Note:** Shield varieties exist.

Date	Mintage	F	VF	XF	Unc	BU
2002				2.50	5.00	7.00

KM# 739   5 PESOS
1.2400 g., Gold, 14 mm. **Subject:** Wonders of the Ancient World **Obv:** Cuban arms **Rev:** Ancient lighthouse of Alexandria

Date	Mintage	F	VF	XF	Unc	BU
2005 Proof	5,000	Value: 80.00				

KM# 740   5 PESOS
1.2400 g., Gold, 14 mm. **Subject:** Wonders of the Ancient World **Obv:** Cuban arms **Rev:** Colossus of Rhodes

Date	Mintage	F	VF	XF	Unc	BU
2005 Proof	5,000	Value: 55.00				

KM# 741   5 PESOS
1.2400 g., Gold, 14 mm. **Subject:** Wonders of the Ancient World **Obv:** Cuban arms **Rev:** Hanging Gardens of Babylon

Date	Mintage	F	VF	XF	Unc	BU
2005 Proof	5,000	Value: 55.00				

KM# 742   5 PESOS
1.2400 g., Gold, 14 mm. **Subject:** Wonders of the Ancient World **Obv:** Cuban arms **Rev:** Egyptian Pyramids

Date	Mintage	F	VF	XF	Unc	BU
2005	5,000	Value: 55.00				

KM# 743   5 PESOS
1.2400 g., Gold, 14 mm. **Subject:** Wonders of the Ancient World **Obv:** Cuban arms **Rev:** Temple of Artemis

Date	Mintage	F	VF	XF	Unc	BU
2005 Proof	5,000	Value: 55.00				

KM# 744   5 PESOS
1.2400 g., Gold, 14 mm. **Subject:** Wonders of the Ancient World **Obv:** Cuban arms **Rev:** Statue of Jupiter

Date	Mintage	F	VF	XF	Unc	BU
2005	5,000	Value: 55.00				

KM# 745   5 PESOS
1.2400 g., Gold, 14 mm. **Subject:** Wonders of the Ancient World **Obv:** Cuban arms **Rev:** Mausoleum of Halicarnas

Date	Mintage	F	VF	XF	Unc	BU
2005 Proof	5,000	Value: 55.00				

KM# 746   5 PESOS
1.2400 g., Gold, 14 mm. **Obv:** Cuban arms **Rev:** Cortes, Montezuma and Aztec Pyramid

Date	Mintage	F	VF	XF	Unc	BU
2005 Proof	15,000	Value: 55.00				

KM# 763   10 PESOS
20.0000 g., 0.9990 Silver 0.6423 oz. ASW, 38 mm.
Subject: Third Globalization Conference **Obv:** Cuban arms **Rev:** World map

Date	Mintage	F	VF	XF	Unc	BU
2001 Proof	100	Value: 200				

KM# 764   10 PESOS
20.0000 g., 0.9990 Silver 0.6423 oz. ASW, 38 mm.
Subject: 40th Anniversary - Battle of Giron **Obv:** Cuban arms **Rev:** Soldiers on tank

Date	Mintage	F	VF	XF	Unc	BU
2001 Proof	3,000	Value: 45.00				

KM# 765   10 PESOS
31.1035 g., 0.9990 Silver 0.9990 oz. ASW, 38 mm.
Subject: 106th Anniversary - Jose Marti's **Obv:** Cuban arms **Rev:** Monument

Date	Mintage	F	VF	XF	Unc	BU
2001 Proof	2,000	Value: 50.00				

KM# 762   10 PESOS
31.1035 g., 0.9990 Silver 0.9990 oz. ASW, 38 mm. **Obv:** Cuban arms **Rev:** Two Bee hummingbirds

Date	Mintage	F	VF	XF	Unc	BU
2001 Proof	20,000	Value: 40.00				

KM# 766   10 PESOS
15.0000 g., 0.9990 Silver 0.4818 oz. ASW, 35 mm.
Subject: Cuban Fauna **Obv:** Cuban arms **Rev:** Red-splashed Sulphur butterfly

Date	Mintage	F	VF	XF	Unc	BU
2001 Proof	5,000	Value: 40.00				

KM# 767   10 PESOS
15.0000 g., 0.9990 Silver 0.4818 oz. ASW, 35 mm.
Subject: Cuban Fauna **Obv:** Cuban arms **Rev:** Cuban Parrot

Date	Mintage	F	VF	XF	Unc	BU
2001 Proof	5,000	Value: 40.00				

KM# 768   10 PESOS
15.0000 g., 0.9990 Silver 0.4818 oz. ASW, 35 mm.
Obv: National arms **Rev:** Cuban (Green) woodpecker

Date	Mintage	F	VF	XF	Unc	BU
2001 Proof	5,000	Value: 40.00				

KM# 769   10 PESOS
15.0000 g., 0.9990 Silver 0.4818 oz. ASW, 35 mm. **Obv:** Cuban arms **Rev:** Multicolor white orchid

Date	Mintage	F	VF	XF	Unc	BU
2001 Proof	5,000	Value: 35.00				

KM# 770   10 PESOS
15.0000 g., 0.9990 Silver 0.4818 oz. ASW, 35 mm. **Subject:** Cuban Flora **Obv:** Cuban arms **Rev:** Multicolor yellow orchid

Date	Mintage	F	VF	XF	Unc	BU
2001 Proof	5,000	Value: 35.00				

KM# 771   10 PESOS
15.0000 g., 0.9990 Silver 0.4818 oz. ASW, 35 mm. **Subject:** Cuban Flora **Obv:** Cuban arms **Rev:** Multicolor pink orchid

Date	Mintage	F	VF	XF	Unc	BU
2001 Proof	5,000	Value: 35.00				

KM# 772   10 PESOS
31.1035 g., 0.9990 Silver 0.9990 oz. ASW, 38 mm. **Obv:** Cuban arms **Rev:** Multicolor Santa Maria

Date	Mintage	F	VF	XF	Unc	BU
2001 Proof	4,000	Value: 55.00				

KM# 773   10 PESOS
15.0000 g., 0.9990 Silver 0.4818 oz. ASW, 35 mm. **Subject:** World Cup Soccer Champions **Obv:** Cuban arms **Rev:** Soccer player and stadium

Date	Mintage	F	VF	XF	Unc	BU
2001 Proof	7,500	Value: 35.00				

KM# 774   10 PESOS
20.0000 g., 0.9990 Silver 0.6423 oz. ASW, 38 mm.
Subject: Cuban Monuments **Obv:** Cuban arms **Rev:** Trinidad street view

Date	Mintage	F	VF	XF	Unc	BU
2001 Proof	5,000	Value: 45.00				

KM# 775   10 PESOS
20.0000 g., 0.9990 Silver 0.6423 oz. ASW, 38 mm.
Subject: Cuban Monuments **Obv:** Cuban arms **Rev:** Havana Cathedral

Date	Mintage	F	VF	XF	Unc	BU
2001 Proof	5,000	Value: 45.00				

KM# 776   10 PESOS
20.0000 g., 0.9990 Silver 0.6423 oz. ASW, 38 mm.
Subject: Cuban Monuments **Obv:** Cuban arms **Rev:** Template building

Date	Mintage	F	VF	XF	Unc	BU
2001 Proof	5,000	Value: 45.00				

KM# 777   10 PESOS
31.1035 g., 0.9990 Silver 0.9990 oz. ASW, 38 mm. **Obv:** Cuban arms **Rev:** Bolivar standing at his birthplace

Date	Mintage	F	VF	XF	Unc	BU
2001 Proof	5,000	Value: 50.00				

KM# 778   10 PESOS
31.1035 g., 0.9990 Silver 0.9990 oz. ASW, 38 mm. **Obv:** Cuban arms **Rev:** Bolivar and map of South America

Date	Mintage	F	VF	XF	Unc	BU
2001 Proof	5,000	Value: 50.00				

KM# 779   10 PESOS
31.1035 g., 0.9990 Silver 0.9990 oz. ASW, 38 mm.
Subject: 180th Anniversary of the Battle of Carabobo
Obv: Cuban arms **Rev:** Bolivar leading troops

Date	Mintage	F	VF	XF	Unc	BU
2001 Proof	5,000	Value: 50.00				

KM# 828   10 PESOS
20.0000 g., 0.9990 Silver 0.6423 oz. ASW **Subject:** XVII World Soccer Championship - Korea and Japan 2002 **Obv:** National arms

Date	Mintage	F	VF	XF	Unc	BU
2001 proof	—	Value: 50.00				

KM# 734   10 PESOS
20.0000 g., 0.9990 Silver 0.6423 oz. ASW, 37.9 mm.
Subject: Olympics **Obv:** Cuban arms **Rev:** Runner and ancient ruins **Edge:** Reeded

Date	Mintage	F	VF	XF	Unc	BU
2002 Proof	—	Value: 35.00				

KM# 780   10 PESOS
20.0000 g., 0.9990 Silver 0.6423 oz. ASW, 38 mm.
Subject: World Cup Soccer Champions **Obv:** Cuban arms **Rev:** Soccer player and map above "CHILE 1962"

Date	Mintage	F	VF	XF	Unc	BU
2002 Proof	7,500	Value: 35.00				

KM# 781   10 PESOS
20.0000 g., 0.9990 Silver 0.6423 oz. ASW, 38 mm.
Subject: World Cup Soccer Champions **Obv:** Cuban arms **Rev:** Soccer player and Cuauhtemoc head below MEXICO 1970

Date	Mintage	F	VF	XF	Unc	BU
2002 Proof	7,500	Value: 35.00				

KM# 782   10 PESOS
20.0000 g., 0.9990 Silver 0.6423 oz. ASW, 38 mm. **Obv:** Cuban arms **Rev:** Vasco De Gama and ship

Date	Mintage	F	VF	XF	Unc	BU
2002 Proof	5,000	Value: 45.00				

KM# 783   10 PESOS
20.0000 g., 0.9990 Silver 0.6423 oz. ASW, 38 mm. **Obv:** Cuban arms **Rev:** Americo Vespucio and ship

Date	Mintage	F	VF	XF	Unc	BU
2002 Proof	5,000	Value: 45.00				

KM# 784   10 PESOS
31.1035 g., 0.9990 Silver 0.9990 oz. ASW, 38 mm.
Subject: Leaders of Communism **Obv:** Cuban arms **Rev:** Head of Mao Tse Tung left

Date	Mintage	F	VF	XF	Unc	BU
2002 Proof	2,000	Value: 50.00				

KM# 785   10 PESOS
31.1035 g., 0.9990 Silver 0.9990 oz. ASW, 38 mm.
Subject: Leaders of Communism **Obv:** Cuban arms **Rev:** Head of Karl Marx 3/4 left

Date	Mintage	F	VF	XF	Unc	BU
2002 Proof	2,000	Value: 50.00				

KM# 786   10 PESOS
31.1035 g., 0.9990 Silver 0.9990 oz. ASW, 38 mm.
Subject: Leaders of Communism **Obv:** Cuban arms **Rev:** Head of Vladimir Lenin right

Date	Mintage	F	VF	XF	Unc	BU
2002 Proof	2,000	Value: 60.00				

KM# 787   10 PESOS
31.1035 g., 0.9990 Silver 0.9990 oz. ASW, 38 mm.
Subject: Leaders of Communism **Obv:** Cuban arms **Rev:** Head of Federico Engels 3/4 right

Date	Mintage	F	VF	XF	Unc	BU
2002 Proof	2,000	Value: 50.00				

KM# 788   10 PESOS
27.0000 g., 0.9990 Silver 0.8672 oz. ASW, 40 mm.
Subject: IBERO-AMERICA Series **Obv:** Circle of arms around Cuban arms **Rev:** Santisima Trinidad ship

Date	Mintage	F	VF	XF	Unc	BU
2002 Proof	14,000	Value: 50.00				

KM# 789   10 PESOS
31.1035 g., 0.9990 Silver 0.9990 oz. ASW, 38 mm.
Subject: Jose Marti's 150th Birthday **Obv:** Cuban arms **Rev:** Numbered infield behind head right

Date	Mintage	F	VF	XF	Unc	BU
2003 Proof	150	Value: 150				

KM# 794   10 PESOS
20.0000 g., 0.9990 Silver 0.6423 oz. ASW, 38 mm.
Subject: Endangered Wildlife **Obv:** Cuban arms **Rev:** Cuban Crocodile

Date	Mintage	F	VF	XF	Unc	BU
2003 Proof	5,000	Value: 50.00				

KM# 795 10 PESOS
20.0000 g., 0.9990 Silver 0.6423 oz. ASW, 38 mm.
Subject: Endangered Wildlife **Obv:** Cuban arms **Rev:** Ocelot

Date	Mintage	F	VF	XF	Unc	BU
2003 Proof	5,000	Value: 50.00				

KM# 792 10 PESOS
20.0000 g., 0.9990 Silver 0.6423 oz. ASW, 38 mm. **Obv:** Cuban arms **Rev:** Che Guevara, 75th Anniversary of Birth

Date	Mintage	F	VF	XF	Unc	BU
2003 Proof	5,000	Value: 45.00				

KM# 791 10 PESOS
20.0000 g., 0.9990 Silver 0.6423 oz. ASW, 38 mm. **Obv:** Cuban arms **Rev:** Sailing ship, Sovereign of the Seas

Date	Mintage	F	VF	XF	Unc	BU
2003 Proof	5,000	Value: 45.00				

KM# 790 10 PESOS
20.0000 g., 0.9990 Silver 0.6423 oz. ASW, 38 mm. **Obv:** Cuban arms **Rev:** Ferdinand Magellan, ship, and astrolab

Date	Mintage	F	VF	XF	Unc	BU
2003 Proof	5,000	Value: 45.00				

KM# 793 10 PESOS
31.1000 g., 0.9990 Silver 0.9988 oz. ASW, 38 mm.
Subject: World Cup Soccer - Germany 2006 **Obv:** Cuban arms **Rev:** 5 soccer players

Date	Mintage	F	VF	XF	Unc	BU
2003 Proof	50,000	Value: 45.00				

KM# 796 10 PESOS
20.0000 g., 0.9990 Silver 0.6423 oz. ASW, 38 mm. **Obv:** Cuban arms **Rev:** John Cabot's portrait in cameo above ship

Date	Mintage	F	VF	XF	Unc	BU
2004 Proof	5,000	Value: 45.00				

KM# 797 10 PESOS
15.0000 g., 0.9990 Silver 0.4818 oz. ASW, 35 mm.
Subject: Hippocampus Kuda **Obv:** Cuban arms **Rev:** Spotted seahorse

Date	Mintage	F	VF	XF	Unc	BU
2004 Proof	5,000	Value: 50.00				

KM# 798 10 PESOS
20.0000 g., 0.9990 Silver 0.6423 oz. ASW, 38 mm. **Obv:** Cuban arms **Rev:** Murphy's Petrel bird on rock

Date	Mintage	F	VF	XF	Unc	BU
2004 Proof	5,000	Value: 50.00				

KM# 799 10 PESOS
20.0000 g., 0.9990 Silver 0.6423 oz. ASW, 38 mm. **Obv:** Cuban arms **Rev:** Cuban Rock Iguana on branch

Date	Mintage	F	VF	XF	Unc	BU
2004 Proof	5,000	Value: 50.00				

KM# 800 10 PESOS
31.1000 g., 0.9990 Silver 0.9988 oz. ASW, 38 mm. **Obv:** Cuban arms **Rev:** Imperial eagle perched on branch

Date	Mintage	F	VF	XF	Unc	BU
2004 Proof	1,000	Value: 55.00				

KM# 801 10 PESOS
31.1000 g., 0.9990 Silver 0.9988 oz. ASW, 38 mm. **Obv:** Cuban arms **Rev:** Bearded vulture in flight

Date	Mintage	F	VF	XF	Unc	BU
2004 Proof	1,000	Value: 55.00				

KM# 802 10 PESOS
31.1000 g., 0.9990 Silver 0.9988 oz. ASW, 38 mm. **Obv:** Cuban arms **Rev:** Iberian Lynx

Date	Mintage	F	VF	XF	Unc	BU
2004 Proof	1,000	Value: 55.00				

KM# 803   10 PESOS
31.1000 g., 0.9990 Silver 0.9988 oz. ASW, 38 mm. **Obv:** Cuban arms **Rev:** 2 grey wolves

Date	Mintage	F	VF	XF	Unc	BU
2004 Proof	1,000	Value: 60.00				

KM# 804   10 PESOS
31.1000 g., 0.9990 Silver 0.9988 oz. ASW, 38 mm. **Obv:** Cuban arms **Rev:** Brown bear

Date	Mintage	F	VF	XF	Unc	BU
2004 Proof	1,000	Value: 60.00				

KM# 805   10 PESOS
31.1000 g., 0.9990 Silver 0.9988 oz. ASW, 38 mm. **Obv:** Cuban arms **Rev:** Peregrine Falcon perches on branch

Date	Mintage	F	VF	XF	Unc	BU
2004 Proof	1,000	Value: 60.00				

KM# 806   10 PESOS
20.0000 g., 0.9990 Silver 0.6423 oz. ASW, 38 mm. **Subject:** Monuments of Cuba **Obv:** Cuban arms **Rev:** University of Havana building

Date	Mintage	F	VF	XF	Unc	BU
2004 Proof	1,500	Value: 50.00				

KM# 807   10 PESOS
20.0000 g., 0.9990 Silver 0.6423 oz. ASW, 38 mm. **Subject:** Monuments of Cuba **Obv:** Cuban arms **Rev:** Fountain of India

Date	Mintage	F	VF	XF	Unc	BU
2004 Proof	1,500	Value: 50.00				

KM# 808   10 PESOS
20.0000 g., 0.9990 Silver 0.6423 oz. ASW, 38 mm. **Subject:** Monuments of Cuba **Obv:** Cuban arms **Rev:** Plaza building

Date	Mintage	F	VF	XF	Unc	BU
2004 Proof	1,500	Value: 50.00				

KM# 809   10 PESOS
27.0000 g., 0.9250 Silver 0.8029 oz. ASW, 40 mm. **Obv:** Cuban arms within circle of arms **Rev:** Portions of the old Havana Wall

Date	Mintage	F	VF	XF	Unc	BU
2005 Proof	12,000	Value: 75.00				

KM# 810   10 PESOS
20.0000 g., 0.9990 Silver 0.6423 oz. ASW, 38 mm. **Subject:** Tobacco **Obv:** Cuban arms **Rev:** Indian showing tobacco to Columbus, ship in background

Date	Mintage	F	VF	XF	Unc	BU
2005 Proof	2,000	Value: 50.00				

KM# 811   10 PESOS
20.0000 g., 0.9250 Silver 0.5948 oz. ASW, 38 mm. **Subject:** Columbus' Ships **Obv:** Cuban arms **Rev:** The Santa Maria under sail

Date	Mintage	F	VF	XF	Unc	BU
2005 Proof	5,000	Value: 45.00				

KM# 812   10 PESOS
20.0000 g., 0.9250 Silver 0.5948 oz. ASW, 38 mm. **Subject:** Columbus' Ships **Obv:** Cuban arms **Rev:** The Nina under sail

Date	Mintage	F	VF	XF	Unc	BU
2005 Proof	5,000	Value: 45.00				

KM# 813   10 PESOS
20.0000 g., 0.9250 Silver 0.5948 oz. ASW, 38 mm. **Subject:** Columbus' Ships **Obv:** Cuban arms **Rev:** The Pinta under sail

Date	Mintage	F	VF	XF	Unc	BU
2005 Proof	5,000	Value: 45.00				

KM# 814   10 PESOS
20.0000 g., 0.9250 Silver 0.5948 oz. ASW, 38 mm. **Obv:** Cuban arms **Rev:** Cuban Solenodon on branch

Date	Mintage	F	VF	XF	Unc	BU
2005 Proof	5,000	Value: 45.00				

KM# 815   10 PESOS
15.0000 g., 0.9990 Silver 0.4818 oz. ASW, 35 mm. **Obv:** Cuban arms **Rev:** Multicolor Solenodon on branch

Date	Mintage	F	VF	XF	Unc	BU
2005 Proof	5,000	Value: 40.00				

KM# 816   10 PESOS
15.0000 g., 0.9250 Silver 0.4461 oz. ASW, 35 mm. **Subject:** Tropical Fish **Obv:** Cuban arms **Rev:** Picassofish (triggerfish)

Date	Mintage	F	VF	XF	Unc	BU
2005 Proof	2,000	Value: 40.00				

KM# 817   10 PESOS
15.0000 g., 0.9250 Silver 0.4461 oz. ASW, 35 mm.
Subject: Tropical Fish **Obv:** Cuban arms **Rev:** Moorish Idol fish

Date	Mintage	F	VF	XF	Unc	BU
2005 Proof	2,000	Value: 40.00				

KM# 818   10 PESOS
15.0000 g., 0.9250 Silver 0.4461 oz. ASW, 35 mm.
Subject: Tropical Fish **Obv:** Cuban arms **Rev:** Regal Angel fish

Date	Mintage	F	VF	XF	Unc	BU
2005 Proof	2,000	Value: 40.00				

KM# 819   10 PESOS
31.1000 g., 0.9250 Silver 0.9249 oz. ASW, 38 mm.
Subject: 400 Years of Quijote **Obv:** Cuban arms **Rev:** Don Quijote and Sancho looking at two windmills

Date	Mintage	F	VF	XF	Unc	BU
2005 Proof	5,000	Value: 50.00				

KM# 820   10 PESOS
31.1000 g., 0.9990 Silver 0.9988 oz. ASW, 38 mm.
Subject: Maximo Gomez Centennial of Death **Obv:** Cuban arms **Rev:** Bust 3/4 left, numbered behind neck

Date	Mintage	F	VF	XF	Unc	BU
2005 Proof	100	Value: 220				

KM# 821   10 PESOS
20.0000 g., 0.9250 Silver 0.5948 oz. ASW, 38 mm.
Subject: XXIX Olympics **Obv:** Cuban arms **Rev:** Baseball player with bat, baseball background

Date	Mintage	F	VF	XF	Unc	BU
2006 Proof	15,000	Value: 45.00				

KM# 822   100 PESOS
31.1000 g., 0.9990 Gold 0.9988 oz. AGW, 38 mm.
Subject: 100th Anniversary - Death of Marti **Obv:** Cuban arms **Rev:** Monument

Date	Mintage	F	VF	XF	Unc	BU
2001 Proof	100	Value: 1,200				

PESO CONVERTIBLE SERIES

KM# 733   CENTAVO
0.7500 g., Aluminum, 16.75 mm. **Obv:** Cuban arms **Rev:** Tower and denomination **Edge:** Plain

Date	Mintage	F	VF	XF	Unc	BU
2001	—	—	—	—	2.00	—
2002	—	—	—	—	2.00	—
2003	—	—	—	—	2.00	—
2005	—	—	—	—	2.00	—

KM# 729   CENTAVO
1.7000 g., Copper Plated Steel, 15 mm. **Obv:** National arms within wreath, denomination below **Rev:** Tower and denomination **Edge:** Reeded

Date	Mintage	F	VF	XF	Unc	BU
2002	—	—	—	—	3.00	—

KM# 575.2   5 CENTAVOS
2.6500 g., Nickel Plated Steel, 18 mm. **Obv:** National arms **Rev:** Casa Colonial **Note:** Coin alignment, recut designs.

Date	Mintage	F	VF	XF	Unc	BU
2002	—	—	—	—	1.00	—
2006	—	—	—	—	1.00	—

KM# 576.2   10 CENTAVOS
3.9400 g., Nickel Plated Steel **Obv:** National arms **Rev:** Castillo de la Fuerza **Note:** Coin alignment, recut designs.

Date	Mintage	F	VF	XF	Unc	BU
2002	—	—	—	—	2.00	—

KM# 577.2   25 CENTAVOS
5.7000 g., Nickel Plated Steel, 23 mm. **Obv:** National arms **Rev:** Trinidad **Note:** Coin alignment.

Date	Mintage	F	VF	XF	Unc	BU
2001	—	—	—	—	3.00	—
2002	—	—	—	—	3.00	—
2003	—	—	—	—	3.00	—
2006	—	—	—	—	3.00	—

KM# 578.2   50 CENTAVOS
7.5000 g., Nickel Plated Steel, 25 mm. **Obv:** Cuban arms **Rev:** Havana Cathedral **Note:** Coin alignment.

Date	Mintage	F	VF	XF	Unc	BU
2002	—	—	—	—	5.00	—

KM# 579.2   PESO
5.0000 g., Nickel Plated Steel, 27 mm. **Obv:** National arms **Rev:** Guama **Note:** Coin alignment.

Date	Mintage	F	VF	XF	Unc	BU
2001	—	—	—	—	5.00	—

MINT SETS

KM#	Date	Mintage	Identification	Issue Price	Mkt Val
MS3	2001 (3)	—	KM#831-833	—	62.50

CYPRUS

The island of Cyprus lies in the eastern Mediterranean Sea 44 miles (71 km.) south of Turkey and 60 miles (97 km.) off the Syrian coast. It is the third largest island in the Mediterranean Sea, having an area of 3,572 sq. mi. (9,251 sq. km.) and a population of 736,636. Capital: Nicosia. Agriculture, light manufacturing and tourism are the chief industries. Citrus fruit, potatoes, footwear and clothing are exported

Cyprus is a member of the Commonwealth of Nations. The president is Chief of State and Head of Government. Cyprus is also a member of the European Union since May 2004.

MINT MARKS
no mint mark - Royal Mint, London, England
H - Birmingham, England

REPUBLIC
REFORM COINAGE
100 Cents = 1 Pound

KM# 53.3   CENT
2.0300 g., Nickel-Brass, 16.48 mm. **Obv:** Shielded arms within altered wreath, date below **Rev:** Stylized bird on a branch, denomination at left **Edge:** Plain

Date	Mintage	F	VF	XF	Unc	BU
2003	5,000,000	—	—	0.10	0.20	0.30
2004 Narrow figures	12,000,000	—	—	0.10	0.20	0.30

KM# 54.3   2 CENTS
2.5800 g., Nickel-Brass, 18.95 mm. **Obv:** Shielded arms within altered wreath, date below **Rev:** Stylized goats, denomination upper right **Edge:** Plain

Date	Mintage	F	VF	XF	Unc	BU
2003	5,000,000	—	—	0.15	0.25	0.35
2004	7,000,000	—	—	0.15	0.25	0.35

KM# 55.3   5 CENTS
3.8000 g., Nickel-Brass, 22 mm. **Obv:** Altered wreath around arms **Rev:** Stylized bulls head above denomination **Edge:** Plain

Date	Mintage	F	VF	XF	Unc	BU
2001	15,000,000	—	—	0.20	0.50	0.75
2004	15,000,000	—	—	0.20	0.50	0.75

KM# 56.3   10 CENTS
5.5700 g., Nickel-Brass, 24.4 mm. **Obv:** Altered wreath around arms **Rev:** Decorative vase, denomination above

Date	Mintage	F	VF	XF	Unc	BU
2002	10,000,000	—	—	0.35	0.75	1.00
2004 Narrow figures	7,000,000	—	—	0.35	0.75	1.00

KM# 62.2   20 CENTS
7.7500 g., Nickel-Brass, 27 mm. **Obv:** Altered wreath around arms **Rev:** Head left, denomination at right

Date	Mintage	F	VF	XF	Unc	BU
2001	15,000,000	—	—	—	1.00	1.50
2004	4,000,000	—	—	—	1.00	1.50

KM# 66   50 CENTS
7.0000 g., Copper-Nickel, 26.11 mm. **Subject:** Abduction of Europa **Obv:** National arms, date below **Rev:** Female figure riding bull right within square, denomination below **Edge:** Plain **Shape:** 7-sided

Date	Mintage	F	VF	XF	Unc	BU
2002	7,000,000	—	—	—	2.50	3.25
2004	5,000,000	—	—	—	2.50	3.25

KM# 75   POUND
28.2800 g., Copper-Nickel, 38.6 mm. **Subject:** Cyprus Joins the European Union **Obv:** National arms **Rev:** Map in center with Triton trumpeting through a seashell **Edge:** Plain

Date	Mintage	F	VF	XF	Unc	BU
2004	3,000	—	—	—	20.00	30.00

KM# 75a   POUND
28.2800 g., 0.9250 Silver 0.8410 oz. ASW, 38.6 mm. **Subject:** Cyprus Joins the European Union **Obv:** National arms **Rev:** Map and Triton trumpeting through a sea shell **Edge:** Plain

Date	Mintage	F	VF	XF	Unc	BU
2004 Proof	3,000	Value: 60.00				

KM# 76   POUND
28.2700 g., Copper-Nickel, 38.5 mm. **Obv:** National arms **Rev:** Mediterranean Monk Seal **Edge:** Plain

Date	Mintage	F	VF	XF	Unc	BU
2005 Proof	4,000	Value: 40.00				

KM# 76a   POUND
28.2800 g., 0.9250 Silver 0.8410 oz. ASW **Obv:** National arms **Rev:** Mediterranean Monk Seal **Edge:** Plain

Date	Mintage	F	VF	XF	Unc	BU
2005	4,000	Value: 50.00				

KM# 77   POUND
28.2800 g., Copper-Nickel, 38.6 mm. **Obv:** National arms **Rev:** Thistle-like flowers **Edge:** Plain

Date	Mintage	F	VF	XF	Unc	BU
2006 Proof-like	6,000	Value: 30.00				

KM# 77a   POUND
28.2800 g., 0.9250 Silver 0.8410 oz. ASW **Obv:** National arms **Rev:** Thistle-like flowers **Edge:** Plain

Date	Mintage	F	VF	XF	Unc	BU
2006	3,000	Value: 75.00				

KM# 86   POUND
28.2800 g., Copper-Nickel, 38.6 mm. **Subject:** 50th Anniversary Treaty of Rome **Obv:** National arms **Rev:** Open Treaty Book **Edge:** Plain

Date	Mintage	F	VF	XF	Unc	BU
2007 Proof-like	10,000	Value: 25.00				

KM# 87   20 POUNDS
7.9880 g., Gold, 22.05 mm. **Obv:** National arms **Rev:** Greek god Triton, trumpeter (messenger) of the deep sea below outlined map of Cyprus

Date	Mintage	F	VF	XF	Unc	BU
2004 Proof	1,500	Value: 500				

EURO COINAGE
European Union Issues

KM# 78   EURO CENT
2.2700 g., Copper Plated Steel, 16.2 mm. **Obv:** Two Mouflons **Rev:** Large value at left, globe at lower right **Edge:** Plain

Date	Mintage	F	VF	XF	Unc	BU
2008	—	—	—	—	0.35	0.50
2009	—	—	—	—	0.35	0.50

KM# 79   2 EURO CENT
3.0300 g., Copper Plated Steel, 18.7 mm. **Obv:** Two Mouflons **Rev:** Large value at left, globe at lower right **Edge:** Plain

Date	Mintage	F	VF	XF	Unc	BU
2008	—	—	—	—	0.50	0.75
2009	—	—	—	—	0.50	0.75

KM# 80   5 EURO CENT
3.8600 g., Copper Plated Steel, 21.2 mm. **Obv:** Two Mouflons **Rev:** Large value at left, globe at lower right **Edge:** Plain

Date	Mintage	F	VF	XF	Unc	BU
2008	—	—	—	—	1.00	1.25
2009	—	—	—	—	1.00	1.25

KM# 81   10 EURO CENT
4.0700 g., Brass, 19.7 mm. **Obv:** Early sailing boat **Rev:** Modified outline of Europe at left, large value at right

Date	Mintage	F	VF	XF	Unc	BU
2008	—	—	—	—	1.25	1.50
2009	—	—	—	—	1.25	1.50

KM# 82   20 EURO CENT
5.7300 g., Brass, 22.1 mm. **Obv:** Early sailing boat **Rev:** Modified outline of Europe at left, large value at right **Edge:** Notched

Date	Mintage	F	VF	XF	Unc	BU
2008	—	—	—	—	1.50	2.00

KM# 83   50 EURO CENT
7.8100 g., Brass, 24.2 mm. **Obv:** Early sailing boat **Rev:** Modified outline of Europe at left, large value at right **Edge:** Reeded

Date	Mintage	F	VF	XF	Unc	BU
2008	—	—	—	—	2.00	2.50
2009	—	—	—	—	2.00	2.50

KM# 84   EURO
7.5000 g., Bi-Metallic Copper-Nickel center in Brass ring, 23.2 mm. **Obv:** Ancient cross shaped idol discovered in the village of Pomos in the distrct of Paphos. **Rev:** Large value at left, modified outline of Europe at right **Edge:** Segmented reeding

Date	Mintage	F	VF	XF	Unc	BU
2008	—	—	—	—	3.50	5.00
2009	—	—	—	—	3.50	5.00

KM# 85   2 EURO
8.5200 g., Bi-Metallic Brass center in Copper-Nickel ring, 25.7 mm. **Obv:** Ancient cross shaped idol discovered in the village of Pomos in the distrct of Paphos. **Rev:** Large value at left, modified outline of Europe at right

Date	Mintage	F	VF	XF	Unc	BU
2008	—	—	—	—	5.00	7.00
2009	—	—	—	—	5.00	7.00

KM# 89   2 EURO
8.5200 g., Bi-Metallic Brass in copper-nickel ring **Subject:** 10th Anniversary of Euro **Obv:** Ancient statue wearing a cross found in Solol **Rev:** Childs drawing of a stick figure and 2E

Date	Mintage	F	VF	XF	Unc	BU
2009	—	—	—	—	5.00	7.00
2009 Proof						

KM# 88   5 EURO
28.2800 g., 0.9250 Silver 0.8410 oz. ASW, 38.61 mm. **Subject:** Entry into Euro Zone **Obv:** National arms **Rev:** Euro band around outlined Europe and Cyprus **Edge:** Reeded

Date	Mintage	F	VF	XF	Unc	BU
2008 Proof	15,000	Value: 75.00				

CZECH REPUBLIC

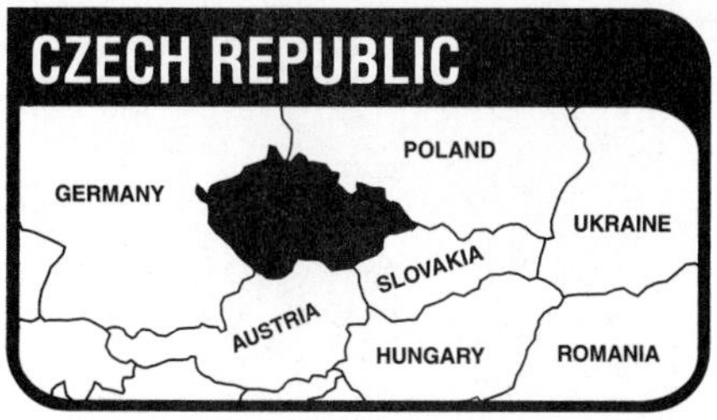

The Czech Republic was formerly united with Slovakia as Czechoslovakia. It is bordered in the west by Germany, to the north by Poland, to the east by Slovakia and to the south by Austria. It consists of 3 major regions: Bohemia, Moravia and Silesia and has an area of 30,450 sq. mi. (78,864 sq. km.) and a population of 10.4 million. Capital: Prague (Praha). Agriculture and livestock are chief occupations while coal deposits are the main mineral resources.

MINT MARKS

(c) - castle = Hamburg
(cr) - cross = British Royal Mint
(l) - leaf = Royal Canadian
(m) - crowned *b* or *CM* = Jablonec nad Nisou
(mk) - *MK* in circle = Kremnica
(o) - broken circle = Vienna (Wien)

MONETARY SYSTEM

1 Koruna = 100 Haleru

REPUBLIC

STANDARD COINAGE

KM# 6 10 HALERU

0.6000 g., Aluminum, 15.5 mm. **Obv:** Crowned Czech lion left, date below **Rev:** Denomination and stylized river **Edge:** Plain **Designer:** Jiri Pradler **Note:** Two varieties of mint marks exist for 1994.

Date	Mintage	F	VF	XF	Unc	BU
2001(m)	40,525,000	—	—	—	0.20	—
2001(m) Proof	2,500	Value: 2.00				
2002(m)	81,496,000	—	—	—	0.20	—
2002(m) Proof	3,490	Value: 2.00				
2003(m)	3,022,350	—	—	—	0.20	—
2003(m) Proof	3,000	Value: 2.00				
2004(m)	—	—	—	—	0.20	—
2004(m) Proof	3,000	Value: 2.00				

KM# 2.3 20 HALERU

0.7400 g., Aluminum **Obv:** Crowned Czech lion left, date above **Rev:** Open 2 in denomination, "h" above angle line **Note:** Medal alignment.

Date	Mintage	F	VF	XF	Unc	BU
2001(m)	44,425,000	—	—	—	0.30	—
2001(m) Proof	2,500	Value: 3.00				
2002(m)	20,000	—	—	—	0.30	—
2002(m) Proof	3,490	Value: 3.00				
2003(m)	22,200	—	—	—	0.30	—
2003(m) Proof	3,000	Value: 3.00				
2004(m)	—	—	—	—	0.30	—
2004(m) Proof	3,000	Value: 3.00				

KM# 3.2 50 HALERU

0.9000 g., Aluminum, 19 mm. **Subject:** Outlined lettering and larger mint mark **Obv:** Crowned Czech lion right, date below **Rev:** Large denomination

Date	Mintage	F	VF	XF	Unc	BU
2001(m)	21,425,000	—	—	—	0.50	—
2001(m) Proof	2,500	Value: 3.00				
2002(m)	26,246,298	—	—	—	0.50	—
2002(m) Proof	3,490	Value: 3.00				
2003(m)	41,548,000	—	—	—	0.50	—
2003(m) Proof	3,000	Value: 3.00				
2004(m)	931,145	—	—	—	0.50	—
2004(m) Proof	4,000	Value: 3.00				
2005(m)	36,800	—	—	—	0.50	—
2005(m) Proof	3,000	Value: 3.00				
2006(m)	40,000	—	—	—	0.50	—
2006(m) Proof	2,500	Value: 3.00				
2007(m)	—	—	—	—	0.50	—
2007(m) Proof	2,500	Value: 3.00				
2008(m)	—	—	—	—	0.50	—
2008(m) Proof	2,500	Value: 3.00				
2009(m)	—	—	—	—	0.50	—
2009(m) Proof	2,500	Value: 3.00				

KM# 3.1 50 HALERU

0.9000 g., Aluminum, 19 mm. **Obv:** Crowned Czech lion left, date below **Rev:** Large denomination **Edge:** Part plain, part milled repeated **Designer:** Vladimir Oppl **Note:** Prev. KM#3.

Date	Mintage	F	VF	XF	Unc	BU
2001(m)	21,425,000	—	—	—	0.50	—
2001(m) Proof	2,500	Value: 3.00				

KM# 7 KORUNA

Nickel Clad Steel, 20 mm. **Obv:** Crowned Czech lion left, date below **Rev:** Denomination above crown **Edge:** Milled **Designer:** Jarmila Truhlikova-Spevakova **Note:** Two varieties of mint marks exist for 1996. 2000-03 have two varieties in the artist monogram.

Date	Mintage	F	VF	XF	Unc	BU
2001(m)	15,938,353	—	—	—	0.60	—
2001(m) Proof	2,500	Value: 4.00				
2002(m)	26,244,666	—	—	—	0.60	—
2002(m) Proof	3,490	Value: 4.00				
2003(m)	36,877,440	—	—	—	0.60	—
2003(m) Proof	3,000	Value: 4.00				
2004(m)	30,500	—	—	—	0.60	—
2004(m) Proof	4,000	Value: 4.00				
2005(m)	—	—	—	—	0.60	—
2005(m) Proof	3,000	Value: 6.00				
2006(m)	35,864	—	—	—	0.60	—
2006(m) Proof	2,500	Value: 6.00				
2007(m)	—	—	—	—	0.60	—
2007(m) Proof	2,500	Value: 6.00				
2008(m)	—	—	—	—	0.60	—
2008(m) Proof	2,500	Value: 6.00				
2009(m)	—	—	—	—	0.60	—
2009(m) Proof	2,500	Value: 6.00				

KM# 9 2 KORUN

3.7000 g., Nickel Clad Steel, 21.5 mm. **Obv:** Crowned Czech lion left, date below **Rev:** Large denomination, pendant design at left **Edge:** Plain **Shape:** 11-sided **Designer:** Jarmila Truhlikova-Spevakova **Note:** Two varieties of designer monograms exist for 2001-04.

Date	Mintage	F	VF	XF	Unc	BU
2001(m)	26,117,000	—	—	—	0.65	—
2001(m) Proof	2,500	Value: 5.00				
2002(m)	20,941,084	—	—	—	0.65	—
2002(m) Proof	3,490	Value: 5.00				
2003(m)	20,955,000	—	—	—	0.65	—
2003(m) Proof	3,000	Value: 5.00				
2004(m)	15,658,556	—	—	—	0.65	—
2004(m) Proof	4,000	Value: 5.00				
2005(m)	—	—	—	—	0.65	—
2005(m) Proof	3,000	Value: 5.00				
2006(m)	—	—	—	—	0.65	—
2006(m) Proof	2,500	Value: 5.00				
2007(m)	—	—	—	—	0.65	—
2007(m) Proof	2,500	Value: 5.00				
2008(m)	—	—	—	—	0.65	—
2008(m) Proof	2,500	Value: 5.00				
2009(m)	—	—	—	—	0.65	—
2009(m) Proof	2,500	Value: 5.00				

KM# 8 5 KORUN

4.8000 g., Nickel Plated Steel, 23 mm. **Obv:** Crowned Czech lion left, date below **Rev:** Large denomination, Charles bridge and linden leaf **Edge:** Plain **Designer:** Jiri Harcuba

Date	Mintage	F	VF	XF	Unc	BU
2001(m)	25,000	—	—	—	1.00	—
2001(m) Proof	2,500	Value: 6.00				
2002(m)	21,344,995	—	—	—	1.00	—
2002(m) Proof	3,490	Value: 6.00				
2003(m)	22,000	—	—	—	1.00	—
2003(m) Proof	3,000	Value: 6.00				
2004(m)	34,940	—	—	—	1.00	—
2004(m) Proof	4,000	Value: 6.00				
2005(m)	—	—	—	—	1.00	—
2005(m) Proof	3,000	Value: 6.00				
2006(m)	25,000	—	—	—	1.00	—
2006(m) Proof	2,500	Value: 6.00				
2007(m)	—	—	—	—	1.00	—
2007(m) Proof	2,500	Value: 6.00				
2008(m)	—	—	—	—	1.00	—
2008(m) Proof	2,500	Value: 6.00				
2009(m)	—	—	—	—	1.00	—
2009(m) Proof	2,500	Value: 6.00				

KM# 4 10 KORUN

7.6200 g., Copper Plated Steel, 24.5 mm. **Obv:** Crowned Czech lion left, date below **Rev:** Brno Cathedral, denomination below **Edge:** Milled **Designer:** Ladislav Kozak **Note:** Position of designer's initials on reverse change during the 1995 strike.

Date	Mintage	F	VF	XF	Unc	BU
2001(m)	25,000	—	—	—	1.50	—
2001(m) Proof	2,500	Value: 7.00				
2002(m)	20,156	—	—	—	1.50	—
2002(m) Proof	3,490	Value: 7.00				
2003(m)	18,747,000	—	—	—	1.50	—
2003(m) Proof	3,000	Value: 7.00				
2004(m)	2,255,740	—	—	—	1.50	—
2004(m) Proof	4,000	Value: 7.00				
2005(m)	—	—	—	—	1.50	—
2005(m) Proof	3,000	Value: 7.00				
2006(m)	—	—	—	—	1.50	—
2006(m) Proof	2,500	Value: 7.00				
2007(m)	—	—	—	—	1.50	—
2007(m) Proof	2,500	Value: 7.00				
2008(m)	—	—	—	—	1.50	—
2008(m) Proof	2,500	Value: 7.00				
2009(m)	—	—	—	—	1.50	—
2009(m) Proof	2,500	Value: 7.00				

KM# 5 20 KORUN

8.4300 g., Brass Plated Steel, 26 mm. **Obv:** Crowned Czech lion left, date below **Rev:** St. Wenceslas (Duke Vaclav) on horse **Edge:** Plain **Shape:** 13-sided **Designer:** Vladimir Oppl **Note:** Two varieties of mint marks and style of 9's exist for 1997.

Date	Mintage	F	VF	XF	Unc	BU
2001(m)	25,000	—	—	—	2.50	—
2001(m) Proof	2,500	Value: 10.00				
2002(m)	20,996,500	—	—	—	2.50	—
2002(m) Proof	3,490	Value: 10.00				
2003(m)	22,000	—	—	—	2.50	—
2003(m) Proof	3,000	Value: 10.00				
2004(m)	8,249,507	—	—	—	2.50	—
2004(m) Proof	4,000	Value: 10.00				
2005(m)	—	—	—	—	2.50	—
2005(m) Proof	3,000	Value: 10.00				
2006(m)	—	—	—	—	2.50	—
2006(m) Proof	2,500	Value: 10.00				
2007(m)	—	—	—	—	2.50	—
2007(m) Proof	2,500	Value: 10.00				
2008(m)	—	—	—	—	2.50	—
2008(m) Proof	2,500	Value: 10.00				

Date	Mintage	F	VF	XF	Unc	BU
2009(m)	—	—	—	—	2.50	
2009(m) Proof	2,500	Value: 10.00				

KM# 1   50 KORUN
9.7000 g., Bi-Metallic Brass plated Steel center in Copper plated Steel ring, 27.5 mm. **Obv:** Crowned Czech lion left **Rev:** Prague city view **Edge:** Plain **Designer:** Ladislav Kozak

Date	Mintage	F	VF	XF	Unc	BU
2001(m)	16,000	—	—	—	9.00	—
2001(m) Proof	2,500	Value: 20.00				
2002(m)	16,771	—	—	—	9.00	—
2002(m) Proof	3,490	Value: 20.00				
2003(m)	22,000	—	—	—	9.00	—
2003(m) Proof	3,000	Value: 20.00				
2004(m)	34,555	—	—	—	9.00	—
2004(m) Proof	4,000	Value: 20.00				
2005(m)	—	—	—	—	9.00	—
2005(m) Proof	3,000	Value: 20.00				
2006(m)	—	—	—	—	9.00	—
2006(m) Proof	2,500	Value: 20.00				
2007(m)	—	—	—	—	9.00	—
2007(m) Proof	2,500	Value: 20.00				
2008(m)	—	—	—	—	9.00	—
2008(m) Proof	2,500	Value: 20.00				
2009(m)	—	—	—	—	9.00	—
2009(m) Proof	2,500	Value: 20.00				

KM# 58   200 KORUN
13.0000 g., 0.9000 Silver 0.3761 oz. ASW, 31 mm. **Subject:** Frantisek Skroup **Obv:** Quartered, elongated arms above date **Rev:** Portrait and name **Designer:** Jiri Harcuba **Note:** 1,480 pieces uncirculated and 13 proof remelted.

Date	Mintage	F	VF	XF	Unc	BU
ND(2001)	12,909	—	—	—	15.00	17.00
Note: Reeded edge						
ND(2001) Proof	3,200	Value: 30.00				
Note: CESKA NARODNI BANKA * 0.900 *						

KM# 51   200 KORUN
13.0000 g., 0.9000 Silver 0.3761 oz. ASW, 31 mm. **Subject:** Jaroslav Seifert **Obv:** Quartered arms above denomination **Rev:** Head right, dates at left **Designer:** Ladislav Kozak **Note:** 1,680 pieces uncirculated and 2 proof remelted.

Date	Mintage	F	VF	XF	Unc	BU
ND(2001)	12,870	—	—	—	15.00	17.00
Note: Reeded edge						
ND(2001) Proof	3,199	Value: 30.00				
Note: CESKA NARODNI BANKA * 0.900 *						

KM# 53   200 KORUN
13.0000 g., 0.9000 Silver 0.3761 oz. ASW, 31 mm. **Subject:** 250th Anniversary - Death of Kilian Ignac Dientzenhofer

---

Obv: Quartered arms, denomination at right **Rev:** Doorway and caliper **Designer:** Petr Pyciak **Note:** 1,840 pieces uncirculated and 104 proof remelted.

Date	Mintage	F	VF	XF	Unc	BU
ND(2001)	12,744	—	—	—	15.00	17.00
Note: Reeded edge						
ND(2001) Proof	3,373	Value: 30.00				
Note: CESKA NARODNI BANKA * 0.900 *						

KM# 54   200 KORUN
13.0000 g., 0.9000 Silver 0.3761 oz. ASW, 31 mm. **Subject:** Euro Currency System **Obv:** National arms **Rev:** Prague gros coin design **Designer:** Josef Safarik **Note:** 134 pieces uncirculated and 1 proof remelted.

Date	Mintage	F	VF	XF	Unc	BU
ND(2001)	13,867	—	—	—	15.00	17.00
ND(2001) Proof	4,000	Value: 28.00				
Note: CESKA NARODNI BANKA * 0.900 *						

KM# 52   200 KORUN
13.0000 g., 0.9000 Silver 0.3761 oz. ASW, 31 mm. **Subject:** Soccer **Obv:** Quartered arms on square, denomination below **Rev:** Rampant lion on soccer ball **Designer:** Milena Blaskova **Note:** 2,350 pieces uncirculated and 1 proof remelted.

Date	Mintage	F	VF	XF	Unc	BU
ND(2001)	13,324	—	—	—	15.00	17.00
ND(2001) Proof	3,900	Value: 28.00				
Note: CESKA NARODNI BANKA * 0.900 *						

KM# 59   200 KORUN
13.0000 g., 0.9000 Silver 0.3761 oz. ASW, 31 mm. **Subject:** Mikolas Ales **Obv:** Four coats of arms above denomination **Rev:** Horse and rider **Edge:** Reeded **Designer:** Petr Pycian **Note:** 573 pieces uncirculated and 139 proof remelted.

Date	Mintage	F	VF	XF	Unc	BU
ND(2002)	12,473	—	—	—	15.00	17.00
ND(2002)(m) Proof	4,400	Value: 28.00				

KM# 57   200 KORUN
13.0000 g., 0.9000 Silver 0.3761 oz. ASW, 30.9 mm. **Subject:** Jiri of Podebrady **Obv:** Overlapped arms **Rev:** Head right **Designer:** Michal Vitanovswky **Note:** 1,200 pieces uncirculated and 5 proof remelted.

Date	Mintage	F	VF	XF	Unc	BU
ND(2002)	12,750	—	—	—	15.00	17.00
Note: Reeded edge						

Date	Mintage	F	VF	XF	Unc	BU
ND(2002) Proof	3,600	Value: 28.00				
Note: CESKA NARDONI BANKA * 0.900 *						

KM# 56   200 KORUN
13.0000 g., 0.9000 Silver 0.3761 oz. ASW, 30.9 mm. **Subject:** Emil Holub **Obv:** National arms, eagles and lions, denomination below **Rev:** Traveler and African dancers **Designer:** Ladislav Kozak **Note:** 1,350 pieces uncirculated and 7 proof remelted.

Date	Mintage	F	VF	XF	Unc	BU
ND(2002)	12,635	—	—	—	15.00	17.00
Note: Reeded edge						
ND(2002) Proof	3,600	Value: 28.00				
Note: CESKA NARODNI BANKA * 0.900 *						

KM# 55   200 KORUN
13.0000 g., 0.9000 Silver 0.3761 oz. ASW, 31 mm. **Subject:** St. Zdislava **Obv:** Old and new arms form diamond above denomination **Rev:** Saint feeding sick person **Designer:** Michal Vitanovsky **Note:** 865 pieces uncirculated remelted.

Date	Mintage	F	VF	XF	Unc	BU
ND(2002)	12,706	—	—	—	15.00	17.00
Note: Reeded edge						
ND(2002) Proof	3,600	Value: 28.00				
Note: CESKA NARODNI BANKA * 0.900 *						

KM# 60   200 KORUN
13.1400 g., 0.9000 Silver 0.3802 oz. ASW, 31 mm. **Subject:** Jaroslav Vrchlicky **Obv:** Denomination and quill **Obv. Designer:** Jiri Harcuba **Rev:** Bust with hat facing **Rev. Designer:** Pavel Jekl **Note:** 889 pieces uncirculated and 5 proof remelted.

Date	Mintage	F	VF	XF	Unc	BU
ND(2003)	11,975	—	—	—	15.00	17.00
Note: Reeded						
ND(2003) Proof	3,700	Value: 28.00				
Note: Plain with CESKA NARODNI BANKA *Ag 0.900* 13g*						

KM# 62   200 KORUN
13.0000 g., 0.9000 Silver 0.3761 oz. ASW, 30.9 mm. **Subject:** Josef Thomayer **Obv:** National arms **Obv. Designer:** Ladislav Kozak **Rev:** Portrait **Rev. Designer:** Josef Oplistil **Edge:** Reeded **Note:** 783 uncirculated and 12 proof were remelted.

Date	Mintage	F	VF	XF	Unc	BU
ND(2003)	11,975	—	—	—	15.00	17.00
ND(2003) Proof	4,000	Value: 28.00				

KM# 63   200 KORUN
13.0000 g., 0.9000 Silver 0.3761 oz. ASW, 31 mm. **Subject:** Tabor-Bechyne Electric Railway **Obv:** Head left **Rev:** Railroad station scene **Designer:** Ladislav Kozak **Note:** 808 Uncirculated were remelted.

Date	Mintage	F	VF	XF	Unc	BU
ND(2003)	11,975	—	—	—	16.00	18.00

Note: Reeded edge

ND(2003) Proof	4,100	Value: 28.00

Note: Plain edge with CESKA NARODNI BANKA * Ag 0.900 * 13g

KM# 64 200 KORUN
13.0000 g., 0.9000 Silver 0.3761 oz. ASW, 31 mm. **Subject:** Bohemian Skiers' Union **Obv:** Head 3/4 left **Rev:** Skier **Designer:** Ladislav Kozak **Note:** 680 Uncirculated and 13 proof were remelted.

Date	Mintage	F	VF	XF	Unc	BU
ND(2003)	11,975	—	—	—	16.00	18.00

Note: Reeded edge

ND(2003) Proof	4,300	Value: 28.00

Note: Plain edge with CESKA NARODNI BANKA * Ag 0.900 * 13g

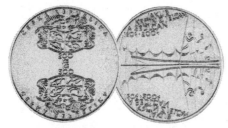

KM# 70 200 KORUN
13.1000 g., 0.9000 Silver 0.3790 oz. ASW, 30.8 mm.
Subject: 300th Anniversary - Death of pond builder Jakub Krcin
Obv: Coat of arms above value with reflected design below
Rev: Two fishermen in boat with reflection on water below
Designer: Vladimir Oppl **Note:** 656 uncirculated remelted.

Date	Mintage	F	VF	XF	Unc	BU
ND(2004)(m)	11,975	—	—	—	16.00	18.00

Note: Reeded

ND(2004) Proof	4,000	Value: 28.00

Note: Plain with CESKA NARODNI BANKA *Ag 0.900* 13g*

KM# 71 200 KORUN
13.1000 g., 0.9000 Silver 0.3790 oz. ASW **Subject:** Entry into the European Union

Date	Mintage	F	VF	XF	Unc	BU
2004	10,000	—	—	—	16.00	18.00

Note: Reeded

2004 Proof	8,800	Value: 28.00

KM# 72 200 KORUN
13.1000 g., 0.9000 Silver 0.3790 oz. ASW **Subject:** Prokop Divis

Date	Mintage	F	VF	XF	Unc	BU
2004	10,975	—	—	—	16.00	18.00

Note: Reeded

2004 Proof	3,900	Value: 28.00

KM# 73 200 KORUN
13.1000 g., 0.9000 Silver 0.3790 oz. ASW **Subject:** Leos Janacek

Date	Mintage	F	VF	XF	Unc	BU
2004	10,975	—	—	—	16.00	18.00

Note: Reeded

2004 Proof	4,100	Value: 28.00

KM# 74 200 KORUN
13.1000 g., 0.9000 Silver 0.3790 oz. ASW **Subject:** Kralice Bible

Date	Mintage	F	VF	XF	Unc	BU
2004	10,975	—	—	—	16.00	18.00

Note: Reeded

2004 Proof	5,000	Value: 28.00

KM# 77 200 KORUN
13.0000 g., 0.9000 Silver 0.3761 oz. ASW, 31 mm.
Rev: Lightning Conductor

Date	Mintage	F	VF	XF	Unc	BU
2004	—	—	—	—	16.00	18.00

Note: Reeded

2004 Proof	—	Value: 28.00

Note: Plain edge with CESKA NARODNI BANKA * Ag 0.900 * 13g *

KM# 78 200 KORUN
13.0000 g., 0.9000 Silver 0.3761 oz. ASW, 31 mm.
Subject: 100th Anniversary of Jan Werich and Jiri Voskovec

Date	Mintage	F	VF	XF	Unc	BU
2005	—	—	—	—	16.00	18.00

2005 Proof	—	Value: 30.00

KM# 79 200 KORUN
13.0000 g., 0.9000 Silver 0.3761 oz. ASW, 31 mm.
Subject: 100th Anniversary of Production of 1st Car in Malada Boleslov

Date	Mintage	F	VF	XF	Unc	BU
2005	—	—	—	—	16.00	18.00

2006 Proof	—	Value: 28.00

KM# 80 200 KORUN
13.0000 g., 0.9000 Silver 0.3761 oz. ASW, 31 mm.
Subject: 450th Anniversary - Birth of Mikulas Dacicky

Date	Mintage	F	VF	XF	Unc	BU
2005	—	—	—	—	16.00	18.00

2005 Proof	—	Value: 28.00

KM# 84 200 KORUN
13.0000 g., 0.9000 Silver 0.3761 oz. ASW, 31 mm.
Subject: 700th Anniversary - Death of Wenceslas III **Obv:** Sword between two shields positioned top-to-top **Rev:** King Wenceslas III between two shields **Designer:** Vojtech Dostal

Date	Mintage	F	VF	XF	Unc	BU
2006	11,500	—	—	—	16.00	18.00

2006 Proof	7,500	Value: 28.00

KM# 85 200 KORUN
13.0000 g., 0.9000 Silver 0.3761 oz. ASW, 31 mm.
Subject: 100th Anniversary - Birth of Jaroslav Jezek
Obv: Musical score **Rev:** Caricature looking at score
Designer: Josef Oplistil

Date	Mintage	F	VF	XF	Unc	BU
2006(m)	11,500	—	—	—	16.00	18.00
2006(m) Proof	20,000	Value: 28.00				

KM# 81 200 KORUN
13.0000 g., 0.9000 Silver 0.3761 oz. ASW, 31 mm.
Subject: 250th Anniversary - Birth of F.J. Gerstner

Date	Mintage	F	VF	XF	Unc	BU
2006	—	—	—	—	16.00	18.00

2006 Proof	—	Value: 28.00

KM# 82 200 KORUN
13.0000 g., 0.9000 Silver 0.3761 oz. ASW, 31 mm.
Subject: 150th Anniversary - School of Glass Making in Kamenicky Senov **Obv:** Image of National Arms within glass cube **Rev:** Artistic image within glass cube **Designer:** Zuzana Hubena

Date	Mintage	F	VF	XF	Unc	BU
2006	12,000	—	—	—	16.00	18.00

2006 Proof	7,500	Value: 28.00

KM# 83 200 KORUN
13.0000 g., 0.9000 Silver 0.3761 oz. ASW, 31 mm.
Subject: 500th Anniversary - Death of Matej Rejsek

Date	Mintage	F	VF	XF	Unc	BU
2006	—	—	—	—	16.00	18.00

2006 Proof	—	Value: 28.00

KM# 91 200 KORUN
13.0000 g., 0.9000 Silver 0.3761 oz. ASW, 31 mm.
Subject: Founding of Jednota Bratska

Date	Mintage	F	VF	XF	Unc	BU
2007	—	—	—	—	20.00	22.00

2007 Proof	—	Value: 32.00

KM# 92 200 KORUN
13.0000 g., 0.9000 Silver 0.3761 oz. ASW, 31 mm.
Subject: Charles Budge Cornerstone

Date	Mintage	F	VF	XF	Unc	BU
2007	—	—	—	—	20.00	22.00

2007 Proof	—	Value: 32.00

KM# 93 200 KORUN
13.0000 g., 0.9000 Silver 0.3761 oz. ASW, 31 mm.
Subject: Jarmila Novotná, birth

Date	Mintage	F	VF	XF	Unc	BU
2007	—	—	—	—	20.00	22.00

2007 Proof	—	Value: 32.00

KM# 94 200 KORUN
13.0000 g., 0.9000 Silver 0.3761 oz. ASW, 31 mm.
Subject: Earth Satellite Launch

Date	Mintage	F	VF	XF	Unc	BU
2007	—	—	—	—	20.00	22.00

2007 Proof	—	Value: 32.00

KM# 97 200 KORUN
13.0000 g., 0.9000 Silver 0.3761 oz. ASW, 31 mm.
Subject: Charles IV Vineyard Planting decresc

Date	Mintage	F	VF	XF	Unc	BU
2008	—	—	—	—	20.00	22.00

2008 Proof	—	Value: 32.00

KM# 98 200 KORUN
13.0000 g., 0.9000 Silver 0.3761 oz. ASW **Subject:** Josef Hlavka Death Centennial **Obv:** Wing over architectural element **Rev:** Bearded portrait facing

Date	Mintage	F	VF	XF	Unc	BU
2008	—	—	—	—	20.00	22.00

2008 Proof	—	Value: 32.00

KM# 99 200 KORUN
13.0000 g., 0.9000 Silver 0.3761 oz. ASW, 31 mm.
Subject: Schengen Convention **Obv:** Arms
Obv. Designer: Zbynek Fojtu

Date	Mintage	F	VF	XF	Unc	BU
2008	9,800	—	—	—	20.00	22.00
2008 Proof	16,000	Value: 32.00				

KM# 100 200 KORUN
13.0000 g., 0.9000 Silver 0.3761 oz. ASW, 31 mm.
Subject: Viktor Ponrepo 150th Anniversary **Obv:** Tripod camera
Rev: Mustache and top hat

Date	Mintage	F	VF	XF	Unc	BU
2008	—	—	—	—	20.00	22.00

2008 Proof	—	Value: 32.00

KM# 101 200 KORUN
13.0000 g., 0.9000 Silver 0.3761 oz. ASW, 31 mm.
Subject: National Technical Museum **Obv:** Steam Locomotive and driving wheel **Rev:** Museum façade and clock face

Date	Mintage	F	VF	XF	Unc	BU
2008	—	—	—	—	20.00	22.00

2008 Proof	—	Value: 32.00

KM# 102 200 KORUN
13.0000 g., 0.9000 Silver 0.3761 oz. ASW, 31 mm.
Subject: 100th Anniversary - Czech Ice Hockey Association
Obv: Hockey Player **Obv. Designer:** Zbynek Fojtu **Rev:** Logo

Date	Mintage	F	VF	XF	Unc	BU
2008	10,600	—	—	—	20.00	22.00
2008 Proof	15,100	Value: 32.00				

KM# 105 200 KORUN
13.0000 g., 0.9000 Silver 0.3761 oz. ASW, 31 mm.
Subject: Czech Presidency to Council of the European Union
Obv: Arms in circle **Rev:** Czech flag and circle of stars

Date	Mintage	F	VF	XF	Unc	BU
2009	13,200	—	—	—	20.00	22.00

KM# 106 200 KORUN
13.0000 g., 0.9000 Silver 0.3761 oz. ASW, 31 mm.
Subject: Nordic World Ski Championships in Liberec **Obv:** Logo with skis **Rev:** Cross country skiers and ski jumpers

Date	Mintage	F	VF	XF	Unc	BU
2009	11,000	—	—	—	20.00	22.00
2009	15,200	Value: 32.00				

KM# 107 200 KORUN
13.0000 g., 0.9000 Silver 0.3761 oz. ASW, 31 mm.
Subject: North Pole Exploration **Obv:** Facing Explorer **Rev:** Sled and Northern Lights **Rev. Designer:** Jiri Venecek

Date	Mintage	F	VF	XF	Unc	BU
2009	10,500	—	—	—	20.00	22.00
2009 Proof	17,600	Value: 32.00				

KM# 108 200 KORUN
13.0000 g., 0.9000 Silver 0.3761 oz. ASW, 31 mm.
Subject: Rabbi Jehuda Löw

Date	Mintage	F	VF	XF	Unc	BU
2009	—	—	—	—	20.00	22.00
2009 Proof	—	Value: 32.00				

KM# 109 200 KORUN
13.0000 g., 0.9000 Silver 0.3761 oz. ASW, 31 mm.
Subject: Kepler's Planetary Motion Laws

Date	Mintage	F	VF	XF	Unc	BU
2009	—	—	—	—	20.00	22.00
2009 Proof	—	Value: 32.00				

KM# 112 200 KORUN
13.0000 g., 0.9000 Silver 0.3761 oz. ASW, 31 mm.
Subject: Astronomical Clock, Prague

Date	Mintage	F	VF	XF	Unc	BU
2010	—	—	—	—	16.00	18.00
2010 Proof	—	Value: 28.00				

KM# 113 200 KORUN
13.0000 g., 0.9000 Silver 0.3761 oz. ASW, 31 mm.
Subject: Gustav Mahler

Date	Mintage	F	VF	XF	Unc	BU
2010	—	—	—	—	16.00	18.00
2010 Proof	—	Value: 28.00				

KM# 114 200 KORUN
13.0000 g., 0.9000 Silver 0.3761 oz. ASW, 31 mm.
Subject: Alfons Mucha

Date	Mintage	F	VF	XF	Unc	BU
2010	—	—	—	—	16.00	18.00
2010 Proof	—	Value: 28.00				

KM# 115 200 KORUN
13.0000 g., 0.9000 Silver 0.3761 oz. ASW, 31 mm.
Subject: John of Luxenboug

Date	Mintage	F	VF	XF	Unc	BU
2010	—	—	—	—	16.00	18.00
2010 Proof	—	Value: 28.00				

KM# 116 200 KORUN
13.0000 g., 0.9000 Silver 0.3761 oz. ASW, 31 mm.
Subject: Karel Zeman

Date	Mintage	F	VF	XF	Unc	BU
2010	—	—	—	—	16.00	18.00
2010 Proof	—	Value: 28.00				

GOLD BULLION COINAGE

KM# 65 2000 KORUN
6.2200 g., 0.9999 Gold 0.1999 oz. AGW, 20 mm.
Subject: Romanesque - Znojmo Rotunda **Obv:** Three heraldic animals **Rev:** Farmer and round building **Designer:** Jiri Harbuca

Date	Mintage	F	VF	XF	Unc	BU
ND(2001)	2,500	—	—	—	—	250
Note: Reeded edge						
ND(2001) Proof	2,997	Value: 265				
Note: Plain edge						

KM# 66 2000 KORUN
6.2200 g., 0.9999 Gold 0.1999 oz. AGW, 20 mm.
Subject: Gothic - Cloister of the Vyssi Brod Monastery
Obv: Three heraldic animals above Gothic design **Rev:** Man holding church building model **Designer:** Michal Vitanovsky

Date	Mintage	F	VF	XF	Unc	BU
2001	2,197	—	—	—	—	250
Note: Reeded edge						
2001 Proof	2,997	Value: 265				
Note: Plain edge						

KM# 67 2000 KORUN
6.2200 g., 0.9999 Gold 0.1999 oz. AGW, 20 mm.
Subject: Gothic - Fountain in Kutna Hora **Obv:** Three heraldic animals **Rev:** Fountain enclosure **Designer:** Josef Oplistil

Date	Mintage	F	VF	XF	Unc	BU
2002	2,197	—	—	—	—	250
Note: Reeded edge						
2002	2,997	Value: 265				
Note: Plain edge						

KM# 61 2000 KORUN
6.2200 g., 0.9999 Gold 0.1999 oz. AGW, 20 mm.
Subject: Renaissance - Litomysl Castle **Obv:** Three heraldic animals above mermaid **Rev:** Aerial castle view and mythical creature **Designer:** Jiri Venecek

Date	Mintage	F	VF	XF	Unc	BU
2002	2,097	—	—	—	—	250
Note: Reeded edge						
2002 Proof	3,097	Value: 265				
Note: Plain edge						

KM# 68 2000 KORUN
6.2200 g., 0.9999 Gold 0.1999 oz. AGW, 20 mm.
Subject: Renaissance - Slavonice House Gables **Obv:** Three heraldic animals above city view **Rev:** City arms **Designer:** Jiri Harcuba

Date	Mintage	F	VF	XF	Unc	BU
2003	1,997	—	—	—	—	250
Note: Reeded edge						
2003 Proof	1,497	Value: 275				
Note: Plain edge						

KM# 69 2000 KORUN
6.2200 g., 0.9999 Gold 0.1999 oz. AGW, 20 mm.
Subject: Baroque - Buchlovice Palace **Obv:** Three heraldic animals above palace **Rev:** Palace view **Designer:** Jakub Venecek

Date	Mintage	F	VF	XF	Unc	BU
2003	1,997	—	—	—	—	250
Note: Reeded edge						
2003 Proof	3,197	Value: 265				
Note: Plain edge						

KM# 75 2000 KORUN
6.2200 g., 0.9999 Gold 0.1999 oz. AGW, 20 mm.
Obv: Ornamental porch below three heraldic animals
Rev: Hluboka Castle with coat of arms in foreground

Date	Mintage	F	VF	XF	Unc	BU
2004	2,500	—	—	—	—	250
Note: Reeded edge						
2004 Proof	3,500	Value: 265				
Note: Plain edge						

KM# 86 2000 KORUN
6.2200 g., 0.9990 Gold 0.1998 oz. AGW, 20 mm.
Subject: Kacina Castle

Date	Mintage	F	VF	XF	Unc	BU
2004	—	—	—	—	—	250
2004 Proof	—	Value: 275				

KM# 87 2000 KORUN
6.2200 g., 0.9990 Gold 0.1998 oz. AGW, 20 mm.
Subject: Lazne Bohdanec Spa

Date	Mintage	F	VF	XF	Unc	BU
2005	—	—	—	—	—	250
2005 Proof	—	Value: 275				

KM# 88 2000 KORUN
6.2200 g., 0.9990 Gold 0.1998 oz. AGW, 20 mm.
Subject: Dancing house in Prague

Date	Mintage	F	VF	XF	Unc	BU
2005	—	—	—	—	—	250
2005 Proof	—	Value: 275				

KM# 76 2500 KORUN
31.1040 g., Bi-Metallic .9999 Gold 7.776g center in .999 Silver 23.328g ring, 40 mm. **Subject:** Czech entry into the European Union **Obv:** Value within circle of shields **Rev:** "1.5.2004" within circle of dates and text **Edge:** Lettered **Edge Lettering:** " CNB * Ag 0.999 * 23,328 g * Au 999.9 * 7,776g * "

Date	Mintage	F	VF	XF	Unc	BU
ND (2004) Proof	10,000	Value: 325				

KM# 89 2500 KORUN
7.7770 g., 0.9990 Gold 0.2498 oz. AGW, 22 mm. **Subject:** Hand Paper Mill at Velke Losiny

Date	Mintage	F	VF	XF	Unc	BU
2006	—	—	—	—	325	—
2006	—	Value: 350				

KM# 90 2500 KORUN
7.7850 g., 0.9990 Gold 0.2500 oz. AGW, 22 mm.
Subject: Observatory at Prague Klementinum **Obv:** Sun's rays thru clouds **Obv. Designer:** Josef Oplistil **Rev:** Building tower, rays and moon **Rev. Designer:** Jesef Oplistil **Note:** Prev. KM#86.

Date	Mintage	F	VF	XF	Unc	BU
2006	2,100	—	—	—	—	325
2006 Proof	3,800	Value: 350				

KM# 95 2500 KORUN
7.7770 g., 0.9990 Gold 0.2498 oz. AGW, 22 mm.
Subject: Serciny Mine at Phibram-Brezove Hory

Date	Mintage	F	VF	XF	Unc	BU
2007	—	—	—	—	325	—
2007 Proof	—	Value: 350				

KM# 96 2500 KORUN
7.7770 g., 0.9990 Gold 0.2498 oz. AGW, 22 mm.
Subject: Water mill at Slup

Date	Mintage	F	VF	XF	Unc	BU
2007	—	—	—	—	325	—
2007 Proof	— Value: 350					

KM# 103 2500 KORUN
7.7800 g., 0.9990 Gold 0.2499 oz. AGW, 22 mm.
Subject: Stadlec Suspension Bridge **Obv:** Side view of bridge
Rev: View of bridge thru arch

Date	Mintage	F	VF	XF	Unc	BU
2008	—	—	—	—	325	—
2008 Proof	— Value: 350					

KM# 104 2500 KORUN
7.7800 g., 0.9990 Gold 0.2499 oz. AGW **Subject:** Pilzen
Brewery **Obv:** View of copper vats **Rev:** View of façade and
wooden barrels

Date	Mintage	F	VF	XF	Unc	BU
2008	—	—	—	—	325	—
2008 Proof	— Value: 350					

KM# 110 2500 KORUN
7.7770 g., 0.9990 Gold 0.2498 oz. AGW, 22 mm. **Subject:** Elbe
Sluice under Strelcov Castle

Date	Mintage	F	VF	XF	Unc	BU
2009	—	—	—	—	325	—
2009	— Value: 350					

KM# 111 2500 KORUN
7.7770 g., 0.9990 Gold 0.2498 oz. AGW, 32 mm.
Subject: Windmill at Ruprechtov

Date	Mintage	F	VF	XF	Unc	BU
2009	—	—	—	—	350	—
2009	— Value: 350					

KM# 117 2500 KORUN
7.7700 g., 0.9990 Gold 0.2496 oz. AGW, 22 mm.
Subject: Hammer Mill

Date	Mintage	F	VF	XF	Unc	BU
2010	—	—	—	—	—	325
2010 Proof	— Value: 350					

KM# 118 2500 KORUN
7.7700 g., 0.9990 Gold 0.2496 oz. AGW, 22 mm.
Subject: Michael Mine

Date	Mintage	F	VF	XF	Unc	BU
2010	—	—	—	—	—	325
2010 Proof	— Value: 350					

MINT SETS

KM#	Date	Mintage	Identification	Issue Price	Mkt Val
MS13	2001 (9)	—	KM#1, 2.3, 3.2, 4-9 Tyn Church	—	17.50
MS14	2002 (9)	—	KM#1, 2.3, 3.2, 4-9 Nato Summit	—	17.50
MS15	2004 (8)	5,000	KM#1, 3.2, 4-5, 7-9, plus Smetna/Dvorak Medal and CD	—	17.50
MS16	2004 (7)	—	KM#1, 3.2, 4-5, 7-9 IIHF Hockey Year	—	16.00
MS17	2007 (7)	—	KM#1, 3.2, 4-5, 7-9. Unesco package	—	16.00
MS18	2007 (14)	10,000	KM#1, 3.2, 4-5, 7-9. Natural beauties with Slovakia coins	—	35.00
MS19	2008 (8)	6,000	KM#1, 3.2, 4-5, 7-9. Soccer medal and package	—	17.50
MS20	2009 (8)	10,000	KM#1, 3.2, 4-5, 7-9 plus brass medal Southern Bohemia	—	17.50

PROOF SETS

KM#	Date	Mintage	Identification	Issue Price	Mkt Val
PS6	2001 (9)	2,500	KM#1, 2.3, 3-9	35.00	65.00
PS7	2002 (9)	3,490	KM#1, 2.3, 3.2, 4-9	35.00	65.00
PS8	2003 (9)	3,000	KM#1, 2.3, 3.2, 4-9	35.00	65.00
PS9	2004 (7)	4,000	KM#1, 3.2, 4-5, 7-9	35.00	60.00
PS10	2005 (7)	—	KM#1, 3.2, 4-5, 7-9, and silver strike of Czechoslovakia KM4	—	85.00
PS11	2006 (7)	—	KM#1, 3.2, 4-5, 7-9, and silver strike of Czechoslovakia KM2	—	85.00
PS12	2007 (7)	—	KM#1, 3.2, 4-5, 7-9, and silver Unesco medal	—	85.00
PS13	2008 (7)	2,500	KM#1, 3.2, 4-5, 7-9 and silver medal	—	85.00
PS14	2009 (8)	2,500	KM#1, 3.2, 4-5, 7-9 and silver medal	—	85.00

DENMARK

The Kingdom of Denmark (Danmark), a constitutional monarchy located at the mouth of the Baltic Sea, has an area of 16,639 sq. mi. (43,070 sq. km.) and a population of 5.2 million. Capital: Copenhagen. Most of the country is arable. Agriculture is conducted by large farms served by cooperatives. The largest industries are food processing, iron and metal, and shipping. Machinery, meats (chiefly bacon), dairy products and chemicals are exported.

As a result of a referendum held September 28, 2000, the currency of the European Monetary Union, the Euro, will not be introduced in Denmark in the foreseeable future.

RULER
Margrethe II, 1972—

MINT MARKS
(h) - Copenhagen, heart

MINT OFFICIALS' INITIALS
Copenhagen

Letter	Date	Name
LG	1989-2001	Laust Grove

MONEYERS' INITIALS
Copenhagen

Letter	Date	Name
A	1986-	Johan Alkjaer (designer)
HV	1986-	Hanne Varming (sculptor)
JP	1989-	Jan Petersen

MONETARY SYSTEM
100 Øre = 1 Krone

KINGDOM

DECIMAL COINAGE
100 Øre = 1 Krone; 1874-present

KM# 868.1 25 ORE
2.8000 g., Bronze, 17.5 mm. **Ruler:** Margrethe II **Obv:** Large crown divides date above, initial to right of country name
Rev: Denomination, small heart above, mint mark and initials LG-JP below **Note:** Beginning in 1996 and ending with 1998, the words "DANMARK" and "ØRE" have raised edges. Heart mint mark under "ØRE"; Prev. KM#868.

Date	Mintage	F	VF	XF	Unc	BU
2001 LG; JP; A	10,530,000	—	—	—	0.20	—

KM# 868.2 25 ORE
2.8000 g., Bronze, 17.5 mm. **Ruler:** Margrethe II **Obv:** Large crown divides date above **Rev:** Denomination, small heart above **Edge:** Plain **Note:** Without initials

Date	Mintage	F	VF	XF	Unc	BU
2002	12,000,000	—	—	—	0.15	—
2003	17,590,000	—	—	—	0.15	—
2004	7,040,304	—	—	—	0.15	—
2004 Proof	3,000	Value: 12.00				
2005	—	—	—	—	0.15	—
2005 Proof	— Value: 12.00					
2006	—	—	—	—	0.15	—
2006 Proof	— Value: 12.00					
2007	—	—	—	—	0.15	—
2007 Proof	— Value: 12.00					
2008	—	—	—	—	2.00	—
2008 Proof	— Value: 25.00					

KM# 866.2 50 ORE
4.3000 g., Bronze, 21.5 mm. **Ruler:** Margrethe II **Obv:** Large crown divides date above, initial to right of country name **Rev:** Large heart above value, mint mark and initials LG-JP below **Note:** Beginning in 1996 and ending with 1998, the words "DANMARK" and "ØRE" have raised edges. Heart mint mark under the word "ØRE".

Date	Mintage	F	VF	XF	Unc	BU
2001 LG; JP; A	12,270,000	—	—	—	0.35	—

KM# 866.3 50 ORE
4.3000 g., Bronze, 21.5 mm. **Ruler:** Margrethe II **Obv:** Large crown divides date above **Rev:** Small heart above denomination **Edge:** Plain **Note:** No initials

Date	Mintage	F	VF	XF	Unc	BU
2002	3,900,000	—	—	—	0.30	—
2003	8,817,000	—	—	—	0.30	—
2004	10,040,706	—	—	—	0.30	—
2004 Proof	3,000	Value: 15.00				
2005	—	—	—	—	0.25	—
2005 Proof	— Value: 15.00					
2006	—	—	—	—	0.25	—
2006 Proof	— Value: 15.00					
2007	—	—	—	—	0.25	—
2007 Proof	— Value: 15.00					
2008	—	—	—	—	0.25	—
2008 Proof	— Value: 15.00					
2009 In sets only	—	—	—	—	0.25	—
2009 Proof	— Value: 15.00					

KM# 873.1 KRONE
3.6000 g., Copper-Nickel, 20.25 mm. **Ruler:** Margrethe II **Obv:** 3 crowned MII monograms around center hole, date, mint mark, and initials LG-JP-A below **Rev:** Wave design surrounds center hole, value above, hearts flank **Note:** Prev. KM#873.

Date	Mintage	F	VF	XF	Unc	BU
2001 LG; JP; A	14,640,000	—	—	—	0.80	—

KM# 873.2 KRONE
3.6000 g., Copper-Nickel, 20.25 mm. **Ruler:** Margrethe II **Obv:** 3 crowned MII monograms around center hole, date below **Rev:** Design surounds center hole, value above, hearts flank **Edge:** Reeded **Note:** Without initials

Date	Mintage	F	VF	XF	Unc	BU
2002	9,000,000	—	—	—	0.60	—
2003	5,231,000	—	—	—	0.60	—
2004	16,139,596	—	—	—	0.60	—
2004 Proof	3,000	Value: 18.00				
2005	—	—	—	—	0.60	—
2005 Proof	— Value: 18.00					
2006	—	—	—	—	0.60	—
2006 Proof	— Value: 18.00					
2007	—	—	—	—	0.60	—
2007 Proof	— Value: 18.00					
2008	—	—	—	—	0.60	—
2008 Proof	— Value: 18.00					
2009	—	—	—	—	0.60	—
2009 Proof	— Value: 18.00					

KM# 874.1 2 KRONER

5.9000 g., Copper-Nickel, 24.5 mm. **Ruler:** Margrethe II **Obv:** 3 crowned MII monograms around center hole, date and initials LG-JP-A below **Rev:** Design surrounds center hole, denomination above, hearts flank **Note:** Prev. KM#874.

Date	Mintage	F	VF	XF	Unc	BU
2001 LG; JP; A	11,180,000	—	—	—	0.80	—

KM# 874.2 2 KRONER

5.9000 g., Copper-Nickel, 24.50 mm. **Ruler:** Margrethe II **Obv:** 3 crowned MII monograms around center hole, date and initials LGpJP-A below **Rev:** Wave design surrounds center hole, denomination above, hearts flank **Edge:** Reeded and plain sections **Note:** Without initials

Date	Mintage	F	VF	XF	Unc	BU
2002	60,159,000	—	—	—	0.80	—
2004	7,381,531	—	—	—	0.80	—
2004 Proof	3,000	Value: 22.00				
2005	—	—	—	—	0.80	—
2005 Proof	—	Value: 22.00				
2006	—	—	—	—	0.80	—
2006 Proof	—	Value: 22.00				
2007	—	—	—	—	0.80	—
2007 Proof	—	Value: 22.00				
2008	—	—	—	—	0.80	—
2008 Proof	—	Value: 22.00				
2009 In sets only	—	—	—	—	0.80	—
2009 Proof	—	Value: 22.00				

KM# 869.1 5 KRONER

9.2000 g., Copper-Nickel, 28.5 mm. **Ruler:** Margrethe II **Obv:** 3 crowned MII monograms around center hole, date and initials LG-JP-A below **Rev:** Wave design surrounds center hole, denomination above, hearts flank **Note:** Large and small date varieties exist.

Date	Mintage	F	VF	XF	Unc	BU
2001 LG; JP; A	5,700,000	—	—	—	2.50	—

KM# 869.2 5 KRONER

9.2000 g., Copper-Nickel, 28.5 mm. **Ruler:** Margrethe II **Obv:** 3 crowned MII monograms around center hole, date below **Rev:** Wave design surrounds center hole, denomination above, hearts flank **Edge:** Reeded **Note:** Without initials

Date	Mintage	F	VF	XF	Unc	BU
2002	5,980,000	—	—	—	2.25	—
2004	1,415,925	—	—	—	2.25	—
2004 Proof	3,000	Value: 30.00				
2005	—	—	—	—	2.25	—
2005 Proof	—	Value: 30.00				
2006	—	—	—	—	2.25	—
2006 Proof	—	Value: 30.00				
2007	—	—	—	—	2.25	—
2007 Proof	—	Value: 30.00				
2008	—	—	—	—	2.25	—
2008 Proof	—	Value: 30.00				
2009	—	—	—	—	2.25	—
2009 Proof	—	Value: 30.00				

KM# 887.1 10 KRONER

7.0000 g., Aluminum-Bronze, 23.35 mm. **Ruler:** Margrethe II **Obv:** Crowned head right within inner circle, date, initials LG-JP-A below, mint mark after II in title **Obv. Legend:** MARGRETHE II - DANMARKS DRONNING **Obv. Designer:** Mogens Moller **Rev:** Crowned arms within inner circle above denomination **Edge:** Plain

Date	Mintage	F	VF	XF	Unc	BU
2001(h) LG; JP; A	4,800,000	—	—	—	4.00	—

KM# 887.2 10 KRONER

7.1000 g., Aluminum-Bronze, 23.35 mm. **Ruler:** Margrethe II **Obv:** Crowned bust right, mint mark after II in title **Obv. Legend:** MARGRETHE II - DANMARKS DRONNING **Obv. Designer:** Mogens Moller **Rev:** Crowned arms and denomination **Edge:** Plain **Note:** Without initials

Date	Mintage	F	VF	XF	Unc	BU
2002(h)	7,299,900	—	—	—	4.00	—

KM# 896 10 KRONER

7.0000 g., Aluminum-Bronze, 23.4 mm. **Ruler:** Margrethe II **Obv:** Crowned bust right within circle, date below **Obv. Legend:** MARGRETHE II - DANMARKS DRONNING **Rev:** Crowned arms above denomination **Edge:** Plain **Designer:** Mogens Moller

Date	Mintage	F	VF	XF	Unc	BU
2004(h)	5,835,426	—	—	—	4.00	—
2004(h) Proof	—	Value: 35.00				
2005(h)	—	—	—	—	4.00	—
2005(h) Proof	—	Value: 35.00				
2006(h)	—	—	—	—	4.00	—
2006(h) Proof	—	Value: 35.00				
2007(h)	—	—	—	—	4.00	—
2007(h) Proof	—	Value: 35.00				
2008(h)	—	—	—	—	3.25	—
2008(h) Proof	—	Value: 35.00				
2009(h)	—	—	—	—	3.25	—
2009(h) Proof	—	Value: 35.00				

KM# 898 10 KRONER

7.0000 g., Aluminum-Bronze, 23.35 mm. **Ruler:** Margrethe II **Subject:** Hans Christian Andersen's Ugly duckling story **Obv:** Crowned bust right within circle, date below **Obv. Legend:** MARGRETHE II - DANMARKS DRONNING **Rev:** Swan and reflection on water within circle, value below **Rev. Designer:** Hans Pauli Olsen **Edge:** Plain

Date	Mintage	F	VF	XF	Unc	BU
2005(h)	1,200,000	—	—	—	4.00	—

KM# 906 10 KRONER

31.1000 g., 0.9990 Silver 0.9988 oz. ASW, 38 mm. **Ruler:** Margrethe II **Subject:** Hans Christian Andersen's The Ugly Duckling **Obv:** Crowned bust right **Obv. Legend:** MARGRETHE II - DANMARKS DRONNING **Rev:** Swan and reflection on water **Rev. Designer:** Hans Pauli Olsen

Date	Mintage	F	VF	XF	Unc	BU
2005(h)	75,000	—	—	—	—	45.00

KM# 907 10 KRONER

8.6500 g., 0.9000 Gold 0.2503 oz. AGW, 22 mm. **Ruler:** Margrethe II **Subject:** Hans Christian Andersen's The Ugly Duckling **Obv:** Crowned bust right **Obv. Legend:** MARGRETHE II - DANMARKS DRONNING **Rev:** Swan and reflection on water **Rev. Designer:** Hans Pauli Olsen

Date	Mintage	F	VF	XF	Unc	BU
2005(h)	7,035	—	—	—	—	420

KM# 900 10 KRONER

7.0000 g., Aluminum-Bronze, 23.35 mm. **Ruler:** Margrethe II **Subject:** Hans Christian Andersen's Little Mermaid **Obv:** Crowned bust right within circle, date below **Obv. Legend:** MARGRETHE II - DANMARKS DRONNING **Rev:** Little Mermaid **Rev. Designer:** Tina Maria Nielsen **Edge:** Plain

Date	Mintage	F	VF	XF	Unc	BU
2005(h)	1,200,000	—	—	—	4.00	—

KM# 908 10 KRONER

31.1000 g., 0.9990 Silver 0.9988 oz. ASW, 38 mm. **Ruler:** Margrethe II **Subject:** Hans Christian Andersen's Little Mermaid **Obv:** Crowned bust right, date below **Obv. Legend:** MARGRETHE II - DANMARKS DRONNING **Rev:** Little Mermaid **Rev. Designer:** Tina Maria Nielsen

Date	Mintage	F	VF	XF	Unc	BU
2005(h)	40,220	—	—	—	—	45.00

KM# 911 10 KRONER

8.6500 g., 0.9000 Gold 0.2503 oz. AGW, 22 mm. **Ruler:** Margrethe II **Subject:** Hans Christian Andersen's Little Mermaid **Obv:** Crowned bust right **Obv. Legend:** MARGRETHE II - DANMARKS DRONNING **Rev:** Little Mermaid **Rev. Designer:** Tina Maria Nielsen

Date	Mintage	F	VF	XF	Unc	BU
2005(h)	4,220	—	—	—	—	450

KM# 903 10 KRONER

7.1000 g., Aluminum-Bronze, 23.35 mm. **Ruler:** Margrethe II **Subject:** H.C. Andersen's "The Shadow" **Obv:** Crowned bust right within circle, date below **Obv. Legend:** MARGRETHE II - DANMARKS DRONNING **Rev:** Stylized figures **Rev. Designer:** Bjørn Nørgaard **Edge:** Plain

Date	Mintage	F	VF	XF	Unc	BU
2006(h)	1,200,000	—	—	—	4.00	—

KM# 909 10 KRONER

31.1000 g., 0.9990 Silver 0.9988 oz. ASW, 38 mm. **Ruler:** Margrethe II **Subject:** H.C. Andersen's "Skyggen" (The Shadow) **Obv:** Crowned bust right **Obv. Legend:** MARGRETHE II - DANMARKS DRONNING **Rev:** Stylized figures **Rev. Designer:** Bjørn Nørgaard

Date	Mintage	F	VF	XF	Unc	BU
2006(h)	22,317	—	—	—	—	45.00

KM# 910 10 KRONER

8.6500 g., 0.9000 Gold 0.2503 oz. AGW, 22 mm. **Ruler:** Margrethe II **Subject:** H.C. Andersen's "Skyggen" (The Shadow) **Obv:** Crowned bust right **Obv. Legend:** MARGRETHE II - DANMARKS DRONNING **Rev:** Stylized figures **Rev. Designer:** Bjørn Nørgaard

Date	Mintage	F	VF	XF	Unc	BU
2006(h)	5,000	—	—	—	—	400

KM# 914a 10 KRONER

31.1000 g., 0.9990 Silver 0.9988 oz. ASW, 38 mm. **Ruler:** Margrethe II **Subject:** Hans Christian Andersen's Snow Queen **Obv:** Crowned bust right **Obv. Legend:** MARGRETHE II - DANMARKS DRONNING **Rev:** Ice pieces **Rev. Designer:** Øivind Nygaard

Date	Mintage	F	VF	XF	Unc	BU
2006(h)	40,000	—	—	—	—	45.00

KM# 914b 10 KRONER

8.6500 g., 0.9000 Gold 0.2503 oz. AGW, 22 mm. **Ruler:** Margrethe II **Subject:** The Snow Queen **Obv:** Crowned bust right **Obv. Legend:** MARGRETHE II - DANMARKS DRONNING **Obv. Designer:** Mogens Møller **Rev:** Ice pieces **Rev. Designer:** Øivind Nygaard

Date	Mintage	F	VF	XF	Unc	BU
2006(h)	4,000	—	—	—	—	420

KM# 914 10 KRONER

7.1000 g., Aluminum-Bronze, 23.25 mm. **Ruler:** Margrethe II **Subject:** Hans Christian Andersen's Snow Queen **Obv:** Crowned bust right. **Obv. Legend:** MARGRETHE II - DANMARKS DRONNING **Rev:** Ice pieces **Rev. Designer:** Ølivind Nygaard

Date	Mintage	F	VF	XF	Unc	BU
2006(h)	1,200,000	—	—	—	4.00	—

KM# 923a 10 KRONER

31.1000 g., 0.9990 Silver 0.9988 oz. ASW, 38 mm. **Ruler:** Margrethe II **Subject:** H.C. Anderson's 'The Nightengale' **Rev:** Bird **Rev. Designer:** Torben Ebbesen

Date	Mintage	F	VF	XF	Unc	BU
2007 Proof	30,000	Value: 45.00				

KM# 916 10 KRONER
7.1000 g., Aluminum-Bronze, 23.35 mm. **Ruler:** Margrethe II
Subject: Polar Year **Obv:** Head with tiara right **Obv. Legend:**
MARGRETHE II - DANMARKS DRONNING **Rev:** Polar bear
facing, walking on ice flow **Rev. Legend:** POLARÅR 2007-2009
Edge: Plain

Date	Mintage	F	VF	XF	Unc	BU
2007(h)	1,200,000	—	—	—	4.00	—

KM# 923 10 KRONER
Aluminum-Bronze, 23.35 mm. **Ruler:** Margrethe II
Subject: H.C. Anderson's 'The Nightingale' **Rev:** Bird
Rev. Designer: Torben Ebbesen

Date	Mintage	F	VF	XF	Unc	BU
2007 Unc	1,200,000	—	—	—	4.00	—

KM# 923b 10 KRONER
8.6500 g., 0.9000 Gold 0.2503 oz. AGW, 22 mm.
Ruler: Margrethe II **Subject:** H.C. Anderson's 'The Nightengale'
Rev: Bird **Rev. Designer:** Torben Ebbesen

Date	Mintage	F	VF	XF	Unc	BU
2007	3,075	—	—	—	—	400

KM# 925 10 KRONER
7.2000 g., Aluminum-Bronze, 23.35 mm. **Ruler:** Margrethe II
Obv: Head with tiara right **Rev:** Outlined globe
Rev. Legend: POLARÅR 2007-2009 **Edge:** Plain

Date	Mintage	F	VF	XF	Unc	BU
2008(h)	1,200,000	—	—	—	4.00	—

KM# 932 10 KRONER
Aluminum-Bronze, 23.5 mm. **Ruler:** Margrethe II **Rev:** Ice
scape, Northern Lights **Rev. Designer:** Morten Straede

Date	Mintage	F	VF	XF	Unc	BU
2009	1,200,000	—	—	—	4.00	—

KM# 888.1 20 KRONER
9.3000 g., Aluminum-Bronze **Ruler:** Margrethe II **Obv:** Crowned
bust right within circle, date and initials LG-JP-A below, mint
mark after II in legend **Obv. Legend:** MARGRETHE II -
DANMARKS DRONNING **Rev:** Crowned arms within ornaments
and value **Edge:** Alternate reeded and plain sections
Designer: Mogens Moller

Date	Mintage	F	VF	XF	Unc	BU
2001(h) LG; JP; A	2,900,000	—	—	—	6.25	—

KM# 889 20 KRONER
9.3000 g., Aluminum-Bronze, 27 mm. **Ruler:** Margrethe II
Subject: Danish Towers **Obv:** Crowned bust right within circle
date below, mint mark after II in legend **Obv. Legend:**
MARGRETHE II - DANMARKS DRONNING **Rev:** Aarhus City
Hall **Rev. Designer:** Lis Nogel **Edge:** Reeded and plain sections

Date	Mintage	F	VF	XF	Unc	BU
2002(h)	1,000,000	—	—	—	6.50	—

KM# 888.2 20 KRONER
9.3000 g., Aluminum-Bronze, 27 mm. **Ruler:** Margrethe II
Obv: Crowned bust right within circle, mint mark after II in legend
Obv. Legend: MARGRETHE II - DANMARKS DRONNING
Rev: Crowned arms within ornaments and value **Edge:** Alternate
reeded and plain sections **Designer:** Mogens Møller **Note:** Without
initials.

Date	Mintage	F	VF	XF	Unc	BU
2002(h)	5,500,000	—	—	—	6.00	—

KM# 890 20 KRONER
9.3000 g., Aluminum-Bronze, 27 mm. **Ruler:** Margrethe II
Subject: Danish towers **Obv:** Crowned bust right within circle,
mint mark and date **Obv. Legend:** MARGRETHE II -
DANMARKS DRONNING **Rev:** Copenhagen Old Stock
Exchange spire with four intertwined dragon tails **Rev. Designer:**
Karin Lorentzen **Edge:** Alternate reeded and plain sections

Date	Mintage	F	VF	XF	Unc	BU
2003(h)	1,000,000	—	—	—	6.00	—

KM# 891 20 KRONER
9.3000 g., Aluminum-Bronze, 27 mm. **Ruler:** Margrethe II
Obv: Crowned bust right within circle, mint mark and date
Obv. Legend: MARGRETHE II - DANMARKS DRONNING
Rev: Crowned arms above denomination **Rev. Designer:**
Mogens M?ller **Edge:** Alternate reeded and plain sections

Date	Mintage	F	VF	XF	Unc	BU
2003(h)	5,720,000	—	—	—	6.00	—
2004(h)	6,922,182	—	—	—	6.00	—
2004(h) Proof	3,000	Value: 50.00				
2005(h)	—	—	—	—	6.00	—
2005(h) Proof	—	Value: 50.00				
2006(h)	—	—	—	—	6.00	—
2006(h) Proof	—	Value: 50.00				
2007(h)	—	—	—	—	6.00	—
2007(h) Proof	—	Value: 50.00				
2008(h)	—	—	—	—	6.00	—
2008(h) Proof	—	Value: 50.00				
2009(h)	—	—	—	—	6.00	—
2009(h) Proof	—	Value: 50.00				

KM# 892 20 KRONER
9.3100 g., Aluminum-Bronze, 27 mm. **Ruler:** Margrethe II
Subject: Danish towers **Obv:** Crowned bust right within circle,
mint mark and date **Obv. Legend:** MARGRETHE II -
DANMARKS DRONNING **Rev:** Christiansborg Castle
(parliament) tower and Danish flag **Rev. Designer:** Hans Pauli
Olsen **Edge:** Alternate reeded and plain sections

Date	Mintage	F	VF	XF	Unc	BU
2003(h)	1,000,000	—	—	—	6.00	—

KM# 893 20 KRONER
9.3100 g., Aluminum-Bronze, 27 mm. **Ruler:** Margrethe II
Subject: Danish towers **Obv:** Crowned bust right within circle,
date below **Obv. Legend:** MARGRETHE II - DANMARKS
DRONNING **Rev:** Gåsetårnet tower **Rev. Designer:** Tina Maria
Nielsen **Edge:** Alternate reeded and plain sections

Date	Mintage	F	VF	XF	Unc	BU
2004(h)	1,200,000	—	—	—	6.00	—

KM# 894 20 KRONER
9.3100 g., Aluminum-Bronze, 27 mm. **Ruler:** Margrethe II
Subject: Crown Prince's Wedding **Obv:** Crowned bust right
within circle, date below **Obv. Legend:** MARGRETHE II -
DANMARKS DRONNING **Rev:** Crown Prince Frederik and
Crown Princess Mary **Rev. Designer:** Karin Lorentzen
Edge: Alternate reeded and plain sections

Date	Mintage	F	VF	XF	Unc	BU
2004(h)	1,200,000	—	—	—	6.00	—

KM# 897 20 KRONER
Aluminum-Bronze, 27 mm. **Ruler:** Margrethe II **Subject:** Danish
towers **Obv:** Crowned bust right within circle, date below
Obv. Legend: MARGRETHE II - DANMARKS DRONNING
Rev: Svaneke water tower, Bornholm **Rev. Designer:** Morten
Straede **Edge:** Alternate reeded and plain sections

Date	Mintage	F	VF	XF	Unc	BU
2004(h)	1,200,000	—	—	—	6.00	—

KM# 899 20 KRONER
9.3000 g., Aluminum-Bronze, 27 mm. **Ruler:** Margrethe II
Subject: Danish Towers **Obv:** Crowned bust right within circle,
date below **Obv. Legend:** MARGRETHE II - DANMARKS
DRONNING **Rev:** Landet Kirke, with elements from the story of
Elvira Madigan and Sixten Sparre, including a revolver among
leaves of chestnut-trees **Rev. Designer:** Øivind Nygaard
Edge: Segmented reeding

Date	Mintage	F	VF	XF	Unc	BU
2005(h)	1,200,000	—	—	—	6.00	—

KM# 901 20 KRONER
9.3000 g., Aluminum-Bronze, 27 mm. **Ruler:** Margrethe II
Subject: Danish Towers **Obv:** Crowned bust right w/ circle, date
below **Obv. Legend:** MARGRETHE II - DANMARKS DRONNING
Rev: Lighthouse of Nolsoy (Faeroe Islands) **Rev. Designer:** Hans
Pauli Olsen **Edge:** Alternate plain and reeded segments

Date	Mintage	F	VF	XF	Unc	BU
2005(h)	1,200,000	—	—	—	6.00	—

KM# 902   20 KRONER
9.3300 g., Aluminum-Bronze, 27 mm. **Ruler:** Margrethe II
Subject: Danish Towers **Obv:** Crowned bust right within circle,
date below **Obv. Legend:** MARGRETHE II - DANMARKS
DRONNING **Rev:** Gråsten Castle Bell Tower **Rev. Designer:**
Sys Hindsbo **Edge:** Segmented reeding

Date	Mintage	F	VF	XF	Unc	BU
2006(h)	1,200,000	—	—	—	6.00	—

KM# 913   20 KRONER
9.3000 g., Aluminum-Bronze, 27 mm. **Ruler:** Margrethe II
Subject: Danish Towers **Obv:** Crowned bust right within circle,
date below **Obv. Legend:** MARGRETHE II - DANMARKS
DRONNING **Rev:** The Greenland Cairns: Nukaritt/Three
Brothers **Rev. Legend:** TRE BRØDRE **Rev. Designer:** Niels
Motzfeldt **Edge:** Alternate plain and reeded segments

Date	Mintage	F	VF	XF	Unc	BU
2006(h)	1,200,000	—	—	—	6.00	—

KM# 919   20 KRONER
9.3000 g., Aluminum-Bronze, 26.94 mm. **Ruler:** Margrethe II
Subject: Danish towers **Obv:** Bust with tiarra right **Obv. Legend:**
MARGRETHE II - DANMARKS DRONNING **Rev:** City Hall in
Copenhagen **Rev. Legend:** KØBENHAVNS RÅDHUS
Edge: Alternate plain and reeded segments

Date	Mintage	F	VF	XF	Unc	BU
2007(h)	1,200,000	—	—	—	6.00	—

KM# 920   20 KRONER
9.3000 g., Aluminum-Bronze, 27 mm. **Ruler:** Margrethe II
Series: Danish ships **Obv:** Crowned bust right
Obv. Legend: MARGRETHE II - DANMARKS DRONNING
Rev: Sailing ship Jylland **Rev. Legend:** FREGATTEN - JYLLAND
Edge: Segmented reeding

Date	Mintage	F	VF	XF	Unc	BU
2007(h)	1,200,000	—	—	—	6.00	—

KM# 921   20 KRONER
9.3000 g., Aluminum-Bronze, 27 mm. **Ruler:** Margrethe II
Series: Danish ships **Subject:** The Galathea 3 expedition
Obv: Crowned bust right **Obv. Legend:** MARGRETHE II -
DANMARKS DRONNING **Rev:** Ship Vaedderen, route map in
background **Rev. Legend:** VAEDDEREN **Edge:** Segmented
reeding

Date	Mintage	F	VF	XF	Unc	BU
2007(h)	1,200,000	—	—	—	6.00	—

KM# 926   20 KRONER
9.3000 g., Aluminum-Bronze, 27 mm. **Ruler:** Margrethe II
Obv: Head with tiarra right **Rev:** World's first ocean-going diesel-
engine merchant ship, built 1912 **Rev. Legend:** SELANDIA
Edge: Segmented reeding

Date	Mintage	F	VF	XF	Unc	BU
2008(h)	1,200,000	—	—	—	8.00	6.00
2008(h) Proof	1,500	Value: 85.00				

KM# 927   20 KRONER
9.3000 g., 27.0000 Aluminum-Bronze 8.0727 oz., 26.9 mm.
Ruler: Margrethe II **Subject:** Voyage to Dublin, Ireledn, with full
size replica Viking ship, HAVHINGSTEN **Obv:** Crowned bust right
Obv. Legend: MARGRETHE II - DANMARKS DRONNING
Rev: HAVHINGSTEN at sea **Rev. Designer:** Erik Varming

Date	Mintage	F	VF	XF	Unc	BU
2008	1,200,000	—	—	—	6.00	—
2008 Proof	1,500	Value: 85.00				

KM# 928   20 KRONER
9.3000 g., Aluminum-Bronze, 27 mm. **Ruler:** Margrethe II
Rev: Royal Yacht Dannebrog **Rev. Designer:** Henrik Wiberg

Date	Mintage	F	VF	XF	Unc	BU
2008 Unc	1,200,000	—	—	—	4.00	—
2008 Proof	1,500	Value: 85.00				

KM# 935   20 KRONER
9.3000 g., Aluminum-Bronze **Ruler:** Margrethe II **Obv:** Crowned
bust right **Obv. Legend:** MARGRETHE II - DANMARKS
DRONNING **Rev:** Lightship XVII (built 1895) on duty

Date	Mintage	F	VF	XF	Unc	BU
2009	1,200,000	—	—	—	6.00	—
2009 Proof	1,500	Value: 85.00				

KM# 936   20 KRONER
9.3000 g., Aluminum-Bronze **Ruler:** Margrethe II **Obv:** Crowned
bust facing right **Rev:** FAERØBÅD (Boat of Faeroe Islands)
Designer: Hans Pauli Olsen

Date	Mintage	F	VF	XF	Unc	BU
2009	900,000	—	—	—	6.00	—
2009	1,500	Value: 85.00				

KM# 917   100 KRONER
31.0000 g., 0.9990 Silver 0.9956 oz. ASW, 38 mm.
Ruler: Margrethe II **Subject:** Polar Year 2007-2009
Obv: Crowned bust right **Obv. Legend:** MARGRETHE II -
DANMARKS DRONNING **Rev:** Polar bear facing, walking on ice
flow **Rev. Legend:** POLARÅR 2007-2009

Date	Mintage	F	VF	XF	Unc	BU
2007(h)	35,000	—	—	—	—	55.00

KM# 930   100 KRONER
31.1000 g., 0.9990 Silver 0.9988 oz. ASW, 38 mm. **Ruler:**
Margrethe II **Subject:** Sirius Patrol **Rev:** Globe and dog sled

Date	Mintage	F	VF	XF	Unc	BU
2008	35,000	—	—	—	—	50.00

KM# 933   100 KRONER
31.1000 g., 0.9990 Silver 0.9988 oz. ASW, 38 mm.
Ruler: Margrethe II **Rev:** Ice scape, Northern Lights
Rev. Designer: Morten Straede

Date	Mintage	F	VF	XF	Unc	BU
2009	—	—	—	—	—	50.00

KM# 895   200 KRONER
31.1000 g., 0.9990 Silver 0.9988 oz. ASW, 38.3 mm.
Ruler: Margrethe II **Subject:** Wedding of Crown Prince
Obv: Crowned bust within circle, date below **Obv. Legend:**
MARGRETHE II - DANMARKS DRONNING **Rev:** Crown Prince
Frederik and Crown Princess Mary **Rev. Designer:** Karin
Lorentzen **Edge:** Plain **Note:** No initials.

Date	Mintage	F	VF	XF	Unc	BU
2004(h)	125,000	—	—	—	—	60.00

KM# 929   500 KRONUR
31.1000 g., 0.9990 Silver 0.9988 oz. ASW, 38 mm.
Ruler: Margrethe II **Rev:** Royal Yacht Dannebrog
Rev. Designer: Henrik Wiberg

Date	Mintage	F	VF	XF	Unc	BU
2008	60,000	—	—	—	—	115

KM# 918   1000 KRONER
0.9000 Gold, 22.00 mm. **Ruler:** Margrethe II **Subject:** Polar
Year 2007-2009 **Obv:** Crowned bust right **Obv. Legend:**
MARGRETHE II - DANMARKS DRONNING **Rev:** Polar bear
facing, walking on ice flow **Rev. Legend:** POLARÅR 2007-2009
Note: Struck from gold from Greenland having a small polar bear
to right of denomination.

Date	Mintage	F	VF	XF	Unc	BU
2007(h) Proof	6,000	Value: 475				

KM# 931   1000 KRONER
8.6500 g., 0.9000 Gold 0.2503 oz. AGW, 22 mm.
Ruler: Margrethe II **Subject:** Sirius Patrol **Rev:** Globe and dog
sled

Date	Mintage	F	VF	XF	Unc	BU
2008 Proof	—	Value: 475				

KM# 934   1000 KRONER
8.6500 g., 0.9000 Gold 0.2503 oz. AGW, 22 mm.
Ruler: Margrethe II **Rev:** Ice scape, Northern Lights
Rev. Designer: Morten Straede

Date	Mintage	F	VF	XF	Unc	BU
2009 Proof	—	Value: 475				

MINT SETS

KM#	Date	Mintage	Identification	Issue Price	Mkt Val
MS46	2001 (5)	28,000	KM866.2, 868, 869, 873, 874, 887, 888	15.00	37.50
MS47	2002 (7)	28,000	KM866.3, 868.2, 869.2, 873.2, 874.2, 887.2, 888.2	17.50	35.00
MS48	2003 (6)	35,000	KM866.3, 868.2, 873.2, 889, 890, 891	17.50	35.00
MS49	2004 (8)	35,000	KM#866.3, 868.2, 869.2, 873.2, 874.2, 891, 895, 896, plus medal in Nordic gold	34.50	75.00
MS50	2005 (8)	31,000	KM#866.3, 868.2, 869.2, 873.2, 874.2, 896, 891, 898, plus medal	34.50	45.00
MS51	2006 (7)	35,000	KM#866.2, 868.2, 869.2, 873.2, 874.2, 896, 902, plus medal in Nordic Gold	40.00	45.00

KM#	Date	Mintage	Identification	Issue Price	Mkt Val
MS52	2007 (7)	6,000	KM#866.2, 868.2, 869.2, 873.2, 874.2, 891, 896 Children's set with medal in .925 Silver	46.00	50.00

PROOF SETS

KM#	Date	Mintage	Identification	Issue Price	Mkt Val
PS1	2004 (8)	3,000	KM#866.3, 868.2, 869.2, 873.2, 874.2, 896, 891, plus Wedding medal in .925 Silver	150	250
PS2	2005 (8)	3,500	KM866.3, 868.2, 869.2, 873.2, 874.2, 896, 891 and 1801 Battle of Copenhagen medal in .925 Silver	150	185
PS3	2006 (8)	2,500	KM#866.3, 868.2, 869.2, 873.2, 874.2, 896, 891 and 1691 Floating Dock medal in .925 Silver	160	185
PS4	2007 (8)	2,000	KM#866.3, 868.2, 869.2, 873.2, 874.2, 896, 891, plus Galathea medal in .925 silver	160	185
PS5	2008 (8)	—	KM#866.3, 868.2, 869.2, 873.2, 874.2, 896, 891, plus medal	—	200

DJIBOUTI

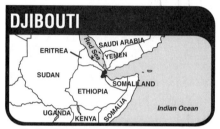

The Republic of Djibouti (formerly French Somaliland and the French Overseas Territory of Afars and Issas), located in northeast Africa at the Bab el Mandeb Strait connecting the Suez Canal and the Red Sea with the Gulf of Aden and the Indian Ocean, has an area of 8,950 sq. mi. (22,000 sq. km.) and a population of 421,320. Capital: Djibouti. The tiny nation has less than one sq. mi. of arable land, and no natural resources except salt, sand, and camels. The commercial activities of the transshipment port of Djibouti and the Addis Abada-Djibouti railroad are the basis of the economy. Salt, fish and hides are exported.

REPUBLIC

STANDARD COINAGE

KM# 34   10 FRANCS
3.4000 g., Copper-Nickel, 20.9 mm.   **Obv:** National arms **Rev:** Chimpanzee **Edge:** Plain

Date	Mintage	F	VF	XF	Unc	BU
2003	—	—	—	—	2.00	4.00

KM# 23   10 FRANCS
3.0000 g., Aluminum-Bronze, 20 mm.   **Obv:** National arms within wreath, date below **Rev:** Boats on water, denomination above **Rev. Designer:** Lucien Bazor **Note:** Varieties exist.

Date	Mintage	F	VF	XF	Unc	BU
2007(a)	—	—	—	—	2.50	4.50

KM# 24   20 FRANCS
4.0000 g., Aluminum-Bronze, 23.5 mm.   **Obv:** National arms within wreath, date below **Rev:** Boats on water, denomination above **Rev. Designer:** Lucien Bazor **Note:** Varieties exist.

Date	Mintage	F	VF	XF	Unc	BU
2007(a)	—	—	—	—	2.50	4.50

KM# 25   50 FRANCS
7.0500 g., Copper-Nickel, 25.7 mm.   **Obv:** National arms within wreath, date below **Rev:** Pair of dromedary camels right, denomination above **Rev. Designer:** Raymond Joly

Date	Mintage	F	VF	XF	Unc	BU
2007(a)	—	—	—	—	6.00	9.00

KM# 38   100 FRANCS
Silver, 35 mm.   **Subject:** 25th Anniversary of Independence **Obv:** Small national arms on state flag **Obv. Legend:** REPUBLIQUE DE DJIBOUTI **Rev:** UNITÉ in color **Rev. Legend:** UNITÉ ... ÉGALITÉ ... PAIX

Date	Mintage	F	VF	XF	Unc	BU
ND(2002)	—	—	—	—	—	125

KM# 39   100 FRANCS
Silver, 35 mm.   **Subject:** 25th Anniversary of Independence **Obv:** Small national arms on state flag **Obv. Legend:** REPUBLIQUE DE DJIBOUTI **Rev:** É/GAL/ITÉ in color **Rev. Legend:** UNITÉ ... ÉGALITÉ ... PAIX

Date	Mintage	F	VF	XF	Unc	BU
AH(2002)	—	—	—	—	—	125

KM# 40   100 FRANCS
Silver, 35 mm.   **Subject:** 25th Anniversary of Independence **Obv:** Small national arms on state flag **Obv. Legend:** REPUBLIQUE DE DJIBOUTI **Rev:** PAI/X in color **Rev. Legend:** UNITÉ ... ÉGALITÉ ... PAIX

Date	Mintage	F	VF	XF	Unc	BU
ND(2002)	—	—	—	—	—	125

KM# 26   100 FRANCS
12.0000 g., Copper-Nickel, 30 mm.   **Obv:** National arms within wreath, date below **Rev:** Pair of dromedary camels right, denomination above **Rev. Designer:** Raymond Joly

Date	Mintage	F	VF	XF	Unc	BU
2004(a)	—	—	—	2.25	7.00	9.00
2007(a)	—	—	—	—	7.00	9.00

KM# 41   250 FRANCS
22.2000 g., 0.9000 Silver 0.6423 oz. ASW **Obv:** National arms **Obv. Legend:** REPUBLIQUE DE DJIBOUTI **Rev:** Two dromedary camels right **Rev. Legend:** UNITÉ - ÉGALITÉ - PAIX

Date	Mintage	F	VF	XF	Unc	BU
2002(a) Proof	—	Value: 75.00				

DOMINICAN REPUBLIC

The Dominican Republic, which occupies the eastern two-thirds of the island of Hispaniola, has an area of 18,704 sq. mi. (48,734 sq. km.) and a population of 7.9 million. Capital: Santo Domingo. The largely agricultural economy produces sugar, coffee, tobacco and cocoa. Tourism and casino gaming are also a rising source of revenue.

REPUBLIC

REFORM COINAGE

100 Centavos = 1 Peso Oro

KM# 80.2   PESO
6.4900 g., Copper-Zinc, 25 mm.   **Subject:** Juan Pablo Duarte **Obv:** National arms and denomination **Rev:** DUARTE below bust, date below **Note:** Coin die alignment.

Date	Mintage	F	VF	XF	Unc	BU
2002	—	—	—	—	2.00	2.50
2005	—	—	—	—	2.00	2.50

KM# 90   PESO
12.5000 g., Copper-Nickel, 30.6 mm.   **Obv:** Pan American Games logo **Rev:** National arms and denomination **Edge:** Reeded

Date	Mintage	F	VF	XF	Unc	BU
2003 Proof	—	Value: 15.00				

KM# 89   5 PESOS
6.0600 g., Bi-Metallic Stainless Steel center in Brass ring, 23 mm. **Subject:** Sanchez **Obv:** National arms and denomination **Rev:** Portrait facing within circle, date below **Edge:** Segmented reeding

Date	Mintage	F	VF	XF	Unc	BU
2002	—	—	—	—	2.50	3.00
2005	—	—	—	—	2.50	3.00
2007	—	—	—	—	2.50	3.00

KM# 106   10 PESOS
8.2000 g., Bi-Metallic Brass center in Copper-Nickel ring, 27 mm. **Obv:** Value at left of national arms **Obv. Legend:** • REPUBLICA DOMINICANA • **Rev:** Bust of General Mella facing **Rev. Legend:** BANCO CENTRAL DE LA REPUBLICA DOMINICANA **Edge:** Segmented reeding

Date	Mintage	F	VF	XF	Unc	BU
2005	—	—	—	—	6.00	8.00

KM# 107   25 PESOS
8.5600 g., Copper-Nickel, 28.82 mm.   **Obv:** Value at left of national arms **Obv. Legend:** REPUBLICA DOMINICANA **Rev:** Bust of General Luperon facing **Rev. Legend:** BANCO CENTRAL DE LA REPUBLICA DOMINICANA **Rev. Inscription:** HEROE DE LA RESTAURACION **Edge:** Reeded

Date	Mintage	F	VF	XF	Unc	BU
2005	—	—	—	—	5.00	7.00

EAST CARIBBEAN STATES

The East Caribbean States, formerly the British Caribbean Territories (Eastern Group), formed a currency board in 1950 to provide the constituent territories of Trinidad & Tobago, Barbados, British Guiana (now Guyana), British Virgin Islands, Anguilla, St. Kitts, Nevis, Antigua, Dominica, St. Lucia, St. Vincent and Grenada with a common currency, thereby permitting withdrawal of the regular British Pound currency. This was dissolved in 1965 and after the breakup, the East Caribbean Territories, a grouping including Barbados, the Leeward and Windward Islands, came into being. Coinage of the dissolved 'Eastern Group' continues to circulate. Paper currency of the East Caribbean Authority was first issued in 1965 and although Barbados withdrew from the group they continued using them prior to 1973 when Barbados issued a decimal coinage.

A series of 4-dollar coins tied to the FAO coinage program were released in 1970 under the name of the Caribbean Development Bank by eight loosely federated island groupings in the eastern Caribbean. These issues are listed individually in this volume under Antigua, Barbados, Dominica, Grenada, Montserrat, St. Kitts, St. Lucia and St. Vincent.

EAST CARIBBEAN STATES

STANDARD COINAGE

100 Cents = 1 Dollar

KM# 34   CENT
1.0300 g., Aluminum, 18.42 mm.   **Ruler:** Elizabeth II
Obv: Crowned head right **Obv. Designer:** Ian Rank-Broadley
Rev: Denomination **Edge:** Plain

Date	Mintage	F	VF	XF	Unc	BU
2002	—	—	—	—	0.20	0.30
2004	—	—	—	—	0.20	0.30
2008	—	—	—	—	0.20	0.30

KM# 35   2 CENTS
1.4200 g., Aluminum, 21.46 mm.   **Ruler:** Elizabeth II
Obv: Crowned head right **Obv. Designer:** Ian Rank-Broadley
Rev: Denomination **Edge:** Plain

Date	Mintage	F	VF	XF	Unc	BU
2002	—	—	—	—	0.25	0.35
2004	—	—	—	—	0.25	0.35

KM# 36   5 CENTS
1.7400 g., Aluminum, 23 mm.   **Ruler:** Elizabeth II **Obv:** Crowned head right **Obv. Designer:** Ian Rank-Broadley
Rev: Denomination **Edge:** Plain

Date	Mintage	F	VF	XF	Unc	BU
2002	—	—	—	—	0.30	0.45
2004	—	—	—	—	0.30	0.45

KM# 37   10 CENTS
Copper-Nickel, 18.06 mm.   **Ruler:** Elizabeth II **Obv:** Crowned head right **Obv. Designer:** Ian Rank-Broadley **Rev:** Sir Francis Drake's Golden Hind and denomination **Edge:** Reeded

Date	Mintage	F	VF	XF	Unc	BU
2002	—	—	—	—	0.40	0.60

KM# 38   25 CENTS
6.4000 g., Copper-Nickel, 24 mm.   **Ruler:** Elizabeth II
Obv: Crowned head right **Obv. Designer:** Ian Rank-Broadley
Rev: Sir Francis Drake's Golden Hind and denomination
Edge: Reeded

Date	Mintage	F	VF	XF	Unc	BU
2002	—	—	—	—	0.50	0.75
2007	—	—	—	—	0.50	0.75

KM# 39   DOLLAR
7.9000 g., Copper-Nickel, 26.5 mm.   **Ruler:** Elizabeth II
Obv: Crowned head right **Obv. Designer:** Ian Rank-Broadley
Rev: Sir Francis Drake's Golden Hind and denomination
Edge: Alternating plain and reeded

Date	Mintage	F	VF	XF	Unc	BU
2002	—	—	—	—	2.00	3.00
2007	—	—	—	—	2.00	3.00

KM# 40   DOLLAR
28.2800 g., Copper-Nickel Gilt, 38.6 mm.   **Ruler:** Elizabeth II
Subject: Golden Jubilee Monarchs **Obv:** Crowned head right
Obv. Designer: Ian Rank-Broadley **Rev:** Henry III (1216-1277)
Edge: Reeded

Date	Mintage	F	VF	XF	Unc	BU
2002	5,000	—	—	—	22.50	25.00

KM# 42   DOLLAR
28.2800 g., Copper-Nickel Gilt, 38.6 mm.   **Ruler:** Elizabeth II
Subject: Golden Jubilee Monarchs **Obv:** Crowned head right
Obv. Designer: Ian Rank-Broadley **Rev:** Edward III (1327-1377)
Edge: Reeded

Date	Mintage	F	VF	XF	Unc	BU
2002	5,000	—	—	—	22.50	25.00

KM# 44   DOLLAR
28.2800 g., Copper-Nickel Gilt, 38.6 mm.   **Ruler:** Elizabeth II
Subject: Golden Jubilee Monarchs **Obv:** Crowned head right
Obv. Designer: Ian Rank-Broadley **Rev:** George III (1760-1820)
Edge: Reeded

Date	Mintage	F	VF	XF	Unc	BU
2002	5,000	—	—	—	22.50	25.00

KM# 46   DOLLAR
28.2800 g., Copper-Nickel Gilt, 38.6 mm.   **Ruler:** Elizabeth II
Subject: Golden Jubilee Monarchs **Obv:** Crowned head right
Obv. Designer: Ian Rank-Broadley **Rev:** Queen Victoria (1837-1901) **Edge:** Reeded

Date	Mintage	F	VF	XF	Unc	BU
2002	5,000	—	—	—	22.50	25.00

KM# 48   DOLLAR
28.2800 g., Copper-Nickel Gilt, 38.6 mm.   **Ruler:** Elizabeth II
Subject: Golden Jubilee Monarchs **Obv:** Crowned head right
Obv. Designer: Ian Rank-Broadley **Rev:** Queen Elizabeth II (1952-) **Edge:** Reeded

Date	Mintage	F	VF	XF	Unc	BU
2002	5,000	—	—	—	22.50	25.00

KM# 86   DOLLAR
27.7300 g., Copper-Nickel, 38.5 mm.   **Ruler:** Elizabeth II
Subject: Coronation Jubilee **Obv:** Crowned head right
Obv. Designer: Ian Rank-Broadley **Rev:** Fireworks display above building **Edge:** Reeded

Date	Mintage	F	VF	XF	Unc	BU
2002	—	—	—	—	10.00	12.00

KM# 58   DOLLAR
7.9800 g., Copper-Nickel, 26.5 mm.   **Ruler:** Elizabeth II
Subject: 25th Anniversary **Obv:** Head right **Rev:** Motto within wreath

Date	Mintage	F	VF	XF	Unc	BU
2008	500,000	—	—	—	—	5.00

KM# 51   2 DOLLARS
56.5600 g., Copper-Nickel Gilt, 38.6 mm.   **Ruler:** Elizabeth II
Subject: British Military Leaders **Obv:** Crowned head right
Obv. Designer: Ian Rank-Broadley **Rev:** Wellington's portrait and battle scene **Edge:** Reeded

Date	Mintage	F	VF	XF	Unc	BU
2002 Proof	10,000	Value: 45.00				

KM# 54   2 DOLLARS
56.5600 g., Copper-Nickel Gilt, 38.6 mm.   **Ruler:** Elizabeth II
Subject: British Military Leaders **Obv:** Crowned head right
Obv. Designer: Ian Rank-Broadley **Rev:** Admiral Nelson's portrait and naval battle scene **Edge:** Reeded

Date	Mintage	F	VF	XF	Unc	BU
2003 Proof	10,000	Value: 45.00				

KM# 57   2 DOLLARS
56.5600 g., Copper-Nickel Gilt, 38.6 mm.   **Ruler:** Elizabeth II
Subject: British Military Leaders **Obv:** Crowned head right
Obv. Designer: Ian Rank-Broadley **Rev:** Churchill's portrait and air battle scene **Edge:** Reeded

Date	Mintage	F	VF	XF	Unc	BU
2003 Proof	10,000	Value: 45.00				

KM# 41   10 DOLLARS
28.2800 g., 0.9250 Silver with gold cameo 0.8410 oz. ASW,
38.6 mm.   **Ruler:** Elizabeth II **Subject:** Golden Jubilee Monarchs
Obv: Crowned head right **Obv. Designer:** Ian Rank-Broadley
Rev: Henry III (1216-1272) **Edge:** Reeded

Date	Mintage	F	VF	XF	Unc	BU
2002 Proof	10,000	Value: 65.00				

KM# 41a   10 DOLLARS
39.9400 g., 0.9166 Gold 1.1770 oz. AGW, 38.6 mm.
Ruler: Elizabeth II **Subject:** Golden Jubilee Monarchs
Obv: Crowned head right **Obv. Designer:** Ian Rank-Broadley
Rev: Henry III (1216-1272) **Edge:** Reeded

Date	Mintage	F	VF	XF	Unc	BU
2002 Proof	100	Value: 1,500				

KM# 43   10 DOLLARS
28.2800 g., 0.9250 Silver 0.8410 oz. ASW, 38.6 mm.
Ruler: Elizabeth II **Subject:** Golden Jubile Monarchs
Obv: Crowned head right **Obv. Designer:** Ian Rank-Broadley
Rev: Edward III (1327-1377) **Edge:** Reeded

Date	Mintage	F	VF	XF	Unc	BU
2002 Proof	10,000	Value: 65.00				

KM# 43a   10 DOLLARS
39.9400 g., 0.9166 Gold 1.1770 oz. AGW, 38.6 mm.
Ruler: Elizabeth II **Subject:** Golden Jubilee Monarchs
Obv: Crowned head right **Obv. Designer:** Ian Rank-Broadley
Rev: Edward III (1327-1377) **Edge:** Reeded

Date	Mintage	F	VF	XF	Unc	BU
2002 Proof	100	Value: 1,500				

KM# 45   10 DOLLARS
28.2800 g., 0.9250 Silver with gold cameo 0.8410 oz. ASW,
38.6 mm.   **Ruler:** Elizabeth II **Subject:** Golden Jubilee Monarchs **Obv:** Crowned head right **Obv. Designer:** Ian Rank-Broadley **Rev:** George III (1760-1820) **Edge:** Reeded

Date	Mintage	F	VF	XF	Unc	BU
2002 Proof	10,000	Value: 65.00				

KM# 45a   10 DOLLARS
39.9400 g., 0.9166 Gold 1.1770 oz. AGW, 38.6 mm.
Ruler: Elizabeth II **Subject:** Golden Jubilee Monarchs
Obv: Crowned head right **Obv. Designer:** Ian Rank-Broadley
Rev: George III (1760-1820) **Edge:** Reeded

Date	Mintage	F	VF	XF	Unc	BU
2002 Proof	100	Value: 1,500				

KM# 47   10 DOLLARS
28.2800 g., 0.9250 Silver with partial gold plating 0.8410 oz.
ASW, 38.6 mm.   **Ruler:** Elizabeth II **Subject:** Golden Jubilee Monarchs **Obv:** Crowned head right **Obv. Designer:** Ian Rank-Broadley **Rev:** Queen Victoria (1837-1901) **Edge:** Reeded

Date	Mintage	F	VF	XF	Unc	BU
2002 Proof	10,000	Value: 65.00				

KM# 47a   10 DOLLARS
39.9400 g., 0.9166 Gold 1.1770 oz. AGW, 38.6 mm.
Ruler: Elizabeth II **Subject:** Golden Jubilee Monarchs
Obv: Crowned head right **Obv. Designer:** Ian Rank-Broadley
Rev: Queen Victoria (1837-1901) **Edge:** Reeded

Date	Mintage	F	VF	XF	Unc	BU
2002 Proof	100	Value: 1,500				

KM# 49   10 DOLLARS
28.2800 g., 0.9250 Silver with gold cameo 0.8410 oz. ASW,
38.6 mm.   **Ruler:** Elizabeth II **Subject:** Golden Jubilee Monarchs
Obv: Crowned head right **Obv. Designer:** Ian Rank-Broadley
Rev: Queen Elizabeth II (1952-) **Edge:** Reeded

Date	Mintage	F	VF	XF	Unc	BU
2002 Proof	10,000	Value: 65.00				

KM# 49a   10 DOLLARS
39.9400 g., 0.9166 Gold 1.1770 oz. AGW, 38.6 mm.
Ruler: Elizabeth II **Subject:** Golden Jubilee Monarchs
Obv: Crowned head right **Obv. Designer:** Ian Rank-Broadley
Rev: Queen Elizabeth II (1952-) **Edge:** Reeded

Date	Mintage	F	VF	XF	Unc	BU
2002 Proof	100	Value: 1,500				

KM# 59   10 DOLLARS
Silver partially gilt, 39 mm. **Ruler:** Elizabeth II **Obv:** Head right, partially gilt **Rev:** Fireworks display above building

Date	Mintage	F	VF	XF	Unc	BU
2002 Proof	—	Value: 40.00				

EAST TIMOR

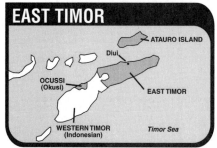

East Timor, population: 522,433, area: 7332 sq. miles, capital: Dili, is primarily located on the eastern half of the island of Timor, just northwest of Australia at the eastern end of the Indonesian archipelago. Formerly a Portuguese colony, Timor declared its independence from Portugal on November 28, 1975. After nine short days of fledgling autonomy, a guerilla faction sympathetic to the Indonesian territorial claim to East Timor seized the government. On July 17, 1976 the Provisional government enacted a law, which dissolved the free republic and made East Timor the 24th province of Indonesia. Violent rule and civil unrest plagued the province, with great loss of life and extreme damage to property and natural resources until independence was again achieved with United Nations assistance during a period from 1999 to 2002. Emerging as the Democratic Republic of Timor-Leste and commonly known as East Timor the country has worked, with international assistance to rebuild its decimated infrastructure. Natural resources waiting to be tapped include rich oil reserves, though current exports are most dependent on coffee, sandalwood and marble. The first coins of the new republic were issued in 2003.

DEMOCRATIC REPUBLIC OF TIMOR-LESTE

DECIMAL COINAGE

KM# 1   CENTAVO
3.1000 g., Nickel Clad Steel, 17 mm. **Obv:** Nautilus above date **Rev:** Denomination within circle **Edge:** Plain **Designer:** Jose Bandeira

Date	Mintage	F	VF	XF	Unc	BU
2003	1,500,000	—	—	—	1.50	2.50
2003 Proof	12,500	Value: 7.00				
2004	1,500,000	—	—	—	1.50	2.50

KM# 2   5 CENTAVOS
4.0500 g., Nickel Clad Steel, 18.8 mm. **Obv:** Rice plant above date **Rev:** Denomination within circle **Edge:** Plain **Designer:** Jose Bandeira

Date	Mintage	F	VF	XF	Unc	BU
2003	1,500,000	—	—	—	2.00	3.00
2003 Proof	12,500	Value: 9.00				
2004	1,500,000	—	—	—	2.00	3.00

KM# 3   10 CENTAVOS
5.1100 g., Nickel Clad Steel, 20.8 mm. **Obv:** Rooster left above date **Rev:** Denomination within circle **Edge:** Plain **Designer:** Jose Bandeira

Date	Mintage	F	VF	XF	Unc	BU
2003	2,500,000	—	—	—	2.50	4.00
2003 Proof	12,500	Value: 12.00				
2004	2,500,000	—	—	—	2.50	4.00

KM# 4   25 CENTAVOS
5.8700 g., Copper-Zinc-Nickel, 21.3 mm. **Obv:** Sail boat above date **Rev:** Denomination within circle **Edge:** Reeded **Designer:** Jose Bandeira

Date	Mintage	F	VF	XF	Unc	BU
2003	1,500,000	—	—	—	3.50	5.00
2003 Proof	12,500	Value: 15.00				
2004	1,500,000	—	—	—	3.50	5.00

KM# 5   50 CENTAVOS
6.5000 g., Copper-Zinc-Nickel, 25 mm. **Obv:** Coffee plant with beans above date **Rev:** Denomination within circle **Edge:** Reeded **Designer:** Jose Bandeira

Date	Mintage	F	VF	XF	Unc	BU
2003	1,000,000	—	—	—	5.00	7.00
2003 Proof	12,500	Value: 20.00				
2004	1,000,000	—	—	—	5.00	7.00

MINT SETS

KM#	Date	Mintage	Identification	Issue Price	Mkt Val
MS1	2003 (5)	25,000	KM#1-5	27.84	35.00

PROOF SETS

KM#	Date	Mintage	Identification	Issue Price	Mkt Val
PS1	2003 (5)	12,500	KM#1-5	57.25	65.00

ECUADOR

The Republic of Ecuador, located astride the equator on the Pacific Coast of South America, has an area of 105,037 sq. mi. (283,560 sq. km.) and a population of 10.9 million. Capital: Quito. Agriculture is the mainstay of the economy but there are appreciable deposits of minerals and petroleum. It is one of the world's largest exporters of bananas and balsa wood. Coffee, cacao, sugar and petroleum are also valuable exports.

REPUBLIC

REFORM COINAGE
100 Centavos = 1 Dollar

KM# 104   CENTAVO (Un)
2.5200 g., Brass, 19 mm. **Obv:** Map of the Americas within circle **Rev:** Denomination **Edge:** Plain

Date	Mintage	F	VF	XF	Unc	BU
2003	—	—	—	—	0.20	0.40
2004	—	—	—	—	0.20	0.40

KM# 104a   CENTAVO (Un)
2.4200 g., Copper Plated Steel, 19 mm. **Obv:** Map of the Americas **Rev:** Denomination **Edge:** Plain

Date	Mintage	F	VF	XF	Unc	BU
2003	—	—	—	—	0.30	0.50

KM# 115   SUCRE (Un)
8.3600 g., 0.9000 Gold 0.2419 oz. AGW, 22 mm.
Subject: Homage to Jefferson Pérez Quezada **Obv:** National arms **Obv. Legend:** BANCO CENTRAL DEL ECUADOR **Rev:** 3/4 length figure of Perez running **Rev. Legend:** BICAMPEON MUNDIAL - CAMPEON OLIMPICO ATLANTA 1996

Date	Mintage	F	VF	XF	Unc	BU
2006	—	Value: 380				

KM# 112   25000 SUCRES
27.1000 g., 0.9250 Silver 0.8059 oz. ASW, 40 mm.
Subject: IBERO-AMERICA Series **Obv:** Coats of arms **Rev:** Balsawood sailing raft **Edge:** Reeded

Date	Mintage	F	VF	XF	Unc	BU
2002 Proof	—	Value: 60.00				

KM# 113   25000 SUCRES
27.0000 g., 0.9250 Silver 0.8029 oz. ASW, 40 mm.
Obv: National arms **Rev:** Capital building in Quito **Edge:** Reeded

Date	Mintage	F	VF	XF	Unc	BU
2004 Proof	1,000	Value: 50.00				

KM# 114   25000 SUCRES
27.2000 g., 0.9250 Silver 0.8089 oz. ASW, 40 mm.
Subject: 2006 World Cup Soccer **Obv:** National arms **Rev:** Ecuadorian Soccer player torso holding a soccer ball **Edge:** Reeded

Date	Mintage	F	VF	XF	Unc	BU
ND(2006) Proof	—	Value: 40.00				

EGYPT

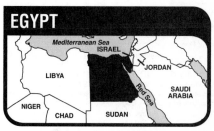

The Arab Republic of Egypt, located on the northeastern corner of Africa, has an area of 385,229 sq. mi. (1,1001,450 sq. km.) and a population of 62.4 million. Capital: Cairo. Although Egypt is an almost rainless expanse of desert, its economy is predominantly agricultural. Cotton, rice and petroleum are exported. Other main sources of income are revenues from the Suez Canal, remittances of Egyptian workers abroad and tourism.

ARAB REPUBLIC
AH1391- / 1971- AD

DECIMAL COINAGE

KM# 941   5 PIASTRES
1.9500 g., Brass, 18 mm. **Obv:** Denomination divides dates below, legend above **Rev:** Antique pottery vase **Edge:** Plain

Date	Mintage	F	VF	XF	Unc	BU
AH1425-2004	—	—	—	—	1.50	—

KM# 922   10 PIASTRES
4.5200 g., Copper-Nickel, 24.8 mm. **Subject:** National Women's Council **Obv:** Value **Rev:** Woman standing next to Sphinx **Edge:** Reeded

Date	Mintage	F	VF	XF	Unc	BU
AH1425-2004	—	—	—	—	1.50	—

KM# 990   10 PIASTRES
3.4100 g., Nickel Plated Steel, 19.03 mm.   **Obv:** Text, date and value **Rev:** Mosque

Date	Mintage	F	VF	XF	Unc	BU
AH1429 (2008)	—					1.50

KM# 923   20 PIASTRES
6.0000 g., Copper-Nickel, 26.8 mm.   **Subject:** National Women's Council **Obv:** Value **Rev:** Woman standing next to Sphinx **Edge:** Reeded

Date	Mintage	F	VF	XF	Unc	BU
AH1425-2004	—	—	—	—	2.50	

KM# 942.1   50 PIASTRES
6.5000 g., Brass, 25 mm.   **Obv:** Value **Rev:** Bust of Cleopatra left **Edge:** Reeded **Note:** Non-magnetic.

Date	Mintage	F	VF	XF	Unc	BU
AH1426-2005	—	—	—	1.20	3.00	4.00

KM# 942.2   50 PIASTRES
6.5000 g., Brass Plated Steel, 23 mm.   **Rev:** Bust of Cleopatra left **Edge:** Reeded **Note:** Magnetic

Date	Mintage	F	VF	XF	Unc	BU
AH1428-2007	—	—	—	—	—	1.50

KM# 903   1/2 POUND
4.0000 g., 0.8750 Gold 0.1125 oz. AGW, 18 mm.   **Subject:** Egyptian Museum Centennial **Obv:** Value **Rev:** Building **Edge:** Reeded

Date	Mintage	F	VF	XF	Unc	BU
AH1423-2002	—	—	—	—	250	—

KM# 930   POUND
15.0000 g., 0.7200 Silver 0.3472 oz. ASW, 35 mm.   **Subject:** National Women's Council **Obv:** Value **Rev:** Woman standing next to Sphinx **Edge:** Reeded

Date	Mintage	F	VF	XF	Unc	BU
AH1421-2001	600	—	—	—	45.00	

KM# 936   POUND
8.0000 g., 0.8750 Gold 0.2250 oz. AGW, 24 mm.   **Subject:** 50th Anniversary of Egyptian Revolution **Obv:** Value **Rev:** Soldier with flag, pyramids and radiant sun **Edge:** Reeded

Date	Mintage	F	VF	XF	Unc	BU
AH1423-2002	400	—	—	—	—	400

KM# 938   POUND
8.0000 g., 0.8750 Gold 0.2250 oz. AGW, 24 mm.   **Subject:** Alexandria Library **Obv:** Cufic text in center **Rev:** Arched inscription above slanted library roof **Edge:** Reeded

Date	Mintage	F	VF	XF	Unc	BU
AH1423-2002	750	—	—	—	—	400

KM# 904   POUND
15.0000 g., 0.7200 Silver 0.3472 oz. ASW, 35 mm.   **Subject:** Egyptian Museum Centennial **Obv:** Value **Rev:** Building, centennial numerals in background **Edge:** Reeded

Date	Mintage	F	VF	XF	Unc	BU
AH1423-2002	1,500	—	—	—	35.00	40.00

KM# 905   POUND
8.0000 g., 0.8750 Gold 0.2250 oz. AGW, 24 mm.   **Subject:** Egyptian Museum Centennial **Obv:** Value **Rev:** Building, centennial numerals in background **Edge:** Reeded

Date	Mintage	F	VF	XF	Unc	BU
AH1423-2002	300	—	—	—	—	400

KM# 909   POUND
15.0000 g., 0.7200 Silver 0.3472 oz. ASW, 35 mm.   **Subject:** International Ear, Nose and Throat Conference **Obv:** King Tut's Gold Mask **Rev:** "IFOS" on world map **Edge:** Reeded

Date	Mintage	F	VF	XF	Unc	BU
AH1423-2002	2,500	—	—	—	30.00	35.00

KM# 910   POUND
15.0000 g., 0.7200 Silver 0.3472 oz. ASW, 35 mm.   **Subject:** 50th Anniversary of Egyptian Revolution **Obv:** Value **Rev:** Soldier with flag **Edge:** Reeded

Date	Mintage	F	VF	XF	Unc	BU
AH1423-2002	1,500	—	—	—	35.00	40.00

KM# 912   POUND
15.0000 g., 0.7200 Silver 0.3472 oz. ASW, 35 mm.   **Subject:** Alexandria Library **Obv:** Legend and inscription **Rev:** Inscribed arches above library roof **Edge:** Reeded

Date	Mintage	F	VF	XF	Unc	BU
AH1423-2002	8,000	—	—	—	30.00	35.00

KM# 913   POUND
15.0000 g., 0.7200 Silver 0.3472 oz. ASW, 35 mm.   **Subject:** Body Building Championships **Obv:** Arabic and English legends **Rev:** Mr. Universe cartoon **Edge:** Reeded

Date	Mintage	F	VF	XF	Unc	BU
AH1423-2002	1,000	—	—	—	30.00	35.00

KM# 955   POUND
8.0000 g., 0.8750 Gold 0.2250 oz. AGW, 24 mm.   **Subject:** Golden Jubilee Ein Shams University **Obv:** Value **Rev:** Obelisk with bird standing at left and right **Edge:** Reeded

Date	Mintage	F	VF	XF	Unc	BU
AH1422-2002	400	—	—	—	350	—

KM# 956   POUND
8.0000 g., 0.8750 Gold 0.2250 oz. AGW, 24 mm.   **Subject:** Police Day **Obv:** Police eagle with wings spread, value **Rev:** Police badge **Edge:** Reeded

Date	Mintage	F	VF	XF	Unc	BU
AH1422-2002	400	—	—	—	350	—

KM# 957   POUND
8.0000 g., 0.8750 Gold 0.2250 oz. AGW, 24 mm.   **Subject:** 30th Anniversary October War Victory **Obv:** Value **Rev:** Soldier holding flag on top of pyramid **Edge:** Reeded

Date	Mintage	F	VF	XF	Unc	BU
AH1424-2003	200	—	—	—	375	—

KM# 958   POUND
8.0000 g., 0.8750 Gold 0.2250 oz. AGW, 24 mm.   **Series:** Value **Subject:** Radio and Television Festival **Obv:** Modern abstract design **Edge:** Reeded

Date	Mintage	F	VF	XF	Unc	BU
AH1424-2003	1,000	—	—	—	325	—

KM# 959   POUND
8.0000 g., 0.8750 Gold 0.2250 oz. AGW, 24 mm.   **Subject:** 50th Anniversary El Gomhoreya Newspaper - Hosni Mubarak **Obv:** Value **Rev:** Bust facing at left, building in background **Edge:** Reeded

Date	Mintage	F	VF	XF	Unc	BU
AH1424-2003	400	—	—	—	350	—

KM# 915   POUND
15.0000 g., 0.7200 Silver 0.3472 oz. ASW, 35 mm.   **Subject:** 30th Anniversary of the October War **Obv:** Value, dates and legend **Rev:** Soldier with flag above pyramids **Edge:** Reeded

Date	Mintage	F	VF	XF	Unc	BU
AH1424-2003	1,000	—	—	—	30.00	35.00

KM# 917   POUND
15.0000 g., 0.7200 Silver 0.3472 oz. ASW, 35 mm.   **Subject:** 25th Anniversary of the Commerce Society **Obv:** Value, dates and legend **Rev:** Radiant sun above lattice work **Edge:** Reeded

Date	Mintage	F	VF	XF	Unc	BU
AH1424-2003	1,200	—	—	—	30.00	35.00

KM# 924   POUND
15.0000 g., 0.7200 Silver 0.3472 oz. ASW, 35 mm.   **Subject:** 90th Anniversary Scouts **Obv:** Value **Rev:** Combined scouting badge **Edge:** Reeded

Date	Mintage	F	VF	XF	Unc	BU
AH1425-2004	2,000	—	—	—	30.00	35.00

KM# 960 POUND
8.0000 g., 0.8750 Gold 0.2250 oz. AGW, 24 mm.
Subject: Golden Jubilee Military Production **Obv:** Value
Rev: Ancient chariot, horse and rider left **Edge:** Reeded

Date	Mintage	F	VF	XF	Unc	BU
AH1425-2004	750	—	—	—	325	—

KM# 934 POUND
15.0000 g., 0.7250 Silver 0.3496 oz. ASW, 35 mm.
Subject: Golden Jubilee - Military Production **Obv:** Value
Rev: Ancient chariot, horse and rider **Edge:** Reeded

Date	Mintage	F	VF	XF	Unc	BU
AH1425-2004	1,000	—	—	—	30.00	35.00

KM# 940 POUND
8.5000 g., Bi-Metallic Brass center in Copper-Nickel ring,
25.1 mm. **Obv:** Value **Rev:** King Tutankhaman's gold mask
Edge: Reeded

Date	Mintage	F	VF	XF	Unc	BU
AH1426-2005	—	—	—	—	3.00	5.00
AH1428-2007	—	—	—	—	3.00	5.00

KM# 965 POUND
15.0000 g., 0.7200 Silver 0.3472 oz. ASW, 35 mm.
Subject: Golden Jubilee Suez Canal Nationalization **Obv:** Value
Rev: Large "50" above government buildings **Edge:** Reeded

Date	Mintage	F	VF	XF	Unc	BU
AH1427-2006	1,750	—	—	—	—	40.00

KM# 966 POUND
15.0000 g., 0.7200 Silver 0.3472 oz. ASW, 35 mm. **Subject:** 60th
Anniversary UNESCO **Obv:** Value **Rev:** Logo **Edge:** Reeded

Date	Mintage	F	VF	XF	Unc	BU
AH1427-2006	800	—	—	—	—	125

KM# 967 POUND
15.0000 g., 0.7200 Silver 0.3472 oz. ASW, 35 mm.
Subject: 13th General Population Census **Obv:** Value
Rev: Stylized couple leaning left at left **Edge:** Reeded

Date	Mintage	F	VF	XF	Unc	BU
AH1427-2006	2,000	—	—	—	—	50.00

KM# 961 POUND
8.0000 g., 0.8750 Gold 0.2250 oz. AGW, 24 mm.
Subject: World Environment Day **Obv:** Value **Rev:** Stylized tree,
emblem at left, bird standing at right **Edge:** Reeded

Date	Mintage	F	VF	XF	Unc	BU
AH1427-2006	200	—	—	—	375	—

KM# 962 POUND
8.0000 g., 0.8750 Gold 0.2250 oz. AGW, 24 mm.
Subject: Golden Jubilee Suez Canal Nationalization **Obv:** Value
Rev: Large "50" above government buildings **Edge:** Reeded

Date	Mintage	F	VF	XF	Unc	BU
AH1427-2006	1,000	—	—	—	325	—

KM# 963 POUND
8.0000 g., 0.8750 Gold 0.2250 oz. AGW, 24 mm. **Subject:** Silver
Jubilee Egyptian Enviromental Protection **Obv:** Value **Rev:** World
globe **Edge:** Reeded

Date	Mintage	F	VF	XF	Unc	BU
AH1428-2007	300	—	—	—	350	—

KM# 964 POUND
8.0000 g., 0.8750 Gold 0.2250 oz. AGW, 24 mm.
Subject: Diamond Jubilee Air Force **Obv:** Value **Rev:** Air Force
emblem **Edge:** Reeded

Date	Mintage	F	VF	XF	Unc	BU
AH1428-2007	130	—	—	—	500	—

KM# 968 POUND
15.0000 g., 0.7200 Silver 0.3472 oz. ASW, 35 mm.
Subject: 100th Anniversary Ahly Club **Obv:** Value **Rev:** Large
"100" with linked zeroes **Edge:** Reeded

Date	Mintage	F	VF	XF	Unc	BU
AH1428-2007	5,000	—	—	—	—	50.00

KM# 940a POUND
8.5000 g., Bi-Metallic Brass center in Nickel ring, 25.1 mm.
Obv: Value at center **Rev:** King Tutankhaman's gold mask
Note: Magnetic

Date	Mintage	F	VF	XF	Unc	BU
AH1428/2007	—	—	—	—	3.00	5.00

KM# 944 POUND
15.0000 g., 0.7200 Silver 0.3472 oz. ASW, 35.00 mm.
Subject: Air Force Diamond Jubilee **Obv:** Value **Rev:** Air Force
insignia **Edge:** Reeded

Date	Mintage	F	VF	XF	Unc	BU
AH1428-2007	—	—	—	—	—	50.00

KM# 931 5 POUNDS
17.5000 g., 0.7200 Silver 0.4051 oz. ASW, 37 mm.
Subject: National Women's Council **Obv:** Value **Rev:** Woman
standing next to Sphinx **Edge:** Reeded

Date	Mintage	F	VF	XF	Unc	BU
AH1421-2001	600	—	—	—	55.00	60.00

KM# 932 5 POUNDS
17.5000 g., 0.7200 Silver 0.4051 oz. ASW, 37 mm.
Subject: 50th Anniversary of the National Police **Obv:** Value and
police logo **Rev:** Ceremonial design **Edge:** Reeded

Date	Mintage	F	VF	XF	Unc	BU
AH1422-2002	750	—	—	—	45.00	50.00

KM# 906 5 POUNDS
17.5000 g., 0.7200 Silver 0.4051 oz. ASW, 37 mm.
Subject: Egyptian Museum Centennial **Obv:** Value
Rev: Building, centennial numerals in background **Edge:** Reeded

Date	Mintage	F	VF	XF	Unc	BU
AH1423-2002	1,500	—	—	—	40.00	45.00

KM# 907 5 POUNDS
26.0000 g., 0.8750 Gold 0.7314 oz. AGW, 33 mm.
Subject: Egyptian Museum Centennial **Obv:** Value
Rev: Building, centennial numerals in background **Edge:** Reeded

Date	Mintage	F	VF	XF	Unc	BU
AH1423-2002	250	—	—	—	950	1,000

KM# 911 5 POUNDS
17.5500 g., 0.9250 Silver 0.5219 oz. ASW, 37 mm.
Subject: 50th Anniversary of the Egyptian Revolution **Obv:** Value
Rev: Soldier with flag **Edge:** Reeded

Date	Mintage	F	VF	XF	Unc	BU
AH1423-2002	1,500	—	—	—	40.00	45.00

KM# 914 5 POUNDS
17.5000 g., 0.7200 Silver 0.4051 oz. ASW, 37 mm.
Subject: Body Building Championships **Obv:** Arabic and English
legends **Rev:** Mr. Universe cartoon **Edge:** Reeded

Date	Mintage	F	VF	XF	Unc	BU
AH1423-2002	800	—	—	—	35.00	40.00

KM# 916 5 POUNDS
17.5000 g., 0.7200 Silver 0.4051 oz. ASW, 37 mm.
Subject: 30th Anniversary of the October War **Obv:** Value and
legend **Rev:** Soldier with flag above pyramids **Edge:** Reeded

Date	Mintage	F	VF	XF	Unc	BU
AH1424-2003	800	—	—	—	35.00	40.00

KM# 918 5 POUNDS
17.5000 g., 0.7200 Silver 0.4051 oz. ASW, 37 mm. **Obv:** Value
and legend **Rev:** Geo-Physical Institute **Edge:** Reeded

Date	Mintage	F	VF	XF	Unc	BU
AH1424-2003	800	—	—	—	35.00	40.00

KM# 919 5 POUNDS
17.5000 g., 0.7200 Silver 0.4051 oz. ASW, 37 mm.
Subject: 50th Anniversary of the Republic **Obv:** Value and
legend **Rev:** Portrait and building **Edge:** Reeded

Date	Mintage	F	VF	XF	Unc	BU
AH1424-2003	3,000	—	—	—	35.00	40.00

KM# 920 5 POUNDS
17.5000 g., 0.7200 Silver 0.4051 oz. ASW, 37 mm.
Subject: 25th Anniversary of the Delta Bank **Obv:** Value and
legend **Rev:** Delta on world globe **Edge:** Reeded

Date	Mintage	F	VF	XF	Unc	BU
AH1424-2004	1,500	—	—	—	35.00	40.00

KM# 925 5 POUNDS
17.5000 g., 0.7200 Silver 0.4051 oz. ASW, 37 mm. **Obv:** Value
Rev: Balance scale **Edge:** Reeded

Date	Mintage	F	VF	XF	Unc	BU
AH1425-2004	3,300	—	—	—	35.00	40.00

KM# 974 5 POUNDS
17.5000 g., 0.7200 Silver 0.4051 oz. ASW, 37 mm.
Subject: Golden Jubilee Cairo Mint **Obv:** Value **Rev:** National
arms above mint building **Edge:** Reeded

Date	Mintage	F	VF	XF	Unc	BU
AH1425-2004	1,750	—	—	—	—	50.00

KM# 933 5 POUNDS
17.5000 g., 0.7200 Silver 0.4051 oz. ASW, 37 mm. **Subject:** 90th Anniversary - Egyptian Scouts Organization - 1914-2004 **Obv:** Value **Rev:** Combined scouting emblem **Edge:** Reeded

Date	Mintage	F	VF	XF	Unc	BU
AH1425-2004	—	—	—	—	35.00	40.00

KM# 935 5 POUNDS
17.5000 g., 0.7200 Silver 0.4051 oz. ASW, 37 mm. **Subject:** Golden Jubilee - Military Production **Obv:** Value **Rev:** Ancient chariot, horse and rider left **Edge:** Reeded

Date	Mintage	F	VF	XF	Unc	BU
AH1425-2004	800	—	—	—	35.00	40.00

KM# 975 5 POUNDS
17.5000 g., 0.7200 Silver 0.4051 oz. ASW, 37 mm. **Subject:** 60th Anniversary Arab League **Obv:** Value **Rev:** Logo in center of ornate background **Edge:** Reeded

Date	Mintage	F	VF	XF	Unc	BU
AH1426-2005	2,000	—	—	—	—	60.00

KM# 976 5 POUNDS
17.5000 g., 0.7200 Silver 0.4051 oz. ASW **Subject:** World Environment Day **Obv:** Value **Rev:** Stylized tree with logo at left, bird at right **Edge:** Reeded **Shape:** 37

Date	Mintage	F	VF	XF	Unc	BU
AH1427-2006	1,000	—	—	—	—	80.00

KM# 977 5 POUNDS
17.5000 g., 0.7200 Silver 0.4051 oz. ASW, 35 mm. **Subject:** Golden jubilee Suez Canal Nationalization **Obv:** Value **Rev:** Large "50" above government buildings **Edge:** Reeded

Date	Mintage	F	VF	XF	Unc	BU
AH1427-2006	1,750	—	—	—	—	50.00

KM# 978 5 POUNDS
17.5000 g., 0.7200 Silver 0.4051 oz. ASW, 37 mm. **Subject:** 60th Anniversary UNESCO **Obv:** Value **Rev:** Logo **Edge:** Reeded

Date	Mintage	F	VF	XF	Unc	BU
AH1427-2006	800	—	—	—	—	125

KM# 979 5 POUNDS
17.5000 g., 0.7200 Silver 0.4051 oz. ASW, 37 mm. **Subject:** Diamond Jubilee Academy of Arab Language **Obv:** Value **Rev:** Globe on open book **Edge:** Reeded

Date	Mintage	F	VF	XF	Unc	BU
AH1427-2006	1,000	—	—	—	—	80.00

KM# 980 5 POUNDS
17.5000 g., 0.7200 Silver 0.4051 oz. ASW, 37 mm. **Subject:** 13th General Population Census **Obv:** Circle with inscription in center **Rev:** Stylized couple leaning left at left **Edge:** Reeded

Date	Mintage	F	VF	XF	Unc	BU
AH1427-2006	1,500	—	—	—	—	75.00

KM# 981 5 POUNDS
17.5000 g., 0.7200 Silver 0.4051 oz. ASW, 37 mm. **Subject:** 100th Anniversary Ahly Club **Obv:** Value **Rev:** Large "100" With linked zeroes **Edge:** Reeded

Date	Mintage	F	VF	XF	Unc	BU
AH1428-2007	3,000	—	—	—	—	50.00

KM# 982 5 POUNDS
17.5000 g., 0.7200 Silver 0.4051 oz. ASW, 37 mm. **Subject:** Diamond Jubilee Court of Cassation **Obv:** Balance scale above inscriptions **Rev:** Court building **Edge:** Reeded

Date	Mintage	F	VF	XF	Unc	BU
AH1428-2007	450	—	—	—	—	150

KM# 983 5 POUNDS
17.5000 g., 0.7200 Silver 0.4051 oz. ASW, 37 mm. **Subject:** Silver Jubilee Enviromental Protection Agency **Obv:** Value **Rev:** World globe **Edge:** Reeded

Date	Mintage	F	VF	XF	Unc	BU
AH1428-2007	1,300	—	—	—	—	60.00

KM# 984 5 POUNDS
17.5000 g., 0.7200 Silver 0.4051 oz. ASW, 37 mm. **Subject:** 11th Arab Sports Championship - Egypt **Obv:** Value **Rev:** Stylized player on map of Arab countries **Edge:** Reeded

Date	Mintage	F	VF	XF	Unc	BU
AH1428-2007	6,300	—	—	—	—	50.00

KM# 943 5 POUNDS
17.5000 g., 0.7200 Silver 0.4051 oz. ASW, 37 mm. **Subject:** 11th Pan-Arab Games **Obv:** Value **Rev:** Logo with outlined map of Arab nations in background **Edge:** Reeded

Date	Mintage	F	VF	XF	Unc	BU
AH1428-2007	6,300	—	—	—	—	35.00

KM# 945 5 POUNDS
17.5000 g., 0.7200 Silver 0.4051 oz. ASW, 37 mm. **Subject:** Air Force Diamond Jubilee **Obv:** Value **Rev:** Air Force insignia **Edge:** Reeded

Date	Mintage	F	VF	XF	Unc	BU
AH1428-2007	600	—	—	—	—	60.00

KM# 908 10 POUNDS
40.0000 g., 0.8750 Gold 1.1252 oz. AGW, 37 mm. **Subject:** Egyptian Museum Centennial **Obv:** Denomination **Rev:** Building, centennial numerals in background **Edge:** Reeded

Date	Mintage	F	VF	XF	Unc	BU
AH1423-2002	150	—	—	—	1,450	—

KM# 989 10 POUNDS
40.0000 g., 0.8750 Gold 1.1252 oz. AGW, 37 mm. **Subject:** Golden Jubilee Police Day **Obv:** Eagle left with wings spread **Rev:** Police emblem **Edge:** Reeded

Date	Mintage	F	VF	XF	Unc	BU
AH1422-2002	150	—	—	—	1,450	—

KM# 985 10 POUNDS
40.0000 g., 0.8750 Gold 1.1252 oz. AGW, 37 mm. **Subject:** 50th Anniversary El Gomhoreya News **Obv:** Value **Rev:** Bust of Hosni Mubarak facing at left, building in background **Edge:** Reeded

Date	Mintage	F	VF	XF	Unc	BU
AH1424-2003	50	—	—	—	1,600	—

KM# 986 10 POUNDS
40.0000 g., 0.8750 Gold 1.1252 oz. AGW, 37 mm. **Subject:** Golden Jubilee Military Production **Obv:** Value **Rev:** Ancient chariot, horse and rider left **Edge:** Reeded

Date	Mintage	F	VF	XF	Unc	BU
AH1425-2004	85	—	—	—	1,550	—

KM# 987 10 POUNDS
40.0000 g., 0.8750 Gold 1.1252 oz. AGW, 37 mm. **Subject:** 60th Anniversary Arab League **Obv:** Value **Rev:** Emblem at center, ornate background **Edge:** Reeded

Date	Mintage	F	VF	XF	Unc	BU
AH1426-2005	50	—	—	—	1,600	—

KM# 988 10 POUNDS
40.0000 g., 0.8750 Gold 1.1252 oz. AGW, 37 mm. **Subject:** Diamond Jubilee Air Force **Obv:** Value **Rev:** Air Force emblem **Edge:** Reeded

Date	Mintage	F	VF	XF	Unc	BU
AH1428-2007	25	—	—	—	1,800	—

ESTONIA

The Republic of Estonia (formerly the Estonian Soviet Socialist Republic of the U.S.S.R.) is the northernmost of the three Baltic States in Eastern Europe. It has an area of 17,462 sq. mi. (45,100 sq. km.) and a population of 1.6 million. Capital: Tallinn. Agriculture and dairy farming are the principal industries. Butter, eggs, bacon, timber and petroleum are exported.

MODERN REPUBLIC
1991 - present
STANDARD COINAGE

KM# 22 10 SENTI
1.8500 g., Copper-Aluminum-Nickel, 17.1 mm. **Obv:** National arms **Rev:** Denomination **Rev. Legend:** EESTI VABARIIK **Edge:** Plain

Date	Mintage	F	VF	XF	Unc	BU
2002	—	—	—	0.20	0.50	0.75
2006	—	—	—	0.20	0.50	0.75
2008	—	—	—	0.20	0.50	0.75

KM# 23a 20 SENTI
2.0000 g., Nickel Plated Steel, 18.9 mm. **Obv:** National arms **Rev:** Denomination **Rev. Legend:** EESTI VABARIIK **Edge:** Plain

Date	Mintage	F	VF	XF	Unc	BU
2003	—	—	—	0.30	0.75	1.00
2004	—	—	—	0.30	0.75	1.00
2006	—	—	—	0.30	0.75	1.00

KM# 24 50 SENTI
2.9000 g., Brass, 19.5 mm. **Obv:** National arms **Rev:** Denomination **Rev. Legend:** EESTI VABARIIK **Edge:** Plain

Date	Mintage	F	VF	XF	Unc	BU
2004	—	—	—	0.40	1.00	1.35
2006	—	—	—	0.40	1.00	1.35
2007	—	—	—	0.40	1.00	1.35

KM# 35 KROON
5.0000 g., Brass, 23.5 mm. **Obv:** National arms **Rev:** Large, thick denomination **Rev. Legend:** EESTI VABARIIK **Edge:** Segmented reeding

Date	Mintage	F	VF	XF	Unc	BU
2001	—	—	—	0.50	1.25	1.75
2003	—	—	—	0.50	1.25	1.75
2006	—	—	—	0.50	1.25	1.75

KM# 44 KROON
4.8000 g., Brass, 23.21 mm. **Obv:** National arms **Rev:** Stylized plant in circle **Rev. Legend:** EESTI VABARIIK **Edge:** Segmented reeding

Date	Mintage	F	VF	XF	Unc	BU
2008	—	—	—	0.50	1.25	1.75

KM# 38 10 KROONI
28.2800 g., 0.9990 Silver 0.9083 oz. ASW, 38.6 mm. **Subject:** Tartu University **Obv:** National arms **Rev:** Building in oval, value at left **Edge:** Reeded

Date	Mintage	F	VF	XF	Unc	BU
2002 Proof	10,000	Value: 28.00				

KM# 40 10 KROONI
28.2800 g., 0.9990 Silver 0.9083 oz. ASW, 38.6 mm. **Subject:** Estonian Flag **Obv:** National arms **Rev:** Round multicolor flag design **Edge:** Reeded

Date	Mintage	F	VF	XF	Unc	BU
2004 Proof	10,000	Value: 28.00				

KM# 42 10 KROONI
28.2800 g., 0.9990 Silver 0.9083 oz. ASW, 38.6 mm. **Subject:** Torino Winter Olympics **Obv:** National arms **Rev:** Gold inset cross country skier in semi-circle above Olympic flame **Edge:** Reeded

Date	Mintage	F	VF	XF	Unc	BU
2006 Proof	5,000	Value: 42.50				

KM# 46 10 KROONI
28.2800 g., 0.9990 Silver 0.9083 oz. ASW, 38.61 mm.
Subject: 90th Anniversary of Independence **Obv:** National arms
Obv. Legend: EESTI VARBARIIK **Rev:** Wiiralt oak tree
Edge: Plain **Designer:** Heino Prunsvelt

Date	Mintage	F	VF	XF	Unc	BU
2008 Proof	10,000	Value: 48.00				

KM# 48 10 KROONI
28.2800 g., 0.9990 Silver 0.9083 oz. ASW, 38.61 mm.
Subject: Olympics **Obv:** Arms **Rev:** Torch and geometric patterns

Date	Mintage	F	VF	XF	Unc	BU
2008 Proof	—	Value: 40.00				

KM# 49 10 KROONI
24.1000 g., 0.9990 Silver 0.7740 oz. ASW, 38.61 mm.
Subject: National Museum **Obv:** Shield in star **Rev:** Design in star

Date	Mintage	F	VF	XF	Unc	BU
2008 Proof	—	Value: 40.00				

KM# 51 10 KROONI
31.1050 g., 0.9990 Silver 0.9990 oz. ASW, 40.6 mm.
Subject: Song and Dance Festival

Date	Mintage	F	VF	XF	Unc	BU
2009 Proof	—	Value: 40.00				

KM# 50 50 KROONI
8.6400 g., 0.9990 Gold 0.2775 oz. AGW, 22 mm. **Obv:** Shield **Rev:** Windmill

Date	Mintage	F	VF	XF	Unc	BU
2008 Proof	—	Value: 400				

KM# 39 100 KROONI
7.7760 g., 0.9999 Gold 0.2500 oz. AGW **Subject:** Monetary Reform **Obv:** National arms **Rev:** Cross design **Edge:** Reeded

Date	Mintage	F	VF	XF	Unc	BU
2002	2,000	—	—	—	—	350

KM# 41 100 KROONI
7.7760 g., 0.9999 Gold 0.2500 oz. AGW, 21.9 mm.
Subject: Olympic Games **Obv:** National arms **Rev:** Olympic flame above rings in center **Edge:** Reeded

Date	Mintage	F	VF	XF	Unc	BU
2004	5,000	—	—	—	—	325

KM# 43 100 KROONI
28.2800 g., 0.9990 Silver 0.9083 oz. ASW, 38.6 mm.
Subject: National Opera **Obv:** National arms **Rev:** Building front
Edge: Plain

Date	Mintage	F	VF	XF	Unc	BU
2006 Proof	10,000	Value: 42.50				

KM# 45 100 KROONI
7.7800 g., 0.9999 Gold 0.2501 oz. AGW **Subject:** 15th Anniversary Reintroduction of the Estonian Kroon **Obv:** National arms **Obv. Legend:** EESTI VARBARIIK **Rev:** Cornflower **Rev. Legend:** KROONI TAAS- / KEHTESTAMISE / 15. AASTAPAEV
Edge: Plain **Shape:** Triangular **Designer:** Ivar Sakk

Date	Mintage	F	VF	XF	Unc	BU
2007 Prooflike	6,000	—	—	—	—	475

KM# 47 100 KROONI
7.7750 g., 0.9990 Platinum 0.2497 oz. APW, 18 mm.
Subject: 90th Anniversary of Republic **Rev:** Three buds on wire

Date	Mintage	F	VF	XF	Unc	BU
2008 Proof	3,000	Value: 600				

KM# 52 100 KROONI
7.7800 g., 0.9990 Gold 0.2499 oz. AGW, 22 mm. **Subject:** Song and dance festival **Obv:** Arms

Date	Mintage	F	VF	XF	Unc	BU
2009 Proof	—	Value: 350				

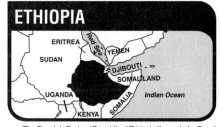

ETHIOPIA

The People's Federal Republic of Ethiopia (formerly the Peoples Democratic Republic and the Empire of Ethiopia), Africa's oldest independent nation, faces the Red Sea in East-Central Africa. The country has an area of 424,214 sq. mi. (1,004,390 sq. km.) and a population of 56 million people who are divided among 40 tribes that speak some 270 languages and dialects. Capital: Addis Ababa. The economy is predominantly agricultural and pastoral. Gold and platinum are mined and petroleum fields are being developed. Coffee, oilseeds, hides and cereals are exported.

DATING

Ethiopian coinage is dated by the Ethiopian Era calendar (E.E.), which commenced 7 years and 8 months after the advent of A.D. dating.

EXAMPLE
1900   (10 and 9 = 19 x 100)
  36   (Add 30 and 6)
1936 E.E.
    8   (Add)
1943/4 AD

PEOPLES DEMOCRATIC REPUBLIC
DECIMAL COINAGE

100 Santeems (Cents) = 1 Birr (Dollar)

100 Matonas = 100 Santeems

KM# 44.3 5 CENTS
3.0000 g., Copper-Zinc, 20 mm. **Obv:** Large lion head, right **Rev:** Denomination left of figure **Designer:** Stuart Devlin

Date	Mintage	F	VF	XF	Unc	BU
EE1996(2004)	—	—	—	—	—	1.00

KM# 45.3 10 CENTS
4.5000 g., Copper-Zinc, 23 mm. **Obv:** Large lion head right **Rev:** Mountain Nyala, denomination at right **Designer:** Stuart Devlin

Date	Mintage	F	VF	XF	Unc	BU
EE1996 (2004)	—	—	—	—	—	1.25
	—	—	—	—	—	1.25

KM# 46.3 25 CENTS
3.7000 g., Copper-Nickel, 21.45 mm. **Obv:** Large lion head right **Rev:** Man and woman with arms raised divide denomination **Designer:** Stuart Devlin

Date	Mintage	F	VF	XF	Unc	BU
EE1996 (2004)	—	—	—	—	—	1.25

FALKLAND ISLANDS

The Colony of the Falkland Islands and Dependencies, a British colony located in the South Atlantic about 500 miles northeast of Cape Horn, has an area of 4,700 sq. mi. (12,170 sq. km.) and a population of 2,121. East Falkland, West Falkland, South Georgia, and South Sandwich are the largest of the 200 islands. Capital: Stanley. Sheep grazing is the main industry. Wool, whale oil, and seal oil are exported.

RULER
British

MONETARY SYSTEM
100 Pence = 1 Pound

BRITISH COLONY
DECIMAL COINAGE

KM# 130 PENNY
Bronze Plated Steel **Ruler:** Elizabeth II **Obv:** Head with tiara right **Obv. Legend:** QUEEN ELIZABETH THE SECOND **Rev:** Two Gentoo penguins flank value **Rev. Legend:** FALKLAND ISLANDS **Edge:** Plain

Date	Mintage	F	VF	XF	Unc	BU
2004	—	—	—	—	0.50	0.75

KM# 131 2 PENCE
Bronze Plated Steel **Ruler:** Elizabeth II **Obv:** Head with tiara right **Obv. Legend:** QUEEN ELIZABETH THE SECOND **Rev:** Upland goose alighting, value above **Rev. Legend:** FALKLAND ISLANDS **Edge:** Plain

Date	Mintage	F	VF	XF	Unc	BU
2004	—	—	—	—	0.50	1.00

KM# 132   5 PENCE
Copper-Nickel   **Ruler:** Elizabeth II **Obv:** Head with tiara right
Obv. Legend: QUEEN ELIZABETH THE SECOND **Rev:** Black-browed Albatross in flight, value below **Rev. Legend:** FALKLAND
- ISLANDS **Edge:** Reeded

Date	Mintage	F	VF	XF	Unc	BU
2004	—	—	—	—	0.75	1.00

KM# 133   10 PENCE
Copper-Nickel   **Ruler:** Elizabeth II **Obv:** Head with tiara right
Obv. Legend: QUEEN ELIZABETH THE SECOND **Rev:** Ursine
seal with cub, value below **Rev. Legend:** FALKLAND ISLANDS

Date	Mintage	F	VF	XF	Unc	BU
2004	—	—	—	—	1.50	3.00

KM# 134   20 PENCE
Copper-Nickel   **Ruler:** Elizabeth II **Obv:** Head with tiara right
Obv. Legend: QUEEN ELIZABETH THE SECOND
Rev: Romney marsh sheep standing left, value above
Rev. Legend: FALKLAND ISLANDS **Rev. Designer:** Robert
Elderton **Edge:** Plain **Shape:** 7-sided

Date	Mintage	F	VF	XF	Unc	BU
2004	—	—	—	—	2.00	4.00

KM# 70   50 PENCE
29.1000 g., Copper-Nickel, 38.6 mm.   **Ruler:** Elizabeth II
Subject: Centennial of Queen Victoria's Death **Obv:** Crowned
bust right, denomination below **Obv. Designer:** Raphael Maklouf
Rev: Crowned head left, three dates **Edge:** Reeded

Date	Mintage	F	VF	XF	Unc	BU
2001	—	—	—	—	6.00	7.00

KM# 70a   50 PENCE
28.2800 g., 0.9250 Silver 0.8410 oz. ASW, 38.6 mm.
Ruler: Elizabeth II **Obv:** Crowned bust right, denomination below
Rev: Crowned head left, three dates **Edge:** Reeded

Date	Mintage	F	VF	XF	Unc	BU
2001 Proof	10,000	Value: 50.00				

KM# 70b   50 PENCE
47.5400 g., 0.9166 Gold 1.4009 oz. AGW, 38.6 mm.
Ruler: Elizabeth II **Subject:** Centennial of Queen Victoria's
Death **Obv:** Crowned bust right, denomination below
Rev: Victoria's crowned bust left, three dates **Edge:** Reeded

Date	Mintage	F	VF	XF	Unc	BU
2001 Proof	100	Value: 1,750				

KM# 71   50 PENCE
29.1000 g., Copper-Nickel, 38.6 mm.   **Ruler:** Elizabeth II
Subject: Queen Elizabeth's 75th Birthday **Obv:** Crowned bust
right, denomination below **Obv. Designer:** Raphael Maklouf
Rev: Bust of Queen Elizabeth II left **Edge:** Reeded

Date	Mintage	F	VF	XF	Unc	BU
2001	—	—	—	—	6.00	7.00

KM# 71b   50 PENCE
47.5400 g., 0.9160 Gold 1.4000 oz. AGW **Ruler:** Elizabeth II
Subject: Queen Elizabeth's 75th Birthday **Obv:** Crowned bust
right, denomination below **Rev:** Bust of Queen Elizabeth II left

Date	Mintage	F	VF	XF	Unc	BU
2001 Proof	Est. 100	Value: 1,750				

KM# 86   50 PENCE
28.2800 g., Copper-Nickel, 38.6 mm.   **Ruler:** Elizabeth II
Obv: Crowned bust right, denomination below **Rev:** Edward IV
(1461-83) with Rose Ryal gold coin design **Rev. Designer:**
Willem Vis **Edge:** Reeded

Date	Mintage	F	VF	XF	Unc	BU
2001	—	—	—	—	9.00	10.00

KM# 86a   50 PENCE
28.2800 g., 0.9250 Silver 0.8410 oz. ASW, 38.6 mm.
Ruler: Elizabeth II **Obv:** Crowned bust right, denomination below
Rev: Edward IV (1461-83) with gold-plated Rose Ryal gold coin
design **Edge:** Reeded

Date	Mintage	F	VF	XF	Unc	BU
2001 Proof	5,000	Value: 50.00				

KM# 87   50 PENCE
28.2800 g., Copper-Nickel, 38.6 mm.   **Ruler:** Elizabeth II
Obv: Crowned bust right, denomination below **Rev:** Henry VII
(1485-1509) with 1489 Gold Sovereign coin design
Rev. Designer: Willem Vis **Edge:** Reeded

Date	Mintage	F	VF	XF	Unc	BU
2001	—	—	—	—	9.00	10.00

KM# 87a   50 PENCE
28.2800 g., 0.9250 Silver 0.8410 oz. ASW, 38.6 mm.
Ruler: Elizabeth II **Obv:** Crowned bust right, denomination below
Rev: Henry VII (1485-1509) with gold-plated 1489 gold Sovereign
coin design **Edge:** Reeded

Date	Mintage	F	VF	XF	Unc	BU
2001 Proof	5,000	Value: 50.00				

KM# 88   50 PENCE
28.2800 g., Copper-Nickel, 38.6 mm.   **Ruler:** Elizabeth II
Obv: Crowned bust right, denomination below **Rev:** Charles II
(1660-85) with 1663 gold Guinea coin design
Rev. Designer: Willem Vis **Edge:** Reeded

Date	Mintage	F	VF	XF	Unc	BU
2001	—	—	—	—	9.00	10.00

KM# 88a   50 PENCE
28.2800 g., 0.9250 Silver 0.8410 oz. ASW, 38.6 mm.
Ruler: Elizabeth II **Obv:** Crowned bust right, denomination below
Rev: Charles II (1660-85) with gold-plated Gold Guinea coin
design **Edge:** Reeded

Date	Mintage	F	VF	XF	Unc	BU
2001 Proof	5,000	Value: 50.00				

KM# 89   50 PENCE
28.2800 g., Copper-Nickel, 38.6 mm.   **Ruler:** Elizabeth II
Obv: Crowned bust right, denomination below **Rev:** Queen
Victoria with Gold Sovereign coin design **Rev. Designer:** Willem
Vis **Edge:** Reeded

Date	Mintage	F	VF	XF	Unc	BU
2001	—	—	—	—	9.00	10.00

KM# 89a   50 PENCE
28.2800 g., 0.9250 Silver 0.8410 oz. ASW, 38.6 mm.
Ruler: Elizabeth II **Obv:** Crowned bust right, denomination below
Rev: Queen Victoria with gold-plated Gold Sovereign coin design
Edge: Reeded

Date	Mintage	F	VF	XF	Unc	BU
2001 Proof	5,000	Value: 50.00				

KM# 73.1   50 PENCE
28.1300 g., Copper-Nickel, 38.6 mm.   **Ruler:** Elizabeth II
Subject: Queen's Golden Jubilee **Obv:** Crowned head right,
denomination below **Rev:** Queen Elizabeth II on throne in inner
circle below multicolor bunting **Edge:** Reeded

Date	Mintage	F	VF	XF	Unc	BU
2002(2001) Proof	—	Value: 8.00				

KM# 73.2   50 PENCE
Copper-Nickel   **Ruler:** Elizabeth II **Subject:** Queen's Golden
Jubilee **Obv:** Crowned bust right, denomination below **Rev:** With
plain bunting

Date	Mintage	F	VF	XF	Unc	BU
2002	—	—	—	—	6.00	7.00

KM# 73a.1   50 PENCE
28.2800 g., 0.9250 Silver 0.8410 oz. ASW, 38.6 mm.
Ruler: Elizabeth II **Subject:** Queen's Golden Jubilee
Obv: Crowned bust right, denomination below **Rev:** Queen on
throne below multicolor bunting **Edge:** Reeded

Date	Mintage	F	VF	XF	Unc	BU
2002 Proof	25,000	Value: 45.00				

KM# 73a.2   50 PENCE
Silver **Ruler:** Elizabeth II **Obv:** Crowned bust right, denomination
below **Rev:** With plain bunting

Date	Mintage	F	VF	XF	Unc	BU
2002 Proof	—	Value: 45.00				

KM# 73b.1   50 PENCE
39.9400 g., 0.9166 Gold 1.1770 oz. AGW, 38.6 mm.
Ruler: Elizabeth II **Obv:** Crowned bust right, denomination below
Rev: Crowned queen with scepter and orb below multicolor
bunting **Edge:** Reeded

Date	Mintage	F	VF	XF	Unc	BU
2002 Proof	150	Value: 1,500				

KM# 74.1   50 PENCE
28.1300 g., Copper-Nickel, 38.6 mm.   **Ruler:** Elizabeth II
Subject: Queen's Golden Jubilee **Obv:** Crowned bust right,

denomination below **Obv. Designer:** Raphael Maklouf
Rev: Queen on horse half left in inner circle below multicolor
bunting **Edge:** Reeded

Date	Mintage	F	VF	XF	Unc	BU
2002(2001) Proof	—			—	Value: 8.00	

KM# 74.2 50 PENCE
Copper-Nickel **Ruler:** Elizabeth II **Subject:** Queen's Golden
Jubilee **Obv:** Crowned bust right, denomination below **Rev:** With
plain bunting

Date	Mintage	F	VF	XF	Unc	BU
2002	—	—	—	—	7.00	8.00

KM# 74a.1 50 PENCE
28.2800 g., 0.9250 Silver 0.8410 oz. ASW, 38.6 mm.
Ruler: Elizabeth II **Subject:** Queen's Golden Jubilee
Obv: Crowned bust right, denomination below **Rev. Designer:**
Queen on horse below multicolor bunting **Edge:** Reeded

Date	Mintage	F	VF	XF	Unc	BU
2002 Proof	25,000				Value: 45.00	

KM# 74a.2 50 PENCE
0.9250 Silver **Ruler:** Elizabeth II **Subject:** Queen's Golden
Jubilee **Obv:** Crowned bust right, denomination below **Rev:** With
plain bunting

Date	Mintage	F	VF	XF	Unc	BU
2002 Proof	—				Value: 45.00	

KM# 74b.1 50 PENCE
39.9400 g., 0.9166 Gold 1.1770 oz. AGW, 38.6 mm.
Ruler: Elizabeth II **Subject:** Queen's Golden Jubilee
Obv: Crowned bust right, denomination below **Rev:** Queen on
horseback below multicolored bunting **Edge:** Reeded

Date	Mintage	F	VF	XF	Unc	BU
2002 Proof	150				Value: 1,500	

KM# 74b.2 50 PENCE
Gold **Ruler:** Elizabeth II **Obv:** Crowned bust right, denomination
below **Rev:** With plain bunting

Date	Mintage	F	VF	XF	Unc	BU
2002 Proof	—				Value: 1,475	

KM# 75.1 50 PENCE
28.1300 g., Copper-Nickel, 38.6 mm. **Ruler:** Elizabeth II
Subject: Queen's Golden Jubilee **Obv:** Crowned bust right,
denomination below **Rev:** Queen Elizabeth II talking into
microphone below multicolor bunting **Edge:** Reeded

Date	Mintage	F	VF	XF	Unc	BU
2002(2001) Proof	—				Value: 8.00	

KM# 75.2 50 PENCE
Copper-Nickel **Ruler:** Elizabeth II **Subject:** Queen's Golden
Jubilee **Obv:** Crowned bust right, denomination below **Rev:** With
plain bunting

Date	Mintage	F	VF	XF	Unc	BU
2002	—	—	—	—	6.00	7.00

KM# 75a.1 50 PENCE
28.2800 g., 0.9250 Silver 0.8410 oz. ASW, 38.6 mm.
Ruler: Elizabeth II **Subject:** Queen's Golden Jubilee
Obv: Crowned bust right, denomination below **Rev:** Queen
speaking into a radio microphone below multicolored bunting
Edge: Reeded

Date	Mintage	F	VF	XF	Unc	BU
2002 Proof	25,000				Value: 45.00	

KM# 75a.2 50 PENCE
Silver **Ruler:** Elizabeth II **Subject:** Queen's Golden Jubilee
Obv: Crowned bust right, denomination below **Rev:** With plain
bunting

Date	Mintage	F	VF	XF	Unc	BU
2002 Proof	—				Value: 45.00	

KM# 75b.1 50 PENCE
39.9400 g., 0.9166 Gold 1.1770 oz. AGW, 38.6 mm.
Ruler: Elizabeth II **Subject:** Queen's Golden Jubilee
Obv: Crowned bust right, denomination below **Rev:** Elizabeth
speaking into a radio microphone below multicolored bunting
Edge: Reeded

Date	Mintage	F	VF	XF	Unc	BU
2002 Proof	50				Value: 1,500	

KM# 75b.2 50 PENCE
Gold **Ruler:** Elizabeth II **Subject:** Queen's Golden Jubilee
Obv: Crowned bust right, denomination below **Rev:** With plain
bunting

Date	Mintage	F	VF	XF	Unc	BU
2002 Proof	—				Value: 1,475	

KM# 76.1 50 PENCE
28.1300 g., Copper-Nickel, 38.6 mm. **Ruler:** Elizabeth II
Subject: Queen's Golden Jubilee **Obv:** Crowned bust right,
denomination below **Rev:** Queen walking to left in front of a crowd
below multicolored bunting **Edge:** Reeded

Date	Mintage	F	VF	XF	Unc	BU
2002(2001) Proof	—				Value: 8.00	

KM# 76.2 50 PENCE
Copper-Nickel **Ruler:** Elizabeth II **Subject:** Queen's Golden
Jubilee **Obv:** Crowned bust right, denomination below **Rev:** With
plain bunting

Date	Mintage	F	VF	XF	Unc	BU
2002	—	—	—	—	6.00	7.00

KM# 76a.1 50 PENCE
28.2800 g., 0.9250 Silver 0.8410 oz. ASW, 38.6 mm.
Ruler: Elizabeth II **Subject:** Queen's Golden Jubilee
Obv: Crowned bust right, denomination below **Rev:** Queen
standing before crowd below multicolored bunting **Edge:** Reeded

Date	Mintage	F	VF	XF	Unc	BU
2002 Proof	15,000				Value: 45.00	

KM# 76a.2 50 PENCE
Silver **Ruler:** Elizabeth II **Subject:** Queen's Golden Jubilee
Obv: Crowned bust right, denomination below **Rev:** With plain
bunting

Date	Mintage	F	VF	XF	Unc	BU
2002 Proof	—				Value: 45.00	

KM# 76b.1 50 PENCE
39.9400 g., 0.9166 Gold 1.1770 oz. AGW, 38.6 mm.
Ruler: Elizabeth II **Subject:** Queen's Golden Jubilee **Obv:**
Crowned bust right, denomination below **Rev:** Queen standing
before a crowd below multicolored bunting **Edge:** Reeded

Date	Mintage	F	VF	XF	Unc	BU
2002 Proof	50				Value: 1,500	

KM# 76b.2 50 PENCE
Gold **Ruler:** Elizabeth II **Subject:** Queen's Golden Jubilee **Obv:**
Crowned bust right, denomination below **Rev:** With plain bunting

Date	Mintage	F	VF	XF	Unc	BU
2002 Proof	—				Value: 1,475	

KM# 77.1 50 PENCE
28.1300 g., Copper-Nickel, 38.6 mm. **Ruler:** Elizabeth II
Subject: Queen's Golden Jubilee **Obv:** Crowned bust right,
denomination below **Obv. Designer:** Raphael Maklouf **Rev:**
Conjoined busts of Queen Elizabeth, Prince Charles, Prince William
facing left in inner circle below multicolor bunting **Edge:** Reeded

Date	Mintage	F	VF	XF	Unc	BU
2002(2001) Proof	—				Value: 8.00	

KM# 77.2 50 PENCE
Copper-Nickel **Ruler:** Elizabeth II **Subject:** Queen's Golden
Jubilee **Obv:** Crowned bust right, denomination below **Rev:** With
plain bunting

Date	Mintage	F	VF	XF	Unc	BU
2002	—	—	—	—	6.00	7.00

KM# 77a.1 50 PENCE
28.2800 g., 0.9250 Silver 0.8410 oz. ASW, 38.6 mm.
Ruler: Elizabeth II **Subject:** Queen's Golden Jubilee
Obv: Crowned bust right, denomination below **Rev:** Queen,
Prince Charles and Prince William below multicolor bunting
Edge: Reeded

Date	Mintage	F	VF	XF	Unc	BU
2002 Proof	15,000				Value: 45.00	

KM# 77a.2 50 PENCE
Silver **Ruler:** Elizabeth II **Subject:** Queen's Golden Jubilee **Obv:**
Crowned bust right, denomination below **Rev:** With plain bunting

Date	Mintage	F	VF	XF	Unc	BU
2002 Proof	—				Value: 45.00	

KM# 77b.1 50 PENCE
39.9400 g., 0.9166 Gold 1.1770 oz. AGW, 38.6 mm. **Ruler:**
Elizabeth II **Subject:** Queen's Golden Jubilee **Obv:** Crowned
bust right, denomination below **Rev:** Elizabeth II, Prince Charles
and his son William below multicolored bunting **Edge:** Reeded

Date	Mintage	F	VF	XF	Unc	BU
2002 Proof	50				Value: 1,500	

KM# 77b.2 50 PENCE
Gold **Ruler:** Elizabeth II **Obv:** Crowned bust right, denomination
below **Rev:** With plain bunting

Date	Mintage	F	VF	XF	Unc	BU
2002 Proof	—				Value: 1,475	

KM# 78.1 50 PENCE
28.1300 g., Copper-Nickel, 38.6 mm. **Ruler:** Elizabeth II
Subject: Queen's Golden Jubilee **Obv:** Crowned bust right,
denomination below **Rev:** Royal coach below multicolor bunting
Edge: Reeded

Date	Mintage	F	VF	XF	Unc	BU
2002 Proof	—				Value: 8.00	

KM# 78.2 50 PENCE
Copper-Nickel **Ruler:** Elizabeth II **Subject:** Queen's Golden
Jubilee **Obv:** Crowned bust right, denomination below **Rev:** With
plain bunting

Date	Mintage	F	VF	XF	Unc	BU
2002	—	—	—	—	6.00	7.00

KM# 78a.1 50 PENCE
28.2800 g., 0.9250 Silver 0.8410 oz. ASW, 38.6 mm.
Ruler: Elizabeth II **Subject:** Queen's Golden Jubilee
Obv: Crowned bust right, denomination below **Rev:** Coronation
coach below multicolor bunting **Edge:** Reeded

Date	Mintage	F	VF	XF	Unc	BU
2002 Proof	15,000				Value: 45.00	

KM# 78b.1 50 PENCE
39.9400 g., 0.9166 Gold 1.1770 oz. AGW, 38.6 mm.
Ruler: Elizabeth II **Subject:** Queen's Golden Jubilee
Obv: Crowned bust right, denomination below **Rev:** Coronation
coach below multicolor bunting **Edge:** Reeded

Date	Mintage	F	VF	XF	Unc	BU
2002 Proof	150				Value: 1,500	

KM# 78b.2 50 PENCE
Gold **Ruler:** Elizabeth II **Subject:** Queen's Golden Jubilee
Obv: Crowned bust right, denomination below **Rev:** With plain
bunting

Date	Mintage	F	VF	XF	Unc	BU
2002 Proof	—				Value: 1,475	

KM# 79.1 50 PENCE
28.1300 g., Copper-Nickel, 38.6 mm. **Ruler:** Elizabeth II
Subject: Queen's Golden Jubilee **Obv:** Crowned bust right,
denomination below **Rev:** Scepter and orb below multicolor
bunting **Edge:** Reeded

Date	Mintage	F	VF	XF	Unc	BU
2002 Proof	—				Value: 8.00	

KM# 79.2 50 PENCE
Copper-Nickel **Ruler:** Elizabeth II **Subject:** Queen's Golden
Jubilee **Obv:** Crowned bust right, denomination below **Rev:** With
plain bunting

Date	Mintage	F	VF	XF	Unc	BU
2002	—	—	—	—	6.00	7.00

KM# 79a.1 50 PENCE
28.2800 g., 0.9250 Silver 0.8410 oz. ASW, 38.6 mm.
Ruler: Elizabeth II **Subject:** Queen's Golden Jubilee
Obv: Crowned bust right, denomination below **Rev:** Orb and
scepter below multicolor bunting **Edge:** Reeded

Date	Mintage	F	VF	XF	Unc	BU
2002 Proof	15,000				Value: 45.00	

KM# 79a.2   50 PENCE
Silver **Ruler:** Elizabeth II **Subject:** Queen's Golden Jubilee
Obv: Crowned bust right, denomination below **Rev:** With plain
bunting

Date	Mintage	F	VF	XF	Unc	BU
2002 Proof	—	Value: 45.00				

KM# 79b.1   50 PENCE
39.9400 g., 0.9166 Gold 1.1770 oz. AGW, 38.6 mm.
Ruler: Elizabeth II **Subject:** Queen's Golden Jubilee
Obv: Crowned bust right, denomination below **Rev:** Orb and
scepter below multicolor bunting **Edge:** Reeded

Date	Mintage	F	VF	XF	Unc	BU
2002 Proof	150	Value: 1,500				

KM# 79b.2   50 PENCE
Gold **Ruler:** Elizabeth II **Subject:** Queen's Golden Jubilee
Obv: Crowned bust right, denomination below **Rev:** With plain
bunting

Date	Mintage	F	VF	XF	Unc	BU
2002 Proof	—	Value: 1,475				

KM# 80.1   50 PENCE
28.1300 g., Copper-Nickel, 38.6 mm. **Ruler:** Elizabeth II
Subject: Queen's Golden Jubilee **Obv:** Crowned bust right,
denomination below **Obv. Designer:** Raphael Maklouf
Rev: Crown below multicolor bunting **Edge:** Reeded

Date	Mintage	F	VF	XF	Unc	BU
2002 Proof	—	Value: 8.00				

KM# 80.2   50 PENCE
Copper-Nickel **Ruler:** Elizabeth II **Subject:** Queen's Golden
Jubilee **Obv:** Crowned bust right, denomination below **Rev:** With
plain bunting

Date	Mintage	F	VF	XF	Unc	BU
2002	—	—	—	—	6.00	7.00

KM# 80a.1   50 PENCE
28.2800 g., 0.9250 Silver 0.8410 oz. ASW, 38.6 mm.
Ruler: Elizabeth II **Subject:** Queen's Golden Jubilee
Obv: Crowned bust right, denomination below **Rev:** Crown below
multicolor bunting **Edge:** Reeded

Date	Mintage	F	VF	XF	Unc	BU
2002 Proof	15,000	Value: 45.00				

KM# 80a.2   50 PENCE
Silver **Ruler:** Elizabeth II **Subject:** Queen's Golden Jubilee
Obv: Crowned bust right, denomination below **Rev:** With plain
bunting

Date	Mintage	F	VF	XF	Unc	BU
2002 Proof	—	Value: 45.00				

KM# 80b.1   50 PENCE
39.9400 g., 0.9166 Gold 1.1770 oz. AGW, 38.6 mm.
Ruler: Elizabeth II **Subject:** Queen's Golden Jubilee
Obv: Crowned bust right, denomination below **Rev:** Crown below
multicolor bunting **Edge:** Reeded

Date	Mintage	F	VF	XF	Unc	BU
2002 Proof	150	Value: 1,500				

KM# 80b.2   50 PENCE
Gold **Ruler:** Elizabeth II **Subject:** Queen's Golden Jubilee
Obv: Crowned bust right, denomination below **Rev:** With plain
bunting

Date	Mintage	F	VF	XF	Unc	BU
2002 Proof	—	Value: 1,475				

KM# 81.1   50 PENCE
28.1300 g., Copper-Nickel, 38.6 mm. **Ruler:** Elizabeth II
Subject: Queen's Golden Jubilee **Obv:** Crowned bust right,
denomination below **Rev:** Throne below multicolor bunting
Edge: Reeded

Date	Mintage	F	VF	XF	Unc	BU
2002 Proof	—	Value: 8.00				

KM# 81.2   50 PENCE
Copper-Nickel **Ruler:** Elizabeth II **Subject:** Queen's Golden
Jubilee **Obv:** Crowned bust right, denomination below **Rev:** With
plain bunting

Date	Mintage	F	VF	XF	Unc	BU
2002	—	—	—	—	6.00	7.00

KM# 81a.1   50 PENCE
28.2800 g., 0.9250 Silver 0.8410 oz. ASW, 38.6 mm.
Ruler: Elizabeth II **Subject:** Queen's Golden Jubilee
Obv: Crowned bust right, denomination below **Rev:** Coronation
throne below multicolor bunting **Edge:** Reeded

Date	Mintage	F	VF	XF	Unc	BU
2002 Proof	15,000	Value: 45.00				

KM# 81a.2   50 PENCE
Silver **Ruler:** Elizabeth II **Subject:** Queen's Golden Jubilee
Obv: Crowned bust right, denomination below **Rev:** With plain
bunting

Date	Mintage	F	VF	XF	Unc	BU
2002 Proof	—	Value: 45.00				

KM# 81b.1   50 PENCE
39.9400 g., 0.9166 Gold 1.1770 oz. AGW, 38.6 mm.
Ruler: Elizabeth II **Subject:** Queen's Golden Jubilee
Obv: Crowned bust right, denomination below **Rev:** Coronation
Throne below multicolored bunting **Edge:** Reeded

Date	Mintage	F	VF	XF	Unc	BU
2002 Proof	150	Value: 1,500				

KM# 81b.2   50 PENCE
Gold **Ruler:** Elizabeth II **Obv:** Crowned bust right, denomination
below **Rev:** With plain bunting

Date	Mintage	F	VF	XF	Unc	BU
2002 Proof	—	Value: 1,475				

KM# 82.1   50 PENCE
28.1300 g., Copper-Nickel, 38.6 mm. **Ruler:** Elizabeth II
Subject: Queen's Golden Jubilee **Obv:** Crowned bust right,
denomination below **Rev:** Queen on throne below multicolor
bunting **Edge:** Reeded

Date	Mintage	F	VF	XF	Unc	BU
2002 Proof	—	—	—	—	6.00	7.00

KM# 82.2   50 PENCE
Copper-Nickel **Ruler:** Elizabeth II **Subject:** Queen's Golden
Jubilee **Obv:** Crowned bust right, denomination below **Rev:** With
plain bunting

Date	Mintage	F	VF	XF	Unc	BU
2002	—	—	—	—	6.00	7.00

KM# 82a.1   50 PENCE
28.2800 g., 0.9250 Silver 0.8410 oz. ASW, 38.6 mm.
Ruler: Elizabeth II **Subject:** Queen's Golden Jubilee
Obv: Crowned bust right, denomination below **Rev:** Queen on
throne below multicolor bunting **Edge:** Reeded

Date	Mintage	F	VF	XF	Unc	BU
2002 Proof	15,000	Value: 45.00				

KM# 82a.2   50 PENCE
Silver **Ruler:** Elizabeth II **Subject:** Queen's Golden Jubilee
Obv: Crowned bust right, denomination below **Rev:** With plain
bunting

Date	Mintage	F	VF	XF	Unc	BU
2002 Proof	—	Value: 45.00				

KM# 82b.1   50 PENCE
39.9400 g., 0.9166 Gold 1.1770 oz. AGW, 38.6 mm.
Ruler: Elizabeth II **Subject:** Queen's Golden Jubilee
Obv: Crowned bust right, denomination below **Rev:** Queen
seated on throne below multicolor bunting **Edge:** Reeded

Date	Mintage	F	VF	XF	Unc	BU
2002 Proof	50	Value: 1,500				

KM# 82b.2   50 PENCE
Gold **Ruler:** Elizabeth II **Subject:** Queen's Golden Jubilee
Obv: Crowned bust right, denomination below **Rev:** With plain
bunting

Date	Mintage	F	VF	XF	Unc	BU
2002 Proof	—	Value: 1,475				

KM# 83.1   50 PENCE
28.1300 g., Copper-Nickel, 38.6 mm. **Ruler:** Elizabeth II
Subject: Queen's Golden Jubilee **Obv:** Crowned bust right,
denomination below **Obv. Designer:** Raphael Maklouf
Rev: Queen and young family below multicolor bunting
Edge: Reeded

Date	Mintage	F	VF	XF	Unc	BU
2002 Proof	—	—	—	—	6.00	7.00

KM# 83a.1   50 PENCE
28.2800 g., 0.9250 Silver 0.8410 oz. ASW, 38.6 mm.
Ruler: Elizabeth II **Subject:** Queen's Golden Jubilee
Obv: Crowned bust right, denomination below **Rev:** Royal family
below multicolor bunting **Edge:** Reeded

Date	Mintage	F	VF	XF	Unc	BU
2002 Proof	15,000	Value: 45.00				

KM# 83a.2   50 PENCE
Silver **Ruler:** Elizabeth II **Subject:** Queen's Golden Jubilee
Obv: Crowned bust right, denomination below **Rev:** With plain
bunting

Date	Mintage	F	VF	XF	Unc	BU
2002 Proof	—	Value: 45.00				

KM# 83b.1   50 PENCE
39.9400 g., 0.9166 Gold 1.1770 oz. AGW, 38.6 mm.
Ruler: Elizabeth II **Subject:** Queen's Golden Jubilee
Obv: Crowned bust right, denomination below **Rev:** Royal Family
below multicolor bunting **Edge:** Reeded

Date	Mintage	F	VF	XF	Unc	BU
2002 Proof	50	Value: 1,500				

KM# 83b.2   50 PENCE
Gold **Ruler:** Elizabeth II **Subject:** Queen's Golden Jubilee
Obv: Crowned bust right, denomination below **Rev:** With plain
bunting

Date	Mintage	F	VF	XF	Unc	BU
2002 Proof	—	Value: 1,475				

KM# 84.1   50 PENCE
28.1300 g., Copper-Nickel, 38.6 mm. **Ruler:** Elizabeth II
Subject: Queen's Golden Jubilee **Obv:** Crowned bust right,
denomination below **Rev:** Queens head and tree house below
multicolor bunting **Edge:** Reeded

Date	Mintage	F	VF	XF	Unc	BU
2002 Proof	—	Value: 8.00				

KM# 84.2   50 PENCE
Copper-Nickel **Ruler:** Elizabeth II **Subject:** Queen's Golden
Jubilee **Obv:** Crowned bust right, denomination below **Rev:** With
plain bunting

Date	Mintage	F	VF	XF	Unc	BU
2002	—	—	—	—	6.00	7.00

KM# 84a.1   50 PENCE
28.2800 g., 0.9250 Silver 0.8410 oz. ASW, 38.6 mm.
Ruler: Elizabeth II **Subject:** Queen's Golden Jubilee
Obv: Crowned bust right, denomination below **Rev:** Queen and
tree house below multicolor bunting **Edge:** Reeded

Date	Mintage	F	VF	XF	Unc	BU
2002 Proof	25,000	Value: 45.00				

KM# 84a.2   50 PENCE
Silver **Ruler:** Elizabeth II **Subject:** Queen's Golden Jubilee
Obv: Crowned bust right, denomination below **Rev:** With plain
bunting

Date	Mintage	F	VF	XF	Unc	BU
2002 Proof	—	Value: 45.00				

KM# 84b.1   50 PENCE
39.9400 g., 0.9166 Gold 1.1770 oz. AGW, 38.6 mm.
Ruler: Elizabeth II **Subject:** Queen's Golden Jubilee
Obv: Crowned bust right, denomination below **Rev:** Queen and
tree house below multicolor bunting **Edge:** Reeded

Date	Mintage	F	VF	XF	Unc	BU
2002 Proof	50	Value: 1,500				

KM# 84b.2 50 PENCE
Gold **Ruler:** Elizabeth II **Subject:** Queen's Golden Jubilee
Obv: Crowned bust right, denomination below **Rev:** With plain
bunting

Date	Mintage	F	VF	XF	Unc	BU
2002 Proof	—	Value: 1,475				

KM# 91b.2 50 PENCE
39.9400 g., 0.9160 Gold 1.1762 oz. AGW, 38.6 mm.
Ruler: Elizabeth II **Obv:** Crowned bust right, denomination below
Rev: With plain bunting **Edge:** Reeded

Date	Mintage	F	VF	XF	Unc	BU
2002 Proof	—	Value: 1,475				

KM# 93b.2 50 PENCE
39.9400 g., 0.9160 Gold 1.1762 oz. AGW, 38.6 mm.
Ruler: Elizabeth II **Obv:** Crowned bust right, denomination below
Rev: With plain bunting **Edge:** Reeded

Date	Mintage	F	VF	XF	Unc	BU
2002 Proof	—	Value: 1,475				

KM# 90 50 PENCE
28.2800 g., Copper-Nickel, 38.6 mm. **Ruler:** Elizabeth II
Obv: Crowned bust right, denomination below **Rev:** Conjoined
busts of Elizabeth and Philip below multicolor bunting
Edge: Reeded

Date	Mintage	F	VF	XF	Unc	BU
2002	—	—	—	—	6.00	7.00

KM# 90a.1 50 PENCE
28.2800 g., 0.9250 Silver 0.8410 oz. ASW, 38.6 mm.
Ruler: Elizabeth II **Obv:** Crowned bust right, denomination below
Rev: Elizabeth and Philip below multicolor bunting **Edge:** Reeded

Date	Mintage	F	VF	XF	Unc	BU
2002 Proof	15,000	Value: 45.00				

KM# 90a.2 50 PENCE
28.2800 g., 0.9250 Silver 0.8410 oz. ASW, 38.6 mm.
Ruler: Elizabeth II **Obv:** Crowned bust right, denomination below
Rev: With plain bunting

Date	Mintage	F	VF	XF	Unc	BU
2002 Proof	—	Value: 45.00				

KM# 90b.1 50 PENCE
39.9400 g., 0.9160 Gold 1.1762 oz. AGW, 38.6 mm.
Ruler: Elizabeth II **Obv:** Crowned bust right, denomination below
Rev: Elizabeth and Philip below multicolor bunting **Edge:** Reeded

Date	Mintage	F	VF	XF	Unc	BU
2002 Proof	50	Value: 1,500				

KM# 90b.2 50 PENCE
39.9400 g., 0.9160 Gold 1.1762 oz. AGW, 38.6 mm.
Ruler: Elizabeth II **Obv:** Crowned bust right, denomination below
Rev: With plain bunting **Edge:** Reeded

Date	Mintage	F	VF	XF	Unc	BU
2002 Proof	—	Value: 1,475				

KM# 92 50 PENCE
28.2800 g., Copper-Nickel, 38.6 mm. **Ruler:** Elizabeth II
Obv: Crowned bust right, denomination below **Rev:** Queen and
St. Paul's Cathedral dome below multicolor bunting
Edge: Reeded

Date	Mintage	F	VF	XF	Unc	BU
2002	—	—	—	—	6.00	7.00

KM# 92a.1 50 PENCE
28.2800 g., 0.9250 Silver 0.8410 oz. ASW, 38.6 mm.
Ruler: Elizabeth II **Obv:** Crowned bust right, denomination below
Rev: Queen and St. Paul's Cathedral dome below multicolor
bunting **Edge:** Reeded

Date	Mintage	F	VF	XF	Unc	BU
2002 Proof	15,000	Value: 45.00				

KM# 92a.2 50 PENCE
28.2800 g., 0.9250 Silver 0.8410 oz. ASW, 38.6 mm.
Ruler: Elizabeth II **Obv:** Crowned bust right, denomination below
Rev: With plain bunting **Edge:** Reeded

Date	Mintage	F	VF	XF	Unc	BU
2002 Proof	—	Value: 45.00				

KM# 92b.1 50 PENCE
39.9400 g., 0.9160 Gold 1.1762 oz. AGW, 38.6 mm.
Ruler: Elizabeth II **Obv:** Crowned bust right, denomination below
Rev: Queen and St. Paul's Cathedral dome below multicolor
bunting **Edge:** Reeded

Date	Mintage	F	VF	XF	Unc	BU
2002 Proof	50	Value: 1,500				

KM# 92b.2 50 PENCE
39.9400 g., 0.9160 Gold 1.1762 oz. AGW, 38.6 mm.
Ruler: Elizabeth II **Obv:** Crowned bust right, denomination below
Rev: With plain bunting **Edge:** Reeded

Date	Mintage	F	VF	XF	Unc	BU
2002 Proof	—	Value: 1,475				

KM# 94 50 PENCE
28.2800 g., Copper-Nickel, 38.6 mm. **Ruler:** Elizabeth II
Obv: Crowned bust right, denomination below **Rev:** Elizabeth
and Prince Charles at flower show below multicolor bunting
Edge: Reeded

Date	Mintage	F	VF	XF	Unc	BU
2002	—	—	—	—	6.00	7.00

KM# 94a.1 50 PENCE
28.2800 g., 0.9250 Silver 0.8410 oz. ASW, 38.6 mm.
Ruler: Elizabeth II **Obv:** Crowned bust right, denomination below
Rev: Queen and Prince Charles at flower show below multicolor
bunting **Edge:** Reeded

Date	Mintage	F	VF	XF	Unc	BU
2002 Proof	15,000	Value: 45.00				

KM# 94a.2 50 PENCE
28.2800 g., 0.9250 Silver 0.8410 oz. ASW, 38.6 mm.
Ruler: Elizabeth II **Obv:** Crowned bust right, denomination below
Rev: With plain bunting **Edge:** Reeded

Date	Mintage	F	VF	XF	Unc	BU
2002 Proof	—	Value: 45.00				

KM# 94b.1 50 PENCE
39.9400 g., 0.9160 Gold 1.1762 oz. AGW, 38.6 mm.
Ruler: Elizabeth II **Obv:** Crowned bust right, denomination below
Rev: Queen and Prince Charles at flower show below multicolor
bunting **Edge:** Reeded

Date	Mintage	F	VF	XF	Unc	BU
2002 Proof	50	Value: 1,500				

KM# 94b.2 50 PENCE
39.9400 g., 0.9160 Gold 1.1762 oz. AGW, 38.6 mm.
Ruler: Elizabeth II **Obv:** Crowned bust right, denomination below
Rev: With plain bunting **Edge:** Reeded

Date	Mintage	F	VF	XF	Unc	BU
2002 Proof	—	Value: 1,475				

KM# 91 50 PENCE
28.2800 g., Copper-Nickel, 38.6 mm. **Ruler:** Elizabeth II
Obv: Crowned bust right, denomination below **Rev:** Queen and
Aborigine dancers below multicolor bunting **Edge:** Reeded

Date	Mintage	F	VF	XF	Unc	BU
2002	—	—	—	—	6.00	7.00

KM# 91a.1 50 PENCE
28.2800 g., 0.9250 Silver 0.8410 oz. ASW, 38.6 mm.
Ruler: Elizabeth II **Obv:** Crowned bust right, denomination below
Rev: Queen and Aborigine dancers below multicolor bunting
Edge: Reeded

Date	Mintage	F	VF	XF	Unc	BU
2002 Proof	15,000	Value: 45.00				

KM# 91a.2 50 PENCE
28.2800 g., 0.9250 Silver 0.8410 oz. ASW, 38.6 mm.
Ruler: Elizabeth II **Obv:** Crowned bust right, denomination below
Rev: With plain bunting **Edge:** Reeded

Date	Mintage	F	VF	XF	Unc	BU
2002 Proof	—	Value: 45.00				

KM# 91b.1 50 PENCE
39.9400 g., 0.9160 Gold 1.1762 oz. AGW, 38.6 mm.
Ruler: Elizabeth II **Obv:** Crowned bust right, denomination below
Rev: Queen and Aborigine dancers below multicolor bunting
Edge: Reeded

Date	Mintage	F	VF	XF	Unc	BU
2002 Proof	50	Value: 1,500				

KM# 93 50 PENCE
28.2800 g., Copper-Nickel, 38.6 mm. **Ruler:** Elizabeth II
Obv: Crowned bust right, denomination below **Rev:** Elizabeth
and Philip in coronation coach below multicolor bunting
Edge: Reeded

Date	Mintage	F	VF	XF	Unc	BU
2002	—	—	—	—	6.00	7.00

KM# 93a.1 50 PENCE
28.2800 g., 0.9250 Silver 0.8410 oz. ASW, 38.6 mm.
Ruler: Elizabeth II **Obv:** Crowned bust right, denomination below
Rev: Elizabeth and Philip in coronation coach below multicolor
bunting **Edge:** Reeded

Date	Mintage	F	VF	XF	Unc	BU
2002 Proof	15,000	Value: 45.00				

KM# 93a.2 50 PENCE
28.2800 g., 0.9250 Silver 0.8410 oz. ASW, 38.6 mm.
Ruler: Elizabeth II **Obv:** Crowned bust right, denomination below
Rev: With plain bunting **Edge:** Reeded

Date	Mintage	F	VF	XF	Unc	BU
2002 Proof	—	Value: 45.00				

KM# 93b.1 50 PENCE
39.9400 g., 0.9160 Gold 1.1762 oz. AGW, 38.6 mm.
Ruler: Elizabeth II **Obv:** Crowned bust right, denomination below
Rev: Elizabeth and Philip in coronation coach below multicolor
bunting **Edge:** Reeded

Date	Mintage	F	VF	XF	Unc	BU
2002 Proof	50	Value: 1,500				

KM# 95 50 PENCE
28.2800 g., Copper-Nickel, 38.6 mm. **Ruler:** Elizabeth II
Obv: Crowned bust right, denomination below **Rev:** Elizabeth
and Philip on balcony below multicolor bunting **Edge:** Reeded

Date	Mintage	F	VF	XF	Unc	BU
2002	—	—	—	—	6.00	7.00

KM# 95a.1 50 PENCE
28.2800 g., 0.9250 Silver 0.8410 oz. ASW, 38.6 mm.
Ruler: Elizabeth II **Obv:** Crowned bust right, denomination below
Rev: Elizabeth and Philip on balcony below colored bunting
Edge: Reeded

Date	Mintage	F	VF	XF	Unc	BU
2002 Proof	15,000	Value: 45.00				

KM# 95a.2 50 PENCE
28.2800 g., 0.9250 Silver 0.8410 oz. ASW, 38.6 mm.
Ruler: Elizabeth II **Obv:** Crowned bust right, denomination below
Rev: With plain bunting **Edge:** Reeded

Date	Mintage	F	VF	XF	Unc	BU
2002 Proof	—	Value: 45.00				

KM# 95b.1 50 PENCE
39.9400 g., 0.9160 Gold 1.1762 oz. AGW, 38.6 mm.
Ruler: Elizabeth II **Obv:** Crowned bust right, denomination below
Rev: Elizabeth and Philip on balcony below multicolor bunting
Edge: Reeded

Date	Mintage	F	VF	XF	Unc	BU
2002 Proof	50	Value: 1,500				

KM# 95b.2 50 PENCE
39.9400 g., 0.9160 Gold 1.1762 oz. AGW, 38.6 mm.
Ruler: Elizabeth II **Obv:** Crowned bust right, denomination below
Rev: With plain bunting **Edge:** Reeded

Date	Mintage	F	VF	XF	Unc	BU
2002 Proof	—	Value: 1,475				

KM# 96 50 PENCE
28.2800 g., Copper-Nickel, 38.6 mm. **Ruler:** Elizabeth II
Obv: Crowned bust right, denomination below **Rev:** Multicolor
jets below multicolor bunting **Edge:** Reeded

Date	Mintage	F	VF	XF	Unc	BU
2002	—	—	—	—	6.00	7.00

KM# 96a.1 50 PENCE
28.2800 g., 0.9250 Silver 0.8410 oz. ASW, 38.6 mm.
Ruler: Elizabeth II **Obv:** Crowned bust right, denomination below
Rev: Multicolor jets below multicolor bunting **Edge:** Reeded

Date	Mintage	F	VF	XF	Unc	BU
2002 Proof	15,000	Value: 45.00				

KM# 96a.2 50 PENCE
28.2800 g., 0.9250 Silver 0.8410 oz. ASW, 38.6 mm.
Ruler: Elizabeth II **Obv:** Crowned bust right, denomination below
Rev: With plain bunting **Edge:** Reeded

Date	Mintage	F	VF	XF	Unc	BU
2002 Proof	—	Value: 45.00				

KM# 96b.1 50 PENCE
39.9400 g., 0.9160 Gold 1.1762 oz. AGW, 38.6 mm.
Ruler: Elizabeth II **Obv:** Crowned bust right, denomination below
Rev: Multicolor jets below multicolor bunting **Edge:** Reeded

Date	Mintage	F	VF	XF	Unc	BU
2002 Proof	50	Value: 1,500				

KM# 96b.2 50 PENCE
39.9400 g., 0.9160 Gold 1.1762 oz. AGW, 38.6 mm.
Ruler: Elizabeth II **Obv:** Crowned bust right, denomination below
Rev: With plain bunting **Edge:** Reeded

Date	Mintage	F	VF	XF	Unc	BU
2002 Proof	—	Value: 1,475				

KM# 97 50 PENCE
28.2800 g., Copper-Nickel, 38.6 mm. **Ruler:** Elizabeth II
Obv: Crowned bust right, denomination below **Rev:** Queen and
fireworks below multicolor bunting **Edge:** Reeded

Date	Mintage	F	VF	XF	Unc	BU
2002	—	—	—	—	6.00	7.00

KM# 97a.1 50 PENCE
28.2800 g., 0.9250 Copper-Nickel 0.8410 oz., 38.6 mm.
Ruler: Elizabeth II **Obv:** Crowned bust right, denomination below
Rev: Queen and fireworks below multicolor bunting
Edge: Reeded

Date	Mintage	F	VF	XF	Unc	BU
2002 Proof	15,000	Value: 45.00				

KM# 97a.2 50 PENCE
28.2800 g., 0.9250 Silver 0.8410 oz. ASW, 38.6 mm.
Ruler: Elizabeth II **Obv:** Crowned bust right, denomination below
Rev: With plain bunting **Edge:** Reeded

Date	Mintage	F	VF	XF	Unc	BU
2002 Proof	—	Value: 45.00				

KM# 97b.1 50 PENCE
39.9400 g., 0.9160 Gold 1.1762 oz. AGW, 38.6 mm.
Ruler: Elizabeth II **Obv:** Crowned bust right, denomination below
Rev: Queen and fireworks below multicolor bunting
Edge: Reeded

Date	Mintage	F	VF	XF	Unc	BU
2002 Proof	50	Value: 1,500				

KM# 97b.2 50 PENCE
39.9400 g., 0.9160 Gold 1.1762 oz. AGW, 38.6 mm.
Ruler: Elizabeth II **Obv:** Crowned bust right, denomination below
Rev: With plain bunting **Edge:** Reeded

Date	Mintage	F	VF	XF	Unc	BU
2002 Proof	—	Value: 1,475				

KM# 98 50 PENCE
28.2800 g., Copper-Nickel, 38.6 mm. **Ruler:** Elizabeth II
Obv: Crowned bust right, denomination below **Rev:** UK map and
flags below multicolor bunting **Edge:** Reeded

Date	Mintage	F	VF	XF	Unc	BU
2002	—	—	—	—	6.00	7.00

KM# 98a.1 50 PENCE
28.2800 g., 0.9250 Silver 0.8410 oz. ASW, 38.6 mm.
Ruler: Elizabeth II **Obv:** Crowned bust right, denomination below
Rev: UK and four flags below multicolor bunting **Edge:** Reeded

Date	Mintage	F	VF	XF	Unc	BU
2002 Proof	15,000	Value: 45.00				

KM# 98a.2 50 PENCE
28.2800 g., 0.9250 Silver 0.8410 oz. ASW, 38.6 mm.
Ruler: Elizabeth II **Obv:** Crowned bust right, denomination below
Rev: With plain bunting **Edge:** Reeded

Date	Mintage	F	VF	XF	Unc	BU
2002 Proof	—	Value: 45.00				

KM# 98b.1 50 PENCE
39.9400 g., 0.9160 Gold 1.1762 oz. AGW, 38.6 mm. **Ruler:**
Elizabeth II **Obv:** Crowned bust right, denomination below **Rev:**
UK map and four flags below multicolor bunting **Edge:** Reeded

Date	Mintage	F	VF	XF	Unc	BU
2002 Proof	50	Value: 1,500				

KM# 98b.2 50 PENCE
39.9400 g., 0.9160 Gold 1.1762 oz. AGW, 38.6 mm.
Ruler: Elizabeth II **Obv:** Crowned bust right, denomination below
Rev: With plain bunting **Edge:** Reeded

Date	Mintage	F	VF	XF	Unc	BU
2002 Proof	—	Value: 1,475				

KM# 99 50 PENCE
28.2800 g., Copper-Nickel, 38.6 mm. **Ruler:** Elizabeth II
Obv: Crowned bust right, denomination below **Rev:** Queen and
two Commonwealth Games athletes below multicolor bunting
Edge: Reeded

Date	Mintage	F	VF	XF	Unc	BU
2002	—	—	—	—	6.00	7.00

KM# 99a.1 50 PENCE
28.2800 g., 0.9250 Silver 0.8410 oz. ASW, 38.6 mm.
Ruler: Elizabeth II **Obv:** Crowned bust right, denomination below
Rev: Queen and two Commonwealth Games athletes below
multicolor bunting **Edge:** Reeded

Date	Mintage	F	VF	XF	Unc	BU
2002 Proof	15,000	Value: 45.00				

KM# 99a.2 50 PENCE
28.2800 g., 0.9250 Silver 0.8410 oz. ASW, 38.6 mm.
Ruler: Elizabeth II **Obv:** Crowned bust right, denomination below
Rev: With plain bunting **Edge:** Reeded

Date	Mintage	F	VF	XF	Unc	BU
2002 Proof	—	Value: 45.00				

KM# 99b.1 50 PENCE
39.9400 g., 0.9160 Gold 1.1762 oz. AGW, 38.6 mm.
Ruler: Elizabeth II **Obv:** Crowned bust right, denomination below
Rev: Queen and two Commonwealth Games athletes below
multicolor bunting **Edge:** Reeded

Date	Mintage	F	VF	XF	Unc	BU
2002 Proof	50	Value: 1,500				

KM# 99b.2 50 PENCE
39.9400 g., 0.9160 Gold 1.1762 oz. AGW, 38.6 mm.
Ruler: Elizabeth II **Obv:** Crowned bust right, denomination below
Rev: With plain bunting **Edge:** Reeded

Date	Mintage	F	VF	XF	Unc	BU
2002 Proof	—	Value: 1,475				

KM# 100 50 PENCE
28.2800 g., Copper-Nickel, 38.6 mm. **Ruler:** Elizabeth II
Obv: Crowned bust right, denomination below **Rev:** Royal Ascot
Carriage scene below multicolor bunting **Edge:** Reeded

Date	Mintage	F	VF	XF	Unc	BU
2002	—	—	—	—	6.00	7.00

KM# 100a.1 50 PENCE
28.2800 g., 0.9250 Silver 0.8410 oz. ASW, 38.6 mm.
Ruler: Elizabeth II **Obv:** Crowned bust right, denomination below
Rev: Royal Ascot Carriage scene below multicolor bunting
Edge: Reeded

Date	Mintage	F	VF	XF	Unc	BU
2002 Proof	15,000	Value: 45.00				

KM# 100a.2 50 PENCE
28.2800 g., 0.9250 Silver 0.8410 oz. ASW, 38.6 mm.
Ruler: Elizabeth II **Obv:** Crowned bust right, denomination below
Rev: With plain bunting **Edge:** Reeded

Date	Mintage	F	VF	XF	Unc	BU
2002 Proof	—	Value: 45.00				

KM# 100b.1 50 PENCE
39.9400 g., 0.9160 Gold 1.1762 oz. AGW, 38.6 mm.
Ruler: Elizabeth II **Obv:** Crowned bust right, denomination below
Rev: Royal Ascot Carriage scene below multicolor bunting
Edge: Reeded

Date	Mintage	F	VF	XF	Unc	BU
2002 Proof	50	Value: 1,500				

KM# 100b.2 50 PENCE
39.9400 g., 0.9160 Gold 1.1762 oz. AGW, 38.6 mm.
Ruler: Elizabeth II **Obv:** Crowned bust right, denomination below
Rev: With plain bunting **Edge:** Reeded

Date	Mintage	F	VF	XF	Unc	BU
2002 Proof	—	Value: 1,475				

KM# 101 50 PENCE
28.2800 g., Copper-Nickel, 38.6 mm. **Ruler:** Elizabeth II
Obv: Crowned bust right, denomination below **Rev:** Queen and
two hockey players below multicolor bunting **Edge:** Reeded

Date	Mintage	F	VF	XF	Unc	BU
2002	—	—	—	—	6.00	7.00

KM# 101a.1 50 PENCE
28.2800 g., 0.9250 Silver 0.8410 oz. ASW, 38.6 mm.
Ruler: Elizabeth II **Obv:** Crowned bust right, denomination below
Rev: Queen and two hockey players below multicolor bunting
Edge: Reeded

Date	Mintage	F	VF	XF	Unc	BU
2002 Proof	15,000	Value: 45.00				

KM# 101a.2 50 PENCE
28.2800 g., 0.9250 Silver 0.8410 oz. ASW, 38.6 mm.
Ruler: Elizabeth II **Obv:** Crowned bust right, denomination below
Rev: With plain bunting **Edge:** Reeded

Date	Mintage	F	VF	XF	Unc	BU
2002 Proof	—	Value: 45.00				

KM# 101b.1 50 PENCE
39.9400 g., 0.9160 Gold 1.1762 oz. AGW, 38.6 mm.
Ruler: Elizabeth II **Obv:** Crowned bust right, denomination below
Rev: Queen and two hockey players below multicolor bunting
Edge: Reeded

Date	Mintage	F	VF	XF	Unc	BU
2002 Proof	50	Value: 1,500				

KM# 101b.2 50 PENCE
39.9400 g., 0.9160 Gold 1.1762 oz. AGW, 38.6 mm.
Ruler: Elizabeth II **Obv:** Crowned bust right, denomination below
Rev: With plain bunting **Edge:** Reeded

Date	Mintage	F	VF	XF	Unc	BU
2002 Proof	—	Value: 1,475				

KM# 102   50 PENCE
28.2800 g., Copper-Nickel, 38.6 mm. **Ruler:** Elizabeth II
Obv: Crowned bust right, denomination below **Obv. Designer:**
Raphael Maklouf **Rev:** Queen Mother as a young lady and as an
elderly lady **Rev. Designer:** Willem Vis **Edge:** Reeded

Date	Mintage	F	VF	XF	Unc	BU
ND(2002)	—	—	—	—	9.00	10.00

KM# 102a   50 PENCE
28.2800 g., 0.9250 Silver 0.8410 oz. ASW, 38.6 mm.
Ruler: Elizabeth II **Obv:** Crowned bust right, denomination below
Rev: Queen Mother as a young lady and as an elderly lady
Edge: Reeded

Date	Mintage	F	VF	XF	Unc	BU
ND(2002) Proof	10,000	Value: 45.00				

KM# 135   50 PENCE
Copper-Nickel **Ruler:** Elizabeth II **Obv:** Young bust right

Date	Mintage	F	VF	XF	Unc	BU
2004	—	—	—	—	5.00	7.50

KM# 149   50 PENCE
28.2800 g., 0.9250 Silver 0.8410 oz. ASW, 38.6 mm.
Ruler: Elizabeth II **Subject:** Queen's 80th Birthday **Obv:** Head
with tiara right - gilt **Obv. Legend:** QUEEN ELIZABETH II -
FALKLAND ISLANDS **Obv. Designer:** Ian Rank-Broadley **Rev:**
Elizabeth seated at left, Queen Mother at right holding baby

Date	Mintage	F	VF	XF	Unc	BU
2006 Proof	—	Value: 40.00				

KM# 136   POUND
Nickel-Brass **Ruler:** Elizabeth II **Obv:** Crowned bust right

Date	Mintage	F	VF	XF	Unc	BU
2004	—	—	—	—	3.50	5.00

KM# 137   2 POUNDS
11.9800 g., Bi-Metallic Copper-Nickel center in Nickel-Brass ring
Ruler: Elizabeth II **Obv:** Head with tiara right **Obv. Legend:**
QUEEN ELIZABETH THE SECOND **Rev:** Sun and map
surrounded by wildlife **Rev. Designer:** Matthew Bonaccorsi
Edge: Reeded and lettered **Edge Lettering:** 30 YEARS OF
FALKLAND ISLANDS COINAGE

Date	Mintage	F	VF	XF	Unc	BU
2004	—	—	—	—	5.00	10.00	12.00

KM# 103   25 POUNDS
7.8100 g., 0.9999 Gold 0.2511 oz. AGW, 22 mm. **Ruler:**
Elizabeth II **Obv:** Crowned bust right, denomination below **Obv.**
Designer: Raphael Maklouf **Rev:** Queen Mother as a young lady
and as an elderly lady **Rev. Designer:** Willem Vis **Edge:** Reeded

Date	Mintage	F	VF	XF	Unc	BU
ND(2002) Proof	1,000	Value: 325				

CROWN COINAGE

KM# 141   1/5 CROWN
6.2200 g., 0.9999 Gold 0.1999 oz. AGW **Ruler:** Elizabeth II
Subject: Diamond Wedding Anniversary **Obv:** Conjoined busts
with Prince Philip right **Obv. Legend:** QUEEN ELIZABETH II -
FALKLAND ISLANDS **Rev:** Bride and groom standing facing at
wedding cake; .01 carat x 1.3mm diamond embedded at top
Rev. Legend: Diamond Wedding of H.M. Queen Elizabeth II &
H.R.H. Prince Philip **Edge:** Reeded

Date	Mintage	F	VF	XF	Unc	BU
2007PM Proof	—	Value: 450				

KM# 129   CROWN
Copper-Nickel **Ruler:** Elizabeth II **Rev:** Nelson and the H.M.S.
Victory

Date	Mintage	F	VF	XF	Unc	BU
2005	—	—	—	—	10.00	12.00

KM# 138   CROWN
Copper-Nickel **Ruler:** Elizabeth II **Rev:** Winston Churchill

Date	Mintage	F	VF	XF	Unc	BU
2007	—	—	—	—	15.00	17.50

KM# 139   CROWN
Copper-Nickel **Ruler:** Elizabeth II **Rev:** Queen Elizabeth I

Date	Mintage	F	VF	XF	Unc	BU
2007	—	—	—	—	15.00	17.50

KM# 140   CROWN
Copper-Nickel **Ruler:** Elizabeth II **Rev:** Charles Darwin

Date	Mintage	F	VF	XF	Unc	BU
2007	—	—	—	—	15.00	17.50

KM# 142   CROWN
Copper-Nickel **Ruler:** Elizabeth II **Subject:** Diamond Wedding
Anniversary **Obv:** Conjoined busts with Prince Philip right
Obv. Legend: QUEEN ELIZABETH II - FALKLAND ISLANDS
Rev: King George VI standing at left giving Philip standing at right
his consent to a contract of matrimony **Rev. Legend:** Diamond
Wedding of H.M. Queen Elizabeth II & H.R.H. Prince Philip
Edge: Reeded

Date	Mintage	F	VF	XF	Unc	BU
2007PM	—	—	—	—	17.00	20.00

KM# 142a   CROWN
0.9167 Silver **Ruler:** Elizabeth II **Subject:** Diamond Wedding
Anniversary **Obv:** Conjoined busts with Prince Philip right
Obv. Legend: QUEEN ELIZABETH II - FALKLAND ISLANDS
Rev: King George VI, standing at left, giving Philip, standing at right,
his consent to a contract of matrimony **Rev. Legend:** Diamond
Wedding of H.M. Queen Elizabeth II & H.R.H. Prince Philip
Edge: Reeded

Date	Mintage	F	VF	XF	Unc	BU
2007PM	—	Value: 35.00				

KM# 143   CROWN
Copper-Nickel **Ruler:** Elizabeth II **Subject:** Diamond Wedding
Anniversary **Obv:** Conjoined busts with Prince Philip right
Obv. Legend: QUEEN ELIZABETH II - FALKLAND ISLANDS
Rev: Bride and groom standing facing at wedding cake
Rev. Legend: Diamond Wedding of H.M. Queen Elizabeth II &
H.R.H. Prince Philip **Edge:** Reeded

Date	Mintage	F	VF	XF	Unc	BU
2007PM	—	—	—	—	17.00	20.00

KM# 144   CROWN
Copper-Nickel **Ruler:** Elizabeth II **Subject:** Diamond Wedding
Anniversary **Obv:** Conjoined busts with Prince Philip right
Obv. Legend: QUEEN ELIZABETH II - FALKLAND ISLANDS
Rev: Bridesmaids and Page Boys **Rev. Legend:** Diamond
Wedding of H.M. Queen Elizabeth II & H.R.H. Prince Philip
Edge: Reeded

Date	Mintage	F	VF	XF	Unc	BU
2007PM	—	—	—	—	17.00	20.00

KM# 144a   CROWN
0.9167 Silver **Ruler:** Elizabeth II **Subject:** Diamond Wedding
Anniversary **Obv:** Conjoined busts with Prince Philip right
Obv. Legend: QUEEN ELIZABETH II - FALKLAND ISLANDS
Rev: Bridesmaids and Page Boys **Rev. Legend:** Diamond
Wedding of H.M. Queen Elizabeth II & H.R.H. Prince Philip
Edge: Reeded

Date	Mintage	F	VF	XF	Unc	BU
2007PM Proof	—	Value: 35.00				

KM# 145   CROWN
Copper-Nickel **Ruler:** Elizabeth II **Subject:** Diamond Wedding
Anniversary **Obv:** Conjoined busts with Prince Philip right
Obv. Legend: QUEEN ELIZABETH II - FALKLAND ISLANDS
Rev: Buckingham Palace facade **Rev. Legend:** Diamond
Wedding of H.M. Queen Elizabeth II & H.R.H. Prince Philip
Edge: Reeded

Date	Mintage	F	VF	XF	Unc	BU
2007PM	—	—	—	—	17.00	20.00

KM# 146   CROWN
Copper-Nickel **Ruler:** Elizabeth II **Subject:** 10th Anniversary -
Death of Princess Diana **Obv:** Bust with tiara right
Obv. Legend: QUEEN ELIZABETH II - FALKLAND ISLANDS
Rev: Bust of Princess Diana facing 3/4 right **Rev. Legend:** 1961
- 1997 • DIANA — PRINCESS OF WALES **Edge:** Reeded

Date	Mintage	F	VF	XF	Unc	BU
2007PM	—	—	—	—	17.00	20.00

KM# 146a   CROWN
0.9167 Silver **Ruler:** Elizabeth II **Subject:** 10th Anniversary
Death of Princess Diana **Obv:** Bust with tiara right
Obv. Legend: QUEEN ELIZABETH II - FALKLAND ISLANDS
Rev: Bust of Princess Diana facing 3/4 right **Rev. Legend:** 1961
- 1997 ? DIANA ? PRINCESS OF WALES **Edge:** Reeded

Date	Mintage	F	VF	XF	Unc	BU
2007PM Proof	—	Value: 75.00				

KM# 147   CROWN
Copper-Nickel, 38 mm. **Ruler:** Elizabeth II **Subject:** 20th
Anniversary - Falkland Islands Fishery **Obv:** Bust right of Queen
Elizabeth II **Rev:** Shortfin Squid (Illex Argentinca) **Edge:** Reeded

Date	Mintage	F	VF	XF	Unc	BU
2007PM	—	—	—	17.00		

KM# 148   CROWN
Copper-Nickel, 39 mm. **Ruler:** Elizabeth II **Subject:** Scouting
Centennial **Obv:** Crowned bust right **Obv. Legend:** QUEEN
ELIZABETH II FALKLAND ISLANDS 2007 **Rev:** Baden-Powell
bust 3/4 left, scout saluting, tent flanking within circle on animal
tracks **Rev. Legend:** 1857 ROBERT BADEN-POWELL 1941
ONE CROWN **Edge:** Reeded

Date	Mintage	F	VF	XF	Unc	BU
2007PM	—	—	—	—	12.50	15.00

KM# 148a   CROWN
28.2800 g., 0.9250 Silver 0.8410 oz. ASW, 38.5 mm.
Ruler: Elizabeth II **Subject:** Scouting Centennial **Obv:** Crowned
bust right **Obv. Legend:** QUEEN ELIZABETH II FALKLAND
ISLANDS 2007 **Rev:** Baden-Powell bust 3/4 facing left, scout
saluting and tent flanking, within circle of animal tracks and rope
Rev. Legend: 1857 ROBERT BADEN-POWELL 1941 ONE
CROWN **Edge:** Reeded

Date	Mintage	F	VF	XF	Unc	BU
2007PM Proof	—	Value: 65.00				

KM# 143a   CROWN
0.9167 Silver **Ruler:** Elizabeth II **Subject:** Diamond Wedding
Anniversary **Obv:** Conjoined busts with Prince Philip right
Obv. Legend: QUEEN ELIZABETH II - FALKLAND ISLANDS
Rev: Bride and groom standing facing at wedding cake
Rev. Legend: Diamond Wedding of H.M. Queen Elizabeth II &
H.R.H. Prince Philip **Edge:** Reeded

Date	Mintage	VG	F	VF	XF	Unc
2007PM Proof	—	Value: 35.00				

KM# 150   CROWN
28.2800 g., Copper-Nickel, 38.6 mm. **Ruler:** Elizabeth II
Subject: Royal Air Force

Date	Mintage	F	VF	XF	Unc	BU
2008	—	—	—	—	—	12.00

PIEFORTS

PIEFORTS

KM#	Date	Mintage	Identification	Mkt Val
P18	2001	500	50 Pence. 0.9250 Silver. 56.5600 g. 38.6 mm. Reeded edge. Proof KM#86a.	90.00
P19	2001	500	50 Pence. 0.9250 Silver. 56.5600 g. 38.6 mm. Reeded edge.	90.00
P20	2001	500	50 Pence. 0.9250 Silver. 56.5600 g. 38.6 mm. Reeded edge.	90.00
P21	2001	500	50 Pence. 0.9250 Silver. 56.5600 g. 38.6 mm. Reeded edge.	90.00
P4	2001	500	50 Pence. 0.9250 Silver. 56.5600 g. 38.6 mm. Reeded edge.	100
P5	2001	500	50 Pence. 0.9250 Silver. 56.5600 g. 38.6 mm. Reeded edge. Proof KM#70a.	100
P6	2002	500	50 Pence. 0.9250 Silver. 56.5600 g. 38.6 mm. Reeded edge. Proof KM#73a.	90.00
P7	2002	500	50 Pence. 0.9250 Silver. 56.5600 g. 38.6 mm. Reeded edge. Proof KM#74a.	90.00
P8	2002	500	50 Pence. 0.9250 Silver. 56.5600 g. 38.6 mm. Reeded edge. Proof KM#75a.	90.00
P9	2002	500	50 Pence. 0.9250 Silver. 56.5600 g. 38.6 mm. Reeded edge. Proof KM#76a.	90.00
P10	2002	500	50 Pence. 0.9250 Silver. 56.5600 g. 38.6 mm. Reeded edge. Proof KM#77a.	90.00

KM#	Date	Mintage	Identification	Mkt Val
P11	2002	500	50 Pence. 0.9250 Silver. 56.5600 g. 38.6 mm. Reeded edge. Proof KM#78a.	90.00
P12	2002	500	50 Pence. 0.9250 Silver. 56.5600 g. 38.6 mm. Reeded edge. Proof KM#79a.	90.00
P13	2002	500	50 Pence. 0.9250 Silver. 56.5600 g. 38.6 mm. Reeded edge. Proof KM#80a.	90.00
P14	2002	500	50 Pence. 0.9250 Silver. 56.5600 g. 38.6 mm. Reeded edge. Proof KM#81a.	90.00
P15	2002	500	50 Pence. 0.9250 Silver. 56.5600 g. 38.6 mm. Reeded edge. Proof KM#82a.	90.00
P16	2002	500	50 Pence. 0.9250 Silver. 56.5600 g. 38.6 mm. Reeded edge. Proof KM#83a.	90.00
P17	2002	500	50 Pence. 0.9250 Silver. 56.5600 g. 38.6 mm. Reeded edge. Proof KM#84a.	90.00
P22	ND(2002)	500	50 Pence. 0.9250 Silver. 56.5600 g. 38.6 mm. Reeded edge. Proof KM#102a.	90.00

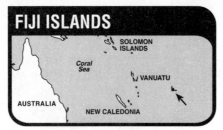

FIJI ISLANDS

The Republic of Fiji consists of about 320 islands located in the southwestern Pacific 1,100 miles (1,770 km.) north of New Zealand. The islands have a combined area of 7,056 sq. mi. (18,274 sq. km.) and a population of 772,891. Capital: Suva. Fiji's economy is based on agriculture and mining. Sugar, coconut products, manganese, and gold are exported. Fiji is a member of the Commonwealth of Nations, but has been subject to periodic short suspensions.

MINT MARK
(o) - Royal Canadian Mint, Ottawa

REPUBLIC
DECIMAL COINAGE
100 Cents = 1 Dollar

KM# 49a CENT
1.5400 g., Copper Plated Zinc, 17.5 mm. **Ruler:** Elizabeth II
Obv: Crowned head right, date at right **Rev:** Tanoa kava bowl divides denomination

Date	Mintage	F	VF	XF	Unc	BU
2001(o)	—	—	—	—	0.20	0.65
2002(o)	5,880,000	—	—	—	0.20	0.65
2003(o)	8,030,000	—	—	—	0.20	0.65
2004(o)	8,840,000	—	—	—	0.20	0.65
2005(o)	9,720,000	—	—	—	0.20	0.65

KM# 50a 2 CENTS
3.1100 g., Copper Plated Zinc, 21.1 mm. **Ruler:** Elizabeth II
Obv: Crowned head right, date at right **Rev:** Palm fan and denomination

Date	Mintage	F	VF	XF	Unc	BU
2001(o)	2,830,000	—	—	—	0.30	0.85
2002(o)	5,000,000	—	—	—	0.30	0.85
2003(o)	6,410,000	—	—	—	0.30	0.85
2004(o)	7,050,000	—	—	—	0.30	0.85
2005(o)	7,760,000	—	—	—	0.30	0.85

KM# 119 5 CENTS
2.3700 g., Nickel Bonded Steel, 19.5 mm. **Ruler:** Elizabeth II
Obv: Crowned head right **Rev:** Fijian drum - Lali divides denomination **Edge:** Plain

Date	Mintage	F	VF	XF	Unc	BU
2009	—	—	—	—	0.75	1.00

KM# 52a 10 CENTS
4.7600 g., Nickel Bonded Steel, 23.6 mm. **Ruler:** Elizabeth II
Obv: Crowned head right **Rev:** Throwing club - ula tava tava

Date	Mintage	F	VF	XF	Unc	BU
2006	—	—	—	—	1.00	1.25

KM# 120 10 CENTS
Nickel Clad Steel, 21 mm. **Ruler:** Elizabeth II **Obv:** Crowned head right **Rev:** Throwing club - ula tava tava **Edge:** Serrated

Date	Mintage	F	VF	XF	Unc	BU
2009	—	—	—	—	1.00	1.25

KM# 95 20 CENTS
11.2400 g., Copper-Nickel, 28.5 mm. **Ruler:** Elizabeth II
Obv: Crowned head right, date at right **Obv. Designer:** Raphael Maklouf **Rev:** South Pacific Games flame logo **Edge:** Reeded
Note: Prooflike examples issued in special cards.

Date	Mintage	F	VF	XF	Unc	BU
2003	1,540,000	—	—	—	1.50	2.50
2003 Prooflike	—	—	—	—	—	6.00

KM# 121 20 CENTS
Nickel Clad Steel, 24 mm. **Ruler:** Elizabeth II **Obv:** Crowned head right **Rev:** Tabua, a ceremonial whale's tooth divides denomination **Edge:** Segmented Reeding

Date	Mintage	F	VF	XF	Unc	BU
2009	—	—	—	0.35	1.25	1.50

KM# 122 50 CENTS
Nickel Clad Steel, 27 mm. **Ruler:** Elizabeth II **Obv:** Crowned head right **Edge:** Rough **Shape:** 12-sided

Date	Mintage	F	VF	XF	Unc	BU
2009	—					

KM# 114 DOLLAR
31.1050 g., 0.9990 Silver 0.9990 oz. ASW, 40.7 mm.
Ruler: Elizabeth II **Subject:** Sputnik I, 50th Anniversary **Rev:** Multicolor earth, satellite rocket

Date	Mintage	F	VF	XF	Unc	BU
2007 Prooflike	6,000	—	—	—	—	100

KM# 115 DOLLAR
31.1050 g., 0.9990 Silver 0.9990 oz. ASW **Ruler:** Elizabeth II
Subject: Birds of Fiji **Rev:** Multicolor - blue crested broadbill

Date	Mintage	F	VF	XF	Unc	BU
2008 Prooflike	4,000	—	—	—	—	90.00

KM# 116 DOLLAR
31.1050 g., 0.9990 Silver 0.9990 oz. ASW **Ruler:** Elizabeth II
Subject: Birds of Fiji **Rev:** Multicolor collared lory

Date	Mintage	F	VF	XF	Unc	BU
2008 Prooflike	4,000	—	—	—	—	90.00

KM# 117 DOLLAR
31.1050 g., 0.9990 Silver 0.9990 oz. ASW **Ruler:** Elizabeth II
Subject: Birds of Fiji **Rev:** Multicolor - Island Thrush

Date	Mintage	F	VF	XF	Unc	BU
2008 Prooflike	4,000	—	—	—	—	90.00

KM# 118 DOLLAR
31.1050 g., 0.9990 Silver 0.9990 oz. ASW **Ruler:** Elizabeth II
Subject: Birds of Fiji **Rev:** Multicolor white collared kingfisher

Date	Mintage	F	VF	XF	Unc	BU
2008 Prooflike	4,000	—	—	—	—	90.00

KM# 108 2 DOLLARS
10.0000 g., 0.9250 Silver 0.2974 oz. ASW **Ruler:** Elizabeth II
Subject: XVIII FIFA World Football Champ. - Germany 2006
Obv: Crowned head right **Obv. Legend:** ELIZABETH II - FIJI **Rev:** World cup

Date	Mintage	F	VF	XF	Unc	BU
2004 Proof	50,000	Value: 22.00				

KM# 93 5 DOLLARS
1.5550 g., 0.9999 Gold 0.0500 oz. AGW **Ruler:** Elizabeth II
Obv: Crowned head right, date at right **Rev:** Arms

Date	Mintage	F	VF	XF	Unc	BU
2002	3,000	Value: 75.00				

KM# 115A 5 DOLLARS
1.5600 g., 0.9999 Gold 0.0501 oz. AGW, 13.9 mm.
Ruler: Elizabeth II **Rev:** Coat of Arms

Date	Mintage	F	VF	XF	Unc	BU
2002 Proof	3,000	Value: 220				

KM# 82 10 DOLLARS
31.6200 g., 0.9250 Silver 0.9403 oz. ASW, 38.6 mm.
Ruler: Elizabeth II **Obv:** Crowned head right, date at right
Obv. Designer: Raphael Maklouf **Rev:** William Bligh's - HMS Providence **Edge:** Reeded

Date	Mintage	F	VF	XF	Unc	BU
2001 Proof	—	Value: 40.00				

KM# 83 10 DOLLARS
28.2800 g., 0.9250 Silver 0.8410 oz. ASW, 38.6 mm.
Ruler: Elizabeth II **Subject:** Queen Elizabeth II - 50 Years of Reign **Obv:** Queen's head right, gilded **Rev:** Cloth draped sword hilt, legend and denomination **Rev. Legend:** Defender of the Faith... **Rev. Designer:** Robert Low **Edge:** Reeded

Date	Mintage	F	VF	XF	Unc	BU
2002 Proof	15,000	Value: 40.00				

KM# 84   10 DOLLARS
28.2800 g., 0.9250 Silver 0.8410 oz. ASW, 38.6 mm.
Ruler: Elizabeth II **Subject:** Queen Elizabeth II - 50th Year of Reign **Obv:** Head right, gilded **Rev:** Four man chorus, legend, and denomination **Rev. Legend:** Westminster Abbey June 1953.
Rev. Designer: Robert Low **Edge:** Reeded

Date	Mintage	F	VF	XF	Unc	BU
2002 Proof	15,000	Value: 40.00				

KM# 94   10 DOLLARS
3.1100 g., 0.9999 Gold 0.1000 oz. AGW   **Ruler:** Elizabeth II
Obv: Crowned head right, date at right **Rev:** Arms **Edge:** Reeded

Date	Mintage	F	VF	XF	Unc	BU
2002 Proof	2,000	Value: 125				

KM# 101   10 DOLLARS
31.1000 g., 0.9990 Silver 0.9988 oz. ASW, 40 mm.
Ruler: Elizabeth II **Series:** Save the Whales **Obv:** Crowned head right, date at right **Obv. Legend:** ELIZABETH II - FIJI **Rev:** Sperm Whale on mother-of-pearl inset **Edge:** Plain

Date	Mintage	F	VF	XF	Unc	BU
2002 Proof	2,000	Value: 85.00				

KM# 104   10 DOLLARS
28.2800 g., 0.9250 Silver 0.8410 oz. ASW, 38.6 mm.
Ruler: Elizabeth II **Series:** Endangered Wildlife **Obv:** Crowned head right **Obv. Legend:** ELIZABETH II - FIJI **Rev:** Head of Peregrine Falcon right

Date	Mintage	F	VF	XF	Unc	BU
2002 Proof	—	Value: 40.00				

KM# 105   10 DOLLARS
28.2800 g., 0.9250 Silver 0.8410 oz. ASW, 38.6 mm.
Ruler: Elizabeth II **Obv:** Crowned head right **Obv. Legend:** ELIZABETH II - FIJI **Rev:** Sailing ship "Vostok"

Date	Mintage	F	VF	XF	Unc	BU
2002 Proof	—	Value: 40.00				

KM# 106   10 DOLLARS
1.2400 g., 0.9999 Gold 0.0399 oz. AGW, 13.88 mm.
Ruler: Elizabeth II **Obv:** Crowned head right **Obv. Legend:** ELIZABETH II - FIJI **Rev:** Sailing ship at left, naval bust 3/4 left at right **Rev. Legend:** HMS INVESTIGATOR * MATTHEW FLINDERS **Edge:** Reeded

Date	Mintage	F	VF	XF	Unc	BU
2002 Proof	—	Value: 65.00				

KM# 114A   10 DOLLARS
3.1100 g., 0.9999 Gold 0.1000 oz. AGW, 16 mm.
Ruler: Elizabeth II **Rev:** Coat of Arms

Date	Mintage	F	VF	XF	Unc	BU
2002 Proof	2,000	Value: 350				

KM# 113   10 DOLLARS
1.2400 g., Gold, 13.91 mm. **Ruler:** Elizabeth II **Subject:** Lost Treasure of King Richard **Obv:** Crowned head right **Rev:** Bust of King Richard facing **Edge:** Reeded

Date	Mintage	F	VF	XF	Unc	BU
2003 Proof	—	Value: 65.00				

KM# 107   10 DOLLARS
28.2600 g., 0.9250 Silver 0.8404 oz. ASW, 38.61 mm.
Ruler: Elizabeth II **Obv:** Crowned head right **Obv. Legend:** ELIZABETH II - FIJI **Obv. Designer:** Raphael Maklouf **Rev:** Sailing ship at left, naval bust 3/4 left at right **Rev. Legend:** HMS INVESTIGATOR * MATTHEW FLINDERS **Edge:** Reeded

Date	Mintage	F	VF	XF	Unc	BU
2003 Proof	—	Value: 40.00				

KM# 109   10 DOLLARS
Silver   **Ruler:** Elizabeth II **Subject:** XXVIII Summer Olympics - Athens 2004 **Obv:** Crowned head right **Obv. Legend:** ELIZABETH II - FIJI **Rev:** Regatta

Date	Mintage	F	VF	XF	Unc	BU
2004 Proof	—	Value: 40.00				

KM# 110   10 DOLLARS
Copper-Nickel-Zinc, 38.6 mm. **Ruler:** Elizabeth II **Subject:** XVIII FIFA World Football Championship - Gemany 2006 **Obv:** Crowned head right **Obv. Legend:** ELIZABETH II - FIJI **Rev:** Digital countdown clock

Date	Mintage	F	VF	XF	Unc	BU
2005	50,000	—	—	—	—	45.00

KM# 111   10 DOLLARS
1.2400 g., 0.9999 Gold 0.0399 oz. AGW   **Ruler:** Elizabeth II **Subject:** 500th Anniversary Death of Christopher Columbus **Obv:** Crowned head right **Obv. Legend:** ELIZABETH II - FIJI **Rev:** Sailing ship "Santa Maria"

Date	Mintage	F	VF	XF	Unc	BU
2006 Proof	15,000	Value: 65.00				

KM# 125   10 DOLLARS
31.1050 g., 0.9990 Silver 0.9990 oz. ASW   **Ruler:** Elizabeth II **Obv:** Crowned head right **Rev:** Yes we can!

Date	Mintage	F	VF	XF	Unc	BU
2009 Proof	—	Value: 45.00				

KM# 112   25 DOLLARS
155.5000 g., 0.9990 Silver 4.9942 oz. ASW   **Ruler:** Elizabeth II **Obv:** Crowned head right **Obv. Legend:** ELIZABETH II - FIJI **Rev:** Sailing ship "Vostok"

Date	Mintage	F	VF	XF	Unc	BU
2002 Proof	—	Value: 185				

KM# 99   100 DOLLARS
7.7800 g., 0.5850 Gold 0.1463 oz. AGW   **Ruler:** Elizabeth II **Subject:** 2006 FIFA World Cup - Germany **Obv:** Crowned head right, date at right **Rev:** World Cup **Edge:** Reeded

Date	Mintage	F	VF	XF	Unc	BU
2003 Proof	25,000	Value: 200				

FINLAND

The Republic of Finland, the third most northerly state of the European continent, has an area of 130,559 sq. mi. (338,127 sq. km.) and a population of 5.1 million. Capital: Helsinki. Lumbering, shipbuilding, metal and woodworking are the leading industries. Paper, timber, wood pulp, plywood and metal products are exported.

MONETARY SYSTEM
100 Pennia = 1 Markka

MINT MARKS
No mm – Helsinki
M – 1987-2006
FI – FINLAND – 2007-

MINT OFFICIALS' INITIALS

Letter	Date	Name
J-M	2002	Toivo Jaatinen & Raimo Makkonen
L-M	2000-03	Maija Lavonen & Raimo Makkonen
K-M	2004	Heli Kauhanen & Raimo Makkonen
K-M	2005-2006	Tapio Kettunen & Raimo Makkonen
M-M	2002-2006	Pertti Mäkinen & Raimo Makkonen
N-M	2001	Antti Neuvonen & Raimo Makkonen
P-M	2003	Matti Peltokangas & Raimo Makkonen
P-M	2001, 2005-2007	Reijo Paavilainen & Raimo Makkonen
S-M	2003	Anneli Sigriläinen & Raimo Makkonen
VV-M	2002	Erkki Vainio & Hannu Veijalainen & Raimo Makkonen

REPUBLIC
REFORM COINAGE

KM# 65   10 PENNIA
1.8000 g., Copper-Nickel, 16.3 mm. **Obv:** Flower pods and stems, date at right **Rev:** Denomination to right of honeycombs **Designer:** Antti Neuvonen

Date	Mintage	F	VF	XF	Unc	BU
2001 M	25,000,000	—	—	—	1.00	1.50
2001 M Proof	—	Value: 7.00				

KM# 66   50 PENNIA
3.3000 g., Copper-Nickel, 19.7 mm. **Obv:** Polar bear, date below **Rev:** Denomination above flower heads **Designer:** Antti Neuvonen

Date	Mintage	F	VF	XF	Unc	BU
2001 M	200,000	—	—	0.20	1.00	1.50
2001 M Proof	—	Value: 8.00				

KM# 76   MARKKA
5.0000 g., Aluminum-Bronze, 22.2 mm. **Obv:** Rampant lion left within circle, date below **Rev:** Ornaments flank denomination within circle

Date	Mintage	F	VF	XF	Unc	BU
2001 M	200,000	—	—	0.35	0.75	1.00
2001 M Proof	—	Value: 10.00				

KM# 95   MARKKA
8.6400 g., 0.7500 Gold 0.2083 oz. AGW, 22 mm. **Subject:** Last Markka Coin **Obv:** Rampant lion with sword left **Rev:** Stylized tree with roots **Edge:** Reeded **Designer:** Reijo Paavilainen

Date	Mintage	F	VF	XF	Unc	BU
2001M P-M Proof	55,000	Value: 275				

KM# 106   MARKKA
6.1000 g., Copper-Nickel, 24 mm. **Subject:** Remembrance Markka **Obv:** Rampant lion with sword left **Rev:** Denomination and pine tree **Edge:** Plain **Designer:** Antti Neuvonen **Note:** This coin is encased in acrylic resin and sealed in a display card.

Date	Mintage	F	VF	XF	Unc	BU
2001M N-M	500,000	—	—	—	5.00	6.50

KM# 73   5 MARKKAA
5.5000 g., Copper-Aluminum-Nickel, 24.5 mm. **Obv:** Lake Saimaa ringed seal, date below **Rev:** Denomination, dragonfly and lily pad leaves

Date	Mintage	F	VF	XF	Unc	BU
2001 M	200,000	—	—	—	4.00	6.00
2001 M Proof	—	Value: 12.00				

KM# 77   10 MARKKAA
8.8000 g., Bi-Metallic Brass center in Copper-Nickel ring, 27.25 mm.   **Obv:** Capercaillie bird within circle, date above **Rev:** Denomination and branches

Date	Mintage	F	VF	XF	Unc	BU
2001 M	200,000	—	—	3.00	5.00	6.00
2001 M Proof	—	Value: 18.00				

KM# 96   25 MARKKAA
20.2000 g., Bi-Metallic Brass center in Copper-Nickel ring, 35 mm.   **Subject:** First Nordic Ski Championship, "Lahti 2001" **Obv:** Stylized woman's face **Rev:** Female torso, landscape **Edge:** Plain **Designer:** Jarkko Roth

Date	Mintage	F	VF	XF	Unc	BU
2001M Prooflike	100,000	—	—	—	—	30.00

KM# 97   100 MARKKAA
31.0000 g., 0.9250 Silver 0.9219 oz. ASW, 35 mm.   **Subject:** Aino Ackte **Obv:** Partial portrait **Rev:** High heel boot and trouser bottom **Edge:** Plain **Designer:** Timo Rytkönen.

Date	Mintage	F	VF	XF	Unc	BU
2001M	33,000	—	—	—	30.00	40.00
2001M Proof	12,000	Value: 50.00				

EURO COINAGE
European Union Issues

KM# 98   EURO CENT
2.3000 g., Copper Plated Steel, 16.3 mm.   **Obv:** Rampant lion left surrounded by stars, date at left **Obv. Designer:** Heikki Häiväoja **Rev:** Denomination and globe **Rev. Designer:** Luc Luycx **Edge:** Plain

Date	Mintage	F	VF	XF	Unc	BU
2001M	500,000	—	—	—	10.00	—
2001M Proof	15,000	—	—	—	—	—
2002M	659,000	—	—	—	5.00	—
2002M Proof	13,000	Value: 15.00				
2003M	6,790,000	—	—	—	1.00	—
2003M Proof	14,500	Value: 15.00				
2004M	9,690,000	—	—	—	1.00	—
2004M Proof	5,000	Value: 15.00				
2005M	5,800,000	—	—	—	1.00	—
2005M Proof	3,000	Value: 15.00				
2006M	4,000,000	—	—	—	1.00	—
2006M Proof	3,300	Value: 15.00				
2007FI	3,000,000	—	—	—	1.00	—
2007FI Proof	—	Value: 15.00				
2008FI	—	—	—	—	1.00	—
2009FI	—	—	—	—	1.00	—

KM# 99   2 EURO CENT
3.0000 g., Copper Plated Steel, 18.8 mm.   **Obv:** Rampant lion surrounded by stars, date at left **Obv. Designer:** Heikki Häiväoja **Rev:** Denomination and globe **Rev. Designer:** Luc Luycx **Edge:** Grooved

Date	Mintage	F	VF	XF	Unc	BU
2001M	500,000	—	—	—	10.00	—
2001M Proof	15,000	Value: 15.00				
2002M	659,000	—	—	—	5.00	—
2002M Proof	13,000	Value: 15.00				
2003M	6,790,000	—	—	—	5.00	—
2003M Proof	14,500	Value: 15.00				
2004M	8,024,000	—	—	—	5.00	—
2004M Proof	5,000	Value: 15.00				
2005M	5,800,000	—	—	—	5.00	—
2005M Proof	3,000	Value: 15.00				
2006M	4,000,000	—	—	—	5.00	—
2006M Proof	3,300	Value: 15.00				
2007FI	3,000,000	—	—	—	5.00	—
2007FI Proof	—	Value: 15.00				
2008FI	—	—	—	—	5.00	—
2009FI	—	—	—	—	5.00	—

KM# 100   5 EURO CENT
3.9400 g., Copper Plated Steel, 21.3 mm.   **Obv:** Rampant lion left surrounded by stars, date at left **Obv. Designer:** Heikki Häiväoja **Rev:** Denomination and globe **Rev. Designer:** Luc Luycx **Edge:** Plain

Date	Mintage	F	VF	XF	Unc	BU
2001M	213,756,000	—	—	—	0.50	—
2001M Proof	15,000	Value: 15.00				
2002M	101,824,000	—	—	—	0.50	—
2002M Proof	13,000	Value: 15.00				
2003M	790,000	—	—	—	1.00	—
2003M Proof	14,500	Value: 15.00				
2004M	629,000	—	—	—	1.00	—
2004M Proof	5,000	Value: 15.00				
2005M	800,000	—	—	—	1.00	—
2005M Proof	3,000	Value: 15.00				
2006M	1,000,000	—	—	—	1.00	—
2006M Proof	3,000	Value: 15.00				
2007FI	1,000,000	—	—	—	1.00	—
2007FI Proof	—	Value: 15.00				
2008FI	—	—	—	—	1.00	—
2009FI	—	—	—	—	1.00	—

KM# 101   10 EURO CENT
4.0000 g., Brass, 19.7 mm.   **Obv:** Rampant lion left surrounded by stars, date at left **Obv. Designer:** Heikki Häiväoja **Rev:** Denomination and map **Rev. Designer:** Luc Luycx **Edge:** Reeded

Date	Mintage	F	VF	XF	Unc	BU
2001M	14,730,000	—	—	—	10.00	—
2001M Proof	15,000	Value: 18.00				
2002M	1,499,000	—	—	—	2.50	—
2002M Proof	13,000	Value: 18.00				
2003M	790,000	—	—	—	2.50	—
2003M Proof	14,500	Value: 18.00				
2004M	629,000	—	—	—	2.50	—
2004M Proof	5,000	Value: 18.00				
2005M	800,000	—	—	—	2.50	—
2005M Proof	3,000	Value: 18.00				
2006M	1,000,000	—	—	—	2.50	—
2006M Proof	3,300	Value: 18.00				

KM# 126   10 EURO CENT
4.1000 g., Brass, 19.8 mm.   **Obv:** Rampant lion surrounded by stars **Obv. Designer:** Heikki Häiväoja **Rev:** Relief map of Western Europe, stars, lines and value **Rev. Designer:** Luc Luycx **Edge:** Reeded

Date	Mintage	F	VF	XF	Unc	BU
2007FI	1,000,000	—	—	—	2.50	—
2007FI Proof	—	—	—	—	—	—
2008FI	—	—	—	—	2.50	—
2009FI	—	—	—	—	2.50	—

KM# 102   20 EURO CENT
5.7300 g., Brass, 22.2 mm.   **Obv:** Rampant lion left surrounded by stars, date at left **Obv. Designer:** Heikki Häiväoja **Rev:** Denomination and map **Rev. Designer:** Luc Luycx **Edge:** Notched

Date	Mintage	F	VF	XF	Unc	BU
2001M	121,763,000	—	—	—	1.75	—
2001M Proof	15,000	Value: 20.00				
2002M	100,759,000	—	—	—	1.75	—
2002M Proof	13,000	Value: 20.00				
2003M	790,000	—	—	—	1.75	—
2003M Proof	14,500	Value: 20.00				
2004M	629,000	—	—	—	1.75	—
2004M Proof	5,000	Value: 20.00				
2005M	800,000	—	—	—	1.75	—
2005M Proof	3,000	Value: 20.00				
2006M	1,000,000	—	—	—	1.75	—
2006M Proof	3,300	Value: 20.00				

KM# 127   20 EURO CENT
5.7000 g., Brass, 22.3 mm.   **Obv:** Rampant lion surrounded by stars **Obv. Designer:** Heikki Häiväoja **Rev:** Relief map of Western Europe, stars, lines and value **Rev. Designer:** Luc Luycx **Edge:** Notched

Date	Mintage	F	VF	XF	Unc	BU
2007FI	1,000,000	—	—	—	1.75	—
2007FI Proof	—	—	—	—	—	—
2008FI	—	—	—	—	1.75	—
2009FI	—	—	—	—	1.75	—

KM# 103   50 EURO CENT
7.8100 g., Brass, 24.2 mm.   **Obv:** Rampant lion left surrounded by stars, date at left **Obv. Designer:** Heikki Häiväoja **Rev:** Denomination and map **Rev. Designer:** Luc Luycx **Edge:** Reeded

Date	Mintage	F	VF	XF	Unc	BU
2001M	4,432,000	—	—	—	7.50	—
2001M Proof	15,000	Value: 22.00				
2002M	1,147,000	—	—	—	5.00	—
2002M Proof	13,000	Value: 22.00				
2003M	790,000	—	—	—	5.00	—
2003M Proof	14,500	Value: 22.00				
2004M	629,000	—	—	—	5.00	—
2004M Proof	5,000	Value: 22.00				
2005M	4,800,000	—	—	—	5.00	—
2005M Proof	3,000	Value: 22.00				
2006M	6,850,000	—	—	—	5.00	—
2006M Proof	3,300	Value: 22.00				

KM# 128   50 EURO CENT
7.9000 g., Brass, 24.3 mm.   **Obv:** Rampant lion surrounded by stars **Obv. Designer:** Heikki Häiväoja **Rev:** Relief map of Western Europe, stars, lines and value **Rev. Designer:** Luc Luycx **Edge:** Reeded

Date	Mintage	F	VF	XF	Unc	BU
2007FI	1,000,000	—	—	—	5.00	—
2007FI Proof	—	—	—	—	—	—
2008FI	—	—	—	—	5.00	—
2009FI	—	—	—	—	5.00	—

KM# 104 EURO

7.5000 g., Bi-Metallic Copper-nickel center in Brass ring, 23.2 mm. **Obv:** 2 flying swans, date below, surrounded by stars on outer ring **Obv. Designer:** Pertti Mäkinen **Rev:** Denomination and map **Rev. Designer:** Luc Luycx **Edge:** Reeded and plain sections

Date	Mintage	F	VF	XF	Unc	BU
2001M	13,862,000	—	—	—	3.00	—
2001M Proof	15,000	Value: 25.00				
2002M	14,114,000	—	—	—	6.50	—
2002M Proof	13,000	Value: 25.00				
2003M	790,000	—	—	—	6.50	—
2003M Proof	14,500	Value: 25.00				
2004M	5,529,000	—	—	—	6.50	—
2004M Proof	5,000	Value: 25.00				
2005M	7,935,000	—	—	—	6.50	—
2005M Proof	3,000	Value: 25.00				
2006M	1,705,000	—	—	—	6.50	—
2006M Proof	3,300	Value: 25.00				

KM# 129 EURO

7.5000 g., Bi-Metallic Copper-Nickel center in Brass ring, 23.2 mm. **Obv:** 2 flying swans surrounded by stars on outer ring **Obv. Designer:** Pertti Mäekinen **Rev:** Relief map of western Europe, stars, lines and value **Rev. Designer:** Luc Luycx **Edge:** Reeded and plain sections

Date	Mintage	F	VF	XF	Unc	BU
2007FI	1,000,000	—	—	—	6.50	—
2007FI Proof	—	—	—	—	—	—
2008FI	—	—	—	—	6.50	—
2009FI	—	—	—	—	6.50	—

KM# 105 2 EURO

8.5200 g., Bi-Metallic Brass center in Copper-nickel ring, 25.6 mm. **Obv:** 2 cloudberry flowers surrounded by stars on outer ring **Obv. Designer:** Raimo Heino **Rev:** Denomination and map **Rev. Designer:** Luc Luycx **Edge:** Reeded and lettered **Edge Lettering:** SUOMI FINLAND

Date	Mintage	F	VF	XF	Unc	BU
2001M	29,132,000	—	—	—	4.00	—
2001M Proof	15,000	Value: 30.00				
2002M	1,386,000	—	—	—	7.50	—
2002M Proof	13,000	Value: 30.00				
2003M	9,080,000	—	—	—	5.00	—
2003M Proof	14,500	Value: 30.00				
2004M	9,029,000	—	—	—	5.00	—
2004M Proof	5,000	Value: 30.00				
2005M	8,800,000	—	—	—	5.00	—
2005M Proof	3,000	Value: 30.00				
2006M	11,000,000	—	—	—	5.00	—
2006M Proof	3,300	Value: 30.00				

KM# 114 2 EURO

8.5200 g., Bi-Metallic, 25.6 mm. **Subject:** EU Expansion **Obv:** Stylized flower **Obv. Designer:** Pertti Mäkinen **Rev:** Denomination and map **Rev. Designer:** Luc Luycx **Edge:** Reeded and lettered

Date	Mintage	F	VF	XF	Unc	BU
2004 M-M	1,000,000	—	—	—	10.00	11.50
2004 Proof	—	—	—	—	—	—

KM# 119 2 EURO

8.5200 g., Bi-Metallic Brass center in Copper-Nickel ring, 25.6 mm. **Subject:** 60th Anniversary - Finland - UN **Obv:** Dove on a puzzle **Rev:** Denomination over map **Edge:** Reeded and lettered **Edge Lettering:** "YK 1945-2005 FN"

Date	Mintage	F	VF	XF	Unc	BU
2005M K-M	2,000,000	—	—	—	6.00	7.50

KM# 125 2 EURO

8.5200 g., Bi-Metallic Brass center in Copper-Nickel ring, 25.6 mm. **Subject:** Centennial of Universal Suffrage **Obv:** Two faces **Obv. Designer:** Pertti Mäkinen **Rev:** Value and map **Rev. Designer:** Luc Luycx **Edge:** Reeded and lettered **Edge Lettering:** "SUOMI FINLAND"

Date	Mintage	F	VF	XF	Unc	BU
ND (2006)M M-M	2,500,000	—	—	—	6.00	7.50

KM# 130 2 EURO

8.3200 g., Bi-Metallic Brass center in Copper-nickel ring, 25.8 mm. **Obv:** 2 cloudberry flowers surrounded by stars on outer ring **Obv. Designer:** Raimo Heino **Rev:** Relief map of Western Europe, stars, lines and value **Rev. Designer:** Luc Luycx **Edge:** Reeded and lettered **Edge Lettering:** SUOMI FINLAND

Date	Mintage	F	VF	XF	Unc	BU
2007FI	8,600,000	—	—	—	6.00	7.50
2007FI Proof	—	—	—	—	—	—
2008FI	—	—	—	—	6.00	7.50
2009FI	—	—	—	—	6.00	7.50

KM# 138 2 EURO

8.5200 g., Bi-Metallic Copper-Nickel center in Brass ring, 25.72 mm. **Subject:** 50th Anniversary Treaty of Rome **Obv:** Open treaty book **Rev:** Large value at left, modified outline of Europe at right **Edge:** Reeded and lettered

Date	Mintage	F	VF	XF	Unc	BU
2007	—	—	—	—	7.00	9.00

KM# 139 2 EURO

8.5200 g., Bi-Metallic Brass center in Copper-Nickel ring, 25.6 mm. **Subject:** 90th Anniversary of Independence

Date	Mintage	F	VF	XF	Unc	BU
2007	—	—	—	—	—	6.00

KM# 143 2 EURO

Bi-Metallic Brass Center in copper-nickel ring, 25.6 mm. **Subject:** Universal Declariation of Human Rights **Obv:** Human figure within heart in landscape

Date	Mintage	F	VF	XF	Unc	BU
2008	1,500,000	—	—	—	6.00	7.50

KM# 149 2 EURO

8.5000 g., Bi-Metallic, 25.6 mm. **Subject:** Autonomy, 200th Anniversary **Obv:** Classical Pyramid

Date	Mintage	F	VF	XF	Unc	BU
2009	1,600,000	—	—	—	6.00	7.50

KM# 144 2 EURO

Bi-Metallic, 25.6 mm. **Subject:** EMU 60th Anniversary **Obv:** Stick figure and E symbol

Date	Mintage	F	VF	XF	Unc	BU
2009	1,400,000	—	—	—	6.00	7.50
2009 Proof	25,000	—	—	—	—	—

KM# 111 5 EURO

20.1000 g., Bi-Metallic Copper-Nickel center in Brass ring, 34.9 mm. **Subject:** Ice Hockey World Championships **Obv:** Summer landscape and denomination **Rev:** Three hockey sticks and a puck **Edge:** Plain **Designer:** Pertti Mäkinen

Date	Mintage	F	VF	XF	Unc	BU
2003M M-M	150,000	—	—	—	15.00	20.00

KM# 118 5 EURO

19.8000 g., Bi-Metallic Brass center in Copper-Nickel ring, 35 mm. **Subject:** 10th Anniversary - IAAF World Championships in Athletics **Obv:** Female javelin thrower, denomination **Rev:** Running feet **Edge:** Plain **Designer:** Tapio Kettunen

Date	Mintage	F	VF	XF	Unc	BU
2005M K-M	170,000	—	—	—	15.00	20.00
2005M K-M Proof	5,000	Value: 25.00				

KM# 123 5 EURO

18.7000 g., Copper, 35 mm. **Subject:** 150th Anniversary - Demilitarization of Aland **Obv:** Boat, Dove of Peace on the helm **Rev:** Tree **Edge Lettering:** AHVENANMAAN DEMILITARISOINTI 150 VUOTTA* **Designer:** Pertti Mäkinen

Date	Mintage	F	VF	XF	Unc	BU
2006 M-M	55,000	—	—	—	20.00	25.00

KM# 131 5 EURO
9.8100 g., Bi-Metallic Copper-Nickel center in Brass ring, 27.25 mm. **Subject:** Finland Presidency of European Union **Obv:** Letter decorations with 2006 and SUOMI-FINLAND **Rev:** 5 EURO below letter decoration **Designer:** Reijo Paavilainen

Date	Mintage	F	VF	XF	Unc	BU
2006M P-M	100,000	—	—	—	15.00	20.00

KM# 135 5 EURO
19.8000 g., Bi-Metallic Brass center in Copper-Nickel ring, 35 mm. **Subject:** 30th Anniversary of Finland's Independence **Designer:** Reijo Paavilainen

Date	Mintage	F	VF	XF	Unc	BU
2007 P	130,000	—	—	—	15.00	20.00
2007 P Proof	20,000	Value: 25.00				

KM# 146 5 EURO
19.8000 g., Silver, 35 mm. **Subject:** Indiependence, 90th Anniversary **Obv:** Petroglif of a longboat **Obv. Designer:** Reijo Paavilainen

Date	Mintage	F	VF	XF	Unc	BU
2007 Proof	—	Value: 35.00				

KM# 141 5 EURO
Bi-Metallic Copper-Nickel center in Brass ring, 34.9 mm. **Obv:** Science and Research

Date	Mintage	F	VF	XF	Unc	BU
2008	25,000	—	—	—	15.00	20.00
2008 Proof	20,000	Value: 25.00				

KM# 107 10 EURO
27.4000 g., 0.9250 Silver 0.8148 oz. ASW, 38.6 mm. **Subject:** 50th Anniversary - Helsinki Olympics **Obv:** Flames and denomination above globe with map of Finland **Obv. Designer:** Erkki Vainio **Rev:** Tower and partial coin design **Rev. Designer:** Hannu Veijalainen **Edge:** Plain

Date	Mintage	F	VF	XF	Unc	BU
2002M VV-M	10,000	—	—	—	28.00	30.00
2002M VV-M Proof	34,800	Value: 32.00				

KM# 108 10 EURO
27.4000 g., 0.9250 Silver 0.8148 oz. ASW, 38.6 mm. **Subject:** Elias Lönnrot **Obv:** Ribbon with stars **Rev:** Quill and signature **Edge:** Plain **Designer:** Pertti Mäkinen

Date	Mintage	F	VF	XF	Unc	BU
2002M M-M	40,000	—	—	—	28.00	30.00
2002M M-M Proof	40,000	Value: 32.00				

KM# 110 10 EURO
27.4000 g., 0.9250 Silver 0.8148 oz. ASW, 38.6 mm. **Subject:** Anders Chydenius **Obv:** Stylized design **Rev:** Name and book **Edge:** Plain **Designer:** Tero Lounas

Date	Mintage	F	VF	XF	Unc	BU
2003M L-M	30,000	—	—	—	32.00	35.00
2003M Proof	30,000	Value: 40.00				

KM# 112 10 EURO
27.4000 g., 0.9250 Silver 0.8148 oz. ASW, 38.6 mm. **Subject:** Mannerheim and St. Petersburg **Obv:** Head 3/4 facing **Rev:** Fortress, denomination at right **Designer:** Anneli Sipiläinen

Date	Mintage	F	VF	XF	Unc	BU
2003 S-M	6,000	—	—	—	35.00	37.50
2003 S-M Proof	29,000	Value: 55.00				

KM# 115 10 EURO
27.4000 g., 0.9250 Silver 0.8148 oz. ASW, 38.6 mm. **Subject:** 200th Birthday of Johan Ludwig Runeberg **Obv:** Head of Runeberg **Rev:** Text of 1831 Helsingfors Tidningar newspaper **Designer:** Heli Kauhanen

Date	Mintage	F	VF	XF	Unc	BU
2004 K-M	6,400	—	—	—	32.00	35.00
2004 K-M Proof	600	Value: 45.00				

KM# 116 10 EURO
27.4000 g., 0.9250 Silver 0.8148 oz. ASW, 38.6 mm. **Subject:** Tove Jansson **Obv:** Three "muumi" figures **Rev:** Head of Tove Jansson **Edge:** Pertti Mäkinen

Date	Mintage	F	VF	XF	Unc	BU
2004 M-M	50,000	—	—	—	32.00	35.00
2004 M-M Proof	20,000	Value: 45.00				

KM# 120 10 EURO
25.5000 g., 0.9250 Silver 0.7583 oz. ASW, 38.6 mm. **Subject:** 60 years of Peace **Obv:** Dove of peace **Rev:** Flowering plant **Designer:** Pertti Mäkinen

Date	Mintage	F	VF	XF	Unc	BU
2005 M-M	55,000	—	—	—	32.00	35.00
2005 Proof	5,000	Value: 45.00				

KM# 122 10 EURO
25.5000 g., 0.9250 Silver 0.7583 oz. ASW, 38.6 mm. **Subject:** Unknown Soldier and Finnish Film Art **Obv:** Trench **Rev:** Soldier with helmet on top of a film **Designer:** Reijo Paavilainen

Date	Mintage	F	VF	XF	Unc	BU
2005 P-M	25,000	—	—	—	35.00	37.50
2005 P-M Proof	15,000	Value: 50.00				

KM# 124 10 EURO
25.5000 g., 0.9250 Silver 0.7583 oz. ASW, 38.6 mm. **Subject:** 200th Birthday - Johan Vilhelm Snellman **Obv:** Sun rising over the lake **Rev:** Snellman **Designer:** Tapio Kettunen

Date	Mintage	F	VF	XF	Unc	BU
2006 K-M	—	—	—	—	32.00	35.00
2006 K-M Proof	—	Value: 45.00				

KM# 132 10 EURO
25.5000 g., 0.9250 Silver 0.7583 oz. ASW, 38.6 mm. **Subject:** 100th Anniversary of Parliamentary Reform **Obv:** Two stylist heads female and male with text SUOMI FINLAND 10 EURO **Rev:** Male and female fingers inserting ballot paper into ballot box with text 100V EDUSKUNTAUUDISTUS 2006 **Edge Lettering:** LANTDAGSREFORMEN 1906 **Designer:** Pertti Mäkinen

Date	Mintage	F	VF	XF	Unc	BU
2006M M-M	40,000	—	—	—	32.00	35.00
2006M M-M Proof	20,000	Value: 45.00				

KM# 134 10 EURO
25.5000 g., 0.9250 Silver 0.7583 oz. ASW, 38.6 mm. **Subject:** A.E. Nordenskiöld and the Northeast Passage **Designer:** Reijo Paavilainen

Date	Mintage	F	VF	XF	Unc	BU
2007M P	7,000	—	—	—	32.00	35.00
2007M P Proof	33,000	Value: 45.00				

KM# 136 10 EURO
25.5000 g., 0.9250 Silver 0.7583 oz. ASW, 38.6 mm. **Subject:** Mikael Agricola - Finnish Language **Designer:** Reijo Paavilainen

Date	Mintage	F	VF	XF	Unc	BU
2007 P	6,000	—	—	—	32.00	35.00
2007 P Proof	24,000	Value: 45.00				

KM# 140 10 EURO
27.4000 g., 0.9250 Silver 0.8148 oz. ASW, 38.6 mm. **Subject:** Finnish Flag

Date	Mintage	F	VF	XF	Unc	BU
2008	9,000	—	—	—	28.00	30.00
2008 Proof	26,000	Value: 32.00				

KM# 142 10 EURO
27.4000 g., 0.9250 Silver 0.8148 oz. ASW, 36.8 mm. **Subject:** Mika Waltari

Date	Mintage	F	VF	XF	Unc	BU
2008	5,000	—	—	—	28.00	30.00
2008 Proof	15,000	Value: 32.00				

KM# 148 10 EURO
27.4000 g., 0.9250 Silver 0.8148 oz. ASW, 38.6 mm. **Subject:** Fredrik Pacius **Obv:** Opening notes to kung Karls Jakt, first opera of Pacius **Rev:** Stage curtian opening

Date	Mintage	F	VF	XF	Unc	BU
2009	—	—	—	—	35.00	37.50

KM# 121 20 EURO
1.7300 g., 0.9000 Gold 0.0501 oz. AGW, 13.9 mm. **Subject:** 10th Anniversary - IAAF World Championships in Athletics **Obv:** Helsinki Stadium **Rev:** Two faces **Designer:** Pertti Mäkinen

Date	Mintage	F	VF	XF	Unc	BU
2005 M-M Proof	30,000	Value: 100				

KM# 113 50 EURO
13.2000 g., Bi-Metallic .750 Gold center in .925 Silver ring, 27.25 mm. **Subject:** Finnish art and design **Obv:** Snowflake design within box, beaded circle surrounds **Rev:** Snowflake design within beaded circle **Designer:** Matti Peltokangas

Date	Mintage	F	VF	XF	Unc	BU
2003 P-M Proof	10,600	Value: 320				

KM# 133 50 EURO
12.8000 g., Tri-Metallic 0.750 Gold 0.125 Silver 0.125 Copper center in 0.925 Silver and 0.075 Copper ring, 27.25 mm. **Subject:** Finland Presidency of European Union **Obv:** Letter decorations with 2006 and SUOMI-FINLAND **Rev:** 50 EURO below letter decoration **Designer:** Reijo Paavilainen

Date	Mintage	F	VF	XF	Unc	BU
2006M P-M Proof	8,000	Value: 320				

KM# 109 100 EURO
8.6400 g., 0.9000 Gold 0.2500 oz. AGW, 22 mm. **Subject:** Lapland **Obv:** Small tree and mountain stream **Rev:** Lake landscape beneath the midnight sun **Edge:** Plain with serial number **Designer:** Toivo Jaatinen

Date	Mintage	F	VF	XF	Unc	BU
2002M J-M Proof	25,000	Value: 325				

KM# 117 100 EURO
8.6400 g., 0.9000 Gold 0.2500 oz. AGW, 22 mm. **Subject:** 150th Birthday of Albert Edelfelt **Obv:** Flower **Rev:** Head of Edelfelt **Designer:** Pertti Mäkinen

Date	Mintage	F	VF	XF	Unc	BU
2004 M-M Proof	8,500	Value: 345				

KM# 137 100 EURO
8.4800 g., 0.9170 Gold 0.2500 oz. AGW **Subject:** 90th Anniversary of Finland's Independence **Obv:** Finland and the years of independence **Rev:** Abstract composition **Designer:** Reijo Paavilainen

Date	Mintage	F	VF	XF	Unc	BU
2007 P	—	—	—	—	325	315
2007 P Proof	—	Value: 350				

KM# 147 100 EURO
8.4800 g., Gold, 22 mm. **Subject:** Independence, 90th Anniversary **Obv:** Abstract composition **Obv. Designer:** Reijo Paavilainen **Rev:** Dates and script

Date	Mintage	F	VF	XF	Unc	BU
2007 Proof	—	Value: 325				

KM# 145 100 EURO
6.7800 g., 0.9170 Gold 0.1999 oz. AGW, 22 mm. **Subject:** Diet of Porvod

Date	Mintage	F	VF	XF	Unc	BU
2009 Proof	7,500	Value: 280				

MINT SETS

KM#	Date	Mintage	Identification	Issue Price	Mkt Val
MS58	2001 (5)	20,000	KM#65, 66, 73, 76, 77 plus 1865 coin design medal	18.00	20.00
MS59	2001 (5)	—	KM#65, 66, 73, 76, 77, medal (Johan Vilhelm Snellman)	—	20.00
MS60	2002 (8)	—	KM#98-105, medal (Church)	—	35.00
MS61	2003 (8)	—	KM#98-105	—	32.50
MS62	2004 (8)	—	KM#98-105, medal	—	32.50
MS63	2004/II (8)	—	KM#98-105, 114, medal	—	35.00
MS64	2005 (8)	—	KM#98-105, medal	—	32.50
MS65	2005/II (9)	—	KM#98-105, 118	—	45.00
MS66	2006 (9)	55,000	KM#98-105, 119	—	40.00
MS67	2006/II (9)	—	KM#98-105, 125	—	40.00

PROOF SETS

KM#	Date	Mintage	Identification	Issue Price	Mkt Val
PS9	2001 (5)	—	KM#65-66, 73, 76-77, medal (Suomen Markka 1864-2001)	—	60.00
PS10	2002 (8)	8,000	KM#98-105, gold medal (National Theater)	—	550
PS11	2002 (8)	—	KM#98-105, Silver medal	—	185
PS12	2003 (8)	—	KM#98-105	—	165
PS13	2004 (9)	5,000	KM#98-105, 114, medal	—	225
PS14	2005 (9)	3,000	KM#98-105, 118	—	200
PS15	2006 (10)	3,300	KM#98-105, 125, medal (Salmon)	—	200

FRANCE

The French Republic, largest of the West European nations, has an area of 210,026 sq. mi. (547,030 sq. km.) and a population of 58.1 million. Capital: Paris. Agriculture, manufacturing, tourist industry and financial services are the most important elements of France's diversified economy. Textiles and clothing, steel products, machinery and transportation equipment, chemicals, pharmaceuticals, nuclear electricity, agricultural products and wine are exported.

ENGRAVER GENERALS' PRIVY MARKS

Mark	Desc.	Date	Name
	Horseshoe	2000-2002	Gérard Buquoy
	SL Heart-shaped monogram	2002-2003	Serge Levet
	French horn w/starfish in water	2003	Hubert Larivière

MINT DIRECTORS' PRIVY MARKS
Some modern coins struck from dies produced at the Paris Mint have the 'A' mint mark. In the absence of a mint mark, the cornucopia privy mark serves to attribute a coin to Paris design.

A – Paris, Central Mint

MODERN REPUBLICS
1870-

REFORM COINAGE
Commencing 1960

1 Old Franc = 1 New Centime;
100 New Centimes = 1 New Franc

KM# 928 CENTIME
1.6500 g., Chrome-Steel, 15 mm. **Obv:** Cursive legend surrounds grain sprig **Rev:** Cursive denomination, date at top **Edge:** Plain **Designer:** Atelier de Paris **Note:** 1991-1993 dated coins, non-Proof, exist in both coin and medal alignment. Values given here are for medal alignment examples. Pieces struck in coin alignment have been traded for as much as $50.00.

Date	Mintage	F	VF	XF	Unc	BU
2001 In sets only	—	—	—	—	—	1.50
2001 Proof	—	Value: 2.00				

KM# 928a CENTIME
2.5000 g., 0.7500 Gold 0.0603 oz. AGW **Obv:** Cursive legend surrounds grain sprig, medallic alignment **Rev:** Cursive denomination, date above, medallic alignment **Edge:** Plain **Note:** Last Centime.

Date	Mintage	F	VF	XF	Unc	BU
2001	Est. 7,492	—	—	—	—	140

KM# 933 5 CENTIMES
2.0000 g., Copper-Aluminum-Nickel, 17 mm. **Obv:** Liberty bust left **Obv. Designer:** Henri Lagrifoul **Rev:** Denomination above date, grain sprig below, laurel branch at left **Rev. Designer:** Adrien Dieudonne **Edge:** Plain **Note:** 1991-1993 dated coins, non-Proof exist in both coin and medal alignment.

Date	Mintage	F	VF	XF	Unc	BU
2001 In sets only	—				1.50	2.50
2001 Proof	—	Value: 1.00				

KM# 929 10 CENTIMES
3.0000 g., Copper-Aluminum-Nickel, 20 mm. **Obv:** Liberty bust left **Obv. Designer:** Henri Lagriffoul **Rev:** Denomination above date, grain sprig below, laurel branch at left **Rev. Designer:** Adrien Dieudonne **Edge:** Plain **Note:** Without mint mark. 1991-1993 dated coins, non-Proof, exist in both coin and medal alignment.

Date	Mintage	F	VF	XF	Unc	BU
2001 In sets only	—					3.00
2001 Proof	—	Value: 1.00				

KM# 930 20 CENTIMES
4.0000 g., Copper-Aluminum-Nickel, 23.5 mm. **Obv:** Liberty bust left **Obv. Designer:** Henri Lagriffoul **Rev:** Denomination above date, grain sprig below, laurel branch at left **Rev. Designer:** Adrien Dieudonne **Edge:** Plain **Note:** Without mint mark. 1991-1993 dated coins, non-Proof, exist in both coin and medal alignment.

Date	Mintage	F	VF	XF	Unc	BU
2001 In sets only	—					3.00
2001 Proof	—	Value: 1.00				

KM# 931.1 1/2 FRANC
4.5000 g., Nickel, 19.5 mm. **Obv:** The seed sower **Rev:** Laurel divides denomination and date **Edge:** Reeded **Designer:** Louis Oscar Roty **Note:** Without mint mark.

Date	Mintage	F	VF	XF	Unc	BU
2001 In sets only	—				2.00	3.00

KM# 931.2 1/2 FRANC
4.5000 g., Nickel, 19.5 mm. **Obv:** Modified sower, engraver's signature: "O. ROTY" preceded by "D'AP" **Rev:** Laurel divides date and denomination **Edge:** Plain

Date	Mintage	F	VF	XF	Unc	BU
2001	—	—	—	—	0.40	0.60
2001 Proof	—	Value: 1.50				

KM# 925.2 FRANC
6.0000 g., Nickel, 24 mm. **Obv:** Modified sower, engraver's signature: O. ROTY, preceded by D'AP **Rev:** Laurel divides date and denomination **Edge:** Plain

Date	Mintage	F	VF	XF	Unc	BU
2001	—	—	—	—	0.40	0.60
2001 Proof	—	Value: 2.50				

KM# 925.1a FRANC
8.0000 g., 0.7500 Gold 0.1929 oz. AGW, 24 mm. **Obv:** The seed sower **Rev:** Laurel divides date and denomination **Edge:** Reeded **Designer:** Louis Oscar Roty **Note:** Medallic alignment.

Date	Mintage	F	VF	XF	Unc	BU
2001	Est. 9,941	—	—	—	245	275

KM# 1290   FRANC
17.7700 g., 0.9800 Silver 0.5599 oz. ASW   **Subject:** The Last Franc **Obv:** Legend on polished field **Obv. Legend:** UN ULTIME FRANC **Rev:** Number "1" on polished field **Edge Lettering:** REPUBLIQUE FRANCAISE STARCK LIBERTE EGALITE FRATERNITE (2001). **Note:** The coin is intentionally warped and the edge inscription is very faint. Struck at Paris Mint.

Date	Mintage	F	VF	XF	Unc	BU
2001 Matte	49,838				Value: 75.00	

KM# 1290a   FRANC
26.1000 g., 0.7500 Gold 0.6293 oz. AGW   **Subject:** The Last Franc **Obv:** Legend on polished field **Obv. Legend:** UN ULTIME FRANC **Rev:** Number "1" on polished field **Edge Lettering:** REPUBLIQUE FRANCAISE. STARCK. LIBERTE. EGALITE. FRATERNITE (cornucopia) 2001 **Note:** This coin has an intentionally warped surface and the edge inscription is very weak.

Date	Mintage	F	VF	XF	Unc	BU
2001 Matte	4,963	—	—	—	800	825

KM# 925.1   FRANC
6.0000 g., Nickel, 24 mm. **Obv:** The seed sower **Obv. Designer:** Louis Oscar Roty **Rev:** Laurel branch divides denomination and date **Edge:** Reeded **Note:** Without mint mark.

Date	Mintage	F	VF	XF	Unc	BU
2001	20,000,000	—	—	—	0.40	0.60

KM# 942.1   2 FRANCS
7.5000 g., Nickel, 26.5 mm.   **Obv:** The seed sower **Rev:** Denomination on branches, date below **Edge:** Wide reeded **Designer:** Louis Oscar Roty

Date	Mintage	F	VF	XF	Unc	BU
2001 Bee	—	—	—	—	0.75	1.25

KM# 942.2   2 FRANCS
7.5000 g., Nickel, 26.5 mm. **Obv:** The seed sower **Rev:** Denomination on branches, date below **Edge:** Plain

Date	Mintage	F	VF	XF	Unc	BU
2001	—	—	—	—	0.75	1.25
2001 Proof	—	Value: 3.50				

KM# 926a.1   5 FRANCS
10.0000 g., Nickel Clad Copper-Nickel, 29 mm.   **Obv:** The seed sower **Rev:** Branches divide denomination and date **Edge:** Reeded **Designer:** Raymond Joly

Date	Mintage	F	VF	XF	Unc	BU
2001 In sets only	—	—	—	—	5.00	7.50

KM# 926a.2   5 FRANCS
6.5000 g., Nickel Clad Copper-Nickel, 29 mm. **Obv:** Modified sower, engraver's signature: "O. ROTY" preceded by "D'AP" **Rev:** Branches divide date and denomination **Edge:** Plain

Date	Mintage	F	VF	XF	Unc	BU
2001	—	—	—	—	1.65	2.50
2001 Proof	—	Value: 6.50				

KM# 1309   5 FRANCS
12.0000 g., 0.9000 Silver 0.3472 oz. ASW, 29 mm. **Subject:** Last Year of the Franc **Obv:** The seed sower **Rev:** Denomination and date **Edge:** Lettered **Edge Lettering:** " * LIBERTY * EGALITE * FRATERNITE * "

Date	Mintage	F	VF	XF	Unc	BU
2001	25,000			—	22.50	25.00

KM# 1265.1   6.55957 FRANCS
13.0000 g., 0.9000 Silver 0.3761 oz. ASW   **Subject:** Last Year of the French Franc **Obv:** French and other European euro currency equivalents **Rev:** Europa allegorical portrait, date below, "last year of the franc" logo after the date **Edge:** Reeded

Date	Mintage	F	VF	XF	Unc	BU
2001	Est. 20,000			—	18.00	20.00

KM# 1265.2   6.55957 FRANCS
22.2000 g., 0.9000 Silver 0.6423 oz. ASW   **Obv:** French and other European euro currency equivalents **Rev:** Europa allegorical portrait, date below, "last year of the franc" logo after the date **Edge:** Plain

Date	Mintage	F	VF	XF	Unc	BU
2001 Proof	Est. 10,000	Value: 35.00				

KM# 1276   6.55957 FRANCS
22.2000 g., 0.9000 Silver 0.6423 oz. ASW   **Subject:** Mottos **Obv:** Denomination **Rev:** FRATERNITE in red letters **Edge:** Reeded

Date	Mintage	F	VF	XF	Unc	BU
2001 Proof	2,171	Value: 40.00				

KM# 1277   6.55957 FRANCS
22.2000 g., 0.9000 Silver 0.6423 oz. ASW   **Subject:** Mottos **Obv:** Denomination **Rev:** EGALITE in white letters

Date	Mintage	F	VF	XF	Unc	BU
2001 Proof	2,190	Value: 40.00				

KM# 1278   6.55957 FRANCS
22.2000 g., 0.9000 Silver 0.6423 oz. ASW   **Subject:** Mottos **Obv:** Denomination **Rev:** LIBERTE in white letters

Date	Mintage	F	VF	XF	Unc	BU
2001 Proof	2,259	Value: 40.00				

KM# 964.2   10 FRANCS
Aluminum-Bronze, 23 mm.   **Obv:** Winged figure divides RF **Rev:** Patterned denomination above date **Edge:** Plain

Date	Mintage	F	VF	XF	Unc	BU
2001	—			—	6.00	7.50
2001 Proof	—	Value: 15.00				

KM# 1268   10 FRANCS
22.2000 g., 0.9000 Silver 0.6423 oz. ASW   **Subject:** Monuments of France - Palace of Versailles **Obv:** Stylized French map **Rev:** 1/2 bust of Louis XIV at right, internal and external palace views at left **Edge:** Plain

Date	Mintage	F	VF	XF	Unc	BU
2001 Proof	Est. 2,561	Value: 35.00				

KM# 1270   10 FRANCS
22.2000 g., 0.9000 Silver 0.6423 oz. ASW   **Subject:** Monuments of France - Arch of Triumph **Obv:** Stylized French map **Rev:** Arch of Triumph on the Champs Elysees partial close up and aerial views

Date	Mintage	F	VF	XF	Unc	BU
2001 Proof	Est. 2,882	Value: 35.00				

KM# 1272   10 FRANCS
22.2000 g., 0.9000 Silver 0.6423 oz. ASW   **Subject:** Monuments of France - Notre Dame Cathedral **Obv:** Stylized French map **Rev:** Gargoyle at left, cathedral views at right

Date	Mintage	F	VF	XF	Unc	BU
2001 Proof	Est. 2,877	Value: 35.00				

KM# 1274   10 FRANCS
22.2000 g., 0.9000 Silver 0.6423 oz. ASW   **Subject:** Monuments of France - Eiffel Tower **Obv:** Stylized French map **Rev:** Two tower views

Date	Mintage	F	VF	XF	Unc	BU
2001 Proof	Est. 3,888	Value: 35.00				

KM# 1008.2   20 FRANCS
9.0000 g., Tri-Metallic Copper-Aluminum-Nickel center, Nickel inner ring, Copper-Aluminum-Nickel outer ring, 27 mm. **Obv:** Mont St. Michel **Rev:** Patterned denomination above date **Edge:** 5 milled bands, reeded or plain

Date	Mintage	F	VF	XF	Unc	BU
2001	—		—	—	8.00	10.00
2001 Proof	—	Value: 25.00				

KM# 1266   65.5997 FRANCS
8.4500 g., 0.9200 Gold 0.2499 oz. AGW   **Subject:** Last Year of the French Franc **Obv:** French and other European euro currency equivalents **Rev:** Europa allegorical portrait, date below, "last year of the franc" logo after the date **Edge:** Reeded

Date	Mintage	F	VF	XF	Unc	BU
2001 Proof	3,000	Value: 325				

KM# 1269   100 FRANCS
17.0000 g., 0.9200 Gold 0.5028 oz. AGW   **Subject:** Palace of Versailles **Obv:** Stylized French map **Rev:** Louis XIV with internal and external palace views **Edge:** Plain

Date	Mintage	F	VF	XF	Unc	BU
2001 Proof	105	Value: 650				

KM# 1271   100 FRANCS
17.0000 g., 0.9200 Gold 0.5028 oz. AGW   **Obv:** Champs-Elysees **Rev:** Arch of Triumph partial close up and aerial views

Date	Mintage	F	VF	XF	Unc	BU
2001 Proof	115	Value: 635				

KM# 1273   100 FRANCS
17.0000 g., 0.9200 Gold 0.5028 oz. AGW   **Obv:** Notre-Dame Cathedral **Rev:** Gargoyle and cathedral views

Date	Mintage	F	VF	XF	Unc	BU
2001 Proof	116	Value: 635				

KM# 1275   100 FRANCS
17.0000 g., 0.9200 Gold 0.5028 oz. AGW   **Obv:** Eiffel Tower **Rev:** Two tower views

Date	Mintage	F	VF	XF	Unc	BU
2001 Proof	170	Value: 625				

KM# 1267   655.957 FRANCS
31.1035 g., 0.9990 Gold 0.9990 oz. AGW   **Subject:** Last Year of the French Franc **Obv:** French and other European euro currency equivalents **Rev:** Europa allegorical portrait, date below, "last year of the franc" logo after the date **Edge:** Plain

Date	Mintage	F	VF	XF	Unc	BU
2001 Proof	2,000	Value: 1,250				

KM# 1267.1   655.957 FRANCS
155.5175 g., 0.9990 Gold 4.9948 oz. AGW   **Obv:** French and other European euro currency equivalents **Rev:** Europa allegorical portrait, date below, "last year of the franc" after the date **Edge:** Plain

Date	Mintage	F	VF	XF	Unc	BU
2001 Proof	99	Value: 6,250				

KM# 1279   655.957 FRANCS
17.0000 g., 0.9200 Gold 0.5028 oz. AGW   **Subject:** Motto Series **Obv:** Denomination **Rev:** FRATERNITE **Edge:** Reeded

Date	Mintage	F	VF	XF	Unc	BU
2001 Proof	62	Value: 650				

KM# 1280 655.957 FRANCS
17.0000 g., 0.9200 Gold 0.5028 oz. AGW **Subject:** Motto Series
Obv: Denomination **Rev:** EGALITE

Date	Mintage	F	VF	XF	Unc	BU
2001 Proof	64	Value: 650				

KM# 1281 655.957 FRANCS
17.0000 g., 0.9200 Gold 0.5028 oz. AGW **Subject:** Motto Series
Obv: Denomination **Rev:** LIBERTE

Date	Mintage	F	VF	XF	Unc	BU
2001 Proof	63	Value: 650				

EURO COINAGE
European Union Issues

KM# 1282 EURO CENT
2.2700 g., Copper Plated Steel, 16.3 mm. **Obv:** Human face
Obv. Designer: Fabienne Courtiade **Rev:** Denomination and
globe **Rev. Designer:** Luc Luycx **Edge:** Plain

Date	Mintage	F	VF	XF	Unc	BU
2001	300,681,580	—	—	—	0.35	0.50
2001 Proof	15,000	Value: 10.00				
2002	200,000	—	—	—	—	10.00
2002 Proof	21,453	Value: 8.00				
2003	160,017,000	—	—	—	1.00	1.50
2003 Proof	40,000	Value: 8.00				
2004	400,032,000	—	—	—	0.35	0.50
2004 Proof	20,000	Value: 10.00				
2005	240,320,000	—	—	—	0.35	0.50
2005 Proof	10,000	Value: 12.00				
2006	343,078,000	—	—	—	0.35	0.50
2006 Proof	10,000	Value: 12.00				
2007	300,058,000	—	—	—	0.35	0.50
2007 Proof	7,500	Value: 14.00				
2008	462,757,000	—	—	—	0.35	0.50
2008 Proof	7,500	Value: 14.00				
2009	404,050,500	—	—	—	0.35	0.50
2009 Proof	7,500	Value: 14.00				

KM# 1283 2 EURO CENT
3.0300 g., Copper Plated Steel, 18.7 mm. **Obv:** Human face
Obv. Designer: Fabienne Courtiade **Rev:** Denomination and
globe **Rev. Designer:** Luc Luycx **Edge:** Grooved

Date	Mintage	F	VF	XF	Unc	BU
2001	249,101,580	—	—	—	0.50	0.75
2001 Proof	15,000	Value: 10.00				
2002 In sets only	100,000	—	—	—	—	12.50
2002 Proof	21,453	Value: 8.00				
2003	160,175,000	—	—	—	1.25	2.00
2003 Proof	40,000	Value: 8.00				
2004	300,024,000	—	—	—	—	1.00
2004 Proof	20,000	Value: 10.00				
2005	2,603,202,000	—	—	—	—	1.00
2005 Proof	10,000	Value: 12.00				
2006	283,276,000	—	—	—	—	1.00
2006 Proof	10,000	Value: 12.00				
2007	213,258,000	—	—	—	—	1.00
2007 Proof	7,500	Value: 14.00				
2008	386,557,000	—	—	—	—	1.00
2008 Proof	7,500	Value: 14.00				
2009	317,050,500	—	—	—	—	1.00
2009 Proof	7,500	Value: 14.00				

KM# 1284 5 EURO CENT
3.8600 g., Copper Plated Steel, 21.2 mm. **Obv:** Human face
Obv. Designer: Fabienne Courtiade **Rev:** Denomination and
globe **Rev. Designer:** Luc Luycx **Edge:** Plain

Date	Mintage	F	VF	XF	Unc	BU
2001	217,324,477	—	—	—	0.75	1.25
2001 Proof	15,000	Value: 12.00				
2002	186,400,000	—	—	—	0.75	1.25
2002 Proof	21,453	Value: 10.00				
2003	101,175,000	—	—	—	1.00	1.50
2003 Proof	40,000	Value: 10.00				
2004	60,162,000	—	—	—	—	1.25
2004 Proof	20,000	Value: 12.00				
2005	20,320,000	—	—	—	—	1.25
2005 Proof	10,000	Value: 14.00				
2006	132,078,000	—	—	—	—	1.25
2006 Proof	10,000	Value: 14.00				

Date	Mintage	F	VF	XF	Unc	BU
2007	130,058,000	—	—	—	—	1.25
2007 Proof	7,500	Value: 16.00				
2008	218,257,000	—	—	—	—	1.25
2008 Proof	7,500	Value: 16.00				
2009	184,550,500	—	—	—	—	1.25
2009 Proof	7,500	Value: 16.00				

KM# 1524 5 EURO CENT
163.8000 g., 0.9500 Silver 5.0028 oz. ASW, 50 mm.
Subject: Euro 5th Anniversary **Obv:** Sower

Date	Mintage	F	VF	XF	Unc	BU
2007 Proof	500	Value: 325				

KM# 1538 5 EURO CENT
1.2400 g., 0.9990 Gold 0.0398 oz. AGW, 14 mm. **Subject:** 5th
Republic, 50th Anniversary **Obv:** Sower **Rev:** de Gaulle head right

Date	Mintage	F	VF	XF	Unc	BU
2008 Proof	20,000	Value: 75.00				

KM# 1285 10 EURO CENT
4.0700 g., Brass, 19.7 mm. **Obv:** The seed sower divides date
and RF **Obv. Designer:** Laurent Jorb **Rev:** Denomination and
map **Rev. Designer:** Luc Luycx **Edge:** Reeded

Date	Mintage	F	VF	XF	Unc	BU
2001	144,513,261	—	—	—	1.25	2.00
2001 Proof	15,000	Value: 12.00				
2002	206,700,000	—	—	—	0.75	1.25
2002 Proof	21,453	Value: 10.00				
2003	180,875,000	—	—	—	1.25	2.00
2003 Proof	40,000	Value: 10.00				
2004	5,000,000	—	—	—	—	1.50
2004 In sets only	140,000					
2004 Proof	20,000	Value: 12.00				
2005	45,120,000	—	—	—	—	1.50
2005 Proof	10,000	Value: 14.00				
2006	60,278,000	—	—	—	—	1.50
2006 Proof	10,000	Value: 14.00				

KM# 1410 10 EURO CENT
4.0700 g., Brass, 19.7 mm. **Obv:** Sower **Obv. Designer:**
Laurent Jorb **Rev:** Relief map of Western Europe, stars, lines
and value **Rev. Designer:** Luc Luycx **Edge:** Reeded

Date	Mintage	F	VF	XF	Unc	BU
2007	90,158,000	—	—	—	—	1.50
2007 Proof	7,500	Value: 14.00				
2008	178,757,000	—	—	—	—	1.50
2008 Proof	7,500	Value: 14.00				
2009	142,550,500	—	—	—	—	1.50
2009 Proof	7,500	Value: 14.00				

KM# 1286 20 EURO CENT
5.7300 g., Brass, 22.2 mm. **Obv:** The seed sower divides date
and RF **Obv. Designer:** Laurent Jorb **Rev:** Denomination and
map **Rev. Designer:** Luc Luycx **Edge:** Notched

Date	Mintage	F	VF	XF	Unc	BU
2001	256,342,108	—	—	—	1.00	1.50
2001 Proof	15,000	Value: 14.00				
2002	192,100,000	—	—	—	1.00	1.50
2002 Proof	21,453	Value: 12.00				
2003 In sets only	180,000	—	—	—	—	9.50
2003 Proof	40,000	Value: 12.00				
2004 In sets only	160,000	—	—	—	—	9.50
2004 Proof	20,000	Value: 14.00				
2005 In sets only	120,000	—	—	—	—	9.50
2005 Proof	10,000	Value: 16.00				
2006 In sets only	67,600	—	—	—	—	9.50
2006 Proof	10,000	Value: 16.00				

KM# 1411 20 EURO CENT
5.7300 g., Brass, 22.2 mm. **Obv:** Sower **Obv. Designer:**
Laurent Jorb **Rev:** Relief map of Western Europe, stars, lines
and value **Rev. Designer:** Luc Luycx **Edge:** Notched

Date	Mintage	F	VF	XF	Unc	BU
2007	40,258,000	—	—	—	—	1.50
2007 Proof	7,500	Value: 14.00				
2008	25,557,000	—	—	—	—	1.50
2008 Proof	7,500	Value: 14.00				

Date	Mintage	F	VF	XF	Unc	BU
2009	82,550,500	—	—	—	—	1.50
2009 Proof	7,500	Value: 14.00				

KM# 1521 20 EURO CENT
17.0000 g., 0.9200 Gold 0.5028 oz. AGW, 31 mm.
Subject: Asterix **Rev:** Asterix and Cleopatria

Date	Mintage	F	VF	XF	Unc	BU
2007 Proof	500	Value: 650				

KM# 1529 20 EURO CENT
163.8000 g., 0.9500 Silver 5.0028 oz. ASW, 50 mm.
Subject: French Presidency of European Union **Obv:** Text within
stars **Rev:** Europa head and flags

Date	Mintage	F	VF	XF	Unc	BU
2008 Proof	500	Value: 250				

KM# 1540 20 EURO CENT
163.8000 g., 0.9500 Silver 5.0028 oz. ASW, 50 mm.
Subject: 5th Republic, 50th Anniversary **Obv:** Sower **Rev:** de
Gaulle head right

Date	Mintage	F	VF	XF	Unc	BU
2008 Proof	500	Value: 250				

KM# 1293 1/4 EURO
12.5000 g., Copper-Aluminum-Nickel, 30 mm.
Subject: Childrens Design **Obv:** Euro globe with children
Rev: Denomination and stars **Edge:** Plain

Date	Mintage	F	VF	XF	Unc	BU
2002	1,000,000	—	—	—	6.50	8.50

KM# 1300 1/4 EURO
13.0000 g., 0.9000 Silver 0.3761 oz. ASW, 30 mm.
Subject: Europa **Obv:** Eight French euro coin designs
Rev: Portrait and flags design of 6.55957 francs coin KM-1265
Edge: Reeded

Date	Mintage	F	VF	XF	Unc	BU
2002	20,000	—	—	—	18.00	22.00

KM# 1293a 1/4 EURO
13.0000 g., 0.9000 Silver 0.3761 oz. ASW, 30 mm.
Subject: Childrens Design **Obv:** Euro globe with children
Rev: Denomination **Edge:** Plain

Date	Mintage	F	VF	XF	Unc	BU
2002 Proof	10,000	Value: 45.00				

KM# 1331 1/4 EURO
3.1100 g., 0.9990 Gold 0.0999 oz. AGW, 15 mm.
Subject: Children's Design **Obv:** Euro globe with children
Rev: Denomination **Edge:** Plain

Date	Mintage	F	VF	XF	Unc	BU
2002 Proof	5,000	Value: 140				

KM# 1350 1/4 EURO
3.1100 g., 0.9999 Gold 0.1000 oz. AGW, 15 mm. **Obv:** Obverse design of first one franc coin **Rev:** Reverse design of first one franc coin **Edge:** Plain

Date	Mintage	F	VF	XF	Unc	BU
2003 Proof	5,000	Value: 140				

KM# 1372 1/4 EURO
22.2000 g., 0.9000 Silver 0.6423 oz. ASW, 37 mm.
Obv: Sammuel de Champlain **Rev:** Sail ship **Edge:** Plain

Date	Mintage	F	VF	XF	Unc	BU
2004	20,000	—	—	—	27.50	32.50

KM# 1390 1/4 EURO
13.0000 g., 0.9000 Silver 0.3761 oz. ASW, 30 mm.
Subject: European Union Expansion **Obv:** Partial face and flags **Rev:** Puzzle map **Edge:** Plain

Date	Mintage	F	VF	XF	Unc	BU
2004	20,000	—	—	—	20.00	25.00

KM# 1402 1/4 EURO
11.0000 g., Copper-Aluminum-Nickel, 30 mm. **Subject:** Jules Verne **Obv:** Various scenes from Jules Verne's novels **Rev:** Jules Verne's portrait left of value and date

Date	Mintage	F	VF	XF	Unc	BU
2005	50,000	—	—	—	—	10.00

KM# 1442 1/4 EURO
22.2000 g., 0.9000 Silver 0.6423 oz. ASW, 37 mm. **Obv:** Bust of Franklin facing slightly right at left, his diplomatic and technical successes at right **Obv. Legend:** BENJAMIN FRANKLIN 1706-2006 **Obv. Inscription:** AMI DE LA FRANCE **Rev:** French flag at left, American flag at right **Rev. Inscription:** PHILOSOPHE / DIPLOMATE / ÉCRIVAIN / SAVANT

Date	Mintage	F	VF	XF	Unc	BU
2006	15,000	—	—	—	30.00	35.00

KM# 1445 1/4 EURO
22.2000 g., 0.9000 Silver 0.6423 oz. ASW, 37 mm.
Subject: Marshall Bernadotte under Napoleon **Rev:** Military bust facing 3/4 left at right, building in backgound at right **Rev. Legend:** LIBERTÉ / ÉGALITÉ / FRATERNITÉ - KARL XIV JOHAN ROI DE SUÉDE

Date	Mintage	F	VF	XF	Unc	BU
2006 Proof	10,000	—	—	—	30.00	35.00

KM# 1457 1/4 EURO
22.2000 g., 0.9000 Silver 0.6423 oz. ASW, 37 mm.
Subject: Hèpitaux de France Foundation **Obv:** Foundation logo **Rev:** TGV train, money box on outlined map of France

Date	Mintage	F	VF	XF	Unc	BU
2006	50,000	—	—	—	—	30.00

KM# 1415 1/4 EURO
22.2000 g., 0.9000 Silver 0.6423 oz. ASW, 37 mm. **Obv:** Jean de la Fontaine, value, Chinese astrological animals, date, Paris mint privy marks but without national identification **Rev:** Dog in wreath **Edge:** Reeded **Note:** Anonymous coinage

Date	Mintage	F	VF	XF	Unc	BU
2006	10,000	—	—	—	30.00	35.00

KM# 1417 1/4 EURO
22.2000 g., 0.9000 Silver 0.6423 oz. ASW, 37 mm. **Obv:** Jean de la Fontaine, value, Chinese astrological animals, date, Paris mint privy marks but without national identification **Rev:** Pig in wreath **Edge:** Reeded **Note:** anonymous issue

Date	Mintage	F	VF	XF	Unc	BU
2007	10,000	—	—	—	30.00	35.00

KM# 1419 1/4 EURO
13.0000 g., 0.9000 Silver 0.3761 oz. ASW, 30 mm. **Obv:** Military bust of Lafayette facing 3/4 left **Obv. Legend:** LA FAYETTE. HÉROS DELA RÉVOLUTION AMÉRICAINE **Obv. Inscription:** 1757/1854 at left, RF monogram at right **Rev:** Sailing ship L' Hermione **Rev. Legend:** LA FAYETTE, HERO OF THE AMERICAN REVOLUTION **Edge:** Plain

Date	Mintage	F	VF	XF	Unc	BU
2007 (a) Proof-like	5,000	—	—	—	30.00	35.00

KM# 1421 1/4 EURO
15.0000 g., 0.9000 Silver 0.4340 oz. ASW **Subject:** 90th Anniversary Death of Degas **Obv:** Ballerina "The Star" at left **Obv. Inscription:** *Degas* **Rev:** Paint brushes and oils multicolor at left, self portrait at right **Rev. Inscription:** LIBERTÉ / ÉGALITÉ / FRATERNITÉ **Shape:** rectangular, 30 x 21 mm

Date	Mintage	F	VF	XF	Unc	BU
2007	5,000	—	—	—	40.00	45.00

KM# 1461 1/4 EURO
13.0000 g., 0.9000 Silver 0.3761 oz. ASW, 30 mm.
Subject: Sebastien Le Prestre de Vauban, 300th Anniversary of Death **Obv:** Arms above funeral coach, book at left **Rev:** Vauban standing; plans of fortress

Date	Mintage	F	VF	XF	Unc	BU
2007 Proof	5,000	Value: 20.00				

KM# 1483 1/4 EURO
13.0000 g., 0.9000 Silver 0.3761 oz. ASW, 37 mm.
Subject: 2007 Rugby World Cup **Obv:** Two Rugby players **Rev:** Logo and goal

Date	Mintage	F	VF	XF	Unc	BU
2007	5,000	—	—	—	30.00	35.00

KM# 1498 1/4 EURO
13.0000 g., 0.9000 Silver 0.3761 oz. ASW, 30 x 21 mm.
Subject: Edgar Degas, 90th Anniversary of Death **Obv:** Degas painting of dancer **Rev:** Multicolor brushes, Degas portrait **Shape:** Rectangle

Date	Mintage	F	VF	XF	Unc	BU
2007	5,000	—	—	—	—	50.00

KM# 1570 1/4 EURO
15.0000 g., 0.9000 Silver 0.4340 oz. ASW, 30 x 21 mm.
Subject: Edward Manet **Obv:** Manet's "Olympia" painting **Rev:** Multicolor paint brushes and Manet's portrait **Shape:** Rectangle

Date	Mintage	F	VF	XF	Unc	BU
2008	10,000	—	—	—	—	65.00

KM# 1572 1/4 EURO
22.2000 g., 0.9000 Silver 0.6423 oz. ASW, 37 mm.
Subject: Lunar New Year - Year of the Rat **Obv:** Bust of Jean de la Fontaine and twelve awards **Rev:** Rat within border

Date	Mintage	F	VF	XF	Unc	BU
2008	10,000	—	—	—	—	35.00

KM# 1287 50 EURO CENT
7.8100 g., Brass, 24.2 mm. **Obv:** The seed sower divides date and RF **Obv. Designer:** Laurent Jorb **Rev:** Denomination and map **Rev. Designer:** Luc Luycx **Edge:** Reeded

Date	Mintage	F	VF	XF	Unc	BU
2001	276,287,274	—	—	—	1.25	2.00
2001 Proof	15,000	Value: 15.00				
2002	226,500,000	—	—	—	1.25	2.00
2002 Proof	21,453	Value: 14.00				
2003 In sets only	180,000	—	—	—	—	11.50
2003 Proof	40,000	Value: 14.00				
2004 In sets only	160,000	—	—	—	—	11.50
2004 Proof	20,000	Value: 15.00				
2005 In sets only	120,000	—	—	—	—	11.50
2005 Proof	10,000	Value: 17.00				
2006 In sets only	67,600	—	—	—	—	11.50
2006 Proof	10,000	Value: 17.00				

KM# 1412 50 EURO CENT
7.8100 g., Brass, 24.2 mm. **Obv:** Sower **Obv. Designer:** Laurent Jorb **Rev:** Relief map of Western Europe, stars, lines and value **Rev. Designer:** Luc Luycx **Edge:** Reeded

Date	Mintage	F	VF	XF	Unc	BU
2007 In sets only	58,000	—	—	—	—	11.50
2007 Proof	7,500	Value: 16.00				
2008 In sets only	57,000	—	—	—	—	2.00
2008 Proof	7,500	Value: 16.00				
2009	—	—	—	—	—	2.00
2009 In sets only	50,500	—	—	—	—	
2009 Proof	7,500	Value: 16.00				

KM# 1288 EURO
7.5000 g., Bi-Metallic Copper-Nickel center in Brass ring, 23.3 mm. **Obv:** Stylized tree divides RF within circle, date below **Obv. Designer:** Joaquin Jimenez **Rev:** Denomination and map **Rev. Designer:** Luc Luycx **Edge:** Reeded and plain sections

Date	Mintage	F	VF	XF	Unc	BU
2001	150,251,624	—	—	—	2.75	4.00
2001 Proof	15,000	Value: 18.00				
2002	129,400,000	—	—	—	2.50	3.75
2002 Proof	21,453	Value: 16.00				
2003 In sets only	100,000	—	—	—	8.00	12.50
2003 Proof	20,000	Value: 18.00				
2004 In sets only	160,000	—	—	—	—	2.50
2004 Proof	20,000	Value: 18.00				
2005 In sets only	120,000	—	—	—	—	2.50
2005 Proof	10,000	Value: 20.00				
2006 In sets only	78,000	—	—	—	—	2.50
2006 Proof	10,000	Value: 20.00				

KM# 1413 EURO
7.5000 g., Bi-Metallic Copper-Nickel center in Brass ring, 23.3 mm. **Obv:** Stylized tree **Obv. Designer:** Joaquin Jimenz **Rev:** Relief map of Western Europe, stars, lines and value **Rev. Designer:** Luc Luycx **Edge:** Reeded and plain sections

Date	Mintage	F	VF	XF	Unc	BU
2007 In sets only	58,000	—	—	—	—	11.50
2007 Proof	7,500	Value: 20.00				
2008 In sets only	57,000	—	—	—	—	2.50
2008 Proof	7,500	Value: 20.00				
2009	—	—	—	—	—	2.50

Date	Mintage	F	VF	XF	Unc	BU
2009 In sets only	50,500	—	—	—	—	—
2009 Proof	7,500	Value: 20.00				

KM# 1464 EURO
155.5500 g., 0.9500 Silver 4.7508 oz. ASW, 50 mm.
Subject: Sebastien Le Prestre de Vauban, 300th Anniversary of Death

Date	Mintage	F	VF	XF	Unc	BU
2007 Proof	500	Value: 325				

KM# 1470 EURO
17.0000 g., 0.9200 Gold 0.5028 oz. AGW, 31 mm. **Subject:** Le Petit Prince, 60th Anniversary **Obv:** Prince standing with rabbit

Date	Mintage	F	VF	XF	Unc	BU
2007 Proof	2,000	Value: 750				

KM# 1486 EURO
17.0000 g., 0.9200 Gold 0.5028 oz. AGW, 31 mm.
Subject: 2007 Rugby World Cup **Obv:** Two players and goal **Rev:** Logo and goal

Date	Mintage	F	VF	XF	Unc	BU
2007 Proof	500	Value: 650				

KM# 1490 EURO
22.0000 g., 0.9000 Silver 0.6366 oz. ASW **Subject:** Unesco **Obv:** Great Wall of China

Date	Mintage	F	VF	XF	Unc	BU
2007 Proof	5,000	Value: 45.00				

KM# 1491 EURO
8.4500 g., 0.9200 Gold 0.2499 oz. AGW, 22 mm.
Subject: Unesco **Obv:** Crest Wall of China **Rev:** Unesco Building and emblem

Date	Mintage	F	VF	XF	Unc	BU
2007 Proof	500	Value: 350				

KM# 1492 EURO
22.0000 g., 0.9000 Silver 0.6423 oz. ASW, 37 mm.
Subject: Point Neuf 400th Anniversary **Obv:** Monuments of France logo **Rev:** Point Neuf Bridge, Paris Mint Museum

Date	Mintage	F	VF	XF	Unc	BU
2007 Proof	3,000	Value: 80.00				

KM# 1493 EURO
8.4500 g., 0.9200 Gold 0.2499 oz. AGW, 22 mm. **Subject:** Point Neuf, 400th Anniversary **Obv:** Monuments of France logo **Rev:** Point Neuf Brudge, Paris Mint Building

Date	Mintage	F	VF	XF	Unc	BU
2007 Proof	500	Value: 400				

KM# 1495 EURO
8.4500 g., 0.9200 Gold 0.2499 oz. AGW, 22 mm.
Subject: Cannes Film Festival **Obv:** Cinema screen and stage, Golden Palm Award

Date	Mintage	F	VF	XF	Unc	BU
2007 Proof	500	Value: 375				

KM# 1514 EURO
17.0000 g., 0.9200 Gold 0.5028 oz. AGW, 31 mm.
Subject: Stanislas Lesczynski **Obv:** Bust, shield **Rev:** Palac Stanislas - Nancy

Date	Mintage	F	VF	XF	Unc	BU
2007 Proof	500	Value: 650				

KM# 1587 EURO
8.4500 g., 0.9200 Gold 0.2499 oz. AGW, 22 mm. **Subject:** Court of Human Rights, 50th Anniversary **Obv:** Sower left **Rev:** Text

Date	Mintage	F	VF	XF	Unc	BU
2009P Proof	500	Value: 350				

KM# 1599 EURO
155.5500 g., 0.9990 Gold 4.9942 oz. AGW, 50 mm.
Subject: Concorde 40th Anniversary **Obv:** Concorde in flight **Rev:** Tail emblems

Date	Mintage	F	VF	XF	Unc	BU
2009P Proof	99	Value: 6,250				

KM# 1332 1-1/2 EURO
22.2000 g., 0.9000 Silver 0.6423 oz. ASW, 37 mm. **Obv:** Victor Hugo, denomination and map **Rev:** Multicolor "Gavroche" **Edge:** Plain

Date	Mintage	F	VF	XF	Unc	BU
2002 Proof	10,000	Value: 52.50				

KM# 1301 1-1/2 EURO
22.2000 g., 0.9000 Silver 0.6423 oz. ASW, 37 mm. **Subject:** Europa **Obv:** Eight French euro coins design **Rev:** Portrait and flags design of 6.55957 francs KM-1265 **Edge:** Plain

Date	Mintage	F	VF	XF	Unc	BU
2002 Proof	50,000	Value: 40.00				

KM# 1305 1-1/2 EURO
22.2000 g., 0.9000 Silver 0.6423 oz. ASW, 37 mm.
Subject: French Landmarks **Obv:** French map **Rev:** Le Mont St. Michel **Edge:** Plain

Date	Mintage	F	VF	XF	Unc	BU
2002 Proof	10,000	Value: 45.00				

KM# 1307 1-1/2 EURO
22.2000 g., 0.9000 Silver 0.6423 oz. ASW, 37 mm.
Subject: French Landmarks **Obv:** French map **Rev:** La Butte Montmartre **Edge:** Plain

Date	Mintage	F	VF	XF	Unc	BU
2002 Proof	10,000	Value: 42.50				

KM# 1310 1-1/2 EURO
22.2000 g., 0.9000 Silver 0.6423 oz. ASW, 37 mm.
Subject: First West to East Transatlantic Flight **Obv:** Denomination, map and Lindbergh portrait **Rev:** Spirit of St. Louis (airplane) and map **Edge:** Plain

Date	Mintage	F	VF	XF	Unc	BU
2002 Proof	10,000	Value: 45.00				

KM# 1321 1-1/2 EURO
22.2000 g., 0.9000 Silver 0.6423 oz. ASW, 37 mm. **Obv:** Tour de France logo **Rev:** Cyclist going left **Edge:** Plain

Date	Mintage	F	VF	XF	Unc	BU
2003 Proof	150,000	Value: 50.00				

KM# 1322 1-1/2 EURO
22.2000 g., 0.9000 Silver 0.6423 oz. ASW, 37 mm. **Obv:** Tour de France logo **Rev:** Group of cyclists and Arch de Triumph **Edge:** Plain

Date	Mintage	F	VF	XF	Unc	BU
2003 (Ht) Proof	150,000	Value: 50.00				

KM# 1323 1-1/2 EURO
22.2000 g., 0.9000 Silver 0.6423 oz. ASW, 37 mm. **Obv:** Tour de France logo **Rev:** Two cyclists and spectators **Edge:** Plain

Date	Mintage	F	VF	XF	Unc	BU
2003 (Ht) Proof	150,000	Value: 50.00				

KM# 1324 1-1/2 EURO
22.2000 g., 0.9000 Silver 0.6423 oz. ASW, 37 mm. **Obv:** Tour de France logo **Rev:** Two groups of cyclists **Edge:** Plain

Date	Mintage	F	VF	XF	Unc	BU
2003 (Ht) Proof	150,000	Value: 50.00				

KM# 1325 1-1/2 EURO
22.2000 g., 0.9000 Silver 0.6423 oz. ASW, 37 mm. **Obv:** Tour de France logo **Rev:** Cyclists, stopwatch and gears **Edge:** Plain

Date	Mintage	F	VF	XF	Unc	BU
2003 (Ht) Proof	150,000	Value: 50.00				

KM# 1336 1-1/2 EURO
22.2000 g., 0.9000 Silver 0.6423 oz. ASW, 37 mm. **Obv:** Jefferson and Napoleon with Louisiana Purchase map **Rev:** Jazz musician, mansion and river boat **Edge:** Plain

Date	Mintage	F	VF	XF	Unc	BU
2003 Proof	10,000	Value: 50.00				

KM# 1338 1-1/2 EURO
22.2000 g., 0.9000 Silver 0.6423 oz. ASW, 37 mm. **Obv:** Curved cross design with multiple values **Rev:** Goddess Europa and flags **Edge:** Plain

Date	Mintage	F	VF	XF	Unc	BU
2003 Proof	40,000	Value: 47.50				

KM# 1341 1-1/2 EURO
22.2000 g., 0.9000 Silver 0.6423 oz. ASW, 37 mm.
Obv: Denomination and compass face **Rev:** SS Normandie and New York City **Edge:** Plain

Date	Mintage	F	VF	XF	Unc	BU
2003 Proof	15,000	Value: 50.00				

KM# 1343 1-1/2 EURO
22.2000 g., 0.9000 Silver 0.6423 oz. ASW, 37 mm.
Obv: Denomination and compass face **Rev:** Airplane and Tokyo Geisha **Edge:** Plain

Date	Mintage	F	VF	XF	Unc	BU
2003 Proof	15,000	Value: 50.00				

KM# 1345 1-1/2 EURO
22.2000 g., 0.9000 Silver 0.6423 oz. ASW, 37 mm. **Obv:** Paul Gauguin **Rev:** Native woman **Edge:** Plain

Date	Mintage	F	VF	XF	Unc	BU
2003 Proof	15,000	Value: 50.00				

KM# 1351 1-1/2 EURO
22.2000 g., 0.9000 Silver 0.6423 oz. ASW, 37 mm.
Obv: Obverse design of first one franc coin **Rev:** Reverse design of first one franc coin **Edge:** Plain

Date	Mintage	F	VF	XF	Unc	BU
2003 Proof	15,000	Value: 47.50				

KM# 1353 1-1/2 EURO
22.2000 g., 0.9000 Silver 0.6423 oz. ASW, 37 mm. **Obv:** Mona Lisa **Rev:** Leonardo da Vinci **Edge:** Plain

Date	Mintage	F	VF	XF	Unc	BU
2003 Proof	10,000	Value: 50.00				

KM# 1355 1-1/2 EURO
22.2000 g., 0.9000 Silver 0.6423 oz. ASW, 37 mm. **Obv:** Map and denomination **Rev:** Chateau Chambord **Edge:** Plain

Date	Mintage	F	VF	XF	Unc	BU
2003 Proof	10,000	Value: 47.50				

KM# 1357 1-1/2 EURO
22.2000 g., 0.9000 Silver 0.6423 oz. ASW, 37 mm.
Obv: Denomination in swirling design **Rev:** Multicolor Hansel and Gretel, witch and house **Edge:** Plain

Date	Mintage	F	VF	XF	Unc	BU
2003 Proof	10,000	Value: 50.00				

KM# 1359 1-1/2 EURO
22.2000 g., 0.9000 Silver 0.6423 oz. ASW, 37 mm.
Obv: Denomination in swirling design **Rev:** Multicolor Alice in Wonderland **Edge:** Plain

Date	Mintage	F	VF	XF	Unc	BU
2003 Proof	10,000	Value: 50.00				

KM# 1361 1-1/2 EURO
22.2000 g., 0.9000 Silver 0.6423 oz. ASW, 37 mm. **Obv:** Pierre de Coubertin **Rev:** Olympic runners **Edge:** Plain

Date	Mintage	F	VF	XF	Unc	BU
2003 Proof	50,000	Value: 47.50				

KM# 1364 1-1/2 EURO
22.2000 g., 0.9000 Silver 0.6423 oz. ASW, 37 mm. **Obv:** Map with denomination **Rev:** Avignon Popes Palace **Edge:** Plain

Date	Mintage	F	VF	XF	Unc	BU
2004 Proof	10,000	Value: 47.50				

KM# 1373 1-1/2 EURO
22.2000 g., 0.9000 Silver 0.6423 oz. ASW, 37 mm. **Obv:** Emile Loubet and King Edward VII **Rev:** Marianne and Britannia **Edge:** Plain

Date	Mintage	F	VF	XF	Unc	BU
2004 Proof	10,000	Value: 45.00				

KM# 1374 1-1/2 EURO
22.2000 g., 0.9000 Silver 0.6423 oz. ASW, 37 mm. **Obv:** Soccer ball and denomination **Rev:** Rooster and quill **Edge:** Plain

Date	Mintage	F	VF	XF	Unc	BU
2004 Proof	25,000	Value: 50.00				

KM# 1378 1-1/2 EURO
22.2000 g., 0.9000 Silver 0.6423 oz. ASW, 37 mm.
Obv: Compass rose **Rev:** Ocean liner **Edge:** Plain

Date	Mintage	F	VF	XF	Unc	BU
2004 Proof	10,000	Value: 45.00				

KM# 1380 1-1/2 EURO
22.2000 g., 0.9000 Silver 0.6423 oz. ASW, 37 mm.
Obv: Compass rose **Rev:** Trans-Siberian Railroad **Edge:** Plain

Date	Mintage	F	VF	XF	Unc	BU
2004 Proof	10,000	Value: 45.00				

KM# 1382   1-1/2 EURO
22.2000 g., 0.9000 Silver 0.6423 oz. ASW, 37 mm.
Obv: Compass rose **Rev:** Half-track vehicle **Edge:** Plain

Date	Mintage	F	VF	XF	Unc	BU
2004 Proof	10,000	Value: 45.00				

KM# 1384   1-1/2 EURO
22.2000 g., 0.9000 Silver 0.6423 oz. ASW, 37 mm.
Obv: Compass rose **Rev:** Biplane airliner **Edge:** Plain

Date	Mintage	F	VF	XF	Unc	BU
2004 Proof	10,000	Value: 45.00				

KM# 1386   1-1/2 EURO
22.2000 g., 0.9000 Silver 0.6423 oz. ASW, 37 mm. **Obv:** Statue of Liberty **Rev:** F.A. Bartholdi **Edge:** Plain

Date	Mintage	F	VF	XF	Unc	BU
2004 Proof	15,000	Value: 45.00				

KM# 1391   1-1/2 EURO
22.2000 g., 0.9000 Silver 0.6423 oz. ASW, 37 mm.
Subject: European Union Expansion **Obv:** Partial face and flags
Rev: Puzzle map **Edge:** Plain

Date	Mintage	F	VF	XF	Unc	BU
2004 Proof	40,000	Value: 40.00				

KM# 1366   1-1/2 EURO
22.2000 g., 0.9000 Silver 0.6423 oz. ASW, 37 mm. **Obv:** Book, eagle and denomination **Rev:** Napoleon and coronation scene in background **Edge:** Plain

Date	Mintage	F	VF	XF	Unc	BU
2004 Proof	20,000	Value: 45.00				

KM# 1369   1-1/2 EURO
22.2000 g., 0.9000 Silver 0.6423 oz. ASW, 37 mm.
Obv: Soldiers and Normandy invasion scene **Rev:** "D-DAY" above denomination **Edge:** Plain

Date	Mintage	F	VF	XF	Unc	BU
2004 Proof	20,000	Value: 50.00				

KM# 1423   1-1/2 EURO
22.2000 g., 0.9000 Silver 0.6423 oz. ASW, 37 mm.
Subject: Biathlon **Rev:** Skier at right facing 3/4 left, mountain peaks in background **Rev. Inscription:** JEUX D'HIVER

Date	Mintage	F	VF	XF	Unc	BU
2005 Proof	30,000	Value: 45.00				

KM# 1425   1-1/2 EURO
22.2000 g., 0.9000 Silver 0.6423 oz. ASW, 37 mm.
Series: Jules Verne **Subject:** From the Earth to the Moon
Rev: Crowd observing at lower left, volcano erupting above, moon at upper right, Verne in spaceship at lower right, factory chimneys belching smoke in bachground **Rev. Legend:** DE LA TERRE… LA LUNE

Date	Mintage	F	VF	XF	Unc	BU
2005 Proof	5,000	Value: 60.00				

KM# 1427   1-1/2 EURO
22.2000 g., 0.9000 Silver 0.6423 oz. ASW, 37 mm. **Rev:** Kitty and poodle at table at cafe, multicolor **Rev. Legend:** Hello Kitty

Date	Mintage	F	VF	XF	Unc	BU
2005 Proof	4,000	Value: 60.00				

KM# 1428   1-1/2 EURO
22.2000 g., 0.9000 Silver 0.6423 oz. ASW, 37 mm. **Rev:** Kitty on the Champs-Elysees, multicolor **Rev. Legend:** Hello Kitty

Date	Mintage	F	VF	XF	Unc	BU
2005 Proof	4,000	Value: 60.00				

KM# 1431   1-1/2 EURO
22.2000 g., 0.9000 Silver 0.6423 oz. ASW, 37 mm.
Subject: Bicentennial Victory at Austerlitz **Rev:** Battle scene
Rev. Legend: LIBERTÉ ÉGALITÉ FRATERNITÉ

Date	Mintage	F	VF	XF	Unc	BU
2005 Proof	15,000	Value: 50.00				

KM# 1434   1-1/2 EURO
22.2000 g., 0.9000 Silver 0.6423 oz. ASW, 37 mm.
Subject: 50th Anniversary of the Europe flag **Rev:** Stars at left, partial flag at center right

Date	Mintage	F	VF	XF	Unc	BU
2005 Proof	15,000	Value: 50.00				

KM# 1436   1-1/2 EURO
, 37 mm. **Subject:** Centenary Law of Dec. 9, 1905 **Obv:** "Sower" left in ring of stars

Date	Mintage	F	VF	XF	Unc	BU
2005 Proof	15,000	Value: 50.00				
2006 Proof	10,000	Value: 50.00				

KM# 1438   1-1/2 EURO
22.2900 g., 0.9000 Silver 0.6449 oz. ASW, 37 mm.
Series: Jules Verne **Subject:** 20,000 leagues under the sea
Rev: Submarine above plants and divers **Rev. Legend:** VINGT MILLE LIEUES SOUS LES MERS

Date	Mintage	F	VF	XF	Unc	BU
2005 Proof	5,000	Value: 60.00				

KM# 1440   1-1/2 EURO
22.2000 g., 0.9000 Silver 0.6423 oz. ASW, 37 mm.
Subject: 150th Anniversary of Classification of Bordeax Wines
Rev: Stylized female with grapes between various names of wines at her feet

Date	Mintage	F	VF	XF	Unc	BU
2005 Proof	5,000	Value: 60.00				

KM# 1441   1-1/2 EURO
22.2000 g., 0.9000 Silver 0.6423 oz. ASW, 37 mm.
Subject: 60th Anniversary - End of World War II **Rev:** Doves in flight **Rev. Inscription:** L'EUROPE FAIT LA PAIX

Date	Mintage	F	VF	XF	Unc	BU
2005 Proof	50,000	Value: 40.00				

KM# 1453   1-1/2 EURO
22.2000 g., 0.9000 Silver 0.6423 oz. ASW, 37 mm.
Subject: 100th Anniversary - Death of Paul Cézanne **Obv:** Self portrait **Obv. Inscription:** PAUL / CÉZANNE **Rev:** "The Card Players" **Rev. Legend:** LIBERTÉ ÉGALITÉ FRATERNITÉ

Date	Mintage	F	VF	XF	Unc	BU
2006 Proof	5,000	Value: 60.00				

KM# 1455   1-1/2 EURO
22.2000 g., 0.9000 Silver 0.6423 oz. ASW, 37 mm. **Obv:** Map of the Basilica **Rev:** Bust of Pope Benoît with arms outstretched facing 3/4 right at lower left, Basilica in background
Rev. Legend: 500 ANS de la BASILIQUE SAINT-PIERRE

Date	Mintage	F	VF	XF	Unc	BU
2006 Proof	5,000	Value: 60.00				

KM# 1456   1-1/2 EURO
22.2000 g., 0.9000 Silver 0.6423 oz. ASW, 37 mm. **Rev:** Half of Arc at left, eternal flame above WW I plaque at right
Rev. Legend: ARC DE TRIOMPHE

Date	Mintage	F	VF	XF	Unc	BU
2006 Proof	10,000	Value: 50.00				

KM# 1458   1-1/2 EURO
22.2000 g., 0.9000 Silver 0.6423 oz. ASW, 37 mm.
Subject: 300th Anniversary - Completion of the Dome of Les Invalides **Rev:** Dome between Jules-Hardouin Mansart at left, Louis XIV at right **Rev. Legend:** SAINT-LOUIS - DES INVALIDES **Rev. Inscription:** 28/AOÛT - 1706

Date	Mintage	F	VF	XF	Unc	BU
2006 Proof	10,000	Value: 50.00				

KM# 1444   1-1/2 EURO
22.2000 g., 0.9200 Silver 0.6566 oz. ASW, 37 mm. **Subject:** 100th Anniversary - French Grand Prix **Obv:** Steering wheel with early race car in upper segment, two gauges at lower left, R / F at lower right **Obv. Legend:** LE MANS 1906 - CENTENAIRE du 1er GRAND PRIX de l'AUTOMOBILE CLUB de FRANCE
Rev: Modern racing car's steering wheel **Rev. Legend:** MAGNY-COURS

Date	Mintage	F	VF	XF	Unc	BU
2006 Proof	5,000	Value: 60.00				

KM# 1447   1-1/2 EURO
22.2000 g., 0.9000 Silver 0.6423 oz. ASW, 37 mm.
Obv: Strogoff on horseback wielding sword, city at left, soldiers at lower left, calvalry at right **Obv. Legend:** MICHEL STROGOFF
Rev: Head of Verne facing 3/4 right at left center, instruments and anchor in curved band **Rev. Legend:** 1828 JULES VERNE 1905 - LIBERTÉ . ÉGALITÉ . FRATERNITÉ

Date	Mintage	F	VF	XF	Unc	BU
2006 Proof	500	Value: 100				

KM# 1450 1-1/2 EURO
22.2000 g., 0.9000 Silver 0.6423 oz. ASW, 37 mm. **Subject:** Jules Verne **Obv:** Hot air balloon, parrots at left, native masks at lower left, foliage at right, native huts below, map of Africa in background **Obv. Legend:** CINQ SEMAINES EN BALLOON **Rev:** Head of Verne facing 3/4 right at left center, instruments and anchor in curved band **Rev. Legend:** 1828 JULES VERNE 1905

Date	Mintage	F	VF	XF	Unc	BU
2006 Proof	5,000	Value: 60.00				

KM# 1452 1-1/2 EURO
22.2000 g., 0.9000 Silver 0.6423 oz. ASW, 37 mm. **Subject:** Formula 1 World Championship **Obv:** Race car outline on checkerboard background **Obv. Legend:** LIBERTÉ ÉGALITÉ FRATERNITÉ **Rev:** Race car outline in victory sprays with star **Rev. Legend:** RENAULT - CHAMPION DU MONDE FIA 2005 DESCONSTRUCTEURS DE FORMULE 1

Date	Mintage	F	VF	XF	Unc	BU
2006 Proof	10,000	Value: 50.00				

KM# 1501 1-1/2 EURO
22.2000 g., 0.9000 Silver 0.6423 oz. ASW, 37 mm. **Subject:** Georges Pompendev Center, 30th Anniversary

Date	Mintage	F	VF	XF	Unc	BU
2007 Proof	—	Value: 50.00				

KM# 1484 1-1/2 EURO
22.2000 g., 0.9000 Silver 0.6423 oz. ASW, 37 mm. **Subject:** 2007 Rugby World Cup **Obv:** Two players and goal **Rev:** Logo and goal

Date	Mintage	F	VF	XF	Unc	BU
2007 Proof	5,000	Value: 40.00				

KM# 1462 1-1/2 EURO
22.0000 g., 0.9000 Silver 0.6366 oz. ASW, 37 mm. **Subject:** Sebastien Le Prestre de Vauban, 300th Anniversary of Death

Date	Mintage	F	VF	XF	Unc	BU
2007 Proof	30,000	Value: 40.00				

KM# 1465 1-1/2 EURO
22.2000 g., 0.9000 Silver 0.6423 oz. ASW, 37 mm. **Subject:** Le Petit Prince, 60th Anniversary **Obv:** Prince standing, multicolor

Date	Mintage	F	VF	XF	Unc	BU
2007 Proof	3,000	Value: 40.00				

KM# 1467 1-1/2 EURO
22.2000 g., 0.9000 Silver 0.6423 oz. ASW, 37 mm. **Subject:** Le Petit Prince, 60th Anniversary **Obv:** Prince lying in field, multicolor

Date	Mintage	F	VF	XF	Unc	BU
2007 Proof	3,000	Value: 40.00				

KM# 1469 1-1/2 EURO
22.2000 g., 0.9000 Silver 0.6423 oz. ASW, 37 mm. **Subject:** Le Petite Prince, 60th Anniversary **Obv:** Prince standing with rabbit, multicolor

Date	Mintage	F	VF	XF	Unc	BU
2007 Proof	—	Value: 45.00				

KM# 1473 1-1/2 EURO
22.2000 g., 0.9000 Silver 0.6423 oz. ASW, 37 mm. **Subject:** Paul E. Victor, 100th birthday **Obv:** International polar year logo **Rev:** Bust at left, Islands

Date	Mintage	F	VF	XF	Unc	BU
2007 Proof	5,000	Value: 45.00				

KM# 1475 1-1/2 EURO
22.2000 g., 0.9000 Silver 0.6423 oz. ASW, 37 mm. **Obv:** Formula 1 race car on checkered background **Rev:** Legend in wreath on checkered background

Date	Mintage	F	VF	XF	Unc	BU
2007//2006 Proof	5,000	Value: 45.00				

KM# 1477 1-1/2 EURO
22.2000 g., 0.9000 Silver 0.6423 oz. ASW, 37 mm. **Subject:** 29th Summer Olympic Games Beijing **Obv:** Rider on horseback, globe map of China **Rev:** Equestrian jump over orienteal fence

Date	Mintage	F	VF	XF	Unc	BU
2007 Proof	10,000	Value: 45.00				

KM# 1479 1-1/2 EURO
22.2000 g., 0.9000 Silver 0.6423 oz. ASW, 37 mm. **Subject:** Airbus A380 **Obv:** Airplane **Rev:** Europa head and flags

Date	Mintage	F	VF	XF	Unc	BU
2007 Proof	5,000	Value: 40.00				

KM# 1488 1-1/2 EURO
22.2000 g., 0.9000 Silver 0.6423 oz. ASW, 37 mm. **Obv:** Christian Dior bust **Rev:** Dior Museum building

Date	Mintage	F	VF	XF	Unc	BU
2007 Proof	3,000	Value: 75.00				

KM# 1505 1-1/2 EURO
22.2000 g., 0.9000 Silver 0.6423 oz. ASW, 37 mm. **Subject:** George Remir Centennial **Obv:** Wand and sparkles **Rev:** Tin Tin and the Professor calculus in multicolor

Date	Mintage	F	VF	XF	Unc	BU
2007 Proof	10,000	Value: 60.00				

KM# 1506 1-1/2 EURO
22.2000 g., 0.9000 Silver 0.6423 oz. ASW, 37 mm. **Subject:** Georges Remi Centennial **Obv:** Wand and sparkles **Rev:** Tin Tin and Captain Haddock in multicolor

Date	Mintage	F	VF	XF	Unc	BU
2007 Proof	10,000	Value: 65.00				

KM# 1507 1-1/2 EURO
22.2000 g., 0.9000 Silver 0.6423 oz. ASW, 37 mm. **Subject:** Georges Remi Centennial **Obv:** Wand and sparkles **Rev:** Tin Tin and Chang in multicolor

Date	Mintage	F	VF	XF	Unc	BU
2007 Proof	10,000	Value: 65.00				

KM# 1511 1-1/2 EURO
22.2000 g., 0.9000 Silver 0.6423 oz. ASW, 37 mm. **Subject:** Aristides de Sousa Mendes, Portuguese diplomat **Obv:** Bust right **Rev:** Plaque

Date	Mintage	F	VF	XF	Unc	BU
2007 Proof	3,000	Value: 45.00				

KM# 1516 1-1/2 EURO
22.2000 g., 0.9000 Silver 0.6423 oz. ASW, 37 mm. **Subject:** Asterix **Rev:** The banquet

Date	Mintage	F	VF	XF	Unc	BU
2007 Proof	3,000	Value: 45.00				

KM# 1517 1-1/2 EURO
22.2000 g., 0.9000 Silver 0.6423 oz. ASW, 37 mm. **Subject:** Asterix **Rev:** The posion

Date	Mintage	F	VF	XF	Unc	BU
2007 Proof	3,000	Value: 45.00				

KM# 1518 1-1/2 EURO
27.2000 g., 0.9000 Silver 0.7870 oz. ASW, 37 mm. **Subject:** Asterix **Rev:** The Chase

Date	Mintage	F	VF	XF	Unc	BU
2007 Proof	3,000	Value: 45.00				

KM# 1527 1-1/2 EURO
22.2000 g., 0.9000 Silver 0.6423 oz. ASW, 37 mm. **Subject:** French Presidency of European Union **Obv:** Text written stars **Rev:** Europa head and flags

Date	Mintage	F	VF	XF	Unc	BU
2008 Proof	10,000	Value: 50.00				

KM# 1532 1-1/2 EURO
22.2000 g., 0.9000 Silver 0.6423 oz. ASW **Subject:** Eurpean Parliament, 50th Anniversary **Obv:** Map of EU within stars **Rev:** European Parlament Building in Strasboury **Shape:** 37

Date	Mintage	F	VF	XF	Unc	BU
2008 Proof	30,000	Value: 50.00				

KM# 1537 1-1/2 EURO
22.2000 g., 0.9000 Silver 0.6423 oz. ASW, 37 mm. **Subject:** 5th Republic, 50th Anniversasry **Obv:** Sower **Rev:** deGaulle head right

Date	Mintage	F	VF	XF	Unc	BU
2008 Proof	10,000	Value: 50.00				

KM# 1543 1-1/2 EURO
22.2000 g., 0.9000 Silver 0.6423 oz. ASW, 37 mm. **Subject:** 29th Summer Olympic Games - Beijing **Obv:** Swimmer and globe **Rev:** Diver and oriental screen

Date	Mintage	F	VF	XF	Unc	BU
2008 Proof	10,000	Value: 65.00				

KM# 1546 1-1/2 EURO
22.2000 g., 0.9000 Silver 0.6423 oz. ASW, 37 mm. **Subject:** UEFA **Obv:** French soccer team **Rev:** UEFA logo

Date	Mintage	F	VF	XF	Unc	BU
2008 Proof	5,000	Value: 50.00				

KM# 1548 1-1/2 EURO
22.2000 g., 0.9000 Silver 0.6423 oz. ASW, 37 mm. **Subject:** Franco - Japanese Relators, 150th Anniversary **Obv:** Eillfel Tower and Kimono forming logo **Rev:** Delacroix "La Liberte"

Date	Mintage	F	VF	XF	Unc	BU
2008 Proof	5,000	Value: 65.00				

KM# 1549 1-1/2 EURO
22.2000 g., 0.9000 Silver 0.6423 oz. ASW, 37 mm. **Subject:** Franco - Japanese Relators - 150th Anniversary **Obv:** Eillfel Tower and Kimono forming logo **Rev:** Ichikawa Ebizo IV portrait painting

Date	Mintage	F	VF	XF	Unc	BU
2008 Proof	5,000	Value: 65.00				

KM# 1550 1-1/2 EURO
22.2000 g., 0.9000 Silver 0.6423 oz. ASW, 37 mm. **Subject:** Franco - Japanese Relators - 150th Anniversary **Obv:** Eillfel Tower and Kimono forming logo **Rev:** Scenes of Paris and Tokyo - Eillfel Tower and Pagoda Sensoji

Date	Mintage	F	VF	XF	Unc	BU
2008 Proof	5,000	Value: 65.00				

KM# 1551 1-1/2 EURO
22.2000 g., 0.9000 Silver 0.6423 oz. ASW, 37 mm. **Subject:** Franco - Japanese Relators - 150th Anniversary **Obv:** Eillfel Tower and Kimono forming logo **Rev:** Japanese csh coin of "Kanei Tsuho"

Date	Mintage	F	VF	XF	Unc	BU
2008 Proof	5,000	Value: 65.00				

KM# 1555 1-1/2 EURO
22.2000 g., 0.9000 Silver 0.6423 oz. ASW, 37 mm. **Subject:** André Citronën **Obv:** First front wheel drive auto **Rev:** Bust 1/4 left

Date	Mintage	F	VF	XF	Unc	BU
2008 Proof	5,000	Value: 60.00				

KM# 1558 1-1/2 EURO
22.2000 g., 0.9000 Silver 0.6423 oz. ASW, 37 mm. **Subject:** Rouen Armada **Obv:** Cape Horn, sextant, hour glass **Rev:** Sailing ship

Date	Mintage	F	VF	XF	Unc	BU
2008 Proof	5,000	Value: 65.00				

KM# 1561 1-1/2 EURO
22.2000 g., 0.9000 Silver 0.6423 oz. ASW **Subject:** Lourdes, 150th Anniversary **Obv:** Church of Notre Dame at Lourdes **Rev:** Cross with Pope John Paul II, Pope Benedict XVI and Bernadette Soubirous in quadrants

Date	Mintage	F	VF	XF	Unc	BU
2008 Proof	15,000	Value: 60.00				

KM# 1574 1-1/2 EURO
22.2000 g., 0.9000 Silver 0.6423 oz. ASW, 37 mm. **Subject:** UNESCO - Grand Canyon **Obv:** Grand Canyon **Rev:** UNESCO logos

Date	Mintage	F	VF	XF	Unc	BU
2008 Proof	5,000	Value: 65.00				

KM# 1576 1-1/2 EURO
22.2000 g., 0.9000 Silver 0.6423 oz. ASW, 37 mm. **Subject:** International Polar Year **Obv:** IPY logo **Rev:** Emperor Penguin and map of Antartica

Date	Mintage	F	VF	XF	Unc	BU
2008 Proof	5,000	Value: 60.00				

KM# 1578 1-1/2 EURO
22.2000 g., 0.9000 Silver 0.6423 oz. ASW, 37 mm. **Subject:** Spirou, 70th Anniversary **Obv:** Character Spirou in thoguht **Rev:** 70th Anniversary logo

Date	Mintage	F	VF	XF	Unc	BU
2008 Proof	10,000	Value: 60.00				

KM# 1633 1-1/2 EURO
11.0000 g., Copper-Aluminum-Nickel, 30 mm. **Obv:** Stadium view, soccer player **Rev:** Shield of Olympique Lyonnais

Date	Mintage	F	VF	XF	Unc	BU
2009	25,000	—	—	—	—	20.00

KM# 1289 2 EURO
8.5200 g., Bi-Metallic Brass center in Copper-Nickel ring, 25.6 mm. **Obv:** Stylized tree divides RF within circle, date below **Obv. Designer:** Joaquin Jimenez **Rev:** Denomination and map **Rev. Designer:** Luc Luycx **Edge:** Reeding with 2's and stars

Date	Mintage	F	VF	XF	Unc	BU
2001	237,950,793	—	—	—	3.75	6.00
2001 Proof	15,000	Value: 20.00				
2002	153,700,000	—	—	—	3.75	6.00
2002 Proof	21,453	Value: 18.00				
2003 In sets only	180,000	—	—	—	—	13.50
2003 Proof	40,000	Value: 20.00				
2004 In sets only	160,000	—	—	—	—	13.50
2004 Proof	20,000	Value: 20.00				
2005 In sets only	120,000	—	—	—	—	13.50
2005 Proof	10,000	Value: 20.00				
2006 In sets only	67,600	—	—	—	—	13.50
2006 Proof	10,000	Value: 20.00				

KM# 1414 2 EURO
8.5200 g., Bi-Metallic Brass center in Copper-Nickel ring, 25.6 mm. **Obv:** Stylized tree **Obv. Designer:** Joaquin Jimenez **Rev:** Relief map of Western Europe, stars, lines and value **Rev. Designer:** Luc Luycx **Edge:** Reeding with 2's and stars

Date	Mintage	F	VF	XF	Unc	BU
2007 In sets only	58,000	—	—	—	—	15.00
2007 Proof	7,500	Value: 25.00				
2008 In sets only	57,000	—	—	—	—	6.00
2008 Proof	7,500	Value: 25.00				
2009	—	—	—	—	—	6.00
2009 In sets only	50,500	—	—	—	—	—
2009 Proof	7,500	Value: 25.00				

KM# 1460 2 EURO
Bi-Metallic Brass center in Copper-Nickel ring **Subject:** Treaty of Rome 50th Anniversary

Date	Mintage	F	VF	XF	Unc	BU
2007	9,600,000	—	—	—	—	6.50

KM# 1459 2 EURO
8.4700 g., Bi-Metallic, 25.74 mm. **Subject:** European Union Presidency **Obv:** Inscription **Obv. Inscription:** PRÉSIDENCE / FRANÇAISE / UNION / EUROPÉENNE / RF **Rev:** Large value "2" at left, modified map of Europe at right **Edge:** Reeded with incuse stars

Date	Mintage	F	VF	XF	Unc	BU
2008(a)	20,100,000	—	—	—	—	6.50

KM# 1542 2 EURO
8.5000 g., Bi-Metallic Brass center in copper-nickel ring, 25.75 mm. **Subject:** 5th Republic, 50th Anniversary **Obv:** Text within stars **Rev:** Value at left, relief map of the EU at right

Date	Mintage	F	VF	XF	Unc	BU
2008	10,000,000	—	—	—	6.50	—
2008 Sets only	20,000	—	—	—	—	20.00
2008 Proof	10,000	Value: 40.00				

KM# 1590 2 EURO
8.5000 g., Bi-Metallic Brass Center in Copper-nickel ring, 25.7 mm. **Obv:** EMU 10th Anniversary **Rev:** Stick figure and E design

Date	Mintage	F	VF	XF	Unc	BU
2009P	—	—	—	—	—	10.00
2009P Proof	10,000	Value: 15.00				

KM# 1347 5 EURO
24.9000 g., 0.9000 Bi-Metallic .900 Silver 22.2g planchet with .750 Gold 2.7g insert 0.7205 oz., 37 mm. **Obv:** The seed sower on gold insert **Rev:** Denomination and map **Edge:** Plain

Date	Mintage	F	VF	XF	Unc	BU
2002 Proof	10,000	Value: 475				

KM# 1371 5 EURO
24.9000 g., Bi-Metallic .750 Gold 2.7 g insert on .900 Silver 22.2g planchet, 37 mm. **Obv:** The seed sower on gold insert **Rev:** French face map and denomination **Edge:** Plain

Date	Mintage	F	VF	XF	Unc	BU
2004 Proof	3,000	Value: 500				

KM# 1523 5 EURO
22.2000 g., 0.9000 Silver 0.6423 oz. ASW, 37 mm. **Subject:** Euro - 5th Anniversary **Obv:** Sower

Date	Mintage	F	VF	XF	Unc	BU
2007 Proof	5,000	Value: 50.00				

KM# 1525 5 EURO
1.2400 g., 0.9990 Gold 0.0398 oz. AGW, 14 mm. **Subject:** Euro 5th Anniversary **Obv:** Sower

Date	Mintage	F	VF	XF	Unc	BU
2007 Proof	20,000	Value: 75.00				

KM# 1526 5 EURO
31.1050 g., 0.9200 Gold 0.9200 oz. AGW, 31 mm. **Subject:** Euro 5th Anniversary **Obv:** Sower

Date	Mintage	F	VF	XF	Unc	BU
2007 Proof	500	Value: 1,150				

KM# 1534 5 EURO
10.0000 g., 0.5000 Silver 0.1607 oz. ASW, 27 mm. **Obv:** Sower, full length **Rev:** Value within hexagon design

Date	Mintage	F	VF	XF	Unc	BU
2008 Proof	2,000,000	Value: 15.00				

KM# 1566 5 EURO
22.2000 g., 0.9000 Silver 0.6423 oz. ASW, 37 mm. **Subject:** Gabrielle Chanel **Obv:** Bust right in hat **Rev:** Value on "Matelassé" pattern

Date	Mintage	F	VF	XF	Unc	BU
2008 Proof	10,000	Value: 65.00				

KM# 1567 5 EURO
8.4500 g., 0.9200 Gold 0.2499 oz. AGW, 22 mm. **Subject:** Gabrielle Chanel **Obv:** Portrait in hat, right **Rev:** Value on "Matelassé" pattern

Date	Mintage	F	VF	XF	Unc	BU
2008 Proof	500	Value: 350				

KM# 1568 5 EURO
163.8000 g., 0.9500 Silver 5.0028 oz. ASW, 50 mm. **Subject:** Gabrielle Chanel **Obv:** Portrait in hat, right **Rev:** Vlaue on "Matelassé" pattern

Date	Mintage	F	VF	XF	Unc	BU
2008 Proof	500	Value: 350				

KM# 1586 5 EURO
1.2400 g., 0.9990 Gold 0.0398 oz. AGW, 13.9 mm. **Subject:** Court of Human Rights, 50th Anniversary **Obv:** Sower left **Rev:** Text

Date	Mintage	F	VF	XF	Unc	BU
2009P Proof	10,000	Value: 60.00				

KM# 1625 5 EURO
15.0000 g., 0.9000 Silver 0.4340 oz. ASW, 30 x 21 mm. **Subject:** Monet **Obv:** Le Bassin Aux Nympheas, 1900 painting **Rev:** Multicolor pallet and brushes, portrait **Shape:** Rectangle

Date	Mintage	F	VF	XF	Unc	BU
2009P Proof	20,000	Value: 30.00				

KM# 1627 5 EURO
22.2000 g., 0.9000 Silver 0.6423 oz. ASW, 37 mm. **Subject:** Year of the Ox **Obv:** Oxen within Asia screen garden **Rev:** Portrait of La Fontaine

Date	Mintage	F	VF	XF	Unc	BU
2009P Proof	10,000	Value: 30.00				

KM# 1302 10 EURO
8.4500 g., 0.9990 Gold 0.2714 oz. AGW, 22 mm. **Subject:** Europa **Obv:** Eight French euro coin designs **Rev:** Portrait and flags design of 6.55957 francs KM-1265 **Edge:** Reeded

Date	Mintage	F	VF	XF	Unc	BU
2002 Proof	3,000	Value: 350				

KM# 1326 10 EURO
8.4500 g., 0.9200 Gold 0.2499 oz. AGW, 22 mm. **Obv:** Tour de France logo **Rev:** Cyclist going left **Edge:** Reeded

Date	Mintage	F	VF	XF	Unc	BU
2003 (Ht) Proof	5,000	Value: 350				

KM# 1327 10 EURO
8.4500 g., 0.9200 Gold 0.2499 oz. AGW, 22 mm. **Obv:** Tour de France logo **Rev:** Group of cyclists and Arch de Triumph **Edge:** Reeded

Date	Mintage	F	VF	XF	Unc	BU
2003A Proof	5,000	Value: 350				

KM# 1328 10 EURO
8.4500 g., 0.9200 Gold 0.2499 oz. AGW, 22 mm. **Obv:** Tour de France logo **Rev:** Two cyclists and spectators **Edge:** Reeded

Date	Mintage	F	VF	XF	Unc	BU
2003A Proof	5,000	Value: 350				

KM# 1329 10 EURO
8.4500 g., 0.9200 Gold 0.2499 oz. AGW, 22 mm. **Obv:** Tour de France logo **Rev:** Two groups of cyclists **Edge:** Reeded

Date	Mintage	F	VF	XF	Unc	BU
2003A Proof	5,000	Value: 350				

KM# 1330 10 EURO
8.4500 g., 0.9200 Gold 0.2499 oz. AGW, 22 mm. **Obv:** Tour de France logo **Rev:** Cyclist, stop watch and gears **Edge:** Reeded

Date	Mintage	F	VF	XF	Unc	BU
2003A Proof	5,000	Value: 350				

KM# 1348 10 EURO
8.4500 g., 0.9200 Gold 0.2499 oz. AGW, 22 mm. **Obv:** The seed sower **Rev:** Denomination and map **Edge:** Plain

Date	Mintage	F	VF	XF	Unc	BU
2003 Proof	15,000	Value: 350				

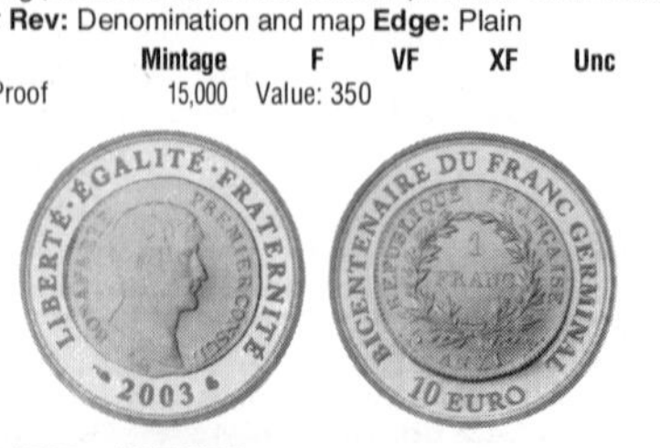

KM# 1352 10 EURO
8.4500 g., 0.9200 Gold 0.2499 oz. AGW, 22 mm. **Obv:** Obverse design of first one franc coin **Rev:** Reverse design of first one franc coin **Edge:** Plain

Date	Mintage	F	VF	XF	Unc	BU
2003 Proof	10,000	Value: 350				

KM# 1362 10 EURO
8.4500 g., 0.9200 Gold 0.2499 oz. AGW, 22 mm. **Obv:** Pierre de Coubertin **Rev:** Olympic runners **Edge:** Plain

Date	Mintage	F	VF	XF	Unc	BU
2003 Proof	15,000	Value: 350				

KM# 1367 10 EURO
6.4100 g., 0.9000 Gold 0.1855 oz. AGW, 22 mm. **Obv:** Book, denomination and eagle **Rev:** Napoleon and coronation scene **Edge:** Plain

Date	Mintage	F	VF	XF	Unc	BU
2004 Proof	5,000	Value: 350				

KM# 1375 10 EURO
8.4500 g., 0.9200 Gold 0.2499 oz. AGW, 22 mm. **Obv:** Half soccer ball and denomination **Rev:** Eiffel tower and soccer balls **Edge:** Plain

Date	Mintage	F	VF	XF	Unc	BU
2004 Proof	10,000	Value: 350				

KM# 1392 10 EURO
8.4500 g., 0.9200 Gold 0.2499 oz. AGW, 22 mm. **Subject:** European Union Expansion **Obv:** Partial face and flags **Rev:** Puzzle map **Edge:** Reeded

Date	Mintage	F	VF	XF	Unc	BU
2004 Proof	5,000	Value: 350				

KM# 1403 10 EURO
8.4500 g., 0.9200 Gold 0.2499 oz. AGW, 22 mm. **Subject:** Jules Verne **Obv:** Various scenes from Verne's novel "Around The World in 80 Days" **Rev:** Jules Verne's portrait left of value and date

Date	Mintage	F	VF	XF	Unc	BU
2005 Proof	2,000	Value: 350				

KM# 1424 10 EURO
8.4500 g., 0.9200 Gold 0.2499 oz. AGW, 22 mm. **Subject:** Biathlon **Rev:** Skier at right facing 3/4 left, mountain peaks in background **Rev. Inscription:** JEUX D'HIVER

Date	Mintage	F	VF	XF	Unc	BU
2005 Proof	—	Value: 350				

KM# 1426 10 EURO
8.4500 g., 0.9200 Gold 0.2499 oz. AGW, 22 mm. **Series:** Jules Verne **Subject:** From the earth to the moon **Rev:** Crowd observing at lower left, volcano erupting above, moon at upper right, Verne in spaceship at lower right, chimneys belching smoke in backgroud **Rev. Legend:** DE LA TERRE À LA LUNE

Date	Mintage	F	VF	XF	Unc	BU
2005 Proof	2,000	Value: 350				

KM# 1429 10 EURO
8.4500 g., 0.9200 Gold 0.2499 oz. AGW, 22 mm. **Rev:** Kitty at the Spectacle, multicolor **Rev. Legend:** Hello Kitty

Date	Mintage	F	VF	XF	Unc	BU
2005 Proof	1,000	Value: 375				

KM# 1432 10 EURO
6.4100 g., 0.9000 Gold 0.1855 oz. AGW, 21 mm. **Subject:** Bicentennial - Victory at Austerlitz **Rev:** Battle scene **Rev. Legend:** LIBERTÉ ÉGALITÉ FRATERNITÉ

Date	Mintage	F	VF	XF	Unc	BU
2005 Proof	3,000	Value: 350				

KM# 1435 10 EURO
8.4500 g., 0.9200 Gold 0.2499 oz. AGW, 22 mm. **Subject:** 50th Anniversary - Flag of Europe **Rev:** Stars at left, partial flag at center right

Date	Mintage	F	VF	XF	Unc	BU
2005 Proof	3,000	Value: 350				

KM# 1439 10 EURO
8.4500 g., 0.9200 Gold 0.2499 oz. AGW, 22 mm. **Series:** Jules Verne **Subject:** 20,000 Leagues Under the Sea **Rev:** Submarine above plants and divers **Rev. Legend:** VINGT MILLE LIEUES SOUS LES MERS

Date	Mintage	F	VF	XF	Unc	BU
2005 Proof	2,000	Value: 350				

KM# 1446 10 EURO
8.4500 g., 0.9200 Gold 0.2499 oz. AGW, 22 mm. **Subject:** Marshal Bernadotte under Napoleon **Rev:** Military bust facing 3/4 right at left, building in backgound at right **Rev. Legend:** LIBERTÉ GALITÉ FRATERNITÉ - KARL XIV JOHAN ROI DE SUÉDE11

Date	Mintage	F	VF	XF	Unc	BU
2006 Proof	1,000	Value: 375				

KM# 1448 10 EURO
8.4500 g., 0.9200 Gold 0.2499 oz. AGW, 22 mm. **Subject:** 20,000 Leagues Under the Sea **Obv:** Strogoff horseback wielding a sword, city at left, soldiers at lower left, calvary at right - the Tartars, Siberia and the Tsar's Army **Obv. Legend:** MICHEL STROGOFF **Rev:** Head of Verne facing 3/4 right at left center, instruments and anchor in curved band **Rev. Legend:** 1828 JULES VERNE 1905

Date	Mintage	F	VF	XF	Unc	BU
2006 Proof	500	Value: 400				

KM# 1449 10 EURO
8.4500 g., 0.9200 Gold 0.2499 oz. AGW, 22 mm. **Subject:** 20,000 Leagues Under the Sea **Obv:** Hot air balloon, parrots at left, native masks below left, foliage at right, huts below, map of Africa in background. **Obv. Legend:** CINQ SEMAINES EN BALLON **Rev:** Head of Verne facing 3/4 right at left center, instruments and anchor in curved band **Rev. Legend:** 1828 JULES VERNE 1905 - LIBERTÉ . ÉGALITÉ . FRATERNITÉ

Date	Mintage	F	VF	XF	Unc	BU
2006 Proof	500	Value: 400				

KM# 1451 10 EURO
8.4500 g., 0.9200 Gold 0.2499 oz. AGW, 22 mm. **Subject:** 100th Anniversary - French Grand Prix **Obv:** Steering wheel with early race car in upper segment, two gauges at lower left, R / F at lower right **Obv. Legend:** LE MANS 1906 - CENTENAIRE du 1er GRAND PRIX de l'AUTOMOBILE CLUB de FRANCE **Rev. Legend:** MAGNY-COURS

Date	Mintage	F	VF	XF	Unc	BU
2006 Proof	500	Value: 400				

KM# 1416 10 EURO
8.4500 g., 0.9200 Gold 0.2499 oz. AGW, 22 mm. **Obv:** Jean de la Fontaine, value, Chinese astrological animals, date, Paris mint privy marks but without national identification **Rev:** Dog in wreath **Edge:** Reeded **Note:** Anonymous issue

Date	Mintage	F	VF	XF	Unc	BU
2006 Proof	500	Value: 400				

KM# 1418 10 EURO
8.4500 g., 0.9200 Gold 0.2499 oz. AGW, 22 mm. **Obv:** Jean de la Fontaine, value, Chinese astrological animals, date, Paris mint privy marks but without national identification **Rev:** Pig in wreath **Edge:** Reeded **Note:** anonymous issue

Date	Mintage	F	VF	XF	Unc	BU
2007 Proof	500	Value: 400				

KM# 1502 10 EURO
8.4500 g., 0.9200 Gold 0.2499 oz. AGW, 22 mm. **Subject:** Georges Pompendev Center, 30th Anniversary

Date	Mintage	F	VF	XF	Unc	BU
2007 Proof	—	Value: 350				

KM# 1420 10 EURO
8.4500 g., 0.9200 Gold 0.2499 oz. AGW, 22 mm. **Obv:** Military bust of Lafayette facing 3/4 left **Obv. Legend:** LA FAYETTE. HÉROS DELA RÉVOLUTION AMÉRICAINE **Obv. Inscription:** 1757/1854 at left, RF monogram at right **Rev:** Sailing ship L' Hermione **Rev. Legend:** LA FAYETTE, HERO OF THE AMERICAN REVOLUTION **Edge:** Plain

Date	Mintage	F	VF	XF	Unc	BU
2007 (a) Proof	500	Value: 400				

KM# 1463 10 EURO
8.4500 g., 0.9200 Gold 0.2499 oz. AGW, 22 mm. **Subject:** Sebastien Le Prestre de Vauban, 300th Anniversary of Death

Date	Mintage	F	VF	XF	Unc	BU
2007 Proof	3,000	Value: 400				

KM# 1474 10 EURO
8.4500 g., 0.9200 Gold 0.2499 oz. AGW, 22 mm. **Subject:** Paul E. Victor, 100th birthday **Obv:** International polar year logo **Rev:** Bust at left, Islands

Date	Mintage	F	VF	XF	Unc	BU
2007 500	—	—	—	—	—	400

KM# 1476 10 EURO
8.4500 g., 0.9200 Gold 0.2499 oz. AGW, 22 mm. **Obv:** Formula 1 race car on checkered background **Rev:** Legend in wreath on checkered background

Date	Mintage	F	VF	XF	Unc	BU
2007//2006 Proof	500	Value: 400				

KM# 1478 10 EURO
8.4500 g., 0.9200 Gold 0.2499 oz. AGW, 22 mm. **Subject:** 29th Summer Olympic Games Beijing **Obv:** Rider on horseback, globe map of China **Rev:** Equestrian jump over oriental fence

Date	Mintage	F	VF	XF	Unc	BU
2007 Proof	500	Value: 400				

KM# 1480 10 EURO
8.4500 g., 0.9200 Gold 0.2499 oz. AGW, 22 mm. **Subject:** Airbus A380 **Obv:** Airplane **Rev:** Europa head and flags

Date	Mintage	F	VF	XF	Unc	BU
2007 Proof	1,000	Value: 400				

KM# 1485 10 EURO
8.4500 g., 0.9200 Gold 0.2499 oz. AGW, 22 mm. **Subject:** 2007 Rugby World Cup **Obv:** Two players and goal **Rev:** Logo and goal

Date	Mintage	F	VF	XF	Unc	BU
2007 Proof	500	Value: 425				

KM# 1489 10 EURO
8.4500 g., 0.9200 Gold 0.2499 oz. AGW, 22 mm. **Obv:** Christian Dior **Rev:** Dior Museum building

Date	Mintage	F	VF	XF	Unc	BU
2007 Proof	500	Value: 375				

KM# 1508 10 EURO
8.4500 g., 0.9200 Gold 0.2499 oz. AGW, 22 mm. **Subject:** Georges Remi Centennial **Obv:** Wand and sparkles **Rev:** Tin Tin raising cap

Date	Mintage	F	VF	XF	Unc	BU
2007 Proof	1,000	Value: 350				

KM# 1512 10 EURO
8.4500 g., 0.9200 Gold 0.2499 oz. AGW, 22 mm. **Subject:** Aristides de Sousa Mendes, Portuguese diplomat **Obv:** Bust right **Rev:** Plaque

Date	Mintage	F	VF	XF	Unc	BU
2007 Proof	500	Value: 375				

KM# 1519 10 EURO
8.4500 g., 0.9200 Gold 0.2499 oz. AGW, 22 mm. **Subject:** Asterix **Rev:** Character with torch

Date	Mintage	F	VF	XF	Unc	BU
2007 Proof	500	Value: 375				

KM# 1544 10 EURO
8.4500 g., 0.9200 Gold 0.2499 oz. AGW, 22 mm. **Subject:** 29th Summer Olympic Games - Beijing **Obv:** Swimmer and globe **Rev:** Diver and oriental screen

Date	Mintage	F	VF	XF	Unc	BU
2008 Proof	1,000	Value: 350				

KM# 1528 10 EURO
8.4500 g., 0.9200 Gold 0.2499 oz. AGW, 22 mm. **Subject:** French Presidency of European Union **Obv:** Text within stars **Rev:** Europa head and flags

Date	Mintage	F	VF	XF	Unc	BU
2008 Proof	1,000	Value: 350				

KM# 1533 10 EURO
8.4500 g., 0.9200 Gold 0.2499 oz. AGW, 22 mm. **Subject:** European Parliament, 50th Anniversary **Obv:** Map of EU within stars **Rev:** European Parliament Building in Strasbourg

Date	Mintage	F	VF	XF	Unc	BU
2008 Proof	3,000	Value: 350				

KM# 1539 10 EURO
8.4500 g., 0.9990 Gold 0.2714 oz. AGW, 22 mm. **Subject:** 5th Repbulic, 50th Anniversary **Obv:** Sower **Rev:** de Gaulle head right

Date	Mintage	F	VF	XF	Unc	BU
2008 Proof	1,000	Value: 350				

KM# 1547 10 EURO
8.4500 g., 0.9200 Gold 0.2499 oz. AGW, 22 mm. **Subject:** UEFA **Obv:** French soccer team **Rev:** UEFA logo

Date	Mintage	F	VF	XF	Unc	BU
2008 Proof	500	Value: 350				

KM# 1552 10 EURO
8.4500 g., 0.9200 Gold 0.2499 oz. AGW, 22 mm. **Subject:** Freanco - Japanese Relators - 150th Anniversary **Obv:** Eillfel Tower and Kimono forming logo **Rev:** Delacroix's "La Liberte"

Date	Mintage	F	VF	XF	Unc	BU
2008 Proof	3,000	Value: 350				

KM# 1553 10 EURO
8.4500 g., 0.9200 Gold 0.2499 oz. AGW, 22 mm. **Subject:** Franco - Japanese Relators - 150th Anniversary **Obv:** Eillfel Tower and Kimono forming logo **Rev:** "Ichikawa Ebizo IV" portrait painting

Date	Mintage	F	VF	XF	Unc	BU
2008 Proof	3,000	Value: 350				

KM# 1554 10 EURO
8.4500 g., 0.9200 Gold 0.2499 oz. AGW, 22 mm. **Subject:** Franco - Japanese Relators - 150th Anniversary **Obv:** Eillfel Tower and Kimono forming logo **Rev:** Japanese cash coin from "Kanci Tsuho"

Date	Mintage	F	VF	XF	Unc	BU
2008 Proof	3,000	Value: 350				

KM# 1556 10 EURO
0.4500 g., 0.9200 Gold 0.0133 oz. AGW, 22 mm. **Subject:** André Citronë **Obv:** First front wheel drive auto **Rev:** Bust 1/4 left

Date	Mintage	F	VF	XF	Unc	BU
2008 Proof	500	Value: 365				

KM# 1559 10 EURO
8.4500 g., 0.9200 Gold 0.2499 oz. AGW, 22 mm. **Subject:** Rouen Armada **Obv:** Cape Hown, sextant, hour glass **Edge:** Sailing ship

Date	Mintage	F	VF	XF	Unc	BU
2008 Proof	500	Value: 365				

KM# 1562 10 EURO
8.4500 g., 0.9200 Gold 0.2499 oz. AGW, 22 mm. **Subject:** Lourdes, 150th Anniversary **Obv:** Church of Notre Dame at Lourdes **Rev:** Cross with Pope John Paul II, Pope Benedict XVI and Bernadette Soubirous in quadrants

Date	Mintage	F	VF	XF	Unc	BU
2008 Proof	1,000	Value: 350				

KM# 1573 10 EURO
8.4500 g., 0.9200 Gold 0.2499 oz. AGW, 22 mm. **Subject:** Lunar New Year - Year of the Rat **Obv:** Bust of Jean de la Fontaine and twelve awards **Rev:** Rat within border

Date	Mintage	F	VF	XF	Unc	BU
2008 Proof	500	Value: 365				

KM# 1575 10 EURO
8.4500 g., 0.9200 Gold 0.2499 oz. AGW, 22 mm. **Subject:** UNESCO - Grand Canyon **Obv:** Grand Canyon **Rev:** UNESCO logos

Date	Mintage	F	VF	XF	Unc	BU
2008 Proof	500	Value: 365				

KM# 1577 10 EURO
8.4500 g., 0.9200 Gold 0.2499 oz. AGW, 22 mm. **Subject:** International Polar Year **Obv:** IPY logo **Rev:** Emperor Penguin and map of Antartica

Date	Mintage	F	VF	XF	Unc	BU
2008 Proof	500	Value: 365				

KM# 1579 10 EURO
8.4500 g., 0.9200 Gold 0.2499 oz. AGW, 22 mm. **Subject:** Spirou, 70th Anniversary **Obv:** Character Spirou in thought **Rev:** 70th Aniversary logo

Date	Mintage	F	VF	XF	Unc	BU
2008 Proof	500	Value: 365				

KM# 1591 10 EURO
27.2000 g., 0.9000 Silver 0.7870 oz. ASW, 37 mm. **Subject:** Europa - Fall of Berlin Wall **Obv:** Brandenburg gate and doves in flight **Rev:** Head facing and flags

Date	Mintage	F	VF	XF	Unc	BU
2009P Proof	10,000	Value: 30.00				

KM# 1580 10 EURO
12.0000 g., 0.9000 Silver 0.3472 oz. ASW, 29 mm. **Obv:** Modernistic sower advancing right **Rev:** Wreath and value

Date	Mintage	F	VF	XF	Unc	BU
2009P	2,000,000	—	—	—	—	12.50

KM# 1584 10 EURO
22.2000 g., 0.9000 Silver 0.6423 oz. ASW, 37 mm. **Subject:** Court of Human Rights, 50th Anniversary **Obv:** Sower left **Rev:** Text

Date	Mintage	F	VF	XF	Unc	BU
2009P Proof	10,000	Value: 30.00				

KM# 1596 10 EURO
22.2000 g., 0.9000 Silver 0.6423 oz. ASW, 37 mm. **Subject:** Concorde 40th Anniversary **Obv:** Concorde in flight **Rev:** Tail emblems

Date	Mintage	F	VF	XF	Unc	BU
2009P Proof	3,000	Value: 30.00				

KM# 1601 10 EURO
20.8900 g., 0.9000 Silver 0.6044 oz. ASW, 37 mm. **Obv:** Eiffel Tower Structure **Rev:** Gustave Eiffel at left

Date	Mintage	F	VF	XF	Unc	BU
2009P Proof	10,000	Value: 30.00				

KM# 1606 10 EURO
27.2000 g., 0.9000 Silver 0.7870 oz. ASW, 37 mm. **Subject:** Bugatti 100th Anniversary **Obv:** Ettore Bugatti at left **Rev:** Race car and quilt motif

Date	Mintage	F	VF	XF	Unc	BU
2009P Proof	10,000	Value: 30.00				

KM# 1611 10 EURO
22.2000 g., 0.9000 Silver 0.6423 oz. ASW, 37 mm. **Subject:** Curie Institute, 100th Anniversary

Date	Mintage	F	VF	XF	Unc	BU
2009P Proof	10,000	Value: 30.00				

KM# 1616   10 EURO
27.2000 g., 0.9000 Silver 0.7870 oz. ASW, 37 mm.
Subject: Unesco site - The Kremlin in Moscow **Obv:** Wall Tower and cathedral

Date	Mintage	F	VF	XF	Unc	BU
2009P Proof	20,000	Value: 30.00				

KM# 1621   10 EURO
22.2000 g., 0.9000 Silver 0.6423 oz. ASW, 37 mm. **Subject:** International Year of Astronomy **Obv:** Footprint on the moon

Date	Mintage	F	VF	XF	Unc	BU
2009P Proof	10,000	Value: 30.00				

KM# 1629   10 EURO
22.2000 g., 0.9000 Silver 0.6423 oz. ASW, 37 mm.
Subject: Comic strip heroes **Obv:** Wanted posted **Rev:** Luckey Luke on horseback

Date	Mintage	F	VF	XF	Unc	BU
2009P Proof	5,000	Value: 30.00				

KM# 1631   10 EURO
22.2000 g., 0.9000 Silver 0.6423 oz. ASW, 37 mm. **Obv:** Soccer player **Rev:** Shield of Stade Francais

Date	Mintage	F	VF	XF	Unc	BU
2009P Proof	5,000	Value: 30.00				

KM# 1634   10 EURO
27.2000 g., 0.9000 Silver 0.7870 oz. ASW, 37 mm.
Subject: Alpine skiing **Obv:** Globe and downhill skier **Rev:** Downhill skier on mountainside

Date	Mintage	F	VF	XF	Unc	BU
2009P Proof	10,000	Value: 28.00				

KM# 1636   10 EURO
22.2000 g., 0.9000 Silver 0.6423 oz. ASW, 37 mm.
Subject: FIFA World Cup, South Africa **Obv:** Soccer player on field **Rev:** Soccerball, map of Africa, Prorea flower

Date	Mintage	F	VF	XF	Unc	BU
2009P Proof	15,000	Value: 30.00				

KM# A1450   15 EURO
31.0000 g., 0.9000 Silver 0.8970 oz. ASW, 31 mm.
Rev: Pantheon

Date	Mintage	F	VF	XF	Unc	BU
2007 Proof	7,500	Value: 75.00				

KM# 1535   15 EURO
15.0000 g., 0.9000 Silver 0.4340 oz. ASW, 31 mm. **Obv:** Sower, half length advancing right **Rev:** Value within hexagon

Date	Mintage	F	VF	XF	Unc	BU
2008 Proof	500,000	Value: 45.00				

KM# 1306   10 EURO
17.0000 g., 0.9200 Gold 0.5028 oz. AGW, 31 mm.
Subject: French Landmarks **Obv:** French map **Rev:** Le Mont St. Michel **Edge:** Plain

Date	Mintage	F	VF	XF	Unc	BU
2002 Proof	1,000	Value: 650				

KM# 1308   20 EURO
17.0000 g., 0.9200 Gold 0.5028 oz. AGW, 31 mm.
Subject: French Landmarks **Obv:** French map **Rev:** La Butte Montmartre **Edge:** Plain

Date	Mintage	F	VF	XF	Unc	BU
2002 Proof	1,000	Value: 650				

KM# 1333   20 EURO
17.0000 g., 0.9200 Gold 0.5028 oz. AGW, 31 mm. **Obv:** Victor Hugo, denomination and map **Rev:** "Gavroche" **Edge:** Plain

Date	Mintage	F	VF	XF	Unc	BU
2002 Proof	2,000	Value: 625				

KM# 1334   20 EURO
17.0000 g., 0.9200 Gold 0.5028 oz. AGW, 31 mm. **Obv:** Tour de France logo **Rev:** Cyclist going left **Edge:** Plain

Date	Mintage	F	VF	XF	Unc	BU
2003 Proof	5,000	Value: 625				

KM# 1337   20 EURO
17.0000 g., 0.9200 Gold 0.5028 oz. AGW, 31 mm.
Obv: Jefferson and Napoleon with Louisiana Purchase map **Rev:** Jazz musician, mansion and river boat **Edge:** Plain

Date	Mintage	F	VF	XF	Unc	BU
2003 Proof	1,000	Value: 650				

KM# 1339   20 EURO
17.0000 g., 0.9200 Gold 0.5028 oz. AGW, 31 mm. **Obv:** Curved cross design with multiple values **Rev:** Goddess Europa and flags **Edge:** Plain

Date	Mintage	F	VF	XF	Unc	BU
2003 Proof	3,000	Value: 625				

KM# 1342   20 EURO
17.0000 g., 0.9200 Gold 0.5028 oz. AGW, 31 mm.
Obv: Denomination and compass face **Rev:** SS Normandie and New York City skyline **Edge:** Plain

Date	Mintage	F	VF	XF	Unc	BU
2003 Proof	1,000	Value: 625				

KM# 1344   20 EURO
17.0000 g., 0.9200 Gold 0.5028 oz. AGW, 31 mm.
Obv: Denomination and compass face **Rev:** Airplane and Tokyo Geisha **Edge:** Plain

Date	Mintage	F	VF	XF	Unc	BU
2003 Proof	1,000	Value: 625				

KM# 1346   20 EURO
17.0000 g., 0.9200 Gold 0.5028 oz. AGW, 31 mm. **Obv:** Paul Gauguin **Rev:** Native woman **Edge:** Plain

Date	Mintage	F	VF	XF	Unc	BU
2003 Proof	2,000	Value: 650				

KM# 1349   20 EURO
17.0000 g., 0.9200 Gold 0.5028 oz. AGW, 31 mm. **Obv:** The seed sower **Rev:** Denomination and map **Edge:** Plain

Date	Mintage	F	VF	XF	Unc	BU
2003 Proof	5,000	Value: 675				

KM# 1354   20 EURO
17.0000 g., 0.9200 Gold 0.5028 oz. AGW, 31 mm. **Obv:** Mona Lisa **Rev:** Leonardo da Vinci and denomination **Edge:** Plain

Date	Mintage	F	VF	XF	Unc	BU
2003 Proof	1,000	Value: 650				

KM# 1356   20 EURO
17.0000 g., 0.9200 Gold 0.5028 oz. AGW, 31 mm. **Obv:** Map and denomination **Rev:** Chateau Chambord **Edge:** Plain

Date	Mintage	F	VF	XF	Unc	BU
2003 Proof	1,000	Value: 625				

KM# 1358   20 EURO
17.0000 g., 0.9200 Gold 0.5028 oz. AGW, 31 mm.
Obv: Denomination in swirling design **Rev:** Hansel and Gretel, witch and house **Edge:** Plain

Date	Mintage	F	VF	XF	Unc	BU
2003 Proof	1,000	Value: 650				

KM# 1360   20 EURO
17.0000 g., 0.9200 Gold 0.5028 oz. AGW, 31 mm.
Obv: Denomination in swirling design **Rev:** Alice in Wonderland **Edge:** Plain

Date	Mintage	F	VF	XF	Unc	BU
2003 Proof	1,000	Value: 650				

KM# 1363   20 EURO
17.0000 g., 0.9200 Gold 0.5028 oz. AGW, 31 mm. **Obv:** Pierre de Coubertin **Rev:** Olympic runners **Edge:** Plain

Date	Mintage	F	VF	XF	Unc	BU
2003 Proof	3,000	Value: 625				

KM# 1365   20 EURO
17.0000 g., 0.9200 Gold 0.5028 oz. AGW, 31 mm. **Obv:** Map with denomination **Rev:** Avignon Popes Palace **Edge:** Plain

Date	Mintage	F	VF	XF	Unc	BU
2004 Proof	1,000	Value: 675				

KM# 1370   20 EURO
17.0000 g., 0.9200 Gold 0.5028 oz. AGW, 31 mm. **Obv:** Soldiers and Normandy invasion scene **Rev:** "D-DAY" above denomination **Edge:** Plain

Date	Mintage	F	VF	XF	Unc	BU
2004 Proof	2,000	Value: 675				

KM# 1376   20 EURO
17.0000 g., 0.9200 Gold 0.5028 oz. AGW, 31 mm. **Subject:** Centenary Law of Dec. 9, 1905 **Obv:** "Sower" left in ring of stars **Rev:** Denomination and French map face design **Edge:** Plain

Date	Mintage	F	VF	XF	Unc	BU
2004 Proof	3,000	Value: 625				
2006 Proof	1,000	Value: 650				

KM# 1379   20 EURO
17.0000 g., 0.9200 Gold 0.5028 oz. AGW, 31 mm.
Obv: Compass rose **Rev:** Ocean liner **Edge:** Plain

Date	Mintage	F	VF	XF	Unc	BU
2004 Proof	1,000	Value: 650				

KM# 1381   20 EURO
17.0000 g., 0.9200 Gold 0.5028 oz. AGW, 31 mm.
Obv: Compass rose **Rev:** Trans-Siberian Railroad **Edge:** Plain

Date	Mintage	F	VF	XF	Unc	BU
2004 Proof	1,000	Value: 635				

KM# 1383   20 EURO
17.0000 g., 0.9200 Gold 0.5028 oz. AGW, 31 mm.
Obv: Compass rose **Rev:** Half-track vehicle **Edge:** Plain

Date	Mintage	F	VF	XF	Unc	BU
2004 Proof	1,000	Value: 635				

KM# 1385   20 EURO
17.0000 g., 0.9200 Gold 0.5028 oz. AGW, 31 mm.
Obv: Compass rose **Rev:** Biplane airliner **Edge:** Plain

Date	Mintage	F	VF	XF	Unc	BU
2004 Proof	1,000	Value: 635				

KM# 1387   20 EURO
155.5000 g., 0.9500 Silver 4.7493 oz. ASW, 50 mm.
Obv: Statue of Liberty **Rev:** F. A. Bartholdi **Edge:** Plain

Date	Mintage	F	VF	XF	Unc	BU
2004 Proof	999	Value: 175				

KM# 1388   20 EURO
17.0000 g., 0.9200 Gold 0.5028 oz. AGW, 31 mm. **Obv:** Statue of Liberty **Rev:** F. A. Bartholdi **Edge:** Plain

Date	Mintage	F	VF	XF	Unc	BU
2004 Proof	2,000	Value: 650				

KM# 1393   20 EURO
17.0000 g., 0.9200 Gold 0.5028 oz. AGW, 31 mm.
Subject: European Union Expansion **Obv:** Partial face and flags **Rev:** Puzzle map **Edge:** Plain

Date	Mintage	F	VF	XF	Unc	BU
2004 Proof	3,000	Value: 650				

KM# 1433   20 EURO
17.0000 g., 0.9200 Gold 0.5028 oz. AGW, 31 mm.
Subject: Bicentennial Victory at Austerlitz **Rev:** Battle scene **Rev. Legend:** LIBERTÉ ÉGALITÉ FRATERNITÉ

Date	Mintage	F	VF	XF	Unc	BU
2005 Proof	5,000	Value: 625				

KM# 1437   20 EURO
17.0000 g., 0.9200 Gold 0.5028 oz. AGW, 31 mm.
Subject: Centenary - Law of Dec. 9, 1905 **Obv:** "Sower" at left in ring of stars

Date	Mintage	F	VF	XF	Unc	BU
2005 Proof	1,500	Value: 650				

KM# 1454   20 EURO
155.5000 g., 0.9500 Silver 4.7493 oz. ASW, 50 mm.
Subject: 100th Anniversary - Paul Cézanne's death **Obv:** Self portrait **Rev:** "The Card Players" **Rev. Legend:** LIBERTÉ ÉGALITÉ FRATERNITÉ

Date	Mintage	F	VF	XF	Unc	BU
2006 Proof	500	Value: 200				

KM# 1443 20 EURO
155.5200 g., 0.9500 Silver 4.7499 oz. ASW, 50 mm. **Obv:** Bust of Franklin facing slightly right at left, his diplomatic and technical successes at right **Obv. Legend:** BENJAMIN FRANKLIN 1706-2006 **Obv. Inscription:** AMI DE LA FRANCE

Date	Mintage	F	VF	XF	Unc	BU
2006 Proof	500	Value: 200				

KM# 1520 20 EURO
155.5000 g., 0.9500 Silver 4.7493 oz. ASW, 50 mm.
Subject: Asterix **Rev:** Character running downhill

Date	Mintage	F	VF	XF	Unc	BU
2007 Proof	500	Value: 325				

KM# 1468 20 EURO
17.0000 g., 0.9200 Gold 0.5028 oz. AGW, 31 mm. **Subject:** Le Petit Prince, 60th Anniversary **Obv:** Prince lying in field

Date	Mintage	F	VF	XF	Unc	BU
2007 Proof	2,000	Value: 700				

KM# 1471 20 EURO
155.5500 g., 0.9500 Silver 4.7508 oz. ASW, 50 mm. **Obv:** Two dragons in flight **Rev:** Merlin and Excalibur

Date	Mintage	F	VF	XF	Unc	BU
2007 Proof	500	Value: 300				

KM# 1472 20 EURO
17.0000 g., 0.9200 Silver 0.5028 oz. ASW, 31 mm. **Obv:** Two dragons in flight **Rev:** Merlin & Excalibur

Date	Mintage	F	VF	XF	Unc	BU
2007 Proof	500	Value: 750				

KM# 1494 20 EURO
155.5500 g., 0.9500 Silver 4.7508 oz. ASW, 50 mm.
Subject: Point Neuf - 400th Anniversary **Obv:** Moments of France logo **Rev:** Point Neuf Bridge and Paris Mint Building

Date	Mintage	F	VF	XF	Unc	BU
2007 Proof	500	Value: 300				

KM# 1496 20 EURO
155.5500 g., 0.9500 Silver 4.7508 oz. ASW, 50 mm.
Subject: Cannes Film Festival, 60th Anniversary **Obv:** Cinema screen and stage, Golden Palm Award

Date	Mintage	F	VF	XF	Unc	BU
2007 Proof	500	Value: 300				

KM# 1499 20 EURO
17.0000 g., 0.9200 Gold 0.5028 oz. AGW, 30 x 21 mm.
Subject: Edgar Degas, 90th Anniversary of Seuth **Obv:** Degas painting of dancer **Rev:** Brushes and Degas portrait
Shape: Rectangle

Date	Mintage	F	VF	XF	Unc	BU
2007 Proof	500	Value: 750				

KM# 1509 20 EURO
100.0000 g., 0.9500 Silver 3.0542 oz. ASW, 49 mm.
Subject: Georges Remi Centennial **Rev:** Tin Tin and Snowy

Date	Mintage	F	VF	XF	Unc	BU
2007 Proof	500	Value: 325				

KM# 1513 20 EURO
155.5000 g., 0.9500 Silver 4.7493 oz. ASW, 50 mm.
Subject: Stanislas Leszczynski **Obv:** Bust and shield
Rev: Palace Stanislas - Nancy

Date	Mintage	F	VF	XF	Unc	BU
2007 Proof	500	Value: 325				

KM# 1541 20 EURO
17.0000 g., 0.9205 Gold 0.5031 oz. AGW, 31 mm. **Subject:** 5th Republic, 50th Anniversary **Obv:** Sower **Rev:** de Gaulle head right

Date	Mintage	F	VF	XF	Unc	BU
2008 Proof	500	Value: 950				

KM# 1557 20 EURO
163.8000 g., 0.9500 Silver 5.0028 oz. ASW, 50 mm.
Subject: André Citronë **Obv:** First front wheel drive auto
Rev: Bust 1/4 left

Date	Mintage	F	VF	XF	Unc	BU
2008 Proof	500	Value: 325				

KM# 1560 20 EURO
163.8000 g., 0.9500 Silver 5.0028 oz. ASW, 50 mm.
Subject: Rouen Armada **Obv:** Cape Horn, sextant, hour glass
Rev: Sailing ship

Date	Mintage	F	VF	XF	Unc	BU
2008 Proof	—	Value: 350				

KM# 1563 20 EURO
163.8000 g., 0.9500 Silver 5.0028 oz. ASW, 50 mm.
Subject: Lourdes, 150th Anniversary **Obv:** Church of Notre Dame at Lourdes **Rev:** Cross with Pope John Paul II, Pope Benedict XVI and Bernadette Soubirous in quadrants

Date	Mintage	F	VF	XF	Unc	BU
2008 Proof	500	Value: 300				

KM# 1571 20 EURO
17.0000 g., 0.9200 Gold 0.5028 oz. AGW, 30 x 21 mm.
Subject: Edward Manet **Obv:** Manet's "Olympia" painting
Rev: Paint brushes and Manet's portrait **Shape:** Rectangle

Date	Mintage	F	VF	XF	Unc	BU
2008 Proof	500	Value: 700				

KM# 1602 20 EURO
44.4000 g., 0.9000 Silver 1.2847 oz. ASW, 37 mm. **Obv:** Eiffel Tower Structure **Rev:** Gustave Eiffel at left

Date	Mintage	F	VF	XF	Unc	BU
2009P Proof	5,000	Value: 100				

KM# 1607 20 EURO
44.4000 g., 0.9000 Silver 1.2847 oz. ASW, 37 mm.
Subject: Bugatti 100th Anniversary **Obv:** Ettore Bugatti at left
Rev: Race car and grill motif

Date	Mintage	F	VF	XF	Unc	BU
2009P Proof	5,000	Value: 100				

KM# 1612 20 EURO
44.4000 g., 0.9000 Silver 1.2847 oz. ASW, 37 mm.
Subject: Curie Institute, 100th Anniversary

Date	Mintage	F	VF	XF	Unc	BU
2009P Proof	5,000	Value: 50.00				

KM# 1581 25 EURO
18.0000 g., 0.9000 Silver 0.5208 oz. ASW, 33 mm.
Obv: Modernistic sower advancing right **Rev:** Value and wreath

Date	Mintage	F	VF	XF	Unc	BU
2009P	250,000	—	—	—	—	25.00

KM# 1303 50 EURO
31.0000 g., 0.9990 Gold 0.9956 oz. AGW, 37 mm.
Subject: Europa **Obv:** Eight French euro coin designs
Rev: Portrait and flags design of 6.55957 francs KM-1265
Edge: Plain

Date	Mintage	F	VF	XF	Unc	BU
2002 Proof	2,000	Value: 1,250				

KM# 1335 50 EURO
31.1000 g., 0.9990 Gold 0.9988 oz. AGW, 37 mm. **Obv:** Tour de France logo **Rev:** Cyclist going left **Edge:** Plain

Date	Mintage	F	VF	XF	Unc	BU
2003 Proof	5,000	Value: 1,250				

KM# 1340 50 EURO
1000.0000 g., 0.9500 Silver 30.541 oz. ASW, 100 mm.
Obv: Curved cross design with multiple values **Rev:** Goddess Europa and flags **Edge:** Plain with three line inscription at six o'clock

Date	Mintage	F	VF	XF	Unc	BU
2003 Proof	2,000	Value: 650				

KM# 1368 50 EURO
31.1000 g., 0.9990 Gold 0.9988 oz. AGW, 37 mm. **Obv:** Book, denomination and eagle **Rev:** Napoleon and coronation scene
Edge: Plain

Date	Mintage	F	VF	XF	Unc	BU
2004 Proof	2,000	Value: 1,300				

KM# 1394 50 EURO
31.1040 g., 0.9990 Gold 0.9990 oz. AGW, 37 mm.
Subject: European Union Expansion **Obv:** Partial face and flags
Rev: Puzzle map **Edge:** Plain

Date	Mintage	F	VF	XF	Unc	BU
2004 Proof	2,000	Value: 1,300				

KM# 1430 50 EURO
31.1040 g., 0.9990 Gold 0.9990 oz. AGW, 37 mm. **Rev:** Kitty and Daniel in Versailles **Rev. Legend:** Hello Kitty

Date	Mintage	F	VF	XF	Unc	BU
2005 Proof	1,000	Value: 1,350				

KM# 1466 50 EURO
31.1050 g., 0.9990 Gold 0.9990 oz. AGW, 37 mm. **Subject:** Le Petit, Prince 60th Anniversary **Obv:** Prince standing

Date	Mintage	F	VF	XF	Unc	BU
2007 Proof	2,000	Value: 1,250				

KM# 1481 50 EURO
31.1000 g., 0.9990 Gold 0.9988 oz. AGW, 37 mm.
Subject: Airbus A380 **Obv:** Airplane **Rev:** Europa and flags

Date	Mintage	F	VF	XF	Unc	BU
2007 Proof	500	Value: 1,400				

KM# 1487 50 EURO
1000.0000 g., 0.9500 Silver 30.541 oz. ASW **Subject:** 2007 Rugby World Cup **Obv:** Two players and goal **Rev:** Logo and goal **Shape:** Oval

Date	Mintage	F	VF	XF	Unc	BU
2007 Proof	299	Value: 1,200				

KM# 1510 50 EURO
31.1050 g., 0.9990 Gold 0.9990 oz. AGW, 37 mm.
Subject: Georges Remi Centennial **Obv:** Wand and sparkles
Rev: Tin Tin and dog Snowy

Date	Mintage	F	VF	XF	Unc	BU
2007 Proof	500	Value: 1,250				

KM# 1522 50 EURO
3.1050 g., 0.9990 Gold 0.0997 oz. AGW, 37 mm.
Subject: Asterix **Rev:** Asterix and the Butcher of Arverne

Date	Mintage	F	VF	XF	Unc	BU
2007 Proof	500	Value: 1,250				

KM# 1530 50 EURO
31.1040 g., 0.9990 Gold 0.9990 oz. AGW, 37 mm.
Subject: French Presidency of the Euopean Union **Obv:** Text within stars **Rev:** Europa head within flags

Date	Mintage	F	VF	XF	Unc	BU
2008 Proof	500	Value: 1,250				

KM# 1564 50 EURO
31.1040 g., 0.9990 Gold 0.9990 oz. AGW, 37 mm.
Subject: Lourdes, 150th Anniversary **Obv:** Church of Notre Dame at Lourdes **Rev:** Cross with Pope John Paul II, Pope Benedict XVI and Bernadette Soubirous in quadrants

Date	Mintage	F	VF	XF	Unc	BU
2008 Proof	500	Value: 1,250				

KM# 1603 50 EURO
163.8000 g., 0.9200 Silver 4.8448 oz. ASW, 50 mm. **Obv:** Eiffel Tower Structure **Rev:** Gustave Eiffel at left

Date	Mintage	F	VF	XF	Unc	BU
2009P Proof	1,000	Value: 250				

KM# 1597 50 EURO
163.8000 g., 0.9500 Silver 5.0028 oz. ASW, 50 mm.
Subject: Concorde 40th Anniversary **Obv:** Concorde in flight
Rev: Tail emblems

Date	Mintage	F	VF	XF	Unc	BU
2009P Proof	1,000	Value: 250				

KM# 1585 50 EURO
163.8000 g., 0.9500 Silver 5.0028 oz. ASW, 50 mm.
Subject: Court of Human Rights, 50th Anniversary **Obv:** Sower left **Rev:** Text

Date	Mintage	F	VF	XF	Unc	BU
2009P Proof	500	Value: 200				

KM# 1592 50 EURO
8.4500 g., 0.9200 Gold 0.2499 oz. AGW, 22 mm.
Subject: Europa - Fall of Berlin Wall **Obv:** Brandenburg gate and doves in flight **Rev:** Head facing and flags

Date	Mintage	F	VF	XF	Unc	BU
2009P	1,000	Value: 355				

KM# 1598 50 EURO
8.4500 g., 0.9200 Gold 0.2499 oz. AGW, 22 mm.
Subject: Concorde 40th Anniversary **Obv:** Concorde in flight
Rev: Tail emblems

Date	Mintage	F	VF	XF	Unc	BU
2009P Proof	3,000	Value: 325				

KM# 1604 50 EURO
8.4500 g., 0.9200 Gold 0.2499 oz. AGW, 22 mm. **Obv:** Eiffel Tower Structure **Rev:** Gustave Eiffel at left

Date	Mintage	F	VF	XF	Unc	BU
2009P Proof	1,000	Value: 350				

KM# 1608 50 EURO
163.8000 g., 0.9500 Silver 5.0028 oz. ASW, 50 mm.
Subject: Bugatti 100th Anniversary **Obv:** Ettore Bugatti at left
Rev: Race car and grill motif

Date	Mintage	F	VF	XF	Unc	BU
2009P Proof	500	Value: 250				

KM# 1609 50 EURO
8.4500 g., 0.9200 Gold 0.2499 oz. AGW, 22 mm.
Subject: Bugatti 100th Anniversary **Obv:** Ettore Bugatti at left
Rev: Race car and grill motif

Date	Mintage	F	VF	XF	Unc	BU
2009P Proof	1,000	Value: 350				

KM# 1613 50 EURO
163.8000 g., 0.9500 Silver 5.0028 oz. ASW, 30 mm.
Subject: Curie Institute, 100th Anniversary

Date	Mintage	F	VF	XF	Unc	BU
2009P Proof	500	Value: 250				

KM# 1614 50 EURO
8.4500 g., 0.9200 Gold 0.2499 oz. AGW, 22 mm. **Subject:** Curie Institute, 100th Anniversary

Date	Mintage	F	VF	XF	Unc	BU
2009P Proof	1,000	Value: 350				

KM# 1618 50 EURO
8.4500 g., 0.9200 Gold 0.2499 oz. AGW, 22 mm.
Subject: Unesco site - the Kremlin in Moscow **Obv:** Wall Tower and cathedral

Date	Mintage	F	VF	XF	Unc	BU
2009P Proof	1,000	Value: 350				

KM# 1622 50 EURO
163.8000 g., 0.9500 Silver 5.0028 oz. ASW, 50 mm. **Subject:** International Year of Astronomy **Obv:** Footprint on the moon

Date	Mintage	F	VF	XF	Unc	BU
2009P Proof	500	Value: 250				

KM# 1623 50 EURO
8.4500 g., 0.9200 Gold 0.2499 oz. AGW, 22 mm. **Subject:** International Year of Astronomy **Obv:** Footprint on the moon

Date	Mintage	F	VF	XF	Unc	BU
2009P Proof	1,000	Value: 350				

KM# 1628 50 EURO
8.4500 g., 0.9200 Gold 0.2499 oz. AGW, 22 mm. **Subject:** Year of the Ox **Obv:** Oxen within Asian screen **Rev:** Portrait of LaFontaine

Date	Mintage	F	VF	XF	Unc	BU
2009P Proof	500	Value: 375				

KM# 1630 50 EURO
8.4500 g., 0.9200 Gold 0.2499 oz. AGW, 22 mm. **Subject:** Comic strip heroes **Obv:** Wanted Poster **Rev:** Lucky Luke on horseback

Date	Mintage	F	VF	XF	Unc	BU
2009P Proof	1,000	Value: 350				

KM# 1632 50 EURO
8.4500 g., 0.9200 Gold 0.2499 oz. AGW, 22 mm. **Obv:** Rugby player **Rev:** State Francais

Date	Mintage	F	VF	XF	Unc	BU
2009P Proof	500	Value: 375				

KM# 1635 50 EURO
8.4500 g., 0.9200 Gold 0.2499 oz. AGW, 22 mm. **Subject:** Alpine skiing **Obv:** Globe/downhill skier **Rev:** Skier on mountainside

Date	Mintage	F	VF	XF	Unc	BU
2009P Proof	1,000	Value: 350				

KM# 1637 50 EURO
163.8000 g., 0.9500 Silver 5.0028 oz. ASW, 50 mm. **Subject:** FIFA World Cup, South Africa 2010 **Obv:** Soccer player on field **Rev:** Soccerball, Map of Africa, Protrea flower

Date	Mintage	F	VF	XF	Unc	BU
2009P Proof	500	Value: 250				

KM# 1638 50 EURO
8.4500 g., 0.9200 Gold 0.2499 oz. AGW, 22 mm. **Subject:** FIFA World Cup, South Africa 2010 **Obv:** Soccer Player on field **Rev:** Soccerball, Map of Africa, Protea flower

Date	Mintage	F	VF	XF	Unc	BU
2009P Proof	7,500	Value: 325				

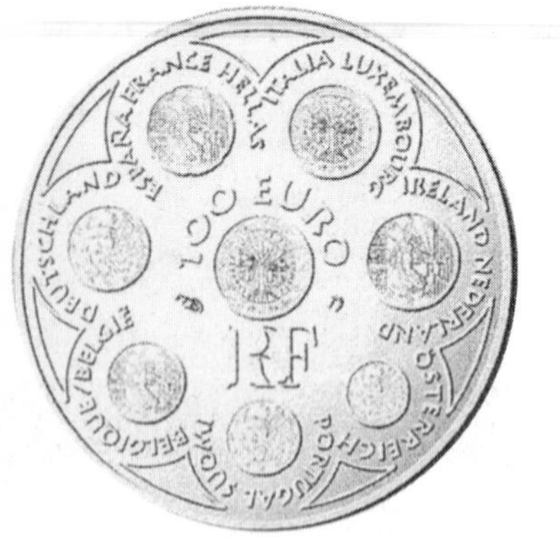

KM# 1304 100 EURO
155.5175 g., 0.9990 Gold 4.9948 oz. AGW, 50 mm. **Subject:** Europa **Obv:** Eight French euro coin designs **Rev:** Portrait and flags design of 6.55957 francs KM-1265 **Edge:** Plain

Date	Mintage	F	VF	XF	Unc	BU
2002 Proof	99	Value: 6,500				

KM# 1377 100 EURO
155.5175 g., 0.9990 Gold 4.9948 oz. AGW, 50 mm. **Subject:** D-Day 60th Anniversary **Obv:** Soldiers and Normandy invasion scene **Rev:** "D-Day" inscription above denomination **Edge:** Plain

Date	Mintage	F	VF	XF	Unc	BU
2004 Proof	299	Value: 6,250				

KM# 1389 100 EURO
155.5000 g., 0.9990 Gold 4.9942 oz. AGW, 50 mm. **Obv:** Statue of Liberty **Rev:** F. A. Bartholdi **Edge:** Plain

Date	Mintage	F	VF	XF	Unc	BU
2004 Proof	99	Value: 6,350				

KM# 1395 100 EURO
155.5500 g., 0.9990 Gold 4.9958 oz. AGW, 50 mm. **Subject:** European Union Expansion **Obv:** Partial face and flags **Rev:** Puzzle map **Edge:** Plain

Date	Mintage	F	VF	XF	Unc	BU
2004 Proof	99	Value: 6,350				

KM# 1482 100 EURO
155.5500 g., 0.9990 Gold 4.9958 oz. AGW, 50 mm. **Subject:** Airbus A380 **Rev:** Europa head and flags

Date	Mintage	F	VF	XF	Unc	BU
2007 Proof	99	Value: 6,350				

KM# 1497 100 EURO
155.5000 g., 0.9990 Gold 4.9942 oz. AGW, 50 mm. **Subject:** Cannes Film Festival, 60th Anniversary **Obv:** Cinema screen and stage, Golden Palm Award

Date	Mintage	F	VF	XF	Unc	BU
2007 Proof	99	Value: 6,250				

KM# 1531 100 EURO
155.5000 g., 0.9990 Gold 4.9942 oz. AGW, 50 mm. **Subject:** French Presidency of the European Union **Obv:** Text within stars **Rev:** Europa head and flags

Date	Mintage	F	VF	XF	Unc	BU
2008 Proof	99	Value: 6,250				

KM# 1536 100 EURO
3.1000 g., 0.9990 Gold 0.0996 oz. AGW, 15 mm. **Obv:** Sower, full length **Rev:** Hexagon

Date	Mintage	F	VF	XF	Unc	BU
2008 Proof	—	Value: 150				

KM# 1545 100 EURO
155.5000 g., 0.9990 Gold 4.9942 oz. AGW, 50 mm. **Subject:** 29th Summer Olympic Games - Beijing **Obv:** Swimmer and globe **Rev:** Diver and oriental screen

Date	Mintage	F	VF	XF	Unc	BU
2008 Proof	99	Value: 6,250				

KM# 1565 100 EURO
155.5000 g., 0.9990 Gold 4.9942 oz. AGW, 50 mm. **Subject:** Lourdes, 150th Anniversary **Obv:** Church of Notre Dame at Lourdes **Rev:** Cross with Pope John Paul II, Pope Benedict XVI and Bernadette Soubirous in quadrants

Date	Mintage	F	VF	XF	Unc	BU
2008 Proof	99	Value: 6,250				

KM# 1582 100 EURO
3.1000 g., 0.9990 Gold 0.0996 oz. AGW, 15 mm.
Obv: Modernistic sower advancing right **Rev:** Value and wreath

Date	Mintage	F	VF	XF	Unc	BU
2009P	50,000	—	—	—	—	150

KM# 1588 100 EURO
17.0000 g., 0.9200 Gold 0.5028 oz. AGW, 31 mm. **Subject:** Court of Human Rights, 50th Anniversary **Obv:** Sower left **Rev:** Text

Date	Mintage	F	VF	XF	Unc	BU
2009P Proof	500	Value: 650				

KM# 1626 100 EURO
17.0000 g., 0.9200 Gold 0.5028 oz. AGW, 30 x 21 mm.
Subject: Renoir **Obv:** Le dejuner des canotiers, 1881 painting **Rev:** Brushes and portrait **Shape:** Rectangle

Date	Mintage	F	VF	XF	Unc	BU
2009P Proof	500	Value: 650				

KM# 1589 200 EURO
31.1040 g., 0.9990 Gold 0.9990 oz. AGW, 37 mm. **Subject:** Court of Human Rights - 50th Ann.y **Obv:** Sower left **Rev:** Text

Date	Mintage	F	VF	XF	Unc	BU
2009P Proof	500	Value: 1,275				

KM# 1593 200 EURO
31.1040 g., 0.9990 Gold 0.9990 oz. AGW, 37 mm.
Subject: Europa - Fall of Berlin Wall **Obv:** Brandenburg gate and doves in flight **Rev:** Head facing and flags

Date	Mintage	F	VF	XF	Unc	BU
2009P Proof	500	Value: 1,275				

KM# 1624 200 EURO
31.1040 g., 0.9990 Gold 0.9990 oz. AGW, 37 mm.
Subject: International Year of Astronomy **Obv:** Footprint on the moon

Date	Mintage	F	VF	XF	Unc	BU
2009P Proof	1,000	Value: 1,275				

KM# 1639 200 EURO
31.1040 g., 0.9990 Gold 0.9990 oz. AGW, 37 mm.
Subject: FIFA World Cup, South Africa 2010 **Obv:** Soccer player on field **Rev:** Soccerball, Map of Africa, Protea flower **Shape:** 37

Date	Mintage	F	VF	XF	Unc	BU
2009P Proof	500	Value: 1,275				

KM# 1583 250 EURO
8.4500 g., 0.9200 Gold 0.2499 oz. AGW, 22 mm.
Obv: Modernistic sower advancing right **Rev:** Value and wreath

Date	Mintage	F	VF	XF	Unc	BU
2009P	25,000	—	—	—	—	350

KM# 1396 500 EURO
1000.0000 g., 0.9990 Gold 32.117 oz. AGW, 85 mm.
Subject: European Union Expansion **Obv:** Partial face and flags **Rev:** Puzzle map **Edge:** Plain **Note:** Illustration reduced.

Date	Mintage	F	VF	XF	Unc	BU
2004 Proof, Rare	20	—	—	—	—	—

KM# 1594 500 EURO
155.5000 g., 0.9990 Gold 4.9942 oz. AGW, 50 mm.
Subject: Europa - Fall of Berlin Wall **Obv:** Brandenburg gate and doves in flight **Rev:** Head facing and flags

Date	Mintage	F	VF	XF	Unc	BU
2009P Proof	99	Value: 6,250				

KM# 1605 500 EURO
155.5000 g., 0.9990 Gold 4.9942 oz. AGW, 50 mm. **Obv:** Eiffel Tower Structure **Rev:** Gustave Eiffel at left

Date	Mintage	F	VF	XF	Unc	BU
2009P Proof	99	Value: 6,250				

KM# 1610 500 EURO
155.5000 g., 0.9990 Gold 4.9942 oz. AGW, 50 mm.
Subject: Bugatti 100th Anniversary **Obv:** Ettore Bugatti at left **Rev:** Race car and grill motif

Date	Mintage	F	VF	XF	Unc	BU
2009P Proof	99	Value: 6,250				

KM# 1615 500 EURO
155.5000 g., 0.9990 Gold 4.9942 oz. AGW, 50 mm.
Subject: Curie Institute, 100th Anniversary

Date	Mintage	F	VF	XF	Unc	BU
2009P Proof	99	Value: 6,250				

KM# 1619 500 EURO
155.5000 g., 0.9990 Gold 4.9942 oz. AGW, 50 mm.
Subject: Unesco site - The Kremlin in Moscow **Obv:** Wall Tower and cathedral

Date	Mintage	F	VF	XF	Unc	BU
2009P Proof	99	Value: 6,250				

KM# 1640 500 EURO
155.5000 g., 0.9990 Gold 4.9942 oz. AGW, 50 mm.
Subject: FIFA World Cup, South Africa 2010 **Obv:** Soccer player on field **Rev:** Soccerball, Map of Africa, Protea flower

Date	Mintage	F	VF	XF	Unc	BU
2009P Proof	99	Value: 6,250				

KM# 1595 1000 EURO
311.0000 g., 0.9990 Gold 9.9885 oz. AGW, 65 mm.
Subject: Europa - Fall of Berlin Wall **Obv:** Brandenburg gate and doves in flight **Rev:** Head facing and flags

Date	Mintage	F	VF	XF	Unc	BU
2009P Proof	20	Value: 13,500				

KM# 1600 1000 EURO
311.0000 g., 0.9990 Gold 9.9885 oz. AGW, 65 mm.
Subject: Concorde 40 Anniversary **Obv:** Concorde in flight **Rev:** Tail emblems

Date	Mintage	F	VF	XF	Unc	BU
2009P Proof	20	Value: 13,500				

KM# 1620 5000 EURO
1000.0000 g., 0.9990 Gold 32.117 oz. AGW, 85 mm.
Subject: Unesco site - The Kremlin in Moscow **Obv:** Wall Tower and cathedral

Date	Mintage	F	VF	XF	Unc	BU
2009P Proof	39	Value: 42,000				

MINT SETS

KM#	Date	Mintage	Identification	Issue Price	Mkt Val
MS20	2001 (2)	10,000	KM#925.1a, 928a	—	425
MS21	2001 (8)	35,000	KM#1282-1289	20.25	20.00
MS22	2002 (8)	35,000	KM#1282-1289	20.25	40.00
MS23	2003 (8)	—	KM#1282-89	—	55.00
MS24	2004 (8)	—	KM#1282-1289	—	45.00
MS25	2005 (8)	—	KM#1282-1289	—	45.00
MS26	2005 (8)	40,000	KM#1282-1289 Moebius set plus token	45.00	45.00
MS27	2005 (8)	10,000	KM1282-1289, French Memories - Bordeaux	45.00	45.00
MS28	2006 (8)	70,000	KM#1282-1289	36.50	42.50
MS29	2006 (8)	500	KM#1282-1289, Denver, Colorado special ANA Coin Convention Set	45.00	70.00
MS30	2006 (8)	500	KM#1282-1289, Berlin Coin Fair set	45.00	55.00

KM#	Date	Mintage	Identification	Issue Price	Mkt Val
MS31	2006 (8)	500	KM1282-1289, Pierre Curie set	45.00	50.00
MS32	2006 (8)	500	KM#1282-1289, Musee de la Monnaie set	45.00	50.00
MS33	2006 (8)	500	KM#1282-1289, Journees du Patrimoine set	45.00	50.00
MS34	2006 (8)	500	KM#1282-1289, Bourgogne set	45.00	50.00
MS35	2006 (8)	500	KM#1282-1289, "Coree set" (Korea)	45.00	50.00
MS36	2006 (8)	500	KM#1282-1289, Nord Pas-de-Calais set	45.00	50.00
MS37	2006 (8)	500	KM#1282-1289, Jacques Chirac set	45.00	50.00
MS38	2006 (8)	500	KM#1282-1289, Mitterand & Khol	45.00	50.00
MS39	2006 (8)	500	KM#1282-1289, Birthday 1 set	45.00	45.00
MS40	2006 (8)	500	KM#1282-1289, Birthday 2 set	45.00	45.00
MS41	2006 (8)	500	KM#1282-1289, Tokyo set	45.00	50.00
MS42	2006 (8)	500	KM#1282-1289, Viaduc de Millau set	45.00	50.00
MS43	2006 (8)	500	KM#1282-1289, Ile-de-France set	45.00	50.00

PROOF SETS

KM#	Date	Mintage	Identification	Issue Price	Mkt Val
PS21	2001 (8)	15,000	KM#1282-1289	59.00	125
PS22	2002 (8)	40,000	KM#1282-1289	59.00	110
PS23	2003 (5)	150,000	KM#1321, 1322, 1323, 1324, 1325	—	260
PS24	2003 (5)	5,000	KM#1326, 1327, 1328, 1329, 1330	—	1,800

FRENCH POLYNESIA

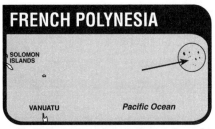

The Territory of French Polynesia (formerly French Oceania) has an area of 1,544 sq. mi. (3,941 sq. km.) and a population of 220,000. It is comprised of the same five archipelagoes that were grouped administratively to form French Oceania.

The colony of French Oceania became the Territory of French Polynesia by act of the French National Assembly in March, 1957. In Sept. of 1958 it voted in favor of the new constitution of the Fifth Republic, thereby electing to remain within the new French Community.

Picturesque, mountainous Tahiti, the setting of many tales of adventure and romance, is one of the most inspiringly beautiful islands in the world. Robert Louis Stevenson called it 'God's sweetest works'. It was there that Paul Gaugin, one of the pioneers of the Impressionist movement, painted the brilliant, exotic pictures that later made him famous. The arid coral atolls of Tuamotu comprise the most economically valuable area of French Polynesia. Pearl oysters thrive in the warm, limpid lagoons, and extensive portions of the atolls are valuable phosphate rock.

RULER
French

MINT MARK
(a) - Paris, privy marks only

MONETARY SYSTEM
100 Centimes = 1 Franc

FRENCH OVERSEAS TERRITORY

DECIMAL COINAGE

KM# 11   FRANC
1.3000 g., Aluminum, 23 mm. **Obv:** Seated Liberty with torch and cornucopia right, date below, legend added flanking figure's feet **Obv. Legend:** I. E. O. M. **Obv. Designer:** G.B.L. Bazor **Rev:** Legend and island scene divide denomination

Date	Mintage	F	VF	XF	Unc	BU
2001(a)	2,900,000	—	—	—	0.50	1.00
2002(a)	1,600,000	—	—	—	0.50	1.00
2003(a)	4,200,000	—	—	—	0.50	1.00
2004(a)	2,400,000	—	—	—	0.50	1.00
2005(a)	—	—	—	—	0.50	1.00
2006(a)	2,100,000	—	—	—	0.50	1.00
2007(a) Coin rotation	3,400,000	—	—	—	0.50	1.00
2007(a) Medal rotation	Inc. above	—	—	—	—	30.00
2008(a)	4,800,000	—	—	—	0.50	1.00

KM# 10   2 FRANCS
2.3000 g., Aluminum, 27 mm. **Obv:** Seated Liberty with torch and cornucopia right, date below, legend added flanking figure's feet **Obv. Legend:** I. E. O. M. **Obv. Designer:** G.B.L. Bazor **Rev:** Legend and island scene divide denomination

Date	Mintage	F	VF	XF	Unc	BU
2001(a)	2,400,000	—	—	—	0.75	1.50
2002(a)	2,500,000	—	—	—	0.75	1.50
2003(a)	3,200,000	—	—	—	0.75	1.50
2004(a)	3,000,000	—	—	—	0.75	1.50
2005(a)	900,000	—	—	—	0.75	1.50
2006(a)	1,600,000	—	—	—	0.75	1.50
2007(a)	640,000	—	—	—	0.75	1.50
2008(a)	1,900,000	—	—	—	0.75	1.50

KM# 12   5 FRANCS
3.7500 g., Aluminum, 31 mm. **Obv:** Seated Liberty with torch and cornucopia right, date below, legend added flanking figure's feet **Obv. Legend:** I. E. O. M. **Obv. Designer:** G.B.L. Bazor **Rev:** Legend and island divide denomination

Date	Mintage	F	VF	XF	Unc	BU
2001(a)	1,600,000	—	—	—	1.00	2.00
2002(a)	400,000	—	—	—	1.00	2.00
2003(a)	1,000,000	—	—	—	1.00	2.00
2004(a)	600,000	—	—	—	1.00	2.00
2005(a)	600,000	—	—	—	1.00	2.00
2006(a)	720,000	—	—	—	1.00	2.00
2007(a)	1,000,000	—	—	—	1.00	2.00
2008(a)	1,060,000	—	—	—	1.00	2.00

KM# 8   10 FRANCS
6.0000 g., Nickel, 24 mm. **Obv:** Capped head left, date and legend below **Obv. Legend:** I. E. O. M. **Obv. Designer:** R. Joly **Rev:** Native art, denomination below **Rev. Designer:** A. Guzman

Date	Mintage	F	VF	XF	Unc	BU
2001(a)	500,000	—	—	—	1.25	2.75
2002(a)	600,000	—	—	—	1.25	2.75
2003(a)	1,000,000	—	—	—	1.25	2.75
2004(a)	600,000	—	—	—	1.25	2.75
2005(a)	200,000	—	—	—	1.25	2.75
2006(a)	620,000	—	—	—	1.25	2.75
2007(a)	800,000	—	—	—	1.25	2.75
2008(a)	820,000	—	—	—	1.25	2.75

KM# 9   20 FRANCS
10.0000 g., Nickel, 28.3 mm. **Obv:** Capped head left, date and legend below **Obv. Legend:** I. E. O. M. **Obv. Designer:** R. Joly **Rev:** Flowers, vanilla shoots, bread fruit **Rev. Designer:** A. Guzman

KM# 13   50 FRANCS
15.0000 g., Nickel, 33 mm. **Obv:** Capped head left, date and legend below **Obv. Legend:** I. E. O. M. **Obv. Designer:** R. Joly **Rev:** Denomination above Moorea Harbor **Rev. Designer:** A. Guzman

Date	Mintage	F	VF	XF	Unc	BU
2001(a)	300,000	—	—	—	2.00	4.00
2002(a)	—	—	—	—	2.00	4.00
2003(a)	240,000	—	—	—	2.00	4.00
2004(a)	100,000	—	—	—	2.00	4.00
2005(a)	100,000	—	—	—	2.00	4.00
2006(a)	15,000	—	—	—	2.00	4.00
2007(a)	310,000	—	—	—	2.00	4.00
2008(a)	200,000	—	—	—	2.00	4.00
2009(a)	—	—	—	—	2.00	4.00

KM# 14   100 FRANCS
10.0000 g., Nickel-Bronze, 30 mm. **Obv:** Capped head left, date below **Obv. Legend:** I. E. O. M. **Obv. Designer:** R. Joly **Rev:** Denomination above Moorea Harbor **Rev. Designer:** A. Guzman

Date	Mintage	F	VF	XF	Unc	BU
2001(a)	200,000	—	—	—	3.00	5.00
2002(a)	—	—	—	—	3.00	5.00
2003(a)	600,000	—	—	—	2.75	5.00
2004(a)	450,000	—	—	—	2.75	5.00
2005(a)	300,000	—	—	—	2.75	5.00
2006(a)	200,000	—	—	—	2.75	5.00
2007(a)	650,000	—	—	—	2.75	5.00
2008(a)	690,000	—	—	—	2.75	5.00
2009(a)	—	—	—	—	2.75	5.00

(20 FRANCS, KM# 9 table)

Date	Mintage	F	VF	XF	Unc	BU
2001(a)	500,000	—	—	—	1.75	3.25
2002(a)	—	—	—	—	1.75	3.25
2003(a)	700,000	—	—	—	1.75	3.00
2004(a)	600,000	—	—	—	1.75	3.00
2005(a)	30,000	—	—	—	20.00	30.00
2006(a)	300,000	—	—	—	1.75	3.00
2007(a)	450,000	—	—	—	1.75	3.00
2008(a)	610,000	—	—	—	1.75	3.00

MINT SETS

KM#	Date	Mintage	Identification	Issue Price	Mkt Val
MS1	2001 (7)	3,000	KM#8-14	—	22.50
MS2	2002 (7)	5,000	KM#8-14	—	22.50
MS3	2003 (7)	3,000	KM#8-14	—	22.50

GEORGIA

Georgia (formerly the Georgian Social Democratic Republic under the U.S.S.R.), is bounded by the Black Sea to the west and by Turkey, Armenia and Azerbaijan. It occupies the western part of Transcaucasia covering an area of 26,900 sq. mi. (69,700 sq.

km.) and a population of 5.7 million. Capitol: Tbilisi. Hydro-electricity, minerals, forestry and agriculture are the chief industries.

Germano-- Georgian treaty was signed on May 28, 1918, followed by a Turko-Georgian peace treaty on June 4. The end of WW I and the collapse of the central powers allowed free The collapse of the U.S.S.R. allowed full transition to independence and on April 9, 1991 a unanimous vote declared the republic an independent state based on its original treaty of independence of May 1918.

REPUBLIC

STANDARD COINAGE
100 Thetri = 1 Lari

KM# 89 50 THETRI
6.5200 g., Copper-Nickel, 24 mm. **Obv:** National arms
Rev: Value **Edge:** Reeded and lettered

Date	Mintage	F	VF	XF	Unc	BU
2006	—				3.00	4.00

KM# 90 LARI
7.8500 g., Copper-Nickel, 26.2 mm. **Obv:** National arms
Rev: Value **Edge:** Reeded and lettered

Date	Mintage	F	VF	XF	Unc	BU
2006	—				5.00	6.50

KM# 92 2 LARI
12.9200 g., Copper-Nickel, 31 mm. **Obv:** Trophy cup, value and date **Rev:** UFFA Winners Cup and soccer player **Edge:** Plain

Date	Mintage	F	VF	XF	Unc	BU
2006 Proof	—	Value: 18.00				

KM# 94 2 LARI
8.0600 g., Bi-Metallic Brass center in Copper-Nickel ring, 26.99 mm. **Obv:** National arms **Rev:** Large value **Edge:** Reeded and lettered

Date	Mintage	F	VF	XF	Unc	BU
2006	—				7.50	9.00

KM# 93 3 LARI
13.1200 g., Copper-Nickel, 31 mm. **Obv:** Three oil wells
Rev: Map with "Baku-Tbilisi-Ceyhan" route **Edge:** Lettered

Date	Mintage	F	VF	XF	Unc	BU
2006 Proof	—	Value: 25.00				

GERMANY-FEDERAL REPUBLIC

The Federal Republic of Germany, located in north-central Europe, has an area of 137,744 sq. mi. (356,910sq. km.) and a population of 81.1 million. Capital: Berlin. The economy centers about one of the world's foremost industrial establishments. Machinery, motor vehicles, iron, steel, yarns and fabrics are exported.

MINT MARKS
A - Berlin
D - Munich
F - Stuttgart
G - Karlsruhe
J - Hamburg

MONETARY SYSTEM
100 Pfennig = 1 Deutsche Mark (DM)

FEDERAL REPUBLIC

STANDARD COINAGE

KM# 105 PFENNIG
2.0000 g., Copper Plated Steel, 16.5 mm. **Obv:** Five oak leaves, date below **Obv. Legend:** BUNDES REPUBLIK DEUTSCHLAND **Rev:** Denomination

Date	Mintage	F	VF	XF	Unc	BU
2001A In sets only	130,000	—			5.00	—
2001A Proof	78,000	Value: 5.00				
2001D In sets only	130,000	—			5.00	—
2001D Proof	78,000	Value: 5.00				
2001F In sets only	130,000	—			5.00	—
2001F Proof	78,000	Value: 5.00				
2001G In sets only	130,000	—			5.00	—
2001G Proof	78,000	Value: 5.00				
2001J In sets only	130,000	—			5.00	—
2001J Proof	78,000	Value: 5.00				

KM# 106a 2 PFENNIG
2.9000 g., Bronze Clad Steel, 19.25 mm. **Obv:** Five oak leaves, date below **Rev:** Denomination

KM# 107 5 PFENNIG
3.0000 g., Brass Plated Steel, 18.5 mm. **Obv:** Five oak leaves, date below **Obv. Legend:** BUNDES REPUBLIK DEUTSCHLAND **Rev:** Denomination

Date	Mintage	F	VF	XF	Unc	BU
2001A In sets only	130,000	—			5.00	—
2001A Proof	78,000	Value: 5.00				
2001D In sets only	130,000	—			5.00	—
2001D Proof	78,000	Value: 5.00				
2001F In sets only	130,000	—			5.00	—
2001F Proof	78,000	Value: 5.00				
2001G In sets only	130,000	—			5.00	—
2001G Proof	78,000	Value: 5.00				
2001J In sets only	130,000	—			5.00	—
2001J Proof	78,000	Value: 5.00				

KM# 108 10 PFENNIG
4.0000 g., Brass Plated Steel, 21.5 mm. **Obv:** Five oak leaves, date below **Obv. Legend:** BUNDES REPUBLIK DEUTSCHLAND **Rev:** Denomination **Edge:** Plain

Date	Mintage	F	VF	XF	Unc	BU
2001A In sets only	130,000	—			5.00	—
2001A Proof	78,000	Value: 5.00				
2001D In sets only	130,000	—			5.00	—
2001D Proof	78,000	Value: 5.00				
2001F In sets only	130,000	—			5.00	—

Date	Mintage	F	VF	XF	Unc	BU
2001F Proof	78,000	Value: 5.00				
2001G In sets only	130,000	—	—	—	5.00	—
2001G Proof	78,000	Value: 5.00				
2001J In sets only	130,000	—	—	—	5.00	—
2001J Proof	78,000	Value: 5.00				

KM# 109.2 50 PFENNIG
3.5000 g., Copper-Nickel, 20 mm. **Obv:** Denomination
Rev: Woman planting an oak seedling **Edge:** Plain

Date	Mintage	F	VF	XF	Unc	BU
2001A In sets only	130,000	—	—	—	10.00	—
2001A Proof	78,000	Value: 10.00				
2001D In sets only	130,000	—	—	—	10.00	—
2001D Proof	78,000	Value: 10.00				
2001F In sets only	130,000	—	—	—	10.00	—
2001F Proof	78,000	Value: 10.00				
2001G In sets only	130,000	—	—	—	10.00	—
2001G Proof	78,000	Value: 10.00				
2001J In sets only	130,000	—	—	—	10.00	—
2001J Proof	78,000	Value: 10.00				

KM# 110 MARK
5.5000 g., Copper-Nickel, 23.5 mm. **Obv:** Eagle
Rev: Denomination flanked by oak leaves, date below

Date	Mintage	F	VF	XF	Unc	BU
2001A In sets only	130,000	—	—	—	15.00	—
2001A Proof	78,000	Value: 15.00				
2001D In sets only	130,000	—	—	—	15.00	—
2001D Proof	78,000	Value: 15.00				
2001F In sets only	130,000	—	—	—	15.00	—
2001F Proof	78,000	Value: 15.00				
2001G In sets only	130,000	—	—	—	15.00	—
2001G Proof	78,000	Value: 15.00				
2001J In sets only	130,000	—	—	—	15.00	—
2001J Proof	78,000	Value: 15.00				

KM# 203 MARK
11.8500 g., 0.9990 Gold 0.3806 oz. AGW, 23.5 mm. **Subject:**
Retirement of the Mark Currency **Obv:** Eagle **Rev:** Denomination
flanked by oak leaves, date below **Edge:** Arabeskes

Date	Mintage	F	VF	XF	Unc	BU
2001A Proof	200,000	Value: 500				
2001D Proof	200,000	Value: 500				
2001G Proof	200,000	Value: 500				
2001J Proof	200,000	Value: 500				
2001F Proof	200,000	Value: 500				

KM# 170 2 MARK
7.0000 g., Copper-Nickel Clad Nickel, 26.75 mm.
Subject: Ludwig Erhard **Obv:** Eagle above denomination
Rev: Head facing divides dates **Edge Lettering:** EINIGKEIT
UND RECHT UND FREIHEIT

Date	Mintage	F	VF	XF	Unc	BU
2001A In sets only	130,000	—	—	—	10.00	—
2001A Proof	78,000	Value: 10.00				
2001D In sets only	130,000	—	—	—	10.00	—
2001D Proof	78,000	Value: 10.00				
2001F In sets only	130,000	—	—	—	10.00	—
2001F Proof	78,000	Value: 10.00				
2001G In sets only	130,000	—	—	—	10.00	—
2001G Proof	78,000	Value: 10.00				

Date	Mintage	F	VF	XF	Unc	BU
2001J In sets only	130,000	—	—	—	10.00	—
2001J Proof	78,000	Value: 10.00				

KM# 175 2 MARK
7.0400 g., Copper-Nickel Clad Nickel, 26.8 mm. **Subject:** Franz
Joseph Strauss **Obv:** Eagle above denomination **Rev:** Head left
divides dates **Edge Lettering:** EINIGKEIT UND RECHT UND
FREIHEIT

Date	Mintage	F	VF	XF	Unc	BU
2001A In sets only	130,000	—	—	—	10.00	—
2001A Proof	78,000	Value: 10.00				
2001D In sets only	130,000	—	—	—	10.00	—
2001D Proof	78,000	Value: 10.00				
2001F In sets only	130,000	—	—	—	10.00	—
2001F Proof	78,000	Value: 10.00				
2001G In sets only	130,000	—	—	—	10.00	—
2001G Proof	78,000	Value: 10.00				
2001J In sets only	130,000	—	—	—	10.00	—
2001J Proof	78,000	Value: 10.00				

KM# 183 2 MARK
7.0000 g., Copper-Nickel Clad Nickel, 26.75 mm. **Subject:** Willy
Brandt **Obv:** Eagle above denomination **Rev:** Head facing
divides dates **Edge Lettering:** EINIGKEIT UND RECHT UND
FREIHEIT

Date	Mintage	F	VF	XF	Unc	BU
2001A In sets only	130,000	—	—	—	10.00	—
2001A Proof	78,000	Value: 10.00				
2001D In sets only	130,000	—	—	—	10.00	—
2001D Proof	78,000	Value: 10.00				
2001F In sets only	130,000	—	—	—	10.00	—
2001F Proof	78,000	Value: 10.00				
2001G In sets only	130,000	—	—	—	10.00	—
2001G Proof	78,000	Value: 10.00				
2001J In sets only	130,000	—	—	—	10.00	—
2001J Proof	78,000	Value: 10.00				

KM# 140.1 5 MARK
10.0000 g., Copper-Nickel Clad Nickel, 29 mm.
Obv: Denomination within rounded square **Rev:** Eagle above
date **Edge Lettering:** EINIGKEIT UND RECHT UND FREIHEIT

Date	Mintage	F	VF	XF	Unc	BU
2001A In sets only	130,000	—	—	—	30.00	—
2001A Proof	78,000	Value: 30.00				
2001D In sets only	130,000	—	—	—	30.00	—
2001D Proof	78,000	Value: 30.00				
2001F In sets only	130,000	—	—	—	30.00	—
2001F Proof	78,000	Value: 30.00				
2001G In sets only	130,000	—	—	—	30.00	—
2001G Proof	78,000	Value: 30.00				
2001J In sets only	130,000	—	—	—	30.00	—
2001J Proof	78,000	Value: 30.00				

COMMEMORATIVE COINAGE

KM# 204 10 MARK
15.5000 g., 0.9250 Silver 0.4609 oz. ASW, 32.5 mm.
Obv: Imperial eagle above denomination **Rev:** Naval Museum,
Stralsund **Edge Lettering:** "OHNE WASSER KEIN LEBEN"

Date	Mintage	F	VF	XF	Unc	BU
2001A	2,500,000	—	—	—	10.00	12.00
2001A Proof	160,000	Value: 16.00				
2001D Proof	160,000	Value: 16.00				
2001F Proof	160,000	Value: 16.00				
2001G Proof	160,000	Value: 16.00				
2001J Proof	160,000	Value: 16.00				

KM# 205 10 MARK
15.5000 g., 0.9250 Silver 0.4609 oz. ASW, 32.5 mm.
Subject: 200th Anniversary - Birth of Albert Gustav Lortzing
Obv: Stylized eagle above denomination **Rev:** Portrait and music
Edge Lettering: "WILDSCHUETZ * UNDINE" ZAR UND
ZIMMERMANN"

Date	Mintage	F	VF	XF	Unc	BU
2001A Proof	160,000	Value: 16.00				
2001D Proof	160,000	Value: 16.00				
2001F Proof	160,000	Value: 16.00				
2001G Proof	160,000	Value: 16.00				
2001J	2,500,000	—	—	—	10.00	12.00
2001J Proof	160,000	Value: 16.00				

KM# 206 10 MARK
15.5000 g., 0.9250 Silver 0.4609 oz. ASW, 32.5 mm.
Subject: Federal Court of Constitution: 50th Anniversary
Obv: Stylized eagle above denomination **Rev:** Justice holding
books and scale **Edge:** Lettered

Date	Mintage	F	VF	XF	Unc	BU
2001A Proof	160,000	Value: 16.00				
2001D Proof	160,000	Value: 16.00				
2001F Proof	160,000	Value: 16.00				
2001G	2,500,000	—	—	—	10.00	12.00
2001G Proof	160,000	Value: 16.00				
2001J Proof	160,000	Value: 16.00				

EURO COINAGE
European Union Issues

KM# 207 EURO CENT
2.2700 g., Copper Plated Steel, 16.3 mm. **Obv:** Oak leaves
Obv. Designer: Rolf Lederbogen **Rev:** Denomination and globe
Rev. Designer: Luc Luycx **Edge:** Plain

Date	Mintage	F	VF	XF	Unc	BU
2002A	770,000,000	—	—	—	0.35	—
2002A Proof	130,000	Value: 1.00				
2002D	805,350,000	—	—	—	0.35	—
2002D Proof	130,000	Value: 1.00				
2002F	902,660,000	—	—	—	0.35	—
2002F Proof	130,000	Value: 1.00				
2002G	537,100,000	—	—	—	0.35	—

Date	Mintage	F	VF	XF	Unc	BU
2002G Proof	130,000	Value: 1.00				
2002J	833,100,000	—	—	—	0.35	—
2002J Proof	130,000	Value: 1.00				
2003A In sets only	180,000	—	—	—	4.50	—
2003A Proof	150,000	Value: 1.00				
2003D In sets only	180,000	—	—	—	4.50	—
2003D Proof	150,000	Value: 1.00				
2003F In sets only	180,000	—	—	—	4.50	—
2003F Proof	150,000	Value: 1.00				
2003G In sets only	180,000	—	—	—	4.50	—
2003G Proof	150,000	Value: 1.00				
2003J In sets only	180,000	—	—	—	4.50	—
2003J Proof	150,000	Value: 1.00				
2004A	280,000,000	—	—	—	0.35	—
2004A Proof	—	Value: 1.00				
2004D	294,000,000	—	—	—	0.35	—
2004D Proof	—	Value: 1.00				
2004F	336,000,000	—	—	—	0.35	—
2004F Proof	—	Value: 1.00				
2004G	196,000,000	—	—	—	0.35	—
2004G Proof	—	Value: 1.00				
2004J	294,000,000	—	—	—	0.35	—
2004J Proof	—	Value: 1.00				
2005A	120,000,000	—	—	—	0.35	—
2005A Proof	—	Value: 1.00				
2005D	126,000,000	—	—	—	0.35	—
2005D Proof	—	Value: 1.00				
2005F	144,000,000	—	—	—	0.35	—
2005F Proof	—	Value: 1.00				
2005G	84,000,000	—	—	—	0.35	—
2005G Proof	—	Value: 1.00				
2005J	126,000,000	—	—	—	0.35	—
2005J Proof	—	Value: 1.00				
2006A In sets only	—	—	—	—	4.50	—
2006A Proof	—	Value: 1.00				
2006D In sets only	—	—	—	—	4.50	—
2006D Proof	—	Value: 1.00				
2006F In sets only	—	—	—	—	4.50	—
2006F Proof	—	Value: 1.00				
2006G In sets only	—	—	—	—	4.50	—
2006G Proof	—	Value: 1.00				
2006J In sets only	—	—	—	—	4.50	—
2006J Proof	—	Value: 1.00				
2007A	119,400,000	—	—	—	0.35	—
2007A Proof	—	Value: 1.00				
2007D	125,370,000	—	—	—	0.35	—
2007D Proof	—	Value: 1.00				
2007F	143,280,000	—	—	—	0.35	—
2007F Proof	—	Value: 1.00				
2007G	83,580,000	—	—	—	0.35	—
2007G Proof	—	Value: 1.00				
2007J	125,370,000	—	—	—	0.35	—
2007J Proof	—	Value: 1.00				
2008A	101,200,000	—	—	—	0.35	—
2008A Proof	—	Value: 1.00				
2008D	106,300,000	—	—	—	0.35	—
2008D Proof	—	Value: 1.00				
2008F	121,400,000	—	—	—	0.35	—
2008F Proof	—	Value: 1.00				
2008G	70,800,000	—	—	—	0.35	—
2008G Proof	—	Value: 1.00				
2008J	106,300,000	—	—	—	0.35	—
2008J Proof	—	Value: 1.00				
2009A	—	—	—	—	0.35	—
2009A Proof	—	Value: 1.00				
2009D	—	—	—	—	0.35	—
2009D Proof	—	Value: 1.00				
2009F	—	—	—	—	0.35	—
2009F Proof	—	Value: 1.00				
2009G	—	—	—	—	0.35	—
2009G Proof	—	Value: 1.00				
2009J	—	—	—	—	0.35	—
2009J Proof	—	Value: 1.00				

KM# 208 2 EURO CENT

3.1000 g., Copper Plated Steel, 18.8 mm. **Obv:** Oak leaves **Obv. Designer:** Rolf Lederbogen **Rev:** Denomination and globe **Rev. Designer:** Luc Luycx **Edge:** Grooved

Date	Mintage	F	VF	XF	Unc	BU
2002A	460,000,000	—	—	—	0.50	—
2002A Proof	130,000	Value: 1.50				
2002D	436,100,000	—	—	—	0.50	—
2002D Proof	130,000	Value: 1.50				
2002F	495,960,000	—	—	—	0.50	—
2002F Proof	130,000	Value: 1.50				
2002G	311,900,000	—	—	—	0.50	—
2002G Proof	130,000	Value: 1.50				
2002J	419,274,000	—	—	—	0.50	—
2002J Proof	130,000	Value: 1.50				
2003A	100,000,000	—	—	—	0.50	—
2003A Proof	150,000	Value: 1.50				
2003D	151,855,000	—	—	—	0.50	—
2003D Proof	150,000	Value: 1.50				
2003F	175,400,000	—	—	—	0.50	—
2003F Proof	150,000	Value: 1.50				
2003G	80,200,000	—	—	—	0.50	—
2003G Proof	150,000	Value: 1.50				
2003J	168,681,000	—	—	—	0.50	—
2003J Proof	150,000	Value: 1.50				
2004A	127,000,000	—	—	—	0.50	—
2004A Proof	—	Value: 1.50				
2004D	133,495,000	—	—	—	0.50	—
2004D Proof	—	Value: 1.50				
2004F	152,400,000	—	—	—	0.50	—
2004F Proof	—	Value: 1.50				
2004G	88,900,000	—	—	—	0.50	—
2004G Proof	—	Value: 1.50				
2004J	133,350,000	—	—	—	0.50	—
2004J Proof	—	Value: 1.50				
2005A	17,000,000	—	—	—	0.50	—
2005A Proof	—	Value: 1.50				
2005D	17,850,000	—	—	—	0.50	—
2005D Proof	—	Value: 1.50				
2005F	20,400,000	—	—	—	0.50	—
2005F Proof	—	Value: 1.50				
2005G	11,900,000	—	—	—	0.50	—
2005G Proof	—	Value: 1.50				
2005J	17,850,000	—	—	—	0.50	—
2005J Proof	—	Value: 1.50				
2006A	108,000,000	—	—	—	0.50	—
2006A Proof	—	Value: 1.50				
2006D	113,400,000	—	—	—	0.50	—
2006D Proof	—	Value: 1.50				
2006F	129,600,000	—	—	—	0.50	—
2006F Proof	—	Value: 1.50				
2006G	75,600,000	—	—	—	0.50	—
2006G Proof	—	Value: 1.50				
2006J	148,400,000	—	—	—	0.50	—
2006J Proof	—	Value: 1.50				
2007A	100,000,000	—	—	—	0.50	—
2007A Proof	—	Value: 1.50				
2007D	105,000,000	—	—	—	0.50	—
2007D Proof	—	Value: 1.50				
2007F	120,000,000	—	—	—	0.50	—
2007F Proof	—	Value: 1.50				
2007G	70,000,000	—	—	—	0.50	—
2007G Proof	—	Value: 1.50				
2007J	105,000,000	—	—	—	0.50	—
2007J Proof	—	Value: 1.50				
2008A	80,000,000	—	—	—	0.50	—
2008A Proof	—	Value: 1.50				
2008D	84,000,000	—	—	—	0.50	—
2008D Proof	—	Value: 1.50				
2008F	96,000,000	—	—	—	0.50	—
2008F Proof	—	Value: 1.50				
2008G	56,000,000	—	—	—	0.50	—
2008G Proof	—	Value: 1.50				
2008J	84,000,000	—	—	—	0.50	—
2008J Proof	—	Value: 1.50				
2009A	—	—	—	—	0.50	—
2009A Proof	—	Value: 1.50				
2009D	—	—	—	—	0.50	—
2009D Proof	—	Value: 1.50				
2009F	—	—	—	—	0.50	—
2009F Proof	—	Value: 1.50				
2009G	—	—	—	—	0.50	—
2009G Proof	—	Value: 1.50				
2009J	—	—	—	—	0.50	—
2009J Proof	—	Value: 1.50				

KM# 209 5 EURO CENT

4.0000 g., Copper Plated Steel, 21.3 mm. **Obv:** Oak leaves **Obv. Designer:** Rolf Lederbogen **Rev:** Denomination and globe **Rev. Designer:** Luc Luycx **Edge:** Plain

Date	Mintage	F	VF	XF	Unc	BU
2002A	475,000,000	—	—	—	0.75	—
2002A Proof	130,000	Value: 2.00				
2002D	495,700,000	—	—	—	0.75	—
2002D Proof	130,000	Value: 2.00				
2002F	563,710,000	—	—	—	0.75	—
2002F Proof	130,000	Value: 2.00				
2002G	328,400,000	—	—	—	0.75	—
2002G Proof	130,000	Value: 2.00				
2002J	501,850,000	—	—	—	0.75	—
2002J Proof	130,000	Value: 2.00				
2003A In sets only	180,000	—	—	—	4.50	—
2003A Proof	150,000	Value: 2.00				
2003D In sets only	180,000	—	—	—	4.50	—
2003D Proof	150,000	Value: 2.00				
2003F In sets only	180,000	—	—	—	4.50	—
2003F Proof	150,000	Value: 2.00				
2003G In sets only	180,000	—	—	—	4.50	—
2003G Proof	150,000	Value: 2.00				
2003J In sets only	180,000	—	—	—	4.50	—
2003J Proof	150,000	Value: 2.00				
2004A	112,000,000	—	—	—	0.75	—
2004A Proof	—	Value: 2.00				
2004D	117,600,000	—	—	—	0.75	—
2004D Proof	—	Value: 2.00				
2004F	134,400,000	—	—	—	0.75	—
2004F Proof	—	Value: 2.00				
2004G	78,400,000	—	—	—	0.75	—
2004G Proof	—	Value: 2.00				
2004J	117,600,000	—	—	—	0.75	—
2004J Proof	—	Value: 2.00				
2005A	44,000,000	—	—	—	0.75	—
2005A Proof	—	Value: 2.00				
2005D	46,200,000	—	—	—	0.75	—
2005D Proof	—	Value: 2.00				
2005F	52,800,000	—	—	—	0.75	—
2005F Proof	—	Value: 2.00				
2005G	30,800,000	—	—	—	0.75	—
2005G Proof	—	Value: 2.00				
2005J	46,200,000	—	—	—	0.75	—
2005J Proof	—	Value: 2.00				
2006A	27,000,000	—	—	—	0.75	—
2006A Proof	—	Value: 2.00				
2006D	28,350,000	—	—	—	0.75	—
2006D Proof	—	Value: 2.00				
2006F	32,400,000	—	—	—	0.75	—
2006F Proof	—	Value: 2.00				
2006G	18,900,000	—	—	—	0.75	—
2006G Proof	—	Value: 2.00				
2006J	28,350,000	—	—	—	0.75	—
2006J Proof	—	Value: 2.00				
2007A	52,400,000	—	—	—	0.75	—
2007A Proof	—	Value: 2.00				
2007D	55,020,000	—	—	—	0.75	—
2007D Proof	—	Value: 2.00				
2007F	62,880,000	—	—	—	0.75	—
2007F Proof	—	Value: 2.00				
2007G	38,680,000	—	—	—	0.75	—
2007G Proof	—	Value: 2.00				
2007J	55,020,000	—	—	—	0.75	—
2007J Proof	—	Value: 2.00				
2008A	29,200,000	—	—	—	0.75	—
2008A Proof	—	Value: 2.00				
2008D	30,700,000	—	—	—	0.75	—
2008D Proof	—	Value: 2.00				
2008F	35,000,000	—	—	—	0.75	—
2008F Proof	—	Value: 2.00				
2008G	20,400,000	—	—	—	0.75	—
2008G Proof	—	Value: 2.00				
2008J	30,700,000	—	—	—	0.75	—
2008J Proof	—	Value: 2.00				
2009A	—	—	—	—	0.75	—
2009A Proof	—	Value: 2.00				
2009D	—	—	—	—	0.75	—
2009D Proof	—	Value: 2.00				
2009F	—	—	—	—	0.75	—
2009F Proof	—	Value: 2.00				
2009G	—	—	—	—	0.75	—
2009G Proof	—	Value: 2.00				
2009J	—	—	—	—	0.75	—
2009J Proof	—	Value: 2.00				

KM# 210 10 EURO CENT

4.0000 g., Brass, 19.7 mm. **Obv:** Brandenburg Gate **Obv. Designer:** Reinhard Heinsdorff **Rev:** Denomination and map **Rev. Designer:** Luc Luycx **Edge:** Reeded

Date	Mintage	F	VF	XF	Unc	BU
2002A	696,000,000	—	—	—	0.75	—
2002A Proof	130,000	Value: 2.00				
2002D	722,050,000	—	—	—	0.75	—
2002D Proof	130,000	Value: 2.00				
2002F	788,860,000	—	—	—	0.75	—
2002F Proof	130,000	Value: 2.00				
2002G	545,500,000	—	—	—	0.75	—
2002G Proof	130,000	Value: 2.00				
2002J	694,150,000	—	—	—	0.75	—
2002J Proof	130,000	Value: 2.00				
2003A	50,655,000	—	—	—	1.25	—
2003A Proof	150,000	Value: 2.00				
2003D	34,000,000	—	—	—	1.25	—
2003D Proof	150,000	Value: 2.00				
2003F	6,000,000	—	—	—	1.50	—
2003F Proof	150,000	Value: 2.00				
2003G	13,500,000	—	—	—	1.25	—
2003G Proof	150,000	Value: 2.00				
2003J	25,500,000	—	—	—	1.25	—
2003J Proof	150,000	Value: 2.00				
2004A In sets only	—	—	—	—	1.25	—
2004A Proof	—	Value: 2.00				
2004D	28,190,000	—	—	—	1.25	—
2004D Proof	—	Value: 2.00				
2004F	51,360,000	—	—	—	1.25	—
2004F Proof	—	Value: 2.00				
2004G	15,460,000	—	—	—	1.25	—
2004G Proof	—	Value: 2.00				
2004J In sets only	—	—	—	—	1.25	—
2004J Proof	—	Value: 2.00				
2005A In sets only	—	—	—	—	1.25	—
2005A Proof	—	Value: 2.00				
2005D In sets only	—	—	—	—	1.25	—
2005D Proof	—	Value: 2.00				
2005F In sets only	—	—	—	—	1.25	—
2005F Proof	—	Value: 2.00				

Date	Mintage	F	VF	XF	Unc	BU
2005G In sets only	—	—	—	—	1.25	—
2005G Proof	—	Value: 2.00				
2005J In sets only	—	—	—	—	1.25	—
2005J Proof	—	Value: 2.00				
2006A In sets only	—	—	—	—	1.25	—
2006A Proof	—	Value: 2.00				
2006D In sets only	—	—	—	—	1.25	—
2006D Proof	—	Value: 2.00				
2006F In sets only	—	—	—	—	1.25	—
2006F Proof	—	Value: 2.00				
2006G In sets only	—	—	—	—	1.25	—
2006G Proof	—	Value: 2.00				
2006J In sets only	—	—	—	—	1.25	—
2006J Proof	—	Value: 2.00				

KM# 254 10 EURO CENT

4.0000 g., Brass, 19.7 mm. **Obv:** Brandenburg Gate **Obv. Designer:** Reinhard Heinsdorff **Rev:** Relief map of Western Europe, stars, lines and value **Rev. Designer:** Luc Luycx **Edge:** Reeded

Date	Mintage	F	VF	XF	Unc	BU
2007A In sets only	—	—	—	—	1.25	—
2007A Proof	—	Value: 2.00				
2007D In sets only	—	—	—	—	1.25	—
2007D Proof	—	Value: 2.00				
2007F In sets only	—	—	—	—	1.25	—
2007F Proof	—	Value: 2.00				
2007G In sets only	—	—	—	—	1.25	—
2007G Proof	—	Value: 2.00				
2007J In sets only	—	—	—	—	1.25	—
2007J Proof	—	Value: 2.00				
2008A In sets only	—	—	—	—	1.25	—
2008A Proof	—	Value: 2.00				
2008D In sets only	—	—	—	—	1.25	—
2008D Proof	—	Value: 2.00				
2008F In sets only	—	—	—	—	1.25	—
2008F Proof	—	Value: 2.00				
2008G In sets only	—	—	—	—	1.25	—
2008G Proof	—	Value: 2.00				
2008J In sets only	—	—	—	—	1.25	—
2008J Proof	—	Value: 2.00				
2009A	—	—	—	—	1.25	—
2009A Proof	—	Value: 2.00				
2009D	—	—	—	—	1.25	—
2009D Proof	—	Value: 2.00				
2009F	—	—	—	—	1.25	—
2009F Proof	—	Value: 2.00				
2009G	—	—	—	—	1.25	—
2009G Proof	—	Value: 2.00				
2009J	—	—	—	—	1.25	—
2009J Proof	—	Value: 2.00				

KM# 211 20 EURO CENT

5.7400 g., Brass, 22.2 mm. **Obv:** Brandenburg Gate **Obv. Designer:** Reinhard Heinsdorff **Rev:** Denomination and map **Rev. Designer:** Luc Luycx **Edge:** Notched

Date	Mintage	F	VF	XF	Unc	BU
2002A	378,000,000	—	—	—	1.00	—
2002A Proof	130,000	Value: 3.00				
2002D	367,100,000	—	—	—	1.00	—
2002D Proof	130,000	Value: 3.00				
2002F	423,760,000	—	—	—	1.00	—
2002F Proof	130,000	Value: 3.00				
2002G	252,100,000	—	—	—	1.00	—
2002G Proof	130,000	Value: 3.00				
2002J	441,000,000	—	—	—	1.00	—
2002J Proof	130,000	Value: 3.00				
2003A	42,000,000	—	—	—	1.00	—
2003A Proof	150,000	Value: 3.00				
2003D	24,100,000	—	—	—	1.00	—
2003D Proof	150,000	Value: 3.00				
2003F	82,000,000	—	—	—	1.00	—
2003F Proof	150,000	Value: 3.00				
2003G	24,829,000	—	—	—	1.00	—
2003G Proof	150,000	Value: 3.00				
2003J In sets only	180,000	—	—	—	4.50	—
2003J Proof	150,000	Value: 3.00				
2004A In sets only	—	—	—	—	4.50	—
2004A Proof	—	Value: 3.00				
2004D	33,600,000	—	—	—	2.50	—
2004D Proof	—	Value: 3.00				
2004F In sets only	—	—	—	—	4.50	—
2004F Proof	—	Value: 3.00				
2004G In sets only	—	—	—	—	4.50	—
2004G Proof	—	Value: 3.00				
2004J In sets only	—	—	—	—	4.50	—
2004J Proof	—	Value: 3.00				
2005A	8,000,000	—	—	—	1.00	—
2005A Proof	—	Value: 3.00				
2005D	24,700,000	—	—	—	1.00	—
2005D Proof	—	Value: 3.00				
2005F	9,600,000	—	—	—	1.00	—
2005F Proof	—	Value: 3.00				
2005G	5,600,000	—	—	—	1.00	—

Date	Mintage	F	VF	XF	Unc	BU
2005G Proof	—	Value: 3.00				
2005J	8,400,000	—	—	—	1.00	—
2005J Proof	—	Value: 3.00				
2006A	39,000,000	—	—	—	1.00	—
2006A Proof	—	Value: 3.00				
2006D	40,950,000	—	—	—	1.00	—
2006D Proof	—	Value: 3.00				
2006F	46,800,000	—	—	—	1.00	—
2006F Proof	—	Value: 3.00				
2006G	27,300,000	—	—	—	1.00	—
2006G Proof	—	Value: 3.00				
2006J	40,950,000	—	—	—	1.00	—
2006J Proof	—	Value: 3.00				

KM# 255 20 EURO CENT

5.7300 g., Brass, 22.2 mm. **Obv:** Brandenburg Gate **Obv. Designer:** Reinhard Heinsdorff **Rev:** Relief map of Western Europe, stars, lines and value **Rev. Designer:** Luc Luycx **Edge:** Notched

Date	Mintage	F	VF	XF	Unc	BU
2007A	21,600,000	—	—	—	1.00	—
2007A Proof	—	Value: 3.00				
2007D	22,680,000	—	—	—	1.00	—
2007D Proof	—	Value: 3.00				
2007F	25,920,000	—	—	—	1.00	—
2007F Proof	—	Value: 3.00				
2007G	15,120,000	—	—	—	1.00	—
2007G Proof	—	Value: 3.00				
2007J	22,930,000	—	—	—	1.00	—
2007J Proof	—	Value: 3.00				
2008A	15,800,000	—	—	—	1.00	—
2008A Proof	—	Value: 3.00				
2008D	16,600,000	—	—	—	1.00	—
2008D Proof	—	Value: 3.00				
2008F	19,000,000	—	—	—	1.00	—
2008F Proof	—	Value: 3.00				
2008G	11,100,000	—	—	—	1.00	—
2008G Proof	—	Value: 3.00				
2008J	16,300,000	—	—	—	1.00	—
2008J Proof	—	Value: 3.00				
2009A	—	—	—	—	1.00	—
2009A Proof	—	Value: 3.00				
2009D	—	—	—	—	1.00	—
2009D Proof	—	Value: 3.00				
2009F	—	—	—	—	1.00	—
2009F Proof	—	Value: 3.00				
2009G	—	—	—	—	1.00	—
2009G Proof	—	Value: 3.00				
2009J	—	—	—	—	1.00	—
2009J Proof	—	Value: 3.00				

KM# 212 50 EURO CENT

7.8100 g., Brass, 24.2 mm. **Obv:** Brandenburg Gate **Obv. Designer:** Reinhard Heinsdorff **Rev:** Denomination and map **Rev. Designer:** Luc Luycx **Edge:** Reeded

Date	Mintage	F	VF	XF	Unc	BU
2002A	337,600,000	—	—	—	1.75	—
2002A Proof	130,000	Value: 4.00				
2002D	370,340,000	—	—	—	1.75	—
2002D Proof	130,000	Value: 4.00				
2002F	432,000,000	—	—	—	1.75	—
2002F Proof	130,000	Value: 4.00				
2002G	257,860,000	—	—	—	1.75	—
2002G Proof	130,000	Value: 4.00				
2002J	375,467,000	—	—	—	1.75	—
2002J Proof	130,000	Value: 4.00				
2003A In sets only	180,000	—	—	—	4.50	—
2003A Proof	150,000	Value: 4.00				
2003D In sets only	180,000	—	—	—	4.50	—
2003D Proof	150,000	Value: 4.00				
2003F In sets only	180,000	—	—	—	4.50	—
2003F Proof	150,000	Value: 4.00				
2003G In sets only	180,000	—	—	—	4.50	—
2003G Proof	150,000	Value: 4.00				
2003J	39,600,000	—	—	—	1.75	—
2003J Proof	150,000	Value: 4.00				
2004A	82,255,000	—	—	—	1.75	—
2004A Proof	—	Value: 4.00				
2004D	70,760,000	—	—	—	1.75	—
2004D Proof	—	Value: 4.00				
2004F	73,520,000	—	—	—	1.75	—
2004F Proof	—	Value: 4.00				
2004G	37,440,000	—	—	—	1.75	—
2004G Proof	—	Value: 4.00				
2004J In sets only	—	—	—	—	1.75	—
2004J Proof	—	Value: 4.00				
2005A In sets only	—	—	—	—	1.50	—
2005A Proof	—	Value: 4.00				
2005D In sets only	—	—	—	—	1.50	—
2005D Proof	—	Value: 4.00				
2005F In sets only	—	—	—	—	1.50	—
2005F Proof	—	Value: 4.00				
2005G In sets only	—	—	—	—	1.50	—

Date	Mintage	F	VF	XF	Unc	BU
2005G Proof	—	Value: 4.00				
2005J In sets only	—	—	—	—	1.50	—
2005J Proof	—	Value: 4.00				
2006A In sets only	—	—	—	—	1.50	—
2006A Proof	—	Value: 4.00				
2006D In sets only	—	—	—	—	1.50	—
2006D Proof	—	Value: 4.00				
2006F In sets only	—	—	—	—	1.50	—
2006F Proof	—	Value: 4.00				
2006G In sets only	—	—	—	—	1.50	—
2006G Proof	—	Value: 4.00				
2006J In sets only	—	—	—	—	1.50	—
2006J Proof	—	Value: 4.00				

KM# 256 50 EURO CENT

7.8100 g., Brass, 24.2 mm. **Obv:** Brandenburg Gate **Obv. Designer:** Reinhard Heinsdorff **Rev:** Relief map of Western Europe, stars, lines and value **Rev. Designer:** Luc Luycx **Edge:** Reeded

Date	Mintage	F	VF	XF	Unc	BU
2007A In sets only	—	—	—	—	1.50	—
2007A Proof	—	Value: 4.00				
2007D In sets only	—	—	—	—	1.50	—
2007D Proof	—	Value: 4.00				
2007F In sets only	—	—	—	—	1.50	—
2007F Proof	—	Value: 4.00				
2007G In sets only	—	—	—	—	1.50	—
2007G Proof	—	Value: 4.00				
2007J In sets only	—	—	—	—	1.50	—
2007J Proof	—	Value: 4.00				
2008A In sets only	—	—	—	—	1.50	—
2008A Proof	—	Value: 4.00				
2008D In sets only	—	—	—	—	1.50	—
2008D Proof	—	Value: 4.00				
2008F In sets only	—	—	—	—	1.50	—
2008F Proof	—	Value: 4.00				
2008G In sets only	—	—	—	—	1.50	—
2008G Proof	—	Value: 4.00				
2008J In sets only	—	—	—	—	1.50	—
2008J Proof	—	Value: 4.00				
2009A	—	—	—	—	1.50	—
2009A Proof	—	Value: 4.00				
2009D	—	—	—	—	1.50	—
2009D Proof	—	Value: 4.00				
2009F	—	—	—	—	1.50	—
2009F Proof	—	Value: 4.00				
2009G	—	—	—	—	1.50	—
2009G Proof	—	Value: 4.00				
2009J	—	—	—	—	1.50	—
2009J Proof	—	Value: 4.00				

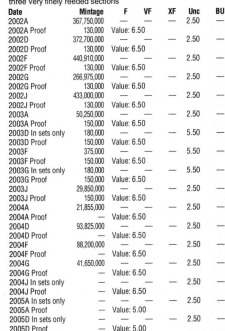

KM# 213 EURO

7.5000 g., Bi-Metallic Copper-Nickel center in Brass ring, 23.3 mm. **Obv:** Stylized eagle **Obv. Designer:** Heinz Sneschana Russewa-Hover **Rev:** Denomination over map **Rev. Designer:** Luc Luycx **Edge:** Three normally reeded and three very finely reeded sections

Date	Mintage	F	VF	XF	Unc	BU
2002A	367,750,000	—	—	—	2.50	—
2002A Proof	130,000	Value: 6.50				
2002D	372,700,000	—	—	—	2.50	—
2002D Proof	130,000	Value: 6.50				
2002F	440,910,000	—	—	—	2.50	—
2002F Proof	130,000	Value: 6.50				
2002G	266,975,000	—	—	—	2.50	—
2002G Proof	130,000	Value: 6.50				
2002J	433,000,000	—	—	—	2.50	—
2002J Proof	130,000	Value: 6.50				
2003A	50,250,000	—	—	—	2.50	—
2003A Proof	150,000	Value: 6.50				
2003D In sets only	180,000	—	—	—	5.50	—
2003D Proof	150,000	Value: 6.50				
2003F	375,000	—	—	—	5.50	—
2003F Proof	150,000	Value: 6.50				
2003G In sets only	180,000	—	—	—	5.50	—
2003G Proof	150,000	Value: 6.50				
2003J	29,850,000	—	—	—	2.50	—
2003J Proof	150,000	Value: 6.50				
2004A	21,855,000	—	—	—	2.50	—
2004A Proof	—	Value: 6.50				
2004D	93,825,000	—	—	—	2.50	—
2004D Proof	—	Value: 6.50				
2004F	88,200,000	—	—	—	2.50	—
2004F Proof	—	Value: 6.50				
2004G	41,650,000	—	—	—	2.50	—
2004G Proof	—	Value: 6.50				
2004J In sets only	—	—	—	—	2.50	—
2004J Proof	—	Value: 6.50				
2005A In sets only	—	—	—	—	2.50	—
2005A Proof	—	Value: 5.00				
2005D In sets only	—	—	—	—	2.50	—
2005D Proof	—	Value: 5.00				
2005F In sets only	—	—	—	—	2.50	—
2005F Proof	—	Value: 5.00				

Date	Mintage	F	VF	XF	Unc	BU
2005G In sets only	—	—	—	—	2.50	—
2005G Proof	—	Value: 5.00				
2005J	59,840,000	—	—	—	2.50	—
2005J Proof	—	Value: 5.00				
2006A In sets only	—	—	—	—	2.50	—
2006A Proof	—	Value: 5.00				
2006D In sets only	—	—	—	—	2.50	—
2006D Proof	—	Value: 5.00				
2006F In sets only	—	—	—	—	2.50	—
2006F Proof	—	Value: 5.00				
2006G In sets only	—	—	—	—	2.50	—
2006G Proof	—	Value: 5.00				
2006J In sets only	—	—	—	—	2.50	—
2006J Proof	—	Value: 5.00				

KM# 257 EURO

7.5000 g., Bi-Metallic Copper-Nickel center in Brass ring, 23.3 mm. **Obv:** Stylized eagle **Obv. Designer:** Heinz Sneschana Russewa-Hover **Rev:** Relief map of Western Europe, stars, lines and value **Rev. Designer:** Luc Luycx **Edge:** Three normally reeded and three very finely reeded sections

Date	Mintage	F	VF	XF	Unc	BU
2007A In sets only	—	—	—	—	2.50	—
2007A Proof	—	Value: 5.00				
2007D In sets only	—	—	—	—	2.50	—
2007D Proof	—	Value: 5.00				
2007F In sets only	—	—	—	—	2.50	—
2007F Proof	—	Value: 5.00				
2007G In sets only	—	—	—	—	2.50	—
2007G Proof	—	Value: 5.00				
2007J In sets only	—	—	—	—	2.50	—
2007J Proof	—	Value: 5.00				
2008A In sets only	—	—	—	—	2.50	—
2008A Proof	—	Value: 5.00				
2008D In sets only	—	—	—	—	2.50	—
2008D Proof	—	Value: 5.00				
2008F In sets only	—	—	—	—	2.50	—
2008F Proof	—	Value: 5.00				
2008G In sets only	—	—	—	—	2.50	—
2008G Proof	—	Value: 5.00				
2008J In sets only	—	—	—	—	2.50	—
2008J Proof	—	Value: 5.00				
2009A	—	—	—	—	2.50	—
2009A Proof	—	Value: 5.00				
2009D	—	—	—	—	2.50	—
2009D Proof	—	Value: 5.00				
2009F	—	—	—	—	2.50	—
2009F Proof	—	Value: 5.00				
2009G	—	—	—	—	2.50	—
2009G Proof	—	Value: 5.00				
2009J	—	—	—	—	2.50	—
2009J Proof	—	Value: 5.00				

KM# 214 2 EURO

8.5200 g., Bi-Metallic Brass center in Copper-Nickel ring, 25.72 mm. **Obv:** Stylized eagle **Obv. Designer:** Heinz Sneschana Russewa-Hover **Rev:** Denomination and map **Rev. Designer:** Luc Luycx **Edge:** Reeded and "EINIGKEIT UND RECHT UND FREIHEIT"

Date	Mintage	F	VF	XF	Unc	BU
2002A	238,775,000	—	—	—	4.50	—
2002A Proof	130,000	Value: 12.50				
2002D	231,400,000	—	—	—	4.50	—
2002D Proof	130,000	Value: 12.50				
2002F	264,610,000	—	—	—	4.50	—
2002F Proof	130,000	Value: 12.50				
2002G	181,050,000	—	—	—	4.50	—
2002G Proof	130,000	Value: 12.50				
2002J	257,718,000	—	—	—	4.50	—
2002J Proof	130,000	Value: 12.50				
2003A	20,475,000	—	—	—	4.50	—
2003A Proof	150,000	Value: 12.50				
2003D	16,269,000	—	—	—	4.50	—
2003D Proof	150,000	Value: 12.50				
2003F	24,575,000	—	—	—	4.50	—
2003F Proof	150,000	Value: 12.50				
2003G	29,425,000	—	—	—	4.50	—
2003G Proof	150,000	Value: 12.50				
2003J	20,100,000	—	—	—	4.50	—
2003J Proof	150,000	Value: 12.50				
2004A	31,565,000	—	—	—	4.50	—
2004A Proof	—	Value: 12.50				
2004D	28,146,000	—	—	—	4.50	—
2004D Proof	—	Value: 12.50				
2004F In sets only	—	—	—	—	4.50	—
2004F Proof	—	Value: 12.50				
2004G In sets only	—	—	—	—	4.50	—
2004G Proof	—	Value: 12.50				
2004J	5,630,000	—	—	—	4.50	—
2004J Proof	—	Value: 12.50				
2005A In sets only	—	—	—	—	4.50	—
2005A Proof	—	Value: 10.00				
2005D In sets only	—	—	—	—	4.50	—
2005D Proof	—	Value: 10.00				
2005F In sets only	—	—	—	—	4.50	—
2005F Proof	—	Value: 10.00				
2005G In sets only	—	—	—	—	4.50	—
2005G Proof	—	Value: 10.00				
2005J In sets only	—	—	—	—	4.50	—
2005J Proof	—	Value: 10.00				
2006A In sets only	—	—	—	—	4.50	—
2006A Proof	—	Value: 10.00				
2006D In sets only	—	—	—	—	4.50	—

Date	Mintage	F	VF	XF	Unc	BU
2006D Proof	—	Value: 10.00				
2006F In sets only	—	—	—	—	4.50	—
2006F Proof	—	Value: 10.00				
2006G In sets only	—	—	—	—	4.50	—
2006G Proof	—	Value: 10.00				
2006J In sets only	—	—	—	—	4.50	—
2006J Proof	—	Value: 10.00				

KM# 253 2 EURO

8.5200 g., Bi-Metallic Brass center in Copper-Nickel ring **Obv:** Towered city gate **Obv. Legend:** BUNDESREPULIK DEUTSCHLAND **Obv. Inscription:** SCHLESWIG- / HOLSTEIN **Rev:** Denomination over map

Date	Mintage	F	VF	XF	Unc	BU
2006A	6,000,000	—	—	—	5.00	—
2006A Proof	70,000	Value: 10.00				
2006D	6,300,000	—	—	—	5.00	—
2006D Proof	70,000	Value: 10.00				
2006F	7,250,000	—	—	—	5.00	—
2006F Proof	70,000	Value: 10.00				
2006G	4,200,000	—	—	—	5.00	—
2006G Proof	70,000	Value: 10.00				
2006J	6,300,000	—	—	—	5.00	—
2006J Proof	70,000	Value: 10.00				

KM# 259 2 EURO

8.4500 g., Bi-Metallic Brass center in Copper-Nickel ring, 25.72 mm. **Subject:** 50th Anniversary Treaty of Rome **Obv:** Open treaty book **Obv. Legend:** BUNDESREPUBLIK DEUTSCHLAND **Rev:** Large value at left, modified outline of Europe at right **Edge:** Reeded and lettered **Edge Lettering:** EINIGKEIT UND RECHT UND FREIHEIT

Date	Mintage	F	VF	XF	Unc	BU
2007A	1,000,000	—	—	—	4.00	5.00
2007A Proof	155,000	Value: 10.00				
2007D	14,500,000	—	—	—	4.00	5.50
2007D Prrof	155,000	Value: 10.00				
2007F	8,000,000	—	—	—	4.00	5.50
2007F Proof	155,000	Value: 10.00				
2007G	5,000,000	—	—	—	4.00	5.50
2007G Proof	155,000	Value: 10.00				
2007J	1,500,000	—	—	—	4.00	5.50
2007J Proof	155,000	Value: 10.00				

KM# 260 2 EURO

8.4000 g., Bi-Metallic Brass center in Copper-Nickel ring, 25.72 mm. **Obv:** City buildings, Mecklenburg's Schwerin Castle **Obv. Legend:** BUNDESREPUBLIK DEUTSCHLAND **Obv. Inscription:** MECKLENBURG- / VORPOMMERN **Rev:** Large value at left, modified map of Europe at right **Edge:** Reeded and lettered **Edge Lettering:** EINIGKEIT UND RECHT UND FREIHEIT

Date	Mintage	F	VF	XF	Unc	BU
2007A	1,040,000	—	—	—	4.00	5.50
2007A Proof	70,000	Value: 10.00				
2007D	11,840,000	—	—	—	4.00	5.50
2007D Proof	70,000	Value: 10.00				
2007F	11,850,000	—	—	—	4.00	5.50
2007F Proof	70,000	Value: 10.00				
2007G	4,200,000	—	—	—	4.00	5.50
2007G Proof	70,000	Value: 10.00				
2007J	1,070,000	—	—	—	4.00	5.50
2007J Proof	70,000	Value: 10.00				

KM# 261 2 EURO

8.4700 g., Bi-Metallic Brass center in Copper-Nickel ring., 25.75 mm. **Obv:** Hamburg Cathedral **Obv. Legend:** BUNDESREPUBLIK DEUTSCHLAND **Obv. Inscription:** HAMBURG **Rev:** Large value at left, modified outline of Europe at right **Edge:** Reeded and lettered **Edge Lettering:** EINIGKEIT UND RECHT UND FREIHEIT

Date	Mintage	F	VF	XF	Unc	BU
2008A	1,000,000	—	—	—	4.00	5.50
2008A Proof	—	Value: 10.00				
2008D	8,900,000	—	—	—	4.00	5.50
2008D Proof	—	Value: 10.00				
2008F	9,600,000	—	—	—	4.00	5.50
2008F Proof	—	Value: 10.00				
2008G	4,200,000	—	—	—	4.00	5.50
2008G Proof	—	Value: 10.00				
2008J	6,300,000	—	—	—	4.00	5.50
2008J Proof	—	Value: 10.00				

KM# 258 2 EURO

8.5200 g., Bi-Metallic Brass center in Copper-Nickel ring, 25.6 mm. **Obv:** Stylized eagle **Obv. Designer:** Heinz Sneschana Russewa-Hover **Rev:** Relief map of Western Europe, stars, lines and value **Rev. Designer:** Luc Luycx **Edge:** Reeded and lettered **Edge Lettering:** EINIGKEIT UND RECHT UND FREIHEIT

Date	Mintage	F	VF	XF	Unc	BU
2008A In sets only	—	—	—	—	4.50	—
2008A Proof	—	Value: 10.00				
2008D In sets only	—	—	—	—	4.50	—
2008D Proof	—	Value: 10.00				
2008F In sets only	—	—	—	—	4.50	—
2008F Proof	—	Value: 10.00				
2008G In sets only	—	—	—	—	4.50	—
2008G Proof	—	Value: 10.00				
2008J In sets only	—	—	—	—	4.50	—
2008J Proof	—	Value: 10.00				
2009A	—	—	—	—	4.50	—
2009A Proof	—	Value: 10.00				
2009D	—	—	—	—	4.50	—
2009D Proof	—	Value: 10.00				
2009F	—	—	—	—	4.50	—
2009F Proof	—	Value: 10.00				
2009G	—	—	—	—	4.50	—
2009G Proof	—	Value: 10.00				
2009J	—	—	—	—	4.50	—
2009J Proof	—	Value: 10.00				

KM# 277 2 EURO

8.5000 g., Bi-Metallic Brass center in copper-nickel ring **Obv:** Stick figure and E symbol

Date	Mintage	F	VF	XF	Unc	BU
2009A	—	—	—	—	4.50	5.00
2009A Proof	—	Value: 10.00				
2009D	—	—	—	—	4.50	5.00
2009D Proof	—	Value: 10.00				
2009F	—	—	—	—	4.50	5.00
2009F Proof	—	Value: 10.00				
2009G	—	—	—	—	4.50	5.00
2009G Proof	—	Value: 10.00				
2009J	—	—	—	—	4.50	5.00
2009J Proof	—	Value: 10.00				

KM# 276 2 EURO

Bi-Metallic Brass center in copper-nickel ring **Obv:** Church in Saarbrücken **Rev:** Value and map

Date	Mintage	F	VF	XF	Unc	BU
2009A	—	—	—	—	4.50	—
2009D	—	—	—	—	4.50	—
2009F	—	—	—	—	4.50	—
2009G	—	—	—	—	4.50	—
2009J	—	—	—	—	4.50	—

KM# 285 2 EURO

8.5000 g., Bi-Metallic, 25.72 mm. **Subject:** Berlin

Date	Mintage	F	VF	XF	Unc	BU
2010A	—	—	—	—	4.50	5.00
2010A Proof	—	Value: 10.00				
2010D	—	—	—	—	4.50	5.00
2010A Proof	—	Value: 10.00				
2010F	—	—	—	—	4.50	5.00
2010F Proof	—	Value: 10.00				
2010G	—	—	—	—	4.50	5.00
2010G Proof	—	Value: 10.00				
2010J	—	—	—	—	4.50	5.00
2010J Proof	—	Value: 10.00				

KM# 215 10 EURO

18.0000 g., 0.9250 Silver 0.5353 oz. ASW, 32.5 mm. **Subject:** Introduction of the Euro Currency **Obv:** Stylized round eagle **Rev:** Euro symbol and map **Edge Lettering:** IM ZEICHEN DER EINIGUNG EUROPAS

Date	Mintage	F	VF	XF	Unc	BU
2002F	2,000,000	—	—	—	20.00	22.00
2002F Proof	400,000	Value: 25.00				

KM# 216   10 EURO
18.0000 g., 0.9250 Silver 0.5353 oz. ASW, 32.5 mm.
Subject: Berlin Subway Centennial **Obv:** Stylized squarish eagle **Rev:** Elevated and subterranean train views **Edge Lettering:** HISTORISCH UND ZUKUNFTS WEISEND

Date	Mintage	F	VF	XF	Unc	BU
2002D	2,000,000	—	—	—	20.00	22.00
2002D Proof	400,000	Value: 25.00				

KM# 217   10 EURO
18.0000 g., 0.9250 Silver 0.5353 oz. ASW, 32.5 mm.
Subject: "Documenta Kassel" Art Exposition **Obv:** Stylized eagle above inscription **Rev:** Exposition logo **Edge Lettering:** ART (in nine languages)

Date	Mintage	F	VF	XF	Unc	BU
2002J	2,000,000	—	—	—	20.00	22.00
2002J Proof	400,000	Value: 25.00				

KM# 218   10 EURO
18.0000 g., 0.9250 Silver 0.5353 oz. ASW, 32.5 mm.
Subject: Museum Island, Berlin **Obv:** Stylized eagle **Rev:** Aerial view of museum complex **Edge Lettering:** FREISTÄTTE FUR KÜNST UND WISSENSCHAFT

Date	Mintage	F	VF	XF	Unc	BU
2002A	2,000,000	—	—	—	20.00	22.00
2002A Proof	280,000	Value: 30.00				

KM# 219   10 EURO
18.0000 g., 0.9250 Silver 0.5353 oz. ASW, 32.5 mm.
Subject: 50 Years - German Television **Obv:** Stylized eagle silhouette **Rev:** Television screen silhouette **Edge Lettering:** BILDUNG UNTERHALTUNG INFORMATION

Date	Mintage	F	VF	XF	Unc	BU
2002G	2,000,000	—	—	—	20.00	22.00
2002G Proof	290,000	Value: 30.00				

KM# 222   10 EURO
18.0000 g., 0.9250 Silver 0.5353 oz. ASW, 32.5 mm.
Subject: Justus von Liebig **Obv:** Eagle above denomination **Rev:** Liebig's portrait **Edge Lettering:** FORSCHEN . LEHREN . ANWENDEN ..

Date	Mintage	F	VF	XF	Unc	BU
2003J	2,050,000	—	—	—	20.00	22.00
2003J Proof	350,000	Value: 30.00				

KM# 227   10 EURO
18.0000 g., 0.9250 Silver 0.5353 oz. ASW, 32.5 mm.   **Obv:** Stylized eagle above denomination **Rev:** Gottfried Semper and floor plan **Edge:** Lettered **Edge Lettering:** "ARCHITEKT. FORSCHER. KOSMOPOLIT. DEMOKRAT."

Date	Mintage	F	VF	XF	Unc	BU
2003G	2,050,000	—	—	—	18.50	20.00
2003G Proof	350,000	Value: 22.50				

KM# 223   10 EURO
18.0000 g., 0.9250 Silver 0.5353 oz. ASW, 32.5 mm.   **Subject:** World Cup Soccer **Obv:** Stylized round eagle above denomination **Rev:** German map on soccer ball **Edge:** Lettered **Edge Lettering:** "DIE WELT ZU GAST BEI FREUNDEN A. D. F. G.J ." **Note:** Mint is determined by which letter "E" in the edge inscription has a short center bar. If the first letter "E" has the short center bar the coin is from the Berlin mint. Second "E"= Munich, third "E"=Stuttgart, fourth "E"=Karlsruhe, fifth "E"=Hamburg

Date	Mintage	F	VF	XF	Unc	BU
2003A	710,000	—	—	—	20.00	22.00
2003A Proof	80,000	Value: 30.00				
2003D	710,000	—	—	—	20.00	22.00
2003D Proof	80,000	Value: 30.00				
2003F	710,000	—	—	—	20.00	22.00
2003F Proof	80,000	Value: 30.00				
2003G	710,000	—	—	—	20.00	22.00
2003G Proof	80,000	Value: 30.00				
2003J	710,000	—	—	—	20.00	22.00
2003J Proof	80,000	Value: 30.00				

KM# 224   10 EURO
18.0000 g., 0.9250 Silver 0.5353 oz. ASW, 32.5 mm.
Subject: Ruhr Industrial District **Obv:** Stylized eagle, denomination below **Rev:** Various city views **Edge:** Lettered **Edge Lettering:** "RUHRPOTT KULTURLANDSCHAFT"

Date	Mintage	F	VF	XF	Unc	BU
2003F	2,050,000	—	—	—	20.00	22.00
2003F Proof	350,000	Value: 30.00				

KM# 226   10 EURO
18.0000 g., 0.9250 Silver 0.5353 oz. ASW, 32.5 mm.
Subject: 50th Anniversary of the Ill-fated East German Revolution **Obv:** Stylized eagle, denomination at left **Rev:** Tank tracks over slogans **Edge:** Lettered **Edge Lettering:** "ERINNERUNG AN DEN VOLKSAUFSTAND IN DER DDR"

Date	Mintage	F	VF	XF	Unc	BU
2003A	2,050,000	—	—	—	20.00	22.00
2003A Proof	350,000	Value: 30.00				

KM# 225   10 EURO
18.0000 g., 0.9250 Silver 0.5353 oz. ASW, 32.5 mm.
Subject: German Museum München Centennial **Obv:** Stylized eagle, denomination at left **Rev:** Abstract design **Edge Lettering:** SAMMELN • AUSSTELLEN • FORSCHEN • BILDEN •

Date	Mintage	F	VF	XF	Unc	BU
2003D	2,050,000	—	—	—	20.00	22.00
2003D Proof	350,000	Value: 30.00				

KM# 230   10 EURO
18.0000 g., 0.9250 Silver 0.5353 oz. ASW, 32.5 mm.
Obv: Stylized eagle, stars and denomination **Rev:** Bauhaus Dessau geometric shapes design **Edge:** Lettered **Edge Lettering:** "KUNST TECHNIK LEHRE"

Date	Mintage	F	VF	XF	Unc	BU
2004A	1,800,000	—	—	—	20.00	22.00
2004A Proof	300,000	Value: 25.00				

KM# 232   10 EURO
18.0000 g., 0.9250 Silver 0.5353 oz. ASW, 32.5 mm.
Obv: Stylized eagle and denomination **Rev:** Geese flying over Wattenmeer National Park **Edge:** Lettered **Edge Lettering:** "MEERESGRUND TRIFFT HORIZONT"

Date	Mintage	F	VF	XF	Unc	BU
2004J	—	—	—	—	20.00	22.00
2004J Proof	—	Value: 25.00				

KM# 233   10 EURO
18.0000 g., 0.9250 Silver 0.5353 oz. ASW, 32.5 mm.
Obv: Stylized eagle **Rev:** Eduard Moerike **Edge:** Lettered **Edge Lettering:** "OHNE DAS SCHÖNE WAS SOLL DER GEWINN"

Date	Mintage	F	VF	XF	Unc	BU
2004F	—	—	—	—	22.00	—
2004F Proof	—	Value: 25.00				

KM# 234   10 EURO
18.0000 g., 0.9250 Silver 0.5353 oz. ASW, 32.5 mm.
Obv: Stylized eagle, denomination below **Rev:** Space station above the earth **Edge:** Lettered **Edge Lettering:** "RAUMFAHRT VERBINDET DIE WELT"

Date	Mintage	F	VF	XF	Unc	BU
2004D	1,800,000	—	—	—	20.00	22.00
2004D Proof	300,000	Value: 25.00				

KM# 231   10 EURO
18.0000 g., 0.9250 Silver 0.5353 oz. ASW, 32.5 mm.
Obv: Stylized eagle above denomination **Rev:** European Union country names and dates **Edge:** Lettered **Edge Lettering:** "FREUDE SCHÖNER GÖTTERFUNKEN"

Date	Mintage	F	VF	XF	Unc	BU
2004F	—	—	—	—	20.00	22.00
2004F Proof	—	Value: 25.00				
2004G	—	—	—	—	20.00	22.00
2004G Proof	—	Value: 25.00				

KM# 229   10 EURO
18.0000 g., 0.9250 Silver 0.5353 oz. ASW, 32.5 mm.
Obv: Stylized eagle, denomination below **Rev:** Soccer ball orbiting the earth **Edge:** Lettered **Edge Lettering:** "DIE WELT ZU GAST BEI FREUNDEN A D F G J" **Note:** Soccer Series: Mint determination same as KM-223.

Date	Mintage	F	VF	XF	Unc	BU
2004A	800,000	—	—	—	25.00	—
2004A Proof	80,000	Value: 22.00				
2004D	800,000	—	—	—	25.00	—
2004D Proof	80,000	Value: 22.00				
2004F	800,000	—	—	—	25.00	—
2004F Proof	80,000	Value: 22.00				
2004G	800,000	—	—	—	25.00	—
2004G Proof	80,000	Value: 22.00				
2004J	800,000	—	—	—	25.00	—
2004J Proof	80,000	Value: 22.00				

KM# 238   10 EURO
18.0000 g., 0.9250 Silver 0.5353 oz. ASW, 32.5 mm.
Subject: Albert Einstein **Obv:** Stylized eagle within circle, denomination below **Rev:** E=mc2 on a sphere resting on a net **Edge Lettering:** "NICHT AUFHOREN ZU FRAGEN"

Date	Mintage	F	VF	XF	Unc	BU
2005J	1,800,000	—	—	—	20.00	22.00
2005J Proof	300,000	Value: 25.00				

KM# 239   10 EURO
18.0000 g., 0.9250 Silver 0.5353 oz. ASW, 32.5 mm.
Subject: Friedrich von Schiller **Obv:** Stylized eagle **Rev:** Schiller portrait **Edge Lettering:** "ERNST IST DAS LEBEN. HEITER IST DIE KUNST"

Date	Mintage	F	VF	XF	Unc	BU
2005G	1,800,000	—	—	—	18.00	20.00
2005G Proof	300,000	Value: 22.00				

KM# 240   10 EURO
18.0000 g., 0.9250 Silver 0.5353 oz. ASW, 32.5 mm.
Subject: Magdeburg **Obv:** Stylized eagle, denomination below **Rev:** Church flanked by landmarks and objects **Edge Lettering:** MAGADOBURG 805..MAGDEBURG 2005..

Date	Mintage	F	VF	XF	Unc	BU
2005A	1,800,000	—	—	—	18.00	20.00
2005A Proof	300,000	Value: 22.00				

KM# 241   10 EURO
18.0000 g., 0.9250 Silver 0.5353 oz. ASW, 32.5 mm.
Subject: Bavarian Forest National Park **Obv:** Stylized eagle **Rev:** Various park scenes **Edge:** Lettered

Date	Mintage	F	VF	XF	Unc	BU
2005D	1,800,000	—	—	—	18.00	20.00
2005D Proof	300,000	Value: 22.00				

KM# 242   10 EURO
18.0000 g., 0.9250 Silver 0.5353 oz. ASW, 32.5 mm.
Subject: Bertha von Suttner **Obv:** Stylized eagle above stars **Rev:** Suttner's portrait **Edge:** Lettered **Edge Lettering:** "EIPHNH PAX FRIEDEN" twice

Date	Mintage	F	VF	XF	Unc	BU
2005F	1,800,000	—	—	—	18.00	20.00
2005F Proof	300,000	Value: 22.00				

KM# 243   10 EURO
18.0000 g., 0.9250 Silver 0.5353 oz. ASW, 32.5 mm.
Subject: World Cup Soccer **Obv:** Round stylized eagle **Rev:** Ball and legs seen through a net **Edge Lettering:** DIE WELT ZU GAST BEI FREUNDEN

Date	Mintage	F	VF	XF	Unc	BU
2005A	800,000	—	—	—	18.00	20.00
2005A Proof	80,000	Value: 25.00				
2005D	800,000	—	—	—	18.00	20.00
2005D Proof	80,000	Value: 25.00				
2005F	800,000	—	—	—	18.00	20.00
2005F Proof	80,000	Value: 25.00				
2005G	800,000	—	—	—	18.00	20.00
2005G Proof	80,000	Value: 25.00				
2005J	800,000	—	—	—	18.00	20.00
2005J Proof	80,000	Value: 25.00				

KM# 245   10 EURO
18.0000 g., 0.9250 Silver 0.5353 oz. ASW, 32.5 mm. **Subject:** Karl Friedrich Schinkel **Obv:** Stylized eagle **Rev:** Kneeling brick layer **Edge Lettering:** DER MENSCH BILDE SICH IN ALLEM SCHÖN

Date	Mintage	F	VF	XF	Unc	BU
2006F	1,600,000	—	—	—	20.00	22.00
2006F Proof	300,000	Value: 25.00				

KM# 246   10 EURO
18.0000 g., 0.9250 Silver 0.5353 oz. ASW, 32.5 mm.
Subject: Dresden **Obv:** Stylized eagle **Rev:** City view and reflection **Edge Lettering:** 1206 1485 1547 1697 1832 1945 1989 2006

Date	Mintage	F	VF	XF	Unc	BU
2006A	1,600,000	—	—	—	18.00	20.00
2006A Proof	300,000	Value: 22.00				

KM# 247   10 EURO
18.0000 g., 0.9250 Silver 0.5353 oz. ASW, 32.5 mm.
Subject: Hanseatic League **Obv:** Stylized eagle **Rev:** Old sail boat **Edge Lettering:** Wandel durch Handel - von der Hanse nach Europa

Date	Mintage	F	VF	XF	Unc	BU
2006J	1,600,000	—	—	—	18.00	20.00
2006J Proof	300,000	Value: 22.00				

KM# 248   10 EURO
18.0000 g., 0.9250 Silver 0.5353 oz. ASW, 32.5 mm.
Subject: Mozart **Obv:** Stylized eagle, music and denomination above **Rev:** Bust left, dates above **Edge Lettering:** --   MOZART -- DIE WELT HAT EINEN SINN

Date	Mintage	F	VF	XF	Unc	BU
2006D	1,600,000	—	—	—	18.00	20.00
2006D Proof	265,000	Value: 22.00				

KM# 249   10 EURO
18.0000 g., 0.9250 Silver 0.5353 oz. ASW, 32.5 mm.
Subject: World Cup Soccer **Obv:** Stylized eagle **Rev:** Brandenburg Gate on ball on globe **Edge Lettering:** DIE WELT ZU GAST BEI FREUNDEN - ADFGJ **Note:** Mint is determined by which letter "E" in the edge inscription has a short center bar. If the first letter "E" has the short center bar the coin is from the Berlin mint. Second "E"= Munich, third "E"=Stuttgart, fourth "E"=Karlsruhe, fifth "E"=Hamburg

Date	Mintage	F	VF	XF	Unc	BU
2006A	800,000	—	—	—	18.00	20.00
2006A Proof	80,000	Value: 25.00				
2006D	800,000	—	—	—	18.00	20.00
2006D Proof	80,000	Value: 25.00				
2006F	800,000	—	—	—	18.00	20.00
2006F Proof	80,000	Value: 25.00				
2006G	800,000	—	—	—	18.00	20.00
2006G Proof	80,000	Value: 25.00				
2006J	800,000	—	—	—	18.00	20.00
2006J Proof	80,000	Value: 25.00				

KM# 263   10 EURO
18.0000 g., 0.9250 Silver 0.5353 oz. ASW, 32.5 mm.
Subject: Saarland, 50th Anniversary of German control **Obv:** Eagle **Rev:** Modern town view, four stylized heads

Date	Mintage	F	VF	XF	Unc	BU
2007G	1,600,000	—	—	—	20.00	22.00
2007G Proof	300,000	Value: 30.00				

KM# 264   10 EURO
18.0000 g., 0.9250 Silver 0.5353 oz. ASW, 32.5 mm.
Subject: Treaty of Rome, 50th Anniversary **Obv:** Eagle **Rev:** Map of Central Europe and stars

Date	Mintage	F	VF	XF	Unc	BU
2007F	1,600,000	—	—	—	20.00	22.00
2007F Proof	300,000	Value: 30.00				

KM# 265   10 EURO
18.0000 g., 0.9250 Silver 0.5353 oz. ASW, 32.5 mm.
Subject: Wilhelm Busch, 175th Anniversary of Birth **Obv:** Eagle within square **Rev:** Portrait of Busch, characters Helene, Max and Moritz flanking

Date	Mintage	F	VF	XF	Unc	BU
2007D	1,600,000	—	—	—	20.00	22.00
2007D	300,000	Value: 30.00				

KM# 266   10 EURO
18.0000 g., 0.9250 Silver 0.5353 oz. ASW, 32.5 mm.
Subject: Deutsche Bundesbank, 50th Aniversary **Obv:** Eagle on rectangle design **Rev:** Buildings on graph

Date	Mintage	F	VF	XF	Unc	BU
2007J	1,600,000	—	—	—	20.00	22.00
2007J Proof	300,000	Value: 30.00				

KM# 268   10 EURO
18.0000 g., 0.9250 Silver 0.5353 oz. ASW, 32.5 mm.
Subject: Eagle **Rev:** St. Elisabeth von Thuringen

Date	Mintage	F	VF	XF	Unc	BU
2007A	150,000	—	—	—	20.00	22.00
2007A	70,000	Value: 30.00				

KM# 271   10 EURO
18.0000 g., 0.9250 Silver 0.5353 oz. ASW, 32.5 mm.
Subject: Franz Kafka, 125th Anniversary of Birth **Obv:** Eagle **Rev:** Prague Cathedral, writings & portrait **Edge Lettering:** EIN KÄFIG GING EINEN VOGEL SUCHENS

Date	Mintage	F	VF	XF	Unc	BU
2008G	500,000	—	—	—	20.00	22.00
2008G Proof	260,000	Value: 30.00				

KM# 272   10 EURO
18.0000 g., 0.9250 Silver 0.5353 oz. ASW, 32.5 mm.
Subject: Max Planck, 150th Anniversary of Birth **Obv:** Eagle **Rev:** Graph and portrait **Edge Lettering:** DEM ANWENDEN MUSS DAS + ERENNEN VORAUSGEHEN

Date	Mintage	F	VF	XF	Unc	BU
2008F	1,500,000	—	—	—	20.00	22.00
2008F Proof	260,000	Value: 30.00				

KM# 273   10 EURO
18.0000 g., 0.9250 Silver 0.5353 oz. ASW **Subject:** Carl Spitzweg - 200th Anniversary of Birth **Obv:** Eagle **Rev:** Spitzweg reclining in bed with books, umbrella above **Edge Lettering:** ACH, DIE VERGANGENHEIT IST SCHÖN **Shape:** 32.5

Date	Mintage	F	VF	XF	Unc	BU
2008D	1,500,000	—	—	—	20.00	22.00
2008D Proof	260,000	Value: 30.00				

KM# 274   10 EURO
18.0000 g., 0.9250 Silver 0.5353 oz. ASW, 32.5 mm. **Subject:** Gorch Fock II, 50th Anniversary **Obv:** Eagle **Rev:** Naval training sailing ship Gorch Fock II **Edge Lettering:** SEEFAHRT 1ST NOT

Date	Mintage	F	VF	XF	Unc	BU
2008J	—	—	—	—	20.00	22.00
2008J Proof	—	Value: 30.00				

KM# 279   10 EURO
18.0000 g., 0.9250 Silver 0.5353 oz. ASW, 32.5 mm.
Subject: IAAF World Championships - Berlin **Obv:** Eagle and value **Rev:** Female javelin thrower in stadium

Date	Mintage	F	VF	XF	Unc	BU
2009A	—	—	—	—	20.00	18.00
2009A Proof	—	Value: 25.00				
2009D	—	—	—	—	20.00	18.00
2009D Proof	—	Value: 25.00				
2009F	—	—	—	—	20.00	18.00
2009F Proof	—	Value: 25.00				
2009G	—	—	—	—	20.00	18.00
2009G Proof	—	Value: 25.00				
2009J	—	—	—	—	20.00	18.00
2009J Proof	—	Value: 25.00				

KM# 280   10 EURO
18.0000 g., 0.9250 Silver 0.5353 oz. ASW, 32.5 mm. **Subject:** Kepler's laws - 400th Anniversary **Obv:** Eagle above value **Rev:** Portrait and geometric diagram demonstrating planetary orbits

Date	Mintage	F	VF	XF	Unc	BU
2009G	1,500,000	—	—	—	18.00	20.00
2009G Proof	200,000	Value: 25.00				

KM# 281   10 EURO
18.0000 g., 0.9250 Silver 0.5353 oz. ASW, 32.5 mm. **Subject:** International Aerospace Expo 100th Anniversary **Obv:** Eagle above value **Rev:** Plane landing, montage of plane development

Date	Mintage	F	VF	XF	Unc	BU
2009G	1,500,000	—	—	—	18.00	20.00
2009G Proof	200,000	Value: 25.00				

KM# 282   10 EURO
18.0000 g., 0.9250 Silver 0.5353 oz. ASW, 32.5 mm. **Subject:** Leipzig University - 600th Anniversary **Obv:** Eagle above value **Rev:** University seal, portrait of Gottfried Wilhelm Leibniz

Date	Mintage	F	VF	XF	Unc	BU
2009A	15,000,000	—	—	—	18.00	20.00
2009G Proof	200,000	Value: 25.00				

KM# 281a   10 EURO
18.0000 g., 0.9250 Silver partially gilt 0.5353 oz. ASW, 32.5 mm. **Subject:** International air travel, 100 Anniversary **Obv:** Stylized eagle **Rev:** Airplanes, partially gilt

Date	Mintage	F	VF	XF	Unc	BU
2009D Proof	10,000	Value: 50.00				

KM# 284   10 EURO
18.0000 g., 0.9250 Silver 0.5353 oz. ASW, 32.5 mm. **Subject:** Marion Countess Donhoff - 100th Anniversary of Birth **Obv:** Eagle and value **Rev:** Profile right

Date	Mintage	F	VF	XF	Unc	BU
2009J	1,500,000	—	—	—	18.00	20.00
2009J Proof	200,000	Value: 25.00				

KM# 283   10 EURO
18.0000 g., 0.9250 Silver 0.5353 oz. ASW, 32.5 mm. **Subject:** Youth hostels - 100th Anniversary **Obv:** Eagle and value **Rev:** Stylized mountain, Alternal hostel in Westphalia

Date	Mintage	F	VF	XF	Unc	BU
2009G	1,500,000	—	—	—	20.00	18.00
2009G Proof	200,000	Value: 25.00				

KM# 287   10 EURO
18.0000 g., 0.9250 Silver 0.5353 oz. ASW, 32.5 mm. **Subject:** Porcelain Production, 300th Anniversary

Date	Mintage	F	VF	XF	Unc	BU
2010G Proof	200,000	Value: 20.00				
2010G	1,500,000	—	—	—	—	15.00

KM# 288   10 EURO
18.0000 g., 0.9250 Silver 0.5353 oz. ASW, 32.5 mm. **Subject:** Robert Schumann - 200th Birth Anniversary

Date	Mintage	F	VF	XF	Unc	BU
2010G	1,500,000	—	—	—	—	15.00
2010G Proof	200,000	Value: 20.00				

KM# 289   10 EURO
18.0000 g., 0.9250 Silver 0.5353 oz. ASW, 32.5 mm. **Subject:** Konrad Zuse, 100th Birth Anniversary

Date	Mintage	F	VF	XF	Unc	BU
2010	1,500,000	—	—	—	—	15.00
2010 Proof	200,000	Value: 20.00				

KM# 290   10 EURO
18.0000 g., 0.9250 Silver 0.5353 oz. ASW, 32.5 mm. **Subject:** German Unification, 20th Anniversary

Date	Mintage	F	VF	XF	Unc	BU
2010	1,500,000	—	—	—	—	15.00
2010 Proof	200,000	Value: 20.00				

KM# 220   100 EURO
15.5500 g., 0.9990 Gold 0.4994 oz. AGW, 28 mm. **Subject:** Introduction of the Euro Currency **Obv:** Stylized round eagle **Rev:** Euro symbol and arches **Edge:** Reeded

Date	Mintage	F	VF	XF	Unc	BU
2002A Proof	100,000	Value: 650				
2002D Proof	100,000	Value: 650				
2002F Proof	100,000	Value: 650				
2002G Proof	100,000	Value: 650				
2002J Proof	100,000	Value: 650				

KM# 228   100 EURO
15.5000 g., 0.9999 Gold 0.4983 oz. AGW, 28 mm. **Obv:** Stylized eagle, denomination below **Rev:** Quedlinburg Abbey in monogram **Edge:** Reeded

Date	Mintage	F	VF	XF	Unc	BU
2003A Proof	100,000	Value: 650				
2003D Proof	100,000	Value: 650				
2003F Proof	100,000	Value: 650				
2003G Proof	100,000	Value: 650				
2003J Proof	100,000	Value: 650				

KM# 235   100 EURO
15.5500 g., 0.9999 Gold 0.4999 oz. AGW, 28 mm. **Obv:** Stylized eagle, denomination below **Rev:** Bamberg city view **Edge:** Reeded

Date	Mintage	F	VF	XF	Unc	BU
2004A Proof	80,000	Value: 650				
2004D Proof	80,000	Value: 650				
2004F Proof	80,000	Value: 650				
2004G Proof	80,000	Value: 650				
2004J Proof	80,000	Value: 650				

KM# 236   100 EURO
15.5500 g., 0.9990 Gold 0.4994 oz. AGW **Subject:** UNESCO - Weimar **Obv:** Stylized eagle **Rev:** Historical City of Weimar buildings **Edge:** Reeded

Date	Mintage	F	VF	XF	Unc	BU
2006A Proof	80,000	Value: 650				
2006D Proof	80,000	Value: 650				
2006F Proof	80,000	Value: 650				
2006G Proof	80,000	Value: 650				
2006J Proof	80,000	Value: 650				

KM# 237   100 EURO
15.5500 g., 0.9990 Gold 0.4994 oz. AGW, 28 mm. **Subject:** Soccer - Germany 2006 **Obv:** Round stylized eagle **Rev:** Aerial view of stadium

Date	Mintage	F	VF	XF	Unc	BU
2005A Proof	70,000	Value: 650				
2005D Proof	70,000	Value: 650				
2005F Proof	70,000	Value: 650				
2005G Proof	70,000	Value: 650				
2005J Proof	70,000	Value: 650				

KM# 267   100 EURO
15.5500 g., 0.9990 Gold 0.4994 oz. AGW, 28 mm. **Subject:** UNESCO City - Lubeck **Obv:** Eagle **Rev:** City view

Date	Mintage	F	VF	XF	Unc	BU
2007A	70,000	Value: 650				
2007D	70,000	Value: 650				
2007F	70,000	Value: 650				
2007G	70,000	Value: 650				
2007J	70,000	Value: 650				

KM# 270   100 EURO
15.5500 g., 0.9990 Gold 0.4994 oz. AGW, 28 mm. **Subject:** UNESCO - Goslar **Obv:** Eagle **Edge:** Reeded

Date	Mintage	F	VF	XF	Unc	BU
2008A	64,000	Value: 650				
2008D	64,000	Value: 650				
2008F	64,000	Value: 650				
2008G	64,000	Value: 650				
2008J	64,000	Value: 650				

KM# 278   100 EURO
15.5000 g., 0.9990 Gold 0.4978 oz. AGW, 28 mm. **Subject:** Trier - Unesco Heritage Site **Obv:** Eagle and denomination **Rev:** Riverside montage of buildings **Edge:** Reeded

Date	Mintage	F	VF	XF	Unc	BU
2009D Proof	100,000	Value: 650				
2009F Proof	100,000	Value: 650				
2009G Proof	100,000	Value: 650				
2009J Proof	100,000	Value: 650				
2009A Proof	100,000	Value: 650				

KM# 286   100 EURO
15.5500 g., 0.9990 Gold 0.4994 oz. AGW, 28 mm. **Subject:** Wurzburg residence and court garden - Unesco site

Date	Mintage	F	VF	XF	Unc	BU
2010A Proof	—	Value: 650				
2010D Proof	—	Value: 650				
2010F Proof	—	Value: 650				
2010G Proof	—	Value: 650				
2010J Proof	—	Value: 650				

KM# 221   200 EURO
31.1000 g., 0.9990 Gold 0.9988 oz. AGW, 32.5 mm. **Subject:** Introduction of the Euro Currency **Obv:** Stylized round eagle **Rev:** Euro symbol and arches **Edge Lettering:** IM...ZEICHEN...DER...EINIGUNG...EUROPAS

Date	Mintage	F	VF	XF	Unc	BU
2002A Proof	20,000	Value: 1,350				
2002D Proof	20,000	Value: 1,350				
2002F Proof	20,000	Value: 1,350				
2002G Proof	20,000	Value: 1,350				
2002J Proof	20,000	Value: 1,350				

MINT SETS

KM#	Date	Mintage	Identification	Issue Price	Mkt Val
MS119	2001A (10)	130,000	KM105,106a,107-108,109.2,110,140.1,170,175,183	—	40.00
MS120	2001D (10)	130,000	KM105,106a,107-108,109.2,110,140.1,170,175,183	—	40.00
MS121	2001F (10)	130,000	KM105,106a,107-108, 109.2,110,140.1,170,175,183	—	40.00
MS122	2001G (10)	130,000	KM105,106a,107-108,109.2,110,140.1,170,175,183	—	40.00
MS123	2001J (10)	130,000	KM105,106a,107-108,109.2,110,140.1,170,175,183	—	40.00
MS124	2002A (8)	145,000	KM#207-214	—	20.00
MS125	2002D (8)	145,000	KM#207-214	—	20.00
MS126	2002F (8)	145,000	KM#207-214	—	20.00
MS127	2002G (8)	145,000	KM#207-214	—	20.00
MS128	2002J (8)	145,000	KM#207-214	—	20.00
MS129	2003A (8)	180,000	KM#207-214	—	20.00
MS130	2003D (8)	180,000	KM#207-214	—	20.00
MS131	2003F (8)	180,000	KM#207-214	—	20.00
MS132	2003G (8)	180,000	KM#207-214	—	20.00
MS133	2003J (8)	180,000	KM#207-214	—	20.00
MS134	2004A (8)	—	KM#207-214	—	20.00
MS135	2004D (8)	—	KM#207-214	—	20.00
MS136	2004F (8)	—	KM#207-214	—	20.00
MS137	2004G (8)	—	KM#207-214	—	20.00
MS138	2004J (8)	—	KM#207-214	—	20.00
MS139	2005A (8)	—	KM#207-214	—	25.00
MS140	2005D (8)	—	KM#207-214	—	25.00
MS141	2005F (8)	—	KM#207-214	—	25.00
MS142	2005G (8)	—	KM#207-214	—	25.00
MS143	2005J (8)	—	KM#207-214	—	25.00

PROOF SETS

KM#	Date	Mintage	Identification	Issue Price	Mkt Val
PS150	2001A (10)	78,000	KM105,106a,107-108,109.2,110,140.1,170,175,183	—	110
PS151	2001D (10)	78,000	KM105,106a,107-108,109.2,110,140.1,170,175,183	—	110
PS152	2001F (10)	78,000	KM105,106a,107-108, 110, 140.1,170,175,183	—	110
PS153	2001G (10)	78,000	KM105,106a,107-108, 109.2,110,140.1,170,175,183	—	110
PS154	2001J (10)	78,000	KM105,106a,107-108, 109.2,110,140.1,170,175,183	—	110
PS155	2002A (8)	130,000	KM#207-214	—	35.00
PS156	2002D (8)	130,000	KM#207-214	—	35.00
PS157	2002F (8)	130,000	KM#207-214	—	35.00
PS158	2002G (8)	130,000	KM#207-214	—	35.00
PS159	2002J (8)	130,000	KM#207-214	—	35.00
PS160	2003A (8)	150,000	KM#207-214	—	35.00
PS161	2003D (8)	150,000	KM#207-214	—	35.00
PS162	2003F (8)	150,000	KM#207-214	—	35.00
PS163	2003G (8)	150,000	KM#207-214	—	35.00
PS164	2003J (8)	150,000	KM#207-214	—	35.00
PS165	2004A (8)	—	KM#207-214	—	35.00
PS166	2004D (8)	—	KM#207-214	—	35.00
PS167	2004F (8)	—	KM#207-214	—	35.00
PS168	2004G (8)	—	KM#207-214	—	35.00
PS169	2004J (8)	—	KM#207-214	—	35.00
PS170	2005A (8)	—	KM#207-214	—	30.00
PS171	2005D (8)	—	KM#207-214	—	30.00
PS172	2005F (8)	—	KM#207-214	—	30.00
PS173	2005G (8)	—	KM#207-214	—	30.00
PS174	2005J (8)	—	KM#207-214	—	30.00

GHANA

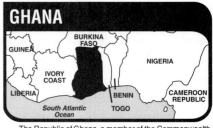

The Republic of Ghana, a member of the Commonwealth of Nations situated on the West Coast of Africa between Ivory Coast and Togo, has an area of 92,100 sq. mi. (238,540 sq. km.) and a population of 14 million, almost entirely African. Capital: Accra. Cocoa (the major crop), coconuts, palm kernels and coffee are exported. Mining, second in importance to agriculture, is concentrated on gold, manganese and industrial diamonds.

MONETARY SYSTEM
1 Cedi = 100 Pesewas, 1965-2007
1 (new) Cedi = 10,000 (old) Cedis, 2007-

REPUBLIC
DECIMAL COINAGE

KM# 36   10 CEDIS
4.4100 g., Copper-Nickel, 22.9 mm. **Obv:** National arms divides date and denomination **Rev:** Gorilla family **Edge:** Plain

Date	Mintage	F	VF	XF	Unc	BU
2003	—	—	—	—	1.50	2.00

REFORM COINAGE
2007-

KM# 37   PESEWA
1.8200 g., Copper Clad Steel, 17 mm. **Obv:** National arms **Obv. Legend:** GHANA **Rev:** Modern arch bridge **Edge:** Plain

Date	Mintage	F	VF	XF	Unc	BU
2007	—	—	—	—	—	0.75

KM# 38   5 PESEWAS
2.5000 g., Nickel Clad Steel, 18 mm. **Obv:** National arms **Obv. Legend:** GHANA **Rev:** Native male blowing horn **Edge:** Plain

Date	Mintage	F	VF	XF	Unc	BU
2007	—	—	—	—	—	1.25

KM# 39 10 PESEWAS
3.2300 g., Nickel Clad Steel, 20.4 mm. **Obv:** National arms
Obv. Legend: GHANA **Rev:** Open book, pen **Edge:** Reeded

Date	Mintage	F	VF	XF	Unc	BU
2007	—	—	—	—	—	2.50

KM# 40 20 PESEWAS
4.4000 g., Nickel Clad Steel, 23.5 mm. **Obv:** National arms
Obv. Legend: GHANA **Rev:** Split open fruit **Edge:** Plain

Date	Mintage	F	VF	XF	Unc	BU
2007	—	—	—	—	—	3.50

KM# 41 50 PESEWAS
6.0800 g., Nickel Clad Steel, 26.4 mm. **Obv:** National arms
Obv. Legend: GHANA **Rev:** 1/2 length figure of native woman
facing **Edge:** Reeded

Date	Mintage	F	VF	XF	Unc	BU
2007	—	—	—	—	—	6.00

KM# 42 CEDI
7.4000 g., Bi-Metallic Brass center in Nickel Clad Steel ring,
28 mm. **Obv:** National arms **Obv. Legend:** GHANA
Rev: Balance scale in sprays **Edge:** Segmented reeding

Date	Mintage	F	VF	XF	Unc	BU
2007	—	—	—	—	—	10.00

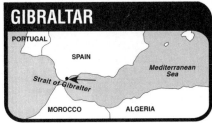

GIBRALTAR

The British Colony of Gibraltar, located at the southernmost
point of the Iberian Peninsula, has an area of 2.25 sq. mi. (6.5 sq.
km.) and a population of 29,651. Capital (and main town): Gibraltar. Aside from its strategic importance as guardian of the western
entrance to the Mediterranean Sea, Gibraltar is also a free port
and a British naval base.

RULERS
British

MINT MARKS
PM - Pobjoy Mint
PMM – Pobjoy Mint (only appears on coins dated 2000)

**NOTE: ALL coins for 1988 –2003 include the PM mint mark
except the 2000 dated circulation pieces which instead
have PMM.**

MINT PRIVY MARKS
U - Unc finish

MONETARY SYSTEM
100 Pence = 1 Pound

BRITISH COLONY

DECIMAL COINAGE
100 Pence = 1 Pound

KM# 773 PENNY
3.5200 g., Bronze Plated Steel, 20.4 mm. **Ruler:** Elizabeth II
Obv: Head with tiara right **Obv. Designer:** Ian Rank-Broadley
Rev: Barbary partridge left divides denomination

Date	Mintage	F	VF	XF	Unc	BU
2001 AA	—	—	—	—	0.35	0.50
2002 AA	—	—	—	—	0.35	0.50
2003 AA	—	—	—	—	0.35	0.50

KM# 1046 PENNY
3.5400 g., Copper Plated Steel, 20.02 mm. **Ruler:** Elizabeth II
Subject: 300th Anniversary **Obv:** Crowned bust right
Obv. Designer: Raphael Maklouf **Rev:** Monkey **Rev. Designer:**
Philip Nathan **Edge:** Plain

Date	Mintage	F	VF	XF	Unc	BU
2004	—	—	—	—	0.30	0.50

KM# 774 2 PENCE
Bronze Plated Steel, 20.4 mm. **Ruler:** Elizabeth II **Obv:** Head
with tiara right **Obv. Designer:** Ian Rank-Broadley

Date	Mintage	F	VF	XF	Unc	BU
2001 AA	—	—	—	—	0.50	0.85
2001PM AB	—	—	—	—	0.50	0.85

KM# 1044 2 PENCE
7.0400 g., Copper Plated Steel, 25.4 mm. **Ruler:** Elizabeth II
Subject: 300th Anniversary **Obv:** Crowned bust right
Obv. Designer: Ralphael Maklouf **Rev:** Four old keys
Rev. Designer: Philip Nathan **Edge:** Plain

Date	Mintage	F	VF	XF	Unc	BU
2004	—	—	—	—	0.50	0.65

KM# 1065 2 PENCE
7.2000 g., Copper Plated Steel, 25.9 mm. **Ruler:** Elizabeth II
Subject: Operation torch, 1942

Date	Mintage	F	VF	XF	Unc	BU
2007	—	—	—	—	—	3.00

KM# 775 5 PENCE
3.1000 g., Copper-Nickel, 18 mm. **Ruler:** Elizabeth II **Obv:** Head
with tiara right **Obv. Designer:** Ian Rank-Broadley **Rev:** Barbary
Ape left divides denomination

Date	Mintage	F	VF	XF	Unc	BU
2001	—	—	—	—	0.60	0.75

KM# 1049 5 PENCE
3.2500 g., Copper-Nickel, 18 mm. **Ruler:** Elizabeth II
Subject: Tercentenary 1704-2004 **Obv:** Elizabeth II
Obv. Designer: Raphael Maklouf **Rev:** British Royal Sceptre
Rev. Designer: Philip Nathan **Edge:** Reeded

Date	Mintage	F	VF	XF	Unc	BU
2004PM	—	—	—	—	—	1.50

KM# 776 10 PENCE
6.5000 g., Copper-Nickel, 24.5 mm. **Ruler:** Elizabeth II
Obv: Head with tiara right, date below **Obv. Designer:** Ian
Rank-Broadley **Rev:** Denomination below building

Date	Mintage	F	VF	XF	Unc	BU
2001	—	—	—	—	1.00	1.25

KM# 1047 10 PENCE
6.4200 g., Copper-Nickel, 24.4 mm. **Ruler:** Elizabeth II
Subject: 300th Anniversary **Obv:** Elizabeth II **Obv. Designer:**
Raphael Maklouf **Rev:** Three military officers planning Operation
Torch 1942 **Rev. Designer:** Philip Nathan **Edge:** Reeded

Date	Mintage	F	VF	XF	Unc	BU
2004	—	—	—	—	0.75	1.00

KM# 777 20 PENCE
5.0000 g., Copper-Nickel, 21.4 mm. **Ruler:** Elizabeth II
Obv: Head with tiara right, date below **Obv. Designer:** Ian Rank-
Broadley **Rev:** Our Lady of Europa, denomination below and right
Rev. Designer: Alfred Ryman **Shape:** 7-sided

Date	Mintage	F	VF	XF	Unc	BU
2001 AA	—	—	—	—	1.50	2.00

KM# 1048 20 PENCE
4.9400 g., Copper-Nickel, 21.4 mm. **Ruler:** Elizabeth II
Subject: 300th Anniversary **Obv:** Crowned buat right
Obv. Designer: Raphael Maklouf **Rev:** Neanderthal skull found
in Gibraltar in 1848 **Rev. Designer:** Philip Nathan **Edge:** Plain
Shape: 7-sided

Date	Mintage	F	VF	XF	Unc	BU
2004	—	—	—	—	1.00	1.50

KM# 971 50 PENCE
8.0000 g., Copper-Nickel, 27.3 mm. **Ruler:** Elizabeth II
Subject: Christmas **Obv:** Head with tiara right, date below
Obv. Designer: Ian Rank-Broadley **Rev:** Three wise men
Edge: Plain **Shape:** 7-sided

Date	Mintage	F	VF	XF	Unc	BU
2001 BB	30,000	—	—	—	10.00	12.00

KM# 971a 50 PENCE
8.0000 g., 0.9250 Silver 0.2379 oz. ASW, 27.3 mm.
Ruler: Elizabeth II **Obv:** Head with tiara right, date below
Obv. Designer: Ian Rank-Broadley **Rev:** Three wise men
Edge: Plain **Shape:** 7-sided

Date	Mintage	F	VF	XF	Unc	BU
2001 Proof	5,000	Value: 35.00				

KM# 971b 50 PENCE
8.0000 g., 0.9167 Gold 0.2358 oz. AGW, 27.3 mm.
Ruler: Elizabeth II **Obv:** Head with tiara right, date below
Obv. Designer: Ian Rank-Broadley **Rev:** Three wise men
Edge: Plain **Shape:** 7-sided

Date	Mintage	F	VF	XF	Unc	BU
2001 Proof	250	Value: 645				

KM# 778 50 PENCE
8.0000 g., Copper-Nickel, 27.3 mm. **Ruler:** Elizabeth II
Obv: Head with tiara right **Obv. Designer:** Ian Rank-Broadley
Rev: Dolphins surround denomination **Edge:** Plain
Shape: 7-sided

Date	Mintage	F	VF	XF	Unc	BU
2001 AA	—	—	—	—	4.50	5.50
2001 AB	—	—	—	—	4.50	5.50

KM# 1026 50 PENCE
8.0000 g., Copper-Nickel, 27.3 mm. **Ruler:** Elizabeth II **Subject:** Christmas **Obv:** Head with tiara right, date below **Obv. Designer:** Ian Rank-Broadley **Rev:** Shepherds **Edge:** Plain **Shape:** 7-sided

Date	Mintage	F	VF	XF	Unc	BU
2002PM BB	30,000	—	—	—	10.00	12.00

KM# 1026a 50 PENCE
8.0000 g., 0.9250 Silver 0.2379 oz. ASW, 27.3 mm. **Ruler:** Elizabeth II **Subject:** Christmas **Obv:** Head with tiara right, date below **Obv. Designer:** Ian Rank-Broadley **Rev:** Two Shepherds **Edge:** Plain **Shape:** 7-sided

Date	Mintage	F	VF	XF	Unc	BU
2002PM Proof	2,002	Value: 35.00				

KM# 1063a 50 PENCE
8.0000 g., 0.9250 Silver 0.2379 oz. ASW, 27.3 mm. **Ruler:** Elizabeth II **Subject:** Christmas **Obv. Designer:** Ian Rank-Broadley **Rev:** Joseph & Mary

Date	Mintage	F	VF	XF	Unc	BU
2003PM BB	—	—	—	—	10.00	12.00

KM# 1063 50 PENCE
8.0000 g., Copper-Nickel **Ruler:** Elizabeth II **Series:** Christmas **Obv:** Head with tiara right, date below **Obv. Designer:** Ian Rank-Broadley **Rev:** Joseph & Mary **Shape:** 27.3

Date	Mintage	F	VF	XF	Unc	BU
2003PM BB	—	—	—	—	10.00	12.00

KM# 1050 50 PENCE
8.0000 g., Copper-Nickel, 27.3 mm. **Ruler:** Elizabeth II **Subject:** Tercentenary 1704-2004 **Obv:** Elizabeth II **Obv. Designer:** Raphael Maklouf **Rev:** HMS Victory sailing past Gibraltar **Rev. Designer:** Philip Nathan **Edge:** Plain **Shape:** Seven sided

Date	Mintage	F	VF	XF	Unc	BU
2004PM	—	—	—	—	—	3.00

KM# 1066 50 PENCE
8.0000 g., Copper-Nickel, 27.3 mm. **Ruler:** Elizabeth II **Subject:** Christmas **Shape:** 7-sided

Date	Mintage	F	VF	XF	Unc	BU
2004	—	—	—	—	10.00	12.00

KM# 1067 50 PENCE
8.0000 g., Copper-Nickel, 27.3 mm. **Ruler:** Elizabeth II **Subject:** Christmas **Shape:** 7-sided

Date	Mintage	F	VF	XF	Unc	BU
2005	—	—	—	—	10.00	12.00

KM# 1068 50 PENCE
8.0000 g., Copper-Nickel, 27.3 mm. **Ruler:** Elizabeth II **Subject:** Christmas **Shape:** 7-sided

Date	Mintage	F	VF	XF	Unc	BU
2006	—	—	—	—	10.00	12.00

KM# 1069 50 PENCE
8.0000 g., Copper-Nickel, 27.3 mm. **Ruler:** Elizabeth II **Subject:** Christmas **Shape:** 7-sided

Date	Mintage	F	VF	XF	Unc	BU
2007	—	—	—	—	10.00	12.00

KM# 1070 50 PENCE
8.0000 g., Copper-Nickel, 27.3 mm. **Ruler:** Elizabeth II **Subject:** Christmas **Shape:** 7-sided

Date	Mintage	F	VF	XF	Unc	BU
2008	—	—	—	—	10.00	12.00

KM# 1071 50 PENCE
8.0000 g., Copper-Nickel, 27.3 mm. **Ruler:** Elizabeth II **Subject:** Christmas **Shape:** 7-sided

Date	Mintage	F	VF	XF	Unc	BU
2009	—	—	—	—	10.00	12.00

KM# 988 1/25 CROWN
1.2240 g., 0.9990 Gold 0.0393 oz. AGW, 13.92 mm. **Ruler:** Elizabeth II **Subject:** Peter Rabbit Centennial **Obv:** Crowned bust right **Rev:** Peter Rabbit **Edge:** Reeded

Date	Mintage	F	VF	XF	Unc	BU
2002 Proof	5,000	Value: 60.00				

KM# 988a 1/25 CROWN
1.2240 g., 0.9990 Platinum 0.0393 oz. APW, 13.92 mm. **Ruler:** Elizabeth II **Subject:** Peter Rabbit Centennial **Obv:** Crowned bust right **Rev:** Peter Rabbit **Edge:** Reeded

Date	Mintage	F	VF	XF	Unc	BU
2002 Proof	3,000	Value: 95.00				

KM# 1016 1/25 CROWN
1.2441 g., 0.9999 Gold 0.0400 oz. AGW, 13.92 mm. **Ruler:** Elizabeth II **Subject:** Peter Pan **Obv:** Crowned bust right **Rev:** Peter Pan and Tinkerbell flying above city **Edge:** Reeded

Date	Mintage	F	VF	XF	Unc	BU
2002 Proof	10,000	Value: 55.00				

KM# 989 1/10 CROWN
3.1100 g., 0.9990 Gold 0.0999 oz. AGW, 17.95 mm. **Ruler:** Elizabeth II **Subject:** Peter Rabbit Centennial **Obv:** Crowned bust right **Rev:** Peter Rabbit **Edge:** Reeded

Date	Mintage	F	VF	XF	Unc	BU
2002 Proof	5,000	Value: 125				

KM# 989a 1/10 CROWN
3.1100 g., 0.9990 Platinum 0.0999 oz. APW, 17395 mm. **Ruler:** Elizabeth II **Subject:** Peter Rabbit Centennial **Obv:** Crowned bust right **Rev:** Peter Rabbit **Edge:** Reeded

Date	Mintage	F	VF	XF	Unc	BU
2002 Proof	2,000	Value: 225				

KM# 1017 1/10 CROWN
3.1104 g., 0.9999 Gold 0.1000 oz. AGW, 17.95 mm. **Ruler:** Elizabeth II **Subject:** Peter Pan **Obv:** Crowned bust right **Rev:** Peter Pan and Tinkerbell flying above city **Edge:** Reeded

Date	Mintage	F	VF	XF	Unc	BU
2002 Proof	7,500	Value: 125				

KM# 902 1/5 CROWN
6.2200 g., 0.9999 Gold 0.1999 oz. AGW, 22 mm. **Ruler:** Elizabeth II **Subject:** Queen Mother **Obv:** Bust with tiara right **Obv. Designer:** Ian Rank-Broadley **Rev:** 1953 Coronation scene **Edge:** Reeded

Date	Mintage	F	VF	XF	Unc	BU
2001 Proof	5,000	Value: 250				

KM# 903 1/5 CROWN
6.2200 g., 0.9999 Gold 0.1999 oz. AGW **Ruler:** Elizabeth II **Obv:** Bust with tiara right **Obv. Designer:** Ian Rank-Broadley **Rev:** Queen Mother and Prince Charles in 1954

Date	Mintage	F	VF	XF	Unc	BU
2001 Proof	5,000	Value: 250				

KM# 909 1/5 CROWN
6.2200 g., 0.9999 Gold 0.1999 oz. AGW, 22 mm. **Ruler:** Elizabeth II **Series:** Victorian Era - Victoria's Coronation 1838 **Obv:** Bust with tiara right **Obv. Designer:** Ian Rank-Broadley **Rev:** 1838 Coronation scene **Edge:** Reeded

Date	Mintage	F	VF	XF	Unc	BU
2001 Proof	5,000	Value: 250				

KM# 909.1 1/5 CROWN
6.2200 g., 0.9999 Gold 0.1999 oz. AGW, 22 mm. **Ruler:** Elizabeth II **Series:** Victorian Era **Obv:** Bust with tiara right **Obv. Designer:** Ian Rank-Broadley **Rev:** 1838 Coronation scene with a tiny emerald set in the field below the 1838 date **Edge:** Reeded

Date	Mintage	F	VF	XF	Unc	BU
2001 Proof	2,001	Value: 260				

KM# 911.1 1/5 CROWN
6.2200 g., 0.9999 Gold 0.1999 oz. AGW, 22 mm. **Ruler:** Elizabeth II **Series:** Victorian Era - Empress of India 1876 **Obv:** Bust with tiara right **Obv. Designer:** Ian Rank-Broadley **Rev:** Crowned portrait of Victoria and two elephants **Edge:** Reeded

Date	Mintage	F	VF	XF	Unc	BU
2001 Proof	5,000	Value: 250				

KM# 911.2 1/5 CROWN
6.2200 g., 0.9999 Gold 0.1999 oz. AGW, 22 mm. **Ruler:** Elizabeth II **Series:** Victorian Era - Empress of India 1876 **Obv:** Bust with tiara right **Obv. Designer:** Ian Rank-Broadley **Rev:** Tiny ruby set in the field behind Victoria's head **Edge:** Reeded

Date	Mintage	F	VF	XF	Unc	BU
2001 Proof	2,001	Value: 260				

KM# 913.1 1/5 CROWN
6.2200 g., 0.9999 Gold 0.1999 oz. AGW, 22 mm. **Ruler:** Elizabeth II **Series:** Victorian Era - Diamond Jubilee 1897 **Obv:** Bust with tiara right **Obv. Designer:** Ian Rank-Broadley **Rev:** Victoria's cameo portrait above naval ships **Edge:** Reeded

Date	Mintage	F	VF	XF	Unc	BU
2001 Proof	5,000	Value: 250				

KM# 913.2 1/5 CROWN
6.2200 g., 0.9999 Gold 0.1999 oz. AGW, 22 mm. **Ruler:** Elizabeth II **Series:** Victorian Era - Diamond Jubilee 1897 **Obv:** Bust with tiara right **Obv. Designer:** Ian Rank-Broadley **Rev:** Tiny diamond set at the top of the fourth mast **Edge:** Reeded

Date	Mintage	F	VF	XF	Unc	BU
2001 Proof	2,001	Value: 260				

KM# 915.1 1/5 CROWN
6.2200 g., 0.9999 Gold 0.1999 oz. AGW, 22 mm. **Ruler:** Elizabeth II **Series:** Victorian Era - Victoria's Death 1901 **Obv:** Bust with tiara right **Obv. Designer:** Ian Rank-Broadley **Rev:** Victoria's cameo portrait and Osborne Manor **Edge:** Reeded

Date	Mintage	F	VF	XF	Unc	BU
2001 Proof	5,000	Value: 250				

KM# 915.2 1/5 CROWN
6.2200 g., 0.9999 Gold 0.1999 oz. AGW, 22 mm. **Ruler:** Elizabeth II **Series:** Victorian Era - Victoria's Death 1901 **Obv:** Bust with tiara right **Obv. Designer:** Ian Rank-Broadley **Rev:** Tiny sapphire set in the field between the towers **Edge:** Reeded

Date	Mintage	F	VF	XF	Unc	BU
2001 Proof	2,001	Value: 260				

KM# 917 1/5 CROWN
6.2200 g., 0.9999 Gold 0.1999 oz. AGW, 22 mm. **Ruler:** Elizabeth II **Series:** Victorian Era - Prince Albert and the Great Exhibition 1851 **Obv:** Bust with tiara right **Obv. Designer:** Ian Rank-Broadley **Rev:** Albert's cameo portrait and the exhibit hall **Edge:** Reeded

Date	Mintage	F	VF	XF	Unc	BU
2001 Proof	5,000	Value: 250				

KM# 919 1/5 CROWN
6.2200 g., 0.9999 Gold 0.1999 oz. AGW, 22 mm. **Ruler:** Elizabeth II **Series:** Victorian Era - Isambard K. Brunel **Obv:** Bust with tiara right **Obv. Designer:** Ian Rank-Broadley **Rev:** Portrait in top hat and railroad bridge **Edge:** Reeded

Date	Mintage	F	VF	XF	Unc	BU
2001 Proof	5,000	Value: 250				

KM# 921 1/5 CROWN
6.2200 g., 0.9999 Gold 0.1999 oz. AGW, 22 mm. **Ruler:** Elizabeth II **Series:** Victorian Era - Charles Dickens **Obv:** Bust with tiara right **Obv. Designer:** Ian Rank-Broadley **Rev:** Portrait and scene from "Oliver Twist" **Edge:** Reeded

Date	Mintage	F	VF	XF	Unc	BU
2001 Proof	5,000	Value: 250				

KM# 923 1/5 CROWN
6.2200 g., 0.9999 Gold 0.1999 oz. AGW, 22 mm. **Ruler:** Elizabeth II **Series:** Victorian Era - Charles Darwin **Obv:** Bust with tiara right **Obv. Designer:** Ian Rank-Broadley **Rev:** Portrait, ship and a squatting aboriginal figure **Edge:** Reeded

Date	Mintage	F	VF	XF	Unc	BU
2001 Proof	5,000	Value: 250				

KM# 925 1/5 CROWN
6.2200 g., 0.9999 Gold 0.1999 oz. AGW, 22 mm. **Ruler:** Elizabeth II **Series:** Mythology of the Solar System **Obv:** Queens portrait **Rev:** Standing goddess with snake basket **Edge:** Reeded

Date	Mintage	F	VF	XF	Unc	BU
2001 Proof	5,000	Value: 250				

KM# 926 1/5 CROWN
Bi-Metallic 0.925 Silver center in 0.999 Gold ring, 32.25 mm. **Ruler:** Elizabeth II **Series:** Mythology of the Solar System **Obv:** Bust with tiara right **Obv. Designer:** Ian Rank-Broadley **Rev:** Standing goddess with snake basket **Edge:** Reeded

Date	Mintage	F	VF	XF	Unc	BU
2001 In Proof sets only	999	Value: 375				

KM# 929.1 1/5 CROWN
6.2200 g., 0.9999 Gold 0.1999 oz. AGW, 22 mm. **Ruler:** Elizabeth II **Series:** Mythology of the Solar System - Sun **Obv:** Bust with tiara right **Obv. Designer:** Ian Rank-Broadley **Rev:** Helios in chariot and the sun **Edge:** Reeded

Date	Mintage	F	VF	XF	Unc	BU
2001 Proof	5,000	Value: 250				

KM# 929.2 1/5 CROWN
6.2200 g., 0.9999 Gold 0.1999 oz. AGW, 22 mm. **Ruler:** Elizabeth II **Series:** Mythology of the Solar System **Obv:** Bust with tiara right **Obv. Designer:** Ian Rank-Broadley **Rev:** Fiery hologram in the sun **Edge:** Reeded

Date	Mintage	F	VF	XF	Unc	BU
2001 In Proof sets only	999	Value: 350				

KM# 931.1 1/5 CROWN
6.2200 g., 0.9999 Gold 0.1999 oz. AGW, 22 mm. **Ruler:** Elizabeth II **Series:** Mythology of the Solar System - Moon **Obv:** Bust with tiara right **Obv. Designer:** Ian Rank-Broadley **Rev:** Goddess Diana and the moon **Edge:** Reeded

Date	Mintage	F	VF	XF	Unc	BU
2001 Proof	5,000	Value: 250				

KM# 931.2 1/5 CROWN
6.2200 g., 0.9999 Gold 0.1999 oz. AGW, 22 mm. **Ruler:** Elizabeth II **Series:** Mythology of the Solar System - Moon **Obv:** Bust with tiara right **Obv. Designer:** Ian Rank-Broadley **Rev:** Small pearl set in the moon **Edge:** Reeded

Date	Mintage	F	VF	XF	Unc	BU
2001 In Proof sets only	999	Value: 350				

KM# 933.1 1/5 CROWN
6.2200 g., 0.9999 Gold 0.1999 oz. AGW, 22 mm. **Ruler:** Elizabeth II **Series:** Mythology of the Solar System - Atlas **Obv:** Bust with tiara right **Obv. Designer:** Ian Rank-Broadley **Rev:** Atlas carrying the earth **Edge:** Reeded

Date	Mintage	F	VF	XF	Unc	BU
2001 Proof	5,000	Value: 250				

KM# 933.2 1/5 CROWN
6.2200 g., 0.9999 Gold 0.1999 oz. AGW, 22 mm. **Ruler:** Elizabeth II **Series:** Mythology of the Solar System - Atlas **Obv:** Bust with tiara right **Obv. Designer:** Ian Rank-Broadley **Rev:** Tiny diamond set in the earth **Edge:** Reeded

Date	Mintage	F	VF	XF	Unc	BU
2001 In Proof sets only	999	Value: 350				

KM# 935 1/5 CROWN
6.2200 g., 0.9999 Gold 0.1999 oz. AGW, 22 mm. **Ruler:** Elizabeth II **Series:** Mythology of the Solar System - Neptune **Obv:** Bust with tiara right **Obv. Designer:** Ian Rank-Broadley **Rev:** Seated god with trident and ringed planet **Edge:** Reeded

Date	Mintage	F	VF	XF	Unc	BU
2001 Proof	5,000	Value: 250				

KM# 937 1/5 CROWN
6.2200 g., 0.9999 Gold 0.1999 oz. AGW, 22 mm. **Ruler:** Elizabeth II **Series:** Mythology of the Solar System - Jupiter **Obv:** Bust with tiara right **Obv. Designer:** Ian Rank-Broadley **Rev:** Seated god with lightning bolts and a planet **Edge:** Reeded

Date	Mintage	F	VF	XF	Unc	BU
2001 Proof	5,000	Value: 250				

KM# 939 1/5 CROWN
6.2200 g., 0.9999 Gold 0.1999 oz. AGW, 22 mm. **Ruler:** Elizabeth II **Series:** Mythology of the Solar System - Mars **Obv:** Bust with tiara right **Obv. Designer:** Ian Rank-Broadley **Rev:** Standing Roman solider and a planet **Edge:** Reeded

Date	Mintage	F	VF	XF	Unc	BU
2001 Proof	5,000	Value: 250				

KM# 941 1/5 CROWN
6.2200 g., 0.9999 Gold 0.1999 oz. AGW, 22 mm.
Ruler: Elizabeth II **Series:** Mythology of the Solar System - Mercury **Obv:** Bust with tiara right **Obv. Designer:** Ian Rank-Broadley **Rev:** Seated god with caduceus and a planet **Edge:** Reeded

Date	Mintage	F	VF	XF	Unc	BU
2001 Proof	5,000	Value: 250				

KM# 943 1/5 CROWN
6.2200 g., 0.9999 Gold 0.1999 oz. AGW, 22 mm.
Ruler: Elizabeth II **Series:** Mythology of the Solar System - Uranus **Obv:** Bust with tiara right **Obv. Designer:** Ian Rank-Broadley **Rev:** Seated god with scepter **Edge:** Reeded

Date	Mintage	F	VF	XF	Unc	BU
2001 Proof	5,000	Value: 250				

KM# 945 1/5 CROWN
6.2200 g., 0.9999 Gold 0.1999 oz. AGW, 22 mm.
Ruler: Elizabeth II **Series:** Mythology of the Solar System - Saturn **Obv:** Bust with tiara right **Obv. Designer:** Ian Rank-Broadley **Rev:** Seated god with long handled sickle and a ringed planet **Edge:** Reeded

Date	Mintage	F	VF	XF	Unc	BU
2001 Proof	5,000	Value: 250				

KM# 947 1/5 CROWN
6.2200 g., 0.9999 Gold 0.1999 oz. AGW, 22 mm.
Ruler: Elizabeth II **Series:** Mythology of the Solar System - Pluto **Obv:** Bust with tiara right **Obv. Designer:** Ian Rank-Broadley **Rev:** Seated god with dogs and a planet **Edge:** Reeded

Date	Mintage	F	VF	XF	Unc	BU
2001 Proof	5,000	Value: 250				

KM# 949 1/5 CROWN
6.2200 g., 0.9999 Gold 0.1999 oz. AGW, 22 mm.
Ruler: Elizabeth II **Series:** Mythology of the Solar System - Venus **Obv:** Bust with tiara right **Obv. Designer:** Ian Rank-Broadley **Rev:** Goddess seated on a half shell **Edge:** Reeded

Date	Mintage	F	VF	XF	Unc	BU
2001 Proof	5,000	Value: 250				

KM# 951 1/5 CROWN
6.2200 g., 0.9999 Gold 0.1999 oz. AGW, 22 mm. **Ruler:** Elizabeth II **Subject:** Queen's 76th Birthday **Obv:** Bust with tiara right **Obv. Designer:** Ian Rank-Broadley **Rev:** Queen in Order of the Garter robes with a tiny inset diamond **Edge:** Reeded

Date	Mintage	F	VF	XF	Unc	BU
2001 Proof	2,001	Value: 260				

KM# 954 1/5 CROWN
6.2200 g., 0.9999 Gold 0.1999 oz. AGW, 22 mm. **Ruler:** Elizabeth II **Series:** Victorian Age Part II - Victoria's Accession to the Throne **Obv:** Bust with tiara right **Obv. Designer:** Ian Rank-Broadley **Rev:** Victoria learning of her accession **Edge:** Reeded

Date	Mintage	F	VF	XF	Unc	BU
2001 Proof	5,000	Value: 250				

KM# 956 1/5 CROWN
6.2200 g., 0.9999 Gold 0.1999 oz. AGW, 22 mm.
Ruler: Elizabeth II **Series:** Victorian Age Part II - Royal Family **Rev:** Victoria and Albert seated with children **Edge:** Reeded

Date	Mintage	F	VF	XF	Unc	BU
2001 Proof	5,000	Value: 250				

KM# 958 1/5 CROWN
6.2200 g., 0.9999 Gold 0.1999 oz. AGW, 22 mm.
Ruler: Elizabeth II **Series:** Victorian Age Part II - Victoria in Scotland **Obv:** Bust with tiara right **Obv. Designer:** Ian Rank-Broadley **Rev:** Victoria on horse and servant **Edge:** Reeded

Date	Mintage	F	VF	XF	Unc	BU
2001 Proof	5,000	Value: 250				

KM# 960 1/5 CROWN
6.2200 g., 0.9999 Gold 0.1999 oz. AGW, 22 mm.
Ruler: Elizabeth II **Series:** Victorian Age Part II **Obv:** Bust with tiara right **Obv. Designer:** Ian Rank-Broadley **Rev:** Portraits of Gladstone and Disaraeli **Edge:** Reeded

Date	Mintage	F	VF	XF	Unc	BU
2001 Proof	5,000	Value: 250				

KM# 962 1/5 CROWN
6.2200 g., 0.9999 Gold 0.1999 oz. AGW, 22 mm.
Ruler: Elizabeth II **Series:** Victorian Age Part II **Obv:** Bust with tiara right **Obv. Designer:** Ian Rank-Broadley **Rev:** Florence Nightingale holding lantern **Edge:** Reeded

Date	Mintage	F	VF	XF	Unc	BU
2001 Proof	5,000	Value: 250				

KM# 964 1/5 CROWN
6.2200 g., 0.9999 Gold 0.1999 oz. AGW, 22 mm.
Ruler: Elizabeth II **Series:** Victorian Age Part II **Obv:** Bust with tiara right **Obv. Designer:** Ian Rank-Broadley **Rev:** Lord Tennyson with the Light Brigade in background **Edge:** Reeded

Date	Mintage	F	VF	XF	Unc	BU
2001 Proof	5,000	Value: 250				

KM# 966 1/5 CROWN
6.2200 g., 0.9999 Gold 0.1999 oz. AGW, 22 mm.
Ruler: Elizabeth II **Series:** Victorian Age Part II **Obv:** Bust with tiara right **Obv. Designer:** Ian Rank-Broadley **Rev:** Stanley meeting Dr. Livingstone **Edge:** Reeded

Date	Mintage	F	VF	XF	Unc	BU
2001 Proof	5,000	Value: 250				

KM# 968 1/5 CROWN
6.2200 g., 0.9999 Gold 0.1999 oz. AGW, 22 mm.
Ruler: Elizabeth II **Series:** Victorian Age Part II **Obv:** Bust with tiara right **Rev:** Bronte sisters **Edge:** Reeded

Date	Mintage	F	VF	XF	Unc	BU
2001 Proof	5,000	Value: 250				

KM# 978 1/5 CROWN
6.2200 g., 0.9990 Gold 0.1998 oz. AGW, 22 mm.
Ruler: Elizabeth II **Subject:** Queen Mother's Life **Obv:** Bust right **Rev:** Prince William's christening scene **Edge:** Reeded

Date	Mintage	F	VF	XF	Unc	BU
2002 Proof	5,000	Value: 250				

KM# 980 1/5 CROWN
6.2200 g., 0.9999 Gold 0.1999 oz. AGW, 22 mm.
Ruler: Elizabeth II **Subject:** World Cup Soccer **Obv:** Bust right **Rev:** Two players about to collide **Edge:** Reeded

Date	Mintage	F	VF	XF	Unc	BU
2002 Proof	5,000	Value: 250				

KM# 982 1/5 CROWN
6.2200 g., 0.9999 Gold 0.1999 oz. AGW, 22 mm.
Ruler: Elizabeth II **Subject:** World Cup Soccer **Obv:** Bust right **Rev:** Two players facing viewer **Edge:** Reeded

Date	Mintage	F	VF	XF	Unc	BU
2002 Proof	5,000	Value: 250				

KM# 984 1/5 CROWN
6.2200 g., 0.9999 Gold 0.1999 oz. AGW, 22 mm.
Ruler: Elizabeth II **Subject:** World Cup Soccer **Obv:** Bust right **Rev:** Two horizontal players **Edge:** Reeded

Date	Mintage	F	VF	XF	Unc	BU
2002 Proof	5,000	Value: 250				

KM# 986 1/5 CROWN
6.2200 g., 0.9999 Gold 0.1999 oz. AGW, 22 mm.
Ruler: Elizabeth II **Subject:** World Cup Soccer **Obv:** Bust right **Rev:** Two players moving to the left **Edge:** Reeded

Date	Mintage	F	VF	XF	Unc	BU
2002 Proof	5,000	Value: 250				

KM# 990 1/5 CROWN
6.2200 g., 0.9990 Gold 0.1998 oz. AGW, 22 mm.
Ruler: Elizabeth II **Subject:** Peter Rabbit Centennial **Obv:** Bust right **Rev:** Peter Rabbit **Edge:** Reeded

Date	Mintage	F	VF	XF	Unc	BU
2002 Proof	3,500	Value: 250				

KM# 990a 1/5 CROWN
6.2200 g., 0.9990 Platinum 0.1998 oz. APW, 22 mm.
Ruler: Elizabeth II **Subject:** Peter Rabbit Centennial **Obv:** Bust right **Rev:** Peter Rabbit **Edge:** Reeded

Date	Mintage	F	VF	XF	Unc	BU
2002 Proof	1,500	Value: 450				

KM# 993 1/5 CROWN
6.2200 g., 0.3750 Gold 0.0750 oz. AGW, 22 mm.
Ruler: Elizabeth II **Subject:** Queen's Golden Jubilee **Obv:** Bust with tiara right **Obv. Designer:** Ian Rank-Broadley **Rev:** Royal couple and tree house **Edge:** Reeded

Date	Mintage	F	VF	XF	Unc	BU
2002 Proof	5,000	Value: 95.00				

KM# 993a 1/5 CROWN
6.2200 g., 0.9999 Gold 0.1999 oz. AGW, 22 mm.
Ruler: Elizabeth II **Subject:** Queen's Golden Jubilee **Obv:** Bust with tiara right **Obv. Designer:** Ian Rank-Broadley **Rev:** Royal couple and tree house **Edge:** Reeded

Date	Mintage	F	VF	XF	Unc	BU
2002 Proof	2,002	Value: 250				

KM# 995 1/5 CROWN
6.2200 g., 0.3750 Gold 0.0750 oz. AGW, 22 mm.
Ruler: Elizabeth II **Subject:** Queen's Golden Jubilee **Obv:** Bust with tiara right **Obv. Designer:** Ian Rank-Broadley **Rev:** Royal coach **Edge:** Reeded

Date	Mintage	F	VF	XF	Unc	BU
2002 Proof	5,000	Value: 95.00				

KM# 995a 1/5 CROWN
6.2200 g., 0.9999 Gold 0.1999 oz. AGW, 22 mm.
Ruler: Elizabeth II **Subject:** Queen's Golden Jubilee **Obv:** Bust with tiara right **Obv. Designer:** Ian Rank-Broadley **Rev:** Royal coach **Edge:** Reeded

Date	Mintage	F	VF	XF	Unc	BU
2002 Proof	2,002	Value: 250				

KM# 997 1/5 CROWN
6.2200 g., 0.3750 Gold 0.0750 oz. AGW, 22 mm.
Ruler: Elizabeth II **Subject:** Queen's Golden Jubilee **Obv:** Bust with tiara right **Obv. Designer:** Ian Rank-Broadley **Rev:** Queen holding baby **Edge:** Reeded

Date	Mintage	F	VF	XF	Unc	BU
2002 Proof	5,000	Value: 95.00				

KM# 997a 1/5 CROWN
6.2200 g., 0.9999 Gold 0.1999 oz. AGW, 22 mm.
Ruler: Elizabeth II **Subject:** Queen's Golden Jubilee **Obv:** Bust with tiara right **Obv. Designer:** Ian Rank-Broadley **Rev:** Queen holding baby **Edge:** Reeded

Date	Mintage	F	VF	XF	Unc	BU
2002 Proof	2,002	Value: 250				

KM# 999 1/5 CROWN
6.2200 g., 0.3750 Gold 0.0750 oz. AGW, 22 mm. **Ruler:** Elizabeth II **Subject:** Queen's Golden Jubilee **Obv:** Bust with tiara right **Obv. Designer:** Ian Rank-Broadley **Rev:** Yacht under Tower bridge **Edge:** Reeded

Date	Mintage	F	VF	XF	Unc	BU
2002 Proof	5,000	Value: 95.00				

KM# 999a 1/5 CROWN
6.2200 g., 0.9999 Gold 0.1999 oz. AGW, 22 mm.
Ruler: Elizabeth II **Subject:** Queen's Golden Jubilee **Obv:** Bust with tiara right **Obv. Designer:** Ian Rank-Broadley **Rev:** Yacht under Tower bridge **Edge:** Reeded

Date	Mintage	F	VF	XF	Unc	BU
2002 Proof	2,002	Value: 250				

KM# 1001 1/5 CROWN
6.2200 g., 0.9999 Gold 0.1999 oz. AGW, 22 mm.
Ruler: Elizabeth II **Subject:** Queen's Golden Jubilee **Obv:** Bust with tiara right **Obv. Designer:** Ian Rank-Broadley **Rev:** Crown jewels inset with a tiny diamond, ruby, sapphire and emerald **Edge:** Reeded

Date	Mintage	F	VF	XF	Unc	BU
2002 Proof	2,002	Value: 250				

KM# 1003 1/5 CROWN
6.2200 g., Electrum Special alloy of equal parts of gold and silver, 22 mm. **Ruler:** Elizabeth II **Series:** Ancient Coins **Obv:** Bust with tiara right **Obv. Designer:** Ian Rank-Broadley **Rev:** Head of Athena left **Edge:** Reeded **Note:** From a Mysia electrum coin c.520BC.

Date	Mintage	F	VF	XF	Unc	BU
2002 Proof	3,500	Value: 100				

KM# 1005 1/5 CROWN
6.2200 g., Electrum Special alloy of equal parts of gold and silver., 22 mm. **Ruler:** Elizabeth II **Series:** Ancient Coins **Obv:** Bust with tiara right **Obv. Designer:** Ian Rank-Broadley **Rev:** Head of Hercules right **Edge:** Reeded **Note:** From a Lesbos coin c. 480-450 BC.

Date	Mintage	F	VF	XF	Unc	BU
2002 Proof	3,500	Value: 100				

KM# 1007 1/5 CROWN
6.2200 g., 0.9990 Electrum Special alloy of equal parts of gold and silver. 0.1998 oz., 22 mm. **Ruler:** Elizabeth II **Series:** Ancient Coins **Obv:** Bust with tiara right **Obv. Designer:** Ian Rank-Broadley **Rev:** Pegasus **Edge:** Reeded **Note:** From a Lampsakos electrum coin c. 450 BC.

Date	Mintage	F	VF	XF	Unc	BU
2002 Proof	3,500	Value: 100				

KM# 1009 1/5 CROWN
6.2200 g., Electrum Special Alloy of equal parts of gold and silver., 22 mm. **Ruler:** Elizabeth II **Series:** Ancient Coins **Obv:** Bust with tiara right **Obv. Designer:** Ian Rank-Broadley **Rev:** Lion and bull facing **Edge:** Reeded **Note:** From a Kroisos "sic" coin c. 560-546 BC.

Date	Mintage	F	VF	XF	Unc	BU
2002 Proof	3,500	Value: 100				

KM# 1012 1/5 CROWN
6.2200 g., 0.9999 Gold 0.1999 oz. AGW, 22 mm.
Ruler: Elizabeth II **Subject:** Queen Mother **Obv:** Bust with tiara right **Obv. Designer:** Ian Rank-Broadley **Rev:** Queen Mother trout fishing **Edge:** Reeded

Date	Mintage	F	VF	XF	Unc	BU
2002 Proof	5,000	Value: 250				

KM# 1014 1/5 CROWN
6.2200 g., 0.9999 Gold 0.1999 oz. AGW, 22 mm.
Ruler: Elizabeth II **Subject:** Princess Diana **Obv:** Bust right **Rev:** Diana's portrait **Edge:** Reeded

Date	Mintage	F	VF	XF	Unc	BU
2002 Proof	5,000	Value: 250				

KM# 1018 1/5 CROWN
6.2200 g., 0.9999 Gold 0.1999 oz. AGW, 22 mm.
Ruler: Elizabeth II **Subject:** Peter Pan **Obv:** Bust right **Rev:** Peter Pan and Tinkerbell flying above city **Edge:** Reeded

Date	Mintage	F	VF	XF	Unc	BU
2002 Proof	5,000	Value: 250				

KM# 1020 1/5 CROWN
6.2200 g., 0.9999 Gold 0.1999 oz. AGW, 22 mm.
Ruler: Elizabeth II **Subject:** Grand Masonic Lodge **Obv:** Bust right **Rev:** Masonic seal above Gibraltar **Edge:** Reeded

Date	Mintage	F	VF	XF	Unc	BU
2002 Proof	5,000	Value: 250				

KM# 991 1/2 CROWN
15.5500 g., 0.9990 Gold 0.4994 oz. AGW, 30 mm.
Ruler: Elizabeth II **Subject:** Peter Rabbit Centennial **Obv:** Bust right **Rev:** Peter Rabbit **Edge:** Reeded

Date	Mintage	F	VF	XF	Unc	BU
2002 Proof	1,000	Value: 625				

KM# 1002 1/2 CROWN
15.5500 g., 0.9999 Gold 0.4999 oz. AGW, 30 mm.
Ruler: Elizabeth II **Subject:** Queen's Golden Jubilee **Obv:** Bust with tiara right **Obv. Designer:** Ian Rank-Broadley **Rev:** Crown jewels inset with a tiny diamond, ruby, sapphire and emerald **Edge:** Reeded

Date	Mintage	F	VF	XF	Unc	BU
2002 Proof	999	Value: 625				

KM# 1004 1/2 CROWN
15.5500 g., Electrum Special alloy of equal parts of gold/silver., 32.2 mm. **Ruler:** Elizabeth II **Series:** Ancient Coins **Obv:** Bust w/tiara right **Obv. Designer:** Ian Rank-Broadley **Rev:** Athena left **Edge:** Reeded **Note:** From a Mysia electrum coin c. 520 BC.

Date	Mintage	F	VF	XF	Unc	BU
2002 Proof	2,000	Value: 220				

KM# 1006 1/2 CROWN
15.5500 g., Electrum Special alloy of equal parts of gold and silver., 32.2 mm. **Ruler:** Elizabeth II **Series:** Ancient Coins **Obv:** Bust with tiara right **Obv. Designer:** Ian Rank-Broadley **Rev:** Head of Hercules right **Edge:** Reeded **Note:** From a Lesbos coin c. 480-450 BC.

Date	Mintage	F	VF	XF	Unc	BU
2002 Proof	2,000	Value: 220				

KM# 1008 1/2 CROWN
15.5500 g., Gold With Silver Special alloy of equal parts of gold and silver., 32.2 mm. **Ruler:** Elizabeth II **Series:** Ancient Coins **Obv:** Bust with tiara right **Obv. Designer:** Ian Rank-Broadley **Rev:** Pegasus **Edge:** Reeded **Note:** From a Lampsakos electrum coin c. 450 BC.

Date	Mintage	F	VF	XF	Unc	BU
2002 Proof	2,000	Value: 220				

KM# 1010 1/2 CROWN
15.5500 g., Electrum Special alloy of equal parts of gold and silver., 32.2 mm. **Ruler:** Elizabeth II **Series:** Ancient Coins **Obv:** Bust with tiara right **Obv. Designer:** Ian Rank-Broadley **Rev:** Lion and bull facing **Edge:** Reeded **Note:** From a Kroisos [sic] coin c. 560-546 BC.

Date	Mintage	F	VF	XF	Unc	BU
2002 Proof	2,000	Value: 220				

KM# 1056 CROWN
31.1000 g., 0.9990 Tri-Metallic Center: silver, Ring: silver-gilt, Outer ring: silver-pearl black 0.9988 oz., 38.60 mm. **Ruler:** Elizabeth II **Subject:** 21st Century **Obv:** Crowned bust right **Obv. Legend:** GIBRALTER • ELIZABETH II **Rev:** Helmeted cross at center flanked by satellites, archaic sailing ship below **Rev. Legend:** 21st CENTURY **Edge:** Reeded

Date	Mintage	F	VF	XF	Unc	BU
2001 Proof	2,001	Value: 600				

KM# 904 CROWN
28.2800 g., Copper-Nickel, 38.6 mm. **Ruler:** Elizabeth II **Subject:** The Life of Queen Elizabeth - The Queen Mother **Obv:** Bust with tiara right **Obv. Designer:** Ian Rank-Broadley **Rev:** 1953 Coronation scene **Edge:** Reeded

Date	Mintage	F	VF	XF	Unc	BU
2001	—	—	—	—	10.00	12.00

KM# 904a CROWN
28.2800 g., 0.9250 Silver 0.8410 oz. ASW, 38.6 mm. **Ruler:** Elizabeth II **Subject:** The Life of Queen Elizabeth - The Queen Mother **Obv:** Bust with tiara right **Obv. Designer:** Ian Rank-Broadley **Rev:** 1953 Coronation scene **Edge:** Reeded

Date	Mintage	F	VF	XF	Unc	BU
2001 Proof	10,000	Value: 47.50				

KM# 905 CROWN
28.2800 g., Copper-Nickel, 38.6 mm. **Ruler:** Elizabeth II **Subject:** The Life of Queen Elizabeth - The Queen Mother **Obv:** Bust with tiara right **Obv. Designer:** Ian Rank-Broadley **Rev:** Queen Mother with Prince Charles in 1954 **Edge:** Reeded

Date	Mintage	F	VF	XF	Unc	BU
2001	—	—	—	—	10.00	12.00

KM# 905a CROWN
28.2800 g., 0.9250 Silver 0.8410 oz. ASW, 38.6 mm. **Ruler:** Elizabeth II **Subject:** The Life of Queen Elizabeth - The Queen Mother **Obv:** Bust with tiara right **Obv. Designer:** Ian Rank-Broadley **Rev:** Queen Mother with Prince Charles in 1954 **Edge:** Reeded

Date	Mintage	F	VF	XF	Unc	BU
2001 Proof	10,000	Value: 47.50				

KM# 906 CROWN
28.2800 g., Copper-Nickel, 38.6 mm. **Ruler:** Elizabeth II **Subject:** 21st Century **Obv:** Crowned bust right, date below **Obv. Designer:** Raphael Maklouf **Rev:** Celtic cross, Viking ship and modern technological items **Edge:** Reeded

Date	Mintage	F	VF	XF	Unc	BU
2001	—	—	—	—	10.00	12.00

KM# 906a CROWN
31.1035 g., 0.9990 Silver 0.9990 oz. ASW, 38.6 mm. **Ruler:** Elizabeth II **Subject:** 21st Century **Obv:** Crowned bust right, date below **Obv. Designer:** Raphael Maklouf **Rev:** Celtic cross, Viking ship and modern technological items **Edge:** Reeded **Note:** 31.1035 .999 Silver, 1.0000 ASW with a gold plated inner ring and a blackened outer ring.

Date	Mintage	F	VF	XF	Unc	BU
2001 Proof	2,001	Value: 47.50				

KM# 906b CROWN
31.1000 g., Tri-Metallic Center .9995 Platinum 5.2g. Inner Ring .9999 Gold 14.2g. Outer Ring .999 Silver 11.7g **Ruler:** Elizabeth II **Subject:** 21st Century **Obv:** Crowned bust right, date below **Obv. Designer:** Raphael Maklouf **Rev:** Celtic cross, Viking ship and modern technological items

Date	Mintage	F	VF	XF	Unc	BU
2001 Proof	999	Value: 650				

KM# 910 CROWN
28.2800 g., Copper-Nickel, 38.6 mm. **Ruler:** Elizabeth II **Series:** The Victorian Age **Obv:** Bust with tiara right **Obv. Designer:** Ian Rank-Broadley **Rev:** 1838 Coronation of Queen Victoria **Edge:** Reeded

Date	Mintage	F	VF	XF	Unc	BU
2001	—	—	—	—	10.00	12.00

KM# 910a CROWN
28.2800 g., 0.9250 Silver 0.8410 oz. ASW, 38.6 mm. **Ruler:** Elizabeth II **Series:** Victorian Era **Obv:** Bust with tiara right **Obv. Designer:** Ian Rank-Broadley **Rev:** 1838 Coronation scene **Edge:** Reeded

Date	Mintage	F	VF	XF	Unc	BU
2001 Proof	10,000	Value: 47.50				

KM# 912 CROWN
Copper-Nickel, 38.6 mm. **Ruler:** Elizabeth II **Series:** Victorian Era - Empress of India 1876 **Obv:** Bust with tiara right **Obv. Designer:** Ian Rank-Broadley **Rev:** Crowned portrait of Victoria and two elephants

Date	Mintage	F	VF	XF	Unc	BU
2001	—	—	—	—	10.00	12.00

KM# 912a CROWN
28.2800 g., 0.9250 Silver 0.8410 oz. ASW **Ruler:** Elizabeth II **Series:** The Victorian Age - Empress of India 1876 **Obv:** Bust with tiara right **Obv. Designer:** Ian Rank-Broadley **Rev:** Crowned portrait of Victoria and two elephants

Date	Mintage	F	VF	XF	Unc	BU
2001 Proof	10,000	Value: 47.50				

KM# 914 CROWN
Copper-Nickel, 38.6 mm. **Ruler:** Elizabeth II **Series:** Victorian Era
- Diamond Jubilee **Obv:** Bust with tiara right **Obv. Designer:** Ian
Rank-Broadley **Rev:** Victoria's cameo portrait above naval ships

Date	Mintage	F	VF	XF	Unc	BU
2001	—			—	10.00	12.00

KM# 914a CROWN
28.2800 g., 0.9250 Silver 0.8410 oz. ASW **Ruler:** Elizabeth II
Series: The Victorian Age - Diamond Jubilee 1897 **Obv:** Bust
with tiara right **Obv. Designer:** Ian Rank-Broadley **Rev:** Victoria's
cameo above naval ships, Spithead Review

Date	Mintage	F	VF	XF	Unc	BU
2001 Proof	10,000	Value: 47.50				

KM# 920 CROWN
Copper-Nickel, 38.6 mm. **Ruler:** Elizabeth II **Series:** The
Victorian Age **Obv:** Bust with tiara right **Obv. Designer:** Ian Rank-
Broadley **Rev:** 1/2 bust of Isambard K. Brunel half left in front of
railroad bridge

Date	Mintage	F	VF	XF	Unc	BU
2001	—			—	10.00	12.00

KM# 920a CROWN
28.2800 g., 0.9250 Silver 0.8410 oz. ASW, 38.6 mm.
Ruler: Elizabeth II **Series:** Victorian Era **Obv:** Bust with tiara right
Rev: 1/2 bust of Isambard K. Brunel half left in front of railroad
bridge

Date	Mintage	F	VF	XF	Unc	BU
2001 Proof	10,000	Value: 47.50				

KM# 927 CROWN
28.2800 g., Copper-Nickel, 38.6 mm. **Ruler:** Elizabeth II
Series: Mythology of the Solar System **Obv:** Bust with tiara right
Obv. Designer: Ian Rank-Broadley **Rev:** Standing goddess with
snake basket **Edge:** Reeded

Date	Mintage	F	VF	XF	Unc	BU
2001	—			—	10.00	12.00

KM# 927a CROWN
28.2800 g., 0.9250 Silver 0.8410 oz. ASW, 38.6 mm.
Ruler: Elizabeth II **Series:** Mythology of the Solar System
Obv: Bust with tiara right **Obv. Designer:** Ian Rank-Broadley
Rev: Standing goddess with snake basket **Edge:** Reeded

Date	Mintage	F	VF	XF	Unc	BU
2001 Proof	10,000	Value: 47.50				

KM# 928 CROWN
Bi-Metallic Titanium center in Silver ring, 32.25 mm.
Ruler: Elizabeth II **Series:** Mythology of the Solar System
Obv: Bust with tiara right **Obv. Designer:** Ian Rank-Broadley
Rev: Standing goddess with snake basket **Edge:** Reeded

Date	Mintage	F	VF	XF	Unc	BU
2001 In Proof sets only	2,001	Value: 100				

KM# 916 CROWN
Copper-Nickel, 38.6 mm. **Ruler:** Elizabeth II **Series:** The
Victorian Age - Victoria's Death 1901 **Obv:** Bust with tiara right
Obv. Designer: Ian Rank-Broadley **Rev:** Victoria's cameo
portrait and Osborne Manor

Date	Mintage	F	VF	XF	Unc	BU
2001	—			—	10.00	12.00

KM# 916a CROWN
28.2800 g., 0.9250 Silver 0.8410 oz. ASW, 38.6 mm.
Ruler: Elizabeth II **Series:** The Victorian Age - Victoria's Death
1901 **Obv:** Bust with tiara right **Obv. Designer:** Ian Rank-
Broadley **Rev:** Victoria's cameo portrait and Osborne Manor

Date	Mintage	F	VF	XF	Unc	BU
2001 Proof	10,000	Value: 47.50				

KM# 918 CROWN
Copper-Nickel, 38.6 mm. **Ruler:** Elizabeth II **Series:** The
Victorian Age - Prince Albert and the Great Exhibition 1851
Obv: Bust with tiara right **Obv. Designer:** Ian Rank-Broadley
Rev: Albert's cameo portrait and the exhibit hall

Date	Mintage	F	VF	XF	Unc	BU
2001 Proof	5,000	Value: 175				

KM# 922 CROWN
Copper-Nickel, 38.6 mm. **Ruler:** Elizabeth II **Series:** The
Victorian Age **Obv:** Bust with tiara right **Obv. Designer:** Ian Rank-
Broadley **Rev:** 1/2 length bust of Charles Dickens half left, scene
from "Oliver Twist" in background

Date	Mintage	F	VF	XF	Unc	BU
2001	—			—	10.00	12.00

KM# 922a CROWN
28.2800 g., 0.9250 Silver 0.8410 oz. ASW, 38.6 mm.
Series: The Victorian Age **Obv:** Bust with tiara right
Obv. Designer: Ian Rank-Broadley **Rev:** 1/2 length bust of
Charles Dickens half left, scene from "Oliver Twist" in background

Date	Mintage	F	VF	XF	Unc	BU
2001 Proof	10,000	Value: 47.50				

KM# 930 CROWN
Copper-Nickel, 38.6 mm. **Ruler:** Elizabeth II **Series:** Mythology
of the Solar System - Sun **Obv:** Bust with tiara right **Obv.**
Designer: Ian Rank-Broadley **Rev:** Helios in chariot and the sun

Date	Mintage	F	VF	XF	Unc	BU
2001	—			—	10.00	12.00

KM# 930a CROWN
28.2800 g., 0.9250 Silver 0.8410 oz. ASW, 38.6 mm.
Ruler: Elizabeth II **Series:** Mythology of the Solar System - Sun
Obv: Bust with tiara right **Obv. Designer:** Ian Rank-Broadley
Rev: Helios in chariot and the sun

Date	Mintage	F	VF	XF	Unc	BU
2001 Proof	10,000	Value: 47.50				

KM# 930a.1 CROWN
28.2800 g., 0.9250 Silver 0.8410 oz. ASW **Ruler:** Elizabeth II
Series: Mythology of the Solar System - Sun **Obv:** Bust with tiara
right **Obv. Designer:** Ian Rank-Broadley **Rev:** Fiery hologram in
the sun

Date	Mintage	F	VF	XF	Unc	BU
2001 In Proof sets only	2,001	Value: 87.50				

KM# 918a CROWN
28.2800 g., 0.9250 Silver 0.8410 oz. ASW, 38.6 mm.
Ruler: Elizabeth II **Series:** The Victorian Age - Prince Albert and
the Great Exhibition 1851 **Obv:** Bust with tiara right
Obv. Designer: Ian Rank-Broadley **Rev:** Albert's cameo portrait
and the exhibit hall

Date	Mintage	F	VF	XF	Unc	BU
2001 Proof	10,000	Value: 47.50				

KM# 924 CROWN
Copper-Nickel, 38.6 mm. **Ruler:** Elizabeth II **Series:** The
Victorian Age **Obv:** Bust with tiara right **Obv. Designer:** Ian Rank-
Broadley **Rev:** 3/4-length figure of Charles Darwin right, ship and
a squatting aboriginal figure

Date	Mintage	F	VF	XF	Unc	BU
2001	—			—	10.00	12.00

KM# 924a CROWN
28.2800 g., 0.9250 Silver 0.8410 oz. ASW, 38.6 mm.
Ruler: Elizabeth II **Series:** The Victorian Age **Obv:** Bust with tiara
right **Obv. Designer:** Ian Rank-Broadley **Rev:** 3/4-length figure
of Charles Darwin right, ship and a squatting aboriginal figure

Date	Mintage	F	VF	XF	Unc	BU
2001 Proof	10,000	Value: 47.50				

KM# 932 CROWN
Copper-Nickel, 38.6 mm. **Ruler:** Elizabeth II **Series:** Mythology of
the Solar System - Moon **Obv:** Bust with tiara right **Obv. Designer:**
Ian Rank-Broadley **Rev:** Goddess Diana and the moon

Date	Mintage	F	VF	XF	Unc	BU
2001	—			—	10.00	12.00

KM# 932a CROWN
28.2800 g., 0.9250 Silver 0.8410 oz. ASW, 38.6 mm.
Ruler: Elizabeth II **Series:** Mythology of the Solar System - Moon
Obv: Bust with tiara right **Obv. Designer:** Ian Rank-Broadley
Rev: Goddess Diana and the moon

Date	Mintage	F	VF	XF	Unc	BU
2001 Proof	10,000	Value: 47.50				

KM# 932a.1 CROWN
28.2800 g., 0.9250 Silver 0.8410 oz. ASW, 38.6 mm.
Ruler: Elizabeth II **Series:** Mythology of the Solar System - Moon
Obv: Bust with tiara right **Obv. Designer:** Ian Rank-Broadley
Rev: Small pearl set in the moon

Date	Mintage	F	VF	XF	Unc	BU
2001 In Proof sets only	2,001	Value: 87.50				

KM# 934 CROWN
Copper-Nickel **Ruler:** Elizabeth II **Series:** Mythology of the Solar System - Atlas **Obv:** Bust with tiara right **Obv. Designer:** Ian Rank-Broadley **Rev:** Atlas carrying the earth

Date	Mintage	F	VF	XF	Unc	BU
2001	—	—	—	—	10.00	12.00

KM# 934a CROWN
28.2800 g., 0.9250 Silver 0.8410 oz. ASW, 38.6 mm.
Ruler: Elizabeth II **Series:** Mythology of the Solar System - Atlas
Obv: Bust with tiara right **Obv. Designer:** Ian Rank-Broadley
Rev: Atlas carrying the earth

Date	Mintage	F	VF	XF	Unc	BU
2001 Proof	10,000	Value: 47.50				

KM# 934a.1 CROWN
28.2800 g., 0.9250 Silver 0.8410 oz. ASW, 38.6 mm.
Ruler: Elizabeth II **Series:** Mythology of the Solar System - Atlas
Obv: Bust with tiara right **Rev:** Fancy diamond set in the earth

Date	Mintage	F	VF	XF	Unc	BU
2001 In Proof sets only	2,001	Value: 87.50				

KM# 936 CROWN
Copper-Nickel, 38.6 mm. **Ruler:** Elizabeth II **Series:** Mythology of the Solar System **Obv:** Bust with tiara right **Obv. Designer:** Ian Rank-Broadley **Rev:** Seated Neptune with trident and ringed planet

Date	Mintage	F	VF	XF	Unc	BU
2001	—	—	—	—	10.00	12.00

KM# 936a CROWN
28.2800 g., 0.9250 Silver 0.8410 oz. ASW, 38.6 mm.
Ruler: Elizabeth II **Series:** Mythology of the Solar System
Obv: Bust with tiara right **Obv. Designer:** Ian Rank-Broadley
Rev: Seated Neptune with trident and ringed planet

Date	Mintage	F	VF	XF	Unc	BU
2001 Proof	10,000	Value: 47.50				

KM# 938 CROWN
Copper-Nickel, 38.6 mm. **Ruler:** Elizabeth II **Series:** Mythology of the Solar System **Obv:** Bust with tiara right **Obv. Designer:**
Ian Rank-Broadley **Rev:** Seated Jupiter with lightening bolts and a planet

Date	Mintage	F	VF	XF	Unc	BU
2001	—	—	—	—	10.00	12.00

KM# 938a CROWN
28.2800 g., 0.9250 Silver 0.8410 oz. ASW, 38.6 mm.
Ruler: Elizabeth II **Series:** Mythology of the Solar System
Obv: Bust with tiara right **Obv. Designer:** Ian Rank-Broadley
Rev: Seated Jupiter with lightening bolts and a planet

Date	Mintage	F	VF	XF	Unc	BU
2001 Proof	10,000	Value: 47.50				

KM# 940 CROWN
Copper-Nickel, 38.6 mm. **Ruler:** Elizabeth II **Series:** Mythology of the Solar System - Mars **Obv:** Bust with tiara right **Obv. Designer:** Ian Rank-Broadley **Rev:** Standing Roman soldier and a planet

Date	Mintage	F	VF	XF	Unc	BU
2001	—	—	—	—	10.00	12.00

KM# 940a CROWN
28.2800 g., 0.9250 Silver 0.8410 oz. ASW, 38.6 mm.
Ruler: Elizabeth II **Series:** Mythology of the Solar System - Mars
Obv: Bust with tiara right **Obv. Designer:** Ian Rank-Broadley
Rev: Standing Roman soldier and a planet

Date	Mintage	F	VF	XF	Unc	BU
2001 Proof	10,000	Value: 47.50				

KM# 942 CROWN
Copper-Nickel, 38.6 mm. **Ruler:** Elizabeth II **Series:** Mythology of the Solar System **Obv:** Bust with tiara right **Obv. Designer:** Ian Rank-Broadley **Rev:** Seated Mercury with caduceus and a planet

Date	Mintage	F	VF	XF	Unc	BU
2001	—	—	—	—	10.00	12.00

KM# 942a CROWN
28.2800 g., 0.9250 Silver 0.8410 oz. ASW, 38.6 mm.
Ruler: Elizabeth II **Series:** Mythology of the Solar System
Obv: Bust with tiara right **Obv. Designer:** Ian Rank-Broadley
Rev: Seated Mercury with caduceus and a planet

Date	Mintage	F	VF	XF	Unc	BU
2001 Proof	10,000	Value: 47.50				

KM# 944 CROWN
Copper-Nickel, 38.6 mm. **Ruler:** Elizabeth II **Series:** Mythology of the Solar System **Obv:** Bust with tiara right **Obv. Designer:** Ian Rank-Broadley **Rev:** Seated Uranus with scepter

Date	Mintage	F	VF	XF	Unc	BU
2001	—	—	—	—	10.00	12.00

KM# 944a CROWN
28.2800 g., 0.9250 Silver 0.8410 oz. ASW, 38.6 mm.
Ruler: Elizabeth II **Series:** Mythology of the Solar System
Obv: Bust with tiara right **Obv. Designer:** Ian Rank-Broadley
Rev: Seated Uranus with scepter

Date	Mintage	F	VF	XF	Unc	BU
2001 Proof	10,000	Value: 47.50				

KM# 946 CROWN
Copper-Nickel, 38.6 mm. **Ruler:** Elizabeth II **Series:** Mythology of the Solar System **Obv:** Bust with tiara right **Obv. Designer:** Ian Rank-Broadley **Rev:** Seated Saturn with long handled sickle and a ringed planet

Date	Mintage	F	VF	XF	Unc	BU
2001	—	—	—	—	10.00	12.00

KM# 946a CROWN
28.2800 g., 0.9250 Silver 0.8410 oz. ASW, 38.6 mm.
Ruler: Elizabeth II **Series:** Mythology of the Solar System
Obv: Bust with tiara right **Obv. Designer:** Ian Rank-Broadley
Rev: Seated Saturn with long handled sickle and a ringed planet

Date	Mintage	F	VF	XF	Unc	BU
2001 Proof	10,000	Value: 47.50				

KM# 948 CROWN
Copper-Nickel, 38.6 mm. **Ruler:** Elizabeth II **Series:** Mythology of the Solar System **Obv:** Bust with tiara right **Obv. Designer:** Ian Rank-Broadley **Rev:** Seated Pluto with dogs and planet

Date	Mintage	F	VF	XF	Unc	BU
2001	—	—	—	—	10.00	12.00

KM# 948a CROWN
28.2800 g., 0.9250 Silver 0.8410 oz. ASW, 38.6 mm.
Ruler: Elizabeth II **Series:** Mythology of the Solar System
Obv: Bust with tiara right **Obv. Designer:** Ian Rank-Broadley
Rev: Seated Pluto with dogs and planet

Date	Mintage	F	VF	XF	Unc	BU
2001 Proof	10,000	Value: 47.50				

KM# 950 CROWN
Copper-Nickel, 38.6 mm. **Ruler:** Elizabeth II **Series:** Mythology of the Solar System **Obv:** Bust with tiara right **Obv. Designer:** Ian Rank-Broadley **Rev:** Venus seated on a half shell

Date	Mintage	F	VF	XF	Unc	BU
2001	—	—	—	—	10.00	12.00

KM# 950a CROWN
28.2800 g., 0.9250 Silver 0.8410 oz. ASW, 38.6 mm.
Ruler: Elizabeth II **Series:** Mythology of the Solar System
Obv: Bust with tiara right **Obv. Designer:** Ian Rank-Broadley
Rev: Venus seated on a half shell

Date	Mintage	F	VF	XF	Unc	BU
2001 Proof	10,000	Value: 47.50				

KM# 952 CROWN

28.2800 g., Copper-Nickel, 38.6 mm. **Ruler:** Elizabeth II
Subject: Queen's 75th Birthday **Obv:** Bust with tiara right
Obv. Designer: Ian Rank-Broadley **Rev:** Queen in Order of
Garter robes **Edge:** Reeded

Date	Mintage	F	VF	XF	Unc	BU
2001	—	—	—	—	10.00	12.00

KM# 952a CROWN

28.2800 g., 0.9250 Silver 0.8410 oz. ASW, 38.6 mm.
Ruler: Elizabeth II **Subject:** Queen's 75th Birthday **Obv:** Bust
with tiara right **Obv. Designer:** Ian Rank-Broadley **Rev:** Queen
in Order of Garter robes **Edge:** Reeded

Date	Mintage	F	VF	XF	Unc	BU
2001 Proof	10,000	Value: 47.50				

KM# 955 CROWN

28.2800 g., Copper-Nickel, 38.6 mm. **Ruler:** Elizabeth II
Series: Victorian Age Part II **Obv:** Bust with tiara right
Obv. Designer: Ian Rank-Broadley **Rev:** Victoria learning of her
accession **Edge:** Reeded

Date	Mintage	F	VF	XF	Unc	BU
2001	—	—	—	—	10.00	12.00

KM# 955a CROWN

28.2800 g., 0.9250 Silver 0.8410 oz. ASW, 38.6 mm.
Ruler: Elizabeth II **Series:** Victorian Age Part II **Obv:** Bust with
tiara right **Obv. Designer:** Ian Rank-Broadley **Rev:** Victoria
learning of her accession **Edge:** Reeded

Date	Mintage	F	VF	XF	Unc	BU
2001 Proof	10,000	Value: 47.50				

KM# 957 CROWN

Copper-Nickel, 38.6 mm. **Ruler:** Elizabeth II **Series:** Victorian
Age Part II - Royal Family **Obv:** Bust with tiara right
Obv. Designer: Ian Rank-Broadley **Rev:** Victoria and Albert
seated with children **Edge:** Reeded

Date	Mintage	F	VF	XF	Unc	BU
2001	—	—	—	—	10.00	12.00

KM# 957a CROWN

28.2800 g., 0.9250 Silver 0.8410 oz. ASW, 38.6 mm.
Ruler: Elizabeth II **Series:** Victorian Age Part II - Royal Family
Obv: Bust with tiara right **Obv. Designer:** Ian Rank-Broadley
Rev: Victoria and Albert seated with children **Edge:** Reeded

Date	Mintage	F	VF	XF	Unc	BU
2001 Proof	10,000	Value: 47.50				

KM# 959 CROWN

Copper-Nickel, 38.6 mm. **Ruler:** Elizabeth II **Series:** Victorian
Age Part II - Victoria in Scotland **Obv:** Bust with tiara right
Obv. Designer: Ian Rank-Broadley **Rev:** Victoria on horse with
servant **Edge:** Reeded

Date	Mintage	F	VF	XF	Unc	BU
2001	2,001	—	—	—	10.00	12.00

KM# 959a CROWN

28.2800 g., 0.9250 Silver 0.8410 oz. ASW, 38.6 mm.
Ruler: Elizabeth II **Series:** Victorian Age Part II - Victoria in
Scotland **Obv:** Bust with tiara right **Obv. Designer:** Ian Rank-
Broadley **Rev:** Victoria on horse with servant **Edge:** Reeded

Date	Mintage	F	VF	XF	Unc	BU
2001 Proof	10,000	Value: 47.50				

KM# 961 CROWN

Copper-Nickel, 38.6 mm. **Ruler:** Elizabeth II **Series:** Victorian
Age Part II - Gladstone and Disraeli **Obv:** Bust with tiara right
Obv. Designer: Ian Rank-Broadley **Rev:** Portraits of both
politicians **Edge:** Reeded

Date	Mintage	F	VF	XF	Unc	BU
2001	—	—	—	—	10.00	12.00

KM# 961a CROWN

28.2800 g., 0.9250 Silver 0.8410 oz. ASW, 38.6 mm.
Ruler: Elizabeth II **Series:** Victorian Age Part II - Gladstone and
Disraeli **Obv:** Bust with tiara right **Obv. Designer:** Ian Rank-
Broadley **Rev:** Portraits of both politicians **Edge:** Reeded

Date	Mintage	F	VF	XF	Unc	BU
2001 Proof	10,000	Value: 47.50				

KM# 963 CROWN

Copper-Nickel, 38.6 mm. **Ruler:** Elizabeth II **Series:** Victorian Age
Part II **Obv:** Bust with tiara right **Obv. Designer:** Ian Rank-Broadley
Rev: Florence Nightingale holding lantern **Edge:** Reeded

Date	Mintage	F	VF	XF	Unc	BU
2001	—	—	—	—	10.00	12.00

KM# 963a CROWN

28.2800 g., 0.9250 Silver 0.8410 oz. ASW, 38.6 mm.
Ruler: Elizabeth II **Series:** Victorian Age Part II **Obv:** Bust with
tiara right **Obv. Designer:** Ian Rank-Broadley **Rev:** Florence
Nightingale holding lantern **Edge:** Reeded

Date	Mintage	F	VF	XF	Unc	BU
2001 Proof	10,000	Value: 47.50				

KM# 965 CROWN

Copper-Nickel, 38.6 mm. **Ruler:** Elizabeth II **Series:** Victorian
Age Part II **Obv:** Bust with tiara right **Obv. Designer:** Ian Rank-
Broadley **Rev:** Lord Tennyson with the Light Brigade in
background **Edge:** Reeded

Date	Mintage	F	VF	XF	Unc	BU
2001	—	—	—	—	10.00	12.00

KM# 965a CROWN

28.2800 g., 0.9250 Silver 0.8410 oz. ASW, 38.6 mm.
Ruler: Elizabeth II **Series:** Victorian Age Part II **Obv:** Bust with
tiara right **Obv. Designer:** Ian Rank-Broadley **Rev:** Lord
Tennyson with the Light Brigade in background **Edge:** Reeded

Date	Mintage	F	VF	XF	Unc	BU
2001 Proof	10,000	Value: 47.50				

KM# 967 CROWN

Copper-Nickel, 38.6 mm. **Ruler:** Elizabeth II **Series:** Victorian
Age Part II **Obv:** Bust with tiara right **Obv. Designer:** Ian Rank-
Broadley **Rev:** Stanley meeting Dr. Livingstone **Edge:** Reeded

Date	Mintage	F	VF	XF	Unc	BU
2001	—	—	—	—	10.00	12.00

KM# 967a CROWN

28.2800 g., 0.9250 Silver 0.8410 oz. ASW, 38.6 mm.
Ruler: Elizabeth II **Series:** Victorian Age Part II **Obv:** Bust with
tiara right **Obv. Designer:** Ian Rank-Broadley **Rev:** Stanley
meeting Dr. Livingstone **Edge:** Reeded

Date	Mintage	F	VF	XF	Unc	BU
2001 Proof	10,000	Value: 47.50				

KM# 969 CROWN

Copper-Nickel, 38.6 mm. **Ruler:** Elizabeth II **Series:** Victorian
Age Part II **Obv:** Bust with tiara right **Obv. Designer:** Ian
Broadley **Rev:** Bronte sisters **Edge:** Reeded

Date	Mintage	F	VF	XF	Unc	BU
2001	—	—	—	—	10.00	12.00

KM# 969a CROWN

28.2800 g., 0.9250 Silver 0.8410 oz. ASW, 38.6 mm. **Ruler:**
Elizabeth II **Series:** Victorian Age Part II **Obv:** Bust w/ tiara right
Obv. Designer: Ian Rank-Broadley **Rev:** Bronte sisters
Edge: Reeded

Date	Mintage	F	VF	XF	Unc	BU
2001 Proof	10,000	Value: 47.50				

KM# 1061 CROWN
31.1000 g., Electrum Special alloy of equal parts of gold and silver. **Ruler:** Elizabeth II **Series:** Ancient Coins **Obv:** Crowned bust right **Rev:** Lion and bull facing **Note:** From a Kroisos [sic] coin c. 560-546 BC.

Date	Mintage	F	VF	XF	Unc	BU
2002 Proof	—	Value: 600				

KM# 1060 CROWN
31.1000 g., Electrum Special alloy of equal parts of gold and silver. **Ruler:** Elizabeth II **Series:** Ancient Coins. **Obv:** Crowned bust right **Rev:** Lion and bull facing **Note:** From a Lampsakos electrum coin c. 450 BC.

Date	Mintage	F	VF	XF	Unc	BU
2002 Proof	—	Value: 600				

KM# 1059 CROWN
31.1000 g., Electrum Special alloy of equal parts of gold/silver. **Ruler:** Elizabeth II **Series:** Ancient Coins **Obv:** Crowned bust right **Rev:** Head of Hercules right **Note:** Lesbos coin c. 480-450

Date	Mintage	F	VF	XF	Unc	BU
2002 Proof	—	Value: 600				

KM# 1058 CROWN
31.1000 g., 1.0000 Electrum Special alloy of equal parts of gold and silver. 0.9998 oz. **Ruler:** Elizabeth II **Series:** Ancient Coins **Obv:** Crowned head right **Rev:** Head of Athena left **Note:** From a Mysia electrum coin c. 520 BC.

Date	Mintage	F	VF	XF	Unc	BU
2002 Proof	—	Value: 600				

KM# 979 CROWN
28.2800 g., Copper-Nickel, 38.6 mm. **Ruler:** Elizabeth II **Subject:** Queen Mother's Life **Obv:** Bust with tiara right **Obv. Designer:** Ian Rank-Broadley **Rev:** Christening of Prince William **Edge:** Reeded

Date	Mintage	F	VF	XF	Unc	BU
2002	—	—	—	—	10.00	12.00

KM# 979a CROWN
28.2800 g., 0.9250 Silver 0.8410 oz. ASW, 38.6 mm. **Ruler:** Elizabeth II **Subject:** Queen Mother's Life **Obv:** Bust with tiara right **Obv. Designer:** Ian Rank-Broadley **Rev:** Prince William's christening **Edge:** Reeded

Date	Mintage	F	VF	XF	Unc	BU
2002 Proof	10,000	Value: 47.50				

KM# 981 CROWN
28.2800 g., Copper-Nickel, 38.6 mm. **Ruler:** Elizabeth II **Subject:** World Cup Soccer **Obv:** Bust with tiara right **Obv. Designer:** Ian Rank-Broadley **Rev:** Two players about to collide **Edge:** Reeded

Date	Mintage	F	VF	XF	Unc	BU
2002	—	—	—	—	10.00	11.50

KM# 981a CROWN
28.2800 g., 0.9250 Silver 0.8410 oz. ASW, 38.6 mm. **Ruler:** Elizabeth II **Subject:** World Cup Soccer **Obv:** Bust with tiara right **Obv. Designer:** Ian Rank-Broadley **Rev:** Two players about to collide **Edge:** Reeded

Date	Mintage	F	VF	XF	Unc	BU
2002 Proof	10,000	Value: 47.50				

KM# 983 CROWN
28.2800 g., Copper-Nickel, 38.6 mm. **Ruler:** Elizabeth II **Subject:** World Cup Soccer **Obv:** Bust with tiara right **Obv. Designer:** Ian Rank-Broadley **Rev:** Two players facing viewer **Edge:** Reeded

Date	Mintage	F	VF	XF	Unc	BU
2002	—	—	—	—	10.00	11.50

KM# 983a CROWN
28.2800 g., 0.9250 Silver 0.8410 oz. ASW, 38.6 mm. **Ruler:** Elizabeth II **Subject:** World Cup Soccer **Obv:** Bust with tiara right **Obv. Designer:** Ian Rank-Broadley **Rev:** Two players facing viewer **Edge:** Reeded

Date	Mintage	F	VF	XF	Unc	BU
2002 Proof	10,000	Value: 47.50				

KM# 985 CROWN
28.2800 g., Copper-Nickel, 38.6 mm. **Ruler:** Elizabeth II **Subject:** World Cup Soccer **Obv:** Bust with tiara right **Obv. Designer:** Ian Rank-Broadley **Rev:** Two horizontal players **Edge:** Reeded

Date	Mintage	F	VF	XF	Unc	BU
2002	—	—	—	—	10.00	11.50

KM# 985a CROWN
28.2800 g., 0.9250 Silver 0.8410 oz. ASW, 38.6 mm. **Ruler:** Elizabeth II **Subject:** World Cup Soccer **Obv:** Bust with tiara right **Obv. Designer:** Ian Rank-Broadley **Rev:** Two horizontal players **Edge:** Reeded

Date	Mintage	F	VF	XF	Unc	BU
2002 Proof	10,000	Value: 47.50				

KM# 987 CROWN
28.2800 g., Copper-Nickel, 38.6 mm. **Ruler:** Elizabeth II **Subject:** World Cup Soccer **Obv:** Bust with tiara right **Obv. Designer:** Ian Rank-Broadley **Rev:** Two players moving to left **Edge:** Reeded

Date	Mintage	F	VF	XF	Unc	BU
2002	—	—	—	—	10.00	11.50

KM# 987a CROWN
28.2800 g., 0.9250 Silver 0.8410 oz. ASW, 38.6 mm. **Ruler:** Elizabeth II **Subject:** World Cup Soccer **Obv:** Bust with tiara right **Obv. Designer:** Ian Rank-Broadley **Rev:** Two players moving to left **Edge:** Reeded

Date	Mintage	F	VF	XF	Unc	BU
2002 Proof	10,000	Value: 47.50				

KM# 992.1 CROWN
28.2800 g., Copper-Nickel, 38.6 mm. **Ruler:** Elizabeth II **Subject:** Peter Rabbit Centennial **Obv:** Bust with tiara right **Obv. Designer:** Ian Rank-Broadley **Rev:** Peter Rabbit **Edge:** Reeded

Date	Mintage	F	VF	XF	Unc	BU
2002	—	—	—	—	10.00	12.00

KM# 992a CROWN
28.2800 g., 0.9250 Silver 0.8410 oz. ASW, 38.6 mm. **Ruler:** Elizabeth II **Subject:** Peter Rabbit Centennial **Obv:** Bust with tiara right **Obv. Designer:** Ian Rank-Broadley **Rev:** Peter Rabbit **Edge:** Reeded

Date	Mintage	F	VF	XF	Unc	BU
2002 Proof	10,000	Value: 47.50				

KM# 992.2 CROWN
Copper-Nickel **Ruler:** Elizabeth II **Obv:** Bust with tiara right **Obv. Designer:** Ian Rank-Broadley **Rev:** Peter Rabbit in multi-color

Date	Mintage	F	VF	XF	Unc	BU
2002	—	—	—	—	10.00	12.00

KM# 994 CROWN
28.2800 g., Copper-Nickel, 38.6 mm. **Ruler:** Elizabeth II **Subject:** Queen's Golden Jubilee **Obv:** Bust with tiara right **Obv. Designer:** Ian Rank-Broadley **Rev:** Royal couple and tree house **Edge:** Reeded

Date	Mintage	F	VF	XF	Unc	BU
2002	—	—	—	—	10.00	12.00

KM# 994a CROWN
Yellow Brass, 38.6 mm. **Ruler:** Elizabeth II **Subject:** Queen's Golden Jubilee **Obv:** Bust with tiara right **Obv. Designer:** Ian Rank-Broadley **Rev:** Royal couple and tree house **Edge:** Reeded

Date	Mintage	F	VF	XF	Unc	BU
2002 Proof	15,000	Value: 20.00				

KM# 994b CROWN
28.2800 g., 0.9250 Gold Clad Silver 0.8410 oz., 38.6 mm. **Ruler:** Elizabeth II **Subject:** Queen's Golden Jubilee **Obv:** Bust with tiara right **Obv. Designer:** Ian Rank-Broadley **Rev:** Royal couple and tree house **Edge:** Reeded

Date	Mintage	F	VF	XF	Unc	BU
2002 Proof	10,000	Value: 50.00				

KM# 996 CROWN

28.2800 g., Copper-Nickel, 38.6 mm. **Ruler:** Elizabeth II
Subject: Queen's Golden Jubilee **Obv:** Bust with tiara right
Obv. Designer: Ian Rank-Broadley **Rev:** Royal coach
Edge: Reeded

Date	Mintage	F	VF	XF	Unc	BU
2002	—	—	—	—	10.00	12.00

KM# 996a CROWN

Yellow Brass, 38.6 mm. **Ruler:** Elizabeth II **Subject:** Queen's
Golden Jubilee **Obv:** Bust with tiara right **Obv. Designer:** Ian
Rank-Broadley **Rev:** Royal coach **Edge:** Reeded

Date	Mintage	F	VF	XF	Unc	BU
2002 Proof	15,000	Value: 20.00				

KM# 996b CROWN

28.2800 g., 0.9250 Gold Clad Silver 0.8410 oz., 38.6 mm.
Ruler: Elizabeth II **Subject:** Queen's Golden Jubilee **Obv:** Bust
with tiara right **Obv. Designer:** Ian Rank-Broadley **Rev:** Royal
coach **Edge:** Reeded

Date	Mintage	F	VF	XF	Unc	BU
2002 Proof	10,000	Value: 50.00				

KM# 998 CROWN

28.2800 g., Copper-Nickel, 38.6 mm. **Ruler:** Elizabeth II
Subject: Queen's Golden Jubilee **Obv:** Bust with tiara right
Obv. Designer: Ian Rank-Broadley **Rev:** Royal couple w/baby
Edge: Reeded

Date	Mintage	F	VF	XF	Unc	BU
2002	—	—	—	—	10.00	12.00

KM# 998a CROWN

Yellow Brass, 38.6 mm. **Ruler:** Elizabeth II **Subject:** Queen's
Golden Jubilee **Obv:** Bust with tiara right **Obv. Designer:** Ian
Rank-Broadley **Rev:** Royal couple with baby **Edge:** Reeded

Date	Mintage	F	VF	XF	Unc	BU
2002 Proof	15,000	Value: 20.00				

KM# 998b CROWN

28.2800 g., 0.9250 Gold Clad Silver 0.8410 oz., 38.6 mm.
Ruler: Elizabeth II **Subject:** Queen's Golden Jubilee **Obv:** Bust
with tiara right **Obv. Designer:** Ian Rank-Broadley **Rev:** Royal
couple with baby **Edge:** Reeded

Date	Mintage	F	VF	XF	Unc	BU
2002 Proof	1,000	Value: 50.00				

KM# 1000 CROWN

28.2800 g., Copper-Nickel, 38.6 mm. **Ruler:** Elizabeth II
Subject: Queen's Golden Jubilee **Obv:** Bust w/tiara righ
Obv. Designer: Ian Rank-Broadley **Rev:** Royal yacht under Tower
bridge **Edge:** Reeded

Date	Mintage	F	VF	XF	Unc	BU
2002	—	—	—	—	10.00	12.00

KM# 1000a CROWN

Yellow Brass, 38.6 mm. **Ruler:** Elizabeth II **Subject:** Queen's
Golden Jubilee **Obv:** Bust with tiara right **Obv. Designer:** Ian Rank-
Broadley **Rev:** Royal yacht under Tower bridge **Edge:** Reeded

Date	Mintage	F	VF	XF	Unc	BU
2002 Proof	15,000	Value: 20.00				

KM# 1000b CROWN

28.2800 g., 0.9250 Gold Clad Silver 0.8410 oz., 38.6 mm.
Ruler: Elizabeth II **Subject:** Queen's Golden Jubilee **Obv:** Bust
with tiara right **Obv. Designer:** Ian Rank-Broadley **Rev:** Royal
yacht under Tower bridge **Edge:** Reeded

Date	Mintage	F	VF	XF	Unc	BU
2002 Proof	10,000	Value: 50.00				

KM# 1013 CROWN

28.2800 g., Copper-Nickel dark patina, 38.6 mm.
Ruler: Elizabeth II **Subject:** Death of Queen Mother **Obv:** Bust
with tiara right **Obv. Designer:** Ian Rank-Broadley **Rev:** Queen
Mother trout fishing **Edge:** Reeded

Date	Mintage	F	VF	XF	Unc	BU
2002	—	—	—	—	10.00	12.00

KM# 1013a CROWN

28.2800 g., 0.9250 Silver 0.8410 oz. ASW, 38.6 mm.
Ruler: Elizabeth II **Subject:** Queen Mother **Obv:** Bust with tiara
right **Obv. Designer:** Ian Rank-Broadley **Rev:** Queen Mother trout
fishing **Edge:** Reeded **Note:** Obv. and rev. have blackened legends.

Date	Mintage	F	VF	XF	Unc	BU
2002 Proof	5,000	Value: 175				

KM# 1015 CROWN

28.2800 g., Copper-Nickel, 38.6 mm. **Ruler:** Elizabeth II
Subject: Princess Diana **Obv:** Bust with tiara right
Obv. Designer: Ian Rank-Broadley **Rev:** Diana's portrait
Edge: Reeded

Date	Mintage	F	VF	XF	Unc	BU
2002	—	—	—	—	10.00	12.00

KM# 1015a CROWN

28.2800 g., 0.9250 Silver 0.8410 oz. ASW, 38.6 mm.
Ruler: Elizabeth II **Subject:** Princess Diana **Obv:** Bust with tiara
right **Obv. Designer:** Ian Rank-Broadley **Rev:** Diana's portrait
Edge: Reeded

Date	Mintage	F	VF	XF	Unc	BU
2002 Proof	10,000	Value: 47.50				

KM# 1019 CROWN

28.2800 g., Copper-Nickel, 38.6 mm. **Ruler:** Elizabeth II
Subject: Peter Pan **Obv:** Bust with tiara right **Obv. Designer:**
Ian Rank-Broadley **Rev:** Peter Pan and Tinkerbell flying above
city **Edge:** Reeded

Date	Mintage	F	VF	XF	Unc	BU
2002	—	—	—	—	10.00	12.00

KM# 1019a CROWN

28.2800 g., 0.9250 Silver 0.8410 oz. ASW, 38.6 mm.
Ruler: Elizabeth II **Subject:** Peter Pan **Obv:** Bust with tiara right
Obv. Designer: Ian Rank-Broadley **Rev:** Peter Pan and
Tinkerbell flying above city **Edge:** Reeded

Date	Mintage	F	VF	XF	Unc	BU
2002 Proof	10,000	Value: 47.50				

KM# 1021 CROWN

28.2800 g., Copper-Nickel, 38.6 mm. **Ruler:** Elizabeth II
Subject: Grand Masonic Lodge **Obv:** Bust with tiara right
Obv. Designer: Ian Rank-Broadley **Rev:** Masonic seal above
Gibraltar **Edge:** Reeded

Date	Mintage	F	VF	XF	Unc	BU
2002 Proof	5,000	Value: 10.00				

KM# 1021a CROWN

28.2800 g., 0.9250 Silver 0.8410 oz. ASW, 38.6 mm.
Ruler: Elizabeth II **Subject:** Grand Masonic Lodge **Obv:** Bust
with tiara right **Obv. Designer:** Ian Rank-Broadley **Rev:** Masonic
seal above Gibraltar **Edge:** Reeded

Date	Mintage	F	VF	XF	Unc	BU
2002 Proof	10,000	Value: 47.50				

KM# 1025 CROWN

28.2800 g., Copper-Nickel, 38.6 mm. **Ruler:** Elizabeth II
Subject: Calpe Conference **Obv:** Bust with tiara right
Obv. Designer: Ian Rank-Broadley **Rev:** Crossed flags and arms
Edge: Reeded

Date	Mintage	F	VF	XF	Unc	BU
2002PM	—	—	—	—	10.00	12.00

KM# 1025a CROWN

28.2800 g., 0.9250 Silver 0.8410 oz. ASW, 38.6 mm.
Ruler: Elizabeth II **Subject:** Calpe Conference **Obv:** Bust with
tiara right **Obv. Designer:** Ian Rank-Broadley **Rev:** Crossed flags
and arms **Edge:** Reeded

Date	Mintage	F	VF	XF	Unc	BU
2002PM Proof	10,000	Value: 47.50				

KM# 1052 CROWN

Copper-Nickel **Ruler:** Elizabeth II **Subject:** 2004 Athens
Olympics **Rev:** Horse jumping left

Date	Mintage	F	VF	XF	Unc	BU
2003	—	—	—	—	10.00	12.00

KM# 1053 CROWN
Copper-Nickel **Ruler:** Elizabeth II **Subject:** 2004 Athens
Olympics **Rev:** Javelin thrower

Date	Mintage	F	VF	XF	Unc	BU
2003	—	—	—	—	10.00	12.00

KM# 1054 CROWN
Copper-Nickel **Ruler:** Elizabeth II **Subject:** 2004 Athens
Olympics **Rev:** Field Hockey

Date	Mintage	F	VF	XF	Unc	BU
2003	—	—	—	—	10.00	12.00

KM# 1055 CROWN
Copper-Nickel **Ruler:** Elizabeth II **Subject:** 2004 Athens
Olympics **Rev:** Wrestlers

Date	Mintage	F	VF	XF	Unc	BU
2003	—	—	—	—	10.00	12.00

KM# 1035 CROWN
28.2800 g., Copper-Nickel, 38.6 mm. **Ruler:** Elizabeth II
Subject: 1700th Anniversary - Death of St. George **Obv:** Bust
with tiara right **Obv. Designer:** Ian Rank-Broadley **Rev:** St.
George and the dragon **Edge:** Reeded

Date	Mintage	F	VF	XF	Unc	BU
2003	—	—	—	—	9.00	10.00

KM# 1035a CROWN
28.2800 g., 0.9250 Silver 0.8410 oz. ASW, 38.6 mm.
Ruler: Elizabeth II **Subject:** 1700th Anniversary - Death of St.
George **Obv:** Bust with tiara right **Obv. Designer:** Ian Rank-
Broadley **Rev:** St. George and the dragon **Edge:** Reeded

Date	Mintage	F	VF	XF	Unc	BU
2003 Proof	10,000	Value: 47.50				

KM# 1039 CROWN
28.3000 g., Copper-Nickel, 38.6 mm. **Ruler:** Elizabeth II
Subject: Peter Rabbit **Obv:** Bust with tiara right
Obv. Designer: Ian Rank-Broadley **Rev:** Peter Rabbit holding
carrot **Edge:** Reeded

Date	Mintage	F	VF	XF	Unc	BU
2003PM	—	—	—	—	9.00	10.00

KM# 1040 CROWN
28.2800 g., Copper-Nickel, 38.6 mm. **Ruler:** Elizabeth II
Subject: Centennial of Powered Flight **Obv:** Queens portrait
Rev: Stealth bomber within circles of WWI and WWII planes
Edge: Reeded

Date	Mintage	F	VF	XF	Unc	BU
2003PM	—	—	—	—	10.00	12.00

KM# 1040a CROWN
31.1000 g., Tri-Metallic .9995 Platinum 5.2g center in .9999 Gold
14.2 g ring within .999 Silver 11.7 g outer ring, 38.6 mm.
Ruler: Elizabeth II **Subject:** Centennial of Powered Flight
Obv: Queens portrait **Rev:** Stealth bomber within circles of WWI
and WWII planes **Edge:** Reeded

Date	Mintage	F	VF	XF	Unc	BU
2003PM Proof	999	Value: 1,000				

KM# 1041 CROWN
28.2800 g., Copper-Nickel, 38.6 mm. **Ruler:** Elizabeth II
Subject: 50th Anniversary of Coronation **Obv:** Queens portrait
Rev: Buckingham Palace **Edge:** Reeded

Date	Mintage	F	VF	XF	Unc	BU
2003PM	—	—	—	—	10.00	12.00

KM# 1034 2 CROWN
41.5000 g., Bi-Metallic .999 Silver 11.5g. star shaped center in
Copper outer ring, 50 mm. **Ruler:** Elizabeth II **Subject:** Euro's
First Anniversary **Obv:** Crowned bust right within star silhouette

Rev: Europa riding a bull, stars and star silhouette in background
Edge: Reeded

Date	Mintage	F	VF	XF	Unc	BU
2003PM Proof	3,500	Value: 100				

KM# 1034a 2 CROWN
50.0000 g., Bi-Metallic .9999 Gold 20g star shaped center in
Copper outer ring, 50 mm. **Ruler:** Elizabeth II **Subject:** 1st
Anniversary - Euro **Obv:** Crowned bust right within star silhouette
Rev: Europa riding the bull, stars and star silhouette in
background **Edge:** Reeded

Date	Mintage	F	VF	XF	Unc	BU
2003PM Proof	2,003	Value: 800				

KM# 1034b 2 CROWN
56.3000 g., Bi-Metallic .9999 Gold 20.8g star shaped center in a
.999 Silver 35.5g outer ring, 50 mm. **Ruler:** Elizabeth II
Subject: 1st Anniversary - Euro **Obv:** Crowned bust right within
star silhouette **Rev:** Europa riding the bull, stars and star
silhouette in background **Edge:** Reeded

Date	Mintage	F	VF	XF	Unc	BU
2003PM Proof	2,003	Value: 850				

KM# 907 5 CROWN
Tri-Metallic Center .9995 Platinum 26.9g. Inner Ring .9999 Gold
73.41g. Outer Ring .999 Silver 55.19g, 50 mm. **Ruler:**
Elizabeth II **Subject:** 21st Century **Obv:** Crowned bust right, date
below **Obv. Designer:** Raphael Maklouf **Rev:** Celtic cross, Viking
ship and modern technological items **Edge:** Reeded

Date	Mintage	F	VF	XF	Unc	BU
2001 Proof	199	Value: 5,250				

KM# 1042 5 CROWN
155.5500 g., 0.9990 Silver 4.9958 oz. ASW, 65 mm.
Ruler: Elizabeth II **Subject:** 50th Anniversary of Coronation
Obv: Queens portrait **Rev:** Buckingham Palace with tiny .01ct ruby,
diamond and sapphire inserts above the main entrance
Edge: Reeded

Date	Mintage	F	VF	XF	Unc	BU
2003PM Proof	2,003	Value: 175				

KM# 1045 32 CROWNS
1000.0000 g., 0.9990 Silver 32.117 oz. ASW **Ruler:** Elizabeth II
Subject: Beatrix Potter's Peter Rabbit **Obv:** Bust with tiara right
Obv. Designer: Ian Rank-Broadley **Rev:** Multicolor Peter Rabbit
holding carrot, with blue coat and red slippers

Date	Mintage	F	VF	XF	Unc	BU
2003 Proof	1,000	Value: 750				

KM# 869 POUND
9.5000 g., Nickel-Brass, 22.5 mm. **Ruler:** Elizabeth II
Obv: Head with tiara right **Obv. Designer:** Ian Rank-Broadley
Rev: Gibraltar castle and key

Date	Mintage	F	VF	XF	Unc	BU
2001 AA	—	—	—	—	3.50	4.50
2001 AB	—	—	—	—	3.50	4.50
2002 AC	—	—	—	—	3.50	4.50

KM# 1036 POUND
9.5000 g., Nickel-Brass, 22 mm. **Ruler:** Elizabeth II
Subject: 1700th Anniversary - Death of St. George **Obv:** Bust
with tiara right **Rev:** St. George and the dragon **Edge:** Reeded

Date	Mintage	F	VF	XF	Unc	BU
2003	—	—	—	—	9.00	10.00

KM# 1051 POUND
9.5000 g., Nickel-Brass, 22.5 mm. **Ruler:** Elizabeth II
Subject: Tercentenary 1704-2004 **Obv:** Elizabeth II
Obv. Designer: Raphael Maklouf **Rev:** Old cannon set for a
downhill target **Rev. Designer:** Philip Nathan **Edge:** Reeded

Date	Mintage	F	VF	XF	Unc	BU
2004PM	—	—	—	—	—	4.00

KM# 970 2 POUNDS
Bi-Metallic Steel Copper-Nickel center in Brass ring, 28.4 mm.
Ruler: Elizabeth II **Subject:** Bicentennial of the Union Jack
Obv: Head with tiara right **Obv. Designer:** Ian Rank-Broadley
Rev: Standing Britannia wearing flag as a cape **Edge:** Reeded

Date	Mintage	F	VF	XF	Unc	BU
2001 AA	—	—	—	—	10.00	12.00

KM# 970a 2 POUNDS
12.0000 g., 0.9990 Bi-Metallic Silver center in Gold plated Silver
ring 0.3854 oz., 28.4 mm. **Ruler:** Elizabeth II **Subject:**
Bicentennial of the Union Jack **Obv:** Head with tiara right
Obv. Designer: Ian Rank-Broadley **Rev:** Standing Britannia
wearing flag as a cape **Edge:** Reeded

Date	Mintage	F	VF	XF	Unc	BU
2001	7,500	—	—	—	30.00	35.00

KM# 1043 2 POUNDS
12.0600 g., Bi-Metallic Copper-Nickel center in Brass ring,
28.3 mm. **Ruler:** Elizabeth II **Obv:** Head with tiara right
Obv. Designer: Ian Rank-Broadley **Rev:** Old cannon
Edge: Reeded

Date	Mintage	F	VF	XF	Unc	BU
2003PM	—	—	—	—	10.00	12.00

KM# 1057 2 POUNDS
9.5000 g., Nickel-Brass, 22.5 mm. **Ruler:** Elizabeth II
Subject: Tercentenary 1704-2004 **Obv:** Elizabeth II
Obv. Designer: Raphael Maklouf **Rev:** Old cannon set for a
downhill target **Rev. Designer:** Philip Nathan **Edge:** Reeded

Date	Mintage	F	VF	XF	Unc	BU
2004PM	—	—	—	—	—	4.00

KM# 953 5 POUNDS
20.0000 g., Virenium, 36.1 mm. **Ruler:** Elizabeth II
Subject: Gibraltar Chronicle 200 Years **Obv:** Head with tiara right
Obv. Designer: Ian Rank-Broadley **Rev:** Naval battle scene with
newspaper in background **Edge:** Reeded

Date	Mintage	F	VF	XF	Unc	BU
2001	—	—	—	—	15.00	18.00

KM# 953a 5 POUNDS
23.5000 g., 0.9250 Silver 0.6988 oz. ASW, 36.1 mm. **Ruler:**
Elizabeth II **Subject:** Gibraltar Chronicle 200 Years **Obv:** Head
with tiara right **Obv. Designer:** Ian Rank-Broadley **Rev:** Naval
battle scene with newspaper in background **Edge:** Reeded

Date	Mintage	F	VF	XF	Unc	BU
2001 Proof	10,000	Value: 50.00				

KM# 953b 5 POUNDS
39.8300 g., 0.9167 Gold 1.1738 oz. AGW, 36.1 mm. **Ruler:**
Elizabeth II **Subject:** Gibraltar Chronicle 200 Years **Obv:** Head
with tiara right **Obv. Designer:** Ian Rank-Broadley **Rev:** Naval
battle scene with newspaper in background **Edge:** Reeded

Date	Mintage	F	VF	XF	Unc	BU
2001 Proof	850	Value: 1,500				

KM# 1011 5 POUNDS
20.0000 g., Virenium, 36.1 mm. **Ruler:** Elizabeth II **Subject:**
Queen's Golden Jubilee **Obv:** Head with tiara right **Obv. Designer:**
Ian Rank-Broadley **Rev:** Coronation scene **Edge:** Reeded

Date	Mintage	F	VF	XF	Unc	BU
2002	—	—	—	—	15.00	18.00

KM# 1011a 5 POUNDS
23.5000 g., 0.9250 Silver 0.6988 oz. ASW, 36.1 mm.
Ruler: Elizabeth II **Subject:** Queen's Golden Jubilee **Obv:** Head
with tiara right **Obv. Designer:** Ian Rank-Broadley
Rev: Coronation scene **Edge:** Reeded

Date	Mintage	F	VF	XF	Unc	BU
2002 Proof	10,000	Value: 50.00				

KM# 1011b 5 POUNDS
39.8300 g., 0.9166 Gold 1.1737 oz. AGW, 36.1 mm. **Ruler:**
Elizabeth II **Subject:** Queen's Golden Jubilee **Obv:** Head w/ tiara
right **Obv. Designer:** Ian Rank-Broadley **Rev:** Coronation scene
Edge: Reeded

Date	Mintage	F	VF	XF	Unc	BU
2002 Proof	850	Value: 1,500				

KM# 1064 5 POUNDS
Silver, 38 mm. **Ruler:** Elizabeth II **Subject:** 20th Anniversary,
Battle of Trafalgar **Rev:** Two naval vessels **Edge:** Reeded

Date	Mintage	F	VF	XF	Unc	BU
2005 Proof	—	Value: 40.00				

SOVEREIGN COINAGE

KM# 1037 1/5 SOVEREIGN
1.2200 g., 0.9999 Gold 0.0392 oz. AGW, 13.92 mm. **Ruler:**
Elizabeth II **Subject:** Death of St. George **Obv:** Bust with tiara
right **Obv. Designer:** Ian Rank-Broadley **Rev:** St. George and
the dragon **Edge:** Reeded

Date	Mintage	F	VF	XF	Unc	BU
2003 Proof	10,000	Value: 55.00				

KM# 1038 SOVEREIGN
6.2200 g., 0.9999 Gold 0.1999 oz. AGW, 22 mm.
Ruler: Elizabeth II **Subject:** Death of St. George **Obv:** Bust with
tiara right **Obv. Designer:** Ian Rank-Broadley **Rev:** St. George
and the dragon **Edge:** Reeded

Date	Mintage	F	VF	XF	Unc	BU
2003 Proof	5,000	Value: 250				

ROYAL COINAGE

KM# 896 1/25 ROYAL
1.2441 g., 0.9999 Gold 0.0400 oz. AGW, 13.92 mm.
Ruler: Elizabeth II **Subject:** Bullion **Obv:** Bust with tiara right
Obv. Designer: Ian Rank-Broadley **Rev:** Two cherubs
Edge: Reeded

Date	Mintage	F	VF	XF	Unc	BU
2001	—	—	—	—	50.00	—
2001 Proof	1,000	Value: 60.00				

KM# 972 1/25 ROYAL
1.2440 g., 0.9990 Gold 0.0400 oz. AGW, 13.92 mm.
Ruler: Elizabeth II **Subject:** Cherubs **Obv:** Bust with tiara right
Obv. Designer: Ian Rank-Broadley **Rev:** Two cherubs shooting
arrrows **Edge:** Reeded

Date	Mintage	F	VF	XF	Unc	BU
2002	—	—	—	—	50.00	—
2002 Proof	1,000	Value: 60.00				

KM# 1027 1/25 ROYAL
1.2440 g., 0.9990 Gold 0.0400 oz. AGW, 13.92 mm.
Ruler: Elizabeth II **Obv:** Bust with tiara right **Obv. Designer:** Ian
Rank-Broadley **Rev:** Cherub with crossed arms **Edge:** Reeded

Date	Mintage	F	VF	XF	Unc	BU
2003PM	—	—	—	—	50.00	—
2003PM Proof	—	Value: 60.00				

KM# 897 1/10 ROYAL
3.1100 g., 0.9999 Gold 0.1000 oz. AGW, 18 mm.
Ruler: Elizabeth II **Subject:** Bullion **Obv:** Bust with tiara right
Obv. Designer: Ian Rank-Broadley **Rev:** Two cherubs
Edge: Reeded

Date	Mintage	F	VF	XF	Unc	BU
2001	—	—	—	—	—	125
2001 Proof	1,000	Value: 135				

KM# 973 1/10 ROYAL
3.1100 g., 0.9990 Gold 0.0999 oz. AGW, 17.95 mm.
Ruler: Elizabeth II **Subject:** Cherubs **Obv:** Bust with tiara right
Obv. Designer: Ian Rank-Broadley **Rev:** Two cherubs shooting
arrows **Edge:** Reeded

Date	Mintage	F	VF	XF	Unc	BU
2002	—	—	—	—	—	125
2002 Proof	1,000	Value: 135				

KM# 1028 1/10 ROYAL
3.1100 g., 0.9999 Gold 0.1000 oz. AGW, 17.95 mm.
Ruler: Elizabeth II **Obv:** Bust with tiara right **Obv. Designer:** Ian
Rank-Broadley **Rev:** Cherub with crossed arms **Edge:** Reeded

Date	Mintage	F	VF	XF	Unc	BU
2003PM	—	—	—	—	—	125
2003PM Proof	—	Value: 135				

KM# 898 1/5 ROYAL
6.2200 g., 0.9990 Gold 0.1998 oz. AGW, 22 mm.
Ruler: Elizabeth II **Subject:** Bullion **Obv:** Bust with tiara right
Obv. Designer: Ian Rank-Broadley **Rev:** Two cherubs
Edge: Reeded

Date	Mintage	F	VF	XF	Unc	BU
2001	—	—	—	—	—	250
2001 Proof	1,000	Value: 265				

KM# 974 1/5 ROYAL
6.2200 g., 0.9990 Gold 0.1998 oz. AGW, 22 mm. **Ruler:**
Elizabeth II **Obv:** Bust with tiara right **Obv. Designer:** Ian Rank-
Broadley **Rev:** Two cherubs shooting arrows **Edge:** Reeded

Date	Mintage	F	VF	XF	Unc	BU
2002	—	—	—	—	—	250
2002 Proof	1,000	Value: 265				

KM# 1029 1/5 ROYAL
6.2200 g., 0.9999 Gold 0.1999 oz. AGW, 22 mm. **Ruler:**
Elizabeth II **Obv:** Bust with tiara right **Obv. Designer:** Ian Rank-
Broadley **Rev:** Cherub with crossed arms **Edge:** Reeded

Date	Mintage	F	VF	XF	Unc	BU
2003PM	—	—	—	—	—	250
2003PM Proof	—	Value: 265				

KM# 899 1/2 ROYAL
15.5517 g., 0.9999 Gold 0.4999 oz. AGW, 30 mm. **Ruler:**
Elizabeth II **Subject:** Bullion **Obv:** Bust with tiara right **Obv.
Designer:** Ian Rank-Broadley **Rev:** Two cherubs **Edge:** Reeded

Date	Mintage	F	VF	XF	Unc	BU
2001	—	—	—	—	—	625
2001 Proof	1,000	Value: 640				

KM# 975 1/2 ROYAL
15.5510 g., 0.9990 Gold 0.4995 oz. AGW, 30 mm. **Ruler:**
Elizabeth II **Obv:** Bust with tiara right **Obv. Designer:** Ian Rank-
Broadley **Rev:** Two cherubs shooting arrows **Edge:** Reeded

Date	Mintage	F	VF	XF	Unc	BU
2002	—	—	—	—	—	625
2002 Proof	1,000	Value: 640				

KM# 1030 1/2 ROYAL
15.5510 g., 0.9999 Gold 0.4999 oz. AGW, 30 mm. **Ruler:**
Elizabeth II **Obv:** Bust with tiara right **Obv. Designer:** Ian Rank-
Broadley **Rev:** Cherub with crossed arms **Edge:** Reeded

Date	Mintage	F	VF	XF	Unc	BU
2003PM	—	—	—	—	—	625
2003PM Proof	—	Value: 640				

KM# 900 ROYAL
28.2800 g., Copper-Nickel, 38.6 mm. **Ruler:** Elizabeth II
Obv: Bust with tiara right **Obv. Designer:** Ian Rank-Broadley
Rev: Two cherubs **Edge:** Reeded

Date	Mintage	F	VF	XF	Unc	BU
2001	—	—	—	—	—	10.00	12.00

KM# 900a ROYAL
31.1035 g., 0.9990 Silver 0.9990 oz. ASW **Ruler:** Elizabeth II
Obv: Bust with tiara right **Obv. Designer:** Ian Rank-Broadley
Rev: Two cherubs

Date	Mintage	F	VF	XF	Unc	BU
2001 Proof	10,000	Value: 47.50				

KM# 901 ROYAL
31.1035 g., 0.9999 Gold 0.9999 oz. AGW, 32.7 mm.
Ruler: Elizabeth II **Subject:** Bullion **Obv:** Bust with tiara right
Obv. Designer: Ian Rank-Broadley **Rev:** Two cherubs
Edge: Reeded

Date	Mintage	F	VF	XF	Unc	BU
2001	—	—	—	—	—	1,250	1,300
2001 Proof	1,000	Value: 1,350				

KM# 976 ROYAL
28.2800 g., Copper-Nickel, 38.6 mm. **Ruler:** Elizabeth II
Obv: Bust with tiara right **Obv. Designer:** Ian Rank-Broadley
Rev: Two cherubs shooting arrows **Edge:** Reeded

Date	Mintage	F	VF	XF	Unc	BU
2002	—	—	—	—	10.00	12.00

KM# 976a ROYAL
31.1035 g., 0.9990 Silver 0.9990 oz. ASW **Ruler:** Elizabeth II
Obv: Bust with tiara right **Obv. Designer:** Ian Rank-Broadley
Rev: Two cherubs shooting arrows **Edge:** Reeded

Date	Mintage	F	VF	XF	Unc	BU
2002 Proof	1,000	Value: 47.50				

KM# 977 ROYAL
31.1035 g., 0.9990 Gold 0.9990 oz. AGW, 32.7 mm. **Ruler:**
Elizabeth II **Obv:** Bust with tiara right **Obv. Designer:** Ian Rank-Broadley **Rev:** Two cherubs shooting arrows **Edge:** Reeded

Date	Mintage	F	VF	XF	Unc	BU
2002	—	—	—	—	1,250	1,300
2002 Proof	1,000	Value: 1,350				

KM# 1031 ROYAL
28.2800 g., Copper-Nickel, 38.6 mm. **Ruler:** Elizabeth II
Obv: Bust with tiara right **Obv. Designer:** Ian Rank-Broadley
Rev: Cherub with crossed arms **Edge:** Reeded

Date	Mintage	F	VF	XF	Unc	BU
2003PM	—	—	—	—	10.00	12.00

KM# 1031a ROYAL
28.2800 g., 0.9990 Silver 0.9083 oz. ASW, 38.6 mm.
Ruler: Elizabeth II **Obv:** Bust with tiara right **Obv. Designer:** Ian Rank-Broadley **Rev:** Cherub with crossed arms **Edge:** Reeded

Date	Mintage	F	VF	XF	Unc	BU
2003PM Proof	10,000	Value: 47.50				

KM# 1032 ROYAL
31.1035 g., 0.9999 Gold 0.9999 oz. AGW, 32.7 mm.
Ruler: Elizabeth II **Obv:** Bust with tiara right **Obv. Designer:** Ian Rank-Broadley **Rev:** Cherub with crossed arms **Edge:** Reeded

Date	Mintage	F	VF	XF	Unc	BU
2003PM	—	—	—	—	1,250	1,300
2003PM Proof	—	Value: 1,350				

PROOF SETS

KM#	Date	Mintage	Identification	Issue Price	Mkt Val
PS29	2001 (5)	1,000	KM#896-899, 901	—	2,500
PS30	2003 (5)	1,000	KM#1027-30, 1032	—	2,500

GREAT BRITAIN

The United Kingdom of Great Britain and Northern Ireland, located off the northwest coast of the European continent, has an area of 94,227 sq. mi. (244,820 sq. km.) and a population of 54 million. Capital: London. The economy is based on industrial activity and trading. Machinery, motor vehicles, chemicals, and textile yarns and fabrics are exported.

By the mid-20th century, most of the territories formerly comprising the British Empire had gained independence, and the empire had evolved into the Commonwealth of Nations, an association of equal and autonomous states, which enjoy special trade interests. The Commonwealth is presently composed of 54 member nations, including the United Kingdom. All recognize the British monarch as head of the Commonwealth. Sixteen continue to recognize the British monarch as Head of State. They are: United Kingdom, Antigua and Barbuda, Australia, Bahamas, Barbados, Belize, Canada, Grenada, Jamaica, New Zealand, Papua New Guinea, St. Christopher & Nevis, Saint Lucia, Saint Vincent and the Grenadines, Solomon Islands, and Tuvalu. Elizabeth II is personally, and separately, the Queen of the sovereign, independent countries just mentioned. There is no other British connection between the several individual, national sovereignties, except that High Commissioners represent them each instead of ambassadors in each other's countries.

RULERS
Elizabeth II, 1952--

MINT MARKS
H - Heaton
KN - King's Norton

KINGDOM
PRE-DECIMAL COINAGE

KM# 898 PENNY
0.4713 g., 0.9250 Silver 0.0140 oz. ASW, 11 mm.
Ruler: Elizabeth II **Obv:** Laureate bust right **Obv. Designer:** Mary Gillick **Rev:** Crowned value in sprays divides date within wreath **Edge:** Reeded

Date	Mintage	F	VF	XF	Unc	BU
2001 Prooflike	1,132	—	—	—	50.00	55.00
2002 Prooflike	1,681	—	—	—	50.00	55.00
2003 Prooflike	1,608	—	—	—	55.00	60.00
2004 Prooflike	1,613	—	—	—	55.00	60.00
2005 Prooflike	1,685	—	—	—	55.00	60.00
2006 Prooflike	1,937	—	—	—	55.00	60.00
2006 Proof	—	—	—	—	—	—
2007 Prooflike	1,822	—	—	—	55.00	60.00
2008 Prooflike	1,833	—	—	—	55.00	60.00
2009 Prooflike	—	—	—	—	55.00	60.00

KM# 898a PENNY
0.9167 Gold **Ruler:** Elizabeth II **Obv:** Laureate bust right
Obv. Designer: Mary Gillick **Rev:** Crowned denomination divides date within wreath

Date	Mintage	F	VF	XF	Unc	BU
2002 Proof	—	Value: 1,000				

KM# 899 2 PENCE
0.9426 g., 0.9250 Silver 0.0280 oz. ASW, 13 mm.
Ruler: Elizabeth II **Obv:** Laureate bust right **Obv. Legend:** Without BRITT OMN **Obv. Designer:** Mary Gillick **Rev:** Crowned value in sprays divides date within wreath **Edge:** Reeded

Date	Mintage	F	VF	XF	Unc	BU
2001 Prooflike	1,132	—	—	—	55.00	60.00
2002 Prooflike	1,681	—	—	—	55.00	60.00
2003 Prooflike	1,608	—	—	—	60.00	65.00
2004 Prooflike	1,613	—	—	—	60.00	65.00
2005 Prooflike	1,685	—	—	—	60.00	65.00
2006 Prooflike	1,937	—	—	—	60.00	65.00
2006 Proof	—	—	—	—	—	—
2007 Prooflike	1,822	—	—	—	60.00	65.00
2008 Prooflike	1,833	—	—	—	60.00	65.00
2009 Prooflike	—	—	—	—	60.00	65.00

KM# 899a 2 PENCE
0.9167 Gold **Ruler:** Elizabeth II **Series:** Maundy Sets
Obv: Laureate bust right **Obv. Legend:** Without BRITT OMN
Obv. Designer: Mary Gillick **Rev:** Crowned denomination divides date within wreath

Date	Mintage	F	VF	XF	Unc	BU
2002 Proof	—	Value: 1,100				

KM# 901 3 PENCE
1.4138 g., 0.9250 Silver 0.0420 oz. ASW, 16 mm.
Ruler: Elizabeth II **Obv:** Laureate bust right **Obv. Legend:** without BRITT OMN **Obv. Designer:** Mary Gillick **Rev:** Crowned value in sprays divides date within wreath **Edge:** Reeded

Date	Mintage	F	VF	XF	Unc	BU
2001 Prooflike	1,132	—	—	—	58.00	62.00
2002 Prooflike	1,681	—	—	—	58.00	62.00
2003 Prooflike	1,608	—	—	—	60.00	65.00
2004 Prooflike	1,613	—	—	—	60.00	65.00
2005 Prooflike	1,685	—	—	—	60.00	65.00
2006 Prooflike	1,937	—	—	—	60.00	65.00
2006 Proof	—	—	—	—	—	—
2007 Prooflike	1,822	—	—	—	60.00	65.00
2008 Prooflike	1,833	—	—	—	60.00	65.00
2009 Prooflike	—	—	—	—	60.00	65.00

KM# 901a 3 PENCE
0.9167 Gold **Ruler:** Elizabeth II **Obv:** Laureate bust right
Obv. Legend: Without RITT OMN **Obv. Designer:** Mary Gillick
Rev: Crowned denomination divides date within wreath

Date	Mintage	F	VF	XF	Unc	BU
2002 Proof	—	Value: 1,150				

KM# 902 4 PENCE (Groat)
1.8851 g., 0.9250 Silver 0.0561 oz. ASW, 18 mm.
Ruler: Elizabeth II **Obv:** Laureate bust right **Obv. Legend:** without BRITT OMN **Rev:** Crowned denomination divides date within wreath **Edge:** Reeded

Date	Mintage	F	VF	XF	Unc	BU
2001 Prooflike	1,132	—	—	—	58.00	62.00
2002 Prooflike	1,681	—	—	—	58.00	62.00
2003 Prooflike	1,608	—	—	—	60.00	65.00
2004 Prooflike	1,613	—	—	—	60.00	65.00
2005 Prooflike	1,685	—	—	—	60.00	65.00
2006 Prooflike	1,937	—	—	—	60.00	65.00
2006 Proof	—	—	—	—	—	—
2007 Prooflike	1,822	—	—	—	60.00	65.00
2008 Prooflike	1,833	—	—	—	60.00	65.00
2009 Prooflike	—	—	—	—	60.00	65.00

KM# 902a 4 PENCE
0.9167 Gold **Ruler:** Elizabeth II **Obv:** Laureate bust right
Obv. Legend: Without BRITT OMN **Rev:** Crowned denomination divides date within wreath

Date	Mintage	F	VF	XF	Unc	BU
2002 Proof	—	Value: 1,250				

DECIMAL COINAGE

1971-1981: 100 New Pence = 1 Pound;
1982-present: 100 Pence = 1 Pound

KM# 986 PENNY
3.5900 g., Copper Plated Steel, 20.34 mm. **Ruler:** Elizabeth II
Obv: Head with tiara right **Obv. Designer:** Ian Rank-Broadley
Rev: Crowned portcullis **Rev. Designer:** Christopher Ironside
Edge: Plain

Date	Mintage	F	VF	XF	Unc	BU
2001	928,698,000	—	—	—	0.20	—
2002	601,446,000	—	—	—	0.20	—
2003	539,436,000	—	—	—	0.20	—
2003 Proof	43,513	Value: 3.25				
2004	739,764,000	—	—	—	0.20	—
2004 Proof	35,020	Value: 3.25				
2005	536,318,000	—	—	—	0.20	—
2005 Proof	40,563	Value: 3.25				
2006	524,605,000	—	—	—	0.20	—
2006 Proof	—	Value: 3.25				
2007	548,002,000	—	—	—	0.20	—
2007 Proof	—	Value: 3.25				
2008	180,600,000	—	—	—	—	2.00

KM# 986c PENNY
0.9167 Gold **Ruler:** Elizabeth II **Obv:** Head with tiara right
Obv. Designer: Ian Rank-Broadley **Rev:** Crowned portcullis
Rev. Designer: Christopher Ironside

Date	Mintage	F	VF	XF	Unc	BU
2002 Proof	—	Value: 700				
2008 Proof	2,008	Value: 500				

KM# 986a PENNY
3.5000 g., Bronze, 20.3 mm. **Ruler:** Elizabeth II **Obv:** Head with tiara right **Obv. Designer:** Ian Rank-Broadley **Rev:** Crowned portcullis **Edge:** Plain **Note:** Issued in sets only

Date	Mintage	F	VF	XF	Unc	BU
2002 Proof	—	Value: 2.00				
2003 Proof	—	Value: 2.00				
2004 Proof	100,000	Value: 2.00				

KM# 1107 PENNY
3.5900 g., Copper Plated Steel, 20.3 mm. **Ruler:** Elizabeth II **Obv:** Head with tiara right **Rev:** Partial arms - lion and harp

Date	Mintage	F	VF	XF	Unc	BU
2008	386,830,000	—	—	—	—	0.20
2008 Proof	—	Value: 3.50				
2009	Est. 500,000					0.20
2009 Proof	—	Value: 3.50				

KM# 986b PENNY
3.5600 g., 0.9250 Silver 0.1059 oz. ASW, 20.3 mm. **Ruler:** Elizabeth II **Obv:** Head with tiara right **Obv. Designer:** Ian Rank-Broadley **Rev:** Crowned portcullis **Rev. Designer:** Christopher Ironside **Edge:** Plain

Date	Mintage	F	VF	XF	Unc	BU
2008 Proof	10,000	Value: 16.50				

KM# 987 2 PENCE
7.1400 g., Copper Plated Steel, 25.86 mm. **Ruler:** Elizabeth II **Obv:** Head with tiara right **Obv. Designer:** Ian Rank-Broadley **Rev:** Welsh plumes and crown **Rev. Designer:** Christopher Ironside **Edge:** Plain

Date	Mintage	F	VF	XF	Unc	BU
2001	551,880,000	—	—	—	0.25	—
2002	168,556,000	—	—	—	0.25	—
2003	260,225,000	—	—	—	0.25	—
2003 Proof	43,513	Value: 3.25				
2004	356,396,000	—	—	—	0.25	—
2004 Proof	35,020	Value: 3.25				
2005	280,396,000	—	—	—	0.25	—
2005 Proof	40,563	Value: 3.25				
2006	170,637,000	—	—	—	0.25	—
2006 Proof	—	Value: 3.25				
2007	254,500,000	—	—	—	0.25	—
2007 Proof	—	Value: 3.25				
2008	10,600,000	—	—	—	—	2.00

KM# 987a 2 PENCE
Bronze, 25.91 mm. **Ruler:** Elizabeth II **Obv:** Head with tiara right **Obv. Designer:** Ian Rank-Broadley **Rev:** Welsh plumes and crown **Rev. Designer:** Christopher Ironside

Date	Mintage	F	VF	XF	Unc	BU
2002 Proof	—	Value: 2.50				
2003 Proof	—	Value: 2.50				
2004 Proof	100,000	Value: 2.50				

KM# 987c 2 PENCE
0.9167 Gold, 25.91 mm. **Ruler:** Elizabeth II **Subject:** Queen's Golden Jubilee - 1952-2002 **Obv:** Head with tiara right **Obv. Designer:** Ian Rank-Broadley **Rev:** Welsh plumes and crown **Rev. Designer:** Christopher Ironside

Date	Mintage	F	VF	XF	Unc	BU
2002 Proof	—	Value: 800				
2008 Proof	2,008	Value: 600				

KM# 1108 2 PENCE
7.1000 g., 25.8600 Copper Plated Steel 5.9028 oz., 25.86 mm. **Ruler:** Elizabeth II **Obv:** Head with tiara right **Rev:** Partial arms lion

Date	Mintage	F	VF	XF	Unc	BU
2008	129,530,000	—	—	—	—	0.25
2008 Proof	—	Value: 3.25				
2009	—	—	—	—	—	0.25
2009 Proof	—	Value: 3.25				

KM# 987b 2 PENCE
7.1200 g., 0.9250 Silver 0.2117 oz. ASW, 25.9 mm. **Ruler:** Elizabeth II **Obv:** Head with tiara right **Obv. Designer:** Ian Rank-Broadley **Rev:** Welsh plumes and crown **Rev. Designer:** Christopher Ironside **Edge:** Plain

Date	Mintage	F	VF	XF	Unc	BU
2008 Proof	10,000	Value: 17.50				

KM# 988 5 PENCE
3.2500 g., Copper-Nickel, 18 mm. **Ruler:** Elizabeth II **Obv:** Head with tiara right **Obv. Designer:** Ian Rank-Broadley **Rev:** Crowned thistle

Date	Mintage	F	VF	XF	Unc	BU
2001	337,930,000	—	—	—	0.30	—
2001 Proof	100,000	Value: 3.00				
2002	219,258,000	—	—	—	0.30	—
2002 Proof	—	Value: 3.00				
2003	333,230,000	—	—	—	0.30	—
2003 Proof	43,513	Value: 3.00				
2004	271,810,000	—	—	—	0.30	—
2004 Proof	35,020	Value: 3.00				
2005	236,212,000	—	—	—	0.30	—
2005 Proof	40,563	Value: 3.00				
2006	317,697,000	—	—	—	0.30	—
2006 Proof	—	Value: 3.00				
2007	246,720,000	—	—	—	0.30	—
2007 Proof	—	Value: 3.00				
2008	86,400,000	—	—	—	—	3.00

KM# 988b 5 PENCE
0.9167 Gold, 18 mm. **Ruler:** Elizabeth II **Obv:** Head with tiara right **Obv. Designer:** Ian Rank-Broadley **Rev:** Crowned thistle

Date	Mintage	F	VF	XF	Unc	BU
2002 Proof	—	Value: 400				
2008 Proof	—	Value: 350				

KM# 1109 5 PENCE
3.2500 g., Copper-Nickel, 18 mm. **Ruler:** Elizabeth II **Obv:** Head with tiara right **Rev:** Partial arms - center

Date	Mintage	F	VF	XF	Unc	BU
2008	109,460,000	—	—	—	0.30	—
2008 Proof	—	Value: 3.00				
2009	Est. 500,000	—	—	—	0.30	—
2009 Proof	—	Value: 3.00				

KM# 988a 5 PENCE
3.2500 g., 0.9250 Silver 0.0966 oz. ASW, 18 mm. **Ruler:** Elizabeth II **Obv:** Head with tiara right **Obv. Designer:** Ian Rank-Broadley **Rev:** Crowned thistle **Rev. Designer:** Christopher Ironside **Edge:** Reeded

Date	Mintage	F	VF	XF	Unc	BU
2008 Proof	10,000	Value: 20.00				

KM# 989 10 PENCE
6.5000 g., Copper-Nickel, 24.5 mm. **Ruler:** Elizabeth II **Obv:** Head with tiara right **Obv. Designer:** Ian Rank-Broadley **Rev:** Crowned lion prancing left **Rev. Designer:** Christopher Ironside

Date	Mintage	F	VF	XF	Unc	BU
2001	129,281,000	—	—	—	0.40	—
2001 Proof	100,000	Value: 3.25				
2002	80,934,000	—	—	—	0.40	—
2002 Proof	—	Value: 3.25				
2003	88,118,000	—	—	—	0.40	—
2003 Proof	43,513	Value: 3.25				
2004	99,602,000	—	—	—	0.40	—
2004 Proof	35,020	Value: 3.25				

Date	Mintage	F	VF	XF	Unc	BU
2005	69,604,000	—	—	—	0.40	—
2005 Proof	40,563	Value: 3.25				
2006	118,803,000	—	—	—	0.40	—
2006 Proof	—	Value: 3.25				
2007	72,720,000	—	—	—	0.40	—
2007 Proof	—	Value: 3.25				
2008	9,720,000	—	—	—	—	3.00

KM# 989b 10 PENCE
0.9167 Gold, 24.5 mm. **Ruler:** Elizabeth II **Obv:** Head with tiara right **Obv. Designer:** Ian Rank-Broadley **Rev:** Crowned lion prancing left **Rev. Designer:** Christopher Ironside

Date	Mintage	F	VF	XF	Unc	BU
2002 Proof	—	Value: 650				
2008 Proof	2,008	Value: 550				

KM# 1110 10 PENCE
6.5000 g., Copper-Nickel, 24.5 mm. **Ruler:** Elizabeth II **Obv:** Head with tiara right **Rev:** Partial arms - two lions

Date	Mintage	F	VF	XF	Unc	BU
2008	53,900,000	—	—	—	—	0.40
2008 Proof	—	Value: 3.25				
2009	Est. 500,000	—	—	—	—	0.40
2009 Proof	—	Value: 3.25				

KM# 989a 10 PENCE
6.5000 g., 0.9250 Silver 0.1933 oz. ASW, 24.5 mm. **Ruler:** Elizabeth II **Obv:** Head with tiara right **Obv. Designer:** Ian Rank-Broadley **Rev:** Crowned lion prancing left **Rev. Designer:** Christopher Ironside **Edge:** Reeded

Date	Mintage	F	VF	XF	Unc	BU
2008 Proof	10,000	Value: 17.50				

KM# 990 20 PENCE
5.0000 g., Copper-Nickel, 21.4 mm. **Ruler:** Elizabeth II **Obv:** Head with tiara right **Obv. Designer:** Ian Rank-Broadley **Rev:** Crowned rose **Rev. Designer:** William Gardner **Shape:** 7-sided

Date	Mintage	F	VF	XF	Unc	BU
2001	148,122,500	—	—	—	0.60	—
2001 Proof	100,000	Value: 3.25				
2002	93,360,000	—	—	—	0.60	—
2002 Proof	100,000	Value: 3.25				
2003	153,383,750	—	—	—	0.60	—
2003 Proof	43,513	Value: 3.25				
2004	120,212,500	—	—	—	0.60	—
2004 Proof	35,020	Value: 3.25				
2005	124,488,750	—	—	—	0.60	—
2005 Proof	40,563	Value: 3.25				
2006	114,800,000	—	—	—	0.60	—
2006 Proof	—	Value: 3.25				
2007	117,075,000	—	—	—	0.60	—
2007 Proof	—	Value: 3.25				
2008	11,900,000	—	—	—	—	3.00

KM# 990b 20 PENCE
0.9167 Gold, 21.4 mm. **Ruler:** Elizabeth II **Obv:** Head with tiara right **Obv. Designer:** Ian Rank-Broadley **Rev:** Crowned rose **Rev. Designer:** William Gardner **Shape:** 7-sided

Date	Mintage	F	VF	XF	Unc	BU
2002 Proof	—	Value: 500				
2008 Proof	2,008	Value: 450				

KM# 1111 20 PENCE

5.0000 g., Copper-Nickel, 21.4 mm. **Ruler:** Elizabeth II **Obv:** Head with tiara right **Rev:** Partial arms - lions tails **Shape:** 7-sided

Date	Mintage	F	VF	XF	Unc	BU
2008	81,920,000	—	—	—	—	0.60
2008 Proof	—	Value: 3.25				
2009	Est. 500,000	—	—	—	—	0.60
2009 Proof	—	Value: 3.25				

KM# 990a 20 PENCE

5.0000 g., 0.9250 Silver 0.1487 oz. ASW, 21.4 mm. **Ruler:** Elizabeth II **Obv:** Head with tiara right **Obv. Designer:** Ian Rank-Broadley **Rev:** Crowned rose **Rev. Designer:** William Gardner **Edge:** Plain **Shape:** 7-sided

Date	Mintage	F	VF	XF	Unc	BU
2008 Proof	10,000	Value: 18.50				

KM# 1122 20 PENCE

5.0000 g., Copper-Nickel, 21.4 mm. **Ruler:** Elizabeth II **Obv:** Head right. Obverse of KM#990 **Rev:** Arms part. Reverse of KM#1111 **Note:** Mule.

Date	Mintage	F	VF	XF	Unc	BU
ND(2009)	—	—	—	—	—	—

KM# 991 50 PENCE

8.0000 g., Copper-Nickel, 27.3 mm. **Ruler:** Elizabeth II **Obv:** Head with tiara right **Obv. Designer:** Ian Rank-Broadley **Rev:** Britannia seated right **Rev. Designer:** Christopher Ironside **Shape:** 7-sided

Date	Mintage	F	VF	XF	Unc	BU
2001	85,000,000	—	—	—	1.75	—
2001 Proof	100,000	Value: 2.50				
2002	23,907,500	—	—	—	1.75	—
2002 Proof	—	Value: 2.50				
2003	23,583,000	—	—	—	1.75	—
2003 Proof	43,513	Value: 2.50				
2004	35,315,500	—	—	—	1.75	—
2004 Proof	35,020	Value: 2.50				
2005	25,363,500	—	—	—	1.75	—
2005 Proof	40,563	Value: 2.50				
2006	24,567,000	—	—	—	1.75	—
2006 Proof	—	Value: 2.50				
2007	53,000,000	—	—	—	1.75	—
2007 Proof	—	Value: 2.50				
2008	700,000	—	—	—	—	5.00

KM# 991b 50 PENCE

0.9167 Gold, 27.3 mm. **Ruler:** Elizabeth II **Obv:** Head with tiara right **Obv. Designer:** Ian Rank-Broadley **Rev:** Britannia seated right **Rev. Designer:** Christopher Ironside **Shape:** 7-sided

Date	Mintage	F	VF	XF	Unc	BU
2002 Proof	—	Value: 650				
2008 Proof	—	Value: 600				

KM# 1036 50 PENCE

8.0000 g., Copper-Nickel, 27.3 mm. **Ruler:** Elizabeth II **Subject:** Woman's Suffrage **Obv:** Head with tiara right **Obv. Designer:** Ian Rank-Broadley **Rev:** Standing woman with banner **Edge:** Plain **Shape:** 7-sided

Date	Mintage	F	VF	XF	Unc	BU
2003	3,124,030	—	—	—	2.50	3.50
2003 Proof	35,513	Value: 9.50				

KM# 1036a 50 PENCE

8.0000 g., 0.9250 Silver 0.2379 oz. ASW, 27.3 mm. **Ruler:** Elizabeth II **Obv:** Head with tiara right **Obv. Designer:** Ian Rank-Broadley **Rev:** Standing woman with banner **Edge:** Plain **Shape:** 7-sided

Date	Mintage	F	VF	XF	Unc	BU
2003 Proof	6,267	Value: 45.00				

KM# 1036b 50 PENCE

15.5000 g., 0.9166 Gold 0.4568 oz. AGW, 27.3 mm. **Ruler:** Elizabeth II **Obv:** Head with tiara right **Obv. Designer:** Ian Rank-Broadley **Rev:** Standing woman with banner **Edge:** Plain **Shape:** 7-sided

Date	Mintage	F	VF	XF	Unc	BU
2003 Proof	942	Value: 650				

KM# 1047 50 PENCE

8.0000 g., Copper-Nickel, 27.3 mm. **Ruler:** Elizabeth II **Subject:** Roger Bannister's Four Minute Mile **Obv:** Head with tiara right **Obv. Designer:** Ian Rank-Broadley **Rev:** Running legs, stop watch and value **Edge:** Plain

Date	Mintage	F	VF	XF	Unc	BU
2004	9,032,500	—	—	—	5.00	6.00
2004 Proof	35,020	Value: 7.50				

KM# 1047a 50 PENCE

8.0000 g., 0.9250 Silver 0.2379 oz. ASW **Ruler:** Elizabeth II **Subject:** The First Four Minute Mile **Obv:** Head with tiara right **Obv. Designer:** Ian Rank-Broadley **Rev:** Running legs, stop watch and value

Date	Mintage	F	VF	XF	Unc	BU
2009 Proof	4,924	Value: 45.00				

KM# 1050 50 PENCE

8.0000 g., Copper-Nickel, 27.3 mm. **Ruler:** Elizabeth II **Obv:** Head with tiara right **Obv. Designer:** Ian Rank-Broadley **Rev:** Text from the first English dictionary by Samuel Johnson **Edge:** Plain

Date	Mintage	F	VF	XF	Unc	BU
2005	17,649,000	—	—	—	2.50	3.50
2005 Proof	40,563	Value: 6.00				

KM# 1050a 50 PENCE

8.0000 g., 0.9250 Silver 0.2379 oz. ASW, 27.3 mm. **Ruler:** Elizabeth II **Subject:** First English Dictionary **Obv:** Head with tiara right **Obv. Designer:** Ian Rank-Broadley **Rev:** Sample page from Johnson's 1755 dictionary **Edge:** Plain **Shape:** 7-sided

Date	Mintage	F	VF	XF	Unc	BU
2005 Proof	4,029	Value: 45.00				

KM# 1050b 50 PENCE

15.5000 g., 0.9167 Gold 0.4568 oz. AGW, 27.3 mm. **Ruler:** Elizabeth II **Subject:** 1st English Dictionary **Obv:** Head with tiara right **Obv. Designer:** Ian Rank-Broadley **Rev:** Sample page from Johnson's 1755 dictionary **Edge:** Plain **Shape:** 7-sided

Date	Mintage	F	VF	XF	Unc	BU
2005 Proof	1,000	Value: 650				

KM# 1057 50 PENCE

8.0000 g., Copper-Nickel, 27.3 mm. **Ruler:** Elizabeth II **Obv:** Head with tiara right **Obv. Designer:** Ian Rank-Broadley **Rev:** Victoria Cross obverse and reverse views **Edge:** Plain **Shape:** 7-sided

Date	Mintage	F	VF	XF	Unc	BU
2006	12,087,000	—	—	—	5.00	6.00
2006 Proof	Est. 50,000	Value: 7.50				
2007 Proof	—	Value: 7.50				

KM# 1058 50 PENCE

8.0000 g., Copper-Nickel, 27.3 mm. **Ruler:** Elizabeth II **Obv:** Head with tiara right **Obv. Designer:** Ian Rank-Broadley **Rev:** Heroic Act scene with cross shape in background **Edge:** Plain **Shape:** 7-sided

Date	Mintage	F	VF	XF	Unc	BU
2006	10,000,500	—	—	—	5.00	6.00
2006 Proof	Est. 50,000	Value: 7.50				
2007 Proof	—	Value: 7.50				

KM# 1073 50 PENCE

8.0000 g., Copper-Nickel, 27.3 mm. **Ruler:** Elizabeth II **Subject:** Centennial of Scouting **Obv:** Bust right **Rev:** Fleur de Lis Scouting emblem superimposed on globe **Edge:** Plain **Shape:** 7-sided

Date	Mintage	F	VF	XF	Unc	BU
2007	7,710,750	—	—	—	—	5.00
2007 Proof	Est. 50,000	Value: 7.50				

KM# 1073a 50 PENCE

8.0000 g., 0.9250 Silver 0.2379 oz. ASW, 27.3 mm. **Ruler:** Elizabeth II **Subject:** Scouting Centennial **Obv:** Elizabeth II **Rev:** Fleur de Lis Scouting emblem superimposed on globe **Edge:** Plain **Shape:** 7-sided

Date	Mintage	F	VF	XF	Unc	BU
2007 Proof	12,500	Value: 60.00				

KM# 1073b 50 PENCE

15.5000 g., 0.9166 Gold 0.4568 oz. AGW, 27.3 mm. **Ruler:** Elizabeth II **Subject:** Scouting Centennial **Obv:** Elizabeth II **Rev:** Fleur de Lis Scouting emblem superimposed on globe **Edge:** Plain **Shape:** 7-sided

Date	Mintage	F	VF	XF	Unc	BU
2007 Proof	1,250	Value: 675				

KM# 1112 50 PENCE

8.0000 g., Copper-Nickel, 27.3 mm. **Ruler:** Elizabeth II **Obv:** Head with tiara right **Rev:** Partial shield - bottom center **Shape:** 7-sided

Date	Mintage	F	VF	XF	Unc	BU
2008	12,320,000	—	—	—	—	1.75
2008 Proof	—	Value: 3.50				
2009	Est. 500,000	—	—	—	—	1.75
2009 Proof	—	Value: 3.50				

KM# 1114 50 PENCE

8.0000 g., Copper-Nickel, 27.3 mm. **Ruler:** Elizabeth II **Subject:** Botanical Gardens at Kew **Obv:** Head with tiara right **Rev:** Vine and tower 1759-2009

Date	Mintage	F	VF	XF	Unc	BU
2009	Est. 500,000	—	—	—	—	5.00
2009 Proof	—	Value: 7.50				

KM# 1119 50 PENCE

8.0000 g., 0.9250 Silver 0.2379 oz. ASW, 27.3 mm. **Ruler:** Elizabeth II **Subject:** Royal Botanical Gardens at Kew, 250th Anniversary **Obv:** Head right **Obv. Designer:** Ian rank-Broadley **Rev:** Chinese pagoda with vines **Rev. Designer:** Christopher Le Brun **Shape:** 7-sided

Date	Mintage	F	VF	XF	Unc	BU
2009 Proof	7,500	Value: 45.00				

KM# 1119a 50 PENCE

15.5000 g., 0.9160 Gold 0.4565 oz. AGW, 27.3 mm. **Ruler:** Elizabeth II **Subject:** Royal otanical Gardens at Kew, 250th Anniversary **Obv:** Head right **Obv. Designer:** Ian Rank-Broadley **Rev:** Chinese pagoda with vines **Rev. Designer:** Christopher Le Brun **Shape:** 7-sided

Date	Mintage	F	VF	XF	Unc	BU
2009 Proof	1,000	Value: 650				

KM# 1013 POUND

9.5000 g., Nickel-Brass, 22.5 mm. **Ruler:** Elizabeth II **Subject:** Northern Ireland **Obv:** Head with tiara right **Obv. Designer:** Ian Rank-Broadley **Rev:** Celtic style cross **Rev. Designer:** Norman Sillman **Edge:** Reeding **Edge Lettering:** DECUS ET TUTAMEN

Date	Mintage	F	VF	XF	Unc	BU
2001	63,968,065	—	—	—	4.00	5.00
2001 Proof	—	Value: 6.00				

KM# 1013a POUND

9.5000 g., 0.9250 Silver 0.2825 oz. ASW, 22.5 mm. **Ruler:** Elizabeth II **Subject:** Northern Ireland **Obv:** Head with tiara right **Obv. Designer:** Ian Rank-Broadley **Rev:** Celtic cross design **Edge:** Reeded **Edge Lettering:** DECUS ET TUTAMEN

Date	Mintage	F	VF	XF	Unc	BU
2001 Proof	25,000	Value: 40.00				

KM# 1030 POUND

9.5000 g., Nickel-Brass, 22.5 mm. **Ruler:** Elizabeth II **Obv:** Head with tiara right **Obv. Designer:** Ian Rank-Broadley **Rev:** Three lions **Rev. Designer:** Norman Sillman **Edge:** Reeded **Edge Lettering:** DECUS ET TUTAMEN

Date	Mintage	F	VF	XF	Unc	BU
2002	77,818,000	—	—	—	5.00	6.00
2002 Proof	100,000	Value: 7.00				

KM# 1030a POUND

9.5000 g., 0.9250 Silver 0.2825 oz. ASW, 22.5 mm. **Ruler:** Elizabeth II **Obv:** Head with tiara right **Obv. Designer:** Ian Rank-Broadley **Rev:** Three lions **Edge:** Reeded **Edge Lettering:** DECUS ET TUTAMEN

Date	Mintage	F	VF	XF	Unc	BU
2002 Proof	—	Value: 40.00				

KM# 1030b POUND

0.9167 Gold, 22.5 mm. **Ruler:** Elizabeth II **Obv:** Head with tiara right **Obv. Designer:** Ian Rank-Broadley **Rev:** Three lions left **Rev. Designer:** Norman Sillman **Edge:** Reeded **Edge Lettering:** DECUS ET TUTAMEN

Date	Mintage	F	VF	XF	Unc	BU
2002 Proof	—	Value: 750				

KM# 993 POUND

9.5000 g., Nickel-Brass, 22.5 mm. **Ruler:** Elizabeth II **Obv:** Head with tiara right **Obv. Designer:** Ian Rank-Broadley **Rev:** Shield of Great Britain within Garter, crowned and supported **Rev. Designer:** Eric Sewell **Edge Lettering:** DECUS ET TUTAMEN

Date	Mintage	F	VF	XF	Unc	BU
2003	61,596,500	—	—	—	5.00	6.00
2003 Proof	43,513	Value: 7.50				
2008	3,910,000	—	—	—	5.00	6.00

KM# 1048a POUND

9.5000 g., 0.9250 Silver 0.2825 oz. ASW, 22.5 mm. **Obv:** Elizabeth II **Rev:** Forth Rail Bridge **Edge:** Ornamented and reeded

Date	Mintage	F	VF	XF	Unc	BU
2004 Proof	Est. 20,000	Value: 45.00				

KM# 1048 POUND

9.5000 g., Nickel-Brass, 22.5 mm. **Ruler:** Elizabeth II **Obv:** Head with tiara right **Obv. Designer:** Ian Rank-Broadley **Rev:** "Forth Rail Bridge" in Scotland **Edge:** Reeded and lettered **Edge Lettering:** "NEMO ME IMPUNE LACESSIT"

Date	Mintage	F	VF	XF	Unc	BU
2004	39,162,000	—	—	—	6.00	7.50
2004 Proof	35,020	Value: 9.00				

KM# 1048b POUND

19.6190 g., 0.9166 Gold 0.5781 oz. AGW, 22.5 mm. **Ruler:** Elizabeth II **Obv:** Elizabeth II **Rev:** Forth Rail Bridge **Edge:** Ornamented and reeded

Date	Mintage	F	VF	XF	Unc	BU
2004 Proof	Est. 1,500	Value: 750				

KM# 1051 POUND

9.5000 g., Nickel-Brass, 22.5 mm. **Ruler:** Elizabeth II **Obv:** Head with tiara right **Obv. Designer:** Ian Rank-Broadley **Rev:** Menai Bridge in Wales **Edge:** Reeded and lettered **Edge Lettering:** PLEIDOL WYF I'M GWLAD

Date	Mintage	F	VF	XF	Unc	BU
2005	99,429,500	—	—	—	5.00	6.00
2005 Proof	40,563	Value: 10.00				

KM# 1051a POUND

9.5000 g., 0.9250 Silver 0.2825 oz. ASW, 22.5 mm. **Ruler:** Elizabeth II **Obv:** Head with tiara right **Obv. Designer:** Ian Rank-Broadley **Rev:** Menai Bridge **Edge Lettering:** 'PLEIDOL WYF I'M GWLAD"

Date	Mintage	F	VF	XF	Unc	BU
2005 Proof	Est. 15,000	Value: 45.00				

KM# 1051b POUND

19.6190 g., 0.9167 Gold 0.5782 oz. AGW, 22.5 mm. **Ruler:** Elizabeth II **Obv:** Head with tiara right **Obv. Designer:** Ian Rank-Broadley **Rev:** Menai Bridge **Edge Lettering:** 'PLEIDOL WYF I'M GWLAD"

Date	Mintage	F	VF	XF	Unc	BU
2005 Proof	Est. 1,500	Value: 750				

KM# 1051a.2 POUND

9.5000 g., 0.9250 Silver 0.2825 oz. ASW, 22.5 mm. **Ruler:** Elizabeth II **Obv:** Elizabeth II **Rev:** Menai Suspension Bridge **Edge:** Ornamented and reeded

Date	Mintage	F	VF	XF	Unc	BU
2005 Proof	Est. 20,000	Value: 45.00				

KM# 1051b.2 POUND

19.6190 g., 0.9166 Gold 0.5781 oz. AGW, 22.5 mm. **Ruler:** Elizabeth II **Obv:** Elizabeth II **Rev:** Menai Suspension Bridge **Edge:** Ornamented and reeded

Date	Mintage	F	VF	XF	Unc	BU
2005 Proof	Est. 1,500	Value: 750				

KM# 1059 POUND

9.6000 g., Nickel-Brass, 23 mm. **Ruler:** Elizabeth II **Obv:** Head with tiara right **Obv. Designer:** Ian Rank-Broadley **Rev:** Egyptian Arch Bridge at Newry, Northern Ireland **Edge:** Reeded and lettered

Date	Mintage	F	VF	XF	Unc	BU
2006	38,938,000	—	—	—	8.00	9.00
2006 Proof	50,000	Value: 10.00				
2007 Proof	—	Value: 10.00				

KM# 1059a POUND

9.5000 g., 0.9250 Silver 0.2825 oz. ASW, 22.5 mm. **Ruler:** Elizabeth II **Obv:** Head with tiara right **Obv. Designer:** Ian Rank-Broadley **Rev:** Egyptian Arch Bridge **Edge Lettering:** "DECUS ET TUTAMEN"

Date	Mintage	F	VF	XF	Unc	BU
2006 Proof	Est. 20,000	Value: 50.00				

KM# 1059a.2 POUND

9.5000 g., 0.9250 Silver 0.2825 oz. ASW, 22.5 mm. **Ruler:** Elizabeth II **Obv:** Elizabeth II **Rev:** Egyptian Arch Bridge **Edge:** Ornamented and reeded

Date	Mintage	F	VF	XF	Unc	BU
2006 Proof	Est. 20,000	Value: 45.00				

KM# 1059b POUND

19.6190 g., 0.9167 Gold 0.5782 oz. AGW, 22.5 mm. **Ruler:** Elizabeth II **Obv:** Head with tiara right **Obv. Designer:** Ian Rank-Broadley **Rev:** Egyptian Arch Bridge **Edge Lettering:** "DECUS ET TUTAMEN"

Date	Mintage	F	VF	XF	Unc	BU
2006 Proof	—	Value: 775				

KM# 1059b.2 POUND

19.6190 g., 0.9166 Gold 0.5781 oz. AGW, 22.5 mm. **Ruler:** Elizabeth II **Obv:** Elizabeth II **Rev:** Egyptian Arch Bridge **Edge:** Ornamented and reeded

Date	Mintage	F	VF	XF	Unc	BU
2006 Proof	Est. 1,500	Value: 750				

KM# 1074a POUND

9.5000 g., 0.9250 Silver 0.2825 oz. ASW, 22.5 mm. **Ruler:** Elizabeth II **Obv:** Elizabeth II **Rev:** Gateshead Millennium Bridge **Edge:** Ornamented and reeded

Date	Mintage	F	VF	XF	Unc	BU
2007 Proof	Est. 20,000	Value: 45.00				

KM# 1074b POUND

19.6190 g., 0.9166 Gold 0.5781 oz. AGW, 22.5 mm. **Ruler:** Elizabeth II **Obv:** Elizabeth II **Rev:** Gateshead Millennium Bridge **Edge:** Ornamented and reeded

Date	Mintage	F	VF	XF	Unc	BU
2007 Proof	Est. 1,500	Value: 750				

KM# 1074 POUND

9.5000 g., Nickel-Brass, 22.5 mm. **Ruler:** Elizabeth II **Obv:** Head with tiara right **Obv. Designer:** Ian Rank-Broadley **Rev:** Gateshead Millennium Bridge **Edge:** Reeded and lettered

Date	Mintage	F	VF	XF	Unc	BU
2007	26,180,160	—	—	—	7.00	8.00
2007 Proof	Est. 50,000	Value: 10.00				

KM# 993a POUND

9.5000 g., 0.9250 Silver 0.2825 oz. ASW, 22.5 mm. **Ruler:** Elizabeth II **Obv:** Head with tiara right **Obv. Designer:** Ian Rank-Broadley **Rev:** Shield of Great Britain within Garter, crowned and supported **Rev. Designer:** Eric Sewell

Date	Mintage	F	VF	XF	Unc	BU
2008 Proof	Est. 10,000	Value: 40.00				

KM# 993b POUND

19.6000 g., 0.9167 Gold 0.5776 oz. AGW, 22.5 mm. **Ruler:** Elizabeth II **Obv:** Head with tiara right **Rev:** Shield of Great Britain withing Garter, crowned and supported **Edge Lettering:** DECUS ET TUTAMEN

Date	Mintage	F	VF	XF	Unc	BU
2008 Proof	Est. 2,008	Value: 750				

KM# 1113 POUND

9.5000 g., Nickel-Brass, 22.5 mm. **Ruler:** Elizabeth II **Obv:** Head with tiara right **Rev:** Full shield of Great Britain

Date	Mintage	F	VF	XF	Unc	BU
2008	29,433,000	—	—	—	4.00	5.00
2008 Proof	—	Value: 6.00				
2009	Est. 300,000	—	—	—	4.00	5.00
2009 Proof	—	Value: 6.00				

KM# 994 2 POUNDS

12.0000 g., Bi-Metallic Copper-Nickel center in Nickel-Brass ring, 28.4 mm. **Ruler:** Elizabeth II **Obv:** Head with tiara right within circle **Obv. Designer:** Ian Rank-Broadley **Rev:** Celtic design within circle **Rev. Designer:** Bruce Rushin **Edge Lettering:** STANDING ON THE SHOULDERS OF GIANTS

Date	Mintage	F	VF	XF	Unc	BU
2001	34,984,750	—	—	—	6.00	8.50
2001 Proof	—	Value: 10.00				
2002	13,024,750	—	—	—	6.00	8.50
2002 Proof	—	Value: 10.00				
2003	17,531,250	—	—	—	6.00	8.50
2003 Proof	43,513	Value: 10.00				
2004	11,981,500	—	—	—	6.00	8.50
2004 Proof	35,020	Value: 10.00				
2005	3,837,250	—	—	—	6.00	8.50
2005 Proof	40,563	Value: 10.00				
2006	16,715,000	—	—	—	6.00	8.50
2006 Proof	—	Value: 10.00				
2007	10,270,000	—	—	—	6.00	8.50
2007 Proof	—	Value: 10.00				
2008	15,346,000	—	—	—	6.00	8.00

KM# 1014 2 POUNDS

11.9700 g., Bi-Metallic Copper-Nickel center in Nickel-Brass ring, 28.4 mm. **Ruler:** Elizabeth II **Subject:** First Transatlantic Radio Transmission **Obv:** Head with tiara right within circle **Obv. Designer:** Ian Rank-Broadley **Rev:** Symbolic design **Rev. Designer:** Robert Evans **Edge:** Reeded and inscribed **Edge Lettering:** WIRELESS BRIDGES THE ATLANTIC... MARCONI... 1901

Date	Mintage	F	VF	XF	Unc	BU
2001	4,558,000	—	—	—	6.00	7.00
2001 Proof	—	Value: 10.00				

KM# 1014a 2 POUNDS

24.0000 g., 0.9250 Silver Silver center in Gold plated ring 0.7137 oz. ASW, 28.4 mm. **Ruler:** Elizabeth II **Subject:** First Transatlantic Radio Transmission **Obv:** Head with tiara right within circle **Obv. Designer:** Ian Rank-Broadley **Rev:** Symbolic design **Rev. Designer:** Robert Evans **Edge:** Reeded and inscribed **Edge Lettering:** "WIRELESS BRIDGES THE ATLANTIC...MARCONI 1901..."

Date	Mintage	F	VF	XF	Unc	BU
2001 Proof	25,000	Value: 35.00				

KM# 1014b 2 POUNDS

15.9700 g., 0.9166 Gold Yellow gold plated Red Gold center in Red Gold ring 0.4706 oz. AGW, 28.4 mm. **Ruler:** Elizabeth II **Subject:** First Transatlantic Radio Transmission **Obv:** Head with tiara right **Obv. Designer:** Ian Rank-Broadley **Rev:** Symbolic design **Rev. Designer:** Robert Evans

Date	Mintage	F	VF	XF	Unc	BU
2001 Proof	1,500	Value: 600				

KM# 994c 2 POUNDS

15.9800 g., 0.9167 Gold 0.4710 oz. AGW, 28.35 mm. **Ruler:** Elizabeth II **Obv:** Head with tiara right within circle **Obv. Designer:** Ian Rank-Broadley **Rev:** Celtic design within circle **Rev. Designer:** Bruce Rushin

Date	Mintage	F	VF	XF	Unc	BU
2002 Proof	—	Value: 750				

KM# 1031 2 POUNDS

12.0000 g., Bi-Metallic Copper-Nickel center in Nickel-Brass ring, 28.4 mm. **Ruler:** Elizabeth II **Subject:** 17th Commonwealth Games - Manchester, England **Obv:** Head with tiara right **Obv. Designer:** Ian Rank-Broadley **Rev:** Runner breaking ribbon at finish line, national flag of England in circle behind athlete **Rev. Designer:** Matthew Bonaccorsi **Edge:** Reeded and lettered **Edge Lettering:** SPIRIT OF FRIENDSHIP MANCHESTER 2002

Date	Mintage	F	VF	XF	Unc	BU
2002	650,500	—	—	—	6.00	7.00
2002 Proof	—	Value: 8.75				

KM# 1031a 2 POUNDS

12.0000 g., 0.9250 Silver Silver center in Gold plated ring 0.3569 oz. ASW, 28.4 mm. **Ruler:** Elizabeth II **Subject:** Commonwealth Games - England **Obv:** Head with tiara right **Obv. Designer:** Ian Rank-Broadley **Rev:** Runner breaking ribbon at finish line **Rev. Designer:** Matthew Bonaccorsi **Edge:** Reeded and lettered

Date	Mintage	F	VF	XF	Unc	BU
2002 Proof	10,000	Value: 40.00				

KM# 1031b 2 POUNDS

15.9800 g., 0.9160 Gold Yellow gold center in Red Gold ring 0.4706 oz. AGW, 28.4 mm. **Ruler:** Elizabeth II **Subject:** Commonwealth Games - England **Obv:** Head with tiara right **Obv. Designer:** Ian Rank-Broadley **Rev:** Runner breaking ribbon at finish line **Rev. Designer:** Matthew Bonaccorsi **Edge:** Reeded and lettered

Date	Mintage	F	VF	XF	Unc	BU
2002 Proof	500	Value: 650				

KM# 1032 2 POUNDS

12.0000 g., Bi-Metallic Copper-Nickel center in Nickel-Brass ring, 28.4 mm. **Ruler:** Elizabeth II **Subject:** 17th Commonwealth Games - Manchester, England **Obv:** Head with tiara right **Obv. Designer:** Ian Rank-Broadley **Rev:** Runner breaking ribbon at finish line, national flag of Scotland in circle behind athlete **Rev. Designer:** Matthew Bonaccorsi **Edge:** Reeded and lettered

Date	Mintage	F	VF	XF	Unc	BU
2002	771,750	—	—	—	5.00	6.00
2002 Proof	—	Value: 8.75				

KM# 1032a 2 POUNDS

12.0000 g., 0.9250 Silver Silver center with Gold plated ring 0.3569 oz. ASW, 28.4 mm. **Ruler:** Elizabeth II **Subject:** Commonwealth Games - Scotland **Obv:** Head with tiara right **Obv. Designer:** Ian Rank-Broadley **Rev:** Runner breaking ribbon at finish line **Rev. Designer:** Matthew Bonaccorsi **Edge:** Reeded and lettered

Date	Mintage	F	VF	XF	Unc	BU
2002 Proof	10,000	Value: 30.00				

KM# 1032b 2 POUNDS

15.9800 g., 0.9160 Gold Yellow gold center in Red Gold ring 0.4706 oz. AGW, 28.4 mm. **Ruler:** Elizabeth II **Subject:** Commonwealth Games - Scotland **Obv:** Head with tiara right **Obv. Designer:** Ian Rank-Broadley **Rev:** Runner breaking ribbon at finish line **Rev. Designer:** Matthew Bonaccorsi **Edge:** Reeded and lettered

Date	Mintage	F	VF	XF	Unc	BU
2002 Proof	500	Value: 550				

KM# 1033 2 POUNDS

12.0000 g., Bi-Metallic Copper-Nickel center in Nickel-Brass ring, 28.4 mm. **Ruler:** Elizabeth II **Subject:** 17th Commonwealth Games - Manchester, England **Obv:** Head with tiara right **Obv. Designer:** Ian Rank-Broadley **Rev:** Runner breaking ribbon at finish line, national flag of Wales in circle behind athlete **Rev. Designer:** Matthew Bonaccorsi **Edge:** Reeded and lettered **Edge Lettering:** SPIRIT OF FRIENDSHIP MANCHESTER 2002

Date	Mintage	F	VF	XF	Unc	BU
2002	588,500	—	—	—	6.00	7.00
2002 Proof	—	Value: 8.75				

KM# 1033a 2 POUNDS

12.0000 g., 0.9250 Silver Silver center in Gold plated ring 0.3569 oz. ASW, 28.4 mm. **Ruler:** Elizabeth II **Subject:** Commonwealth Games - Wales **Obv:** Head with tiara right **Obv. Designer:** Ian Rank-Broadley **Rev:** Runner breaking ribbon at finish line **Rev. Designer:** Matthew Bonaccorsi **Edge:** Reeded and lettered

Date	Mintage	F	VF	XF	Unc	BU
2002 Proof	10,000	Value: 30.00				

KM# 1033b 2 POUNDS

15.9800 g., 0.9160 Gold Yellow Gold center in Red Gold ring 0.4706 oz. AGW, 28.4 mm. **Ruler:** Elizabeth II **Subject:** Commonwealth Games - Wales **Obv:** Head with tiara right **Obv. Designer:** Ian Rank-Broadley **Rev:** Runner breaking ribbon at finish line **Rev. Designer:** Matthew Bonaccorsi **Edge:** Reeded and lettered

Date	Mintage	F	VF	XF	Unc	BU
2002 Proof	500	Value: 550				

KM# 1034 2 POUNDS

12.0000 g., Bi-Metallic Copper-Nickel center in Nickel-Brass ring, 28.4 mm. **Ruler:** Elizabeth II **Subject:** 17th Commonwealth Games - Manchester, England **Obv:** Head with tiara right **Obv. Designer:** Ian Rank-Broadley **Rev:** Runner breaking ribbon at finish line, national flag of Northern Ireland in circle behind athlete **Rev. Designer:** Matthew Bonaccorsi **Edge:** Reeded and lettered **Edge Lettering:** SPIRIT OF FRIENDSHIP MANCHESTER 2002

Date	Mintage	F	VF	XF	Unc	BU
2002	485,500	—	—	—	6.00	7.00
2002 Proof	—	Value: 8.75				

KM# 1034a 2 POUNDS

12.0000 g., 0.9250 Silver Silver center in Gold plated ring 0.3569 oz. ASW, 28.4 mm. **Ruler:** Elizabeth II **Subject:** Commonwealth Games - Northern Ireland **Obv:** Head with tiara right **Obv. Designer:** Ian Rank-Broadley **Rev:** Runner breaking ribbon at finish line **Rev. Designer:** Matthew Bonaccorsi **Edge:** Reeded and lettered

Date	Mintage	F	VF	XF	Unc	BU
2002 Proof	10,000	Value: 30.00				

KM# 1034b 2 POUNDS

15.9800 g., 0.9160 Gold Yellow Gold center in Red Gold ring 0.4706 oz. AGW, 28.4 mm. **Ruler:** Elizabeth II **Subject:** Commonwealth Games - Northern Ireland **Obv:** Head with tiara right **Obv. Designer:** Ian Rank-Broadley **Rev:** Runner breaking ribbon at finish line **Rev. Designer:** Matthew Bonaccorsi **Edge:** Reeded and lettered

Date	Mintage	F	VF	XF	Unc	BU
2002 Proof	500	Value: 650				

KM# 1037 2 POUNDS

12.0000 g., Bi-Metallic Copper-Nickel center in Nickel-Brass ring, 28.4 mm. **Ruler:** Elizabeth II **Subject:** 50th Anniversary of the Discovery of DNA **Obv:** Head with tiara right **Obv. Designer:** Ian Rank-Broadley **Rev:** DNA Double Helix **Rev. Designer:** John Mills **Edge:** Reeded and inscribed **Edge Lettering:** DEOXYRIBONUCLEIC ACID

Date	Mintage	F	VF	XF	Unc	BU
ND(2003)	4,299,000	—	—	—	7.00	8.00
ND(2003) Proof	43,513	Value: 10.00				

KM# 1037a 2 POUNDS

12.0000 g., 0.9250 Silver Silver center in Gold plated ring 0.3569 oz. ASW, 28.4 mm. **Ruler:** Elizabeth II **Obv:** Head with tiara right **Obv. Designer:** Ian Rank-Broadley **Rev:** DNA Double Helix **Rev. Designer:** John Mills **Edge:** Reeded and lettered

Date	Mintage	F	VF	XF	Unc	BU
ND(2003) Proof	11,204	Value: 30.00				

KM# 1037b 2 POUNDS

15.9800 g., 0.9167 Gold Yellow gold center in Red gold ring 0.4710 oz. AGW, 28.4 mm. **Ruler:** Elizabeth II **Obv:** Head with tiara right **Obv. Designer:** Ian Rank-Broadley **Rev:** DNA Double Helix **Rev. Designer:** John Mills **Edge:** Reeded and lettered

Date	Mintage	F	VF	XF	Unc	BU
ND2003 Proof	1,500	Value: 650				

KM# 1049 2 POUNDS

12.0000 g., Bi-Metallic Nickel-Brass center in Copper-Nickel ring, 28.4 mm. **Ruler:** Elizabeth II **Subject:** Richard Trevithick, Inventor of the First Steam Locomotive **Obv:** Head with tiara right **Obv. Designer:** Ian Rank-Broadley **Rev:** First steam locomotive **Edge:** Reeded and lettered **Edge Lettering:** 2004 R. TREVITHICK 1804 INVENTION-INDUSTRY-PROGRESS

Date	Mintage	F	VF	XF	Unc	BU
2004	5,004,500	—	—	—	7.50	8.50
2004 Proof	35,020	Value: 10.00				

KM# 1049a 2 POUNDS

12.0000 g., 0.9250 Silver Silver center in Gold plated ring 0.3569 oz. ASW, 28.4 mm. **Ruler:** Elizabeth II **Obv:** Head with tiara right **Obv. Designer:** Ian Rank-Broadley **Rev:** First steam locomotive **Edge:** Reeded and lettered

Date	Mintage	F	VF	XF	Unc	BU
2004	1,923	—	—	—	—	25.00
2004 Proof	19,233	Value: 30.00				

KM# 1049b 2 POUNDS

15.9800 g., 0.9166 Gold Yellow Gold center in Red Gold ring 0.4709 oz. AGW, 28.4 mm. **Ruler:** Elizabeth II **Obv:** Head with tiara right **Obv. Designer:** Ian Rank-Broadley **Rev:** First steam locomotive **Edge:** Reeded and lettered

Date	Mintage	F	VF	XF	Unc	BU
2004 Proof	1,500	Value: 650				

KM# 1052 2 POUNDS

12.0000 g., Bi-Metallic Nickel-Brass center in Copper-Nickel ring, 28.4 mm. **Ruler:** Elizabeth II **Subject:** 400th Anniversary - The Gunpowder Plot **Obv:** Head with tiara right **Obv. Designer:** Ian Rank-Broadley **Rev:** Circular design of Royal scepters, swords and crosiers **Rev. Designer:** Peter Forster **Edge:** Reeded and lettered **Edge Lettering:** REMEMBER REMEMBER THE FIFTH OF NOVEMBER

Date	Mintage	F	VF	XF	Unc	BU
ND(2005)	5,140,500	—	—	—	6.00	7.00
ND(2005) Proof	40,563	Value: 9.00				

KM# 1056 2 POUNDS

Bi-Metallic Nickel-Brass center in Copper-Nickel ring, 28.4 mm. **Ruler:** Elizabeth II **Subject:** 60th Anniversary of the End of WW II **Obv:** Head with tiara right **Obv. Designer:** Ian Rank-Broadley **Rev:** St. Paul's Cathedral amid search light beams **Rev. Designer:** Robert Elderton **Edge:** Reeded and lettered **Edge Lettering:** IN VICTORY MAGNANIMITY IN PEACE GOODWILL

Date	Mintage	F	VF	XF	Unc	BU
ND (2005)	10,191,000	—	—	—	8.00	9.50

KM# 1056a 2 POUNDS

12.0000 g., 0.9250 Silver Silver center in Gold-plated ring 0.3569 oz. ASW, 28.4 mm. **Ruler:** Elizabeth II **Subject:** 60th Anniversary of the End of WWII **Obv:** Crowned head right **Obv. Designer:** Ian Rank-Broadley **Rev:** St. Paul's Cathedral amid search light beams **Rev. Designer:** Robert Elderton **Edge:** Reeded and lettered **Edge Lettering:** IN VICTORY MAGNANIMITY IN PEACE GOODWILL

Date	Mintage	F	VF	XF	Unc	BU
ND(2005) Proof	25,000	Value: 30.00				

KM# 1056b 2 POUNDS

Gold **Ruler:** Elizabeth II **Subject:** 60th Anniversary of the End of WWII **Obv:** Crowned head right **Obv. Designer:** Ian Rank-Broadley **Rev:** St. Paul's Cathedral amid search light beams **Rev. Designer:** Robert Elderton **Edge:** Reeded and lettered **Edge Lettering:** IN VICTORY MAGNANIMITY IN PEACE GOODWILL

Date	Mintage	F	VF	XF	Unc	BU
ND(2005) Proof	2,924	—	—	—	—	—

KM# 1060 2 POUNDS

12.0000 g., Bi-Metallic Copper-Nickel center in Nickel-Brass ring, 28.4 mm. **Ruler:** Elizabeth II **Subject:** 200th Birthday of Engineer Isambard Kingdom Brunel **Obv:** Head with tiara right **Obv. Designer:** Ian Rank-Broadley **Rev:** Isambard Brunel **Edge:** Lettered

Date	Mintage	F	VF	XF	Unc	BU
2006	7,925,250	—	—	—	16.00	18.00
2006 Proof	Est. 50,000	Value: 35.00				
2007 Proof	—	Value: 35.00				

KM# 1061 2 POUNDS

12.0000 g., Bi-Metallic Copper-Nickel center in Nickel-Brass ring, 28.4 mm. **Ruler:** Elizabeth II **Subject:** Engineering Achievements of Isambard Kingdom Brunel **Obv:** Head with tiara right **Obv. Designer:** Ian Rank-Broadley **Rev:** Paddington Station structural supports **Edge:** Lettered

Date	Mintage	F	VF	XF	Unc	BU
2006	7,452,250	—	—	—	16.00	17.50
2006 Proof	Est. 50,000	Value: 20.00				
2007 Proof	—	Value: 20.00				

KM# 1075 2 POUNDS

12.0000 g., Bi-Metallic Copper-Nickel center in Brass ring, 28.4 mm. **Ruler:** Elizabeth II **Subject:** 200th Anniversary of the Abolition of the Slave Trade **Obv:** Bust right **Rev:** Chain crossing 1807 date **Edge:** Reeded and lettered

Date	Mintage	F	VF	XF	Unc	BU
2007	8,445,000	—	—	—	—	6.00
2007 Proof	Est. 50,000	Value: 9.00				

KM# 1075a 2 POUNDS

12.0000 g., 0.9250 Silver Silver center in Gold plated ring 0.3569 oz. ASW, 28.4 mm. **Ruler:** Elizabeth II **Subject:** Abolition of the Slave Trade **Obv:** Elizabeth II right **Rev:** Zero in 1807 date as a broken chain link **Edge:** Reeded and lettered

Date	Mintage	F	VF	XF	Unc	BU
2007 Proof	Est. 10,000	Value: 55.00				

KM# 1075b 2 POUNDS

15.9700 g., 0.9166 Gold Yellow Gold center in Red Gold ring 0.4706 oz. AGW, 28.4 mm. **Ruler:** Elizabeth II **Subject:** Abolition of the Slave Trade **Obv:** Elizabeth II right **Rev:** Zero in 1807 date as a broken chain link **Edge:** Reeded and lettered

Date	Mintage	F	VF	XF	Unc	BU
2007 Proof	Est. 1,000	Value: 765				

KM# 1076 2 POUNDS
12.0000 g., Bi-Metallic Copper-Nickel center in Nickel-Brass ring,
28.4 mm. **Ruler:** Elizabeth II **Subject:** 300th Anniversary of the
Act of Union of England and Scotland **Obv:** Bust right
Rev: Combination of British and Scottish arms **Edge:** Reeded
and lettered

Date	Mintage	F	VF	XF	Unc	BU
2007	7,545,000	—	—	—	—	6.00
2007 Proof	Est. 50,000	Value: 9.00				

KM# 1076a 2 POUNDS
12.0000 g., 0.9250 Silver Silver center in Gold Plated ring
0.3569 oz. ASW, 28.4 mm. **Ruler:** Elizabeth II **Subject:** 300th
Anniv. Union of Scotland and England **Obv:** Elizabeth II
Rev: Combined English and Scottish arms **Edge:** Reeded and
lettered **Edge Lettering:** TVEATVR VNITA DEUS

Date	Mintage	F	VF	XF	Unc	BU
2007 Proof	Est. 10,000	Value: 55.00				

KM# 1076b 2 POUNDS
15.9800 g., 0.9166 Gold Yellow Gold center in Red Gold ring
0.4709 oz. AGW, 28.4 mm. **Ruler:** Elizabeth II **Subject:** 300th
Anniv. Union of Scotland and England **Obv:** Elizabeth II
Rev: Combined English and Scottish arms **Edge:** Reeded and
lettered **Edge Lettering:** TVEATVR VNITA DEUS

Date	Mintage	F	VF	XF	Unc	BU
2007 Proof	750	Value: 765				

KM# 1105 2 POUNDS
12.0000 g., Bi-Metallic Copper-nickel center in brass ring,
28.4 mm. **Ruler:** Elizabeth II **Subject:** London 1908 - Olympics
Obv: Head with tiara right **Rev:** Sprint track

Date	Mintage	F	VF	XF	Unc	BU
2008	910,000	—	—	—	—	6.00
Note: Most still at banks, very few circulated.						
2008 Proof	—	Value: 9.00				

KM# 1106 2 POUNDS
12.0000 g., Bi-Metallic Copper-Nickel center in Brass ring, 28.4 mm.
Ruler: Elizabeth II **Subject:** Beijing - London Olympic Flag handoff
Obv: Head w/ tiara right **Rev:** London 2012 Games Flag hand off
Edge Lettering: I CALL UPON THE YOUTH OF THE WORLD

Date	Mintage	F	VF	XF	Unc	BU
2008	910,000	—	—	—	—	6.00
2008 Proof	Est. 250,000	Value: 45.00				

KM# 1115 2 POUNDS
12.0000 g., Bi-Metallic, 28.4 mm. **Ruler:** Elizabeth II **Obv:** Head
with tiara right **Rev:** Darwin and ape heads facing

Date	Mintage	F	VF	XF	Unc	BU
2009	Est. 300,000	—	—	—	16.00	18.00
2009 Proof	—	Value: 20.00				

KM# 1116 2 POUNDS
12.0000 g., Bi-Metallic, 28.4 mm. **Ruler:** Elizabeth II **Subject:**
Robert Burns' 250th Birth Ann. **Obv:** Head with tiara right **Rev:** Text

Date	Mintage	F	VF	XF	Unc	BU
2009	300,000	—	—	—	16.00	18.00
2009 Proof	—	Value: 20.00				

KM# 1116a 2 POUNDS
Gold **Ruler:** Elizabeth II **Subject:** Robert Burns Ann. **Rev:** Text

Date	Mintage	F	VF	XF	Unc	BU
2009 Proof	—	Value: 600				

KM# 1120 2 POUNDS
15.9800 g., 0.9160 Gold 0.4706 oz. AGW, 28.4 mm.
Ruler: Elizabeth II **Subject:** Countdown to 2010 London
Olympics **Obv:** Head right **Obv. Designer:** Ian rank-Broadley
Rev: handoff of the Olympic flag **Edge Lettering:** I CALL UPON
THE YOUTH OF THE WORLD

Date	Mintage	F	VF	XF	Unc	BU
2009 Proof	3,000	Value: 650				

KM# 1015 5 POUNDS
28.2800 g., Copper-Nickel, 38.6 mm. **Ruler:** Elizabeth II
Subject: Centennial of Queen Victoria's death **Obv:** Head with
tiara right **Obv. Designer:** Ian Rank-Broadley **Rev:** Young portrait
from stamp, within industrial "V" **Rev. Designer:** Mary Milner
Dickens, William Wyon **Edge:** Reeded

Date	Mintage	F	VF	XF	Unc	BU
2001	851,500	—	—	—	14.00	16.00
2001 Proof	—	Value: 20.00				

KM# 1015a 5 POUNDS
28.2800 g., 0.9250 Silver 0.8410 oz. ASW, 38.6 mm. **Ruler:**
Elizabeth II **Subject:** Centennial of Queen Victoria **Obv:** Head
with tiara right **Obv. Designer:** Ian Rank-Broadley **Rev:** Queen
Victoria's portrait within "V" **Rev. Designer:** Mary Milner Dickens

Date	Mintage	F	VF	XF	Unc	BU
2001 Proof	—	Value: 65.00				

KM# 1015b 5 POUNDS
39.9400 g., 0.9167 Gold 1.1771 oz. AGW **Ruler:** Elizabeth II
Subject: Centennial of Queen Victoria **Obv:** Head with tiara right
Obv. Designer: Ian Rank-Broadley **Rev:** Queen Victoria's
portrait within "V" **Rev. Designer:** Mary Milner Dickens

Date	Mintage	F	VF	XF	Unc	BU
2001 Proof	1,000	Value: 1,600				

KM# 1024 5 POUNDS
28.2800 g., Copper-Nickel, 38.6 mm. **Ruler:** Elizabeth II
Subject: Queen's Golden Jubilee of Reign **Obv:** Crowned bust
in royal garb right **Rev:** Queen on horse **Edge:** Reeded

Date	Mintage	F	VF	XF	Unc	BU
2002	3,688,000	—	—	—	12.50	14.50
Note: Mintage figure included KM#1035						
2002 Proof	—	Value: 20.00				

KM# 1024a 5 POUNDS
28.2800 g., 0.9250 Silver 0.8410 oz. ASW, 38.6 mm.
Ruler: Elizabeth II **Subject:** Queen's Golden Jubilee of Reign
Obv: Crowned bust in royal garb right **Rev:** Queen on horse
Edge: Reeded

Date	Mintage	F	VF	XF	Unc	BU
2002 Proof	—	Value: 50.00				

KM# 1024b 5 POUNDS
39.9400 g., 0.9167 Gold 1.1771 oz. AGW, 38.6 mm.
Ruler: Elizabeth II **Subject:** Queen's Golden Jubilee of Reign
Obv: Crowned bust in royal garb right **Rev:** Queen on horse left
Edge: Reeded

Date	Mintage	F	VF	XF	Unc	BU
2002 Proof	—	Value: 1,500				

KM# 1035 5 POUNDS
28.2800 g., Copper-Nickel, 38.6 mm. **Ruler:** Elizabeth II
Subject: Queen Mother **Obv:** Head with tiara right
Obv. Designer: Ian Rank-Broadley **Rev:** Queen Mother's portrait
in wreath **Rev. Designer:** Avril Vaughan **Edge:** Reeded

Date	Mintage	F	VF	XF	Unc	BU
ND(2002)	—	—	—	—	15.00	—
Note: Mintage included with 1024b, 2002						
ND(2002) Proof	—	Value: 20.00				

KM# 1035a 5 POUNDS
28.2800 g., Silver, 38.6 mm. **Ruler:** Elizabeth II **Subject:** Queen
Mother **Obv:** Head with tiara right **Obv. Designer:** Ian Rank-
Broadley **Rev:** Queen Mother's portrait in wreath **Rev. Designer:**
Avril Vaughan **Edge:** Reeded

Date	Mintage	F	VF	XF	Unc	BU
ND(2002) Proof	25,000	Value: 50.00				

KM# 1035b 5 POUNDS
39.9400 g., 0.9167 Gold 1.1771 oz. AGW, 38.6 mm.
Ruler: Elizabeth II **Subject:** Queen Mother **Obv:** Head with tiara
right **Obv. Designer:** Ian Rank-Broadley **Rev:** Queen Mother's
portrait in wreath **Rev. Designer:** Avril Vaughan **Edge:** Reeded

Date	Mintage	F	VF	XF	Unc	BU
ND(2002) Proof	3,000	Value: 1,500				

KM# 1038 5 POUNDS
28.2800 g., Copper-Nickel, 38.6 mm. **Ruler:** Elizabeth II
Subject: Queen's Golden Jubilee **Obv:** Queen's stylized portrait
Rev: Childlike lettering **Edge:** Reeded **Designer:** Tom Phillips

Date	Mintage	F	VF	XF	Unc	BU
2003	1,307,147	—	—	—	12.50	14.50
2003 Proof	43,513	Value: 20.00				

KM# 1038a 5 POUNDS
28.2800 g., 0.9250 Silver 0.8410 oz. ASW, 38.6 mm.
Ruler: Elizabeth II **Subject:** Queen's Golden Jubilee
Obv: Stylized Queens portrait **Rev:** Childlike lettering
Edge: Reeded **Designer:** Tom Phillips

Date	Mintage	F	VF	XF	Unc	BU
2003 Proof	28,758	Value: 50.00				

KM# 1038b 5 POUNDS
39.9400 g., 0.9166 Gold 1.1770 oz. AGW, 38.6 mm.
Ruler: Elizabeth II **Subject:** Queen's Golden Jubilee
Obv: Stylized Queens portrait **Rev:** Childlike lettering
Edge: Reeded **Designer:** Tom Phillips

Date	Mintage	F	VF	XF	Unc	BU
2003 Proof	1,896	Value: 1,500				

KM# 1055 5 POUNDS
28.2800 g., Copper-Nickel, 38.6 mm. **Ruler:** Elizabeth II
Subject: Entente Cordiale **Obv:** Head with tiara right
Obv. Designer: Ian Rank-Broadley **Rev:** Britannia and Marianne
Edge: Reeded

Date	Mintage	F	VF	XF	Unc	BU
2004	1,205,594	—	—	—	15.00	17.50
2004 Proof	51,527	Value: 20.00				

KM# 1055a 5 POUNDS
28.2800 g., 0.9250 Silver 0.8410 oz. ASW, 38.6 mm.
Ruler: Elizabeth II **Subject:** Entente Cordiale **Obv:** Head with
tiara right **Obv. Designer:** Ian Rank-Broadley **Rev:** Britannia and
Marianne **Edge:** Reeded

Date	Mintage	F	VF	XF	Unc	BU
2004 Proof	11,295	Value: 50.00				

KM# 1055b 5 POUNDS
39.9400 g., 0.9167 Gold 1.1771 oz. AGW, 38.6 mm.
Ruler: Elizabeth II **Subject:** Entente Cordiale **Obv:** Head with
tiara right **Obv. Designer:** Ian Rank-Broadley **Rev:** Britannia and
Marianne **Edge:** Reeded

Date	Mintage	F	VF	XF	Unc	BU
2004 Proof	926	Value: 1,500				

KM# 1055c 5 POUNDS
94.2000 g., 0.9995 Platinum 3.0270 oz. APW, 38.6 mm.
Ruler: Elizabeth II **Subject:** Entente Cordiale **Obv:** Head with
tiara right **Obv. Designer:** Ian Rank-Broadley **Rev:** Britannia and
Marianne **Edge:** Reeded

Date	Mintage	F	VF	XF	Unc	BU
2004 Proof	501	Value: 7,000				

KM# 1053   5 POUNDS
28.2800 g., Copper-Nickel, 38.6 mm.   **Ruler:** Elizabeth II
Subject: Battle of Trafalgar **Obv:** Head with tiara right
Obv. Legend: ELIZABETH•II D•G•REG•F•D **Obv. Designer:**
Ian Rank-Broadley **Rev:** HMS Victory and HMS Temeraire at
Trafalgar **Rev. Legend:** TRAFALGAR **Rev. Designer:** Clive
Duncan **Edge:** Reeded

Date	Mintage	F	VF	XF	Unc	BU
2005	1,075,516	—	—	—	12.50	16.50
2005 Proof	40,563	Value: 18.50				

KM# 1053a   5 POUNDS
28.2800 g., 0.9250 Silver 0.8410 oz. ASW, 38.6 mm.
Ruler: Elizabeth II **Subject:** Battle of Trafalgar **Obv:** Head with
tiara right **Obv. Legend:** ELIZABETH • II D • G • REG • F • D
Obv. Designer: Ian Rank-Broadley **Rev:** Ships HMS Victory and
Temeraire at Trafalgar **Rev. Legend:** TRAFALGAR
Rev. Designer: Clive Duncan **Edge:** Reeded

Date	Mintage	F	VF	XF	Unc	BU
2005 Proof	21,448	Value: 60.00				

KM# 1053b   5 POUNDS
39.9400 g., 0.9167 Gold 1.1771 oz. AGW, 38.6 mm.
Ruler: Elizabeth II **Subject:** Battle of Trafalgar **Obv:** Head with
tiara right **Obv. Legend:** ELIZABETH • II D • G • REG • F • D
Obv. Designer: Ian Rank-Broadley **Rev:** Ships HMS Victory and
Temeraire at Trafalgar **Rev. Legend:** TRAFALGAR
Rev. Designer: Clive Duncan **Edge:** Reeded

Date	Mintage	F	VF	XF	Unc	BU
2005 Proof	1,805	Value: 1,550				

KM# 1054   5 POUNDS
28.2800 g., Copper-Nickel, 38.6 mm.   **Ruler:** Elizabeth II
Obv: Head with tiara right **Obv. Legend:** ELIZABETH • II D • G
• REG • F • D **Obv. Designer:** Ian Rank-Broadley **Rev:** Uniformed
facing 1/2 bust of Admiral Horatio Nelson **Rev. Legend:**
HORATIO NELSON **Edge:** Reeded

Date	Mintage	F	VF	XF	Unc	BU
2005	—	—	—	—	15.00	16.50

Note: Mintage included with KM#1053b, 2005.

Date	Mintage	F	VF	XF	Unc	BU
2005 Proof	40,563	Value: 18.50				

KM# 1054a   5 POUNDS
28.2800 g., 0.9250 Silver 0.8410 oz. ASW, 38.6 mm.
Ruler: Elizabeth II **Obv:** Queen's head with tiara right
Obv. Legend: ELIZABETH•II D•G•REG•F•D **Obv. Designer:**
Ian Rank-Broadley **Rev:** Uniformed facing 1/2 bust of Admiral
Horatio Nelson **Rev. Legend:** HORATIO NELSON

Date	Mintage	F	VF	XF	Unc	BU
2005 Proof	12,852	Value: 60.00				

KM# 1054b   5 POUNDS
39.9400 g., 0.9167 Gold 1.1771 oz. AGW, 38.6 mm. **Obv:** Queen's
head with tiara right **Obv. Legend:** ELIZABETH • II D • G • REG
• F • D **Rev:** Uniformed facing 1/2 bust of Admiral Horatio Nelson
Rev. Legend: HORATIO NELSON

Date	Mintage	F	VF	XF	Unc	BU
2005 Proof	1,700	Value: 1,500				

KM# 1062   5 POUNDS
28.2800 g., Copper-Nickel, 38.6 mm.   **Ruler:** Elizabeth II
Obv: Head with tiara right **Obv. Designer:** Ian Rank-Broadley
Rev: Three bannered trumpets **Edge:** Reeded

Date	Mintage	F	VF	XF	Unc	BU
2006	—	—	—	—	20.00	22.00
2006 Proof	Est. 50,000	Value: 27.00				
2007 Proof	—	Value: 27.00				

KM# 1062a   5 POUNDS
28.2800 g., 0.9250 Silver 0.8410 oz. ASW   **Ruler:** Elizabeth II
Subject: Queen's 80th Birthday Celebration **Obv:** Queens head
right **Obv. Legend:** ELIZABETH • II D • G • REG • F • D
Obv. Designer: Ian Rank-Broadley **Rev:** Three bannered
trumpets **Rev. Legend:** VIVAT REGINA **Edge:** Reeded

Date	Mintage	F	VF	XF	Unc	BU
2006 Proof	—	Value: 65.00				

KM# 1062b   5 POUNDS
39.9400 g., 0.9167 Gold 1.1771 oz. AGW, 38.6 mm.
Ruler: Elizabeth II **Subject:** Queen's 80th Birthday Celebration
Obv: Queen's head with tiara right **Obv. Legend:** ELIZABETH •
II D • G • REG • F • D **Obv. Designer:** Ian Rank-Broadley
Rev: Three bannered trumpets **Rev. Legend:** VIVAT REGINA
Edge: Reeded

Date	Mintage	F	VF	XF	Unc	BU
2006 Proof	—	Value: 1,500				

KM# 1077   5 POUNDS
28.2800 g., Copper-Nickel, 38.6 mm.   **Ruler:** Elizabeth II
Subject: Queen's 60th Wedding Anniversary **Obv:** Queen
Elizabeth II and Prince Philip **Rev:** Westminster Abbey's North
Rose Window **Edge:** Reeded

Date	Mintage	F	VF	XF	Unc	BU
2007	—	—	—	—	—	20.00
2007 Proof	Est. 50,000	Value: 30.00				

KM# 1077a   5 POUNDS
28.2800 g., 0.9250 Silver 0.8410 oz. ASW, 38.6 mm.
Ruler: Elizabeth II **Subject:** 60th Wedding Anniversary
Obv: Elizabeth II and Prince Philip **Rev:** Westminster Abbey's
North Rose Window **Edge Lettering:** MY STRENGTH AND
STAY

Date	Mintage	F	VF	XF	Unc	BU
ND (2007) Proof	Est. 35,000	Value: 70.00				

KM# 1077b   5 POUNDS
39.9400 g., 0.9166 Gold 1.1770 oz. AGW, 28.4 mm.
Ruler: Elizabeth II **Subject:** 60th Wedding Ann. **Obv:** Elizabeth
II and Prince Philip **Rev:** Westminster Abbey's North Rose
Window **Edge Lettering:** MY STRENGTH AND STAY

Date	Mintage	F	VF	XF	Unc	BU
ND (2007) Proof	Est. 2,500	Value: 1,550				

KM# 1103   5 POUNDS
28.2800 g., Copper-Nickel, 38.6 mm.   **Ruler:** Elizabeth II
Subject: Charles, Prince of Wales 60th Birthday **Obv:** Head with
tiara right **Rev:** Head right of Prince Charles

Date	Mintage	F	VF	XF	Unc	BU
2008	500,000	—	—	—	12.50	16.50
2008 Proof	—	Value: 18.50				

KM# 1104   5 POUNDS
28.2800 g., Copper-Nickel, 38.6 mm.   **Ruler:** Elizabeth II
Subject: Elizabeth I Accession 1558-2008 **Obv:** Head with tiara
right **Rev:** Bust of Elizabeth I

Date	Mintage	F	VF	XF	Unc	BU
2008	500,000	—	—	—	12.50	16.50
2008 Proof	—	Value: 18.50				

KM# 1121   5 POUNDS
28.2800 g., Copper-Nickel, 38.61 mm.   **Ruler:** Elizabeth II
Subject: Countdown to 2012 London Olympics **Obv:** Bust right
Obv. Designer: Ian Rank-Broadley **Rev:** Swimmer, stopwatch
Rev. Designer: Claire Aldridge

Date	Mintage	F	VF	XF	Unc	BU
2009	500,000	—	—	—	—	20.00
2009 Proof	—	Value: 30.00				

KM# 1121a   5 POUNDS
28.2800 g., 0.9250 Silver 0.8410 oz. ASW, 38.61 mm.
Ruler: Elizabeth II **Subject:** Countdown to the 2010 London
Olympics **Obv:** Bust right **Obv. Designer:** Ian Rank-Broadley
Rev: Swimmer, stopwatch **Rev. Designer:** Claire Aldridge

Date	Mintage	F	VF	XF	Unc	BU
2009 Proof	30,000	Value: 70.00				

SOVEREIGN COINAGE

KM# 1117   1/4 SOVEREIGN
2.0000 g., 0.9170 Gold 0.0590 oz. AGW   **Ruler:** Elizabeth II
Obv: Head with tiara right **Rev:** St. George slaying dragon

Date	Mintage	F	VF	XF	Unc	BU
2009	—	—	—	—	—	90.00
2009 Proof	—	Value: 125				
2010	—	—	—	—	—	90.00

KM# 1001   1/2 SOVEREIGN
3.9900 g., 0.9170 Gold 0.1176 oz. AGW   **Ruler:** Elizabeth II
Obv: Head with tiara right **Obv. Designer:** Ian Rank-Broadley
Rev: St. George slaying the dragon

Date	Mintage	F	VF	XF	Unc	BU
2001	94,763	—	—	—	—	150
2001 Proof	10,000	Value: 160				
2002	61,347	—	—	—	—	150
2003	47,818	—	—	—	—	150
2003 Proof	14,750	Value: 160				
2004	34,924	—	—	—	—	150
2006	30,299	—	—	—	—	150
2006 Proof	8,500	Value: 170				
2007	75,000	—	—	—	—	150
2007 Proof	7,500	Value: 195				
2008	75,000	—	—	—	—	170
2008 Proof	7,500	Value: 195				
2009	75,000	—	—	—	—	170
2009 Proof	7,500	Value: 195				
2010	—	—	—	—	—	170

KM# 1025 1/2 SOVEREIGN
3.9900 g., 0.9167 Gold 0.1176 oz. AGW, 19.3 mm.
Ruler: Elizabeth II **Subject:** Queen Elizabeth II's Golden Jubilee
Obv: Head with tiara right **Obv. Designer:** Ian Rank-Broadley
Rev: Crowned arms within wreath, date below **Edge:** Reeded

Date	Mintage	F	VF	XF	Unc	BU
2002 Proof	18,000	Value: 175				

KM# 1064 1/2 SOVEREIGN
3.9940 g., 0.9167 Gold 0.1177 oz. AGW, 19.3 mm. **Ruler:**
Elizabeth II **Obv:** Head with tiara right **Obv. Designer:** Ian Rank-Broadley **Rev:** Knight fighting dragon with sword **Edge:** Reeded

Date	Mintage	F	VF	XF	Unc	BU
2005	30,299	—	—	—	—	150
2005 Proof	12,500	Value: 175				

KM# 1002 SOVEREIGN
7.9881 g., 0.9170 Gold 0.2355 oz. AGW **Ruler:** Elizabeth II
Obv: Head with tiara right **Obv. Designer:** Ian Rank-Broadley
Rev: St. George slaying the dragon

Date	Mintage	F	VF	XF	Unc	BU
2001	49,462	—	—	—	—	300
2001 Proof	15,000	Value: 320				
2002	75,264	—	—	—	—	300
2003	43,230	—	—	—	—	300
2003 Proof	19,750	Value: 320				
2004	30,688	—	—	—	—	300
2006	45,542	—	—	—	—	300
2006 Proof	16,000	Value: 325				
2007	75,000	—	—	—	—	300
2007 Proof	12,500	Value: 345				
2008	75,000	—	—	—	—	300
2008 Proof	12,500	Value: 345				
2009	75,000	—	—	—	—	300
2009 Proof	12,500	Value: 345				
2010	—	—	—	—	—	300

KM# 1026 SOVEREIGN
7.9800 g., 0.9167 Gold 0.2352 oz. AGW, 22 mm.
Ruler: Elizabeth II **Subject:** Queen Elizabeth II's Golden Jubilee
Obv: Head with tiara right **Obv. Designer:** Ian Rank-Broadley
Rev: Crowned arms within wreath, date below **Edge:** Reeded

Date	Mintage	F	VF	XF	Unc	BU
2002	71,815	—	—	—	—	300
2002 Proof	20,500	Value: 320				

KM# 1065 SOVEREIGN
7.9880 g., 0.9176 Gold 0.2356 oz. AGW, 22.05 mm. **Ruler:**
Elizabeth II **Obv:** Head with tiara right **Obv. Designer:** Ian Rank-Broadley **Rev:** Knight fighting dragon with sword **Edge:** Reeded

Date	Mintage	F	VF	XF	Unc	BU
2005	45,542	—	—	—	—	300
2005 Proof	17,500	Value: 320				

KM# 1027 2 POUNDS
15.9700 g., 0.9167 Gold 0.4707 oz. AGW, 28.4 mm.
Ruler: Elizabeth II **Subject:** Queen Elizabeth II's Golden Jubilee
Obv: Head with tiara right **Obv. Designer:** Ian Rank-Broadley
Rev: Crowned arms within wreath, date below **Edge:** Reeded

Date	Mintage	F	VF	XF	Unc	BU
2002 Proof	8,000	Value: 600				

KM# 1066 2 POUNDS
15.9760 g., 0.9167 Gold 0.4708 oz. AGW, 28.4 mm. **Ruler:**
Elizabeth II **Obv:** Head with tiara right **Obv. Designer:** Ian Rank-Broadley **Rev:** Knight fighting dragon with sword **Edge:** Reeded

Date	Mintage	F	VF	XF	Unc	BU
2005 Proof	5,000	Value: 600				

KM# 1072 2 POUNDS
15.9700 g., 0.9167 Gold 0.4707 oz. AGW, 28.4 mm. **Ruler:**
Elizabeth II **Obv:** Head with tiara right **Obv. Designer:** Ian Rank-Broadley **Rev:** St. George slaying the Dragon **Edge:** Reeded

Date	Mintage	F	VF	XF	Unc	BU
2006 Proof	3,500	Value: 600				
2007 Proof	2,500	Value: 620				
2008 Proof	2,500	Value: 620				
2009 Proof	2,500	Value: 620				

KM# 1003 5 POUNDS
39.9400 g., 0.9170 Gold 1.1775 oz. AGW, 36 mm. **Ruler:**
Elizabeth II **Obv:** Head with tiara right **Obv. Designer:** Ian Rank-Broadley **Rev:** St. George slaying dragon **Edge:** Reeded

Date	Mintage	F	VF	XF	Unc	BU
2001 Proof	1,000	Value: 1,600				
2003 Proof	2,250	Value: 1,500				
2004	1,000	—	—	—	—	1,650
2006	1,000	—	—	—	—	1,600
2006 Proof	1,750	Value: 1,500				
2007 Proof	1,750	Value: 1,650				
2008 Proof	1,750	Value: 1,650				
2009 Proof	1,750	Value: 1,650				

KM# 1028 5 POUNDS
39.9400 g., 0.9167 Gold 1.1771 oz. AGW, 36 mm.
Ruler: Elizabeth II **Subject:** Queen Elizabeth II's Golden Jubilee
Obv: Head with tiara right **Obv. Designer:** Ian Rank-Broadley
Rev: Crowned arms within wreath **Edge:** Reeded

Date	Mintage	F	VF	XF	Unc	BU
2002 Proof	3,000	Value: 1,500				

KM# 1067 5 POUNDS
39.9400 g., 0.9167 Gold 1.1771 oz. AGW, 36 mm.
Ruler: Elizabeth II **Obv:** Head with tiara right
Obv. Designer: Ian Rank-Broadley **Rev:** Knight fighting dragon with sword **Edge:** Reeded

Date	Mintage	F	VF	XF	Unc	BU
2005 Proof	2,500	Value: 1,500				

BULLION COINAGE

All proof issues have designers name as P. Nathan. The uncirculated issues use only Nathan.

KM# 1016 20 PENCE
3.2400 g., 0.9584 Silver 0.0998 oz. ASW, 16.5 mm.
Ruler: Elizabeth II **Subject:** Britannia Bullion **Obv:** Head w/tiara
right **Obv. Designer:** Ian Rank-Broadley **Rev:** Una and Lion
Edge: Reeded

Date	Mintage	F	VF	XF	Unc	BU
2001 Proof	15,000	Value: 25.00				

KM# 1079 20 PENCE
3.2400 g., 0.9584 Silver 0.0998 oz. ASW, 16.5 mm.
Ruler: Elizabeth II **Obv:** Head with tiara right **Rev:** Britannia
standing **Edge:** Reeded

Date	Mintage	F	VF	XF	Unc	BU
2002 Proof	—	Value: 25.00				
2004 Proof	—	Value: 25.00				
2006 Proof	—	Value: 25.00				

KM# 1044 20 PENCE
3.2400 g., 0.9584 Silver 0.0998 oz. ASW, 16.5 mm. **Ruler:**
Elizabeth II **Obv:** Head with tiara right **Obv. Designer:** Ian Rank-Broadley **Rev:** Britannia portrait behind wavy lines **Edge:** Reeded

Date	Mintage	F	VF	XF	Unc	BU
2003 Proof	5,000	Value: 35.00				

KM# 1085 20 PENCE
3.2400 g., 0.9584 Silver 0.0998 oz. ASW, 16.5 mm.
Ruler: Elizabeth II **Obv:** Head with tiara right **Rev:** Britannia
seated with shield left **Edge:** Reeded

Date	Mintage	F	VF	XF	Unc	BU
2005 Proof	—	Value: 25.00				

KM# 1088 20 PENCE
3.2400 g., 0.9584 Silver 0.0998 oz. ASW, 16.5 mm.
Ruler: Elizabeth II **Obv:** Head with tiara right **Rev:** Britannia
seated with reclining lion right **Edge:** Reeded

Date	Mintage	F	VF	XF	Unc	BU
2007 Proof	—	Value: 25.00				

KM# 1095 20 PENCE
3.2400 g., 0.9584 Silver 0.0998 oz. ASW, 16.5 mm. **Ruler:**
Elizabeth II **Obv:** Head with tiara right **Rev:** Britannia standing
facing left with trident, flowing garment, shield **Edge:** Reeded

Date	Mintage	F	VF	XF	Unc	BU
2008 Proof	—	Value: 35.00				

KM# 1017 50 PENCE
8.1100 g., 0.9584 Silver 0.2499 oz. ASW, 27.3 mm.
Ruler: Elizabeth II **Subject:** Britannia Bullion **Obv:** Head with
tiara right **Obv. Designer:** Ian Rank-Broadley **Rev:** Una and Lion
Edge: Reeded

Date	Mintage	F	VF	XF	Unc	BU
2001 Proof	5,000	Value: 25.00				

KM# 1080 50 PENCE
8.1100 g., 0.9584 Silver 0.2499 oz. ASW, 22 mm. **Obv:** Head
with tiara right **Rev:** Britannia standing **Edge:** Reeded

Date	Mintage	F	VF	XF	Unc	BU
2002 Proof	—	Value: 35.00				
2004 Proof	—	Value: 35.00				
2006 Proof	—	Value: 35.00				

KM# 1045 50 PENCE
8.1100 g., 0.9584 Silver 0.2499 oz. ASW, 22 mm. **Ruler:**
Elizabeth II **Obv:** Head with tiara right **Obv. Designer:** Ian Rank-Broadley **Rev:** Britannia portrait behind wavy lines **Edge:** Reeded

Date	Mintage	F	VF	XF	Unc	BU
2003 Proof	5,000	Value: 35.00				

KM# 1086 50 PENCE
8.1100 g., 0.9584 Silver 0.2499 oz. ASW, 22 mm.
Ruler: Elizabeth II **Obv:** Head with tiara right **Rev:** Britannia
seated with shield left **Edge:** Reeded

Date	Mintage	F	VF	XF	Unc	BU
2005 Proof	—	Value: 35.00				

KM# 1089 50 PENCE
8.1100 g., 0.9584 Silver 0.2499 oz. ASW, 22 mm.
Ruler: Elizabeth II **Obv:** Head with tiara right **Rev:** Britannia
seated with reclining lion right **Edge:** Reeded

Date	Mintage	F	VF	XF	Unc	BU
2007 Proof	—	Value: 35.00				

KM# 1096 50 PENCE
8.1100 g., 0.9584 Silver 0.2499 oz. ASW, 22 mm.
Ruler: Elizabeth II **Obv:** Head with tiara right **Rev:** Britannia
standing facing left with trident, flowing garment, shield
Edge: Reeded

Date	Mintage	F	VF	XF	Unc	BU
2008 Proof	—	Value: 45.00				

KM# 1018 POUND
16.2200 g., 0.9584 Silver 0.4998 oz. ASW, 27 mm.
Ruler: Elizabeth II **Subject:** Britannia Bullion **Obv:** Head with
tiara right **Obv. Designer:** Ian Rank-Broadley **Rev:** Una and Lion"
Edge: Reeded

Date	Mintage	F	VF	XF	Unc	BU
2001 Proof	5,000	Value: 40.00				

KM# 1081 POUND
16.2200 g., 0.9584 Silver 0.4998 oz. ASW, 27 mm.
Ruler: Elizabeth II **Obv:** Head with tiara right **Rev:** Britannia
standing **Edge:** Reeded

Date	Mintage	F	VF	XF	Unc	BU
2002 Proof	—	Value: 50.00				
2004 Proof	—	Value: 50.00				
2006 Proof	—	Value: 50.00				

KM# 1046   POUND
16.2200 g., 0.9584 Silver 0.4998 oz. ASW, 27 mm. **Ruler:**
Elizabeth II **Obv:** Head with tiara right **Obv. Designer:** Ian Rank-
Broadley **Rev:** Britannia portrait behind wavy lines **Edge:** Reeded

Date	Mintage	F	VF	XF	Unc	BU
2003 Proof	5,000	Value: 50.00				

KM# 1087   POUND
16.2200 g., 0.9584 Silver 0.4998 oz. ASW, 27 mm.
Ruler: Elizabeth II **Obv:** Head with tiara right **Rev:** Britannia
seated with shield left **Edge:** Reeded

Date	Mintage	F	VF	XF	Unc	BU
2005 Proof	—	Value: 50.00				

KM# 1090   POUND
16.2200 g., 0.9584 Silver 0.4998 oz. ASW, 27 mm.
Ruler: Elizabeth II **Obv:** Head with tiara right **Rev:** Britannia
seated with reclining lion right **Edge:** Reeded

Date	Mintage	F	VF	XF	Unc	BU
2007 Proof	—	Value: 50.00				

KM# 1097   POUND
16.2200 g., 0.9584 Silver 0.4998 oz. ASW, 27 mm. **Ruler:**
Elizabeth II **Obv:** Head with tiara right **Rev:** Britannia standing
facing left with trident, flowing garment, shield **Edge:** Reeded

Date	Mintage	F	VF	XF	Unc	BU
2008 Proof	—	Value: 60.00				

KM# 1019   2 POUNDS
32.4500 g., 0.9584 Silver 0.9998 oz. ASW, 40 mm.
Ruler: Elizabeth II **Subject:** Britannia Bullion **Obv:** Head with
tiara right **Obv. Designer:** Ian Rank-Broadley **Rev:** Una and Lion
Edge: Reeded

Date	Mintage	F	VF	XF	Unc	BU
2001	100,000	—	—	—	28.00	32.00
2001 Proof	10,000	Value: 55.00				

KM# 1029   2 POUNDS
32.5400 g., 0.9580 Silver 1.0022 oz. ASW, 40 mm.
Ruler: Elizabeth II **Obv:** Head with tiara right
Obv. Designer: Ian Rank-Broadley **Rev:** Standing Britannia
Rev. Designer: Philip Nathan **Edge:** Reeded

Date	Mintage	F	VF	XF	Unc	BU
2002	36,543	—	—	—	—	28.00
2002 Proof	—	Value: 50.00				
2004	100,000	—	—	—	—	28.00
2004 Proof	2,174	Value: 50.00				
2006	100,000	—	—	—	—	28.00
2006 Proof	2,529	Value: 50.00				

KM# 1039   2 POUNDS
32.4500 g., 0.9580 Silver 0.9994 oz. ASW, 40 mm. **Ruler:**
Elizabeth II **Subject:** Britannia Bullion **Obv:** Head w/tiara right **Obv.**
Designer: Ian Rank-Broadley **Rev:** Britannia portrait behind wavy
puzzle-like lines **Rev. Designer:** Philip Nathan **Edge:** Reeded

Date	Mintage	F	VF	XF	Unc	BU
2003	73,271	—	—	—	—	28.00
2003 Proof	2,016	Value: 60.00				

KM# 1063   2 POUNDS
32.4500 g., 0.9580 Silver 0.9994 oz. ASW, 40 mm.
Ruler: Elizabeth II **Obv:** Head with tiara right **Obv. Designer:**
Ian Rank-Broadley **Rev:** Seated Britannia **Rev. Designer:** Philip
Nathan **Edge:** Reeded

Date	Mintage	F	VF	XF	Unc	BU
2005	100,000	—	—	—	—	28.00
2005 Proof	1,539	Value: 65.00				

KM# 1000a   2 POUNDS
32.4500 g., 0.9580 Silver 0.9994 oz. ASW, 40 mm. **Ruler:**
Elizabeth II **Subject:** Golden Silhouette Britannias **Obv:** Head with
tiara right **Obv. Designer:** Ian Rank-Broadley **Rev:** Gold plated
Britannia in chariot **Rev. Designer:** Philip Nathan **Edge:** Reeded

Date	Mintage	F	VF	XF	Unc	BU
2006 Proof	3,000	Value: 100				

KM# 1029a   2 POUNDS
32.4500 g., 0.9580 Silver 0.9994 oz. ASW, 40 mm.
Ruler: Elizabeth II **Subject:** Golden Silhouette Britannias
Obv: Head with tiara right **Obv. Designer:** Ian Rank-Broadley
Rev: Gold plated Britannia standing with shield **Edge:** Reeded

Date	Mintage	F	VF	XF	Unc	BU
2006 Proof	3,000	Value: 100				

KM# 1039a   2 POUNDS
32.4500 g., 0.9580 Silver 0.9994 oz. ASW, 40 mm.
Ruler: Elizabeth II **Subject:** Golden Silhouette Britannias
Obv: Head with tiara right **Obv. Designer:** Ian Rank-Broadley
Rev: Gold plated Britannia head **Edge:** Reeded

Date	Mintage	F	VF	XF	Unc	BU
2006 Proof	3,000	Value: 100				

KM# 1063a   2 POUNDS
32.4500 g., 0.9580 Gold 0.9994 oz. AGW, 40 mm.
Ruler: Elizabeth II **Subject:** Golden Silhouette Britannias
Obv: Head with tiara right **Obv. Designer:** Ian Rank-Broadley
Rev: Gold plated Britannia seated **Edge:** Reeded

Date	Mintage	F	VF	XF	Unc	BU
2006 Proof	3,000	Value: 100				

KM# 1019a   2 POUNDS
32.4500 g., 0.9580 Silver 0.9994 oz. ASW, 40 mm.
Ruler: Elizabeth II **Subject:** Golden Silhouette Britannias
Obv: Head with tiara right **Obv. Designer:** Ian Rank-Broadley
Rev: Gold plated Britannia and Lion **Edge:** Reeded

Date	Mintage	F	VF	XF	Unc	BU
2006 Proof	3,000	Value: 100				

KM# 1078   2 POUNDS
32.4500 g., 0.9580 Silver 0.9994 oz. ASW, 40 mm. **Ruler:**
Elizabeth II **Subject:** Britannia series **Obv:** Elizabeth II **Rev:** Seated,
bareheaded Britannia w/recumbent lion at her feet **Edge:** Reeded

Date	Mintage	F	VF	XF	Unc	BU
2007	100,000	—	—	—	—	35.00
2007 Proof	2,500	Value: 65.00				

KM# 1098   2 POUNDS
32.4500 g., 0.9584 Silver 0.9998 oz. ASW, 40 mm. **Ruler:**
Elizabeth II **Obv:** Head with tiara right **Rev:** Britannia standing
facing left with trident, flowing garment, shield **Edge:** Reeded

Date	Mintage	F	VF	XF	Unc	BU
2008	—	—	—	—	—	35.00
2008 Proof	—	Value: 80.00				

KM# 1000   2 POUNDS
32.5400 g., 0.9580 Silver 1.0022 oz. ASW, 40 mm.
Ruler: Elizabeth II **Obv:** Head with tiara right **Obv. Designer:**
Rank-Broadley **Rev:** Britannia in chariot **Edge:** Reeded

Date	Mintage	F	VF	XF	Unc	BU
2009	—	—	—	—	—	30.00

KM# 1020   10 POUNDS
3.4100 g., 0.9167 Gold 0.1005 oz. AGW, 16.5 mm. **Ruler:**
Elizabeth II **Subject:** Britannia Bullion **Obv:** Head with tiara right
Obv. Designer: Ian Rank-Broadley **Rev:** Stylized "Britannia and
the Lion" **Rev. Designer:** Philip Nathan **Edge:** Reeded

Date	Mintage	F	VF	XF	Unc	BU
2001	1,100	—	—	—	BV+16%	
2001 Proof	1,557	Value: 150				

KM# 1008   10 POUNDS
3.4100 g., 0.9167 Gold 0.1005 oz. AGW, 16.5 mm. **Ruler:**
Elizabeth II **Obv:** Head with tiara right **Obv. Designer:** Ian Rank-
Broadley **Rev:** Britannia standing **Rev. Designer:** Philip Nathan
Edge: Reeded

Date	Mintage	F	VF	XF	Unc	BU
2002 Proof	1,500	Value: 150				
2004	—	—	—	—	BV+16%	

Date	Mintage	F	VF	XF	Unc	BU
2004 Proof	—	Value: 200				
2006	—	—	—	—	—	BV+16%
2006 Proof	—	Value: 150				

KM# 1040 10 POUNDS

3.4100 g., 0.9167 Gold 0.1005 oz. AGW, 16.5 mm. **Ruler:** Elizabeth II **Obv:** Head with tiara right **Obv. Designer:** Ian Rank-Broadley **Rev:** Britannia portrait behind wavy lines **Rev. Designer:** Philip Nathan **Edge:** Reeded

Date	Mintage	F	VF	XF	Unc	BU
2003	—	—	—	—	BV+16%	—
2003 Proof	4,000	Value: 150				

KM# 1068 10 POUNDS

3.4100 g., 0.9167 Gold 0.1005 oz. AGW, 16.5 mm. **Ruler:** Elizabeth II **Obv:** Head with tiara right **Obv. Designer:** Ian Rank-Broadley **Rev:** Seated Britannia **Rev. Designer:** Philip Nathan **Edge:** Reeded

Date	Mintage	F	VF	XF	Unc	BU
2005 Proof	1,225	Value: 165				

KM# 1091 10 POUNDS

3.4100 g., 0.9167 Gold 0.1005 oz. AGW, 16.5 mm. **Ruler:** Elizabeth II **Obv:** Head with tiara right **Rev:** Britannia seated with reclining lion right **Edge:** Reeded

Date	Mintage	F	VF	XF	Unc	BU
2007 Proof	—	Value: 175				

KM# 1091a 10 POUNDS

0.9999 Platinum APW **Ruler:** Elizabeth II **Obv:** Head with tiara right **Rev:** Britannia seated with reclining lion right **Edge:** Reeded **Edge Lettering:** 16.5

Date	Mintage	F	VF	XF	Unc	BU
2007 Proof	—	Value: 450				

KM# 1099 10 POUNDS

3.4100 g., 0.9167 Gold 0.1005 oz. AGW, 16.5 mm. **Ruler:** Elizabeth II **Obv:** Head with tiara right **Rev:** Britannia standing facing left with trident, flowing garment, shield **Edge:** Reeded

Date	Mintage	F	VF	XF	Unc	BU
2008 Proof	—	Value: 200				

KM# 1099a 10 POUNDS

0.9999 Platinum APW, 16.5 mm. **Ruler:** Elizabeth II **Obv:** Head with tiara right **Rev:** Britannia standing facing left with trident, flowing garment, shield **Edge:** Reeded

Date	Mintage	F	VF	XF	Unc	BU
2008 Proof	—	Value: 450				

KM# 1021 25 POUNDS

8.5100 g., 0.9167 Gold 0.2508 oz. AGW, 22 mm. **Ruler:** Elizabeth II **Subject:** Britannia Bullion **Obv:** Head with tiara right **Obv. Designer:** Ian Rank-Broadley **Rev:** Stylized "Britannia and the Lion" **Rev. Designer:** Philip Nathan **Edge:** Reeded

Date	Mintage	F	VF	XF	Unc	BU
2001	1,100	—	—	—	BV+25%	—
2001 Proof	1,500	Value: 400				

KM# 1009 25 POUNDS

8.5100 g., 0.9167 Gold 0.2508 oz. AGW, 22 mm. **Ruler:** Elizabeth II **Obv:** Head with tiara right **Obv. Designer:** Ian Rank-Broadley **Rev:** Britannia standing **Rev. Designer:** Philip Nathan **Edge:** Reeded

Date	Mintage	F	VF	XF	Unc	BU
2002 Proof	750	Value: 400				
2004	—	—	—	—	BV+15%	—
2004 Proof	750	Value: 450				
2006	—	—	—	—	BV+15%	—
2006 Proof	1,000	Value: 450				

KM# 1041 25 POUNDS

8.5100 g., 0.9167 Gold 0.2508 oz. AGW, 22 mm. **Ruler:** Elizabeth II **Obv:** Head with tiara right **Obv. Designer:** Ian Rank-Broadley **Rev:** Britannia portrait behind wavy lines **Rev. Designer:** Philip Nathan **Edge:** Reeded

Date	Mintage	F	VF	XF	Unc	BU
2003	604	—	—	—	BV+25%	—
2003 Proof	3,250	Value: 400				

KM# 1069 25 POUNDS

8.5100 g., 0.9167 Gold 0.2508 oz. AGW, 22 mm. **Ruler:** Elizabeth II **Obv:** Head with tiara right **Obv. Designer:** Ian Rank-Broadley **Rev:** Seated Britannia **Rev. Designer:** Philip Nathan **Edge:** Reeded

Date	Mintage	F	VF	XF	Unc	BU
2005 Proof	2,750	Value: 420				

KM# 1092 25 POUNDS

8.5100 g., 0.9167 Gold 0.2508 oz. AGW, 22 mm. **Ruler:** Elizabeth II **Obv:** Head with tiara right **Rev:** Britannia seated with reclining lion right **Edge:** Reeded

Date	Mintage	F	VF	XF	Unc	BU
2007 Proof	—	Value: 420				

KM# 1092a 25 POUNDS

0.9999 Platinum APW, 22 mm. **Ruler:** Elizabeth II **Obv:** Head with tiara right **Rev:** Britannia seated with reclining lion right **Edge:** Reeded

Date	Mintage	F	VF	XF	Unc	BU
2007 Proof	—	Value: 750				

KM# 1100 25 POUNDS

8.5100 g., 0.9167 Gold 0.2508 oz. AGW, 22 mm. **Ruler:** Elizabeth II **Obv:** Head with tiara right **Rev:** Britannia standing facing left with trident, flowing garment, shield **Edge:** Reeded

Date	Mintage	F	VF	XF	Unc	BU
2008 Proof	—	Value: 450				

KM# 1100a 25 POUNDS

0.9999 Platinum APW, 22 mm. **Ruler:** Elizabeth II **Obv:** Head with tiara right **Rev:** Britannia standing facing left with trident, flowing garment, shield **Edge:** Reeded

Date	Mintage	F	VF	XF	Unc	BU
2008 Proof	—	Value: 750				

KM# 1022 50 POUNDS

17.0200 g., 0.9167 Gold 0.5016 oz. AGW, 27 mm. **Ruler:** Elizabeth II **Subject:** Britannia Bullion **Obv:** Head with tiara right **Obv. Designer:** Ian Rank-Broadley **Rev:** Stylized "Britannia and the Lion" **Rev. Designer:** Philip Nathan **Edge:** Reeded

Date	Mintage	F	VF	XF	Unc	BU
2001	600	—	—	—	BV+25%	—
2001 Proof	1,000	Value: 750				

KM# 1010 50 POUNDS

17.0300 g., 0.9167 Gold 0.5019 oz. AGW, 27 mm. **Ruler:** Elizabeth II **Obv:** Head with tiara right **Obv. Designer:** Ian Rank-Broadley **Rev:** Britannia standing **Rev. Designer:** Philip Nathan **Edge:** Reeded

Date	Mintage	F	VF	XF	Unc	BU
2002 Proof	1,000	Value: 750				
2004	—	—	—	—	—	BV+15%
2004 Proof	—	Value: 775				
2006	—	—	—	—	—	BV+15%
2006 Proof	—	Value: 775				

KM# 1042 50 POUNDS

17.0200 g., 0.9167 Gold 0.5016 oz. AGW, 27 mm. **Ruler:** Elizabeth II **Obv:** Head with tiara right **Obv. Designer:** Ian Rank-Broadley **Rev:** Britannia portrait behind wavy lines **Rev. Designer:** Philip Nathan **Edge:** Reeded

Date	Mintage	F	VF	XF	Unc	BU
2003	—	—	—	—	BV+15%	—
2003 Proof	2,500	Value: 750				

KM# 1070 50 POUNDS

17.0300 g., 0.9167 Gold 0.5019 oz. AGW, 27 mm. **Ruler:** Elizabeth II **Obv:** Head with tiara right **Obv. Designer:** Ian Rank-Broadley **Rev:** Seated Britannia **Rev. Designer:** Philip Nathan **Edge:** Reeded

Date	Mintage	F	VF	XF	Unc	BU
2005 Proof	2,000	Value: 750				

KM# 1093 50 POUNDS

17.0250 g., 0.9167 Gold 0.5017 oz. AGW, 27 mm. **Ruler:** Elizabeth II **Obv:** Head with tiara right **Rev:** Britannia seated with reclining lion right **Edge:** Reeded

Date	Mintage	F	VF	XF	Unc	BU
2007 Proof	—	Value: 800				

KM# 1093a 50 POUNDS

0.9999 Platinum APW, 27 mm. **Ruler:** Elizabeth II **Obv:** Head with tiara right **Rev:** Britannia seated with reclining lion right **Edge:** Reeded

Date	Mintage	F	VF	XF	Unc	BU
2007 Proof	—	Value: 1,700				

KM# 1101 50 POUNDS

17.0250 g., 0.9167 Gold 0.5017 oz. AGW, 27 mm. **Ruler:** Elizabeth II **Obv:** Head with tiara right **Rev:** Britannia standing facing left with trident, flowing garment, shield **Edge:** Reeded

Date	Mintage	F	VF	XF	Unc	BU
2008 Proof	—	Value: 800				

KM# 1101a 50 POUNDS

0.9999 Platinum APW, 27 mm. **Ruler:** Elizabeth II **Obv:** Head with tiara right **Rev:** Britannia standing facing left with trident, flowing garment, shield **Edge:** Reeded

Date	Mintage	F	VF	XF	Unc	BU
2008 Proof	—	Value: 1,700				

KM# 1023 100 POUNDS

34.0500 g., 0.9167 Gold 1.0035 oz. AGW, 32.7 mm. **Ruler:** Elizabeth II **Subject:** Britannia Bullion **Obv:** Head with tiara right **Obv. Designer:** Ian Rank-Broadley **Rev:** Stylized "Britannia and the Lion" **Rev. Designer:** Philip Nathan **Edge:** Reeded

Date	Mintage	F	VF	XF	Unc	BU
2001	900	—	—	—	BV+15%	—
2001 Proof	1,000	Value: 1,500				

KM# 1011 100 POUNDS

34.0500 g., 0.9167 Gold 1.0035 oz. AGW, 32.7 mm. **Ruler:** Elizabeth II **Obv:** Head with tiara right **Obv. Designer:** Ian Rank-Broadley **Rev:** Britannia standing **Rev. Designer:** Philip Nathan **Edge:** Reeded

Date	Mintage	F	VF	XF	Unc	BU
2002	—	—	—	—	—	BV+15%
2002 Proof	1,000	Value: 1,500				
2004	—	—	—	—	—	BV+15%
2004 Proof	—	Value: 1,500				

Date	Mintage	F	VF	XF	Unc	BU
2006	—	—	—	—	—	BV+15%
2006 Proof	—	Value: 1,500				

KM# 1043 100 POUNDS

34.0500 g., 0.9167 Gold 1.0035 oz. AGW, 32.7 mm. **Ruler:** Elizabeth II **Obv:** Head with tiara right **Obv. Designer:** Ian Rank-Broadley **Rev:** Britannia portrait behind wavy lines **Rev. Designer:** Philip Nathan **Edge:** Reeded

Date	Mintage	F	VF	XF	Unc	BU
2003	—	—	—	—	BV+15%	—
2003 Proof	1,500	Value: 1,500				

KM# 1071 100 POUNDS

34.0500 g., 0.9167 Gold 1.0035 oz. AGW, 32.7 mm. **Ruler:** Elizabeth II **Obv:** Head with tiara right **Obv. Designer:** Ian Rank-Broadley **Rev:** Seated Britannia **Edge:** Reeded

Date	Mintage	F	VF	XF	Unc	BU
2005	—	—	—	—	BV+15%	—
2005 Proof	1,500	Value: 1,500				

KM# 1094 100 POUNDS

34.0500 g., 0.9167 Gold 1.0035 oz. AGW, 32.7 mm. **Ruler:** Elizabeth II **Obv:** Head with tiara right **Rev:** Britannia seated with reclining lion right **Edge:** Reeded

Date	Mintage	F	VF	XF	Unc	BU
2007	—	—	—	—	BV+15%	—
2007 Proof	—	Value: 1,500				

KM# 1094a 100 POUNDS

0.9999 Platinum APW, 32.7 mm. **Ruler:** Elizabeth II **Obv:** Head with tiara right **Rev:** Britannia seated with reclining lion right **Edge:** Reeded

Date	Mintage	F	VF	XF	Unc	BU
2007 Proof	—	Value: 2,900				

KM# 1102 100 POUNDS

34.0500 g., 0.9167 Gold 1.0035 oz. AGW, 32.7 mm. **Ruler:** Elizabeth II **Obv:** Head with tiara right **Rev:** Britannia standing facing left with trident, flowing garment, shield **Edge:** Reeded

Date	Mintage	F	VF	XF	Unc	BU
2008	—	—	—	—	BV+15%	—
2008 Proof	—	Value: 1,500				

KM# 1102a 100 POUNDS

0.9999 Platinum APW, 32.7 mm. **Ruler:** Elizabeth II **Obv:** Head with tiara right **Rev:** Britannia standing facing left with trident, flowing garment, shield **Edge:** Reeded

Date	Mintage	F	VF	XF	Unc	BU
2008 Proof	—	Value: 2,900				

PIEFORTS

KM#	Date	Mintage	Identification	Mkt Val
P32	2004	10,000	2 Pounds. 0.9250 Bi-Metallic. 24.0000 g. 28.4 mm. Queen Elizabeth II. First steam locomotive. Reeded and lettered edge.	—
P33	2007	—	50 Pence. 0.9250 Silver. 16.0000 g. 27.3 mm. Elizabeth II. Fleur de Lis Scouting emblem. Plain edge.	—
P34	2007	250	5 Pounds. 0.9995 Platinum. 94.2000 g. 38.6 mm. Elizabeth II and Prince Philip. North Rose window of Westminster Abbey.	7,500
P35	2007	5,000	5 Pounds. 0.9250 Silver. 56.5600 g. 38.6 mm. Elizabeth II and Prince Philip. Westminster Abbey's North Rose Window. KM#1075a.	125
P36	2007	3,000	Pound. 0.9250 Silver. 19.0000 g. 22.5 mm. Elizabeth II. Gateshead Millennium Bridge. KM#1074a.	75.00
P37	2007	3,000	2 Pounds. 0.9250 Silver. 24.0000 g. 28.4 mm. Elizabeth II. 1807 Date and broken chain. KM#1075a.	80.00
P38	2007	3,000	2 Pounds. 0.9250 Silver. 24.0000 g. 28.4 mm. Elizabeth II. Combined English and Scottish arms. KM#1076a.	80.00
P39	2005	—	5 Pounds. 0.9250 Silver. KM#1053a.	70.00
P40	2005	—	5 Pounds. 0.9250 Silver. KM#1054a.	70.00
P41	2006	—	5 Pounds. 0.9250 Silver. KM#1062a.	70.00
P42	2009	—	5 Pounds. 0.9250 Silver. 56.5600 g. KM#1121a.	170

MAUNDY SETS

KM#	Date	Mintage	Identification	Issue Price	Mkt Val
MDS260	2001 (4)	1,132	KM#898-899, 901-902. Westminster Abbey	—	250
MDS261	2002 (4)	1,681	KM#898-899, 901-902. Canterbury Cathedral	—	250
MDS262	2003 (4)	1,601	KM#898-899, 901-902. Gloucester Cathedral	—	265
MDS263	2004 (4)	1,613	KM#898-899, 901-902. Liverpool Cathedral	—	265
MDS264	2005 (4)	1,685	KM#898-899,901-902 Wakefield Cathedral	—	265
MDS265	2006 (4)	1,937	KM#898-899, 901-902; Guilford Cathedral	—	265
MDS266	2007 (4)	1,953	KM#898-899, 901-902; Manchester Cathedral	—	265
MDS267	2008 (4)	—	KM#898-899, 901-902; St. Patrick's Cathedral	—	265

MINT SETS

KM#	Date	Mintage	Identification	Issue Price	Mkt Val
MS129	2001 (9)	57,741	KM#986-991, 994, 1013-1015 B.U. set	22.50	25.00
MS130	2001 (9)	—	KM#986-991, 994, 1013-1014 Wedding Collection	27.50	25.00
MS131	2001 (9)	—	KM#986-991, 994, 1013-1014 Baby Gift Set	27.50	25.00
MS132	2002 (8)	60,539	KM#986-991, 994, 1030	22.50	20.00
MS133	2002 (8)	—	KM#986-991, 994, 1030 Wedding Collection	27.50	20.00
MS134	2002 (8)	—	KM#986-991, 994, 1030 Baby Gift Set	27.50	20.00
MS135	2003 (10)	—	KM#986-991, 993, 994, 1036-1037 BU Set	22.50	35.00
MS136	2003 (10)	—	KM#986-991, 993, 994, 1036-1037 Wedding Collection	27.50	30.00
MS137	2003 (10)	—	KM#986-991, 993, 994, 1036-1037 Baby Gift Set	27.50	30.00
MSA135	2004 (10)	46,032	KM#986-991, 994, 1047-1049 BU Set	—	35.00
MSB135	2004 (10)	4,214	KM#986-991, 994, 1047-1049, 1055 Wedding Collection	—	35.00
MSC135	2004 (10)	34,371	KM#986-991, 994, 1047-1049, 1055 Baby Gift Set	—	35.00
MS138	2005 (10)	—	KM#986-991, 994, 1050-1052	26.50	30.00
MS139	2005 (10)	—	KM#986-991, 994, 1050-1052 Baby Gift Set	36.50	35.00
MS140	2005 (3)	—	KM#1050-1052 New Coinage Set	16.25	17.50
MS141	2005 (2)	—	KM#1053-1054 Trafalgar Set	36.00	35.00
MS142	2006 (10)	—	KM#986-990, 1057-1061	30.00	60.00
MS143	2006 (10)	—	KM#986-990, 1057-1061 Baby Gift Set	38.50	60.00
MS144	2007 (6)	—	KM#986-991	—	10.00

PROOF SETS

KM#	Date	Mintage	Identification	Issue Price	Mkt Val
PS117	2001 (4)	1,000	KM#1001-1003,1014a	1,645	2,250
PS118	2001 (4)	5,000	KM#1016-1019	—	150
PS127	2001 (10)	10,000	KM#986-991, 994, 1013-1015 Executive Proof Set in display case	115	60.00
PS128	2001 (10)	30,000	KM#986-991, 994, 1013-1015 Deluxe Proof Set in red leather case	72.50	60.00
PS129	2001 (10)	28,244	KM#986-991, 994, 1013-1015 Standard Proof Set in simple case	50.00	60.00
PS130	2001 (10)	1,351	KM#986-991, 994, 1013-1015 Gift Proof Set with a pack of occasion cards	65.00	60.00
PS131	2002 (9)	5,000	KM#986-991, 994, 1024, 1030 Executive Proof Set	100	60.00
PS119	2001 (9)	1,000	KM#1020-1023	1,595	2,850
PS116	2001 (3)	1,500	KM#1001-1002, 1014a	795	525
PSA119	2001 (3)	1,500	KM#1001, 1002, 1014b	—	525
PSB119	2001 (4)	1,000	KM#1001, 1002, 1014b, 1015b	—	2,700
PS120	2002 (3)	5,000	KM#1025-1027	795	1,125
PS121	2002 (3)	3,000	KM#1025-1028	1,645	2,300
PS126	2002 (4)	1,000	KM#1008-1011	1,600	2,850
PS132	2002 (9)	30,000	KM#986-991, 994, 1024, 1030 Deluxe Proof Set	70.00	55.00
PS133	2002 (9)	30,884	KM#986-991, 994, 1024, 1030 Standard Proof Set	48.00	55.00
PS134	2002 (9)	1,544	KM#986-991, 994, 1024, 1030 Gift Proof Set	62.40	55.00
PS160	2002 (4)	—	KM#1029, 1079-1081	—	175
PSA135	2002 (13)	—	KM#898a, 899a, 901a, 902a, 986c, 987c, 988b, 989b, 990b, 991b, 1030b, 994c, 1024b Queen Elizabeth II - Golden Jubilee 1952-2002, set is struck in gold (including Maundy set), in presentation box	—	11,250
PS122	2002 (4)	3,358	KM#1031-1034; Standard Set	34.95	35.00
PS123	2002 (4)	673	KM#1031-1034; Display Set	44.95	40.00

KM#	Date	Mintage	Identification	Issue Price	Mkt Val
PS124	2002 (4)	2,553	KM#1031a-1034a; Display Set	120	135
PS125	2002 (4)	315	KM#1031b-1034b; Display Set	1,675	2,450
PS135	2003 (11)	5,000	KM#986-991, 993, 994, 1036-1038 Executive Proof Set	100	85.00
PS136	2003 (11)	14,863	KM#986-991, 993, 994, 1036-1038 Deluxe Proof Set	72.00	80.00
PS137	2003 (11)	23,650	KM#986-991, 993, 994, 1036-1038 Standard Proof Set	50.00	80.00
PS161	2003 (3)	1,250	KM#1040-1043	—	2,800
PSA138	2003 (4)	3,669	KM#1039, 1044-1046	—	180
PS162	2004 (4)	—	KM#1029, 1079-1081	—	175
PS165	2006 (4)	—	KM#1029, 1079-1081	—	175
PSB138	2004 (11)	4,101	KM#986-991, 994, 1047-1049, 1055 Executive Proof Set	—	80.00
PSC138	2004 (11)	12,968	KM#986-991, 994, 1047-1049, 1055 Deluxe Proof Set	—	80.00
PSD138	2004 (11)	17,951	KM#986-991, 994, 1047-1049, 1055 Standard Proof Set	—	80.00
PS163	2004 (4)	973	KM#1008-1011	—	3,000
PS138	2005 (12)	4,290	KM#986-991, 994, 1050-1054 Executive Set	146	95.00
PS139	2005 (12)	14,899	KM#986-991, 994, 1050-1054 Deluxe Proof Set	80.00	95.00
PS140	2005 (12)	21,374	KM#986-991, 994, 1050-1054, Standard Proof Set	60.00	95.00
PS141	2005 (3)	417	KM#1068-1070	850	1,350
PS142	2005 (4)	1,439	KM#1068-1071	1,895	2,850
PS143	2005 (3)	2,500	KM#1064-1066	820	1,100
PS144	2005 (4)	2,500	KM#1064-1067	1,925	2,600
PS145	2005 (2)	—	P39, P40	—	175
PS164	2005 (4)	2,360	KM#1063, 1085-1087	—	185
PS149	2006 (5)	3,000	KM#1000a, 1012a, 1018a, 1039, 1063a	475	525
PS150	2006 (3)	1,750	KM#1001, 1002, 1072	1,015	1,100
PS151	2006 (4)	1,750	KM#1001-1003, 1072	2,091	2,600
PS166	2006 (4)	—	KM#1008-1011	—	2,900
PS146	2006 (13)	5,000	KM#986-991, 994, 1057-1062 Executive Proof Set, wooden case	—	140
PS147	2006 (13)	15,000	KM#986-991, 994, 1057-1062 Deluxe Proof Set	82.50	140
PS148	2006 (13)	30,000	KM#986-991, 994, 1057-1062 Standard Proof Set	65.00	140
PS152	2007 (13)	30,000	KM#986-991, 994, 1057-1062	65.00	140
PS153	2007 (4)	1,750	KM#1001-1003, 1072	—	2,850
PS154	2007 (3)	750	KM#1001-1002, 1072	—	1,175
PS156	2007 (5)	3,000	KM#P33, P35-P38	450	500
PS167	2007 (4)	—	KM#1078, 1088-1090	—	185
PS168	2007 (4)	—	KM#1091-1094	—	2,950
PS169	2007 (4)	—	KM#1091a-1094a	—	5,850
PS155	2007 (2)	5,000	KM#1001-1002	—	550
PS170	2008 (4)	—	KM#1095-1098	—	225
PS171	2008 (4)	—	KM#1099-1102	—	3,000
PS172	2008 (4)	—	KM#1099a-1102a	—	5,850

GREECE

The Hellenic (Greek) Republic is situated in southeastern Europe on the southern tip of the Balkan Peninsula. The republic includes many islands, the most important of which are Crete and the Ionian Islands. Greece (including islands) has an area of 50,944 sq. mi. (131,940 sq. km.) and a population of 10.3 million. Capital: Athens. Greece is still largely agricultural. Tobacco, cotton, fruit and wool are exported.

MINT MARKS
(a) - Paris, privy marks only
A - Paris
B - Vienna
E – Madrid
F – Pessac, France
(p) – Poissy – Thunderbolt
S – Vantaa (Suomi), Finland
(an) = Anthemion – Greek National Mint, Athens

MONETARY SYSTEM
100 Lepta = 1 Drachma

REPUBLIC

DECIMAL COINAGE

KM# 132   10 DRACHMES
7.6000 g., Copper-Nickel, 26 mm. **Obv:** Atom design **Rev:** Head of Democritus left

Date	Mintage	F	VF	XF	Unc	BU
2002	—	—	0.25	0.50	1.25	2.50

EURO COINAGE
European Union Issues

The Greek Euro coinage series contains the denomination in Lepta as well.

KM# 181   EURO CENT
2.2700 g., Copper Plated Steel, 16.2 mm. **Obv:** Ancient Athenian trireme **Obv. Designer:** George Stamatopoulos **Rev:** Denomination and globe **Rev. Designer:** Luc Luycx **Edge:** Plain

Date	Mintage	F	VF	XF	Unc	BU
2002	101,000,000	—	—	—	0.35	—
2002 F in star	15,000,000	—	—	—	1.25	—
2003	35,200,000	—	—	—	0.35	—
2003 Proof	7,000,000	—	—	—	—	—
2004	50,000,000	—	—	—	0.35	—
2005	15,000,000	—	—	—	0.35	—
2006	45,000,000	—	—	—	0.35	—
2007	60,000,000	—	—	—	0.35	—
2008	24,000,000	—	—	—	0.35	—
2009	—	—	—	—	0.35	—

KM# 182   2 EURO CENT
3.0300 g., Copper Plated Steel, 18.7 mm. **Obv:** Corvette sailing ship **Obv. Designer:** George Stamatopoulos **Rev:** Denomination and globe **Rev. Designer:** Luc Luycx **Edge:** Grooved

Date	Mintage	F	VF	XF	Unc	BU
2002	176,000,000	—	—	—	0.50	—
2002 F in star	18,000,000	—	—	—	1.00	—
2003	10,000,000	—	—	—	0.50	—
2003 Proof	500,000	—	—	—	—	—
2004	25,000,000	—	—	—	0.50	—
2005	15,000,000	—	—	—	0.50	—
2006	45,000,000	—	—	—	0.50	—
2007	25,000,103	—	—	—	0.50	—
2008	68,000,000	—	—	—	0.50	—
2009	—	—	—	—	0.50	—

KM# 183   5 EURO CENT
3.8600 g., Copper Plated Steel, 21.2 mm. **Obv:** Freighter **Obv. Designer:** George Stamatopoulos **Rev:** Denomination and globe **Rev. Designer:** Luc Luycx **Edge:** Plain

Date	Mintage	F	VF	XF	Unc	BU
2002	211,000,000	—	—	—	1.00	—
2002 F in star	90,000,000	—	—	—	1.25	—
2003	750,000	—	—	—	1.00	—
2003 Proof	—	—	—	—	—	—
2004	250,000	—	—	—	1.00	—
2005	1,000,000	—	—	—	1.00	—
2006	50,000,000	—	—	—	1.00	—
2007	55,005,598	—	—	—	1.00	—
2008	50,000,000	—	—	—	1.00	—
2009	—	—	—	—	1.00	—

KM# 184   10 EURO CENT
4.0700 g., Brass, 19.7 mm. **Obv:** Bust of Rhgas Feriaou's half right **Obv. Designer:** George Stamatopoulos **Rev:** Denomination and map **Rev. Designer:** Luc Luycx **Edge:** Reeded

Date	Mintage	F	VF	XF	Unc	BU
2002	138,000,000	—	—	—	1.25	—
2002 F in star	100,000,000	—	—	—	2.00	—

Date	Mintage	F	VF	XF	Unc	BU
2003	600,000	—	—	—	1.25	—
2003 Proof	—	—	—	—	—	—
2004	10,000,000	—	—	—	1.25	—
2005	25,000,000	—	—	—	1.25	—
2006	45,000,000	—	—	—	1.25	—

KM# 211 10 EURO CENT

4.0700 g., Brass, 19.25 mm. **Obv:** Bust of Rhgas Feriaou's half right **Obv. Designer:** George Stamatopoulos **Rev:** Relief map of Western Europe, stars, lines and value **Rev. Designer:** Luc Luycx **Edge:** Reeded

Date	Mintage	F	VF	XF	Unc	BU
2007	63,000,000	—	—	—	1.25	—
2008	40,000,000	—	—	—	1.25	—
2009	—	—	—	—	1.25	—

KM# 185 20 EURO CENT

5.7300 g., Brass, 22.25 mm. **Obv:** Bust of John Kapodistrias half right **Obv. Designer:** George Stamatopoulos **Rev:** Denomination and map **Rev. Designer:** Luc Luycx **Edge:** Notched

Date	Mintage	F	VF	XF	Unc	BU
2002	209,000,000	—	—	—	1.25	—
2002 E in star	120,000,000	—	—	—	2.25	—
2003	800,000	—	—	—	1.25	—
2003 Proof	—	—	—	—	—	—
2004	500,000	—	—	—	1.25	—
2005	1,000,000	—	—	—	1.25	—
2006	1,000,000	—	—	—	1.25	—

KM# 212 20 EURO CENT

5.7300 g., Brass, 22.1 mm. **Obv:** Bust of John Kapodistrias' half right **Obv. Designer:** George Stamatopoulos **Rev:** Relief map of Western Europe, stars, lines and value **Rev. Designer:** Luc Luycx **Edge:** Notched

Date	Mintage	F	VF	XF	Unc	BU
2007	1,000,000	—	—	—	1.25	—
2008	—	—	—	—	1.25	—

KM# 186 50 EURO CENT

7.8100 g., Brass, 24.2 mm. **Obv:** Bust of El. Venizelos half left **Obv. Designer:** George Stamatopoulos **Rev:** Denomination and map **Rev. Designer:** Luc Luycx **Edge:** Reeded

Date	Mintage	F	VF	XF	Unc	BU
2002	93,000,000	—	—	—	1.50	—
2002 F in star	70,000,000	—	—	—	2.50	—
2003	700,000	—	—	—	1.50	—
2003 Proof	—	—	—	—	—	—
2004	500,000	—	—	—	1.50	—
2005	1,000,000	—	—	—	1.50	—
2006	1,000,000	—	—	—	1.50	—

KM# 213 50 EURO CENT

7.8100 g., Brass, 24.2 mm. **Obv:** Bust of El. Venizelos half left **Obv. Designer:** George Stamatopoulos **Rev:** Relief map of Western Europe, stars, lines and value **Rev. Designer:** Luc Luycx **Edge:** Reeded

Date	Mintage	F	VF	XF	Unc	BU
2007	1,000,000	—	—	—	1.00	1.50
2008	—	—	—	—	1.00	1.50
2009	—	—	—	—	1.00	1.50

KM# 187 EURO

7.5000 g., Bi-Metallic Copper-Nickel center in Brass ring, 23.2 mm. **Obv:** Ancient Athenian coin design **Obv. Designer:** George Stamatopoulos **Rev:** Denomination and map **Rev. Designer:** Luc Luycx **Edge:** Reeded and plain sections

Date	Mintage	F	VF	XF	Unc	BU
2002	61,500,000	—	—	—	4.00	—
2002 S in star	50,000,000	—	—	—	6.00	—
2003	11,000,000	—	—	—	7.50	—
2003 Proof	—	—	—	—	—	—
2004	10,000,000	—	—	—	5.00	—
2005	10,000,000	—	—	—	5.00	—
2006	10,000,000	—	—	—	5.00	—

KM# 214 EURO

7.5000 g., Bi-Metallic Copper-Nickel center in Brass ring, 23.2 mm. **Obv:** Ancient Athenian coin design **Obv. Designer:** George Stamatopoulos **Rev:** Relief map of Western Europe, stars, lines and value **Rev. Designer:** Luc Luycx **Edge:** Reeded and plain sections

Date	Mintage	F	VF	XF	Unc	BU
2007	24,000,000	—	—	—	3.00	4.00
2008	—	—	—	—	3.00	4.00
2009	—	—	—	—	3.00	4.00

KM# 188 2 EURO

8.5200 g., Bi-Metallic Brass center in Copper-Nickel ring, 25.7 mm. **Obv:** Europa seated on a bull **Obv. Designer:** George Stamatopoulos **Rev:** Denomination and map **Rev. Designer:** Luc Luycx **Edge:** Reeded with Greek letters and stars

Date	Mintage	F	VF	XF	Unc	BU
2002	75,400,000	—	—	—	4.00	—
2002 S in star	70,000,000	—	—	—	6.50	—
2003	550,000	—	—	—	20.00	—
2003 Proof	—	—	—	—	—	—
2004 In sets only	30,000	—	—	—	50.00	—
2005	1,000,000	—	—	—	4.00	—
2006	1,000,000	—	—	—	4.00	—

KM# 209 2 EURO

8.5200 g., Bi-Metallic Brass center in Copper-Nickel ring., 25.7 mm. **Subject:** 2004 Olympics **Obv:** Discus thrower **Rev:** Denomination and map **Edge:** Reeded and lettered **Edge Lettering:** Greek

Date	Mintage	F	VF	XF	Unc	BU
2004	49,500,000	—	—	—	4.00	6.00
2004 Prooflike	500,000	—	—	—	—	15.00

KM# 215 2 EURO

8.5200 g., Bi-Metallic Brass center in Copper-Nickel ring, 25.7 mm. **Obv:** Europa seated on a bull **Obv. Designer:** George Stamatopoulos **Rev:** Relief map of Western Europe, stars, lines and value **Rev. Designer:** Luc Luycx **Edge:** Reeded with Greek letters and stars

Date	Mintage	F	VF	XF	Unc	BU
2007 In sets only	15,000	—	—	—	—	25.00
2008	—	—	—	—	3.00	10.00
2009	—	—	—	—	3.00	5.00

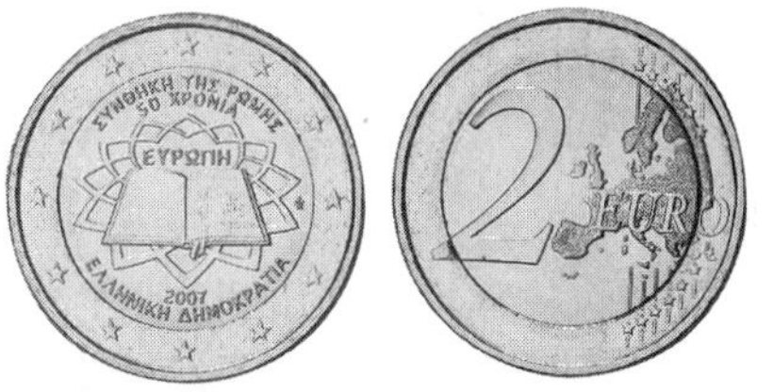

KM# 216 2 EURO

8.5500 g., Bi-Metallic Brass center in Copper-Nickel ring, 25.72 mm. **Subject:** 50th Anniversary - Treaty of Rome **Obv:** Open treaty book **Rev:** Large value at left, modified outline of Europe at right **Edge:** Reeded and lettered

Date	Mintage	F	VF	XF	Unc	BU
2007	4,000,000	—	—	—	—	9.00

KM# 227 2 EURO

8.5500 g., Bi-Metallic Brass center in Copper-Nickel ring, 25.72 mm. **Subject:** European Monetary Union, 10th Anniversary **Obv:** Stick figure and Euro symbol

Date	Mintage	F	VF	XF	Unc	BU
2009	—	—	—	—	—	5.00

KM# 191 10 EURO

34.0000 g., 0.9250 Silver 1.0111 oz. ASW, 40 mm. **Subject:** Olympics **Obv:** Olympic rings in wreath above value within circle of stars **Rev:** Ancient and modern discus throwers **Edge:** Plain

Date	Mintage	F	VF	XF	Unc	BU
ND(2003) Proof	68,000	Value: 60.00				

KM# 193 10 EURO

34.0000 g., 0.9250 Silver 1.0111 oz. ASW, 40 mm. **Subject:** Olympics **Obv:** Olympic rings in wreath above value within circle of stars **Rev:** Ancient and modern javelin throwers **Edge:** Plain

Date	Mintage	F	VF	XF	Unc	BU
ND(2003) Proof	68,000	Value: 60.00				

KM# 194 10 EURO

34.0000 g., 0.9250 Silver 1.0111 oz. ASW, 40 mm. **Subject:** Olympics **Obv:** Olympic rings in wreath above value within circle of stars **Rev:** Ancient and modern long jumpers **Edge:** Plain

Date	Mintage	F	VF	XF	Unc	BU
ND(2003) Proof	68,000	Value: 60.00				

KM# 196 10 EURO

34.0000 g., 0.9250 Silver 1.0111 oz. ASW, 40 mm. **Subject:** Olympics **Obv:** Olympic rings in wreath above value within circle of stars **Rev:** Ancient and modern relay runners **Edge:** Plain

Date	Mintage	F	VF	XF	Unc	BU
ND(2003) Proof	68,000	Value: 60.00				

KM# 197 10 EURO

34.0000 g., 0.9250 Silver 1.0111 oz. ASW, 40 mm. **Subject:** Olympics **Obv:** Olympic rings in wreath above value within circle of stars **Rev:** Ancient and modern horsemen **Edge:** Plain

Date	Mintage	F	VF	XF	Unc	BU
ND(2003) Proof	68,000	Value: 60.00				

KM# 199 10 EURO

34.0000 g., 0.9250 Silver 1.0111 oz. ASW, 40 mm. **Subject:** Olympics **Obv:** Olympic rings in wreath above value within circle of stars **Rev:** Modern ribbon dancer and two ancient female acrobats **Edge:** Plain

Date	Mintage	F	VF	XF	Unc	BU
ND(2003) Proof	68,000	Value: 60.00				

KM# 200 10 EURO

34.0000 g., 0.9250 Silver 1.0111 oz. ASW, 40 mm. **Subject:** Olympics **Obv:** Olympic rings in wreath above value within a circle of stars **Rev:** Ancient and modern female swimmers **Edge:** Plain

Date	Mintage	F	VF	XF	Unc	BU
ND(2003) Proof	68,000	Value: 60.00				

KM# 208 10 EURO

9.7500 g., 0.9250 Silver 0.2899 oz. ASW, 28.25 mm. **Subject:** Greek Presidency of E. U. **Obv:** National arms in wreath above value **Rev:** Stylized document design **Edge:** Notched

Date	Mintage	F	VF	XF	Unc	BU
2003 Proof	50,000	Value: 55.00				

KM# 190 10 EURO

34.0000 g., 0.9250 Silver 1.0111 oz. ASW, 40 mm. **Subject:** Olympics **Obv:** Olympic rings in wreath above value within circle of stars **Rev:** Ancient and modern runners **Edge:** Plain **Note:** Olympics

Date	Mintage	F	VF	XF	Unc	BU
ND (2003) Proof	68,000	Value: 60.00				

KM# 202 10 EURO

34.0000 g., 0.9250 Silver 1.0111 oz. ASW, 40 mm. **Subject:** Olympics **Obv:** Olympic rings in wreath above value within circle of stars **Rev:** Ancient and modern weight lifters **Edge:** Plain

Date	Mintage	F	VF	XF	Unc	BU
ND(2004) Proof	68,000	Value: 60.00				

KM# 203 10 EURO

34.0000 g., 0.9250 Silver 1.0111 oz. ASW, 40 mm. **Subject:** Olympics **Obv:** Olympic rings in wreath above value within circle of stars **Rev:** Ancient and modern wrestlers **Edge:** Plain

Date	Mintage	F	VF	XF	Unc	BU
ND(2004) Proof	68,000	Value: 60.00				

KM# 205 10 EURO

34.0000 g., 0.9250 Silver 1.0111 oz. ASW, 40 mm. **Subject:** Olympics **Obv:** Olympic rings in wreath above value within circle of stars **Rev:** Ancient and modern handball players **Edge:** Plain

Date	Mintage	F	VF	XF	Unc	BU
ND(2004) Proof	68,000	Value: 60.00				

KM# 206 10 EURO

34.0000 g., 0.9250 Silver 1.0111 oz. ASW, 40 mm. **Subject:** Olympics **Obv:** Olympic rings in wreath above value within circle of stars **Rev:** Ancient and modern soccer players **Edge:** Plain

Date	Mintage	F	VF	XF	Unc	BU
ND(2004) Proof	68,000	Value: 60.00				

KM# 217 10 EURO

9.7500 g., 0.9250 Silver 0.2899 oz. ASW **Obv:** National arms above stylized flowers **Rev:** Four Titans above flowers in camp

Date	Mintage	F	VF	XF	Unc	BU
2005 Proof	25,000	Value: 45.00				

KM# 218 10 EURO

9.7500 g., 0.9250 Silver 0.2899 oz. ASW, 28.25 mm. **Subject:** PATRA - European Capitol of Culture - Achaia **Obv:** National arms at upper right, stylized bridge below **Rev:** PATRA logo **Edge:** Plain

Date	Mintage	F	VF	XF	Unc	BU
2006 Proof	—	Value: 50.00				

KM# 219 10 EURO

34.0000 g., 0.9250 Silver 1.0111 oz. ASW, 40.00 mm. **Obv:** National arms above stylizes flowers **Rev:** Outline of Greece at left, statue of Zeus, flowers at right **Edge:** Plain

Date	Mintage	F	VF	XF	Unc	BU
2006 Proof	5,000	Value: 55.00				

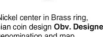

KM# 220 10 EURO
34.0000 g., 0.9250 Silver 1.0111 oz. ASW, 40.00 mm.
Subject: National Parks - Mount Olympus - International
Biosphere Reserve **Obv:** National arms above stylized flowers
Rev: Archaeological outline of Dion City above landscape
Edge: Plain

Date	Mintage	F	VF	XF	Unc	BU
2006 Proof	5,000	Value: 55.00				

KM# 221 10 EURO
34.0000 g., 0.9250 Silver 1.0111 oz. ASW, 40.00 mm. **Subject:**
National Parks - Arkoudorema River in Southern Pindos - Valia Kalda
Obv: National arms above denomination **Rev:** Outlined map at upper left,
bird perched on stalk, flowers at center right **Edge:** Plain

Date	Mintage	F	VF	XF	Unc	BU
2007 Proof	5,000	Value: 60.00				

KM# 222 10 EURO
34.0000 g., 0.9250 Silver 1.0111 oz. ASW, 40.00 mm.
Subject: National Parks - Valia Kalda - Southern Pindos
Obv: National arms on stylized tree **Rev:** Tree line **Edge:** Plain

Date	Mintage	F	VF	XF	Unc	BU
2007 Proof	5,000	Value: 60.00				

KM# 223 10 EURO
9.7500 g., 0.9250 Silver 0.2899 oz. ASW, 28.25 mm.
Subject: 30th Anniversary Death of Maria Callas, Operatic
Soprano **Obv:** National arms above denomination, facsimile
signature below, music scores in background **Rev:** Bust of M.
Callas right **Edge:** Plain **Shape:** Spanish Flower

Date	Mintage	F	VF	XF	Unc	BU
2007 Proof	5,000	Value: 50.00				

KM# 224 10 EURO
9.7500 g., 0.9250 Silver 0.2899 oz. ASW, 28.25 mm.
Subject: 50th Anniversary death of Nikos Kazantzakis, Author
Obv: National arms above denomination, facsimile signature
below **Rev:** Head of N. Kazantzakis facing 3/4 left **Edge:** Plain
Shape: Spanish Flower

Date	Mintage	F	VF	XF	Unc	BU
2007 Proof	5,000	Value: 50.00				

KM# 225 10 EURO
9.7500 g., 0.9250 Silver 0.2899 oz. ASW, 28.25 mm.
Subject: Acropolis Museum **Obv:** Panoramic view of the
Acropolis **Rev:** Pediment sculpture

Date	Mintage	F	VF	XF	Unc	BU
2008	10,000	—	—	—	—	50.00

KM# 226 10 EURO
9.7500 g., 0.9250 Silver 0.2899 oz. ASW **Subject:** Yannis Ritsos

Date	Mintage	F	VF	XF	Unc	BU
2008 Proof	—	Value: 50.00				

KM# 228 10 EURO
34.0000 g., 0.9250 Silver 1.0111 oz. ASW, 40 mm.
Subject: Astronomy

Date	Mintage	F	VF	XF	Unc	BU
2009 Proof	—	Value: 45.00				

KM# 210 20 EURO
24.0000 g., 0.9250 Silver 0.7137 oz. ASW, 37 mm.
Subject: Bank of Greece 75th Anniversary **Obv:** Value **Rev:** Flag

Date	Mintage	F	VF	XF	Unc	BU
2003	10,000	—	—	—	—	27.00
2003 Proof	1,000	Value: 55.00				

KM# 192 100 EURO
0.9999 Gold, 25 mm. **Subject:** Olympics **Obv:** Olympic rings in
wreath above value within circle of stars **Rev:** Knossos Palace
Edge: Plain

Date	Mintage	F	VF	XF	Unc	BU
ND(2003) Proof	28,000	Value: 575				

KM# 195 100 EURO
10.0000 g., 0.9999 Gold 0.3215 oz. AGW, 25 mm.
Subject: Olympics **Obv:** Olympic rings in wreath above value
within circle of stars **Rev:** Krypte archway **Edge:** Plain

Date	Mintage	F	VF	XF	Unc	BU
ND(2003) Proof	28,000	Value: 575				

KM# 198 100 EURO
10.0000 g., 0.9999 Gold 0.3215 oz. AGW, 25 mm.
Subject: Olympics **Obv:** Olympic rings in wreath above value
within circle of stars **Rev:** Panathenean Stadium **Edge:** Plain

Date	Mintage	F	VF	XF	Unc	BU
ND(2003) Proof	28,000	Value: 575				

KM# 201 100 EURO
10.0000 g., 0.9999 Gold 0.3215 oz. AGW, 25 mm.
Subject: Olympics **Obv:** Olympic rings in wreath above value
within circle of stars **Rev:** Zappeion Mansion **Edge:** Plain

Date	Mintage	F	VF	XF	Unc	BU
ND(2003) Proof	28,000	Value: 575				

KM# 204 100 EURO
10.0000 g., 0.9999 Gold 0.3215 oz. AGW, 25 mm.
Subject: Olympics **Obv:** Olympic rings in wreath above value
within circle of stars **Rev:** Acropolis **Edge:** Plain

Date	Mintage	F	VF	XF	Unc	BU
ND(2004) Proof	28,000	Value: 575				

KM# 207 100 EURO
10.0000 g., 0.9999 Gold 0.3215 oz. AGW, 25 mm.
Subject: Olympics **Obv:** Olympic rings in wreath above value
within circle of stars **Rev:** Academy of Athens **Edge:** Plain

Date	Mintage	F	VF	XF	Unc	BU
ND(2004) Proof	28,000	Value: 575				

MINT SETS

KM#	Date	Mintage Identification	Issue Price	Mkt Val
MS6	2002 (8)	50,000 KM#181-188	—	30.00

KM#	Date	Mintage	Identification	Issue Price	Mkt Val
MS7	2002F (8)	5,000	KM#181-188 Issued by Ministry of Finance	—	300
MS8	2003 (8)	—	KM#181-188	—	40.00
MS9	2003 (9)	—	KM#181-188, 208	—	80.00
MS11	2004 (8)	20,000	KM#181-188 2004 Discobole commemorating Olympic Games in Athens	—	65.00
MS12	2005 (8)	25,000	KM#181-188	—	35.00
MS13	2005 (9)	25,000	KM#181-188, 220 Mount Olympus as a National Park	—	70.00
MS14	2006 (9)	25,000	KM#181-188 (2005), 220 Aegina - Korinth set	28.00	70.00
MS15	2006 (9)	25,000	KM#181-188, 218 Patras - Cultural Capital of Europe	50.00	70.00
MS16	2007 (8)	15,000	KM#181-183, 211-215, 224 Ancient Coins of the Aegean Sea	—	50.00
MS17	2007 (9)	15,000	KM#181-183, 211-215, 224 Nikos Kazantzakis	50.00	75.00
MS18	2007 (9)	15,000	KM#181-183, 211-215, 223 Maria Callas	50.00	95.00

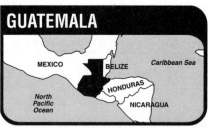

GUATEMALA

The Republic of Guatemala, the northernmost of the five
Central American republics, has an area of 42,042 sq. mi.
(108,890 sq. km.) and a population of 10.7 million. Capital: Guatemala City. The economy of Guatemala is heavily dependent on
agriculture, however, the country is rich in nickel resources which
are being developed. Coffee, cotton and bananas are exported.

Guatemala, once the site of an ancient Mayan civilization,
was conquered by Pedro de Alvarado, the resourceful lieutenant
of Cortes who undertook the conquest from Mexico. Cruel but
strategically skillful, he progressed rapidly along the Pacific
coastal lowlands to the highland plain of Quetzaltenango where
the decisive battle for Guatemala was fought. After routing the
Indian forces, he established the city of Guatemala in 1524. The
Spanish Captaincy-General of Guatemala included all Central
America but Panama. Guatemala declared its independence of
Spain in 1821 and was absorbed into the Mexican empire of
Augustin Iturbide (1822-23). From 1823 to 1839 Guatemala was
a constituent state of the Central American Republic. Upon dis-
solution of that confederation, Guatemala proclaimed itself an
independent republic. Like El Salvador, Guatemala suffered from
internal strife between right-wing, US-backed military government and leftist indigenous peoples from ca. 1954 to ca. 1997.

MINT MARKS
(L) – London, Royal Mint

REPUBLIC

REFORM COINAGE

100 Centavos = 1 Quetzal

KM# 276.6 5 CENTAVOS
1.6000 g., Copper-Nickel, 16 mm. **Obv:** National arms, smaller
sized emblem, no dots by date **Obv. Legend:** REPUBLICA DE
GUATEMALA 1997 **Rev:** Kapok tree center, value at right, ground
below **Note:** Varieties exist.

Date	Mintage	F	VF	XF	Unc	BU
2006	—	—	—	0.15	0.30	0.50

KM# 277.6 10 CENTAVOS
3.2000 g., Copper-Nickel, 21 mm. **Obv:** National arms, small
letters in legend **Obv. Legend:** REPUBLICA DE GUATEMALA
Rev: Monolith **Note:** Varieties exist.

Date	Mintage	F	VF	XF	Unc	BU
2006	—	—	0.15	0.25	0.75	1.00

KM# 283 50 CENTAVOS
5.5400 g., Brass, 24.2 mm. **Obv:** National arms **Rev:** Whitenun
orchid (lycaste skinneri var. alba orchidaceae) **Edge:** Reeded

Date	Mintage	F	VF	XF	Unc	BU
2001	—	—	—	0.50	1.25	1.75
2007	—	—	—	0.50	1.25	1.75

KM# 284 QUETZAL
11.1000 g., Brass, 28.9 mm. **Obv:** National arms **Rev:** PAZ
above stylized dove **Edge:** Reeded

Date	Mintage	F	VF	XF	Unc	BU
2001 Small letters	—	—	—	1.00	2.50	3.00

KM# 287 QUETZAL
31.1035 g., 0.9999 Silver 0.9999 oz. ASW, 30 mm.
Subject: Canonization of Brother Pedro Betancourt
Obv: National arms **Rev:** Standing monk **Edge:** Plain

Date	Mintage	F	VF	XF	Unc	BU
ND(2002) Proof	6,000	Value: 50.00				

KM# 288 QUETZAL
Silver **Subject:** Discovery of the Americas **Obv:** Shields around
inner circle holding arms with date below **Rev:** Nature with fish
in canoe

Date	Mintage	F	VF	XF	Unc	BU
2002 Proof	—	Value: 55.00				

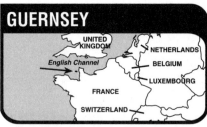

GUERNSEY

The Bailiwick of Guernsey, a British crown dependency
located in the English Channel 30 miles (48 km.) west of Normandy, France, has an area of 30 sq. mi. (194 sq. km.)(including
the isles of Alderney, Jethou, Herm, Brechou, and Sark), and a
population of 54,000. Capital: St. Peter Port. Agriculture and cattle breeding are the main occupations.

Guernsey is administered by its own laws and customs.
Unless the island is mentioned specifically, acts passed by the
British Parliament are not applicable to Guernsey. During World
War II, German troops occupied the island from June 30, 1940
till May 9,1945.

RULER
British

BRITISH DEPENDENCY

DECIMAL COINAGE
100 Pence = 1 Pound

KM# 89 PENNY
3.5300 g., Copper Plated Steel, 20.3 mm. **Ruler:** Elizabeth II **Obv:** Head with tiara right **Obv. Designer:** Ian Rank-Broadley **Rev:** Edible crab **Rev. Designer:** Robert Elderton **Edge:** Plain

Date	Mintage	F	VF	XF	Unc	BU
2003	1,302,600	—	—	—	0.35	1.00
2006	1,731,000	—	—	—	0.35	0.75

KM# 96 2 PENCE
7.2000 g., Copper Plated Steel, 25.9 mm. **Ruler:** Elizabeth II **Obv:** Head with tiara, shield at left **Obv. Designer:** Ian Rank-Broadley **Rev:** Guernsey cows **Rev. Designer:** Robert Elderton **Edge:** Plain

Date	Mintage	F	VF	XF	Unc	BU
2003	662,600	—	—	—	0.50	1.00
2006	1,322,000	—	—	—	0.50	1.00

KM# 97 5 PENCE
3.2500 g., Copper-Nickel, 18 mm. **Ruler:** Elizabeth II **Obv:** Head with tiara right **Obv. Designer:** Ian Rank-Broadley **Rev:** Sailboat **Rev. Designer:** Robert Elderton **Edge:** Reeded

Date	Mintage	F	VF	XF	Unc	BU
2003	292,600	—	—	—	0.45	0.65
2006	1,217,000	—	—	—	0.45	0.65

KM# 149 10 PENCE
6.4400 g., Copper-Nickel, 24.5 mm. **Ruler:** Elizabeth II **Obv:** Crowned head right **Obv. Designer:** Ian Rank-Broadley **Rev:** Tomato plant **Rev. Designer:** Robert Elderton **Edge:** Reeded

Date	Mintage	F	VF	XF	Unc	BU
2003	32,600	—	—	—	0.60	0.85
2006	26,000	—	—	—	0.60	0.85

KM# 90 20 PENCE
5.1000 g., Copper-Nickel, 21.4 mm. **Ruler:** Elizabeth II **Obv:** Head with tiara right, small arms at left **Obv. Designer:** Ian Rank-Broadley **Rev:** Island map within cogwheel **Rev. Designer:** Robert Elderton **Shape:** 7-sided

Date	Mintage	F	VF	XF	Unc	BU
2003	732,600	—	—	—	0.90	1.25
2006	16,250	—	—	—	0.90	1.25
2009	—	—	—	—	0.90	1.25

KM# 145 50 PENCE
7.9700 g., Copper-Nickel, 27.3 mm. **Ruler:** Elizabeth II **Subject:** Coronation Jubilee **Obv:** Head with tiara right **Obv. Designer:** Ian Rank-Broadley **Rev:** Queen on horseback **Edge:** Plain **Shape:** 7-sided

Date	Mintage	F	VF	XF	Unc	BU
2003	—	—	—	—	1.50	2.50

KM# 145a 50 PENCE
8.1000 g., 0.9250 Silver 0.2409 oz. ASW, 27.3 mm. **Ruler:** Elizabeth II **Subject:** Coronation Jubilee **Obv:** Head with tiara right **Obv. Designer:** Ian Rank-Broadley **Rev:** Queen on horseback **Edge:** Plain **Shape:** 7-sided

Date	Mintage	F	VF	XF	Unc	BU
2003 Proof	—	Value: 25.00				

KM# 146 50 PENCE
7.9700 g., Copper-Nickel, 27.3 mm. **Ruler:** Elizabeth II **Subject:** Coronation Jubilee **Obv:** Head with tiara right **Rev:** Queen on throne **Edge:** Plain **Shape:** 7-sided

Date	Mintage	F	VF	XF	Unc	BU
2003	—	—	—	—	1.50	2.50

KM# 146a 50 PENCE
8.1000 g., 0.9250 Silver 0.2409 oz. ASW, 27.3 mm. **Ruler:** Elizabeth II **Subject:** Coronation Jubilee **Obv:** Head with tiara right **Rev:** Queen on throne **Edge:** Plain **Shape:** 7-sided

Date	Mintage	F	VF	XF	Unc	BU
2003 Proof	—	Value: 25.00				

KM# 147 50 PENCE
7.9700 g., Copper-Nickel, 27.3 mm. **Ruler:** Elizabeth II **Subject:** Coronation Jubilee **Obv:** Head with tiara right **Rev:** Crown **Edge:** Plain **Shape:** 7-sided

Date	Mintage	F	VF	XF	Unc	BU
2003	—	—	—	—	1.50	2.50
2006	—	—	—	—	1.50	2.50

KM# 147a 50 PENCE
8.1000 g., 0.9250 Silver 0.2409 oz. ASW, 27.3 mm. **Ruler:** Elizabeth II **Subject:** Coronation Jubilee **Obv:** Head with tiara right **Rev:** Crown **Edge:** Plain **Shape:** 7-sided

Date	Mintage	F	VF	XF	Unc	BU
2003 Proof	—	Value: 25.00				

KM# 148 50 PENCE
7.9700 g., Copper-Nickel, 27.3 mm. **Ruler:** Elizabeth II **Subject:** Coronation Jubilee **Obv:** Head with tiara right **Rev:** Crowned ERII monogram **Edge:** Plain **Shape:** 7-sided

Date	Mintage	F	VF	XF	Unc	BU
2003	—	—	—	—	1.50	2.50

KM# 148a 50 PENCE
8.1000 g., 0.9250 Silver 0.2409 oz. ASW, 27.3 mm. **Ruler:** Elizabeth II **Subject:** Coronation Jubilee **Obv:** Head with tiara right **Rev:** Crowned ERII monogram **Edge:** Plain **Shape:** 7-sided

Date	Mintage	F	VF	XF	Unc	BU
2003 Proof	—	Value: 25.00				

KM# 156 50 PENCE
7.9700 g., Copper-Nickel, 27.3 mm. **Ruler:** Elizabeth II **Obv:** Head with tiara right **Rev:** Crossed flowers **Edge:** Plain **Shape:** 7-sided

Date	Mintage	F	VF	XF	Unc	BU
2003	—	—	—	—	1.75	2.75
2006	19,000	—	—	—	1.75	2.75
2008	—	—	—	—	1.75	2.75

KM# 110 POUND
9.5000 g., Nickel-Brass, 22.5 mm. **Ruler:** Elizabeth II **Subject:** Circulation Type **Obv:** Head with tiara right **Obv. Designer:** Ian Rank-Broadley **Rev:** Denomination **Edge:** Reeded

Date	Mintage	F	VF	XF	Unc	BU
2001	175,000	—	—	—	2.50	3.50
2003	46,600	—	—	—	2.50	3.50
2006	11,000	—	—	—	2.50	3.50

KM# 111 POUND
9.5000 g., 0.9250 Silver 0.2825 oz. ASW, 22.5 mm. **Subject:** Queen's 75th Birthday **Obv:** Head with tiara right **Rev:** Queen's portrait in wreath **Edge:** Reeded

Date	Mintage	F	VF	XF	Unc	BU
2001 Proof	50,000	Value: 25.00				

KM# 142 POUND
30.9300 g., 0.9250 Silver 0.9198 oz. ASW, 38.6 mm. **Ruler:** Elizabeth II **Obv:** Head with tiara right **Obv. Designer:** Ian Rank-Broadley **Rev:** 1/2-bust of William, Duke of Normandy holding sword at left **Edge:** Reeded

Date	Mintage	F	VF	XF	Unc	BU
2002	—	—	—	—	35.00	45.00

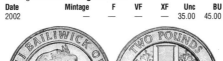

KM# 83 2 POUNDS
12.0000 g., Bi-Metallic Copper-Nickel center in Nickel-Brass ring, 28.35 mm. **Ruler:** Elizabeth II **Obv:** Head with tiara right **Obv. Designer:** Ian Rank-Broadley **Rev:** Latent image arms on cross **Rev. Designer:** Alan Copp **Edge:** BAILIWICK OF GUERNSEY

Date	Mintage	F	VF	XF	Unc	BU
2003	19,600	—	—	—	8.50	10.00
2006	9,500	—	—	—	8.50	10.00

KM# 106 5 POUNDS
28.2800 g., Copper-Nickel, 38.6 mm. **Ruler:** Elizabeth II **Subject:** Queen Victoria Centennial **Obv:** Head with tiara right **Obv. Designer:** Ian Rank-Broadley **Rev:** Bust of Queen Victoria left **Edge:** Reeded

Date	Mintage	F	VF	XF	Unc	BU
2001	12,754	—	—	—	7.50	8.50
2001 Proof	30,000	Value: 20.00				

KM# 106a 5 POUNDS
28.2800 g., 0.9250 Silver 0.8410 oz. ASW, 38.6 mm. **Ruler:** Elizabeth II **Subject:** Queen Victoria 1837-1901 **Obv:** Head with tiara right **Obv. Designer:** Ian Rank-Broadley **Rev:** Bust of Queen Victoria left **Edge:** Reeded

Date	Mintage	F	VF	XF	Unc	BU
2001 Proof	10,000	Value: 47.50				

KM# 108 5 POUNDS
28.0000 g., Copper-Nickel, 38.6 mm. **Ruler:** Elizabeth II **Subject:** Queen Elizabeth's 75th Birthday **Obv:** Head with tiara right **Obv. Designer:** Ian Rank-Broadley **Rev:** Queen's portrait in wreath **Edge:** Reeded

Date	Mintage	F	VF	XF	Unc	BU
2001	14,000	—	—	—	6.00	7.00

KM# 108a 5 POUNDS
28.2800 g., 0.9250 Silver 0.8410 oz. ASW, 38.6 mm. **Ruler:** Elizabeth II **Subject:** Queen's 75th Birthday **Obv:** Head with tiara right **Obv. Designer:** Ian Rank-Broadley **Rev:** Queen's portrait in wreath **Edge:** Reeded

Date	Mintage	F	VF	XF	Unc	BU
2001 Proof	20,000	Value: 55.00				

KM# 114 5 POUNDS
28.2800 g., Copper-Nickel, 38.6 mm. **Ruler:** Elizabeth II **Subject:** 19th Century Monarchy **Obv:** Head with tiara right **Obv. Designer:** Ian Rank-Broadley **Rev:** Four portraits **Edge:** Reeded

Date	Mintage	F	VF	XF	Unc	BU
2001	5,700	—	—	—	11.50	12.50

KM# 114a 5 POUNDS
28.2800 g., 0.9250 Silver 0.8410 oz. ASW, 38.6 mm. **Ruler:** Elizabeth II **Obv:** Head with tiara right **Obv. Designer:** Ian Rank-Broadley **Rev:** Four portraits **Edge:** Reeded

Date	Mintage	F	VF	XF	Unc	BU
2001 Proof	10,000	Value: 55.00				

KM# 115 5 POUNDS
1.1300 g., 0.9170 Gold 0.0333 oz. AGW, 13.9 mm. **Ruler:** Elizabeth II **Subject:** 19th Century Monarchy **Obv:** Head with tiara right **Obv. Designer:** Ian Rank-Broadley **Rev:** Four portraits **Edge:** Reeded

Date	Mintage	F	VF	XF	Unc	BU
2001 Proof	—	Value: 65.00				

KM# 117 5 POUNDS
1.1300 g., 0.9170 Gold 0.0333 oz. AGW, 13.9 mm. **Ruler:** Elizabeth II **Subject:** Queen Victoria 1837-1901 **Obv:** Head with tiara right **Obv. Designer:** Ian Rank-Broadley **Rev:** Queen Victoria's portrait **Edge:** Reeded

Date	Mintage	F	VF	XF	Unc	BU
2001 Proof	300	Value: 65.00				

KM# 118 5 POUNDS
1.1300 g., 0.9170 Gold 0.0333 oz. AGW, 13.9 mm. **Ruler:** Elizabeth II **Subject:** Queen's 75th Birthday **Obv:** Head with tiara right **Obv. Designer:** Ian Rank-Broadley **Rev:** Queen's portrait in wreath **Edge:** Reeded

Date	Mintage	F	VF	XF	Unc	BU
2001 Proof	250	Value: 65.00				

KM# 114b 5 POUNDS
39.9400 g., 0.9166 Gold 1.1770 oz. AGW, 38.6 mm.
Ruler: Elizabeth II **Subject:** 19th Century Monarchy **Obv:** Head with tiara right **Obv. Designer:** Ian Rank-Broadley **Rev:** Four royal portraits **Edge:** Reeded

Date	Mintage	F	VF	XF	Unc	BU
2001 Proof	200	Value: 1,500				

KM# 119 5 POUNDS
27.7100 g., Copper-Nickel, 38.6 mm. **Ruler:** Elizabeth II **Subject:** The Golden Jubilee **Obv:** Head with tiara right **Obv. Designer:** Ian Rank-Broadley **Rev:** The queen in her coach **Edge:** Reeded

Date	Mintage	F	VF	XF	Unc	BU
2002	9,250	—	—	—	16.50	18.00

KM# 119a 5 POUNDS
28.2800 g., Base Metal Gilt Gold plated copper-nickel, 38.6 mm. **Ruler:** Elizabeth II **Subject:** Golden Jubilee **Obv:** Head with tiara right **Obv. Designer:** Ian Rank-Broadley **Rev:** Queen in coach **Edge:** Reeded

Date	Mintage	F	VF	XF	Unc	BU
2002	50,000	—	—	—	15.00	16.50

KM# 119b 5 POUNDS
28.2800 g., 0.9250 Silver 0.8410 oz. ASW, 38.6 mm. **Ruler:** Elizabeth II **Subject:** Queen's Golden Jubilee **Obv:** Head with tiara right **Obv. Designer:** Ian Rank-Broadley **Rev:** Queen in her coach **Edge:** Reeded **Note:** Previous KM#119a.

Date	Mintage	F	VF	XF	Unc	BU
2002 Proof	20,000	Value: 50.00				

KM# 119c 5 POUNDS
39.9400 g., 0.9166 Gold 1.1770 oz. AGW, 38.6 mm. **Ruler:** Elizabeth II **Subject:** Golden Jubilee **Obv:** Head with tiara right **Obv. Designer:** Ian Rank-Broadley **Rev:** Queen in coach **Edge:** Reeded

Date	Mintage	F	VF	XF	Unc	BU
2002 Proof	250	Value: 1,500				

KM# 121 5 POUNDS
27.7100 g., Copper-Nickel, 38.6 mm. **Ruler:** Elizabeth II **Subject:** Queen's Golden Jubilee **Obv:** Head with tiara right **Obv. Designer:** Ian Rank-Broadley **Rev:** Trooping the Colors scene **Edge:** Reeded

Date	Mintage	F	VF	XF	Unc	BU
2002	2,000	—	—	—	17.50	20.00

KM# 121a 5 POUNDS
28.2800 g., 0.9250 Silver 0.8410 oz. ASW, 38.6 mm. **Ruler:** Elizabeth II **Subject:** Queen's Golden Jubilee **Obv:** Head with tiara right **Obv. Designer:** Ian Rank-Broadley **Rev:** Trooping the Colors scene **Edge:** Reeded

Date	Mintage	F	VF	XF	Unc	BU
2002 Proof	20,000	Value: 50.00				

KM# 121b 5 POUNDS
39.9400 g., 0.9166 Gold 1.1770 oz. AGW, 38.6 mm. **Ruler:** Elizabeth II **Subject:** Golden Jubilee **Obv:** Head with tiara right **Obv. Designer:** Ian Rank-Broadley **Rev:** Trooping the Colors scene **Edge:** Reeded

Date	Mintage	F	VF	XF	Unc	BU
2002 Proof	250	Value: 1,500				

KM# 122 5 POUNDS
28.2800 g., Copper-Nickel, 38.6 mm. **Ruler:** Elizabeth II **Subject:** Princess Diana **Obv:** Head with tiara right **Obv. Designer:** Ian Rank-Broadley **Rev:** World and children behind cameo portrait of Diana **Edge:** Reeded

Date	Mintage	F	VF	XF	Unc	BU
2002	4,231	—	—	—	13.50	15.00

KM# 122a 5 POUNDS
28.2800 g., 0.9250 Silver 0.8410 oz. ASW **Ruler:** Elizabeth II **Subject:** Princess Diana **Obv:** Head with tiara right **Obv. Designer:** Ian Rank-Broadley **Rev:** World and children behind Diana's cameo portrait **Edge:** Reeded

Date	Mintage	F	VF	XF	Unc	BU
2002 Proof	20,000	Value: 45.00				

KM# 122b 5 POUNDS
39.9400 g., 0.9167 Gold 1.1771 oz. AGW, 1.1771 mm. **Ruler:** Elizabeth II **Subject:** Princess Diana **Obv:** Head with tiara right **Obv. Designer:** Ian Rank-Broadley **Rev:** World and children behind Diana's cameo portrait **Edge:** Reeded

Date	Mintage	F	VF	XF	Unc	BU
2002 Proof	100	Value: 1,600				

KM# 124 5 POUNDS
28.2800 g., Copper-Nickel, 38.6 mm. **Ruler:** Elizabeth II **Subject:** 18th Century British Monarchy **Obv:** Head with tiara right **Obv. Designer:** Ian Rank-Broadley **Rev:** Five royal portraits **Edge:** Reeded

Date	Mintage	F	VF	XF	Unc	BU
2002	1,300	—	—	—	15.00	16.50

KM# 124a 5 POUNDS
28.2800 g., 0.9250 Silver 0.8410 oz. ASW, 38.6 mm. **Ruler:** Elizabeth II **Subject:** 18th Century British Monarchy **Obv:** Head with tiara right **Obv. Designer:** Ian Rank-Broadley **Rev:** Five royal portraits **Edge:** Reeded

Date	Mintage	F	VF	XF	Unc	BU
2002 Proof	10,000	Value: 50.00				

KM# 124b 5 POUNDS
39.9400 g., 0.9166 Gold 1.1770 oz. AGW, 38.6 mm. **Ruler:** Elizabeth II **Subject:** 18th Century British Monarchy **Obv:** Head with tiara right **Obv. Designer:** Ian Rank-Broadley **Rev:** Five royal portraits **Edge:** Reeded

Date	Mintage	F	VF	XF	Unc	BU
2002 Proof	200	Value: 1,500				

KM# 125 5 POUNDS
1.1300 g., 0.9166 Gold 0.0333 oz. AGW, 13.9 mm. **Ruler:** Elizabeth II **Subject:** 18th Century British Monarchy **Obv:** Head with tiara right **Obv. Designer:** Ian Rank-Broadley **Rev:** Five royal portraits **Edge:** Reeded **Note:** Prev. KM#124b.

Date	Mintage	F	VF	XF	Unc	BU
2002 Proof	55	Value: 70.00				

KM# 127 5 POUNDS
28.2800 g., Copper-Nickel, 38.6 mm. **Ruler:** Elizabeth II **Subject:** Queen Mother **Obv:** Head with tiara right **Obv. Designer:** Ian Rank-Broadley **Rev:** The late Queen Mother's portrait **Edge:** Reeded

Date	Mintage	F	VF	XF	Unc	BU
2002	1,750	—	—	—	15.00	16.50
2002 Proof	1,680	Value: 20.00				

KM# 127a 5 POUNDS
28.2800 g., 0.9250 Silver 0.8410 oz. ASW, 38.6 mm. **Ruler:** Elizabeth II **Subject:** Queen Mother **Obv:** Head with tiara right **Obv. Designer:** Ian Rank-Broadley **Rev:** The late Queen Mother's portrait **Edge:** Reeded

Date	Mintage	F	VF	XF	Unc	BU
2002 Proof	15,000	Value: 50.00				

KM# 127b 5 POUNDS
39.9400 g., 0.9166 Gold 1.1770 oz. AGW, 38.6 mm. **Ruler:** Elizabeth II **Subject:** Queen Mother **Obv:** Head with tiara right **Obv. Designer:** Ian Rank-Broadley **Rev:** Queen Mother's portrait **Edge:** Reeded

Date	Mintage	F	VF	XF	Unc	BU
2002 Proof	250	Value: 1,500				

KM# 128 5 POUNDS
1.1300 g., 0.9166 Gold 0.0333 oz. AGW, 13.9 mm. **Ruler:** Elizabeth II **Subject:** Queen Mother **Obv:** Head with tiara right **Obv. Designer:** Ian Rank-Broadley **Rev:** The late Queen Mother's portrait **Edge:** Reeded

Date	Mintage	F	VF	XF	Unc	BU
2002 Proof	—	Value: 65.00				

KM# 129 5 POUNDS
28.2800 g., Copper-Nickel, 38.6 mm. **Ruler:** Elizabeth II **Subject:** The Duke of Wellington **Obv:** Head with tiara right **Obv. Designer:** Ian Rank-Broadley **Rev:** Portrait with mounted dragoons in background **Edge:** Reeded

Date	Mintage	F	VF	XF	Unc	BU
2002	675	—	—	—	22.50	25.00

KM# 129a 5 POUNDS
28.2800 g., 0.9250 Silver 0.8410 oz. ASW, 38.6 mm. **Ruler:** Elizabeth II **Subject:** The Duke of Wellington **Obv:** Head with tiara right **Obv. Designer:** Ian Rank-Broadley **Rev:** Portrait with multicolor mounted dragoons in background **Rev. Designer:** Willem Vis **Edge:** Reeded

Date	Mintage	F	VF	XF	Unc	BU
2002 Proof	15,000	Value: 50.00				

KM# 129b 5 POUNDS
39.9400 g., 0.9166 Gold 1.1770 oz. AGW, 38.6 mm. **Ruler:** Elizabeth II **Subject:** Duke of Wellington **Obv:** Head with tiara right **Obv. Designer:** Ian Rank-Broadley **Rev:** Wellington's portrait with multicolor cavalry scene **Edge:** Reeded

Date	Mintage	F	VF	XF	Unc	BU
2002 Proof	200	Value: 1,500				

KM# 130 5 POUNDS
1.1300 g., 0.9166 Gold 0.0333 oz. AGW, 13.9 mm. **Ruler:** Elizabeth II **Subject:** The Duke of Wellington **Obv:** Head with tiara right **Obv. Designer:** Ian Rank-Broadley **Rev:** Portrait with mounted dragoons in background **Edge:** Reeded

Date	Mintage	F	VF	XF	Unc	BU
2002 Proof	—	Value: 65.00				

KM# 143 5 POUNDS
28.2800 g., Copper-Nickel, 38.6 mm. **Ruler:** Elizabeth II
Obv: Head with tiara right **Obv. Designer:** Ian Rank-Broadley
Rev: Prince William wearing sweater **Edge:** Reeded

Date	Mintage	F	VF	XF	Unc	BU
2003	—	—	—	17.50	20.00	

KM# 143a 5 POUNDS
28.2800 g., 0.9250 Silver 0.8410 oz. ASW, 38.6 mm.
Ruler: Elizabeth II **Obv:** Head with tiara right **Obv. Designer:**
Ian Rank-Broadley **Rev:** Prince William wearing sweater
Edge: Reeded

Date	Mintage	F	VF	XF	Unc	BU
2003 Proof	5,000	Value: 47.50				

KM# 143b 5 POUNDS
39.9400 g., 0.9166 Gold 1.1770 oz. AGW, 38.6 mm.
Ruler: Elizabeth II **Obv:** Head with tiara right **Obv. Designer:**
Ian Rank-Broadley **Rev:** Prince William wearing sweater
Edge: Reeded

Date	Mintage	F	VF	XF	Unc	BU
2003 Proof	200	Value: 1,500				

KM# 158 5 POUNDS
28.2800 g., Copper-Nickel, 38.7 mm. **Ruler:** Elizabeth II
Subject: Golden Hind **Obv:** Head with tiara right **Obv. Designer:**
Ian Rank-Broadley **Rev:** The Golden Hind ship **Edge:** Reeded

Date	Mintage	F	VF	XF	Unc	BU
2003	300	—	—	—	25.00	

KM# 159 5 POUNDS
Copper-Nickel **Ruler:** Elizabeth II **Subject:** 17th Century Monarchs
Obv: Head with tiara right **Obv. Designer:** Ian Rank-Broadley

Date	Mintage	F	VF	XF	Unc	BU
2003	500	—	—	—	22.50	

KM# 160 5 POUNDS
Copper-Nickel **Ruler:** Elizabeth II **Subject:** Royal Navy - H. Nelson
Obv: Head with tiara right **Obv. Designer:** Ian Rank-Broadley

Date	Mintage	F	VF	XF	Unc	BU
2003	550	—	—	—	22.50	

KM# 175 5 POUNDS
28.2800 g., Nickel-Brass, 38 mm. **Ruler:** Elizabeth II
Subject: History of the Royal Navy **Rev:** Two naval vessels and
Horatis Nelson, flag in color

Date	Mintage	F	VF	XF	Unc	BU
2003 Proof	—	Value: 40.00				

KM# 176 5 POUNDS
28.3200 g., Silver, 38 mm. **Ruler:** Elizabeth II **Subject:** History
of the Royal Navy **Rev:** HMS Invincible, flag in color

Date	Mintage	F	VF	XF	Unc	BU
2004 Proof	—	—	—	—	40.00	

KM# 161 5 POUNDS
Copper-Nickel **Ruler:** Elizabeth II **Subject:** 16th Century
Monarchs **Obv:** Head with tiara right **Obv. Designer:** Ian Rank-Broadley

Date	Mintage	F	VF	XF	Unc	BU
2004	500	—	—	—	22.50	

KM# 162 5 POUNDS
Copper-Nickel **Ruler:** Elizabeth II **Subject:** Mallard Locomotive
Obv: Head with tiara right **Obv. Designer:** Ian Rank-Broadley

Date	Mintage	F	VF	XF	Unc	BU
2004	2,193	—	—	—	17.50	

KM# 163 5 POUNDS
Copper-Nickel **Ruler:** Elizabeth II **Subject:** City of Truro Train
Obv: Head with tiara right **Obv. Designer:** Ian Rank-Broadley

Date	Mintage	F	VF	XF	Unc	BU
2004	500	—	—	—	22.50	

KM# 164 5 POUNDS
Copper-Nickel **Ruler:** Elizabeth II **Subject:** The Boat Train
Obv: Head with tiara right **Obv. Designer:** Ian Rank-Broadley

Date	Mintage	F	VF	XF	Unc	BU
2004	250	—	—	—	25.00	

KM# 165 5 POUNDS
Copper-Nickel **Ruler:** Elizabeth II **Subject:** Train Spotter
Obv: Head with tiara right **Obv. Designer:** Ian Rank-Broadley

Date	Mintage	F	VF	XF	Unc	BU
2004	300	—	—	—	25.00	

KM# 166 5 POUNDS
Copper-Nickel **Ruler:** Elizabeth II **Subject:** Royal Navy - Henry
VIII **Obv:** Head with tiara right **Obv. Designer:** Ian Rank-Broadley

Date	Mintage	F	VF	XF	Unc	BU
2004	300	—	—	—	25.00	

KM# 167 5 POUNDS
Copper-Nickel **Ruler:** Elizabeth II **Subject:** Royal Navy - Invincible
Obv: Head with tiara right **Obv. Designer:** Ian Rank-Broadley

Date	Mintage	F	VF	XF	Unc	BU
2004	300	—	—	—	25.00	

KM# 150 5 POUNDS
28.2800 g., Copper-Nickel, 38.6 mm. **Ruler:** Elizabeth II
Subject: D-Day **Obv:** Head with tiara right **Obv. Designer:** Ian
Rank-Broadley **Rev:** British troops storming ashore **Edge:** Reeded

Date	Mintage	F	VF	XF	Unc	BU
2004	65,611	—	—	—	15.00	16.50

KM# 154 5 POUNDS
28.2800 g., 0.9250 Silver 0.8410 oz. ASW, 38.6 mm.
Ruler: Elizabeth II **Subject:** D-Day **Obv:** Head with tiara right
Obv. Designer: Ian Rank-Broadley **Rev:** British soldier
advancing to left **Edge:** Reeded

Date	Mintage	F	VF	XF	Unc	BU
2004 Proof	10,000	Value: 85.00				

KM# 154a 5 POUNDS
39.9400 g., 0.9167 Gold 1.1771 oz. AGW, 38.6 mm.
Ruler: Elizabeth II **Subject:** D-Day **Obv:** Head with tiara right
Obv. Designer: Ian Rank-Broadley **Rev:** British soldier
advancing to left **Edge:** Reeded

Date	Mintage	F	VF	XF	Unc	BU
2004 Proof	500	Value: 1,475				

KM# 155 5 POUNDS
28.2800 g., Copper-Nickel, 38.6 mm. **Ruler:** Elizabeth II
Subject: 150th Anniversary of the Crimean War **Obv:** Head with
tiara right **Obv. Designer:** Ian Rank-Broadley **Rev:** Sgt. Luke
O'Connor, first army Victoria Cross winner, above Battle of Alma
scene with multicolor flag **Edge:** Reeded

Date	Mintage	F	VF	XF	Unc	BU
2004 plain	—	—	—	—	25.00	27.50
2004 partial color	1,060	—	—	—	25.00	27.50

KM# 155a 5 POUNDS
28.2800 g., 0.9250 Silver 0.8410 oz. ASW, 38.6 mm.
Ruler: Elizabeth II **Obv:** Head with tiara right **Obv. Designer:** Ian
Rank-Broadley **Rev:** Sgt. Luke O'Conner, first army Victoria Cross
winner, above Battle of Alma scene with multicolor flag
Edge: Reeded

Date	Mintage	F	VF	XF	Unc	BU
2004 Proof	10,000	Value: 85.00				

KM# 155b 5 POUNDS
39.9400 g., 0.9166 Gold 1.1770 oz. AGW, 38.6 mm.
Ruler: Elizabeth II **Obv:** Head with tiara right **Obv. Designer:** Ian
Rank-Broadley **Rev:** Sgt. Luke O'Connor, first army Victoria Cross
winner, above Battle of Alma scene with multicolor flag
Edge: Reeded

Date	Mintage	F	VF	XF	Unc	BU
2004 Proof	500	Value: 1,475				

KM# 168a 5 POUNDS
28.2800 g., 0.9250 Silver 0.8410 oz. ASW, 38.6 mm.
Ruler: Elizabeth II **Subject:** End of WWII **Obv:** Head with tiara
right **Obv. Designer:** Ian Rank-Broadley **Rev:** Churchill and
George VI **Edge:** Reeded

Date	Mintage	F	VF	XF	Unc	BU
2005 Proof	5,000	Value: 85.00				

KM# 168b 5 POUNDS
39.9400 g., 0.9167 Gold 1.1771 oz. AGW, 38.6 mm.
Ruler: Elizabeth II **Subject:** End of WWII **Obv:** Head with tiara
right **Obv. Designer:** Ian Rank-Broadley **Rev:** Churchill and
George VI **Edge:** Reeded

Date	Mintage	F	VF	XF	Unc	BU
2005 Proof	150	Value: 1,500				

KM# 169a 5 POUNDS
39.9400 g., 0.9167 Gold 1.1771 oz. AGW, 38.6 mm.
Ruler: Elizabeth II **Subject:** WWII Liberation **Obv:** Head with
tiara right **Obv. Designer:** Ian Rank-Broadley **Rev:** Soldiers and
waving crowd **Edge:** Reeded

Date	Mintage	F	VF	XF	Unc	BU
2005 Proof	150	Value: 1,500				

KM# 170 5 POUNDS
28.2800 g., 0.9250 Silver 0.8410 oz. ASW, 38.6 mm.
Ruler: Elizabeth II **Subject:** Queen's 80th Birthday **Obv:** Head with tiara right - gilt **Obv. Legend:** ELIZABETH II BAILIWICK OF GUERNSEY **Obv. Designer:** Ian Rank-Broadley **Rev:** Bust at left looking upwards, tower and florals at upper right

Date	Mintage	F	VF	XF	Unc	BU
2006 Proof	—	Value: 40.00				

KM# 173 5 POUNDS
28.2800 g., 0.9250 Silver 0.8410 oz. ASW **Ruler:** Elizabeth II **Subject:** FIFA - XVIII World Football Championship - Germany 2006 **Rev:** Wembley Stadium

Date	Mintage	F	VF	XF	Unc	BU
2006 Proof	50,000	Value: 60.00				

KM# 116 10 POUNDS
141.7500 g., 0.9990 Silver 4.5526 oz. ASW, 65 mm.
Ruler: Elizabeth II **Subject:** 19th Century Monarchy **Obv:** Head with tiara right **Obv. Designer:** Ian Rank-Broadley **Rev:** Four portraits **Edge:** Reeded

Date	Mintage	F	VF	XF	Unc	BU
2001 Proof	950	Value: 200				

KM# 126 10 POUNDS
155.5175 g., 0.9990 Silver 4.9948 oz. ASW, 65 mm.
Ruler: Elizabeth II **Subject:** British Monarchy 18th Century **Obv:** Head with tiara right **Obv. Designer:** Ian Rank-Broadley **Rev:** Five royal portraits **Edge:** Reeded

Date	Mintage	F	VF	XF	Unc	BU
2002 Proof	950	Value: 200				

KM# 151 10 POUNDS
155.5170 g., 0.9250 Silver 4.6248 oz. ASW, 65 mm.
Ruler: Elizabeth II **Subject:** D-Day **Obv:** Head with tiara right **Obv. Designer:** Ian Rank-Broadley **Rev:** British troops storming ashore **Edge:** Reeded

Date	Mintage	F	VF	XF	Unc	BU
2004 Proof	1,944	Value: 400				

KM# 107 25 POUNDS
7.8100 g., 0.9170 Gold 0.2302 oz. AGW, 22 mm.
Ruler: Elizabeth II **Subject:** Queen Victoria Centennial **Obv:** Head with tiara right **Obv. Designer:** Ian Rank-Broadley **Rev:** Queen Victoria's portrait **Edge:** Reeded

Date	Mintage	F	VF	XF	Unc	BU
2001 Proof	2,500	Value: 300				

KM# 112 25 POUNDS
7.8100 g., 0.9170 Gold 0.2302 oz. AGW, 22 mm.
Ruler: Elizabeth II **Subject:** Queen's 75th Birthday **Obv:** Head with tiara right **Obv. Designer:** Ian Rank-Broadley **Rev:** Queen's portrait in wreath **Edge:** Reeded

Date	Mintage	F	VF	XF	Unc	BU
2001 Proof	5,000	Value: 285				

KM# 123 25 POUNDS
7.9800 g., 0.9167 Gold 0.2352 oz. AGW, 22.05 mm.
Ruler: Elizabeth II **Subject:** Princess Diana **Obv:** Head with tiara right **Obv. Designer:** Ian Rank-Broadley **Rev:** Diana's cameo portrait in wreath **Edge:** Reeded

Date	Mintage	F	VF	XF	Unc	BU
2002 Proof	2,500	Value: 300				

KM# 131 25 POUNDS
7.8100 g., 0.9166 Gold 0.2301 oz. AGW, 22 mm.
Ruler: Elizabeth II **Subject:** The Duke of Wellington **Obv:** Head with tiara right **Obv. Designer:** Ian Rank-Broadley **Rev:** Portrait with mounted dragoons in the background **Edge:** Reeded

Date	Mintage	F	VF	XF	Unc	BU
2002 Proof	2,500	Value: 285				

KM# 139 25 POUNDS
7.9800 g., 0.9166 Gold 0.2352 oz. AGW, 22 mm.
Ruler: Elizabeth II **Subject:** Golden Jubilee **Obv:** Head with tiara right **Obv. Designer:** Ian Rank-Broadley **Rev:** Queen in coach **Edge:** Reeded

Date	Mintage	F	VF	XF	Unc	BU
2002 Proof	5,000	Value: 300				

KM# 140 25 POUNDS
7.9800 g., 0.9166 Gold 0.2352 oz. AGW, 22 mm.
Ruler: Elizabeth II **Subject:** Queen Mother **Obv:** Head with tiara right **Obv. Designer:** Ian Rank-Broadley **Rev:** Queen Mother's portrait **Edge:** Reeded

Date	Mintage	F	VF	XF	Unc	BU
2002 Proof	2,500	Value: 300				

KM# 141 25 POUNDS
7.9800 g., 0.9166 Gold 0.2352 oz. AGW, 22 mm.
Ruler: Elizabeth II **Subject:** Golden Jubilee **Obv:** Head with tiara right **Obv. Designer:** Ian Rank-Broadley **Rev:** Trooping the Colors scene **Edge:** Reeded

Date	Mintage	F	VF	XF	Unc	BU
2003 Proof	5,000	Value: 300				

KM# 172 25 POUNDS
7.9800 g., 0.9166 Gold 0.2352 oz. AGW **Ruler:** Elizabeth II **Obv:** Head with tiara right **Rev:** Bust of Prince William facing **Edge:** Reeded

Date	Mintage	F	VF	XF	Unc	BU
2003 Proof	—	Value: 285				

KM# 152 25 POUNDS
7.9800 g., 0.9167 Gold 0.2352 oz. AGW, 22 mm.
Ruler: Elizabeth II **Subject:** D-Day **Obv:** Head with tiara right **Obv. Designer:** Ian Rank-Broadley **Rev:** Advancing British soldier **Edge:** Reeded

Date	Mintage	F	VF	XF	Unc	BU
2004 Proof	500	Value: 325				

KM# 174 25 POUNDS
7.9800 g., 0.9166 Gold 0.2352 oz. AGW **Ruler:** Elizabeth II **Subject:** FIFA - XVIII World Football Championship - Germany 2006 **Rev:** Wembley Stadium

Date	Mintage	F	VF	XF	Unc	BU
2006 Proof	2,500	Value: 300				

KM# 144 50 POUNDS
1000.0000 g., 0.9250 Silver 29.738 oz. ASW, 100 mm.
Ruler: Elizabeth II **Obv:** Head with tiara right **Obv. Designer:** Ian Rank-Broadley **Rev:** Prince William wearing sweater **Edge:** Reeded

Date	Mintage	F	VF	XF	Unc	BU
2003 Proof	500	Value: 995				

KM# 153 50 POUNDS
1000.0000 g., 0.9250 Silver 29.738 oz. ASW, 100 mm.
Ruler: Elizabeth II **Subject:** D-Day **Obv:** Head with tiara right **Obv. Designer:** Ian Rank-Broadley **Rev:** British troops storming ashore **Edge:** Reeded

Date	Mintage	F	VF	XF	Unc	BU
2004 Proof	600	Value: 1,200				

PIEFORTS

KM#	Date	Mintage	Identification	Mkt Val
P3	2002	100	5 Pounds. 0.9166 Gold. 79.8900 g. 38.6 mm. Queen's portrait. Queen in coach. Reeded edge.	2,950

MINT SETS

KM#	Date	Mintage	Identification	Issue Price	Mkt Val
MS10	2003 (8)	—	KM#83, 89-90, 96-97, 110, 148-49	—	22.50
MS11	2004 (1)	—	Guernsey KM#155, Alderney KM#43, Jersey KM#126, 150th Anniversary of the Crimean War	—	80.00

GUYANA

The Cooperative Republic of Guyana, is situated on the northeast coast of South America, has an area of 83,000 sq. mi. (214,970 sq. km.) and a population of 729,000. Capital: Georgetown. The economy is basically agrarian. Sugar, rice and bauxite are exported.

The original area of Essequibo and Demerary, which included present-day Suriname, French Guiana, and parts of Brazil and Venezuela was sighted by Columbus in 1498. Guyana became a republic on Feb. 23, 1970. It is a member of the Commonwealth of Nations. The president is the Chief of State. The prime minister is the Head of Government. Guyana is a member of the Caribbean Community and Common Market (CARICOM).

REPUBLIC

DECIMAL COINAGE

KM# 50 DOLLAR
2.4000 g., Copper Plated Steel, 16.96 mm. **Obv:** Helmeted and supported arms **Obv. Designer:** Sean Thomas **Rev:** Hand gathering rice **Rev. Designer:** Jean Thomas **Edge:** Reeded

Date	Mintage	F	VF	XF	Unc	BU
2001	—	—	—	0.30	0.50	0.65
2002	—	—	—	0.30	0.50	0.65

KM# 51 5 DOLLARS
3.7800 g., Copper Plated Steel, 20.5 mm. **Obv:** Helmeted and supported arms **Rev:** Sugar cane **Rev. Designer:** Selayn Cambridge **Edge:** Reeded

Date	Mintage	F	VF	XF	Unc	BU
2002	—	—	—	—	0.75	1.00
2005	—	—	—	—	0.75	1.00

KM# 52 10 DOLLARS
5.0000 g., Nickel Plated Steel, 23 mm. **Obv:** Helmeted and supported arms **Rev:** Gold mining scene **Rev. Designer:** Ignatias Adams **Edge:** Reeded **Shape:** 7-sided

Date	Mintage	F	VF	XF	Unc	BU
2007	—	—	—	0.75	1.25	1.50

KM# 54 1000 DOLLARS
28.2800 g., 0.9250 Silver partially gilt 0.8410 oz. ASW, 38.6 mm.
Subject: Bank of Guyana, 40th Anniversary **Obv:** Arms **Rev:** Bank building, partially gilt

Date	Mintage	F	VF	XF	Unc	BU
2005 Proof	1,000	Value: 65.00				

HAITI

The Republic of Haiti, which occupies the western one-third of the island of Hispaniola in the Caribbean Sea between Puerto Rico and Cuba, has an area of 10,714 sq. mi. (27,750 sq. km.)

and a population of 6.5 million. Capital: Port-au-Prince. The economy is based on agriculture; but light manufacturing and tourism are increasingly important. Coffee, bauxite, sugar, essential oils and handicrafts are exported.

The French language is used on Haitian coins although it is spoken by only about 10% of the populace. A form of Creole is the language of the Haitians.

MINT MARKS
A - Paris
(a) - Paris, privy marks only
R - Rome

REPUBLIC
DECIMAL COINAGE

100 Centimes = 1 Gourde

KM# 155   GOURDE
6.3000 g., Brass Plated Steel, 23 mm.   **Obv:** Citadelle de Roi Christophe **Shape:** 7-sided

Date	Mintage	F	VF	XF	Unc	BU
2003	—	—	—	—	1.75	2.00

HONDURAS

MEXICO	BELIZE	Caribbean Sea
North Pacific Ocean	GUATEMALA	NICARAGUA
	EL SALVADOR	

The Republic of Honduras, situated in Central America alongside El Salvador, between Nicaragua and Guatemala, has an area of 43,277 sq. mi. (112,090 sq. km.) and a population of 5.6 million. Capital: Tegucigalpa. Agriculture, mining (gold and silver), and logging are the major economic activities, with increasing tourism and emerging petroleum resource discoveries. Precious metals, bananas, timber and coffee are exported.

From 1933 to 1940 General Tiburcio Carias Andino was dictator president of the Republic. Since 1990 democratic practices have become more consistent.

MINT MARKS
T.G. - Yoro
T.L. – Comayagua

MONETARY SYSTEM
100 Centavos = 1 Lempira

REPUBLIC
REFORM COINAGE

KM# 72.4   5 CENTAVOS
3.2500 g., Brass, 21 mm.   **Obv:** National arms **Rev:** Value in circle within sprays **Edge:** Plain

Date	Mintage	F	VF	XF	Unc	BU
2002	—	—	—	0.10	0.25	0.35
2003	—	—	—	0.10	0.25	0.35
2005	—	—	—	0.10	0.25	0.35

KM# 76.3   10 CENTAVOS
5.9700 g., Brass, 26 mm.   **Obv:** National arms, without clouds behind pyramid **Rev:** Denomination within circle, wreath surrounds

Date	Mintage	F	VF	XF	Unc	BU
2002	—	—	0.10	0.20	0.45	0.65

Date	Mintage	F	VF	XF	Unc	BU
2003	—	—	0.10	0.20	0.45	0.65
2005	—	—	0.10	0.20	0.45	0.65

KM# 76.4   10 CENTAVOS
6.2000 g., Brass, 25.95 mm.   **Obv:** National arms, slightly larger legend, large date **Rev:** Value in circle within wreath **Edge:** Plain

Date	Mintage	F	VF	XF	Unc	BU
2006	—	—	—	0.15	0.35	0.45

KM# 84a.2   50 CENTAVOS
5.1800 g., Nickel Plated Steel, 24 mm.   **Obv:** National arms **Rev:** Head of Chief Lempira left within circle **Edge:** Reeded

Date	Mintage	F	VF	XF	Unc	BU
2005	—	—	0.15	0.35	0.90	1.25

HONG KONG

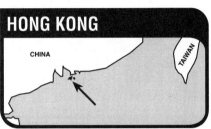

Hong Kong, a former British colony, reverted to control of the People's Republic of China on July 1, 1997 as a Special Administrative Region. It is situated at the mouth of the Canton or Pearl River 90 miles (145 km.) southeast of Canton, has an area of 403 sq. mi. (1,040 sq. km.) and an estimated population of 6.3 million. Capital: Victoria. The free port of Hong Kong, the commercial center of the Far East, is a trans-shipment point for goods destined for China and the countries of the Pacific Rim. Light manufacturing and tourism are important components of the economy.

SPECIAL ADMINISTRATION REGION (S.A.R.)
DECIMAL COINAGE

KM# 80   50 DOLLARS
35.4300 g., 0.9250 Silver Gold plated center 1.0536 oz. ASW, 40 mm.   **Series:** Five Blessings **Obv:** Bauhinia flower **Rev:** Jade Ju-I

Date	Mintage	F	VF	XF	Unc	BU
2002 Proof	60,000	Value: 80.00				

KM# 81   50 DOLLARS
35.4300 g., 0.9250 Silver Gold plated center 1.0536 oz. ASW, 40 mm.   **Series:** Five Blessings **Obv:** Bauhinia flower **Rev:** Fish

Date	Mintage	F	VF	XF	Unc	BU
2002 Proof	60,000	Value: 80.00				

KM# 82   50 DOLLARS
35.2500 g., 0.9250 Silver Gold plated center 1.0483 oz. ASW, 40 mm.   **Series:** Five Blessings **Obv:** Bauhinia flower **Rev:** Horses

Date	Mintage	F	VF	XF	Unc	BU
2002 Proof	60,000	Value: 80.00				

KM# 83   50 DOLLARS
35.3400 g., 0.9250 Silver Gold plated center 1.0509 oz. ASW, 40 mm.   **Series:** Five Blessings **Obv:** Bauhinia flower **Rev:** Peony flower

Date	Mintage	F	VF	XF	Unc	BU
2002 Proof	60,000	Value: 80.00				

KM# 84   50 DOLLARS
35.1400 g., 0.9250 Silver Gold plated center 1.0450 oz. ASW, 40 mm.   **Series:** Five Blessings **Obv:** Bauhinia flower **Rev:** Windmills

Date	Mintage	F	VF	XF	Unc	BU
2002 Proof	60,000	Value: 80.00				

PROOF SETS

KM#	Date	Mintage	Identification	Issue Price	Mkt Val
PS8	2002 (5)	60,000	KM#80-84 plus 7.8g, .9999, AGW .2508, 25mm gold medal	370	600

HUNGARY

	CZECH REPUBLIC	UKRAINE
GERMANY	SLOVAKIA	
	AUSTRIA	
SLOVENIA	CROATIA	ROMANIA
ITALY	BOSNIA SERBIA	

The Republic of Hungary, located in central Europe, has an area of 35,929 sq. mi. (93,030 sq. km.) and a population of 10.7 million. Capital: Budapest. The economy is based on agriculture, bauxite and a rapidly expanding industrial sector. Machinery, chemicals, iron and steel, and fruits and vegetables are exported.

MINT MARKS
BP - Budapest

MONETARY SYSTEM
100 Filler = 1 Forint

SECOND REPUBLIC
1989-present
DECIMAL COINAGE

KM# 692   FORINT
2.0500 g., Brass, 16.5 mm. **Obv:** Crowned shield
Rev: Denomination

Date	Mintage	F	VF	XF	Unc	BU
2001BP	—	—	—	—	0.10	0.25
2001BP Proof	3,000	Value: 3.75				
2002BP	—	—	—	—	0.10	0.25
2002BP Proof	3,000	Value: 3.75				
2003BP	—	—	—	—	0.10	0.25
2003BP Proof	7,000	Value: 3.50				
2004BP	—	—	—	—	0.10	0.25
2004BP Proof	7,000	Value: 3.50				
2005BP	—	—	—	—	0.10	0.25
2005BP Proof	—	Value: 3.50				
2006BP	—	—	—	—	0.10	0.25
2006BP Proof	—	Value: 3.50				
2007 Proof	—	Value: 3.50				
2008 Proof	—	Value: 3.50				

KM# 693   2 FORINT
3.1000 g., Copper-Nickel, 19 mm. **Obv:** Native flower:
Colchicum Hungaricum **Rev:** Denomination

Date	Mintage	F	VF	XF	Unc	BU
2001BP	—	—	—	—	0.20	0.35
2001BP Proof	3,000	Value: 4.25				
2002BP	—	—	—	—	0.20	0.35
2002BP Proof	3,000	Value: 4.25				
2003BP	—	—	—	—	0.20	0.35
2003BP Proof	7,000	Value: 4.00				
2004BP	—	—	—	—	0.20	0.35
2004BP Proof	7,000	Value: 4.00				
2005BP	—	—	—	—	0.20	0.35
2005BP Proof	—	Value: 4.00				
2006BP	—	—	—	—	0.20	0.35
2006BP Proof	—	Value: 4.00				
2007 Proof	—	Value: 4.00				
2008 Proof	—	Value: 4.00				

KM# 694   5 FORINT
4.2000 g., Brass, 21.5 mm. **Obv:** Great White Egret
Rev: Denomination

Date	Mintage	F	VF	XF	Unc	BU
2001BP	—	—	—	—	1.00	1.50
2001BP Proof	3,000	Value: 5.00				
2002BP	—	—	—	—	1.00	1.50
2002BP Proof	3,000	Value: 5.00				
2003BP	—	—	—	—	1.00	1.50
2003BP Proof	7,000	Value: 4.50				
2004BP	—	—	—	—	1.00	1.50
2004BP Proof	7,000	Value: 4.50				
2005BP	—	—	—	—	1.00	1.50
2005BP Proof	—	Value: 4.50				
2006BP	—	—	—	—	1.00	1.50
2006BP Proof	—	Value: 4.50				
2007 Proof	—	Value: 4.50				
2008 Proof	—	Value: 4.50				

KM# 695   10 FORINT
6.1000 g., Copper-Nickel Clad Brass, 25 mm. **Obv:** Crowned
shield **Rev:** Denomination

Date	Mintage	F	VF	XF	Unc	BU
2001BP	—	—	—	—	1.00	2.50
2001BP Proof	3,000	Value: 5.50				

Date	Mintage	F	VF	XF	Unc	BU
2002BP	—	—	—	—	1.00	2.50
2002BP Proof	3,000	Value: 5.50				
2003BP	—	—	—	—	1.00	2.50
2003BP Proof	7,000	Value: 5.00				
2004BP	—	—	—	—	1.00	2.50
2004BP Proof	7,000	Value: 5.00				
2005BP	—	—	—	—	1.00	2.50
2005BP Proof	—	Value: 5.00				
2006BP	—	—	—	—	1.00	2.50
2006BP Proof	—	Value: 5.00				
2007 Proof	—	Value: 5.00				
2008 Proof	—	Value: 5.00				

KM# 779   10 FORINT
6.1000 g., Copper-Nickel, 24.8 mm. **Obv:** Jozsef Attila
Rev: Value **Edge:** Segmented reeding

Date	Mintage	F	VF	XF	Unc	BU
2005BP	20,000	—	—	—	2.50	3.00
2005BP Proof	7,000	Value: 3.50				

KM# 696   20 FORINT
7.0000 g., Nickel-Brass, 26.3 mm. **Obv:** Hungarian Iris
Rev: Denomination

Date	Mintage	F	VF	XF	Unc	BU
2001BP	—	—	—	—	1.50	2.00
2001BP Proof	3,000	Value: 4.50				
2002BP	—	—	—	—	1.50	2.00
2002BP Proof	3,000	Value: 4.50				
2003BP	—	—	—	—	1.50	2.00
2003BP Proof	7,000	Value: 4.00				
2004BP	—	—	—	—	1.50	2.00
2004BP Proof	7,000	Value: 4.00				
2005BP	—	—	—	—	1.50	2.00
2005BP Proof	—	Value: 4.00				
2006BP	—	—	—	—	1.50	2.00
2006BP Proof	—	Value: 4.00				
2007 Proof	—	Value: 4.00				
2008 Proof	—	Value: 4.00				

KM# 768   20 FORINT
6.9400 g., Nickel-Brass, 26.4 mm. **Obv:** Deak Ferenc
Rev: Denomination **Edge:** Reeded

Date	Mintage	F	VF	XF	Unc	BU
2003BP	993,000	—	—	—	1.50	2.00
2003BP Proof	7,000	Value: 4.00				

KM# 697   50 FORINT
7.8000 g., Copper-Nickel Clad Brass, 27.5 mm. **Obv:** Saker
falcon **Rev:** Denomination

Date	Mintage	F	VF	XF	Unc	BU
2001BP	—	—	—	—	3.00	4.00
2001BP Proof	3,000	Value: 6.00				
2002BP	—	—	—	—	3.00	3.50
2002BP Proof	3,000	Value: 5.50				
2003BP	—	—	—	—	3.00	3.50
2003BP Proof	7,000	Value: 5.00				

Date	Mintage	F	VF	XF	Unc	BU
2004BP	—	—	—	—	3.00	3.50
2004BP Proof	7,000	Value: 5.00				
2005BP	—	—	—	—	3.00	3.50
2005BP Proof	—	Value: 5.00				
2006BP	—	—	—	—	3.00	3.50
2006BP Proof	—	Value: 5.00				
2007 Proof	—	Value: 5.00				
2008 Proof	—	Value: 5.00				

KM# 773   50 FORINT
7.7000 g., Copper-Nickel Clad Brass, 27.5 mm. **Obv:** National arms
above Euro Union star circle **Rev:** Denomination **Edge:** Plain

Date	Mintage	F	VF	XF	Unc	BU
2004BP	993,000	—	—	—	3.00	3.50
2004BP Proof	7,000	Value: 6.00				

KM# 780   50 FORINT
7.7000 g., Copper-Nickel, 27.4 mm. **Subject:** International
Childrens Safety Service **Obv:** Stylized crying child
Rev: Denomination **Edge:** Plain

Date	Mintage	F	VF	XF	Unc	BU
2005BP	2,000,000	—	—	—	3.00	3.50

KM# 788   50 FORINT
7.7000 g., Copper-Nickel, 27.4 mm. **Obv:** Hungarian Red Cross
125th Anniversary seal above date and country name **Rev:** Value
Edge: Plain

Date	Mintage	F	VF	XF	Unc	BU
2006BP	2,000,000	—	—	—	—	3.50

KM# 789   50 FORINT
7.7000 g., Copper-Nickel, 27.4 mm. **Subject:** 1956 Revolution
Obv: Holed flag with Parliament building in background
Rev: Value **Edge:** Plain

Date	Mintage	F	VF	XF	Unc	BU
2006BP	2,000,000	—	—	—	—	3.50

KM# 805   50 FORINT
7.7000 g., Copper-Nickel, 27.4 mm. **Subject:** Celebrating 50
years of the Treaty of Rome **Obv:** Book logo **Rev:** Value

Date	Mintage	F	VF	XF	Unc	BU
2007	2,000,000	—	—	—	0.50	—
2007 Proof	5,000	Value: 3.50				

KM# 760   100 FORINT
8.0000 g., Bi-Metallic Stainless Steel center in Brass plated Steel
ring, 23.7 mm. **Subject:** Lajos Kossuth **Obv:** Head right within
circle **Rev:** Denomination within circle **Edge:** Reeded

Date	Mintage	F	VF	XF	Unc	BU
2002BP	997,000	—	—	—	2.00	2.50
2002BP Proof	3,000	Value: 5.00				

KM# 721 100 FORINT (Szaz)

Bi-Metallic Brass plated Steel center in Stainless Steel ring, 23.6 mm. **Obv:** Crowned shield **Rev:** Denomination

Date	Mintage	F	VF	XF	Unc	BU
2001BP	—	—	—	—	3.50	5.00
2001BP Proof	3,000	Value: 8.00				
2002BP	—	—	—	—	3.50	5.00
2002BP Proof	3,000	Value: 8.00				
2003BP	—	—	—	—	3.50	5.00
2003BP Proof	7,000	Value: 7.50				
2004BP	—	—	—	—	3.50	5.00
2004BP Proof	7,000	Value: 7.50				
2005BP	—	—	—	—	3.50	5.00
2005BP Proof	—	Value: 7.50				
2006BP	—	—	—	—	3.50	5.00
2006BP Proof	—	Value: 7.50				
2007 Proof	—	Value: 7.50				
2008 Proof	—	Value: 7.50				

KM# 754 200 FORINT

9.4000 g., Brass, 29.2 mm. **Subject:** Childrens Literature: Ludas Matyi **Obv:** Denomination **Rev:** Man holding a goose **Edge:** Plain

Date	Mintage	F	VF	XF	Unc	BU
2001BP	12,000	—	—	—	7.50	9.00
2001BP Proof	5,000	Value: 15.00				

KM# 755 200 FORINT

Brass, 29.2 mm. **Subject:** Childrens Literature: Janos Vitez **Obv:** Denomination **Rev:** Soldier riding a flying bird **Edge:** Plain

Date	Mintage	F	VF	XF	Unc	BU
2001BP	12,000	—	—	—	7.50	9.00
2001BP Proof	5,000	Value: 15.00				

KM# 756 200 FORINT

Brass, 29.2 mm. **Subject:** Childrens Literature: Toldi **Obv:** Denomination **Rev:** Knight kicking a boat off the shore **Edge:** Plain

Date	Mintage	F	VF	XF	Unc	BU
2001BP	12,000	—	—	—	7.50	9.00
2001BP Proof	5,000	Value: 15.00				

KM# 757 200 FORINT

Brass, 29.2 mm. **Subject:** Childrens Literature: A Pal Utcai Fiuk **Obv:** Denomination **Rev:** Two men and cordwood **Edge:** Plain

Date	Mintage	F	VF	XF	Unc	BU
2001	12,000	—	—	—	7.50	9.00
2001 Proof	5,000	Value: 15.00				

KM# 764 500 FORINT

13.9000 g., Copper-Nickel **Subject:** Farkas Kempelen's Chess Machine **Obv:** Denomination, letters A-H and numbers 1-8 repeated along edges **Rev:** Robotic human form chess playing machine built in 1769 **Edge:** Plain **Shape:** Square, 28.43 x 28.43 mm

Date	Mintage	F	VF	XF	Unc	BU
2002BP	5,000	—	—	—	15.00	18.00
2002BP Proof	5,000	Value: 25.00				

KM# 765 500 FORINT

13.8000 g., Copper-Nickel **Subject:** Rubik's Cube **Obv:** Inscription on Rubik's Cube design **Rev:** Rubik's Cube with inscription **Edge:** Plain **Shape:** Square, 28.43 x 28.43 mm

Date	Mintage	F	VF	XF	Unc	BU
2002BP Proof	5,000	Value: 30.00				
2002BP	5,000	—	—	—	16.00	20.00

KM# 781 500 FORINT

14.0000 g., Copper-Nickel **Obv:** Old wheel **Rev:** First Hungarian Post Office motor vehicle **Edge:** Plain **Shape:** Square **Note:** 28.43 x 28.43mm

Date	Mintage	F	VF	XF	Unc	BU
2005BP	5,000	—	—	—	16.00	20.00
2005BP Proof	10,000	Value: 30.00				

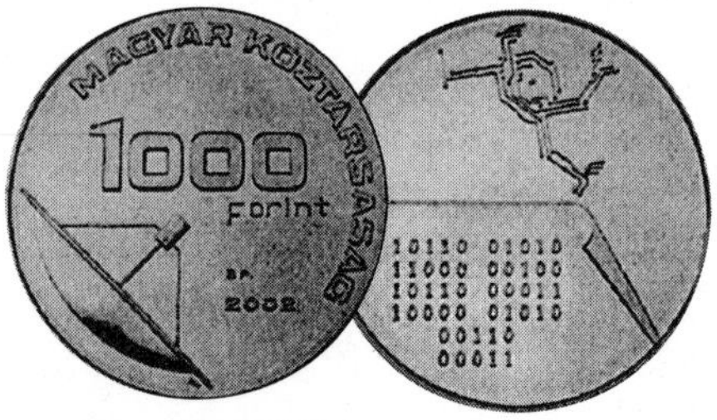

KM# 766 1000 FORINT

19.5000 g., Bronze Hollow coin unscrews to open **Obv:** Denomination and satellite dish **Rev:** Mercury

Date	Mintage	F	VF	XF	Unc	BU
2002BP	15,000	—	—	—	15.00	16.50

KM# 787 1000 FORINT

13.8100 g., Copper-Nickel, 28.3 mm. **Obv:** Value and partial front view of antique automobile **Rev:** Model T Ford **Edge:** Plain **Shape:** Square

Date	Mintage	F	VF	XF	Unc	BU
2006BP Proof	10,000	Value: 25.00				
2006BP	10,000	—	—	—	15.00	18.00

KM# 797 1000 FORINT

14.0000 g., Copper-Nickel, 28.43 x 28.43 mm. **Subject:** 125th Anniversary - Birth of János Adorján **Obv:** Early two cylinder aircraft motor with propeller **Obv. Legend:** MAGYAR / KOZTARSASAG **Obv. Designer:** Balozs Bi **Rev:** Early monoplane **Rev. Legend:** ADORJAN JANOS / AZ ELSO SIKERES MAGYAR / REPULOGEP TERVEZOJE **Edge:** Plain **Shape:** Square

Date	Mintage	F	VF	XF	Unc	BU
2007BP	10,000	—	—	—	15.00	18.00
2007BP Proof	10,000	Value: 25.00				

KM# 809 1000 FORINT

14.0000 g., Copper-Nickel, 28.43x28.43 mm. **Subject:** Telephone Herald **Edge:** Plain **Shape:** Square **Designer:** Áron Bohus

Date	Mintage	F	VF	XF	Unc	BU
2008	10,000	—	—	—	15.00	18.00
2008 Proof	15,000	Value: 25.00				

KM# 818 1000 FORINT

14.0000 g., Copper-Nickel, 28.4x28.4 mm. **Subject:** Laszlo Jozsef Biro, Inventor of the ball point pen **Obv:** Ball point pen schematic **Obv. Designer:** Gyorgy Szabo **Rev:** Bust facing **Shape:** Square

Date	Mintage	F	VF	XF	Unc	BU
2010BP	10,000	—	—	—	12.00	15.00
2010BP Proof	10,000	Value: 25.00				

KM# 752 3000 FORINT

31.4600 g., 0.9250 Silver 0.9356 oz. ASW, 38.5 mm. **Subject:** Hungarian Silver Coinage Millennium **Obv:** Denomination in ornamental frame **Rev:** Thaler design circa 1500 portraying Ladislaus I (1077-95) with the title of saint **Edge:** Reeding over "1001-2001" **Edge Lettering:** BP • NX • KB • HX • GY • F • AF • MM • C +

Date	Mintage	F	VF	XF	Unc	BU
2001BP	5,000	—	—	—	35.00	37.50
2001BP Proof	5,000	Value: 40.00				

KM# 759   3000 FORINT
31.8000 g., 0.9250 Silver 0.9457 oz. ASW, 38.7 mm.
Subject: Centennial of First Hungarian Film "The Dance"
Obv: Denomination **Rev:** Two dancers on film **Edge:** Reeded

Date	Mintage	F	VF	XF	Unc	BU
2001BP	3,500	—	—	—	37.50	40.00
2001BP Proof	3,500	Value: 45.00				

KM# 761   3000 FORINT
31.3300 g., 0.9250 Silver 0.9317 oz. ASW, 38.6 mm.
Subject: Hortobagy National Park **Obv:** Landscape,
denomination **Rev:** Hungarian Grey Longhorn bull **Edge:** Reeded

Date	Mintage	F	VF	XF	Unc	BU
2002BP	5,000	—	—	—	32.00	35.00
2002BP Proof	5,000	Value: 45.00				

KM# 767   3000 FORINT
31.4600 g., 0.9250 Silver 0.9356 oz. ASW **Subject:** 100th
Anniversary - Birth of Kovacs Margit (1902-1977)
Obv: Denomination **Rev:** The "Trumpet of Judgement Day"

Date	Mintage	F	VF	XF	Unc	BU
2002BP	4,000	—	—	—	38.00	40.00
2002BP Proof	4,000	Value: 48.00				

KM# 762   3000 FORINT
31.4600 g., 0.9250 Silver 0.9356 oz. ASW, 38.5 mm. **Subject:**
200th Anniversary - National Library **Obv:** Small coat of arms in
ornate frame **Rev:** Interior view of library **Edge:** Reeded

Date	Mintage	F	VF	XF	Unc	BU
2002BP Proof	3,000	Value: 40.00				
2002BP	3,000	—	—	—	35.00	37.50

KM# 763   3000 FORINT
31.4600 g., 0.9250 Silver 0.9356 oz. ASW, 38.5 mm.
Subject: Janos Bolyai's publication of his "Appendix"
Obv: Circular graph **Rev:** Signature above 7-line inscription,
name and dates **Edge:** Reeded

Date	Mintage	F	VF	XF	Unc	BU
2002BP Proof	3,000	Value: 40.00				
2002BP	3,000	—	—	—	35.00	37.50

KM# 817   3000 FORINT
10.0000 g., 0.9250 Silver 0.2974 oz. ASW **Subject:** Ferenc
Kazinczy, 250th Anniversary of Birth **Obv:** Quill pen and rolled
document **Rev:** Bust facing **Rev. Designer:** E. Tamás Soltra

Date	Mintage	F	VF	XF	Unc	BU
2009	5,000	—	—	—	15.00	18.00
2009 Proof	5,000	Value: 25.00				

KM# 751   4000 FORINT
31.4600 g., 0.9250 Silver 0.9356 oz. ASW, 26.4 x 39.6 mm.
Subject: Godollo Artist Colony Centennial **Obv:** Denomination
Rev: "Sisters" stained glass window design **Edge:** Plain
Shape: Vertical rectangle

Date	Mintage	F	VF	XF	Unc	BU
2001BP	4,000	—	—	—	40.00	42.50
2001BP Proof	4,000	Value: 50.00				

KM# 769   5000 FORINT
31.4600 g., 0.9250 Silver 0.9356 oz. ASW, 38.6 mm.
Subject: Budapest Philharmonic Orchestra **Obv:** Crowned arms
in wreath **Rev:** Four coin-like portraits of Erkel, Dohnanyi, Bartók
and Kodaly **Edge:** Reeded

Date	Mintage	F	VF	XF	Unc	BU
2003BP Proof	4,000	Value: 42.50				
2003BP	4,000	—	—	—	37.50	40.00

KM# 770   5000 FORINT
31.4600 g., 0.9250 Silver 0.9356 oz. ASW, 38.6 mm. **Subject:**
100th Anniversary - Birth of Neumann Janos **Obv:** Denomination
and binary number date **Rev:** Neumann Janos **Edge:** Reeded

Date	Mintage	F	VF	XF	Unc	BU
2003BP Proof	3,000	Value: 45.00				
2003BP	3,000	—	—	—	40.00	42.50

KM# 771   5000 FORINT
31.4600 g., 0.9250 Silver 0.9356 oz. ASW, 38.6 mm.
Subject: Rakoczi's War of Liberation **Obv:** Transylvanian ducat
design above country name, value and date **Rev:** Kuruc
cavalryman with sword and trumpet **Edge:** Reeded

Date	Mintage	F	VF	XF	Unc	BU
2003BP	3,000	—	—	—	45.00	47.50
2003BP Proof	3,000	Value: 50.00				

KM# 772   5000 FORINT
31.4600 g., 0.9250 Silver 0.9356 oz. ASW, 38.6 mm.
Subject: World Heritage in Hungary - Holloko **Obv:** Holloko
castle ruins above country name, value and date **Rev:** Village
view behind woman in folk costume **Edge:** Reeded

Date	Mintage	F	VF	XF	Unc	BU
2003BP	5,000	—	—	—	42.50	45.00
2003BP Proof	5,000	Value: 50.00				

KM# 774   5000 FORINT
31.4600 g., 0.9250 Silver 0.9356 oz. ASW, 38.6 mm.
Obv: Value **Rev:** Two Olympic boxers **Edge:** Reeded

Date	Mintage	F	VF	XF	Unc	BU
2004BP	3,000	—	—	—	45.00	47.50
2004BP Proof	9,000	Value: 50.00				

KM# 775 5000 FORINT
31.4600 g., 0.9250 Silver 0.9356 oz. ASW, 38.6 mm.
Obv: "Solomon Tower" above value **Rev:** Visegrad Castle with the Solomon Tower **Edge:** Reeded

Date	Mintage	F	VF	XF	Unc	BU
2004BP	4,000	—	—	—	45.00	47.50
2004BP Proof	4,000	Value: 50.00				

KM# 776 5000 FORINT
31.4600 g., 0.9250 Silver 0.9356 oz. ASW, 38.6 mm.
Obv: Value and country name above Euro Union stars **Rev:** Mythical stag seen through an ornate window **Edge:** Reeded

Date	Mintage	F	VF	XF	Unc	BU
2004BP Proof	10,000	Value: 50.00				

KM# 778 5000 FORINT
31.4600 g., 0.9250 Silver 0.9356 oz. ASW, 38.6 mm.
Subject: Ancient Christian Necropolis at Pecs **Obv:** Value and ancient artifact **Rev:** Interior view of tomb **Edge:** Reeded

Date	Mintage	F	VF	XF	Unc	BU
2004BP	5,000	—	—	—	40.00	42.00
2004BP Proof	5,000	Value: 45.00				

KM# 782 5000 FORINT
31.4600 g., 0.9250 Silver 0.9356 oz. ASW, 38.6 mm. **Obv:** Bat flying above value **Rev:** Interior cave view **Edge:** Reeded

Date	Mintage	F	VF	XF	Unc	BU
2005BP	5,000	—	—	—	45.00	50.00
2005BP Proof	5,000	Value: 55.00				

KM# 783 5000 FORINT
31.4600 g., 0.9250 Silver 0.9356 oz. ASW, 38.6 mm.
Obv: Hungarian National Bank building **Rev:** Ignac Alpar and life dates **Edge:** Reeded

Date	Mintage	F	VF	XF	Unc	BU
ND (2005)BP	3,000	—	—	—	45.00	47.50
ND (2005)BP Proof	3,000	Value: 50.00				

KM# 784 5000 FORINT
31.4600 g., 0.9250 Silver 0.9356 oz. ASW, 38.6 mm.
Obv: Knight on horse with lance **Rev:** Diosgyor Castle **Edge:** Reeded

Date	Mintage	F	VF	XF	Unc	BU
2005BP	4,000	—	—	—	45.00	47.50
2005BP Proof	4,000	Value: 50.00				

KM# 785 5000 FORINT
31.4600 g., 0.9250 Silver 0.9356 oz. ASW, 38.6 mm.
Obv: Large building above value **Rev:** Karoli Gaspar Reformed (Calvinist) University seal **Edge:** Reeded

Date	Mintage	F	VF	XF	Unc	BU
2005BP	3,000	—	—	—	45.00	47.50
2005BP Proof	3,000	Value: 50.00				

KM# 786 5000 FORINT
31.4600 g., 0.9250 Silver 0.9356 oz. ASW, 38.6 mm. **Obv:** Coin design of a Transylvanian KM-10 thaler reverse dated 1605 **Rev:** Stephan Bocskai (1557-1606) **Edge:** Reeded

Date	Mintage	F	VF	XF	Unc	BU
2005BP	3,000	—	—	—	42.50	45.00
2005BP Proof	3,000	Value: 50.00				

KM# 790 5000 FORINT
31.4600 g., 0.9250 Silver 0.9356 oz. ASW, 38.61 mm.
Series: Masterpieces of Ecclesiastical Architecture **Obv:** View of interior of dome **Obv. Legend:** MAGYAR KÖZTÁRSASÁG **Obv. Designer:** István Péter Bartos **Rev:** Basilica facade **Rev. Legend:** ESZTERGOMI BAZILIKA

Date	Mintage	F	VF	XF	Unc	BU
2006BP	2,500	—	—	—	47.50	50.00
2006BP Proof	3,500	Value: 55.00				

KM# 791 5000 FORINT
31.4600 g., 0.9250 Silver 0.9356 oz. ASW, 38.61 mm. **Subject:** 125th Anniversary - Birth of Béla Bartók **Obv:** Transylvanian

woodcarving **Obv. Legend:** MAGYAR KÖZTÁRSASÁG **Obv. Designer:** György Kiss **Rev:** Bust of Bartók right, Euro star behind **Edge:** Reeded and lettered **Edge Lettering:** Bartók Béla repeated three times

Date	Mintage	F	VF	XF	Unc	BU
2006BP Proof	25,000	Value: 35.00				

KM# 792 5000 FORINT
31.4600 g., 0.9250 Silver 0.9356 oz. ASW, 38.61 mm.
Series: Heritage Sites **Obv:** Great White Egret in flight **Obv. Legend:** MAGYAR - KÖZTÁRSASÁG **Obv. Designer:** Virág Szabó **Rev:** Landscape, Schneeberg Mountain above Esterházy palace facade

Date	Mintage	F	VF	XF	Unc	BU
2006BP	5,000	—	—	—	42.50	45.00
2006BP Proof	5,000	Value: 50.00				

KM# 793 5000 FORINT
31.4600 g., 0.9250 Silver 0.9356 oz. ASW, 38.61 mm.
Series: Hungarian Castles **Subject:** Hungarian Castles **Obv:** Portrait of Ilona Zrinyi **Obv. Legend:** MAGYAR KÖZTÁRSASÁG **Obv. Designer:** Enikö Szöllössy **Rev:** Munkács Castle

Date	Mintage	F	VF	XF	Unc	BU
2006BP	4,000	—	—	—	42.50	45.00
2006BP Proof	4,000	Value: 50.00				

KM# 794 5000 FORINT
31.4600 g., 0.9250 Silver 0.9356 oz. ASW, 38.61 mm.
Subject: 500th Anniversary - Victory in Nándorfehévár **Obv:** Decorative sword hilt **Obv. Legend:** MAGYAR KÖZTÁRSASÁG **Obv. Designer:** E. Tamás Soltra **Rev:** János Hunyadi in armor at left, John Capistrano in monk's garb at right **Rev. Inscription:** NÁNDORFEHÉRVÁRI / DIADAL

Date	Mintage	F	VF	XF	Unc	BU
2006BP	2,500	—	—	—	42.50	45.00
2006BP Proof	3,500	Value: 50.00				

KM# 795   5000 FORINT
31.4600 g., 0.9250 Silver 0.9356 oz. ASW, 38.61 mm. **Subject:** 50th Anniversary - Hungarian Revolution **Obv:** 1956 repeated in stone blocks at right **Obv. Legend:** MAGYAR KÖZTÁRSASÁG **Obv. Designer:** Attila Rónay **Rev:** 1956 repeated in stone blocks at left, freedom fighter's flag at center **Rev. Legend:** MAGYAR FORRADALOM ÉS SZABADSÁGHARC

Date	Mintage	F	VF	XF	Unc	BU
2006BP	5,000	—	—	—	42.50	45.00
2006BP Proof	5,000	Value: 50.00				

KM# 798   5000 FORINT
31.4600 g., 0.9250 Silver 0.9356 oz. ASW, 38.61 mm. **Series:** Hungarian Castles **Obv:** Walled tower **Obv. Inscription:** MAGYAR / KÖZTÁRSASÁG **Obv. Designer:** György Kiss **Rev:** Gyula castle **Rev. Inscription:** GYULAI / VÁR

Date	Mintage	F	VF	XF	Unc	BU
2007BP	4,000	—	—	—	50.00	55.00
2007BP Proof	4,000	Value: 60.00				

KM# 799   5000 FORINT
31.4600 g., 0.9250 Silver 0.9356 oz. ASW, 38.61 mm. **Subject:** 200th Anniversary - Birth of Count Lajos Batthyány **Obv:** Seal dated 1848 with crowned arms above Batthyány's autograph **Obv. Legend:** MAGYAR KÖZTÁRSASÁG **Obv. Designer:** Márta Csikai **Rev:** 1/2 length figure of Batthyány facing **Rev. Legend:** BATTHYÁNY LAJOS

Date	Mintage	FVF	XF	Unc	BU
2007BP Proof	20,000	Value: 35.00			

KM# 800   5000 FORINT
31.4600 g., 0.9250 Silver 0.9356 oz. ASW, 38.61 mm. **Subject:** 125th Anniversary - Birth of Zoltán Kodály **Obv:** Gramophone **Obv. Legend:** MAGYAR KÖZTÁRSASÁG **Obv. Designer:** Gábor Gáti **Rev:** Bust of Kodály facing 3/4 right

Date	Mintage	F	VF	XF	Unc	BU
2007BP	4,000	—	—	—	42.50	45.00
2007BP Proof	6,000	Value: 50.00				

KM# 802   5000 FORINT
31.4600 g., 0.9250 Silver 0.9356 oz. ASW, 38.61 mm. **Subject:** 800th Anniversary - Birth of St. Elizabeth **Obv:** Stylized image of St. Elizabeth feeding the hungry **Obv. Inscription:** Magyar / Köztárszág **Rev:** 3/4 length figure of St. Elizabeth seated facing holding roses and bread rolls in her lap

Date	Mintage	F	VF	XF	Unc	BU
2007BP	4,000	—	—	—	52.50	55.00
2007BP Proof	4,000	Value: 57.50				

KM# 804   5000 FORINT
31.4600 g., 0.9250 Silver 0.9356 oz. ASW, 38.61 mm. **Subject:** Great Reformed Church - Debrecen **Obv:** Church interior **Obv. Legend:** MAGYAR KOZTARSASAG **Rev:** Church facade **Rev. Legend:** DEBRECENI REFORMATUS NAGYTEMPLOM **Edge:** Plain **Shape:** 12-sided **Designer:** SZ.EGYED Emma

Date	Mintage	F	VF	XF	Unc	BU
2007BP	4,000	—	—	—	42.50	45.00
2007BP Proof	6,000	Value: 50.00				

KM# 811   5000 FORINT
31.4600 g., 0.9250 Silver 0.9356 oz. ASW, 38.6 mm. **Subject:** Europa heritage site Tokaj Wine Region **Obv:** Value within grape wreath **Rev:** Tokaj Hill and TV tower **Rev. Designer:** Gábor Gáti **Edge:** Reeded

Date	Mintage	F	VF	XF	Unc	BU
2008BP	5,000	—	—	—	—	30.00
2008BP Proof	15,000	Value: 35.00				

KM# 806   5000 FORINT
31.4600 g., 0.9250 Silver 0.9356 oz. ASW, 38.61 mm. **Obv:** Grape wreath rim with denomination, legend & mintmark inside **Rev:** Tokaj hill, TV tower, grapefield with a village & church **Edge:** Milled **Designer:** Gáti Gábor

Date	Mintage	F	VF	XF	Unc	BU
2008	5,000	—	—	—	—	40.00
2008 Proof	15,000	Value: 45.00				

KM# 807   5000 FORINT
31.4600 g., 0.9250 Silver 0.9356 oz. ASW, 38.61 mm. **Subject:** Castle of the Siklós **Obv:** Castle, tower, Franciscan monastery & church **Rev:** Castle of the Siklós **Designer:** Szöllössy Enikö

Date	Mintage	F	VF	XF	Unc	BU
2008	4,000	—	—	—	—	45.00
2008 Proof	6,000	Value: 50.00				

KM# 808   5000 FORINT
31.4600 g., 0.9250 Silver 0.9356 oz. ASW, 38.61 mm. **Subject:** 29th Summer Olympics **Obv:** Coat of arms over water **Rev:** Water polo player **Rev. Designer:** Gábor Kereszthury **Edge:** Milled

Date	Mintage	F	VF	XF	Unc	BU
2008	4,000	—	—	—	—	40.00
2008 Proof	14,000	Value: 45.00				

KM# 810   5000 FORINT
31.4600 g., 0.9250 Silver 0.9356 oz. ASW, 38.61 mm. **Subject:** Centenery birth of Ede Teller **Obv:** Diagram of Deuterium-tritium fusion reaction **Rev:** Portrait Ede Teller **Designer:** Mihály Fritz

Date	Mintage	F	VF	XF	Unc	BU
2008	4,000	—	—	—	—	45.00
2008 Proof	6,000	Value: 50.00				

KM# 812   5000 FORINT
31.4600 g., 0.9250 Silver 0.9356 oz. ASW **Subject:** Miklós Badnóti, 100th Anniversary of Birth **Obv:** Value **Rev:** Bust in suit facing **Rev. Designer:** Gábor Gáti

Date	Mintage	F	VF	XF	Unc	BU
2009	4,000	—	—	—	—	30.00
2009 Proof	4,000	Value: 40.00				

KM# 813   5000 FORINT
14.0000 g., Copper-Nickel, 28.4 mm. **Subject:** Donat Banki, 150th Anniversary of Birth **Obv:** Denomination view of crossflow turbine **Rev:** Portrait facing in suit **Shape:** Square

Date	Mintage	F	VF	XF	Unc	BU
2009	10,000	—	—	—	—	15.00
2009 Proof	10,000	Value: 20.00				

KM# 814   5000 FORINT
31.4600 g., 0.9250 Silver 0.9356 oz. ASW, 38.6 mm. **Subject:** Dohany Street Synagogue, 150th Anniversary **Obv:** Mosaic **Obv. Designer:** György Szabó **Rev:** Facade **Shape:** Scalloped

Date	Mintage	F	VF	XF	Unc	BU
2009	4,000	—	—	—	—	30.00
2009 Proof	4,000	Value: 40.00				

KM# 815   5000 FORINT
31.4600 g., 0.9250 Silver 0.9356 oz. ASW, 38.61 mm. **Subject:** Budapest - World Heritage Site **Obv:** Street scene **Rev:** Panoramic view of Danube and Parliament **Rev. Designer:** Mihály Fritz

Date	Mintage	F	VF	XF	Unc	BU
2009	5,000	—	—	—	—	30.00
2009 Proof	5,000	Value: 40.00				

KM# 819 5000 FORINT
31.4600 g., 0.9250 Silver 0.9356 oz. ASW, 38.6 mm.
Subject: Kosztolanyi Dezso, 125th Anniversary of birth
Obv: Architectural element of stone **Rev:** Portrait

Date	Mintage	F	VF	XF	Unc	BU
2010BP	3,000	—	—	45.00	40.00	
2010BP Proof	5,000	Value: 50.00				

KM# 820 5000 FORINT
31.4700 g., 0.9250 Silver 0.9359 oz. ASW, 39.6x26.4 mm.
Subject: Orseg National Park **Obv:** Butterfly **Obv. Designer:**
Gabor Gati **Rev:** Traditional rural buildings **Shape:** Rectangle

Date	Mintage	F	VF	XF	Unc	BU
2010BP	3,000	—	—	40.00	45.00	
2010BP Proof	5,000	Value: 50.00				

KM# 821 5000 FORINT
31.4600 g., 0.9250 Silver 0.9356 oz. ASW, 38.6 mm.
Subject: European Watersports Championships **Obv:** Value and
waves **Obv. Designer:** Attila Ronay **Rev:** Swimmer with butterfly
stroke

Date	Mintage	F	VF	XF	Unc	BU
2010BP	4,000	—	—	40.00	45.00	
2010BP Proof	6,000	Value: 50.00				

KM# 822 5000 FORINT
0.5000 g., 0.9990 Gold 0.0161 oz. AGW, 11 mm.
Subject: Ferenc Erkel - 200th Anniversary of birth
Obv: Denomination **Obv. Designer:** Laszlo Szlavics **Rev:** Large
bust facing

Date	Mintage	F	VF	XF	Unc	BU
2010BP Proof	10,000	Value: 50.00				

KM# 823 5000 FORINT
31.4600 g., 0.9250 Silver 0.9356 oz. ASW, 38.6 mm.
Subject: Ferenc Erkel, 200th Anniversary of birth **Obv:** House
Obv. Designer: Gyorgy Kiss **Rev:** Bust facing, signature below

Date	Mintage	F	VF	XF	Unc	BU
2010 PROOF	5,000	Value: 50.00				

KM# 753 20000 FORINT
6.9820 g., 0.9860 Gold 0.2213 oz. AGW, 22 mm.
Subject: Hungarian Coinage Millennium **Obv:** Denomination
Rev: Hammered coinage minting scene above old coin design
Edge: Plain

Date	Mintage	F	VF	XF	Unc	BU
2001BP Proof	3,000	Value: 275				

KM# 777 50000 FORINT
13.9640 g., 0.9860 Gold 0.4426 oz. AGW, 25 mm. **Obv:** Value
and country name above Euro Union stars **Rev:** Mythical stag
seen through ornate window **Edge:** Reeded

Date	Mintage	F	VF	XF	Unc	BU
2004BP Proof	7,000	Value: 550				

KM# 803 50000 FORINT
10.0000 g., 0.9860 Gold 0.3170 oz. AGW, 25 mm.
Subject: 550th Anniversary - Enthronement of Matthias Hunyadi
Obv: Raven holding a ring in its beak **Rev:** Portrait of Mátyás
Hunyadi based on a marble relief **Edge:** Smooth
Designer: László Szlávics, Jr.

Date	Mintage	F	VF	XF	Unc	BU
2008 Proof	5,000	Value: 400				

KM# 816 50000 FORINT
10.0000 g., 0.9860 Gold 0.3170 oz. AGW, 25 mm.
Subject: Ferenc Kazinczy, 250th Anniversary of Birth **Obv:** Value
and classical fagade **Obv. Designer:** Enikö Szölössy **Rev:** Bust
at left

Date	Mintage	F	VF	XF	Unc	BU
2009 Proof	5,000	Value: 400				

KM# 825 5000 FORINT
6.9820 g., 0.9860 Gold 0.2213 oz. AGW, 22 mm. **Subject:** St.
Stephen and St. Emeric **Obv:** Medieval document **Obv.
Designer:** Eniko Szollossy **Rev:** St. Stephen and prince standing

Date	Mintage	F	VF	XF	Unc	BU
2010BP Proof	5,000	—	—			

KM# 758 100000 FORINT
31.1040 g., 0.9860 Gold 0.9860 oz. AGW, 37 mm.
Subject: Saint Stephen **Obv:** Angels crowning coat of arms
Rev: King seated on throne **Edge:** Reeded

Date	Mintage	F	VF	XF	Unc	BU
2001BP Proof	3,000	Value: 1,250				

KM# 796 100000 FORINT
20.9460 g., 0.9860 Gold 0.6640 oz. AGW, 38.61 mm.
Subject: 50th Anniversary - Hungarian Revolution **Obv:** 1956
repeated in cut out stone **Rev:** 1956 repeated in cut out stone
with two freedom fighter's flags

Date	Mintage	F	VF	XF	Unc	BU
2006BP Proof	5,000	Value: 850				

KM# 824 500,000 FORINT
63.8280 g., 0.9860 Gold 2.0233 oz. AGW, 46 mm. **Subject:** St.
Stephan and St. Emeric **Obv:** Medieval document **Obv. Designer:**
Eniko Szollossy **Rev:** King and prince standing **Note:** 18 Ducats

Date	Mintage	F	VF	XF	Unc	BU
2010BP Proof	500	Value: 2,750				

MINT SETS

KM#	Date	Mintage	Identification	Issue Price	Mkt Val
MS32	2001 (7)	—	KM#692-697, 721	—	16.50
MS33	2002 (8)	—	KM#692, 693, 694, 695, 696, 697, 721, 760	—	18.00
MS34	2003 (8)	—	KM#692, 693, 694, 695, 696, 697, 721, 768	—	17.50
MS35	2004 (8)	—	KM#692, 693, 694, 695, 696, 697, 721, 773	—	19.00
MS36	2005 (8)	—	KM#692-697, 721, 779 Magyarorszag Penzemei	—	20.00
MS37	2006 (7)	—	KM#692-697, 721, plus silver 1946 KM532	—	17.50

PROOF SETS

KM#	Date	Mintage	Identification	Issue Price	Mkt Val
PS26	2001 (7)	—	KM#692-697, 721	35.00	37.50
PS27	2002 (8)	—	KM#692-697, 721, 760	—	42.50
PS28	2003 (8)	—	KM#692-697, 721, 768	—	40.00
PS29	2004 (8)	—	KM#692-697, 721, 773	—	40.00
PS30	2005 (8)	7,000	KM#692-697, 721, 779	—	37.50
PS31	2006 (7)	—	KM#692-697, 721	—	35.00
PS32	2007 (8)	—	KM#692-697, 721, 805	—	40.00
PS33	2008 (7)	—	KM#692-697, 721	—	35.00

ICELAND

The Republic of Iceland, an island of recent volcanic origin
in the North Atlantic east of Greenland and immediately south of
the Arctic Circle, has an area of 39,768 sq. mi. (103,000 sq. km.)
and a population of just over 300,000. Capital: Reykjavik. Fishing
is the chief industry and accounts for a little less than 60 percent
of the exports.

REPUBLIC

REFORM COINAGE
100 Old Kronur = 1 New Krona

KM# 27a KRONA
4.0000 g., Nickel Plated Steel, 21.5 mm. **Obv:** Giant facing
Rev: Cod **Edge:** Reeded

Date	Mintage	F	VF	XF	Unc	BU
2003	5,144,000	—	—	—	0.75	1.50
2005	5,000,000	—	—	—	0.75	1.50
2006	10,000,000	—	—	—	0.75	1.50
2007	10,000,000	—	—	—	0.75	1.50

KM# 28a 5 KRONUR
5.6000 g., Nickel Clad Steel, 24.5 mm. **Obv:** Quartered design
of Eagle, dragon, bull and giant **Rev:** Two dolphins leaping left
Edge: Reeded

Date	Mintage	F	VF	XF	Unc	BU
2005	2,000,000	—	—	—	2.00	3.00
2007	10,000,000	—	—	—	2.00	3.00

KM# 29.1a 10 KRONUR
8.0000 g., Nickel Clad Steel, 27.5 mm. **Obv:** Quartered design
of Eagle, dragon, bull and giant **Rev:** Four capelins left
Edge: Reeded

Date	Mintage	F	VF	XF	Unc	BU
2004	2,000,000	—	—	—	1.75	2.50
2005	4,505,000	—	—	—	1.75	2.50
2006	7,800,000	—	—	—	1.75	2.50

KM# 31 50 KRONUR
8.2500 g., Nickel-Brass, 23 mm. **Obv:** Quartered design of
eagle, dragon, bull and giant **Rev:** Crab **Edge:** Reeded
Designer: Throstur MLagnusson

Date	Mintage	F	VF	XF	Unc	BU
2001	2,000,000	—	—	—	4.00	5.00
2005	2,000,000	—	—	—	4.00	5.00

KM# 35 100 KRONUR
8.5000 g., Nickel-Brass, 25.5 mm. **Obv:** Quartered design of
Eagle, dragon, bull and giant **Rev:** Lumpfish left **Edge:** Reeded
Designer: Throstur Magnusson

Date	Mintage	F	VF	XF	Unc	BU
2001	2,140,000	—	—	—	6.00	7.00
2004	2,400,000	—	—	—	6.00	7.00
2006	2,000,000	—	—	—	6.00	7.00
2007	3,000,000	—	—	—	6.00	7.00

INDIA - REPUBLIC

The Republic of India, a subcontinent jutting southward from
the mainland of Asia, has an area of 1,269,346 sq. mi. (3,287,590
sq. km.) and a population of over 900 million, second only to that
of the People's Republic of China. Capital: New Delhi. India's
economy is based on agriculture and industrial activity. Engineering goods, cotton apparel and fabrics, handicrafts, tea, iron
and steel are exported.

The Republic of India is a member of the Common-wealth
of Nations. The president is the Chief of State. The prime minister
is the Head of Government.

MINT MARKS

(Mint marks usually appear directly below the date.)
B - Mumbai (Bombay), proof issues only
(B) - Mumbai (Bombay), diamond
(C) - Calcutta, no mint mark
(H) - Hyderabad, star (1963--)
M - Mumbai (Bombay), proof only after 1996
(N) - Noida, dot
(T) - Taegu (Korea), star below first or last date digit

REPUBLIC

DECIMAL COINAGE

KM# 368   2 PAISE

5.8000 g., Stainless Steel, 26.97 mm. **Subject:** Louis Braile, 200th Anniversary of Birth

Date	Mintage	F	VF	XF	Unc	BU
2009(C)	—	—	—	—	0.50	1.25

KM# 54   25 PAISE

2.8200 g., Stainless Steel, 19 mm. **Obv:** Small Asoka lion pedestal **Rev:** Rhinoceros left **Edge:** Plain **Note:** Varieties of date size exist.

Date	Mintage	F	VF	XF	Unc	BU
2001(B)	—	—	0.10	0.20	1.00	—
2001(C)	—	—	0.10	0.20	1.00	—
2001(H)	—	—	0.15	0.25	1.00	—
2002(B)	—	—	0.15	0.25	1.00	—
2002(C)	—	—	0.15	0.25	1.00	—
2002(H)	—	—	0.25	0.40	1.00	—

KM# 69   50 PAISE

3.8000 g., Stainless Steel, 22 mm. **Subject:** Parliament Building in New Delhi **Obv:** Denomination **Rev:** Building

Date	Mintage	F	VF	XF	Unc	BU
2001(B)	—	—	0.15	0.25	0.50	—
2001(C)	—	—	0.15	0.25	0.50	—
2001(H)	—	—	0.20	0.40	0.75	—
2001(N)	—	—	0.15	0.25	0.50	—
2002(B)	—	—	0.15	0.25	0.50	—
2002(C)	—	—	0.15	0.25	0.50	—
2002(N)	—	—	0.15	0.25	0.50	—
2002(H)	—	—	0.15	0.25	0.50	—
2003(B)	—	—	0.15	0.25	0.50	—
2003(N)	—	—	0.15	0.25	0.50	—
2003(C)	—	—	0.15	0.25	0.50	—

KM# 92.2   RUPEE

4.9000 g., Stainless Steel, 25 mm. **Obv:** Asoka lion pedestal **Rev:** Denomination and date, grain ears flank **Edge:** Plain **Note:** Mint mark varieties exist.

Date	Mintage	F	VF	XF	Unc	BU
2001(H)	—	—	0.15	0.30	0.45	—

Note: Small and large mint mark exist, doubled left or right of wheat stalks

Date	Mintage	F	VF	XF	Unc	BU
2001(B)	—	—	0.15	0.30	0.45	—
2001(C)	—	—	0.15	0.30	0.45	—
2001(K)	—	—	0.15	0.30	0.45	—
2001(N)	—	—	0.15	0.30	0.45	—
2002(N)	—	—	0.15	0.30	0.45	—
2002(B)	—	—	0.15	0.30	0.45	—
2002(C)	—	—	0.15	0.30	0.45	—
2002(H)	—	—	0.15	0.30	0.45	—
2003(B)	—	—	0.15	0.30	0.45	—
2003(C)	—	—	0.15	0.30	0.45	—
2003(H)	—	—	0.15	0.30	0.45	—
2004(B)	—	—	0.15	0.30	0.45	—
2004H	—	—	0.15	0.30	0.45	—
2004(C)	—	—	0.15	0.30	0.45	—

KM# 313   RUPEE

4.9500 g., Stainless Steel, 25 mm. **Subject:** 100th Anniversary Birth of Jaya Prakash Narayan **Obv:** Asoka column **Rev:** Bust of Jaya Prakash Narayan slightly left **Edge:** Plain

Date	Mintage	F	VF	XF	Unc	BU
2002(B)	—	—	0.45	0.75	1.00	—
2002(B) Proof	—	Value: 3.00				
2002(H)	—	—	0.45	0.75	1.00	—

KM# 314   RUPEE

4.9500 g., Stainless Steel, 25 mm. **Subject:** Maharana Pratap **Edge:** Plain

Date	Mintage	F	VF	XF	Unc	BU
2003(B)	—	—	0.45	0.75	1.00	—
2003(B) Proof	—	Value: 2.50				
2003(H)	—	—	0.45	0.75	1.00	—

KM# 316   RUPEE

4.8500 g., Stainless Steel, 25 mm. **Obv:** Asoka lions **Rev:** 3/4 length military figure Veer Durgadass with spear left **Edge:** Plain

Date	Mintage	F	VF	XF	Unc	BU
2003(B)	—	—	0.50	0.80	1.25	—
2003(B) Proof	—	Value: 2.50				
2003(H)	—	—	0.50	0.80	1.25	—

KM# 321   RUPEE

5.0000 g., Stainless Steel, 24.9 mm. **Subject:** 150th Anniversary of the Indian Postal Service **Obv:** Asoka lions above value **Rev:** Partial postage stamp design **Edge:** Grooved

Date	Mintage	F	VF	XF	Unc	BU
2004	—	—	—	—	2.00	—
2004 Proof	—	Value: 3.50				

KM# 322   RUPEE

4.9500 g., Stainless Steel, 24.8 mm. **Obv:** Asoka lions and value **Rev:** Cross dividing four dots **Edge:** Plain

Date	Mintage	F	VF	XF	Unc	BU
2005(C)	—	—	—	—	2.00	—
2007(H)	—	—	—	—	2.00	—

KM# 331   RUPEE

4.9000 g., Stainless Steel, 25 mm. **Subject:** Bharata Natyam Dance Expressions **Obv:** Asoka lion pedestal **Rev:** Gesture of hand with thumb up **Edge:** Plain

Date	Mintage	F	VF	XF	Unc	BU
2007(N)	—	—	—	0.40	1.00	—
2008(N)	—	—	—	0.40	1.00	—

KM# 121.5   2 RUPEES

6.0600 g., Copper-Nickel, 26 mm. **Subject:** National Integration **Obv:** Type C **Rev:** Flag on map **Edge:** Plain **Note:** 11-sided

Date	Mintage	F	VF	XF	Unc	BU
2001(B)	—	—	0.30	0.50	1.00	—
2001(C)	—	—	0.30	0.50	1.00	—
2001(H)	—	—	0.30	0.50	1.00	—
2002(B)	—	—	0.30	0.50	1.00	—
2002(C)	—	—	0.30	0.50	1.00	—
2002(H)	—	—	0.30	0.50	1.00	—
2002(N)	—	—	0.30	0.50	1.00	—
2003(B)	—	—	0.30	0.50	1.00	—
2003(C)	—	—	0.30	0.50	1.00	—
2003(H)	—	—	0.30	0.50	1.00	—

KM# 121.3   2 RUPEES

6.0000 g., Copper-Nickel, 26 mm. **Subject:** National Integration **Obv:** Type A **Rev:** Flag on map **Edge:** Plain **Shape:** 11-sided **Note:** Reduced size, non magnetic.

Date	Mintage	F	VF	XF	Unc	BU
2001(B)	—	—	0.30	0.50	1.00	—
2001(C)	—	—	0.30	0.50	1.00	—
2002(C)	—	—	0.30	0.50	1.00	—
2003(C)	—	—	0.30	0.50	1.00	—

KM# 303   2 RUPEES

6.2400 g., Copper-Nickel, 25.7 mm. **Subject:** 100th Anniversary Birth of Dr. Syama P. Mookerjee **Obv:** Asoka lion pedestal above denomination, type B **Rev:** Bust of Dr. Mookerjee right **Edge:** Plain

Date	Mintage	F	VF	XF	Unc	BU
2001(C)	—	—	1.25	2.00	3.00	—
2001(N)	—	—	1.25	2.00	3.00	—
2001(C) Proof	—	Value: 7.50				

KM# 305   2 RUPEES

6.1000 g., Copper-Nickel, 25.7 mm. **Subject:** St. Tukaram **Obv:** Asoka column above value **Rev:** Seated musician **Shape:** Eleven sided

Date	Mintage	F	VF	XF	Unc	BU
2002(B)	—	—	0.75	1.25	2.00	—
2002(C)	—	—	0.75	1.25	2.00	—

KM# 346 2 RUPEES
6.0000 g., Copper-Nickel, 26 mm. **Subject:** Sant Tukaram (film about poet) **Obv:** Asoka column **Edge:** Plain **Shape:** 11-sided

Date	Mintage	F	VF	XF	Unc	BU
2002(C)	—	—	—	2.00	3.00	—
2002(C) Proof	—	Value: 5.00				

KM# 307 2 RUPEES
6.0500 g., Copper-Nickel **Subject:** 150th Anniversary - Indian Railways **Obv:** Asoka column above value **Rev:** Cartoon elephant holding railroad lantern **Edge:** Plain **Shape:** 11-sided

Date	Mintage	F	VF	XF	Unc	BU
2003(B)	—	—	0.75	1.25	2.00	—
2003(C)	—	—	0.75	1.25	2.00	—
2003(C) Proof	—	Value: 5.00				

KM# 334 2 RUPEES
6.0000 g., Copper-Nickel, 26 mm. **Subject:** 150th Anniversary Telecommunications **Obv:** Asoka lions **Rev:** Cartoon bird standing holding cell phone **Edge:** Plain **Shape:** 11-sided

Date	Mintage	F	VF	XF	Unc	BU
2004(B)	—	—	—	—	2.00	—
2004(B) Proof	—	Value: 5.00				

KM# 326 2 RUPEES
5.8000 g., Stainless Steel **Obv:** Asoka Pillar and value in center **Rev:** Cross with U-shaped arms and dots **Edge:** Plain **Note:** Size varies 26.75 - 27.07 mm

Date	Mintage	F	VF	XF	Unc	BU
2005(B)	—	—	—	0.50	1.35	—
2005(C)	—	—	—	0.50	1.35	—
2006(B) small date	—	—	—	0.40	1.00	—
2006(B) large date	—	—	—	0.40	1.00	—
2006(H)	—	—	—	0.40	1.00	—
2006(N)	—	—	—	0.40	1.00	—
2007(B)	—	—	—	0.40	1.00	—
2007(H)	—	—	—	0.40	1.00	—

KM# 327 2 RUPEES
5.8000 g., Stainless Steel, 27 mm. **Obv:** Asoka Pillar at center **Obv. Inscription:** INDIA in Hindi and English **Rev:** Hasta Mudra - hand gesture from the dance Bharata Natyam **Edge:** Plain

Date	Mintage	F	VF	XF	Unc	BU
2007(B)	—	—	—	0.50	1.25	—
2007(C)	—	—	—	0.50	1.25	—
2008(N)	—	—	—	0.50	1.25	—

KM# 350 2 RUPEES
6.0000 g., Stainless Steel, 26.9 mm. **Subject:** 75th Anniversary Indian Air Force **Obv:** Asoka column **Rev:** Planes in flight **Edge:** Plain **Shape:** 11-sided

Date	Mintage	F	VF	XF	Unc	BU
2007(C)	—	—	—	2.00	3.00	—
2007(C) Proof	—	Value: 5.00				

KM# 364 2 RUPEES
5.8000 g., Stainless Steel, 26.97 mm. **Subject:** St. Alphonsa **Obv:** Asoka column **Rev:** Bust facing

Date	Mintage	F	VF	XF	Unc	BU
2009	—	—	—	—	0.50	1.25

KM# 366 2 RUPEES
5.8000 g., Stainless Steel, 26.97 mm. **Subject:** C. A. Annadurai

Date	Mintage	F	VF	XF	Unc	BU
2009	—	—	—	—	0.50	1.25

KM# 154.1 5 RUPEES
9.3000 g., Copper-Nickel, 23.4 mm. **Obv:** Asoka lion pedestal **Rev:** Denomination flanked by flowers **Edge:** Security **Note:** (C) - Calcutta mint has issued 2 distinctly different security edge varieties every year 1992-2003 with large dots and thick center line, w/small dots and narrow center line.

Date	Mintage	F	VF	XF	Unc	BU
2001(B)	—	—	0.25	0.50	1.00	—
2001(C) Plain 1	—	—	0.25	0.50	1.00	—
2001(C) Serif 1	—	—	1.00	2.00	3.00	—
2001(H)	—	—	0.30	0.60	1.50	—
2002(C)	—	—	0.25	0.50	1.00	—
2002(N)	—	—	0.25	0.50	1.00	—
2003(C)	—	—	0.25	0.50	1.00	—

KM# 154.2 5 RUPEES
8.9100 g., Copper-Nickel, 23 mm. **Obv:** Asoka lion pedestal **Rev:** Denomination flanked by flowers **Edge:** Milled

Date	Mintage	F	VF	XF	Unc	BU
2001(C)	—	—	8.00	10.00	15.00	—
2002(C)	—	—	8.00	10.00	15.00	—
2003(C)	—	—	8.00	10.00	15.00	—

KM# 154.4 5 RUPEES
Copper-Nickel, 23 mm. **Obv:** Asoka lion pedestal as seen on 2 Rupees, KM#121.5 **Rev:** Denomination flanked by flowers

Date	Mintage	F	VF	XF	Unc	BU
2001(B)	—	—	0.25	0.50	1.00	—
2002(B)	—	—	0.25	0.50	1.00	—
2003(B)	—	—	0.25	0.50	1.00	—
2004(B)	—	—	0.25	0.50	1.00	—

KM# 304 5 RUPEES
9.0700 g., Copper-Nickel, 23.19 mm. **Subject:** 2600th Anniversary Birth of Bhagwan Mahavir **Obv:** Asoka column above denomination **Rev:** Swastika above hand in irregular frame **Edge:** Security

Date	Mintage	F	VF	XF	Unc	BU
2001(B)	—	—	1.00	2.00	3.00	5.00
2001(B) Proof	—	Value: 6.50				
2001(N)	—	—	1.00	2.00	3.00	5.00

KM# 308 5 RUPEES
8.9200 g., Copper-Nickel, 23.1 mm. **Subject:** Dadabhai Naroji **Obv:** Asoka column above value **Rev:** Bust of Dadabhai Naroji 3/4 right **Edge:** Security

Date	Mintage	F	VF	XF	Unc	BU
ND(2003)(B)	—	—	1.00	1.75	3.00	5.00

KM# 317.1 5 RUPEES
8.8000 g., Copper-Nickel, 23.1 mm. **Obv:** Asoka lions **Rev:** K. Kamaraj above life dates **Edge:** Security

Date	Mintage	F	VF	XF	Unc	BU
ND(2003)(B)	—	—	1.00	1.75	3.00	5.00
ND(2003)(B) Proof	—	Value: 7.50				
ND(2003)(H)	—	—	1.25	2.00	3.50	5.50
ND(2003)(C)	—	—	1.00	1.75	3.00	5.00

KM# 317.2 5 RUPEES
8.8000 g., Copper-Nickel, 23.1 mm. **Obv:** Asoka lion pedestal **Rev:** K. Kamaraj above life dates **Edge:** Reeded

Date	Mintage	F	VF	XF	Unc	BU
ND (2003)(H)	—	—	5.00	7.00	11.00	—

KM# 329 5 RUPEES
9.0700 g., Bi-Metallic Brass center in Copper-Nickel ring, 23.25 mm. **Obv:** Asoka column, value below **Rev:** Bust of Shastri 3/4 left **Rev. Legend:** LALBAHADUR SHASTRI BIRTH CENTENARY **Edge:** Security

Date	Mintage	F	VF	XF	Unc	BU
ND(2004)	—	—	—	—	3.50	5.00

KM# 336 5 RUPEES
9.0000 g., Copper-Nickel, 23 mm. **Subject:** 100th Anniversary Birth of Lal Bahadur Shastri **Obv:** Asoka lions **Rev:** Bust of Lal Bahadur Shastri 3/4 right **Edge:** Security

Date	Mintage	F	VF	XF	Unc	BU
ND(2004)(C)	—	—	—	—	3.50	5.00
ND(2004)(C) Proof	—	Value: 8.00				

KM# 325 5 RUPEES
8.8500 g., Copper-Nickel, 23 mm. **Subject:** 75th Anniversary Dandi March **Obv:** Asoka column **Rev:** Ghandi leading marchers **Edge:** Security type

Date	Mintage	F	VF	XF	Unc	BU
ND (2005)(B)	—	—	—	—	3.00	5.00
ND (2005)(B) Proof	—	Value: 7.50				

KM# 324 5 RUPEES
8.8500 g., Copper-Nickel, 23 mm. **Obv:** Asoka column **Rev:** Bust of Mahatma Basaveshwara slightly left **Edge:** Security

Date	Mintage	F	VF	XF	Unc	BU
ND(2006)(B)	—	—	0.40	1.00	3.00	5.00
ND(2006)(B) Proof	—	Value: 6.00				

KM# 356 5 RUPEES
6.0300 g., Stainless Steel, 22.9 mm. **Subject:** Tilak "Jee" **Note:** Withdrawn.

Date	Mintage	F	VF	XF	Unc	BU
2006	—	—	—	—	10.00	15.00

KM# 352   5 RUPEES
9.0000 g., Copper-Nickel **Subject:** Mahatma Basveshwara

Date	Mintage	F	VF	XF	Unc	BU
2006	—	—	—	—	—	2.50

KM# 354   5 RUPEES
6.0300 g., Stainless Steel, 22.8 mm. **Subject:** O.N.G.C., 50th Anniversary **Obv:** Asoka column above value

Date	Mintage	F	VF	XF	Unc	BU
ND(2006)(H)	—	—	—	—	4.00	5.00

KM# 355   5 RUPEES
9.5000 g., Copper-Nickel, 23.1 mm. **Subject:** Jagathguru Sree Narayana Guruden

Date	Mintage	F	VF	XF	Unc	BU
2006	—	—	—	—	3.00	5.00

KM# 357   5 RUPEES
6.0300 g., Stainless Steel, 22.9 mm. **Series:** Asoka column **Subject:** State Bank of India

Date	Mintage	F	VF	XF	Unc	BU
ND(2006)(H)	—	—	—	—	4.00	5.00

KM# 328   5 RUPEES
9.5000 g., Copper-Nickel, 23.10 mm. **Subject:** 150th Anniversary Birth of L. B. G. Tilak **Obv:** Asoka Lion pedestal **Rev:** Bust of Tilak facing slightly right **Edge:** Security

Date	Mintage	F	VF	XF	Unc	BU
2007(B)	—	—	—	—	3.50	5.00

KM# 330   5 RUPEES
6.0300 g., Stainless Steel, 22.88 mm. **Subject:** Information Technology **Obv:** Asoka column **Rev:** Waves **Edge:** Security

Date	Mintage	F	VF	XF	Unc	BU
2007(B)	—	—	—	—	4.00	5.00
2007(H)	—	—	—	—	4.00	5.00
2007(N)	—	—	—	—	4.00	5.00
2008(B)	—	—	—	—	4.00	5.00
2008(H)	—	—	—	—	4.00	5.00
2008(K)	—	—	—	—	4.00	5.00
2008(N)	—	—	—	—	4.00	5.00

KM# 336a   5 RUPEES
6.0300 g., Stainless Steel, 22.9 mm. **Subject:** Lal Bahadur Shastri

Date	Mintage	F	VF	XF	Unc	BU
2008	—	—	—	—	4.00	5.00
2009	—	—	—	—	4.00	5.00

KM# 352a   5 RUPEES
6.0000 g., Stainless Steel **Subject:** Mahatma Basveshwara

Date	Mintage	F	VF	XF	Unc	BU
2008	—	—	—	—	—	2.50

KM# 355a   5 RUPEES
6.0300 g., Stainless Steel, 22.9 mm. **Subject:** Jagadguru Shree Narayan Guru

Date	Mintage	F	VF	XF	Unc	BU
2008	—	—	—	—	4.00	5.00

KM# 358   5 RUPEES
6.0300 g., Nickel-Bronze, 22.9 mm. **Subject:** FIST

Date	Mintage	F	VF	XF	Unc	BU
2008	—	—	—	—	4.00	5.00

KM# 359   5 RUPEES
6.0300 g., Stainless Steel **Subject:** First War of Independence

Date	Mintage	F	VF	XF	Unc	BU
2008	—	—	—	—	4.00	5.00

KM# 361   5 RUPEES
6.0300 g., Stainless Steel, 22.9 mm. **Subject:** Dandi March

Date	Mintage	F	VF	XF	Unc	BU
2008	—	—	—	—	4.00	5.00

KM# 362   5 RUPEES
6.0300 g., Stainless Steel, 22.9 mm. **Subject:** SBI, 200th Anniversary

Date	Mintage	F	VF	XF	Unc	BU
2008	—	—	—	—	4.00	5.00

KM# 365   5 RUPEES
6.0300 g., Stainless Steel, 22.9 mm. **Subject:** St. Alphonsa, 100th Anniversary **Obv:** Asoka column **Rev:** Bust facing

Date	Mintage	F	VF	XF	Unc	BU
2009	—	—	—	—	4.00	5.00

KM# 367   5 RUPEES
6.0300 g., Stainless Steel, 22.9 mm. **Subject:** C. N. Annadurai, 100th Anniversary of Birth

Date	Mintage	F	VF	XF	Unc	BU
2009	—	—	—	—	4.00	5.00

KM# 309   10 RUPEES
12.5000 g., Copper-Nickel, 31 mm. **Subject:** 100th Anniversary Birth of Dr. Syama P. Mookerjee **Obv:** Asoka lion pedestal **Rev:** Bust of Dr. Mookerjee 1/2 right **Edge:** Reeded

Date	Mintage	F	VF	XF	Unc	BU
2001(C)	—	—	—	—	9.00	10.00
2001(C) Proof	—	Value: 15.00				

KM# 344   10 RUPEES
12.5000 g., Copper-Nickel, 31 mm. **Subject:** 100th Anniversary Birth of Jaya Prakash Narayan **Obv:** Asoka column **Rev:** Bust of Jaya Prakash Narayan slightly left **Edge:** Reeded

Date	Mintage	F	VF	XF	Unc	BU
2002(B)	—	—	—	—	9.00	10.00
2002(B) Proof	—	Value: 15.00				

KM# 347   10 RUPEES
12.5000 g., Copper-Nickel, 31 mm. **Subject:** Sant Tukaram (film about poet) **Obv:** Asoka column **Edge:** Reeded

Date	Mintage	F	VF	XF	Unc	BU
2002(C)	—	—	—	—	9.00	10.00
2002(C) Proof	—	Value: 15.00				

KM# 319   10 RUPEES
12.5000 g., Copper-Nickel, 31 mm. **Obv:** Asoka lion pedestal **Rev:** Bust of Maharana Pratap left

Date	Mintage	F	VF	XF	Unc	BU
2003(B)	—	—	—	—	9.00	10.00
2003(B) Proof	—	Value: 15.00				

KM# 332   10 RUPEES
12.5000 g., Copper-Nickel, 31 mm. **Obv:** Asoka lions **Rev:** 3/4 length military figure Veer Durgadass with spear left **Edge:** Reeded

Date	Mintage	F	VF	XF	Unc	BU
2003(B)	—	—	—	—	9.00	10.00
2003(B) Proof	—	Value: 15.00				

KM# 353   10 RUPEES
7.7000 g., Bi-Metallic Copper-Nickel center in Brass ring, 27 mm. **Subject:** Unity in Diversity **Obv:** Ashoka Pillar **Rev:** Four heads sharing a common body

Date	Mintage	F	VF	XF	Unc	BU
2006	—	—	—	—	—	2.50

KM# 363   10 RUPEES
7.7000 g., Bi-Metallic Copper-Nickel center in Brass ring, 27 mm. **Subject:** Information Technology **Obv:** Asoka column **Rev:** Large 10, rays above

Date	Mintage	F	VF	XF	Unc	BU
2008	—	—	—	—	17.00	20.00

KM# 310   50 RUPEES
30.0000 g., Copper-Nickel, 39 mm. **Subject:** 100th Anniversary Birth of Dr. Syama P. Mookerjee **Obv:** Asoka lion pedestal **Rev:** Bust of Dr. Mookerjee 1/2 right **Edge:** Reeded

Date	Mintage	F	VF	XF	Unc	BU
2001(C)	—	—	—	—	17.00	20.00
2001(C) Proof	—	Value: 30.00				

KM# 348   50 RUPEES
30.0000 g., Copper-Nickel, 39 mm. **Subject:** Sant Tukaram (film about poet) **Obv:** Asoka column **Edge:** Reeded

Date	Mintage	F	VF	XF	Unc	BU
2002(C)	—	—	—	—	15.00	17.00
2002(C) Proof	—	Value: 35.00				

KM# 311   100 RUPEES
35.0000 g., 0.5000 Silver 0.5626 oz. ASW, 44 mm. **Subject:** 10th Anniversary Dr, Syama P. Mookerjee **Obv:** Asoka lion pedestal **Rev:** Bust of Dr. Mookerjee1/2 right **Edge:** Reeded

Date	Mintage	F	VF	XF	Unc	BU
2001(C)	—	—	—	—	40.00	45.00
2001(C) Proof	—	Value: 70.00				

KM# 312   100 RUPEES
35.0000 g., 0.5000 Silver 0.5626 oz. ASW, 44 mm. **Subject:** 2600th Anniversary Birth of Bhagwan Mahavir **Obv:** Asoka lion pedestal **Rev:** Swastika above hand in irregular frame **Edge:** Reeded

Date	Mintage	F	VF	XF	Unc	BU
2001(B)	—	—	—	—	40.00	45.00
2001(B) Proof	—	Value: 70.00				

KM# 345   100 RUPEES
35.0000 g., 0.5000 Silver 0.5626 oz. ASW, 44 mm. **Subject:** 100th Anniversary Birth of Jaya Prakash Narayan **Obv:** Asoka column **Rev:** Bust of Jaya Prakash Narayan slightly left **Edge:** Reeded

Date	Mintage	F	VF	XF	Unc	BU
2002(B)	—	—	—	—	40.00	45.00
2002(B) Proof	—	Value: 70.00				

KM# 349   100 RUPEES
35.0000 g., 0.5000 Silver 0.5626 oz. ASW, 44 mm. **Subject:** Sant Tukaram (film about poet) **Obv:** Asoka column **Edge:** Reeded

Date	Mintage	F	VF	XF	Unc	BU
2002(C)	—	—	—	—	40.00	45.00
2002(C) Proof	—	Value: 70.00				

KM# 340   100 RUPEES
35.0000 g., 0.5000 Silver 0.5626 oz. ASW, 44 mm. **Subject:** 150th Anniversary Indian Railways **Obv:** Asoka column **Rev:** Cartoon elephant holding railroad lantern **Edge:** Reeded

Date	Mintage	F	VF	XF	Unc	BU
2003(C)	—	—	—	—	40.00	45.00
2003(C) Proof	—	Value: 70.00				

KM# 318   100 RUPEES
35.0000 g., 0.5000 Silver 0.5626 oz. ASW, 44 mm. **Obv:** Asoka lion pedestal **Rev:** K. Kamaraj above life dates **Edge:** Reeded

Date	Mintage	F	VF	XF	Unc	BU
ND(2003)(B)	—	—	—	—	40.00	45.00
ND(2003)(B) Proof	—	Value: 70.00				

KM# 320   100 RUPEES
35.0000 g., 0.5000 Silver 0.5626 oz. ASW, 44 mm. **Obv:** Asoka lion pedestal **Rev:** Bust of Maharana Pratap left **Edge:** Reeded

Date	Mintage	F	VF	XF	Unc	BU
2003(B)	—	—	—	—	40.00	45.00
2003(B) Proof	—	Value: 70.00				

KM# 333   100 RUPEES
35.0000 g., 0.5000 Silver 0.5626 oz. ASW, 44 mm. **Obv:** Asoka lions **Rev:** 3/4 length military figure Veer Durgadass with spear left **Edge:** Reeded

Date	Mintage	F	VF	XF	Unc	BU
2003(B)	—	—	—	—	40.00	45.00
2003(B) Proof	—	Value: 70.00				

KM# 335 100 RUPEES

35.0000 g., 0.5000 Silver 0.5626 oz. ASW, 44 mm.
Subject: 150th Anniversary Telecommunications **Obv:** Asoka lions **Rev:** Cartoon bird standing holding cell phone
Edge: Reeded

Date	Mintage	F	VF	XF	Unc	BU
2004(B)	—	—	—	—	40.00	45.00
2004(B) Proof	—	Value: 70.00				

KM# 337 100 RUPEES

35.0000 g., 0.5000 Silver 0.5626 oz. ASW, 44 mm. **Subject:** 100th Anniversary Birth of Lal Bahadur Shasti **Obv:** Asoka lions **Rev:** Bust of Lal Bahadur Shastri 3/4 left **Edge:** Reeded

Date	Mintage	F	VF	XF	Unc	BU
ND(2004)(C)	—	—	—	—	40.00	45.00
ND(2004)(C) Proof	—	Value: 70.00				

KM# 343 100 RUPEES

35.0000 g., 0.5000 Silver 0.5626 oz. ASW, 44 mm.
Subject: 150th Anniversary Indian Postal Service **Obv:** Asoka column **Rev:** Partial postage stamp design **Edge:** Reeded

Date	Mintage	F	VF	XF	Unc	BU
2004	—	—	—	—	40.00	45.00
2004 Proof	—	Value: 70.00				

KM# 338 100 RUPEES

35.0000 g., 0.5000 Silver 0.5626 oz. ASW, 44 mm.
Subject: 75th Anniversary Dandi March **Obv:** Asoka lions **Rev:** Ghandi leading marchers **Edge:** Reeded

Date	Mintage	F	VF	XF	Unc	BU
ND(2005)(B)	—	—	—	—	40.00	45.00
ND(2005)(B) Proof	—	Value: 70.00				

KM# 339 100 RUPEES

35.0000 g., 0.5000 Silver 0.5626 oz. ASW, 44 mm. **Obv:** Asoka column **Rev:** Bust of Mahatma Basaveshwara slightly left
Edge: Reeded

Date	Mintage	F	VF	XF	Unc	BU
ND(2006)B	—	—	—	—	40.00	45.00
ND(2006)B Proof	—	Value: 70.00				

KM# 351 100 RUPEES

35.0000 g., 0.5000 Silver 0.5626 oz. ASW, 44 mm.
Subject: 75th Anniversary Indian Air Force **Obv:** Asoka column
Edge: Reeded

Date	Mintage	F	VF	XF	Unc	BU
2007(C)	—	—	—	—	40.00	45.00
2007(C) Proof	—	Value: 70.00				

KM# 369 100 RUPEES

35.0000 g., 0.5000 Silver 0.5626 oz. ASW, 44 mm.
Subject: Louis Braile, 200th Anniversary of Birth

Date	Mintage	F	VF	XF	Unc	BU
2009	—	—	—	—	40.00	45.00

PROOF SETS

KM#	Date	Mintage Identification	Issue Price	Mkt Val
PS56	2001 (4)	— KM#303, 309, 310, 311	—	125
PS57	2001 (2)	— KM#304, 312	—	80.00
PS58	2002B (3)	— KM#313, 344, 345	—	90.00
PS59	2002(C) (4)	— KM#346-349	—	130
PS60	2003 (3)	— KM#314, 319, 320	—	90.00
PS61	2003B (3)	— KM#316, 332, 333	—	90.00
PS62	2003(C) (2)	— KM#307, 340	—	80.00
PS63	ND(2003) (2)	— KM#317.1,318	—	80.00
PS64	2004 (2)	— KM#321, 343	—	75.00
PS65	2004B (2)	— KM#334, 335	—	80.00
PS66	2004(C) (2)	— KM#336, 337	—	80.00
PS67	2005B (2)	— KM#325, 338	—	80.00
PS68	2006B (2)	— KM#324, 339	—	80.00
PS69	2007 (2)	— KM#350, 351	—	80.00

The Republic of Indonesia, the world's largest archipelago, extends for more than 3,000 miles (4,827 km.) along the equator from the mainland of southeast Asia to Australia. The 17,508 islands comprising the archipelago have a combined area of 788,425 sq. mi. (1,919,440 sq. km.) and a population of 205 million, including East Timor. On August 30, 1999, the Timorese majority voted for independence. The Inter FET (International Forces for East Timor) is now in charge of controlling the chaotic situation. Capitol: Jakarta. Petroleum, timber, rubber, and coffee are exported.

Modern coinage issued by the Republic of Indonesia includes separate series for West Irian and for the Riau Archipelago, an area of small islands between Singapore and Sumatra.

MONETARY SYSTEM
100 Sen = 1 Rupiah

REPUBLIC
STANDARD COINAGE

KM# 60 50 RUPIAH

1.3600 g., Aluminum, 19.95 mm. **Obv:** National emblem
Rev: Black-naped Oriole **Edge:** Plain

Date	Mintage	F	VF	XF	Unc	BU
2001	—	—	—	—	0.30	1.00
2002	—	—	—	—	0.30	1.00

KM# 61 100 RUPIAH

1.7900 g., Aluminum, 23 mm. **Obv:** National emblem **Rev:** Palm Cockatoo **Edge:** Plain

Date	Mintage	F	VF	XF	Unc	BU
2001	—	—	—	—	0.75	1.25
2002	—	—	—	—	0.75	1.25
2003	—	—	—	—	0.75	1.25
2004	—	—	—	—	0.75	1.25
2005	—	—	—	—	0.75	1.25

KM# 66 200 RUPIAH

2.4000 g., Aluminum, 25 mm. **Obv:** National arms **Rev:** Balinese starling bird above value **Edge:** Plain

Date	Mintage	F	VF	XF	Unc	BU
2003	—	—	—	—	1.00	1.50

KM# 59   500 RUPIAH
5.3700 g., Aluminum-Bronze, 24 mm. **Obv:** National emblem
Rev: Denomination

Date	Mintage	F	VF	XF	Unc	BU
2001	—	—	—	—	1.75	2.25
2002	—	—	—	—	1.75	2.25
2003	—	—	—	—	1.75	2.25

KM# 67   500 RUPIAH
3.0500 g., Aluminum, 27.2 mm. **Obv:** National arms
Rev: Jasmine flower above value **Edge:** Segmented reeding

Date	Mintage	F	VF	XF	Unc	BU
2003	—	—	—	—	2.00	2.50

KM# 64   25000 RUPIAH
28.2800 g., 0.9250 Silver 0.8410 oz. ASW, 38.6 mm.
Subject: Centennial of Sukarno's Birth **Obv:** National arms
Rev: Uniformed bust of Sukarno **Edge:** Reeded

Date	Mintage	F	VF	XF	Unc	BU
2001 Proof	500	Value: 120				

KM# 65   500,000 RUPIAH
15.0000 g., 0.9990 Gold 0.4818 oz. AGW, 28.2 mm.
Subject: Centennial of Sukarno's Birth **Obv:** National arms
Rev: Head left **Edge:** Reeded

Date	Mintage	F	VF	XF	Unc	BU
2001 Proof	500	Value: 650				

IRAN

The Islamic Republic of Iran, located between the Caspian Sea and the Persian Gulf in southwestern Asia, has an area of 636,296 sq. mi. (1,648,000 sq. km.) and a population of 59.7 million. Capital: Tehran. Although predominantly an agricultural state, Iran depends heavily on oil for foreign exchange. Crude oil, carpets and agricultural products are exported.

In 1931 the Kingdom of Persia became known as the Kingdom of Iran. In 1979 the monarchy was toppled and an Islamic Republic proclaimed.

TITLES

دار الخلافة

Dar al-Khilafat

RULERS
Islamic Republic, SH1358-/1979-AD

MINT NAME

طهران

Tehran

تفليس

Tiflis

MINT MARKS
H - Heaton (Birmingham)
L - Leningrad (St. Petersburg)

COIN DATING
Iranian coins were dated according to the Moslem lunar calendar until March 21, 1925 (AD), when dating was switched to a new calendar based on the solar year, indicated by the notation SH. The monarchial calendar system was adopted in 1976 = MS2535 and was abandoned in 1978 = MS2537. The previously used solar year calendar was restored at that time.

MONETARY SYSTEM
20 Shahis = 1 Rial (100 Dinars)

ISLAMIC REPUBLIC

MILLED COINAGE

KM# 1260   50 RIALS
Copper-Nickel, 26 mm.   **Subject:** Shrine of Hazrat Masumah
Obv: Value and date **Rev:** Shrine within beaded circle
Edge: Reeded

Date	Mintage	F	VF	XF	Unc	BU
SH1380 (2001)	—	—	2.50	3.50	5.00	—
SH1382 (2003)	—	—	2.50	3.50	5.00	—

KM# 1266   50 RIALS
3.5100 g., Aluminum-Bronze, 20.1 mm.   **Obv:** Value and date
Rev: Hazrat Masumah Shrine **Edge:** Reeded **Mint:** Tehran

Date	Mintage	F	VF	XF	Unc	BU
SH1382(2003)	—	—	—	—	50.00	—
SH1383(2004)	—	—	—	—	2.50	—
SH1384(2005)	—	—	—	—	2.50	—
SH1385(2006)	—	—	—	—	2.50	—

KM# 1261.2   100 RIALS
Copper-Nickel, 29 mm. **Obv:** Value and date **Rev:** Shrine within designed border **Note:** Thick denomination and numerals

Date	Mintage	F	VF	XF	Unc	BU
SH1380 (2001)	—	—	—	—	6.50	—
SH1382 (2003)	—	—	—	—	6.50	—

KM# 1267   100 RIALS
4.6200 g., Aluminum-Bronze, 22.9 mm. **Obv:** Value, date divides wreath below **Rev:** Imam Reza Shrine **Edge:** Reeded
Mint: Tehran

Date	Mintage	F	VF	XF	Unc	BU
SH1382(2003)	—	—	—	—	50.00	—
SH1383(2004)	—	—	—	—	3.50	—
SH1384(2005)	—	—	—	—	3.50	—
SH1385(2006)	—	—	—	—	3.50	—

KM# 1262   250 RIALS
10.7000 g., Bi-Metallic Copper-Nickel center in Brass ring, 28.3 mm. **Obv:** Value within circle, inscription and date divide wreath **Rev:** Stylized flower within circle and wreath

Date	Mintage	F	VF	XF	Unc	BU
SH1381 (2002)	—	—	—	—	7.50	—
SH1382 (2003)	—	—	—	—	7.50	—

KM# 1268   250 RIALS
5.5000 g., Copper-Nickel, 24.6 mm. **Obv:** Value, date below divides sprays **Rev:** Stylized flower within sprays **Edge:** Plain
Mint: Tehran

Date	Mintage	F	VF	XF	Unc	BU
SH1382(2003)	—	—	—	—	50.00	—
SH1383(2004)	—	—	—	—	4.50	—
SH1384(2005)	—	—	—	—	4.50	—
SH1385(2006)	—	—	—	—	4.50	—

KM# 1268a   250 RIALS
Aluminum-Bronze **Obv:** Value, date below divides sprays **Rev:** Stylized flower within sprays **Mint:** Tehran

Date	Mintage	F	VF	XF	Unc	BU
SH1386(2007)	—	—	—	—	4.50	—

KM# 1269   500 RIALS
8.9100 g., Bi-Metallic Aluminum-Bronze center in Copper-Nickel ring, 27.1 mm. **Obv:** Value **Rev:** Bird and flowers **Edge:** Reeded
Mint: Tehran

Date	Mintage	F	VF	XF	Unc	BU
SH1382(2003)	—	—	—	—	50.00	—
SH1383(2004)	—	—	—	—	6.00	—
SH1384(2005)	—	—	—	—	6.00	—
SH1385(2006)	—	—	—	—	6.00	—

KM# 1269a   500 RIALS
Aluminum-Bronze **Obv:** Value in ornamental circle **Rev:** Bird and flowers **Mint:** Tehran

Date	Mintage	F	VF	XF	Unc	BU
SH1386(2007)	—	—	—	—	6.00	—

REFORM COINAGE

KM# 1270   250 RIALS
2.8000 g., Copper-Nickel, 18.5 mm. **Rev:** Feyziyeh School

Date	Mintage	F	VF	XF	Unc	BU
SH1388 (2009)	—	—	—	—	—	5.00

KM# 1271 500 RIALS
3.9000 g., Copper-Nickel, 20.6 mm. **Rev:** Saadi Tomb

Date	Mintage	F	VF	XF	Unc	BU
SH1388 (2009)	—	—	—	—	—	6.00

KM# 1272 1000 RIALS
5.8000 g., Copper-Nickel, 23.7 mm. **Rev:** Khajou Bridge in Isfahan

Date	Mintage	F	VF	XF	Unc	BU
SH1388 (2009)	—	—	—	—	—	12.00

BULLION COINAGE

Issued by the National Bank of Iran

KM# 1250.2 1/2 AZADI
4.0680 g., 0.9000 Gold 0.1177 oz. AGW **Obv:** Legend larger
Obv. Legend: "Spring of Freedom"

Date	Mintage	F	VF	XF	Unc	BU
SH1381 (2002)	—	—	—	—	160	—
SH1383 (2004)	—	—	—	—	160	—

IRAQ

The Republic of Iraq, historically known as Mesopotamia, is located in the Near East and is bordered by Kuwait, Iran, Turkey, Syria, Jordan and Saudi Arabia. It has an area of 167,925 sq. mi. (434,920 sq. km.) and a population of 19 million. Capital: Baghdad. The economy of Iraq is based on agriculture and petroleum. Crude oil accounted for 94 percent of the exports before the war with Iran began in 1980.

Mesopotamia was the site of a number of flourishing civilizations of antiquity - Sumeria, Assyria, Babylonia, Parthia, Persia and the Biblical cities of Ur, Ninevehand and Babylon. Desired because of its favored location, which embraced the fertile alluvial plains of the Tigris and Euphrates Rivers, Mesopotamia - 'land between the rivers'- was conquered by Cyrus the Great of Persia, Alexander of Macedonia and by Arabs who made the legendary city of Baghdad the capital of the ruling caliphate. Suleiman the Magnificent conquered Mesopotamia for Turkey in1534, and it formed part of the Ottoman Empire until 1623, and from 1638 to 1917. Great Britain, given a League of Nations mandate over the territory in 1920, recognized Iraq as a kingdom in 1922. Iraq became an independent constitutional monarchy presided over by the Hashemite family, direct descendants of the prophet Mohammed, in 1932. In 1958, the army-led revolution of July 14 overthrew the monarchy and proclaimed a republic.

MONETARY SYSTEM

Falus, Fulus	Fals, Fils	Falsan

50 Fils = 1 Dirham
200 Fils = 1 Riyal
1000 Fils = 1 Dinar (Pound)

REPUBLIC

DECIMAL COINAGE

KM# 175 25 DINARS
2.5000 g., Copper Plated Steel, 17.4 mm. **Obv:** Value **Rev:** Map
Edge: Plain

Date	Mintage	F	VF	XF	Unc	BU
AH1425-2004	—	—	—	0.30	0.75	1.00

KM# 176 50 DINARS
4.3400 g., Brass Plated Steel, 22 mm. **Obv:** Value and legend
Rev: Map **Edge:** Plain

Date	Mintage	F	VF	XF	Unc	BU
AH1425-2004	—	—	—	0.50	1.20	1.60

KM# 177 100 DINARS
4.3000 g., Stainless Steel, 22 mm. **Obv:** Value **Rev:** Map
Edge: Reeded

Date	Mintage	F	VF	XF	Unc	BU
AH1425-2004	—	—	—	0.80	2.00	2.50

IRELAND REPUBLIC

The Republic of Ireland, which occupies five-sixths of the island of Ireland located in the Atlantic Ocean west of Great Britain, has an area of 27,136 sq. mi. (70,280 sq. km.) and a population of 4.3 million. Capital: Dublin. Agriculture and dairy farming are the principal industries. Meat, livestock, dairy products and textiles are exported.

REPUBLIC

EURO COINAGE
European Union Issues

KM# 32 EURO CENT
2.2700 g., Copper Plated Steel, 16.25 mm. **Obv:** Harp
Obv. Designer: Jarlath Hayes **Rev:** Denomination and globe
Rev. Designer: Luc Luycx **Edge:** Plain

Date	Mintage	F	VF	XF	Unc	BU
2002	404,339,788	—	—	—	0.35	—
2003	67,902,182	—	—	—	0.35	—
2004	174,833,634	—	—	—	0.35	—
2005	126,964,391	—	—	—	0.35	—
2006	105,413,273	—	—	—	0.35	—
2006 Proof	5,000	Value: 15.00				
2007	18,515,843	—	—	—	0.35	—
2007 Proof	10,000	Value: 12.00				
2008	—	—	—	—	0.35	—
2009	—	—	—	—	0.35	—
2009 Proof	—	Value: 12.00				

KM# 33 2 EURO CENT
3.0000 g., Copper Plated Steel, 18.75 mm. **Obv:** Harp
Obv. Designer: Jarlath Hayes **Rev:** Denomination and globe
Rev. Designer: Luc Luycx **Edge:** Plain with groove

Date	Mintage	F	VF	XF	Unc	BU
2002	354,643,386	—	—	—	0.50	—
2003	177,290,034	—	—	—	0.50	—
2004	143,004,694	—	—	—	0.50	—
2005	72,544,884	—	—	—	0.50	—
2006	26,568,597	—	—	—	0.50	—
2006 Proof	5,000	Value: 15.00				
2007	84,291,248	—	—	—	0.50	—
2007 Proof	10,000	Value: 12.00				
2008	—	—	—	—	0.50	—
2009	—	—	—	—	0.50	—
2009 Proof	—	Value: 12.00				

KM# 34 5 EURO CENT
4.0000 g., Copper Plated Steel, 19.60 mm. **Obv:** Harp
Obv. Designer: Jarlath Hayes **Rev:** Denomination and globe
Rev. Designer: Luc Luycx **Edge:** Plain

Date	Mintage	F	VF	XF	Unc	BU
2002	456,270,848	—	—	—	0.75	—
2003	48,352,370	—	—	—	0.75	—
2004	80,354,322	—	—	—	0.75	—
2005	56,454,380	—	—	—	0.75	—
2006	88,003,370	—	—	—	0.75	—
2006 Proof	5,000	Value: 18.00				
2007	36,225,742	—	—	—	0.75	—
2007 Proof	10,000	Value: 15.00				
2008	—	—	—	—	0.75	—
2009	—	—	—	—	0.75	—
2009 Proof	—	Value: 15.00				

KM# 35 10 EURO CENT
4.0700 g., Aluminum-Bronze, 19.75 mm. **Obv:** Harp
Obv. Designer: Jarlath Hayes **Rev:** Denomination and map
Rev. Designer: Luc Luycx **Edge:** Reeded

Date	Mintage	F	VF	XF	Unc	BU
2002	275,913,000	—	—	—	1.00	—
2003	133,815,907	—	—	—	1.00	—
2004	34,092,712	—	—	—	1.00	—
2005	4,652,786	—	—	—	1.00	—
2006	9,208,411	—	—	—	1.00	—
2006 Proof	5,000	Value: 18.00				

KM# 47 10 EURO CENT
4.0700 g., Aluminum-Bronze, 19.75 mm. **Obv:** Harp **Obv. Designer:** Jarlath Hayes **Rev:** Relief map of Western Europe, stars, lines and map **Rev. Designer:** Luc Luycx **Edge:** Reeded

Date	Mintage	F	VF	XF	Unc	BU
2007	54,434,307	—	—	—	1.00	—
2007 Proof	10,000	Value: 15.00				
2008	—	—	—	—	1.00	—
2009	—	—	—	—	1.00	—
2009 Proof	—	Value: 15.00				

KM# 36 20 EURO CENT
5.7300 g., Aluminum-Bronze, 22.25 mm. **Obv:** Harp
Obv. Designer: Jarlath Hayes **Rev:** Denomination and map
Rev. Designer: Luc Luycx **Edge:** Notched

Date	Mintage	F	VF	XF	Unc	BU
2002	234,575,562	—	—	—	1.25	—
2003	57,142,221	—	—	—	1.25	—
2004	32,421,447	—	—	—	1.25	—
2005	37,798,942	—	—	—	1.25	—
2006	10,357,229	—	—	—	1.25	—
2006 Proof	5,000	Value: 20.00				

KM# 48 20 EURO CENT
5.7300 g., Aluminum-Bronze, 22.25 mm. **Obv:** Harp **Obv. Designer:** Jarlath Hayes **Rev:** Relief map of Western Europe, stars, lines and value **Rev. Designer:** Luc Luycx **Edge:** Notched

Date	Mintage	F	VF	XF	Unc	BU
2007	12,953,789	—	—	—	1.25	—
2007 Proof	10,000	Value: 18.00				
2008	—	—	—	—	1.25	—
2009	—	—	—	—	1.25	—
2009 Proof	—	Value: 18.00				

KM# 37 50 EURO CENT
7.8100 g., Aluminum-Bronze, 24.25 mm. **Obv:** Harp
Obv. Designer: Jarlath Hayes **Rev:** Denomination and map
Edge: Reeded

Date	Mintage	F	VF	XF	Unc	BU
2002	144,144,592	—	—	—	1.50	—
2003	11,811,926	—	—	—	1.50	—
2004	6,748,912	—	—	—	1.50	—
2005	17,253,568	—	—	—	1.50	—
2006	961,135	—	—	—	1.50	—
2006 Proof	5,000					

KM# 49   50 EURO CENT
7.8100 g., Aluminum-Bronze, 24.25 mm. **Obv:** Harp **Obv. Designer:** Jarlath Hayes **Rev:** Relief map of Western Europe, stars, lines and value **Rev. Designer:** Luc Luycx **Edge:** Reeded

Date	Mintage	F	VF	XF	Unc	BU
2007	4,991,002	—	—	—	1.50	—
2007 Proof	10,000	Value: 20.00				
2008	—	—	—	—	1.50	—
2009	—	—	—	—	1.50	—
2009 Proof	—	Value: 20.00				

KM# 38   EURO
7.5000 g., Bi-Metallic Copper-Nickel center in Brass ring, 23.25 mm. **Obv:** Harp **Obv. Designer:** Jarlath Hayes **Rev:** Denomination and map **Rev. Designer:** Luc Luycx **Edge:** Reeded and plain sections

Date	Mintage	F	VF	XF	Unc	BU
2002	135,139,737	—	—	—	2.75	—
2003	2,520,000	—	—	—	2.75	—
2004	1,632,990	—	—	—	2.75	—
2005	6,769,777	—	—	—	2.75	—
2006	4,023,722	—	—	—	2.75	—
2006 Proof	5,000	Value: 25.00				

KM# 50   EURO
7.5000 g., Bi-Metallic Copper-Nickel center in Brass ring, 23.25 mm. **Obv:** Harp **Obv. Designer:** Jarlath Hayes **Rev:** Relief map of Western Europe, stars, lines and value **Rev. Designer:** Luc Luycz **Edge:** Reeded and plain sections

Date	Mintage	F	VF	XF	Unc	BU
2007	1,850,049	—	—	—	2.75	—
2007 Proof	10,000	Value: 22.00				
2008	—	—	—	—	2.75	—
2009	—	—	—	—	2.75	—
2009 Proof	—	Value: 22.00				

KM# 39   2 EURO
8.5200 g., Bi-Metallic Brass center in Copper-Nickel ring, 25.7 mm. **Obv:** Harp **Obv. Designer:** Jarlath Hayes **Rev:** Denomination and map **Rev. Designer:** Luc Luycx **Edge:** Reeded with 2's and stars

Date	Mintage	F	VF	XF	Unc	BU
2002	90,548,166	—	—	—	4.00	—
2003	2,631,076	—	—	—	4.00	—
2004	3,738,186	—	—	—	4.00	—
2005	11,982,981	—	—	—	4.00	—
2006	3,860,519	—	—	—	4.00	—
2006 Proof	5,000	Value: 28.00				

KM# 51   2 EURO
8.5200 g., Bi-Metallic Brass center in Copper-Nickel ring, 25.7 mm. **Obv:** Harp **Obv. Designer:** Jarlath Hayes **Rev:** Relief map of Western Europe, stars, lines and value **Rev. Designer:** Luc Luycx **Edge:** Reeded with 2's and stars

Date	Mintage	F	VF	XF	Unc	BU
2007	—	—	—	—	4.00	—
2007 Proof	10,000	Value: 25.00				
2008	—	—	—	—	4.00	—
2009	—	—	—	—	4.00	—
2009 Proof	—	Value: 25.00				

KM# 53   2 EURO
8.4500 g., Bi-Metallic Brass senter in Copper-Nickel ring, 25.72 mm. **Subject:** 50th Anniversary Treaty of Rome **Obv:** Open treaty book **Rev:** Large value at left, modified outline of Europe at right **Edge:** Reeded with stars and 2's

Date	Mintage	F	VF	XF	Unc	BU
2007 Proof	—	Value: 25.00				
2007	—	—	—	—	—	10.00

KM# 62   2 EURO
8.5200 g., Bi-Metallic Brass center in Copper-Nickel ring, 25.72 mm. **Subject:** EMU, 10th Anniversary

Date	Mintage	F	VF	XF	Unc	BU
2009	5,000,000	—	—	—	—	10.00

KM# 40   5 EURO
14.1900 g., Copper-Nickel, 28.4 mm. **Subject:** Special Olympics **Obv:** Harp **Obv. Designer:** Jarlath Hayes **Rev:** Multicolor games logo **Edge:** Reeded

Date	Mintage	F	VF	XF	Unc	BU
2003	35,000	—	—	—	15.00	18.00
2003 Proof	25,000	Value: 25.00				

KM# 56   5 EURO
8.5200 g., 0.9250 Silver 0.2534 oz. ASW, 28 mm. **Subject:** International Polar Year **Obv:** Harp within wreath **Rev:** Ernest Shackleton, Tom Crean and The Endurance in distance **Rev. Designer:** Tom Ryan **Edge:** Reeded

Date	Mintage	F	VF	XF	Unc	BU
2008 Proof	5,000	Value: 90.00				

KM# 41   10 EURO
28.3000 g., 0.9250 Silver 0.8416 oz. ASW, 38.6 mm. **Subject:** Special Olympics **Obv:** Gold highlighted harp, 2003, Eire **Obv. Designer:** Jarlath Hayes **Rev:** Gold highlighted games logo **Edge:** Reeded

Date	Mintage	F	VF	XF	Unc	BU
2003 Proof	30,000	Value: 45.00				

KM# 42   10 EURO
28.3400 g., 0.9250 Silver 0.8428 oz. ASW, 38.6 mm. **Subject:** EU Presidency **Obv:** 2004, Eire, Harp **Rev:** Stylized Celtic swan **Rev. Designer:** Thomas Emmet Mullins **Edge:** Reeded

Date	Mintage	F	VF	XF	Unc	BU
2004 Proof	50,000	Value: 40.00				

KM# 44   10 EURO
28.2800 g., 0.9250 Silver 0.8410 oz. ASW, 38.6 mm. **Subject:** Sir William R. Hamilton **Obv:** Eire, 2005, Harp **Rev:** Triangle in circle of Greek letters used as math symbols **Rev. Designer:** Michael Guilfoyle **Edge:** Reeded

Date	Mintage	F	VF	XF	Unc	BU
2005 Proof	30,000	Value: 40.00				

KM# 45   10 EURO
28.5000 g., 0.9250 Silver 0.8475 oz. ASW, 38.6 mm. **Subject:** Samuel Beckett 1906-1989 **Obv:** 2006, Eire, Harp **Rev:** Face, value and play scene **Edge:** Reeded

Date	Mintage	F	VF	XF	Unc	BU
2006 Proof	35,000	Value: 50.00				

KM# 58   10 EURO
28.2800 g., 0.9250 Silver 0.8410 oz. ASW, 38.6 mm. **Subject:** European Culture - Ireland **Obv:** Irish map **Rev:** Celtic design **Rev. Designer:** Mary Gregoriy

Date	Mintage	F	VF	XF	Unc	BU
2007 Proof	35,000	Value: 55.00				

KM# 54   10 EURO
28.2800 g., Silver, 38.61 mm. **Subject:** Skellig Michael Island **Rev:** Birds and 12 stars above island **Rev. Legend:** SCEILIG MHICHIL **Rev. Designer:** Michael Guilfoyle

Date	Mintage	F	VF	XF	Unc	BU
2008 Proof	25,000	Value: 65.00				

KM# 60   10 EURO
28.2800 g., 0.9250 Silver 0.8410 oz. ASW, 38.61 mm. **Subject:** First currency, 80th Anniversary **Obv. Designer:** Emmet Mullins

Date	Mintage	F	VF	XF	Unc	BU
2009 Proof	15,000	Value: 55.00				

KM# 52   15 EURO
24.0000 g., 0.9250 Silver 0.7137 oz. ASW, 37 mm. **Obv:** Stylized clover with date and harp **Rev:** Ivan Mestroviae's Seated Woman with Harp design **Rev. Designer:** Damir Matavsic **Edge:** Plain **Note:** Illustration reduced.

Date	Mintage	F	VF	XF	Unc	BU
2007 Proof	10,000	Value: 75.00				

Note: 8,000 were sold in a single coin case. 1,000 were sold in a two coin set with the corresponding Croatian coin, as an Ireland set. An additional 1,000 were sold with the corresponding Croatian coin as a Croatia set. coins in both sets were the same but the packaging was different.

KM# 63 15 EURO
24.0000 g., 0.9250 Silver 0.7137 oz. ASW **Subject:** Gaelic Athletics, 125 years

Date	Mintage	F	VF	XF	Unc	BU
2009 Proof	10,000	Value: 75.00				

KM# 46 20 EURO
1.2400 g., 0.9990 Gold 0.0398 oz. AGW, 14 mm. **Subject:** Samuel Beckett 1906-1989 **Obv:** 2006, Eire, Harp **Rev:** Face, value and play **Edge:** Reeded

Date	Mintage	F	VF	XF	Unc	BU
2006 Proof	20,000	Value: 80.00				

KM# 59 20 EURO
1.2400 g., 0.9990 Gold 0.0398 oz. AGW, 14 mm. **Subject:** European Culture - Ireland **Obv:** Map **Rev:** Celtic design

Date	Mintage	F	VF	XF	Unc	BU
2007 Proof	25,000	Value: 90.00				

KM# 55 20 EURO
1.2440 g., Gold, 13.92 mm. **Subject:** Skellig Michael Island **Rev:** Birds and 12 stars above island **Rev. Legend:** SCEILIG MHICHIL

Date	Mintage	F	VF	XF	Unc	BU
2008 Proof	15,000	Value: 95.00				

KM# 61 20 EURO
1.2400 g., 0.9990 Gold 0.0398 oz. AGW, 14 mm. **Subject:** First currency, 80th Anniversary **Obv. Designer:** Emmet Mullins

Date	Mintage	F	VF	XF	Unc	BU
2009 Proof	15,000	Value: 85.00				

KM# 57 100 EURO
15.5500 g., 0.9990 Gold 0.4994 oz. AGW, 28 mm. **Subject:** International Polar Year **Obv:** Harp within wreath **Rev:** Ernest Shackleton, Tom Crean and The Endurance in distance **Rev. Designer:** Tom Ryan **Edge:** Reeded

Date	Mintage	F	VF	XF	Unc	BU
2008 Proof	—	Value: 750				

MINT SETS

KM#	Date	Mintage	Identification	Issue Price	Mkt Val
MS10	2002 (8)	20,000	KM#32-39	16.00	200
MS11	2003 (8)	30,000	KM#32-39	20.00	65.00
MS12	2003 (9)	35,000	KM#32-40 Special Olympics	25.00	90.00
MS13	2004 (8)	40,000	KM#32-39	25.00	45.00
MS14	2005 (8)	50,000	KM#32-39 Heywood Gardens	29.00	40.00
MS15	2006 (8)	40,000	KM#32-39 Glenveagh National Park and Castle	26.00	40.00
MS16	2006 (8)	—	KM#32-39 Boy Baby Set	35.00	42.50
MS17	2006 (8)	—	KM#32-39 Girl Baby Set	35.00	42.50
MS18	2007 (8)	20,000	KM#32-34, 47-51 Aran Islands	29.00	30.00
MS19	2007 (8)	—	KM#32-34, 47-51 Boy Baby Set	—	30.00
MS20	2007 (8)	—	KM#32-34, 47-51 Girl Baby Set	—	30.00
MS21	2007 (9)	20,000	KM#32-34, 47-51, 53	—	30.00
MS22	2008 (8)	30,000	KM#32-34, 47-51 Newgrange	—	30.00
MS23	2008 (8)	—	KM#32-34, 47-51 Boy Baby Set	—	30.00
MS24	2008 (8)	—	KM#32-34, 47-51 Girl Baby Set	—	30.00
MS25	2009 (8)	25,000	KM#32-34, 47-51 GAA 125th Anniversary	—	30.00
MS26	2009 (8)	—	KM#32-34, 47-51 Boy Baby Set	—	30.00
MS27	2009 (8)	—	KM#32-34, 47-51 Girl Baby Set	—	30.00

PROOF SETS

KM#	Date	Mintage	Identification	Issue Price	Mkt Val
PS6	2006 (8)	5,000	KM#32-39	125	165
PS7	2006 (2)	—	KM#45, 46	—	135
PS8	2007 (9)	10,000	KM#32-34, 47-51, 53	—	165
PS9	2009 (9)	—	KM#32-34, 47-51, 58 GAA 125th Anniversary	—	200
PS10	2009 (9)	5,000	KM#32-34, 47-51, 61.	—	225
PS11	2009 (2)	5,000	KM#60, 61. Ploughman Bank Note	—	150

ISLE OF MAN

The Isle of Man, a dependency of the British Crown located in the Irish Sea equidistant from Ireland, Scotland and England, has an area of 227 sq. mi. (588 sq. km.) and a population of 68,000. Capital: Douglas. Agriculture, dairy farming, fishing and tourism are the chief industries.

MINT MARK
PM - Pobjoy Mint

BRITISH DEPENDENCY
DECIMAL COINAGE
100 Pence = 1 Pound

KM# 1036 PENNY
3.5600 g., Bronze Plated Steel, 20.32 mm. **Ruler:** Elizabeth II **Obv:** Head with tiara right with small triskeles dividing legend **Obv. Designer:** Ian Rank-Broadley **Rev:** Ruins **Edge:** Plain

Date	Mintage	F	VF	XF	Unc	BU
2001PM AA	—	—	—	—	0.25	0.45
2001PM AC	—	—	—	—	0.25	0.45
2002PM AA	—	—	—	—	0.25	0.45
2002PM AE	—	—	—	—	0.25	0.45
2003PM AA	—	—	—	—	0.25	0.45
2003PM AE	—	—	—	—	0.25	0.45

KM# 1253 PENNY
3.5600 g., Copper Plated Steel, 20.3 mm. **Ruler:** Elizabeth II **Obv:** Head with tiara right **Rev:** Santon War Memorial **Edge:** Reeded

Date	Mintage	F	VF	XF	Unc	BU
2004 AA	—	—	—	—	0.25	0.45
2004PM AB	—	—	—	—	0.25	0.45
2005PM AA	—	—	—	—	0.25	0.45
2005PM AB	—	—	—	—	0.25	0.45
2006PM AA	—	—	—	—	0.25	0.45
2006PM AB	—	—	—	—	0.25	0.45
2007PM AA	—	—	—	—	0.25	0.45
2007PM AB	—	—	—	—	0.25	0.45

KM# 1037 2 PENCE
7.0400 g., Brass Plated Steel, 25.9 mm. **Ruler:** Elizabeth II **Obv:** Head with tiara right **Obv. Designer:** Ian Rank-Broadley **Rev:** Sailboat **Edge:** Plain

Date	Mintage	F	VF	XF	Unc	BU
2001PM AA	—	—	—	—	0.40	0.60
2001PM AB	—	—	—	—	0.40	0.60
2001PM AC	—	—	—	—	0.40	0.60
2002PM AA	—	—	—	—	0.40	0.60
2002PM AB	—	—	—	—	0.40	0.60
2002PM AC	—	—	—	—	0.40	0.60
2002PM AF	—	—	—	—	0.40	0.60
2003PM AA	—	—	—	—	0.40	0.60
2003PM AF	—	—	—	—	0.40	0.60

KM# 1254 2 PENCE
7.1200 g., Copper Plated Steel, 25.9 mm. **Ruler:** Elizabeth II **Obv:** Head with tiara right **Obv. Designer:** Ian Rank-Broadley **Rev:** Albert Tower **Edge:** Reeded

Date	Mintage	F	VF	XF	Unc	BU
2004PM AA	—	—	—	—	0.40	0.60
2004PM AB	—	—	—	—	0.40	0.60
2005PM AA	—	—	—	—	0.40	0.60
2005PM AB	—	—	—	—	0.40	0.60
2006PM AA	—	—	—	—	0.40	0.60
2006PM AB	—	—	—	—	0.40	0.60
2007PM AA	—	—	—	—	0.40	0.60
2007PM AB	—	—	—	—	0.40	0.60

KM# 1038 5 PENCE
3.2500 g., Copper-Nickel, 18 mm. **Ruler:** Elizabeth II **Obv:** Head with tiara right **Obv. Designer:** Ian Rank-Broadley **Rev:** Gaut's Cross **Edge:** Reeded

Date	Mintage	F	VF	XF	Unc	BU
2001PM AA	—	—	—	—	0.75	1.00
2002PM AA	—	—	—	—	0.75	1.00
2002PM AC	—	—	—	—	0.75	1.00
2003PM AA	—	—	—	—	0.75	1.00
2003PM AD	—	—	—	—	0.75	1.00

KM# 1255 5 PENCE
3.2500 g., Copper-Nickel, 18 mm. **Ruler:** Elizabeth II **Obv:** Head with tiara right **Obv. Designer:** Ian Rank-Broadley **Rev:** Tower of Refuge **Edge:** Reeded

Date	Mintage	F	VF	XF	Unc	BU
2004 AA	—	—	—	—	0.75	1.00
2004PM AB	—	—	—	—	0.75	1.00
2005PM AA	—	—	—	—	0.75	1.00
2005PM AB	—	—	—	—	0.75	1.00
2006PM AA	—	—	—	—	0.75	1.00
2006PM AB	—	—	—	—	0.75	1.00
2007PM AA	—	—	—	—	0.75	1.00
2007PM AB	—	—	—	—	0.75	1.00

KM# 1039 10 PENCE
6.5000 g., Copper-Nickel, 24.5 mm. **Ruler:** Elizabeth II **Obv:** Head with tiara right **Obv. Designer:** Ian Rank-Broadley **Rev:** Cathedral **Edge:** Reeded

Date	Mintage	F	VF	XF	Unc	BU
2001PM AA	—	—	—	—	1.00	1.50
2002PM AA	—	—	—	—	1.00	1.50
2003PM AA	—	—	—	—	1.00	1.50

KM# 1256 10 PENCE
6.5000 g., Copper-Nickel, 24.5 mm. **Ruler:** Elizabeth II **Obv:** Head with tiara right **Obv. Designer:** Ian Rank-Broadley **Rev:** Chicken Rock Lighthouse **Edge:** Reeded

Date	Mintage	F	VF	XF	Unc	BU
2004PM AA	—	—	—	—	1.00	1.50
2004PM AB	—	—	—	—	1.00	1.50
2005PM AA	—	—	—	—	1.00	1.50
2005PM AB	—	—	—	—	1.00	1.50
2006PM AA	—	—	—	—	1.00	1.50
2006PM AB	—	—	—	—	1.00	1.50
2007PM AA	—	—	—	—	1.00	1.50
2007PM AB	—	—	—	—	1.00	1.50

KM# 1040 20 PENCE
5.0000 g., Copper-Nickel, 21.4 mm. **Ruler:** Elizabeth II **Subject:** Rushen Abbey **Obv:** Head with tiara right **Obv. Designer:** Ian Rank-Broadley **Rev:** Monk writing **Edge:** Plain **Shape:** 7-sided

Date	Mintage	F	VF	XF	Unc	BU
2001PM AA	—	—	—	—	1.50	2.00
2002PM AA	—	—	—	—	1.50	2.00
2002PM AB	—	—	—	—	1.50	2.00
2003PM AA	—	—	—	—	1.50	2.00
2003PM BA	—	—	—	—	1.50	2.00

KM# 1257 20 PENCE
5.0000 g., Copper-Nickel, 21.5 mm. **Ruler:** Elizabeth II **Obv:** Head with tiara right **Obv. Designer:** Ian Rank-Broadley **Rev:** Castle Rushen Clock **Edge:** Plain **Shape:** 7-sided

Date	Mintage	F	VF	XF	Unc	BU
2004PM AA	—	—	—	—	1.50	2.00
2004PM AB	—	—	—	—	1.50	2.00
2005PM AA	—	—	—	—	1.50	2.00
2005PM AB	—	—	—	—	1.50	2.00
2006PM AA	—	—	—	—	1.50	2.00
2006PM AB	—	—	—	—	1.50	2.00
2007PM AA	—	—	—	—	1.50	2.00
2007PM AB	—	—	—	—	1.50	2.00

KM# 1041 50 PENCE
8.0000 g., Copper-Nickel, 27.3 mm. **Ruler:** Elizabeth II **Obv:** Head with tiara right **Obv. Designer:** Ian Rank-Broadley **Rev:** Stylized crucifix **Edge:** Plain **Shape:** 7-sided

Date	Mintage	F	VF	XF	Unc	BU
2001PM AA	—	—	—	—	2.25	2.75
2002PM AA	—	—	—	—	2.25	2.75
2003PM AA	—	—	—	—	2.25	2.75

KM# 1105 50 PENCE
8.0000 g., Copper-Nickel, 27.3 mm. **Ruler:** Elizabeth II **Subject:** Christmas **Obv:** Head with tiara right **Obv. Designer:** Ian Rank-Broadley **Rev:** Postman and children **Edge:** Plain **Shape:** 7-sided

Date	Mintage	F	VF	XF	Unc	BU
2001PM BB	30,000	—	—	—	4.50	6.00

KM# 1105a 50 PENCE
8.0000 g., 0.9250 Silver 0.2379 oz. ASW, 27.3 mm. **Ruler:** Elizabeth II **Obv:** Head with tiara right **Rev:** Postman and children **Edge:** Plain **Shape:** 7-sided

Date	Mintage	F	VF	XF	Unc	BU
2001PM Proof	5,000	Value: 35.00				

KM# 1105b 50 PENCE
8.0000 g., 0.9167 Gold 0.2358 oz. AGW, 27.3 mm. **Ruler:** Elizabeth II **Obv:** Head with tiara right **Rev:** Postman and children **Edge:** Plain **Shape:** 7-sided

Date	Mintage	F	VF	XF	Unc	BU
2001PM Proof	250	Value: 500				

KM# 1160 50 PENCE
8.0000 g., Copper-Nickel, 27.3 mm. **Ruler:** Elizabeth II **Subject:** Christmas **Obv:** Head with tiara right **Obv. Designer:** Ian Rank-Broadley **Rev:** Scrooge in bed **Edge:** Plain **Shape:** 7-sided

Date	Mintage	F	VF	XF	Unc	BU
2002BB PM	30,000	—	—	—	4.50	6.00

KM# 1160a 50 PENCE
8.0000 g., 0.9250 Silver 0.2379 oz. ASW, 27.3 mm. **Ruler:** Elizabeth II **Subject:** Christmas **Obv:** Head with tiara right **Rev:** Scrooge in bed **Edge:** Plain **Shape:** 7-sided

Date	Mintage	F	VF	XF	Unc	BU
2002PM Proof	5,000	Value: 35.00				

KM# 1160b 50 PENCE
8.0000 g., 0.9167 Gold 0.2358 oz. AGW, 27.3 mm. **Ruler:** Elizabeth II **Subject:** Christmas **Obv:** Head with tiara right **Rev:** Scrooge in bed **Edge:** Plain **Shape:** 7-sided

Date	Mintage	F	VF	XF	Unc	BU
2002PM Proof	250	Value: 500				

KM# 1183 50 PENCE
8.0000 g., Copper-Nickel, 27.3 mm. **Ruler:** Elizabeth II **Obv:** Head with tiara right **Obv. Designer:** Ian Rank-Broadley **Rev:** "The Snowman and James" **Edge:** Plain **Shape:** 7-sided

Date	Mintage	F	VF	XF	Unc	BU
2003PM BB	10,000	—	—	—	6.50	8.00

KM# 1183a 50 PENCE
8.0000 g., 0.9250 Silver 0.2379 oz. ASW, 27.3 mm. **Ruler:** Elizabeth II **Subject:** Christmas **Obv:** Head with tiara right **Rev:** "The Snowman and James" **Edge:** Plain **Shape:** 7-sided

Date	Mintage	F	VF	XF	Unc	BU
2003PM Proof	3,000	Value: 35.00				

KM# 1183b 50 PENCE
8.0000 g., 0.9167 Gold 0.2358 oz. AGW, 27.3 mm. **Ruler:** Elizabeth II **Obv:** Head with tiara right **Rev:** "The Snowman and James" **Edge:** Plain **Shape:** 7-sided

Date	Mintage	F	VF	XF	Unc	BU
2003PM Proof	100	Value: 500				

KM# 1258 50 PENCE
8.0000 g., Copper-Nickel, 21.5 mm. **Ruler:** Elizabeth II **Obv:** Head with tiara right **Obv. Designer:** Ian Rank-Broadley **Rev:** Milner's Tower **Edge:** Plain **Shape:** 7-sided

Date	Mintage	F	VF	XF	Unc	BU
2004PM AA	—	—	—	—	2.25	2.75
2004PM AB	—	—	—	—	2.25	2.75
2005PM AA	—	—	—	—	2.25	2.75
2005PM AB	—	—	—	—	2.25	2.75
2006PM AA	—	—	—	—	2.25	2.75
2006PM AB	—	—	—	—	2.25	2.75
2007PM AA	—	—	—	—	2.25	2.75
2007PM AB	—	—	—	—	2.25	2.75

KM# 1293 50 PENCE
Copper-Nickel **Ruler:** Elizabeth II **Obv:** Queen's new portrait **Rev:** Tourist Trophy Races

Date	Mintage	F	VF	XF	Unc	BU
2004PM AA	—	—	—	—	6.00	7.00

KM# 1262 50 PENCE
8.0000 g., Copper-Nickel, 27.3 mm. **Ruler:** Elizabeth II **Subject:** Christmas **Obv:** Head with tiara right **Obv. Designer:** Ian Rank-Broadley **Rev:** Laxey Wheel **Edge:** Plain **Shape:** 7-sided

Date	Mintage	F	VF	XF	Unc	BU
2004PM AA	—	—	—	—	6.00	7.00
2004PM BA	30,000	—	—	—	6.00	7.00

KM# 1262a 50 PENCE
9.1852 g., 0.9250 Silver 0.2732 oz. ASW, 27.3 mm. **Ruler:** Elizabeth II **Subject:** Christmas **Obv:** Head with tiara right **Rev:** Laxey Wheel **Edge:** Plain **Shape:** 7-sided

Date	Mintage	F	VF	XF	Unc	BU
2004PM Proof	5,000	Value: 35.00				

KM# 1262b 50 PENCE
15.4074 g., 0.9167 Gold 0.4541 oz. AGW, 27.3 mm. **Ruler:** Elizabeth II **Subject:** Christmas **Obv:** Head with tiara right **Rev:** Laxey Wheel **Edge:** Plain **Shape:** 7-sided

Date	Mintage	F	VF	XF	Unc	BU
2004PM Proof	250	Value: 625				

KM# 1294 50 PENCE
Copper-Nickel **Ruler:** Elizabeth II **Obv:** Queen's new portrait **Rev:** Christmas scene

Date	Mintage	F	VF	XF	Unc	BU
2005	—	—	—	—	6.50	8.00

KM# 1320.1 50 PENCE
8.0000 g., Copper-Nickel, 27.3 mm. **Ruler:** Elizabeth II **Series:** 12 Days of Christmas **Obv:** Head with tiara right **Obv. Legend:** ISLE OF MAN - ELIZABETH II **Obv. Designer:** Ian Rank-Broadley **Rev:** Partridge in a Pear Tree **Rev. Legend:** CHRISTMAS **Edge:** Plain **Shape:** 7-sided

Date	Mintage	F	VF	XF	Unc	BU
2005PM AA	30,000	—	—	—	—	16.00

KM# 1320.2 50 PENCE
8.0000 g., Copper-Nickel, 27.3 mm. **Ruler:** Elizabeth II **Series:** 12 Days of Christmas **Obv:** Head with tiara right **Obv. Legend:** ISLE OF MAN - ELIZABETH II **Obv. Designer:** Ian Rank-Broadley **Rev:** Partidge in a Pear Tree multicolor **Rev. Legend:** CHRISTMAS **Edge:** Plain **Shape:** 7-sided

Date	Mintage	F	VF	XF	Unc	BU
2005PM	Inc. above	—	—	—	—	20.00

KM# 1320.1a 50 PENCE
9.1825 g., 0.9250 Silver 0.2731 oz. ASW, 27.3 mm. **Ruler:** Elizabeth II **Series:** 12 Days of Christmas **Obv:** Head with tiara right **Obv. Legend:** ISLE OF MAN - ELIZABETH II **Obv. Designer:** Ian Rank-Broadley **Rev:** Partridge in a Pear Tree **Rev. Legend:** CHRISTMAS **Edge:** Plain **Shape:** 7-sided

Date	Mintage	F	VF	XF	Unc	BU
2005PM Proof	—	Value: 35.00				

KM# 1320.2a 50 PENCE
8.0000 g., 0.9250 Silver 0.2379 oz. ASW, 27.3 mm. **Ruler:** Elizabeth II **Series:** 12 Days of Christmas **Obv:** Head with tiara right **Obv. Legend:** ISLE OF MAN - ELIZABETH II **Obv. Designer:** Ian Rank-Broadley **Rev:** Partridge in a Pear Tree multicolor **Rev. Legend:** CHRISTMAS **Edge:** Plain **Shape:** 7-sided

Date	Mintage	F	VF	XF	Unc	BU
2005PM Proof	—	Value: 35.00				

KM# 1320b 50 PENCE
0.9167 Gold, 27.3 mm. **Ruler:** Elizabeth II **Series:** 12 Days of Christmas **Obv:** Head with tiara right **Obv. Legend:** ISLE OF MAN - ELIZABETH II **Obv. Designer:** Ian Rank-Broadley **Rev:** Partridge in a Pear Tree **Rev. Legend:** CHRISTMAS **Edge:** Plain **Shape:** 7-sided

Date	Mintage	F	VF	XF	Unc	BU
2005PM Proof	—	Value: 600				

KM# 1321.1 50 PENCE
8.0000 g., Copper-Nickel, 27.3 mm. **Ruler:** Elizabeth II **Series:** 12 Days of Christmas **Obv:** Head with tiara right **Obv. Legend:** ISLE OF MAN - ELIZABETH II **Obv. Designer:** Ian Rank-Broadley **Rev:** Two Turtle Doves **Rev. Legend:** CHRISTMAS **Edge:** Plain **Shape:** 7-sided

Date	Mintage	F	VF	XF	Unc	BU
2006PM AA	—	—	—	—	6.00	7.00

KM# 1321.2 50 PENCE
8.0000 g., Copper-Nickel, 27.3 mm. **Ruler:** Elizabeth II **Series:** 12 Days of Christmas **Obv:** Head with tiara right **Obv. Legend:** ISLE OF MAN - ELIZABETH II **Obv. Designer:** Ian Rank-Broadley **Rev:** 2 Turtle Doves multicolor **Rev. Legend:** CHRISTMAS **Edge:** Plain **Shape:** 7-sided

Date	Mintage	F	VF	XF	Unc	BU
2006PM	—	—	—	—	8.00	10.00

KM# 1321.1a 50 PENCE
0.9250 Silver, 27.3 mm. **Ruler:** Elizabeth II **Series:** 12 Days of Christmas **Obv:** Head with tiara right **Obv. Legend:** ISLE OF MAN - ELIZABETH II **Obv. Designer:** Ian Rank-Broadley **Rev:** Two Turtle Doves **Rev. Legend:** CHRISTMAS **Edge:** Plain **Shape:** 7-sided

Date	Mintage	F	VF	XF	Unc	BU
2006PM Proof	—	Value: 35.00				

KM# 1321.2a 50 PENCE
0.9250 Silver, 27.3 mm. **Ruler:** Elizabeth II **Series:** 12 Days of Christmas **Obv:** Head with tiara right **Obv. Legend:** ISLE OF MAN - ELIZABETH II **Obv. Designer:** Ian Rank-Broadley **Rev:** 2 Turtle Doves multicolor **Rev. Legend:** CHRISTMAS **Edge:** Plain **Shape:** 7-sided

Date	Mintage	F	VF	XF	Unc	BU
2006PM Proof	—	Value: 40.00				

KM# 1321b 50 PENCE
0.9167 Gold, 27.3 mm. **Ruler:** Elizabeth II **Series:** 12 Days of Christmas **Obv:** Head with tiara right **Obv. Legend:** ISLE OF MAN - ELIZABETH II **Obv. Designer:** Ian Rank-Broadley **Rev:** 2 Turtle Doves **Rev. Legend:** CHRISTMAS **Edge:** Plain **Shape:** 7-sided

Date	Mintage	F	VF	XF	Unc	BU
2006PM Proof	—	Value: 600				

KM# 1322.1 50 PENCE
8.0000 g., Copper-Nickel, 27.3 mm. **Ruler:** Elizabeth II **Series:** 12 Days of Christmas **Obv:** Head with tiara right **Obv. Legend:** ISLE OF MAN - ELIZABETH II **Obv. Designer:** Ian Rank-Broadley **Rev:** 3 French Hens **Rev. Legend:** CHRISTMAS **Edge:** Plain **Shape:** 7-sided

Date	Mintage	F	VF	XF	Unc	BU
2007PM	—	—	—	—	6.00	7.00

KM# 1322.2 50 PENCE
8.0000 g., Copper-Nickel, 27.3 mm. **Ruler:** Elizabeth II **Series:** 12 Days of Christmas **Obv:** Head with tiara right **Obv. Legend:** ISLE OF MAN - ELIZABETH II **Obv. Designer:** Ian Rank-Broadley **Rev:** 3 French Hens multicolor **Rev. Legend:** CHRISTMAS **Edge:** Plain **Shape:** 7-sided

Date	Mintage	F	VF	XF	Unc	BU
2007PM	—	—	—	—	8.00	10.00

KM# 1322.1a 50 PENCE
0.9250 Silver, 27.3 mm. **Ruler:** Elizabeth II **Series:** 12 Days of Christmas **Obv:** Head with tiara right **Obv. Legend:** ISLE OF MAN - ELIZABETH II **Obv. Designer:** Ian Rank-Broadley **Rev:** 3 French Hens **Rev. Legend:** CHRISTMAS **Edge:** Plain **Shape:** 7-sided

Date	Mintage	F	VF	XF	Unc	BU
2007PM Proof	—	Value: 35.00				

KM# 1322.2a 50 PENCE
0.9250 Silver, 27.3 mm. **Ruler:** Elizabeth II **Series:** 12 Days of Christmas **Obv:** Head with tiara right **Obv. Legend:** ISLE OF MAN - ELIZABETH II **Obv. Designer:** Ian Rank-Broadley **Rev:** 3 French Hens multicolor **Rev. Legend:** CHRISTMAS **Edge:** Plain **Shape:** 7-sided

Date	Mintage	F	VF	XF	Unc	BU
2007PM Proof	—	Value: 40.00				

KM# 1322b 50 PENCE
0.9167 Gold, 27.3 mm. **Ruler:** Elizabeth II **Series:** 12 Days of Christmas **Obv:** Head with tiara right **Obv. Legend:** ISLE OF MAN - ELIZABETH II **Obv. Designer:** Ian Rank-Broadley **Rev:** 3 French Hens **Rev. Legend:** CHRISTMAS **Edge:** Plain **Shape:** 7-sided

Date	Mintage	F	VF	XF	Unc	BU
2007PM Proof	250	Value: 600				

KM# 1393 50 PENCE
8.0000 g., Copper-Nickel, 27.3 mm. **Ruler:** Elizabeth II **Subject:** Christmas **Shape:** 7-sided

Date	Mintage	F	VF	XF	Unc	BU
2008	—	—	—	—	10.00	12.00

KM# 1372 50 PENCE
8.0000 g., Copper-Nickel, 27.3 mm. **Ruler:** Elizabeth II **Subject:** Honda, 50th Anniversary TT

Date	Mintage	F	VF	XF	Unc	BU
2009	—	—	—	—	—	9.00

KM# 1394 50 PENCE
8.0000 g., Copper-Nickel, 27.3 mm. **Ruler:** Elizabeth II **Subject:** Christmas **Shape:** 7-sided

Date	Mintage	F	VF	XF	Unc	BU
2009	—	—	—	—	10.00	12.00

KM# 1128 60 PENCE
Bi-Metallic Bronze finished base metal with a silver finished rotator on reverse., 38.6 mm. **Ruler:** Elizabeth II **Subject:** Euro Currency Converter **Obv:** Head with tiara right **Obv. Designer:** Ian Rank-Broadley **Rev:** Rotating map with cut out arrow revealing the Euro equivalent of the country's currency to which the arrow is pointed **Edge:** Reeded

Date	Mintage	F	VF	XF	Unc	BU
2002	15,000	—	—	—	20.00	22.50

KM# 1042 POUND
9.5000 g., Brass, 22.5 mm. **Ruler:** Elizabeth II **Subject:** Millennium Bells **Obv:** Head with tiara right **Obv. Designer:** Ian Rank-Broadley **Rev:** Triskeles and three bells **Edge:** Reeded and plain sections

Date	Mintage	F	VF	XF	Unc	BU
2001PM AA	—	—	—	—	4.00	5.00
2002PM AA	—	—	—	—	4.00	5.00
2003PM AA	—	—	—	—	4.00	5.00

KM# 1259 POUND
9.5000 g., Nickel-Brass, 22.5 mm. **Ruler:** Elizabeth II **Obv:** Head with tiara right **Obv. Designer:** Ian Rank-Broadley **Rev:** St. John's Chapel **Edge:** Reeded and Plain Sections

Date	Mintage	F	VF	XF	Unc	BU
2004PM	—	—	—	—	4.00	5.00
2004PM AA	—	—	—	—	4.00	5.00
2004PM AB	—	—	—	—	4.00	5.00
2004PM AC	—	—	—	—	4.00	5.00
2005PM AA	—	—	—	—	4.00	5.00
2005PM AB	—	—	—	—	4.00	5.00
2006PM AA	—	—	—	—	4.00	5.00
2006PM AB	—	—	—	—	4.00	5.00
2007PM AA	—	—	—	—	4.00	5.00
2007PM AB	—	—	—	—	4.00	5.00

KM# 1043 2 POUNDS
12.0000 g., Bi-Metallic Copper-Nickel center in Brass ring, 28.4 mm. **Ruler:** Elizabeth II **Subject:** Thorwald's Cross **Obv:** Head with tiara right within beaded circle **Obv. Designer:** Ian Rank-Broadley **Rev:** Ancient drawing within circle **Edge:** Reeded

Date	Mintage	F	VF	XF	Unc	BU
2001PM AA	—	—	—	—	6.50	7.50
2002PM AA	—	—	—	—	6.50	7.50
2003PM AA	—	—	—	—	6.50	7.50
2003PM AB	—	—	—	—	6.50	7.50

KM# 1260 2 POUNDS
12.0000 g., Bi-Metallic Copper-Nickel center in Brass ring, 28.4 mm. **Ruler:** Elizabeth II **Obv:** Head with tiara right **Obv. Designer:** Ian Rank-Broadley **Rev:** Round Tower of Peel Castle **Edge:** Reeded

Date	Mintage	F	VF	XF	Unc	BU
2004PM AA	—	—	—	—	6.50	7.50
2005PM AA	—	—	—	—	6.50	7.50
2006PM AA	—	—	—	—	6.50	7.50
2007PM AA	—	—	—	—	6.50	7.50
2007PM AB	—	—	—	—	6.50	7.50

KM# 1044 5 POUNDS
20.1000 g., Virenium, 36.5 mm. **Ruler:** Elizabeth II **Subject:** St. Patrick's Hymn **Obv:** Head with tiara right **Obv. Designer:** Ian Rank-Broadley **Rev:** Stylized cross design **Edge:** Reeded and plain sections

Date	Mintage	F	VF	XF	Unc	BU
2001PM AA	—	—	—	—	15.00	16.50
2002PM AA	—	—	—	—	15.00	16.50
2003PM AA	—	—	—	—	15.00	16.50

KM# 1261 5 POUNDS
20.1000 g., Virenium, 36 mm. **Ruler:** Elizabeth II **Obv:** Head with tiara right **Obv. Designer:** Ian Rank-Broadley **Rev:** Laxey Wheel **Edge:** Reeded

Date	Mintage	F	VF	XF	Unc	BU
2004PM AA	—	—	—	—	15.00	16.50
2005PM AA	—	—	—	—	15.00	16.50
2006PM AA	—	—	—	—	15.00	16.50
2007PM AA	—	—	—	—	15.00	16.50
2007PM AB	—	—	—	—	15.00	16.50

CROWN SERIES

Pobjoy Mint Key

KM# 1129 1/32 CROWN
1.0000 g., 0.9720 Gold 0.0312 oz. AGW, 9.8 mm. **Ruler:** Elizabeth II **Subject:** Queen's Golden Jubilee **Obv:** Head with tiara right **Obv. Designer:** Ian Rank-Broadley **Rev:** Seated crowned Queen holding sceptre at her coronation **Edge:** Plain

Date	Mintage	F	VF	XF	Unc	BU
2002 Prooflike	—	—	—	—	—	40.00

KM# 1058 1/25 CROWN
1.2440 g., 0.9999 Gold 0.0400 oz. AGW, 13.92 mm. **Ruler:** Elizabeth II **Subject:** Year of the Snake **Obv:** Bust with tiara right **Obv. Designer:** Ian Rank-Broadley **Rev:** Snake **Edge:** Reeded

Date	Mintage	F	VF	XF	Unc	BU
2001 Proof	20,000	Value: 55.00				

KM# 1067 1/25 CROWN
1.2440 g., 0.9999 Gold 0.0400 oz. AGW, 13.9 mm. **Ruler:** Elizabeth II **Subject:** Somali Kittens **Obv:** Head with tiara right **Obv. Designer:** Ian Rank-Broadley **Rev:** Two kittens **Edge:** Reeded

Date	Mintage	F	VF	XF	Unc	BU
2001	—	—	—	—	—	55.00
2001 Proof	1,000	Value: 60.00				

KM# 1067a 1/25 CROWN
1.2441 g., 0.9995 Platinum 0.0400 oz. APW, 13.9 mm. **Ruler:** Elizabeth II **Subject:** Somali Kittens **Obv:** Head with tiara right **Obv. Designer:** Ian Rank-Broadley **Rev:** Two kittens **Edge:** Reeded

Date	Mintage	F	VF	XF	Unc	BU
2001	—	—	—	—	—	95.00

KM# 1086 1/25 CROWN
1.2441 g., 0.9999 Gold 0.0400 oz. AGW, 13.9 mm. **Ruler:** Elizabeth II **Subject:** Harry Potter **Obv:** Bust with tiara right **Obv. Designer:** Ian Rank-Broadley **Rev:** Boy with magic wand **Edge:** Reeded

Date	Mintage	F	VF	XF	Unc	BU
2001 Proof	10,000	Value: 55.00				

KM# 1088 1/25 CROWN
1.2441 g., 0.9999 Gold 0.0400 oz. AGW, 13.9 mm. **Ruler:** Elizabeth II **Series:** Harry Potter **Subject:** Journey to Hogwarts School **Obv:** Bust with tiara right **Obv. Designer:** Ian Rank-Broadley **Rev:** Boat full of children going to Hogwarts School **Edge:** Reeded

Date	Mintage	F	VF	XF	Unc	BU
2001 Proof	10,000	Value: 55.00				

KM# 1090 1/25 CROWN
1.2441 g., 0.9999 Gold 0.0400 oz. AGW, 13.9 mm. **Ruler:** Elizabeth II **Series:** Harry Potter **Subject:** First Quidditch Match **Obv:** Bust with tiara right **Obv. Designer:** Ian Rank-Broadley **Rev:** Harry flying a broom **Edge:** Reeded

Date	Mintage	F	VF	XF	Unc	BU
2001 Proof	10,000	Value: 55.00				

KM# 1092 1/25 CROWN
1.2441 g., 0.9999 Gold 0.0400 oz. AGW, 13.9 mm. **Ruler:** Elizabeth II **Series:** Harry Potter **Subject:** Birth of Norbert **Obv:** Bust with tiara right **Obv. Designer:** Ian Rank-Broadley **Edge:** Reeded

Date	Mintage	F	VF	XF	Unc	BU
2001 Proof	10,000	Value: 55.00				

KM# 1094 1/25 CROWN
1.2441 g., 0.9999 Gold 0.0400 oz. AGW, 13.9 mm. **Ruler:** Elizabeth II **Series:** Harry Potter **Subject:** School **Obv:** Bust with tiara right **Obv. Designer:** Ian Rank-Broadley **Rev:** Harry in Potions class **Edge:** Reeded

Date	Mintage	F	VF	XF	Unc	BU
2001 Proof	10,000	Value: 55.00				

KM# 1096 1/25 CROWN
1.2441 g., 0.9999 Gold 0.0400 oz. AGW, 13.9 mm. **Ruler:** Elizabeth II **Series:** Harry Potter **Subject:** Keys **Obv:** Bust with tiara right **Obv. Designer:** Ian Rank-Broadley **Rev:** Harry chasing a quidditch **Edge:** Reeded

Date	Mintage	F	VF	XF	Unc	BU
2001 Proof	10,000	Value: 55.00				

KM# 1098 1/25 CROWN
1.2441 g., 0.9999 Gold 0.0400 oz. AGW, 13.9 mm. **Ruler:** Elizabeth II **Subject:** Year of the Horse **Obv:** Bust with tiara right **Obv. Designer:** Ian Rank-Broadley **Rev:** Two horses **Edge:** Reeded

Date	Mintage	F	VF	XF	Unc	BU
2002 Proof	20,000	Value: 55.00				

KM# 1107 1/25 CROWN
1.2440 g., 0.9990 Gold 0.0400 oz. AGW, 13.92 mm. **Ruler:** Elizabeth II **Subject:** Bengal Cat **Obv:** Head with tiara right **Obv. Designer:** Ian Rank-Broadley **Rev:** Cat and kitten **Edge:** Reeded

Date	Mintage	F	VF	XF	Unc	BU
2002	—	—	—	—	—	55.00
2002 Proof	1,000	Value: 60.00				

KM# 1107a 1/25 CROWN
1.2440 g., 0.9990 Platinum 0.0400 oz. APW, 13.92 mm. **Ruler:** Elizabeth II **Subject:** Bengal Cat **Obv:** Head with tiara right **Obv. Designer:** Ian Rank-Broadley **Rev:** Cat and kitten **Edge:** Reeded

Date	Mintage	F	VF	XF	Unc	BU
2002 Proof	—	Value: 85.00				

KM# 1145 1/25 CROWN
1.2440 g., 0.9999 Gold 0.0400 oz. AGW, 13.92 mm. **Ruler:** Elizabeth II **Subject:** Harry Potter Series **Obv:** Bust with tiara right **Obv. Designer:** Ian Rank-Broadley **Rev:** Harry and friends making Polyjuice potion **Edge:** Reeded

Date	Mintage	F	VF	XF	Unc	BU
2002PM Proof	10,000	Value: 55.00				

KM# 1143 1/25 CROWN
1.2440 g., 0.9999 Gold 0.0400 oz. AGW, 13.92 mm. **Ruler:** Elizabeth II **Subject:** Harry Potter **Obv:** Bust with tiara right **Obv. Designer:** Ian Rank-Broadley **Rev:** Tom Riddle twirling Harry's magic wand **Edge:** Reeded

Date	Mintage	F	VF	XF	Unc	BU
2002PM Proof	10,000	Value: 55.00				

KM# 1147 1/25 CROWN
1.2440 g., 0.9999 Gold 0.0400 oz. AGW **Ruler:** Elizabeth II **Subject:** Harry Potter **Obv:** Bust with tiara right **Obv. Designer:** Ian Rank-Broadley **Rev:** Harry arrives at the Burrow in a flying car **Edge:** Reeded

Date	Mintage	F	VF	XF	Unc	BU
2002PM Proof	10,000	Value: 55.00				

KM# 1149 1/25 CROWN
1.2440 g., 0.9999 Gold 0.0400 oz. AGW, 13.92 mm. **Ruler:** Elizabeth II **Subject:** Harry Potter Series **Obv:** Bust with tiara right **Obv. Designer:** Ian Rank-Broadley **Rev:** Harry retrieves Gryffindor sword from snake **Edge:** Reeded

Date	Mintage	F	VF	XF	Unc	BU
2002PM Proof	10,000	Value: 55.00				

KM# 1151 1/25 CROWN
1.2240 g., 0.9999 Gold 0.0393 oz. AGW, 13.92 mm. **Ruler:** Elizabeth II **Series:** Harry Potter **Obv:** Bust with tiara right **Obv. Designer:** Ian Rank-Broadley **Rev:** Harry and Ron encounter the spider Aragog **Edge:** Reeded

Date	Mintage	F	VF	XF	Unc	BU
2002PM Proof	10,000	Value: 55.00				

KM# 1153 1/25 CROWN
1.2440 g., 0.9999 Gold 0.0400 oz. AGW, 13.92 mm. **Ruler:** Elizabeth II **Series:** Harry Potter **Obv:** Bust with tiara right **Obv. Designer:** Ian Rank-Broadley **Rev:** Harry in hospital **Edge:** Reeded

Date	Mintage	F	VF	XF	Unc	BU
2002PM Proof	10,000	Value: 55.00				

KM# 1186 1/25 CROWN
1.2440 g., 0.9999 Gold 0.0400 oz. AGW, 13.9 mm. **Ruler:** Elizabeth II **Subject:** Lord of the Rings **Obv:** Bust with tiara right **Obv. Designer:** Ian Rank-Broadley **Rev:** Man with short sword **Edge:** Reeded

Date	Mintage	F	VF	XF	Unc	BU
2003PM Proof	6,000	Value: 55.00				

KM# 1161 1/25 CROWN
1.2440 g., 0.9999 Gold 0.0400 oz. AGW, 13.92 mm. **Ruler:** Elizabeth II **Subject:** Cat **Obv:** Head with tiara right **Obv. Designer:** Ian Rank-Broadley **Rev:** Two Balinese kittens **Edge:** Reeded

Date	Mintage	F	VF	XF	Unc	BU
2003PM	—	—	—	—	—	55.00
2003PM Proof	—	Value: 60.00				

KM# 1161a 1/25 CROWN
1.2440 g., 0.9995 Platinum 0.0400 oz. APW, 13.92 mm. **Ruler:** Elizabeth II **Subject:** Cat **Obv:** Head with tiara right **Obv. Designer:** Ian Rank-Broadley **Rev:** Two Balinese kittens **Edge:** Reeded

Date	Mintage	F	VF	XF	Unc	BU
2003PM Proof	—	Value: 85.00				

KM# 1167 1/25 CROWN
1.2441 g., 0.9999 Gold 0.0400 oz. AGW, 13.9 mm. **Ruler:** Elizabeth II **Subject:** Year of the Goat **Obv:** Head with tiara right **Obv. Designer:** Ian Rank-Broadley **Rev:** Three goats **Edge:** Reeded

Date	Mintage	F	VF	XF	Unc	BU
2003PM Proof	20,000	Value: 55.00				

KM# 1203 1/25 CROWN
1.2440 g., 0.9999 Gold 0.0400 oz. AGW, 14 mm. **Ruler:** Elizabeth II **Obv:** Bust with tiara right **Obv. Designer:** Ian Rank-Broadley **Rev:** Harry Potter and patron fighting off a spectre **Edge:** Reeded

Date	Mintage	F	VF	XF	Unc	BU
2004PM Proof	2,500	Value: 60.00				

KM# 1205 1/25 CROWN
1.2440 g., 0.9999 Gold 0.0400 oz. AGW, 14 mm. **Ruler:** Elizabeth II **Obv:** Bust with tiara right **Obv. Designer:** Ian Rank-Broadley **Rev:** Harry Potter in the shrieking shack **Edge:** Reeded

Date	Mintage	F	VF	XF	Unc	BU
2004PM Proof	2,500	Value: 60.00				

KM# 1207 1/25 CROWN
1.2440 g., 0.9999 Gold 0.0400 oz. AGW, 14 mm. **Ruler:** Elizabeth II **Obv:** Bust with tiara right **Obv. Designer:** Ian Rank-Broadley **Rev:** Harry Potter and Professor Dumbledore **Edge:** Reeded

Date	Mintage	F	VF	XF	Unc	BU
2004PM Proof	2,500	Value: 60.00				

KM# 1209 1/25 CROWN
1.2440 g., 0.9999 Gold 0.0400 oz. AGW, 14 mm. **Ruler:** Elizabeth II **Obv:** Bust with tiara right **Obv. Designer:** Ian Rank-Broadley **Rev:** Sirius Black on flying griffin **Edge:** Reeded

Date	Mintage	F	VF	XF	Unc	BU
2004PM Proof	2,500	Value: 60.00				

KM# 1211 1/25 CROWN
1.2440 g., 0.9999 Gold 0.0400 oz. AGW, 14 mm. **Ruler:** Elizabeth II **Obv:** Head with tiara right **Obv. Designer:** Ian Rank-Broadley **Rev:** Three Olympic Swimmers **Edge:** Reeded

Date	Mintage	F	VF	XF	Unc	BU
2004PM Proof	5,000	Value: 55.00				

KM# 1213 1/25 CROWN
1.2440 g., 0.9999 Gold 0.0400 oz. AGW, 14 mm. **Ruler:** Elizabeth II **Obv:** Head with tiara right **Obv. Designer:** Ian Rank-Broadley **Rev:** Three Olympic Cyclists **Edge:** Reeded

Date	Mintage	F	VF	XF	Unc	BU
2004PM Proof	5,000	Value: 55.00				

KM# 1215 1/25 CROWN
1.2440 g., 0.9999 Gold 0.0400 oz. AGW, 14 mm. **Ruler:** Elizabeth II **Obv:** Head with tiara right **Obv. Designer:** Ian Rank-Broadley **Rev:** Three Olympic Runners **Edge:** Reeded

Date	Mintage	F	VF	XF	Unc	BU
2004PM Proof	5,000	Value: 55.00				

KM# 1217 1/25 CROWN
1.2440 g., 0.9999 Gold 0.0400 oz. AGW, 14 mm. **Ruler:** Elizabeth II **Obv:** Head with tiara right **Obv. Designer:** Ian Rank-Broadley **Rev:** Three Olympic Sail Boarders **Edge:** Reeded

Date	Mintage	F	VF	XF	Unc	BU
2004PM Proof	5,000	Value: 55.00				

KM# 1240 1/25 CROWN
1.2440 g., 0.9999 Gold 0.0400 oz. AGW, 14 mm. **Ruler:** Elizabeth II **Obv:** Head with tiara right **Obv. Designer:** Ian Rank-Broadley **Rev:** Monkey **Edge:** Reeded

Date	Mintage	F	VF	XF	Unc	BU
2004PM Proof	20,000	Value: 55.00				

KM# 1247 1/25 CROWN
1.2440 g., 0.9999 Gold 0.0400 oz. AGW, 14 mm. **Ruler:** Elizabeth II **Obv:** Head with tiara right **Obv. Designer:** Ian Rank-Broadley **Rev:** Two Tonkinese cats **Edge:** Reeded

Date	Mintage	F	VF	XF	Unc	BU
2004PM	—	—	—	—	—	55.00
2004PM Proof	1,000	Value: 60.00				

KM# 1269 1/25 CROWN
1.2440 g., 0.9999 Gold 0.0400 oz. AGW, 13.92 mm. **Ruler:** Elizabeth II **Obv:** Bust with tiara right **Obv. Designer:** Ian Rank-Broadley **Rev:** Himalayan cat and two kittens **Edge:** Reeded

Date	Mintage	F	VF	XF	Unc	BU
2005PM Proof	—	Value: 60.00				

KM# 1269a 1/25 CROWN
1.2440 g., 0.9950 Platinum 0.0398 oz. APW, 13.92 mm. **Ruler:** Elizabeth II **Obv:** Bust with tiara right **Obv. Designer:** Ian Rank-Broadley **Rev:** Himalayan cat and two kittens **Edge:** Reeded

Date	Mintage	F	VF	XF	Unc	BU
2005PM Proof	—	Value: 90.00				

KM# 1340 1/25 CROWN
1.2441 g., 0.9999 Gold 0.0400 oz. AGW **Ruler:** Elizabeth II **Obv:** Bust with tiara right **Obv. Designer:** Ian Rank-Broadley **Rev:** Three Exotic Shorthair cats sitting facing **Edge:** Reeded

Date	Mintage	F	VF	XF	Unc	BU
2006PM	—	—	—	—	—	100

KM# 1343 1/25 CROWN
1.2441 g., 0.9999 Gold 0.0400 oz. AGW **Ruler:** Elizabeth II **Obv:** Bust with tiara right **Obv. Legend:** ELIZABETH II - ISLE OF MAN **Obv. Designer:** Ian Rank-Broadley **Rev:** Ragdoll cat with two kittens sitting facing **Edge:** Reeded

Date	Mintage	F	VF	XF	Unc	BU
2007PM	—	—	—	—	—	100

KM# 1349 1/25 CROWN
1.2440 g., 0.9999 Gold 0.0400 oz. AGW **Ruler:** Elizabeth II **Subject:** The tale of Peter Rabbit **Obv:** Bust with tiara right **Obv. Legend:** ELIZABETH II - ISLE OF MAN **Obv. Designer:** Ian Rank-Broadley **Rev:** Peter walking with friends **Edge:** Reeded

Date	Mintage	F	VF	XF	Unc	BU
2007PM	—	—	—	—	—	110

KM# 1308 1/25 CROWN
1.2441 g., 0.9999 Gold 0.0400 oz. AGW **Ruler:** Elizabeth II **Subject:** 100th Anniversary of Scouting **Obv:** Bust with tiara right **Obv. Legend:** ELIZABETH II - ISLE OF MAN **Rev:** 3/4 length figure of Robert Baden-Powell standing facing 3/4 left, Fleur-de-lys below, images of scouting at left and right **Rev. Legend:** CENTENARY OF SCOUTING **Edge:** Reeded

Date	Mintage	F	VF	XF	Unc	BU
2007PM Proof	—	Value: 300				

KM# 1314 1/25 CROWN
1.2200 g., 0.9999 Gold AGW 0.0400 0.0392 oz. AGW, 13.92 mm. **Ruler:** Elizabeth II **Obv:** Bust with tiara right **Obv. Legend:** ELIZABETH II - ISLE OF MAN **Rev:** Two swans facing **Edge:** Reeded

Date	Mintage	F	VF	XF	Unc	BU
2007 Proof	10,000	Value: 55.00				

KM# 1383 1/25 CROWN
1.2400 g., 0.9999 Gold 0.0399 oz. AGW, 13.92 mm. **Ruler:** Elizabeth II **Obv:** Bust right **Rev:** Chinchilla cat and kitten

Date	Mintage	F	VF	XF	Unc	BU
2009	—	—	—	—	—	60.00
2009 Proof	1,000	Value: 75.00				

KM# 1387 1/25 CROWN
1.2400 g., 0.9950 Platinum 0.0397 oz. APW, 13.92 mm. **Ruler:** Elizabeth II **Obv:** Bust right **Rev:** Chinchilla cat and kitten

Date	Mintage	F	VF	XF	Unc	BU
2009	—	—	—	—	—	75.00

KM# 1059 1/10 CROWN
3.1100 g., 0.9999 Gold 0.1000 oz. AGW, 17.95 mm. **Ruler:** Elizabeth II **Subject:** Year of the Snake **Obv:** Bust with tiara right **Obv. Designer:** Ian Rank-Broadley **Rev:** Snake **Edge:** Reeded

Date	Mintage	F	VF	XF	Unc	BU
2001 Proof	15,000	Value: 125				

KM# 1068 1/10 CROWN
3.1100 g., 0.9999 Gold 0.1000 oz. AGW, 18 mm. **Ruler:** Elizabeth II **Obv:** Head with tiara right **Obv. Designer:** Ian Rank-Broadley **Rev:** Somali kittens **Edge:** Reeded

Date	Mintage	F	VF	XF	Unc	BU
2001	—	—	—	—	—	125
2001 Proof	1,000	Value: 130				

KM# 1068a 1/10 CROWN
3.1100 g., 0.9995 Platinum 0.0999 oz. APW, 18 mm. **Ruler:** Elizabeth II **Obv:** Head with tiara right **Obv. Designer:** Ian Rank-Broadley **Rev:** Somali kittens **Edge:** Reeded

Date	Mintage	F	VF	XF	Unc	BU
2001 Proof	—	Value: 200				

KM# 1328 1/10 CROWN
3.1100 g., 0.9990 Gold 0.0999 oz. AGW **Ruler:** Elizabeth II **Subject:** Harry Potter **Obv:** Bust right **Obv. Designer:** Ian Rank-Broadley **Rev:** Boy with magic wand **Edge:** Reeded

Date	Mintage	F	VF	XF	Unc	BU
2001 Proof	7,500	Value: 125				

KM# 1329 1/10 CROWN
3.1100 g., 0.9990 Gold 0.0999 oz. AGW **Ruler:** Elizabeth II **Subject:** Harry Potter - Journey to Hogwarts **Obv:** Bust right **Rev:** Boat full of children going to Hogwarts School **Edge:** Reeded

Date	Mintage	F	VF	XF	Unc	BU
2001 Proof	7,500	Value: 125				

KM# 1330 1/10 CROWN
3.1100 g., 0.9990 Gold 0.0999 oz. AGW **Ruler:** Elizabeth II **Subject:** Harry Potter **Obv:** Bust right **Obv. Designer:** Ian Rank-Broadley **Rev:** Harry flying on a broomstick **Edge:** Reeded

Date	Mintage	F	VF	XF	Unc	BU
2001 Proof	7,500	Value: 125				

KM# 1331 1/10 CROWN
3.1100 g., 0.9990 Gold 0.0999 oz. AGW **Ruler:** Elizabeth II **Subject:** Harry Potter **Obv:** Bust right **Obv. Designer:** Ian Rank-Broadley **Rev:** Birth of Norbert the dragon **Edge:** Reeded

Date	Mintage	F	VF	XF	Unc	BU
2001 Proof	7,500	Value: 125				

KM# 1332 1/10 CROWN
3.1100 g., 0.9990 Gold 0.0999 oz. AGW **Ruler:** Elizabeth II **Subject:** Harry Potter **Obv:** Bust right **Obv. Designer:** Ian Rank-Broadley **Rev:** Harry in Potions class **Edge:** Reeded

Date	Mintage	F	VF	XF	Unc	BU
2001 Proof	7,500	Value: 125				

KM# 1333 1/10 CROWN
3.1100 g., 0.9990 Gold 0.0999 oz. AGW **Ruler:** Elizabeth II **Subject:** Harry Potter **Obv:** Bust right **Obv. Designer:** Ian Rank-Broadley **Rev:** Harry chasing a snitch **Edge:** Reeded

Date	Mintage	F	VF	XF	Unc	BU
2001 Proof	7,500	Value: 125				

KM# 1099 1/10 CROWN
3.1100 g., 0.9999 Gold 0.1000 oz. AGW, 17.95 mm. **Ruler:** Elizabeth II **Subject:** Year of the Horse **Obv:** Bust with tiara right **Obv. Designer:** Ian Rank-Broadley **Rev:** Two horses **Edge:** Reeded

Date	Mintage	F	VF	XF	Unc	BU
2002 Proof	15,000	Value: 125				

KM# 1155 1/10 CROWN
3.1100 g., 0.9999 Gold 0.1000 oz. AGW, 17.95 mm. **Ruler:** Elizabeth II **Subject:** Queen's Golden Jubilee **Obv:** Queen's portrait **Rev:** Queen on horse **Edge:** Reeded

Date	Mintage	F	VF	XF	Unc	BU
2002PM Proof	500	Value: 125				

KM# 1108 1/10 CROWN
3.1100 g., 0.9990 Gold 0.0999 oz. AGW, 17.95 mm. **Ruler:** Elizabeth II **Subject:** Bengal Cat **Obv:** Head with tiara right **Obv. Designer:** Ian Rank-Broadley **Rev:** Cat and kitten **Edge:** Reeded

Date	Mintage	VG	F	VF	XF	Unc
2002	—	—	—	—	—	—
2002 Proof	—	Value: 130				

KM# 1108a 1/10 CROWN
3.1100 g., 0.9990 Platinum 0.0999 oz. APW, 17.95 mm. **Ruler:** Elizabeth II **Subject:** Bengal Cat **Obv:** Head with tiara right **Obv. Designer:** Ian Rank-Broadley **Rev:** Cat and kitten **Edge:** Reeded

Date	Mintage	F	VF	XF	Unc	BU
2002	—	—	—	—	—	210

KM# 1162 1/10 CROWN
3.1100 g., 0.9999 Gold 0.1000 oz. AGW, 17.95 mm. **Ruler:** Elizabeth II **Subject:** Cat **Obv:** Head with tiara right **Obv. Designer:** Ian Rank-Broadley **Rev:** Two Balinese kittens **Edge:** Reeded

Date	Mintage	F	VF	XF	Unc	BU
2003PM	—	—	—	—	—	125
2003PM Proof	—	Value: 130				

KM# 1162a 1/10 CROWN
3.1100 g., 0.9995 Platinum 0.0999 oz. APW, 17.95 mm. **Ruler:** Elizabeth II **Subject:** Cat **Obv:** Head with tiara right **Obv. Designer:** Ian Rank-Broadley **Rev:** Two Balinese kittens **Edge:** Reeded

Date	Mintage	F	VF	XF	Unc	BU
2003PM	—	—	—	—	—	210

KM# 1168 1/10 CROWN
3.1100 g., 0.9999 Gold 0.1000 oz. AGW, 17.95 mm. **Ruler:** Elizabeth II **Subject:** Year of the Goat **Obv:** Bust with tiara right **Obv. Designer:** Ian Rank-Broadley **Rev:** Three goats **Edge:** Reeded

Date	Mintage	F	VF	XF	Unc	BU
2003PM Proof	—	Value: 125				

KM# 1187 1/10 CROWN
3.1100 g., 0.9999 Gold 0.1000 oz. AGW, 18 mm. **Ruler:** Elizabeth II **Subject:** Lord of the Rings **Obv:** Bust with tiara right **Obv. Designer:** Ian Rank-Broadley **Rev:** Aragorn with broad sword **Edge:** Reeded

Date	Mintage	F	VF	XF	Unc	BU
2003PM Proof	4,500	Value: 125				

KM# 1241 1/10 CROWN
3.1100 g., 0.9999 Gold 0.1000 oz. AGW, 18 mm. **Ruler:** Elizabeth II **Obv:** Head with tiara right **Obv. Designer:** Ian Rank-Broadley **Rev:** Monkey **Edge:** Reeded

Date	Mintage	F	VF	XF	Unc	BU
2004PM Proof	15,000	Value: 125				

KM# 1248 1/10 CROWN
3.1100 g., 0.9999 Gold 0.1000 oz. AGW, 18 mm. **Ruler:** Elizabeth II **Obv:** Head with tiara right **Obv. Designer:** Ian Rank-Broadley **Rev:** Two Tonkinese cats **Edge:** Reeded

Date	Mintage	F	VF	XF	Unc	BU
2004PM	—	—	—	—	—	125
2004PM Proof	1,000	Value: 130				

KM# 1270 1/10 CROWN
3.1100 g., 0.9999 Gold 0.1000 oz. AGW, 18 mm. **Ruler:** Elizabeth II **Obv:** Bust with tiara right **Obv. Designer:** Ian Rank-Broadley **Rev:** Himalayan cat and two kittens **Edge:** Reeded

Date	Mintage	F	VF	XF	Unc	BU
2005PM Proof	—	Value: 125				

KM# 1270a 1/10 CROWN
3.1100 g., 0.9950 Platinum 0.0995 oz. APW, 18 mm. **Ruler:** Elizabeth II **Obv:** Queen Elizabeth II **Rev:** Himalayan cat and two kittens **Edge:** Reeded

Date	Mintage	F	VF	XF	Unc	BU
2005PM Proof	—	Value: 235				

KM# 1341 1/10 CROWN
3.1100 g., 0.9999 Gold 0.1000 oz. AGW **Ruler:** Elizabeth II **Obv:** Bust with tiara right **Obv. Designer:** Ian Rank-Broadley **Rev:** Three Exotic Shorthair cats sitting facing **Edge:** Reeded

Date	Mintage	F	VF	XF	Unc	BU
2006PM	—	—	—	—	—	170

KM# 1350 1/10 CROWN
3.1100 g., 0.9999 Gold 0.1000 oz. AGW **Ruler:** Elizabeth II **Subject:** The Tale of Peter Rabbit **Obv:** Bust with tiara right **Obv. Legend:** ELIZABETH II - ISLE OF MAN **Obv. Designer:** Ian Rank-Broadley **Rev:** Peter walking with friends **Edge:** Reeded

Date	Mintage	F	VF	XF	Unc	BU
2007PM	—	—	—	—	—	180

KM# 1344 1/10 CROWN
3.1100 g., 0.9999 Gold 0.1000 oz. AGW **Ruler:** Elizabeth II **Obv:** Bust with tiara right **Obv. Legend:** ELIZABETH II - ISLE OF MAN **Obv. Designer:** Ian Rank-Broadley **Rev:** Ragdoll cat with two kittens sitting facing **Edge:** Reeded

Date	Mintage	F	VF	XF	Unc	BU
2007PM	—	—	—	—	—	170

KM# 1382 1/10 CROWN
3.1100 g., 0.9999 Gold 0.1000 oz. AGW, 17.95 mm. **Ruler:** Elizabeth II **Obv:** Bust right **Rev:** Chinchilla cat and kitten

Date	Mintage	F	VF	XF	Unc	BU
2009 Proof	1,000	Value: 150				
2009	—	—	—	—	—	130

KM# 1386 1/10 CROWN
3.1100 g., 0.9950 Platinum 0.0995 oz. APW, 17.95 mm. **Ruler:** Elizabeth II **Obv:** Bust right **Rev:** Chinchilla cat and kitten

Date	Mintage	F	VF	XF	Unc	BU
2009	—	—	—	—	—	175

KM# 1060 1/5 CROWN
6.2200 g., 0.9999 Gold 0.1999 oz. AGW, 22 mm. **Ruler:** Elizabeth II **Subject:** Year of the Snake **Obv:** Bust with tiara right **Obv. Designer:** Ian Rank-Broadley **Rev:** Snake **Edge:** Reeded

Date	Mintage	F	VF	XF	Unc	BU
2001 Proof	12,000	Value: 250				

KM# 1069 1/5 CROWN
6.2200 g., 0.9999 Gold 0.1999 oz. AGW, 22 mm. **Ruler:** Elizabeth II **Obv:** Head with tiara right **Obv. Designer:** Ian Rank-Broadley **Rev:** Two Somali kittens **Edge:** Reeded

Date	Mintage	F	VF	XF	Unc	BU
2001	—	—	—	—	—	250
2001 Proof	1,000	Value: 260				

KM# 1069a 1/5 CROWN
6.2200 g., 0.9995 Platinum 0.1999 oz. APW, 22 mm. **Ruler:** Elizabeth II **Obv:** Head with tiara right **Obv. Designer:** Ian Rank-Broadley **Rev:** Somali kittens **Edge:** Reeded

Date	Mintage	F	VF	XF	Unc	BU
2001	—	—	—	—	—	400

KM# 1074 1/5 CROWN
6.2200 g., 0.9999 Gold 0.1999 oz. AGW, 22 mm. **Ruler:** Elizabeth II **Subject:** Queen Mother **Obv:** Head with tiara right **Obv. Designer:** Ian Rank-Broadley **Rev:** 1948 Silver wedding anniversary **Edge:** Reeded

Date	Mintage	F	VF	XF	Unc	BU
2001 Proof	5,000	Value: 250				

KM# 1075 1/5 CROWN
6.2200 g., 0.9999 Gold 0.1999 oz. AGW, 22 mm. **Ruler:** Elizabeth II **Subject:** Queen Mother **Obv:** Head with tiara right **Obv. Designer:** Ian Rank-Broadley **Rev:** 1948 holding baby Prince Charles **Edge:** Reeded

Date	Mintage	F	VF	XF	Unc	BU
2001 Proof	5,000	Value: 250				

KM# 1078 1/5 CROWN
6.2200 g., 0.9999 Gold 0.1999 oz. AGW, 22 mm. **Ruler:** Elizabeth II **Subject:** Martin Frobisher **Obv:** Head with tiara right **Obv. Designer:** Ian Rank-Broadley **Rev:** Portrait, ship and map **Edge:** Reeded

Date	Mintage	F	VF	XF	Unc	BU
2001 Proof	5,000	Value: 250				

KM# 1079 1/5 CROWN
6.2200 g., 0.9999 Gold 0.1999 oz. AGW, 22 mm. **Ruler:** Elizabeth II **Subject:** Ronald Amundsen **Obv:** Head with tiara right **Obv. Designer:** Ian Rank-Broadley **Rev:** Portrait, ship and dirigible **Edge:** Reeded

Date	Mintage	F	VF	XF	Unc	BU
2001 Proof	5,000	Value: 250				

KM# 1082 1/5 CROWN

6.2200 g., 0.9999 Gold 0.1999 oz. AGW, 22 mm. **Ruler:** Elizabeth II **Subject:** Queen's 75th Birthday **Obv:** Head with tiara right **Obv. Designer:** Ian Rank-Broadley **Rev:** Flower bouquet with a tiny diamond mounted on the bow of the ribbon **Edge:** Reeded

Date	Mintage	F	VF	XF	Unc	BU
2001 Proof	2,000	Value: 300				

KM# 1334 1/5 CROWN

6.1500 g., 0.9990 Gold 0.1975 oz. AGW, 21.78 mm. **Ruler:** Elizabeth II **Subject:** Harry Potter **Obv:** Bust right **Obv. Designer:** Ian Rank-Broadley **Rev:** Harry with magic wand **Edge:** Reeded

Date	Mintage	F	VF	XF	Unc	BU
2001 Proof	5,000	Value: 250				

KM# 1335 1/5 CROWN

6.1500 g., 0.9990 Gold 0.1975 oz. AGW, 21.78 mm. **Ruler:** Elizabeth II **Subject:** Harry Potter - Journey to Hogwarts School **Obv:** Bust right **Obv. Designer:** Ian Rank-Broadley **Rev:** Boat full of children going to Hogwarts School **Edge:** Reeded

Date	Mintage	F	VF	XF	Unc	BU
2001 Proof	5,000	Value: 250				

KM# 1336 1/5 CROWN

6.1500 g., 0.9990 Gold 0.1975 oz. AGW, 21.78 mm. **Ruler:** Elizabeth II **Subject:** Harry Potter - First Quidditch Match **Obv:** Bust right **Obv. Designer:** Ian Rank-Broadley **Rev:** Harry flying a broom in a quidditch match **Edge:** Reeded

Date	Mintage	F	VF	XF	Unc	BU
2001 Proof	5,000	Value: 250				

KM# 1337 1/5 CROWN

6.1500 g., 0.9990 Gold 0.1975 oz. AGW, 21.78 mm. **Ruler:** Elizabeth II **Subject:** Harry Potter **Obv:** Bust right **Obv. Designer:** Ian Rank-Broadley **Rev:** Birth of Norbert, the dragon **Edge:** Reeded

Date	Mintage	F	VF	XF	Unc	BU
2001 Proof	5,000	Value: 250				

KM# 1338 1/5 CROWN

6.1500 g., 0.9990 Gold 0.1975 oz. AGW, 21.78 mm. **Ruler:** Elizabeth II **Subject:** Harry Potter **Obv:** Bust right **Obv. Designer:** Ian Rank-Broadley **Rev:** Harry in Potions class **Edge:** Reeded

Date	Mintage	F	VF	XF	Unc	BU
2001 Proof	5,000	Value: 250				

KM# 1339 1/5 CROWN

6.1500 g., 0.9990 Gold 0.1975 oz. AGW, 21.78 mm. **Ruler:** Elizabeth II **Subject:** Harry Potter **Obv:** Bust right **Obv. Designer:** Ian Rank-Broadley **Rev:** Harry chasing a jeweled snitch **Edge:** Reeded

Date	Mintage	F	VF	XF	Unc	BU
2001 Proof	5,000	Value: 250				

KM# 1156 1/5 CROWN

6.2200 g., 0.9990 Gold 0.1998 oz. AGW, 22 mm. **Ruler:** Elizabeth II **Subject:** Queen's Golden Jubilee **Obv:** Queen's portrait **Rev:** Queen on horse **Edge:** Reeded

Date	Mintage	F	VF	XF	Unc	BU
2002PM Proof	500	Value: 265				

KM# 1117 1/5 CROWN

6.2200 g., 0.9990 Gold 0.1998 oz. AGW, 22 mm. **Ruler:** Elizabeth II **Subject:** Queen Mother's Love of Horses **Obv:** Bust with tiara right **Obv. Designer:** Ian Rank-Broadley **Rev:** Queen Mother and horse **Edge:** Reeded

Date	Mintage	F	VF	XF	Unc	BU
2002 Proof	5,000	Value: 250				

KM# 1109 1/5 CROWN

6.2200 g., 0.9990 Gold 0.1998 oz. AGW, 22 mm. **Ruler:** Elizabeth II **Subject:** Bengal Cat **Obv:** Head with tiara right **Obv. Designer:** Ian Rank-Broadley **Rev:** Cat and kitten **Edge:** Reeded

Date	Mintage	VG	F	VF	XF	Unc
2002	—	—	—	—	—	—
2002 Proof	1,000	Value: 260				

KM# 1109a 1/5 CROWN

6.2200 g., 0.9990 Platinum 0.1998 oz. APW, 22 mm. **Ruler:** Elizabeth II **Subject:** Bengal Cat **Obv:** Head with tiara right **Obv. Designer:** Ian Rank-Broadley **Rev:** Cat and kitten **Edge:** Reeded

Date	Mintage	F	VF	XF	Unc	BU
2002	—	—	—	—	—	400

KM# 1100 1/5 CROWN

6.2200 g., 0.9999 Gold 0.1999 oz. AGW, 22 mm. **Ruler:** Elizabeth II **Subject:** Year of the Horse **Obv:** Bust with tiara right **Obv. Designer:** Ian Rank-Broadley **Rev:** Two horses **Edge:** Reeded

Date	Mintage	F	VF	XF	Unc	BU
2002 Proof	12,000	Value: 250				

KM# 1113 1/5 CROWN

6.2200 g., 0.9990 Gold 0.1998 oz. AGW, 22 mm. **Ruler:** Elizabeth II **Subject:** Olympics - Salt Lake City **Obv:** Bust with tiara right **Obv. Designer:** Ian Rank-Broadley **Rev:** Skier, torch and flag **Edge:** Reeded

Date	Mintage	F	VF	XF	Unc	BU
2002 Proof	5,000	Value: 250				

KM# 1114 1/5 CROWN

6.2200 g., 0.9990 Gold 0.1998 oz. AGW **Ruler:** Elizabeth II **Subject:** Olympics - Salt Lake City **Obv:** Bust with tiara righ t **Obv. Designer:** Ian Rank-Broadley **Rev:** Bobsled, torch and stadium **Edge:** Reeded

Date	Mintage	F	VF	XF	Unc	BU
2002 Proof	5,000	Value: 250				

KM# 1120 1/5 CROWN

6.2200 g., 0.9990 Gold 0.1998 oz. AGW, 22 mm. **Ruler:** Elizabeth II **Subject:** World Cup 2002 Japan - Korea **Obv:** Bust with tiara right **Obv. Designer:** Ian Rank-Broadley **Rev:** Player running right **Edge:** Reeded

Date	Mintage	F	VF	XF	Unc	BU
2002 Proof	5,000	Value: 250				

KM# 1122 1/5 CROWN

6.2200 g., 0.9990 Gold 0.1998 oz. AGW, 22 mm. **Ruler:** Elizabeth II **Subject:** World Cup 2002 Japan - Korea **Obv:** Bust with tiara right **Obv. Designer:** Ian Rank-Broadley **Rev:** Player kicking to right **Edge:** Reeded

Date	Mintage	F	VF	XF	Unc	BU
2002 Proof	5,000	Value: 250				

KM# 1124 1/5 CROWN

6.2200 g., 0.9990 Gold 0.1998 oz. AGW, 22 mm. **Ruler:** Elizabeth II **Subject:** World Cup 2002 Japan - Korea **Obv:** Head with tiara right **Obv. Designer:** Ian Rank-Broadley **Rev:** Player kicking to left **Edge:** Reeded

Date	Mintage	F	VF	XF	Unc	BU
2002 Proof	5,000	Value: 250				

KM# 1126 1/5 CROWN

6.2200 g., 0.9990 Gold 0.1998 oz. AGW, 22 mm. **Ruler:** Elizabeth II **Subject:** World Cup 2002 Japan - Korea **Obv:** Head with tiara right **Obv. Designer:** Ian Rank-Broadley **Rev:** Player running to left **Edge:** Reeded

Date	Mintage	F	VF	XF	Unc	BU
2002 Proof	5,000	Value: 250				

KM# 1130 1/5 CROWN

6.2200 g., 0.3750 Gold 0.0750 oz. AGW, 22 mm. **Ruler:** Elizabeth II **Subject:** Elizabeth II's Golden Jubilee **Obv:** Bust with tiara right **Obv. Designer:** Ian Rank-Broadley **Rev:** Seated crowned Queen holding scepter at her coronation **Edge:** Reeded

Date	Mintage	F	VF	XF	Unc	BU
2002 Proof	2,002	Value: 95.00				

KM# 1132 1/5 CROWN

6.2200 g., 0.3750 Gold 0.0750 oz. AGW, 22 mm. **Ruler:** Elizabeth II **Subject:** Elizabeth II's Golden Jubilee **Obv:** Bust with tiara right **Obv. Designer:** Ian Rank-Broadley **Rev:** Queen on horse **Edge:** Reeded

Date	Mintage	F	VF	XF	Unc	BU
2002 Proof	2,002	Value: 95.00				

KM# 1134 1/5 CROWN

6.2200 g., 0.3750 Gold 0.0750 oz. AGW, 22 mm. **Ruler:** Elizabeth II **Subject:** Elizabeth II's Golden Jubilee **Obv:** Head with tiara right **Obv. Designer:** Ian Rank-Broadley **Rev:** Queen with dog **Edge:** Reeded

Date	Mintage	F	VF	XF	Unc	BU
2002 Proof	2,002	Value: 95.00				

KM# 1136 1/5 CROWN

6.2200 g., 0.3750 Gold 0.0750 oz. AGW, 22 mm. **Ruler:** Elizabeth II **Subject:** Elizabeth II's Golden Jubilee **Obv:** Bust with tiara right **Obv. Designer:** Ian Rank-Broadley **Rev:** Queen at war memorial **Edge:** Reeded

Date	Mintage	F	VF	XF	Unc	BU
2002 Proof	2,002	Value: 95.00				

KM# 1138 1/5 CROWN

6.2200 g., 0.9990 Gold 0.1998 oz. AGW, 22 mm. **Ruler:** Elizabeth II **Subject:** Queen Mother **Obv:** Bust with tiara right **Obv. Designer:** Ian Rank-Broadley **Rev:** Queen Mother and Castle May **Edge:** Reeded

Date	Mintage	F	VF	XF	Unc	BU
2002 Proof	5,000	Value: 250				

KM# 1140 1/5 CROWN

6.2200 g., 0.9999 Gold 0.1999 oz. AGW, 22 mm. **Ruler:** Elizabeth II **Subject:** Princess Diana **Obv:** Bust with tiara right **Obv. Designer:** Ian Rank-Broadley **Rev:** Diana's portrait **Edge:** Reeded

Date	Mintage	F	VF	XF	Unc	BU
2002 Proof	5,000	Value: 250				

KM# 1163 1/5 CROWN

6.2200 g., 0.9999 Gold 0.1999 oz. AGW, 22 mm. **Ruler:** Elizabeth II **Subject:** Cat **Obv:** Head with tiara right **Obv. Designer:** Ian Rank-Broadley **Rev:** Two Balinese kittens **Edge:** Reeded

Date	Mintage	F	VF	XF	Unc	BU
2003PM	—	—	—	—	—	250
2003PM Proof	—	Value: 260				

KM# 1163a 1/5 CROWN

6.2200 g., 0.9995 Platinum 0.1999 oz. APW, 22 mm. **Ruler:** Elizabeth II **Subject:** Cat **Obv:** Head with tiara right **Obv. Designer:** Ian Rank-Broadley **Rev:** Two Balinese kittens **Edge:** Reeded

Date	Mintage	F	VF	XF	Unc	BU
2003PM	—	—	—	—	—	400

KM# 1169 1/5 CROWN

6.2200 g., 0.9999 Gold 0.1999 oz. AGW, 22 mm. **Ruler:** Elizabeth II **Subject:** Year of the Goat **Obv:** Bust with tiara right **Obv. Designer:** Ian Rank-Broadley **Rev:** Three goats **Edge:** Reeded

Date	Mintage	F	VF	XF	Unc	BU
2003PM Proof	—	Value: 250				

KM# 1175 1/5 CROWN

6.2200 g., 0.9999 Gold 0.1999 oz. AGW, 22 mm. **Ruler:** Elizabeth II **Subject:** Olympics **Obv:** Bust with tiara right **Obv. Designer:** Ian Rank-Broadley **Rev:** Swimmers **Edge:** Reeded

Date	Mintage	F	VF	XF	Unc	BU
2003PM Proof	5,000	Value: 250				

KM# 1177 1/5 CROWN

6.2200 g., 0.9999 Gold 0.1999 oz. AGW, 22 mm. **Ruler:** Elizabeth II **Subject:** Olympics **Obv:** Bust with tiara right **Obv. Designer:** Ian Rank-Broadley **Rev:** Runners **Edge:** Reeded

Date	Mintage	F	VF	XF	Unc	BU
2003PM Proof	5,000	Value: 250				

KM# 1179 1/5 CROWN

6.2200 g., 0.9999 Gold 0.1999 oz. AGW, 22 mm. **Ruler:** Elizabeth II **Subject:** Olympics **Obv:** Bust with tiara right **Obv. Designer:** Ian Rank-Broadley **Rev:** Bicyclists **Edge:** Reeded

Date	Mintage	F	VF	XF	Unc	BU
2003PM Proof	5,000	Value: 250				

KM# 1181 1/5 CROWN

6.2200 g., 0.9999 Gold 0.1999 oz. AGW, 22 mm. **Ruler:** Elizabeth II **Subject:** Olympics **Obv:** Head with tiara right **Obv. Designer:** Ian Rank-Broadley **Rev:** Sail Boarders **Edge:** Reeded

Date	Mintage	F	VF	XF	Unc	BU
2003PM Proof	—	Value: 250				

KM# 1188 1/5 CROWN

6.2200 g., 0.9999 Gold 0.1999 oz. AGW, 22 mm. **Ruler:** Elizabeth II **Subject:** Lord of the Rings **Obv:** Bust with tiara right **Obv. Designer:** Ian Rank-Broadley **Rev:** Legolas **Edge:** Reeded

Date	Mintage	F	VF	XF	Unc	BU
2003PM Proof	3,500	Value: 250				

KM# 1223 1/5 CROWN

6.2200 g., 0.9999 Gold 0.1999 oz. AGW, 22 mm. **Ruler:** Elizabeth II **Obv:** Bust with tiara right **Obv. Designer:** Ian Rank-Broadley **Rev:** D-Day Invasion Plan Map **Edge:** Reeded

Date	Mintage	F	VF	XF	Unc	BU
2004PM Proof	5,000	Value: 250				

KM# 1225 1/5 CROWN

6.2200 g., 0.9999 Gold 0.1999 oz. AGW, 22 mm. **Ruler:** Elizabeth II **Obv:** Bust with tiara right **Obv. Designer:** Ian Rank-Broadley **Rev:** Victoria Cross and battle scene **Edge:** Reeded

Date	Mintage	F	VF	XF	Unc	BU
2004PM Proof	5,000	Value: 250				

KM# 1227 1/5 CROWN

6.2200 g., 0.9999 Gold 0.1999 oz. AGW, 22 mm. **Ruler:** Elizabeth II **Obv:** Bust with tiara right **Obv. Designer:** Ian Rank-Broadley **Rev:** Silver Star and battle scene **Edge:** Reeded

Date	Mintage	F	VF	XF	Unc	BU
2004PM Proof	5,000	Value: 250				

KM# 1229 1/5 CROWN

6.2200 g., 0.9999 Gold 0.1999 oz. AGW, 22 mm. **Ruler:** Elizabeth II **Obv:** Bust with tiara right **Obv. Designer:** Ian Rank-Broadley **Rev:** George Cross and rescue scene **Edge:** Reeded

Date	Mintage	F	VF	XF	Unc	BU
2004PM Proof	5,000	Value: 250				

KM# 1231 1/5 CROWN

6.2200 g., 0.9999 Gold 0.1999 oz. AGW, 22 mm. **Ruler:** Elizabeth II **Obv:** Bust with tiara right **Obv. Designer:** Ian Rank-Broadley **Rev:** White Rose of Finland Medal and battle scene **Edge:** Reeded

Date	Mintage	F	VF	XF	Unc	BU
2004PM Proof	5,000	Value: 250				

KM# 1233 1/5 CROWN

6.2200 g., 0.9999 Gold 0.1999 oz. AGW, 22 mm. **Ruler:** Elizabeth II **Obv:** Bust with tiara right **Obv. Designer:** Ian Rank-Broadley **Rev:** The Norwegian War Medal and naval battle scene **Edge:** Reeded

Date	Mintage	F	VF	XF	Unc	BU
2004PM Proof	5,000	Value: 250				

KM# 1235 1/5 CROWN

6.2200 g., 0.9999 Gold 0.1999 oz. AGW, 22 mm. **Ruler:** Elizabeth II **Obv:** Bust with tiara right **Obv. Designer:** Ian Rank-Broadley **Rev:** French Croix de Guerre and Partisan battle scene **Edge:** Reeded

Date	Mintage	F	VF	XF	Unc	BU
2004PM Proof	5,000	Value: 250				

KM# 1249.1 1/5 CROWN

6.2200 g., 0.9999 Gold 0.1999 oz. AGW, 22 mm. **Ruler:** Elizabeth II **Obv:** Head with tiara right **Obv. Designer:** Ian Rank-Broadley **Rev:** Two Tonkinese cats **Edge:** Reeded

Date	Mintage	F	VF	XF	Unc	BU
2004PM Proof	1,000	Value: 260				
2004PM	—	—	—	—	—	250

KM# 1249.2 1/5 CROWN

6.2200 g., 0.9999 Gold 0.1999 oz. AGW, 22 mm. **Ruler:** Elizabeth II **Obv:** Head with tiara right **Obv. Designer:** Ian Rank-Broadley **Rev:** Two multicolor Tonkinese cats **Edge:** Reeded

Date	Mintage	F	VF	XF	Unc	BU
2004PM Proof	—	Value: 250				

KM# 1198 1/5 CROWN

6.2200 g., 0.9990 Palladium 0.1998 oz., 22 mm. **Ruler:** Elizabeth II **Subject:** Palladium Bicentennial **Obv:** Head with tiara right **Obv. Designer:** Ian Rank-Broadley **Rev:** Athena **Edge:** Reeded

Date	Mintage	F	VF	XF	Unc	BU
2004PM Proof	999	Value: 200				

KM# 1271 1/5 CROWN

6.2200 g., 0.9999 Gold 0.1999 oz. AGW, 22 mm. **Ruler:** Elizabeth II **Obv:** Bust with tiara right **Obv. Designer:** Ian Rank-Broadley **Rev:** Himalayan cat and two kittens **Edge:** Reeded

Date	Mintage	F	VF	XF	Unc	BU
2005PM Proof	—	Value: 260				

KM# 1271a 1/5 CROWN

6.2200 g., 0.9950 Platinum 0.1990 oz. APW, 22 mm. **Ruler:** Elizabeth II **Obv:** Bust with tiara right **Obv. Designer:** Ian Rank-Broadley **Rev:** Himalayan cat and two kittens **Edge:** Reeded

Date	Mintage	F	VF	XF	Unc	BU
2005PM Proof	—	Value: 400				

KM# 1295 1/5 CROWN

6.2200 g., 0.9999 Gold 0.1999 oz. AGW, 22 mm. **Ruler:** Elizabeth II **Subject:** Battles that Changed the World **Obv:** Elizabeth II **Rev:** Trojan War scene **Edge:** Reeded

Date	Mintage	F	VF	XF	Unc	BU
2006PM Proof	5,000	Value: 250				

KM# 1297 1/5 CROWN

6.2200 g., 0.9999 Gold 0.1999 oz. AGW, 22 mm. **Ruler:** Elizabeth II **Subject:** Battles that Changed the World **Obv:** Elizabeth II **Rev:** Battle of Arbela scene **Edge:** Reeded

Date	Mintage	F	VF	XF	Unc	BU
2006PM Proof	5,000	Value: 250				

KM# 1299 1/5 CROWN

6.2200 g., 0.9999 Gold 0.1999 oz. AGW, 22 mm. **Ruler:** Elizabeth II **Subject:** Battles that Changed the World **Obv:** Elizabeth II **Rev:** Battle of Thapsus scene **Edge:** Reeded

Date	Mintage	F	VF	XF	Unc	BU
2006PM Proof	5,000	Value: 250				

KM# 1301 1/5 CROWN

6.2200 g., 0.9999 Gold 0.1999 oz. AGW, 22 mm. **Ruler:** Elizabeth II **Subject:** Battles that Changed the World **Obv:** Elizabeth II **Rev:** Battle of Cologne scene **Edge:** Reeded

Date	Mintage	F	VF	XF	Unc	BU
2006PM Proof	5,000	Value: 250				

KM# 1303 1/5 CROWN

6.2200 g., 0.9999 Gold 0.1999 oz. AGW, 22 mm. **Ruler:** Elizabeth II **Subject:** Battles that Changed the World **Obv:** Elizabeth II **Rev:** Siege of Valencia scene **Edge:** Reeded

Date	Mintage	F	VF	XF	Unc	BU
2006PM Proof	5,000	Value: 250				

KM# 1305 1/5 CROWN

6.2200 g., 0.9999 Gold 0.1999 oz. AGW, 22 mm. **Ruler:** Elizabeth II **Subject:** Battles that Changed the World **Obv:** Elizabeth II **Rev:** Battle of Agincourt scene **Edge:** Reeded

Date	Mintage	F	VF	XF	Unc	BU
2006PM Proof	5,000	Value: 250				

KM# 1342 1/5 CROWN

6.2200 g., 0.9999 Gold 0.1999 oz. AGW **Ruler:** Elizabeth II **Obv:** Bust with tiara right **Obv. Designer:** Ian Rank-Broadley **Rev:** Three Exotic Shorthair cats sitting facing **Edge:** Reeded

Date	Mintage	F	VF	XF	Unc	BU
2006PM	—	—	—	—	—	330

KM# 1345 1/5 CROWN

6.2200 g., 0.9999 Gold 0.1999 oz. AGW **Ruler:** Elizabeth II **Obv:** Bust with tiara right **Obv. Legend:** ELIZABETH II - ISLE OF MAN **Obv. Designer:** Ian Rank-Broadley **Rev:** Ragdoll cat with two kittens sitting facing **Edge:** Reeded

Date	Mintage	F	VF	XF	Unc	BU
2007PM	—	—	—	—	—	330

KM# 1351.1 1/5 CROWN

6.2200 g., 0.9999 Gold 0.1999 oz. AGW **Ruler:** Elizabeth II **Subject:** The Tale of Peter Rabbit **Obv:** Bust with tiara right **Obv. Legend:** ELIZABETH II - ISLE OF MAN **Obv. Designer:** Ian Rank-Broadley **Rev:** Peter walking with friends **Edge:** Reeded

Date	Mintage	F	VF	XF	Unc	BU
2007PM	—	—	—	—	—	340

KM# 1351.2 1/5 CROWN

6.2200 g., 0.9999 Gold 0.1999 oz. AGW **Ruler:** Elizabeth II **Subject:** The Tale of Peter Rabbit **Obv:** Bust with tiara right **Obv. Legend:** ELIZABETH II - ISLE OF MAN **Obv. Designer:** Ian Rank-Broadley **Rev:** Peter walking with friends **Edge:** Reeded

Date	Mintage	F	VF	XF	Unc	BU
2007PM	—	—	—	—	—	355

KM# 1309 1/5 CROWN

6.2200 g., 0.9999 Gold 0.1999 oz. AGW **Ruler:** Elizabeth II **Subject:** 100th Anniversary of Scouting **Obv:** Bust with tiara right **Obv. Legend:** ELIZABETH II - ISLE OF MAN **Rev:** 3/4 length figure of Robert Baden-Powell standing facing 3/4 left, Fleur-de-lys below, images of scouting at left and right **Rev. Legend:** CENTERARY OF SCOUTING **Edge:** Reeded

Date	Mintage	F	VF	XF	Unc	BU
2007 Proof	—	Value: 250				

KM# 1352 1/5 CROWN

6.2200 g., 0.9999 Gold 0.1999 oz. AGW, 22 mm. **Ruler:** Elizabeth II **Subject:** Prince Charles 60th Birthday **Obv:** Bust with tiara right **Obv. Legend:** ELIZABETH II - ISLE OF MAN **Obv. Designer:** Ian Rank-Broadley **Rev:** Heads of Charles, Princes William and Henry right **Edge:** Reeded

Date	Mintage	F	VF	XF	Unc	BU
2008PM Proof	5,000	Value: 260				

KM# 1381 1/5 CROWN

6.2200 g., 0.9999 Gold 0.1999 oz. AGW **Ruler:** Elizabeth II **Obv:** Bust right **Rev:** Chinchilla cat and kitten

Date	Mintage	F	VF	XF	Unc	BU
2009	—	—	—	—	—	275
2009 Proof	1,000	Value: 350				

KM# 1385 1/4 CROWN

6.2200 g., 0.9950 Platinum 0.1990 oz. APW, 22 mm. **Ruler:** Elizabeth II **Series:** Bust right **Obv:** Chinchilla cat and kitten

Date	Mintage	F	VF	XF	Unc	BU
2009	—	—	—	—	—	375

KM# 1061 1/2 CROWN

15.5517 g., 0.9999 Gold 0.4999 oz. AGW, 30 mm. **Ruler:** Elizabeth II **Subject:** Year of the Snake **Obv:** Bust with tiara right **Obv. Designer:** Ian Rank-Broadley **Rev:** Snake **Edge:** Reeded

Date	Mintage	F	VF	XF	Unc	BU
2001 Proof	6,000	Value: 650				

KM# 1070 1/2 CROWN

15.5517 g., 0.9999 Gold 0.4999 oz. AGW, 30 mm. **Ruler:** Elizabeth II **Obv:** Head with tiara right **Obv. Designer:** Ian Rank-Broadley **Rev:** Two Somali kittens **Edge:** Reeded

Date	Mintage	F	VF	XF	Unc	BU
2001	—	—	—	—	—	625
2001 Proof	1,000	Value: 640				

KM# 1071 1/2 CROWN

15.5517 g., 0.9995 Platinum 0.4997 oz. APW, 27 mm. **Ruler:** Elizabeth II **Obv:** Head with tiara right **Obv. Designer:** Ian Rank-Broadley **Rev:** Two Somali kittens **Edge:** Reeded

Date	Mintage	F	VF	XF	Unc	BU
2001	—	—	—	—	—	875

KM# 1157 1/2 CROWN

15.5510 g., 0.9990 Gold 0.4995 oz. AGW, 30 mm. **Ruler:** Elizabeth II **Subject:** Queen's Golden Jubilee **Obv:** Queen's portrait **Rev:** Queen on horse **Edge:** Reeded

Date	Mintage	F	VF	XF	Unc	BU
2002PM Proof	500	Value: 650				

KM# 1101 1/2 CROWN

15.5500 g., 0.9999 Gold 0.4999 oz. AGW, 30 mm. **Ruler:** Elizabeth II **Subject:** Year of the Horse **Obv:** Bust with tiara right **Obv. Designer:** Ian Rank-Broadley **Rev:** Two horses **Edge:** Reeded

Date	Mintage	F	VF	XF	Unc	BU
2002 Proof	6,000	Value: 640				

KM# 1110 1/2 CROWN

15.5510 g., 0.9990 Gold 0.4995 oz. AGW, 30 mm. **Ruler:** Elizabeth II **Subject:** Bengal Cat **Obv:** Head with tiara right **Obv. Designer:** Ian Rank-Broadley **Rev:** Cat and kitten **Edge:** Reeded

Date	Mintage	VG	F	VF	XF	Unc
2002	—	—	—	—	—	—
2002 Proof	1,000	Value: 640				

KM# 1110a 1/2 CROWN

6.2200 g., 0.9990 Platinum 0.1998 oz. APW, 30 mm. **Ruler:** Elizabeth II **Subject:** Bengal Cat **Obv:** Head with tiara right **Obv. Designer:** Ian Rank-Broadley **Rev:** Cat and kitten **Edge:** Reeded

Date	Mintage	F	VF	XF	Unc	BU
2002	—	—	—	—	—	525

KM# 1164 1/2 CROWN

15.5510 g., 0.9999 Gold 0.4999 oz. AGW, 30 mm. **Ruler:** Elizabeth II **Subject:** Cat **Obv:** Head with tiara right **Obv. Designer:** Ian Rank-Broadley **Rev:** Two Balinese kittens **Edge:** Reeded

Date	Mintage	F	VF	XF	Unc	BU
2003PM	—	—	—	—	—	625
2003PM Proof	—	Value: 640				

KM# 1164a 1/2 CROWN

15.5510 g., 0.9995 Platinum 0.4997 oz. APW, 30 mm. **Ruler:** Elizabeth II **Subject:** Cat **Obv:** Head with tiara right **Obv. Designer:** Ian Rank-Broadley **Rev:** Two Balinese kittens **Edge:** Reeded

Date	Mintage	F	VF	XF	Unc	BU
2003PM	—	—	—	—	—	875

KM# 1170 1/2 CROWN

15.5500 g., 0.9999 Gold 0.4999 oz. AGW, 30 mm. **Ruler:** Elizabeth II **Subject:** Year of the Goat **Obv:** Bust with tiara right **Obv. Designer:** Ian Rank-Broadley **Rev:** Three goats **Edge:** Reeded

Date	Mintage	F	VF	XF	Unc	BU
2003PM Proof	—	Value: 640				

KM# 1189 1/2 CROWN

15.5510 g., 0.9999 Gold 0.4999 oz. AGW, 30 mm. **Ruler:** Elizabeth II **Subject:** Lord of the Rings **Obv:** Bust with tiara right **Obv. Designer:** Ian Rank-Broadley **Rev:** Gimli with two battle axes **Edge:** Reeded

Date	Mintage	F	VF	XF	Unc	BU
2003PM Proof	1,000	Value: 650				

KM# 1243 1/2 CROWN

15.5520 g., 0.9999 Gold 0.4999 oz. AGW, 30 mm. **Ruler:** Elizabeth II **Obv:** Head with tiara right **Obv. Designer:** Ian Rank-Broadley **Rev:** Monkey **Edge:** Reeded

Date	Mintage	F	VF	XF	Unc	BU
2004PM Proof	6,000	Value: 640				

KM# 1250 1/2 CROWN

15.5520 g., 0.9999 Gold 0.4999 oz. AGW, 30 mm. **Ruler:** Elizabeth II **Obv:** Head with tiara right **Obv. Designer:** Ian Rank-Broadley **Rev:** Two Tonkinese cats **Edge:** Reeded

Date	Mintage	F	VF	XF	Unc	BU
2004PM Proof	1,000	Value: 650				
2004PM	—	—	—	—	—	625

KM# 1199 1/2 CROWN

15.5500 g., 0.9990 Bi-Metallic .999 Palladium 6.3g center in .9999 Gold 9.25 g ring 0.4994 oz., 30 mm. **Ruler:** Elizabeth II **Subject:** Palladium Bicentennial **Obv:** Bust with tiara right **Obv. Designer:** Ian Rank-Broadley **Rev:** Athena **Edge:** Reeded

Date	Mintage	F	VF	XF	Unc	BU
2004PM Proof	500	Value: 775				

KM# 1272 1/2 CROWN

15.5510 g., 0.9999 Gold 0.4999 oz. AGW, 27 mm. **Ruler:** Elizabeth II **Obv:** Bust with tiara right **Obv. Designer:** Ian Rank-Broadley **Rev:** Himalayan cat and two kittens **Edge:** Reeded

Date	Mintage	F	VF	XF	Unc	BU
2005PM Proof	—	Value: 640				

KM# 1272a 1/2 CROWN

15.5510 g., 0.9950 Platinum 0.4975 oz. APW, 27 mm. **Ruler:** Elizabeth II **Obv:** Bust with tiara right **Obv. Designer:** Ian Rank-Broadley **Rev:** Himalayan cat and two kittens **Edge:** Reeded

Date	Mintage	F	VF	XF	Unc	BU
2005PM	—	—	—	—	—	850
2005PM Proof	—	Value: 900				

KM# 1346 1/2 CROWN

15.5500 g., 0.9999 Gold 0.4999 oz. AGW **Ruler:** Elizabeth II **Obv:** Bust with tiara right **Obv. Legend:** ELIZABETH II - ISLE OF MAN **Obv. Designer:** Ian Rank-Broadley **Rev:** Ragdoll cat with two kittens sitting facing **Edge:** Reeded

Date	Mintage	F	VF	XF	Unc	BU
2007PM	—	—	—	—	—	650

KM# 1380 1/2 CROWN

15.5500 g., 0.9999 Gold 0.4999 oz. AGW, 30 mm. **Ruler:** Elizabeth II **Obv:** Bust right **Rev:** Chinchilla cat and kitten

Date	Mintage	F	VF	XF	Unc	BU
2009	—	—	—	—	—	650
2009 Proof	1,000	Value: 700				

KM# 1384 1/2 CROWN

15.5500 g., 0.9950 Platinum 0.4974 oz. APW, 27 mm. **Ruler:** Elizabeth II **Obv:** Bust right **Rev:** Chinchilla cat and kitten

Date	Mintage	F	VF	XF	Unc	BU
2009	—	—	—	—	—	850

KM# 1073 CROWN

31.1035 g., 0.9999 Gold 0.9999 oz. AGW, 32.7 mm. **Ruler:** Elizabeth II **Subject:** Somali Kittens **Obv:** Bust with tiara right **Obv. Designer:** Ian Rank-Broadley **Rev:** Two kittens **Edge:** Reeded

Date	Mintage	F	VF	XF	Unc	BU
2001	—	—	—	—	—	1,250
2001 Proof	1,000	Value: 1,300				

KM# 1076 CROWN

28.2800 g., Copper-Nickel, 38.6 mm. **Ruler:** Elizabeth II **Subject:** Queen Mother **Obv:** Bust with tiara right **Obv. Designer:** Ian Rank-Broadley **Rev:** 1948 Silver wedding anniversary **Edge:** Reeded

Date	Mintage	F	VF	XF	Unc	BU
2001	—	—	—	—	10.00	12.00

KM# 1076a CROWN

28.2800 g., 0.9250 Silver 0.8410 oz. ASW, 38.6 mm. **Ruler:** Elizabeth II **Subject:** Queen Mother **Obv:** Bust with tiara right **Obv. Designer:** Ian Rank-Broadley **Rev:** 1948 Silver wedding anniversary **Edge:** Reeded

Date	Mintage	F	VF	XF	Unc	BU
2001 Proof	10,000	Value: 47.50				

KM# 1077 CROWN

Copper-Nickel, 38.6 mm. **Ruler:** Elizabeth II **Subject:** Queen Mother **Obv:** Bust with tiara right **Obv. Designer:** Ian Rank-Broadley **Rev:** 1948 holding baby Prince Charles **Edge:** Reeded

Date	Mintage	F	VF	XF	Unc	BU
2001	—	—	—	—	10.00	12.00

KM# 1077a CROWN
28.2800 g., 0.9250 Silver 0.8410 oz. ASW, 38.6 mm.
Ruler: Elizabeth II **Subject:** Queen Mother **Obv:** Head with tiara right **Obv. Designer:** Ian Rank-Broadley **Rev:** 1948 holding baby Prince Charles **Edge:** Reeded

Date	Mintage	F	VF	XF	Unc	BU
2001 Proof	10,000	Value: 47.50				

KM# 1080 CROWN
Copper-Nickel, 38.6 mm. **Ruler:** Elizabeth II **Subject:** Martin Frobisher **Obv:** Bust w/tiara right **Obv. Designer:** Ian Rank-Broadley **Rev:** Bust at left, ship at right and map below **Edge:** Reeded

Date	Mintage	F	VF	XF	Unc	BU
2001	—	—	—	—	10.00	12.00

KM# 1080a CROWN
28.2800 g., 0.9250 Silver 0.8410 oz. ASW, 38.6 mm.
Ruler: Elizabeth II **Subject:** Martin Frobisher **Obv:** Bust of Queen Elizabeth II right **Obv. Designer:** Ian Rank-Broadley **Edge:** Reeded

Date	Mintage	F	VF	XF	Unc	BU
2001 Proof	10,000	Value: 47.50				

KM# 1081 CROWN
Copper-Nickel, 38.6 mm. **Ruler:** Elizabeth II **Subject:** Roald Amundsen **Obv:** Bust with tiara right **Obv. Designer:** Ian Rank-Broadley **Rev:** Bust at right, ship at center, dirigible above at left **Edge:** Reeded

Date	Mintage	F	VF	XF	Unc	BU
2001	—	—	—	—	10.00	12.00

KM# 1081a CROWN
28.2800 g., 0.9250 Silver 0.8410 oz. ASW, 38.6 mm.
Ruler: Elizabeth II **Subject:** Roald Amundsen **Obv:** Bust with tiara right **Obv. Designer:** Ian Rank-Broadley **Rev:** Bust at right, ship at center, dirigible at upper left **Edge:** Reeded

Date	Mintage	F	VF	XF	Unc	BU
2001 Proof	10,000	Value: 47.50				

KM# 1085 CROWN
28.2800 g., Copper-Nickel, 38.6 mm. **Ruler:** Elizabeth II **Subject:** Joey Dunlop (1952-2000) **Obv:** Bust w/tiara right **Obv. Designer:** Ian Rank-Broadley **Rev:** Motorcycle racer **Edge:** Reeded

Date	Mintage	F	VF	XF	Unc	BU
2001 Black finish	—	—	—	—	10.00	12.00

KM# 1085a CROWN
28.2800 g., 0.9250 Silver 0.8410 oz. ASW, 38.6 mm. **Ruler:** Elizabeth II **Subject:** Joey Dunlop (1952-2000) **Obv:** Bust with tiara right **Obv. Designer:** Ian Rank-Broadley **Rev:** Motorcycle racer **Edge:** Reeded

Date	Mintage	F	VF	XF	Unc	BU
2001 Proof	10,000	Value: 47.50				

KM# 1083 CROWN
28.2800 g., Copper-Nickel, 38.6 mm. **Ruler:** Elizabeth II **Subject:** Queen's 75th Birthday **Obv:** Bust with tiara right **Obv. Designer:** Ian Rank-Broadley **Rev:** Flower bouquet **Edge:** Reeded

Date	Mintage	F	VF	XF	Unc	BU
2001	—	—	—	—	14.00	16.00

KM# 1083a CROWN
28.2800 g., 0.9250 Silver 0.8410 oz. ASW, 38.6 mm.
Ruler: Elizabeth II **Subject:** Queen's 75th Birthday **Obv:** Bust with tiara right **Obv. Designer:** Ian Rank-Broadley **Rev:** Flower bouquet **Edge:** Reeded

Date	Mintage	F	VF	XF	Unc	BU
2001 Proof	10,000	Value: 50.00				

KM# 1087 CROWN
28.2800 g., Copper-Nickel, 38.6 mm. **Ruler:** Elizabeth II **Series:** Harry Potter **Obv:** Bust with tiara right **Obv. Designer:** Ian Rank-Broadley **Rev:** Harry with magic wand **Edge:** Reeded

Date	Mintage	F	VF	XF	Unc	BU
2001	—	—	—	—	10.00	12.00

KM# 1087a CROWN
28.2800 g., 0.9250 Silver 0.8410 oz. ASW, 38.6 mm.
Ruler: Elizabeth II **Series:** Harry Potter **Obv:** Bust with tiara right **Obv. Designer:** Ian Rank-Broadley **Rev:** Harry with magic wand **Edge:** Reeded

Date	Mintage	F	VF	XF	Unc	BU
2001 Proof	15,000	Value: 47.50				

KM# 1089 CROWN
28.2800 g., Copper-Nickel, 38.6 mm. **Ruler:** Elizabeth II **Series:** Harry Potter **Subject:** Journey to Hogwart's **Obv:** Bust with tiara right **Obv. Designer:** Ian Rank-Broadley **Rev:** Boat full of children going to Hogwart's **Edge:** Reeded

Date	Mintage	F	VF	XF	Unc	BU
2001	—	—	—	—	10.00	12.00

KM# 1089a CROWN
28.2800 g., 0.9250 Silver 0.8410 oz. ASW, 38.6 mm.
Ruler: Elizabeth II **Series:** Harry Potter **Obv:** Bust with tiara right **Obv. Designer:** Ian Rank-Broadley **Rev:** Boat full of children going to Hogwart's **Edge:** Reeded

Date	Mintage	F	VF	XF	Unc	BU
2001 Proof	15,000	Value: 47.50				

KM# 1091 CROWN
Copper-Nickel **Ruler:** Elizabeth II **Series:** Harry Potter **Subject:** First Quidditch Match **Obv:** Bust with tiara right **Obv. Designer:** Ian Rank-Broadley **Rev:** Harry flying his Nimbus 2000

Date	Mintage	F	VF	XF	Unc	BU
2001	—	—	—	—	10.00	12.00

KM# 1091a CROWN
28.2800 g., 0.9250 Silver 0.8410 oz. ASW **Ruler:** Elizabeth II **Series:** Harry Potter **Subject:** First Quidditch Match **Obv:** Bust with tiara right **Obv. Designer:** Ian Rank-Broadley **Rev:** Harry flying his Nimbus 2000

Date	Mintage	F	VF	XF	Unc	BU
2001 Proof	15,000	Value: 47.50				

KM# 1093 CROWN
Copper-Nickel **Ruler:** Elizabeth II **Series:** Harry Potter **Subject:** Birth of Norbert **Obv:** Bust with tiara right **Obv. Designer:** Ian Rank-Broadley **Rev:** Hagrid and children watching Norbert hatch

Date	Mintage	F	VF	XF	Unc	BU
2001	—	—	—	—	10.00	14.00

KM# 1093a CROWN
28.2800 g., 0.9250 Silver 0.8410 oz. ASW **Ruler:** Elizabeth II **Series:** Harry Potter **Subject:** Birth of Norbert **Obv:** Bust with tiara right **Obv. Designer:** Ian Rank-Broadley **Rev:** Hagrid and children watching Norbert hatch

Date	Mintage	F	VF	XF	Unc	BU
2001 Proof	15,000	Value: 47.50				

KM# 1095 CROWN
Copper-Nickel **Ruler:** Elizabeth II **Series:** Harry Potter **Subject:** School **Obv:** Bust with tiara right **Obv. Designer:** Ian Rank-Broadley **Rev:** Harry in Potions class

Date	Mintage	F	VF	XF	Unc	BU
2001	—	—	—	—	10.00	12.00

KM# 1095a CROWN
28.2800 g., 0.9250 Silver 0.8410 oz. ASW **Ruler:** Elizabeth II **Series:** Harry Potter **Subject:** School **Obv:** Bust with tiara right **Obv. Designer:** Ian Rank-Broadley **Rev:** Harry in Potions class

Date	Mintage	F	VF	XF	Unc	BU
2001 Proof	15,000	Value: 47.50				

KM# 1097 CROWN
Copper-Nickel, 38.72 mm. **Ruler:** Elizabeth II **Series:** Harry Potter **Obv:** Bust with tiara right **Obv. Designer:** Ian Rank-Broadley **Rev:** Harry catching a flying jeweled key **Edge:** Reeded

Date	Mintage	F	VF	XF	Unc	BU
2001	—	—	—	—	10.00	12.00

KM# 1097a   CROWN
28.2800 g., 0.9250 Silver 0.8410 oz. ASW, 38.71 mm.
Ruler: Elizabeth II **Series:** Harry Potter **Obv:** Bust with tiara right
Obv. Designer: Ian Rank-Broadley **Rev:** Harry catching a flying
jeweled key **Edge:** Reeded

Date	Mintage	F	VF	XF	Unc	BU
2001 Proof	15,000	Value: 47.50				

KM# 1062   CROWN
28.2800 g., Copper-Nickel, 38.6 mm.   **Ruler:** Elizabeth II
Subject: Year of the Snake **Obv:** Bust with tiara right
Obv. Designer: Ian Rank-Broadley **Rev:** Snake **Edge:** Reeded

Date	Mintage	F	VF	XF	Unc	BU
2001	—	—	—	—	10.00	15.00

KM# 1062a   CROWN
28.2800 g., 0.9250 Silver 0.8410 oz. ASW, 38.6 mm.   **Ruler:**
Elizabeth II **Subject:** Year of the Snake **Obv:** Head with tiara right
Obv. Designer: Ian Rank-Broadley **Rev:** Snake **Edge:** Reeded

Date	Mintage	F	VF	XF	Unc	BU
2001 Proof	30,000	Value: 47.50				

KM# 1063   CROWN
31.1035 g., 0.9999 Gold 0.9999 oz. AGW, 32.7 mm.   **Ruler:**
Elizabeth II **Subject:** Year of the Snake **Obv:** Bust with tiara right
Obv. Designer: Ian Rank-Broadley **Rev:** Snake **Edge:** Reeded

Date	Mintage	F	VF	XF	Unc	BU
2001 Proof	2,000	Value: 1,250				

KM# 1072   CROWN
28.2800 g., Copper-Nickel, 38.6 mm.   **Ruler:** Elizabeth II
Subject: Somali Kittens **Obv:** Bust with tiara right **Obv.**
Designer: Ian Rank-Broadley **Rev:** Two kittens **Edge:** Reeded

Date	Mintage	F	VF	XF	Unc	BU
2001	—	—	—	—	11.00	15.00

KM# 1072a   CROWN
31.1035 g., 0.9990 Silver 0.9990 oz. ASW, 38.6 mm.
Ruler: Elizabeth II **Subject:** Somali Kittens **Obv:** Bust with tiara
right **Obv. Designer:** Ian Rank-Broadley **Rev:** Two kittens
Edge: Reeded

Date	Mintage	F	VF	XF	Unc	BU
2001 Proof	50,000	Value: 47.50				

KM# 1102   CROWN
28.2800 g., Copper-Nickel, 38.6 mm.   **Ruler:** Elizabeth II
Subject: Year of the Horse **Obv:** Bust with tiara right **Obv.**
Designer: Ian Rank-Broadley **Rev:** Two horses **Edge:** Reeded

Date	Mintage	F	VF	XF	Unc	BU
2002	—	—	—	—	12.00	15.00

KM# 1102a   CROWN
28.2800 g., 0.9250 Silver 0.8410 oz. ASW, 38.6 mm.
Ruler: Elizabeth II **Subject:** Year of the Horse **Obv:** Bust with
tiara right **Obv. Designer:** Ian Rank-Broadley **Rev:** Two horses
Edge: Reeded

Date	Mintage	F	VF	XF	Unc	BU
2002 Proof	30,000	Value: 47.50				

KM# 1103   CROWN
31.1000 g., 0.9999 Gold 0.9997 oz. AGW   **Ruler:** Elizabeth II
Subject: Year of the Horse **Obv:** Bust with tiara right
Obv. Designer: Ian Rank-Broadley

Date	Mintage	F	VF	XF	Unc	BU
2002 Proof	2,000	Value: 1,250				

KM# 1111   CROWN
28.2800 g., Copper-Nickel, 38.6 mm.   **Ruler:** Elizabeth II
Subject: Bengal Cat **Obv:** Bust with tiara right **Obv. Designer:**
Ian Rank-Broadley **Rev:** Cat and kitten **Edge:** Reeded

Date	Mintage	F	VF	XF	Unc	BU
2002	—	—	—	—	12.50	14.00

KM# 1111a   CROWN
31.1035 g., 0.9990 Silver 0.9990 oz. ASW, 38.6 mm.
Ruler: Elizabeth II **Subject:** Bengal Cat **Obv:** Bust with tiara right
Obv. Designer: Ian Rank-Broadley **Rev:** Cat and kitten
Edge: Reeded

Date	Mintage	F	VF	XF	Unc	BU
2002 Proof	10,000	Value: 47.50				

KM# 1112   CROWN
31.1035 g., 0.9990 Gold 0.9990 oz. AGW, 33 mm.
Ruler: Elizabeth II **Subject:** Bengal Cat **Obv:** Bust with tiara right
Obv. Designer: Ian Rank-Broadley **Rev:** Cat and kitten
Edge: Reeded

Date	Mintage	F	VF	XF	Unc	BU
2002	—	—	—	—	—	1,250
2002 Proof	1,000	Value: 1,300				

KM# 1115   CROWN
28.2800 g., Copper-Nickel, 38.6 mm.   **Ruler:** Elizabeth II
Subject: Olympics - Salt Lake City **Obv:** Bust with tiara right
Obv. Designer: Ian Rank-Broadley **Rev:** Skier, torch and flag
Edge: Reeded

Date	Mintage	F	VF	XF	Unc	BU
2002	—	—	—	—	10.00	12.00

KM# 1115a   CROWN
28.2800 g., 0.9250 Silver 0.8410 oz. ASW, 38.6 mm.
Ruler: Elizabeth II **Subject:** Olympics - Salt Lake City **Obv:** Bust
with tiara right **Obv. Designer:** Ian Rank-Broadley **Rev:** Skier,
torch and flag **Edge:** Reeded

Date	Mintage	F	VF	XF	Unc	BU
2002 Proof	10,000	Value: 47.50				

KM# 1116   CROWN
28.2800 g., Copper-Nickel, 38.6 mm.   **Ruler:** Elizabeth II
Subject: Olympics - Salt Lake City **Obv:** Bust with tiara right
Obv. Designer: Ian Rank-Broadley **Rev:** Bobsled, torch and
stadium **Edge:** Reeded

Date	Mintage	F	VF	XF	Unc	BU
2002	—	—	—	—	10.00	12.00

KM# 1116a   CROWN
28.2800 g., 0.9250 Silver 0.8410 oz. ASW, 38.6 mm.
Ruler: Elizabeth II **Subject:** Olympics - Salt Lake City **Obv:** Bust
with tiara right **Obv. Designer:** Ian Rank-Broadley **Rev:** Bobsled,
torch and stadium **Edge:** Reeded

Date	Mintage	F	VF	XF	Unc	BU
2002 Proof	10,000	Value: 47.50				

KM# 1118   CROWN
28.2800 g., Copper-Nickel, 38.6 mm.   **Ruler:** Elizabeth II
Subject: Queen Mother's Love of Horses **Obv:** Bust with tiara
right **Obv. Designer:** Ian Rank-Broadley **Rev:** Queen Mother and
horse **Edge:** Reeded

Date	Mintage	F	VF	XF	Unc	BU
2002	—	—	—	—	10.00	12.00

KM# 1118a   CROWN
28.2800 g., Silver, 38.6 mm.   **Ruler:** Elizabeth II **Subject:** Queen
Mother's Love of Horses **Obv:** Bust with tiara right **Obv.**
Designer: Ian Rank-Broadley **Rev:** Queen Mother and horse
Edge: Reeded

Date	Mintage	F	VF	XF	Unc	BU
2002 Proof	10,000	Value: 47.50				

KM# 1119 CROWN
35.0000 g., 0.7500 Gold 0.8439 oz. AGW, 38.6 mm.
Ruler: Elizabeth II **Subject:** Golden Jubilee **Obv:** Bust with tiara right **Obv. Designer:** Ian Rank-Broadley **Rev:** Queen Elizabeth II's young laureate bust right **Rev. Designer:** Mary Gillick **Edge:** Reeded **Note:** Red Gold center in a White Gold inner ring within a Yellow Gold outer ring.

Date	Mintage	F	VF	XF	Unc	BU
2002 Proof	999	Value: 1,100				

KM# 1121 CROWN
28.2800 g., Copper-Nickel, 38.6 mm. **Ruler:** Elizabeth II **Subject:** World Cup 2002 Japan - Korea **Obv:** Bust w/tiara right **Obv. Designer:** Ian Rank-Broadley **Rev:** Player running right **Edge:** Reeded

Date	Mintage	F	VF	XF	Unc	BU
2002	—	—	—	—	10.00	12.00

KM# 1121a CROWN
28.2800 g., 0.9250 Silver 0.8410 oz. ASW, 38.6 mm.
Ruler: Elizabeth II **Subject:** World Cup 2002 Japan - Korea **Obv:** Bust with tiara right **Obv. Designer:** Ian Rank-Broadley **Rev:** Player running right **Edge:** Reeded

Date	Mintage	F	VF	XF	Unc	BU
2002 Proof	10,000	Value: 47.50				

KM# 1123 CROWN
28.2800 g., Copper-Nickel, 38.6 mm. **Ruler:** Elizabeth II **Subject:** World Cup 2002 Japan - Korea **Obv:** Bust with tiara right **Obv. Designer:** Ian Rank-Broadley **Rev:** Player kicking to right **Edge:** Reeded

Date	Mintage	F	VF	XF	Unc	BU
2002	—	—	—	—	10.00	12.00

KM# 1123a CROWN
28.2800 g., 0.9250 Silver 0.8410 oz. ASW, 38.6 mm.
Ruler: Elizabeth II **Subject:** World Cup 2002 Japan - Korea **Obv:** Bust with tiara right **Obv. Designer:** Ian Rank-Broadley **Rev:** Player kicking to right **Edge:** Reeded

Date	Mintage	F	VF	XF	Unc	BU
2002 Proof	10,000	Value: 47.50				

KM# 1125 CROWN
28.2800 g., Copper-Nickel, 38.6 mm. **Ruler:** Elizabeth II **Subject:** World Cup 2002 Japan - Korea **Obv:** Bust with tiara right **Obv. Designer:** Ian Rank-Broadley **Rev:** Player kicking to left **Edge:** Reeded

Date	Mintage	F	VF	XF	Unc	BU
2002	—	—	—	—	10.00	12.00

KM# 1125a CROWN
28.2800 g., 0.9250 Silver 0.8410 oz. ASW, 38.6 mm.
Ruler: Elizabeth II **Subject:** World Cup 2002 Japan - Korea **Obv:** Bust with tiara right **Rev:** Player kicking to left **Edge:** Reeded

Date	Mintage	F	VF	XF	Unc	BU
2002 Proof	10,000	Value: 47.50				

KM# 1127 CROWN
28.2800 g., Copper-Nickel, 38.6 mm. **Ruler:** Elizabeth II **Subject:** World Cup 2002 Japan - Korea **Obv:** Bust with tiara right **Obv. Designer:** Ian Rank-Broadley **Rev:** Player running to left **Edge:** Reeded

Date	Mintage	F	VF	XF	Unc	BU
2002	—	—	—	—	10.00	12.00

KM# 1127a CROWN
28.2800 g., 0.9250 Silver 0.8410 oz. ASW, 38.6 mm.
Ruler: Elizabeth II **Subject:** World Cup 2002 Japan - Korea **Obv:** Bust with tiara right **Obv. Designer:** Ian Rank-Broadley **Rev:** Player running to left **Edge:** Reeded

Date	Mintage	F	VF	XF	Unc	BU
2002 Proof	10,000	Value: 47.50				

KM# 1131 CROWN
28.2800 g., Copper-Nickel, 38.6 mm. **Ruler:** Elizabeth II **Subject:** Queen Elizabeth II's Golden Jubilee **Obv:** Bust with tiara right **Obv. Designer:** Ian Rank-Broadley **Rev:** Seated crowned Queen holding scepter at her coronation **Edge:** Reeded

Date	Mintage	F	VF	XF	Unc	BU
2002	—	—	—	—	10.00	12.00

KM# 1131a CROWN
28.2800 g., Gold Color Base Metal, 38.6 mm. **Ruler:** Elizabeth II **Subject:** Queen Elizabeth II's Golden Jubilee **Obv:** Bust with tiara right **Obv. Designer:** Ian Rank-Broadley **Rev:** Seated crowned Queen holding scepter at her coronation **Edge:** Reeded

Date	Mintage	F	VF	XF	Unc	BU
2002	15,000	—	—	—	10.00	12.00

KM# 1131b CROWN
28.2800 g., 0.9250 Gold Clad Silver 0.8410 oz., 38.6 mm.
Ruler: Elizabeth II **Subject:** Queen Elizabeth II's Golden Jubilee **Obv:** Bust with tiara right **Obv. Designer:** Ian Rank-Broadley **Rev:** Seated crowned Queen holding scepter at her coronation **Edge:** Reeded

Date	Mintage	F	VF	XF	Unc	BU
2002 Proof	10,000	Value: 47.50				

KM# 1133 CROWN
28.2800 g., Copper-Nickel, 38.6 mm. **Ruler:** Elizabeth II **Subject:** Queen Elizabeth II's Golden Jubilee **Obv:** Bust with tiara right **Obv. Designer:** Ian Rank-Broadley **Rev:** Queen on horse **Edge:** Reeded

Date	Mintage	F	VF	XF	Unc	BU
2002	—	—	—	—	10.00	12.00

KM# 1133a CROWN
28.2800 g., Gold Color Base Metal, 38.6 mm. **Ruler:** Elizabeth II **Subject:** Queen Elizabeth II's Golden Jubilee **Obv:** Bust with tiara right **Obv. Designer:** Ian Rank-Broadley **Rev:** Queen on horse **Edge:** Reeded

Date	Mintage	F	VF	XF	Unc	BU
2002	15,000	—	—	—	10.00	12.00

KM# 1133b CROWN
28.2800 g., 0.9250 Gold Clad Silver 0.8410 oz., 38.6 mm.
Ruler: Elizabeth II **Subject:** Queen Elizabeth II's Golden Jubilee **Obv:** Bust with tiara right **Obv. Designer:** Ian Rank-Broadley **Rev:** Queen on horse half left **Edge:** Reeded

Date	Mintage	F	VF	XF	Unc	BU
2002 Proof	10,000	Value: 47.50				

KM# 1135 CROWN
28.2800 g., Copper-Nickel, 38.6 mm. **Ruler:** Elizabeth II **Subject:** Queen Elizabeth II's Golden Jubilee **Obv:** Bust with tiara right **Obv. Designer:** Ian Rank-Broadley **Rev:** Queen with her pet Corgi **Edge:** Reeded

Date	Mintage	F	VF	XF	Unc	BU
2002	—	—	—	—	10.00	12.00

KM# 1135a CROWN
28.2800 g., Gold Color Base Metal, 38.6 mm. **Ruler:** Elizabeth II **Subject:** Queen Elizabeth II's Golden Jubilee **Obv:** Bust with tiara right **Obv. Designer:** Ian Rank-Broadley **Rev:** Seated Queen with her pet Corgi **Edge:** Reeded

Date	Mintage	F	VF	XF	Unc	BU
2002	15,000	—	—	—	10.00	12.00

KM# 1135b CROWN
28.2800 g., 0.9250 Gold Clad Silver 0.8410 oz., 38.6 mm.
Ruler: Elizabeth II **Subject:** Queen Elizabeth II's Golden Jubilee **Obv:** Bust with tiara right **Obv. Designer:** Ian Rank-Broadley **Rev:** Queen with her pet Corgi **Edge:** Reeded

Date	Mintage	F	VF	XF	Unc	BU
2002 Proof	10,000	Value: 47.50				

KM# 1137 CROWN
28.2800 g., Copper-Nickel, 38.6 mm. **Ruler:** Elizabeth II
Subject: Queen Elizabeth II's Golden Jubilee **Obv:** Bust with
tiara right **Obv. Designer:** Ian Rank-Broadley **Rev:** Queen at war
memorial **Edge:** Reeded

Date	Mintage	F	VF	XF	Unc	BU
2002	—	—	—	—	10.00	12.00

KM# 1137a CROWN
28.2800 g., Gold Color Base Metal, 38.6 mm. **Ruler:** Elizabeth II
Subject: Queen Elizabeth II's Golden Jubilee **Obv:** Bust with
tiara right **Obv. Designer:** Ian Rank-Broadley **Rev:** Queen at war
memorial **Edge:** Reeded

Date	Mintage	F	VF	XF	Unc	BU
2002	15,000	—	—	—	10.00	12.00

KM# 1137b CROWN
28.2800 g., Gold Clad Silver, 38.6 mm. **Ruler:** Elizabeth II
Subject: Queen Elizabeth II's Golden Jubilee **Obv:** Bust with
tiara right **Obv. Designer:** Ian Rank-Broadley **Rev:** Queen at war
memorial **Edge:** Reeded

Date	Mintage	F	VF	XF	Unc	BU
2002 Proof	10,000	Value: 47.50				

KM# 1139 CROWN
Copper-Nickel dark patina, 38.6 mm. **Ruler:** Elizabeth II
Subject: Queen Mother **Obv:** Bust with tiara right
Obv. Designer: Ian Rank-Broadley **Rev:** Queen Mother and
Castle May **Edge:** Reeded

Date	Mintage	F	VF	XF	Unc	BU
2002	—	—	—	—	10.00	12.00

KM# 1139a CROWN
28.2800 g., 0.9250 Silver 0.8410 oz. ASW, 38.6 mm.
Ruler: Elizabeth II **Obv:** Head with tiara right with blackened
legends **Obv. Designer:** Ian Rank-Broadley **Rev:** Queen Mother
standing at left in front of Castle May with blackened legends

Date	Mintage	F	VF	XF	Unc	BU
2002 Proof	10,000	Value: 47.50				

KM# 1141 CROWN
28.2800 g., Copper-Nickel, 38.6 mm. **Ruler:** Elizabeth II
Subject: Princess Diana **Obv:** Bust with tiara right **Obv. Designer:**
Ian Rank-Broadley **Rev:** Diana's bust facing **Edge:** Reeded

Date	Mintage	F	VF	XF	Unc	BU
2002	—	—	—	—	10.00	12.00

KM# 1141a CROWN
28.2800 g., 0.9250 Silver 0.8410 oz. ASW, 38.6 mm.
Ruler: Elizabeth II **Subject:** Princess Diana **Obv:** Bust with tiara
right **Obv. Designer:** Ian Rank-Broadley **Rev:** Diana facing
Edge: Reeded

Date	Mintage	F	VF	XF	Unc	BU
2002 Proof	10,000	Value: 47.50				

KM# 1144 CROWN
28.2800 g., Copper-Nickel, 38.6 mm. **Ruler:** Elizabeth II
Series: Harry Potter **Obv:** Bust with tiara right **Obv. Designer:**
Ian Rank-Broadley **Rev:** Tom Riddle twirling Harry's magic wand
Edge: Reeded

Date	Mintage	F	VF	XF	Unc	BU
2002PM	—	—	—	—	10.00	12.00

KM# 1144a CROWN
28.2800 g., 0.9250 Silver 0.8410 oz. ASW, 28.6 mm.
Ruler: Elizabeth II **Series:** Harry Potter **Obv:** Bust with tiara right
Obv. Designer: Ian Rank-Broadley **Rev:** Tom Riddle twirling
Harry's magic wand **Edge:** Reeded

Date	Mintage	F	VF	XF	Unc	BU
2002PM Proof	15,000	Value: 50.00				

KM# 1146 CROWN
28.2800 g., Copper-Nickel, 38.6 mm. **Ruler:** Elizabeth II
Series: Harry Potter **Obv:** Bust with tiara right **Obv. Designer:**
Ian Rank-Broadley **Rev:** Harry and friends making Polyjuice
potion **Edge:** Reeded

Date	Mintage	F	VF	XF	Unc	BU
2002PM	—	—	—	—	10.00	12.00

KM# 1146a CROWN
28.2800 g., 0.9250 Silver 0.8410 oz. ASW, 38.6 mm.
Ruler: Elizabeth II **Series:** Harry Potter **Obv:** Bust with tiara right
Obv. Designer: Ian Rank-Broadley **Rev:** Harry Potter and friends
making Polyjuice potion **Edge:** Reeded

Date	Mintage	F	VF	XF	Unc	BU
2002PM Proof	15,000	Value: 50.00				

KM# 1148 CROWN
28.2800 g., Copper-Nickel, 38.6 mm. **Ruler:** Elizabeth II
Series: Harry Potter **Obv:** Bust with tiara right **Obv. Designer:**
Ian Rank-Broadley **Rev:** Harry arrives at the Burrow in a flying
car **Edge:** Reeded

Date	Mintage	F	VF	XF	Unc	BU
2002PM	—	—	—	—	10.00	12.00

KM# 1148a CROWN
28.2800 g., 0.9250 Silver 0.8410 oz. ASW, 38.6 mm.
Ruler: Elizabeth II **Series:** Harry Potter **Obv:** Bust with tiara right
Obv. Designer: Ian Rank-Broadley **Rev:** Harry arrives at the
Burrow in a flying car **Edge:** Reeded

Date	Mintage	F	VF	XF	Unc	BU
2002PM Proof	15,000	Value: 50.00				

KM# 1150 CROWN
28.2800 g., Copper-Nickel, 38.6 mm. **Ruler:** Elizabeth II
Series: Harry Potter **Obv:** Bust with tiara right **Obv. Designer:**
Ian Rank-Broadley **Rev:** Harry retrieves Gryffindor sword from
sorting hat **Edge:** Reeded

Date	Mintage	F	VF	XF	Unc	BU
2002PM	—	—	—	—	10.00	12.00

KM# 1150a CROWN
28.2800 g., 0.9250 Silver 0.8410 oz. ASW, 38.6 mm.
Ruler: Elizabeth II **Series:** Harry Potter **Obv:** Bust with tiara right
Obv. Designer: Ian Rank-Broadley **Rev:** Harry retrieves
Gryffindor sword from sorting hat **Edge:** Reeded

Date	Mintage	F	VF	XF	Unc	BU
2002PM Proof	15,000	Value: 50.00				

KM# 1152 CROWN
28.2800 g., Copper-Nickel, 38.6 mm. **Ruler:** Elizabeth II
Series: Harry Potter **Obv:** Bust with tiara right **Obv. Designer:**
Ian Rank-Broadley **Rev:** Harry and Ron encounter the spider
Aragog **Edge:** Reeded

Date	Mintage	F	VF	XF	Unc	BU
2002PM	—	—	—	—	10.00	12.00

KM# 1152a CROWN
28.2800 g., 0.9250 Silver 0.8410 oz. ASW, 38.6 mm.
Ruler: Elizabeth II **Series:** Harry Potter **Obv:** Bust with tiara right
Obv. Designer: Ian Rank-Broadley **Rev:** Harry and Ron
encounter the spider Aragog **Edge:** Reeded

Date	Mintage	F	VF	XF	Unc	BU
2002PM Proof	15,000	Value: 50.00				

KM# 1154 CROWN
28.2800 g., Copper-Nickel, 38.6 mm. **Ruler:** Elizabeth II **Series:**
Harry Potter **Obv:** Bust with tiara right **Obv. Designer:** Ian Rank-
Broadley **Rev:** Harry in hospital with Dobby **Edge:** Reeded

Date	Mintage	F	VF	XF	Unc	BU
2002PM	—	—	—	—	10.00	12.00

KM# 1154a CROWN
28.2800 g., 0.9250 Silver 0.8410 oz. ASW, 38.6 mm.
Ruler: Elizabeth II **Series:** Harry Potter **Obv:** Bust with tiara right
Obv. Designer: Ian Rank-Broadley **Rev:** Harry in hospital with
Dobby **Edge:** Reeded

Date	Mintage	F	VF	XF	Unc	BU
2002PM Proof	15,000	Value: 50.00				

KM# 1185 CROWN
28.2800 g., Copper-Nickel, 38.6 mm. **Ruler:** Elizabeth II
Obv: Bust with tiara right **Obv. Designer:** Ian Rank-Broadley
Rev: Lord of the Rings characters **Edge:** Reeded

Date	Mintage	F	VF	XF	Unc	BU
2003PM	100,000	—	—	—	12.50	14.50

KM# 1185a CROWN
28.2800 g., 0.9250 Silver 0.8410 oz. ASW, 38.6 mm. **Ruler:**
Elizabeth II **Obv:** Bust with tiara right **Obv. Designer:** Ian Rank-
Broadley **Rev:** Lord of the Rings characters **Edge:** Reeded

Date	Mintage	F	VF	XF	Unc	BU
2003PM Proof	10,000	Value: 50.00				

KM# 1190 CROWN
31.1035 g., 0.9999 Gold 0.9999 oz. AGW, 32.7 mm.
Ruler: Elizabeth II **Subject:** Lord of the Rings **Obv:** Bust with
tiara right **Obv. Designer:** Ian Rank-Broadley **Rev:** Man on horse
Edge: Reeded

Date	Mintage	F	VF	XF	Unc	BU
2003PM Proof	1,000	Value: 1,300				

KM# 1191 CROWN
28.2800 g., 0.9250 Silver 0.8410 oz. ASW, 38.6 mm.
Ruler: Elizabeth II **Subject:** Lord of the Rings **Obv:** Bust with
tiara right **Obv. Designer:** Ian Rank-Broadley **Rev:** Man with
short sword **Edge:** Reeded

Date	Mintage	F	VF	XF	Unc	BU
2003PM Proof	5,000	Value: 47.50				

KM# 1192 CROWN
28.2800 g., 0.9250 Silver 0.8410 oz. ASW, 38.6 mm. **Ruler:** Elizabeth II **Subject:** Lord of the Rings **Obv:** Bust with
tiara right **Obv. Designer:** Ian Rank-Broadley **Rev:** Aragorn with
broadsword **Edge:** Reeded

Date	Mintage	F	VF	XF	Unc	BU
2003PM Proof	5,000	Value: 47.50				

KM# 1193 CROWN
28.2800 g., 0.9250 Silver 0.8410 oz. ASW, 38.6 mm. **Ruler:**
Elizabeth II **Subject:** Lord of the Rings **Obv:** Bust with tiara right
Obv. Designer: Ian Rank-Broadley **Rev:** Legolas **Edge:** Reeded

Date	Mintage	F	VF	XF	Unc	BU
2003PM Proof	5,000	Value: 47.50				

KM# 1194 CROWN
28.2800 g., 0.9250 Silver 0.8410 oz. ASW, 38.6 mm.
Ruler: Elizabeth II **Subject:** Lord of the Rings **Obv:** Bust with
tiara right **Obv. Designer:** Ian Rank-Broadley **Rev:** Gimli with
two battle axes **Edge:** Reeded

Date	Mintage	F	VF	XF	Unc	BU
2003PM Proof	5,000	Value: 47.50				

KM# 1195 CROWN
28.2800 g., 0.9250 Silver 0.8410 oz. ASW, 38.6 mm.
Ruler: Elizabeth II **Subject:** Lord of the Rings **Obv:** Bust with
tiara right **Obv. Designer:** Ian Rank-Broadley **Rev:** Man on horse
Edge: Reeded

Date	Mintage	F	VF	XF	Unc	BU
2003PM Proof	5,000	Value: 47.50				

KM# 1165 CROWN
28.2800 g., Copper-Nickel, 38.6 mm. **Ruler:** Elizabeth II
Subject: Cat **Obv:** Bust with tiara right **Obv. Designer:** Ian Rank-
Broadley **Rev:** Two Balinese kittens **Edge:** Reeded

Date	Mintage	F	VF	XF	Unc	BU
2003PM	—	—	—	—	12.00	14.00

KM# 1165a CROWN
31.1035 g., 0.9990 Silver 0.9990 oz. ASW, 38.6 mm. **Ruler:**
Elizabeth II **Subject:** Cat **Obv:** Head with tiara right **Obv. Designer:**
Ian Rank-Broadley **Rev:** Two Balinese kittens **Edge:** Reeded

Date	Mintage	F	VF	XF	Unc	BU
2003PM Proof	50,000	Value: 47.50				

KM# 1166 CROWN
31.1035 g., 0.9999 Gold 0.9999 oz. AGW, 32.7 mm. **Ruler:**
Elizabeth II **Subject:** Cat **Obv:** Head with tiara right **Obv. Designer:**
Ian Rank-Broadley **Rev:** Two Balinese kittens **Edge:** Reeded

Date	Mintage	F	VF	XF	Unc	BU
2003PM	—	—	—	—	—	1,250
2003PM Proof	—	Value: 1,300				

KM# 1171 CROWN
28.2800 g., Copper-Nickel, 38.6 mm. **Ruler:** Elizabeth II
Subject: Year of the Goat **Obv:** Bust with tiara right **Obv.
Designer:** Ian Rank-Broadley **Rev:** Three goats **Edge:** Reeded

Date	Mintage	F	VF	XF	Unc	BU
2003PM	—	—	—	—	12.00	14.00

KM# 1171a CROWN
28.2800 g., 0.9250 Silver 0.8410 oz. ASW, 38.6 mm. **Ruler:**
Elizabeth II **Subject:** Year of the Goat **Obv:** Bust with tiara
right **Obv. Designer:** Ian Rank-Broadley **Rev:** Three goats
Edge: Reeded

Date	Mintage	F	VF	XF	Unc	BU
2003PM Proof	30,000	Value: 47.50				

KM# 1172 CROWN
31.1035 g., 0.9999 Gold 0.9999 oz. AGW, 32.7 mm.
Ruler: Elizabeth II **Subject:** Year of the Goat **Obv:** Bust with tiara
right **Obv. Designer:** Ian Rank-Broadley **Rev:** Three goats
Edge: Reeded

Date	Mintage	F	VF	XF	Unc	BU
2003PM Proof	2,000	Value: 1,250				

KM# 1174 CROWN
28.5300 g., Copper-Nickel, 38.6 mm. **Ruler:** Elizabeth II
Obv: Bust with tiara right **Obv. Designer:** Ian Rank-Broadley
Rev: The Star of India sailing ship **Edge:** Reeded

Date	Mintage	F	VF	XF	Unc	BU
2003PM	—	—	—	—	10.00	12.00

KM# 1176 CROWN
28.2800 g., Copper-Nickel, 38.6 mm. **Ruler:** Elizabeth II
Subject: Olympics **Obv:** Bust with tiara right **Obv. Designer:** Ian
Rank-Broadley **Rev:** Swimmers **Edge:** Reeded

Date	Mintage	F	VF	XF	Unc	BU
2003PM	—	—	—	—	10.00	12.00

KM# 1176a CROWN
28.2800 g., 0.9250 Silver 0.8410 oz. ASW, 38.6 mm. **Ruler:**
Elizabeth II **Subject:** Olympics **Obv:** Bust with tiara right **Obv.
Designer:** Ian Rank-Broadley **Rev:** Swimmers **Edge:** Reeded

Date	Mintage	F	VF	XF	Unc	BU
2003PM Proof	10,000	Value: 47.50				

KM# 1178 CROWN
28.2800 g., Copper-Nickel, 38.6 mm. **Ruler:** Elizabeth II
Subject: Olympics **Obv:** Bust with tiara right **Obv. Designer:** Ian
Rank-Broadley **Rev:** Runners **Edge:** Reeded

Date	Mintage	F	VF	XF	Unc	BU
2003PM	—	—	—	—	10.00	12.00

KM# 1178a CROWN
28.2800 g., 0.9250 Silver 0.8410 oz. ASW, 38.6 mm. **Ruler:**
Elizabeth II **Subject:** Olympics **Obv:** Bust with tiara right **Obv.
Designer:** Ian Rank-Broadley **Rev:** Runners **Edge:** Reeded

Date	Mintage	F	VF	XF	Unc	BU
2003PM Proof	10,000	Value: 47.50				

KM# 1180 CROWN
28.2800 g., Copper-Nickel, 38.6 mm. **Ruler:** Elizabeth II
Subject: Olympics **Obv:** Bust with tiara right **Obv. Designer:** Ian
Rank-Broadley **Rev:** Bicyclists **Edge:** Reeded

Date	Mintage	F	VF	XF	Unc	BU
2003PM	—	—	—	—	10.00	12.00

KM# 1180a CROWN
28.2800 g., 0.9250 Silver 0.8410 oz. ASW, 38.6 mm. **Ruler:**
Elizabeth II **Subject:** Olympics **Obv:** Bust with tiara right **Obv.
Designer:** Ian Rank-Broadley **Rev:** Bicyclists **Edge:** Reeded

Date	Mintage	F	VF	XF	Unc	BU
2003PM Proof	10,000	Value: 47.50				

KM# 1182   CROWN
28.2800 g., Copper-Nickel, 38.6 mm.   **Ruler:** Elizabeth II
Subject: Olympics **Obv:** Bust with tiara right **Obv. Designer:** Ian
Rank-Broadley **Rev:** Sail Boarders **Edge:** Reeded

Date	Mintage	F	VF	XF	Unc	BU
2003PM	—	—	—	—	10.00	12.00

KM# 1182a   CROWN
28.2800 g., 0.9250 Silver 0.8410 oz. ASW, 38.6 mm.   **Ruler:**
Elizabeth II **Subject:** Olympics **Obv:** Bust with tiara right **Obv.
Designer:** Ian Rank-Broadley **Rev:** Sail Boarders **Edge:** Reeded

Date	Mintage	F	VF	XF	Unc	BU
2003PM Proof	10,000	Value: 47.50				

KM# 1196   CROWN
28.4400 g., Copper-Nickel, 38.6 mm.   **Ruler:** Elizabeth II
Obv: Bust with tiara right **Obv. Designer:** Ian Rank-Broadley
Rev: Four pre-1918 airplanes **Edge:** Reeded

Date	Mintage	F	VF	XF	Unc	BU
2003PM	—	—	—	—	10.00	12.00

KM# 1197   CROWN
28.4400 g., Copper-Nickel, 38.6 mm.   **Obv:** Bust with tiara right
Obv. Designer: Ian Rank-Broadley **Rev:** Propeller plain,
Zeppelin and two jet airliners **Edge:** Reeded

Date	Mintage	F	VF	XF	Unc	BU
2003PM	—	—	—	—	10.00	12.00

KM# 1201   CROWN
28.2800 g., Copper-Nickel, 38.6 mm.   **Ruler:** Elizabeth II
Obv: Bust with tiara right **Obv. Designer:** Ian Rank-Broadley
Rev: European Union map within hand held rope circle
Edge: Reeded

Date	Mintage	F	VF	XF	Unc	BU
2004PM	—	—	—	—	10.00	12.00

KM# 1201a   CROWN
28.2800 g., 0.9250 Silver 0.8410 oz. ASW, 38.6 mm.
Ruler: Elizabeth II **Obv:** Bust with tiara right **Obv. Designer:** Ian
Rank-Broadley **Rev:** European Union map within a hand held
rope circle **Edge:** Reeded

Date	Mintage	F	VF	XF	Unc	BU
2004PM Proof	10,000	Value: 50.00				

KM# 1202   CROWN
28.2800 g., Copper-Nickel, 38.6 mm.   **Ruler:** Elizabeth II
Obv: Bust with tiara right **Obv. Designer:** Ian Rank-Broadley
Rev: Harry Potter and patron fighting off a spectre **Edge:** Reeded

Date	Mintage	F	VF	XF	Unc	BU
2004PM	—	—	—	—	15.00	17.00

KM# 1202a   CROWN
28.2800 g., 0.9250 Silver 0.8410 oz. ASW, 38.6 mm.
Ruler: Elizabeth II **Obv:** Bust with tiara right **Obv. Designer:** Ian
Rank-Broadley **Rev:** Harry Potter and patron fighting off a spectre
Edge: Reeded

Date	Mintage	F	VF	XF	Unc	BU
2004PM Proof	10,000	Value: 50.00				

KM# 1204   CROWN
28.2800 g., Copper-Nickel, 38.6 mm.   **Ruler:** Elizabeth II
Obv: Bust with tiara right **Obv. Designer:** Ian Rank-Broadley
Rev: Harry Potter in the shrieking shed **Edge:** Reeded

Date	Mintage	F	VF	XF	Unc	BU
2004PM	—	—	—	—	15.00	17.00

KM# 1204a   CROWN
28.2800 g., 0.9250 Silver 0.8410 oz. ASW, 38.6 mm.   **Ruler:**
Elizabeth II **Obv:** Bust with tiara right **Obv. Designer:** Ian Rank-
Broadley **Rev:** Harry Potter in the shrieking shack **Edge:** Reeded

Date	Mintage	F	VF	XF	Unc	BU
2004PM Proof	10,000	Value: 50.00				

KM# 1206   CROWN
28.2800 g., Copper-Nickel, 38.6 mm.   **Ruler:** Elizabeth II
Obv: Bust with tiara right **Obv. Designer:** Ian Rank-Broadley
Rev: Harry Potter and Professor Dumbledore **Edge:** Reeded

Date	Mintage	F	VF	XF	Unc	BU
2004PM	—	—	—	—	15.00	17.00

KM# 1206a   CROWN
28.2800 g., 0.9250 Silver 0.8410 oz. ASW, 38.6 mm.
Ruler: Elizabeth II **Obv:** Bust with tiara right **Obv. Designer:** Ian
Rank-Broadley **Rev:** Harry Potter and Professor Dumbledore
Edge: Reeded

Date	Mintage	F	VF	XF	Unc	BU
2004PM Proof	10,000	Value: 50.00				

KM# 1208   CROWN
28.2800 g., Copper-Nickel, 38.6 mm.   **Ruler:** Elizabeth II
Obv: Bust with tiara right **Obv. Designer:** Ian Rank-Broadley
Rev: Sirius Black on flying griffin **Edge:** Reeded

Date	Mintage	F	VF	XF	Unc	BU
2004PM	—	—	—	—	15.00	17.00

KM# 1208a   CROWN
28.2800 g., 0.9250 Silver 0.8410 oz. ASW, 38.6 mm.
Ruler: Elizabeth II **Obv:** Bust with tiara right **Obv. Designer:** Ian
Rank-Broadley **Rev:** Sirius Black on flying griffin **Edge:** Reeded

Date	Mintage	F	VF	XF	Unc	BU
2004PM Proof	10,000	Value: 50.00				

KM# 1210   CROWN
28.2800 g., Copper-Nickel, 38.6 mm.   **Ruler:** Elizabeth II
Obv: Bust with tiara right **Obv. Designer:** Ian Rank-Broadley
Rev: Three Olympic Swimmers **Edge:** Reeded

Date	Mintage	F	VF	XF	Unc	BU
2004PM	—	—	—	—	10.00	12.00

KM# 1210a   CROWN
28.2800 g., 0.9250 Silver 0.8410 oz. ASW, 38.6 mm.
Ruler: Elizabeth II **Obv:** Bust with tiara right **Obv. Designer:** Ian
Rank-Broadley **Rev:** Three Olympic Swimmers **Edge:** Reeded

Date	Mintage	F	VF	XF	Unc	BU
2004PM Proof	10,000	Value: 50.00				

KM# 1212   CROWN
28.2800 g., Copper-Nickel, 38.6 mm.   **Ruler:** Elizabeth II
Obv: Bust with tiara right **Obv. Designer:** Ian Rank-Broadley
Rev: Three Olympic Cyclists **Edge:** Reeded

Date	Mintage	F	VF	XF	Unc	BU
2004PM	—	—	—	—	10.00	12.00

KM# 1212a   CROWN
28.2800 g., 0.9250 Silver 0.8410 oz. ASW, 38.6 mm.
Ruler: Elizabeth II **Obv:** Bust with tiara right **Obv. Designer:** Ian
Rank-Broadley **Rev:** Three Olympic Cyclists **Edge:** Reeded

Date	Mintage	F	VF	XF	Unc	BU
2004PM Proof	10,000	Value: 50.00				

KM# 1214   CROWN
28.2800 g., Copper-Nickel, 38.6 mm.   **Ruler:** Elizabeth II
Obv: Bust with tiara right **Obv. Designer:** Ian Rank-Broadley
Rev: Three Olympic Runners **Edge:** Reeded

Date	Mintage	F	VF	XF	Unc	BU
2004PM	—	—	—	—	10.00	12.00

KM# 1214a   CROWN
28.2800 g., 0.9250 Silver 0.8410 oz. ASW, 38.6 mm.   **Ruler:**
Elizabeth II **Obv:** Bust with tiara right **Obv. Designer:** Ian Rank-
Broadley **Rev:** Three Olympic Runners **Edge:** Reeded

Date	Mintage	F	VF	XF	Unc	BU
2004PM Proof	10,000	Value: 50.00				

KM# 1216   CROWN
28.2800 g., Copper-Nickel, 38.6 mm.   **Ruler:** Elizabeth II
Obv: Bust with tiara right **Obv. Designer:** Ian Rank-Broadley
Rev: Three Olympic Sail Boarders **Edge:** Reeded

Date	Mintage	F	VF	XF	Unc	BU
2004PM	—	—	—	—	10.00	12.00

KM# 1216a   CROWN
28.2800 g., 0.9250 Silver 0.8410 oz. ASW, 38.6 mm.
Ruler: Elizabeth II **Obv:** Bust with tiara right **Obv. Designer:** Ian
Rank-Broadley **Rev:** Three Olympic Sail Boarders **Edge:** Reeded

Date	Mintage	F	VF	XF	Unc	BU
2004PM Proof	10,000	Value: 50.00				

KM# 1218   CROWN
28.2800 g., Copper-Nickel, 38.6 mm.   **Ruler:** Elizabeth II
Obv: Bust with tiara right **Obv. Designer:** Ian Rank-Broadley
Rev: Ocean Liner Queen Mary 2 **Edge:** Reeded

Date	Mintage	F	VF	XF	Unc	BU
2004PM	—	—	—	—	15.00	17.00

KM# 1220   CROWN
28.2800 g., Copper-Nickel, 38.6 mm.   **Ruler:** Elizabeth II
Obv: Bust with tiara right **Obv. Designer:** Ian Rank-Broadley
Rev: Lt. Quillan portrait above Battle of Trafalgar scene
Edge: Reeded

Date	Mintage	F	VF	XF	Unc	BU
2004PM	—	—	—	—	15.00	17.00

KM# 1220a   CROWN
28.2800 g., 0.9250 Silver 0.8410 oz. ASW, 38.6 mm.
Ruler: Elizabeth II **Obv:** Bust with tiara right **Obv. Designer:** Ian
Rank-Broadley **Rev:** Lt. Quillan portrait above Battle of Trafalgar
scene **Edge:** Reeded

Date	Mintage	F	VF	XF	Unc	BU
2004PM Proof	10,000	Value: 50.00				

KM# 1221   CROWN
28.2800 g., Copper-Nickel, 38.6 mm.   **Ruler:** Elizabeth II
Obv: Bust with tiara right **Obv. Designer:** Ian Rank-Broadley
Rev: Napoleon and Nelson portraits above Battle of Trafalgar
scene **Edge:** Reeded

Date	Mintage	F	VF	XF	Unc	BU
2004PM	—	—	—	—	15.00	17.00

KM# 1221a   CROWN
28.2800 g., 0.9990 Silver 0.9083 oz. ASW, 38.6 mm.
Ruler: Elizabeth II **Obv:** Bust with tiara right **Obv. Designer:** Ian
Rank-Broadley **Rev:** Napoleon and Nelson portraits above Battle
of Trafalgar scene **Edge:** Reeded

Date	Mintage	F	VF	XF	Unc	BU
2004PM Proof	10,000	Value: 50.00				

KM# 1222 CROWN
28.2800 g., Copper-Nickel, 38.6 mm. **Ruler:** Elizabeth II
Obv: Bust with tiara right **Obv. Designer:** Ian Rank-Broadley
Rev: D-Day Invasion Plan Map **Edge:** Reeded

Date	Mintage	F	VF	XF	Unc	BU
2004PM	—	—	—	—	15.00	17.00

KM# 1222a CROWN
28.2800 g., 0.9250 Silver 0.8410 oz. ASW, 38.6 mm.
Ruler: Elizabeth II **Obv:** Bust with tiara right **Obv. Designer:** Ian
Rank-Broadley **Rev:** D-Day Invasion Plan Map **Edge:** Reeded

Date	Mintage	F	VF	XF	Unc	BU
2004PM Proof	10,000	Value: 50.00				

KM# 1224 CROWN
28.2800 g., Copper-Nickel, 38.6 mm. **Ruler:** Elizabeth II
Obv: Bust with tiara right **Obv. Designer:** Ian Rank-Broadley
Rev: Victoria Cross and battle scene **Edge:** Reeded

Date	Mintage	F	VF	XF	Unc	BU
2004PM	—	—	—	—	15.00	17.00

KM# 1224a CROWN
28.2800 g., 0.9250 Silver 0.8410 oz. ASW, 38.6 mm.
Ruler: Elizabeth II **Obv:** Bust with tiara right **Obv. Designer:** Ian
Rank-Broadley **Rev:** Victoria Cross and battle scene
Edge: Reeded

Date	Mintage	F	VF	XF	Unc	BU
2004PM Proof	10,000	Value: 50.00				

KM# 1226 CROWN
28.2800 g., Copper-Nickel, 38.6 mm. **Ruler:** Elizabeth II
Obv: Bust with tiara right **Obv. Designer:** Ian Rank-Broadley
Rev: Silver Star and battle scene **Edge:** Reeded

Date	Mintage	F	VF	XF	Unc	BU
2004PM	—	—	—	—	15.00	17.00

KM# 1226a CROWN
28.2800 g., 0.9250 Silver 0.8410 oz. ASW, 38.6 mm.
Ruler: Elizabeth II **Obv:** Bust with tiara right **Obv. Designer:** Ian
Rank-Broadley **Rev:** Silver Star and battle scene **Edge:** Reeded

Date	Mintage	F	VF	XF	Unc	BU
2004PM Proof	10,000	Value: 50.00				

KM# 1228 CROWN
28.2800 g., Copper-Nickel, 38.6 mm. **Ruler:** Elizabeth II
Obv: Bust with tiara right **Obv. Designer:** Ian Rank-Broadley
Rev: George Cross and rescue scene **Edge:** Reeded

Date	Mintage	F	VF	XF	Unc	BU
2004PM	—	—	—	—	15.00	17.00

KM# 1228a CROWN
28.2800 g., 0.9250 Silver 0.8410 oz. ASW, 38.6 mm.
Ruler: Elizabeth II **Obv:** Bust with tiara right **Obv. Designer:** Ian
Rank-Broadley **Rev:** George Cross and rescue scene
Edge: Reeded

Date	Mintage	F	VF	XF	Unc	BU
2004PM Proof	10,000	Value: 50.00				

KM# 1230 CROWN
28.2800 g., Copper-Nickel, 38.6 mm. **Ruler:** Elizabeth II
Obv: Bust with tiara right **Obv. Designer:** Ian Rank-Broadley
Rev: White Rose of Finland Medal and battle scene
Edge: Reeded

Date	Mintage	F	VF	XF	Unc	BU
2004PM	—	—	—	—	15.00	17.00

KM# 1230a CROWN
28.2800 g., 0.9250 Silver 0.8410 oz. ASW, 38.6 mm.
Ruler: Elizabeth II **Obv:** Bust with tiara right **Obv. Designer:** Ian
Rank-Broadley **Rev:** White Rose of Finland Medal and battle
scene **Edge:** Reeded

Date	Mintage	F	VF	XF	Unc	BU
2004PM Proof	10,000	Value: 50.00				

KM# 1232 CROWN
28.2800 g., Copper-Nickel, 38.6 mm. **Ruler:** Elizabeth II
Obv: Bust with tiara right **Obv. Designer:** Ian Rank-Broadley
Rev: The Norwegian War Medal and naval battle scene
Edge: Reeded

Date	Mintage	F	VF	XF	Unc	BU
2004PM	—	—	—	—	15.00	17.00

KM# 1232a CROWN
28.2800 g., 0.9250 Silver 0.8410 oz. ASW, 38.6 mm.
Ruler: Elizabeth II **Obv:** Bust with tiara right **Obv. Designer:** Ian
Rank-Broadley **Rev:** The Norwegian War Medal and a naval
battle scene **Edge:** Reeded

Date	Mintage	F	VF	XF	Unc	BU
2004PM Proof	10,000	Value: 50.00				

KM# 1234 CROWN
28.2800 g., Copper-Nickel, 38.6 mm. **Ruler:** Elizabeth II
Obv: Bust with tiara right **Obv. Designer:** Ian Rank-Broadley
Rev: French Croix de Guerre and partisan battle scene
Edge: Reeded

Date	Mintage	F	VF	XF	Unc	BU
2004PM	—	—	—	—	15.00	17.00

KM# 1234a CROWN
28.2800 g., 0.9250 Silver 0.8410 oz. ASW, 38.6 mm.
Ruler: Elizabeth II **Obv:** Bust with tiara right **Obv. Designer:** Ian
Rank-Broadley **Rev:** French Croix de Guerre and partisan battle
scene **Edge:** Reeded

Date	Mintage	F	VF	XF	Unc	BU
2004PM Proof	10,000	Value: 50.00				

KM# 1236 CROWN
28.2800 g., Copper-Nickel, 38.6 mm. **Ruler:** Elizabeth II
Obv: Bust with tiara right **Obv. Designer:** Ian Rank-Broadley
Rev: Multicolor cartoon soccer player **Edge:** Reeded

Date	Mintage	F	VF	XF	Unc	BU
2004PM	—	—	—	—	10.00	12.00

KM# 1236a CROWN
28.2800 g., 0.9250 Silver 0.8410 oz. ASW, 38.6 mm.
Ruler: Elizabeth II **Obv:** Bust with tiara right **Obv. Designer:** Ian
Rank-Broadley **Rev:** Multicolor cartoon soccer player
Edge: Reeded

Date	Mintage	F	VF	XF	Unc	BU
2004PM Proof	7,500	Value: 50.00				

KM# 1237 CROWN
28.2800 g., Copper-Nickel, 38.6 mm. **Ruler:** Elizabeth II
Obv: Bust with tiara right **Obv. Designer:** Ian Rank-Broadley
Rev: Soccer ball in flight **Edge:** Reeded

Date	Mintage	F	VF	XF	Unc	BU
2004PM	—	—	—	—	10.00	12.00

KM# 1237a CROWN
28.2800 g., 0.9250 Silver 0.8410 oz. ASW, 38.6 mm.
Ruler: Elizabeth II **Obv:** Bust with tiara right **Obv. Designer:** Ian
Rank-Broadley **Rev:** Soccer ball in flight **Edge:** Reeded

Date	Mintage	F	VF	XF	Unc	BU
2004PM Proof	7,500	Value: 50.00				

KM# 1238 CROWN
28.2800 g., Copper-Nickel, 38.6 mm. **Ruler:** Elizabeth II
Obv: Bust with tiara right **Obv. Designer:** Ian Rank-Broadley
Rev: Gibbon monkey **Edge:** Reeded

Date	Mintage	F	VF	XF	Unc	BU
2004PM	—	—	—	—	10.00	15.00

KM# 1238a CROWN
28.2800 g., 0.9250 Silver 0.8410 oz. ASW, 38.6 mm.
Ruler: Elizabeth II **Obv:** Bust with tiara right **Obv. Designer:** Ian
Rank-Broadley **Rev:** Monkey **Edge:** Reeded

Date	Mintage	F	VF	XF	Unc	BU
2004PM Proof	30,000	Value: 50.00				

KM# 1239 CROWN
31.1035 g., 0.9999 Gold 0.9999 oz. AGW, 32.7 mm.
Ruler: Elizabeth II **Obv:** Bust with tiara right **Obv. Designer:** Ian
Rank-Broadley **Rev:** Monkey **Edge:** Reeded

Date	Mintage	F	VF	XF	Unc	BU
2004PM Proof	2,000	Value: 1,250				

KM# 1242 CROWN
6.2200 g., 0.9999 Gold 0.1999 oz. AGW, 22 mm.
Ruler: Elizabeth II **Obv:** Bust with tiara right **Obv. Designer:** Ian
Rank-Broadley **Rev:** Monkey **Edge:** Reeded

Date	Mintage	F	VF	XF	Unc	BU
2004PM Proof	12,000	Value: 250				

KM# 1245 CROWN
28.2800 g., Copper-Nickel, 38.6 mm. **Ruler:** Elizabeth II
Subject: Lord of the Rings **Obv:** Bust with tiara right **Obv.
Designer:** Ian Rank-Broadley **Rev:** Nine characters **Edge:** Reeded

Date	Mintage	F	VF	XF	Unc	BU
2004PM	100,000	—	—	—	15.00	17.00

KM# 1245a CROWN
28.2800 g., 0.9250 Silver 0.8410 oz. ASW, 38.6 mm.
Ruler: Elizabeth II **Subject:** Lord of the Rings **Obv:** Bust with
tiara right **Obv. Designer:** Ian Rank-Broadley **Rev:** Nine
characters **Edge:** Reeded

Date	Mintage	F	VF	XF	Unc	BU
2004PM Proof	10,000	Value: 50.00				

KM# 1246.1 CROWN
28.2800 g., Copper-Nickel, 38.6 mm. **Ruler:** Elizabeth II
Obv: Head with tiara right **Obv. Designer:** Ian Rank-Broadley
Rev: Multicolor pair of Tonkinese cats **Edge:** Reeded

Date	Mintage	F	VF	XF	Unc	BU
2004PM	—	—	—	—	14.00	16.00

KM# 1246a.1 CROWN
31.1035 g., 0.9990 Silver 0.9990 oz. ASW, 38.6 mm. **Ruler:**
Elizabeth II **Obv:** Head with tiara right **Obv. Designer:** Ian Rank-
Broadley **Rev:** Two Tonkinese cats **Edge:** Reeded

Date	Mintage	F	VF	XF	Unc	BU
2004PM Proof	50,000	Value: 50.00				

KM# 1246a.2 CROWN
31.1035 g., 0.9990 Silver 0.9990 oz. ASW, 38.6 mm.
Ruler: Elizabeth II **Obv:** Head with tiara right **Obv. Designer:**
Ian Rank-Broadley **Rev:** Two multicolor Tonkinese cats
Edge: Reeded

Date	Mintage	F	VF	XF	Unc	BU
2004PM Proof	—	Value: 55.00				

KM# 1251 CROWN
31.1035 g., 0.9999 Gold 0.9999 oz. AGW, 32.7 mm.
Ruler: Elizabeth II **Obv:** Head with tiara right **Obv. Designer:**
Ian Rank-Broadley **Rev:** Two Tonkinese cats **Edge:** Reeded

Date	Mintage	F	VF	XF	Unc	BU
2004PM	—	—	—	—	—	1,250
2004PM Proof	1,000	Value: 1,300				

KM# 1246.2 CROWN
28.2800 g., Copper-Nickel **Ruler:** Elizabeth II **Obv:** Head with
tiara right **Obv. Designer:** Ian Rank-Broadley **Rev:** Two
multicolor Tonkinese cats **Edge:** Reeded

Date	Mintage	F	VF	XF	Unc	BU
2004PM	—	—	—	—	14.00	16.00

KM# 1266 CROWN
28.3300 g., Copper-Nickel, 38.7 mm. **Ruler:** Elizabeth II
Obv: Bust with tiara right **Obv. Designer:** Ian Rank-Broadley
Rev: Himalayan cat with two kittens **Edge:** Reeded

Date	Mintage	F	VF	XF	Unc	BU
2005PM	—	—	—	—	12.00	14.00

KM# 1266a CROWN
31.1030 g., 0.9990 Silver 0.9989 oz. ASW, 38.6 mm.
Ruler: Elizabeth II **Obv:** Bust with tiara right **Obv. Designer:** Ian
Rank-Broadley **Rev:** Himalayan cat and two kittens
Edge: Reeded

Date	Mintage	F	VF	XF	Unc	BU
2005PM Proof	50,000	Value: 50.00				

KM# 1268 CROWN
31.1030 g., 0.9999 Gold 0.9998 oz. AGW, 32.7 mm. **Ruler:**
Elizabeth II **Obv:** Bust with tiara right **Obv. Designer:** Ian Rank-
Broadley **Rev:** Himalayan cat and two kittens **Edge:** Reeded

Date	Mintage	F	VF	XF	Unc	BU
2005PM Proof	—	Value: 1,250				

KM# 1273 CROWN
28.2800 g., Copper-Nickel, 38.6 mm. **Ruler:** Elizabeth II
Obv: Bust with tiara right **Obv. Designer:** Ian Rank-Broadley
Rev: Harry Potter and the Hungarian Horn Tail, Tri-Wizard
Tournament feat **Edge:** Reeded

Date	Mintage	F	VF	XF	Unc	BU
2005PM	—	—	—	—	15.00	17.00

KM# 1274 CROWN
28.2800 g., Copper-Nickel, 38.6 mm. **Ruler:** Elizabeth II
Subject: 60th Anniversary - End of WW II **Obv:** Bust with tiara right
Obv. Designer: Ian Rank-Broadley **Rev:** Sir Winston Churchill

Date	Mintage	F	VF	XF	Unc	BU
2005	—	—	—	—	10.00	12.00

KM# 1275 CROWN
28.2800 g., Copper-Nickel, 38.6 mm. **Ruler:** Elizabeth II **Subject:**
400th Ann. - Gunpowder plot **Obv:** Bust with tiara right **Obv.
Designer:** Ian Rank-Broadley **Rev:** Tower of London, Beefeaters

Date	Mintage	F	VF	XF	Unc	BU
2005	—	—	—	—	10.00	12.00

KM# 1276 CROWN
28.2800 g., Copper-Nickel, 38.6 mm. **Ruler:** Elizabeth II
Obv: Bust with tiara right **Obv. Designer:** Ian Rank-Broadley **Rev:**
Harry Potter and Tri-Wizard Tourn. feat - Underwater retrieval

Date	Mintage	F	VF	XF	Unc	BU
2005	—	—	—	—	10.00	12.00

KM# 1277 CROWN
28.2800 g., Copper-Nickel, 38.6 mm. **Ruler:** Elizabeth II
Obv: Bust with tiara right **Obv. Designer:** Ian Rank-Broadley
Rev: Harry Potter and pensive

Date	Mintage	F	VF	XF	Unc	BU
2005	—	—	—	—	10.00	12.00

KM# 1278 CROWN
28.2800 g., Copper-Nickel, 38.6 mm. **Ruler:** Elizabeth II
Obv: Bust with tiara right **Obv. Designer:** Ian Rank-Broadley
Rev: Harry Potter and portkey

Date	Mintage	F	VF	XF	Unc	BU
2005	—	—	—	—	10.00	12.00

KM# 1291 CROWN
28.2800 g., Copper-Nickel, 38.6 mm. **Ruler:** Elizabeth II **Subject:** Trafalgar - 300th Ann. **Obv:** Bust with tiara right **Obv. Designer:** Ian Rank-Broadley **Rev:** Nelson at Battle of Copenhagen

Date	Mintage	F	VF	XF	Unc	BU
2005	—	—	—	—	10.00	12.00

KM# 1279 CROWN
28.2800 g., Copper-Nickel, 38.6 mm. **Ruler:** Elizabeth II
Subject: The Battle of Cape St. Vincent **Obv:** Bust with tiara right
Obv. Designer: Ian Rank-Broadley **Rev:** Naval battle scene

Date	Mintage	F	VF	XF	Unc	BU
2005	—	—	—	—	10.00	12.00

KM# 1280 CROWN
28.2800 g., Copper-Nickel, 38.6 mm. **Ruler:** Elizabeth II
Subject: Nelson Funeral Procession **Obv:** Bust with tiara right
Obv. Designer: Ian Rank-Broadley **Rev:** Thames and Greenwich view

Date	Mintage	F	VF	XF	Unc	BU
2005	—	—	—	—	10.00	12.00

KM# 1281 CROWN
Copper-Nickel **Ruler:** Elizabeth II **Subject:** Battle of the Nile
Obv: Bust with tiara right **Obv. Designer:** Ian Rank-Broadley
Rev: Naval battle

Date	Mintage	F	VF	XF	Unc	BU
2005	—	—	—	—	10.00	12.00

KM# 1282 CROWN
28.2800 g., Copper-Nickel, 38.6 mm. **Ruler:** Elizabeth II
Subject: Norway Independence **Obv:** Bust with tiara right
Obv. Designer: Ian Rank-Broadley **Rev:** Three swords

Date	Mintage	F	VF	XF	Unc	BU
2005	—	—	—	—	10.00	12.00

KM# 1283 CROWN
28.2800 g., Copper-Nickel, 38.6 mm. **Ruler:** Elizabeth II
Subject: Nelson - Trafalgar 300th Anniversary
Obv. Designer: Ian Rank-Broadley **Rev:** Nelson portrait

Date	Mintage	F	VF	XF	Unc	BU
2005	—	—	—	—	10.00	12.00

KM# 1284 CROWN
28.2800 g., Copper-Nickel, 38.6 mm. **Ruler:** Elizabeth II
Subject: Battle of Trafalgar **Obv. Designer:** Ian Rank-Broadley
Rev: Naval battle scene

Date	Mintage	F	VF	XF	Unc	BU
2005	—	—	—	—	10.00	12.00

KM# 1285 CROWN
28.2800 g., Copper-Nickel, 38.6 mm. **Ruler:** Elizabeth II
Subject: Steam Packet - King Orry III **Obv:** Bust with tiara right
Obv. Designer: Ian Rank-Broadley **Rev:** Ship view

Date	Mintage	F	VF	XF	Unc	BU
2005	—	—	—	—	10.00	12.00

KM# 1286 CROWN
28.2800 g., Copper-Nickel, 38.6 mm. **Ruler:** Elizabeth II
Subject: Isle of Man Steam Packet Company - 175th Anniversary
Obv: Bust with tiara right **Obv. Designer:** Ian Rank-Broadley
Rev: Modern and early ferry

Date	Mintage	F	VF	XF	Unc	BU
2005	—	—	—	—	10.00	12.00

KM# 1287 CROWN
28.2800 g., Copper-Nickel, 38.6 mm. **Ruler:** Elizabeth II
Rev: Motorcycle right

Date	Mintage	F	VF	XF	Unc	BU
2005	—	—	—	—	10.00	12.00

KM# 1288 CROWN
28.2800 g., Copper-Nickel, 38.6 mm. **Ruler:** Elizabeth II
Rev: Motorcycle forward

Date	Mintage	F	VF	XF	Unc	BU
2005	—	—	—	—	10.00	12.00

KM# 1289 CROWN
28.2800 g., Copper-Nickel, 38.6 mm. **Ruler:** Elizabeth II
Subject: Ugly Duckling story **Obv:** Bust with tiara right
Obv. Designer: Ian Rank-Broadley **Rev:** Farm animals

Date	Mintage	F	VF	XF	Unc	BU
2005	—	—	—	—	12.00	14.00

KM# 1290b CROWN
28.2800 g., 0.9250 Silver 0.8410 oz. ASW, 38.6 mm.
Ruler: Elizabeth II **Obv:** Bust with tiara right **Obv. Designer:** Ian Rank-Broadley **Rev:** Three Exotic Shorthair cats sitting facing
Edge: Reeded

Date	Mintage	F	VF	XF	Unc	BU
2006PM	—	—	—	—	15.00	25.00

KM# 1296 CROWN
28.2800 g., Copper-Nickel, 38.6 mm. **Ruler:** Elizabeth II
Subject: Battles that Changed the World **Obv:** Elizabeth II
Rev: Trojan War scene **Edge:** Reeded

Date	Mintage	F	VF	XF	Unc	BU
2006PM	—	—	—	—	10.00	12.00

KM# 1296a CROWN
28.2800 g., 0.9250 Silver 0.8410 oz. ASW, 38.6 mm.
Ruler: Elizabeth II **Subject:** Battles that Changed the World
Obv: Elizabeth II **Rev:** Trojan War scene **Edge:** Reeded

Date	Mintage	F	VF	XF	Unc	BU
2006PM Proof	10,000	Value: 47.50				

KM# 1298 CROWN
28.2800 g., Copper-Nickel, 38.6 mm. **Ruler:** Elizabeth II
Subject: Battles that Changed the World **Obv:** Elizabeth II
Rev: Battle of Arbela scene **Edge:** Reeded

Date	Mintage	F	VF	XF	Unc	BU
2006PM	—	—	—	—	10.00	12.00

KM# 1298a CROWN
28.2800 g., 0.9250 Silver 0.8410 oz. ASW, 38.6 mm.
Ruler: Elizabeth II **Subject:** Battles that Changed the World
Obv: Elizabeth II **Rev:** Battle of Arbela scene **Edge:** Reeded

Date	Mintage	F	VF	XF	Unc	BU
2006PM Proof	10,000	Value: 47.50				

KM# 1300 CROWN
28.2800 g., Copper-Nickel, 38.6 mm. **Ruler:** Elizabeth II
Subject: Battles that Changed the World **Obv:** Elizabeth II
Rev: Battle of Thapsus scene **Edge:** Reeded

Date	Mintage	F	VF	XF	Unc	BU
2006PM	—	—	—	—	10.00	12.00

KM# 1300a CROWN
28.2800 g., 0.9250 Silver 0.8410 oz. ASW, 38.6 mm.
Ruler: Elizabeth II **Subject:** Battles that Changed the World
Obv: Elizabeth II **Rev:** Battle of Thapsus scene **Edge:** Reeded

Date	Mintage	F	VF	XF	Unc	BU
2006PM Proof	10,000	Value: 47.50				

KM# 1302 CROWN
28.2800 g., Copper-Nickel, 38.6 mm. **Ruler:** Elizabeth II
Subject: Battles that Changed the World **Obv:** Elizabeth II
Rev: Battle of Cologne scene **Edge:** Reeded

Date	Mintage	F	VF	XF	Unc	BU
2006PM	—	—	—	—	10.00	12.00

KM# 1302a CROWN
28.2800 g., 0.9250 Silver 0.8410 oz. ASW, 38.6 mm.
Ruler: Elizabeth II **Subject:** Battles that Changed the World
Obv: Elizabeth II **Rev:** Battle of Cologne scene **Edge:** Reeded

Date	Mintage	F	VF	XF	Unc	BU
2006PM Proof	10,000	Value: 47.50				

KM# 1304 CROWN
28.2800 g., Copper-Nickel, 38.6 mm. **Ruler:** Elizabeth II
Subject: Battles that Changed the World **Obv:** Elizabeth II
Rev: Siege of Valencia scene **Edge:** Reeded

Date	Mintage	F	VF	XF	Unc	BU
2006PM	—	—	—	—	10.00	12.00

KM# 1304a CROWN
28.2800 g., 0.9250 Silver 0.8410 oz. ASW, 38.6 mm.
Ruler: Elizabeth II **Subject:** Battles that Changed the World
Obv: Elizabeth II **Rev:** Siege of Valencia scene **Edge:** Reeded

Date	Mintage	F	VF	XF	Unc	BU
2006PM Proof	10,000	Value: 47.50				

KM# 1306 CROWN
28.2800 g., Copper-Nickel, 38.6 mm. **Ruler:** Elizabeth II
Subject: Battles that Changed the World **Obv:** Elizabeth II
Rev: Battle of Agincourt scene **Edge:** Reeded

Date	Mintage	F	VF	XF	Unc	BU
2006PM	—	—	—	—	10.00	12.00

KM# 1306a CROWN
28.2800 g., 0.9250 Silver 0.8410 oz. ASW, 38.6 mm.
Ruler: Elizabeth II **Subject:** Battles that Changed the World
Obv: Elizabeth II **Rev:** Battle of Agincourt scene **Edge:** Reeded

Date	Mintage	F	VF	XF	Unc	BU
2006PM Proof	10,000	Value: 47.50				

KM# 1323.1 CROWN
28.2800 g., Copper-Nickel, 38.60 mm. **Ruler:** Elizabeth II
Subject: Hans Christian Anderson's Fairy Tales **Obv:** Bust with
tiarra right **Obv. Legend:** ELIZABETH II - ISLE OF MAN
Obv. Designer: Ian Rank-Broadley **Rev:** Three bears startling
Goldilocks in bed **Rev. Legend:** Goldilocks and the Three Bears
Edge: Reeded

Date	Mintage	F	VF	XF	Unc	BU
2006PM	—	—	—	—	—	35.00

KM# 1323.2 CROWN
28.2800 g., Copper-Nickel, 38.60 mm. **Ruler:** Elizabeth II
Subject: Hans Christian Anderson's Fairy Tales **Obv:** Bust with
tiara right **Obv. Legend:** ELIZABETH II - ISLE OF MAN
Obv. Designer: Ian Rank-Broadley **Rev:** Three bears startling
Goldilocks in bed multicolor **Rev. Legend:** Goldilocks and the
Three Bears **Edge:** Reeded

Date	Mintage	F	VF	XF	Unc	BU
2006PM	—	—	—	—	—	40.00

KM# 1323.1a CROWN
28.2800 g., 0.9250 Silver 0.8410 oz. ASW, 38.60 mm.
Ruler: Elizabeth II **Subject:** Hans Christian Anderson's Fairy
Tales **Obv:** Bust with tiara right **Obv. Legend:** ELIZABETH II -
ISLE OF MAN **Obv. Designer:** Ian Rank-Broadley **Rev:** Three
bears startling Goldilocks in bed **Rev. Legend:** Goldilocks and
the Three Bears **Edge:** Reeded

Date	Mintage	F	VF	XF	Unc	BU
2006PM Proof	—	Value: 80.00				

KM# 1323.2a CROWN
28.2800 g., 0.9250 Silver 0.8410 oz. ASW, 38.60 mm.
Ruler: Elizabeth II **Subject:** Hans Christian Anderson's Fairy
Tales **Obv:** Bust with tiara right **Obv. Legend:** ELIZABETH II -
ISLE OF MAN **Obv. Designer:** Ian-Rank-Broadley **Rev:** Three
bears startling Goldilocks in bed multicolor **Rev. Legend:**
Goldilocks and the Three Bears **Edge:** Reeded

Date	Mintage	F	VF	XF	Unc	BU
2006PM Proof	—	Value: 100				

KM# 1290a CROWN
28.2800 g., Copper-Nickel, 38.6 mm. **Ruler:** Elizabeth II
Obv: Bust with tiara right **Obv. Designer:** Ian Rank-Broadley
Rev: Three Exotic Shorthair cats sitting facing **Edge:** Reeded

Date	Mintage	F	VF	XF	Unc	BU
2006PM	—	—	—	—	12.00	14.00

KM# 1290c CROWN
31.1030 g., 0.9999 Gold 0.9998 oz. AGW **Ruler:** Elizabeth II
Obv: Bust with tiara right **Obv. Designer:** Ian Rank-Broadley
Rev: Three Exotic Shorthair cats sitting facing, multicolor
Edge: Reeded

Date	Mintage	F	VF	XF	Unc	BU
2006PM	—	—	—	—	—	1,350

KM# 1347 CROWN
31.1030 g., 0.9999 Gold 0.9998 oz. AGW **Ruler:** Elizabeth II
Obv: Bust with tiara right **Obv. Legend:** ELIZABETH II - ISLE
OF MAN **Obv. Designer:** Ian Rank-Broadley **Rev:** Ragdoll cat
with two kittens sitting facing **Edge:** Reeded

Date	Mintage	F	VF	XF	Unc	BU
2007PM	—	—	—	—	—	1,350

KM# 1348.1 CROWN
Copper-Nickel **Ruler:** Elizabeth II **Subject:** The Tale of Peter
Rabbit **Obv:** Bust with tiara right **Obv. Legend:** ELIZABETH II -
ISLE OF MAN **Obv. Designer:** Ian Rank-Broadley **Rev:** Peter
walking with friends **Edge:** Reeded

Date	Mintage	F	VF	XF	Unc	BU
2007PM	—	—	—	—	—	30.00

KM# 1348.2 CROWN

Copper-Nickel **Ruler:** Elizabeth II **Subject:** The Tale of Peter Rabbit **Obv:** Bust with tiara right **Obv. Legend:** ELIZABETH II - ISLE OF MAN **Obv. Designer:** Ian Rank-Broadley **Rev:** Peter walking with friends, multicolor **Edge:** Reeded

Date	Mintage	F	VF	XF	Unc	BU
2007PM	—	—	—	—	—	35.00

KM# 1348.1a CROWN

0.9250 Silver **Ruler:** Elizabeth II **Subject:** The Tale of Peter Rabbit **Obv:** Bust with tiara right **Obv. Legend:** ELIZABETH II - ISLE OF MAN **Obv. Designer:** Ian Rank-Broadley **Rev:** Peter walking with friends **Edge:** Reeded

Date	Mintage	F	VF	XF	Unc	BU
2007PM Proof	—	Value: 85.00				

KM# 1348.2a CROWN

0.9250 Silver **Ruler:** Elizabeth II **Subject:** The Tale of Peter Rabbit **Obv:** Bust with tiara right **Obv. Legend:** ELIZABETH II - ISLE OF MAN **Obv. Designer:** Ian Rank-Broadley **Rev:** Peter walking with friends, multicolor **Edge:** Reeded

Date	Mintage	F	VF	XF	Unc	BU
2007PM Proof	—	Value: 100				

KM# 1307 CROWN

28.2800 g., Copper-Nickel, 38.6 mm. **Ruler:** Elizabeth II **Rev:** Ragdoll cat and kittens

Date	Mintage	F	VF	XF	Unc	BU
2007	—	—	—	—	15.00	18.00

KM# 1310 CROWN

28.2800 g., Copper-Nickel, 38.6 mm. **Ruler:** Elizabeth II **Subject:** 100th Anniversary of Scouting **Obv:** Bust with tiara right **Obv. Legend:** ELIZABETH II - ISLE OF MAN **Rev:** 3/4 length figure of Robert Baden-Powell standing facing 3/4 left, Fleur-de-lys below, images of scouting at left and right **Rev. Legend:** CENTENARY OF SCOUTING **Edge:** Reeded

Date	Mintage	F	VF	XF	Unc	BU
2007	—	—	—	—	17.00	20.00

KM# 1311 CROWN

28.2800 g., 0.9167 Silver 0.8334 oz. ASW **Ruler:** Elizabeth II **Subject:** 100th Anniversary of Scouting **Obv:** Bust with tiara right **Obv. Legend:** ELIZABETH II - ISLE OF MAN **Rev:** 3/4 length figure of Robert Baden-Powell standing facing 3/4 left, Fleur-de-lys below, images of scouting at left and right **Rev. Legend:** CENTENARY OF SCOUTING **Edge:** Reeded

Date	Mintage	F	VF	XF	Unc	BU
2007 Proof	—	Value: 75.00				

KM# 1312 CROWN

0.7500 Gold Yellow, white and red Gold **Ruler:** Elizabeth II **Subject:** Diamond Wedding Ann. **Obv:** Bust with tiara right **Obv. Legend:** ELIZABETH II - ISLE OF MAN **Rev:** Crowned pair of doves surrounded by a leek, thistle, rose and shamrock **Edge:** Reeded

Date	Mintage	F	VF	XF	Unc	BU
2007 Proof	—	Value: 2,000				

KM# 1313 CROWN

28.2800 g., Copper-Nickel, 38.60 mm. **Ruler:** Elizabeth II **Obv:** Bust with tiara right **Obv. Legend:** ELIZABETH II - ISLE OF MAN **Rev:** Two swans facing **Edge:** Reeded

Date	Mintage	F	VF	XF	Unc	BU
2007	—	—	—	—	15.00	18.00

KM# 1315 CROWN

28.2800 g., 0.9167 Silver 0.8334 oz. ASW, 38.60 mm. **Ruler:** Elizabeth II **Obv:** Bust with tiara right **Obv. Legend:** ELIZABETH II - ISLE OF MAN **Rev:** Two swans facing **Edge:** Reeded

Date	Mintage	F	VF	XF	Unc	BU
2007 Proof	10,000	Value: 75.00				

KM# 1316 CROWN

28.2800 g., Copper-Nickel, 38.6 mm. **Ruler:** Elizabeth II **Subject:** Diamond Wedding Anniversary **Obv:** Conjoined busts with Philip right **Obv. Legend:** ELIZABETH II - ISLE OF MAN **Rev:** Bridal bouquet of white orchids **Rev. Legend:** Diamond Wedding of H.M. Queen Elizabeth II & H.R.H. Prince Philip **Edge:** Reeded

Date	Mintage	F	VF	XF	Unc	BU
2007	—	—	—	—	15.00	18.00

KM# 1316a CROWN

28.2800 g., 0.9167 Silver 0.8334 oz. ASW **Ruler:** Elizabeth II **Subject:** Diamond Wedding Anniversary **Obv:** Conjoined busts with Philip right **Obv. Legend:** ELIZABETH II - ISLE OF MAN **Rev:** Bridal bouquet of white orchids **Rev. Legend:** Diamond Wedding of H.M. Queen Elizabeth II & H.R.H. Prince Philip **Edge:** Reeded

Date	Mintage	F	VF	XF	Unc	BU
2007 Proof	—	Value: 75.00				

KM# 1317 CROWN

28.2800 g., Copper-Nickel **Ruler:** Elizabeth II **Subject:** Diamond Wedding Anniversary **Obv:** Conjoined busts with Philip right **Obv. Legend:** ELIZABETH II - ISLE OF MAN **Rev:** Westminster Abbey **Rev. Legend:** Diamond Wedding of H.M. Queen Elizabeth II & H.R.H. Prince Philip **Edge:** Reeded

Date	Mintage	F	VF	XF	Unc	BU
2007	—	—	—	—	15.00	18.00

KM# 1317a CROWN

28.2800 g., 0.9167 Silver 0.8334 oz. ASW **Ruler:** Elizabeth II **Subject:** Diamond Wedding Anniversary **Obv:** Conjoined busts with Philip right **Obv. Legend:** ELIZABETH II - ISLE OF MAN **Rev:** Westminster Abbey **Rev. Legend:** Diamond Wedding of H.M. Queen Elizabeth II & H.R.H. Prince Philip **Edge:** Reeded

Date	Mintage	F	VF	XF	Unc	BU
2007 Proof	—	Value: 75.00				

KM# 1318 CROWN

28.2800 g., Copper-Nickel, 38.6 mm. **Ruler:** Elizabeth II **Subject:** Diamond Wedding Anniversary **Obv:** Conjoined busts with Philip right **Obv. Legend:** ELIZABETH II - ISLE OF MAN **Rev:** Royal Family of five standing facing **Rev. Legend:** Diamond Wedding of H.M. Queen Elizabeth II & H.R.H. Prince Philip **Edge:** Reeded

Date	Mintage	F	VF	XF	Unc	BU
2007	—	—	—	—	15.00	18.00

KM# 1318a CROWN

28.2800 g., 0.9167 Silver 0.8334 oz. ASW, 38.6 mm. **Ruler:** Elizabeth II **Subject:** Diamond Wedding Ann. **Obv:** Conjoined busts w/Philip right **Obv. Legend:** ELIZABETH II - ISLE OF MAN **Rev:** Royal Family of five standing facing **Rev. Legend:** Diamond Wedding of H.M. Queen Elizabeth II & H.R.H. Prince Philip **Edge:** Reeded

Date	Mintage	F	VF	XF	Unc	BU
2007 Proof	—	Value: 75.00				

KM# 1319 CROWN

28.2800 g., Copper-Nickel, 38.6 mm. **Ruler:** Elizabeth II **Subject:** Diamond Wedding Anniversary **Obv:** Conjoined busts with Philip right **Obv. Legend:** ELIZABETH II - ISLE OF MAN **Rev:** Bride and groom standing facing **Rev. Legend:** Diamond Wedding of H.M. Queen Elizabeth II & H.R.H. Prince Philip **Edge:** Reeded

Date	Mintage	F	VF	XF	Unc	BU
2007	—	—	—	—	15.00	18.00

KM# 1319a CROWN

28.2800 g., 0.9167 Silver 0.8334 oz. ASW, 38.6 mm. **Ruler:** Elizabeth II **Subject:** Diamond Wedding Ann. **Obv:** Conjoined busts with Philip right **Obv. Legend:** ELIZABETH II - ISLE OF MAN **Rev:** Bride/groom standing facing **Rev. Legend:** Diamond Wedding of H.M. Queen Elizabeth II & H.R.H. Prince Philip **Edge:** Reeded

Date	Mintage	F	VF	XF	Unc	BU
2007 Proof	—	Value: 75.00				

KM# 1325.1 CROWN

28.2800 g., Copper-Nickel, 38.60 mm. **Ruler:** Elizabeth II **Subject:** Hans Christian Anderson's Fairy Tales **Obv:** Bust with tiara right **Obv. Legend:** ELIZABETH II - ISLE OF MAN **Obv. Designer:** Ian Rank-Broadley **Rev:** Wolf at right trying to blow pig's house down, two pigs fleeing above in background **Rev. Legend:** Three Little Pigs **Edge:** Reeded

Date	Mintage	F	VF	XF	Unc	BU
2007PM	—	—	—	—	—	35.00

KM# 1325.2 CROWN

28.2800 g., Copper-Nickel, 38.60 mm. **Ruler:** Elizabeth II **Subject:** Hans Christian Anderson's Fairy Tales **Obv:** Bust with tiara right **Obv. Legend:** ELIZABETH II - ISLE OF MAN **Obv. Designer:** Ian Rank-Broadley **Rev:** Wolf at right trying to blow pig's house down, two pigs fleeing above in backgound multicolor **Rev. Legend:** Three Little Pigs **Edge:** Reeded

Date	Mintage	F	VF	XF	Unc	BU
2007PM	—	—	—	—	—	40.00

KM# 1325.1a CROWN

28.2800 g., 0.9250 Silver 0.8410 oz. ASW, 38.60 mm. **Ruler:** Elizabeth II **Subject:** Hans Christian Anderson's Fairy Tales **Obv:** Bust with tiara right **Obv. Legend:** ELIZABETH II - ISLE OF MAN **Obv. Designer:** Ian Rank-Broadley **Rev:** Wolf at right trying to blow pig's house down, two pigs fleeing above in background **Rev. Legend:** Three Little Pigs **Edge:** Reeded

Date	Mintage	F	VF	XF	Unc	BU
2007PM Proof	—	Value: 80.00				

KM# 1325.2a CROWN

28.2800 g., 0.9250 Silver 0.8410 oz. ASW, 38.60 mm. **Ruler:** Elizabeth II **Subject:** Hans Christian Anderson's Fairy Tales **Obv:** Bust with tiara right **Obv. Legend:** ELIZABETH II - ISLE OF MAN **Obv. Designer:** Ian Rank-Broadley **Rev:** Wolf at right trying to blow pig's house down, two pigs fleeing above in background multicolor **Rev. Legend:** Three Little Pigs **Edge:** Reeded

Date	Mintage	F	VF	XF	Unc	BU
2007PM Proof	—	Value: 100				

KM# 1324.1 CROWN

28.2800 g., Copper-Nickel, 38.60 mm. **Ruler:** Elizabeth II **Subject:** Hans Christian Anderson's Fairy Tales **Obv:** Bust with tiara right **Obv. Legend:** ELIZABETH II - ISLE OF MAN **Obv. Designer:** Ian Rank-Broadley **Rev:** Prince awakening Sleeping Beauty, castle in background **Rev. Legend:** Sleeping Beauty **Edge:** Reeded

Date	Mintage	F	VF	XF	Unc	BU
2007PM	—	—	—	—	—	35.00

KM# 1324.1a CROWN

28.2800 g., 0.9250 Silver 0.8410 oz. ASW, 38.60 mm. **Ruler:** Elizabeth II **Subject:** Hans Christian Anderson's Fairy Tales **Obv:** Bust with tiara right **Obv. Legend:** ELIZABETH II - ISLE OF MAN **Obv. Designer:** Ian Rank-Broadley **Rev:** Prince wakening Sleeping Beauty, castle in background **Rev. Legend:** Sleeping Beauty **Edge:** Reeded

Date	Mintage	F	VF	XF	Unc	BU
2007PM Proof	—	Value: 80.00				

KM# 1324.2 CROWN

28.2800 g., Copper-Nickel, 38.60 mm. **Ruler:** Elizabeth II **Subject:** Hans Christian Anderson's Fairy Tales **Obv:** Bust with tiara right **Obv. Legend:** ELIZABET II - ISLE OF MAN **Obv. Designer:** Ian Rank-Broadley **Rev:** Prince awakening Sleeping Beauty, castle in background multicolor **Rev. Legend:** Sleeping Beauty **Edge:** Reeded

Date	Mintage	F	VF	XF	Unc	BU
2007PM	—	—	—	—	—	40.00

KM# 1324.2a CROWN

28.2800 g., 0.9250 Silver 0.8410 oz. ASW, 38.60 mm. **Ruler:** Elizabeth II **Subject:** Hans Christian Anderson's Fairy Tales **Obv:** Bust with tiara right **Obv. Legend:** ELIZABETH II - ISLE OF MAN **Obv. Designer:** Ian Rank-Broadley **Rev:** Prince awakening Sleeping Beauty, castle in background multicolor **Rev. Legend:** Sleeping Beauty **Edge:** Reeded

Date	Mintage	F	VF	XF	Unc	BU
2007PM Proof	—	Value: 100				

KM# 1353 CROWN

28.2800 g., Copper-Nickel, 38.6 mm. **Ruler:** Elizabeth II **Subject:** Prince Charles 60th Birthday **Obv:** Bust with tiara right **Obv. Legend:** ELIZABETH II - ISLE OF MAN **Obv. Designer:** Ian Rank-Broadley **Rev:** Heads of Charles, Princes William and Henry right **Edge:** Reeded

Date	Mintage	F	VF	XF	Unc	BU
2008PM	—	—	—	—	10.00	12.00

KM# 1353a CROWN

28.2800 g., 0.9250 Silver 0.8410 oz. ASW, 38.6 mm. **Ruler:** Elizabeth II **Subject:** Prince Charles 60th Birthday **Obv:** Bust with tiara right **Obv. Legend:** ELIZABETH II - ISLE OF MAN **Obv. Designer:** Ian Rank-Broadley **Rev:** Heads of Charles, Princes William and Henry right **Edge:** Reeded

Date	Mintage	F	VF	XF	Unc	BU
2008PM Proof	10,000	Value: 50.00				

KM# 1373 CROWN

28.2800 g., Copper-Nickel, 38.6 mm. **Ruler:** Elizabeth II **Rev:** Berlin Wall and Brandenburg Gate

Date	Mintage	F	VF	XF	Unc	BU
2009	—	—	—	—	15.00	18.00

KM# 1373a CROWN

28.2800 g., 0.9250 Silver 0.8410 oz. ASW, 38.6 mm. **Ruler:** Elizabeth II **Rev:** Berlin Wall and Brandenenberg Gate

Date	Mintage	F	VF	XF	Unc	BU
2009 Proof	10,000	Value: 35.00				

KM# 1374 CROWN

28.2800 g., Copper-Nickel, 38.6 mm. **Ruler:** Elizabeth II **Subject:** Terra Cotta Army **Obv:** Bust right **Rev:** Making of the Soldier

Date	Mintage	F	VF	XF	Unc	BU
2009	—	—	—	—	12.00	15.00

KM# 1374a CROWN

28.2800 g., 0.9250 Silver 0.8410 oz. ASW, 38.6 mm. **Ruler:** Elizabeth II **Subject:** Terra Cotta Army **Obv:** Bust right **Rev:** Making of the Soldier

Date	Mintage	F	VF	XF	Unc	BU
2009 Proof	10,000	Value: 35.00				

KM# 1375 CROWN

6.2200 g., 0.9999 Gold 0.1999 oz. AGW, 22 mm. **Ruler:** Elizabeth II **Subject:** Terra Cotta Army **Obv:** Bust right **Rev:** Making of the Soldier

Date	Mintage	F	VF	XF	Unc	BU
2009 Proof	5,000	Value: 300				

KM# 1376   CROWN
28.2800 g., 0.9250 Copper-Nickel 0.8410 oz., 38.6 mm.
Ruler: Elizabeth II **Subject:** Terra Cotta Army **Obv:** Bust right
Rev: Making of the Horse

Date	Mintage	F	VF	XF	Unc	BU
2009	—	—	—	—	12.00	15.00

KM# 1376a   CROWN
28.2800 g., 0.9250 Silver 0.8410 oz. ASW, 38.6 mm.
Ruler: Elizabeth II **Subject:** Terra Cotta Army **Obv:** Bust right
Rev: Making of the Horse

Date	Mintage	F	VF	XF	Unc	BU
2009 Proof	10,000	Value: 35.00				

KM# 1377   CROWN
6.2200 g., 0.9999 Gold 0.1999 oz. AGW, 22 mm.
Ruler: Elizabeth II **Subject:** Terra Cotta Army **Obv:** Bust right
Rev: Making of the Horse

Date	Mintage	F	VF	XF	Unc	BU
2009 Proof	5,000	Value: 300				

KM# 1378.1   CROWN
28.2800 g., Copper-Nickel, 38.6 mm. **Ruler:** Elizabeth II
Obv: Bust right **Rev:** Chinchilla cat and kitten

Date	Mintage	F	VF	XF	Unc	BU
2009	—	—	—	—	15.00	18.00

KM# 1378.2   CROWN
28.2800 g., Copper-Nickel, 38.6 mm. **Ruler:** Elizabeth II
Obv: Bust right **Rev:** Multicolor chinchilla cat and kitten

Date	Mintage	F	VF	XF	Unc	BU
2009	—	—	—	—	25.00	

KM# 1378.1a   CROWN
31.1000 g., 0.9990 Silver 0.9988 oz. ASW, 38.6 mm.
Ruler: Elizabeth II **Obv:** Bust right **Rev:** Chinchilla cat and kitten

Date	Mintage	F	VF	XF	Unc	BU
2009 Proof	10,000	Value: 35.00				

KM# 1378.2a   CROWN
31.1050 g., 0.9999 Silver 0.9999 oz. ASW, 38.6 mm.
Ruler: Elizabeth II **Obv:** Bust right **Rev:** Multicolor chinchilla cat and kitten

Date	Mintage	F	VF	XF	Unc	BU
2009	—	—	—	—	—	35.00

KM# 1379   CROWN
31.1050 g., 0.9999 Gold 0.9999 oz. AGW, 32.7 mm.
Ruler: Elizabeth II **Obv:** Bust right **Rev:** Chinchilla cat and kitten

Date	Mintage	F	VF	XF	Unc	BU
2009	—	—	—	—	—	1,250
2009 Proof	1,000	Value: 1,300				

KM# 1388   CROWN
31.1050 g., 0.9999 Gold 0.9999 oz. AGW, 45x31.1 mm.
Ruler: Elizabeth II **Subject:** Harold Carter, 70th Anniversary of death **Obv:** Bust right **Rev:** Pharoh and Anubis carving, encased with sand **Shape:** Pyramid

Date	Mintage	F	VF	XF	Unc	BU
2009 Proof	250	Value: 1,400				

KM# 1389   CROWN
31.1030 g., 0.9990 Silver 0.9989 oz. ASW, 56.2x40.7 mm.
Ruler: Elizabeth II **Subject:** Harold Carter, 70th Anniversary of death **Obv:** Bust right **Rev:** Pharoh and Anubis, encased with sand **Shape:** Prymaid

Date	Mintage	F	VF	XF	Unc	BU
2009	3,000	—	—	—	—	50.00

KM# 1390   CROWN
28.2800 g., Copper-Nickel, 38.6 mm. **Ruler:** Elizabeth II
Subject: Concorde test flight, 40th Anniversary **Obv:** Bust right
Rev: Concorde and five world landmarks

Date	Mintage	F	VF	XF	Unc	BU
2009	—	—	—	—	15.00	18.00

KM# 1390a   CROWN
28.2800 g., 0.9250 Silver 0.8410 oz. ASW, 38.6 mm. **Ruler:**
Elizabeth II **Subject:** Corcorde test flight, 40th Anniversary
Obv: Bust right **Rev:** Concorde and five world landmarks

Date	Mintage	F	VF	XF	Unc	BU
2009 Proof	10,000	Value: 35.00				

KM# 1391   CROWN
28.2800 g., Copper-Nickel, 38.6 mm. **Ruler:** Elizabeth II
Obv: Bust right **Rev:** Henry VIII

Date	Mintage	F	VF	XF	Unc	BU
2009	—	—	—	—	15.00	18.00

KM# 1391a   CROWN
28.2800 g., 0.9250 Silver 0.8410 oz. ASW, 38.6 mm.
Ruler: Elizabeth II **Obv:** Bust right **Rev:** Henry VIII

Date	Mintage	F	VF	XF	Unc	BU
2009 Proof	10,000	Value: 35.00				

KM# 1392   CROWN
28.2800 g., Copper-Nickel, 38.6 mm. **Ruler:** Elizabeth II
Subject: FIFA World Cup - South Africa **Obv:** Bust right

Date	Mintage	F	VF	XF	Unc	BU
2009	—	—	—	—	15.00	18.00

KM# 1392a   CROWN
28.2800 g., 0.9250 Silver 0.8410 oz. ASW, 38.6 mm. **Ruler:**
Elizabeth II **Subject:** FIFA World Cup - South Africa **Obv:** Bust right

Date	Mintage	F	VF	XF	Unc	BU
2009 Proof	10,000	Value: 35.00				

KM# 1200   2 CROWNS
62.2000 g., 0.9990 Palladium 1.9977 oz., 40 mm.
Ruler: Elizabeth II **Subject:** Discovery of Palladium Bicentennial
Obv: Bust with tiara right **Obv. Designer:** Ian Rank-Broadley
Rev: Pallas Athena left **Edge:** Reeded

Date	Mintage	F	VF	XF	Unc	BU
2004PM Proof	300	Value: 900				

KM# 1064   5 CROWN
155.5175 g., 0.9999 Gold 4.9993 oz. AGW, 65 mm. **Ruler:**
Elizabeth II **Subject:** Year of the Snake **Obv:** Bust with tiara right
Obv. Designer: Ian Rank-Broadley **Rev:** Snake **Edge:** Reeded

Date	Mintage	F	VF	XF	Unc	BU
2001 Proof	250	Value: 6,250				

KM# 1104   5 CROWN
155.5100 g., 0.9999 Gold 4.9991 oz. AGW, 65 mm.
Ruler: Elizabeth II **Subject:** Year of the Horse **Obv:** Bust with tiara right **Obv. Designer:** Ian Rank-Broadley **Rev:** Two horses **Edge:** Reeded

Date	Mintage	F	VF	XF	Unc	BU
2002 Proof	250	Value: 6,250				

KM# 1173   5 CROWN
155.5100 g., 0.9999 Gold 4.9991 oz. AGW, 65 mm.
Ruler: Elizabeth II **Subject:** Year of the Goat **Obv:** Bust with tiara right **Obv. Designer:** Ian Rank-Broadley **Rev:** Three goats **Edge:** Reeded

Date	Mintage	F	VF	XF	Unc	BU
2003PM Proof	250	Value: 6,250				

KM# 1244   5 CROWN
155.5175 g., 0.9999 Gold 4.9993 oz. AGW, 65 mm.
Ruler: Elizabeth II **Obv:** Bust with tiara right **Obv. Designer:** Ian Rank-Broadley **Rev:** Monkey **Edge:** Reeded

Date	Mintage	F	VF	XF	Unc	BU
2004PM Proof	250	Value: 6,250				

KM# 1219   64 CROWNS
2000.0000 g., 0.9990 Silver 64.234 oz. ASW, 140 mm. **Ruler:**
Elizabeth II **Obv:** Bust with tiara right **Obv. Designer:** Ian Rank-Broadley **Rev:** Ocean Liner Queen Mary 2 **Edge:** Reeded

Date	Mintage	F	VF	XF	Unc	BU
2004PM Proof	500	Value: 1,400				

KM# 1142   100 CROWNS
3000.0000 g., 0.9999 Silver 96.438 oz. ASW, 130 mm.
Ruler: Elizabeth II **Subject:** Queen's Golden Jubilee **Obv:** Bust
with tiara right **Obv. Designer:** Ian Rank-Broadley **Rev:** Queen on horse **Edge:** Reeded **Note:** Illustration reduced.

Date	Mintage	F	VF	XF	Unc	BU
2002 Proof	500	Value: 2,000				

KM# 1184   130 CROWNS
4000.0000 g., 0.9990 Silver 128.46 oz. ASW, 130 mm.
Ruler: Elizabeth II **Obv:** Bust with tiara right **Obv. Designer:** Ian Rank-Broadley **Rev:** Gold clad cameo portrait of Elizabeth I with a .035ct ruby inset on her forehead all within a circle of portraits **Edge:** Reeded

Date	Mintage	F	VF	XF	Unc	BU
2003PM Proof	500	Value: 2,750				

GOLD BULLION COINAGE
Angel Issues

KM# 1106   1/20 ANGEL
1.5552 g., 0.9999 Gold 0.0500 oz. AGW, 15 mm.
Ruler: Elizabeth II **Obv:** Bust with tiara right **Obv. Designer:** Ian Rank-Broadley **Rev:** St. Michael slaying dragon, three crown privy mark at right **Edge:** Reeded

Date	Mintage	F	VF	XF	Unc	BU
2001 (3c) Proof	1,000	Value: 70.00				
2002 Proof	—	Value: 70.00				

Note: With candy cane privy mark

KM# 393   1/20 ANGEL
1.5551 g., 0.9999 Gold 0.0500 oz. AGW **Ruler:** Elizabeth II
Obv: Crowned bust right **Obv. Designer:** Raphael Maklouf
Rev: Archangel Michael slaying dragon right

Date	Mintage	F	VF	XF	Unc	BU
2001	—	—	—	—	—	70.00
2001 Proof	—	Value: 75.00				
2001 Proof	—	Value: 80.00				
Note: Privy mark: 3 Kings						
2002	—	—	—	—	—	70.00
2002 Proof	—	Value: 75.00				
2002 Proof	—	Value: 80.00				
Note: Privy mark: Candy						
2003	—	—	—	—	—	70.00
2003 Proof	—	Value: 75.00				
2003 Proof	—	Value: 80.00				
Note: Privy mark: Candy						
2004	—	—	—	—	—	70.00
2004 Proof	—	Value: 75.00				
2004 Proof	—	Value: 80.00				
Note: Privy mark: Partridge in a Pear Tree						
2005	—	—	—	—	—	70.00
2005 Proof	—	Value: 75.00				
2005 Proof	—	Value: 80.00				
Note: Privy mark: 2 Turtle doves						
2006	—	—	—	—	—	70.00
2006 Proof	—	Value: 75.00				
2006 Proof	—	Value: 80.00				
Note: Privy mark: 4 Calling birds						
2007	—	—	—	—	—	70.00
2007 Proof	—	Value: 75.00				
2007 Proof	—	Value: 80.00				
Note: Privy mark: 4 Calling birds						

KM# 1252   1/20 ANGEL
1.5550 g., 0.9999 Gold 0.0500 oz. AGW, 15 mm. **Ruler:** Elizabeth II
Obv: Bust with tiara right **Obv. Designer:** Ian Rank-Broadley
Rev: St. Michael and Christmas privy mark **Edge:** Reeded

Date	Mintage	F	VF	XF	Unc	BU
2004PM Proof	1,000	Value: 70.00				

KM# 394   1/10 ANGEL
3.1103 g., 0.9999 Gold 0.1000 oz. AGW **Ruler:** Elizabeth II
Obv: Crowned bust right **Obv. Designer:** Raphael Maklouf
Rev: Archangel Michael

Date	Mintage	F	VF	XF	Unc	BU
2001 Proof	—	Value: 130				
2001	—	—	—	—	—	125
2002 Proof	—	Value: 130				
2002	—	—	—	—	—	125
2003 Proof	—	Value: 130				
2003	—	—	—	—	—	125
2004 Proof	—	Value: 130				
2004	—	—	—	—	—	125

Date	Mintage	F	VF	XF	Unc	BU
2005 Proof	—	Value: 130				
2005	—	—	—	—	—	125

KM# 395 1/4 ANGEL
7.7758 g., 0.9999 Gold 0.2500 oz. AGW **Ruler:** Elizabeth II
Obv: Crowned bust right **Obv. Designer:** Raphael Maklouf
Rev: Archangel Michael slaying dragon

Date	Mintage	F	VF	XF	Unc	BU
2001 Proof	—	Value: 325				
2001	—	—	—	—	—	315
2002 Proof	—	Value: 325				
2002	—	—	—	—	—	315
2003 Proof	—	Value: 325				
2003	—	—	—	—	—	315
2004 Proof	—	Value: 325				
2004	—	—	—	—	—	315
2005 Proof	—	Value: 325				
2005	—	—	—	—	—	315

KM# 397 ANGEL
31.1035 g., 0.9999 Gold 0.9999 oz. AGW **Ruler:** Elizabeth II
Obv: Crowned bust right **Obv. Designer:** Raphael Maklouf
Rev: Archangel Michael slaying dragon right

Date	Mintage	F	VF	XF	Unc	BU
2001 Proof	—	Value: 1,300				
2001	—	—	—	—	—	1,250
2002 Proof	—	Value: 1,300				
2002	—	—	—	—	—	1,250
2003 Proof	—	Value: 1,300				
2003	—	—	—	—	—	1,250
2004 Proof	—	Value: 1,300				
2004	—	—	—	—	—	1,250
2005 Proof	—	Value: 1,300				
2005	—	—	—	—	—	1,250
2006 Proof	500	Value: 1,300				
2006	—	—	—	—	—	1,250
2007 Proof	—	Value: 1,300				
2007	—	—	—	—	—	1,250

KM# 397.1 ANGEL
31.1035 g., 0.9990 Gold 0.9990 oz. AGW **Ruler:** Elizabeth II
Obv: Crowned bust right **Obv. Designer:** Raphael Maklouf
Rev: Archangel Michael slaying dragon right

Date	Mintage	F	VF	XF	Unc	BU
2006 Proof, High Relief	Est. 1,000	Value: 1,300				
2007 Proof, High Relief	Est. 1,000	Value: 1,300				

MINT SETS

KM#	Date	Mintage	Identification	Issue Price	Mkt Val
MS30	2001 (8)	—	KM#1036-1043	—	22.50
MS31	2001 (9)	—	KM#1036-1044	—	40.00
MS32	2002 (8)	—	KM#1036-1043	—	22.50
MS33	2002 (9)	—	KM#1036-1044	—	40.00
MS34	2003 (8)	—	KM#1036-1043	—	22.50
MS35	2003 (9)	—	KM#1036-1044	—	40.00
MS36	2004 (8)	—	KM#1253-1260	—	25.00
MS37	2004 (9)	—	KM#1253-1261	—	40.00
MS38	2005 (8)	—	KM#1253-1260	—	22.50
MS39	2005 (9)	—	KM#1253-1261	—	40.00
MS40	2006 (8)	—	MS#1253-1261	35.00	25.00
MS41	2006 (9)	—	KM1253-1261	42.50	40.00
MS42	2007 (8)	—	KM#1253-1260	35.00	22.50
MS43	2007 (9)	—	KM1253-1261	42.50	40.00

PROOF SETS

KM#	Date	Mintage	Identification	Issue Price	Mkt Val
PS59	2001 (5)	1,000	KM#1067-1070, 1073	—	2,450
PS60	2003 (3)	—	KM#1186, 1187, 1188	—	450
PS61	2003 (5)	—	KM#1186, 1187, 1188, 1189, 1190 w/gold ring	—	1,400
PS62	2003 (5)	—	KM#1191-1195 w/gold-plated silver ring	—	245

KM#	Date	Mintage	Identification	Issue Price	Mkt Val
PS63	2004 (5)	1,000	KM#1247, 1248, 1249.1, 1250, 1251	—	2,450

ISRAEL

The state of Israel, a Middle Eastern republic at the eastern end of the Mediterranean Sea, bounded by Lebanon on the north, Syria on the northeast, Jordan on the east, and Egypt on the southwest, has an area of 9,000sq. mi. (20,770 sq. km.) and a population of 6 million. Capital: Jerusalem. Finished diamonds, chemicals, citrus, textiles, minerals, electronic and transportation equipment are exported.

HEBREW COIN DATING
Modern Israel's coins carry Hebrew dating formed from a combination of the 22 consonant letters of the Hebrew alphabet and read from right to left. The Jewish calendar dates back more than 5700 years; but five millenniums are assumed in the dating of coins (until 1981). Thus, the year 5735 (1975AD) appears as 735, with the first two characters from the right indicating the number of years in hundreds; tav (400), plus shin (300). The next is lamedh (30), followed by a separation mark which has the appearance of double quotation marks, then heh (5).

The Star of David is not a mintmark. It appears only on some coins sold by the Israel Government Coins and Medals Corporation Ltd., which is owned by the Israel government, and is a division of the Prime Minister's office and sole distributor to collectors. The Star of David was first used in 1971 on the science coin to signify that it was minted in Jerusalem, but was later used by different mint facilities.

AD Date		Jewish Era
2001	התשס"א	5761
2002	התשס"ב	5762
2003	התשס"ג	5763
2004	התשס"ד	5764
2005	התשס"ה	5765
2006	התשס"ו	5766
2007	התשס"ז	5767
2008	התשס"ח	5768
2009	התשס"ט	5769
2010	התש"ע	5770

MINT MARKS

מ

(m) - Mem

(o) - Ottawa

(s) - San Francisco

None – Jerusalem

REPUBLIC
REFORM COINAGE
100 Agorot = 1 New Sheqel
1,000 Sheqalim = 1 New Sheqel

September 4, 1985

KM# 157 5 AGOROT
2.9500 g., Aluminum-Bronze, 19.45 mm. **Obv:** Ancient coin **Rev:** Value within lined square **Edge:** Plain

Date	Mintage	F	VF	XF	Unc	BU
JE5761 (2001)(sl)	6,144,000	—	—	—	0.15	—
JE5762 (2002)(sl)	6,144,000	—	—	—	0.15	—
JE5764 (2004)	—	—	—	—	0.15	—
JE5765 (2005)	—	—	—	—	0.15	—
JE5766 (2006)	—	—	—	—	0.15	—
JE5767 (2007)	—	—	—	—	0.15	—

KM# 172 5 AGOROT
3.0000 g., Alum.-Bronze, 14.5 mm. **Subject:** Hanukka **Obv:** Ancient coin **Rev:** Value within lined square **Note:** JE5754-576 coins contain the Star of David mint mark; the JE5747-5753 coins do not.

Date	Mintage	F	VF	XF	Unc	BU
JE5761 (2001)(u)	4,000	—	—	—	2.50	—
Note: In sets only						
JE5762 (2002)(u)	4,000	—	—	—	2.50	—
Note: In sets only						
JE5763 (2003)(u)	3,000	—	—	—	3.00	—
Note: In sets only						
JE5764 (2004)(u)	3,000	—	—	—	3.00	—
Note: In sets only						
JE5765 (2005)(u)	2,500	—	—	—	3.00	—
Note: In sets only						
JE5766 (2006)(u)	3,000	—	—	—	3.00	—
Note: In sets only						
JE5767 (2007)(u)	3,000	—	—	—	3.00	—
Note: In sets only						
JE5768 (2008)(u)	3,000	—	—	—	3.00	—
Note: In sets only						

KM# 158 10 AGOROT
4.0000 g., Aluminum-Bronze, 22 mm. **Obv:** Menorah **Rev:** Value within lined square **Edge:** Plain

Date	Mintage	F	VF	XF	Unc	BU
JE5761 (2001)(sl)	46,140,000	—	—	—	0.20	—
Note: Sides of central part of zero are rounded.						
JE5761 (2001)(so)	32,256,000	—	—	—	0.20	—
Note: Sides of central part of zero are straight.						
JE5762 (2002)(w)	4,608,000	—	—	—	0.20	—
JE5763 (2003)(sl)	22,980,000	—	—	—	0.20	—
JE5764 (2004)	—	—	—	—	0.20	—
JE5765 (2005)	—	—	—	—	0.20	—
JE5766 (2006)	—	—	—	—	0.20	—
JE5767 (2007)	—	—	—	—	0.20	—
JEJE5768 (2008)	—	—	—	—	0.20	—

KM# 173 10 AGOROT
4.0700 g., Aluminum-Bronze, 22 mm. **Subject:** Hanukka **Obv:** Menorah **Rev:** Value within lined square **Note:** JE5754-5769 have the Star of David mint mark, JE5747-5753 coins do not.

Date	Mintage	F	VF	XF	Unc	BU
JE5761 (2001)(u)	4,000	—	—	—	3.00	—
Note: In sets only						
JE5762 (2002)(u)	4,000	—	—	—	3.00	—
Note: In sets only						
JE5763 (2003)(u)	3,000	—	—	—	3.00	—
Note: In sets only						
JE5764 (2004)(u)	3,000	—	—	—	3.00	—
Note: In sets only						
JE5765 (2005)(u)	2,500	—	—	—	3.00	—
Note: In sets only						
JE5766 (2006)(u)	3,000	—	—	—	3.00	—
Note: In sets only						
JE5767 (2007)(u)	3,000	—	—	—	3.00	—
Note: In sets only						
JE5768 (2008)(u)	3,000	—	—	—	3.00	—
Note: In sets only						
JE5769 (2009)	1,800	—	—	—	3.50	—
Note: In sets only						

KM# 174   1/2 NEW SHEQEL
6.5000 g., Aluminum-Bronze, 26 mm. **Subject:** Hanukka
Obv: Value **Rev:** Lyre **Note:** Coins dated JE5754-5769 have the
Star of David mint mark; the coins dated JE5747-5753 do not.

Date	Mintage	F	VF	XF	Unc	BU
JE5761 (2001)(u)	4,000	—	—	—	3.50	
Note: In sets only						
JE5762 (2002)(u)	4,000	—	—	—	3.50	
Note: In sets only						
JE5763 (2003)(u)	3,000	—	—	—	3.50	
Note: In sets only						
JE5764 (2004)(u)	3,000	—	—	—	3.50	
Note: In sets only						
JE5765 (2005)(u)	2,500	—	—	—	3.50	
Note: In sets only						
JE5766 (2006)(u)	3,000	—	—	—	3.50	
Note: In sets only						
JE5767 (2007)(u)	3,000	—	—	—	3.50	
Note: In sets only						
JE5768 (2008)(u)	3,000	—	—	—	3.50	
Note: In sets only						
JE5769 (2009)	1,800	—	—	—	3.50	
Note: In sets only						

KM# 354   1/2 NEW SHEQEL
6.5000 g., Copper-Aluminum-Nickel, 25.5 mm. **Subject:**
Hanukka **Obv:** Denomination **Rev:** Curacao Hanukka lamp
Edge: Plain **Shape:** 12-sided **Note:** Struck for sets only

Date	Mintage	F	VF	XF	Unc	BU
JE5761 (2001)(u)	4,000	—	—	—	11.00	

KM# 159   1/2 NEW SHEQEL
6.5200 g., Aluminum-Bronze, 25.95 mm. **Obv:** Value **Rev:** Lyre
Edge: Plain

Date	Mintage	F	VF	XF	Unc	BU
JE5762 (2002)(so)	2,880,000	—	—	—	0.75	—
JE5762 (2002)(v)	5,760,000	—	—	—	0.75	—
Note: Length of fraction line is 4 or 4.5 mm. But which mint produced which coin is not known.						
JE5763 (2003)		—	—	—	0.75	—
JE5764 (2004)(so)	2,640,000	—	—	—	0.75	—
JE5765 (2005)		—	—	—	0.75	—
JE5766 (2006)		—	—	—	0.75	—
JE5767 (2007)		—	—	—	0.75	—
5768 (2008)		—	—	—	0.75	—

KM# 355   1/2 NEW SHEQEL
6.5000 g., Copper-Aluminum-Nickel, 25.5 mm. **Obv:** Value
Rev: Yemenite Hanukka Lamp **Edge:** Twelve plain sections
Note: Struck for sets only

Date	Mintage	F	VF	XF	Unc	BU
JE5762 (2002)(u)	4,000	—	—	—	11.00	

KM# 389   1/2 NEW SHEQEL
6.5000 g., Copper-Aluminum-Nickel, 25.5 mm. **Obv:** Value
Rev: Polish Hanukka Lamp **Edge:** Plain **Shape:** 12-sided
Note: Struck for sets only

Date	Mintage	F	VF	XF	Unc	BU
JE5763 (2003)(u)	3,000	—	—	—	12.00	
Note: Even though not a proof, the coin has a mem						

KM# 390   1/2 NEW SHEQEL
6.5000 g., Copper-Aluminum-Nickel, 25.5 mm. **Obv:** Value
Rev: Iraqi Hanukka Lamp **Edge:** Plain **Shape:** 12-sided
Note: Struck for sets only

Date	Mintage	F	VF	XF	Unc	BU
JE5764 (2004)(u)	3,000	—	—	—	12.00	

KM# 391   1/2 NEW SHEQEL
6.5000 g., Copper-Aluminum-Nickel, 25.5 mm. **Obv:** Value
Rev: Syrian Hanukka Lamp **Edge:** Plain **Shape:** 12-sided
Note: Struck for sets only

Date	Mintage	F	VF	XF	Unc	BU
JE5765 (2005)(u)	2,500	—	—	—	12.00	

KM# 415   1/2 NEW SHEQEL
6.5000 g., Copper-Aluminum-Nickel, 25.5 mm. **Obv:** Value and
mini-Hanukka Lamp **Rev:** Dutch Hanukka Lamp **Edge:** Plain
Shape: 12-sided **Note:** Struck for sets only

Date	Mintage	F	VF	XF	Unc	BU
JE5766 (2006)(u)	3,000	—	—	—	12.00	

KM# 422   1/2 NEW SHEQEL
6.5000 g., Copper-Aluminum-Nickel, 25.5 mm. **Obv:** Value and
mini-Hanukka Lamp **Rev:** Corfu (Greek) Hanukka Lamp
Edge: Plain **Shape:** 12-sided **Note:** Struck for sets only

Date	Mintage	F	VF	XF	Unc	BU
JE5767 (2007)(u)	3,000	—	—	—	12.00	

KM# 434   1/2 NEW SHEQEL
6.5000 g., Copper-Aluminum-Nickel, 26 mm. **Subject:** Hanukka
Obv: Value, date, inscriptions and menorah **Rev:** Egyptian
Hanukka lamp **Shape:** 12-sided **Note:** Struck for sets only

Date	Mintage	F	VF	XF	Unc	BU
JE5768 (2008)(u)	3,000	—	—	—	12.00	

KM# 466   1/2 NEW SHEQEL
6.5000 g., Copper-Aluminum-Nickel, 26 mm. **Subject:** Hanukka
Obv: Value, date, inscriptions and menorah **Rev:** Algerian
Hanukka Lamp **Edge:** Plain **Shape:** 12-sided **Note:** Struck for
sets only

Date	Mintage	F	VF	XF	Unc	BU
JE5770 (2010)(u)	1,800	—	—	—	12.00	

KM# 436   1/2 NEW SHEQEL
6.5000 g., Copper-Aluminum-Nickel, 26 mm. **Subject:** Hanukka
Obv: Value, date, inscriptions and menorah **Rev:** Prague
Hanukka Lamp **Shape:** 12-sided **Note:** Struck for sets only

Date	Mintage	F	VF	XF	Unc	BU
JEJE5769 (2009)	1,800	—	—	—	12.00	

KM# 160a   NEW SHEQEL
3.4500 g., Nickel Clad Steel, 17.97 mm. **Obv:** Value **Rev:** Lily,
state emblem and ancient Hebrew inscription **Edge:** Plain

Date	Mintage	F	VF	XF	Unc	BU
JE5761 (2001)(h)	9,648,000	—	—	—	1.00	
JE5762 (2002)(h)	18,816,000	—	—	—	1.00	
JE5763 (2003)(v)	10,198,500	—	—	—	1.00	
JE5765 (2005)		—	—	—	1.00	
JE5766 (2006)		—	—	—	1.00	
Note: Coin alignment error exists. Value: $150.						
JE5767 (2007)		—	—	—	1.00	

KM# 344   NEW SHEQEL
14.4000 g., 0.9250 Silver 0.4282 oz. ASW, 30 mm.
Subject: Anniversary - Independence Day and Education
Obv: Denomination **Rev:** Pomegranate full of symbols - Hebrew
'ABC-123', etc. **Rev. Designer:** Asher Kalderon **Edge:** Plain

Date	Mintage	F	VF	XF	Unc	BU
JE5761-2001(u)	1,653	—	—	—	—	35.00
Prooflike						

KM# 351   NEW SHEQEL
14.4000 g., 0.9250 Silver 0.4282 oz. ASW, 30 mm. **Subject:** Music
Obv: National arms and denom. **Rev:** Musical inst.. **Edge:** Plain

Date	Mintage	F	VF	XF	Unc	BU
JE5761-2001(u)	1,182	—	—	—	—	30.00

KM# 163   NEW SHEQEL
4.0500 g., Copper-Nickel, 18 mm. **Subject:** Hanukka
Obv: Value **Rev:** Lily **Note:** Coins dated JE5754-5769 have the
Star of David mint mark; the JE5746-5753 coins do not.

Date	Mintage	F	VF	XF	Unc	BU
JE5761 (2001)(u)	4,000	—	—	—	4.00	
Note: In sets only						
JE5762 (2002)(u)	4,000	—	—	—	4.00	
Note: In sets only						
JE5763 (2003)(u)	3,000	—	—	—	4.00	
Note: In sets only						
JE5764 (2004)(u)	3,000	—	—	—	4.00	
Note: In sets only						
JE5765 (2005)(u)	2,500	—	—	—	4.00	
Note: In sets only						
JE5766 (2006)(u)	3,000	—	—	—	4.00	
Note: In sets only						
JE5767 (2007)(u)	3,000	—	—	—	4.00	
Note: In sets only						
JE5768 (2008)(u)	3,000	—	—	—	4.00	
Note: In sets only.						

Date	Mintage	F	VF	XF	Unc	BU
JEJE59769 (2009)	1,800	—	—	—	4.00	
Note: In sets only						

KM# 356   NEW SHEQEL
14.4000 g., 0.9250 Silver 0.4282 oz. ASW, 30 mm.
Subject: Independence - Volunteering **Obv:** Denomination
Rev: Heart in hands **Edge:** Plain

Date	Mintage	F	VF	XF	Unc	BU
JE5762-2002(o)	1,364	—	—	—	—	30.00
Prooflike						

KM# 359   NEW SHEQEL
14.4000 g., 0.9250 Silver 0.4282 oz. ASW, 30 mm.
Subject: Tower of Babel **Obv:** National arms in spiral inscription
Rev: Tower of Hebrew verses **Edge:** Plain

Date	Mintage	F	VF	XF	Unc	BU
JE5762 (2002)(o)	1,312	—	—	—	—	30.00
Prooflike						

KM# 371   NEW SHEQEL
14.4000 g., 0.9250 Silver 0.4282 oz. ASW, 30 mm. **Subject:** Space
Exploration **Obv:** "Ofeq" satellite in orbit **Rev:** "Shavit" rocket
Edge Lettering: Hebrew: "In memory of Ilan Ramon and his
colleagues in the Columbia"

Date	Mintage	F	VF	XF	Unc	BU
JE5763-2003(v)	Est. 1,233	—	—	—	—	40.00

KM# 374   NEW SHEQEL
14.4000 g., 0.9250 Silver 0.4282 oz. ASW, 30 mm. **Obv:** Value
Rev: Jacob and Rachel floating in air **Edge:** Plain

Date	Mintage	F	VF	XF	Unc	BU
JE5763-2003(v)	Est. 2,000	—	—	—	—	30.00

KM# 380   NEW SHEQEL
14.4000 g., 0.9250 Silver 0.4282 oz. ASW, 30 mm. **Obv:** Value
Rev: Parent and child **Edge:** Plain

Date	Mintage	F	VF	XF	Unc	BU
JE5764-2004(u)	Est. 1,446	—	—	—	—	30.00

KM# 383 NEW SHEQEL
14.4000 g., 0.9250 Silver 0.4282 oz. ASW, 30 mm. **Obv:** Four windsurfers, value and national arms **Rev:** Eight windsurfers **Edge:** Plain

Date	Mintage	F	VF	XF	Unc	BU
JE5764-2004(v) Prooflike	Est. 2,000	—	—	—	—	30.00

KM# 386 NEW SHEQEL
14.4000 g., 0.9250 Silver 0.4282 oz. ASW, 30 mm.
Subject: Biblical Burning Bush **Obv:** Burning twig and value **Rev:** Burning Bush **Edge:** Plain

Date	Mintage	F	VF	XF	Unc	BU
JE5764-2004(v)	Est. 1,274	—	—	—	—	30.00

KM# 377 NEW SHEQEL
14.4000 g., 0.9250 Silver 0.4282 oz. ASW, 30 mm. **Obv:** Value **Rev:** Architectural design **Edge:** Plain **Note:** With enamel.

Date	Mintage	F	VF	XF	Unc	BU
JE5764-2004(u)	Est. 930	—	—	—	—	30.00

KM# 405 NEW SHEQEL
1.2440 g., 0.9990 Gold 0.0400 oz. AGW, 13.92 mm. **Obv:** Value **Rev:** Jacob and Rachel floating in air **Edge:** Reeded

Date	Mintage	F	VF	XF	Unc	BU
JE5764 (2004) Proof	—	Value: 75.00				

KM# 405a NEW SHEQEL
1.2440 g., 0.9990 Gold 0.0400 oz. AGW, 13.92 mm. **Obv:** Value **Rev:** Jacob and Rachel floating in arc. Arabic legend Israel is mispelled **Edge:** Reeded

Date	Mintage	F	VF	XF	Unc	BU
JE5764 (2004) Proof	682	Value: 120				

KM# 406 NEW SHEQEL
14.4000 g., 0.9250 Silver 0.4282 oz. ASW, 30 mm.
Subject: FIFA 2006 World Cup **Obv:** Value and soccer ball **Rev:** Map and soccer ball **Edge:** Plain

Date	Mintage	F	VF	XF	Unc	BU
JE5764-2004(u)	Est. 2,800	—	—	—	—	40.00

Note: Issued in 2006

KM# 412 NEW SHEQEL
14.4000 g., 0.9250 Silver 0.4282 oz. ASW, 30 mm.
Subject: Naomi Shemer **Obv:** Value **Rev:** Portrait of Naomi Shemer **Edge:** Plain

Date	Mintage	F	VF	XF	Unc	BU
JE5765-2005(u)	Est. 1,800	—	—	—	—	45.00

KM# 396 NEW SHEQEL
14.4000 g., 0.9250 Silver 0.4282 oz. ASW, 30 mm.
Subject: Einstein's Relativity Theory **Obv:** Concentric circles above equation **Rev:** Value above signature

Date	Mintage	F	VF	XF	Unc	BU
JE5765-2005(v) Prooflike	2,800	—	—	—	—	40.00

KM# 399 NEW SHEQEL
14.4000 g., 0.9250 Silver 0.4282 oz. ASW, 30 mm. **Subject:** Moses and the Ten Commandments **Obv:** Ten Commandments and value **Rev:** Moses and the Ten Commandments

Date	Mintage	F	VF	XF	Unc	BU
JE5765-2005(u) Prooflike	Est. 2,800	—	—	—	—	40.00

KM# 402 NEW SHEQEL
14.4000 g., 0.9250 Silver 0.4282 oz. ASW, 30 mm.
Subject: Israel 57th Anniversary **Obv:** Value and olive branch **Rev:** Twisted olive tree

Date	Mintage	F	VF	XF	Unc	BU
JE5765-2005(u) Prooflike	Est. 1,800	—	—	—	—	45.00

KM# 409 NEW SHEQEL
14.4000 g., 0.9250 Silver 0.4282 oz. ASW, 30 mm. **Series:** Biblical Art **Subject:** Abraham and the Three Angels **Obv:** Value and stars **Rev:** Abraham and the three angels **Edge:** Reeded

Date	Mintage	F	VF	XF	Unc	BU
JE5766-2006(ig)	Est. 1,800	—	—	—	—	45.00

KM# 416 NEW SHEQEL
14.4000 g., 0.9250 Silver 0.4282 oz. ASW, 30 mm.
Series: Independence Day **Subject:** Higher Education in Israel **Obv:** Value and design **Rev:** Symbols of Science, Humanities, Technology and Mathematics **Edge:** Plain

Date	Mintage	F	VF	XF	Unc	BU
JE5766-2006(ig)	Est. 1,200	—	—	—	—	45.00

KM# 419 NEW SHEQEL
14.4000 g., 0.9250 Silver 0.4282 oz. ASW, 30 mm.
Subject: UNESCO World Heritage Site; White City of Tel Aviv **Obv:** Value and Bauhaus building **Rev:** Fall of Bauhaus style building and UNESCO symbol **Edge:** Plain

Date	Mintage	F	VF	XF	Unc	BU
JE5766-2006(ig)	Est. 1,200	—	—	—	—	50.00

KM# 423 NEW SHEQEL
14.4000 g., 0.9250 Silver 0.4282 oz. ASW, 30 mm.
Subject: Independence Day - Performing Arts in Israel
Obv: Value, state emblem and inscriptions **Rev:** Stylized actor, dancer and musician and inscription in Hebrew, English and Arabic, Performing Arts in Israel **Edge:** Plain

Date	Mintage	F	VF	XF	Unc	BU
JE5767-2007(ig)	Est. 1,200	—	—	—	—	50.00

KM# 426 NEW SHEQEL
14.4000 g., 0.9250 Silver 0.4282 oz. ASW, 30 mm.
Subject: 2008 Olympics - Judo **Obv:** Value, state emblem, judo belt and inscriptions **Rev:** 2 judo athletes and inscriptions in Hebrew, English and Arabic **Edge:** Plain

Date	Mintage	F	VF	XF	Unc	BU
JE5767-2007(u)	Est. 2,800	—	—	—	—	50.00

KM# 429 NEW SHEQEL
14.4000 g., 0.9250 Silver 0.4282 oz. ASW, 30 mm.
Subject: Biblical Art - Isaiah, Wolf with the Lamb **Obv:** Value, state emblem and inscriptions in Hebrew, English and Arabic **Obv. Inscription:** And the Wolf shall dwell with the Lamb **Rev:** Wolf and lamb lying together under a tree **Edge:** Plain

Date	Mintage	F	VF	XF	Unc	BU
JE5767-2007(v)	Est. 1,800	—	—	—	—	55.00

KM# 437 NEW SHEQEL
1.2440 g., 0.9990 Gold 0.0400 oz. AGW, 13.92 mm.
Series: Biblical Art **Subject:** Abraham and the Angels
Obv: Value, state emblem and Moses in Hebrew **Rev:** Abraham greeting three angels **Edge:** Reeded

Date	Mintage	F	VF	XF	Unc	BU
JE5767-2007 Proof	5,000	Value: 92.00				

KM# 438 NEW SHEQEL
1.2440 g., 0.9990 Gold 0.0400 oz. AGW, 13.92 mm.
Series: Biblical Art **Subject:** Moses and the Ten Commandments **Obv:** Value, state emblem and Moses in Hebrew **Rev:** Moses holding the Ten Commandments **Edge:** Reeded

Date	Mintage	F	VF	XF	Unc	BU
JE5767-2007 Proof	5,000	Value: 92.00				

KM# 439 NEW SHEQEL
14.4000 g., 0.9250 Silver 0.4282 oz. ASW, 30 mm.
Series: Israeli Nobel Prize Laureates **Subject:** Shmuel Yosef Agnon **Obv:** Value, state emblem, outline of Agnon **Rev:** Portrait of Agnon **Edge:** Plain

Date	Mintage	F	VF	XF	Unc	BU
JE5768-2008	666	—	—	—	—	55.00

KM# 440 NEW SHEQEL
1.2440 g., 0.9990 Gold 0.0400 oz. AGW, 13.92 mm.
Series: Biblical Art **Subject:** Isaiah, Wolf with the Lamb
Obv: Value, state emblem, and inscriptions **Rev:** Wolf and lamb lying under tree **Edge:** Reeded

Date	Mintage	F	VF	XF	Unc	BU
JEJE5768-2008 Proof	5,000	Value: 92.00				

KM# 441 NEW SHEQEL
14.4000 g., 0.9250 Silver 0.4282 oz. ASW, 30mm mm.
Series: Independence Day **Subject:** Israel's Sixtieth Anniversary **Obv:** Value, state emblem and inscriptions including "Independence Day" **Rev:** "60" the zero is shaped like a pomegranite and a dove

Date	Mintage	F	VF	XF	Unc	BU
JE5768-2008	1,800	—	—	—	—	60.00

KM# 442 NEW SHEQEL
14.4000 g., 0.9250 Silver 0.4282 oz. ASW, 30mm mm.
Subject: Israel Defense Forces Reserves **Obv:** Triangle, state emblem and inscription **Rev:** Teddy bear pendant over soldier's ID tag

Date	Mintage	F	VF	XF	Unc	BU
JE5768-2008	1,200	—	—	—	—	60.00

KM# 443 NEW SHEQEL
1.2440 g., 0.9990 Gold 0.0400 oz. AGW, 13.92 mm.
Series: Biblical Art **Subject:** Parting of the Red Sea **Obv:** Value, state emblem and inscriptions **Rev:** Israelites passing through the Red Sea **Edge:** Reeded

Date	Mintage	F	VF	XF	Unc	BU
JE5769-2008 Proof	5,000	Value: 98.00				

KM# 444 NEW SHEQEL
14.4000 g., 0.9250 Silver 0.4282 oz. ASW, 30 mm.
Series: Biblical Art **Subject:** Parting of the Red Sea **Obv:** Value, state emblem and inscriptions **Rev:** Israelites passing through the Red Sea

Date	Mintage	F	VF	XF	Unc	BU
JE5769-2008	1,800	—	—	—	—	60.00

KM# 453 NEW SHEQEL
14.4000 g., 0.9250 Silver 0.4282 oz. ASW, 30 mm.
Subject: UNESCO World Heritage Sites Masada **Obv:** Value, state emblem, image of Masada **Rev:** View of Masada, UNESCO emblem, World Heritage Site emblem **Edge:** Plain

Date	Mintage	F	VF	XF	Unc	BU
JE5769 (2009)(u) Prooflike	1,800	—	—	—	—	60.00

KM# 456 NEW SHEQEL
14.4000 g., 0.9250 Silver 0.4282 oz. ASW, 30 mm.
Subject: Israel's sixty-first anniversary **Obv:** Value, state emblem, finch **Rev:** Three birds, hoopoe, warbler and finch **Edge:** Plain

Date	Mintage	F	VF	XF	Unc	BU
JE5769 (2009)(u) Prooflike	1,800	—	—	—	—	60.00

KM# 459 NEW SHEQEL
14.4000 g., 0.9250 Silver 0.4282 oz. ASW, 30 mm.
Subject: 2010 FIFA World Cup South Africa **Obv:** Soccer Player, ball, outline of globe, value, state emblem **Rev:** Soccer ball with design **Edge:** Plain

Date	Mintage	F	VF	XF	Unc	BU
JE5769 (2009)(u) Prooflike	1,800	—	—	—	—	55.00

KM# 462 NEW SHEQEL
1.2440 g., 0.9990 Gold 0.0400 oz. AGW, 13.92 mm.
Series: Biblical Art **Subject:** Samson and the Lion **Obv:** Small stylized palm tree, value, state emblem **Rev:** Stylized Samson wrestling a lion and small stylized palm tree **Edge:** Reeded

Date	Mintage	F	VF	XF	Unc	BU
JE5769 (2009)(u) Proof	Est. 5,000	Value: 100				

KM# 463 NEW SHEQEL
14.4000 g., 0.9250 Silver 0.4282 oz. ASW, 30 mm.
Series: Biblical Art **Subject:** Samson and the Lion **Obv:** Small stylized palm tree, value, state emblem **Rev:** Stylized Samson wrestling a lion and small stylized palm tree **Edge:** Plain

Date	Mintage	F	VF	XF	Unc	BU
JE5769 (2009)(u) Prooflike	Est. 1,800	—	—	—	—	60.00

KM# 468 NEW SHEQEL
14.4000 g., 0.9250 Silver 0.4282 oz. ASW, 30 mm.
Series: Unesco Heritage Set **Subject:** Old Akko **Obv:** Coast of Wall **Rev:** Old city streets and buildings

Date	Mintage	F	VF	XF	Unc	BU
JE5770 (2010)(u) Prooflike	1,800	—	—	—	—	—

KM# 450 10 SHEQALIM
16.9600 g., 0.9170 Gold 0.5000 oz. AGW, 30 mm.
Series: Independence Day **Subject:** Israel's 60th Anniversary **Obv:** Value, state emblem and inscription "Independence Day" **Rev:** "60" the zero is shaped like a pomegranite and a dove **Edge:** Reeded

Date	Mintage	F	VF	XF	Unc	BU
JE5768-2008 Proof	444	Value: 850				

KM# 352 2 NEW SHEQALIM
28.8000 g., 0.9250 Silver 0.8565 oz. ASW, 38.7 mm.
Subject: Music **Obv:** National arms and denomination **Rev:** Musical instruments **Edge:** Reeded

Date	Mintage	F	VF	XF	Unc	BU
JE5761-2001(u) Proof	1,747	Value: 55.00				

KM# 349   2 NEW SHEQALIM
28.8000 g., 0.9250 Silver 0.8565 oz. ASW, 38.7 mm.
Subject: Wildlife **Obv:** Acacia tree **Rev:** Ibex **Edge:** Reeded

Date	Mintage	F	VF	XF	Unc	BU
JE5761-2000(u)	2,000	Value: 55.00				
Proof						

KM# 345   2 NEW SHEQALIM
28.8000 g., 0.9250 Silver 0.8565 oz. ASW, 38.7 mm.
Subject: Independence Day and Education **Obv:** Denomination
Rev: Pomegranate full of symbols **Edge:** Reeded **Designer:**
Asher Kalderon

Date	Mintage	F	VF	XF	Unc	BU
JE5761-2001(u)	1,847	Value: 55.00				
Proof						

KM# 357   2 NEW SHEQALIM
28.8000 g., 0.9250 Silver 0.8565 oz. ASW, 38.7 mm.
Subject: Independence - Volunteering **Obv:** Denomination
Rev: Heart in hands **Edge:** Reeded

Date	Mintage	F	VF	XF	Unc	BU
JE5762-2002(o)	1,426	Value: 55.00				
Proof						

KM# 360   2 NEW SHEQALIM
28.8000 g., 0.9250 Silver 0.8565 oz. ASW, 38.7 mm.
Subject: Tower of Babel **Obv:** National arms in spiral inscription
Rev: Tower of Hebrew verses **Edge:** Reeded

Date	Mintage	F	VF	XF	Unc	BU
JE5762-2002(o)	1,295	Value: 55.00				
Proof						

KM# 372   2 NEW SHEQALIM
28.8000 g., 0.9250 Silver 0.8565 oz. ASW, 38.7 mm.
Subject: Space Exploration **Obv:** "Amos" satellite in orbit
Rev: "Shavit" rocket **Edge Lettering:** Hebrew: "In memory of Ilan
Ramon and his colleagues in the Columbia"

Date	Mintage	F	VF	XF	Unc	BU
JE5763-2003(v)	Est. 1,249	Value: 60.00				
Proof						

KM# 375   2 NEW SHEQALIM
28.8000 g., 0.9250 Silver 0.8565 oz. ASW, 38.7 mm.
Obv: Value **Rev:** Figures floating in air above flower and sheep
Edge: Reeded

Date	Mintage	F	VF	XF	Unc	BU
JE5763-2003(u)	Est. 2,000	Value: 55.00				
Proof						

KM# 378   2 NEW SHEQALIM
28.8000 g., 0.9250 Silver 0.8565 oz. ASW, 38.7 mm.
Obv: Value and enameled shapes **Rev:** Architectural design
Edge: Reeded

Date	Mintage	F	VF	XF	Unc	BU
JE5764-2004(u)	Est. 1,084	Value: 55.00				
Proof						

KM# 381   2 NEW SHEQALIM
28.8000 g., 0.9250 Silver 0.8565 oz. ASW, 38.7 mm.
Obv: Value and stylized human shapes **Rev:** Stylized parent and
child **Edge:** Reeded

Date	Mintage	F	VF	XF	Unc	BU
JE5764-2004(u)	Est. 1,182	Value: 55.00				
Proof						

KM# 384   2 NEW SHEQALIM
28.8000 g., 0.9250 Silver 0.8565 oz. ASW, 38.7 mm. **Obv:** Four
windsurfers, value and national arms **Rev:** Eight windsurfers
Edge: Reeded

Date	Mintage	F	VF	XF	Unc	BU
JE5764-2004(v)	2,800	Value: 55.00				
Proof						

KM# 387   2 NEW SHEQALIM
28.8000 g., 0.9250 Silver 0.8565 oz. ASW, 38.7 mm.
Subject: Biblical Burning Bush **Obv:** Burning twig and value
Rev: Burning Bush **Edge:** Reeded

Date	Mintage	F	VF	XF	Unc	BU
JE5764-2004(v)	Est. 1,354	Value: 55.00				
Proof						

KM# 407   2 NEW SHEQALIM
28.8000 g., 0.9250 Silver 0.8565 oz. ASW, 38.7 mm.
Subject: FIFA 2006 World Cup **Obv:** Value and soccer ball
Rev: Map and soccer ball **Edge:** Reeded

Date	Mintage	F	VF	XF	Unc	BU
JE5764-2004(u)	Est. 5,000	Value: 65.00				
Proof						

Note: Issued in 2006

KM# 413   2 NEW SHEQALIM
28.8000 g., 0.9250 Silver 0.8565 oz. ASW, 38.7 mm.
Subject: Noami Sherner **Obv:** Value **Rev:** Portrait of Naomi
Shemer **Edge:** Reeded

Date	Mintage	F	VF	XF	Unc	BU
JE5765-2005	Est. 1,800	Value: 60.00				
Proof						

KM# 397   2 NEW SHEQALIM
28.8000 g., 0.9250 Silver 0.8565 oz. ASW, 38.7 mm.
Subject: Einstein's Relativity Theory **Obv:** Concentric circles
above equation **Rev:** Value above signature

Date	Mintage	F	VF	XF	Unc	BU
JE5765-2005(v)	2,800	Value: 60.00				
Proof						

KM# 400   2 NEW SHEQALIM
28.8000 g., 0.9250 Silver 0.8565 oz. ASW, 38.7 mm. **Subject:**
Moses and Ten Commandments **Obv:** Ten Commandments and
value **Rev:** Moses and Ten Commandments

Date	Mintage	F	VF	XF	Unc	BU
JE5765-2005(u)	Est. 1,800	Value: 60.00				
Proof						

KM# 403   2 NEW SHEQALIM
28.8000 g., 0.9250 Silver 0.8565 oz. ASW, 38.7 mm.
Subject: Israel 57th Anniversary **Obv:** Value and olive branch
Rev: Twisted olive tree **Edge:** Reeded

Date	Mintage	F	VF	XF	Unc	BU
JE5765-2005(u)	Est. 1,800	Value: 60.00				
Proof						

KM# 435   2 NEW SHEQALIM
5.6000 g., Nickel Plated Steel, 21.48 mm. **Obv:** Large value
Rev: Small national arms above stylized double cornucopiae
Edge: Segmented reeding

Date	Mintage	F	VF	XF	Unc	BU
JE5765(2005)	—	—	—	—	1.50	—

KM# 417 2 NEW SHEQALIM
28.8000 g., 0.9250 Silver 0.8565 oz. ASW, 38.7 mm. **Series:** Independence Day **Subject:** Higher Education in Israel **Obv:** Value and design **Rev:** Symbols of Science, Humanities, Technology and Mathematics **Edge:** Reeded

Date	Mintage	F	VF	XF	Unc	BU
JE5766-2006(ig) Proof	Est. 1,200	Value: 65.00				

KM# 410 2 NEW SHEQALIM
28.8000 g., 0.9250 Silver 0.8565 oz. ASW, 38.7 mm. **Series:** Biblical Art **Subject:** Abraham and the Three Angels **Obv:** Value and stars **Rev:** Abraham and the three angels **Edge:** Reeded

Date	Mintage	F	VF	XF	Unc	BU
JE5766-2006(ig) Proof	Est. 2,800	Value: 65.00				

KM# 420 2 NEW SHEQALIM
28.8000 g., 0.9250 Silver 0.8565 oz. ASW, 38.7 mm. **Subject:** UNESCO World Heritage Site, White Cityof Tel Aviv **Obv:** Value and Bauhaus building **Rev:** Fall of Bauhaus building and UNESCO symbl **Edge:** Reeded

Date	Mintage	F	VF	XF	Unc	BU
JE5766-2006(ig) Proof	Est. 1,200	Value: 75.00				

KM# 424 2 NEW SHEQALIM
Silver, 38.7 mm. **Subject:** Performing Arts in Israel **Obv:** Value, state emblem and inscriptions **Rev:** Stylized actor, dancer and musician and inscription in Hebrew, English and Arabiv **Edge:** Reeded

Date	Mintage	F	VF	XF	Unc	BU
JE5767-2007(ig) Proof	Est. 1,200	Value: 75.00				

KM# 427 2 NEW SHEQALIM
28.8000 g., 0.8565 Silver 0.7930 oz. ASW, 38.7 mm. **Subject:** 2008 Olympics - Judo **Obv:** Value, state emblem, judo belt and inscriptions **Rev:** 2 judo athletes and inscriptions **Edge:** Reeded

Date	Mintage	F	VF	XF	Unc	BU
JE5767-2007(u) Proof	Est. 6,000	Value: 75.00				

KM# 430 2 NEW SHEQALIM
28.8000 g., 0.8565 Silver 0.7930 oz. ASW, 38.7 mm. **Subject:** Biblical Art - Isaiah, Wolf with the Lamb **Obv:** Value, state emblem and inscriptions in Hebrew, English and Arabic **Obv. Inscription:** And the Wolf shall dwell with the Lamb **Rev:** Wolf and lamb lying together under a tree **Edge:** Reeded

Date	Mintage	F	VF	XF	Unc	BU
JE5767-2007(v) Proof	Est. 2,800	Value: 80.00				

KM# 432 2 NEW SHEQALIM
5.7000 g., Nickel Plated Steel, 21.6 mm. **Subject:** Hanukka **Obv:** Value, date, inscriptions and menorah **Rev:** Double cornucopiae (horns of plenty) draped in ribbons and filled with fruit and grain including a pomegranate **Edge:** Plain with 4 notches

Date	Mintage	F	VF	XF	Unc	BU
JE5768 (2008)(u) In sets only	3,000	—	—	—	5.00	—
JE5769-2009 In sets only	1,800	—	—	—	5.00	—

KM# 433 2 NEW SHEQALIM
5.7000 g., Nickel Plated Steel, 21.6 mm. **Obv:** Value, date and inscriptions **Rev:** Double cornucopiae (horns of plenty) draped in ribbons and filled with fruit and grain including a pomegranate **Edge:** Plain with 4 notches

Date	Mintage	F	VF	XF	Unc	BU
JE5768 (2008)(u)	—	—	—	—	1.50	—

KM# 445 2 NEW SHEQALIM
28.8000 g., 0.8565 Silver 0.7930 oz. ASW, 38.7 mm. **Series:** Israeli Nobel Prize Laureates **Subject:** Shmuel Yosef Agnon **Obv:** Value, state emblem and outline of Agnon **Rev:** Portrait of Agnon **Edge:** Reeded

Date	Mintage	F	VF	XF	Unc	BU
JE5768-2008 Proof	666	Value: 80.00				

KM# 446 2 NEW SHEQALIM
28.8000 g., 0.8565 Silver 0.7930 oz. ASW, 38.7 mm. **Series:** Independence Day **Subject:** Israel's 60th Anniversary **Obv:** Value, state emblem and inscription "Independence Day" **Rev:** "60" the zero is shaped like a pomegranate and a dove

Date	Mintage	F	VF	XF	Unc	BU
JE5768-2008 Proof	1,800	Value: 85.00				

KM# 447 2 NEW SHEQALIM
28.8000 g., 0.8565 Silver 0.7930 oz. ASW, 38.7 mm. **Subject:** Israel Defense Forces Reserves **Obv:** Traingle, state emblem and inscription **Rev:** Teddy bear pendant over a soldier's ID tag

Date	Mintage	F	VF	XF	Unc	BU
JE5768-2008 Proof	1,200	Value: 85.00				

KM# 448 2 NEW SHEQALIM
28.8000 g., 0.8565 Silver 0.7930 oz. ASW, 38.7 mm. **Series:** Biblical Art **Subject:** Parting of the Red Sea **Obv:** Value, state emblem and inscriptions **Rev:** Israelites passing throught the Red Sea **Edge:** Reeded

Date	Mintage	F	VF	XF	Unc	BU
JE5769-2008 1800	—	Value: 86.00				

KM# 454 2 NEW SHEQALIM
28.8000 g., 0.9250 Silver 0.8565 oz. ASW, 38.7 mm. **Subject:** UNESCO World Heritage sites Masada **Obv:** Value, state emblem, image of Masada **Rev:** View of Masada, UNESCO emblem, World Heritage Site emblem **Edge:** Reeded

Date	Mintage	F	VF	XF	Unc	BU
JE5769 (2009)(u) Proof	1,800	Value: 90.00				

KM# 457 2 NEW SHEQALIM
28.8000 g., 0.9250 Silver 0.8565 oz. ASW, 38.7 mm. **Subject:** Israel's sixty-first anniversary **Obv:** Value, state emblem, hoopoe **Rev:** Three birds, hoopoe, warbler and finch **Edge:** Reeded

Date	Mintage	F	VF	XF	Unc	BU
JE5769 (2009)(u) Proof	2,800	Value: 90.00				

KM# 460 2 NEW SHEQALIM
28.8000 g., 0.9250 Silver 0.8565 oz. ASW, 38.7 mm. **Subject:** 2010 FIFA World Cup South Africa **Obv:** Soccer Player, ball, outline of globe **Rev:** Soccer player with design **Edge:** Reeded

Date	Mintage	F	VF	XF	Unc	BU
JE5769 (2009)(u) Proof	Est. 5,000	Value: 90.00				

KM# 464 2 NEW SHEQALIM
28.8000 g., 0.9250 Silver 0.8565 oz. ASW, 38.7 mm. **Series:** Biblical Art **Subject:** Samson and the Lion **Obv:** Small stylized palm tree, value, state emblem **Rev:** Stylized Samson wrestling with a lion and small stylized palm tree **Edge:** Reeded

Date	Mintage	F	VF	XF	Unc	BU
JE5769 (2009)(u) Proof	Est. 2,800	Value: 90.00				

KM# 469 2 NEW SHEQALIM
28.8000 g., 0.9250 Silver 0.8565 oz. ASW, 38.7 mm. **Series:** Unesco Heritage Site **Subject:** Old Akko **Obv:** Coastal World **Rev:** Old city streets and buildings

Date	Mintage	F	VF	XF	Unc	BU
JE5770 (2010)(u) Proof	1,800	—	—	—	—	—

KM# 207 5 NEW SHEQALIM
8.1800 g., Copper-Nickel, 24 mm. **Obv:** Value **Rev:** Ancient column capitol **Edge:** Plain **Shape:** 12-sided

Date	Mintage	F	VF	XF	Unc	BU
JE5762 (2002)(o)	4,464,000	—	—	—	3.75	—
Note: The JE5762 coins are practically round.						
JE5765 (2005)	—	—	—	—	3.00	—
JE5766 (2006)	—	—	—	—	3.00	—
JE5768-2008	—	—	—	—	3.00	—

KM# 217 5 NEW SHEQALIM
8.1800 g., Copper-Nickel, 24 mm. **Obv:** Value, small menorah and inscription Hanukka **Rev:** Ancient column capitol **Note:** Coins dated JE5754-5769 have the Star of David mint mark; the JE5751-5753 coins do not.

Date	Mintage	F	VF	XF	Unc	BU
JE5762 (2002)(u)	4,000	—	—	—	7.00	—
Note: In sets only						
JE5763 (2003)(u)	3,000	—	—	—	8.00	—
Note: In sets only						
JE5764 (2004)(u)	3,000	—	—	—	8.00	—
Note: In sets only						
JE5765 (2005)(u)	2,500	—	—	—	8.00	—
Note: In sets only						
JE5766 (2006)(u)	3,000	—	—	—	8.00	—
Note: In sets only						
JE5767 (2007)(u)	3,000	—	—	—	8.00	—
Note: In sets only						
JE5768 (2008)(u)	3,000	—	—	—	8.00	—
Note: In sets only						
JE5769 (2009)	1,800	—	—	—	8.00	—
Note: In sets only						

KM# 408 5 NEW SHEQALIM
7.7770 g., 0.9990 Gold 0.2498 oz. AGW, 27 mm. **Subject:** FIFA 2006 World Cup **Obv:** Value and soccer ball **Rev:** Map and soccer ball **Edge:** Reeded **Note:** Issued in 2006

Date	Mintage	F	VF	XF	Unc	BU
JE5764-2004(u) Proof	Est. 777	Value: 400				

KM# 461 5 NEW SHEQALIM
7.7700 g., 0.9990 Gold 0.2496 oz. AGW, 27 mm. **Subject:** 2010 FIFA World Cup South Africa **Obv:** Soccer Player, ball, outline of globe **Rev:** Soccer ball with design **Edge:** Reeded

Date	Mintage	F	VF	XF	Unc	BU
JE5769 (2009)(u) Proof	Est. 888	Value: 450				

KM# 315 10 NEW SHEQALIM
7.0000 g., Bi-Metallic Aureate bonded Bronze center in Nickel bonded Steel ring, 22.5 mm. **Subject:** Hanukka **Obv:** Value, text and menorah within circle and vertical lines **Rev:** Palm tree and baskets within half beaded circle

Date	Mintage	F	VF	XF	Unc	BU
JE5761 (2001)(u)	4,000	—	—	—	9.00	—
Note: In sets only						
JE5762 (2002)(u)	4,000	—	—	—	9.00	—
Note: In sets only						
JE5763 (2003)(u)	3,000	—	—	—	10.00	—
Note: In sets only						
JE5764 (2004)(u)	3,000	—	—	—	10.00	—
Note: In sets only						
JE5765 (2005)(u)	2,500	—	—	—	10.00	—
Note: In sets only						
JE5766 (2006)(u)	3,000	—	—	—	10.00	—
Note: In sets only						
JE5767 (2007)(u)	3,000	—	—	—	10.00	—
Note: In sets only						
JE5768 (2008)(u)	3,000	—	—	—	10.00	—
Note: In sets only						
JE5769 (2009)	1,800	—	—	—	10.00	—
Note: In sets only						

KM# 346 10 NEW SHEQALIM
16.9600 g., 0.9170 Gold 0.5000 oz. AGW, 30 mm. **Subject:** Independence Day and Education **Obv:** Value **Rev:** Pomegranate full of symbols - Hebrew for 'ABC - 123', etc. **Edge:** Reeded **Designer:** Asher Kalderon

Date	Mintage	F	VF	XF	Unc	BU
JE5761-2001(u) Proof	660	Value: 700				

KM# 353 10 NEW SHEQALIM
16.9600 g., 0.9170 Gold 0.5000 oz. AGW, 30 mm. **Subject:** Music **Obv:** National arms and value **Rev:** Musical instruments **Edge:** Reeded

Date	Mintage	F	VF	XF	Unc	BU
JE5761-2001(u) Proof	766	Value: 700				

KM# 358 10 NEW SHEQALIM
16.9600 g., 0.9166 Gold 0.4998 oz. AGW, 30 mm. **Subject:** Independence - Volunteering **Obv:** Value **Rev:** Heart in hands **Edge:** Reeded

Date	Mintage	F	VF	XF	Unc	BU
JE5762-2002(o) Proof	617	Value: 650				

KM# 361 10 NEW SHEQALIM
16.9600 g., 0.9170 Gold 0.5000 oz. AGW, 30 mm.
Subject: Tower of Babel **Obv:** National arms in spiral inscription
Rev: Tower of Hebrew verses **Edge:** Reeded

Date	Mintage	F	VF	XF	Unc	BU
JE5762-2002(o)	750	Value: 700				
Proof						

KM# 270 10 NEW SHEQALIM
7.0000 g., Bi-Metallic Aureate bonded Bronze center in Nickel
bonded Steel ring, 22.95 mm. **Obv:** Value, vertical lines and text
within circle **Rev:** Palm tree and baskets within half beaded circle
Edge: Reeded

Date	Mintage	F	VF	XF	Unc	BU
JE5762 (2002)(h)	4,749,000	—	—	—	5.00	
JE5765 (2005)		—	—	—	5.00	
Note: Coin alignment error exists. Value: $350.						
JE5766 (2006)		—	—	—	5.00	

KM# 373 10 NEW SHEQALIM
16.9600 g., 0.9170 Gold 0.5000 oz. AGW, 30 mm.
Subject: Space Exploration **Obv:** "Eros" satellite in orbit
Rev: "Shavit" rocket **Edge Lettering:** Hebrew: In memory of Ilan
Ramon and his colleagues in the Columbia"

Date	Mintage	F	VF	XF	Unc	BU
JE5763-2003(v)	573	Value: 650				
Proof						

KM# 376 10 NEW SHEQALIM
16.9600 g., 0.9170 Gold 0.5000 oz. AGW, 30 mm. **Obv:** Value
Rev: Jacob and Rachel floating in air above tree and sheep
Edge: Reeded

Date	Mintage	F	VF	XF	Unc	BU
JE5763-2003(u)	686	Value: 700				
Proof						

KM# 379 10 NEW SHEQALIM
16.9600 g., 0.9170 Gold 0.5000 oz. AGW, 30 mm. **Obv:** Value
Rev: Architectural design **Edge:** Reeded

Date	Mintage	F	VF	XF	Unc	BU
JE5764-2004(u)	555	Value: 700				
Proof						

KM# 382 10 NEW SHEQALIM
16.9600 g., 0.9170 Gold 0.5000 oz. AGW, 30 mm. **Obv:** Value
Rev: Stylized parent and child **Edge:** Reeded

Date	Mintage	F	VF	XF	Unc	BU
JE5764-2004(u)	539	Value: 700				
Proof						

KM# 385 10 NEW SHEQALIM
16.9600 g., 0.9170 Gold 0.5000 oz. AGW, 30 mm. **Obv:** Four
windsurfers, value and national arms **Rev:** Eight windsurfers
Edge: Reeded

Date	Mintage	F	VF	XF	Unc	BU
JE5764-2004(v)	555	Value: 700				
Proof						

KM# 388 10 NEW SHEQALIM
16.9600 g., 0.9170 Gold 0.5000 oz. AGW, 30 mm.
Subject: Biblical Burning Bush **Obv:** Burning twig and value
Rev: Burning Bush **Edge:** Reeded

Date	Mintage	F	VF	XF	Unc	BU
JE5764-2004(v)	555	Value: 700				
Proof						

KM# 398 10 NEW SHEQALIM
16.9600 g., 0.9166 Gold 0.4998 oz. AGW, 30 mm.
Subject: Einstein's Relativity Theory **Obv:** Concentric circles
above equation **Rev:** Value above signature

Date	Mintage	F	VF	XF	Unc	BU
JE5765-2005(v)	555	Value: 750				
Proof						

KM# 401 10 NEW SHEQALIM
16.9600 g., 0.9166 Gold 0.4998 oz. AGW, 30 mm. **Series:**
Biblical Art **Subject:** Moses and Ten Commandments **Obv:** Ten
Commandments and value **Rev:** Moses and Ten Command.

Date	Mintage	F	VF	XF	Unc	BU
JE5765-2005(u)	555	Value: 700				
Proof						

KM# 404 10 NEW SHEQALIM
16.9600 g., 0.9166 Gold 0.4998 oz. AGW, 30 mm. **Series:**
Independence Day **Subject:** Israel 57th Anniversary **Obv:** Value
and olive branch **Rev:** Twisted olive tree **Edge:** Reeded

Date	Mintage	F	VF	XF	Unc	BU
JE5765-2005(u)	555	Value: 650				
Proof						

KM# 414 10 NEW SHEQALIM
16.9600 g., 0.9170 Gold 0.5000 oz. AGW, 30 mm. **Subject:** Naomi
Shemer **Obv:** Value **Rev:** Portrait of Naomi Shemer **Edge:** Reeded

Date	Mintage	F	VF	XF	Unc	BU
JE5765-2005(u)	Est. 555	Value: 650				
Proof						

KM# 418 10 NEW SHEQALIM
16.9600 g., 0.9170 Gold 0.5000 oz. AGW, 30 mm.
Series: Independence Day **Subject:** Higher Education in Israel
Obv: Value and design **Rev:** Symbols of Science, Humanities,
Technology and Mathematics **Edge:** Reeded

Date	Mintage	F	VF	XF	Unc	BU
JE5766-2006(ig)	Est. 444	Value: 675				
Proof						

KM# 411 10 NEW SHEQALIM
16.9600 g., 0.9170 Gold 0.5000 oz. AGW, 30 mm.
Subject: Abraham and the Three Angels **Obv:** Value and stars
Rev: Abraham and the three angels **Edge:** Reeded

Date	Mintage	F	VF	XF	Unc	BU
JE5766-2006(ig)	Est. 555	Value: 725				
Proof						

KM# 421 10 NEW SHEQALIM
16.9600 g., 0.9170 Gold 0.5000 oz. AGW, 30 mm.
Subject: UNESCO World Heritage Site, White City Tel Aviv
Obv: Value and Bauhaus building **Rev:** Face of Bauhaus building
and UNESCO symbol **Edge:** Reeded

Date	Mintage	F	VF	XF	Unc	BU
JE5766-2006(ig)	Est. 555	Value: 700				
Proof						

KM# 425 10 NEW SHEQALIM
16.9600 g., 0.9170 Gold 0.5000 oz. AGW, 30 mm.
Subject: Independence Day - Performing Arts in Israel
Obv: Value, state emblem and inscriptions **Rev:** Stylized actor,
dancer and musician and inscription in Hebrew, English and
Arabic, "Performing Arts in Israel" **Edge:** Reeded

Date	Mintage	F	VF	XF	Unc	BU
JE5767-2007(ig)	Est. 444	Value: 750				
Proof						

KM# 428 10 NEW SHEQALIM
16.9600 g., 0.9170 Gold 0.5000 oz. AGW, 30 mm.
Subject: 2008 Olympics - Judo **Obv:** Value, state emblem, judo
belt and inscriptions **Rev:** 2 judo athletes and inscriptions in
Hebrew, English and Arabic **Edge:** Reeded

Date	Mintage	F	VF	XF	Unc	BU
5767-2007(u)	Est. 555	Value: 750				
Proof						

KM# 431 10 NEW SHEQALIM
16.9600 g., 0.9170 Gold 0.5000 oz. AGW, 30 mm.
Subject: Biblical Art - Isaiah, Wolf with the Lamb **Obv:** Value,
state emblem and inscriptions in Hebrew, English and Arabic
Obv. Inscription: And the Wolf shall dwell with the Lamb
Rev: Wolf and lamb lying together under a tree **Edge:** Reeded

Date	Mintage	F	VF	XF	Unc	BU
JE5767-2007(v)	Est. 555	Value: 800				
Proof						

KM# 452 10 NEW SHEQALIM
16.9600 g., 0.9170 Gold 0.5000 oz. AGW, 30 mm.
Series: Biblical Art **Subject:** Parting of the Red Sea **Obv:** Value,
state emblem and inscriptions **Rev:** Israelites passing through
the Red Sea

Date	Mintage	F	VF	XF	Unc	BU
JE5769-2008	555	Value: 830				
Proof						

KM# 449 10 NEW SHEQALIM
16.9600 g., 0.9170 Gold 0.5000 oz. AGW, 30 mm.
Series: Israeli Nobel Prize Laureates **Subject:** Shmuel Yosef
Agnon **Obv:** Value, state emblem and outline of Agnon **Rev:**
Portrait of Agnon **Edge:** Reeded

Date	Mintage	F	VF	XF	Unc	BU
JE5768-2008	—	Value: 800				
Proof						

KM# 451 10 NEW SHEQALIM
16.9600 g., 0.9170 Gold 0.5000 oz. AGW, 30 mm.
Subject: Israel Defense Force Reserves **Obv:** Value over a
triangle, state emblem and inscriptions **Rev:** Teddy bear pendant
over a soldier's ID tag **Edge:** Reeded

Date	Mintage	F	VF	XF	Unc	BU
JE5768-2008	444	Value: 850				
Proof						

KM# 455 10 NEW SHEQALIM
16.9600 g., 0.9170 Gold 0.5000 oz. AGW, 30 mm.
Subject: UNESCO World Heritage Sites Masada **Obv:** Value,
state emblem, image of Masada **Rev:** View of Masada, UNESCO
emblem, World Heritage Site Emblem **Edge:** Reeded

Date	Mintage	F	VF	XF	Unc	BU
JE5679 (2009)(u)	555	Value: 875				
Proof						

KM# 458 10 NEW SHEQALIM
16.9600 g., 0.9170 Gold 0.5000 oz. AGW, 30 mm. **Subject:**
Israel's sixty-first anniversary **Obv:** Value, state emblem, warbler
Rev: Three birds, hoopoe, warbler and finch **Edge:** Reeded

Date	Mintage	F	VF	XF	Unc	BU
JE5769 (2009)(u) Proof	650	Value: 875				

KM# 465 10 NEW SHEQALIM
16.9600 g., 0.9170 Gold 0.5000 oz. AGW, 30 mm.
Series: Biblical Art **Subject:** Samson and the Lion **Obv:** Small
stylized palm tree, value, state emblem **Rev:** Stylized Samson
wrestling a lion, stylized palm tree **Edge:** Reeded

Date	Mintage	F	VF	XF	Unc	BU
JE5769 (2009)(u) Proof	Est. 555	Value: 875				

KM# 470 10 NEW SHEQALIM
16.9600 g., 0.9170 Gold 0.5000 oz. AGW, 30 mm.
Series: Unesco Heritage site **Subject:** Old Akko **Obv:** Coastal
World **Rev:** Old city streets and buildings

Date	Mintage	F	VF	XF	Unc	BU
JE5770 (2010)(u)	555	—	—	—	—	—
Proof						

BULLION COINAGE

KM# 467 20 NEW SHEQALIM
31.1000 g., 0.9990 Gold 0.9988 oz. AGW, 32 mm. **Obv:** State emblem above lion. **Rev:** Tower of David near the Jaffa Gate in Jerusalem

Date	Mintage	F	VF	XF	Unc	BU
JE5770 (2010)(u)	3,600					

MINT SETS

KM#	Date	Mintage	Identification	Issue Price	Mkt Val
MS60	JE5761 (2001) (7)	4,000	KM#163, 172-174, 217, 315, 354 (plastic case)	—	37.00
MS63	JE5761-5762 (2001-2002) (9)	3,000	KM#157, 158, 160a (JE5761), 157-159, 160a, 207, 270 (JE5762) (folder)	—	30.00
MSA67	JE5761-5763 (2001-2003) (6)	3,000	KM#157-159, 169a, 207, 270 (various dates) (folder) (Bank of Israel Jubilee; given or sold to Bank of Israel employees and VIP guests, not go to the general public)	—	45.00
MS62	JE5762 (2002) (7)	—	KM#163, 172-174, 217, 315, 355 (plastic case)	—	40.00
MS65	JE5763 (2003) (7)	300	KM#163, 172-174, 217, 315, 389 (plastic case)	—	42.00
MS67	JE5764 (2004) (7)	3,000	KM#163, 172-174, 217, 315, 390 (plastic case)	—	40.00
MS70	JE5764-5765 (2004-05) (6)	3,000	KM#158, 159 (JE5764), 157, 160a, 207, 270 (JE5765) (folder)	39.00	35.00
MS69	JE5765 (2005) (7)	2,500	KM#163, 172-174, 217, 315, 391 (plastic case)	—	42.00
MS71	JE5766 (2006) (7)	2,700	KM#163, 172-174, 217, 315, 415 (folder)	42.00	45.00
MS72	JE5766 (2006) (7)	2,000	KM#163, 172-174, 217, 315, 415 (plastic case)	39.00	35.00
MS73	JE5766 (2006) (6)	2,000	KM#157-159, 160a, 207, 270 (folder)	39.00	35.00
MSB74	JE5767-5768 (2007-08) (8)	1,000	KM#157-159, 160a (JE5767), 158, 159, 207, 433 (JE5768) (folder)	46.00	46.00
MS74	JE5767 (2007) (7)	3,000	KM#163, 172-174, 217, 315, 422 (folder)	42.00	42.00
MSA74	JE5768 (2008) (8)	3,000	KM#163, 172-174, 217, 315, 432, 434 (folder)	43.00	45.00
MSC74	2009 (6)	1,800	KM#163, 173, 174, 217, 315, 432 (folder)	43.00	43.00

MINT SETS NON-STANDARD METALS

KM#	Date	Mintage	Identification	Issue Price	Mkt Val
MS58	JE5761-62 (2001-02) (9)	3,000	KM#157 (2 pcs), 158 (2 pcs), 159, 160a (2 pcs), 207, 270 mixed date set	—	—
MS59	JE5761 (2001) (7)	4,000	KM#163, 172-174, 217, 315, 354 (folder)	39.00	38.00
MS61	JE5762 (2002) (7)	4,000	KM#163, 172-174, 217, 315, 355 (folder)	39.00	40.00
MS64	JE5763 (2003) (7)	3,000	KM#163, 172-174, 217, 315, 389 (folder)	39.00	39.00
MS66	JE5764 (2004) (7)	3,000	KM#163, 172-174, 217, 315, 390 (folder)	39.00	40.00
MS68	JE5765 (2005) (7)	2,500	KM#163, 172-174, 217, 315, 391 (folder)	39.00	40.00

ITALY

The Italian Republic, a 700-mile-long peninsula extending into the heart of the Mediterranean Sea, has an area of 116,304 sq. mi. (301,230 sq. km.) and a population of 60 million. Capital: Rome. The economy centers around agriculture, manufacturing, forestry and fishing. Machinery, textiles, clothing and motor vehicles are exported.

MINT

R - Rome

REPUBLIC
DECIMAL COINAGE

KM# 91 LIRA
0.6200 g., Aluminum, 17 mm. **Obv:** Balance scales **Rev:** Cornucopia, value and date **Designer:** Giuseppe Romagnoli **Note:** The 1968-1969 and 1982-2001 dates were issued in sets only.

Date	Mintage	F	VF	XF	Unc	BU
2001R	100,000	—	—	—	20.00	—
2001R Proof	10,000	Value: 40.00				

KM# 219 LIRA
11.0000 g., 0.8350 Silver 0.2953 oz. ASW, 29 mm. **Subject:** History of the Lira - Lira of 1946 (KM#87) **Obv:** Head with laureate left within circle **Rev:** Apple on branch within circle flanked by sprigs **Edge:** Reeded **Note:** This is a Lira Series reproducing an old coin design in the center of each coin.

Date	Mintage	F	VF	XF	Unc	BU
2001R	50,000	—	—	—	70.00	
2001R Proof	6,100	Value: 220				

KM# 220 LIRA
6.0000 g., 0.8350 Silver 0.1611 oz. ASW, 24 mm. **Subject:** History of the Lira - Lira of 1951 (KM#91) **Obv:** Balance scale within circle **Rev:** Value and cornucopia within circle **Edge:** Reeded **Note:** This is a Lira Series reproducing an old coin design in the center of each coin.

Date	Mintage	F	VF	XF	Unc	BU
2001R	50,000	—	—	—	70.00	
2001R Proof	6,100	Value: 220				

KM# 87a LIRA
8.0000 g., 0.9000 Gold 0.2315 oz. AGW, 21.6 mm. **Obv:** Ceres **Rev:** Orange on branch **Edge:** Plain **Note:** Official Restrike

Date	Mintage	F	VF	XF	Unc	BU
1946 (2006)R Proof	1,999	Value: 400				

KM# 91a LIRA
4.0000 g., 0.9000 Gold 0.1157 oz. AGW, 17.2 mm. **Obv:** Balance scale **Rev:** Cornucopia, date and value **Edge:** Plain **Note:** Official Restrike

Date	Mintage	F	VF	XF	Unc	BU
1951 (2006)R Proof	1,999	Value: 250				

KM# 94 2 LIRE
0.8000 g., Aluminum **Obv:** Honey bee **Rev:** Olive branch and value **Designer:** G. Romagnoli **Note:** The 1968-1969 and 1982-2001 dates were issued in sets only.

Date	Mintage	F	VF	XF	Unc	BU
2001R	100,000	—	—	—	18.00	—
2001R Proof	10,000	Value: 40.00				

KM# 88a 2 LIRE
11.0000 g., 0.9000 Gold 0.3183 oz. AGW, 24.1 mm. **Obv:** Farmer plowing field **Rev:** Wheat ear **Edge:** Plain **Note:** Official Restrike

Date	Mintage	F	VF	XF	Unc	BU
1946 (2006)R Proof	1,999	Value: 700				

KM# 94a 2 LIRE
5.0000 g., 0.9000 Gold 0.1447 oz. AGW, 18.3 mm. **Obv:** Honey bee **Rev:** Olive branch **Edge:** Reeded **Note:** Official Restrike

Date	Mintage	F	VF	XF	Unc	BU
1953 (2006)R Proof	1,999	Value: 300				

KM# 92 5 LIRE
1.0350 g., Aluminum, 20.12 mm. **Obv:** Rudder **Rev:** Dolphin and value **Edge:** Plain **Designer:** Giuseppe Romagnoli

Date	Mintage	F	VF	XF	Unc	BU
2001R	100,000	—	—	—	12.00	—
2001R Proof	10,000	Value: 20.00				

KM# 89a 5 LIRE
16.0000 g., 0.9000 Gold 0.4630 oz. AGW, 26.7 mm. **Obv:** Italia with torch **Rev:** Bunch of grapes **Edge:** Reeded **Note:** Official Restrike

Date	Mintage	F	VF	XF	Unc	BU
1946 (2006)R Proof	1,999	Value: 1,000				

KM# 92a 5 LIRE
6.0000 g., 0.9000 Gold 0.1736 oz. AGW, 20.2 mm. **Obv:** Rudder **Rev:** Dolphin and value **Edge:** Plain **Note:** Official Restrike

Date	Mintage	F	VF	XF	Unc	BU
1951 (2006)R Proof	1,999	Value: 400				

KM# 93 10 LIRE
1.6000 g., Aluminum, 23.25 mm. **Obv:** Plow **Rev:** Value within wheat ears **Edge:** Plain **Designer:** Giuseppe Romagnoli

Date	Mintage	F	VF	XF	Unc	BU
2001R	100,000	—	—	—	12.00	—
2001R Proof	10,000	Value: 35.00				

KM# 90a 10 LIRE
19.0000 g., 0.9000 Gold 0.5498 oz. AGW, 29 mm. **Obv:** Pegasus **Rev:** Olive branch **Edge:** Lettered **Edge Lettering:** REPVBBLICA ITALIANA **Note:** Official Restrike

Date	Mintage	F	VF	XF	Unc	BU
1946 (2006)R Proof	1,999	Value: 1,000				

KM# 93a 10 LIRE
10.0000 g., 0.9000 Gold 0.2893 oz. AGW, 23.3 mm. **Obv:** Plow **Rev:** Value within wheat ears **Edge:** Plain **Note:** Official Restrike

Date	Mintage	F	VF	XF	Unc	BU
1951 (2006)R Proof	1,999	Value: 600				

KM# 97.2 20 LIRE
3.6000 g., Aluminum-Bronze, 19.63 mm. **Obv:** Wheat sprigs within head left **Rev:** Oak leaves divide value and date **Edge:** Plain **Designer:** Pietro Giampaoli

Date	Mintage	F	VF	XF	Unc	BU
2001R	100,000	—	—	—	12.00	—
2001R Proof	10,000	Value: 35.00				

KM# 97.1a 20 LIRE
8.0000 g., 0.9000 Gold 0.2315 oz. AGW, 21.3 mm. **Obv:** Head laureate left **Rev:** Oak leaves divides date and value **Edge:** Reeded **Note:** Official Restrike

Date	Mintage	F	VF	XF	Unc	BU
1957 (2006)R Proof	1,999	Value: 500				

KM# 183 50 LIRE
Copper-Nickel, 19 mm. **Obv:** Turreted head left **Rev:** Large value within wreath of produce **Designer:** L. Cretara

Date	Mintage	F	VF	XF	Unc	BU
2001R	100,000	—	—	—	10.00	—
2001R Proof	10,000	Value: 18.00				

KM# 95.1a 50 LIRE
14.0000 g., 0.9000 Gold 0.4051 oz. AGW, 24.8 mm. **Obv:** Italia **Rev:** Vulcan **Edge:** Reeded **Note:** Official Restrike

Date	Mintage	F	VF	XF	Unc	BU
1954 (2006)R Proof	1,999	Value: 550				

KM# 183a 50 LIRE
9.0000 g., 0.9000 Gold 0.2604 oz. AGW, 19.2 mm. **Obv:** Roma **Rev:** Value within wreath **Edge:** Plain **Note:** Official Restrike

Date	Mintage	F	VF	XF	Unc	BU
1996 (2006)R Proof	1,999	Value: 500				

KM# 159 100 LIRE
Copper-Nickel, 22 mm. **Obv:** Turreted head left **Rev:** Large value within circle flanked by sprigs **Designer:** Laura Cretara

Date	Mintage	F	VF	XF	Unc	BU
2001R	100,000	—	—	—	12.00	—
2001R Proof	10,000	Value: 35.00				

KM# 96.1a 100 LIRE
18.0000 g., 0.9000 Gold 0.5208 oz. AGW, 27.8 mm. **Obv:** Ancient athlete **Rev:** Minerva standing **Edge:** Reeded **Note:** Official Restrike

Date	Mintage	F	VF	XF	Unc	BU
1955 (2006)R Proof	1,999	Value: 1,000				

KM# 159a 100 LIRE
9.0000 g., 0.9000 Gold 0.2604 oz. AGW, 22 mm. **Obv:** Turreted head left **Rev:** Large value within circle flanked by sprigs **Edge:** Segmented reeding **Note:** Official Restrike

Date	Mintage	F	VF	XF	Unc	BU
1993 (2006)R Proof	1,999	Value: 500				

KM# 105 200 LIRE
5.0000 g., Aluminum-Bronze, 24 mm. **Obv:** Head right **Rev:** Value within gear **Designer:** M. Vallucci

Date	Mintage	F	VF	XF	Unc	BU
2001R	100,000	—	—	—	18.00	—
2001R Proof	10,000	Value: 40.00				

KM# 105a 200 LIRE
11.0000 g., 0.9000 Gold 0.3183 oz. AGW, 24 mm. **Obv:** Head right **Rev:** Value within gear **Edge:** Reeded **Note:** Official Restrike

Date	Mintage	F	VF	XF	Unc	BU
1977 (2006)R Proof	1,999	Value: 700				

KM# 98 500 LIRE
11.0000 g., 0.8350 Silver 0.2953 oz. ASW, 29.3 mm. **Obv:** Columbus' ships **Obv. Designer:** Guido Veroi **Rev:** Bust left within wreath **Rev. Designer:** Pietro Giampaoli **Edge:** Dates in raised lettering

Date	Mintage	F	VF	XF	Unc	BU
2001R	100,000	—	—	—	40.00	—
2001R Proof	10,000	Value: 200				

KM# 111 500 LIRE
6.8000 g., Bi-Metallic Bronzital center in Acmonital ring, 25.8 mm. **Obv:** Head left within circle **Rev:** Plaza within circle flanked by sprigs **Designer:** Cretara

Date	Mintage	F	VF	XF	Unc	BU
2001R	100,000	—	—	—	12.00	—
2001R Proof	10,000	Value: 35.00				

KM# 98a 500 LIRE
18.0000 g., 0.9000 Gold 0.5208 oz. AGW, 29 mm. **Obv:** Columbus' ships **Rev:** Bust left within wreath **Edge:** Lettered **Edge Lettering:** REPVBBLICA ITALIANA *** 1958*** **Note:** Official Restrike

Date	Mintage	F	VF	XF	Unc	BU
1958 (2006)R Proof	1,999	Value: 1,000				

KM# 99a 500 LIRE
18.0000 g., 0.9000 Gold 0.5208 oz. AGW, 29 mm. **Obv:** Seated Italia **Rev:** Lady **Edge:** Lettered **Edge Lettering:** "1 CENTENARIO VNITA'D'ITALIA * 1861-1961* " **Note:** Official Restrike

Date	Mintage	F	VF	XF	Unc	BU
1961 (2006)R Proof	1,999	Value: 1,000				

KM# 100a 500 LIRE
18.0000 g., 0.9000 Gold 0.5208 oz. AGW, 29 mm. **Obv:** Dante **Rev:** Hell **Edge:** Lettered **Edge Lettering:** "7 CENTENARIO DELLA NASCITA DI DANTE" **Note:** Official Restrike

Date	Mintage	F	VF	XF	Unc	BU
1965 (2006)R Proof	1,999	Value: 1,000				

KM# 111a 500 LIRE
14.0000 g., Bi-Metallic .750 Gold center in .900 Gold ring, 25.8 mm. **Obv:** Head left within circle **Rev:** Plaza within circle flanked by sprigs **Edge:** Segmented reeding **Note:** Official Restrike

Date	Mintage	F	VF	XF	Unc	BU
1982 (2006)R Proof	1,999	Value: 270				

KM# 194 1000 LIRE
Bi-Metallic Copper-Nickel center in Aluminum-Bronze ring, 27 mm. **Subject:** European Union **Obv:** Head left within circle **Obv. Designer:** Laura Cretara **Rev:** Corrected map with United Germany within globe design **Rev. Designer:** Pernazza

Date	Mintage	F	VF	XF	Unc	BU
2001R	100,000	—	—	—	10.00	—
2001R Proof	10,000	Value: 35.00				

KM# 236 1000 LIRE
14.6000 g., 0.8350 Silver 0.3919 oz. ASW, 31.4 mm. **Obv:** Giuseppe Verdi **Rev:** Building **Designer:** E. L. Frapiccini

Date	Mintage	F	VF	XF	Unc	BU
2001R	115,000	—	—	—	50.00	—
2001R Proof	10,000	Value: 100				

KM# 190a 1000 LIRE
17.0000 g., 0.9000 Gold 0.4919 oz. AGW, 27 mm. **Obv:** Roma **Rev:** European map **Edge:** Segmented reeding **Note:** Official Restrike

Date	Mintage	F	VF	XF	Unc	BU
1997 (2006)R Proof	1,999	Value: 650				

KM# 101a 1000 LIRE
24.0000 g., 0.9000 Gold 0.6944 oz. AGW, 31.4 mm. **Obv:** Concordia **Rev:** Geometric shape above value **Edge:** Lettered **Edge Lettering:** "REPVBBLICA ITALIANA" **Note:** Official restrike.

Date	Mintage	F	VF	XF	Unc	BU
1970 (2006)R Proof	1,999	Value: 1,200				

KM# 234 50000 LIRE
7.5000 g., 0.9000 Gold 0.2170 oz. AGW, 20 mm. **Subject:** 250th Anniversary - Palace of Caserta **Obv:** Front view of palace **Rev:** Fountain, date and denomination **Designer:** L. De Simoni

Date	Mintage	F	VF	XF	Unc	BU
2001R Proof	6,200	Value: 450				

KM# 233 100000 LIRE
15.0000 g., 0.9000 Gold 0.4340 oz. AGW, 25 mm. **Subject:** 700th Anniversary - Pulpit at the Church of St. Andrea a Pistoia **Obv:** Full pulpit **Rev:** Enlarged detail of the pulpit **Designer:** C. Momoni

Date	Mintage	F	VF	XF	Unc	BU
2001R Proof	4,500	Value: 850				

EURO COINAGE
European Union Issues

KM# 210 EURO CENT
2.3000 g., Copper Plated Steel, 16.3 mm. **Obv:** Castle del Monte **Obv. Designer:** Eugenio Drutti **Rev:** Value and globe **Rev. Designer:** Luc Luycx **Edge:** Plain

Date	Mintage	F	VF	XF	Unc	BU
2002R	1,348,899,500	—	—	—	0.25	—
2003R	9,629,000	—	—	—	0.35	—
2003R Proof	12,000	Value: 10.00				

Date	Mintage	F	VF	XF	Unc	BU
2004R	100,000,000	—	—	—	0.25	—
2004R Proof	12,000	Value: 7.00				
2005R	180,000,000	—	—	—	0.35	—
2005R Proof	12,000	Value: 5.00				
2006R	159,000,000	—	—	—	0.25	—
2006R Proof	12,000	Value: 5.00				
2007R	215,000,000	—	—	—	0.25	—
2007R Proof	12,000	Value: 5.00				
2008R	180,000,000	—	—	—	0.25	—
2008R Proof	—	Value: 5.00				
2009R	—	—	—	—	0.25	—
2009R Proof	—	Value: 5.00				

KM# 211 2 EURO CENT
3.0300 g., Copper Plated Steel, 18.7 mm. **Obv:** Observation tower in Turin **Obv. Designer:** Luciana de Simoni **Rev:** Value and globe **Rev. Designer:** Luc Luycx **Edge:** Plain

Date	Mintage	F	VF	XF	Unc	BU
2002R	1,099,166,250	—	—	—	0.25	—
2003R	21,817,000	—	—	—	0.25	—
2003R Proof	12,000	Value: 10.00				
2004R	120,000,000	—	—	—	0.25	—
2004R Proof	12,000	Value: 7.00				
2005R	120,000,000	—	—	—	0.25	—
2005R Proof	12,000	Value: 5.00				
2006R	196,000,000	—	—	—	0.25	—
2006R Proof	12,000	Value: 5.00				
2007R	140,000,000	—	—	—	0.25	—
2007R Proof	12,000	Value: 5.00				
2008R	135,000,000	—	—	—	0.25	—
2008R Proof	—	Value: 5.00				
2009R	—	—	—	—	0.25	—
2009R Proof	—	Value: 5.00				

KM# 212 5 EURO CENT
3.9500 g., Copper Plated Steel, 19.64 mm. **Obv:** Colosseum **Obv. Designer:** Lorenzo Frapiccini **Rev:** Value and globe **Rev. Designer:** Luc Luycx **Edge:** Plain

Date	Mintage	F	VF	XF	Unc	BU
2002R	1,341,742,204	—	—	—	0.25	—
2003R	1,960,000	—	—	—	10.00	—
2003R Proof	12,000	Value: 20.00				
2004R	10,000,000	—	—	—	0.25	—
2004R Proof	12,000	Value: 8.00				
2005R	70,000,000	—	—	—	0.25	—
2005R Proof	12,000	Value: 6.00				
2006R	119,000,000	—	—	—	0.25	—
2006R Proof	12,000	Value: 6.00				
2007R	85,000,000	—	—	—	0.25	—
2007R Proof	12,000	Value: 6.00				
2008R	90,000,000	—	—	—	0.25	—
2008R Proof	—	Value: 6.00				
2009R	—	—	—	—	0.25	—
2009R Proof	—	Value: 6.00				

KM# 213 10 EURO CENT
4.1000 g., Brass, 19.8 mm. **Obv:** Venus by Botticelli **Obv. Designer:** Claudia Momoni **Rev:** Value and map **Rev. Designer:** Luc Luycx **Edge:** Reeded

Date	Mintage	F	VF	XF	Unc	BU
2002R	1,142,383,000	—	—	—	0.25	—
2003R	29,976,000	—	—	—	0.50	—
2003R Proof	12,000	Value: 15.00				
2004R	5,000,000	—	—	—	10.00	—
2004R Proof	12,000	Value: 10.00				
2005R	100,000,000	—	—	—	0.50	—
2005R Proof	12,000	Value: 7.00				
2006R	180,000,000	—	—	—	0.50	—
2006R Proof	12,000	Value: 7.00				
2007R	105,000,000	—	—	—	0.50	—
2007R Proof	12,000	Value: 7.00				

KM# 247 10 EURO CENT

4.0700 g., Brass, 19.7 mm. **Obv:** Venus by Botticelli **Obv. Designer:** Claudia Momoni **Rev:** Relief Map of Western Europe, stars, lines and value **Rev. Designer:** Luc Luycx **Edge:** Reeded

Date	Mintage	F	VF	XF	Unc	BU
2008R	—	—	—	—	0.25	—
2009R	—	—	—	—	0.25	—

KM# 214 20 EURO CENT

5.7300 g., Brass, 22.1 mm. **Obv:** Futuristic sculpture **Obv. Designer:** Maria Cassol **Rev:** Value and map **Rev. Designer:** Luc Luycx **Edge:** Notched

Date	Mintage	F	VF	XF	Unc	BU
2002R	1,411,836,000	—	—	—	0.30	—
2003R	26,155,000	—	—	—	0.30	—
2003R Proof	12,000	Value: 16.00				
2004R	5,000,000	—	—	—	0.50	—
2004R Proof	12,000	Value: 14.00				
2005R	5,000,000	—	—	—	5.00	—
2005R Proof	12,000	Value: 8.00				
2006R	5,000,000	—	—	—	5.00	—
2006R Proof	12,000	Value: 8.00				
2007R	5,000,000	—	—	—	0.50	—
2007R Proof	12,000	Value: 8.00				

KM# 288 20 EURO CENT

6.4510 g., 0.9000 Gold 0.1867 oz. AGW, 21 mm. **Subject:** European Arts - Germany

Date	Mintage	F	VF	XF	Unc	BU
2006R	—	—	—	—	—	450

KM# 248 20 EURO CENT

5.7300 g., Brass, 22.1 mm. **Obv:** Futuristic sculpture **Obv. Designer:** Maria Cassoll **Rev:** Relief map of Western Europe, stars, lines and value **Rev. Designer:** Luc Luycx **Edge:** Reeded

Date	Mintage	F	VF	XF	Unc	BU
2008R	—	—	—	—	1.00	—
2009R	—	—	—	—	1.00	—

KM# 215 50 EURO CENT

7.8100 g., Brass, 24.2 mm. **Obv:** Sculpture of Marcus Aurelius on horseback **Obv. Designer:** Roberto Mauri **Rev:** Value and map **Rev. Designer:** Luc Luycx **Edge:** Reeded

Date	Mintage	F	VF	XF	Unc	BU
2002R	1,136,718,000	—	—	—	0.80	—
2003R	44,825,000	—	—	—	1.00	—
2003R Proof	12,000	Value: 18.00				
2004R	5,000,000	—	—	—	4.00	—
2004R Proof	12,000	Value: 16.00				
2005R	5,000,000	—	—	—	1.00	—
2005R Proof	12,000	Value: 10.00				
2006R	5,000,000	—	—	—	1.00	—
2006R Proof	12,000	Value: 10.00				
2007R	5,000,000	—	—	—	1.00	—
2007R Proof	12,000	Value: 10.00				

KM# 249 50 EURO CENT

7.8100 g., Brass, 24.2 mm. **Obv:** Sculpture of Marcus Aurelius on horseback **Obv. Designer:** Roberto Mauri **Rev:** Relief map of Western Europe, stars, lines and value **Rev. Designer:** Luc Luycx **Edge:** Reeded

Date	Mintage	F	VF	XF	Unc	BU
2008R	—	—	—	—	1.25	—
2009R	—	—	—	—	1.25	—

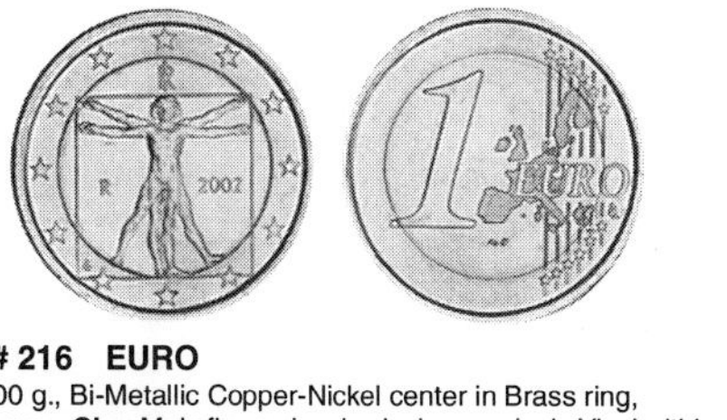

KM# 216 EURO

7.5000 g., Bi-Metallic Copper-Nickel center in Brass ring, 23.2 mm. **Obv:** Male figure drawing by Leonardo da Vinci within circle of stars **Obv. Designer:** Laura Cretara **Rev:** Value and map within circle **Rev. Designer:** Luc Luycx **Edge:** Reeded and plain sections

Date	Mintage	F	VF	XF	Unc	BU
2002R	966,025,300	—	—	—	1.60	—
2003R	66,474,000	—	—	—	2.00	—
2003R Proof	12,000	Value: 20.00				
2004R	5,000,000	—	—	—	5.00	—
2004R Proof	12,000	Value: 18.00				
2005R	5,000,000	—	—	—	5.00	—

Date	Mintage	F	VF	XF	Unc	BU
2005R Proof	12,000	Value: 15.00				
2006R	108,000,000	—	—	—	2.00	—
2006R Proof	12,000	Value: 15.00				
2007R	135,000,000	—	—	—	2.00	—
2007R Proof	12,000	Value: 15.00				

KM# 290 EURO

8.5200 g., Bi-Metallic Brass center in copper-nickel ring

Date	Mintage	F	VF	XF	Unc	BU
2007R	—	—	—	—	—	6.00

KM# 294 EURO

18.0000 g., 0.9250 Silver 0.5353 oz. ASW, 32 mm. **Subject:** Arturo Toscani - 50th Aniversary Death

Date	Mintage	F	VF	XF	Unc	BU
2007R	—	—	—	—	—	62.00

KM# 250 EURO

7.5000 g., Bi-Metallic Copper-Nickel center in Brass ring, 23.2 mm. **Obv:** Male figure drawing by Leonardo da Vinci **Obv. Designer:** Laura Cretara **Rev:** Relief map of Western Europe, stars, lines and value **Rev. Designer:** Luc Luycx **Edge:** Reeded and plain sections

Date	Mintage	F	VF	XF	Unc	BU
2008R	—	—	—	—	2.50	—
2009R	—	—	—	—	2.50	—

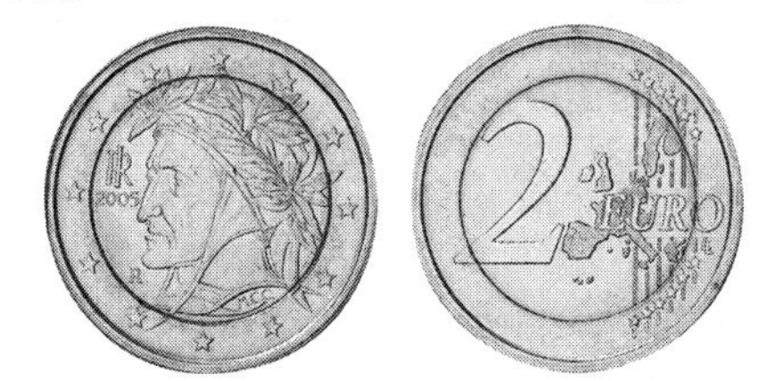

KM# 217 2 EURO

8.5200 g., Bi-Metallic Brass center in Copper-Nickel ring, 25.7 mm. **Obv:** Head left within circle **Obv. Designer:** Maria Colanieri **Rev:** Value and map within circle **Rev. Designer:** Luc Luycx **Edge:** Reeded **Edge Lettering:** 2's and stars

Date	Mintage	F	VF	XF	Unc	BU
2002R	463,702,000	—	—	—	4.00	—
2003R	36,160,000	—	—	—	4.00	—
2003R Proof	12,000	Value: 25.00				
2004R	7,000,000	—	—	—	6.00	—
2004R Proof	12,000	Value: 22.00				
2005R	62,000,000	—	—	—	4.00	—
2005R Proof	12,000	Value: 20.00				
2006R	10,000,000	—	—	—	4.00	—
2006R Proof	12,000	Value: 20.00				
2007R	5,000,000	—	—	—	5.00	—
2007R Proof	12,000	Value: 20.00				

KM# 237 2 EURO

8.5300 g., Bi-Metallic Aluminum-Bronze center in Copper-Nickel ring, 25.7 mm. **Obv:** World Food Program globe within circle **Rev:** Value and map within circle **Edge:** Reeded and lettered **Edge Lettering:** 2's and stars

Date	Mintage	F	VF	XF	Unc	BU
2004R	16,000,000	—	—	—	5.00	—

KM# 245 2 EURO

8.5200 g., Bi-Metallic Brass center in Copper-Nickel ring, 25.6 mm. **Subject:** European Constitution **Obv:** Europa holding an open book while sitting on a bull within circle **Rev:** Value and map within circle **Edge:** Reeding over stars and 2's

Date	Mintage	F	VF	XF	Unc	BU
2005R	18,000,000	—	—	—	4.00	—

KM# 246 2 EURO

8.5100 g., Bi-Metallic Brass center in Copper-Nickel ring, 25.7 mm. **Subject:** Torino Winter Olympics **Obv:** Skier and other designs within circle **Rev:** Value and map within circle **Edge:** Reeded with stars and 2's

Date	Mintage	F	VF	XF	Unc	BU
2006R	40,000,000	—	—	—	4.00	—

KM# 280 2 EURO

8.5200 g., Bi-Metallic Brass center, copper-nickel ring **Subject:** Turin Olympics

Date	Mintage	F	VF	XF	Unc	BU
2006R	—	—	—	—	—	4.00

KM# 311 2 EURO

8.5500 g., Bi-Metallic Brass center in Copper-Nickel ring, 25.72 mm. **Subject:** Treaty of Rome, 50th Anniversary

Date	Mintage	F	VF	XF	Unc	BU
2007R	—	—	—	—	—	5.00

KM# 251 2 EURO

8.5200 g., Bi-Metallic Brass center in Copper-Nickel ring, 25.7 mm. **Obv:** Bust of Dante Aligheri **Obv. Designer:** Maria Colanieri **Rev:** Relief map of Western Europe, stars, lines and value **Rev. Designer:** Luc Luycx **Edge:** Reeded **Edge Lettering:** 2's and stars

Date	Mintage	F	VF	XF	Unc	BU
2008R	—	—	—	—	4.00	—
2009R	—	—	—	—	4.00	—

KM# 301 2 EURO

8.5200 g., Bi-Metallic Brass center in copper-nickel ring **Subject:** Declaration of Rights

Date	Mintage	F	VF	XF	Unc	BU
2008R	—	—	—	—	—	6.00

KM# 310 2 EURO

8.5200 g., Bi-Metallic Brass center in Copper-Nickel ring, 25.7 mm. **Subject:** Louis Braille **Obv:** Hand reading book in braille font

Date	Mintage	F	VF	XF	Unc	BU
2009R	—	—	—	—	—	6.00

KM# 314 2 EURO

0.9250 Silver, 32 mm. **Subject:** World Aquatics Championships **Obv:** River God reclining **Rev:** Two swimmers

Date	Mintage	F	VF	XF	Unc	BU
2009R	5,500	—	—	—	—	50.00

KM# 312 2 EURO

8.5500 g., Bi-Metallic Brass center in Copper-Nickel ring, 25.72 mm. **Subject:** European Monetrary Union, 10th Anniversary **Obv:** Stick figure and Euro symbol

Date	Mintage	F	VF	XF	Unc	BU
2009R	—	—	—	—	—	5.00

KM# 252 5 EURO

18.0000 g., 0.9250 Silver 0.5353 oz. ASW, 32 mm. **Subject:** People in Europe

Date	Mintage	F	VF	XF	Unc	BU
2003R	25,000	—	—	—	35.00	—
2003R Proof	8,000	Value: 65.00				

KM# 253 5 EURO

18.0000 g., 0.9250 Silver 0.5353 oz. ASW, 32 mm. **Subject:** Work in Europe

Date	Mintage	F	VF	XF	Unc	BU
2003R	50,000	—	—	—	35.00	—
2003R Proof	12,000	Value: 65.00				

KM# 238 5 EURO

18.0000 g., 0.9250 Silver 0.5353 oz. ASW, 32 mm. **Subject:** World Cup Soccer - Germany 2006 **Obv:** Santa Croce Square in Florence **Rev:** Soccer ball and world globe design

Date	Mintage	F	VF	XF	Unc	BU
2004R Proof	35,000	Value: 100				

KM# 239 5 EURO

18.0000 g., 0.9250 Silver 0.5353 oz. ASW, 32 mm. **Subject:** Madam Butterfly **Obv:** La Scala Opera House, where Madam Butterfly was first performed there in 1904 **Rev:** Geisha

Date	Mintage	F	VF	XF	Unc	BU
2004R	30,000	—	—	—	35.00	—
2004R Proof	12,000	Value: 60.00				

KM# 254 5 EURO

18.0000 g., 0.9250 Silver 0.5353 oz. ASW, 32 mm. **Subject:** 50th Anniversary of Italian Television

Date	Mintage	F	VF	XF	Unc	BU
2004R	40,000	—	—	—	35.00	—
2004R Proof	15,000	Value: 65.00				

KM# 255 5 EURO

18.0000 g., 0.9250 Silver 0.5353 oz. ASW, 32 mm. **Subject:** 85th Birthday of Federico Fellini

Date	Mintage	F	VF	XF	Unc	BU
2005R	35,000	—	—	—	30.00	—
2005R Proof	22,000	Value: 60.00				

KM# 256 5 EURO

18.0000 g., 0.9250 Silver 0.5353 oz. ASW, 32 mm. **Subject:** 2006 Olympic Winter Games Torino Ski Jump

Date	Mintage	F	VF	XF	Unc	BU
2005R	35,000	—	—	—	30.00	—
2005R Proof	40,000	Value: 60.00				

KM# 257 5 EURO

18.0000 g., 0.9250 Silver 0.5353 oz. ASW, 32 mm. **Subject:** 2006 Olympic Winter Games Cross Country Skiing

Date	Mintage	F	VF	XF	Unc	BU
2005R	35,000	—	—	—	30.00	—
2005R Proof	40,000	Value: 50.00				

KM# 266 5 EURO

18.0000 g., 0.9250 Silver 0.5353 oz. ASW, 32 mm. **Subject:** 2006 Olympic Games Torino Figure Skating

Date	Mintage	F	VF	XF	Unc	BU
2005	40,000	—	—	—	30.00	—
2005 Proof	—	Value: 50.00				

KM# 291 5 EURO

18.0000 g., 0.9250 Silver 0.5353 oz. ASW, 32 mm. **Subject:** Kyoto Agreement - 5th Anniversary

Date	Mintage	F	VF	XF	Unc	BU
2007R	—	—	—	—	—	62.00

KM# 292 5 EURO

18.0000 g., 0.9250 Silver 0.5353 oz. ASW, 32 mm. **Subject:** Giuseppe Garibaldi - 200th Anniversary Birth

Date	Mintage	F	VF	XF	Unc	BU
2007R	—	—	—	—	—	62.00

KM# 293 5 EURO
18.0000 g., 0.9250 Silver 0.5353 oz. ASW, 32 mm.
Subject: Aitero Spinelini 100th Birthday

Date	Mintage	F	VF	XF	Unc	BU
2007R	—	—	—	—	—	62.00

KM# 281 5 EURO
18.0000 g., 0.9250 Silver 0.5353 oz. ASW, 32 mm.
Subject: Italian Republic - 60th Anniversary

Date	Mintage	F	VF	XF	Unc	BU
2008R	—	—	—	—	—	62.00
2008R Proof	—	Value: 65.00				

KM# 282 5 EURO
18.0000 g., 0.9250 Silver 0.5353 oz. ASW, 32 mm.
Subject: FIFA World Cup

Date	Mintage	F	VF	XF	Unc	BU
2008R	—	—	—	—	—	62.00
2008R Proof	—	Value: 65.00				

KM# 303 5 EURO
18.0000 g., 0.9250 Silver 0.5353 oz. ASW, 32 mm.
Subject: Anna Magnani - 100th Birthday

Date	Mintage	F	VF	XF	Unc	BU
2008R	—	—	—	—	—	62.00

KM# 304 5 EURO
18.0000 g., 0.9250 Silver 0.5353 oz. ASW, 32 mm.
Subject: Italian Constitution - 60th Anniversary

Date	Mintage	F	VF	XF	Unc	BU
2008	—	—	—	—	—	48.00

KM# 313 5 EURO
18.0000 g., 0.9250 Silver 0.5353 oz. ASW, 32 mm.
Subject: Giro d'Italy - Cycling Race Centennial **Obv:** Two cyclists
Rev: Bicycle and map of Italy

Date	Mintage	F	VF	XF	Unc	BU
2009R Proof	—	Value: 50.00				

KM# 315 5 EURO
18.0000 g., 0.9250 Silver 0.5353 oz. ASW, 32 mm.
Subject: Herculaneum Discovery, 300th Anniversary **Obv:** Four dogs nipping at horse **Rev:** Female statue

Date	Mintage	F	VF	XF	Unc	BU
2009R Proof	—	Value: 50.00				

KM# 258 10 EURO
22.0000 g., 0.9250 Silver 0.6542 oz. ASW, 34 mm.
Subject: People In Europe

Date	Mintage	F	VF	XF	Unc	BU
2003	25,000	—	—	—	70.00	—
2003R Proof	8,000	Value: 120				

KM# 259 10 EURO
22.0000 g., 0.9250 Silver 0.6542 oz. ASW, 34 mm.
Subject: Italian Presidency of E.U.

Date	Mintage	F	VF	XF	Unc	BU
2003R	40,000	—	—	—	45.00	—
2003R Proof	8,000	Value: 120				

KM# 240 10 EURO
22.0000 g., 0.9250 Silver 0.6542 oz. ASW, 34 mm.
Subject: City of Genoa **Obv:** Sculpture and art works **Rev:** Tower and harbor map

Date	Mintage	F	VF	XF	Unc	BU
2004R	30,000	—	—	—	55.00	—
2004R Proof	12,000	Value: 70.00				

KM# 241 10 EURO
22.0000 g., 0.9250 Silver 0.6542 oz. ASW, 34 mm.
Subject: Giacomo Puccini **Obv:** Puccini wearing hat **Rev:** Stage, music and quill

Date	Mintage	F	VF	XF	Unc	BU
2004R	30,000	—	—	—	70.00	—
2004R Proof	12,000	Value: 100				

KM# 260 10 EURO
22.0000 g., 0.9250 Silver 0.6542 oz. ASW, 34 mm.
Subject: 2006 Olympic Winter Games Torino Alpine Skiing

Date	Mintage	F	VF	XF	Unc	BU
2005R	40,000	—	—	—	60.00	—
2005R Proof	40,000	Value: 80.00				

KM# 261 10 EURO
22.0000 g., 0.9250 Silver 0.6542 oz. ASW, 34 mm.
Subject: 2006 Olympic Winter Games Torino Ice Hockey

Date	Mintage	F	VF	XF	Unc	BU
2005R	35,000	—	—	—	60.00	—
2005R Proof	40,000	Value: 80.00				

KM# 262 10 EURO
22.0000 g., 0.9250 Silver 0.6542 oz. ASW, 34 mm.
Subject: 2006 Olympic Winter Games Torino Speed Skating

Date	Mintage	F	VF	XF	Unc	BU
2005R	35,000	—	—	—	60.00	—
2005R Proof	40,000	Value: 80.00				

KM# 268 10 EURO
22.0000 g., 0.9250 Silver 0.6542 oz. ASW, 34 mm.
Subject: 60th Anniversary UN "ONU"

Date	Mintage	F	VF	XF	Unc	BU
2005	25,000	—	—	—	50.00	—

KM# 271 10 EURO
22.0000 g., 0.9250 Silver 0.6542 oz. ASW, 34 mm.
Subject: Peace and Freedom In Europe

Date	Mintage	F	VF	XF	Unc	BU
2005 Proof	20,000	Value: 55.00				

KM# 283 10 EURO
22.0000 g., 0.9250 Silver 0.6542 oz. ASW, 34 mm.
Subject: FIFA World Cup - Germany

Date	Mintage	F	VF	XF	Unc	BU
2006R	—	—	—	—	—	75.00

KM# 284 10 EURO
22.0000 g., 0.9250 Silver 0.6542 oz. ASW **Subject:** Andre Martenga - 500th Anniversary

Date	Mintage	F	VF	XF	Unc	BU
2006R	—	—	—	—	—	75.00

KM# 285 10 EURO
22.0000 g., 0.9250 Silver 0.6542 oz. ASW, 34 mm.
Subject: Leonardo da Vinci

Date	Mintage	F	VF	XF	Unc	BU
2006R	—	—	—	—	—	75.00

KM# 286 10 EURO
22.0000 g., 0.9250 Silver 0.6542 oz. ASW, 34 mm.
Subject: UNICEF 60th Anniversary

Date	Mintage	F	VF	XF	Unc	BU
2006R	—	—	—	—	—	75.00

KM# 295 10 EURO
22.0000 g., 0.9250 Silver 0.6542 oz. ASW, 34 mm.
Subject: Treaty of Rome, 50th Anniversary

Date	Mintage	F	VF	XF	Unc	BU
2007R	—	—	—	—	—	75.00

KM# 296 10 EURO
22.0000 g., 0.9250 Silver 0.6542 oz. ASW, 34 mm.
Subject: Antonia Canova - 250th Anniversary Birth

Date	Mintage	F	VF	XF	Unc	BU
2007R	—	—	—	—	—	75.00

KM# 297 10 EURO
22.0000 g., 0.9250 Silver 0.6542 oz. ASW, 34 mm.
Subject: Mint of Rome - 100th Anniversary

Date	Mintage	F	VF	XF	Unc	BU
2007R	—	—	—	—	—	75.00

KM# 305 10 EURO
22.0000 g., 0.9250 Silver 0.6542 oz. ASW, 34 mm.
Subject: Andrea Palladio - 500th Birthday

Date	Mintage	F	VF	XF	Unc	BU
2008	—	—	—	—	—	75.00

KM# 306 10 EURO
22.0000 g., 0.9250 Silver 0.6542 oz. ASW, 34 mm.
Subject: University of Perugia - 700th Anniversary

Date	Mintage	F	VF	XF	Unc	BU
2008	—	—	—	—	—	75.00

KM# 316 10 EURO
0.9250 Silver, 34 mm. **Subject:** International Year of Astronomy **Obv:** Head right **Rev:** Astrological instruments

Date	Mintage	F	VF	XF	Unc	BU
2009R Proof	9,000	Value: 75.00				

KM# 317 10 EURO
22.0000 g., 0.9250 Silver 0.6542 oz. ASW, 34 mm.
Subject: Guglielmo Maroni's Nobel Peace Prize **Obv:** Bust and steamship **Rev:** Telegraph machine

Date	Mintage	F	VF	XF	Unc	BU
2009R Proof	18,000					

KM# 318 10 EURO
22.0000 g., 0.9250 Silver 0.6542 oz. ASW, 34 mm.
Subject: Annibale Carracci, 400th Anniversary **Obv:** 1/2 length figure standing **Rev:** Historical cart

Date	Mintage	F	VF	XF	Unc	BU
2009R Proof	18,000					

KM# 319 10 EURO
22.0000 g., 0.9250 Silver 0.6542 oz. ASW, 34 mm.
Subject: Futurist movement, 100th Anniversary **Obv:** Building design **Rev:** Round sculpture

Date	Mintage	F	VF	XF	Unc	BU
2009R Proof	7,000	Value: 75.00				

KM# 263 20 EURO
6.4510 g., 0.9000 Gold 0.1867 oz. AGW, 21 mm. **Subject:** Arts in Europe - Italy

Date	Mintage	F	VF	XF	Unc	BU
2003R Proof	6,000	Value: 360				

KM# 242 20 EURO
6.4510 g., 0.9000 Gold 0.1867 oz. AGW, 21 mm. **Obv:** Arts In Europe: Belgium **Rev:** Flying bird obscuring a man's face

Date	Mintage	F	VF	XF	Unc	BU
2004R Proof	6,000	Value: 300				

KM# 243 20 EURO
6.4510 g., 0.9000 Gold 0.1867 oz. AGW, 21 mm.
Subject: World Cup Soccer - Germany 2006 **Obv:** Mascot **Rev:** Soccer ball and world globe

Date	Mintage	F	VF	XF	Unc	BU
2004R Proof	7,500	Value: 360				

KM# 265 20 EURO
6.4510 g., 0.9000 Gold 0.1867 oz. AGW, 54 mm. **Subject:** 2006 Olympic Winter Games Torino Porte Palatine Gate

Date	Mintage	F	VF	XF	Unc	BU
2005R Proof	10,000	Value: 350				

KM# 267 20 EURO
6.4510 g., 0.9000 Gold 0.1867 oz. AGW, 21 mm. **Subject:** 2006 Olympic Games Torino Madama Palace

Date	Mintage	F	VF	XF	Unc	BU
2005 Proof	10,000	Value: 350				

KM# 269 20 EURO
6.4510 g., 0.9000 Gold 0.1867 oz. AGW, 21 mm. **Subject:** 2006 Olympic Games Torino Stupinigi Palace

Date	Mintage	F	VF	XF	Unc	BU
2005 Proof	10,000	Value: 350				

KM# 272 20 EURO
6.4510 g., 0.9000 Gold 0.1867 oz. AGW, 21 mm. **Subject:** Art In Europe - Finland

Date	Mintage	F	VF	XF	Unc	BU
2005 Proof	5,000	Value: 400				

KM# 287 20 EURO
6.4510 g., 0.9000 Gold 0.1867 oz. AGW, 21 mm. **Subject:** FIFA World Cup

Date	Mintage	F	VF	XF	Unc	BU
2006R	—	—	—	—	—	450

KM# 298 20 EURO
6.4510 g., 0.9000 Gold 0.1867 oz. AGW, 21 mm.
Subject: Treaty of Rome - 50th Anniversary

Date	Mintage	F	VF	XF	Unc	BU
2007R	—	—	—	—	—	450

KM# 299 20 EURO
6.4510 g., 0.9000 Gold 0.1867 oz. AGW, 21 mm.
Subject: European Art - Iceland

Date	Mintage	F	VF	XF	Unc	BU
2007R	—	—	—	—	—	450

KM# 307 20 EURO
6.4510 g., 0.9000 Gold 0.1867 oz. AGW, 21 mm.
Subject: Andrea Palladio - 500th Birthday

Date	Mintage	F	VF	XF	Unc	BU
2008	—	—	—	—	—	450

KM# 308 20 EURO
6.4510 g., 0.9000 Gold 0.1867 oz. AGW, 21 mm. **Subject:** Arts in Europe - Netherlands

Date	Mintage	F	VF	XF	Unc	BU
2008	—	—	—	—	—	450

KM# 320 20 EURO
6.4500 g., 0.9000 Gold 0.1866 oz. AGW, 21 mm.
Subject: Guglielmo Marconi, 100th Anniversary **Obv:** Bust and steamship **Rev:** Telegraph machine

Date	Mintage	F	VF	XF	Unc	BU
2009R Proof	5,000	Value: 350				

KM# 321 20 EURO
6.4500 g., 0.9000 Gold 0.1866 oz. AGW, 21 mm. **Subject:** Arts in Europe - Great Britain **Obv:** Sailing ship **Rev:** Venus by Edward B. Jones

Date	Mintage	F	VF	XF	Unc	BU
2009R Proof	2,500	Value: 350				

KM# 264 50 EURO
16.1300 g., 0.9000 Gold 0.4667 oz. AGW, 28 mm.
Subject: Arts in Europe - Austria

Date	Mintage	F	VF	XF	Unc	BU
2003R Proof	6,000	Value: 700				

KM# 244 50 EURO
16.1300 g., 0.9000 Gold 0.4667 oz. AGW, 28 mm. **Obv:** Arts In Europe: Denmark **Rev:** Angel carrying away two children

Date	Mintage	F	VF	XF	Unc	BU
2004R Proof	6,000	Value: 700				

KM# 270 50 EURO
16.1300 g., 0.9000 Gold 0.4667 oz. AGW, 28 mm.
Subject: 2006 Olympic Games Torino Emanuele Filiberto

Date	Mintage	F	VF	XF	Unc	BU
2005 Proof	6,000	Value: 650				

KM# 273 50 EURO
16.1300 g., 0.9000 Gold 0.4667 oz. AGW, 28 mm. **Subject:** Art In Europe - France

Date	Mintage	F	VF	XF	Unc	BU
2005 Proof	5,000	Value: 700				

KM# 274 50 EURO
16.1300 g., 0.9000 Gold 0.4667 oz. AGW, 28 mm.
Subject: 2006 Olympic Games Torino Olympic Torch

Date	Mintage	F	VF	XF	Unc	BU
2006 Proof	5,000	Value: 700				

KM# 289 50 EURO
16.1300 g., 0.9000 Gold 0.4667 oz. AGW, 28 mm.
Subject: European Arts - Greece

Date	Mintage	F	VF	XF	Unc	BU
2006R	—	—	—	—	—	800

KM# 300 50 EURO
16.1300 g., 0.9000 Gold 0.4667 oz. AGW, 28 mm.
Subject: European Art - Norway

Date	Mintage	F	VF	XF	Unc	BU
2007R	—	—	—	—	—	800

KM# 309 50 EURO
16.1300 g., 0.9000 Gold 0.4667 oz. AGW, 28 mm.
Subject: Arts in Europe - Portugal

Date	Mintage	F	VF	XF	Unc	BU
2008	—	—	—	—	—	800

KM# 322 50 EURO
6.1300 g., 0.9000 Gold 0.1774 oz. AGW, 28 mm. **Subject:** Arts in Europe - Spain **Obv:** Sailing ship **Rev:** Sagrada Familia of Antoni Gaudí

Date	Mintage	F	VF	XF	Unc	BU
2009R Proof	2,000	Value: 800				

MINT SETS

KM#	Date	Mintage	Identification	Issue Price	Mkt Val
MS39	2001 (12)	125,200	KM#91-94, 97.2, 98, 105, 111, 159, 183, 194, 236	—	225
MS40	2002 (8)	50,000	KM#210-217	—	22.00
MS41	2003 (8)	50,000	KM#210-217	—	30.00
MS42	2003 (9)	50,000	KM#210-217, 253	—	70.00
MS43	2004 (8)	40,000	KM#210-217	—	35.00
MS44	2004 (9)	40,000	KM#210-217, 254	—	65.00
MS45	2005 (8)	35,000	KM#210-217	—	35.00
MS46	2005 (9)	35,000	KM#210-217, 255	—	65.00
MS47	2006 (8)	25,000	KM#210-217	—	30.00
MS48	2007 (8)	—	KM#210-217	—	30.00
MS49	2008 (8)	—	KM#210-216, 301	—	45.00
MS50	2008 (9)	—	KM#210-217, 281	—	75.00

PROOF SETS

KM#	Date	Mintage	Identification	Issue Price	Mkt Val
PS25	2001 (12)	10,000	KM#91-94, 97.2, 98, 105, 111, 159, 183, 194, 236	—	635
PS26	2003 (9)	12,000	KM#210-217, 253	—	200
PS27	2004 (9)	15,000	KM#210-217, 254	—	170
PS28	2005 (9)	12,000	KM#210-217, 255	—	135
PS29	2006 (9)	10,000	KM#210-217	—	75.00
PS30	2007 (8)	—	KM#210-217	—	75.00
PS31	2008 (9)	—	KM#210-217, 282	—	140

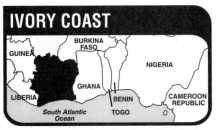

IVORY COAST

The Republic of the Ivory Coast, (Cote d'Ivoire), a former French Overseas territory located on the south side of the African bulge between Liberia and Ghana, has an area of 124,504 sq. mi. (322,463 sq. km.) and a population of 11.8 million. Capital: Yamoussoukro. The predominantly agricultural economy is one of Africa's most prosperous. Coffee, tropical woods, cocoa, and bananas are exported.

REPUBLIC

DECIMAL COINAGE

KM# 6 100 FRANCS
25.0000 g., 0.9250 Silver 0.7435 oz. ASW, 38.6 mm.
Rev: Mamouth and embedded tooth fragment

Date	Mintage	F	VF	XF	Unc	BU
2010 Proof	2,500	Value: 50.00				

JAMAICA

Jamaica is situated in the Caribbean Sea 90 miles south of Cuba, has an area of 4,244 sq. mi. (10,990 sq. km.) and a population of 2.1 million. Capital: Kingston. The economy is founded chiefly on mining, tourism and agriculture. Aluminum, bauxite, sugar, rum and molasses are exported.

Jamaica is a member of the Commonwealth of Nations. Elizabeth II is the Head of State, as Queen of Jamaica.

MINT MARKS
C - Royal Canadian Mint, Ottawa
H - Heaton

MONETARY SYSTEM
100 Cents = 1 Dollar

COMMONWEALTH

DECIMAL COINAGE

KM# 64 CENT
1.2000 g., Aluminum, 20.05 mm. **Ruler:** Elizabeth II **Series:** F.A.O. **Obv:** National arms **Obv. Legend:** JAMAICA **Rev:** Ackee fruit above value **Edge:** Plain **Shape:** 12-sided **Designer:** Christopher Ironside

Date	Mintage	F	VF	XF	Unc	BU
2002	—	—	—	0.25	0.50	0.75
2002 Proof	500	Value: 1.00				

KM# 146.2 10 CENTS
2.4500 g., Copper Plated Steel, 17 mm. **Ruler:** Elizabeth II **Series:** National Heroes **Subject:** Paul Bogle **Obv:** National arms **Obv. Legend:** JAMAICA **Rev:** Bust facing **Edge:** Plain **Note:** Reduced size.

Date	Mintage	F	VF	XF	Unc	BU
2002	—	—	—	0.25	0.50	0.75
2002 Proof	500	Value: 2.00				
2003	—	—	—	0.25	0.50	0.75

KM# 167 25 CENTS
3.6100 g., Copper Plated Steel, 20 mm. **Ruler:** Elizabeth II **Series:** National Heroes **Subject:** Marcus Garvey **Obv:** National arms **Obv. Legend:** JAMAICA **Rev:** Head 1/4 right **Edge:** Plain

Date	Mintage	F	VF	XF	Unc	BU
2002	—	—	—	0.25	0.50	0.75
2002 Proof	500	Value: 3.00				
2003	—	—	—	0.25	0.50	0.75

KM# 164 DOLLAR
2.9100 g., Nickel Clad Steel, 18.5 mm. **Ruler:** Elizabeth II **Series:** National Heroes **Subject:** Sir Alexander Bustamante **Obv:** National arms **Obv. Legend:** JAMAICA **Rev:** Bust facing **Edge:** Plain **Shape:** 7-sided

Date	Mintage	F	VF	XF	Unc	BU
2002	—	—	—	0.40	1.00	1.50
2002 Proof	500	Value: 4.00				
2003	—	—	—	0.40	1.00	1.50
2005	—	—	—	0.40	1.00	1.50
2006	—	—	—	0.40	1.00	1.50

KM# 189 DOLLAR
2.9000 g., Nickel Clad Steel, 18.5 mm. **Ruler:** Elizabeth II **Rev:** Sir Alexander Bustamante

Date	Mintage	F	VF	XF	Unc	BU
2009	—	—	—	—	1.00	1.50

KM# 163 5 DOLLARS
Steel, 21.5 mm. **Ruler:** Elizabeth II **Series:** National Heroes **Subject:** Norman Manley **Obv:** National arms **Obv. Legend:** JAMAICA **Rev:** Head left

Date	Mintage	F	VF	XF	Unc	BU
2002	—	—	—	1.50	2.50	3.50
2002 Proof	500	Value: 5.00				

KM# 181 10 DOLLARS
5.9400 g., Stainless Steel **Ruler:** Elizabeth II **Series:** National Heroes **Subject:** George William Gordon **Obv:** National arms **Obv. Legend:** JAMAICA **Rev:** Bust facing **Edge:** Plain **Shape:** Scalloped **Note:** Diameter varies: 24-24.6.

Date	Mintage	F	VF	XF	Unc	BU
2002	—	—	—	1.50	3.00	4.00
2002 Proof	500	Value: 9.00				
2005	—	—	—	1.50	3.00	4.00

KM# 190 10 DOLLARS
5.9400 g., Stainless Steel, 24.6 mm. **Ruler:** Elizabeth II **Obv:** Arms **Rev:** George William Gordon

Date	Mintage	F	VF	XF	Unc	BU
2009	—	—	—	—	6.00	7.50

KM# 182 20 DOLLARS
7.8000 g., Bi-Metallic Copper-Nickel center in Brass ring, 23 mm. **Ruler:** Elizabeth II **Series:** National Heroes **Subject:** Marcus Garvey **Obv:** Value above national arms within circle **Obv. Legend:** JAMAICA **Rev:** Head 1/4 right within circle **Edge:** Alternate reeding and plain

Date	Mintage	F	VF	XF	Unc	BU
2001	—	—	—	1.50	3.00	4.00
2002	—	—	—	1.50	3.00	4.00
2002 Proof	500	Value: 15.00				

KM# 186 25 DOLLARS
28.2800 g., 0.9250 Silver 0.8410 oz. ASW, 38.6 mm. **Ruler:** Elizabeth II **Subject:** UNICEF **Obv:** Arms with supporters **Rev:** Two boys above "Pals" **Edge:** Reeded

Date	Mintage	F	VF	XF	Unc	BU
2001 Proof	—	Value: 55.00				

KM# 185 25 DOLLARS
28.2800 g., 0.9250 Silver 0.8410 oz. ASW, 38.6 mm. **Ruler:** Elizabeth II **Subject:** IAAF World Junior Championships **Obv:** Arms with supporters and value **Rev:** Female runner **Edge:** Reeded

Date	Mintage	F	VF	XF	Unc	BU
2002 Proof	5,500	Value: 60.00				

KM# 184   50 DOLLARS
28.4500 g., 0.9250 Silver 0.8461 oz. ASW, 38.6 mm.
Ruler: Elizabeth II **Subject:** Millennium **Obv:** Arms with
supporters **Rev:** Family within radiant sun **Edge:** Reeded

Date	Mintage	F	VF	XF	Unc	BU
ND(2002) Proof	5,000	Value: 50.00				

PROOF SETS

KM#	Date	Mintage	Identification	Issue Price	Mkt Val
PS33	2002 (8)	500	KM#64, 146.2, 163, 164, 167, 181, 182, 185	99.00	100

JAPAN

Japan, a constitutional monarchy situated off the east coast
of Asia, has an area of 145,809 sq. mi. (377,835 sq. km.) and a
population of 123.2 million. Capital: Tokyo. Japan, one of the
major industrial nations of the world, exports machinery, motor
vehicles, electronics and chemicals.

Japanese coinage of concern to this catalog includes those
issued for the Ryukyu Islands (also called Liuchu), a chain of
islands extending southwest from Japan toward Taiwan (For-
mosa), before the Japanese government converted the islands
into a prefecture under the name Okinawa. Many of the provinces
of Japan issued their own definitive coinage under the Shogunate.

RULERS

Emperors

Akihito (Heisei), 1989-

Years 1 –　　平　成

NOTE: The personal name of the emperor is followed by the
name that he chose for his regnal era.

MONETARY UNITS

Rin　　厘

Sen　　銭

Yen　　円 or 圓 or 圓

DATING

Year

2

x10

3

Reading right to left,
3x10+2 = 32 year

Meiji

Dai Nippon
Great Japan

EMPIRE
REFORM COINAGE

Y# 95.2   YEN
1.0000 g., Aluminum, 20 mm.   **Ruler:** Akihito **Obv:** Sprouting
branch divides authority and value **Rev:** Value within circles
above date **Edge:** Plain

Date	Mintage	F	VF	XF	Unc	BU
Yr,13(2001)	7,786,000	—	—	0.70	1.25	1.50
Yr.13(2001) Proof	238,000	Value: 3.00				
Yr.14(2002)	9,425,000	—	—	—	—	0.50
Yr.14(2002) Proof	242,000	Value: 3.00				
Yr.15(2003)	117,131,000	—	—	—	—	0.50
Yr.15(2003) Proof	275,000	Value: 3.00				
Yr.16(2004)	52,623,000	—	—	—	—	0.50
Yr.16(2004) Proof	280,000	Value: 3.00				
Yr.17(2005)	29,761,000	—	—	—	—	0.50
Yr.17(2005) Proof	258,000	Value: 3.00				
Yr.18(2006)	129,347,000	—	—	—	—	0.50
Yr.18(2006) Proof	247,000	Value: 3.00				
Yr.19(2007)	223,702,200	—	—	—	—	0.50
Yr.19(2007) Proof	201,800	Value: 3.00				
Yr.20(2008)	—	—	—	—	—	0.50
Yr.20(2008) Proof	—	Value: 3.00				
Yr.21(2009)	—	—	—	—	—	0.50
Yr.21(2009) Proof	—	Value: 3.00				
Yr.22(2010)	—	—	—	—	—	0.50
Yr.22(2010) Proof	—	Value: 3.00				

Y# 96.2   5 YEN
3.7500 g., Brass, 22 mm.   **Ruler:** Akihito **Obv:** Hole in center
flanked by a seed leaf with authority on top and date below
Rev: Gear design around center hole with bending rice stalk
above value in horizontal lines below

Date	Mintage	F	VF	XF	Unc	BU
Yr.13(2001)	77,787,000	—	—	—	—	0.35
Yr.13(2001) Proof	238,000	Value: 1.75				
Yr.14(2002)	143,420,000	—	—	—	—	0.35
Yr.14(2002) Proof	242,000	Value: 1.75				
Yr.15(2003)	102,031,000	—	—	—	—	0.35
Yr.15(2003) Proof	275,000	Value: 1.75				
Yr.16(2004)	70,623,000	—	—	—	—	0.35
Yr.16(2004) Proof	280,000	Value: 1.75				
Yr.17(2005)	15,761,000	—	—	—	—	0.35
Yr.17(2005) Proof	258,000	Value: 1.75				
Yr.18(2006)	9,347,000	—	—	—	—	0.35
Yr.18(2006) Proof	247,000	Value: 1.75				
Yr.19(2007)	9,702,200	—	—	—	—	0.35
Yr.19(2007) Proof	201,800	Value: 1.75				
Yr.20(2008)	—	—	—	—	—	0.35
Yr.20(2008) Proof	—	Value: 1.75				
Yr.21(2009)	—	—	—	—	—	0.35
Yr.21(2009) Proof	—	Value: 1.75				
Yr.22(2010)	—	—	—	—	—	0.35
Yr.22(2010) Proof	—	Value: 1.75				

Y# 97.2   10 YEN
4.5000 g., Bronze, 23.5 mm.   **Ruler:** Akihito **Obv:** Temple divides
authority and value **Rev:** Value within wreath

Date	Mintage	F	VF	XF	Unc	BU
Yr.13(2001)	541,786,000	—	—	—	—	0.45
Yr.13(2001) Proof	238,000	Value: 1.75				
Yr.14(2002)	455,425,000	—	—	—	—	0.45
Yr.14(2002) Proof	242,000	Value: 1.75				
Yr.15(2003)	551,131,000	—	—	—	—	0.45
Yr.15(2003) Proof	275,000	Value: 1.75				
Yr.16(2004)	592,623,000	—	—	—	—	0.45
Yr.16(2004) Proof	280,000	Value: 1.75				
Yr.17(2005)	503,761,000	—	—	—	—	0.45
Yr.17(2005) Proof	258,000	Value: 1.75				
Yr.18(2006)	440,347,000	—	—	—	—	0.45
Yr.18(2006) Proof	247,000	Value: 1.75				
Yr.19(2007)	388,702,200	—	—	—	—	0.45
Yr.19(2007) Proof	201,800	Value: 1.75				
Yr.20(2008)	—	—	—	—	—	0.45
Yr.20(2008) Proof	—	Value: 1.75				
Yr.21(2009)	—	—	—	—	—	0.45
Yr.21(2009) Proof	—	Value: 1.75				
Yr.22(2010)	—	—	—	—	—	0.45
Yr.22(2010) Proof	—	Value: 1.75				

Y# 101.2   50 YEN
4.0000 g., Copper-Nickel, 21 mm.   **Ruler:** Akihito **Obv:** Center
hole flanked by chrysanthemums, authority at top and value
below **Rev:** Value above hole in center

Date	Mintage	F	VF	XF	Unc	BU
Yr.13(2001)	7,786,000	—	—	—	—	3.00
Yr.13(2001) Proof	238,000	Value: 4.00				
Yr.14(2002)	11,425,000	—	—	—	—	5.00
Yr.14(2002) Proof	242,000	Value: 7.00				
Yr.15(2003)	10,131,000	—	—	—	—	5.00
Yr.15(2003) Proof	275,000	Value: 7.00				
Yr.16(2004)	9,623,000	—	—	—	—	5.00
Yr.16(2004) Proof	280,000	Value: 7.00				
Yr.17(2005)	9,761,000	—	—	—	—	5.00
Yr.17(2005) Proof	258,000	Value: 7.00				
Yr.18(2006)	10,347,000	—	—	—	—	5.00
Yr.18(2006) Proof	247,000	Value: 7.00				
Yr.19(2007)	9,702,200	—	—	—	—	5.00
Yr.19(2007) Proof	201,800	Value: 7.00				
Yr.20(2008)	—	—	—	—	—	5.00
Yr.20(2008) Proof	—	Value: 7.00				
Yr.21(2009)	—	—	—	—	—	5.00
Yr.21(2009) Proof	—	Value: 7.00				
Yr.22(2010)	—	—	—	—	—	5.00
Yr.22(2010) Proof	—	Value: 7.00				

Y# 98.2   100 YEN
4.8000 g., Copper-Nickel, 22.6 mm.   **Ruler:** Akihito **Obv:** Cherry
blossoms **Rev:** Large numeral 100, date in western numerals

Date	Mintage	F	VF	XF	Unc	BU
Yr.13(2001)	7,786,000	—	—	—	—	7.50
Yr.13(2001) Proof	238,000	Value: 10.00				
Yr.14(2002)	10,425,000	—	—	—	—	5.00
Yr.14(2002) Proof	242,000	Value: 8.00				
Yr.15(2003)	98,131,000	—	—	—	—	2.00
Yr.15(2003) Proof	275,000	Value: 5.00				
Yr.16(2004)	204,623,000	—	—	—	—	2.00
Yr.16(2004) Proof	280,000	Value: 5.00				
Yr.17(2005)	299,761,000	—	—	—	—	2.00
Yr.17(2005) Proof	258,000	Value: 5.00				
Yr.18(2006)	216,347,000	—	—	—	—	2.00
Yr.18(2006) Proof	247,000	Value: 5.00				
Yr.19(2007)	129,702,200	—	—	—	—	2.00
Yr.19(2007) Proof	201,800	Value: 5.00				
Yr.20(2008)	—	—	—	—	—	2.00
Yr.20(2008) Proof	—	Value: 5.00				
Yr.21(2009)	—	—	—	—	—	2.00
Yr.21(2009) Proof	—	Value: 5.00				

Date	Mintage	F	VF	XF	Unc	BU
Yr.22(2010)	—	—	—	—	—	2.00
Yr.22(2010) Proof	—	Value: 5.00				

Y# 125   500 YEN
7.0000 g., Nickel-Brass, 26.5 mm. **Ruler:** Akihito **Obv:** Pawlownia flower and highlighted legends **Rev:** Value with latent zeros
Edge: Slanted reeding

Date	Mintage	F	VF	XF	Unc	BU
Yr.13(2001)	607,813,000	—	—	—	—	9.00
Yr.13(2001) Proof	238,000	Value: 15.00				
Yr.14(2002)	504,419,000	—	—	—	—	9.00
Yr.14(2002) Proof	242,000	Value: 15.00				
Yr.15(2003)	438,130,000	—	—	—	—	9.00
Yr.15(2003) Proof	275,000	Value: 15.00				
Yr.16(2004)	356,623,000	—	—	—	—	9.00
Yr.16(2004) Proof	280,000	Value: 15.00				
Yr.17(2005)	334,762,000	—	—	—	—	9.00
Yr.17(2005) Proof	258,000	Value: 15.00				
Yr.18(2006)	381,346,000	—	—	—	—	9.00
Yr.18(2006) Proof	247,000	Value: 15.00				
Yr.19(2007)	401,701,200	—	—	—	—	9.00
Yr.19(2007) Proof	201,800	Value: 15.00				
Yr.20(2008)	—	—	—	—	—	9.00
Yr.20(2008) Proof	—	Value: 15.00				
Yr.21(2009)	—	—	—	—	—	9.00
Yr.21(2009) Proof	—	Value: 15.00				
Yr.22(2010)	—	—	—	—	—	9.00
Yr.22(2010) Proof	—	Value: 15.00				

Y# 126   500 YEN
7.0000 g., Copper-Zinc-Nickel, 26.5 mm. **Ruler:** Akihito **Subject:** World Cup Soccer - Europe & Africa **Obv:** Four players and map background **Rev:** Games logo within shooting star wreath **Edge:** Reeded

Date	Mintage	VG	F	VF	XF	BU
Yr.14(2002)	10,000,000	—	—	—	—	10.00

Y# 127   500 YEN
7.0000 g., Copper-Zinc-Nickel, 26.5 mm. **Ruler:** Akihito **Subject:** World Cup Soccer - Asia & Oceania **Obv:** Three players and map background **Rev:** Games logo within shooting star wreath **Edge:** Reeded

Date	Mintage	VG	F	VF	XF	BU
Yr. 14(2002)	10,000,000	—	—	—	—	10.00

Y# 128   500 YEN .
7.0000 g., Copper-Zinc-Nickel, 26.5 mm. **Ruler:** Akihito **Subject:** World Cup Soccer - North & South America **Obv:** Four players and map background **Rev:** Games logo **Edge:** Reeded

Date	Mintage	VG	F	VF	XF	BU
Yr. 14 (2002)	10,000,000	—	—	—	—	10.00

Y# 133   500 YEN
7.0000 g., Copper-Zinc-Nickel, 26.5 mm. **Ruler:** Akihito **Subject:** Expo 2005 - Aichi, Japan **Obv:** Pacific map an globe **Rev:** Circular Expo logo

Date	Mintage	VG	F	VF	XF	BU
Yr. 17(2005)	8,241,000	—	—	—	—	10.00

Y# 134   500 YEN
15.6000 g., 0.9990 Silver 0.5010 oz. ASW, 28 mm.
Ruler: Akihito **Subject:** Chubu International Airport **Obv:** Aircraft wing in flight over airport **Rev:** Aircraft silhouettes over maps

Date	Mintage	F	VF	XF	Unc	BU
Yr. 17(2005) Proof	50,000	Value: 85.00				

Y# 137   500 YEN
7.0000 g., Copper-Zinc-Nickel, 26.5 mm. **Ruler:** Akihito **Subject:** 50th Anniversary of Japanese Antarctic Research **Obv:** Ship and two dogs **Rev:** Map of Antarctica **Edge:** Helical ridges

Date	Mintage	F	VF	XF	Unc	BU
Yr.19(2007)	6,600,000	—	—	—	—	12.00

Y# 152   500 YEN
7.0000 g., Copper-Nickel-Zinc, 26.5 mm. **Ruler:** Akihito **Subject:** Japanese - Brazil Immigration Centennial **Obv:** Ship and map of Brazil **Rev:** Cherry Blosoms and grape clusterb

Date	Mintage	F	VF	XF	Unc	BU
Yr.21(2008)	4,800,000	—	—	—	—	10.00

Y# 145   500 YEN
7.1000 g., Bi-Metallic Copper-nickel center in brass ring, 26.5 mm. **Ruler:** Akihito **Subject:** Shimane Prefecture **Obv:** Bell shaped bronze vessel, artifact from Kamoiwakura **Rev:** Cash coin

Date	Mintage	F	VF	XF	Unc	BU
Yr.20(2008)	1,970,000	—	—	—	—	15.00

Y# 139   500 YEN
7.0000 g., Copper-Zinc-Nickel, 26.5 mm. **Ruler:** Akihito **Subject:** Centenary of Japanese immigration to Brazil/Japan-Brazil year of exchange **Obv:** Ship **Rev:** Crossed sprigs of cherry and coffee **Note:** Prev. #Y143.

Date	Mintage	F	VF	XF	Unc	BU
Yr. 20 (2008)	—	—	—	—	—	15.00

Y# 141   500 YEN
7.1000 g., Bi-Metallic, 26.5 mm. **Ruler:** Akihito **Subject:** Hokkaido Prefecture **Obv:** Lake Toya and the former Hokkaido Government Building

Date	Mintage	F	VF	XF	Unc	BU
Yr.20(2008)	2,100,000	—	—	—	—	15.00

Y# 143   500 YEN
7.1000 g., Bi-Metallic Copper-nickel center in brass ring, 26.5 mm. **Ruler:** Akihito **Subject:** Kyoto Prefecture **Obv:** Scebe frin ab antique illustrated version of the Tale of Genji **Rev:** Cash coin

Date	Mintage	F	VF	XF	Unc	BU
Yr.20(2008)	2,050,000	—	—	—	—	15.00

Y# 151   500 YEN
7.0000 g., Copper-Nickel-Zinc, 26.5 mm. **Ruler:** Akihito **Subject:** Japanese - Brazil Imigration Centennial **Obv:** Commemorative statue in Santos Port **Note:** Recalled

Date	Mintage	F	VF	XF	Unc	BU
yr.20(2008)	4,800,000	—	—	—	—	15.00

Y# 147   500 YEN
7.1000 g., Bi-Metallic, 26.5 mm. **Ruler:** Akihito **Subject:** Nagano Prefecture **Obv:** Zenkoji Temple and ox

Date	Mintage	F	VF	XF	Unc	BU
Yr.21(2009)	1,830,000	—	—	—	—	15.00
Yr.21(2009) Proof	—	Value: 50.00				

Y# 149   500 YEN
7.1000 g., Bi-Metallic, 26.5 mm. **Ruler:** Akihito **Subject:** Niigata Prefecture **Obv:** Two Japanese crested ibises and rice terrace

Date	Mintage	F	VF	XF	Unc	BU
Yr.21(2009)	—	—	—	—	—	15.00
Yr.21(2009) Proof	—	Value: 50.00				

Y# 153   500 YEN
7.1000 g., Bi-Metallic, 26.5 mm. **Ruler:** Akihito **Subject:** Ibarai Prefecteture **Obv:** Kairakuen Garden and plum tree **Rev:** Cast Japanese coin

Date	Mintage	F	VF	XF	Unc	BU
Yr.21(2009)	1,870,000	—	—	—	—	15.00
Yr.21(2009) Proof	—	Value: 50.00				

Y# 155   500 YEN
7.1000 g., Bi-Metallic, 26.5 mm. **Ruler:** Akihito **Subject:** Nara Prefecture **Obv:** Kentishi-sen -Ship of the Japanese envoy to China in Tang Dynasty **Rev:** Cast Japanese coin

Date	Mintage	F	VF	XF	Unc	BU
Yr.21(2009)	1,800,000	—	—	—	—	15.00
Yr.21(2009) Proof	—	Value: 50.00				

Y# 157   500 YEN
7.0000 g., Nickel-Brass, 26.5 mm. **Ruler:** Akihito **Subject:** 20th Anniversary of Emperor's Enthronement **Obv:** Imperial chrysthantem crest **Rev:** Chrysthantem blosums

Date	Mintage	F	VF	XF	Unc	BU
Yr.21(2009)	9,950,000	—	—	—	—	12.50
Yr.21(2009) Proof	50,000	Value: 30.00				

Y# 159   500 YEN
7.0000 g., Bi-Metallic, 26.5 mm. **Ruler:** Akihito **Subject:** Kochi Prefecture

Date	Mintage	F	VF	XF	Unc	BU
Yr.22(2010)	—	—	—	—	—	15.00
Yr.22(2010) Proof	—	Value: 50.00				

Y# 161   500 YEN
7.0000 g., Bi-Metallic, 26.5 mm. **Ruler:** Akihito **Subject:** Gifu Prefecture

Date	Mintage	F	VF	XF	Unc	BU
Yr.22(2010)	—	—	—	—	—	15.00
Yr.22(2010) Proof	—	Value: 50.00				

Y# 163   500 YEN
7.0000 g., Bi-Metallic, 26.5 mm. **Ruler:** Akihito **Subject:** Fukui Prefecture

Date	Mintage	F	VF	XF	Unc	BU
Yr.22(2010)	—	—	—	—	—	15.00
Yr.22(2010) Proof	—	Value: 50.00				

Y# 129   1000 YEN
31.1000 g., 0.9990 Silver 0.9988 oz. ASW, 40 mm.
Ruler: Akihito **Subject:** World Cup Soccer **Obv:** Trophy within flower sprigs **Rev:** Games logo flanked by players **Edge:** Reeded

Date	Mintage	F	VF	XF	Unc	BU
Yr. 14 (2002) Proof	100,000	Value: 200				

Y# 132   1000 YEN
31.1000 g., 0.9990 Silver 0.9988 oz. ASW, 40 mm.
Ruler: Akihito **Subject:** 50th Anniversary of the reversion of the Amami Islands **Obv:** Lily and bird in multicolor enamel **Rev:** Map of the Amami-shoto

Date	Mintage	F	VF	XF	Unc	BU
Yr. 15 (2003) Proof	50,000	Value: 220				

Y# 131   1000 YEN
31.1000 g., 0.9990 Silver 0.9988 oz. ASW, 40 mm.   **Ruler:** Akihito **Subject:** 5th Winter Asian Games, Aomori **Obv:** Skier and skater **Rev:** Three red apples and multicolor games logo

Date	Mintage	VG	F	VF	XF	BU
Yr.15 (2003) Proof	50,000	Value: 625				

Y# 135   1000 YEN
31.1000 g., 0.9990 Silver 0.9988 oz. ASW, 40 mm.   **Ruler:** Akihito **Subject:** Expo 2005 **Obv:** Blue and white enamel Pacific map in wreath **Rev:** Expo logo

Date	Mintage	F	VF	XF	Unc	BU
Yr. 16(2004) Proof	70,000	Value: 165				

Y# 138   1000 YEN
31.1000 g., 1.0000 Silver 0.9998 oz. ASW, 40 mm.
Ruler: Akihito **Subject:** 50th Anniversary of Japan's Entry into the United Nations **Obv:** Globe and plum blossom wreath (enameled blue, pink and green) **Rev:** UN emblem

Date	Mintage	F	VF	XF	Unc	BU
Yr.18(2006) Proof	70,000	Value: 165				

Y# 140   1000 YEN
31.1000 g., 0.9990 Silver 0.9988 oz. ASW, 40 mm.   **Ruler:** Akihito **Obv:** Dual multicolor rainbows **Obv. Inscription:** SKILLS / 2007 **Rev:** Mount Fuji **Rev. Legend:** International Skills Festival for All, Japan **Edge:** Helical ridges **Note:** Prev. #Y142.

Date	Mintage	F	VF	XF	Unc	BU
Yr.19(2007) Proof	80,000	Value: 75.00				

Y# 142   1000 YEN
31.1000 g., 0.9990 Silver 0.9988 oz. ASW, 40 mm.
Ruler: Akihito **Subject:** Hokkaido Prefecture **Obv:** Lake Toya and two multicolor red-crowned cranes in flight **Rev:** Cherry blossoms and crescent

Date	Mintage	F	VF	XF	Unc	BU
Yr.20(2008) Proof	100,000	Value: 120				

Y# 144   1000 YEN
31.1000 g., 0.9990 Silver 0.9988 oz. ASW, 40 mm.
Ruler: Akihito **Subject:** Kyoto Prefecture **Obv:** Multicolor scene from an antique illustrated version of the Tale of Genji **Rev:** Cherry blossoms and crescent

Date	Mintage	F	VF	XF	Unc	BU
Yr.20(2008) Proof	100,000	Value: 120				

Y# 146   1000 YEN
31.1000 g., 0.9990 Silver 0.9988 oz. ASW, 40 mm.
Ruler: Akihito **Subject:** Shimane Prefecture **Obv:** Multicolor peony flowers and Otoriosame chogin coin **Rev:** Cherry blossoms and crescent

Date	Mintage	F	VF	XF	Unc	BU
Yr.20(2008) Proof	100,000	Value: 115				

Y# 154   1000 YEN
31.1000 g., 0.9990 Silver 0.9988 oz. ASW   **Ruler:** Akihito
Subject: Ibarki Prefecture **Obv:** Multicolor H-II launch vehicle and Mt. Tsukuba **Rev:** Snow crystals, moon and cherry blossom

Date	Mintage	F	VF	XF	Unc	BU
Yr.21(2008) Proof	100,000	Value: 95.00				

Y# 156   1000 YEN
31.1000 g., 0.9990 Silver 0.9988 oz. ASW   **Ruler:** Akihito
Subject: Nara Prefecture **Obv:** Daigokuden audience hall in multicolor, cherry blossoms and Kemari (ancient ball players) **Rev:** Snow crystal, moon and cherry blossoms

Date	Mintage	F	VF	XF	Unc	BU
Yr.21(2008) Proof	100,000	Value: 90.00				

Y# 148   1000 YEN
31.1000 g., 0.9990 Silver 0.9988 oz. ASW, 40 mm.
Ruler: Akihito **Subject:** Nagano Prefecture **Obv:** Multicolor Japan Alps and Kamikochi

Date	Mintage	F	VF	XF	Unc	BU
Yr.21(2009) Proof	100,000	Value: 80.00				

Y# 150   1000 YEN
31.1000 g., 0.9990 Silver 0.9988 oz. ASW, 40 mm.
Ruler: Akihito **Subject:** Niigata Prefecture **Obv:** Two Japanese creasted ibis and Sado Island

Date	Mintage	F	VF	XF	Unc	BU
Yr.21(2009) Proof	100,000	Value: 85.00				

Y# 160   1000 YEN
31.1000 g., 0.9990 Silver 0.9988 oz. ASW, 40 mm.
Ruler: Akihito **Subject:** Kochi Prefecture

Date	Mintage	F	VF	XF	Unc	BU
Yr.22(2010) Proof	100,000	Value: 80.00				

Y# 162   1000 YEN
31.1000 g., 0.9990 Silver 0.9988 oz. ASW, 40 mm.
Ruler: Akihito **Subject:** Gifu Prefecture

Date	Mintage	F	VF	XF	Unc	BU
Yr.22(2010) Proof	100,000	Value: 80.00				

Y# 164   1000 YEN
31.1000 g., 0.9990 Silver 0.9988 oz. ASW, 40 mm.
Ruler: Akihito **Subject:** Fukui Prefecture

Date	Mintage	F	VF	XF	Unc	BU
Yr.22(2010) Proof	100,000	Value: 80.00				

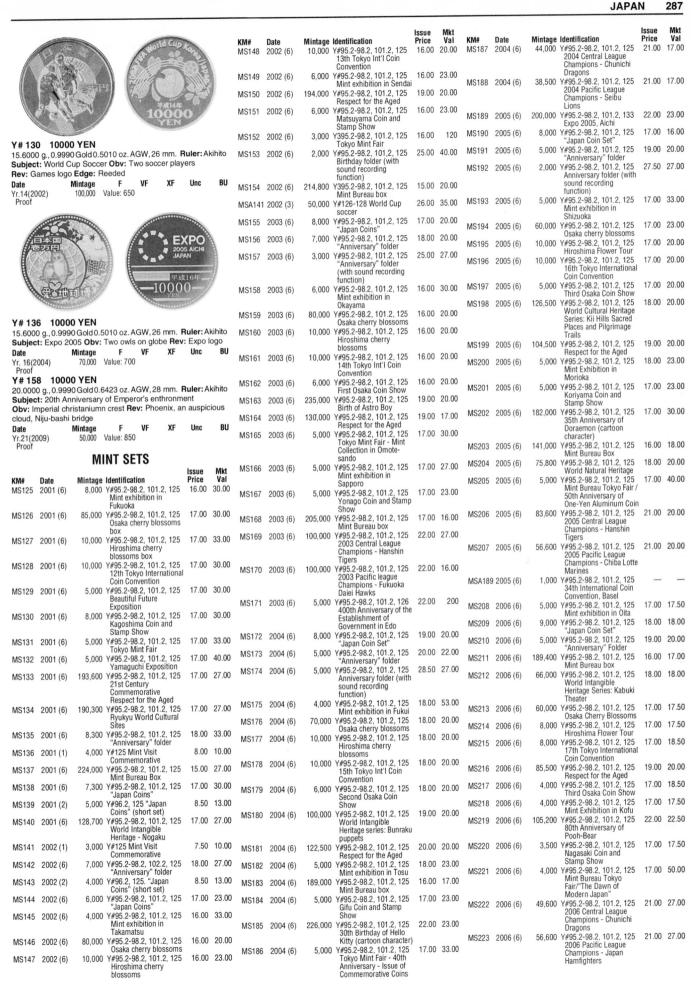

Y# 130 10000 YEN
15.6000 g., 0.9990 Gold 0.5010 oz. AGW, 26 mm. **Ruler:** Akihito
Subject: World Cup Soccer **Obv:** Two soccer players
Rev: Games logo **Edge:** Reeded

Date	Mintage	F	VF	XF	Unc	BU
Yr.14(2002) Proof	100,000	Value: 650				

Y# 136 10000 YEN
15.6000 g., 0.9990 Gold 0.5010 oz. AGW, 26 mm. **Ruler:** Akihito
Subject: Expo 2005 **Obv:** Two owls on globe **Rev:** Expo logo

Date	Mintage	F	VF	XF	Unc	BU
Yr. 16(2004) Proof	70,000	Value: 700				

Y# 158 10000 YEN
20.0000 g., 0.9990 Gold 0.6423 oz. AGW, 28 mm. **Ruler:** Akihito
Subject: 20th Anniversary of Emperor's enthronment
Obv: Imperial christaniumn crest **Rev:** Phoenix, an auspicious cloud, Niju-bashi bridge

Date	Mintage	F	VF	XF	Unc	BU
Yr.21(2009) Proof	50,000	Value: 850				

MINT SETS

KM#	Date	Mintage	Identification	Issue Price	Mkt Val
MS125	2001 (6)	8,000	Y#95.2-98.2, 101.2, 125 Mint exhibition in Fukuoka	16.00	30.00
MS126	2001 (6)	85,000	Y#95.2-98.2, 101.2, 125 Osaka cherry blossoms box	17.00	30.00
MS127	2001 (6)	10,000	Y#95.2-98.2, 101.2, 125 Hiroshima cherry blossoms box	17.00	33.00
MS128	2001 (6)	10,000	Y#95.2-98.2, 101.2, 125 12th Tokyo International Coin Convention	17.00	30.00
MS129	2001 (6)	5,000	Y#95.2-98.2, 101.2, 125 Beautiful Future Exposition	17.00	30.00
MS130	2001 (6)	8,000	Y#95.2-98.2, 101.2, 125 Kagoshima Coin and Stamp Show	17.00	30.00
MS131	2001 (6)	5,000	Y#95.2-98.2, 101.2, 125 Tokyo Mint Fair	17.00	33.00
MS132	2001 (6)	5,000	Y#95.2-98.2, 101.2, 125 Yamaguchi Exposition	17.00	40.00
MS133	2001 (6)	193,600	Y#95.2-98.2, 101.2, 125 21st Century Commemorative Respect for the Aged	17.00	27.00
MS134	2001 (6)	190,300	Y#95.2-98.2, 101.2, 125 Ryukyu World Cultural Sites	17.00	27.00
MS135	2001 (6)	8,300	Y#95.2-98.2, 101.2, 125 "Anniversary" folder	18.00	33.00
MS136	2001 (1)	4,000	Y#125 Mint Visit Commemorative	8.00	10.00
MS137	2001 (6)	224,000	Y#95.2-98.2, 101.2, 125 Mint Bureau Box	15.00	27.00
MS138	2001 (6)	7,300	Y#95.2-98.2, 101.2, 125 "Japan Coins"	17.00	30.00
MS139	2001 (2)	5,000	Y#96.2, 125 "Japan Coins" (short set)	8.50	13.00
MS140	2001 (6)	128,700	Y#95.2-98.2, 101.2, 125 World Intangible Heritage - Nogaku	17.00	27.00
MS141	2002 (1)	3,000	Y#125 Mint Visit Commemorative	7.50	10.00
MS142	2002 (6)	7,000	Y#95.2-98.2, 102.2, 125 "Anniversary" folder	18.00	27.00
MS143	2002 (2)	4,000	Y#96.2, 125. "Japan Coins" (short set)	8.50	13.00
MS144	2002 (6)	6,000	Y#95.2-98.2, 101.2, 125 "Japan Coins"	17.00	23.00
MS145	2002 (6)	4,000	Y#95.2-98.2, 101.2, 125 Mint exhibition in Takamatsu	16.00	33.00
MS146	2002 (6)	80,000	Y#95.2-98.2, 101.2, 125 Osaka cherry blossoms	16.00	20.00
MS147	2002 (6)	10,000	Y#95.2-98.2, 101.2, 125 Hiroshima cherry blossoms	16.00	23.00

KM#	Date	Mintage	Identification	Issue Price	Mkt Val
MS148	2002 (6)	10,000	Y#95.2-98.2, 101.2, 125 13th Tokyo Int'l Coin Convention	16.00	20.00
MS149	2002 (6)	6,000	Y#95.2-98.2, 101.2, 125 Mint exhibition in Sendai	16.00	23.00
MS150	2002 (6)	194,000	Y#95.2-98.2, 101.2, 125 Respect for the Aged	19.00	20.00
MS151	2002 (6)	6,000	Y#95.2-98.2, 101.2, 125 Matsuyama Coin and Stamp Show	16.00	23.00
MS152	2002 (6)	3,000	Y395.2-98.2, 101.2, 125 Tokyo Mint Fair	16.00	120
MS153	2002 (6)	2,000	Y#95.2-98.2, 101.2, 125 Birthday folder (with sound recording function)	25.00	40.00
MS154	2002 (6)	214,800	Y395.2-98.2, 101.2, 125 Mint Bureau box	15.00	20.00
MSA141	2002 (3)	50,000	Y#126-128 World Cup soccer	26.00	35.00
MS155	2003 (6)	8,000	Y#95.2-98.2, 101.2, 125 "Japan Coins"	17.00	20.00
MS156	2003 (6)	7,000	Y#95.2-98.2, 101.2, 125 "Anniversary" folder	18.00	20.00
MS157	2003 (6)	3,000	Y#95.2-98.2, 101.2, 125 "Anniversary" folder (with sound recording function)	25.00	27.00
MS158	2003 (6)	6,000	Y#95.2-98.2, 101.2, 125 Mint exhibition in Okayama	16.00	30.00
MS159	2003 (6)	80,000	Y#95.2-98.2, 101.2, 125 Osaka cherry blossoms	16.00	20.00
MS160	2003 (6)	10,000	Y#95.2-98.2, 101.2, 125 Hiroshima cherry blossoms	16.00	20.00
MS161	2003 (6)	10,000	Y#95.2-98.2, 101.2, 125 14th Tokyo Int'l Coin Convention	16.00	20.00
MS162	2003 (6)	6,000	Y#95.2-98.2, 101.2, 125 First Osaka Coin Show	16.00	20.00
MS163	2003 (6)	235,000	Y#95.2-98.2, 101.2, 125 Birth of Astro Boy	19.00	20.00
MS164	2003 (6)	130,000	Y#95.2-98.2, 101.2, 125 Respect for the Aged	19.00	17.00
MS165	2003 (6)	5,000	Y#95.2-98.2, 101.2, 125 Tokyo Mint Fair - Mint Collection in Omote-sando	17.00	30.00
MS166	2003 (6)	5,000	Y#95.2-98.2, 101.2, 125 Mint exhibition in Sapporo	17.00	27.00
MS167	2003 (6)	5,000	Y#95.2-98.2, 101.2, 125 Yonago Coin and Stamp Show	17.00	23.00
MS168	2003 (6)	205,000	Y#95.2-98.2, 101.2, 125 Mint Bureau box	17.00	16.00
MS169	2003 (6)	100,000	Y#95.2-98.2, 101.2, 125 2003 Central League Champions - Hanshin Tigers	22.00	27.00
MS170	2003 (6)	100,000	Y#95.2-98.2, 101.2, 125 2003 Pacific league Champions - Fukuoka Daiei Hawks	22.00	16.00
MS171	2003 (6)	5,000	Y#95.2-98.2, 101.2, 126 400th Anniversary of the Establishment of Government in Edo	22.00	200
MS172	2004 (6)	8,000	Y#95.2-98.2, 101.2, 125 "Japan Coin Set"	19.00	20.00
MS173	2004 (6)	5,000	Y#95.2-98.2, 101.2, 125 "Anniversary" folder	20.00	22.00
MS174	2004 (6)	5,000	Y#95.2-98.2, 101.2, 125 Anniversary folder (with sound recording function)	28.50	27.00
MS175	2004 (6)	4,000	Y#95.2-98.2, 101.2, 125 Mint exhibition in Fukui	18.00	53.00
MS176	2004 (6)	70,000	Y#95.2-98.2, 101.2, 125 Osaka cherry blossoms	18.00	20.00
MS177	2004 (6)	10,000	Y#95.2-98.2, 101.2, 125 Hiroshima cherry blossoms	18.00	20.00
MS178	2004 (6)	10,000	Y#95.2-98.2, 101.2, 125 15th Tokyo Int'l Coin Convention	18.00	20.00
MS179	2004 (6)	6,000	Y#95.2-98.2, 101.2, 125 Second Osaka Coin Show	18.00	20.00
MS180	2004 (6)	100,000	Y#95.2-98.2, 101.2, 125 World Intangible Heritage series: Bunraku puppets	19.00	20.00
MS181	2004 (6)	122,500	Y#95.2-98.2, 101.2, 125 Respect for the Aged	20.00	20.00
MS182	2004 (6)	5,000	Y#95.2-98.2, 101.2, 125 Mint exhibition in Tosu	18.00	23.00
MS183	2004 (6)	189,000	Y#95.2-98.2, 101.2, 125 Mint Bureau box	16.00	17.00
MS184	2004 (6)	5,000	Y#95.2-98.2, 101.2, 125 Gifu Coin and Stamp Show	17.00	23.00
MS185	2004 (6)	226,000	Y#95.2-98.2, 101.2, 125 30th Birthday of Hello Kitty (cartoon character)	22.00	23.00
MS186	2004 (6)	5,000	Y#95.2-98.2, 101.2, 125 Tokyo Mint Fair - 40th Anniversary - Issue of Commemorative Coins	17.00	33.00

KM#	Date	Mintage	Identification	Issue Price	Mkt Val
MS187	2004 (6)	44,000	Y#95.2-98.2, 101.2, 125 2004 Central League Champions - Chunichi Dragons	21.00	17.00
MS188	2004 (6)	38,500	Y#95.2-98.2, 101.2, 125 2004 Pacific League Champions - Seibu Lions	21.00	17.00
MS189	2005 (6)	200,000	Y#95.2-98.2, 101.2, 133 Expo 2005, Aichi	22.00	23.00
MS190	2005 (6)	8,000	Y#95.2-98.2, 101.2, 125 "Japan Coin Set"	17.00	16.00
MS191	2005 (6)	5,000	Y#95.2-98.2, 101.2, 125 "Anniversary" folder	19.00	20.00
MS192	2005 (6)	2,000	Y#95.2-98.2, 101.2, 125 Anniversary folder (with sound recording function)	27.50	27.00
MS193	2005 (6)	5,000	Y#95.2-98.2, 101.2, 125 Mint exhibition in Shizuoka	17.00	33.00
MS194	2005 (6)	60,000	Y#95.2-98.2, 101.2, 125 Osaka cherry blossoms	17.00	23.00
MS195	2005 (6)	10,000	Y#95.2-98.2, 101.2, 125 Hiroshima Flower Tour	17.00	20.00
MS196	2005 (6)	10,000	Y#95.2-98.2, 101.2, 125 16th Tokyo International Coin Convention	17.00	20.00
MS197	2005 (6)	5,000	Y#95.2-98.2, 101.2, 125 Third Osaka Coin Show	17.00	20.00
MS198	2005 (6)	126,500	Y#95.2-98.2, 101.2, 125 World Cultural Heritage Series: Kii Hills Sacred Places and Pilgrimage Trails	18.00	20.00
MS199	2005 (6)	104,500	Y#95.2-98.2, 101.2, 125 Respect for the Aged	19.00	20.00
MS200	2005 (6)	5,000	Y#95.2-98.2, 101.2, 125 Mint Exhibition in Morioka	18.00	23.00
MS201	2005 (6)	5,000	Y#95.2-98.2, 101.2, 125 Koriyama Coin and Stamp Show	17.00	23.00
MS202	2005 (6)	182,000	Y#95.2-98.2, 101.2, 125 35th Anniversary of Doraemon (cartoon character)	17.00	30.00
MS203	2005 (6)	141,000	Y#95.2-98.2, 101.2, 125 Mint Bureau Box	16.00	18.00
MS204	2005 (6)	75,800	Y#95.2-98.2, 101.2, 125 World Natural Heritage	18.00	20.00
MS205	2005 (6)	5,000	Y#95.2-98.2, 101.2, 125 Mint Bureau Tokyo Fair / 50th Anniversary of One-Yen Aluminum Coin	17.00	40.00
MS206	2005 (6)	83,600	Y#95.2-98.2, 101.2, 125 2005 Central League Champions - Hanshin Tigers	21.00	20.00
MS207	2005 (6)	56,600	Y#95.2-98.2, 101.2, 125 2005 Pacific League Champions - Chiba Lotte Marines	21.00	20.00
MSA189	2005 (6)	1,000	Y#95.2-98.2, 101.2, 125 34th International Coin Convention, Basel	—	—
MS208	2006 (6)	5,000	Y#95.2-98.2, 101.2, 125 Mint exhibition in Oita	17.00	17.50
MS209	2006 (6)	9,000	Y#95.2-98.2, 101.2, 125 "Japan Coin Set"	18.00	18.00
MS210	2006 (6)	5,000	Y#95.2-98.2, 101.2, 125 "Anniversary" Folder	19.00	20.00
MS211	2006 (6)	189,400	Y#95.2-98.2, 101.2, 125 Mint Bureau box	16.00	17.00
MS212	2006 (6)	66,000	Y#95.2-98.2, 101.2, 125 World Intangible Heritage Series: Kabuki Theater	18.00	18.00
MS213	2006 (6)	60,000	Y#95.2-98.2, 101.2, 125 Osaka Cherry Blossoms	17.00	17.50
MS214	2006 (6)	8,000	Y#95.2-98.2, 101.2, 125 Hiroshima Flower Tour	17.00	17.50
MS215	2006 (6)	8,000	Y#95.2-98.2, 101.2, 125 17th Tokyo International Coin Convention	18.00	18.50
MS216	2006 (6)	85,500	Y#95.2-98.2, 101.2, 125 Respect for the Aged	19.00	20.00
MS217	2006 (6)	4,000	Y#95.2-98.2, 101.2, 125 Third Osaka Coin Show	17.00	18.50
MS218	2006 (6)	4,000	Y#95.2-98.2, 101.2, 125 Mint Exhibition in Kofu	17.00	17.50
MS219	2006 (6)	105,200	Y#95.2-98.2, 101.2, 125 80th Anniversary of Pooh-Bear	22.00	22.50
MS220	2006 (6)	3,500	Y#95.2-98.2, 101.2, 125 Nagasaki Coin and Stamp Show	17.00	17.50
MS221	2006 (6)	4,000	Y#95.2-98.2, 101.2, 125 Mint Bureau Tokyo Fair/"The Dawn of Modern Japan"	17.00	50.00
MS222	2006 (6)	49,600	Y#95.2-98.2, 101.2, 125 2006 Central League Champions - Chunichi Dragons	21.00	27.00
MS223	2006 (6)	56,600	Y#95.2-98.2, 101.2, 125 2006 Pacific League Champions - Japan Hamfighters	21.00	27.00

KM#	Date	Mintage	Identification	Issue Price	Mkt Val
MS224	2007 (6)	180,000	Y#95.2-98.2, 101.2, 137 50th Anniversary of Japanese Antarctic Research	23.00	30.00
MS225	2007 (6)	4,000	Y#95.2-98.2, 101.2, 125 Mint exhibition in Tsukuba	17.00	18.00
MS226	2007 (6)	8,000	Y#95.2-98.2, 101.2, 125 "Japan Coin Set"	18.00	20.00
MS227	2007 (6)	5,700	Y#95.2-98.2, 101.2, 125 "Anniversary" folder	19.00	20.00
MS228	2007 (6)	150,000	Y#95.2-98.2, 101.2, 125 Mint Bureau box	16.00	18.00
MS229	2007 (6)	82,200	Y#95.2-98.2, 101.2, 125 "Gongitsune" 75th Anniversary of Publication	22.00	25.00
MS230	2007 (6)	7,000	Y#95.2-98.2, 101.2, 125 Hiroshima Flower Tour	18.00	—
MS231	2007 (6)	60,000	Y#95.2-98.2, 101.2, 125 Osaka cherry blossoms	17.00	18.00
MS232	2007 (6)	6,000	Y#95.2-98.2, 101.2, 125 18th Tokyo International Coin Convention	17.00	18.00
MS233	2007 (6)	4,000	Y#95.2-98.2, 101.2, 125 Fifth Osaka Coin Show	17.00	18.00
MS234	2007 (6)	76,500	Y#95.2-98.2, 101.2, 125 Rose of Versailles, Lady Oscar	22.00	25.00
MS235	2007 (6)	2,720	Y#95.2-98.2, 101.2, 125 Mint exhibition in Matsue	17.00	18.00
MS236	2007 (6)	4,000	Y#95.2-98.2, 101.2, 125 Nagoya Coin and Stamp Show	17.00	18.00
MS237	2007 (6)	69,000	Y#95.2-98.2, 101.2, 125 Respect for the Aged	19.00	20.00
MS238	2007 (6)	4,000	Y#95.2-98.2, 101.2, 125 Mint Bureau Tokyo Fair/50th anniversary of introduction of the 100-yen coin	17.00	18.00
MS239	2007 (6)	45,200	Y#95.2-98.2, 101.2, 125 2007 Central League Champions - Yomiuri Giants	21.00	22.00
MS240	2007 (6)	36,500	Y#95.2-98.2, 101.2, 125 2007 Pacific League Champions - Japan Hamfighters	21.00	22.00
MS241	2007 (6)	74,500	Y#95.2-98.2, 101.2, 125 World Cultural Heritage Series: Iwami Silver Mines Ruins and Cultural Landscape	18.00	20.00
MS242	2008 (6)	4,000	Y#95.2-98.2, 101.2, 125, Mint exhibition in Miyazaki	18.00	20.00
MS243	2008 (6)	—	Y95.2-98.2, 101.2, 125, "Japan Coin Set"	19.00	20.00
MS244	2008 (6)	—	Y95.2-98.2, 101.2, 125, "Anniversary" folder	20.00	20.00
MS245	2008 (6)	150,000	Y95.2-98.2, 101.2, 125, Mint Bureau Box	17.00	20.00
MS246	2008 (6)	4,500	Y95.2-98.2, 101.2, 125, Hiroshima Flower Tour	18.00	20.00
MS247	2008 (6)	60,000	Y95.2-98.2, 101.2, 125, Osaka cherry blossoms	18.00	20.00
MS248	2008 (6)	5,500	Y95.2-98.2, 101.2, 125, 19th Tokyo International Coin Convention	18.00	20.00
MS249	2008 (6)	3,786	Y25.2-98.2, 101.2, 125, G8 Finance Ministers' meeting, Osaka	18.00	18.00
MS250	2008 (6)	3,500	Y95.2-98.2, 101.2, 125, Sixth Osaka Coin Show.	18.00	20.00
MS251	2008 (6)	1,792	Y95.2-98.2, 101.2, 125, Kobe Coin and Stamp Exposition.	18.00	18.00
MS252	2008 (6)	142,000	Y95.2-98.2, 101.2, 125, Japan-Brazil Year of Exchange and Centenary of Japanese Immigration to Brazil	24.00	25.00
MS253	2008 (6)	100,000	Y95.2-98.2, 101.2, 125, Children's song coin set, Red Dragonfly.	23.00	25.00

PROOF SETS

KM#	Date	Mintage	Identification	Issue Price	Mkt Val
PS32	2001 (6)	138,000	Y#95.2-98.2, 101.2, 125 Mint Bureau Box	62.50	47.00
PS33	2001 (6)	100,000	Y#95.2-98.2, 101.2, 125 Old Type Coin Series (Trade dollar medallet)	62.50	53.00
PS38	2002 (2)	50,000	Y#129, 130 World Cup	385	550
PS34	2002 (6)	144,000	Y#95.2-98.2, 101.2, 125 Mint Bureau box	62.50	53.00
PS35	2002 (6)	3,000	Y#95.2-98.2, 101.2, 125 15th Anniversary of Proof Sets	62.50	100
PS36	2002 (6)	95,000	Y#95.2-98.2, 101.2, 125 Techno medal set	62.50	53.00
PS39	2003 (6)	98,400	Y#95.2-98.2, 101.2, 125 Mint Bureau box, with date plaquette	67.50	53.00
PS40	2003 (6)	90,000	Y#95.2-98.2, 101.2, 125 Astro Boy	115	100

KM#	Date	Mintage	Identification	Issue Price	Mkt Val
PS41	2003 (6)	5,000	Y#95.2-98.2, 101.2, 125 Tokyo Mint Fair - Mint Collection in Omote-Sando	67.50	100
PS42	2003 (6)	70,000	Y#95.2-98.2, 101.2, 125 Mickey Mouse	125	120
PS43	2003 (6)	5,000	Y#95.2-98.2, 101.2, 125 400th Anniversary - Establishment of Government in Edo	67.50	165
PS50	2004 (2)	35,000	Y#135-136 Expo 2005, Aichi	425	500
PS44	2004 (6)	94,900	Y#95.2-98.2, 101.2, 125 Mint Bureau box with date plaquette	71.00	60.00
PS45	2004 (6)	13,100	Y#95.2-98.2, 101.2, 125 Mint Bureau box without date plaquette	70.00	100
PS46	2004 (6)	60,000	Y#95.2-98.2, 101.2, 125 70h Anniversary - Pro Baseball	120	145
PS47	2004 (6)	60,000	Y#95.2-98.2, 101.2, 125 Techno Medal Series 2	71.00	60.00
PS48	2004 (6)	50,000	Y#95.2-98.2, 101.2, 125 30th Birthday of Hello Kitty (cartoon character)	120	150
PS49	2004 (6)	5,000	Y#95.2-98.2, 101.2, 125 Tokyo Mint Fair - 40th Anniversary - Issue of Commemorative Coins	71.00	100
PSA40	2003 (6)	6,600	Y#95.2-98.2, 101.2, 125 Mint Bureau Box without Date Plaquette	66.00	100
PS51	2005 (6)	76,700	Y#95.2-98.2, 101.2, 125 Mint Bureau Box with date plaquette	71.00	65.00
PS52	2005 (6)	10,000	Y#95.2-98.2, 101.2, 125 Mint Bureau Box without date plaquette	70.00	100
PS53	2005 (6)	60,000	Y#95.2-98.2, 101.2, 125 35th Anniversary of Doraemon (cartoon character)	125	170
PS54	2005 (6)	34,000	Y#95.2-98.2, 101.2, 125 50th Anniversary of One-Yen Aluminum Coin	125	170
PS55	2005 (6)	30,000	Y#95.2-98.2, 101.2, 125 50th Anniversary of the Pencil Rocket	125	100
PS56	2005 (6)	47,300	Y#95.2-98.2, 101.2, 125 Techno Medal Series #3	71.00	65.00
PS62	2006 (6)	4,000	Y#95.2-98.2, 101.2, 125 Mint Bureau Tokyo Fair/"The Dawn of Modern Japan"	71.00	150
PS57	2006 (6)	63,420	Y#95.2-98.2, 101.2, 125 Mint Bureau box with date plaquette	71.00	65.00
PS58	2006 (6)	8,700	Y#95.2-98.2, 101.2, 125 Mint Bureau Box without date plaquette	70.00	65.00
PS59	2006 (6)	35,000	Y#95.2-98.2, 101.2, 125 120th Anniversary of Cherry Blossom Viewing at the Mint	125	125
PS60	2006 (6)	46,000	Y#95.2-98.2, 101.2, 125 includes Australian 1oz Silver coin KM#838 Australia-Japan Year of Exchange	128	145
PS61	2006 (6)	49,900	Y#95.2-98.2, 101.2, 125 50th Anniversary of Debut of Ishihara Yujiro (film actor)	125	120
PS63	2007 (6)	40,000	Y#95.2-98.2, 101.2, 125 20-yen Gold Coin Memorial	125	150
PS64	2007 (6)	53,200	Y#95.2-98.2, 101.2, 125 Mint Bureau box, with date plaquette	71.00	75.00
PS65	2007 (6)	7,000	Y#95.2-98.2, 101.2, 125 Mint Bureau box, without date plaquette	70.00	75.00
PS66	2007 (6)	35,000	Y#95.2-98.2, 101.2, 125 60th Anniversary of Resumption of Cherry Blossom Viewing (at the Mint)	125	125
PS67	2007 (6)	40,100	Y#95.2-98.2, 101.2, 125 Sakamoto Ryohma (pre-Meiji loyalist, assassinated 1867)	125	125
PS68	2007 (6)	33,500	Y#95.2-98.2, 101.2, 125 11th IAAF World Championships in Athletics, Osaka (plus silver medal)	125	125
PS69	2007 (6)	3,000	Y#95.2-98.2, 101.2, 125 Mint Bureau Tokyo Fair/50th anniversary of introduction of the 100-yen coin	71.00	75.00
PS70	2007 (6)	30,000	Y#95.2-98.2, 101.2, 125 Japan-New Zealand Friendship (with NZ KM#232 coin)	125	125
PSA39	2007 (6)	—	Y#95.2-98.2, 101.2, 125 Mint Bureau box, without date plaquette	66.00	100

KM#	Date	Mintage	Identification	Issue Price	Mkt Val
PS71	2008 (6)	60,000	Y#95.2-95.2, 101.2, 125, Mint Bureau box with date plaquette	75.00	75.00
PS72	2008 (6)	—	Y95.2-98.2, 101.2, 125, Mint Bureau box without date plaquette	73.50	75.00
PS73	2008 (6)	35,000	Y95.2-98.2, 101.2, 125, Cherry blossom viewing (at the mint)	130	130
PS74	2008 (6)	30,000	Y95.2-98.2, 101.2, 125, 150th Anniversary of Japanese-French relations (with French 1.5 euro coin KM1550.)	130	130
PS75	2008 (6)	50,000	Y95.2-98.2, 101.2, 125, 1300th Anniversary of the Wado Kaichin coin (with a silver replica of it)	100	100

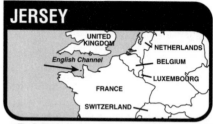

JERSEY

The Bailiwick of Jersey, a British Crown dependency located in the English Channel 12 miles (19 km.) west of Normandy, France, has an area of 45 sq. mi. (117 sq. km.) and a population of 74,000. Capital: St. Helier. The economy is based on agriculture and cattle breeding – the importation of cattle is prohibited to protect the purity of the island's world-famous strain of milk cows.

The island together with the Bailiwick of Guernsey, is the only part of the Dutchy of Normandy belonging to the British Crown, has been a possession of Britain since the Norman conquest of 1066. Jersey is administered by its own laws and customs. Unless the island is mentioned specifically, acts passed by the British Parliament are not applicable to Jersey. During WW II, German troops occupied the island from 1940 to 1945.

RULER
British

MINT MARK
H - Heaton, Birmingham

BRITISH DEPENDENCY

DECIMAL COINAGE
100 New Pence = 1 Pound

KM# 103   PENNY
3.5000 g., Copper Plated Steel, 20.3 mm. **Ruler:** Elizabeth II
Obv: Crowned head right **Obv. Designer:** Ian Rank-Broadley
Rev: Le Hoeq Watchtower, St. Clement **Edge:** Plain

Date	Mintage	F	VF	XF	Unc	BU
2002	1,500,000	—	—	0.15	0.65	—
2003	1,485,000	—	—	0.15	0.65	—
2005	—	—	—	0.15	0.65	—
2006	—	—	—	0.15	0.65	—
2008	—	—	—	0.15	0.65	—

KM# 104   2 PENCE
7.1000 g., Copper Plated Steel, 25.91 mm. **Ruler:** Elizabeth II
Obv: Head with tiara right **Obv. Designer:** Ian Rank-Broadley
Rev: L'Hermitage, St. Helier **Edge:** Plain

Date	Mintage	F	VF	XF	Unc	BU
2002	1,250,000	—	—	0.20	0.65	—
2003	10,000	—	—	0.20	0.65	—
2005	—	—	—	0.20	0.65	—
2006	—	—	—	0.20	0.65	—
2008	—	—	—	0.20	0.65	—

KM# 105 5 PENCE
3.2900 g., Copper-Nickel, 18 mm. **Ruler:** Elizabeth II **Obv:** Head with tiara right **Obv. Designer:** Ian Rank-Broadley **Rev:** Seymour Tower, Grouville, L'Avathigon **Edge:** Reeded

Date	Mintage	F	VF	XF	Unc	BU
2002	1,200,000	—	—	0.20	0.65	—
2003	1,002,000	—	—	0.20	0.65	—
2005	—	—	—	0.20	0.65	—
2006	—	—	—	0.20	0.65	—
2008	—	—	—	0.20	0.65	—

KM# 106 10 PENCE
Copper-Nickel, 24.5 mm. **Ruler:** Elizabeth II **Obv:** Head with tiara right **Obv. Designer:** Ian Rank-Broadley **Rev:** La Hougne Bie, Faldouet, St. Martin

Date	Mintage	F	VF	XF	Unc	BU
2002	500,000	—	—	—	1.25	—
2003	10,000	—	—	—	1.25	—
2006	—	—	—	—	1.25	—
2007	—	—	—	—	1.25	—

KM# 107 20 PENCE
Copper-Nickel, 21.4 mm. **Ruler:** Elizabeth II **Obv:** Head with tiara right **Obv. Designer:** Ian Rank-Broadley

Date	Mintage	F	VF	XF	Unc	BU
2002	515,000	—	—	—	1.00	1.25
2003	10,000	—	—	—	1.00	1.25
2005	—	—	—	—	1.00	1.25
2006	—	—	—	—	1.00	1.25
2007	—	—	—	—	1.00	1.25
2009	—	—	—	—	1.00	1.25

KM# 108 50 PENCE
Copper-Nickel, 27.3 mm. **Ruler:** Elizabeth II **Obv:** Crowned bust right **Obv. Designer:** Ian Rank-Broadley **Rev:** Gothic gate arch **Edge:** Plain

Date	Mintage	F	VF	XF	Unc	BU
2003	—	—	—	1.00	2.50	3.00
2005	—	—	—	1.00	2.50	3.00
2006	—	—	—	1.00	2.50	3.00
2009	—	—	—	1.00	2.50	3.00

KM# 123 50 PENCE
8.0000 g., Copper-Nickel, 27.3 mm. **Ruler:** Elizabeth II **Subject:** Golden Coronation Anniversary **Obv:** Crowned head right **Rev:** Coronation scene **Edge:** Plain **Shape:** 7-sided

Date	Mintage	F	VF	XF	Unc	BU
2003	10,000	—	—	—	2.50	3.00

KM# 123a 50 PENCE
8.0000 g., 0.9250 Silver 0.2379 oz. ASW, 27.3 mm. **Ruler:** Elizabeth II **Subject:** Golden Coronation Anniversary **Obv:** Crowned head right **Rev:** Coronation scene **Edge:** Plain **Shape:** 7-sided

Date	Mintage	F	VF	XF	Unc	BU
2003 Proof	15,000	Value: 25.00				

KM# 101 POUND
9.5000 g., Nickel-Brass, 22.5 mm. **Ruler:** Elizabeth II **Obv:** Head with tiara right **Obv. Designer:** Ian Rank-Broadley **Rev:** Schooner, Resolute **Rev. Designer:** Robert Evans **Edge Lettering:** CAESAREA INSULA

Date	Mintage	F	VF	XF	Unc	BU
2003	10,000	—	—	—	4.00	4.50
2005	—	—	—	—	4.00	4.50
2006	—	—	—	—	4.00	4.50

KM# 102 2 POUNDS
12.0000 g., Bi-Metallic Copper-Nickel center in Nickel-Brass ring, 28.35 mm. **Ruler:** Elizabeth II **Obv:** Head with tiara right **Obv. Designer:** Ian Rank-Broadley **Rev:** Latent image value within circle of assorted shields **Rev. Designer:** Alan Copp **Edge Lettering:** CAESAREA INSULA

Date	Mintage	F	VF	XF	Unc	BU
2003	10,000	—	—	—	10.00	12.00
2006	—	—	—	—	10.00	12.00

KM# 111 5 POUNDS
28.2800 g., Copper-Nickel, 38.6 mm. **Ruler:** Elizabeth II **Subject:** Princess Diana **Obv:** Crowned head right **Rev:** Diana's cameo above people **Edge:** Reeded

Date	Mintage	F	VF	XF	Unc	BU
2002	—	—	—	—	13.50	15.00

KM# 111a 5 POUNDS
28.2800 g., 0.9250 Silver 0.8410 oz. ASW, 38.6 mm. **Ruler:** Elizabeth II **Subject:** Princess Diana **Obv:** Crowned head right **Rev:** Diana's cameo above people **Edge:** Reeded

Date	Mintage	F	VF	XF	Unc	BU
2002 Proof	20,000	Value: 40.00				

KM# 111b 5 POUNDS
39.9400 g., 0.9167 Gold 1.1771 oz. AGW, 38.6 mm. **Ruler:** Elizabeth II **Subject:** Princess Diana **Obv:** Crowned head right **Rev:** Diana's cameo above people **Edge:** Reeded

Date	Mintage	F	VF	XF	Unc	BU
2002 Proof	100	Value: 1,500				

KM# 113 5 POUNDS
28.2800 g., Copper-Nickel, 38.6 mm. **Ruler:** Elizabeth II **Subject:** Queen Mother **Obv:** Crowned head right **Obv. Designer:** Ian Rank-Broadley **Rev:** Queen Mother's bust right (circa 1918) **Rev. Legend:** HER MAJESTY QUEEN ELIZABETH THE QUEEN MOTHER **Edge:** Reeded

Date	Mintage	F	VF	XF	Unc	BU
2002	—	—	—	—	13.50	15.00

KM# 113a 5 POUNDS
28.2800 g., 0.9250 Silver 0.8410 oz. ASW, 38.6 mm. **Ruler:** Elizabeth II **Subject:** Queen Mother **Obv:** Crowned head right **Obv. Designer:** Ian Rank-Broadley **Rev:** Queen Mother's bust right, (circa 1918) **Rev. Legend:** HER MAJESTY QUEEN ELIZABETH THE QUEEN MOTHER **Edge:** Reeded

Date	Mintage	F	VF	XF	Unc	BU
2002 Proof	15,000	Value: 50.00				

KM# 113b 5 POUNDS
39.9400 g., 0.9166 Gold 1.1770 oz. AGW, 38.6 mm. **Ruler:** Elizabeth II **Subject:** Queen Mother **Obv:** Crowned head right **Obv. Designer:** Ian Rank-Broadley **Rev:** Queen Mother's bust right, (circa 1918) **Rev. Legend:** HER MAJESTY QUEEN ELIZABETH THE QUEEN MOTHER **Edge:** Reeded

Date	Mintage	F	VF	XF	Unc	BU
2002 Proof	250	Value: 1,350				

KM# 115 5 POUNDS
28.2800 g., Copper-Nickel, 38.6 mm. **Ruler:** Elizabeth II **Subject:** Golden Jubilee **Obv:** Crowned head right **Rev:** Abbey procession scene **Rev. Designer:** Robert Evans **Edge:** Reeded

Date	Mintage	F	VF	XF	Unc	BU
2002	—	—	—	—	13.50	15.00

KM# 115a 5 POUNDS
28.2800 g., 0.9250 Silver 0.8410 oz. ASW, 38.6 mm. **Ruler:** Elizabeth II **Subject:** Golden Jubilee **Obv:** Crowned head right **Rev:** Abbey procession scene **Edge:** Reeded

Date	Mintage	F	VF	XF	Unc	BU
2002 Proof	20,000	Value: 50.00				

KM# 115b 5 POUNDS
39.9400 g., 0.9166 Gold 1.1770 oz. AGW, 38.6 mm. **Ruler:** Elizabeth II **Subject:** Golden Jubilee **Obv:** Crowned head right **Rev:** Abbey procession scene **Edge:** Reeded

Date	Mintage	F	VF	XF	Unc	BU
2002 Proof	100	Value: 1,500				

KM# 117 5 POUNDS
28.2800 g., Copper-Nickel, 38.6 mm. **Ruler:** Elizabeth II **Subject:** Duke of Wellington **Obv:** Crowned head right **Rev:** Wellington's portrait with multicolor infantry scene **Rev. Designer:** Willem Vis **Edge:** Reeded

Date	Mintage	F	VF	XF	Unc	BU
2002	—	—	—	—	13.50	15.00

KM# 117a 5 POUNDS
28.2800 g., 0.9250 Silver 0.8410 oz. ASW, 38.6 mm. **Ruler:** Elizabeth II **Subject:** Duke of Wellington **Obv:** Crowned head right **Rev:** Wellington's portrait with multicolor infantry scene **Edge:** Reeded

Date	Mintage	F	VF	XF	Unc	BU
2002 Proof	15,000	Value: 50.00				

KM# 117b 5 POUNDS
39.9400 g., 0.9166 Gold 1.1770 oz. AGW, 38.6 mm. **Ruler:** Elizabeth II **Subject:** Duke of Wellington **Obv:** Crowned head right **Rev:** Wellington's portrait with multicolor infantry scene **Edge:** Reeded

Date	Mintage	F	VF	XF	Unc	BU
2002 Proof	200	Value: 1,400				

KM# 119 5 POUNDS
28.2800 g., Copper-Nickel, 38.6 mm. **Ruler:** Elizabeth II **Subject:** Golden Jubilee **Obv:** Crowned head right **Rev:** Honor guard and memorial **Edge:** Reeded

Date	Mintage	F	VF	XF	Unc	BU
2003	—	—	—	—	13.50	15.00

KM# 119a 5 POUNDS
28.2800 g., 0.9250 Silver 0.8410 oz. ASW, 38.6 mm. **Ruler:** Elizabeth II **Subject:** Golden Jubilee **Obv:** Crowned head right **Rev:** Honor guard and monument **Edge:** Reeded

Date	Mintage	F	VF	XF	Unc	BU
2003 Proof	20,000	Value: 50.00				

KM# 119b 5 POUNDS
39.9400 g., 0.9166 Gold 1.1770 oz. AGW, 38.6 mm. **Ruler:** Elizabeth II **Subject:** Golden Jubilee **Obv:** Crowned head right **Rev:** Honor guard and monument **Edge:** Reeded

Date	Mintage	F	VF	XF	Unc	BU
2003 Proof	250	Value: 1,350				

KM# 121 5 POUNDS
28.2800 g., Copper-Nickel, 38.6 mm. **Ruler:** Elizabeth II **Obv:** Crowned head right **Rev:** Bust of Prince William facing and crowned arms with supporters **Edge:** Reeded

Date	Mintage	F	VF	XF	Unc	BU
2003	—	—	—	—	16.50	18.00

KM# 121a 5 POUNDS
28.2800 g., 0.9250 Silver 0.8410 oz. ASW, 38.6 mm. **Ruler:** Elizabeth II **Obv:** Crowned head right **Rev:** Bust of Prince William facing and crowned arms with supporters **Edge:** Reeded

Date	Mintage	F	VF	XF	Unc	BU
2003 Proof	5,000	Value: 47.50				

KM# 121b 5 POUNDS
39.9400 g., 0.9166 Gold 1.1770 oz. AGW, 38.6 mm. **Ruler:** Elizabeth II **Obv:** Crowned head right **Rev:** Bust of Prince William facing and crowned arms with supporters **Edge:** Reeded

Date	Mintage	F	VF	XF	Unc	BU
2003 Proof	200	Value: 1,400				

KM# 130 5 POUNDS
28.2800 g., 0.9250 Silver 0.8410 oz. ASW, 38.6 mm. **Ruler:** Elizabeth II **Subject:** Drake **Obv:** Crowned head right **Rev:** Naval leader Sir Francis Drake

Date	Mintage	F	VF	XF	Unc	BU
2003 Proof	—	Value: 75.00				

KM# 131 5 POUNDS
28.2800 g., 0.9250 Silver 0.8410 oz. ASW, 38.6 mm. **Ruler:** Elizabeth II **Subject:** Sovereign Of The Seas **Obv:** Crowned head right **Rev:** The Sovereign of the Seas ship

Date	Mintage	F	VF	XF	Unc	BU
2003 Proof	—	Value: 75.00				

KM# 132 5 POUNDS
28.2800 g., 0.9250 Silver 0.8410 oz. ASW, 38.6 mm. **Ruler:** Elizabeth II **Subject:** John Fisher **Obv:** Crowned head right **Rev:** WWI Naval leader Sir John Fisher

Date	Mintage	F	VF	XF	Unc	BU
2003 Proof	—	Value: 75.00				

KM# 133 5 POUNDS
28.2800 g., 0.9250 Silver 0.8410 oz. ASW, 38.6 mm. **Ruler:** Elizabeth II **Subject:** HMS Victory **Obv:** Crowned head right **Rev:** Nelson's flag ship HMS Victory

Date	Mintage	F	VF	XF	Unc	BU
2003 Proof	—	Value: 75.00				

KM# 134 5 POUNDS
28.2800 g., 0.9250 Silver 0.8410 oz. ASW, 38.6 mm. **Ruler:** Elizabeth II **Subject:** Cunningham **Obv:** Crowned head right **Rev:** WWII Admiral Andrew B. Cunningham

Date	Mintage	F	VF	XF	Unc	BU
2003 Proof	—	Value: 75.00				

KM# 135 5 POUNDS
28.2800 g., 0.9250 Silver 0.8410 oz. ASW, 38.6 mm. **Ruler:** Elizabeth II **Subject:** Conqueror **Obv:** Crowned head right **Rev:** Submarine HMS Conqueror

Date	Mintage	F	VF	XF	Unc	BU
2003 Proof	—	Value: 75.00				

KM# 144 5 POUNDS
28.2800 g., 0.9250 Silver 0.8410 oz. ASW, 38.61 mm. **Ruler:** Elizabeth II **Subject:** History of the Royal Navy **Obv:** Head left with tiarra **Obv. Legend:** ELIZABETH II BALIWICK - OF JERSEY **Rev:** Five heads of King Alfred the Great, Sir Francis Drake, Admirals Horatio Nelson, John Fisher and John Woodward at five ships **Edge:** Reeded

Date	Mintage	F	VF	XF	Unc	BU
2003 Proof	—	Value: 75.00				

KM# 139 5 POUNDS
28.2800 g., 0.9250 Silver 0.8410 oz. ASW, 38.6 mm. **Ruler:** Elizabeth II **Subject:** Driver and Fireman **Obv:** Crowned head right **Rev:** Familiar image from the Golden Age of Steam: the driver and fireman

Date	Mintage	F	VF	XF	Unc	BU
2004 Proof	—	Value: 75.00				

KM# 124   5 POUNDS
28.2800 g., Copper-Nickel, 38.6 mm. **Ruler:** Elizabeth II
Obv: Crowned head right **Rev:** British Horsa gliders in flight
Rev. Designer: David Cornell **Edge:** Reeded **Note:** D-Day

Date	Mintage	F	VF	XF	Unc	BU
2004	—	—	—	—	15.00	17.00

KM# 124a   5 POUNDS
28.2800 g., 0.9250 Silver 0.8410 oz. ASW, 38.6 mm.
Ruler: Elizabeth II **Obv:** Crowned head right **Rev:** British Horsa
gliders in flight

Date	Mintage	F	VF	XF	Unc	BU
2004 Proof	10,000	Value: 85.00				

KM# 124b   5 POUNDS
39.9400 g., 0.9167 Gold 1.1771 oz. AGW, 38.6 mm.
Ruler: Elizabeth II **Obv:** Crowned head right **Rev:** British Horsa
gliders in flight

Date	Mintage	F	VF	XF	Unc	BU
2004 Proof	500	Value: 1,350				

KM# 126   5 POUNDS
28.2800 g., Copper-Nickel, 38.6 mm. **Ruler:** Elizabeth II
Subject: 150th Anniversary of the Crimean War **Obv:** Crowned
head right **Rev:** Charge of the Light Brigade scene with one blue
uniform behind the Earl of Cardigan **Edge:** Reeded

Date	Mintage	F	VF	XF	Unc	BU
2004 plain	—	—	—	—	25.00	27.50
2004 partial color	—	—	—	—	25.00	27.50

KM# 126a   5 POUNDS
28.2800 g., 0.9250 Silver 0.8410 oz. ASW, 38.6 mm.
Ruler: Elizabeth II **Obv:** Crowned head right **Rev:** Charge of the
Light Brigade scene with one blue uniform behind the Earl of
Cardigan **Edge:** Reeded

Date	Mintage	F	VF	XF	Unc	BU
2004 Proof	10,000	Value: 85.00				

KM# 126b   5 POUNDS
39.9400 g., 0.9166 Gold 1.1770 oz. AGW, 38.6 mm.
Ruler: Elizabeth II **Obv:** Crowned head right **Rev:** Charge of the
Light Brigade scene with one blue uniform behind the Earl of
Cardigan **Edge:** Reeded

Date	Mintage	F	VF	XF	Unc	BU
2004 Proof	500	Value: 1,350				

KM# 136   5 POUNDS
28.2800 g., 0.9250 Silver 0.8410 oz. ASW, 38.6 mm.
Ruler: Elizabeth II **Subject:** Coronation **Obv:** Crowned head
right **Rev:** The Pacific Class Coronation

Date	Mintage	F	VF	XF	Unc	BU
2004 Proof	—	Value: 75.00				

KM# 137   5 POUNDS
28.2800 g., 0.9250 Silver 0.8410 oz. ASW, 38.6 mm.
Ruler: Elizabeth II **Subject:** Flying Scotsman **Obv:** Crowned
head right **Rev:** Famous Flying Scotsman Locomotive, designed
by Sir Nigel Gresley

Date	Mintage	F	VF	XF	Unc	BU
2004 Proof	—	Value: 75.00				

KM# 138   5 POUNDS
28.2800 g., 0.9250 Silver 0.8410 oz. ASW, 38.6 mm.
Ruler: Elizabeth II **Subject:** Golden Arrow **Obv:** Crowned head
right **Rev:** The Golden Arrow, which ran from London to Dover
en route to Paris

Date	Mintage	F	VF	XF	Unc	BU
2004 Proof	—	Value: 75.00				

KM# 140   5 POUNDS
28.2800 g., 0.9250 Silver 0.8410 oz. ASW, 38.6 mm.
Ruler: Elizabeth II **Subject:** Tunnel **Obv:** Crowned head right
Rev: Familiar image from the Golden Age of Steam: A locomotive
steaming out of a tunnel

Date	Mintage	F	VF	XF	Unc	BU
2004	—	Value: 75.00				

KM# 141   5 POUNDS
28.2800 g., 0.9250 Silver 0.8410 oz. ASW, 38.6 mm.
Ruler: Elizabeth II **Subject:** Evening Star **Obv:** Crowned head
right **Rev:** The Evening Star - representing the last British Rail
Steam Locomotive

Date	Mintage	F	VF	XF	Unc	BU
2004 Proof	—	Value: 75.00				

KM# 127   5 POUNDS
Copper-Nickel **Ruler:** Elizabeth II **Subject:** Battle of Trafalgar
Obv: Crowned head right

Date	Mintage	F	VF	XF	Unc	BU
2005	—	—	—	—	7.50	10.00

KM# 127a   5 POUNDS
28.2800 g., 0.9250 Silver 0.8410 oz. ASW, 38.6 mm.
Ruler: Elizabeth II **Subject:** Nelson Trafalger **Obv:** Crowned
head right **Rev:** 200th Anniversary of the Battle of Trafalgar,
image of Nelson with a gilded ship in the background

Date	Mintage	F	VF	XF	Unc	BU
2005 Proof	—	Value: 75.00				

KM# 128   5 POUNDS
Copper-Nickel **Ruler:** Elizabeth II **Subject:** 60th Anniversary -
End of WW II **Obv:** Crowned head right **Obv. Designer:** Ian Rank-
Broadley **Rev:** Big Ben Tower

Date	Mintage	F	VF	XF	Unc	BU
2005	—	—	—	—	7.50	10.00

KM# 128a   5 POUNDS
28.2800 g., 0.9250 Silver 0.8410 oz. ASW, 38.6 mm.
Ruler: Elizabeth II **Subject:** WWII Liberation **Obv:** Crowned
head right **Rev:** Big Ben Tower **Edge:** Reeded

Date	Mintage	F	VF	XF	Unc	BU
2005 Proof	5,000	Value: 85.00				

KM# 128b   5 POUNDS
39.9400 g., 0.9167 Gold 1.1771 oz. AGW, 38.6 mm.
Ruler: Elizabeth II **Subject:** WWII Liberation **Obv:** Crowned
head right **Rev:** Big Ben Tower **Edge:** Reeded

Date	Mintage	F	VF	XF	Unc	BU
2005 Proof	150	Value: 1,400				

KM# 129   5 POUNDS
Copper-Nickel **Ruler:** Elizabeth II **Subject:** WW II Liberation
Obv: Crowned head right **Rev:** Returning evacuees
Edge: Reeded

Date	Mintage	F	VF	XF	Unc	BU
2005	—	—	—	—	7.50	10.00

KM# 129a   5 POUNDS
39.9400 g., 0.9167 Gold 1.1771 oz. AGW, 38.6 mm.
Ruler: Elizabeth II **Subject:** WWII Liberation **Obv:** Crowned
head right **Rev:** Returning evacuees **Edge:** Reeded

Date	Mintage	F	VF	XF	Unc	BU
2005 Proof	150	Value: 1,450				

KM# 142   5 POUNDS
28.2800 g., 0.9250 Silver 0.8410 oz. ASW, 38.6 mm.
Ruler: Elizabeth II **Subject:** Queen's 80th Birthday **Obv:** Head
with tiara right - gilt **Obv. Legend:** ELIZABETH II BAILIWICK -
OF JERSEY **Obv. Designer:** Ian Rank-Broadley **Rev:** Queen
horseback facing

Date	Mintage	F	VF	XF	Unc	BU
2006 Proof	—	Value: 40.00				

KM# 145   5 POUNDS
28.2800 g., 0.9250 Silver 0.8410 oz. ASW, 38.6 mm.
Ruler: Elizabeth II **Subject:** Elizabeth II's 80th Birthday
Obv: Head with tiara right **Obv. Legend:** ELIZABETH II
BAILIWICK - OF JERSEY **Obv. Designer:** Ian Rank-Broadley
Rev: Queen on horseback **Edge:** Reeded

Date	Mintage	F	VF	XF	Unc	BU
2006 Proof	—	Value: 40.00				

KM# 146   5 POUNDS
28.2800 g., 0.9250 Silver 0.8410 oz. ASW, 38.6 mm.
Ruler: Elizabeth II **Subject:** Battle of Agincourt, 1415 **Obv:** Head
right **Rev:** Archers and horsemen

Date	Mintage	F	VF	XF	Unc	BU
2009 Proof	2,500	Value: 50.00				

KM# 143   10 POUNDS
155.5000 g., 0.9250 Silver partially gilt 4.6243 oz. ASW, 65 mm.
Ruler: Elizabeth II **Subject:** 50th Anniversary of Coronation
Obv: Queens silver portrait on gold plated fields **Rev:** Crown and
scepter above arms, gold plated **Rev. Designer:** Marcel Canioni

Date	Mintage	F	VF	XF	Unc	BU
2003	2,000	—	—	—	125	145

KM# 147   10 POUNDS
155.5000 g., 0.9250 Silver partially gilt 4.6243 oz. ASW, 65 mm.
Ruler: Elizabeth II **Obv:** Head right **Rev:** St. George slaying
dragon, partially gilt

Date	Mintage	F	VF	XF	Unc	BU
2009 Proof	450	Value: 350				

KM# 112   25 POUNDS
7.9800 g., 0.9167 Gold 0.2352 oz. AGW, 22.05 mm.
Ruler: Elizabeth II **Subject:** Princess Diana **Obv:** Crowned head
right **Rev:** Diana's portrait **Edge:** Reeded

Date	Mintage	F	VF	XF	Unc	BU
2002 Proof	2,500	Value: 325				

KM# 114   25 POUNDS
7.9800 g., 0.9166 Gold 0.2352 oz. AGW, 22 mm.
Ruler: Elizabeth II **Subject:** Queen Mother **Obv:** Crowned head
right **Rev:** Queen Mother's portrait circa 1918 **Edge:** Reeded

Date	Mintage	F	VF	XF	Unc	BU
2002 Proof	2,500	Value: 325				

KM# 116   25 POUNDS
7.9800 g., 0.9166 Gold 0.2352 oz. AGW, 22 mm.
Ruler: Elizabeth II **Subject:** Golden Jubilee **Obv:** Crowned head
right **Rev:** Abbey procession scene **Edge:** Reeded

Date	Mintage	F	VF	XF	Unc	BU
2002 Proof	2,500	Value: 325				

KM# 118   25 POUNDS
7.9800 g., 0.9166 Gold 0.2352 oz. AGW, 22 mm. **Ruler:**
Elizabeth II **Subject:** Duke of Wellington **Obv:** Crowned head
right **Rev:** Wellington's portrait with infantry scene **Edge:** Reeded

Date	Mintage	F	VF	XF	Unc	BU
2002 Proof	2,500	Value: 325				

KM# 120   25 POUNDS
7.9800 g., 0.9166 Gold 0.2352 oz. AGW, 22 mm.
Ruler: Elizabeth II **Subject:** Golden Jubilee **Obv:** Crowned head
right **Rev:** Honor guard and monument **Edge:** Reeded

Date	Mintage	F	VF	XF	Unc	BU
2003 Proof	5,000	Value: 300				

KM# 125   25 POUNDS
7.9800 g., 0.9167 Gold 0.2352 oz. AGW, 22 mm.
Ruler: Elizabeth II **Subject:** D-Day **Obv:** Crowned head right
Rev: British Horsa gliders in flight **Edge:** Reeded

Date	Mintage	F	VF	XF	Unc	BU
2004 Proof	500	Value: 350				

KM# 122   50 POUNDS
1000.0000 g., 0.9250 Silver 29.738 oz. ASW, 100 mm.
Ruler: Elizabeth II **Obv:** Crowned head right **Rev:** Bust facing
and crowned arms with supporters **Edge:** Reeded

Date	Mintage	F	VF	XF	Unc	BU
2003 Proof	500	Value: 995				

KAZAKHSTAN

PIEFORTS

KM#	Date	Mintage	Identification	Mkt Val
P3	2002	100	5 Pounds. 0.9166 Gold. 56.5600 g. 38.6 mm. Queen's portrait. Abbey procession scene. Reeded edge. Underweight piefort	1,600

MINT SETS

KM#	Date	Mintage	Identification	Issue Price	Mkt Val
MS7	2004 (1)	—	Jersey KM#126, Guernsey KM#155, Alderney KM#43, 150th Anniversary of the Crimean War	—	85.00

JORDAN

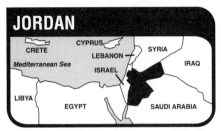

The Hashemite Kingdom of Jordan, a constitutional monarchy in southwest Asia, has an area of 37,738 sq. mi.(91,880 sq. km.) and a population of 3.5 million. Capital: Amman. Agriculture and tourism comprise Jordan's economic base. Chief exports are phosphates, tomatoes and oranges.

RULER
Abdullah Ibn Al-Hussein, 1999-

MONETARY SYSTEM
100 Piastres = 1 Dinar

KINGDOM
DECIMAL COINAGE

KM# 73   5 PIASTRES
5.0000 g., Nickel Clad Steel, 25.8 mm.   **Ruler:** Abdullah Ibn Al-Hussein **Obv:** Bust right **Rev:** Value to left within lines below date with written value at lower right **Edge:** Milled

Date	Mintage	F	VF	XF	Unc	BU
AH1427-2006	—	—	—	—	1.50	2.00
AH1429-2008	—	—	—	—	1.50	2.00

KM# 74   10 PIASTRES
8.0000 g., Nickel Clad Steel, 28 mm.   **Ruler:** Abdullah Ibn Al-Hussein **Obv:** Bust right **Rev:** Value at left within lines below date with written value at lower right **Edge:** Milled

Date	Mintage	F	VF	XF	Unc	BU
AH1425-2004	—	—	—	—	1.75	3.50

KM# 83   1/4 DINAR
7.4000 g., Nickel-Brass   **Ruler:** Abdullah Ibn Al-Hussein **Obv:** Bust right **Edge:** Plain

Date	Mintage	F	VF	XF	Unc	BU
AH1425-2004	—	—	—	—	2.00	3.00
AH1427-2006	—	—	—	—	2.00	3.00
AH1429-2008	—	—	—	—	2.00	3.00

KM# 79   1/2 DINAR
9.6700 g., Bi-Metallic Copper-Nickel center in Brass ring, 29 mm. **Ruler:** Abdullah Ibn Al-Hussein **Obv:** Bust right within circle **Rev:** Value in center of circled wreath **Edge:** Plain **Shape:** 7-sided

Date	Mintage	F	VF	XF	Unc	BU
AH1429-2008	—	—	—	—	3.00	4.00

KM# 75   3 DINARS
28.5000 g., Brass, 40 mm.   **Ruler:** Abdullah Ibn Al-Hussein **Subject:** Amman: Arabic Culture Capital **Obv:** Bust right **Rev:** Building **Edge:** Milled

Date	Mintage	F	VF	XF	Unc	BU
AH1423//2002	2,000	—	—	—	120	—

Note: Only 500 sold to collectors. Rest were taken by Amman municipality as official gifts

KM# 86   5 DINARS
120.0000 g., Bronze, 60 mm.   **Ruler:** Abdullah Ibn Al-Hussein **Subject:** Selection of Petra as one of the new Seven Wonders of the World **Obv:** King Abdullah II and Queen Rania **Rev:** Petra **Edge:** Milled

Date	Mintage	F	VF	XF	Unc	BU
AH1428-2008 Proof	500	Value: 160				

KM# 84   10 DINARS
120.0000 g., 0.9990 Silver 3.8541 oz. ASW, 60 mm. **Ruler:** Abdullah Ibn Al-Hussein **Subject:** 60th Anniversary of Jordan's Independence **Obv:** King Abdullah I and Independence speech **Rev:** The National Assembly building **Edge:** Milled

Date	Mintage	F	VF	XF	Unc	BU
2006 Proof	250	Value: 250				

Note: Issued primarily for use as official state gifts

KM# 88   10 DINARS
31.1050 g., 0.9990 Silver 0.9990 oz. ASW, 40 mm. **Ruler:** Abdullah Ibn Al-Hussein **Subject:** Accession, 10th Anniversary **Obv:** Bust **Rev:** Arms

Date	Mintage	F	VF	XF	Unc	BU
2009 Proof	2,250	Value: 150				

KM# 87   20 DINARS
120.0000 g., 0.9990 Silver 3.8541 oz. ASW, 60 mm. **Ruler:** Abdullah Ibn Al-Hussein **Subject:** Selection of Petra as one of the new Seven Wonders of the World **Obv:** King Abdullah II and Queen Rania **Rev:** Petra **Edge:** Milled

Date	Mintage	F	VF	XF	Unc	BU
AH1428-2008 Proof	500	Value: 260				

KM# 89   50 DINARS
16.9600 g., 0.9990 Gold 0.5447 oz. AGW, 30 mm. **Ruler:** Abdullah Ibn Al-Hussein **Subject:** Accession, 10th Anniversary **Obv:** Bust **Rev:** Arms

Date	Mintage	F	VF	XF	Unc	BU
2009 Proof	1,750	Value: 700				

KM# 85   60 DINARS
72.7500 g., 0.9170 Gold 2.1447 oz. AGW, 40 mm. **Ruler:** Abdullah Ibn Al-Hussein **Subject:** 60th Anniversary of Jordan's Independence **Obv:** King Abdullah II **Rev:** Treasury in Petra **Edge:** Milled

Date	Mintage	F	VF	XF	Unc	BU
2006 Proof	250	Value: 2,750				

Note: Issued primarily for use as official state gifts

MINT SETS

KM#	Date	Mintage	Identification	Issue Price	Mkt Val
MS4	2000-2004 (5)	—	KM#73-74, 78.1, 79, 83	—	20.00

PROOF SETS

KM#	Date	Mintage	Identification	Issue Price	Mkt Val
PS14	2006 (2)	250	KM#84-85	—	3,000
PS15	2008 (2)	—	KM#86-87	—	400

KAZAKHSTAN

The Republic of Kazakhstan (formerly Kazakhstan S.S.R.) is bordered to the west by the Caspian Sea and Russia, to the north by Russia, in the east by the Peoples Republic of China and in the south by Uzbekistan and Kirghizia. It has an area of 1,049,155 sq. mi. (2,717,300 sq. km.) and a population of 16.7 million. Capital: Astana. Rich in mineral resources including coal, tungsten, copper, lead, zinc and manganese with huge oil and natural gas reserves. Agriculture is very important, (it previously represented 20 percent of the total arable acreage of the combined U.S.S.R.) Non-ferrous metallurgy, heavy engineering and chemical industries are leaders in its economy.

MONETARY SYSTEM
100 Tyin = 1 Tenge

REPUBLIC
DECIMAL COINAGE

KM# 23   TENGE
1.6000 g., Brass, 15 mm.   **Obv:** National emblem **Rev:** Value flanked by designs **Edge:** Plain

Date	Mintage	F	VF	XF	Unc	BU
2002	—	—	—	—	0.50	0.85
2004	—	—	—	—	0.50	0.85
2005	—	—	—	—	0.50	0.85

KM# 64   2 TENGE
1.8200 g., Brass, 16 mm.   **Obv:** National emblem **Rev:** Value flanked by designs **Edge:** Plain

Date	Mintage	F	VF	XF	Unc	BU
2005	—	—	—	—	0.65	1.20
2006	—	—	—	—	0.65	1.20

KM# 24   5 TENGE
2.2000 g., Brass, 17.3 mm.   **Obv:** National emblem **Rev:** Value flanked by designs

Date	Mintage	F	VF	XF	Unc	BU
2002	—	—	—	—	0.50	0.85
2004	—	—	—	—	0.50	0.85
2005	—	—	—	—	0.50	0.85
2006	—	—	—	—	0.50	0.85

KM# 25   10 TENGE
2.8000 g., Brass, 19.6 mm.   **Obv:** National emblem **Rev:** Value above design

Date	Mintage	F	VF	XF	Unc	BU
2002	—	—	—	—	0.75	1.25
2004	—	—	—	—	0.75	1.25
2005	—	—	—	—	0.75	1.25
2006	—	—	—	—	0.75	1.25

KM# 26   20 TENGE
2.8600 g., Copper-Nickel, 18.3 mm.   **Obv:** National emblem **Rev:** Value above design **Edge:** Segmented reeding **Edge Lettering:** * CTO TENGE * Y 3 TENGE

Date	Mintage	F	VF	XF	Unc	BU
2002	—	—	—	—	1.00	1.75
2006	—	—	—	—	1.00	1.75

KM# 40 50 TENGE
11.5000 g., Copper-Nickel, 31 mm. **Obv:** Eagle superimposed on ornate 10 **Edge:** Reeded and plain sections

Date	Mintage	F	VF	XF	Unc	BU
2001	—	—	—	—	4.00	6.50

KM# 41 50 TENGE
11.2000 g., Copper-Nickel, 31.1 mm. **Subject:** Gabiden Mustafin **Obv:** National emblem above value **Rev:** Bust 1/4 left **Edge:** Segmented reeding

Date	Mintage	F	VF	XF	Unc	BU
ND(2002)	—	—	—	—	4.00	6.50

KM# 27 50 TENGE
4.7000 g., Copper-Nickel, 23.1 mm. **Obv:** National emblem **Rev:** Value above design

Date	Mintage	F	VF	XF	Unc	BU
2002	—	—	—	—	2.00	3.50

KM# 69 50 TENGE
Copper-Nickel, 31 mm. **Subject:** Gabit Mosrepov **Obv:** Symbol and value

Date	Mintage	F	VF	XF	Unc	BU
2002	—	—	—	—	4.00	6.50

KM# 70 50 TENGE
Copper-Nickel, 31 mm. **Subject:** 200th Anniversary of Makhambet Utemisov **Obv:** Symbol and value

Date	Mintage	F	VF	XF	Unc	BU
2003	—	—	—	—	4.00	6.50

KM# 54 50 TENGE
11.5000 g., Copper-Nickel, 31.1 mm. **Obv:** National emblem above value **Rev:** Painter Abylichan Kasteev (1904-1973) **Edge:** Reeded and plain sections

Date	Mintage	F	VF	XF	Unc	BU
2004	—	—	—	—	4.00	6.50

KM# 65 50 TENGE
11.5000 g., Copper-Nickel, 31.1 mm. **Subject:** Alken Margulan **Obv:** National emblem above value **Rev:** Bust facing **Edge:** Segmented reeding

Date	Mintage	F	VF	XF	Unc	BU
2004	—	—	—	—	4.00	6.50

KM# 58 50 TENGE
11.5000 g., Copper-Nickel, 31.1 mm. **Subject:** 10th Anniversary of the Constitution **Obv:** National emblem above value **Rev:** National emblem within circle above book **Edge:** Segmented reeding

Date	Mintage	F	VF	XF	Unc	BU
2005	—	—	—	—	4.00	6.50

KM# 71 50 TENGE
10.9500 g., Copper-Nickel, 31 mm. **Subject:** 60 Years Victory WWII **Obv:** Symbol and value

Date	Mintage	F	VF	XF	Unc	BU
2005	—	—	—	—	4.00	6.50

KM# 79 50 TENGE
11.2200 g., Copper-Nickel, 31 mm. **Subject:** 20th Anniversary **Obv:** National arms above value **Rev:** Happy woman **Edge:** Segmented reeding

Date	Mintage	F	VF	XF	Unc	BU
ND (2006)	—	—	—	—	4.00	6.50

KM# 73 50 TENGE
11.3700 g., Copper-Nickel, 31 mm. **Obv:** Human figure and solar system **Rev:** Astronaut and solar system **Edge:** Segmented reeding

Date	Mintage	F	VF	XF	Unc	BU
2006	50,000	—	—	—	4.00	6.00

KM# 74 50 TENGE
11.3700 g., Copper-Nickel, 31 mm. **Obv:** National arms on tapestry **Rev:** Woman with baby in cradle **Edge:** Segmented reeding

Date	Mintage	F	VF	XF	Unc	BU
2006	—	—	—	—	4.00	6.00

KM# 75 50 TENGE
11.3700 g., Copper-Nickel, 31 mm. **Obv:** National arms **Rev:** Altai Snowcock **Edge:** Segmented reeding

Date	Mintage	F	VF	XF	Unc	BU
2006	50,000	—	—	—	4.00	6.00

KM# 76 50 TENGE
11.3700 g., Copper-Nickel, 31 mm. **Obv:** National arms **Rev:** Altyn Kyran Order Grand Collar and Badge **Edge:** Segmented reeding

Date	Mintage	F	VF	XF	Unc	BU
2006	50,000	—	—	—	4.00	6.00

KM# 77 50 TENGE
11.3700 g., Copper-Nickel, 31 mm. **Obv:** National arms **Rev:** Altyn Kyran Order Breast Star **Edge:** Segmented reeding

Date	Mintage	F	VF	XF	Unc	BU
2006	50,000	—	—	—	4.00	6.00

KM# 78 50 TENGE
11.3700 g., Copper-Nickel, 31 mm. **Obv:** National arms **Rev:** Zhubanov bust and music score **Edge:** Segmented reeding

Date	Mintage	F	VF	XF	Unc	BU
2006	50,000	—	—	—	4.00	6.00

KM# 80 50 TENGE
10.8900 g., Copper-Nickel, 31.10 mm. **Subject:** 50th Anniversary Launch of Sputnik I **Obv:** Stylized view of solar system **Obv. Legend:** REPUBLIC OF KAZAKHSTAN **Rev:** Sputnik I in space, earth in background **Rev. Legend:** THE FIRST SPACE SATELLITE OF THE EARTH **Edge:** Segmented reeding

Date	Mintage	F	VF	XF	Unc	BU
ND(2007)	—	—	—	—	4.00	6.00

KM# 81 50 TENGE
11.1100 g., Copper-Nickel, 31 mm. **Obv:** National arms, value below **Obv. Legend:** КАЗАКСТАН.... **Rev:** Eurasian Spoonbill standing left **Rev. Legend:** ... • PLATALEA LEUCORODIA **Edge:** Segmented reeding

Date	Mintage	F	VF	XF	Unc	BU
2007	—	—	—	—	4.00	6.00

KM# 83   50 TENGE
10.8800 g., Copper-Nickel, 31.07 mm.   **Obv:** National arms
Rev: Spoonbill standing **Rev. Legend:** ... ? PLATALEA
LEUCORODIA **Edge:** Segmented reeding

Date	Mintage	F	VF	XF	Unc	BU
2007	—	—	—	—	5.00	7.00

KM# 86   50 TENGE
Copper-Nickel, 31 mm.   **Obv:** National Arms

Date	Mintage	F	VF	XF	Unc	BU
2008 Proof	—	Value: 6.00				

KM# 132   50 TENGE
Copper-Nickel, 31 mm.   **Subject:** Betashar **Obv:** Arms **Rev:** Two
figures standing

Date	Mintage	F	VF	XF	Unc	BU
2009	50,000	—	—	—	—	10.00

KM# 135   50 TENGE
0.5000 g., 0.9990 Gold 0.0161 oz. AGW, 11 mm.   **Obv:** Value
Rev: Cat head sculpture

Date	Mintage	F	VF	XF	Unc	BU
2009 Proof	14,000	—	—	—	—	50.00

KM# 140   50 TENGE
Copper-Nickel, 31 mm.   **Obv:** Arms **Rev:** Parassat medal
insignia

Date	Mintage	F	VF	XF	Unc	BU
2009	50,000	—	—	—	—	10.00

KM# 141   50 TENGE
Copper-Nickel   **Obv:** Arms **Rev:** Porcupine advancing right
Shape: 31

Date	Mintage	F	VF	XF	Unc	BU
2009	50,000	—	—	—	—	10.00

KM# 144   50 TENGE
Copper-Nickel, 31 mm.   **Obv:** Man standing in solor system
Rev: Apollo-Soyuz space craft

Date	Mintage	F	VF	XF	Unc	BU
2009	50,000	—	—	—	—	10.00

KM# 145   50 TENGE
Copper-Nickel, 31 mm.   **Obv:** Arms **Rev:** Star of the Order of
Dostyk

Date	Mintage	F	VF	XF	Unc	BU
2009	50,000	—	—	—	—	10.00

KM# 146   50 TENGE
Copper-Nickel, 31 mm.   **Subject:** T. Bassenov, 100th Anniversary
of Birth **Obv:** Arms **Rev:** Bust at right, architectural column

Date	Mintage	F	VF	XF	Unc	BU
2009	50,000	—	—	—	—	10.00

KM# 152   50 TENGE
0.5000 g., 0.9990 Gold 0.0161 oz. AGW, 11 mm.   **Subject:**
Ahalavlinky Treasure **Obv:** Value **Rev:** Historical jewlery design

Date	Mintage	F	VF	XF	Unc	BU
2009 Proof	14,000	Value: 40.00				

KM# 39   100 TENGE
6.2300 g., Bi-Metallic Copper-Nickel center in Brass ring,
24.4 mm.   **Obv:** National emblem **Rev:** Value within lined circle
flanked by designs **Edge:** Reeding over incuse value

Date	Mintage	F	VF	XF	Unc	BU
2002	—	—	—	—	3.50	5.50
2004	—	—	—	—	3.50	5.50
2005	—	—	—	—	3.50	5.50
2006	—	—	—	—	3.50	5.50
2007	—	—	—	—	3.50	5.50

KM# 49   100 TENGE
6.4000 g., Bi-Metallic Copper-Nickel center in Brass ring,
24.5 mm.   **Obv:** Stylized chicken **Rev:** Value within lined circle
flanked by designs **Edge:** Reeded and lettered

Date	Mintage	F	VF	XF	Unc	BU
2003	100,000	—	—	—	4.00	6.50

KM# 50   100 TENGE
6.4000 g., Bi-Metallic Copper-Nickel center in Brass ring,
24.5 mm.   **Obv:** Stylized panther **Rev:** Value within lined circle
flanked by designs **Edge:** Reeded and lettered

Date	Mintage	F	VF	XF	Unc	BU
2003	100,000	—	—	—	4.00	6.50

KM# 51   100 TENGE
6.4000 g., Bi-Metallic Copper-Nickel center in Brass ring,
24.5 mm.   **Obv:** Stylized wolf's head **Rev:** Value within lined
circle flanked by designs **Edge:** Reeded and lettered

Date	Mintage	F	VF	XF	Unc	BU
2003	100,000	—	—	—	4.00	6.50

KM# 52   100 TENGE
6.4000 g., Bi-Metallic Copper-Nickel center in Brass ring,
24.5 mm.   **Obv:** Stylized sheep's head **Rev:** Value within lined
circle flanked by designs **Edge:** Reeded and lettered

Date	Mintage	F	VF	XF	Unc	BU
2003	100,000	—	—	—	4.00	6.50

KM# 120   100 TENGE
1.2400 g., 0.9990 Gold 0.0398 oz. AGW   **Subject:** King Kroisos
Obv: Arms **Rev:** Head left, coin, temple

Date	Mintage	F	VF	XF	Unc	BU
2004 Proof	—	Value: 75.00				

KM# 116   100 TENGE
31.1000 g., 0.9250 Silver 0.9249 oz. ASW, 37 mm.   **Subject:**
Olympics **Obv:** Arms and stylized stadium **Rev:** Two cyclists

Date	Mintage	F	VF	XF	Unc	BU
2004 Proof	—	—	—	—	—	—

KM# 119 100 TENGE
31.1000 g., 0.9250 Silver 0.9249 oz. ASW, 37mm mm.
Subject: FIFA World Cup, Germany **Obv:** Arms and stylized
stadium **Rev:** Two soccer players and large ball

Date	Mintage	F	VF	XF	Unc	BU
2004 Proof	—	Value: 50.00				

KM# 121 100 TENGE
1.2400 g., 0.9990 Gold 0.0398 oz. AGW **Subject:** King Midas
Rev: King Midas reclining on bench

Date	Mintage	F	VF	XF	Unc	BU
2004 Proof	—	Value: 75.00				

KM# 122 100 TENGE
1.2400 g., 0.9990 Gold 0.0398 oz. AGW **Subject:** Ancient
Turkestan **Obv:** Arms **Rev:** Camel carivan and building

Date	Mintage	F	VF	XF	Unc	BU
2004 Proof	—	Value: 75.00				

KM# 57 100 TENGE
6.4000 g., Bi-Metallic Copper-Nickel center in Brass ring,
24.5 mm. **Subject:** 60th Anniversary of the UN **Obv:** UN logo
as part of the number 60 **Rev:** Value within lined circle flanked
by designs **Edge:** Reeded and lettered

Date	Mintage	F	VF	XF	Unc	BU
2005	—			—	5.00	7.50

KM# 95 100 TENGE
31.1050 g., 0.9250 Silver 0.9250 oz. ASW, 38.61 mm.
Subject: Baiturramman Mosque **Rev:** Mosque and reflecting
pool

Date	Mintage	F	VF	XF	Unc	BU
2006 (2008) Proof	6,000	Value: 90.00				

KM# 98 100 TENGE
31.1050 g., 0.9250 Silver 0.9250 oz. ASW, 38.61 mm.
Subject: Zahir Mosque **Rev:** Mosque

Date	Mintage	F	VF	XF	Unc	BU
2006 Proof	6,000	Value: 90.00				

KM# 96 100 TENGE
31.1050 g., 0.9250 Silver 0.9250 oz. ASW, 38.61 mm.
Subject: Faisal Mosque, Islamabad **Rev:** Mosque

Date	Mintage	F	VF	XF	Unc	BU
2006 (2008) Proof	6,000	Value: 90.00				

KM# 97 100 TENGE
31.1050 g., 0.9250 Silver 0.9250 oz. ASW, 38.61 mm. **Subject:**
Hodja Akhmed Yassavi Mausoleum Turkestan **Rev:** Mausoleum

Date	Mintage	F	VF	XF	Unc	BU
2006 (2008) Proof	6,000	Value: 90.00				

KM# 110 100 TENGE
31.1050 g., 0.9250 Silver 0.9250 oz. ASW, 38.61 mm.
Subject: Chingis Khan **Rev:** Khan on horseback facing

Date	Mintage	F	VF	XF	Unc	BU
2008 Proof	13,000	Value: 65.00				

KM# 125 100 TENGE
31.1050 g., 0.9250 Silver 0.9250 oz. ASW, 38.61 mm.
Subject: Attila the Hun **Rev:** Medallic Profile right

Date	Mintage	F	VF	XF	Unc	BU
2009 Proof	13,000	Value: 75.00				

KM# 126 100 TENGE
31.1050 g., 0.9250 Silver 0.9250 oz. ASW, 38.61 mm.
Subject: 2010 Olympics **Rev:** Ski jumper and Vancouver skyline

Date	Mintage	F	VF	XF	Unc	BU
2009 Proof	12,000	Value: 50.00				

KM# 134 100 TENGE
31.1000 g., 0.9990 Silver partially gilt 0.9988 oz. ASW **Subject:**
Caracal **Obv:** Arms **Rev:** Caracal cat head facing, partially gilt

Date	Mintage	F	VF	XF	Unc	BU
2009 Proof	13,000			—	50.00	

KM# 136 100 TENGE
1.2400 g., 0.9990 Gold 0.0398 oz. AGW, 13.9 mm. **Obv:** Value
Rev: Cat head sculpture

Date	Mintage	F	VF	XF	Unc	BU
2009 Proof	9,500	—	—	—	80.00	

KM# 147 100 TENGE
31.1000 g., 0.9250 Silver 0.9249 oz. ASW, 38.6 mm. **Obv:** Arms
Rev: Tiger advancing right

Date	Mintage	F	VF	XF	Unc	BU
2009 Proof	13,000	Value: 40.00				

KM# 151   100 TENGE
31.1000 g., 0.9990 Silver 0.9988 oz. ASW, 38.61 mm.
Subject: World Cup, South Africa **Obv:** Arms and stadium
Rev: Soccer Player, gilt ball

Date	Mintage	F	VF	XF	Unc	BU
2009 Proof	—	—	—	—	—	40.00

KM# 153   100 TENGE
1.2400 g., 0.9990 Gold 0.0398 oz. AGW, 13.92 mm.   **Subject:**
Zhalavlinky Treasure **Obv:** Arms **Rev:** Historic jewelery design

Date	Mintage	F	VF	XF	Unc	BU
2009 Proof	9,500	Value: 75.00				

KM# 66   500 TENGE
24.0000 g., 0.9250 Silver 0.7137 oz. ASW, 37 mm.   **Obv:** Man
seated under tree playing stringed instrument **Rev:** Stringed
instrument, musical notes

Date	Mintage	F	VF	XF	Unc	BU
2001 Proof	—	Value: 45.00				

KM# 37   500 TENGE
23.9000 g., 0.9250 Silver 0.7107 oz. ASW, 37 mm.
Subject: Wildlife **Obv:** Value **Rev:** Female Saiga with two babies
Edge: Plain

Date	Mintage	F	VF	XF	Unc	BU
2001 Proof	3,000	Value: 90.00				

KM# 38   500 TENGE
23.8100 g., 0.9250 Silver 0.7081 oz. ASW, 36.9 mm.
Subject: 10 Years of Independence **Obv:** Monument and flag
Rev: National emblem within design above value **Edge:** Plain

Date	Mintage	F	VF	XF	Unc	BU
2001 Proof	3,000	Value: 125				

KM# 55   500 TENGE
24.0000 g., 0.9250 Silver 0.7137 oz. ASW, 37 mm.   **Obv:** Value
Rev: Altai Mountain petroglyph **Edge:** Plain

Date	Mintage	F	VF	XF	Unc	BU
2001 Proof	3,000	Value: 175				

KM# 112   500 TENGE
24.0000 g., 0.9250 Silver 0.7137 oz. ASW   **Subject:** Applied art,
stringed instrument **Obv:** Man seated under tree **Rev:** Stringed
instrument and notes

Date	Mintage	F	VF	XF	Unc	BU
2001 Proof	—	Value: 40.00				

KM# 42   500 TENGE
23.9000 g., 0.9250 Silver 0.7107 oz. ASW, 37 mm.
Subject: Music **Obv:** Musician and value divided by tree
Rev: Musical instruments **Edge:** Plain

Date	Mintage	F	VF	XF	Unc	BU
2002 Proof	—	Value: 165				

KM# 43   500 TENGE
23.9000 g., 0.9250 Silver 0.7107 oz. ASW, 37 mm.   **Subject:**
Prehistoric Art **Obv:** Value **Rev:** Prehistoric cave art **Edge:** Plain

Date	Mintage	F	VF	XF	Unc	BU
2002 Proof	3,000	Value: 140				

KM# 44   500 TENGE
23.9000 g., 0.9250 Silver 0.7107 oz. ASW, 37 mm.
Subject: Bighorn Sheep **Obv:** Value **Rev:** Kazakhstan Argali
Ram **Edge:** Plain

Date	Mintage	F	VF	XF	Unc	BU
2002 Proof	3,000	Value: 120				

KM# 113   500 TENGE
24.0000 g., 0.9250 Silver 0.7137 oz. ASW, 37 mm.
Subject: Petroglyph **Obv:** Value on traditional weave pattern
Rev: Horse petroglyph

Date	Mintage	F	VF	XF	Unc	BU
2002 Proof	—	Value: 50.00				

KM# 53   500 TENGE
24.0000 g., 0.9250 Silver 0.7137 oz. ASW, 37 mm.   **Obv:** Value
Rev: Great Bustard bird standing on ground **Edge:** Plain

Date	Mintage	F	VF	XF	Unc	BU
2003 Proof	3,000	Value: 75.00				

KM# 56   500 TENGE
24.0000 g., 0.9250 Silver 0.7137 oz. ASW, 37 mm.   **Subject:**
Applied Arts **Obv:** Folk Dancer **Rev:** Cultural artifacts **Edge:** Plain

Date	Mintage	F	VF	XF	Unc	BU
2003 Proof	3,000	Value: 80.00				

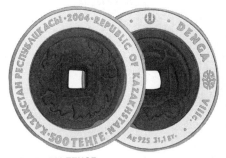

KM# 59   500 TENGE
31.1000 g., 0.9250 Bi-Metallic Blackend silver center in proof
silver ring 0.9249 oz., 38.6 mm.   **Subject:** "Denga" **Obv:** Black
square holed coin design above value **Rev:** Black square holed
coin design and metal content statement **Edge:** Reeded

Date	Mintage	F	VF	XF	Unc	BU
2004 Proof	5,000	Value: 90.00				

KM# 117   500 TENGE
31.1000 g., 0.9250 Silver partially gilt 0.9249 oz. ASW, 38.6 mm.
Obv: Three riders **Rev:** Golden deer ornament **Shape:** 12-sided

Date	Mintage	F	VF	XF	Unc	BU
2004 Proof	—	Value: 50.00				

KM# 60   500 TENGE
24.0000 g., 0.9250 Silver 0.7137 oz. ASW, 37 mm. **Obv:** Value
Rev: Prehistoric art horseman **Edge:** Plain

Date	Mintage	F	VF	XF	Unc	BU
2005 Proof	3,000	Value: 70.00				

KM# 61   500 TENGE
24.0000 g., 0.9250 Silver 0.7137 oz. ASW, 37 mm. **Obv:** Value
Rev: Two Goitered Gazelles **Edge:** Plain

Date	Mintage	F	VF	XF	Unc	BU
2005 Proof	3,000	Value: 70.00				

KM# 62   500 TENGE
31.1000 g., 0.9250 Silver 0.9249 oz. ASW, 38.6 mm.
Obv: Horse race and value **Rev:** Gold plated tiger **Edge:** Plain
Shape: 12-sided

Date	Mintage	F	VF	XF	Unc	BU
2005 Proof	5,000	Value: 120				

KM# 63   500 TENGE
31.1000 g., 0.9250 Bi-Metallic Blackened Silver center in proof
Silver ring 0.9249 oz., 38.6 mm.   **Subject:** "Drakhma" coin
Obv: Old coin design **Rev:** Old coin design **Edge:** Reeded

Date	Mintage	F	VF	XF	Unc	BU
2005 Proof	5,000	Value: 65.00				

KM# 72   500 TENGE
31.1000 g., 0.9250 Silver 0.9249 oz. ASW, 38.6 mm.
Obv: Horse race and value **Rev:** Gold plated rider **Edge:** Plain

Date	Mintage	F	VF	XF	Unc	BU
2005 Proof	5,000	Value: 100				

KM# 123   500 TENGE
31.1000 g., 0.9250 Silver partially gilt 0.9249 oz. ASW, 38.6 mm.
Obv: Three riders **Rev:** Tiger head sculpture **Shape:** 12-sided

Date	Mintage	F	VF	XF	Unc	BU
2005 Proof	—	Value: 50.00				

KM# 124   500 TENGE
24.0000 g., 0.9250 Silver 0.7137 oz. ASW, 37 mm. **Subject:**
Zhoshi Khan Mausoleum **Rev:** 3/4 view of building facade

Date	Mintage	F	VF	XF	Unc	BU
2005 Proof	—	Value: 50.00				

KM# 84   500 TENGE
31.1000 g., 0.9250 Bi-Metallic Blackened Silver center in proof
Silver ring. 0.9249 oz., 38.6 mm. **Subject:** "Dirkhem" coin **Obv:**
Old coin design **Rev:** Old coin design **Edge:** Reeded

Date	Mintage	F	VF	XF	Unc	BU
2006 Proof	5,000	Value: 65.00				

KM# 82   500 TENGE
41.4000 g., Bi-Metallic Sterling Silver ring., 38.61 mm.
Subject: 50th Anniversary Launch of Sputnik I **Obv:** Stylized view
of our solar system, multicolor **Obv. Legend:** REPUBLIC OF
KAZAKHSTAN **Rev:** Sputnik I in space, earth in background,
multicolor **Rev. Legend:** THE FIRST SPACE SATELLITE OF
THE EARTH **Edge:** Reeded

Date	Mintage	F	VF	XF	Unc	BU
ND(2007) Proof	4,000	Value: 100				

KM# 85   500 TENGE
31.1000 g., 0.9250 Bi-Metallic Blackened Silver center in proof
Silver ring. 0.9249 oz., 38.6 mm. **Subject:** "Otyrar" coin
Obv: Old coin design **Rev:** Old coin design **Edge:** Reeded

Date	Mintage	F	VF	XF	Unc	BU
2007 Proof	4,000	Value: 75.00				

KM# 87   500 TENGE
24.0000 g., 0.9250 Silver 0.7137 oz. ASW, 38.6 mm.
Obv: Value **Rev:** Terekin Valley - noble deer petraglyph

Date	Mintage	F	VF	XF	Unc	BU
2007 Proof	3,000	Value: 90.00				

KM# 88   500 TENGE
31.1000 g., 0.9250 Silver 0.9249 oz. ASW **Subject:** Movement
series - myth **Obv:** Value within square **Rev:** Design

Date	Mintage	F	VF	XF	Unc	BU
2007 Proof	4,000	Value: 80.00				

KM# 89   500 TENGE
31.1000 g., 0.9250 Silver 0.9249 oz. ASW, 38.6 mm.
Subject: Gold of the Romans **Obv:** Four horseman **Rev:** Gilt
Roman seal ring **Shape:** 12-sided

Date	Mintage	F	VF	XF	Unc	BU
2007 Proof	5,000	Value: 100				

KM# 93   500 TENGE
24.0000 g., 0.9250 Silver 0.7137 oz. ASW, 38.6 mm.
Subject: Spoon billed duck **Obv:** Value **Rev:** Duck in reeds

Date	Mintage	F	VF	XF	Unc	BU
2007 Proof	3,000	Value: 85.00				

KM# 101   500 TENGE
31.1050 g., 0.9250 Silver 0.9250 oz. ASW, 38.61 mm.
Subject: Nomad Gold **Rev:** Diadem fragment **Shape:** 12-sided

Date	Mintage	F	VF	XF	Unc	BU
2008 Proof	5,000	Value: 100				

KM# 90   500 TENGE
31.1000 g., 0.9250 Silver 0.9249 oz. ASW, 38.6 mm. **Obv:** State
emblem **Rev:** Church

Date	Mintage	F	VF	XF	Unc	BU
2007 Proof	4,000	Value: 75.00				

KM# 94   500 TENGE
31.1050 g., 0.9250 Silver 0.9250 oz. ASW, 38.6 mm. **Subject:**
National currency, 15th Anniversary **Obv:** Three coin designs

Date	Mintage	F	VF	XF	Unc	BU
2008 Proof	5,000	Value: 75.00				

KM# 102   500 TENGE
31.1050 g., 0.9250 Silver 0.9250 oz. ASW, 38.61 mm.
Subject: Kalmykov **Rev:** Fantasy scene

Date	Mintage	F	VF	XF	Unc	BU
2008 Proof	4,000	Value: 80.00				

KM# 91   500 TENGE
31.1000 g., 0.9250 Silver 0.9249 oz. ASW, 38.6 mm. **Obv:** State
emblem **Rev:** Traditional family

Date	Mintage	F	VF	XF	Unc	BU
2007 Proof	4,000	Value: 70.00				

KM# 99   500 TENGE
31.1050 g., 0.9250 Silver 0.9250 oz. ASW, 38.61 mm.
Subject: Eurasic Capitals - Astana **Rev:** Skyline montage

Date	Mintage	F	VF	XF	Unc	BU
2008 Proof	5,000	Value: 75.00				

KM# 103   500 TENGE
31.1050 g., 0.9250 Silver 0.9250 oz. ASW, 38.61 mm.
Subject: Kyz Kuu **Rev:** Two horseback riders

Date	Mintage	F	VF	XF	Unc	BU
2008 Proof	4,000	Value: 80.00				

KM# 92   500 TENGE
31.1000 g., 0.9250 Silver 0.9249 oz. ASW, 38.6 mm.
Obv: Leaves **Rev:** Tree growth rings, multicolor seeds

Date	Mintage	F	VF	XF	Unc	BU
2007 Proof	4,000	Value: 80.00				

KM# 100   500 TENGE
24.0000 g., 0.9250 Silver 0.7137 oz. ASW, 38.61 mm.
Subject: Tien Shan - Brown Bear **Rev:** Bear seated

Date	Mintage	F	VF	XF	Unc	BU
2008 Proof	3,000	Value: 85.00				

KM# 104   500 TENGE
31.1050 g., 0.9250 Silver 0.9250 oz. ASW, 38.61 mm.
Subject: Linum Olgae **Rev:** Flowers

Date	Mintage	F	VF	XF	Unc	BU
2008 Proof	4,000	Value: 100				

KM# 105   500 TENGE
31.1050 g., 0.9250 Silver 0.9250 oz. ASW, 38.61 mm.
Subject: National Currency, 15th Anniversary **Rev:** Coin and bank note montage

Date	Mintage	F	VF	XF	Unc	BU
2008 Proof	5,000	Value: 75.00				

KM# 106   500 TENGE
24.0000 g., 0.9250 Silver 0.7137 oz. ASW, 38.6x28.8 mm.
Subject: Papilio Alexanor **Rev:** Two butterflies **Shape:** oval

Date	Mintage	F	VF	XF	Unc	BU
2008 Proof	4,000	Value: 115				

KM# 107   500 TENGE
31.1050 g., 0.9250 Silver 0.9250 oz. ASW, 38.61 mm.
Subject: Saraichik Coin **Rev:** Coin of the 14th Century

Date	Mintage	F	VF	XF	Unc	BU
2008 Proof	5,000	Value: 75.00				

KM# 108   500 TENGE
41.4000 g., Bi-Metallic Silver and Titanium, 38.61 mm.
Subject: Vostok **Rev:** Space ship

Date	Mintage	F	VF	XF	Unc	BU
2008 Proof	4,000	Value: 110				

KM# 109   500 TENGE
31.1050 g., 0.9250 Silver 0.9250 oz. ASW, 38.61 mm.
Subject: Zharkent Mosque **Rev:** Mosque

Date	Mintage	F	VF	XF	Unc	BU
2008 Proof	400	Value: 75.00				

KM# 118   500 TENGE
24.0000 g., 0.9250 Silver 0.7137 oz. ASW, 37 mm.
Subject: Kazakhstan Railroads, 100th Anniversary **Obv:** Arms **Rev:** Modern train and Steam locomotive, country route map in background

Date	Mintage	F	VF	XF	Unc	BU
2008 Proof	—	Value: 50.00				

KM# 131   500 TENGE
31.1050 g., 0.9250 Silver 0.9250 oz. ASW, 38.61 mm.
Subject: Almaty Aport **Rev:** Apple tree branch and flower

Date	Mintage	F	VF	XF	Unc	BU
2009 Proof	4,000	Value: 80.00				

KM# 149   500 TENGE
31.1050 g., 0.9250 Silver 0.9250 oz. ASW, 38.61 mm.
Subject: Balkhash Tiger **Rev:** Tiger on the hunt

Date	Mintage	F	VF	XF	Unc	BU
2009 Proof	5,000	Value: 75.00				

KM# 133   500 TENGE
31.1050 g., 0.9990 Silver 0.9990 oz. ASW, 38.61 mm.
Subject: Betashar **Rev:** Two figures standing

Date	Mintage	F	VF	XF	Unc	BU
2009 Proof	4,000	Value: 75.00				

KM# 139   500 TENGE
31.1050 g., 0.9250 Silver 0.9250 oz. ASW, 38.6 mm.
Subject: Nur-Astana Mosque **Rev:** Mosque

Date	Mintage	F	VF	XF	Unc	BU
2009 Proof	4,000	Value: 75.00				

KM# 142   500 TENGE
24.0000 g., 0.9250 Silver 0.7137 oz. ASW, 38.61 mm.
Rev: Porcupine left with quills raised

Date	Mintage	F	VF	XF	Unc	BU
2009 Proof	3,000	Value: 90.00				

KM# 143   500 TENGE
31.1050 g., 0.9990 Silver 0.9990 oz. ASW, 38.61 mm. **Rev:** Satir head facing **Shape:** 12-sided

Date	Mintage	F	VF	XF	Unc	BU
2009 Proof	5,000	Value: 100				

KM# 130 500 TENGE
41.1000 g., Bi-Metallic Silver and Titanium, 38.61 mm.
Subject: Apollo - Soyoz Missions **Rev:** Spacecraft docked in orbit above the earth

Date	Mintage	F	VF	XF	Unc	BU
2009 Proof	4,000	Value: 115				

KM# 137 500 TENGE
31.1050 g., 0.9250 Silver 0.9250 oz. ASW, 38.61 mm.
Subject: Coin of Almaty **Rev:** 13th Century coin

Date	Mintage	F	VF	XF	Unc	BU
2009 Proof	4,000	Value: 100				

KM# 127 500 TENGE
7.7800 g., 0.9990 Gold 0.2499 oz. AGW, 25 mm.
Subject: Olympics - Biathlon **Obv:** Arms and stylized stadium **Rev:** Biathlon, skier and shooter

Date	Mintage	F	VF	XF	Unc	BU
2009 Proof	5,000	Value: 350				

KM# 128 500 TENGE
31.1000 g., 0.9990 Gold 0.9988 oz. AGW, 38.6 mm. **Subject:** Almaty Aport **Obv:** Value and leaves **Rev:** Apples and flower

Date	Mintage	F	VF	XF	Unc	BU
2009 Proof	4,000	—	—	—	—	50.00

KM# 129 500 TENGE
31.1000 g., 0.9250 Silver 0.9249 oz. ASW, 36.6 mm.
Subject: Alpamys Batyr **Obv:** Arms **Rev:** Historical figure

Date	Mintage	F	VF	XF	Unc	BU
2009 Proof	5,000	Value: 50.00				

KM# 138 500 TENGE
24.0000 g., 0.9250 Silver 0.7137 oz. ASW, 28.61x28.81 mm.
Subject: Flamingo **Obv:** Partial butterfly **Rev:** Pair of flamings standing in holographic water **Shape:** Vertical oval

Date	Mintage	F	VF	XF	Unc	BU
2009 Proof	4,000	Value: 40.00				

KM# 148 500 TENGE
7.7800 g., 0.9990 Gold 0.2499 oz. AGW, 21.87 mm. **Rev:** Tiger walking right

Date	Mintage	F	VF	XF	Unc	BU
2009 Proof	3,000	Value: 350				

KM# 150 500 TENGE
7.7800 g., 0.9990 Gold 0.2499 oz. AGW, 25 mm.
Subject: Uncia **Obv:** Arms **Rev:** Tiger head left

Date	Mintage	F	VF	XF	Unc	BU
2009 Proof	5,000	Value: 350				

KM# 68 1000 TENGE
7.7800 g., 0.9990 Gold 0.2499 oz. AGW, 20 mm. **Obv:** Two winged ibexes **Rev:** Ancient warrior **Edge:** Reeded

Date	Mintage	F	VF	XF	Unc	BU
2001 Proof	—	Value: 350				

KM# 114 1000 TENGE
67.2500 g., 0.9250 Silver 1.9999 oz. ASW, 50 mm.
Subject: National Currency, 10th Anniversary **Obv:** Flag, multicolor **Rev:** Coin and bank note designs

Date	Mintage	F	VF	XF	Unc	BU
2003 Proof	—	Value: 100				

KM# 115 1000 TENGE
67.2500 g., 0.9250 Silver 1.9999 oz. ASW, 50 mm.
Subject: National Currency, 10th Anniversary **Obv:** Arms, gilt and blue enamel **Rev:** Coin montage

Date	Mintage	F	VF	XF	Unc	BU
2003 Proof	—	Value: 100				

KM# 67 5000 TENGE
1000.0000 g., 0.9250 Silver 29.738 oz. ASW, 100 mm.
Subject: 10th Anniversary of Independence **Obv:** National arms above value **Rev:** Monument statue

Date	Mintage	F	VF	XF	Unc	BU
2001 Proof	—	Value: 650				

BULLION COINAGE

KM# 157 TENGE
3.1100 g., 0.9990 Gold 0.0999 oz. AGW **Obv:** Arms **Rev:** Tiger standing right on rock

Date	Mintage	F	VF	XF	Unc	BU
2009	—	—	—	—	—	150

KM# 161 TENGE
31.1050 g., 0.9990 Silver 0.9990 oz. ASW, 38.61 mm.
Obv: Arms **Rev:** Tiger standing right on rock

Date	Mintage	F	VF	XF	Unc	BU
2009	—	—	—	—	—	30.00

KM# 160   2 TENGE
64.2100 g., 0.9990 Silver 2.0622 oz. ASW **Obv:** Arms
Rev: Tiger standing right on rock **Shape:** 50

Date	Mintage	F	VF	XF	Unc	BU
2009	—	—	—	—	—	50.00

KM# 159   5 TENGE
155.0000 g., 0.9990 Silver 4.9782 oz. ASW, 65 mm. **Obv:** Arms
Rev: Tiger standing right on rock

Date	Mintage	F	VF	XF	Unc	BU
2009	—	—	—	—	—	125

KM# 158   10 TENGE
31.1050 g., 0.9990 Silver 0.9990 oz. ASW **Obv:** Arms
Rev: Tiger standing right on rock

Date	Mintage	F	VF	XF	Unc	BU
2009	—	—	—	—	—	30.00

KM# 156   20 TENGE
7.7800 g., 0.9990 Gold 0.2499 oz. AGW **Obv:** Arms **Rev:** Tiger
standing right on rock

Date	Mintage	F	VF	XF	Unc	BU
2009	—	—	—	—	—	350

KM# 155   50 TENGE
15.5500 g., 0.9990 Gold 0.4994 oz. AGW, 25 mm. **Obv:** Arms
Rev: Tiger standing right on rock

Date	Mintage	F	VF	XF	Unc	BU
2009	—	—	—	—	—	650

KM# 154   100 TENGE
31.1050 g., 0.9990 Gold 0.9990 oz. AGW, 32 mm. **Obv:** Arms
Rev: Tiger standing right on rock

Date	Mintage	F	VF	XF	Unc	BU
2009	—	—	—	—	—	1,300

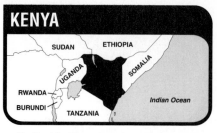

The Republic of Kenya, located on the east coast of Central
Africa, has an area of 224,961 sq. mi (582,650 sq. km.) and a population of 20.1 million. Capital: Nairobi. The predominantly agricultural country exports coffee, tea and petroleum products.
    Independence was attained on Dec. 12, 1963. Kenya
became a republic in 1964. It is a member of the Commonwealth
of Nations. The president is Chief of State and Head of Government.

MONETARY SYSTEM
100 Cents = 1 Shilling

REPUBLIC
STANDARD COINAGE

KM# 39   5 CENTS
Copper Clad Steel **Subject:** First President **Obv:** National arms
Rev: Bust of Mzee Jomo Kenyatta left **Note:** Initially a planned
issue, abandoned prior to release for circulation.

Date	Mintage	F	VF	XF	Unc	BU
2005	—					

KM# 40   10 CENTS
Copper Clad Steel **Subject:** First President **Obv:** National arms
Rev: Bust of Mzee Jomo Kenyatta left **Note:** Initially a planned
issue, abandoned prior to release for circulation.

Date	Mintage	F	VF	XF	Unc	BU
2005	—					

KM# 41   50 CENTS
Copper Clad Steel **Subject:** First President **Obv:** National arms,
value **Rev:** Bust of Mwee Jomo Kenyatta left

Date	Mintage	F	VF	XF	Unc	BU
2005	—				0.60	0.80

KM# 34   SHILLING
5.4600 g., Nickel Clad Steel, 23.9 mm. **Subject:** First President
Obv: Value above national arms **Rev:** Bust of President Mzee
Jomo Kenyata left **Edge:** Segmented reeding

Date	Mintage	F	VF	XF	Unc	BU
2005	—	—	—	—	0.80	1.20

KM# 37   5 SHILLINGS
3.7000 g., Bi-Metallic Brass center in Copper-Nickel ring,
19.49 mm. **Subject:** First President **Obv:** Value above national
arms **Obv. Legend:** REPUBLIC OF KENYA **Rev:** Bust of
President Mzee Jomo Kenyatta left **Edge:** Reeded

Date	Mintage	F	VF	XF	Unc	BU
2005	—	—	—	0.60	1.50	2.00

KM# 35   10 SHILLINGS
5.0300 g., Bi-Metallic Copper-Nickel center in Aluminum-Nickel-Bronze ring, 22.95 mm.   **Subject:** First President **Obv:** Value above national arms **Obv. Legend:** REPUBLIC OF KENYA **Rev:** Bust of Mzee Jomo Kenyatta left **Edge:** Reeded

Date	Mintage	F	VF	XF	Unc	BU
2005	—	—	—	0.90	2.25	3.00

KM# 36   20 SHILLINGS
9.0200 g., Bi-Metallic Aluminum-Nickel-Bronze center in copper-Nickel ring, 25.97 mm.   **Subject:** First President **Obv:** Large value above national arms **Obv. Legend:** REPUBLIC OF KENYA **Rev:** Bust of President Mzee Jomo Kenyatta left **Edge:** Segmented reeding

Date	Mintage	F	VF	XF	Unc	BU
2005	—	—	—	1.20	3.00	4.00

KM# 33   40 SHILLINGS
11.1000 g., Bi-Metallic Copper-Nickel center in Aluminum-Nickel-Bronze ring, 27.4 mm.   **Obv:** Bust of H. E. Mwai Kibaki facing **Rev:** National arms, value below **Edge:** Reeded and lettered **Edge Lettering:** "40 YEARS OF INDEPENDENCE" **Note:** Issued December 11, 2003.

Date	Mintage	F	VF	XF	Unc	BU
ND(2003)	—	—	—	—	6.00	7.50

KM# 38   1000 SHILLINGS
31.1030 g., 0.9250 Silver 0.9249 oz. ASW, 38.61 mm.
Subject: 40th Anniversary Independence **Obv:** National arms **Rev:** Bust of President H. E. Mwai Kibaki facing

Date	Mintage	F	VF	XF	Unc	BU
ND(2003) Proof	—	Value: 60.00				

KIRIBATI

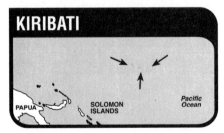

The Republic of Kiribati (formerly the Gilbert Islands), consists of 30 coral atolls and islands spread over more than one million sq. mi. (2,590,000 sq. km.) of the southwest Pacific Ocean, has an area of 332 sq. mi. (717 sq. km.) and a population of 64,200. Capital: Bairiki, on Tarawa. In addition to the Gilbert Islands proper, Kiribati includes Ocean Island, the Central and Southern Line Islands, and the Phoenix Islands, though possession of Canton and Enderbury of the Phoenix Islands is disputed with the United States. Most families engage in subsistence fishing. Copra and phosphates are exported, mostly to Australia and New Zealand.

Kiribati is a member of the Commonwealth of Nations. The President is the Head of State and Head of Government.

MONETARY SYSTEM
100 Cents = 1 Dollar

REPUBLIC
DECIMAL COINAGE

KM# 40   5 CENTS
4.2400 g., Brass, 22.9 mm.   **Obv:** National arms **Rev:** Gorilla **Edge:** Reeded

Date	Mintage	F	VF	XF	Unc	BU
2003	—	—	—	—	1.00	1.50

NORTH KOREA

The Democratic Peoples Republic of Korea, situated in northeastern Asia on the northern half of the Korean peninsula between the Peoples Republic of China and the Republic of Korea, has an area of 46,540 sq. mi. (120,540 sq. km.) and a population of 20 million. Capital: Pyongyang. The economy is based on heavy industry and agriculture. Metals, minerals and farm produce are exported.

MONETARY SYSTEM
100 Chon = 1 Won

MINT
Pyongyang

DATING
In the year 2001 the North Korean adopted the "Juche" dating system which is based on the birth year of Kim Il Sung, founder of North Korea. He was born in 1911. "Quel" refers to month and "Quil" refers to day. 9 Quel 3 Quil refers to September 3rd. The western dates on these coins follow the "Juche" date in parenthesis.

PEOPLES REPUBLIC
DECIMAL COINAGE

KM# 183   1/2 CHON
2.1600 g., Aluminum, 27.02 mm.   **Obv:** State arms **Rev:** Horse **Edge:** Plain

Date	Mintage	F	VF	XF	Unc	BU
2002	—	—	—	—	1.25	1.50

KM# 184   1/2 CHON
2.1600 g., Aluminum, 27.02 mm.   **Obv:** State arms **Rev:** Orangutan **Edge:** Plain

Date	Mintage	F	VF	XF	Unc	BU
2002	—	—	—	—	1.25	1.50

KM# 185   1/2 CHON
2.1600 g., Aluminum, 27.02 mm.   **Obv:** State arms **Rev:** Leopard **Edge:** Plain

Date	Mintage	F	VF	XF	Unc	BU
2002	—	—	—	—	1.25	1.50

KM# 186   1/2 CHON
2.1600 g., Aluminum, 27.02 mm.   **Obv:** State arms **Rev:** Two giraffes **Edge:** Plain

Date	Mintage	F	VF	XF	Unc	BU
2002	—	—	—	—	1.25	1.50

KM# 187   1/2 CHON
2.1600 g., Aluminum, 27.02 mm.   **Obv:** State arms **Rev:** Helmeted guineafowl **Edge:** Plain

Date	Mintage	F	VF	XF	Unc	BU
2002	—	—	—	—	1.25	1.50

KM# 188   1/2 CHON
2.1600 g., Aluminum, 27.02 mm.   **Obv:** State arms **Rev:** Mamushi pit viper **Edge:** Plain

Date	Mintage	F	VF	XF	Unc	BU
2002	—	—	—	—	1.25	1.50

KM# 189   1/2 CHON
2.1600 g., Aluminum, 27.02 mm.   **Obv:** State arms **Rev:** Bighorn sheep **Edge:** Plain

Date	Mintage	F	VF	XF	Unc	BU
2002	—	—	—	—	1.25	1.50

KM# 190   1/2 CHON
2.1600 g., Aluminum, 27.02 mm.   **Obv:** State arms **Rev:** Hippopotamus **Edge:** Plain

Date	Mintage	F	VF	XF	Unc	BU
2002	—	—	—	—	1.25	1.50

KM# 191   1/2 CHON

2.1600 g., Aluminum, 27.02 mm. **Subject:** FAO **Obv:** State arms
Rev: Ancient ship **Edge:** Plain

Date	Mintage	F	VF	XF	Unc	BU
2002	—	—	—	—	1.25	1.50

KM# 192   1/2 CHON

2.1600 g., Aluminum, 27.02 mm. **Subject:** FAO **Obv:** State arms
Rev: Archaic ship **Edge:** Plain

Date	Mintage	F	VF	XF	Unc	BU
2002	—	—	—	—	1.25	1.50

KM# 193   1/2 CHON

2.1600 g., Aluminum, 27.02 mm. **Subject:** FAO **Obv:** State arms
Rev: Modern train **Edge:** Plain

Date	Mintage	F	VF	XF	Unc	BU
2002	—	—	—	—	1.25	1.50

KM# 194   1/2 CHON

2.1600 g., Aluminum, 27.02 mm. **Subject:** FAO **Obv:** State arms
Rev: Jet airliner **Edge:** Plain

Date	Mintage	F	VF	XF	Unc	BU
2002	—	—	—	—	1.25	1.50

KM# 195   CHON

4.6300 g., Brass, 21.7 mm. **Subject:** FAO **Obv:** State arms
Rev: Antique steam locomotive **Edge:** Plain

Date	Mintage	F	VF	XF	Unc	BU
2002	—	—	—	—	1.50	1.75

KM# 196   CHON

4.6300 g., Brass, 21.7 mm. **Subject:** FAO **Obv:** State arms
Rev: Antique automobile **Edge:** Plain

Date	Mintage	F	VF	XF	Unc	BU
2002	—	—	—	—	1.50	1.75

KM# 197   2 CHON

6.0400 g., Copper-Nickel, 24.2 mm. **Subject:** FAO **Obv:** State
arms **Rev:** Antique touring car **Edge:** Plain

Date	Mintage	F	VF	XF	Unc	BU
2002	—	—	—	—	2.00	2.50

KM# 162.2   WON

7.0000 g., Aluminum, 40 mm. **Obv:** State arms, date above
value **Rev:** Radiant Korean map and landmarks **Edge:** Plain

Date	Mintage	F	VF	XF	Unc	BU
2001 Proof	—	Value: 15.00				

KM# 351   WON

7.0000 g., Aluminum, 40 mm. **Obv:** State arms, date and value
below **Rev:** North Korean Arch of Triumph **Edge:** Plain

Date	Mintage	F	VF	XF	Unc	BU
2001 Proof	—	Value: 12.00				

KM# 352   WON

28.6000 g., Brass, 40.1 mm. **Obv:** State arms, value below
Rev: North Korean Arch of Triumph **Edge:** Plain

Date	Mintage	F	VF	XF	Unc	BU
2001 Proof	—	Value: 15.00				

KM# 353   WON

6.4500 g., Aluminum, 40 mm. **Obv:** State arms, value below
Rev: N. Korean landmarks and tourists above ship **Edge:** Plain

Date	Mintage	F	VF	XF	Unc	BU
2001 Proof	—	Value: 12.00				

KM# 354   WON

27.6300 g., Brass, 40 mm. **Obv:** State arms, date and value
below **Rev:** N. Korean landmarks and tourists above ship
Edge: Plain

Date	Mintage	F	VF	XF	Unc	BU
2001 Proof	—	Value: 15.00				

KM# 355   WON

6.7500 g., Aluminum, 40 mm. **Obv:** State arms, value below
Rev: Temple of Heaven above Hong Kong city view below
Edge: Plain

Date	Mintage	F	VF	XF	Unc	BU
ND Proof	—	Value: 12.00				

KM# 356   WON

28.1000 g., Brass, 40 mm. **Obv:** State arms, date and value
below **Rev:** Temple of Heaven above, Hong Kong city view below
Edge: Plain

Date	Mintage	F	VF	XF	Unc	BU
2001 Proof	—	Value: 15.00				

KM# 294a   WON

6.7500 g., Aluminum, 40 mm. **Obv:** State arms **Rev:** Antique
ceramics **Edge:** Plain

Date	Mintage	F	VF	XF	Unc	BU
2001 Proof	—	Value: 15.00				

KM# 358   WON

6.7500 g., Aluminum, 40 mm. **Obv:** State arms **Rev:** Old fort
Edge: Plain

Date	Mintage	F	VF	XF	Unc	BU
2001 Proof	—	Value: 12.00				

KM# 358a   WON

28.1000 g., Brass, 40 mm. **Obv:** State arms **Rev:** Old fort

Date	Mintage	F	VF	XF	Unc	BU
2001 Proof	—	Value: 15.00				

KM# 359   WON

7.0000 g., Aluminum, 40.1 mm. **Obv:** State arms **Rev:** Old
couple above dates 1945-2000 **Edge:** Plain

Date	Mintage	F	VF	XF	Unc	BU
2001 Proof	—	Value: 12.00				

KM# 359a   WON

27.8000 g., Brass, 40.1 mm. **Obv:** State arms **Rev:** Old couple
above dates 1945-2000 **Edge:** Plain

Date	Mintage	F	VF	XF	Unc	BU
2001 Proof	—	Value: 15.00				

KM# 360   WON

27.8000 g., Brass, 40.1 mm. **Obv:** State arms **Rev:** Blue Dragon
Edge: Plain

Date	Mintage	F	VF	XF	Unc	BU
2001 Proof	—	Value: 20.00				

KM# 361   WON

7.0000 g., Aluminum, 40.1 mm. **Obv:** State arms **Rev:** Head
3/4 left divides dates (1904-1997) flanked by sprigs **Edge:** Plain

Date	Mintage	F	VF	XF	Unc	BU
2001 Proof	—	Value: 12.00				

KM# 361a   WON

27.8000 g., Brass, 40.1 mm. **Obv:** State arms **Rev:** Head 3/4
left divides dates(1904-1997) flanked by sprigs **Edge:** Plain

Date	Mintage	F	VF	XF	Unc	BU
2001 Proof	—	Value: 15.00				

KM# 362 WON
7.0000 g., Aluminum, 40.1 mm. **Obv:** State arms **Rev:** Children flying a kite **Edge:** Plain

Date	Mintage	F	VF	XF	Unc	BU
2001 Proof	—				Value: 15.00	

KM# 362a WON
27.8000 g., Brass, 40.1 mm. **Obv:** State arms **Rev:** Children flying a kite **Edge:** Plain

Date	Mintage	F	VF	XF	Unc	BU
2001 Proof	—				Value: 17.50	

KM# 363 WON
7.0000 g., Aluminum, 40.1 mm. **Obv:** State arms **Rev:** Children on seesaw **Edge:** Plain

Date	Mintage	F	VF	XF	Unc	BU
2001 Proof	—				Value: 15.00	

KM# 363a WON
27.8000 g., Brass, 40.1 mm. **Obv:** State arms **Rev:** Children on seesaw **Edge:** Plain

Date	Mintage	F	VF	XF	Unc	BU
2001 Proof	—				Value: 17.50	

KM# 364 WON
7.0000 g., Aluminum, 40.1 mm. **Obv:** State arms **Rev:** Children wrestling **Edge:** Plain

Date	Mintage	F	VF	XF	Unc	BU
2001 Proof	—				Value: 15.00	

KM# 364a WON
27.8000 g., Brass, 40.1 mm. **Obv:** State arms **Rev:** Children wrestling **Edge:** Plain

Date	Mintage	F	VF	XF	Unc	BU
2001 Proof	—					

KM# 365 WON
7.0000 g., Aluminum, 40.1 mm. **Obv:** State arms **Rev:** Girl on swing **Edge:** Plain

Date	Mintage	F	VF	XF	Unc	BU
2001 Proof	—				Value: 15.00	

KM# 365a WON
27.8000 g., Brass, 40.1 mm. **Obv:** State arms **Rev:** Girl on swing **Edge:** Plain

Date	Mintage	F	VF	XF	Unc	BU
2001 Proof	—				Value: 17.50	

KM# 366 WON
7.0000 g., Aluminum, 40.1 mm. **Obv:** State arms **Rev:** Girls jumping rope **Edge:** Plain

Date	Mintage	F	VF	XF	Unc	BU
2001 Proof	—				Value: 15.00	

KM# 366a WON
27.8000 g., Brass, 40.1 mm. **Obv:** State arms **Rev:** Girls jumping rope **Edge:** Plain

Date	Mintage	F	VF	XF	Unc	BU
2001 Proof	—				Value: 17.50	

KM# 367 WON
8.7000 g., Aluminum, 40.4 mm. **Obv:** State arms **Rev:** "Kumdang-2 Injection" in center square on leaves **Edge:** Plain

Date	Mintage	F	VF	XF	Unc	BU
2001 Proof	—				Value: 15.00	

KM# 367a WON
26.5400 g., Brass, 40.2 mm. **Obv:** State arms **Rev:** "Kumdang-2 Injection" in center square on leaves **Edge:** Plain

Date	Mintage	F	VF	XF	Unc	BU
2001 Proof	—				Value: 17.50	

KM# 368 WON
27.6100 g., Brass, 40.2 mm. **Obv:** State arms **Rev:** Bust facing divides dates(1912-1994) above sprigs **Edge:** Plain

Date	Mintage	F	VF	XF	Unc	BU
JU90-2001 Proof	—				Value: 17.50	

KM# 369 WON
6.5500 g., Aluminum, 40.4 mm. **Obv:** State arms **Rev:** Train at left, couple below jet plane at right **Edge:** Plain

Date	Mintage	F	VF	XF	Unc	BU
2001 Proof	—				Value: 15.00	

KM# 370 WON
27.5600 g., Brass, 40.1 mm. **Obv:** State arms **Rev:** Train at left, couple below jet plane at right **Edge:** Plain

Date	Mintage	F	VF	XF	Unc	BU
2001 Proof	—				Value: 17.50	

KM# 371 WON
5.0500 g., Aluminum, 35 mm. **Obv:** State arms **Rev:** Hong Kong city view **Edge:** Plain

Date	Mintage	F	VF	XF	Unc	BU
2001 Proof	—				Value: 10.00	

KM# 372   WON
6.4000 g., Aluminum, 40 mm. **Obv:** State arms **Rev:** Bust with beard facing flanked by text **Edge:** Plain

Date	Mintage	F	VF	XF	Unc	BU
2001 Proof	—	Value: 12.00				

KM# 372a   WON
27.7000 g., Brass, 40 mm. **Obv:** State arms **Rev:** Bust with beard facing flanked by text **Edge:** Plain

Date	Mintage	F	VF	XF	Unc	BU
2001 Proof	—	Value: 15.00				

KM# 373   WON
6.9000 g., Aluminum, 40 mm. **Subject:** 1996 Olympics **Obv:** State arms **Rev:** Two green gymnasts and multicolor flame **Edge:** Plain

Date	Mintage	F	VF	XF	Unc	BU
2001 Proof	—	Value: 15.00				

KM# 374   WON
7.0000 g., Aluminum, 40 mm. **Obv:** State arms **Rev:** Taedong Gatehouse **Edge:** Plain

Date	Mintage	F	VF	XF	Unc	BU
2001 Proof	—	Value: 15.00				

KM# 375   WON
8.5000 g., Aluminum, 40.2 mm. **Obv:** State arms **Rev:** Tourists above volcano crater **Edge:** Plain

Date	Mintage	F	VF	XF	Unc	BU
JU90-2001 Proof	—	Value: 10.00				

KM# 238a   WON
7.1400 g., Aluminum, 40.1 mm. **Obv:** State arms **Rev:** Tiger and cub **Edge:** Plain

Date	Mintage	F	VF	XF	Unc	BU
2001 Proof	—	Value: 17.00				

KM# 376   WON
7.1000 g., Aluminum, 40.1 mm. **Subject:** 1996 Olympics **Obv:** State arms **Rev:** Horse jumping **Edge:** Plain

Date	Mintage	F	VF	XF	Unc	BU
2001 Proof	—	Value: 15.00				

KM# 377   WON
7.0000 g., Aluminum, 40.1 mm. **Subject:** 1996 Olympics **Obv:** State arms **Rev:** Four runners **Edge:** Plain

Date	Mintage	F	VF	XF	Unc	BU
2001 Proof	—	Value: 15.00				

KM# 378   WON
6.8400 g., Aluminum, 40.1 mm. **Obv:** State arms **Rev:** Monument flanked by multicolor flags and flowers **Edge:** Plain

Date	Mintage	F	VF	XF	Unc	BU
2001 Proof	—	Value: 12.00				

KM# 379   WON
6.6000 g., Aluminum, 40.1 mm. **Obv:** State arms **Rev:** Olympic diver **Edge:** Plain

Date	Mintage	F	VF	XF	Unc	BU
2001 Proof	—	Value: 15.00				

KM# 380   WON
6.9100 g., Aluminum, 40.1 mm. **Obv:** State arms **Rev:** Olympic handball player **Edge:** Plain

Date	Mintage	F	VF	XF	Unc	BU
2001 Proof	—	Value: 15.00				

KM# 381   WON
7.1100 g., Aluminum, 40.2 mm. **Obv:** State arms **Rev:** Olympic high bar gymnast **Edge:** Plain

Date	Mintage	F	VF	XF	Unc	BU
2001 Proof	—	Value: 15.00				

KM# 381a   WON
28.8200 g., Brass, 40.1 mm. **Obv:** State arms **Rev:** Olympic high bar gymnast **Edge:** Plain

Date	Mintage	F	VF	XF	Unc	BU
2001 Proof	—	Value: 17.50				

KM# 382   WON
6.5000 g., Aluminum, 40.1 mm. **Obv:** State arms **Rev:** Olympic archer **Edge:** Plain

Date	Mintage	F	VF	XF	Unc	BU
2001 Proof	—	Value: 15.00				

KM# 382a   WON
27.4100 g., Brass, 40.2 mm. **Obv:** State arms **Rev:** Olympic archer **Edge:** Plain

Date	Mintage	F	VF	XF	Unc	BU
2001 Proof	—	Value: 17.50				

KM# 383 WON
7.1000 g., Aluminum, 40.1 mm. **Obv:** State arms **Rev:** Olympic hurdler **Edge:** Plain

Date	Mintage	F	VF	XF	Unc	BU
2001 Proof	—	Value: 15.00				

KM# 383a WON
28.0000 g., Brass, 40.1 mm. **Obv:** State arms **Rev:** Olympic hurdler **Edge:** Plain

Date	Mintage	F	VF	XF	Unc	BU
2001 Proof	—	Value: 17.50				

KM# 384 WON
7.1500 g., Aluminum, 40.1 mm. **Obv:** State arms **Rev:** Kim Il Sung's birthplace side view **Edge:** Plain

Date	Mintage	F	VF	XF	Unc	BU
JU90-2001 Proof	—	Value: 15.00				

KM# 385 WON
7.0000 g., Aluminum, 40.1 mm. **Obv:** State arms **Rev:** Mt. Kumgang Fairy playing flute **Edge:** Plain

Date	Mintage	F	VF	XF	Unc	BU
2001 Proof	—	Value: 12.00				

KM# 385a WON
28.1600 g., Brass, 40.2 mm. **Obv:** State arms **Rev:** Mt. Kumgang Fairy playing flute **Edge:** Plain

Date	Mintage	F	VF	XF	Unc	BU
2001 Proof	—	Value: 15.00				

KM# 290 WON
28.2000 g., Brass, 40.1 mm. **Obv:** State arms **Rev:** Bust facing above flower sprigs **Edge:** Plain

Date	Mintage	F	VF	XF	Unc	BU
JU90-2001 Proof	—	Value: 20.00				

KM# 291 WON
28.2000 g., Brass, 40.1 mm. **Obv:** State arms **Rev:** Bust facing divides dates (1917-1949) above flower sprigs **Edge:** Plain

Date	Mintage	F	VF	XF	Unc	BU
JU90-2001 Proof	—	Value: 20.00				

KM# 293 WON
28.2000 g., Brass, 40.2 mm. **Obv:** State arms **Rev:** Olympic runners **Edge:** Crude reeding

Date	Mintage	F	VF	XF	Unc	BU
2001 Proof	—	Value: 20.00				

KM# 294 WON
28.2000 g., Brass, 40.2 mm. **Obv:** State arms **Rev:** Antique porcelain objects **Edge:** Plain

Date	Mintage	F	VF	XF	Unc	BU
2001 Proof	—	Value: 20.00				

KM# 458 WON
Brass, 35 mm. **Subject:** Tall ships **Obv:** Arms **Rev:** Krugenstern

Date	Mintage	F	VF	XF	Unc	BU
2001 Proof	—	Value: 8.00				

KM# 459 WON
Brass, 35 mm. **Subject:** Return of Hong Kong **Obv:** Arms **Rev:** Architecture

Date	Mintage	F	VF	XF	Unc	BU
2001 Proof	—	Value: 6.50				

KM# 460 WON
Brass, 35 mm. **Subject:** Return of Hong Kong **Obv:** Skyline **Rev:** Dragon boat

Date	Mintage	F	VF	XF	Unc	BU
2001 Proof	—	Value: 12.00				

KM# 461 WON
Brass **Subject:** 2002 Olympics **Obv:** Arms **Rev:** Speedskater

Date	Mintage	F	VF	XF	Unc	BU
2001 Proof	—	Value: 10.00				

KM# 462 WON
Aluminum, 40 mm. **Subject:** Tae Kwon do **Obv:** Arms **Rev:** Two sportsmen

Date	Mintage	F	VF	XF	Unc	BU
2001 Proof	—	Value: 8.00				

KM# 463 WON
Aluminum, 40 mm. **Obv:** Arms **Rev:** Multicolor flowers

Date	Mintage	F	VF	XF	Unc	BU
2001 Proof	—	Value: 8.00				

KM# 464 WON
Aluminum, 40 mm. **Obv:** Arms **Rev:** Wood pecker on branch (Dryocopus Javensis)

Date	Mintage	F	VF	XF	Unc	BU
2001 Proof	—	Value: 8.00				

KM# 465 WON
Aluminum, 35 mm. **Obv:** Arms **Rev:** Zhou Enlai portrait facing

Date	Mintage	F	VF	XF	Unc	BU
2001 Proof	—	Value: 8.00				

KM# 466 WON
Aluminum, 40 mm. **Obv:** Arms **Rev:** Buddha seated, facing

Date	Mintage	F	VF	XF	Unc	BU
2001 Proof	—	Value: 7.00				

KM# 467 WON
Brass **Obv:** Arms **Rev:** Buddha seated, facing

Date	Mintage	F	VF	XF	Unc	BU
2001 Proof	—	Value: 10.00				

KM# 468 WON
Brass **Obv:** Arms **Rev:** Couple embracing, 1945-2000

Date	Mintage	F	VF	XF	Unc	BU
ND(2001) Proof	—	Value: 10.00				

KM# 236a WON
7.0000 g., Aluminum, 40 mm. **Obv:** State arms **Rev:** "Hyonmu" **Edge:** Plain

Date	Mintage	F	VF	XF	Unc	BU
2001 Proof	—	Value: 17.50				

KM# 452 WON
27.4400 g., Brass, 40 mm. **Obv:** State arms **Rev:** Early sailing ship **Rev. Legend:** • HISTORY OF SEAFARING • MERCHANTMAN - THE DPR KOREA . KORYO PERIOD . 918-1392 **Edge:** Plain

Date	Mintage	F	VF	XF	Unc	BU
2001 Proof	—	Value: 9.00				

KM# 157 WON
6.7000 g., Aluminum, 40 mm. **Subject:** Seafaring Ships **Obv:** State arms **Rev:** Cruise ship below sryilized head left profile **Edge:** Plain

Date	Mintage	F	VF	XF	Unc	BU
JU90-2001 Proof	—	Value: 10.00				

KM# 157a WON
29.0500 g., Brass, 40.2 mm. **Obv:** State arms **Rev:** Cruise ship below stylized head profile left **Edge:** Plain

Date	Mintage	F	VF	XF	Unc	BU
2001 Proof	—	Value: 17.50				

KM# 158   WON
16.2000 g., Brass, 35 mm.   **Subject:** First Nobel Prize Winner in Literature **Obv:** State arms **Rev:** Half length seated bust left flanked by shelves and books **Edge:** Plain

Date	Mintage	F	VF	XF	Unc	BU
ND(2001) Proof	—	Value: 10.00				

KM# 158a   WON
17.0000 g., Copper-Nickel, 35 mm.   **Subject:** First Nobel Prize Winner in Literature - Sully Prudhomme **Obv:** State arms **Rev:** Half length seated bust left flanked by shelves and books **Edge:** Plain

Date	Mintage	F	VF	XF	Unc	BU
ND(2001) Proof	2,000	Value: 100				

KM# 159   WON
16.2000 g., Brass, 35 mm.   **Subject:** First Nobel Prize in Physics **Obv:** State arms **Rev:** Bust 3/4 right at left with same person seated in lab at right **Edge:** Plain

Date	Mintage	F	VF	XF	Unc	BU
ND(2001) Proof	—	Value: 10.00				

KM# 159a   WON
17.0000 g., Copper-Nickel, 35 mm.   **Subject:** First Nobel Prize Winner in Physics - Wilhelm C. Roentgen **Obv:** State arms **Rev:** Bust 3/4 right at left with same person seated in lab at right **Edge:** Plain

Date	Mintage	F	VF	XF	Unc	BU
ND(2001) Proof	2,000	Value: 100				

KM# 160   WON
16.2000 g., Brass, 35 mm.   **Subject:** Nipponia Nippon **Obv:** State arms **Rev:** Two nest building Japanese ibis **Edge:** Plain

Date	Mintage	F	VF	XF	Unc	BU
JU90-2001 Proof	—	Value: 15.00				

KM# 160a   WON
17.0000 g., Copper-Nickel, 35 mm.   **Subject:** Wildlife **Obv:** State arms **Rev:** Two nesting Japanese Ibis birds **Edge:** Plain

Date	Mintage	F	VF	XF	Unc	BU
JU2001 Proof	200	Value: 100				

KM# 160b   WON
5.3500 g., Aluminum, 35.1 mm.   **Obv:** State arms **Rev:** Two nest building Japanese Ibis birds **Edge:** Plain

Date	Mintage	F	VF	XF	Unc	BU
JU90-2001 Proof	—	Value: 15.00				

KM# 202   WON
17.0000 g., Copper-Nickel, 35 mm.   **Subject:** School Ships **Obv:** State arms **Rev:** SS Krusenstern **Edge:** Plain

Date	Mintage	F	VF	XF	Unc	BU
ND(2001) Proof	200	Value: 100				

KM# 204   WON
17.0000 g., Copper-Nickel, 35 mm.   **Subject:** Wildlife **Obv:** State arms **Rev:** Two standing Japanese Ibis birds **Edge:** Plain

Date	Mintage	F	VF	XF	Unc	BU
JU90-2001 Proof	100	Value: 150				

KM# 207   WON
17.0000 g., Copper-Nickel, 35 mm.   **Subject:** Wildlife **Obv:** State arms **Rev:** Two Korean Longtail Gorals **Edge:** Plain

Date	Mintage	F	VF	XF	Unc	BU
JU90-2001 Proof	200	Value: 100				

KM# 207a   WON
16.0500 g., Brass, 35 mm.   **Obv:** State arms **Rev:** Two Longtail Gorals **Edge:** Plain

Date	Mintage	F	VF	XF	Unc	BU
JU90-2001 Proof	—	Value: 12.50				

KM# 207b   WON
5.3500 g., Aluminum, 35.1 mm.   **Obv:** State arms **Rev:** Two Longtail Gorals **Edge:** Plain

Date	Mintage	F	VF	XF	Unc	BU
JU90-2001 Proof	—	Value: 10.00				

KM# 209   WON
17.0000 g., Copper-Nickel, 35 mm.   **Subject:** First Nobel Prize Winner in Medicine - Emil A. von Behring **Obv:** State arms **Rev:** Lab beaker divides half length figures facing each other **Edge:** Plain

Date	Mintage	F	VF	XF	Unc	BU
ND(2001) Proof	2,000	Value: 100				

KM# 210   WON
17.0000 g., Copper-Nickel, 35 mm.   **Subject:** First Nobel Prize Winner in Peace - Henri Dunant **Obv:** State arms **Rev:** Bust facing at left, war wounded at right **Edge:** Plain

Date	Mintage	F	VF	XF	Unc	BU
ND(2001) Proof	2,000	Value: 100				

KM# 211   WON
17.0000 g., Copper-Nickel, 35 mm.   **Subject:** First Nobel Prize Winner in Chemistry - Jacobus Van't Hoff **Obv:** State arms **Rev:** Standing figures in lab scene **Edge:** Plain

Date	Mintage	F	VF	XF	Unc	BU
ND(2001) Proof	2,000	Value: 100				

KM# 212   WON
17.0000 g., Copper-Nickel, 35 mm.   **Subject:** First Nobel Prize Winner in Peace - Frederic Passy **Obv:** State arms **Rev:** Head left at right with allegorical scene at left **Edge:** Plain

Date	Mintage	F	VF	XF	Unc	BU
ND(2001) Proof	2,000	Value: 100				

KM# 232   WON
28.1100 g., Brass, 40 mm.   **Obv:** State arms **Rev:** White-bellied woodpecker **Edge:** Plain

Date	Mintage	F	VF	XF	Unc	BU
2001 Proof	—	Value: 27.50				

KM# 233   WON
28.1100 g., Brass, 40 mm.   **Obv:** State arms **Rev:** Black grouse **Edge:** Plain

Date	Mintage	F	VF	XF	Unc	BU
2001 Proof	—	Value: 27.50				

KM# 234 WON
28.1100 g., Brass, 40 mm. **Obv:** State arms **Rev:** Sand grouse
Edge: Plain

Date	Mintage	F	VF	XF	Unc	BU
2001 Proof	—			Value: 27.50		

KM# 239 WON
28.1100 g., Brass, 40 mm. **Obv:** State arms **Rev:** Brontosaurus
Edge: Plain

Date	Mintage	F	VF	XF	Unc	BU
2001 Proof	—			Value: 27.50		

KM# 305 WON
28.2000 g., Brass, 40.2 mm. **Obv:** State arms **Rev:** Tomb of
King Kong Min **Edge:** Plain

Date	Mintage	F	VF	XF	Unc	BU
JU91-2002 Proof	—			Value: 20.00		

KM# 235 WON
28.1100 g., Brass, 40 mm. **Obv:** State arms **Rev:** Fairy Pitta
bird **Edge:** Plain

Date	Mintage	F	VF	XF	Unc	BU
2001 Proof	—			Value: 27.50		

KM# 247 WON
26.9500 g., Brass, 40 mm. **Obv:** State arms **Rev:** Soldier
watching an air raid on a Yalu River bridge **Edge:** Plain

Date	Mintage	F	VF	XF	Unc	BU
2001 Proof	—			Value: 20.00		

KM# 306 WON
7.1000 g., Aluminum, 40 mm. **Obv:** State arms **Rev:** Two horses
within circle of animals **Edge:** Plain **Note:** Prev. KM#398.

Date	Mintage	F	VF	XF	Unc	BU
2002 Proof	—			Value: 20.00		

KM# 306a WON
28.2000 g., Brass, 40.2 mm. **Obv:** State arms **Rev:** Two horses
within circle of animals **Edge:** Plain

Date	Mintage	F	VF	XF	Unc	BU
2002 Proof	—			Value: 20.00		

KM# 236 WON
28.1100 g., Brass, 40 mm. **Obv:** State arms **Rev:** Mythical
"Hyonmu" **Edge:** Plain

Date	Mintage	F	VF	XF	Unc	BU
2001 Proof	—			Value: 27.50		

KM# 248 WON
7.0000 g., Aluminum, 40 mm. **Obv:** State arms **Rev:** Multicolor
rabbit and hearts **Edge:** Plain **Note:** Year of the Rabbit

Date	Mintage	F	VF	XF	Unc	BU
2001 Proof	—			Value: 20.00		

KM# 470 WON
Brass, 35 mm. **Subject:** 2004 Olympics **Obv:** Arms **Rev:** Three
Karate Sportsmen

Date	Mintage	F	VF	XF	Unc	BU
2002 Proof	—			Value: 6.50		

KM# 471 WON
Brass **Obv:** Arms **Rev:** Bridge

Date	Mintage	F	VF	XF	Unc	BU
2002 (91) Proof	—			Value: 7.50		

KM# 472 WON
Brass, 40 mm. **Obv:** Arms **Rev:** Tomb of King Kong Min

Date	Mintage	F	VF	XF	Unc	BU
2002 Proof	—			Value: 7.50		

KM# 473 WON
Aluminum, 40 mm. **Obv:** Arms **Rev:** Tomb of King Tong My Ong

Date	Mintage	F	VF	XF	Unc	BU
2002 Proof	—			Value: 7.50		

KM# 474 WON
Brass **Obv:** Arms **Rev:** Family about to hug

Date	Mintage	F	VF	XF	Unc	BU
2002 Proof	—			Value: 10.00		

KM# 475 WON
Brass, 40 mm. **Obv:** Arms **Rev:** Three people in group hug

Date	Mintage	F	VF	XF	Unc	BU
2002 Proof	—			Value: 10.00		

KM# 476 WON
Brass **Obv:** Arms **Rev:** Four dragons around map of North Korea

Date	Mintage	F	VF	XF	Unc	BU
2002 Proof	—			Value: 10.00		

KM# 308 WON
6.9000 g., Aluminum, 40 mm. **Obv:** State arms **Rev:** Arirang
dancer with cranes flying above **Edge:** Plain **Note:** Prev. KM#390.

Date	Mintage	F	VF	XF	Unc	BU
JU91-(2002) Proof	—			Value: 15.00		

KM# 308a WON
28.2000 g., Brass, 40.2 mm. **Subject:** Arirang **Obv:** State arms
Rev: Performers and flying cranes **Edge:** Plain

Date	Mintage	F	VF	XF	Unc	BU
JU91-(2002) Proof	—			Value: 20.00		

KM# 237 WON
28.1100 g., Brass, 40 mm. **Obv:** State arms **Rev:** Blue Dragon
Edge: Plain

Date	Mintage	F	VF	XF	Unc	BU
2001 Proof	—			Value: 27.50		

KM# 238 WON
28.1100 g., Brass, 40 mm. **Obv:** State arms **Rev:** Two tigers
Edge: Plain

Date	Mintage	F	VF	XF	Unc	BU
2001 Proof	—			Value: 27.50		

KM# 310a WON
28.2000 g., Brass, 40.2 mm. **Obv:** State arms **Rev:** Tomb of
King Tongmyong **Edge:** Plain

Date	Mintage	F	VF	XF	Unc	BU
JU91-2002 Proof	—			Value: 15.00		

KM# 313 WON
6.7000 g., Aluminum, 40 mm. **Obv:** State arms **Rev:** Arirang dancer **Edge:** Plain **Note:** Prev. KM#389.

Date	Mintage	F	VF	XF	Unc	BU
JU91-(2002) Proof	—				Value: 15.00	

KM# 313a WON
28.2000 g., Brass, 40.2 mm. **Subject:** Arirang **Obv:** State arms **Rev:** Dancer with upheld arms **Edge:** Plain

Date	Mintage	F	VF	XF	Unc	BU
JU91-(2002) Proof	—				Value: 20.00	

KM# 388 WON
7.1000 g., Aluminum, 40 mm. **Obv:** State arms **Rev:** Arirang dancer Silhouette **Edge:** Plain

Date	Mintage	F	VF	XF	Unc	BU
2002 Proof	—				Value: 15.00	

KM# 391 WON
7.1000 g., Aluminum, 40 mm. **Obv:** State arms **Rev:** Arirang ribbon dancer **Edge:** Plain

Date	Mintage	F	VF	XF	Unc	BU
JU91-2002 Proof	—				Value: 15.00	

KM# 392 WON
7.0000 g., Aluminum, 40 mm. **Obv:** State arms **Rev:** May Day Stadium **Edge:** Plain

Date	Mintage	F	VF	XF	Unc	BU
JU91-2002 Proof	—				Value: 12.00	

KM# 392a WON
28.5000 g., Brass, 40.1 mm. **Obv:** State arms **Rev:** May Day Stadium **Edge:** Plain

Date	Mintage	F	VF	XF	Unc	BU
JU91-2002 Proof	—				Value: 15.00	

KM# 393 WON
7.1000 g., Aluminum, 40 mm. **Obv:** State arms **Rev:** Woman floating above stadium **Edge:** Plain

Date	Mintage	F	VF	XF	Unc	BU
JU91-2002 Proof	—				Value: 15.00	

KM# 393a WON
28.2000 g., Brass, 40 mm. **Obv:** State arms **Rev:** Woman floating above stadium **Edge:** Plain

Date	Mintage	F	VF	XF	Unc	BU
JU91-2002 Proof	—				Value: 17.50	

KM# 394 WON
27.5000 g., Brass, 40 mm. **Obv:** State arms **Rev:** Ribbon dancer with Korea shaped ribbon **Edge:** Plain

Date	Mintage	F	VF	XF	Unc	BU
JU91-2002 Proof	—				Value: 17.50	

KM# 395 WON
27.5000 g., Brass, 40 mm. **Obv:** State arms **Rev:** Dancer in the shape of Korea **Edge:** Plain

Date	Mintage	F	VF	XF	Unc	BU
JU91-2002 Proof	—				Value: 17.50	

KM# 396 WON
7.0000 g., Aluminum, 40 mm. **Obv:** State arms **Rev:** Bust with hat facing divides dates(1337-1392) above building foundation **Edge:** Plain

Date	Mintage	F	VF	XF	Unc	BU
JU91-2002 Proof	—				Value: 15.00	

KM# 397 WON
7.0000 g., Aluminum, 40 mm. **Obv:** State arms **Rev:** Victorious athletes hugging **Edge:** Plain

Date	Mintage	F	VF	XF	Unc	BU
JU91-(2002) Proof	—				Value: 10.00	

KM# 397a WON
28.2400 g., Brass, 40 mm. **Obv:** State arms **Rev:** Victorious athletes hugging **Edge:** Plain

Date	Mintage	F	VF	XF	Unc	BU
JU91-(2002) Proof	—				Value: 12.50	

KM# 399 WON
4.8600 g., Aluminum, 35 mm. **Obv:** State arms **Rev:** Cantering horse **Edge:** Plain

Date	Mintage	F	VF	XF	Unc	BU
JU91-(2002) Proof	—				Value: 15.00	

KM# 399a WON
16.9300 g., Brass, 35 mm. **Obv:** State arms **Rev:** Cantering horse **Edge:** Plain

Date	Mintage	F	VF	XF	Unc	BU
JU91-(2002) Proof	—				Value: 15.00	

KM# 400 WON
5.1000 g., Aluminum, 35 mm. **Obv:** State arms **Rev:** Two wrestlers **Edge:** Plain

Date	Mintage	F	VF	XF	Unc	BU
JU91-(2002) Proof	—				Value: 12.50	

KM# 400a WON
16.5000 g., Brass, 35 mm. **Obv:** State arms **Rev:** Two wrestlers
Edge: Plain

Date	Mintage	F	VF	XF	Unc	BU
JU91-(2002) Proof	—	Value: 15.00				

KM# 310 WON
Aluminum **Obv:** State arms **Rev:** Tomb of King Tongmyong

Date	Mintage	F	VF	XF	Unc	BU
2002 Proof	—	Value: 12.00				

KM# 264 WON
28.4700 g., Brass, 40 mm. **Obv:** State arms **Rev:** Sheep within circle of animals **Edge:** Plain

Date	Mintage	F	VF	XF	Unc	BU
2003 Proof	—	Value: 22.00				

KM# 323a WON
28.1000 g., Brass, 40.2 mm. **Obv:** State arms **Rev:** Turtle-shaped armoured ship of 1592 **Edge:** Plain

Date	Mintage	F	VF	XF	Unc	BU
JU92-2003 Proof	—	Value: 20.00				

KM# 323 WON
6.9400 g., Aluminum, 40 mm. **Obv:** State arms **Rev:** Turtle shaped armoured ship of 1592 **Edge:** Plain

Date	Mintage	F	VF	XF	Unc	BU
JU92-2003 Proof	—	Value: 15.00				

KM# 319 WON
9.6200 g., Aluminum, 40 mm. **Obv:** State arms **Rev:** Helmeted head with two antenna-like horns on the helmet **Edge:** Plain

Date	Mintage	F	VF	XF	Unc	BU
JU92-2003 Proof	—	Value: 15.00				

KM# 319a WON
28.2000 g., Brass, 40.2 mm. **Obv:** State arms **Rev:** Helmeted head with two antenna-like horns on helmet **Edge:** Plain

Date	Mintage	F	VF	XF	Unc	BU
JU92-(2003) Proof	—	Value: 17.50				

KM# 403a WON
22.1000 g., Brass, 40 mm. **Obv:** State arms **Rev:** Armored bust facing wearing winged helmet (948-1031) **Edge:** Plain

Date	Mintage	F	VF	XF	Unc	BU
JU92-2003 Proof	—	Value: 17.50				

KM# 404 WON
9.6300 g., Aluminum, 40 mm. **Obv:** State arms **Rev:** Armored bust wearing a horned helmet **Edge:** Plain

Date	Mintage	F	VF	XF	Unc	BU
JU92-2003 Proof	—	Value: 15.00				

KM# 404a WON
22.2500 g., Brass, 40 mm. **Obv:** State arms **Rev:** Armored bust wearing a horned helmet **Edge:** Plain

Date	Mintage	F	VF	XF	Unc	BU
JU92-2003 Proof	—	Value: 17.50				

KM# 405 WON
7.0000 g., Aluminum, 40 mm. **Obv:** State arms **Rev:** Ram within circle of animals **Edge:** Plain

Date	Mintage	F	VF	XF	Unc	BU
2003 Proof	—	Value: 15.00				

KM# 405a WON
28.4400 g., Brass, 40 mm. **Obv:** State arms **Rev:** Ram within circle of animals **Edge:** Plain

Date	Mintage	F	VF	XF	Unc	BU
2003 Proof	—	Value: 17.50				

KM# 406 WON
10.1500 g., Aluminum, 40 mm. **Obv:** State arms **Rev:** Children kicking a shuttlecock **Edge:** Plain

Date	Mintage	F	VF	XF	Unc	BU
JU92-2003 Proof	—	Value: 15.00				

KM# 406a WON
24.6300 g., Brass, 40 mm. **Obv:** State arms **Rev:** Children kicking a shuttlecock **Edge:** Plain

Date	Mintage	F	VF	XF	Unc	BU
JU92-2003 Proof	—	Value: 17.50				

KM# 407a WON
23.1000 g., Brass, 40 mm. **Obv:** State arms **Rev:** Children playing jacks **Edge:** Plain

Date	Mintage	F	VF	XF	Unc	BU
JU92-2003 Proof	—	Value: 17.50				

KM# 408a WON
24.5600 g., Brass, 40 mm. **Obv:** State arms **Rev:** Children spinning tops **Edge:** Plain

Date	Mintage	F	VF	XF	Unc	BU
JU92-2003 Proof	—	Value: 17.50				

KM# 410a WON
24.6400 g., Brass, 40 mm. **Obv:** State arms **Rev:** Large dome building **Edge:** Plain

Date	Mintage	F	VF	XF	Unc	BU
JU92-2003 Proof	—	Value: 17.50				

KM# 265 WON
17.7000 g., Brass, 23.2 x 40.1 mm. **Obv:** State arms **Rev:** White-tufted-ear Marmoset **Edge:** Plain

Date	Mintage	F	VF	XF	Unc	BU
2004	—	Value: 27.50				

KM# 266   WON
17.7000 g., Brass, 23.2 x 40.1 mm.   **Obv:** State arms **Rev:**
Cercopjthecus Mitis monkey **Edge:** Plain

Date	Mintage	F	VF	XF	Unc	BU
2004 Proof	—	Value: 27.50				

KM# 267   WON
17.7000 g., Brass, 23.2 x 40.1 mm.   **Obv:** State arms **Rev:** Two
Saguinus Midas monkeys **Edge:** Plain

Date	Mintage	F	VF	XF	Unc	BU
2004 Proof	—	Value: 27.50				

KM# 330   WON
9.9200 g., Aluminum, 45 mm.   **Obv:** State arms **Rev:** Mountain
cabin **Edge:** Plain **Note:** Prev. KM#411.

Date	Mintage	F	VF	XF	Unc	BU
JU93-(2004) Proof	—	Value: 15.00				

KM# 330a   WON
26.4500 g., Brass, 45 mm.   **Obv:** State arms **Rev:** Mountain
cabin **Edge:** Plain

Date	Mintage	F	VF	XF	Unc	BU
JU93-(2004) Proof	—	Value: 20.00				

KM# 331   WON
10.0000 g., Aluminum, 45 mm.   **Obv:** State arms **Rev:** Kim Il
Sung's birthplace, front view **Edge:** Plain **Note:** Prev. KM#412.

Date	Mintage	F	VF	XF	Unc	BU
JU93-(2004) Proof	—	Value: 15.00				

KM# 331a   WON
26.4500 g., Brass, 45 mm.   **Obv:** State arms **Rev:** Sung's birth
place, front view **Edge:** Plain

Date	Mintage	F	VF	XF	Unc	BU
JU93-(2004) Proof	—	Value: 20.00				

KM# 332   WON
10.0000 g., Aluminum, 45 mm.   **Obv:** State arms **Rev:** Kim Il
Sung's birthplace, side view **Edge:** Plain **Note:** Prev. KM#413.

Date	Mintage	F	VF	XF	Unc	BU
JU93-(2004) Proof	—	Value: 15.00				

KM# 332a   WON
26.4500 g., Brass, 45 mm.   **Obv:** State arms **Rev:** Sung's
birthplace, side view **Edge:** Plain

Date	Mintage	F	VF	XF	Unc	BU
JU93-(2004) Proof	—	Value: 20.00				

KM# 333   WON
26.4500 g., Brass, 45 mm.   **Obv:** State arms **Rev:** Kim Jung
Sook facing **Edge:** Plain

Date	Mintage	F	VF	XF	Unc	BU
JU93-2004 Proof	—	Value: 22.50				

KM# 334   WON
26.4500 g., Brass, 45 mm.   **Obv:** State arms **Rev:** Uniformed
bust facing **Edge:** Plain

Date	Mintage	F	VF	XF	Unc	BU
JU93-2004 Proof	—	Value: 22.50				

KM# 335   WON
26.4500 g., Brass, 45 mm.   **Obv:** State arms **Rev:** Uniformed
bust facing **Edge:** Plain

Date	Mintage	F	VF	XF	Unc	BU
JU93-2004 Proof	—	Value: 22.50				

KM# 336   WON
10.1000 g., Aluminum, 45 mm.   **Obv:** State arms **Rev:** Kim Il
Sung flower, orchid **Edge:** Plain **Note:** Prev. KM#414.

Date	Mintage	F	VF	XF	Unc	BU
JU93-(2004) Proof	—	Value: 15.00				

KM# 336a   WON
26.4500 g., Brass, 45 mm.   **Obv:** State arms **Rev:** Orchids
Edge: Plain

Date	Mintage	F	VF	XF	Unc	BU
JU93-(2004) Proof	—	Value: 20.00				

KM# 337 WON
10.1000 g., Aluminum, 45 mm. **Obv:** State arms **Rev:** Kim Jong
Il flower, peony **Edge:** Plain **Note:** Prev. KM#415.

Date	Mintage	F	VF	XF	Unc	BU
JU93-2004 Proof	—				Value: 15.00	

KM# 337a WON
26.4500 g., Brass, 45 mm. **Obv:** State arms **Rev:** Peony flower
Edge: Plain

Date	Mintage	F	VF	XF	Unc	BU
JU93-(2004) Proof	—				Value: 20.00	

KM# 338 WON
9.9300 g., Aluminum, 45 mm. **Obv:** State arms **Rev:** Jin Dal
Lae flower, Rose of Sharon **Edge:** Plain **Note:** Prev. KM#416.

Date	Mintage	F	VF	XF	Unc	BU
JU93-(2004) Proof	—				Value: 15.00	

KM# 338a WON
26.4500 g., Brass, 45 mm. **Obv:** State arms **Rev:** Rose of
Sharon flowers **Edge:** Plain

Date	Mintage	F	VF	XF	Unc	BU
JU93-(2004) Proof	—				Value: 20.00	

KM# 483 WON
Copper-Nickel **Subject:** Uzgn Monument **Obv:** Arms **Rev:** Map
and building

Date	Mintage	F	VF	XF	Unc	BU
2008 Proof	—				Value: 15.00	

KM# 249 2 WON
7.0000 g., 0.9990 Silver 0.2248 oz. ASW, 30 mm. **Obv:** State
arms **Rev:** Two multicolor pandas **Edge:** Plain

Date	Mintage	F	VF	XF	Unc	BU
2003 Proof	—				Value: 30.00	

KM# 417 2 WON
24.6600 g., Brass, 31.6x45.75 mm. **Obv:** State arms **Rev:** Half
length uniformed figure standing in land rover saluting below
dates 1904-2004 **Edge:** Plain **Shape:** Rectangle

Date	Mintage	F	VF	XF	Unc	BU
ND(2004) Proof	—				Value: 25.00	

KM# 339 3 WON
12.5500 g., Aluminum, 50.1 mm. **Obv:** Korean map **Rev:** Huh
Jun, Chosun doctor with books **Edge:** Plain

Date	Mintage	F	VF	XF	Unc	BU
JU93-2004 Proof	—				Value: 20.00	

KM# 339a 3 WON
40.5300 g., Brass, 50.2 mm. **Obv:** Korean map **Rev:** Bust facing
to left of books **Edge:** Plain

Date	Mintage	F	VF	XF	Unc	BU
JU93-(2004) Proof	—				Value: 25.00	

KM# 203 5 WON
15.0000 g., 0.9990 Silver 0.4818 oz. ASW, 35 mm. **Subject:**
School Ships **Obv:** State arms **Rev:** SS Krusenstern **Edge:** Plain

Date	Mintage	F	VF	XF	Unc	BU
ND(2001) Proof	500				Value: 75.00	

KM# 205 5 WON
15.0000 g., 0.9990 Silver 0.4818 oz. ASW, 35 mm.
Subject: Wildlife **Obv:** State arms **Rev:** Two standing Japanese
Ibis birds **Edge:** Plain

Date	Mintage	F	VF	XF	Unc	BU
JU90-2001 Proof	100				Value: 200	

KM# 206 5 WON
15.0000 g., 0.9990 Silver 0.4818 oz. ASW, 35 mm.
Subject: Wildlife **Obv:** State arms **Rev:** Two nesting Japanese
Ibis birds **Edge:** Plain

Date	Mintage	F	VF	XF	Unc	BU
JU90-2001 Proof	3,000				Value: 50.00	

KM# 208 5 WON
15.0000 g., 0.9990 Silver 0.4818 oz. ASW, 35 mm. **Subject:** Wildlife
Obv: State arms **Rev:** Two Korean Longtail Gorals **Edge:** Plain

Date	Mintage	F	VF	XF	Unc	BU
JU90-2001 Proof	3,000				Value: 50.00	

KM# 219 5 WON
14.9600 g., 0.9990 Silver 0.4805 oz. ASW, 35 mm. **Obv:** State
arms **Rev:** Dragon ship **Edge:** Plain

Date	Mintage	F	VF	XF	Unc	BU
2001 Proof	5,000				Value: 35.00	

KM# 226   5 WON
20.0000 g., 0.9990 Silver 0.6423 oz. ASW, 33.8 mm. **Subject:**
Olympics **Obv:** State arms **Rev:** Hurdler **Edge:** Reeded

Date	Mintage	F	VF	XF	Unc	BU
2001 Proof	—	Value: 35.00				

KM# 240   5 WON
14.9400 g., 0.9990 Silver 0.4798 oz. ASW, 35 mm. **Obv:** State
arms **Rev:** "Orca" (Killer Whale) **Edge:** Plain

Date	Mintage	F	VF	XF	Unc	BU
2001 Proof	—	Value: 60.00				

KM# 241   5 WON
14.9200 g., 0.9990 Silver 0.4792 oz. ASW, 35 mm. **Obv:** State
arms **Rev:** Orca and Eco-Tourists in boat **Edge:** Plain

Date	Mintage	F	VF	XF	Unc	BU
2001 Proof	—	Value: 60.00				

KM# 242   5 WON
14.8700 g., 0.9990 Silver 0.4776 oz. ASW, 35 mm. **Obv:** State
arms **Rev:** "Pottwal" (Sperm Whale) **Edge:** Plain

Date	Mintage	F	VF	XF	Unc	BU
2001 Proof	—	Value: 60.00				

KM# 243   5 WON
14.9500 g., 0.9990 Silver 0.4802 oz. ASW, 35 mm. **Obv:** State
arms **Rev:** "Buckelwal" (Humpback Whale) **Edge:** Plain

Date	Mintage	F	VF	XF	Unc	BU
2001 Proof	—	Value: 60.00				

KM# 244   5 WON
14.9300 g., 0.9990 Silver 0.4795 oz. ASW, 35 mm. **Obv:** State
arms **Rev:** "Groenlandwal" (Greenland Right Whale) **Edge:** Plain

Date	Mintage	F	VF	XF	Unc	BU
2001 Proof	—	Value: 60.00				

KM# 245   5 WON
14.9500 g., 0.9990 Silver 0.4802 oz. ASW, 35 mm. **Obv:** State
arms **Rev:** "Blauwal" (Blue Whale) **Edge:** Plain

Date	Mintage	F	VF	XF	Unc	BU
2001 Proof	—	Value: 60.00				

KM# 246   5 WON
14.9600 g., 0.9990 Silver 0.4805 oz. ASW, 35 mm. **Obv:** State
arms **Rev:** "Grindwal" (Pilot Whale) **Edge:** Plain

Date	Mintage	F	VF	XF	Unc	BU
2001 Proof	—	Value: 60.00				

KM# 250   5 WON
14.9600 g., 0.9990 Silver 0.4805 oz. ASW, 35 mm.
Subject: Return of Hong Kong to China **Obv:** State arms
Rev: City view **Edge:** Plain

Date	Mintage	F	VF	XF	Unc	BU
2001 Proof	—	Value: 18.00				

KM# 251   5 WON
14.9000 g., 0.9990 Silver 0.4785 oz. ASW, 35 mm. **Subject:** Year
of the Horse **Obv:** State arms **Rev:** Cantering horse **Edge:** Plain

Date	Mintage	F	VF	XF	Unc	BU
2002 Proof	—	Value: 30.00				

KM# 252   5 WON
14.9200 g., 0.9990 Silver 0.4792 oz. ASW, 35 mm. **Subject:**
Korean Games **Obv:** State arms **Rev:** Two wrestlers **Edge:** Plain

Date	Mintage	F	VF	XF	Unc	BU
JU91-2002 Proof	—	Value: 18.00				

KM# 303   5 WON
15.0000 g., 0.9990 Silver 0.4818 oz. ASW, 35 mm. **Obv:** State
arms **Rev:** Janggo dancer **Edge:** Segmented reeding

Date	Mintage	F	VF	XF	Unc	BU
JU91-2002 Proof	—	Value: 30.00				

KM# 304   5 WON
15.0000 g., 0.9990 Silver 0.4818 oz. ASW, 35 mm. **Obv:** State
arms **Rev:** Armored Knight **Edge:** Segmented reeding

Date	Mintage	F	VF	XF	Unc	BU
JU91-2002 Proof	—	Value: 30.00				

KM# 327   5 WON
20.0000 g., 0.9990 Silver 0.6423 oz. ASW, 35 mm. **Obv:** State
arms **Rev:** "Turtle Boat" of 1592 **Edge:** Segmented reeding

Date	Mintage	F	VF	XF	Unc	BU
JU92-2003 Proof	—	Value: 30.00				

KM# 328   5 WON
20.0000 g., 0.9990 Silver 0.6423 oz. ASW, 35 mm. **Obv:** State
arms **Rev:** Olympic fencers **Edge:** Segmented reeding

Date	Mintage	F	VF	XF	Unc	BU
JU92-2003 Proof	—	Value: 30.00				

KM# 329   5 WON
20.0000 g., 0.9990 Silver 0.6423 oz. ASW, 35 mm. **Obv:** State
arms **Rev:** Three wild horses **Edge:** Segmented reeding

Date	Mintage	F	VF	XF	Unc	BU
JU92-2003 Proof	—	Value: 30.00				

KM# 220   7 WON
20.0000 g., 0.9990 Silver 0.6423 oz. ASW, 38 mm.
Subject: 2002 Olympics **Obv:** State arms **Rev:** Two speed
skaters **Edge:** Plain

Date	Mintage	F	VF	XF	Unc	BU
2001 Proof	10,000	Value: 40.00				

KM# 221   7 WON
20.0000 g., 0.9990 Silver 0.6423 oz. ASW, 38 mm. **Subject:**
Endangered Wildlife **Obv:** State arms **Rev:** White-tailed sea
Eagle **Edge:** Plain

Date	Mintage	F	VF	XF	Unc	BU
2001 Proof	10,000	Value: 30.00				

KM# 477   7 WON
20.0000 g., Bi-Metallic Silver center in Brass ring. **Obv:** Arms
Rev: Stadium along river

Date	Mintage	F	VF	XF	Unc	BU
2004 Proof	—	Value: 55.00				

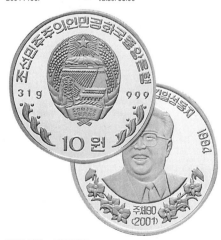

KM# 292   10 WON
31.0000 g., 0.9990 Silver 0.9956 oz. ASW, 40.2 mm. **Obv:** State
arms **Rev:** Bust facing flanked by dates (1912-1994) above flower
sprigs **Edge:** Plain

Date	Mintage	F	VF	XF	Unc	BU
JU90-2001 Proof	—	Value: 35.00				

KM# 295   10 WON
31.0000 g., 0.9990 Silver 0.9956 oz. ASW, 40.2 mm. **Obv:** State
arms **Rev:** Mountain cabin **Edge:** Plain

Date	Mintage	F	VF	XF	Unc	BU
JU90-2001 Proof	—	Value: 35.00				

KM# 296   10 WON
31.0000 g., 0.9990 Silver 0.9956 oz. ASW, 40.2 mm. **Obv:** State
arms **Rev:** "KUMDANG - 2 INJECTION" in center of leaves **Edge:**
Plain

Date	Mintage	F	VF	XF	Unc	BU
2001 Proof	—	Value: 35.00				

KM# 297   10 WON
31.0000 g., 0.9990 Silver 0.9956 oz. ASW, 40.2 mm. **Obv:** State
arms **Rev:** Train scene and a couple below a jet liner **Rev.**
Legend: ...1945 - 2001... **Edge:** Plain

Date	Mintage	F	VF	XF	Unc	BU
ND(2001) Proof	—	Value: 35.00				

KM# 298   10 WON
31.0000 g., 0.9990 Silver 0.9956 oz. ASW, 40.2 mm. **Obv:** State
arms **Rev:** Cruise ship below stylized head left profile **Edge:** Plain

Date	Mintage	F	VF	XF	Unc	BU
JU90-2001 Proof	—	Value: 40.00				

KM# 299   10 WON
31.0000 g., 0.9990 Silver 0.9956 oz. ASW, 40.2 mm. **Obv:** State
arms **Rev:** Old fortress **Edge:** Plain

Date	Mintage	F	VF	XF	Unc	BU
JU90-2001 Proof	—	Value: 37.50				

KM# 300   10 WON
31.0000 g., 0.9990 Silver 0.9956 oz. ASW, 40.2 mm. **Obv:** State
arms **Rev:** Landmarks, flag and tourist couple above cruise ship
Edge: Plain

Date	Mintage	F	VF	XF	Unc	BU
JU90-2001 Proof	—	Value: 35.00				

KM# 301   10 WON
31.0000 g., 0.9990 Silver 0.9956 oz. ASW, 40.2 mm. **Obv:** State
arms **Rev:** Conjoined half length figures facing shaking hands
Edge: Plain

Date	Mintage	F	VF	XF	Unc	BU
JU90-2001 Proof	—	Value: 35.00				

KM# 302   10 WON
31.0000 g., 0.9990 Silver 0.9956 oz. ASW, 40.1 mm. **Obv:** State
arms **Rev:** Great East Gate **Edge:** Plain

Date	Mintage	F	VF	XF	Unc	BU
JU90-2001 Proof	—	Value: 37.50				

KM# 357   10 WON
31.0000 g., 0.9990 Silver 0.9956 oz. ASW, 40.2 mm. **Obv:** State
arms **Rev:** Antique ceramic items **Edge:** Plain

Date	Mintage	F	VF	XF	Unc	BU
2001 Proof	—	Value: 35.00				

KM# 386   10 WON
30.7600 g., 0.9990 Silver 0.9879 oz. ASW, 40.1 mm. **Obv:** State
arms **Rev:** Kim Jung Sook facing flanked by dates (1917-1949)
above flower sprigs **Edge:** Plain

Date	Mintage	F	VF	XF	Unc	BU
JU90-2001 Proof	—	Value: 37.50				

KM# 387   10 WON
30.7600 g., 0.9990 Silver 0.9879 oz. ASW, 40.1 mm. **Obv:** State
arms **Rev:** Bust facing above flower sprigs **Edge:** Plain

Date	Mintage	F	VF	XF	Unc	BU
JU90-2001 Proof	—	Value: 37.50				

KM# 152   10 WON
31.0000 g., 0.9990 Silver 0.9956 oz. ASW, 39.8 mm.
Subject: Asian Money Fair **Obv:** State arms **Rev:** Two snakes
Edge: Reeded and plain sections

Date	Mintage	F	VF	XF	Unc	BU
2001 Proof	—	Value: 60.00				

KM# 153   10 WON
31.0000 g., 0.9990 Silver 0.9956 oz. ASW, 39.8 mm.
Subject: Tortoise-Serpent **Obv:** State arms **Rev:** Mythical
creature **Edge:** Reeded and plain sections

Date	Mintage	F	VF	XF	Unc	BU
2001 Proof	—	Value: 55.00				

KM# 227   10 WON
31.0600 g., 0.9250 Silver 0.9237 oz. ASW, 39.9 mm.
Subject: General Ri Sun Sin **Obv:** State arms **Rev:** Helmeted
head 1/4 left **Edge:** Reeded

Date	Mintage	F	VF	XF	Unc	BU
2001 Proof	—	Value: 37.50				

KM# 253   10 WON
31.1100 g., 0.9990 Silver 0.9992 oz. ASW, 40.2 mm. **Obv:** State
arms **Rev:** Head 3/4 left flanked by dates (1904-1997) above
flower sprigs **Edge:** Plain

Date	Mintage	F	VF	XF	Unc	BU
2001	—	Value: 35.00				

KM# 469   10 WON
31.1050 g., 0.9250 oz. ASW   **Obv:** Arms
Rev: General Ri Sun Sin

Date	Mintage	F	VF	XF	Unc	BU
2001 Proof	—	Value: 40.00				

KM# 231   10 WON
31.0000 g., 0.9990 Silver 0.9956 oz. ASW, 39.9 mm.
Subject: Kim III Sung **Obv:** State arms **Rev:** Bust facing
Edge: Segmented reeding

Date	Mintage	F	VF	XF	Unc	BU
JU91-2002 Proof	—	Value: 40.00				

KM# 254   10 WON
30.7700 g., 0.9990 Silver 0.9882 oz. ASW, 40.15 mm.
Obv: State arms **Rev:** Bust facing and his tomb **Edge:** Plain

Date	Mintage	F	VF	XF	Unc	BU
JU91-2002 Proof	—	Value: 32.00				

KM# 255   10 WON
30.9400 g., 0.9990 Silver 0.9937 oz. ASW, 40.2 mm.
Subject: Jongmongju and Sonjukgyo **Obv:** State arms
Rev: Head with hat facing above building foundation **Edge:** Plain

Date	Mintage	F	VF	XF	Unc	BU
JU91-2002 Proof	—	Value: 32.00				

KM# 401   10 WON
31.0000 g., 0.9990 Silver 0.9956 oz. ASW, 40.1 mm. **Obv:** State
arms **Rev:** Arirang dancer **Edge:** Plain

Date	Mintage	F	VF	XF	Unc	BU
JU91-2002 Proof	—	Value: 35.00				

KM# 402   10 WON
31.0000 g., 0.9990 Silver 0.9956 oz. ASW, 40.1 mm. **Obv:** State
arms **Rev:** Arirang ribbon dancer **Edge:** Plain

Date	Mintage	F	VF	XF	Unc	BU
JU91-2002 Proof	—	Value: 35.00				

KM# 307   10 WON
31.0000 g., 0.9990 Silver 0.9956 oz. ASW, 40.1 mm. **Obv:** State arms **Rev:** Two horses within a circle of animals **Edge:** Plain

Date	Mintage	F	VF	XF	Unc	BU
2002 Proof	—	Value: 35.00				

KM# 309   10 WON
31.0000 g., 0.9990 Silver 0.9956 oz. ASW, 40.2 mm.
Subject: Arirang **Obv:** State arms **Rev:** Performers and flying cranes **Edge:** Plain

Date	Mintage	F	VF	XF	Unc	BU
JU91-2002 Proof	—	Value: 35.00				

KM# 311   10 WON
31.0000 g., 0.9990 Silver 0.9956 oz. ASW, 40.2 mm. **Obv:** State arms **Rev:** Tomb of King Tongmyong **Edge:** Plain

Date	Mintage	F	VF	XF	Unc	BU
JU91-2002 Proof	—	Value: 35.00				

KM# 312   10 WON
31.0000 g., 0.9990 Silver 0.9956 oz. ASW, 40.2 mm. **Obv:** State arms **Rev:** Tomb of King Kong Min **Edge:** Plain

Date	Mintage	F	VF	XF	Unc	BU
JU91-2002 Proof	—	Value: 35.00				

KM# 314   10 WON
31.0000 g., 0.9990 Silver 0.9956 oz. ASW, 40.2 mm. **Subject:** Arirang **Obv:** State arms **Rev:** Stylized dancer **Edge:** Plain

Date	Mintage	F	VF	XF	Unc	BU
2002 Proof	—	Value: 35.00				

KM# 315   10 WON
31.0000 g., 0.9990 Silver 0.9956 oz. ASW, 40.2 mm. **Obv:** State arms **Rev:** Korean map shaped dancer **Edge:** Plain

Date	Mintage	F	VF	XF	Unc	BU
JU91-2002 Proof	—	Value: 37.50				

KM# 316   10 WON
31.0000 g., 0.9990 Silver 0.9956 oz. ASW, 40.2 mm. **Obv:** State arms **Rev:** Korean map shaped ribbon dancer **Edge:** Plain

Date	Mintage	F	VF	XF	Unc	BU
JU91-2002 Proof	—	Value: 37.50				

KM# 317   10 WON
31.0000 g., 0.9990 Silver 0.9956 oz. ASW, 40.2 mm. **Obv:** State arms **Rev:** Victorious athletes hugging **Edge:** Plain

Date	Mintage	F	VF	XF	Unc	BU
JU91-2002 Proof	—	Value: 35.00				

KM# 318   10 WON
31.0000 g., 0.9990 Silver 0.9956 oz. ASW, 40.2 mm. **Obv:** State arms **Rev:** Woman floating above arena **Edge:** Plain

Date	Mintage	F	VF	XF	Unc	BU
JU91-2002 Proof	—	Value: 35.00				

KM# 320   10 WON
31.0000 g., 0.9990 Silver 0.9956 oz. ASW, 40.2 mm. **Obv:** State arms **Rev:** Helmeted head with two antenna-like horns on helmet **Edge:** Plain

Date	Mintage	F	VF	XF	Unc	BU
JU92-2003 Proof	—	Value: 37.50				

KM# 321   10 WON
31.0000 g., 0.9990 Silver 0.9956 oz. ASW, 40.2 mm. **Obv:** State arms **Rev:** Helmeted head with horns **Edge:** Plain

Date	Mintage	F	VF	XF	Unc	BU
JU92-2003 Proof	—	Value: 37.50				

KM# 322   10 WON
31.0000 g., 0.9990 Silver 0.9956 oz. ASW, 40.2 mm. **Obv:** State arms **Rev:** Armored bust facing (948-1031) wearing winged helmet **Edge:** Plain

Date	Mintage	F	VF	XF	Unc	BU
JU92-2003 Proof	—	Value: 37.50				

KM# 324   10 WON
31.0000 g., 0.9990 Silver 0.9956 oz. ASW, 40.2 mm. **Obv:** State arms **Rev:** Turtle-shaped armoured ship of 1592 **Edge:** Plain

Date	Mintage	F	VF	XF	Unc	BU
JU92-2003	—	Value: 35.00				
Proof						

KM# 325   10 WON
31.0000 g., 0.9990 Silver 0.9956 oz. ASW, 40.2 mm. **Obv:** State arms **Rev:** Children playing jacks **Edge:** Plain

Date	Mintage	F	VF	XF	Unc	BU
JU92-2003 Proof	—	Value: 35.00				

KM# 326   10 WON
31.0000 g., 0.9990 Silver 0.9956 oz. ASW, 40.2 mm. **Obv:** State arms **Rev:** Children kicking a shuttlecock **Edge:** Plain

Date	Mintage	F	VF	XF	Unc	BU
JU92-2003 Proof	—	Value: 35.00				

KM# 409   10 WON
30.9400 g., 0.9990 Silver 0.9937 oz. ASW, 40 mm. **Obv:** State arms **Rev:** Children spinning tops **Edge:** Plain

Date	Mintage	F	VF	XF	Unc	BU
JU92-2003 Proof	—	Value: 35.00				

KM# 453   10 WON
31.0000 g., 0.9990 Silver 0.9956 oz. ASW **Subject:** FIFA World Championship - Germany 2006 **Obv:** National arms **Rev:** Two hands holding up cup in rays at lower right, two small players at left. **Rev. Legend:** WORLD CUP **Rev. Inscription:** FIFA

Date	Mintage	F	VF	XF	Unc	BU
JU92-2003 Proof	—	Value: 50.00				

KM# 418   10 WON
31.0000 g., 0.9990 Silver 0.9956 oz. ASW, 39.7 mm. **Obv:** State arms **Rev:** Ibis standing in water **Edge:** Segmented reeding

Date	Mintage	F	VF	XF	Unc	BU
JU93-2004 Proof	—	Value: 45.00				

KM# 342   10 WON
31.0000 g., 0.9990 Silver 0.9956 oz. ASW, 40 mm. **Obv:** State arms **Rev:** Domed building **Edge:** Plain

Date	Mintage	F	VF	XF	Unc	BU
JU93-2004 Proof	—	Value: 37.50				

KM# 343   10 WON
31.0000 g., 0.9990 Silver 0.9956 oz. ASW, 40 mm. **Obv:** State arms **Rev:** Pigeon on branch **Edge:** Segmented reeding

Date	Mintage	F	VF	XF	Unc	BU
JU93-2004 Proof	—	Value: 40.00				

KM# 344   10 WON
31.0000 g., 0.9990 Silver 0.9956 oz. ASW, 40 mm. **Obv:** State arms **Rev:** Two Leiothrix birds **Edge:** Segmented reeding

Date	Mintage	F	VF	XF	Unc	BU
JU93-2004 Proof	—	Value: 40.00				

KM# 345   10 WON
31.0000 g., 0.9990 Silver 0.9956 oz. ASW, 40 mm. **Obv:** State arms **Rev:** Two cranes standing in water **Edge:** Segmented reeding

Date	Mintage	F	VF	XF	Unc	BU
JU93-2004 Proof	—	Value: 42.00				

KM# 346   10 WON
31.0000 g., 0.9990 Silver 0.9956 oz. ASW, 40 mm. **Obv:** State arms **Rev:** Curlew bird **Edge:** Segmented reeding

Date	Mintage	F	VF	XF	Unc	BU
JU93-2004 Proof	—	Value: 40.00				

KM# 347   10 WON
31.0000 g., 0.9990 Silver 0.9956 oz. ASW, 40 mm. **Obv:** State arms **Rev:** Goshawk on branch **Edge:** Segmented reeding

Date	Mintage	F	VF	XF	Unc	BU
JU93-2004 Proof	—	Value: 40.00				

KM# 420   10 WON
30.9100 g., 0.9990 Silver 0.9927 oz. ASW, 40 mm. **Subject:** End of WWII 60th Anniversary **Obv:** State arms **Rev:** Multicolor radiant map, doves, rainbow and inscription **Edge:** Plain

Date	Mintage	F	VF	XF	Unc	BU
JU94-2005 Proof	—	Value: 35.00				

KM# 425   10 WON
1.6700 g., Aluminum, 23 mm. **Obv:** State arms **Rev:** Value

Date	Mintage	F	VF	XF	Unc	BU
JU94(2005)	—	—	—	—	1.00	1.25

KM# 256 20 WON
42.0600 g., 0.9990 Silver 1.3509 oz. ASW, 45.1 mm. **Obv:** State arms **Rev:** Rose of sharon flower **Edge:** Plain

Date	Mintage	F	VF	XF	Unc	BU
JU93-2004 Proof	—	Value: 50.00				

KM# 257 20 WON
42.0100 g., 0.9990 Silver 1.3492 oz. ASW, 45.1 mm. **Obv:** State arms **Rev:** Peony flower **Edge:** Plain

Date	Mintage	F	VF	XF	Unc	BU
JU93-2004 Proof	—	Value: 50.00				

KM# 258 20 WON
41.9200 g., 0.9990 Silver 1.3464 oz. ASW, 45.1 mm. **Obv:** State arms **Rev:** Orchid flowers **Edge:** Plain

Date	Mintage	F	VF	XF	Unc	BU
JU93-2004 Proof	—	Value: 50.00				

KM# 259 20 WON
42.0000 g., 0.9990 Silver 1.3489 oz. ASW, 45.1 mm. **Obv:** State arms **Rev:** Kim Il Sung's birth place, side view **Edge:** Plain

Date	Mintage	F	VF	XF	Unc	BU
JU93-2004 Proof	—	Value: 50.00				

KM# 260 20 WON
41.6200 g., 0.9990 Silver 1.3367 oz. ASW, 45.1 mm. **Obv:** State arms **Rev:** Mountain cabin **Edge:** Plain

Date	Mintage	F	VF	XF	Unc	BU
JU93-2004 Proof	—	Value: 50.00				

KM# 261 20 WON
41.9100 g., 0.9990 Silver 1.3460 oz. ASW, 45.1 mm. **Obv:** State arms **Rev:** Kim Il Sung's birth place, front view **Edge:** Plain

Date	Mintage	F	VF	XF	Unc	BU
JU93-2004 Proof	—	Value: 50.00				

KM# 340 20 WON
31.0000 g., 0.9990 Silver 0.9956 oz. ASW, 39.8 mm. **Obv:** State arms **Rev:** Conjoined half length figures facing shaking hands **Edge:** Segmented reeding

Date	Mintage	F	VF	XF	Unc	BU
2004 Proof	—	Value: 45.00				

KM# 341 20 WON
31.0000 g., 0.9990 Silver 0.9956 oz. ASW, 39.8 mm. **Obv:** State arms **Rev:** Bust facing **Edge:** Segmented reeding

Date	Mintage	F	VF	XF	Unc	BU
2004 Proof	—	Value: 45.00				

KM# 419 20 WON
31.0000 g., 0.9990 Silver 0.9956 oz. ASW, 39.75 mm. **Subject:** Historic Pyongyang Meeting **Obv:** State arms **Rev:** Half length figures facing each other shaking hands, English legend **Edge:** Segmented reeding

Date	Mintage	F	VF	XF	Unc	BU
2004 Proof	—	Value: 45.00				

KM# 478 20 WON
27.3000 g., Brass, 40 mm. **Obv:** Temple **Rev:** Multicolor rooster right

Date	Mintage	F	VF	XF	Unc	BU
2005 Proof	—	Value: 10.00				

KM# 479 20 WON
31.1050 g., 0.9990 Silver 0.9990 oz. ASW **Obv:** Arms **Rev:** A puppy, dog's head facing

Date	Mintage	F	VF	XF	Unc	BU
2005 Proof	—	Value: 40.00				

KM# 480 20 WON
23.7000 g., Brass, 40 mm. **Obv:** Temple **Rev:** Multicolor german shepard

Date	Mintage	F	VF	XF	Unc	BU
2006 Proof	—				Value: 10.00	

KM# 481 20 WON
Brass **Obv:** Arms **Rev:** Bejeweled female head

Date	Mintage	F	VF	XF	Unc	BU
2006 Proof	—				Value: 10.00	

KM# 482 20 WON
27.3000 g., Brass, 40 mm. **Obv:** Temple **Rev:** Multicolor pig and pigletts

Date	Mintage	F	VF	XF	Unc	BU
2007 Proof	—				Value: 10.00	

KM# 484 20 WON
27.3000 g., Brass, 40 mm. **Obv:** Temple **Rev:** Multicolor goat left

Date	Mintage	F	VF	XF	Unc	BU
2008 Proof	—				Value: 10.00	

KM# 485 20 WON
27.3000 g., Brass, 40 mm. **Obv:** Temple **Rev:** Multicolor snake and flowers

Date	Mintage	F	VF	XF	Unc	BU
2008 Proof	—				Value: 10.00	

KM# 486 20 WON
27.3000 g., Brass, 40 mm. **Obv:** Temple **Rev:** Multicolor, two rabbits

Date	Mintage	F	VF	XF	Unc	BU
2008 Proof	—				Value: 10.00	

KM# 487 20 WON
27.3000 g., Brass, 40 mm. **Obv:** Temple **Rev:** Multicolro two white rats

Date	Mintage	F	VF	XF	Unc	BU
2008 Proof	—				Value: 10.00	

KM# 488 20 WON
27.3000 g., Brass, 40 mm. **Obv:** Temple **Rev:** Multicolor monkey seated on branch

Date	Mintage	F	VF	XF	Unc	BU
2008 Proof	—				Value: 10.00	

KM# 489 20 WON
27.3000 g., Brass, 40 mm. **Obv:** Temple **Rev:** Multicolor tiger

Date	Mintage	F	VF	XF	Unc	BU
2008 Proof	—				Value: 10.00	

KM# 490 20 WON
27.3000 g., Brass, 40 mm. **Obv:** Temple **Rev:** Multicolor horse prancing right

Date	Mintage	F	VF	XF	Unc	BU
2008 Proof	—				Value: 10.00	

KM# 491 20 WON
27.3000 g., Brass, 40 mm. **Obv:** Temple **Rev:** Multicolor two oxen

Date	Mintage	F	VF	XF	Unc	BU
2008 Proof	—				Value: 10.00	

KM# 262 50 WON
69.6300 g., 0.9990 Silver 2.2363 oz. ASW, 50 mm. **Obv:** Korean map **Rev:** Huh Jun Chosun doctor with books **Edge:** Plain

Date	Mintage	F	VF	XF	Unc	BU
JU93-2004 Proof	—				Value: 85.00	

KM# 426 50 WON
2.0100 g., Aluminum, 25 mm. **Obv:** State arms **Rev:** Value

Date	Mintage	F	VF	XF	Unc	BU
JU94-2005	—	—	—	—	1.20	1.50

KM# 427 100 WON
2.2700 g., Aluminum, 27 mm. **Obv:** State arms **Rev:** Value

Date	Mintage	F	VF	XF	Unc	BU
JU94-2005	—	—	—	—	1.35	1.75

KM# 445 200 WON
5.1900 g., 0.9990 Silver 0.1667 oz. ASW, 30.00 mm. **Series:** Endangered Wildlife **Obv:** Fortress Gate **Rev:** Polar Bear standing facing **Rev. Legend:** URSUS MARITIMUS **Edge:** Plain

Date	Mintage	F	VF	XF	Unc	BU
2007 Proof	5,000				Value: 28.00	

KM# 441 500 WON
12.0000 g., 0.9990 Silver 0.3854 oz. ASW, 38.00 mm. **Subject:** 170th Anniversary First Public Railway St. Petersburg - Zarskoje Selo **Obv:** Fortress Gate **Rev:** First train arriving **Edge:** Plain

Date	Mintage	F	VF	XF	Unc	BU
ND(2007) Proof	5,000				Value: 70.00	

KM# 447 500 WON
12.0000 g., 0.9990 Silver 0.3854 oz. ASW, 38.00 mm. **Subject:** 150th Anniversay Birth of Ziolkowski and 50th Anniversary Launch of Sputnik I **Obv:** Fortress Gate **Rev:** Bust of Ziolkowski facing 3/4 right at lower left, Sputnik circling earth at upper right **Edge:** Plain

Date	Mintage	F	VF	XF	Unc	BU
ND(2007) Proof	5,000				Value: 65.00	

KM# 443 500 WON
12.0000 g., 0.9990 Silver 0.3854 oz. ASW, 38.00 mm. **Subject:** Lunar Year of the Rat **Obv:** Fortress Gate **Rev:** Two rats within circle of Lunar figures **Edge:** Plain

Date	Mintage	F	VF	XF	Unc	BU
2008	—	—	—	—	—	50.00
2008 Proof	5,000				Value: 70.00	

KM# 428 700 WON
15.5500 g., 0.9990 Silver tigereye colored center 0.4994 oz. ASW, 30.00 mm. **Series:** European Union Euro Commemoratives **Obv:** National arms **Rev:** Schleswig-Holstein City gate in relief in tigereye **Edge:** Plain

Date	Mintage	F	VF	XF	Unc	BU
2006 Proof	3,000				Value: 70.00	

KM# 429 700 WON
15.5500 g., 0.9990 Silver tigereye colored center 0.4994 oz. ASW, 30.00 mm. **Series:** European Union Euro Commemoratives **Obv:** National arms **Rev:** Vatican in relief in tigereye **Edge:** Plain

Date	Mintage	F	VF	XF	Unc	BU
2006 Proof	3,000				Value: 70.00	

KM# 430 700 WON
15.5500 g., 0.9990 Silver tigereye colored center 0.4994 oz. ASW, 30.00 mm. **Series:** European Union Euro Commemoratives **Obv:** National arms **Rev:** Male Olympic statue - discus - Athens in relief in tigereye **Edge:** Plain

Date	Mintage	F	VF	XF	Unc	BU
2006 Proof	3,000				Value: 70.00	

KM# 431 700 WON
15.5500 g., 0.9990 Silver tigereye colored center 0.4994 oz. ASW, 30.00 mm. **Series:** European Union Euro Commemoratives **Obv:** National arms **Rev:** 50th Anniversary Austrian States Treaty in relief in tigereye **Edge:** Plain

Date	Mintage	F	VF	XF	Unc	BU
2006 Proof	3,000				Value: 70.00	

KM# 432 700 WON
15.5500 g., 0.9990 Silver tigereye colored center 0.4994 oz. ASW, 30.00 mm. **Series:** European Union Euro Commemoratives **Obv:** National arms **Rev:** Don Quixote in relief in tigereye **Edge:** Plain

Date	Mintage	F	VF	XF	Unc	BU
2006 Proof	3,000				Value: 70.00	

KM# 433 700 WON
15.5500 g., 0.9990 Silver tigereye colored center 0.4994 oz. ASW, 30.00 mm. **Series:** European Union Euro Commemoratives **Obv:** National arms **Rev:** Head of Henri, Grand Duke of Luxembourg at left facing right, crowned H at right in relief in tigereye **Edge:** Plain

Date	Mintage	F	VF	XF	Unc	BU
2006 Proof	3,000				Value: 70.00	

KM# 434 700 WON
15.5500 g., 0.9990 Silver tigereye colored center 0.4994 oz. ASW, 30 mm. **Series:** European Union Euro Commemoratives **Obv:** National arms **Rev:** Italian FAO logo in relief in tigereye **Edge:** Plain

Date	Mintage	F	VF	XF	Unc	BU
2006 Proof	3,000				Value: 70.00	

KM# 435 700 WON
15.5500 g., 0.9990 Silver tigereye colored center 0.4994 oz.
ASW, 30 mm. **Series:** European Union Euro Commemoratives
Obv: National arms **Rev:** Finland - stylized flower in relief in
tigereye **Edge:** Plain

Date	Mintage	F	VF	XF	Unc	BU
2006 Proof	3,000	Value: 70.00				

KM# 436 700 WON
15.5500 g., 0.9990 Silver tigereye colored center 0.4994 oz.
ASW, 30 mm. **Series:** European Union Euro Commemoratives
Obv: National arms **Rev:** Conjoined heads of Grand Duke Henri
of Luxembourg and King Albert of Belgium left in relief in tigereye
Edge: Plain

Date	Mintage	F	VF	XF	Unc	BU
2006 Proof	3,000	Value: 70.00				

KM# 437 700 WON
15.5500 g., 0.9990 Silver tigereye colored center 0.4994 oz.
ASW, 30 mm. **Series:** European Union Euro Commemoratives
Obv: National arms **Rev:** San Marino - bust of Bartolomeo
Borghesi slightly right in relief in tigereye **Edge:** Plain

Date	Mintage	F	VF	XF	Unc	BU
2006 Proof	3,000	Value: 70.00				

KM# 438 700 WON
15.5500 g., 0.9990 Silver tigereye colored center 0.4994 oz.
ASW, 30 mm. **Series:** European Union Euro Commemoratives
Obv: National arms **Rev:** Vatican - World Youth Day in Cologne
Edge: Plain

Date	Mintage	F	VF	XF	Unc	BU
2006 Proof	3,000	Value: 70.00				

KM# 439 700 WON
15.5500 g., 0.9990 Silver tigereye colored center 0.4994 oz.
ASW, 30 mm. **Series:** European Union Euro Commemoratives
Obv: National arms **Rev:** San Marino - Year of Physics design
in relief in tigereye **Edge:** Plain

Date	Mintage	F	VF	XF	Unc	BU
2006 Proof	3,000	Value: 70.00				

KM# 440 1000 WON
20.0000 g., 0.9990 Silver 0.6423 oz. ASW, 38 mm.
Obv: National arms **Rev:** Arctic animals with map of North Pole
in background **Rev. Legend:** INTERNATIONAL POLAR YEAR
/ ARCTIC ANIMALS **Edge:** Plain

Date	Mintage	F	VF	XF	Unc	BU
ND(2007) Proof	—	Value: 85.00				

KM# 446 1000 WON
20.0000 g., 0.9990 Silver 0.6423 oz. ASW, 38 mm.
Series: Endangered Wildlife **Obv:** Fortress Gate **Rev:** Polar Bear
standing facing **Rev. Legend:** URSUS MAITIMUS **Edge:** Plain

Date	Mintage	F	VF	XF	Unc	BU
2007 Proof	5,000	Value: 70.00				

KM# 442 15000 WON
7.7800 g., 0.9990 Gold 0.2499 oz. AGW, 26 mm. **Subject:** 170th
Anniversary First Public Railway St. Petersburg - Zarskoje Selo
Obv: Fortress Gate **Rev:** First train arriving **Edge:** Plain

Date	Mintage	F	VF	XF	Unc	BU
ND(2007) Proof	2,000	Value: 425				

KM# 448 15000 WON
7.7800 g., 0.9990 Gold 0.2499 oz. AGW, 26 mm. **Subject:** 150th
Anniversary Birth of Ziolkowski and 50th Anniversary Launch of
Sputnik I **Obv:** Fortress Gate **Rev:** Bust of Ziolkowski facing 3/4
right at lower left, Sputnik circling earth at top right **Edge:** Plain

Date	Mintage	F	VF	XF	Unc	BU
ND(2007) Proof	2,000	Value: 425				

KM# 444 15000 WON
7.7800 g., 0.9990 Gold 0.2499 oz. AGW, 26 mm.
Subject: Lunar Year of the Rat **Obv:** Fortress Gate **Rev:** Two
rats within circle of Lunar figures **Edge:** Plain

Date	Mintage	F	VF	XF	Unc	BU
2008 Proof	2,000	Value: 425				

KOREA-SOUTH

The Republic of Korea, situated in northeastern Asia on the
southern half of the Korean peninsula between North Korea and
the Korean Strait, has an area of 38,025 sq. mi. (98,480 sq. km.)
and a population of 42.5 million. Capital: Seoul. The economy is
based on agriculture and light and medium industry. Some of the
world's largest oil tankers are built here. Automobiles, plywood,
electronics, and textile products are exported.

NOTE: For earlier coinage see Korea.

MINT
KOMSCO - Korea Minting and Security Printing Corporation

REPUBLIC

REFORM COINAGE
10 Hwan = 1 Won

KM# 31 WON
0.7290 g., Aluminum, 17.2 mm. **Obv:** Rose of Sharon
Rev: Value and date

Date	Mintage	F	VF	XF	Unc	BU
2001	130,000	—	—	—	0.15	0.25
2002	122,000	—	—	—	0.15	0.25
2003	20,000	—	—	—	0.15	0.25
2004	25,500	—	—	—	0.15	0.25
2005	38,000	—	—	—	0.15	0.25
2006	53,000	—	—	—	0.15	0.25
2007	53,000	—	—	—	0.15	0.25

KM# 32 5 WON
2.9500 g., Brass, 20.4 mm. **Obv:** Iron-clad turtle boat **Rev:** Value
and date

Date	Mintage	F	VF	XF	Unc	BU
2001	130,000	—	—	0.10	0.20	0.30
2002	120,000	—	—	0.10	0.20	0.30
2003	20,000	—	—	0.10	0.20	0.30
2004	25,500	—	—	0.10	0.20	0.30
2005	38,000	—	—	0.10	0.20	0.30
2006	53,000	—	—	0.10	0.20	0.30
2007	53,000	—	—	0.10	0.20	0.30

KM# 33.2 10 WON
4.0600 g., Brass **Obv:** Pagoda at Pul Guk Temple **Rev:** Thicker
value below date

Date	Mintage	F	VF	XF	Unc	BU
2001	345,000,000	—	—	0.10	0.35	0.50
2002	100,000,000	—	—	0.10	0.35	0.50
2003	128,000,000	—	—	0.10	0.35	0.50
2004	135,000,000	—	—	0.10	0.35	0.50
2005	250,000,000	—	—	0.10	0.35	0.50

KM# 33.2a 10 WON
1.2200 g., Aluminum-Bronze, 18 mm. **Obv:** Pagoda at Pul Guk
Temple **Rev:** Value below date

Date	Mintage	F	VF	XF	Unc	BU
2006	109,200,000	—	—	—	0.10	0.35
2007	—	—	—	—	0.10	0.35
2008	—	—	—	—	0.10	0.35

KM# 103 10 WON
1.3500 g., Copper Plated Aluminum, 18 mm. **Obv:** Pagoda at
Pul Guk Temple **Rev:** Value below date **Edge:** Plain
Mint: KOMSCO **Note:** Prev. KM #106.

Date	Mintage	F	VF	XF	Unc	BU
2006	40,800,000	—	—	0.10	0.20	0.25
2007	210,000,000	—	—	0.10	0.20	0.25
2008	—	—	—	0.10	0.20	0.25

KM# 34 50 WON
4.1600 g., Copper-Nickel, 21.16 mm. **Series:** F.A.O. **Obv:** Text
below sagging oat sprig **Rev:** Value and date **Note:** Die varieties
exist.

Date	Mintage	F	VF	XF	Unc	BU
2001	102,000,000	—	—	0.10	0.35	1.00
2002	100,000,000	—	—	0.10	0.35	0.50
2003	169,000,000	—	—	0.10	0.35	0.50
2004	100,000,000	—	—	0.10	0.45	1.00
2005	90,000,000	—	—	0.10	0.35	0.50
2006	120,000,000	—	—	0.10	0.35	0.50
2007	50,000,000	—	—	0.10	0.35	0.50
2008	—	—	—	0.10	0.35	0.50

KM# 35.2 100 WON
5.4200 g., Copper-Nickel, 24 mm. **Obv:** Bust with hat facing
Rev: Value and date

Date	Mintage	F	VF	XF	Unc	BU
2001	470,000,000	—	0.25	0.50	1.00	3.00
2002	490,000,000	—	0.15	0.25	0.55	1.00
2003	415,000,000	—	0.15	0.25	0.55	1.00
2004	250,000,000	—	0.15	0.25	0.55	1.00
2005	205,000,000	—	0.15	0.25	0.55	1.00
2006	310,000,000	—	0.15	0.25	0.55	0.75
2007	240,000,000	—	0.15	0.25	0.55	0.75
2008	—	—	0.15	0.25	0.55	0.75

KM# 27 500 WON
7.7000 g., Copper-Nickel, 26.5 mm. **Obv:** Manchurian crane
Rev: Value and date

Date	Mintage	F	VF	XF	Unc	BU
2001	113,000,000	—	—	1.00	2.50	5.00
2002	110,000,000	—	—	1.00	2.50	5.00

Date	Mintage	F	VF	XF	Unc	BU
2003	122,000,000	—	—	1.00	2.50	5.00
2004	45,000,000	—	—	1.00	2.50	5.00
2005	105,000,000	—	—	1.00	2.50	5.00
2006	170,000,000	—	—	1.00	2.50	5.00
2007	70,000,000	—	—	1.00	2.50	5.00
2008	—	—	—	1.00	2.50	5.00

KM# 89   1000 WON
12.0000 g., Brass, 32 mm. **Series:** World Cup Soccer
Obv: FIFA World Cup logo **Rev:** Mascot soccer player
Edge: Reeded **Mint:** Seoul

Date	Mintage	F	VF	XF	Unc	BU
2001	102,000	—	—	—	10.00	12.00

KM# 90   10000 WON
31.1035 g., 0.9990 Silver 0.9990 oz. ASW, 35 mm.
Series: World Cup Soccer **Subject:** Gwangju Stadium
Obv: Multicolor soccer logo **Rev:** Player heading the ball
Edge: Reeded **Mint:** Seoul

Date	Mintage	F	VF	XF	Unc	BU
2001 Proof	37,000	Value: 45.00				

KM# 91   10000 WON
31.1035 g., 0.9990 Silver 0.9990 oz. ASW, 35 mm.
Series: World Sup Soccer **Subject:** Busan Stadium
Obv: Multicolor soccer logo **Rev:** Player kicking the ball
Edge: Reeded **Mint:** Seoul

Date	Mintage	F	VF	XF	Unc	BU
2001 Proof	37,000	Value: 45.00				

KM# 92   10000 WON
31.1035 g., 0.9990 Silver 0.9990 oz. ASW, 35 mm.
Series: World Cup Soccer **Subject:** Daegu Stadium
Obv: Multicolor soccer logo **Rev:** Player controlling the ball
Edge: Reeded **Mint:** Seoul

Date	Mintage	F	VF	XF	Unc	BU
2001 Proof	37,000	Value: 45.00				

KM# 93   10000 WON
31.1035 g., 0.9990 Silver 0.9990 oz. ASW, 35 mm.
Series: World Cup Soccer **Subject:** Suwon Stadium
Obv: Multicolor soccer logo **Rev:** Player kicking the ball
Edge: Reeded **Mint:** Seoul

Date	Mintage	F	VF	XF	Unc	BU
2001 Proof	37,000	Value: 45.00				

KM# 98   10000 WON
31.1035 g., 0.9990 Silver 0.9990 oz. ASW, 35 mm. **Obv:** Multicolor FIFA World Cup logo **Rev:** Player "Heading" ball
Edge: Reeded **Mint:** Seoul

Date	Mintage	F	VF	XF	Unc	BU
2002 Proof	—	Value: 45.00				

KM# 99   10000 WON
31.1035 g., 0.9990 Silver 0.9990 oz. ASW, 35 mm. **Obv:** Multicolor FIFA World Cup logo **Rev:** Goalie catching ball
Edge: Reeded **Mint:** Seoul

Date	Mintage	F	VF	XF	Unc	BU
2002 Proof	—	Value: 45.00				

KM# 100   10000 WON
31.1035 g., 0.9990 Silver 0.9990 oz. ASW, 35 mm. **Obv:** Multicolor FIFA World Cup logo **Rev:** Player's legs kicking ball
Edge: Reeded **Mint:** Seoul

Date	Mintage	F	VF	XF	Unc	BU
2002 Proof	—	Value: 45.00				

KM# 101   10000 WON
31.1035 g., 0.9990 Silver 0.9990 oz. ASW, 35 mm. **Obv:** Multicolor FIFA World Cup logo **Rev:** Two players legs and ball
Edge: Reeded **Mint:** Seoul

Date	Mintage	F	VF	XF	Unc	BU
2002 Proof	—	Value: 45.00				

KM# 94   20000 WON
15.5518 g., 0.9990 Gold 0.4995 oz. AGW, 28 mm.
Series: World Cup Soccer **Obv:** Soccer logo **Rev:** World Cup soccer trophy **Edge:** Reeded **Mint:** Seoul

Date	Mintage	F	VF	XF	Unc	BU
2001 Proof	20,000	Value: 650				

KM# 97   20000 WON
20.7000 g., Silver, 35 mm. **Obv:** Blue circle with APEC, 2005 Korea at bottom at upper center, Vista Pacific Economic Cooperation and value below **Rev:** APEC on World map at upper center, building below with Korean words below it

Date	Mintage	F	VF	XF	Unc	BU
2005 Proof	10,000	Value: 65.00				

KM# 102   20000 WON
20.7000 g., 0.9990 Silver 0.6648 oz. ASW **Subject:** 60th Anniversary of Independence **Obv:** Adult hand reaching out towards child's hand **Mint:** KOMSCO **Note:** Prev. KM #103.

Date	Mintage	F	VF	XF	Unc	BU
2005 Proof	10,000	Value: 65.00				

KM# 104   20000 WON
19.0000 g., 0.9990 Silver 0.6102 oz. ASW **Subject:** 560th Year of Hangeul - Alphabet **Obv:** Early alphabet characters
Obv. Legend: THE BANK OF KOREA **Rev:** Modern alphabet characters **Shape:** Round with square center hole
Mint: KOMSCO

Date	Mintage	F	VF	XF	Unc	BU
2006 Proof	—	Value: 75.00				

KM# 105   20000 WON
19.0000 g., 0.9990 Silver 0.6102 oz. ASW, 33.00 mm.
Series: Traditional Folk Dance **Subject:** Talchum - Mask Dances **Obv:** Mask at center surrounded by 6 other masks **Obv. Legend:** THE BANK OF KOREA **Rev:** Mask dancer at left center **Edge:** Plain **Shape:** 12-sided **Mint:** KOMSCO **Note:** Prev. KM #102.

Date	Mintage	F	VF	XF	Unc	BU
2007 Proof	50,000	Value: 75.00				

KM# 106   20000 WON
19.0000 g., 0.9990 Silver 0.6102 oz. ASW, 33 mm.
Subject: Mask dance **Rev:** Ganggangsullae ("Circle dance")
Shape: 12-sided **Mint:** KOMSCO

Date	Mintage	F	VF	XF	Unc	BU
2008 Proof	50,000	Value: 75.00				

KM# 108   20000 WON
19.0000 g., 0.9000 Silver 0.5498 oz. ASW, 33 mm.
Subject: Mask dance **Rev:** Youngsan Juldarigi (Tug of War)
Mint: KOMSCO

Date	Mintage	F	VF	XF	Unc	BU
2009 Proof	50,000	Value: 75.00				

KM# 95   30000 WON
31.1035 g., 0.9990 Gold 0.9990 oz. AGW, 35 mm.
Series: World Cup Soccer **Obv:** Soccer logo **Rev:** Nude soccer player flanked by other players **Edge:** Reeded **Mint:** Seoul

Date	Mintage	F	VF	XF	Unc	BU
2001 Proof	12,000	Value: 1,275				

KM# 107   30000 WON
Silver **Subject:** Flag, 60th Anniversary **Obv:** Flag **Rev:** Multicolor 60 logo **Mint:** KOMSCO

Date	Mintage	F	VF	XF	Unc	BU
2008 Proof	—	Value: 75.00				

MINT SETS

KM#	Date	Mintage	Identification	Issue Price	Mkt Val
MS8	2001 (7)	—	KM#27, 31, 32, 33.2, 34, 35.2, 89	10.00	20.00

PROOF SETS

KM#	Date	Mintage Identification	Issue Price	Mkt Val
PS10	2001 (6)	2,002 KM#90-95	—	2,100

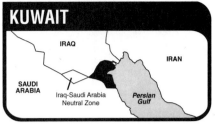

KUWAIT

The State of Kuwait, a constitutional monarchy located on the Arabian Peninsula at the northwestern corner of the Persian Gulf, has an area of 6,880 sq. mi. (17,820 sq. km.) and a population of 1.7 million. Capital: Kuwait. Petroleum, the basis of the economy, provides 95 percent of the exports.

RULERS
Al Sabah Dynasty
Jabir Ibn Ahmad, 1977-2006
Sabah Al Ahmad Al Sabah, 2006-

MONETARY SYSTEM
1000 Fils = 1 Dinar

SOVEREIGN EMIRATE
MODERN COINAGE

KM# 9a FILS
2.4100 g., 0.9250 Silver 0.0717 oz. ASW, 17 mm. **Ruler:** Jabir Ibn Ahmad **Obv:** Value within circle **Rev:** Ship with sails

Date	Mintage	F	VF	XF	Unc	BU
AH1429-2008 Proof	—	Value: 65.00				

KM# 9c FILS
2.4100 g., 0.9250 Silver Gilt 0.0717 oz. ASW, 17 mm. **Obv:** Value within circle **Rev:** Dhow, dates below

Date	Mintage	F	VF	XF	Unc	BU
AH1429-2008 Proof	—	Value: 70.00				

KM# 10 5 FILS
2.5000 g., Nickel-Brass, 19.5 mm. **Ruler:** Jabir Ibn Ahmad **Obv:** Value within circle **Rev:** Dhow, dates below

Date	Mintage	F	VF	XF	Unc	BU
AH1422-2001	—	—	0.10	0.20	0.40	—
AH1424-2003	—	—	0.10	0.20	0.40	—
AH1426-2005	—	—	0.10	0.20	0.40	—

KM# 10a 5 FILS
3.0100 g., 0.9250 Silver 0.0895 oz. ASW, 19.5 mm. **Ruler:** Jabir Ibn Ahmad **Obv:** Value within circle **Rev:** Ship with sails

Date	Mintage	F	VF	XF	Unc	BU
AH1429-2008 Proof	—	Value: 70.00				

KM# 10c 5 FILS
3.0100 g., 0.9250 Silver Gilt 0.0895 oz. ASW, 19.5 mm. **Obv:** Value in circle **Rev:** Dhow, dates below

Date	Mintage	F	VF	XF	Unc	BU
AH1429-2008 Proof	—	Value: 75.00				

KM# 11 10 FILS
3.7500 g., Nickel-Brass, 21 mm. **Ruler:** Jabir Ibn Ahmad **Obv:** Value within circle **Rev:** Dhow, dates below

Date	Mintage	F	VF	XF	Unc	BU
AH1422-2001	—	—	0.15	0.25	0.75	—
AH1424-2003	—	—	0.15	0.25	0.75	—
AH1426-2005	—	—	0.15	0.25	0.75	—

KM# 11a 10 FILS
4.3500 g., 0.9250 Silver 0.1294 oz. ASW, 21 mm. **Ruler:** Jabir Ibn Ahmad **Obv:** Value within circle **Rev:** Ship with sails

Date	Mintage	F	VF	XF	Unc	BU
AH1429-2008 Proof	—	Value: 75.00				

KM# 11c 10 FILS
4.3500 g., 0.9250 Silver Gilt 0.1294 oz. ASW, 21 mm. **Obv:** Value within circle **Rev:** Dhow, dates below

Date	Mintage	F	VF	XF	Unc	BU
AH1429-2008 Proof	—	Value: 80.00				

KM# 12c 20 FILS
Stainless Steel, 20 mm. **Ruler:** Jabir Ibn Ahmad **Obv:** Value **Rev:** Dhow, dates below

Date	Mintage	F	VF	XF	Unc	BU
AH1422-2001	—	—	0.20	0.35	1.00	—
AH1424-2003	—	—	0.20	0.35	1.00	—
AH1426-2005	—	—	0.20	0.35	1.00	—

KM# 12 20 FILS
3.0000 g., Copper-Nickel, 20 mm. **Ruler:** Jabir Ibn Ahmad **Obv:** Value within circle **Rev:** Dhow, dates below **Note:** Varieties exist.

Date	Mintage	F	VF	XF	Unc	BU
AH1424-2003	—	—	0.20	0.45	2.00	—
AH1426-2005	—	—	0.20	0.45	2.00	—

KM# 12a 20 FILS
3.3700 g., 0.9250 Silver 0.1002 oz. ASW, 20 mm. **Ruler:** Jabir Ibn Ahmad **Obv:** Value within circle **Rev:** Dhow, dates below

Date	Mintage	F	VF	XF	Unc	BU
AH1429-2008 Proof	—	Value: 80.00				

KM# 12d 20 FILS
3.3700 g., 0.9250 Silver Gilt 0.1002 oz. ASW, 20 mm. **Obv:** Value within circle **Rev:** Dhow, dates below

Date	Mintage	F	VF	XF	Unc	BU
1429-2008 Proof	—	Value: 85.00				

KM# 13 50 FILS
4.5000 g., Copper-Nickel, 23 mm. **Ruler:** Jabir Ibn Ahmad **Obv:** Value within circle **Rev:** Dhow, dates below

Date	Mintage	F	VF	XF	Unc	BU
AH1424-2003	—	—	0.25	0.35	1.00	—
AH1426-2005	—	—	0.25	0.35	1.00	—
AH1427-2006	—	—	0.25	0.35	1.00	—

KM# 13a 50 FILS
5.0700 g., 0.9250 Silver 0.1508 oz. ASW, 23 mm. **Ruler:** Jabir Ibn Ahmad **Obv:** Value within circle **Rev:** Ship with sails

Date	Mintage	F	VF	XF	Unc	BU
AH1429-2008 Proof	—	Value: 85.00				

KM# 13c 50 FILS
5.0700 g., 0.9250 Silver Gilt 0.1508 oz. ASW, 23 mm. **Obv:** Value within circle **Rev:** Dhow, dates below

Date	Mintage	F	VF	XF	Unc	BU
1429-2008 Proof	—	Value: 90.00				

KM# 14 100 FILS
6.5000 g., Copper-Nickel, 26 mm. **Ruler:** Jabir Ibn Ahmad **Obv:** Value within circle **Rev:** Dhow, dates below

Date	Mintage	F	VF	XF	Unc	BU
AH1424-2003	—	—	0.50	0.75	1.50	—
AH1426-2005	—	—	0.50	0.75	1.50	—

KM# 14a 100 FILS
7.3400 g., 0.9250 Silver 0.2183 oz. ASW, 26 mm. **Ruler:** Jabir Ibn Ahmad **Obv:** Value within circle **Rev:** Ship with sails

Date	Mintage	F	VF	XF	Unc	BU
AH1429-2008 Proof	—	Value: 90.00				

KM# 14c 100 FILS
7.3400 g., 0.9250 Silver Gilt 0.2183 oz. ASW, 26 mm. **Obv:** Value within circle **Rev:** Dhow, dates below

Date	Mintage	F	VF	XF	Unc	BU
1429-2008 Proof	—	Value: 100				

PROOF SETS

KM#	Date	Mintage Identification	Issue Price	Mkt Val
PS5	2008 (6)	— KM#9a-14a	—	450
PS6	2008 (6)	— KM#9c-11c, 12d, 13c-14c	—	500

KYRGYZSTAN

The Republic of Kyrgyzstan, (formerly Kirghiz S.S.R., a Union Republic of the U.S.S.R.), is an independent state since Aug. 31, 1991, a member of the United Nations and of the C.I.S. It was the last state of the Union Republics to declare its sovereignty. Capital: Bishkek (formerly Frunze).

MONETARY SYSTEM
100 Tiyin = 1 Som

REPUBLIC
STANDARD COINAGE

KM# 11 TIYIN
1.0000 g., Aluminum-Bronze, 13.98 mm. **Obv:** National arms **Rev:** Flower at left of value **Edge:** Reeded **Note:** Prev. KM #8.

Date	Mintage	F	VF	XF	Unc	BU
2008 In sets only	95,000	—	—	—	0.65	1.00

KM# 12 10 TIYIN
1.3300 g., Brass Plated Steel, 14.94 mm. **Obv:** National arms **Rev:** Flower at left of value **Edge:** Plain **Note:** Prev. KM #9.

Date	Mintage	F	VF	XF	Unc	BU
2008	—	—	—	—	0.85	1.50

KM# 13 50 TIYIN
1.8600 g., Brass Plated Steel, 16.94 mm. **Obv:** National arms **Rev:** Flower at left of value **Edge:** Plain **Note:** Prev. KM #10.

Date	Mintage	F	VF	XF	Unc	BU
2008	—	—	—	—	1.25	2.00

KM# 19 SOM
12.0000 g., Copper-Nickel, 30 mm. **Series:** Great Silk Road **Subject:** Tashrabat **Obv:** Arms **Rev:** Fortress

Date	Mintage	F	VF	XF	Unc	BU
2008 Prooflike	5,000	—	—	—	12.00	20.00

KM# 14 SOM
2.5700 g., Nickel Plated Steel, 18.96 mm. **Obv:** National arms **Rev:** Symbol at left of denomination **Edge:** Reeded **Note:** Prev. KM #11.

Date	Mintage	F	VF	XF	Unc	BU
2008	—	—	—	—	1.50	2.25

KM# 21   SOM

12.0000 g., Copper-Nickel, 30 mm. **Subject:** Uzgen Architectural Complex **Obv:** Arms **Rev:** Tower and building - map above

Date	Mintage	F	VF	XF	Unc	BU
2008 Prooflike	5,000	—	—	—	12.00	20.00

KM# 35   SOM

12.0000 g., Copper-Nickel, 30 mm. **Series:** Great Silk Road **Subject:** Burana Tower **Rev:** Tower and map

Date	Mintage	F	VF	XF	Unc	BU
2008 Prooflike	5,000	—	—	—	12.00	20.00

KM# 20   SOM

28.2800 g., Copper-Nickel, 30 mm. **Series:** Great Silk Road **Subject:** Uzgen architecture complex

Date	Mintage	F	VF	XF	Unc	BU
2009 Proof	5,000	—	—	—	12.00	20.00

KM# 31   SOM

12.0000 g., Copper-Nickel, 30 mm. **Series:** Great Silk Road **Subject:** Suilaman Mountain

Date	Mintage	F	VF	XF	Unc	BU
2009 Prooflike	5,000	—	—	—	12.00	20.00

KM# 33   SOM

12.0000 g., Copper-Nickel, 30 mm. **Series:** Great Silk Road **Subject:** Lake Issykkul

Date	Mintage	F	VF	XF	Unc	BU
2009 Prooflike	5,000	—	—	—	15.00	25.00

KM# 15   3 SOM

3.1800 g., Nickel Plated Steel, 20.97 mm. **Obv:** National arms **Rev:** Symbol above right of denomination **Edge:** Reeded **Note:** Prev. KM# 12.

Date	Mintage	F	VF	XF	Unc	BU
2008	—	—	—	—	1.25	2.00

KM# 16   5 SOM

4.2800 g., Nickel Plated Steel, 22.95 mm. **Obv:** National arms **Rev:** Symbol at right of value **Edge:** Reeded **Note:** Prev. KM# 13.

Date	Mintage	F	VF	XF	Unc	BU
2008	—	—	—	—	1.50	2.50

KM# 4   10 SOM

28.2800 g., 0.9250 Silver 0.8410 oz. ASW, 38.6 mm. **Subject:** Tenth Anniversary of Republic **Obv:** National arms within circle **Rev:** Value and Khan Tengri mountain **Edge:** Reeded **Note:** Prev. KM #3.

Date	Mintage	F	VF	XF	Unc	BU
2001 Proof	1,000	Value: 175				

KM# 5   10 SOM

28.2800 g., 0.9250 Silver 0.8410 oz. ASW, 38.6 mm. **Subject:** International Year of the mountains **Obv:** National arms **Rev:** Edelweiss flower and mountain **Edge:** Reeded **Note:** Prev. KM #4.

Date	Mintage	F	VF	XF	Unc	BU
2002 Proof	1,000	Value: 125				

KM# 6   10 SOM

28.2800 g., 0.9250 Silver 0.8410 oz. ASW, 38.6 mm. **Subject:** International Year of the mountains **Obv:** National arms **Rev:** Argali Ram head and mountain **Edge:** Reeded **Note:** Prev. KM #5.

Date	Mintage	F	VF	XF	Unc	BU
2002 Proof	1,000	Value: 125				

KM# 7   10 SOM

28.2800 g., 0.9250 Silver partially gilt 0.8410 oz. ASW, 38.6 mm. **Subject:** Genesis of the Kyrgyz Statehood **Obv:** Arms **Rev:** Classical designs

Date	Mintage	F	VF	XF	Unc	BU
2003 Proof	1,000	Value: 250				

KM# 8   10 SOM

28.2800 g., 0.9250 Silver 0.8410 oz. ASW, 38.6 mm. **Subject:** 60 Years of Great Victory **Rev:** Figure of a mother, eternal light, Victory Memorial complex **Note:** Prev. KM #6.

Date	Mintage	F	VF	XF	Unc	BU
2005 Proof	1,000	Value: 100				

KM# 9   10 SOM

28.2800 g., 0.8250 Silver partially gilt 0.7501 oz. ASW, 38.6 mm. **Series:** Great Silk Road **Subject:** Tashrabat **Note:** Prev. KM #7.

Date	Mintage	F	VF	XF	Unc	BU
2005 Proof	1,500	Value: 100				

KM# 10   10 SOM

28.2800 g., 0.9250 Silver 0.8410 oz. ASW, 38.6 mm. **Subject:** Shanghai Cooperation **Obv:** Arms **Rev:** Multicolor logo of the Shanghai Cooperation Organization

Date	Mintage	F	VF	XF	Unc	BU
2007 Proof	1,000	Value: 150				

KM# 22 10 SOM
28.2800 g., 0.9250 Silver partially gilt 0.8410 oz. ASW, 38.6 mm.
Series: Great Silk Road **Subject:** Uzgen Architectural Complex

Date	Mintage	F	VF	XF	Unc	BU
2007 Proof	1,500	Value: 100				

KM# 18 10 SOM
28.2800 g., 0.9250 Silver partially gilt 0.8410 oz. ASW, 38.6 mm.
Series: Great Silk Road **Subject:** Burana Tower **Rev:** Buildings with partial gilting

Date	Mintage	F	VF	XF	Unc	BU
2008 Proof	1,500	Value: 100				

KM# 23 10 SOM
28.2800 g., 0.9250 Silver 0.8410 oz. ASW, 38.6 mm.
Series: Capitals of the Eurasia Economic Community
Subject: City of Bishkek **Obv:** National emblem **Rev:** Horseman statue, multicolor logo

Date	Mintage	F	VF	XF	Unc	BU
2008 Proof	2,500	Value: 90.00				

KM# 24 10 SOM
28.2800 g., 0.9250 Silver 0.8410 oz. ASW, 38.6 mm.
Rev: Chynqyz Aytmatov

Date	Mintage	F	VF	XF	Unc	BU
2009 Proof	2,000	Value: 75.00				

KM# 25 10 SOM
28.2800 g., 0.9250 Silver 0.8410 oz. ASW, 38.6 mm.
Series: Chinqiz Aitmatov's work's **Rev:** Jamila

Date	Mintage	F	VF	XF	Unc	BU
2009 Proof	3,000	Value: 75.00				

KM# 26 10 SOM
28.2800 g., 0.9250 Silver 0.8410 oz. ASW, 38.6 mm.
Series: Chinqiz Aitmatov's works **Rev:** Duishen

Date	Mintage	F	VF	XF	Unc	BU
2009 Proof	3,000	Value: 75.00				

KM# 27 10 SOM
28.2800 g., 0.9250 Silver 0.8410 oz. ASW, 38.6 mm.
Series: Chinqiz Aitmatov's works **Rev:** Mother field

Date	Mintage	F	VF	XF	Unc	BU
2009 Proof	3,000	Value: 75.00				

KM# 28 10 SOM
28.2800 g., 0.9250 Silver 0.8410 oz. ASW, 38.5 mm.
Series: Chinqiz Aitmatov's works **Rev:** Farewell, Gulsary!

Date	Mintage	F	VF	XF	Unc	BU
2009 Proof	3,000	Value: 75.00				

KM# 29 10 SOM
28.2800 g., 0.9250 Silver 0.8410 oz. ASW, 38.5 mm.
Series: Chinqiz Aitmatov's works **Rev:** The white ship

Date	Mintage	F	VF	XF	Unc	BU
2009 Proof	3,000	Value: 75.00				

KM# 32 10 SOM
28.2800 g., 0.9250 Silver Partially gilt 0.8410 oz. ASW, 38.6 mm.
Series: Great Silk Road **Subject:** Suliman Mountain

Date	Mintage	F	VF	XF	Unc	BU
2009 Proof	1,500	Value: 100				

KM# 34 10 SOM
28.2800 g., 0.9250 Silver partially gilt 0.8410 oz. ASW, 38.6 mm.
Series: Great Silk Road **Subject:** Lake Issykkul

Date	Mintage	F	VF	XF	Unc	BU
2009 Proof	1,500	Value: 100				

MINT SETS

KM#	Date	Mintage Identification	Issue Price	Mkt Val
MS1	2008 (6)	— KM#11-16	—	30.00

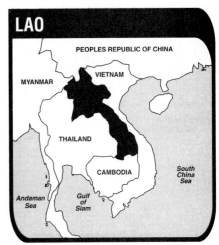

LAO

The Lao Peoples Democratic Republic, located on the Indo-Chinese Peninsula between the Socialist Republic of Vietnam and the Kingdom of Thailand, has an area of 91,428 sq. mi. (236,800 km.) and a population of 3.6 million. Capital Vientiane. Agriculture employs 95 per cent of the people. Tin, lumber and coffee are exported.

PEOPLES DEMOCRATIC REPUBLIC

STANDARD COINAGE
100 Att = 1 Kip

KM# 85   1000 KIP
31.5000 g., 0.9990 Silver 1.0117 oz. ASW, 38.5 mm.
Subject: Olympics **Obv:** State emblem **Rev:** Freestyle skier
Edge: Reeded

Date	Mintage	F	VF	XF	Unc	BU
2001 Proof	—	Value: 45.00				

KM# 96   1000 KIP
31.4500 g., 0.9990 Silver 1.0101 oz. ASW, 38.5 mm. **Obv:** State emblem **Rev:** Soccer player **Edge:** Reeded

Date	Mintage	F	VF	XF	Unc	BU
2001 Proof	—	Value: 45.00				

KM# 86   15000 KIP
20.0000 g., 0.9250 Silver 0.5948 oz. ASW, 38.7 mm.
Subject: Year of the Horse **Obv:** State emblem **Rev:** Multicolor horse **Edge:** Reeded

Date	Mintage	F	VF	XF	Unc	BU
2002 Proof	9,500	Value: 45.00				

KM# 87   15000 KIP
20.0000 g., 0.9250 Silver 0.5948 oz. ASW, 38.7 mm.
Subject: Year of the Horse **Obv:** State emblem **Rev:** Horse with multicolor holographic background **Edge:** Reeded

Date	Mintage	F	VF	XF	Unc	BU
2002 Proof	9,500	Value: 50.00				

KM# 94   15000 KIP
20.0000 g., 0.9990 Silver 0.6423 oz. ASW, 38.7 mm. **Obv:** State emblem **Rev:** Multicolor Golden Monkey **Edge:** Reeded

Date	Mintage	F	VF	XF	Unc	BU
2004 Proof	2,300	Value: 50.00				

KM# 98   15000 KIP
Silver, 38.7 mm. **Issuer:** Bank of Lao PDR **Obv:** National arms **Obv. Legend:** THE LAO PEOPLE'S DEMOCRATIC REPUBLIC **Rev:** Statue of Mazu with stylized Phoenix at left and right **Rev. Legend:** GODDESS OF THE SEA **Edge:** Reeded

Date	Mintage	F	VF	XF	Unc	BU
2006 Proof	6,888	Value: 60.00				

KM# 88   60000 KIP
155.5175 g., 0.9250 Silver 4.6248 oz. ASW, 65 mm.
Subject: Year of the Horse **Obv:** State emblem **Rev:** Multicolor horse **Edge:** Reeded

Date	Mintage	F	VF	XF	Unc	BU
2002 Proof	1,000	Value: 200				

KM# 89   100000 KIP
15.5518 g., 0.9999 Gold 0.4999 oz. AGW, 27 mm. **Subject:** Year of the Horse **Obv:** State emblem **Rev:** Horse **Edge:** Reeded

Date	Mintage	F	VF	XF	Unc	BU
2002	2,000	Value: 625				

KM# 95   100000 KIP
15.5518 g., 0.9990 Gold 0.4995 oz. AGW, 27 mm. **Obv:** State emblem **Rev:** Black Gibbon on holographic background **Edge:** Reeded

Date	Mintage	F	VF	XF	Unc	BU
2004 Proof	888	Value: 650				

KM# 90   1000000 KIP
155.5175 g., 0.9999 Gold 4.9993 oz. AGW, 55 mm.
Subject: Year of the Horse **Obv:** State emblem **Rev:** Horse with multicolor holographic background **Edge:** Reeded

Date	Mintage	F	VF	XF	Unc	BU
2002 Proof	500	Value: 6,000				

KM# 99   1000000 KIP
155.5150 g., 0.9999 Gold 4.9992 oz. AGW, 55.0 mm.
Issuer: Bank of Lao PDR **Obv:** National arms **Obv. Legend:** THE LAO PEOPLE'S DEMOCRATIC REPUBLIC **Rev:** Multilatent color bust of Lord Buddha "Fo Guang Pu Zhao" facing with diamond insert in forehead **Edge:** Reeded

Date	Mintage	F	VF	XF	Unc	BU
2006 Proof	99	Value: 6,250				

PROOF SETS

KM#	Date	Mintage	Identification	Issue Price	Mkt Val
PS7	2000-2001 (3)	3,500	KM#74-76	138	200
PS8	2000-2001 (3)	500	KM#74-76	214	300
PS9	2000-2001 (2)	800	KM#78, 83	—	950

LATVIA

The Republic of Latvia, the central Baltic state in east Europe, has an area of 24,749 sq. mi. (43,601 sq. km.) and a population of *2.6 million. Capital: Riga. Livestock raising and manufacturing are the chief industries. Butter, bacon, fertilizers and telephone equipment are exported.

MODERN REPUBLIC
1991-present
STANDARD COINAGE
100 Santimu = 1 Lats

KM# 15   SANTIMS
1.6000 g., Copper Clad Steel, 15.65 mm. **Obv:** National arms **Rev:** Value flanked by diamonds below lined arch **Edge:** Plain

Date	Mintage	F	VF	XF	Unc	BU
2003	30,000,000	—	—	0.10	0.30	0.40
2005	20,000,000	—	—	0.10	0.30	0.40
2007	25,000,000	—	—	0.10	0.30	0.40
2008	75,000,000	—	—	0.10	0.30	0.40

KM# 21   2 SANTIMI
1.9000 g., Copper Clad Steel, 17 mm. **Obv:** National arms **Rev:** Lined arch above value flanked by diamonds **Edge:** Plain

Date	Mintage	F	VF	XF	Unc	BU
2006	18,000,000	—	—	0.15	0.45	0.60
2007	30,000,000	—	—	0.15	0.45	0.60
2009	50,000,000	—	—	0.15	0.45	0.60

KM# 16   5 SANTIMI
2.5000 g., Copper-Nickel-Zinc, 18.5 mm. **Obv:** National arms **Obv. Legend:** LATVIJAS REPUBLIKA **Rev:** Lined arch above value flanked by diamonds **Edge:** Plain

Date	Mintage	F	VF	XF	Unc	BU
2006	8,000,000	—	—	0.30	0.75	1.00
2007	15,000,000	—	—	0.30	0.75	1.00
2009	10,000,000	—	—	0.30	0.75	1.00

KM# 17   10 SANTIMU
3.2500 g., Copper-Nickel-Zinc, 19.9 mm. **Obv:** National arms **Rev:** Lined arch above value flanked by diamonds

Date	Mintage	F	VF	XF	Unc	BU
2008	15,000,000	—	—	0.45	1.10	1.50

KM# 22.1   20 SANTIMU
4.0000 g., Copper-Zinc-Nickel, 21.5 mm. **Obv:** National arms **Rev:** Lined arch above value flanked by diamonds **Edge:** Plain
Note: 1.5mm thick.

Date	Mintage	F	VF	XF	Unc	BU
2007	15,000,000	—	—	0.60	1.50	2.00
2009	10,000,000	—	—	0.60	1.50	2.00

KM# 13   50 SANTIMU
3.5000 g., Copper-Nickel, 18.73 mm. **Obv:** National arms **Rev:** Triple sprig above value **Edge:** Reeded

Date	Mintage	F	VF	XF	Unc	BU
2007	4,000,000	—	—	1.70	3.00	4.00
2009	10,000,000	—	—	1.70	3.00	4.00

KM# 70   100 SANTIMU
31.4700 g., 0.9250 Silver 0.9359 oz. ASW, 38.6 mm.
Obv: Baron von Muenchausen with chain of birds around a dog with a lantern hanging from its tail. **Rev:** Baron von Muenchausen and dog hunting a circle of animals **Edge Lettering:** LATVIJAS BANKA LATVIJAS REPUBLIKA

Date	Mintage	F	VF	XF	Unc	BU
2005 Proof	Est. 5,000	Value: 45.00				

KM# 49   LATS
31.4700 g., 0.9250 Silver 0.9359 oz. ASW, 38.6 mm.
Subject: Hanseatic City of Cesis **Obv:** City arms **Rev:** Sailing ship above, inverted walled city view below **Edge Lettering:** LATVIJAS REPUBLIKA • LATVIJAS BANKA

Date	Mintage	F	VF	XF	Unc	BU
2001 Proof	Est. 15,000	Value: 70.00				

KM# 50   LATS
31.4700 g., 0.9250 Silver 0.9359 oz. ASW **Series:** Ice Hockey **Obv:** Arms with supporters **Rev:** Hockey player

Date	Mintage	F	VF	XF	Unc	BU
2001 Proof	Est. 25,000	Value: 90.00				

KM# 51 LATS
31.4700 g., 0.9250 Silver 0.9359 oz. ASW, 38.6 mm.
Series: Roots - Heaven **Obv:** Stylized design **Rev:** Styilized woman holding sun **Edge:** Plain

Date	Mintage	F	VF	XF	Unc	BU
2001 Proof	Est. 5,000	Value: 50.00				

KM# 54 LATS
4.8000 g., Copper-Nickel, 21.75 mm. **Obv:** Arms with supporters **Rev:** Stork above value **Edge Lettering:** LATVIJAS BANKA LATVIJAS BANKA

Date	Mintage	F	VF	XF	Unc	BU
2001	250,000	—	—	7.00	12.00	15.00

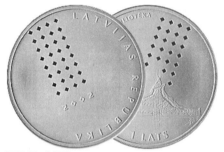

KM# 55 LATS
31.4700 g., 0.9250 Silver 0.9359 oz. ASW, 38.6 mm.
Subject: National Library **Obv:** Country name and diamonds pattern **Rev:** Library building sketch and diamonds design **Edge Lettering:** GAISMU SAUCA - GAISMA AUSA

Date	Mintage	F	VF	XF	Unc	BU
2002 Proof	Est. 5,000	Value: 80.00				

KM# 56 LATS
15.0000 g., 0.9250 Silver 0.4461 oz. ASW, 28 mm.
Subject: "Fortune" **Obv:** Totally gold plated sun above country name **Rev:** Waning moon, date and value **Edge:** Plain

Date	Mintage	F	VF	XF	Unc	BU
2002 Proof	Est. 5,000	Value: 250				

KM# 52 LATS
31.4700 g., 0.9250 Silver 0.9359 oz. ASW, 38.6 mm.
Series: Roots - Destiny **Obv:** Stylized design **Rev:** Apple tree and landscape **Edge:** Plain

Date	Mintage	F	VF	XF	Unc	BU
2002 Proof	Est. 5,000	Value: 85.00				

KM# 53 LATS
31.4700 g., 0.9250 Silver 0.9359 oz. ASW, 38.6 mm.
Subject: Hanseatic City of Kuldiga **Obv:** City arms **Rev:** City view and ships **Edge:** Lettered

Date	Mintage	F	VF	XF	Unc	BU
2002 Proof	Est. 15,000	Value: 80.00				

KM# 57 LATS
31.4700 g., 0.9250 Silver 0.9359 oz. ASW, 38.6 mm.
Subject: Olympics 2004 **Obv:** Arms with supporters **Rev:** Ancient wrestlers **Edge Lettering:** LATVIJAS BANKA • LATVIJAS BANKA

Date	Mintage	F	VF	XF	Unc	BU
2002 Proof	Est. 26,000	Value: 70.00				

KM# 60 LATS
31.4700 g., 0.9250 Silver 0.9359 oz. ASW, 38.6 mm.
Obv: Crowned arms above partially built ship **Rev:** Hemp weighing scene with Iron foundry and brick wall in background **Edge Lettering:** REPUBLIKA LATVIJAS • BANKA LATVIJA

Date	Mintage	F	VF	XF	Unc	BU
2003 Proof	Est. 5,000	Value: 70.00				

KM# 71 LATS
31.4700 g., 0.9250 Silver 0.9359 oz. ASW, 38.6 mm. **Subject:** Vidzeme **Obv:** Crowned arms above horse drawn wagon **Rev:** Two men sawing wood **Edge Lettering:** Rahapaja Oy

Date	Mintage	F	VF	XF	Unc	BU
ND (2003) Proof	—	Value: 50.00				
2004 Proof	Est. 5,000	Value: 50.00				

KM# 72 LATS
31.4700 g., 0.9250 Silver 0.9359 oz. ASW, 38.6 mm. **Subject:** Latgale **Obv:** Madonna and Child above landscape **Rev:** Man sowing seeds and an angel **Edge Lettering:** Rahapaja Oy

Date	Mintage	F	VF	XF	Unc	BU
ND (2003) Proof	—	Value: 50.00				
2004 Proof	Est. 5,000	Value: 50.00				

KM# 75 LATS
31.4700 g., 0.9250 Silver 0.9359 oz. ASW, 38.61 mm.
Obv: Coat of arms **Rev:** St. Simanis Church with VALMIERA and reflection of sailing ship **Edge:** LATVIJAS REPUBLIKA • LATVIJAS BANKA

Date	Mintage	F	VF	XF	Unc	BU
2003 Proof	Est. 15,000	Value: 50.00				

KM# 58 LATS
4.8000 g., Copper-Nickel, 21.75 mm. **Obv:** Arms with supporters **Rev:** Ant above value **Edge Lettering:** LATVIJAS BANKA

Date	Mintage	F	VF	XF	Unc	BU
2003	250,000	—	—	5.00	6.50	8.00

KM# 64 LATS
31.4700 g., 0.9250 Silver 0.9359 oz. ASW, 38.6 mm.
Subject: Latvian European Union Membership **Obv:** Arms with supporters **Rev:** P.S. LATVIJA-ES 2004 above value **Edge Lettering:** LATVIJAS BANKA • LATVIJAS BANKA

Date	Mintage	F	VF	XF	Unc	BU
2004 Proof	Est. 15,000	Value: 80.00				

KM# 61 LATS
4.8000 g., Copper-Nickel, 21.75 mm. **Obv:** Arms with supporters **Rev:** Child with shovel above value **Edge Lettering:** LATVIJAS BANKA • LATVIJAS BANKA

Date	Mintage	F	VF	XF	Unc	BU
2004	500,000	—	—	2.00	4.00	6.00

KM# 62 LATS
17.1500 g., Bi-Metallic Dark Blue Niobium 7.15g center in .900 Silver 10g ring, 34 mm. **Obv:** Heraldic Rose **Rev:** Astronomical Clock **Edge:** Plain

Date	Mintage	F	VF	XF	Unc	BU
2004	Est. 5,000	—	—	—	55.00	65.00

KM# 63 LATS
31.4700 g., 0.9250 Silver 0.9359 oz. ASW, 38.6 mm. **Obv:** Arms with supporters **Rev:** World Cup Soccer player **Edge Lettering:** LATVIJA three times

Date	Mintage	F	VF	XF	Unc	BU
2004 Proof	Est. 50,000	Value: 70.00				

KM# 67 LATS
4.8000 g., Copper-Nickel, 21.75 mm. **Obv:** National arms **Obv. Legend:** LATVIJAS REPUBLIKA **Rev:** Mushroom above value **Edge Lettering:** LATVIJAS BANKA • LATVIJAS BANKA

Date	Mintage	F	VF	XF	Unc	BU
2004	500,000	—	—	2.00	4.00	5.00

KM# 68 LATS
31.4700 g., 0.9250 Silver 0.9359 oz. ASW, 38.6 mm. **Obv:** Mountains and value **Rev:** Laser picture of Janis Plieksans, pseudonym "Rainis" the mountain climbing poet, dramatist and patriot. **Edge Lettering:** LATVIJAS BANKA • LATVIJAS REPUBLIKA

Date	Mintage	F	VF	XF	Unc	BU
2005 Proof	Est. 5,000	Value: 45.00				

KM# 69 LATS
31.4700 g., 0.9250 Silver 0.9359 oz. ASW, 38.6 mm. **Obv:** National arms **Rev:** Bobsled **Edge Lettering:** LATVIJA repeated 3 times

Date	Mintage	F	VF	XF	Unc	BU
2005 Proof	Est. 15,000	Value: 45.00				

KM# 65 LATS
4.8000 g., Copper-Nickel, 21.75 mm. **Obv:** Arms with supporters **Rev:** Weathercock (from the spire of Riga's St. Peter Church) above value **Edge Lettering:** LATVIJAS BANKA • LATVIJAS BANKA

Date	Mintage	F	VF	XF	Unc	BU
2005	500,000	—	—	2.00	6.00	7.00

KM# 76 LATS
31.4700 g., 0.9250 Silver 0.9359 oz. ASW, 38.61 mm. **Obv:** Large coat of arms, date below **Rev:** Two hockey players viewed from above, RIGA 2006 on either side with hockey puck in center **Edge:** LATVIJA seperated by rhombic dots

Date	Mintage	F	VF	XF	Unc	BU
2005 Proof	Est. 5,000	Value: 50.00				

KM# 77 LATS
31.4700 g., 9.2500 Silver 9.3586 oz. ASW, 38.61 mm. **Obv:** Coat of arms **Rev:** Koknese castle on top with moon and sun on sides, reflection of Hanseatic Castle and ship on bottom **Edge Lettering:** LATVIJAS REPUBLIKA • LATVIJAS BANKA

Date	Mintage	F	VF	XF	Unc	BU
2005 Proof	Est. 15,000	Value: 45.00				

KM# 81 LATS
1.1500 g., Gold, 13.91 mm. **Obv:** Ribbon design **Obv. Legend:** RIGAS / LATVIJAS REPUBLIKA **Rev:** Stone face **Edge:** Reeded

Date	Mintage	F	VF	XF	Unc	BU
2005 Proof	—	Value: 65.00				

KM# 66 LATS
4.8000 g., Copper-Nickel, 21.75 mm. **Obv:** National arms **Obv. Legend:** LATVIJAS REPUBLIKA **Rev:** Pretzel above value **Edge Lettering:** LATVIJAS BANKA • LATVIJAS BANKA

Date	Mintage	F	VF	XF	Unc	BU
2005	500,000	—	—	2.00	4.00	6.00

KM# 73 LATS
4.8000 g., Copper-Nickel, 21.75 mm. **Subject:** Summer Solstice **Obv:** National arms **Rev:** Head wearing leaves above value **Edge Lettering:** LATVIJAS BANKA

Date	Mintage	F	VF	XF	Unc	BU
2006	500,000	—	—	2.00	4.00	6.00

KM# 74 LATS
4.8000 g., Copper-Nickel, 21.75 mm. **Obv:** National arms **Rev:** Pine cone above value **Edge Lettering:** LATVIJAS BANKA • LATVIJAS BANKA

Date	Mintage	F	VF	XF	Unc	BU
2006	1,000,000	—	—	2.00	5.00	6.00

KM# 78 LATS
31.4700 g., 0.9250 Silver 0.9359 oz. ASW, 38.61 mm. **Obv:** Stylized bonfire flames **Obv. Legend:** janvāris 1991 **Rev:** Latvian mythological hero with raised sword against the background of concrete block barricades, rising sun behind **Edge Lettering:** LATVIJAS BANKA

Date	Mintage	F	VF	XF	Unc	BU
2006 Proof	—	Value: 45.00				

KM# 79 LATS
31.4700 g., 0.9250 Silver 0.9359 oz. ASW, 38.61 mm. **Obv:** Starry sky on left with value on right side **Rev:** Portrait of Krisjanis Barons on right side and starry sky on left **Edge Lettering:** LATVIJAS BANKA • LATVIJAS REPUBLIKA

Date	Mintage	F	VF	XF	Unc	BU
2006 Proof	—	Value: 45.00				

KM# 80 LATS
31.4700 g., 0.9250 Silver 0.9359 oz. ASW, 38.61 mm. **Obv:** Seagull flying above water on left, value on right **Rev:** Portrait of Krisjanis Valdemars on right with sea on left **Edge Lettering:** LATVIJAS BANKA • LATVIJAS REPUBLIKA

Date	Mintage	F	VF	XF	Unc	BU
2006 Proof	—	Value: 45.00				

KM# 82 LATS
31.4700 g., 0.9250 Silver 0.9359 oz. ASW, 38.61 mm. **Obv:** Outline of Latvia with three stars above **Obv. Inscription:** LATVIJAS REPUBLIKA **Rev:** Two crossed swords outlined against the sun **Rev. Inscription:** NO ZOBENA SAULE LECA **Edge:** Plain

Date	Mintage	F	VF	XF	Unc	BU
2006 Proof	—	Value: 45.00				

KM# 83 LATS
31.4700 g., 0.9250 Silver 0.9359 oz. ASW, 38.61 mm. **Obv:** Coat of arms, date and value below **Obv. Inscription:** ROOP top, 1 LATS bottom **Rev:** Lielstraupe castle church top, reflection of Hanseatic ship with trees on both sides on bottom **Edge Lettering:** LATVIJAS REPUBLIKA • LATVIJAS BANKA

Date	Mintage	F	VF	XF	Unc	BU
2006 Proof	—	Value: 45.00				

KM# 84 LATS
27.0000 g., 0.9990 Silver 0.8672 oz. ASW, 38.61 mm. **Obv:** Arabic O in center of haptagon against an oriental background **Rev:** Roman I in center of heptagon **Shape:** 7-sided **Designer:** Ilmars Blumbergs and Janis Struplis

Date	Mintage	F	VF	XF	Unc	BU
2006 Proof	2,006	Value: 400				

KM# 12 LATS
4.8000 g., Copper-Nickel, 21.75 mm. **Obv:** Arms with supporters **Rev:** Salmon above value

Date	Mintage	F	VF	XF	Unc	BU
2007	7,000,000	—	—	2.00	4.00	7.00
2008	25,000,000	—	—	2.00	4.00	7.00

KM# 85 LATS
4.8000 g., Copper-Nickel, 21.75 mm. **Obv:** National arms **Obv. Legend:** LATVIJAS REPUBLIKA **Rev:** Snowman **Edge Lettering:** LATVIJAS BANKA

Date	Mintage	F	VF	XF	Unc	BU
2007	1,000,000	—	—	2.00	4.00	6.00

KM# 86 LATS

4.8000 g., Copper-Nickel, 21.75 mm. **Obv:** National arms
Obv. Legend: LATVIJAS REPUBLIKA **Rev:** Medieval owl
figurine **Edge Lettering:** LATVIJAS BANKA

Date	Mintage	F	VF	XF	Unc	BU
2007	1,000,000	—	—	2.00	4.00	6.00

KM# 87 LATS

31.4700 g., 0.9250 Silver 0.9359 oz. ASW, 38.6 mm.
Obv: Fragment of a large coat of arms **Rev:** Large coat of arms
broken into fragments **Designer:** Ivo Grundulis and Ligita
Franckevica

Date	Mintage	F	VF	XF	Unc	BU
2007 Proof	—	Value: 65.00				

KM# 88 LATS

31.4700 g., 0.9250 Silver 0.9359 oz. ASW, 38.6 mm.
Obv: Large coat of arms **Rev:** Sun with its rays forming the red-
white-red flag of the Republic **Designer:** Ivo Grundulis and Ligita
Franckevica

Date	Mintage	F	VF	XF	Unc	BU
2007 Proof	—	Value: 65.00				

KM# 89 LATS

31.4700 g., 0.9250 Silver 0.9359 oz. ASW, 38.6 mm.
Obv: Horse and sword within pendant **Rev:** Gauja Valley with
the Turaida Castle and Sigulda Castle **Edge Lettering:**
LATVIJAS REPUBLIKA • LATVIJAS BANKS **Designer:** Arvids
Priedite and Janis Strupulis

Date	Mintage	F	VF	XF	Unc	BU
2007 Proof	—	Value: 65.00				

KM# 90 LATS

17.1500 g., Bi-Metallic Dark Purple, 34 mm. **Obv:** Heraldic rose
at center **Rev:** Outer ring signs of the zodiac, inner circle different
evolutionary stages of the plant world **Designer:** Laimonis
Senbergs and Janis Strupulis

Date	Mintage	F	VF	XF	Unc	BU
2007	—	—	—	—	50.00	60.00

KM# 91 LATS

1.2442 g., 0.9990 Gold 0.0400 oz. AGW, 13.92 mm. **Obv:** Small
coat of arms **Rev:** Logo of the publishing house Zelta abele
Designer: Laimonis Senbergs and Janis Strupulis

Date	Mintage	F	VF	XF	Unc	BU
2007 Proof	—	Value: 65.00				

KM# 97 LATS

31.4700 g., 0.9250 Silver 0.9359 oz. ASW, 38.6 mm.
Subject: Coin of life **Obv:** Golden heart-shaped leaves
Obv. Designer: Ilmars Blumbergs and Ligita Franckevica
Rev: Mother holding gilt wrapped child

Date	Mintage	F	VF	XF	Unc	BU
2007 Proof	—	Value: 80.00				

KM# 98 LATS

22.0000 g., 0.9250 Silver 0.6542 oz. ASW, 35 mm.
Subject: Luckey Coin **Obv:** Cat on rooftop **Rev:** Man on ladder
Edge Lettering: LATVIJAS BANKA (dots) LATVIJAS BANKA

Date	Mintage	F	VF	XF	Unc	BU
2008 Proof	5,000	Value: 45.00				

KM# 99 LATS

31.4700 g., 0.9250 Silver 0.9359 oz. ASW, 38.6 mm.
Subject: 90th Anniversary of Statehood **Obv:** First Arms of the
Republic **Rev:** Two children holding multicolor flag

Date	Mintage	F	VF	XF	Unc	BU
2008 Proof	5,000	Value: 80.00				

KM# 92 LATS

4.8000 g., Copper-Nickel, 21.75 mm. **Obv:** National arms
Obv. Legend: LATVIJAS REPUBLIKA **Rev:** Water Lily
Edge Lettering: LATVIJAS BANKA

Date	Mintage	F	VF	XF	Unc	BU
2008	1,000,000	—	—	2.00	4.00	6.00

KM# 93 LATS

12.4000 g., Copper-Nickel, 30 mm. **Obv:** Woman walking
holding flowers **Rev:** Man walking holding wreath
Edge Lettering: DZIESMAI SODIEN LIELA DIENA
Designer: Arvids Priedite and Ligita Franckevica

Date	Mintage	F	VF	XF	Unc	BU
2008	—	—	—	—	7.00	9.00

KM# 93a LATS

31.4700 g., 0.9250 Silver 0.9359 oz. ASW, 38.61 mm.
Obv: Woman walking holding flowers **Rev:** Man walking holding
wreath **Edge Lettering:** DZIESMAI SODIEN LIELA DIENA
Designer: Arvids Priedite and Ligita Franckevica

Date	Mintage	F	VF	XF	Unc	BU
2008 Proof	10,000	Value: 65.00				

KM# 94 LATS

31.4700 g., 0.9250 Silver 0.9359 oz. ASW **Obv:** Hanseatic city
seal with coat of arms **Rev:** Limbazi Castle ruins and St. Johns
Church with reflection of Hanseatic Ship on lower half
Edge Lettering: LATVIJAS REPUBLIKA • LATVIJAS BANKA
Shape: 38.61 **Designer:** Gunars Krollis and Janis Strupulis

Date	Mintage	F	VF	XF	Unc	BU
2008 Proof	5,000	Value: 65.00				

KM# 95 LATS

31.4700 g., 0.9250 Silver 0.9359 oz. ASW, 38.6 mm. **Obv:**
Three stars and stylized basket ball design **Rev:** Two basketball
players and a jump shot **Edge Lettering:** LATVIJAS BANKA •
LATVIJAS REPUBLIKA **Designer:** Franceska Kirke and Ligita
Franckevica

Date	Mintage	F	VF	XF	Unc	BU
2008 Proof	5,000	—	—	—	—	45.00

KM# 101 LATS

4.8000 g., Copper-Nickel, 21.75 mm. **Subject:** Namejs ring
Obv: National Arms **Rev:** Ring **Rev. Designer:** Ilze Libiete and
Baiba Sime **Edge Lettering:** LATVIJAS BANKA

Date	Mintage	F	VF	XF	Unc	BU
2009	1,000,000	—	—	2.00	4.00	6.00

KM# 100   LATS
20.0000 g., 0.9250 Silver 0.5948 oz. ASW, 34 mm.
Subject: My Dream Coin **Obv:** State Arms **Rev:** Piglet

Date	Mintage	F	VF	XF	Unc	BU
2009 Proof	—	Value: 50.00				

KM# 102   LATS
31.4700 g., 0.9250 Silver 0.9359 oz. ASW, 38.6 mm.
Subject: Time of the Surveyors, Novel's 130th Anniversary
Obv: Brali Kaudzites standing **Rev:** Six figures forming spokes
of wheel **Edge Lettering:** LATVIJAS REPUBLICA LATVIJAS
BANKA **Designer:** Laimonis Senbergs and Ligita Franckevica

Date	Mintage	F	VF	XF	Unc	BU
2009 Proof	—	Value: 50.00				

KM# 103   LATS
31.4700 g., 0.9250 Silver 0.9359 oz. ASW, 38.6 mm.
Subject: University of Latvia **Obv:** Oak tree within wreath,
partially multicolor **Rev:** Owl standing on open book, University
building in background **Designer:** Arvids Predite and Ligita
Frackevica

Date	Mintage	F	VF	XF	Unc	BU
2009 Proof	—	Value: 50.00				

KM# 104   LATS
26.0000 g., 0.9250 Silver 0.7732 oz. ASW, 32x32 mm.
Subject: Coin of Water **Obv:** Water droplets **Rev:** Snowflake
crystal **Shape:** Square **Designer:** Ilmars Blumbergs and Janis
Strupulis

Date	Mintage	F	VF	XF	Unc	BU
2009 Proof	—	Value: 50.00				

KM# 105   LATS
4.8000 g., Copper-Nickel, 21.75 mm. **Subject:** Christmas Tree,
500th Anniversary **Obv:** Three children in folktale costumes
Rev: Man walking with cut tree in moonlight, cat jumping from tree

Date	Mintage	F	VF	XF	Unc	BU
2009	1,000,000	—	—	—	4.00	8.00

KM# 38   2 LATI
9.5000 g., Bi-Metallic Brass center in Copper-Nickel ring.,
26.3 mm. **Obv:** Arms with supporters within circle **Rev:** Cow
above value within circle **Edge Lettering:** LATVIJAS BANKA

Date	Mintage	F	VF	XF	Unc	BU
2003 In sets only	30,000				—	12.00
2009	2,000,000	—	—	7.00	8.00	9.00

KM# 59   5 LATI
1.2442 g., 0.9999 Gold 0.0400 oz. AGW, 13.92 mm. **Obv:** Bust
right **Rev:** Arms with supporters above value **Edge:** Reeded
Note: Remake of the popular KM-9 design

Date	Mintage	F	VF	XF	Unc	BU
2003 Proof	Est. 20,000	Value: 120				

KM# 96   20 LATI
10.0000 g., 0.9990 Gold 0.3212 oz. AGW, 22 mm.
Obv: Womans head covered with scarf **Rev:** Vessel with a milk
bottle, apple, jug of milk, bread & knife on table **Designer:** Tedors
Zalkalns and Ligita Franckevica

Date	Mintage	F	VF	XF	Unc	BU
2008	5,000	—	—	—	—	650

LEBANON

The Republic of Lebanon, situated on the eastern shore of
the Mediterranean Sea between Syria and Israel, has an area of
4,015 sq. mi. (10,400 sq. km.) and a population of 3.5 million.
Capital: Beirut. The economy is based on agriculture, trade and
tourism. Fruit, other foodstuffs and textiles are exported.

MONETARY SYSTEM
100 Piastres = 1 Livre (Pound)

REPUBLIC
STANDARD COINAGE

KM# 40   25 LIVRES
2.8200 g., Nickel Plated Steel, 20.5 mm. **Obv:** Large value on
cedar tree **Rev:** Value within square design **Rev. Legend:**
BANQUE DU LIBAN **Edge:** Plain

Date	Mintage	F	VF	XF	Unc	BU
2002	—	—	—	0.30	0.80	1.20

KM# 38a   100 LIVRES
4.0500 g., Nickel, 22.48 mm. **Obv:** Arabic legend above large
value on cedar tree **Rev:** Two banners above large value "100"
Rev. Legend: BANQUE DU LIBAN **Edge:** Plain

Date	Mintage	F	VF	XF	Unc	BU
2003	—	—	—	0.60	1.50	2.00

KM# 38b   100 LIVRES
4.0700 g., Copper Plated Steel, 22.49 mm. **Obv:** Arabic legend
above large value on cedar tree **Rev:** Two banners above large
value "100" **Rev. Legend:** BANQUE DU LIBAN **Edge:** Plain

Date	Mintage	F	VF	XF	Unc	BU
2006	—	—	—	0.60	1.50	2.00

KM# 38   100 LIVRES
4.0000 g., Brass, 22.5 mm. **Obv:** Arabic legend above large
value on cedar tree **Rev:** Two banners above large value "100"
Rev. Legend: BANQUE DU LIBAN **Edge:** Plain

Date	Mintage	F	VF	XF	Unc	BU
2006	—	—	—	0.65	1.50	2.00

KM# 36   250 LIVRES
5.3000 g., Aluminum-Nickel-Bronze, 23.5 mm. **Obv:** Arabic
legend above large value on cedar tree **Rev:** Large 250 within
eliptical border design **Edge:** Reeded

Date	Mintage	F	VF	XF	Unc	BU
2003	—	—	—	0.75	1.85	2.50
2006	—	—	—	0.75	1.85	2.50

KM# 39   500 LIVRES
6.0600 g., Nickel Clad Steel, 24.5 mm. **Obv:** Arabic legend
above large value on cedar tree **Rev:** Large value "500", thick
segmented circular border **Rev. Legend:** BANQUE DU LIBAN
Edge: Plain

Date	Mintage	F	VF	XF	Unc	BU
2003	—			0.90	2.25	3.00

LESOTHO

The Kingdom of Lesotho, a constitutional monarchy located
within the east-central part of the Republic of South Africa, has an
area of 11,720 sq. mi. (30,350 sq. km.) and a population of 1.5 million. Capital: Maseru. The economy is based on subsistence agriculture and livestock raising. Wool, mohair, and cattle are exported.

Lesotho (formerly Basutoland) was sparsely populated until
the end of the 16th century. Between the 16th and 19th centuries
an influx of refugees from tribal wars led to the development of a
distinct Basotho group. During the reign of tribal chief Mashoeshoe I (1823-70), a series of wars with the Orange Free State
resulted in the loss of large areas of territory to South Africa.
Mashoeshoe appealed to the British for help, and Basutoland was
constituted a native state under British protection. In 1871 it was
annexed to Cape Colony, but was restored to direct control by the
Crown in 1884. From 1884 to 1959 legislative and executive
authority was vested in a British High Commissioner. The constitution of 1959 recognized the expressed wish of the people for
independence, which was attained on Oct.4, 1966.

Lesotho is a member of the Commonwealth of Nations. The
king is Head of State.

RULERS
Moshoeshoe II, 1995-

KINGDOM
STANDARD COINAGE
100 Licente/Lisente = 1 Maloti/Loti

KM# 62   5 LICENTE (Lisente)
1.6400 g., Brass Plated Steel, 15 mm. **Ruler:** Letsie III
Obv: Arms with supporters **Rev:** Single pine tree among grass,
hills and value

Date	Mintage	F	VF	XF	Unc	BU
2006	—	—	—	0.35	0.75	1.00

LIBERIA

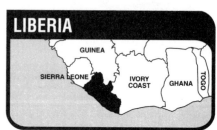

The Republic of Liberia, located on the southern side of the
West African bulge between Sierra Leone and Ivory Coast, has an
area of 38,250 sq. mi. (111,370 sq. km) and a population of
2.2 million. Capital: Monrovia. The major industries are agriculture, mining and lumbering. Iron ore, diamonds, rubber, coffee
and coca are exported.

MINT MARKS
PM - Pobjoy Mint

MONETARY SYSTEM
100 Cents = 1 Dollar

REPUBLIC

STANDARD COINAGE

100 Cents = 1 Dollar

KM# 618   5 CENTS
5.0200 g., Copper-Nickel, 23.8 mm. **Obv:** National arms
Rev: Chimpanzee family **Edge:** Plain

Date	Mintage	F	VF	XF	Unc	BU
2003	—	—	—	—	1.50	2.00

KM# 651   5 DOLLARS
14.5600 g., Copper-Nickel, 33.1 mm. **Obv:** National arms
Rev: Japanese "Zero" flying over Pearl Harbor **Edge:** Reeded

Date	Mintage	F	VF	XF	Unc	BU
2001	—	—	—	—	10.00	12.00

KM# 568   5 DOLLARS
14.6300 g., Copper-Nickel, 33.1 mm. **Subject:** Battle of
Gettysburg **Obv:** National arms **Rev:** Cannon and crossed flags
divides busts facing **Edge:** Reeded **Note:** This also exists in an
obverse denominated type for $2,000. Also see KM828.

Date	Mintage	F	VF	XF	Unc	BU
2001B	—	—	—	—	12.00	14.00

KM# 494   5 DOLLARS
8.5000 g., 0.9999 Silver 0.2732 oz. ASW, 30 mm.
Subject: Soccer **Obv:** National arms **Rev:** Soccer player divides
circle **Edge:** Reeded

Date	Mintage	F	VF	XF	Unc	BU
2002 Proof	3,000	Value: 30.00				

KM# 829   5 DOLLARS
14.9400 g., Copper-Nickel, 32.9 mm. **Subject:** 12th Anniversary
Columbia Space Shuttle **Obv:** National arms **Rev:** Astronaut,
space shuttle **Edge:** Reeded

Date	Mintage	F	VF	XF	Unc	BU
2003	—	—	—	—	8.00	10.00

KM# 831   5 DOLLARS
15.5500 g., 0.9990 Niobium 0.4994 oz., 38 mm. **Series:** From
ancient to Modern Sports **Obv:** National arms **Rev:** Discus
throwers **Edge:** Plain

Date	Mintage	F	VF	XF	Unc	BU
2004	2,004	—	—	—	—	15.00

KM# 832   5 DOLLARS
15.5500 g., 0.9990 Niobium 0.4994 oz., 38 mm. **Series:** From
Ancient to Modern Sports **Obv:** National arms **Rev:** Javelin
throwers **Edge:** Plain

Date	Mintage	F	VF	XF	Unc	BU
2004	2,004	—	—	—	—	15.00

KM# 833   5 DOLLARS
15.5500 g., 0.9990 Niobium 0.4994 oz., 38 mm. **Series:** From
ancient to Modern Sports **Obv:** National arms **Rev:** Broad
jumpers **Edge:** Plain

Date	Mintage	F	VF	XF	Unc	BU
2004	2,004	—	—	—	—	15.00

KM# 834   5 DOLLARS
15.5500 g., 0.9990 Niobium 0.4994 oz., 38 mm. **Series:** From
Ancient to Modern Sports **Obv:** National arms **Rev:** Runners
Edge: Plain

Date	Mintage	F	VF	XF	Unc	BU
2004	2,004	—	—	—	—	15.00

KM# 835   5 DOLLARS
15.5500 g., 0.9990 Niobium 0.4994 oz., 38 mm. **Series:** From
Ancient to Modern Sports **Obv:** National arms **Rev:** Wrestlers
Edge: Plain

Date	Mintage	F	VF	XF	Unc	BU
2004	2,004	—	—	—	—	15.00

KM# 664   5 DOLLARS
6.4000 g., Bi-Metallic Brass center in Copper-Nickel ring,
25.7 mm. **Obv:** National arms **Rev:** Pope and cathedral within
circle **Edge:** Reeded

Date	Mintage	F	VF	XF	Unc	BU
2005	—	—	—	—	12.00	14.00

KM# 809   5 DOLLARS
25.9500 g., Silver, 39.97 mm. **Subject:** Papal visits to Africa
Obv: National arms **Rev:** !/2 length multicolor figure of Pope John
Paul II at center left, outlined map of Africa at center right in
background **Edge:** Reeded

Date	Mintage	F	VF	XF	Unc	BU
2005 Proof	—	Value: 20.00				

KM# 810   5 DOLLARS
25.7200 g., Silver, 39.92 mm. **Obv:** National arms **Rev:** St.
Peter's square in background, multicolor bust of Pope Benedict
XVI in oval frame at upper right **Edge:** Reeded

Date	Mintage	F	VF	XF	Unc	BU
2005 Proof	—	Value: 25.00				

KM# 865   5 DOLLARS
7.7800 g., Niobium partially gilt, 35 mm. **Subject:** 10th
Anniversary of the Euro - San Marino **Rev:** Castle

Date	Mintage	F	VF	XF	Unc	BU
2006 Proof	10,000	Value: 50.00				

KM# 866   5 DOLLARS
7.7800 g., Niobium partially gilt, 35 mm. **Subject:** 10th
Anniversary of the Euro - Slovakia **Rev:** Bratislava Castle

Date	Mintage	F	VF	XF	Unc	BU
2006 Proof	10,000	Value: 50.00				

KM# 867   5 DOLLARS
7.7800 g., Niobium partially gilt, 35 mm. **Subject:** 10th
Anniversary of the Euro - Latvia **Rev:** Old Buildings

Date	Mintage	F	VF	XF	Unc	BU
2006 Proof	10,000	Value: 50.00				

KM# 868   5 DOLLARS
7.7800 g., Niobium partially gilt, 35 mm. **Subject:** 10th
Anniversary of the Euro - Monaco **Rev:** Ariel view of Principality

Date	Mintage	F	VF	XF	Unc	BU
2006 Proof	10,000	Value: 50.00				

KM# 869   5 DOLLARS
7.7800 g., Niobium partially gilt, 35 mm. **Subject:** 10th
Anniversary of the Euro - Slovenia **Rev:** Hill-top buildings

Date	Mintage	F	VF	XF	Unc	BU
2006 Proof	10,000	Value: 50.00				

KM# 724   5 DOLLARS
26.3000 g., Silver Plated Bronze, 38.6 mm. **Obv:** National arms
Rev: Multicolor Pope John Paul II with cross **Edge:** Reeded

Date	Mintage	F	VF	XF	Unc	BU
2007 Proof	—	Value: 30.00				

KM# 733   5 DOLLARS
27.0000 g., Copper-Nickel Silvered and Gilt, 38.61 mm.
Subject: The Black Madonna of Czestochowa **Obv:** Arms
Obv. Legend: REPUBLIC OF LIBERIA **Rev:** 1/2 length figure of
Madonna facing with child

Date	Mintage	F	VF	XF	Unc	BU
2007 Proof	1,000	Value: 40.00				

KM# 863   5 DOLLARS
27.0000 g., Silver Plated Copper, 38.6 mm. **Rev:** Pope John
Paul II holding croizer, multicolor

Date	Mintage	F	VF	XF	Unc	BU
2007 Proof	1,000	Value: 40.00				

KM# 513   10 DOLLARS
28.5000 g., Copper-Nickel, 38.6 mm. **Series:** Moments of
Freedom **Subject:** Hungarian Revolution of 1848 **Obv:** National
arms **Rev:** Multicolor heroic scene **Edge:** Reeded

Date	Mintage	F	VF	XF	Unc	BU
2001 Proof	9,999	Value: 10.00				

KM# 491   10 DOLLARS
25.2500 g., 0.9250 Silver 0.7509 oz. ASW, 36.8 mm.
Subject: Illusion **Obv:** National arms **Rev:** Stylized head with
glasses facing **Edge:** Plain **Shape:** 10-sided

Date	Mintage	F	VF	XF	Unc	BU
2001 Proof	5,000	Value: 35.00				

KM# 777   10 DOLLARS
14.5500 g., Copper-Nickel, 32 mm. **Subject:** 43rd President of
USA **Obv:** National arms **Obv. Legend:** REPUBLIC OF LIBERIA
Rev: George W. Bush, flag in background

Date	Mintage	F	VF	XF	Unc	BU
2001 Proof	—	Value: 10.00				

KM# 822   10 DOLLARS
1.2400 g., Gold, 13.68 mm. **Obv:** National arms **Rev:** Bust of
Marlene Dietrich facing **Edge:** Reeded

Date	Mintage	F	VF	XF	Unc	BU
2001 Proof	—	Value: 50.00				

KM# 493   10 DOLLARS
770.0000 g., Copper, 100 mm.   **Subject:** Wreck of the Princess Louisa **Obv:** National arms **Rev:** Sailing ship **Edge:** Reeded **Note:** Illustration reduced. With an encased glass shard recovered from the wreck site of the Princess Louisa.

Date	Mintage	F	VF	XF	Unc	BU
2001	2,000	—	—	—	225	—

KM# 510   10 DOLLARS
33.2400 g., Copper Gilt, 40.1 mm.   **Obv:** National arms **Rev:** Multicolor holographic bald eagle **Edge:** Reeded

Date	Mintage	F	VF	XF	Unc	BU
2001	20,000	—	—	—	—	35.00

KM# 537   10 DOLLARS
28.5000 g., Copper-Nickel, 38.6 mm.   **Subject:** Moments of Freedom **Obv:** National arms **Rev:** Multicolor Buddha, spelled "Budha" on the coin **Edge:** Reeded

Date	Mintage	F	VF	XF	Unc	BU
2001 Proof	9,999	Value: 10.00				

KM# 538   10 DOLLARS
28.5000 g., Copper-Nickel, 38.6 mm.   **Subject:** Moments of Freedom **Obv:** National arms **Rev:** Multicolor Battle of Marathon scene **Edge:** Reeded

Date	Mintage	F	VF	XF	Unc	BU
2001 Proof	9,999	Value: 10.00				

KM# 539   10 DOLLARS
28.5000 g., Copper-Nickel, 38.6 mm.   **Series:** Moments of Freedom **Obv:** National arms **Rev:** Multicolor founding of Liberia design **Edge:** Reeded

Date	Mintage	F	VF	XF	Unc	BU
2001 Proof	9,999	Value: 10.00				

KM# 540   10 DOLLARS
28.5000 g., Copper-Nickel, 38.6 mm.   **Series:** Moments of Freedom **Obv:** National arms **Rev:** Multicolor portrait of Constantine I **Edge:** Reeded

Date	Mintage	F	VF	XF	Unc	BU
2001 Proof	9,999	Value: 10.00				

KM# 541   10 DOLLARS
28.5000 g., Copper-Nickel, 38.6 mm.   **Series:** Moments of Freedom **Obv:** National arms **Rev:** Multicolor William Tell statue **Edge:** Reeded

Date	Mintage	F	VF	XF	Unc	BU
2001 Proof	9,999	Value: 10.00				

KM# 542   10 DOLLARS
28.5000 g., Copper-Nickel, 38.6 mm.   **Series:** Moments of Freedom **Obv:** National arms **Rev:** Multicolor bust facing **Edge:** Reeded

Date	Mintage	F	VF	XF	Unc	BU
2001 Proof	9,999	Value: 10.00				

KM# 543   10 DOLLARS
28.5000 g., Copper-Nickel, 38.6 mm.   **Series:** Moments of Freedom **Obv:** National arms **Rev:** Multicolor head with headdress and battle scene **Edge:** Reeded

Date	Mintage	F	VF	XF	Unc	BU
2001 Proof	9,999	Value: 10.00				

KM# 544   10 DOLLARS
28.5000 g., Copper-Nickel, 38.6 mm.   **Series:** Moments of Freedom **Obv:** National arms **Rev:** Multicolor Brandenburg Gate scene **Edge:** Reeded

Date	Mintage	F	VF	XF	Unc	BU
2001 Proof	9,999	Value: 10.00				

KM# 545   10 DOLLARS
28.5000 g., Copper-Nickel, 38.6 mm.   **Series:** Moments of Freedom **Obv:** National arms **Rev:** Multicolor half length figure facing **Edge:** Reeded

Date	Mintage	F	VF	XF	Unc	BU
2001 Proof	9,999	Value: 10.00				

KM# 546   10 DOLLARS
28.5000 g., Copper-Nickel, 38.6 mm.   **Series:** Moments of Freedom **Obv:** National arms **Rev:** Multicolor Sitting Bull portrait **Edge:** Reeded

Date	Mintage	F	VF	XF	Unc	BU
2001 Proof	9,999	Value: 10.00				

KM# 547   10 DOLLARS
28.5000 g., Copper-Nickel, 38.6 mm.   **Series:** Moments of Freedom **Obv:** National arms **Rev:** Multicolor Declaration of Independence scene **Edge:** Reeded

Date	Mintage	F	VF	XF	Unc	BU
2001 Proof	9,999	Value: 10.00				

KM# 548   10 DOLLARS
28.5000 g., Copper-Nickel, 38.6 mm.   **Series:** Moments of Freedom **Obv:** National arms **Rev:** Multicolor allegorical woman **Edge:** Reeded

Date	Mintage	F	VF	XF	Unc	BU
2001 Proof	9,999	Value: 10.00				

KM# 549   10 DOLLARS
28.5000 g., Copper-Nickel, 38.6 mm.   **Series:** Moments of Freedom **Obv:** National arms **Rev:** Multicolor bust looking down **Edge:** Reeded

Date	Mintage	F	VF	XF	Unc	BU
2001 Proof	9,999	Value: 10.00				

KM# 550   10 DOLLARS
28.5000 g., Copper-Nickel, 38.6 mm.   **Series:** Moments of Freedom **Obv:** National arms **Rev:** Multicolor picture of a soldier at the moment he is shot in battle **Edge:** Reeded

Date	Mintage	F	VF	XF	Unc	BU
2001 Proof	9,999	Value: 10.00				

KM# 551   10 DOLLARS
28.5000 g., Copper-Nickel, 38.6 mm.   **Series:** Moments of Freedom **Obv:** National arms **Rev:** Multicolor inmates behind wire fence scene **Edge:** Reeded

Date	Mintage	F	VF	XF	Unc	BU
2001 Proof	9,999	Value: 10.00				

KM# 552   10 DOLLARS
28.5000 g., Copper-Nickel, 38.6 mm.   **Series:** Moments of Freedom **Obv:** National arms **Rev:** Multicolor Iwo Jima flag raising scene **Edge:** Reeded

Date	Mintage	F	VF	XF	Unc	BU
2001 Proof	9,999	Value: 10.00				

KM# 553   10 DOLLARS
28.5000 g., Copper-Nickel, 38.6 mm.   **Series:** Moments of Freedom **Obv:** National arms **Rev:** Multicolor UN logo and dove **Edge:** Reeded

Date	Mintage	F	VF	XF	Unc	BU
2001 Proof	9,999	Value: 10.00				

KM# 554   10 DOLLARS
28.5000 g., Copper-Nickel, 38.6 mm.   **Series:** Moments of Freedom **Obv:** National arms **Rev:** Multicolor Solzhenitsyn portrait **Edge:** Reeded

Date	Mintage	F	VF	XF	Unc	BU
2001 Proof	9,999	Value: 10.00				

KM# 555   10 DOLLARS
28.5000 g., Copper-Nickel, 38.6 mm.   **Series:** Moments of Freedom **Obv:** National arms **Rev:** Multicolor Spartacus and troops **Edge:** Reeded

Date	Mintage	F	VF	XF	Unc	BU
2001 Proof	9,999	Value: 12.00				

KM# 556   10 DOLLARS
28.5000 g., Copper-Nickel, 38.6 mm.   **Series:** Moments of Freedom **Obv:** National arms **Rev:** Multicolor Soviet tank in Prague **Edge:** Reeded

Date	Mintage	F	VF	XF	Unc	BU
2001 Proof	9,999	Value: 10.00				

KM# 557   10 DOLLARS
28.5000 g., Copper-Nickel, 38.6 mm.   **Series:** Moments of Freedom **Obv:** National arms **Rev:** Multicolor Bastille scene **Edge:** Reeded

Date	Mintage	F	VF	XF	Unc	BU
2001 Proof	9,999	Value: 10.00				

KM# 558 10 DOLLARS
28.5000 g., Copper-Nickel, 38.6 mm. **Series:** Moments of Freedom **Obv:** National arms **Rev:** Multicolor Nelson Mandela and fist **Edge:** Reeded

Date	Mintage	F	VF	XF	Unc	BU
2001 Proof	9,999	Value: 10.00				

KM# 559 10 DOLLARS
28.5000 g., Copper-Nickel, 38.6 mm. **Series:** Moments of Freedom **Obv:** National arms **Rev:** Multicolor circuit board and world globe **Edge:** Reeded

Date	Mintage	F	VF	XF	Unc	BU
2001 Proof	9,999	Value: 10.00				

KM# 654 10 DOLLARS
15.3300 g., Copper-Nickel, 33.2 mm. **Obv:** National arms **Rev:** "GEORGE W. BUSH..." No value at bottom **Edge:** Reeded

Date	Mintage	F	VF	XF	Unc	BU
2002	—	—	—	—	—	10.00

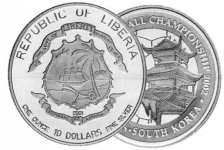

KM# 705 10 DOLLARS
31.1035 g., 0.9990 Silver 0.9990 oz. ASW, 38.6 mm. **Subject:** 2002 World Football Championship - Japan - South Korea **Obv:** National arms **Rev:** Pagoda superimposed on a soccer ball, legend around **Edge:** Reeded

Date	Mintage	F	VF	XF	Unc	BU
2002 Proof	—	Value: 45.00				

KM# 806 10 DOLLARS
14.3000 g., Copper-Nickel, 33.11 mm. **Obv:** National arms **Rev:** Bust of President Bush facing at left, soldier standing at right facing, flag in background **Rev. Legend:** America's Fight For Freedom **Edge:** Reeded

Date	Mintage	F	VF	XF	Unc	BU
2002	—	—	—	—	10.00	12.00

KM# 807 10 DOLLARS
26.3000 g., Copper-Nickel, 40.36 mm. **Subject:** America's First Ladies **Obv:** National arms **Rev:** Bust of Jacqueline Kennedy facing, small oval portrait of President John F. Kennedy at right **Edge:** Reeded

Date	Mintage	F	VF	XF	Unc	BU
2003 Proof	—	Value: 15.00				

KM# 824 10 DOLLARS
14.6000 g., Copper-Nickel, 33 mm. **Subject:** Abraham Lincoln **Obv:** National arms **Rev:** Bust facing at left, Lincoln Memorial in background **Edge:** Reeded

Date	Mintage	F	VF	XF	Unc	BU
2003 Proof	20,000	Value: 12.00				

KM# 708 10 DOLLARS
25.1000 g., 0.9250 Silver 0.7464 oz. ASW, 38.6 mm. **Obv:** National arms **Rev:** Clipper ship "Flying Cloud" **Edge:** Reeded

Date	Mintage	F	VF	XF	Unc	BU
2003 Proof	—	Value: 35.00				

KM# 602 10 DOLLARS
25.0000 g., 0.9250 Silver 0.7435 oz. ASW, 38.6 mm. **Obv:** National arms **Rev:** Icarus and Daedalus in flight **Edge:** Reeded

Date	Mintage	F	VF	XF	Unc	BU
2003 Proof	—	Value: 35.00				

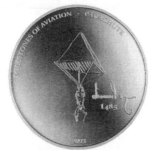

KM# 603 10 DOLLARS
25.0000 g., 0.9250 Silver 0.7435 oz. ASW, 38.6 mm. **Obv:** National arms **Rev:** First parachute **Edge:** Reeded

Date	Mintage	F	VF	XF	Unc	BU
2003 Proof	—	Value: 35.00				

KM# 604 10 DOLLARS
25.0000 g., 0.9250 Silver 0.7435 oz. ASW, 38.6 mm. **Obv:** National arms **Rev:** Montgolfier ballon **Edge:** Reeded

Date	Mintage	F	VF	XF	Unc	BU
2003 Proof	—	Value: 35.00				

KM# 605 10 DOLLARS
25.0000 g., 0.9250 Silver 0.7435 oz. ASW, 38.6 mm. **Obv:** National arms **Rev:** Otto v. Lillenthal **Edge:** Reeded

Date	Mintage	F	VF	XF	Unc	BU
2003 Proof	—	Value: 35.00				

KM# 606 10 DOLLARS
25.0000 g., 0.9250 Silver 0.7435 oz. ASW, 38.6 mm. **Obv:** National arms **Rev:** Wright Brothers **Edge:** Reeded

Date	Mintage	F	VF	XF	Unc	BU
2003 Proof	—	Value: 35.00				

KM# 607 10 DOLLARS
25.0000 g., 0.9250 Silver 0.7435 oz. ASW, 38.6 mm. **Obv:** National arms **Rev:** Mach 1- Bell X **Edge:** Reeded

Date	Mintage	F	VF	XF	Unc	BU
2003 Proof	—	Value: 35.00				

KM# 608 10 DOLLARS
25.0000 g., 0.9250 Silver 0.7435 oz. ASW, 38.6 mm. **Obv:** National arms **Rev:** The Concorde **Edge:** Reeded

Date	Mintage	F	VF	XF	Unc	BU
2003 Proof	—	Value: 35.00				

KM# 823 10 DOLLARS
1.2300 g., Gold, 13.88 mm. **Subject:** 2006 World Football championship Gernany **Obv:** National arms **Rev:** Football at lower left, stadium at center **Rev. Legend:** DEUTSCHLAND 2006 **Edge:** Reeded

Date	Mintage	F	VF	XF	Unc	BU
2004 Proof	—	Value: 50.00				

KM# 611 10 DOLLARS
62.2070 g., 0.9990 Silver 1.9979 oz. ASW, 50 mm. **Obv:** National arms left of window design with Tiffany Glass inlay **Rev:** Window design with Tiffany Glass inlay **Edge:** Plain

Date	Mintage	F	VF	XF	Unc	BU
2004	999	—	—	—	—	125

KM# 740 10 DOLLARS
20.0000 g., 0.9990 Silver partially gilt 0.6423 oz. ASW, 38.00 mm. **Series:** Endangered Wildlife **Obv:** National arms **Obv. Legend:** REPUBLIC OF LIBERIA **Rev:** Gilt Siberian Tiger with diamonds inset in eyes **Rev. Legend:** RUSSIA **Edge:** Plain

Date	Mintage	F	VF	XF	Unc	BU
2004 Proof	5,000	Value: 175				

KM# 741 10 DOLLARS
20.0000 g., 0.9990 Silver partially gilt 0.6423 oz. ASW,
38.00 mm. **Series:** Endangered Wildlife **Obv:** National arms
Obv. Legend: REPUBLIC OF LIBERIA **Rev:** Two gilt Hyacinth
Macaws perched on branch with diamond insets in eyes
Rev. Legend: BRAZIL **Edge:** Plain

Date	Mintage	F	VF	XF	Unc	BU
2004 Proof	5,000	Value: 175				

KM# 742 10 DOLLARS
20.0000 g., 0.9990 Silver partially gilt 0.6423 oz. ASW,
38.00 mm. **Series:** Endangered Wildlife **Obv:** National arms
Obv. Legend: REPUBLIC OF LIBERIA **Rev:** Gilt young Giant
Panda seated eating bamboo shoots **Rev. Legend:** CHINA
Edge: Plain

Date	Mintage	F	VF	XF	Unc	BU
2004 Proof	5,000	Value: 175				

KM# 743 10 DOLLARS
20.0000 g., 0.9990 Silver partially gilt 0.6423 oz. ASW,
38.00 mm. **Subject:** Endangered Wildlife **Obv:** National arms
Obv. Legend: REPUBLIC OF LIBERIA **Rev:** Two gilt Bald
Eagles. one perched at left, one alighting at center right
Rev. Legend: USA **Edge:** Plain

Date	Mintage	F	VF	XF	Unc	BU
2004 Proof	5,000	Value: 175				

KM# 744 10 DOLLARS
20.0000 g., 0.9990 Silver partially gilt 0.6423 oz. ASW, 38 mm.
Series: Endangered Wildlife **Obv:** National arms **Obv. Legend:**
REPUBLIC OF LIBERIA **Rev:** Gilt Puma standing with diamonds
inset in eyes **Rev. Legend:** MEXICO **Edge:** Plain

Date	Mintage	F	VF	XF	Unc	BU
2004 Proof	5,000	Value: 175				

KM# 745 10 DOLLARS
20.0000 g., 0.9990 Silver partially gilt 0.6423 oz. ASW, 38 mm.
Series: Endangered Wildlife **Obv:** National arms **Obv. Legend:**
REPUBLIC OF LIBERIA **Rev:** Gilt Red-ruffed Lemur on branch
with diamonds inset in eyes **Rev. Legend:** MADAGASCAR
Edge: Plain

Date	Mintage	F	VF	XF	Unc	BU
2004 Proof	5,000	Value: 175				

KM# 746 10 DOLLARS
20.0000 g., 0.9990 Silver partially gilt 0.6423 oz. ASW, 38 mm.
Series: Endangered Wildlife **Obv:** National arms **Obv. Legend:**
REPUBLIC OF LIBERIA **Rev:** Two gilt Andean Condors, one
lifting off at center, one perched at right **Rev. Legend:** CHILE
Edge: Plain

Date	Mintage	F	VF	XF	Unc	BU
2004 Proof	5,000	Value: 175				

KM# 747 10 DOLLARS
20.0000 g., 0.9990 Silver partially gilt 0.6423 oz. ASW, 38 mm.
Series: Endangered Wildlife **Obv:** National arms **Obv. Legend:**
REPUBLIC OF LIBERIA **Rev:** Two gilt Yellow-eyed Penguins
standing facing with diamonds inset in eyes **Rev. Legend:** NEW
ZEALAND **Edge:** Plain

Date	Mintage	F	VF	XF	Unc	BU
2004 Proof	5,000	Value: 175				

KM# 748 10 DOLLARS
20.0000 g., 0.9990 Silver partially gilt 0.6423 oz. ASW, 38 mm.
Series: Endangered Wildlife **Obv:** National arms
Obv. Legend: REPUBLIC OF LIBERIA **Rev:** Gilt African lion
standing facing with diamonds inset in eyes **Rev. Legend:**
SOUTH AFRICA **Edge:** Plain

Date	Mintage	F	VF	XF	Unc	BU
2004 Proof	5,000	Value: 175				

KM# 749 10 DOLLARS
20.0000 g., 0.9990 Silver partially gilt 0.6423 oz. ASW, 38 mm.
Series: Endangered Wildlife **Obv:** National arms **Obv. Legend:**
REPUBLIC OF LIBERIA **Rev:** Two gilt perched Kookaburras with
diamonds inset in eyes **Rev. Legend:** AUSTRALIA **Edge:** Plain

Date	Mintage	F	VF	XF	Unc	BU
2004 Proof	5,000	Value: 175				

KM# 750 10 DOLLARS
20.0000 g., 0.9990 Silver partially gilt 0.6423 oz. ASW, 38 mm.
Series: Endangered Wildlife **Obv:** National arms **Obv. Legend:**
REPUBLIC OF LIBERIA **Rev:** Gilt Polar Bear standing facing
with diamonds inset in eyes **Rev. Legend:** CANADA **Edge:** Plain

Date	Mintage	F	VF	XF	Unc	BU
2004 Proof	5,000	Value: 175				

KM# 751 10 DOLLARS
20.0000 g., 0.9990 Silver partially gilt 0.6423 oz. ASW
Series: Endangered Wildlife **Obv:** National arms **Obv. Legend:**
REPUBLIC OF LIBERIA **Rev:** Gilt perched Blakiston's Fish-owl
with diamonds inset in eyes **Rev. Legend:** JAPAN

Date	Mintage	F	VF	XF	Unc	BU
2004 Proof	5,000	Value: 175				

KM# 808 10 DOLLARS
14.5800 g., Copper-Nickel, 32.98 mm. **Obv:** National arms
Rev: Bust of President Ronald Reagon facing, flag in background
Edge: Reeded

Date	Mintage	F	VF	XF	Unc	BU
2004	—	—	—	—	8.00	10.00

KM# 830 10 DOLLARS

15.6200 g., Copper-Nickel, 33.3 mm. **Obv:** National arms **Rev:** Flag at left, bust of 43rd President George W. Bush facing at right **Edge:** Reeded

Date	Mintage	F	VF	XF	Unc	BU
2004	—	—	—	—	10.00	12.00

KM# 738 10 DOLLARS

27.1900 g., Copper-Nickel, 43 mm. **Subject:** Death of Pope John-Paul II **Edge:** Reeded

Date	Mintage	F	VF	XF	Unc	BU
2005	—	—	—	—	12.00	14.00

KM# 739.1 10 DOLLARS

25.0000 g., 0.9250 Silver 0.7435 oz. ASW **Subject:** Death of Pope John-Paul II **Rev:** Silhouette of John-Paul gilt, backgound in Ruthenium

Date	Mintage	F	VF	XF	Unc	BU
2005	7,500	—	—	—	—	60.00

KM# 739.2 10 DOLLARS

25.0000 g., 0.9250 Silver 0.7435 oz. ASW **Subject:** Death of Pope John-Paul II **Rev:** Silhouette of John-Paul gilt, blackened background

Date	Mintage	F	VF	XF	Unc	BU
2005	7,500	—	—	—	—	47.50

KM# 752 10 DOLLARS

20.0000 g., 0.9990 Silver partially gilt 0.6423 oz. ASW, 38 mm. **Series:** Endangered Wildlife **Obv:** National arms **Obv. Legend:** REPUBLIC OF LIBERIA **Rev:** Gilt Koala perched on branch with diamonds inset in eyes **Rev. Legend:** AUSTRALIA **Edge:** Plain

Date	Mintage	F	VF	XF	Unc	BU
2005 Proof	5,000	Value: 150				

KM# 753 10 DOLLARS

20.0000 g., 0.9990 Silver partially gilt 0.6423 oz. ASW, 38 mm. **Series:** Endangered Wildlife **Obv:** National arms **Obv. Legend:** REPUBLIC OF LIBERIA **Rev:** Two perched gilt Yellow-eared Conures with diamonds inset in eyes **Rev. Legend:** COLOMBIA **Edge:** Plain

Date	Mintage	F	VF	XF	Unc	BU
2005 Proof	5,000	Value: 150				

KM# 754 10 DOLLARS

20.0000 g., 0.9990 Silver partially gilt 0.6423 oz. ASW, 38 mm. **Series:** Endangered Wildlife **Obv:** National arms **Obv. Legend:** REPUBLIC OF LIBERIA **Rev:** Gilt Iberian Lynx standing facing with diamonds inset in eyes **Rev. Legend:** SPAIN **Edge:** Plain

Date	Mintage	F	VF	XF	Unc	BU
2005 Proof	5,000	Value: 150				

KM# 755 10 DOLLARS

20.0000 g., 0.9990 Silver partially gilt 0.6423 oz. ASW, 38 mm. **Series:** Endangered Wildlife **Obv:** National arms **Obv. Legend:** REPUBLIC OF LIBERIA **Rev:** Two perched gilt Yellow-crested Cockatoos **Rev. Legend:** INDONESIA **Edge:** Plain

Date	Mintage	F	VF	XF	Unc	BU
2005 Proof	5,000	Value: 150				

KM# 756 10 DOLLARS

20.0000 g., 0.9990 Silver partially gilt 0.6423 oz. ASW, 38 mm. **Series:** Endangered Wildlife **Obv:** National arms **Obv. Legend:** REPUBLIC OF LIBERIA **Rev:** Gilt Jaguar resting on branch with diamonds inset in eyes **Rev. Legend:** BELIZE **Edge:** Plain

Date	Mintage	F	VF	XF	Unc	BU
2005 Proof	5,000	Value: 150				

KM# 757 10 DOLLARS

20.0000 g., 0.9990 Silver partially gilt 0.6423 oz. ASW, 38 mm. **Series:** Endangered Wildlife **Obv:** National arms **Obv. Legend:** REPUBLIC OF LIBERIA **Rev:** Two perched gilt Plate-billed Mountain Toucans with diamonds inset in eyes **Rev. Legend:** ECUADOR **Edge:** Plain

Date	Mintage	F	VF	XF	Unc	BU
2005 Proof	5,000	Value: 150				

KM# 758 10 DOLLARS

20.0000 g., 0.9990 Silver partially gilt 0.6423 oz. ASW, 38 mm. **Series:** Endangered Wildlife **Obv:** National arms **Obv. Legend:** REPUBLIC OF LIBERIA **Rev:** Gilt Red Panda resting facing with diamonds inset in eyes **Rev. Legend:** INDIA **Edge:** Plain

Date	Mintage	F	VF	XF	Unc	BU
2005 Proof	5,000	Value: 150				

KM# 759 10 DOLLARS

20.0000 g., 0.9990 Silver partially gilt 0.6423 oz. ASW, 38 mm. **Series:** Endangered Wildlife **Obv:** National arms **Obv. Legend:** REPUBLIC OF LIBERIA **Rev:** Two perched gilt Resplendent Quetzals with diamonds inset in eyes **Rev. Legend:** GUATEMALA **Edge:** Plain

Date	Mintage	F	VF	XF	Unc	BU
2005 Proof	5,000	Value: 150				

KM# 760 10 DOLLARS

20.0000 g., 0.9990 Silver partially gilt 0.6423 oz. ASW, 38 mm. **Series:** Endangered Wildlife **Obv:** National arms **Obv. Legend:** REPUBLIC OF LIBERIA **Rev:** Gilt Snow Leopard standing left looking back with diamonds inset in eyes **Rev. Legend:** NEPAL **Edge:** Plain

Date	Mintage	F	VF	XF	Unc	BU
2005 Proof	5,000	Value: 150				

KM# 761 10 DOLLARS

20.0000 g., 0.9990 Silver partially gilt 0.6423 oz. ASW, 38 mm. **Series:** Endangered Wildlife **Obv:** National arms **Obv. Legend:** REPUBLIC OF LIBERIA **Rev:** Gilt Fossa standing right on branch facing with diamonds inset in eyes **Rev. Legend:** MADAGASCAR **Edge:** Plain

Date	Mintage	F	VF	XF	Unc	BU
2005 Proof	5,000	Value: 150				

KM# 762 10 DOLLARS

20.0000 g., 0.9990 Silver partially gilt 0.6423 oz. ASW, 38 mm. **Series:** Endangered Wildlife **Obv:** National arms **Obv. Legend:** REPUBLIC OF LIBERIA **Rev:** Two gilt Chilean Flamingos standing left with diamonds inset in eyes **Rev. Legend:** ARGENTINA **Edge:** Plain

Date	Mintage	F	VF	XF	Unc	BU
2005 Proof	5,000	Value: 150				

KM# 763 10 DOLLARS

20.0000 g., 0.9990 Silver partially gilt 0.6423 oz. ASW, 38 mm. **Series:** Endangered Wildlife **Obv:** National arms **Obv. Legend:** REPUBLIC OF LIBERIA **Rev:** Two gilt White-winged ducks, one standing, one swimming right with diamonds inset in eyes **Rev. Legend:** THAILAND **Edge:** Plain

Date	Mintage	F	VF	XF	Unc	BU
2005 Proof	5,000	Value: 150				

KM# 860 10 DOLLARS

25.0000 g., 0.9250 Silver 0.7435 oz. ASW, 38.6 mm. **Subject:** Poison frogs **Rev:** Green Frog, multicolor

Date	Mintage	F	VF	XF	Unc	BU
2005 Proof	2,500	Value: 40.00				

KM# 861 10 DOLLARS

25.0000 g., 0.9250 Silver 0.7435 oz. ASW, 38.6 mm. **Subject:** Poison frogs **Rev:** Red frog, multicolor

Date	Mintage	F	VF	XF	Unc	BU
2005 Proof	2,500	Value: 40.00				

KM# 862 10 DOLLARS

25.0000 g., 0.9250 Silver 0.7435 oz. ASW, 38.6 mm. **Subject:** Poison frog **Rev:** Blue frog, multicolor

Date	Mintage	F	VF	XF	Unc	BU
2005 Proof	2,500	Value: 40.00				

KM# 864 10 DOLLARS

0.5000 g., 0.5850 Gold 0.0094 oz. AGW, 11 mm. **Subject:** 25th Anniversary of the Krugerrand **Obv:** Shield **Rev:** Paul Krueger bust left

Date	Mintage	F	VF	XF	Unc	BU
2005 Proof	—	Value: 35.00				

KM# 843 10 DOLLARS

0.7300 g., 0.9990 Gold 0.0234 oz. AGW, 11 mm. **Obv:** Arms **Rev:** John F. Kennedy head left

Date	Mintage	F	VF	XF	Unc	BU
2006 Proof	20,000	Value: 35.00				

KM# 764 10 DOLLARS

20.0000 g., 0.9990 Silver partially gilt 0.6423 oz. ASW, 38 mm. **Series:** Endangered Wildlife **Obv:** National arms **Obv. Legend:** REPUBLIC OF LIBERIA **Rev:** Gilt Crested Genet on branch facing with diamonds inset in eyes **Rev. Legend:** CAMEROON **Edge:** Plain

Date	Mintage	F	VF	XF	Unc	BU
2006 Proof	5,000	Value: 150				

KM# 765 10 DOLLARS

20.0000 g., 0.9990 Silver partially gilt 0.6423 oz. ASW, 38 mm. **Series:** Endangered Wildlife **Obv:** National arms **Obv. Legend:** REPUBLIC OF LIBERIA **Rev:** Two gilt Dalmatian Pelicans, one swimming, one standing with diamonds inset in eyes **Rev. Legend:** MONTENEGRO **Edge:** Plain

Date	Mintage	F	VF	XF	Unc	BU
2006 Proof	5,000	Value: 150				

KM# 766 10 DOLLARS

20.0000 g., 0.9990 Silver partially gilt 0.6423 oz. ASW, 38 mm. **Series:** Endangered Wildlife **Obv:** National arms **Obv. Legend:** REPUBLIC OF LIBERIA **Rev:** Gilt Hairy-bared Dwarf Lemue standing on branch with diamonds inset in eyes **Rev. Legend:** MADAGASCAR **Edge:** Plain

Date	Mintage	F	VF	XF	Unc	BU
2006 Proof	5,000	Value: 150				

KM# 767 10 DOLLARS

20.0000 g., 0.9990 Silver partially gilt 0.6423 oz. ASW, 38 mm. **Series:** Endangered Wildlife **Obv:** National arms **Obv. Legend:** REPUBLIC OF LIBERIA **Rev:** Two gilt Visayan Tarictics perched on branches with diamonds inset in eyes **Rev. Legend:** Philippines **Edge:** Plain

Date	Mintage	F	VF	XF	Unc	BU
2006 Proof	5,000	Value: 150				

KM# 768 10 DOLLARS

20.0000 g., 0.9990 Silver partially gilt 0.6423 oz. ASW, 38 mm. **Series:** Endangered Wildlife **Obv:** National arms **Obv. Legend:** REPUBLIC OF LIBERIA **Rev:** Two gilt Ethiopian Wolves, one seated, one laying with diamonds inset in eyes **Rev. Legend:** ETHIOPIA **Edge:** Plain

Date	Mintage	F	VF	XF	Unc	BU
2006 Proof	5,000	Value: 150				

KM# 769 10 DOLLARS

20.0000 g., 0.9990 Silver partially gilt 0.6423 oz. ASW, 38 mm. **Series:** Endangered Wildlife **Obv:** National arms **Obv. Legend:** REPUBLIC OF LIBERIA **Rev:** Two gilt Kakapos perched on a branch with diamonds inset in eyes **Rev. Legend:** NEW ZEALAND **Edge:** Plain

Date	Mintage	F	VF	XF	Unc	BU
2006 Proof	5,000	Value: 150				

KM# 770 10 DOLLARS

20.0000 g., 0.9990 Silver partially gilt 0.6423 oz. ASW, 38 mm. **Series:** Endangered Wildlife **Obv:** National arms **Obv. Legend:** REPUBLIC OF LIBERIA **Rev:** Gilt Spectacled Bear standing with diamonds inset in eyes **Rev. Legend:** BOLIVIA **Edge:** Plain

Date	Mintage	F	VF	XF	Unc	BU
2006 Proof	5,000	Value: 150				

KM# 771 10 DOLLARS

20.0000 g., 0.9990 Silver partially gilt 0.6423 oz. ASW, 38 mm. **Series:** Endangered Wildlife **Obv:** National arms **Obv. Legend:** REPUBLIC OF LIBERIA **Rev:** Two gilt Mauritius Kestrels perched on branch with diamonds inset in eyes **Rev. Legend:** MAURITIUS **Edge:** Plain

Date	Mintage	F	VF	XF	Unc	BU
2006 Proof	5,000	Value: 150				

KM# 772 10 DOLLARS

20.0000 g., 0.9990 Silver Partially gilt 0.6423 oz. ASW, 38 mm. **Series:** Endangered Wildlife **Obv:** National arms **Obv. Legend:** REPUBLIC OF LIBERIA **Rev:** Two gilt Mhorr Gazelles, one standing, one resting with diamonds inset in eyes **Rev. Legend:** MALI **Edge:** Plain

Date	Mintage	F	VF	XF	Unc	BU
2006 Proof	5,000	Value: 150				

KM# 773 10 DOLLARS

20.0000 g., 0.9990 Silver partially gilt 0.6423 oz. ASW, 38 mm. **Series:** Endangered Wildlife **Obv:** National arms **Obv. Legend:** REPUBLIC OF LIBERIA **Rev:** Two gilt Blue Lorikeets perched on branches with diamonds inset in eyes **Rev. Legend:** FRENCH POLYNESIA **Edge:** Plain

Date	Mintage	F	VF	XF	Unc	BU
2006 Proof	5,000	Value: 150				

KM# 774 10 DOLLARS

20.0000 g., 0.9990 Silver partially gilt 0.6423 oz. ASW, 38 mm. **Series:** Endangered Wildlife **Obv:** National arms **Obv. Legend:** REPUBLIC OF LIBERIA **Rev:** Gilt resting Arabian Leopard with diamonds inset in eyes **Rev. Legend:** SAUDI ARABIA **Edge:** Plain

Date	Mintage	F	VF	XF	Unc	BU
2006 Proof	5,000	Value: 150				

KM# 775 10 DOLLARS

20.0000 g., 0.9990 Silver partially gilt 0.6423 oz. ASW, 38 mm. **Series:** Endangered Wildlife **Obv:** National arms **Obv. Legend:** REPUBLIC OF LIBERIA **Rev:** Two gilt Hawaiian Geese standing with diamonds inset in eyes **Rev. Legend:** USA **Edge:** Plain

Date	Mintage	F	VF	XF	Unc	BU
2006 Proof	5,000	Value: 150				

KM# 827 10 DOLLARS

14.6000 g., Copper-Nickel, 33 mm. **Subject:** Abraham Lincoln **Obv:** National arms **Rev:** Bust facing 3/4 right **Edge:** Reeded

Date	Mintage	F	VF	XF	Unc	BU
2006 Proof	50,000	Value: 10.00				

KM# 725 10 DOLLARS

3.1100 g., 0.9990 Gold 0.0999 oz. AGW, 16 mm. **Obv:** National arms **Rev:** Leopard head **Edge:** Reeded

Date	Mintage	F	VF	XF	Unc	BU
2007 Proof	120	Value: 160				

KM# 734 10 DOLLARS

25.0000 g., 0.9250 Silver 0.7435 oz. ASW, 38.61 mm. **Subject:** The Black Madonna of Czestochowa **Obv:** Arms **Obv. Legend:** REPUBLIC OF LIBERIA **Rev:** 1/2 length figure of Madonna facing with child

Date	Mintage	F	VF	XF	Unc	BU
2007 Proof	1,000	Value: 65.00				

KM# 643 20 DOLLARS
15.5500 g., 0.9990 Silver 0.4994 oz. ASW, 30.4 mm. **Obv:** St. Peter's Basilica **Rev:** Bust of Pope facing **Edge:** Reeded

Date	Mintage	F	VF	XF	Unc	BU
2001S Proof	—	Value: 25.00				

KM# 650 20 DOLLARS
19.9100 g., 0.9990 Silver 0.6395 oz. ASW, 40 mm. **Obv:** National arms **Rev:** Bust of Charles Lindbergh facing and plane **Edge:** Reeded

Date	Mintage	F	VF	XF	Unc	BU
2001 Proof	—	Value: 40.00				

KM# 715 20 DOLLARS
20.0000 g., 0.9990 Silver 0.6423 oz. ASW, 40.3 mm. **Series:** American History **Obv:** National arms **Rev:** First Continental Congress in prayer **Edge:** Reeded

Date	Mintage	F	VF	XF	Unc	BU
2001 Proof	20,000	Value: 25.00				

KM# 716 20 DOLLARS
20.0000 g., 0.9990 Silver 0.6423 oz. ASW, 40.3 mm. **Series:** American History **Obv:** National arms **Rev:** U.S. Constitution Ratification, text in stars of folded flag **Edge:** Reeded

Date	Mintage	F	VF	XF	Unc	BU
2001 Proof	20,000	Value: 25.00				

KM# 717 20 DOLLARS
20.0000 g., 0.9990 Silver 0.6423 oz. ASW, 40.3 mm. **Series:** American History **Obv:** National arms **Rev:** Washington's Inauguration scene **Edge:** Reeded

Date	Mintage	F	VF	XF	Unc	BU
2001 Proof	20,000	Value: 25.00				

KM# 718 20 DOLLARS
20.0000 g., 0.9990 Silver 0.6423 oz. ASW, 40.3 mm. **Series:** American History **Obv:** National arms **Rev:** Appomattox Courthouse surrender scene with Lee and Grant **Edge:** Reeded

Date	Mintage	F	VF	XF	Unc	BU
2001 Proof	20,000	Value: 25.00				

KM# 719 20 DOLLARS
20.0000 g., 0.9990 Silver 0.6423 oz. ASW, 40.3 mm. **Series:** American History **Obv:** National arms **Rev:** Prohibition, hatchet, barrels and bottles destruction **Edge:** Reeded

Date	Mintage	F	VF	XF	Unc	BU
2001 Proof	20,000	Value: 25.00				

KM# 720 20 DOLLARS
20.0000 g., 0.9990 Silver 0.6423 oz. ASW, 40.3 mm. **Series:** American History **Obv:** National arms **Rev:** Cuban Missile Crisis, Castro, Khrushchev, Kennedy, missiles and map **Edge:** Reeded

Date	Mintage	F	VF	XF	Unc	BU
2001 Proof	20,000	Value: 25.00				

KM# 721 20 DOLLARS
20.0000 g., 0.9990 Silver 0.6423 oz. ASW, 40.3 mm. **Series:** American History **Obv:** National arms **Rev:** First Man on Moon, Armstrong and Lander **Edge:** Reeded

Date	Mintage	F	VF	XF	Unc	BU
2001 Proof	20,000	Value: 25.00				

KM# 722 20 DOLLARS
20.0000 g., 0.9990 Silver 0.6423 oz. ASW, 40.3 mm. **Series:** American History **Obv:** National arms **Rev:** Desert Storm, soldier, helicopter, rocket launcher etc. **Edge:** Reeded

Date	Mintage	F	VF	XF	Unc	BU
2001 Proof	20,000	Value: 25.00				

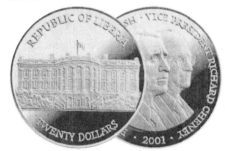

KM# 514 20 DOLLARS
31.1035 g., 0.9990 Silver 0.9990 oz. ASW, 38.2 mm. **Subject:** Bush-Cheney Inauguration **Obv:** White House **Rev:** Conjoined busts right **Edge:** Reeded

Date	Mintage	F	VF	XF	Unc	BU
2001 Proof	—	Value: 45.00				

KM# 616 20 DOLLARS
31.2000 g., 0.9990 Silver gilt 1.0021 oz. ASW, 38.7 mm. **Obv:** National arms **Rev:** Diamond studded scorpion (scorpio) **Edge:** Reeded

Date	Mintage	F	VF	XF	Unc	BU
2002 Proof	—	Value: 60.00				

KM# 617 20 DOLLARS
31.2000 g., 0.9990 Silver gilt 1.0021 oz. ASW, 38.7 mm. **Obv:** National arms **Rev:** Diamond studded archer (sagittarius) **Edge:** Reeded

Date	Mintage	F	VF	XF	Unc	BU
2002 Proof	—	Value: 60.00				

KM# 825 20 DOLLARS
20.0000 g., Silver, 40 mm. **Series:** America's First Ladies **Subject:** Mary Todd Lincoln **Obv:** National arms **Rev:** Bust facing slightly left at center left, oval portrait of Abraham Lincoln at right **Edge:** Reeded

Date	Mintage	F	VF	XF	Unc	BU
2003 Proof	20,000	Value: 27.50				

KM# 826 20 DOLLARS
20.0000 g., Silver, 40 mm. **Series:** History of America **Subject:** Emancipation Proclamation **Obv:** National arms **Rev:** Lincoln seated with seven politicians gathered **Edge:** Reeded

Date	Mintage	F	VF	XF	Unc	BU
2004 Proof	20,000	Value: 37.50				

KM# 634 25 DOLLARS
0.7300 g., 0.9990 Gold 0.0234 oz. AGW, 11.1 mm. **Obv:** National arms **Rev:** Joan of Arc **Edge:** Reeded

Date	Mintage	F	VF	XF	Unc	BU
2001 Proof	—	Value: 35.00				

KM# 666 25 DOLLARS
1.5200 g., Gold, 13.68 mm. **Subject:** Abraham Lincoln **Obv:** National arms **Rev:** Statue of Lincoln seated **Edge:** Reeded

Date	Mintage	F	VF	XF	Unc	BU
2001 Proof	—	Value: 65.00				

KM# 667 25 DOLLARS
0.7300 g., 0.9990 Gold 0.0234 oz. AGW, 11 mm. **Obv:** National arms **Rev:** Mount Rushmore **Edge:** Reeded

Date	Mintage	F	VF	XF	Unc	BU
2001 Proof	20,000	Value: 45.00				

KM# 669 25 DOLLARS
0.7300 g., 0.9990 Gold 0.0234 oz. AGW, 11 mm. **Subject:** Abraham Lincoln **Obv:** National arms **Rev:** Bust facing at right, Lincoln Memorial in background **Edge:** Reeded

Date	Mintage	F	VF	XF	Unc	BU
2002 Proof	20,000	Value: 45.00				

KM# 730 25 DOLLARS
0.0234 g., 0.9990 Gold 0.0008 oz. AGW **Obv:** Shield **Rev:** Map of Germany and stars

Date	Mintage	F	VF	XF	Unc	BU
2003B Proof	—	Value: 35.00				

KM# 804 25 DOLLARS
1.2500 g., 0.9990 Gold 0.0401 oz. AGW, 14.5 x 9 mm. **Subject:** R. M. S. Titanic - Expedition 2000 **Obv:** National arms **Obv. Legend:** REPUBLIC OF LIBERIA **Rev:** Titanic with small piece of recovered coal embedded in hull. **Edge:** Reeded **Shape:** Oval

Date	Mintage	F	VF	XF	Unc	BU
2005 Proof	—	Value: 65.00				

KM# 731 50 DOLLARS
222.0800 g., 0.9990 Silver 7.1326 oz. ASW, 80.04 mm. **Subject:** Japanese Attack on Pearl Harbor **Obv:** National arms **Obv. Legend:** REPUBLIC OF LIBERIA **Rev:** USA flag hologram at upper left, bust of Franklin D. Roosevelt facing above Japanese aircraft attacking ship in harbor **Rev. Legend:** REMEMBERING PEARL HARBOR - DECEMBER 7, 1941

Date	Mintage	F	VF	XF	Unc	BU
2001 Proof	—	Value: 175				

KM# 495 50 DOLLARS
907.0000 g., 0.9990 Silver 29.130 oz. ASW, 100 mm.
Subject: Wreck of the Princess Louisa **Obv:** National arms and value **Rev:** Ship under sail **Edge:** Reeded **Note:** Each coin has a cob coin recovered from the wreck site encased in a hole with clear resin. Illustration reduced.

Date	Mintage	F	VF	XF	Unc	BU
2001	500	—	—	—	625	

KM# 776 50 DOLLARS
93.3000 g., 0.9990 Silver partially gilt 2.9965 oz. ASW, 65.00 mm. **Series:** Endangered Wildlife **Obv:** National arms **Obv. Legend:** REPUBLIC OF LIBERIA **Rev:** Two gilt Cheetahs, one sitting, one resting with diamonds inset in eyes **Rev. Legend:** TANZANIA **Edge:** Plain

Date	Mintage	F	VF	XF	Unc	BU
2005 Proof	999	Value: 400				

KM# 726 50 DOLLARS
62.2070 g., 0.9990 Silver 1.9979 oz. ASW, 50 mm.
Obv: National arms **Rev:** Leopard lying across a map of Africa **Edge:** Reeded

Date	Mintage	F	VF	XF	Unc	BU
2007 Proof	500	Value: 85.00				

KM# 844 100 DOLLARS
1000.0000 g., 0.9990 Silver 32.117 oz. ASW **Subject:** Tanks of QWorld War II - T-34

Date	Mintage	F	VF	XF	Unc	BU
2008 Proof	1,000	Value: 1,500				

KM# 845 100 DOLLARS
1000.0000 g., 0.9990 Silver 32.117 oz. ASW **Subject:** Tanks of World War II - VI-Tiger

Date	Mintage	F	VF	XF	Unc	BU
2008 Proof	1,000	Value: 1,500				

KM# 846 100 DOLLARS
1000.0000 g., 0.9990 Silver 32.117 oz. ASW, 120 mm.
Obv: Arms **Rev:** St. Paul standing, events of his life around

Date	Mintage	F	VF	XF	Unc	BU
2008 Proof	1,000	Value: 2,000				

KM# 727 2500 DOLLARS
155.5175 g., 0.9990 Gold 4.9948 oz. AGW, 60 mm.
Obv: National arms **Rev:** Leopard lying across a map of Africa **Edge:** Reeded

Date	Mintage	F	VF	XF	Unc	BU
2007 Proof	48	Value: 6,500				

PATTERNS
Including off metal strikes

KM#	Date	Mintage Identification	Mkt Val

| Pn58 | 2001 | — 10 Dollars. Copper-Nickel. 29.2500 g. 38.2 mm. National arms. "9-11" Flag raising scene. Plain edge. | 125 |

| Pn59 | 2001 | — 20 Dollars. Silver Plated Base Metal. 5.3100 g. 20 mm. National arms. "9-11" Flag raising scene. Plain edge. | 75.00 |

| Pn60 | 2001 | — 100 Dollars. Base Metal Gilt. 3.4200 g. 16 mm. National arms. "9-11" Flag raising scene. Plain edge. | 50.00 |

LIECHTENSTEIN

The Principality of Liechtenstein, located in central Europe on the east bank of the Rhine between Austria and Switzerland, has an area of 62 sq. mi. (160 sq. km.) and a population of 27,200. Capital: Vaduz. The economy is based on agriculture and light manufacturing. Canned goods, textiles, ceramics and precision instruments are exported.

RULERS
Prince Hans Adam II, 1990-

MINT MARKS
B - Bern

PRINCIPALITY

REFORM COINAGE
100 Rappen = 1 Frank

Y# 24 10 FRANKEN
29.9500 g., 0.9000 Silver 0.8666 oz. ASW, 37.3 mm.
Ruler: Prince Hans Adam II **Subject:** 200 Years of Sovereignty **Obv:** Vertical inscription between crowned arms and value **Rev:** Johann I (1760-1836) **Edge:** Reeded

Date	Mintage	F	VF	XF	Unc	BU
ND (2006)B Proof	—	Value: 55.00				

KM# 25 50 FRANKEN
8.8800 g., 0.9990 Gold 0.2852 oz. AGW **Ruler:** Prince Hans Adam II **Subject:** 200th Anniversary of Sovereignty

Date	Mintage	F	VF	XF	Unc	BU
ND (2006)B Proof	—	Value: 450				

LITHUANIA

The Republic of Lithuania, southernmost of the Baltic states in east Europe, has an area of 25,174 sq. mi. (65,201 sq. km.) and a population of *3.6 million. Capital: Vilnius. The economy is based on livestock raising and manufacturing. Hogs, cattle, hides and electric motors are exported.

Lithuania declared its independence March 11, 1990 and it was recognized by the United States on Sept. 2, 1991, followed by the Soviet government in Moscow on Sept. 6. They were seated in the UN General Assembly on Sept. 17, 1991.

MODERN REPUBLIC

REFORM COINAGE
100 Centas = 1 Litas

KM# 106 10 CENTU
2.6700 g., Brass, 17 mm. **Obv:** National arms **Rev:** Value **Edge:** Reeded

Date	Mintage	F	VF	XF	Unc	BU
2003 In sets only	—	—	—	—	—	0.40
2003 Proof	10,000	Value: 0.75				
2006	—	—	—	—	—	0.40
2006 Proof	2,000	Value: 45.00				
2007	—	—	—	—	—	0.40
2008	—	—	—	—	—	0.40
2008 Proof-like	200	—	—	—	—	5.00
2009	—	—	—	—	—	0.40
2009 Proof-like	500	—	—	—	—	3.00

KM# 107 20 CENTU
4.7700 g., Brass, 20.43 mm. **Obv:** National arms **Rev:** Value **Edge:** Reeded

Date	Mintage	F	VF	XF	Unc	BU
2003 In sets only	—	—	—	—	—	1.50
2003 Proof	10,000	Value: 1.00				
2007	—	—	—	—	—	1.00
2008	—	—	—	—	—	1.00
2008 Proof-like	200	—	—	—	—	5.00
2009	—	—	—	—	—	1.00
2009 Proof-like	500	—	—	—	—	3.00

KM# 108 50 CENTU
6.0000 g., Brass **Obv:** National arms **Rev:** Value within designed circle

Date	Mintage	F	VF	XF	Unc	BU
2003 In mint sets	—	—	—	—	—	2.00
2003 Proof	10,000	Value: 1.50				
2008	—	—	—	—	1.00	1.50
2008 Proof-like	200	—	—	—	—	5.00
2009	—	—	—	—	1.00	1.50
2009 Proof-like	500	—	—	—	—	3.00

KM# 111 LITAS

6.1800 g., Copper-Nickel, 22.3 mm. **Obv:** National arms
Rev: Value within circle above lined designs **Edge:** Reeded

Date	Mintage	F	VF	XF	Unc	BU
2001	—	—	—	—	1.50	2.00
2002	—	—	—	—	1.50	2.00
2003 In mint sets	—	—	—	—	—	3.00
2003 Proof	10,000	Value: 3.00				
2008	—	—	—	—	1.50	2.00
2008 Proof-like	200	—	—	—	—	5.00
2009	—	—	—	—	1.50	2.00
2009 Proof-like	500	—	—	—	—	4.00

KM# 137 LITAS

6.1500 g., Copper-Nickel, 22.2 mm. **Subject:** 425th Anniversary
- University of Vilnius **Obv:** Knight on horse within rope wreath
Rev: Building within court yard **Edge:** Segmented reeding

Date	Mintage	F	VF	XF	Unc	BU
2004	200,000	—	—	—	4.00	6.00

KM# 142 LITAS

6.4100 g., Copper-Nickel, 22.35 mm. **Obv:** Knight on horse
within circle **Rev:** Palace **Edge:** Segmented reeding

Date	Mintage	F	VF	XF	Unc	BU
2005	1,000,000	—	—	—	4.00	5.00

KM# 162 LITAS

6.2500 g., Copper-Nickel, 22.3 mm. **Subject:** Vilnius - European
Culture Capital **Obv:** National Arms **Rev:** Femal figure standing
at easle

Date	Mintage	F	VF	XF	Unc	BU
2009	1,000,000	—	—	—	4.00	5.00

KM# 112 2 LITAI

7.5000 g., Bi-Metallic Brass center in Copper-Nickel ring, 25 mm.
Obv: National arms within circle **Rev:** Value within circle
Edge: Segmented reeding

Date	Mintage	F	VF	XF	Unc	BU
2001	—	—	—	—	2.25	3.00
2002	—	—	—	—	2.25	3.00
2003 In sets only	—	—	—	—	—	4.00
2003 Proof	10,000	Value: 3.50				
2008	—	—	—	—	2.25	3.00
2008 Proof-like	200	—	—	—	—	5.00
2009	—	—	—	—	2.25	3.00
2009 Proof-like	500	—	—	—	—	4.00

KM# 132 5 LITAI

28.2800 g., 0.9250 Silver 0.8410 oz. ASW, 38.6 mm.
Series: Endangered Wildlife **Obv:** Knight on horse **Rev:** Barn
owl in flight **Edge Lettering:** LIETUVOS BANKAS

Date	Mintage	F	VF	XF	Unc	BU
2002 Proof	3,000	Value: 150				

KM# 113 5 LITAI

10.2600 g., Bi-Metallic Copper-Nickel ring in Brass center,
22.5 mm. **Obv:** National arms within circle **Rev:** Value within
circle **Edge Lettering:** PENKI LITAI

Date	Mintage	F	VF	XF	Unc	BU
2003 In sets only	—	—	—	—	—	9.00
2003 Proof	10,000	Value: 9.00				
2008	—	—	—	—	5.50	7.50
2008 Proof-like	200	—	—	—	—	10.00
2009	—	—	—	—	5.00	7.50
2009 Proof-like	500	—	—	—	—	9.00

KM# 131 10 LITU

13.1500 g., Copper-Nickel, 28.7 mm. **Obv:** Knight on horse on
shield within aerial harbor view **Rev:** Shield within city view
Edge Lettering: KLAIPEDAI - 75 (twice)

Date	Mintage	F	VF	XF	Unc	BU
2002 Proof	5,000	Value: 25.00				

KM# 157 10 LITU

1.2440 g., 0.9990 Gold 0.0400 oz. AGW, 13.9 mm. **Obv:** Town
gate **Rev:** Mathematical arc **Rev. Legend:** Sectio Aurea

Date	Mintage	F	VF	XF	Unc	BU
2007 Proof	7,000	Value: 60.00				

KM# 160 10 LITU

1.2400 g., 0.9990 Gold 0.0398 oz. AGW, 13.92 mm.
Obv: Castle gate **Rev:** Geometric design

Date	Mintage	F	VF	XF	Unc	BU
2007LMK Proof	7,000	Value: 75.00				

KM# 129 50 LITU

28.2800 g., 0.9250 Silver 0.8410 oz. ASW, 38.61 mm.
Subject: Motiejus Valancius' 200th Birthday **Obv:** Knight on
horse within shield above church and landscape **Rev:** Bust facing
Edge Lettering: LIETUVISKAS ZODIS RASTAS IR TIKEJMAS
TAUTOS GYVASTIS

Date	Mintage	F	VF	XF	Unc	BU
2001 Proof	2,000	Value: 100				

KM# 130 50 LITU

28.2800 g., 0.9250 Silver 0.8410 oz. ASW, 38.61 mm.
Subject: Jonas Basanavicius (1851-1927) **Obv:** Knight on horse
Rev: Jonas Basanavicius **Edge Lettering:** KAD AUSRAI
AUSTANT PRAVISTU IR LIETUVOS DVASIA

Date	Mintage	F	VF	XF	Unc	BU
2001 Proof	2,000	Value: 90.00				

KM# 133 50 LITU

28.2800 g., 0.9250 Silver 0.8410 oz. ASW, 38.61 mm.
Series: Historical Architecture **Obv:** Republic of Lithuania coat
of arms **Rev:** Trakai Island Castle **Edge Lettering:** ISTORIJOS
IR ARCHITEKTUROS PAMINKLAI

Date	Mintage	F	VF	XF	Unc	BU
2002 Proof	1,500	Value: 100				

KM# 134 50 LITU

28.2800 g., 0.9250 Silver 0.8410 oz. ASW, 38.6 mm.
Obv: Knight on horse above value **Rev:** Vilnius Cathedral
Edge Lettering: ISTORIJOS IR ARCHITEKTUROS PAMINKLAI

Date	Mintage	F	VF	XF	Unc	BU
2003 Proof	1,500	Value: 110				

KM# 135 50 LITU

28.2800 g., 0.9250 Silver 0.8410 oz. ASW, 38.6 mm.
Subject: Olympics **Obv:** Knight on horse above value
Rev: Stylized cyclists **Edge Lettering:** XXVIII OLIMPIADOS
ZAIDYNEMS

Date	Mintage	F	VF	XF	Unc	BU
2003 Proof	2,000	Value: 140				

KM# 138   50 LITU
28.2800 g., 0.9250 Silver 0.8410 oz. ASW, 38.6 mm.
Series: Historical Architecture **Subject:** 425th Anniversary -
University of Vilnius **Obv:** Knight on horse **Rev:** Old university
buildings **Edge:** Lettered **Edge Lettering:** ISTORIJOS IR
ARCHITEKTUROS PAMINKLAI

Date	Mintage	F	VF	XF	Unc	BU
2004 Proof	2,000	Value: 120				

KM# 139   50 LITU
28.2800 g., 0.9250 Silver 0.8410 oz. ASW, 38.6 mm.
Obv: Knight on horse **Rev:** Pazaislis Monastery **Edge:** Lettered
Edge Lettering: ISTORIJOS IR ARCHITEKTUROS PAMINKLAI

Date	Mintage	F	VF	XF	Unc	BU
2004 Proof	1,500	Value: 140				

KM# 140   50 LITU
28.2800 g., 0.9250 Silver 0.8410 oz. ASW, 38.6 mm.
Subject: First Lithuanian Statute of 1529 **Obv:** Knight on horse
Rev: Seated and kneeling figures **Edge:** Lettered
Edge Lettering: "BUKIME TEISES VERGAI, KAD GALETUME
NAUDOTIS LAISVEMIS"

Date	Mintage	F	VF	XF	Unc	BU
2004 Proof	1,000	Value: 200				

KM# 141   50 LITU
28.2800 g., 0.9250 Silver 0.8410 oz. ASW, 38.6 mm. **Subject:**
Curonian Spit **Obv:** Knight on horse **Rev:** Shifting sand dunes
design **Edge:** Ornamented pattern from Neringa emblem

Date	Mintage	F	VF	XF	Unc	BU
2004 Proof	2,000	Value: 170				

KM# 143   50 LITU
28.2800 g., 0.9250 Silver ASW 0.8410 0.8410 oz. ASW,
38.6 mm. **Series:** Historical Architecture **Obv:** Denar coin with
Knight on horse **Rev:** Kernavé hill fort **Edge Lettering:**
ISTORIJOS IR ARCHITEKTUROS PAMINKLAI

Date	Mintage	F	VF	XF	Unc	BU
2005 Proof	2,000	Value: 140				

KM# 147   50 LITU
28.2800 g., 0.9250 Silver 0.8410 oz. ASW, 38.6 mm.
Subject: 1905 Lithuanian Congress **Obv:** Knight on horse
Rev: Legend and inscription **Edge:** Ornamented

Date	Mintage	F	VF	XF	Unc	BU
2005 Proof	1,500	Value: 220				

KM# 144   50 LITU
28.2800 g., 0.9250 Silver 0.8410 oz. ASW, 38.6 mm.
Subject: 150th Anniversary - National Museum **Obv:** Trio of
ancient Lithuanian coins **Rev:** Man blowing horn
Edge Lettering: PRO PUBLICO BONO

Date	Mintage	F	VF	XF	Unc	BU
2005 Proof	1,500	Value: 325				

KM# 145   50 LITU
28.2800 g., 0.9250 Silver 0.8410 oz. ASW, 38.6 mm.
Subject: Knight on horse and cross **Rev:** Cardinal Vincentas
Sladkevicius **Edge Lettering:** LET OUR LIFE BE BUILT ON
GOODNESS AND HOPE

Date	Mintage	F	VF	XF	Unc	BU
2005 Proof	2,000	Value: 90.00				

KM# 148   50 LITU
28.2800 g., 0.9250 Silver 0.8410 oz. ASW, 38.6 mm.
Obv: National arms on forest background **Rev:** Lynx prowling
Edge: Stylized lynx paw prints

Date	Mintage	F	VF	XF	Unc	BU
2006 Proof	3,000	Value: 175				

KM# 149   50 LITU
28.2800 g., 0.9250 Silver 0.8410 oz. ASW, 38.6 mm.
Obv: National arms against castle wall background
Rev: Medininkai Castle **Edge Lettering:** ISTORIJOS IR
ARCHITEKTUROS PAMINKLAI

Date	Mintage	F	VF	XF	Unc	BU
2006 Proof	2,500	Value: 80.00				

KM# 151   50 LITU
28.2800 g., 0.9250 Silver 0.8410 oz. ASW, 38.61 mm.
Subject: 1831 Uprising **Obv:** Small national arms above battle
scene **Obv. Legend:** LIETUVA **Rev:** Bust of Pliaterytè facing
Rev. Legend: EMILIJA PLIATERYTÈ **Edge Lettering:** 1831 *
SUKILIMAS **Designer:** Giedrius Paulauskis

Date	Mintage	F	VF	XF	Unc	BU
2006 Proof	2,500	Value: 80.00				

KM# 152   50 LITU
28.2800 g., 0.9250 Silver 0.8410 oz. ASW, 38.6 mm.
Subject: XXIX Olympics 2008 - Beijing **Obv:** National arms
Obv. Legend: LIETUVA **Rev:** Stylized swimmer right
Rev. Legend: PEKINAS

Date	Mintage	F	VF	XF	Unc	BU
2007 Proof	5,000	Value: 75.00				

KM# 161 50 LITU
28.2800 g., 0.9250 Silver 0.8410 oz. ASW, 38.6 mm.
Subject: Panemune Castle **Obv:** Shield and fortress detail
Rev: Castle towers

Date	Mintage	F	VF	XF	Unc	BU
2007LMK Proof	5,000	Value: 40.00				

KM# 153 50 LITU
28.2800 g., 0.9250 Silver 0.8410 oz. ASW, 38.6 mm. **Series:**
European Cultural Heritage **Obv:** National arms surrounded by
seven archaic crosses **Obv. Legend:** LIETUVA **Rev:** Circular
latent image surrounded by seven archaic crosses

Date	Mintage	F	VF	XF	Unc	BU
2008 Proof	10,000	Value: 50.00				

KM# 155 50 LITU
28.2800 g., 0.9250 Silver 0.8410 oz. ASW, 38.6 mm.
Obv: National arms **Obv. Legend:** LIETUVA **Rev:** Partial castle
wall, towers **Rev. Legend:** KAUNO PILIS
Rev. Designer: Giedrius Paulauskis

Date	Mintage	F	VF	XF	Unc	BU
2008 Proof	10,000	Value: 45.00				

KM# 154 50 LITU
28.2800 g., 0.9250 Silver 0.8410 oz. ASW, 38.6 mm.
Subject: 550th Anniversary Birth of St. Casimer **Obv:** National
arms on shield **Obv. Legend:** LIETUVA **Rev:** St. Casimer
standing holding flowers **Rev. Legend:** SV. KAZIMIERAS
Rev. Designer: Giedrius Paulauskis

Date	Mintage	F	VF	XF	Unc	BU
2008 Proof	5,000	Value: 75.00				

KM# 159 50 LITU
28.2800 g., 0.9250 Silver 0.8410 oz. ASW, 38.6 mm.
Subject: Lithuania Nature **Obv:** National Arms **Rev:** Bee

Date	Mintage	F	VF	XF	Unc	BU
2008 Proof	10,000	Value: 80.00				

KM# 163 50 LITU
28.2800 g., 0.9250 Silver 0.8410 oz. ASW, 38.6 mm.
Subject: Vilnius - European Culture Capital **Obv:** National Arms
Rev: Female figure standing at easle

Date	Mintage	F	VF	XF	Unc	BU
2009 Proof	10,000	Value: 80.00				

KM# 164 50 LITU
28.2800 g., 0.9250 Silver 0.8410 oz. ASW, 38.6 mm.
Subject: Tytuvenai **Obv:** National Arms in Shield **Rev:** Tytuvenai
Church facade at left

Date	Mintage	F	VF	XF	Unc	BU
2009 Proof	10,000	Value: 80.00				

KM# 165 50 LITU
28.2800 g., 0.9250 Silver 0.8410 oz. ASW, 38.6 mm.
Subject: Nature, Naktiziede **Obv:** Knight on horseback left
Rev: Flowers

Date	Mintage	F	VF	XF	Unc	BU
2009LMK Proof	—	Value: 40.00				

KM# 158 100 LITU
7.7800 g., 0.9990 Gold 0.2499 oz. AGW, 22.3 mm.
Subject: Use of the Name Lithuania Millenium **Obv:** Linear
National Arms **Rev:** Circular Legend

Date	Mintage	F	VF	XF	Unc	BU
2007 Proof	5,000	Value: 325				

KM# 168 100 LITU
7.7800 g., 0.9990 Gold 0.2499 oz. AGW, 22.3 mm.
Subject: 1000th Anniversary of Name Lithuania **Obv:** Knight on
horseback left, stick figure **Rev:** Legend in concentric circle

Date	Mintage	F	VF	XF	Unc	BU
2007LMK Proof	5,000	Value: 350				

KM# 156 100 LITU
7.7800 g., 0.9999 Gold 0.2501 oz. AGW, 22.3 mm.
Subject: Millennium of name "Lithuania" **Obv:** Stylized national
arms **Obv. Legend:** LIETUVA **Rev:** Partial parchment
Rev. Legend: LIETUVOS DIDZIOJI KUNIGAIKSTYSTS

Date	Mintage	F	VF	XF	Unc	BU
2008 Proof	10,000	Value: 350				

KM# 167 100 LITU
7.7800 g., 0.9999 Gold 0.2499 oz. AGW, 22.3 mm.
Subject: Lithuania Millenium **Obv:** National Arms **Rev:** Text

Date	Mintage	F	VF	XF	Unc	BU
2009 Proof	10,000	Value: 350				

KM# 166 100 LITU
7.7800 g., 0.9990 Gold 0.2499 oz. AGW, 22.3 mm.
Subject: 1000th Anniversary of Name Lithuania **Obv:** Linear
knight **Rev:** Timeline

Date	Mintage	F	VF	XF	Unc	BU
2009LMK Proof	10,000	Value: 350				

KM# 136 200 LITU
15.0000 g., Bi-Metallic .900 Gold 7.9g. center in a .925 Silver
7.1g. ring, 27 mm. **Subject:** 750th Anniversary - King Mindaugas
Obv: Knight on horse **Obv. Legend:** LIETUVA **Rev:** Seated King
Rev. Legend: MINDAUGO KARUNAVIMAS **Edge Lettering:**
LIETUVOS KARALYSTE 1253

Date	Mintage	F	VF	XF	Unc	BU
2003 Proof	2,000	Value: 1,200				

KM# 146 500 LITU
31.1000 g., 0.9999 Gold 0.9997 oz. AGW, 32.5 mm.
Obv: Knight on horse **Rev:** Palace **Edge:** Plain

Date	Mintage	F	VF	XF	Unc	BU
2005 Proof	1,000	Value: 1,400				

MINT SETS

KM#	Date	Mintage	Identification	Issue Price	Mkt Val
MS4	2003 (6)	10,000	KM#106-108, 111-113	7.50	20.00
MS5	2008 (9)	4,000	KM#85-87, 106-108, 111-113 KM#85-87 are dated 1991.	30.00	20.00

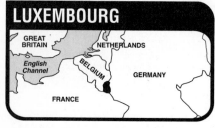

LUXEMBOURG

The Grand Duchy of Luxembourg is located in western Europe between Belgium, Germany and France, has an area of 1,103 sq. mi. (2,586 sq. km.) and a population of 377,100. Capital: Luxembourg. The economy is based on steel.

RULER
Henri, 2000-

MINT MARKS
A - Paris
(b) - Brussels, privy marks only
H – Gunzburg
(n) – lion - Namur
(u) - Utrecht, privy marks only

GRAND DUCHY

EURO COINAGE
European Economic Community Issues

KM# 75   EURO CENT
2.3000 g., Copper Plated Steel, 16.3 mm.   **Ruler:** Henri
Obv: Head right **Obv. Designer:** Yvette Gastauer-Claire
Rev: Value and globe **Rev. Designer:** Luc Luycx **Edge:** Plain

Date	Mintage	F	VF	XF	Unc	BU
2002(u)	34,557,500	—	—	—	0.35	0.50
2002(u) Proof	1,500	Value: 3.00				
2003(u)	1,500,000	—	—	—	0.50	0.75
2003(u) Proof	1,500	Value: 3.00				
2004(u)	21,001,000	—	—	—	0.35	0.50
2004(u) Proof	1,500	Value: 3.00				
2005(u)	7,000,000	—	—	—	0.35	0.50
2005(u) Proof	1,500	Value: 3.00				
2006(u)	4,000,000	—	—	—	0.35	0.50
2006(u) Proof	2,000	Value: 4.00				
2007(a)	6,000,000	—	—	—	0.35	0.50
2007(a) Proof	2,500	Value: 4.00				
2008(a)	10,000,000	—	—	—	0.35	0.50
2008(a) Proof	2,500	Value: 4.00				
2009(a)	4,000,000	—	—	—	0.35	0.50
2009(a) Proof	2,500	Value: 4.00				
2010	6,000,000	—	—	—	0.35	0.50
2010 Proof	—	Value: 4.00				

KM# 76   2 EURO CENT
3.0000 g., Copper Plated Steel, 18.7 mm.   **Ruler:** Henri
Obv: Head right **Obv. Designer:** Yvette Gastauer-Claire **Rev:** Value and globe **Rev. Designer:** Luc Luycx **Edge:** Grooved

Date	Mintage	F	VF	XF	Unc	BU
2002(u)	35,917,500	—	—	—	0.50	0.75
2002(u) Proof	1,500	Value: 5.00				
2003(u)	1,500,000	—	—	—	0.65	0.85
2003(u) Proof	1,500	Value: 5.00				
2004(u)	20,001,000	—	—	—	0.50	0.75
2004(u) Proof	1,500	Value: 5.00				
2005(u)	13,000,000	—	—	—	0.50	0.75
2005(u) Proof	1,500	Value: 5.00				
2006(u)	4,000,000	—	—	—	0.50	0.75
2006(u) Proof	2,000	Value: 6.00				
2007(a)	8,000,000	—	—	—	0.50	0.75
2007(a) Proof	2,500	Value: 6.00				
2008(a)	12,000,000	—	—	—	0.50	0.75
2008(a) Proof	2,500	Value: 6.00				
2009(a)	3,000,000	—	—	—	0.50	0.75
2009(a) Proof	2,500	Value: 6.00				
2010(u)	8,000,000	—	—	—	0.50	0.75
2010(u) Proof	—	Value: 6.00				

KM# 77   5 EURO CENT
3.9000 g., Copper Plated Steel, 21.3 mm.   **Ruler:** Henri
Obv: Head right **Obv. Designer:** Yvette Gastauer-Claire
Rev: Value and globe **Rev. Designer:** Luc Luycx **Edge:** Plain

Date	Mintage	F	VF	XF	Unc	BU
2002(u)	28,917,500	—	—	—	0.75	1.00
2002(u) Proof	1,500	Value: 7.00				
2003(u)	4,500,000	—	—	—	1.00	1.25
2003(u) Proof	1,500	Value: 7.00				
2004(u)	16,001,000	—	—	—	0.75	1.00
2004(u) Proof	1,500	Value: 7.00				
2005(u)	6,000,000	—	—	—	0.75	1.00
2005(u) Proof	1,500	Value: 7.00				
2006(u)	5,000,000	—	—	—	0.75	1.00
2006(u) Proof	2,000	Value: 8.00				
2007(a)	5,000,000	—	—	—	0.75	1.00
2007(a) Proof	2,500	Value: 9.00				
2008(a)	9,000,000	—	—	—	0.75	1.00
2008(a) Proof	2,500	Value: 9.00				
2009(a)	6,000,000	—	—	—	0.75	1.00
2009(a) Proof	2,500	Value: 9.00				
2010(u)	6,000,000	—	—	—	0.75	1.00
2010(u) Proof	—	Value: 9.00				

KM# 78   10 EURO CENT
4.0700 g., Brass, 19.7 mm.   **Ruler:** Henri **Obv:** Grand Duke's portrait **Obv. Designer:** Yvette Gastauer-Claire **Rev:** Value and map **Rev. Designer:** Luc Luycx **Edge:** Reeded

Date	Mintage	F	VF	XF	Unc	BU
2002(u)	25,117,500	—	—	—	0.75	—
2002(u) Proof	1,500	—	—	—	—	—
2003(u)	1,500,000	—	—	—	1.00	—
2003(u) Proof	1,500	—	—	—	—	—
2004(u)	12,001,000	—	—	—	0.75	—
2004(u) Proof	1,500	—	—	—	—	—
2005(u)	2,000,000	—	—	—	0.75	—
2005(u) Proof	1,500	—	—	—	—	—
2006(u)	4,000,000	—	—	—	0.75	—
2006(u) Proof	2,000	—	—	—	—	—

KM# 89   10 EURO CENT
4.1000 g., Brass, 19.8 mm.   **Ruler:** Henri **Obv:** Prince's portrait **Obv. Designer:** Yvette Gastauer-Claire **Rev:** Relief map of Western Europe, stars, lines and value **Rev. Designer:** Luc Luycx **Edge:** Reeded

Date	Mintage	F	VF	XF	Unc	BU
2007(a)	5,000,000	—	—	—	0.75	1.00
2007(a) Proof	2,500	Value: 14.00				
2008(a)	5,000,000	—	—	—	0.75	1.00
2008(a) Proof	2,500	Value: 14.00				
2009(a)	4,000,000	—	—	—	0.75	1.00
2009(a) Proof	2,500	Value: 14.00				
2010(a)	4,000,000	—	—	—	0.75	1.00
2010(a) Proof	—	Value: 14.00				

KM# 79   20 EURO CENT
5.7300 g., Brass, 22.1 mm.   **Ruler:** Henri **Obv:** Grand Duke's portrait **Obv. Designer:** Yvette Gastauer-Claire **Rev:** Value and map **Rev. Designer:** Luc Luycx **Edge:** Notched

Date	Mintage	F	VF	XF	Unc	BU
2002(u)	25,717,500	—	—	—	1.00	—
2002(u) Proof	1,500	—	—	—	—	—
2003(u)	1,500,000	—	—	—	1.25	—
2003(u) Proof	1,500	—	—	—	—	—
2004(u)	14,001,000	—	—	—	1.00	—
2004(u) Proof	1,500	—	—	—	—	—
2005(u)	6,000,000	—	—	—	1.00	—
2005(u) Proof	1,500	—	—	—	—	—
2006(u)	7,000,000	—	—	—	1.00	—
2006(u) Proof	2,000	—	—	—	—	—

KM# 90   20 EURO CENT
5.7000 g., Brass, 22.3 mm.   **Ruler:** Henri **Obv:** Prince's portrait **Obv. Designer:** Yvette Gastauer-Claire **Rev:** Relief map of Western Europe, stars, lines and value **Rev. Designer:** Luc Luycx **Edge:** Notched

Date	Mintage	F	VF	XF	Unc	BU
2007(a)	8,000,000	—	—	—	1.00	1.25
2007(a) Proof	2,500	Value: 16.00				
2008(a)	6,000,000	—	—	—	1.00	1.25
2008(a) Proof	2,500	Value: 16.00				
2009(a)	5,000,000	—	—	—	1.00	1.25
2009(a) Proof	2,500	Value: 16.00				
2010(a)	8,000,000	—	—	—	1.00	1.25
2010(a) Proof	—	Value: 16.00				

KM# 80   50 EURO CENT
7.8100 g., Brass, 24.1 mm.   **Ruler:** Henri **Obv:** Grand Duke's portrait **Obv. Designer:** Yvette Gastauer-Claire **Rev:** Value and map **Rev. Designer:** Luc Luycx **Edge:** Reeded

Date	Mintage	F	VF	XF	Unc	BU
2002(u)	21,917,500	—	—	—	1.25	—
2002(u) Proof	1,500	—	—	—	—	—
2003(u)	2,500,000	—	—	—	1.50	—
2003(u) Proof	1,500	—	—	—	—	—
2004(u)	10,001,000	—	—	—	1.25	—
2004(u) Proof	1,500	—	—	—	—	—
2005(u)	3,000,000	—	—	—	1.25	—
2005(u) Proof	1,500	—	—	—	—	—
2006(u)	3,000,000	—	—	—	1.25	—
2006(u) Proof	2,000	—	—	—	—	—

KM# 91   50 EURO CENT
7.8000 g., Brass, 24.3 mm.   **Ruler:** Henri **Obv:** Prince's portrait **Obv. Designer:** Yvette Gastauer-Claire **Rev:** Relief map of Western Europe, stars, lines and value **Rev. Designer:** Luc Luycx **Edge:** Reeded

Date	Mintage	F	VF	XF	Unc	BU
2007(a)	4,000,000	—	—	—	1.25	1.50
2007(a) Proof	2,500	Value: 18.00				
2008(a)	4,000,000	—	—	—	1.25	1.50
2008(a) Proof	2,500	Value: 18.00				
2009(a)	2,000,000	—	—	—	1.25	1.50
2009(a) Proof	2,500	Value: 18.00				
2010(a)	5,000,000	—	—	—	1.25	1.50
2010(a) Proof	—	Value: 18.00				

KM# 81   EURO
7.5000 g., Bi-Metallic Copper-Nickel center in Brass ring, 23.2 mm.   **Ruler:** Henri **Obv:** Grand Duke's portrait **Obv. Designer:** Yvette Gastauer-Claire **Rev:** Value and map within divided circle **Rev. Designer:** Luc Luycx **Edge:** Segmented reeding

Date	Mintage	F	VF	XF	Unc	BU
2002(u)	21,318,525	—	—	—	2.50	—
2002(u) Proof	1,500	—	—	—	—	—
2003(u)	1,500,000	—	—	—	2.75	—
2003(u) Proof	1,500	—	—	—	—	—
2004(u)	9,001,000	—	—	—	2.50	—
2004(u) Proof	1,500	—	—	—	—	—
2005(u)	2,000,000	—	—	—	2.50	—
2006(u)	1,000,000	—	—	—	2.50	—

KM# 92   EURO
7.5000 g., Bi-Metallic Copper-Nickel center in Brass ring, 23.3 mm.   **Ruler:** Henri **Obv:** Prince's portrait **Obv. Designer:** Yvette Gastauer-Claire **Rev:** Relief map of Western Europe, stars, lines and value **Rev. Designer:** Luc Luycx **Edge:** Segmented reeding

Date	Mintage	F	VF	XF	Unc	BU
2007(a)	480,000	—	—	—	2.25	2.75
2007(a) Proof	2,500	Value: 24.00				
2008(a)	480,000	—	—	—	2.25	2.75
2008(a) Proof	2,500	Value: 24.00				
2009(a)	240,000	—	—	—	2.25	2.75
2009(a) Proof	2,500	Value: 24.00				
2010(a)	1,000,000	—	—	—	2.25	2.75
2010(a) Proof	—	Value: 24.00				

KM# 82 2 EURO

8.5200 g., Bi-Metallic Brass center in Copper-Nickel ring, 25.7 mm. **Ruler:** Henri **Obv:** Grand Duke's portrait **Obv. Designer:** Yvette Gastauer-Claire **Rev:** Value and map within divided circle **Rev. Designer:** Luc Luycx **Edge:** Reeded with 2's and stars

Date	Mintage	F	VF	XF	Unc	BU
2002(u)	18,517,500	—	—	—	3.75	—
2002(u) Proof	1,500	—	—	—	—	—
2003(u)	3,500,000	—	—	—	4.50	—
2003(u) Proof	1,500	—	—	—	—	—
2004(u)	7,553,200	—	—	—	4.00	—
2004(u) Proof	1,500	—	—	—	—	—
2005(u)	3,500,000	—	—	—	4.00	—
2005(u) Proof	1,500	—	—	—	—	—
2006(u)	2,000,000	—	—	—	4.00	—
2006(u) Proof	2,000	—	—	—	—	—

KM# 85 2 EURO

8.5200 g., Bi-Metallic Brass center in Copper-Nickel ring, 25.7 mm. **Ruler:** Henri **Obv:** Head right and crowned monogram within 1/2 star circle **Rev:** Value and map within divided circle

Date	Mintage	F	VF	XF	Unc	BU
2004(u)	2,447,800	—	—	—	7.00	9.00
2004(u) Prooflike	10,000	—	—	—	—	50.00
2004(u) Proof	1,500	—	—	—	—	—

KM# 87 2 EURO

8.5200 g., Bi-Metallic Brass center in Copper-Nickel ring, 25.7 mm. **Ruler:** Henri **Obv:** Conjoined heads right within circle **Rev:** Value and map within divided circle **Edge:** Reeding over stars and 2's

Date	Mintage	F	VF	XF	Unc	BU
2005(u)	2,720,000	—	—	—	7.00	9.00
2005(u) Prooflike	10,000	—	—	—	—	75.00
2005(u) Proof	1,500	—	—	—	—	—

KM# 88 2 EURO

8.5000 g., Bi-Metallic Brass center in Copper-Nickel ring, 25.7 mm. **Ruler:** Henri **Obv:** Conjoined heads right within circle and star border **Rev:** Value and map within divided circle **Edge:** Reeding over 2's and stars

Date	Mintage	F	VF	XF	Unc	BU
2006(u)	1,052,000	—	—	—	7.00	9.00
2006(u) Prooflike	10,000	—	—	—	—	32.00
2006(u) Proof	2,000	—	—	—	—	—

KM# 93 2 EURO

8.5000 g., Bi-Metallic Brass center in Copper-Nickel ring, 25.8 mm. **Ruler:** Henri **Obv:** Prince's portrait **Obv. Designer:** Yvette Gastauer-Claire **Rev:** Relief map of Western Europe, stars, lines and value **Rev. Designer:** Luc Luycx **Edge:** Reeded with 2's and stars

Date	Mintage	F	VF	XF	Unc	BU
2007(a)	4,000,000	—	—	—	4.00	5.00
2007(a) Proof	2,500	Value: 28.00				
2008(a)	6,000,000	—	—	—	4.00	5.00
2008(a) Proof	2,500	Value: 28.00				
2009(a)	240,000	—	—	—	6.00	7.50
2009(a) Proof	2,500	Value: 30.00				
2010(a)	3,500,000	—	—	—	4.00	5.00
2010(a) Proof	—	Value: 30.00				

KM# 94 2 EURO

Bi-Metallic Brass center in Copper-Nickel ring, 25.71 mm. **Ruler:** Henri **Subject:** 50th Anniversary Treaty of Rome **Obv:** Open treaty book with latent image on left hand page **Obv. Legend:** LËTZEBUERG **Rev:** Large value at left, modified outline of Europe at right **Edge:** Reeded with 2's and stars

Date	Mintage	F	VF	XF	Unc	BU
2007(a)	2,047,000	—	—	—	6.50	9.00
2007(a) Prooflike	15,000	—	—	—	—	25.00
2007(a) Proof	2,500	Value: 30.00				

KM# 95 2 EURO

8.5400 g., Bi-Metallic Brass center in Copper-Nickel ring, 25.71 mm. **Ruler:** Henri **Obv:** Palace in background at left, head 3/4 left at right **Obv. Legend:** L?TZEBUERG **Rev:** Large value at left, modified outline of Europe at right **Edge:** Reeded with 2's and stars

Date	Mintage	F	VF	XF	Unc	BU
2007(a)	1,000,000	—	—	—	6.50	9.00
2007(a) Prooflike	15,000	—	—	—	—	25.00
2007(a) Proof	2,500	—	—	—	—	—

KM# 96 2 EURO

8.5200 g., Bi-Metallic Brass center in Copper-Nickel ring, 25.71 mm. **Ruler:** Henri **Obv:** Head at left, Chateau de Berg at right **Obv. Legend:** L?TZEBUERG **Rev:** Large value at left, modified outline of Europe at right **Edge:** Reeded with 2's and stars

Date	Mintage	F	VF	XF	Unc	BU
2008(a)	1,000,000	—	—	4.00	5.00	6.25

KM# 106 2 EURO

8.5000 g., Bi-Metallic Brass center in copper-nickel ring **Ruler:** Henri **Subject:** 90th Anniversary of Grand Duchess Charlotte **Obv:** Conjoint bust of Charlotte and Henri

Date	Mintage	F	VF	XF	Unc	BU
2009	—	—	—	—	7.00	9.00
2009 Proof	—	Value: 15.00				

KM# 107 2 EURO

8.5000 g., Bi-Metallic Brass center in copper-nickel ring **Ruler:** Henri **Subject:** European Monetary Union - 10th Anniversary **Obv:** Stick figure and E emblem

Date	Mintage	F	VF	XF	Unc	BU
2009	—	—	—	—	5.00	6.00
2009 Proof	—	Value: 10.00				

KM# 84 5 EURO

6.2200 g., 0.9990 Gold 0.1998 oz. AGW, 20 mm. **Ruler:** Henri **Subject:** European Central Bank **Obv:** Grand Duke Henri **Rev:** Building

Date	Mintage	F	VF	XF	Unc	BU
2003(u) Proof	20,000	Value: 250				

KM# 108 5 EURO

Bi-Metallic, 34 mm. **Ruler:** Henri **Subject:** Castle of Vianden **Obv:** Head right **Rev:** Castle view

Date	Mintage	F	VF	XF	Unc	BU
2009	7,500	—	—	—	—	120

KM# 109 5 EURO

Bi-Metallic Nordic gold center in silver ring, 34 mm. **Ruler:** Henri **Subject:** Common Kestrel **Obv:** Head right **Rev:** Bird

Date	Mintage	F	VF	XF	Unc	BU
2009 Proof	3,000	Value: 60.00				

KM# 112 5 EURO

Bi-Metallic, 34 mm. **Ruler:** Henri **Obv:** Head right **Rev:** Falcon

Date	Mintage	F	VF	XF	Unc	BU
2009 Proof	3,000	Value: 50.00				

KM# 111 5 EURO

Bi-Metallic, 34 mm. **Ruler:** Henri **Subject:** Chateau d'Esch sur sure **Obv:** Head right **Rev:** Chateau view

Date	Mintage	F	VF	XF	Unc	BU
2010 Prooflike	3,000	—	—	—	—	100

KM# 113 700 EURO CENTS

0.9250 Silver, 34 mm. **Ruler:** Henri **Subject:** Marriage of John of Luxembourg

Date	Mintage	F	VF	XF	Unc	BU
2010 Proof	3,000	Value: 75.00				

KM# 97 10 EURO

3.1100 g., 0.9990 Gold 0.0999 oz. AGW, 25.71 mm. **Ruler:** Henri **Subject:** Culture **Obv:** Head right **Rev:** Hellenic sculpture head

Date	Mintage	F	VF	XF	Unc	BU
2004 Proof	5,000	Value: 125				

KM# 99 10 EURO

8.0000 g., Bi-Metallic Titanium center in silver ring, 26 mm. **Ruler:** Henri **Subject:** State Bank 150th Anniversary **Obv:** Head right **Rev:** Bank Plaza

Date	Mintage	F	VF	XF	Unc	BU
2006	7,500	—	—	—	—	140

KM# 101 10 EURO

3.1100 g., 0.9990 Gold 0.0999 oz. AGW, 16 mm. **Ruler:** Henri **Obv:** Head right **Rev:** Wild pig of Titelberg

Date	Mintage	F	VF	XF	Unc	BU
2006 Proof	5,000	Value: 125				

KM# 110 10 EURO

3.1100 g., 0.9990 Gold 0.0999 oz. AGW, 16 mm. **Ruler:** Henri **Subject:** Deer of Orval's Refuge **Obv:** Head right **Rev:** Stag seated, flower in background

Date	Mintage	F	VF	XF	Unc	BU
2007 Proof	3,000	Value: 135				

KM# 104 10 EURO

10.3700 g., 0.9990 Gold 0.3331 oz. AGW, 23 mm. **Ruler:** Henri **Subject:** Banque Central - 10th Anniversary **Obv:** Head right **Rev:** Old and ndw bank buildings

Date	Mintage	F	VF	XF	Unc	BU
2008 Proof	1,250	Value: 425				

KM# 114 10 EURO

0.9250 Silver, 34 mm. **Ruler:** Henri **Subject:** Schengen Accord, 25th Anniversary **Obv:** Head right **Rev:** Building

Date	Mintage	F	VF	XF	Unc	BU
2010 Prooflike	3,000	—	—	—	—	110

KM# 102 20 EURO

13.5000 g., Bi-Metallic Titanium center in silver ring, 34 mm. **Ruler:** Henri **Obv:** Three heads facing **Rev:** Council D'Etat building

Date	Mintage	F	VF	XF	Unc	BU
2006	4,000	—	—	—	—	120

KM# 83 25 EURO

22.8500 g., 0.9250 Silver 0.6795 oz. ASW, 37 mm. **Ruler:** Henri **Subject:** European Court System **Obv:** Grand Duke Henri **Rev:** Sword scale on law book

Date	Mintage	F	VF	XF	Unc	BU
2002(u) Proof	20,000	Value: 100				

KM# 86 25 EURO

22.8500 g., 0.9250 Silver 0.6795 oz. ASW, 37 mm. **Ruler:** Henri **Subject:** European Parliament **Obv:** Grand Duke Henri **Rev:** Parliament

Date	Mintage	F	VF	XF	Unc	BU
2004(u) Proof	20,000	Value: 100				

KM# 98 25 EURO

22.8000 g., 0.9250 Silver 0.6780 oz. ASW, 37 mm. **Ruler:** Henri **Subject:** EU Presidency **Obv:** Head right **Rev:** Conseil de l'Union builing in Brussels

Date	Mintage	F	VF	XF	Unc	BU
2005 Proof	10,000	Value: 100				

KM# 100 25 EURO

22.8000 g., 0.9250 Silver 0.6780 oz. ASW, 37 mm. **Ruler:** Henri **Obv:** Head right **Rev:** European Commission building "Berlaymont" in Brussels

Date	Mintage	F	VF	XF	Unc	BU
2006 Proof	5,000	Value: 110				

KM# 103 25 EURO

22.8500 g., 0.9250 Silver 0.6795 oz. ASW, 37 mm. **Ruler:** Henri **Subject:** European Court of Auditors 30th Anniversary

Date	Mintage	F	VF	XF	Unc	BU
2007 Proof	3,000	Value: 80.00				

KM# 105 25 EURO

22.8500 g., 0.9250 Silver 0.6795 oz. ASW, 37 mm. **Ruler:** Henri **Subject:** European Investment Bank

Date	Mintage	F	VF	XF	Unc	BU
2008 Proof	4,000	Value: 80.00				

MINT SETS

KM#	Date	Mintage	Identification	Issue Price	Mkt Val
MS7	2005 (9)	20,000	KM#75-82, 87	40.00	65.00
MS8	2006 (9)	15,000	KM#75-82, 88	40.00	65.00

MACAO

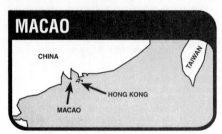

The Province of Macao, a Portuguese overseas province located in the South China Sea 40 miles southwest of Hong Kong, consists of the peninsula of Macao and the islands of Taipa and Coloane. It has an area of 6.2 sq. mi.(16 sq. km.) and a population of 500,000. Capital: Macao. Macao's economy is based on light industry, commerce, tourism, fishing, and gold trading - Macao is one of the entirely free markets for gold in the world. Cement, textiles, fireworks, vegetable oils, and metal products are exported.

In 1987, Portugal and China agreed that Macao would become a Chinese Territory in 1999. In December of 1999, Macao became a special administrative zone of China.

MINT MARKS
(p) - Pobjoy Mint
(s) - Singapore Mint

Pobjoy Mint	Singapore Mint

SPECIAL ADMINISTRATIVE REGION (S.A.R.)

STANDARD COINAGE
100 Avos = 1 Pataca

KM# 70   10 AVOS
1.3800 g., Brass, 17 mm.   **Obv:** MACAU written at center with date below **Rev:** Crowned lion dance scene above value flanked by mint marks **Designer:** Justino Lei

Date	Mintage	F	VF	XF	Unc	BU
2005	—	—	—	—	0.75	1.25
2007	—	—	—	—	0.75	1.25

KM# 72   50 AVOS
4.5900 g., Brass, 23 mm.   **Obv:** MACAU written across center of globe with date below **Rev:** The dragon dance led by a man **Designer:** Justino Lei

Date	Mintage	F	VF	XF	Unc	BU
2003	—	—	—	—	1.50	2.50
2005	—	—	—	—	1.50	2.50

KM# 57   PATACA
9.1800 g., Copper-Nickel, 25.98 mm.   **Obv:** MACAU written across center of globe with date below **Rev:** Guia Fortress adn Chapel of Our Lady of Guia **Edge:** Reeded **Designer:** Justino Lei

Date	Mintage	F	VF	XF	Unc	BU
2003	—	—	—	0.60	1.50	2.00
2005	—	—	—	0.60	1.50	2.00

KM# 56   5 PATACAS
10.1000 g., Copper-Nickel   **Obv:** MACAU written across center of globe with date below **Rev:** Chinese junk, ruins of St. Paul's Cathedral in background **Edge:** Plain **Shape:** 12-sided **Designer:** Justino Lei

Date	Mintage	F	VF	XF	Unc	BU
2003	—	—	—	—	6.50	10.00
2005	—	—	—	—	6.50	10.00
2007	—	—	—	—	6.50	10.00

KM# 142   20 PATACAS
31.1050 g., 0.9990 Silver 0.9990 oz. ASW, 40.7 mm.   **Subject:** Year of the Rat **Obv:** A Ma Temple **Rev:** Rat, multicolor flowers at right

Date	Mintage	F	VF	XF	Unc	BU
2008 Proof	6,000	Value: 130				

KM# 145   20 PATACAS
31.1050 g., 0.9990 Silver 0.9990 oz. ASW, 40.7 mm.   **Subject:** Year of the Ox **Obv:** Moorish Barracks **Rev:** Ox, multicolor flowers at right

Date	Mintage	F	VF	XF	Unc	BU
2009 Proof	—	Value: 50.00				

KM# 128   50 PATACAS
28.2800 g., 0.9250 Silver partially gilt 0.8410 oz. ASW   **Subject:** 1st World Championship Grand Prix **Rev:** Two race cars - gilt

Date	Mintage	F	VF	XF	Unc	BU
2003 Proof	5,000	Value: 75.00				

KM# 102   100 PATACAS
28.2800 g., 0.9250 Silver 0.8410 oz. ASW   **Subject:** Year of the Snake **Obv:** Church facade **Rev:** Snake

Date	Mintage	F	VF	XF	Unc	BU
2001 Proof	4,000	Value: 55.00				

KM# 107   100 PATACAS
28.2800 g., 0.9250 Silver 0.8410 oz. ASW, 38.6 mm.   **Subject:** Year of the Horse **Obv:** Church facade flanked by stars **Rev:** Horse above value **Edge:** Reeded

Date	Mintage	F	VF	XF	Unc	BU
2002 Proof	4,000	Value: 45.00				

KM# 122   100 PATACAS
28.2800 g., 0.9250 Silver 0.8410 oz. ASW **Subject:** 5th Anniversary Return of Macao to China

Date	Mintage	F	VF	XF	Unc	BU
2004 Proof	10,000	Value: 60.00				

KM# 130   100 PATACAS
28.2800 g., 0.9250 Silver 0.8410 oz. ASW **Series:** Lunar **Subject:** Year of the Monkey

Date	Mintage	F	VF	XF	Unc	BU
2004	1,000	—	—	—	—	60.00
2004 Proof	4,000	Value: 75.00				

KM# 134   100 PATACAS
28.2800 g., 0.9250 Silver 0.8410 oz. ASW **Series:** Lunar **Subject:** Year of the Rooster **Rev:** Stylized rooster walking left

Date	Mintage	F	VF	XF	Unc	BU
2005 Proof	—	Value: 90.00				

KM# 137   100 PATACAS
28.2800 g., 0.9250 Silver 0.8410 oz. ASW **Subject:** IV East Asian Games - FRIENDSHIP

Date	Mintage	F	VF	XF	Unc	BU
2005 Proof	6,000	Value: 75.00				

KM# 139   100 PATACAS
28.2800 g., 0.9250 Silver 0.8410 oz. ASW **Series:** Lunar **Subject:** Year of the Dog **Rev:** Stylized dog standing left

Date	Mintage	F	VF	XF	Unc	BU
2006 Proof	—	Value: 90.00				

KM# 143   100 PATACAS
155.5000 g., 0.9990 Silver 4.9942 oz. ASW, 65 mm.   **Subject:** Year of the Rat **Obv:** A Ma Temple **Rev:** Rat, multicolor flowers at right **Note:** Illustration reduced.

Date	Mintage	F	VF	XF	Unc	BU
2008 Proof	500	Value: 250				

KM# 146 100 PATACAS
155.5000 g., 0.9990 Silver 4.9942 oz. ASW, 65 mm.
Subject: Year of the Ox **Obv:** Moorish Barracks **Rev:** Ox,
multicolor flowers at right **Note:** Illustration reduced.

Date	Mintage	F	VF	XF	Unc	BU
2009 Proof	500	Value: 250				

KM# 123 200 PATACAS
28.2800 g., 0.9250 Silver partially gilt. 0.8410 oz. ASW
Subject: 5th Anniversary Return of Macao to China

Date	Mintage	F	VF	XF	Unc	BU
2004 Proof	10,000	Value: 75.00				

KM# 138 200 PATACAS
28.2800 g., 0.9250 Silver partially gilt 0.8410 oz. ASW
Subject: IV East Asian Games **Rev:** U-N-I-T-Y in blocks at left -
bottom. logo at upper right

Date	Mintage	F	VF	XF	Unc	BU
2005 Proof	6,000	Value: 120				

KM# 103 250 PATACAS
3.9900 g., 0.9167 Gold 0.1176 oz. AGW **Subject:** Year of the
Snake **Obv:** Church facade **Rev:** Snake

Date	Mintage	F	VF	XF	Unc	BU
2001 Proof	2,500	Value: 175				

KM# 108 250 PATACAS
3.9900 g., 0.9167 Gold 0.1176 oz. AGW, 19.3 mm.
Subject: Year of the Horse **Obv:** Church of St. Paul facade
Rev: Horse above value **Edge:** Reeded

Date	Mintage	F	VF	XF	Unc	BU
2002 Proof	2,500	Value: 175				

KM# 119 250 PATACAS
3.9900 g., 0.9167 Gold 0.1176 oz. AGW, 19.3 mm.
Subject: Year of the Goat **Obv:** Church facade **Rev:** Goat above
value **Edge:** Reeded

Date	Mintage	F	VF	XF	Unc	BU
2003 Proof	2,500	Value: 175				

KM# 131 250 PATACAS
3.9900 g., 0.9167 Gold 0.1176 oz. AGW **Series:** Lunar
Subject: Year of the Monkey

Date	Mintage	F	VF	XF	Unc	BU
2004 Proof	2,500	Value: 255				

KM# 135 250 PATACAS
2.8300 g., 0.9990 Gold 0.0909 oz. AGW **Series:** Lunar
Subject: Year of the Rooster **Rev:** Stylized rooster walking left

Date	Mintage	F	VF	XF	Unc	BU
2005 Proof	—	Value: 255				

KM# 140 250 PATACAS
3.1100 g., 0.9990 Gold 0.0999 oz. AGW **Series:** Lunar **Subject:**
Year of the Dog **Rev:** Stylized dog standing left - multicolor

Date	Mintage	F	VF	XF	Unc	BU
2006 Proof	—	Value: 255				

KM# 148 250 PATACAS
7.7900 g., 0.9990 Gold 0.2502 oz. AGW **Subject:** Year of the
Rat **Obv:** Temple **Rev:** Rat and multicolor flowers at right

Date	Mintage	F	VF	XF	Unc	BU
2008 Proof	—	Value: 325				

KM# 144 250 PATACAS
7.7700 g., 0.9990 Gold 0.2496 oz. AGW **Subject:** Year of the
Rat **Obv:** A Ma Temple **Rev:** Rat, multicolor flowers at right

Date	Mintage	F	VF	XF	Unc	BU
2009 Proof	—	Value: 350				

KM# 147 250 PATACAS
7.7700 g., 0.9990 Gold 0.2496 oz. AGW **Subject:** Year of the
Ox **Obv:** Moorish Barracks **Rev:** Ox, multicolor flowers at right

Date	Mintage	F	VF	XF	Unc	BU
2009 Proof	—	Value: 350				

KM# 104 500 PATACAS
7.9900 g., 0.9167 Gold 0.2355 oz. AGW **Subject:** Year of the
Snake **Obv:** Church facade **Rev:** Snake

Date	Mintage	F	VF	XF	Unc	BU
2001 Proof	2,500	Value: 300				

KM# 109 500 PATACAS
7.9800 g., 0.9167 Gold 0.2352 oz. AGW, 22.05 mm.
Subject: Year of the Horse **Obv:** Church facade **Rev:** Horse
above value **Edge:** Reeded

Date	Mintage	F	VF	XF	Unc	BU
2002 Proof	2,500	Value: 300				

KM# 120 500 PATACAS
7.9800 g., 0.9167 Gold 0.2352 oz. AGW, 22 mm. **Subject:** Year
of the Goat **Obv:** Church facade **Rev:** Goat above value
Edge: Reeded

Date	Mintage	F	VF	XF	Unc	BU
2003 Proof	2,500	Value: 300				

KM# 129 500 PATACAS
7.9600 g., 0.9167 Gold 0.2346 oz. AGW **Subject:** 1st World
Championship Grand Prix **Rev:** Two race cars

Date	Mintage	F	VF	XF	Unc	BU
2003 Proof	2,000	Value: 300				

KM# 124 500 PATACAS
62.2060 g., 0.9990 Silver partially gilt 1.9979 oz. ASW
Subject: 5th Anniversary Return of Macao to China

Date	Mintage	F	VF	XF	Unc	BU
2004 Proof	1,000	Value: 120				

KM# 132 500 PATACAS
7.9800 g., 0.9167 Gold 0.2352 oz. AGW **Series:** Lunar
Subject: Year of the Monkey

Date	Mintage	F	VF	XF	Unc	BU
2004 Proof	2,500	Value: 320				

KM# 136 500 PATACAS
7.9600 g., 0.9990 Gold 0.2557 oz. AGW **Series:** Lunar
Subject: Year of the Rooster **Rev:** Stylized rooster walking left

Date	Mintage	F	VF	XF	Unc	BU
2005 Proof	—	Value: 375				

KM# 141 500 PATACAS
7.9600 g., 0.9990 Gold 0.2557 oz. AGW **Series:** Lunar
Subject: Year of the Dog **Rev:** Stylized dog standing left

Date	Mintage	F	VF	XF	Unc	BU
2006 Proof	—	Value: 375				

KM# 105 1000 PATACAS
16.9760 g., 0.9167 Gold 0.5003 oz. AGW **Subject:** Year of the
Snake **Obv:** Church facade flanked by stars **Rev:** Snake

Date	Mintage	F	VF	XF	Unc	BU
2001 Proof	4,000	Value: 625				

KM# 110 1000 PATACAS
15.9700 g., 0.9167 Gold 0.4707 oz. AGW, 28.4 mm.
Subject: Year of the Horse **Obv:** Church facade **Rev:** Horse
above value **Edge:** Reeded

Date	Mintage	F	VF	XF	Unc	BU
2002 Proof	4,000	Value: 600				

KM# 118 1000 PATACAS
28.2800 g., 0.9250 Silver 0.8410 oz. ASW, 38.6 mm.
Subject: Year of the Goat **Obv:** Church facade **Rev:** Goat above
value **Edge:** Reeded

Date	Mintage	F	VF	XF	Unc	BU
2003 Proof	4,000	Value: 45.00				

KM# 121 1000 PATACAS
15.9760 g., 0.9170 Gold 0.4710 oz. AGW **Subject:** Year of the
Goat **Obv:** Church facade flanked by stars **Rev:** Goat above value
Edge: Reeded

Date	Mintage	F	VF	XF	Unc	BU
2003 Proof	4,000	Value: 600				

KM# 125 1000 PATACAS
155.5150 g., 0.9990 Silver 4.9947 oz. ASW **Subject:** 5th
Anniversary Return of Macao to China

Date	Mintage	F	VF	XF	Unc	BU
2004 Proof	3,000	Value: 310				

KM# 133 1000 PATACAS
15.9800 g., 0.9167 Gold 0.4710 oz. AGW **Series:** Lunar
Subject: Year of the Monkey

Date	Mintage	F	VF	XF	Unc	BU
2004	500	—	—	—	620	—
2004 Proof	4,000	Value: 610				

KM# 126 2000 PATACAS
155.5150 g., 0.9990 Silver partially gilt 4.9947 oz. ASW
Subject: 5th Anniversary Return of Macao to China

Date	Mintage	F	VF	XF	Unc	BU
2004 Proof	1,500	Value: 300				

PROOF SETS

KM#	Date	Mintage	Identification	Issue Price	Mkt Val
PS16	2001 (3)	2,500	KM#103-105	849	1,100
PS17	2002 (3)	4,000	KM#108-110	849	1,100
PS18	2003 (3)	2,500	KM#119-121	849	1,100

MACEDONIA

The Republic of Macedonia is land-locked, and is bordered
in the north by Yugoslavia, to the east by Bulgaria, in the south
by Greece and to the west by Albania and has an area of 9,781
sq. mi. (25,713 sq. km.) and a population at the 1991 census was
2,038,847, of which the predominating ethnic groups were Mace-
donians. The capital is Skopje.

On Nov. 20, 1991 parliament promulgated a new constitution, and declared its independence on Nov.20, 1992, but failed
to secure EC and US recognition owing to Greek objections to
use of the name *Macedonia*. On Dec. 11, 1992, the UN Security
Council authorized the expedition of a small peacekeeping force
to prevent hostilities spreading into Macedonia.

There is a 120-member single-chamber National Assembly.

REPUBLIC

STANDARD COINAGE

KM# 2 DENAR
5.1500 g., Brass, 23.7 mm. **Obv:** Pyrenean mountain dog
Obv. Legend: РЕПУБЛИКА МАКЕДОНИЈА **Rev:** Radiant value
Edge: Plain

Date	Mintage	F	VF	XF	Unc	BU
2001	12,874,000	—	0.20	0.35	1.50	4.00
2006	—	—	—	—	1.25	3.75

KM# 3 2 DENARI
5.1500 g., Brass, 23.7 mm. **Obv:** Trout above water
Obv. Legend: РЕПУБЛИКА МАКЕДОНИЈА **Rev:** Radiant value
Edge: Plain

Date	Mintage	F	VF	XF	Unc	BU
2001	11,672,000	—	0.25	0.50	1.25	3.00
2006	—	—	0.25	0.50	1.00	2.50

KM# 4   5 DENARI
7.2500 g., Brass, 27.5 mm. **Obv:** European lynx
Obv. Legend: РЕПУБЛИКА МАКЕДОНИЈА **Rev:** Radiant value
Edge: Plain

Date	Mintage	F	VF	XF	Unc	BU
2001	6,921,000	—	0.35	0.75	1.75	3.50
2006	—	—	—	—	1.50	3.00

KM# 13   10 DENARI
10.0000 g., 0.9160 Gold 0.2945 oz. AGW, 27 mm.
Subject: 10th Anniversary of Independence **Obv:** Value in circle within radiant map **Rev:** Grape vine

Date	Mintage	F	VF	XF	Unc	BU
2001	1,000	—	—	—	375	400

KM# 31   10 DENARI
Brass **Obv:** Peacock **Rev:** Value within rays

Date	Mintage	F	VF	XF	Unc	BU
2008	—	—	—	—	—	2.00

KM# 22   60 DENARI
6.0000 g., 0.9160 Gold 0.1767 oz. AGW, 23.8 mm.
Subject: 100th Anniversary - Statehood **Obv:** Monument above value within circle **Rev:** Djorce Petrov

Date	Mintage	F	VF	XF	Unc	BU
2003	500	—	—	—	225	245

KM# 23   60 DENARI
6.0000 g., 0.9160 Gold 0.1767 oz. AGW, 23.8 mm.
Subject: 100th Anniversary - Statehood **Obv:** Monument above value within circle **Rev:** Krste Petkov-Misirkov

Date	Mintage	F	VF	XF	Unc	BU
2003	500	—	—	—	225	245

KM# 24   60 DENARI
6.0000 g., 0.9160 Gold 0.1767 oz. AGW, 23.8 mm.
Subject: 100th Anniversary - Statehood **Obv:** Monument above value within circle **Rev:** Metodije Andonov

Date	Mintage	F	VF	XF	Unc	BU
2003	500	—	—	—	225	245

KM# 25   60 DENARI
6.0000 g., 0.9160 Gold 0.1767 oz. AGW, 23.8 mm.
Subject: 100th Anniversary - Statehood **Obv:** Monument above value within circle **Rev:** Mihailo Apostolski

Date	Mintage	F	VF	XF	Unc	BU
2003	500	—	—	—	225	245

KM# 26   60 DENARI
6.0000 g., 0.9160 Gold 0.1767 oz. AGW, 23.8 mm.
Subject: 100th Anniversary - Statehood **Obv:** Monument above value within circle **Rev:** Blaze Koneski

Date	Mintage	F	VF	XF	Unc	BU
2003	500	—	—	—	225	245

KM# 21   60 DENARI
8.0000 g., 0.9160 Gold 0.2356 oz. AGW, 23.8 mm.
Subject: 50th Anniversary of separation from Greece **Obv:** The Monifest **Rev:** Monastery

Date	Mintage	F	VF	XF	Unc	BU
2004	500	—	—	—	300	325

KM# 32   50 DENARI
Brass **Obv:** Classical female bust right **Rev:** Value within rays

Date	Mintage	F	VF	XF	Unc	BU
2008	—	—	—	—	—	2.00

KM# 14   100 DENARI
16.0000 g., 0.9250 Silver 0.4758 oz. ASW, 32 mm.
Subject: 100th Anniversary of Statehood **Obv:** Monument above value within circle **Rev:** Cherry tree canon divides circle

Date	Mintage	F	VF	XF	Unc	BU
2003	500	—	—	—	600	625

KM# 14a   100 DENARI
18.0000 g., 0.9160 Gold 0.5301 oz. AGW, 32 mm.
Subject: 100th Anniversary of Statehood **Obv:** Monument above value within circle **Rev:** Cherry tree canon divides circle

Date	Mintage	F	VF	XF	Unc	BU
2003	500	—	—	—	650	700

KM# 15   100 DENARI
6.0000 g., 0.9160 Gold 0.1767 oz. AGW, 23.8 mm.
Subject: 100th Anniversary of Statehood **Obv:** Monument above value within circle **Rev:** Bust facing within circle

Date	Mintage	F	VF	XF	Unc	BU
2003	500	—	—	—	225	245

KM# 16   100 DENARI
6.0000 g., 0.9160 Gold 0.1767 oz. AGW, 23.8 mm.
Subject: 100th Anniversary of Statehood **Obv:** Monument above value within circle **Rev:** Head with hat facing within circle

Date	Mintage	F	VF	XF	Unc	BU
2003	500	—	—	—	225	245

KM# 17   100 DENARI
6.0000 g., 0.9160 Gold 0.1767 oz. AGW, 23.8 mm.
Subject: 100th Anniversary of Statehood **Obv:** Monument above value within circle **Rev:** Head facing within circle

Date	Mintage	F	VF	XF	Unc	BU
2003	500	—	—	—	225	245

KM# 18   100 DENARI
6.0000 g., 0.9160 Gold 0.1767 oz. AGW, 23.8 mm.
Subject: 100th Anniversary of Statehood **Obv:** Monument above value within circle **Rev:** Bust left within circle

Date	Mintage	F	VF	XF	Unc	BU
2003	500	—	—	—	225	245

KM# 19   100 DENARI
6.0000 g., 0.9160 Gold 0.1767 oz. AGW, 23.8 mm.
Subject: 100th Anniversary of Statehood **Obv:** Monument above value within circle **Rev:** Bust right within circle

Date	Mintage	F	VF	XF	Unc	BU
2003	500	—	—	—	225	245

KM# 28   100 DENARI
7.0000 g., 0.9250 Silver 0.2082 oz. ASW **Obv:** Monument
Rev: Jan Sandanski bust facing

Date	Mintage	F	VF	XF	Unc	BU
2003 Proof	1,000	Value: 60.00				

KM# 29   100 DENARI
7.0000 g., 0.9250 Silver 0.2082 oz. ASW **Obv:** Monument
Rev: Nikola Karev bust facing

Date	Mintage	F	VF	XF	Unc	BU
2003 Proof	1,000	Value: 60.00				

KM# 30   100 DENARI
7.0000 g., 0.9250 Silver 0.2082 oz. ASW **Obv:** Monument
Rev: Pitu Guli bust facing

Date	Mintage	F	VF	XF	Unc	BU
2003 Proof	1,000	Value: 60.00				

The Democratic Republic of Madagascar, an independent member of the French Community located in the Indian Ocean 250 miles (402 km.) off the southeast coast of Africa, has an area of 226,656 sq. mi. (587,040 sq. km.) and a population of 10 million. Capital: Antananarivo. The economy is primarily agricultural; large bauxite deposits are being developed. Coffee, vanilla, graphite, and rice are exported.

MONETARY SYSTEM
100 Centimes = 1 Franc

MINT MARKS
(a) - Paris, privy marks only
SA - Pretoria

MALAGASY REPUBLIC
STANDARD COINAGE
1 Ariary = 100 Iraimbilanja

KM# 8   FRANC
2.4000 g., Stainless Steel **Obv:** Poinsettia **Rev:** Value within horns of ox head above sprigs

Date	Mintage	F	VF	XF	Unc	BU
2002(a)	—	0.15	0.20	0.40	1.45	—

REPUBLIC
STANDARD COINAGE

KM# 25.2   50 ARIARY
10.2600 g., Stainless Steel, 30.63 mm. **Obv:** Star above value within sprays **Rev:** Avenue of the Baobabs **Rev. Inscription:** Motto C **Edge:** Plain **Shape:** 11-sided

Date	Mintage	F	VF	XF	Unc	BU
2005	—	—	—	2.40	6.00	—

STANDARD COINAGE
1 Ariary = 100 Iraimbilanja

KM# 28   10 FRANCS (2 Ariary)
4.3400 g., Bronze (Red To Yellow), 21.9 mm. **Obv:** Monkey
Obv. Legend: BANKY FOIBEN'I MADAGASIKARA **Rev:** Value within steer horns flanked by sprigs **Edge:** Plain

Date	Mintage	F	VF	XF	Unc	BU
2003	—	—	—	1.00	2.50	3.50

KM# 29 ARIARY
4.9300 g., Stainless Steel, 22 mm. **Obv:** Flower **Obv. Legend:** BANKY FOIBEN'I MADAGASIKARA **Rev:** Value within steer horns above sprigs **Edge:** Plain

Date	Mintage	F	VF	XF	Unc	BU
2004(a)	—	—	—	0.90	2.25	3.00

KM# 30 2 ARIARY
3.2300 g., Copper Plated Steel, 21 mm. **Obv:** Plant **Obv. Legend:** BANKY FOIBEN'I MADAGASIKARA **Rev:** Value within steer horns flanked by sprigs **Edge:** Reeded

Date	Mintage	F	VF	XF	Unc	BU
2003	—	—	—	0.90	2.25	3.00

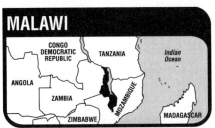

MALAWI

The Republic of Malawi (formerly Nyasaland), located in southeastern Africa to the west of Lake Malawi (Nyasa), has an area of 45,745 sq. mi. (118,480 sq. km.) and a population of 7 million. Capital: Lilongwe. The economy is predominantly agricultural. Tobacco, tea, peanuts and cotton are exported.

REPUBLIC

DECIMAL COINAGE
100 Tambala = 1 Kwacha

KM# 33a TAMBALA
Copper Plated Steel, 17.3 mm. **Obv:** Arms with supporters **Rev:** 2 Talapia fish **Edge:** Plain

Date	Mintage	F	VF	XF	Unc	BU
2003	—	—	—	—	1.00	1.50

KM# 34a 2 TAMBALA
Copper Plated Steel, 20.3 mm. **Obv:** Arms with supporters **Rev:** Paradise whydah bird divides date and value, designer's initials "P.V." **Edge:** Plain

Date	Mintage	F	VF	XF	Unc	BU
2003	—	—	—	—	1.00	1.50

KM# 32.2 5 TAMBALA
Nickel Plated Steel, 19.35 mm. **Obv:** Arms with supporters **Rev:** Purple heron, value, designer's initials "P.V."

Date	Mintage	F	VF	XF	Unc	BU
2003	—	—	—	—	2.50	3.00

KM# 27 10 TAMBALA
5.6200 g., Nickel Plated Steel, 23.6 mm. **Obv:** Bust right **Rev:** Bundled corncobs divide date and value **Rev. Designer:** Paul Vincze

Date	Mintage	F	VF	XF	Unc	BU
2003	—	—	—	—	2.25	3.00

KM# 29 20 TAMBALA
7.5200 g., Nickel Clad Steel, 26.5 mm. **Obv:** Bust right **Rev:** Elephants **Rev. Designer:** Paul Vincze

Date	Mintage	F	VF	XF	Unc	BU
2003	—	—	—	—	3.75	4.50

KM# 30 50 TAMBALA
4.4000 g., Brass Plated Steel, 22 mm. **Obv:** Bust right **Rev:** Arms with supporters **Shape:** 7-sided

Date	Mintage	F	VF	XF	Unc	BU
2003	—	—	—	—	4.50	5.00

KM# 66 50 TAMBALA
4.4000 g., Brass Plated Steel, 22 mm. **Obv:** State arms and supporters with country name below **Rev:** Zebras with date above and value below **Shape:** 7-sided

Date	Mintage	F	VF	XF	Unc	BU
2004	—	—	—	—	4.50	5.00

KM# 28 KWACHA
9.0000 g., Brass Plated Steel, 26 mm. **Obv:** Bust right **Rev:** Fish eagle

Date	Mintage	F	VF	XF	Unc	BU
2003	—	—	—	—	7.00	10.00

KM# 65 KWACHA
Brass Plated Steel, 26 mm. **Obv:** State arms, country name **Rev:** Fish eagle, date

Date	Mintage	F	VF	XF	Unc	BU
2004	—	—	—	—	2.50	3.50

KM# 59 5 KWACHA
Brass, 45x27.5 mm. **Obv:** National arms, date and value **Rev:** USS Coral Sea aircraft carrier **Edge:** Plain

Date	Mintage	F	VF	XF	Unc	BU
2005 Proof	—	Value: 18.50				

KM# 62 5 KWACHA
Brass, 45x27.5 mm. **Obv:** National arms, date and value **Rev:** Ship USSR Molotov **Edge:** Plain

Date	Mintage	F	VF	XF	Unc	BU
2005 Proof	—	Value: 18.50				

KM# 63 5 KWACHA
Brass, 45x27.5 mm. **Obv:** National arms, date and value **Rev:** Ship USS Missouri **Edge:** Plain

Date	Mintage	F	VF	XF	Unc	BU
2005 Proof	—	Value: 18.50				

KM# 64 5 KWACHA
Brass, 45x27.5 mm. **Obv:** National arms, date and value **Rev:** Ship HMS Hood **Edge:** Plain

Date	Mintage	F	VF	XF	Unc	BU
2005 Proof	—	Value: 18.50				

KM# 44 5 KWACHA
22.0000 g., Silver Plated Copper-Nickel, 40 mm. **Subject:** Asian Zodiac Animals **Obv:** Queen Elizabeth II above Zambian arms **Rev:** Multicolor stylized rat **Edge:** Reeded

Date	Mintage	F	VF	XF	Unc	BU
2005 Prooflike	835	—	—	—	—	12.50

KM# 45 5 KWACHA
22.0000 g., Silver Plated Copper-Nickel, 40 mm. **Subject:** Asian Zodiac Animals **Obv:** Queen Elizabeth II above Zambian arms **Rev:** Multicolor stylized ox **Edge:** Reeded

Date	Mintage	F	VF	XF	Unc	BU
2005 Prooflike	835	—	—	—	—	12.50

KM# 46 5 KWACHA
22.0000 g., Silver Plated Copper-Nickel, 40 mm. **Subject:** Asian Zodiac Animals **Obv:** Queen Elizabeth II above Zambian arms **Rev:** Multicolor stylized tiger **Edge:** Reeded

Date	Mintage	F	VF	XF	Unc	BU
2005 Prooflike	835	—	—	—	—	12.50

KM# 47 5 KWACHA
22.0000 g., Silver Plated Copper-Nickel, 40 mm. **Subject:** Asian Zodiac Animals **Obv:** Queen Elizabeth II above Zambian arms **Rev:** Multicolor stylized rabbit **Edge:** Reeded

Date	Mintage	F	VF	XF	Unc	BU
2005 Prooflike	835	—	—	—	—	12.50

KM# 48 5 KWACHA
22.0000 g., Silver Plated Copper-Nickel, 40 mm. **Subject:** Asian Zodiac Animals **Obv:** Queen Elizabeth II above Zambian arms **Rev:** Multicolor stylized dragon **Edge:** Reeded

Date	Mintage	F	VF	XF	Unc	BU
2005 Prooflike	835	—	—	—	—	12.50

KM# 49 5 KWACHA
22.0000 g., Silver Plated Copper-Nickel, 40 mm. **Subject:** Asian Zodiac Animals **Obv:** Queen Elizabeth II above Zambian arms **Rev:** Multicolor stylized snake **Edge:** Reeded

Date	Mintage	F	VF	XF	Unc	BU
2005 Prooflike	835	—	—	—	—	12.50

KM# 50 5 KWACHA
22.0000 g., Silver Plated Copper-Nickel, 40 mm. **Subject:** Asian Zodiac Animals **Obv:** Queen Elizabeth II above Zambian arms **Rev:** Multicolor stylized horse **Edge:** Reeded

Date	Mintage	F	VF	XF	Unc	BU
2005 Prooflike	835	—	—	—	—	12.50

KM# 51 5 KWACHA
22.0000 g., Silver Plated Copper-Nickel, 40 mm. **Subject:** Asian Zodiac Animals **Obv:** Queen Elizabeth II above Zambian arms **Rev:** Multicolor stylized goat **Edge:** Reeded

Date	Mintage	F	VF	XF	Unc	BU
2005 Prooflike	835	—	—	—	—	12.50

KM# 52 5 KWACHA
22.0000 g., Silver Plated Copper-Nickel, 40 mm. **Subject:** Asian Zodiac Animals **Obv:** Queen Elizabeth II above Zambian arms **Rev:** Multicolor stylized monkey **Edge:** Reeded

Date	Mintage	F	VF	XF	Unc	BU
2005 Proolike	835	—	—	—	—	12.50

KM# 53 5 KWACHA
22.0000 g., Silver Plated Copper-Nickel, 40 mm. **Subject:** Asian Zodiac Animals **Obv:** Queen Elizabeth II above Zambian arms **Rev:** Multicolor stylized rooster **Edge:** Reeded

Date	Mintage	F	VF	XF	Unc	BU
2005 Prooflike	835	—	—	—	—	12.50

KM# 54 5 KWACHA
22.0000 g., Silver Plated Copper-Nickel, 40 mm. **Subject:** Asian Zodiac Animals **Obv:** Queen Elizabeth II above Zambian arms **Rev:** Multicolor stylized dog **Edge:** Reeded

Date	Mintage	F	VF	XF	Unc	BU
2005 Prooflike	835	—	—	—	—	12.50

KM# 55 5 KWACHA
22.0000 g., Silver Plated Copper-Nickel, 40 mm. **Subject:** Asian Zodiac Animals **Obv:** Queen Elizabeth II above Zambian arms **Rev:** Multicolor stylized pig **Edge:** Reeded

Date	Mintage	F	VF	XF	Unc	BU
2005 Prooflike	835	—	—	—	—	12.50

KM# 57 5 KWACHA
10.2500 g., Bi-Metallic Copper-Nickel ring and Nickel-Brass center, 27 mm. **Obv:** State arms and supporters with country name below **Obv. Legend:** MALAWI **Rev:** Fisherman at work with date above and value below **Edge:** Reeded

Date	Mintage	F	VF	XF	Unc	BU
2006	—	—	—	—	3.50	5.00

KM# 39 10 KWACHA
29.1000 g., Copper-Nickel, 38.7 mm. **Subject:** Soccer World Championship **Obv:** Arms with supporters **Rev:** Soccer players **Edge:** Reeded

Date	Mintage	F	VF	XF	Unc	BU
2002 Proof	—	Value: 50.00				

KM# 42 10 KWACHA
19.7400 g., 0.9990 Silver 0.6340 oz. ASW, 29.9 mm. **Subject:** XXVII Olympic Games - Athens 2004 **Obv:** Arms with supporters divides date **Obv. Legend:** REPUBLIC OF MALAWI **Rev:** Two rowers within circle flanked by sprigs **Edge:** Reeded

Date	Mintage	F	VF	XF	Unc	BU
2003 Proof	—	Value: 40.00				

KM# 80 10 KWACHA
24.0000 g., 0.9990 Silver 0.7708 oz. ASW, 38.5 mm. **Obv:** Arms **Rev:** Pope John Paul II in mitre and vestments

Date	Mintage	F	VF	XF	Unc	BU
2003 Proof	—	Value: 15.00				

KM# 61 10 KWACHA
29.1500 g., Copper-Nickel silver plated, 38.7 mm.
Subject: Endangered Wildlife **Obv:** National arms
Rev: Multicolor Leopard with cub **Edge:** Reeded

Date	Mintage	F	VF	XF	Unc	BU
2004 Proof	—	—	—	—	—	—

KM# 86 10 KWACHA
29.1500 g., Copper-Nickel silver plated, 38.7 mm.
Subject: Endangered Wildlife **Obv:** National arms
Rev: Multicolor Lion and cub **Edge:** Reeded

Date	Mintage	F	VF	XF	Unc	BU
2004 Proof	— Value: 10.00					

KM# 60 10 KWACHA
29.1500 g., Copper-Nickel silver plated, 38.7 mm.
Subject: Endangered Wildlife **Obv:** National arms
Rev: Multicolor Zebra and colt **Edge:** Reeded

Date	Mintage	F	VF	XF	Unc	BU
2004 Proof	—	—	—	—	—	—

KM# 84 10 KWACHA
29.1400 g., Copper-Nickel, 38.7 mm. **Obv:** National arms
Rev: Multicolor elephant and calf **Edge:** Reeded

Date	Mintage	F	VF	XF	Unc	BU
2004 Proof	— Value: 10.00					

KM# 89 10 KWACHA
29.1500 g., Copper-Nickel silver plated, 38.7 mm. **Obv:** National arms **Rev:** Multicolor Deer and fawn **Edge:** Reeded

Date	Mintage	F	VF	XF	Unc	BU
2004 Proof	— Value: 10.00					

KM# 90 10 KWACHA
29.1500 g., Copper-Nickel silver plated, 38.7 mm. **Obv:** National arms **Rev:** Multicolor Giraffe and her calf **Edge:** Reeded

Date	Mintage	F	VF	XF	Unc	BU
2004 Proof	— Value: 10.00					

KM# 81 10 KWACHA
Copper-Nickel silver plated **Obv:** Arms **Rev:** Chevrotain advancing left

Date	Mintage	F	VF	XF	Unc	BU
2005 Proof	— Value: 12.50					

KM# 82 10 KWACHA
Copper-Nickel silver plated **Obv:** Arms **Rev:** Lemur on branch

Date	Mintage	F	VF	XF	Unc	BU
2005 Proof	— Value: 12.50					

KM# 83 10 KWACHA
Copper-Nickel silver plated **Obv:** Arms **Rev:** Pigmy Hippo

Date	Mintage	F	VF	XF	Unc	BU
2005 Proof	— Value: 12.50					

KM# 88 10 KWACHA
Copper-Nickel **Obv:** Arms **Rev:** Oryx in photo insert

Date	Mintage	F	VF	XF	Unc	BU
2005	—	—	—	—	—	20.00

KM# 71 10 KWACHA
23.5000 g., Silver Plated Copper-Nickel, 39 mm.
Subject: Endangered wildlife **Obv:** National arms **Rev:** Tree pangolin (Manis Tricuspis)

Date	Mintage	F	VF	XF	Unc	BU
2005 Proof	— Value: 12.50					

KM# 87 10 KWACHA
Copper-Nickel **Obv:** Arms **Rev:** Monkeys in photo insert

Date	Mintage	F	VF	XF	Unc	BU
2005 Proof	—					

KM# 58 10 KWACHA
15.1000 g., Bi-Metallic Copper-Nickel center with Nickel-Brass ring, 28.04 mm. **Obv:** State arms and supporters with country name below **Obv. Legend:** MALAWI **Rev:** Farm worker harvesting **Edge:** Coarse reeding

Date	Mintage	F	VF	XF	Unc	BU
2006	—	—	—	—	4.50	6.00

KM# 56 20 KWACHA
31.1000 g., 0.9988 Silver 0.9988 oz. ASW, 38.6 mm.
Series: The Big Five **Obv:** National arms **Rev:** Two water buffalo on green malachite center insert **Edge:** Plain

Date	Mintage	F	VF	XF	Unc	BU
2004 Proof	3,000 Value: 55.00					

KM# 67 20 KWACHA
31.1000 g., 0.9990 Silver 0.9988 oz. ASW, 38.6 mm.
Series: The Big Five **Obv:** National arms **Rev:** Elephant family on Haematite (blood stone) center insert **Edge:** Plain

Date	Mintage	F	VF	XF	Unc	BU
2004 Proof	3,000 Value: 55.00					

KM# 68 20 KWACHA
31.1000 g., 0.9990 Silver 0.9988 oz. ASW, 38.6 mm.
Series: The Big Five **Obv:** National arms **Rev:** Leopard family on hawk or falconeye center insert **Edge:** Plain

Date	Mintage	F	VF	XF	Unc	BU
2004 Proof	3,000 Value: 55.00					

KM# 69 20 KWACHA
31.1000 g., 0.9990 Silver 0.9988 oz. ASW, 38.6 mm.
Series: The Big Five **Obv:** National arms **Rev:** Lion family on tigereye center insert **Edge:** Plain

Date	Mintage	F	VF	XF	Unc	BU
2004 Proof	3,000 Value: 55.00					

KM# 70 20 KWACHA
31.1000 g., 0.9990 Silver 0.9988 oz. ASW, 38.6 mm.
Series: The Big Five **Obv:** National arms **Rev:** Rhinoceros family on heliotrope center insert **Edge:** Plain

Date	Mintage	F	VF	XF	Unc	BU
2004 Proof	3,000 Value: 55.00					

KM# 74 20 KWACHA
0.5000 g., 0.9990 Gold 0.0161 oz. AGW **Subject:** Springbnok, 40 years, first design

Date	Mintage	F	VF	XF	Unc	BU
2007 Proof	— Value: 70.00					

KM# 75 20 KWACHA
0.5000 g., 0.9990 Gold 0.0161 oz. AGW **Subject:** Springbok, 40th Anniversary, second desgin

Date	Mintage	F	VF	XF	Unc	BU
2007 Proof	— Value: 70.00					

KM# 76 20 KWACHA
0.5000 g., 0.9990 Gold 0.0161 oz. AGW **Subject:** Springbok, 40th Anniversary, third design

Date	Mintage	F	VF	XF	Unc	BU
2007 Proof	— Value: 70.00					

KM# 77 40 KWACHA
1.0000 g., 0.9990 Gold 0.0321 oz. AGW **Rev:** Springbok

Date	Mintage	F	VF	XF	Unc	BU
2008 Proof	— Value: 100					

KM# 78 40 KWACHA
1.0000 g., 0.9990 Palladium 0.0321 oz. **Rev:** Springbok

Date	Mintage	F	VF	XF	Unc	BU
2008 Proof	— Value: 75.00					

KM# 79 40 KWACHA
1.0000 g., 0.9990 Platinum 0.0321 oz. APW **Rev:** Springbok

Date	Mintage	F	VF	XF	Unc	BU
2008 Proof	— Value: 125					

KM# 43   50 KWACHA
141.2100 g., Bronze with Gold Plated center and Silver Plated ring, 65 mm.   **Subject:** Republic of China **Obv:** Large building above value within circle **Rev:** Conjoined busts facing within circle **Edge:** Reeded **Note:** Illustration reduced.

Date	Mintage	F	VF	XF	Unc	BU
2004 Proof	1,000	Value: 75.00				

KM# 85   50 KWACHA
62.2100 g., 0.9990 Silver 1.9980 oz. ASW, 42x42 mm.   **Obv:** Arms **Rev:** White lion with crystal inserts in eyes **Shape:** Square

Date	Mintage	F	VF	XF	Unc	BU
2009 Proof	2,500	Value: 175				

PATTERNS
Including off metal strikes

KM#	Date	Mintage	Identification	Mkt Val

| Pn2 | 2002 | — | 10 Kwacha. Copper-Nickel. 29.0200 g. 38.7 mm. National arms. Alexander the Great. Reeded edge. | — |

KM#	Date	Mintage	Identification		Mkt Val

| Pn3 | 2002 | — | 10 Kwacha. Copper-Nickel. 29.0200 g. 38.7 mm. National arms. Olympic torch under two world globes. Reeded edge. | — |

| Pn4 | 2002 | — | 10 Kwacha. Copper-Nickel. 29.0200 g. 38.7 mm. National arms. "MILLENNIUM" above Mona Lisa like portrait. Reeded edge. | — |

| Pn5 | 2003 | — | 10 Kwacha. Silver Plated. 29.4500 g. 38.7 mm. National arms. Trans-Siberian Express train. Reeded edge. | — |

| Pn6 | 2003 | — | 10 Kwacha. Silver Plated. 29.4500 g. 38.7 mm. National arms. Blesbok antelope. Reeded edge. | — |

| Pn7 | 2003 | — | 10 Kwacha. Copper-Nickel. 29.0200 g. 38.7 mm. National arms. Eland antelope. Reeded edge. | — |

KM#	Date	Mintage	Identification		Mkt Val

| Pn8 | 2003 | — | 10 Kwacha. Copper-Nickel. 29.0200 g. 38.7 mm. National arms. Kudu antelope. Reeded edge. | — |

| Pn15 | ND (2004) | — | 10 Kwacha. Silver Plated. 29.2200 g. 38.7 mm. National arms. Multicolor pair of birds with chick. Reeded edge. | 15.00 |

MALAYSIA

The independent limited constitutional monarchy of Malaysia, which occupies the southern part of the Malay Peninsula in Southeast Asia and the northern part of the island of Borneo, has an area of 127,316 sq. mi. (329,750 sq. km.) and a population of 15.4 million. Capital: Kuala Lumpur. The economy is based on agriculture, mining and forestry. Rubber, tin, timber and palm oil are exported.

Malaysia came into being on Sept. 16, 1963, as a federation of Malaya (Johore, Kelantan, Kedah, Perlis, Trengganu, Negri-Sembilan, Pahang, Perak, Selangor, Penang, Malacca), Singapore, Sabah (British North Borneo) and Sarawak. Following two serious racial riots involving Malays and Chinese, Singapore withdrew from the federation on Aug. 9, 1965. Malaysia is a member of the Commonwealth of Nations.

CONSTITUTIONAL MONARCHY

STANDARD COINAGE
100 Sen = 1 Ringgit (Dollar)

KM# 49   SEN
1.8000 g., Bronze Clad Steel, 17.66 mm.   **Obv:** Value divides date below flower blossom **Obv. Legend:** BANK NEGARA MALAYSIA **Rev:** Drum **Edge:** Plain

Date	Mintage	F	VF	XF	Unc	BU
2001	213,645,000	—	—	—	0.15	0.25
2002	185,220,000	—	—	—	0.15	0.25
2003	235,350,000	—	—	—	0.15	0.25
2004	227,700,000	—	—	—	0.15	0.25
2005	437,400,000	—	—	—	0.15	0.25
2006	328,050,000	—	—	—	0.15	0.25
2007		—	—	—	0.15	0.25

KM# 162 SEN
Brass **Subject:** 200th Anniversary Malaysian Police Force
Obv: Police badge **Obv. Legend:** BANK NEGARA MALAYSIA
Rev: Two hands clasped in sprays

Date	Mintage	F	VF	XF	Unc	BU
2007	20,000	—	—	—	—	5.50

KM# 50 5 SEN
1.4000 g., Copper-Nickel, 16.28 mm. **Obv:** Value divides date below flower blossom **Obv. Legend:** BANK NEGARA MALAYSIA **Rev:** Top with string **Edge:** Reeded

Date	Mintage	F	VF	XF	Unc	BU
2001	94,617,472	—	—	—	0.15	0.25
2002	85,316,000	—	—	—	0.15	0.25
2003	75,690,000	—	—	—	0.15	0.25
2004	11,520,000	—	—	—	0.15	0.25
2005	119,520,000	—	—	—	0.15	0.25
2006	87,120,000	—	—	—	0.15	0.25
2007	—	—	—	—	0.15	0.25

KM# 51 10 SEN
2.8200 g., Copper-Nickel, 19.43 mm. **Obv:** Value divides date below flower blossom **Obv. Legend:** BANK NEGARA MALAYSIA **Rev:** Ceremonial table **Edge:** Reeded

Date	Mintage	F	VF	XF	Unc	BU
2001	313,422,000	—	—	—	0.25	0.40
2002	290,451,948	—	—	—	0.25	0.40
2003	8,640,000	—	—	—	0.25	0.40
2004	170,640,000	—	—	—	0.25	0.40
2005	316,800,000	—	—	—	0.25	0.40
2006	304,560,000	—	—	—	0.25	0.40
2007	—	—	—	—	0.25	0.40

KM# 52 20 SEN
5.6900 g., Copper-Nickel, 23.57 mm. **Obv:** Value divides date below flower blossom **Obv. Legend:** BANK NEGARA MALAYSIA **Rev:** Basket with food and utensils **Edge:** Reeded

Date	Mintage	F	VF	XF	Unc	BU
2001	278,802,000	—	—	—	0.35	0.50
2002	131,279,881	—	—	—	0.35	0.50
2003	—	—	—	—	0.35	0.50
2004	96,840,000	—	—	—	0.35	0.50
2005	209,700,000	—	—	—	0.35	0.50
2006	155,880,000	—	—	—	0.35	0.50
2007	—	—	—	—	0.35	0.50

KM# 77 25 SEN
9.1400 g., Brass, 30 mm. **Series:** Endangered Species **Obv:** Logo left, value right **Rev:** Sumatran Rhinoceros **Edge:** Reeded

Date	Mintage	F	VF	XF	Unc	BU
2003	—	—	—	—	—	4.00

KM# 78 25 SEN
9.1400 g., Brass, 30 mm. **Series:** Endangered Species **Obv:** Logo left, value right **Rev:** Elephant **Edge:** Reeded

Date	Mintage	F	VF	XF	Unc	BU
2003	—	—	—	—	—	4.00

KM# 79 25 SEN
9.1400 g., Brass, 30 mm. **Series:** Endangered Species **Obv:** Logo left, value right **Rev:** Orangutan **Edge:** Reeded

Date	Mintage	F	VF	XF	Unc	BU
2003	—	—	—	—	—	4.00

KM# 80 25 SEN
9.1400 g., Brass, 30 mm. **Series:** Endangered Species **Obv:** Logo left, value right **Rev:** Sumatran Tiger **Edge:** Reeded

Date	Mintage	F	VF	XF	Unc	BU
2003	—	—	—	—	—	4.00

KM# 81 25 SEN
9.1400 g., Brass, 30 mm. **Series:** Endangered Species **Obv:** Logo left, value right **Rev:** Slow Loris on branch **Edge:** Reeded

Date	Mintage	F	VF	XF	Unc	BU
2003	—	—	—	—	—	4.00

KM# 82 25 SEN
9.1400 g., Brass, 30 mm. **Series:** Endangered Species **Obv:** Logo left, value right **Rev:** Barking Deer **Edge:** Reeded

Date	Mintage	F	VF	XF	Unc	BU
2003	—	—	—	—	—	4.00

KM# 83 25 SEN
9.1400 g., Brass, 30 mm. **Series:** Endangered Species **Obv:** Logo left, value right **Rev:** Malayan Tapir **Edge:** Reeded

Date	Mintage	F	VF	XF	Unc	BU
2003	—	—	—	—	—	4.00

KM# 84 25 SEN
9.1400 g., Brass, 30 mm. **Series:** Endangered Species **Obv:** Logo left, value right **Rev:** Serow **Edge:** Reeded

Date	Mintage	F	VF	XF	Unc	BU
2003	—	—	—	—	—	4.00

KM# 85 25 SEN
9.1400 g., Brass, 30 mm. **Series:** Endangered Species **Obv:** Logo left, value right **Rev:** Sambar Deer **Edge:** Reeded

Date	Mintage	F	VF	XF	Unc	BU
2003	—	—	—	—	—	4.00

KM# 86 25 SEN
9.1400 g., Brass, 30 mm. **Series:** Endangered Species **Obv:** Logo left, value right **Rev:** Seated Proboscis Monkey flanked by sprigs **Edge:** Reeded

Date	Mintage	F	VF	XF	Unc	BU
2003	—	—	—	—	—	4.00

KM# 87 25 SEN
9.1400 g., Brass, 30 mm. **Series:** Endangered Species **Obv:** Logo left, value right **Rev:** Gaur **Edge:** Reeded

Date	Mintage	F	VF	XF	Unc	BU
2003	—	—	—	—	—	4.00

KM# 88 25 SEN
9.1400 g., Brass, 30 mm. **Series:** Endangered Species **Obv:** Logo left, value right **Rev:** Clouded Leopard **Edge:** Reeded

Date	Mintage	F	VF	XF	Unc	BU
2003	—	—	—	—	—	4.00

KM# 89 25 SEN
9.1400 g., Brass, 30 mm. **Series:** Endangered Species **Obv:** Logo left, value right **Obv. Legend:** BANK NEGARA MALAYSIA - SIRI HAIWAN TERANCAM **Rev:** Straw-headed Bulbul bird (Barau-Barau) **Edge:** Reeded

Date	Mintage	F	VF	XF	Unc	BU
2004	—	—	—	—	—	9.00
2005	—	—	—	—	—	9.00

KM# 90   25 SEN
9.1400 g., Brass, 30 mm.   **Series:** Endangered Species
Obv: Logo left, value right **Obv. Legend:** BANK NEGARA
MALAYSIA - SIRI HAIWAN TERANCAM **Rev:** Great Argus
Pheasant (Kuang Raya) **Edge:** Reeded

Date	Mintage	F	VF	XF	Unc	BU
2004	—	—	—	—	—	4.00
2005	40,000	—	—	—	—	4.00

KM# 91   25 SEN
9.1400 g., Brass, 30 mm.   **Series:** Endangered Species
Obv: Logo left, value right **Obv. Legend:** BANK NEGARA
MALAYSIA - SIRI HAIWAN TERANCAM **Rev:** White-collared
Kingfisher (Pekaka Sungai) **Edge:** Reeded

Date	Mintage	F	VF	XF	Unc	BU
2004	—	—	—	—	—	4.00
2005	40,000	—	—	—	—	4.00

KM# 92   25 SEN
9.1400 g., Brass, 30 mm.   **Series:** Endangered Species
Obv: Logo left, value right **Obv. Legend:** BANK NEGARA
MALAYSIA - SIRI HAIWAN TERANCAM **Rev:** White-bellied Sea
Eagle (Lang Siput) perched on branch **Edge:** Reeded

Date	Mintage	F	VF	XF	Unc	BU
2004	—	—	—	—	—	4.00
2005	40,000	—	—	—	—	4.00

KM# 93   25 SEN
9.1600 g., Brass, 30 mm.   **Series:** Endangered Species
Obv: Logo left, value right **Obv. Legend:** BANK NEGARA
MALAYSIA - SIRI HAIWAN TERANCAM **Rev:** Asian Fairy
Bluebird (Dendang Gajah) **Edge:** Reeded

Date	Mintage	F	VF	XF	Unc	BU
2004	40,000	—	—	—	—	4.00
2005	40,000	—	—	—	—	4.00

KM# 94   25 SEN
9.1600 g., Brass, 30 mm.   **Series:** Endangered Species
Obv: Logo left, value right **Obv. Legend:** BANK NEGARA
MALAYSIA - SIRI HAIWAN TERANCAM **Rev:** Rhinoceros
Hornbill bird (Enggang Badak) **Edge:** Reeded

Date	Mintage	F	VF	XF	Unc	BU
2004	40,000	—	—	—	—	4.00
2005	40,000	—	—	—	—	4.00

KM# 95   25 SEN
9.1600 g., Brass, 30 mm.   **Series:** Endangered Species
Obv: Logo left, value right **Obv. Legend:** BANK NEGARA
MALAYSIA - SIRI HAIWAN TERANCAM **Rev:** Nicobar Pigeon
(Merpati Emas) **Edge:** Reeded

Date	Mintage	F	VF	XF	Unc	BU
2004	40,000	—	—	—	—	4.00
2005	40,000	—	—	—	—	4.00

KM# 96   25 SEN
9.1600 g., Brass, 30 mm.   **Series:** Endangered Species
Obv: Logo left, value right **Obv. Legend:** BANK NEGARA
MALAYSIA - SIRI HAIWAN TERANCAM **Rev:** Two Crested
Wood Partridges (Siul Berjambul) **Edge:** Reeded

Date	Mintage	F	VF	XF	Unc	BU
2004	40,000	—	—	—	—	4.00
2005	40,000	—	—	—	—	4.00

KM# 97   25 SEN
9.1600 g., Brass, 30 mm.   **Series:** Endangered Species
Obv: Logo left, value right **Obv. Legend:** BANK NEGARA
MALAYSIA - SIRI HAIWAN TERANCAM **Rev:** Black and Red
Broadbill bird (Takau Rakit) **Edge:** Reeded

Date	Mintage	F	VF	XF	Unc	BU
2004	40,000	—	—	—	—	4.00
2005	40,000	—	—	—	—	4.00

KM# 98   25 SEN
9.1600 g., Brass, 30 mm.   **Series:** Endangered Species
Obv: Logo left, value right **Obv. Legend:** BANK NEGARA
MALAYSIA - SIRI HAIWAN TERANCAM **Rev:** Green Imperial
Pigeon (Pergam Besar) on branch **Edge:** Reeded

Date	Mintage	F	VF	XF	Unc	BU
2004	40,000	—	—	—	—	4.00
2005	40,000	—	—	—	—	4.00

KM# 99   25 SEN
9.1600 g., Brass, 30 mm.   **Series:** Endangered Species
Obv: Logo left, value right **Obv. Legend:** BANK NEGARA
MALAYSIA - SIRI HAIWAN TERANCAM **Rev:** Great Egret
(Bangau Besar) **Edge:** Reeded

Date	Mintage	F	VF	XF	Unc	BU
2004	40,000	—	—	—	—	4.00
2005	40,000	—	—	—	—	4.00

KM# 100   25 SEN
9.1600 g., Brass, 30 mm.   **Series:** Endangered Species
Obv: Logo left, value right **Obv. Legend:** BANK NEGARA
MALAYSIA - SIRI HAIWAN TERANCAM **Rev:** Brown Shrike
(Tirjup Tanah) on branch **Edge:** Reeded

Date	Mintage	F	VF	XF	Unc	BU
2004	40,000	—	—	—	—	4.00
2005	40,000	—	—	—	—	4.00

KM# 103   25 SEN
Brass, 34 mm.   **Series:** Endangered Species **Obv:** Logo and
value **Obv. Legend:** BANK NEGARA MALAYSIA - SIRI HAIWAN
TERANCAM **Rev:** Green turtle (Penyu Agar)

Date	Mintage	F	VF	XF	Unc	BU
2006	40,000	—	—	—	—	4.00

KM# 102   25 SEN
Brass, 34 mm.   **Series:** Endangered Species **Obv:** Logo and
value **Obv. Legend:** BANK NEGARA MALAYSIA - SIRI HAIWAN
TERANCAM **Rev:** Leatherback turtle (Penyu Belimbing)

Date	Mintage	F	VF	XF	Unc	BU
2006	40,000	—	—	—	—	4.00

KM# 101   25 SEN
Brass, 34 mm.   **Series:** Endangered Species **Obv:** Logo and
value **Obv. Legend:** BANK NEGARA MALAYSIA - SIRI HAIWAN
TERANCAM **Rev:** Olive Ridley Turtle (Pengu Lipas)

Date	Mintage	F	VF	XF	Unc	BU
2006	40,000	—	—	—	—	4.00

KM# 104   25 SEN
Brass, 34 mm.   **Series:** Endangered Species **Obv:** Logo and
value **Obv. Legend:** BANK NEGARA MALAYSIA - SIRI HAIWAN
TERANCAM **Rev:** Hawksbill turtle (Penyu Karah)

Date	Mintage	F	VF	XF	Unc	BU
2006	40,000	—	—	—	—	4.00

KM# 105   25 SEN
15.5000 g., Brass, 34 mm.   **Series:** Endangered Species **Obv:**
Logo and value **Obv. Legend:** BANK NEGARA MALAYSIA - SIRI
HAIWAN TERANCAM **Rev:** Dugong manatee **Edge:** Reeded

Date	Mintage	F	VF	XF	Unc	BU
2006	40,000	—	—	—	—	4.00

KM# 106 25 SEN
15.5000 g., Brass, 34 mm. **Series:** Endangered Species
Obv: Logo and value **Obv. Legend:** BANK NEGARA MALAYSIA
- SIRI HAIWAN TERANCAM **Rev:** Whale Shark (Jerung Paus)
Edge: Reeded

Date	Mintage	F	VF	XF	Unc	BU
2006	40,000	—	—	—	—	4.00

KM# 107 25 SEN
15.5000 g., Brass, 34 mm. **Series:** Endangered Species **Obv:**
Logo and value **Obv. Legend:** BANK NEGARA MALAYSIA - SIRI
HAIWAN TERANCAM **Rev:** Irraddy Dolphin (Lumba-Lumba
Empesut) **Edge:** Reeded

Date	Mintage	F	VF	XF	Unc	BU
2006	40,000	—	—	—	—	4.00

KM# 108 25 SEN
15.5000 g., Brass, 34 mm. **Series:** Endangered Species
Obv: Logo and value **Obv. Legend:** BANK NEGARA MALAYSIA
- SIRI HAIWAN TERANCAM **Rev:** Bottlenose Dolphin (Lumba
Lumba) **Edge:** Reeded

Date	Mintage	F	VF	XF	Unc	BU
2006	40,000	—	—	—	—	4.00

KM# 109 25 SEN
15.5000 g., Brass, 34 mm. **Series:** Endangered Species
Obv: Logo and value **Obv. Legend:** BANK NEGARA MALAYSIA
- SIRI HAIWAN TERANCAM **Rev:** Siamese Crocodile (Buaya
Siam) **Edge:** Reeded

Date	Mintage	F	VF	XF	Unc	BU
2006	40,000	—	—	—	—	4.00

KM# 110 25 SEN
15.5000 g., Brass, 34 mm. **Series:** Endangered Species
Obv: Logo and value **Obv. Legend:** BANK NEGARA MALAYSIA
- SIRI HAIWAN TERANCAM **Rev:** Indopacific Crocodile (Buaya
Tembaga) **Edge:** Reeded

Date	Mintage	F	VF	XF	Unc	BU
2006	40,000	—	—	—	—	4.00

KM# 111 25 SEN
15.5000 g., Brass, 34 mm. **Series:** Endangered Species
Obv: Logo and value **Obv. Legend:** BANK NEGARA MALAYSIA
- SIRI HAIWAN TERANCAM **Rev:** Malayan Gharial (Buaya
Julong) **Edge:** Reeded

Date	Mintage	F	VF	XF	Unc	BU
2006	40,000	—	—	—	—	4.00

KM# 112 25 SEN
15.5000 g., Brass, 34 mm. **Series:** Endangered Species **Obv:**
Logo and value **Obv. Legend:** BANK NEGARA MALAYSIA - SIRI
HAIWAN TERANCAM **Rev:** Painted Terrapin turtle (Tuntung
Laut) **Edge:** Reeded

Date	Mintage	F	VF	XF	Unc	BU
2006	40,000	—	—	—	—	4.00

KM# 53 50 SEN
9.2800 g., Copper-Nickel, 27.78 mm. **Obv:** Value divides date
below flower blossom **Obv. Legend:** BANK NEGARA
MALAYSIA **Rev:** Ceremonial kite **Edge Lettering:** BANK
NEGARA MALAYSIA (twice)

Date	Mintage	F	VF	XF	Unc	BU
2001	67,371,000	—	—	—	0.65	0.85
2002	61,928,000	—	—	—	0.65	0.85
2003	32,580,000	—	—	—	0.65	0.85
2004	37,890,000	—	—	—	0.65	0.85
2005	691,680,006	—	—	—	0.65	0.85
2006	19,480,006	—	—	—	0.65	0.85

KM# 71 RINGGIT
16.8000 g., Copper-Nickel, 33.7 mm. **Subject:** XXI SEA Games
Obv: Games logo **Rev:** Cartoon mascot **Edge:** Reeded

Date	Mintage	F	VF	XF	Unc	BU
2001	200,000	—	—	—	3.00	5.00

KM# 165 RINGGIT
10.4000 g., Copper Plated Zinc, 26 mm. **Subject:** 10th Men's
Hockey World Cup **Obv:** Logo **Obv. Legend:** BANK NEGARA
MALAYSIA **Rev:** 2 stylized players **Rev. Legend:** KEJOHANAN
HOKI LELAKI PIALA DUNIA **Edge:** Reeded

Date	Mintage	F	VF	XF	Unc	BU
2002	100,000	—	—	—	—	6.00

KM# 168 RINGGIT
Brass **Subject:** 45th National Day **Obv:** Buildings, tower, metro
liner **Obv. Legend:** BANK NEGARA MALAYSIA **Rev:** Stylized
waving flag **Rev. Legend:** 45 TAHUN MERDEKA

Date	Mintage	F	VF	XF	Unc	BU
2002	10,000	—	—	—	—	5.50

KM# 74 RINGGIT
16.8000 g., Copper-Nickel, 33.7 mm. **Subject:** Coronation of
Agong XII **Obv:** Head with headdress facing **Rev:** Arms with
supporters within sprigs **Edge:** Reeded **Note:** Prev. KM#72.

Date	Mintage	F	VF	XF	Unc	BU
ND(2002)	100,000	—	—	—	4.00	6.00

KM# 171 RINGGIT
Brass **Subject:** XIII NAM Summit **Obv:** Modern building, plaza
Obv. Legend: MALAYSIA - BANK NEGARA MALAYSIA
Rev: Stylized dove in rays **Rev. Legend:** XIII CONFERENCE
OF HEADS OF STATE OR GOVERNMENT OF THE NON-
ALIGNED MOVEMENT

Date	Mintage	F	VF	XF	Unc	BU
2003	9,400	—	—	—	—	5.50

KM# 174 RINGGIT
Brass **Subject:** LIMA - 7th Bi-annual Langkawi Island Trade
Fair **Obv:** Jet fighter plane above naval missile corvette **Obv.
Legend:** BANK NEGARA MALAYSIA **Rev:** Logo **Rev. Legend:**
LANGKAWI INTERNATIONAL MARITIME & AEROSPACE

Date	Mintage	F	VF	XF	Unc	BU
2003	25,000	—	—	—	—	5.50

KM# 177 RINGGIT
Brass **Subject:** 10th Session Islamic Summit Conference **Obv:**
Circular Arabic text **Obv. Legend:** BANK NEGARA MALAYSIA
Rev: Symmetrical design **Rev. Legend:** PERSIDANGAN
KETUA-KETUA NEGARASLAM

Date	Mintage	F	VF	XF	Unc	BU
2003	25,000	—	—	—	—	5.50

KM# 114 RINGGIT
Copper-Nickel **Subject:** Century of Tunku Abdul Rahman
Obv: National arms **Obv. Legend:** BANK NEGARA MALAYSIA
- BAPA KEMERDEKAAN **Rev:** 3/4 length figure of Tunku Abdul
Rahman left with right hand raised **Rev. Legend:** Y. T. M. TUNKU
ABDUL RAHMAN PUTRA AL-HAJ

Date	Mintage	F	VF	XF	Unc	BU
2005	25,000	—	—	—	—	4.00

KM# 132 RINGGIT
Brass **Subject:** 30th Annual Meeting Islamic Development Bank
Obv: Circular Arabic text **Obv. Legend:** BANK NEGARA
MALYSIA - MESYUARAT TAHUNAN BANK PEMBANCUNAN
ISLAM KE - 30 **Rev:** Logo

Date	Mintage	F	VF	XF	Unc	BU
2005	20,000	—	—	—	—	6.00

KM# 135 RINGGIT
Copper-Nickel **Subject:** 11th ASEAN Summit **Obv:** Twin towers
center right **Obv. Legend:** BANK NEGARA MALAYSIA -
SIDANG KEMUNCAK ASEAN KE-11 **Rev:** Logo

Date	Mintage	F	VF	XF	Unc	BU
2005	20,000	—	—	—	—	5.00

KM# 138 RINGGIT

Bi-Metallic **Subject:** Songket - The Regal Heritage **Obv:** Stylized flower - Bunga Ketola **Obv. Legend:** BANK NEGARA MALAYSIA **Rev:** Floral pattern below inscription

Date	Mintage	F	VF	XF	Unc	BU
2005	20,000	—	—	—	—	5.00

KM# 141 RINGGIT

Brass **Subject:** 50th Anniversary Mara Technology University **Obv:** Large "50" with horizontal lines in background **Obv. Legend:** BANK NEGARA MALAYSIA - JUBLI EMAS UITM **Rev:** Logo **Rev. Legend:** Universiti Teknologi Mara

Date	Mintage	F	VF	XF	Unc	BU
ND(2006)	12,050	—	—	—	—	5.00

KM# 144 RINGGIT

Brass **Subject:** 50th Anniversary P. Felda **Obv:** 1/2 length figure of Felda 3/4 right **Obv. Legend:** BANK NEGARA MALYSIA **Rev:** Two opposed hands holding symbol **Rev. Legend:** MENEMPA KEJAYAAN

Date	Mintage	F	VF	XF	Unc	BU
2006	10,000	—	—	—	—	5.00

KM# 147 RINGGIT

Brass **Subject:** 9th Malaysian Plan **Obv:** Bust 3/4 right **Obv. Legend:** BANK NEGARA MALAYSIA - CEMERLANG GEMILANG TERBILANg **Rev:** Globe logo **Rev. Legend:** RANCANGAN MALAYSIA KE SEMBILAN

Date	Mintage	F	VF	XF	Unc	BU
2006	10,000	—	—	—	—	5.50

KM# 155 RINGGIT

8.8000 g., Brass, 30 mm. **Subject:** Bank Negara Malaysia, 50th Anniversary **Obv:** Bank logo **Rev:** 14-pointed star

Date	Mintage	F	VF	XF	Unc	BU
2009	13,700	—	—	—	—	5.50

KM# 159 RINGGIT

8.0000 g., Brass, 30 mm. **Subject:** Parliament, 50th Anniversary **Obv:** National Arms and 2 maces **Rev:** Parliament Building

Date	Mintage	F	VF	XF	Unc	BU
2009	10,450	—	—	—	—	5.50

KM# 72 10 RINGGIT

21.7000 g., 0.9250 Silver 0.6453 oz. ASW, 35.7 mm. **Subject:** XXI SEA Games **Obv:** Games logo **Rev:** Cartoon mascot **Edge:** Reeded

Date	Mintage	F	VF	XF	Unc	BU
2001 Proof	3,000	Value: 60.00				

KM# 75 10 RINGGIT

21.7000 g., 0.9250 Silver 0.6453 oz. ASW, 35.7 mm. **Subject:** Coronation of Agong XII **Obv:** Head with headdress facing **Rev:** Arms with supporters within sprigs **Edge:** Reeded

Date	Mintage	F	VF	XF	Unc	BU
ND(2002) Proof	10,000	Value: 80.00				

KM# 166 10 RINGGIT

16.8000 g., 0.9250 Silver 0.4996 oz. ASW, 32 mm. **Subject:** 10th Men's Hockey World Cup **Obv:** Official logo of the World Cup games **Obv. Legend:** BANK NEGARA MALAYSIA **Rev:** 2 stylized players in front of the Kuala Lumpur skyline **Rev. Legend:** KEJOHANAN HOKI LELAKI PIALA

Date	Mintage	F	VF	XF	Unc	BU
2002 Proof	3,000	Value: 85.00				

KM# 169 10 RINGGIT

0.9250 Silver **Subject:** 45th National Day **Obv:** Buildings, tower, metro liner **Obv. Legend:** BANK NEGARA MALAYSIA **Rev:** Stylized waving flag **Rev. Legend:** 45 TAHUN MERDEKA

Date	Mintage	F	VF	XF	Unc	BU
2002 Proof	1,800	Value: 70.00				

KM# 172 10 RINGGIT

0.9250 Silver **Subject:** XIII NAM Summit **Obv:** Modern building, plaza **Obv. Legend:** MALAYSIA - BANK NEGARA MALAYSIA **Rev:** Stylized dove in rays **Rev. Legend:** XIII CONFERENCE OF HEADS OF STATE OR GOVERNMENT OF THE NON-ALIGNED MOVEMENT

Date	Mintage	F	VF	XF	Unc	BU
2003 Proof	—	Value: 70.00				

KM# 175 10 RINGGIT

0.9250 Silver **Subject:** LIMA - 7th bi-annual Langkawi Island Trade Fair **Obv:** Jet fighter plane above naval missile corvette **Obv. Legend:** BANK NEGARA MALAYSIA **Rev:** Logo **Rev. Legend:** LANGKAWI INTERNATIONAL MARITIME & SPACE

Date	Mintage	F	VF	XF	Unc	BU
2003 Proof	—	Value: 70.00				

KM# 178 10 RINGGIT

0.9250 Silver **Subject:** 10th Session Islamic Summit Conference **Obv:** Circular Arabic Text **Obv. Legend:** BANK NEGARA MALAYSIA **Rev:** Symmetrical pattern **Rev. Legend:** PERSIDANGAN KETUA - KETUA NEGARA ISLAM

Date	Mintage	F	VF	XF	Unc	BU
2003 Proof	—	Value: 70.00				

KM# 115 10 RINGGIT

0.9250 Silver **Subject:** Century of Tunku Abdul Rahman **Obv:** National arms **Obv. Legend:** BANK NEGARA MALAYSIA - BAPA KEMERDEKAAN **Rev:** 3/4 length figure of Tunku Abdul Rahman left with right hand raised **Rev. Legend:** Y. T. M. TUNKU ABDUL RAHMAN PUTRA AL-HAJ

Date	Mintage	F	VF	XF	Unc	BU
2005 Proof	—	Value: 65.00				

KM# 136 10 RINGGIT

21.7000 g., Silver, 35.7 mm. **Subject:** 11th ASEAN Summit **Obv:** Twin towers center right **Obv. Legend:** BANK NEGARA MALAYSIA - SIDANG KEMUNCAK ASEAN KE-11 **Rev:** Logo

Date	Mintage	F	VF	XF	Unc	BU
2005 Proof	250	Value: 80.00				

KM# 139 10 RINGGIT

21.7000 g., Silver, 35.7 mm. **Subject:** Songket - The Regal Heritage **Obv:** Uniform pattern - Bunga Bintang **Obv. Legend:** BANK NEGARA MALAYSIA **Rev:** Floral pattern below inscription

Date	Mintage	F	VF	XF	Unc	BU
2005 Proof	—	Value: 80.00				

KM# 142 10 RINGGIT

21.7000 g., Silver, 35.7 mm. **Subject:** 50th Anniversary Mara Technology Universit **Obv:** Large "50" with horizontal lines in background **Obv. Legend:** BANK NEGARA MALAYSIA - JUBLI EMAS UITM **Rev:** Logo **Rev. Legend:** Universiti Teknologi Mara

Date	Mintage	F	VF	XF	Unc	BU
ND(2006) Proof	—	Value: 80.00				

KM# 145 10 RINGGIT

31.1100 g., Silver, 40 mm. **Subject:** 50th Anniversary P. Felda **Obv:** Outlined map of South East Asia above logo **Obv. Legend:** BANK NEGARA MALAYSIA **Rev:** Monument at left, Felda with 4 others at right **Rev. Legend:** MENEMPA KEJAYAAN

Date	Mintage	F	VF	XF	Unc	BU
2006 Proof	—	Value: 75.00				

KM# 148 10 RINGGIT

21.0000 g., Silver, 35.7 mm. **Subject:** 9th Malaysian Plan **Obv:** Bust 3/4 right **Obv. Legend:** BANK NEGARA MALAYSIA - CEMERLANG GEMILANG TERBILANG **Rev:** Globe logo **Rev. Legend:** RANCANGAN MALAYSIA KE SEMBILAN

Date	Mintage	F	VF	XF	Unc	BU
2006 Proof	—	Value: 60.00				

KM# 163 10 RINGGIT

21.0000 g., Silver, 35.70 mm. **Subject:** 200th Anniversary Malaysian Police Force **Obv:** Police badge **Obv. Legend:** BANK NEGARA MALAYSIA **Rev:** Two hands clasped in sprays

Date	Mintage	F	VF	XF	Unc	BU
2007 Proof	—	Value: 60.00				

KM# 156 10 RINGGIT

21.0000 g., 0.9250 Silver 0.6245 oz. ASW, 35.7 mm. **Subject:** Bank Negara Malaysia, 50th Anniversary **Obv:** Bank logo **Rev:** 14-pointed star

Date	Mintage	F	VF	XF	Unc	BU
2009 Proof	4,000	Value: 65.00				

KM# 160 10 RINGGIT

21.0000 g., 0.9250 Silver 0.6245 oz. ASW, 35.7 mm. **Subject:** Parliament, 50th Anniversary **Obv:** National Arms and 2 maces **Rev:** Parliament Building

Date	Mintage	F	VF	XF	Unc	BU
2009 Proof	500	Value: 50.00				

KM# 133 20 RINGGIT

31.1000 g., Silver, 40 mm. **Subject:** 30th Annual Meeting Islamic Development Bank **Obv:** Mosque **Obv. Legend:** BANK NEGARA MALAYSIA **Rev:** Logo

Date	Mintage	F	VF	XF	Unc	BU
2005 Proof	1,000	Value: 70.00				

KM# 157 50 RINGGIT

10.0700 g., 0.9990 Gold 0.3234 oz. AGW, 25 mm. **Subject:** Bank Negara Malaysia, 50th Anniversary **Obv:** Bank logo **Rev:** 14-pointed star

Date	Mintage	F	VF	XF	Unc	BU
2009 Proof	500	Value: 425				

KM# 73 100 RINGGIT

8.6000 g., 0.9160 Gold 0.2533 oz. AGW, 22 mm. **Subject:** XXI SEA Games **Obv:** Games logo **Rev:** Cartoon mascot **Edge:** Reeded

Date	Mintage	F	VF	XF	Unc	BU
2001 Proof	500	Value: 500				

KM# 76 100 RINGGIT

8.6000 g., 0.9160 Gold 0.2533 oz. AGW, 22 mm. **Subject:** Coronation of Agong XII **Obv:** Head with headdress facing **Rev:** Arms with supporters within sprigs **Edge:** Reeded

Date	Mintage	F	VF	XF	Unc	BU
ND(2002) Proof	300	Value: 500				

KM# 167 100 RINGGIT

9.0000 g., 0.9000 Gold 0.2604 oz. AGW, 22 mm. **Subject:** 10th Men's Hockey World Cup **Obv:** Logo **Obv. Legend:** BANK NEGARA MALAYSIA **Rev:** 2 stylized players in front of Kuala Lumpur skyline **Rev. Legend:** KEJOHANAN HOKI LELAKI PIALA

Date	Mintage	F	VF	XF	Unc	BU
2002 Proof	1,000	Value: 550				

KM# 170 100 RINGGIT

8.6000 g., 0.9999 Gold 0.2765 oz. AGW **Subject:** 45th National Day **Obv:** Buildings, tower, metro liner **Obv. Legend:** BANK NEGARA MALAYSIA **Rev:** Stylized waving flag **Rev. Legend:** 45 TAHUN MERDEKA

Date	Mintage	F	VF	XF	Unc	BU
2002 Proof	300	Value: 550				

KM# 173 100 RINGGIT

8.6000 g., 0.9999 Gold 0.2765 oz. AGW, 22 mm. **Subject:** XIII NAM Summit **Obv:** Modern building, plaza **Obv. Legend:** MALAYSIA - BANK NEGARA MALAYSIA **Rev:** Stylized dove in rays **Rev. Legend:** XIII CONFERENCE OF HEADS OF STATE OR GOVERNMENT OF THE NON-ALIGNED MOVEMENT

Date	Mintage	F	VF	XF	Unc	BU
2003 Proof	—	Value: 550				

KM# 176 100 RINGGIT

8.6000 g., 0.9999 Gold 0.2765 oz. AGW, 22 mm. **Subject:** LIMA - 7th bi-annual Langkawi Island Trade Fair **Obv:** Jet fighter plane above naval missile corvette **Obv. Legend:** BANK NEGARA MALAYSIA **Rev:** Logo **Rev. Legend:** LANGKAWI INTERNATIONAL MARITIME & AEROSPACE

Date	Mintage	F	VF	XF	Unc	BU
2003 Proof	50	Value: 950				

KM# 179 100 RINGGIT

8.6000 g., 0.9999 Gold 0.2765 oz. AGW, 22 mm. **Obv:** Circular Arabic text **Obv. Legend:** BANK NEGARA MALAYSIA **Rev:** Symmetrical design **Rev. Legend:** PERSIDANGAN KETUA - KETUA NEGARA ISLAM

Date	Mintage	F	VF	XF	Unc	BU
2003 Proof	200	Value: 650				

KM# 116 100 RINGGIT

0.9999 Gold **Subject:** Century of Tunku Abdul Rahman **Obv:** National arms **Obv. Legend:** BANK NEGARA MALAYSIA - BAPA KEMERDEKAAN **Rev:** 3/4 length figure of Tunku Abdul Rahman left with right hand raised **Rev. Legend:** Y. T. M. TUNKU ABDUL RAHMAN PUTRA AL-HAJ

Date	Mintage	F	VF	XF	Unc	BU
2005 Proof	100	Value: 650				

KM# 137 100 RINGGIT

8.6000 g., Gold, 22 mm. **Subject:** 11th ASEAN Summit **Obv:** Twin towers center right **Obv. Legend:** BANK NEGARA MALAYSIA - SIDANG KEMUNCAK ASEAN KE-11 **Rev:** Logo

Date	Mintage	F	VF	XF	Unc	BU
2005 Proof	150	Value: 600				

KM# 140 100 RINGGIT

8.6000 g., Gold, 22 mm. **Subject:** Songket - The Regal Heritage **Obv:** Uniform pattern - Tampur Kesemak **Obv. Legend:** BANK NEGARA MALAYSIA **Rev:** Floral pattern below inscription

Date	Mintage	F	VF	XF	Unc	BU
2005 Proof	150	Value: 700				

KM# 143 100 RINGGIT

8.6000 g., Gold, 22 mm. **Subject:** 50th Anniversary Mara Technology University **Obv:** Large "50" with horizontal lines in background **Obv. Legend:** BANK NEGARA MALAYSIA - JUBLI EMAS UITM **Rev:** Logo **Rev. Legend:** Universiti Teknologi Mara

Date	Mintage	F	VF	XF	Unc	BU
ND(2006) Proof	300	Value: 550				

KM# 146 100 RINGGIT

9.0000 g., Gold, 22 mm. **Subject:** 50th Anniversary P. Felda **Obv:** 1/2 length figure of Felda 3/4 right **Obv. Legend:** BANK NEGARA MALAYSIA **Rev:** Stylized palm tree at left, rubber tree trunk at right **Rev. Legend:** MENEMPA KEJAYAAN

Date	Mintage	F	VF	XF	Unc	BU
2006 Proof	200	Value: 550				

KM# 149 100 RINGGIT

7.9600 g., Gold, 22 mm. **Subject:** 9th Malaysian Plan **Obv:** Bust 3/4 right **Obv. Legend:** BANK NEGARA MALAYSIA - CEMERLANG GEMILANG TERBILANG **Rev:** Globe logo **Rev. Legend:** RANCANGAN MALAYSIA KE SEMBILAN

Date	Mintage	F	VF	XF	Unc	BU
2006 Proof	500	Value: 550				

KM# 164 100 RINGGIT

7.9600 g., Gold, 22 mm. **Subject:** 200th Anniversary Malaysian Police Force **Obv:** Police badge **Obv. Legend:** BANK NEGARA MALAYSIA **Rev:** Two hands clasped in sprays

Date	Mintage	F	VF	XF	Unc	BU
2007 Proof	500	Value: 550				

KM# 158 100 RINGGIT

7.9600 g., 0.9990 Gold 0.2557 oz. AGW, 22 mm. **Subject:** Bank Negara Malaysia, 50th Anniversary **Obv:** Bank logo **Rev:** 14-pointed star

Date	Mintage	F	VF	XF	Unc	BU
2009 Proof	350	Value: 425				

KM# 134 200 RINGGIT

15.5500 g., Gold, 28 mm. **Subject:** 30th Annual Meeting Islamic Development Bank **Obv:** Mosque in rays **Obv. Legend:** BANK NEGARA MALAYSIA **Rev:** Logo

Date	Mintage	F	VF	XF	Unc	BU
2005 Proof	500	Value: 650				

PROOF SETS

KM#	Date	Mintage	Identification	Issue Price	Mkt Val
PS19	2003 (2)	300	KM#171, 172	—	90.00
PS20	2003 (3)	300	KM#171-173	—	500
PS21	2003 (2)	300	KM#174, 175	—	90.00
PS22	2003 (3)	100	KM#174-176	—	1,000
PS23	2003 (2)	500	KM#177, 178	—	90.00
PS24	2003 (3)	250	KM#177-179	—	600
PS25	2005 (2)	300	KM#114, 115	—	80.00
PS26	2005 (3)	100	KM#114-116	—	600
PS27	2005 (2)	1,000	KM#132, 133	—	80.00
PS28	2005 (3)	500	KM#132-134	—	725
PS29	2005 (2)	200	KM#135, 136	—	90.00
PS30	2005 (3)	150	KM#135-137	—	500
PS31	2005 (2)	150	KM#138, 139	—	90.00
PS32	2005 (3)	150	KM#138-140	—	550
PS33	2006 (2)	300	KM#141, 142	—	90.00
PS34	2006 (3)	300	KM#141-143	—	550
PS35	2006 (2)	500	KM#144, 145	—	90.00
PS36	2006 (3)	500	KM#144-146	—	550
PS37	2006 (2)	300	KM#147, 148	—	60.00
PS38	2006 (3)	500	KM#147-149	—	520
PS39	2007 (2)	200	KM#162, 163	—	90.00
PS40	2007 (3)	200	KM#162-164	—	550

MALDIVE ISLANDS

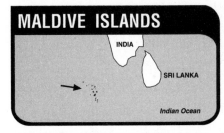

The Republic of Maldives, an archipelago of 2,000 coral islets in the northern Indian Ocean 417 miles (671 km.) west of Ceylon, has an area of 116 sq. mi. (298 sq. km.)and a population of 189,000. Capital: Male. Fishing employs 95% of the male work force. Dried fish, copra and coir yarn are exported.

The Maldive Islands were visited by Arab traders and converted to Islam in 1153. After being harassed in the 16th and 17th centuries by Mopla pirates of the Malabar coast and Portuguese raiders, the Maldivians voluntarily placed themselves under the suzerainty of Ceylon. In 1887 the islands became an internally self-governing British protectorate and a nominal dependency of Ceylon. Traditionally a sultanate, the Maldives became a republic in 1953 but restored the sultanate in 1954. The Sultanate of the Maldive Islands attained complete internal and external autonomy on July 26, 1965, and on Nov. 11, 1968, again became a republic. The Maldives is a member of the Commonwealth of Nations.

2ND REPUBLIC

STANDARD COINAGE
100 Laari = 1 Rufiyaa

KM# 68 LAARI
0.4700 g., Aluminum, 18.2 mm. **Obv:** Value **Rev:** Palm tree within circle **Rev. Designer:** Maizan Hassan Manik and Ahmed Abbas **Edge:** Plain

Date	Mintage	F	VF	XF	Unc	BU
AH1423-2002	—	—	—	0.10	0.15	0.20

KM# 70 10 LAARI
1.9500 g., Aluminum, 23 mm. **Obv:** Value **Rev:** Maldivian sailing ship - Odi **Rev. Designer:** Maizan Hassan Manik and Ahmed Abbas **Shape:** Scalloped

Date	Mintage	F	VF	XF	Unc	BU
AH1422-2001	—	—	—	0.10	0.20	0.30

KM# 73b RUFIYAA
6.5400 g., Nickel Plated Steel, 25.8 mm. **Obv:** Value **Obv. Legend:** REPUBLIC OF MALDIVES **Rev:** National arms **Edge:** Reeded

Date	Mintage	F	VF	XF	Unc	BU
AH1428-2007	—	—	—	0.50	2.00	3.00

KM# 88 2 RUFIYAA
11.7000 g., Brass, 25.47 mm. **Obv:** Value **Rev:** Pacific triton sea shell **Edge:** Reeded and lettered **Edge Lettering:** REPUBLIC OF MALDIVES

Date	Mintage	F	VF	XF	Unc	BU
AH1428-2007	—	—	—	2.25	5.50	7.50

MALTA

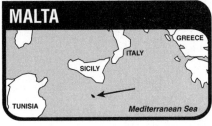

The Republic of Malta, an independent parliamentary democracy, is situated in the Mediterranean Sea between Sicily and North Africa. With the islands of Gozo and Comino, Malta has an area of 124 sq. mi. (320 sq. km.) and a population of 386,000. Capital: Valletta. Malta has no proven mineral resources, an agriculture insufficient to its needs, and a small, but expanding, manufacturing facility. Clothing, textile yarns and fabrics, and knitted wear are exported.

For more than 3,500 years Malta was ruled, in succession by Phoenicians, Carthaginians, Romans, Arabs, Normans, the Knights of Malta, France and Britain. Napoleon seized Malta by treachery in 1798. The French were ousted by a Maltese insurrection assisted by Britain, and in 1814 Malta, of its own free will, became a part of the British Empire. Malta obtained full independence in Sept., 1964; electing to remain within the Commonwealth with the British monarch as the nominal head of state.

Malta became a republic on Dec. 13, 1974, but remained a member of the Commonwealth of Nations. The president is Chief of State. The prime minister is the Head of Government.

REPUBLIC

DECIMAL COINAGE
10 Mils = 1 Cent; 100 Cents = 1 Pound

KM# 5 2 MILS
0.9500 g., Aluminum, 20.3 mm. **Obv:** Maltese cross **Rev:** Value within 3/4 wreath **Shape:** Scalloped **Designer:** Envin Cremona

Date	Mintage	F	VF	XF	Unc	BU
2005 In sets only	—	—	—	—	—	4.00
2006 In sets only	—	—	—	—	—	4.00
2007 In sets only	—	—	—	—	—	4.00

REFORM COINAGE
1982 - Present

10 Mils = 1 Cent; 100 Cents = 1 Lira = (Pound)

KM# 93 CENT
2.8000 g., Copper-Zinc, 18.53 mm. **Obv:** Crowned shield within sprigs **Obv. Designer:** Galea Bason **Rev:** Common Weasel below value **Edge:** Plain

Date	Mintage	F	VF	XF	Unc	BU
2001	—	—	0.40	0.50	1.00	—
2002 In sets only	—	—	—	—	1.00	—
2004	—	—	0.40	0.50	0.75	—
2005 In sets only	—	—	—	—	1.00	—
2006 In sets only	—	—	—	—	1.00	—
2007 In sets only	—	—	—	—	1.00	—

KM# 94 2 CENTS
2.2400 g., Copper-Zinc, 17.8 mm. **Obv:** Crowned shield within sprigs **Obv. Designer:** Galea Bason **Rev:** Olive branch and value

Date	Mintage	F	VF	XF	Unc	BU
2002	—	—	0.75	1.00	1.25	—
2004	—	—	0.75	1.00	1.25	—
2005	—	—	—	—	1.25	—
2006 In sets only	—	—	—	—	1.25	—
2007 In sets only	—	—	—	—	1.25	—

KM# 95 5 CENTS
3.5100 g., Copper-Nickel, 20 mm. **Obv:** Crowned shield within sprigs **Obv. Designer:** Galea Bason **Rev:** Freshwater Crab and value **Edge:** Reeded

Date	Mintage	F	VF	XF	Unc	BU
2001	—	—	0.75	1.00	1.25	2.00
2005 In sets only	—	—	—	—	—	2.00
2006 In sets only	—	—	—	—	—	2.00
2007 In sets only	—	—	—	—	—	2.00

KM# 96 10 CENTS
5.0000 g., Copper-Nickel, 22 mm. **Obv:** Crowned shield within sprigs **Obv. Designer:** Galea Bason **Rev:** Dolphin fish and value

Date	Mintage	F	VF	XF	Unc	BU
2005	—	—	1.25	1.50	2.00	—
2006 In sets only	—	—	—	—	2.00	—
2007 In sets only	—	—	—	—	2.00	—

KM# 97 25 CENTS
6.2300 g., Copper-Nickel, 25 mm. **Obv:** Crowned shield within sprigs **Obv. Designer:** Galea Bason **Rev:** Ghirlanda flower and value

Date	Mintage	F	VF	XF	Unc	BU
2001	—	—	2.25	2.50	3.00	—
2005	—	—	2.25	2.50	3.00	—
2006 In sets only	—	—	—	—	3.00	—
2007 In sets only	—	—	—	—	3.00	—

KM# 98 50 CENTS
7.9500 g., Copper-Nickel, 26.9 mm. **Obv:** Crowned shield within sprigs **Obv. Designer:** Galea Bason **Rev:** Tulliera plant and value

Date	Mintage	F	VF	XF	Unc	BU
2001	—	—	2.50	5.00	10.00	—
2005 In sets only	—	—	—	—	10.00	—
2006 In sets only	—	—	—	—	10.00	—
2007 In sets only	—	—	—	—	10.00	—

KM# 99 LIRA
13.0900 g., Nickel, 30 mm. **Obv:** Crowned shield within sprigs **Obv. Designer:** Galea Bason **Rev:** Merill bird and value **Rev. Designer:** Noel Galea

Date	Mintage	F	VF	XF	Unc	BU
2005	—	—	—	4.50	6.50	12.00
2006 In sets only	—	—	—	—	—	12.00
2007 In sets only	—	—	—	—	—	12.00

KM# 117 5 LIRI
28.2800 g., 0.9250 Silver 0.8410 oz. ASW, 38.6 mm. **Obv:** Crowned shield within sprigs **Rev:** Enrico Mizzi right **Edge:** Reeded

Date	Mintage	F	VF	XF	Unc	BU
2001 Proof	2,000	Value: 80.00				

KM# 118 5 LIRI
28.2800 g., 0.9250 Silver 0.8410 oz. ASW, 38.6 mm. **Obv:** Crowned shield within sprigs **Rev:** Nicolo Isouard left **Edge:** Reeded

Date	Mintage	F	VF	XF	Unc	BU
2002 Proof	2,000	Value: 80.00				

KM# 120 5 LIRI
28.2800 g., 0.9250 Silver 0.8410 oz. ASW, 38.6 mm. **Obv:** Crowned shield within sprigs **Rev:** Sir Adriano Dingli as Grand Commander of the St. Michael and George Order **Edge:** Reeded

Date	Mintage	F	VF	XF	Unc	BU
2003 Proof	2,000	Value: 80.00				

KM# 121 5 LIRI
28.2800 g., 0.9250 Silver 0.8410 oz. ASW, 38.6 mm. **Obv:** Crowned shield within sprigs **Rev:** Painter Giuseppe Cali with palette **Edge:** Reeded

Date	Mintage	F	VF	XF	Unc	BU
2004 Proof	2,000	Value: 120				

KM# 123 5 LIRI
28.2800 g., 0.9250 Silver 0.8410 oz. ASW, 38.61 mm. **Subject:** 450th Anniversary of Jean de la Valette appointed Grand master **Rev:** de la Vallete standing facing left, city of Valletta map at lower left

Date	Mintage	F	VF	XF	Unc	BU
ND(2007) Proof	25,000	Value: 75.00				

KM# 119 10 LIRI
1.2400 g., 0.9990 Gold 0.0398 oz. AGW, 13.92 mm. **Obv:** Crowned shield within sprigs **Rev:** Xprunara sailboat **Edge:** Reeded

Date	Mintage	F	VF	XF	Unc	BU
2002 Prooflike	Est. 25,000	—	—	—	—	130

KM# 122 25 LIRI
3.9940 g., 0.9167 Gold 0.1177 oz. AGW, 19.3 mm. **Subject:** Accession to the European Union **Obv:** Crowned shield within sprigs **Rev:** Maltese flag under European Union star circle **Edge:** Reeded

Date	Mintage	F	VF	XF	Unc	BU
2004 Proof	6,000	Value: 290				

KM# 124 25 LIRI
6.5000 g., 0.9200 Gold 0.1923 oz. AGW, 21 mm. **Subject:** 450th Anniversary Jean de la Valette Appointed as Grand Master **Rev:** de la Valette standing facing left, city of Valletta map at lower left

Date	Mintage	F	VF	XF	Unc	BU
ND(2007) Proof	2,500	Value: 350				

EURO COINAGE

KM# 125 EURO CENT
Copper Plated Steel **Obv:** Doorway **Rev:** Denomination and globe

Date	Mintage	F	VF	XF	Unc	BU
2008	—	—	—	—	—	1.00

KM# 126 2 EURO CENT
Copper Plated Steel **Obv:** Doorway **Rev:** Denomination and globe

Date	Mintage	F	VF	XF	Unc	BU
2008	—	—	—	—	—	0.70

KM# 127 5 EURO CENT
Copper Plated Steel **Obv:** Doorway **Rev:** Denomination and globe

Date	Mintage	F	VF	XF	Unc	BU
2008	—	—	—	—	—	0.70

KM# 128 10 EURO CENT
Aluminum-Bronze **Obv:** Crowned shield within wreath

Date	Mintage	F	VF	XF	Unc	BU
2008	—	—	—	—	—	1.00

KM# 129 20 EURO CENT
Aluminum-Brass **Obv:** Crowned shield within wreath **Rev:** Denomination and Map of Western Europe **Edge:** Notched

Date	Mintage	F	VF	XF	Unc	BU
2008	—	—	—	—	—	1.50

KM# 130 50 EURO CENT
Aluminum-Brass **Obv:** Crowned shield within wreath **Rev:** Relief map of Western Europe **Edge:** Notched

Date	Mintage	F	VF	XF	Unc	BU
2008	—	—	—	—	—	2.00

KM# 131 EURO
Bi-Metallic Copper-Nickel center in Brass ring **Obv:** Maltese Cross **Rev:** Value and relief map of Europe

Date	Mintage	F	VF	XF	Unc	BU
2008	—	—	—	—	—	4.00

KM# 132 2 EURO
Bi-Metallic Brass center in Copper-Nickel ring **Obv:** Maltese Cross **Rev:** Value and Relief Map of Western Europe

Date	Mintage	F	VF	XF	Unc	BU
2008	—	—	—	—	—	6.00

KM# 134 2 EURO
Bi-Metallic Brass center in Copper-Nickel ring **Subject:** E.M.U. 70th Anniversary **Obv:** Stick figure and large E symbol

Date	Mintage	F	VF	XF	Unc	BU
2009	—	—	—	—	—	6.00

KM# 136 10 EURO
28.2800 g., 0.9250 Silver 0.8410 oz. ASW, 38.6 mm. **Subject:** Auberge de Castille **Rev:** Building tower

Date	Mintage	F	VF	XF	Unc	BU
2008 Proof	18,000	Value: 50.00				

KM# 133 10 EURO
28.2800 g., 0.9250 Silver 0.8410 oz. ASW, 38.6 mm. **Rev:** La Castellania, Merchant's Street, Valletta

Date	Mintage	F	VF	XF	Unc	BU
2009 Proof	15,000	Value: 50.00				

KM# 137 50 EURO
6.5000 g., 0.9160 Gold 0.1914 oz. AGW, 21 mm. **Subject:** Auberge de Castille **Rev:** Building tower

Date	Mintage	F	VF	XF	Unc	BU
2008 Proof	3,000	Value: 275				

KM# 135 50 EURO
6.5000 g., 0.9160 Gold 0.1914 oz. AGW, 21 mm. **Rev:** La Castellania, Merchant's Street, Valletta

Date	Mintage	F	VF	XF	Unc	BU
2009 Proof	3,000	Value: 275				

MINT SETS

KM#	Date	Mintage	Identification	Issue Price	Mkt Val
MS26	2005 (8)	—	KM#5, 93-99	—	35.00
MS27	2006 (8)	—	KM#5, 93-99	—	37.50
MS28	2007 (8)	—	KM#5, 93-99	—	45.00

MARSHALL ISLANDS

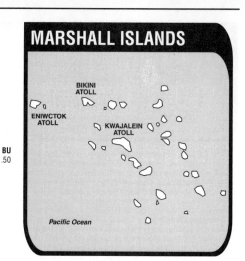

The Republic of the Marshall Islands, an archipelago which is one of the four island groups that make up what is commonly known as Micronesia, consists of 33 coral atolls comprised of over 1,150 islands or islets. It is located east of the Caroline Islands and west-northwest of the Gilbert Islands halfway between Hawaii and Australia. The Ratak chain to the east and the Ralik chain to the west comprise a total land area of 70 sq. mi. (181 sq. km.) with a population of 25,000 of which about 10% includes Americans who work at the Kwajalein Missile Range. Majuro Atoll is the government and commercial center of the Republic.

A constitutional government was formed on May 1, 1979 with Amata Kabua being elected as the head of the government. On October 1, 1986, the United States notified the United Nations that the Marshall Islands were to be recognized as a separate nation.

MINT MARKS
M - Medallic Art Co.
R - Roger Williams Mint, Rhode Island
S - Sunshine Mining Co. Mint, Idaho

REPUBLIC
NON-CIRCULATING COLLECTOR COINAGE

The USA dollar is the current monetary system. Recently, the coinage has had limited redemption policies enforced.

KM# 495 50 DOLLARS
31.1600 g., 0.9990 Silver 1.0008 oz. ASW, 39 mm. **Obv:** State seal **Rev:** Long-snouted Spinner Dolphins **Edge:** Reeded **Note:** Legal tender status questionable

Date	Mintage	F	VF	XF	Unc	BU
2002S Proof	—	Value: 60.00				

MAURITANIA

The Islamic Republic of Mauritania, located in northwest Africa bounded by Western Sahara, Mali, Algeria, Senegal and the Atlantic Ocean, has an area of 397,955 sq. mi. (1,030,700 sq. km.) and a population of 1.9 million. Capital: Nouakchott. The economy centers on herding, agriculture, fishing and mining. Iron ore, copper concentrates and fish products are exported.

On June 28, 1973, in a move designed to emphasize its non-alignment with France, Mauritania converted its currency from the old French-supported C.F.A. franc unit to a new unit called the Ouguiya.

MONETARY SYSTEM
5 Khoums = 1 Ouguiya

REPUBLIC
STANDARD COINAGE

KM# 6 OUGUIYA
3.6000 g., Copper-Nickel-Aluminum, 21 mm. **Obv:** National emblem divides date above value **Obv. Legend:** BANQUE CENTRALE DE MAURITANIE **Rev:** Star and crescent divide sprigs with legend below value, all within circle **Edge:** Reeded

Date	Mintage	F	VF	XF	Unc	BU
AH1423//2003	—	—	—	0.50	1.25	2.00

KM# 3 5 OUGUIYA
5.8800 g., Copper-Nickel-Aluminum, 25 mm. **Obv:** National emblem divides date above value **Obv. Legend:** BANQUE CENTRALE DE MAURITANIE **Rev:** Star and crescent divide sprigs below value within circle **Edge:** Plain

Date	Mintage	F	VF	XF	Unc	BU
AH1423//2003	—	—	—	1.75	3.50	5.00
AH1425//2004	—	—	—	1.75	3.50	5.00

KM# 3a 5 OUGUIYA
6.0000 g., Copper Plated Steel, 25 mm. **Obv:** National emblem divides date above value **Obv. Legend:** BANQUE CENTRALE DE MAURITANIE **Rev:** Star and crescent divides sprigs below value within circle **Edge:** Plain

Date	Mintage	F	VF	XF	Unc	BU
AH1425//2004	—	—	0.50	1.00	2.00	3.00
AH1426//2005	—	—	0.50	1.00	2.00	3.00

KM# 4 10 OUGUIYA
6.0000 g., Copper-Nickel, 25 mm. **Obv:** National emblem divides date above value **Obv. Legend:** BANQUE CENTRALE DE MAURITANIE **Rev:** Crescent and star divide sprigs below value within circle **Edge:** Reeded

Date	Mintage	F	VF	XF	Unc	BU
AH1423//2003	—	—	—	2.00	4.00	5.50
AH1425//2004	—	—	—	2.00	4.00	5.50

KM# 4a 10 OUGUIYA
5.8000 g., Nickel Plated Steel, 25 mm. **Obv:** National emblem divides date above value **Obv. Legend:** BANQUE CENTRALE DE MAURITANIE **Rev:** Crescent and star divides sprigs below value within circle **Edge:** Reeded

Date	Mintage	F	VF	XF	Unc	BU
AH1425//2004	—	—	—	1.25	3.00	4.50
AH1426//2005	—	—	—	1.25	3.00	4.50

KM# 5 20 OUGUIYA
8.0000 g., Copper-Nickel, 28 mm. **Obv:** National emblem divides date above value **Obv. Legend:** BANQUE CENTRALE DE MAURITANIE **Rev:** Star and crescent divide sprigs below value within circle **Edge:** Reeded

Date	Mintage	F	VF	XF	Unc	BU
AH1423//2003	—	—	—	3.00	6.00	8.00
AH1425//2004	—	—	—	3.00	6.00	8.00

KM# 5a 20 OUGUIYA
7.8000 g., Nickel Plated Steel, 28.05 mm. **Obv:** National emblem divides date above value **Obv. Legend:** BANQUE CENTRALE DE MAURITANIE **Rev:** Star and crescent divide sprigs below value within circle **Edge:** Reeded

Date	Mintage	F	VF	XF	Unc	BU
AH1425//2004	—	—	—	2.00	4.00	6.00
AH1426//2005	—	—	—	2.00	4.00	6.00

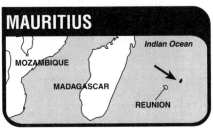

MAURITIUS

The Republic of Mauritius, is located in the Indian Ocean 500 miles (805 km.) east of Madagascar, has an area of 790 sq. mi. (1,860 sq. km.) and a population of 1 million. Capital: Port Louis. Sugar provides 90 percent of the export revenue.

Mauritius became independent on March 12, 1968. It is a member of the Commonwealth of Nations.

REPUBLIC
STANDARD COINAGE

100 Cents = 1 Rupee

KM# 52 5 CENTS
3.0000 g., Copper Plated Steel **Obv:** Value within beaded circle **Rev:** Bust of Sir Seewoosagur Ramgoolam 3/4 right

Date	Mintage	F	VF	XF	Unc	BU
2003	—	—	—	0.10	0.35	0.50
2004	—	—	—	0.10	0.35	0.50
2005	—	—	—	0.10	0.35	0.50
2007	—	—	—	0.10	0.35	0.50

KM# 53 20 CENTS
3.0000 g., Nickel Plated Steel, 19 mm. **Obv:** Value within beaded circle **Rev:** Bust of Sir Seewoosagur Ramgoolam 3/4 right

Date	Mintage	F	VF	XF	Unc	BU
2001	—	—	—	0.20	0.50	0.75
2003	—	—	—	0.20	0.50	0.75
2004	—	—	—	0.20	0.50	0.75
2005	—	—	—	0.20	0.50	0.75
2007	—	—	—	0.20	0.50	0.75

KM# 54 1/2 RUPEE
5.9000 g., Nickel Plated Steel, 23.6 mm. **Obv:** Stag left **Rev:** Bust of Sir Seewoosagur Ramgoolam 3/4 right **Rev. Designer:** G. E. Kruger-Gray

Date	Mintage	F	VF	XF	Unc	BU
2002	—	—	—	0.60	1.50	2.00
2003	—	—	—	0.60	1.50	2.00
2004	—	—	—	0.60	1.50	2.00
2005	—	—	—	0.60	1.50	2.00
2007	—	—	—	0.60	1.50	2.00

KM# 55 RUPEE
7.5000 g., Copper-Nickel, 26.6 mm. **Obv:** Shield divides date above value **Rev:** Bust of Sir Seewoosagur Ramgoolam 3/4 right **Rev. Designer:** G.E. Kruger-Gray

Date	Mintage	F	VF	XF	Unc	BU
2002	—	—	—	0.65	1.65	2.75
2004	—	—	—	0.65	1.65	2.75
2005	—	—	—	0.65	1.65	2.75
2007	—	—	—	0.65	1.65	2.75

KM# 66 20 RUPEES
10.1000 g., Bi-Metallic Copper-Nickel center in Aluminum-Bronze ring, 27.96 mm. **Obv:** Modern tower **Rev:** Bust of Sir Seewoosagur Ramgoolam KT 3/4 right **Edge:** Reeded

Date	Mintage	F	VF	XF	Unc	BU
2007	—	—	—	2.00	5.00	7.00

KM# 65 100 RUPEES
36.5700 g., 0.9250 Silver 1.0875 oz. ASW, 43.9 mm. **Obv:** National arms, date below **Obv. Legend:** MAURITIUS ONE HUNDRED RUPEES **Rev:** Bust of Gandhi 3/4 right **Rev. Legend:** MAHATMA GANDHI CENTENARY OF ARRIVAL IN MAURITIUS **Edge:** Reeded

Date	Mintage	F	VF	XF	Unc	BU
2001 Proof	—	Value: 125				

REFORM COINAGE

KM# 67 1500 RUPEES
7.7800 g., 0.9990 Platinum 0.2499 oz. APW, 25 mm. **Subject:** Sir Seewoosagur Ramgoolan **Obv:** Portrait **Rev:** State House **Edge:** Plain

Date	Mintage	F	VF	XF	Unc	BU
2009 Proof	—	Value: 425				

MEXICO

U.S.A.

Gulf of Mexico

North Pacific Ocean

CUBA

BELIZE

GUATEMALA

Caribbean Sea

The United States of Mexico, located immediately south of the United States has an area of 759,529 sq. mi. (1,967,183 sq. km.) and an estimated population of 100 million. Capital: Mexico City. The economy is based on agriculture, manufacturing and mining. Oil, cotton, silver, coffee, and shrimp are exported.

UNITED STATES

REFORM COINAGE
1 New Peso = 1000 Old Pesos

KM# 546 5 CENTAVOS
1.5900 g., Stainless Steel, 15.58 mm. **Obv:** National arms **Rev:** Large value **Edge:** Plain

Date	Mintage	F	VF	XF	Unc	BU
2001Mo	34,811,000	—	—	0.15	0.20	0.50
2002Mo	14,901,000	—	—	0.15	0.20	0.50

KM# 547 10 CENTAVOS
2.0300 g., Stainless Steel, 17 mm. **Obv:** National arms, eagle left **Rev:** Value

Date	Mintage	F	VF	XF	Unc	BU
2001	618,061,000	—	—	0.20	0.25	0.30
2002	463,968,000	—	—	0.20	0.25	0.30
2003Mo	378,938,000	—	—	0.20	0.25	0.30
2004	393,705,000	—	—	0.20	0.25	0.30
2005	488,773,000	—	—	0.20	0.25	0.30
2006	473,261,000	—	—	0.20	0.25	0.30
2007	473,261,000	—	—	0.20	0.25	0.30
2008	109,731,000	—	—	0.20	0.25	0.30
2009	—	—	—	0.20	0.25	0.30

KM# 548 20 CENTAVOS
Aluminum-Bronze, 19 mm. **Obv:** National arms, eagle left **Rev:** Value and date within 3/4 wreath **Shape:** 12-sided

Date	Mintage	F	VF	XF	Unc	BU
2001	234,360,000	—	—	0.25	0.35	0.40
2002Mo	229,256,000	—	—	0.25	0.35	0.40
2003Mo	149,518,000	—	—	0.25	0.35	0.40
2004	174,351,000	—	—	0.25	0.35	0.40
2005	204,444,000	—	—	0.25	0.35	0.40
2006	234,263,000	—	—	0.25	0.35	0.40
2007	234,301,000	—	—	0.25	0.35	0.40
2008	59,778,000	—	—	0.25	0.35	0.40
2009	—	—	—	0.25	0.35	0.40

KM# 549 50 CENTAVOS
4.4000 g., Aluminum-Bronze, 22 mm. **Obv:** National arms, eagle left **Rev:** Value and date within 1/2 designed wreath **Shape:** 12-sided

Date	Mintage	F	VF	XF	Unc	BU
2001	199,006,000	—	—	0.45	0.75	1.00
2002	94,552,000	—	—	0.45	0.75	1.00
2003Mo	124,522,000	—	—	0.45	0.75	1.00
2004	154,434,000	—	—	0.45	0.75	1.00
2005	179,304,000	—	—	0.45	0.75	1.00
2006	234,142,000	—	—	0.45	0.75	1.00

Date	Mintage	F	VF	XF	Unc	BU
2007	253,634,000	—	—	0.45	0.75	1.00
2008	79,760,000	—	—	0.45	0.75	1.00
2009	—	—	—	0.45	0.75	1.00

KM# 603 PESO
3.9500 g., Bi-Metallic Aluminumn-Bronze center in Stainless-steel ring, 21.1 mm. **Obv:** National arms, eagle left within circle **Rev:** Value and date within circle **Note:** Similar to KM#550 but without N.

Date	Mintage	F	VF	XF	Unc	BU
2001Mo	208,576,000	—	—	—	1.25	2.75
2002Mo	119,541,000	—	—	—	1.25	2.75
2003Mo	169,320,000	—	—	—	1.25	2.75
2004	208,611,000	—	—	—	1.25	2.75
2005	253,924,000	—	—	—	1.25	2.75
2006	289,834,000	—	—	—	1.25	2.75
2007	368,408,000	—	—	—	1.25	2.75
2008	99,687,000	—	—	—	1.25	2.75
2009	—	—	—	—	1.25	2.75

KM# 604 2 PESOS
5.2100 g., Bi-Metallic Aluminum-Bronze center in Stainless Steel ring, 23 mm. **Obv:** National arms, eagle left within circle **Rev:** Value and date within center circle of assorted emblems **Note:** Similar to KM#551, but denomination without N.

Date	Mintage	F	VF	XF	Unc	BU
2001Mo	74,563,000	—	—	—	2.35	4.00
2002Mo	74,547,000	—	—	—	2.35	4.00
2003Mo	39,814,000	—	—	—	2.35	4.00
2004	89,496,000	—	—	—	2.35	4.00
2005	94,532,000	—	—	—	2.35	4.00
2006	144,123,000	—	—	—	2.35	4.00
2007	129,422,000	—	—	—	2.35	4.00
2008	49,801,000	—	—	—	2.35	4.00
2009	—	—	—	—	2.35	4.00

KM# 651 5 PESOS
31.1710 g., 0.9990 Silver 1.0011 oz. ASW, 40 mm. **Series:** Endangered Wildlife **Obv:** National arms in center of past and present arms **Rev:** Manatee, value and date **Edge:** Reeded

Date	Mintage	F	VF	XF	Unc	BU
2001	50,000	—	—	—	40.00	50.00

KM# 653 5 PESOS
31.1710 g., 0.9990 Silver 1.0011 oz. ASW, 40 mm. **Subject:** Aguila Arpia **Obv:** National arms in center of past and present arms **Rev:** Crowned Harpy Eagle perched on branch

Date	Mintage	F	VF	XF	Unc	BU
2001	50,000	—	—	—	40.00	50.00

KM# 654 5 PESOS
31.1710 g., 0.9990 Silver 1.0011 oz. ASW, 40 mm. **Series:** Endangered Wildlife **Subject:** Oso Negro **Obv:** National arms in center of past and present arms **Rev:** Black bear, value and date

Date	Mintage	F	VF	XF	Unc	BU
2001	50,000	—	—	—	40.00	50.00

KM# 658 5 PESOS
31.1710 g., 0.9990 Silver 1.0011 oz. ASW, 40 mm. **Series:** Endangered Wildlife **Obv:** National arms in center of past and present arms **Rev:** Jaguar, value and date

Date	Mintage	F	VF	XF	Unc	BU
2001	50,000	—	—	—	40.00	50.00

KM# 659 5 PESOS
31.1710 g., 0.9990 Silver 1.0011 oz. ASW, 40 mm. **Series:** Endangered Wildlife **Obv:** National arms in center of past and present arms **Rev:** Prairie dog, value and date

Date	Mintage	F	VF	XF	Unc	BU
2001	50,000	—	—	—	40.00	50.00

KM# 660 5 PESOS
31.1710 g., 0.9990 Silver 1.0011 oz. ASW, 40 mm. **Series:** Endangered Wildlife **Obv:** National arms in center of past and present arms **Rev:** Volcano rabbit, value and date

Date	Mintage	F	VF	XF	Unc	BU
2001	50,000	—	—	—	40.00	50.00

KM# 605 5 PESOS
Bi-Metallic Aluminum-Bronze center in Stainless Steel ring, 25.5 mm. **Obv:** National arms, eagle left within circle **Rev:** Value within circle **Note:** Similar to KM#552 but denomination without N.

Date	Mintage	F	VF	XF	Unc	BU
2001Mo	79,169,000	—	—	3.00	5.00	7.50
2002Mo	34,754,000	—	—	3.00	5.00	7.50
2003Mo	54,676,000	—	—	3.00	5.00	7.50
2004	89,518,000	—	—	3.00	5.00	7.50
2005	94,482,000	—	—	3.00	5.00	7.50
2006	89,447,000	—	—	3.00	5.00	7.50
2007	123,382,000	—	—	3.00	5.00	7.50
2008	9,939,000	—	—	3.00	5.00	7.50
2009	—	—	—	3.00	5.00	7.50

KM# 678 5 PESOS
27.0000 g., 0.9250 Silver 0.8029 oz. ASW, 40 mm. **Subject:** Ibero-America: Acapulco Galleon **Obv:** National arms in center of past and present arms **Rev:** Spanish galleon with Pacific Ocean background and trading scene in foreground **Edge:** Reeded

Date	Mintage	F	VF	XF	Unc	BU
2003Mo Proof	5,000	Value: 90.00				

KM# 765 5 PESOS
31.1035 g., 0.9250 Silver 0.9250 oz. ASW, 40 mm. **Subject:** Palacio de Bellas Artes **Obv:** Mexican Eagle and Snake **Rev:** Palace of Fine Arts **Edge:** Reeded

Date	Mintage	F	VF	XF	Unc	BU
2005Mo Proof	—	Value: 90.00				

KM# 769 5 PESOS
15.5518 g., 0.9990 Silver 0.4995 oz. ASW, 33 mm. **Subject:** Monetary Reform of 1905 **Obv:** Mexican Eagle and Snake **Rev:** Cap and rays coin design

Date	Mintage	F	VF	XF	Unc	BU
2005Mo Proof	—	Value: 45.00				

KM# 770 5 PESOS
31.1035 g., 0.9990 Silver 0.9990 oz. ASW, 40 mm. **Subject:** World Cup Soccer **Obv:** Mexican Eagle and Snake **Rev:** Mayan Pelota player and soccer ball

Date	Mintage	F	VF	XF	Unc	BU
2006Mo Proof	40,000	Value: 65.00				

KM# 805 5 PESOS
31.1050 g., 0.9250 Silver 0.9250 oz. ASW **Obv:** Eagle on cactus **Rev:** Mayan ball game

Date	Mintage	F	VF	XF	Unc	BU
2006 Proof	—	Value: 75.00				

KM# 636 10 PESOS
10.3500 g., Bi-Metallic Copper-Nickel center in Brass ring, 28 mm. **Series:** Millennium **Obv:** National arms **Obv. Legend:** ESTADOS UNIDOS MEXICANOS **Rev:** Aztec carving **Edge:** Lettered **Edge Lettering:** ANO and date repeated 3 times

Date	Mintage	F	VF	XF	Unc	BU
2001Mo	44,768,000	—	—	5.00	7.50	10.00
2002Mo	44,721,000	—	—	5.00	7.50	10.00

Date	Mintage	F	VF	XF	Unc	BU
2004Mo	74,739,000	—	—	5.00	7.50	10.00
2005Mo	64,635,000	—	—	5.00	7.50	10.00
2006Mo	84,575,000	—	—	5.00	7.50	10.00
2007	89,678,000	—	—	5.00	7.50	10.00
2008	24,896,000	—	—	5.00	7.50	10.00
2009	—	—	—	5.00	7.50	10.00

KM# 766 10 PESOS
31.1035 g., 0.9990 Silver 0.9990 oz. ASW, 40 mm.
Subject: Cervantes Festival **Obv:** Mexican Eagle and Snake
Rev: Don Quixote **Edge:** Reeded

Date	Mintage	F	VF	XF	Unc	BU
2005Mo Proof	—	Value: 75.00				

KM# 768 10 PESOS
31.1035 g., 0.9990 Silver 0.9990 oz. ASW, 40 mm.
Subject: 470th Anniversary - Mexico City Mint **Obv:** Mexican
Eagle and Snake **Rev:** Antique coin press

Date	Mintage	F	VF	XF	Unc	BU
2005Mo Proof	—	Value: 65.00				

KM# 755 10 PESOS
31.1040 g., 0.9990 Silver 0.9990 oz. ASW, 40 mm.
Obv: National arms **Rev:** Baja California del Norte arms

Date	Mintage	F	VF	XF	Unc	BU
2005 Proof	—	Value: 75.00				

KM# 763 10 PESOS
31.1040 g., 0.9990 Silver 0.9990 oz. ASW, 40 mm.
Obv: National arms **Rev:** Benito Juarez **Edge:** Reeded

Date	Mintage	F	VF	XF	Unc	BU
2006Mo Proof	—	Value: 75.00				

KM# 637 20 PESOS
Bi-Metallic Copper-Nickel center within Brass ring, 32 mm.
Subject: Xiuhtecuhtli **Obv:** National arms, eagle left within circle
Rev: Aztec with torch within spiked circle

Date	Mintage	F	VF	XF	Unc	BU
2001	2,478,000	—	—	—	16.00	18.00

KM# 638 20 PESOS
Bi-Metallic Copper-Nickel center within Brass ring, 32 mm.
Obv: National arms, eagle left within circle **Rev:** Head 1/4 right
within circle

Date	Mintage	F	VF	XF	Unc	BU
2001	2,515,000	—	—	—	16.00	18.50

KM# 704 20 PESOS
62.4000 g., 0.9990 Silver 2.0041 oz. ASW, 48.1 mm.
Subject: 400th Anniversary of Don Quijote de la Manchia
Obv: National arms **Rev:** Skeletal figure horseback with spear
galloping right **Edge:** Plain

Date	Mintage	F	VF	XF	Unc	BU
ND(2005)Mo Proof	10,000	Value: 85.00				

KM# 767 20 PESOS
62.4000 g., 0.9990 Silver 2.0041 oz. ASW, 48 mm.
Subject: 80th Anniversary - Bank of Mexico **Obv:** National arms
Rev: 100 Peso banknote design of 1925

Date	Mintage	F	VF	XF	Unc	BU
2005Mo	—	—	—	—	—	50.00
2005Mo Proof	—	Value: 90.00				

KM# 705 100 PESOS
33.7400 g., Bi-Metallic .925 Silver center in Aluminum-Bronze
ring, 39 mm. **Subject:** 400th Anniversary of Don Quijote de la
Manchia **Obv:** National arms **Obv. Legend:** ESTADOS UNIDOS
MEXICANOS **Rev:** Sekeletal figure Horseback with spear
galloping right **Edge:** Segmented reeding

Date	Mintage	F	VF	XF	Unc	BU
2005Mo	726,833	—	—	—	25.00	32.00
2005Mo Proof	3,761	Value: 75.00				

KM# 730 100 PESOS
33.8250 g., Bi-Metallic .925 Silver 20.1753g center in Aluminum-
Bronze ring, 39.9 mm. **Subject:** Monetary Reform Centennial
Obv: National arms **Rev:** Radiant Liberty Cap divides date above
value within circle **Edge:** Segmented reeding

Date	Mintage	F	VF	XF	Unc	BU
2005Mo	49,716	—	—	—	40.00	45.00
2005Mo Proof	—	Value: 75.00				

KM# 731 100 PESOS
33.8250 g., Bi-Metallic .925 Silver 20.1753g center in Aluminum-
Bronze ring, 39.9 mm. **Subject:** Mexico City Mint's 470th
Anniversary **Obv:** National arms **Rev:** Screw press, value and
date within circle **Edge:** Segmented reeding

Date	Mintage	F	VF	XF	Unc	BU
2005Mo	49,895	—	—	—	40.00	45.00
2005Mo Proof	—	Value: 95.00				

KM# 732 100 PESOS
33.8250 g., Bi-Metallic .925 Silver 20.1753g center in Aluminum-
Bronze ring, 39.9 mm. **Subject:** Bank of Mexico's 80th

Anniversary **Obv:** National arms **Rev:** Back design of the 1925
hundred peso note **Edge:** Segmented reeding

Date	Mintage	F	VF	XF	Unc	BU
2005Mo	49,712	—	—	—	40.00	45.00
2005Mo Proof	—	Value: 95.00				

KM# 764 100 PESOS
33.7000 g., Bi-Metallic .925 Silver 20.1753g center in Aluminum-
Bronze ring **Subject:** 200th Anniversary Birth of Benito Juarez
Garcia **Obv:** National arms **Rev:** Bust 1/4 left within circle

Date	Mintage	F	VF	XF	Unc	BU
2006Mo	49,913	—	—	—	40.00	45.00

KM# 771 50000 PESOS
0.9990 Gold, 23 mm. **Subject:** World Cup Soccer **Obv:** Mexican
Eagle and Snake **Rev:** Kneeling Mayan Pelota player and soccer
ball

Date	Mintage	F	VF	XF	Unc	BU
2006Mo Proof	—	Value: 600				

REFORM COINAGE
State Commemoratives

KM# 679 10 PESOS
31.1040 g., 0.9990 Silver 0.9990 oz. ASW, 39.9 mm.
Series: First **Subject:** 180th Anniversary of Federation
Obv: National arms **Obv. Legend:** ESTADOS UNIDOS
MEXICANOS **Rev:** State Arms **Rev. Legend:** ESTADO DE
ZACATECAS **Edge:** Reeded

Date	Mintage	F	VF	XF	Unc	BU
2003Mo Proof	10,000	Value: 70.00				

KM# 680 10 PESOS
31.1040 g., 0.9990 Silver 0.9990 oz. ASW, 39.9 mm.
Series: First **Subject:** 180th Anniversary of Federation
Obv: National arms **Obv. Legend:** ESTADO UNIDOS
MEXICANOS **Rev:** State arms **Rev. Legend:** ESTADO DE
YUCATÁN **Edge:** Reeded

Date	Mintage	F	VF	XF	Unc	BU
2003Mo Proof	10,000	Value: 70.00				

KM# 681   10 PESOS
31.1040 g., 0.9990 Silver 0.9990 oz. ASW, 39.9 mm.
Series: First **Subject:** 180th Anniversary of Federation
Obv: National arms **Obv. Legend:** ESTADOS UNIDOS
MEXICANOS **Rev:** State arms **Rev. Legend:** ESTADO DE
VERACRUZ-LLAVE **Edge:** Reeded

Date	Mintage	F	VF	XF	Unc	BU
2003Mo Proof	10,000	Value: 70.00				

KM# 685   10 PESOS
31.1040 g., 0.9990 Silver 0.9990 oz. ASW, 39.9 mm.
Series: First **Subject:** 180th Anniversary of Federation
Obv: National arms **Obv. Legend:** ESTADOS UNIDOS
MEXICANOS **Rev:** State arms **Rev. Legend:** ESTADO DE
SONORA **Edge:** Reeded **Note:** Mexican States: Sonora

Date	Mintage	F	VF	XF	Unc	BU
2004Mo Proof	10,000	Value: 70.00				

KM# 733   10 PESOS
31.1040 g., 0.9990 Silver 0.9990 oz. ASW, 39.9 mm.
Series: First **Subject:** 180th Anniversary of Federation
Obv: National arms **Obv. Legend:** ESTADOS UNIDOS
MEXICANOS **Rev:** State arms **Rev. Legend:** ESTADO DE
QUERÉTARO ARTEAGA **Edge:** Reeded

Date	Mintage	F	VF	XF	Unc	BU
2004 Proof	10,000	Value: 70.00				

KM# 682   10 PESOS
31.1040 g., 0.9990 Silver 0.9990 oz. ASW, 39.9 mm.
Series: First **Subject:** 180th Anniversary of Frederation
Obv: National arms **Obv. Legend:** ESTADOS UNIDOS
MEXICANOS **Rev:** State arms **Rev. Legend:** ESTADO DE
TLAXCALA **Edge:** Reeded

Date	Mintage	F	VF	XF	Unc	BU
2003Mo Proof	10,000	Value: 70.00				

KM# 686   10 PESOS
31.1040 g., 0.9990 Silver 0.9990 oz. ASW, 39.9 mm. **Series:**
First **Subject:** 180th Anniversary of Federation **Obv:** National
arms **Obv. Legend:** ESTADOS UNIDOS DE MEXICANOS **Rev:**
State arms **Rev. Legend:** ESTADO DE SINALOA **Edge:** Reeded
Note: Mexican States: Sinaloa

Date	Mintage	F	VF	XF	Unc	BU
2004Mo Proof	10,000	Value: 70.00				

KM# 737   10 PESOS
31.1040 g., 0.9990 Silver 0.9990 oz. ASW, 39.9 mm.
Series: First **Subject:** 180th Anniversary of Federation
Obv: National arms **Obv. Legend:** ESTADOS UNIDOS
MEXICANOS **Rev:** State arms **Rev. Legend:** ESTADO DE
PUEBLA **Edge:** Reeded

Date	Mintage	F	VF	XF	Unc	BU
2004Mo Proof	10,000	Value: 70.00				

KM# 683   10 PESOS
31.1040 g., 0.9990 Silver 0.9990 oz. ASW, 39.9 mm.
Series: First **Subject:** 180th Anniversary of Federation
Obv: National arms **Obv. Legend:** ESTADOS UNIDOS
MEXICANOS **Rev:** State arms **Rev. Legend:** ESTADO DE
TAMAULIPAS **Edge:** Reeded

Date	Mintage	F	VF	XF	Unc	BU
2004Mo Proof	10,000	Value: 70.00				

KM# 687   10 PESOS
31.1040 g., 0.9990 Silver 0.9990 oz. ASW, 39.9 mm.
Series: First **Subject:** 180th Anniversary of Federation
Obv: National arms **Obv. Legend:** ESTADOS UNIDOS
MEXICANOS **Rev:** State arms **Rev. Legend:** ESTADO DE SAN
LUIS POTOSÍ **Edge:** Reeded

Date	Mintage	F	VF	XF	Unc	BU
2004Mo Proof	10,000	Value: 70.00				

KM# 739   10 PESOS
31.1040 g., 0.9990 Bi-Metallic 0.9990 oz., 39.9 mm.
Series: First **Subject:** 180th Anniversary of Federation
Obv: National arms **Obv. Legend:** ESTADOS UNIDOS
MEXICANOS **Rev:** State arms **Rev. Legend:** ESTADO DE
OAXACA **Edge:** Reeded

Date	Mintage	F	VF	XF	Unc	BU
2004Mo Proof	10,000	Value: 70.00				

KM# 684   10 PESOS
31.1040 g., 0.9990 Silver 0.9990 oz. ASW, 39.9 mm.
Series: First **Subject:** 180th Anniversary of Federation
Obv: National arms **Obv. Legend:** ESTADOS UNIDOS DE
MEXICANOS **Rev:** State arms **Rev. Legend:** ESTADO DE
TABASCO **Edge:** Reeded

Date	Mintage	F	VF	XF	Unc	BU
2004Mo Proof	10,000	Value: 70.00				

KM# 735   10 PESOS
31.1040 g., 0.9990 Silver 0.9990 oz. ASW, 39.9 mm.
Series: First **Subject:** 180th Anniversary of Federation
Obv: National arms **Obv. Legend:** ESTADOS UNIDOS
MEXICANOS **Rev:** State arms **Rev. Legend:** ESTADO DE
QUINTANA ROO

Date	Mintage	F	VF	XF	Unc	BU
2004 Proof	10,000	Value: 70.00				

KM# 741   10 PESOS
31.1040 g., 0.9990 Silver 0.9990 oz. ASW, 39.9 mm.
Series: First **Subject:** 180th Anniversary of Federation
Obv: National arms **Obv. Legend:** ESTADOS UNIDOS
MEXICANOS **Rev:** State arms **Rev. Legend:** ESTADO DE
NUEVO LEÓN **Edge:** Reeded

Date	Mintage	F	VF	XF	Unc	BU
2004Mo Proof	10,000	Value: 70.00				

KM# 743   10 PESOS
31.1040 g., 0.9990 Silver 0.9990 oz. ASW, 39.9 mm.
Series: First **Subject:** 180th Anniversary of Federation
Obv: National arms **Obv. Legend:** ESTADOS UNIDOS
MEXICANOS **Rev:** State arms **Rev. Legend:** ESTADO DE
NAYARIT **Edge:** Reeded

Date	Mintage	F	VF	XF	Unc	BU
2004Mo Proof	10,000	Value: 70.00				

KM# 749   10 PESOS
31.1040 g., 0.9990 Silver 0.9990 oz. ASW, 39.9 mm.
Series: First **Subject:** 180th Anniversary of Federation
Obv: National arms **Obv. Legend:** ESTADOS UNIDOS
MEXICANOS **Rev:** State arms **Rev. Legend:** ESTADO DE
JALISCO **Edge:** Reeded

Date	Mintage	F	VF	XF	Unc	BU
2004Mo Proof	10,000	Value: 70.00				

KM# 708   10 PESOS
31.1040 g., 0.9990 Silver 0.9990 oz. ASW, 39.9 mm.
Series: First **Subject:** 180th Anniversary of Federation
Obv: National arms **Obv. Legend:** ESTADOS UNIDOS
MEXICANOS **Rev:** State arms **Rev. Legend:** ESTADO DE
DURANGO **Edge:** Reeded

Date	Mintage	F	VF	XF	Unc	BU
2005Mo Proof	10,000	Value: 70.00				

KM# 745   10 PESOS
31.1040 g., 0.9990 Silver 0.9990 oz. ASW, 39.9 mm.
Series: First **Subject:** 180th Anniversary of Federation
Obv: National arms **Obv. Legend:** ESTADOS UNIDOS
MEXICANOS **Rev:** State arms **Rev. Legend:** ESTADO DE
MORELOS **Edge:** Reeded

Date	Mintage	F	VF	XF	Unc	BU
2004Mo Proof	10,000	Value: 70.00				

KM# 711   10 PESOS
31.1040 g., 0.9990 Silver 0.9990 oz. ASW, 39.9 mm.
Series: First **Subject:** 180th Anniversary of Federation
Obv: National arms **Obv. Legend:** ESTADOS UNIDOS
MEXICANOS **Rev:** State arms **Rev. Legend:** ESTADO DE
HIDALGO **Edge:** Reeded

Date	Mintage	F	VF	XF	Unc	BU
2005Mo Proof	10,000	Value: 70.00				

KM# 707   10 PESOS
31.1040 g., 0.9990 Silver 0.9990 oz. ASW, 39.9 mm.
Series: First **Subject:** 180th Anniversary of Federation
Obv: National arms **Obv. Legend:** ESTADOS UNIDOS
MEXICANOS **Rev:** Federal District arms **Rev. Legend:**
DISTRITO FEDERAL **Edge:** Reeded

Date	Mintage	F	VF	XF	Unc	BU
2005Mo Proof	10,000	Value: 70.00				

KM# 796   10 PESOS
31.1040 g., 0.9990 Silver 0.9990 oz. ASW, 39.9 mm.
Series: First **Subject:** 180th Anniversary of Federation
Obv: National arms **Obv. Legend:** ESTADOS UNIDOS
MEXICANOS **Rev:** State arms **Rev. Legend:** ESTADO DE
MICHOACÁN DE OCAMPO **Edge:** Reeded

Date	Mintage	F	VF	XF	Unc	BU
2004Mo Proof	10,000	Value: 70.00				

KM# 710   10 PESOS
31.1040 g., 0.9990 Silver 0.9990 oz. ASW, 39.9 mm.
Series: First **Subject:** 180th Anniversary of Federation
Obv: National arms **Obv. Legend:** ESTADOS UNIDOS
MEXICANOS **Rev:** State arms **Rev. Legend:** ESTADO DE
GUERRERO **Edge:** Reeded

Date	Mintage	F	VF	XF	Unc	BU
2005Mo Proof	10,000	Value: 70.00				

KM# 753   10 PESOS
31.1040 g., 0.9990 Silver 0.9990 oz. ASW, 39.9 mm.
Series: First **Subject:** 180th Anniversary of Federation
Obv: National arms **Obv. Legend:** ESTADOS UNIDOS
MEXICANOS **Rev:** State arms **Rev. Legend:** ESTADO DE
CHIHUAHUA **Edge:** Reeded

Date	Mintage	F	VF	XF	Unc	BU
2005Mo Proof	10,000	Value: 70.00				

KM# 747   10 PESOS
31.1040 g., 0.9990 Silver 0.9990 oz. ASW, 39.9 mm.
Series: First **Subject:** 180th Anniversary of Federation
Obv: National arms **Obv. Legend:** ESTADOS UNIDOS
MEXICANOS **Rev:** State arms **Rev. Legend:** ESTADO DE
MÉXICO **Edge:** Reeded

Date	Mintage	F	VF	XF	Unc	BU
2004Mo Proof	10,000	Value: 70.00				

KM# 709   10 PESOS
31.1040 g., 0.9990 Silver 0.9990 oz. ASW, 39.9 mm.
Series: First **Subject:** 180th Anniversary of Federation
Obv: National arms **Obv. Legend:** ESTADOS UNIDOS
MEXICANOS **Rev:** State arms **Rev. Legend:** ESTADO DE
GUANAJUATO **Edge:** Reeded

Date	Mintage	F	VF	XF	Unc	BU
2005Mo Proof	10,000	Value: 70.00				

KM# 706   10 PESOS
31.1040 g., 0.9990 Silver 0.9990 oz. ASW, 39.9 mm.
Series: First **Subject:** 180th Anniversary of Federation
Obv: National arms **Obv. Legend:** ESTADOS UNIDOS
MEXICANOS **Rev:** State arms **Rev. Legend:** ESTADO DE
CHIAPAS **Edge:** Reeded

Date	Mintage	F	VF	XF	Unc	BU
2005Mo Proof	10,000	Value: 70.00				

KM# 728   10 PESOS
31.1040 g., 0.9990 Silver 0.9990 oz. ASW, 39.9 mm.
Series: First **Subject:** 180th Anniversary of Federation
Obv: National arms **Obv. Legend:** ESTADOS UNIDOS
MEXICANOS **Rev:** State arms **Rev. Legend:** ESTADO DE
COLIMA **Edge:** Reeded

Date	Mintage	F	VF	XF	Unc	BU
2005Mo Proof	10,000	Value: 70.00				

KM# 751   10 PESOS
31.1040 g., 0.9990 Silver 0.9990 oz. ASW, 39.9 mm.
Series: First **Subject:** 180th Anniversary of Federation
Obv: National arms **Obv. Legend:** ESTADOS UNIDOS
MEXICANOS **Rev:** State arms **Rev. Legend:** ESTADO DE
COAHUILA DE ZARAGOZA **Edge:** Reeded

Date	Mintage	F	VF	XF	Unc	BU
2005Mo Proof	10,000	Value: 70.00				

KM# 726   10 PESOS
31.1040 g., 0.9990 Silver 0.9990 oz. ASW, 39.9 mm.
Series: First **Subject:** 180th Anniversary of Federation
Obv: National arms **Obv. Legend:** ESTADOS UNIDOS
MEXICANOS **Rev:** State arms **Rev. Legend:** ESTADO DE
CAMPECHE **Edge:** Reeded

Date	Mintage	F	VF	XF	Unc	BU
2005Mo Proof	10,000	Value: 70.00				

KM# 724   10 PESOS
31.1040 g., 0.9990 Silver 0.9990 oz. ASW, 39.9 mm.
Series: First **Subject:** 180th Anniversary of Federation
Obv: National arms **Obv. Legend:** ESTADOS UNIDOS
MEXICANOS **Rev:** State arms **Rev. Legend:** ESTADO DE BAJA
CALIFORNIA SUR **Edge:** Reeded

Date	Mintage	F	VF	XF	Unc	BU
2005Mo Proof	10,000	Value: 70.00				

KM# 722   10 PESOS
31.1040 g., 0.9990 Silver 0.9990 oz. ASW, 39.9 mm.
Series: First **Subject:** 180th Anniversary of Federation
Obv: National arms **Obv. Legend:** ESTADOS UNIDOS
MEXICANOS **Rev:** State arms **Rev. Legend:** ESTADO DE BAJA
CALIFORNIA **Edge:** Reeded

Date	Mintage	F	VF	XF	Unc	BU
2005Mo Proof	10,000	Value: 70.00				

KM# 720   10 PESOS
31.1040 g., 0.9990 Silver 0.9990 oz. ASW, 39.9 mm.
Series: First **Subject:** 180th Anniversary of Federation
Obv: National arms **Obv. Legend:** ESTADOS UNIDOS
MEXICANOS **Rev:** State arms **Rev. Legend:** ESTADO DE
AGUASCALIENTES **Edge:** Reeded

Date	Mintage	F	VF	XF	Unc	BU
2005Mo Proof	10,000	Value: 70.00				

KM# 718   10 PESOS
31.1040 g., 0.9990 Silver 0.9990 oz. ASW, 40 mm.
Series: Second **Obv:** National arms **Obv. Legend:** ESTADOS
UNIDOS MEXICANOS **Rev:** Facade of the San Marcos garden
above sculpture of national emblem at left, San Antonio Temple
at right **Rev. Legend:** AGUASCALIENTES **Edge:** Reeded

Date	Mintage	F	VF	XF	Unc	BU
2005Mo Proof	6,000	Value: 65.00				

KM# 757   10 PESOS
31.1040 g., 0.9990 Silver 0.9990 oz. ASW, 40 mm.
Series: Second **Obv:** National arms **Obv. Legend:** ESTADOS
UNIDOS MEXICANOS **Rev:** Rams head, mountain outline in
background **Rev. Legend:** BAJA CALIFORNIA - GOBIERNO
DEL ESTADO **Edge:** Reeded

Date	Mintage	F	VF	XF	Unc	BU
2005Mo Proof	6,000	Value: 65.00				

KM# 761   10 PESOS
31.1040 g., 0.9990 Silver 0.9990 oz. ASW, 40 mm.
Series: Second **Obv:** National arms **Obv. Legend:** ESTADOS
UNIDOS MEXICANOS **Rev:** Outlined map of peninsula at center,
cave painting of deer behind, cactus at right **Rev. Legend:**
ESTADO DE BAJA CALIFORNIA SUR **Edge:** Reeded

Date	Mintage	F	VF	XF	Unc	BU
2006Mo Proof	6,000	Value: 65.00				

KM# 759   10 PESOS
31.1040 g., 0.9990 Silver 0.9990 oz. ASW, 40 mm.
Series: Second **Obv:** National arms **Obv. Legend:** ESTADOS
UNIDOS MEXICANOS **Rev:** Jade mask - Calakmul, Campeche
Rev. Legend: ESTADO DE CAMPECHE **Edge:** Reeded

Date	Mintage	F	VF	XF	Unc	BU
2006Mo Proof	6,000	Value: 65.00				

KM# 780   10 PESOS
31.1040 g., 0.9990 Silver 0.9990 oz. ASW, 40 mm.
Series: Second **Obv:** National arms **Obv. Legend:** ESTADOS
UNIDOS MEXICANOS **Rev:** Outlined map with turtle, mine cart
above grapes at center, Friendship dam above Christ of the
Nodas at left, chimneys above crucibles and bell tower of
Santiago's cathedral at right **Rev. Inscription:** COAHUILA DE
ZARAGOZA **Edge:** Reeded

Date	Mintage	F	VF	XF	Unc	BU
2006Mo Proof	6,000	Value: 65.00				

KM# 776   10 PESOS
31.1040 g., 0.9990 Silver 0.9990 oz. ASW, 40 mm.
Series: Second **Obv:** National arms **Obv. Legend:** ESTADOS
UNIDOS MEXICANOS **Rev:** State arms at lower center, Nevado
de Colima and Volcan de Fuego volcanos in background **Rev.
Legend:** *Colima* **Rev. Inscription:** GENEROSO **Edge:** Reeded

Date	Mintage	F	VF	XF	Unc	BU
2006Mo Proof	6,000	Value: 65.00				

KM# 772 10 PESOS
31.1040 g., 0.9990 Silver 0.9990 oz. ASW, 40 mm.
Series: Second **Obv:** National arms **Obv. Legend:** ESTADOS
UNIDOS MEXICANOS **Rev:** Head of Pakal, ancient Mayan king,
Palenque **Rev. Legend:** ESTADO DE CHIAPAS - CABEZA
MAYA DEL REY PAKAL, PALENQUE **Edge:** Reeded

Date	Mintage	F	VF	XF	Unc	BU
2006Mo Proof	6,000	Value: 65.00				

KM# 774 10 PESOS
31.1040 g., 0.9990 Silver 0.9990 oz. ASW, 40 mm.
Series: Second **Obv:** National arms **Obv. Legend:** ESTADOS
UNIDOS MEXICANOS **Rev:** Angel of Liberty
Rev. Legend: MÉXICO - ANGEL DE LA LIBERTAD,
CHIHUAHUA **Edge:** Reeded

Date	Mintage	F	VF	XF	Unc	BU
2006Mo Proof	6,000	Value: 65.00				

KM# 778 10 PESOS
31.1040 g., 0.9990 Silver 0.9990 oz. ASW, 40 mm. **Series:**
Second **Obv:** National arms **Obv. Legend:** ESTADOS UNIDOS
MEXICANOS **Rev:** National Palace **Rev. Legend:** DISTRITO
FEDERAL - ANTIGUO AYUNTAMIENTO **Edge:** Reeded

Date	Mintage	F	VF	XF	Unc	BU
2006Mo Proof	6,000	Value: 65.00				

KM# 786 10 PESOS
31.1040 g., 0.9990 Silver 0.9990 oz. ASW, 40 mm.
Series: Second **Obv:** National arms **Obv. Legend:** ESTADOS
UNIDOS MEXICANOS **Rev:** Tree **Rev. Legend:** PRIMERA
RESERVA NACIONAL FORESTAL - DURANGO **Edge:** Reeded

Date	Mintage	F	VF	XF	Unc	BU
2006Mo Proof	6,000	Value: 65.00				

KM# 788 10 PESOS
31.1040 g., 0.9990 Silver 0.9990 oz. ASW, 40 mm.
Series: Second **Obv:** National arms **Obv. Legend:** ESTADOS

UNIDOS MEXICANOS **Rev:** State arms at center, statue of
Miguel Hidalgo at left, monument to Pípila at lower right
Rev. Inscription: *Guanajuato* **Edge:** Reeded

Date	Mintage	F	VF	XF	Unc	BU
2006Mo Proof	6,000	Value: 65.00				

KM# 790 10 PESOS
31.1040 g., 0.9990 Silver 0.9990 oz. ASW, 40 mm.
Series: Second **Obv:** National arms **Obv. Legend:** ESTADOS
UNIDOS MEXICANOS **Rev:** Stylized portrait of Vicente Guerrero
at left, church of Taxco at upper center, Acapulco's la Quebrada
with diver above Christmas Eve flower and mask
Rev. Legend: GUERRERO **Edge:** Reeded

Date	Mintage	F	VF	XF	Unc	BU
2006Mo Proof	6,000	Value: 65.00				

KM# 792 10 PESOS
31.1040 g., 0.9990 Silver 0.9990 oz. ASW, 40 mm.
Series: Second **Obv:** National arms **Obv. Legend:** ESTADOS
UNIDOS MEXICANOS **Rev:** Monument of Pachuca Hidalgo
Rev. Inscription: *RELOJ / MONUMENTAL / DE / PACHUCA /
HIDALGO - La / Bella / Airosa* **Edge:** Reeded

Date	Mintage	F	VF	XF	Unc	BU
2006Mo Proof	6,000	Value: 65.00				

KM# 794 10 PESOS
31.1040 g., 0.9990 Silver 0.9990 oz. ASW, 40 mm.
Series: Second **Obv:** National arms **Obv. Legend:** ESTADOS
UNIDOS MEXICANOS **Rev:** Hospicio Cabañas orphanage
Rev. Legend: ESTADO DE JALISCCO **Edge:** Reeded

Date	Mintage	F	VF	XF	Unc	BU
2006Mo Proof	6,000	Value: 65.00				

KM# 830 10 PESOS
31.1040 g., 0.9990 Silver 0.9990 oz. ASW, 40 mm.
Series: Second **Obv:** National arms **Obv. Legend:** ESTADOS

UNIDOS MEXICANOS **Rev:** Pyramid de la Loona (Moon)
Rev. Legend: ESTADO DE MEXICO **Edge:** Reeded

Date	Mintage	F	VF	XF	Unc	BU
2006Mo Proof	6,000	Value: 65.00				

KM# 831 10 PESOS
31.1040 g., 0.9990 Silver 0.9990 oz. ASW, 40 mm. **Series:**
Second **Obv:** National arms **Obv. Legend:** ESTADOS UNIDOS
MEXICANOS **Rev:** Four Monarch butterflies **Rev. Legend:**
ESTADO DE MICHOACÁN **Edge:** Reeded

Date	Mintage	F	VF	XF	Unc	BU
2006Mo Proof	6,000	Value: 65.00				

KM# 832 10 PESOS
31.1040 g., 0.9990 Silver 0.9990 oz. ASW, 40 mm.
Series: Second **Obv:** National arms **Obv. Legend:** ESTADOS
UNIDOS MEXICANOS **Rev:** 1/2 length figure of Chinelo (local
dancer) at right, Palacio de Cortes in background
Rev. Inscription: ESTADO DE / MORELOS **Edge:** Reeded

Date	Mintage	F	VF	XF	Unc	BU
2006Mo Proof	6,000	Value: 65.00				

KM# 833 10 PESOS
31.1040 g., 0.9990 Silver 0.9990 oz. ASW, 40 mm.
Series: Second **Obv:** National arms **Obv. Legend:** ESTADOS
UNIDOS MEXICANOS **Rev:** Isle de Mexcaltitlán **Rev. Legend:**
ESTADO DE NAYARIT **Edge:** Reeded

Date	Mintage	F	VF	XF	Unc	BU
2007Mo Proof	6,000	Value: 65.00				

KM# 834 10 PESOS
31.1040 g., 0.9990 Silver 0.9990 oz. ASW, 40 mm.
Series: Second **Obv:** National arms **Obv. Legend:** ESTADOS
UNIDOS MEXICANOS **Rev:** Old foundry in Parque Fundidora
(public park) at right, Cerro de la Silla (Saddle Hill) in background
Rev. Legend: ESTADO DE NUEVO LEÓN **Edge:** Reeded

Date	Mintage	F	VF	XF	Unc	BU
2007Mo Proof	6,000	Value: 65.00				

KM# 835 10 PESOS

31.1040 g., 0.9990 Silver 0.9990 oz. ASW, 40 mm.
Series: Second **Obv:** National arms **Obv. Legend:** ESTADOS
UNIDOS MEXICANOS **Rev:** Teatro Macedonio Alcala (theater)
Rev. Legend: OAXACA **Edge:** Reeded

Date	Mintage	F	VF	XF	Unc	BU
2007Mo Proof	6,000	Value: 65.00				

KM# 836 10 PESOS

31.1040 g., 0.9990 Silver 0.9990 oz. ASW, 40 mm.
Series: Second **Obv:** National arms **Obv. Legend:** ESTADOS
UNIDOS MEXICANOS **Rev:** Talavera porcelain dish
Rev. Legend: ESTADO DE PUEBLA **Edge:** Reeded

Date	Mintage	F	VF	XF	Unc	BU
2007Mo Proof	6,000	Value: 65.00				

KM# 837 10 PESOS

31.1040 g., 0.9990 Silver 0.9990 oz. ASW, 40 mm.
Series: Second **Obv:** National arms **Obv. Legend:** ESTADOS
UNIDOS MEXICANOS **Rev:** Mask at left, rays above state arms
at center, Mayan ruins at right **Rev. Legend:** QUINTANA ROO
Edge: Reeded

Date	Mintage	F	VF	XF	Unc	BU
2007Mo Proof	6,000	Value: 65.00				

KM# 838 10 PESOS

31.1040 g., 0.9990 Silver 0.9990 oz. ASW, 40 mm.
Series: Second **Obv:** National arms **Obv. Legend:** ESTADOS
UNIDOS MEXICANOS **Rev:** Acueduct of Querétaro at left,
church of Santa Rosa de Viterbo at right **Rev. Legend:** ESTADO
DE QUERÉTARO ARTEAGA **Edge:** Reeded

Date	Mintage	F	VF	XF	Unc	BU
2007Mo Proof	6,000	Value: 65.00				

KM# 839 10 PESOS

31.1040 g., Silver, 40 mm. **Series:** Second **Obv:** National arms
Obv. Legend: ESTADOS UNIDOS MEXICANOS **Rev:** Facade
of Caja Real **Rev. Legend:** • SAN LUIS POTOSÍ • **Edge:** Reeded

Date	Mintage	F	VF	XF	Unc	BU
2007Mo Proof	6,000	Value: 65.00				

KM# 840 10 PESOS

31.1040 g., 0.9990 Silver 0.9990 oz. ASW, 40 mm. **Series:**
Second **Obv:** National arms **Obv. Legend:** ESTADOS UNIDOS
MEXICANOS **Rev:** Shield on pile of cactus fruits **Rev. Legend:**
ESTADO DE SINALOA - LUGAR DE PITAHAYAS **Edge:** Reeded

Date	Mintage	F	VF	XF	Unc	BU
2007Mo Proof	6,000	Value: 65.00				

KM# 841 10 PESOS

31.1040 g., 0.9990 Silver 0.9990 oz. ASW, 40 mm.
Series: Second **Obv:** National arms **Obv. Legend:** ESTADOS
UNIDOS MEXICANOS **Rev:** Local in Dance of the Deer at left,
cactus at right, mountains in background **Rev. Legend:** ESTADO
DE SONORA **Edge:** Reeded

Date	Mintage	F	VF	XF	Unc	BU
2007Mo Proof	6,000	Value: 65.00				

KM# 842 10 PESOS

31.1040 g., 0.9990 Silver 0.9990 oz. ASW, 40 mm.
Series: Second **Obv:** National arms **Obv. Legend:** ESTADOS
UNIDOS MEXICANOS **Rev:** Fuente de los Pescadores
(fisherman fountain) at lower left, giant head from the Olmec-pre-
Hispanic culture at right, Planetario Tabasco in background
Rev. Legend: TABASCO **Edge:** Reeded

Date	Mintage	F	VF	XF	Unc	BU
2007Mo Proof	6,000	Value: 65.00				

KM# 843 10 PESOS

31.1040 g., 0.9990 Silver 0.9990 oz. ASW, 40 mm.
Series: Second **Obv:** National arms **Obv. Legend:** ESTADOS
UNIDOS MEXICANOS **Rev:** Ridge - Cerro Del Bernal, Gonzáles
Rev. Legend: TAMAULIPAS **Edge:** Reeded

Date	Mintage	F	VF	XF	Unc	BU
2007Mo Proof	6,000	Value: 65.00				

KM# 844 10 PESOS

31.1040 g., 0.9990 Silver 0.9990 oz. ASW, 40 mm.
Series: Second **Obv:** National arms **Obv. Legend:** ESTADOS
UNIDOS MEXICANOS **Rev:** Basílica de Ocotlán at left, state
arms above Capilla Abierta, Plaza de Toros Ranchero Aguilar
below, Exconvento de San Francisco at right **Rev. Legend:**
ESTADO DE TLAXCALA **Edge:** Reeded

Date	Mintage	F	VF	XF	Unc	BU
2007Mo Proof	6,000	Value: 65.00				

KM# 845 10 PESOS

31.1040 g., 0.9990 Silver 0.9990 oz. ASW, 40 mm.
Series: Second **Obv:** National arms **Obv. Legend:** ESTADOS
UNIDOS MEXICANOS **Rev:** Pyramid of El Tajín **Rev. Legend:**
• VERACRUZ • - • DE IGNACIO DE LA LLAVE • **Edge:** Reeded

Date	Mintage	F	VF	XF	Unc	BU
2007Mo Proof	6,000	Value: 65.00				

KM# 846 10 PESOS

31.1030 g., 0.9990 Silver 0.9989 oz. ASW, 40 mm.
Series: Second **Obv:** National arms **Obv. Legend:** ESTADOS
UNIDOS MEXICANOS **Rev:** Stylized pyramid of Chichén-Itzá
Rev. Legend: Castillo de Chichén Itzá **Rev. Inscription:**
YUCATÁN **Edge:** Reeded

Date	Mintage	F	VF	XF	Unc	BU
2007Mo Proof	6,000	Value: 65.00				

KM# 847 10 PESOS
31.1040 g., 0.9990 Silver 0.9990 oz. ASW, 40 mm.
Series: Second **Obv:** National arms **Obv. Legend:** ESTADOS
UNIDOS MEXICANOS **Rev:** Cable car above Monumento al
Minero at left, Catedral de Zacatecas at center right
Rev. Legend: Zacatecas **Edge:** Reeded

Date	Mintage	F	VF	XF	Unc	BU
2007Mo Proof	6,000	Value: 65.00				

KM# 688 100 PESOS
33.9400 g., Bi-Metallic .925 Silver 20.1753g center in Aluminum-
Bronze ring, 39.04 mm. **Series:** First **Subject:** 180th
Anniversary of Federation **Obv:** National arms **Obv. Legend:**
ESTADOS UNIDOS MEXICANOS **Rev:** State arms
Rev. Legend: ESTADO DE ZACATECAS **Edge:** Segmented
reeding

Date	Mintage	F	VF	XF	Unc	BU
2003Mo	244,900	—	—	—	40.00	50.00

KM# 696 100 PESOS
29.1690 g., Bi-Metallic .999 Gold 17.154g center in .999 Silver
12.015g ring, 34.5 mm. **Series:** First **Subject:** 180th Anniversary
of Federation **Obv:** National arms **Obv. Legend:** ESTADOS
UNIDOS MEXICANOS **Rev:** State arms **Rev. Legend:** ESTADO
DE ZACATECAS **Edge:** Segmented reeding

Date	Mintage	F	VF	XF	Unc	BU
2003Mo Proof	1,000	Value: 750				

KM# 689 100 PESOS
33.9400 g., Bi-Metallic .925 Silver 20.1753g center in Aluminum-
Bronze ring, 39.04 mm. **Series:** First **Subject:** 180th
Anniversary of Federation **Obv:** National arms **Obv. Legend:**
ESTADOS UNIDOS MEXICANOS **Rev:** State arms **Rev.
Legend:** ESTADO DE YUCATÁN **Edge:** Segmented reeding

Date	Mintage	F	VF	XF	Unc	BU
2003Mo	235,763	—	—	—	40.00	50.00

KM# 697 100 PESOS
29.1690 g., Bi-Metallic .999 Gold 17.154g center in .999 Silver
12.015g ring, 34.5 mm. **Series:** First **Subject:** 180th Anniversary
of Federation **Obv:** National arms **Obv. Legend:** ESTADOS
UNIDOS MEXICANOS **Rev:** State arms **Rev. Legend:** ESTADO
DE YUCATÁN **Edge:** Segmented reeding

Date	Mintage	F	VF	XF	Unc	BU
2003Mo Proof	1,000	Value: 750				

KM# 690 100 PESOS
33.9400 g., Bi-Metallic .925 Silver 20.1753g center in Aluminum-
Bronze ring, 39.04 mm. **Series:** First **Subject:** 180th
Anniversary of Federation **Obv:** National arms **Obv. Legend:**
ESTADOS UNIDOS MEXICANOS **Rev:** State arms
Rev. Legend: ESTADO DE VERACRUZ-LLAVE
Edge: Segmented reeding

Date	Mintage	F	VF	XF	Unc	BU
2003Mo	248,810	—	—	—	40.00	50.00

KM# 698 100 PESOS
29.1690 g., Bi-Metallic .999 Gold 17.154g center in .999 Silver
12.015g ring, 34.5 mm. **Series:** First **Subject:** 180th Anniversary
of Federation **Obv:** National arms **Obv. Legend:** ESTADOS
UNIDOS MEXICANOS **Rev:** State arms **Rev. Legend:** ESTADO
DE VERACRUZ-LLAVE **Edge:** Segmented reeding

Date	Mintage	F	VF	XF	Unc	BU
2003Mo Proof	1,000	Value: 750				

KM# 691 100 PESOS
33.9400 g., Bi-Metallic .925 Silver 20.1753g center in Aluminum-
Bronze ring, 39.9 mm. **Series:** First **Subject:** 180th Anniversary
of Federation **Obv:** National arms **Obv. Legend:** ESTADOS
UNIDOS MEXICANOS **Rev:** State arms **Rev. Legend:** ESTADO
DE TLAXCALA **Edge:** Segmented reeding

Date	Mintage	F	VF	XF	Unc	BU
2003Mo	248,976	—	—	—	35.00	40.00

KM# 699 100 PESOS
29.1690 g., Bi-Metallic .999 Gold 17.154g center in .999 Silver
12.015g ring, 34.5 mm. **Series:** First **Subject:** 180th Anniversary
of Federation **Obv:** National arms **Obv. Legend:** ESTADOS
UNIDOS MEXICANOS **Rev:** State arms **Rev. Legend:** ESTADO
DE TLAXCALA **Edge:** Segmented reeding

Date	Mintage	F	VF	XF	Unc	BU
2003Mo Proof	1,000	Value: 750				

KM# 692 100 PESOS
33.9400 g., Bi-Metallic .925 Silver 20.1753g center in Aluminum-
Bronze ring, 39.04 mm. **Series:** First **Subject:** 180th
Anniversary of Federation **Obv:** National arms **Obv. Legend:**
ESTADOS UNIDOS MEXICANOS **Rev:** State arms **Rev. Legend:** ESTADO
DE TAMAULIPAS **Edge:** Segmented reeding

Date	Mintage	F	VF	XF	Unc	BU
2004Mo	249,398	—	—	—	35.00	40.00

KM# 700 100 PESOS
29.1690 g., Bi-Metallic .999 Gold 17.154g center in .999 Silver
12.015g ring, 34.5 mm. **Series:** First **Subject:** 180th Anniversary
of Federation **Obv:** National arms **Obv. Legend:** ESTADOS
UNIDOS MEXICANOS **Rev:** State arms **Rev. Legend:** ESTADO
DE TAMAULIPAS **Edge:** Segmented reeding

Date	Mintage	F	VF	XF	Unc	BU
2004Mo Proof	1,000	Value: 750				

KM# 693 100 PESOS
33.9400 g., Bi-Metallic .925 Silver 20.1753g center in Aluminum-
Bronze ring, 39.04 mm. **Series:** First **Subject:** 180th
Anniversary of Federation **Obv:** National arms **Obv. Legend:**
ESTADOS UNIDOS MEXICANOS **Rev:** State arms **Rev.
Legend:** ESTADO DE TABASCO **Edge:** Segmented reeding

Date	Mintage	F	VF	XF	Unc	BU
2004Mo	249,318	—	—	—	35.00	40.00

KM# 701 100 PESOS
29.1690 g., Bi-Metallic .999 Gold 17.154g center in .999 Silver
12.015g ring, 34.5 mm. **Series:** First **Subject:** 180th Anniversary
of Federation **Obv:** National arms **Obv. Legend:** ESTADOS
UNIDOS MEXICANOS **Rev:** State arms **Rev. Legend:** ESTADO
DE TABASCO **Edge:** Segmented reeding

Date	Mintage	F	VF	XF	Unc	BU
2004Mo Proof	1,000	Value: 750				

KM# 694 100 PESOS
33.9400 g., Bi-Metallic .925 Silver 20.1753g center in Aluminum-
Bronze ring, 39.04 mm. **Series:** First **Subject:** 180th
Anniversary of Federation **Obv:** National arms **Obv. Legend:**
ESTADOS UNIDOS MEXICANOS **Rev:** State arms **Rev.
Legend:** ESTADO DE SONORA **Edge:** Segmented reeding

Date	Mintage	F	VF	XF	Unc	BU
2004Mo	249,300	—	—	—	35.00	40.00

KM# 702 100 PESOS
29.1690 g., Bi-Metallic .999 Gold 17.154g center in .999 Silver
12.015g ring, 34.5 mm. **Series:** First **Subject:** 180th Anniversary
of Federation **Obv:** National arms **Obv. Legend:** ESTADOS
UNIDOS MEXICANOS **Rev:** State arms **Rev. Legend:** ESTADO
DE SONORA **Edge:** Segmented reeding

Date	Mintage	F	VF	XF	Unc	BU
2004Mo Proof	1,000	Value: 750				

KM# 695 100 PESOS
33.9400 g., Bi-Metallic .925 Silver 20.1753g center in Aluminum-
Bronze ring, 39.04 mm. **Series:** First **Subject:** 180th
Anniversary of Federation **Obv:** National arms **Obv. Legend:**
ESTADOS UNIDOS MEXICANOS **Rev:** State arms **Rev.
Legend:** ESTADO DE SINALOA **Edge:** Segmented reeding

Date	Mintage	F	VF	XF	Unc	BU
2004Mo	244,722	—	—	—	35.00	40.00

KM# 703 100 PESOS
29.1690 g., Bi-Metallic .999 Gold 17.154g center in .999 Silver
12.015g ring, 34.5 mm. **Series:** First **Subject:** 180th Anniversary
of Federation **Obv:** National arms **Obv. Legend:** ESTADOS
UNIDOS MEXICANOS **Rev:** State arms **Rev. Legend:** ESTADO
DE SINALOA **Edge:** Segmented reeding

Date	Mintage	F	VF	XF	Unc	BU
2004Mo Proof	1,000	Value: 750				

KM# 803 100 PESOS

33.9400 g., Bi-Metallic .925 Silver 20.1753g center in Aluminum-Bronze ring, 39.04 mm. **Series:** First **Subject:** 180th Anniversary of Federation **Obv:** National arms **Obv. Legend:** ESTADOS UNIDOS MEXICANOS **Rev:** State arms **Rev. Legend:** ESTADO DE SAN LUIS POTOSÍ **Edge:** Segmented reeding

Date	Mintage	F	VF	XF	Unc	BU
2004Mo	249,662	—	—	—	35.00	40.00

KM# 806 100 PESOS

29.1690 g., Bi-Metallic .999 Gold 17.154g center in .999 silver 12.015 ring, 34.5 mm. **Series:** First **Subject:** 180th Anniversary of Federation **Obv:** National arms **Obv. Legend:** ESTADOS UNIDOS MEXICANOS **Rev:** State arms **Rev. Legend:** ESTADO DE SAN LUIS POTOSÍ **Edge:** Segmented reeding

Date	Mintage	F	VF	XF	Unc	BU
2004Mo Proof	1,000	Value: 750				

KM# 738 100 PESOS

33.9400 g., Bi-Metallic .925 Silver 20.1753g center in Aluminum-Bronze ring, 39.04 mm. **Series:** First **Subject:** 180th Anniversary of Federation **Obv:** National arms **Obv. Legend:** ESTADOS UNIDOS MEXICANOS **Rev:** State arms **Rev. Legend:** ESTADO DE PUEBLA **Edge:** Segmented reeding

Date	Mintage	F	VF	XF	Unc	BU
2004Mo	248,850	—	—	—	35.00	40.00

KM# 809 100 PESOS

Bi-Metallic .999 Gold 17.154g center in .999 Silver 12.015g ring, 34.5 mm. **Series:** First **Subject:** 180th Anniversary of Federation **Obv:** National arms **Obv. Legend:** ESTADOS UNIDOS MEXICANOS **Rev:** State arms **Rev. Legend:** ESTADO DE PUEBLA **Edge:** Segmented reeding

Date	Mintage	F	VF	XF	Unc	BU
2004Mo Proof	1,000	Value: 750				

KM# 744 100 PESOS

33.9400 g., Bi-Metallic .925 Silver 20.1753g center in Aluminum-Bronze ring, 39.04 mm. **Series:** First **Subject:** 180th Anniversary of Federation **Obv:** National arms **Obv. Legend:** ESTADOS UNIDOS MEXICANOS **Rev:** State arms **Rev. Legend:** ESTADO DE NAYARIT **Edge:** Segmented reeding

Date	Mintage	F	VF	XF	Unc	BU
2004Mo	248,305	—	—	—	35.00	40.00

KM# 812 100 PESOS

29.1690 g., Bi-Metallic .999 Gold 17.154g center in .999 Silver 12.015g ring, 34.5 mm. **Series:** First **Subject:** 180th Anniversary of Federation **Obv:** National arms **Obv. Legend:** ESTADOS UNIDOS MEXICANOS **Rev:** State arms **Rev. Legend:** ESTADO DE NAYARIT **Edge:** Segmented reeding

Date	Mintage	F	VF	XF	Unc	BU
2004Mo Proof	1,000	Value: 750				

KM# 736 100 PESOS

33.9400 g., Bi-Metallic .925 Silver 20.1753g center in Aluminum-Bronze ring, 39.04 mm. **Series:** First **Subject:** 180th Anniversary of Federation **Obv:** National arms **Obv. Legend:** ESTADOS UNIDOS MEXICANOS **Rev:** State arms **Rev. Legend:** ESTADO DE QUINTANA ROO **Edge:** Segmented reeding

Date	Mintage	F	VF	XF	Unc	BU
2004Mo	249,134	—	—	—	35.00	40.00

KM# 807 100 PESOS

29.1690 g., Bi-Metallic .999 Gold 17.154g center in .999 Silver 12.015g ring, 34.5 mm. **Series:** First **Subject:** 180th Anniversary of Federation **Obv:** National arms **Obv. Legend:** ESTADOS UNIDOS MEXICANOS **Rev:** State arms **Rev. Legend:** ESTADO DE QUINTANA ROO **Edge:** Segmented reeding

Date	Mintage	F	VF	XF	Unc	BU
2004Mo Proof	1,000	Value: 750				

KM# 740 100 PESOS

33.9400 g., Bi-Metallic .925 Silver 20.1753g center in Aluminum-Bronze ring, 39.04 mm. **Series:** First **Subject:** 180th Anniversary of Federation **Obv:** National arms **Obv. Legend:** ESTADOS UNIDOS MEXICANOS **Rev:** State arms **Rev. Legend:** ESTADO DE OAXACA **Edge:** Segmented reeding

Date	Mintage	F	VF	XF	Unc	BU
2004Mo	249,589	—	—	—	35.00	40.00

KM# 810 100 PESOS

29.1690 g., Bi-Metallic .999 Gold 17.154g center in .999 Silver 12.015g ring, 34.5 mm. **Series:** First **Subject:** 180th Anniversary of Federation **Obv:** National arms **Obv. Legend:** ESTADOS UNIDOS MEXICANOS **Rev:** State arms **Rev. Legend:** ESTADO DE OAXACA **Edge:** Segmented reeding

Date	Mintage	F	VF	XF	Unc	BU
2004Mo Proof	1,000	Value: 750				

KM# 746 100 PESOS

33.9400 g., Bi-Metallic .925 Silver 20.1753g center in Aluminum-Bronze ring, 39.04 mm. **Series:** First **Subject:** 180th Anniversary of Federation **Obv:** National arms **Obv. Legend:** ESTADOS UNIDOS MEXICANOS **Rev:** State arms **Rev. Legend:** ESTADO DE MORELOS **Edge:** Segmented reeding

Date	Mintage	F	VF	XF	Unc	BU
2004Mo	249,260	—	—	—	35.00	40.00

KM# 813 100 PESOS

29.1690 g., Bi-Metallic .999 Gold 17.154g center in .999 Silver 12.015g ring, 34.5 mm. **Series:** First **Subject:** 180th Anniversary of Federation **Obv:** National arms **Obv. Legend:** ESTADOS UNIDOS MEXICANOS **Rev:** State arms **Rev. Legend:** ESTADO DE MORELOS **Edge:** Segmented reeding

Date	Mintage	F	VF	XF	Unc	BU
2004Mo Proof	1,000	Value: 750				

KM# 734 100 PESOS

33.9400 g., Bi-Metallic .925 Silver 20.1753g center in Aluminum-Bronze ring, 39.04 mm. **Series:** First **Subject:** 180th Anniversary of Federation **Obv:** National arms **Obv. Legend:** ESTADOS UNIDOS MEXICANOS **Rev:** State arms **Rev. Legend:** ESTADO DE QUERÉTARO ARTEAGA **Edge:** Segmented reeding

Date	Mintage	F	VF	XF	Unc	BU
2004Mo	249,263	—	—	—	35.00	40.00

KM# 808 100 PESOS

29.1690 g., Bi-Metallic .999 Gold 17.154g center in .999 Silver 12.015g ring, 34.5 mm. **Series:** First **Subject:** 180th Anniversary of Federation **Obv:** National arms **Obv. Legend:** ESTADOS UNIDOS MEXICANOS **Rev:** State arms **Rev. Legend:** ESTADO DE QUERÉTARO ARTEAGA **Edge:** Segmented reeding

Date	Mintage	F	VF	XF	Unc	BU
2004Mo Proof	1,000	Value: 750				

KM# 742 100 PESOS

33.9400 g., Bi-Metallic .925 Silver 20.1753g center in Aluminum-Bronze ring, 39.04 mm. **Series:** First **Subject:** 180th Anniversary of Federation **Obv:** National arms **Obv. Legend:** ESTADOS UNIDOS MEXICANOS **Rev:** State arms **Rev. Legend:** ESTADO DE NUEVO LEÓN **Edge:** Segmented reeding

Date	Mintage	F	VF	XF	Unc	BU
2004Mo	249,199	—	—	—	35.00	40.00

KM# 811 100 PESOS

29.1690 g., Bi-Metallic .999 Gold 17.154g center in .999 Silver 12.015g ring, 34.5 mm. **Series:** First **Subject:** 180th Anniversary of Federation **Obv:** National arms **Obv. Legend:** ESTADOS UNIDOS MEXICANOS **Rev:** State arms **Rev. Legend:** ESTADO DE NUEVO LEÓN **Edge:** Segmented reeding

Date	Mintage	F	VF	XF	Unc	BU
2004Mo Proof	1,000	Value: 750				

KM# 804 100 PESOS

33.9400 g., Bi-Metallic o.925 Silver 20.1763g center in Aluminum-Bronze ring, 39.04 mm. **Series:** First **Subject:** 180th Anniversary of Federation **Obv:** National arms **Obv. Legend:** ESTADOS UNIDOS MEXICANOS **Rev:** State arms **Rev. Legend:** ESTADO DE MICHOACÁN DE OCAMPO **Edge:** Segmented reeding

Date	Mintage	F	VF	XF	Unc	BU
2004Mo	249,492	—	—	—	35.00	40.00

KM# 814 100 PESOS

29.1690 g., Bi-Metallic .999 Gold 17.154g center in .999 12.015g ring, 34.5 mm. **Series:** First **Subject:** 180th Anniversary of Federation **Obv:** National arms **Obv. Legend:** ESTADOS UNIDOS MEXICANOS **Rev:** State arms **Rev. Legend:** ESTADO DE MICHOACÁN DE OCAMPO **Edge:** Segmented reeding

Date	Mintage	F	VF	XF	Unc	BU
2004Mo Proof	1,000	Value: 750				

KM# 748   100 PESOS
33.9400 g., Bi-Metallic .925 Silver 20.1753g center in Aluminum-Bronze ring, 39.04 mm. **Series:** First **Subject:** 180th Anniversary of Federation **Obv:** National arms **Obv. Legend:** ESTADOS UNIDOS MEXICANOS **Rev:** State arms **Rev. Legend:** ESTADO DE MÉXICO **Edge:** Segmented reeding

Date	Mintage	F	VF	XF	Unc	BU
2004Mo	249,800	—	—	—	35.00	40.00

KM# 815   100 PESOS
29.1690 g., Bi-Metallic .999 Gold 17.154 center in .999 Silver 12.015 ring, 34.5 mm. **Series:** First **Subject:** 180th Anniversary of Federation **Obv:** National arms **Obv. Legend:** ESTADOS UNIDOS MEXICANOS **Rev:** State arms **Rev. Legend:** ESTADO DE MÉXICO **Edge:** Segmented reeding

Date	Mintage	F	VF	XF	Unc	BU
2004Mo Proof	1,000	Value: 750				

KM# 716   100 PESOS
33.9400 g., Bi-Metallic .925 Silver center in Brass ring, 39.04 mm. **Series:** First **Subject:** 180th Anniversary of Federation **Obv:** National arms **Obv. Legend:** ESTADOS UNIDOS MEXICANOS **Rev:** State arms **Rev. Legend:** ESTADO DE GUERRERO **Edge:** Segmented reeding

Date	Mintage	F	VF	XF	Unc	BU
2005Mo	248,850	—	—	—	35.00	40.00

KM# 818   100 PESOS
29.1690 g., Bi-Metallic .999 Gold 17.154g center in .999 Silver 12.015 ring, 34.5 mm. **Series:** First **Subject:** 180th Anniversary of Federation **Obv:** National arms **Obv. Legend:** ESTADOS UNIDOS MEXICANOS **Rev:** State arms **Rev. Legend:** ESTADO DE GUERRERO **Edge:** Segmented reeding

Date	Mintage	F	VF	XF	Unc	BU
2005Mo Proof	1,000	Value: 750				

KM# 713   100 PESOS
33.9400 g., Bi-Metallic .925 Silver 20.1753g center in Brass ring, 39.04 mm. **Series:** First **Subject:** 180th Anniversary of Federation **Obv:** National arms **Obv. Legend:** ESTADOS UNIDOS MEXICANOS **Rev:** Federal District arms **Rev. Legend:** DISTRITO FEDERAL **Edge:** Segmented reeding

Date	Mintage	F	VF	XF	Unc	BU
2005Mo	249,461	—	—	—	35.00	40.00

KM# 821   100 PESOS
29.1690 g., Bi-Metallic .999 Gold 17.154g center in .999 Silver 12.015g ring, 34.5 mm. **Series:** First **Subject:** 180th Anniversary of Federation **Obv:** National arms **Obv. Legend:** ESTADOS UNIDOS MEXICANOS **Rev:** Federal District arms **Rev. Legend:** DISTRITO FEDERAL **Edge:** Segmented reeding

Date	Mintage	F	VF	XF	Unc	BU
2005Mo Proof	1,000	Value: 750				

KM# 750   100 PESOS
33.9400 g., Bi-Metallic .925 Silver 20.1753g center in Aluminum-Bronze ring, 39.04 mm. **Series:** First **Subject:** 180th Anniversary of Federation **Obv:** National arms **Obv. Legend:** ESTADOS UNIDOS MEXICANOS **Rev:** State arms **Rev. Legend:** ESTADO DE JALISCO **Edge:** Segmented reeding

Date	Mintage	F	VF	XF	Unc	BU
2004Mo	249,115	—	—	—	35.00	40.00

KM# 816   100 PESOS
29.1690 g., Bi-Metallic .999 Gold 17.154g center in .999 Silver 12.015g ring, 34.5 mm. **Series:** First **Subject:** 180th Anniversary of Federation **Obv:** National arms **Obv. Legend:** ESTADOS UNIDOS MEXICANOS **Rev:** State arms **Rev. Legend:** ESTADO DE JALISCO **Edge:** Segmented reeding

Date	Mintage	F	VF	XF	Unc	BU
2004Mo Proof	1,000	Value: 750				

KM# 715   100 PESOS
33.9400 g., Bi-Metallic .925 Silver center in Brass ring, 39.04 mm. **Series:** First **Subject:** 180th Anniversary of Federation **Obv:** National arms **Obv. Legend:** ESTADOS UNIDOS MEXICANOS **Rev:** State arms **Rev. Legend:** ESTADO DE GUANAJUATO **Edge:** Segmented reeding

Date	Mintage	F	VF	XF	Unc	BU
2005Mo	249,489	—	—	—	35.00	40.00

KM# 819   100 PESOS
29.1690 g., Bi-Metallic .999 Gold 17.154g center in .999 Silver 12.015g ring, 34.5 mm. **Series:** First **Subject:** 180th Anniversary of Federation **Obv:** National arms **Obv. Legend:** ESTADOS UNIDOS MEXICANOS **Rev:** State arms **Rev. Legend:** ESTADO DE GUANAJUATO **Edge:** Segmented reeding

Date	Mintage	F	VF	XF	Unc	BU
2005Mo Proof	1,000	Value: 750				

KM# 754   100 PESOS
33.9400 g., Bi-Metallic .925 Silver 20.1753g center in Aluminum-Bronze ring, 39.04 mm. **Series:** First **Subject:** 180th Anniversary of Federation **Obv:** National arms **Obv. Legend:** ESTADOS UNIDOS MEXICANOS **Rev:** State arms **Rev. Legend:** ESTADO DE CHIHUAHUA **Edge:** Segmented reeding

Date	Mintage	F	VF	XF	Unc	BU
2005Mo	249,102	—	—	—	35.00	40.00

KM# 822   100 PESOS
29.1690 g., Bi-Metallic .999 Gold 17.154g center in .999 Silver 12.015g ring, 34.5 mm. **Series:** First **Subject:** 180th Anniversary of Federation **Obv:** National arms **Obv. Legend:** ESTADOS UNIDOS MEXICANOS **Rev:** State arms **Rev. Legend:** ESTADO DE CHIHUAHUA **Edge:** Segmented reeding

Date	Mintage	F	VF	XF	Unc	BU
2005Mo Proof	1,000	Value: 750				

KM# 717   100 PESOS
33.9400 g., Bi-Metallic .925 Silver center in Brass ring, 39.04 mm. **Series:** First **Subject:** 180th Anniversary of Federation **Obv:** National arms **Obv. Legend:** ESTADOS UNIDOS MEXICANOS **Rev:** State arms **Rev. Legend:** ESTADO DE HIDALGO **Edge:** Segmented reeding

Date	Mintage	F	VF	XF	Unc	BU
2005Mo	249,820	—	—	—	35.00	40.00

KM# 817   100 PESOS
29.1690 g., Bi-Metallic .999 Gold 17.154g center in .999 Silver 12.015g ring, 34.5 mm. **Series:** First **Subject:** 180th Anniversary of Federation **Obv:** National arms **Obv. Legend:** ESTADOS UNIDOS MEXICANOS **Rev:** State arms **Rev. Legend:** ESTADO DE HIDALGO **Edge:** Segmented reeding

Date	Mintage	F	VF	XF	Unc	BU
2005Mo Proof	1,000	Value: 750				

KM# 714   100 PESOS
33.9400 g., Bi-Metallic .925 Silver center in Brass ring, 39.04 mm. **Series:** First **Subject:** 180th Anniversary of Federation **Obv:** National arms **Obv. Legend:** ESTADOS UNIDOS MEXICANOS **Rev:** State arms **Rev. Legend:** ESTADO DE DURANGO **Edge:** Segmented reeding

Date	Mintage	F	VF	XF	Unc	BU
2005Mo	249,774	—	—	—	35.00	40.00

KM# 820   100 PESOS
29.1690 g., Bi-Metallic .999 Gold 17.154g center in .999 silver 12.015g ring, 34.5 mm. **Series:** First **Subject:** 180th Anniversary of Federation **Obv:** National arms **Obv. Legend:** ESTADOS UNIDOS MEXICANOS **Rev:** State arms **Rev. Legend:** ESTADO DE DURANGO **Edge:** Segmented reeding

Date	Mintage	F	VF	XF	Unc	BU
2005Mo Proof	1,000	Value: 750				

KM# 712   100 PESOS
33.9400 g., Bi-Metallic .925 Silver 20.1753g center in Brass ring, 39.04 mm. **Series:** First **Subject:** 180th Anniversary of Federation **Obv:** National arms **Obv. Legend:** ESTADOS UNIDOS MEXICANOS **Rev:** State arms **Rev. Legend:** ESTADO DE CHIAPAS **Edge:** Segmented reeding

Date	Mintage	F	VF	XF	Unc	BU
2005Mo	249,417	—	—	—	35.00	40.00

KM# 823   100 PESOS
29.1690 g., Bi-Metallic .999 Gold 17.154g center in .999 Silver 12.015g ring, 34.5 mm. **Series:** First **Subject:** 180th Anniversary of Federation **Obv:** National arms **Obv. Legend:** ESTADOS UNIDOS MEXICANOS **Rev:** State arms **Rev. Legend:** ESTADO DE CHIAPAS **Edge:** Segmented reeding

Date	Mintage	F	VF	XF	Unc	BU
2005Mo Proof	1,000	Value: 750				

KM# 729   100 PESOS
33.8250 g., Bi-Metallic .925 Silver 20.1753g center in Aluminum-Bronze ring, 39.04 mm. **Series:** First **Subject:** 180th Anniversary of Federation **Obv:** National arms **Obv. Legend:** ESTADOS UNIDOS MEXICANOS **Rev:** State arms **Rev. Legend:** ESTADO DE COLIMA **Edge:** Segmented reeding

Date	Mintage	F	VF	XF	Unc	BU
2005Mo	248,850	—	—	—	35.00	40.00

KM# 824   100 PESOS
29.1690 g., Bi-Metallic .999 Gold 17.154g center in .999 Silver 12.015g ring, 34.5 mm. **Series:** First **Subject:** 180th Anniversary of Federation **Obv:** National arms **Obv. Legend:** ESTADOS UNIDOS MEXICANOS **Rev:** State arms **Rev. Legend:** ESTADO DE COLIMA **Edge:** Segmented reeding

Date	Mintage	F	VF	XF	Unc	BU
2005Mo Proof	1,000	Value: 750				

KM# 752   100 PESOS
33.9400 g., Bi-Metallic .925 Silver 20.1753g center in Aluminum-Bronze ring, 39.04 mm. **Series:** First **Subject:** 180th Anniversary of Federation **Obv:** National arms **Obv. Legend:** ESTADOS UNIDOS MEXICANOS **Rev:** State arms **Rev. Legend:** ESTADO DE COAHUILA DE ZARAGOZA **Edge:** Segmented reeding

Date	Mintage	F	VF	XF	Unc	BU
2005Mo	247,991	—	—	—	35.00	40.00

KM# 825   100 PESOS
29.1690 g., Bi-Metallic .999 Gold 17.154g center in .999 Silver 12.015g ring, 34.5 mm. **Series:** First **Subject:** 180th Anniversary of Federation **Obv:** National arms **Obv. Legend:** ESTADOS UNIDOS MEXICANOS **Rev:** State arms **Rev. Legend:** ESTADO DE COAHUILA DE ZARAGOZA **Edge:** Segmented reeding

Date	Mintage	F	VF	XF	Unc	BU
2005Mo Proof	1,000	Value: 825				

KM# 727   100 PESOS
33.9400 g., Bi-Metallic .925 Silver 20.1753g center in Aluminum-Bronze ring, 39.04 mm. **Series:** First **Subject:** 180th Anniversary of Federation **Obv:** National arms **Obv. Legend:** ESTADOS UNIDOS MEXICANOS **Rev:** State arms **Rev. Legend:** ESTADO DE CAMPECHE **Edge:** Segmented reeding

Date	Mintage	F	VF	XF	Unc	BU
2005Mo	249,040	—	—	—	35.00	40.00

KM# 826   100 PESOS
29.1690 g., Bi-Metallic .999 Gold 17.154g center in .999 Silver 12.015g ring, 34.5 mm. **Series:** First **Subject:** 180th Anniversary of Federation **Obv:** National arms **Obv. Legend:** ESTADOS UNIDOS MEXICANOS **Rev:** State arms **Rev. Legend:** ESTADO DE CAMPECHE **Edge:** Segmented reeding

Date	Mintage	F	VF	XF	Unc	BU
2005Mo Proof	1,000	Value: 750				

KM# 725   100 PESOS
33.9400 g., Bi-Metallic .925 Silver 20.1753g center in Aluminum-Bronze ring, 39.04 mm. **Series:** First **Subject:** 180th Anniversary of Federation **Obv:** National arms **Obv. Legend:** ESTADOS UNIDOS MEXICANOS **Rev:** State arms **Rev. Legend:** ESTADO DE BAJA CALIFORNIA SUR **Edge:** Segmented reeding

Date	Mintage	F	VF	XF	Unc	BU
2005Mo	249,585	—	—	—	35.00	40.00

KM# 827   100 PESOS
29.1690 g., Bi-Metallic .999 Gold 17.154g center in .999 Silver 12.015g ring, 34.5 mm. **Series:** First **Subject:** 180th Anniversary of Federation **Obv:** National arms **Obv. Legend:** ESTADOS UNIDOS MEXICANOS **Rev:** State arms **Rev. Legend:** ESTADO DE BAJA CALIFORNIA SUR **Edge:** Segmented reeding

Date	Mintage	F	VF	XF	Unc	BU
2005Mo Proof	—	Value: 750				

KM# 723   100 PESOS
33.9400 g., Bi-Metallic .925 Silver 20.1753g center in Aluminum-Bronze ring, 39.04 mm. **Series:** First **Subject:** 180th Anniversary of Federation **Obv:** National arms **Obv. Legend:** ESTADOS UNIDOS MEXICANOS **Rev:** State arms **Rev. Legend:** ESTADO DE BAJA CALIFORNIA **Edge:** Segmented reeding

Date	Mintage	F	VF	XF	Unc	BU
2005Mo	249,263	—	—	—	35.00	40.00

KM# 828   100 PESOS
29.1690 g., Bi-Metallic .999 Gold 17.154g center in .999 Silver 12.015g ring, 34.5 mm. **Series:** First **Subject:** 180th Anniversary of Federation **Obv:** National arms **Obv. Legend:** ESTADOS UNIDOS MEXICANOS **Rev:** State arms **Rev. Legend:** ESTADO DE BAJA CALIFORNIA **Edge:** Segmented reeding

Date	Mintage	F	VF	XF	Unc	BU
2005Mo Proof	1,000	Value: 750				

KM# 721   100 PESOS
33.9400 g., Bi-Metallic .925 Silver 20.1753g center in Aluminum-Bronze ring, 39.04 mm. **Series:** First **Subject:** 180th Anniversary of Federation **Obv:** National arms **Obv. Legend:** ESTADOS UNIDOS MEXICANOS **Rev:** Estados de Aguascalientes state arms **Rev. Legend:** ESTADO DE AGUASCALIENTES **Edge:** Segmented reeding

Date	Mintage	F	VF	XF	Unc	BU
2005Mo	248,410	—	—	—	35.00	40.00

KM# 829   100 PESOS
29.1690 g., Bi-Metallic .999 Gold 17.154g center in .999 Silver 12.015g ring, 34.5 mm. **Series:** First **Subject:** 180th Anniversary of Federation **Obv:** National arms **Obv. Legend:** ESTADOS UNIDOS MEXICANOS **Rev:** State arms **Rev. Legend:** ESTADO DE AGUASCALIENTES **Edge:** Segmented reeding

Date	Mintage	F	VF	XF	Unc	BU
2005Mo Proof	1,000	Value: 750				

KM# 719   100 PESOS
33.8250 g., Bi-Metallic .925 Silver 20.1753g center in Aluminum-Bronze ring, 39.04 mm. **Series:** Second **Obv:** National arms **Obv. Legend:** ESTADOS UNIDOS MEXICANOS **Rev:** Facade of the San Marcos garden above sculpture of national emblem at left, San Antonio Temple at right **Rev. Legend:** AGUASCALIENTES **Edge:** Segmented reeding

Date	Mintage	F	VF	XF	Unc	BU
2005Mo	149,705	—	—	—	25.00	30.00

KM# 862   100 PESOS
29.1690 g., Bi-Metallic .999 Gold 17.154g center in .999 Silver 12.015g ring, 34.5 mm. **Series:** Second **Obv:** National arms **Obv. Legend:** ESTADOS UNIDOS MEXICANOS **Rev:** Facade of the San Marcos garden above sculpture of national emblem at left, San Antonio temple at right **Rev. Legend:** AGUASCALUENTES **Edge:** Segmented reeding

Date	Mintage	F	VF	XF	Unc	BU
2005Mo Proof	600	Value: 750				

KM# 758   100 PESOS
33.9400 g., Bi-Metallic .925 Silver 20.1753g center in Aluminum-Bronze ring, 39.04 mm. **Series:** Second **Obv:** National arms **Obv. Legend:** ESTADOS UNIDOS MEXICANOS **Rev:** Ram's head and value within circle **Rev. Legend:** BAJA CALIFORNIA - GOBIERNO DEL ESTADO **Edge:** Segmented reeding

Date	Mintage	F	VF	XF	Unc	BU
2005Mo	—	—	—	—	25.00	30.00

KM# 863   100 PESOS
29.1690 g., Bi-Metallic .999 Gold 17.154g center in .999 Silver 12.015g ring, 34.5 mm. **Series:** Second **Obv:** National arms **Obv. Legend:** ESTTADOS UNIDOS MEXICANOS **Rev:** Ram's head, mountain outline in background **Rev. Legend:** BAJA CALIFORNIA - GOBIERNO DEL ESTADO **Edge:** Segmented reeding

Date	Mintage	F	VF	XF	Unc	BU
2005Mo Proof	600	Value: 750				

KM# 762   100 PESOS
33.9400 g., Bi-Metallic .925 Silver 20.175g center in Aluminum-Bronze ring, 39.04 mm. **Series:** Second **Obv:** National arms **Obv. Legend:** ESTADOS UNIDOS MEXICANOS **Rev:** Outlined map of peninsula at center, cave painting of deer behind, cactus at right **Rev. Legend:** ESTADO DE BAJA CALIFORNIA SUR **Edge:** Segmented reeding

Date	Mintage	F	VF	XF	Unc	BU
2005Mo	149,152	—	—	—	25.00	30.00

KM# 864 100 PESOS

29.1690 g., Bi-Metallic .999 Gold 17.154g center in .999 Silver 12.015g ring, 34.5 mm. **Series:** Second **Obv:** National arms **Obv. Legend:** ESTADOS UNIDOS MEXICANOS **Rev:** Outlined map of peninsula at center, cave painting of deer behind, cactus at right **Rev. Legend:** ESTADO DE BAJA CALIFORNIA SUR **Edge:** Segmented reeding

Date	Mintage	F	VF	XF	Unc	BU
2006Mo Proof	600	Value: 750				

KM# 760 100 PESOS

33.9400 g., Bi-Metallic .925 Silver 20.1753g center in Aluminum-Bronze ring, 39.04 mm. **Series:** Second **Subject:** Estado de Campeche **Obv:** National arms **Obv. Legend:** ESTADOS UNIDOS MEXICANOS **Rev:** Jade mask - Calakmul, Campeche **Rev. Legend:** ESTADO DE CAMPECHE **Edge:** Segmented reeding

Date	Mintage	F	VF	XF	Unc	BU
2006Mo	—	—	—	—	25.00	30.00

KM# 865 100 PESOS

29.1690 g., Bi-Metallic .999 Gold 17.154g center in .999 Silver 12.015g ring, 34.5 mm. **Series:** Second **Obv:** National arms **Obv. Legend:** ESTADOS UNIDOS MEXICANOS **Rev:** Jade mask - Calakmul, Campeche **Rev. Legend:** ESTADO DE CAMPECHE **Edge:** Segmented reeding

Date	Mintage	F	VF	XF	Unc	BU
2006Mo Proof	600	Value: 750				

KM# 781 100 PESOS

33.7000 g., Bi-Metallic .925 Silver 20.1753g center in Aluminum-Bronze ring, 39.04 mm. **Series:** Second **Obv:** National arms **Obv. Legend:** ESTADOS UNIDOS MEXICANOS **Rev:** Outlined map with turtle, mine cart above grapes at center, Friendship Dam above Christ of the Nodas at left, chimneys above crucibles and bell tower of Santiago's cathedral at right **Rev. Legend:** COAHUILA DE ZARAGOZA **Edge:** Segmented reeding

Date	Mintage	F	VF	XF	Unc	BU
2006Mo	—	—	—	—	25.00	30.00

KM# 866 100 PESOS

29.1690 g., Bi-Metallic .999 Gold 17.154g center in .999 Silver 12.015g ring, 34.5 mm. **Series:** Second **Obv:** National arms **Obv. Legend:** ESTADOS UNIDOS MEXICANOS **Rev:** Outlined map with turtle, mine cart above grapes at center, Friendship dam above Christ of the Nodas at left, chimneys above crucibles and bell tower of Santiago's cathedral at right **Rev. Inscription:** COAHUILA DE ZARAGOZA **Edge:** Segmented reeding

Date	Mintage	F	VF	XF	Unc	BU
2006Mo Proof	600	Value: 750				

KM# 777 100 PESOS

33.9400 g., Bi-Metallic .925 Silver 20.1753g center in Aluminum-Bronze ring, 39.04 mm. **Series:** Second **Obv:** National arms **Obv. Legend:** ESTADOS UNIDOS MEXICANOS **Rev:** State arms at lower center, Nevado de Colima and Volcan de Fuego volcanos in background **Rev. Legend:** Colima **Rev. Inscription:** GENEROSO **Edge:** Segmented reeding

Date	Mintage	F	VF	XF	Unc	BU
2006Mo	149,041	—	—	—	25.00	30.00

KM# 867 100 PESOS

29.1690 g., Bi-Metallic .999 Gold 17.154g center in .999 Silver 12.015g ring, 34.5 mm. **Series:** Second **Obv:** National arms **Obv. Legend:** ESTADOS UNIDOS MEXICANOS **Rev:** State arms at lower center, Nevado de Colima and Volcan de Fuego volcanos in background **Rev. Legend:** Colima **Rev. Inscription:** GENEROSO **Edge:** Segmented reeding

Date	Mintage	F	VF	XF	Unc	BU
2006Mo Proof	600	Value: 750				

KM# 773 100 PESOS

33.9400 g., Bi-Metallic .925 Silver 20.1753g center in Aluminum-Bronze ring, 39.04 mm. **Series:** Second **Obv:** National arms **Obv. Legend:** ESTADOS UNIDOS MEXICANOS **Rev:** Head of Pakal, ancient Mayan king, Palenque **Rev. Legend:** ESTADO DE CHIAPAS - CABEZA MAYA DEL REY PAKAL, PALENQUE **Edge:** Segmented reeding

Date	Mintage	F	VF	XF	Unc	BU
2006Mo	149,491	—	—	—	25.00	30.00

KM# 868 100 PESOS

29.1690 g., Bi-Metallic .999 Gold 17.154g center in .999 Silver 12.015g ring, 34.5 mm. **Series:** Second **Obv:** National arms **Obv. Legend:** ESTADOS UNIDOS MEXICANOS **Rev:** Head of Pakal, ancient Mayan king, Palenque **Rev. Legend:** ESTADO DE CHIAPAS - CABEZA MAYA DEL REY PAKAL, PALENQUE **Edge:** Segmented reeding

Date	Mintage	F	VF	XF	Unc	BU
2006Mo Proof	600	Value: 750				

KM# 775 100 PESOS

33.9400 g., Bi-Metallic .925 Silver 20.1753g center in Aluminum-Bronze ring, 39.04 mm. **Series:** Second **Obv:** National arms **Obv. Legend:** ESTADOS UNIDOS MEXICANOS **Rev:** Angel of Liberty **Rev. Legend:** MÉXICO - ANGEL DE LA LIBERTAD, CHIHUAHUA **Edge:** Segmented reeding

Date	Mintage	F	VF	XF	Unc	BU
2006Mo	149,557	—	—	—	25.00	30.00

KM# 869 100 PESOS

29.1690 g., Bi-Metallic .999 Gold 17.154g center in .999 Silver 12.015g ring, 34.5 mm. **Series:** Second **Obv:** National arms **Obv. Legend:** ESTADOS UNIDOS MEXICANOS **Rev:** Angel of Liberty **Rev. Legend:** MÉXICO - ANGEL DE LA LIBERTAD, CHIHUAHUA **Edge:** Segmented reeding

Date	Mintage	F	VF	XF	Unc	BU
2006Mo Proof	600	Value: 750				

KM# 779 100 PESOS

33.9400 g., Bi-Metallic .925 Silver 20.1753g center in Aluminum-Bronze ring, 39.04 mm. **Series:** Second **Obv:** National arms **Obv. Legend:** ESTADOS UNIDOS MEXICANOS **Rev:** National Palace **Rev. Legend:** DISTRITO FEDERAL - ANTIGUO AYUNTAMIENTO **Edge:** Segmented reeding

Date	Mintage	F	VF	XF	Unc	BU
2006Mo	149,525	—	—	—	25.00	30.00

KM# 870 100 PESOS

29.1690 g., Bi-Metallic .999 Gold 17.154g center in .999 Silver 12.015g ring, 34.5 mm. **Series:** Second **Obv:** National arms **Obv. Legend:** ESTADOS UNIDOS MEXICANOS **Rev:** National palace **Rev. Legend:** DISTRITO FEDERAL - ANTIGUO AYUNTAMIENTO **Edge:** Segmented reeding

Date	Mintage	F	VF	XF	Unc	BU
2006Mo Proof	600	Value: 750				

KM# 787 100 PESOS

33.9400 g., Bi-Metallic .925 Silver 20.1753g center in Brass ring, 39.04 mm. **Series:** Second **Obv:** National arms **Obv. Legend:** ESTADOS UNIDOS MEXICANOS **Rev:** Tree **Rev. Legend:** PRIMERA RESERVA NACIONAL FORESTAL - DURANGO **Edge:** Segmented reeding

Date	Mintage	F	VF	XF	Unc	BU
2006Mo	149,034	—	—	—	25.00	30.00

KM# 871 100 PESOS

29.1690 g., Bi-Metallic .999 Gold 17.154g center in .999 Silver 12.015g ring, 34.5 mm. **Series:** Second **Obv:** National arms **Obv. Legend:** ESYADOS UNIDOS MEXICANOS **Rev:** Tree **Rev. Legend:** PRIMERA RESERVA NACIONAL RORESTAL - DURANGO **Edge:** Segmented reeding

Date	Mintage	F	VF	XF	Unc	BU
2006Mo Proof	600	Value: 750				

KM# 789 100 PESOS

33.9400 g., Bi-Metallic .925 Silver 20.1753g center in Brass ring, 39.04 mm. **Series:** Second **Obv:** National arms **Obv. Legend:** ESTADOS UNIDOS MEXICANOS **Rev:** State arms at center, statue of Miguel Hidalgo at left, monument to Pipla at lower right **Rev. Inscription:** Guanajuato **Edge:** Segmented reeding

Date	Mintage	F	VF	XF	Unc	BU
2006Mo	149,921	—	—	—	25.00	30.00

KM# 872 100 PESOS

29.1690 g., Bi-Metallic .999 Gold 17.154g center in .999 Silver 12.015g ring, 34.50 mm. **Series:** Second **Obv:** National arms **Obv. Legend:** ESTADOS UNIDOS MEXICANOS **Rev:** State arms at lower center, statue of Miguel Hidalgo at left, monument to Pipila at lower right **Rev. Inscription:** Guanajauto **Edge:** Segmented reeding

Date	Mintage	F	VF	XF	Unc	BU
2006Mo Proof	600	Value: 750				

KM# 791   100 PESOS

33.9400 g., Bi-Metallic .925 Silver 20.1753g center in Brass ring, 39.04 mm.   **Series:** Second **Obv:** National arms **Obv. Legend:** ESTADOS UNIDOS MEXICANOS **Rev:** Stylized portrait of Vicente Guerrero at left, church of Taxco at upper center, Acapulco's la Quebrada with diver above Christmas Eve flower and mask **Rev. Legend:** GUERRERO **Edge:** Segmented reeding

Date	Mintage	F	VF	XF	Unc	BU
2006Mo	149,675	—	—	—	25.00	30.00

KM# 873   100 PESOS

29.1690 g., Bi-Metallic .999 Gold 17.154g center in .999 Silver 12.015g ring, 34.5 mm.   **Series:** Second **Obv:** National arms **Obv. Legend:** ESTADOS UNIDOS MEXICANOS **Rev:** Stylized portrait of Vicente Guerrero at left, church of Taxco at upper center, Acapulco's la Quebrada with diver over Christmas Eve flower and mask **Rev. Legend:** GUERRERO **Edge:** Segmented reeding

Date	Mintage	F	VF	XF	Unc	BU
2006Mo Proof	600	Value: 750				

KM# 793   100 PESOS

33.9400 g., Bi-Metallic .925 Silver 20.1753g center in Aluminum-Bronze ring, 39.04 mm.   **Series:** Second **Obv:** National arms **Obv. Legend:** ESTADOS UNIDOS MEXICANOS **Rev:** Monument of Pachuca Hidalgo **Rev. Inscription:** *RELOJ / MONUMENTAL / DE / PACHUCA / HIDALGO - La / Bella / Airosa* **Edge:** Segmented reeding

Date	Mintage	F	VF	XF	Unc	BU
2006Mo	149,273	—	—	—	25.00	30.00

KM# 874   100 PESOS

29.1690 g., Bi-Metallic .999 Gold 17.154g center in .999 Silver 12.015g ring, 34.5 mm.   **Series:** Second **Obv:** National arms **Obv. Legend:** ESTADOS UNIDOS MEXICANOS **Rev:** Monument of Pachuca Hidalgo **Rev. Inscription:** *RELOJ / MONUMENTAL / DE / PACHUCA / HIDALGO* **Edge:** Segmented reeding

Date	Mintage	F	VF	XF	Unc	BU
2006Mo Proof	600	Value: 750				

KM# 795   100 PESOS

33.9400 g., Bi-Metallic .925 Silver 20.1753g center in Brass ring, 39.04 mm.   **Series:** Second **Obv:** National arms **Obv. Legend:** ESTADOS UNIDOS MEXICANOS **Rev:** Hospicio Cabañas orphanage **Rev. Legend:** ESTADO DE JALISCO **Edge:** Segmented reeding

Date	Mintage	F	VF	XF	Unc	BU
2006Mo	149,750	—	—	—	25.00	30.00

KM# 875   100 PESOS

29.1690 g., Bi-Metallic .999 Gold 17.154g center in .999 Silver 12.015g ring, 34.5 mm.   **Series:** Second **Obv:** National arms **Obv. Legend:** ESTADOS UNIDOS MEXICANOS **Rev:** Hospicio Cabañas orphanage **Rev. Legend:** ESTADO DE JALISCO **Edge:** Segmented reeding

Date	Mintage	F	VF	XF	Unc	BU
2006Mo Proof	600	Value: 750				

KM# 802   100 PESOS

33.9400 g., Bi-Metallic .925 Silver 20.1753g center in Aluminum-Bronze ring, 33.7, 39.04 mm.   **Series:** Second **Obv:** National arms **Obv. Legend:** ESTADOS UNIDOS MEXICANOS **Rev:** Pyramid de la Loona (moon) **Rev. Legend:** ESTADO DE MÉXICO **Edge:** Segmented reeding

Date	Mintage	F	VF	XF	Unc	BU
2006Mo	149,377	—	—	—	25.00	30.00

KM# 876   100 PESOS

29.1690 g., Bi-Metallic .999 Gold 17.154g center in .999 Silver 12.015g ring, 34.5 mm.   **Series:** Second **Obv:** National arms **Obv. Legend:** ESTADOS UNIDOS MEXICANOS **Rev:** Pyramid de la Looona (moon) **Rev. Legend:** ESTADO DE MÉXICO **Edge:** Segmented reeding

Date	Mintage	F	VF	XF	Unc	BU
2006Mo Proof	600	Value: 750				

KM# 785   100 PESOS

33.9400 g., Bi-Metallic .925 Silver 20.1753g center in Aluminum-Bronze ring, 33.7, 39.04 mm.   **Series:** Second **Obv:** National arms **Obv. Legend:** ESTADOS UNIDOS MEXICANOS **Rev:** Four Monarch butterflies **Rev. Legend:** ESTADO DE MICHOACÁN **Edge:** Segmented reeding

Date	Mintage	F	VF	XF	Unc	BU
2006Mo	149,730	—	—	—	25.00	30.00

KM# 877   100 PESOS

29.1690 g., Bi-Metallic .999 Gold 17.154g center in .999 Silver 12.015g ring, 34.5 mm.   **Series:** Second **Obv:** National arms **Obv. Legend:** ESTADOS UNIDOS MEXICANOS **Rev:** Four Monarch butterflies **Rev. Legend:** ESTADO DE MICHOACÁN **Edge:** Segmented reeding

Date	Mintage	F	VF	XF	Unc	BU
2006Mo Proof	600	Value: 750				

KM# 800   100 PESOS

33.9400 g., Bi-Metallic .925 Silver 20.1753g center in Aluminum-Bronze ring, 33.7, 39.04 mm.   **Series:** Second **Obv:** National arms **Obv. Legend:** ESTADOS UNIDOS MEXICANOS **Rev:** 1/2 length figure of Chinelo (local dancer) at right, Palacio de Cortes in background **Rev. Inscription:** ESTADO DE / MORELOS **Edge:** Segmented reeding

Date	Mintage	F	VF	XF	Unc	BU
2006Mo	149,648	—	—	—	25.00	30.00

KM# 878   100 PESOS

29.1690 g., Bi-Metallic .999 Gold 17.154g center in .999 Silver 12.015g ring, 34.5 mm.   **Series:** Second **Obv:** National arms **Obv. Legend:** ESTADOS UNIDOS MEXICANOS **Rev:** 1/2 length figure of Chinelo (local dancer) at right, Palacio de Cortes in background **Rev. Inscription:** ESTADO DE / MORELOS **Edge:** Segmented reeding

Date	Mintage	F	VF	XF	Unc	BU
2006Mo Proof	600	Value: 750				

KM# 798   100 PESOS

33.9400 g., 33.8250 Bi-Metallic 0.925 Silver 20.1753g center in Aluminum-Bronze ring 36.908 oz., 39.04 mm.   **Series:** Second **Obv:** National arms **Obv. Legend:** ESTADOS UNIDOS MEXICANOS **Rev:** Isle de Mexcaltitlán **Rev. Legend:** ESTADO DE NAYARIT **Edge:** Segmented reeding

Date	Mintage	F	VF	XF	Unc	BU
2007Mo	149,560	—	—	—	25.00	30.00

KM# 879   100 PESOS

29.1690 g., Bi-Metallic .999 Gold 17.154g center in .999 12.015g ring, 34.5 mm.   **Series:** Second **Obv:** National arms **Obv. Legend:** ESTADOS UNIDOS MEXICANOS **Rev:** Isle de Mexcaltitlán **Rev. Legend:** ESTADO DE NAYARIT **Edge:** Segmented reeding

Date	Mintage	F	VF	XF	Unc	BU
2007Mo Proof	600	Value: 750				

KM# 848   100 PESOS

33.9400 g., Bi-Metallic .925 Silver 20.1753 center in Aluminum-Bronze ring, 39.04 mm.   **Series:** Second **Obv:** National arms **Obv. Legend:** ESTADOS UNIDOS MEXICANOS **Rev:** Old foundry in Parque Fundidora (public park) at right, Cerro de la Silla (Saddle Hill) in background **Rev. Legend:** ESTADO DE NUEVO LÉON **Edge:** Segmented reeding

Date	Mintage	F	VF	XF	Unc	BU
2007Mo	149,425	—	—	—	25.00	30.00

KM# 880   100 PESOS

29.1690 g., Bi-Metallic .999 Gold 17.154g center in .999 Silver 12.015g ring, 34.5 mm.   **Series:** Second **Obv:** National arms **Obv. Legend:** ESTADOS UNIDOS MEXICANOS **Rev:** Old foundry in Parque Fundidora (public park) at right, Cerro de la Silla (Saddle hill) in background **Rev. Legend:** ESTADO DE NUEVO LÉON **Edge:** Segmented reeding

Date	Mintage	F	VF	XF	Unc	BU
2007Mo Proof	600	Value: 750				

KM# 849   100 PESOS

33.9400 g., Bi-Metallic .925 Silver 20.1753g center in Aluminum-Bronze ring, 39.04 mm.   **Series:** Second **Obv:** National arms **Obv. Legend:** ESTADOS UNIDOS MEXICANOS **Rev:** Teatro Macedonio Alcala (theater) **Rev. Legend:** OAXACA **Edge:** Segmented reeding

Date	Mintage	F	VF	XF	Unc	BU
2007Mo	149,892	—	—	—	25.00	30.00

KM# 881   100 PESOS

29.1690 g., Bi-Metallic .999 Gold 17.154g center in .999 Silver 12.015g ring, 34.50 mm.   **Series:** Second **Obv:** National arms **Obv. Legend:** ESTADOS UNIDOS MEXICANOS **Rev:** Teatro Macedonio Alcala (theater) **Rev. Legend:** OAXACA **Edge:** Segmented reeding

Date	Mintage	F	VF	XF	Unc	BU
2007Mo Proof	600	Value: 750				

KM# 850 100 PESOS
33.9400 g., Bi-Metallic .925 Silver 20.1753g center in Aluminum-Bronze ring, 39.04 mm. **Series:** Second **Obv:** National arms **Obv. Legend:** ESTADOS UNIDOS MEXICANOS **Rev:** Talavera porcelain dish **Rev. Legend:** ESTADO DE PUEBLA **Edge:** Segmented reeding

Date	Mintage	F	VF	XF	Unc	BU
2007Mo	149,474	—	—	—	25.00	30.00

KM# 882 100 PESOS
29.1690 g., Bi-Metallic .999 Gold 17.154g center in .999 Silver 12.015g ring, 34.5 mm. **Series:** Second **Obv:** National arms **Obv. Legend:** ESTADOS UNIDOS MEXICANOS **Rev:** Talavera porcelain dish **Rev. Legend:** ESTADO DE PUEBLA **Edge:** Segmented reeding

Date	Mintage	F	VF	XF	Unc	BU
2007Mo Proof	600	Value: 750				

KM# 853 100 PESOS
33.9400 g., Bi-Metallic .925 Silver 20.1753g center in Aluminum-Bronze ring, 39.04 mm. **Series:** Second **Obv:** National arms **Obv. Legend:** ESTADOS UNIDOS MEXICANOS **Rev:** Facade of Caja Real **Rev. Legend:** • SAN LUIS POTOSÍ • **Edge:** Segmented reeding

Date	Mintage	F	VF	XF	Unc	BU
2007Mo	148,750	—	—	—	25.00	30.00

KM# 885 100 PESOS
29.1690 g., Bi-Metallic .999 Gold 17.154g center in .999 Silver 12.015 ring, 34.5 mm. **Series:** Second **Obv:** National arms **Obv. Legend:** ESTADOS UNIDOS MEXICANOS **Rev:** Facade of Caja Real **Rev. Legend:** • SAN LUIS POTOSÍ • **Edge:** Segmented reeding

Date	Mintage	F	VF	XF	Unc	BU
2007Mo Proof	600	Value: 750				

KM# 856 100 PESOS
33.9400 g., Bi-Metallic .925 Silver 20.1753 center in Aluminum-Bronze ring, 39.04 mm. **Series:** Second **Obv:** National arms **Obv. Legend:** ESTADOS UNIDOS MEXICANOS **Rev:** Fuente de los Pescadores (fisherman fountain) at lower left, giant head from the Olmec-pre-Hispanic culture at right, Planetario Tabasco in background **Rev. Legend:** TABASCO **Edge:** Segmented reeding

Date	Mintage	F	VF	XF	Unc	BU
2007Mo	149,715	—	—	—	25.00	30.00

KM# 888 100 PESOS
29.1690 g., Bi-Metallic .999 Gold 17.154g center in .999 Silver 12.015g ring, 34.5 mm. **Series:** Second **Obv:** National arms **Obv. Legend:** ESTADOS UNIDOS MEXICANOS **Rev:** Fuente de los Pescadores (fisherman fountain) at lower left, giant head from the Olmec-pre-Hispanic culture at right, Planetario Tabasco in background **Rev. Legend:** TABASCO **Edge:** Segmented reeding

Date	Mintage	F	VF	XF	Unc	BU
2007Mo Proof	600	Value: 750				

KM# 851 100 PESOS
33.9400 g., Bi-Metallic .925 Silver 20.1753g center in Aluminum-Bronze ring, 39.04 mm. **Series:** Second **Obv:** National arms **Obv. Legend:** ESTADOS UNIDOS MEXICANOS **Rev:** Mask at left, rays above state arms at center, Mayan ruins at right **Rev. Legend:** QUINTANA ROO **Edge:** Segmented reeding

Date	Mintage	F	VF	XF	Unc	BU
2007Mo	149,582	—	—	—	25.00	30.00

KM# 883 100 PESOS
29.1690 g., Bi-Metallic .999 Gold 17.154g center in .999 Silver 12.015g ring, 34.5 mm. **Series:** Second **Obv:** National arms **Obv. Legend:** ESTADOS UNIDOS MEXICANOS **Rev:** Mask at left, rays above state arms at center, Mayan ruins at right **Rev. Legend:** QUINTANA ROO **Edge:** Segmented reeding

Date	Mintage	F	VF	XF	Unc	BU
2007Mo Proof	600	Value: 750				

KM# 854 100 PESOS
33.9400 g., Bi-Metallic .925 Silver 20.1753g center in Aluminum-Bronze ring, 39.04 mm. **Series:** Second **Obv:** National arms **Obv. Legend:** ESTADOS UNIDOS MEXICANOS **Rev:** Shield on pile of cactus fruits **Rev. Legend:** ESTADO DE SINALOA - LUGAR DE PITAHAYAS **Edge:** Segmented reeding

Date	Mintage	F	VF	XF	Unc	BU
2007Mo	149,032	—	—	—	25.00	30.00

KM# 886 100 PESOS
29.1690 g., Bi-Metallic .999 Gold 17.154 center in .999 Silver 12.015g ring, 34.5 mm. **Series:** Second **Obv:** National arms **Obv. Legend:** ESTADOS UNIDOS MEXICANOS **Rev:** Shield on pile of cactus fruits **Rev. Legend:** ESTADO DE SINALOA - LUGAR DE PITAHAYES **Edge:** Segmented reeding

Date	Mintage	F	VF	XF	Unc	BU
2007Mo Proof	600	Value: 750				

KM# 857 100 PESOS
33.9400 g., Bi-Metallic .925 Silver 20.1753g center in Aluminum-Bronze ring, 39.04 mm. **Series:** Second **Obv:** National arms **Obv. Legend:** ESTADOS UNIDOS MEXICANOS **Rev:** Ridge - Cerro Del Bernal, Gonzáles **Rev. Legend:** TAMAULIPAS **Edge:** Segmented reeding

Date	Mintage	F	VF	XF	Unc	BU
2007Mo	149,776	—	—	—	25.00	30.00

KM# 889 100 PESOS
29.1690 g., Bi-Metallic .999 Gold 17.154g center in .999 Silver 12.015g ring, 34.5 mm. **Series:** Second **Obv:** National arms **Obv. Legend:** ESTADOS DE MEXICANOS **Rev:** Ridge - Cerro Del Bernal, Gonzáles **Rev. Legend:** TAMAULIPAS **Edge:** Segmented reeding

Date	Mintage	F	VF	XF	Unc	BU
2007Mo Proof	600	Value: 750				

KM# 852 100 PESOS
33.9400 g., Bi-Metallic .925 Silver 20.1753 center in Aluminum-Bronze ring, 39.04 mm. **Series:** Second **Obv:** National arms **Obv. Legend:** ESTADOS UNIDOS MEXICANOS **Rev:** Aqueduct of Querétaro at left, church of Santa Rosa de Viterbo at right **Rev. Legend:** ESTADO DE QUERÉTARO ARTEAGA **Edge:** Segmented reeding

Date	Mintage	F	VF	XF	Unc	BU
2007Mo	149,127	—	—	—	25.00	30.00

KM# 884 100 PESOS
29.1690 g., Bi-Metallic .999 Gold 17.154g center in .999 Silver 12.015g ring, 34.5 mm. **Series:** Second **Obv:** National arms **Obv. Legend:** ESTADOS UNIDOS MEXICANOS **Rev:** Aqueduct of Querétaro at left, church of Santa Rosa de Viterbo at right **Rev. Legend:** ESTADO DE QUERÉTARO ARTEAGA **Edge:** Segmented reeding

Date	Mintage	F	VF	XF	Unc	BU
2007Mo Proof	600	—	—	—	—	750

KM# 855 100 PESOS
33.9400 g., Bi-Metallic .925 Silver 20.1753g center in Aluminum-Bronze ring, 39.04 mm. **Series:** Second **Obv:** National arms **Obv. Legend:** ESTADOS UNIDOS MEXICANOS **Rev:** Local in Dance of the Deer at left, cactus at right, mountains in background **Rev. Legend:** ESTADO DE SONORA **Edge:** Segmented reeding

Date	Mintage	F	VF	XF	Unc	BU
2007Mo	149,891	—	—	—	25.00	30.00

KM# 887 100 PESOS
29.1690 g., Bi-Metallic .999 Gold 17.154g center in .999 Silver 12.015g ring, 34.5 mm. **Series:** Second **Obv:** National arms **Obv. Legend:** ESTADOS UNIDOS MEXICANOS **Rev:** Local in Dance of the Deer at left, cactus at right, mountains in background **Rev. Legend:** ESTADO DE SONORA **Edge:** Segmented reeding

Date	Mintage	F	VF	XF	Unc	BU
2007Mo Proof	600	Value: 750				

KM# 858 100 PESOS
33.9400 g., Bi-Metallic .925 Silver 20.1753g center in Aluminum-Bronze ring, 39.04 mm. **Series:** Second **Obv:** National arms **Obv. Legend:** ESTADOS UNIDOS MEXICANOS **Rev:** Basilica de Ocotlán at left, state arms above Capilla Abierta, Plaza de Toros Ranchero Aguilar below, Exconvento de San Francisco at right **Rev. Legend:** ESTADO DE TLAXCALA **Edge:** Segmented reeding

Date	Mintage	F	VF	XF	Unc	BU
2007Mo	149,465	—	—	—	25.00	30.00

KM# 890 100 PESOS
29.1690 g., Bi-Metallic .999 Gold 17.154g center in .999 Silver 12.015g ring, 34.5 mm. **Series:** Second **Obv:** National arms **Obv. Legend:** ESTADOS UNIDOS MEXICANOS **Rev:** Basilica de Ocotlán at left, state arms above Capilla Abierta, Plaza de Toros Ranchero Aguilar below, Exconvento de San Francisco at right **Rev. Legend:** ESTADO DE TLAXCALA **Edge:** Segmented reeding

Date	Mintage	F	VF	XF	Unc	BU
2007Mo Proof	600	Value: 750				

KM# 859 100 PESOS
33.9400 g., Bi-Metallic .912 Silver 20.1753g center in Aluminum-Bronze ring, 39.04 mm. **Series:** Second **Obv:** National arms **Obv. Legend:** ESTADOS UNIDOS MEXICANOS **Rev:** Pyramid of El Tajín **Rev. Legend:** • VERACRUZ • - • DE IGNACIO DE LA LLAVE • **Edge:** Segmented reeding

Date	Mintage	F	VF	XF	Unc	BU
2007Mo	149,703	—	—	—	25.00	30.00

KM# 891 100 PESOS
29.1690 g., Bi-Metallic .999 Gold 17.154g center in .999 Silver 12.015g ring, 34.5 mm. **Series:** Second **Obv:** National arms **Obv. Legend:** ESTADOS UNIDOS MEXICANOS **Rev:** Pyramid of El Tajín **Rev. Legend:** • VERACRUZ • - • DE IGNACIO DE LA LLAVE • **Edge:** Segmented reeding

Date	Mintage	F	VF	XF	Unc	BU
2007Mo Proof	600	Value: 750				

KM# 860 100 PESOS
33.9400 g., Bi-Metallic .925 Silver 20.1753 center in Aluminum-Bronze ring, 39.04 mm. **Series:** Second **Obv:** National arms **Obv. Legend:** ESTADOS UNIDOS MEXICANOS **Rev:** Stylized pyramid of Chichén Itzá **Rev. Legend:** Castillo de Chichén Itzá **Edge:** Segmented reeding

Date	Mintage	F	VF	XF	Unc	BU
2007Mo	149,579	—	—	—	25.00	30.00

KM# 892 100 PESOS
29.1690 g., Bi-Metallic .999 Gold 17.154g center in .999 Silver 12.015g ring, 34.5 mm. **Series:** Second **Obv:** National arms **Obv. Legend:** ESTADOS UNIDOS MEXICANOS **Rev:** Stylized pyramid of Chichén-Itzá **Rev. Inscription:** YUCATÁN **Edge:** Segmented reeding

Date	Mintage	F	VF	XF	Unc	BU
2007Mo Proof	600	Value: 750				

KM# 861 100 PESOS
33.9400 g., Bi-Metallic .925 Silver 20.1753g center in Aluminum-Bronze ring, 39.04 mm. **Series:** Second **Obv:** National arms **Obv. Legend:** ESTADOS UNIDOS MEXICANOS **Rev:** Cable car above Monumento al Minero at left, Cathedral of Zacatecas at center right **Rev. Legend:** ZACATECAS **Edge:** Segmented reeding

Date	Mintage	F	VF	XF	Unc	BU
2007Mo	148,833	—	—	—	25.00	30.00

KM# 893 100 PESOS
29.1690 g., Bi-Metallic .999 Gold 17.154g center in .999 Silver 12.015g ring, 34.5 mm. **Series:** Second **Obv:** National arms **Obv. Legend:** ESTADOS UNIDOS MEXICANOS **Rev:** Cable car above Monumento al Minero at left, Cathedral de Zacatecas at center right **Rev. Legend:** Zacatecas **Edge:** Segmented reeding

Date	Mintage	F	VF	XF	Unc	BU
2007Mo Proof	600	Value: 750				

SILVER BULLION COINAGE
Libertad Series

KM# 609 1/20 ONZA (1/20 Troy Ounce of Silver)
1.5551 g., 0.9990 Silver 0.0499 oz. ASW **Obv:** National arms, eagle left **Rev:** Winged Victory

Date	Mintage	F	VF	XF	Unc	BU
2001Mo	23,750	—	—	—	—	12.00
2001Mo Proof	3,200	Value: 15.00				
2002Mo	55,000	—	—	—	—	8.00
2002Mo Proof	1,200	Value: 13.00				
2003Mo	35,000	—	—	—	—	8.00
2003Mo Proof	3,015	Value: 13.00				
2004Mo	35,000	—	—	—	—	8.00
2004Mo Proof	5,285	Value: 13.00				
2005Mo	16,525	—	—	—	—	8.00
2005Mo Proof	1,500	Value: 12.00				
2006Mo	20,000	—	—	—	—	8.00
2006Mo Proof	3,300	Value: 12.00				
2007Mo	—	—	—	—	—	8.00
2007Mo Proof	—	Value: 12.00				
2008Mo	—	—	—	—	—	8.00
2008Mo Proof	—	Value: 12.00				
2009Mo	—	—	—	—	—	8.00
2009Mo Proof	—	Value: 12.00				
2010Mo	—	—	—	—	—	8.00
2010Mo Proof	—	Value: 12.00				

KM# 610 1/10 ONZA (1/10 Troy Ounce of Silver)
3.1103 g., 0.9990 Silver 0.0999 oz. ASW **Obv:** National arms, eagle left **Rev:** Winged Victory

Date	Mintage	F	VF	XF	Unc	BU
2001Mo	23,750	—	—	—	—	14.00
2001Mo Proof	3,200	Value: 18.00				
2002Mo	45,000	—	—	—	—	10.00
2002Mo Proof	1,200	Value: 15.00				
2003Mo	5,000	—	—	—	—	10.00
2003Mo Proof	3,500	Value: 15.00				
2004Mo	22,277	—	—	—	—	10.00
2004Mo Proof	3,500	Value: 15.00				
2005Mo	7,086	—	—	—	—	10.00
2005Mo Proof	2,500	Value: 14.00				
2006Mo	15,000	—	—	—	—	10.00
2006Mo Proof	3,000	Value: 14.00				
2007Mo	—	—	—	—	—	10.00
2007Mo Proof	—	Value: 14.00				
2008Mo	—	—	—	—	—	10.00
2008Mo Proof	—	Value: 14.00				
2009Mo	—	—	—	—	—	10.00
2009Mo Proof	—	Value: 14.00				
2010Mo	—	—	—	—	—	10.00
2010Mo Proof	—	Value: 14.00				

KM# 611 1/4 ONZA (1/4 Troy Ounce of Silver)
7.7758 g., 0.9990 Silver 0.2497 oz. ASW **Obv:** National arms, eagle left **Rev:** Winged Victory

Date	Mintage	F	VF	XF	Unc	BU
2001Mo	23,750	—	—	—	—	18.00
2001Mo Proof	2,850	Value: 22.00				
2002Mo	45,000	—	—	—	—	13.50
2002Mo Proof	1,200	Value: 20.00				
2003Mo	7,000	—	—	—	—	13.50
2003Mo Proof	3,500	Value: 20.00				
2004Mo	30,000	—	—	—	—	13.50
2004Mo Proof	3,900	Value: 20.00				
2005Mo	1,901	—	—	—	—	13.50

Date	Mintage	F	VF	XF	Unc	BU
2005Mo Proof	1,500	Value: 18.50				
2006Mo	15,000	—	—	—	—	13.00
2006Mo Proof	2,900	Value: 18.50				
2007Mo	—	—	—	—	—	13.00
2007Mo Proof	—	Value: 18.50				
2008Mo	—	—	—	—	—	13.00
2008Mo Proof	—	Value: 18.50				
2009Mo	—	—	—	—	—	13.00
2009Mo Proof	—	Value: 18.50				
2010Mo	—	—	—	—	—	13.00
2010Mo	—	Value: 18.50				

KM# 612 1/2 ONZA (1/2 Troy Ounce of Silver)
15.5517 g., 0.9990 Silver 0.4995 oz. ASW **Obv:** National arms, eagle left **Rev:** Winged Victory

Date	Mintage	F	VF	XF	Unc	BU
2001Mo	20,000	—	—	—	—	22.00
2001Mo Proof	1,000	Value: 30.00				
2002Mo	45,000	—	—	—	—	18.00
2002Mo Proof	2,800	Value: 25.00				
2003Mo	15,000	—	—	—	—	18.00
2003Mo Proof	3,000	Value: 25.00				
2004Mo	24,000	—	—	—	—	18.00
2004Mo Proof	4,300	Value: 25.00				
2005Mo	8,126	—	—	—	—	18.00
2005Mo Proof	1,500	Value: 22.00				
2006Mo	15,000	—	—	—	—	18.00
2006Mo Proof	2,900	Value: 22.00				
2007Mo	—	—	—	—	—	18.00
2007Mo Proof	—	Value: 22.00				
2008Mo	—	—	—	—	—	18.00
2008Mo Proof	—	Value: 22.00				
2009Mo	—	—	—	—	—	18.00
2009Mo Proof	—	Value: 22.00				
2010Mo	—	—	—	—	—	18.00
2010Mo Proof	—	Value: 22.00				

KM# 639 ONZA (Troy Ounce of Silver)
31.1000 g., 0.9990 Silver 0.9988 oz. ASW **Subject:** Libertad **Obv:** National arms, eagle left within center of past and present arms **Rev:** Winged Victory **Edge:** Reeded

Date	Mintage	F	VF	XF	Unc	BU
2001Mo	768,600	—	—	—	—	30.00
2001Mo Proof	4,100	Value: 70.00				
2002Mo	955,000	—	—	—	—	28.00
2002Mo Proof	1,700	Value: 75.00				
2003Mo	678,869	—	—	—	—	28.00
2003Mo Proof	5,000	Value: 65.00				
2004Mo	560,412	—	—	—	—	37.50
2004Mo Proof	5,300	Value: 65.00				
2005Mo	600,007	—	—	—	—	45.00
2005Mo Proof	1,500	Value: 75.00				
2006Mo	300,000	—	—	—	—	28.00
2006Mo Proof	4,000	Value: 70.00				
2007Mo	—	—	—	—	—	47.50
2007Mo Proof	—	Value: 75.00				
2008Mo	—	—	—	—	—	32.50
2008Mo Proof	—	Value: 75.00				
2009Mo	—	—	—	—	—	37.50
2009Mo Proof	—	Value: 75.00				
2010Mo	—	—	—	—	—	37.50
2010Mo Proof	—	Value: 70.00				

KM# 614 2 ONZAS (2 Troy Ounces of Silver)
62.2070 g., 0.9990 Silver 1.9979 oz. ASW, 48 mm. **Subject:** Libertad **Obv:** National arms, eagle left within center of past and present arms **Rev:** Winged Victory **Edge:** Reeded

Date	Mintage	F	VF	XF	Unc	BU
2001Mo	1,600	—	—	—	—	60.00
2001Mo Proof	1,350	Value: 80.00				
2002Mo	9,000	—	—	—	—	55.00
2002Mo Proof	400	Value: 95.00				
2003Mo	9,000	—	—	—	—	55.00
2003Mo Proof	400	Value: 95.00				
2004Mo	11,349	—	—	—	—	50.00
2004Mo Proof	1,360	Value: 80.00				
2005Mo	1,200	—	—	—	—	50.00
2005Mo Proof	740	Value: 75.00				
2006Mo	5,800	—	—	—	—	50.00
2006Mo Proof	1,100	Value: 75.00				
2007Mo	—	—	—	—	—	50.00
2007Mo Proof	—	Value: 85.00				
2008Mo	—	—	—	—	—	55.00
2008Mo Proof	—	Value: 85.00				
2009Mo	—	—	—	—	—	55.00
2009Mo Proof	—	Value: 85.00				
2010Mo Proof	—	Value: 95.00				

KM# 615 5 ONZAS (5 Troy Ounces of Silver)
155.5175 g., 0.9990 Silver 4.9948 oz. ASW, 65 mm. **Subject:** Libertad **Obv:** National arms, eagle left within center of past and present arms **Rev:** Winged Victory **Edge:** Reeded **Note:** Illustration reduced.

Date	Mintage	F	VF	XF	Unc	BU
2001Mo	3,120	—	—	—	—	110
2001Mo Proof	1,450	Value: 200				

Date	Mintage	F	VF	XF	Unc	BU
2002Mo	5,500	—	—	—	—	110
2002Mo Proof	400	Value: 200				
2003Mo	5,500	—	—	—	—	100
2003Mo Proof	495	Value: 150				
2004Mo	6,324	—	—	—	—	100
2004Mo Proof	1,805	Value: 135				
2005Mo	790	—	—	—	—	125
2005Mo Proof	900	Value: 135				
2006Mo	3,000	—	—	—	—	100
2006Mo Proof	1,000	Value: 160				
2007Mo	—	—	—	—	—	100
2007Mo Proof	—	Value: 125				
2008Mo	—	—	—	—	—	125
2008Mo Proof	—	Value: 165				
2009Mo	—	—	—	—	—	135
2009Mo Proof	—	Value: 165				

KM# 677 KILO (32.15 Troy Ounces of Silver)
999.9775 g., 0.9990 Silver 32.116 oz. ASW, 110 mm. **Subject:** Collector Bullion **Obv:** National arms in center of past and present arms **Rev:** Winged Victory **Edge:** Reeded

Date	Mintage	F	VF	XF	Unc	BU
2001Mo Prooflike	—	—	—	—	—	1,480
2002Mo Prooflike	1,100	—	—	—	—	1,150
2003Mo Prooflike	2,234	—	—	—	—	1,100
2004Mo Prooflike	500	—	—	—	—	1,200
2005Mo Prooflike	874	—	—	—	—	1,150
2006Mo Prooflike	—	—	—	—	—	1,100
2007Mo Prooflike	—	—	—	—	—	1,100
2008Mo Prooflike	—	—	—	—	—	1,100
2009Mo Prooflike	—	—	—	—	—	1,100

GOLD BULLION COINAGE

KM# 671 1/20 ONZA (1/20 Ounce of Pure Gold)
1.5551 g., 0.9990 Gold 0.0499 oz. AGW, 16 mm. **Obv:** National arms, eagle left **Rev:** Winged Victory **Edge:** Reeded **Note:** Design similar to KM#609. Value estimates do not include the high taxes and surcharges added to the issue prices by the Mexican Government.

Date	Mintage	F	VF	XF	Unc	BU
2002Mo	5,000	Value: BV+30%				
2003Mo	300	Value: BV+30%				
2004Mo	6,318	Value: BV+30%				
2005Mo	1,520	Value: BV+30%				
2005Mo Proof	200	Value: BV+35%				
2006Mo	3,200	Value: BV+30%				
2006Mo Proof	520	Value: BV+35%				
2007Mo	—	Value: BV+35%				

KM# 672 1/10 ONZA (1/10 Ounce of Pure Gold)
3.1103 g., 0.9990 Gold 0.0999 oz. AGW, 20 mm. **Obv:** National arms, eagle left **Rev:** Winged Victory **Edge:** Reeded **Note:** Design similar to KM#610. Value estimates do not include the high taxes and surcharges added to the issue prices by the Mexican Government.

Date	Mintage	F	VF	XF	Unc	BU
2002Mo	5,000	Value: BV+20%				
2003Mo	300	—	—	—	—	—
2004Mo	2,500	Value: BV+20%				
2005Mo	500	Value: BV+20%				
2005Mo Proof	200	Value: BV+22%				
2006Mo	2,500	Value: BV+20%				
2006Mo Proof	520	Value: BV+22%				
2007Mo	—	Value: BV+20%				

KM# 673 1/4 ONZA (1/4 Ounce of Pure Gold)
7.7758 g., 0.9990 Gold 0.2497 oz. AGW, 26.9 mm. **Obv:** National arms, eagle left **Rev:** Winged Victory **Edge:** Reeded **Note:** Design similar to KM#611. Value estimates do not include the high taxes and surcharges added to the issue prices by the Mexican Government.

Date	Mintage	F	VF	XF	Unc	BU
2002Mo	5,000	Value: BV+12%				
2003Mo	300	—	—	—	—	—
2004Mo	2,000	Value: BV+12%				
2004Mo Proof	1,000	Value: BV+15%				
2005Mo	500	Value: BV+12%				
2005Mo Proof	1,800	Value: BV+15%				
2006Mo	1,500	Value: BV+12%				
2006Mo Proof	2,120	Value: BV+12%				
2007Mo	—	Value: BV+12%				

KM# 674 1/2 ONZA (1/2 Ounce of Pure Gold)
15.5517 g., 0.9990 Gold 0.4995 oz. AGW, 32.9 mm. **Obv:** National arms, eagle left **Rev:** Winged Victory **Edge:** Reeded **Note:** Design similar to KM#612. Value estimates do not include the high taxes and surcharges added to the issue prices by the Mexican Government.

Date	Mintage	F	VF	XF	Unc	BU
2002Mo	5,000	Value: BV+8%				
2003Mo	300	—	—	—	—	—
2004Mo	1,000	Value: BV+8%				
2005Mo	500	Value: BV+8%				
2005Mo Proof	200	Value: BV+12%				
2006Mo	500	Value: BV+8%				
2006Mo Proof	520	Value: BV+12%				
2007Mo	—	Value: BV+8%				

KM# 675 ONZA (Ounce of Pure Gold)
31.1035 g., 0.9990 Gold 0.9990 oz. AGW, 40 mm. **Obv:** National arms, eagle left **Rev:** Winged Victory **Edge:** Reeded **Note:** Design similar to KM#639. Value estimates do not include the high taxes and surcharges added to the issue prices by the Mexican Government.

Date	Mintage	F	VF	XF	Unc	BU
2002Mo	15,000	Value: BV+3%				
2003Mo	500	Value: BV+3%				
2004Mo	4,810	Value: BV+3%				
2004Mo Proof	150	Value: BV+5%				
2005Mo	2,000	Value: BV+3%				
2005Mo Proof	50	Value: BV+5%				
2006Mo	4,000	Value: BV+3%				
2006Mo Proof	520	Value: BV+5%				

BANK SETS

Hard Case Sets unless otherwise noted.

KM#	Date	Mintage	Identification	Issue Price	Mkt Val
BS38	2001 (10)	—	KM#546-549, 603-605, 636-638 Set in folder	—	30.00
BS39	2002 (8)	—	KM#546-549, 603-605, 616 Set in folder	—	30.00
BS40	2003 (6)	—	KM#547-549, 603-605 Set in folder	—	30.00

MOLDOVA

The Republic of Moldova (formerly the Moldavian S.S.R.) is bordered in the north, east and south by the Ukraine and on the west by Romania. It has an area of 13,000 sq.mi. (33,700 sq.km.) and a population of 4.4 million. The capital is Chisinau. Agricultural products are mainly cereals, grapes, tobacco, sugar beets and fruits. Food processing, clothing, building materials and agricultural machinery manufacturing dominate industry.

MONETARY SYSTEM
100 Bani = 1 Leu

REPUBLIC
DECIMAL COINAGE

KM# 1 BAN
0.6800 g., Aluminum, 14.5 mm. **Obv:** National arms **Rev:** Value divides date above monogram **Edge:** Plain

Date	Mintage	F	VF	XF	Unc	BU
2004	—	—	—	—	0.25	0.50
2006	—	—	—	—	0.25	0.50

KM# 2 5 BANI
0.8000 g., Aluminum, 16 mm. **Obv:** National arms **Rev:** Monogram divides sprigs below value and date **Edge:** Plain

Date	Mintage	F	VF	XF	Unc	BU
2001	—	—	—	0.15	0.35	0.50
2002	—	—	—	0.15	0.35	0.50
2003	—	—	—	0.15	0.35	0.50
2004	—	—	—	0.15	0.35	0.50
2005	—	—	—	0.15	0.35	0.50
2006	—	—	—	0.15	0.35	0.50
2008	—	—	—	0.15	0.35	0.50

KM# 7 10 BANI
0.8400 g., Aluminum, 16.6 mm. **Obv:** National arms **Rev:** Value, date and monogram **Edge:** Plain

Date	Mintage	F	VF	XF	Unc	BU
2001	—	—	—	—	0.40	0.60
2002	—	—	—	—	0.40	0.60
2003	—	—	—	—	0.40	0.60
2004	—	—	—	—	0.40	0.60
2005	—	—	—	—	0.40	0.60
2006	—	—	—	—	0.40	0.60
2008	—	—	—	—	0.40	0.60

KM# 3   25 BANI

0.9200 g., Aluminum, 17.5 mm. **Obv:** National arms
Rev: Monogram divides sprigs below value and date **Edge:** Plain

Date	Mintage	F	VF	XF	Unc	BU
2001	—	—	—	—	0.20	0.50	0.75
2002	—	—	—	—	0.20	0.50	0.75
2003	—	—	—	—	0.20	0.50	0.75
2004	—	—	—	—	0.20	0.50	0.75
2005	—	—	—	—	0.20	0.50	0.75
2006	—	—	—	—	0.20	0.50	0.75
2008	—	—	—	—	0.20	0.50	0.75

KM# 10   50 BANI

3.1000 g., Brass Clad Steel, 19 mm. **Obv:** National arms
Rev: Value and date within grapevine **Edge:** Reeded

Date	Mintage	F	VF	XF	Unc	BU
2003	—	—	—	—	1.50	2.00
2005	—	—	—	—	1.50	2.00
2008	—	—	—	—	1.50	2.00

KM# 12   10 LEI

13.5000 g., 0.9250 Silver 0.4015 oz. ASW, 24.5 mm.
Obv: National arms above value **Rev:** European wildcat within circle **Edge:** Plain

Date	Mintage	F	VF	XF	Unc	BU
2001 Proof	1,000	Value: 65.00				

KM# 13   10 LEI

13.5000 g., 0.9250 Silver 0.4015 oz. ASW, 24.5 mm.
Obv: National arms above value **Rev:** Green Woodpecker on tree within circle **Edge:** Plain

Date	Mintage	F	VF	XF	Unc	BU
2001 Proof	1,000	Value: 60.00				

KM# 19   10 LEI

13.4500 g., 0.9250 Silver 0.4000 oz. ASW, 24.5 mm.
Obv: National arms above value **Rev:** European Mink within circle **Edge:** Plain

Date	Mintage	F	VF	XF	Unc	BU
2003 Proof	500	Value: 65.00				

KM# 20   10 LEI

13.4500 g., 0.9250 Silver 0.4000 oz. ASW, 24.5 mm.
Obv: National arms above value **Rev:** Black Storks within circle **Edge:** Plain

Date	Mintage	F	VF	XF	Unc	BU
2003 Proof	500	Value: 65.00				

KM# 25   10 LEI

25.0000 g., Nickel Plated Brass, 30 mm. **Subject:** Wine Holiday
Obv: National arms above value **Rev:** Wine grapes, goblet and flask **Edge:** Plain

Date	Mintage	F	VF	XF	Unc	BU
2003 Proof	—	Value: 12.50				

KM# 22   10 LEI

13.5000 g., 0.9250 Silver 0.4015 oz. ASW, 24.5 mm.
Obv: National arms above value **Rev:** Pine Marten within circle **Edge:** Plain

Date	Mintage	F	VF	XF	Unc	BU
2004 Proof	500	Value: 65.00				

KM# 29   10 LEI

25.0000 g., Nickel Plated Brass, 30 mm. **Subject:** European Women's Chess Championship **Obv:** Arms, date at top, value at bottom **Obv. Legend:** REPUBLICA - 2005 - MOLDOVA **Rev:** 2 chess figures on board at left, map at right **Rev. Inscription:** 2005 CHISINAU **Edge:** Plain

Date	Mintage	F	VF	XF	Unc	BU
2005 Proof	—	Value: 12.50				

KM# 30   10 LEI

13.5000 g., 0.9250 Silver 0.4015 oz. ASW, 24.5 mm.
Obv: Arms, value below **Obv. Legend:** REPUBLICA MOLDOVA **Rev:** Imperial eagle on branch, legend follows the coin circumference **Edge:** Plain

Date	Mintage	F	VF	XF	Unc	BU
2005 Proof	500	Value: 65.00				

KM# 33   10 LEI

13.5000 g., 0.9250 Silver 0.4015 oz. ASW, 24.5 mm.
Obv: Arms, value below **Obv. Legend:** REPUBLICA - 2006 - MOLDOVA **Rev:** Bustard on vegetal background, legend around circumference using Latin name **Edge:** Plain

Date	Mintage	F	VF	XF	Unc	BU
2006 Proof	500	Value: 65.00				

KM# 38   10 LEI

13.5000 g., 0.9250 Silver 0.4015 oz. ASW, 24.5 mm.
Rev: Common ground squirrel

Date	Mintage	F	VF	XF	Unc	BU
2006 Proof	500	Value: 60.00				

KM# 43   10 LEI

13.5000 g., 0.9250 Silver 0.4015 oz. ASW, 24.5 mm. **Rev:** White water lilly

Date	Mintage	F	VF	XF	Unc	BU
2008 Proof	500	Value: 60.00				

KM# 47   20 LEI

13.5000 g., 0.9250 Silver 0.4015 oz. ASW, 22 mm.
Subject: Assumption of the Virgin Mary

Date	Mintage	F	VF	XF	Unc	BU
2009 Proof	1,000	Value: 40.00				

KM# 36   50 LEI

16.5000 g., 0.9250 Silver 0.4907 oz. ASW, 30 mm.
Subject: Vazile Alecsandri, 180th Anniversary **Obv:** Arms **Rev:** Bust and landscape

Date	Mintage	F	VF	XF	Unc	BU
2001 Proof	1,000	Value: 40.00				

KM# 17   50 LEI

16.5000 g., 0.9250 Silver 0.4907 oz. ASW, 30 mm.
Obv: National arms above value **Rev:** Constantin Brancusi and building **Edge:** Plain

Date	Mintage	F	VF	XF	Unc	BU
2001 Proof	1,000	Value: 65.00				

KM# 18   50 LEI

16.5000 g., 0.9250 Silver 0.4907 oz. ASW, 30 mm.
Obv: National arms above value **Rev:** Vasile Alecsandri with book and landscape **Edge:** Plain

Date	Mintage	F	VF	XF	Unc	BU
2001 Proof	1,000	Value: 65.00				

KM# 21   50 LEI

16.5000 g., 0.9250 Silver 0.4907 oz. ASW, 29.8 mm.
Subject: Effigy of Dimitrie Cantemir **Obv:** National arms above value **Rev:** Bust facing flanked by dates and scroll **Edge:** Plain

Date	Mintage	F	VF	XF	Unc	BU
2003 Proof	500	Value: 165				

KM# 14   50 LEI

16.5500 g., 0.9250 Silver 0.4922 oz. ASW, 29.9 mm.
Subject: Effigy of Miron Costin **Obv:** National arms above value **Rev:** Bust with hat 1/4 right flanked by dates and books **Edge:** Plain

Date	Mintage	F	VF	XF	Unc	BU
2003 Proof	500	Value: 165				

KM# 23   50 LEI

16.5000 g., 0.9250 Silver 0.4907 oz. ASW, 30 mm.
Obv: National arms above value **Rev:** Bust of Bishop facing holding scepter **Edge:** Plain

Date	Mintage	F	VF	XF	Unc	BU
2004 Proof	500	Value: 90.00				

KM# 31   50 LEI

16.5000 g., 0.9250 Silver 0.4907 oz. ASW, 30 mm.
Subject: 415th Anniversary - Birth of Grigore Ureche **Obv:** Arms, date divides legend at top, value below, **Obv. Legend:** REPUBLICA MOLDOVA **Rev:** Bust faces right, scroll with feather pen at right, inscription on scroll **Rev. Legend:** GRIGORE URECHE **Rev. Inscription:** Letopisetul Tarii Moldovei **Edge:** Plain

Date	Mintage	F	VF	XF	Unc	BU
2005 Proof	—	Value: 120				

KM# 34   50 LEI

16.5000 g., 0.9250 Silver 0.4907 oz. ASW, 30 mm.
Subject: 200th Anniversary - Birth of Alexandru Donici
Obv: Arms, date divides legend above, value below **Obv. Legend:** REPUBLICA MOLDOVA **Rev:** Bust of Donici facing, life dates on ribbon below **Rev. Legend:** ALEXANDRU DONICI

Date	Mintage	F	VF	XF	Unc	BU
2006 Proof	—	Value: 120				

KM# 40   50 LEI

16.5000 g., 0.9250 Silver 0.4907 oz. ASW, 30 mm.
Subject: Metropolitian Varilaam **Rev:** Bust 3/4 right

Date	Mintage	F	VF	XF	Unc	BU
2007 Proof	500	Value: 120				

KM# 41   50 LEI
16.5000 g., 0.9250 Silver 0.4907 oz. ASW, 30 mm.
Subject: Pottery Tradition **Rev:** Hand modeling clay vessel on pottery wheel

Date	Mintage	F	VF	XF	Unc	BU
2007 Proof	500	Value: 60.00				

KM# 44   50 LEI
16.5000 g., 0.9250 Silver 0.4907 oz. ASW, 30 mm.
Subject: Oak tree in Stefan **Rev:** Oak tree

Date	Mintage	F	VF	XF	Unc	BU
2008 Proof	500	Value: 75.00				

KM# 45   50 LEI
16.5000 g., 0.9250 Silver 0.4907 oz. ASW, 30 mm.
Subject: Cooper trade **Rev:** Barrell maker

Date	Mintage	F	VF	XF	Unc	BU
2008 Proof	500	Value: 55.00				

KM# 48   50 LEI
16.5000 g., 0.9250 Silver 0.4907 oz. ASW, 30 mm.
Subject: Geodezic arc of Struve **Rev:** Map

Date	Mintage	F	VF	XF	Unc	BU
2009 Proof	500	Value: 75.00				

KM# 49   50 LEI
16.5000 g., 0.9250 Silver 0.4907 oz. ASW, 30 mm.
Subject: Rule of Vasile Lupu **Rev:** Open book and coat-of-arms

Date	Mintage	F	VF	XF	Unc	BU
2009 Proof	500	Value: 75.00				

KM# 50   50 LEI
16.5000 g., 0.9250 Silver 0.4907 oz. ASW, 30 mm. **Subject:** Traditional weaving **Rev:** Woman seated at weaving frame

Date	Mintage	F	VF	XF	Unc	BU
2009 Proof	500	Value: 70.00				

KM# 16   100 LEI
31.1000 g., 0.9250 Silver 0.9249 oz. ASW, 37 mm.
Subject: 10th Anniversary of Independence **Obv:** National arms above value **Rev:** Arch monument within circle above value and sprigs **Edge:** Plain

Date	Mintage	F	VF	XF	Unc	BU
2001 Proof	1,000	Value: 220				

KM# 26   100 LEI
7.8000 g., 0.9999 Gold 0.2507 oz. AGW, 24 mm. **Obv:** National arms above value **Rev:** King Stephan the Great (1456-1504) **Edge:** Plain

Date	Mintage	F	VF	XF	Unc	BU
2004 Proof	—	Value: 350				

KM# 32   100 LEI
31.1000 g., 0.9250 Silver 0.9249 oz. ASW, 37 mm.
Subject: Burebista - King of Dacians **Obv:** Arms, date divides legend at top, value below **Obv. Legend:** REPUBLICA MOLDOVA **Rev:** Bust of Burebista at left, battle scene of Geto-Dacians with Romans at right **Rev. Legend:** BUREBISTA REGELE DACILOR **Edge:** Plain

Date	Mintage	F	VF	XF	Unc	BU
2005 Proof	500	Value: 300				

KM# 35   100 LEI
31.1000 g., 0.9250 Silver 0.9249 oz. ASW, 37 mm. **Subject:** 15th Anniversary - Independence Proclamation of the Republic of Moldova **Obv:** Arms, date divides legend above, value below **Obv. Legend:** REPUBLICA MOLDOVA **Rev:** Map of Moldova within stars in inner circle, legend around **Rev. Legend:** PROCLAMAREA INDEPENDENTEI / 1991-2006 **Edge:** Plain

Date	Mintage	F	VF	XF	Unc	BU
2006 Proof	500	Value: 500				

KM# 37   100 LEI
31.1050 g., 0.9250 Silver 0.9250 oz. ASW, 37 mm. **Subject:** National Bank, 15th Anniversary **Obv:** Arms **Rev:** Bank building and coins

Date	Mintage	F	VF	XF	Unc	BU
2006 Proof	500	Value: 140				

KM# 39   100 LEI
31.1050 g., 0.9990 Silver 0.9990 oz. ASW, 37 mm.
Subject: National Bank, 15th Anniversary **Rev:** Bank building

Date	Mintage	F	VF	XF	Unc	BU
2006 Proof	500	Value: 140				

KM# 42   100 LEI
31.1050 g., 0.9250 Silver 0.9250 oz. ASW, 37 mm.
Subject: Petru Rares **Rev:** Bust 3/4 right

Date	Mintage	F	VF	XF	Unc	BU
2007 Proof	500	Value: 450				

KM# 46   100 LEI
31.1050 g., 0.9250 Silver 0.9250 oz. ASW, 37 mm. **Subject:** Antioh Cantemir **Rev:** Half-length figure standing 3/4 left

Date	Mintage	F	VF	XF	Unc	BU
2008 Proof	1,000	Value: 100				

KM# 51   100 LEI
22.5000 g., 0.9250 Silver 0.6691 oz. ASW, 34 mm. **Subject:** Moldovan Chronicals, 15-18 Centuries **Rev:** Man seated writing

Date	Mintage	F	VF	XF	Unc	BU
2009 Proof	1,000	Value: 90.00				

MONACO

The Principality of Monaco, located on the Mediterranean coast nine miles from Nice, has an area of 0.58 sq. mi. (1.9 sq. km.) and a population of 26,000. Capital: Monaco-Ville. The economy is based on tourism and the manufacture of cosmetics, gourmet foods and highly specialized electronics. Monaco also derives its revenue from a tobacco monopoly and the sale of postage stamps for philatelic purpose. Gambling in Monte Carlo accounts for only a small fraction of the country's revenue.

RULERS
Rainier III, 1949-2005
Albert II, 2005-

MINT PRIVY MARKS
(a) - Paris (privy marks only)
   Horseshoe - 2001 and 2002
   Heart – 2002-2003
   French Horn with starfish in water – 2003-
(p) - Thunderbolt - Poissy

MONETARY SYSTEM
100 Euro Cents = 1 Euro

PRINCIPALITY

EURO COINAGE

KM# 167 EURO CENT

2.2700 g., Copper Plated Steel, 16.2 mm. **Ruler:** Rainier III **Obv:** Crowned arms **Obv. Designer:** Robert Cochet **Rev:** Value and globe **Rev. Designer:** Luc Luycx **Edge:** Plain

Date	Mintage	F	VF	XF	Unc	BU
2001(a)	327,200	—	—	—	20.00	35.00
2001(a) Proof	3,500	Value: 75.00				
2002(a) In sets only	40,000	—	—	—	—	75.00
2003(a)	—	—	—	—	—	10.00
2004(a) Proof	14,999	Value: 25.00				
2005(a) Proof	35,000	Value: 50.00				
2009(a)	—	—	—	—	—	10.00

KM# 188 EURO CENT

2.2700 g., Copper Plated Steel, 16.2 mm. **Ruler:** Albert II **Obv:** Crowned arms within circle of stars **Rev:** Value and globe

Date	Mintage	F	VF	XF	Unc	BU
2006 Proof	11,180	Value: 30.00				
2007	—	—	—	—	—	30.00

KM# 168 2 EURO CENT

3.0300 g., Copper Plated Steel, 18.7 mm. **Ruler:** Rainier III **Obv:** Crowned arms **Obv. Designer:** Robert Cochet **Rev:** Value and globe **Rev. Designer:** Luc Luycx **Edge:** Grooved

Date	Mintage	F	VF	XF	Unc	BU
2001(a)	393,400	—	—	—	15.00	30.00
2001(a) Proof	3,500	Value: 85.00				
2002(a) In sets only	40,000	—	—	—	—	85.00
2003(a)	—	—	—	—	—	10.00
2004(a) Proof	14,999	Value: 35.00				
2005(a) Proof	35,000	Value: 50.00				
2009(a)	—	—	—	—	—	10.00

KM# 189 2 EURO CENT

3.0600 g., Copper Plated Steel, 18.7 mm. **Ruler:** Albert II **Obv:** Crowned arms within circle of stars **Rev:** Value and globe

Date	Mintage	F	VF	XF	Unc	BU
2006 Proof	11,260	Value: 25.00				
2007	—	—	—	—	—	25.00

KM# 169 5 EURO CENT

3.8600 g., Copper-Nickel Plated Steel, 21.2 mm. **Ruler:** Rainier III **Obv:** Crowned arms **Obv. Designer:** Robert Cochet **Rev:** Value and globe **Rev. Designer:** Luc Luycx **Edge:** Plain

Date	Mintage	F	VF	XF	Unc	BU
2001(a)	320,000	—	—	—	20.00	35.00
2001(a) Proof	3,500	Value: 95.00				
2002(a) In sets only	40,000	—	—	—	—	85.00
2003(a)	—	—	—	—	—	15.00
2004(a) Proof	14,999	Value: 45.00				
2005(a) Proof	35,000	Value: 55.00				
2009(a)	—	—	—	—	—	15.00

KM# 170 10 EURO CENT

4.0700 g., Brass, 19.7 mm. **Ruler:** Rainier III **Obv:** Knight on horse **Obv. Designer:** R. Baron **Rev:** Value and map **Rev. Designer:** Luc Luycx **Edge:** Reeded

Date	Mintage	F	VF	XF	Unc	BU
2001(a)	320,000	—	—	—	15.00	25.00
2001(a) Proof	3,500	Value: 110				
2002(a)	407,200	—	—	—	8.00	12.00
2003(a)	100,800	—	—	—	12.00	16.00
2004(a) Proof	14,999	Value: 50.00				

KM# 181 10 EURO CENT

4.0700 g., Brass, 19.7 mm. **Ruler:** Albert II **Obv:** Crowned AA monogram **Rev:** Relief map of Western Europe, stars, lines and value **Rev. Designer:** Luc Luycx **Edge:** Reeded

Date	Mintage	F	VF	XF	Unc	BU
2006(a) Proof	11,180	Value: 50.00				
2009(a)	—	—	—	—	12.00	16.00

KM# 191 10 EURO CENT

Brass **Ruler:** Albert II **Obv:** Crowned AA monogram **Rev:** Relief map of western Europe, stars, lines and value

Date	Mintage	F	VF	XF	Unc	BU
2007 (a)	—	—	—	—	—	—

KM# 171 20 EURO CENT

5.7300 g., Brass, 22.1 mm. **Ruler:** Rainier III **Obv:** Knight on horse **Rev:** Value and map **Edge:** Notched **Designer:** R. Baron

Date	Mintage	F	VF	XF	Unc	BU
2001(a)	386,400	—	—	—	15.00	20.00
2001(a) Proof	3,500	Value: 120				
2002(a)	376,000	—	—	—	12.00	16.00
2003(a)	100,000	—	—	—	12.00	16.00
2004(a) Proof	14,999	Value: 60.00				

KM# 182 20 EURO CENT

5.7300 g., Brass, 22.1 mm. **Ruler:** Albert II **Obv:** Crowned AA monogram **Obv. Designer:** R. Baron **Rev:** Relief map of Western Europe, stars, lines and value **Edge:** Notched

Date	Mintage	F	VF	XF	Unc	BU
2006(a) Proof	11,180	Value: 60.00				
2009(a)	—	—	—	—	12.00	16.00

KM# 192 20 EURO CENT

Brass **Ruler:** Albert II **Obv:** Crowned AA monogram **Rev:** Relief map of western Europe, stars, lines and value

Date	Mintage	F	VF	XF	Unc	BU
2007 (a)	—	—	—	—	—	—

KM# 172 50 EURO CENT

7.8100 g., Brass **Ruler:** Rainier III **Obv:** Knight on horse **Obv. Designer:** R. Baron **Rev:** Value and map **Rev. Designer:** Luc Luycx **Edge:** Reeded

Date	Mintage	F	VF	XF	Unc	BU
2001 (a)	320,000	—	—	—	15.00	30.00
2001 (a) Proof	3,500	Value: 130				
2002 (a)	364,000	—	—	—	8.00	12.00
2003 (a)	100,000	—	—	—	12.00	16.00
2004 (a) Proof	14,999	Value: 65.00				

KM# 183 50 EURO CENT

7.8100 g., Brass **Ruler:** Albert II **Obv:** Crowned AA monogram **Obv. Designer:** R. Baron **Rev:** Relief map of Western Europe, stars, lines and value **Rev. Designer:** Luc Luycx **Edge:** Reeded

Date	Mintage	F	VF	XF	Unc	BU
2006(a)	11,180	Value: 65.00				
2009(a)	—	—	—	—	12.00	16.00

KM# 193 50 EURO CENT

Brass **Ruler:** Albert II **Obv:** Crowned AA monogram **Rev:** Relief map of western Europe, stars, lines and values

Date	Mintage	F	VF	XF	Unc	BU
2007 (a)	—	—	—	—	—	—

KM# 173 EURO

7.5000 g., Bi-Metallic Copper-Nickel center in Brass ring, 23.2 mm. **Ruler:** Rainier III **Obv:** Conjoined heads of Prince Ranier and Crown Prince Albert right within circle **Obv. Designer:** Henri Thiebaud **Rev:** Value and map **Rev. Designer:** Luc Luycx **Edge:** Reeded and plain sections

Date	Mintage	F	VF	XF	Unc	BU
2001(a)	991,100	—	—	—	10.00	12.00
2001(a) Proof	3,500	Value: 145				
2002(a)	512,500	—	—	—	11.00	14.00
2003(a)	135,000	—	—	—	13.50	18.50
2004(a) Proof	14,999	Value: 75.00				

KM# 184 EURO

7.5000 g., Bi-Metallic Copper-Nickel center in Brass ring, 23.2 mm. **Ruler:** Albert II **Obv:** Head right of Prince Albert **Rev:** Relief map of Western Europe, stars, lines and value **Rev. Designer:** Luc Luycx **Edge:** Reeded and plain sections

Date	Mintage	F	VF	XF	Unc	BU
2006(a) Proof	11,180	Value: 75.00				
2009(a)	—	—	—	—	11.00	14.00

KM# 194 EURO

Bi-Metallic Copper nickel center in brass ring **Ruler:** Albert II **Obv:** Head right **Rev:** Relief map of western Europe, stars, lines and value

Date	Mintage	F	VF	XF	Unc	BU
2007 (a)	—	—	—	—	—	—

KM# 174 2 EURO

8.5200 g., Bi-Metallic Brass center in Copper-Nickel ring, 25.7 mm. **Ruler:** Rainier III **Obv:** Head right within circle flanked by stars **Obv. Designer:** Pierre Givaudin **Rev:** Value and map **Rev. Designer:** Luc Luycx **Edge:** Reeding over "2's" and stars

Date	Mintage	F	VF	XF	Unc	BU
2001(a)	919,800	—	—	—	14.00	25.00
2001(a) Proof	3,500	Value: 165				
2002(a)	496,000	—	—	—	15.00	18.00
2003(a)	228,000	—	—	—	17.50	22.50
2004(a) Proof	14,999	Value: 95.00				

KM# 185 2 EURO

8.5200 g., Bi-Metallic Brass center in Copper-Nickel ring, 25.7 mm. **Ruler:** Albert II **Obv:** Prince Albert's head right **Rev:** Relief map of Western Europe, stars, lines and value **Rev. Designer:** Luc Luycx **Edge:** Reeding over 2's and stars

Date	Mintage	F	VF	XF	Unc	BU
2006(a) Proof	11,180	Value: 120				
2009(a)	—	—	—	—	15.00	18.00

KM# 186 2 EURO

8.5200 g., Bi-Metallic Brass center in Copper-Nickel ring., 25.75 mm. **Ruler:** Albert II **Subject:** 25th Anniversary Death of Princess Grace **Obv:** Head of Princess Grace left **Rev:** Relief map of Western Europe, stars, lines and value **Edge:** Reeded

Date	Mintage	F	VF	XF	Unc	BU
2007(a)	20,000	—	—	—	850	1,250

KM# 195 2 EURO

Bi-Metallic Brass center in copper nickel ring **Ruler:** Albert II **Obv:** Head right **Rev:** Relief map of western Europe, stars, lines and values

Date	Mintage	F	VF	XF	Unc	BU
2007 (a)	—	—	—	—	—	—

KM# 180 5 EURO

12.0000 g., 0.9000 Silver 0.3472 oz. ASW, 29 mm. **Ruler:** Rainier III **Obv:** Bust right **Rev:** Saint standing

Date	Mintage	F	VF	XF	Unc	BU
2004 (a) Proof	14,999	Value: 150				

KM# 190 5 EURO

3.9000 g., Copper Plated Steel, 21.2 mm. **Ruler:** Albert II **Obv:** Crowned arms within circle of stars **Rev:** Value and globe

Date	Mintage	F	VF	XF	Unc	BU
2006 Proof	11,180	Value: 30.00				
2007	—	—	—	—	—	30.00

KM# 178 10 EURO

25.0000 g., 0.9250 Silver 0.7435 oz. ASW, 37 mm. **Ruler:** Rainier III **Obv:** Conjoined busts of Prince Ranier and Crown Prince Albert right **Rev:** Arms

Date	Mintage	F	VF	XF	Unc	BU
2003(a) Proof	4,000	Value: 465				

KM# 187 10 EURO

3.2200 g., 0.9000 Gold 0.0932 oz. AGW **Ruler:** Albert II **Subject:** Death of Rainier III **Obv:** Principality arms **Rev:** Head of Rainier III right

Date	Mintage	F	VF	XF	Unc	BU
2005(a) Proof	3,313	Value: 550				

KM# 177 20 EURO

18.0000 g., 0.9250 Gold 0.5353 oz. AGW, 32 mm. **Ruler:** Rainier III **Obv:** Bust right **Rev:** Arms

Date	Mintage	F	VF	XF	Unc	BU
2002(a) Proof	10,000	Value: 1,100				

KM# 179 100 EURO

29.0000 g., 0.9000 Gold 0.8391 oz. AGW **Ruler:** Rainier III **Obv:** Bust right **Rev:** Knight on horse

Date	Mintage	F	VF	XF	Unc	BU
2003(a) Proof	1,000	Value: 3,250				

MINT SETS

KM#	Date	Mintage	Identification	Issue Price	Mkt Val
MS1	2001 (8)	20,000	KM#167-174, exercise caution, as privately packaged and deceptively false sets are known	35.00	450
MS2	2002 (8)	40,000	KM#167-174, exercise caution, as partial sets, privately packaged and deceptively false sets are known	35.00	425

PROOF SETS

KM#	Date	Mintage	Identification	Issue Price	Mkt Val
PS1	2001 (8)	3,500	KM#167-174	—	1,000
PS2	2004 (9)	14,999	KM#167-174, 180	—	600
PS3	2005 (3)	35,000	KM#167-169	—	155

MONGOLIA

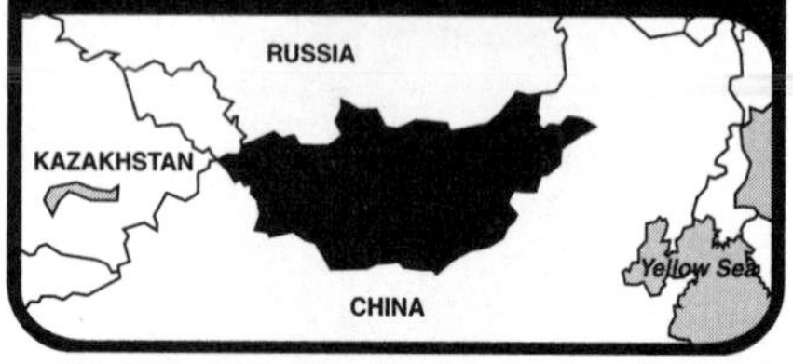

The State of Mongolia, (formerly the Mongolian Peoples Republic) a landlocked country in central Asia between Russia and the People's Republic of China, has an area of 604,250 sq. mi. (1,565,000 sq. km.) and a population of 2.26 million. Capital: Ulaan Baator. Animal herds and flocks are the chief economic asset. Wool, cattle, butter, meat and hides are exported.

For earlier issues see Russia - Tannu Tuva.

MONETARY SYSTEM
100 Mongo = 1 Tugrik

STATE

DECIMAL COINAGE

KM# 254 100 TUGRIK

25.0000 g., 0.9250 Silver 0.7435 oz. ASW **Obv:** Arms **Rev:** Yin-Yang symbol

Date	Mintage	F	VF	XF	Unc	BU
2007 Proof	—	Value: 25.00				

KM# 282 250 TUGRIK
15.5000 g., 0.9250 Silver 0.4609 oz. ASW, 33 mm. **Subject:**
Zodiac - Capricorn **Rev:** Seated goat left, partially gilt

Date	Mintage	F	VF	XF	Unc	BU
2007	7,000	—	—	—	—	25.00

KM# 283 250 TUGRIK
15.5000 g., 0.9250 Silver 0.4609 oz. ASW, 33 mm. **Subject:**
Zodiac - Aquarius **Rev:** Man pouring water, partially gilt

Date	Mintage	F	VF	XF	Unc	BU
2007	7,000	—	—	—	—	25.00

KM# 284 250 TUGRIK
15.5000 g., 0.9250 Silver 0.4609 oz. ASW, 33 mm.
Subject: Zodiac - Piceis **Rev:** Two fish partially gilt

Date	Mintage	F	VF	XF	Unc	BU
2007	7,000	—	—	—	—	25.00

KM# 285 250 TUGRIK
15.5000 g., 0.9250 Silver 0.4609 oz. ASW, 33 mm.
Subject: Zodiac - Aries **Rev:** Ram seated partially gilt

Date	Mintage	F	VF	XF	Unc	BU
2007	7,000	—	—	—	—	25.00

KM# 286 250 TUGRIK
15.5000 g., 0.9250 Silver 0.4609 oz. ASW, 33 mm.
Subject: Zodiac - Taurus **Rev:** Bull, partially gilt

Date	Mintage	F	VF	XF	Unc	BU
2007	7,000	—	—	—	—	25.00

KM# 287 250 TUGRIK
15.5000 g., 0.9250 Silver 0.4609 oz. ASW, 33 mm.
Subject: Zodiac - Gemini **Rev:** Twins, partially gilt

Date	Mintage	F	VF	XF	Unc	BU
2007	7,000	—	—	—	—	25.00

KM# 288 250 TUGRIK
15.5000 g., 0.9250 Silver 0.4609 oz. ASW, 33 mm.
Subject: Zodiac - Cancer **Rev:** Crab - partially gilt

Date	Mintage	F	VF	XF	Unc	BU
2007	7,000	—	—	—	—	25.00

KM# 289 250 TUGRIK
15.5000 g., 0.9250 Silver 0.4609 oz. ASW, 33 mm.
Subject: Zodiac - Leo **Rev:** Lion walking left, partially gilt

Date	Mintage	F	VF	XF	Unc	BU
2007	7,000	—	—	—	—	25.00

KM# 290 250 TUGRIK
15.5000 g., 0.9250 Silver 0.4609 oz. ASW, 33 mm.
Subject: Zodiac - Virgo **Rev:** Female, partially gilt

Date	Mintage	F	VF	XF	Unc	BU
2007	7,000	—	—	—	—	25.00

KM# 291 250 TUGRIK
15.5000 g., 0.9250 Silver 0.4609 oz. ASW, 33 mm.
Subject: Zodiac - Libra **Rev:** Scales, partially gilt

Date	Mintage	F	VF	XF	Unc	BU
2007	7,000	—	—	—	—	25.00

KM# 292 250 TUGRIK
15.5000 g., 0.9250 Silver 0.4609 oz. ASW, 33 mm.
Subject: Zodiac - Scorpio **Rev:** Scorpion, partially gilt

Date	Mintage	F	VF	XF	Unc	BU
2007	7,000	—	—	—	—	25.00

KM# 293 250 TUGRIK
15.5000 g., 0.9250 Silver 0.4609 oz. ASW, 33 mm.
Subject: Zodiac - Sagitarius **Rev:** Centar, partailly gilt

Date	Mintage	F	VF	XF	Unc	BU
2007	7,000	—	—	—	—	25.00

KM# 300 250 TUGRIK
15.5000 g., 0.9990 Silver 0.4978 oz. ASW, 33 mm.
Subject: Moscow Waterworks **Rev:** Building in multicolor,
aqueduct in background

Date	Mintage	F	VF	XF	Unc	BU
2007	1,000	—	—	—	—	35.00

KM# 301 250 TUGRIK
15.5000 g., 0.9990 Silver 0.4978 oz. ASW, 33 mm.
Subject: Moscow Metro **Rev:** Subway train, multicolor

Date	Mintage	F	VF	XF	Unc	BU
2007	1,000	—	—	—	—	35.00

KM# 270 250 TUGRIK
15.5500 g., 0.9250 Silver 0.4624 oz. ASW, 37 mm.
Subject: Baby Boy **Obv:** Arms **Rev:** Baby seated on flower,
multicolor **Shape:** Heart

Date	Mintage	F	VF	XF	Unc	BU
2008 Proof	2,500	Value: 40.00				

KM# 271 250 TUGRIK
15.5500 g., 0.9250 Silver 0.4624 oz. ASW, 37 mm. **Subject:**
Baby Girl **Obv:** Arms **Rev:** Baby Girl on flower **Shape:** Heart

Date	Mintage	F	VF	XF	Unc	BU
2008 Proof	2,500	Value: 40.00				

KM# 189 500 TUGRIK
25.0000 g., 0.9250 Silver 0.7435 oz. ASW, 38.7 mm.
Obv: National emblem above value **Rev:** Protoceratops
Andrewsi **Edge:** Reeded

Date	Mintage	F	VF	XF	Unc	BU
2001 Proof	2,500	Value: 40.00				

KM# 190 500 TUGRIK
25.0000 g., 0.9250 Silver 0.7435 oz. ASW **Obv:** National
emblem above value **Rev:** Velociraptor Mongoliensis

Date	Mintage	F	VF	XF	Unc	BU
2001 Proof	2,500	Value: 40.00				

KM# 191 500 TUGRIK
25.0000 g., 0.9250 Silver 0.7435 oz. ASW **Series:** Olympics **Obv:** National emblem above value **Rev:** Speed skater

Date	Mintage	F	VF	XF	Unc	BU
2001 Proof	15,000		Value: 25.00			

KM# 192 500 TUGRIK
25.0000 g., 0.9250 Silver 0.7435 oz. ASW **Series:** Olympics **Obv:** National emblem above value **Rev:** Cross-country skiers

Date	Mintage	F	VF	XF	Unc	BU
2001 Proof	20,000		Value: 22.50			

KM# 195 500 TUGRIK
Copper-Nickel, 22.1 mm. **Subject:** Sukhe-Bataar **Obv:** National emblem and value **Rev:** Crowned head facing **Edge:** Plain

Date	Mintage	F	VF	XF	Unc	BU
2001	—	—	—	—	2.50	3.00

KM# 238 500 TUGRIK
20.0000 g., 0.9250 Silver 0.5948 oz. ASW **Subject:** Gobi Desert Brown Bear **Obv:** Arms **Rev:** Bear standing on rock in stream

Date	Mintage	F	VF	XF	Unc	BU
2001 Proof	—		Value: 25.00			

KM# 239 500 TUGRIK
31.1050 g., 0.9990 Silver 0.9990 oz., 38.5 mm. **Subject:** Year of the Snake **Rev:** Snake

Date	Mintage	F	VF	XF	Unc	BU
2001 Proof	—		Value: 65.00			

KM# 239a 500 TUGRIK
31.1050 g., 0.9990 Silver partially gilt 0.9990 oz. ASW **Subject:** Year of the Snake **Obv:** Arms **Rev:** Snake, gilt

Date	Mintage	F	VF	XF	Unc	BU
2001 Proof	—		Value: 75.00			

KM# 241 500 TUGRIK
31.1050 g., 0.9990 Silver 0.9990 oz. ASW, 38.5 mm. **Subject:** Year of the Horse **Obv:** Arms **Rev:** Horse

Date	Mintage	F	VF	XF	Unc	BU
2002 Proof	—		Value: 65.00			

KM# 241a 500 TUGRIK
31.1050 g., 0.9990 Silver partially gilt 0.9990 oz. ASW, 38.5 mm. **Subject:** Year of the Horse **Rev:** Horse, gilt

Date	Mintage	F	VF	XF	Unc	BU
2002 Proof	—		Value: 75.00			

KM# 200 500 TUGRIK
25.5700 g., 0.9250 Silver 0.7604 oz. ASW, 38.5 mm. **Subject:** Marco Polo, Homeward **Obv:** National emblem above value **Rev:** Five-masted sailing junk **Edge:** Reeded

Date	Mintage	F	VF	XF	Unc	BU
2003 Proof	5,000		Value: 45.00			

KM# 205 500 TUGRIK
25.0000 g., 0.9250 Silver 0.7435 oz. ASW, 38.6 mm. **Obv:** National emblem above value **Rev:** Medallion divides busts **Edge:** Reeded

Date	Mintage	F	VF	XF	Unc	BU
2003 Proof	5,000		Value: 55.00			

KM# 206 500 TUGRIK
1.2440 g., 0.9999 Gold 0.0400 oz. AGW, 13.92 mm. **Obv:** National emblem above value **Rev:** Five masted sailing junk **Edge:** Reeded

Date	Mintage	F	VF	XF	Unc	BU
2003 Proof	25,000		Value: 50.00			

KM# 207 500 TUGRIK
1.2440 g., 0.9999 Gold 0.0400 oz. AGW, 13.92 mm. **Obv:** National emblem above value **Rev:** Medallion divides busts **Edge:** Reeded

Date	Mintage	F	VF	XF	Unc	BU
2003 Proof	25,000		Value: 55.00			

KM# 204 500 TUGRIK
25.0000 g., 0.9250 Silver 0.7435 oz. ASW, 38 mm. **Obv:** National emblem above value **Rev:** Wolf within full moon **Edge:** Reeded

Date	Mintage	F	VF	XF	Unc	BU
2003 Proof	10,000		Value: 55.00			

KM# 229 500 TUGRIK
31.1050 g., 0.9990 Silver 0.9990 oz. ASW **Obv:** Arms above legend **Rev:** Ram standing left

Date	Mintage	F	VF	XF	Unc	BU
2003	—	—	—	—		65.00

KM# 229a 500 TUGRIK
31.1050 g., 0.9990 Silver partialy gilt 0.9990 oz. ASW, 38.5 mm. **Subject:** Year of the Ram **Obv:** Arms **Rev:** Ram standing left, gilt

Date	Mintage	F	VF	XF	Unc	BU
2003 Proof	—		Value: 75.00			

KM# 208 500 TUGRIK
25.0000 g., 0.9250 Silver 0.7435 oz. ASW, 38 mm. **Obv:** National emblem above value **Rev:** Holographic Osprey catching fish **Edge:** Reeded

Date	Mintage	F	VF	XF	Unc	BU
2004 Proof	5,000		Value: 50.00			

KM# 218 500 TUGRIK
31.2400 g., 0.9990 Silver 1.0033 oz. ASW, 38.59 mm. **Series:** Chinese Lunar **Subject:** Year of the Monkey **Obv:** National emblem **Rev:** Monkey seated on branch - gilt, border of scampering monkeys **Edge:** Reeded

Date	Mintage	F	VF	XF	Unc	BU
ND(2004) Proof	20,000		Value: 35.00			

KM# 219 500 TUGRIK
1.2400 g., 0.9999 Gold 0.0399 oz. AGW **Series:** Chinese Lunar **Subject:** Year of the Monkey **Obv:** National emblem **Rev:** Monkey seated on branch

Date	Mintage	F	VF	XF	Unc	BU
ND(2004) Proof	—		Value: 55.00			

KM# 244 500 TUGRIK
31.1050 g., 0.9990 Silver 0.9990 oz. ASW, 38.5 mm. **Subject:** Year of the Monkey **Rev:** Monkey

Date	Mintage	F	VF	XF	Unc	BU
2004 Proof	—		Value: 65.00			

KM# 244a 500 TUGRIK
31.1050 g., 0.9990 Silver partially gilt 0.9990 oz. ASW, 38.5 mm. **Subject:** Year of the Monkey **Obv:** Arms **Rev:** Monkey, gilt

Date	Mintage	F	VF	XF	Unc	BU
2004 Proof	—		Value: 75.00			

KM# 209 500 TUGRIK
24.9300 g., 0.9250 Bi-Metallic Niobium Leopard shape center in .925 Silver oval 0.7414 oz., 30 mm. **Obv:** National emblem above value **Rev:** Snow Leopard **Edge:** Reeded **Shape:** Oval

Date	Mintage	F	VF	XF	Unc	BU
2005 Proof	5,000		Value: 75.00			

KM# 210 500 TUGRIK
31.1035 g., 0.9990 Silver 0.9990 oz. ASW, 35x35 mm. **Obv:** Bronze plated horse and rider on antiqued silver with national emblem and value **Rev:** Bronze plated horse and rider on antiqued silver above date **Edge:** Reeded **Shape:** Square

Date	Mintage	F	VF	XF	Unc	BU
2005	2,500	—	—	—	65.00	70.00

KM# 210a 500 TUGRIK
31.1035 g., 0.9990 Silver 0.9990 oz. ASW, 35x35 mm.
Obv: Gold plated horse and rider with national emblem and value
Rev: Gold plated horse and rider above date **Edge:** Reeded

Date	Mintage	F	VF	XF	Unc	BU
2005 Proof	2,500		Value: 75.00			

KM# 246 500 TUGRIK
31.1050 g., 0.9990 Silver 0.9990 oz. ASW, 38.5 mm.
Subject: Year of the Rooster **Obv:** Arms **Rev:** Rooster standing right

Date	Mintage	F	VF	XF	Unc	BU
2005 Proof	—		Value: 65.00			

KM# 246a 500 TUGRIK
31.1050 g., 0.9990 Silver 0.9990 oz. ASW, 38.5 mm.
Subject: Year of the Rooster **Obv:** Arms **Rev:** Rooster, gilt

Date	Mintage	F	VF	XF	Unc	BU
2005 Proof	—		Value: 75.00			

KM# 230 500 TUGRIK
25.0000 g., 0.9250 Silver 0.7435 oz. ASW **Rev:** Swan with crystal insert

Date	Mintage	F	VF	XF	Unc	BU
2006 Proof	—		Value: 60.00			

KM# 231 500 TUGRIK
25.0000 g., 0.9250 Silver 0.7435 oz. ASW **Rev:** Gobi bear head with crystal inserts

Date	Mintage	F	VF	XF	Unc	BU
2006 Proof	—		Value: 100			

KM# 248 500 TUGRIK
25.0000 g., 0.9250 Silver 0.7435 oz. ASW **Subject:** Long Eared Jerboa **Obv:** Arms **Rev:** Long eared jerboa, crystal eyes **Shape:** 38.6

Date	Mintage	F	VF	XF	Unc	BU
2006 Proof	2,500		Value: 40.00			

KM# 249 500 TUGRIK
25.0000 g., 0.9250 Silver 0.7435 oz. ASW, 38.6 mm. **Obv:** Arms **Rev:** Scorpion, crystal tail point

Date	Mintage	F	VF	XF	Unc	BU
2006 Proof	2,500		Value: 40.00			

KM# 250 500 TUGRIK
25.0000 g., 0.9250 Silver 0.7435 oz. ASW, 38.6 mm. **Rev:** Tiger, head facing, crystal eyes

Date	Mintage	F	VF	XF	Unc	BU
2006 Proof	2,500		Value: 40.00			

KM# 251 500 TUGRIK
31.1050 g., 0.9990 Silver 0.9990 oz. ASW, 38.5 mm.
Subject: Year of the Dog **Obv:** Arms **Rev:** Dog standing

Date	Mintage	F	VF	XF	Unc	BU
2006 Proof	—		Value: 40.00			

KM# 251a 500 TUGRIK
31.1050 g., 0.9990 Silver 0.9990 oz. ASW, 38.5 mm.
Subject: Year of the Dog **Obv:** Arms **Rev:** Dog standing, gilt

Date	Mintage	F	VF	XF	Unc	BU
2006 Proof	—		Value: 65.00			

KM# 260 500 TUGRIK
25.0000 g., 0.9250 Silver 0.7435 oz. ASW, 38.6 mm.
Subject: Great Mongolian State, 800th Anniversary **Obv:** Arms **Rev:** Chinggis Khan and black pennant

Date	Mintage	F	VF	XF	Unc	BU
2006 Proof	2,500		Value: 50.00			

KM# 261 500 TUGRIK
25.0000 g., 0.9250 Silver 0.7435 oz. ASW, 38.61 mm.
Subject: Great Mongolian State, 800th Anniversary **Obv:** Arms **Rev:** Nine white pennants

Date	Mintage	F	VF	XF	Unc	BU
2006 Proof	2,500		Value: 50.00			

KM# 212 500 TUGRIK
31.1050 g., 0.9990 Silver 0.9990 oz. ASW, 38 mm. **Obv:** Arms and value **Rev:** Wolverine head facing with diamonds in eyes **Rev. Inscription:** WILDLIFE PROTECTION GULO GULO

Date	Mintage	F	VF	XF	Unc	BU
2007	—	—	—	—	—	95.00

KM# 265 500 TUGRIK
31.1050 g., 0.9990 Silver 0.9990 oz. ASW, 38.61 mm.
Subject: Society Space exploration **Obv:** Arms **Rev:** Sputnik, rocket, three figures

Date	Mintage	F	VF	XF	Unc	BU
2007 Proof	1,000		Value: 75.00			

KM# 266 500 TUGRIK
31.1050 g., 0.9990 Silver 0.9990 oz. ASW, 38.61 mm.
Subject: Soviet Space Exploration **Rev:** Laika, first dog in space

Date	Mintage	F	VF	XF	Unc	BU
2007 Proof	500		Value: 75.00			

KM# 267 500 TUGRIK
31.1050 g., 0.9990 Silver 0.9990 oz. ASW, 38.61 mm.
Subject: Soviet Space Exploration **Obv:** Arms **Rev:** Sputnik

Date	Mintage	F	VF	XF	Unc	BU
2007 Proof	500		Value: 75.00			

KM# 268 500 TUGRIK
31.1050 g., 0.9990 Silver 0.9990 oz. ASW, 38.61 mm. **Subject:** Soviet Space Exploration **Obv:** Arms **Rev:** Yuri Gagarin

Date	Mintage	F	VF	XF	Unc	BU
2007 Proof	500		Value: 75.00			

KM# 269 500 TUGRIK
31.1050 g., 0.9990 Silver 0.9990 oz. ASW, 38.61 mm. **Subject:** Soviety Space Exploration **Obv:** Arms **Rev:** Mir space station

Date	Mintage	F	VF	XF	Unc	BU
2007 Proof	1,000		Value: 75.00			

KM# 222 500 TUGRIK
25.0000 g., 0.9250 Silver 0.7435 oz. ASW, 38.61 mm. **Subject:** Wonders of the World **Obv:** Arms **Rev:** Multicolor Chichen Itza

Date	Mintage	F	VF	XF	Unc	BU
2008	2,500	—	—	—	—	70.00

KM# 223 500 TUGRIK
25.0000 g., 0.9250 Silver 0.7435 oz. ASW, 38.6 mm.
Subject: Wonders of the World **Obv:** Arms **Rev:** Multicolor Treasury at Petra

Date	Mintage	F	VF	XF	Unc	BU
2008	2,500	—	—	—	—	70.00

KM# 224 500 TUGRIK
25.0000 g., 0.9250 Silver 0.7435 oz. ASW, 38.61 mm. **Subject:** Wonders of the World **Obv:** Arms **Rev:** Multicolor Taj Mahal

Date	Mintage	F	VF	XF	Unc	BU
2008	2,500	—	—	—	—	70.00

KM# 225 500 TUGRIK
25.0000 g., 0.9250 Silver 0.7435 oz. ASW, 38.61 mm. **Subject:** Wonders of the World **Obv:** Arms **Rev:** Multicolor Machu Picchu

Date	Mintage	F	VF	XF	Unc	BU
2008	2,500	—	—	—	—	70.00

KM# 226 500 TUGRIK
25.0000 g., 0.9250 Silver 0.7435 oz. ASW, 38.61 mm.
Subject: Wonders of the World **Obv:** Arms **Rev:** Multicolor Great Wall of China

Date	Mintage	F	VF	XF	Unc	BU
2008	2,500	—	—	—	—	70.00

KM# 227 500 TUGRIK
25.0000 g., 0.9250 Silver 0.7435 oz. ASW, 38.61 mm.
Subject: Wonders of the World **Obv:** Arms **Rev:** Multicolor Colosseum in Rome

Date	Mintage	F	VF	XF	Unc	BU
2008	2,500	—	—	—	—	70.00

KM# 228 500 TUGRIK
25.0000 g., 0.9250 Silver 0.7435 oz. ASW, 38.61 mm.
Subject: Wonders of the World **Obv:** Arms **Rev:** Multicolor Christ the Redeemer statue in Rio

Date	Mintage	F	VF	XF	Unc	BU
2008	2,500	—	—	—	—	70.00

KM# 213 500 TUGRIK
31.1000 g., 0.9990 Silver 0.9988 oz. ASW, 39mm mm.
Subject: Year of the Rat **Obv:** National emblem, value below **Rev:** Three rats in grass **Edge:** Reeded

Date	Mintage	F	VF	XF	Unc	BU
2008	20,000	—	—	—	—	35.00

KM# 213a 500 TUGRIK
31.1000 g., 0.9990 Silver 0.9988 oz. ASW, 39.0 mm.
Subject: Year of the Rat **Obv:** National emblem, value below **Rev:** Three gilt rats in grass **Edge:** Reeded

Date	Mintage	F	VF	XF	Unc	BU
2008 Proof	5,000		Value: 45.00			

KM# 255 500 TUGRIK
25.0000 g., 0.9250 Silver 0.7435 oz. ASW, 38.6 mm.
Subject: Frederic Chopin **Obv:** Arms **Rev:** Bust right, color keyboard vertical in center

Date	Mintage	F	VF	XF	Unc	BU
2008 Proof	1,000		Value: 90.00			

KM# 256 500 TUGRIK
31.1050 g., 0.9990 Silver 0.9990 oz. ASW, 38.6 mm.
Subject: Year of the Rat **Obv:** Arms **Rev:** Two mice

Date	Mintage	F	VF	XF	Unc	BU
2008 Proof	—		Value: 50.00			

KM# 256a 500 TUGRIK
31.1050 g., 0.9990 Silver partially gilt 0.9990 oz. ASW, 38.6 mm.
Subject: Year of the Rat **Obv:** Arms **Rev:** Two mice, gilt

Date	Mintage	F	VF	XF	Unc	BU
2008 Proof	—		Value: 60.00			

KM# 272 500 TUGRIK
25.0000 g., 0.9250 Silver 0.7435 oz. ASW, 38.6 mm.
Series: Mongolian Olympians, Baatarjav **Obv:** Arms

Date	Mintage	F	VF	XF	Unc	BU
2008 Proof	2,500		Value: 40.00			

KM# 273 500 TUGRIK
25.0000 g., 0.9250 Silver 0.7435 oz. ASW, 38.61 mm.
Subject: Mongolian Olympians - Badar-Uugan

Date	Mintage	F	VF	XF	Unc	BU
2008 Proof	2,500		Value: 40.00			

KM# 274 500 TUGRIK
25.0000 g., 0.9990 Silver 0.8029 oz. ASW, 38.61 mm.
Subject: Mongolian Olympians - Serdamba

Date	Mintage	F	VF	XF	Unc	BU
2008 Proof	2,500		Value: 40.00			

KM# 275 500 TUGRIK
25.0000 g., 0.9250 Silver 0.7435 oz. ASW, 38.61 mm.
Subject: Mongolian Olympians - Tuvshinbayar

Date	Mintage	F	VF	XF	Unc	BU
2008 Proof	2,500		Value: 40.00			

KM# 276 500 TUGRIK
25.0000 g., 0.9250 Silver 0.7435 oz. ASW, 38.61 mm.
Subject: Mongolian Olympians - Gundegmaa

Date	Mintage	F	VF	XF	Unc	BU
2008 Proof	2,500		Value: 40.00			

KM# 279 500 TUGRIK
0.5000 g., 0.9990 Gold 0.0161 oz. AGW, 11 mm.
Subject: Mongolian Olympic Sports - Archery

Date	Mintage	F	VF	XF	Unc	BU
2008 Proof	15,000	—	—	—	—	40.00

KM# 280 500 TUGRIK
25.0000 g., 0.9250 Silver 0.7435 oz. ASW, 38.61 mm.
Obv: Arms **Rev:** Two snow leopards, multicolor

Date	Mintage	F	VF	XF	Unc	BU
2008 Proof	2,500		Value: 40.00			

KM# 281 500 TUGRIK
25.0000 g., 0.9250 Silver 0.7435 oz. ASW, 38.61 mm.
Obv: Arms **Rev:** The Almas, multicolor changing insert

Date	Mintage	F	VF	XF	Unc	BU
2008 Proof	2,500		Value: 40.00			

KM# 258 500 TUGRIK
31.1050 g., 0.9990 Silver 0.9990 oz. ASW, 38.6 mm.
Subject: Year of the Ox **Obv:** Arms **Rev:** Ox

Date	Mintage	F	VF	XF	Unc	BU
2009 Proof	—		Value: 50.00			

KM# 258a   500 TUGRIK
31.1050 g., 0.9990 Silver partially gilt 0.9990 oz. ASW, 38.6 mm.
Subject: Year of the Ox **Obv:** Arms **Rev:** Ox, gilt

Date	Mintage	F	VF	XF	Unc	BU
2009 Proof	—		Value: 60.00			

KM# 199   1000 TUGRIK
31.1100 g., 0.9250 Silver 0.9252 oz. ASW, 38.6 mm. **Obv:**
National emblem above value **Obv. Inscription:** Denomination
spelled "TOGROG" **Rev:** Head facing **Edge:** Reeded

Date	Mintage	F	VF	XF	Unc	BU
2002	17,000	—	—	—	30.00	35.00

KM# 233   1000 TUGRIK
Gold **Rev:** Snow leopard

Date	Mintage	F	VF	XF	Unc	BU
2005 Proof	—		Value: 76.00			

KM# 253   1000 TUGRIK
1.2400 g., 0.9990 Gold 0.0398 oz. AGW **Subject:** Mozart
Obv: Arms **Rev:** Portrait and profile heads above building

Date	Mintage	F	VF	XF	Unc	BU
2006 Proof	—		Value: 60.00			

KM# 262   1000 TUGRIK
1.2400 g., 0.9990 Gold 0.0398 oz. AGW, 13.92 mm. **Obv:** Arms
Rev: Scorpion

Date	Mintage	F	VF	XF	Unc	BU
2006 Proof	25,000		Value: 75.00			

KM# 263   1000 TUGRIK
1.2400 g., 0.9990 Silver 0.0398 oz. ASW, 13.9 mm. **Obv:** Arms
Rev: Long-eared Jerboa

Date	Mintage	F	VF	XF	Unc	BU
2006 Proof	—		Value: 75.00			

KM# 264   1000 TUGRIK
1.2400 g., 0.9990 Gold 0.0398 oz. AGW, 13.9 mm. **Obv:** Arms
Rev: Gobi Bear

Date	Mintage	F	VF	XF	Unc	BU
2006 Proof	25,000		Value: 75.00			

KM# 294   1000 TUGRIK
62.2000 g., 0.9990 Silver 1.9977 oz. ASW, 50 mm. **Rev:** Tsarina
Catherina multicolor

Date	Mintage	F	VF	XF	Unc	BU
2007 Proof	500		Value: 75.00			

KM# 295   1000 TUGRIK
62.2000 g., 0.9990 Silver 1.9977 oz. ASW, 50 mm. **Rev:** Tsar
Nicholas I, multicolor

Date	Mintage	F	VF	XF	Unc	BU
2007 Proof	500		Value: 75.00			

KM# 296   1000 TUGRIK
62.2000 g., 0.9990 Silver 1.9977 oz. ASW, 50 mm. **Rev:** Tsar
Nicholas II

Date	Mintage	F	VF	XF	Unc	BU
2007 Proof	500		Value: 75.00			

KM# 297   1000 TUGRIK
62.2000 g., 0.9990 Silver 1.9977 oz. ASW, 50 mm. **Rev:** Tsar
Ivan IV, multicolor

Date	Mintage	F	VF	XF	Unc	BU
2007 Proof	500		Value: 75.00			

KM# 298   1000 TUGRIK
62.2000 g., 0.9990 Silver 1.9977 oz. ASW, 50 mm. **Rev:** Tsar
Peter I, multicolor

Date	Mintage	F	VF	XF	Unc	BU
2007 Proof	500		Value: 75.00			

KM# 299   1000 TUGRIK
62.2000 g., 0.9990 Silver 1.9977 oz. ASW, 50 mm. **Rev:** Tsar
Yuri

Date	Mintage	F	VF	XF	Unc	BU
2007 Proof	500		Value: 75.00			

KM# 214   1000 TUGRIK
1.2400 g., 0.9990 Gold 0.0398 oz. AGW, 14.0 mm.
Subject: Year of the Rat **Obv:** National emblem, value below
Edge: Reeded

Date	Mintage	F	VF	XF	Unc	BU
2008 Proof	10,000		Value: 60.00			

KM# 277   1000 TUGRIK
1.2400 g., 0.9990 Gold 0.0398 oz. AGW, 13.92 mm. **Subject:**
Mongolian Olympic Sports - Boxing **Rev:** Two fighters in the ring

Date	Mintage	F	VF	XF	Unc	BU
2008 Proof	15,000		Value: 75.00			

KM# 278   1000 TUGRIK
1.2400 g., 0.9990 Gold 0.0398 oz. AGW, 13.92 mm. **Subject:**
Mongolian Olympic Sports - Judo **Rev:** Judo athlete getting fliped

Date	Mintage	F	VF	XF	Unc	BU
2008 Proof	15,000		Value: 75.00			

KM# 240   2500 TUGRIK
7.7700 g., 0.9990 Gold 0.2496 oz. AGW **Subject:** Year of the
Snake **Obv:** Arms **Rev:** Snake

Date	Mintage	F	VF	XF	Unc	BU
2001 Proof	2,000		Value: 340			

KM# 242   2500 TUGRIK
7.7000 g., 0.9990 Gold 0.2473 oz. AGW **Subject:** Year of the
Horse **Obv:** Arms **Rev:** Year of the Horse

Date	Mintage	F	VF	XF	Unc	BU
2002 Proof	—		Value: 340			

KM# 243   2500 TUGRIK
155.5000 g., 0.9990 Silver partially gilt 4.9942 oz. ASW, 65 mm.
Subject: Year of the Ram **Obv:** Arms **Rev:** Ram standing left, gilt

Date	Mintage	F	VF	XF	Unc	BU
2003 Proof	4,000	Value: 325				

KM# 245   2500 TUGRIK
155.5000 g., 0.9990 Silver partially gilt 4.9942 oz. ASW, 65 mm.
Subject: Year of the Monkey **Obv:** Arms **Rev:** Monkey, gilt

Date	Mintage	F	VF	XF	Unc	BU
2004 Proof	4,000	Value: 325				

KM# 220   2500 TUGRIK
7.7800 g., 0.9999 Gold 0.2501 oz. AGW **Series:** Chinese Lunar
Subject: Year of the Monkey **Obv:** National emblem
Rev: Monkey seated on branch **Edge:** Reeded

Date	Mintage	F	VF	XF	Unc	BU
ND(2004) Proof	2,000	Value: 375				

KM# 247   2500 TUGRIK
155.5000 g., 0.9990 Silver partially gilt 4.9942 oz. ASW, 65 mm.
Subject: Year of the Rooster **Obv:** Arms **Rev:** Rooster, gilt

Date	Mintage	F	VF	XF	Unc	BU
2005 Proof	4,000	Value: 325				

KM# 252   2500 TUGRIK
155.5000 g., 0.9990 Silver partially gilt 4.9942 oz. ASW, 65 mm.
Subject: Year of the Dog **Obv:** Arms **Rev:** Dog standing, gilt

Date	Mintage	F	VF	XF	Unc	BU
2006 Proof	—	Value: 325				

KM# 257   2500 TUGRIK
155.5000 g., 0.9990 Silver partially gilt 4.9942 oz. ASW, 65 mm.
Subject: Year of the Rat **Obv:** Arms **Rev:** Two mice, gilt

Date	Mintage	F	VF	XF	Unc	BU
2008 Proof	—	Value: 325				

KM# 259   2500 TUGRIK
155.5000 g., 0.9990 Silver partially gilt 4.9942 oz. ASW, 65 mm.
Subject: Year of the Ox **Obv:** Arms **Rev:** Ox, gilt

Date	Mintage	F	VF	XF	Unc	BU
2009 Proof	—	Value: 325				

KM# 198   5000 TUGRIK
155.5000 g., 0.9990 Silver 4.9942 oz. ASW, 40x90 mm.
Subject: Year of the Horse **Obv:** National emblem above value to left of Palace Museum **Rev:** Five multicolor running horses **Edge:** Plain **Note:** Round-cornered rectangle. Photo reduced.

Date	Mintage	F	VF	XF	Unc	BU
2002 Proof	—	Value: 175				

KM# 232   5000 TUGRIK
155.5000 g., 0.9990 Silver 4.9942 oz. ASW, 40x90 mm.
Rev: Three sumo wrestlers, multicolor **Shape:** Rectangle
Note: Illustration reduced.

Date	Mintage	F	VF	XF	Unc	BU
2005 Proof	—	Value: 300				

KM# 221   1.0000 TUGRIK
3000.0000 g., 0.9990 Silver 96.351 oz. ASW **Series:** Chinese Lunar **Subject:** Year of the Monkey **Obv:** National emblem **Rev:** Monkey seated on branch

Date	Mintage	F	VF	XF	Unc	BU
ND(2004) Proof	—	Value: 2,250				

KM# 215   1.0000 TUGRIK
3000.0000 g., 0.9990 Silver 96.351 oz. ASW, 130.0 mm.
Subject: Year of the Rat **Obv:** National emblem, value below **Rev:** Three rats in grass **Edge:** Reeded **Note:** Serial number on edge.

Date	Mintage	F	VF	XF	Unc	BU
2008 Proof	500	Value: 2,250				

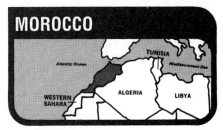

MOROCCO

The Kingdom of Morocco, situated on the northwest corner of Africa, has an area of 432,620 sq. mi. (710,850 sq. km.) and a population of 36 million. Capital: Rabat. The economy is essentially agricultural. Phosphates, fresh and preserved vegetables, canned fish, and raw materials are exported.

KINGDOM
Mohammed VI
AH1420/1999AD

REFORM COINAGE
100 Santimat = 1 Dirham

Y# 116   1/2 DIRHAM
4.0000 g., Copper-Nickel, 21 mm. **Obv:** Crowned arms with supporters **Rev:** Value, design theme "telecommunications and new technologies" **Edge:** Reeded

Date	Mintage	F	VF	XF	Unc	BU
AH1423-2002	—	—	—	—	2.00	3.00

Y# 117   DIRHAM
6.0000 g., Copper-Nickel, 24 mm. **Obv:** Head 3/4 left **Rev:** Crowned arms with supporters above value **Edge:** Reeded

Date	Mintage	F	VF	XF	Unc	BU
AH1423-2002	—	—	—	—	3.00	5.00

Y# 112   5 SANTIMAT
2.5000 g., Brass, 17.5 mm. **Obv:** Crowned arms with supporters **Rev:** Value, flower and dates **Edge:** Plain

Date	Mintage	F	VF	XF	Unc	BU
AH1423-2002	—	—	—	—	0.50	1.00

Y# 114   10 SANTIMAT
3.0000 g., Brass, 19.8 mm. **Obv:** Crowned arms with supporters **Rev:** Value, design of "sport and solidarity" **Edge:** Reeded

Date	Mintage	F	VF	XF	Unc	BU
AH1423-2002	—	—	—	—	1.00	2.00

Y# 115   20 SANTIMAT
4.0000 g., Brass, 23 mm. **Obv:** Crowned arms with supporters **Rev:** Value, design of "tourist and craftsmen trade"
Edge: Reeded

Date	Mintage	F	VF	XF	Unc	BU
AH1423-2002	—	—	—	—	1.50	3.00

Y# 118   2 DIRHAMS
7.3000 g., Copper-Nickel, 25.9 mm. **Obv:** Head 3/4 left within octagon shape **Rev:** Crowned arms with supporters above value within octogon shape **Edge:** Reeded

Date	Mintage	F	VF	XF	Unc	BU
AH1423-2002	—	—	—	—	4.00	6.00

Y# 109   5 DIRHAMS
7.5300 g., Bi-Metallic Brass center in Copper-Nickel ring, 25 mm. **Obv:** Head 3/4 left **Rev:** Crowned arms with supporters above value **Edge:** Segmented reeding

Date	Mintage	F	VF	XF	Unc	BU
AH1423-2002	—	—	—	—	6.00	9.00

Y# 124   5 DIRHAMS
Bi-Metallic **Obv:** King Hassan II 1903-2000 **Rev:** Coat of arms

Date	Mintage	F	VF	XF	Unc	BU
2002	—	—	—	—	6.00	9.00

Y# 110   10 DIRHAMS
9.0000 g., Bi-Metallic Copper-Nickel center in Brass ring, 26.9 mm. **Obv:** Head 3/4 left **Rev:** Crowned arms with supporters above value **Edge:** Reeded

Date	Mintage	F	VF	XF	Unc	BU
AH1423-2002	—	—	—	—	10.00	15.00

Y# 107   250 DIRHAMS
25.0000 g., 0.9250 Silver 0.7435 oz. ASW, 37 mm.
Subject: Inauguration of Mohammed VI 2nd Anniversary **Obv:** Head 3/4 left **Rev:** Crowned arms with supporters above value **Edge:** Reeded

Date	Mintage	F	VF	XF	Unc	BU
AH1422-2001	—	—	—	—	55.00	70.00

Y# 95   250 DIRHAMS
25.0000 g., 0.9250 Silver 0.7435 oz. ASW, 37 mm.
Subject: World Children's Day **Obv:** Head 3/4 left **Rev:** Children standing on open book within globe **Edge:** Reeded

Date	Mintage	F	VF	XF	Unc	BU
AH1422-2001	—	—	—	—	55.00	70.00
AH1422-2001 Proof	—	Value: 90.00				

Y# 95a   250 DIRHAMS
25.0000 g., 0.9999 Gold 0.8037 oz. AGW, 37 mm.
Subject: World Children's Day **Obv:** Head 3/4 left **Rev:** Two children standing on an open book within globe **Edge:** Reeded
Note: Prev. Y#95.

Date	Mintage	F	VF	XF	Unc	BU
AH1422-2001 Proof	2,800	Value: 925				

Y# 108   250 DIRHAMS
25.0000 g., 0.9250 Silver 0.7435 oz. ASW, 37 mm.
Subject: Mohammed VI's Inauguration 3rd Anniversary
Obv: Head 3/4 left **Rev:** Crowned arms with supporters above
value **Edge:** Reeded **Note:** Slightly different legend of Y-107

Date	Mintage	F	VF	XF	Unc	BU
AH1423-2002	—			—	55.00	70.00
AH1423-2002 Proof	—	Value: 90.00				

Y# 113   250 DIRHAMS
25.0000 g., 0.9250 Silver 0.7435 oz. ASW, 37 mm.
Subject: Marriage of King Mohamed VI, July 12, 2002 **Obv:** Head
3/4 left **Rev:** Crown above radiant flowers **Edge:** Reeded

Date	Mintage	F	VF	XF	Unc	BU
ND (2002) Proof	—	Value: 90.00				

Y# 119   250 DIRHAMS
25.0000 g., Silver, 37 mm. **Subject:** Birth of Crown Prince
Moulay Al Hassan **Obv:** Head 3/4 left **Rev:** Crowned arms with
supporters above value

Date	Mintage	F	VF	XF	Unc	BU
ND (2003) Proof	—	Value: 90.00				

Y# 120   250 DIRHAMS
25.0000 g., Silver, 37 mm. **Subject:** 50th Anniversary - Kingdom
Obv: Conjoined heads right **Rev:** Crowned arms with supporters
above value

Date	Mintage	F	VF	XF	Unc	BU
AH1424-2003	—			—	55.00	70.00
AH1424-2003 Proof	—	Value: 90.00				

Y# 111   250 DIRHAMS
25.0000 g., 0.9250 Silver 0.7435 oz. ASW, 37 mm.
Subject: Mohammed VI's Inauguration 4th Anniversary **Obv:**
Head 3/4 left **Rev:** Crowned arms with supporters above value
Edge: Reeded **Note:** Virtually identical to Y-107 and Y-108.

Date	Mintage	F	VF	XF	Unc	BU
AH1424-2003	—			—	55.00	70.00

Y# 122   250 DIRHAMS
25.0000 g., 0.9250 Silver 0.7435 oz. ASW, 37 mm. **Subject:**
5th Anniversary of Mohammed VI's Reign **Obv:** Head 3/4 left,
national arms **Rev:** Crowned arms with supporters above value
Edge: Reeded **Note:** Vitually identical to Y-107, 108 and 111.

Date	Mintage	F	VF	XF	Unc	BU
AH1425-2004	—			—	55.00	70.00

Y# 121   250 DIRHAMS
25.0000 g., Silver, 37 mm. **Subject:** Year of Handicapped
Persons **Obv:** Head 3/4 left **Rev:** Stylized figures

Date	Mintage	F	VF	XF	Unc	BU
AH1425-2004	—			—	55.00	70.00

Y# 123   250 DIRHAMS
25.0000 g., Silver, 37 mm. **Subject:** 30th Anniversary - Green
March **Obv:** Head 3/4 left **Rev:** Men marching left with flags aloft

Date	Mintage	F	VF	XF	Unc	BU
AH1426-2005	—			—	55.00	70.00

MOZAMBIQUE

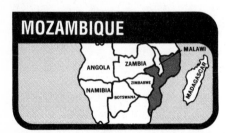

The Republic of Mozambique, a former overseas province of
Portugal, stretches for 1,430 miles (2,301 km.) along the southeast
coast of Africa, has an area of 302,330 sq. mi. (801,590 sq. km.)
and a population of 14.1 million, 99 % of whom are native Africans
of the Bantu tribes. Capital: Maputo. Agriculture is the chief industry. Cashew nuts, cotton, sugar, copra and tea are exported.

Mozambique became a member of the Commonwealth of
Nations in November 1995. The President is Head of State; the
Prime Minister is Head of Government.

REPUBLIC
REFORM COINAGE
100 Centavos = 1 Metical; 1994

KM# 130   1000 METICAIS
25.7100 g., 0.9800 Silver 0.8100 oz. ASW, 38.5 mm.
Subject: Pedro De Covilha, 1498 **Obv:** National arms within
circle **Rev:** Sailing ship within circle **Edge:** Reeded

Date	Mintage	F	VF	XF	Unc	BU
2003 Proof	—	Value: 40.00				

KM# 131   10000 METICAIS
8.0400 g., Bi-Metallic Stainless Steel center in Brass ring,
26.6 mm. **Obv:** National arms within circle **Rev:** Rhino within
circle **Edge:** Segmented reeding

Date	Mintage	F	VF	XF	Unc	BU
2003	—		3.50	5.00	7.50	12.00

REFORM COINAGE
(New) Metical = 1,000 Meticals; 2005

KM# 132   CENTAVO
2.0000 g., Copper Plated Steel, 15 mm. **Obv:** Bank logo, date
Obv. Legend: BANCO DE MOÇAMBIQUE **Rev:** Rhinoceros
standing left, value **Rev. Designer:** Michael Guilfoyle
Edge: Reeded

Date	Mintage	F	VF	XF	Unc	BU
2006	—	—	—	—	0.15	0.25

KM# 133   5 CENTAVOS
2.3000 g., Copper Plated Steel, 19 mm. **Obv:** Bank logo, date
Obv. Legend: BANCO DE MOÇAMBIQUE **Rev:** Cheetah
standing left, value **Rev. Designer:** Michael Guilfoyle
Edge: Reeded

Date	Mintage	F	VF	XF	Unc	BU
2006	—	—	—	0.10	0.25	0.35

KM# 134   10 CENTAVOS
3.0600 g., Brass Plated Steel, 17 mm. **Obv:** Bank logo, date
Obv. Legend: BANCO DE MOÇAMBIQUE **Rev:** Farmer
cultivating with tractor, value **Rev. Designer:** Michael Guilfoyle
Edge: Reeded

Date	Mintage	F	VF	XF	Unc	BU
2006	—	—	—	0.15	0.35	0.50

KM# 135   20 CENTAVOS
4.1000 g., Brass Plated Steel, 20 mm. **Obv:** Bank logo, date
Obv. Legend: BANCO DE MOÇAMBIQUE **Rev:** Cotton plant,
value **Rev. Designer:** Michael Guilfoyle **Edge:** Reeded

Date	Mintage	F	VF	XF	Unc	BU
2006	—	—	—	0.20	0.50	0.75

KM# 136   50 CENTAVOS
5.7400 g., Brass Plated Steel, 23 mm.   **Obv:** Bank logo, date
Obv. Legend: BANCO DE MOÇAMBIQUE **Rev:** Giant Kingfisher
perched on branch, value **Rev. Designer:** Michael Guilfoyle
Edge: Reeded

Date	Mintage	F	VF	XF	Unc	BU
2006	—			0.50	1.25	1.75

KM# 137   METICAL
5.3000 g., Nickel Plated Steel, 21 mm. **Obv:** Bank logo, date
Obv. Legend: BANCO DE MOÇAMBIQUE **Rev:** Young woman
seated left writing, value **Rev. Designer:** Michael Guilfoyle
Edge: Plain **Shape:** 7-sided

Date	Mintage	F	VF	XF	Unc	BU
2006	—			0.45	1.10	1.50

KM# 138   2 METICAIS
6.0000 g., Nickel Plated Steel, 24 mm. **Obv:** Bank logo, date **Obv.
Legend:** BANCO DE MOÇAMBIQUE **Rev:** Coelacanth fish, value
Rev. Designer: Michael Guilfoyle **Edge:** Segmented reeding

Date	Mintage	F	VF	XF	Unc	BU
2006	—	—	—	0.75	1.80	2.50

KM# 139   5 METICAIS
6.5000 g., Nickel Plated Steel, 27 mm. **Obv:** Bank logo, date **Obv.
Legend:** BANCO DE MOÇAMBIQUE **Rev:** Timbila (similar to a
xylophone), value **Rev. Designer:** Michael Guilfoyle **Edge:** Reeded

Date	Mintage	F	VF	XF	Unc	BU
2006	—	—	—	1.20	3.00	4.00

KM# 140   10 METICAIS
7.5100 g., Bi-Metallic Nickel Clad Steel center in Brass ring.,
24.92 mm. **Obv:** Bank logo **Obv. Legend:** BANCO • DE •
MOÇAMBIQUE **Rev:** Modern bank building, value below
Rev. Designer: Michael Guilfoyle **Edge:** Reeded

Date	Mintage	F	VF	XF	Unc	BU
2006	—	—	—	1.50	3.75	5.00

NAGORNO-KARABAKH

Nagorno-Karabakh, an ethnically Armenian enclave inside Azerbaijan (pop., 1991 est.: 193,000), SW region. It occupies an area of 1,700 sq mi (4,400 square km) on the NE flank of the Kara-bakh Mountain Range, with the capital city of Stepanakert.

Russia annexed the area from Persia in 1813, and in 1923 it was established as an autonomous province of the Azerbaijan S.S.R. In 1988 the region's ethnic Armenian majority demonstrated against Azerbaijani rule, and in 1991, after the breakup of the U.S.S.R. brought independence to Armenia and Azerbaijan, war broke out between the two ethnic groups. On January 8, 1992 the leaders of Nagorno-Karabakh declared independence as the Republic of Mountainous Karabakh (RMK). Since 1994, following a cease-fire, ethnic Armenians have held Karabakh, though officially it remains part of Azerbaijan. Karabakh remains sovereign, but the political and military condition is volatile and tensions frequently flare into skirmishes.

Its marvelous nature and geographic situation, have all facilitated Karabakh to be a center of science, poetry and, especially, of the musical culture of Azerbaijan.

MONETARY SYSTEM
100 Luma = 1 Dram

REPUBLIC

STANDARD COINAGE

KM# 6   50 LUMA
0.9500 g., Aluminum, 19.8 mm. **Obv:** National arms **Rev:** Horse cantering left **Edge:** Plain

Date	Mintage	F	VF	XF	Unc	BU
2004	—	—	—	—	1.00	1.25

KM# 7   50 LUMA
0.9500 g., Aluminum, 19.8 mm. **Obv:** National arms **Rev:** Gazelle **Edge:** Plain

Date	Mintage	F	VF	XF	Unc	BU
2004	—	—	—	—	1.00	1.25

KM# 8   DRAM
1.1300 g., Aluminum, 21.7 mm. **Obv:** National arms **Rev:** Pheasant **Edge:** Plain

Date	Mintage	F	VF	XF	Unc	BU
2004	—	—	—	—	1.00	1.25

KM# 9   DRAM
1.1200 g., Aluminum, 21.7 mm. **Obv:** National arms **Rev:** 1/2-length Saint facing **Edge:** Plain

Date	Mintage	F	VF	XF	Unc	BU
2004	—	—	—	—	1.00	1.25

KM# 10   DRAM
1.1300 g., Aluminum, 21.7 mm. **Obv:** National arms **Rev:** Cheetah facing **Edge:** Plain

Date	Mintage	F	VF	XF	Unc	BU
2004	—	—	—	—	1.00	1.25

KM# 11   5 DRAMS
4.4000 g., Brass, 21.8 mm. **Obv:** National arms **Rev:** Church **Edge:** Plain

Date	Mintage	F	VF	XF	Unc	BU
2004	—	—	—	—	1.00	1.50

KM# 12   5 DRAMS
4.5000 g., Brass, 21.8 mm. **Obv:** National arms **Rev:** Monument faces **Edge:** Plain

Date	Mintage	F	VF	XF	Unc	BU
2004	—	—	—	—	1.00	1.50

KM# 23   1000 DRAMS
31.4300 g., 0.9990 Silver 1.0094 oz. ASW, 38.9 mm. **Obv:** National arms **Rev:** Archer **Edge:** Plain

Date	Mintage	F	VF	XF	Unc	BU
2003 Proof	—	Value: 75.00				

KM# 24   1000 DRAMS
31.3300 g., 0.9990 Silver 1.0062 oz. ASW, 38.39 mm. **Series:** Armenian architectural sculpture **Obv:** National arms **Rev:** Church of the Holy Cross at Aghthamar, Turkey **Edge:** Plain

Date	Mintage	F	VF	XF	Unc	BU
2003 Proof	—	Value: 75.00				

KM# 25   1000 DRAMS
31.3000 g., 0.9990 Silver 1.0053 oz. ASW, 38.92 mm. **Obv:** National arms **Rev:** Bust of Kevork Chavoush 3/4 left **Edge:** Plain

Date	Mintage	F	VF	XF	Unc	BU
2004 Proof	—	Value: 75.00				

KM# 19   1000 DRAMS
31.3700 g., 0.9990 Silver 1.0075 oz. ASW, 38.9 mm. **Obv:** National arms **Rev:** Leopard head facing **Edge:** Plain

Date	Mintage	F	VF	XF	Unc	BU
2004 Proof	—	Value: 75.00				

KM# 19a   1000 DRAMS
31.3700 g., 0.9990 Silver Gilt 1.0075 oz. ASW, 38.9 mm. **Obv:** National arms **Rev:** Leopard head facing **Edge:** Plain

Date	Mintage	F	VF	XF	Unc	BU
2004 Proof	—	Value: 85.00				

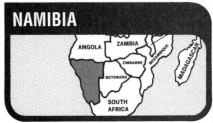

KM# 20   1000 DRAMS
31.3700 g., 0.9990 Silver 1.0075 oz. ASW, 38.9 mm. **Obv:** National arms **Rev:** Standing Brown Bear **Edge:** Plain

Date	Mintage	F	VF	XF	Unc	BU
2004 Proof	—	Value: 75.00				

KM# 20a   1000 DRAMS
31.3700 g., 0.9990 Silver Gilt 1.0075 oz. ASW, 38.9 mm. **Obv:** National arms **Rev:** Standing Brown Bear **Edge:** Plain

Date	Mintage	F	VF	XF	Unc	BU
2004 Proof	—	Value: 85.00				

KM# 21   1000 DRAMS
31.3700 g., 0.9990 Silver 1.0075 oz. ASW, 38.9 mm. **Obv:** National arms **Rev:** Eagle head within circle **Edge:** Plain

Date	Mintage	F	VF	XF	Unc	BU
2004 Proof	—	Value: 75.00				

KM# 21a   1000 DRAMS
31.3700 g., 0.9990 Silver Gilt 1.0075 oz. ASW, 38.9 mm. **Obv:** National arms **Rev:** Eagle head within circle **Edge:** Plain

Date	Mintage	F	VF	XF	Unc	BU
2004 Proof	—	Value: 85.00				

KM# 22   1000 DRAMS
31.1200 g., 0.9990 Silver 0.9995 oz. ASW, 38.9 mm. **Obv:** National arms **Rev:** 1918 Genocide Victims Monument **Edge:** Plain

Date	Mintage	F	VF	XF	Unc	BU
2004 Proof	—	Value: 65.00				

NAMIBIA

The Republic of Namibia, once the German colonial territory of German South West Africa, and later South West Africa, is situated on the Atlantic coast of southern Africa, bounded on the north by Angola, on the east by Botswana, and on the south by South Africa. It has an area of 318,261 sq. mi. (824,290 sq. km.) and a population of *1.4 million. Capital: Windhoek. Diamonds, copper, lead, zinc, and cattle are exported.

On June 17, 1985 the Transitional Government of National Unity was installed. Negotiations were held in 1988 between Angola, Cuba, and South Africa reaching a peaceful settlement on Aug. 5, 1988. By April 1989 Cuban troops were to withdraw from Angola and South African troops from Namibia. The Transitional Government resigned on Feb. 28, 1988 for the upcoming elections of the constituent assembly in Nov. 1989. Independence was finally achieved on March 12, 1990 within the Commonwealth of Nations. The President is the Head of State; the Prime Minister is Head of Government.

MONETARY SYSTEM
100 Cents = 1 Namibia Dollar

REPUBLIC
DECIMAL COINAGE

KM# 1 5 CENTS
2.2000 g., Nickel Plated Steel, 17 mm. **Obv:** National arms **Rev:** Value left, aloe plant within 3/4 sun design

Date	Mintage	F	VF	XF	Unc	BU
2002	—	—	—	0.20	0.50	0.75
2007	—	—	—	0.20	0.50	0.75

KM# 2 10 CENTS
3.4000 g., Nickel Plated Steel, 21.5 mm. **Obv:** National arms **Rev:** Camelthorn tree right, partial sun design left, value below

Date	Mintage	F	VF	XF	Unc	BU
2002	—	—	—	0.35	1.00	1.25

KM# 4 DOLLAR
5.0000 g., Brass, 22.4 mm. **Obv:** National arms **Rev:** Value divides Bateleur eagle at right, partial sun design at left

Date	Mintage	F	VF	XF	Unc	BU
2002	—	—	—	1.25	3.50	6.00
2006	—	—	—	1.25	3.50	6.00

NAURU

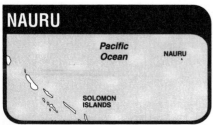

The Republic of Nauru, formerly Pleasant Island, is an island republic in the western Pacific Ocean west of the Gilbert Islands. It has an area of 8-1/2 sq. mi. and a population of 7,254. It is known for its phosphate deposits. Nauru is a special member of the Commonwealth of Nations.

MONETARY SYSTEM
100 Cents = 1 (Australian) Dollar

REPUBLIC
DECIMAL COINAGE

KM# 38 DOLLAR
27.0000 g., Silver Plated Copper, 38.6 mm. **Subject:** Guardian Angel **Obv:** Arms **Rev:** Angel standing, swarovski crystals in hair

Date	Mintage	F	VF	XF	Unc	BU
2009 Proof	10,000	Value: 25.00				

KM# 36 5 DOLLARS
0.5000 g., 0.9990 Gold 0.0161 oz. AGW, 11 mm. **Subject:** Kaiser Wilhelm **Obv:** Arms **Rev:** Bust right

Date	Mintage	F	VF	XF	Unc	BU
2008 Proof	—	Value: 60.00				

KM# 37 5 DOLLARS
0.5000 g., 0.9990 Gold 0.0161 oz. AGW, 11 mm. **Subject:** Christmas **Obv:** Arms **Rev:** Bells ringing

Date	Mintage	F	VF	XF	Unc	BU
2008 Proof	—	Value: 60.00				

KM# 39 5 DOLLARS
0.5000 g., 0.9990 Gold 0.0161 oz. AGW **Issuer:** 11 **Subject:** Christmas **Obv:** Arms **Rev:** Teddy bear seated

Date	Mintage	F	VF	XF	Unc	BU
2009 Proof	—	Value: 50.00				

KM# 18 10 DOLLARS
31.1000 g., 0.9990 Silver 0.9988 oz. ASW **Subject:** Discontinuation of the German Mark **Obv:** National arms **Obv. Legend:** BANK OF NAURU

Date	Mintage	F	VF	XF	Unc	BU
2001 Proof	—	Value: 60.00				

KM# 13 10 DOLLARS
31.2500 g., 0.9990 Silver 71.5 x 72 1.0037 oz. ASW, 72 mm. **Subject:** First Euro Coinage **Obv:** National arms, matte finish **Rev:** Denomination, inscription and partially gold-plated 1 Euro reverse coin design, Proof finish **Edge:** Plain **Shape:** Like a map

Date	Mintage	F	VF	XF	Unc	BU
2002 Proof	—	Value: 60.00				

KM# 15 10 DOLLARS
31.1000 g., 0.9990 Silver 0.9988 oz. ASW, 40 mm. **Series:** Save the Whales **Obv:** National arms **Obv. Legend:** BANK OF NAURU **Rev:** Blue Whale on mother-of-pearl insert **Edge:** Plain

Date	Mintage	F	VF	XF	Unc	BU
2002 Proof	2,000	Value: 85.00				

KM# 14 10 DOLLARS
34.6000 g., 0.9250 Silver with gold plated or gold attachment 1.0289 oz. ASW, 38.5 mm. **Subject:** Brandenburg Gate **Obv:** National arms **Rev:** Brandenburg Gate **Edge:** Plain **Note:** Gold color 1mm thick

Date	Mintage	F	VF	XF	Unc	BU
2002 Proof/Matte	—	Value: 110				

KM# 19 10 DOLLARS
31.1000 g., 0.9990 Silver 0.9988 oz. ASW **Subject:** European Union - Mark and Euro **Obv:** National arms **Obv. Legend:** BANK OF NAURU

Date	Mintage	F	VF	XF	Unc	BU
2003 Proof	5,000	Value: 60.00				

KM# 20 10 DOLLARS
1.2400 g., 0.9990 Gold 0.0398 oz. AGW, 13.92 mm. **Subject:** First Anniversary of the Euro **Obv:** National arms **Obv. Legend:** BANK OF NAURU **Rev:** Euro symbol **Edge:** Reeded

Date	Mintage	F	VF	XF	Unc	BU
2003 Proof	—	Value: 65.00				

KM# 21 10 DOLLARS
1.2400 g., 0.9990 Gold 0.0398 oz. AGW **Subject:** Treasure of Priamos in Troja **Obv:** National arms **Obv. Legend:** BANK OF NAURU

Date	Mintage	F	VF	XF	Unc	BU
2003 Proof	—	Value: 75.00				

KM# 22 10 DOLLARS
1.2400 g., 0.9990 Gold 0.0398 oz. AGW **Subject:** Treasure of Nibelungen **Obv:** National arms **Obv. Legend:** BANK OF NAURU

Date	Mintage	F	VF	XF	Unc	BU
2003 Proof	—	Value: 75.00				

KM# 23 10 DOLLARS
30.9500 g., Silver With removable gold or gilt 2.6g Reichstag building attachment with 2004/ NAURU 0077 on reverse **Subject:** European Monuments **Obv:** National arms

Obv. Legend: BANK OF NAURU **Rev. Legend:** GERMANY - DEUTSCHER REICHSTAG **Edge:** Plain

Date	Mintage	F	VF	XF	Unc	BU
2003	—	Value: 110				
Proof/Matte						

KM# 24   10 DOLLARS
Silver With removable gold or gilt attachment **Series:** European Monuments **Subject:** Palazzo Pubblico in San Marino **Obv:** National arms **Obv. Legend:** BANK OF NAURU **Edge:** Plain

Date	Mintage	F	VF	XF	Unc	BU
2005	—	Value: 110				
Proof/Matte						

KM# 25   10 DOLLARS
1.2400 g., 0.9990 Gold 0.0398 oz. AGW **Subject:** East Gothic stylized eagle broach from Domagnano, Italy in National Museum in Nuremburg **Obv:** National arms **Obv. Legend:** BANK OF NAURU

Date	Mintage	F	VF	XF	Unc	BU
2005 Proof	25,000	Value: 75.00				

KM# 35   10 DOLLARS
31.1050 g., 0.9990 Silver 0.9990 oz. ASW **Subject:** German Railways, 150th Anniversary **Obv:** National Arms **Rev:** Baureihi "01"

Date	Mintage	F	VF	XF	Unc	BU
2005 Proof	—	Value: 30.00				

KM# 26   10 DOLLARS
1.2400 g., 0.9990 Gold 0.0398 oz. AGW **Subject:** Angela Dorothea Merkel, Chancellor of Germany **Obv:** National arms **Obv. Legend:** BANK OF NAURU

Date	Mintage	F	VF	XF	Unc	BU
2005 Proof	—	Value: 75.00				

KM# 27   10 DOLLARS
1.2400 g., 0.9990 Gold 0.0398 oz. AGW **Subject:** Konrad Adenauer at 1949 demonstration **Obv:** National arms **Obv. Legend:** BANK OF NAURU

Date	Mintage	F	VF	XF	Unc	BU
2006 Proof	15,000	Value: 75.00				

KM# 28   10 DOLLARS
1.2400 g., 0.9990 Gold 0.0398 oz. AGW **Subject:** Volkswagen **Obv:** National arms **Obv. Legend:** BANK OF NAURU

Date	Mintage	F	VF	XF	Unc	BU
2006 Proof	—	Value: 75.00				

KM# 29   10 DOLLARS
1.2400 g., 0.9990 Gold 0.0398 oz. AGW **Subject:** Conrad Schumann in Berlin 1961 **Obv:** National arms **Obv. Legend:** BANK OF NAURU

Date	Mintage	F	VF	XF	Unc	BU
2006 Proof	—	Value: 75.00				

KM# 30   10 DOLLARS
1.2400 g., 0.9990 Gold 0.0398 oz. AGW **Subject:** Olympic Stadium in Munich 1972 **Obv:** National arms **Obv. Legend:** BANK OF NAURU

Date	Mintage	F	VF	XF	Unc	BU
2006 Proof	—	Value: 75.00				

KM# 31   10 DOLLARS
1.2400 g., 0.9990 Gold 0.0398 oz. AGW **Subject:** Independent Activists 1980 **Obv:** National arms **Obv. Legend:** BANK OF NAURU

Date	Mintage	F	VF	XF	Unc	BU
2006 Proof	—	Value: 75.00				

KM# 32   10 DOLLARS
1.2400 g., 0.9990 Gold 0.0398 oz. AGW **Subject:** Brandenburg Gate in Berlin 1990 **Obv. Legend:** BANK OF NAURU

Date	Mintage	F	VF	XF	Unc	BU
2006 Proof	—	Value: 75.00				

KM# 33   10 DOLLARS
1.2400 g., 0.9990 Gold 0.0398 oz. AGW **Subject:** European Union 2002 **Obv:** National arms **Obv. Legend:** BANK OF NAURU

Date	Mintage	F	VF	XF	Unc	BU
2006 Proof	—	Value: 75.00				

KM# 34   10 DOLLARS
1.2400 g., 0.9990 Gold 0.0398 oz. AGW **Subject:** Johannes Rau, German President, 1999-2004 **Obv:** National arms **Obv. Legend:** BANK OF NAURU

Date	Mintage	F	VF	XF	Unc	BU
2006 Proof	—	Value: 75.00				

NEPAL

The Kingdom of Nepal, the world's only surviving Hindu kingdom, is a landlocked country occupying the southern slopes of the Himalayas. It has an area of 56,136 sq. mi. (140,800 sq. km.) and a population of 18 million. Capital: Kathmandu. Nepal has deposits of coal, copper, iron and cobalt, but they are largely unexploited. Agriculture is the principal economic activity. Rice, timber and jute are exported, with tourism being the other major foreign exchange earner.

On June 2, 2001 tragedy struck the royal family when Crown Prince Dipendra used an assault rifle to kill his father, mother and other members of the royal family as the result of a dispute over his current lady friend. He died 48 hours later, as King, from self inflicted gunshot wounds. Gyanendra began his second reign as King (his first was a short time as a toddler, 1950-51).

DATING

Bikram Samvat Era (VS)
From 1888AD most copper coins were dated in the Bikram Samvat (VS) era. To convert take VS date - 57 =AD date. Coins with this era have VS before the year in the listing. Tthis era is used for all coins struck in Nepal since 1911AD.

RULER

SHAH DYNASTY

ज्ञानेन्दबीर विक्रम

Gyanendra Bir Bikram
VS2058-/2001-AD

NUMERALS
Nepal has used more variations of numerals on their coins than any other nation. The most common are illustrated in the numeral chart in the introduction. The chart below illustrates some variations encompassing the last four centuries.

१ २ ३ ४ ५ ६ ७ ८ ९ ०

NUMERICS

One	एक
Two	द्इ
Ten	दसा
Twenty-five	पचीसा
Fifty	पचासा
Hundred	सय

DENOMINATIONS

Rupee	रुपैयाँ

Legend on reverse

श्री श्री श्री गोरखनाथ
Shri Shri Shri Gorakhanatha in 8 petals

KINGDOM

Gyanendra Bir Bikram
VS2058-2064 / 2001- 2007AD

DECIMAL COINAGE
100 Paisa = 1 Rupee

KM# 1173   10 PAISA
Aluminum, 17 mm. **Obv:** Royal crown **Edge:** Plain

Date	Mintage	F	VF	XF	Unc	BU
VS2058 (2001)	—	—	—	—	1.00	1.50

KM# 1148   25 PAISA
Aluminum, 20 mm. **Obv:** Royal crown **Edge:** Plain

Date	Mintage	F	VF	XF	Unc	BU
VS2058 (2001)	—	—	—	—	0.50	0.75
VS2059 (2002)	—	—	—	—	0.50	0.75
VS2060 (2003)	—	—	—	—	0.50	0.75

KM# 1149   50 PAISA
Aluminum, 22.5 mm. **Obv:** Royal crown **Rev:** Swayambhunath **Edge:** Plain

Date	Mintage	F	VF	XF	Unc	BU
VS2058 (2001)	—	—	—	—	0.50	0.75
VS2059 (2002)	—	—	—	—	0.50	0.75

KM# 1179   50 PAISA
1.4100 g., Aluminum, 22.5 mm. **Obv:** Crown above crossed flags **Rev:** Swayambhunath **Edge:** Plain

Date	Mintage	F	VF	XF	Unc	BU
VS2060 (2003)	—	—	—	—	0.40	0.50
VS2061 (2004)	—	—	—	—	0.40	0.50

KM# 1150.2   RUPEE
Brass Plated Steel **Obv:** Traditional design **Rev:** Small (7mm high) temple, small (4mm) "1" **Edge:** Plain **Note:** Magnetic.

Date	Mintage	F	VF	XF	Unc	BU
VS2058 (2001)	—	—	—	—	1.00	1.50
VS2059 (2002)	—	—	—	—	1.00	1.50
VS2060 (2003)	—	—	—	—	1.00	1.50

KM# 1150.1   RUPEE
Brass Plated Steel **Rev:** Large (8mm) temple, medium '1' (4.5mm) **Edge:** Reeded **Note:** Non-magnetic.

Date	Mintage	F	VF	XF	Unc	BU
VS2058 (2001)	—	—	—	—	1.00	1.50

KM# 1150.3   RUPEE
3.9600 g., Brass, 20 mm. **Obv:** Traditional design **Rev:** Small (6.5mm high) temple, small (4mm) "1" **Edge:** Plain

Date	Mintage	F	VF	XF	Unc	BU
VS2058 (2001)	—	—	—	—	0.50	0.75

KM# 1150.4   RUPEE
3.9600 g., Brass Plated Steel, 20 mm. **Obv:** Traditional design **Rev:** Small (7mm high) temple, large (5.5mm) "1" **Note:** Magnetic.

Date	Mintage	F	VF	XF	Unc	BU
VS2059 (2002)	—	—	—	—	1.00	1.50
VS2060 (2003)	—	—	—	—	1.00	1.50

KM# 1180   RUPEE
3.9600 g., Brass Plated Steel, 20 mm. **Obv:** Traditional design **Rev:** Wagheshwari Temple **Edge:** Plain **Note:** "1" in denomination of a different style.

Date	Mintage	F	VF	XF	Unc	BU
VS2061 (2004)	—	—	—	—	0.75	1.00

KM# 1187   RUPEE
3.9400 g., Brass Plated Steel, 19.95 mm. **Obv:** Traditional design **Rev:** Talwarahi Temple **Edge:** Plain

Date	Mintage	F	VF	XF	Unc	BU
VS2062(2005)	—	—	—	0.50	1.20	1.60

KM# 1181   RUPEE
4.0000 g., Brass Plated Steel, 20 mm. **Obv:** Traditional design **Rev:** Sri Talbarahi Temple with outline mountain scene behind **Edge:** Plain

Date	Mintage	F	VF	XF	Unc	BU
VS 2062 (2005)	—	—	—	—	—	1.00

KM# 1170   2 RUPEES
4.9400 g., Brass, 25 mm.   **Obv:** Traditional square design
Rev: People with flag celebrating 50 Years of Democracy
Edge: Plain

Date	Mintage	F	VF	XF	Unc	BU
VS2058(2001)	—	—	—	—	0.50	0.75

KM# 1151.2   2 RUPEES
Brass, 25 mm.   **Obv:** Traditional design **Rev:** Three domed building **Edge:** Plain

Date	Mintage	F	VF	XF	Unc	BU
VS2058 (2001)	—	—	—	—	1.50	2.00
VS2059 (2002)	—	—	—	—	1.50	2.00
VS2060 (2003)	—	—	—	—	1.50	2.00

KM# 1151.1   2 RUPEES
5.0700 g., Brass Plated Steel, 25 mm.   **Obv:** Traditional design
Rev: Three domed building **Edge:** Plain **Note:** Edge varieties exist. Prev. KM#1151. Magnetic.

Date	Mintage	F	VF	XF	Unc	BU
VS2060 (2003)	—	—	—	—	1.50	2.00

KM# 1151.1a   2 RUPEES
6.7000 g., Silver, 25 mm.   **Obv:** Traditional design **Rev:** Three domed building **Edge:** Plain

Date	Mintage	F	VF	XF	Unc	BU
VS2060(2003)	—	—	—	—	100	

KM# 1188   2 RUPEES
5.0000 g., Brass Plated Steel, 24.93 mm.   **Obv:** Farmer plowing with water buffalos **Rev:** Mount Everest **Edge:** Plain

Date	Mintage	F	VF	XF	Unc	BU
VS2063(2006)	—	—	—	1.50	2.75	3.50

KM# 1159   25 RUPEE
8.3600 g., Copper-Nickel, 29.1 mm.   **Obv:** Crowned bust right
Rev: Traditional design **Edge:** Plain

Date	Mintage	F	VF	XF	Unc	BU
VS2058 (2001)	—	—	—	—	4.00	5.00
VS2059 (2002)	—	—	—	—	4.00	5.00

KM# 1164   25 RUPEE
8.6000 g., Copper-Nickel, 29.1 mm.   **Subject:** Silver Jubilee
Obv: Traditional design **Rev:** Stylized face design **Edge:** Plain

Date	Mintage	F	VF	XF	Unc	BU
VS2060 (2003)	—	—	—	—	4.00	5.00

KM# 1183   25 RUPEE
8.5500 g., Copper-Nickel, 29.1 mm.   **Subject:** World Hindu Federation **Obv:** Traditional design **Edge:** Plain

Date	Mintage	F	VF	XF	Unc	BU
VS2062 (2005)	—	—	—	—	4.00	5.00

KM# 1160   50 RUPEE
20.1000 g., Brass, 37.7 mm.   **Subject:** 50th Anniversary of Scouting in Nepal **Obv:** Traditional design **Rev:** Scouting emblem within beaded wreath **Edge:** Plain

Date	Mintage	F	VF	XF	Unc	BU
VS2059 (2002)	—	—	—	—	9.00	10.00

KM# 1182   50 RUPEE
8.6000 g., Copper-Nickel, 29 mm.   **Subject:** Golden Jubilee of Supreme Court **Obv:** Traditional design **Rev:** Supreme Court building **Edge:** Plain

Date	Mintage	F	VF	XF	Unc	BU
VS2063 (2006)	—	—	—	—	6.00	9.00

KM# 1157   100 RUPEE
20.0000 g., Brass, 38.7 mm.   **Subject:** Buddha **Obv:** Traditional design **Rev:** Seated Buddha teaching five seated monks **Edge:** Reeded

Date	Mintage	F	VF	XF	Unc	BU
VS2058 (2001)	30,000	—	—	—	10.00	12.00

KM# 1162   200 RUPEE
18.1000 g., 0.5000 Silver 0.2910 oz. ASW, 29.6 mm.
Subject: 50th Anniversary of Civil Service **Obv:** Traditional design **Rev:** Crown above flags and value **Edge:** Plain

Date	Mintage	F	VF	XF	Unc	BU
VS2058 (2001)	—	—	—	—	20.00	25.00

KM# 1161   200 RUPEE
18.1000 g., 0.5000 Silver 0.2910 oz. ASW, 29.6 mm.   **Subject:** 50th Anniversary of the Nepal Chamber of Commerce **Obv:** Traditional design **Rev:** Swastika within rotary gear **Edge:** Plain

Date	Mintage	F	VF	XF	Unc	BU
VS2059 (2002)	—	—	—	—	20.00	25.00

KM# 1171   250 RUPEE
18.0000 g., 0.5000 Silver 0.2893 oz. ASW, 29 mm.
Subject: 2600th Anniversary of Bhagawan Mahavir **Obv:** Traditional design **Rev:** Haloed head above value **Edge:** Plain

Date	Mintage	F	VF	XF	Unc	BU
VS2058 (2001)	—	—	—	—	25.00	30.00

KM# 1176   250 RUPEE
17.8300 g., 0.5000 Silver 0.2866 oz. ASW, 31.6 mm.
Subject: Marwadi, non-profit making organization **Obv:** Traditional design **Rev:** Swastika within circle **Edge:** Reeded

Date	Mintage	F	VF	XF	Unc	BU
VS2060 (2003)	—	—	—	—	25.00	30.00

KM# 1184   250 RUPEE
18.0000 g., Silver, 32 mm.   **Subject:** 400th Anniversary of Guru Granth Sahib **Obv:** Traditional design **Rev:** Holy Book of Sikhs **Edge:** Reeded

Date	Mintage	F	VF	XF	Unc	BU
VS2061 (2004)	—	—	—	—	25.00	30.00

KM# 1174   300 RUPEE
22.5000 g., 0.5000 Silver 0.3617 oz. ASW, 31.8 mm.
Subject: Economic Growth Through Export **Obv:** Traditional design **Rev:** Two joined hands in front of globe **Edge:** Reeded

Date	Mintage	F	VF	XF	Unc	BU
VS2060 (2003)	—	—	—	—	20.00	25.00

KM# 1177   500 RUPEE
23.0000 g., 0.9000 Silver 0.6655 oz. ASW, 31.7 mm.
Subject: Management Education 50th Anniversary **Obv:** Traditional design **Rev:** Six point star outline **Edge:** Reeded

Date	Mintage	F	VF	XF	Unc	BU
VS2060 (2003)	—	—	—	—	25.00	30.00

KM# 1163 500 RUPEE
23.3400 g., 0.9000 Silver 0.6753 oz. ASW, 32 mm.
Subject: 50th Anniversary of the Conquest of Mt. Everest
Obv: Traditional design **Rev:** Mountain and map above value
Edge: Reeded

Date	Mintage	F	VF	XF	Unc	BU
VS2060 (2003)	—	—	—	—	25.00	30.00

KM# 1185 500 RUPEE
20.1000 g., Silver, 32 mm. **Subject:** 50th Anniversary of Nepal-
United Nations **Obv:** Traditional design **Rev:** Head of the late
King Mahendra Bir Birkam **Edge:** Reeded

Date	Mintage	F	VF	XF	Unc	BU
VS2062	—	—	—	—	25.00	30.00

KM# 1175 1000 RUPEE
35.0000 g., Silver, 40 mm. **Subject:** 100 Years - Rotary Club
Edge: Reeded

Date	Mintage	F	VF	XF	Unc	BU
VS2062 (2005)	—	—	—	—	45.00	50.00

KM# 1178 1000 RUPEE
35.2000 g., 0.5000 Silver 0.5658 oz. ASW, 40 mm.
Subject: Rastriya Bank 50th Anniversary **Obv:** Traditional
square design **Rev:** Bank seal above value **Edge:** Reeded

Date	Mintage	F	VF	XF	Unc	BU
VS2062 (2005)	—	—	—	—	25.00	30.00

KM# 1158 1500 RUPEE
20.0000 g., 0.9250 Silver 0.5948 oz. ASW, 38.7 mm.
Subject: Buddha **Obv:** Traditional design **Rev:** Seated Buddha
teaching five seated monks **Edge:** Reeded

Date	Mintage	F	VF	XF	Unc	BU
VS2058 (2001) Proof	15,000	Value: 32.50				

KM# 1172 2000 RUPEE
31.2000 g., 0.7200 Silver 0.7222 oz. ASW, 40 mm. **Subject:**
Gyanendra's Accession to the Throne **Obv:** Crowned bust right
Rev: Upright sword above value in circular design **Edge:** Reeded

Date	Mintage	F	VF	XF	Unc	BU
VS2058 (2001)	—	—	—	—	40.00	45.00

KM# 1201 2000 RUPEE
31.1050 g., 0.9990 Silver 0.9990 oz. ASW, 40 mm.
Subject: Conquest of Mt. Everest 50th Anniversary **Rev:** Sir
Edmond Hillary and Tenzing Norgay at Summit

Date	Mintage	F	VF	XF	Unc	BU
VS2061 (2003) Proof	8,000	Value: 80.00				

ASARFI GOLD COINAGE
(Asarphi)

Fractional designations are approximate for this series.
Actual Gold Weight (AGW) is used to identify each type.

KM# 1200 ASARPHI
7.7700 g., 0.9999 Gold 0.2498 oz. AGW, 22 mm.
Subject: Conquest of Mt. Everest **Rev:** Sir Edward Hillary and
Tenzing Norgay at Summit

Date	Mintage	F	VF	XF	Unc	BU
VS2060 (2003)	2,000	—	—	—	800	—

KM# 1153 0.3G ASARPHI
0.3000 g., 0.9999 Gold 0.0096 oz. AGW, 7 mm.
Subject: Buddha **Obv:** Traditional design **Rev:** Seated Buddha
Edge: Plain

Date	Mintage	VG	F	VF	XF	BU
VS2058 (2001)	30,000	—	—	—	—	16.00

KM# 1154 1/25-OZ. ASARFI
1.2441 g., 0.9999 Gold 0.0400 oz. AGW, 13.92 mm.
Subject: Buddha **Obv:** Traditional design **Rev:** Seated Buddha
Edge: Reeded

Date	Mintage	VG	F	VF	XF	BU
VS2058 (2001)	25,000	—	—	—	—	50.00

KM# 1191 2000 RUPEE
31.2000 g., 0.9250 Silver 0.9278 oz. ASW, 38.61 mm. **Subject:**
2006 FIFA World Cup - Germany **Obv:** Traditional design

Date	Mintage	F	VF	XF	Unc	BU
VS2063 (2006)	—	—	—	—	40.00	45.00

KM# 1155 1/10-OZ. ASARFI
3.1104 g., 0.9999 Gold 0.1000 oz. AGW, 17.95 mm.
Subject: Buddha **Obv:** Traditional design **Rev:** Seated Buddha
Edge: Reeded

Date	Mintage	VG	F	VF	XF	BU
VS2058 (2001)	15,000	—	—	—	—	125

KM# 1156 1/2-OZ. ASARFI
15.5518 g., 0.9999 Gold 0.4999 oz. AGW, 27 mm.
Subject: Buddha **Obv:** Traditional design **Rev:** Seated Buddha
Edge: Reeded

Date	Mintage	VG	F	VF	XF	BU
VS2058 (2001) Proof	2,500	Value: 625				

SECULAR STATE

Gyanendra Bir Bikram
VS2058-2064 / 2001- 2007AD

DECIMAL COINAGE
100 Paisa = 1 Rupee

KM# 1186 25 RUPEE
8.5000 g., Copper-Nickel, 29 mm. **Subject:** 125th Anniversary
- First Nepal Postal Stamp Issue **Obv:** Features image of
legendary 1 Anna stamp **Rev:** Traditional mailman on the reverse

Date	Mintage	F	VF	XF	Unc	BU
VS2063 (2006)	—	—	—	—	7.00	9.00
VS2064 (2006)	—	—	—	—	7.00	9.00

DEMOCRATIC REPUBLIC

DECIMAL COINAGE
100 Paisa = 1 Rupee

KM# 1204 RUPEE
Brass Plated Steel, 19 mm. **Obv:** Mt. Everest within square
Rev: Map of Nepal

Date	Mintage	F	VF	XF	Unc	BU
2008	—	—	—	—	2.00	3.50

KM# 1205 2 RUPEES
Obv: Mt. Everest at center **Rev:** Farmer plowing field

Date	Mintage	F	VF	XF	Unc	BU
BE2063	—	—	—	—	6.00	7.50

KM# 1189 50 RUPEE
8.6000 g., Copper-Nickel, 29 mm. **Subject:** 250th Anniversary
Hindu festival "Kimari Jatra" **Obv:** Kumari Temple at Durbar
Square in Kathmandu **Rev:** Bust of Goddess Kumari facing
Edge: Plain

Date	Mintage	F	VF	XF	Unc	BU
VS2064 (2006)	—	—	—	—	8.00	10.00

KM# 1190 500 RUPEE
14.1900 g., 0.5000 Silver 0.2281 oz. ASW, 32 mm.
Subject: 250th Anniversary Hindu festival "Kimari Jatra"
Obv: Kumari Temple at Durbar Square in Kathmandu **Rev:** Bust
of Goddess Kumari facing **Edge:** Reeded

Date	Mintage	F	VF	XF	Unc	BU
VS2064 (2007)	—	—	—	—	25.00	30.00

NETHERLANDS

The Kingdom of the Netherlands, a country of western
Europe fronting on the North Sea and bordered by Belgium and
Germany, has an area of 15,770 sq. mi. (41,500 sq. km.) and a
population of 16.1 million. Capital: Amsterdam, but the seat of
government is at The Hague. The economy is based on dairy
farming and a variety of industrial activities. Chemicals, yarns and
fabrics, and meat products are exported.

NOTE: Excepting the World War II issues struck at U.S.
mints, all of the modern coins were struck at the Utrecht Mint and
bear the caduceus mint mark of that facility. They also bear the
mintmasters' marks.

RULERS

KINGDOM OF THE NETHERLANDS

Beatrix, 1980—

MINT PRIVY MARKS

Utrecht

Date	Privy Mark
1806-present	Caduceus

MINTMASTERS' PRIVY MARKS
Utrecht Mint

Date	Privy Mark
2001	Wine tendril w/grapes
2002	Wine tendril w/grapes and star
2003	Sails of a clipper

NOTE: A star adjoining the privy mark indicates that the
piece was struck at the beginning of the term of office of a successor. (The star was used only if the successor had not chosen
his own mark yet.)
NOTE: Since October 1999, the Dutch Mint has taken the
title of Royal Dutch Mint.

MONETARY SYSTEM

Until January 29, 2002
100 Cents = 1 Gulden
Since January 1, 2002
100 Euro Cents = 1 Euro

KINGDOM

DECIMAL COINAGE

KM# 202 5 CENTS
3.5000 g., Bronze, 21 mm. **Ruler:** Beatrix **Obv:** Head left with
vertical inscription **Rev:** Value within vertical lines **Edge:** Plain
Designer: Bruno Ninaber Van Eyben

Date	Mintage	F	VF	XF	Unc	BU
2001 Proof	17,000	Value: 4.00				
2001	15,815,000	—	—	—	—	0.40

KM# 203 10 CENTS
1.5000 g., Nickel, 15 mm. **Ruler:** Beatrix **Obv:** Head left with vertical inscription **Rev:** Value and vertical lines **Edge:** Reeded **Designer:** Bruno Ninaber Van Eyben

Date	Mintage	F	VF	XF	Unc	BU
2001	25,600,000	—	—	—	—	0.50
2001 Proof	17,000	Value: 4.00				

KM# 204 25 CENTS
3.0000 g., Nickel, 19 mm. **Ruler:** Beatrix **Obv:** Head left with vertical inscription **Obv. Inscription:** Beatrix/Konincin Der/Nederlanden **Rev:** Value within vertical and horizontal lines **Edge:** Reeded **Designer:** Bruno Ninaber van Eyben

Date	Mintage	F	VF	XF	Unc	BU
2001 Proof	17,000	Value: 6.00				
2001	11,515,000	—	—	—	0.20	0.60

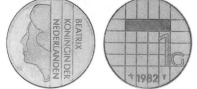

KM# 205 GULDEN
6.0000 g., Nickel, 25 mm. **Ruler:** Beatrix **Obv:** Head left with vertical inscription **Rev:** Value within vertical and horizontal lines **Edge Lettering:** GOD * ZIJ * MET * ONS * **Designer:** Bruno Ninaber von Eyben

Date	Mintage	F	VF	XF	Unc	BU
2001	6,414,500	—	—	—	—	1.25
2001 Proof	17,000	Value: 7.50				

KM# 233 GULDEN
6.0000 g., Nickel, 25 mm. **Ruler:** Beatrix **Obv:** Head left within inscription **Obv. Designer:** Geerten Verheus and Michael Raedecker **Rev:** Child art design **Rev. Designer:** Tim van Melis **Edge Lettering:** GOD ZIJ MET ONS

Date	Mintage	F	VF	XF	Unc	BU
2001	16,009,000	—	—	—	—	4.00
2001 Prooflike	32,000	—	—	—	—	6.00

KM# 205a GULDEN
7.1000 g., 0.9250 Silver 0.2111 oz. ASW **Ruler:** Beatrix **Obv:** Head left with vertical inscription **Rev:** Value within vertical and horizontal lines **Edge Lettering:** GOD*ZIJ*MET*OMS*

Date	Mintage	F	VF	XF	Unc	BU
2001 Prooflike	200,000	—	—	—	—	10.00

KM# 205c GULDEN
13.2000 g., 0.9990 Gold 0.4239 oz. AGW **Ruler:** Beatrix **Obv:** Head left with vertical inscription **Rev:** Value within vertical and horizontal lines **Edge:** Plain, missing lettering

Date	Mintage	F	VF	XF	Unc	BU
2001 Prooflike	Est. 500	—	—	—	—	550

KM# 205b GULDEN
13.2000 g., 0.9990 Gold 0.4239 oz. AGW **Ruler:** Beatrix **Obv:** Head left with vertical inscription **Rev:** Value within vertical and horizontal lines **Edge Lettering:** GOD*ZIJ*MET*ONS*
Note: Prev. KM#205a.

Date	Mintage	F	VF	XF	Unc	BU
2001 Prooflike	25,500	—	—	—	—	525

Note: Mintage includes KM#205c.

KM# 233a GULDEN
7.1000 g., 0.9250 Silver 0.2111 oz. ASW, 25 mm. **Ruler:** Beatrix **Obv:** Head left within inscription **Rev:** Child art design **Edge Lettering:** GOD * ZIJ * MET * ONS *

Date	Mintage	F	VF	XF	Unc	BU
2001 Prooflike	360	—	—	—	—	2,400

Note: Given as gifts to workers at the mint

KM# 233b GULDEN
13.2000 g., 0.9990 Gold 0.4239 oz. AGW, 25 mm. **Ruler:** Beatrix **Obv:** Head left within inscription **Obv. Designer:** G. Verheus and M. Raedecker **Rev:** Child art design **Rev. Designer:** T. van Melis **Note:** 98 of 100 pieces melted down, with 2 known in museum collections.

Date	Mintage	F	VF	XF	Unc	BU
2001 Prooflike; Rare	100	—	—	—	—	—

KM# 206 2-1/2 GULDEN
10.0000 g., Nickel, 29 mm. **Ruler:** Beatrix **Obv:** Head left with vertical inscription **Rev:** Value within horizontal, vertical and diagonal lines **Edge Lettering:** GOD * ZIJ * MET * ONS * **Designer:** Bruno Ninaber van Eyben

Date	Mintage	F	VF	XF	Unc	BU
2001	315,000	—	—	—	—	12.00
2001 Proof	17,000	Value: 16.00				

KM# 210 5 GULDEN
9.2500 g., Bronze Clad Nickel, 23.5 mm. **Ruler:** Beatrix **Obv:** Head left with vertical inscription **Rev:** Value within horizontal, vertical and diagonal lines **Edge:** GOD * ZIJ * MET * ONS * **Designer:** Bruno Ninaber van Eyben

Date	Mintage	F	VF	XF	Unc	BU
2001 Proof	17,000	Value: 15.50				
2001	115,000	—	—	—	—	10.00

EURO COINAGE
European Union Issues

KM# 234 EURO CENT
2.3000 g., Copper Plated Steel, 16.2 mm. **Ruler:** Beatrix **Obv:** Head left among stars **Obv. Designer:** Bruno Ninaber van Eyben **Rev:** Value and globe **Rev. Designer:** Luc Luycx **Edge:** Plain

Date	Mintage	F	VF	XF	Unc	BU
2001	179,300,000	—	—	—	0.35	0.50
2001 Proof	16,500	—	—	—	—	—
2002	800,000	—	—	—	1.00	1.25
2002 Proof	16,500	Value: 5.00				
2003	58,100,000	—	—	—	0.50	0.75
2003 Proof	13,000	Value: 4.00				
2004	113,900,000	—	—	—	0.50	0.75
2004 Proof	5,000	Value: 4.00				
2005	413,000	—	—	—	1.50	2.00
2005 Proof	5,000	Value: 4.00				
2006	200,000	—	—	—	1.50	2.00
2006 Proof	3,500	Value: 4.00				
2007	225,000	—	—	—	1.50	2.00
2007 Proof	10,000	Value: 3.50				
2008	162,500	—	—	—	1.50	2.00
2008 Proof	10,000	Value: 3.50				
2009	—	—	—	—	1.50	2.00
2009 Proof	—	Value: 3.50				
2010	—	—	—	—	1.50	2.00

KM# 235 2 EURO CENT
3.0600 g., Copper Plated Steel, 18.7 mm. **Ruler:** Beatrix **Obv:** Head left among stars **Obv. Designer:** Bruno Ninaber van Eyben **Rev:** Value and globe **Rev. Designer:** Luc Luycx **Edge:** Grooved

Date	Mintage	F	VF	XF	Unc	BU
2001	145,800,000	—	—	—	0.50	0.75
2001 Proof	16,500	—	—	—	—	—
2002	53,100,000	—	—	—	0.75	1.00
2002 Proof	16,500	—	—	—	—	—
2003	151,200,000	—	—	—	0.50	0.75
2003 Proof	13,000	—	—	—	—	—
2004	115,622,000	—	—	—	0.50	0.75

Date	Mintage	F	VF	XF	Unc	BU
2004 Proof	5,000	Value: 4.00				
2005	413,000	—	—	—	1.50	2.00
2005 Proof	5,000	Value: 4.00				
2006	200,000	—	—	—	1.50	2.00
2006 Proof	3,500	Value: 4.00				
2007	225,000	—	—	—	1.50	2.00
2007 Proof	10,000	Value: 3.50				
2008	162,500	—	—	—	1.50	2.00
2008 Proof	10,000	Value: 3.50				
2009	—	—	—	—	1.50	2.00
2009 Proof	—	Value: 3.50				
2010	—	—	—	—	1.50	2.00

KM# 236 5 EURO CENT
3.9200 g., Copper Plated Steel, 21.25 mm. **Ruler:** Beatrix **Obv:** Head left among stars **Obv. Designer:** Bruno Ninaber van Eyben **Rev:** Value and globe **Rev. Designer:** Luc Luycx **Edge:** Plain

Date	Mintage	F	VF	XF	Unc	BU
2001	205,900,000	—	—	—	0.50	0.75
2001 Proof	16,500	—	—	—	—	—
2002	900,000	—	—	—	1.75	2.25
2002 Proof	16,500	—	—	—	—	—
2003	1,400,000	—	—	—	1.50	2.00
2003 Proof	13,000	—	—	—	—	—
2004	306,000	—	—	—	2.00	2.50
2004 Proof	5,000	Value: 4.00				
2005	80,413,000	—	—	—	1.00	1.25
2005 Proof	5,000	Value: 4.00				
2006	60,100,000	—	—	—	1.00	1.25
2006 Proof	3,500	Value: 4.00				
2007	78,625,000	—	—	—	1.00	1.25
2007 Proof	10,000	Value: 3.50				
2008	—	—	—	—	1.00	1.25
2008 Proof	10,000	Value: 3.50				
2009	—	—	—	—	1.00	1.25
2009 Proof	—	Value: 3.50				
2010	—	—	—	—	1.00	1.25

KM# 237 10 EURO CENT
4.1000 g., Brass, 19.7 mm. **Ruler:** Beatrix **Obv:** Head left among stars **Obv. Designer:** Bruno Ninaber van Eyben **Rev:** Value and map **Rev. Designer:** Luc Luycx

Date	Mintage	F	VF	XF	Unc	BU
2001	193,500,000	—	—	—	0.75	1.00
2001 Proof	16,500	—	—	—	—	—
2002	800,000	—	—	—	1.50	2.00
2002 Proof	16,500	—	—	—	—	—
2003	1,200,000	—	—	—	1.50	2.00
2003 Proof	13,000	—	—	—	—	—
2004	262,000	—	—	—	2.00	2.50
2004 Proof	5,000	Value: 6.00				
2005	363,000	—	—	—	1.75	2.25
2005 Proof	5,000	Value: 6.00				
2006	150,000	—	—	—	1.75	2.25
2006 Proof	3,500	Value: 6.00				

KM# 268 10 EURO CENT
4.1000 g., Brass, 19.7 mm. **Ruler:** Beatrix **Obv:** Head of Queen Beatrix left **Obv. Designer:** Bruno Ninaber van Eybew **Rev:** Relief map of Western Europe, stars, lines and value **Rev. Designer:** Luc Luycx

Date	Mintage	F	VF	XF	Unc	BU
2007	180,000	—	—	—	1.75	2.50
2007 Proof	10,000	Value: 5.00				
2008	130,000	—	—	—	1.75	2.50
2008 Proof	10,000	Value: 5.00				
2009	—	—	—	—	1.75	2.50
2009 Proof	—	Value: 5.00				
2010	—	—	—	—	1.75	2.50

Date	Mintage	F	VF	XF	Unc	BU
2008	81,250	—	—	—	6.00	8.00
2008 Proof	10,000	—	—	—	—	—
2009	—	—	—	—	6.00	8.00
2009 Proof	—	—	—	—	—	—
2010	—	—	—	—	6.00	8.00

KM# 238 20 EURO CENT
5.7400 g., Brass, 22.2 mm. **Ruler:** Beatrix **Obv:** Head left among stars **Obv. Designer:** Bruno Ninaber van Eyben **Rev:** Value and map **Rev. Designer:** Luc Luycx **Edge:** Notched

Date	Mintage	F	VF	XF	Unc	BU
2001	97,600,000	—	—	—	1.00	1.25
2001 Proof	16,500	—	—	—	—	—
2002	51,200,000	—	—	—	1.75	2.25
2002 Proof	16,500	—	—	—	—	—
2003	58,200,000	—	—	—	1.75	2.25
2003 Proof	13,000	—	—	—	—	—
2004	20,430,000	—	—	—	2.00	2.50
2004 Proof	5,000	Value: 8.00				
2005	363,000	—	—	—	2.50	3.00
2005 Proof	5,000	Value: 8.00				
2006	150,000	—	—	—	2.50	3.00
2006 Proof	3,500	Value: 8.00				

KM# 269 20 EURO CENT
5.7000 g., Brass, 22.2 mm. **Ruler:** Beatrix **Obv:** Head of Queen Beatrix left **Obv. Designer:** Bruno Ninaber van Eybew **Rev:** Relief map of Western Europe, stars, lines and value **Rev. Designer:** Luc Luycx **Edge:** Notched

Date	Mintage	F	VF	XF	Unc	BU
2007	180,000	—	—	—	2.50	3.00
2007 Proof	10,000	Value: 7.00				
2008	130,000	—	—	—	2.50	3.00
2008 Proof	10,000	Value: 7.00				
2009	—	—	—	—	2.50	3.00
2009 Proof	—	Value: 7.00				
2010	—	—	—	—	2.50	3.00

KM# 239 50 EURO CENT
7.8000 g., Brass, 24.2 mm. **Ruler:** Beatrix **Obv:** Head left among stars **Obv. Designer:** Bruno Ninaber van Eyben **Rev:** Value and map **Rev. Designer:** Luc Luycx **Edge:** Notched

Date	Mintage	F	VF	XF	Unc	BU
2001	94,500,000	—	—	—	1.25	1.50
2001 Proof	16,500	—	—	—	—	—
2002	80,900,000	—	—	—	1.25	1.50
2002 Proof	16,500	—	—	—	—	—
2003	1,200,000	—	—	—	2.00	2.50
2003 Proof	13,000	—	—	—	—	—
2004	269,000	—	—	—	2.25	2.75
2004 Proof	5,000	Value: 10.00				
2005	363,000	—	—	—	2.00	2.50
2005 Proof	5,964	Value: 10.00				
2006	150,000	—	—	—	2.00	2.50
2006 Proof	3,500	Value: 10.00				

KM# 270 50 EURO CENT
7.8000 g., Brass, 24.2 mm. **Ruler:** Beatrix **Obv:** Head of Quen Beatrix left **Obv. Designer:** Bruno Ninaber van Eybew **Rev:** Relief map of Western Europe, stars, lines and value **Rev. Designer:** Luc Luycx **Edge:** Notched

Date	Mintage	F	VF	XF	Unc	BU
2007	180,000	—	—	—	2.00	2.75
2007 Proof	10,000	Value: 9.00				
2008	162,500	—	—	—	2.00	2.75
2008 Proof	10,000	Value: 9.00				
2009	—	—	—	—	2.00	2.75
2009 Proof	—	Value: 9.00				
2010	—	—	—	—	2.00	2.75

KM# 240 EURO
7.5000 g., Bi-Metallic Copper-Nickel center in Brass ring, 23.2 mm. **Ruler:** Beatrix **Obv:** Half head left within 1/2 circle and star border, name within vertical lines **Obv. Designer:** Bruno Ninaber van Eyben **Rev:** Value and map within circle **Rev. Designer:** Luc Luycx **Edge:** Segmented reeding

Date	Mintage	F	VF	XF	Unc	BU
2001	67,900,000	—	—	—	2.50	3.00
2001 Proof	16,500	—	—	—	—	—
2002	20,100,000	—	—	—	3.25	3.75
2002 Proof	16,500	—	—	—	—	—
2003	1,400,000	—	—	—	3.50	4.00
2003 Proof	13,000	—	—	—	—	—
2004	235,000	—	—	—	5.00	6.00
2004 Proof	5,000	Value: 15.00				
2005	288,000	—	—	—	4.00	5.00
2005 Proof	5,964	Value: 15.00				
2006	100,000	—	—	—	4.00	5.00
2006 Proof	3,500	Value: 15.00				

KM# 271 EURO
7.5000 g., Bi-Metallic Copper-Nickel center in Brass ring, 23.2 mm. **Ruler:** Beatrix **Obv:** Queen's profile left **Obv. Designer:** Bruno Ninaber van Eybew **Rev:** Relief map of Western Europe, stars, lines and value **Edge:** Segmented reeding

Date	Mintage	F	VF	XF	Unc	BU
2007	112,500	—	—	—	4.00	5.00
2007 Proof	10,000	Value: 14.50				
2008	81,250	—	—	—	4.00	5.00
2008 Proof	10,000	Value: 14.50				
2009	—	—	—	—	4.00	5.00
2009 Proof	—	Value: 14.50				
2010	—	—	—	—	4.00	5.00

KM# 241 2 EURO
8.5000 g., Bi-Metallic Brass center in Copper-Nickel ring, 25.7 mm. **Ruler:** Beatrix **Obv:** Profile left within 1/2 circle and star border, name within vertical lines **Obv. Designer:** Bruno Ninaber van Eyben **Rev:** Value and map within circle **Rev. Designer:** Luc Luycx **Edge Lettering:** GOD * ZIJ *MET * ONS *

Date	Mintage	F	VF	XF	Unc	BU
2001	140,500,000	—	—	—	4.00	5.00
2001 Proof	16,500	—	—	—	—	—
2002	37,200,000	—	—	—	4.50	5.50
2002 Proof	16,500	—	—	—	—	—
2003	1,200,000	—	—	—	5.50	6.50
2003 Proof	13,000	—	—	—	—	—
2004	245,000	—	—	—	7.00	9.00
2004 Proof	5,000	Value: 18.00				
2005	288,000	—	—	—	6.00	8.00
2005 Proof	5,964	Value: 18.00				
2006	100,000	—	—	—	6.00	8.00
2006 Proof	3,500	Value: 18.00				

KM# 272 2 EURO
8.5000 g., Bi-Metallic Brass center in Copper-Nickel ring, 25.7 mm. **Ruler:** Beatrix **Obv:** Queen's profile left **Obv. Designer:** Bruno Ninaber van Eybew **Rev:** Relief map of Western Europe, stars, lines and value **Rev. Designer:** Luc Luycx **Edge Lettering:** GOD * ZIJ * MET * ONS *

Date	Mintage	F	VF	XF	Unc	BU
2007	112,500	—	—	—	6.00	8.00
2007 Proof	10,000					

KM# 273 2 EURO
8.5000 g., Bi-Metallic Brass center in Copper-Nickel ring, 25.69 mm. **Ruler:** Beatrix **Subject:** 50th Anniversary Treaty of Rome **Obv:** Open treaty book **Rev:** Large value at left, modified outline of Europe at right **Edge Lettering:** GOD * ZU * MET * ONS * **Note:** 15,000 BU coins are in a Benelux set

Date	Mintage	F	VF	XF	Unc	BU
2007	6,515,000	—	—	—	6.00	9.00
2007 Proof	10,000	Value: 22.00				

KM# 281 2 EURO
8.5000 g., Bi-Metallic Brass center in copper-nickel ring, 25.69 mm. **Ruler:** Beatrix **Subject:** European Monetary Union, 10th Anniversary **Rev:** Stick figure and euro symbol **Edge Lettering:** *GOD *ZIJ *MET *ONS

Date	Mintage	F	VF	XF	Unc	BU
2009	5,300,000	—	—	—	4.50	15.00
2009 Proof	10,000	Value: 60.00				

KM# 245 5 EURO
11.9000 g., 0.9250 Silver 0.3539 oz. ASW, 29 mm. **Ruler:** Beatrix **Subject:** Vincent Van Gogh **Obv:** Head facing **Rev:** Tilted head facing **Edge Lettering:** GOD * ZIJ * MET * ONS * **Designer:** K. Martens

Date	Mintage	F	VF	XF	Unc	BU
ND(2003)	1,000,000	—	—	—	7.00	8.00
ND(2003) Prooflike	100,000	—	—	—	—	20.00

KM# 252 5 EURO
11.9000 g., 0.9250 Silver 0.3539 oz. ASW **Ruler:** Beatrix **Subject:** New EEC member countries **Obv:** Head left **Obv. Designer:** M. Mieras and H. Mieras **Rev:** Names of old and new member countries **Edge:** GOD * ZIJ * MET * ONS *

Date	Mintage	F	VF	XF	Unc	BU
2004	600,000	—	—	—	—	10.00
2004 Proof	55,000	Value: 40.00				

KM# 253 5 EURO
11.9000 g., 0.9250 Silver 0.3539 oz. ASW **Ruler:** Beatrix **Subject:** 50th Anniversary - End of colonization of Netherlands Antilles **Obv:** Head left **Obv. Designer:** R. Luijters **Rev:** Fruit and date within beaded circle **Edge Lettering:** GOD * ZIJ * MET * ONS *

Date	Mintage	F	VF	XF	Unc	BU
2004	650,000	—	—	—	10.00	12.00
2004 Proof	26,900	Value: 35.00				

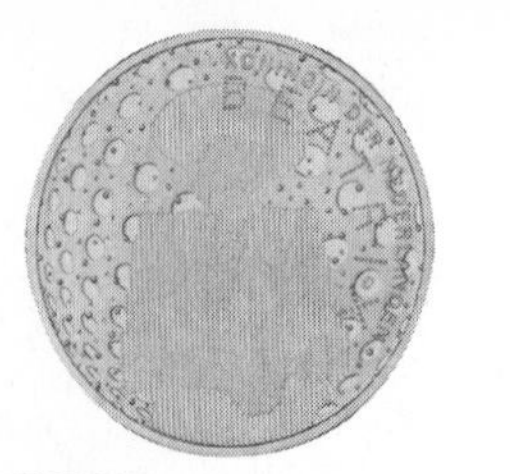

KM# 254 5 EURO

11.9100 g., 0.9250 Silver 0.3542 oz. ASW, 29 mm.
Ruler: Beatrix **Subject:** 60th Anniversary of Liberation
Obv: Queen's image **Rev:** Value and dots **Edge Lettering:** GOD * ZIJ * MET * ONS * **Designer:** Suzan Drummen

Date	Mintage	F	VF	XF	Unc	BU
2005	630,000	—	—	—	12.00	15.00
2005 Proof	40,000	Value: 45.00				

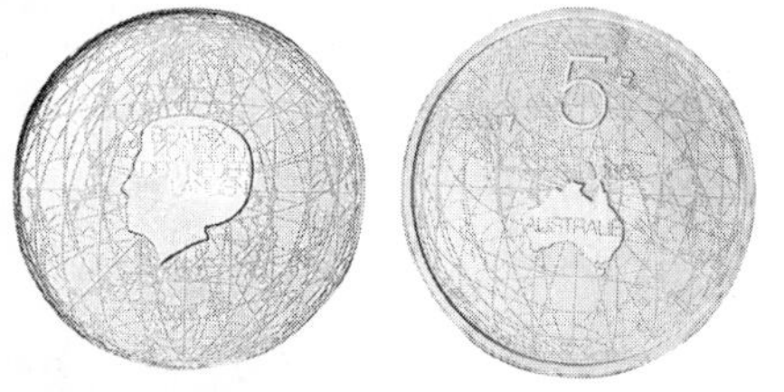

KM# 255 5 EURO

11.9000 g., 0.9250 Silver 0.3539 oz. ASW, 29 mm.
Ruler: Beatrix **Obv:** Queen's silhouette centered on a world globe **Rev:** Value above Australia on a world globe **Edge Lettering:** GOD * ZIJ * MET * ONS * **Designer:** Irma Boom

Date	Mintage	F	VF	XF	Unc	BU
2006	500,000	—	—	—	12.00	15.00
2006 Proof	22,500	Value: 40.00				

KM# 266 5 EURO

11.9000 g., 0.9250 Silver 0.3539 oz. ASW, 28.9 mm.
Ruler: Beatrix **Obv:** Queen Beatrix **Rev:** Rembrandt
Edge Lettering: GOD * Z IJ * MET * ONS * **Designer:** Berend Strik

Date	Mintage	F	VF	XF	Unc	BU
ND(2006)	655,000	—	—	—	10.00	15.00
ND(2006) Proof	35,000	Value: 35.00				

KM# 267 5 EURO

11.9000 g., 0.9250 Silver 0.3539 oz. ASW, 29 mm.
Ruler: Beatrix **Subject:** 200th Anniversary of Taxes
Obv: Queen's portrait **Rev:** Circles with dates 1806-2006
Designer: Hennie Bouwe

Date	Mintage	F	VF	XF	Unc	BU
2006	359,189	—	—	—	10.00	20.00
2006 Prooflike	40,000	—	—	—	—	25.00
2006 Proof	15,000	Value: 45.00				

KM# 277 5 EURO

11.9000 g., 0.9250 Silver 0.3539 oz. ASW, 29 mm.
Ruler: Beatrix **Subject:** M.A. de Ruyter, 400th Anniversary of Birth **Obv:** Head 1/4 left **Obv. Designer:** Martyn Engelbregt
Rev: Head 1/4 right

Date	Mintage	F	VF	XF	Unc	BU
2007	520,500	—	—	—	25.00	35.00
2007 Proof	17,500	Value: 45.00				

KM# 279 5 EURO

15.5000 g., 0.9250 Silver 0.4609 oz. ASW, 33 mm.
Ruler: Beatrix **Subject:** Architecture **Obv:** Portrait facing
Rev: Books around map of the Netherlands **Designer:** Stani Michiels

Date	Mintage	F	VF	XF	Unc	BU
2008 Proof	25,000	Value: 45.00				

KM# 279a 5 EURO

10.5000 g., Silver Plated Copper, 29 mm. **Ruler:** Beatrix
Obv: Portrait facing **Rev:** Architecture books around map of the Netherlands

Date	Mintage	F	VF	XF	Unc	BU
2008	350,000	—	—	—	10.00	12.50

KM# 282 5 EURO

15.5000 g., 0.9250 Silver 0.4609 oz. ASW, 33 mm.
Ruler: Beatrix **Subject:** Manhattan 400th Anniversary
Obv: Bottom tip of Manhattan Island today **Rev:** Bottom tip of Manhattan Island in 1609 **Designer:** Ronald van Tienhoven

Date	Mintage	F	VF	XF	Unc	BU
2009 Proof	25,000	Value: 45.00				

KM# 282a 5 EURO

10.5000 g., Silver Plated Copper, 29 mm. **Ruler:** Beatrix
Subject: Manhattan 400th Anniversary **Obv:** Tip of Manhattan Island today **Rev:** Tip of Manhattan Island in 1609
Designer: Ronald van Tienhoven

Date	Mintage	F	VF	XF	Unc	BU
2009	350,000	—	—	—	10.00	12.50

KM# 287 5 EURO

15.5000 g., 0.9250 Silver 0.4609 oz. ASW, 33 mm.
Ruler: Beatrix **Subject:** Netherlands-Japanese Friendship

Date	Mintage	F	VF	XF	Unc	BU
2009 Proof	45,000	Value: 40.00				

KM# 287a 5 EURO

10.5000 g., Silver Plated Copper, 29 mm. **Ruler:** Beatrix
Subject: Netherlands-Japanese Friendship

Date	Mintage	F	VF	XF	Unc	BU
2009	350,000	—	—	—	10.00	12.50

KM# 243 10 EURO

17.8000 g., 0.9250 Silver 0.5293 oz. ASW, 33 mm.
Ruler: Beatrix **Subject:** Crown Prince's Wedding **Obv:** Head left **Rev:** Two facing silhouettes **Edge:** Plain **Designer:** H. van Houwelingen

Date	Mintage	F	VF	XF	Unc	BU
2002	1,000,000	—	—	—	15.00	40.00
2002 Prooflike	100,000	—	—	—	—	55.00
2002 Proof	80,000	Value: 60.00				

KM# 244 10 EURO

6.7200 g., 0.9000 Gold 0.1944 oz. AGW, 22.5 mm.
Ruler: Beatrix **Subject:** Crown Prince's Wedding **Obv:** Head left **Rev:** Two facing silhouettes **Edge:** Reeded **Designer:** J. van Houwelingen

Date	Mintage	F	VF	XF	Unc	BU
2002 Prooflike	33,000	—	—	—	—	245

KM# 246 10 EURO

6.7200 g., 0.9000 Gold 0.1944 oz. AGW, 22.5 mm.
Ruler: Beatrix **Subject:** Vincent Van Gogh **Obv:** Head facing
Rev: Tilted head facing **Edge:** Reeded **Designer:** K. Martens

Date	Mintage	F	VF	XF	Unc	BU
ND(2003) Prooflike	20,000	—	—	—	—	275

KM# 247 10 EURO

6.7200 g., 0.9000 Gold 0.1944 oz. AGW, 22.5 mm. **Ruler:** Beatrix **Subject:** New EEC members **Obv:** Head left **Rev:** Value and legend **Edge:** Reeded **Designer:** M. Mieras and H. Mieras

Date	Mintage	F	VF	XF	Unc	BU
2004 Proof	6,000	Value: 600				

KM# 251 10 EURO

6.7200 g., 0.9000 Gold 0.1944 oz. AGW, 22.5 mm.
Ruler: Beatrix **Subject:** 50 Years of Domestic Autonomy, 1954-2004 (for Netherlands Antilles) **Obv:** Small head left **Rev:** Fruit and date within beaded circle **Edge:** Reeded **Designer:** Rudy Luijters

Date	Mintage	F	VF	XF	Unc	BU
2004 Proof	3,800	Value: 550				

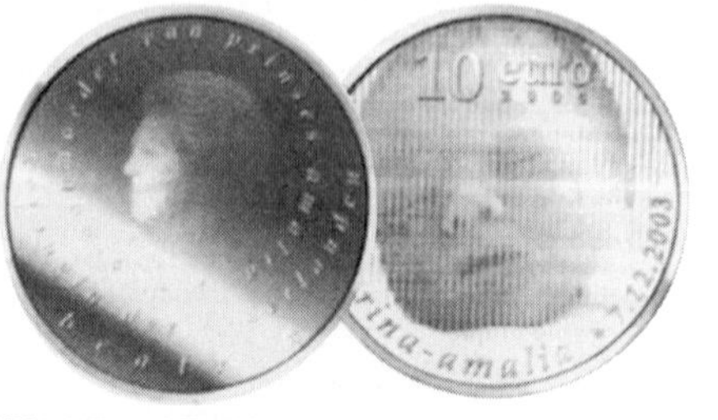

KM# 248 10 EURO

17.8000 g., 0.9250 Silver 0.5293 oz. ASW, 33 mm.
Ruler: Beatrix **Obv:** Head left **Rev:** Multi-views of Prince Willem-Alexander, Princess Catherina-Amalia and Princess Maxima

Date	Mintage	F	VF	XF	Unc	BU
2004	1,000,000	—	—	—	—	18.00
2004 Proof	50,000	Value: 40.00				

KM# 261 10 EURO

17.8000 g., 0.9250 Silver 0.5293 oz. ASW, 33 mm.
Ruler: Beatrix **Subject:** Silver Jubilee of Reign **Obv:** Queen's photo **Rev:** Queen taking oath photo **Edge Lettering:** GOD * ZIJ * MET * ONS * **Designer:** Germaine Kruip

Date	Mintage	F	VF	XF	Unc	BU
2005	1,000,000	—	—	—	—	20.00
2005 Proof	59,754	Value: 40.00				

KM# 264 10 EURO

6.7200 g., 0.9000 Gold 0.1944 oz. AGW, 22.5 mm.
Ruler: Beatrix **Subject:** 60th Anniversary of Liberation
Obv: Queen and dots **Rev:** Value and dots **Edge:** Reeded
Designer: Suzan Drummen

Date	Mintage	F	VF	XF	Unc	BU
2005 Proof	6,000	Value: 500				

KM# 289 10 EURO

6.7200 g., 0.9000 Gold 0.1944 oz. AGW, 29 mm. **Ruler:** Beatrix
Series: Tax Services, 200th Anniversary **Rev:** Florin of 1807

Date	Mintage	F	VF	XF	Unc	BU
2006 Proof	5,500	Value: 400				

KM# 290 10 EURO

6.7200 g., 0.9000 Gold 0.1944 oz. AGW, 29 mm. **Ruler:** Beatrix
Subject: Netherlands-Australian Friendship

Date	Mintage	F	VF	XF	Unc	BU
2006 Proof	3,500	Value: 600				

KM# 278 10 EURO

6.7200 g., 0.9000 Gold 0.1944 oz. AGW, 29 mm. **Ruler:** Beatrix
Subject: M.A. de Ruyter, 400th Birthday **Obv:** Head 1/4 left
Rev: Head 1/4 right **Designer:** Martyn Engelbregt

Date	Mintage	F	VF	XF	Unc	BU
2007 Proof	7,000	Value: 275				

KM# 280 10 EURO

6.7200 g., 0.9000 Gold 0.1944 oz. AGW, 22.5 mm.
Ruler: Beatrix **Subject:** Architecture **Obv:** Portrait facing
Rev: Architecture books around map of the Netherlands
Designer: Stani Michiels

Date	Mintage	F	VF	XF	Unc	BU
2008 Proof	8,000	Value: 300				

KM# 283 10 EURO

6.7200 g., 0.9000 Gold 0.1944 oz. AGW, 22.5 mm.
Ruler: Beatrix **Subject:** Dutch settlement of Manhattan, NY 400th Anniversary **Obv:** Bottom tip of Manhattan Island today **Rev:** Bottom tip of Manhattan Island in 1609 **Designer:** Ronald van Tienhoven

Date	Mintage	F	VF	XF	Unc	BU
2009 Proof	6,500	Value: 350				

KM# 288 10 EURO

6.7200 g., 0.9000 Gold 0.1944 oz. AGW, 22.5 mm.
Ruler: Beatrix **Subject:** Netherlands-Japanese Friendship

Date	Mintage	F	VF	XF	Unc	BU
2009 Proof	9,000	Value: 300				

KM# 291 10 EURO

6.7200 g., 0.9000 Gold 0.1944 oz. AGW, 29 mm. **Ruler:** Beatrix
Subject: Rembrant, 400th Anniversary of Birth **Rev:** Self-portrait

Date	Mintage	F	VF	XF	Unc	BU
2009 Proof	8,500	Value: 300				

KM# 249 20 EURO

8.5000 g., 0.9000 Gold 0.2459 oz. AGW, 25 mm. **Ruler:** Beatrix
Subject: Birth of Crown-Princess - Catharina-Amalia - July 12, 2003 **Obv:** Bust left **Rev:** Holographic images: left, Princess Maxima; front, Princess Catharina-Amalia; right, Prince Willem-Alexander **Edge:** Reeded

Date	Mintage	F	VF	XF	Unc	BU
2004 Proof	5,345	Value: 530				

KM# 262 20 EURO

8.5000 g., 0.9000 Gold 0.2459 oz. AGW, 25 mm. **Ruler:** Beatrix
Subject: Silver Jubilee of Reign **Obv:** Queen's photo **Rev:** Queen taking oath photo **Edge:** Reeded **Designer:** Germaine Kruip

Date	Mintage	F	VF	XF	Unc	BU
2005 Proof	5,001	Value: 450				

KM# 250 50 EURO

13.4400 g., 0.9000 Gold 0.3889 oz. AGW, 27 mm.
Ruler: Beatrix **Subject:** Birth of Crown-Princess - Catharina-Amalia - July 12, 2003 **Obv:** Bust left **Rev:** Holographic images: left, Princess Maxima; front, Princess Catharina-Amalia; right, Prince Willem-Alexander **Edge:** Reeded

Date	Mintage	F	VF	XF	Unc	BU
2004 Proof	3,500	Value: 675				

KM# 263 50 EURO

13.4400 g., 0.9000 Gold 0.3889 oz. AGW, 27 mm.
Ruler: Beatrix **Subject:** Silver Jubilee of Reign **Obv:** Queen's photo **Rev:** Queen taking oath photo **Edge:** Reeded
Designer: Germaine Kruip

Date	Mintage	F	VF	XF	Unc	BU
2005 Proof	3,500	Value: 675				

TRADE COINAGE

KM# 190.2 DUCAT

3.4940 g., 0.9830 Gold 0.1104 oz. AGW **Ruler:** Beatrix
Obv: Knight divides date with larger letters in legend
Rev: Inscription within decorated square

Date	Mintage	F	VF	XF	Unc	BU
2001 Proof	7,500	Value: 150				
2002 Proof	3,400	Value: 175				
2003 Proof	3,800	Value: 175				
2004 Proof	2,120	Value: 250				
2005 Proof	2,243	Value: 175				
2006 Proof	2,097	Value: 175				
2007 Proof	2,250	Value: 175				
2008 Proof	3,260	Value: 165				
2009 Proof	3,500	Value: 165				
2010 Proof	—	Value: 165				

KM# 211 2 DUCAT
6.9880 g., 0.9830 Gold 0.2208 oz. AGW, 26 mm. **Ruler:** Beatrix
Obv: Knight divides date within beaded circle **Rev:** Inscription within decorated square

Date	Mintage	F	VF	XF	Unc	BU
2002 Proof	6,650	Value: 300				
2003 Proof	4,500	Value: 300				
2004 Proof	2,015	Value: 300				
2005 Proof	3,500	Value: 300				
2006 Proof	1,800	Value: 300				
2007 Proof	2,000	Value: 300				
2008 Proof	2,100	Value: 300				
2009 Proof	2,500	Value: 300				
2010 Proof	—	Value: 300				

SILVER BULLION COINAGE

KM# 242 SILVER DUCAT
28.2500 g., 0.8730 Silver 0.7929 oz. ASW, 40 mm.
Ruler: Beatrix **Obv:** Crowned shield **Rev:** Armored Knight with sword divides date and circle, shield in front **Edge:** Reeded
Note: Utrecht coin design circa 1659 based on KM#48.

Date	Mintage	F	VF	XF	Unc	BU
2001 Proof	9,000	Value: 30.00				

KM# 256 SILVER DUCAT
28.2500 g., 0.8730 Silver 0.7929 oz. ASW, 40 mm.
Ruler: Beatrix **Obv:** Crowned shield **Rev:** Armored Knight with Gelderland arms **Edge:** Reeded

Date	Mintage	F	VF	XF	Unc	BU
2002 Proof	9,400	Value: 30.00				

KM# 257 SILVER DUCAT
28.2500 g., 0.8730 Silver 0.7929 oz. ASW, 40 mm.
Ruler: Beatrix **Obv:** Crowned shield **Rev:** Armored Knight with sword holding arms of Holland **Edge:** Reeded

Date	Mintage	F	VF	XF	Unc	BU
2003 Proof	4,100	Value: 45.00				

KM# 258 SILVER DUCAT
28.2500 g., 0.8730 Silver 0.7929 oz. ASW, 40 mm.
Ruler: Beatrix **Obv:** Crowned shield **Rev:** Armored Knight holding sword with Zeeland arms **Edge:** Reeded

Date	Mintage	F	VF	XF	Unc	BU
2004 Proof	4,109	Value: 45.00				

KM# 259 SILVER DUCAT
28.2500 g., 0.8730 Silver 0.7929 oz. ASW, 40 mm.
Ruler: Beatrix **Obv:** Crowned shield **Rev:** Armored Knight holding sword with Friesland arms **Edge:** Reeded

Date	Mintage	F	VF	XF	Unc	BU
2005 Proof	4,000	Value: 45.00				

KM# 260 SILVER DUCAT
28.2500 g., 0.8730 Silver 0.7929 oz. ASW, 40 mm.
Ruler: Beatrix **Obv:** Crowned shield **Rev:** Armored Knight holding sword with Groningen arms **Edge:** Reeded

Date	Mintage	F	VF	XF	Unc	BU
2006 Proof	4,000	Value: 45.00				

KM# 275 SILVER DUCAT
28.2500 g., 0.8730 Silver 0.7929 oz. ASW, 40 mm.
Ruler: Beatrix **Obv:** Crowned shield **Rev:** Armed Knight holding sword with Overyssel arms **Edge:** Reeded

Date	Mintage	F	VF	XF	Unc	BU
2007 Proof	3,500	Value: 45.00				

KM# 276 SILVER DUCAT
28.2500 g., 0.8730 Silver 0.7929 oz. ASW, 40 mm.
Ruler: Beatrix **Obv:** Crowned shield **Rev:** Jan I standing holding sword with Noord-Brabant arms **Edge:** Reeded

Date	Mintage	F	VF	XF	Unc	BU
2008 Proof	3,000	Value: 45.00				

KM# 292 SILVER DUCAT
28.2500 g., 0.8730 Silver 0.7929 oz. ASW, 40 mm. **Ruler:** Beatrix **Subject:** Northern Brabant **Obv:** Crowned shield **Rev:** John I, Count of Brabant standing with shield **Edge:** Reeded

Date	Mintage	F	VF	XF	Unc	BU
2008 Proof	—	Value: 65.00				

KM# 284 SILVER DUCAT
28.2500 g., 0.8730 Silver 0.7929 oz. ASW, 40 mm. **Ruler:** Beatrix **Rev:** Jan I standing with sword and Gelderland arms

Date	Mintage	F	VF	XF	Unc	BU
2009 Proof	3,000	Value: 55.00				

KM# 293 SILVER DUCAT
28.2500 g., 0.8730 Silver 0.7929 oz. ASW, 40 mm. **Ruler:** Beatrix **Subject:** Limburg **Obv:** Crowned shield **Rev:** Philips II of Montmorency, Count of Horne, standing **Edge:** Reeded

Date	Mintage	F	VF	XF	Unc	BU
2009 Proof	—	Value: 65.00				

KM# 285 SILVER DUCAT
28.2500 g., 0.8750 Silver 0.7947 oz. ASW, 40 mm. **Ruler:** Beatrix **Obv:** Willaim of Orange standing with Zuid-Holland arms

Date	Mintage	F	VF	XF	Unc	BU
2010 Proof	—	Value: 55.00				

KM# 286 SILVER DUCAT
28.2500 g., 0.8750 Silver 0.7947 oz. ASW, 40 mm.
Ruler: Beatrix **Obv:** Floris V standing with Noord Holland arms

Date	Mintage	F	VF	XF	Unc	BU
2010 Proof	—	Value: 55.00				

PATTERNS
Including off metal strikes

KM#	Date	Mintage	Identification	Mkt Val
Pn162	2001	—	Gulden. Nickel. Medal rotation	—
Pn166	2001	—	Euro. Brass. KM240	—
Pn165	2001	—	2 Euro Cent. Nickel.	100

MINT SETS

KM#	Date	Mintage	Identification	Issue Price	Mkt Val
MS109	2001 (6)	120,000	KM#202-206, 210 Introduction Euro-coins, no medal	15.00	16.00
MS110	2001 (6)	3,400	KM#202-206, 210 Queen Juliana	17.50	40.00
MS111	2001 (6)	100	KM#202-206, 210 Queen Juliana (error) in these sets are 5 or 25 cents or 5 guilden coins dated 2000	17.50	150
MS112	2001 (6)	1,000	KM#202-206, 210 BOLEGO-VOK	—	60.00
MS113	2001 (6)	1,000	KM#202-206, 210 De Akerendam II, with a silver 2 stuiver coin from the wreck	125	145

KM#	Date	Mintage	Identification	Issue Price	Mkt Val
MS114	2001 (6)	1,000	KM#202-206, 210 United Seven Provinces Groningen	40.00	40.00
MS115	2001 (6)	1,000	KM#202-206, 210 United Seven Provinces Utrecht	40.00	40.00
MS116	2001 (6)	21,000	KM#202-206, 210 Baby set + bear medal	15.50	17.50
MS117	2001 (6)	1,015	KM#202-206, 210 Onderlinge "s-Grdevenhage"	—	70.00
MS121	2001 (8)	68,000	KM#234-241 Charity set, disabled sport	15.00	17.00
MS4	2001 (6)	85,000	KM#202-206, 210	12.00	8.00
MS5	2001 (8)	68,000	KM#234-241 Charity set, Disabled Sports	15.00	8.00
MS10	2002 (8)	3,500	KM#234-241 plus medal Queen Beatrix set	20.00	110
MS11	2002 (8)	2,002	KM#234-241 plus medal 10th Day of the Mint	22.00	150
MS12	2002 (8)	10,000	KM#234-241 plus medal VOC set I	22.00	20.00
MS122	2002 (8)	105,000	KM#234-241 Charity set, blind escort dogs fund	15.00	17.00
MS123	2002 (8)	59,500	KM#234-241 Last FDS-set	15.00	17.00
MS124	2002 (8)	25,000	KM#234-241 Baby set + bear medal	15.50	25.00
MS125	2002 (8)	10,000	KM#234-241 Wedding-set + medal	15.50	35.00
MS126	2002 (8)	3,500	KM#234-241 Queen Beatrix + medal	20.00	110
MS127	2002 (8)	2,002	KM#234-241 10th day of the Mint + medal	22.00	175
MS128	2002 (8)	10,000	KM#234-241 VOC set I + medal	22.00	35.00
MS129	2002 (8)	10,000	KM#234-241 VOC set II + medal	22.00	25.00
MS13	2002 (8)	10,000	KM#234-241 plus medal VOC set II	22.00	20.00
MS130	2002 (8)	10,000	KM#234-241 VOC set III + medal	22.00	25.00
MS131	2002 (8)	10,000	KM#234-241 VOC set IV + medal	22.00	25.00
MS132	2002 (8)	3,000	KM#234-241 BVC + medal	30.00	40.00
MS133	2002 (8)	9,200	KM#234-241 10 Euro + poststamp	30.00	30.00
MS134	2002 (8)	2,500	KM#234-241VVV-Iris gift set	20.00	40.00
MS135	2002 (8)	1,000	KM#234-241 Theo Peters (Christmas) + medal	99.00	90.00
MS14	2002 (9)	10,000	KM#234-241 plus medal VOC set III	22.00	20.00
MS15	2002 (8)	10,000	KM#234-241 plus medal VOC set IV	22.00	20.00
MS16	2002 (8)	3,000	KM#234-241 plus medal BVC	30.00	40.00
MS17A	2002 (8)	2,500	KM#234-241 VVV - Irisgitftset	20.00	40.00
MS18	2002 (8)	1,000	KM#234-241 plus medal Theo Peters (Christmas)	99.00	60.00
MS6	2002 (8)	105,000	KM#234-241 Charity set, Blind Escort Dogs Fund	15.00	10.00
MS7	2002 (8)	59,500	KM#234-241 Last FDC set	15.00	10.00
MS8	2002 (8)	25,000	KM#234-241 plus bear medal Baby set	15.50	25.00
MS9	2002 (8)	10,000	KM#234-241 plus medal Wedding Set	15.50	35.00
MS17	2002 (1)	9,200	KM#243 plus stamp	30.00	30.00
MS136	2003 (8)	75,000	KM#234-241 Charity set, epilepsy fund	15.50	17.00
MS137	2003 (8)	15,000	KM#234-241 Information set Denmark	20.00	40.00
MS138	2003 (8)	10,000	KM#234-241 VVV-Iris gift set	20.00	25.00
MS139	2003 (8)	10,000	KM#234-241 VOC set V + medal	22.00	25.00
MS140	2003 (8)	10,000	KM#234-241 VOC set VI + medal	42.00	45.00
MS141	2003 (8)	2,003	KM#234-241 Day of the mint + medal	25.00	140
MS142	2003 (8)	1,000	KM#234-241 Theo Peters jubilee set + bi-colour medal	—	30.00
MS143	2003 (8)	100	KM#234-241 Theo Peters jubilee set + silver medal	70.00	70.00
MS144	2003 (8)	25	KM#234-241 Theo Peters jubilee set + golden medal	400	410
MS145	2003 (8)	25,000	KM#234-241 Baby set + bear medal	20.00	25.00
MS146	2003 (8)	15,000	KM#234-241 Wedding-set + medal	20.00	25.00
MS147	2003 (8)	1,000	KM#234-241 Theo Peters Christmas set + bi-colour medal	—	30.00
MS148	2003 (8)	150	KM#234-241 Theo Peters Christmas set + silver medal	70.00	70.00
MS149	2003 (8)	50	KM#234-241 Theo Peters Christmas set + golden medal	400	400
MS150	2003 (8)	3,500	KM#234-241 Mint masters I + medal	20.00	60.00
MS151	2003 (8)	1,000	KM#234-241 World Money Fair Basel	20.00	130
MS152	2003 (8)	15,000	KM#234-241 Information set Hungaria	20.00	40.00
MS153	2003 (8)	20,000	KM#234-241 Royal birthset of Princess Catharina-Amalia December 7 + silver medal	22.00	25.00
MS154	2003 (8)	10,000	KM#234-241 Benelux set, with Belgium (8) KM#224-231 and Luxembourg (8) KM#75-81	40.00	45.00

KM#	Date	Mintage	Identification	Issue Price	Mkt Val
MS155	2003 (8)	10,000	KM#234-241 Charles V set + medal, with Germany (8) KM#207-214, Spain (8) KM#1040-1047, Belgium (8) KM#224-231, and Austria (8) KM#3082-3089	85.00	85.00
MS19	2003 (8)	75,000	KM#234-241 Charity set, Epilepsy fund	15.50	10.00
MS20	2003 (8)	15,000	KM#234-241 Information set Denmark	20.00	40.00
MS21	2003 (9)	10,000	KM#234-241 VVV - Irisgiftset	15.50	20.00
MS22	2003 (8)	10,000	KM#234-241 plus medal VOC set V	22.00	25.00
MS23	2003 (8)	10,000	KM#234-241 plus medal VOC set VI	42.00	45.00
MS24	2003 (7)	2,003	KM#234-241 plus medal Day of the Mint	25.00	100
MS25	2003 (8)	1,000	KM#234-241 plus bi-color medal Theo Peters Jubilee set	—	20.00
MS26	2003 (7)	100	KM#234-241 plus silver medal Theo Peters Jubilee set	70.00	50.00
MS27	2003 (8)	25	KM#234-241 plus golden medal Theo Peters Jubilee set	400	250
MS28	2003 (8)	25,000	KM#234-241 plus bear medal Baby set	20.00	25.00
MS29	2003 (8)	15,000	KM#234-241 plus medal Wedding set	20.00	25.00
MS30	2003 (8)	1,000	KM#234-241 plus silver medal Theo Peters Christmas set	—	20.00
MS31	2003 (8)	150	KM#234-241 plus silver medal Theo Peters Christmas set	70.00	50.00
MS32	2003 (8)	50	KM#234-241 plus golden medal Theo Peters Christmas set	400	275
MS33	2003	3,500	KM#234-241 plus medal Mintmasters I	20.00	60.00
MS34	2003 (8)	1,000	KM#234-241 World Money Fair	20.00	100
MS35	2003 (8)	15,000	KM234-241 Information Set Hungaria	20.00	25.00
MS36	2003 (8)	20,000	KM#234-241 plus silver medal Royal Birth of Princess Catharina-Amalia	22.00	25.00
MS37	2003 (16)	10,000	KM#234-241 and Luxembourg KM#75-81, 40 Benelux Set	40.00	45.00
MS38	2003 (40)	10,000	KM#224-231 plus Germany KM#207-214 plus Spain KM#1040-1047 plus Belgium KM#224-231 and Austria KM#3082-3089 Charles V Set	85.00	85.00
MS156	2004 (8)	3,500	KM#234-241 Mintmasters II + medal	20.00	60.00
MS157	2004 (8)	10,000	KM#234-241 Wedding-set + medal	18.00	20.00
MS158	2004 (8)	20,000	KM#234-241 Baby set + bear medal	20.00	25.00
MS159	2004 (8)	1,000	KM#234-241 World Money Fair Basel	20.00	110
MS160	2004 (8)	35,000	KM#234-241 Benelux: Belgium, Netherlands + Luxembourg. With silver medal	60.00	60.00
MS161	2004 (8)	10,000	KM#234-241 Queen Juliana-set + silver guilder KM#184 and 30mm silver medal	25.00	28.00
MS162	2004 (8)	1,500	KM#234-241 Theo Peters Christmas set + bi-colour medal	30.00	30.00
MS163	2004 (8)	3,500	KME234-241 VVV-Iris gift set	20.00	25.00
MS164	2004 (8)	150	KM#234-241 Theo Peters Christmas set + silver medal	100	100
MS165	2004 (8)	50	KM#234-241 Theo Peters Christmas set + golden medal	500	500
MS166	2004 (8)	50,000	KM#234-241 Charity set, Fire-burn Centre	18.00	22.00
MS167	2004 (8)	2,004	KM#234-241 Day of the Mint + medal	25.00	150
MS170	2005 (8)	10,000	KM#234-241 Wedding-set + medal	18.00	—
MS39	2004 (8)	3,500	KM#234-241 plus medal Mintmasters II	20.00	60.00
MS40	2004 (8)	10,000	KM#234-241 Wedding set plus medal	18.00	—
MS41	2004 (9)	20,000	KM#234-241 Baby set plus bear medal	20.00	25.00
MS42	2004 (8)	1,000	KM#234-241 Basel World Money Fair	20.00	110
MS43	2004 (24)	35,000	KM#234-241 and Luxembourg KM#75-81 plus Belgium KM#224-231 Benelux set with silver medal	60.00	60.00
MS44	2004 (10)	10,000	KM#234-241 Queen Juliana set plus silver guilder, KM#184 and 30mm silver medal	25.00	28.00
MS45	2004 (9)	1,500	KM#234-241 Theo Peters Christmas set plus bi-color medal	30.00	30.00
MS46	2004 (8)	3,500	KM#234-241 VVV - Iris gift set	20.00	25.00
MS47	2004 (9)	150	KM#234-241 Theo Peters Christmas set plus silver medal	100	100
MS48	2004 (9)	50	KM#234-241 Theo Peters Christmas set plus golden medal	500	500
MS49	2004 (8)	50,000	KM#234-241 Fire - Burn Centre Charity set	18.00	22.00
MS50	2004 (9)	—	KM#234-241 Day of the Mint plus medal	25.00	150
MS168	2005 (8)	3,500	KM#234-241 Mintmasters III + medal	20.00	60.00
MS169	2005 (8)	2,005	KM#234-241 Day of the Mint + medal	25.00	150
MS171	2005 (8)	20,000	KM#234-241 Baby set + bear medal	20.00	25.00
MS172	2005 (8)	20,000	KM#234-241 Nijntje-set (Dick Bruna) + medal	18.00	20.00
MS173	2005 (8)	55,000	KM#234-241 Charity set: Princess Beatrix Fonds	18.00	22.00
MS174	2005 (8)	20,000	KM#234-241 Beneluz: Belgium, Netherlands + Luxembourg. With silver medal	60.00	60.00
MS175	2005 (8)	1,000	KM#234-241 World Money Fair Basel	25.00	110
MS176	2005 (8)	15,000	KM#234-241 60th Anniversary Liberation + Canadian 25 ct	35.00	35.00
MS177	2005 (8)	1,000	KM#234-241 Theo Peters Christmas set + bi-colour medal	30.00	30.00
MS178	2005 (8)	100	KM#234-241 Theo Peters Christmas set + silver medal	120	120
MS179	2005 (8)	25	KM#234-241 Theo Peters Christmas set + golden medal	550	550
MS51	2005 (9)	3,500	KM#234-241 Mintmasters III plus medal	20.00	60.00
MS52	2005 (9)	—	KM#234-241 Day of the Mint plus medal	25.00	150
MS53	2005 (9)	10,000	KM#234-241 Wedding set plus medal	18.00	20.00
MS54	2005 (9)	20,000	KM#234-241 Baby set plus bear medal	20.00	25.00
MS55	2005 (9)	20,000	KM#234-241 Nijntje set (Dick Bruna) plus medal	18.00	20.00
MS56	2005 (8)	55,000	KM#234-241 Charity set: Princess Beatrix Fonds	18.00	22.00
MS57	2005 (24)	20,000	KM#234-241, Belgium 224-231, Luxembourg 75-81 Benelux set: Belgium, Netherlands plus Luxembourg with silver medal	60.00	60.00
MS58	2005 (8)	1,000	KM#234-241 World Money Fair, Basel	25.00	110
MS59	2005 (8)	15,000	KM#234-241 60th Anniversary Liberation plus Canadian 25 cent	35.00	35.00
MS60	2005 (9)	1,000	KM#234-241 Theo Peters Christmas set plus bi-color medal	30.00	30.00
MS61	2005 (9)	100	KM#234-241 Theo Peters Christmas set plus silver medal	120	80.00
MS62	2005 (9)	25	KM#234-241 Theo Peters Christmas set plus golden medal	550	300
XMS2	2005 (7)	—	X#Pn23-29	—	30.00
MS180	2006 (8)	3,500	KM#234-241 Mintmasters IV + medal	20.00	40.00
MS181	2006 (8)	4,000	KM#234-241 5 sets with a Rembrandt silver medal and one set with the Rembrandt 5 euro coin	250	250
MS182	2006 (8)	500	KM#234-241 5 sets with a Rembrandt silver medal and one set with the Rembrandt 10 euro coin	900	900
MS183	2006 (8)	45,000	KM#234-241 Charity set: (Kika)	18.00	22.00
MS184	2006 (8)	2,750	KM#234-241 Baby set boy + bear medal	20.00	25.00
MS185	2006 (8)	100	KM#234-241 Baby set boy + silver medal	—	95.00
MS186	2006 (8)	25	KM#234-241 Baby set boy + gold medal	—	500
MS187	2006 (8)	2,750	KM#234-241 Baby set girl + bear medal	20.00	25.00
MS188	2006 (8)	100	KM#234-241 Baby set girl + silver medal	—	95.00
MS189	2006 (8)	25	KM#234-241 Baby set girl + gold medal	—	500
MS190	2006 (8)	15,000	KM#234-241 Beneluz: Belgium, Netherlands + Luxembourg. With silver medal	65.00	65.00
MS192	2006 (8)	1,050	KM#234-241 Wedding-set + medal	22.00	25.00
MS193	2006 (8)	1,500	KM#234-241 Christmas set Royal Dutch Mint	30.00	30.00
MS194	2006 (8)	600	KM#234-241 Theo Peters Christmas set + bi-colour medal	35.00	40.00
MS195	2006 (8)	100	KM#234-241 Christmas set + silver medal	150	150
MS196	2006 (8)	25	KM#234-241 Christmas set + golden medal	650	650
MS197	2006 (8)	1,000	KM#234-241 Berlin Coin Fair	25.00	45.00
MS198	2006 (8)	2,006	KM#234-241 Day of the Mint + medal	25.00	120
MS199	2006 (8)	10,000	KM#234-241 200 years coins in Kingdom Holland	25.00	20.00
MS200	2007 (8)	3,500	KM#234-236, 268-272 Mintmasters V + medal	20.00	40.00
MS63	2006 (10)	3,500	KM#234-241 Mintmasters IV plus medal	20.00	40.00
MS64	2006 (10)	4,000	KM#234-241 5 sets plus a Rembrandt silver medal and 1 set with a Rembrandt 5 Euro coin (6x8)	250	210
MS65	2006 (10)	500	KM#234-241 5 sets with Rembrandt silver medal and one set with Rembrandt 10 euro coin (6x8)	900	900
MS66	2006 (8)	45,000	KM#234-241 Charity set: Kika	18.00	10.00
MS67	2006 (9)	2,750	KM#231-241 Baby set boy plus bear medal	20.00	25.00
MS68	2006 (9)	100	KM#234-241 Baby set boy plus silver medal	—	95.00
MS69	2006 (8)	25	KM#234-241 Baby set boy plus gold medal	—	500
MS70	2006 (9)	2,750	KM#234-241 Baby set girl plus bear medal	20.00	25.00
MS71	2006 (8)	100	KM#234-241 Baby set girl plus silver medal	—	95.00
MS72	2006 (9)	25	KM#234-241 Baby set girl, plus gold medal	—	500
MS73	2006 (9)	15,000	KM#234-241 Benelux set: Belgium, 224-231, Luxembourg 75-81 plus Netherlands	65.00	65.00
MS74	2006 (9)	1,050	KM#234-241 Wedding set plus medal	22.00	25.00
MS75	2006 (8)	1,500	KM#234-241 Royal Dutch Mint Christmas set	30.00	25.00
MS76	2006 (9)	600	KM#234-241 Theo Peters Christmas set plus bi-color medal	35.00	40.00
MS77	2006 (9)	100	KM#234-241 Christmas set plus silver medal	150	100
MS78	2006 (9)	25	KM#234-241 Christmas set plus golden medal	650	400
MS79	2006 (8)	1,000	KM#234-241 Berlin Coin Fair	25.00	45.00
MS80	2006 (9)	—	KM#234-241 Day of the Mint set plus medal	25.00	120
MS81	2006 (8)	10,000	KM#234-241 200 Years of Coins in Kingdom of Holland	25.00	20.00
MS201	2007 (8)	100	KM#234-236, 268-272 Mintmasters V + silver medal	—	600
MS202	2007 (8)	3,500	KM#234-236, 268-272 5 sets Michiel de Ruyter + silver medal and one set with the Michiel de Ruyter 5 euro coin BU	250	250
MS203	2007 (8)	500	KM#234-236, 268-272 5 sets Michiel de Ruyter + silver medal and one set with the Michiel de Ruyter 10 euro coin	900	900
MS204	2007 (8)	40,000	KM#234-236, 268-272 Charity set	18.00	22.00
MS205	2007 (8)	3,000	KM#234-236, 268-272 Baby set boy + bear medal	20.00	25.00
MS206	2007 (8)	100	KM#234-236, 268-272 Baby set boy + silver medal	—	95.00
MS207	2007 (8)	3,000	KM#234-236, 268-272 Baby set girl + bear medal	20.00	25.00
MS208	2007 (8)	100	KM#234-236, 268-272 Baby set girl + silver medal	—	95.00
MS209	2007 (8)	15,000	KM#234-236, 268-272 Benelux: Belgium, Netherlands + Luxembourg. With silver medal + 3x 2 Euro Rome Treaty	75.00	75.00
MS210	2007 (8)	1,050	KM#234-236, 268-272 Wedding-set + medal	22.00	25.00
MS211	2007 (8)	1,000	KM#234-236, 268-272 Christmas set + bi-colour medal	35.00	40.00
MS212	2007 (8)	100	KM#234-236, 268-272 Christmas set + silver medal	150	150
MS213	2007 (8)	25	KM#234-236, 268-272 Christmas set + golden medal	650	650
MS214	2007 (8)	500	KM#234-236, 268-272 Berlin Coin Fair	25.00	90.00
MS215	2007 (8)	2,007	KM#234-236, 268-272 Day of the Mint + medal	25.00	100
MS216	2007 (8)	5,000	KM#234-236, 268-272 200 years of Royal predicate	25.00	28.00
MS224	2008 (8)	12,500	KM#234-236, 268-272 Benelux: Belgium, Netherlands + Luxembourg. With silver medal	75.00	75.00
MS82	2007 (9)	3,500	KM#234-236, 268-272 Mintmasters V plus medal	20.00	40.00
MS83	2007 (9)	100	KM#234-236, 268-272 Mintmasters V plus silver medal	—	500
MS84	2007 (8)	3,500	KM#234-236, 268-272 Michiel de Ruyter sets, 1 plus silver medal and 1 set with Ruyter's 5 euro coin	—	250
MS85	2007 (8)	500	KM#234-236, 268-272 Michiel de Ruyter sets, 1 set with silver medal and 1 set with Ruyter's 10 euro coin	900	900
MS86	2007 (8)	40,000	KM#234-236, 268-272 National set	18.00	22.00
MS87	2007 (9)	3,000	KM#234-236, 268-272 Baby set boy plus bear medal	20.00	25.00

KM#	Date	Mintage	Identification	Issue Price	Mkt Val
MS88	2007 (9)	100	KM#234-236, 268-272 Baby set boy plus silver medal	—	95.00
MS89	2007 (9)	3,000	KM#234-236, 268-272 Baby set girl plus bear medal	20.00	25.00
MS90	2007 (9)	100	KM#234-236, 268-272 Baby set girl plus silver medal	—	95.00
MS92	2007 (9)	1,050	KM#234-236, 268-272 Wedding set plus medal	22.00	25.00
MS93	2007 (9)	1,000	KM#234-236, 268-272 Christmas set plus bi-color medal	35.00	40.00
MS94	2007 (9)	100	KM#234-236, 268-272 Christmas set plus silver medal	150	150
MS95	2007 (9)	25	KM#234-236, 268-272 Christmas set plus golden medal	650	650
MS96	2007 (8)	1,000	KM#234-236, 268-272 Berlin Coin Fair	25.00	75.00
MS97	2007 (8)	—	KM#234-236, 268-272 Day of the Mint plus medal	25.00	100
MS98	2007 (8)	5,000	KM#234-236, 268-272 200 Years of Royal Predicate	25.00	28.00
MS217	2008 (8)	3,500	KM#234-236, 268-272 Mintmasters VI + medal	20.00	40.00
MS218	2008 (8)	100	KM#234-236, 268-272 Mintmasters VI + silver medal	20.00	500
MS219	2008 (8)	40,000	KM#234-236, 268-272 National set	20.00	22.00
MS220	2008 (8)	2,500	KM#234-236, 268-272 Baby set boy + bear medal	25.00	25.00
MS221	2008 (8)	100	KM#234-236, 268-272 Baby set boy + silver medal	65.00	65.00
MS222	2008 (8)	2,500	KM#234-236, 268-272 Baby set girl + bear medal	25.00	25.00
MS223	2008 (8)	100	KM#234-236, 268-272 Baby set girl + silver medal	65.00	65.00
MS225	2008 (8)	1,250	KM#234-236, 268-272 Wedding-set + medal	22.00	25.00
MS226	2008 (8)	500	KM#234-236, 268-272 Christmas set + bi-colour medal	35.00	40.00
MS227	2008 (8)	50	KM#234-236, 268-272 Christmas set + silver medal	130	135
MS228	2008 (8)	25	KM#234-236, 268-272 Christmas set + golden medal	850	850
MS229	2008 (8)	500	KM#234-236, 268-272 Berlin Coin Fair	25.00	75.00
MS230	2008 (8)	2,008	KM#234-236, 268-272 Day of the Mint + medal	25.00	80.00
MS231	2008 (8)	5,000	KM#234-236, 268-272 150 year Queen Emma + silver medal	32.00	35.00
MS232	2008 (8)	500	KM#234-236, 268-272 Theo Peters Jubilation set + bi-colour medal	35.00	40.00
MS233	2008 (8)	50	KM#234-236, 268-272 Theo Peters Jubilation set + silver medal	130	135
MS234	2008 (8)	25	KM#234-236, 268-272 Theo Peters Jubilation set + golden medal	850	850
MS235	2008 (8)	500	KM#234-236, 268-272 5 sets "2 centuries Amsterdam capitol of the Netherlands" + gold plated silver medals and one set with the golden Arctecture 10 euro coin	900	850

PROOF SETS

KM#	Date	Mintage	Identification	Issue Price	Mkt Val
PS76	2003 (8)	2,000	KM#234-241 Frigateship "The Netherland" + silver medal and numbered ingot. "Mintmaster Set" in wooden box	125	125
PS54	2001 (6)	17,000	KM#202-206, 210 Booklet 5 Guilder	50.00	50.00
PS55	2001 (2)	500	KM#190.2, 242 Gold and Silver Ducat	50.00	120
PS63	2001 (7)	17,000	KM#202-207, 210 Booklet 5 guilder	50.00	60.00
PS64	2001 (2)	500	KM#190.2, 242 Gold + silver ducat	—	230
PS56	2002 (2)	—	KM#190.2, 211 Golden Ducats	—	230
PS57	2002 (3)	—	KM#190.2, 211, 232 Golden Ducats and Silver Ducat	—	270
PS65	2002 (2)	—	KM#190.2, 211 Golden ducats	—	230
PS66	2002 (3)	—	KM#190.2, 211, 256 Golden ducats + silver ducat	—	270
PS58	2003 (2)	—	KM#190.2, 211 Golden ducats in wooden box	230	230
PS59	2003 (8)	2,000	KM#234-241 Frigate "The Netherland" and silver medal and numbered ingot	85.00	125
PS67	2003 (2)	—	KM#190.2, 211 Golden ducats in wooden box	230	230
PS68	2004 (8)	5,000	KM#234-241 Proofset in wooden box	60.00	65.00
PS77	2004 (8)	1,000	KM#234-241 Value transport over sea during the eighty year of war + silver medal and numbered ingot. "Mintmaster Set" in wooden box	125	125
PS70	2005 (2)	2,500	KM#254, 264 60 years of freedom 5 Euro (silver) and 10 Euro (gold)	—	180
PS69	2005 (8)	5,000	KM#234-241 Proofset in wooden box	60.00	65.00
PS78	2005 (8)	1,000	KM#234-241 Value transport over sea 1650-1750 + silver medal and numbered ingot. "Mintmaster Set" in wooden box	125	125
PS71	2006 (8)	3,500	KM#234-241	—	60.00
PS79	2006 (8)	1,500	KM#234-241 Plus silver medal and numbered ingot. "Mintmaster Set" in wooden box	125	125
PS74	2007 (8)	10,000	KM#234-236, 268-272 Proofset, including 2 Euro Rome Treaty KM#273	—	60.00
PS75	2008 (8)	10,000	KM#234-236, 268-272	—	60.00

PROOF-LIKE SETS (PL)

KM#	Date	Mintage	Identification	Issue Price	Mkt Val
PL12	2001 (8)	16,500	KM#234-241	50.00	40.00
PL3	2001 (8)	16,500	KM#234-241	50.00	40.00
PL13	2002 (2)	—	KM#243-244 Wedding set (10 Euro silver and gold) in plastic box	145	150
PL14	2002 (2)	—	KM#243-244 Wedding set in wooden box	145	160
PL15	2002 (8)	16,500	KM#234-241	50.00	40.00
PL4	2002 (2)	—	KM#243, 244 Wedding set (10 Euro in silver and gold) in plastic box	145	250
PL5	2002 (2)	—	KM#243, 244 Wedding set in wooden box	145	200
PL6	2002 (8)	15,500	KM#234-241	50.00	40.00
PL16	2003 (8)	16,500	KM#234-241	50.00	40.00
PL7	2003 (8)	10,000	KM#234-241	50.00	40.00
PL8	2004 (8)	10,000	KM#234-241	—	50.00
PL9	2005 (8)	10,000	KM#234-241	—	50.00

SELECT SETS (FLEUR DE COIN)

KM#	Date	Mintage	Identification	Issue Price	Mkt Val
SS90	2001 (6)	120,000	KM#202-206, 210 Introduction to Euro Coins	15.00	10.00
SS91	2001 (6)	3,400	KM#202-206, 210 Queen Julianna Medal	17.50	30.00
SS92	2001 (6)	100	KM#202-206, 210 Queen Julianna Medal; some coins dated 2000 in error	17.50	150
SS93	2001 (6)	1,000	KM#202-206, 210 BOLEGO - VOK	—	60.00
SS94	2001 (6)	1,000	KM#202-206, 210, 2 Stuiver coin from the wreck of the De Akerendam II	125	60.00
SS95	2001 (6)	1,000	KM#202-206, 210 United Provinces, Groningen Medal	40.00	25.00
SS96	2001 (6)	21,000	KM#202-206, 210 Baby set plus bear medal	15.50	17.50
SS97	2001 (6)	1,015	KM#202-206, 210 Onderlinge "'s-Gravenhage"	70.00	100

SPECIMEN FDC SETS (FLEUR DE COIN)

KM#	Date	Mintage	Identification	Issue Price	Mkt Val
SS95A	2001 (6)	1,000	KM202-206, 210 United Provinces, Utrecht Medal	40.00	40.00

NETHERLANDS ANTILLES

The Netherlands Antilles, comprises two groups of islands in the West Indies: Aruba (until 1986), Bonaire and Curacao and their dependencies near the Venezuelan coast and St. Eustatius, Saba, and the southern part of St. Martin (*St. Maarten*) southeast of Puerto Rico. The island group has an area of 371 sq. mi. (960 sq. km.) and a population of 225,000. Capital: Willemstad. Chief industries are the refining of crude oil and tourism. Petroleum products and phosphates are exported.

RULERS
Beatrix, 1980-

MINT MARKS
Y – York Mint

Utrecht Mint
(privy marks only)

Date	Privy Mark
2001	Wine tendril with grapes
2002	Wine tendril with grapes and star
2003	Sails of a clipper

MONETARY SYSTEM
100 Cents = 1 Gulden

DUTCH ADMINISTRATION

DECIMAL COINAGE

KM# 32 CENT
0.7000 g., Aluminum, 14 mm. **Ruler:** Beatrix **Obv:** Orange blossom within circle **Rev:** Value within circle of geometric designed border **Edge:** Reeded

Date	Mintage	F	VF	XF	Unc	BU
2001(u)	12,806,500	—	—	0.10	0.20	0.50
2002(u) In sets only	6,000	—	—	—	—	1.25
2003(u)	19,604,000	—	—	0.10	0.20	0.50
2004(u) In sets only	7,100	—	—	—	—	0.50
2005(u)	—	—	—	0.10	0.20	0.50
2006(u)	—	—	—	0.10	0.20	0.50
2007(u)	—	—	—	0.10	0.20	0.50
2008(u)	—	—	—	0.10	0.20	0.50
2009(u)	—	—	—	0.10	0.20	0.50

KM# 33 5 CENTS
1.2000 g., Aluminum, 16 mm. **Ruler:** Beatrix **Obv:** Orange blossom within circle **Rev:** Value within circle, geometric designed border **Edge:** Reeded

Date	Mintage	F	VF	XF	Unc	BU
2001	2,006,500	—	—	0.20	0.60	0.75
2002 In sets only	6,000	—	—	—	—	2.50
2003	3,104,000	—	—	0.30	0.60	0.75
2004	2,402,100	—	—	0.30	0.50	0.75
2005	—	—	—	0.30	0.50	0.75
2006	—	—	—	0.30	0.50	0.75
2007	—	—	—	0.30	0.50	0.75
2008	—	—	—	0.30	0.50	0.75
2009	—	—	—	0.30	0.50	0.75

KM# 34 10 CENTS
3.0000 g., Nickel Bonded Steel, 18 mm. **Ruler:** Beatrix **Obv:** Orange blossom within circle **Rev:** Value within circle, geometric designed border **Edge:** Reeded

Date	Mintage	F	VF	XF	Unc	BU
2001 In sets only	11,500	—	—	—	—	3.00
2002 In sets only	6,000	—	—	—	—	3.00
2003	2,104,000	—	—	0.50	1.00	1.75
2004	2,202,100	—	—	0.50	1.00	1.75
2005	—	—	—	0.50	1.00	1.75
2006	—	—	—	0.50	1.00	1.75
2007	—	—	—	0.50	1.00	1.75
2008	—	—	—	0.50	1.00	1.75
2009	—	—	—	0.50	1.00	1.75

KM# 35 25 CENTS
3.5000 g., Nickel Bonded Steel, 20.2 mm. **Ruler:** Beatrix **Obv:** Orange blossom within circle **Rev:** Value within circle, geometric designed border **Edge:** Reeded

Date	Mintage	F	VF	XF	Unc	BU
2001 In sets only	11,500	—	—	—	—	3.00
2002 In sets only	6,000	—	—	—	—	3.00
2003	1,404,000	—	—	0.50	1.25	1.50

Date	Mintage	F	VF	XF	Unc	BU
2004	1,502,100	—	—	0.50	1.25	1.50
2005	—	—	—	0.50	1.25	1.50
2006	—	—	—	0.50	1.25	1.50
2007	—	—	—	0.50	1.25	1.50
2008	—	—	—	0.50	1.25	1.50
2009	—	—	—	0.50	1.25	1.50

KM# 36   50 CENTS
5.0000 g., Aureate Steel, 24 mm. **Ruler:** Beatrix **Obv:** Orange blossom within circle, designed border **Rev:** Value within circle of pearls and shell border **Edge:** Plain **Shape:** 4-sided

Date	Mintage	F	VF	XF	Unc	BU
2001 In sets only	11,500	—	—	—	—	4.00
2002 In sets only	6,000	—	—	—	—	6.00
2003 In sets only	9,000	—	—	—	—	4.00
2004 In sets only	7,100	—	—	—	—	6.00
2005	—	—	—	0.75	3.00	4.00
2006	—	—	—	0.75	3.00	4.00
2007	—	—	—	0.75	3.00	4.00
2008	—	—	—	0.75	3.00	4.00
2009	—	—	—	0.75	3.00	4.00

KM# 37   GULDEN
6.0000 g., Aureate Steel, 24 mm. **Ruler:** Beatrix **Obv:** Head left **Rev:** Crowned shield divides value above date and ribbon **Edge Lettering:** GOD * ZIJ * MET * ONS *

Date	Mintage	F	VF	XF	Unc	BU
2001 In sets only	11,500	—	—	—	—	4.00
2002 In sets only	6,000	—	—	—	—	6.00
2003	504,000	—	—	0.75	3.00	4.00
2004 In sets only	7,100	—	—	—	—	6.00
2005	—	—	—	0.75	3.00	4.00
2006	—	—	—	0.75	3.00	4.00
2007	—	—	—	0.75	3.00	4.00
2008	—	—	—	0.75	3.00	4.00
2009	—	—	—	0.75	3.00	4.00

KM# 38   2-1/2 GULDEN
9.0000 g., Aureate Steel, 28 mm. **Ruler:** Beatrix **Obv:** Head left **Rev:** Crowned shield divides value above date and ribbon **Edge Lettering:** GOD * ZIJ * MET * ONS *

Date	Mintage	F	VF	XF	Unc	BU
2001 In sets only	11,500	—	—	—	—	6.00
2002 In sets only	6,000	—	—	—	—	8.00
2003 In sets only	9,000	—	—	—	—	6.00
2004 In sets only	7,100	—	—	—	—	6.00
2005	—	—	—	1.00	5.00	6.00
2006	—	—	—	1.00	5.00	6.00
2007	—	—	—	1.00	5.00	6.00
2008	—	—	—	1.00	5.00	6.00
2009	—	—	—	1.00	5.00	6.00

KM# 43   5 GULDEN
11.0000 g., Brass Plated Steel, 26 mm. **Ruler:** Beatrix **Obv:** Head left **Rev:** Crowned shield divides value above date and ribbon **Edge Lettering:** GOD * ZIJ * MET * ONS *

Date	Mintage	F	VF	XF	Unc	BU
2001 In sets only	9,500	—	—	—	—	7.50
2002 In sets only	6,000	—	—	—	—	7.50
2003 In sets only	7,000	—	—	—	—	7.50
2004	102,100	—	—	1.00	4.00	5.00
2005	—	—	—	1.00	4.00	5.00
2006	—	—	—	1.00	4.00	5.00
2007	—	—	—	1.00	4.00	5.00
2008	—	—	—	1.00	4.00	5.00
2009	—	—	—	1.00	4.00	5.00

KM# 74   5 GULDEN
11.9000 g., 0.9250 Silver 0.3539 oz. ASW, 29 mm. **Ruler:** Beatrix **Subject:** 50th Anniversary - Charter for the Kingdom of Netherlands including Aruba as third party **Obv:** Head left **Rev:** Triangular design with hands writing signatures around value **Edge Lettering:** GOD * ZIJ * MET * ONS * **Designer:** Ans Mezas-Hummelink

Date	Mintage	F	VF	XF	Unc	BU
2004(u) Proof	4,000	Value: 30.00				

KM# 74.1   5 GULDEN
11.0000 g., Aureate Bonded Steel, 26 mm. **Ruler:** Beatrix **Subject:** 50th Anniversary - End To Dutch Colonial Rule **Obv:** Head left **Rev:** Triangular signatures around value **Edge Lettering:** GOD * ZIJ * MET * ONS *

Date	Mintage	F	VF	XF	Unc	BU
2004	10,000	—	—	—	—	8.00

KM# 76   5 GULDEN
11.9000 g., 0.9250 Silver 0.3539 oz. ASW, 29 mm. **Ruler:** Beatrix **Subject:** Queen's Silver Jubilee **Obv:** Head left **Rev:** Child art and value **Edge Lettering:** GOD * ZIJ * MET * ONS *

Date	Mintage	F	VF	XF	Unc	BU
2005(u) Proof	4,000	Value: 32.00				

KM# 76.1   5 GULDEN
11.0000 g., Aureate Bonded Steel, 26 mm. **Ruler:** Beatrix **Subject:** Queen's Silver Jubilee **Obv:** Head left **Rev:** Child art and value **Edge Lettering:** GOD * ZIJ * MET * ONS *

Date	Mintage	F	VF	XF	Unc	BU
2005	10,000	—	—	—	—	8.00

KM# 49   10 GULDEN
31.1035 g., 0.9250 Silver 0.9250 oz. ASW, 40 mm. **Ruler:** Beatrix **Subject:** Gold Trade Coins: Sulla Aureus **Obv:** Crowned shield divides value above date and ribbon **Rev:** Bust facing with two gold coins at lower left **Edge:** Plain

Date	Mintage	F	VF	XF	Unc	BU
2001(u) Proof	589	Value: 55.00				

KM# 50   10 GULDEN
31.1035 g., 0.9250 Silver 0.9250 oz. ASW, 40 mm. **Ruler:** Beatrix **Subject:** Gold Trade Coins: Constantin I Solidus **Obv:** Crowned shield divides value above date and ribbon **Rev:** Bust facing with two gold coins at lower right **Edge:** Plain

Date	Mintage	F	VF	XF	Unc	BU
2001(u) Proof	578	Value: 65.00				

KM# 51   10 GULDEN
31.1035 g., 0.9250 Silver 0.9250 oz. ASW, 40 mm. **Ruler:** Beatrix **Subject:** Gold Trade Coins: Clovis I Tremississfiorino d'oro **Obv:** Crowned shield divides value above date and ribbon **Rev:** Bust facing with two gold coins **Edge:** Plain

Date	Mintage	F	VF	XF	Unc	BU
2001(u) Proof	566	Value: 55.00				

KM# 52   10 GULDEN
31.1035 g., 0.9250 Silver 0.9250 oz. ASW, 40 mm. **Ruler:** Beatrix **Subject:** Gold Trade Coins: Cosimo de'Medici Fiorino d'oro **Obv:** Crowned shield divides value above date and ribbon **Rev:** Bust facing with two gold coins **Edge:** Plain

Date	Mintage	F	VF	XF	Unc	BU
2001(u) Proof	575	Value: 55.00				

KM# 53   10 GULDEN
31.1035 g., 0.9250 Silver 0.9250 oz. ASW, 40 mm. **Ruler:** Beatrix **Subject:** Gold Trade Coins: Dandolo Ducato d'Oro **Obv:** Crowned shield divides value above date and ribbon **Rev:** Bust facing with two gold coins **Edge:** Plain

Date	Mintage	F	VF	XF	Unc	BU
2001(u) Proof	490	Value: 55.00				

KM# 54   10 GULDEN
31.1035 g., 0.9250 Silver 0.9250 oz. ASW, 40 mm. **Ruler:** Beatrix **Subject:** Gold Trade Coins: Philips IV Ecu d'or la chaise **Obv:** Crowned shield divides value above date and ribbon **Rev:** Bust facing with two gold coins **Edge:** Plain

Date	Mintage	F	VF	XF	Unc	BU
2001(u) Proof	460	Value: 55.00				

KM# 55   10 GULDEN
31.1035 g., 0.9250 Silver 0.9250 oz. ASW, 40 mm. **Ruler:** Beatrix **Subject:** Gold Trade Coins: Edward III Nobel **Obv:** Crowned shield divides value above date and ribbon **Rev:** Crowned bust facing with two gold coins **Edge:** Plain

Date	Mintage	F	VF	XF	Unc	BU
2001(u) Proof	575	Value: 65.00				

KM# 56   10 GULDEN
31.1035 g., 0.9250 Silver 0.9250 oz. ASW, 40 mm. **Ruler:** Beatrix **Subject:** Gold Trade Coins: Carolus IV Rhine Gold Guilder **Obv:** Crowned shield divides value above date and ribbon **Rev:** Bust facing with two gold coins **Edge:** Plain

Date	Mintage	F	VF	XF	Unc	BU
2001(u) Proof	430	Value: 75.00				

KM# 57   10 GULDEN
31.1035 g., 0.9250 Silver 0.9250 oz. ASW, 40 mm. **Ruler:** Beatrix **Subject:** Gold Trade Coins: John II Franc d'or a cheval **Obv:** Crowned shield divides value above date and ribbon **Rev:** Bust facing with two gold coins **Edge:** Plain

Date	Mintage	F	VF	XF	Unc	BU
2001(u) Proof	464	Value: 55.00				

KM# 58   10 GULDEN
31.1035 g., 0.9250 Silver 0.9250 oz. ASW, 40 mm. **Ruler:** Beatrix **Subject:** Gold Trade Coins: Philip the Good Adriesguilder **Obv:** Crowned shield divides value above date and ribbon **Rev:** Bust facing with two gold coins **Edge:** Plain

Date	Mintage	F	VF	XF	Unc	BU
2001(u) Proof	250	Value: 110				

KM# 59   10 GULDEN
31.1035 g., 0.9250 Silver 0.9250 oz. ASW, 40 mm. **Ruler:** Beatrix **Subject:** Gold Trade Coins: Louis XI Ecu d'or au soleil **Obv:** Crowned shield divides value above date and ribbon **Rev:** Bust facing with two gold coins **Edge:** Plain

Date	Mintage	F	VF	XF	Unc	BU
2001(u) Proof	450	Value: 65.00				

KM# 60   10 GULDEN
31.1035 g., 0.9250 Silver 0.9250 oz. ASW, 40 mm. **Ruler:** Beatrix **Subject:** Gold Trade Coins: Elisabeth I Sovereign **Obv:** Crowned shield divides value above date and ribbon **Rev:** Bust facing with two gold coins **Edge:** Plain

Date	Mintage	F	VF	XF	Unc	BU
2001(u) Proof	450	Value: 55.00				

KM# 61 10 GULDEN
31.1035 g., 0.9250 Silver 0.9250 oz. ASW, 40 mm.
Ruler: Beatrix **Subject:** Gold Trade Coins: Carolus V Carolus
Guilder **Obv:** Crowned shield divides value above date and ribbon
Rev: Bust facing with two gold coins **Edge:** Plain

Date	Mintage	F	VF	XF	Unc	BU
2001(u) Proof	440	Value: 65.00				

KM# 62 10 GULDEN
31.1035 g., 0.9250 Silver 0.9250 oz. ASW, 40 mm.
Ruler: Beatrix **Subject:** Gold Trade Coins: Philips II Real
Obv: Crowned shield divides value above date and ribbon
Rev: Bust facing with two gold coins **Edge:** Plain

Date	Mintage	F	VF	XF	Unc	BU
2001(u) Proof	440	Value: 55.00				

KM# 63 10 GULDEN
31.1035 g., 0.9250 Silver 0.9250 oz. ASW, 40 mm.
Ruler: Beatrix **Subject:** Gold Trade Coins: Maurits Ducat
Obv: Crowned shield divides value above date and ribbon
Rev: Bust facing with two gold coins **Edge:** Plain

Date	Mintage	F	VF	XF	Unc	BU
2001(u) Proof	443	Value: 55.00				

KM# 64 10 GULDEN
31.1035 g., 0.9250 Silver 0.9250 oz. ASW, 40 mm.
Ruler: Beatrix **Subject:** Gold Trade Coins: Isabella and Albrecht
Double Albertin **Obv:** Crowned shield divides value above date
and ribbon **Rev:** Conjoined busts facing with two gold coins
Edge: Plain

Date	Mintage	F	VF	XF	Unc	BU
2001(u) Proof	490	Value: 55.00				

KM# 65 10 GULDEN
31.1035 g., 0.9250 Silver 0.9250 oz. ASW, 40 mm.
Ruler: Beatrix **Subject:** Gold Trade Coins: William III Golden
Rider **Obv:** Crowned shield divides value above date and ribbon
Rev: Bust facing with two gold coins **Edge:** Plain

Date	Mintage	F	VF	XF	Unc	BU
2001(u) Proof	440	Value: 55.00				

KM# 66 10 GULDEN
31.1035 g., 0.9250 Silver 0.9250 oz. ASW, 40 mm.
Ruler: Beatrix **Subject:** Gold Trade Coins: Louis XIII Louis d'or
Obv: Crowned shield divides value above date and ribbon
Rev: Bust facing with two gold coins **Edge:** Plain

Date	Mintage	F	VF	XF	Unc	BU
2001(u) Proof	440	Value: 55.00				

KM# 67 10 GULDEN
31.1035 g., 0.9250 Silver 0.9250 oz. ASW, 40 mm.
Ruler: Beatrix **Subject:** Gold Trade Coins: Catharina the Great
Rubel **Obv:** Crowned shield divides value above date and ribbon
Rev: Crowned laureate bust facing with two gold coins
Edge: Plain

Date	Mintage	F	VF	XF	Unc	BU
2001(u) Proof	560	Value: 55.00				

KM# 68 10 GULDEN
31.1035 g., 0.9250 Silver 0.9250 oz. ASW, 40 mm.
Ruler: Beatrix **Subject:** Gold Trade Coins: Maria Theresia
Double Sovereign **Obv:** Crowned shield divides value above date
and ribbon **Rev:** Bust facing with two gold coins **Edge:** Plain

Date	Mintage	F	VF	XF	Unc	BU
2001(u) Proof	440	Value: 55.00				

KM# 69 10 GULDEN
31.1035 g., 0.9250 Silver 0.9250 oz. ASW, 40 mm.
Ruler: Beatrix **Subject:** Gold Trade Coins: Napolean Bonaparte
20 Franc **Obv:** Crowned shield divides value above date and
ribbon **Rev:** Bust facing with two gold coins **Edge:** Plain

Date	Mintage	F	VF	XF	Unc	BU
2001(u) Proof	555	Value: 55.00				

KM# 70 10 GULDEN
31.1035 g., 0.9250 Silver 0.9250 oz. ASW, 40 mm.
Ruler: Beatrix **Series:** Gold Trade Coins: Wilhelmina Golden 10
Guilder **Obv:** Crowned shield divides value above date and ribbon
Rev: Bust facing with two gold coins **Edge:** Plain

Date	Mintage	F	VF	XF	Unc	BU
2001(u) Proof	440	Value: 55.00				

KM# 71 10 GULDEN
31.1035 g., 0.9250 Silver 0.9250 oz. ASW, 40 mm.
Ruler: Beatrix **Subject:** Gold Trade Coins: George III Sovereign
Obv: Crowned shield divides value above date and ribbon
Rev: Bust facing with two gold coins **Edge:** Plain

Date	Mintage	F	VF	XF	Unc	BU
2001(u) Proof	440	Value: 55.00				

KM# 72 10 GULDEN
31.1035 g., 0.9250 Silver 0.9250 oz. ASW, 40 mm.
Ruler: Beatrix **Subject:** Gold Trade Coins: Albert I Belgium 20
Franc **Obv:** Crowned shield divides value above date and ribbon
Rev: Bust facing with two gold coins **Edge:** Plain

Date	Mintage	F	VF	XF	Unc	BU
2001(u) Proof	490	Value: 55.00				

KM# 75 10 GULDEN
6.7200 g., 0.9000 Gold 0.1944 oz. AGW **Ruler:** Beatrix
Subject: 50th Anniversary - End to Dutch Colonial Rule
Obv: Head left **Rev:** Triangular signatures around value
Edge: Reeded **Designer:** Ans Mezas-Hummelink

Date	Mintage	F	VF	XF	Unc	BU
2004 Proof	1,000	Value: 250				

KM# 77 10 GULDEN
6.7200 g., 0.9000 Gold 0.1944 oz. AGW, 22.5 mm.
Ruler: Beatrix **Subject:** Queen's Silver Jubilee **Obv:** Head left
Rev: Child art and value **Edge:** Reeded

Date	Mintage	F	VF	XF	Unc	BU
2005(u) Proof	1,500	Value: 240				

KM# 78 10 GULDEN
1.2442 g., 0.9990 Gold 0.0400 oz. AGW, 13.92 mm.
Ruler: Beatrix **Subject:** Year of the dolphin **Obv:** Head left
Obv. Legend: BEATRIX KONINGIN DER NEDERLANDEN
Rev: Stylized outlines of birds above dolphins at sunset
Rev. Legend: NEDERLANDSE ANTILLEN - JAAR VAN DE
DOLFIJN **Edge:** Reeded

Date	Mintage	F	VF	XF	Unc	BU
2007(u) Proof	5,000	Value: 120				
		INA Issue				

MINT SETS

KM#	Date	Mintage	Identification	Issue Price	Mkt Val
MS22	2001 (8)	6,500	KM#32-38, 43	15.00	18.50
MS23	2002 (8)	6,000	KM#32-38, 43	15.00	27.50
MS24	2003 (8)	4,000	KM#32-38, 43	15.00	20.00
MS25	2004 (8)	2,100	KM32-38, 43	15.00	20.00
MS26	2005 (8)	3,500	KM32-38, 43	17.00	17.50
MS27	2006 (8)	2,000	KM#32-38, 43	20.00	20.00
MS28	2007 (8)	2,000	KM#32-38, 43	20.00	20.00
MS29	2008 (8)	—	KM#32-38, 43	21.00	21.00

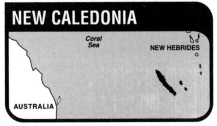

The French Associated State of New Caledonia is a group
of about 25 islands in the South Pacific. They are situated about
750 miles (1,207 km.) east of Australia. The territory, which
includes the dependencies of Isle des Pins, Loyalty Islands, Isle
Huon, Isles Belep, Isles Chesterfield, Isle Walpole, Wallis and
Futuna Islands and has a total land area of 7,358 sq. mi.(19,060
sq. km.) and a population of *156,000. Capital: Noumea. The
islands are rich in minerals; New Caledonia has some of the
world's largest known deposit of nickel. Nickel, nickel castings,
coffee and copra are exported.

MINT MARK
Paris, privy marks only

MONETARY SYSTEM
100 Centimes = 1 Franc

FRENCH OVERSEAS TERRITORY
DECIMAL COINAGE

KM# 10 FRANC
1.3000 g., Aluminum, 23 mm. **Obv:** Seated figure holding torch,
legend added **Obv. Legend:** I. E. O. M. **Rev:** Kagu bird within
sprigs below value **Designer:** G.B.L. Bazor

Date	Mintage	F	VF	XF	Unc	BU
2001(a)	100,000	—	—	0.15	0.50	1.25
2002(a)	1,200,000	—	—	0.15	0.50	1.25
2003(a)	2,000,000	—	—	0.15	0.50	1.25
2004(a)	1,200,000	—	—	0.15	0.50	1.25
2005(a)	700,000	—	—	0.15	0.50	1.25
2006(a)	1,600,000	—	—	—	0.50	1.25
2007(a)	2,000,000	—	—	—	0.50	1.25
2008(a)	2,800,000	—	—	—	0.50	1.25

KM# 14 2 FRANCS
2.2000 g., Aluminum, 27 mm. **Obv:** Seated figure holding torch,
legend added **Obv. Legend:** I. E. O. M. **Rev:** Kagu bird and value
within sprigs

Date	Mintage	F	VF	XF	Unc	BU
2001(a)	800,000	—	—	0.25	0.75	1.50
2002(a)	1,200,000	—	—	0.25	0.75	1.50
2003(a)	2,400,000	—	—	0.20	0.65	1.50
2004(a)	200,000	—	—	0.20	0.65	1.50
2005(a)	530,000	—	—	0.20	0.65	1.50
2006(a)	1,200,000	—	—	—	0.65	1.50
2007(a)	600,000	—	—	—	0.65	1.50
2008(a)	2,400,000	—	—	—	0.65	1.50

KM# 16 5 FRANCS
3.7500 g., Aluminum, 31 mm. **Obv:** Seated figure holding torch,
legend added **Obv. Legend:** I. E. O. M. **Rev:** Kagu bird and value
within sprigs **Designer:** G.B.L. Bazor

Date	Mintage	F	VF	XF	Unc	BU
2001(a)	600,000	—	—	0.50	1.00	2.00
2002(a)	480,000	—	—	0.50	1.00	2.00
2003(a)	700,000	—	—	0.40	1.00	2.00
2004(a)	1,000,000	—	—	0.40	1.00	2.00
2005(a)	360,000	—	—	0.40	1.00	2.00
2006(a)	480,000	—	—	0.40	1.00	2.00
2007(a)	960,000	—	—	—	1.00	2.00
2008	1,700,000	—	—	—	1.00	2.00

KM# 11 10 FRANCS
6.0000 g., Nickel, 24 mm. **Obv:** Liberty head left **Obv. Legend:**
I. E. O. M. **Rev:** Sailboat above value **Designer:** R. Joly

Date	Mintage	F	VF	XF	Unc	BU
2001(a)	100,000	—	—	0.65	1.25	2.75
2002(a)	200,000	—	—	0.65	1.25	2.75
2003(a)	800,000	—	—	0.65	1.25	2.75
2004(a)	600,000	—	—	0.65	1.25	2.75
2005(a)	64,000	—	—	0.65	1.25	2.75
2006(a)	60,000	—	—	0.65	1.25	2.75

Date	Mintage	F	VF	XF	Unc	BU
2007(a)	1,000,000	—	—	—	1.25	2.75
2008(a)	1,200,000	—	—	—	1.25	2.75

KM# 12   20 FRANCS
10.0000 g., Nickel, 28.5 mm.   **Obv:** Liberty head left
Obv. Legend: I. O. E. M. **Rev:** Three ox heads above value
Designer: R. Joly

Date	Mintage	F	VF	XF	Unc	BU
2001(a)	150,000	—	—	1.00	1.75	3.25
2002(a)	250,000	—	—	1.00	1.75	3.25
2003(a)	250,000	—	—	1.00	1.75	3.25
2004(a)	500,000	—	—	1.00	1.75	3.25
2005(a)	300,000	—	—	1.00	1.75	3.25
2006(a)	300,000	—	—	1.00	1.75	3.25
2007(a)	800,000	—	—	—	1.75	3.25
2008(a)	800,000	—	—	—	1.75	3.25

KM# 13   50 FRANCS
15.0000 g., Nickel, 33 mm.   **Obv:** Liberty head left
Obv. Legend: I. E. O. M. **Rev:** Hut above value in center of palm
and pine trees **Designer:** R. Joly

Date	Mintage	F	VF	XF	Unc	BU
2001(a)	100,000	—	—	1.25	2.00	4.00
2002(a)	—	—	—	1.25	2.00	4.00
2003(a)	75,000	—	—	1.25	2.00	4.00
2004(a)	150,000	—	—	1.25	2.00	4.00
2005(a)	54,000	—	—	1.25	2.00	4.00
2006(a)	75,000	—	—	1.25	2.00	4.00
2007(a)	225,000	—	—	—	2.00	4.00
2008(a)	375,000	—	—	—	2.00	4.00

KM# 15   100 FRANCS
10.0000 g., Nickel-Bronze, 30 mm.   **Obv:** Liberty head left
Rev: Hut above value in center of palm and pine trees
Designer: R. Joly

Date	Mintage	F	VF	XF	Unc	BU
2001(a)	100,000	—	—	1.50	3.00	5.00
2002(a)	620,000	—	—	1.50	3.00	6.00
2003(a)	500,000	—	—	1.50	3.00	5.00
2004(a)	500,000	—	—	1.50	3.00	5.00
2005(a)	180,000	—	—	1.50	3.00	5.00
2006(a)	300,000	—	—	1.50	3.00	5.00
2007(a)	800,000	—	—	—	3.00	5.00
2008(a)	1,100,000	—	—	—	3.00	5.00

MINT SETS

KM#	Date	Mintage	Identification	Issue Price	Mkt Val
MS1	2001 (7)	3,000	KM#10-16	—	30.00
MS2	2002 (7)	5,000	KM#10-16	—	25.00
MS3	2004 (7)	3,000	KM#10-16	—	30.00

NEW ZEALAND

New Zealand, a parliamentary state located in the Southwest Pacific 1,250 miles (2,011 km.) east of Australia, has an area of 103,883 sq. mi. (268,680 sq. km.) and a population of *3.4 million. Capital: Wellington. Wool, meat, dairy products and some manufactured items are exported.

Decimal Currency was introduced in 1967 with special sets commemorating the last issues of pound sterling (1965) and the first of the decimal issues. Since then dollars and sets of coins have been issued nearly every year.

New Zealand is a founding member of the Commonwealth of Nations. Elizabeth II is the Head of State as the Queen of New Zealand; the Prime Minister is the Head of Government.

RULER
British

STATE
DECIMAL COINAGE
100 Cents = 1 Dollar

(c) Royal Australian Mint, Canberra

(l) Royal Mint, Llantrisant

(o) Royal Canadian Mint, Ottawa

(m) B.H. Mayer, Germany

(n) Norwegian Mint, Kongsberg

(p) South African Mint, Pretoria

(v) Valcambi SA, Switzerland

(w) Perth Mint, Western Australia

KM# 116   5 CENTS
2.8000 g., Copper-Nickel, 19.4 mm.   **Ruler:** Elizabeth II
Obv: Head with tiara right **Obv. Designer:** Ian Rank-Broadley
Rev: Value below tuatara **Rev. Designer:** James Berry
Edge: Reeded **Note:** Many recalled and melted in 2006.

Date	Mintage	F	VF	XF	Unc	BU
2001(l)	20,000,000	—	—	0.10	0.50	1.00
2001(c) In sets only	2,910	—	—	—	4.00	5.00
2001(c) Proof	1,364	Value: 3.00				
2002(l)	40,500,000	—	—	0.10	0.50	1.00
2002(c) In sets only	3,000	—	—	—	5.00	6.00
2002(c) Proof	1,500	Value: 3.00				
2003(l)	30,000,000	—	—	—	0.50	1.00
2003(c) In sets only	1,496	—	—	—	5.00	6.00
2003 Proof	3,000	Value: 3.00				
2004(l)	15,000,000	—	—	—	2.00	3.00

Note: All but 48,000 melted. Many of these survivors have recently come onto the NZ market in bulk.

Date	Mintage	F	VF	XF	Unc	BU
2004(c) In sets only	2,800	—	—	—	20.00	30.00
2004(c) Proof	1,750	Value: 3.00				
2005(c) In sets only	3,000	—	—	—	8.00	12.00
2005(c) Proof	2,250	Value: 3.00				
2006(c) In sets only	3,000	—	—	—	8.00	12.00
2006(c) Proof	—	Value: 3.00				

KM# 117   10 CENTS
5.6600 g., Copper-Nickel, 23.62 mm.   **Ruler:** Elizabeth II
Obv: Head with tiara right **Obv. Designer:** Ian Rank-Broadley
Rev: Value above koruru **Rev. Designer:** James Berry
Note: Many recalled and melted in 2006.

Date	Mintage	F	VF	XF	Unc	BU
2001(l)	10,000,000	—	—	0.10	0.30	0.50
2001(c) In sets only	2,910	—	—	—	6.00	8.00
2001(c) Proof	1,364	Value: 4.00				
2002(l)	10,000,000	—	—	0.10	0.30	0.50
2002(c) Proof	1,500	Value: 4.00				

Date	Mintage	F	VF	XF	Unc	BU
2002(c) In sets only	3,000	—	—	—	3.00	5.00
2003(l)	13,000,000	—	—	0.10	0.30	0.50
2003(c) In sets only	3,000	—	—	—	5.00	8.00
2003(l) Proof	1,496	Value: 4.00				
2004(l)	6,500,000	—	—	—	0.30	0.50
2004(c) In sets only	3,000	—	—	—	5.00	8.00
2004(c) Proof	1,750	Value: 4.00				
2005	2,000,000	—	—	—	30.00	40.00

Note: All but 28,000 melted

Date	Mintage	F	VF	XF	Unc	BU
2005(c) In sets only	3,000	—	—	—	20.00	30.00
2005(c) Proof	2,250	Value: 4.00				
2006(c) In sets only	3,000	—	—	—	10.00	15.00
2006(c) Proof	2,100	Value: 4.00				

KM# 117a   10 CENTS
3.3100 g., Copper Plated Steel, 20.5 mm.   **Ruler:** Elizabeth II
Obv: Head with tiara right **Obv. Designer:** Ian Rank-Broadley
Rev: Value above koruru

Date	Mintage	F	VF	XF	Unc	BU
2006(o)	140,200,000	—	—	—	0.20	0.40
2007(o)	15,000,000	—	—	—	—	—
2007(c) In sets only	5,000	—	—	—	—	5.00
2007(c) Proof	3,500	Value: 4.00				
2008(l) In sets only	4,000	—	—	—	—	5.00
2008(l) Proof	3,000	Value: 4.00				
2009(o)	30,000,000	—	—	—	0.20	0.40
2009(w) In Sets only	2,000	—	—	—	—	5.00
2009(w) Proof	1,500	Value: 4.00				

KM# 234   10 CENTS
3.3100 g., Copper Plated Steel, 20.5 mm.   **Ruler:** Elizabeth II
Obv: Head with tiara right **Obv. Designer:** Ian Rank-Broadley
Rev: Tuatara right **Edge:** Plain

Date	Mintage	F	VF	XF	Unc	BU
2007(c) In sets only	15,000	—	—	—	0.50	5.00

KM# 118   20 CENTS
11.3100 g., Copper-Nickel, 28.58 mm.   **Ruler:** Elizabeth II
Obv: Head with tiara right **Obv. Designer:** Ian Rank-Broadley
Rev: Value below Pukaki **Rev. Designer:** R.M. Conly **Note:** Many
recalled and melted in 2006.

Date	Mintage	F	VF	XF	Unc	BU
2001(c) Proof	1,364	Value: 10.00				
2001(c) In sets only	2,910	—	—	—	—	4.00
2002(l)	7,000,000	—	—	—	0.50	—
2002(c) In sets only	3,000	—	—	—	—	5.00
2002(c) Proof	1,500	Value: 10.00				
2003(c) In sets only	3,000	—	—	—	—	4.00
2003(c) Proof	3,000	Value: 10.00				
2004(l)	8,500,000	—	—	—	0.50	—
2004(c) In sets only	2,800	—	—	—	—	5.00
2004(c) Proof	1,750	Value: 10.00				
2005(l)	4,000,000	—	—	—	—	15.00

Note: All but 178,000 melted

Date	Mintage	F	VF	XF	Unc	BU
2005(c) In sets only	3,000	—	—	—	—	5.00
2005(c) Proof	2,250	Value: 10.00				
2006(c) In sets only	3,000	—	—	—	—	5.00
2006(c) Proof	2,100	Value: 10.00				

KM# 118a   20 CENTS
4.0000 g., Copper-Nickel Plated Steel, 21.75 mm.
Ruler: Elizabeth II **Obv:** Head with tiara right
Obv. Designer: Ian Rank-Broadley **Rev:** Value below Pukaki
Rev. Designer: R.M. Conly **Shape:** Scalloped

Date	Mintage	F	VF	XF	Unc	BU
2006(o)	116,600,000	—	—	—	0.40	0.65
2007(c) In sets only	5,000	—	—	—	—	7.00
2007(c) Proof	4,000	Value: 8.00				
2008(o)	80,000,000	—	—	—	0.40	0.65
2008(I) In sets only	4,000	—	—	—	—	7.00
2008(I) Proof	3,000	Value: 8.00				
2009(w) In sets only	2,000	—	—	—	—	7.00
2009(w) Proof	1,500	Value: 8.00				

KM# 119 50 CENTS
13.6100 g., Copper-Nickel, 31.75 mm. **Ruler:** Elizabeth II
Obv: Head with tiara right **Obv. Designer:** Ian Rank-Broadley
Rev: Ship, H.M.S. Endeavour **Rev. Designer:** James Berry
Note: Many recalled and melted in 2006.

Date	Mintage	F	VF	XF	Unc	BU
2001(I)	5,000,000	—	—	—	1.00	—
2001(c) In sets only	2,910	—	—	—	—	4.00
2001(c) Proof	1,364	Value: 5.00				
2002(I)	3,000,000	—	—	0.50	1.00	—
2002(c) In sets only	3,000	—	—	—	—	4.00
2002(c) Proof	1,500	Value: 5.00				
2003(I)	2,500,000	—	—	0.50	1.00	—
2003(c) In sets only	3,000	—	—	—	—	4.00
2003(c) Proof	1,496	Value: 5.00				
2004(I)	2,000,000	—	—	—	1.00	—
2004(c) In sets only	2,800	—	—	—	—	4.00
2004(c) Proof	1,750	Value: 5.00				
2005(I)	1,000,000	—	—	—	7.50	—
Note: All but 503,800 melted						
2005(c) In sets only	3,000	—	—	—	—	4.00
2005(c) Proof	2,250	Value: 5.00				
2006(c) In sets only	3,000	—	—	—	—	4.00
2006(c) Proof	2,100	Value: 5.00				

KM# 135 50 CENTS
13.6100 g., Copper-Nickel, 31.75 mm. **Ruler:** Elizabeth II
Subject: Lord of the Rings **Obv:** Head with tiara right
Obv. Designer: Ian Rank-Broadley **Rev:** Frodo's head facing to
left of vine and value **Rev. Designer:** Matthew Bonaccorsi
Edge: Reeded

Date	Mintage	F	VF	XF	Unc	BU
2003(I)	41,221	—	—	—	—	15.00

KM# 136 50 CENTS
13.6100 g., Copper-Nickel, 31.75 mm. **Ruler:** Elizabeth II
Subject: Lord of the Rings **Obv:** Head with tiara right
Obv. Designer: Ian Rank-Broadley **Rev:** Head of Gandalf with
hat facing and value **Rev. Designer:** Matthew Bonaccorsi
Edge: Reeded

Date	Mintage	F	VF	XF	Unc	BU
2003(I)	41,221	—	—	—	—	15.00

KM# 137 50 CENTS
13.6100 g., Copper-Nickel, 31.75 mm. **Ruler:** Elizabeth II
Subject: Lord of the Rings **Obv:** Head with tiara right
Obv. Designer: Ian Rank-Broadley **Rev:** Head of Aragorn facing
and value **Rev. Designer:** Matthew Bonaccorsi **Edge:** Reeded

Date	Mintage	F	VF	XF	Unc	BU
2003(I)	41,221	—	—	—	—	15.00

KM# 138 50 CENTS
13.6100 g., Copper-Nickel, 31.75 mm. **Ruler:** Elizabeth II
Subject: Lord of the Rings **Obv:** Head with tiara right
Obv. Designer: Ian Rank-Broadley **Rev:** Head of Gollum facing
and value **Rev. Designer:** Matthew Bonaccorsi **Edge:** Reeded

Date	Mintage	F	VF	XF	Unc	BU
2003(I)	38,400	—	—	—	—	15.00

KM# 139 50 CENTS
13.6100 g., Copper-Nickel, 31.75 mm. **Ruler:** Elizabeth II
Subject: Lord of the Rings **Obv:** Head with tiara right
Obv. Designer: Ian Rank-Broadley **Rev:** Saruman, value
Rev. Designer: Matthew Bonaccorsi **Edge:** Reeded

Date	Mintage	F	VF	XF	Unc	BU
2003(I)	38,400	—	—	—	—	15.00

KM# 140 50 CENTS
13.6100 g., Copper-Nickel, 31.75 mm. **Ruler:** Elizabeth II
Subject: Lord of the Rings **Obv:** Head with tiara right
Obv. Designer: Ian Rank-Broadley **Rev:** Head of Sauron left and
value **Rev. Designer:** Matthew Bonaccorsi **Edge:** Reeded

Date	Mintage	F	VF	XF	Unc	BU
2003(I)	38,400	—	—	—	—	15.00

KM# 235 50 CENTS
13.6100 g., Copper-Nickel, 31.75 mm. **Ruler:** Elizabeth II
Subject: Lord of the Rings **Obv:** Head with tiara right
Obv. Designer: Ian Rank-Broadley **Rev:** Boromir
Rev. Designer: Matthew Bonaccorsi

Date	Mintage	F	VF	XF	Unc	BU
2003(I)	6,889	—	—	—	—	18.00

KM# 236 50 CENTS
13.6100 g., Copper-Nickel, 31.75 mm. **Ruler:** Elizabeth II
Subject: Lord of the Rings **Obv:** Head with tiara right
Obv. Designer: Ian Rank-Broadley **Rev:** Gimli
Rev. Designer: Matthew Bonaccorsi

Date	Mintage	F	VF	XF	Unc	BU
2003(I)	6,889	—	—	—	—	18.00

KM# 237 50 CENTS
13.6100 g., Copper-Nickel, 31.75 mm. **Ruler:** Elizabeth II
Subject: Lord of the Rings **Obv:** Head with tiara right
Obv. Designer: Ian Rank-Broadley **Rev:** Legolas
Rev. Designer: Matthew Bonaccorsi

Date	Mintage	F	VF	XF	Unc	BU
2003(I)	6,889	—	—	—	—	18.00

KM# 238 50 CENTS
13.6100 g., Copper-Nickel, 31.75 mm. **Ruler:** Elizabeth II
Subject: Lord of the Rings **Obv:** Head with tiara right
Obv. Designer: Ian Rank-Broadley **Rev:** Merry
Rev. Designer: Matthew Bonaccorsi

Date	Mintage	F	VF	XF	Unc	BU
2003(I)	6,889	—	—	—	—	18.00

KM# 239 50 CENTS
13.6100 g., Copper-Nickel, 31.75 mm. **Ruler:** Elizabeth II
Subject: Lord of the Rings **Obv:** Head with tiara right
Obv. Designer: Ian Rank-Broadley **Rev:** Pippin
Rev. Designer: Matthew Bonaccorsi

Date	Mintage	F	VF	XF	Unc	BU
2003(I)	6,889	—	—	—	—	18.00

KM# 240 50 CENTS
13.6100 g., Copper-Nickel, 31.75 mm. **Ruler:** Elizabeth II
Subject: Lord of the Rings **Obv:** Head with tiara right
Obv. Designer: Ian Rank-Broadley **Rev:** Sam
Rev. Designer: Matthew Bonaccorsi

Date	Mintage	F	VF	XF	Unc	BU
2003(I)	6,889	—	—	—	—	18.00

KM# 241 50 CENTS
13.6100 g., Copper-Nickel, 31.75 mm. **Ruler:** Elizabeth II
Subject: Lord of the Rings **Obv:** Head with tiara right
Obv. Designer: Ian Rank-Broadley **Rev:** Arwen
Rev. Designer: Matthew Bonaccorsi

Date	Mintage	F	VF	XF	Unc	BU
2003(I)	4,068	—	—	—	—	20.00

KM# 242 50 CENTS
13.6100 g., Copper-Nickel, 31.75 mm. **Ruler:** Elizabeth II
Subject: Lord of the Rings **Obv:** Head with tiara right
Obv. Designer: Ian Rank-Broadley **Rev:** Elrond
Rev. Designer: Matthew Bonaccorsi

Date	Mintage	F	VF	XF	Unc	BU
2003(I)	4,068	—	—	—	—	20.00

KM# 243 50 CENTS
13.6100 g., Copper-Nickel, 31.75 mm. **Ruler:** Elizabeth II
Subject: Lord of the Rings **Obv:** Head with tiara right
Obv. Designer: Ian Rank-Broadley **Rev:** Eowyn
Rev. Designer: Matthew Bonaccorsi

Date	Mintage	F	VF	XF	Unc	BU
2003(I)	4,068	—	—	—	—	20.00

KM# 244 50 CENTS
13.6100 g., Copper-Nickel, 31.75 mm. **Ruler:** Elizabeth II
Subject: Lord of the Rings **Obv:** Head with tiara right
Obv. Designer: Ian Rank-Broadley **Rev:** Galadriel
Rev. Designer: Matthew Bonaccorsi

Date	Mintage	F	VF	XF	Unc	BU
2003(I)	4,068	—	—	—	—	20.00

KM# 245 50 CENTS
13.6100 g., Copper-Nickel, 31.75 mm. **Ruler:** Elizabeth II
Subject: Lord of the Rings **Obv:** Head with tiara right
Obv. Designer: Ian Rank-Broadley **Rev:** An Orc
Rev. Designer: Matthew Bonaccorsi

Date	Mintage	F	VF	XF	Unc	BU
2003(I)	4,068	—	—	—	—	20.00

KM# 246 50 CENTS
13.6100 g., Copper-Nickel, 31.75 mm. **Ruler:** Elizabeth II
Subject: Lord of the Rings **Obv:** Head with tiara right
Obv. Designer: Ian Rank-Broadley **Rev:** Treebeard
Rev. Designer: Matthew Bonaccorsi

Date	Mintage	F	VF	XF	Unc	BU
2003(I)	4,068	—	—	—	—	20.00

KM# 119a 50 CENTS
5.0000 g., Nickel Plated Steel, 24.75 mm. **Ruler:** Elizabeth II
Obv: Head with tiara right **Rev:** Ship, H.M.S. Endeavour
Rev. Designer: James Berry

Date	Mintage	F	VF	XF	Unc	BU
2006(o)	70,200,000	—	—	—	0.75	1.00
2007(c) In sets only	5,000	—	—	—	—	8.00
2007(c) Proof	3,500	Value: 10.00				
2008(I) In sets only	4,000	—	—	—	—	8.00
2008(I) Proof	3,000	Value: 10.00				
2009(o)	20,000,000	—	—	—	0.75	1.00
2009(w) In sets only	2,000	—	—	—	—	8.00
2009(w) Proof	1,500	Value: 10.00				

KM# 279 50 CENTS
Aluminum-Bronze, 38.74 mm. **Ruler:** Elizabeth II
Subject: Narnia **Obv:** Head with tiara right **Obv. Designer:** Ian
Rank-Broadley **Rev:** Peter **Rev. Designer:** W. Pietranik

Date	Mintage	F	VF	XF	Unc	BU
2006(c)	20,000	—	—	—	—	6.00

KM# 280   50 CENTS

Aluminum-Bronze, 38.74 mm.   **Ruler:** Elizabeth II **Subject:** Narnia **Obv:** Head with tiara right **Obv. Designer:** Ian Rank-Broadley **Rev. Designer:** Susan **Rev. Designer:** W. Pietranik

Date	Mintage	F	VF	XF	Unc	BU
2006(c)	20,000	—	—	—	—	6.00

KM# 281   50 CENTS

Aluminum-Bronze, 38.74 mm.   **Ruler:** Elizabeth II **Subject:** Narnia **Obv:** Head with tiara right **Obv. Designer:** Ian Rank-Broadley **Rev. Designer:** Edmund **Rev. Designer:** W. Pietranik

Date	Mintage	F	VF	XF	Unc	BU
2006(c)	20,000	—	—	—	—	6.00

KM# 282   50 CENTS

Aluminum-Bronze, 38.74 mm.   **Ruler:** Elizabeth II **Subject:** Narnia **Obv:** Head with tiara right **Obv. Designer:** Ian Rank-Broadley **Rev. Designer:** Lucy **Rev. Designer:** W. Pietranik

Date	Mintage	F	VF	XF	Unc	BU
2006(c)	20,000	—	—	—	—	6.00

KM# 283   50 CENTS

Aluminum-Bronze, 38.74 mm.   **Ruler:** Elizabeth II **Subject:** Narnia **Obv:** Head with tiara right **Obv. Designer:** Ian Rank-Broadley **Rev. Designer:** Mr. Tumnus **Rev. Designer:** W. Pietranik

Date	Mintage	F	VF	XF	Unc	BU
2006(c)	20,000	—	—	—	—	6.00

KM# 284   50 CENTS

Aluminum-Bronze, 38.74 mm.   **Ruler:** Elizabeth II **Subject:** Narnia **Obv:** Head with tiara right **Obv. Designer:** Ian Rank-Broadley **Rev. Designer:** Ginarrbrik **Rev. Designer:** W. Pietranik

Date	Mintage	F	VF	XF	Unc	BU
2006(c)	20,000	—	—	—	—	6.00

KM# 120   DOLLAR

8.0000 g., Aluminum-Bronze **Ruler:** Elizabeth II **Obv:** Head with tiara right **Obv. Designer:** Ian Rank-Broadley **Rev:** Kiwi bird within sprigs **Rev. Designer:** R. Maurice Conly
Edge: Segmented reeding

Date	Mintage	F	VF	XF	Unc	BU
2001(c) In sets only	2,910	—	—	—	—	4.00
2001(c) Proof	1,364	Value: 5.00				
2002(I)	8,000,000	—	—	—	1.00	2.50
2002(c) In sets only	4,000	—	—	—	—	4.00
2002(c) Proof	1,500	Value: 5.00				
2003(I)	4,000,000	—	—	—	1.00	2.50
2003(c) In sets only	5,000	—	—	—	—	4.00
2003(c) Proof	1,750	Value: 5.00				
2004(I)	2,700,000	—	—	—	1.00	2.50
2004(c) In sets only	3,500	—	—	—	—	4.00
2004(c) Proof	2,250	Value: 5.00				
2005(I)	2,000,000	—	—	—	1.00	2.50
2005(c) In sets only	4,000	—	—	—	—	4.00
2005(c) Proof	2,250	Value: 5.00				
2006(c) In sets only	3,000	—	—	—	—	4.00
2006(c) Proof	2,100	Value: 5.00				
2007(c)	—	—	—	—	—	4.00
2007(c) Proof	—	Value: 5.00				
2008(I)	6,000,000	—	—	—	1.00	2.50
2008(I) In sets only	4,000	—	—	—	—	4.00
2008(I) Proof	3,000	Value: 5.00				
2009(w) In sets only	2,000	—	—	—	—	4.00
2009(w) Proof	1,500	Value: 5.00				

KM# 141   DOLLAR

28.2800 g., Aluminum-Bronze, 38.61 mm.   **Ruler:** Elizabeth II **Subject:** Lord of the Rings **Obv:** Head with tiara right **Obv. Designer:** Ian Rank-Broadley **Rev:** Inscribed ring around value **Rev. Designer:** Matthew Bonaccorsi **Edge:** Reeded

Date	Mintage	F	VF	XF	Unc	BU
2003(I)	30,081	—	—	—	—	15.00

Note: Mintage includes 10,454 in sets.

KM# 141a   DOLLAR

28.2800 g., 0.9250 Silver 0.8410 oz. ASW, 38.61 mm.   **Ruler:** Elizabeth II **Obv:** Head with tiara right **Obv. Designer:** Ian Rank-Broadley **Rev:** Gold-plated ring and edge **Edge:** Reeded

Date	Mintage	F	VF	XF	Unc	BU
2003(I) Proof	39,244	Value: 70.00				

KM# 142   DOLLAR

28.2800 g., Aluminum-Bronze, 38.61 mm.   **Ruler:** Elizabeth II **Subject:** Lord of the Rings **Obv:** Head with tiara right **Obv. Designer:** Ian Rank-Broadley **Rev:** Head of Frodo looking down above inscription **Rev. Designer:** Matthew Bonaccorsi **Edge:** Reeded

Date	Mintage	F	VF	XF	Unc	BU
2003(I)	10,454	—	—	—	—	10.00

KM# 143   DOLLAR

28.2800 g., Aluminum-Bronze, 38.61 mm.   **Ruler:** Elizabeth II **Subject:** Lord of the Rings **Obv:** Head with tiara right **Obv. Designer:** Ian Rank-Broadley **Rev:** View of Sauron, value **Rev. Designer:** Matthew Bonaccorsi **Edge:** Reeded

Date	Mintage	F	VF	XF	Unc	BU
2003(I)	10,454	—	—	—	—	10.00

KM# 247   DOLLAR

28.2800 g., 0.9250 Silver 0.8410 oz. ASW, 38.61 mm.   **Ruler:** Elizabeth II **Subject:** Lord of the Rings **Obv:** Head with tiara right **Obv. Designer:** Ian Rank-Broadley **Rev:** Aragorn's Coronation **Rev. Designer:** Matthew Bonaccorsi

Date	Mintage	F	VF	XF	Unc	BU
2003(I) Proof	3,057	Value: 70.00				

KM# 248   DOLLAR

28.2800 g., 0.9250 Silver 0.8410 oz. ASW, 38.61 mm.   **Ruler:** Elizabeth II **Subject:** Lord of the Rings **Obv:** Head with tiara right **Obv. Designer:** Ian Rank-Broadley **Rev:** King Theoden **Rev. Designer:** Matthew Bonaccorsi

Date	Mintage	F	VF	XF	Unc	BU
2003(I) Proof	2,022	Value: 70.00				

KM# 249   DOLLAR

28.2800 g., 0.9250 Silver 0.8410 oz. ASW, 38.61 mm.   **Ruler:** Elizabeth II **Subject:** Lord of the Rings **Obv:** Head with tiara right **Obv. Designer:** Ian Rank-Broadley **Rev:** Flight to the Ford **Rev. Designer:** Matthew Bonaccorsi

Date	Mintage	F	VF	XF	Unc	BU
2003(I) Proof	2,020	Value: 70.00				

KM# 250   DOLLAR

28.2800 g., 0.9250 Silver 0.8410 oz. ASW, 38.61 mm.   **Ruler:** Elizabeth II **Subject:** Lord of the Rings **Obv:** Head with tiara right **Obv. Designer:** Ian Rank-Broadley **Rev:** Mirror of Galadriel **Rev. Designer:** Matthew Bonaccorsi

Date	Mintage	F	VF	XF	Unc	BU
2003(I) Proof	2,036	Value: 70.00				

KM# 251   DOLLAR

28.2800 g., 0.9250 Silver 0.8410 oz. ASW, 38.61 mm.   **Ruler:** Elizabeth II **Subject:** Lord of the Rings **Obv:** Head with tiara right **Obv. Designer:** Ian Rank-Broadley **Rev:** Frodo offering ring to Nazgul **Rev. Designer:** Matthew Bonaccorsi

Date	Mintage	F	VF	XF	Unc	BU
2003(I) Proof	1,784	Value: 70.00				

KM# 252 DOLLAR
28.2800 g., 0.9250 Silver 0.8410 oz. ASW, 38.61 mm.
Ruler: Elizabeth II **Subject:** Lord of the Rings **Obv:** Head with tiara right **Obv. Designer:** Ian Rank-Broadley **Rev:** Bridge of Kazad-Dum **Rev. Designer:** Matthew Bonaccorsi

Date	Mintage	F	VF	XF	Unc	BU
2003(I) Proof	952	Value: 70.00				

KM# 253 DOLLAR
28.2800 g., 0.9250 Silver 0.8410 oz. ASW, 38.61 mm.
Ruler: Elizabeth II **Subject:** Lord of the Rings **Obv:** Head with tiara right **Obv. Designer:** Ian Rank-Broadley **Rev:** Shelob's Lair **Rev. Designer:** Matthew Bonaccorsi

Date	Mintage	F	VF	XF	Unc	BU
2003(I) Proof	917	Value: 70.00				

KM# 254 DOLLAR
28.2800 g., 0.9250 Silver 0.8410 oz. ASW, 38.61 mm.
Ruler: Elizabeth II **Subject:** Lord of the Rings **Obv:** Head with tiara right **Obv. Designer:** Ian Rank-Broadley **Rev:** Taming of Smeagol **Rev. Designer:** Matthew Bonaccorsi

Date	Mintage	F	VF	XF	Unc	BU
2003(I) Proof	1,017	Value: 70.00				

KM# 255 DOLLAR
28.2800 g., 0.9250 Silver 0.8410 oz. ASW, 38.61 mm.
Ruler: Elizabeth II **Subject:** Lord of the Rings **Obv:** Head with tiara right **Obv. Designer:** Ian Rank-Broadley **Rev:** Dark Lord's Tower and the Eye **Rev. Designer:** Matthew Bonaccorsi

Date	Mintage	F	VF	XF	Unc	BU
2003(I) Proof	1,002	Value: 70.00				

KM# 256 DOLLAR
28.2800 g., 0.9250 Silver 0.8410 oz. ASW, 38.61 mm.
Ruler: Elizabeth II **Subject:** Lord of the Rings **Obv:** Head with tiara right **Obv. Designer:** Ian Rank-Broadley **Rev:** Knife in the Dark **Rev. Designer:** Matthew Bonaccorsi

Date	Mintage	F	VF	XF	Unc	BU
2003(I) Proof	967	Value: 70.00				

KM# 257 DOLLAR
28.2800 g., 0.9250 Silver 0.8410 oz. ASW, 38.61 mm.
Ruler: Elizabeth II **Subject:** Lord of the Rings **Obv:** Head with tiara right **Obv. Designer:** Ian Rank-Broadley **Rev:** Gandalf and Saruman **Rev. Designer:** Matthew Bonaccorsi

Date	Mintage	F	VF	XF	Unc	BU
2003(I) Proof	867	Value: 70.00				

KM# 258 DOLLAR
28.2800 g., 0.9250 Silver 0.8410 oz. ASW, 38.61 mm.
Ruler: Elizabeth II **Subject:** Lord of the Rings **Obv:** Head with tiara right **Obv. Designer:** Ian Rank-Broadley **Rev:** Council of Elrond **Rev. Designer:** Matthew Bonaccorsi

Date	Mintage	F	VF	XF	Unc	BU
2003(I) Proof	1,204	Value: 70.00				

KM# 259 DOLLAR
28.2800 g., 0.9250 Silver 0.8410 oz. ASW, 38.61 mm.
Ruler: Elizabeth II **Subject:** Lord of the Rings **Obv:** Head with tiara right **Obv. Designer:** Ian Rank-Broadley **Rev:** Helm's Deep **Rev. Designer:** Matthew Bonaccorsi

Date	Mintage	F	VF	XF	Unc	BU
2003(I) Proof	967	Value: 70.00				

KM# 260 DOLLAR
28.2800 g., 0.9250 Silver 0.8410 oz. ASW, 38.61 mm.
Ruler: Elizabeth II **Subject:** Lord of the Rings **Obv:** Head with tiara right **Obv. Designer:** Ian Rank-Broadley **Rev:** Frodo & Co. at Mt. Doom **Rev. Designer:** Matthew Bonaccorsi

Date	Mintage	F	VF	XF	Unc	BU
2003(I) Proof	917	Value: 70.00				

KM# 261 DOLLAR
28.2800 g., 0.9250 Silver 0.8410 oz. ASW, 38.61 mm.
Ruler: Elizabeth II **Subject:** Lord of the Rings **Obv:** Head with tiara right **Obv. Designer:** Ian Rank-Broadley **Rev:** Departure of Boromir **Rev. Designer:** Matthew Bonaccorsi

Date	Mintage	F	VF	XF	Unc	BU
2003(I) Proof	917	Value: 70.00				

KM# 262 DOLLAR
28.2800 g., 0.9250 Silver 0.8410 oz. ASW, 38.61 mm.
Ruler: Elizabeth II **Subject:** Lord of the Rings **Obv:** Head with tiara right **Obv. Designer:** Ian Rank-Broadley **Rev:** Meeting of Treebeard **Rev. Designer:** Matthew Bonaccorsi

Date	Mintage	F	VF	XF	Unc	BU
2003(I) Proof	867	Value: 70.00				

KM# 263 DOLLAR
28.2800 g., 0.9250 Silver 0.8410 oz. ASW, 38.61 mm.
Ruler: Elizabeth II **Subject:** Lord of the Rings **Obv:** Head with tiara right **Obv. Designer:** Ian Rank-Broadley **Rev:** Battle of Minas Tirith / Pelenor Fields **Rev. Designer:** Matthew Bonaccorsi

Date	Mintage	F	VF	XF	Unc	BU
2003(I) Proof	867	Value: 70.00				

KM# 264 DOLLAR
28.2800 g., 0.9250 Silver 0.8410 oz. ASW, 38.61 mm.
Ruler: Elizabeth II **Subject:** Lord of the Rings **Obv:** Head with tiara right **Obv. Designer:** Ian Rank-Broadley **Rev:** Gandalf Reappears **Rev. Designer:** Matthew Bonaccorsi

Date	Mintage	F	VF	XF	Unc	BU
2003(I) Proof	967	Value: 70.00				

KM# 265 DOLLAR
28.2800 g., 0.9250 Silver 0.8410 oz. ASW, 38.61 mm.
Ruler: Elizabeth II **Subject:** Lord of the Rings **Obv:** Head with tiara right **Obv. Designer:** Ian Rank-Broadley **Rev:** Army of the Dead **Rev. Designer:** Matthew Bonaccorsi

Date	Mintage	F	VF	XF	Unc	BU
2003(I) Proof	917	Value: 70.00				

KM# 266 DOLLAR
28.2800 g., 0.9250 Silver 0.8410 oz. ASW, 38.61 mm.
Ruler: Elizabeth II **Subject:** Lord of the Rings **Obv:** Head with tiara right **Obv. Designer:** Ian Rank-Broadley **Rev:** Travel to the Undying Lands **Rev. Designer:** Matthew Bonaccorsi

Date	Mintage	F	VF	XF	Unc	BU
2003(I) Proof	867	Value: 70.00				

KM# 267 DOLLAR
28.2800 g., 0.9250 Silver 0.8410 oz. ASW, 38.61 mm.
Ruler: Elizabeth II **Subject:** Lord of the Rings **Obv:** Head with tiara right **Obv. Designer:** Ian Rank-Broadley **Rev:** Great River **Rev. Designer:** Matthew Bonaccorsi

Date	Mintage	F	VF	XF	Unc	BU
2003(I) Proof	867	Value: 70.00				

KM# 268 DOLLAR
28.2800 g., 0.9250 Silver 0.8410 oz. ASW, 38.61 mm.
Ruler: Elizabeth II **Subject:** Lord of the Rings **Obv:** Head with tiara right **Obv. Designer:** Ian Rank-Broadley **Rev:** Death of the Witch King **Rev. Designer:** Matthew Bonaccorsi

Date	Mintage	F	VF	XF	Unc	BU
2003(I) Proof	867	Value: 70.00				

KM# 269 DOLLAR
28.2800 g., 0.9250 Silver 0.8410 oz. ASW, 38.61 mm.
Ruler: Elizabeth II **Subject:** Lord of the Rings **Obv:** Head with tiara right **Obv. Designer:** Ian Rank-Broadley **Rev:** March of the Oliphants **Rev. Designer:** Matthew Bonaccorsi

Date	Mintage	F	VF	XF	Unc	BU
2003(I) Proof	867	Value: 70.00				

KM# 152 DOLLAR
31.1350 g., 0.9990 Silver 1.0000 oz. ASW, 40 mm.
Ruler: Elizabeth II **Obv:** Crowned head right **Rev:** Little spotted kiwi **Edge:** Reeded

Date	Mintage	F	VF	XF	Unc	BU
2004(c)	2,500	—	—	—	—	45.00
2004(c) Proof	2,000	Value: 50.00				

Note: Includes 500 struck in 2008 for sets.

KM# 153 DOLLAR
31.6350 g., 0.9990 Silver 1.0160 oz. ASW, 40.6 mm.
Ruler: Elizabeth II **Obv:** Crowned head right **Obv. Designer:** Ian Rank-Broadley **Rev:** Rowi Kiwi **Edge:** Reeded

Date	Mintage	F	VF	XF	Unc	BU
2005(w)	10,000	—	—	—	—	40.00
2005(w)	4,000	Value: 60.00				

KM# 153a DOLLAR
31.6350 g., 0.9990 Silver 1.0160 oz. ASW, 38.74 mm.
Ruler: Elizabeth II **Rev:** Kiwi

Date	Mintage	F	VF	XF	Unc	BU
2005(w) Proof	2,700	Value: 80.00				

Note: Mintage includes 500 struck in 2008 for sets.

2005(w) Proof	5,000	Value: 50.00				

Note: Each has different packaging.

KM# 154 DOLLAR
31.1350 g., 0.9990 Silver 1.0000 oz. ASW, 40 mm.
Ruler: Elizabeth II **Subject:** ANZAC **Obv:** Crowned head right **Rev:** Soldiers superimposed on a colored flag **Edge:** Reeded

Date	Mintage	F	VF	XF	Unc	BU
2005(w) Proof	15,000	Value: 110				

KM# 155 DOLLAR
20.0000 g., Aluminum-Bronze, 38.74 mm. **Ruler:** Elizabeth II **Subject:** ANZAC **Obv:** Crowned head right **Rev:** New Zealand soldier playing bugle in front of War Memorial **Edge:** Reeded

Date	Mintage	F	VF	XF	Unc	BU
2005(w)	15,000	—	—	—	—	25.00

KM# 156 DOLLAR
28.2800 g., Aluminum-Bronze, 38.61 mm. **Ruler:** Elizabeth II **Subject:** Lions Rugby Tour **Obv:** Crowned head right **Rev:** Rugby player, Lions crest and New Zealand map **Rev. Designer:** Michael Guilfoyle

Date	Mintage	F	VF	XF	Unc	BU
2005(I)	15,000	—	—	—	—	20.00

KM# 156a DOLLAR
28.2800 g., 0.9250 Silver 0.8410 oz. ASW, 38.61 mm.
Ruler: Elizabeth II **Series:** Rugby player, Lions crest & New Zealand map **Subject:** Lions Rugby Tour **Obv:** Crowned head right **Obv. Designer:** Ian Rank-Broadley **Rev. Designer:** Michael Guilfoyle **Edge:** Reeded

Date	Mintage	F	VF	XF	Unc	BU
2005(I) Proof	5,000	Value: 50.00				

KM# 159 DOLLAR
20.0000 g., Aluminum-Bronze, 38.74 mm. **Ruler:** Elizabeth II **Subject:** King Kong **Obv:** Crowned head right **Obv. Designer:** Ian Rank-Broadley **Rev:** King Kong **Edge:** Reeded

Date	Mintage	F	VF	XF	Unc	BU
2005(w)	7,000	—	—	—	—	20.00

KM# 160 DOLLAR
20.0000 g., Aluminum-Bronze, 38.74 mm. **Ruler:** Elizabeth II **Subject:** King Kong **Obv:** Crowned head right **Rev:** Multicolored King Kong **Edge:** Reeded

Date	Mintage	F	VF	XF	Unc	BU
2005(w)	4,000	—	—	—	—	35.00

KM# 161 DOLLAR
20.0000 g., Aluminum-Bronze, 38.74 mm. **Ruler:** Elizabeth II **Subject:** King Kong **Obv:** Crowned head right **Rev:** Carl Denham and camera in multicolor **Edge:** Reeded

Date	Mintage	F	VF	XF	Unc	BU
2005	4,000	—	—	—	—	35.00

KM# 162 DOLLAR
20.0000 g., Aluminum-Bronze, 38.74 mm. **Ruler:** Elizabeth II **Subject:** King Kong **Obv:** Crowned head right **Rev:** Ann Darrow and Jack Driscoll multicolored **Edge:** Reeded

Date	Mintage	F	VF	XF	Unc	BU
2005	4,000	—	—	—	—	35.00

KM# 164 DOLLAR
31.1350 g., 0.9990 Silver partially gold plated 1.0000 oz. ASW, 40.6 mm. **Ruler:** Elizabeth II **Obv:** Crowned head right **Rev:** King Kong partially gold plated

Date	Mintage	F	VF	XF	Unc	BU
2005(w) Proof	3,000	Value: 70.00				

KM# 276 DOLLAR
20.0000 g., Aluminum-Bronze, 38.74 mm. **Ruler:** Elizabeth II **Subject:** Emblem **Obv:** Head with tiara right **Obv. Designer:** Ian Rank-Broadley **Rev:** Rowi and chick inside patterned ring

Date	Mintage	F	VF	XF	Unc	BU
2005(w)	20,000	—	—	—	—	25.00

KM# 158 DOLLAR
28.2800 g., 0.9990 Silver 0.9083 oz. ASW, 38.61 mm.
Ruler: Elizabeth II **Subject:** FIFA **Obv:** Crowned head right **Obv. Designer:** Ian Rank-Broadley **Rev:** Soccer player, silver fern and map **Rev. Designer:** Michael McHalick

Date	Mintage	F	VF	XF	Unc	BU
2006(v) Proof	7,500	Value: 50.00				

KM# 285 DOLLAR
31.1000 g., 0.9990 Silver with gold highlights 0.9988 oz. ASW, 40 mm. **Ruler:** Elizabeth II **Subject:** Narnia **Obv:** Head with tiara right **Obv. Designer:** Ian Rank-Broadley **Rev:** White Witch

Date	Mintage	F	VF	XF	Unc	BU
2006(c) Proof	2,000	Value: 70.00				

KM# 286 DOLLAR
20.0000 g., Aluminum-Bronze, 38.74 mm. **Ruler:** Elizabeth II **Subject:** Narnia **Obv:** Head with tiara right **Obv. Designer:** Ian Rank-Broadley **Rev:** Asian, lion standing right

Date	Mintage	F	VF	XF	Unc	BU
2006(c)	8,000	—	—	—	—	20.00

KM# 287 DOLLAR
31.1350 g., 0.9990 Silver With Gold highlights 1.0000 oz. ASW, 40 mm. **Ruler:** Elizabeth II **Subject:** Narnia **Obv:** Head with tiara right **Obv. Designer:** Ian Rank-Broadley **Rev:** Asian

Date	Mintage	F	VF	XF	Unc	BU
2006(c) Proof	4,320	Value: 70.00				

KM# 288 DOLLAR
31.1350 g., 0.9990 Silver 1.0000 oz. ASW, 40 mm.
Ruler: Elizabeth II **Subject:** Narnia **Obv:** Head with tiara right **Obv. Designer:** Ian Rank-Broadley **Rev:** Wardrobe from the Lion, Witch and Wardrobe series

Date	Mintage	F	VF	XF	Unc	BU
2006(c) Proof	1,000	Value: 70.00				

KM# 289 DOLLAR
20.0000 g., Aluminum-Bronze, 38.74 mm. **Ruler:** Elizabeth II **Subject:** Queen's 80th birthday **Obv:** Head with tiara right **Obv. Designer:** Ian Rank-Broadley **Rev:** Heraldic arms **Rev. Designer:** Philip O'Shea

Date	Mintage	F	VF	XF	Unc	BU
2006	2,000	—	—	—	—	30.00

KM# 290 DOLLAR
31.1350 g., 0.9990 Silver 1.0000 oz. ASW, 38.74 mm.
Ruler: Elizabeth II **Subject:** Queen's 80th birthday **Obv:** Head with tiara right **Obv. Designer:** Ian Rank-Broadley **Rev:** Heraldic arms **Rev. Designer:** Philip O'Shea

Date	Mintage	F	VF	XF	Unc	BU
2006 Proof	1,500	—	—	—	—	—

KM# 291 DOLLAR
31.1350 g., 0.9990 Silver 1.0000 oz. ASW, 40 mm.
Ruler: Elizabeth II **Obv:** Head with tiara right **Obv. Designer:** Ian Rank-Broadley **Rev:** North Island Brown Kiwi **Edge:** Reeded

Date	Mintage	F	VF	XF	Unc	BU
2006(w)	3,000	—	—	—	—	50.00

KM# 291a DOLLAR
31.1350 g., 0.9990 Silver 1.0000 oz. ASW, 40 mm.
Ruler: Elizabeth II **Obv:** Head with tiara right **Obv. Designer:** Ian Rank-Broadley **Rev:** North Island Brown Kiwi **Edge:** Reeded

Date	Mintage	F	VF	XF	Unc	BU
2006(w) Proof	2,000	Value: 80.00				

Note: Mintage includes 500 struck in 2008 for sets.

KM# 293 DOLLAR
20.0000 g., Aluminum-Bronze, 38.74 mm. **Ruler:** Elizabeth II
Subject: NZ Gold Rushes - West Coast **Obv:** Head with tiara
right **Obv. Designer:** Ian Rank-Broadley **Rev:** 1860s miners

Date	Mintage	F	VF	XF	Unc	BU
2006(w)	1,500	—	—	—	—	30.00

KM# 294 DOLLAR
31.1350 g., 0.9990 Silver with gold highlights 1.0000 oz. ASW,
40.60 mm. **Ruler:** Elizabeth II **Subject:** NZ Gold Rushes -
Thames/Coromandel **Obv:** Head with tiara righ
Obv. Designer: Ian Rank-Broadley **Rev:** Gold panning

Date	Mintage	F	VF	XF	Unc	BU
2006(w) Proof	3,000	Value: 90.00				

KM# 232 DOLLAR
31.1350 g., 0.9990 Silver 1.0000 oz. ASW, 40 mm.
Ruler: Elizabeth II **Subject:** Aoraki - Mount Cook, Japanese
Friendship **Obv:** Head with tiara right **Obv. Legend:** NEW
ZEALAND - ELIZABETH II **Rev:** Flowers in bloom, Mount
Cook in background multicolor **Note:** Also released in a Japanese
proof set.

Date	Mintage	F	VF	XF	Unc	BU
2007(j) Proof	70,000	Value: 90.00				

KM# 296 DOLLAR
1.2440 g., 0.9990 Gold 0.0400 oz. AGW, 13.92 mm.
Ruler: Elizabeth II **Subject:** 50th anniversary of Scott Base
Obv: Head with tiara right **Obv. Designer:** Ian Rank-Broadley
Rev: Scott Base, Antarctica and International Polar Year logo

Date	Mintage	F	VF	XF	Unc	BU
2007(m) Proof	10,000	Value: 100				

KM# 297 DOLLAR
31.1350 g., 0.9990 Silver 1.0000 oz. ASW, 40 mm.
Ruler: Elizabeth II **Subject:** 50th anniversary of Scott Base
Obv: Head with tiara right **Obv. Designer:** Ian Rank-Broadley
Rev: Scott Base, Antarctica and International Polar Year logo

Date	Mintage	F	VF	XF	Unc	BU
2007(m) Proof	10,000	Value: 80.00				

KM# 298 DOLLAR
28.2800 g., 0.9250 Silver 0.8410 oz. ASW, 38.61 mm.
Ruler: Elizabeth II **Subject:** Scouting centenary **Obv:** Head with
tiara right **Obv. Designer:** Ian Rank-Broadley

Date	Mintage	F	VF	XF	Unc	BU
2007(I) Proof	1,500	Value: 80.00				

KM# 299 DOLLAR
28.2800 g., Copper-Nickel, 38.61 mm. **Ruler:** Elizabeth II
Subject: Scouting centenary **Obv:** Head with tiara right
Obv. Designer: Ian Rank-Broadley

Date	Mintage	F	VF	XF	Unc	BU
2007(I)	1,900	—	—	—	—	50.00

KM# 300 DOLLAR
31.1350 g., 0.9990 Silver 1.0000 oz. ASW, 40 mm.
Ruler: Elizabeth II **Obv:** Head with tiara right
Obv. Designer: Ian Rank-Broadley **Rev:** Great Spotted Kiwi
Rev. Designer: Chris Waind **Edge:** Reeded

Date	Mintage	F	VF	XF	Unc	BU
2007(m)	4,000	—	—	—	—	50.00

KM# 300a DOLLAR
31.1350 g., 0.9990 Silver 1.0000 oz. ASW, 40 mm.
Ruler: Elizabeth II **Obv:** Head with tiara right
Obv. Designer: Ian Rank-Broadley **Rev:** Great Spotted Kiwi
Rev. Designer: Chris Waind **Edge:** Reeded

Date	Mintage	F	VF	XF	Unc	BU
2007(m) Proof	3,000	Value: 100				

Note: Mintage includes 500 struck in 2008 for sets.

KM# 302 DOLLAR
31.1350 g., Copper-Nickel, 40 mm. **Ruler:** Elizabeth II
Subject: Elizabeth & Philip Diamond Wedding **Obv:** Head with
tiara right **Obv. Designer:** Ian Rank-Broadley **Rev:** Royal crests
Rev. Designer: Phillip O'Shea **Edge:** Reeded

Date	Mintage	F	VF	XF	Unc	BU
2007(m)	1,600	—	—	—	—	30.00

KM# 302a DOLLAR
31.1050 g., 0.9990 Silver 0.9990 oz. ASW, 40 mm.
Ruler: Elizabeth II **Subject:** Elizabeth & Philip Diamond Wedding
Obv: Head with tiara right **Obv. Designer:** Ian Rank-Broadley
Rev: Royal crests **Rev. Designer:** Phillip O'Shea **Edge:** Reeded

Date	Mintage	F	VF	XF	Unc	BU
2007(m) Proof	1,500	Value: 80.00				

KM# 321 DOLLAR
30.8000 g., Brass, 30 mm. **Ruler:** Elizabeth II **Rev:** Sir Edmond
Hillary with Mt. Everest **Edge:** Reeded **Note:** Sold in a PNC cover
only

Date	Mintage	F	VF	XF	Unc	BU
2008(w)	4,000	—	—	—	—	20.00

KM# 309 DOLLAR
31.1350 g., 0.9990 Silver 1.0000 oz. ASW, 40 mm.
Ruler: Elizabeth II **Obv:** Head with tiara right
Obv. Designer: Ian Rank-Broadley **Rev:** Haast Tokeoka Kiwi

Date	Mintage	F	VF	XF	Unc	BU
2008(w)	8,000	—	—	—	—	60.00

KM# 309a DOLLAR
31.1350 g., 0.9990 Silver 1.0000 oz. ASW, 40 mm.
Ruler: Elizabeth II **Obv:** Head with tiara right
Obv. Designer: Ian Rank-Broadley **Rev:** Haast tokoeka kiwi

Date	Mintage	F	VF	XF	Unc	BU
2008(w) Proof	5,000	Value: 85.00				

Note: Includes 500 for 2004-2008 sets.

KM# 311 DOLLAR
31.1350 g., 0.9990 Silver 1.0000 oz. ASW, 40.6 mm.
Ruler: Elizabeth II **Subject:** Sir Edmund Hillary **Obv:** Head with
tiara right **Obv. Designer:** Ian Rank-Broadley **Rev:** Hillary with
Mt. Everest in background

Date	Mintage	F	VF	XF	Unc	BU
2008(w) Proof	10,000	Value: 90.00				

KM# 322 DOLLAR
31.1350 g., 0.9990 Silver 1.0000 oz. ASW, 40 mm.
Ruler: Elizabeth II **Subject:** Icons of New Zealand **Rev:** Kiwi with
map of New Zealand **Edge:** Reeded

Date	Mintage	F	VF	XF	Unc	BU
2009(m)	10,000	—	—	—	—	50.00
2009(m) Proof	7,500	Value: 80.00				

KM# 323 DOLLAR
31.1350 g., 0.9990 Silver 1.0000 oz. ASW, 40 mm.
Ruler: Elizabeth II **Obv:** Bust right **Obv. Designer:** Ian Rank-
Broadley **Rev:** Southern right whale **Rev. Designer:** Ken Wright
Edge: Reeded

Date	Mintage	F	VF	XF	Unc	BU
2009(m) Prooflike	11,500	—	—	—	—	70.00

KM# 324 DOLLAR
31.1350 g., 0.9990 Silver 1.0000 oz. ASW, 40 mm. **Ruler:**
Elizabeth II **Rev:** Haast's Eagle **Rev. Designer:** Ken Wright

Date	Mintage	F	VF	XF	Unc	BU
2009(m) Prooflike	11,500	—	—	—	—	80.00

KM# 325 DOLLAR
31.1350 g., 0.9990 Silver 1.0000 oz. ASW, 40 mm.
Ruler: Elizabeth II **Rev:** Giant Moa **Rev. Designer:** Ken Wright

Date	Mintage	F	VF	XF	Unc	BU
2009(m) Prooflike	1,500	—	—	—	—	80.00

KM# 326 DOLLAR
31.1350 g., 0.9990 Silver 1.0000 oz. ASW, 40 mm.
Ruler: Elizabeth II **Rev:** Colossal squid **Edge:** Reeded

Date	Mintage	F	VF	XF	Unc	BU
2009(m) Prooflike	1,500	—	—	—	—	80.00

KM# 327 DOLLAR
31.1350 g., 0.9990 Silver 1.0000 oz. ASW, 40 mm.
Ruler: Elizabeth II **Rev:** Giant weta **Rev. Designer:** Ken Wright
Edge: Reeded

Date	Mintage	F	VF	XF	Unc	BU
2009(m) Prooflike	1,500	—	—	—	—	80.00

KM# 328 DOLLAR
26.4500 g., Copper-Nickel, 39.19 mm. **Ruler:** Elizabeth II
Subject: Reserve Bank of New Zealand, 75th Anniversary
Rev: Tui and Kowhai as on 1940-65 bronze penny

Date	Mintage	F	VF	XF	Unc	BU
2009(o)	2,000	—	—	—	—	30.00

KM# 331 DOLLAR
31.1050 g., 0.9990 Silver 0.9990 oz. ASW, 40 mm.
Ruler: Elizabeth II **Subject:** Icons of New Zealand
Obv. Designer: Ian Rank Broadley **Rev:** Kiwi and Southern
Cross **Edge:** Reeded

Date	Mintage	F	VF	XF	Unc	BU
2010(m)	Est. 12,500	—	—	—	—	60.00
2010(m) Proof	Est. 8,500	Value: 90.00				

KM# 333 DOLLAR
31.1050 g., 0.9990 Silver 0.9990 oz. ASW, 40 mm.
Ruler: Elizabeth II **Subject:** 2010 FIFA World Cup
Obv. Designer: Ian Rank Broadley **Rev:** Soccer player with
stylized NS koru **Edge:** Reeded

Date	Mintage	F	VF	XF	Unc	BU
2010	10,000	—	—	—	—	100

Note: Mintage includes 1500 in NZ Post packaging.

KM# 121 2 DOLLARS
10.0000 g., Aluminum-Bronze, 26.5 mm. **Ruler:** Elizabeth II
Obv: Head with tiara right **Obv. Designer:** Ian Rank-Broadley
Rev: White heron (kotuku) above value **Rev. Designer:** R.
Maurice Conly

Date	Mintage	F	VF	XF	Unc	BU
2001(I)	3,000,000	—	—	—	2.50	5.00
2001(c) In sets only	2,910	—	—	—	—	6.00
2001(c) Proof	2,000	Value: 7.50				
2002(I)	6,000,000	—	—	—	2.50	5.00
2002(c) In sets only	3,000	—	—	—	—	6.00
2002(c) Proof	2,000	Value: 7.50				
2003(I)	6,000,000	—	—	—	2.50	5.00
2003(c) In sets only	3,000	—	—	—	—	6.00
2003(c) Proof	3,000	Value: 7.50				
2004 Proof	3,500	Value: 7.50				
2004(c) In sets only	2,800	—	—	—	—	5.00
2005(I)	5,000,000	—	—	—	2.50	5.00
2005(c) In sets only	3,000	—	—	—	—	6.00
2005(c) Proof	3,000	Value: 7.50				
2006(c) In sets only	3,000	—	—	—	—	6.00
2006(c) Proof	2,100	Value: 7.50				
2007(c)	—	—	—	—	—	6.00
2007(c) Proof	4,000	Value: 7.50				
2008(I) In sets only	4,000	—	—	—	—	6.00
2008(I) Proof	3,000	Value: 7.50				
2009(w) In sets only	2,000	—	—	—	—	6.00
2009(w) Proof	1,500	Value: 7.50				

KM# 128 5 DOLLARS
28.2800 g., Copper-Nickel, 38.6 mm. **Ruler:** Elizabeth II
Subject: Kereru Bird **Obv:** Head with tiara right **Obv. Designer:**
Ian Rank-Broadley **Rev:** Wood Pigeon on branch **Edge:** Reeded

Date	Mintage	F	VF	XF	Unc	BU
2001(I)	1,500	—	—	—	25.00	—

KM# 128a 5 DOLLARS
28.2800 g., 0.9990 Silver 0.9083 oz. ASW **Ruler:** Elizabeth II
Obv: Head with tiara right **Obv. Designer:** Ian Rank-Broadley
Rev: Pigeon on branch

Date	Mintage	F	VF	XF	Unc	BU
2001 Proof	1,000	Value: 80.00				

KM# 149 5 DOLLARS
28.2800 g., Copper-Nickel, 38.6 mm. **Ruler:** Elizabeth II
Subject: Royal Visit (canceled after coin issue) **Obv:** Crowned
head right **Obv. Designer:** Ian Rank-Broadley **Rev:** Queen with
flowers and two girls **Edge:** Reeded

Date	Mintage	F	VF	XF	Unc	BU
2001	—	—	—	—	—	20.00

KM# 149a 5 DOLLARS
28.2800 g., 0.9250 Silver 0.8410 oz. ASW, 38.6 mm.
Ruler: Elizabeth II **Subject:** Royal Visit (canceled after coin
issue) **Obv:** Head with tiara right **Obv. Designer:** Ian Rank-
Broadley **Rev:** Queen with flowers and two girls **Edge:** Reeded

Date	Mintage	F	VF	XF	Unc	BU
2001 Proof	2,000	Value: 100				

Note: 200 issued in stamp cover

KM# 131 5 DOLLARS
28.2800 g., Copper-Nickel, 38.6 mm. **Ruler:** Elizabeth II
Subject: Architectural Heritage **Obv:** Head with tiara right
Obv. Designer: Ian Rank-Broadley **Rev:** Auckland Sky Tower
Edge: Reeded

Date	Mintage	F	VF	XF	Unc	BU
2002(I)	3,000	—	—	—	12.50	—

Note: 500 pieces were housed in a stamp cover

KM# 131a 5 DOLLARS
28.2800 g., 0.9250 Silver 0.8410 oz. ASW, 38.6 mm.
Ruler: Elizabeth II **Subject:** Architectural Heritage **Obv:** Head with tiara right **Obv. Designer:** Ian Rank-Broadley **Rev:** Auckland Sky Tower **Edge:** Reeded

Date	Mintage	F	VF	XF	Unc	BU
2002(l)	2,000	—	—	—	—	Value: 37.50

Note: 500 pieces were housed in a stamp cover

KM# 145 5 DOLLARS
27.2200 g., Copper-Nickel, 38.74 mm. **Ruler:** Elizabeth II **Obv:** Head with tiara right **Obv. Designer:** Ian Rank-Broadley **Rev:** Hector's Dolphins jumping out of the water **Rev. Designer:** Michael McHalick **Edge:** Reeded

Date	Mintage	F	VF	XF	Unc	BU
2002(c)	4,000	—	—	—	30.00	—

Note: 500 pieces were housed in a stamp covers

KM# 145a 5 DOLLARS
27.2220 g., 0.9990 Silver 0.8743 oz. ASW **Ruler:** Elizabeth II **Obv:** Head with tiara right **Obv. Designer:** Ian Rank-Broadley **Rev:** Two Hector's Dolphins jumping out of the water **Edge:** Reeded

Date	Mintage	F	VF	XF	Unc	BU
2002(c)	Est. 2,000	—	—	—	—	100

Note: 500 in stamp covers

KM# 151 5 DOLLARS
28.2800 g., 0.9250 Silver Gilt 0.8410 oz. ASW, 38.61 mm.
Ruler: Elizabeth II **Subject:** Queen's Jubilee **Obv:** Gilt head with tiara right **Obv. Designer:** Ian Rank-Broadley **Rev:** Scepter with "Great Star of Africa' at left of vertical band with crowns and shields **Rev. Designer:** Robert Lowe **Edge:** Reeded

Date	Mintage	F	VF	XF	Unc	BU
2002(l) Proof	25,000	—	—	—	Value: 80.00	

Note: 100 pieces were housed in a stamp cover, value $85

KM# 272a 5 DOLLARS
28.2800 g., 0.9250 Silver 0.8410 oz. ASW, 38.61 mm.
Ruler: Elizabeth II **Subject:** America's Cup **Obv:** Head with tiara right **Obv. Designer:** Ian Rank-Broadley **Rev:** Yachts **Rev. Designer:** Michael McHalick

Date	Mintage	F	VF	XF	Unc	BU
2002(l) Proof	4,000	—	—	—	Value: 50.00	

Note: Includes 500 in stamp cover, value $50.

KM# 272 5 DOLLARS
28.2800 g., Copper-Nickel, 38.61 mm. **Ruler:** Elizabeth II **Subject:** America's cup **Rev. Designer:** Michael McHalick

Date	Mintage	F	VF	XF	Unc	BU
2002(l)	6,000	—	—	—	—	20.00

KM# 132 5 DOLLARS
26.7000 g., Copper-Nickel, 38.6 mm. **Ruler:** Elizabeth II **Obv:** Head with tiara right **Rev:** Giant Kokopu fish divides circle **Edge:** Reeded **Designer:** Michael McHalick

Date	Mintage	F	VF	XF	Unc	BU
2003(c)	2,400	—	—	—	12.00	27.50

Note: Includes 400 issued in a stamp cover.

KM# 132a 5 DOLLARS
28.2800 g., 0.9990 Silver Gold plated 0.9083 oz. ASW, 38.6 mm.
Ruler: Elizabeth II **Obv:** Head with tiara right **Obv. Designer:** Ian Rank-Broadley **Rev:** Giant Kokopu fish **Edge:** Reeded

Date	Mintage	F	VF	XF	Unc	BU
2003(c) Proof	1,700	—	—	—	Value: 75.00	

Note: Includes 200 issued in a stamp cover

KM# 133 5 DOLLARS
26.7200 g., Copper-Nickel, 38.6 mm. **Ruler:** Elizabeth II **Subject:** Chatham Island Taiko **Obv:** Head with tiara right **Obv. Designer:** Ian Rank-Broadley **Rev:** Magenta Petrel **Edge:** Reeded

Date	Mintage	F	VF	XF	Unc	BU
2004(2003)	1,350	—	—	—	—	27.50

KM# 147 5 DOLLARS
28.2300 g., 0.9250 Silver 0.8395 oz. ASW, 38.6 mm.
Ruler: Elizabeth II **Subject:** 50th Anniversary of Coronation **Obv:** Gold plated crowned head right **Obv. Designer:** Ian Rank-Broadley **Rev:** Crown above fern and flowers **Edge:** Reeded

Date	Mintage	F	VF	XF	Unc	BU
2003 Proof	25,000	—	—	—	Value: 80.00	

Note: Includes 100 issued in a stamp cover

KM# 133a 5 DOLLARS
28.2800 g., 0.9990 Silver 0.9083 oz. ASW, 38.74 mm.
Ruler: Elizabeth II **Obv:** Head with tiara right **Obv. Designer:** Ian Rank-Broadley **Rev:** Chatham Island Taiko

Date	Mintage	F	VF	XF	Unc	BU
2004 Proof	1,300	—	—	—	Value: 60.00	

KM# 146 5 DOLLARS
27.2200 g., Copper-Nickel, 38.74 mm. **Ruler:** Elizabeth II **Obv:** Head with tiara right **Obv. Designer:** Ian Rank-Broadley **Rev:** Fiordland Crested Penguin **Edge:** Reeded

Date	Mintage	F	VF	XF	Unc	BU
2005(2004)	4,000	—	—	—	25.00	30.00

KM# 146a 5 DOLLARS
27.2200 g., 0.9990 Silver 0.8742 oz. ASW, 38.74 mm.
Ruler: Elizabeth II **Obv:** Head with tiara right **Obv. Designer:** Ian Rank-Broadley **Rev:** Fiordland Crested Penguin **Edge:** Reeded

Date	Mintage	F	VF	XF	Unc	BU
2005	3,500	—	—	—	—	50.00

KM# 148 5 DOLLARS
27.2200 g., Copper-Nickel, 38.74 mm. **Ruler:** Elizabeth II **Obv:** Head with tiara right **Obv. Designer:** Ian Rank-Broadley **Rev:** Falcon on tree stump **Edge:** Reeded

Date	Mintage	F	VF	XF	Unc	BU
2006	4,000	—	—	—	—	30.00

KM# 148a 5 DOLLARS
28.2800 g., 0.9990 Silver 0.9083 oz. ASW, 38.74 mm.
Ruler: Elizabeth II **Obv:** Head with tiara right **Obv. Designer:** Ian Rank-Broadley **Rev:** New Zealand Falcon on tree stump **Edge:** Reeded

Date	Mintage	F	VF	XF	Unc	BU
2006 Proof	2,500	—	—	—	Value: 50.00	

KM# 150 5 DOLLARS
27.2200 g., Copper-Nickel, 38.74 mm. **Ruler:** Elizabeth II **Subject:** Tuatara **Obv:** Head with tiara right **Obv. Designer:** Ian

Rank-Broadley **Rev:** Tuatara (Sphenodon punctatus), a lizard-like reptile **Edge:** Reeded

Date	Mintage	F	VF	XF	Unc	BU
2007(c)	3,000	—	—	—	—	30.00

KM# 150a 5 DOLLARS
28.2800 g., 0.9990 Silver 0.9083 oz. ASW, 38.74 mm.
Ruler: Elizabeth II **Subject:** Tuatara **Obv:** Head with tiara right **Obv. Designer:** Ian Rank-Broadley **Rev:** Tuatara right **Edge:** Reeded

Date	Mintage	F	VF	XF	Unc	BU
2007(c) Proof	4,000	—	—	—	Value: 80.00	

KM# 233 5 DOLLARS
28.2800 g., 0.9990 Silver 0.9083 oz. ASW, 38.6 mm.
Ruler: Elizabeth II **Subject:** Hamilton's frog **Obv:** Head with tiara right **Obv. Legend:** NEW ZEALAND - ELIZABETH II **Obv. Designer:** Ian Rank-Broadley **Rev:** Frog perched on branch at left center **Rev. Designer:** Chris Waind

Date	Mintage	F	VF	XF	Unc	BU
2008	4,000	—	—	—	—	30.00

KM# 233a 5 DOLLARS
28.2800 g., 0.9990 Silver 0.9083 oz. ASW, 38.61 mm.
Ruler: Elizabeth II **Rev:** Hamilton's frog **Rev. Designer:** Chris Waind **Edge:** Reeded

Date	Mintage	F	VF	XF	Unc	BU
2008(l) Proof	4,000	—	—	—	Value: 90.00	

Note: Mintage includes 1500 struck in 2009

KM# 329 5 DOLLARS
22.0000 g., Copper-Nickel, 38.60 mm. **Ruler:** Elizabeth II **Obv. Designer:** Ian Rank-Broadley **Rev:** Kakapo **Rev. Designer:** Ken Wright **Edge:** Reeded

Date	Mintage	F	VF	XF	Unc	BU
2009(w)	2,000	—	—	—	—	30.00

KM# 329a 5 DOLLARS
31.1350 g., 0.9990 Silver 1.0000 oz. ASW, 38.61 mm.
Ruler: Elizabeth II **Rev:** Kakapo **Rev. Designer:** Ken Wright

Date	Mintage	F	VF	XF	Unc	BU
2009(w) Proof	4,000	—	—	—	Value: 90.00	

KM# 129 10 DOLLARS
3.8879 g., 0.9990 Gold 0.1249 oz. AGW, 18 mm.
Ruler: Elizabeth II **Obv:** Head with tiara right **Obv. Designer:** Ian Rank-Broadley **Rev:** Salvage ship above value **Edge:** Reeded

Date	Mintage	F	VF	XF	Unc	BU
2001 Proof	600	—	—	—	Value: 155	

KM# 130 10 DOLLARS
7.7759 g., 0.9990 Gold 0.2497 oz. AGW, 22 mm. **Ruler:** Elizabeth II **Obv:** Head with tiara right **Obv. Designer:** Ian Rank-Broadley **Rev:** Ship above value **Edge:** Reeded

Date	Mintage	F	VF	XF	Unc	BU
2001 Proof	600	—	—	—	Value: 315	

KM# 273 10 DOLLARS
Nickel-Brass gold plated, 28.4 mm. **Ruler:** Elizabeth II **Subject:** America's Cup **Obv:** Head with tiara right **Obv. Designer:** Ian Rank-Broadley **Rev:** Map, cup and yachts **Rev. Designer:** Michael McHalick

Date	Mintage	F	VF	XF	Unc	BU
2002(l)	5,000	—	—	—	—	45.00

KM# 274 10 DOLLARS
15.5520 g., 0.9990 Gold 0.4995 oz. AGW, 28.4 mm.
Ruler: Elizabeth II **Subject:** America's Cup **Obv:** Head with tiara right **Obv. Designer:** Ian Rank-Broadley **Rev:** Map, cup and yachts **Rev. Designer:** Michael McHalick

Date	Mintage	F	VF	XF	Unc	BU
2002(l) Proof	900	Value: 625				

KM# 144 10 DOLLARS
39.9400 g., 0.9170 Gold 1.1775 oz. AGW, 38.61 mm.
Ruler: Elizabeth II **Subject:** Lord of the Rings **Obv:** Head with tiara right **Obv. Designer:** Ian Rank-Broadley **Rev:** The One Ring **Rev. Designer:** Matthew Bonaccorsi **Edge:** Reeded

Date	Mintage	F	VF	XF	Unc	BU
2003(l) Proof	1,198	Value: 1,500				

KM# 270 10 DOLLARS
39.9400 g., 0.9170 Gold 1.1775 oz. AGW, 38.61 mm.
Ruler: Elizabeth II **Subject:** Lord of the Rings **Obv:** Head with tiara right **Obv. Designer:** Ian Rank-Broadley **Rev:** Frodo **Rev. Designer:** Matthew Bonaccorsi **Edge:** Reeded

Date	Mintage	F	VF	XF	Unc	BU
2003(l) Proof	142	Value: 1,500				

KM# 271 10 DOLLARS
39.9400 g., 0.9170 Gold 1.1775 oz. AGW, 38.61 mm.
Ruler: Elizabeth II **Subject:** Lord of the Rings **Obv:** Head with tiara right **Obv. Designer:** Ian Rank-Broadley **Rev:** Sauron **Rev. Designer:** Matthew Bonaccorsi **Edge:** Reeded

Date	Mintage	F	VF	XF	Unc	BU
2003(l) Proof	142	Value: 1,500				

KM# 275 10 DOLLARS
38.5000 g., 0.9170 Gold 1.1350 oz. AGW, 38.61 mm.
Ruler: Elizabeth II **Subject:** Pukaki **Obv:** Head with tiara right **Obv. Designer:** Ian Rank-Broadley **Rev:** Statue of Pukaki **Edge:** Reeded

Date	Mintage	F	VF	XF	Unc	BU
2004(l) Proof	300	Value: 3,500				
2004(l) NW RB Proof	2	—	—	—	—	—

Note: Initials added for presention to Ngati Whakaue (Maori tribe) and the Reserve Bank.

KM# 157 10 DOLLARS
7.7700 g., 0.9990 Gold 0.2496 oz. AGW, 20.1 mm.
Ruler: Elizabeth II **Subject:** ANZAC **Obv:** Crowned head right **Rev:** Soldiers from Chun uk Bair battle with rifles and bayonets **Edge:** Reeded

Date	Mintage	F	VF	XF	Unc	BU
2005(w) Proof	1,000	Value: 600				

KM# 165 10 DOLLARS
7.9880 g., 0.9170 Gold 0.2355 oz. AGW, 22.05 mm.
Ruler: Elizabeth II **Subject:** Lions Rugby Tour **Obv:** Crowned head right **Edge:** Reeded

Date	Mintage	F	VF	XF	Unc	BU
2005(l) Proof	1,000	Value: 300				

KM# 295 10 DOLLARS
31.1350 g., 0.9990 Gold 1.0000 oz. AGW, 34 mm.
Ruler: Elizabeth II **Subject:** Narnia **Obv:** Head with tiara right **Obv. Designer:** Ian Rank-Broadley **Rev:** Asian

Date	Mintage	F	VF	XF	Unc	BU
2006 Proof	365	Value: 1,600				

KM# 307 10 DOLLARS
7.7770 g., 0.9990 Gold 0.2498 oz. AGW, 20 mm.
Ruler: Elizabeth II **Subject:** Queen's 80th birthday **Obv:** Head with tiara right **Obv. Designer:** Ian Rank-Broadley **Rev:** Heraldic arms **Rev. Designer:** Phillip O'Shea

Date	Mintage	F	VF	XF	Unc	BU
2006 Proof	500	Value: 325				

KM# 308 10 DOLLARS
15.5540 g., 0.9990 Gold 0.4996 oz. AGW, 25.10 mm.
Ruler: Elizabeth II **Subject:** Gold Rushes - Otago **Obv:** Head with tiara right **Obv. Designer:** Ian Rank-Broadley **Rev:** Picks, shovels and nuggets

Date	Mintage	F	VF	XF	Unc	BU
2006(w) Proof	500	Value: 625				

KM# 304 10 DOLLARS
7.7750 g., 0.9990 Gold 0.2497 oz. AGW, 26 mm. **Ruler:** Elizabeth II **Subject:** Elizabeth & Philip Diamond Wedding Anniversary **Obv:** Head with tiara right **Obv. Designer:** Ian Rank-Broadley **Rev:** Royal crests **Rev. Designer:** Phillip O'Shea

Date	Mintage	F	VF	XF	Unc	BU
2007(m) Proof	300	Value: 500				

KM# 305 10 DOLLARS
31.1350 g., 0.9170 Gold 0.9179 oz. AGW, 38.61 mm.
Ruler: Elizabeth II **Subject:** Scouting centenary **Obv:** Head with tiara right **Obv. Designer:** Ian Rank-Broadley

Date	Mintage	F	VF	XF	Unc	BU
2007(l) Proof	150	Value: 1,800				

KM# 306 10 DOLLARS
7.7855 g., 0.9990 Gold 0.2500 oz. AGW, 20.6 mm.
Ruler: Elizabeth II **Subject:** Sir Edmund Hilary **Obv:** Head with tiara right **Obv. Designer:** Ian Rank-Broadley **Rev:** Ed Hilary with Mt. Everest in background

Date	Mintage	F	VF	XF	Unc	BU
2008(w) Proof	1,953	Value: 520				

KM# 330 10 DOLLARS
7.7750 g., 0.9990 Gold 0.2497 oz. AGW, 26 mm.
Ruler: Elizabeth II **Subject:** Icons of New Zealand **Rev:** Kiwi and map of New Zealand **Edge:** Reeded

Date	Mintage	F	VF	XF	Unc	BU
2009(m) Proof	1,500	Value: 575				

KM# 332 10 DOLLARS
7.7750 g., 0.9990 Gold 0.2497 oz. AGW, 26. mm. **Ruler:** Elizabeth II **Subject:** Icons of New Zealand **Obv. Designer:** Ian Rank Broadley **Rev:** Kiwi and Southern Cross **Edge:** Reeded

Date	Mintage	F	VF	XF	Unc	BU
2010(m) Proof	1,800	—	—	—	—	650

MINT SETS

KM#	Date	Mintage	Identification	Issue Price	Mkt Val
MS50	2001 (7)	2,910	KM#116-121, 128	18.50	70.00
MS51	2002 (7)	3,000	KM#116-121, 145. Hector's dolphin.	18.00	60.00
MS52	2003 (7)	3,000	KM#116-121, 132. Giant Kokopu.	18.00	120
MS53	2003 (6)	34,332	KM#135-140. Lord of the Rings, Light vs. Dark set.	19.95	100
MS54	2003 (9)	2,821	KM#135-137; 235-240. Fellowship of the Ring.	—	175
MS55	2003 (18)	4,068	KM#135-140; 235-246. Lord of the Rings. Character collection.	—	325
MS57	2004 (7)	2,800	KM#116-121, 133. Taiko.	33.00	150
MS60	2003-5-6 (7)	5,000	Mixed Set for Change over to smaller size coins. KM#116 (2003); 117-119 (2005); KM#117a-119a (2006).	7.50	70.00
MS56	2003 (3)	10,454	KM#141, 142, 143. Lord of the Rings. Battle for the Ring set.	29.95	35.00
MS58	2005 (7)	3,000	KM#116-121; 146. Crested Penguin.	33.00	120
MS59	2006 (7)	3,000	KM#116-121; 148. Falcon.	33.00	110
MS61	2007 (6)	5,000	KM#117a-119a; 120-121; 150. Tuatara.	33.00	55.00
MS62	2008 (6)	4,000	KM#117a-119a; 120-121; 233. Hamilton's frog.	37.50	50.00
MS63	2009 (6)	2,000	KM#117a-119a; 120-121; 329. Kakapo.	—	50.00
MS64	2009 (5)	1,500	KM#323-327. Giants of New Zealand.	—	400

PROOF SETS

KM#	Date	Mintage	Identification	Issue Price	Mkt Val
PS45	2001 (7)	1,366	KM#116-121, 128a	49.25	220
PS46	2001 (2)	600	KM#129-130	400	450
PS47	2001 (7)	1,500	KM#116-121, 128a	60.00	250
PS48	2003 (1)	810	KM#141a and 5 others.	—	—
PS49	2003	—	Five coins as per PS48, less 141a	—	—
PS50	2003 (3)	133	KM#144; 270; 271. Lord of the Rings. Gold set.	—	4,200
PS51	2003 (2)	9	KM#270; 271. Lord of the Rings.	—	2,800
PS52	2003 (7)	1,496	KM#116-121, 132a.	60.00	230
PS53	2004 (7)	1,750	KM#116-121, 133. Chatham Islands Taiko	—	200
PS54	2005 (7)	2,250	KM#116-121; 146a. Crested Penguin.	88.00	120
PS55	2006 (7)	2,100	KM#116-121; 148a. Falcon.	90.00	125
PS56	2006 (3)	1,000	KM#285; 287; 288.	—	225
PS57	2007 (6)	3,500	KM#117a-119a; 120-121; 150a. Tuatara.	88.00	90.00
PS58	2007 (7)	69,000	KM#232, NZ Aoraki dollar and Japan 95.2; 96.2; 97.2; 98.2; 101.2; 125.	115	—
PS59	2008 (6)	3,000	KM#117a-119a; 120-121; 233a. Hamilton's frog.	94.00	95.00
PS60	2004-08 (5)	500	KM#152; 153a; 291a; 300a; 309a. Kiwi.	375	500
PS61	2009 (6)	1,500	KM#117a-119a; 120-121; 329a. Kakapo.	—	95.00

NICARAGUA

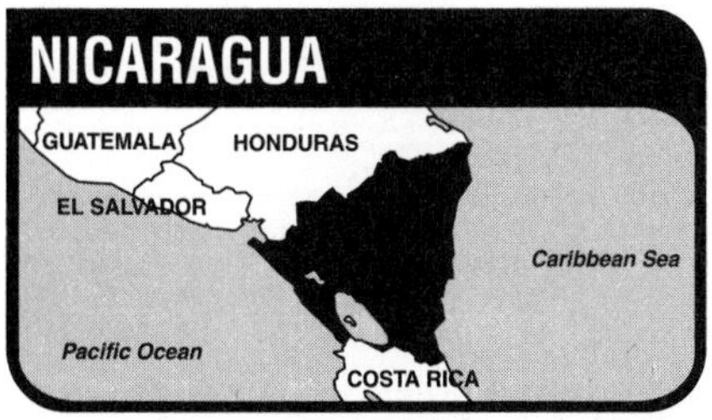

The Republic of Nicaragua, situated in Central America between Honduras and Costa Rica, has an area of 50,193 sq. mi. (129,494 sq. km.).

Columbus sighted the coast of Nicaragua on Sept. 12,1502 during the course of his last voyage of discovery. It was first visited in 1522 by conquistadors from Panama, under the command of Gil Gonzalez. Francisco Hernandez de Cordoba established the first settlements in 1524 at Granada and Leon. Nicaragua was incorporated, for administrative purpose, in the Captaincy General of Guatemala, which included every Central American state but Panama. On September 15, 1821 the Captaincy General of Guatemala declared itself and all the Central American provinces independent of Spain. The next year Nicaragua united with the Mexican Empire of Augustin de Iturbide, only to join in 1823 the federation of the Central American Republic. Within Nicaragua rival cities or juntas such as Leon, Granada and El Viejo vied for power, wealth and influence, often attacking each other at will. To further prove their legitimacy as well as provide an acceptable circulating coinage in those turbulent times (1821-1825), provisional mints functioned intermittently at Granada, Leon and El Viejo. The early coinage reflected traditional but crude Spanish colonial cob-style designs. Nicaragua's first governor was Pedro Arias Davila, appointed on June 1, 1827. When the federation was dissolved, Nicaragua declared itself an independent republic on April 30, 1838.

Dissension between the Liberals and Conservatives of the contending cities kept Nicaragua in turmoil, which made it possible for William Walker to make himself President in 1855. The two major political parties finally united to drive him out and in 1857 he was expelled. A relative peace followed, but by 1912, Nicaragua had requested the U.S. Marines to restore order, which began a U.S. involvement that lasted until the Good Neighbor Policy was adopted in 1933.

MINT MARKS
HF - Huguenin Freres, Le Locle, Switzerland
Mo - Mexico City

MONETARY SYSTEM
100 Centavos = 1 Peso

REPUBLIC

DECIMAL COINAGE

KM# 97 5 CENTAVOS
3.0000 g., Copper Plated Steel, 18.5 mm. **Obv:** National arms **Rev:** Value within circle **Edge:** Plain

Date	Mintage	F	VF	XF	Unc	BU
2002	—	—	—	—	0.25	0.50

KM# 98 10 CENTAVOS
4.0000 g., Brass Plated Steel, 20.5 mm. **Obv:** National arms **Rev:** Value within circle **Edge:** Reeded and plain sections

Date	Mintage	F	VF	XF	Unc	BU
2002	—	—	—	—	0.45	0.85

KM# 99 25 CENTAVOS
5.0000 g., Brass Plated Steel, 23.25 mm. **Obv:** National arms **Rev:** Value within circle **Edge:** Reeded and plain sections

Date	Mintage	F	VF	XF	Unc	BU
2002	—	—	—	—	0.65	1.25

KM# 104 25 CENTAVOS
Brass **Obv:** Arms **Rev:** Value at center **Rev. Legend:** EN DIOS CONFIAMOS

Date	Mintage	F	VF	XF	Unc	BU
2007	—	—	—	—	1.50	2.50

KM# 89 CORDOBA
6.2000 g., Nickel Clad Steel, 25 mm. **Obv:** National emblem **Rev:** Value above sprigs within circle

Date	Mintage	F	VF	XF	Unc	BU
2002	—	—	—	—	2.50	3.00

KM# 101   CORDOBA
6.2700 g., Nickel Clad Steel, 24.9 mm.   **Obv:** National arms
Rev: Large value "1" **Rev. Legend:** EN DIOS CONFIAMOS
Edge: Reeded

Date	Mintage	F	VF	XF	Unc	BU
2002	—	0.35	0.90	2.25	3.00	

KM# 100   10 CORDOBAS
27.1200 g., 0.9250 Silver 0.8065 oz. ASW, 40 mm.
Subject: Ibero-America **Obv:** National arms in circle of arms
Rev: Sail boat **Edge:** Reeded

Date	Mintage	F	VF	XF	Unc	BU
2002 Proof	—	Value: 45.00				

KM# 102   10 CORDOBAS
8.4700 g., Brass Plated Steel, 26.5 mm.   **Obv:** National arms
Rev: Value at upper left, circular latent image BCN below, statue
of Andrés Castro at right **Edge Lettering:** B C N repeated 4 times

Date	Mintage	F	VF	XF	Unc	BU
2007	—	—	—	—	4.00	

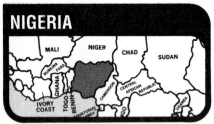

NIGERIA

Nigeria, situated on the Atlantic coast of West Africa has an
area of 356,669 sq. mi. (923,770 sq. km.). Nigeria is a member
of the Commonwealth of Nations. The President is the Head of
State and the Head of Government.

FEDERAL REPUBLIC

DECIMAL COINAGE
100 Kobo = 1 Naira

KM# 17   KOBO
4.6700 g., Brass, 23.2 mm.   **Obv:** Arms with supporters
Rev: Monkey musicians below value **Edge:** Reeded

Date	Mintage	F	VF	XF	Unc	BU
2003	—	—	—	—	15.00	20.00

KM# 13.3   50 KOBO
3.5000 g., Nickel Clad Steel, 19.44 mm.   **Obv:** Arms with
supporters **Obv. Legend:** FEDERAL REPUBLIC of NIGERIA
Rev: Value at left, corn cob and stalk at right **Edge:** Plain
Note: Reduced size.

Date	Mintage	F	VF	XF	Unc	BU
2006	—	—	—	—	1.00	1.35

KM# 18   NAIRA
5.4300 g., Bi-Metallic Brass center in Stainless Steel ring,
21.48 mm.   **Obv:** National arms **Obv. Legend:** FEDERAL
REPUBLIC OF NIGERIA **Rev:** Small bust of Herbert Macaulay
above value **Edge:** Plain

Date	Mintage	F	VF	XF	Unc	BU
2006	—	—	—	—	2.00	3.00

KM# 19   2 NAIRA
7.4800 g., Bi-Metallic Stainless Steel center in Copper-Brass
ring, 25.99 mm.   **Obv:** National arms **Obv. Legend:** FEDERAL
REPUBLIC OF NIGERIA **Rev:** Large value, National Assembly
in background **Edge:** Coarse reeding

Date	Mintage	F	VF	XF	Unc	BU
2006	—	—	—	—	3.00	4.00

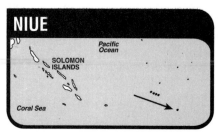

NIUE

Niue, or Savage Island, a dependent state of New Zealand
is located in the Pacific Ocean east of Tonga and southeast of
Samoa. The size is 100 sq. mi. (260 sq. km.) with a population
of *2,000. Chief village and port is Alofi. Bananas and copra are
exported.

MINT MARK
PM - Pobjoy Mint

NEW ZEALAND
DEPENDENT STATE

DECIMAL COINAGE

KM# 193   5 CENTS
4.3000 g., Copper Plated Bronze, 19 mm.   **Ruler:** Elizabeth II
Obv: Head right **Rev:** Two whales

Date	Mintage	F	VF	XF	Unc	BU
2009	—	—	—	—	1.00	2.00
2010	—	—	—	—	1.00	2.00

KM# 194   10 CENTS
5.8000 g., Copper Plated Bronze, 22 mm.   **Ruler:** Elizabeth II
Obv: Head right **Rev:** Coconut crab **Edge:** Reeded

Date	Mintage	F	VF	XF	Unc	BU
2009	—	—	—	—	1.50	2.00
2010	—	—	—	—	1.50	2.00

KM# 195   20 CENTS
7.3000 g., Nickel Plated Bronze, 25 mm.   **Ruler:** Elizabeth II
Obv: Head right **Rev:** Two scuba divers and coral

Date	Mintage	F	VF	XF	Unc	BU
2009	—	—	—	—	2.00	4.00
2010	—	—	—	—	2.00	4.00

KM# 189   50 CENTS
15.5000 g., 0.9990 Silver 0.4978 oz. ASW   **Ruler:** Elizabeth II
Subject: Year of the Pig **Obv:** Head right **Rev:** Multicolor pig

Date	Mintage	F	VF	XF	Unc	BU
2007 Proof	—	Value: 50.00				

KM# 196   50 CENTS
9.3000 g., Nickel Plated Bronze, 28 mm.   **Ruler:** Elizabeth II
Obv: Head right **Rev:** Outrigger canoe **Edge:** Segmented reeding

Date	Mintage	F	VF	XF	Unc	BU
2009	—	—	—	—	5.00	7.50
2010	—	—	—	—	5.00	7.50

KM# 207   DOLLAR
35.0000 g., Copper-Nickel, 50 mm.   **Ruler:** Elizabeth II **Obv:**
Shield **Rev:** Fan of four queens cut corners of Hearts - Clubs

Date	Mintage	F	VF	XF	Unc	BU
ND (2001) Antique	—	—	—	—	—	25.00

KM# 123   DOLLAR
28.2800 g., Copper-Nickel, 38.6 mm.   **Ruler:** Elizabeth II
Subject: Snoopy as an Ace **Obv:** Crowned head right **Rev:**
Snoopy flying his dog house **Edge:** Reeded

Date	Mintage	F	VF	XF	Unc	BU
2001	100,000	—	—	—	3.00	4.50

KM# 128   DOLLAR
28.2800 g., Copper-Nickel, 38.6 mm.   **Ruler:** Elizabeth II
Series: Pokemon **Obv:** Crowned shield within sprigs
Rev: Bulbasaur **Edge:** Reeded

Date	Mintage	F	VF	XF	Unc	BU
2001	100,000	—	—	—	12.00	14.00

KM# 129   DOLLAR
7.7700 g., 0.9990 Silver 0.2496 oz. ASW, 22 mm.
Ruler: Elizabeth II **Series:** Pokemon **Obv:** Crowned shield within
sprigs **Rev:** Bulbasaur **Edge:** Reeded

Date	Mintage	F	VF	XF	Unc	BU
2001 Proof	20,000	Value: 8.00				

KM# 131   DOLLAR
28.2800 g., Copper-Nickel, 38.6 mm.   **Ruler:** Elizabeth II
Series: Pokemon **Obv:** Crowned shield within sprigs
Rev: Charmander **Edge:** Reeded

Date	Mintage	F	VF	XF	Unc	BU
2001	100,000	—	—	—	12.00	14.00

KM# 132   DOLLAR
7.7700 g., 0.9990 Silver 0.2496 oz. ASW, 22 mm.
Ruler: Elizabeth II **Series:** Pokemon **Obv:** Crowned shield within
sprigs **Rev:** Charmander **Edge:** Reeded

Date	Mintage	F	VF	XF	Unc	BU
2001 Proof	20,000	Value: 8.00				

KM# 134 DOLLAR

28.2800 g., Copper-Nickel, 38.6 mm. **Ruler:** Elizabeth II
Series: Pokemon **Obv:** Crowned shield within sprigs
Rev: Meowth **Edge:** Reeded

Date	Mintage	F	VF	XF	Unc	BU
2001	100,000	—	—	—	12.00	14.00

KM# 135 DOLLAR

7.7700 g., 0.9990 Silver 0.2496 oz. ASW, 22 mm.
Ruler: Elizabeth II **Series:** Pokemon **Obv:** Crowned shield within sprigs **Rev:** Meowth **Edge:** Reeded

Date	Mintage	F	VF	XF	Unc	BU
2001 Proof	20,000	Value: 8.00				

KM# 137 DOLLAR

28.2800 g., Copper-Nickel, 38.6 mm. **Ruler:** Elizabeth II
Series: Pokemon **Obv:** Crowned shield within sprigs
Rev: Pikachu **Edge:** Reeded

Date	Mintage	F	VF	XF	Unc	BU
2001	100,000	—	—	—	12.00	14.00

KM# 138 DOLLAR

7.7700 g., 0.9990 Silver 0.2496 oz. ASW, 22 mm.
Ruler: Elizabeth II **Series:** Pokemon **Obv:** Crowned shield within sprigs **Rev:** Pikachu **Edge:** Reeded

Date	Mintage	F	VF	XF	Unc	BU
2001 Proof	20,000	Value: 8.00				

KM# 140 DOLLAR

28.2800 g., Copper-Nickel, 38.6 mm. **Ruler:** Elizabeth II
Series: Pokemon **Obv:** Crowned shield within sprigs
Rev: Squirtle **Edge:** Reeded

Date	Mintage	F	VF	XF	Unc	BU
2001	100,000	—	—	—	12.00	14.00

KM# 141 DOLLAR

7.7700 g., 0.9990 Silver 0.2496 oz. ASW, 22 mm.
Ruler: Elizabeth II **Series:** Pokemon **Obv:** Crowned shield within sprigs **Rev:** Squirtle **Edge:** Reeded

Date	Mintage	F	VF	XF	Unc	BU
2001 Proof	20,000	Value: 8.00				

KM# 208 DOLLAR

35.0000 g., Copper-Nickel, 50 mm. **Ruler:** Elizabeth II **Obv:** Shield **Rev:** Fan of four queens, cut corners of Spades, Diamonds

Date	Mintage	F	VF	XF	Unc	BU
ND (2001) Antique	—	—	—	—	—	25.00

KM# 146 DOLLAR

28.2800 g., Copper-Nickel, 38.6 mm. **Ruler:** Elizabeth II
Subject: Pokemon Series **Obv:** Crowned shield within sprigs
Rev: Pikachu **Edge:** Reeded

Date	Mintage	F	VF	XF	Unc	BU
2002PM	100,000	—	—	—	3.00	4.50

KM# 151 DOLLAR

28.2800 g., Copper-Nickel, 38.6 mm. **Ruler:** Elizabeth II
Subject: Pokemon Series **Obv:** Crowned shield within sprigs
Rev: Pichu **Edge:** Reeded

Date	Mintage	F	VF	XF	Unc	BU
2002PM	100,000	—	—	—	3.00	4.50

KM# 156 DOLLAR

28.2800 g., Copper-Nickel, 38.6 mm. **Ruler:** Elizabeth II
Subject: Pokemon Series **Obv:** Crowned shield within sprigs
Rev: Mewtwo **Edge:** Reeded

Date	Mintage	F	VF	XF	Unc	BU
2002PM	100,000	—	—	—	3.00	4.50

KM# 161 DOLLAR

28.2800 g., Copper-Nickel, 38.6 mm. **Ruler:** Elizabeth II
Subject: Pokemon Series **Obv:** Crowned shield within sprigs
Rev: Entei **Edge:** Reeded

Date	Mintage	F	VF	XF	Unc	BU
2002PM	100,000	—	—	—	3.00	4.50

KM# 166 DOLLAR

28.2800 g., Copper-Nickel, 38.6 mm. **Ruler:** Elizabeth II
Subject: Pokemon Series **Obv:** Crowned shield within sprigs
Rev: Celebi **Edge:** Reeded

Date	Mintage	F	VF	XF	Unc	BU
2002PM	100,000	—	—	—	3.00	4.50

KM# 186 DOLLAR

31.1050 g., 0.9990 Silver 0.9990 oz. ASW **Ruler:** Elizabeth II
Subject: Marshalls of China's Army, 50th Anniversary **Obv:** Head right **Rev:** Multicolor scene of military men

Date	Mintage	F	VF	XF	Unc	BU
2005	1,000	—	—	—	—	50.00

KM# 187 DOLLAR

31.1050 g., 0.9990 Silver 0.9990 oz. ASW **Ruler:** Elizabeth II
Subject: World War II, 60th Anniversary **Obv:** Bust right
Rev: Multicolor badge

Date	Mintage	F	VF	XF	Unc	BU
2005	1,000	—	—	—	—	50.00

KM# 188 DOLLAR

31.1050 g., 0.9990 Silver 0.9990 oz. ASW **Ruler:** Elizabeth II
Series: Bust right **Obv:** Multicolor image of two astronauts, rocket and map of China

Date	Mintage	F	VF	XF	Unc	BU
2005 Proof	—	Value: 65.00				

KM# 176 DOLLAR

28.2800 g., 0.9250 Silver 0.8410 oz. ASW **Ruler:** Elizabeth II
Obv: Tiarra head of Elizabeth II right at left, multicolor Van Gogh's painting "Starry Night" with 3 zircon crystals as stars at center right. **Obv. Inscription:** ELIZABETH II - NIUE ISLAND **Rev:** Van Gogh's painting "Vase with Twelve Sunflowers" at left, self portrait of artist with brush at upper right **Rev. Inscription:** VAN GOGH / Vincent **Edge:** Plain **Shape:** Rectangular, 39.94 x 27.97 mm

Date	Mintage	F	VF	XF	Unc	BU
2007 Proof	10,000	Value: 85.00				

KM# 201 DOLLAR

28.2800 g., 0.9250 Silver 0.8410 oz. ASW, 38.61 mm. **Ruler:** Elizabeth II **Subject:** Amber Road **Obv:** Roman cart and map, Elizabeth II head at lower left **Rev:** Church, goblet, ancient coin, amber insert **Rev. Legend:** ELBLAG SZLAK BURSZTYNOWY

Date	Mintage	F	VF	XF	Unc	BU
2008 Antique finish	10,000	—	—	—	—	80.00

KM# 202 DOLLAR

28.2800 g., 0.9250 Silver 0.8410 oz. ASW, 38.61 mm. **Ruler:** Elizabeth II **Subject:** Amber Road **Obv:** Roman cart, map, Elizabeth II head at lower left **Rev:** Antonius Pius coins, Nepture statue, mine shaft, amber insert **Rev. Legend:** GDANSK SZLAK BURSZTYNOWY

Date	Mintage	F	VF	XF	Unc	BU
2008 Antique finish	10,000	—	—	—	—	80.00

KM# 203 DOLLAR

28.2800 g., 0.9250 Silver 0.8410 oz. ASW, 38.61 mm. **Ruler:** Elizabeth II **Subject:** Amber Road **Obv:** Roman cart, map, Elizabeth II head at lower left **Rev:** Castle, roman coin, squid, amber insert **Rev. Legend:** KALINGRAD SZLAK BURSZTYNOWY

Date	Mintage	F	VF	XF	Unc	BU
2008 Antique finish	10,000	—	—	—	—	140

KM# 204 DOLLAR

28.2800 g., 0.9990 Silver 0.9083 oz. ASW, 38.61 mm.
Ruler: Elizabeth II **Subject:** Amber Road **Rev:** Kalingrad, amber insert **Rev. Legend:** SZLAK BURSZTYNOWY KALINGRAD

Date	Mintage	F	VF	XF	Unc	BU
2008 Antique finish	10,000	—	—	—	—	125

KM# 211 DOLLAR

28.2800 g., 0.9250 Silver 0.8410 oz. ASW, 28x40 mm.
Ruler: Elizabeth II **Obv:** Head of Elizabeth II at lower left, Portrait of Lautrec at top right **Rev:** Toulouse-Lautrec and can-can girl

Date	Mintage	F	VF	XF	Unc	BU
2008 Proof	15,000	Value: 65.00				

KM# 197 DOLLAR

17.3000 g., Copper Plated Bronze, 32 mm. **Ruler:** Elizabeth II
Obv: Head right **Rev:** Swordfish **Edge:** Reeded

Date	Mintage	F	VF	XF	Unc	BU
2009	—	—	—	—	7.50	12.50

KM# 192 DOLLAR

31.1050 g., 0.9990 Silver 0.9990 oz. ASW **Ruler:** Elizabeth II
Subject: Year of the Ox **Obv:** Head right **Rev:** Multicolor ox

Date	Mintage	F	VF	XF	Unc	BU
2009 Proof	10,000	Value: 70.00				

KM# 198 DOLLAR

17.3000 g., Copper Plated Bronze, 32 mm. **Ruler:** Elizabeth II
Obv: Head right **Rev:** Taro leaves **Edge:** Reeded

Date	Mintage	F	VF	XF	Unc	BU
2010	—	—	—	—	7.50	12.50

KM# 190 2 DOLLARS

1.5000 g., 0.9990 Gold 0.0482 oz. AGW **Ruler:** Elizabeth II
Subject: Year of the Pig **Obv:** Head right **Rev:** Multicolor pig

Date	Mintage	F	VF	XF	Unc	BU
2007 Proof	—	Value: 90.00				

KM# 205 2 DOLLARS

31.1050 g., 0.9990 Silver 0.9990 oz. ASW, 40.7 mm.
Ruler: Elizabeth II **Subject:** Peoples Republic of China, 60th Anniversary **Rev:** Dragon and scenes of China in multicolor

Date	Mintage	F	VF	XF	Unc	BU
2008 Proof	6,888	Value: 150				

KM# 185 2 DOLLARS

31.1050 g., 0.9990 Silver Partially gilt 0.9990 oz. ASW, 40 mm.
Ruler: Elizabeth II **Subject:** Year of the Ox **Rev:** Gilt ox advancing left

Date	Mintage	F	VF	XF	Unc	BU
2009 Proof	20,000	Value: 75.00				

KM# 199 2 DOLLARS

25.0000 g., 0.9250 Silver 0.7435 oz. ASW, 38.6 mm.
Ruler: Elizabeth II **Rev:** Two spinner dolphins leaping, swarovski crystal chip in eye

Date	Mintage	F	VF	XF	Unc	BU
2009 Proof	2,500	Value: 45.00				

KM# 200 2 DOLLARS

0.5000 g., 0.9990 Gold 0.0161 oz. AGW, 11 mm. **Ruler:** Elizabeth II **Rev:** Two spinner dolphins leaping out of the water

Date	Mintage	F	VF	XF	Unc	BU
2009 Proof	10,000	Value: 50.00				

KM# 209 2 DOLLARS

1.0000 g., 0.9000 Gold 0.0289 oz. AGW **Ruler:** Elizabeth II
Subject: Frederic Chopin **Obv:** Elizabeth II head right
Rev: Chopin bust and autograph

Date	Mintage	F	VF	XF	Unc	BU
2009 Proof	10,000	Value: 100				

KM# 210 2 DOLLARS

31.1050 g., 0.9990 Silver 0.9990 oz. ASW, 40.7 mm.
Ruler: Elizabeth II **Obv:** Head right **Rev:** Two black swans, multicolor **Rev. Designer:** LOVE IS PRECIOUS

Date	Mintage	F	VF	XF	Unc	BU
2009 Proof	10,000	Value: 80.00				

KM# 206 2 DOLLARS

31.1050 g., 0.9990 Silver 0.9990 oz. ASW, 40.7 mm.
Ruler: Elizabeth II **Rev:** Two white swans

Date	Mintage	F	VF	XF	Unc	BU
2010 Proof	10,000	—	—	—	—	50.00

KM# 191 5 DOLLARS

15.5000 g., 0.9000 Gold 0.4485 oz. AGW, 27 mm. **Ruler:** Elizabeth II **Subject:** Amber road **Obv:** Bust and Roman cart **Rev:** Kaliningrad Castle, Roman coin, Amber insert

Date	Mintage	F	VF	XF	Unc	BU
2008 Proof	2,000	Value: 575				

KM# 124   10 DOLLARS
28.2800 g., 0.9250 Silver 0.8410 oz. ASW, 38.6 mm.
Ruler: Elizabeth II **Subject:** Snoopy as an Ace **Obv:** Crowned head right **Rev:** Snoopy flying his dog house **Edge:** Reeded

Date	Mintage	F	VF	XF	Unc	BU
2001 Proof	10,000	Value: 18.50				

KM# 130   10 DOLLARS
28.2800 g., 0.9250 Silver 0.8410 oz. ASW, 38.6 mm.
Ruler: Elizabeth II **Series:** Pokeman **Obv:** Crowned shield within sprigs **Rev:** Bulbasaur **Edge:** Reeded

Date	Mintage	F	VF	XF	Unc	BU
2001 Proof	10,000	Value: 17.50				

KM# 133   10 DOLLARS
28.2800 g., 0.9250 Silver 0.8410 oz. ASW, 38.6 mm.
Ruler: Elizabeth II **Series:** Pokeman **Obv:** Crowned shield within sprigs **Rev:** Charmander **Edge:** Reeded

Date	Mintage	F	VF	XF	Unc	BU
2001 Proof	10,000	Value: 17.50				

KM# 136   10 DOLLARS
28.2800 g., 0.9250 Silver 0.8410 oz. ASW, 38.6 mm.
Ruler: Elizabeth II **Series:** Pokeman **Obv:** Crowned shield within sprigs **Rev:** Meowth **Edge:** Reeded

Date	Mintage	F	VF	XF	Unc	BU
2001 Proof	10,000	Value: 17.50				

KM# 139   10 DOLLARS
28.2800 g., 0.9250 Silver 0.8410 oz. ASW, 38.6 mm.
Ruler: Elizabeth II **Series:** Pokeman **Obv:** Crowned shield within sprigs **Rev:** Pikachu **Edge:** Reeded

Date	Mintage	F	VF	XF	Unc	BU
2001 Proof	10,000	Value: 17.50				

KM# 142   10 DOLLARS
28.2800 g., 0.9250 Silver 0.8410 oz. ASW, 38.6 mm.
Ruler: Elizabeth II **Series:** Pokeman **Obv:** Crowned shield within sprigs **Rev:** Squirtle **Edge:** Reeded

Date	Mintage	F	VF	XF	Unc	BU
2001 Proof	10,000	Value: 17.50				

KM# 147   10 DOLLARS
28.2800 g., 0.9250 Silver 0.8410 oz. ASW, 38.6 mm.
Ruler: Elizabeth II **Subject:** Pokémon Series **Obv:** Crowned shield within sprigs **Rev:** Pikachu **Edge:** Reeded

Date	Mintage	F	VF	XF	Unc	BU
2002PM Proof	10,000	Value: 17.50				

KM# 152   10 DOLLARS
28.2800 g., 0.9250 Silver 0.8410 oz. ASW, 38.6 mm.
Ruler: Elizabeth II **Subject:** Pokémon Series **Obv:** Crowned shield within sprigs **Rev:** Pichu **Edge:** Reeded

Date	Mintage	F	VF	XF	Unc	BU
2002PM Proof	10,000	Value: 17.50				

KM# 157   10 DOLLARS
28.2800 g., 0.9250 Silver 0.8410 oz. ASW, 38.6 mm.
Ruler: Elizabeth II **Subject:** Pokémon Series **Obv:** Crowned shield within sprigs **Rev:** Mewtwo **Edge:** Reeded

Date	Mintage	F	VF	XF	Unc	BU
2002PM Proof	10,000	Value: 17.50				

KM# 162   10 DOLLARS
28.2800 g., 0.9250 Silver 0.8410 oz. ASW, 38.6 mm.
Ruler: Elizabeth II **Subject:** Pokémon Series **Obv:** Crowned shield within sprigs **Rev:** Entei **Edge:** Reeded

Date	Mintage	F	VF	XF	Unc	BU
2002PM Proof	10,000	Value: 17.50				

KM# 167   10 DOLLARS
28.2800 g., 0.9250 Silver 0.8410 oz. ASW, 38.6 mm.
Ruler: Elizabeth II **Subject:** Pokémon Series **Obv:** Crowned shield within sprigs **Rev:** Celebi **Edge:** Reeded

Date	Mintage	F	VF	XF	Unc	BU
2002PM Proof	10,000	Value: 17.50				

KM# 125   20 DOLLARS
1.2400 g., 0.9999 Gold 0.0399 oz. AGW, 13.9 mm.
Ruler: Elizabeth II **Subject:** Snoopy as an Ace **Obv:** Crowned head right **Rev:** Snoopy flying his dog house **Edge:** Reeded

Date	Mintage	F	VF	XF	Unc	BU
2001 Proof	10,000	Value: 50.00				

KM# 148   20 DOLLARS
1.2400 g., 0.9999 Gold 0.0399 oz. AGW, 13.92 mm.
Ruler: Elizabeth II **Subject:** Pokémon Series **Obv:** Crowned shield within sprigs **Rev:** Pikachu **Edge:** Reeded

Date	Mintage	F	VF	XF	Unc	BU
2002PM Proof	10,000	Value: 50.00				

KM# 153   20 DOLLARS
1.2400 g., 0.9999 Gold 0.0399 oz. AGW, 13.9 mm.
Ruler: Elizabeth II **Subject:** Pokémon Series **Obv:** Crowned shield within sprigs **Rev:** Pichu **Edge:** Reeded

Date	Mintage	F	VF	XF	Unc	BU
2002PM Proof	10,000	Value: 50.00				

KM# 158   20 DOLLARS
1.2400 g., 0.9999 Gold 0.0399 oz. AGW, 13.92 mm.
Ruler: Elizabeth II **Subject:** Pokémon Series **Obv:** Crowned shield within sprigs **Rev:** Mewtwo **Edge:** Reeded

Date	Mintage	F	VF	XF	Unc	BU
2002PM Proof	10,000	Value: 50.00				

KM# 163   20 DOLLARS
1.2400 g., 0.9999 Gold 0.0399 oz. AGW, 13.9 mm.
Ruler: Elizabeth II **Subject:** Pokémon Series **Obv:** Crowned shield within sprigs **Rev:** Entei **Edge:** Reeded

Date	Mintage	F	VF	XF	Unc	BU
2002PM Proof	10,000	Value: 50.00				

KM# 168   20 DOLLARS
1.2400 g., 0.9999 Gold 0.0399 oz. AGW, 13.9 mm.
Ruler: Elizabeth II **Subject:** Pokémon Series **Obv:** Crowned shield within sprigs **Rev:** Celebi **Edge:** Reeded

Date	Mintage	F	VF	XF	Unc	BU
2002PM Proof	10,000	Value: 50.00				

KM# 126   50 DOLLARS
3.1100 g., 0.9999 Gold 0.1000 oz. AGW, 17.9 mm.
Ruler: Elizabeth II **Subject:** Snoopy as an Ace **Obv:** Crowned head right **Rev:** Snoopy flying his dog house **Edge:** Reeded

Date	Mintage	F	VF	XF	Unc	BU
2001 Proof	7,500	Value: 125				

KM# 149   50 DOLLARS
3.1100 g., 0.9999 Gold 0.1000 oz. AGW, 17.9 mm.
Ruler: Elizabeth II **Subject:** Pokémon Series **Obv:** Crowned shield within sprigs **Rev:** Pikachu **Edge:** Reeded

Date	Mintage	F	VF	XF	Unc	BU
2002PM Proof	7,500	Value: 125				

KM# 154   50 DOLLARS
3.1100 g., 0.9999 Gold 0.1000 oz. AGW, 17.9 mm.
Ruler: Elizabeth II **Subject:** Pokémon Series **Obv:** Crowned shield within sprigs **Rev:** Pichu **Edge:** Reeded

Date	Mintage	F	VF	XF	Unc	BU
2002PM Proof	7,500	Value: 125				

KM# 159   50 DOLLARS
3.1100 g., 0.9999 Gold 0.1000 oz. AGW, 17.9 mm.
Ruler: Elizabeth II **Subject:** Pokémon Series **Obv:** Crowned shield within sprigs **Rev:** Mewtwo **Edge:** Reeded

Date	Mintage	F	VF	XF	Unc	BU
2002PM Proof	7,500	Value: 125				

KM# 164   50 DOLLARS
3.1100 g., 0.9999 Gold 0.1000 oz. AGW, 17.9 mm.
Ruler: Elizabeth II **Subject:** Pokémon Series **Obv:** Crowned shield within sprigs **Rev:** Entei **Edge:** Reeded

Date	Mintage	F	VF	XF	Unc	BU
2002PM Proof	7,500	Value: 125				

KM# 169   50 DOLLARS
3.1100 g., 0.9999 Gold 0.1000 oz. AGW, 17.9 mm.
Ruler: Elizabeth II **Subject:** Pokémon Series **Obv:** Crowned shield within sprigs **Rev:** Celebi **Edge:** Reeded

Date	Mintage	F	VF	XF	Unc	BU
2002PM Proof	7,500	Value: 125				

KM# 127   100 DOLLARS
6.2200 g., 0.9999 Gold 0.1999 oz. AGW, 22 mm.
Ruler: Elizabeth II **Subject:** Snoopy as an Ace **Obv:** Crowned head right **Rev:** Snoopy flying his dog house **Edge:** Reeded

Date	Mintage	F	VF	XF	Unc	BU
2001 Proof	5,000	Value: 250				

KM# 150   100 DOLLARS
6.2200 g., 0.9999 Gold 0.1999 oz. AGW, 22 mm.
Ruler: Elizabeth II **Subject:** Pokémon Series **Obv:** Crowned shield within sprigs **Rev:** Pikachu **Edge:** Reeded

Date	Mintage	F	VF	XF	Unc	BU
2002PM Proof	5,000	Value: 250				

KM# 155   100 DOLLARS
6.2200 g., 0.9999 Gold 0.1999 oz. AGW, 22 mm.
Ruler: Elizabeth II **Subject:** Pokémon Series **Obv:** Crowned shield within sprigs **Rev:** Pichu **Edge:** Reeded

Date	Mintage	F	VF	XF	Unc	BU
2002PM Proof	5,000	Value: 250				

KM# 160   100 DOLLARS
6.2200 g., 0.9999 Gold 0.1999 oz. AGW, 22 mm.
Ruler: Elizabeth II **Subject:** Pokémon Series **Obv:** Crowned shield within sprigs **Rev:** Mewtwo **Edge:** Reeded

Date	Mintage	F	VF	XF	Unc	BU
2002PM Proof	5,000	Value: 250				

KM# 165   100 DOLLARS
6.2200 g., 0.9999 Gold 0.1999 oz. AGW, 22 mm.
Ruler: Elizabeth II **Subject:** Pokémon Series **Obv:** Crowned shield within sprigs **Rev:** Entei **Edge:** Reeded

Date	Mintage	F	VF	XF	Unc	BU
2002PM Proof	5,000	Value: 250				

KM# 170   100 DOLLARS
6.2200 g., 0.9999 Gold 0.1999 oz. AGW, 22 mm.
Ruler: Elizabeth II **Subject:** Pokémon Series **Obv:** Crowned shield within sprigs **Rev:** Celebi **Edge:** reeded

Date	Mintage	F	VF	XF	Unc	BU
2002PM Proof	5,000	Value: 250				

MINT SETS

KM#	Date	Mintage	Identification	Issue Price	Mkt Val
MS1	2009 (5)	20,000	KM#193-197	—	35.00
MS2	2010 (5)	20,000	KM193-196, 198	—	35.00

NORWAY

The Kingdom of Norway (*Norge, Noreg*), a constitutional monarchy located in northwestern Europe, has an area of 150,000sq. mi. (324,220 sq. km.), including the island territories of Spitzbergen (Svalbard) and Jan Mayen, and a population of *4.2 million. Capital: Oslo (Christiania). The diversified economic base of Norway includes shipping, fishing, forestry, agriculture, and manufacturing. Nonferrous metals, paper and paperboard, paper pulp, iron, steel and oil are exported.

RULER
Harald V, 1991-

MINT MARK
(h) - Crossed hammers – Kongsberg

MONETARY SYSTEM
100 Ore = 1 Krone

KINGDOM

DECIMAL COINAGE

KM# 460   50 ORE
3.6000 g., Bronze, 18.49 mm.   **Ruler:** Harald V **Obv:** Crown
Rev: Stylized animal and value **Edge:** Plain **Designer:** Grazyna Jolanta Linday

Date	Mintage	VG	F	VF	XF	BU
2001 without star	16,848,250	—	—	—	—	0.40
2001 with star	13,291,750	—	—	—	—	0.40
2001 Proof	—	Value: 10.00				
2002	—	—	—	—	—	0.40
2002 Proof	—	Value: 10.00				
2003	—	—	—	—	—	0.40
2003 Proof	—	Value: 10.00				
2004	—	—	—	—	—	0.40
2004 Proof	—	Value: 10.00				
2005	4,963,000	—	—	—	—	0.40
2005 Proof	—	Value: 10.00				
2006	30,227,000	—	—	—	—	0.40
2006 Proof	—	Value: 10.00				
2007	20,117,000	—	—	—	—	0.40
2007 Proof	—	Value: 10.00				
2008	19,391,000	—	—	—	—	0.40
2008 Proof	—	Value: 10.00				
2009	9,903,000	—	—	—	—	0.40
2009 Proof	—	Value: 10.00				
2010	—	—	—	—	—	0.40
2010 Proof	—	Value: 10.00				

KM# 462   KRONE
4.3000 g., Copper-Nickel, 21 mm.   **Ruler:** Harald V **Obv:** Crowned monograms form cross within circle with center hole
Rev: Bird on vine above center hole date and value below

Date	Mintage	VG	F	VF	XF	BU
2001 without star	43,128,650	—	—	—	—	0.65
2001 with star	7,355,350	—	—	—	—	0.75
2001 Proof	—	Value: 10.00				
2002	—	—	—	—	—	0.65
2002 Proof	—	Value: 10.00				
2003	—	—	—	—	—	0.65
2003 Proof	—	Value: 10.00				
2004	—	—	—	—	—	0.65
2004 Proof	—	Value: 10.00				
2005	25,648,000	—	—	—	—	0.65
2005 Proof	—	Value: 10.00				
2006	63,129,000	—	—	—	—	0.65
2006 Proof	—	Value: 10.00				
2007	47,108,000	—	—	—	—	0.65
2007 Proof	—	Value: 10.00				
2008	46,047,000	—	—	—	—	0.65
2008 Proof	—	Value: 10.00				
2009	50,055,000	—	—	—	—	0.65

Date	Mintage	VG	F	VF	XF	BU
2009 Proof	—	Value: 10.00				
2010	—	—	—	—	—	0.65
2010 Proof	—	Value: 10.00				

KM# 463   5 KRONER
7.8500 g., Copper-Nickel, 26 mm.   **Ruler:** Harald V
Subject: Order of St. Olaf **Obv:** Hole at center of order chain **Rev:** Center hole divides sprigs, value above and date below

Date	Mintage	VG	F	VF	XF	BU
2001	460,000	—	—	—	—	2.00
2001 Proof	—	Value: 12.50				
2002	—	—	—	—	—	1.50
2002 Proof	—	Value: 12.50				
2003	—	—	—	—	—	1.50
2003 Proof	—	Value: 12.50				
2004	—	—	—	—	—	1.50
2004 Proof	—	Value: 12.50				
2005	503,000	—	—	—	—	1.50
2005 Proof	—	Value: 12.50				
2006	509,000	—	—	—	—	1.50
2006 Proof	—	Value: 12.50				
2007	9,152,000	—	—	—	—	1.50
2007 Proof	—	Value: 12.50				
2008	5,502,000	—	—	—	—	1.50
2008 Proof	—	Value: 12.50				
2009	10,020,000	—	—	—	—	1.50
2009 Proof	—	Value: 12.50				
2010	—	—	—	—	—	1.50
2010 Proof	—	Value: 12.50				

KM# 457   10 KRONER
6.8000 g., Copper-Zinc-Nickel, 24 mm.   **Ruler:** Harald V
Obv: Head right **Rev:** Stylized church rooftop, value and date **Designer:** Ingrid Austlid Rise

Date	Mintage	VG	F	VF	XF	BU
2001 without star	9,837,500	—	—	—	—	3.50
2001 with star	10,000	—	—	—	—	7.50
2001 Proof	—	Value: 10.00				
2002	—	—	—	—	—	3.50
2002 Proof	—	Value: 10.00				
2003	—	—	—	—	—	3.50
2003 Proof	—	Value: 10.00				
2004	—	—	—	—	—	3.50
2004 Proof	—	Value: 10.00				
2005	466,000	—	—	—	—	3.50
2005 Proof	—	Value: 10.00				
2006	497,000	—	—	—	—	3.50
2006 Proof	—	Value: 10.00				
2007	474,000	—	—	—	—	3.50
2007 Proof	—	Value: 10.00				
2008	565,000	—	—	—	—	3.50
2008 Proof	—	Value: 10.00				
2009	475,000	—	—	—	—	3.50
2009 Proof	—	Value: 10.00				
2010	—	—	—	—	—	3.50
2010 Proof	—	Value: 10.00				

KM# 453   20 KRONER
9.9000 g., Copper-Zinc-Nickel, 27.5 mm.   **Ruler:** Harald V
Obv: Head right **Rev:** Value above 1/2 ancient boat **Designer:** Ingrid Austlid Rise

Date	Mintage	VG	F	VF	XF	BU
2001	4,178,010	—	—	—	—	6.50
2001 Proof	—	Value: 25.00				
2002	—	—	—	—	—	6.50
2002 Proof	—	Value: 25.00				
2003	—	—	—	—	—	6.50
2003 Proof	—	Value: 25.00				
2004	—	—	—	—	—	6.50

Date	Mintage	VG	F	VF	XF	BU
2004 Proof	—	Value: 25.00				
2005	553,000	—	—	—	—	6.50
2005 Proof	—	Value: 25.00				
2006	1,000,000	—	—	—	—	6.50
2006 Proof	—	Value: 22.50				
2007	493,000	—	—	—	—	6.50
2007 Proof	—	Value: 25.00				
2008	481,000	—	—	—	—	6.50
2008 Proof	—	Value: 25.00				
2009	473,000	—	—	—	—	6.50
2009 Proof	—	Value: 25.00				
2010	—	—	—	—	—	6.50
2010 Proof	—	Value: 25.00				

KM# 471   20 KRONER
9.7300 g., Nickel-Brass, 27.4 mm.   **Ruler:** Harald V
Subject: Niels Henrik Abel **Obv:** Head right **Rev:** Pair of glasses, dates and value within mathematical graphs **Edge:** Plain

Date	Mintage	F	VF	XF	Unc	BU
2002	—	—	—	—	10.00	12.50

KM# 478   20 KRONER
9.9000 g., Copper-Zinc-Nickel, 27.5 mm.   **Ruler:** Harald V
Subject: First Norwegian Railroad **Obv:** Head right **Rev:** Switch track and value **Edge:** Plain

Date	Mintage	F	VF	XF	Unc	BU
2004	10,000	—	—	—	17.50	20.00
2004 Proof	—	Value: 25.00				

KM# 479   20 KRONER
9.9000 g., Copper-Zinc-Nickel, 27.5 mm.   **Ruler:** Harald V
Obv: Head right **Rev:** Henrik Ibsen characture walking left, signature **Rev. Designer:** Nina Sundbye **Edge:** Plain

Date	Mintage	F	VF	XF	Unc	BU
2006	10,000	—	—	—	10.00	12.50

KM# 469   100 KRONER
33.6000 g., 0.9250 Silver 0.9992 oz. ASW, 39 mm.
Ruler: Harald V **Subject:** Nobel Peace Prize Centennial
Obv: Rampant crowned lion left holding axe **Rev:** Head left **Edge:** Plain

Date	Mintage	F	VF	XF	Unc	BU
2001 Proof	Est. 50,000	Value: 85.00				

KM# 472   100 KRONER
33.8000 g., 0.9250 Silver 1.0052 oz. ASW, 39 mm.
Ruler: Harald V **Subject:** 1905 Independence from Sweden
Obv: Three kings **Rev:** Farm field **Edge:** Plain

Date	Mintage	F	VF	XF	Unc	BU
2003 Proof	65,000	Value: 70.00				

KM# 474   100 KRONER
33.8000 g., 0.9250 Silver 1.0052 oz. ASW, 39 mm.
Ruler: Harald V **Subject:** 1905 Liberation **Obv:** Three kings
Rev: Off shore ocean oil well **Edge:** Plain

Date	Mintage	F	VF	XF	Unc	BU
2004 Proof	65,000	Value: 70.00				

KM# 476   100 KRONER
33.8000 g., 0.9250 Silver 1.0052 oz. ASW, 39 mm.
Ruler: Harald V **Obv:** Three kings **Rev:** Circuit board **Edge:** Plain

Date	Mintage	F	VF	XF	Unc	BU
2005 Proof	—	Value: 70.00				

KM# 480   200 KRONER
16.8500 g., 0.9250 Silver 0.5011 oz. ASW, 32 mm.
Ruler: Harald V **Subject:** Henrik Wergeland, 200th Birth Anniversary **Obv:** Head right **Rev:** Specticles and signature
Rev. Designer: Enzo Finger

Date	Mintage	F	VF	XF	Unc	BU
2008 Proof	40,000	Value: 100				

KM# 481 200 KRONER
16.8500 g., 0.9250 Silver 0.5011 oz. ASW, 32 mm.
Ruler: Harald V **Subject:** Knut Hamsun 150th Birth Anniversary
Obv: Crowned shield **Rev:** Streppled portrait, novel text and signature **Rev. Designer:** Enzo Finger

Date	Mintage	F	VF	XF	Unc	BU
2009 Proof	40,000	Value: 100				

KM# 470 1500 KRONER
16.9600 g., 0.9170 Gold 0.5000 oz. AGW, 27 mm.
Ruler: Harald V **Subject:** Nobel Peace Prize Centennial
Obv: Head right **Rev:** Reverse design of the prize medal
Edge: Plain

Date	Mintage	VG	F	VF	XF	BU
ND(2001) Matte Proof	7,500	Value: 650				

KM# 473 1500 KRONER
16.9600 g., 0.9170 Gold 0.5000 oz. AGW, 27 mm.
Ruler: Harald V **Subject:** 1905 Liberation **Obv:** Three kings **Rev:** Various leaf types **Edge:** Plain

Date	Mintage	F	VF	XF	Unc	BU
2003 Proof	10,000	Value: 625				

KM# 475 1500 KRONER
16.9600 g., 0.9170 Gold 0.5000 oz. AGW, 27 mm.
Ruler: Harald V **Subject:** 1905 Liberation **Obv:** Three kings **Rev:** Liquid drops on hard surface **Edge:** Plain

Date	Mintage	F	VF	XF	Unc	BU
2004 Proof	10,000	Value: 625				

KM# 477 1500 KRONER
16.9600 g., 0.9170 Gold 0.5000 oz. AGW, 27 mm. **Ruler:** Harald V **Obv:** Three kings **Rev:** Binary language **Edge:** Plain

Date	Mintage	F	VF	XF	Unc	BU
2005 Proof	—	Value: 625				

MINT SETS

KM#	Date	Mintage	Identification	Issue Price	Mkt Val
MS59	2001 (5)	55,000	KM453, 457, 460, 462, 463. Folder.	20.00	25.00
MS60	2001 (5)	30,000	KM453, 457, 460, 462, 463. Baby gift set.	18.00	30.00
MS61	2001 (5)	2,000	KM453, 457, 460, 462, 463 plus medal.	27.00	27.00
MS62	2001 (5)	—	KM453, 457, 460, 462, 463. Sandhill.	—	30.00
MS63	2002 (6)	55,000	KM#453, 457, 460, 462, 463, 471	—	32.00
MS64	2003 (5)	55,000	KM#453, 457, 460, 462, 463	—	30.00
MS65	2004 (6)	55,000	KM#453, 457, 460, 462, 463, 478	—	32.00
MS66	2005 (5)	55,000	KM#453, 457, 460, 462, 463	—	30.00

PROOF SETS

KM#	Date	Mintage	Identification	Issue Price	Mkt Val
PS13	2002 (6)	10,000	KM#453, 457, 460, 462, 463, 471	—	110
PS14	2003 (5)	10,000	KM#453, 457, 460, 42, 463	—	100
PS15	2004 (6)	10,000	KM#453, 457, 460, 462, 463, 478	—	110
PS16	2005 (5)	10,000	KM#453, 457, 460, 462, 463	—	100

OMAN

The Sultanate of Oman (formerly Muscat and Oman), an independent monarchy located in the southeastern part of the Arabian Peninsula, has an area of 82,030 sq. mi. (212,460 sq. km.) and a population of *1.3 million. Capital: Muscat. The economy is based on agriculture, herding and petroleum. Petroleum products, dates, fish and hides are exported.

RULER:
Qaboos ibn al-Sa'id, AH1390-/1970AD-

SULTANATE
REFORM COINAGE
1000 Baisa = 1 Omani Rial

KM# 150 5 BAISA
2.6500 g., Bronze Clad Steel, 19 mm. **Ruler:** Qabus bin Sa'id AH1390-/1970AD- **Obv:** National arms **Rev:** Value and dates

Date	Mintage	F	VF	XF	Unc	BU
AH1429-2008	—	—	—	0.20	0.50	0.75

KM# 151 10 BAISA
4.0400 g., Bronze Clad Steel, 22.5 mm. **Ruler:** Qabus bin Sa'id AH1390-/1970AD- **Obv:** National arms **Rev:** Value and both dates

Date	Mintage	F	VF	XF	Unc	BU
AH1429-2008	—	—	—	0.30	0.75	1.00

KM# 152 25 BAISA
3.0300 g., Copper-Nickel, 18 mm. **Ruler:** Qabus bin Sa'id AH1390-/1970AD- **Obv:** National arms **Rev:** Value and both dates **Edge:** Plain

Date	Mintage	F	VF	XF	Unc	BU
AH1428-2008	—	—	0.15	0.35	0.90	1.25
AH1429-2009	—	—	0.15	0.35	0.90	1.25

KM# 152a 25 BAISA
2.6300 g., Nickel Clad Steel, 17.95 mm. **Ruler:** Qabus bin Sa'id AH1390-/1970AD- **Obv:** National arms **Rev:** Value with both dates **Edge:** Reeded

Date	Mintage	F	VF	XF	Unc	BU
AH1428-2008	—	—	—	0.35	0.90	1.25

KM# 153 50 BAISA
6.4000 g., Copper-Nickel, 24 mm. **Ruler:** Qabus bin Sa'id AH1390-/1970AD- **Obv:** National arms **Rev:** Value with both dates **Edge:** Reeded

Date	Mintage	F	VF	XF	Unc	BU
AH1429-2008	—	—	0.25	0.60	1.50	2.00

KM# 153a 50 BAISA
5.5700 g., Nickel Clad Steel, 23.96 mm. **Ruler:** Qabus bin Sa'id AH1390-/1970AD- **Obv:** National arms **Rev:** Value with both dates **Edge:** Reeded

Date	Mintage	F	VF	XF	Unc	BU
AH1428-2008	—	—	—	0.60	1.50	2.00

KM# 154 OMANI RIAL
28.2800 g., 0.9250 Silver 0.8410 oz. ASW, 38.6 mm.
Ruler: Qabus bin Sa'id AH1390-/1970AD- **Subject:** 31st National Day and Environment Year **Obv:** National arms **Rev:** Multicolor map design **Edge:** Reeded

Date	Mintage	F	VF	XF	Unc	BU
2001 Proof	105	Value: 150				
2001	500	—	—	—	90.00	—

KM# 154a OMANI RIAL
37.8000 g., 0.9160 Gold 1.1132 oz. AGW, 38.6 mm.
Ruler: Qabus bin Sa'id AH1390-/1970AD- **Subject:** 31st National Day and Environment Year **Obv:** National arms **Rev:** Multicolor map design **Edge:** Reeded

Date	Mintage	F	VF	XF	Unc	BU
2001 Proof	105	Value: 1,550				
2001	350	—	—	—	1,400	—

KM# 156 OMANI RIAL
28.2800 g., 0.9250 Silver 0.8410 oz. ASW, 38.7 mm.
Ruler: Qabus bin Sa'id AH1390-/1970AD- **Series:** Environment Collection **Obv:** National arms **Rev:** Hoopoe bird standing right multicolor

Date	Mintage	F	VF	XF	Unc	BU
2002 Proof	1,000	Value: 75.00				

KM# 157 OMANI RIAL
28.2800 g., 0.9250 Silver 0.8410 oz. ASW, 38.7 mm.
Ruler: Qabus bin Sa'id AH1390-/1970AD- **Series:** Environment Collection **Obv:** National arms **Rev:** Dolphin right multicolor

Date	Mintage	F	VF	XF	Unc	BU
2002 Proof	1,000	Value: 75.00				

KM# 158 OMANI RIAL
28.2800 g., 0.9250 Silver 0.8410 oz. ASW, 38.7 mm.
Ruler: Qabus bin Sa'id AH1390-/1970AD- **Series:** Environment Collection **Obv:** National arms **Rev:** Turtle left multicolor

Date	Mintage	F	VF	XF	Unc	BU
2002 Proof	1,000	Value: 75.00				

KM# 159 OMANI RIAL
28.2800 g., 0.9250 Silver 0.8410 oz. ASW, 38.7 mm.
Ruler: Qabus bin Sa'id AH1390-/1970AD- **Series:** Environment Collection **Obv:** National arms **Rev:** Flower multicolor

Date	Mintage	F	VF	XF	Unc	BU
2002 Proof	1,000	Value: 75.00				

KM# 160 OMANI RIAL
28.2800 g., 0.9250 Silver 0.8410 oz. ASW, 38.7 mm.
Ruler: Qabus bin Sa'id AH1390-/1970AD- **Series:** Environment Collection **Obv:** National arms **Rev:** Ibex standing left multicolor

Date	Mintage	F	VF	XF	Unc	BU
2002 Proof	1,000	Value: 75.00				

KM# 161 OMANI RIAL
28.2800 g., 0.9250 Silver 0.8410 oz. ASW, 38.7 mm.
Ruler: Qabus bin Sa'id AH1390-/1970AD- **Series:** Environment Collection **Obv:** National arms **Rev:** Butterfly multicolor

Date	Mintage	F	VF	XF	Unc	BU
2002 Proof	1,000	Value: 75.00				

KM# 162 OMANI RIAL
28.2800 g., 0.9250 Silver 0.8410 oz. ASW, 38.7 mm.
Ruler: Qabus bin Sa'id AH1390-/1970AD- **Subject:** Population Census - December, 2003

Date	Mintage	F	VF	XF	Unc	BU
2003 Rare	—	—	—	—	—	—

KM# 155 OMANI RIAL
28.2800 g., 0.9250 Silver 0.8410 oz. ASW, 38.6 mm.
Ruler: Qabus bin Sa'id AH1390-/1970AD- **Subject:** The Sindibad Voyage, 1980/1981 **Obv:** National arms **Rev:** Sailing ship below map within circle **Edge:** Reeded

Date	Mintage	F	VF	XF	Unc	BU
2003 Proof	—	Value: 65.00				

KM# 163 OMANI RIAL

28.2800 g., 0.9250 Silver 0.8410 oz. ASW, 38.7 mm.
Ruler: Qabus bin Sa'id AH1390-/1970AD- **Subject:** 35th
National Day **Obv:** Oman Map

Date	Mintage	F	VF	XF	Unc	BU
AH1427-2005	—	—	—	—	100	120

KM# 164 OMANI RIAL

28.2800 g., 0.9250 Silver 0.8410 oz. ASW, 38.7 mm.
Ruler: Qabus bin Sa'id AH1390-/1970AD- **Subject:** 40th
Anniversary of First Oil Export from Oman

Date	Mintage	F	VF	XF	Unc	BU
2007	—	—	—	—	90.00	100

KM# 165 OMANI RIAL

28.2800 g., 0.9250 Silver 0.8410 oz. ASW, 38.7 mm.
Ruler: Qabus bin Sa'id AH1390-/1970AD- **Subject:** 29th Gulf
Congress - Muscat 2008

Date	Mintage	F	VF	XF	Unc	BU
2008	—	—	—	—	100	120

KM# 166 OMANI RIAL

28.2800 g., 0.9250 Silver 0.8410 oz. ASW, 38.7 mm.
Ruler: Qabus bin Sa'id AH1390-/1970AD- **Subject:** 19th
Arabian Gulf Cup

Date	Mintage	F	VF	XF	Unc	BU
2008	—	—	—	—	250	—

PAKISTAN

The Islamic Republic of Pakistan, located on the Indian sub-continent between India and Afghanistan, has an area of 310,404 sq. mi. (803,940 sq. km.) and a population of 130 million. Capital: Islamabad. Pakistan is mainly an agricultural land although the industrial base is expanding rapidly. Yarn, textiles, cotton, rice, medical instruments, sports equipment and leather are exported.

TITLE

پاکستان

Pakistan

ISLAMIC REPUBLIC

DECIMAL COINAGE

100 Paisa = 1 Rupee

KM# 62 RUPEE

4.0000 g., Bronze, 20 mm. **Obv:** Head of Jinnah facing left
Rev: Mosque above value **Edge:** Reeded

Date	Mintage	F	VF	XF	Unc	BU
2001	—	0.20	0.25	0.35	0.65	0.75
2002	—	0.20	0.25	0.35	0.65	0.75
2003	—	0.20	0.25	0.35	0.65	0.75
2004	—	0.20	0.25	0.35	0.65	0.75
2005	—	0.20	0.25	0.35	0.65	0.75
2006	—	0.20	0.25	0.35	0.65	0.75

KM# 67 RUPEE

Aluminum **Obv:** Head left **Rev:** Mosque

Date	Mintage	F	VF	XF	Unc	BU
2007	—	—	—	—	—	2.00

KM# 67a RUPEE

1.7500 g., Aluminum, 20 mm.

Date	Mintage	F	VF	XF	Unc	BU
2008	—	—	—	—	—	2.00

KM# 64 2 RUPEES

5.0000 g., Nickel-Brass, 22.5 mm. **Obv:** Crescent, star and date
above sprigs **Rev:** Value below mosque and clouds
Edge: Reeded

Date	Mintage	F	VF	XF	Unc	BU
2001	—	0.20	0.30	0.45	0.85	1.00
2002	—	0.20	0.30	0.45	0.85	1.00
2003	—	0.20	0.30	0.45	0.85	1.00
2004	—	0.20	0.30	0.45	0.85	1.00
2005	—	0.20	0.30	0.45	0.85	1.00
2006	—	0.20	0.30	0.45	0.85	1.00

KM# 68 2 RUPEES

Aluminum **Obv:** Star and crescent, wheat ears below
Rev: Mosque

Date	Mintage	F	VF	XF	Unc	BU
2007	—	—	—	—	—	2.00

KM# 68a 2 RUPEES

2.6000 g., Aluminum, 22.5 mm.

Date	Mintage	F	VF	XF	Unc	BU
2008	—	—	—	—	—	2.00

KM# 65 5 RUPEES

6.5000 g., Copper-Nickel, 24 mm. **Obv:** Cresent, star and date
above sprays **Rev:** Value within star design and sprigs
Edge: Reeded

Date	Mintage	F	VF	XF	Unc	BU
2002	—	0.50	1.00	1.50	3.00	3.25
2003	—	0.50	1.00	1.50	3.00	3.25
2004	—	0.50	1.00	1.50	3.00	3.25
2005	—	0.50	1.00	1.50	3.00	3.25

KM# 66 10 RUPEES

7.5000 g., Copper-Nickel, 27.5 mm. **Obv:** Cresent, star and date
above sprays **Rev:** Flowers and inscription
Rev. Inscription: Year of Fatima Jinnah **Edge:** Reeded

Date	Mintage	F	VF	XF	Unc	BU
2003	200,000	—	—	4.00	6.50	7.50

KM# 69 10 RUPEES

8.2500 g., Copper-Nickel, 27.5 mm. **Subject:** Benazir Bhutto
Obv: Star and cresent, wheat wreath below **Rev:** Bust facing,
Urdu script legend above

Date	Mintage	F	VF	XF	Unc	BU
2008	300,000	—	—	—	—	5.00

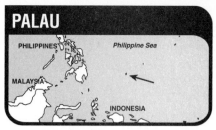

PALAU

The Republic of Palau, a group of about 100 islands and islets, is generally considered a part of the Caroline Islands. It is located about 1,000 miles southeast of Manila and about the same distance southwest of Saipan and has an area of 179 sq. mi. and a population of 12,116. Capital: Koror.

REPUBLIC

MILLED COINAGE

KM# 86 DOLLAR

1.2441 g., 0.9999 Gold 0.0400 oz. AGW, 13.94 mm. **Subject:**
Marine Life Protection **Obv:** Prone Mermaid **Rev:** Two fish

Date	Mintage	F	VF	XF	Unc	BU
2001 Proof	—	Value: 55.00				

KM# 87 DOLLAR

1.2441 g., 0.9999 Gold 0.0400 oz. AGW, 13.94 mm.
Subject: Marine Life Protection **Obv:** Seated Mermaid with
raised arm above value **Rev:** Two glittering fish

Date	Mintage	F	VF	XF	Unc	BU
2001 Proof	—	Value: 55.00				

KM# 88 DOLLAR

1.2441 g., 0.9999 Gold 0.0400 oz. AGW, 13.94 mm.
Subject: Marine Life Protection **Obv:** Figurehead Mermaid and
value **Rev:** Moorish Idol fish

Date	Mintage	F	VF	XF	Unc	BU
2001 Proof	—	Value: 55.00				

KM# 89 DOLLAR

1.2441 g., 0.9999 Gold 0.0400 oz. AGW, 13.94 mm.
Subject: Marine Life Protection **Obv:** Figurehead Mermaid and
value **Rev:** Moorish Idol fish

Date	Mintage	F	VF	XF	Unc	BU
2001 Proof	—	Value: 55.00				

KM# 60 DOLLAR

26.8000 g., Copper-Nickel, 37.2 mm. **Subject:** Marine Life
Protection **Obv:** Seated Mermaid with raised arm above value
Rev: Two glittering fish **Edge:** Reeded

Date	Mintage	F	VF	XF	Unc	BU
2001 Proof	—	Value: 30.00				

KM# 61   DOLLAR
26.8000 g., Copper-Nickel, 37.2 mm.   **Subject:** Marine Life Protection **Obv:** Prone Mermaid above value **Rev:** Two glittering fish **Edge:** Reeded

Date	Mintage	F	VF	XF	Unc	BU
2001 Proof	—	Value: 32.50				

KM# 62   DOLLAR
26.8000 g., Copper-Nickel, 37.2 mm.   **Subject:** Marine Life Protection **Obv:** Figurehead mermaid and value **Rev:** Moorish-Idol fish **Edge:** Reeded

Date	Mintage	F	VF	XF	Unc	BU
2001 Proof	—	Value: 30.00				

KM# 52   DOLLAR
26.8600 g., Copper-Nickel, 37.3 mm.   **Subject:** Marine Life Protection **Obv:** Mermaid figurehead and value **Rev:** Multicolor jellyfish **Edge:** Reeded

Date	Mintage	F	VF	XF	Unc	BU
2001 Proof	—	Value: 30.00				

KM# 253   DOLLAR
1.2500 g., 0.9990 Gold 0.0401 oz. AGW, 13.9 mm. **Obv:** Mermaid body-surfing wave **Rev:** Blue angelfish

Date	Mintage	F	VF	XF	Unc	BU
2001 Proof	—	Value: 60.00				

KM# 254   DOLLAR
1.2400 g., 0.9990 Gold 0.0398 oz. AGW, 13.9 mm. **Obv:** Large breasted mermaid on beach **Rev:** Emperor Angelfish

Date	Mintage	F	VF	XF	Unc	BU
2001 Proof	—	Value: 60.00				

KM# 56   DOLLAR
26.8000 g., Copper-Nickel, 37.2 mm.   **Subject:** Marine Life Protection **Obv:** Mermaid figurehead and value **Rev:** Multicolor fish scene **Edge:** Reeded

Date	Mintage	F	VF	XF	Unc	BU
2002 Proof	—	Value: 32.50				

KM# 57   DOLLAR
26.8000 g., Copper-Nickel, 37.2 mm.   **Subject:** Marine Life Protection **Obv:** Mermaid figurehead on approaching ship **Rev:** Multicolor reflective fish scene under an acrylic layer **Edge:** Reeded

Date	Mintage	F	VF	XF	Unc	BU
2002 Proof	—	Value: 37.50				

KM# 63   DOLLAR
26.8000 g., Copper-Nickel, 37.2 mm.   **Subject:** Marine Life Protection **Obv:** Figurehead mermaid and value **Rev:** Blue Tang Fish **Edge:** Reeded

Date	Mintage	F	VF	XF	Unc	BU
2002 Proof	—	Value: 37.50				

KM# 64   DOLLAR
26.8000 g., Copper-Nickel, 37.2 mm.   **Subject:** Marine Life Protection **Obv:** Figurehead mermaid and value **Rev:** Multicolor whales **Edge:** Reeded

Date	Mintage	F	VF	XF	Unc	BU
2002 Proof	—	Value: 37.50				

KM# 65   DOLLAR
26.8000 g., Copper-Nickel, 37.2 mm.   **Subject:** Marine Life Protection **Obv:** Mermaid washing hair and value **Rev:** Multicolor jellyfish **Edge:** Reeded

Date	Mintage	F	VF	XF	Unc	BU
2002 Proof	—	Value: 37.50				

KM# 90   DOLLAR
1.2441 g., 0.9999 Gold 0.0400 oz. AGW, 13.94 mm. **Subject:** Marine Life Protection **Obv:** Figurehead Mermaid and value **Rev:** Multicolor whales

Date	Mintage	F	VF	XF	Unc	BU
2002 Proof	—	Value: 55.00				

KM# 91   DOLLAR
1.2441 g., 0.9999 Gold 0.0400 oz. AGW, 13.94 mm. **Subject:** Marine Life Protection **Obv:** Figurehead Mermaid and value **Rev:** Pufferfish

Date	Mintage	F	VF	XF	Unc	BU
2002 Proof	—	Value: 55.00				

KM# 92   DOLLAR
1.2441 g., 0.9999 Gold 0.0400 oz. AGW, 13.94 mm. **Subject:** Marine Life Protection **Obv:** Seated Mermaid with both arms raised and value **Rev:** Jellyfish

Date	Mintage	F	VF	XF	Unc	BU
2002 Proof	—	Value: 55.00				

KM# 93   DOLLAR
1.2441 g., 0.9999 Gold 0.0400 oz. AGW, 13.94 mm. **Subject:** Marine Life Protection **Obv:** Figurehead Mermaid and value **Rev:** Blue Tang Fish

Date	Mintage	F	VF	XF	Unc	BU
2002 Proof	—	Value: 55.00				

KM# 94   DOLLAR
1.2441 g., 0.9999 Gold 0.0400 oz. AGW, 13.94 mm. **Subject:** Marine Life Protection **Obv:** Figurehead mermaid and value **Rev:** Lionfish

Date	Mintage	F	VF	XF	Unc	BU
2002 Proof	—	Value: 55.00				

KM# 95   DOLLAR
1.2441 g., 0.9999 Gold 0.0400 oz. AGW, 13.94 mm. **Subject:** Marine Life Protection **Obv:** Mermaid riding dolphin and value **Rev:** Starfish

Date	Mintage	F	VF	XF	Unc	BU
2003 Proof	—	Value: 55.00				

KM# 96   DOLLAR
1.2441 g., 0.9999 Gold 0.0400 oz. AGW, 13.94 mm. **Subject:** Marine Life Protection **Obv:** Seated Mermaid on shell and value **Rev:** Multicolor Orca **Edge:** Reeded   Proof

Date	Mintage	F	VF	XF	Unc	BU
2003 Proof	—	Value: 55.00				

KM# 97   DOLLAR
1.2441 g., 0.9999 Gold 0.0400 oz. AGW, 13.94 mm. **Subject:** Marine Life Protection **Obv:** Mermaid under radiant sun and value **Rev:** Crab

Date	Mintage	F	VF	XF	Unc	BU
2003 Proof	—	Value: 55.00				

KM# 98   DOLLAR
1.2441 g., 0.9999 Gold 0.0400 oz. AGW, 13.94 mm. **Subject:** Marine Life Protection **Obv:** Mermaid riding turtle and value **Rev:** Two glittering fish

Date	Mintage	F	VF	XF	Unc	BU
2003 Proof	—	Value: 55.00				

KM# 66 DOLLAR
26.8000 g., Copper-Nickel, 37.2 mm. **Subject:** Marine Life Protection **Obv:** Mermaid under sun and value **Rev:** Orange crab **Edge:** Reeded

Date	Mintage	F	VF	XF	Unc	BU
2003 Proof	—	Value: 37.50				

KM# 67 DOLLAR
26.8000 g., Copper-Nickel, 37.2 mm. **Subject:** Marine Life Protection **Obv:** Mermaid riding turtle and value **Rev:** Two glittering fish **Edge:** Reeded

Date	Mintage	F	VF	XF	Unc	BU
2003 Proof	—	Value: 37.50				

KM# 68 DOLLAR
26.8000 g., Copper-Nickel, 37.2 mm. **Subject:** Marine Life Protection **Obv:** Seated Mermaid on shell and value **Rev:** Multicolor Orca **Edge:** Reeded

Date	Mintage	F	VF	XF	Unc	BU
2003 Proof	—	Value: 37.50				

KM# 69 DOLLAR
26.8000 g., Copper-Nickel, 37.2 mm. **Subject:** Marine Life Protection **Obv:** Mermaid playing shell guitar and value **Rev:** Green fish **Edge:** Reeded

Date	Mintage	F	VF	XF	Unc	BU
2003 Proof	—	Value: 37.50				

KM# 256 DOLLAR
Copper-Nickel, 38.6 mm. **Obv:** Mermaid on dolphin **Rev:** Red starfish - multicolor

Date	Mintage	F	VF	XF	Unc	BU
2003	—	—	—	—	—	25.00

KM# 70 DOLLAR
26.8000 g., Copper-Nickel, 37.2 mm. **Subject:** Marine Life Protection **Obv:** Seated Mermaid on rock and value **Rev:** School of blue fish **Edge:** Reeded

Date	Mintage	F	VF	XF	Unc	BU
2004 Proof	—	Value: 37.50				

KM# 71 DOLLAR
26.8000 g., Copper-Nickel, 37.2 mm. **Subject:** Marine Life Protection **Obv:** Side view of Mermaid facing right and value **Rev:** Clownfish **Edge:** Reeded

Date	Mintage	F	VF	XF	Unc	BU
2004 Proof	—	Value: 37.50				

KM# 72 DOLLAR
26.8000 g., Copper-Nickel, 37.2 mm. **Subject:** Marine Life Protection **Obv:** Mermaid flanked by dolphins **Rev:** Multicolor dolphin head **Edge:** Reeded

Date	Mintage	F	VF	XF	Unc	BU
2004 Proof	—	Value: 37.50				

KM# 123 DOLLAR
Copper-Nickel, 37.2 mm. **Subject:** Marine Life Protection **Obv:** Mermaid seated inside a giant conch shell **Rev:** Puffer fish **Edge:** Reeded

Date	Mintage	F	VF	XF	Unc	BU
2004 Proof	—	Value: 35.00				

KM# 124 DOLLAR
Copper-Nickel, 37.2 mm. **Subject:** Marine Life Protection **Obv:** Seated Mermaid **Rev:** Sea turtle **Edge:** Reeded

Date	Mintage	F	VF	XF	Unc	BU
2004 Proof	—	Value: 50.00				

KM# 99 DOLLAR
1.2441 g., 0.9999 Gold 0.0400 oz. AGW, 13.94 mm. **Subject:** Marine Life Protection **Obv:** Mermaid under radiant sun and value **Rev:** Clownfish

Date	Mintage	F	VF	XF	Unc	BU
2004 Proof	—	Value: 55.00				

KM# 100 DOLLAR
1.2441 g., 0.9999 Gold 0.0400 oz. AGW, 13.94 mm. **Subject:** Marine Life Protection **Obv:** Mermaid flanked by dolphins **Rev:** Multicolor dolphin head

Date	Mintage	F	VF	XF	Unc	BU
2004 Proof	—	Value: 55.00				

KM# 101 DOLLAR
1.2441 g., 0.9999 Gold 0.0400 oz. AGW, 13.94 mm. **Subject:** Marine Life Protection **Obv:** Mermaid sitting in a shell listening to a conch shell **Rev:** Sea Horse

Date	Mintage	F	VF	XF	Unc	BU
2005 Proof	—	Value: 55.00				

KM# 139 DOLLAR
26.8000 g., Copper-Nickel, 37.2 mm. **Subject:** Marine Life - Protection **Obv:** Mermaid fixing hair, dolphin jumping **Rev:** School of fish

Date	Mintage	F	VF	XF	Unc	BU
2005	—	—	—	—	—	37.50

KM# 140 DOLLAR
26.8000 g., Copper-Nickel **Subject:** Marine Life - Protection **Obv:** Mermaid seated in shell, listening to shell **Rev:** Multicolor sea horse

Date	Mintage	F	VF	XF	Unc	BU
2005	—	—	—	—	—	37.50

KM# 141 DOLLAR
26.8000 g., Copper-Nickel **Subject:** Marine Life - Protection **Obv:** Mermaid and dolphin **Rev:** Multicolor fish scene

Date	Mintage	F	VF	XF	Unc	BU
2005	—	—	—	—	—	37.50

KM# 255 DOLLAR
Copper-Nickel, 38.6 mm. **Obv:** Mermaid seated on rock **Rev:** Stingray - multicolor

Date	Mintage	F	VF	XF	Unc	BU
2005	—	—	—	—	—	25.00

KM# 125 DOLLAR
Copper-Nickel, 37.2 mm. **Subject:** Marine Life Protection **Obv:** Mermaid with head tilted back **Rev:** Barracuda

Date	Mintage	F	VF	XF	Unc	BU
2006 Proof	—	Value: 37.50				

KM# 126 DOLLAR
Copper-Nickel, 37.2 mm. **Subject:** Marine Life Protection **Obv:** Two mermaids **Rev:** Parrot fish

Date	Mintage	F	VF	XF	Unc	BU
2006 Proof	—	Value: 50.00				

KM# 127   DOLLAR
Copper-Nickel, 37.2 mm.   **Subject:** Marine Life Protection
Obv: Mermaid swimming downward **Rev:** Hog Fish
Edge: Reeded

Date	Mintage	F	VF	XF	Unc	BU
2006 Proof	—	Value: 32.50				

KM# 128   DOLLAR
Copper-Nickel, 37.2 mm.   **Subject:** Marine Life Protection
Obv: Seated mermaid with bird perched on outstretched hand
Rev: Mahi Mahi **Edge:** Reeded

Date	Mintage	F	VF	XF	Unc	BU
2006 Proof	—	Value: 47.50				

KM# 129   DOLLAR
Copper-Nickel, 37.2 mm.   **Subject:** Marine Life Protection
Obv: Mermaid, sailing ship and sun **Rev:** Box Fish **Edge:** Reeded

Date	Mintage	F	VF	XF	Unc	BU
2006 Proof	—	Value: 45.00				

KM# 142   DOLLAR
20.0000 g., 0.9990 Silver 0.6423 oz. ASW   **Obv:** Arms
Rev: Snowflake with blue crystal

Date	Mintage	F	VF	XF	Unc	BU
2006 Proof	2,500	Value: 60.00				

KM# 257   DOLLAR
25.0000 g., 0.9250 Silver 0.7435 oz. ASW, 38.6 mm.   **Obv:** Arms
Rev: White pearl in shell **Shape:** Heart

Date	Mintage	F	VF	XF	Unc	BU
2006 Proof	500	Value: 35.00				

KM# 144   DOLLAR
27.0000 g., 0.9250 Silver 0.8029 oz. ASW   **Obv:** Shield
Rev: Multicolor John Paul II waving

Date	Mintage	F	VF	XF	Unc	BU
2007 Proof	—	Value: 25.00				

KM# 145   DOLLAR
1.2440 g., 0.9990 Gold 0.0400 oz. AGW, 13.92 mm.
Subject: Marine Life - Protection **Obv:** Nepture and mermaid
seated on rocks **Rev:** Tropical fish

Date	Mintage	F	VF	XF	Unc	BU
2007 Proof	—	Value: 75.00				

KM# 150   DOLLAR
25.0000 g., 0.9250 Silver 0.7435 oz. ASW   **Subject:** Pacific
Wildlife **Obv:** Shield **Rev:** Multicolor seahorse

Date	Mintage	F	VF	XF	Unc	BU
2007 Proof	—	Value: 70.00				

KM# 116   DOLLAR
25.7000 g., Silver Plated Bronze, 38.6 mm.   **Obv:** National arms
Rev: Multicolor Pope John Paul II with cross **Edge:** Reeded

Date	Mintage	F	VF	XF	Unc	BU
2007 Proof	—	Value: 32.50				

KM# 118   DOLLAR
27.0000 g., Copper-Nickel, 38.61 mm.   **Series:** Marine Life
Protection **Obv:** Neptune reclining with trident, mermaid at his
side **Obv. Legend:** REPUBLIC OF PALAU **Rev:** Multicolor
Doctor Fish

Date	Mintage	F	VF	XF	Unc	BU
2007 Proof	5,000	Value: 32.50				

KM# 121   DOLLAR
27.0000 g., Copper-Nickel, 38.61 mm.   **Obv:** Shield with
Neptune holding trident, mermaid reclining at his side,
RAINBOW'S / END below **Obv. Legend:** REPUBLIC OF PALAU
Rev: Red racing car 3/4 left **Rev. Legend:** FERRARI - 60 YEARS
ANNIVERSARY

Date	Mintage	F	VF	XF	Unc	BU
ND(2007) Proof	5,000	Value: 32.50				

KM# 120   DOLLAR
0.5000 g., 0.9990 Gold 0.0161 oz. AGW, 11.0 mm.   **Obv:** Shield
with Neptune holding trident, mermaid reclining at his side,
RAINBOW'S / END below **Obv. Legend:** REPUBLIC OF PALAU
Shape: 4-leaf clover **Note:** Uniface

Date	Mintage	F	VF	XF	Unc	BU
2007 Proof	25,000	Value: 45.00				

KM# 258   DOLLAR
25.0000 g., 0.9990 Silver 0.8029 oz. ASW   **Subject:** Pacific
Wildlife **Rev:** Seahorse - prism

Date	Mintage	F	VF	XF	Unc	BU
2007 Proof	—	Value: 35.00				

KM# 154   DOLLAR
26.8000 g., Copper-Nickel silver plated, 38.61 mm.
Subject: 150th Anniversary of the Appriations **Obv:** Shield
Rev: Statue of Our Lady of Lourdes and holy water vile

Date	Mintage	F	VF	XF	Unc	BU
2008 Proof	—	Value: 20.00				

KM# 155   DOLLAR
26.8000 g., Copper-Nickel, 37.2 mm.   **Subject:** Dealer Button
Obv: Shield **Rev:** Vegas Chips and cards, Ace of Clubs corner cut

Date	Mintage	F	VF	XF	Unc	BU
2008	—	—	—	—	—	20.00

KM# 156   DOLLAR
26.8000 g., Copper-Nickel, 37.2 mm.   **Subject:** Dealer Buttons
Obv: Shield **Rev:** Vegas Chips and cards, Ace of Diamonds
corner cut

Date	Mintage	F	VF	XF	Unc	BU
2008	—	—	—	—	—	20.00

KM# 157   DOLLAR
26.8000 g., Copper-Nickel, 37.2 mm.   **Subject:** Dear Buttons
Obv: Shield **Rev:** Vegas Chips and cards, Ace of Heats corner cut

Date	Mintage	F	VF	XF	Unc	BU
2008	—	—	—	—	—	20.00

KM# 158   DOLLAR
26.8000 g., Copper-Nickel, 37.2 mm.   **Obv:** Shield **Rev:** Vegas
chips and cards, Ace of Spades corner cut

Date	Mintage	F	VF	XF	Unc	BU
2008	—	—	—	—	—	20.00

KM# 159   DOLLAR
1.2400 g., 0.9990 Gold 0.0398 oz. AGW, 13.9 mm.
Subject: St. Francis of Assisi **Obv:** Shield **Rev:** Bust facing

Date	Mintage	F	VF	XF	Unc	BU
2008 Proof	—	Value: 75.00				

KM# 160   DOLLAR
1.2440 g., 0.9900 Gold 0.0396 oz. AGW, 13.9 mm.
Subject: St, Francis of Assisi **Obv:** Shield **Rev:** Multicolor bust
facing

Date	Mintage	F	VF	XF	Unc	BU
2008	—	—	—	—	—	80.00

KM# 161   DOLLAR
0.5000 g., 0.9990 Gold 0.0161 oz. AGW, 11 mm.   **Obv:** Shield
Rev: Multicolor poppy **Shape:** Irregular

Date	Mintage	F	VF	XF	Unc	BU
2008	—	—	—	—	—	50.00

KM# 162   DOLLAR
0.5000 g., 0.9990 Gold 0.0161 oz. AGW   **Subject:** Everlasting
love **Obv:** Shield **Rev:** Heart **Shape:** Heart

Date	Mintage	F	VF	XF	Unc	BU
2008	—	—	—	—	—	50.00

KM# 163   DOLLAR
1.2440 g., 0.9990 Gold 0.0400 oz. AGW   **Subject:** Marine Life-
Protection **Obv:** Neptune and mermaid seated on rock **Rev:** Grey
reef shark

Date	Mintage	F	VF	XF	Unc	BU
2008 Proof	1,500	Value: 80.00				

KM# 164   DOLLAR
26.8000 g., Copper-Nickel, 37.2 mm.   **Subject:** Endangered
Wildlife **Obv:** Shield **Rev:** Multicolor Tiger shark

Date	Mintage	F	VF	XF	Unc	BU
2008	—	—	—	—	—	30.00

KM# 165   DOLLAR
26.8000 g., Copper-Nickel, 37.2 mm.   **Subject:** Endangered
Wildlife **Obv:** Shield **Rev:** Multicolor Hawksbill turtle

Date	Mintage	F	VF	XF	Unc	BU
2008	—	—	—	—	—	30.00

KM# 166   DOLLAR
26.8000 g., Copper-Nickel, 37.2 mm.   **Subject:** Endangered
Wildlife **Obv:** Shield **Rev:** Multicolored Regal angelfish swimming
right

Date	Mintage	F	VF	XF	Unc	BU
2008 Proof	—	Value: 20.00				

KM# 167 DOLLAR
26.8000 g., Copper-Nickel, 37.2 mm. **Subject:** Endangered
Wildlife **Obv:** Shield **Rev:** Multicolor Spiny lobster

Date	Mintage	F	VF	XF	Unc	BU
2008 Proof	—				Value: 20.00	

KM# 259 DOLLAR
0.5000 g., 0.9990 Gold 0.0161 oz. AGW, 11 mm.
Subject: Sitting bull **Obv:** Shield **Rev:** Portrait facing

Date	Mintage	F	VF	XF	Unc	BU
2008 Proof	—				Value: 60.00	

KM# 177 DOLLAR
1.2440 g., 0.9990 Gold 0.0400 oz. AGW, 13.9 mm. **Obv:** Shield
Rev: Madonna and child

Date	Mintage	F	VF	XF	Unc	BU
ND(2009) Proof	25,000				Value: 80.00	

KM# 178 DOLLAR
1.2440 g., 0.9990 Gold 0.0400 oz. AGW, 13.9 mm.
Subject: FIAA World Cup - South Africa **Obv:** Shield **Rev:** Soccer
ball, South African flag and Water Buffalo

Date	Mintage	F	VF	XF	Unc	BU
2009 Proof	—				Value: 75.00	

KM# 222 DOLLAR
27.0000 g., Silver Plated Copper, 38.6 mm. **Rev:** Lighthouse of
Alexandria, multicolor

Date	Mintage	F	VF	XF	Unc	BU
2009 Prooflike	5,000	—	—	—	—	20.00

KM# 223 DOLLAR
27.0000 g., Silver Plated Copper, 38.6 mm. **Rev:** Zeus statue,
multicolor

Date	Mintage	F	VF	XF	Unc	BU
2009 Prooflike	—	—	—	—	—	20.00

KM# 224 DOLLAR
27.0000 g., Silver Plated Copper, 38.6 mm. **Rev:** Hanging
Garden of Babylon, multicolor

Date	Mintage	F	VF	XF	Unc	BU
2009 Prooflike	5,000	—	—	—	—	20.00

KM# 225 DOLLAR
27.0000 g., Silver Plated Copper, 38.6 mm. **Rev:** Mausoleum,
multicolor

Date	Mintage	F	VF	XF	Unc	BU
2009 Prooflike	5,000	—	—	—	—	20.00

KM# 226 DOLLAR
27.0000 g., Silver Plated Copper, 38.6 mm. **Rev:** Pyramids,
multicolor

Date	Mintage	F	VF	XF	Unc	BU
2009 Prooflike	5,000	—	—	—	—	20.00

KM# 227 DOLLAR
27.0000 g., Silver Plated Copper, 38.6 mm. **Rev:** Artemis
temple, multicolor

Date	Mintage	F	VF	XF	Unc	BU
2009 Prooflike	5,000	—	—	—	—	20.00

KM# 228 DOLLAR
27.0000 g., Silver Plated Copper, 38.6 mm. **Rev:** Colosus of
Rhodes, multicolor

Date	Mintage	F	VF	XF	Unc	BU
2009 Prooflike	5,000	—	—	—	—	20.00

KM# 229 DOLLAR
27.0000 g., Silver Plated Copper, 38.6 mm. **Subject:** Dugatti -
Casey Stoner **Rev:** Motorcycle left, multicolor

Date	Mintage	F	VF	XF	Unc	BU
2009 Prooflike	2,008	—	—	—	—	25.00

KM# 230 DOLLAR
27.0000 g., Silver Plated Copper, 38.6 mm. **Subject:** Dugatti -
Troy Bayliss **Rev:** Motorcycle, multicolor

Date	Mintage	F	VF	XF	Unc	BU
2009 Prooflike	2,008	—	—	—	—	25.00

KM# 233 DOLLAR
27.0000 g., Copper-Nickel, 38.6 mm. **Subject:** Marine Life
Protection **Obv:** Neptune standing, two mermaids below
Rev: Lionfish, multicolor

Date	Mintage	F	VF	XF	Unc	BU
2009 Prooflike	5,000	—	—	—	—	25.00

KM# 234 DOLLAR
1.0000 g., 0.9990 Gold 0.0321 oz. AGW, 13.9 mm.
Subject: Marine Life Protection **Rev:** Lionfish

Date	Mintage	F	VF	XF	Unc	BU
2009 Proof	25,000				Value: 65.00	

KM# 235 DOLLAR
0.5000 g., 0.9990 Gold 0.0161 oz. AGW, 11.8 mm.
Subject: Augustus Aureus **Rev:** Head laureate right

Date	Mintage	F	VF	XF	Unc	BU
MMIX (2009)	15,000	—	—	—	—	30.00

KM# 236 DOLLAR
0.5000 g., 0.9990 Gold 0.0161 oz. AGW, 11.8 mm.
Subject: Germanicus Dupondius **Rev:** General in quadriga right

Date	Mintage	F	VF	XF	Unc	BU
MMIX (2009)	15,000	—	—	—	—	30.00

KM# 237 DOLLAR
0.5000 g., 0.9990 Gold 0.0161 oz. AGW, 11.8 mm.
Subject: Julius Caesar Denarius **Rev:** Head laureate right

Date	Mintage	F	VF	XF	Unc	BU
MMIX (2009)	15,000	—	—	—	—	30.00

KM# 238 DOLLAR
0.5000 g., 0.9990 Gold 0.0161 oz. AGW, 11.8 mm.
Subject: Brutus Denarius **Rev:** Cap flanked by two daggers

Date	Mintage	F	VF	XF	Unc	BU
MMIX (2009)	15,000	—	—	—	—	30.00

KM# 239 DOLLAR
1.2400 g., 0.9990 Gold 0.0398 oz. AGW, 13.9 mm. **Subject:**
Salesian Order, 150th Anniversary **Rev:** Don Bosco facing

Date	Mintage	F	VF	XF	Unc	BU
2009 Proof	15,000				Value: 65.00	

KM# 240 DOLLAR
0.5000 g., 0.9990 Gold 0.0161 oz. AGW, 11 mm. **Rev:** Pebbled
Shape: 5-pointed star

Date	Mintage	F	VF	XF	Unc	BU
ND (2009)	25,000	—	—	—	—	30.00

KM# 241 DOLLAR
1.2400 g., 0.9990 Gold 0.0398 oz. AGW, 13.9 mm.
Subject: Fontana de Trevi **Rev:** Fountain and building facade

Date	Mintage	F	VF	XF	Unc	BU
2009 Proof	15,000					65.00

KM# 244 DOLLAR
0.5000 g., 0.9990 Gold 0.0161 oz. AGW, 11.8 mm.
Subject: First didrachm **Rev:** Twins sucking at she-wolf

Date	Mintage	F	VF	XF	Unc	BU
MMIX (2009)	15,000	—	—	—	—	30.00

KM# 245 DOLLAR
0.5000 g., 0.9990 Gold 0.0161 oz. AGW, 11.8 mm.
Subject: Claudius aureus **Rev:** Head laureate right

Date	Mintage	F	VF	XF	Unc	BU
MMIX (2009)	15,000	—	—	—	—	30.00

KM# 246 DOLLAR
0.5000 g., 0.9990 Gold 0.0161 oz. AGW, 11.8 mm.
Subject: Tiberius aureus **Rev:** Head laureate right

Date	Mintage	F	VF	XF	Unc	BU
MMIX (2009)	15,000	—	—	—	—	30.00

KM# 247 DOLLAR
0.5000 g., 0.9990 Gold 0.0161 oz. AGW, 11.8 mm.
Subject: Caligula aureus **Rev:** Head laureate right

Date	Mintage	F	VF	XF	Unc	BU
MMIX (2009)	15,000	—	—	—	—	30.00

KM# 260 DOLLAR
Silver Plated Copper **Subject:** 2000th Anniversary Teutobury
Forest Battle **Obv:** Shield **Rev:** Warrior in forest battle, multicolor

Date	Mintage	F	VF	XF	Unc	BU
MMIX (2009) Proof	2,500				Value: 30.00	

KM# 261 DOLLAR
25.0000 g., 0.9990 Silver 0.8029 oz. ASW, 38.6 mm.
Subject: Pacific Wildlife **Obv:** Arms **Rev:** Barn Swallow - prism

Date	Mintage	F	VF	XF	Unc	BU
2009 Proof	2,500				Value: 35.00	

KM# 262 DOLLAR
25.0000 g., 0.9990 Silver 0.8029 oz. ASW, 38.6 mm.
Subject: Pacific Wildlife **Obv:** Arms **Rev:** Gecko on rock - prism

Date	Mintage	F	VF	XF	Unc	BU
2009 Proof	2,500				Value: 35.00	

KM# 263 DOLLAR
0.5000 g., 0.9990 Gold 0.0161 oz. AGW, 11 mm. **Rev:** 4-leaf
clover, green

Date	Mintage	F	VF	XF	Unc	BU
2009	—	—	—	—	—	65.00

KM# 266 DOLLAR
25.0000 g., 0.9250 Silver 0.7435 oz. ASW **Subject:** Battle of
Grimwald **Rev:** Vyautas and Jagiello busts **Shape:** Square

Date	Mintage	F	VF	XF	Unc	BU
2010 Proof	—				Value: 40.00	

KM# 267 DOLLAR
25.0000 g., 0.9990 Silver 0.8029 oz. ASW **Subject:** Battle of
Grimwald **Rev:** Warrior on horseback, multicolor **Shape:** Square

Date	Mintage	F	VF	XF	Unc	BU
2010 Proof	2,500				Value: 40.00	

KM# 268 DOLLAR
25.0000 g., 0.9990 Silver 0.8029 oz. ASW **Subject:** Battle of
Grimwald **Rev:** Knight kneeling, multicolor **Shape:** Square

Date	Mintage	F	VF	XF	Unc	BU
2010 Proof	2,500				Value: 40.00	

KM# 130 2 DOLLARS
10.0000 g., 0.9990 Silver 0.3212 oz. ASW, 30.0 mm.
Obv: Shield with Neptune holding trident, mermaid reclining at
his side **Obv. Legend:** REPUBLIC OF PALAU **Rev:** Red racing
car 3/4 right **Rev. Legend:** FERRARI - 60 YEARS
ANNIVERSARY

Date	Mintage	F	VF	XF	Unc	BU
ND(2007) Proof	2,500				Value: 55.00	

KM# 131 2 DOLLARS
10.0000 g., 0.9990 Silver 0.3212 oz. ASW, 30.0 mm.
Obv: Shield with Neptune holding trident, mermaid reclining at
his side **Obv. Legend:** REPUBLIC OF PALAU **Rev:** Red racing
car 3/4 right **Rev. Legend:** FERRARI - 60 YEARS
ANNIVERSARY

Date	Mintage	F	VF	XF	Unc	BU
ND(2007) Proof	2,500				Value: 55.00	

KM# 132 2 DOLLARS
10.0000 g., 0.9990 Silver 0.3212 oz. ASW, 30.00 mm.
Obv: Shield with Neptune holding trident, mermaid reclining at
his side **Obv. Legend:** REPUBLIC OF PALAU **Rev:** Red racing
car front view **Rev. Legend:** FERRARI - 60 YEARS
ANNIVERSARY

Date	Mintage	F	VF	XF	Unc	BU
ND(2007) Proof	2,500				Value: 55.00	

KM# 133 2 DOLLARS
10.0000 g., 0.9990 Silver 0.3212 oz. ASW, 30.0 mm.
Obv: Shield with Neptune holding trident, mermaid reclining at
his side **Obv. Legend:** REPUBLIC OF PALAU **Rev:** Looking
down on red racing car approaching in turn **Rev. Legend:**
FERRARI - 60 YEARS ANNIVERSARY

Date	Mintage	F	VF	XF	Unc	BU
ND(2007) Proof	2,500				Value: 55.00	

KM# 134 2 DOLLARS
10.0000 g., 0.9990 Silver 0.3212 oz. ASW, 30.0 mm. **Obv:**
Shield with Neptune holding trident, reclining mermaid at his side
Obv. Legend: REPUBLIC OF PALAU **Rev:** Front view of red
racing car **Rev. Legend:** FERRARI - 60 YEARS ANNIVERSARY

Date	Mintage	F	VF	XF	Unc	BU
ND(2007) Proof	2,500				Value: 55.00	

KM# 135 2 DOLLARS
10.0000 g., 0.9990 Silver 0.3212 oz. ASW, 30.0 mm. **Obv:**
Shield with Neptune holding trident, mermaid reclining at his side
Obv. Legend: REPUBLIC OF PALAU **Rev:** Red racing car
approaching 3/4 right **Rev. Legend:** FERRARI - 60 YEARS
ANNIVERSARY

Date	Mintage	F	VF	XF	Unc	BU
ND(2007) Proof	2,500				Value: 55.00	

KM# 53 5 DOLLARS
25.0000 g., 0.9000 Silver 0.7234 oz. ASW, 37.2 mm.
Series: Marine Life Protection **Obv:** Neptune **Rev:** Multicolor
jellyfish **Edge:** Reeded

Date	Mintage	F	VF	XF	Unc	BU
2001 Proof	—				Value: 75.00	

KM# 75 5 DOLLARS
25.0000 g., 0.9000 Silver 0.7234 oz. ASW, 37.2 mm.
Subject: Marine Life Protection **Obv:** Neptune behind
Polynesian ship and value **Rev:** Moorish-Idol fish **Edge:** Reeded

Date	Mintage	F	VF	XF	Unc	BU
2001 Proof	—				Value: 75.00	

KM# 76 5 DOLLARS
Silver, 37.2 mm. **Subject:** Marine Life Protection **Obv:** Neptune riding seahorse and value **Rev:** Fish **Edge:** Reeded

Date	Mintage	F	VF	XF	Unc	BU
2001 Proof	—	Value: 75.00				

KM# 115 5 DOLLARS
25.0000 g., 0.9000 Silver 0.7234 oz. ASW, 37.2 mm.
Subject: Marine Life Protection **Obv:** Neptune waist deep in water above value with mermaid to the left and behind **Rev:** Multicolor iridescent fish scene **Edge:** Reeded

Date	Mintage	F	VF	XF	Unc	BU
2001 Proof	—	Value: 70.00				

KM# 77 5 DOLLARS
25.0000 g., 0.9000 Silver 0.7234 oz. ASW, 37.2 mm.
Subject: Marine Life Protection **Obv:** Neptune in shell boat **Rev:** Blue Tang Fish **Edge:** Reeded

Date	Mintage	F	VF	XF	Unc	BU
2002 Proof	—	Value: 75.00				

KM# 78 5 DOLLARS
25.0000 g., 0.9000 Silver 0.7234 oz. ASW, 37.2 mm.
Subject: Marine Life Protection **Obv:** Neptune in sea chariot **Rev:** Multicolor whales **Edge:** Reeded

Date	Mintage	F	VF	XF	Unc	BU
2002 Proof	—	Value: 75.00				

KM# 79 5 DOLLARS
25.0000 g., 0.9000 Silver 0.7234 oz. ASW, 37.2 mm.
Subject: Marine Life Protection **Obv:** Zeus and value **Rev:** Multicolor puffer fish **Edge:** Reeded

Date	Mintage	F	VF	XF	Unc	BU
2002 Proof	—	Value: 75.00				

KM# 80 5 DOLLARS
25.0000 g., 0.9000 Silver 0.7234 oz. ASW, 37.2 mm.
Subject: Marine Life Protection **Obv:** Neptune standing behind Polynesian ship **Rev:** Multicolor Jellyfish **Edge:** Reeded

Date	Mintage	F	VF	XF	Unc	BU
2002 Proof	—	Value: 70.00				

KM# 102 5 DOLLARS
25.0000 g., 0.9000 Silver 0.7234 oz. ASW, 32 mm.
Subject: Marine Life Protection **Obv:** Neptune in sea chariot with two merhorses **Rev:** Two multicolor reflective fish

Date	Mintage	F	VF	XF	Unc	BU
2002 Proof	—	Value: 60.00				

KM# 103 5 DOLLARS
25.0000 g., 0.9000 Silver 0.7234 oz. ASW, 32 mm.
Subject: Marine Life Protection **Obv:** Neptune standing in waves **Rev:** Multicolor starfish

Date	Mintage	F	VF	XF	Unc	BU
2003 Proof	—	Value: 60.00				

KM# 104 5 DOLLARS
25.0000 g., 0.9000 Silver 0.7234 oz. ASW, 32 mm.
Subject: Marine Life Protection **Obv:** Neptune standing in sea chariot **Rev:** Two multicolor reflective fish

Date	Mintage	F	VF	XF	Unc	BU
2003 Proof	—	Value: 60.00				

KM# 105 5 DOLLARS
25.0000 g., 0.9000 Silver 0.7234 oz. ASW, 32 mm.
Subject: Marine Life Protection **Rev:** Multicolor Orca

Date	Mintage	F	VF	XF	Unc	BU
2003 Proof	—	Value: 60.00				

KM# 106 5 DOLLARS
25.0000 g., 0.9000 Silver 0.7234 oz. ASW, 32 mm.
Subject: Marine Life Protection **Obv:** Neptune in sea chariot **Rev:** Multicolor Napoleon Fish

Date	Mintage	F	VF	XF	Unc	BU
2003 Proof	—	Value: 60.00				

KM# 107 5 DOLLARS
25.0000 g., 0.9000 Silver 0.7234 oz. ASW, 32 mm.
Subject: Marine Life Protection **Obv:** Neptune seated behind mermaid **Rev:** Multicolor school of sweetlips fish

Date	Mintage	F	VF	XF	Unc	BU
2004 Proof	—	Value: 60.00				

KM# 108 5 DOLLARS
25.0000 g., 0.9000 Silver 0.7234 oz. ASW, 32 mm.
Subject: Marine Life Protection **Obv:** Standing Neptune and ship **Rev:** Multicolor Porcupine fish

Date	Mintage	F	VF	XF	Unc	BU
2004 Proof	—	Value: 75.00				

KM# 109 5 DOLLARS
25.0000 g., 0.9000 Silver 0.7234 oz. ASW, 32 mm.
Subject: Marine Life Protection **Obv:** Neptune in sea chariot **Rev:** Multicolor Loggerhead turtle

Date	Mintage	F	VF	XF	Unc	BU
2004 Proof	—	Value: 75.00				

KM# 110 5 DOLLARS
25.0000 g., 0.9000 Silver 0.7234 oz. ASW, 32 mm.
Subject: Marine Life Protection **Obv:** Neptune and merhorse **Rev:** Multicolor dolphin head

Date	Mintage	F	VF	XF	Unc	BU
2004 Proof	—	Value: 75.00				

KM# 81 5 DOLLARS
25.0000 g., 0.9000 Silver 0.7234 oz. ASW, 37.2 mm.
Subject: Marine Life Protection **Obv:** Neptune with treasure chest **Rev:** Clownfish **Edge:** Reeded

Date	Mintage	F	VF	XF	Unc	BU
2004 Proof	—	Value: 75.00				

KM# 111 5 DOLLARS
25.0000 g., 0.9000 Silver 0.7234 oz. ASW, 32 mm.
Subject: Marine Life Protection **Obv:** Neptune flanked by mermaids **Rev:** Multicolor sea horse

Date	Mintage	F	VF	XF	Unc	BU
2005 Proof	—	Value: 75.00				

KM# 113 5 DOLLARS
25.0000 g., 0.9000 Silver 0.7234 oz. ASW, 32 mm.
Subject: Marine Life Protection **Obv:** Neptune flanked by mermaids **Rev:** Multicolor fish with ring-like stripes **Edge:** Reeded

Date	Mintage	F	VF	XF	Unc	BU
2005 Proof	—	Value: 75.00				

KM# 114 5 DOLLARS
25.0000 g., 0.9000 Silver 0.7234 oz. ASW, 32 mm. **Subject:** Marine Life Protection **Obv:** Neptune in shell boat talking to a dolphin **Rev:** Multicolor reef fish scene **Edge:** Reeded

Date	Mintage	F	VF	XF	Unc	BU
2006 Proof	—	Value: 75.00				

KM# 143 5 DOLLARS
25.0000 g., 0.9250 Silver with meteorite insert. 0.7435 oz. ASW
Subject: Nantan Meteorite fall, May 1516 **Obv:** Shield
Rev: Farmer and oxen plowing field, meteorite insert

Date	Mintage	F	VF	XF	Unc	BU
2006 Proof	2,500	Value: 75.00				

KM# 185 5 DOLLARS
24.8500 g., 0.9990 Silver 0.7981 oz. ASW, 38.61 mm.
Rev: Black pearl oyster

Date	Mintage	F	VF	XF	Unc	BU
2006 Proof	2,500	Value: 300				

KM# 186 5 DOLLARS
25.0000 g., 0.9990 Silver 0.8029 oz. ASW, 38.61 mm.
Subject: Pacific Wildlife **Rev:** Rainbow Lorikeet head left

Date	Mintage	F	VF	XF	Unc	BU
2006 Proof	5,000	Value: 50.00				

KM# 187 5 DOLLARS
25.0000 g., 0.9990 Silver 0.8029 oz. ASW, 38.61 mm.
Subject: Pacific Wildlife **Rev:** Eclectus Parrot head right

Date	Mintage	F	VF	XF	Unc	BU
2006 Proof	5,000	Value: 50.00				

KM# 188 5 DOLLARS
25.0000 g., 0.9990 Silver 0.8029 oz. ASW, 38.61 mm.
Subject: Pacific Wildlife **Rev:** Fruit dove head right

Date	Mintage	F	VF	XF	Unc	BU
2006 Proof	5,000	Value: 50.00				

KM# 189 5 DOLLARS
31.1050 g., 0.9990 Silver 0.9990 oz. ASW, 38.61 mm.
Subject: One ounce of luck **Rev:** Four-leaf clover

Date	Mintage	F	VF	XF	Unc	BU
2006 Proof	5,000	Value: 50.00				

KM# 190 5 DOLLARS
25.0000 g., 0.9250 Silver 0.7435 oz. ASW, 38.61 mm. **Subject:** Dream Island **Rev:** Pacific island scene - beach, boat and sunset

Date	Mintage	F	VF	XF	Unc	BU
2006 Proof	5,000	Value: 50.00				

KM# 151 5 DOLLARS
25.0000 g., 0.9250 Silver 0.7435 oz. ASW, 38.6 mm. **Subject:** Pacific Wildlife **Obv:** Shield **Rev:** Multicolor nautilus shell

Date	Mintage	F	VF	XF	Unc	BU
2007 Proof	—	Value: 70.00				

KM# 152 5 DOLLARS
25.0000 g., 0.9250 Silver 0.7435 oz. ASW **Subject:** Pacific Wildlife **Obv:** Shield **Rev:** Multicolor starfish

Date	Mintage	F	VF	XF	Unc	BU
2007 Proof	—	Value: 70.00				

KM# 153   5 DOLLARS
25.0000 g., 0.9250 Silver 0.7435 oz. ASW   **Subject:** Good heavens! **Obv:** Multicolor devil and angel child **Shape:** Heart

Date	Mintage	F	VF	XF	Unc	BU
2007 Proof	2,500	Value: 65.00				

KM# 119   5 DOLLARS
25.0000 g., 0.9000 Silver 0.7234 oz. ASW, 38.61 mm. **Series:** Marine Life Protection **Obv:** Neptune reclining with trident, mermaid at his side **Obv. Legend:** REPUBLIC OF PALAU **Rev:** Multicolor Doctor Fish

Date	Mintage	F	VF	XF	Unc	BU
2007 Proof	1,500	Value: 120				

KM# 122   5 DOLLARS
25.0000 g., 0.5000 Silver 0.4019 oz. ASW, 38.61 mm. **Obv:** Shield with Neptune holding trident, mermaid reclining at his side, RAINBOW'S / End below **Obv. Legend:** REPUBLIC OF PALAU **Rev:** Red racing car 3/4 right **Rev. Legend:** FERRARI - 60 YEARS ANNIVERSARY

Date	Mintage	F	VF	XF	Unc	BU
ND(2007) Proof	2,500	Value: 75.00				

KM# 136   5 DOLLARS
25.0000 g., 0.9250 Silver 0.7435 oz. ASW   **Series:** Pacific Wildlife **Obv:** National arms **Obv. Legend:** REPUBLIC OF PALAU **Rev:** Saltwater Crocodile with green crystal eye

Date	Mintage	F	VF	XF	Unc	BU
2007 Proof	2,500	Value: 75.00				

KM# 138   5 DOLLARS
24.7000 g., Silver, 38.6 mm.   **Series:** Marine Life Protection **Obv:** National arms with Neptune and mermaid **Rev:** Pearl in oyster shell - multicolor **Edge:** Reeded

Date	Mintage	F	VF	XF	Unc	BU
2007 Proof	2,500	Value: 200				

KM# 137   5 DOLLARS
24.7000 g., 0.9250 Silver 0.7345 oz. ASW, 38.5 mm. **Obv:** Outrigger canoe above shield **Obv. Legend:** REPUBLIC OF PALAU **Rev:** Pearl in colorized shell **Rev. Legend:** MARINE LIFE PROTECTION / Pearl of the sea **Edge:** Reeded

Date	Mintage	F	VF	XF	Unc	BU
2008 Proof	2,500	Value: 125				

KM# 168   5 DOLLARS
25.0000 g., 0.9250 Silver 0.7435 oz. ASW, 30x45 mm. **Obv:** Shield **Rev:** Don Quiote in armor **Shape:** Vertical oval

Date	Mintage	F	VF	XF	Unc	BU
2008 Proof	—	Value: 70.00				

KM# 169   5 DOLLARS
25.0000 g., 0.9250 Silver 0.7435 oz. ASW   **Subject:** Pacific Wildlife **Obv:** Shield **Rev:** Multicolor hologram, blue butterfly (Papilio Pericles) **Shape:** 37.2

Date	Mintage	F	VF	XF	Unc	BU
2008 Proof	2,500	Value: 60.00				

KM# 170   5 DOLLARS
25.0000 g., 0.9250 Silver 0.7435 oz. ASW, 37.2 mm. **Subject:** Pacific Wildlife **Obv:** Shield **Rev:** Multicolor sulphur butterfly (Hebomoia Leucippe)

Date	Mintage	F	VF	XF	Unc	BU
2008 Proof	2,500	Value: 60.00				

KM# 171   5 DOLLARS
25.0000 g., 0.9250 Silver 0.7435 oz. ASW, 37.2 mm. **Subject:** Pacific Wildlife **Obv:** Shield **Rev:** Multicolor hologram, butterfly

Date	Mintage	F	VF	XF	Unc	BU
2008 Proof	2,500	Value: 70.00				

KM# 172   5 DOLLARS
25.0000 g., 0.9250 Silver 0.7435 oz. ASW, 38.6 mm. **Subject:** Telescope, 400th Anniversary **Obv:** Shield **Rev:** Hans Lippersheg, lens insert

Date	Mintage	F	VF	XF	Unc	BU
2008 Matte finish	1,608	—	—	—	—	70.00

KM# 173   5 DOLLARS
25.0000 g., 0.9250 Silver 0.7435 oz. ASW, 38.6 mm. **Subject:** Telescope, 400th Anniversary **Obv:** Shield **Rev:** The Hubble Telescope, lens insert

Date	Mintage	F	VF	XF	Unc	BU
2008 Matte finish	1,608	—	—	—	—	70.00

KM# 174   5 DOLLARS
Copper-Nickel, 38.6 mm.   **Subject:** Endangered Wildlife **Obv:** Shield **Rev:** Multicolor yellow fish

Date	Mintage	F	VF	XF	Unc	BU
2008 Proof	—	—	—	—	—	20.00

KM# 175   5 DOLLARS
25.0000 g., 0.9250 Silver 0.7435 oz. ASW, 38.6 mm. **Subject:** Everything for you **Obv:** Shield **Rev:** Multicolor, outstretched hand, ribbon above **Shape:** Heart

Date	Mintage	F	VF	XF	Unc	BU
2008 Proof	2,500	Value: 100				

KM# 192   5 DOLLARS
25.0000 g., 0.9250 Silver partially gilt 0.7435 oz. ASW, 30x45 mm.   **Subject:** Illusion Autum leaves **Rev:** Gilt leaf **Shape:** Oval

Date	Mintage	F	VF	XF	Unc	BU
2008 Proof	2,500	Value: 75.00				

KM# 179   5 DOLLARS
25.0000 g., 0.9250 Silver 0.7435 oz. ASW, 38.61 mm. **Subject:** Scent of Paradise **Obv:** Shield **Rev:** Multicolor open coconut, scented

Date	Mintage	F	VF	XF	Unc	BU
2009	2,500	—	—	—	—	65.00

KM# 180   5 DOLLARS
25.0000 g., 0.9250 Silver 0.7435 oz. ASW, 38.5 mm. **Subject:** Jewels of the Sea **Obv:** Shield **Rev:** Multicolor blue oyster with inset pearl

Date	Mintage	F	VF	XF	Unc	BU
2009 Proof	2,500	Value: 125				

KM# 181 5 DOLLARS
25.0000 g., 0.9250 Silver 0.7435 oz. ASW, 38.5 mm.
Subject: Louis Braile, 200th Anniversary of birth **Obv:** Shield
Rev: Portrait of Braile

Date	Mintage	F	VF	XF	Unc	BU
2009 Matte finish	2,500	—	—	—	—	45.00

KM# 182 5 DOLLARS
25.0000 g., 0.9250 Silver 0.7435 oz. ASW **Subject:** Missing you
Obv: Shield **Rev:** Two angels, multicolor, crystal insert
Shape: Heart

Date	Mintage	F	VF	XF	Unc	BU
2009 Proof	2,500	Value: 50.00				

KM# 196 5 DOLLARS
25.0000 g., 0.9250 Silver 0.7435 oz. ASW, 38.61 mm.
Subject: Pacific Wildlife **Rev:** Angelfish

Date	Mintage	F	VF	XF	Unc	BU
2009 Proof	2,500	Value: 45.00				

KM# 197 5 DOLLARS
25.0000 g., 0.9250 Silver 0.7435 oz. ASW, 38.61 mm.
Subject: Pacific Wildlife **Rev:** Barn Swallow

Date	Mintage	F	VF	XF	Unc	BU
2009 Proof	2,500	Value: 45.00				

KM# 198 5 DOLLARS
25.0000 g., 0.9250 Silver 0.7435 oz. ASW, 38.61 mm.
Subject: Pacific Wildlife **Rev:** Gecko

Date	Mintage	F	VF	XF	Unc	BU
2009 Proof	2,500	Value: 45.00				

KM# 199 5 DOLLARS
25.0000 g., 0.9250 Silver 0.7435 oz. ASW, 38.61 mm.
Subject: Exceptional Animals **Rev:** Bird of Paradise

Date	Mintage	F	VF	XF	Unc	BU
2009 Proof	2,500	Value: 60.00				

KM# 200 5 DOLLARS
25.0000 g., 0.9250 Silver 0.7435 oz. ASW, 38.61 mm.
Subject: Exceptional Animals **Rev:** Peacock

Date	Mintage	F	VF	XF	Unc	BU
2009 Proof	2,500	Value: 60.00				

KM# 201 5 DOLLARS
25.0000 g., 0.9250 Silver 0.7435 oz. ASW, 38.61 mm.
Subject: Marine Life Protection **Rev:** Lionfish

Date	Mintage	F	VF	XF	Unc	BU
2009 Proof	1,500	Value: 65.00				

KM# 202 5 DOLLARS
25.0000 g., 0.9990 Silver 0.8029 oz. ASW, 38.61 mm.
Subject: Fall of the Berlin Wall **Rev:** Brandenberg Gate, half with and half without wall

Date	Mintage	F	VF	XF	Unc	BU
2009 Proof	2,009	Value: 80.00				

KM# 203 5 DOLLARS
20.0000 g., 0.9250 Silver 0.5948 oz. ASW, 38.61 mm. **Rev:** Sail training vessel Pamir

Date	Mintage	F	VF	XF	Unc	BU
2009 Proof	2,500	Value: 50.00				

KM# 204 5 DOLLARS
25.0000 g., 0.9250 Silver 0.7435 oz. ASW, 38.61 mm.
Subject: Wonders of the Ancient World **Rev:** Lighthouse at Alexandria

Date	Mintage	F	VF	XF	Unc	BU
2009 Proof	2,500	Value: 65.00				

KM# 205 5 DOLLARS
25.0000 g., 0.9250 Silver 0.7435 oz. ASW **Subject:** Wonders of the Ancient World **Rev:** Statue of Zeus

Date	Mintage	F	VF	XF	Unc	BU
2009 Proof	2,500	Value: 65.00				

KM# 206 5 DOLLARS
25.0000 g., 0.9250 Silver 0.7435 oz. ASW, 38.61 mm.
Subject: Wonders of the Ancient World **Rev:** Hanging Gardens of Babylon

Date	Mintage	F	VF	XF	Unc	BU
2009 Proof	2,500	Value: 65.00				

KM# 207 5 DOLLARS
25.0000 g., 0.9250 Silver 0.7435 oz. ASW, 38.61 mm.
Subject: Wonders of the Ancient World **Rev:** Mausoleum of Halicarnassus

Date	Mintage	F	VF	XF	Unc	BU
2009 Proof	2,500	Value: 65.00				

KM# 208 5 DOLLARS
25.0000 g., 0.9250 Silver 0.7435 oz. ASW, 38.61 mm.
Subject: Wonders of the Ancient World **Rev:** Pyramids of Giza

Date	Mintage	F	VF	XF	Unc	BU
2009 Proof	2,500	Value: 65.00				

KM# 209 5 DOLLARS
25.0000 g., 0.9250 Silver 0.7435 oz. ASW, 38.61 mm.
Subject: Wonders of the Ancient World **Rev:** Temple of Artemis

Date	Mintage	F	VF	XF	Unc	BU
2009 Proof	2,500	Value: 65.00				

KM# 210 5 DOLLARS
25.0000 g., 0.9250 Silver 0.7435 oz. ASW, 38.61 mm.
Subject: Wonders of the Ancient World **Rev:** Colossus of Rhodes

Date	Mintage	F	VF	XF	Unc	BU
2009 Proof	2,500	Value: 65.00				

KM# 211 5 DOLLARS
25.0000 g., 0.9250 Silver 0.7435 oz. ASW, 38.6 mm.
Subject: Flora and Mountains of the Alps **Rev:** Zugspitze and blue flower

Date	Mintage	F	VF	XF	Unc	BU
2009 Proof	2,500	Value: 55.00				

KM# 212 5 DOLLARS
25.0000 g., 0.9250 Silver 0.7435 oz. ASW, 38.61 mm.
Subject: Flora and Mountains of the Alps **Rev:** Grossglockner and white flower

Date	Mintage	F	VF	XF	Unc	BU
2009 Proof	2,500	Value: 55.00				

KM# 213 5 DOLLARS
25.0000 g., 0.9250 Silver 0.7435 oz. ASW, 38.61 mm.
Subject: Flora and Mountains of the Alps **Rev:** Materhorn and pink flower

Date	Mintage	F	VF	XF	Unc	BU
2009 Proof	2,500	Value: 55.00				

KM# 214 5 DOLLARS
25.0000 g., 0.9250 Silver 0.7435 oz. ASW, 38.61 mm.
Subject: Flora and Mountains of the Alps **Rev:** Dachstein and purple flower

Date	Mintage	F	VF	XF	Unc	BU
2009 Proof	2,500	Value: 55.00				

KM# 215 5 DOLLARS
25.0000 g., 0.9250 Silver 0.7435 oz. ASW, 38.61 mm.
Subject: Flora and Mountains of the Alps **Rev:** Mont Blanc and orange flower

Date	Mintage	F	VF	XF	Unc	BU
2009 Proof	2,500	Value: 55.00				

KM# 216 5 DOLLARS
25.0000 g., 0.9250 Silver 0.7435 oz. ASW, 38.61 mm.
Subject: Flora and Mountains of the Alps **Rev:** Watzmann and purple flower

Date	Mintage	F	VF	XF	Unc	BU
2009 Proof	2,500	Value: 55.00				

KM# 217 5 DOLLARS
25.0000 g., 0.9250 Silver 0.7435 oz. ASW, 38.61 mm.
Subject: Flora and Mountains of the Alps **Rev:** Oetscher and yellow flower

Date	Mintage	F	VF	XF	Unc	BU
2009 Proof	2,500	Value: 55.00				

KM# 218 5 DOLLARS
25.0000 g., 0.9250 Silver 0.7435 oz. ASW, 38.61 mm.
Subject: Flora and Mountains of the Alps **Rev:** Piz Buin and pink flower

Date	Mintage	F	VF	XF	Unc	BU
2009 Proof	2,500	Value: 55.00				

KM# 242 5 DOLLARS
20.0000 g., 0.9250 Silver 0.5948 oz. ASW, 38.6 mm.
Subject: Finnish icebreaker Tarmo **Rev:** Ship left in ice pack

Date	Mintage	F	VF	XF	Unc	BU
2009 Proof	2,500	Value: 30.00				

KM# 264 5 DOLLARS
25.0000 g., 0.9250 Silver 0.7435 oz. ASW, 38.61 mm.
Subject: Treasures of the World - Emeralds **Rev:** Mule mine cart and emerald insert

Date	Mintage	F	VF	XF	Unc	BU
2009 Antique	2,000	Value: 50.00				

KM# 265 5 DOLLARS
25.0000 g., 0.9250 Silver 0.7435 oz. ASW, 38.6 mm. **Obv:** Arms **Rev:** Our Lady of the Gate of Dawn, partially gilt

Date	Mintage	F	VF	XF	Unc	BU
2009 Proof	1,000	Value: 50.00				

KM# 248 5 DOLLARS
25.0000 g., 0.9250 Silver 0.7435 oz. ASW, 38.6 mm.
Subject: Marine Life Protection **Rev:** Blue freshwater pearl set within multicolor shell

Date	Mintage	F	VF	XF	Unc	BU
2010 Proof	2,500	Value: 40.00				

KM# 249 5 DOLLARS
25.0000 g., 0.9250 Silver 0.7435 oz. ASW, 38.6 mm.
Subject: Scent of Paradise - Sea breeze fragrance **Rev:** Female surfboarder in multicolor wave

Date	Mintage	F	VF	XF	Unc	BU
2010	2,500	—	—	—	—	50.00

KM# 191 10 DOLLARS
62.2050 g., 0.9990 Silver 1.9979 oz. ASW, 50 mm.
Subject: Tiffany Art **Rev:** Renaissance doorway

Date	Mintage	F	VF	XF	Unc	BU
2007 Matte Proof	999	Value: 260				

KM# 193 10 DOLLARS
62.2100 g., 0.9990 Silver 1.9980 oz. ASW, 50 mm.
Subject: Tiffany Art **Rev:** Mannerism, staircase design

Date	Mintage	F	VF	XF	Unc	BU
2008 Matte Proof	999	Value: 225				

KM# 194 10 DOLLARS
62.2100 g., 0.9990 Silver 1.9980 oz. ASW, 42x42 mm.
Subject: WWII Battleships **Rev:** Japan's Yamato

Date	Mintage	F	VF	XF	Unc	BU
2008 Proof	1,000	Value: 300				

KM# 195 10 DOLLARS
62.2100 g., 0.9990 Silver 1.9980 oz. ASW, 42x42 mm.
Subject: WWII Battleships **Rev:** USS Missouri, gilt eagle above

Date	Mintage	F	VF	XF	Unc	BU
2008 Proof	1,000	Value: 175				

KM# 184 10 DOLLARS
62.2500 g., 0.9990 Silver 1.9993 oz. ASW, 42x42 mm.
Subject: WWII Battleships **Obv:** Shield **Rev:** Bismark, gilt Iron Cross above **Shape:** Square

Date	Mintage	F	VF	XF	Unc	BU
2009 Proof	—	Value: 175				

KM# 219 10 DOLLARS
62.2100 g., 0.9990 Silver 1.9980 oz. ASW, 50 mm.
Subject: Tiffany Art **Rev:** Baroque facade

Date	Mintage	F	VF	XF	Unc	BU
2009 Matte Proof	—	Value: 245				

KM# 220 10 DOLLARS
62.2100 g., 0.9990 Silver 1.9980 oz. ASW, 50 mm. **Rev:** Amber insert

Date	Mintage	F	VF	XF	Unc	BU
2009 Matte Proof	2,500	Value: 225				

KM# 221 10 DOLLARS
62.2100 g., 0.9990 Silver 1.9980 oz. ASW, 42x42 mm.
Subject: WWII Battleship **Rev:** Britians's HMS Prince of Wales, gilt Union Jack above

Date	Mintage	F	VF	XF	Unc	BU
2009 Proof	1,000	Value: 135				

KM# 250 10 DOLLARS
62.2000 g., 0.9990 Silver 1.9977 oz. ASW, 42x42 mm.
Subject: Russian Battleship Marat **Rev:** Battleship sailing left

Date	Mintage	F	VF	XF	Unc	BU
2010 Proof	1,000	Value: 60.00				

KM# 252 10 DOLLARS
64.2100 g., 0.9990 Silver 2.0622 oz. ASW, 50 mm.
Subject: Tiffany Art - Rococo **Obv:** Arms at lower right, glass insert **Rev:** Cherus at left, glass insert

Date	Mintage	F	VF	XF	Unc	BU
2010 Antique	999	—	—	—	—	75.00

KM# 176 20 DOLLARS
164.0000 g., 0.9990 Silver 5.2672 oz. ASW, 63 mm. **Obv:** Auto steering wheel **Rev:** Side sillouette of Corvette 206

Date	Mintage	F	VF	XF	Unc	BU
2008 Proof	—	Value: 125				

KM# 183　500 DOLLARS

77.7000 g., 0.9990 Gold 2.4955 oz. AGW, 42x42 mm.
Obv: Shield **Rev:** Battleship Bismark

Date	Mintage	F	VF	XF	Unc	BU
2009 Proof	77	Value: 3,250				

KM# 243　500 DOLLARS

77.7500 g., 0.9990 Gold 2.4971 oz. AGW, 42x42 mm.
Subject: H.M.S. Prince of Wales **Rev:** Battleship right, Royal Navy flag above

Date	Mintage	F	VF	XF	Unc	BU
2009 Proof	77	Value: 3,250				

KM# 251　500 DOLLARS

77.7500 g., 0.9990 Gold 2.4971 oz. AGW, 42x42 mm.
Subject: Battleship Marat **Rev:** Battleship sailing left

Date	Mintage	F	VF	XF	Unc	BU
2010 Proof	77	Value: 3,250				

PROOF SETS

KM#	Date	Mintage	Identification	Issue Price	Mkt Val
PS4	2007 (6)	2,500	KM#130-135	—	350

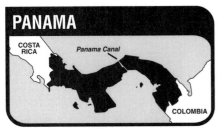

PANAMA

The Republic of Panama, a Central American country situated between Costa Rica and Colombia, has an area of 29,762 sq. mi. (78,200 sq. km.) and a population of *2.4 million. Capital: Panama City. The Panama Canal is the country's biggest asset; servicing world related transit trade and international commerce. Bananas, refined petroleum, sugar and shrimp are exported.

MONETARY SYSTEM
100 Centesimos = 1 Balboa

REPUBLIC

DECIMAL COINAGE

KM# 125　CENTESIMO

2.4400 g., Copper Plated Zinc, 18.96 mm. **Obv:** Written value **Obv. Legend:** REPUBLICA DE PANAMA **Rev:** Native Urraca bust left **Edge:** Plain

Date	Mintage	F	VF	XF	Unc	BU
2001RCM	160,000,000	—	—	—	0.15	0.35

KM# 133　5 CENTESIMOS

5.0000 g., Copper-Nickel, 21.15 mm. **Subject:** Sara Sotillo **Obv:** National coat of arms **Obv. Legend:** REPUBLICA DE PANAMA **Rev:** Head of Sotillo 3/4 right **Edge:** Plain

Date	Mintage	F	VF	XF	Unc	BU
2001RCM	8,000,000	—	—	0.10	0.30	0.50

KM# 127　1/10 BALBOA

2.2800 g., Copper-Nickel Clad Copper, 17.9 mm. **Obv:** National coat of arms **Obv. Legend:** REPUBLICA DE PANAMA **Rev:** Armored bust of Balboa left **Edge:** Reeded

Date	Mintage	F	VF	XF	Unc	BU
2001RCM	15,000,000	—	—	0.15	0.45	0.60
2008RCM	28,000,000	—	—	0.15	0.25	0.50

KM# 135　25 CENTESIMOS

5.5600 g., Copper-Nickel Clad Copper, 24.2 mm. **Obv:** National coat of arms **Obv. Legend:** REPUBLICA DE PANAMA **Rev:** Tower and Spanish ruins **Edge:** Reeded **Note:** Released in 2004

Date	Mintage	F	VF	XF	Unc	BU
2003RCM Proof	2,000	Value: 20.00				
2003RCM	6,000,000	—	—	0.30	1.00	2.00

KM# 136　25 CENTESIMOS

5.6700 g., Copper-Nickel Clad Copper, 24 mm. **Obv:** National coat of arms **Obv. Legend:** REPUBLICA DE PANAMA **Rev:** King's Bridge **Rev. Legend:** Puente Del Rey **Edge:** Reeded

Date	Mintage	F	VF	XF	Unc	BU
2005RCM Proof	2,000	Value: 12.00				
2005RCM	6,000,000	—	—	—	1.50	2.00

KM# 128　1/4 BALBOA

5.6500 g., Copper-Nickel Clad Copper, 24.25 mm. **Obv:** National coat of arms **Subject:** 1/4 Balboa **Rev:** Armored bust of Balboa left **Edge:** Reeded

Date	Mintage	F	VF	XF	Unc	BU
2001RCM	12,000,000	—	—	0.35	0.75	1.25

KM# 137　1/4 BALBOA

Copper-Nickel Clad Copper, 24 mm. **Subject:** Breast Cancer Awareness **Obv:** National coat of arms **Obv. Legend:** REPUBLICA DE PANAMA **Rev:** Ribbon **Rev. Legend:** Protegete Mujer **Edge:** Reeded

Date	Mintage	F	VF	XF	Unc	BU
2008RCM	14,000,000	—	—	—	1.00	1.50

Note: Also available in a laminated Breast Cancer Awareness pink bookmark

KM# 137a　1/4 BALBOA

5.6700 g., Copper-Nickel Clad Copper, 24.26 mm. **Subject:** Breast Cancer Awareness **Obv:** National coat of arms **Obv. Legend:** REPUBLICA DE PANAMA **Rev:** Pink Ribbon **Rev. Legend:** Protegete Mujer **Edge:** Reeded

Date	Mintage	F	VF	XF	Unc	BU
2008RCM Proof, pink colored ribbon	2,500	Value: 100				

Note: Pink ribbon proof issued in red plush case with black cardboard sleeve with printed pink ribbon

KM# 138　1/4 BALBOA

Copper-Nickel Clad Copper, 24 mm. **Subject:** 50th Anniversary of the Children's Hospital **Obv:** National coat of arms **Obv. Legend:** REPUBLICA DE PANAMA **Rev:** Children's Hospital **Edge:** Reeded

Date	Mintage	F	VF	XF	Unc	BU
2008	6,000,000	—	—	—	1.50	2.00

KM# 138a　1/4 BALBOA

Copper-Nickel Clad Copper, 24.26 mm. **Subject:** 50th Anniversary of the Children's Hospital **Obv:** National coat of arms **Obv. Legend:** REPUBLICA DE PANAMA **Rev:** Children's Hospital **Edge:** Reeded

Date	Mintage	F	VF	XF	Unc	BU
2008RCM Proof	1,000	Value: 25.00				

KM# 139　50 CENTESIMOS

11.3400 g., Copper-Nickel Clad Copper, 30.6 mm. **Subject:** Centenary of the National Bank of Panama **Obv:** National coat of arms **Obv. Legend:** REPUBLICA DE PANAMA **Rev:** BNP Building - Banco National de Panama **Rev. Legend:** BANCO NACIONAL DE PANAMA CENTENARIO **Edge:** Reeded

Date	Mintage	F	VF	XF	Unc	BU
2009RCM	2,000,000	—	—	—	2.00	2.75

KM# 139a　50 CENTESIMOS

11.3400 g., Copper-Nickel Clad Copper, 30.61 mm. **Subject:** Centenary - National Bank of Panama **Obv:** National coat of arms **Obv. Legend:** REPUBLICA DE PANAMA **Rev:** BNP building - 1904-2004 **Rev. Legend:** BANCO NACIONAL DE PANAMA CENTENARIO **Edge:** Reeded

Date	Mintage	F	VF	XF	Unc	BU
2009RCM Proof	2,000	Value: 50.00				

KM# 129　1/2 BALBOA

11.3000 g., Copper-Nickel Clad Copper, 30.54 mm. **Obv:** National coat of arms **Obv. Legend:** REPUBLICA DE PANAMA **Rev:** Armored bust of Balboa left **Edge:** Reeded

Date	Mintage	F	VF	XF	Unc	BU
2001RCM	600,000	—	—	1.00	2.25	4.00
2008RCM	5,800,000	—	—	0.75	1.50	2.50

KM# 134　BALBOA

22.6800 g., Copper-Nickel, 38 mm. **Obv:** Bust of President Mireya Moscoso left, flanked by dates of her presidency **Rev:** Flag and canal scene **Edge:** Reeded

Date	Mintage	F	VF	XF	Unc	BU
2004RCM Proof	2,000	Value: 60.00				
2004RCM	348,000	—	—	1.30	3.25	10.00

PAPUA NEW GUINEA

Papua New Guinea occupies the eastern half of the island of New Guinea. It lies north of Australia near the equator and borders on West Irian. The country, which includes nearby Bismark archipelago, Buka and Bougainville, has an area of 178,260 sq. mi. (461,690 sq. km.) and a population of 3.7 million that is divided into more than 1,000 separate tribes, speaking more than 700 mutually unintelligible languages. Capital: Port Moresby. The economy is agricultural, and exports copra, rubber, cocoa, coffee, tea, gold and copper

Papua New Guinea is a member of the Commonwealth of Nations. Elizabeth II is Head of State, as Queen of Papua New Guinea.

CONSTITUTIONAL MONARCHY
Commonwealth of Nations
STANDARD COINAGE

100 Toea = 1 Kina

KM# 1   TOEA
2.0000 g., Bronze, 17.65 mm. **Obv:** National emblem
Obv. Designer: Richard Renninger **Rev:** Butterfly and value
Rev. Designer: Herman de Roos **Edge:** Plain

Date	Mintage	F	VF	XF	Unc	BU
2001	—	—	—	0.25	1.00	10.00
2002	—	—	—	0.15	1.00	10.00
2004	—	—	—	0.10	1.00	10.00

KM# 2   2 TOEA
4.1000 g., Bronze, 21.6 mm. **Obv:** National emblem
Obv. Designer: Richard Renninger **Rev:** Lion fish
Rev. Designer: William Shoyer **Edge:** Plain

Date	Mintage	F	VF	XF	Unc	BU
2001	—	—	—	0.30	0.75	12.00
2002	—	—	—	0.25	0.60	12.00
2004	—	—	—	0.15	0.45	12.00

KM# 3a   5 TOEA
2.5500 g., Nickel Plated Steel, 19.53 mm. **Obv:** National emblem **Rev:** Plateless turtle **Edge:** Reeded

Date	Mintage	F	VF	XF	Unc	BU
2002	—	—	—	0.50	1.25	2.50
2005	—	—	—	0.40	1.00	2.00

KM# 4   10 TOEA
5.6700 g., Copper-Nickel, 23.72 mm. **Obv:** National emblem
Obv. Designer: Richard Renninger **Rev:** Cuscus and value
Rev. Designer: Herman DeRoos **Edge:** Reeded

Date	Mintage	F	VF	XF	Unc	BU
2001	—	Value: 2.50					

KM# 4a   10 TOEA
5.1600 g., Nickel Plated Steel, 23.72 mm. **Obv:** National emblem **Rev:** Cuscus and value **Edge:** Reeded

Date	Mintage	F	VF	XF	Unc	BU
2002	—	—	—	0.80	2.00	3.00
2004	—	—	—	0.80	2.00	3.00
2006	—	—	—	0.60	1.50	2.50

KM# 5a   20 TOEA
10.1300 g., Nickel Plated Steel, 28.65 mm. **Obv:** National emblem **Rev:** Bennett's Cassowary and value **Edge:** Reeded

Date	Mintage	F	VF	XF	Unc	BU
2004	—	—	—	0.80	2.00	3.00
2005	—	—	—	0.80	2.00	3.00

KM# 6a   KINA
14.6100 g., Nickel Plated Steel, 33.28 mm. **Obv:** Native design **Obv. Designer:** Richard Renninger **Rev:** Two Salt Water Crocodiles **Rev. Designer:** William Shoyer **Edge:** Reeded

Date	Mintage	F	VF	XF	Unc	BU
2002	—	—	—	1.60	4.00	5.00
2004	—	—	—	1.40	3.50	4.50

KM# 6b   KINA
11.1300 g., Nickel Plated Steel, 30 mm. **Obv:** Native design **Obv. Designer:** Richard Renninger **Rev:** Two Salt Water Crocodiles **Rev. Designer:** William Shoyer **Edge:** Reeded

Date	Mintage	F	VF	XF	Unc	BU
2005	—	—	—	1.20	3.00	4.00

KM# 51   2 KINA
Bi-Metallic Brass center in Copper-Nickel ring **Subject:** 35th Anniversary **Obv:** Bird of Pariaise

Date	Mintage	F	VF	XF	Unc	BU
2008	—	—	—	—	—	5.00

PARAGUAY

The Republic of Paraguay, a landlocked country in the heart of South America surrounded by Argentina, Bolivia and Brazil, has an area of 157,048 sq. mi. (406,750 sq. km.) and a population of *4.5 million, 95 percent of whom are of mixed Spanish and Indian descent. Capital: Asuncion. The country is predominantly agrarian, with no important mineral deposits or oil reserves. Meat, timber, hides, oilseeds, tobacco and cotton account for 70 percent of Paraguay's export revenue.

During the Triple Alliance War (1864-1870) in which Paraguay faced Argentina, Brazil and Uruguay, Asuncion's ladies gathered in an Assembly on Feb. 24, 1867 and decided to give up their jewelry in order to help the national defense. The President of the Republic, Francisco Solano Lopez accepted the offering and ordered one twentieth of it be used to mint the first Paraguayan gold coins according to the Decree of the 11th of Sept.1867.

Two dies were made, one by Bouvet, and another by an American, Leonard Charles, while only the die made by Bouvet was eventually used.

MINT MARK
HF – LeLocle (Swiss)

REPUBLIC
REFORM COINAGE
100 Centimos = 1 Guarani

KM# 197   GUARANI
27.0000 g., 0.9250 Silver 0.8029 oz. ASW, 39.7 mm. **Subject:** 50th Anniversary of the Central Bank **Obv:** Naval gunship **Obv. Legend:** REPUBLICA DEL PARAGUAY **Obv. Inscription:** CAÑONERO PARAGUAY **Rev:** Bank building within circle **Rev. Legend:** BANCO CENTRAL DEL PARAGUAY **Edge:** Reeded

Date	Mintage	F	VF	XF	Unc	BU
2002 Proof	3,000	Value: 75.00					

KM# 199   GUARANI
26.8600 g., 0.9250 Silver 0.7988 oz. ASW, 40.03 mm.
Series: 5th Ibero-America **Subject:** Encounter of the Two Worlds **Obv:** National arms in center with ten national arms in outer circle **Obv. Legend:** REPUBLICA DEL PARAGUAY **Rev:** Native in canoe with outline of South America in background at left, early sailing ship at loewer right. **Rev. Legend:** ENCUENTRO DE DOS MUNDOS **Edge:** Reeded

Date	Mintage	F	VF	XF	Unc	BU
2002 Proof	—	Value: 42.50					

KM# 200   GUARANI
27.0000 g., 0.9250 Silver 0.8029 oz. ASW **Subject:** 60th Anniversary of Currency Reform **Obv:** National arms **Obv. Legend:** REPUBLICA DEL PARAGUAY **Rev:** Outline map of Paraguay **Edge:** Reeded

Date	Mintage	F	VF	XF	Unc	BU
2003 Proof	—	Value: 80.00					

KM# 201 GUARANI
26.9000 g., 0.9250 Silver 0.8000 oz. ASW, 40.04 mm.
Subject: FIFA - XVIII World Football Championship - Germany 2006 **Obv:** National arms **Obv. Legend:** REPUBLICA DEL PARAGUAY **Rev:** Two opponents after ball **Rev. Legend:** COPA MUNDIAL DE LA FIFA - ALEMANIA 2006 **Edge:** Reeded

Date	Mintage	F	VF	XF	Unc	BU
2003 Proof	50,000	Value: 60.00				

KM# 202 GUARANI
27.0000 g., 0.9250 Silver 0.8029 oz. ASW **Subject:** FIFA - XVIII World Football Championship - Germany 2006 **Obv:** National arms **Obv. Legend:** REPUBLICA DEL PARAGUAY **Rev:** Ball in goal **Edge:** Reeded

Date	Mintage	F	VF	XF	Unc	BU
2004 Proof	50,000	Value: 60.00				

KM# 204 GUARANI
27.0000 g., 0.9250 Silver 0.8029 oz. ASW **Series:** 6th Ibero-America **Subject:** Encounter of the Two Worlds **Obv:** National arms in center with ten national arms in outer circle **Obv. Legend:** REPUBLICA DEL PARAGUAY **Rev:** Church of the Most Holy, Trinidad in Yaguarón **Rev. Legend:** ENCUENTRO DE DOS MUNDOS - IGLESIA DE LA SANTISIMA TRINIDAD **Edge:** Reeded

Date	Mintage	F	VF	XF	Unc	BU
2005 Proof	—	Value: 50.00				

KM# 191a 50 GUARANIES
Brass Plated Steel **Obv:** Uniformed bust facing **Rev:** Value above river dam **Note:** Magnetic

Date	Mintage	F	VF	XF	Unc	BU
2005	10,000,000	—	—	—	0.75	1.00

KM# 191b 50 GUARANIES
1.0100 g., Aluminum, 18.98 mm. **Obv:** Bust of Major General J.F. Estigarribia facing **Obv. Legend:** REPUBLICA DEL PARAGUAY **Rev:** Acaray River Dam **Rev. Inscription:** REPRESA ACARAY **Edge:** Plain **Note:** Reduced size

Date	Mintage	F	VF	XF	Unc	BU
2006	25,000,000	—	—	—	1.00	2.00
2008	—	—	—	—	1.00	2.00

KM# 177a 100 GUARANIES
5.4500 g., Brass Plated Steel **Obv:** Bust of General Jose E. Dias facing **Obv. Legend:** REPUBLICA DEL PARAGUAY **Rev:** Ruins of Humaita **Rev. Inscription:** RUINAS DE HUMAITA 1865/70 **Note:** Reduced weight and thickness.

Date	Mintage	F	VF	XF	Unc	BU
2004	15,000,000	—	—	—	1.50	2.00
2005	10,000,000	—	—	—	1.50	2.00

KM# 177b 100 GUARANIES
3.6600 g., Nickel-Steel, 20.94 mm. **Obv:** Bust of General Jose E. Dias facing **Obv. Legend:** REPUBLICA DEL PARAGUAY **Rev:** Ruins of Humaita **Rev. Inscription:** RUINAS DE HUMAITA 1865/70 **Edge:** Plain

Date	Mintage	F	VF	XF	Unc	BU
2006	30,000,000	—	—	—	1.50	2.00
2007	25,000,000	—	—	—	1.50	2.00
2008	—	—	—	—	1.50	2.00

KM# 195 500 GUARANIES
7.8200 g., Brass Plated Steel **Obv:** Head of General Bernardino Caballero facing **Obv. Legend:** REPUBLICA DEL PARAGUAY **Rev:** Bank above value within circle **Rev. Legend:** BANCO CENTRAL DEL PARAGUAY

Date	Mintage	F	VF	XF	Unc	BU
2002	15,000,000	—	—	—	2.50	3.00
2005	5,000,000	—	—	—	2.50	3.00

KM# 195a 500 GUARANIES
4.8000 g., Nickel-Steel, 23 mm. **Obv:** Head of General Bernardino Caballero facing **Obv. Legend:** REPUBLICA DEL PARAGUAY **Rev:** Bank above value in circle **Rev. Legend:** BANCO CENTRAL DEL PARAGUAY **Edge:** Plain

Date	Mintage	F	VF	XF	Unc	BU
2006	12,000,000	—	—	—	2.00	2.50
2007	25,000,000	—	—	—	2.00	2.50
2008	—	—	—	—	2.00	2.50

KM# 198 MIL (1000) GUARANIES
6.0700 g., Nickel-Steel, 25 mm. **Obv:** Bust of Major General Francisco Solano Lopez facing **Obv. Legend:** REPUBLICA DEL PARAGUAY **Rev:** National Heroes Pantheon **Rev. Legend:** BANCO CENTRAL DEL PARAGUAY **Rev. Inscription:** PANTEON NACIONAL / DE LOS HEROES **Edge:** Plain

Date	Mintage	F	VF	XF	Unc	BU
2006	25,000,000	—	—	—	3.00	4.00
2007	35,000,000	—	—	—	3.00	4.00
2008	—	—	—	—	3.00	4.00

KM# 203 1500 GUARANIES
6.7000 g., 0.9990 Gold 0.2152 oz. AGW **Subject:** XVIII World Football Championship - Germany 2006 **Obv:** National arms **Obv. Legend:** REPUBLICA DEL PARAGUAY **Rev:** Ball in goal

Date	Mintage	F	VF	XF	Unc	BU
2004 Proof	25,000	Value: 450				

PERU

The Republic of Peru, located on the Pacific coast of South America, has an area of 496,225 sq. mi. (1,285,220sq. km.) and a population of *21.4 million. Capital: Lima. The diversified economy includes mining, fishing and agriculture. Fishmeal, copper, sugar, zinc and iron ore are exported.

MINT MARKS
L, LIMAE (monogram), Lima (monogram), LIMA = Lima

NOTE: The LIMAE monogram appears in three forms. The early LM monogram form looks like a dotted L with M. The later LIMAE monogram has all the letters of LIMAE more readily distinguishable. The third form appears as an M monogram during early Republican issues.

REPUBLIC
REFORM COINAGE
1/M Intis = 1 Nuevo Sol; 100 (New) Centimos = 1 Nuevo Sol

KM# 303.4 CENTIMO
1.8800 g., Brass, 15.9 mm. **Obv:** National arms, accent mark above "u" **Rev:** Without Braille dots, no Chavez **Edge:** Plain **Note:** LIMA monogram is mint mark.

Date	Mintage	F	VF	XF	Unc	BU
2001LIMA	—	—	—	—	0.25	0.40
2002LIMA	—	—	—	—	0.25	0.40
2004LIMA	—	—	—	—	0.25	0.40
2005LIMA	—	—	—	—	0.25	0.40
2006LIMA	—	—	—	—	0.25	0.40

KM# 303.4a CENTIMO
0.8300 g., Aluminum, 16 mm. **Obv:** National arms **Rev:** Value flanked by designs **Edge:** Plain **Note:** LIMA monogram is mint mark.

Date	Mintage	F	VF	XF	Unc	BU
2005LIMA	—	—	—	—	0.25	0.40
2006LIMA	—	—	—	—	0.50	0.75
2007LIMA	—	—	—	—	0.50	0.75
2008LIMA	—	—	—	—	0.50	0.75

KM# 304.4 5 CENTIMOS
2.6900 g., Brass, 18.01 mm. **Obv:** National arms, accent above "u" **Rev:** Without Braille dots, with accent above "e" **Edge:** Plain **Note:** LIMA monogram is mint mark.

Date	Mintage	F	VF	XF	Unc	BU
2001LIMA	—	—	—	—	0.35	0.50
2002LIMA	—	—	—	—	0.35	0.50
2005LIMA	—	—	—	—	0.35	0.50
2006LIMA	—	—	—	—	0.35	0.50

KM# 304.4a 5 CENTIMOS
1.0200 g., Aluminum, 18 mm. **Obv:** National arms **Edge:** Plain **Note:** LIMA monogram is mint mark.

Date	Mintage	F	VF	XF	Unc	BU
2007LIMA	—	—	—	—	0.50	0.75
2008LIMA	—	—	—	—	0.50	0.75

KM# 305.4 10 CENTIMOS
3.5000 g., Brass, 20.47 mm. **Obv:** National arms, accent above "u" **Rev:** Without braille dots, accent above "e" **Edge:** Plain **Note:** LIMA monogram is mint mark.

Date	Mintage	F	VF	XF	Unc	BU
2001LIMA	—	—	—	—	0.65	0.85
2002LIMA	—	—	—	—	0.65	0.85
2003LIMA	—	—	—	—	0.65	0.85
2004LIMA	—	—	—	—	0.65	0.85
2005LIMA	—	—	—	—	0.65	0.85
2006LIMA	—	—	—	—	0.65	0.85
2007LIMA	—	—	—	—	0.65	0.85
2008LIMA	—	—	—	—	0.65	0.85

KM# 306.4   20 CENTIMOS
4.5300 g., Brass, 23 mm. **Obv:** National arms, accent above "u"
Rev: Without braille dots, accent above "e" **Edge:** Plain
Note: LIMA monogram is mint mark.

Date	Mintage	F	VF	XF	Unc	BU
2001LIMA	—	—	—	—	0.85	1.20
2002LIMA	—	—	—	—	0.85	1.20
2004LIMA	—	—	—	—	0.85	1.20
2006LIMA	—	—	—	—	0.85	1.20
2007LIMA	—	—	—	—	0.85	1.20
2008LIMA	—	—	—	—	0.85	1.20

KM# 307.4   50 CENTIMOS
5.5200 g., Copper-Nickel, 22 mm. **Obv:** National arms, accent
above "u" **Rev:** Without braille, accent above "e" **Edge:** Reeded
Note: LIMA monogram is mint mark.

Date	Mintage	F	VF	XF	Unc	BU
2001LIMA	—	—	—	—	1.50	1.75
2002LIMA	—	—	—	—	1.50	1.75
2003LIMA	—	—	—	—	1.50	1.75
2004LIMA	—	—	—	—	1.50	1.75
2006LIMA	—	—	—	—	1.50	1.75
2007LIMA	—	—	—	—	1.50	1.75
2008LIMA	—	—	—	—	1.50	1.75

KM# 308.4   NUEVO SOL
7.3000 g., Copper-Nickel, 25.5 mm. **Obv:** National arms, accent
above "u" **Rev:** Without braille, accent above "e" **Edge:** Reeded
Note: LIMA monogram is mint mark.

Date	Mintage	F	VF	XF	Unc	BU
2001LIMA	—	—	—	—	2.50	3.00
2002LIMA	—	—	—	—	2.50	3.00
2003LIMA	—	—	—	—	2.50	3.00
2004LIMA	—	—	—	—	2.50	3.00
2005LIMA	—	—	—	—	2.50	3.00
2006LIMA	—	—	—	—	2.50	3.00
2007LIMA	—	—	—	—	2.50	3.00
2008LIMA	—	—	—	—	2.50	3.00

KM# 329   NUEVO SOL
33.6250 g., 0.9250 Silver 0.9999 oz. ASW, 37 mm.
Subject: 450th Anniversary - San Marcos University
Obv: National arms **Rev:** University seal and building
Edge: Reeded **Note:** LIMA monogram is mint mark.

Date	Mintage	F	VF	XF	Unc	BU
2001 Proof	—	Value: 55.00				

KM# 330   NUEVO SOL
33.6250 g., 0.9250 Silver 0.9999 oz. ASW, 37 mm.
Subject: 50th Anniversary - Numismatic Society of Peru
Obv: National arms **Rev:** Stylized design within circle
Edge: Reeded **Note:** LIMA monogram is mint mark.

Date	Mintage	F	VF	XF	Unc	BU
2001 Proof	—	Value: 45.00				

KM# 331   NUEVO SOL
33.6250 g., 0.9250 Silver 0.9999 oz. ASW, 37 mm.
Subject: 200th Anniversary - von Humboldt's visit to Peru
Obv: National arms **Rev:** Seated figure 1/4 left **Edge:** Reeded
Note: LIMA monogram is mint mark.

Date	Mintage	F	VF	XF	Unc	BU
2002 Proof	—	Value: 55.00				

KM# 334   NUEVO SOL
27.0800 g., 0.9250 Silver 0.8053 oz. ASW, 40 mm. **Series:** Fifth
Ibero-America **Obv:** National arms in center with ten national
arms in outer circle **Obv. Legend:** BANCO CENTRAL DE
RESERVA DEL PERÚ **Rev:** Ceramic - Indians in reed boats
Rev. Legend: PERÚ **Edge:** Reeded

Date	Mintage	F	VF	XF	Unc	BU
2002 Proof	—	Value: 60.00				

KM# 332   NUEVO SOL
33.6250 g., 0.9250 Silver 0.9999 oz. ASW, 37 mm.
Subject: 125th Anniversary of the Inmaculate Jesuitas - Lima
College **Obv:** National arms **Rev:** Statue and 3/4 crowned shield
Edge: Reeded **Note:** LIMA monogram is mint mark.

Date	Mintage	F	VF	XF	Unc	BU
2003 Proof	—	Value: 50.00				

KM# 333   NUEVO SOL
33.6250 g., 0.9250 Silver 0.9999 oz. ASW, 37 mm.
Subject: 180th Anniversary of Peru's Congress **Obv:** National
arms **Rev:** Statue in front of building **Edge:** Reeded **Note:** LIMA
monogram is mint mark.

Date	Mintage	F	VF	XF	Unc	BU
2003 Proof	—	Value: 55.00				

KM# 335   NUEVO SOL
Silver **Subject:** FIFA World Cup Soccer **Obv:** Arms within wreath
Rev: Action scene beneath globe **Edge:** Reeded

Date	Mintage	F	VF	XF	Unc	BU
2004 Proof	—	Value: 55.00				

KM# 339   NUEVO SOL
27.0000 g., 0.9250 Silver 0.8029 oz. ASW, 40 mm. **Series:** 6th
Ibero-America **Subject:** Lost city of the Incas **Obv:** National arms
in center with ten national arms in outer ring **Obv. Legend:**
BANCO CENTRAL DE RESERVA DEL PERÚ **Rev:** Village ruins
Rev. Legend: MACHU PICCHU . PERÚ **Edge:** Reeded

Date	Mintage	F	VF	XF	Unc	BU
2005 Proof	—	Value: 60.00				

KM# 313   2 NUEVOS SOLES
5.5800 g., Bi-Metallic Brass center in Steel ring, 22.22 mm.
Obv: National arms within circle **Rev:** Stylized bird in flight to left
of value within circle **Edge:** Plain **Note:** LIMA monogram is mint
mark.

Date	Mintage	F	VF	XF	Unc	BU
2002LIMA	—	—	—	—	4.50	5.00
2003LIMA	—	—	—	—	4.50	5.00
2004LIMA	—	—	—	—	4.50	5.00
2005LIMA	—	—	—	—	4.50	5.00
2006LIMA	—	—	—	—	4.50	5.00
2007LIMA	—	—	—	—	4.50	5.00
2008LIMA	—	—	—	—	4.50	5.00

KM# 316   5 NUEVOS SOLES
6.6700 g., Bi-Metallic Brass center in Steel ring, 24.27 mm.
Obv: National arms within circle **Rev:** Stylized bird in flight to left
of value within circle **Edge:** Plain **Note:** LIMA monogram is mint
mark.

Date	Mintage	F	VF	XF	Unc	BU
2001LIMA	—	—	—	—	6.50	7.00
2002LIMA	—	—	—	—	6.50	7.00
2004LIMA	—	—	—	—	6.50	7.00
2005LIMA	—	—	—	—	6.50	7.00
2006LIMA	—	—	—	—	6.50	7.00
2008LIMA	—	—	—	—	6.50	7.00

PHILIPPINES

The Republic of the Philippines, an archipelago in the western Pacific 500 miles (805 km.) from the southeast coast of Asia,
has an area of 115,830 sq. mi. (300,000 sq. km.) and a population
of *64.9 million. Capital: Manila. The economy of the 7,000-island
group is based on agriculture, forestry and fishing. Timber, coconut products, sugar and hemp are exported.

MINT MARKS
BSP - Bangko Sentral Pilipinas
M, MA - Manila

REPUBLIC
REFORM COINAGE
100 Sentimos = 1 Piso

KM# 270.2 10 CENTIMOS
2.4600 g., Bronze Plated Steel, 16.9 mm. **Obv:** Value high on coin, different font, date **Rev:** Central Bank seal within circle and gear design **Rev. Legend:** BANGKO SENTRAL NG PILIPINAS - 1993 **Edge:** Reeded

Date	Mintage	F	VF	XF	Unc	BU
2006	—			0.10	0.30	0.40

KM# 273 SENTIMO
2.0000 g., Copper Plated Steel **Obv:** Value and date **Rev:** Central bank seal within circle and gear design, 1993 (date Cenral Bank was established) below **Rev. Legend:** BANGKO SENTRAL NG PILIPINAS - 1993

Date	Mintage	F	VF	XF	Unc	BU
2004	—	—	—	—	0.10	0.15
2005	—	—	—	—	0.10	0.15
2006	—	—	—	—	0.10	0.15
2007	—	—	—	—	0.10	0.15
2008	—	—	—	—	0.10	0.15

KM# 268 5 SENTIMOS
1.9000 g., Copper Plated Steel, 15.43 mm. **Obv:** Numeral value around center hole **Rev:** Hole in center with date, bank and name around border, 1993 (date Cenral Bank was established) below **Rev. Legend:** BANGKO CENTRAL NG PILIPINAS - 1993 **Edge:** Plain

Date	Mintage	F	VF	XF	Unc	BU
2001	—	—	—	—	0.20	0.25
2002	—	—	—	—	0.20	0.25
2004	—	—	—	—	0.50	1.00
2005	—	—	—	—	0.20	0.25
2006	—	—	—	—	0.20	0.25
2007	—	—	—	—	0.20	0.25
2008	—	—	—	—	0.20	0.25

KM# 270.1 10 SENTIMOS
2.4600 g., Bronze Plated Steel, 16.9 mm. **Obv:** Value and date **Rev:** Central Bank seal within circle and gear design, 1993 (date Cenral Bank was established) below **Rev. Legend:** BANGKO SENTRAL NG PILIPINAS - 1993 **Edge:** Reeded

Date	Mintage	F	VF	XF	Unc	BU
2002	—	—	—	0.10	0.30	0.40
2004	—	—	—	0.75	1.50	2.50
2005	—	—	—	0.10	0.30	0.40

KM# 271 25 SENTIMOS
3.8000 g., Brass, 20 mm. **Obv:** Value and date **Rev:** Central Bank seal within circle and gear design, 1993 (date Cenral Bank was established) below **Rev. Legend:** BANGKO SENTRAL NG PILIPINAS - 1993 **Edge:** Plain

Date	Mintage	F	VF	XF	Unc	BU
2001	—	—	0.10	0.25	0.60	0.80
2002	—	—	0.10	0.25	0.60	0.80
2003	—	—	0.10	0.25	0.60	0.80

KM# 271a 25 SENTIMOS
Brass Plated Steel, 20 mm. **Obv:** Value and date **Rev:** Central Bank seal within circle and gear design **Rev. Legend:** BANGKO SENTRAL NG PILIPINAS - 1993 **Edge:** Plain

Date	Mintage	F	VF	XF	Unc	BU
2004	—	—	—	0.25	2.00	2.50
2005	—	—	—	0.25	1.00	1.25
2006	—	—	—	0.25	1.00	1.25
2007	—	—	—	0.25	1.00	1.25
2008	—	—	—	0.25	0.50	1.00

KM# 269 PISO
6.0700 g., Copper-Nickel, 24 mm. **Obv:** Head of Jose Rizal right, value and date **Rev:** Bank seal within circle and gear design, 1993 (date Cenral Bank was established) below **Rev. Legend:** BANGKO SENTRAL NG PILIPINAS - 1993 **Edge:** Reeded

Date	Mintage	F	VF	XF	Unc	BU
2001	—	—	0.25	0.50	1.25	1.75
2002	—	—	0.25	0.50	1.25	1.75
2003 Magnetic	—	—	0.25	0.50	2.00	3.25
2003 Non Magnetic	—	—	—	—	—	10.00
2004	—	—	0.50	1.00	5.00	7.00
2006	—	—	0.25	0.50	1.00	1.75
2007	—	—	0.25	0.50	1.00	1.75
2008	—	—	0.25	0.50	1.00	1.75

KM# 269a 2 PISO
5.4000 g., Nickel Plated Steel, 24 mm. **Obv:** Head of Jose Rizal right, value and date **Rev:** Bank seal within circle and gear design **Rev. Legend:** BANGKO SENTRAL NG PILIPINAS - 1993 **Edge:** Reeded

Date	Mintage	F	VF	XF	Unc	BU
2004	—	—	0.20	0.45	1.10	1.50
2005	—	—	0.20	0.45	1.10	1.50
2006	—	—	0.20	0.45	1.10	1.50

KM# 272 5 PISO
7.6700 g., Nickel-Brass, 25.5 mm. **Obv:** Head of Emilio Aguinaldo right, value and date within scalloped border **Rev:** Central Bank seal within circle and gear design within scalloped border, 1993 (date Cenral Bank was established) below **Rev. Legend:** BANGKO SENTRAL NG PILIPINAS - 1993 **Edge:** Plain

Date	Mintage	F	VF	XF	Unc	BU
2001 BSP	—	—	1.00	2.00	3.00	4.50
2002	—	—	0.35	0.70	1.75	3.00
2003	—	—	0.35	0.70	1.75	3.00
2004	—	—	0.50	1.00	5.00	6.00
2005	—	—	0.35	0.70	1.75	4.00
2006	—	—	0.35	0.70	1.75	3.00
2007	—	—	0.35	0.70	1.75	3.00
2008	—	—	0.35	0.70	1.75	3.00

KM# 278 10 PISO
8.7000 g., Bi-Metallic Brass center in Copper-Nickel ring, 26.5 mm. **Obv:** Conjoined heads right within circle **Rev:** Bank seal within circle and gear design, 1993 (date Cenral Bank was established) below **Rev. Legend:** BANGKO SENTRAL NG PILIPINAS - 1993 **Edge:** Plain and reeded sections

Date	Mintage	F	VF	XF	Unc	BU
2001	—	—	0.70	1.40	3.50	4.50
2002	—	—	0.60	1.20	3.00	4.00
2003	—	—	0.60	1.20	3.00	4.00
2004	—	—	0.80	2.00	5.00	8.00
2005	—	—	0.75	1.50	3.75	5.00
2006	—	—	0.60	1.20	3.00	4.00
2007	—	—	0.75	1.50	3.75	5.00
2008	—	—	0.75	1.50	3.75	5.00

MINT SETS

KM#	Date	Mintage	Identification	Issue Price	Mkt Val
MS39	2005 (7)	—	KM#268-273, 278 plus medal	10.00	15.00
MS40	2006 (7)	—	KM#268-273, 278	10.00	15.00

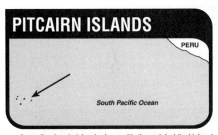

PITCAIRN ISLANDS

PERU

South Pacific Ocean

A small volcanic island, along with the uninhabited islands of Oeno, Henderson, and Ducie, constitute the British Colony of Pitcairn Islands. The main island has an area of about 2 sq. mi. (5 sq. km.) and a population of *68. It is located 1350 miles southeast of Tahiti. The islanders subsist on fishing, garden produce and crops. The sale of postage stamps and carved curios to passing ships brings cash income.

New Zealand currency has been used since July 10, 1967.

BRITISH COLONY
REGULAR COINAGE

KM# 14 DOLLAR
Copper-Nickel **Ruler:** Elizabeth II **Obv:** Bust facing right **Rev:** Queen Mum, Elizabeth II and Margaret facing **Rev. Legend:** 80th Birthday of H.M. Queen Elizabeth II

Date	Mintage	F	VF	XF	Unc	BU
2006	—	—	—	—	12.50	15.00

KM# 45 2 DOLLARS
31.1050 g., 0.9990 Silver 0.9990 oz. ASW, 40.7 mm. **Ruler:** Elizabeth II **Subject:** Year of the Rat **Rev:** Multicolor rat seated right

Date	Mintage	F	VF	XF	Unc	BU
2008 Prooflike	30,000	—	—	—	—	65.00

KM# 46 2 DOLLARS
31.1050 g., 0.9990 Silver 0.9990 oz. ASW, 40.7 mm. **Ruler:** Elizabeth II **Rev:** Multicolor HMAV Bounty under full sail right

Date	Mintage	F	VF	XF	Unc	BU
2008 Prooflike	5,000	—	—	—	—	75.00

KM# 47 2 DOLLARS
31.1050 g., 0.9990 Silver Partially gilt 0.9990 oz. ASW, 40.7 mm. **Ruler:** Elizabeth II **Rev:** HMAV Bounty under full sail right

Date	Mintage	F	VF	XF	Unc	BU
2008 Proof	1,500	Value: 85.00				

KM# 51 2 DOLLARS
31.1050 g., 0.9990 Silver partially gilt 0.9990 oz. ASW, 40.7 mm. **Ruler:** Elizabeth II **Rev:** Captian William Bligh

Date	Mintage	F	VF	XF	Unc	BU
2009 Proof	1,500	Value: 75.00				

KM# 12 5 DOLLARS
31.1000 g., 0.9990 Silver with Mother-of-Pearl inset 0.9988 oz. ASW, 40 mm. **Ruler:** Elizabeth II **Series:** Save the Whales **Obv:** Crowned bust right **Obv. Legend:** ELIZABETH II • PITCAIRN ISLANDS **Rev:** Humpback Whale and date on mother-of-pearl inset **Edge:** Plain

Date	Mintage	F	VF	XF	Unc	BU
2002 Proof	2,000			Value: 85.00		

KM# 50 5 DOLLARS
1.2700 g., 0.9999 Gold 0.0408 oz. AGW, 13.92 mm. **Ruler:** Elizabeth II **Obv:** Crowned bust right **Obv. Legend:** Elizabeth II Pitcairn Islands **Rev:** Bounty Bible and ship

Date	Mintage	F	VF	XF	Unc	BU
2005 Proof	—			Value: 75.00		

KM# 48 10 DOLLARS
1.2440 g., 0.9999 Gold 0.0400 oz. AGW, 22 mm. **Ruler:** Elizabeth II **Rev:** HMAV Bounty under full sail right

Date	Mintage	F	VF	XF	Unc	BU
2008 Proof	10,000			Value: 75.00		

KM# 49 25 DOLLARS
7.7700 g., 0.9990 Gold 0.2496 oz. AGW, 22 mm. **Ruler:** Elizabeth II **Rev:** HMAV Bounty under full sail right

Date	Mintage	F	VF	XF	Unc	BU
2008 Proof	1,000			Value: 375		

POLAND

The Republic of Poland, located in central Europe, has an area of 120,725 sq. mi. (312,680 sq. km.) and a population of *38.2 million. Capital: Warszawa (Warsaw). The economy is essentially agricultural, but industrial activity provides the products for foreign trade. Machinery, coal, coke, iron, steel and transport equipment are exported.

MINT MARKS
MV, MW, MW-monogram - Warsaw Mint, 1965-
CHI - Valcambi, Switzerland
Other letters appearing with date denote the Mintmaster at the time the coin was struck.

REPUBLIC
Democratic
REFORM COINAGE
100 Old Zlotych = 1 Grosz; 10,000 Old Zlotych = 1 Zloty

As far back as 1990, production was initiated for the new 1 Grosz - 1 Zlotych coins for a forthcoming monetary reform. It wasn't announced until the Act of July 7, 1994 and was enacted on January 1, 1995.

Y# 276 GROSZ
1.6400 g., Brass, 15.5 mm. **Obv:** National arms **Obv. Legend:** RZECZPOSPOLITA POLSKA **Rev:** Drooping oak leaf over value **Edge:** Reeded

Date	Mintage	F	VF	XF	Unc	BU
2001MW	210,000,020	—	—	—	0.10	0.20
2002MW	240,000,000	—	—	—	0.10	0.20
2003MW	250,000,000	—	—	—	0.10	0.20
2004MW	300,000,000	—	—	—	0.10	0.20
2005MW	375,000,000	—	—	—	0.10	0.20
2006MW	184,000,000	—	—	—	0.10	0.20
2007MW	330,000,000	—	—	—	0.10	0.20
2008MW	—	—	—	—	0.10	0.20

Y# 277 2 GROSZE
2.1300 g., Brass, 17.5 mm. **Obv:** National arms **Obv. Legend:** RZECZPOSPOLITA POLSKA **Rev:** Drooping oak leaves above value **Edge:** Plain

Date	Mintage	F	VF	XF	Unc	BU
2001MW	86,100,000	—	—	—	0.15	0.25
2002MW	83,910,000	—	—	—	0.15	0.25
2003MW	80,000,000	—	—	—	0.15	0.25
2004MW	100,000,000	—	—	—	0.15	0.25
2005MW	163,003,250	—	—	—	0.15	0.25
2006MW	105,000,000	—	—	—	0.15	0.25
2007MW	160,000,000	—	—	—	0.15	0.25
2008MW	—	—	—	—	0.15	0.25

Y# 278 5 GROSZY
2.5900 g., Brass, 19.5 mm. **Obv:** National arms **Obv. Legend:** RZECZPOSPOLITA POLSKA **Rev:** Value at upper left of oak leaves **Edge:** Segmented reeding

Date	Mintage	F	VF	XF	Unc	BU
2001MW	67,368,000	—	—	—	0.25	0.45
2002MW	67,200,000	—	—	—	0.25	0.45
2003MW	48,000,000	—	—	—	0.25	0.45
2004MW	62,500,000	—	—	—	0.25	0.45
2005MW	113,000,000	—	—	—	0.25	0.45
2006MW	54,000,000	—	—	—	0.25	0.45
2007MW	116,000,000	—	—	—	0.25	0.45
2008MW	—	—	—	—	0.25	0.45

Y# 279 10 GROSZY
2.5500 g., Copper-Nickel, 16.5 mm. **Obv:** National arms **Obv. Legend:** RZECZPOSPOLITA POLSKA **Rev:** Value within wreath

Date	Mintage	F	VF	XF	Unc	BU
2001MW	62,820,000	—	—	—	0.40	0.60
2002MW	10,500,000	—	—	—	0.40	0.60
2003MW	31,500,000	—	—	—	0.40	0.60
2004MW	70,500,000	—	—	—	0.40	0.60
2005MW	94,000,000	—	—	—	0.40	0.60
2006MW	40,000,000	—	—	—	0.40	0.60
2007MW	100,000,000	—	—	—	0.40	0.60

Y# 280 20 GROSZY
3.2200 g., Copper-Nickel, 18.5 mm. **Obv:** National arms **Obv. Legend:** RZECZPOSPOLITA POLSKA **Rev:** Value within artistic design **Edge:** Reeded

Date	Mintage	F	VF	XF	Unc	BU
2001MW	41,980,001	—	—	—	0.65	0.85
2002MW	10,500,000	—	—	—	0.65	0.85
2003MW	20,400,000	—	—	—	0.65	0.85
2004MW	40,000,025	—	—	—	0.65	0.85
2005MW	37,000,000	—	—	—	0.65	0.85
2006MW	35,000,000	—	—	—	0.65	0.85
2007MW	68,000,000	—	—	—	0.65	0.85
2008MW	—	—	—	—	0.65	0.85

Y# 421 2 ZLOTE
8.1500 g., Brass, 27 mm. **Subject:** Michal Siedlecki **Obv:** Crowned eagle with wings open **Rev:** Bust left and art work **Edge:** NBP eight times

Date	Mintage	F	VF	XF	Unc	BU
2001MW	600,000	—	—	—	3.00	5.00

Y# 422 2 ZLOTE
8.1500 g., Brass, 27 mm. **Subject:** Koledicy **Obv:** Crowned eagle with wings open **Rev:** Christmas celebration scene

Date	Mintage	F	VF	XF	Unc	BU
2001MW	600,000	—	—	—	3.00	5.00

Y# 408 2 ZLOTE
8.1500 g., Brass, 27 mm. **Subject:** Wieliczka Salt Mine **Obv:** Crowned eagle with wings open **Rev:** Ancient salt miners

Date	Mintage	F	VF	XF	Unc	BU
2001	500,000	—	—	3.50	7.00	12.00

Y# 410 2 ZLOTE
8.1500 g., Brass, 27 mm. **Subject:** Amber Route **Obv:** Crowned eagle with wings open **Rev:** Ancient Roman coin and map with route marked in stars

Date	Mintage	F	VF	XF	Unc	BU
2001	500,000	—	—	3.50	7.00	12.00

Y# 412 2 ZLOTE
8.1500 g., Brass, 27 mm. **Subject:** 15 Years of the Constitutional Court **Obv:** Crowned eagle with wings open **Rev:** Crowned eagle head and scale **Edge:** * NBP * eight times

Date	Mintage	F	VF	XF	Unc	BU
2001MW	500,000	—	—	—	3.00	5.00

Y# 414 2 ZLOTE
8.1500 g., Brass, 27 mm. **Obv:** Crowned eagle with wings open **Rev:** Butterfly **Edge:** * NBP * eight times

Date	Mintage	F	VF	XF	Unc	BU
2001MW	600,000	—	—	4.00	8.00	15.00

Y# 418 2 ZLOTE
8.1500 g., Brass, 27 mm. **Subject:** Cardinal Stefan Wyszynski **Obv:** Crowned eagle with wings open **Rev:** Bust left wearing mitre **Edge:** "NBP" eight times

Date	Mintage	F	VF	XF	Unc	BU
2001MW	1,200,000	—	—	—	3.00	5.00

Y# 423 2 ZLOTE
8.1500 g., Brass, 27 mm. **Subject:** Jan III Sobieski **Obv:** Crowned eagle with wings open **Rev:** Bust facing **Edge Lettering:** * NBP * eight times

Date	Mintage	F	VF	XF	Unc	BU
2001MW	500,000	—	—	3.50	7.00	12.00

Y# 426 2 ZLOTE
8.1500 g., Brass, 27 mm. **Subject:** Henryk Wieniawski **Obv:** Crowned eagle with wings open **Rev:** Bust left and violin **Edge Lettering:** * NBP * eight times

Date	Mintage	F	VF	XF	Unc	BU
2001MW	600,000	—	—	—	3.00	5.00

Y# 427 2 ZLOTE
8.1500 g., Brass, 27 mm. **Obv:** Crowned eagle with wings open **Rev:** European Pond Turtles **Edge Lettering:** * NBP * eight times

Date	Mintage	F	VF	XF	Unc	BU
2002MW	750,000	—	—	3.50	7.00	12.00

Y# 431 2 ZLOTE
8.1500 g., Brass, 27 mm. **Subject:** Bronislaw Malinowski **Obv:** Crowned eagle with wings open **Rev:** Bust facing and Trobriand Islanders **Edge Lettering:** * NBP * eight times

Date	Mintage	F	VF	XF	Unc	BU
2002MW	680,000	—	—	—	3.50	5.50

Y# 433 2 ZLOTE
8.1500 g., Brass, 27 mm. **Subject:** World Cup Soccer
Obv: National arms **Rev:** Soccer players **Edge Lettering:** * NBP * eight times

Date	Mintage	F	VF	XF	Unc	BU
2002MW	1,000,000	—	—	—	3.00	5.00

Y# 439 2 ZLOTE
8.1000 g., Brass, 26.8 mm. **Subject:** August II (1697-1706, 1709-1733) **Obv:** National arms **Rev:** Head facing
Edge Lettering: * NBP * eight times

Date	Mintage	F	VF	XF	Unc	BU
2002MW	620,000	—	—	—	4.00	7.00

Y# 440 2 ZLOTE
8.1500 g., Brass, 27 mm. **Subject:** Gen. Wladyslaw Anders
Obv: Crowned eagle with wings open **Rev:** Uniformed bust facing and cross **Edge Lettering:** * NBP * eight times

Date	Mintage	F	VF	XF	Unc	BU
2002MW	680,000	—	—	—	3.00	5.00

Y# 443 2 ZLOTE
8.1500 g., Brass, 27 mm. **Subject:** Zamek W. Malborku
Obv: Crowned eagle with wings open **Rev:** Castle
Edge Lettering: * NBP * eight times

Date	Mintage	F	VF	XF	Unc	BU
2002MW	680,000	—	—	—	3.00	5.00

Y# 444 2 ZLOTE
8.1500 g., Brass, 27 mm. **Subject:** Jan Matejko
Obv: Denomination, crowned eagle and artist's palette
Rev: Jester behind portrait **Edge Lettering:** * NBP * eight times

Date	Mintage	F	VF	XF	Unc	BU
2002MW	700,000	—	—	—	3.00	5.00

Y# 445 2 ZLOTE
8.1500 g., Brass, 27 mm. **Subject:** Eels **Obv:** Crowned eagle with wings open **Rev:** Two European eels **Edge Lettering:** * NBP * eight times

Date	Mintage	F	VF	XF	Unc	BU
2003MW	450,000	—	—	6.00	12.00	20.00

Y# 446 2 ZLOTE
7.7500 g., Brass, 27 mm. **Subject:** Children **Obv:** Children and square design above crowned eagle, date and value
Rev: Children on square design **Edge Lettering:** * NBP * eight times **Note:** Center hole.

Date	Mintage	F	VF	XF	Unc	BU
2003MW	2,500,000	—	—	—	4.50	6.50

Y# 447 2 ZLOTE
8.1500 g., Brass, 27 mm. **Subject:** City of Poznan (Posen)
Obv: Crowned eagle with wings open **Rev:** Clock face and tower flanked by goat heads **Edge Lettering:** * NBP * eight times

Date	Mintage	F	VF	XF	Unc	BU
2003MW	600,000	—	—	—	5.00	8.00

Y# 451 2 ZLOTE
8.1500 g., Brass, 27 mm. **Subject:** Easter Monday Festival
Obv: Crowned eagle with wings open **Rev:** Festival scene
Edge Lettering: * NBP * eight times

Date	Mintage	F	VF	XF	Unc	BU
2003MW	600,000	—	—	—	4.00	7.00

Y# 455 2 ZLOTE
8.1500 g., Brass, 27 mm. **Subject:** Petroleum and Gas Industry 150th Anniversary **Obv:** Crowned eagle with wings open
Rev: Portrait and refinery **Edge Lettering:** * NBP * eight times

Date	Mintage	F	VF	XF	Unc	BU
2003MW	600,000	—	—	—	3.50	5.50

Y# 456 2 ZLOTE
8.1500 g., Brass, 27 mm. **Subject:** General B. S. Maczek
Obv: Crowned eagle with wings open **Rev:** Military uniformed portrait **Edge Lettering:** * NBP * eight times

Date	Mintage	F	VF	XF	Unc	BU
2003MW	700,000	—	—	—	3.00	5.00

Y# 465 2 ZLOTE
8.1500 g., Aluminum-Bronze, 27 mm. **Subject:** Pope JohnPaul II
Obv: Small national arms at lower right with cross in background
Obv. Legend: RZECZPOSPOLITA POLSKA **Rev:** Pope in prayer at left, cross in background **Edge Lettering:** * NBP * eight times

Date	Mintage	F	VF	XF	Unc	BU
2003MW	2,000,000	—	—	—	3.00	5.00

Y# 473 2 ZLOTE
8.1500 g., Brass, 27 mm. **Obv:** Crowned eagle with wings open
Rev: Stanislaus Leszcywski **Edge Lettering:** * NBP * eight times

Date	Mintage	F	VF	XF	Unc	BU
2003MW	600,000	—	—	—	3.50	5.50

Y# 477 2 ZLOTE
8.1500 g., Brass, 27 mm. **Obv:** Crowned eagle with wings open and artist's palette **Rev:** Self portrait of Jacek Malczewski
Edge Lettering: * NBP * eight times

Date	Mintage	F	VF	XF	Unc	BU
2003MW	600,000	—	—	—	3.50	5.50

Y# 479 2 ZLOTE
8.1500 g., Brass, 27 mm. **Subject:** 80th Anniversary of the Modern Zloty Currency **Obv:** Crowned eagle with wings open above value **Rev:** Bust left **Edge Lettering:** * NBP * eight times

Date	Mintage	F	VF	XF	Unc	BU
2004MW	800,000	—	—	—	3.00	5.00

Y# 481 2 ZLOTE
8.1500 g., Brass, 27 mm. **Subject:** Poland Joining the European Union **Obv:** Crowned eagle with wings open above value
Rev: Map and stars **Edge Lettering:** * NBP * eight times

Date	Mintage	F	VF	XF	Unc	BU
2004MW	1,000,000	—	—	—	3.00	5.00

Y# 484 2 ZLOTE
8.1500 g., Brass, 27 mm. **Subject:** Dolnoslaskie (Lower Silesian) District **Obv:** Crowned eagle with wings open on map
Rev: Silesian eagle on shield **Edge Lettering:** * NBP * eight times

Date	Mintage	F	VF	XF	Unc	BU
2004MW	700,000	—	—	—	4.00	6.00

Y# 485 2 ZLOTE
8.1500 g., Brass, 27 mm. **Subject:** Kujawsko-Pomorskie District
Obv: Crowned eagle with wings open on map **Rev:** Shield with crowned half eagle and griffin **Edge Lettering:** * NBP * eight times

Date	Mintage	F	VF	XF	Unc	BU
2004MW	750,000	—	—	—	7.00	12.00

Y# 486 2 ZLOTE
8.1500 g., Brass, 27 mm. **Subject:** Lubusk
ie District
Obv: Crowned eagle with wings open on map **Rev:** Shield with stag left **Edge Lettering:** * NBP * eight times

Date	Mintage	F	VF	XF	Unc	BU
2004MW	820,000	—	—	—	3.00	5.00

Y# 487 2 ZLOTE
8.1500 g., Brass, 27 mm. **Subject:** Lodzkie District
Obv: Crowned eagle with wings open on map **Rev:** Shield with two creatures above an eagle **Edge Lettering:** * NBP * eight times

Date	Mintage	F	VF	XF	Unc	BU
2004MW	920,000	—	—	—	3.00	5.00

Y# 488 2 ZLOTE
8.1500 g., Brass, 27 mm. **Subject:** Malopolskie District
Obv: Crowned eagle with wings open on map **Rev:** Shield with crowned eagle **Edge Lettering:** * NBP * eight times

Date	Mintage	F	VF	XF	Unc	BU
2004MW	920,000	—	—	—	3.00	5.00

Y# 489 2 ZLOTE
8.1500 g., Brass, 27 mm. **Subject:** Mazowieckie District
Obv: Crowned eagle with wings open on map **Rev:** Eagle on shield **Edge Lettering:** * NBP * eight times

Date	Mintage	F	VF	XF	Unc	BU
2004MW	920,000	—	—	—	3.00	5.00

Y# 490 2 ZLOTE
8.1500 g., Brass, 27 mm. **Subject:** Podkarpackie District **Obv:** Crowned eagle with wings open on map **Rev:** Shield with iron cross above griffin and lion **Edge Lettering:** * NBP * eight times

Date	Mintage	F	VF	XF	Unc	BU
2004MW	920,000	—	—	—	3.00	5.00

Y# 491 2 ZLOTE
8.1500 g., Brass, 27 mm. **Subject:** Podlaskie District
Obv: Crowned eagle with wings open on map **Rev:** Shield with Polish eagle above Lithuanian knight **Edge Lettering:** * NBP * eight times

Date	Mintage	F	VF	XF	Unc	BU
2004MW	900,000	—	—	—	3.00	5.00

Y# 492 2 ZLOTE
8.1500 g., Brass, 27 mm. **Subject:** Pomorskie District
Obv: Crowned eagle with wings open on map **Rev:** Griffin on shield **Edge Lettering:** * NBP * eight times

Date	Mintage	F	VF	XF	Unc	BU
2004MW	900,000	—	—	—	3.00	5.00

Y# 493 2 ZLOTE
8.1500 g., Brass, 27 mm. **Subject:** Slaskie (Silesia) District
Obv: Crowned eagle with wings open on map **Rev:** Eagle on shield **Edge Lettering:** * NBP * eight times

Date	Mintage	F	VF	XF	Unc	BU
2004MW	960,000	—	—	—	3.00	5.00

Y# 496 2 ZLOTE
8.1500 g., Brass, 27 mm. **Subject:** Warsaw Uprising 60th Anniversary **Obv:** Crowned eagle with wings open
Rev: Resistance symbol on brick wall **Edge Lettering:** * NBP * eight times

Date	Mintage	F	VF	XF	Unc	BU
2004MW	900,000	—	—	—	3.00	5.00

Y# 499 2 ZLOTE
8.1500 g., Brass, 27 mm. **Obv:** Crowned eagle with wings open
Rev: Gen. Stanislaw F. Sosabowski **Edge Lettering:** * NBP * eight times

Date	Mintage	F	VF	XF	Unc	BU
2004MW	850,000	—	—	—	3.00	5.00

Y# 501 2 ZLOTE
8.1500 g., Brass, 27 mm. **Subject:** Polish Police 85th
Anniversary **Obv:** Crowned eagle with wings open **Rev:** Police
badge **Edge Lettering:** * NBP * eight times

Date	Mintage	F	VF	XF	Unc	BU
2004MW	760,000	—	—	—	3.00	5.00

Y# 503 2 ZLOTE
8.1500 g., Brass, 27 mm. **Subject:** Polish Senate **Obv:** Crowned
eagle with wings open **Rev:** Senate eagle and speaker's staff
Edge Lettering: * NBP * eight times

Date	Mintage	F	VF	XF	Unc	BU
2004MW	760,000	—	—	—	3.00	5.00

Y# 505 2 ZLOTE
8.1500 g., Brass, 27 mm. **Obv:** Crowned eagle with wings open
Rev: Aleksander Czekanowski (1833-1876) **Edge Lettering:** *
NBP * eight times

Date	Mintage	F	VF	XF	Unc	BU
2004MW	700,000	—	—	—	3.00	5.00

Y# 507 2 ZLOTE
8.1500 g., Brass, 27 mm. **Obv:** National arms
Obv. Legend: RZECZPOSPOLITA POLSKA **Rev:** Harvest fest
couple in folk costume at left, large group in background at right
Rev. Legend: DOZYNKI **Edge Lettering:** * NBP * eight times

Date	Mintage	F	VF	XF	Unc	BU
2004MW	850,000	—	—	—	3.00	5.00

Y# 509 2 ZLOTE
8.1500 g., Brass, 27 mm. **Subject:** Warsaw Fine Arts Academy
Centennial **Obv:** Crowned eagle with wings open **Rev:** Painter's
hands **Edge Lettering:** * NBP * eight times

Date	Mintage	F	VF	XF	Unc	BU
2004MW	850,000	—	—	—	3.00	5.00

Y# 512 2 ZLOTE
8.1500 g., Brass, 27 mm. **Obv:** Crowned eagle with wings open
and artist's palette **Rev:** Stanislaw Wyspianski (1869-1907)
Edge Lettering: * NBP * eight times

Date	Mintage	F	VF	XF	Unc	BU
2004MW	900,000	—	—	—	3.00	5.00

Y# 516 2 ZLOTE
8.1500 g., Brass, 27 mm. **Subject:** Olympics **Obv:** Crowned
eagle with wings open **Rev:** Ancient runners **Edge Lettering:** *
NBP * eight times

Date	Mintage	F	VF	XF	Unc	BU
2004MW	1,000,000	—	—	—	3.00	5.00

Y# 464 2 ZLOTE
8.1500 g., Brass, 27 mm. **Obv:** Crowned eagle with wings open
Rev: Harbor Porpoises **Edge Lettering:** * NBP * eight times

Date	Mintage	F	VF	XF	Unc	BU
2004MW	800,000	—	—	3.50	7.00	12.00

Y# 607 2 ZLOTE
8.1500 g., Brass, 27 mm. **Obv:** National arms on outlined map
Obv. Legend: RZECZPOSPOLITA POLSKA **Rev:** Region arms
Rev. Legend: WOJEWODZTWO - OPOLSKIE
Edge Lettering: * NBP * eight times

Date	Mintage	F	VF	XF	Unc	BU
2004MW	900,000	—	—	—	3.00	5.00

Y# 514 2 ZLOTE
8.1500 g., Brass, 27 mm. **Obv:** National arms on outlined map
Rev: Wojewodztwo-Lubelskie arms with stag on shield
Edge Lettering: * NBP * eight times

Date	Mintage	F	VF	XF	Unc	BU
2004MW	820,000	—	—	—	—	7.50

Y# 283 2 ZLOTE
5.2100 g., Bi-Metallic Copper-Nickel center in Brass ring,
21.5 mm. **Obv:** National arms within circle **Obv. Legend:**
RZECZPOSPOLITA POLSKA **Rev:** Value flanked by oak leaves

Date	Mintage	F	VF	XF	Unc	BU
2005MW	5,000,000	—	—	—	4.00	4.50
2006MW	5,000,000	—	—	—	4.00	4.50
2007MW	20,000,000	—	—	—	4.00	4.50

Y# 520 2 ZLOTE
8.1500 g., Brass, 27 mm. **Obv:** National arms **Rev:** Owl perched
on nest with owlets **Rev. Legend:** PUCHACZ - Bubo-bubo
Edge Lettering: * NBP * eight times

Date	Mintage	F	VF	XF	Unc	BU
2005MW	990,000	—	—	—	4.00	7.00

Y# 521 2 ZLOTE
8.1500 g., Brass, 27 mm. **Obv:** Crowned eagle with wings open
Rev: Ship within circle **Edge Lettering:** * NBP * eight times

Date	Mintage	F	VF	XF	Unc	BU
2005MW	920,000	—	—	—	3.50	5.50

Y# 522 2 ZLOTE
8.1500 g., Brass, 26.8 mm. **Subject:** Japan's Aichi Expo
Obv: Crowned eagle with wings open **Rev:** Two cranes flying
over Mt. Fuji with rising sun background **Edge Lettering:** * NBP
* eight times

Date	Mintage	F	VF	XF	Unc	BU
2005MW	1,000,000	—	—	—	3.50	5.50

Y# 524 2 ZLOTE
8.1500 g., Brass, 27 mm. **Subject:** Obrony Jasnej Gory
Obv: Crowned eagle with wings open **Rev:** Half length figure left
and bombarded city scene **Edge Lettering:** * NBP * eight times

Date	Mintage	F	VF	XF	Unc	BU
2005MW	1,000,000	—	—	—	4.00	6.00

Y# 525 2 ZLOTE
8.1500 g., Brass, 27 mm. **Subject:** Pope John-Paul II
Obv: National arms **Obv. Legend:** RZECZPOSPOLITA
POLSKA **Rev:** Bust right at left, outline of church steeple at center
right **Edge Lettering:** * NBP * eight times

Date	Mintage	F	VF	XF	Unc	BU
2005MW	4,000,000	—	—	—	4.00	6.00

Y# 527 2 ZLOTE
8.1500 g., Brass, 27 mm. **Obv:** Crowned eagle with wings open
Rev: Bust 1/4 left with horse head and goose at left
Edge Lettering: * NBP * eight times

Date	Mintage	F	VF	XF	Unc	BU
2005MW	850,000	—	—	—	3.00	5.00

Y# 528 2 ZLOTE
8.1500 g., Brass, 27 mm. **Obv:** Crowned eagle above wall
Rev: Kolobrzeg Lighthouse **Edge Lettering:** * NBP * eight times

Date	Mintage	F	VF	XF	Unc	BU
2005MW	1,100,000	—	—	—	3.00	5.00

Y# 529 2 ZLOTE
8.1500 g., Brass, 27 mm. **Obv:** National arms above gateway
Rev: Wioclawek Cathedral **Edge Lettering:** * NBP * eight times

Date	Mintage	F	VF	XF	Unc	BU
2005MW	1,100,000	—	—	—	3.00	5.00

Y# 530 2 ZLOTE
8.1500 g., Brass, 27 mm. **Obv:** National arms **Rev:** Bust of King
Stanislaus Poniatowski right **Edge Lettering:** * NBP * eight times

Date	Mintage	F	VF	XF	Unc	BU
2005MW	990,000	—	—	—	3.00	5.00

Y# 541 2 ZLOTE
8.1500 g., Brass, 27 mm. **Obv:** Eagle, value, palette and paint
brushes **Rev:** Painter Tadeusz Makowski **Edge Lettering:** * NBP
* eight times

Date	Mintage	F	VF	XF	Unc	BU
2005MW	900,000	—	—	—	3.00	5.00

Y# 558 2 ZLOTE
8.1500 g., Brass, 27 mm. **Subject:** 60th Anniversary of WWII
Obv: National arms **Edge Lettering:** * NBP * eight times

Date	Mintage	F	VF	XF	Unc	BU
2005MW	1,000,000	—	—	—	3.00	5.00

Y# 560 2 ZLOTE
8.1500 g., Brass, 27 mm. **Obv:** National arms on outline map
Obv. Legend: RZECZPOSPOLITA POLSKA **Rev:** Region arms
Rev. Legend: WOJEWOZTWO SWIETOKRZYSKIE
Edge Lettering: * NBP * eight times

Date	Mintage	F	VF	XF	Unc	BU
2005MW	900,000	—	—	—	3.00	5.00

Y# 562 2 ZLOTE
8.1500 g., Brass, 27 mm. **Obv:** National arms **Rev:** Region
Wielkopolskie **Edge Lettering:** * NBP * eight times

Date	Mintage	F	VF	XF	Unc	BU
2005MW	940,000	—	—	—	3.00	5.00

Y# 563 2 ZLOTE
8.1500 g., Brass, 27 mm. **Obv:** National arms on outlined map
Obv. Legend: RZECZPOSPOLITA POLSKA **Rev:** Region arms
Rev. Legend: WOJEWODZTWO ZACHODIOPOMORSKIE
Edge Lettering: * NBP * eight times

Date	Mintage	F	VF	XF	Unc	BU
2005	—	—	—	—	3.00	5.00

Y# 564 2 ZLOTE
8.1500 g., Brass, 27 mm. **Obv:** National arms **Rev:** City of
Gniezno **Edge Lettering:** * NBP * eight times

Date	Mintage	F	VF	XF	Unc	BU
2005	1,250,000	—	—	—	3.00	5.00

Y# 565 2 ZLOTE
8.1500 g., Brass, 27 mm. **Obv:** National arms **Rev:** Solidarity
Edge Lettering: * NBP * eight times

Date	Mintage	F	VF	XF	Unc	BU
2005MW	1,000,000	—	—	—	3.00	5.00

Y# 608 2 ZLOTE
8.1500 g., Brass, 27 mm. **Subject:** 500th Anniversary Birth of
Nikolaja Reja **Obv:** National arms **Obv. Legend:**
RZECZPOSPOLITA POLSKA **Rev:** Bust of Reja facing 3/4 right
Edge Lettering: NBP eight times

Date	Mintage	F	VF	XF	Unc	BU
2005	850,000	—	—	—	3.00	5.00

Y# 614 2 ZLOTE
8.1500 g., Brass, 27 mm. **Obv:** National arms on outlined map
Obv. Legend: RZECZPOSPOLITA POLSKA **Rev:** Region arms
Rev. Legend: WOJEWÓDZTWO WARMINSKO - MAZURSKIE
Edge Lettering: * NBP * eight times

Date	Mintage	F	VF	XF	Unc	BU
2005MW	900,000	—	—	—	3.00	5.00

Y# 532 2 ZLOTE
8.1500 g., Brass, 27 mm. **Obv:** National arms **Rev:** St. John's
Night dancer **Edge Lettering:** * NBP * eight times

Date	Mintage	F	VF	XF	Unc	BU
2006MW	1,000,000	—	—	—	2.50	4.00

Y# 534 2 ZLOTE
8.1500 g., Brass, 27 mm. **Obv:** National arms **Rev:** Alpine
Marmot standing **Edge Lettering:** * NBP * eight times

Date	Mintage	F	VF	XF	Unc	BU
2006MW	1,400,000	—	—	—	3.00	6.00

Y# 543 2 ZLOTE
8.1500 g., Brass, 27 mm. **Obv:** Polish Eagle above castle gate
Rev: Bochnia church **Edge Lettering:** * NBP * eight times

Date	Mintage	F	VF	XF	Unc	BU
2006MW	1,100,000	—	—	—	3.00	5.00

Y# 544 2 ZLOTE
8.1500 g., Brass, 27 mm. **Obv:** Polish Eagle above castle gate
Rev: Chelm church **Edge Lettering:** * NBP * eight times

Date	Mintage	F	VF	XF	Unc	BU
2006MW	1,100,000	—	—	—	3.00	5.00

Y# 545 2 ZLOTE
8.1500 g., Brass, 27 mm. **Obv:** Polish Eagle above castle gate
Rev: Chelmno Palace **Edge Lettering:** * NBP * eight times

Date	Mintage	F	VF	XF	Unc	BU
2006MW	1,100,000	—	—	—	3.00	5.00

Y# 546 2 ZLOTE
8.1500 g., Brass, 27 mm. **Obv:** Polish Eagle above castle gate
Rev: Elblag tower **Edge Lettering:** * NBP * eight times

Date	Mintage	F	VF	XF	Unc	BU
2006MW	1,100,000	—	—	—	3.00	5.00

Y# 547 2 ZLOTE
8.1500 g., Brass, 27 mm. **Obv:** Polish Eagle above castle gate
Rev: Castle **Rev. Legend:** KOSCIOL W. HACZOWIE
Edge Lettering: * NBP * eight times

Date	Mintage	F	VF	XF	Unc	BU
2006MW	1,000,000	—	—	—	3.00	5.00

Y# 548 2 ZLOTE
8.1500 g., Brass, 27 mm. **Obv:** National arms above gateway
Rev: Legnica tower and building **Edge Lettering:** * NBP * eight
times

Date	Mintage	F	VF	XF	Unc	BU
2006MW	1,100,000	—	—	—	3.00	5.00

Y# 549 2 ZLOTE
8.1500 g., Brass, 27 mm. **Obv:** Polish Eagle above castle gate
Rev: Pszczyna palace **Edge Lettering:** * NBP * eight times

Date	Mintage	F	VF	XF	Unc	BU
2006MW	1,100,000	—	—	—	3.00	5.00

Y# 550 2 ZLOTE
8.1500 g., Brass, 27 mm. **Obv:** Polish Eagle above castle gate
Rev: Sandomierz palace **Edge Lettering:** * NBP * eight times

Date	Mintage	F	VF	XF	Unc	BU
2006MW	1,100,000	—	—	—	3.00	5.00

Y# 566 2 ZLOTE
8.1500 g., Brass, 27 mm. **Obv:** National arms **Rev:** City of
Jaroslaw **Edge Lettering:** * NBP * eight times

Date	Mintage	F	VF	XF	Unc	BU
2006MW	1,200,000	—	—	—	3.00	5.00

Y# 569 2 ZLOTE
8.1500 g., Brass, 27 mm. **Obv:** National arms **Rev:** Castle Zagan
Edge Lettering: * NBP * eight times

Date	Mintage	F	VF	XF	Unc	BU
2006MW	1,100,000	—	—	—	3.00	5.00

Y# 570 2 ZLOTE
815.0000 g., Brass, 27 mm. **Obv:** National arms above gateway
Rev: City of Nysa **Edge Lettering:** * NBP * eight times

Date	Mintage	F	VF	XF	Unc	BU
2006MW	1,100,000	—	—	—	5.00	3.00

Y# 571 2 ZLOTE
8.1500 g., Brass, 27 mm. **Subject:** 30th Anniversary of June
1976 **Obv:** National arms **Edge Lettering:** * NBP * eight times

Date	Mintage	F	VF	XF	Unc	BU
2006MW	1,000,000	—	—	—	3.00	5.00

Y# 573 2 ZLOTE
8.1500 g., Brass, 27 mm. **Obv:** Polish eagle above wall
Rev: Nowy Sacz church **Edge Lettering:** * NBP * eight times

Date	Mintage	F	VF	XF	Unc	BU
2006MW	1,100,000	—	—	—	3.00	5.00

Y# 574 2 ZLOTE
8.1500 g., Brass, 27 mm. **Subject:** 500th Anniversary of the
Publication of the Statute by Laski **Obv:** National arms above
value **Rev:** Jan Laskjego and book **Edge Lettering:** * NBP * eight
times

Date	Mintage	F	VF	XF	Unc	BU
2006MW	1,000,000	—	—	—	3.00	5.00

Y# 575 2 ZLOTE
8.1500 g., Brass, 27 mm. **Subject:** Aleksander Gierymski
(painter) **Obv:** Palette, brushes at left, national arms at right
Obv. Legend: RZECZPOSPOLITA POLSKA **Rev:** Bust of
Gierymski facing at left, coastline village in background
Edge Lettering: * NBP * eight times

Date	Mintage	F	VF	XF	Unc	BU
2006MW	1,000,000	—	—	—	3.00	5.00

Y# 576 2 ZLOTE
8.1500 g., Brass, 27 mm. **Obv:** National arms **Rev:** Knight on
horseback **Edge Lettering:** * NBP * eight times

Date	Mintage	F	VF	XF	Unc	BU
2006MW	1,000,000	—	—	—	3.00	5.00

Y# 580 2 ZLOTE
8.1500 g., Brass, 27 mm. **Obv:** Polish eagle above wall
Rev: Kalisz building **Edge Lettering:** * NBP * eight times

Date	Mintage	F	VF	XF	Unc	BU
2006MW	1,100,000	—	—	—	3.00	5.00

Y# 582 2 ZLOTE
8.1500 g., Brass, 27 mm. **Obv:** National arms **Obv. Legend:**
RZECZPOSPOLITA POLSKA **Rev:** Queen's head left as on KM-
20, coin design from 1932 **Edge Lettering:** * NBP * eight times

Date	Mintage	F	VF	XF	Unc	BU
2006MW	1,000,000	—	—	—	3.00	5.00

Y# 605 2 ZLOTE
8.1500 g., Brass, 27 mm. **Obv:** National arms **Obv. Legend:**
RZECZPOSPOLITA POLSKA **Rev:** Skier and marksman
standing **Rev. Legend:** XX ZIMOWE IGAZYSKA OLIMPIJSKIE
- TURYN **Edge Lettering:** * NBP * eight times

Date	Mintage	F	VF	XF	Unc	BU
2006MW	1,200,000	—	—	—	3.00	5.00

Y# 606 2 ZLOTE
8.1500 g., Brass, 27 mm. **Obv:** National arms
Obv. Legend: RZECZPOSPOLITA POLSKA **Rev:** Large soccer
ball with fancy linked date 2006 **Rev. Legend:** MISTRZOSTWA
SWIATA W PItCE NOZNEJ NIEMCY - FIFA **Edge Lettering:** *
NBP * eight times

Date	Mintage	F	VF	XF	Unc	BU
2006MW	1,200,000	—	—	—	3.00	5.00

Y# 609 2 ZLOTE
8.1500 g., Brass, 27 mm. **Subject:** 100th Anniversary Warsaw
School of Economics **Obv:** National arms **Obv. Legend:**
RZECZPOSPOLITA POLSKA **Rev:** School facade
Rev. Legend: SZKOLA CLOWNA HANDLOWA W
WARSZAWIE **Rev. Inscription:** Large SGH
Edge Lettering: * NBP * eight times

Date	Mintage	F	VF	XF	Unc	BU
2006MW	1,000,000	—	—	—	3.00	5.00

Y# 577 2 ZLOTE
8.1500 g., Brass, 27 mm. **Obv:** Crowned eagle **Rev:** Kwidzyn
Castle **Edge Lettering:** * NBP * eight times

Date	Mintage	F	VF	XF	Unc	BU
2007MW	1,000,000	—	—	—	3.00	5.00

Y# 578 2 ZLOTE
8.1500 g., Brass, 27 mm. **Obv:** Crowned eagle **Rev:** Grey Seal
and silhouette **Edge Lettering:** * NBP * eight times

Date	Mintage	F	VF	XF	Unc	BU
2007MW	1,000,000	—	—	—	4.00	7.00

Y# 586 2 ZLOTE
8.1500 g., Brass, 27 mm. **Subject:** 75th Anniversary Breaking
the Enigma Code **Obv:** National arms **Obv. Legend:**
RZECZPOSPOLITA POLSKA **Rev:** Enigma machine wheel
Edge Lettering: * NBP * eight times

Date	Mintage	F	VF	XF	Unc	BU
2007MW	900,000	—	—	—	3.00	5.00

Y# 590 2 ZLOTE
8.1500 g., Brass, 27 mm. **Obv:** National arms
Obv. Legend: RZECZPOSPOLITA POLSKA **Rev:** Bust of
Domeyko facing **Rev. Legend:** IGNACY DOMEYKO 1802 - 1889
Edge Lettering: * NBP * eight times

Date	Mintage	F	VF	XF	Unc	BU
2007MW	900,000	—	—	—	3.00	5.00

Y# 592 2 ZLOTE
8.1500 g., Brass, 27 mm. **Subject:** History of Zloty **Obv:** Nike at left, obverse of 5 Zlotych, Y#18, national arms below **Obv. Legend:** RZECZPOLPOLITA POLSKA **Rev:** Spray at left of reverse of 5 Zlotych, Y# 18 **Edge Lettering:** * NBP * eight times

Date	Mintage	F	VF	XF	Unc	BU
2007MW	900,000	—	—	—	3.00	5.00

Y# 594 2 ZLOTE
8.1500 g., Brass, 27 mm. **Subject:** 750th Anniversary Municipality of Krakau **Obv:** National arms **Obv. Legend:** RZECZPOSPOLITA POLSKA **Rev:** Knight standing facing with spear and shield **Edge Lettering:** * NBP * eight times

Date	Mintage	F	VF	XF	Unc	BU
2007MW	900,000	—	—	—	3.00	5.00

Y# 610 2 ZLOTE
8.1500 g., Brass, 27 mm. **Subject:** Artic Explorers Antoni B. Dombrowolski and Henryk Arctowski **Obv:** National arms **Obv. Legend:** RZECZPOSPOLITA POLSKA **Rev:** Explorer's bust facing at bottom, sailing ship in background **Edge Lettering:** * NBP * eight times

Date	Mintage	F	VF	XF	Unc	BU
2007MW	900,000	—	—	—	3.00	5.00

Y# 611 2 ZLOTE
8.1500 g., Brass, 27 mm. **Obv:** National arms **Obv. Legend:** RZECZPOSPOLIYA POLSKA **Rev:** Ciezkozbrojny in armor, horseback left **Rev. Legend:** RYCERZ CIEZKOZBROJNY-XV **Edge Lettering:** * NBP * eight times

Date	Mintage	F	VF	XF	Unc	BU
2007MW	900,000	—	—	—	3.00	5.00

Y# 612 2 ZLOTE
8.1500 g., Brass, 27 mm. **Subject:** 70th Anniversary Death of Szymanowskiego **Obv:** National arms **Obv. Legend:** RZECZPOSPOLITA POLSKA **Rev:** Bust facing 3/4 right at left, music score in background **Rev. Legend:** ROCZNICA URODZIN KAROLA SYMANOWSKIEGO **Edge Lettering:** * NBP * eight times

Date	Mintage	F	VF	XF	Unc	BU
2007MW	900,000	—	—	—	3.00	5.00

Y# 613 2 ZLOTE
8.1500 g., Brass, 27 mm. **Obv:** National arms above gateway **Obv. Legend:** RZECZPOSPOLITA POLSKA **Rev:** Buildings **Rev. Legend:** STARGARD - SZCZECINSKI **Edge Lettering:** * NBP * eight times

Date	Mintage	F	VF	XF	Unc	BU
2007MW	1,000,000	—	—	—	3.00	5.00

Y# 615 2 ZLOTE
8.1500 g., Brass, 27 mm. **Obv:** National arms above gateway **Obv. Legend:** RZECZPOSPOLITA POLSKA **Rev:** Building with branches at left and right **Rev. Legend:** BRZEG **Edge Lettering:** * NBP * eight times

Date	Mintage	F	VF	XF	Unc	BU
2007MW	1,000,000	—	—	—	3.00	5.00

Y# 616 2 ZLOTE
8.1500 g., Brass, 27 mm. **Obv:** National arms above gateway **Obv. Legend:** RZECZPOSPOLITA POLSKA **Rev:** Church **Rev. Legend:** LOMZA **Edge Lettering:** * NBP * eight times

Date	Mintage	F	VF	XF	Unc	BU
2007MW	1,000,000	—	—	—	3.00	5.00

Y# 617 2 ZLOTE
8.1500 g., Brass, 27 mm. **Obv:** National arms above gateway **Obv. Legend:** RZECZPOSPOLITA POLSKA **Rev:** Church **Rev. Legend:** PLOCK **Edge Lettering:** * NBP * eight times

Date	Mintage	F	VF	XF	Unc	BU
2007MW	1,000,000	—	—	—	3.00	5.00

Y# 618 2 ZLOTE
8.1500 g., Brass, 27 mm. **Obv:** National arms above gateway **Obv. Legend:** RZECZPOSPOLITA POLSKA **Rev:** Church **Rev. Legend:** PRZEMYSL **Edge Lettering:** * NBP * eight times

Date	Mintage	F	VF	XF	Unc	BU
2007MW	1,000,000	—	—	—	3.00	5.00

Y# 619 2 ZLOTE
8.1500 g., Brass, 27 mm. **Obv:** National arms above gateway **Obv. Legend:** RZECZPOSPOLITA POLSKA **Rev:** Towered gateway **Rev. Legend:** RACIBÓRZ **Edge Lettering:** * NBP * eight times

Date	Mintage	F	VF	XF	Unc	BU
2007MW	1,000,000	—	—	—	3.00	5.00

Y# 620 2 ZLOTE
8.1500 g., Brass, 27 mm. **Obv:** National arms above gateway **Obv. Legend:** RZECZPOSPOLITA POLSKA **Rev:** Church **Rev. Legend:** SLUPSK **Edge Lettering:** NBP repeated

Date	Mintage	F	VF	XF	Unc	BU
2007MW	1,000,000	—	—	—	3.00	5.00

Y# 621 2 ZLOTE
8.1500 g., Brass, 27 mm. **Obv:** National arms above gateway **Obv. Legend:** RZECZPOSPOLITA POLSKA **Rev:** Church **Rev. Legend:** SWIDNICA **Edge Lettering:** * NBP * eight times

Date	Mintage	F	VF	XF	Unc	BU
2007MW	1,000,000	—	—	—	3.00	5.00

Y# 622 2 ZLOTE
8.1500 g., Brass, 27 mm. **Obv:** National arms **Obv. Legend:** RZECZPOSPOLITA POLSKE **Rev:** Town view **Rev. Legend:** MIASTO SREDNIOWIECZNE - W TORUNIU **Edge Lettering:** * NBP * eight times

Date	Mintage	F	VF	XF	Unc	BU
2007MW	900,000	—	—	—	3.00	5.00

Y# 623 2 ZLOTE
8.1500 g., Brass, 27 mm. **Obv:** National arms above gateway **Obv. Legend:** RZECZPOSPOLITA POLSKA **Rev:** Church **Rev. Legend:** GORZÓW WIELKOPOLSKI **Edge Lettering:** * NBP * eight times

Date	Mintage	F	VF	XF	Unc	BU
2007MW	1,000,000	—	—	—	3.00	5.00

Y# 624 2 ZLOTE
8.1500 g., Brass, 27 mm. **Obv:** National arms above gateway
Obv. Legend: RZECZPOSPOLITA POLSKA **Rev:** Church at
lower right, houses to left, fortress in upper background
Rev. Legend: KLODZKO **Edge Lettering:** * NBP * eight times

Date	Mintage	F	VF	XF	Unc	BU
2007MW	1,000,000	—	—	—	3.00	5.00

Y# 625 2 ZLOTE
8.1500 g., Brass, 27 mm. **Obv:** National arms above gateway
Obv. Legend: RZECZPOSPOLITA POLSKE **Rev:** Church
Rev. Legend: TARNOW **Edge Lettering:** * NBP * eight times

Date	Mintage	F	VF	XF	Unc	BU
2007MW	1,000,000	—	—	—	3.00	5.00

Y# 626 2 ZLOTE
8.1500 g., Brass, 27 mm. **Subject:** Leon Wyczotkowski
Obv: Artist's palette, brushes at left, national arms at right
Obv. Legend: RZECZPOSPOLITA POLSKA **Rev:** Bust facing
Edge Lettering: * NBP * eight times

Date	Mintage	F	VF	XF	Unc	BU
2007MW	900,000	—	—	—	3.00	5.00

Y# 628 2 ZLOTE
8.1500 g., Brass, 27 mm. **Obv:** National arms above gateway
Obv. Legend: RZECZPOSPOLITA POLSKA **Rev:** National arms
ar upper left, Piotrków Tribunal building at lower right
Rev. Legend: PIOTRKÓW - TRYBUNALSKI **Edge Lettering:** *
NBP * eight times

Date	Mintage	F	VF	XF	Unc	BU
2007MW	1,100,000	—	—	0.90	2.25	3.00

Y# 627 2 ZLOTE
8.1500 g., Brass, 27 mm. **Obv:** National arms above flags
Obv. Legend: RZECZPOSPOLITA POLSKA **Obv. Designer:**
Ewa Tyc-Karpinska **Rev:** Peregrine Falcon perched on branch
Rev. Legend: SOKOL WEDROWNY - Falco peregrinus
Rev. Designer: Roussanka Nowakowska **Edge Lettering:** *
NBP * eight times

Date	Mintage	F	VF	XF	Unc	BU
2008MW	1,600,000	—	—	—	3.00	4.00

Y# 629 2 ZLOTE
8.1500 g., Brass, 27 mm. **Subject:** 40th Anniversary "Rocznica"
March **Obv:** National arms above value **Obv. Legend:**
RZECZPOSPOLITA POLSKA **Obv. Designer:** Ewa Tyc-
Karpinska **Rev:** University of Warsaw coat of arms above political
protest marchers **Rev. Designer:** Andrzej Nowakowski
Edge Lettering: * NBP * eight times

Date	Mintage	F	VF	XF	Unc	BU
2008MW	1,400,000	—	—	0.90	2.25	3.00

Y# 630 2 ZLOTE
8.1500 g., Brass, 27 mm. **Obv:** National arms above gateway
Obv. Legend: RZECZPOSPOLITA POLSKA **Rev:** Building
Rev. Legend: LOWICZ **Edge Lettering:** * NBP * eight times

Date	Mintage	F	VF	XF	Unc	BU
2008MW	1,100,000	—	—	0.90	2.25	3.00

Y# 631 2 ZLOTE
8.1500 g., Brass, 27 mm. **Obv:** National arms above gateway
Obv. Legend: RZECZPOSPOLITA POLSKA **Rev:** Monument
Rev. Legend: KONIN **Edge Lettering:** * NBP * eight times

Date	Mintage	F	VF	XF	Unc	BU
2008MW	1,100,000	—	—	0.90	2.25	3.00

Y# 633 2 ZLOTE
8.1500 g., Brass, 27 mm. **Subject:** 65th Anniversary Warsaw
Uprising **Obv:** National arms **Obv. Legend:** RZECZPOSPOLITA
POLSKA **Rev:** Star of David in barbed wire, female freedom fighter
at right. **Rev. Legend:** POWSTANIA W GETCIE
WARSZAWSKKIM 65. ROCZNICA **Edge Lettering:** * NBP * eight
times

Date	Mintage	F	VF	XF	Unc	BU
2008MW	1,750,000	—	—	—	3.00	5.00

Y# 634 2 ZLOTE
8.1500 g., Brass, 27 mm. **Subject:** Zbigniew Herbert
Obv: National arms **Obv. Legend:** RZECZPOSPOLITA
POLSKA **Rev:** Head of Herbert right **Edge Lettering:** * NBP *
eight times

Date	Mintage	F	VF	XF	Unc	BU
2008MW	1,510,000	—	—	—	3.00	4.00

Y# 638 2 ZLOTE
8.1500 g., Brass, 27 mm. **Subject:** Siberian Exiles
Obv: National arms **Obv. Legend:** RZECZPOSPOLITA
POLSKA **Rev:** Bleak forest **Rev. Inscription:** SYBIRACY
Edge Lettering: * NBP * eight times

Date	Mintage	F	VF	XF	Unc	BU
2008MW	1,500,000	—	—	—	3.00	4.00

Y# 641 2 ZLOTE
8.1500 g., Brass, 27 mm. **Subject:** Kazimierz Dolny **Obv:** National
arms **Obv. Legend:** RZECZPOSPOLITA POLSKA **Obv.
Designer:** Ewa Tyc-Karpinska **Rev:** City view **Rev. Designer:** Ewa
Olszewska-Borys **Edge Lettering:** * NBP * eight times

Date	Mintage	F	VF	XF	Unc	BU
2008MW	1,380,000	—	—	—	3.00	4.00

Y# 644 2 ZLOTE
8.1500 g., Brass, 27 mm. **Subject:** 29th Olympic Games Beijing
2008 **Obv:** Eagle **Obv. Designer:** Ewa Tyc-Karpinska **Rev:** Two
rowers in boat & a square **Rev. Designer:** Urszula Walerzak
Edge Lettering: * NBP * eight times

Date	Mintage	F	VF	XF	Unc	BU
2008	2,000,000	—	—	—	3.00	4.00

Y# 648 2 ZLOTE
8.1500 g., Brass, 27 mm. **Subject:** Polish Travellers & Explorers
Obv: Eagle **Obv. Designer:** Ewa Tyc-Karpinska **Rev:** Bust of
Bronislaw Pilsudski **Rev. Designer:** Roussanka Nowakowska
Edge Lettering: * NBP * eight times

Date	Mintage	F	VF	XF	Unc	BU
2008	1,100,000	—	—	—	3.00	4.00

Y# 650 2 ZLOTE
8.1500 g., Brass, 27 mm. **Subject:** 90th Anniversary of
Regaining Freedom **Obv:** Eagle **Obv. Designer:** Ewa Tyc-
Karpinska **Rev:** Order of Polonia Restituta **Rev. Designer:** Ewa
Olszewska-Borys **Edge Lettering:** * NBP * eight times

Date	Mintage	F	VF	XF	Unc	BU
2008	1,200,000	—	—	—	3.00	4.00

Y# 656 2 ZLOTE
8.1500 g., Brass, 27 mm. **Subject:** 450th Anniversary of the
Polish Post **Obv:** Eagle **Obv. Designer:** Ewa Tyc-Karpinska
Rev: Post rider on horse **Rev. Designer:** Robert Kotowicz
Edge: NBP

Date	Mintage	F	VF	XF	Unc	BU
2008	1,400,000	—	—	—	3.00	4.00

Y# 659 2 ZLOTE
8.1500 g., Brass, 27 mm. **Subject:** 400th Anniversary of Polish
settlement in North America **Obv:** Eagle **Obv. Designer:** Ewa
Tyc-Karpinska **Rev:** Man blowing glassware **Rev. Designer:**
Roussanka Nowakowska **Edge Lettering:** * NBP * eight times

Date	Mintage	F	VF	XF	Unc	BU
2008	1,200,000	—	—	—	3.00	4.00

Y# 662 2 ZLOTE
8.1500 g., Brass, 27 mm. **Subject:** 90th Anniversary of the Greater Poland Uprising **Obv:** Eagle **Obv. Designer:** Ewa Tyc-Karpinska **Rev:** Bust of Igancy Jan Paderewski, soldiers at bottom **Rev. Designer:** Urszula Walerzak **Edge Lettering:** * NBP * eight times

Date	Mintage	F	VF	XF	Unc	BU
2008	1,100,000	—	—	—	3.00	4.00

Y# 663 2 ZLOTE
8.1500 g., Brass, 27 mm. **Subject:** Belsko - Biala **Obv:** National arms above gateway **Rev:** Building

Date	Mintage	F	VF	XF	Unc	BU
2008MW	—	—	—	—	3.00	4.00

Y# 673 2 ZLOTE
8.1500 g., Brass, 27 mm. **Subject:** Supreme Chamber of Control, 100th Anniversary **Obv:** National arms above value **Rev:** Building

Date	Mintage	F	VF	XF	Unc	BU
2009MW	1,200,000	—	—	—	3.00	4.00

Y# 675 2 ZLOTE
8.1500 g., Brass, 27 mm. **Subject:** Central Banking, 180th Anniversary **Obv:** National arms above value **Rev:** Five coins

Date	Mintage	F	VF	XF	Unc	BU
2009MW	1,300,000	—	—	—	3.00	4.00

Y# 678 2 ZLOTE
8.1500 g., Brass, 27 mm. **Subject:** Green Lizards **Obv:** National arms above value **Rev:** Two green lizards on rocks (lacerta viridis) **Rev. Legend:** JASZCZURKA

Date	Mintage	F	VF	XF	Unc	BU
2009MW	1,700,000	—	—	—	3.00	4.00

Y# 680 2 ZLOTE
8.1500 g., Brass, 27 mm. **Subject:** General Elections of 1989 **Obv:** National arms above eagle **Rev:** Election notice within wreath

Date	Mintage	F	VF	XF	Unc	BU
2009MW	1,300,000	—	—	—	3.00	4.00

Y# 684 2 ZLOTE
8.1500 g., Brass, 27 mm. **Subject:** Czeslaw Niemen **Obv:** National arms above value **Rev:** Two dimentional facing portrait

Date	Mintage	F	VF	XF	Unc	BU
2009MW	1,400,000	—	—	—	3.00	4.00

Y# 687 2 ZLOTE
8.1500 g., Brass, 27 mm. **Subject:** Poets of the Warsaw uprising, 65th Anniversary **Obv:** National arms above eagle

Date	Mintage	F	VF	XF	Unc	BU
2009MW	1,400,000	—	—	—	3.00	4.00

Y# 690 2 ZLOTE
8.1500 g., Brass, 27 mm. **Subject:** First Cadre March **Obv:** National arms above value **Rev:** Military badge

Date	Mintage	F	VF	XF	Unc	BU
2009MW	1,000,000	—	—	—	3.00	4.00

Y# 692 2 ZLOTE
8.1500 g., Brass, 27 mm. **Subject:** Liquidation of Lodz Ghetto **Obv:** National arms above value **Rev:** Silouette of Ghetto

Date	Mintage	F	VF	XF	Unc	BU
2009MW	1,000,000	—	—	—	3.00	4.00

Y# 694 2 ZLOTE
8.1500 g., Brass, 27 mm. **Subject:** Westerplatte **Obv:** National arms above value **Rev:** Three soldiers and map

Date	Mintage	F	VF	XF	Unc	BU
2009	1,400,000	—	—	—	3.00	4.00

Y# 697 2 ZLOTE
8.1500 g., Brass, 27 mm. **Subject:** Tatar Mountain Rescue **Obv:** National arms above value **Rev:** Mountain climber

Date	Mintage	F	VF	XF	Unc	BU
2009MW	1,400,000	—	—	—	3.00	4.00

Y# 700 2 ZLOTE
8.1500 g., Brass, 27 mm. **Subject:** Fr. Jerzy Popieluszko, 25th Anniversary of Murder **Obv:** National arms above value **Rev:** Portrait and candle memorial

Date	Mintage	F	VF	XF	Unc	BU
2009MW	1,500,000	—	—	—	3.00	4.00

Y# 703 2 ZLOTE
8.1500 g., Brass, 27 mm. **Subject:** Poles saving Jews **Obv:** National arms above value **Rev:** Broken brick wall

Date	Mintage	F	VF	XF	Unc	BU
2009MW	1,400,000	—	—	—	3.00	4.00

Y# 705 2 ZLOTE
8.1500 g., Brass, 27 mm. **Subject:** Wald Strzeminski **Obv:** Artist palet and National arms **Rev:** Portrait at left

Date	Mintage	F	VF	XF	Unc	BU
2009MW	1,300,000	—	—	—	3.00	4.00

Y# 707 2 ZLOTE
8.1500 g., Brass, 27 mm. **Subject:** Polish Underground **Obv:** National arms above value **Rev:** Monogram of resistance and map of Poland

Date	Mintage	F	VF	XF	Unc	BU
2009MW	1,000,000	—	—	—	3.00	4.00

Y# 709 2 ZLOTE
8.1500 g., Brass, 27 mm. **Subject:** Czestochowa **Rev:** Chruch

Date	Mintage	F	VF	XF	Unc	BU
2009MW	—	—	—	—	3.00	4.00

Y# 710 2 ZLOTE

8.1500 g., Brass, 27 mm. **Subject:** Jedrzejow Cistercian Monastery **Rev:** Church

Date	Mintage	F	VF	XF	Unc	BU
2009MW	—				3.00	4.00

Y# 711 2 ZLOTE

8.1500 g., Brass, 27 mm. **Subject:** Trzebnica **Rev:** Building

Date	Mintage	F	VF	XF	Unc	BU
2009MW	—				3.00	4.00

Y# 712 2 ZLOTE

8.1500 g., Brass, 27 mm. **Subject:** Liberation of Auschwitz **Obv:** National arms above value **Rev:** Three prisoners and camp gate sign

Date	Mintage	F	VF	XF	Unc	BU
2010MW	1,000,000	—	—	—	3.00	4.00

Y# 715 2 ZLOTE

8.1500 g., Brass, 27 mm. **Subject:** Vancouver Winter Olympics **Obv:** National arms above value **Rev:** Ski jump athlete

Date	Mintage	F	VF	XF	Unc	BU
2010MW	1,400,000	—	—	—		4.00

Y# 718 2 ZLOTE

8.1500 g., Brass, 27 mm. **Subject:** Imperial Guard **Obv:** National arms above value **Rev:** Napoleonic era mounter soldier

Date	Mintage	F	VF	XF	Unc	BU
2010MW	1,400,000	—	—	—	3.00	4.00

Y# 721 2 ZLOTE

8.1500 g., Brass, 27 mm. **Subject:** Katyn Crime **Obv:** Naitonal arms above value **Rev:** City name above cap

Date	Mintage	F	VF	XF	Unc	BU
2010MW	1,000,000	—	—	—	3.00	4.00

Y# 670 2 ZLOTYCH

8.1500 g., Brass, 27 mm. **Subject:** Polish Calvery **Obv:** National arms above value **Rev:** Hussar Knights, XVII Century

Date	Mintage	F	VF	XF	Unc	BU
2009MW	1,400,000	—	—	—	3.00	4.00

Y# 406 10 ZLOTYCH

14.1400 g., 0.9250 Silver 0.4205 oz. ASW. **Subject:** Year 2001 **Obv:** Crowned eagle with wings open **Rev:** Printed circuit board

Date	Mintage	F	VF	XF	Unc	BU
2001MW Proof	35,000	Value: 75.00				

Y# 413 10 ZLOTYCH

14.1400 g., 0.9250 Silver 0.4205 oz. ASW, 32 mm. **Subject:** 15 Years of the Constitutional Court **Obv:** Crowned eagle suspended from a judge's neck chain **Rev:** Crowned eagle head and balance scale **Edge Lettering:** TRYBUNAL KONSTYTUCYJNY W SLUZBIE PANSTWA PRAWA

Date	Mintage	F	VF	XF	Unc	BU
2001MW Proof	25,000	Value: 65.00				

Y# 419 10 ZLOTYCH

14.1400 g., 0.9250 Silver 0.4205 oz. ASW, 32 mm. **Subject:** Cardinal Stefan Wyszynski **Obv:** Crowned eagle with wings open above ribbon **Rev:** Half length figure facing with raised hands **Edge Lettering:** 100 • ROCZNIA URODZIN

Date	Mintage	F	VF	XF	Unc	BU
2001MW Proof	60,000	Value: 30.00				

Y# 425 10 ZLOTYCH

14.2100 g., 0.9250 Silver 0.4226 oz. ASW, 32 mm. **Subject:** Jan III Sobieski **Obv:** Crowned eagle with wings open **Rev:** 3/4 armored bust facing with army in background **Edge:** Plain

Date	Mintage	F	VF	XF	Unc	BU
2001MW Proof	24,000	Value: 120				

Y# 458 10 ZLOTYCH

14.1400 g., 0.9250 Silver 0.4205 oz. ASW, 32 mm. **Obv:** Crowned eagle with wings open **Rev:** Jan Sobieski, type II **Edge:** Plain

Date	Mintage	F	VF	XF	Unc	BU
2001MW Proof	17,000	Value: 175				

Y# 459 10 ZLOTYCH

14.1400 g., 0.9250 Silver 0.4205 oz. ASW, 32 mm. **Obv:** Three violins **Rev:** Henryk Wieniawski **Edge:** Plain

Date	Mintage	F	VF	XF	Unc	BU
2001MW Proof	28,000	Value: 60.00				

Y# 460 10 ZLOTYCH

14.1400 g., 0.9250 Silver 0.4205 oz. ASW, 32 mm. **Obv:** Crowned eagle with wings open above fish **Rev:** Michal Siedlecki **Edge:** Plain

Date	Mintage	F	VF	XF	Unc	BU
2001MW Proof	26,000	Value: 60.00				

Y# 432 10 ZLOTYCH

14.1400 g., 0.9250 Silver 0.4205 oz. ASW, 32 mm. **Subject:** Bronislaw Malinowski **Obv:** Small crowned eagle with wings open to right of bust facing **Rev:** Trobriand Islands village scene **Edge Lettering:** etnolog, antropolog kultury

Date	Mintage	F	VF	XF	Unc	BU
2002MW Proof	33,500	Value: 35.00				

Y# 434 10 ZLOTYCH

14.1400 g., 0.9250 Silver 0.4205 oz. ASW, 32 mm. **Subject:** World Cup Soccer **Obv:** Crowned eagle with wings open **Rev:** Soccer player **Edge Lettering:** etnolog, antropolog kultury

Date	Mintage	F	VF	XF	Unc	BU
2002MW Proof	55,000	Value: 27.50				

Y# 435 10 ZLOTYCH

14.1400 g., 0.9250 Silver 0.4205 oz. ASW, 32 mm. **Subject:** World Cup Soccer **Obv:** Amber soccer ball inset entering goal net **Rev:** Two soccer players with amber soccer ball inset **Edge Lettering:** etnolog, antropolog kultury

Date	Mintage	F	VF	XF	Unc	BU
2002MW Proof	65,000	Value: 75.00				

Y# 437 10 ZLOTYCH

14.1400 g., 0.9250 Silver 0.4205 oz. ASW, 32 mm. **Subject:** Pope John Paul II **Obv:** Crowned eagle with wings open within two views of praying Pope **Rev:** Pope facing radiant Holy Door **Edge:** Plain

Date	Mintage	F	VF	XF	Unc	BU
2002MW Proof	80,000	Value: 45.00				

Y# 441 10 ZLOTYCH
14.2000 g., 0.9250 Silver 0.4223 oz. ASW, 32 mm.
Subject: Gen. Wladyslaw Anders **Obv:** Crowned eagle with wings open, cross and multicolor flowers **Rev:** Uniformed bust right **Edge:** Plain

Date	Mintage	F	VF	XF	Unc	BU
2002MW Proof	40,000	Value: 120				

Y# 450 10 ZLOTYCH
14.1400 g., 0.9250 Silver 0.4205 oz. ASW, 32 mm.
Subject: August II (1697-1706, 1709-1735) **Obv:** Crowned eagle with wings open **Rev:** Portrait and Order of the White Eagle **Edge:** Plain

Date	Mintage	F	VF	XF	Unc	BU
2002MW Proof	30,000	Value: 90.00				

Y# 453 10 ZLOTYCH
14.1400 g., 0.9250 Silver 0.4205 oz. ASW, 32 mm.
Subject: Great Orchestra of Christmas Charity **Obv:** Large inscribed heart above crowned eagle with wings open **Rev:** Boy playing flute **Edge:** Plain

Date	Mintage	F	VF	XF	Unc	BU
2003MW Proof	47,000	Value: 45.00				

Y# 468 10 ZLOTYCH
14.1400 g., 0.9250 Silver 0.4205 oz. ASW, 32 mm. **Obv:** Tanks on battlefield **Rev:** General Maczek **Edge:** Plain

Date	Mintage	F	VF	XF	Unc	BU
2003MW Proof	44,000	Value: 35.00				

Y# 469 10 ZLOTYCH
14.1400 g., 0.9250 Silver 0.4205 oz. ASW, 32 mm.
Subject: Gas and Oil Industry **Obv:** Crowned eagle and highway leading to city view **Rev:** Portrait and refinery **Edge:** Plain

Date	Mintage	F	VF	XF	Unc	BU
2003MW Proof	43,000	Value: 35.00				

Y# 474 10 ZLOTYCH
14.1400 g., 0.9250 Silver 0.4205 oz. ASW, 32 mm.
Obv: Crowned eagle with wings open **Rev:** Stanislaus I and wife's portrait **Edge:** Plain

Date	Mintage	F	VF	XF	Unc	BU
2003MW Proof	45,000	Value: 35.00				

Y# 475 10 ZLOTYCH
14.1400 g., 0.9250 Silver 0.4205 oz. ASW, 32 mm.
Obv: Crowned eagle with wings open **Rev:** Half-length figure of Stanislaus I with his wife in background **Edge:** Plain

Date	Mintage	F	VF	XF	Unc	BU
2003MW Proof	40,000	Value: 45.00				

Y# 448 10 ZLOTYCH
14.1400 g., 0.9250 Silver 0.4205 oz. ASW, 32 mm.
Subject: City of Poznan (Posen) **Obv:** Old coin design and arched door **Rev:** Old coin design and city view **Edge:** Plain

Date	Mintage	F	VF	XF	Unc	BU
2003MW Proof	39,000	Value: 75.00				

Y# 480 10 ZLOTYCH
14.1400 g., 0.9250 Silver 0.4205 oz. ASW, 32 mm.
Subject: 80th Anniversary of the Modern Zloty Currency **Obv:** Man wearing glasses behind crowned eagle with wings open **Rev:** Bust left **Edge:** Plain

Date	Mintage	F	VF	XF	Unc	BU
2004MW Proof	55,000	Value: 35.00				

Y# 482 10 ZLOTYCH
14.1400 g., 0.9250 Silver 0.4205 oz. ASW, 32 mm.
Subject: Poland Joining the European Union **Obv:** Crowned eagle in blue circle with yellow stars **Rev:** Multicolor European Union and Polish flags **Edge:** Plain

Date	Mintage	F	VF	XF	Unc	BU
2004MW Proof	78,000	Value: 50.00				

Y# 497 10 ZLOTYCH
14.1400 g., 0.9250 Silver 0.4205 oz. ASW, 32 mm.
Subject: Warsaw Uprising 60th Anniversary **Obv:** Crowned eagle and value on resistance symbol **Rev:** Polish soldier wearing captured German helmet **Edge:** Plain

Date	Mintage	F	VF	XF	Unc	BU
2004MW Proof	92,000	Value: 25.00				

Y# 500 10 ZLOTYCH
14.1400 g., 0.9250 Silver 0.4205 oz. ASW, 32 mm. **Obv:** Polish paratrooper badge **Rev:** Gen. Sosabowski and descending paratrooper **Edge:** Plain

Date	Mintage	F	VF	XF	Unc	BU
2004MW Proof	56,000	Value: 25.00				

Y# 502 10 ZLOTYCH
14.1400 g., 0.9250 Silver 0.4205 oz. ASW, 32 mm. **Subject:** Polish Police 85th Anniversary **Obv:** Crowned eagle with wings open **Rev:** Seal partially overlapping police badge **Edge:** Plain

Date	Mintage	F	VF	XF	Unc	BU
2004MW Proof	65,000	Value: 25.00				

Y# 506 10 ZLOTYCH
14.1400 g., 0.9250 Silver 0.4205 oz. ASW, 32 mm.
Obv: Siberian landscape above crowned eagle and value **Rev:** Aleksander Czekanowski (1833-1876) **Edge:** Plain

Date	Mintage	F	VF	XF	Unc	BU
2004MW Proof	45,000	Value: 25.00				

Y# 510 10 ZLOTYCH
14.1400 g., 0.9250 Silver 0.4205 oz. ASW, 32 mm.
Subject: Warsaw Fine Arts Academy Centennial **Obv:** Crowned eagle with wings open within city square **Rev:** Art studio **Edge:** Plain

Date	Mintage	F	VF	XF	Unc	BU
2004MW Proof	75,000	Value: 25.00				

Y# 517 10 ZLOTYCH
14.1400 g., 0.9250 Silver 0.4205 oz. ASW, 32 mm.
Subject: Olympics **Obv:** Crowned eagle with wings open and woman **Rev:** Fencers in front of Parthenon **Edge:** Plain

Date	Mintage	F	VF	XF	Unc	BU
2004MW Proof	70,000	Value: 25.00				

Y# 518 10 ZLOTYCH
14.1400 g., 0.9250 Silver 0.4205 oz. ASW, 32 mm.
Subject: Olympics **Obv:** Crowned eagle with wings open within gold plated center **Rev:** Ancient athlete within gold plated circle **Edge:** Plain

Date	Mintage	F	VF	XF	Unc	BU
2004MW Proof	90,000	Value: 35.00				

Y# 523 10 ZLOTYCH
14.2300 g., 0.9250 Silver 0.4232 oz. ASW, 43.2 x 29.2 mm.
Subject: Japan's Aichi Expo **Obv:** Monument **Rev:** Two cranes **Edge:** Plain **Shape:** Quarter of circle

Date	Mintage	F	VF	XF	Unc	BU
2005MW Proof	80,000	Value: 45.00				

Y# 526 10 ZLOTYCH
14.1400 g., 0.9250 Silver partially gilt 0.4205 oz. ASW, 32.1 mm.
Obv: Crowned eagle with wings open above date and grasping hands **Rev:** Gold plated bust right and church **Edge:** Plain

Date	Mintage	F	VF	XF	Unc	BU
2005MW Proof	—	Value: 30.00				

Y# 537 10 ZLOTYCH
14.1400 g., 0.9250 Silver 0.4205 oz. ASW, 32 mm. **Obv:** Horse drawn carriage **Rev:** Green duck and Konstanty Ildefons Galczynski in top hat **Edge:** Plain

Date	Mintage	F	VF	XF	Unc	BU
2005MW Proof	62,000	Value: 25.00				

Y# 539 10 ZLOTYCH
14.1400 g., 0.9250 Silver 0.4205 oz. ASW, 32 mm.
Obv: Baptismal font and Polish eagle **Rev:** Pope John Paul II and St. Peter's Basilica **Edge:** Plain

Date	Mintage	F	VF	XF	Unc	BU
2005MW Proof	170,000	Value: 30.00				

Y# 552 10 ZLOTYCH
14.1400 g., 0.9250 Silver 0.4205 oz. ASW, 32 mm.
Obv: Crowned eagle above value **Rev:** Stanislaw August Poniatowski and shadow **Edge:** Plain

Date	Mintage	F	VF	XF	Unc	BU
2005MW Proof	60,000	Value: 30.00				

Y# 553 10 ZLOTYCH
14.1400 g., 0.9250 Silver 0.4205 oz. ASW, 32 mm.
Obv: Crowned eagle above value **Rev:** Stanislaw August Poniatowski and crowned monogram **Edge:** Plain

Date	Mintage	F	VF	XF	Unc	BU
2005MW Proof	60,000	Value: 30.00				

Y# 554 10 ZLOTYCH
14.1400 g., 0.9250 Silver 0.4205 oz. ASW, 32 mm.
Subject: End of WWII 60th Anniversary **Obv:** Crowned eagle above soldier silhouettes and value **Rev:** City view in ruins above bird with green sprig **Edge:** Plain

Date	Mintage	F	VF	XF	Unc	BU
2005MW Proof	70,000	Value: 35.00				

Y# 596 10 ZLOTYCH
14.1800 g., 0.9250 Silver 0.4217 oz. ASW, 32 mm.
Subject: 500th Anniversary Birth of M. Reja **Obv:** National arms in oval, value below **Obv. Legend:** RZECZPOSPOLITA POLSKA **Rev:** Bust of Reja 3/4 right **Rev. Legend:** 500. ROCZNICA URODZIN MIKOLAJA REJA **Edge:** Plain

Date	Mintage	F	VF	XF	Unc	BU
2005MW Proof	60,000	Value: 25.00				

Y# 568 10 ZLOTYCH
14.1400 g., 0.9250 Silver 0.4205 oz. ASW, 32 mm. **Obv:** Sail ship and obverse design of Y-31 **Rev:** Reverse design of Y-31 on radiant design **Edge:** Lettered

Date	Mintage	F	VF	XF	Unc	BU
2005MW Proof	61,000	Value: 30.00				

Y# 598 10 ZLOTYCH
14.1500 g., 0.9250 Silver 0.4208 oz. ASW, 32 mm. **Subject:** 30th Anniversary June 1976 **Obv:** National arms divides denomination, split railroad tracks below **Obv. Legend:** RZECZPOSPOLITA POLSKA **Rev:** 3/4 length woman standing with child, outlined row of shielded forces in background **Rev. Legend:** 30. ROCZNICA - CZERWCA 1976 **Edge:** Plain

Date	Mintage	F	VF	XF	Unc	BU
2006MW Proof	56,000	Value: 30.00				

Y# 599 10 ZLOTYCH
14.1800 g., 0.9250 Silver 0.4217 oz. ASW, 32 mm. **Series:** History of the Zloty **Obv:** National arms at upper left, 1932 dated 10 Zlotych obverse at lower right, building facade in background **Obv. Legend:** RZECZPOSPOLITA POLSKA **Rev:** Reverse of 1932 dated coin with head of Queen Jadwiga **Rev. Legend:** DZIEJE ZLOTEGO **Edge:** Plain

Date	Mintage	F	VF	XF	Unc	BU
2006MW Proof	61,000	Value: 40.00				

Y# 555 10 ZLOTYCH
14.1400 g., 0.9250 Silver 0.4205 oz. ASW, 32 mm. **Subject:** 2006 Winter Olympics **Obv:** Snow boarder above crowned eagle **Rev:** Snow boarder **Edge:** Plain

Date	Mintage	F	VF	XF	Unc	BU
2006MW Proof	71,400	Value: 30.00				

Y# 556 10 ZLOTYCH
14.1400 g., 0.9250 Silver 0.4205 oz. ASW, 32.03 mm. **Subject:** 2006 Winter Olympics **Obv:** Small national arms at left, figure skating couple at center **Obv. Legend:** RZECZPOSPOLITA POLSKA **Rev:** Female figure skater **Rev. Legend:** XX ZIMOWE IGRZYSKA OLIMPIJSKIE **Edge:** Plain

Date	Mintage	F	VF	XF	Unc	BU
2006MW Proof	72,000	Value: 30.00				

Y# 600 10 ZLOTYCH
14.1000 g., 0.9250 Silver 0.4193 oz. ASW, 32 mm. **Subject:** 125th Anniversary - Birth of Szymanowskiego **Obv:** Piano keys at left, national arms on music score at right **Obv. Legend:** RZECZPOSPOLITA POLSKA **Rev:** Bust of Szymanowskiego 3/4 left, music composition at back of head and over upper body, dates as hologram at left **Rev. Legend:** 125. ROCZNICA URODZIN KAROLA SZYMANOWSKIEGO **Edge:** Plain

Date	Mintage	F	VF	XF	Unc	BU
2007MW Proof	55,000	Value: 30.00				

Y# 601 10 ZLOTYCH
14.3000 g., 0.9250 Silver 0.4253 oz. ASW, 14 mm. **Subject:** Arctic Explorers **Obv:** Sailing ship at center, national arms at right with denomination below **Obv. Legend:** RZECZPOSPOLITA POLSKA **Rev:** Busts of Henryk Arctowski and Antoni Dobrowolski facing, polar outline map at lower left **Edge:** Plain

Date	Mintage	F	VF	XF	Unc	BU
2007MW Proof	60,000	Value: 30.00				

Y# 602 10 ZLOTYCH
14.0500 g., 0.9250 Silver 0.4178 oz. ASW, 31.95 x 22.39 mm. **Obv:** Helmeted national arms, sword and denomination below **Obv. Legend:** RZECZPOSPOLITA - POLSKA **Rev:** Chivalrous knight on horseback jousting right **Rev. Inscription:** RYCERZ - CIEZKOZBROJNY **Edge:** Plain **Shape:** Rectangular

Date	Mintage	F	VF	XF	Unc	BU
2007MW Proof	57,000	Value: 40.00				

Y# 585 10 ZLOTYCH
14.1400 g., 0.9250 Silver 0.4205 oz. ASW, 32 mm. **Obv:** Mountains, Polish Eagle and value **Rev:** Ignacy Domeyko **Edge:** Plain

Date	Mintage	F	VF	XF	Unc	BU
2007MW Proof	55,000	Value: 30.00				

Y# 587 10 ZLOTYCH
14.1400 g., 0.9250 Silver 0.4205 oz. ASW, 32 mm. **Subject:** 75th Anniversary - Breaking the Enigma Code **Obv:** Polish Eagle on circuit board **Rev:** Segmented letters **Edge:** Lettered

Date	Mintage	F	VF	XF	Unc	BU
2007MW Proof	55,000	Value: 50.00				

Y# 589 10 ZLOTYCH
14.1400 g., 0.9250 Silver 0.4205 oz. ASW, 32 mm. **Obv:** Angel, Polish Eagle and obverse coin design of Y-18 **Rev:** Reverse coin design of Y-18 on wheat ears **Edge:** Plain

Date	Mintage	F	VF	XF	Unc	BU
2007MW Proof	57,000	Value: 40.00				

Y# 595 10 ZLOTYCH
14.1400 g., 0.9250 Silver ASW 0.4205 0.4205 oz. ASW **Subject:** 750th Anniversary Municipality of Krakau **Obv:** City gate tower, national arms at lower right **Obv. Legend:** RZECZPOSPOLITA POLSKA **Rev:** Knight with shield standing facing

Date	Mintage	F	VF	XF	Unc	BU
2007MW Proof	58,000	Value: 50.00				

Y# 645 10 ZLOTYCH
14.4000 g., Silver center gold plated, 32 mm. **Subject:** The 29th Olympic Games Beijing 2008 **Obv:** Chinese ornament & dragon **Rev:** Swimmer **Designer:** Robert Kotowicz

Date	Mintage	F	VF	XF	Unc	BU
2008 Proof	140,000	Value: 40.00				

Y# 632 10 ZLOTYCH
14.1400 g., 0.9250 Silver 0.4205 oz. ASW, 32 mm. **Subject:** 40th Anniversary "Rocznica" March **Obv:** National arms at upper right, manuscript pages fluttering at left **Obv. Legend:** RZECZPOSPOLITA POLSKA **Rev:** Student protesters in front of gates of Warsaw University, military police in silhouette in foreground **Designer:** Andrzej Nowakowski

Date	Mintage	F	VF	XF	Unc	BU
2008MW Proof	118,000	Value: 50.00				

Y# 635   10 ZLOTYCH
14.1000 g., Silver, 32.03 mm. **Subject:** Zbigniew Herbert
Obv: Bust of Herbert 3/4 right at left, national arms at lower right
Rev: Statue of Nike **Edge:** Plain

Date	Mintage	F	VF	XF	Unc	BU
2008MW Proof	—	Value: 40.00				

Y# 639   10 ZLOTYCH
14.1400 g., 0.9250 Silver 0.4205 oz. ASW, 32 mm. **Subject:**
Siberian Exiles **Obv:** Small national arms at left, human outlines
at right **Obv. Legend:** RZECZPOSPOLITA POLSKA **Rev:** Tree
lines with imbedded triangular crystal below **Rev. Inscription:**
SYBIRACY **Edge:** Plain **Designer:** Ewa Tyc-Karpinska

Date	Mintage	F	VF	XF	Unc	BU
2008MW Proof	135,000	Value: 35.00				

Y# 646   10 ZLOTYCH
14.1400 g., Silver, 32 mm. **Subject:** The 29th Olympic Games
Beijing 2008 **Obv:** Square hole & an eagle **Rev:** Square hole &
a windsurfer **Designer:** Urszula Walerzak

Date	Mintage	F	VF	XF	Unc	BU
2008 Proof	150,000	Value: 25.00				

Y# 649   10 ZLOTYCH
14.1400 g., Silver, 32 mm. **Subject:** Polish Travellers &
Explorers **Obv:** Man & woman holding child **Obv. Designer:**
Roussanka Nowakowska **Rev:** Bust of Bronislaw Pilsudski
Rev. Designer: Roussanks Nowakowska

Date	Mintage	F	VF	XF	Unc	BU
2008 Proof	99,000	Value: 30.00				

Y# 655   10 ZLOTYCH
14.1400 g., Silver, 32 mm. **Subject:** 450th Anniversary of the
Polish Post **Obv:** Eatle on top right, post stamp in center with
man on horse **Rev:** Post courier **Designer:** Robert Kotowicz

Date	Mintage	F	VF	XF	Unc	BU
2008 Proof	135,000	Value: 25.00				

Y# 658   10 ZLOTYCH
14.1400 g., Silver, 32 mm. **Subject:** 400th Anniversary of Polish
settlement in North America **Obv:** Man blowing glassware left
Rev: Man blowing glassware right **Designer:** Robert Kotowicz

Date	Mintage	F	VF	XF	Unc	BU
2008 Proof	126,000	Value: 25.00				

Y# 661   10 ZLOTYCH
14.1400 g., Silver, 32 mm. **Subject:** 90th Anniversary of the
Greater Poland Uprising **Obv:** Eagle at top, Commander riding
horse followed by soldiers **Rev:** Rose at left, Bust of Igancy Jan
Paderewski at right **Designer:** Urszula Walerzak

Date	Mintage	F	VF	XF	Unc	BU
2008 Proof	107,000	Value: 30.00				

Y# 695   10 ZLOTYCH
14.1400 g., 0.9250 Silver 0.4205 oz. ASW, 32 mm.
Subject: 70th Anniversary of the start of World War II **Obv:** Eagle
and map of Nazi and Soviet invasion **Rev:** Planes droping bombs
on Wielun

Date	Mintage	F	VF	XF	Unc	BU
2009MW Proof	100,000	Value: 40.00				

Y# 671   10 ZLOTYCH
14.4000 g., 0.9250 Silver 0.4282 oz. ASW, 22x32 mm.
Obv: Eagle, flag and armor **Rev:** Hussar Knights, XVII Century
Shape: Vertical rectangle

Date	Mintage	F	VF	XF	Unc	BU
2009 Proof	100,000	Value: 45.00				

Y# 674   10 ZLOTYCH
14.4000 g., 0.9250 Silver 0.4282 oz. ASW, 32 mm.
Subject: Supreme Chamber, 90th Anniversary **Obv:** Building
Rev: Monogram hologram

Date	Mintage	F	VF	XF	Unc	BU
2009MW Proof	100,000	Value: 45.00				

Y# 676   10 ZLOTYCH
14.4000 g., 0.9250 Silver 0.4282 oz. ASW, 32 mm.
Subject: Central Banking, 180th Anniversary **Obv:** National arms
above building **Rev:** Portrait above banknote

Date	Mintage	F	VF	XF	Unc	BU
2009MW Proof	92,000	Value: 40.00				

Y# 681   10 ZLOTYCH
14.1400 g., 0.9250 Silver 0.4205 oz. ASW, 32 mm.
Subject: General elections of 1989 **Obv:** Eagle **Rev:** Pope John
Paul II and Solidarity banner in color

Date	Mintage	F	VF	XF	Unc	BU
2009MW Proof	100,000	Value: 30.00				

Y# 685   10 ZLOTYCH
14.1400 g., 0.9250 Silver 0.4205 oz. ASW, 29x29 mm.
Subject: Czeslaw Niemen **Obv:** National arms and large portrait
Rev: Female crying **Shape:** Square

Date	Mintage	F	VF	XF	Unc	BU
2009MW Proof	100,000	Value: 40.00				

Y# 686   10 ZLOTYCH
14.1400 g., 0.9250 Silver 0.4205 oz. ASW, 32 mm.
Subject: Cezeslaw Neiman **Obv:** National arms and portrait
Rev: Abstract painting

Date	Mintage	F	VF	XF	Unc	BU
2009MW Proof	100,000	—	—	—	—	40.00

Y# 688   10 ZLOTYCH
14.1400 g., 0.9250 Silver GGold plated center in silver ring
0.4205 oz. ASW, 27 mm. **Subject:** Poets of the Uprising
Obv: National arms **Rev:** Tadeusz Gajcy portrait

Date	Mintage	F	VF	XF	Unc	BU
2009MW Proof	100,000	Value: 40.00				

Y# 689   10 ZLOTYCH
14.1400 g., 0.9250 Silver Silver center in gold plated ring
0.4205 oz. ASW, 32 mm.   **Subject:** Poets of the uprising
Obv: National arms **Rev:** Krzystof Baczynski portrait facing

Date	Mintage	F	VF	XF	Unc	BU
2009MW Proof	100,000	Value: 40.00				

Y# 691   10 ZLOTYCH
14.1400 g., 0.9250 Silver 0.4205 oz. ASW, 32 mm.   **Subject:**
First Cadre Company March **Obv:** National arms and eagle atop
stelle monument **Rev:** Troops marching, song and music

Date	Mintage	F	VF	XF	Unc	BU
2009MW Proof	50,000	Value: 40.00				

Y# 698   10 ZLOTYCH
14.1400 g., 0.9250 Silver 0.4205 oz. ASW, 32 mm.
Series: Tatar Rescues, 100th Anniversary **Obv:** National arms
and logo colorized **Rev:** Mountains and figure of Karlowicz

Date	Mintage	F	VF	XF	Unc	BU
2009MW Proof	100,000	Value: 40.00				

Y# 701   10 ZLOTYCH
14.1400 g., 0.9250 Silver 0.4205 oz. ASW, 32 mm.
Subject: Fr. Jerzy Popielosko, 25th Anniversary of Murder **Obv:**
Rose on monument **Rev:** Statue and tear drop on map of Poland

Date	Mintage	F	VF	XF	Unc	BU
2009MW Proof	100,000	Value: 40.00				

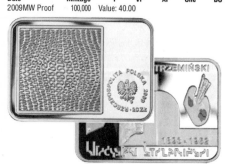

Y# 706   10 ZLOTYCH
28.2800 g., 0.9250 Silver 0.8410 oz. ASW, 40x28 mm.
Subject: Wald Strzeminski **Obv:** Portrait and multicolor palet
Rev: Artwork **Shape:** Rectangle

Date	Mintage	F	VF	XF	Unc	BU
2009MW Proof	100,000	Value: 40.00				

Y# 708   10 ZLOTYCH
14.1400 g., 0.9250 Silver 0.4205 oz. ASW, 32 mm.
Subject: Polish Underground State **Obv:** National arms and
monogram and cloth flag **Rev:** Figure and cloth flag

Date	Mintage	F	VF	XF	Unc	BU
2009MW Proof	50,000	Value: 40.00				

Y# 713   10 ZLOTYCH
14.1400 g., 0.9250 Silver 0.4205 oz. ASW, 32 mm.
Subject: Auschwitz liberation **Obv:** National arms, camp sign
and barbed wire fence **Rev:** Prisoner and barbed wire fence

Date	Mintage	F	VF	XF	Unc	BU
2010MW Proof	80,000	Value: 40.00				

Y# 716   10 ZLOTYCH
14.1400 g., 0.9250 Silver 0.4205 oz. ASW, 32 mm.   **Subject:**
Vancouver Winter Olympics **Obv:** Speedskaters **Rev:** Biathlon

Date	Mintage	F	VF	XF	Unc	BU
2010MW Proof	80,000	Value: 40.00				

Y# 719   10 ZLOTYCH
14.1400 g., 0.9250 Silver 0.4205 oz. ASW, 32x22 mm.
Subject: Napoleonic Imperial Guard **Obv:** National arms and
helmet **Rev:** Mounted Napoleonic Guard member
Shape: Vertical rectangle

Date	Mintage	F	VF	XF	Unc	BU
2010MW Proof	100,000	Value: 40.00				

Y# 722   10 ZLOTYCH
14.1400 g., 0.9250 Silver 0.4205 oz. ASW, 32 mm.
Subject: Katyn Crime **Obv:** National emblem and siluete of a
badge **Rev:** Field of crosses

Date	Mintage	F	VF	XF	Unc	BU
2010MW Antiqued	80,000	—	—	—	40.00	—

Y# 409   20 ZLOTYCH
28.2800 g., 0.9250 Silver 0.8410 oz. ASW, 38.6 mm.
Subject: Wieliezce Salt Mine **Obv:** Crowned eagle with wings
open in center of rock **Rev:** Ancient salt miners **Edge:** Plain

Date	Mintage	F	VF	XF	Unc	BU
2001MW Proof	25,000	Value: 250				

Y# 415   20 ZLOTYCH
28.2800 g., 0.9250 Silver 0.8410 oz. ASW, 38.6 mm.
Obv: Crowned eagle with wings open flanked by flags
Rev: European Swallowtail Butterfly **Edge:** Plain

Date	Mintage	F	VF	XF	Unc	BU
2001MW Proof	27,000	Value: 300				

Y# 411   20 ZLOTYCH
28.2800 g., 0.9250 Silver 0.8410 oz. ASW, 38.6 mm.
Subject: Amber Route **Obv:** Crowned eagle and two ancient
Roman silver cups **Rev:** Piece of amber mounted above an
ancient Roman coin design and map with the route marked with
stars **Edge:** Plain **Note:** Antiqued patina

Date	Mintage	F	VF	XF	Unc	BU
2001MW	30,000	—	—	—	750	—

Y# 424   20 ZLOTYCH
28.7700 g., 0.9250 Silver 0.8556 oz. ASW, 38.6 mm.   **Subject:**
Christmas **Obv:** Ornate city view **Rev:** Celebration scene including
an attached zirconia star **Edge:** Plain **Note:** Antiqued patina.

Date	Mintage	F	VF	XF	Unc	BU
2001MW	55,000	—	—	—	225	—

Y# 457   20 ZLOTYCH
28.2800 g., 0.9250 Silver 0.8410 oz. ASW, 38.6 mm.
Obv: National arms at lower left, castle complex in background
Rev: Malborku castle, reddish-brown ceramic applique,
Rev. Legend: ZAMEK W MALBORKU **Edge:** Plain
Note: Antiqued patina.

Date	Mintage	F	VF	XF	Unc	BU
2002MW	51,000	—	—	—	100	—
Antiqued finish						

Y# 442   20 ZLOTYCH
28.0500 g., 0.9250 Silver 0.8342 oz. ASW **Subject:** Jan Matejko
Obv: Seated figure with crowned eagle at lower right **Rev:** Head
facing with multicolor artist's palette **Edge:** Plain
Shape: Rectangular **Note:** Actual size 40 x 37.9mm.

Date	Mintage	F	VF	XF	Unc	BU
2002MW Proof	57,000	Value: 200				

Y# 428   20 ZLOTYCH
28.2800 g., 0.9250 Silver 0.8410 oz. ASW, 38.6 mm.
Obv: Crowned eagle with wings open flanked by flags
Rev: European Pond Turtles **Edge:** Plain

Date	Mintage	F	VF	XF	Unc	BU
2002 Proof	35,000	Value: 175				

Y# 449   20 ZLOTYCH
28.4700 g., 0.9250 Silver 0.8466 oz. ASW, 38.6 mm.
Obv: Crowned eagle with wings open **Rev:** European Eels and
world globe **Edge:** Plain

Date	Mintage	F	VF	XF	Unc	BU
2003MW Proof	—	Value: 250				

Y# 452   20 ZLOTYCH
28.2800 g., 0.9250 Silver 0.8410 oz. ASW, 38.6 mm.
Subject: Easter Monday Festival **Obv:** Crowned eagle on lace
curtain above lamb and multicolor Easter eggs **Rev:** Festival
scene **Edge:** Plain

Date	Mintage	F	VF	XF	Unc	BU
2003MW Proof	44,000	Value: 100				

Y# 471   20 ZLOTYCH
28.2800 g., 0.9250 Silver 0.8410 oz. ASW, 40 x 40 mm.
Obv: Standing Pope John Paul II **Rev:** Pope"s portrait
Edge: Plain **Shape:** Square

Date	Mintage	F	VF	XF	Unc	BU
2003MW Proof	83,000	Value: 65.00				

Y# 478   20 ZLOTYCH
28.2800 g., 0.9250 Silver 0.8410 oz. ASW **Obv:** "Death" allegory
closing an old man's eyes, national arms at lower right **Rev:** Self
portrait of Jacek Malczewski, palette at lower right multicolor
Edge: Plain **Shape:** Rectangular **Note:** 27.93 x 39.94 mm.

Date	Mintage	F	VF	XF	Unc	BU
2003MW Proof	64,000	Value: 45.00				

Y# 498   20 ZLOTYCH
28.2800 g., 0.9250 Silver 0.8410 oz. ASW, 38.6 mm.
Subject: Lodz Ghetto (1940-1944) **Obv:** Silhouette on wall
Rev: Child with a pot **Edge:** Plain

Date	Mintage	F	VF	XF	Unc	BU
2004MW Matte	64,000	—	—	—	—	40.00

Y# 504   20 ZLOTYCH
28.2800 g., 0.9250 Silver 0.8410 oz. ASW, 38.6 mm.
Subject: Polish Senate **Obv:** Crowned eagle above Senate
chamber **Rev:** Senate eagle and speaker's staff **Edge:** Plain

Date	Mintage	F	VF	XF	Unc	BU
2004MW Proof	67,000	Value: 75.00				

Y# 508   20 ZLOTYCH
28.2800 g., 0.9250 Silver 0.8410 oz. ASW, 38.6 mm.
Obv: Crowned eagle in harvest wreath **Rev:** Harvest fest parade
Edge: Plain

Date	Mintage	F	VF	XF	Unc	BU
2004MW Proof	74,000	Value: 40.00				

Y# 513   20 ZLOTYCH
28.2800 g., 0.9250 Silver 0.8410 oz. ASW, 40x28 mm.
Obv: Mother and children **Rev:** Stanislaw Wyspianski (1869-
1907) **Edge:** Plain

Date	Mintage	F	VF	XF	Unc	BU
2004MW Proof	80,000	Value: 50.00				

Y# 515   20 ZLOTYCH
28.2800 g., 0.9250 Silver 0.8410 oz. ASW, 38.6 mm.
Obv: National arms **Obv. Legend:** RZECZPOSPOLITA
POLSKA **Rev:** 2 Harbor Porpoises **Rev. Legend:** MORSWIN -
Phocoena phocoena **Edge:** Plain

Date	Mintage	F	VF	XF	Unc	BU
2004MW Proof	56,000	Value: 175				

Y# 531   20 ZLOTYCH
28.8400 g., 0.9250 Silver 0.8576 oz. ASW, 38.6 mm.
Obv: Polish eagle above value **Rev:** Eagle Owl with nestlings
Edge: Plain

Date	Mintage	F	VF	XF	Unc	BU
2005MW Proof	61,000	Value: 150				

Y# 542   20 ZLOTYCH
28.2800 g., 0.9250 Silver 0.8410 oz. ASW, 28 x 40 mm.
Obv: Sneak thief stealing from a miser **Rev:** Painter Tadeusz
Makowski **Edge:** Plain **Shape:** Rectangular

Date	Mintage	F	VF	XF	Unc	BU
2005MW Proof	70,000	Value: 50.00				

Y# 597   20 ZLOTYCH
28.5000 g., 0.9250 Silver 0.8475 oz. ASW, 38.5 mm.
Subject: 350 Years, Defence of Góry **Obv:** National arms to right
of outlined Góry **Obv. Legend:** RZECZPOSPOLITA POLSKA
Obv. Inscription: Tutaj zawsze / bylismy woini / JAN PAWEL II
Rev: 1/2 length figure of man at lower right, Góry under
bombardment in background **Rev. Legend:** 350 - LECIE
OBRONY JASNEJ GÓRY **Edge:** Lettered **Edge Lettering:**
CZESTOCHOWA 2005 repeated three times

Date	Mintage	F	VF	XF	Unc	BU
2005MW Proof	69,000	Value: 50.00				

Y# 535   20 ZLOTYCH
28.8400 g., 0.9250 Silver 0.8576 oz. ASW, 38.6 mm.
Obv: Polish eagle above value **Rev:** Alpine Marmot standing
Edge: Plain

Date	Mintage	F	VF	XF	Unc	BU
2006MW Proof	60,000	Value: 125				

Y# 533   20 ZLOTYCH
28.8400 g., 0.9250 Silver 0.8576 oz. ASW, 38.6 mm.
Obv: Polish eagle above value **Rev:** Multicolor holographic spider
web **Edge:** Plain

Date	Mintage	F	VF	XF	Unc	BU
2006MW Proof	65,000	Value: 115				

Y# 604 20 ZLOTYCH

28.1400 g., Silver **Subject:** Aleksander Gierymski **Obv:** National arms at upper right, painting of elderly woman carrying baskets **Rev:** Bust of Gierymski facing at center, harbor scene at right, painter's palette at lower left multicolor **Edge:** Plain **Shape:** Rectangular **Note:** 39.95 x 27.97 mm.

Date	Mintage	F	VF	XF	Unc	BU
2006MW Proof	66,000	Value: 60.00				

Y# 584 20 ZLOTYCH

28.4700 g., 0.9250 Silver 0.8466 oz. ASW, 38.6 mm. **Obv:** Polish Eagle on old wood **Rev:** Multi-color wood behind Haczowie church **Edge:** Plain

Date	Mintage	F	VF	XF	Unc	BU
2006MW Proof	—	Value: 50.00				

Y# 579 20 ZLOTYCH

28.2800 g., 0.9250 Silver 0.8410 oz. ASW, 38.6 mm. **Obv:** Crowned eagle **Rev:** Two Grey Seal females and cub with two silhouettes in background **Edge:** Plain

Date	Mintage	F	VF	XF	Unc	BU
2007MW Proof	58,000	Value: 125				

Y# 603 20 ZLOTYCH

28.2500 g., 0.9250 Silver 0.8401 oz. ASW, 38.5 mm. **Subject:** Medieval Principality of Sredniowiecznew in Torin **Obv:** City arms at right, national arms below walled city gate in background **Obv. Legend:** RZECZPOSPOLITA POLSKA **Rev:** City view **Rev. Legend:** MIASTO SREDNIOWIECZNEW W TORUNIU **Edge:** Plain

Date	Mintage	F	VF	XF	Unc	BU
2007MW Proof	58,000	Value: 55.00				

Y# 636 20 ZLOTYCH

28.3800 g., Silver, 38.6 mm. **Subject:** 65th Anniversary Warsaw Ghetto Uprising **Obv:** Small national arms at left, flames, shattered wall **Obv. Legend:** RZECZPOSPOLITA POLSKA **Rev:** Tree, Star of David, wall in backgound **Rev. Inscription:** 65. ROCZNICA POWSTANIA / W GETCIE WARSZAWSKIM **Edge:** Plain

Date	Mintage	F	VF	XF	Unc	BU
2008MW Proof	—	Value: 45.00				

Y# 642 20 ZLOTYCH

28.2800 g., Silver, 38.61 mm. **Subject:** Kazimierez Dolny **Obv:** Part of a wall and an eagle **Rev:** Houses and a well **Designer:** Ewa Olszewska-Borys

Date	Mintage	F	VF	XF	Unc	BU
2008 Proof	125,000	Value: 45.00				

Y# 637 20 ZLOTYCH

28.2800 g., 0.9250 Silver 0.8410 oz. ASW, 38.61 mm. **Obv:** National arms **Obv. Legend:** RZECZPOSPOLITA POLSKA **Obv. Designer:** Ewa Tyc-Karpinska **Rev:** Peregrine Falcon by 2 chicks in nest at right **Rev. Legend:** SOKOL WEDROWNY - Falco peregrinus **Rev. Designer:** Roussanka Nowakowska **Edge:** Plain

Date	Mintage	F	VF	XF	Unc	BU
2008MW Proof	107,000	Value: 80.00				

Y# 651 20 ZLOTYCH

28.2800 g., Silver, 38.61 mm. **Subject:** 90th Anniversary of Regaining Freedom **Obv:** War decoration left side, eagle top right **Rev:** 3 generals **Designer:** Ewa Olszewska-Borys

Date	Mintage	F	VF	XF	Unc	BU
2008 Proof	110,000	Value: 50.00				

Y# 679 20 ZLOTYCH

28.2800 g., 0.9250 Silver 0.8410 oz. ASW, 38.6 mm. **Subject:** Green Lizard **Obv:** National arms above value **Rev:** Two green lizards in nature

Date	Mintage	F	VF	XF	Unc	BU
2009MW Proof	100,000	Value: 40.00				

Y# 693 20 ZLOTYCH

28.2800 g., 0.9250 Silver 0.8410 oz. ASW, 38.6 mm. **Subject:** Liquidation of the Lotz Ghetto **Obv:** New oak sprig amongst broken bricks **Rev:** Oak tree, bare and with leaves, star of David within

Date	Mintage	F	VF	XF	Unc	BU
2009MW Antiqued	50,000	—	—	—	40.00	—

Y# 704 20 ZLOTYCH

28.2800 g., 0.9250 Silver 0.8410 oz. ASW, 38.6 mm. **Subject:** Poles who saved Jews **Obv:** National arms above broken brick wall **Rev:** Three portraits

Date	Mintage	F	VF	XF	Unc	BU
2009MW Proof	100,000	Value: 40.00				

Y# 682 25 ZLOTYCH

1.0000 g., 0.9000 Gold 0.0289 oz. AGW, 12 mm. **Subject:** General Elections of 1989 **Obv:** National arms above value **Rev:** Solidarity logo

Date	Mintage	F	VF	XF	Unc	BU
2009MW Proof	40,000	Value: 60.00				

Y# 702 37 ZLOTYCH

1.7500 g., 0.9000 Gold 0.0506 oz. AGW, 16 mm. **Subject:** Fr. Jorzy Popieluszko, 25th Anniversary of Murder **Obv:** National arms above large 37 **Rev:** Many hands holding crosses

Date	Mintage	F	VF	XF	Unc	BU
2009MW Proof	60,000	Value: 80.00				

Y# 652 50 ZLOTYCH
3.1300 g., Gold, 18 mm. **Subject:** 90th Annniversary of Regaining Freedom **Obv:** Tomb of the unknown soldier **Rev:** Mounted Commander-In-Chief Jósef Pilsudski **Designer:** Ewa Olszewska-Borys

Date	Mintage	F	VF	XF	Unc	BU
2008 Proof	8,800	Value: 125				

Y# 416 100 ZLOTYCH
8.0000 g., 0.9000 Gold 0.2315 oz. AGW, 21 mm. **Subject:** Wladyslaw I (1320-33) **Obv:** Crowned eagle with wings open **Rev:** Crowned bust facing **Edge:** Plain

Date	Mintage	F	VF	XF	Unc	BU
2001MW Proof	2,000	Value: 875				

Y# 417 100 ZLOTYCH
8.0000 g., 0.9000 Gold 0.2315 oz. AGW, 21 mm. **Subject:** Boleslaw III (1102-1138) **Obv:** Crowned eagle with wings open **Rev:** Pointed crowned bust facing **Edge:** Plain

Date	Mintage	F	VF	XF	Unc	BU
2001MW Proof	2,000	Value: 875				

Y# 462 100 ZLOTYCH
8.0000 g., 0.9000 Gold 0.2315 oz. AGW, 21 mm. **Obv:** Crowned eagle with wings open **Rev:** Jan Sobieski III **Edge:** Plain

Date	Mintage	F	VF	XF	Unc	BU
2001MV Proof	2,200	Value: 875				

Y# 436 100 ZLOTYCH
8.0000 g., 0.9000 Gold 0.2315 oz. AGW, 21 mm. **Subject:** World Cup Soccer **Obv:** Crowned eagle with wings open and world background **Rev:** Soccer player **Edge:** Plain

Date	Mintage	F	VF	XF	Unc	BU
2002MW Proof	4,500	Value: 375				

Y# 429 100 ZLOTYCH
8.0000 g., 0.9000 Gold 0.2315 oz. AGW, 21 mm. **Obv:** Crowned eagle with wings open **Rev:** Crowned bust facing **Edge:** Plain

Date	Mintage	F	VF	XF	Unc	BU
2002MW Proof	2,400	Value: 875				

Y# 430 100 ZLOTYCH
8.0000 g., 0.9000 Gold 0.2315 oz. AGW, 21 mm. **Obv:** Crowned eagle with wings open **Rev:** Crowned bust 1/4 left **Edge:** Plain

Date	Mintage	F	VF	XF	Unc	BU
2002MW Proof	2,200	Value: 875				

Y# 454 100 ZLOTYCH
8.0000 g., 0.9000 Gold 0.2315 oz. AGW, 21 mm. **Obv:** Crowned eagle with wings open **Rev:** Uniformed bust 1/4 left **Edge:** Plain

Date	Mintage	F	VF	XF	Unc	BU
2003MW Proof	2,000	Value: 1,000				

Y# 466 100 ZLOTYCH
8.0000 g., 0.9000 Gold 0.2315 oz. AGW, 21 mm. **Subject:** 750th Anniversary - City Charter **Obv:** Door knocker and church **Rev:** Clock face and tower **Edge:** Plain

Date	Mintage	F	VF	XF	Unc	BU
2003MW Proof	2,100	Value: 750				

Y# 467 100 ZLOTYCH
8.0000 g., 0.9000 Gold 0.2315 oz. AGW, 21 mm. **Obv:** Crowned eagle with wings open **Rev:** Kazimierz IV (1447-1492) **Edge:** Plain

Date	Mintage	F	VF	XF	Unc	BU
2003MW Proof	2,300	Value: 750				

Y# 476 100 ZLOTYCH
8.0000 g., 0.9000 Gold 0.2315 oz. AGW, 21 mm. **Obv:** Crowned eagle with wings open **Rev:** Stanislaus I and eagle **Edge:** Plain

Date	Mintage	F	VF	XF	Unc	BU
2003MW Proof	2,500	Value: 750				

Y# 494 100 ZLOTYCH
8.0000 g., 0.9000 Gold 0.2315 oz. AGW, 21 mm. **Obv:** Crowned eagle with wings open **Rev:** King Przemysi II (1295-1296) **Edge:** Plain

Date	Mintage	F	VF	XF	Unc	BU
2004MW Proof	3,400	Value: 550				

Y# 495 100 ZLOTYCH
8.0000 g., 0.9000 Gold 0.2315 oz. AGW, 21 mm. **Obv:** Crowned eagle with wings open **Rev:** King Zygmunt I (1506-1548) **Edge:** Plain

Date	Mintage	F	VF	XF	Unc	BU
2004MW Proof	3,400	Value: 550				

Y# 540 100 ZLOTYCH
8.0000 g., 0.9000 Gold 0.2315 oz. AGW, 21 mm. **Obv:** St. Peters Basilica dome **Rev:** Pope John Paul II and baptismal font **Edge:** Plain

Date	Mintage	F	VF	XF	Unc	BU
2005MW Proof	18,700	Value: 450				

Y# 581 100 ZLOTYCH
8.0000 g., 0.9000 Gold 0.2315 oz. AGW, 21 mm. **Obv:** Line of soccer players on soccer ball surface with Polish eagle in one of the sections **Rev:** Two soccer players **Edge:** Plain

Date	Mintage	F	VF	XF	Unc	BU
2006MW Proof	—	Value: 300				

Y# 640 100 ZLOTYCH
8.0000 g., 0.9000 Gold 0.2315 oz. AGW, 21 mm. **Subject:** Siberian Exiles **Obv:** Small national arms at left, bleak forest at right **Obv. Legend:** RZECZPOSPOLITA POLSKA **Rev:** Grieving mother with child by tree at lower right, building in background at left **Rev. Legend:** SYBIRACY

Date	Mintage	F	VF	XF	Unc	BU
2008MW Proof	12,000	Value: 285				

Y# 657 100 ZLOTYCH
8.0000 g., 0.9000 Gold 0.2315 oz. AGW, 21 mm. **Subject:** 400th Anniversary of Polish Settlement in North America **Obv:** Eagle in center against wind rose. Outline of Europe & North America. **Obv. Designer:** Roussanka Nowakowska **Rev:** Center wind rose surrounded by 4 men working **Rev. Designer:** Roussanks Nowakowska

Date	Mintage	F	VF	XF	Unc	BU
2008 Proof	9,500	Value: 425				

Y# 699 100 ZLOTYCH
8.0000 g., 0.9000 Gold 0.2315 oz. AGW, 21 mm. **Subject:** Tatar Rescue, 100th Anniversary **Obv:** Figure of Mariusz Zaruski **Rev:** Mountains and reszue helicopter image

Date	Mintage	F	VF	XF	Unc	BU
2009MW Proof	10,000	Value: 325				

Y# 714 100 ZLOTYCH
8.0000 g., 0.9000 Gold 0.2315 oz. AGW, 21 mm. **Subject:** Auschwitz liberation **Obv:** Prisoner and railroad track entrance **Rev:** Buildings

Date	Mintage	F	VF	XF	Unc	BU
2010MW Proof	8,000	Value: 350				

Y# 407 200 ZLOTYCH
Tri-Metallic Gold with Palladium center, Gold with Silver ring, Gold with Copper outer limit, 27 mm. **Subject:** Year 2001 **Obv:** Crowned eagle with wings open within a swirl **Rev:** Couple looking into the future **Edge:** Plain

Date	Mintage	F	VF	XF	Unc	BU
2001MW Proof	4,000	Value: 400				

Y# 420 200 ZLOTYCH
15.5000 g., 0.9000 Gold 0.4485 oz. AGW, 27 mm. **Subject:** Cardinal Stefan Wyszynski **Obv:** Pillar divides arms and eagle **Rev:** Bust left within arch **Edge Lettering:** 100 ROCZNIA URODZIN

Date	Mintage	F	VF	XF	Unc	BU
2001MW Proof	4,500	Value: 500				

Y# 463 200 ZLOTYCH
15.5000 g., 0.9000 Gold 0.4485 oz. AGW, 27 mm. **Obv:** Standing violinist **Rev:** Henry Wieniawski **Edge Lettering:** XII MIEDZYNARODOWY KONKURS SKRZYPCOWY IM HENRYKA WIENIAWSKIEGO

Date	Mintage	F	VF	XF	Unc	BU
2001MW Proof	2,000	Value: 1,150				

Y# 438 200 ZLOTYCH
15.5000 g., 0.9000 Gold 0.4485 oz. AGW, 27 mm. **Subject:** Pope John Paul II **Obv:** Bust left and small eagle with wings open **Rev:** Pope facing radiant Holy Door **Edge:** Plain

Date	Mintage	F	VF	XF	Unc	BU
2002MW Proof	5,000	Value: 1,200				

Y# 470 200 ZLOTYCH
15.5000 g., 0.9000 Gold 0.4485 oz. AGW, 27 mm. **Subject:** Gas and Oil Industry **Obv:** Crowned eagle, oil wells and refinery **Rev:** Scientist at work **Edge:** Plain

Date	Mintage	F	VF	XF	Unc	BU
2003MW Proof	2,100	Value: 1,250				

Y# 472 200 ZLOTYCH
15.5000 g., 0.9000 Gold 0.4485 oz. AGW, 27 mm. **Obv:** Standing Pope John Paul II **Rev:** Seated Pope **Edge:** Plain

Date	Mintage	F	VF	XF	Unc	BU
2003MW Proof	4,900	Value: 1,300				

Y# 483 200 ZLOTYCH
15.5000 g., 0.9000 Gold 0.4485 oz. AGW, 27 mm. **Subject:** Poland Joining the European Union **Obv:** Polish euro coin design elements **Rev:** Polish euro coin design elements **Edge:** Plain

Date	Mintage	F	VF	XF	Unc	BU
2004MW Proof	4,400	Value: 650				

Y# 511 200 ZLOTYCH
15.5000 g., 0.9000 Gold 0.4485 oz. AGW, 27 mm.
Subject: Warsaw Fine Arts Academy Centennial **Obv:** Campus view **Rev:** Statue and building **Edge:** Plain

Date	Mintage	F	VF	XF	Unc	BU
2004MW Proof	5,000	Value: 575				

Y# 519 200 ZLOTYCH
15.5000 g., 0.9000 Gold 0.4485 oz. AGW, 27 mm.
Subject: Olympics **Obv:** Woman and crowned eagle
Rev: Ancient runners painted on pottery **Edge:** Plain

Date	Mintage	F	VF	XF	Unc	BU
2004MW Proof	6,000	Value: 575				

Y# 538 200 ZLOTYCH
15.5000 g., 0.9000 Gold 0.4485 oz. AGW, 27 mm. **Obv:** Horse drawn carriage **Rev:** Konstanty Ildefons Galczynski in top hat **Edge:** Plain

Date	Mintage	F	VF	XF	Unc	BU
2005MW Proof	3,500	Value: 675				

Y# 536 200 ZLOTYCH
15.5000 g., 0.9000 Gold 0.4485 oz. AGW, 27 mm. **Obv:** Chopin
Rev: Nagoya Castle roof tops and Mt. Fuji **Edge:** Plain
Note: Aichi Expo Japan

Date	Mintage	F	VF	XF	Unc	BU
2005MW Proof	4,200	Value: 600				

Y# 672 200 ZLOTYCH
15.5000 g., 0.9000 Gold 0.4485 oz. AGW, 27 mm. **Obv:** Helmet and breastplate **Rev:** Knight of the 15th Century

Date	Mintage	F	VF	XF	Unc	BU
2007 Proof	10,500	Value: 650				

Y# 643 200 ZLOTYCH
15.5000 g., Gold, 27 mm. **Subject:** Zbigniew Herbert
Obv: Eagle and Zbigniew Herbert **Rev:** Mounted statue of Marcus Aurelius **Designer:** Dominika Karpinska-Kopiec

Date	Mintage	F	VF	XF	Unc	BU
2008 Proof	11,200	Value: 575				

Y# 647 200 ZLOTYCH
15.5000 g., Gold, 27 mm. **Series:** The 29th Olympic Games Beijing 2008 **Obv:** Two kites and an eagle **Rev:** Female pole vault jumper **Designer:** Robert Kotowicz

Date	Mintage	F	VF	XF	Unc	BU
2008	—				—	550

Y# 653 200 ZLOTYCH
15.5000 g., Gold, 27 mm. **Subject:** 90th Anniversary of Regaining Freedom **Obv:** Tomb of the unknown soldier
Rev: Mounted Commander-In-Chief Jozef Pilsudski
Designer: Ewa Olszewska-Borys

Date	Mintage	F	VF	XF	Unc	BU
2008 Proof	10,000	Value: 700				

Y# 654 200 ZLOTYCH
15.5000 g., Gold, 27 mm. **Subject:** 450 years of the Polish Post
Obv: Eagle right, bottom against post stamp **Rev:** Horse with rider crossing bridge **Designer:** Robert Kotowicz

Date	Mintage	F	VF	XF	Unc	BU
2008 Proof	11,000	Value: 700				

Y# 660 200 ZLOTYCH
15.5000 g., Gold, 27 mm. **Subject:** 90th Anniversary of the Greater Poland Uprising **Obv:** Eagle at left, eagle at right with chain **Rev:** Charging cavalrymen and German soldiers firing at them **Designer:** Urszula Walerzak

Date	Mintage	F	VF	XF	Unc	BU
2008 Proof	9,400	Value: 700				

Y# 664 200 ZLOTYCH
15.5000 g., 0.9000 Gold 0.4485 oz. AGW, 27 mm.
Subject: Warsaw Ghetto **Obv:** Building on fire, Naitonal arms
Rev: Face looking out from broken brick wall

Date	Mintage	F	VF	XF	Unc	BU
2008MW Proof	12,000	Value: 600				

Y# 665 200 ZLOTYCH
8.0000 g., 0.9000 Gold 0.2315 oz. AGW, 21 mm. **Subject:** Poles in the US, 400th Anniversary **Obv:** National Arms, North America and Europe map, compass **Rev:** Four glass maker views

Date	Mintage	F	VF	XF	Unc	BU
2008MW Proof	9,500	Value: 275				

Y# 696 200 ZLOTYCH
15.1500 g., 0.9000 Gold 0.4384 oz. AGW, 27 mm. **Obv:** Eagle and statue, flames in background **Rev:** Stefan Starzonski, Warsaw Mayor; Burning of the Clock Tower

Date	Mintage	F	VF	XF	Unc	BU
2009 Proof	10,500	Value: 750				

Y# 677 200 ZLOTYCH
15.5000 g., 0.9000 Gold 0.4485 oz. AGW, 27 mm.
Subject: Central Banking, 180th Anniversary **Obv:** National arms above crowned shield **Rev:** Building and portrait

Date	Mintage	F	VF	XF	Unc	BU
2009MW Proof	8,500	Value: 650				

Y# 683 200 ZLOTYCH
15.5000 g., 0.9000 Gold 0.4485 oz. AGW, 27 mm.
Subject: General election of 1989 **Obv:** National arms above shipyard scene **Rev:** Lech Walesa silouette before crowd

Date	Mintage	F	VF	XF	Unc	BU
2009MW Proof	10,000	Value: 650				

Y# 717 200 ZLOTYCH
15.5000 g., 0.9000 Gold 0.4485 oz. AGW, 27 mm.
Subject: Vancouver Winter Olympics **Obv:** Downhill skiing
Rev: Cross Country skiing

Date	Mintage	F	VF	XF	Unc	BU
2010MW Proof	8,000	Value: 650				

Y# 720 200 ZLOTYCH
15.5000 g., 0.9000 Gold 0.4485 oz. AGW, 27 mm.
Subject: Napoleonic Imperial Guard **Obv:** Pile of arms
Rev: Galloping guardsman

Date	Mintage	F	VF	XF	Unc	BU
2010MW Proof	10,500	Value: 650				

GOLD BULLION COINAGE

Y# 292 50 ZLOTYCH
3.1000 g., 0.9999 Gold 0.0997 oz. AGW, 18 mm. **Obv:** Crowned eagle with wings open, all within circle **Rev:** Golden eagle

Date	Mintage	F	VF	XF	Unc	BU
2002	500	—	—	—	BV	210
2004	2,000	—	—	—	BV	150
2006	1,600	—	—	—	BV	160
2007	2,000	—	—	—	BV	150
2008	—	—	—	—	BV	150

Y# 293 100 ZLOTYCH
7.7800 g., 0.9999 Gold 0.2501 oz. AGW, 22 mm. **Obv:** Crowned eagle with wings open, all within circle **Rev:** Golden eagle

Date	Mintage	F	VF	XF	Unc	BU
2002	800	—	—	—	BV	300
2004	1,000	—	—	—	BV	285
2006	900	—	—	—	BV	300
2007	1,500	—	—	—	BV	285
2008	—	—	—	—	BV	285

Y# 294 200 ZLOTYCH
15.5000 g., 0.9000 Gold 0.4485 oz. AGW, 27 mm.
Obv: Crowned eagle with wings open within beaded circle
Rev: Golden eagle

Date	Mintage	F	VF	XF	Unc	BU
2002	1,000	—	—	—	BV	575
2004	1,000	—	—	—	BV	575
2006	900	—	—	—	BV	575
2007	1,500	—	—	—	BV	575
2008	—	—	—	—	BV	575

Y# 295 500 ZLOTYCH
31.1035 g., 0.9999 Gold 0.9999 oz. AGW **Obv:** Crowned eagle with wings open within beaded circle **Rev:** Golden eagle

Date	Mintage	F	VF	XF	Unc	BU
2002	1,000	—	—	—	BV	1,200
2004	2,500	—	—	—	BV	1,150
2006	600	—	—	—	BV	1,300
2007	2,500	—	—	—	BV	1,150
2008	—	—	—	—	BV	1,150

MINT SETS

KM#	Date	Mintage	Identification	Issue Price	Mkt Val
MS5	2007 (11)	2,000	Y#276-284, 465, 525, mixed date set - 1995-2007	39.95	37.50

PORTUGAL

The Portuguese Republic, located in the western part of the Iberian Peninsula in southwestern Europe, has an area of 35,553 sq. mi. (92,080 sq. km.) and a population of *10.5 million. Capital: Lisbon. Portugal's economy is based on agriculture, tourism, minerals, fisheries and a rapidly expanding industrial sector. Textiles account for 33% of the exports and Portuguese wine is world famous. Portugal has become Europe's number one producer of copper and the world's largest producer of cork.

RULER
Republic, 1910 to date

MONETARY SYSTEM
100 Cents = 1 Euro

REPUBLIC
DECIMAL COINAGE

KM# 631a ESCUDO
4.6000 g., 0.9167 Gold 0.1356 oz. AGW, 16 mm. **Subject:** Last Escudo **Obv:** Design above shield with "Au" above top left corner of shield **Rev:** Flower design above value **Edge:** Plain

Date	Mintage	F	VF	XF	Unc	BU
2001INCM	50,000	—	—	—	170	185

KM# 634.1 20 ESCUDOS
6.9000 g., Copper-Nickel, 26.5 mm. **Obv:** Shield divides date with value below **Obv. Legend:** REPUBLICA PORTUGUESA **Rev:** Nautical windrose **Designer:** Euclides Vaz

Date	Mintage	F	VF	XF	Unc	BU
2001INCM	Est. 250,000	—	—	—	2.75	3.50

KM# 733 500 ESCUDOS
13.9600 g., 0.5000 Silver 0.2244 oz. ASW, 30.1 mm. **Subject:** Porto, European Culture Capital **Obv:** National arms and value **Rev:** Stylized design **Edge:** Reeded

Date	Mintage	F	VF	XF	Unc	BU
2001INCM	—	—	—	—	6.50	7.50
2001INCM Proof	10,000	Value: 60.00				

KM# 733a 500 ESCUDOS
Gold **Subject:** Porto, European Culture Capital **Obv:** National arms and value **Rev:** Stylized design **Edge:** Reeded

Date	Mintage	F	VF	XF	Unc	BU
2001INCM Proof	5,000	Value: 450				

KM# 734 1000 ESCUDOS
26.9500 g., 0.5000 Silver 0.4332 oz. ASW, 40 mm. **Obv:** National arms and value **Obv. Legend:** REPUBLICA PORTUGUESA 2001 **Rev:** Soccer ball within net **Rev. Legend:** 10º Campeonato Europeu de Futebol - UEFA Euro 2004 Portugal **Edge:** Reeded

Date	Mintage	F	VF	XF	Unc	BU
2001INCM	50,000	—	—	—	13.50	15.00
2001INCM Proof	—	Value: 75.00				

EURO COINAGE
European Union Issues

KM# 788 1-1/2 EURO
10.3700 g., 0.9990 Gold 0.3331 oz. AGW, 26.5 mm. **Subject:** Numismatics - Marabitino of Sancho II **Obv:** Cross of shields **Rev:** King on horseback

Date	Mintage	F	VF	XF	Unc	BU
2009 Proof	2,500	Value: 620				

KM# 789 1-1/2 EURO
Copper-Nickel, 26.5 mm. **Obv:** Numismatics - Marabitino of Sancho II

Date	Mintage	F	VF	XF	Unc	BU
2009 Proof						

KM# 740 EURO CENT
2.3000 g., Copper Plated Steel, 16.25 mm. **Obv:** Royal seal of 1134 with country name and cross **Obv. Designer:** Vitor Santos **Rev:** Value and globe **Rev. Designer:** Luc Luycx **Edge:** Plain

Date	Mintage	F	VF	XF	Unc	BU
2002INCM	278,106,172	—	—	—	0.35	0.50
2002INCM Proof	15,000	Value: 7.00				
2003INCM	50,000	—	—	—	0.35	0.50
2003INCM Proof	15,000	Value: 7.00				
2004INCM	75,000,000	—	—	—	0.35	0.50
2004INCM Proof	15,000	Value: 7.00				
2005INCM	40,000,000	—	—	—	0.35	0.50
2005INCM Proof	10,000	Value: 7.00				
2006INCM	30,000,000	—	—	—	0.35	0.50
2006INCM Proof	3,000	Value: 7.00				
2007INCM	105,000,000	—	—	—	0.35	0.50
2007INCM Proof	—	Value: 7.00				
2008INCM	75,000,000	—	—	—	0.35	0.50
2008INCM Proof	—	Value: 7.00				
2009INCM	60,000,000	—	—	—	0.35	0.50
2009INCM Proof	—	Value: 7.00				

KM# 741 2 EURO CENT
3.0300 g., Copper Plated Steel, 18.7 mm. **Obv:** Royal seal of 1134 with country name and cross **Obv. Designer:** Vitor Santos **Rev:** Value and globe **Rev. Designer:** Luc Luycx **Edge:** Grooved

Date	Mintage	F	VF	XF	Unc	BU
2002INCM	324,376,590	—	—	—	0.50	0.65
2002INCM Proof	15,000	Value: 9.00				
2003INCM	50,000	—	—	—	—	2.50
Note: In sets only						
2003INCM Proof	15,000	Value: 9.00				
Note: In sets only						
2004INCM	1,000,000	—	—	—	0.50	0.65

KM# 742 5 EURO CENT
3.8600 g., Copper Plated Steel, 21.2 mm. **Obv:** Royal seal of 1134 with country name and cross **Obv. Designer:** Vitor Santos **Rev:** Value and globe **Rev. Designer:** Luc Luycx **Edge:** Plain

Date	Mintage	F	VF	XF	Unc	BU
2004INCM Proof	15,000	Value: 9.00				
2005INCM	10,000,000	—	—	—	0.50	0.65
2005INCM Proof	10,000	Value: 9.00				
2006INCM	1,000,000	—	—	—	0.50	0.65
2006INCM Proof	3,000	Value: 9.00				
2007INCM	10,000,000	—	—	—	0.50	0.65
2007INCM Proof	—	Value: 9.00				
2008INCM	35,000,000	—	—	—	0.50	0.65
2008INCM Proof	—	Value: 9.00				
2009INCM	45,000,000	—	—	—	0.50	0.65
2009INCM Proof	—	Value: 9.00				

KM# 742 5 EURO CENT
3.8600 g., Copper Plated Steel, 21.2 mm. **Obv:** Royal seal of 1134 with country name and cross **Obv. Designer:** Vitor Santos **Rev:** Value and globe **Rev. Designer:** Luc Luycx **Edge:** Plain

Date	Mintage	F	VF	XF	Unc	BU
2002INCM	234,512,047	—	—	—	0.75	1.00
2002INCM Proof	15,000	Value: 10.00				
2003INCM	50,000	—	—	—	—	4.00
Note: In sets only						
2003INCM Proof	15,000	Value: 10.00				
Note: In sets only						
2004INCM	40,000,000	—	—	—	0.75	1.00
2004INCM Proof	15,000	Value: 10.00				
2005INCM	30,000,000	—	—	—	0.75	1.00
2005INCM Proof	10,000	Value: 10.00				
2006INCM	20,000,000	—	—	—	0.75	1.00
2006INCM Proof	3,000	Value: 10.00				
2007INCM	25,000,000	—	—	—	0.75	1.00
2007INCM Proof	—	Value: 10.00				
2008INCM	25,000,000	—	—	—	0.75	1.00
2008INCM Proof	—	Value: 10.00				
2009INCM	25,000,000	—	—	—	0.75	1.00
2009INCM Proof	—	Value: 10.00				

KM# 743 10 EURO CENT
4.0700 g., Brass, 19.7 mm. **Obv:** Royal seal of 1142, country name in circular design **Obv. Designer:** Vitor Santos **Rev:** Value and map **Rev. Designer:** Luc Luycx **Edge:** Reeded

Date	Mintage	F	VF	XF	Unc	BU
2002INCM	220,289,835	—	—	—	0.75	1.00
2002INCM Proof	15,000	Value: 12.00				
2003INCM	6,332,000	—	—	—	1.00	1.50
2003INCM Proof	15,000	Value: 12.00				
Note: In sets only						
2004INCM	1,000,000	—	—	—	1.50	2.00
2004INCM Proof	15,000	Value: 12.00				
2005INCM	1,000,000	—	—	—	1.50	2.00
2005INCM Proof	10,000	Value: 12.00				
2006INCM	1,000,000	—	—	—	1.50	2.00
2006INCM Proof	3,000	Value: 12.00				

KM# 763 10 EURO CENT
4.0700 g., Brass, 19.7 mm. **Obv:** Royal seal of 1142, country name in circular design **Obv. Designer:** Vitor Santos **Rev:** Relief map of Western Europe, stars, lines and value **Rev. Designer:** Luc Luycx **Edge:** Reeded

Date	Mintage	F	VF	XF	Unc	BU
2008INCM	1,000,000	—	—	—	1.50	2.00
2008INCM Proof	—	Value: 12.00				
2009INCM	10,000,000	—	—	—	1.50	2.00
2009INCM Proof	—	Value: 12.00				

KM# 744 20 EURO CENT
5.7300 g., Brass, 22.1 mm. **Obv:** Royal seal of 1142, country name in circular design **Obv. Designer:** Vitor Santos **Rev:** Value and map **Rev. Designer:** Luc Luycx **Edge:** Notched

Date	Mintage	F	VF	XF	Unc	BU
2002INCM	147,411,038	—	—	—	1.00	1.25
2002INCM Proof	15,000	Value: 14.00				
2003INCM	9,493,600	—	—	—	1.25	1.50
2003INCM Proof	15,000	Value: 14.00				
2004INCM	1,000,000	—	—	—	1.50	2.00
2004INCM Proof	15,000	Value: 14.00				
2005INCM	25,000,000	—	—	—	1.50	2.00

Date	Mintage	F	VF	XF	Unc	BU
2005INCM Proof	10,000	Value: 14.00				
2006INCM	20,000,000	—	—	—	1.50	2.00
2006INCM Proof	3,000	Value: 14.00				

KM# 764 20 EURO CENT

5.7300 g., Brass, 22.1 mm. **Obv:** Royal seal of 1142, country name in circular design **Obv. Designer:** Vitor Santos **Rev:** Relief map of Western Europe, stars, lines and value **Rev. Designer:** Luc Luyckx **Edge:** Notched

Date	Mintage	F	VF	XF	Unc	BU
2008INCM	1,000,000	—	—	—	1.50	2.00
2008INCM Proof	—	Value: 14.00				
2009INCM	20,000,000	—	—	—	1.50	2.00
2009INCM Proof	—	Value: 14.00				

KM# 777 1/4 EURO

1.5600 g., 0.9990 Gold 0.0501 oz. AGW, 14 mm. **Series:** Portugal Universal **Subject:** King Alfons I, the Conqueror **Obv:** National arms, value **Obv. Legend:** REPÚBLICA PORTUGUESA **Rev:** Stylized 3/4 length armored figure standing facing **Rev. Legend:** D. AFONSO HENRIQUES **Edge:** Reeded **Note:** Each coin is numbered.

Date	Mintage	F	VF	XF	Unc	BU
2006INCM FDC	30,000	—	—	—	—	125

KM# 787 1/4 EURO

1.5600 g., 0.9990 Gold 0.0501 oz. AGW, 14 mm. **Subject:** Vasco da Gama

Date	Mintage	F	VF	XF	Unc	BU
2009 Proof	30,000	Value: 75.00				

KM# 745 50 EURO CENT

7.8100 g., Brass, 24.2 mm. **Obv:** Royal seal of 1142, country name in circular design **Obv. Designer:** Vitor Santos **Rev:** Value and map **Rev. Designer:** Luc Luyckx **Edge:** Reeded

Date	Mintage	F	VF	XF	Unc	BU
2002INCM	151,947,133	—	—	—	1.50	2.00
2002INCM Proof	15,000	Value: 16.00				
2003INCM	10,353,000	—	—	—	1.50	2.00
2003INCM Proof	15,000	Value: 16.00				

Note: In sets only

Date	Mintage	F	VF	XF	Unc	BU
2004INCM	1,000,000	—	—	—	2.50	3.00
2004INCM Proof	15,000	Value: 16.00				
2005INCM	1,000,000	—	—	—	2.50	3.00
2005INCM Proof	10,000	Value: 16.00				
2006INCM	1,000,000	—	—	—	2.50	3.00
2006INCM Proof	3,000	Value: 16.00				

KM# 765 50 EURO CENT

7.8100 g., Brass, 24.2 mm. **Obv:** Royal seal of 1142, country name in circular design **Obv. Designer:** Vitor Santos **Rev:** Relief map of Western Europe, stars, lines and value **Rev. Designer:** Luc Luyckx **Edge:** Reeded

Date	Mintage	F	VF	XF	Unc	BU
2008INCM	5,000,000	—	—	—	2.50	3.00
2008INCM Proof	—	Value: 16.00				
2009INCM	20,000,000	—	—	—	2.50	3.00
2009INCM Proof	—	Value: 16.00				

KM# 746 EURO

7.5000 g., Bi-Metallic Copper-Nickel center in Brass ring, 23.25 mm. **Obv:** Royal seal of 1144, country name in looped design **Obv. Designer:** Vitor Santos **Rev:** Value and map **Rev. Designer:** Luc Luyckx **Edge:** Alternating plain and milled.

Date	Mintage	F	VF	XF	Unc	BU
2002INCM	100,228,135	—	—	—	2.00	2.50

Note: Variety in the edge milling, 28 or 29.

Date	Mintage	F	VF	XF	Unc	BU
2002INCM Proof	15,000	Value: 18.00				
2003INCM	16,206,875	—	—	—	2.00	2.50
2003INCM Proof	15,000	Value: 18.00				
2004INCM	20,000,000	—	—	—	2.00	2.50
2004INCM Proof	15,000	Value: 18.00				
2005INCM	20,000,000	—	—	—	2.00	2.50
2005INCM Proof	10,000	Value: 18.00				
2006INCM	20,000,000	—	—	—	2.00	2.50
2006INCM Proof	3,000	Value: 18.00				
2007INCM	4,935,400	—	—	—	2.00	2.50

KM# 766 EURO

7.5000 g., Bi-Metallic Copper-Nickel center in Brass ring, 23.2 mm. **Obv:** Royal seal of 1144, country name in looped design **Obv. Designer:** Vitor Santos **Rev:** Relief map of Western Europe, stars, lines and value **Rev. Designer:** Luc Luyckx **Edge:** Reeded and plain sections

Date	Mintage	F	VF	XF	Unc	BU
2008INCM	5,000,000	—	—	—	2.75	3.50
2008INCM Proof	—	Value: 18.00				
2009INCM	20,000,000	—	—	—	2.75	3.50
2009INCM Proof	—	Value: 18.00				

KM# 747 2 EURO

8.5200 g., Bi-Metallic Brass center in Copper-Nickel ring, 25.7 mm. **Obv:** Royal seal of 1144, country name in looped design **Obv. Designer:** Vitor Santos **Rev:** Value and map **Rev. Designer:** Luc Luyckx **Edge:** Reeding over castles and shields

Date	Mintage	F	VF	XF	Unc	BU
2002INCM	61,930,775	—	—	—	3.50	4.00
2002INCM Proof	15,000	Value: 22.00				
2003INCM	5,979,750	—	—	—	4.25	5.00
2003INCM Proof	15,000	Value: 22.00				

Note: In sets only

Date	Mintage	F	VF	XF	Unc	BU
2004INCM	1,000,000	—	—	—	5.50	6.00
2004INCM Proof	15,000	Value: 22.00				
2005INCM	1,000,000	—	—	—	5.50	6.00
2005INCM Proof	10,000	Value: 22.00				
2006INCM	1,000,000	—	—	—	5.50	6.00
2006INCM Proof	3,000	Value: 22.00				

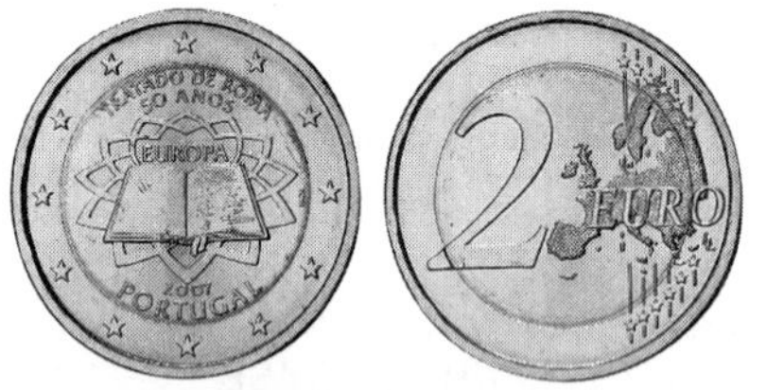

KM# 771 2 EURO

8.4700 g., Bi-Metallic Brass center in Copper-Nickel ring, 25.74 mm. **Subject:** 50th Anniversary Treaty of Rome **Obv:** Open treaty book **Rev:** Large value at left, modified outline of Europe at right **Edge:** Reeded and lettered

Date	Mintage	F	VF	XF	Unc	BU
2007	1,500,000	—	—	—	4.50	6.00
2007 Prooflike	15,000	—	—	—	—	12.50
2007 Proof	5,000	Value: 25.00				

KM# 772 2 EURO

8.4000 g., Bi-Metallic Brass center in Copper-Nickel ring, 25.73 mm. **Subject:** European Union President **Obv:** Large tree, small national arms at lower left **Obv. Inscription:** POR / TV / GAL **Rev:** Large value at left, revised map of Europe at right **Edge:** Reeded with repeated symbols

Date	Mintage	F	VF	XF	Unc	BU
2007	1,250,000	—	—	—	4.50	6.00
2007 Prooflike	15,000	—	—	—	—	12.50
2007 Proof	5,000	Value: 25.00				

KM# 767 2 EURO

8.5200 g., Bi-Metallic Brass center in Copper-Nickel ring, 25.7 mm. **Obv:** Royal seal of 1144, country name in looped design **Obv. Designer:** Vitor Santos **Rev:** Relief map of Western Europe, stars, lines and value **Rev. Designer:** Luc Luyckx **Edge:** Reeding over castles and shields

Date	Mintage	F	VF	XF	Unc	BU
2008INCM	—	—	—	—	5.50	6.00
2008INCM Proof	—	Value: 22.00				
2009INCM	—	—	—	—	5.50	6.00
2009INCM Proof	—	Value: 22.00				

KM# 784 2 EURO

8.5500 g., Bi-Metallic Brass center in Copper-Nickel ring, 25.72 mm. **Subject:** Treaty of Rome, 50th Anniversary

Date	Mintage	F	VF	XF	Unc	BU
2008INCM	—	—	—	—	—	5.00

KM# 785 2 EURO

8.5500 g., Bi-Metallic Brass center in Copper-Nickel ring, 25.72 mm. **Subject:** European monetary Union, 10th Anniversary **Obv:** Stick figure and Euro symbol

Date	Mintage	F	VF	XF	Unc	BU
2009INCM	—	—	—	—	—	5.00

KM# 786 2 EURO

8.5500 g., Bi-Metallic Brass center in Copper-Nickel ring, 25.72 mm. **Subject:** Games of Lusophony

Date	Mintage	F	VF	XF	Unc	BU
2009INCM	—	—	—	—	—	5.00

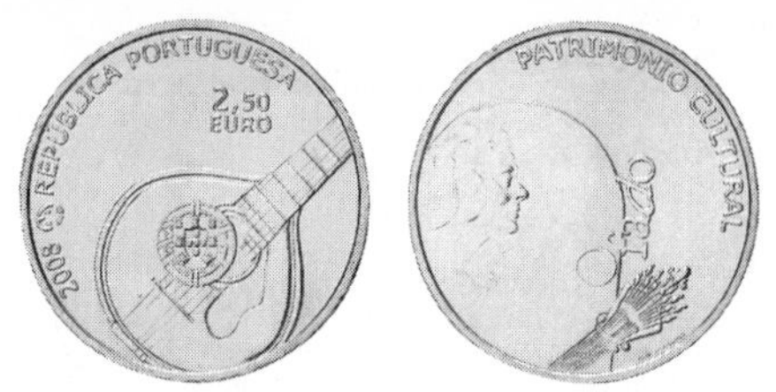

KM# 783 2-1/2 EURO

9.8500 g., Copper-Nickel, 28 mm. **Obv:** Small national arms on stringed instrument at right **Rev:** Fado musician at lower left **Edge:** Coarse reeding

Date	Mintage	F	VF	XF	Unc	BU
2008	150,000	—	—	—	6.00	9.00

KM# 783a 2-1/2 EURO

12.0000 g., 0.9250 Silver 0.3569 oz. ASW, 28 mm. **Obv:** Small national arms on stringed instrument at right **Rev:** Fado musician at lower left

Date	Mintage	F	VF	XF	Unc	BU
2008 Proof	20,000	Value: 60.00				

KM# 790 2-1/2 EURO

Copper-Nickel, 28 mm. **Subject:** Bejing Olympics

Date	Mintage	F	VF	XF	Unc	BU
2008	—	—	—	—	—	—

KM# 791 2-1/2 EURO

Copper-Nickel, 28 mm. **Subject:** Portugese Literature

Date	Mintage	F	VF	XF	Unc	BU
2009	—	—	—	—	—	—

KM# 792 2-1/2 EURO

Copper-Nickel, 28 mm. **Subject:** Hieronymites Monastery - Belém

Date	Mintage	F	VF	XF	Unc	BU
2009	—	—	—	—	—	—

KM# 793 2-1/2 EURO

Copper-Nickel, 28 mm. **Rev. Designer:** Belém Unesco Heritage Site

Date	Mintage	F	VF	XF	Unc	BU
2009	—	—	—	—	—	—

KM# 749 5 EURO

14.0000 g., 0.5000 Silver 0.2250 oz. ASW, 30 mm. **Subject:** 150th Anniversary - First Portuguese Postage Stamp **Obv:** National arms and value within partial stamp design **Rev:** Partial postal stamp design **Edge:** Reeded

Date	Mintage	F	VF	XF	Unc	BU
2003INCM	300,000	—	—	—	30.00	32.50
2003INCM Prooflike	—	—	—	—	—	45.00

KM# 749a 5 EURO

14.0000 g., 0.9250 Silver 0.4163 oz. ASW, 30 mm. **Obv:** National arms and value within partial stamp design **Rev:** Partial postal stamp design

Date	Mintage	F	VF	XF	Unc	BU
2003INCM Proof	20,000	Value: 55.00				

KM# 749b 5 EURO

17.5000 g., 0.9166 Gold 0.5157 oz. AGW, 30 mm. **Obv:** National arms and value within partial stamp design **Rev:** Partial postal stamp design

Date	Mintage	F	VF	XF	Unc	BU
2003INCM Proof	—	Value: 650				

KM# 754 5 EURO

14.0000 g., 0.5000 Silver 0.2250 oz. ASW, 30 mm. **Subject:** Convent of Christ **Obv:** National arms above value flanked by designs **Rev:** Ornate convent window **Edge:** Reeded

Date	Mintage	F	VF	XF	Unc	BU
2004INCM	300,000	—	—	—	30.00	32.50

KM# 754a 5 EURO
14.0000 g., 0.9250 Silver 0.4163 oz. ASW, 30 mm.
Subject: Convent of Christ **Obv:** National arms above value flanked by designs **Rev:** Ornate convent window **Edge:** Reeded

Date	Mintage	F	VF	XF	Unc	BU
2004INCM Proof	10,000				Value: 60.00	

KM# 755 5 EURO
14.0000 g., 0.5000 Silver 0.2250 oz. ASW, 30 mm.
Subject: Historic City of Evora **Obv:** National arms and value on city map silhouette **Rev:** Architectural highlights **Edge:** Reeded

Date	Mintage	F	VF	XF	Unc	BU
2004INCM	300,000	—	—	—	30.00	32.50

KM# 755a 5 EURO
14.0000 g., 0.9250 Silver 0.4163 oz. ASW, 30 mm.
Subject: Historic City of Evora **Obv:** National arms and value on city map silhouette **Rev:** Architectural highlights **Edge:** Reeded

Date	Mintage	F	VF	XF	Unc	BU
2004INCM Proof	10,000				Value: 60.00	

KM# 762 5 EURO
14.0000 g., 0.5000 Silver 0.2250 oz. ASW, 30 mm. **Subject:** 800th Anniversary Birth of Pope John XXI **Obv:** National arms at lower right with archways in backgound **Obv. Legend:** REPUBLICA PORTUGUESA **Rev:** 1/2 length figure of Pope facing at right with staff dividing dates, small shield at left **Edge:** Reeded

Date	Mintage	F	VF	XF	Unc	BU
2005INCM	300,000	—	—	—	30.00	32.50

KM# 762a 5 EURO
14.0000 g., 0.9250 Silver 0.4163 oz. ASW, 30 mm.
Subject: 800th Anniversary Birth of Pope John XXI **Obv:** National arms at lower right with archways in backgound **Obv. Legend:** REPUBLICA PORTUGUESA **Rev:** 1/2 length figure of Pope facing at right with staff dividing dates, small shield at left **Edge:** Reeded

Date	Mintage	F	VF	XF	Unc	BU
2005INCM Proof	15,000				Value: 65.00	

KM# 762b 5 EURO
17.5000 g., 0.9167 Gold 0.5157 oz. AGW, 30 mm.
Subject: 800th Anniversary Birth of Pope John XXI **Obv:** National arms at lower right, archways in background **Obv. Legend:** REPUBLICA PORTUGUESA **Edge:** Reeded

Date	Mintage	F	VF	XF	Unc	BU
2005INCM Proof	7,500				Value: 650	

KM# 760 5 EURO
14.0000 g., 0.5000 Silver 0.2250 oz. ASW, 30 mm.
Obv: National arms within circle **Obv. Legend:** REPUBLICA POTUGUESA **Rev:** Angra do Heroismo - Azores Terceira, emblem above **Rev. Legend:** CENTRO HISTÓRICO DE ANGRA DO HEROISMA **Edge:** Reeded

Date	Mintage	F	VF	XF	Unc	BU
2005	300,000	—	—	—	30.00	32.50

KM# 760a 5 EURO
14.0000 g., 0.9250 Silver 0.4163 oz. ASW, 30 mm.
Obv: National arms within circle **Obv. Legend:** REPUBLICA PORTUGUESA **Rev:** Angra do Heroisma - Azores Terceira, emblem above **Rev. Legend:** CENTRO HISTÓRICO DE ANGRA DO HEROISMA **Edge:** Reeded

Date	Mintage	F	VF	XF	Unc	BU
2005 Proof	10,000				Value: 60.00	

KM# 761 5 EURO
14.0000 g., 0.5000 Silver 0.2250 oz. ASW, 30 mm. **Obv:** Design divides national arms and value **Obv. Legend:** REPUBLICA PORTUGUESA **Rev:** Batalha monastery and emblem **Rev. Legend:** MONTEIRO DA BATALHA **Edge:** Reeded

Date	Mintage	F	VF	XF	Unc	BU
2005	300,000	—	—	—	30.00	32.50

KM# 761a 5 EURO
14.0000 g., 0.9250 Silver 0.4163 oz. ASW, 30 mm. **Obv:** Design divides national arms and value **Obv. Legend:** REPUBLICA PORTUGUESA **Rev:** Batalha monastery and emblem **Rev. Legend:** MONTEIRO DA BATALHA **Edge:** Reeded

Date	Mintage	F	VF	XF	Unc	BU
2005 Proof	10,000				Value: 60.00	

KM# 769 5 EURO
14.0000 g., 0.5000 Silver 0.2250 oz. ASW, 30 mm.
Subject: UNESCO - Cultural preservation **Obv:** National arms above value **Obv. Legend:** REPUBLICA PORTUGUESA **Rev:** Outlined view **Rev. Legend:** PAISAGEM CULTURAL DE SINTRA **Edge:** Reeded

Date	Mintage	F	VF	XF	Unc	BU
2006INCM	300,000	—	—	—	30.00	32.50

KM# 769a 5 EURO
14.0000 g., 0.9250 Silver 0.4163 oz. ASW, 30 mm.
Subject: UNESCO - Cultural preservation **Obv:** National arms above value **Obv. Legend:** REPUBLICA PORTUGUESA **Rev:** Outlined view **Rev. Legend:** PAISAGEM CULTURAL DE SINTRA **Edge:** Reeded

Date	Mintage	F	VF	XF	Unc	BU
2006INCM Proof	10,000				Value: 60.00	

KM# 779 5 EURO
14.0000 g., 0.5000 Silver 0.2250 oz. ASW **Subject:** Alcoba?a Monastery **Obv:** National arms **Obv. Legend:** REP?BLICA PORTUGUESA **Edge:** Reeded

Date	Mintage	F	VF	XF	Unc	BU
2006INCM	300,000	—	—	—	25.00	27.50

KM# 779a 5 EURO
14.0000 g., 0.9250 Silver 0.4163 oz. ASW **Subject:** Alcobaça Monestary **Obv:** National arms **Obv. Legend:** REPÚBLICA PORTUGUESA **Edge:** Reeded

Date	Mintage	F	VF	XF	Unc	BU
2006INCM Proof	10,000				Value: 60.00	

KM# 770a 5 EURO
14.0000 g., 0.9250 Silver 0.4163 oz. ASW, 30 mm.
Subject: World Scouting Centennial **Obv:** National arms, World Scouting emblem **Obv. Legend:** REPUBLICA POTUGUESA 1907 - 2007 CENTENARIO DO ESCUTISMO MUNDIAL **Rev:** Linear portrait of Lord Robert Baden-Powell **Rev. Legend:** UM MUNDO UMA PROMESA **Edge:** Reeded **Designer:** Joao Calvina

Date	Mintage	F	VF	XF	Unc	BU
ND(2007) Proof	10,000				Value: 60.00	

KM# 781 5 EURO
14.0400 g., 0.5000 Silver 0.2257 oz. ASW, 30 mm.
Subject: Equal Opportunities **Obv:** Small national arms above moon shaped arc **Obv. Legend:** República Portuguesa **Rev:** Small 3 persons logo above 12 stars along rim **Rev. Legend:** Ano Europeu da Igualdade de Oportunidades para Todos **Edge:** Reeded

Date	Mintage	F	VF	XF	Unc	BU
2007INCM	75,000	—	—	—	25.00	27.50

KM# 781a 5 EURO
14.0000 g., 0.9250 Silver 0.4163 oz. ASW, 30 mm.
Subject: Equal Opportunities **Obv:** Small national arms above moon shaped arc **Obv. Legend:** República Portuguesa **Rev:** Small 3 persons logo above 12 stars along rim **Rev. Legend:** Ano Europeu da Igualdade de Oportunidades para Todos **Edge:** Reeded

Date	Mintage	F	VF	XF	Unc	BU
2007INCM Proof	6,000				Value: 65.00	

KM# 770 5 EURO
14.0000 g., 0.5000 Silver 0.2250 oz. ASW, 30 mm.
Subject: World Scouting Centennial **Obv:** Portuguese Arms, World Scouting emblem **Obv. Legend:** REPUBLICA PORTUGUESA 1907-2007 CENTENARIO DO ESCUTISMO MUNDIAL **Rev:** Linear portrait of Lord Robert Baden-Powell **Rev. Legend:** UM MUNDO UMA PROMESA **Edge:** Reeded **Designer:** Joao Calvino

Date	Mintage	F	VF	XF	Unc	BU
ND(2007)	70,000	—	—	—	25.00	27.50

KM# 782 5 EURO
13.9500 g., 0.5000 Silver 0.2242 oz. ASW, 30 mm.
Series: UNESCO - World Heritage **Subject:** National Forest Reserve in Madeira Nature Park **Obv:** National arms **Obv. Legend:** REPÚBLICA POTUGUESA **Rev:** Foliage with small UNESCO World Heritage logo at lower right **Rev. Legend:** FLORESTA LAURISSILVA DA MADEIRA **Edge:** Reeded

Date	Mintage	F	VF	XF	Unc	BU
2007INCM	70,000	—	—	—	25.00	27.50

KM# 782a 5 EURO
14.0000 g., 0.9250 Silver 0.4163 oz. ASW, 30 mm.
Series: UNESCO - World Heritage **Subject:** National Forest Reserve in Madeira Nature Park **Obv:** National arms **Obv. Legend:** REPÚBLICA POTUGUESA **Rev:** Foliage with small UNESCO World Heritage logo at lower right **Rev. Legend:** FLORESTA LAURISSILVA DA MADEIRA **Edge:** Reeded

Date	Mintage	F	VF	XF	Unc	BU
2007INCM Proof	7,500				Value: 65.00	

KM# 750a 8 EURO
31.1000 g., 0.9250 Silver 0.9249 oz. ASW, 36 mm.
Obv: National arms, value and flag-covered globe **Rev:** Flag-covered globe and "Euro 2004" soccer games logo

Date	Mintage	F	VF	XF	Unc	BU
2003INCM Prooflike	30,000	—	—	—	—	100
2003INCM Proof	15,000				Value: 165	

KM# 750 8 EURO
21.1000 g., 0.5000 Silver 0.3392 oz. ASW, 36 mm.
Obv: National arms, value and flag-covered globe **Rev:** Flag-covered globe and "Euro 2004" soccer games logo **Edge:** Reeded

Date	Mintage	F	VF	XF	Unc	BU
2003INCM	1,500,000	—	—	—	35.00	37.50

KM# 750b 8 EURO
31.1000 g., 0.9166 Gold 0.9165 oz. AGW, 36 mm.
Obv: National arms, value and flag-covered globe **Rev:** Flag-covered globe and "Euro 2004" soccer games logo

Date	Mintage	F	VF	XF	Unc	BU
2003INCM Proof	10,000				Value: 1,850	

KM# 751 8 EURO
21.1000 g., 0.5000 Silver 0.3392 oz. ASW, 36 mm.
Obv: National arms and value below many bubbles **Rev:** "Euro 2004" soccer games logo below many hearts **Edge:** Reeded

Date	Mintage	F	VF	XF	Unc	BU
2003INCM	1,500,000	—	—	—	35.00	37.50

KM# 751a 8 EURO
31.1000 g., 0.9250 Silver 0.9249 oz. ASW, 36 mm.
Obv: National arms and value below many bubbles **Rev:** "Euro 2004" soccer games logo below many hearts

Date	Mintage	F	VF	XF	Unc	BU
2003INCM Prooflike	—	—	—	—	—	100
2003INCM Proof	15,000	Value: 165				

KM# 751b 8 EURO
31.1000 g., 0.9166 Gold 0.9165 oz. AGW, 36 mm.
Obv: National arms and value below many bubbles **Rev:** "Euro 2004" soccer games logo below many hearts

Date	Mintage	F	VF	XF	Unc	BU
2003INCM Proof	10,000	Value: 1,850				

KM# 752 8 EURO
21.1000 g., 0.5000 Silver 0.3392 oz. ASW, 36 mm.
Obv: National arms and value **Rev:** "Euro 2004" soccer games logo in center with partial text background **Edge:** Reeded

Date	Mintage	F	VF	XF	Unc	BU
2003INCM	1,500,000	—	—	—	35.00	37.50

KM# 752a 8 EURO
31.1000 g., 0.9250 Silver 0.9249 oz. ASW, 36 mm.
Obv: National arms and value **Rev:** "Euro 2004" soccer games logo in center with partial text background

Date	Mintage	F	VF	XF	Unc	BU
2003INCM Prooflike	—	—	—	—	—	100
2003INCM Proof	15,000	Value: 165				

KM# 752b 8 EURO
31.1000 g., 0.9166 Gold 0.9165 oz. AGW, 36 mm.
Obv: National arms and value **Rev:** "Euro 2004" soccer games logo in center with partial text background

Date	Mintage	F	VF	XF	Unc	BU
2003INCM Proof	10,000	Value: 1,850				

KM# 753 8 EURO
21.2200 g., 0.5000 Silver 0.3411 oz. ASW, 36 mm.
Subject: Expansion of the European Union **Obv:** Radiant national arms and value **Rev:** European map **Edge:** Reeded

Date	Mintage	F	VF	XF	Unc	BU
2004INCM	300,000	—	—	—	25.00	27.50

KM# 753a 8 EURO
31.1000 g., 0.9250 Silver 0.9249 oz. ASW, 36 mm.
Subject: Expansion of the European Union **Obv:** Radiant national arms and value **Rev:** European map **Edge:** Reeded

Date	Mintage	F	VF	XF	Unc	BU
2004INCM Proof	35,000	Value: 60.00				

KM# 756 8 EURO
21.0000 g., 0.5000 Silver 0.3376 oz. ASW, 36 mm.
Subject: Euro 2004 Soccer **Obv:** National arms **Rev:** Stylized goal keeper **Edge:** Reeded

Date	Mintage	F	VF	XF	Unc	BU
2004INCM	1,500,000	—	—	—	25.00	27.50

KM# 756a 8 EURO
31.1000 g., 0.9250 Silver 0.9249 oz. ASW, 36 mm.
Subject: Euro 2004 Soccer **Obv:** National arms **Rev:** Stylized goal keeper **Edge:** Reeded

Date	Mintage	F	VF	XF	Unc	BU
2004INCM	30,000	—	—	—	—	80.00
2004INCM Proof	15,000	Value: 150				

KM# 756b 8 EURO
31.1000 g., 0.9166 Gold 0.9165 oz. AGW, 36 mm.
Subject: Euro 2004 Soccer **Obv:** National arms **Rev:** Stylized goal keeper **Edge:** Reeded

Date	Mintage	F	VF	XF	Unc	BU
2004INCM Proof	10,000	Value: 1,850				

KM# 757 8 EURO
21.0000 g., 0.9250 Silver 0.6245 oz. ASW, 36 mm.
Subject: Euro 2004 Soccer **Obv:** National arms **Rev:** Face of player making shot **Edge:** Reeded

Date	Mintage	F	VF	XF	Unc	BU
2004INCM	1,500,000	—	—	—	25.00	27.50

KM# 757a 8 EURO
31.1000 g., 0.9250 Silver 0.9249 oz. ASW, 36 mm.
Subject: Euro 2004 Soccer **Obv:** National arms **Rev:** Face of player making a shot **Edge:** Reeded

Date	Mintage	F	VF	XF	Unc	BU
2004INCM	30,000	—	—	—	—	80.00
2004INCM Proof	15,000	Value: 150				

KM# 757b 8 EURO
31.1000 g., 0.9166 Gold 0.9165 oz. AGW, 36 mm.
Subject: Euro 2004 Soccer **Obv:** National arms **Rev:** Face of player making a shot **Edge:** Reeded

Date	Mintage	F	VF	XF	Unc	BU
2004INCM Proof	10,000	Value: 1,850				

KM# 758 8 EURO
21.0000 g., 0.5000 Silver 0.3376 oz. ASW, 36 mm.
Subject: Euro 2004 Soccer **Obv:** National arms **Rev:** Symbolic explosion of a goal **Edge:** Reeded

Date	Mintage	F	VF	XF	Unc	BU
2004INCM	1,500,000	—	—	—	25.00	27.50

KM# 758a 8 EURO
31.1000 g., 0.9250 Silver 0.9249 oz. ASW, 36 mm.
Subject: Euro 2004 Soccer **Obv:** National arms **Rev:** Symbolic explosion of a goal **Edge:** Reeded

Date	Mintage	F	VF	XF	Unc	BU
2004INCM	30,000	—	—	—	—	80.00
2004INCM Proof	15,000	Value: 150				

KM# 758b 8 EURO
31.1000 g., 0.9166 Gold 0.9165 oz. AGW, 36 mm.
Subject: Euro 2004 Soccer **Obv:** National arms **Rev:** Symbolic explosion of a goal **Edge:** Reeded

Date	Mintage	F	VF	XF	Unc	BU
2004INCM Proof	10,000	Value: 1,850				

KM# 773 8 EURO
21.0000 g., 0.5000 Silver 0.3376 oz. ASW, 36 mm.
Subject: 60th Anniversary End of WW II **Obv:** Quill pens horizontal at left center, national arms at lower righr
Obv. Inscription: REPÚBLICA PORTUGUESA **Rev:** Four quill pens upright, outlined map of Europe in background
Rev. Inscription: FIM DA II GUERRA MUNDIAL **Edge:** Reeded

Date	Mintage	F	VF	XF	Unc	BU
2005INCM	300,000	—	—	—	30.00	32.50

KM# 773a 8 EURO
31.1000 g., 0.9250 Silver 0.9249 oz. ASW, 36 mm.
Subject: 60th Anniversary End of WW II **Obv:** Quill pens horizontal at left center, national arms at lower right
Obv. Inscription: REPÚBLICA PORTUGUESA **Rev:** Four quill pens upright, outlined map of Europe in background
Rev. Inscription: FIM DA II GUERRA MUNDIAL **Edge:** Reeded

Date	Mintage	F	VF	XF	Unc	BU
2005INCM Proof	35,000	Value: 70.00				

KM# 776 8 EURO
20.8000 g., 0.5000 Silver 0.3344 oz. ASW, 36 mm.
Series: Famous Europeans **Subject:** Prince Henry the Navigator **Obv:** Small national arms and shield **Obv. Legend:** REPÚBLICA PORTUGUESA **Rev:** Tiny bust 3/4 right **Edge:** Reeded

Date	Mintage	F	VF	XF	Unc	BU
2006INCM	100,000	—	—	—	30.00	32.50

KM# 776a 8 EURO
31.1000 g., 0.9250 Silver 0.9249 oz. ASW, 36 mm.
Series: Famous Europeans **Subject:** Prince Henry the Navigator **Obv:** Small national arms and shield **Obv. Legend:** REPÚBLICA PORTUGUESA **Rev:** Tiny bust 3/4 right **Edge:** Reeded

Date	Mintage	F	VF	XF	Unc	BU
2006INCM Proof	35,000	Value: 65.00				

KM# 778 8 EURO
21.0000 g., 0.5000 Silver 0.3376 oz. ASW, 36 mm.
Subject: 150th Anniversary Railroad Lisbon - Carregado
Obv: National arms on wavy flag **Obv. Legend:** REPÚBLICA PORTUGUESA **Rev:** Vertical railroad track divides two shields
Rev. Legend: 150 ANOS DA PRIMEIRA LINHA FERREA LISBOA CARREGADO **Edge:** Reeded

Date	Mintage	F	VF	XF	Unc	BU
2006INCM	100,000	—	—	—	32.50	35.00

KM# 778a 8 EURO
31.1000 g., 0.9250 Silver 0.9249 oz. ASW, 36 mm.
Subject: 150th Anniversary Railroad Lisbon - Carregado
Obv: National srms on wavy flag **Obv. Legend:** REPÚBLICA PORTUGUESA **Rev:** Vertical railroad track divides two shields
Rev. Legend: 150 ANOSDA PRIMEIRA LINHA FERREA LISBOA CARREGADO **Edge:** Reeded

Date	Mintage	F	VF	XF	Unc	BU
2006INCM Proof	35,000	Value: 75.00				

KM# 748 10 EURO
27.0000 g., 0.5000 Silver 0.4340 oz. ASW, 40 mm.
Subject: Nautica **Obv:** National arms within circle of assorted shields **Rev:** Sailing ship and sextant **Edge:** Reeded

Date	Mintage	F	VF	XF	Unc	BU
2003INCM	350,000	—	—	—	22.50	25.00

KM# 748a 10 EURO
27.0000 g., 0.9250 Silver 0.8029 oz. ASW, 40 mm.
Obv: National arms within circle of assorted shields **Rev:** Sailing ship and sextant **Edge:** Reeded

Date	Mintage	F	VF	XF	Unc	BU
2003INCM Proof	10,000	Value: 70.00				

KM# 759 10 EURO
27.0000 g., 0.5000 Silver 0.4340 oz. ASW, 40 mm.
Subject: Olympics **Obv:** National arms above stylized value **Rev:** Stylized sail above Olympic rings **Edge:** Reeded

Date	Mintage	F	VF	XF	Unc	BU
2004INCM	350,000	—	—	—	25.00	27.50

KM# 759a 10 EURO
27.0000 g., 0.9250 Silver 0.8029 oz. ASW, 40 mm.
Subject: Olympics **Obv:** National arms above stylized value
Rev: Stylized sail above Olympic rings **Edge:** Reeded

Date	Mintage	F	VF	XF	Unc	BU
2004INCM Proof	15,000		Value: 65.00			

KM# 768 10 EURO
27.0000 g., 0.5000 Silver 0.4340 oz. ASW, 40 mm.
Obv: National arms above value in circle of multi-national coats of arms **Rev:** Church **Edge:** Reeded

Date	Mintage	F	VF	XF	Unc	BU
2005INCM	—	—	—	—		30.00
2005INCM Proof	300,000		Value: 75.00			

KM# 774 10 EURO
27.0000 g., 0.5000 Silver 0.4340 oz. ASW, 40 mm.
Subject: XVIII World Championship Football Games - Germany 2006 **Obv:** National arms above stadium **Obv. Legend:** REPÚBLICA PORTUGUESA **Rev:** Circular legend above sticks representing stadium fans **Rev. Legend:** CAMPEONATO DO MUNDO DE FUTEBOL FIFA ALEMANHA 2006 **Edge:** Reeded

Date	Mintage	F	VF	XF	Unc	BU
2006INCM	100,000	—	—	—	37.50	40.00

KM# 774a 10 EURO
27.0000 g., 0.9250 Silver 0.8029 oz. ASW, 40 mm.
Subject: XVIII World Championship Football Games - Germany 2006 **Obv:** National arms above stadium **Obv. Inscription:** REPÚBLICA PORTUGUESA **Rev:** Circular legend above sticks representing stadium fans **Edge:** Reeded

Date	Mintage	F	VF	XF	Unc	BU
2006INCM Proof	25,000		Value: 85.00			

KM# 775 10 EURO
27.0000 g., 0.5000 Silver 0.4340 oz. ASW, 40 mm.
Subject: 20th Anniversary of Spain and Portugal's membership in the European Union **Obv:** National arms **Obv. Legend:** REPÚBLICA PORTUGUESA **Rev:** Viaduct, outlined map of Europe above **Rev. Legend:** ADESÃO AS COMUNIDADES EUROPIAS **Edge:** Reeded

Date	Mintage	F	VF	XF	Unc	BU
2006INCM	100,000	—	—	—	27.50	30.00

KM# 775a 10 EURO
27.0000 g., 0.9250 Silver 0.8029 oz. ASW, 40 mm.
Subject: 20th Anniversary of Spain and Portugal's membership in European Union **Obv:** National arms **Obv. Legend:** REPÚBLICA PORTUGUESA **Rev:** Viaduct, outlined map of Europe above **Rev. Legend:** ADESÃO AS COMUNIDADES EUROPIAS **Edge:** Reeded

Date	Mintage	F	VF	XF	Unc	BU
2006INCM Proof	25,000		Value: 70.00			

MINT SETS

KM#	Date	Mintage	Identification	Issue Price	Mkt Val
MS32	2002 (8)	50,000	KM#740-747	—	50.00
MS33	2003 (8)	50,000	KM#740-747	—	50.00
MS34	2004 (8)	50,000	KM#740-747	—	45.00
MS35	2005 (8)	30,000	KM#740-747	—	45.00
MS36	2006 (8)	12,500	KM#740-747	—	45.00

PROOF SETS

KM#	Date	Mintage	Identification	Issue Price	Mkt Val
PS45	2002 (8)	15,000	KM#740-747	—	120
PS46	2003 (8)	15,000	kM#740-747	—	110
PS47	2004 (8)	15,000	KM#740-747	—	110
PS48	2005 (8)	10,000	KM#740-747	—	110
PS49	2006 (8)	3,000	KM#740-747	—	110

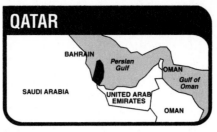

QATAR

The State of Qatar, an emirate in the Persian Gulf between Bahrain and Trucial Oman, has an area of 4,247sq. mi. (11,000 sq. km.) and a population of *469,000. Capital: Doha. Oil is the chief industry and export.

TITLES

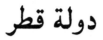

Daulat Qatar

RULERS

Al-Thani Dynasty
Hamad bin Khalifah, 1995-

MONETARY SYSTEM
100 Dirhem = 1 Riyal

STATE
STANDARD COINAGE

KM# 12 5 DIRHAMS
3.8000 g., Bronze, 21.9 mm. **Ruler:** Hamad bin Khalifah
Obv: Arms **Rev:** Value **Edge:** Plain

Date	Mintage	F	VF	XF	Unc	BU
AH1427-2006	—	—	—	0.35	0.90	1.25

KM# 13 10 DIRHAMS
7.5000 g., Bronze, 26.91 mm. **Ruler:** Hamad bin Khalifah
Obv: Arms **Rev:** Value **Edge:** Plain

Date	Mintage	F	VF	XF	Unc	BU
AH1427-2006	—	—	—	0.60	1.50	2.00

KM# 8 25 DIRHAMS
3.5000 g., Copper-Nickel, 19 mm. **Ruler:** Hamad bin Khalifah
Obv: Value **Obv. Legend:** STATE OF QATAR **Rev:** Sail boat and palm trees flanked by beads **Rev. Designer:** Norman Sillman **Edge:** Reeded

Date	Mintage	F	VF	XF	Unc	BU
AH1424-2003	—	—	0.30	0.65	1.50	2.50

KM# 14 25 DIRHAMS
3.5000 g., Copper-Nickel, 19.94 mm. **Ruler:** Hamad bin Khalifah **Obv:** Arms **Rev:** Value **Edge:** Reeded

Date	Mintage	F	VF	XF	Unc	BU
AH1427-2006	—	—	—	0.75	1.85	2.50

KM# 9 50 DIRHAMS
6.5000 g., Copper-Nickel, 24 mm. **Ruler:** Hamad bin Khalifah
Obv: Arms **Obv. Designer:** Norman Sillman **Rev:** Value
Edge: Reeded

Date	Mintage	F	VF	XF	Unc	BU
AH1424-2003	—				2.00	3.00

KM# 15 50 DIRHAMS
6.5000 g., Copper-Nickel, 24.96 mm. **Ruler:** Hamad bin Khalifah **Obv:** Arms **Rev:** Value **Edge:** Reeded

Date	Mintage	F	VF	XF	Unc	BU
AH1427-2006	—	—	—	0.80	2.00	2.75

KM# 16 RIYAL
Aluminum-Bronze **Ruler:** Hamad bin Khalifah **Subject:** 15th Asian Games **Obv:** Arms above value **Rev:** Multicolor Fox on Bicycle, cartoon character

Date	Mintage	F	VF	XF	Unc	BU
2006	—	—	—	—	—	25.00

KM# 34 RIYAL
Aluminum-Bronze, 38.74 mm. **Ruler:** Hamad bin Khalifah
Subject: 15th Asian Games **Obv:** Arms **Rev:** Multicolor mascot with flag

Date	Mintage	F	VF	XF	Unc	BU
2006	25,000	—	—	—	—	25.00

KM# 35 RIYAL
Aluminum-Bronze, 38.74 mm. **Ruler:** Hamad bin Khalifah
Subject: 15th Asian Games **Obv:** Arms **Rev:** Multicolor mascot kicking soccer ball

Date	Mintage	F	VF	XF	Unc	BU
2006	25,000	—	—	—	—	25.00

KM# 36 RIYAL
Aluminum-Bronze, 38.74 mm. **Ruler:** Hamad bin Khalifah
Subject: 15th Asian Games **Obv:** Arms **Rev:** Three multicolor torches

Date	Mintage	F	VF	XF	Unc	BU
2006	25,000	—	—	—	—	25.00

KM# 37 RIYAL
Aluminum-Bronze, 38.74 mm. **Ruler:** Hamad bin Khalifah
Subject: 15th Asian Games **Obv:** Arms **Rev:** Two figures with linked arms

Date	Mintage	F	VF	XF	Unc	BU
2006	25,000	—	—	—	—	25.00

KM# 38 RIYAL
Aluminum-Bronze, 38.74 mm. **Ruler:** Hamad bin Khalifah
Subject: 15th Asian Games **Obv:** Arms **Rev:** Figure with outstretched arms

Date	Mintage	F	VF	XF	Unc	BU
2006	25,000	—	—	—	—	25.00

KM# 25 10 RIYALS
31.1035 g., 0.9990 Silver 0.9990 oz. ASW, 40.5 mm.
Ruler: Hamad bin Khalifah **Subject:** 15th Asian Games
Obv: Arms **Rev:** Runner trailing green color

Date	Mintage	F	VF	XF	Unc	BU
2006 Proof	25,000		Value: 110			

KM# 26   10 RIYALS
31.1035 g., 0.9990 Silver 0.9990 oz. ASW, 40.5 mm.
Ruler: Hamad bin Khalifah **Subject:** 15th Asian Games
Obv: Arms **Rev:** Cyclist trailing red color

Date	Mintage	F	VF	XF	Unc	BU
2006 Proof	25,000	Value: 110				

KM# 27   10 RIYALS
31.1035 g., 0.9990 Silver 0.9990 oz. ASW, 40.5 mm.
Ruler: Hamad bin Khalifah **Subject:** 15th Asian Games
Obv: Arms **Rev:** Soccer player legs on green color

Date	Mintage	F	VF	XF	Unc	BU
2006 Proof	25,000	Value: 110				

KM# 28   10 RIYALS
31.1035 g., 0.9990 Silver 0.9990 oz. ASW, 40.5 mm.
Ruler: Hamad bin Khalifah **Subject:** 15th Asian Games
Obv: Arms **Rev:** Ribbon dancer trailing red color

Date	Mintage	F	VF	XF	Unc	BU
2006 Proof	25,000	Value: 110				

KM# 29   10 RIYALS
31.1035 g., 0.9990 Silver 0.9990 oz. ASW, 40.5 mm.
Ruler: Hamad bin Khalifah **Subject:** 15th Asian Games
Obv: Arms **Rev:** Karate contestants and dark yellow color

Date	Mintage	F	VF	XF	Unc	BU
2006 Proof	25,000	Value: 110				

KM# 30   10 RIYALS
31.1035 g., 0.9990 Silver 0.9990 oz. ASW, 40.5 mm.
Ruler: Hamad bin Khalifah **Subject:** 15th Asian Games
Obv: Arms **Rev:** Swimmer in aqua colored water

Date	Mintage	F	VF	XF	Unc	BU
2006 Proof	25,000	Value: 110				

KM# 31   10 RIYALS
31.1035 g., 0.9990 Silver 0.9990 oz. ASW, 40.5 mm.
Ruler: Hamad bin Khalifah **Subject:** 15th Asian Games
Obv: Arms **Rev:** Table tennis player and orange-brownish color

Date	Mintage	F	VF	XF	Unc	BU
2006 Proof	25,000	Value: 110				

KM# 32   10 RIYALS
31.1035 g., 0.9990 Silver 0.9990 oz. ASW, 40.5 mm.
Ruler: Hamad bin Khalifah **Subject:** 15th Asian Games
Obv: Arms **Rev:** Tennis player and aqua color

Date	Mintage	F	VF	XF	Unc	BU
2006 Proof	25,000	Value: 110				

KM# 33   10 RIYALS
31.1035 g., 0.9990 Silver 0.9990 oz. ASW, 40.5 mm.
Ruler: Hamad bin Khalifah **Subject:** 15th Asian Games
Obv: Arms **Rev:** Volleyball player trailing purple color

Date	Mintage	F	VF	XF	Unc	BU
2006 Proof	25,000	Value: 110				

KM# 17   100 RIYALS
Gold **Ruler:** Hamad bin Khalifah **Subject:** 15th Asian Games
Obv: Arms above value **Rev:** Games mascot Fox on Bicycle cartoon character

Date	Mintage	F	VF	XF	Unc	BU
2006 Proof	Est. 10,000	Value: 525				

KM# 18   100 RIYALS
17.0000 g., 0.9200 Gold 0.5028 oz. AGW, 31 mm.
Ruler: Hamad bin Khalifah **Obv:** Arms **Rev:** Central Bank building **Edge:** Reeded

Date	Mintage	F	VF	XF	Unc	BU
2006 Proof	300	Value: 1,400				

KM# 19   100 RIYALS
10.0000 g., 0.9999 Gold 0.3215 oz. AGW, 24.5 mm.
Ruler: Hamad bin Khalifah **Subject:** 15th Asian Games
Obv: Arms **Rev:** Khalifa Stadium **Edge:** Reeded

Date	Mintage	F	VF	XF	Unc	BU
2006 Proof	—	Value: 600				

KM# 20   100 RIYALS
10.0000 g., 0.9999 Gold 0.3215 oz. AGW, 24.5 mm.
Ruler: Hamad bin Khalifah **Subject:** 15th Asian Games
Obv: Arms **Rev:** Two fighting oryxes **Edge:** Reeded

Date	Mintage	F	VF	XF	Unc	BU
2006 Proof	—	Value: 600				

KM# 21   100 RIYALS
10.0000 g., 0.9999 Gold 0.3215 oz. AGW, 24.5 mm.
Ruler: Hamad bin Khalifah **Subject:** 15th Asian Games
Obv: Arms **Rev:** Falcon bust **Edge:** Reeded

Date	Mintage	F	VF	XF	Unc	BU
2006 Proof	—	Value: 600				

KM# 22   100 RIYALS
10.0000 g., 0.9999 Gold 0.3215 oz. AGW, 24.5 mm.
Ruler: Hamad bin Khalifah **Subject:** 15th Asian Games
Obv: Arms **Rev:** Coffee pot **Edge:** Reeded

Date	Mintage	F	VF	XF	Unc	BU
2006 Proof	—	Value: 600				

KM# 23   100 RIYALS
10.0000 g., 0.9999 Gold 0.3215 oz. AGW, 24.5 mm.
Ruler: Hamad bin Khalifah **Subject:** 15th Asian Games
Obv: Arms **Rev:** Radiant sun **Edge:** Reeded

Date	Mintage	F	VF	XF	Unc	BU
2006 Proof	—	Value: 600				

KM# 11   250 RIYALS
Silver **Ruler:** Hamad bin Khalifah **Subject:** 4th WTO Conference **Obv:** National arms **Rev:** WTO logo, value, date, and legend in English and Islamic

Date	Mintage	F	VF	XF	Unc	BU
AH1422 (2001) Proof	1,000	Value: 650				

KM# 39 300 RIYALS
1000.0000 g., 0.9990 Silver 32.117 oz. ASW, 100.0 mm.
Ruler: Hamad bin Khalifah **Obv:** National arms **Obv. Legend:**
STATE OF QATAR **Rev:** Sports montage around game's logo
Rev. Inscription: 15TH ASIAN GAMES / DOHA 2006
Edge: Plain

Date	Mintage	F	VF	XF	Unc	BU
2006 Proof	5,000	Value: 750				

KM# 24 10000 RIYALS
1000.0000 g., 0.9999 Gold 32.146 oz. AGW, 75.3 mm.
Ruler: Hamad bin Khalifah **Subject:** 15th Asian Games
Obv: Arms **Rev:** Radiant sun **Edge:** Reeded **Note:** Illustration
reduced.

Date	Mintage	F	VF	XF	Unc	BU
2006 Proof	—	Value: 40,000				

ROMANIA

UKRAINE MOLDOVA
SLOVAKIA
HUNGARY
CROATIA
BOSNIA
SERBIA BULGARIA
Black Sea

Romania (formerly the Socialist Republic of Romania), a
country in southeast Europe, has an area of 91,699 sq. mi.
(237,500 sq. km.) and a population of 23.2 million. Capital:
Bucharest. Machinery, foodstuffs, raw minerals and petroleum
products are exported. Heavy industry and oil have become
increasingly important to the economy since 1959. Romania
joined the European Union in January 2007.

MONETARY SYSTEM
100 Bani = 1 Leu

REPUBLIC
STANDARD COINAGE

KM# 115 LEU
2.5200 g., Copper Clad Steel, 19 mm. **Obv:** Value flanked by
sprigs **Rev:** Shield divides date

Date	Mintage	F	VF	XF	Unc	BU
2002 Proof	1,500	Value: 5.00				
2003 Proof	2,000	Value: 5.00				

Date	Mintage	F	VF	XF	Unc	BU
2004 Proof	2,000	Value: 5.00				
2005	—	—	—	—	1.00	—
2005 Proof	—	Value: 6.00				
2006 Proof	1,000	Value: 6.00				

KM# 199 LEU
23.5000 g., Copper Plated Tombac, 37 mm. **Subject:** 130th
Anniversary of Proclamation of Independence **Obv:** Shield and
"The Smardan Assault" painting by Nicolae Grigoresuv
Rev: Meeting of the Parliament

Date	Mintage	F	VF	XF	Unc	BU
2007 Proof	130	Value: 350				

KM# 114 5 LEI
3.3000 g., Nickel Plated Steel, 21 mm. **Obv:** Value flanked by
oak leaves **Rev:** Shield divides date **Edge:** Plain

Date	Mintage	F	VF	XF	Unc	BU
2002 Proof	1,500	Value: 5.00				
2003 Proof	2,000	Value: 5.00				
2004 Proof	—	Value: 5.00				
2005 Proof	—	Value: 5.00				

KM# 200 5 LEI
15.5500 g., 0.9990 Silver 0.4994 oz. ASW, 30 mm.
Subject: 130th Anniversary of Proclamation of Independence
Obv: Shield and "The Smardan Assault" painting by Nicolae
Grigoresuv **Rev:** Meeting of the Parliament

Date	Mintage	F	VF	XF	Unc	BU
2007 Proof	130	Value: 750				

KM# 116 10 LEI
4.7000 g., Nickel Clad Steel, 23 mm. **Obv:** Value within sprigs
Rev: Shield divides date **Edge:** Plain

Date	Mintage	F	VF	XF	Unc	BU
2002 Proof	1,500	Value: 6.00				
2003 Proof	2,000	Value: 6.00				

KM# 233 10 LEI
31.1030 g., Silver, 37 mm. **Subject:** Snagov Monastery
Obv: Shield and saints **Obv. Designer:** Christian Ciomai and
Vasile Gabor **Rev:** Monastery Building

Date	Mintage	F	VF	XF	Unc	BU
2007 Proof	500	Value: 180				

KM# 234 10 LEI
31.1030 g., 0.9990 Silver 0.9989 oz. ASW, 37 mm.
Subject: Romanian Oil Industry, 150th Anniversary **Obv:** Shield,
Mehedinteanu Refinery **Obv. Designer:** Cristian Ciomet and
Vasile Gabor **Rev:** Drilling well and pump jack

Date	Mintage	F	VF	XF	Unc	BU
2007 Proof	500	Value: 140				

KM# 231 10 LEI
31.1030 g., 99.9000 Silver 99.894 oz. ASW, 37 mm. **Subject:**
80th Anniversary Romanian Broadcasting Co. **Obv:** Radio
Romania, years 1928 and 2008, coat of arms **Rev:** Radio set
from 30's, logo of Radio Romania, headphones **Edge:** Reeded

Date	Mintage	F	VF	XF	Unc	BU
2008 Proof	500	Value: 450				

KM# 232 10 LEI
1.2240 g., 99.9000 Gold 3.9312 oz. AGW, 13.9 mm.
Subject: Hoard of Hinova **Obv:** Romanian Coat of Arms,
necklace parts **Rev:** Necklace parts, four bell shaped necklace
parts, muff **Edge:** Reeded

Date	Mintage	F	VF	XF	Unc	BU
2008 Proof	500	Value: 135				

KM# 109 20 LEI
5.0000 g., Brass Clad Steel, 24 mm. **Obv:** Crowned bust of
Prince Stefan Cel Mare facing, flanked by dots **Rev:** Value and
date within half sprigs and dots **Edge:** Plain **Designer:** Constantin
Dumitrescu **Note:** Date varieties exist.

Date	Mintage	F	VF	XF	Unc	BU
2002 Proof	1,500	Value: 7.50				
2003 Proof	2,000	Value: 7.50				

KM# 159 50 LEI
15.5510 g., 0.9990 Silver 0.4995 oz. ASW, 31.1 mm.
Series: Romanian Aviation **Obv:** AVIONUL VUIA 1 - 1906
airplane **Rev:** Traian Vuia **Edge:** Plain **Shape:** Octagonal

Date	Mintage	F	VF	XF	Unc	BU
2001 Proof	500	Value: 200				

KM# 160 50 LEI
15.5510 g., 0.9990 Silver 0.4995 oz. ASW, 31.1 mm.
Series: Romanian Aviation **Obv:** Avionul Coanda 1910, world's
first (?) jet airplane **Rev:** Portrait of Henri Coanda **Edge:** Plain
Shape: Octagonal

Date	Mintage	F	VF	XF	Unc	BU
2001 Proof	500	Value: 200				

KM# 161 50 LEI
15.5510 g., 0.9990 Silver 0.4995 oz. ASW, 27 mm.
Series: Romanian Aviation **Obv:** IAR CV-11 airplane **Rev:** Elie
Carafoli **Edge:** Plain **Shape:** Octagonal

Date	Mintage	F	VF	XF	Unc	BU
2001 Proof	500	Value: 200				

KM# 110 50 LEI
5.9000 g., Brass Clad Steel, 26 mm. **Obv:** Bust left flanked by
dots **Rev:** Sprig divides date and value **Edge:** Plain
Designer: Vasile Gabor

Date	Mintage	F	VF	XF	Unc	BU
2002 Proof	1,500	Value: 8.00				
2003 Proof	2,000	Value: 8.00				

KM# 167 50 LEI
15.5510 g., 0.9990 Silver 0.4995 oz. ASW, 29.5 mm.
Subject: National Parks: Retezat **Obv:** National arms in
triangular design **Rev:** Chamois **Edge:** Plain **Shape:** Rounded
triangle

Date	Mintage	F	VF	XF	Unc	BU
2002 Proof	500	Value: 300				

KM# 168 50 LEI
15.5510 g., 0.9990 Silver 0.4995 oz. ASW, 29.5 mm.
Subject: National Parks: Pictrosul Mare **Obv:** National arms in
triangular design **Rev:** Eagle **Edge:** Plain **Shape:** Rounded
triangle

Date	Mintage	F	VF	XF	Unc	BU
2002 Proof	500	Value: 300				

KM# 169 50 LEI
15.5510 g., 0.9990 Silver 0.4995 oz. ASW, 29.5 mm.
Subject: National Parks: Piatra Craiului **Obv:** National arms in
triangular design **Rev:** Lynx **Edge:** Plain **Shape:** Rounded
triangle

Date	Mintage	F	VF	XF	Unc	BU
2002 Proof	500	Value: 300				

KM# 186 50 LEI
15.5510 g., 0.9990 Silver 0.4995 oz. ASW, 27 mm.
Subject: Birds **Obv:** Stylized water drop **Rev:** Dalmatian Pelicans within circle **Edge:** Plain

Date	Mintage	F	VF	XF	Unc	BU
2003 Proof	500	Value: 120				

KM# 187 50 LEI
15.5510 g., 0.9990 Silver 0.4995 oz. ASW, 27 mm.
Subject: Birds **Obv:** Stylized water drop **Rev:** Great Egret within circle **Edge:** Plain

Date	Mintage	F	VF	XF	Unc	BU
2003 Proof	500	Value: 120				

KM# 188 50 LEI
15.5510 g., 0.9990 Silver 0.4995 oz. ASW, 27 mm.
Subject: Birds **Obv:** Stylized water drop **Rev:** Common Kingfisher within circle **Edge:** Plain

Date	Mintage	F	VF	XF	Unc	BU
2003 Proof	500	Value: 120				

KM# 111 100 LEI
8.7500 g., Nickel Plated Steel, 29 mm. **Obv:** Bust with headdress 1/4 right **Rev:** Value within sprigs **Edge Lettering:** ROMANIA **Designer:** Vasile Gabor

Date	Mintage	F	VF	XF	Unc	BU
2002 Proof	1,500	Value: 8.00				
2003 Proof	2,000	Value: 8.00				
2004 Proof	2,000	Value: 8.00				
2005	—	—	—	—	2.50	—
2005 Proof	2,000	Value: 9.00				
2006 Proof	1,000	Value: 9.00				

KM# 165 100 LEI
1.2240 g., 0.9990 Gold 0.0393 oz. AGW, 13.9 mm.
Subject: History of Gold - "The Apahida Eagle" **Obv:** National arms in ornamental circle above value **Edge:** Plain

Date	Mintage	F	VF	XF	Unc	BU
2003 Proof	2,000	Value: 125				

KM# 198 100 LEI
1.2240 g., 0.9990 Gold 0.0393 oz. AGW, 13.93 mm.
Obv: National arms in wreath **Obv. Legend:** ROMANIA **Rev:** Medieval helmet - "COIF POTANA COTOFENESTI" **Edge:** Reeded

Date	Mintage	F	VF	XF	Unc	BU
2003 Proof	—	Value: 75.00				

KM# 166 100 LEI
1.2240 g., 0.9990 Gold 0.0393 oz. AGW, 14 mm.
Subject: History of Gold - Engolpion **Obv:** National arms and country name above two stylized birds and value **Rev:** Jeweled double headed eagle pendant

Date	Mintage	F	VF	XF	Unc	BU
2004 Proof	1,000	Value: 165				

KM# 201 100 LEI
6.4520 g., 0.9000 Gold 0.1867 oz. AGW, 21 mm. **Subject:** 130th Anniversary of Proclamation of Independence **Obv:** Shield and "The Smardan Assault" painting by Nicole Grigorescu **Rev:** Meeting of the Parliament

Date	Mintage	F	VF	XF	Unc	BU
2007 Proof	130	Value: 5,000				

KM# 235 100 LEI
6.4520 g., 0.9990 Gold 0.2072 oz. AGW, 21 mm.
Subject: Battles of Marasti, Marasesti, Oituz 90th Anniversary **Obv:** Mausoleum of Marasesti **Obv. Designer:** Cristian Ciomei and Vasile Gabor **Rev:** Group of soldiers at Battle of Marasti

Date	Mintage	F	VF	XF	Unc	BU
2007 Proof	250	Value: 600				

KM# 176 500 LEI
6.2200 g., 0.9990 Gold 0.1998 oz. AGW, 23.2 mm. **Subject:** Christian Monuments **Rev:** Mogosoaia Palace **Shape:** Square

Date	Mintage	F	VF	XF	Unc	BU
2001	250	—	—	—	—	600

KM# 170 500 LEI
6.2200 g., 0.9990 Gold 0.1998 oz. AGW, 11.75 mm.
Subject: History of Gold - Treasure of Pietroasa **Rev:** "Big Clip" of Pietroasa

Date	Mintage	F	VF	XF	Unc	BU
2001	250	—	—	—	—	800

KM# 171 500 LEI
6.2200 g., 0.9990 Gold 0.1998 oz. AGW, 11.75 mm.
Subject: History of Gold - Treasure of Pietroasa **Rev:** "Medium Clip" of Pietroasa

Date	Mintage	F	VF	XF	Unc	BU
2001	250	—	—	—	—	800

KM# 172 500 LEI
6.2200 g., 0.9990 Gold 0.1998 oz. AGW, 11.75 mm. **Subject:** History of Gold - Treasure of Pietroasa **Rev:** 12-sided golden bowl

Date	Mintage	F	VF	XF	Unc	BU
2001	250	—	—	—	—	800

KM# 173 500 LEI
6.2200 g., 0.9990 Gold 0.1998 oz. AGW, 11.75 mm.
Subject: History of Gold - Treasure of Pietroasa **Rev:** Pitcher

Date	Mintage	F	VF	XF	Unc	BU
2001	250	—	—	—	—	800

KM# 145 500 LEI
3.7000 g., Aluminum, 25 mm. **Obv:** Shield within sprigs **Rev:** Value within 3/4 wreath **Edge:** Lettered **Edge Lettering:** ROMANIA (three times)

Date	Mintage	F	VF	XF	Unc	BU
2001	—	—	—	0.75	2.00	—
2002 Proof	1,500	Value: 7.00				
2003 Proof	2,000	Value: 7.00				
2004 Proof	2,000	Value: 7.00				
2005	—	—	—	—	3.00	—
2005 Proof	1,000	Value: 8.00				
2006	—	—	—	—	3.00	—
2006 Proof	—	Value: 8.00				

KM# 174 500 LEI
6.2200 g., 0.9990 Gold 0.1998 oz. AGW, 23.2 mm.
Subject: Christian Monuments **Rev:** Bistritz Monastery

Date	Mintage	F	VF	XF	Unc	BU
2002	250	—	—	—	—	600

KM# 175 500 LEI
6.2200 g., 0.9990 Gold 0.1998 oz. AGW, 23.2 mm.
Subject: Christian Monuments **Rev:** Coltea Church

Date	Mintage	F	VF	XF	Unc	BU
2002	250	—	—	—	—	600

KM# 177 500 LEI
31.1030 g., 0.9990 Silver 0.9989 oz. ASW, 37 mm.
Subject: 150th Anniversary - Birth of Ciprian Porumbescu, Composer **Obv:** Partial piano and violin left of National arms and value **Rev:** Portrait and musical score **Edge:** Plain

Date	Mintage	F	VF	XF	Unc	BU
2003 Proof	500	Value: 180				

KM# 178 500 LEI
31.1030 g., 0.9990 Silver 0.9989 oz. ASW, 37 mm.
Subject: 500th Anniversary - Establishment of Bishopric of Ramnic **Obv:** National arms and value above inscription **Rev:** Bishopric's coat-of-arms **Edge:** Plain

Date	Mintage	F	VF	XF	Unc	BU
2003 Proof	500	Value: 180				

KM# 179 500 LEI
31.1030 g., 0.9990 Silver 0.9989 oz. ASW, 37 mm. **Subject:** Romanian Numismatic Society Centennial **Obv:** Cornucopia pouring forth coins, value below **Rev:** Minerva and torch **Rev. Legend:** CENTENARUL SOCIETATII NUMISMATICE ROMANE, 1903-2003 **Edge:** Plain

Date	Mintage	F	VF	XF	Unc	BU
2003 Proof	1,000	Value: 150				

KM# 180 500 LEI
31.1030 g., 0.9990 Silver 0.9989 oz. ASW, 37 mm. **Subject:** 140th Anniversary - University of Bucharest **Obv:** Vertical inscription divides National arms, value and date at left. University emblem at right **Obv. Inscription:** ROMANIA **Rev:** Cameo at right and crowned arms at left above University Building **Rev. Inscription:** Upper: UNIVERSITATEA DIN BUCURESTI / 140 DE ANI; Lower: INTEMEIATA LA 1864 DE / AL IOAN CUZA **Edge:** Plain

Date	Mintage	F	VF	XF	Unc	BU
2004 Proof	500	Value: 300				

KM# 193 500 LEI
31.1035 g., 0.9990 Silver 0.9990 oz. ASW, 37 mm.
Subject: 150th Anniversary - Birth of Anghel Saligny **Obv:** Arms

at left above Cernavoda bridge, inscription, date, and value below **Obv. Inscription:** PODUL DE LA CERNAVODA **Rev:** Bust of bridge builder Anghel Saligny half right, life dates at right, his signature below at left **Edge:** Plain

Date	Mintage	F	VF	XF	Unc	BU
2004 Proof	500	Value: 750				

KM# 163 500 LEI
31.1030 g., 0.9990 Silver 0.9989 oz. ASW, 37 mm. **Subject:** Christian Feudal Art Monuments **Obv:** National arms, date and value at left, belfry tower of church at right **Rev:** Cotroceni Monastery church **Edge:** Plain **Shape:** 10-sided

Date	Mintage	F	VF	XF	Unc	BU
2004 Proof	500	Value: 180				

KM# 164 500 LEI
31.1030 g., 0.9990 Silver 0.9989 oz. ASW, 37 mm. **Subject:** Christian Feudal Art Monuments **Obv:** National arms, bell and value **Rev:** St. Trei Ierarhi church in Iasi **Edge:** Plain **Shape:** 10-sided

Date	Mintage	F	VF	XF	Unc	BU
2004 Proof	500	Value: 180				

KM# 194 500 LEI
31.1035 g., 0.9990 Silver 0.9990 oz. ASW, 37 mm. **Subject:** 125th Anniversary - National Bank **Obv:** National arms and coin design of 5 Lei dated 1880 **Rev:** Bank building **Edge:** Plain

Date	Mintage	F	VF	XF	Unc	BU
2005 Proof	—	Value: 1,500				

KM# 233a 500 LEI
31.1030 g., 0.9990 Gold 0.9989 oz. AGW, 35 mm. **Subject:** Union of 1918 - 90 years

Date	Mintage	F	VF	XF	Unc	BU
2008 Proof	3,000	Value: 1,500				

KM# 153 1000 LEI
2.0000 g., Aluminum, 22.2 mm. **Subject:** Constantin Brancoveanu **Obv:** Value above shield within lined circle **Rev:** Bust with headdress facing **Edge:** Plain with serrated sections

Date	Mintage	VG	F	VF	XF	Unc
2001	—	—	—	—	0.25	2.50
2002	—	—	—	—	0.25	2.50
2002 Proof	1,500	Value: 12.00				
2003	—	—	—	—	0.25	2.50
2003 Proof	2,000	Value: 12.00				
2004	—	—	—	—	0.25	2.50
2004 Proof	2,000	Value: 12.00				
2005	—	—	—	—	0.25	2.50
2005 Proof	—	Value: 13.00				
2006 Proof	1,000	Value: 13.00				

KM# 156 1000 LEI
15.5510 g., 0.9990 Gold 0.4995 oz. AGW, 27 mm. **Subject:** 1900th Anniversary of the First Roman-Dacian War **Obv:** Traian's column and shield **Rev:** Monument divides cameos **Edge:** Plain

Date	Mintage	VG	F	VF	XF	Unc
2001 Proof	500	Value: 1,000				

KM# 181 2000 LEI
25.0000 g., Bi-Metallic .999 Silver, 10g center in .999 Gold, 15g ring, 35 mm. **Subject:** Ion Heliade Radulescu (1802-1872) **Obv:** Lyre at left, national arms at right in divided circle design **Rev:** Ion Heliade Radulescu above signature **Edge:** Reeded

Date	Mintage	F	VF	XF	Unc	BU
2002 Proof	500	Value: 1,200				

KM# 158 5000 LEI
2.5200 g., Aluminum, 23.5 mm. **Obv:** Value and country name **Rev:** Sprig divides date and shield **Edge:** Plain **Shape:** 12-sided

Date	Mintage	F	VF	XF	Unc	BU
2001	—	—	—	—	0.50	—
2002	—	—	—	—	0.50	—
2002 Proof	1,500	Value: 15.00				
2003	—	—	—	—	0.25	—
2003 Proof	2,000	Value: 15.00				
2004	—	—	—	—	0.25	—
2004 Proof	2,000	Value: 16.00				
2005	—	—	—	—	0.25	—
2005 Proof	2,000	Value: 17.00				
2006 Proof	1,000	Value: 17.00				

KM# 162 5000 LEI
31.1035 g., 0.9990 Gold 0.9990 oz. AGW, 35 mm. **Subject:** Constantin Brancusi 125th Anniversary of Birth **Obv:** National arms, value and sculpture **Rev:** Bearded portrait and signature **Edge:** Plain

Date	Mintage	F	VF	XF	Unc	BU
2001 Proof	500	Value: 2,250				

KM# 183 5000 LEI
31.1030 g., 0.9990 Gold 0.9989 oz. AGW, 35 mm. **Subject:** Ion Luca Caragiale, playright (1852-1912) **Obv:** National arms, value and masks of Comedy and Tragedy **Rev:** Portrait **Edge:** Plain

Date	Mintage	F	VF	XF	Unc	BU
2002 Proof	250	Value: 2,750				

KM# 184 5000 LEI
31.1030 g., 0.9990 Gold 0.9989 oz. AGW, 35 mm. **Subject:** Bran Castle (1378-2003) **Obv:** Two coats of arms on shield above value **Rev:** Castle view **Edge:** Plain

Date	Mintage	F	VF	XF	Unc	BU
2003 Proof	250	Value: 2,000				

KM# 185 5000 LEI
31.1030 g., 0.9990 Gold 0.9989 oz. AGW, 35 mm. **Subject:** Stephen the Great **Obv:** National arms, value above coin design in wall **Rev:** Portrait of Stephen and Putna Monastery

Date	Mintage	F	VF	XF	Unc	BU
2004 Proof	250	Value: 2,000				

REFORM COINAGE - 2005
10,000 Old Leu = 1 New Leu

KM# 189 BAN
2.4000 g., Brass Clad Steel, 16.8 mm. **Subject:** Monetary Reform of 2005 **Obv:** National arms flanked by stars **Rev:** Value **Edge:** Plain

Date	Mintage	F	VF	XF	Unc	BU
2005	—	—	—	—	0.30	0.50
2005 Proof	—	Value: 2.50				
2006	—	—	—	—	0.30	0.50
2006 Proof	—	Value: 2.50				
2007	—	—	—	—	0.30	0.50
2007 Proof	—	Value: 2.50				
2008	—	—	—	—	0.30	0.50
2008 Proof	—	Value: 2.50				
2009	—	—	—	—	0.30	0.50

KM# 190 5 BANI
2.8100 g., Copper Plated Steel, 18.2 mm. **Subject:** Monetary Reform of 2005 **Obv:** National arms flanked by stars **Obv. Legend:** ROMANIA **Rev:** Value **Edge:** Reeded

Date	Mintage	F	VF	XF	Unc	BU
2005	—	—	—	—	0.50	0.75
2005 Proof	—	Value: 5.00				
2006	—	—	—	—	0.50	0.75
2006 Proof	—	Value: 5.00				
2007	—	—	—	—	0.50	0.75
2007 Proof	—	Value: 5.00				
2008	—	—	—	—	0.50	0.75
2008 Proof	—	Value: 5.00				
2009	—	—	—	—	0.50	0.75

KM# 191 10 BANI
4.0000 g., Nickel Plated Steel, 20.4 mm. **Subject:** Monetary Reform of 2005 **Obv:** National arms flanked by stars **Obv. Legend:** ROMANIA **Rev:** Value **Edge:** Segmented reeding

Date	Mintage	F	VF	XF	Unc	BU
2005	—	—	—	—	0.65	0.85
2005 Proof	—	Value: 7.00				
2006	—	—	—	—	0.60	0.80
2006 Proof	—	Value: 7.00				
2007	—	—	—	—	0.50	0.75
2007 Proof	—	Value: 7.00				
2008	—	—	—	—	0.50	0.70
2008 Proof	—	Value: 7.00				
2009	—	—	—	—	0.50	0.70

KM# 192 50 BANI
6.1200 g., Brass, 23.6 mm. **Subject:** Monetary Reform of 2005 **Obv:** National arms flanked by stars **Obv. Legend:** ROMANIA **Rev:** Value **Edge:** Lettered **Edge Lettering:** "ROMANIA' twice

Date	Mintage	F	VF	XF	Unc	BU
2005	—	—	—	—	0.85	1.00
2005 Proof	—	Value: 10.00				

Date	Mintage	F	VF	XF	Unc	BU
2006	—	—	—	—	0.75	0.85
2006 Proof	—	Value: 10.00				
2007	—	—	—	—	0.65	0.75
2007 Proof	—	Value: 10.00				
2008	—	—	—	—	0.65	0.75
2008 Proof	—	Value: 10.00				
2009	—	—	—	—	0.65	0.75

KM# 209 LEU
23.5000 g., Copper Plated Tombac, 37 mm. **Subject:** 140th Anniversary Founding Romanian Academy **Edge:** Plain

Date	Mintage	F	VF	XF	Unc	BU
2006 Proof	35	Value: 750				

KM# 220 LEU
23.5000 g., Copper Plated Tombac, 37 mm.
Subject: Centennial - Birth of Mircea Eliade **Obv:** Shield and value **Rev:** Portrait facing **Edge:** Reeded

Date	Mintage	F	VF	XF	Unc	BU
2007 Proof	250	Value: 150				

KM# 223 LEU
23.5000 g., Copper Plated Tombac, 37 mm. **Subject:** Dimitrie Cantemir, (Prince of Moldavia 1710-1711), Scientist
Edge: Reeded

Date	Mintage	F	VF	XF	Unc	BU
2007 Proof	250	Value: 150				

KM# 226 LEU
23.5000 g., Copper Plated Tombac, 37 mm. **Subject:** Stephan the Great **Edge:** Reeded

Date	Mintage	F	VF	XF	Unc	BU
2007 Proof	250	Value: 150				

KM# 208 5 LEI
31.1000 g., 0.9990 Silver 0.9988 oz. ASW, 37 mm.
Subject: 100th Anniversary - Birth of Grigore Vasiliu-Birlic
Edge: Plain

Date	Mintage	F	VF	XF	Unc	BU
2005 Proof	150	Value: 1,500				

KM# 210 5 LEI
31.1000 g., 0.9990 Silver 0.9988 oz. ASW, 37 mm.
Subject: 140th Anniversary Founding Romanian Academy
Edge: Plain

Date	Mintage	F	VF	XF	Unc	BU
2006 Proof	500	Value: 300				

KM# 212 5 LEI
31.1000 g., 0.9990 Silver 0.9988 oz. ASW, 37 mm.
Subject: Christian Feudal Art - "Wooden Church from Ieud-Deal"
Obv: Fragment of mural in Ieud Church depicting Isaac, Abraham and Jacob at top, inscription, value and date in lower half
Obv. Inscription: ROMANIA **Rev:** Front view of Ieud Church against frosted background **Rev. Inscription:** BISERICA DE LEMN IEUD DEAL **Edge:** Plain **Designer:** Cristian Ciornci, Vasilc Gabor

Date	Mintage	F	VF	XF	Unc	BU
2006 Proof	500	Value: 170				

KM# 213 5 LEI
31.1030 g., Silver, 37 mm. **Subject:** 150th Anniversary - Establishment of the European Commission of the Danube
Edge: Plain

Date	Mintage	F	VF	XF	Unc	BU
2006 Proof	500	Value: 170				

KM# 216 5 LEI
31.1030 g., 0.9990 Silver 0.9989 oz. ASW, 37 mm. **Subject:** Church from Densus **Obv:** 14th century icon on which "The Holy Trinity of Densus" was painted at left, arms with value below at center, inscription at right **Obv. Inscription:** ROMANIA
Obv. Designer: Cristian Ciornei and Vasile Gabor **Rev:** Image of Densus Church as from the altar apse, central pillar at right
Rev. Inscription: BISERICA DE LA DENSUS **Edge:** Plain

Date	Mintage	F	VF	XF	Unc	BU
2006 Proof	500	Value: 170				

KM# 236 5 LEI
31.1050 g., 0.9990 Silver 0.9990 oz. ASW, 37 mm.
Subject: Wooden Church of Ievd Deal **Obv:** Fragment of mural painting **Rev:** Front view of church

Date	Mintage	F	VF	XF	Unc	BU
2006 Proof	500	Value: 100				

KM# 217 5 LEI
31.1030 g., 0.9990 Silver 0.9989 oz. ASW, 37 mm.
Subject: Designation of Sibiu as the "European Capital of Culture in 2007" **Obv:** 2 city towers in Sibiu at left, fortress wall connecting them, Potter's Tower in background, coat of arms at right
Obv. Inscription: ROMANIA **Obv. Designer:** Cristian Ciornci and Vasile Gabor **Rev:** City of Sibiu's logo at bottom, 2 line inscription at left, 3 line inscription at right, 4 famous edifices at center **Rev. Inscription:** SIBIU/2007 and CAPITALA / CULTURALA / EUROPEANA **Edge:** Plain

Date	Mintage	F	VF	XF	Unc	BU
2007 Proof	500	Value: 400				

KM# 221 5 LEI
15.5500 g., 0.9990 Silver 0.4994 oz. ASW, 30 mm.
Subject: Centennial - Birth of Mircea Eliade **Obv:** Shield and value **Rev:** Portrait facing **Edge:** Reeded

Date	Mintage	F	VF	XF	Unc	BU
2007 Proof	250	Value: 300				

KM# 224 5 LEI
15.5500 g., 0.9000 Silver 0.4499 oz. ASW, 30 mm.
Subject: Dimitrie Cantemir, (Prince of Moldavia 1710-1711), Scientist **Edge:** Reeded

Date	Mintage	F	VF	XF	Unc	BU
2007 Proof	250	Value: 300				

KM# 227 5 LEI
15.5000 g., 0.9990 Silver 0.4978 oz. ASW, 30 mm.
Subject: Stephan the Great **Edge:** Reeded

Date	Mintage	F	VF	XF	Unc	BU
2007 Proof	250	Value: 300				

KM# 242 5 LEI
15.5500 g., 0.9990 Silver 0.4994 oz. ASW, 30 mm.
Subject: Ovidivs Naso **Rev:** Half-length figure

Date	Mintage	F	VF	XF	Unc	BU
2008 Proof	500	Value: 170				

KM# 207 10 LEI
1.2200 g., 0.9990 Gold 0.0392 oz. AGW, 13.92 mm.
Subject: History of Gold - The Persinari Hoard **Edge:** Plain

Date	Mintage	F	VF	XF	Unc	BU
2005 Proof	1,000	Value: 200				

KM# 203 10 LEI
1.2240 g., 0.9990 Gold 0.0393 oz. AGW, 13.92 mm.
Subject: Histoy of Gold - The Cuculeni Báiceni Hoard
Obv: Romania's Coat of Arms with denomination
Rev: Cheekpiece of the gold helmet in the Cucuteni-Baiceni hoard **Edge:** Milled **Designer:** Cristian Ciornei

Date	Mintage	F	VF	XF	Unc	BU
2006 Proof	500	Value: 250				

KM# 229 10 LEI
31.1030 g., 0.9990 Silver 0.9989 oz. ASW, 37 mm.
Subject: 50th Anniversary - Treaty of Rome **Edge:** Reeded

Date	Mintage	F	VF	XF	Unc	BU
2007 Proof	500	Value: 400				

KM# 240   10 LEI
31.1050 g., 0.9990 Silver 0.9990 oz. ASW, 37 mm.
Subject: Petroleum Industry, 150th Anniversary **Rev:** Oil derrick and pump

Date	Mintage	F	VF	XF	Unc	BU
2007 Proof	500	Value: 150				

KM# 241   10 LEI
31.1050 g., 0.9990 Silver 0.9990 oz. ASW, 37 mm.
Subject: Snagov Monastery **Rev:** Building and bust

Date	Mintage	F	VF	XF	Unc	BU
2007 Proof	500	Value: 170				

KM# 230   10 LEI
31.1000 g., 0.9990 Silver 0.9988 oz. ASW, 37 mm.
Subject: 150th Anniversary of First Postage Stamp **Rev:** "Cap de Bour" (bull's head) stamp **Edge:** Reeded

Date	Mintage	F	VF	XF	Unc	BU
2008 Proof	1,000	Value: 200				

KM# 243   10 LEI
31.1050 g., 0.9990 Silver 0.9990 oz. ASW, 37 mm.
Subject: Romanian Broadcast Company, 80th anniversary
Rev: Radio and headset

Date	Mintage	F	VF	XF	Unc	BU
2008 Proof	500	Value: 300				

KM# 244   10 LEI
31.1050 g., 0.9990 Silver 0.9990 oz. ASW, 37 mm.
Subject: Constin Kirtescu **Rev:** Bust facing

Date	Mintage	F	VF	XF	Unc	BU
2008 Proof	500	Value: 170				

KM# 245   10 LEI
31.1050 g., 0.9990 Silver 0.9990 oz. ASW, 37 mm.
Subject: First printed book in Walachia, 500th Anniversary
Rev: Building and printers at press

Date	Mintage	F	VF	XF	Unc	BU
2008 Proof	500	Value: 170				

KM# 246   10 LEI
31.1050 g., 0.9990 Silver 0.9990 oz. ASW, 37 mm.
Subject: Simon Barnutiu **Rev:** Bust facing

Date	Mintage	F	VF	XF	Unc	BU
2008 Proof	500	Value: 150				

KM# 247   10 LEI
31.1050 g., 0.9990 Silver 0.9990 oz. ASW, 37 mm.
Subject: Cozia Monastery **Rev:** Church building

Date	Mintage	F	VF	XF	Unc	BU
2008 Proof	500	Value: 170				

KM# 248   10 LEI
31.1050 g., 0.9990 Silver 0.9990 oz. ASW, 37 mm.
Subject: Sambata des Sus Monastery **Rev:** Chruch building

Date	Mintage	F	VF	XF	Unc	BU
2008 Proof	500	Value: 170				

KM# 249   10 LEI
31.1050 g., 0.9990 Silver 0.9990 oz. ASW, 37 mm.
Subject: Voronet Monastery **Rev:** Church building

Date	Mintage	F	VF	XF	Unc	BU
2008 Proof	500	Value: 170				

KM# 250   10 LEI
31.1050 g., 0.9990 Silver 0.9990 oz. ASW, 37 mm.
Subject: European Monitary Union, 10th Anniversary **Rev:** Stick figure and Euro symbol

Date	Mintage	F	VF	XF	Unc	BU
2009 Proof	1,000	Value: 150				

KM# 251   10 LEI
31.1050 g., 0.9990 Silver 0.9990 oz. ASW, 37 mm.
Subject: Alexander Macedonski **Rev:** Bust left

Date	Mintage	F	VF	XF	Unc	BU
2009 Proof	500	Value: 150				

KM# 252   10 LEI
31.1050 g., 0.9990 Silver 0.9990 oz. ASW, 37 mm.
Subject: Walachia's establishment as an Archdiocese, 650th Anniversary **Rev:** Archbishop and Cathedral

Date	Mintage	F	VF	XF	Unc	BU
2009 Proof	500	Value: 170				

KM# 253   10 LEI
31.1050 g., 0.9990 Silver 0.9990 oz. ASW, 37 mm.
Subject: Statistical Office, 150th Anniversary **Rev:** Two busts and document

Date	Mintage	F	VF	XF	Unc	BU
2009 Proof	500	Value: 150				

KM# 254   10 LEI
31.1050 g., 0.9990 Silver 0.9990 oz. ASW, 37 mm.
Subject: Bucharest - Giurgiv Railway, 150th Anniversary
Rev: Steam train

Date	Mintage	F	VF	XF	Unc	BU
2009 Proof	500	Value: 170				

KM# 255   10 LEI
31.1050 g., 0.9990 Silver 0.9990 oz. ASW, 37 mm.
Subject: Bucharest, 550th Anniversary **Rev:** Architectural elements

Date	Mintage	F	VF	XF	Unc	BU
2009 Proof	500	Value: 150				

KM# 256   10 LEI
31.1050 g., 0.9990 Silver 0.9990 oz. ASW, 37 mm.
Subject: Constanta Harbor, 100th Anniversary **Rev:** Ship and buildings

Date	Mintage	F	VF	XF	Unc	BU
2009 Proof	500	Value: 150				

KM# 257   10 LEI
31.1050 g., 0.9990 Silver 0.9990 oz. ASW, 37 mm.
Subject: Tropaeum Traiani, 1900th Anniversary **Rev:** Ancient Roman building, Emperor Trajan

Date	Mintage	F	VF	XF	Unc	BU
2009 Proof	500	Value: 150				

KM# 211   50 LEI
6.4500 g., 0.9000 Gold 0.1866 oz. AGW, 21 mm. **Subject:** 140th Anniversary Founding Romanian Academy **Edge:** Plain

Date	Mintage	F	VF	XF	Unc	BU
2006 Proof	35	Value: 3,000				

KM# 222   100 LEI
6.4500 g., 0.9000 Gold 0.1866 oz. AGW, 21 mm.
Subject: Centennial - Birth of Mircea Eliade **Obv:** Shield and value **Rev:** Portrait facing **Edge:** Reeded

Date	Mintage	F	VF	XF	Unc	BU
2007 Proof	250	Value: 900				

KM# 225   100 LEI
6.4500 g., 0.9000 Gold 0.1866 oz. AGW, 21 mm.
Subject: Dimitrie Cantemir, (Prince of Moldavia 1710-1711), Scientist **Edge:** Reeded

Date	Mintage	F	VF	XF	Unc	BU
2007 Proof	250	Value: 900				

KM# 228   100 LEI
6.4520 g., 0.9000 Gold 0.1867 oz. AGW, 21 mm. **Subject:** 550th Anniversary - Ascension Prince Stephen the Great into Moldavia **Edge:** Reeded

Date	Mintage	F	VF	XF	Unc	BU
2007 Proof	250	Value: 900				

KM# 206   500 LEI
31.1000 g., 0.9990 Gold 0.9988 oz. AGW, 35 mm. **Subject:** 50th Anniversary - Death of George Enescu **Edge:** Plain

Date	Mintage	F	VF	XF	Unc	BU
2005 Proof	250	Value: 2,250				

KM# 214   500 LEI
31.1030 g., 0.9990 Gold 0.9989 oz. AGW, 35 mm.
Subject: 350th Anniversary - Establishment of the Patriarchal Cathedral **Edge:** Plain

Date	Mintage	F	VF	XF	Unc	BU
2006 Proof	250	Value: 3,000				

KM# 204   500 LEI
31.1035 g., 0.9990 Gold 0.9990 oz. AGW, 35 mm.
Subject: Romania's Accession to European Union, January 1 2007 **Obv:** Romania's Coat of Arms surrounded by 12 stars of European Union **Rev:** Map of the European Union including Romania **Edge:** Plain **Designer:** Cristian Ciornei

Date	Mintage	F	VF	XF	Unc	BU
2007 Proof	250	Value: 3,000				

KM# 205   500 LEI
31.1035 g., 0.9990 Gold 0.9990 oz. AGW, 35 mm.
Subject: Nicolae Balcescu (1819-1852) **Obv:** Romania's Coat of Arms and **Obv. Inscription:** Justice and Brotherhood **Rev:** Portrait of Nicolae Balcescu **Edge:** Plain

Date	Mintage	F	VF	XF	Unc	BU
2007 Proof	250	Value: 2,250				

MINT SETS

KM#	Date	Mintage	Identification	Issue Price	Mkt Val
MS6	2005 (4)	—	KM#189-192	—	50.00
MS4	2006 (4)	—	KM189-192, plus medal	—	75.00
MS5	2007 (4)	1,000	KM189-192, plus medal	—	60.00

PROOF SETS

KM#	Date	Mintage	Identification	Issue Price	Mkt Val
PS4	2001 (3)	500	KM#159,160,161	80.00	600
PS5	2002 (9)	1,500	KM#109-111, 114-116, 145, 153, 158	20.00	75.00
PS6	2003 (9)	2,000	KM#109-111, 114-116, 145, 153, 158	20.00	75.00
PS7	2003 (3)	500	KM#186-188	—	360
PS8	2004 (2)	500	KM#163, 164	—	360
PS9	2005 (10)	—	KM#111, 115, 145, 153, 158, 189-192 plus medal	—	80.00
PS10	2006 (10)	—	KM#111, 115, 145, 153, 158, 189-192	—	80.00
PS11	2006 (3)	—	KM#209-211	—	4,050
PS12	2007 (3)	—	KM#220-222	—	1,350
PS13	2007 (3)	—	KM#223-225	—	1,350
PS14	2007 (3)	—	KM#226-228	—	1,350
PS15	2007 (5)	—	KM#189-192 plus Silver 75th Anniversary of Rodna Mountains National Park medal	—	50.00
PS16	2004 (5)	—	KM#111, 115, 145, 153, 158	—	50.00
PS17	2008 (4)	—	KM#189-192 plus silver medal Antipa Museum	—	50.00

RUSSIA (U.S.S.R.)

Russia, formerly the central power of the Union of Soviet Socialist Republics and now of the Commonwealth of Independent States occupies the northern part of Asia and the eastern part of Europe, has an area of 17,075,400 sq. km. Capital: Moscow. Exports include iron and steel, crude oil, timber, and nonferrous metals.

In the fall of 1991, events moved swiftly in the Soviet Union. Estonia, Latvia and Lithuania won their independence and were recognized by Moscow, Sept. 6. The Commonwealth of Independent States was formed Dec. 8, 1991 in Mensk by Belarus, Russia and Ukraine. It was expanded at a summit Dec. 21, 1991 to include 11 of the 12 remaining republics (excluding Georgia) of the old U.S.S.R.

RUSSIAN FEDERATION
Issued by РОССИЈСКИЈ БАНК
(Russian Bank)

REFORM COINAGE
January 1, 1998

1,000 Old Roubles = 1 New Rouble

Y# 600 KOPEK
1.5000 g., Copper-Nickel Plated Steel, 15.5 mm. **Obv:** St. George **Obv. Legend:** БАНК РОССИИ **Rev:** Value above vine sprig **Edge:** Plain

Date	Mintage	F	VF	XF	Unc	BU
2001М	—	—	—	—	0.30	0.40
2001СП	—	—	—	—	0.30	0.40
2002М	—	—	—	—	0.30	0.40
2002СП	—	—	—	—	0.30	0.40
2003М	—	—	—	—	0.30	0.40
2003СП	—	—	—	—	0.30	0.40
2004М	—	—	—	—	0.30	0.40
2004СП	—	—	—	—	0.30	0.40
2005М	—	—	—	—	0.30	0.40
2005СП	—	—	—	—	0.30	0.40
2006М	—	—	—	—	0.30	0.40
2006СП	—	—	—	—	0.30	0.40
2007М	—	—	—	—	0.30	0.40
2007СП	—	—	—	—	0.30	.0.40
2008М	—	—	—	—	0.30	0.40
2008СП	—	—	—	—	0.30	0.40
2009М	—	—	—	—	0.30	0.40
2009СП	—	—	—	—	0.30	0.40

Y# 601 5 KOPEKS
2.6000 g., Copper-Nickel Clad Steel, 18.5 mm. **Obv:** St. George **Obv. Legend:** БАНК РОССИИ **Rev:** Value above vine sprig **Edge:** Plain

Date	Mintage	F	VF	XF	Unc	BU
2001М	—	—	—	—	0.40	0.60
2001СП	—	—	—	—	0.40	0.60
2002	—	—	80.00	95.00	120	—
2002М	—	—	—	—	0.40	0.60
2002СП	—	—	—	—	0.40	0.60
2003	—	—	10.00	15.00	25.00	—
2003М	—	—	—	—	0.35	0.50
2003СП	—	—	—	—	0.35	0.50
2004М	—	—	—	—	0.35	0.50
2004СП	—	—	—	—	0.35	0.50
2005М	—	—	—	—	0.35	0.50
2005СП	—	—	—	—	0.35	0.50
2006М	—	—	—	—	0.35	0.50
2006СП	—	—	—	—	0.35	0.50
2007М	—	—	—	—	0.35	0.50
2007СП	—	—	—	—	0.35	0.50
2008М	—	—	—	—	0.35	0.50
2008СП	—	—	—	—	0.35	0.50
2009М	—	—	—	—	0.35	0.50
2009СП	—	—	—	—	0.35	0.50

Y# 601a 5 KOPEKS
Brass Plated Steel **Obv:** St. George on horseback slaying dragon right **Obv. Legend:** БАНК РОССИИ **Rev:** Value above vine sprig **Edge:** Plain

Date	Mintage	F	VF	XF	Unc	BU
2006СП	—	—	—	—	300	—

Y# 602 10 KOPEKS
1.9500 g., Brass, 17.5 mm. **Obv:** St. George horseback right slaying dragon **Rev:** Value above vine sprig **Edge:** Reeded

Date	Mintage	F	VF	XF	Unc	BU
2001М	—	—	—	—	0.50	0.80
2001СП	—	—	—	—	0.50	0.80
2002М	—	—	—	—	0.50	0.80
2002СП	—	—	—	—	0.50	0.80
2003М	—	—	—	—	0.50	0.80
2003СП	—	—	—	—	0.50	0.80
2004М	—	—	—	—	0.50	0.80
2004СП	—	—	—	—	0.50	0.80
2005М	—	—	—	—	0.50	0.80
2005СП	—	—	—	—	0.50	0.80
2006М	—	—	—	—	0.50	0.80
2006СП	—	—	—	—	0.50	0.80

Y# 602a 10 KOPEKS
1.8500 g., Tombac Plated Steel, 17.5 mm. **Obv:** St. George on horseback slaying dragon to right **Obv. Legend:** БАНК РОССИИ **Rev:** Denomination above vine sprig **Edge:** Plain

Date	Mintage	F	VF	XF	Unc	BU
2006М	—	—	—	—	0.50	0.80
2006СП	—	—	—	—	0.50	0.80
2007М	—	—	—	—	0.50	0.80
2007СП	—	—	—	—	0.50	0.80
2008М	—	—	—	—	0.50	0.80
2008СП	—	—	—	—	0.50	0.80
2009М	—	—	—	—	0.50	0.80
2009СП	—	—	—	—	0.50	0.80

Y# 603 50 KOPEKS
2.9000 g., Brass, 19.5 mm. **Obv:** St. George on horseback slaying dragon right **Rev:** Value above vine sprig **Edge:** Reeded

Date	Mintage	F	VF	XF	Unc	BU
2001М Rare	—	—	—	5,000		
2002М	—	—	—	—	1.50	3.00
2002СП	—	—	—	—	1.50	3.00
2003М	—	—	—	—	0.80	1.00
2003СП	—	—	—	—	0.80	1.00
2004М	—	—	—	—	0.80	1.00
2004СП	—	—	—	—	0.80	1.00
2005М	—	—	—	—	0.80	1.00
2005СП	—	—	—	—	0.80	1.00
2006М	—	—	—	—	0.80	1.00
2006СП	—	—	—	—	0.80	1.00

Y# 603a 50 KOPEKS
2.7500 g., Tombac Plated Steel, 19.5 mm. **Obv:** St. George on horseback slaying dragon right **Rev:** Value above vine sprig **Edge:** Plain

Date	Mintage	F	VF	XF	Unc	BU
2006М	—	—	—	—	0.80	1.00
2006СП	—	—	—	—	0.80	1.00
2007М	—	—	—	—	0.80	1.00
2007СП	—	—	—	—	0.80	1.00
2008М	—	—	—	—	0.80	1.00
2008СП	—	—	—	—	0.80	1.00
2009М	—	—	—	—	0.80	1.00
2009СП	—	—	—	—	0.80	1.00

Y# 745   ROUBLE
17.4000 g., 0.9000 Silver 0.5035 oz. ASW, 32.8 mm.
Obv: Double-headed eagle within beaded circle **Rev:** Altai argalia
sheep **Edge:** Reeded

Date	Mintage	F	VF	XF	Unc	BU
2001(sp) Proof	7,500	Value: 45.00				

Y# 746   ROUBLE
17.4000 g., 0.9000 Silver 0.5035 oz. ASW, 32.8 mm.
Obv: Double-headed eagle within beaded circle **Rev:** Beavers
Edge: Reeded

Date	Mintage	F	VF	XF	Unc	BU
2001(sp) Proof	7,500	Value: 45.00				

Y# 604   ROUBLE
3.2500 g., Copper-Nickel-Zinc, 20.5 mm. **Obv:** Double-headed
eagle **Rev:** Value **Edge:** Reeded

Date	Mintage	F	VF	XF	Unc	BU
2001M Rare	—	—	—	—	—	—

Y# 731   ROUBLE
3.2100 g., Copper-Nickel, 20.7 mm. **Obv:** Double-headed eagle
Rev: Stylized design above hologram **Edge:** Reeded

Date	Mintage	F	VF	XF	Unc	BU
2001СПМД	100,000,000	—	—	—	1.50	2.00

Y# 732   ROUBLE
17.4300 g., 0.9000 Silver 0.5043 oz. ASW, 32.8 mm.
Subject: Sturgeon **Obv:** Double-headed eagle within beaded
circle **Rev:** Sakhalin sturgeon and other fish **Edge:** Reeded

Date	Mintage	F	VF	XF	Unc	BU
2001 Proof	7,500	Value: 45.00				

Y# 758   ROUBLE
17.4400 g., 0.9000 Silver 0.5046 oz. ASW, 33 mm.
Obv: Double-headed eagle within beaded circle **Rev:** Chinese
Goral **Edge:** Reeded

Date	Mintage	F	VF	XF	Unc	BU
2002(sp) Proof	10,000	Value: 30.00				

Y# 759   ROUBLE
17.4400 g., 0.9000 Silver 0.5046 oz. ASW, 33 mm.
Obv: Double-headed eagle within beaded circle **Rev:** Sei Whale
Edge: Reeded

Date	Mintage	F	VF	XF	Unc	BU
2002(sp) Proof	10,000	Value: 30.00				

Y# 760   ROUBLE
17.4400 g., 0.9000 Silver 0.5046 oz. ASW, 33 mm.
Subject: Golden Eagle **Obv:** Double-headed eagle within
beaded circle **Rev:** Golden Eagle with nestling **Edge:** Reeded

Date	Mintage	F	VF	XF	Unc	BU
2002(sp) Proof	10,000	Value: 30.00				

Y# 770   ROUBLE
8.5300 g., 0.9250 Silver 0.2537 oz. ASW, 25 mm.
Subject: Ministry of Education **Obv:** Double-headed eagle within
beaded circle **Rev:** Seedling within open book **Edge:** Reeded

Date	Mintage	F	VF	XF	Unc	BU
2002(m) Proof	3,000	Value: 50.00				

Y# 771   ROUBLE
8.5300 g., 0.9250 Silver 0.2537 oz. ASW, 25 mm.
Subject: Ministry of Finances **Obv:** Double-headed eagle within
beaded circle **Rev:** Caduceus in monogram **Edge:** Reeded

Date	Mintage	F	VF	XF	Unc	BU
2002(sp) Proof	3,000	Value: 50.00				

Y# 772   ROUBLE
8.5300 g., 0.9250 Silver 0.2537 oz. ASW, 25 mm.
Subject: Ministry of Economic Development **Obv:** Double-
headed eagle within beaded circle **Rev:** Crowned double-headed
eagle with cornucopia and caduceus **Edge:** Reeded

Date	Mintage	F	VF	XF	Unc	BU
2002(sp) Proof	3,000	Value: 50.00				

Y# 773   ROUBLE
8.5300 g., 0.9250 Silver 0.2537 oz. ASW, 25 mm.
Subject: Ministry of Foreign Affairs **Obv:** Double-headed eagle
within beaded circle **Rev:** Crowned two-headed eagle above
crossed sprigs **Edge:** Reeded

Date	Mintage	F	VF	XF	Unc	BU
2002(sp) Proof	3,000	Value: 50.00				

Y# 774   ROUBLE
8.5300 g., 0.9250 Silver 0.2537 oz. ASW, 25 mm.
Subject: Ministry of Internal Affairs **Obv:** Double-headed eagle
within beaded circle **Rev:** Crowned two-headed eagle with round
breast **Edge:** Reeded

Date	Mintage	F	VF	XF	Unc	BU
2002(sp) Proof	3,000	Value: 50.00				

Y# 775   ROUBLE
8.5300 g., 0.9250 Silver 0.2537 oz. ASW, 25 mm.
Subject: Ministry of Justice **Obv:** Double-headed eagle within
beaded circle **Rev:** Crowned double-headed eagle with column
on breast shield **Edge:** Reeded

Date	Mintage	F	VF	XF	Unc	BU
2002(sp) Proof	3,000	Value: 50.00				

Y# 776   ROUBLE
8.5300 g., 0.9250 Silver 0.2537 oz. ASW, 25 mm.
Subject: Russian Armed Forces **Obv:** Double-headed eagle
within beaded circle **Rev:** Double-headed eagle with crowned top
pointed breast shield **Edge:** Reeded

Date	Mintage	F	VF	XF	Unc	BU
2002(m) Proof	3,000	Value: 50.00				

Y# 833 ROUBLE
3.2500 g., Copper-Nickel-Zinc, 20.5 mm. **Obv:** Two headed
eagle above curved inscription **Rev:** Value and flower
Edge: Reeded

Date	Mintage	F	VF	XF	Unc	BU
2002(m) Mint sets only	15,000	—	—	—	—	—
2002(sp) Mint sets only	15,000	—	—	—	—	—
2003(sp)	15,000	—	—	300	400	500
2005(m)	—	—	—	—	2.00	3.00
2005(sp)	—	—	—	—	2.00	3.00
2006(m)	—	—	—	—	2.00	3.00
2006(sp)	—	—	—	—	2.00	3.00
2007(m)	—	—	—	—	2.00	3.00
2007(sp)	—	—	—	—	2.00	3.00
2008(m)	—	—	—	—	2.00	3.00
2008(sp)	—	—	—	—	2.00	3.00
2009(m)	—	—	—	—	2.00	3.00
2009(sp)	—	—	—	—	2.00	3.00

Y# A834 ROUBLE
7.7800 g., 0.9250 Silver 0.2314 oz. ASW, 0.25 mm.
Subject: St. Petersburg **Obv:** Double-headed eagle within
beaded circle **Rev:** Angel on steeple of Cathedral in fortress

Date	Mintage	F	VF	XF	Unc	BU
2002 Proof	5,000	Value: 25.00				

Y# 835 ROUBLE
7.7800 g., 0.9250 Silver 0.2314 oz. ASW, 25 mm. **Subject:** St.
Petersburg **Obv:** Double-headed eagle within beaded circle
Rev: Sphinx

Date	Mintage	F	VF	XF	Unc	BU
2002 Proof	5,000	Value: 25.00				

Y# 836 ROUBLE
7.7800 g., 0.9250 Silver 0.2314 oz. ASW, 25 mm. **Subject:** St.
Petersburg **Obv:** Double-headed eagle within beaded circle
Rev: Small ship

Date	Mintage	F	VF	XF	Unc	BU
2002 Proof	5,000	Value: 25.00				

Y# 837 ROUBLE
7.7800 g., 0.9250 Silver 0.2314 oz. ASW, 25 mm. **Subject:** St.
Petersburg **Obv:** Double-headed eagle within beaded circle
Rev: Lion

Date	Mintage	F	VF	XF	Unc	BU
2002 Proof	5,000	Value: 25.00				

Y# 838 ROUBLE
7.7800 g., 0.9250 Silver 0.2314 oz. ASW, 25 mm. **Subject:** St.
Petersburg **Obv:** Double-headed eagle within beaded circle
Rev: Horse sculpture

Date	Mintage	F	VF	XF	Unc	BU
2002 Proof	5,000	Value: 25.00				

Y# 839 ROUBLE
7.7800 g., 0.9250 Silver 0.2314 oz. ASW, 25 mm. **Subject:** St.
Petersburg **Obv:** Double-headed eagle within beaded circle
Rev: Griffin

Date	Mintage	F	VF	XF	Unc	BU
2002 Proof	5,000	Value: 25.00				

Y# 814 ROUBLE
17.4000 g., 0.9000 Silver 0.5035 oz. ASW, 32.8 mm.
Obv: Double-headed eagle within beaded circle **Rev:** Arctic foxes
Edge: Reeded

Date	Mintage	F	VF	XF	Unc	BU
2003(sp) Proof	10,000	Value: 30.00				

Y# 816 ROUBLE
17.4000 g., 0.9000 Silver 0.5035 oz. ASW, 32.8 mm.
Obv: Double-headed eagle within beaded circle **Rev:** Pygmy
Cormorant drying its wings **Edge:** Reeded

Date	Mintage	F	VF	XF	Unc	BU
2003(sp) Proof	10,000	Value: 30.00				

Y# 815 ROUBLE
17.4000 g., 0.9000 Silver 0.5035 oz. ASW, 32.8 mm.
Obv: Double-headed eagle within beaded circle **Rev:** Chinese
Softshell turtle **Edge:** Reeded

Date	Mintage	F	VF	XF	Unc	BU
2003(sp) Proof	10,000	Value: 35.00				

Y# 828 ROUBLE
17.2800 g., 0.9000 Silver 0.5000 oz. ASW, 33 mm. **Obv:** Two
headed eagle within beaded circle **Rev:** Amur Forest Cat on
branch **Edge:** Reeded

Date	Mintage	F	VF	XF	Unc	BU
2004(sp) Proof	10,000	Value: 30.00				

Y# 881 ROUBLE
17.2800 g., 0.5000 Silver 0.2778 oz. ASW, 32.8 mm.
Obv: Double-headed eagle within beaded circle **Rev:** Rush Toad
Edge: Reeded

Date	Mintage	F	VF	XF	Unc	BU
2004 Proof	—	Value: 45.00				

Y# 882 ROUBLE
16.8100 g., 0.4999 Silver 0.2702 oz. ASW, 32.8 mm.
Obv: Double-headed eagle within beaded circle **Rev:** Two
Marbled Murrelet sea birds **Edge:** Reeded

Date	Mintage	F	VF	XF	Unc	BU
2005 Proof	—	Value: 30.00				

Y# 883 ROUBLE
16.8100 g., 0.4999 Silver 0.2702 oz. ASW, 32.8 mm.
Obv: Double-headed eagle within beaded circle **Rev:** Asiatic Wild
Dog **Edge:** Reeded

Date	Mintage	F	VF	XF	Unc	BU
2005 Proof	—	Value: 30.00				

Y# 884 ROUBLE
16.8100 g., 0.4999 Silver 0.2702 oz. ASW, 32.8 mm.
Obv: Double-headed eagle within beaded circle **Rev:** Volkhov
Whitefish **Edge:** Reeded

Date	Mintage	F	VF	XF	Unc	BU
2005 Proof	—	Value: 30.00				

Y# 916 ROUBLE
8.5300 g., 0.9250 Silver 0.2537 oz. ASW, 25 mm. **Obv:** Double-
headed eagle **Rev:** Russian Navy Emblem **Edge:** Reeded

Date	Mintage	F	VF	XF	Unc	BU
2005 Proof	10,000	Value: 25.00				

Y# 917 ROUBLE
8.5300 g., 0.9250 Silver 0.2537 oz. ASW, 25 mm. **Obv:** Double-
headed eagle **Rev:** Russian Marine circa 1705 **Edge:** Reeded

Date	Mintage	F	VF	XF	Unc	BU
2005 Proof	10,000	Value: 25.00				

Y# 918 ROUBLE
8.5300 g., 0.9250 Silver 0.2537 oz. ASW, 25 mm. **Obv:** Double-
headed eagle **Rev:** Russian Marine circa 2005 **Edge:** Reeded

Date	Mintage	F	VF	XF	Unc	BU
2005 Proof	10,000	Value: 25.00				

Y# 981 ROUBLE
15.5500 g., 0.9250 Silver 0.4624 oz. ASW, 33 mm. **Obv:** Double headed eagle **Rev:** Mongolian Gazelle **Edge:** Reeded

Date	Mintage	F	VF	XF	Unc	BU
2006 Proof	—	Value: 50.00				

Y# 961 ROUBLE
15.5500 g., 0.9250 Silver 0.4624 oz. ASW, 33 mm. **Obv:** Double headed eagle **Rev:** Red banded snake **Edge:** Reeded

Date	Mintage	F	VF	XF	Unc	BU
2007 Proof	—	Value: 30.00				

Y# 962 ROUBLE
15.5500 g., 0.9250 Silver 0.4624 oz. ASW, 33 mm. **Obv:** Double headed eagle **Rev:** Pallid Harrier in flight

Date	Mintage	F	VF	XF	Unc	BU
2007 Proof	—	Value: 30.00				

Y# 979 ROUBLE
15.5500 g., 0.9250 Silver 0.4624 oz. ASW, 33 mm. **Obv:** Double headed eagle **Rev:** Black caped marmot **Edge:** Reeded

Date	Mintage	F	VF	XF	Unc	BU
2008 Proof	—	Value: 30.00				

Y# 980 ROUBLE
15.5500 g., 0.9250 Silver 0.4624 oz. ASW, 33 mm. **Obv:** Double headed eagle **Rev:** Shemaya fish **Edge:** Reeded

Date	Mintage	F	VF	XF	Unc	BU
2008 Proof	—	Value: 30.00				

Y# 833a ROUBLE
3.0000 g., Nickel Plated Steel, 20.5 mm.

Date	Mintage	F	VF	XF	Unc	BU
2009ММД	—	—	—	—	0.75	1.50
2009СПМД	—	—	—	—	0.75	1.50

Y# 605 2 ROUBLES
5.1000 g., Copper-Nickel-Zinc, 23 mm. **Obv:** Double-headed eagle **Rev:** Value and vine sprig **Edge:** Alternating reeded and smooth

Date	Mintage	F	VF	XF	Unc	BU
2001M Rare	—	—	—	—	—	—

Y# 730 2 ROUBLES
17.0000 g., 0.9250 Silver 0.5055 oz. ASW, 33 mm. **Subject:** V.I. Dal **Obv:** Double-headed eagle **Rev:** Portrait, book, signature, figures **Edge:** Reeded

Date	Mintage	F	VF	XF	Unc	BU
2001(m) Proof	7,500	Value: 40.00				

Y# 675 2 ROUBLES
5.1000 g., Copper-Nickel, 23 mm. **Subject:** Yuri Gagarin **Obv:** Value and date to left of vine sprig **Rev:** Uniformed bust facing **Edge:** Segmented reeding

Date	Mintage	F	VF	XF	Unc	BU
2001	—	—	100	125	175	—
2001ММД	10,000,000	—	—	—	2.00	4.00
2001СПМД	10,000,000	—	—	—	2.00	4.00

Y# 742 2 ROUBLES
17.0000 g., 0.9250 Silver 0.5055 oz. ASW, 33 mm. **Subject:** Zodiac Signs **Obv:** Double-headed eagle within beaded circle **Rev:** Leo **Edge:** Reeded

Date	Mintage	F	VF	XF	Unc	BU
2002(m) Proof	20,000	Value: 35.00				

Y# 834 2 ROUBLES
5.1000 g., Copper-Nickel-Zinc, 23 mm. **Obv:** Two headed eagle above curved inscription **Rev:** Value and flower **Edge:** Segmented reeding

Date	Mintage	F	VF	XF	Unc	BU
2002ММД Mint sets only	15,000	—	—	—	—	—
2002СПМД Mint sets only	15,000	—	—	—	—	—
2003ММД	15,000	—	—	300	400	500
2006ММД	—	—	—	—	4.00	5.00
2006СПМД	—	—	—	—	4.00	5.00
2007ММД	—	—	—	—	4.00	5.00
2007СПМД	—	—	—	—	4.00	5.00
2008ММД	—	—	—	—	4.00	5.00
2008СПМД	—	—	—	—	4.00	5.00
2009ММД	—	—	—	—	4.00	5.00
2009СПМД	—	—	—	—	4.00	5.00

Y# 747 2 ROUBLES
17.0000 g., 0.9250 Silver 0.5055 oz. ASW, 33 mm. **Subject:** Zodiac Signs **Obv:** Double-headed eagle within beaded circle **Rev:** Virgo and stars **Edge:** Reeded

Date	Mintage	F	VF	XF	Unc	BU
2002(m) Proof	20,000	Value: 30.00				

Y# 761 2 ROUBLES
17.0000 g., 0.9250 Silver 0.5055 oz. ASW, 33 mm. **Subject:** Zodiac Signs **Obv:** Double-headed eagle within beaded circle **Rev:** Capricorn **Edge:** Reeded

Date	Mintage	F	VF	XF	Unc	BU
2002(sp) Proof	20,000	Value: 35.00				

Y# 762 2 ROUBLES
17.0000 g., 0.9250 Silver 0.5055 oz. ASW, 33 mm. **Subject:** Zodiac Signs **Obv:** Double-headed eagle within beaded circle **Rev:** Sagittarius **Edge:** Reeded

Date	Mintage	F	VF	XF	Unc	BU
2002(sp) Proof	20,000	Value: 30.00				

Y# 766 2 ROUBLES
17.0000 g., 0.9250 Silver 0.5055 oz. ASW, 33 mm. **Subject:** Zodiac Signs **Obv:** Double-headed eagle within beaded circle **Rev:** Scorpion **Edge:** Reeded

Date	Mintage	F	VF	XF	Unc	BU
2002(m) Proof	20,000	Value: 35.00				

Y# 768 2 ROUBLES
17.0000 g., 0.9250 Silver 0.5055 oz. ASW, 33 mm. **Subject:** Zodiac Signs **Obv:** Double-headed eagle **Rev:** Balance scale **Edge:** Reeded

Date	Mintage	F	VF	XF	Unc	BU
2002(sp) Proof	20,000	Value: 30.00				

Y# 793   2 ROUBLES
17.0000 g., 0.9250 Silver 0.5055 oz. ASW, 33 mm.
Subject: L.P. Orlova **Obv:** Double-headed eagle **Rev:** Head facing **Edge:** Reeded

Date	Mintage	F	VF	XF	Unc	BU
2002(m) Proof	10,000	Value: 25.00				

Y# 803   2 ROUBLES
17.1000 g., 0.9250 Silver 0.5085 oz. ASW, 32.8 mm.
Subject: Zodiac signs **Obv:** Double-headed eagle within beaded circle **Rev:** Pisces **Edge:** Reeded

Date	Mintage	F	VF	XF	Unc	BU
2003(sp) Proof	20,000	Value: 35.00				

Y# 804   2 ROUBLES
17.1000 g., 0.9250 Silver 0.5085 oz. ASW, 32.8 mm.
Subject: Zodiac signs **Obv:** Double-headed eagle within beaded circle **Rev:** Aquarius **Edge:** Reeded

Date	Mintage	F	VF	XF	Unc	BU
2003(m) Proof	20,000	Value: 35.00				

Y# 820   2 ROUBLES
17.0000 g., 0.9250 Silver 0.5055 oz. ASW, 33 mm.
Subject: Zodiac signs **Obv:** Double-headed eagle within beaded circle **Rev:** Cancer Crayfish **Edge:** Reeded

Date	Mintage	F	VF	XF	Unc	BU
2003(sp) Proof	20,000	Value: 35.00				

Y# 840   2 ROUBLES
16.8100 g., 0.9250 Silver 0.4999 oz. ASW, 33 mm. **Rev:** Guil Yarovsky

Date	Mintage	F	VF	XF	Unc	BU
2003(m) Proof	10,000	Value: 20.00				

Y# 841   2 ROUBLES
16.8100 g., 0.9250 Silver 0.4999 oz. ASW, 33 mm. **Rev:** Fedor Tyutchev

Date	Mintage	F	VF	XF	Unc	BU
2003(sp) Proof	10,000	Value: 20.00				

Y# 844   2 ROUBLES
17.0000 g., 0.9250 Silver 0.5055 oz. ASW, 33 mm.
Subject: Zodiac Signs **Obv:** Double-headed eagle within beaded circle **Rev:** Aries

Date	Mintage	F	VF	XF	Unc	BU
2003 Proof	20,000	Value: 25.00				

Y# 845   2 ROUBLES
17.0000 g., 0.9250 Silver 0.5055 oz. ASW **Subject:** Zodiac Signs **Obv:** Double-headed eagle within beaded circle **Rev:** Taurus

Date	Mintage	F	VF	XF	Unc	BU
2003 Proof	20,000	Value: 25.00				

Y# 846   2 ROUBLES
17.0000 g., 0.9250 Silver 0.5055 oz. ASW, 33 mm.
Subject: Zodiac Signs **Obv:** Double-headed eagle within beaded circle **Rev:** Gemini

Date	Mintage	F	VF	XF	Unc	BU
2003 Proof	20,000	Value: 22.50				

Y# 842   2 ROUBLES
16.8100 g., 0.9250 Silver 0.4999 oz. ASW, 33 mm. **Rev:** V. P. Tchkalov

Date	Mintage	F	VF	XF	Unc	BU
2004(m) Proof	7,000	Value: 20.00				

Y# 843   2 ROUBLES
16.8100 g., 0.9250 Silver 0.4999 oz. ASW, 33 mm. **Rev:** Mikhail Glinka

Date	Mintage	F	VF	XF	Unc	BU
2004(m) Proof	7,000	Value: 20.00				

Y# 897   2 ROUBLES
17.0000 g., 0.9250 Silver 0.5055 oz. ASW, 33 mm.
Obv: Double-headed eagle **Rev:** Gemini twins **Edge:** Reeded

Date	Mintage	F	VF	XF	Unc	BU
2005 Proof	20,000	Value: 25.00				

Y# 899   2 ROUBLES
17.0000 g., 0.9250 Silver 0.5055 oz. ASW, 33 mm. **Obv:** Double-headed eagle **Rev:** Cancer Crayfish **Edge:** Reeded

Date	Mintage	F	VF	XF	Unc	BU
2005 Proof	20,000	Value: 30.00				

Y# 901   2 ROUBLES
17.0000 g., 0.9250 Silver 0.5055 oz. ASW, 33 mm.
Obv: Double-headed eagle **Rev:** Leo lion **Edge:** Reeded

Date	Mintage	F	VF	XF	Unc	BU
2005 Proof	20,000	Value: 30.00				

Y# 905   2 ROUBLES
17.0000 g., 0.9250 Silver 0.5055 oz. ASW, 33 mm.
Obv: Double-headed eagle **Rev:** Mikhail Sholokhov with pen in hand **Edge:** Reeded

Date	Mintage	F	VF	XF	Unc	BU
2005 Proof	10,000	Value: 25.00				

Y# 909   2 ROUBLES
17.0000 g., 0.9250 Silver 0.5055 oz. ASW, 33 mm.
Obv: Double-headed eagle **Rev:** Peter Klodt viewing man and horse statue **Edge:** Reeded

Date	Mintage	F	VF	XF	Unc	BU
2005 Proof	10,000	Value: 25.00				

Y# 914   2 ROUBLES
17.0000 g., 0.9250 Silver 0.5055 oz. ASW, 33 mm. **Obv:** Double-headed eagle **Rev:** Virgo standing lady **Edge:** Reeded

Date	Mintage	F	VF	XF	Unc	BU
2005 Proof	20,000	Value: 25.00				

Y# 919   2 ROUBLES
17.0000 g., 0.9250 Silver 0.5055 oz. ASW, 33 mm.
Obv: Double-headed eagle **Rev:** Libra - 2 stylized birds forming a balance scale **Edge:** Reeded

Date	Mintage	F	VF	XF	Unc	BU
2005 Proof	20,000	Value: 25.00				

Y# 921   2 ROUBLES
17.0000 g., 0.9250 Silver 0.5055 oz. ASW, 33 mm.
Obv: Double-headed eagle **Rev:** Scorpio scorpion **Edge:** Reeded

Date	Mintage	F	VF	XF	Unc	BU
2005 Proof	25	Value: 30.00				

Y# 926   2 ROUBLES
17.0000 g., 0.9250 Silver 0.5055 oz. ASW, 33 mm.
Obv: Double-headed eagle **Rev:** Sagittarius the archer **Edge:** Reeded

Date	Mintage	F	VF	XF	Unc	BU
2005 Proof	20,000	Value: 25.00				

Y# 928   2 ROUBLES
17.0000 g., 0.9250 Silver 0.5055 oz. ASW, 33 mm.
Obv: Double-headed eagle **Rev:** Capricorn as half goat and fish
Edge: Reeded

Date	Mintage	F	VF	XF	Unc	BU
2005 Proof	20,000	Value: 30.00				

Y# 930   2 ROUBLES
17.0000 g., 0.9250 Silver 0.5055 oz. ASW, 33 mm.
Obv: Double-headed eagle **Rev:** Pisces as catfish and sturgeon
Edge: Reeded

Date	Mintage	F	VF	XF	Unc	BU
2005 Proof	20,000	Value: 25.00				

Y# 932   2 ROUBLES
17.0000 g., 0.9250 Silver 0.5055 oz. ASW, 33 mm.
Obv: Double-headed eagle **Rev:** Aries ram **Edge:** Reeded

Date	Mintage	F	VF	XF	Unc	BU
2005 Proof	20,000	Value: 25.00				

Y# 934   2 ROUBLES
17.0000 g., 0.9250 Silver 0.5055 oz. ASW, 33 mm.
Obv: Double-headed eagle **Rev:** Taurus bull **Edge:** Reeded

Date	Mintage	F	VF	XF	Unc	BU
2005 Proof	20,000	Value: 30.00				

Y# 936   2 ROUBLES
17.0000 g., 0.9250 Silver 0.5055 oz. ASW, 33 mm. **Obv:** Double-headed eagle **Rev:** Aquarius water carrier **Edge:** Reeded

Date	Mintage	F	VF	XF	Unc	BU
2005 Proof	20,000	Value: 25.00				

Y# 967   2 ROUBLES
17.0000 g., 0.9250 Silver 0.5055 oz. ASW, 33.0 mm.
Subject: 100th Anniversary Birth of Gerasimov **Obv:** Two-headed eagle **Rev:** Gerasimov recreating a man's face
Rev. Legend: М. М. ГЕРАСИМОВ

Date	Mintage	F	VF	XF	Unc	BU
2007(m) Proof	10,000	Value: 30.00				

Y# 968   2 ROUBLES
17.0000 g., 0.9250 Silver 0.5055 oz. ASW, 33.0 mm.
Subject: 150th Anniversary Birth of Tsiolkovsky **Rev:** Bust of Tsiolkovsky 3/4 right at left, scheme of two flight vehicles with earth in background at upper right **Rev. Legend:** К. Э. ЦИОЛКОВСКИJ **Edge:** Reeded

Date	Mintage	F	VF	XF	Unc	BU
2007(m) Proof	10,000	Value: 30.00				

Y# 834a   2 ROUBLES
5.0000 g., Nickel Plated Steel, 23 mm. **Edge:** Segmented reeding

Date	Mintage	F	VF	XF	Unc	BU
2009ММД	—	—	—	—	0.50	0.75
2009СПМД	—	—	—	—	0.50	0.75

Y# 677   3 ROUBLES
34.8800 g., 0.9000 Silver 1.0092 oz. ASW, 39 mm.
Subject: 225 Years - Bolshoi Theater **Obv:** Double-headed eagle
Rev: Standing figures facing **Edge:** Reeded

Date	Mintage	F	VF	XF	Unc	BU
2001 Proof	7,500	Value: 40.00				

Y# 680   3 ROUBLES
34.8800 g., 0.9000 Silver 1.0092 oz. ASW, 39 mm. **Subject:** 40th Anniversary of Manned Space Flight - Yuri Gagarin **Obv:** Double-headed eagle **Rev:** Uniformed bust holding dove **Edge:** Reeded

Date	Mintage	F	VF	XF	Unc	BU
2001 Proof	7,500	Value: 40.00				

Y# 682   3 ROUBLES
34.8800 g., 0.9000 Silver 1.0092 oz. ASW, 39 mm.
Subject: Siberian Exploration **Obv:** Double-headed eagle
Rev: Men riding horses, deer and sleds **Edge:** Reeded

Date	Mintage	F	VF	XF	Unc	BU
2001 Proof	5,000	Value: 45.00				

Y# 733   3 ROUBLES
34.8800 g., 0.9000 Silver 1.0092 oz. ASW, 39 mm. **Subject:** 200th Anniversary of Navigation School **Obv:** Double-headed eagle **Rev:** Navigational tools and building **Edge:** Reeded

Date	Mintage	F	VF	XF	Unc	BU
2001 Proof	5,000	Value: 42.50				

Y# 734   3 ROUBLES
34.8800 g., 0.9000 Silver 1.0092 oz. ASW, 39 mm.
Subject: First Moscow Savings Bank **Obv:** Double-headed eagle
Rev: Beehive above building within circle **Edge:** Reeded

Date	Mintage	F	VF	XF	Unc	BU
2001 Proof	17,500	Value: 40.00				

Y# 735   3 ROUBLES
34.8800 g., 0.9000 Silver 1.0092 oz. ASW, 39 mm.
Subject: State Labor Savings Bank **Obv:** Double-headed eagle
Rev: Dam, passbook and tractor **Edge:** Reeded

Date	Mintage	F	VF	XF	Unc	BU
2001 Proof	17,500	Value: 40.00				

Y# 736   3 ROUBLES
34.8800 g., 0.9000 Silver 1.0092 oz. ASW, 39 mm.
Subject: Savings Bank of the Russian Federation **Obv:** Double-headed eagle **Rev:** Chevrons above building **Edge:** Reeded

Date	Mintage	F	VF	XF	Unc	BU
2001 Proof	17,500	Value: 40.00				

Y# 737   3 ROUBLES
34.8800 g., 0.9000 Silver 1.0092 oz. ASW, 39 mm. **Subject:**
10th Anniversary - Commonwealth of Independent States **Obv:**
Double-headed eagle **Rev:** Hologram below logo **Edge:** Reeded

Date	Mintage	F	VF	XF	Unc	BU
2001 Proof	7,500	Value: 45.00				

Y# 738   3 ROUBLES
34.8800 g., 0.9000 Silver 1.0092 oz. ASW, 39 mm.
Subject: Olympics **Obv:** Double-headed eagle **Rev:** Cross-
country skiers **Edge:** Reeded

Date	Mintage	F	VF	XF	Unc	BU
2002 Proof	25,000	Value: 40.00				

Y# 744   3 ROUBLES
34.8800 g., 0.9000 Silver 1.0092 oz. ASW, 39 mm.
Subject: St. John's Nunnery, St. Petersburg **Obv:** Double-
headed eagle **Rev:** Nunnery and cameo **Edge:** Reeded

Date	Mintage	F	VF	XF	Unc	BU
2002 Proof	5,000	Value: 45.00				

Y# 778   3 ROUBLES
34.8800 g., 0.9000 Silver 1.0092 oz. ASW, 39 mm.
Subject: Kideksha **Obv:** Double-headed eagle **Rev:** Three
churches on river bank **Edge:** Reeded

Date	Mintage	F	VF	XF	Unc	BU
2002(sp) Proof	10,000	Value: 42.50				

Y# 779   3 ROUBLES
34.8800 g., 0.9000 Silver 1.0092 oz. ASW, 39 mm. **Subject:** Iversky Monastery, Valdaiy **Obv:** Double-headed eagle
Rev: Building complex on an island in Lake Valdaiy
Edge: Reeded

Date	Mintage	F	VF	XF	Unc	BU
2002(sp) Proof	10,000	Value: 42.50				

Y# 780   3 ROUBLES
34.8800 g., 0.9000 Silver 1.0092 oz. ASW, 39 mm.
Subject: Miraculous Savior Church **Obv:** Double-headed eagle
Rev: Church with separate bell tower **Edge:** Reeded

Date	Mintage	F	VF	XF	Unc	BU
2002(m) Proof	5,000	Value: 50.00				

Y# 781   3 ROUBLES
34.8800 g., 0.9000 Silver 1.0092 oz. ASW, 39 mm.
Subject: Works of Dionissy **Obv:** Double-headed eagle
Rev: "The Crucifix" **Edge:** Reeded

Date	Mintage	F	VF	XF	Unc	BU
2002(sp) Proof	10,000	Value: 40.00				

Y# 755   3 ROUBLES
34.8800 g., 0.9000 Silver 1.0092 oz. ASW, 39 mm. **Subject:**
Admiral Nakhimov **Obv:** Double-headed eagle **Rev:** Monument,
Admiral with cannon and naval battle scene **Edge:** Reeded

Date	Mintage	F	VF	XF	Unc	BU
2002(sp) Proof	10,000	Value: 40.00				

Y# 787   3 ROUBLES
34.8800 g., 0.9000 Silver 1.0092 oz. ASW, 39 mm.
Subject: World Cup Soccer **Obv:** Double-headed eagle
Rev: Soccer ball within circle of players **Edge:** Reeded

Date	Mintage	F	VF	XF	Unc	BU
2002(sp) Proof	25,000	Value: 35.00				

Y# 756   3 ROUBLES
34.8800 g., 0.9000 Silver 1.0092 oz. ASW, 39 mm.
Subject: Hermitage **Obv:** Double-headed eagle **Rev:** Statues
and arch **Edge:** Reeded

Date	Mintage	F	VF	XF	Unc	BU
2002(sp) Proof	10,000	Value: 42.50				

Y# 885   3 ROUBLES
34.8000 g., 0.9000 Silver 1.0069 oz. ASW, 38.7 mm.
Subject: City of Pskov 1100th Anniversary **Obv:** Double-headed
eagle **Rev:** Walled city view **Edge:** Reeded

Date	Mintage	F	VF	XF	Unc	BU
2003(sp) Proof	—	Value: 55.00				

Y# 801   3 ROUBLES
34.8000 g., 0.9000 Silver 1.0069 oz. ASW, 38.7 mm.
Subject: Veborg **Obv:** Double-headed eagle **Rev:** Sailing ships
and buildings **Edge:** Reeded

Date	Mintage	F	VF	XF	Unc	BU
2003(sp) Proof	10,000	Value: 50.00				

Y# 802   3 ROUBLES
34.7500 g., 0.9000 Silver 1.0055 oz. ASW, 38.7 mm.
Subject: Lunar Calendar **Obv:** National emblem **Rev:** Mountain
goat in crescent **Edge:** Reeded

Date	Mintage	F	VF	XF	Unc	BU
2003(m) Proof	15,000	Value: 50.00				

Y# 805   3 ROUBLES
34.8400 g., 0.9000 Silver 1.0081 oz. ASW, 38.8 mm.
Subject: Zodiac signs **Obv:** Double-headed eagle within beaded
circle **Rev:** Leo **Edge:** Reeded

Date	Mintage	F	VF	XF	Unc	BU
2003(m) Proof	30,000	Value: 50.00				

Y# 806   3 ROUBLES
34.7400 g., 0.9000 Silver 1.0052 oz. ASW, 38.8 mm.
Subject: St. Daniel's Monastery **Obv:** Double-headed eagle
Rev: Statue and monastery **Edge:** Reeded

Date	Mintage	F	VF	XF	Unc	BU
2003(m) Proof	10,000	Value: 45.00				

Y# 807   3 ROUBLES
34.7400 g., 0.9000 Silver 1.0052 oz. ASW, 38.8 mm.
Subject: World Biathlon Championships **Obv:** Double-headed eagle **Rev:** Rifleman and archer on skis **Edge:** Reeded

Date	Mintage	F	VF	XF	Unc	BU
2003(m) Proof	7,500	Value: 40.00				

Y# 808   3 ROUBLES
34.7400 g., 0.9000 Silver 1.0052 oz. ASW, 38.8 mm.
Obv: Double-headed eagle **Rev:** Monastery **Edge:** Reeded

Date	Mintage	F	VF	XF	Unc	BU
2003(m) Proof	10,000	Value: 42.50				

Y# 809   3 ROUBLES
34.7400 g., 0.9000 Silver 1.0052 oz. ASW, 38.8 mm.
Subject: First Kamchatka Expedition **Obv:** Double-headed eagle **Rev:** Natives, fish and ship **Edge:** Reeded

Date	Mintage	F	VF	XF	Unc	BU
2003(sp) Proof	10,000	Value: 37.50				

Y# 810   3 ROUBLES
34.7400 g., 0.9000 Silver 1.0052 oz. ASW, 38.8 mm.
Subject: Zodiac signs **Obv:** Double-headed eagle within beaded circle **Rev:** Virgo **Edge:** Reeded

Date	Mintage	F	VF	XF	Unc	BU
2003(sp)	30,000	Value: 35.00				

Y# 811   3 ROUBLES
34.7400 g., 0.9000 Silver 1.0052 oz. ASW, 38.8 mm.
Subject: Zodiac signs **Obv:** Double-headed eagle within beaded circle **Rev:** Libra **Edge:** Reeded

Date	Mintage	F	VF	XF	Unc	BU
2003(m) Proof	30,000	Value: 35.00				

Y# 812   3 ROUBLES
34.7400 g., 0.9000 Silver 1.0052 oz. ASW, 38.8 mm.
Subject: Diveyevsky Monastery **Obv:** Double-headed eagle **Rev:** Cameo above churches **Edge:** Reeded

Date	Mintage	F	VF	XF	Unc	BU
2003(sp) Proof	10,000	Value: 42.50				

Y# 813   3 ROUBLES
34.7400 g., 0.9000 Silver 1.0052 oz. ASW, 38.8 mm.
Subject: Zodiac Signs **Obv:** Double-headed eagle within beaded circle **Rev:** Scorpio **Edge:** Reeded

Date	Mintage	F	VF	XF	Unc	BU
2003(m) Proof	30,000	Value: 35.00				

Y# 847   3 ROUBLES
34.5600 g., 0.9000 Silver 1.0000 oz. ASW, 39 mm. **Rev:** St. Trinity Monastery

Date	Mintage	F	VF	XF	Unc	BU
2003(sp) Proof	10,000	Value: 40.00				

Y# 848   3 ROUBLES
34.5600 g., 0.9000 Silver 1.0000 oz. ASW, 39 mm.
Subject: Zodiac Signs **Obv:** Double-headed eagle within beaded circle **Rev:** Sagittarius

Date	Mintage	F	VF	XF	Unc	BU
2003(sp) Proof	30,000	Value: 35.00				

Y# 849   3 ROUBLES
34.5600 g., 0.9000 Silver 1.0000 oz. ASW, 39 mm.
Subject: Zodiac Signs **Obv:** Double-headed eagle within beaded circle **Rev:** Capricorn

Date	Mintage	F	VF	XF	Unc	BU
2003(m) Proof	30,000	Value: 35.00				

Y# 850   3 ROUBLES
34.5600 g., 0.9000 Silver 1.0000 oz. ASW, 39 mm.
Subject: Lunar Calendar **Rev:** Monkey

Date	Mintage	F	VF	XF	Unc	BU
2004(m) Proof	15,000	Value: 37.50				

Y# 851   3 ROUBLES
34.5600 g., 0.9000 Silver 1.0000 oz. ASW, 39 mm.
Subject: Zodiac Signs **Obv:** Double-headed eagle within beaded circle **Rev:** Aquarius

Date	Mintage	F	VF	XF	Unc	BU
2004(sp) Proof	30,000	Value: 35.00				

Y# 852   3 ROUBLES
34.5600 g., 0.9000 Silver 1.0000 oz. ASW, 39 mm. **Rev:** Tomsk

Date	Mintage	F	VF	XF	Unc	BU
2004(m) Proof	8,000	Value: 35.00				

Y# 853   3 ROUBLES
34.5600 g., 0.9000 Silver 1.0000 oz. ASW, 39 mm.
Subject: Zodiac Signs **Obv:** Double-headed eagle within beaded circle **Rev:** Pisces

Date	Mintage	F	VF	XF	Unc	BU
2004(m) Proof	30,000	Value: 35.00				

Y# 854   3 ROUBLES
34.5600 g., 0.9000 Silver 1.0000 oz. ASW, 39 mm.
Rev: Epiphany Cathedral, Moscow

Date	Mintage	F	VF	XF	Unc	BU
2004(m) Proof	8,000	Value: 35.00				

Y# 855   3 ROUBLES
34.5600 g., 0.9000 Silver 1.0000 oz. ASW, 39 mm.
Subject: Zodiac Signs **Obv:** Double-headed eagle within beaded circle **Rev:** Aries

Date	Mintage	F	VF	XF	Unc	BU
2004(sp) Proof	30,000	Value: 35.00				

Y# 856   3 ROUBLES
34.5600 g., 0.9000 Silver 1.0000 oz. ASW, 39 mm. **Rev:** Soccer

Date	Mintage	F	VF	XF	Unc	BU
2004(sp) Proof	10,000	Value: 30.00				

Y# 857   3 ROUBLES
34.5600 g., 0.9000 Silver 1.0000 oz. ASW, 39 mm.
Subject: Zodiac Signs **Obv:** Double-headed eagle within beaded circle **Rev:** Taurus

Date	Mintage	F	VF	XF	Unc	BU
2004(sp) Proof	30,000	Value: 35.00				

Y# 858   3 ROUBLES
34.5600 g., 0.9000 Silver 1.0000 oz. ASW, 39 mm.
Rev: Olympic torch

Date	Mintage	F	VF	XF	Unc	BU
2004(m) Proof	20,000	Value: 32.50				

Y# 859   3 ROUBLES
34.5600 g., 0.9000 Silver 1.0000 oz. ASW, 39 mm.
Subject: Zodiac Signs **Obv:** Double-headed eagle within beaded circle **Rev:** Gemini

Date	Mintage	F	VF	XF	Unc	BU
2004(m) Proof	30,000	Value: 35.00				

Y# 860   3 ROUBLES
34.5600 g., 0.9000 Silver 1.0000 oz. ASW, 39 mm.
Subject: Zodiac Signs **Obv:** Double-headed eagle within beaded circle **Rev:** Cancer

Date	Mintage	F	VF	XF	Unc	BU
2004(sp) Proof	30,000	Value: 35.00				

Y# 861   3 ROUBLES
34.5600 g., 0.9000 Silver 1.0000 oz. ASW, 39 mm. **Rev:** Church of the Sign of the Holy Mother of God

Date	Mintage	F	VF	XF	Unc	BU
2004(m) Proof	8,000	Value: 35.00				

Y# 862   3 ROUBLES
34.5600 g., 0.9000 Silver 1.0000 oz. ASW, 39 mm.
Rev: Transfiguration icon

Date	Mintage	F	VF	XF	Unc	BU
2004(m) Proof	8,000	Value: 35.00				

Y# 863   3 ROUBLES
34.5600 g., 0.9000 Silver 1.0000 oz. ASW, 39 mm. **Rev:** Peter I's monetary reform

Date	Mintage	F	VF	XF	Unc	BU
2004(sp) Proof	8,000	Value: 75.00				

Y# 892   3 ROUBLES
33.9400 g., 0.9250 Silver 1.0093 oz. ASW, 39 mm.
Obv: Double-headed eagle **Rev:** Rooster and crescent moon **Edge:** Reeded

Date	Mintage	F	VF	XF	Unc	BU
2005 Proof	15,000	Value: 35.00				

Y# 893   3 ROUBLES
33.9400 g., 0.9250 Silver 1.0093 oz. ASW, 39 mm. **Subject:** 60th Anniversary - Victory Over Germany **Obv:** Double-headed eagle **Rev:** Soldier and wife circa 1945 **Edge:** Reeded

Date	Mintage	F	VF	XF	Unc	BU
2005 Proof	35,000	Value: 35.00				

Y# 903   3 ROUBLES
33.9400 g., 0.9250 Silver 1.0093 oz. ASW, 39 mm.
Obv: Double-headed eagle **Rev:** St. Nicholas Cathedral in Kaliningrad **Edge:** Reeded

Date	Mintage	F	VF	XF	Unc	BU
2005 Proof	10,000	Value: 35.00				

Y# 904   3 ROUBLES
33.9400 g., 0.9250 Silver 1.0093 oz. ASW, 39 mm.
Obv: Double-headed eagle **Rev:** Kropotkin Metro Station in
Moscow **Edge:** Reeded

Date	Mintage	F	VF	XF	Unc	BU
2005 Proof	10,000	Value: 35.00				

Y# 906   3 ROUBLES
33.9400 g., 0.9250 Silver 1.0093 oz. ASW, 39 mm.
Subject: Helsinki Games **Obv:** Double-headed eagle
Rev: Stylized track and field athletes **Edge:** Reeded

Date	Mintage	F	VF	XF	Unc	BU
2005 Proof	10,000	Value: 32.50				

Y# 908   3 ROUBLES
33.9400 g., 0.9250 Silver 1.0093 oz. ASW, 39 mm.
Obv: Double-headed eagle **Rev:** Virgin Monastery in Raifa,
Tatarstan **Edge:** Reeded

Date	Mintage	F	VF	XF	Unc	BU
2005 Proof	10,000	Value: 35.00				

Y# 910   3 ROUBLES
33.9400 g., 0.9250 Silver 1.0093 oz. ASW, 39 mm.
Obv: Double-headed eagle **Rev:** Kazan Theater Building
Edge: Reeded

Date	Mintage	F	VF	XF	Unc	BU
2005 Proof	10,000	Value: 35.00				

Y# 923   3 ROUBLES
33.9400 g., 0.9250 Silver 1.0093 oz. ASW, 39 mm.
Subject: 625th Anniversary - Battle of Kulikovo **Obv:** Double-
headed eagle **Rev:** Carved Lion and Griffin between opposing
armies **Edge:** Reeded

Date	Mintage	F	VF	XF	Unc	BU
2005 Proof	10,000	Value: 35.00				

Y# 955   3 ROUBLES
33.9400 g., 0.9250 Silver 1.0093 oz. ASW, 39 mm.
Subject: Moscow's Lomonosov University **Obv:** Two headed
eagle **Rev:** Lomonosov statue before university building and
Moscow skyline **Edge:** Reeded

Date	Mintage	F	VF	XF	Unc	BU
2005(m) Proof	10,000	Value: 32.50				

Y# 966   3 ROUBLES
33.9400 g., 0.9250 Silver 1.0093 oz. ASW, 39.0 mm. **Subject:**
250th Anniversary Academy of the Arts **Obv:** Two-headed eagle
Rev: Relief image of Minerva group **Rev. Legend:** РОССИЙСКАЯ
- АКАДЕМИЯ ХУДОЖЕСТВ **Edge:** Reeded

Date	Mintage	F	VF	XF	Unc	BU
2007(m) Proof	10,000	Value: 32.50				

Y# 992   3 ROUBLES
Silver **Subject:** Year of the Bull **Obv:** Double headed eagle
Rev: Stylized bull

Date	Mintage	F	VF	XF	Unc	BU
2009 Proof	—	Value: 30.00				

Y# 799   5 ROUBLES
6.4500 g., Copper-Nickel Clad Copper, 25 mm.   **Obv:** Curved
bank name below eagle **Edge:** Segmented reeding

Date	Mintage	F	VF	XF	Unc	BU
2002ММД In sets only	15,000	—	—	—	—	—
2002СПМД In sets only	15,000	—	—	—	—	—
2003ММД	15,000	—	—	150	200	250
2008ММД	—	—	—	—	3.00	4.00
2008СПМД	—	—	—	—	3.00	4.00
2009ММД	—	—	—	—	3.00	4.00
2009СПМД	—	—	—	—	3.00	4.00

Y# 829   5 ROUBLES
47.2400 g., Bi-Metallic .900 Silver 21.34g center in .900 Gold
25.9g ring, 39.5 mm.   **Obv:** Double-headed eagle **Rev:** Uglich
city view **Edge:** Reeded

Date	Mintage	F	VF	XF	Unc	BU
2004(sp) Proof	5,000	Value: 850				

Y# 799a   5 ROUBLES
6.0000 g., Nickel Plated Steel, 25 mm.

Date	Mintage	F	VF	XF	Unc	BU
2009ММД	—	—	—	—	2.00	3.00
2009СПМД	—	—	—	—	2.00	3.00

Y# 676   10 ROUBLES
8.2200 g., Bi-Metallic Copper-Nickel center in Brass ring, 27 mm.
Subject: Yuri Gagarin **Obv:** Value with latent image in zero within
circle and sprigs **Rev:** Helmeted bust 1/4 right **Edge:** Reeding
over denomination

Date	Mintage	F	VF	XF	Unc	BU
2001ММД	10,000,000	—	—	—	4.00	5.00
2001СПМД	10,000,000	—	—	—	4.00	5.00

Y# 686   10 ROUBLES
1.6100 g., 0.9990 Gold 0.0517 oz. AGW, 12 mm.   **Subject:**
Bolshoi Theater 225 Years **Obv:** Double-headed eagle within
circle **Rev:** Building above number 225 **Edge:** Reeded

Date	Mintage	F	VF	XF	Unc	BU
2001 Proof	3,000	Value: 65.00				

Y# 739   10 ROUBLES
8.2200 g., Bi-Metallic Copper-Nickel center in Brass ring, 27 mm.
Subject: Ancient Towns - Derbent **Obv:** Value with latent image
in zero within circle and sprigs **Rev:** Shield above walled city view
Edge: Reeding over denomination

Date	Mintage	F	VF	XF	Unc	BU
2002ММД	5,000,000	—	—	—	4.00	5.00

Y# 740   10 ROUBLES
8.2200 g., Bi-Metallic Copper-Nickel center in Brass ring, 27 mm.
Subject: Ancient Towns - Kostroma **Obv:** Value with latent image
in zero within circle and sprigs **Rev:** Cupola, shield and river view
Edge: Reeding over denomination

Date	Mintage	F	VF	XF	Unc	BU
2002СПМД	5,000,000	—	—	—	4.00	6.00

Y# 741   10 ROUBLES
8.2200 g., Bi-Metallic Copper-Nickel center in Brass ring, 27 mm.
Subject: Ancient Towns - Staraya Russa **Obv:** Value with latent
image in zero within circle and sprigs **Rev:** Shield and cathedral
Edge: Reeding over denomination

Date	Mintage	F	VF	XF	Unc	BU
2002СПМД	5,000,000	—	—	—	4.00	6.00

Y# 748   10 ROUBLES
8.2200 g., Bi-Metallic Copper-Nickel center in Brass ring, 27 mm.
Subject: Ministry of Education **Obv:** Value with latent image in
zero within circle and sprigs **Rev:** Seedling within open book
Edge: Reeding over denomination

Date	Mintage	F	VF	XF	Unc	BU
2002ММД	5,000,000	—	—	—	4.00	6.00

Y# 749   10 ROUBLES
8.2200 g., Bi-Metallic Copper-Nickel center in Brass ring, 27 mm.
Subject: Ministry of Finance **Obv:** Value with latent image in zero
within circle and sprigs **Rev:** Caduceus within monogram
Edge: Reeding over denomination

Date	Mintage	F	VF	XF	Unc	BU
2002СПМД	5,000,000	—	—	—	4.00	6.00

Y# 750   10 ROUBLES
8.2200 g., Bi-Metallic Copper-Nickel center in Brass ring, 27 mm.
Subject: Ministry of Economic Development and Trade
Obv: Value with latent image in zero within circle and sprigs
Rev: Crowned double-headed eagle with cornucopia and
caduceus **Edge:** Reeding over denomination

Date	Mintage	F	VF	XF	Unc	BU
2002СПМД	5,000,000	—	—	—	4.00	6.00

Y# 751   10 ROUBLES
8.2200 g., Bi-Metallic Copper-Nickel center in Brass ring, 27 mm.
Subject: Ministry of Foreign Affairs **Obv:** Value with latent image
in zero within circle and sprigs **Rev:** Crowned double-headed
eagle above crossed sprigs **Edge:** Reeding over denomination

Date	Mintage	F	VF	XF	Unc	BU
2002СПМД	5,000,000	—	—	—	4.00	6.00

Y# 752   10 ROUBLES
8.2200 g., Bi-Metallic Copper-Nickel center in Brass ring, 27 mm. **Subject:** Ministry of Internal Affairs **Obv:** Value with latent image in zero within circle and sprigs **Rev:** Crowned double-headed eagle with round breast shield **Edge:** Reeding over denomination

Date	Mintage	F	VF	XF	Unc	BU
2002ММД	5,000,000	—	—	—	4.00	6.00

Y# 753   10 ROUBLES
8.2200 g., Bi-Metallic Copper-Nickel center in Brass ring, 27 mm. **Subject:** Ministry of Justice **Obv:** Value with latent image in zero within circle and sprigs **Rev:** Crowned double-headed eagle with column on breast shield **Edge:** Reeding over denomination

Date	Mintage	F	VF	XF	Unc	BU
2002СПМД	5,000,000	—	—	—	4.00	6.00

Y# 754   10 ROUBLES
8.2200 g., Bi-Metallic Copper-Nickel center in Brass ring, 27 mm. **Subject:** Russian Armed Forces **Obv:** Value with latent image in zero within circle and sprigs **Rev:** Crowned double-headed eagle with crowned pointed top shield **Edge:** Reeding over denomination

Date	Mintage	F	VF	XF	Unc	BU
2002ММД	5,000,000	—	—	—	4.00	6.00

Y# 817   10 ROUBLES
8.3400 g., Bi-Metallic Copper-Nickel center in Brass ring, 27 mm. **Obv:** Value with latent image in zero within circle and sprigs **Rev:** Murom city view and tilted oval shields within circle **Edge:** Reeded and lettered

Date	Mintage	F	VF	XF	Unc	BU
2003(sp)	5,000,000	—	—	—	4.00	6.00

Y# 800   10 ROUBLES
8.4400 g., Bi-Metallic Copper-Nickel center in Brass ring, 27.1 mm. **Subject:** Pskov **Obv:** Value with latent image in zero within circle and sprigs **Rev:** Shield above walled city **Edge:** Reeding over lettering

Date	Mintage	F	VF	XF	Unc	BU
2003СПМД	5,000,000	—	—	—	4.00	6.00

Y# 818   10 ROUBLES
8.3400 g., Bi-Metallic Copper-Nickel center in Brass ring, 27 mm. **Obv:** Value w/ latent image in zero within circle and sprigs **Rev:** Kasimov city view and shield within circle **Edge:** Reeded and lettered

Date	Mintage	F	VF	XF	Unc	BU
2003СПМД	5,000,000	—	—	—	4.00	6.00

Y# 819   10 ROUBLES
8.3400 g., Bi-Metallic Copper-Nickel center in Brass ring, 27 mm. **Subject:** Dorogobuzh **Obv:** Value with latent image in zero within circle and sprigs **Rev:** Monument, city view and shield within circle **Edge:** Reeded and lettered

Date	Mintage	F	VF	XF	Unc	BU
2003ММД	5,000,000	—	—	—	4.00	6.00

Y# 824   10 ROUBLES
8.4600 g., Bi-Metallic Copper-Nickel center in Brass ring, 27.1 mm. **Subject:** Town of Ryazhsk **Obv:** Value with latent image in zero within circle and sprigs **Obv. Legend:** БАНК РОССИИ **Rev:** City view and crowned shield within circle **Edge:** Reeded and lettered

Date	Mintage	F	VF	XF	Unc	BU
2004ММД					4.00	6.00

Y# 825   10 ROUBLES
8.4600 g., Bi-Metallic Copper-Nickel center in Brass ring, 27.1 mm. **Subject:** Town of Dmitrov **Obv:** Value with latent image in zero within circle and sprigs **Obv. Legend:** БАНК РОССИИ **Rev:** City view and crowned shield within circle **Edge:** Reeded and lettered

Date	Mintage	F	VF	XF	Unc	BU
2004ММД	5,000,000	—	—	—	4.00	6.00

Y# 826   10 ROUBLES
8.4600 g., Bi-Metallic Copper-Nickel center in Brass ring, 27.1 mm. **Subject:** Town of Kem **Obv:** Value with latent image in zero within circle and sprigs **Obv. Legend:** БАНК РОССИИ **Rev:** City view and crowned shield within circle **Edge:** Reeded and lettered

Date	Mintage	F	VF	XF	Unc	BU
2004СПМД	5,000,000	—	—	—	4.00	6.00

Y# 827   10 ROUBLES
8.4000 g., Bi-Metallic Copper-Nickel center in brass ring, 27 mm. **Subject:** Great Victory, 60th Anniversary **Obv:** Value with latent image in zero within circle and sprigs **Rev:** WWII eternal flame monument above date and sprig within circle **Edge:** Reeded and Lettered

Date	Mintage	F	VF	XF	Unc	BU
2005ММД	30,000,000	—	—	—	4.00	6.00
2005СПМД	30,000,000	—	—	—	4.00	6.00

Y# 886   10 ROUBLES
8.2300 g., Bi-Metallic Copper-Nickel center in Brass ring, 27 mm. **Obv:** Value with latent image in zero within circle and sprigs **Rev:** Moscow coat of arms within circle **Edge:** Reeded and lettered

Date	Mintage	F	VF	XF	Unc	BU
2005ММД	10,000,000	—	—	—	4.00	6.00

Y# 887   10 ROUBLES
8.2300 g., Bi-Metallic Copper-Nickel center in Brass ring, 27 mm. **Obv:** Value with latent image in zero within circle and sprigs **Rev:** Leningrad Oblast coat of arms within circle **Edge:** Reeded and lettered

Date	Mintage	F	VF	XF	Unc	BU
2005СПМД	10,000,000	—	—	—	4.00	6.00

Y# 888   10 ROUBLES
8.2300 g., Bi-Metallic Copper-Nickel center in Brass ring, 27 mm. **Obv:** Value with latent image in zero within circle and sprigs **Rev:** Tverskaya arms within circle **Edge:** Reeded and lettered

Date	Mintage	F	VF	XF	Unc	BU
2005ММД	10,000,000	—	—	—	4.00	6.00

Y# 889   10 ROUBLES
8.2300 g., Bi-Metallic Copper-Nickel center in Brass ring, 27 mm. **Obv:** Value with latent image in zero within circle and sprigs **Rev:** Krasnodarskiy Kray coat of arms **Edge:** Reeded and lettered

Date	Mintage	F	VF	XF	Unc	BU
2005	10,000,000	—	—	—	4.00	6.00

Y# 890   10 ROUBLES
8.2300 g., Bi-Metallic Copper-Nickel center in Brass ring, 27 mm. **Obv:** Value with latent image in zero within circle and sprigs **Rev:** Orlovskaya Oblast coat of arms within circle **Edge:** Reeded and lettered

Date	Mintage	F	VF	XF	Unc	BU
2005	10,000,000	—	—	—	4.00	6.00

Y# 891   10 ROUBLES
8.2300 g., Bi-Metallic Copper-Nickel center in Brass ring, 27 mm. **Obv:** Value with latent image in zero within circle and sprigs **Rev:** Tatarstan Republic coat of arms within circle **Edge:** Reeded and lettered

Date	Mintage	F	VF	XF	Unc	BU
2005СПМД	10,000,000	—	—	—	4.00	6.00

Y# 943   10 ROUBLES
8.2300 g., Bi-Metallic Copper-Nickel center in Brass ring, 27.1 mm. **Obv:** Double-headed eagle **Rev:** City of Kazan

Date	Mintage	F	VF	XF	Unc	BU
2005СПМД	5,000,000	—	—	—	4.00	6.00

Y# 944   10 ROUBLES
8.2300 g., Bi-Metallic Copper-Nickel center in Brass ring, 27.1 mm. **Obv:** Double-headed eagle **Rev:** City of Borovsk

Date	Mintage	F	VF	XF	Unc	BU
2005СПМД	5,000,000	—	—	—	4.00	6.00

Y# 945   10 ROUBLES
8.2300 g., Bi-Metallic Copper-Nickel center in Brass ring, 27.1 mm. **Obv:** Double-headed eagle **Rev:** City of Mzensk

Date	Mintage	F	VF	XF	Unc	BU
2005ММД	5,000,000	—	—	—	4.00	6.00

Y# 946   10 ROUBLES
8.2300 g., Bi-Metallic Copper-Nickel center in Brass ring, 27.1 mm. **Obv:** Double-headed eagle **Rev:** City of Kaliningrad

Date	Mintage	F	VF	XF	Unc	BU
2005ММД	5,000,000	—	—	—	4.00	6.00

Y# 938   10 ROUBLES
8.2300 g., Bi-Metallic Copper-Nickel center in Brass ring, 27 mm. **Obv:** Value with latent image in zero within circle and sprigs **Rev:** Republic of Altai arms **Edge:** Lettered and reeded

Date	Mintage	F	VF	XF	Unc	BU
2006СПМД	10,000,000	—	—	—	4.00	6.00

Y# 939   10 ROUBLES
8.2300 g., Bi-Metallic Copper-Nickel center in Brass ring, 27 mm. **Obv:** Value with latent image in zero within circle and sprigs **Rev:** Chita Region arms **Edge:** Lettered and reeded

Date	Mintage	F	VF	XF	Unc	BU
2006СПМД	10,000,000	—	—	—	4.00	6.00

Y# 940 10 ROUBLES

8.2300 g., Bi-Metallic Copper-Nickel center in Brass ring, 27 mm. **Obv:** Value with latent image in zero within circle and sprigs **Rev:** Primorskij Kraj Maritime Territory coat of arms **Edge:** Lettered and reeded

Date	Mintage	F	VF	XF	Unc	BU
2006ММД	10,000,000	—	—	—	4.00	6.00

Y# 941 10 ROUBLES

8.2300 g., Bi-Metallic Copper-Nickel center in Brass ring, 27 mm. **Obv:** Value with latent image in zero within circle and sprigs **Rev:** Sakha (Yakutiya) Republic coat of arms **Edge:** Lettered and reeded

Date	Mintage	F	VF	XF	Unc	BU
2006СПМД	10,000,000	—	—	—	4.00	6.00

Y# 942 10 ROUBLES

8.2300 g., Bi-Metallic Copper-Nickel center in Brass ring, 27 mm. **Obv:** Value with latent image in zero within circle and sprigs **Rev:** Sakhalinskaya Oblast coat of arms **Edge:** Lettered and reeded

Date	Mintage	F	VF	XF	Unc	BU
2006ММД	10,000,000	—	—	—	4.00	6.00

Y# 947 10 ROUBLES

8.2300 g., Bi-Metallic Copper-Nickel center in Brass ring, 27.1 mm. **Obv:** Double-headed eagle **Rev:** City of Belgorod

Date	Mintage	F	VF	XF	Unc	BU
2006ММД	5,000,000	—	—	—	4.00	6.00

Y# 948 10 ROUBLES

8.2300 g., Bi-Metallic Copper-Nickel center in Brass ring, 27.1 mm. **Obv:** Double-headed eagle **Rev:** City of Kargopol

Date	Mintage	F	VF	XF	Unc	BU
2006ММД	5,000,000	—	—	—	4.00	6.00

Y# 949 10 ROUBLES

8.2300 g., Bi-Metallic Copper-Nickel center in Brass ring, 27.1 mm. **Obv:** Double-headed eagle **Rev:** City of Turzhok

Date	Mintage	F	VF	XF	Unc	BU
2006СПМД	5,000,000	—	—	—	4.00	6.00

Y# 963 10 ROUBLES

8.3000 g., Bi-Metallic Copper-Nickel center in Brass ring, 27 mm. **Obv:** Value with latent image in zero within circle and sprays **Rev:** Vologda church **Edge:** Reeded and lettered **Edge Lettering:** Denomination repeated

Date	Mintage	F	VF	XF	Unc	BU
2007ММД	2,500,000	—	—	—	4.00	6.00
2007СПМД	2,500,000	—	—	—	4.00	6.00

Y# 964 10 ROUBLES

8.3000 g., Bi-Metallic Copper-Nickel center in Brass ring, 27 mm. **Obv:** Value with latent image in zero within circle and sprays **Rev:** Veliky Ustyug city view **Edge:** Reeded and lettered **Edge Lettering:** Denomination repeated

Date	Mintage	F	VF	XF	Unc	BU
2007ММД	2,500,000	—	—	—	4.00	6.00
2007СПМД	2,500,000	—	—	—	4.00	6.00

Y# 965 10 ROUBLES

8.3000 g., Bi-Metallic Copper-Nickel center in Brass ring, 27 mm. **Obv:** Value with latent image in zero within circle and sprays **Rev:** Gdov church **Edge:** Reeded and lettered **Edge Lettering:** Denomination repeated

Date	Mintage	F	VF	XF	Unc	BU
2007ММД	2,500,000	—	—	—	4.00	6.00
2007СПМД	2,500,000	—	—	—	4.00	6.00

Y# 970 10 ROUBLES

8.5700 g., Bi-Metallic Copper-Nickel center in Brass ring, 27.08 mm. **Obv:** Value with latent image in zero within circle and sprays **Obv. Legend:** БАНК РОССИИ **Rev:** Rostovskaya Oblast arms **Edge:** Reeded and lettered **Edge Lettering:** Denomination repeated

Date	Mintage	F	VF	XF	Unc	BU
2007СПМД	10,000,000	—	—	—	4.00	6.00

Y# 971 10 ROUBLES

8.5700 g., Bi-Metallic Copper-Nickel center in Brass ring, 27.08 mm. **Obv:** Value with latent image in zero within circle and sprays **Obv. Legend:** БАНК РОССИИ **Rev:** Khakassia Republic arms **Edge:** Reeded and lettered **Edge Lettering:** Denomination repeated

Date	Mintage	F	VF	XF	Unc	BU
2007СПМД	10,000,000	—	—	—	4.00	6.00

Y# 972 10 ROUBLES

8.5700 g., Bi-Metallic Copper-Nickel center in Brass ring, 27.08 mm. **Obv:** Value with latent image in zero within circle and sprays **Obv. Legend:** БАНК РОССИИ **Rev:** Bashkortostan Republic arms **Edge:** Reeded and lettered **Edge Lettering:** Denomination repeated

Date	Mintage	F	VF	XF	Unc	BU
2007ММД	10,000,000	—	—	—	4.00	6.00

Y# 973 10 ROUBLES

8.5700 g., Bi-Metallic Copper-Nickel center in Brass ring, 27.08 mm. **Obv:** Value with latent image in zero within circle and sprays **Obv. Legend:** БАНК РОССИИ **Rev:** Archangelskaya Oblast arms **Edge:** Reeded and lettered **Edge Lettering:** Denomination repeated

Date	Mintage	F	VF	XF	Unc	BU
2007СПМД	10,000,000	—	—	—	4.00	6.00

Y# 974 10 ROUBLES

8.5700 g., Bi-Metallic Copper-Nickel center in brass ring., 27.08 mm. **Obv:** Value with latent image in zero within circle and sprays **Obv. Legend:** БАНК РОССИИ **Rev:** Novosibirskaya Oblast arms **Edge:** Reeded and lettered **Edge Lettering:** Denomination repeated

Date	Mintage	F	VF	XF	Unc	BU
2007ММД	10,000,000	—	—	—	4.00	6.00

Y# 993 10 ROUBLES

Bi-Metallic Copper-Nickel center in Brass ring **Subject:** Lipetskaya Oblast

Date	Mintage	F	VF	XF	Unc	BU
2007ММД	10,000,000	—	—	—	2.00	3.50

Y# 975 10 ROUBLES

8.2000 g., Bi-Metallic Copper-Nickel center in brass ring., 27.1 mm. **Obv:** Value with latent image in zero within circle and sprays **Obv. Legend:** БАНК РОССИИ **Rev:** Udmurtia Republic arms **Rev. Legend:** УДМУРТСКАЯ РЕСПУБЛИКА **Edge:** Reeded and lettered **Edge Lettering:** Denomination repeated

Date	Mintage	F	VF	XF	Unc	BU
2008ММД	5,000,000	—	—	0.90	2.25	3.00
2008СПМД	5,000,000	—	—	0.90	2.25	3.00

Y# 976 10 ROUBLES

8.2800 g., Bi-Metallic Copper-Nickel center in brass ring., 27.1 mm. **Series:** Ancient cities **Subject:** Vladimir **Obv:** Value with latent image in zero within circle and sprays **Obv. Legend:** БАНК РОССИИ **Rev:** Small shield at upper left above city view **Rev. Legend:** ВЛАДИМИР **Edge:** Reeded and lettered **Edge Lettering:** Denomination repeated

Date	Mintage	F	VF	XF	Unc	BU
2008ММД	2,500,000	—	—	0.90	2.25	3.00
2008СПМД	2,500,000	—	—	0.90	2.25	3.00

Y# 977 10 ROUBLES

8.2300 g., Bi-Metallic Copper-Nickel center in Brass ring, 27 mm. **Obv:** Value with latent image in zero within circle and sprays **Obv. Legend:** БАНК РОССИИ **Rev:** Astrakhanskaya Oblast arms **Edge:** Reeded and lettered **Edge Lettering:** Denomination repeated

Date	Mintage	F	VF	XF	Unc	BU
2008ММД	5,000,000	—	—	0.90	2.25	3.00
2008СПМД	5,000,000	—	—	0.90	2.25	3.00

Y# 978 10 ROUBLES

8.1600 g., Bi-Metallic Copper-Nickel center in brass ring, 27 mm. **Obv:** Value with latent image in zero within circle and sprays **Obv. Legend:** БАНК РОССИИ **Rev:** Sverdlovskaya Oblast arms **Edge:** Reeded and lettered **Edge Lettering:** Denomination repeated

Date	Mintage	F	VF	XF	Unc	BU
2008ММД	5,000,000	—	—	0.90	2.25	3.00
2008СПМД	5,000,000	—	—	0.90	2.25	3.00

Y# 986 10 ROUBLES

8.0800 g., Bi-Metallic Copper-Nickel center in Brass ring, 27 mm. **Rev:** Azov town view

Date	Mintage	F	VF	XF	Unc	BU
2008ММД	2,500,000	—	—	—	2.00	3.50
2008СПМД	2,500,000	—	—	—	2.00	3.50

Y# 991 10 ROUBLES

8.0800 g., Bi-Metallic Copper-Nickel center in Brass ring, 27 mm. **Rev:** Kabardino-Balkaria Republic Arms

Date	Mintage	F	VF	XF	Unc	BU
2008ММД	5,000,000	—	—	—	2.00	3.50
2008СПМД	5,000,000	—	—	—	2.00	3.50

Y# 994 10 ROUBLES

Bi-Metallic Copper-Nickel center in Brass ring **Subject:** Priozersk

Date	Mintage	F	VF	XF	Unc	BU
2008ММД	2,500,000	—	—	—	2.00	3.50
2008СПМД	2,500,000	—	—	—	2.00	3.50

Y# 995 10 ROUBLES

Bi-Metallic Copper-Nickel center in Brass ring **Subject:** Smolensk

Date	Mintage	F	VF	XF	Unc	BU
2008ММД	2,500,000	—	—	—	2.00	3.50
2008СПМД	2,500,000	—	—	—	2.00	3.50

Y# 998 10 ROUBLES

5.6300 g., Brass Plated Steel, 22 mm. **Obv:** Double heavded eagle **Rev:** Value

Date	Mintage	F	VF	XF	Unc	BU
2009ММД	—	—	—	—	2.50	4.00
2010ММД	—	—	—	—	2.50	4.00
2010СПМД	—	—	—	—	2.50	4.00

Y# 982 10 ROUBLES

8.0800 g., Bi-Metallic Copper-Nickel center in Brass ring, 27 mm. **Rev:** Kaluga town view

Date	Mintage	F	VF	XF	Unc	BU
2009ММД	2,500,000	—	—	—	2.00	3.50
2009СПМД	2,500,000	—	—	—	2.00	3.50

Y# 983 10 ROUBLES

8.0800 g., Bi-Metallic Copper-Nickel center in Brass ring, 27 mm. **Rev:** Vyborg town view

Date	Mintage	F	VF	XF	Unc	BU
2009ММД	2,500,000	—	—	—	2.00	3.50
2009СПМД	2,500,000	—	—	—	2.00	3.50

Y# 984 10 ROUBLES

8.0800 g., Bi-Metallic Copper-Nickel center in Brass ring, 27 mm. **Rev:** Galich town view

Date	Mintage	F	VF	XF	Unc	BU
2009ММД	2,500,000	—	—	—	2.00	3.50
2009СПМД	2,500,000	—	—	—	2.00	3.50

Y# 985 10 ROUBLES
8.0800 g., Bi-Metallic Copper-Nickel center in Brass ring, 27 mm.
Rev: Kalmykiya Republic arms

Date	Mintage	F	VF	XF	Unc	BU
2009ММД	5,000,000	—	—	—	2.00	3.50
2009СПМД	5,000,000	—	—	—	2.00	3.50

Y# 987 10 ROUBLES
8.0800 g., Bi-Metallic Copper-Nickel center in Brass ring, 27 mm.
Rev: Adygeya Republic arms

Date	Mintage	F	VF	XF	Unc	BU
2009ММД	5,000,000	—	—	—	2.00	3.50
2009СПМД	5,000,000	—	—	—	2.00	3.50

Y# 988 10 ROUBLES
8.0800 g., Bi-Metallic Copper-Nickel center in Brass ring, 27 mm.
Rev: Veliky Novgorod arms

Date	Mintage	F	VF	XF	Unc	BU
2009ММД	2,500,000	—	—	—	2.00	3.50
2009СПМД	2,500,000	—	—	—	2.00	3.50

Y# 989 10 ROUBLES
8.0800 g., Bi-Metallic Copper-Nickel center in Brass ring, 27 mm.
Rev: Jewish Autonomous Oblast Arms

Date	Mintage	F	VF	XF	Unc	BU
2009ММД	5,000,000	—	—	—	2.00	3.50
2009СПМД	5,000,000	—	—	—	2.00	3.50

Y# 996 10 ROUBLES
Bi-Metallic Copper-Nickel center in Brass ring **Subject:** Komi Republic

Date	Mintage	F	VF	XF	Unc	BU
2009СПМД	10,000,000	—	—	—	2.00	3.50

Y# 997 10 ROUBLES
Bi-Metallic Copper-Nickel center in Brass ring
Subject: Kirovskaya Oblast

Date	Mintage	F	VF	XF	Unc	BU
2009СПМД	10,000,000	—	—	—	2.00	3.50

Y# 678 25 ROUBLES
173.2900 g., 0.9000 Silver 5.0141 oz. ASW, 60 mm. **Subject:** Bolshoi Theater 225 Years **Obv:** Double-headed eagle **Rev:** Dancing couple scene **Edge:** Reeded **Note:** Illustration reduced.

Date	Mintage	F	VF	XF	Unc	BU
2001 Proof	2,000	Value: 275				

Y# 683 25 ROUBLES
173.2900 g., 0.9000 Silver 5.0141 oz. ASW, 60 mm.
Subject: Siberian Exploration **Obv:** Double-headed eagle **Rev:** Standing king and river boats **Edge:** Reeded **Note:** Illustration reduced.

Date	Mintage	F	VF	XF	Unc	BU
2001 Proof	1,000	Value: 300				

Y# 794 25 ROUBLES
173.1300 g., 0.9000 Silver 5.0094 oz. ASW, 60.2 mm.
Subject: Foundation of Russian Savings Banks **Obv:** Double-headed eagle **Rev:** Czar Nicholas I and document **Edge:** Reeded

Date	Mintage	F	VF	XF	Unc	BU
2001(m) Proof	10,500	Value: 175				

Y# 687 25 ROUBLES
3.2000 g., 0.9990 Gold 0.1028 oz. AGW, 16 mm.
Subject: Bolshoi Theater **Obv:** Double-headed eagle
Rev: Ballerina **Edge:** Reeded

Date	Mintage	F	VF	XF	Unc	BU
2001 Proof	2,500	Value: 145				

Y# 777 25 ROUBLES
173.2900 g., 0.9000 Silver 5.0141 oz. ASW, 60 mm.
Subject: Czar Alexander I **Obv:** Double-headed eagle
Rev: Head right and crowned double-headed eagle above document text **Edge:** Reeded **Note:** Illustration reduced.

Date	Mintage	F	VF	XF	Unc	BU
2002(m) Proof	1,500	Value: 285				

Y# 785 25 ROUBLES
173.2900 g., 0.9000 Silver 5.0141 oz. ASW, 60 mm. **Subject:** Admiral Nakhimov **Obv:** Double-headed eagle **Rev:** Admiral watching naval battle **Edge:** Reeded **Note:** Illustration reduced.

Date	Mintage	F	VF	XF	Unc	BU
2002(sp) Proof	2,000	Value: 225				

Y# 790 25 ROUBLES
173.2900 g., 0.9000 Silver 5.0141 oz. ASW, 60 mm. **Subject:** Hermitage **Obv:** Double-headed eagle **Rev:** Staircase viewed through doorway **Edge:** Reeded **Note:** Illustration reduced.

Date	Mintage	F	VF	XF	Unc	BU
2002(sp) Proof	2,000	Value: 225				

Y# 743 25 ROUBLES
3.2000 g., 0.9990 Gold 0.1028 oz. AGW, 16 mm.
Subject: Zodiac Signs: **Obv:** Double-headed eagle within beaded circle **Rev:** Leo **Edge:** Reeded

Date	Mintage	F	VF	XF	Unc	BU
2002 Proof	10,000	Value: 145				

Y# 763 25 ROUBLES
3.2000 g., 0.9990 Gold 0.1028 oz. AGW, 16 mm.
Subject: Zodiac Signs **Obv:** Double-headed eagle within beaded circle **Rev:** Capricorn **Edge:** Reeded

Date	Mintage	F	VF	XF	Unc	BU
2002(m)	10,000	—	—	—	—	200

Y# 764 25 ROUBLES
3.2000 g., 0.9990 Gold 0.1028 oz. AGW, 16 mm.
Subject: Zodiac Signs **Obv:** Double-headed eagle within beaded circle **Rev:** Virgo **Edge:** Reeded

Date	Mintage	F	VF	XF	Unc	BU
2002(sp)	10,000	—	—	—	—	200

Y# 765 25 ROUBLES
3.2000 g., 0.9990 Gold 0.1028 oz. AGW, 16 mm.
Subject: Zodiac Signs **Obv:** Double-headed eagle within beaded circle **Rev:** Sagittarius **Edge:** Reeded

Date	Mintage	F	VF	XF	Unc	BU
2002(SP)	10,000	—	—	—	—	200

Y# 767 25 ROUBLES
3.2000 g., 0.9990 Gold 0.1028 oz. AGW, 16 mm.
Subject: Zodiac signs **Obv:** Double-headed eagle within beaded circle **Rev:** Scorpio **Edge:** Reeded

Date	Mintage	F	VF	XF	Unc	BU
2002(m)	10,000	—	—	—	—	200

Y# 769 25 ROUBLES
3.2000 g., 0.9990 Gold 0.1028 oz. AGW **Subject:** Zodiac Signs **Obv:** Double-headed eagle within beaded circle **Rev:** Libra **Edge:** Reeded

Date	Mintage	F	VF	XF	Unc	BU
2002(sp)	10,000	—	—	—	—	200

Y# 821 25 ROUBLES
3.2000 g., 0.9990 Gold 0.1028 oz. AGW, 16 mm.
Subject: Zodiac signs **Obv:** Double-headed eagle within beaded circle **Rev:** Cancer **Edge:** Reeded

Date	Mintage	F	VF	XF	Unc	BU
2003(sp)	50,000	—	—	—	—	200

Y# 864 25 ROUBLES
172.8000 g., 0.9000 Silver 4.9999 oz. ASW, 60 mm. **Rev:** St. Sercius Monastery

Date	Mintage	F	VF	XF	Unc	BU
2003 Proof	2,000	Value: 275				

Y# 865 25 ROUBLES
172.8000 g., 0.9000 Silver 4.9999 oz. ASW, 60 mm.
Rev: Shlisselburg

Date	Mintage	F	VF	XF	Unc	BU
2003(m) Proof	2,000	Value: 275				

Y# 866 25 ROUBLES
172.8000 g., 0.9000 Silver 4.9999 oz. ASW, 60 mm.
Rev: Kamchatka

Date	Mintage	F	VF	XF	Unc	BU
2003	2,000	Value: 275				

Y# 830 25 ROUBLES
177.9600 g., 0.9000 Bi-Metallic .900 Silver 172.78 g planchet with .900 Gold 5.18 g insert 5.1492 oz., 60 mm. **Subject:** Monetary reform of Peter the Great **Obv:** Double-headed eagle **Rev:** Gold insert replicating the obverse and reverse designs of a 1704 one rouble coin **Edge:** Reeded **Note:** Illustration reduced.

Date	Mintage	F	VF	XF	Unc	BU
2004(sp) Proof	1,000	Value: 875				

Y# 867 25 ROUBLES
172.8000 g., 0.9000 Silver 4.9999 oz. ASW, 60 mm.
Rev: Valaam Church

Date	Mintage	F	VF	XF	Unc	BU
2004	1,500	Value: 285				

Y# 898 25 ROUBLES
3.2000 g., 0.9990 Gold 0.1028 oz. AGW, 16 mm. **Obv:** Double-headed eagle **Rev:** Gemini twins **Edge:** Reeded

Date	Mintage	F	VF	XF	Unc	BU
2005	10,000	—	—	—	—	200

Y# 900 25 ROUBLES
3.2000 g., 0.9990 Gold 0.1028 oz. AGW, 16 mm. **Obv:** Double-headed eagle **Rev:** Cancer crawfish **Edge:** Reeded

Date	Mintage	F	VF	XF	Unc	BU
2005 Proof	10,000			Value: 145		

Y# 902 25 ROUBLES
3.2000 g., 0.9990 Gold 0.1028 oz. AGW, 16 mm. **Obv:** Double-headed eagle **Rev:** Leo lion **Edge:** Reeded

Date	Mintage	F	VF	XF	Unc	BU
2005	10,000	—	—	—	—	200

Y# 915 25 ROUBLES
3.2000 g., 0.9990 Gold 0.1028 oz. AGW, 16 mm. **Obv:** Double-headed eagle **Rev:** Virgos standing lady **Edge:** Reeded

Date	Mintage	F	VF	XF	Unc	BU
2005 Proof	10,000			Value: 145		

Y# 920 25 ROUBLES
3.2000 g., 0.9990 Gold 0.1028 oz. AGW, 16 mm. **Obv:** Double-headed eagle **Rev:** Two stylized birds forming balance scale **Edge:** Reeded

Date	Mintage	F	VF	XF	Unc	BU
2005	10,000	—	—	—	—	200

Y# 922 25 ROUBLES
3.2000 g., 0.9990 Gold 0.1028 oz. AGW, 16 mm. **Obv:** Double-headed eagle **Rev:** Scorpio scorpion **Edge:** Reeded

Date	Mintage	F	VF	XF	Unc	BU
2005	10,000	—	—	—	—	200

Y# 927 25 ROUBLES
3.2000 g., 0.9990 Gold 0.1028 oz. AGW, 16 mm. **Obv:** Double-headed eagle **Rev:** Sagittarius the archer **Edge:** Reeded

Date	Mintage	F	VF	XF	Unc	BU
2005	10,000	—	—	—	—	200

Y# 929 25 ROUBLES
3.2000 g., 0.9990 Gold 0.1028 oz. AGW, 16 mm. **Obv:** Double-headed eagle **Rev:** Capricorn as half goat and fish **Edge:** Reeded

Date	Mintage	F	VF	XF	Unc	BU
2005	10,000	—	—	—	—	200

Y# 931 25 ROUBLES
3.2000 g., 0.9990 Gold 0.1028 oz. AGW, 16 mm. **Obv:** Double-headed eagle **Rev:** Pisces as catfish and sturgeon **Edge:** Reeded

Date	Mintage	F	VF	XF	Unc	BU
2005	10,000	—	—	—	—	200

Y# 933 25 ROUBLES
3.2000 g., 0.9990 Gold 0.1028 oz. AGW, 16 mm. **Obv:** Double-headed eagle **Rev:** Aries ram **Edge:** Reeded

Date	Mintage	F	VF	XF	Unc	BU
2005	10,000	—	—	—	—	200

Y# 935 25 ROUBLES
3.2000 g., 0.9990 Gold 0.1028 oz. AGW, 16 mm. **Obv:** Double-headed eagle **Rev:** Taurus bull **Edge:** Reeded

Date	Mintage	F	VF	XF	Unc	BU
2005	10,000	—	—	—	—	200

Y# 937 25 ROUBLES
3.2000 g., 0.9990 Gold 0.1028 oz. AGW, 16 mm. **Obv:** Double-headed eagle **Rev:** Aquarius water carrier **Edge:** Reeded

Date	Mintage	F	VF	XF	Unc	BU
2005	10,000	—	—	—	—	200

Y# 924 25 ROUBLES
169.0000 g., 0.9250 Silver 5.0258 oz. ASW, 60 mm. **Subject:** 625th Anniversary - Battle of Kulikovo **Obv:** Double-headed eagle **Rev:** Mounted warriors above and below crossed swords **Edge:** Reeded **Note:** Illustration reduced.

Date	Mintage	F	VF	XF	Unc	BU
2005 Proof	1,500			Value: 285		

Y# 969 25 ROUBLES
169.0000 g., 0.9250 Silver 5.0258 oz. ASW, 60.00 mm. **Obv:** Two-headed eagle **Rev:** Vyatka St. Trifon Monastery of the Assumption, Kirov **Edge:** Reeded **Note:** Illustration reduced

Date	Mintage	F	VF	XF	Unc	BU
2007(sp) Proof	2,000			Value: 275		

Y# 679 50 ROUBLES
8.7500 g., 0.9990 Gold 0.2810 oz. AGW, 22.6 mm. **Subject:** Bolshoi Theater **Obv:** Double-headed eagle within beaded circle **Rev:** Dueling figures **Edge:** Reeded

Date	Mintage	F	VF	XF	Unc	BU
2001 Proof	2,000			Value: 350		

Y# 684 50 ROUBLES
8.7500 g., 0.9000 Gold 0.2532 oz. AGW, 22.6 mm. **Subject:** Siberian Exploration **Obv:** Double-headed eagle within beaded circle **Rev:** Head with hat 1/4 right and boat **Edge:** Reeded

Date	Mintage	F	VF	XF	Unc	BU
2001 Proof	1,500			Value: 345		

Y# 757 50 ROUBLES
8.6444 g., 0.9000 Gold 0.2501 oz. AGW, 22.6 mm. **Subject:** Olympics **Obv:** Double-headed eagle within beaded circle **Rev:** Figure skater and flying eagle **Edge:** Reeded

Date	Mintage	F	VF	XF	Unc	BU
2002 Proof	3,000			Value: 320		

Y# 782 50 ROUBLES
7.8900 g., 0.9990 Gold 0.2534 oz. AGW, 22.6 mm. **Subject:** Works of Dionissy **Obv:** Double-headed eagle within beaded circle **Rev:** Half-length figure holding child flanked by double headed eagle and church **Edge:** Reeded

Date	Mintage	F	VF	XF	Unc	BU
2002(m) Proof	1,500			Value: 345		

Y# 786 50 ROUBLES
8.7500 g., 0.9000 Gold 0.2532 oz. AGW, 22.6 mm. **Subject:** Admiral Nakhimov **Obv:** Double-headed eagle within beaded circle **Rev:** Bust facing within circle above flags and anchor **Edge:** Reeded

Date	Mintage	F	VF	XF	Unc	BU
2002(sp) Proof	1,500			Value: 345		

Y# 788 50 ROUBLES
8.7500 g., 0.9000 Gold 0.2532 oz. AGW, 22.6 mm. **Subject:** World Cup Soccer **Obv:** Double-headed eagle within beaded circle **Rev:** Stylized player kicking soccer ball **Edge:** Reeded

Date	Mintage	F	VF	XF	Unc	BU
2002(m) Proof	3,000			Value: 320		

Y# 822 50 ROUBLES
7.8900 g., 0.9990 Gold 0.2534 oz. AGW, 22.6 mm. **Subject:** Zodiac Signs **Obv:** Double-headed eagle within beaded circle **Rev:** Virgo **Edge:** Reeded

Date	Mintage	F	VF	XF	Unc	BU
2003(sp)	30,000	—	—	—	—	315

Y# 823 50 ROUBLES
7.8900 g., 0.9990 Gold 0.2534 oz. AGW, 22.6 mm. **Subject:** Zodiac signs **Obv:** Double-headed eagle within beaded circle **Rev:** Libra **Edge:** Reeded

Date	Mintage	F	VF	XF	Unc	BU
2003(m)	30,000	—	—	—	—	315

Y# 868 50 ROUBLES
8.6400 g., 0.9000 Gold 0.2500 oz. AGW, 23 mm. **Rev:** Peter I monetary reform

Date	Mintage	F	VF	XF	Unc	BU
2003(m) Proof	1,500			Value: 335		

Y# 869 50 ROUBLES
8.6400 g., 0.9000 Gold 0.2500 oz. AGW, 23 mm. **Rev:** Ski race

Date	Mintage	F	VF	XF	Unc	BU
2003(m) Proof	1,500			Value: 325		

Y# 870 50 ROUBLES
8.6400 g., 0.9000 Gold 0.2500 oz. AGW, 23 mm. **Rev:** Soccer player

Date	Mintage	F	VF	XF	Unc	BU
2004(sp) Proof	1,000			Value: 350		

Y# 871 50 ROUBLES
8.6400 g., 0.9000 Gold 0.2500 oz. AGW, 23 mm. **Rev:** Olympic athletes

Date	Mintage	F	VF	XF	Unc	BU
2004(m) Proof	2,000			Value: 320		

Y# 872 50 ROUBLES
8.6400 g., 0.9000 Gold 0.2500 oz. AGW, 23 mm. **Rev:** Virgin of the Son Icon

Date	Mintage	F	VF	XF	Unc	BU
2004(m) Proof	1,500			Value: 340		

Y# 894 50 ROUBLES
7.8900 g., 0.9990 Gold 0.2534 oz. AGW, 22.6 mm. **Subject:** 60th Anniversary - Victory Over Germany **Obv:** Double-headed eagle **Rev:** 60th Anniversary - Victory Over Germany medal **Edge:** Reeded

Date	Mintage	F	VF	XF	Unc	BU
2005 Proof	7,000			Value: 320		

Y# 907   50 ROUBLES
7.8900 g., 0.9990 Gold 0.2534 oz. AGW, 22.6 mm.
Subject: Helsinki Games **Obv:** Double-headed eagle
Rev: Stylized track and field athletes **Edge:** Reeded

Date	Mintage	F	VF	XF	Unc	BU
2005 Proof	1,500	Value: 335				

Y# 911   50 ROUBLES
7.8900 g., 0.9990 Gold 0.2534 oz. AGW, 22.6 mm.
Obv: Double-headed eagle **Rev:** Kazan University Building
Edge: Reeded

Date	Mintage	F	VF	XF	Unc	BU
2005 Proof	1,500	Value: 340				

Y# 795   100 ROUBLES
1111.1200 g., 0.9000 Silver 32.149 oz. ASW, 100 mm.
Subject: The Bark Sedov **Obv:** Double-headed eagle **Rev:** Ship flanked by compass and cameo **Edge:** Reeded **Note:** Illustration reduced.

Date	Mintage	F	VF	XF	Unc	BU
2001(m) Proof	500	Value: 2,000				

Y# 681   100 ROUBLES
1111.1000 g., 0.9000 Silver 32.149 oz. ASW, 100 mm.
Subject: 40th Anniversary of Manned Space Flight - Yuri Gagarin **Obv:** Double-headed eagle **Rev:** Astronaut and rocket in space **Edge:** Reeded **Note:** Illustration reduced.

Date	Mintage	F	VF	XF	Unc	BU
2001 Proof	750	Value: 1,800				

Y# 689   100 ROUBLES
1111.1000 g., 0.9000 Silver 32.149 oz. ASW, 100 mm.
Subject: Bolshoi Theater 225 Years **Obv:** Double-headed eagle **Rev:** Casino gambling scene **Edge:** Reeded **Note:** Illustration reduced.

Date	Mintage	F	VF	XF	Unc	BU
2001 Proof	500	Value: 1,850				

Y# 685   100 ROUBLES
17.4500 g., 0.9000 Gold 0.5049 oz. AGW, 30 mm.
Subject: Siberian Exploration **Obv:** Double-headed eagle within beaded circle **Rev:** Head and silhouette left, sailboat and other designs **Edge:** Reeded

Date	Mintage	F	VF	XF	Unc	BU
2001 Proof	1,000	Value: 650				

Y# 688   100 ROUBLES
15.7200 g., 0.9990 Gold 0.5049 oz. AGW, 30 mm. **Subject:** Bolshoi Theater 225 Years **Obv:** Double-headed eagle within beaded circle **Rev:** Three dancers with swords **Edge:** Reeded

Date	Mintage	F	VF	XF	Unc	BU
2001 Proof	1,500	Value: 650				

Y# 783   100 ROUBLES
1111.1200 g., 0.9000 Silver 32.149 oz. ASW, 100 mm.
Subject: Works of Dionissy **Obv:** Double-headed eagle **Rev:** St. Ferapont Monastery in the center of a fresco covered cross **Edge:** Reeded **Note:** Illustration reduced.

Date	Mintage	F	VF	XF	Unc	BU
2002(sp) Prooflike	500	—	—	—	—	900

Y# 789   100 ROUBLES
1111.1200 g., 0.9000 Silver 32.149 oz. ASW, 100 mm.
Subject: World Cup Soccer **Obv:** Double-headed eagle **Rev:** Soccer ball design with map and players **Edge:** Reeded **Note:** Illustration reduced.

Date	Mintage	F	VF	XF	Unc	BU
2002(sp) Proof	500	Value: 1,850				

Y# 791   100 ROUBLES
1111.1200 g., 0.9000 Silver 32.149 oz. ASW, 100 mm.
Subject: Hermitage **Obv:** Double-headed eagle **Rev:** Statues and arches **Edge:** Reeded **Note:** Illustration reduced.

Date	Mintage	F	VF	XF	Unc	BU
2002(sp) Proof	1,000	Value: 1,500				

Y# 792   100 ROUBLES
17.4500 g., 0.9000 Gold 0.5049 oz. AGW, 30 mm.
Subject: Hermitage **Obv:** Double-headed eagle within beaded circle **Rev:** Ancient battle scene sculpted on comb **Edge:** Reeded

Date	Mintage	F	VF	XF	Unc	BU
2002(sp) Proof	1,000	Value: 900				

Y# 873   100 ROUBLES
1111.1200 g., 0.9000 Silver 32.149 oz. ASW, 100 mm. **Rev:** St. Petersburg

Date	Mintage	F	VF	XF	Unc	BU
2003(m) Proof	1,000	Value: 1,650				

Y# 874   100 ROUBLES
17.4500 g., 0.9000 Gold 0.5049 oz. AGW, 30 mm.
Rev: Petrozavodsk

Date	Mintage	F	VF	XF	Unc	BU
2003(m) Proof	1,000	Value: 900				

Y# 875   100 ROUBLES
17.4500 g., 0.9000 Gold 0.5049 oz. AGW, 30 mm.
Rev: Kamchatka

Date	Mintage	F	VF	XF	Unc	BU
2003(sp) Proof	1,500	Value: 850				

Y# 832   100 ROUBLES
17.2800 g., 0.9000 Gold 0.5000 oz. AGW, 30 mm. **Subject:** 2nd Kamchatka Expedition **Obv:** Double-headed eagle **Rev:** Shaman and two seated men **Edge:** Reeded

Date	Mintage	F	VF	XF	Unc	BU
2004(sp) Proof	1,500	Value: 850				

Y# 831   100 ROUBLES
1000.0000 g., 0.9000 Silver 28.934 oz. ASW, 100 mm.
Obv: Double-headed eagle **Rev:** Panel of icons painted by Theophanes the Greek **Edge:** Reeded **Note:** Illustration reduced.

Date	Mintage	F	VF	XF	Unc	BU
2004(sp) Proof	500	Value: 1,850				

Y# 876   100 ROUBLES
1111.1200 g., 0.9000 Silver 32.149 oz. ASW, 100 mm.
Rev: Annunciation Cathedral Iconostasis

Date	Mintage	F	VF	XF	Unc	BU
2004(sp) Proof	500	Value: 2,000				

Y# 895   100 ROUBLES
1083.7400 g., 0.9250 Silver 32.228 oz. ASW, 100 mm.
Subject: 60th Anniversary Victory Over Germany **Obv:** Double-headed eagle **Rev:** Decorated locomotive returning soldiers circa 1945 **Edge:** Reeded **Note:** Illustration reduced.

Date	Mintage	F	VF	XF	Unc	BU
2005 Proof	2,000	Value: 1,750				

Y# 912   100 ROUBLES
1083.7400 g., 0.9250 Silver 32.228 oz. ASW, 100 mm.
Obv: Double-headed eagle **Rev:** Kazan city view with mausoleums **Edge:** Reeded **Note:** Illustration reduced.

Date	Mintage	F	VF	XF	Unc	BU
2005 Proof	500	Value: 1,750				

Y# 925   100 ROUBLES
1083.7400 g., 0.9250 Silver 32.228 oz. ASW, 100 mm.
Subject: 625th Anniversary - Battle of Kulikovo **Obv:** Double-headed eagle **Rev:** Battle of Kulikovo beginning scene
Edge: Reeded **Note:** Illustration reduced.

Date	Mintage	F	VF	XF	Unc	BU
2005 Proof	500	Value: 1,750				

Y# 877   200 ROUBLES
3342.3899 g., 0.9000 Silver 96.710 oz. ASW, 130 mm.
Rev: Peter I monetary reform

Date	Mintage	F	VF	XF	Unc	BU
2003(sp) Proof	300	Value: 4,000				

Y# 796   1000 ROUBLES
156.4000 g., 0.9990 Gold 5.0231 oz. AGW, 50 mm. **Subject:** The Bark Sedov **Obv:** Double-headed eagle **Rev:** Four-masted sailing ship **Edge:** Reeded

Date	Mintage	F	VF	XF	Unc	BU
2001(m) Proof	250	Value: 6,500				

Y# 878   1000 ROUBLES
156.4000 g., 0.9990 Gold 5.0231 oz. AGW, 50 mm. **Rev:** Cronstadt

Date	Mintage	F	VF	XF	Unc	BU
2003(m) Proof	250	Value: 6,500				

Y# 784   10000 ROUBLES
1001.1000 g., 0.9990 Gold 32.152 oz. AGW, 100 mm.
Subject: Works of Dionissy **Obv:** Double-headed eagle
Rev: Interior view of the carved portal of the Virgin of the Nativity Church **Edge:** Reeded **Note:** Illustration reduced.

Date	Mintage	F	VF	XF	Unc	BU
2002(sp) Proof	100	Value: 40,000				

Y# 879   10000 ROUBLES
1001.1000 g., 0.9990 Gold 32.152 oz. AGW, 100 mm.
Rev: St. Petersburg area map

Date	Mintage	F	VF	XF	Unc	BU
2003 Proof	200	Value: 40,000				

Y# 880   10000 ROUBLES
1001.1000 g., 0.9990 Gold 32.152 oz. AGW, 100 mm.
Rev: Church of the Transfiguration of the Savior, Novgorod

Date	Mintage	F	VF	XF	Unc	BU
2004 Proof	100	Value: 40,000				

Y# 896   10000 ROUBLES
1001.1000 g., 0.9990 Gold 32.152 oz. AGW, 100 mm.
Subject: 60th Anniversary - Victory Over Germany **Obv:** Double-headed eagle **Rev:** Soldiers dishonoring captured Nazi flags and standards **Edge:** Reeded **Note:** Illustration reduced.

Date	Mintage	F	VF	XF	Unc	BU
2005 Proof	250	Value: 40,000				

Y# 913   10000 ROUBLES
1001.1000 g., 0.9990 Gold 32.152 oz. AGW, 100 mm.
Obv: Two headed eagle **Rev:** Kazan Kremlin view **Edge:** Reeded **Note:** Illustration reduced.

Date	Mintage	F	VF	XF	Unc	BU
2005 Proof	150	Value: 40,000				

MINT SETS

KM#	Date	Mintage	Identification	Issue Price	Mkt Val
MS44	2002 (7)	—	Y#600-603, 797-799, plus mint medal	7.50	15.00

RWANDA

The Republic of Rwanda, located in central Africa between the Republic of the Congo and Tanzania, has an area of 10,169 sq. mi. (26,340 sq. km.) and a population of 7.3 million. Capital: Kigali. The economy is based on agriculture and mining. Coffee and tin are exported.

For earlier coinage see Belgian Congo, and Rwanda and Burundi.

MINT MARKS
(a) - Paris, privy marks only
(b) - Brussels, privy marks only

MONETARY SYSTEM
100 Centimes = 1 Franc

REPUBLIC

STANDARD COINAGE

KM# 22   FRANC
0.0700 g., Aluminum, 16 mm. **Obv:** National arms
Rev: Sorghum plant **Edge:** Plain

Date	Mintage	F	VF	XF	Unc	BU
2003	—	—	—	0.25	0.65	1.00

KM# 23   5 FRANCS
2.9600 g., Brass Plated Steel, 20 mm. **Obv:** National arms
Rev: Coffee plant **Edge:** Plain

Date	Mintage	F	VF	XF	Unc	BU
2003	—	—	—	0.25	0.65	1.00

KM# 24   10 FRANCS
5.0000 g., Brass Plated Steel, 23.9 mm. **Obv:** National arms
Rev: Banana tree **Edge:** Plain

Date	Mintage	F	VF	XF	Unc	BU
2003	—	—	—	0.45	1.00	1.50

KM# 25   20 FRANCS
3.5000 g., Nickel Clad Steel, 20 mm. **Obv:** National arms
Rev: Coffee plant seedling **Edge:** Reeded

Date	Mintage	F	VF	XF	Unc	BU
2003	—	—	—	—	1.75	2.00

KM# 26   50 FRANCS
5.8000 g., Nickel Clad Steel, 24 mm. **Obv:** National arms
Rev: Ear of corn within husks **Edge:** Reeded

Date	Mintage	F	VF	XF	Unc	BU
2003(a)	—	—	—	—	2.50	4.00

KM# 32   100 FRANCS
Bi-Metallic **Obv:** Shield **Rev:** Value

Date	Mintage	F	VF	XF	Unc	BU
2007	—	—	—	—	5.00	6.50

KM# 28   200 FRANCS
1.0000 g., 0.9990 Gold 0.0321 oz. AGW, 13.9 mm.
Subject: 75th Birthday Dian Fossey **Obv:** National arms
Obv. Legend: BANKI NASIYONALI Y'U RWANDA **Rev:** Fossey facing holding monkey **Edge:** Plain

Date	Mintage	F	VF	XF	Unc	BU
2007 Proof	15,000	Value: 85.00				

KM# 30   500 FRANCS
22.2000 g., 0.9000 Silver 0.6423 oz. ASW **Obv:** National arms
Obv. Legend: BANQUE NATIONALE DU RWANDA **Rev:** Stalk of bananas on leaves

Date	Mintage	F	VF	XF	Unc	BU
2002(a) Proof	500	Value: 85.00				

KM# 31   500 FRANCS
22.2000 g., 0.9000 Silver 0.6423 oz. ASW **Subject:** Euro Parity
Obv: Arms **Rev:** Plant

Date	Mintage	F	VF	XF	Unc	BU
2002 Proof	500	Value: 65.00				

KM# 27   500 FRANCS
20.0000 g., 0.9990 Silver 0.6423 oz. ASW, 38 mm.
Subject: Olympic Games 2008 - Peking, marathon races
Obv: National arms **Obv. Legend:** BANKI NASIYONALI Y'U RWANDA **Rev:** Three male marathon runners, Rwanda Olympic logo at right **Rev. Legend:** JEUX OLYMPIQUES **Edge:** Plain

Date	Mintage	F	VF	XF	Unc	BU
2006 Proof	—	Value: 110				

KM# 29   1000 FRANCS
93.3000 g., 0.9990 Silver And Gold 2.9965 oz., 65 mm.
Obv: National arms **Obv. Legend:** BANKI NASIYONALI Y'U RWANDA **Rev:** Gilt elephant family of four with diamonds inset in eyes **Rev. Legend:** AFRICAN ELEPHANT **Edge:** Plain
Note: Illustration reduced.

Date	Mintage	F	VF	XF	Unc	BU
2007	1,500	—	—	—	—	650
2007 Proof	500	Value: 1,000				

SAHARAWI ARAB D.R.

The Saharawi Arab Democratic Republic, located in northwest Africa has an area of 102,703 sq. mi. and a population (census taken 1974) of 76,425. Formerly known as Spanish Sahara, the area is bounded on the north by Morocco, on the east and southeast by Mauritania, on the northeast by Algeria, and on the west by the Atlantic Ocean. Capital: El Aaium. Agriculture, fishing and mining are the three main industries. Exports are barley, livestock and phosphates. The SADR is a "government in exile". It currently controls about 20% of its claimed territory, the former Spanish colony of Western Sahara; Morocco controls and administers the majority of the territory as its Southern Provinces. SADR claims control over a zone largely bordering Mauritania, described as "the Free Zone," although characterized by Morocco as a buffer zone.

DEMOCRATIC REPUBLIC

STANDARD COINAGE

KM# 51   500 PESETAS
Bi-Metallic Stainless Steel center in Brass ring, 26 mm.
Obv: National arms within circle **Rev:** Two Fennec foxes within circle **Edge:** Segmented reeding

Date	Mintage	F	VF	XF	Unc	BU
2004	5,000	—	—	—	27.50	32.50

KM# 51a   500 PESETAS
Bi-Metallic .999 Silver center in .999 Gold plated .999 Silver ring, 26 mm. **Obv:** National arms within circle **Rev:** Two Fennec foxes within circle **Edge:** Segmented reeded

Date	Mintage	F	VF	XF	Unc	BU
2004	25	—	—	—	250	275

KM# 51b   500 PESETAS
0.9990 Silver, 26 mm. **Obv:** National arms within circle **Rev:** Two Fennec foxes within circle **Edge:** Segmented reeding

Date	Mintage	F	VF	XF	Unc	BU
2004	25	—	—	—	225	250

KM# 52   500 PESETAS
Bi-Metallic Stainless Steel center in Brass ring, 26 mm.
Obv: National arms within circle **Rev:** Independence map divides circle **Edge:** Segmented reeding

Date	Mintage	F	VF	XF	Unc	BU
2004	5,000	—	—	—	30.00	35.00

KM# 52a   500 PESETAS
Bi-Metallic .999 Silver center in .999 Gold plated .999 Silver ring, 26 mm. **Obv:** National arms within circle **Rev:** Independence map divides circle **Edge:** Segmented reeding

Date	Mintage	F	VF	XF	Unc	BU
2004	25	—	—	—	250	275

KM# 52b   500 PESETAS
0.9990 Silver, 26 mm. **Obv:** National arms within circle **Rev:** Independence map divides circle **Edge:** Segmented reeding

Date	Mintage	F	VF	XF	Unc	BU
2004	25	—	—	—	225	250

KM# 54   1000 PESETAS
19.9400 g., 0.9990 Silver 0.6404 oz. ASW, 38.1 mm.
Obv: National arms **Rev:** Soccer player and stadium **Edge:** Plain

Date	Mintage	F	VF	XF	Unc	BU
2002 Proof	—	Value: 35.00				

SAINT HELENA

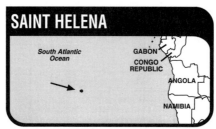

Saint Helena, a British colony located about 1,150 miles (1,850 km.) from the west coast of Africa, has an area of 47 sq. mi. (410 sq. km.) and a population of *7,000. Capital: Jamestown. Flax, lace, and rope are produced for export. Ascension and Tristan da Cunha are dependencies of Saint Helena.

MONETARY SYSTEM
100 Pence = 1 Pound

BRITISH COLONY

STANDARD COINAGE

KM# 19   50 PENCE
38.6000 g., Copper-Nickel, 38.6 mm. **Ruler:** Elizabeth II **Subject:** 75th Birthday of Queen Elizabeth II **Obv:** Crowned bust right **Obv. Designer:** Raphael Maklouf **Rev:** Bust facing within circle and rose sprigs **Edge:** Reeded

Date	Mintage	VG	F	VF	XF	Unc
2001	—	—	—	—	—	8.00

KM# 19a   50 PENCE
28.2800 g., 0.9250 Silver 0.8410 oz. ASW, 38.6 mm.
Ruler: Elizabeth II **Subject:** 75th Birthday of Queen Elizabeth II **Obv:** Crowned bust right **Rev:** Bust facing within circle and rose sprigs **Edge:** Reeded

Date	Mintage	F	VF	XF	Unc	BU
2001 Proof	10,000	Value: 45.00				

KM# 19b   50 PENCE
47.5400 g., 0.9166 Gold 1.4009 oz. AGW, 38.6 mm.
Ruler: Elizabeth II **Subject:** 75th Birthday of Queen Elizabeth II **Obv:** Crowned bust right **Rev:** Bust facing within circle and rose sprigs **Edge:** Reeded

Date	Mintage	F	VF	XF	Unc	BU
2001 Proof	75	Value: 1,800				

KM# 20   50 PENCE
28.5500 g., Copper-Nickel, 38.6 mm. **Ruler:** Elizabeth II **Subject:** Queen Victoria's Death **Obv:** Crowned bust right **Obv. Designer:** Raphael Maklouf **Rev:** Half-length figure facing and ship within circle **Edge:** Reeded

Date	Mintage	VG	F	VF	XF	Unc
2001	—	—	—	—	—	8.00

KM# 20a   50 PENCE
28.2800 g., 0.9250 Silver 0.8410 oz. ASW, 38.6 mm.
Ruler: Elizabeth II **Subject:** Centennial - Death of Queen Victoria **Obv:** Crowned bust right **Rev:** Half-length figure facing and ship within circle **Edge:** Reeded

Date	Mintage	F	VF	XF	Unc	BU
2001 Proof	10,000	Value: 45.00				

KM# 20b   50 PENCE
47.5400 g., 0.9166 Gold 1.4009 oz. AGW, 38.6 mm.
Ruler: Elizabeth II **Subject:** Centennial - Death of Queen Victoria **Obv:** Crowned bust right **Rev:** Half-length figure facing and ship within circle **Edge:** Reeded

Date	Mintage	F	VF	XF	Unc	BU
2001 Proof	100	Value: 1,750				

KM# 23   50 PENCE
28.2800 g., Copper-Nickel, 38.6 mm. **Ruler:** Elizabeth II **Subject:** 50th Anniversary - Queen Elizabeth II's Accession **Obv:** Crowned bust right **Obv. Designer:** Raphael Maklouf **Rev:** Crown on pillow within circle **Edge:** Reeded

Date	Mintage	F	VF	XF	Unc	BU
ND(2002)	—	—	—	—	8.00	10.00

KM# 23a   50 PENCE
28.2800 g., 0.9250 Silver 0.8410 oz. ASW, 38.6 mm.
Ruler: Elizabeth II **Subject:** 50th Anniversary - Queen Elizabeth's Accession **Obv:** Crowned bust right **Rev:** Crown on pillow within circle **Edge:** Reeded

Date	Mintage	F	VF	XF	Unc	BU
ND(2002) Proof	10,000	Value: 35.00				

KM# 24   50 PENCE
28.2800 g., Copper-Nickel, 38.6 mm. **Ruler:** Elizabeth II **Subject:** To Celebrate a Life of Duty, Dignity and Love, 1900-2002 **Obv:** Crowned bust right **Obv. Designer:** Raphael Maklouf **Rev:** Conjoined busts right **Rev. Designer:** Willem Vis **Edge:** Reeded

Date	Mintage	F	VF	XF	Unc	BU
ND(2002)	—	—	—	—	8.00	10.00

KM# 24a   50 PENCE
28.2800 g., 0.9250 Silver 0.8410 oz. ASW, 38.6 mm.
Ruler: Elizabeth II **Subject:** To Celebrate a Life of Duty, Dignity and Love, 1900-2002 **Obv:** Crowned bust right **Rev:** Conjoined busts right **Edge:** Reeded

Date	Mintage	F	VF	XF	Unc	BU
ND(2002) Proof	10,000	Value: 35.00				

KM# 25   50 PENCE
28.2800 g., Copper-Nickel, 38.6 mm. **Ruler:** Elizabeth II **Subject:** 500th Anniversary - Discovery of St. Helena **Obv:** Crowned bust right **Obv. Designer:** Raphael Maklouf **Rev:** Half length figure right and ship above 1502 date **Rev. Designer:** Willem Vis **Edge:** Reeded

Date	Mintage	F	VF	XF	Unc	BU
ND(2002)	—	—	—	—	10.00	12.00

KM# 25a   50 PENCE
28.2800 g., 0.9250 Silver 0.8410 oz. ASW, 38.6 mm.
Ruler: Elizabeth II **Subject:** 500th Anniversary - Discovery of St. Helena **Obv:** Crowned bust right **Rev:** Half length figure right and ship above 1502 date **Edge:** Reeded

Date	Mintage	F	VF	XF	Unc	BU
ND(2002) Proof	5,000	Value: 50.00				

KM# 26 50 PENCE
28.2800 g., Copper-Nickel, 38.6 mm. **Ruler:** Elizabeth II **Obv:** Crowned bust right **Obv. Designer:** Raphael Maklouf **Rev:** Bust 1/4 left, ship HMS Paramour and a comet **Rev. Designer:** Willem Vis **Edge:** Reeded

Date	Mintage	F	VF	XF	Unc	BU
ND(2002)	—	—	—	—	10.00	12.00

KM# 26a 50 PENCE
28.2800 g., 0.9250 Silver 0.8410 oz. ASW, 38.6 mm. **Ruler:** Elizabeth II **Obv:** Crowned bust right **Rev:** Bust 1/4 left, ship HMS Paramour and a comet **Edge:** Reeded

Date	Mintage	F	VF	XF	Unc	BU
ND(2002) Proof	5,000	Value: 50.00				

KM# 27 50 PENCE
28.2800 g., Copper-Nickel, 38.6 mm. **Ruler:** Elizabeth II **Obv:** Crowned bust right **Obv. Designer:** Raphael Maklouf **Rev:** Bust 1/4 right and the HMS Resolution **Rev. Designer:** Willem Vis **Edge:** Reeded

Date	Mintage	F	VF	XF	Unc	BU
ND(2002)	—	—	—	—	10.00	12.00

KM# 27a 50 PENCE
28.2800 g., 0.9250 Silver 0.8410 oz. ASW, 38.6 mm. **Ruler:** Elizabeth II **Obv:** Crowned bust right **Rev:** Bust 1/4 right and the HMS Resolution **Edge:** Reeded

Date	Mintage	F	VF	XF	Unc	BU
ND(2002) Proof	5,000	Value: 50.00				

KM# 28 50 PENCE
28.2800 g., Copper-Nickel, 38.6 mm. **Ruler:** Elizabeth II **Obv:** Crowned bust right **Obv. Designer:** Raphael Maklouf **Rev:** Half length figure facing and the ship HMS Northumberland **Rev. Designer:** Willem Vis **Edge:** Reeded

Date	Mintage	F	VF	XF	Unc	BU
ND(2002)	—	—	—	—	10.00	12.00

KM# 28a 50 PENCE
28.2800 g., 0.9250 Silver 0.8410 oz. ASW, 38.6 mm. **Ruler:** Elizabeth II **Obv:** Queen Elizabeth II **Rev:** Napoleon and the ship HMS Northumberland **Edge:** Reeded

Date	Mintage	F	VF	XF	Unc	BU
ND(2002) Proof	5,000	Value: 50.00				

KM# 29 50 PENCE
28.2800 g., Copper-Nickel, 38.6 mm. **Ruler:** Elizabeth II **Obv:** Crowned bust right **Obv. Designer:** Raphael Maklouf **Rev:** Four conjoined busts left plus the HMS Vanguard **Rev. Designer:** Willem Vis **Edge:** Reeded

Date	Mintage	F	VF	XF	Unc	BU
ND(2002)	—	—	—	—	8.00	10.00

KM# 29a 50 PENCE
28.2800 g., 0.9250 Silver 0.8410 oz. ASW, 38.6 mm. **Ruler:** Elizabeth II **Obv:** Crowned bust right **Rev:** Four conjoined busts left plus the HMS Vanguard **Edge:** Reeded

Date	Mintage	F	VF	XF	Unc	BU
ND(2002) Proof	5,000	Value: 35.00				

KM# 30 50 PENCE
28.2800 g., Copper-Nickel, 38.6 mm. **Ruler:** Elizabeth II **Subject:** 50th Anniversary of Queen Elizabeth's Coronation **Obv:** Crowned bust right **Obv. Designer:** Raphael Maklouf **Rev:** Crowned Queen facing with scepter and orb **Edge:** Reeded

Date	Mintage	F	VF	XF	Unc	BU
ND(2003)	—	—	—	—	10.00	12.00

KM# 30a 50 PENCE
28.2800 g., 0.9250 Silver 0.8410 oz. ASW, 38.6 mm. **Ruler:** Elizabeth II **Subject:** 50th Anniversary - Queen Elizabeth's Coronation **Obv:** Crowned bust right **Rev:** Crowned Queen facing with scepter and orb **Edge:** Reeded

Date	Mintage	F	VF	XF	Unc	BU
ND(2003) Proof	5,000	Value: 50.00				

KM# 30b 50 PENCE
39.9400 g., 0.9166 Gold 1.1770 oz. AGW, 38.6 mm. **Ruler:** Elizabeth II **Subject:** 50th Anniversary of Queen's Coronation **Obv:** Crowned bust right **Rev:** Crowned Queen facing with scepter and orb **Edge:** Reeded

Date	Mintage	F	VF	XF	Unc	BU
ND(2003) Proof	50	Value: 1,850				

KM# 31 50 PENCE
28.2800 g., Copper-Nickel, 38.6 mm. **Ruler:** Elizabeth II **Subject:** 50th Anniversary of Coronation **Obv:** Crowned bust right **Obv. Designer:** Raphael Maklouf **Rev:** Coronation implements **Edge:** Reeded

Date	Mintage	F	VF	XF	Unc	BU
ND(2003)	—	—	—	—	10.00	12.00

KM# 31a 50 PENCE
28.2800 g., 0.9250 Silver 0.8410 oz. ASW, 38.6 mm. **Ruler:** Elizabeth II **Subject:** 50th Anniversary - Queen Elizabeth II's Coronation **Obv:** Crowned bust right **Rev:** Coronation implements **Edge:** Reeded

Date	Mintage	F	VF	XF	Unc	BU
ND(2003) Proof	5,000	Value: 50.00				

KM# 31b 50 PENCE
39.9400 g., 0.9166 Gold 1.1770 oz. AGW, 38.6 mm. **Ruler:** Elizabeth II **Subject:** 50th Anniversary of Coronation **Obv:** Crowned bust right **Rev:** Coronation implements **Edge:** Reeded

Date	Mintage	F	VF	XF	Unc	BU
ND(2003) Proof	50	Value: 1,850				

PIEFORTS

KM#	Date	Mintage	Identification	Mkt Val
P3	ND(2002)	500	50 Pence. 0.9250 Silver. 56.5600 g. 38.6 mm. Reeded edge. Proof.	110

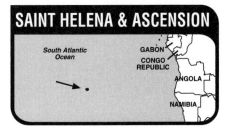

SAINT HELENA & ASCENSION

South Atlantic Ocean — GABON, CONGO REPUBLIC, ANGOLA, NAMIBIA

BRITISH OVERSEAS TERRITORY

STANDARD COINAGE

100 Pence = 1 Pound

KM# 13a PENNY
3.5000 g., Copper Plated Steel, 20.28 mm. **Ruler:** Queen Elizabeth II **Obv:** Crowned head right **Obv. Designer:** Raphael David Maklouf **Rev:** Tuna above value **Rev. Designer:** Michael Hibbit **Edge:** Plain

Date	Mintage	F	VF	XF	Unc	BU
2003	—	—	—	0.15	0.35	0.75

KM# 12a 2 PENCE
Copper Plated Steel **Ruler:** Queen Elizabeth II **Obv:** Crowned head right **Obv. Designer:** Raphael David Maklouf **Rev:** Value below donkey **Rev. Designer:** Mike Hibbit **Shape:** 25.9

Date	Mintage	F	VF	XF	Unc	BU
2003	—	—	—	0.20	0.60	1.25
2006	—	—	—	0.20	0.60	1.25

KM# 22 5 PENCE
Copper-Nickel, 18 mm. **Ruler:** Queen Elizabeth II **Obv:** Crowned head right **Rev:** Giant tortoise **Rev. Designer:** Robert Elderton

Date	Mintage	F	VF	XF	Unc	BU
2003	—	—	—	1.00	2.50	5.00

KM# 23 10 PENCE
Copper-Nickel, 24.5 mm. **Ruler:** Queen Elizabeth II **Obv:** Crowned head right **Obv. Designer:** Raphael David Maklouf **Rev:** Dolphins **Rev. Designer:** Robert Elderton

Date	Mintage	F	VF	XF	Unc	BU
2003	—	—	—	2.00	4.00	6.00
2006	—	—	—	2.00	4.00	6.00

KM# 21 20 PENCE
Copper-Nickel, 21.4 mm. **Ruler:** Queen Elizabeth II **Obv:** Crowned head right **Rev:** Ebony flower **Rev. Designer:** Robert Elderton **Shape:** 7-sided

Date	Mintage	F	VF	XF	Unc	BU
2003	—	—	—	0.75	1.50	2.50

KM# 16 50 PENCE
13.5000 g., Copper-Nickel, 30 mm. **Ruler:** Queen Elizabeth II **Obv:** Crowned head right **Obv. Designer:** Raphael David Maklouf **Rev:** Green sea turtle **Rev. Designer:** Michael Hibbit **Shape:** 7-sided

Date	Mintage	F	VF	XF	Unc	BU
2003	—	—	—	1.50	4.00	6.00
2006	—	—	—	1.50	4.00	6.00

KM# 17 POUND
9.5000 g., Nickel-Brass, 22.5 mm. **Ruler:** Queen Elizabeth II **Obv:** Crowned head right **Obv. Designer:** Raphael David Maklouf **Rev:** Sooty terns (Wideawake birds) **Rev. Designer:** Michael Hibbit

Date	Mintage	F	VF	XF	Unc	BU
2003	—	—	—	2.25	5.00	8.00
2006	—	—	—	2.25	5.00	8.00

KM# 26 2 POUNDS
11.8100 g., Nickel-Brass, 28.3 mm. **Ruler:** Queen Elizabeth II
Obv: Crowned bust right **Obv. Designer:** Raphael Maklouf
Rev: National arms above value **Edge:** Reeded and lettered
Edge Lettering: 500TH ANNIVERSARY

Date	Mintage	F	VF	XF	Unc	BU
2002	—			6.00	10.00	12.50

KM# 25 2 POUNDS
12.0000 g., Bi-Metallic Copper-Nickel center in Brass ring,
28.4 mm. **Ruler:** Queen Elizabeth II **Obv:** Crowned bust right
Obv. Designer: Raphael Maklouf **Rev:** National Arms
Edge: Reeded and lettered **Edge Lettering:** LOYAL AND
FAITHFUL

Date	Mintage	F	VF	XF	Unc	BU
2003	—			9.00	15.00	17.50

SAMOA

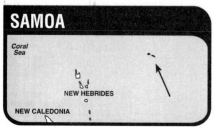

The Independent State of Samoa (formerly Western
Samoa), located in the Pacific Ocean 1,600 miles (2,574 km.)
northeast of New Zealand, has an area of 1,097 sq. mi. (2,860
sq. km.) and a population of *182,000. Capital: Apia. The economy is based on agriculture, fishing and tourism. Copra, cocoa
and bananas are exported.
Samoa is a member of the Commonwealth of Nations. The
Chief Executive is Chief of State. The prime minister is the Head
of Government. The present Head of State, Malietoa Tanumafili
II, holds his position for life. The Legislative Assembly will elect
future Heads of State for 5-year terms.
Samoa, which had used New Zealand coinage, converted to
a decimal coinage in 1967.

RULER
Malietoa Tanumafili II, 1962-2007
Tuiatua Tupua Tamasese Efi, 2007-

MONETARY SYSTEM
100 Sene = 1 Tala

CONSTITUTIONAL
MONARCHY
Commonwealth of Nations

STANDARD COINAGE

KM# 131 5 SENE
2.8400 g., Copper-Nickel, 19.5 mm. **Obv:** Head left
Obv. Designer: T.H. Paget **Rev:** Pineapple and value
Rev. Designer: James Berry **Edge:** Reeded **Note:** "Western"
dropped from country name

Date	Mintage	F	VF	XF	Unc	BU
2002	—	—	—	0.30	0.50	0.75
2006	—	—	—	0.30	0.50	0.75

KM# 132 10 SENE
5.6500 g., Copper-Nickel, 23.6 mm. **Obv:** Head left **Rev:** Taro
leaves and value **Rev. Designer:** James Berry **Edge:** Reeded
Note: "Western" dropped from country name

Date	Mintage	F	VF	XF	Unc	BU
2002	—			0.45	0.75	1.00

KM# 133 20 SENE
11.4000 g., Copper-Nickel, 28.45 mm. **Obv:** Head left
Obv. Designer: T.H. Paget **Rev:** Breadfruits and value
Rev. Designer: James Berry **Edge:** Reeded **Note:** "Western"
dropped from country name

Date	Mintage	F	VF	XF	Unc	BU
2002	—			0.60	1.00	1.50

KM# 134 50 SENE
14.1300 g., Copper-Nickel, 32.3 mm. **Obv:** Head left
Rev: Banana tree and value **Edge:** Reeded **Note:** "Western"
dropped from country name

Date	Mintage	F	VF	XF	Unc	BU
2002	—			1.00	1.75	2.00

KM# 135 TALA
9.5000 g., Brass, 30 mm. **Obv:** Head left **Obv. Designer:** T.H.
Paget **Rev:** National arms above value and banner flanked by
sprigs **Rev. Designer:** Nelson Eustis **Edge:** Reeded
Note: "Western" dropped from country name

Date	Mintage	F	VF	XF	Unc	BU
2002	—			1.50	2.50	3.00

KM# 150 TALA
Goldine Plated Metal **Subject:** Thomas Mann **Obv:** Arms
Rev: Bust facing

Date	Mintage	F	VF	XF	Unc	BU
2009	—				—	30.00

KM# 151 TALA
Goldine Plated Metal **Subject:** Hercules & Hydra

Date	Mintage	F	VF	XF	Unc	BU
2009	—				—	25.00

KM# 152 TALA
Goldine Plated Metal **Subject:** Alhambra

Date	Mintage	F	VF	XF	Unc	BU
2009	—				—	25.00

KM# 153 TALA
Goldine Plated Metal **Rev:** Golden horn

Date	Mintage	F	VF	XF	Unc	BU
2009	—				—	25.00

KM# 154 TALA
Goldine Plated Metal **Rev:** Sphinx

Date	Mintage	F	VF	XF	Unc	BU
2009	—				—	25.00

KM# 155 TALA
Gold **Rev:** Kaiser Wilhelm II

Date	Mintage	F	VF	XF	Unc	BU
2009	—				—	25.00

KM# 156 TALA
Goldine Plated Metal **Rev:** Hagia Sophia

Date	Mintage	F	VF	XF	Unc	BU
2009	—				—	20.00

KM# 137 10 TALA
31.1000 g., 0.9990 Silver with Mother-of-Pearl insert 0.9988 oz.
ASW, 40 mm. **Series:** Save the Whales **Obv:** National arms above
value and banner flanked by sprigs **Obv. Legend:** SAMOA I SISIFO
Rev: Bowhead Whale on mother-of-pearl insert **Edge:** Plain

Date	Mintage	F	VF	XF	Unc	BU
2002 Proof	2,000	Value: 85.00				

KM# 139 10 TALA
31.4700 g., 0.9250 Silver 0.9359 oz. ASW **Subject:** XXVIII
Summer Olympics - Athens **Obv:** National arms **Obv. Legend:**
SAMOA I SISIFO **Rev:** Swimming - two divers

Date	Mintage	F	VF	XF	Unc	BU
2003 Proof	—	Value: 60.00				

KM# 146 10 TALA
1.2300 g., Gold, 13.89 mm. **Obv:** National arms **Obv. Legend:**
SAMOA I SISIFO **Rev:** Bust of Fletcher Christian 3/4 left at left,
sailing ship "H. M. S. Bounty" at right **Edge:** Reeded

Date	Mintage	F	VF	XF	Unc	BU
2003 Proof	—	Value: 55.00				

KM# 140 10 TALA
1.2400 g., 0.9990 Gold 0.0398 oz. AGW **Series:** World
Statesmen **Subject:** Mahatma Gandhi **Obv:** National arms
Obv. Legend: SAMOA I SISIFO

Date	Mintage	F	VF	XF	Unc	BU
2003 Proof	—	Value: 75.00				

KM# 141 10 TALA
1.2400 g., 0.9990 Gold 0.0398 oz. AGW **Series:** World
Statesmen **Subject:** Konrad Adenauer **Obv:** National arms
Obv. Legend: SAMOA I SISIFO

Date	Mintage	F	VF	XF	Unc	BU
2003 Proof	—	Value: 75.00				

KM# 143 10 TALA
28.5800 g., Silver, 38.61 mm. **Obv:** National arms
Obv. Legend: SAMOA I SISIFO **Rev:** Sailing ship "La
Récherche" **Rev. Legend:** JEAN FRANCOIS GALAUP - COMTE
DE LA PEROUSE **Edge:** Reeded

Date	Mintage	F	VF	XF	Unc	BU
2004 Proof	—	Value: 50.00				

KM# 142 10 TALA
1.2400 g., 0.9990 Gold 0.0398 oz. AGW **Subject:** Death of Pope
John-Paul II **Obv:** National arms

Date	Mintage	F	VF	XF	Unc	BU
2005	15,000	—	—	—	—	65.00
2005 Proof	3,300	Value: 75.00				

SAN MARINO

The Republic of San Marino, the oldest and smallest republic in the world is located in north central Italy entirely surrounded by the Province of Emilia-Romagna. It has an area of 24 sq. mi. (60 sq. km.) and a population of *23,000. Capital: San Marino. The principal economic activities are farming, livestock raising, cheese making, tourism and light manufacturing. Building stone, lime, wheat, hides and baked goods are exported. The government derives most of its revenue from the sale of postage stamps for philatelic purposes.

San Marino has its own coinage, but Italian and Vatican City coins and currency are also in circulation.

MINT MARKS
R - Rome

MONETARY SYSTEM
100 Centesimi = 1 Lira

REPUBLIC

STANDARD COINAGE

KM# 424   10 LIRE
1.6000 g., Aluminum, 23.3 mm. **Obv:** Three towers within circle **Rev:** Wheat stalks and value **Edge:** Plain

Date	Mintage	F	VF	XF	Unc	BU
2001R	—	—	—	—	0.35	0.50

KM# 425   20 LIRE
3.6000 g., Aluminum-Bronze, 21.8 mm. **Obv:** Three towers within circle **Rev:** Two dolphins and value **Edge:** Plain

Date	Mintage	F	VF	XF	Unc	BU
2001R	—	—	—	—	1.00	2.00

KM# 426   50 LIRE
4.5000 g., Stainless Steel, 19.2 mm. **Obv:** Three towers within circle **Rev:** Tree and value **Edge:** Plain

Date	Mintage	F	VF	XF	Unc	BU
2001R	—	—	—	—	0.85	1.50

KM# 427   100 LIRE
4.5000 g., Copper-Nickel, 22 mm. **Obv:** Three towers within circle **Rev:** Grasping hands and value **Edge:** Plain and reeded sections

Date	Mintage	F	VF	XF	Unc	BU
2001R	—	—	—	—	1.25	2.00

KM# 428   200 LIRE
5.0000 g., Aluminum-Bronze, 24 mm. **Obv:** Three towers within circle **Rev:** Broken chain, leaves, vines and value **Edge:** Reeded

Date	Mintage	F	VF	XF	Unc	BU
2001R	—	—	—	—	1.50	2.50

KM# 429   500 LIRE
Bi-Metallic Aluminum-Bronze center in Stainless Steel ring, 25.8 mm. **Obv:** Three towers within circle **Rev:** Three different plant stalks and value **Edge:** Reeded and plain sections
Note: 6.8 grams.

Date	Mintage	F	VF	XF	Unc	BU
2001R	—	—	—	—	3.00	3.50

KM# 430   1000 LIRE
8.8000 g., Bi-Metallic Stainless-Steel center in Aluminum-Bronze ring, 27 mm. **Obv:** Three towers within circle **Rev:** Value within circle of birds **Edge:** Reeded and plain sections

Date	Mintage	F	VF	XF	Unc	BU
2001R	—	—	—	—	7.50	10.00

KM# 431   5000 LIRE
18.0000 g., 0.8350 Silver 0.4832 oz. ASW, 32 mm. **Obv:** Three towers within circle **Rev:** Dove on laurel branch above value **Edge:** Reeded and plain sections

Date	Mintage	F	VF	XF	Unc	BU
2001R	—	—	—	—	17.50	27.50

KM# 436   5000 LIRE
18.0000 g., 0.8350 Silver 0.4832 oz. ASW, 32 mm. **Subject:** Last Lire Coinage **Obv:** Crowned arms within sprigs **Rev:** Feather above six old coin designs with value below, all within beaded border **Edge:** Lettered

Date	Mintage	F	VF	XF	Unc	BU
2001R Proof	20,000	Value: 20.00				

KM# 432   10000 LIRE
22.0000 g., 0.8350 Silver 0.5906 oz. ASW, 34 mm. **Subject:** Ferrari **Obv:** Crowned arms within sprigs **Rev:** Race car with "FERRARI" background **Edge:** Reeded and plain sections

Date	Mintage	F	VF	XF	Unc	BU
2001R Proof	20,000	Value: 45.00				

KM# 437   10000 LIRE
22.0000 g., 0.8350 Silver 0.5906 oz. ASW, 34 mm. **Subject:** Last Lire Coinage **Obv:** Crowned arms within sprigs **Rev:** Feather above six old coin designs with value below, all within star border **Edge:** Reeded and plain sections

Date	Mintage	F	VF	XF	Unc	BU
2001R Proof	20,000	Value: 35.00				

KM# 438   10000 LIRE
22.0000 g., 0.8350 Silver 0.5906 oz. ASW, 34 mm. **Subject:** 2nd International Chambers of Commerce Convention **Obv:** Crowned arms within sprigs **Rev:** Mercury running by a computer **Edge:** Reeded and plain sections

Date	Mintage	F	VF	XF	Unc	BU
2001R Proof	20,000	Value: 30.00				

KM# 433   1/2 SCUDO
1.6100 g., 0.9000 Gold 0.0466 oz. AGW, 13.8 mm. **Subject:** Cavaliere **Obv:** Crowned arms within sprigs **Rev:** Horse and rider **Edge:** Reeded

Date	Mintage	F	VF	XF	Unc	BU
2001R Proof	4,500	Value: 75.00				

KM# 434   SCUDO
3.2200 g., 0.9000 Gold 0.0932 oz. AGW, 16 mm. **Subject:** Tiziano **Obv:** Crowned arms within sprigs **Rev:** Bearded bust left **Edge:** Reeded

Date	Mintage	F	VF	XF	Unc	BU
2001R Proof	4,500	Value: 125				

KM# 435   2 SCUDI
6.4400 g., 0.9000 Gold 0.1863 oz. AGW, 21 mm. **Subject:** Flora **Obv:** Crowned arms within sprigs **Rev:** Bust 1/4 left and value **Edge:** Reeded

Date	Mintage	F	VF	XF	Unc	BU
2001R Proof	4,500	Value: 240				

KM# 457   2 SCUDI
6.4516 g., 0.9000 Gold 0.1867 oz. AGW, 21 mm. **Obv:** Crowned arms within sprigs **Rev:** Madonna and Child **Edge:** Reeded

Date	Mintage	F	VF	XF	Unc	BU
2002R Proof	3,000	Value: 245				

KM# 459   2 SCUDI
6.4516 g., 0.9000 Gold 0.1867 oz. AGW, 21 mm. **Obv:** Crowned arms within sprigs **Rev:** Nostradamus above value **Edge:** Reeded

Date	Mintage	F	VF	XF	Unc	BU
2003R Proof	7,500	Value: 235				

KM# 464   2 SCUDI
6.4516 g., 0.9000 Gold 0.1867 oz. AGW, 21 mm. **Subject:** The Domagnano Treasure **Obv:** Crowned arms within sprigs **Rev:** Gothic Eagle Brooch, 5 Mark coin of 1952 **Edge:** Reeded

Date	Mintage	F	VF	XF	Unc	BU
2004R Proof	6,500	Value: 235				

KM# 493   2 SCUDI
6.4100 g., 0.9000 Gold 0.1855 oz. AGW, 21 mm. **Subject:** Pompeo Batoni, 300th Anniversary of Brith **Obv:** Arms **Rev:** Batoni's "San Marino Risolleva la Republica"

Date	Mintage	F	VF	XF	Unc	BU
2008R Proof	2,100	Value: 300				

KM# 439 5 SCUDI
16.9655 g., 0.9166 Gold 0.4999 oz. AGW, 28 mm.
Subject: San Marino's World Bank Membership **Obv:** Crowned arms within sprigs **Rev:** Orchid and bee within globe
Edge: Reeded

Date	Mintage	F	VF	XF	Unc	BU
2001R Proof	4,000	Value: 525				

EURO COINAGE

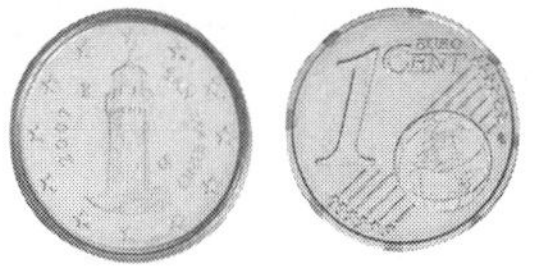

KM# 440 EURO CENT
2.2700 g., Copper Plated Steel, 16.2 mm. **Obv:** "Il Montale" **Obv. Designer:** M. Frantisek Chochola **Rev:** Value and globe **Rev. Designer:** Luc Luycx **Edge:** Plain

Date	Mintage	F	VF	XF	Unc	BU
2002R	125,000	—	—	—	—	40.00
2003R In sets only	70,000	—	—	—	—	42.00
2004R	1,500,000	—	—	—	—	20.00
2005R In sets only	70,000	—	—	—	—	20.00
2006R	2,730,000	—	—	8.00	—	12.00
2007R	—	—	—	8.00	—	12.00
2008R	—	—	—	8.00	—	12.00
2008R Proof	13,000	Value: 10.00				
2009R	—	—	—	8.00	—	12.00
2009R Proof	13,500	Value: 10.00				

KM# 441 2 EURO CENT
3.0300 g., Copper Plated Steel, 18.7 mm. **Obv:** Stefano Gallietti, Liberty fighter **Obv. Designer:** M. Frantisek Chochola **Rev:** Value and globe **Rev. Designer:** Luc Luycx **Edge:** Grooved

Date	Mintage	F	VF	XF	Unc	BU
2002R	125,000	—	—	—	—	40.00
2003R In sets only	70,000	—	—	—	—	42.00
2004R	1,395,000	—	—	—	—	20.00
2005R In sets only	150,000	—	—	—	—	20.00
2006R	2,730,000	—	—	—	8.00	12.00
2007R	—	—	—	—	8.00	12.00
2008R	—	—	—	—	8.00	12.00
2008R Proof	13,000	Value: 10.00				
2009R	—	—	—	—	8.00	12.00
2009R Proof	13,500	Value: 10.00				

KM# 442 5 EURO CENT
3.8600 g., Copper Plated Steel, 21.2 mm. **Obv:** "Guaita" tower **Obv. Designer:** M. Frantisek Chochola **Rev:** Value and globe **Rev. Designer:** Luc Luycx **Edge:** Plain

Date	Mintage	F	VF	XF	Unc	BU
2002R	125,000	—	—	—	—	40.00
2003R In sets only	70,000	—	—	—	—	42.00
2004R	1,000,000	—	—	—	—	20.00
2005R In sets only	70,000	—	—	—	—	20.00
2006R	2,880,000	—	—	—	8.00	12.00
2007R	—	—	—	—	8.00	12.00
2008R	—	—	—	—	8.00	12.00
2008R Proof	13,000	Value: 10.00				
2009R	—	—	—	—	8.00	12.00
2009R Proof	13,500	Value: 10.00				

KM# 443 10 EURO CENT
4.0700 g., Brass, 19.7 mm. **Obv:** Building Basilica del Santo Marinus **Obv. Designer:** M. Frantisek Chochola **Rev:** Map and value **Rev. Designer:** Luc Luycx **Edge:** Reeded

Date	Mintage	F	VF	XF	Unc	BU
2002R	125,000	—	—	—	—	40.00
2003R In sets only	70,000	—	—	—	—	42.00
2004R	180,000	—	—	—	—	22.00
2005R In sets only	70,000	—	—	—	—	22.00
2006R In sets only	65,000	—	—	—	—	20.00
2007R	—	—	—	—	—	18.00

KM# 482 10 EURO CENT
4.0700 g., Brass, 19.7 mm. **Obv:** Basilica de Santo Marinus facade **Rev:** Relief maps of Western Europe, value and stars

Date	Mintage	F	VF	XF	Unc	BU
2008R	—	—	—	—	8.00	12.00
2008R Proof	13,000	Value: 12.00				
2009R	—	—	—	—	8.00	12.00
2009R Proof	13,500	Value: 12.00				

KM# 444 20 EURO CENT
5.7300 g., Brass, 22.1 mm. **Obv:** St. Marinus from a portrait by van Guercino **Obv. Designer:** M. Frantisek Chochola **Rev:** Map and value **Rev. Designer:** Luc Luycx **Edge:** Notched

Date	Mintage	F	VF	XF	Unc	BU
2002R	267,400	—	—	—	18.00	20.00
2003R	430,000	—	—	—	15.00	18.00
2004R In sets only	70,000	—	—	—	15.00	18.00
2005R	310,000	—	—	—	15.00	18.00
2006R In sets only	70,000	—	—	—	15.00	18.00
2007R	—	—	—	—	14.00	16.00

KM# 483 20 EURO CENT
5.7300 g., Brass **Obv:** Saint holding Monte Titano **Rev:** Relief map of Western Europe, value and stars

Date	Mintage	F	VF	XF	Unc	BU
2008R	—	—	—	—	8.00	12.00
2008R Proof	13,000	Value: 15.00				
2009R	—	—	—	—	8.00	12.00
2009R Proof	13,500	Value: 15.00				

KM# 445 50 EURO CENT
7.8100 g., Brass, 24.2 mm. **Obv:** Fortress of San Marino **Obv. Designer:** M. Frantisek Chochola **Rev:** Map and value **Rev. Designer:** Luc Luycx **Edge:** Reeded

Date	Mintage	F	VF	XF	Unc	BU
2002R	230,400	—	—	—	20.00	22.50
2003R	415,000	—	—	—	17.50	20.00
2004R In sets only	70,000	—	—	—	17.50	20.00
2005R	179,000	—	—	—	17.50	20.00
2006R	343,880	—	—	—	15.00	18.00
2007R	—	—	—	—	14.00	16.00

KM# 484 50 EURO CENT
7.8000 g., Brass, 24.2 mm. **Obv:** Buildings on hill top **Rev:** Relief map of Western Europe, value and stars

Date	Mintage	F	VF	XF	Unc	BU
2008R	—	—	—	—	10.00	12.00
2008R Proof	13,000	Value: 13.00				
2009R	—	—	—	—	10.00	12.00
2009R Proof	13,500	Value: 13.00				

KM# 446 EURO
7.5000 g., Bi-Metallic Copper-Nickel center in Brass ring, 23.2 mm. **Obv:** Crowned arms within sprigs and circle within star border **Obv. Designer:** M. Frantisek Chochola **Rev:** Value and map **Rev. Designer:** Luc Luycx **Edge:** Reeded and plain sections

Date	Mintage	F	VF	XF	Unc	BU
2002R	360,800	—	—	—	22.00	25.00
2003R In sets only	70,000	—	—	—	—	45.00
2004R	180,000	—	—	—	—	25.00
2005R In sets only	70,000	—	—	—	—	25.00
2006R In sets only	220,000	—	—	—	—	20.00
2007R	—	—	—	—	—	18.00

KM# 485 EURO
7.5000 g., Bi-Metallic Copper nickel center in brass ring, 23.2 mm. **Obv:** Covered arms within wreath and stars **Rev:** Relief map of Western Europe, value and stars

Date	Mintage	F	VF	XF	Unc	BU
2008R	—	—	—	—	12.00	15.00
2008R Proof	13,000	Value: 15.00				
2009R	—	—	—	—	12.00	15.00
2009R Proof	13,500	Value: 15.00				

KM# 447 2 EURO
8.5200 g., Bi-Metallic Brass center in Copper-Nickel ring, 25.7 mm. **Obv:** Government building **Obv. Designer:** M. Frantisek Chochola **Rev:** Value and map **Rev. Designer:** Luc Luycx **Edge:** Reeded with 2's and stars

Date	Mintage	F	VF	XF	Unc	BU
2002R	255,760	—	—	—	25.00	28.00
2003R In sets only	70,000	—	—	—	—	45.00
2004R In sets only	70,000	—	—	—	—	28.00
2005R In sets only	210,000	—	—	—	—	28.00
2006R In sets only	190,000	—	—	—	—	22.00
2007R	—	—	—	—	—	20.00

KM# 467 2 EURO
8.5000 g., Bi-Metallic Brass center in Copper-Nickel ring, 25.75 mm. **Obv:** Crowned arms within sprigs **Rev:** Bartolomeo Borghesi **Edge:** Alternating stars and 2's

Date	Mintage	F	VF	XF	Unc	BU
2004R	110,000	—	—	—	17.50	30.00

KM# 469 2 EURO
8.5000 g., Bi-Metallic Brass center in Copper-Nickel ring, 25.75 mm. **Obv:** Galileo Galilei at telescope

Date	Mintage	F	VF	XF	Unc	BU
2005R	130,000	—	—	—	35.00	45.00

KM# 478 2 EURO
8.5000 g., Bi-Metallic Brass center in Copper-Nickel ring, 25.75 mm. **Subject:** Christopher Columbus, 500th Anniversary of Death **Obv:** Head of Columbus within border of stars **Rev:** Map and value

Date	Mintage	F	VF	XF	Unc	BU
2006R	120,000	—	—	—	55.00	60.00

KM# 481 2 EURO
8.5000 g., Bi-Metallic Brass center in copper-nickel ring, 27.5 mm. **Subject:** Giuseppe Garibaldi, 200th Anniversary of Birth **Obv:** Half length bust facing **Rev:** Relief map of Western Europe, value and stars

Date	Mintage	F	VF	XF	Unc	BU
2007R	130,000	—	—	—	50.00	55.00

KM# 486 2 EURO
Bi-Metallic Brass center in copper-nickel ring **Obv:** Palace **Rev:** Relief map of Western Europe, value and stars

Date	Mintage	F	VF	XF	Unc	BU
2008R	—	—	—	—	24.00	28.00
2008R Proof	13,000	Value: 20.00				
2009R	—	—	—	—	24.00	28.00
2009R Proof	13,500	Value: 20.00				

KM# 487 2 EURO
8.5000 g., Bi-Metallic Brass center in copper-nickel ring **Subject:** European year of Inter-Cultural dialogue **Obv:** Five figures with arms outstretched, books below **Rev:** Relief map of Western Europe, value and stare

Date	Mintage	F	VF	XF	Unc	BU
2008R	130,000	—	—	—	20.00	25.00

KM# 490 2 EURO
8.5000 g., Bi-Metallic Brass center in Copper-Nickel ring, 27.5 mm. **Subject:** Creativitiy and innovation **Obv:** Chemical flasks and book

Date	Mintage	F	VF	XF	Unc	BU
2009R	—	—	—	—	17.50	30.00

KM# 448 5 EURO
18.0000 g., 0.9250 Silver 0.5353 oz. ASW, 32 mm. **Subject:** Welcome Euro **Obv:** Three plumed towers **Rev:** Circle of roses

Date	Mintage	F	VF	XF	Unc	BU
2002R Proof	37,000	Value: 75.00				

KM# 450 5 EURO
18.0000 g., 0.9250 Silver 0.5353 oz. ASW, 32 mm. **Subject:** 1600th Anniversary of Ravenna **Obv:** National arms **Rev:** Bas-relief wall design **Edge:** Reeded

Date	Mintage	F	VF	XF	Unc	BU
2002R Proof	—	Value: 60.00				

KM# 453 5 EURO
18.0000 g., 0.9250 Silver 0.5353 oz. ASW, 32 mm. **Subject:** 2004 Olympics **Obv:** Stylized three towers **Rev:** Ancient Olympians **Edge:** Reeded

Date	Mintage	F	VF	XF	Unc	BU
2003R Proof	37,766	Value: 50.00				

KM# 452 5 EURO
18.0000 g., 0.9250 Silver 0.5353 oz. ASW, 32 mm. **Obv:** National arms **Rev:** Allegorical depiction of Independence, Tolerance and Liberty

Date	Mintage	F	VF	XF	Unc	BU
2003R	—	—	—	—	35.00	40.00

KM# 468 5 EURO
18.0000 g., 0.9250 Silver 0.5353 oz. ASW, 32 mm. **Obv:** Three towers **Rev:** Antonio Onofri and value

Date	Mintage	F	VF	XF	Unc	BU
2004R	—	—	—	—	45.00	50.00
2005R	—	—	—	—	45.00	50.00

KM# 458 5 EURO
18.0000 g., 0.9250 Silver 0.5353 oz. ASW, 32 mm.
Obv: National arms **Rev:** Value behind Bartolomeo Borghesi

Date	Mintage	F	VF	XF	Unc	BU
2004R	—	—	—	—	—	35.00
2004R Proof	—	Value: 45.00				

KM# 462 5 EURO
18.0000 g., 0.9250 Silver 0.5353 oz. ASW, 32 mm. **Obv:** Three stylized plumed towers **Rev:** Two soccer players

Date	Mintage	F	VF	XF	Unc	BU
2004R Proof	35,000	Value: 45.00				

KM# 472 5 EURO
18.0000 g., 0.9250 Silver 0.5353 oz. ASW, 32 mm. **Obv:** Portrait of Melchiorre Delfico

Date	Mintage	F	VF	XF	Unc	BU
2006R	65,000	—	—	—	30.00	35.00

KM# 476 5 EURO
18.0000 g., 0.9250 Silver 0.5353 oz. ASW, 32 mm.
Subject: Andrea Mantegna, 500th Anniversary of Death
Obv: Three towers **Rev:** Statue of soldier and naked femal

Date	Mintage	F	VF	XF	Unc	BU
2006R Proof	19,000	Value: 40.00				

KM# 473 5 EURO
18.0000 g., 0.9250 Silver 0.5353 oz. ASW, 32 mm.
Subject: Equal Opportunity between the sexes **Obv:** Three plumed towers **Obv. Legend:** REPUBLICA DI SAN MARINO **Rev:** Nude female at left, nude male at right, ribbon across symbols within circle above, value below **Rev. Inscription:** PARI OPPORTITA **Edge:** Reeded

Date	Mintage	F	VF	XF	Unc	BU
2007R	—	—	—	—	30.00	35.00

KM# 474 5 EURO
18.0000 g., 0.9250 Silver 0.5353 oz. ASW, 32 mm.
Subject: 50th Anniversary Death of Toscanini **Obv:** Stylized national arms **Obv. Legend:** REPUBLICA DI SAN MARINO **Rev:** Head of Toscanini left **Edge:** Reeded

Date	Mintage	F	VF	XF	Unc	BU
ND(2007)R Proof	18,000	Value: 35.00				

KM# 449 10 EURO
22.0000 g., 0.9250 Silver 0.6542 oz. ASW, 34 mm.
Subject: Welcome Euro **Obv:** Three plumed towers **Rev:** Infant sleeping in flower

Date	Mintage	F	VF	XF	Unc	BU
2002R Proof	37,000	Value: 100				

KM# 451 10 EURO
22.0000 g., 0.9250 Silver 0.6542 oz. ASW, 34 mm.
Subject: 1600th Anniversary of Ravenna **Obv:** National arms **Rev:** Wall painting

Date	Mintage	F	VF	XF	Unc	BU
2002R Proof	—	Value: 95.00				

KM# 454 10 EURO
22.0000 g., 0.9250 Silver 0.6542 oz. ASW, 34 mm.
Subject: 2004 Olympics **Obv:** Three stylized towers **Rev:** Modern Olympians **Edge:** Segmented reeding

Date	Mintage	F	VF	XF	Unc	BU
2003R Proof	37,766	Value: 75.00				

KM# 463 10 EURO
22.0000 g., 0.9250 Silver 0.6542 oz. ASW, 34 mm. **Obv:** Three stylized plumed towers **Rev:** Two soccer players

Date	Mintage	F	VF	XF	Unc	BU
2004R Proof	30,000	Value: 60.00				

KM# 477 10 EURO
22.0000 g., 0.9250 Silver 0.6542 oz. ASW, 34 mm.
Subject: Antonio Canova **Obv:** Three towers **Rev:** The Three Graces

Date	Mintage	F	VF	XF	Unc	BU
2006R Proof	19,000	Value: 50.00				

KM# 475 10 EURO
22.0000 g., 0.9250 Silver 0.6542 oz. ASW, 34 mm.
Subject: 100th Anniversary - Birthday of Giosuè Carducci
Obv: Stylized national arms **Obv. Legend:** REPUBBLICA DI SAN MARINO **Rev:** 1/2 length figure of Carducci facing with quill pen in hand at table **Rev. Legend:** CARDUCCI **Edge:** Plain and reeded segments

Date	Mintage	F	VF	XF	Unc	BU
ND(2007)R Proof	16,000	Value: 45.00				

KM# 460 20 EURO
6.4510 g., 0.9000 Gold 0.1867 oz. AGW, 21 mm.
Subject: 1600th Anniversary of Ravenna **Obv:** National arms **Rev:** Bas-relief wall design **Edge:** Reeded

Date	Mintage	F	VF	XF	Unc	BU
2002R Proof	4,550	Value: 375				

KM# 455 20 EURO
6.4516 g., 0.9000 Gold 0.1867 oz. AGW, 21 mm. **Obv:** Three plumes **Rev:** Giotto's "Presentation of Jesus at the Temple" **Edge:** Reeded

Date	Mintage	F	VF	XF	Unc	BU
2003R Proof	7,300	Value: 255				

KM# 465 20 EURO
6.4510 g., 0.9000 Gold 0.1867 oz. AGW, 21 mm. **Obv:** Three plumes **Rev:** Marco Polo meeting Kublai Khan **Edge:** Reeded

Date	Mintage	F	VF	XF	Unc	BU
2004R Proof	7,300	Value: 255				

KM# 470 20 EURO
6.4510 g., 0.9000 Gold 0.1867 oz. AGW, 21 mm.
Subject: International Day of Peace **Obv:** Stylized faces and leaves

Date	Mintage	F	VF	XF	Unc	BU
2005R Proof	5,300	Value: 300				

KM# 479 20 EURO
6.4500 g., 0.9000 Gold 0.1866 oz. AGW, 21 mm.
Subject: Giovan Battista Belluzzi, 500th Birthday **Obv:** Crowned shield **Rev:** Fortification plan **Designer:** Guido Veroi

Date	Mintage	F	VF	XF	Unc	BU
2006R Proof	4,500	Value: 300				

KM# 491 20 EURO
6.4500 g., 0.9000 Gold 0.1866 oz. AGW **Subject:** Roman Antiquities **Obv:** Arms **Rev:** Small statue of Mercury

Date	Mintage	F	VF	XF	Unc	BU
2008R Proof	2,100	Value: 300				

KM# 461 50 EURO
16.1290 g., 0.9000 Gold 0.4667 oz. AGW, 28 mm.
Subject: 1600th Anniversary of Ravenna **Obv:** National arms **Rev:** Wall painting **Edge:** Reeded

Date	Mintage	F	VF	XF	Unc	BU
2002R Proof	4,550	Value: 775				

KM# 456 50 EURO
16.1290 g., 0.9000 Gold 0.4667 oz. AGW, 28 mm. **Obv:** Three plumes **Rev:** Giotto's "The Pentecost" **Edge:** Reeded

Date	Mintage	F	VF	XF	Unc	BU
2003R Proof	7,300	Value: 600				

KM# 466 50 EURO
16.1290 g., 0.9000 Gold 0.4667 oz. AGW, 28 mm. **Obv:** Three plumes **Rev:** Marco Polo **Edge:** Reeded

Date	Mintage	F	VF	XF	Unc	BU
2004R Proof	7,300	Value: 600				

KM# 471 50 EURO
16.1290 g., 0.9000 Gold 0.4667 oz. AGW, 28 mm.
Subject: International Day of Peace **Obv:** Group of people gathering

Date	Mintage	F	VF	XF	Unc	BU
2005R Proof	5,300	Value: 650				

KM# 480 50 EURO
16.1300 g., 0.9000 Gold 0.4667 oz. AGW, 28 mm.
Subject: Giovan Batista Belluzzi **Obv:** Crowned shield **Rev:** Bust right **Designer:** Guido Veroi

Date	Mintage	F	VF	XF	Unc	BU
2006R Proof	4,500	Value: 650				

KM# 492 50 EURO
16.1300 g., 0.9000 Gold 0.4667 oz. AGW, 28 mm.
Subject: Antiquities **Obv:** Arms **Rev:** Two bronze fibulae

Date	Mintage	F	VF	XF	Unc	BU
2008R Proof	2,100	Value: 700				

MINT SETS

KM#	Date	Mintage	Identification	Issue Price	Mkt Val
MS61	2001 (8)	2,000	KM424-431	18.00	40.00
MS62	2002 (8)	120,000	KM440-447	—	275
MS63	2003 (9)	—	KM#440-447, 452	55.00	350
MS64	2004 (9)	—	KM#440-447, 458	55.00	220
MS65	2005 (9)	—	KM#440-447, 468	55.00	225
MS66	2006 (9)	65,000	KM#440-447, 472	—	185
MS67	2007 (3)	—	KM#443-444,447	27.50	50.00
MS68	2007 (9)	—	KM#440-447, 473	120	125

PROOF SETS

KM#	Date	Mintage	Identification	Issue Price	Mkt Val
PS14	2001 (3)	4,500	KM433-435	179	390
PSA15	2001 (2)	—	KM436-437	—	—
PS15	2002 (2)	37,000	KM448-449	—	175
PS16	2002 (2)	4,550	KM460-461	—	1,150
PS17	2003 (2)	7,300	KM455-456	—	750
PS18	2004 (2)	7,300	KM465-466	—	780
PS19	2005 (2)	5,300	KM470-471	—	800
PS20	2008 (8)	13,000	KM#440-442, 482-486.	—	135
PS21	2009 (8)	13,500	KM#440-443, 482-486.	—	135

SAUDI ARABIA

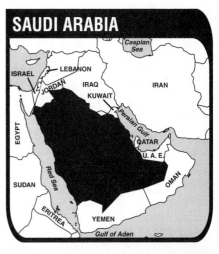

UNITED KINGDOMS

The Kingdom of Saudi Arabia, an independent and absolute hereditary monarchy comprising the former sultanate of Nejd, the old kingdom of Hejaz, Asir and Al Hasa, occupies four-fifths of the Arabian peninsula. The kingdom has an area of 830,000 sq. mi. (2,149,690 sq. km.) and a population of *16.1 million. Capital: Riyadh. The economy is based on oil, which provides 85 percent of Saudi Arabia's revenue.

TITLES

العربية السعودية

Al-Arabiya(t) as-Sa'udiya(t)

المملكة العربية السعودية

Al-Mamlaka(t) al-'Arabiya(t) as-Sa'udiya(t)

RULERS

al Sa'ud Dynasty

Fahad bin Abd Al-Aziz, AH1403-1426/1982-2005AD
Abdullah bin Abdul Aziz, AH1426-/2005AD

KINGDOM

REFORM COINAGE

5 Halala = 1 Ghirsh; 100 Halala = 1 Riyal

KM# 69 5 HALALA (Ghirsh)
Copper-Nickel **Ruler:** Abdullah bin Abdul Aziz AH1426-/2005-AD **Obv:** National emblem at center **Rev:** Legend above inscription in circle, dividing value, date below

Date	Mintage	F	VF	XF	Unc	BU
AH1430(2009)	—		0.15	0.30	0.75	1.00

KM# 62 10 HALALA (2 Ghirsh)
4.0000 g., Copper-Nickel, 21 mm. **Ruler:** Fahad Bin Abd Al-Aziz AH1403-1426/1982-2005AD **Obv:** National emblem at center, legend above and below **Rev:** Legend above inscription in circle dividing value, date below

Date	Mintage	F	VF	XF	Unc	BU
AH1423 (2002)	—		0.15	0.35	0.90	1.00

KM# 70 10 HALALA (2 Ghirsh)
Copper-Nickel **Ruler:** Abdullah bin Abdul Aziz AH1426-/2005-AD **Obv:** National emblem at center **Rev:** Legend above inscription in circle, dividing value, date below

Date	Mintage	F	VF	XF	Unc	BU
AH1430(2009)	—		0.15	0.30	0.80	1.25

KM# 63 25 HALALA (1/4 Riyal)
5.0000 g., Copper-Nickel, 23 mm. **Ruler:** Fahad Bin Abd Al-Aziz AH1403-1426/1982-2005AD **Obv:** National emblem at center, legend above and below **Rev:** Legend above inscription in circle dividing value, date below

Date	Mintage	F	VF	XF	Unc	BU
AH1423 (2002)	—	—	0.20	0.45	1.10	1.50

KM# 71 25 HALALA (1/4 Riyal)
Copper-Nickel **Ruler:** Abdullah bin Abdul Aziz AH1426-/2005-AD **Obv:** National emblem at center **Rev:** Legend above inscription in circle, divides value, date below

Date	Mintage	F	VF	XF	Unc	BU
AH1430(2009)	—	0.10	0.20	0.45	1.10	1.50

KM# 64 50 HALALA (1/2 Riyal)
6.5000 g., Copper-Nickel, 26 mm. **Ruler:** Fahad Bin Abd Al-Aziz AH1403-1426/1982-2005AD **Obv:** National emblem at center, legend above and below **Rev:** Legend above inscription in circle dividing value, date below

Date	Mintage	F	VF	XF	Unc	BU
AH1423 (2002)	—	0.15	0.30	0.75	1.50	2.00

KM# 68 50 HALALA (1/2 Riyal)
6.5000 g., Copper-Nickel **Ruler:** Abdullah bin Abdul Aziz AH1426-/2005-AD **Obv:** National emblem at center **Rev:** Legend above inscription in circle, dividing value, date below

Date	Mintage	F	VF	XF	Unc	BU
AH1427(2006)	—	0.15	0.30	0.60	1.50	2.00
AH1428 (2007)	—	0.15	0.30	0.60	1.50	2.00

KM# 72 100 HALALA (1 Riyal)
Copper-Nickel **Ruler:** Abdullah bin Abdul Aziz AH1426-/2005-AD **Obv:** National emblem at center **Rev:** Legend above inscription, divides value, date below

Date	Mintage	F	VF	XF	Unc	BU
AH1427(2006)	—	—	0.45	0.90	2.25	3.00
AH1429(2008)	—	—	0.45	0.90	2.25	3.00

SERBIA

Serbia, a former inland Balkan kingdom has an area of 34,116 sq. mi. (88,361 sq. km.). Capital: Belgrade.

MINT MARKS
A - Paris
(a) - Paris, privy mark only
H - Birmingham
V - Vienna
БП - (BP) Budapest

MONETARY SYSTEM
100 Para = 1 Dinara
DENOMINATIONS
ПАРА = Para
ПАРЕ = Pare
ДИНАР = Dinar
ДИНАРА = Dinara

REPUBLIC
STANDARD COINAGE

KM# 34 DINAR
4.3300 g., Copper-Zinc-Nickel, 20 mm. **Obv:** National Bank emblem within circle **Rev:** Bank building and value **Edge:** Reeded

Date	Mintage	F	VF	XF	Unc	BU
2003	10,320,000	—	—	0.25	1.00	1.50
2004	—	—	—	0.25	1.00	1.50
2005	—	—	—	0.25	1.00	1.50

KM# 39 DINAR
4.2600 g., Copper-Zinc-Nickel, 20 mm. **Obv:** Crowned and mantled arms **Rev:** National Bank and value **Edge:** Segmented reeding

Date	Mintage	F	VF	XF	Unc	BU
2005	—	—	—	0.25	1.00	1.50
2006	—	—	—	0.25	1.00	1.50
2007	—	—	—	0.25	1.00	1.50
2008	—	—	—	0.25	1.00	1.50
2009	—	—	—	0.25	1.00	1.50

KM# 48 DINAR
4.2000 g., Copper Plated Steel, 20 mm. **Obv:** Arms **Rev:** Nation Bank and value

Date	Mintage	F	VF	XF	Unc	BU
2009	—	—	—	—	1.00	1.50

KM# 35 2 DINARA
5.2400 g., Copper-Zinc-Nickel, 22 mm. **Obv:** National Bank emblem within circle **Rev:** Gracanica Monastery and value **Edge:** Reeded

Date	Mintage	F	VF	XF	Unc	BU
2003	4,688,500	—	—	0.50	2.00	2.50

KM# 46 2 DINARA
5.0000 g., Brass, 22 mm. **Obv:** Crowned and mantled arms **Rev:** Gracanica Monastery and value **Edge:** Segmented reeding

Date	Mintage	F	VF	XF	Unc	BU
2006	—	—	—	0.50	2.00	2.50
2007	—	—	—	0.50	2.00	2.50
2008	—	—	—	0.50	2.00	2.50
2009	—	—	—	0.50	2.00	2.50

KM# 49 2 DINARA
5.0500 g., Copper Plated Steel, 22 mm. **Obv:** Arms **Rev:** Gracanica Monastery and value

Date	Mintage	F	VF	XF	Unc	BU
2009	—	—	—	0.50	2.00	2.50

KM# 36 5 DINARA
5.2400 g., Copper-Zinc-Nickel, 22 mm. **Obv:** National Bank emblem within circle **Rev:** Krusedol Monastery and value **Edge:** Reeded

Date	Mintage	F	VF	XF	Unc	BU
2003	15,170,000	—	0.50	1.00	2.25	3.50

KM# 40 5 DINARA
5.2500 g., Copper-Zinc-Nickel, 24 mm. **Obv:** Crowned and mantled arms **Rev:** Krusedol Monastery and value **Edge:** Segmented reeding

Date	Mintage	F	VF	XF	Unc	BU
2005	—	—	—	0.75	2.00	3.50
2006	—	—	—	0.75	2.00	3.50
2007	—	—	—	0.75	2.00	3.50
2008	—	—	—	0.75	2.00	3.50

KM# 50 5 DINARA
Copper Plated Steel **Obv:** Arms **Rev:** Krusedol Monastery and value

Date	Mintage	F	VF	XF	Unc	BU
2009	—	—	—	0.75	2.00	3.50

KM# 37 10 DINARA
7.7700 g., Copper-Zinc-Nickel, 26 mm. **Obv:** National Bank emblem within circle **Rev:** Studenica Monastery and value **Edge:** Reeded

Date	Mintage	F	VF	XF	Unc	BU
2003	10,160,500	—	0.50	1.00	2.50	3.50

KM# 41 10 DINARA
8.0000 g., Copper-Zinc-Nickel, 26 mm. **Obv:** Crowned and mantled arms **Rev:** Studenica Monastery and value **Edge:** Segmented reeding

Date	Mintage	F	VF	XF	Unc	BU
2005	—	—	—	0.75	2.25	4.00
2006	—	—	—	0.75	2.25	4.00
2007	—	—	—	0.75	2.00	4.00
2008	—	—	—	0.75	2.00	4.00
2009	—	—	—	—	2.00	4.00

KM# 51 10 DINARA
7.7700 g., Copper-Nickel, 26 mm. **Subject:** 25th Summer Universiade, Belgrade **Obv:** Arms **Rev:** Logo

Date	Mintage	F	VF	XF	Unc	BU
2009	500,000	—	—	—	3.00	5.00

KM# 38 20 DINARA
9.0000 g., Copper-Zinc-Nickel, 28 mm. **Obv:** National Bank emblem within circle **Rev:** Temple of St. Sava and value **Edge:** Reeded

Date	Mintage	F	VF	XF	Unc	BU
2003	25,491,500	—	—	0.75	2.25	4.00

KM# 42 20 DINARA
9.0000 g., Copper-Nickel-Zinc, 28 mm. **Obv:** Crowned and mantled Serbian royal arms **Rev:** Nikola Tesla **Edge:** Segmented reeding

Date	Mintage	F	VF	XF	Unc	BU
2006	1,000,000	—	—	0.75	2.25	4.00

KM# 47 20 DINARA
9.1200 g., Copper-Nickel-Zinc, 27.93 mm. **Subject:** Dositej Obradovic, 1742-1811 **Obv:** National arms **Obv. Legend:** РЕПУБЛИКА СРБИЈА - REPUBLIKA SRBIJA **Rev:** Bust facing slightly left **Edge:** Segmented reeding

Date	Mintage	F	VF	XF	Unc	BU
2007	—	—	—	0.75	2.00	3.50

KM# 52 20 DINARA
9.0000 g., Copper-Nickel, 28 mm. **Obv:** Arms **Rev:** Milutin Milankovic portrait

Date	Mintage	F	VF	XF	Unc	BU
2009	500,000	—	—	—	2.00	3.50

KM# 43 1000 DINARA
13.0000 g., 0.9250 Silver 0.3866 oz. ASW, 30 mm.
Obv: Crowned and mantled Serbian royal arms **Rev:** Nikola Tesla **Edge:** Segmented reeding

Date	Mintage	F	VF	XF	Unc	BU
2006 Proof	2,000	Value: 28.00				

KM# 44 5000 DINARA
3.4550 g., 0.9000 Gold 0.1000 oz. AGW, 20 mm. **Obv:** Crowned and mantled Serbian royal arms **Rev:** Nikola Tesla

Date	Mintage	F	VF	XF	Unc	BU
2006 Proof	2,000	Value: 175				

KM# 45 10000 DINARA
8.6400 g., 0.9000 Gold 0.2500 oz. AGW, 25 mm. **Obv:** Crowned and mantled Serbian royal arms **Rev:** Nikola Tesla

Date	Mintage	F	VF	XF	Unc	BU
2006 Proof	1,000	Value: 325				

MINT SETS

KM#	Date	Mintage Identification	Issue Price	Mkt Val
MS1	2003 (5)	— KM34-38	—	10.00
MS2	2005 (3)	— KM39-41	—	10.00
MS3	2006 (5)	— KM#39-42, 46	—	12.00

PROOF SETS

KM#	Date	Mintage Identification	Issue Price	Mkt Val
PS1	2006 (3)	— KM#43-45	—	525

SEYCHELLES

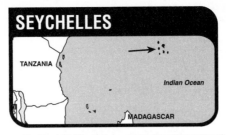

The Republic of Seychelles, an archipelago of 85 granite and coral islands situated in the Indian Ocean 600 miles (965 km.) northeast of Madagascar, has an area of 156 sq. mi. (455 sq. km.) and a population of *70,000. Among these islands are the Aldabra Islands, the Farquhar Group, and Ile Desroches, which the United Kingdom ceded to the Seychelles upon its independence. Capital: Victoria, on Mahe. The economy is based on fishing, a plantation system of agriculture, and tourism. Copra, cinnamon and vanilla are exported.

Seychelles is a member of the Commonwealth of Nations. The president is the Head of State and of the Government.

MINT MARKS
(sa) – M in oval – South African Mint Co.
  (starting in 2000, not PM)
None - British Royal Mint

MONETARY SYSTEM
100 Cents = 1 Rupee

REPUBLIC
STANDARD COINAGE

KM# 46.2 CENT
1.4300 g., Brass, 16.03 mm. **Obv:** Altered coat of arms **Rev:** Mud Crab **Rev. Designer:** Robert Elderton **Edge:** Plain

Date	Mintage	F	VF	XF	Unc	BU
2004	—	—	—	0.15	0.25	0.35

KM# 47.2 5 CENTS
2.0000 g., Brass, 18 mm. **Obv:** Altered coat of arms **Rev:** Tapioca plant **Rev. Designer:** Robert Elderton

Date	Mintage	F	VF	XF	Unc	BU
2003	—	—	—	0.10	0.30	0.50

KM# 47a 5 CENTS
1.9700 g., Brass Plated Steel, 17.97 mm. **Obv:** National arms **Rev:** Tapioca plant **Rev. Designer:** Robert Elderton **Edge:** Plain

Date	Mintage	F	VF	XF	Unc	BU
2007PM	—	—	—	0.10	0.30	0.50

KM# 48.2 10 CENTS
3.3400 g., Brass, 21 mm. **Obv:** Altered coat of arms **Rev:** Yellowfin tuna **Rev. Designer:** Robert Elderton **Edge:** Plain

Date	Mintage	F	VF	XF	Unc	BU
2003	—	—	—	0.10	0.35	1.00	1.50

KM# 48a 10 CENTS
3.3700 g., Brass Plated Steel, 21 mm. **Obv:** National arms **Rev:** Black parrot, value **Edge:** Plain

Date	Mintage	F	VF	XF	Unc	BU
2007PM	—	—	—	0.15	0.30	0.75	1.00

KM# 49a 25 CENTS
2.9700 g., Nickel Clad Steel, 18.9 mm. **Obv:** National arms **Rev:** Black Parrot and value **Edge:** Plain

Date	Mintage	F	VF	XF	Unc	BU
2003PM	—	—	0.15	0.40	1.00	1.25
2007PM	—	—	0.15	0.40	1.00	1.25

KM# 50.2 RUPEE
6.1800 g., Copper-Nickel, 25.46 mm. **Obv:** Altered coat of arms **Rev:** Triton Conch Shell **Rev. Designer:** Suzanne Danielli **Edge:** Reeded

Date	Mintage	F	VF	XF	Unc	BU
2007	—	—	0.25	0.45	1.10	1.50

KM# 118 5 RUPEES
28.2800 g., Copper-Nickel, 38.6 mm. **Subject:** John Paul II memorial **Obv:** National Arms **Rev:** John Paul II in mitre waving

Date	Mintage	F	VF	XF	Unc	BU
2005	—	—	—	—	8.00	10.00

KM# 119 5 RUPEES
28.2800 g., Copper-Nickel, 38.6 mm. **Obv:** National Arms **Rev:** Benedict XVI blessing crowd at St. Peter's Square

Date	Mintage	F	VF	XF	Unc	BU
2005	—	—	—	—	10.00	12.00

KM# 51.2 5 RUPEES
9.0000 g., Copper-Nickel, 29 mm. **Obv:** Altered arms **Rev:** Fruit tree divides value **Rev. Designer:** Frederick Mogford **Edge:** Reeded

Date	Mintage	F	VF	XF	Unc	BU
2007	—	—	0.30	0.70	1.75	2.25

KM# 121 25 RUPEES
28.2800 g., 0.9250 Silver 0.8410 oz. ASW, 38.6 mm. **Obv:** National arms **Rev:** Benedict XVI blessing crowd at St. Peter's Square **Edge:** Reeded

Date	Mintage	F	VF	XF	Unc	BU
2005	—	Value: 50.00				

KM# 120 25 RUPEES
28.2800 g., 0.9250 Silver 0.8410 oz. ASW, 38.6 mm. **Obv:** National arms **Rev:** Description John Paul II in mitre waving **Edge:** Reeded

Date	Mintage	F	VF	XF	Unc	BU
2005 Proof	—	Value: 50.00				

KM# 122 250 RUPEES
6.2200 g., 0.9999 Gold 0.1999 oz. AGW, 22 mm. **Obv:** National arms **Rev:** Description John Paul II in mitre waving **Edge:** Reeded

Date	Mintage	F	VF	XF	Unc	BU
2005 Proof	—	Value: 265				

KM# 123 250 RUPEES
6.2200 g., 0.9999 Gold 0.1999 oz. AGW, 22 mm. **Obv:** National arms **Rev:** Benedict XVI blessing crowd at St. Peter's Square **Edge:** Reeded

Date	Mintage	F	VF	XF	Unc	BU
2005 Proof	—	Value: 265				

SHAWNEE TRIBAL NATION
SOVEREIGN NATION
MILLED COINAGE

KM# 1 DOLLAR
31.2000 g., 0.9999 Silver 1.0030 oz. ASW, 39 mm. **Obv:** Tribal seal **Obv. Legend:** THE SOVEREIGN NATION OF THE SHAWNEE TRIBE **Obv. Designer:** Alex Shagin **Rev:** Bust of Chief Tenskwatawa "The Prophet" 3/4 right **Edge:** Reeded

Date	Mintage	F	VF	XF	Unc	BU
2002	50,000	—	—	—	—	20.00
2002 Proof	20,000	Value: 40.00				

KM# 10 DOLLAR
124.4120 g., 0.9990 Silver 3.9958 oz. ASW

Date	Mintage	F	VF	XF	Unc	BU
2003 Proof	10,000	Value: 175				

KM# 3 DOLLAR
31.2000 g., 0.9999 Silver 1.0030 oz. ASW, 39 mm. **Obv:** Tribal seal **Obv. Legend:** THE SOVEREIGN NATION OF THE SHAWNEE TRIBE **Obv. Designer:** Alex Shagin **Rev:** Lewis, Clark and Drouillard scouting **Edge:** Reeded

Date	Mintage	F	VF	XF	Unc	BU
2003	50,000	—	—	—	—	25.00
2003 Proof	20,000	Value: 45.00				

KM# 5 DOLLAR
31.2000 g., 0.9999 Silver 1.0030 oz. ASW, 39 mm. **Obv:** Tribal seal **Obv. Legend:** THE SOVEREIGN NATION OF THE SHAWNEE TRIBE **Obv. Designer:** Alex Shagin **Rev:** Flag behing Indian Chief and Thomas Jefferson standing, eagle on shield at their feet **Edge:** Reeded

Date	Mintage	F	VF	XF	Unc	BU
2004	50,000	—	—	—	—	20.00
2004 Proof	20,000	Value: 40.00				

KM# 15 DOLLAR
31.3100 g., 0.9990 Silver 1.0056 oz. ASW, 40.6 mm. **Obv:** Tribal seal **Obv. Legend:** THE SOVEREIGN NATION OF THE SHAWNEE TRIBE **Obv. Designer:** A. Shagin **Rev:** Lewis, Clark, Dromillard and Sacagawea in a canoe **Rev. Legend:** EXPEDITION OF DISCOVERY **Edge:** Reeded

Date	Mintage	F	VF	XF	Unc	BU
2005 Proof	20,000	Value: 45.00				
2005	50,000	—	—	—	30.00	—

KM# 20 DOLLAR
31.2100 g., 0.9999 Silver 1.0033 oz. ASW, 40.6 mm. **Obv:** Tribal seal **Obv. Legend:** THE SOVEREIGN NATION OF THE SHAWNEE TRIBE **Obv. Designer:** A. Shagin **Rev:** 1/2 length figure of Tenskwatawa "the prophet" 3/4 left **Rev. Legend:** PROPHET TENSKWATAWA **Edge:** Reeded

Date	Mintage	F	VF	XF	Unc	BU
2006 Proof	20,000	Value: 45.00				
2006	50,000	—	—	—	—	30.00

KM# 24 DOLLAR
31.1050 g., 0.9990 Silver 0.9990 oz. ASW **Rev:** Battle of Wabash

Date	Mintage	F	VF	XF	Unc	BU
2007 Proof	20,000	Value: 50.00				
2007	50,000	—	—	—	—	40.00

KM# 26 DOLLAR
31.1050 g., 0.9990 Silver 0.9990 oz. ASW **Rev:** Battle of Point Pleasant

Date	Mintage	F	VF	XF	Unc	BU
2008	50,000	—	—	—	—	40.00
2008 Proof	20,000	Value: 50.00				

KM# 28 DOLLAR
31.1050 g., 0.9990 Silver 0.9990 oz. ASW **Rev:** Battle of Fallen Timber

Date	Mintage	F	VF	XF	Unc	BU
2009 Proof	20,000	Value: 50.00				
2009	50,000	—	—	—	—	40.00

KM# 2 5 DOLLARS
6.2200 g., 0.9999 Gold 0.1999 oz. AGW, 20 mm. **Obv:** Arms **Obv. Legend:** THE SOVEREIGN NATION OF THE SHAWNEE TRIBE **Obv. Designer:** Alex Shagin **Rev:** Bust of Tecumseh "Shooting Star" 3/4 left **Edge:** Reeded

Date	Mintage	F	VF	XF	Unc	BU
2002 Proof	5,000	Value: 375				

KM# 4 5 DOLLARS
6.2200 g., 0.9999 Gold 0.1999 oz. AGW, 22.5 mm. **Obv:** Arms **Obv. Legend:** THE SOVEREIGN NATION OF THE SHAWNEE TRIBE **Obv. Designer:** Alex Shagin **Rev:** Bust of George Drouillard 3/4 right **Rev. Legend:** GEORGE DROUILLARD SIGN TALKER

Date	Mintage	F	VF	XF	Unc	BU
2003 Proof	5,000	Value: 375				

KM# 6 5 DOLLARS
6.2207 g., 0.9990 Gold 0.1998 oz. AGW, 22 mm. **Obv:** Arms **Obv. Legend:** THE SOVEREIGN NATION OF THE SHAWNEE TRIBE **Rev:** Sacagawea with child and horse **Edge:** Reeded

Date	Mintage	F	VF	XF	Unc	BU
2004 Proof	5,000	Value: 375				

KM# 16 5 DOLLARS
6.3000 g., 0.9999 Gold 0.2025 oz. AGW, 22.5 mm. **Obv:** Tribal seal **Obv. Legend:** THE SOVEREIGN NATION OF THE SHAWNEE TRIBE **Obv. Designer:** A. Shagin **Rev:** Sacagawea with papoose on horseback right **Rev. Legend:** EXPEDITION OF DISCOVERY **Edge:** Reeded

Date	Mintage	F	VF	XF	Unc	BU
2005 Proof	5,000	Value: 375				

KM# 21 5 DOLLARS
6.2500 g., 0.9999 Gold 0.2009 oz. AGW, 22.5 mm. **Obv:** Tribal seal **Obv. Legend:** THE SOVEREIGN NATION OF THE SHAWNEE TRIBE **Obv. Designer:** A. Shagin **Rev:** Bust of Chief Tecumseh 3/4 right **Rev. Legend:** TECVMSEH **Edge:** Reeded

Date	Mintage	F	VF	XF	Unc	BU
2006 Proof	5,000	Value: 375				

KM# 25 5 DOLLARS
6.2500 g., 0.9990 Gold 0.2007 oz. AGW **Rev:** Chief Blue Jacket

Date	Mintage	F	VF	XF	Unc	BU
2007 Proof	5,000	Value: 400				

KM# 27 5 DOLLARS
6.2500 g., 0.9990 Gold 0.2007 oz. AGW **Rev:** Chief Cornstalk

Date	Mintage	F	VF	XF	Unc	BU
2008 Proof	5,000	Value: 400				

KM# 29 5 DOLLARS
6.2500 g., 0.9990 Gold 0.2007 oz. AGW **Rev:** Chief Black-Hoof

Date	Mintage	F	VF	XF	Unc	BU
2009 Proof	5,000	Value: 400				

KM# 7 50 DOLLARS
15.5500 g., 0.9990 Gold 0.4994 oz. AGW **Rev:** George Drouillard

Date	Mintage	F	VF	XF	Unc	BU
2003 Proof	999	Value: 800				

KM# 11 50 DOLLARS
15.5500 g., 0.9990 Gold 0.4994 oz. AGW **Rev:** Sacagawea and child

Date	Mintage	F	VF	XF	Unc	BU
2004 Proof	—	Value: 800				

KM# 17 50 DOLLARS
15.5500 g., 0.9999 Gold 0.4999 oz. AGW, 30.1 mm. **Obv:** Tribal seal **Obv. Legend:** THE SOVEREIGN NATION OF THE SHAWNEE TRIBE **Obv. Designer:** A. Shagin **Rev:** Sacagawea with papoose on horseback right **Rev. Legend:** EXPEDITION OF DISCOVERY **Edge:** Reeded

Date	Mintage	F	VF	XF	Unc	BU
2005 Proof	999	Value: 800				

KM# 8 100 DOLLARS
30.9100 g., 0.9999 Gold 0.9936 oz. AGW, 38.9 mm. **Obv:** Tribal seal **Obv. Legend:** THE SOVEREIGN NATION OF THE SHAWNEE TRIBE **Obv. Designer:** A. Shagin **Rev:** Bust of "Sign Talker" 3/4 right **Rev. Legend:** GEORGE DROILLARD "SIGN TALKER" **Edge:** Milled

Date	Mintage	F	VF	XF	Unc	BU
2003 Proof	999	Value: 1,800				

KM# 12 100 DOLLARS
31.1050 g., 0.9990 Gold 0.9990 oz. AGW **Rev:** Sacagawea and child

Date	Mintage	F	VF	XF	Unc	BU
2004 Proof	—	Value: 1,800				

KM# 18 100 DOLLARS
31.1050 g., 0.9990 Gold 0.9990 oz. AGW **Rev:** Sacagawea and child on horseback

Date	Mintage	F	VF	XF	Unc	BU
2005 Proof	999	Value: 1,800				

KM# 23 100 DOLLARS
62.2100 g., 0.9990 Bi-Metallic 1 oz. gold and 1 oz. silver 1.9980 oz. **Rev:** Lewis and Clark

Date	Mintage	F	VF	XF	Unc	BU
2005 Proof	500	Value: 2,500				

KM# 9 500 DOLLARS
93.5000 g., 0.9999 Gold 3.0057 oz. AGW **Obv:** Tribal seal **Obv. Legend:** THE SOVEREIGN NATION OF THE SHAWNEE TRIBE **Obv. Designer:** A. Shagin **Rev:** Lewis, Clark and Drouillard scouting **Rev. Legend:** LEWIS • CLARK • DROUILLARD **Edge:** Reeded

Date	Mintage	F	VF	XF	Unc	BU
2003 Proof	300	Value: 5,700				

KM# 13 500 DOLLARS
15.5400 g., 0.9990 Platinum 0.4991 oz. APW, 30 mm. **Obv:** Tribal seal **Obv. Legend:** THE SOVEREIGN NATION OF

THE SHAWNEE TRIBE **Obv. Designer:** A. Shagin **Rev:** Flag and shield between standing Chief and Thomas Jefferson **Rev. Legend:** EXPEDITION OF DISCOVERY **Edge:** Reeded

Date	Mintage	F	VF	XF	Unc	BU
2004 Proof	999	Value: 1,250				

KM# 23A 500 DOLLARS
15.5500 g., 0.9990 Platinum 0.4994 oz. APW **Rev:** Shawnee Chief and Thomas Jefferson standing

Date	Mintage	F	VF	XF	Unc	BU
2005 Proof	999	Value: 1,250				

KM# 14 1000 DOLLARS
31.0000 g., 0.9999 Platinum 0.9965 oz. APW, 38.7 mm. **Obv:** Tribal seal **Obv. Legend:** THE SOVEREIGN NATION OF THE SHAWNEE TRIBE **Obv. Designer:** A. Shagin **Rev:** Flag and shield between standing Chief and Thomas Jefferson **Rev. Legend:** EXPEDITION OF DISCOVERY **Edge:** Reeded

Date	Mintage	F	VF	XF	Unc	BU
2004 Proof	300	Value: 3,000				

KM# 22 1000 DOLLARS
31.1050 g., 0.9990 Platinum 0.9990 oz. APW **Rev:** Shawnee Chief and Thomas Jefferson standing

Date	Mintage	F	VF	XF	Unc	BU
2005 Proof	300	Value: 3,000				

SIERRA LEONE

The Republic of Sierra Leone is located in western Africa between Guinea and Liberia, has an area of 27,699 sq. mi. (71,740 sq. km.) and a population of *4.1 million. Capital: Freetown. The economy is predominantly agricultural but mining contributes significantly to export revenues. Diamonds, iron ore, palm kernels, cocoa, and coffee are exported.

Sierra Leone is a member of the Commonwealth of Nations. The president is Chief of State and Head of Government.

MONETARY SYSTEM

Beginning 1964

100 Cents = 1 Leone

REPUBLIC

STANDARD COINAGE

KM# 295 20 LEONES
3.9200 g., Copper-Nickel, 21.7 mm. **Obv:** Value within fish and beaded circle **Rev:** Chimpanzee facing **Edge:** Plain

Date	Mintage	F	VF	XF	Unc	BU
2003	—	—	—	—	0.50	1.25

KM# 302 100 LEONES
28.2800 g., Copper-Nickel, 38.6 mm. **Subject:** 40th Anniversary - Bank of Sierra Leone **Obv:** Bank President Kabbah **Rev:** Lion **Edge:** Reeded

Date	Mintage	F	VF	XF	Unc	BU
ND (2004)PM	5,000	—	—	—	15.00	18.00

KM# 296 500 LEONES
7.2000 g., Bi-Metallic Stainless Steel center in Brass ring, 24 mm. **Obv:** Building within circle **Rev:** Bust with hat facing within circle **Edge:** Plain **Shape:** 10-sided

Date	Mintage	F	VF	XF	Unc	BU
2004	—	—	—	—	7.50	9.00

KM# 346 500 LEONES
28.2800 g., Bronze, 38.6 mm. **Subject:** 40th Anniversary - Bank of Sierra Leone **Obv:** Bank President Kabbah **Rev:** Lion, denomination as "Le 500" **Edge:** Reeded

Date	Mintage	F	VF	XF	Unc	BU
ND(2004)PM	10,000	—	—	—	15.00	18.00

DOLLAR DENOMINATED COINAGE

KM# 222 DOLLAR
28.4900 g., Copper-Nickel, 38.5 mm. **Series:** The Big Five **Obv:** National arms **Rev:** Rhino **Edge:** Reeded

Date	Mintage	F	VF	XF	Unc	BU
2001PM	—	—	—	—	12.50	15.00

KM# 225 DOLLAR
28.4900 g., Copper-Nickel, 38.5 mm. **Series:** The Big Five **Obv:** National arms **Rev:** Lion **Edge:** Reeded

Date	Mintage	F	VF	XF	Unc	BU
2001PM	—	—	—	—	10.00	14.00

KM# 228 DOLLAR
28.4900 g., Copper-Nickel, 38.5 mm. **Series:** The Big Five **Obv:** National arms **Rev:** Leopard **Edge:** Reeded

Date	Mintage	F	VF	XF	Unc	BU
2001PM	—	—	—	—	10.00	14.00

KM# 231 DOLLAR
28.4900 g., Copper-Nickel, 38.5 mm. **Series:** The Big Five **Obv:** National arms **Rev:** Elephants **Edge:** Reeded

Date	Mintage	F	VF	XF	Unc	BU
2001PM	—	—	—	—	10.00	14.00

KM# 234 DOLLAR
28.4900 g., Copper-Nickel, 38.5 mm. **Series:** The Big Five **Obv:** National arms **Rev:** Buffalo **Edge:** Reeded

Date	Mintage	F	VF	XF	Unc	BU
2001PM	—	—	—	—	10.00	14.00

KM# 237 DOLLAR
28.4900 g., Copper-Nickel, 38.5 mm. **Series:** The Big Five **Obv:** National arms **Rev:** All five animals **Edge:** Reeded

Date	Mintage	F	VF	XF	Unc	BU
2001PM	—	—	—	—	10.00	14.00

KM# 241.1 DOLLAR
28.5400 g., Copper-Nickel, 38.65 mm. **Series:** Big Cats **Obv:** National arms **Rev:** Male and female lions **Edge:** Reeded

Date	Mintage	F	VF	XF	Unc	BU
2001PM	—	—	—	—	12.50	15.00

KM# 241.2 DOLLAR
28.5400 g., Copper-Nickel, 38.65 mm. **Series:** Big Cats **Obv:** National arms **Rev:** Multi-colored male and female lions **Edge:** Reeded

Date	Mintage	F	VF	XF	Unc	BU
2001PM	—	—	—	—	15.00	17.50

KM# 242.1 DOLLAR
28.5400 g., Copper-Nickel, 38.65 mm. **Series:** Big Cats **Obv:** National arms **Rev:** Tiger **Edge:** Reeded

Date	Mintage	F	VF	XF	Unc	BU
2001PM	—	—	—	—	10.00	14.00

KM# 242.2 DOLLAR
28.5400 g., Copper-Nickel, 38.65 mm. **Series:** Big Cats **Obv:** National arms **Rev:** Multi-colored Tiger **Edge:** Reeded

Date	Mintage	F	VF	XF	Unc	BU
2001PM	—	—	—	—	15.00	17.50

KM# 243.1 DOLLAR
28.5400 g., Copper-Nickel, 38.65 mm. **Series:** Big Cats **Obv:** National arms **Rev:** Cheetah **Edge:** Reeded

Date	Mintage	F	VF	XF	Unc	BU
2001PM	—	—	—	—	12.50	15.00

KM# 243.2 DOLLAR
28.5400 g., Copper-Nickel, 38.65 mm. **Series:** Big Cats **Obv:** National arms **Rev:** Multi-colored Cheetah **Edge:** Reeded

Date	Mintage	F	VF	XF	Unc	BU
2001PM	—	—	—	—	15.00	17.50

KM# 244.1 DOLLAR
28.5400 g., Copper-Nickel, 38.65 mm. **Series:** Big Cats **Obv:** National arms **Rev:** Cougar **Edge:** Reeded

Date	Mintage	F	VF	XF	Unc	BU
2001PM	—	—	—	—	10.00	14.00

KM# 244.2 DOLLAR
28.5400 g., Copper-Nickel, 38.65 mm. **Series:** Big Cats **Obv:** National arms **Rev:** Multi-colored Cougar **Edge:** Reeded

Date	Mintage	F	VF	XF	Unc	BU
2001PM	—	—	—	—	15.00	17.50

KM# 245.1 DOLLAR
28.5400 g., Copper-Nickel, 38.65 mm. **Series:** Big Cats **Obv:** National arms **Rev:** Black panther **Edge:** Reeded

Date	Mintage	F	VF	XF	Unc	BU
2001PM	—	—	—	—	10.00	14.00

KM# 245.2 DOLLAR
28.5400 g., Copper-Nickel, 38.65 mm. **Series:** Big Cats **Obv:** National arms **Rev:** Multi-colored Black Panther **Edge:** Reeded

Date	Mintage	F	VF	XF	Unc	BU
2001PM	—	—	—	—	15.00	17.50

KM# 198 DOLLAR
28.2800 g., Copper-Nickel, 38.6 mm. **Subject:** Year of the Snake **Obv:** National arms **Rev:** Snake **Edge:** Reeded

Date	Mintage	F	VF	XF	Unc	BU
2001	—	—	—	—	10.00	14.00

KM# 206 DOLLAR
Copper-Nickel **Subject:** P'an Ku **Obv:** National arms **Rev:** Dragon

Date	Mintage	F	VF	XF	Unc	BU
2001	—	—	—	—	10.00	14.00

KM# 214 DOLLAR
Copper-Nickel **Subject:** P'an Ku **Obv:** National arms **Rev:** Dragon and three animals

Date	Mintage	F	VF	XF	Unc	BU
2001	—	—	—	—	10.00	14.00

KM# 256 DOLLAR
28.2800 g., Copper-Nickel, 38.6 mm. **Subject:** Year of the Horse **Obv:** National arms **Rev:** Horse **Edge:** Reeded

Date	Mintage	F	VF	XF	Unc	BU
2002	—	—	—	—	12.50	15.00

KM# 264 DOLLAR
28.2800 g., Copper-Nickel, 38.6 mm. **Subject:** RMS Titanic **Obv:** National arms **Rev:** Titanic at dock **Edge:** Reeded

Date	Mintage	F	VF	XF	Unc	BU
2002	—	—	—	—	10.00	12.00

KM# 268   DOLLAR
28.2800 g., Copper-Nickel, 38.6 mm. **Subject:** Queen's Golden Jubilee **Obv:** National arms **Rev:** Queen Elizabeth II and Prince Philip visiting blacksmiths in Sierra Leone **Edge:** Reeded

Date	Mintage	F	VF	XF	Unc	BU
2002	—	—	—	—	10.00	12.00

KM# 269   DOLLAR
28.2800 g., Copper-Nickel, 38.6 mm. **Subject:** Queen's Golden Jubilee **Obv:** National arms **Rev:** Queen, Prince Charles and Princess Anne **Edge:** Reeded

Date	Mintage	F	VF	XF	Unc	BU
2002	—	—	—	—	10.00	12.00

KM# 276   DOLLAR
28.2800 g., Copper-Nickel, 38.6 mm. **Subject:** British Queen Mother **Obv:** National arms **Rev:** Queen Mother with dog in garden **Edge:** Reeded

Date	Mintage	F	VF	XF	Unc	BU
2002	—	—	—	—	10.00	12.00

KM# 279   DOLLAR
28.2800 g., Copper-Nickel, 38.6 mm. **Subject:** Queen Mother **Obv:** National arms **Rev:** Queen Mother with daughters **Edge:** Reeded

Date	Mintage	F	VF	XF	Unc	BU
2002	—	—	—	—	10.00	12.00

KM# 282   DOLLAR
28.2800 g., Copper-Nickel, 38.6 mm. **Subject:** Queen's Golden Jubilee **Obv:** National arms **Rev:** Queen Elizabeth and a young Prince Charles **Edge:** Reeded

Date	Mintage	F	VF	XF	Unc	BU
2002	—	—	—	—	10.00	12.00

KM# 285   DOLLAR
28.2800 g., Copper-Nickel, 38.6 mm. **Subject:** Queen's Golden Jubilee **Obv:** National arms **Rev:** Queen Elizabeth and Prince Philip **Edge:** Reeded

Date	Mintage	F	VF	XF	Unc	BU
2002	—	—	—	—	10.00	12.00

KM# 288   DOLLAR
28.2800 g., Copper-Nickel, 38.6 mm. **Subject:** Olympics **Obv:** National arms **Rev:** Victory goddess Nike **Edge:** Reeded

Date	Mintage	F	VF	XF	Unc	BU
2003	—	—	—	—	10.00	12.00
2004	—	—	—	—	10.00	12.00

KM# 291   DOLLAR
28.2800 g., Copper-Nickel, 38.6 mm. **Subject:** Olympics **Obv:** National arms **Rev:** Ancient archer **Edge:** Reeded

Date	Mintage	F	VF	XF	Unc	BU
2003	—	—	—	—	10.00	12.00
2004	—	—	—	—	10.00	12.00

KM# 297   DOLLAR
28.2800 g., Copper-Nickel, 38.6 mm. **Obv:** National arms **Rev:** Nelson Mandela **Edge:** Reeded

Date	Mintage	F	VF	XF	Unc	BU
2004	—	—	—	—	15.00	16.50

KM# 300   DOLLAR
28.2800 g., Copper-Nickel, 38.6 mm. **Obv:** National arms **Rev:** Ronald Reagan **Edge:** Reeded

Date	Mintage	F	VF	XF	Unc	BU
2004	—	—	—	—	15.00	16.50

KM# 304   DOLLAR
28.4200 g., Copper-Nickel, 38.6 mm. **Obv:** National arms **Rev:** Giraffe **Edge:** Reeded

Date	Mintage	F	VF	XF	Unc	BU
2005	—	—	—	—	12.00	16.00

KM# 305   DOLLAR
28.4200 g., Copper-Nickel, 38.6 mm. **Obv:** National arms **Rev:** Crocodile **Edge:** Reeded

Date	Mintage	F	VF	XF	Unc	BU
2005	—	—	—	—	12.00	16.00

KM# 306   DOLLAR
28.4200 g., Copper-Nickel, 38.6 mm. **Obv:** National arms **Rev:** Hippo in water **Edge:** Reeded

Date	Mintage	F	VF	XF	Unc	BU
2005	—	—	—	—	12.00	16.00

KM# 307   DOLLAR
28.6200 g., 0.9250 Silver 0.8511 oz. ASW, 38.5 mm. **Obv:** National arms **Rev:** Giraffe **Edge:** Reeded

Date	Mintage	F	VF	XF	Unc	BU
2005 Proof	—	Value: 50.00				

KM# 345   DOLLAR
28.5000 g., Copper-Nickel, 38.58 mm. **Subject:** Death of Prince Rainier III **Obv:** National arms **Rev:** Bust left, small knight horseback right on neck **Edge:** Reeded

Date	Mintage	F	VF	XF	Unc	BU
2005	—	—	—	—	7.00	9.00

KM# 317   DOLLAR
Copper-Nickel **Series:** 60th Anniversary End of WW II **Subject:** Battle of El Alamein **Obv:** National arms **Obv. Legend:** REPUBLIC OF SIERRA LEONE **Rev:** Tank, plane and ground troops

Date	Mintage	F	VF	XF	Unc	BU
2005	—	—	—	—	10.00	12.00

KM# 316   DOLLAR
Copper-Nickel **Series:** 60th Anniversary End of WW II **Subject:** The Battle of the Atlantic **Obv:** National arms **Obv. Legend:** REPUBLIC OF SIERRA LEONE **Rev:** Plane and ship convoy

Date	Mintage	F	VF	XF	Unc	BU
2005	—	—	—	—	10.00	12.00

KM# 319   DOLLAR
Copper-Nickel **Series:** 60th Anniversary End of WW II **Subject:** The Battle of Berlin **Obv:** National arms **Obv. Legend:** REPUBLIC OF SIERRA LEONE **Rev:** Berlin city view, tank

Date	Mintage	F	VF	XF	Unc	BU
2005	—	—	—	—	10.00	12.00

KM# 315   DOLLAR
Copper-Nickel **Series:** 60th Anniversary End of WW II **Subject:** Battle of Britian **Obv:** National arms **Obv. Legend:** REPUBLIC OF SIERRA LEONE **Rev:** Planes in flight

Date	Mintage	F	VF	XF	Unc	BU
2005	—	—	—	—	10.00	12.00

KM# 318 DOLLAR
Copper-Nickel **Series:** 60th Anniversay End of WW II
Subject: Battle of the Bulge **Obv:** National arms **Obv. Legend:**
REPUBLIC OF SIERRA LEONE **Rev:** Forest battle scene

Date	Mintage	F	VF	XF	Unc	BU
2005	—	—	—	—	10.00	12.00

KM# 320 DOLLAR
Copper-Nickel **Series:** 60th Anniversary End of WW II
Subject: The Heavy Water Raids **Obv:** National arms
Obv. Legend: REPUBLIC OF SIERRA LEONE **Rev:** Troops on
skies, factory in ruins

Date	Mintage	F	VF	XF	Unc	BU
2005	—	—	—	—	10.00	12.00

KM# 321 DOLLAR
Copper-Nickel **Obv:** National Arms **Rev:** Mountain Gorillia

Date	Mintage	F	VF	XF	Unc	BU
2005	—	—	—	—	12.00	16.00

KM# 322 DOLLAR
Copper-Nickel **Rev:** John Paul II head left, within ring of the
Stations of the Cross

Date	Mintage	F	VF	XF	Unc	BU
2005	—	—	—	—	10.00	12.00

KM# 323 DOLLAR
Copper-Nickel **Rev:** Benedict XVI and St. Peter's

Date	Mintage	F	VF	XF	Unc	BU
2005	—	—	—	—	10.00	12.00

KM# 324 DOLLAR
Copper-Nickel **Obv:** National Arms **Rev:** Brontosaurus

Date	Mintage	F	VF	XF	Unc	BU
2006	—	—	—	—	12.00	16.00

KM# 308 DOLLAR
28.3700 g., Copper-Nickel, 38.5 mm. **Obv:** National arms
Rev: Stegosaurus **Edge:** Reeded

Date	Mintage	F	VF	XF	Unc	BU
2006	—	—	—	—	—	16.00

KM# 309 DOLLAR
28.3700 g., Copper-Nickel, 38.5 mm. **Obv:** National arms
Rev: Tyrannosaurus Rex **Edge:** Reeded

Date	Mintage	F	VF	XF	Unc	BU
2006	—	—	—	—	—	16.00

KM# 310 DOLLAR
28.3700 g., Copper-Nickel, 38.5 mm. **Obv:** National arms
Rev: Triceratops **Edge:** Reeded

Date	Mintage	F	VF	XF	Unc	BU
2006	—	—	—	—	—	16.00

KM# 311 DOLLAR
28.3700 g., Copper-Nickel, 38.5 mm. **Obv:** National arms
Rev: Lion **Edge:** Reeded

Date	Mintage	F	VF	XF	Unc	BU
2006	—	—	—	—	—	16.00

KM# 312 DOLLAR
28.3700 g., Copper-Nickel, 38.5 mm. **Obv:** National arms
Rev: Dromedary Camel **Edge:** Reeded

Date	Mintage	F	VF	XF	Unc	BU
2006	—	—	—	—	—	16.00

KM# 313 DOLLAR
28.3700 g., Copper-Nickel, 38.63 mm. **Obv:** National arms
Rev: Chimpanzee **Edge:** Reeded

Date	Mintage	F	VF	XF	Unc	BU
2006	—	—	—	—	—	16.00

KM# 314 DOLLAR
28.3700 g., Copper-Nickel, 38.5 mm. **Obv:** National arms
Rev: Impala **Edge:** Reeded

Date	Mintage	F	VF	XF	Unc	BU
2006	—	—	—	—	—	16.00

KM# 326 DOLLAR
Copper-Nickel **Rev:** Cheetah

Date	Mintage	F	VF	XF	Unc	BU
2007	—	—	—	—	—	17.00

KM# 327 DOLLAR
Copper-Nickel **Rev:** Zebra

Date	Mintage	F	VF	XF	Unc	BU
2007	—	—	—	—	—	17.00

KM# 328 DOLLAR
Copper-Nickel **Rev:** Rhino

Date	Mintage	F	VF	XF	Unc	BU
2007	—	—	—	—	—	17.00

KM# 329 DOLLAR
Copper-Nickel **Obv:** Arms **Rev:** African elephant

Date	Mintage	F	VF	XF	Unc	BU
2007	—	—	—	—	—	18.00

KM# 347 DOLLAR
28.3700 g., Copper-Nickel, 38.6 mm. **Series:** Nocternal
Creatures of Africa **Obv:** National arms **Rev:** Duiker Antelope
standing left, facing **Edge:** Reeded **Note:** Blackened finish.

Date	Mintage	F	VF	XF	Unc	BU
2008	—	—	—	—	17.50	—

KM# 348 DOLLAR
28.3700 g., Copper-Nickel, 38.6 mm. **Series:** Nocternal
Creatures of Africa **Obv:** National arms **Rev:** Bush Baby on tree
limb **Edge:** Reeded **Note:** Blackened finish.

Date	Mintage	F	VF	XF	Unc	BU
2008	—	—	—	—	17.50	—

KM# 349 DOLLAR
28.3700 g., Copper-Nickel, 38.6 mm. **Series:** Nocternal
Creatures of Africa **Obv:** National arms **Rev:** Honey Badger
Edge: Reeded **Note:** Blackened finish

Date	Mintage	F	VF	XF	Unc	BU
2008	—	—	—	—	17.50	—

KM# 350 DOLLAR
28.3700 g., Copper-Nickel, 38.6 mm. **Series:** Nocternal
Creatures of Africa **Obv:** National arms. **Rev:** Pygmy
Hippopotamus in water facing **Edge:** Reeded **Note:** Blackened
finish.

Date	Mintage	F	VF	XF	Unc	BU
2008	—	—	—	—	17.50	—

KM# 223 10 DOLLARS
28.2800 g., 0.9250 Silver 0.8410 oz. ASW, 38.6 mm.
Series: The Big Five **Obv:** National arms **Rev:** Rhino and value
within circle **Edge:** Reeded

Date	Mintage	F	VF	XF	Unc	BU
2001 Proof	—	Value: 40.00				

KM# 226 10 DOLLARS
28.2800 g., 0.9250 Silver 0.8410 oz. ASW **Series:** The Big Five
Obv: National arms **Rev:** Lion head and value within circle

Date	Mintage	F	VF	XF	Unc	BU
2001 Proof	Est. 10,000	Value: 40.00				

KM# 229   10 DOLLARS
28.2800 g., 0.9250 Silver 0.8410 oz. ASW **Series:** The Big Five
Obv: National arms **Rev:** Leopard and value within circle

Date	Mintage	F	VF	XF	Unc	BU
2001 Proof	Est. 10,000	Value: 40.00				

KM# 232   10 DOLLARS
28.2800 g., 0.9250 Silver 0.8410 oz. ASW **Series:** The Big Five
Obv: National arms **Rev:** Elephants and value within circle

Date	Mintage	F	VF	XF	Unc	BU
2001 Proof	Est. 10,000	Value: 40.00				

KM# 235   10 DOLLARS
28.2800 g., 0.9250 Silver 0.8410 oz. ASW **Series:** The Big Five
Obv: National arms **Rev:** Buffalo and value within circle

Date	Mintage	F	VF	XF	Unc	BU
2001 Proof	Est. 10,000	Value: 40.00				

KM# 238   10 DOLLARS
28.2800 g., 0.9250 Silver 0.8410 oz. ASW **Series:** The Big Five
Obv: National arms **Rev:** All five animals within circle

Date	Mintage	F	VF	XF	Unc	BU
2001 Proof	Est. 10,000	Value: 40.00				

KM# 246.1   10 DOLLARS
28.2800 g., 0.9250 Silver 0.8410 oz. ASW, 38.6 mm.
Series: Big Cats **Obv:** National arms **Rev:** Male and female lions
Edge: Reeded

Date	Mintage	F	VF	XF	Unc	BU
2001 Proof	10,000	Value: 40.00				

KM# 246.2   10 DOLLARS
28.2800 g., 0.9250 Silver 0.8410 oz. ASW, 38.6 mm.
Series: Big Cats **Obv:** National arms **Rev:** Multi-colored male
and female lions **Edge:** Reeded

Date	Mintage	F	VF	XF	Unc	BU
2001 Proof	—	Value: 50.00				

KM# 247.1   10 DOLLARS
28.2800 g., 0.9250 Silver 0.8410 oz. ASW, 38.6 mm.
Series: Big Cats **Obv:** National arms **Rev:** Tiger **Edge:** Reeded

Date	Mintage	F	VF	XF	Unc	BU
2001 Proof	—	Value: 40.00				

KM# 247.2   10 DOLLARS
28.2800 g., 0.9250 Silver 0.8410 oz. ASW, 38.6 mm.
Series: Big Cats **Obv:** National arms **Rev:** Multi-colored Tiger
Edge: Reeded

Date	Mintage	F	VF	XF	Unc	BU
2001 Proof	—	Value: 50.00				

KM# 248.1   10 DOLLARS
28.2800 g., 0.9250 Silver 0.8410 oz. ASW, 38.6 mm.
Series: Big Cats **Obv:** National arms **Rev:** Cheetah head facing
Edge: Reeded

Date	Mintage	F	VF	XF	Unc	BU
2001 Proof	10,000	Value: 40.00				

KM# 248.2   10 DOLLARS
28.2800 g., 0.9250 Silver 0.8410 oz. ASW, 38.6 mm.
Series: Big Cats **Obv:** National arms **Rev:** Multi-colored Cheetah
head facing **Edge:** Reeded

Date	Mintage	F	VF	XF	Unc	BU
2001 Proof	—	Value: 50.00				

KM# 249.1   10 DOLLARS
28.2800 g., 0.9250 Silver 0.8410 oz. ASW, 38.6 mm.
Series: Big Cats **Obv:** National arms **Rev:** Cougar **Edge:** Reeded

Date	Mintage	F	VF	XF	Unc	BU
2001 Proof	10,000	Value: 40.00				

KM# 249.2   10 DOLLARS
28.2800 g., 0.9250 Silver 0.8410 oz. ASW, 38.6 mm.
Series: Big Cats **Obv:** National arms **Rev:** Multi-colored Cougar
Edge: Reeded

Date	Mintage	F	VF	XF	Unc	BU
2001 Proof	—	Value: 50.00				

KM# 250.1   10 DOLLARS
28.2800 g., 0.9250 Silver 0.8410 oz. ASW, 38.6 mm.
Series: Big Cats **Obv:** National arms **Rev:** Leopard
Edge: Reeded

Date	Mintage	F	VF	XF	Unc	BU
2001 Proof	10,000	Value: 40.00				

KM# 199   10 DOLLARS
28.2800 g., 0.9250 Silver 0.8410 oz. ASW, 38.6 mm.
Subject: Year of the Snake **Obv:** National arms **Rev:** Snake on
bamboo **Edge:** Reeded

Date	Mintage	F	VF	XF	Unc	BU
2001 Proof	Est. 25,000	Value: 50.00				

KM# 207   10 DOLLARS
28.2800 g., 0.9250 Silver 0.8410 oz. ASW **Subject:** P'an Ku
Obv: National arms **Rev:** Dragon

Date	Mintage	F	VF	XF	Unc	BU
2001 Proof	Est. 5,000	Value: 47.50				

KM# 215   10 DOLLARS
28.2800 g., 0.9250 Silver 0.8410 oz. ASW **Subject:** P'an Ku
Obv: National arms **Rev:** Dragon and three animals

Date	Mintage	F	VF	XF	Unc	BU
2001 Proof	Est. 5,000	Value: 47.50				

KM# 250.2   10 DOLLARS
28.2800 g., 0.9250 Silver 0.8410 oz. ASW, 38.6 mm.
Series: Big Cats **Obv:** National arms **Rev:** Multi-colored Leopard
Edge: Reeded

Date	Mintage	F	VF	XF	Unc	BU
2001 Proof	—	Value: 50.00				

KM# 277   10 DOLLARS
28.2800 g., 0.9250 Silver Gold clad 0.8410 oz. ASW, 38.6 mm.
Subject: British Queen Mother **Obv:** National arms **Rev:** Bust
facing in garden with dog within sprigs **Edge:** Reeded

Date	Mintage	F	VF	XF	Unc	BU
2002 Proof	10,000	Value: 47.50				

KM# 280 10 DOLLARS
28.2800 g., 0.9250 Silver Gold clad 0.8410 oz. ASW, 38.6 mm.
Subject: British Queen Mother **Obv:** National arms
Rev: Conjoined busts facing within sprigs **Edge:** Reeded

Date	Mintage	F	VF	XF	Unc	BU
2002 Proof	10,000	Value: 47.50				

KM# 257 10 DOLLARS
28.2800 g., 0.9250 Silver 0.8410 oz. ASW, 38.6 mm.
Subject: Year of the Horse **Obv:** National arms **Rev:** Horse divides circle **Edge:** Reeded

Date	Mintage	F	VF	XF	Unc	BU
2002 Proof	5,000	Value: 50.00				

KM# 265 10 DOLLARS
28.2800 g., 0.9250 Silver 0.8410 oz. ASW, 38.6 mm.
Subject: RMS Titanic **Obv:** National arms **Rev:** Titanic at dock
Edge: Reeded

Date	Mintage	F	VF	XF	Unc	BU
2002 Proof	10,000	Value: 47.50				

KM# 270 10 DOLLARS
28.2800 g., 0.9250 Silver Gold clad 0.8410 oz. ASW, 38.6 mm.
Subject: Queen's Golden Jubilee **Obv:** National arms
Rev: Queen Elizabeth II and Prince Philip visiting blacksmiths in Sierra Leone **Edge:** Reeded

Date	Mintage	F	VF	XF	Unc	BU
2002 Proof	10,000	Value: 50.00				

KM# 271 10 DOLLARS
28.2800 g., 0.9250 Silver Gold clad 0.8410 oz. ASW, 38.6 mm.
Subject: Queen's Golden Jubilee **Obv:** National arms
Rev: Queen Elizabeth II, Prince Charles and Princess Anne
Edge: Reeded

Date	Mintage	F	VF	XF	Unc	BU
2002 Proof	10,000	Value: 50.00				

KM# 283 10 DOLLARS
28.2800 g., 0.9250 Silver Gold clad 0.8410 oz. ASW, 38.6 mm.
Subject: Queen Elizabeth's Golden Jubilee **Obv:** National arms
Rev: Queen and young Prince Charles **Edge:** Reeded

Date	Mintage	F	VF	XF	Unc	BU
2002 Proof	10,000	Value: 47.50				

KM# 286 10 DOLLARS
28.2800 g., 0.9250 Silver Gold clad 0.8410 oz. ASW, 38.6 mm.
Subject: Queen Elizabeth's Golden Jubilee **Obv:** National arms
Rev: Queen and Prince Philip **Edge:** Reeded

Date	Mintage	F	VF	XF	Unc	BU
2002 Proof	10,000	Value: 47.50				

KM# 292 10 DOLLARS
28.2800 g., 0.9250 Silver 0.8410 oz. ASW, 38.6 mm. **Subject:** Olympics **Obv:** National arms **Rev:** Ancient archer **Edge:** Reeded

Date	Mintage	F	VF	XF	Unc	BU
2003 Proof	10,000	Value: 45.00				
2004 Proof	10,000	Value: 45.00				

KM# 289 10 DOLLARS
28.2800 g., 0.9250 Silver 0.8410 oz. ASW, 38.6 mm.
Subject: Olympics **Obv:** National arms **Rev:** Victory goddess
Nike **Edge:** Reeded **Note:** The leone is the official currency of Sierra Leone

Date	Mintage	F	VF	XF	Unc	BU
2003 Proof	10,000	Value: 45.00				
2004 Proof	10,000	Value: 45.00				

KM# 298 10 DOLLARS
28.2800 g., 0.9250 Silver 0.8410 oz. ASW, 38.6 mm.
Obv: National arms **Rev:** Nelson Mandela **Edge:** Reeded

Date	Mintage	F	VF	XF	Unc	BU
2004 Proof	10,000	Value: 50.00				

KM# 301 10 DOLLARS
28.2800 g., 0.9250 Silver 0.8410 oz. ASW, 38.6 mm.
Obv: National arms **Rev:** Ronald Reagan **Edge:** Reeded

Date	Mintage	F	VF	XF	Unc	BU
2004 Proof	10,000	Value: 35.00				

KM# 342 10 DOLLARS
0.9250 Silver **Series:** 60th Anniversary End of WW II
Subject: Battle of the Bulge **Obv:** National arms **Obv. Legend:**
REPUBLIC OF SIERRA LEONE **Rev:** Forest battle scene

Date	Mintage	F	VF	XF	Unc	BU
—	Value: 45.00					

KM# 339 10 DOLLARS
0.9250 g., Silver **Series:** 60th Anniversary of WW II
Subject: Battle of Britain **Obv:** National arms **Obv. Legend:**
REPUBLIC OF SIERRA LEONE **Rev:** Planes in flight

Date	Mintage	F	VF	XF	Unc	BU
2005 Proof	—	Value: 45.00				

KM# 340 10 DOLLARS
0.9250 Silver **Series:** 60th Anniversary End of WW II
Subject: The Battle of the Atlantic **Obv:** National arms
Obv. Legend: REPUBLIC OF SIERRA LEONE **Rev:** Plane and ship convoy

Date	Mintage	F	VF	XF	Unc	BU
2005 Proof	—	Value: 45.00				

KM# 341 10 DOLLARS
0.9250 Silver **Series:** 60th Anniversary End of WW II
Subject: Battle of El Alamein **Obv:** National arms
Obv. Legend: REPUBLIC OF SIERRA LEONE **Rev:** Tank, plane and ground troops

Date	Mintage	F	VF	XF	Unc	BU
2005 Proof	—	Value: 45.00				

KM# 343 10 DOLLARS
0.9250 Silver **Series:** 60th Anniversary End of WW II
Subject: Battle of Berlin **Obv:** National arms **Obv. Legend:**
REPUBLIC OF SIERRA LEONE **Rev:** Berlin city view, tank

Date	Mintage	F	VF	XF	Unc	BU
2005 Proof	—	Value: 45.00				

KM# 344 10 DOLLARS
0.9250 Silver **Series:** 60th Anniversary End of WW II
Subject: The Heavy Water Raids **Obv:** National arms
Obv. Legend: REPUBLIC OF SIERRA LEONE **Rev:** Troops on skies, factory in ruins

Date	Mintage	F	VF	XF	Unc	BU
2005 Proof	—	Value: 45.00				

KM# 330 10 DOLLARS
0.9167 Silver **Series:** Crown Jewels **Obv:** Arms **Obv. Legend:**
REPUBLIC OF SIERRA LEONE **Rev:** Imperial State crown with ruby setting **Rev. Legend:** CROWN JEWELS **Edge:** Reeded

Date	Mintage	F	VF	XF	Unc	BU
2006 Proof	—	Value: 120				

KM# 331 10 DOLLARS
0.9167 Silver **Series:** Crown Jewels **Obv:** Arms
Obv. Legend: REPUBLIC OF SIERRA LEONE **Rev:** Sword of State with sapphire setting **Rev. Legend:** CROWN JEWELS
Edge: Reeded

Date	Mintage	F	VF	XF	Unc	BU
2006 Proof	—	Value: 120				

KM# 332 10 DOLLARS
0.9167 Silver **Series:** Crown Jewels **Obv:** Arms
Obv. Legend: REPUBLIC OF SIERRA LEONE **Rev:** St. Edward's Crown with emerald setting **Rev. Legend:** CROWN JEWELS **Edge:** Reeded

Date	Mintage	F	VF	XF	Unc	BU
2006 Proof	—	Value: 120				

KM# 333 10 DOLLARS
0.9167 Silver **Series:** Crown Jewels **Obv:** Arms
Obv. Legend: REPUBLIC OF SIERRA LEONE **Rev:** Orb and Sceptre with the cross with diamond setting **Rev. Legend:**
CROWN JEWELS **Edge:** Reeded

Date	Mintage	F	VF	XF	Unc	BU
2006 Proof	—	Value: 120				

KM# 334 10 DOLLARS
Copper-Nickel **Subject:** 80th Birthday of Queen Elizabeth II
Obv: Arms **Obv. Legend:** REPUBLIC OF SIERRA LEONE
Rev: Elizabeth II seated giving Christmas message
Rev. Legend: 80th Birthday of H.M. Queen Elizabeth II
Edge: Reeded

Date	Mintage	F	VF	XF	Unc	BU
2006	—	—	—	—	16.50	18.50

KM# 334a 10 DOLLARS
Silver **Subject:** 80th Birthday of Queen Elizabeth II **Obv:** Arms
Obv. Legend: REPUBLIC OF SIERRA LEONE **Rev:** Elizabeth II seated giving Christmas Message **Rev. Legend:** 80th Birthday of H.M. Queen Elizabeth II **Edge:** Reeded

Date	Mintage	F	VF	XF	Unc	BU
2006 Proof	—	Value: 75.00				

KM# 335 10 DOLLARS
Copper-Nickel **Subject:** 80th Bithday of Queen Elizabeth II
Obv: Arms **Obv. Legend:** REPUBLIC OF SIERRA LEONE
Rev: Elizabeth II at 2002 Golden Jubilee celebrations in London, Concorde and Red Arrows doing flypass over Buckingham Palace **Rev. Legend:** 80th Birthday of H.M. Queen Elizabeth II
Edge: Reeded

Date	Mintage	F	VF	XF	Unc	BU
2006	—	—	—	—	16.50	18.50

KM# 335a 10 DOLLARS
0.9167 Silver **Subject:** 80th Birthday of Queen Elizabeth Ii **Obv:** Arms **Obv. Legend:** RIPUBLIC OF SIERRA LEONE **Rev:** Elizabeth II at 2002 Golden Jubilee celebrations in London, Concorde and Red Arrows doing flypass over Buckingham Palace **Rev. Legend:** 80th Birthday of H.M. Queen Elizabeth II **Edge:** Reeded

Date	Mintage	F	VF	XF	Unc	BU
2006 Proof	—	Value: 75.00				

KM# 336 10 DOLLARS
Copper-Nickel **Subject:** 80th Birthday of Queen Elizabeth II **Obv:** Arms **Obv. Legend:** REPUBLIC OF SIERRA LEONE **Rev:** Elizabeth II presenting 1966 Football World Cup to English team **Rev. Legend:** 80th Birthday of H.M. Queen Elizabeth II **Edge:** Reeded

Date	Mintage	F	VF	XF	Unc	BU
2006	—	—	—	—	16.50	18.50

KM# 336a 10 DOLLARS
0.9167 Silver **Subject:** 80th Birthday of Queen Elizabeth II **Obv:** Arms **Obv. Legend:** REPUBLIC OF SIERRA LEONE **Rev:** Elizabeth II presenting 1966 Football World Cup to English team **Rev. Legend:** 80th Birthday of H.M. Queen Elizabeth II **Edge:** Reeded

Date	Mintage	F	VF	XF	Unc	BU
2006 Proof	—	Value: 75.00				

KM# 337 10 DOLLARS
Copper-Nickel **Subject:** 80th Birthday of Queen Elizabeth II **Obv:** Arms **Obv. Legend:** REPUBLIC OF SIERRA LEONE **Rev:** Investiture of Charles as Prince of Wales in 1969 **Rev. Legend:** 80th Birthday of H.M. Queen Elizabeth II **Edge:** Reeded

Date	Mintage	F	VF	XF	Unc	BU
2006	—	—	—	—	16.50	18.50

KM# 337a 10 DOLLARS
0.9167 Silver **Subject:** 80th Birthday of Queen Elizabeth II **Obv:** Arms **Obv. Legend:** REPUBLIC OF SIERRA LEONE **Rev:** Investiture of Charles as Prince of Wales in 1969 **Rev. Legend:** 80th Birthday of H.M. Queen Elizabeth II **Edge:** Reeded

Date	Mintage	F	VF	XF	Unc	BU
2006 Proof	—	Value: 75.00				

KM# 338 10 DOLLARS
Copper-Nickel **Subject:** 10th Anniversary Death of Princess Diana **Obv:** Arms **Obv. Legend:** REPUBLIC OF SIERRA LEONE **Rev:** Diana with sons, Prince William and Prince Harry facing **Rev. Legend:** DIANA — PRINCESS OF WALES **Edge:** Reeded

Date	Mintage	F	VF	XF	Unc	BU
2007	—	—	—	—	16.50	18.50

KM# 338a 10 DOLLARS
0.9167 Silver **Subject:** 10th Anniversary Death of Princess Diana **Obv:** Arms **Obv. Legend:** REPUBLIC OF SIERRA LEONE **Rev:** Diana with sons, Prince William and Prince Harry facing **Rev. Legend:** DIANA — PRINCESS OF WALES **Edge:** Reeded

Date	Mintage	F	VF	XF	Unc	BU
2007 Proof	—	Value: 75.00				

KM# 200 20 DOLLARS
1.2441 g., 0.9990 Gold 0.0400 oz. AGW, 13.9 mm. **Subject:** Year of the Snake **Obv:** National arms **Rev:** Snake **Edge:** Reeded

Date	Mintage	F	VF	XF	Unc	BU
2001 Proof	Est. 50,000	Value: 60.00				

KM# 208 20 DOLLARS
1.2441 g., 0.9990 Gold 0.0400 oz. AGW **Subject:** P'an Ku **Obv:** National arms **Rev:** Dragon

Date	Mintage	F	VF	XF	Unc	BU
2001 Proof	Est. 5,000	Value: 60.00				

KM# 216 20 DOLLARS
1.2441 g., 0.9990 Gold 0.0400 oz. AGW **Subject:** P'an Ku **Obv:** National arms **Rev:** Dragon and three animals

Date	Mintage	F	VF	XF	Unc	BU
2001 Proof	Est. 5,000	Value: 60.00				

KM# 258 20 DOLLARS
1.2400 g., 0.9990 Gold 0.0398 oz. AGW, 13.92 mm. **Subject:** Year of the Horse **Obv:** National arms **Rev:** Horse **Edge:** Reeded

Date	Mintage	F	VF	XF	Unc	BU
2002 Proof	5,000	Value: 60.00				

KM# 272 30 DOLLARS
6.2200 g., 0.3750 Gold 0.0750 oz. AGW, 22 mm. **Subject:** Queen's Golden Jubilee **Obv:** National arms **Rev:** Queen Elizabeth II and Prince Philip **Edge:** Reeded

Date	Mintage	F	VF	XF	Unc	BU
2002 Proof	5,000	Value: 100				

KM# 273 30 DOLLARS
6.2200 g., 0.3750 Gold 0.0750 oz. AGW, 22 mm. **Subject:** Queen's Golden Jubilee **Obv:** National arms **Rev:** Queen Elizabeth II, Prince Charles and Princess Anne **Edge:** Reeded

Date	Mintage	F	VF	XF	Unc	BU
2002 Proof	5,000	Value: 100				

KM# 201 50 DOLLARS
3.1103 g., 0.9990 Gold 0.0999 oz. AGW, 18 mm. **Subject:** Year of the Snake **Obv:** National arms **Rev:** Snake **Edge:** Reeded

Date	Mintage	F	VF	XF	Unc	BU
2001 Proof	Est. 10,000	Value: 125				

KM# 209 50 DOLLARS
3.1103 g., 0.9990 Gold 0.0999 oz. AGW **Subject:** P'an Ku **Obv:** National arms **Rev:** Dragon

Date	Mintage	F	VF	XF	Unc	BU
2001 Proof	Est. 5,000	Value: 125				

KM# 217 50 DOLLARS
3.1103 g., 0.9990 Gold 0.0999 oz. AGW **Subject:** P'an Ku **Obv:** National arms **Rev:** Dragon and three animals

Date	Mintage	F	VF	XF	Unc	BU
2001 Proof	Est. 5,000	Value: 125				

KM# 266 50 DOLLARS
155.5500 g., 0.9999 Silver 5.0003 oz. ASW, 65 mm. **Subject:** RMS Titanic **Obv:** National arms **Rev:** Titanic at dock **Edge:** Reeded

Date	Mintage	F	VF	XF	Unc	BU
2002 Proof	2,000	Value: 150				

KM# 259 50 DOLLARS
3.1100 g., 0.9990 Gold 0.0999 oz. AGW, 17.95 mm. **Subject:** Year of the Horse **Obv:** National arms **Rev:** Horse **Edge:** Reeded

Date	Mintage	F	VF	XF	Unc	BU
2002 Proof	5,000	Value: 125				

KM# 202 100 DOLLARS
6.2200 g., 0.9990 Gold 0.1998 oz. AGW, 22 mm. **Subject:** Year of the Snake **Obv:** National arms **Rev:** Snake **Edge:** Reeded

Date	Mintage	F	VF	XF	Unc	BU
2001 Proof	—	Value: 250				

KM# 210 100 DOLLARS
6.2200 g., 0.9990 Gold 0.1998 oz. AGW **Subject:** P'an Ku **Obv:** National arms **Rev:** Dragon

Date	Mintage	F	VF	XF	Unc	BU
2001 Proof	Est. 10,000	Value: 245				

KM# 218 100 DOLLARS
6.2200 g., 0.9990 Gold 0.1998 oz. AGW **Subject:** P'an Ku **Obv:** National arms **Rev:** Dragon and three animals

Date	Mintage	F	VF	XF	Unc	BU
2001 Proof	Est. 10,000	Value: 245				

KM# 224 100 DOLLARS
6.2200 g., 0.9990 Gold 0.1998 oz. AGW, 22 mm. **Series:** The Big Five **Obv:** National arms **Rev:** Rhino **Edge:** Reeded

Date	Mintage	F	VF	XF	Unc	BU
2001 Proof	Est. 5,000	Value: 235				

KM# 227 100 DOLLARS
6.2200 g., 0.9990 Gold 0.1998 oz. AGW **Series:** The Big Five **Obv:** National arms **Rev:** Lion

Date	Mintage	F	VF	XF	Unc	BU
2001 Proof	Est. 5,000	Value: 235				

KM# 230 100 DOLLARS
6.2200 g., 0.9990 Gold 0.1998 oz. AGW **Series:** The Big Five **Obv:** National arms **Rev:** Leopard

Date	Mintage	F	VF	XF	Unc	BU
2001 Proof	Est. 5,000	Value: 235				

KM# 233 100 DOLLARS
6.2200 g., 0.9990 Gold 0.1998 oz. AGW **Series:** The Big Five **Obv:** National arms **Rev:** Elephants

Date	Mintage	F	VF	XF	Unc	BU
2001 Proof	Est. 5,000	Value: 235				

KM# 236 100 DOLLARS
6.2200 g., 0.9990 Gold 0.1998 oz. AGW **Series:** The Big Five **Obv:** National arms **Rev:** Buffalo

Date	Mintage	F	VF	XF	Unc	BU
2001 Proof	Est. 5,000	Value: 235				

KM# 239 100 DOLLARS
6.2200 g., 0.9990 Gold 0.1998 oz. AGW **Series:** The Big Five **Obv:** National arms **Rev:** All five animals

Date	Mintage	F	VF	XF	Unc	BU
2001 Proof	Est. 5,000	Value: 235				

KM# 251 100 DOLLARS
6.2200 g., 0.9990 Gold 0.1998 oz. AGW, 22 mm. **Series:** Big Cats **Obv:** National arms **Rev:** Male and female lions **Edge:** Reeded

Date	Mintage	F	VF	XF	Unc	BU
2001 Proof	5,000	Value: 235				

KM# 252 100 DOLLARS
6.2200 g., 0.9990 Gold 0.1998 oz. AGW, 22 mm. **Series:** Big Cats **Rev:** Tiger **Edge:** Reeded

Date	Mintage	F	VF	XF	Unc	BU
2001 Proof	5,000	Value: 235				

KM# 253 100 DOLLARS
6.2200 g., 0.9990 Gold 0.1998 oz. AGW, 22 mm. **Series:** Big Cats **Rev:** Cheetah **Edge:** Reeded

Date	Mintage	F	VF	XF	Unc	BU
2001 Proof	5,000	Value: 235				

KM# 254 100 DOLLARS
6.2200 g., 0.9990 Gold 0.1998 oz. AGW, 22 mm. **Series:** Big Cats **Rev:** Cougar **Edge:** Reeded

Date	Mintage	F	VF	XF	Unc	BU
2001 Proof	5,000	Value: 235				

KM# 255 100 DOLLARS
6.2200 g., 0.9990 Gold 0.1998 oz. AGW, 22 mm. **Series:** Big Cats **Rev:** Black panther **Edge:** Reeded

Date	Mintage	F	VF	XF	Unc	BU
2001 Proof	5,000	Value: 235				

KM# 274 100 DOLLARS
6.2200 g., 0.9999 Gold 0.1999 oz. AGW, 22 mm. **Subject:** Queen's Golden Jubilee **Obv:** National arms **Rev:** Queen Elizabeth II and Prince Philip **Edge:** Reeded

Date	Mintage	F	VF	XF	Unc	BU
2002 Proof	2,002	Value: 250				

KM# 275 100 DOLLARS
6.2200 g., 0.9999 Gold 0.1999 oz. AGW, 22 mm. **Subject:** Queen's Golden Jubilee **Obv:** National arms **Rev:** Queen Elizabeth II, Prince Charles and Princess Anne **Edge:** Reeded

Date	Mintage	F	VF	XF	Unc	BU
2002 Proof	5,000	Value: 245				

KM# 284 100 DOLLARS
6.2200 g., 0.9999 Gold 0.1999 oz. AGW, 22 mm. **Subject:** Queen Elizabeth's Golden Jubilee **Obv:** National arms **Rev:** Queen and young Prince Charles **Edge:** Reeded

Date	Mintage	F	VF	XF	Unc	BU
2002 Proof	2,002	Value: 250				

KM# 287 100 DOLLARS
6.2200 g., 0.9999 Gold 0.1999 oz. AGW, 22 mm. **Subject:** Queen Elizabeth's Golden Jubilee **Obv:** National arms **Rev:** Queen and Prince Philip **Edge:** Reeded

Date	Mintage	F	VF	XF	Unc	BU
2002 Proof	2,002	Value: 250				

KM# 278 100 DOLLARS
6.2200 g., 0.9999 Gold 0.1999 oz. AGW, 22 mm. **Subject:** British Queen Mother **Obv:** National arms **Rev:** Queen Mother in garden with dog **Edge:** Reeded

Date	Mintage	F	VF	XF	Unc	BU
2002 Proof	2,000	Value: 250				

KM# 281 100 DOLLARS
6.2200 g., 0.9999 Gold 0.1999 oz. AGW, 22 mm. **Subject:** British Queen Mother **Obv:** National arms **Rev:** Queen Mother with daughters **Edge:** Reeded

Date	Mintage	F	VF	XF	Unc	BU
2002 Proof	2,000	Value: 250				

KM# 260 100 DOLLARS
6.2200 g., 0.9990 Gold 0.1998 oz. AGW, 22 mm. **Subject:** Year of the Horse **Obv:** National arms **Rev:** Horse **Edge:** Reeded

Date	Mintage	F	VF	XF	Unc	BU
2002 Proof	2,000	Value: 250				

KM# 290 100 DOLLARS
6.2200 g., 0.9999 Gold 0.1999 oz. AGW, 22 mm. **Subject:** Olympics **Obv:** National arms **Rev:** Victory goddess Nike **Edge:** Reeded

Date	Mintage	F	VF	XF	Unc	BU
2003 Proof	5,000	Value: 240				
2004 Proof	5,000	Value: 240				

KM# 293 100 DOLLARS
6.2200 g., 0.9999 Gold 0.1999 oz. AGW, 22 mm. **Subject:** Olympics **Obv:** National arms **Rev:** Ancient archer **Edge:** Reeded

Date	Mintage	F	VF	XF	Unc	BU
2003 Proof	5,000	Value: 240				
2004 Proof	5,000	Value: 240				

KM# 267 150 DOLLARS
1000.0000 g., 0.9999 Silver 32.146 oz. ASW, 85 mm. **Subject:** RMS Titanic **Obv:** National arms **Rev:** Titanic at dock **Edge:** Reeded

Date	Mintage	F	VF	XF	Unc	BU
2002 Proof	500	Value: 675				

KM# 203 250 DOLLARS
15.5118 g., 0.9990 Gold 0.4982 oz. AGW, 30 mm. **Subject:** Year of the Snake **Obv:** National arms **Rev:** Snake **Edge:** Reeded

Date	Mintage	F	VF	XF	Unc	BU
2001 Proof	Est. 5,000	Value: 635				

KM# 211 250 DOLLARS
15.5518 g., 0.9990 Gold 0.4995 oz. AGW **Subject:** P'an Ku **Obv:** National arms **Rev:** Dragon

Date	Mintage	F	VF	XF	Unc	BU
2001 Proof	Est. 2,000	Value: 625				

KM# 219 250 DOLLARS
15.5518 g., 0.9990 Gold 0.4995 oz. AGW **Subject:** P'an Ku **Obv:** National arms **Rev:** Dragon and three animals

Date	Mintage	F	VF	XF	Unc	BU
2001 Proof	Est. 2,000	Value: 550				

KM# 261 250 DOLLARS
15.5500 g., 0.9990 Gold 0.4994 oz. AGW, 30 mm. **Subject:** Year of the Horse **Obv:** National arms **Rev:** Horse **Edge:** Reeded

Date	Mintage	F	VF	XF	Unc	BU
2002 Proof	2,000	Value: 625				

KM# 204 500 DOLLARS
31.1035 g., 0.9990 Gold 0.9990 oz. AGW, 32.7 mm. **Subject:** Year of the Snake **Obv:** National arms **Rev:** Snake **Edge:** Reeded

Date	Mintage	F	VF	XF	Unc	BU
2001 Proof	Est. 1,000	Value: 1,300				

KM# 212 500 DOLLARS
31.1035 g., 0.9990 Gold 0.9990 oz. AGW **Subject:** P'an Ku **Obv:** National arms **Rev:** Dragon

Date	Mintage	F	VF	XF	Unc	BU
2001 Proof	Est. 1,000	Value: 1,250				

KM# 220 500 DOLLARS
31.1035 g., 0.9990 Gold 0.9990 oz. AGW **Subject:** P'an Ku **Obv:** National arms **Rev:** Dragon and three animals

Date	Mintage	F	VF	XF	Unc	BU
2001 Proof	Est. 1,000	Value: 1,250				

KM# 262 500 DOLLARS
31.1000 g., 0.9990 Gold 0.9988 oz. AGW, 32.7 mm. **Subject:** Year of the Horse **Obv:** National arms **Rev:** Horse **Edge:** Reeded

Date	Mintage	F	VF	XF	Unc	BU
2002 Proof	1,000	Value: 1,250				

KM# 294 500 DOLLARS
31.1000 g., 0.9999 Gold 0.9997 oz. AGW, 32.7 mm. **Obv:** National arms **Rev:** Multicolor Astro Boy cartoon **Edge:** Reeded

Date	Mintage	F	VF	XF	Unc	BU
2003 Proof	2,003	Value: 1,200				

KM# 299 500 DOLLARS

31.1035 g., 0.9999 Gold 0.9999 oz. AGW, 32.7 mm.
Obv: National arms **Rev:** Nelson Mandela **Edge:** Reeded

Date	Mintage	F	VF	XF	Unc	BU
2004 Proof	—	Value: 1,250				

KM# 205 2500 DOLLARS

155.5175 g., 0.9990 Gold 4.9948 oz. AGW, 50 mm. **Subject:** Year of the Snake **Obv:** National arms **Rev:** Snake **Edge:** Reeded

Date	Mintage	F	VF	XF	Unc	BU
2001 Proof	Est. 250	Value: 6,250				

KM# 213 2500 DOLLARS

155.5175 g., 0.9990 Gold 4.9948 oz. AGW **Subject:** P'an Ku
Obv: National arms **Rev:** Dragon

Date	Mintage	F	VF	XF	Unc	BU
2001 Proof	Est. 250	Value: 6,000				

KM# 263 2500 DOLLARS

155.5100 g., 0.9990 Gold 4.9946 oz. AGW, 50 mm. **Subject:** Year of the Horse **Obv:** National arms **Rev:** Horse **Edge:** Reeded

Date	Mintage	F	VF	XF	Unc	BU
2002 Proof	250	Value: 6,000				

MINT SETS

KM#	Date	Mintage	Identification	Issue Price	Mkt Val
MS2	2006 (4)	—	KM# 334 - 337	65.00	70.00

PROOF SETS

KM#	Date	Mintage	Identification	Issue Price	Mkt Val
PS7	2006 (4)	—	KM# 330 - 333	450	480
PS8	2006 (4)	—	KM# 334a - 337a	300	300

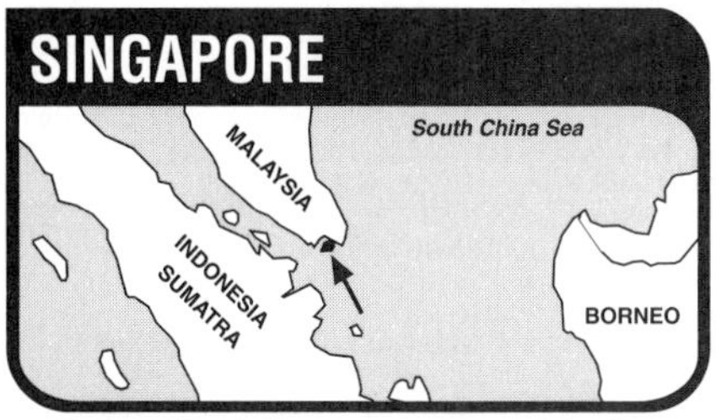

The Republic of Singapore, a member of the Commonwealth of Nations situated off the southern tip of the Malay peninsula, has an area of 224 sq. mi. (633 sq. km.) and a population of *2.7 million. Capital: Singapore. The economy is based on entrepôt trade, manufacturing and oil. Rubber, petroleum products, machinery and spices are exported.

The President is Chief of State. The prime minister is Head of Government.

MINT MARK

sm = "*sm*" - Singapore Mint monogram

REPUBLIC

STANDARD COINAGE

100 Cents = 1 Dollar

KM# 98a CENT

1.8100 g., 0.9250 Silver 0.0538 oz. ASW, 15.9 mm.
Obv: National arms **Rev:** Value divides plants

Date	Mintage	F	VF	XF	Unc	BU
2001sm Proof	10,000	Value: 2.25				
2002sm Proof	10,000	Value: 2.25				
2003sm Proof	—	Value: 2.25				
2004sm Proof	—	Value: 2.25				
2005sm Proof	—	Value: 2.25				
2006sm Proof	—	Value: 2.25				
2007sm Proof	—	Value: 2.25				
2008sm Proof	—	Value: 2.25				
2009sm Proof	—	Value: 2.25				

KM# 98 CENT

1.2400 g., Copper Plated Zinc, 15.9 mm. **Obv:** National arms **Rev:** Value divides plants **Edge:** Plain **Note:** Similar to KM#49 but motto ribbon on arms curves down at center.

Date	Mintage	F	VF	XF	Unc	BU
2001	56,220,000	—	—	—	0.10	0.15
2002	19,003,000	—	—	—	0.10	0.15
2003	—	—	—	—	0.10	0.15
2003 Proof	—	Value: 2.00				
2004	—	—	—	—	0.10	0.15
2004 Proof	20,000	Value: 2.00				
2005	—	—	—	—	0.10	0.15
2006	—	—	—	—	0.10	0.15
2007	—	—	—	—	0.10	0.15
2008	—	—	—	—	0.10	0.15
2009	—	—	—	—	0.10	0.15

KM# 99a 5 CENTS

2.0000 g., 0.9250 Silver 0.0595 oz. ASW, 16.75 mm.
Obv: National arms **Rev:** Fruit salad plant

Date	Mintage	F	VF	XF	Unc	BU
2001sm Proof	10,000	Value: 2.50				
2002sm Proof	10,000	Value: 2.50				
2003sm Proof	—	Value: 2.50				
2004sm Proof	—	Value: 2.50				
2005sm Proof	—	Value: 2.50				
2006sm Proof	—	Value: 2.50				
2007sm Proof	—	Value: 2.50				
2008sm Proof	—	Value: 2.50				
2009sm Proof	—	Value: 2.50				

KM# 99 5 CENTS

1.5600 g., Aluminum-Bronze, 16.75 mm. **Obv:** National arms **Rev:** Fruit salad plant **Edge:** Reeded **Note:** Similar to KM#50 but motto ribbon on arms curves down at center.

Date	Mintage	F	VF	XF	Unc	BU
2001	35,005,000	—	—	—	0.20	0.30
2002	33,556,000	—	—	—	0.20	0.30
2003	35,930,000	—	—	—	0.20	0.30
2003 Proof	—	Value: 3.00				
2004	38,040,000	—	—	—	0.20	0.30
2004 Proof	20,000	Value: 3.00				
2005	56,832,000	—	—	—	0.20	0.30
2006	—	—	—	—	0.20	0.30
2007	—	—	—	—	0.20	0.30
2008	—	—	—	—	0.20	0.30
2009	—	—	—	—	0.20	0.30

KM# 100a 10 CENTS

3.0500 g., 0.9250 Silver 0.0907 oz. ASW, 18.5 mm.
Obv: National arms **Rev:** Star Jasmine plant **Edge:** Reeded

Date	Mintage	F	VF	XF	Unc	BU
2001sm Proof	10,000	Value: 4.00				
2002sm Proof	10,000	Value: 4.00				
2003sm Proof	—	Value: 4.00				
2004sm Proof	—	Value: 4.00				
2005sm Proof	—	Value: 4.00				
2006sm Proof	—	Value: 4.00				
2007sm Proof	—	Value: 4.00				
2008sm Proof	—	Value: 4.00				
2009sm Proof	—	Value: 4.00				

KM# 100 10 CENTS

2.6000 g., Copper-Nickel, 18.5 mm. **Obv:** National arms **Rev:** Star Jasmine plant **Edge:** Reeded **Note:** Similar to KM#51 but motto ribbon on arms curves down at center.

Date	Mintage	F	VF	XF	Unc	BU
2001	70,600,000	—	—	—	0.20	0.30
2002	61,670,000	—	—	—	0.20	0.30
2003	58,990,000	—	—	—	0.20	0.30
2003 Proof	—	Value: 4.00				
2004	59,670,000	—	—	—	0.20	0.30
2004 Proof	20,000	Value: 4.00				
2005	49,960,000	—	—	—	0.20	0.30
2006	—	—	—	—	0.20	0.30
2007	—	—	—	—	0.20	0.30
2008	—	—	—	—	0.20	0.30
2009	—	—	—	—	0.20	0.30

KM# 101a 20 CENTS

5.2400 g., 0.9250 Silver 0.1558 oz. ASW, 21.36 mm.
Obv: National arms **Rev:** Powder puff plant above value
Edge: Reeded

Date	Mintage	F	VF	XF	Unc	BU
2001sm Proof	10,000	Value: 6.50				
2002sm Proof	10,000	Value: 6.50				
2003sm Proof	—	Value: 6.50				
2004sm Proof	—	Value: 6.50				
2005sm Proof	—	Value: 6.50				
2006sm Proof	—	Value: 6.50				
2007sm Proof	—	Value: 6.50				

KM# 101 20 CENTS

4.5000 g., Copper-Nickel, 21.36 mm. **Obv:** National arms **Rev:** Powder puff plant above value **Edge:** Reeded **Note:** Similar to KM#52 but motto ribbon on arms curves down at center.

Date	Mintage	F	VF	XF	Unc	BU
2001	52,050,000	—	—	—	0.60	0.75
2002	48,120,000	—	—	—	0.60	0.75
2003	45,470,000	—	—	—	0.60	0.75
2003	—	Value: 5.00				
2004	44,870,000	—	—	—	0.60	0.75
2004	20,000	Value: 5.00				
2005	—	—	—	—	0.60	0.75
2006	23,310,000	—	—	—	0.60	0.75
2007	—	—	—	—	0.60	0.75
2008	—	—	—	—	0.60	0.75
2009	—	—	—	—	0.60	0.75

KM# 102a 50 CENTS

8.5600 g., 0.9250 Silver 0.2546 oz. ASW, 24.66 mm.
Obv: National arms **Rev:** Yellow Allamanda plant above value

Date	Mintage	F	VF	XF	Unc	BU
2001sm Proof	10,000	Value: 12.00				
2002sm Proof	10,000	Value: 12.00				
2003sm Proof	—	Value: 12.00				
2004sm Proof	—	Value: 12.00				
2005sm Proof	—	Value: 12.00				
2006sm Proof	—	Value: 12.00				
2007sm Proof	—	Value: 12.00				

KM# 102 50 CENTS

7.2900 g., Copper-Nickel, 24.66 mm. **Obv:** National arms **Rev:** Yellow Allamanda plant above value **Edge Lettering:** REPUBLIC OF SINGAPORE (lion's head) **Note:** Similar to KM#53 but motto ribbon on arms curves down at center.

Date	Mintage	F	VF	XF	Unc	BU
2001	30,020,000	—	—	—	0.75	1.00
2002	27,420,000	—	—	—	0.75	1.00
2003	23,650,000	—	—	—	0.75	1.00
2003 Proof	—	Value: 6.00				
2004	24,640,000	—	—	—	0.75	1.00
2004 Proof	20,000	Value: 6.00				
2005	24,996,000	—	—	—	0.75	1.00
2006	—	—	—	—	0.75	1.00
2007	7,680,000	—	—	—	0.75	1.00
2008	—	—	—	—	0.75	1.00
2009	—	—	—	—	0.75	1.00

KM# 103a DOLLAR

8.4273 g., 0.9250 Silver 0.2506 oz. ASW, 22.4 mm.
Obv: National arms **Rev:** Periwinkle flower

Date	Mintage	F	VF	XF	Unc	BU
2001sm Proof	10,000	Value: 15.00				
2002sm Proof	10,000	Value: 15.00				
2003sm Proof	—	Value: 15.00				
2004sm Proof	—	Value: 15.00				
2005sm Proof	—	Value: 15.00				
2006sm Proof	—	Value: 15.00				
2007sm Proof	—	Value: 15.00				

KM# 103 DOLLAR

6.3000 g., Aluminum-Bronze, 22.4 mm. **Obv:** National arms **Rev:** Periwinkle flower **Edge:** Reeded **Note:** Similar to KM#54 but motto ribbon on arms curves down at center.

Date	Mintage	F	VF	XF	Unc	BU
2001	40,840,000	—	—	—	1.50	2.25
2002	35,660,000	—	—	—	1.50	2.25
2003	31,900,000	—	—	—	1.50	2.25
2003 Proof	—	Value: 10.00				
2004	34,380,000	—	—	—	1.50	2.25
2004 Proof	20,000	Value: 10.00				
2005	—	—	—	—	1.50	2.25
2006	25,488,000	—	—	—	1.50	2.25
2007	—	—	—	—	1.50	2.25
2008	—	—	—	—	1.50	2.25
2009	—	—	—	—	1.50	2.25

KM# 184 DOLLAR

Copper-Nickel, 24.6 mm. **Subject:** Old World Charm - Balestier
Obv: Arms with supporters **Rev:** Old buildings **Edge:** Reeded

Date	Mintage	F	VF	XF	Unc	BU
2004sm Prooflike	—	—	—	—	—	10.00

KM# 184a DOLLAR

0.9990 Silver, 24.6 mm. **Subject:** Old World Charm - Balestier
Obv: Arms with supporters **Rev:** Old buildings

Date	Mintage	F	VF	XF	Unc	BU
2004sm Proof	8,000	Value: 27.50				

KM# 190 DOLLAR

Copper-Nickel, 24.6 mm. **Subject:** Old World Charm - Jalan Besar

Date	Mintage	F	VF	XF	Unc	BU
2004sm Prooflike	—	—	—	—	—	10.00

KM# 190a DOLLAR
0.9990 Silver, 24.6 mm. **Subject:** Old World Charm - Jalan Besar

Date	Mintage	F	VF	XF	Unc	BU
2004sm Proof	8,000			Value: 27.50		

KM# 191 DOLLAR
Copper-Nickel, 24.6 mm. **Subject:** Old World Charm - Joo Chiat

Date	Mintage	F	VF	XF	Unc	BU
2004sm Prooflike	—				—	10.00

KM# 191a DOLLAR
0.9990 Silver, 24.6 mm. **Subject:** Old World Charm - Joo Chiat

Date	Mintage	F	VF	XF	Unc	BU
2004sm Proof	8,000			Value: 27.50		

KM# 192 DOLLAR
Copper-Nickel, 24.6 mm. **Subject:** Old World Charm - Tanjong Katong

Date	Mintage	F	VF	XF	Unc	BU
2004sm Prooflike	—				—	10.00

KM# 192a DOLLAR
0.9990 Silver, 24.6 mm. **Subject:** Old World Charm - Tanjong Katong

Date	Mintage	F	VF	XF	Unc	BU
2004sm Proof	8,000			Value: 27.50		

KM# 244 DOLLAR
Copper-Nickel **Series:** Urban Redevelopment **Obv:** National arms **Rev:** Anak Bukit

Date	Mintage	F	VF	XF	Unc	BU
2005sm Prooflike	—		Value: 12.00			

KM# 244a DOLLAR
0.9999 Silver **Series:** Urban Redevelopment **Obv:** National arms **Rev:** Anak Bukit - multicolor

Date	Mintage	F	VF	XF	Unc	BU
2005sm Proof	8,000		Value: 45.00			

KM# 245 DOLLAR
Copper-Nickel **Series:** Urban Redevelopment **Obv:** National arms **Rev:** Coronation

Date	Mintage	F	VF	XF	Unc	BU
2005sm Prooflike	—		Value: 12.00			

KM# 245a DOLLAR
0.9999 Silver **Series:** Urban Redevelopment **Obv:** National arms **Rev:** Coronation - multicolor

Date	Mintage	F	VF	XF	Unc	BU
2005sm Proof	8,000		Value: 45.00			

KM# 246 DOLLAR
Copper-Nickel **Series:** Urban Redevelopment **Obv:** National arms **Rev:** Jalan Leban and Casuarina Road

Date	Mintage	F	VF	XF	Unc	BU
2005sm Prooflike	—		Value: 12.00			

KM# 246a DOLLAR
0.9999 Silver **Series:** Urban Redevelopment **Obv:** National arms **Rev:** Jalan Leban and Casuarina Road - multicolor

Date	Mintage	F	VF	XF	Unc	BU
2005sm Proof	8,000		Value: 45.00			

KM# 247 DOLLAR
Copper-Nickel **Series:** Urban Redevelopment **Obv:** National arms **Rev:** Springleaf

Date	Mintage	F	VF	XF	Unc	BU
2005sm Prooflike	—		Value: 12.00			

KM# 247a DOLLAR
0.9999 Silver **Series:** Urban Redevelopment **Obv:** National arms **Rev:** Springleaf - multicolor

Date	Mintage	F	VF	XF	Unc	BU
2005sm Proof	8,000		Value: 45.00			

KM# 248 DOLLAR
Copper-Nickel **Series:** Urban Redevelopment **Obv:** National arms **Rev:** Thomson Village

Date	Mintage	F	VF	XF	Unc	BU
2005sm Prooflike	—		Value: 12.00			

KM# 248a DOLLAR
0.9999 Silver **Series:** Urban Redevelopment **Obv:** National arms **Rev:** Thomson Village - multicolor

Date	Mintage	F	VF	XF	Unc	BU
2005sm Proof	8,000		Value: 45.00			

KM# 259 DOLLAR
Copper-Nickel **Series:** Urban Redevelopment **Obv:** National arms **Rev:** Changi Village - multicolor

Date	Mintage	F	VF	XF	Unc	BU
2007sm Prooflike	—			—	—	12.50

KM# 262 DOLLAR
Copper-Nickel **Series:** Urban Redevelopment **Obv:** National arms **Rev:** Punggoi Point and Coney Island - multicolor

Date	Mintage	F	VF	XF	Unc	BU
2007sm Prooflike	—			—	—	12.50

KM# 259a DOLLAR
0.9990 Silver **Series:** Urban Redevelopment **Obv:** National arms **Rev:** Changi Village - multicolor

Date	Mintage	F	VF	XF	Unc	BU
2007sm Proof	8,000		Value: 32.50			

KM# 260 DOLLAR
Copper-Nickel **Series:** Urban Redevelopment **Obv:** National arms **Rev:** Pasir Ris Park - multicolor

Date	Mintage	F	VF	XF	Unc	BU
2007sm Prooflike	—			—	—	12.50

KM# 260a DOLLAR
0.9990 Silver **Series:** Urban Redevelopment **Obv:** National arms **Rev:** Pasir Ris Park - multicolor

Date	Mintage	F	VF	XF	Unc	BU
2007sm Proof	8,000		Value: 32.50			

KM# 261 DOLLAR
Copper-Nickel **Series:** Urban Redevelopment **Obv:** National arms **Rev:** Pulau Ubin - multicolor

Date	Mintage	F	VF	XF	Unc	BU
2007sm Prooflike	—			—	—	12.50

KM# 261a DOLLAR
0.9990 Silver **Series:** Urban Redevelopment **Obv:** National arms **Rev:** Pulau Ubin - multicolor

Date	Mintage	F	VF	XF	Unc	BU
2007sm Proof	8,000		Value: 32.50			

KM# 262a DOLLAR
0.9990 Silver **Series:** Urban Redevelopment **Obv:** National arms **Rev:** Punggoi Point and Coney Island - multicolor

Date	Mintage	F	VF	XF	Unc	BU
2007sm Proof	8,000		Value: 32.50			

KM# 291a DOLLAR
Silver **Obv:** Supported arms **Rev:** Multicolor Labrador Nature Reserve

Date	Mintage	F	VF	XF	Unc	BU
2008 Proof	—		Value: 30.00			

KM# 290 DOLLAR
Copper-Nickel **Obv:** Supported arms **Rev:** Multicolor Kent Ridge Park

Date	Mintage	F	VF	XF	Unc	BU
2008 Proof	—		Value: 10.00			

KM# 290a DOLLAR
Silver **Obv:** Supported arms **Rev:** Multicolor Kent Ridge Park

Date	Mintage	F	VF	XF	Unc	BU
2008 Proof	—		Value: 30.00			

KM# 291 DOLLAR
Copper-Nickel **Obv:** Supported arms **Rev:** Multicolor Labrador Nature Reserve

Date	Mintage	F	VF	XF	Unc	BU
2008 Proof	—		Value: 10.00			

KM# 292 DOLLAR
Copper-Nickel **Obv:** Supported arms **Rev:** Multicolor Mount Faber Building

Date	Mintage	F	VF	XF	Unc	BU
2008 Proof	—		Value: 10.00			

KM# 292a DOLLAR
Silver **Obv:** Supported arms **Rev:** Multicolor Mount Faber Building

Date	Mintage	F	VF	XF	Unc	BU
2008 Proof	—		Value: 30.00			

KM# 293 DOLLAR
Copper-Nickel **Obv:** Supported arms **Rev:** Multicolor Telok Blangah Hill Park

Date	Mintage	F	VF	XF	Unc	BU
2008 Proof	—		Value: 10.00			

KM# 293a DOLLAR
Silver **Obv:** Supported arms **Rev:** Multicolor Telok Blangah Hill Park

Date	Mintage	F	VF	XF	Unc	BU
2008 Proof	—		Value: 30.00			

KM# 294 DOLLAR
0.3000 g., 0.9990 Gold 0.0096 oz. AGW, 7 mm. **Subject:** Year of the Ox **Obv:** Supported arms **Rev:** Ox

Date	Mintage	F	VF	XF	Unc	BU
2009	3,000			—	30.00	35.00

KM# 196 2 DOLLARS
Copper-Nickel **Subject:** Tribute to Healthcare Givers **Obv:** National arms **Rev:** Five 3/4 length people standing facing, clinic in background

Date	Mintage	F	VF	XF	Unc	BU
2003sm	—				—	15.00

KM# 196a 2 DOLLARS
0.9990 Silver **Subject:** Tribute to Healthcare Givers **Obv:** National arms **Rev:** Five 3/4 length people standing facing, clinic in background

Date	Mintage	F	VF	XF	Unc	BU
2003sm Proof	10,000		Value: 60.00			

KM# 223 2 DOLLARS
20.0000 g., 0.9990 Silver 0.6423 oz. ASW, 38.70 mm. **Series:** Lunar **Subject:** Year of the Goat **Obv:** National arms **Rev:** Stylized goat standing right facing left

Date	Mintage	F	VF	XF	Unc	BU
2003sm Proof	30,000		Value: 60.00			

KM# 229 2 DOLLARS
20.0000 g., 0.9990 Silver 0.6423 oz. ASW, 38.7 mm. **Series:** Lunar **Subject:** Year of the Monkey **Obv:** National arms **Rev:** Stylized monkey sitting left

Date	Mintage	F	VF	XF	Unc	BU
2004sm Proof	30,000		Value: 60.00			

KM# 234 2 DOLLARS
20.0000 g., Copper-Nickel, 38.7 mm. **Series:** Lunar **Subject:** Year of the Rooster **Obv:** National arms **Rev:** Rooster standing right

Date	Mintage	F	VF	XF	Unc	BU
2005sm Prooflike	—			—	—	15.00

KM# 242 2 DOLLARS
Copper-Nickel **Subject:** 40th National Day Parade **Obv:** National arms **Rev:** Fireworks, parade in government plaza, multicolor

Date	Mintage	F	VF	XF	Unc	BU
2005sm Prooflike	—		Value: 15.00			

KM# 242a 2 DOLLARS
20.0000 g., 0.9999 Silver 0.6429 oz. ASW **Subject:** 40th National Day Parade **Obv:** National arms **Rev:** Fireworks, parade in government plaza

Date	Mintage	F	VF	XF	Unc	BU
2005sm Proof	—		Value: 60.00			

KM# 234a 2 DOLLARS
20.0000 g., 0.9999 Silver 0.6429 oz. ASW, 38.7 mm. **Series:** Lunar **Subject:** Year of the Rooster **Obv:** National arms **Rev:** Stylized rooster standing right

Date	Mintage	F	VF	XF	Unc	BU
2005sm Proof	10,000		Value: 42.50			

KM# 258 2 DOLLARS
Copper-Nickel **Subject:** 41st National Day **Obv:** National arms **Rev:** People in stadium, emblem - multicolor

Date	Mintage	F	VF	XF	Unc	BU
2006sm Prooflike	—		Value: 15.00			

KM# 258a 2 DOLLARS
20.0000 g., 0.9990 Silver 0.6423 oz. ASW **Subject:** 41st National Day **Obv:** National arms **Rev:** People in stadium, emblem - multicolor

Date	Mintage	F	VF	XF	Unc	BU
2006sm Proof	8,000		Value: 60.00			

KM# 250 2 DOLLARS
20.0000 g., Copper-Nickel **Series:** Lunar **Subject:** Year of the Dog **Obv:** National arms **Rev:** Stylized dog standing left

Date	Mintage	F	VF	XF	Unc	BU
2006sm Prooflike	—		Value: 15.00			

KM# 250a 2 DOLLARS
20.0000 g., 0.9999 Silver 0.6429 oz. ASW **Series:** Lunar **Subject:** Year of the Dog **Obv:** National arms **Rev:** Stylized dog standing left

Date	Mintage	F	VF	XF	Unc	BU
2006sm Proof	6,000		Value: 60.00			

KM# 264 2 DOLLARS
Copper-Nickel **Series:** Lunar **Subject:** Year of the Boar **Obv:** National arms **Rev:** Stylized boar running right

Date	Mintage	F	VF	XF	Unc	BU
2007sm Prooflike	—			—	—	12.00

KM# 193 2 DOLLARS
20.0000 g., Copper-Nickel, 38.70 mm. **Subject:** 42nd National Day Parade **Obv:** Arms with supporters **Obv. Legend:** SINGAPURA - SINGAPORE **Rev:** Colored overlay with four children above Marina Bay floating platform **Edge:** Reeded

Date	Mintage	F	VF	XF	Unc	BU
2007 Prooflike	—			—	—	13.50

KM# 193a 2 DOLLARS
20.0000 g., 0.9990 Silver 0.6423 oz. ASW, 38.70 mm. **Subject:** 42nd National Day Parade **Obv:** Arms with supporters **Obv. Legend:** SINGAPURA - SINGAPORE **Rev:** Colored overlay with four children above Marina Bay floating platform **Edge:** Reeded

Date	Mintage	F	VF	XF	Unc	BU
2007 Proof	8,000		Value: 42.50			

KM# 264a 2 DOLLARS
20.0000 g., 0.9990 Silver 0.6423 oz. ASW **Series:** Lunar **Subject:** Year of the Boar **Obv:** National arms **Rev:** Stylized boar running right

Date	Mintage	F	VF	XF	Unc	BU
2007sm Proof	6,000		Value: 40.00			

KM# 270 2 DOLLARS
20.0000 g., Copper-Nickel **Series:** Lunar **Subject:** Year of the Rat **Obv:** National arms **Rev:** Stylized rat lying left

Date	Mintage	F	VF	XF	Unc	BU
2008sm Prooflike	—			—	—	12.50

KM# 270a 2 DOLLARS
20.0000 g., 0.9990 Silver 0.6423 oz. ASW **Series:** Lunar **Subject:** Year of the Rat **Obv:** National arms **Rev:** Stylized rat lying left

Date	Mintage	F	VF	XF	Unc	BU
2008sm Proof	6,000		Value: 42.50			

KM# 287 2 DOLLARS
Copper-Nickel **Subject:** Formula 1 - Singapore Grand Prix **Obv:** Supported arms **Rev:** Formula 1 racecar and skyline

Date	Mintage	F	VF	XF	Unc	BU
2008 Proof	—		Value: 10.00			

KM# 295 2 DOLLARS
Copper-Nickel **Subject:** Year of the Ox **Obv:** Supported arms

Date	Mintage	F	VF	XF	Unc	BU
2009 Prooflike	—			—	—	10.00

KM# 296 2 DOLLARS
20.0000 g., 0.9990 Silver 0.6423 oz. ASW **Subject:** Year of the Ox **Obv:** Supported arms **Rev:** Ox

Date	Mintage	F	VF	XF	Unc	BU
2009 Proof	—		Value: 30.00			

KM# 303 2 DOLLARS
Copper-Nickel **Subject:** Independence, 44th Anniversary

Date	Mintage	F	VF	XF	Unc	BU
2009	8,009			—	—	15.00

KM# 303a 2 DOLLARS
20.0000 g., 0.9990 Silver 0.6423 oz. ASW **Series:** Indpendence, 44th Anniversary

Date	Mintage	F	VF	XF	Unc	BU
2009 Proof	7,009		Value: 40.00			

KM# 104.1a 5 DOLLARS
8.2500 g., 0.9250 Silver 0.2453 oz. ASW **Obv:** National arms **Rev:** Vanda Miss Joaquim flower and value within beaded circle

Date	Mintage	F	VF	XF	Unc	BU
2001sm Proof	—	Value: 25.00				
2002sm Proof	—	Value: 25.00				

KM# 104.2 5 DOLLARS
Bi-Metallic Aluminn-Bronze center in Copper-Nickel ring **Obv:** National arms, date and BCCS logo **Rev:** Flower above value **Edge:** Plain

Date	Mintage	F	VF	XF	Unc	BU
2001sm In sets only	—	—	—	—	—	12.00
2002sm In sets only	—	—	—	—	—	12.00
2003sm	—	—	—	—	—	12.00
2004sm	—	—	—	—	—	12.00
2005sm	—	—	—	—	—	12.00
2006sm	—	—	—	—	—	12.00

KM# 104.2a 5 DOLLARS
8.2500 g., 0.9250 Silver 0.2453 oz. ASW **Obv:** National arms, date and BCCS logo **Rev:** Flower above value **Edge:** Plain

Date	Mintage	F	VF	XF	Unc	BU
2001sm Proof	10,000	Value: 25.00				
2002sm Proof	10,000	Value: 25.00				
2003sm Proof	—	Value: 25.00				
2004sm Proof	—	Value: 25.00				
2005sm Proof	—	Value: 25.00				
2006sm Proof	—	Value: 25.00				

KM# 177a 5 DOLLARS
20.0000 g., 0.9250 Silver 0.5948 oz. ASW, 38.6 mm. **Subject:** Productivity Movement **Obv:** Arms with supporters **Rev:** Spiral design **Edge:** Reeded

Date	Mintage	F	VF	XF	Unc	BU
2001sm Proof	10,000	Value: 50.00				

KM# 177 5 DOLLARS
20.0000 g., Copper-Nickel, 38.6 mm. **Subject:** Productivity Movement **Obv:** Arms with supporters **Rev:** Spiral design **Edge:** Reeded

Date	Mintage	F	VF	XF	Unc	BU
2001sm	20,000	—	—	—	12.50	15.00

KM# 181 5 DOLLARS
20.0000 g., Copper-Nickel, 38.7 mm. **Subject:** Esplanade Theaters on the Bay **Obv:** Arms with supporters **Rev:** Stylized symbolic design **Edge:** Reeded

Date	Mintage	F	VF	XF	Unc	BU
2002sm	—	—	—	—	13.50	16.50

KM# 181a 5 DOLLARS
20.0000 g., 0.9990 Silver 0.6423 oz. ASW, 38.7 mm. **Subject:** Esplanade Theaters on the Bay **Obv:** Arms with supporters **Rev:** Stylized symbolic design **Edge:** Reeded

Date	Mintage	F	VF	XF	Unc	BU
2002sm Proof	10,000	Value: 45.00				

KM# 104.1 5 DOLLARS
Bi-Metallic Aluminum-Bronze center in Copper-Nickel ring **Obv:** National arms **Rev:** Vanda Miss Joaquim flower and value within beaded circle **Shape:** Scalloped

Date	Mintage	F	VF	XF	Unc	BU
2002sm	—	—	—	—	—	15.00

KM# 104.3 5 DOLLARS
Bi-Metallic Aluminum-Bronze center in Copper-Nickel ring **Obv:** National arms above latent image "MAS" **Rev:** Flower and value **Shape:** Scalloped

Date	Mintage	F	VF	XF	Unc	BU
2002sm	—	—	—	—	—	10.00
2003sm	—	—	—	—	—	10.00
2003sm Proof	—	Value: 15.00				
2004sm	—	—	—	—	—	10.00
2004sm Proof	20,000	Value: 15.00				
2005sm	—	—	—	—	—	10.00
2006sm	—	—	—	—	—	10.00
2007sm	—	—	—	—	—	10.00

Date	Mintage	F	VF	XF	Unc	BU
2008sm	—	—	—	—	—	10.00
2009sm	—	—	—	—	—	10.00

KM# 104.3a 5 DOLLARS
8.2500 g., 0.9250 Silver 0.2453 oz. ASW **Obv:** National arms above latent image "MAS" **Rev:** Flower and value **Shape:** Scalloped

Date	Mintage	F	VF	XF	Unc	BU
2003sm Proof	—	Value: 25.00				
2004sm Proof	—	Value: 25.00				
2005sm Proof	—	Value: 25.00				
2006sm Proof	—	Value: 25.00				
2007sm Proof	—	Value: 25.00				

KM# 194 5 DOLLARS
20.0000 g., 0.9990 Silver 0.6423 oz. ASW, 38.7 mm. **Obv:** Arms with supporters **Obv. Legend:** SINGAPURA - SINGAPORE **Rev:** Multicolor Singapore's skyline above world map, golden lion symbol below pointing to location of Singapore **Rev. Legend:** BOARD OF GOVERNORS ANNUAL MEETINGS • SINGAPORE 2006 • INTERNATIONAL MONETARY FUND • WORLD BANK GROUP •

Date	Mintage	F	VF	XF	Unc	BU
2006sm Proof	10,000	Value: 60.00				

KM# 256 5 DOLLARS
20.0000 g., 0.9990 Silver 0.6423 oz. ASW **Series:** Heritage Orchids **Obv:** National arms **Rev:** Vanda Tan Chay Yan - multicolor

Date	Mintage	F	VF	XF	Unc	BU
2006sm Proof	8,000	Value: 60.00				

KM# 257 5 DOLLARS
20.0000 g., 0.9990 Silver 0.6423 oz. ASW **Series:** Heritage Orchids **Obv:** National arms **Rev:** Aranda Majula - multicolor

Date	Mintage	F	VF	XF	Unc	BU
2006sm Proof	8,000	Value: 60.00				

KM# 275 5 DOLLARS
20.0000 g., 0.9990 Silver 0.6423 oz. ASW, 38.7 mm. **Series:** Heritage Orchids **Obv:** National arms **Rev:** Dendrobium Singa Mas - multicolor

Date	Mintage	F	VF	XF	Unc	BU
2007sm Proof	8,000	Value: 45.00				

KM# 276 5 DOLLARS
20.0000 g., 0.9990 Silver 0.6423 oz. ASW, 38.7 mm. **Series:** Heritage Orchids **Obv:** National arms **Rev:** Vanda Mimi Palmar - multicolor

Date	Mintage	F	VF	XF	Unc	BU
2007sm Proof	8,000	Value: 45.00				

KM# 285 5 DOLLARS
20.0000 g., 0.9990 Silver 0.6423 oz. ASW, 38.6 mm. **Subject:** Heritage orchids **Obv:** Supported arms **Rev:** Multicolor yellow orchid - Oncidum Goldiana

Date	Mintage	F	VF	XF	Unc	BU
2008 Proof	—	Value: 25.00				

KM# 286 5 DOLLARS
20.0000 g., 0.9990 Silver 0.6423 oz. ASW, 38.6 mm. **Subject:** Heritage orchids **Obv:** Supported arms **Rev:** Multicolor pink orchid - Aranda Tay Swee Eng

Date	Mintage	F	VF	XF	Unc	BU
2008 Proof	—	Value: 25.00				

KM# 301 5 DOLLARS
20.0000 g., 0.9990 Silver 0.6423 oz. ASW **Subject:** Orchids of Singapore **Obv:** Arms **Rev:** Yellow flower - Spathoglottis Primrose

Date	Mintage	F	VF	XF	Unc	BU
2009 Proof	12,000	Value: 40.00				

KM# 302 5 DOLLARS
20.0000 g., 0.9990 Silver 0.6423 oz. ASW, 38.7 mm. **Subject:** Orchids of Singapore **Obv:** Arms **Rev:** Pink flower - Vanda Amy

Date	Mintage	F	VF	XF	Unc	BU
2009 Proof	12,000	Value: 40.00				

KM# 179 10 DOLLARS
28.0000 g., Copper-Nickel, 40.7 mm. **Series:** Lunar **Subject:** Year of the Snake **Obv:** National arms **Rev:** Stylized snake **Edge:** Reeded

Date	Mintage	F	VF	XF	Unc	BU
2001sm Prooflike	—	—	—	—	—	20.00

KM# 179a 10 DOLLARS
62.2060 g., 0.9990 Silver 1.9979 oz. ASW, 40.7 mm. **Series:** Lunar **Subject:** Year of the Snake **Obv:** National arms **Rev:** Stylized snake **Edge:** Reeded

Date	Mintage	F	VF	XF	Unc	BU
2001sm Proof	35,000	Value: 85.00				

KM# 182 10 DOLLARS
28.0000 g., Copper-Nickel, 40.7 mm. **Series:** Lunar **Subject:** Year of the Horse **Obv:** National arms **Rev:** Stylized horse standing left **Edge:** Reeded

Date	Mintage	F	VF	XF	Unc	BU
2002sm Prooflike	—	—	—	—	—	20.00

KM# 182a 10 DOLLARS
62.2060 g., 0.9990 Silver 1.9979 oz. ASW, 40.7 mm. **Series:** Lunar **Subject:** Year of the Horse **Obv:** National arms **Rev:** Stylized horse standing left **Edge:** Reeded

Date	Mintage	F	VF	XF	Unc	BU
2002sm Proof	35,000	Value: 85.00				

KM# 225 10 DOLLARS
28.0000 g., Copper-Nickel, 40.7 mm. **Series:** Lunar **Subject:** Year of the Goat **Obv:** National arms **Rev:** Stylized goat standing right facing left

Date	Mintage	F	VF	XF	Unc	BU
2003sm Prooflike	—	—	—	—	—	20.00

KM# 225a 10 DOLLARS
62.2060 g., 0.9990 Silver 1.9979 oz. ASW, 40.7 mm. **Series:** Lunar **Subject:** Year of the Goat **Obv:** National arms **Rev:** Stylized goat standing right facing left

Date	Mintage	F	VF	XF	Unc	BU
2003sm Proof	35,000	Value: 85.00				

KM# 187 10 DOLLARS
28.0000 g., Copper-Nickel, 40.7 mm. **Series:** Lunar **Subject:** Year of the Monkey **Obv:** National arms **Rev:** Stylized monkey sitting left **Edge:** Reeded

Date	Mintage	F	VF	XF	Unc	BU
2004sm Prooflike	—	—	—	—	—	20.00

KM# 189 10 DOLLARS
28.0000 g., Copper-Nickel, 40.7 mm. **Subject:** 10th Anniversary China-Singapore Suzhou Industrial Park **Obv:** National arms **Rev:** "Harmony" Sculpture **Edge:** Reeded

Date	Mintage	F	VF	XF	Unc	BU
2004sm Prooflike	7,000	—	—	—	—	20.00

KM# 189a 10 DOLLARS
0.9990 Silver, 40.7 mm. **Subject:** 10th Anniversary China-Singapore Suzhou Industrial Park **Obv:** National arms **Rev:** "Harmony" sculpture **Edge:** Reeded

Date	Mintage	F	VF	XF	Unc	BU
2004sm Proof	5,000	Value: 55.00				

KM# 187a 10 DOLLARS
62.2060 g., 0.9990 Silver 1.9979 oz. ASW, 40.7 mm. **Series:** Lunar **Subject:** Year of the Monkey **Obv:** National arms **Rev:** Stylized monkey sitting left **Edge:** Reeded

Date	Mintage	F	VF	XF	Unc	BU
2004sm Proof	35,000	Value: 85.00				

KM# 236 10 DOLLARS
62.2060 g., 0.9999 Silver 1.9997 oz. ASW, 45 mm. **Series:** Lunar **Subject:** Year of the Rooster **Obv:** National arms **Rev:** Stylized rooster standing right

Date	Mintage	F	VF	XF	Unc	BU
2005sm Proof	30,000	Value: 85.00				

KM# 240 10 DOLLARS
Copper-Nickel **Subject:** National University of Singapore **Obv:** National arms **Rev:** Person, globe and emblem

Date	Mintage	F	VF	XF	Unc	BU
2005sm Prooflike	20,000	—	—	—	—	22.50

KM# 240a 10 DOLLARS
20.0000 g., 0.9999 Silver 0.6429 oz. ASW **Subject:** National University of Singapore **Obv:** National arms **Rev:** Person, globe and emblem

Date	Mintage	F	VF	XF	Unc	BU
2005sm Proof	10,000	Value: 60.00				

KM# 243 10 DOLLARS
31.1030 g., 0.9999 Silver with Gold 2.3g inlay 0.9998 oz. ASW **Subject:** 40th National Day parade **Obv:** National arms **Rev:** Fireworks, parade in government plaza

Date	Mintage	F	VF	XF	Unc	BU
2005sm Proof	1,500	Value: 225				

KM# 252 10 DOLLARS
62.2030 g., 0.9990 Silver 1.9978 oz. ASW **Series:** Lunar **Subject:** Year of the Dog **Obv:** National arms **Rev:** Stylized dog standing left

Date	Mintage	F	VF	XF	Unc	BU
2006sm Proof	30,000	Value: 90.00				

KM# 266 10 DOLLARS
62.2060 g., 0.9990 Silver 1.9979 oz. ASW **Series:** Lunar **Subject:** Year of the Boar **Obv:** National arms **Rev:** Stylized boar running right - multicolor

Date	Mintage	F	VF	XF	Unc	BU
2007sm Proof	30,000	Value: 100				

KM# 272 10 DOLLARS
62.2060 g., 0.9990 Silver 1.9979 oz. ASW **Series:** Lunar **Subject:** Year of the Rat **Obv:** National arms **Rev:** Stylized rat lying left - multicolor

Date	Mintage	F	VF	XF	Unc	BU
2008sm Proof	20,000	Value: 100				

KM# 297 10 DOLLARS
62.2000 g., 0.9990 Silver 1.9977 oz. ASW **Subject:** Year of the Ox **Obv:** Supported arms **Rev:** Multicolor Ox

Date	Mintage	F	VF	XF	Unc	BU
2009 Proof	—	Value: 85.00				

KM# 226 25 DOLLARS
155.5200 g., 0.9990 Silver 4.9949 oz. ASW, 65.00 mm. **Series:** Lunar **Subject:** Year of the Goat **Obv:** National arms **Rev:** Stylized goat standing right facing left

Date	Mintage	F	VF	XF	Unc	BU
2003sm Proof	250	Value: 300				

KM# 231 25 DOLLARS
155.5200 g., 0.9990 Silver 4.9949 oz. ASW, 65 mm. **Series:** Lunar **Subject:** Year of the Monkey **Obv:** National arms **Rev:** Stylized monkey sitting left

Date	Mintage	F	VF	XF	Unc	BU
2004sm Proof	250	Value: 300				

KM# 237 25 DOLLARS
155.5200 g., 0.9999 Silver 4.9994 oz. ASW, 65 mm. **Series:** Lunar **Subject:** Year of the Rooster **Obv:** National arms **Rev:** Stylized rooster standing right

Date	Mintage	F	VF	XF	Unc	BU
2005sm Proof	250	Value: 300				

KM# 253 25 DOLLARS
155.5150 g., 0.9990 Silver 4.9947 oz. ASW **Series:** Lunar **Subject:** Year of the Dog **Obv:** National arms **Rev:** Stylized dog standing right

Date	Mintage	F	VF	XF	Unc	BU
2006sm Proof	250	Value: 350				

KM# 267 25 DOLLARS
155.5150 g., 0.9990 Silver 4.9947 oz. ASW **Series:** Lunar **Subject:** Year of the Boar **Obv:** National arms **Rev:** Stylized boar running right

Date	Mintage	F	VF	XF	Unc	BU
2007sm Proof	250	Value: 360				

KM# 273 25 DOLLARS
155.5150 g., 0.9990 Silver 4.9947 oz. ASW **Series:** Lunar **Subject:** Year of the Rat **Obv:** National arms **Rev:** Stylized rat lying left

Date	Mintage	F	VF	XF	Unc	BU
2008sm Proof	250	Value: 375				

KM# 298 25 DOLLARS
155.5000 g., 0.9990 Silver 4.9942 oz. ASW **Subject:** Year of the Ox **Obv:** Supported arms **Rev:** Ox

Date	Mintage	F	VF	XF	Unc	BU
2009 Proof	—	Value: 250				

KM# 288 50 DOLLARS
Silver **Subject:** Formula 1 - Singapore Grand Prix **Obv:** Supported arms **Rev:** Multicolor race car and skyline

Date	Mintage	F	VF	XF	Unc	BU
2008 Proof	—	Value: 30.00				

KM# 241 100 DOLLARS
31.1030 g., 0.9999 Gold 0.9998 oz. AGW **Subject:** National University of Singapore **Obv:** National arms **Rev:** Person, globe and emblem

Date	Mintage	F	VF	XF	Unc	BU
2005sm Proof	500	Value: 1,150				

KM# 289 100 DOLLARS
Gold **Subject:** Formula 1 - Singapore Grand Prix **Obv:** Supported arms **Rev:** Formula 1 racecar and skyline

Date	Mintage	F	VF	XF	Unc	BU
2008 Proof	—	Value: 300				

KM# 299 100 DOLLARS
31.1050 g., 0.9990 Gold 0.9990 oz. AGW **Subject:** Year of the Ox **Obv:** Supported arms **Rev:** Ox

Date	Mintage	F	VF	XF	Unc	BU
2009 Proof	—	Value: 1,050				

BULLION COINAGE

Lunar Year Issues

KM# 212 DOLLAR
1.5550 g., 0.9999 Gold 0.0500 oz. AGW, 13.9 mm. **Series:** Lunar **Subject:** Year of the Snake **Obv:** National arms **Rev:** Stylized lion's head right, snake privy mark at lower left

Date	Mintage	F	VF	XF	Unc	BU
2001sm Proof	—	Value: 80.00				

KM# 217 DOLLAR
1.5550 g., 0.9999 Gold 0.0500 oz. AGW, 13.9 mm. **Series:** Lunar **Subject:** Year of the Horse **Obv:** National arms **Rev:** Stylized lion's head right, horse privy mark at lower left

Date	Mintage	F	VF	XF	Unc	BU
2002sm Proof	—	Value: 80.00				

KM# 222 DOLLAR
0.3000 g., 0.9999 Gold 0.0096 oz. AGW, 7 mm. **Series:** Lunar **Subject:** Year of the Goat **Obv:** National arms **Rev:** Stylized goat standing right facing left

Date	Mintage	F	VF	XF	Unc	BU
2003sm Prooflike	8,000	—	—	—	—	32.50

KM# 186 DOLLAR
0.3000 g., 0.9999 Gold 0.0096 oz. AGW, 7 mm. **Series:** Lunar **Subject:** Year of the Monkey **Obv:** National arms **Rev:** Stylized monkey sitting left **Edge:** Plain

Date	Mintage	F	VF	XF	Unc	BU
2004 Prooflike	8,000	—	—	—	—	32.50

KM# 233 DOLLAR
0.3000 g., 0.9999 Gold 0.0096 oz. AGW, 7 mm. **Series:** Lunar **Subject:** Year of the Rooster **Obv:** National arms **Rev:** Stylized rooster standing right

Date	Mintage	F	VF	XF	Unc	BU
2005sm Prooflike	8,000	—	—	—	—	32.50

KM# 249 DOLLAR
0.3000 g., 0.9999 Gold 0.0096 oz. AGW **Series:** Lunar **Subject:** Year of the Dog **Obv:** National arms **Rev:** Stylized dog standing left

Date	Mintage	F	VF	XF	Unc	BU
2006sm Prooflike	5,000	—	—	—	—	32.50

KM# 263 DOLLAR
0.3000 g., 0.9999 Gold 0.0096 oz. AGW **Series:** Lunar **Subject:** Year of the Boar **Obv:** National arms **Rev:** Stylized boar running right

Date	Mintage	F	VF	XF	Unc	BU
2007sm Prooflike	5,000	—	—	—	—	32.50

KM# 269 DOLLAR
0.3000 g., 0.9999 Gold 0.0096 oz. AGW **Series:** Lunar **Subject:** Year of the Rat **Obv:** National arms **Rev:** Stylized rat lying left

Date	Mintage	F	VF	XF	Unc	BU
2008sm	3,000	—	—	—	—	30.00

KM# 213 5 DOLLARS
3.1100 g., 0.9999 Gold 0.1000 oz. AGW, 17.9 mm. **Series:** Lunar **Subject:** Year of the Snake **Obv:** National arms **Rev:** Stylized lion's head right, snake privy mark at lower left

Date	Mintage	F	VF	XF	Unc	BU
2001sm Proof	—	Value: 150				

KM# 218 5 DOLLARS
7.7750 g., 0.9999 Gold 0.2499 oz. AGW, 17.9 mm. **Series:** Lunar **Subject:** Year of the Horse **Obv:** National arms **Rev:** Stylized lion's head right, horse privy mark at lower left

Date	Mintage	F	VF	XF	Unc	BU
2002sm Proof	—	Value: 350				

KM# 224 5 DOLLARS
7.7760 g., 0.9999 Gold 0.2500 oz. AGW, 21.9 mm. **Series:** Lunar **Subject:** Year of the Goat **Obv:** National arms **Rev:** Stylized goat standing right facing left

Date	Mintage	F	VF	XF	Unc	BU
2003sm Proof	8,000	Value: 300				

KM# 230 5 DOLLARS
7.7760 g., 0.9999 Gold 0.2500 oz. AGW, 21.9 mm. **Series:** Lunar **Subject:** Year of the Monkey **Obv:** National arms **Rev:** Stylized monkey sitting left

Date	Mintage	F	VF	XF	Unc	BU
2004sm Proof	8,000	Value: 300				

KM# 235 5 DOLLARS
7.7760 g., 0.9999 Gold 0.2500 oz. AGW, 21.9 mm. **Series:** Lunar **Subject:** Year of the Rooster **Obv:** National arms **Rev:** Stylized rooster standing right

Date	Mintage	F	VF	XF	Unc	BU
2005sm Proof	8,000	Value: 300				

KM# 251 5 DOLLARS
7.7750 g., 0.9999 Gold 0.2499 oz. AGW **Series:** Lunar **Subject:** Year of the Dog **Obv:** National arms **Rev:** Stylized dog standing left

Date	Mintage	F	VF	XF	Unc	BU
2006sm Proof	5,000	Value: 315				

KM# 265 5 DOLLARS
7.7750 g., 0.9999 Gold 0.2499 oz. AGW **Series:** Lunar **Subject:** Year of the Boar **Obv:** National arms **Rev:** Stylized boar running right

Date	Mintage	F	VF	XF	Unc	BU
2007sm Proof	5,000	Value: 360				

KM# 271 5 DOLLARS
7.7750 g., 0.9999 Gold 0.2499 oz. AGW **Series:** Lunar **Subject:** Year of the Rat **Obv:** National arms **Rev:** Stylized rat lying left

Date	Mintage	F	VF	XF	Unc	BU
2008sm Proof	2,000	Value: 350				

KM# 214 10 DOLLARS
7.7750 g., 0.9999 Gold 0.2499 oz. AGW, 21.9 mm. **Series:** Lunar **Subject:** Year of the Snake **Obv:** National arms **Rev:** Stylized lion's head right, snake privy mark at lower left

Date	Mintage	F	VF	XF	Unc	BU
2001sm Proof	—	Value: 350				

KM# 219 10 DOLLARS
7.7750 g., 0.9999 Gold 0.2499 oz. AGW, 21.9 mm. **Series:** Lunar **Subject:** Year of the Horse **Obv:** National arms **Rev:** Stylized lion's head right, horse privy mark at lower left

Date	Mintage	F	VF	XF	Unc	BU
2002sm Proof	—	Value: 350				

KM# 185 10 DOLLARS
31.1040 g., 0.9999 Gold 0.9999 oz. AGW, 32.1 mm. **Subject:** 10th Anniversary China-Singapore Suzhou Industrial Park **Obv:** National arms **Rev:** "Harmony" Sculpture **Edge:** Lettered edge

Date	Mintage	F	VF	XF	Unc	BU
2004sm Proof	500	Value: 1,200				

KM# 215 20 DOLLARS
15.5520 g., 0.9999 Gold 0.4999 oz. AGW, 27 mm. **Series:** Lunar **Subject:** Year of the Snake **Obv:** National arms **Rev:** Stylized lion's head right, snake privy mark at lower left

Date	Mintage	F	VF	XF	Unc	BU
2001sm Proof	—	Value: 660				

KM# 220 20 DOLLARS
15.5520 g., 0.9999 Gold 0.4999 oz. AGW, 27 mm. **Series:** Lunar **Subject:** Year of the Horse **Obv:** National arms **Rev:** Stylized lion's head right, horse privy mark at lower left

Date	Mintage	F	VF	XF	Unc	BU
2002sm Proof	—	Value: 660				

KM# 216 50 DOLLARS
31.1030 g., 0.9999 Gold 0.9998 oz. AGW, 32.1 mm. **Series:** Lunar **Subject:** Year of the Snake **Obv:** National arms **Rev:** Stylized lion's head right, snake privy mark at lower left

Date	Mintage	F	VF	XF	Unc	BU
2001sm Proof	—	Value: 1,300				

KM# 221 50 DOLLARS
31.1030 g., 0.9999 Gold 0.9998 oz. AGW, 32.1 mm. **Series:** Lunar **Subject:** Year of the Horse **Obv:** National arms **Rev:** Stylized lion's head right, horse privy mark at lower left

Date	Mintage	F	VF	XF	Unc	BU
2002sm Proof	—	Value: 1,300				

KM# 238 100 DOLLARS
31.1030 g., 0.9999 Gold 0.9998 oz. AGW, 33 mm. **Series:** Lunar **Subject:** Year of the Rooster **Obv:** National arms **Rev:** Stylized rooster standing right

Date	Mintage	F	VF	XF	Unc	BU
2005sm Proof	5,000	Value: 1,200				

KM# 254 100 DOLLARS
31.1030 g., 0.9999 Gold 0.9998 oz. AGW **Series:** Lunar **Subject:** Year of the Dog **Obv:** National arms **Rev:** Stylized dog standing left

Date	Mintage	F	VF	XF	Unc	BU
2006sm Proof	3,000	Value: 1,250				

KM# 268 100 DOLLARS
31.1030 g., 0.9999 Gold 0.9998 oz. AGW **Series:** Lunar **Subject:** Year of the Boar **Obv:** National arms **Rev:** Stylized boar running right

Date	Mintage	F	VF	XF	Unc	BU
2007sm Proof	3,000	Value: 1,250				

KM# 274 100 DOLLARS
31.1030 g., 0.9999 Gold 0.9998 oz. AGW **Series:** Lunar **Subject:** Year of the Rat **Obv:** National arms **Rev:** Stylized rat lying left

Date	Mintage	F	VF	XF	Unc	BU
2008sm Proof	2,000	Value: 1,275				

KM# 239 200 DOLLARS
155.5200 g., 0.9999 Gold 4.9994 oz. AGW, 60 mm. **Series:** Lunar **Subject:** Year of the Rooster **Obv:** National arms **Rev:** Stylized rooster standing right

Date	Mintage	F	VF	XF	Unc	BU
2005sm Proof	200	Value: 6,000				

KM# 255 200 DOLLARS
155.1500 g., 0.9999 Gold 4.9875 oz. AGW **Series:** Lunar **Subject:** Year of the Dog **Obv:** National arms **Rev:** Stylized dog standing left

Date	Mintage	F	VF	XF	Unc	BU
2006sm Proof	200	Value: 6,000				

KM# 300 200 DOLLARS
155.5000 g., 0.9990 Gold 4.9942 oz. AGW **Subject:** Year of the Ox **Obv:** Supported arms **Rev:** Ox

Date	Mintage	F	VF	XF	Unc	BU
2009 Proof	—	Value: 5,750				

KM# 178 250 DOLLARS
31.1035 g., 0.9990 Gold 0.9990 oz. AGW, 32.1 mm. **Subject:** Year of the Snake **Obv:** National arms **Rev:** Stylized snake **Edge:** Reeded

Date	Mintage	F	VF	XF	Unc	BU
2001sm Proof	7,000	Value: 1,250				

KM# 183 250 DOLLARS
31.1035 g., 0.9999 Gold 0.9999 oz. AGW, 32.1 mm. **Subject:** Year of the Horse **Obv:** National arms **Rev:** Horse **Edge:** Reeded

Date	Mintage	F	VF	XF	Unc	BU
2002sm Proof	7,600	Value: 1,250				

KM# 227 250 DOLLARS
31.1030 g., 0.9999 Gold 0.9998 oz. AGW, 32.1 mm. **Series:** Lunar **Subject:** Year of the Goat **Obv:** National arms **Rev:** Stylized goat standing right facing left

Date	Mintage	F	VF	XF	Unc	BU
2003sm Proof	7,000	Value: 1,200				

KM# 188 250 DOLLARS
31.1030 g., 0.9999 Gold 0.9998 oz. AGW, 32.1 mm.
Series: Lunar **Subject:** Year of the Monkey **Obv:** National arms **Rev:** Stylized monkey sitting left **Edge:** Reeded

Date	Mintage	F	VF	XF	Unc	BU
2004sm Proof	7,000	Value: 1,250				

KM# 228 500 DOLLARS
155.5200 g., 0.9999 Gold 4.9994 oz. AGW, 55 mm.
Series: Lunar **Subject:** Year of the Goat **Obv:** National arms **Rev:** Stylized goat standing right facing left

Date	Mintage	F	VF	XF	Unc	BU
2003sm Proof	200	Value: 6,000				

KM# 232 500 DOLLARS
155.5200 g., 0.9999 Gold 4.9994 oz. AGW, 55 mm.
Series: Lunar **Subject:** Year of the Monkey **Obv:** National arms **Rev:** Stylized monkey sitting left

Date	Mintage	F	VF	XF	Unc	BU
2004sm Proof	200	Value: 6,000				

MINT SETS

KM#	Date	Mintage	Identification	Issue Price	Mkt Val
MS39	2002 (7)	—	KM#98-103, 104.3 Hongbao	—	11.00
MS40	2003 (7)	—	KM#98-103, 104.3 Hongbao	—	11.00
MS41	2004 (7)	—	KM#98-103, 104.3 Hongbao	—	11.00
MS42	2005 (7)	—	KM#98-103, 104.3 Hongbao	—	11.00
MS43	2006 (7)	—	KM#98-103, 104.3 Hongbao	—	11.00
MS44	2007 (7)	—	KM98-103, 104.3 Hongbao	10.78	11.00

PROOF SETS

KM#	Date	Mintage	Identification	Issue Price	Mkt Val
PS61	2001 (2)	3,000	KM#179-180 plus copper-nickel ingot	—	100
PS62	2001 (3)	2,000	KM#178-180 plus copper-nickel ingot	—	1,100
PS63	2001 (4)	—	KM#212-215	—	—
PS64	2001 (6)	—	KM#212-216, plus ingot	—	—
PS66	2001 (7)	10,000	KM#98a-103a, 104.2a	—	70.00
PS65	2001 (2)	2,001	KM#177, 177a	—	60.00
PS67	2002 (2)	3,000	KM#182, 182a	—	100
PS68	2002 (3)	2,000	KM#182, 182a, 183	—	1,100
PS69	2002 (2)	2,001	KM#181, 181a	—	60.00
PS70	2002 (3)	2,001	KM#181, 181a, 217	—	100
PS71	2002 (4)	—	KM#217-220	—	—
PS72	2002 (6)	—	KM#217-221 plus ingot	—	—
PS73	2002 (7)	10,000	KM#98a-103a, 104.2a	—	70.00
PS74	2003 (2)	2,003	KM#196, 196a	—	75.00
PS75	2003 (7)	10,000	KM#98a-103a, 104.3a	—	70.00
PS76	2003 (8)	1,000	KM#98a-103a, 104.3a, 196a	—	130
PS77	2003 (2)	88	KM#226, 228	—	5,150
PS78	2003 (2)	3,000	KM#225, 225a	—	100
PS79	2003 (3)	2,000	KM#225, 225a, 227	—	1,100
PS80	2004 (2)	1,000	KM#189, 189a	—	85.00
PS81	2004 (3)	88	KM#185, 189, 189a	—	1,050
PS82	2004 (7)	10,000	KM#98a-103a, 104.3a	—	70.00
PS83	2004 (2)	1,000	KM#184, 184a	—	40.00
PS84	2004 (2)	1,000	KM#190, 190a	—	40.00
PS85	2004 (2)	1,000	KM#191, 191a	—	40.00
PS86	2004 (2)	1,000	KM#192, 192a	—	40.00
PS87	2004 (4)	800	KM#184a, 190a-192a	—	110
PS88	2004 (8)	88	KM#184, 184a, 190, 190a, 191, 191a, 192, 192a	—	150
PS89	2004 (2)	80	KM#231, 232	—	5,150
PS90	2004 (2)	3,000	KM#187, 187a	—	100
PS91	2004 (3)	2,000	KM#187, 187a, 188	—	1,250
PS92	2005 (7)	—	KM#98a-103a, 104.3a	—	70.00
PS93	2005 (2)	3,000	KM#234, 236	—	100
PS94	2005 (2)	88	KM#237, 239	—	5,150
PS95	2005 (3)	2,000	KM#234, 236, 238	—	1,100
PS96	2006 (7)	—	KM#98a-103a, 104.3a	—	70.00
PS97	2006 (2)	8,000	KM#256, 257	—	120
PS101	2007 (2)	3,000	KM#193, 193a	65.00	65.00
PS98	2007 (7)	—	KM#98a-103a, 104.3a	—	70.00
PS99	2007 (4)	800	KM#259a-262a	—	130
PS100	2007 (2)	8,000	KM#275, 276	90.00	90.00

PROOF-LIKE SETS (PL)

KM#	Date	Mintage	Identification	Issue Price	Mkt Val
PL1	2004 (4)	800	KM#184, 190, 191, 192	—	40.00
PL2	2007 (4)	800	KM#259-262	—	50.00

The Republic of Slovakia has an area of 18,923 sq. mi. (49,035 sq. km.) and a population of 4.9 million. Capital: Bratislava. Textiles, steel, and wood products are exported.

MINT MARK

Kremnica Mint

REPUBLIC

STANDARD COINAGE

100 Halierov = 1 Slovak Koruna (Sk)

KM# 17 10 HALIEROV
0.7200 g., Aluminum, 17 mm. **Obv:** Double cross on shield above inscription **Rev:** Church steeple **Edge:** Plain **Designer:** Drahomir Zobek

Date	Mintage	F	VF	XF	Unc	BU
2001	20,330,000	—	—	—	0.35	—
2001 Proof	12,500	Value: 2.50				
2002	37,640,000	—	—	—	0.35	—
2002 Proof	16,100	Value: 1.50				
2003 In sets only	3,000	—	—	—	2.50	—

KM# 17a 10 HALIEROV
2.8500 g., 0.9250 Silver 0.0848 oz. ASW, 17 mm.

Date	Mintage	F	VF	XF	Unc	BU
2004	4,000	—	—	—	—	10.00
2004 Proof	2,000	Value: 15.00				

KM# 18 20 HALIEROV
0.9500 g., Aluminum, 19.5 mm. **Obv:** Double cross on shield above inscription **Rev:** Mountain peak and value **Edge:** Reeded **Designer:** Drahomir Zobek

Date	Mintage	F	VF	XF	Unc	BU
2001	21,920,000	—	—	—	0.45	—
2001 Proof	12,500	Value: 2.50				
2002	36,300,000	—	—	—	0.45	—
2002 Proof	16,100	Value: 1.50				
2003 In sets only	3,000	—	—	—	2.50	—

KM# 18a 20 HALIEROV
3.8700 g., 0.9250 Silver 0.1151 oz. ASW, 19.5 mm.

Date	Mintage	F	VF	XF	Unc	BU
2004	4,000	—	—	—	—	15.00
2004	2,000	Value: 20.00				

KM# 35 50 HALIEROV
2.8000 g., Copper Plated Steel, 18.7 mm. **Obv:** Double cross on shield above inscription **Rev:** Watch tower and value **Edge:** Milled and plain **Designer:** Drahomir Zobek

Date	Mintage	F	VF	XF	Unc	BU
2001	10,400,000	—	—	—	0.60	—
2001 Proof	12,500	Value: 2.50				
2002	11,000,000	—	—	—	0.60	—
2002 Proof	16,100	Value: 1.50				
2003	11,000,000	—	—	—	0.60	—
2004	16,500,000	—	—	—	0.60	—
2004 Proof	—	Value: 1.50				
2005	17,000,000	—	—	—	0.60	—
2006	22,050,000	—	—	—	0.60	—
2006 Proof	—	Value: 1.50				
2007	—	—	—	—	0.60	—
2008	—	—	—	—	0.60	—
2008 Proof	—	Value: 1.50				

KM# 12 KORUNA
3.8500 g., Bronze Clad Steel, 21 mm. **Subject:** 15th Century of Madonna and Child **Obv:** Double cross on shield above inscription **Rev:** Madonna holding child and value **Edge:** Milled **Designer:** Drahomir Zobek

Date	Mintage	F	VF	XF	Unc	BU
2001 In sets only	12,500	—	—	—	1.50	—
2001 Proof	—	Value: 3.00				

Date	Mintage	F	VF	XF	Unc	BU
2002	11,000,000	—	—	—	0.75	—
2002 Proof	16,100	Value: 2.50				
2003 In sets only	14,000	—	—	—	1.50	—
2004 In sets only	—	—	—	—	1.50	—
2004 Proof	—	Value: 2.50				
2005	10,000,000	—	—	—	0.75	—
2005 Proof	—	Value: 2.50				
2006	9,605,000	—	—	—	0.75	—
2006 Proof	—	Value: 2.50				
2007	—	—	—	—	0.75	—
2008	—	—	—	—	0.75	—
2008 Proof	—	Value: 2.50				

KM# 13 2 KORUNA
4.4000 g., Nickel Clad Steel, 21.5 mm. **Obv:** Double cross on shield above inscription **Rev:** Venus statue and value **Designer:** Drahomir Zobek

Date	Mintage	F	VF	XF	Unc	BU
2001	10,668,000	—	—	—	0.85	—
2001 Proof	12,500	Value: 5.00				
2002	11,000,000	—	—	—	0.85	—
2002 Proof	16,100	Value: 2.50				
2003	11,000,000	—	—	—	0.85	—
2004 In sets only	—	—	—	—	2.00	—
2004 Proof	—	Value: 2.50				
2005 In sets only	—	—	—	—	2.00	—
2006 In sets only	—	—	—	—	2.00	—
2006 Proof	—	Value: 2.50				
2007 In sets only	—	—	—	—	2.00	—
2008 In sets only	—	—	—	—	2.00	—
2008 Proof	—	Value: 2.50				

KM# 14 5 KORUNA
5.4000 g., Nickel Clad Steel, 24.75 mm. **Obv:** Double cross on shield above inscription **Rev:** Celtic coin of BIATEC at upper left of value **Edge:** Milled **Designer:** Drahomir Zobek

Date	Mintage	F	VF	XF	Unc	BU
2001 Proof	12,500	Value: 6.00				
2002 Proof	16,100	Value: 5.00				
2003 In sets only	14,000	—	—	—	2.00	—
2004 In sets only	—	—	—	—	2.00	—
2004 Proof	—	Value: 5.00				
2005 In sets only	—	—	—	—	2.00	—
2006 In sets only	—	—	—	—	2.00	—
2006 Proof	—	Value: 5.00				
2007 In sets only	—	—	—	—	2.00	—
2008 In sets only	—	—	—	—	2.00	—
2008 Proof	—	Value: 5.00				

KM# 11.1 10 KORUNA
6.6000 g., Brass, 26.5 mm. **Obv:** Double cross on shield above inscription **Rev:** Bronze cross and value **Designer:** Drahomir Zobek

Date	Mintage	F	VF	XF	Unc	BU
2001 Proof	12,500	Value: 12.50				
2002 Proof	16,100	Value: 10.00				
2003	10,923,000	—	—	—	2.50	—
2004 In sets only	—	—	—	—	4.00	—
2004 Proof	—	Value: 10.00				
2005 In sets only	—	—	—	—	4.00	—

Date	Mintage	F	VF	XF	Unc	BU
2006 In sets only	—	—	—	—	4.00	—
2006 Proof	—	Value: 10.00					
2007 In sets only	—	—	—	—	4.00	—
2008 In sets only	—	—	—	—	4.00	—
2008 Proof	—	Value: 10.00					

KM# 67   20 KORUN
24.4800 g., 0.9250 Silver 0.7280 oz. ASW, 27.1 x 50.6 mm.
Series: Banknotes **Obv:** Prince Pribina (800-861) **Rev:** Nitra
Castle **Edge:** Plain

Date	Mintage	F	VF	XF	Unc	BU
2003 Proof	6,000	Value: 30.00					

KM# 68   50 KORUN
26.6300 g., 0.9250 Silver 0.7919 oz. ASW, 28.2 x 52.8 mm.
Series: Banknotes **Obv:** Saints Cyril and Methodius (814-885)
Rev: Two hands **Edge:** Plain

Date	Mintage	F	VF	XF	Unc	BU
2003 Proof	6,000	Value: 30.00					

KM# 69   100 KORUN
28.8700 g., 0.9250 Silver 0.8585 oz. ASW, 29.3 x 55 mm.
Series: Banknotes **Obv:** The Levoca Madonna **Rev:** St. James
Church in Levoca **Edge:** Plain

Date	Mintage	F	VF	XF	Unc	BU
2003 Proof	—	Value: 35.00					

KM# 59   200 KORUN
20.0000 g., 0.7500 Silver 0.4822 oz. ASW, 34 mm. **Subject:**
Alexander Dubcek **Obv:** Double cross on shield and tree **Obv.**
Designer: Anton Gabrik **Rev:** Head left **Rev. Designer:** Ladislav
Kozak **Edge Lettering:** BUDSKOST SLOBODA DEMOKRACIA

Date	Mintage	F	VF	XF	Unc	BU
2001	12,800	—	—	—	22.00	25.00
2001 Proof	3,000	Value: 60.00					

Note: Unc. examples without edge lettering exist. Value
$800.00.

KM# 60   200 KORUN
20.0000 g., 0.7500 Silver 0.4822 oz. ASW, 34 mm.
Subject: Ludovit Fulla **Obv:** Modern art **Rev:** Head facing in
national colstume, value and dates **Edge:** Lettered
Designer: Emil Fulka **Note:** 1,800 pieces melted.

Date	Mintage	F	VF	XF	Unc	BU
2002 Proof	2,400	Value: 45.00					
2002	11,300	—	—	—	22.00	25.00

KM# 62   200 KORUN
20.3500 g., 0.7500 Silver 0.4907 oz. ASW, 34 mm.
Subject: UNESCO World Heritage site - Vlkolínec **Obv:** Log
building and double cross on shield **Rev:** Wooden tower and value
Edge Lettering: WORLD HERITAGE PATRIMONE MONDIAL
Designer: Pavol Karoly **Note:** 900 pieces melted.

Date	Mintage	F	VF	XF	Unc	BU
2002	11,500	—	—	—	22.00	25.00
2002 Proof	2,800	Value: 45.00					

KM# 66   200 KORUN
20.0000 g., 0.7500 Silver 0.4822 oz. ASW, 34 mm.
Obv: Building below double cross within shield **Rev:** Head facing
and value **Edge:** Lettered **Edge Lettering:** VYTRVALOST A
VERNOST NARODNEMU IDEALU **Note:** 500 pieces
uncirculated melted.

Date	Mintage	F	VF	XF	Unc	BU
2003 Proof	2,700	Value: 45.00					
2003	8,800	—	—	—	22.00	25.00

KM# 65   200 KORUN
20.0000 g., 0.7500 Silver 0.4822 oz. ASW, 34 mm.
Subject: Imrich Karvas **Obv:** Building, national arms and value
Rev: Portrait **Edge:** Lettered **Edge Lettering:**
NARODOHOSPODAR HUMANISTA EUROPAN **Designer:**
Miroslav Ronai **Note:** 500 pieces uncirculated melted.

Date	Mintage	F	VF	XF	Unc	BU
2003	9,800	—	—	—	22.00	25.00
2003 Proof	3,000	Value: 45.00					

KM# 70   200 KORUN
31.2100 g., 0.9250 Silver 0.9281 oz. ASW, 30.4 x 57.2 mm.
Series: Banknotes **Obv:** Head facing and value **Rev:** 18th
Century city view and value **Edge:** Plain

Date	Mintage	F	VF	XF	Unc	BU
2003 Proof	6,000	Value: 40.00					

KM# 75   200 KORUN
20.0000 g., 0.7500 Silver 0.4822 oz. ASW, 34 mm.
Obv: Kempelen's Chess Machine (1770) **Rev:** Inventor Wolfgang
Kemelen (1734-1804) above Bratislava city view
Edge Lettering: VYNALEZCA - TECHNIK - KONSTRUKTER
Designer: Miroslav Ronai

Date	Mintage	F	VF	XF	Unc	BU
2004 Proof	3,200	Value: 45.00					
2004	8,000	—	—	—	22.00	25.00

KM# 76   200 KORUN
20.0000 g., 0.7500 Silver 0.4822 oz. ASW, 34 mm. **Obv:** Church
and town hall below double cross within shield **Rev:** Aerial view
of Bardejov circa 1768 **Edge Lettering:** WORLD HERITAGE -
PATRIMOINE MONDIAL **Designer:** Jan Cernaj

Date	Mintage	F	VF	XF	Unc	BU
2004 Proof	3,600	Value: 45.00					
2004	8,400	—	—	—	22.00	25.00

KM# 77   200 KORUN
18.0000 g., 0.9000 Silver 0.5208 oz. ASW, 34 mm. **Obv:** "The
Segner Wheel" model **Rev:** Bust with fur hat facing within circle
of designs **Edge Lettering:** VYNALEZCA - FYZIK - MATEMATIK
- PEDAGOG **Designer:** Maria Poldaufova

Date	Mintage	F	VF	XF	Unc	BU
2004 Proof	4,700	Value: 45.00				
2004	10,500	—	—	—	22.00	25.00

KM# 78 200 KORUN

20.0000 g., 0.7500 Silver 0.4822 oz. ASW, 34 mm.
Subject: Slovakian entry into the European Union **Obv:** Circle of stars in arch above national arms **Rev:** Map in arch above value **Edge Lettering:** ROZSIRENIE EUROPSKEJ UNIE O DESAT KRAJIN **Designer:** Patrik Kovacovsky

Date	Mintage	F	VF	XF	Unc	BU
2004 Proof	4,700	Value: 45.00				
2004	10,100	—	—	—	22.00	25.00

KM# 81 200 KORUN

18.0000 g., 0.9000 Silver 0.5208 oz. ASW, 34 mm.
Subject: Leopold I Coronation 350th Anniversary **Obv:** Value and partial castle view **Rev:** Coin design of Leopold I in large size legend **Edge Lettering:** BRATISLAVSKE KORUNOVACIE **Designer:** Maria Poldaufova

Date	Mintage	F	VF	XF	Unc	BU
2005 Proof	4,800	Value: 45.00				
2005	8,900	—	—	—	22.00	25.00

KM# 82 200 KORUN

18.0000 g., 0.9000 Silver 0.5208 oz. ASW, 34 mm.
Subject: Treaty of Pressburg **Obv:** Primate's Palace behind French military standard **Rev:** Napoleon and Francis I of Austria **Edge Lettering:** 26 DECEMBER. 5 MIVOSE AN 14 **Designer:** Pavel Karoly

Date	Mintage	F	VF	XF	Unc	BU
2005 Proof	3,400	Value: 45.00				
2005	5,100	—	—	—	22.00	25.00

KM# 87 200 KORUN

18.0000 g., 0.9000 Silver 0.5208 oz. ASW, 34 mm.
Subject: 200th Anniversary Birth of Karol Kuzmány **Obv:** Small national arms at upper left, denomination at center **Obv. Inscription:** SLOVENSKÁ / REPUBLIKA **Rev:** Partial medallic head of Kuzmány facing

Date	Mintage	F	VF	XF	Unc	BU
2006	—	—	—	—	30.00	35.00

KM# 105 200 KORUN

18.0000 g., 0.9000 Silver 0.5208 oz. ASW, 34 mm. **Subject:** Josef M. Petzval, Physicist **Obv:** Lens **Rev:** Bust at left

Date	Mintage	F	VF	XF	Unc	BU
2007 Proof	—	Value: 50.00				

KM# 88 200 KORUN

18.0000 g., 0.9000 Silver 0.5208 oz. ASW, 34 mm.
Subject: 100th Anniversary Birth of Andrej Kmet **Obv:** Small national arms above stylized M-shaped memorial representing the Slovak Museum. **Obv. Legend:** SLOVENSKÁ REPUBLIKA **Obv. Designer:** Stefan Novotny **Rev:** Head of Kmet 3/4 left **Rev. Designer:** Dalibor Schmidt **Edge:** Lettered **Edge Lettering:** POZNÁVAJME KRAJE SVOJE A POZNÁME SAMYCH SEBA

Date	Mintage	F	VF	XF	Unc	BU
2008	8,500	—	—	—	30.00	35.00

KM# 56 500 KORUN

33.6300 g., 0.9250 Silver 1.0000 oz. ASW, 40 mm.
Subject: Mala Fatra National Park **Obv:** National arms center of

---

cross formed by beetles **Rev:** Orchid with mountain background **Edge Lettering:** OCHRANA PRIRODY A KRAJINY **Designer:** Patrik Kovacovsky **Note:** 400 pieces uncirculated melted.

Date	Mintage	F	VF	XF	Unc	BU
2001	10,200	—	—	—	55.00	60.00
2001 Proof	1,800	Value: 80.00				

KM# 57 500 KORUN

31.1035 g., 0.9990 Silver 0.9990 oz. ASW, 45 mm.
Subject: Third Millennium **Obv:** "The Universe" **Rev:** Three hands **Edge:** Plain **Shape:** 3-sided **Designer:** Patrik Kovacovsky **Note:** 400 pieces uncirculated melted.

Date	Mintage	F	VF	XF	Unc	BU
2001	13,000	—	—	—	50.00	55.00
2001 Proof	4,000	Value: 75.00				

KM# 71 500 KORUN

33.6300 g., 0.9250 Silver 1.0000 oz. ASW, 31.5 x 59.4 mm.
Series: Banknotes **Obv:** Head facing and value **Rev:** Bratislava Castle view and value **Edge:** Plain

Date	Mintage	F	VF	XF	Unc	BU
2003 Proof	6,000	Value: 45.00				

KM# 85 500 KORUN

33.6300 g., 0.9250 Silver 1.0000 oz. ASW, 40 mm.
Subject: Slovensky Kras National Park **Obv:** 2 Rock buntings above value **Rev:** Dogs Tooth violet flowers in front of Karst cave interior view **Edge Lettering:** OCHRANA PRIRODY A KRAJINY **Designer:** Maria Poldaufova

Date	Mintage	F	VF	XF	Unc	BU
2005	8,500	—	—	—	—	45.00
2005 Proof	3,600	Value: 70.00				

KM# 84 500 KORUN

33.6300 g., 0.9250 Silver 1.0000 oz. ASW, 40 mm. **Subject:** Muranska Planina National Park **Obv:** Wildflowers and Muran castle ruins **Rev:** Two wild horses **Edge Lettering:** OCHRANA PRIRODY A KRAJINY [flower] **Designer:** Karol Licko

Date	Mintage	F	VF	XF	Unc	BU
2006 Proof	2,800	Value: 70.00				
2006	4,300	—	—	—	—	45.00

KM# 86 500 KORUN

33.6300 g., 0.9250 Silver 1.0000 oz. ASW, 40 mm.
Subject: 450th Anniversary - Construction Fortress at Komárno **Obv:** Early ships, fortress in background, national arms at lower right **Obv. Legend:** SLOVENSKÁ REPUBLIKA **Obv. Designer:** Karol Licko **Rev:** Layout of fortress, horses in battle against Turks below **Rev. Legend:** PEVNOST - KOMÁRNO **Rev. Designer:** Mária Poldaufová **Edge Lettering:** NEC ARTE NEC MARTE - COMORRA in relief

Date	Mintage	F	VF	XF	Unc	BU
2007	4,600	—	—	—	—	45.00
2007 Proof	2,600	Value: 70.00				

KM# 106 500 KORUN

33.6300 g., 0.9250 Silver 1.0000 oz. ASW, 40 mm.
Subject: National Park - Low Tatra Mountains **Obv:** Mountains, flower and shield **Rev:** Bear in pine tree

Date	Mintage	F	VF	XF	Unc	BU
2008	4,300	—	—	—	—	45.00

KM# 63 1000 KORUN

62.2070 g., 0.9990 Silver 1.9979 oz. ASW, 43.6 x 43.6 mm.
Subject: 10th Anniversary of Republic **Obv:** National arms between hands **Rev:** Value above map **Edge:** Segmented reeding **Shape:** Square **Designer:** Milos Vavro

Date	Mintage	F	VF	XF	Unc	BU
2003 Proof	10,000	Value: 80.00				

KM# 72   1000 KORUN
43.9100 g., 0.9250 Bi-Metallic .925 Silver 43.91g planchet with .999 Gold .28g insert 1.3058 oz., 32.6 x 61.6 mm.
Series: Banknotes **Obv:** Head facing and value **Rev:** The Madonna Protector facing and church of Liptovske Sliace **Edge:** Plain **Note:** Illustration reduced.

Date	Mintage	F	VF	XF	Unc	BU
2003 Proof	6,000	Value: 75.00				

KM# 58   5000 KORUN
Tri-Metallic 31.1035, .999 Silver, 1.00 oz ASW with 6.22, .999 Gold, .20 oz AGW and .31, .999 Platinum, .10 oz. APW, 50 mm.
Series: Third Millennium **Obv:** "The Universe" **Rev:** Three hands **Edge:** Plain **Shape:** Triangular **Designer:** Patrik Kovacovsky

Date	Mintage	F	VF	XF	Unc	BU
2001 Proof	8,000	Value: 475				

KM# 61   5000 KORUN
9.5000 g., 0.9000 Gold 0.2749 oz. AGW, 26 mm.
Subject: Vikolinec village - UNESCO historic site **Obv:** Enclosed communal well **Rev:** Window and fence **Edge:** Reeded **Designer:** Maria Poldaufova

Date	Mintage	F	VF	XF	Unc	BU
2002 Proof	7,200	Value: 350				

KM# 73   5000 KORUN
47.6340 g., 0.9250 Bi-Metallic .925 Silver 46.65g planchet with two .9999 Gold inserts .964g in total 1.4165 oz., 33.4 x 63.8 mm.
Series: Banknotes **Obv:** Head facing and value **Rev:** Stefanik's grave monument **Edge:** Plain **Note:** Illustration reduced.

Date	Mintage	F	VF	XF	Unc	BU
2003 Proof	6,000	Value: 125				

KM# 80   5000 KORUN
9.5000 g., 0.9000 Gold 0.2749 oz. AGW, 26 mm.
Subject: Bardejov - UNESCO historic site **Obv:** National arms and value left of Town Hall **Rev:** Zachariah in window frame left of St. Aegidius Church, Bardejov **Edge:** Reeded

Date	Mintage	F	VF	XF	Unc	BU
2004 Proof	9,000	Value: 350				

KM# 83   5000 KORUN
9.5000 g., 0.9000 Gold 0.2749 oz. AGW, 26 mm.
Subject: Leopold I Coronation **Obv:** Mounted Herald with Bratislava Castile in background **Rev:** Leopold I and Crown of St. Stephan **Edge:** Reeded

Date	Mintage	F	VF	XF	Unc	BU
2005 Proof	7,500	Value: 350				

KM# 89   5000 KORUN
9.5000 g., 0.9000 Gold 0.2749 oz. AGW, 26 mm. **Subject:** 400th Anniversary Coronation of King Matthias II **Obv:** Cathedral and Bratislava castle **Obv. Legend:** SLOVENSKÁ - REPUBLIKA **Obv. Designer:** Miroslav and Branislav Ronai **Rev:** 1/2 length figure of Matthias II left, crown in lower foreground, towers of the St. Michael's Gate and franciscan Church in Bratislava in background **Rev. Legend:** KORUNOVÁCIA MATEJA II. / BRATISLAVA **Edge:** Reeded

Date	Mintage	F	VF	XF	Unc	BU
2008 Proof	4,050	Value: 375				

KM# 64   10000 KORUN
18.8350 g., Bi-Metallic 1.555g, .999 Palladium round center in a 15.55g, .900 Gold square, 29.5 x 29.5 mm.   **Subject:** 10th Anniversary of the Republic **Obv:** Young head left within circular inscription above double cross within shield **Rev:** Bratislava castle above value **Edge:** Segmented reeding **Shape:** Square **Designer:** Ludmila Cvengrosova

Date	Mintage	F	VF	XF	Unc	BU
2003 Proof	6,000	Value: 800				

KM# 79   10000 KORUN
24.8828 g., Bi-Metallic .999 Gold 12.4414g 23mm round center in .999 Palladium 12.4414g 40mm pentagon, 40 mm.
Subject: Slovakian entry into the European Union **Obv:** National arms above date in center **Obv. Designer:** Stefan Novotny **Rev:** European map with entry date **Rev. Designer:** Jan Cernaj **Edge:** Plain

Date	Mintage	F	VF	XF	Unc	BU
2004 Proof	7,200	Value: 900				

EURO COINAGE
European Union Issues

KM# 95   EURO CENT
2.3500 g., Copper Plated Steel, 16.2 mm. **Obv:** Krivan Peak in the Tatras, state emblem **Obv. Designer:** Drahomir Zobek **Rev:** Denomination and globe

Date	Mintage	F	VF	XF	Unc	BU
2009	—	—	—	—	0.35	0.50
2009 Proof	—				—	
2010	—	—	—	—	0.35	0.50
2010 Proof	—				—	

KM# 96   2 EURO CENT
3.0700 g., Copper Plated Steel, 18.7 mm. **Obv:** Krivan Peak in the Tatras, state emblem **Obv. Designer:** Drahomir Zobek **Rev:** Denomination and globe

Date	Mintage	F	VF	XF	Unc	BU
2009	—	—	—	—	0.50	0.65
2009 Proof	—				—	
2010	—	—	—	—	0.50	0.65
2010 Proof	—				—	

KM# 97   5 EURO CENT
3.8600 g., Copper Plated Steel, 21.3 mm. **Obv:** Krivan Peak in the Tatras - state emblem **Obv. Designer:** Drahomir Zobek **Rev:** Denomination and globe

Date	Mintage	F	VF	XF	Unc	BU
2009	—	—	—	—	0.75	1.00
2009 Proof	—				—	
2010	—	—	—	—	0.75	1.00
2010 Proof	—				—	

KM# 98   10 EURO CENT
4.0700 g., Brass, 19.8 mm. **Obv:** Bratislava Castle and state emblem **Obv. Designer:** Jan Cernaj and Pavel Karoly **Rev:** Expanded relief map of European Union at left, denomination at right

Date	Mintage	F	VF	XF	Unc	BU
2009	—	—	—	—	0.75	1.00
2009 Proof	—				—	
2010	—	—	—	—	0.75	1.00
2010 Proof	—				—	

KM# 99 20 EURO CENT

5.7300 g., Brass, 22.3 mm. **Obv:** Bratislava Castle and state emblem **Obv. Designer:** Jan Cernaj and Pavel Karoly **Rev:** Expanded relief map of European Union at left, denomination at right

Date	Mintage	F	VF	XF	Unc	BU
2009	—	—	—	—	1.00	1.25
2009 Proof	—	—	—	—	—	—
2010	—	—	—	—	1.00	1.25
2010 Proof	—	—	—	—	—	—

KM# 100 50 EURO CENT

7.8100 g., Brass, 24.2 mm. **Obv:** Bratislava Castle and state shield **Obv. Designer:** Jan Cernaj and Pavel Karoly **Rev:** Expanded relief map of European Union at left, denomination at right

Date	Mintage	F	VF	XF	Unc	BU
2009	—	—	—	—	1.25	1.50
2009 Proof	—	—	—	—	—	—
2010	—	—	—	—	1.25	1.50
2010 Proof	—	—	—	—	—	—

KM# 101 EURO

Bi-Metallic Copper-Nickel center in Brass ring, 23.2 mm.
Obv: Double cross in middle of three hills **Obv. Designer:** Ivan Rehak **Rev:** Value at left, expanded relief map of European Union at right

Date	Mintage	F	VF	XF	Unc	BU
2009	—	—	—	—	2.50	2.75
2009 Proof	—	—	—	—	—	—
2010	—	—	—	—	2.50	2.75
2010 Proof	—	—	—	—	—	—

KM# 102 2 EURO

8.5200 g., Bi-Metallic, 25.7 mm. **Obv:** Double cross on middle of three hills **Obv. Designer:** Ivan Rehak **Rev:** Value at left, expanded map of European Union at left

Date	Mintage	F	VF	XF	Unc	BU
2009	—	—	—	—	5.00	6.00
2009 Proof	—	—	—	—	—	—
2010	—	—	—	—	5.00	6.00
2010 Proof	—	—	—	—	—	—

KM# 103 2 EURO

8.5200 g., Bi-Metallic Brass center in Copper-Nickel ring, 25.7 mm. **Subject:** EMU 10th Anniversary **Obv:** Stick figure and large E symbol **Rev:** Expanded relief map of European Union at left, denomination at right

Date	Mintage	F	VF	XF	Unc	BU
2009	—	—	—	—	6.00	7.50

KM# 107 2 EURO

8.5200 g., Bi-Metallic, 25.72 mm. **Subject:** 17 November 1989, 20th Anniversary **Obv:** Ringing bell **Obv. Designer:** Pavel Karoly

Date	Mintage	F	VF	XF	Unc	BU
2009	1,000,000	—	—	—	6.00	7.50

KM# 108 10 EURO

18.0000 g., 0.9000 Silver 0.5208 oz. ASW, 34 mm.
Subject: Aurel Stodola, 150th Anniversary of birth **Obv:** Turbo generator, national shield **Rev:** Portrait **Edge Lettering:** KONSTRUKTER - VYNALEZCA - PEDAGOG

Date	Mintage	F	VF	XF	Unc	BU
2009	10,100	—	—	—	—	50.00
2009 Proof	13,300	Value: 65.00				

KM# 110 10 EURO

18.0000 g., 0.9000 Silver 0.5208 oz. ASW, 34 mm.
Subject: Wooden Churches of Carpathian Slovakia - UNESCO World Heritage site

Date	Mintage	F	VF	XF	Unc	BU
2010	—	—	—	—	—	50.00
2010 Proof	—	Value: 65.00				

KM# 111 10 EURO

18.0000 g., 0.9000 Silver 0.5208 oz. ASW, 34 mm.
Subject: Martin Kukucin, 150th Anniversary of birth

Date	Mintage	F	VF	XF	Unc	BU
2010	—	—	—	—	—	50.00
2010 Proof	—	Value: 65.00				

KM# 109 20 EURO

Silver **Subject:** National Park - Velka Fatra **Obv:** Fora and national shield **Rev:** Falcon in flight over mountain peak **Designer:** Roman Lugar

Date	Mintage	F	VF	XF	Unc	BU
2009	9,900	—	—	—	—	55.00
2009 Proof	12,600	Value: 70.00				

KM# 112 20 EURO

33.6300 g., 0.9250 Silver 1.0000 oz. ASW, 40 mm.
Subject: Poloniny National Park

Date	Mintage	F	VF	XF	Unc	BU
2010	—	—	—	—	—	55.00
2010 Proof	—	Value: 70.00				

KM# 113 100 EURO

9.5000 g., 0.9000 Gold 0.2749 oz. AGW, 26 mm.
Subject: Wooden Churches of Carpathian Slovakia - UNESCO Heritage Site

Date	Mintage	F	VF	XF	Unc	BU
2010 Proof	—	Value: 350				

MINT SETS

KM#	Date	Mintage	Identification	Issue Price	Mkt Val
MS9	2001 (7)	—	KM#11.1-14, 17-18, 35, plus medal	—	12.00
MS10	2002 (7)	—	KM#11.1-14, 17-18, 35, plus medal	—	12.00
MS11	2003 (7)	—	KM#11.1-14, 17-18, 35, plus medal	—	12.00
MS12	2004 (7)	—	KM#11.1-14, 17, 18, 35 plus medal	—	12.00
MS13	2005 (7)	—	KM#11.1-14, 17, 18, 35 plus medal	—	12.00

KM#	Date	Mintage	Identification	Issue Price	Mkt Val
MS14	2006 (7)	—	KM#11.1-14, 17, 18, 35 plus medal	—	12.00
MS15	2007 (7)	—	KM#11.1-14, 17, 18, 35 plus medal	—	12.00
MS16	2007 (5)	—	KM11.2, 12-14, 35. National parks	—	15.00
MS17	2005 (5)	—	KM#11.1, 12-14, 35, Austrian 2005 KM#3088	—	10.00
MS18	2007 (5)	—	KM#11.1, 12-14, 35.	—	12.00
MS19	2007 (5)	—	KM#11.1, 12-14, 35. National parks packaging	—	15.00
MS20	2007 (5)	—	KM#11.1, 12-14, 35 and a bimetallic medal and cd. Set to commemorate musician Gejza Dusik	—	20.00

PROOF SETS

KM#	Date	Mintage	Identification	Issue Price	Mkt Val
PS1	2000 (7)	900	KM#11.1-14, 17-18, 35	—	90.00
PS2	2001 (7)	12,500	KM#11.1-14, 17-18, 35	—	35.00
PS3	2002 (7)	16,500	KM#11.1-14, 17-18, 35	—	25.00
PS4	2004 (7)	—	KM#11.1, 12-14, 35, silver strikes of 1993, KM#17-18	—	35.00
PS5	2006 (5)	—	KM#11.1, 12-14, 35 and a bimetallic medal for Torino Winter Olympics	—	45.00
PS6	2008 (5)	—	KM#11.1, 12-14, 35 and a bimetallic medal. Issued to commemorate 2008 Peking Olympics	—	45.00

SLOVENIA

The Republic of Slovenia is located northwest of Yugoslavia in the valleys of the Danube River. It has an area of 7,819 sq. mi. and a population of *1.9 million. Capital: Ljubljana. Agriculture is the main industry with large amounts of hops and fodder crops grown as well as many varieties of fruit trees. Sheep raising, timber production and the mining of mercury from one of the country's oldest mines are also very important to the economy. Slovenia joined the European Union in May 2004.

MINT MARKS
Based on last digit in date.
(K) - Kremnitz (Slovakia): open 4, upturned 5
(BP) - Budapest (Hungary): closed 4, down-turned 5

MONETARY SYSTEM
100 Stotinov = 1 Tolar
100 Euro Cents = 1 Euro

REPUBLIC

STANDARD COINAGE
100 Stotinow = 1 Tolar

KM# 7 10 STOTINOV

0.5500 g., Aluminum, 16 mm. **Obv:** Value within square **Rev:** Olm salamander **Edge:** Plain **Note:** Varieties exist.

Date	Mintage	F	VF	XF	Unc	BU
2001 In sets only	1,000	—	—	—	—	3.00
2001 Proof	800	Value: 5.00				
2002 In sets only	1,000	—	—	—	—	3.00
2002 Proof	800	Value: 5.00				
2003 In sets only	1,000	—	—	—	—	3.00
2003 Proof	800	Value: 5.00				
2004 In sets only	1,000	—	—	—	—	3.00
2004 Proof	800	Value: 5.00				
2005 In sets only	3,000	—	—	—	—	2.00
2005 Proof	1,000	Value: 5.00				
2006 In sets only	4,000	—	—	—	—	2.00
2006 Proof	1,000	Value: 5.00				

KM# 8 20 STOTINOV
0.7000 g., Aluminum, 18 mm. **Obv:** Value within square
Rev: Barn owl and value **Edge:** Plain

Date	Mintage	F	VF	XF	Unc	BU
2001 In sets only	1,000	—	—	—	—	4.00
2001 Proof	800	Value: 6.00				
2002 In sets only	1,000	—	—	—	—	4.00
2002 Proof	800	Value: 6.00				
2003 In sets only	1,000	—	—	—	—	4.00
2003 Proof	800	Value: 6.00				
2004 In sets only	1,000	—	—	—	—	4.00
2004 Proof	500	Value: 6.00				
2005 In sets only	3,000	—	—	—	—	3.00
2005 Proof	1,000	Value: 6.00				
2006 In sets only	4,000	—	—	—	—	3.00
2006 Proof	1,000	Value: 6.00				

KM# 3 50 STOTINOV
0.8500 g., Aluminum, 19.9 mm. **Obv:** Value within square
Rev: Bee and value **Edge:** Plain

Date	Mintage	F	VF	XF	Unc	BU
2001 In sets only	1,000	—	—	—	—	6.00
2001 Proof	800	Value: 7.50				
2002 In sets only	1,000	—	—	—	—	6.00
2002 Proof	800	Value: 7.50				
2003 In sets only	1,000	—	—	—	—	6.00
2003 Proof	800	Value: 7.50				
2004 In sets only	1,000	—	—	—	—	6.00
2004 Proof	500	Value: 12.00				
2005 In sets only	3,000	—	—	—	—	4.00
2005 Proof	1,000	Value: 7.00				
2006 In sets only	4,000	—	—	—	—	4.00
2006 Proof	1,000	Value: 7.00				

KM# 4 TOLAR
4.5000 g., Brass, 21.9 mm. **Obv:** Value within circle **Rev:** Three
brown trout **Edge:** Reeded **Note:** Date varieties exist: 1994 =
closed or open "4"; 1995 = serif up and serif down in "5".

Date	Mintage	F	VF	XF	Unc	BU
2001	10,001,000	—	—	—	0.75	1.25
2001 Proof	800	Value: 7.50				
2002 In sets only	1,000	—	—	—	—	5.00
2002 Proof	800	Value: 7.50				
2003 In sets only	1,000	—	—	—	—	5.00
2003 Proof	800	Value: 7.50				
2004	10,001,000	—	—	—	0.75	1.25
2004 (K) In sets only	1,000	—	—	—	—	5.00
Note: 4 open to right						
2004 Proof	500	Value: 8.50				
2005 Proof	3,000	—	—	—	—	4.00
2005 Proof	1,000	Value: 7.50				
2006 In sets only	4,000	—	—	—	—	4.00
2006 Proof	1,000	Value: 7.50				

KM# 5 2 TOLARJA
5.4000 g., Brass, 24 mm. **Obv:** Value within circle **Rev:** Barn
swallow in flight **Edge:** Reeded **Note:** Date varieties exist: 1994
= closed or open "4"; 1995 = serif up and serif down in "5".

Date	Mintage	F	VF	XF	Unc	BU
2001	10,001,000	—	—	—	0.75	1.75
2001 Proof	800	Value: 8.50				
2002 In sets only	1,000	—	—	—	—	7.00
2002 Proof	800	Value: 8.50				
2003 In sets only	1,000	—	—	—	—	7.00
2003 Proof	800	Value: 8.50				

Date	Mintage	F	VF	XF	Unc	BU
2004	10,001,000	—	—	—	0.75	1.50
2004 Proof	500	Value: 8.50				
2005 In sets only	3,000	—	—	—	—	7.00
2005 Proof	1,000	Value: 8.50				
2006 In sets only	4,000	—	—	—	—	7.00
2006 Proof	1,000	Value: 8.50				

KM# 6 5 TOLARJEV
6.4400 g., Brass, 26 mm. **Obv:** Value within circle **Rev:** Head
and horns of ibex **Edge:** Reeded **Note:** Date varieties exist: 1994
= closed or open "4"; 1995 = serif up and serif down in "5".

Date	Mintage	F	VF	XF	Unc	BU
2001 In sets only	1,000	—	—	—	—	8.00
2001 Proof	800	Value: 10.00				
2002 In sets only	1,000	—	—	—	—	8.00
2002 Proof	800	Value: 10.00				
2003 In sets only	1,000	—	—	—	—	8.00
2003 Proof	800	Value: 10.00				
2004 In sets only	1,000	—	—	—	—	8.00
2004 Proof	500	Value: 15.00				
2005 In sets only	3,000	—	—	—	—	7.00
2005 Proof	1,000	Value: 10.00				
2006 In sets only	4,000	—	—	—	—	7.00
2006 Proof	1,000	Value: 10.00				

KM# 41 10 TOLARJEV
5.7500 g., Copper-Nickel, 22 mm. **Obv:** Value within circle
Rev: Stylized rearing horse **Edge:** Reeded

Date	Mintage	F	VF	XF	Unc	BU
2001	29,441,000	—	—	—	2.00	3.50
2001 Proof	800	Value: 12.00				
2002	10,037,000	—	—	—	2.00	3.50
2002 Proof	800	Value: 12.00				
2003 In sets only	1,000	—	—	—	—	5.00
2003 Proof	800	Value: 12.00				
2004	10,001,000	—	—	—	2.00	3.50
2004 Proof	500	Value: 12.00				
2005	6,003,000	—	—	—	2.00	3.50
2005 Proof	1,000	Value: 12.00				
2006	6,001,000	—	—	—	2.00	3.50
2006 Proof	1,000	Value: 12.00				

KM# 51 20 TOLARJEV
6.8500 g., Copper-Nickel, 24 mm. **Obv:** Value within circle
Rev: White Stork **Edge:** Reeded

Date	Mintage	F	VF	XF	Unc	BU
2003	10,001,000	—	—	—	3.50	5.00
2003 Proof	800	Value: 15.00				
2004	10,001,000	—	—	—	3.00	5.00
2004 Proof	500	Value: 15.00				
2005	12,003,000	—	—	—	3.50	5.00
2005 Proof	1,000	Value: 15.00				
2006	4,004,000	—	—	—	3.50	5.00
2006 Proof	1,000	Value: 15.00				

KM# 52 50 TOLARJEV
8.0000 g., Copper-Nickel, 26 mm. **Obv:** Value within circle
Rev: Stylized bull **Edge:** Reeded and plain sections

Date	Mintage	F	VF	XF	Unc	BU
2003	10,001,000	—	—	—	2.50	4.50
2003 Proof	800	Value: 12.00				

Date	Mintage	F	VF	XF	Unc	BU
2004	10,001,000	—	—	—	0.75	1.50
2004 Proof	500	Value: 8.50				
2005 In sets only	3,000	—	—	—	—	7.00
2005 Proof	1,000	Value: 8.50				
2006 In sets only	4,000	—	—	—	—	7.00
2006 Proof	1,000	Value: 8.50				

Date	Mintage	F	VF	XF	Unc	BU
2004	5,001,000	—	—	—	2.50	4.50
2004 Proof	500	Value: 15.00				
2005	8,003,000	—	—	—	2.50	4.50
2005 Proof	1,000	Value: 12.00				
2006 In sets only	4,000	—	—	—	—	6.50
2006 Proof	1,000	Value: 12.00				

KM# 42 100 TOLARJEV
9.1000 g., Copper-Nickel, 28 mm. **Subject:** 10th Anniversary
of Slovenia and the Tolar **Obv:** Value **Rev:** Tree rings and
inscription **Edge:** Reeded

Date	Mintage	F	VF	XF	Unc	BU
2001 Proof	800	Value: 10.00				
2001	500,000	—	—	—	3.00	4.00

KM# 45 500 TOLARJEV
8.5400 g., Bi-Metallic Copper-Nickel center in Brass ring,
28.1 mm. **Subject:** Soccer **Obv:** Value **Rev:** Soccer player and
radiant sun **Edge:** Reeded

Date	Mintage	F	VF	XF	Unc	BU
2002	500,000	—	—	—	5.50	7.50
2002 Proof	800	Value: 12.50				

KM# 50 500 TOLARJEV
8.7200 g., Bi-Metallic Copper-Nickel center in Brass ring,
27.9 mm. **Subject:** European Year of the Disabled **Obv:** Stylized
wheelchair **Rev:** Value **Edge:** Reeded

Date	Mintage	F	VF	XF	Unc	BU
2003 Proof	800	Value: 13.50				
2003	200,000	—	—	—	6.00	8.00

KM# 57 500 TOLARJEV
8.6000 g., Bi-Metallic Copper-Nickel center in Brass ring, 28 mm.
Obv: Value **Rev:** Profile left looking down within mathematical
graph **Edge:** Reeded

Date	Mintage	F	VF	XF	Unc	BU
2004	200,000	—	—	—	6.00	8.00
2004 Proof	500	Value: 20.00				

KM# 63 500 TOLARJEV
8.6500 g., Bi-Metallic Copper-Nickel center in Brass ring,
27.9 mm. **Obv:** Perched falcon and value **Rev:** Horizontal line
in center divides partial suns **Edge:** Reeded

Date	Mintage	F	VF	XF	Unc	BU
2005	103,000	—	—	—	6.25	8.50
2005 Proof	1,000	Value: 12.00				

KM# 65   500 TOLARJEV
8.6000 g., Bi-Metallic Copper-Nickel center in Brass ring, 28 mm. **Obv:** Value **Rev:** Anton Tomaz Linhart's silhouette above life dates **Edge:** Reeded

Date	Mintage	F	VF	XF	Unc	BU
2006	104,000	—	—	—	6.00	8.00
2006 Proof	1,000	Value: 12.00				

KM# 43   2000 TOLARJEV
15.0000 g., 0.9250 Silver 0.4461 oz. ASW, 32 mm. **Subject:** 10th Anniversary of Slovenia and the Tolar **Obv:** Value **Rev:** Tree rings and inscription **Edge:** Reeded

Date	Mintage	F	VF	XF	Unc	BU
2001 Proof	3,000	Value: 35.00				

KM# 46   2500 TOLARJEV
15.0000 g., 0.9250 Silver 0.4461 oz. ASW, 32 mm. **Subject:** Soccer **Obv:** Value **Rev:** Soccer player and radiant sun **Edge:** Reeded

Date	Mintage	F	VF	XF	Unc	BU
2002 Proof	2,500	Value: 35.00				

KM# 48   2500 TOLARJEV
15.0000 g., 0.9250 Silver 0.4461 oz. ASW, 32 mm. **Subject:** 35th Chess Olympiad **Obv:** Rearing horse and reflection **Rev:** Chess pieces in starting positions and reflection **Edge:** Reeded **Designer:** MNiljenko Licul and Jan Cernaj

Date	Mintage	F	VF	XF	Unc	BU
2002 Proof	1,000	Value: 45.00				

KM# 53   2500 TOLARJEV
15.0000 g., 0.9250 Silver 0.4461 oz. ASW, 32 mm. **Subject:** European Year of the Disabled **Obv:** Value **Rev:** Stylized wheel chair **Edge:** Reeded

Date	Mintage	F	VF	XF	Unc	BU
2003 Proof	1,500	Value: 40.00				

KM# 55   5000 TOLARJEV
15.0000 g., 0.9250 Silver 0.4461 oz. ASW, 32 mm. **Subject:** 60th Anniversary of the Slovenian Assembly **Obv:** Value in partial star design **Rev:** Dates in partial star design **Edge:** Reeded

Date	Mintage	F	VF	XF	Unc	BU
2003 Proof	1,500	Value: 40.00				

KM# 58   5000 TOLARJEV
15.0000 g., 0.9250 Silver 0.4461 oz. ASW, 32 mm. **Obv:** Value **Rev:** Facial profile left looking down within mathematical graph **Edge:** Reeded

Date	Mintage	F	VF	XF	Unc	BU
2004 Proof	1,500	Value: 50.00				

KM# 60   5000 TOLARJEV
15.0000 g., 0.9250 Silver 0.4461 oz. ASW, 32 mm. **Subject:** 1000th Anniversary Town of Bled **Obv:** Value **Rev:** Castle and towers silhouette **Edge:** Reeded

Date	Mintage	F	VF	XF	Unc	BU
2004 Proof	1,500	Value: 50.00				

KM# 62   5000 TOLARJEV
15.1000 g., 0.9250 Silver 0.4490 oz. ASW, 32 mm. **Subject:** Slovenian Film Centennial **Obv:** Value above a director's clapboard **Rev:** Film segment **Edge:** Reeded

Date	Mintage	F	VF	XF	Unc	BU
2005 Proof	—	Value: 47.50				

KM# 64   5000 TOLARJEV
15.1000 g., 0.9250 Silver 0.4490 oz. ASW, 32 mm. **Obv:** Perched falcon above value **Rev:** Diagonal center line divides partial suns **Edge:** Reeded

Date	Mintage	F	VF	XF	Unc	BU
2005 Proof	—	Value: 47.50				

KM# 91   5000 TOLARJEV
15.0000 g., 0.9250 Silver 0.4461 oz. ASW, 32 mm. **Subject:** 1000th Anniversary, mention of town of Bled, 2nd issue

Date	Mintage	F	VF	XF	Unc	BU
2006 Proof	1,000	Value: 55.00				

KM# 92   5000 TOLARJEV
15.0000 g., 0.9000 Silver 0.4340 oz. ASW, 32 mm. **Subject:** Anton Tomaz Linhart, 250th Anniversary of Birth

Date	Mintage	F	VF	XF	Unc	BU
2006 Proof	5,000	Value: 45.00				

KM# 93   5000 TOLARJEV
15.0000 g., 0.9250 Silver 0.4461 oz. ASW, 32 mm. **Subject:** Anton Askerc, 150th Anniversary of birth

Date	Mintage	F	VF	XF	Unc	BU
2006 Proof	5,000	Value: 45.00				

KM# 44   20000 TOLARJEV
7.0000 g., 0.9000 Gold 0.2025 oz. AGW, 24 mm. **Subject:** 10th Anniversary of Slovenia and the Tolar **Obv:** Value **Rev:** Tree rings and inscription **Edge:** Reeded

Date	Mintage	F	VF	XF	Unc	BU
2001 Proof	1,000	Value: 285				

KM# 47   20000 TOLARJEV
7.0000 g., 0.9000 Gold 0.2025 oz. AGW, 24 mm. **Subject:** World Cup Soccer **Obv:** Value **Rev:** Soccer player and rising sun **Edge:** Reeded

Date	Mintage	F	VF	XF	Unc	BU
2002 Proof	500	Value: 300				

KM# 49   20000 TOLARJEV
7.0000 g., 0.9000 Gold 0.2025 oz. AGW, 24 mm. **Subject:** 35th Chess Olympiad **Obv:** Rearing horse and reflection **Rev:** Chess pieces in starting positions and reflection **Edge:** Reeded

Date	Mintage	F	VF	XF	Unc	BU
2002 Proof	500	Value: 320				

KM# 54   25000 TOLARJEV
7.0000 g., 0.9000 Gold 0.2025 oz. AGW, 24 mm. **Subject:** European Year of the Disabled **Obv:** Value **Rev:** Stylized wheel chair **Edge:** Reeded

Date	Mintage	F	VF	XF	Unc	BU
2003 Proof	300	Value: 325				

KM# 56 25000 TOLARJEV
7.0000 g., 0.9000 Gold 0.2025 oz. AGW, 24 mm. **Subject:** 60th Anniversary of the Slovenian Assembly **Obv:** Value in partial star design **Rev:** Dates in partial star design **Edge:** Reeded

Date	Mintage	F	VF	XF	Unc	BU
2003 Proof	300	Value: 325				

KM# 59 25000 TOLARJEV
7.0000 g., 0.9000 Gold 0.2025 oz. AGW, 24 mm. **Subject:** 250th Anniversary of Jurij Vega's Birth **Obv:** Value **Rev:** Facial profile left looking down within mathematical graph **Edge:** Reeded

Date	Mintage	F	VF	XF	Unc	BU
2004 Proof	300	Value: 325				

KM# 61 25000 TOLARJEV
7.0000 g., 0.9000 Gold 0.2025 oz. AGW, 24 mm.
Subject: 1000th Anniversary Town of Bled **Obv:** Value **Rev:** Castle and towers silhouette **Edge:** Reeded

Date	Mintage	F	VF	XF	Unc	BU
2004 Proof	300	Value: 325				

KM# 66 25000 TOLARJEV
7.0000 g., 0.9000 Gold 0.2025 oz. AGW, 24 mm.
Subject: Centennial of Slovene Sokol Association **Obv:** Perched falcon above value **Rev:** Rising sun and reflection **Edge:** Reeded

Date	Mintage	F	VF	XF	Unc	BU
2005 Proof	1,000	Value: 300				

KM# 67 25000 TOLARJEV
7.0000 g., 0.9000 Gold 0.2025 oz. AGW, 24 mm.
Subject: Centennial of Slovene Film **Obv:** Value above clapboard **Rev:** Film segment **Edge:** Reeded

Date	Mintage	F	VF	XF	Unc	BU
2005 Proof	1,000	Value: 300				

KM# 83 25000 TOLARJEV
7.0000 g., 0.9000 Gold 0.2025 oz. AGW, 24 mm.
Subject: Anton Askerc **Edge:** Reeded

Date	Mintage	F	VF	XF	Unc	BU
2006 Proof	—	Value: 350				

KM# 84 25000 TOLARJEV
7.0000 g., 0.9000 Gold 0.2025 oz. AGW, 24 mm.
Subject: Anton Tomaz Linhart **Edge:** Reeded

Date	Mintage	F	VF	XF	Unc	BU
2006 Proof	—	Value: 350				

KM# 90 25000 TOLARJEV
7.0000 g., 0.9000 Gold 0.2025 oz. AGW, 24 mm.
Subject: 1000th Anniversary, Town of Bled mention, 2nd issue

Date	Mintage	F	VF	XF	Unc	BU
2006 Proof	500	Value: 300				

EURO COINAGE

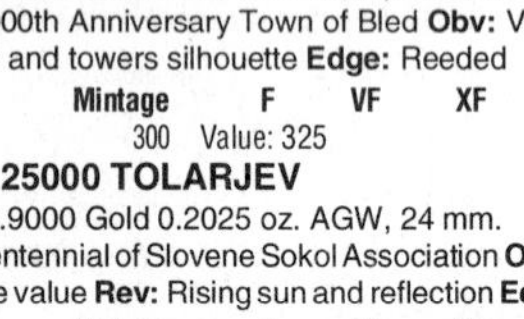

KM# 68 EURO CENT
2.2700 g., Copper Plated Steel, 16.2 mm. **Obv:** White Stork **Obv. Legend:** SLOVENIJA, star between each letter **Rev:** Value and globe **Edge:** Plain

Date	Mintage	F	VF	XF	Unc	BU
2007	—	—	—	—	0.25	0.35
2008	—	—	—	—	0.25	0.35
2009	—	—	—	—	0.25	0.35
2010	—	—	—	—	0.25	0.35
2010 Proof	5,000	Value: 3.00				

KM# 69 2 EURO CENT
3.0000 g., Copper Plated Steel, 18.7 mm. **Obv:** Princely stone of power in consciousness **Obv. Legend:** SLOVENIJA, star between each letter **Rev:** Value and globe **Edge:** Grooved

Date	Mintage	F	VF	XF	Unc	BU
2007	—	—	—	—	0.50	0.65
2008	—	—	—	—	0.50	0.65
2009	—	—	—	—	0.50	0.65
2010	—	—	—	—	0.50	0.65
2010 Proof	5,000	Value: 4.00				

KM# 70 5 EURO CENT
3.8600 g., Copper Plated Steel, 21.3 mm. **Obv:** Sower of Seeds - and stars **Obv. Legend:** SLOVENIJA, star between each letter **Rev:** Value and globe **Edge:** Plain

Date	Mintage	F	VF	XF	Unc	BU
2007	—	—	—	—	0.75	1.00
2008	—	—	—	—	0.75	1.00
2009	—	—	—	—	0.75	1.00
2010	—	—	—	—	0.75	1.00
2010 Proof	5,000	Value: 5.00				

KM# 71 10 EURO CENT
4.0000 g., Brass, 19.7 mm. **Obv:** Plecnik's unrealised plans for Parliament building **Obv. Legend:** SLOVENIJA, star between each letter **Rev:** Value and map **Edge:** Reeded

Date	Mintage	F	VF	XF	Unc	BU
2007	—	—	—	—	1.00	1.25
2008	—	—	—	—	1.00	1.25
2009	—	—	—	—	1.00	1.25
2010	—	—	—	—	1.00	1.25
2010 Proof	5,000	Value: 6.00				

KM# 72 20 EURO CENT
5.7300 g., Brass, 22.3 mm. **Obv:** Two Lipizzaner horses prancing left **Obv. Legend:** SLOVENIJA, star between each letter **Rev:** Value and map **Edge:** Notched

Date	Mintage	F	VF	XF	Unc	BU
2007	—	—	—	—	1.25	1.50
2008	—	—	—	—	1.25	1.50
2009	—	—	—	—	1.25	1.50
2010	—	—	—	—	1.25	1.50
2010 Proof	5,000	Value: 7.00				

KM# 73 50 EURO CENT
7.8100 g., Brass, 24.2 mm. **Obv:** Mountain and stars **Rev:** Value and map **Edge:** Reeded

Date	Mintage	F	VF	XF	Unc	BU
2007	—	—	—	—	1.50	2.00
2008	—	—	—	—	1.50	2.00
2009	—	—	—	—	1.50	2.00
2010	—	—	—	—	1.50	2.00
2010 Proof	5,000	Value: 8.00				

KM# 74 EURO
7.5000 g., Bi-Metallic Copper-Nickel center in Brass ring, 23.2 mm. **Obv:** Bearded Primoz Trubar **Rev:** Value and map **Edge:** Segmented reeding

Date	Mintage	F	VF	XF	Unc	BU
2007	—	—	—	—	2.50	3.50
2008	—	—	—	—	2.50	3.50
2009	—	—	—	—	2.50	3.50
2010	—	—	—	—	2.50	3.50
2010 Proof	5,000	Value: 15.00				

KM# 75 2 EURO
8.5200 g., Bi-Metallic Brass center in Copper-Nickel ring, 25.7 mm. **Obv:** France Preseren silhouette and signature **Rev:** Value and map **Edge:** Reeded and lettered

Date	Mintage	F	VF	XF	Unc	BU
2007	—	—	—	—	4.00	5.00
2008	—	—	—	—	4.00	5.00
2009	—	—	—	—	4.00	5.00
2010	—	—	—	—	4.00	5.00
2010 Proof	5,000	Value: 20.00				

KM# 80 2 EURO
Bi-Metallic Aluminum-Bronze center in Copper-Nickel ring **Subject:** 500th Anniversary Birth of Primoz Tubar **Obv:** Bust of Trubar left at right **Rev:** Large "2" at left, modified map of Europe at right **Edge:** Reeded

Date	Mintage	F	VF	XF	Unc	BU
2008	—	—	—	—	6.00	8.00

KM# 82 2 EURO
8.5200 g., Bi-Metallic, 25.7 mm. **Subject:** European Monetary Union, 10th Anniversary **Obv:** Stick figure and large E symbol **Rev:** Value at left, modified map of Europe at left

Date	Mintage	F	VF	XF	Unc	BU
2009	—	—	—	—	5.00	6.00

KM# 81 3 EURO
Bi-Metallic **Subject:** Six Month Term as President of the EU 2008 **Obv:** Field of stars representing EU membership **Rev:** Pinwheel

Date	Mintage	F	VF	XF	Unc	BU
2008	—	—	—	—	8.00	10.00

KM# 85 3 EURO
Bi-Metallic **Subject:** First Airplane, 100th Anniversary

Date	Mintage	F	VF	XF	Unc	BU
2009	—	—	—	—	8.00	10.00

KM# 76 30 EURO
15.0000 g., 0.9250 Silver 0.4461 oz. ASW, 32 mm.
Subject: 250th Anniversary Birth of Valentin Vodnik **Obv:** Value **Obv. Legend:** SLOVENIJA **Rev:** Large bust of Vodnik left

Date	Mintage	F	VF	XF	Unc	BU
2008 Proof	—	Value: 65.00				

KM# 78 30 EURO
15.0000 g., 0.9250 Silver 0.4461 oz. ASW, 32 mm.
Subject: EU President **Obv:** EU membership stars **Obv. Legend:** SLOVENIJA **Rev:** Pinwheel 5-pointed star

Date	Mintage	F	VF	XF	Unc	BU
2008 Proof	—	Value: 60.00				

KM# 86 30 EURO
15.0000 g., 0.9250 Silver 0.4461 oz. ASW, 32 mm.
Subject: First Airplane, 100th Anniversary

Date	Mintage	F	VF	XF	Unc	BU
2009 Proof	8,000	Value: 60.00				

KM# 88 30 EURO
15.0000 g., 0.9250 Silver 0.4461 oz. ASW, 32 mm.
Subject: Zoran Music, painter

Date	Mintage	F	VF	XF	Unc	BU
2009 Proof	—	Value: 70.00				

KM# 77 100 EURO
7.0000 g., 0.9000 Gold 0.2025 oz. AGW, 24 mm. **Subject:** 250th Anniversary Birth of Valentin Vodnik **Obv:** Value **Obv. Legend:** SLOVENIJA **Rev:** Large bust of Vodnik left

Date	Mintage	F	VF	XF	Unc	BU
2008 Proof	—	Value: 325				

KM# 79 100 EURO
7.0000 g., 0.9000 Gold 0.2025 oz. AGW, 24 mm. **Subject:** EU President **Obv:** EU membership stars **Obv. Legend:** SLOVENIJA **Rev:** Pinwheel 5-pointed star

Date	Mintage	F	VF	XF	Unc	BU
2008 Proof	—	Value: 300				

KM# 87 100 EURO
7.0000 g., 0.9000 Gold 0.2025 oz. AGW, 24 mm. **Subject:** First Airplane, 100th Anniversary

Date	Mintage	F	VF	XF	Unc	BU
2009 Proof	6,000	Value: 300				

KM# 89 100 EURO
7.0000 g., 0.9000 Gold 0.2025 oz. AGW, 24 mm. **Subject:** Zoran Music, painter

Date	Mintage	F	VF	XF	Unc	BU
2009 Proof	—	Value: 300				

MINT SETS

KM#	Date	Mintage	Identification	Issue Price	Mkt Val
MS10	2001 (7)	1,000	KM#3-8, 41	20.00	40.00
MS11	2002 (8)	1,000	KM#3-8, 41, 45	—	40.00
MS12	2003 (10)	1,000	KM#3-8, 41, 50-52	—	40.00
MS13	2004 (10)	1,000	KM#3-8, 41, 51, 52, 57	—	45.00
MS14	2005 (9)	3,000	KM#3-8, 41, 51, 52	25.00	45.00
MS15	2006 (10)	4,000	KM#3-8, 41, 51, 52, 65	25.00	50.00

PROOF SETS

KM#	Date	Mintage	Identification	Issue Price	Mkt Val
PS13	2001 (8)	800	KM#3-8, 41, 42	—	55.00
PS14	2002 (8)	800	KM#3-8, 41, 45	—	58.00
PS15	2003 (10)	800	KM#3-8, 41, 50-52	22.50	100
PS16	2004 (10)	500	KM#3-8, 41, 51-52, 57	—	120
PS17	2005 (10)	1,000	KM#3-8, 41, 51-52, 63	—	95.00
PS18	2006 (10)	1,000	KM#3-8, 41, 51-52, 65	—	95.00

SOLOMON ISLANDS

The Solomon Islands are made up of about 200 islands. They are located in the southwest Pacific east of Papua New Guinea, have an area of 10,983 sq. mi. (28,450 sq. km.) and a population of *552,000. Capital: Honiara. The most important islands of the Solomon chain are Guadalcanal (scene of some of the fiercest fighting of World War II), Malaitia, New Georgia, Florida, Vella Lavella, Choiseul, Rendova, San Cristobal, the Lord Howe group, the Santa Cruz islands, and the Duff group. Copra is the only important cash crop but it is hoped that timber will become an economic factor.

Solomon Islands is a member of the Commonwealth of Nations. Queen Elizabeth II is Head of State, as Queen of the Solomon Islands.

RULER
British

MONETARY SYSTEM
100 Cents = 1 Dollar

COMMONWEALTH NATION
STANDARD COINAGE

KM# 24 CENT
2.3000 g., Bronze Plated Steel, 17.53 mm. **Ruler:** Elizabeth II **Obv:** Crowned head right **Obv. Legend:** ELIZABETH II - SOLOMON ISLANDS **Rev:** Food bowl divides value **Edge:** Plain

Date	Mintage	F	VF	XF	Unc	BU
2005	—				0.35	0.75

KM# 25 2 CENTS
Bronze Plated Steel, 21.6 mm. **Ruler:** Elizabeth II **Obv:** Crowned head right **Obv. Legend:** ELIZABETH II - SOLOMON ISLANDS **Rev:** Eagle spirit below value **Rev. Designer:** David Thomas **Edge:** Plain

Date	Mintage	F	VF	XF	Unc	BU
2005	—				0.35	0.75
2006	—				0.35	0.75

KM# 26a 5 CENTS
Nickel Plated Steel, 18.40 mm. **Ruler:** Elizabeth II **Obv:** Crowned bust right **Obv. Legend:** ELIZABETH II - SOLOMON ISLANDS **Rev:** Value at left, native mask at center right **Rev. Designer:** David Thomas

Date	Mintage	F	VF	XF	Unc	BU
2005	—				0.50	1.00

KM# 27a 10 CENTS
Nickel Plated Steel, 23.6 mm. **Ruler:** Elizabeth II **Subject:** Ngorieru **Obv:** Crowned head right **Obv. Legend:** ELIZABETH II - SOLOMON ISLANDS **Rev:** Sea spirit divides value **Rev. Designer:** David Thomas **Edge:** Reeded

Date	Mintage	F	VF	XF	Unc	BU
2005	—				0.65	1.00

KM# 28 20 CENTS
11.2500 g., Nickel Plated Steel, 28.5 mm. **Ruler:** Elizabeth II **Obv:** Crowned head right **Obv. Legend:** ELIZABETH II - SOLOMON ISLANDS **Rev:** Malaita pendant design within circle, denomination appears twice in legend **Rev. Designer:** David Thomas **Edge:** Reeded

Date	Mintage	F	VF	XF	Unc	BU
2005	—	—	—	—	0.85	1.25

KM# 29 50 CENTS
10.0000 g., Copper-Nickel, 29.5 mm. **Ruler:** Elizabeth II **Obv:** Crowned head right **Obv. Legend:** ELIZABETH II - SOLOMON ISLANDS **Rev:** Arms with supporters **Edge:** Plain **Shape:** 12-sided **Note:** Circulation type.

Date	Mintage	F	VF	XF	Unc	BU
2005	—	—	—	—	2.00	3.00

KM# 72 DOLLAR
13.4500 g., Copper-Nickel, 30 mm. **Ruler:** Elizabeth II **Obv:** Crowned head right **Obv. Legend:** ELIZABETH II - SOLOMON ISLANDS **Rev:** Sea spirit statue divides value **Rev. Designer:** David Thomas **Edge:** Plain **Shape:** 7-sided

Date	Mintage	F	VF	XF	Unc	BU
2005	—	—	—	—	2.50	4.00

KM# 83 2 DOLLARS
62.2700 g., 0.9990 Silver 1.9999 oz. ASW, 50.3 mm. **Subject:** Regional Assistance Mission to Solomon Islands **Obv:** Crowned head right **Rev:** Dove outline over multicolor islands in a sea of country names **Edge:** Reeded

Date	Mintage	F	VF	XF	Unc	BU
2005 Proof	2,500	Value: 75.00				

KM# 113 5 DOLLARS
28.2800 g., 0.9250 Silver partially gilt 0.8410 oz. ASW, 38.6 mm. **Ruler:** Elizabeth II **Obv:** Bust right gilt **Rev:** Orb

Date	Mintage	F	VF	XF	Unc	BU
2002 Proof	20,000	Value: 30.00				

KM# 75 5 DOLLARS
28.2800 g., Copper-Nickel, 38.6 mm. **Obv:** Crowned head right **Obv. Designer:** Raphael Maklouf **Rev:** F-117A Nighthawk Stealth fighter plane **Edge:** Reeded

Date	Mintage	F	VF	XF	Unc	BU
2003	—	—	—	—	5.00	7.00

KM# 76 5 DOLLARS
28.2800 g., Copper-Nickel, 38.6 mm. **Obv:** Crowned head right **Obv. Designer:** Raphael Maklouf **Rev:** Concorde supersonic airliner **Edge:** Reeded

Date	Mintage	F	VF	XF	Unc	BU
2003	—	—	—	—	5.00	7.00

KM# 84   5 DOLLARS
31.1035 g., 0.9990 Silver 0.9990 oz. ASW, 38.6 mm.
Obv: Maklouf's portrait of Elizabeth II **Rev:** Gold plated pig
Edge: Reeded **Note:** Year of the Pig

Date	Mintage	F	VF	XF	Unc	BU
2007	10,000	—	—	—	—	50.00

KM# 85   5 DOLLARS
31.1035 g., 0.9990 Silver 0.9990 oz. ASW, 38.6 mm.
Obv: Maklouf's portrait of Elizabeth II **Rev:** Dark red pig and piglet
Edge: Reeded **Note:** Year of the Pig

Date	Mintage	F	VF	XF	Unc	BU
2007	10,000	—	—	—	—	50.00

KM# 86   10 DOLLARS
28.3600 g., Silver, 38.6 mm. **Obv:** Crowned bust right
Obv. Legend: ELIZABETH II - SOLOMON ISLANDS **Rev:** Bust
of Mendana facing at left, early sailing ship at center - right
Rev. Legend: ALVARO DE MENDANA **Edge:** Reeded

Date	Mintage	F	VF	XF	Unc	BU
2004 Proof	—	Value: 50.00				

KM# 96   10 DOLLARS
1.2200 g., 0.9990 Gold 0.0392 oz. AGW, 14 mm. **Ruler:**
Elizabeth II **Subject:** Wonders of the Ancient World **Obv:** Head
right **Rev:** Mausoleum of Mauussollos of Halicarnassus

Date	Mintage	F	VF	XF	Unc	BU
2007 Proof	7,000	Value: 65.00				

KM# 97   10 DOLLARS
1.2200 g., 0.9990 Gold 0.0392 oz. AGW, 14 mm.
Ruler: Elizabeth II **Subject:** Wonders of the Ancient World
Obv: Head right **Rev:** Taj Mahal

Date	Mintage	F	VF	XF	Unc	BU
2007 7000	—	Value: 65.00				

KM# 98   10 DOLLARS
1.2200 g., 0.9990 Gold 0.0392 oz. AGW, 14 mm.
Ruler: Elizabeth II **Subject:** Wonders of the Ancient World
Obv: Head right **Rev:** Treasury at Petra

Date	Mintage	F	VF	XF	Unc	BU
2007 Proof	7,000	Value: 65.00				

KM# 99   10 DOLLARS
1.2200 g., 0.9990 Gold 0.0392 oz. AGW, 14 mm.
Ruler: Elizabeth II **Subject:** Wonders of the Ancient World
Obv: Head right **Rev:** Colleseum in Rome

Date	Mintage	F	VF	XF	Unc	BU
2007 Proof	7,000	Value: 65.00				

KM# 100   10 DOLLARS
1.2200 g., 0.9990 Gold 0.0392 oz. AGW, 14 mm.
Ruler: Elizabeth II **Subject:** Wonders of the Ancient World
Obv: Head right **Rev:** Inca's Machu Kicuhu

Date	Mintage	F	VF	XF	Unc	BU
2007 Proof	7,000	Value: 65.00				

KM# 101   10 DOLLARS
1.2200 g., 0.9990 Gold 0.0392 oz. AGW, 14 mm.
Ruler: Elizabeth II **Subject:** Wonders of the Ancient World
Obv: Head right **Rev:** Chichen Itza

Date	Mintage	F	VF	XF	Unc	BU
2007 Proof	7,000	Value: 65.00				

KM# 102   10 DOLLARS
1.2200 g., 0.9990 Gold 0.0392 oz. AGW, 14 mm.
Ruler: Elizabeth II **Subject:** Wonders of the World **Obv:** Head
right **Rev:** Great wall of China

Date	Mintage	F	VF	XF	Unc	BU
2007 Proof	7,000	Value: 65.00				

KM# 103   10 DOLLARS
1.2200 g., 0.9990 Gold 0.0392 oz. AGW, 14 mm.
Ruler: Elizabeth II **Subject:** Wonders of the World **Rev:** Christ
Statue in Rio

Date	Mintage	F	VF	XF	Unc	BU
2007 Proof	7,000	Value: 65.00				

KM# 104   10 DOLLARS
1.2200 g., Gold, 14 mm. **Ruler:** Elizabeth II **Subject:** Seven
Wonders of the World **Obv:** Head right **Rev:** Giza Prymids

Date	Mintage	F	VF	XF	Unc	BU
2009 Proof	7,500	Value: 65.00				

KM# 105   10 DOLLARS
1.2200 g., 0.9990 Gold 0.0392 oz. AGW, 14 mm.
Ruler: Elizabeth II **Subject:** Seven Wonders of the World
Obv: Head right **Rev:** Colossus of Rhodes

Date	Mintage	F	VF	XF	Unc	BU
2009 Proof	7,500	Value: 65.00				

KM# 106   10 DOLLARS
1.2200 g., 0.9990 Gold 0.0392 oz. AGW, 14 mm.
Ruler: Elizabeth II **Subject:** Seven Wonders of the World
Obv: Head right **Rev:** Statue of Zeus at Olympia

Date	Mintage	F	VF	XF	Unc	BU
2009 Proof	7,500	Value: 65.00				

KM# 107   10 DOLLARS
1.2200 g., 0.9990 Gold 0.0392 oz. AGW, 14 mm.
Ruler: Elizabeth II **Subject:** Seven Wonders of the World
Obv: Head right **Rev:** Temple of Artemis at Ephesus

Date	Mintage	F	VF	XF	Unc	BU
2009 Proof	7,500	Value: 65.00				

KM# 108   10 DOLLARS
1.2200 g., 0.9990 Gold 0.0392 oz. AGW, 14 mm.
Ruler: Elizabeth II **Subject:** Seven Wonders of the World
Obv: Head right **Rev:** Hanging Gardens of Bablyon

Date	Mintage	F	VF	XF	Unc	BU
2009 Proof	7,500	Value: 65.00				

KM# 109   10 DOLLARS
1.2200 g., 0.9990 Gold 0.0392 oz. AGW, 14 mm.
Ruler: Elizabeth II **Subject:** Seven Wonders of the World
Obv: Head right **Rev:** Lighthouse at Alexandria

Date	Mintage	F	VF	XF	Unc	BU
2009 Proof	7,500	Value: 65.00				

KM# 110   10 DOLLARS
1.2200 g., 0.9990 Gold 0.0392 oz. AGW, 14 mm.
Ruler: Elizabeth II **Subject:** Seven Wonders of the World
Obv: Head right

Date	Mintage	F	VF	XF	Unc	BU
2009 Proof	7,500	Value: 65.00				

KM# 90   25 DOLLARS
31.1050 g., 0.9990 Silver 0.9990 oz. ASW, 36.6 mm. **Ruler:**
Elizabeth II **Obv:** Head right **Rev:** Wright Brother's 1903 Flyer

Date	Mintage	F	VF	XF	Unc	BU
2003 Proof	—	Value: 40.00				

KM# 91   25 DOLLARS
31.1050 g., 0.9990 Silver 0.9990 oz. ASW, 36.6 mm.
Ruler: Elizabeth II **Obv:** Head right **Rev:** AN-225 Mriya

Date	Mintage	F	VF	XF	Unc	BU
2003 Proof	—	Value: 40.00				

KM# 92   25 DOLLARS
31.1050 g., 0.9990 Silver 0.9990 oz. ASW, 36.6 mm.
Ruler: Elizabeth II **Obv:** Head right **Rev:** Spitfire

Date	Mintage	F	VF	XF	Unc	BU
2003 Proof	—	Value: 40.00				

KM# 93   25 DOLLARS
31.1050 g., 0.9990 Silver 0.9990 oz. ASW **Ruler:** Elizabeth II
Subject: Trafalgar **Obv:** Head right **Rev:** H.M.S. Victory

Date	Mintage	F	VF	XF	Unc	BU
2005 Proof	—	Value: 40.00				

KM# 114   25 DOLLARS
0.9250 Silver gilt, 50 mm. **Ruler:** Elizabeth II **Rev:** Wright flier
of 1903

Date	Mintage	F	VF	XF	Unc	BU
2005 Proof	—	Value: 75.00				

KM# 87   25 DOLLARS
0.9250 Silver **Ruler:** Elizabeth II **Obv:** Crowned bust right
Obv. Legend: ELIZABETH II - SOLOMON ISLANDS **Rev:** 3/4
length figures of Elizabeth and Prince Philip facing

Date	Mintage	F	VF	XF	Unc	BU
2006 Proof	—	Value: 45.00				

KM# 95   25 DOLLARS
31.1050 g., 0.9990 Silver partially gilt 0.9990 oz. ASW
Ruler: Elizabeth II **Obv:** Head right, partially gilt **Rev:** Queen
Elizabeth II and WWII Red Cross Nurse, gilt 80 above.

Date	Mintage	F	VF	XF	Unc	BU
2006 Proof	—	Value: 40.00				

KM# 87a   25 DOLLARS
31.1050 g., 0.9990 Silver partially gilt 0.9990 oz. ASW
Ruler: Elizabeth II **Obv:** Head right, partially gilt **Rev:** Wedding
of Elizabeth II and Philip. Gothic window behind, gilt 80 above.

Date	Mintage	F	VF	XF	Unc	BU
2006 Proof	—	Value: 45.00				

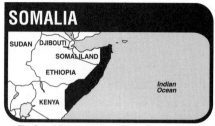

SOMALIA

The Somali Democratic Republic consists of the former Italian Somaliland and is located on the coast of the eastern projection of the African continent commonly referred to as the "Horn". It has an area of 178,201 sq. mi. (461,657 sq. km.) and a population of *8.2 million. Capital: Mogadishu. The economy is pastoral and agricultural. Livestock, bananas and hides are exported.

The Northern Somali National Movement (SNM) declared a secession of the northwestern Somaliland Republic on May 17, 1991, which is not recognized by the Somali Democratic Republic.

TITLE
Al-Jumhuriya(t)as - Somaliya(t)

REPUBLIC OF SOMALIA
STANDARD COINAGE

100 Centesimi = 1 Scellino

KM# 45   5 SHILLING / SCELLINI
1.2900 g., Aluminum, 21 mm. **Series:** F.A.O. **Obv:** Crowned
arms with supporters **Rev:** Elephant **Edge:** Plain

Date	Mintage	F	VF	XF	Unc	BU
2002	—	—	—	—	1.50	1.75

KM# 159   10 SHILLINGS
25.1500 g., Copper-Nickel, 38.66 mm. **Series:** Marine Life
Protection **Obv:** National arms **Rev:** Two fish multicolor
Edge: Reeded

Date	Mintage	F	VF	XF	Unc	BU
2003 Proof	—	Value: 10.00				

KM# 155   25 SHILLINGS
28.1000 g., Copper-Nickel, 38.73 mm. **Subject:** The life of Pope
John-Paul II **Obv:** National arms **Obv. Legend:** SOMALI
REPUBLIC **Rev:** Pope John-Paul II in window at the Vatican
Edge: Plain

Date	Mintage	F	VF	XF	Unc	BU
2004	—	—	—	—	6.00	7.00

KM# 156   25 SHILLINGS

28.1000 g., Copper-Nickel, 38.73 mm.   **Subject:** Life of Pope John Paul II **Obv:** National arms **Obv. Legend:** SOMALI REPUBLIC **Rev:** Pope traveling in special vehicle **Edge:** Plain

Date	Mintage	F	VF	XF	Unc	BU
2004	—	—	—	—	6.00	7.00

KM# 157   25 SHILLINGS

28.1000 g., Copper-Nickel, 38.73 mm. **Subject:** The life of Pope John-Paul II **Obv:** National arms **Obv. Legend:** SOMALI REPUBLIC **Rev:** Pope blessing Mother Teresa **Edge:** Plain

Date	Mintage	F	VF	XF	Unc	BU
2004	—	—	—	—	6.00	7.00

KM# 164   25 SHILLINGS

25.8000 g., Copper-Nickel, 38.77 mm.   **Obv:** National arms **Obv. Legend:** SOMALI REPUBLIC **Rev:** Black rhinoceros walking left **Edge:** Reeded

Date	Mintage	F	VF	XF	Unc	BU
2006	—	—	—	—	9.00	12.00

KM# 165   25 SHILLINGS

25.8000 g., Copper-Nickel, 38.77 mm.   **Obv:** National arms **Rev:** Red Kite perched on branch **Edge:** Reeded

Date	Mintage	F	VF	XF	Unc	BU
2006	—	—	—	—	12.00	14.00

KM# 103   25 SHILLINGS / SCELLINI

4.3700 g., Brass, 21.8 mm.   **Subject:** Soccer **Obv:** Crowned arms with supporters **Rev:** Soccer player **Edge:** Plain

Date	Mintage	F	VF	XF	Unc	BU
2001	—	—	—	—	1.25	1.50

KM# 111   50 SHILLINGS

3.9000 g., Nickel Clad Steel, 21.9 mm.   **Obv:** Crowned arms with supporters **Rev:** Mandrill **Edge:** Plain

Date	Mintage	F	VF	XF	Unc	BU
2002	—	—	—	—	0.85	1.25

KM# 161   50 SHILLINGS

1.2000 g., Gold, 13.88 mm.   **Subject:** Gold of the Pharaohs **Obv:** National arms **Obv. Legend:** SOMALI REPUBLIC **Rev:** King Tutankhaman's death mask **Edge:** Reeded

Date	Mintage	F	VF	XF	Unc	BU
2002 Proof	—	Value: 75.00				

KM# 109   100 SHILLINGS

10.5000 g., 0.9990 Silver 0.3372 oz. ASW, 30.1 mm. **Subject:** Soccer **Obv:** Crowned arms with supporters **Rev:** Multicolor soccer player and Brandenburg Gate **Edge:** Reeded

Date	Mintage	F	VF	XF	Unc	BU
2001 Proof	—	Value: 20.00				

KM# 112   100 SHILLINGS

3.5400 g., Brass, 18.8 mm.   **Obv:** Crowned arms with supporters above value **Rev:** Bust with headdress facing **Edge:** Plain

Date	Mintage	F	VF	XF	Unc	BU
2002	—	—	—	—	1.50	2.50

KM# 110   250 SHILLINGS

31.1050 g., 0.9990 Silver 0.9990 oz. ASW, 40 mm. **Subject:** Queen of Sheba **Obv:** Crowned arms with supporters **Rev:** Crowned bust 1/4 right **Edge:** Reeded

Date	Mintage	F	VF	XF	Unc	BU
2002	—	—	—	—	25.00	30.00

KM# 158   250 SHILLINGS

20.0500 g., Silver, 38.59 mm.   **Obv:** National arms **Obv. Legend:** SOMALI REPUBLIC **Rev:** Laureate bust of Julius Caesar 3/4 left **Edge:** Reeded

Date	Mintage	F	VF	XF	Unc	BU
2002 Proof	—	Value: 30.00				

KM# 169   250 SHILLINGS

Silver   **Obv:** Arms **Rev:** Soccer player, Brazil

Date	Mintage	F	VF	XF	Unc	BU
2002	—	—	—	—	—	20.00

KM# 160   250 SHILLINGS

20.5000 g., Silver, 38.56 mm.   **Subject:** Wembley Goal - England 1966 **Obv:** National arms **Obv. Legend:** SOMALI REPUBLIC **Rev:** 3 soccer players at goal **Edge:** Reeded

Date	Mintage	F	VF	XF	Unc	BU
2003 Proof	—	Value: 25.00				

KM# 121   250 SHILLINGS

20.1200 g., Silver Plated Base Metal, 38.5 mm.   **Obv:** Crowned arms with supporters **Rev:** Multicolor Pope John Paul II and mountains **Edge:** Reeded

Date	Mintage	F	VF	XF	Unc	BU
2005 Proof	—	Value: 16.50				

KM# 123   250 SHILLINGS

20.1200 g., Silver Plated Base Metal, 38.5 mm.   **Obv:** Crowned arms with supporters **Rev:** Multicolor Pope John Paul II kissing bible **Edge:** Reeded

Date	Mintage	F	VF	XF	Unc	BU
2005 Proof	—	Value: 16.50				

KM# 125   250 SHILLINGS

20.1200 g., Silver Plated Base Metal, 38.5 mm.   **Obv:** Crowned arms with supporters **Rev:** Multicolor Pope John Paul II with flowers **Edge:** Reeded

Date	Mintage	F	VF	XF	Unc	BU
2005 Proof	—	Value: 16.50				

KM# 127   250 SHILLINGS
20.1200 g., Silver Plated Base Metal, 38.5 mm. **Obv:** Crowned arms with supporters **Rev:** Multicolor Pope John Paul II saying mass **Edge:** Reeded

Date	Mintage	F	VF	XF	Unc	BU
2005 Proof	—	Value: 16.50				

KM# 129   250 SHILLINGS
20.1200 g., Silver Plated Base Metal, 38.5 mm. **Obv:** Crowned arms with supporters **Rev:** Multicolor Pope John Paul II with cardinals **Edge:** Reeded

Date	Mintage	F	VF	XF	Unc	BU
2005 Proof	—	Value: 16.50				

KM# 131   250 SHILLINGS
20.1200 g., Silver Plated Base Metal, 38.5 mm. **Obv:** Crowned arms with supporters **Rev:** Pope John Paul II with red vestments **Edge:** Reeded

Date	Mintage	F	VF	XF	Unc	BU
2005 Proof	—	Value: 16.50				

KM# 133   250 SHILLINGS
20.1200 g., Silver Plated Base Metal, 38.5 mm. **Obv:** Crowned arms with supporters **Rev:** Pope John Paul II in white with skull cap **Edge:** Reeded

Date	Mintage	F	VF	XF	Unc	BU
2005 Proof	—	Value: 16.50				

KM# 135   250 SHILLINGS
20.1200 g., Silver Plated Base Metal, 38.5 mm. **Obv:** Crowned arms with supporters **Rev:** Multicolor Pope John Paul II leaning head on staff **Edge:** Reeded

Date	Mintage	F	VF	XF	Unc	BU
2005 Proof	—	Value: 16.50				

KM# 137   250 SHILLINGS
20.1200 g., Silver Plated Base Metal, 38.5 mm. **Obv:** Crowned arms with supporters **Rev:** Multicolor Pope John Paul II with staff facing left **Edge:** Reeded

Date	Mintage	F	VF	XF	Unc	BU
2005 Proof	—	Value: 16.50				

KM# 139   250 SHILLINGS
20.1200 g., Silver Plated Base Metal, 38.5 mm. **Obv:** Crowned arms with supporters **Rev:** Multicolor Pope John Paul II with staff facing half right **Edge:** Reeded

Date	Mintage	F	VF	XF	Unc	BU
2005 Proof	—	Value: 16.50				

KM# 143   250 SHILLINGS
Copper-Nickel **Obv:** Crowned shield **Obv. Legend:** SOMALI REPUBLIC / 250 SHILLINGS **Rev:** Color applique, German Shephard **Rev. Legend:** YEAR OF THE DOG / 2006 **Edge:** Reeded

Date	Mintage	F	VF	XF	Unc	BU
2006	—	—	—	—	—	12.50

KM# 144   250 SHILLINGS
Copper-Nickel **Obv:** Crowned shield **Obv. Legend:** SOMALI REPUBLIC / 250 SHILLINGS **Rev:** Color applique, Dachsund **Rev. Legend:** YEAR OF THE DOG / 2006 **Edge:** Reeded

Date	Mintage	F	VF	XF	Unc	BU
2006	—	—	—	—	—	12.50

KM# 145   250 SHILLINGS
Copper-Nickel **Obv:** Crowned shield **Obv. Legend:** SOMALI REPUBLIC / 250 SHILLINGS **Rev:** Color applique, Yorkshire Terrier **Rev. Legend:** YEAR OF THE DOG / 2006 **Edge:** Reeded

Date	Mintage	F	VF	XF	Unc	BU
2006	—	—	—	—	—	12.50

KM# 146   250 SHILLINGS
Copper-Nickel **Obv:** Crowned shield **Obv. Legend:** SOMALI REPUBLIC / 250 SHILLINGS **Rev:** Color applique, Scottie (small white) **Rev. Legend:** YEAR OF THE DOG / 2006 **Edge:** Reeded

Date	Mintage	F	VF	XF	Unc	BU
2006	—	—	—	—	—	12.50

KM# 147   250 SHILLINGS
Copper-Nickel **Obv:** Crowned shield **Obv. Legend:** SOMALI REPUBLIC / 250 SHILLINGS **Rev:** Color applique, Wire-haired Terrier **Rev. Legend:** YEAR OF THE DOG / 2006 **Edge:** Reeded

Date	Mintage	F	VF	XF	Unc	BU
2006	—	—	—	—	—	12.50

KM# 148 250 SHILLINGS
Copper-Nickel **Obv:** Crowned shield **Obv. Legend:** SOMALI REPUBLIC / 250 SHILLINGS **Rev:** Color applique, Bulldog **Rev. Legend:** YEAR OF THE DOG / 2006 **Edge:** Reeded

Date	Mintage	F	VF	XF	Unc	BU
2006	—	—	—	—	—	12.50

KM# 149 250 SHILLINGS
Copper-Nickel **Obv:** Crowned shield **Obv. Legend:** SOMALI REPUBLIC / 250 SHILLINGS **Rev:** Color applique, Golden Retriever **Rev. Legend:** YEAR OF THE DOG **Edge:** Reeded

Date	Mintage	F	VF	XF	Unc	BU
2006	—	—	—	—	—	12.50

KM# 150 250 SHILLINGS
Copper-Nickel **Obv:** Crowned shield **Obv. Legend:** SOMALI REPUBLIC / 250 SHILLINGS **Rev:** Color applique, St. Bernard **Rev. Legend:** YEAR OF THE DOG / 2006 **Edge:** Reeded

Date	Mintage	F	VF	XF	Unc	BU
2006	—	—	—	—	—	12.50

KM# 151 250 SHILLINGS
Copper-Nickel **Obv:** Crowned shield **Obv. Legend:** SOMALI REPUBLIC / 250 SHILLINGS **Rev:** Color applique, Rottweiler **Rev. Legend:** YEAR OF THE DOG / 2006 **Edge:** Reeded

Date	Mintage	F	VF	XF	Unc	BU
2006	—	—	—	—	—	12.50

KM# 152 250 SHILLINGS
Copper-Nickel **Obv:** Crowned shield **Obv. Legend:** SOMALI REPUBLIC / 250 SHILLINGS **Rev:** Color applique, Basset Hound **Rev. Legend:** YEAR OF THE DOG / 2006 **Edge:** Reeded

Date	Mintage	F	VF	XF	Unc	BU
2006	—	—	—	—	—	12.50

KM# 153 250 SHILLINGS
Copper-Nickel **Obv:** Crowned shield **Obv. Legend:** SOMALI REPUBLIC / 250 SHILLINGS **Rev:** Color applique, Sheep Dog **Rev. Legend:** YEAR OF THE DOG / 2006 **Edge:** Reeded

Date	Mintage	F	VF	XF	Unc	BU
2006	—	—	—	—	—	12.50

KM# 154 250 SHILLINGS
Copper-Nickel **Obv:** Crowned shield **Obv. Legend:** SOMALI REPUBLIC / 250 SHILLINGS **Rev:** Color applique, Cocker Spaniel **Rev. Legend:** YEAR OF THE DOG / 2006 **Edge:** Reeded

Date	Mintage	F	VF	XF	Unc	BU
2006	—	—	—	—	—	12.50

KM# 170 250 SHILLINGS
Copper-Nickel Gilt, 38 mm. **Obv:** Arms in cartouche **Rev:** Gold mask of Tutankahamun, enameled

Date	Mintage	F	VF	XF	Unc	BU
2008	—	—	—	—	—	17.50

KM# 122 500 SHILLINGS
18.8400 g., Silver Plated Base Metal, 34.1 mm. **Obv:** Crowned arms with supporters **Rev:** Multicolor Pope John Paul II and mountains **Edge:** Plain **Shape:** Square with round corners

Date	Mintage	F	VF	XF	Unc	BU
2005 Proof	—	Value: 16.50				

KM# 124 500 SHILLINGS
18.8400 g., Silver Plated Base Metal, 34.1 mm. **Obv:** Crowned arms with supporters **Rev:** Multicolor Pope John Paul II kissing bible **Edge:** Plain **Shape:** Square with round corners

Date	Mintage	F	VF	XF	Unc	BU
2005 Proof	—	Value: 16.50				

KM# 126 500 SHILLINGS
18.8400 g., Silver Plated Base Metal, 34.1 mm. **Obv:** Crowned arms with supporters **Rev:** Multicolor Pope John Paul II with flowers **Edge:** Plain **Shape:** Square with round corners

Date	Mintage	F	VF	XF	Unc	BU
2005 Proof	—	Value: 20.00				

KM# 128 500 SHILLINGS
18.1400 g., Silver Plated Base Metal, 34.1 mm. **Obv:** Crowned arms with supporters **Rev:** Multicolor Pope John Paul II saying mass **Edge:** Plain **Shape:** Square with round corners

Date	Mintage	F	VF	XF	Unc	BU
2005 Proof	—	Value: 16.50				

KM# 130 500 SHILLINGS
18.8400 g., Silver Plated Base Metal, 34.1 mm. **Obv:** Crowned arms with supporters **Rev:** Multicolor Pope John Paul II with cardinals **Edge:** Plain **Shape:** Square with round corners

Date	Mintage	F	VF	XF	Unc	BU
2005 Proof	—	Value: 16.50				

KM# 132 500 SHILLINGS
18.8400 g., Silver Plated Base Metal, 34.1 mm. **Obv:** Crowned arms with supporters **Rev:** Pope John Paul II with red vestments **Edge:** Plain **Shape:** Square with round corners

Date	Mintage	F	VF	XF	Unc	BU
2005 Proof	—	Value: 16.50				

KM# 134   500 SHILLINGS
18.8400 g., Silver Plated Base Metal, 34.1 mm. **Obv:** Crowned arms with supporters **Rev:** Pope John Paul II in white with skull cap **Edge:** Plain **Shape:** Square with round corners

Date	Mintage	F	VF	XF	Unc	BU
2005 Proof	—	Value: 16.50				

KM# 136   500 SHILLINGS
18.8400 g., Silver Plated Base Metal, 34.1 mm. **Obv:** Crowned arms with supporters **Rev:** Multicolor Pope John Paul II leaning head on staff **Edge:** Plain **Shape:** Square with round corners

Date	Mintage	F	VF	XF	Unc	BU
2005 Proof	—	Value: 16.50				

KM# 138   500 SHILLINGS
18.8400 g., Silver Plated Base Metal, 34.1 mm. **Obv:** Crowned arms with supporters **Rev:** Multicolor Pope John Paul II with staff facing left **Edge:** Plain **Shape:** Square with round corners

Date	Mintage	F	VF	XF	Unc	BU
2005 Proof	—	Value: 16.50				

KM# 140   500 SHILLINGS
18.8400 g., Silver Plated Base Metal, 34.1 mm. **Obv:** Crowned arms with supporters **Rev:** Multicolor Pope John Paul II with staff facing half right **Edge:** Plain **Shape:** Square with round corners

Date	Mintage	F	VF	XF	Unc	BU
2005 Proof	—	Value: 16.50				

KM# 163   1000 SHILLINGS
31.2700 g., 0.9990 Silver 1.0043 oz. ASW, 38.54 mm. **Series:** African Wildlife **Obv:** National arms **Obv. Legend:** SOMALI REPUBLIC **Rev:** Elephant standing facing - gilt **Edge:** Reeded

Date	Mintage	F	VF	XF	Unc	BU
2004 Proof	—	Value: 30.00				

KM# 180   1000 SHILLINGS
31.1050 g., 0.9990 Silver 0.9990 oz. ASW, 39 mm. **Obv:** Arms **Rev:** Elephant, mountian in background. Multicolor

Date	Mintage	F	VF	XF	Unc	BU
2006	—	—	—	—	—	35.00

KM# 177   1000 SHILLINGS
31.1050 g., 0.9990 Silver partially gilt 0.9990 oz. ASW, 38 mm. **Rev:** Elephant, mountain, partially gilt

Date	Mintage	F	VF	XF	Unc	BU
2006	—	Value: 55.00				

KM# 178   1000 SHILLINGS
31.1050 g., 0.9990 Silver 0.9990 oz. ASW, 38 mm. **Obv:** Arms **Rev:** Elephant and mountain

Date	Mintage	F	VF	XF	Unc	BU
2006	—	—	—	—	—	45.00

REFORM COINAGE

100 Senti = 1 Shilling

KM# 175   20 SHILLINGS
0.6200 g., 0.9990 Gold 0.0199 oz. AGW **Obv:** Arms **Rev:** Mom and baby elephant

Date	Mintage	F	VF	XF	Unc	BU
2007 Proof	—	Value: 50.00				

KM# 166   25 SHILLINGS
Silver **Obv:** Arms **Rev:** Mozart, multicolor

Date	Mintage	F	VF	XF	Unc	BU
2001	—	—	—	—	—	30.00

KM# 182   100 SHILLINGS
31.1050 g., 0.9990 Silver 0.9990 oz. ASW, 39 mm. **Obv:** Arms **Rev:** Mom and baby elephant, multicolor

Date	Mintage	F	VF	XF	Unc	BU
2007	—	—	—	—	—	35.00

KM# 167   100 SHILLINGS
31.1050 g., 0.9990 Silver partially gilt 0.9990 oz. ASW **Obv:** Arms **Rev:** Heard of six elephants

Date	Mintage	F	VF	XF	Unc	BU
2008	—	—	—	—	—	25.00

KM# 176   200 SHILLINGS
0.6200 g., 0.9990 Gold 0.0199 oz. AGW **Obv:** Arms **Rev:** Elephant head left

Date	Mintage	F	VF	XF	Unc	BU
2005 Proof	—	Value: 50.00				

KM# 168   250 SHILLINGS
Silver **Obv:** Arms **Rev:** Victoria, gothic crown

Date	Mintage	F	VF	XF	Unc	BU
2001 Proof	—	Value: 20.00				

KM# 162   250 SHILLINGS
1.2700 g., Gold, 13.90 mm. **Obv:** National arms **Obv. Legend:** SOMALI REPUBLIC **Rev:** Bust of Hans Rühmann facing **Edge:** Reeded

Date	Mintage	F	VF	XF	Unc	BU
2002 Proof	—	Value: 75.00				

KM# 171   250 SHILLINGS
Copper-Nickel Gilt, 38 mm. **Obv:** Arms within cartouche **Rev:** Udjat eye, enameled

Date	Mintage	F	VF	XF	Unc	BU
2008	—	—	—	—	—	40.00

KM# 172   250 SHILLINGS
Copper-Nickel **Obv:** Arms within cartouche **Rev:** Statue of Ptah, enameled

Date	Mintage	F	VF	XF	Unc	BU
2008	—	—	—	—	—	20.00

KM# 173   250 SHILLINGS
Copper-Nickel Gilt, 38 mm. **Obv:** Arms in cartouche **Rev:** Jcarab Pectoral necklace, enameled

Date	Mintage	F	VF	XF	Unc	BU
2008	—	—	—	—	—	20.00

KM# 174   250 SHILLINGS
Copper-Nickel Gilt, 38 mm. **Obv:** Arms within cartouche **Rev:** Statue of Horus the Elder

Date	Mintage	F	VF	XF	Unc	BU
2008	—	—	—	—	—	20.00

KM# 179   1000 SHILLINGS
31.1050 g., 0.9990 Silver 0.9990 oz. ASW, 39 mm. **Obv:** Arms **Rev:** Elephant head left, multicolor

Date	Mintage	F	VF	XF	Unc	BU
2005	—	—	—	—	—	35.00

KM# 181   1000 SHILLINGS
31.1050 g., 0.9990 Silver 0.9990 oz. ASW, 39 mm. **Obv:** Arms **Rev:** Heard of six elephants, multicolor

Date	Mintage	F	VF	XF	Unc	BU
2008	—	—	—	—	—	35.00

SOMALILAND

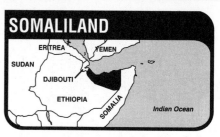

The Somaliland Republic consists of the former British Somaliland Protectorate and is located on the coast of the northeastern projection of the African continent commonly referred to as the "Horn" on the southwestern end of the Gulf of Aden. Bordered by Ethiopia to the west and south and Somalia to the east. It has an area of 68,000* sq. mi. (176,000* sq. km). Capital: Hargeysa. It is mostly arid and mountainous except for the gulf shoreline.

The northern Somali National Movement (SNM) declared a secession of the Somaliland Republic on May 17, 1991, which is not recognized by the Somali Democratic Republic.

REPUBLIC

SHILLING COINAGE

KM# 4   5 SHILLINGS
1.4500 g., Aluminum, 21.9 mm. **Obv:** Value **Rev:** Bust of Sir Richard F. Burton - explorer, divides dates **Edge:** Plain

Date	Mintage	F	VF	XF	Unc	BU
2002	—	—	—	—	1.25	1.50

KM# 5   5 SHILLINGS
1.4500 g., Aluminum, 21.9 mm. **Obv:** Value **Rev:** Rooster **Edge:** Plain

Date	Mintage	F	VF	XF	Unc	BU
2002	—	—	—	—	1.00	1.25

KM# 19   5 SHILLINGS
1.2400 g., Aluminum, 22 mm. **Obv:** Elephant with calf walking right **Obv. Legend:** REPUBLIC OF SOMALILAND **Rev:** Value **Rev. Legend:** BAANKA SOMALILAND **Edge:** Plain

Date	Mintage	F	VF	XF	Unc	BU
2005	—	—	—	—	1.25	1.50

KM# 3   10 SHILLINGS
3.5100 g., Brass, 17.7 mm. **Obv:** Vervet Monkey **Rev:** Value **Edge:** Plain

Date	Mintage	F	VF	XF	Unc	BU
2002	—	—	—	—	0.65	1.25

KM# 7   10 SHILLINGS
4.8000 g., Stainless Steel, 24.9 mm. **Obv:** Value **Rev:** Aquarius the water carrier **Edge:** Plain

Date	Mintage	F	VF	XF	Unc	BU
2006	—	—	—	—	1.00	1.25

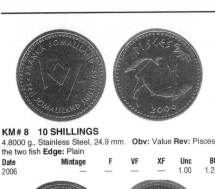

KM# 8 10 SHILLINGS
4.8000 g., Stainless Steel, 24.9 mm. **Obv:** Value **Rev:** Pisces
the two fish **Edge:** Plain

Date	Mintage	F	VF	XF	Unc	BU
2006	—	—	—	—	1.00	1.25

KM# 9 10 SHILLINGS
4.8000 g., Stainless Steel, 24.9 mm. **Obv:** Value **Rev:** Aries the
ram **Edge:** Plain

Date	Mintage	F	VF	XF	Unc	BU
2006	—	—	—	—	1.00	1.25

KM# 10 10 SHILLINGS
4.8000 g., Stainless Steel, 24.9 mm. **Obv:** Value **Rev:** Taurus
the bull **Edge:** Plain

Date	Mintage	F	VF	XF	Unc	BU
2006	—	—	—	—	1.00	1.25

KM# 11 10 SHILLINGS
4.8000 g., Stainless Steel, 24.9 mm. **Obv:** Value **Rev:** Gemini
twins **Edge:** Plain

Date	Mintage	F	VF	XF	Unc	BU
2006	—	—	—	—	1.00	1.25

KM# 12 10 SHILLINGS
4.8000 g., Stainless Steel, 24.9 mm. **Obv:** Value **Rev:** Cancer
the crab **Edge:** Plain

Date	Mintage	F	VF	XF	Unc	BU
2006	—	—	—	—	1.00	1.25

KM# 13 10 SHILLINGS
4.8000 g., Stainless Steel, 24.9 mm. **Obv:** Value **Rev:** Leo the
lion **Edge:** Plain

Date	Mintage	F	VF	XF	Unc	BU
2006	—	—	—	—	1.00	1.25

KM# 14 10 SHILLINGS
4.8000 g., Stainless Steel, 24.9 mm. **Obv:** Value **Rev:** Virgo as
a winged woman **Edge:** Plain

Date	Mintage	F	VF	XF	Unc	BU
2006	—	—	—	—	1.00	1.25

KM# 15 10 SHILLINGS
4.8000 g., Stainless Steel, 24.9 mm. **Obv:** Value **Rev:** Libra
balance scale **Edge:** Plain

Date	Mintage	F	VF	XF	Unc	BU
2006	—	—	—	—	1.00	1.25

KM# 16 10 SHILLINGS
4.8000 g., Stainless Steel, 24.9 mm. **Obv:** Value **Rev:** Scorpio
the scorpion **Edge:** Plain

Date	Mintage	F	VF	XF	Unc	BU
2006	—	—	—	—	1.00	1.25

KM# 17 10 SHILLINGS
4.8000 g., Stainless Steel, 24.9 mm. **Obv:** Value
Rev: Sagittarius the archer **Edge:** Plain

Date	Mintage	F	VF	XF	Unc	BU
2006	—	—	—	—	1.00	1.25

KM# 18 10 SHILLINGS
4.8000 g., Stainless Steel, 24.9 mm. **Obv:** Value **Rev:** Capricorn
the goat **Edge:** Plain

Date	Mintage	F	VF	XF	Unc	BU
2006	—	—	—	—	1.00	1.25

KM# 6 20 SHILLINGS
3.8700 g., Stainless Steel, 21.8 mm. **Obv:** Value
Rev: Greyhound dog **Edge:** Plain

Date	Mintage	F	VF	XF	Unc	BU
2002	—	—	—	—	1.00	1.50

KM# 2 1000 SHILLINGS
31.2700 g., 0.9990 Silver 1.0043 oz. ASW. 38.8 mm.
Obv: Crowned arms with supporters **Rev:** Bust with hat 3/4 right
Edge: Reeded

Date	Mintage	F	VF	XF	Unc	BU
2002	—	—	—	—	45.00	50.00

SOUTH AFRICA

The Republic of South Africa, located at the southern tip of
Africa, has an area of 471,445 sq. mi. (1,221,043 sq. km.) and a
population of *30.2 million. Capitals: Administrative, Pretoria;
Legislative, Cape Town; Judicial, Bloemfontein. Manufacturing,
mining and agriculture are the principal industries. Exports
include wool, diamonds, gold, and metallic ores.
  The apartheid era ended April 27, 1994 with the first democratic election for all people of South Africa. Nelson Mandela
was inaugurated President May 10, 1994, and South Africa was
readmitted into the Commonwealth of Nations.
  South African coins and currency bear inscriptions in tribal
languages, Afrikaans and English.

MONETARY SYSTEM
100 Cents = 1 Rand

MINT MARKS
GRC + paw print = Gold Reef City Mint

REPUBLIC

STANDARD COINAGE
100 Cents = 1 Rand

KM# 221 CENT
1.5000 g., Copper Plated Steel, 15 mm. **Obv:** New national arms
Obv. Legend: ISEWULA AFRIKA **Obv. Designer:** A.L.
Sutherland **Rev:** Value divides two sparrows **Rev. Designer:** W.
Lumley **Edge:** Plain

Date	Mintage	F	VF	XF	Unc	BU
2001	—	—	—	0.15	0.35	0.50
2001 Proof	3,678	Value: 5.00				

KM# 222 2 CENTS
3.0000 g., Copper Plated Steel, 18 mm. **Obv:** New national arms
Obv. Legend: AFURIKA TSHIPEMBE **Rev:** Eagle with fish in
talons divides value **Edge:** Plain **Designer:** A.L. Sutherland

Date	Mintage	F	VF	XF	Unc	BU
2001	—	—	—	—	0.50	0.75
2001 Proof	3,678	Value: 6.00				

KM# 223 5 CENTS
4.4200 g., Copper Plated Steel, 21 mm. **Obv:** New national arms
Obv. Legend: AFRIKA DZONGA **Obv. Designer:** A.L.
Sutherland **Rev:** Value and Blue crane **Rev. Designer:** G.
Richard **Edge:** Plain

Date	Mintage	F	VF	XF	Unc	BU
2001	—	—	0.10	0.25	0.65	1.00
2001 Proof	—	Value: 5.00				

KM# 268 5 CENTS
4.5000 g., Copper Plated Steel, 21 mm. **Obv:** New national arms **Obv. Legend:** Ningizimu Afrika **Obv. Designer:** A.L. Sutherland **Rev:** Value and Blue crane **Rev. Designer:** G. Richard **Edge:** Plain

Date	Mintage	F	VF	XF	Unc	BU
2002	—	—	—	0.30	0.75	1.00
2002 Proof	3,250	Value: 5.00				

KM# 324 5 CENTS
4.5000 g., Copper Plated Steel, 21 mm. **Obv:** New national arms **Obv. Legend:** Afrika Dzonga **Rev:** Blue crane and denomination **Edge:** Plain

Date	Mintage	F	VF	XF	Unc	BU
2003	—	—	—	0.30	0.75	1.00
2003 Proof	2,909	Value: 5.00				

KM# 325 5 CENTS
4.5000 g., Copper Plated Steel, 21 mm. **Obv:** New national arms **Obv. Legend:** South Africa **Rev:** Value and Blue crane **Edge:** Plain

Date	Mintage	F	VF	XF	Unc	BU
2004	—	—	—	0.20	0.50	0.75
2004 Proof	1,935	Value: 5.00				

KM# 291 5 CENTS
4.5000 g., Copper Plated Steel, 21 mm. **Obv:** New national arms **Obv. Legend:** Aforika Borwa **Rev:** Value and Blue crane **Edge:** Plain

Date	Mintage	F	VF	XF	Unc	BU
2005	—	—	—	0.20	0.50	0.75
2005 Proof	—	Value: 5.00				

KM# 486 5 CENTS
4.5000 g., Copper Plated Steel, 21 mm. **Obv:** National arms **Obv. Legend:** Afrika Borwa **Rev:** Value and blue crane

Date	Mintage	F	VF	XF	Unc	BU
2006	—	—	—	—	0.50	0.75
2006 Proof	—	Value: 5.00				

KM# 340 5 CENTS
4.5100 g., Copper Plated Steel, 20.9 mm. **Obv:** New national arms **Obv. Legend:** Suid- Afrika **Rev:** Value at left, Blue Crane at right **Edge:** Plain

Date	Mintage	F	VF	XF	Unc	BU
2007	—	—	—	0.20	0.50	0.75
2007 Proof	—	Value: 5.00				

KM# 497 5 CENTS
4.5000 g., Copper Plated Steel, 21 mm. **Obv:** National arms **Obv. Legend:** uMzantsi Afrika **Rev:** Value and Blue crane

Date	Mintage	F	VF	XF	Unc	BU
2008	—	—	—	—	0.75	1.00
2008 Proof	—	Value: 5.00				

KM# 224 10 CENTS
2.0000 g., Bronze Plated Steel, 16 mm. **Obv:** New national arms **Obv. Legend:** AFRIKA DZONGA **Obv. Designer:** A.L. Sutherland **Rev:** Arum Lily and value **Rev. Designer:** R.C. McFarlane **Edge:** Reeded

Date	Mintage	F	VF	XF	Unc	BU
2001	—	—	—	0.30	0.60	1.00
2001 Proof	3,678	Value: 6.00				

KM# 269 10 CENTS
2.0000 g., Bronze Plated Steel, 16 mm. **Obv:** New national arms **Obv. Legend:** Afrika Dzonga **Obv. Designer:** A.L. Sutherland **Rev:** Arum Lily and value **Rev. Designer:** R.C. McFarlane **Edge:** Reeded

Date	Mintage	F	VF	XF	Unc	BU
2002	—	—	—	0.30	0.75	1.00
2002 Proof	3,250	Value: 6.00				

KM# 347 10 CENTS
2.0000 g., Bronze Plated Steel, 16 mm. **Obv:** New national arms **Obv. Legend:** South Africa **Rev:** Arum lily and value **Edge:** Reeded

Date	Mintage	F	VF	XF	Unc	BU
2003	—	—	—	0.30	0.75	1.00
2003 Proof	2,909	Value: 6.00				

KM# 326 10 CENTS
2.0000 g., Bronze Plated Steel, 16 mm. **Obv:** new national arms **Obv. Legend:** Aforika Borwa **Rev:** Arum lily and value

Date	Mintage	F	VF	XF	Unc	BU
2004	—	—	—	0.30	0.75	1.00
2004 Proof	1,935	Value: 6.00				

KM# 292 10 CENTS
2.0000 g., Bronze Plated Steel, 16 mm. **Obv:** New national arms **Obv. Legend:** Afrika Borwa **Rev:** Arum Lily and value **Edge:** Reeded

Date	Mintage	F	VF	XF	Unc	BU
2005	—	—	—	0.30	0.75	1.00
2005	—	Value: 6.00				

KM# 487 10 CENTS
2.0000 g., Bronze Plated Steel, 16 mm. **Obv:** National arms **Obv. Legend:** Suid-Afrika **Rev:** Arum lily and value

Date	Mintage	F	VF	XF	Unc	BU
2006	—	—	—	—	0.75	1.00
2006 Proof	—	Value: 6.00				

KM# 341 10 CENTS
2.0000 g., Bronze Plated Steel, 15.95 mm. **Obv:** New national arms **Obv. Legend:** uMzantsi - Afrika **Rev:** Alum lily at left, value at right **Edge:** Reeded

Date	Mintage	F	VF	XF	Unc	BU
2007	—	—	—	0.30	0.75	1.00
2007 Proof	—	Value: 6.00				

KM# 498 10 CENTS
2.0000 g., Bronze Plated Steel, 16 mm. **Obv:** National arms **Obv. Legend:** iNingizimu Afrika **Rev:** Arum lily and value

Date	Mintage	F	VF	XF	Unc	BU
2008	—	—	—	—	0.75	1.00
2008 Proof	—	Value: 8.00				

KM# 499 10 CENTS
2.0000 g., Bronze Plated Steel, 16 mm. **Obv:** National arms **Obv. Legend:** iNingizimu Afrika **Rev:** Arum lily and value

Date	Mintage	F	VF	XF	Unc	BU
2008	—	—	—	—	0.75	1.00
2008 Proof	—	Value: 6.00				

KM# 225 20 CENTS
3.5000 g., Bronze Plated Steel, 19 mm. **Obv:** New national arms **Obv. Legend:** AFERIKA BORWA **Obv. Designer:** A.L. Sutherland **Rev:** Protea flower and value **Edge:** Reeded

Date	Mintage	F	VF	XF	Unc	BU
2001	—	—	—	0.35	0.90	1.20
2001 Proof	3,678	Value: 7.00				

KM# 270 20 CENTS
3.5000 g., Bronze Plated Steel, 19 mm. **Obv:** New national arms **Obv. Legend:** South Africa **Obv. Designer:** A.L. Sutherland **Rev:** Protea flower and value **Rev. Designer:** S. Erasmus **Edge:** Reeded

Date	Mintage	F	VF	XF	Unc	BU
2002	—	—	—	0.35	0.90	1.20
2002 Proof	3,250	Value: 7.00				

KM# 327 20 CENTS
3.5000 g., Bronze Plated Steel, 19 mm. **Obv:** New national arms **Obv. Legend:** Aforika Borwa **Rev:** Protea flower and value

Date	Mintage	F	VF	XF	Unc	BU
2003	—	—	—	0.35	0.90	1.20
2003 Proof	2,909	Value: 7.00				

KM# 328 20 CENTS
3.5000 g., Bronze Plated Steel, 19 mm. **Obv:** New national arms **Obv. Legend:** Afrika Borwa **Rev:** Protea flower and value **Edge:** Reeded

Date	Mintage	F	VF	XF	Unc	BU
2004	—	—	—	0.35	0.90	1.20
2004 Proof	1,935	Value: 7.00				

KM# 293 20 CENTS
3.5000 g., Bronze Plated Steel, 19 mm. **Obv:** New national arms **Obv. Legend:** Suid-Afrika **Rev:** Protea flower and value **Edge:** Reeded **Shape:** Round

Date	Mintage	F	VF	XF	Unc	BU
2005	—	—	—	0.35	0.90	1.20
2005 Proof	—	Value: 7.00				

KM# 488 20 CENTS
3.5000 g., Bronze Plated Steel, 19 mm. **Obv:** National arms **Obv. Legend:** uMzantsi Afrika **Rev:** Protea flower and value

Date	Mintage	F	VF	XF	Unc	BU
2006	—	—	—	—	0.90	1.20
2006 Proof	—	Value: 7.00				

KM# 342 20 CENTS
3.4800 g., Bronze Plated Steel, 19 mm. **Obv:** New national arms **Obv. Legend:** iNingizimu Afrika **Rev:** Protea flower and value **Edge:** Reeded

Date	Mintage	F	VF	XF	Unc	BU
2007	—	—	—	0.35	0.90	1.20
2007 Proof	—	Value: 7.00				

KM# 226 50 CENTS
5.0000 g., Bronze Plated Steel, 22 mm. **Obv:** New national arms **Obv. Legend:** AFERIKA BORWA **Obv. Designer:** A.L. Sutherland **Rev:** Strelitzia plant, value **Rev. Designer:** Linda Lotriet **Edge:** Reeded

Date	Mintage	F	VF	XF	Unc	BU
2001	1,152,000	—	—	0.50	1.20	1.60
2001	3,678	Value: 8.00				

KM# 271 50 CENTS
5.0000 g., Brass Plated Steel, 22 mm. **Obv:** New national arms **Obv. Legend:** Aforika Borwa **Obv. Designer:** A.L. Sutherland **Rev:** Strelitzia plant **Rev. Designer:** Linda Lotriet **Edge:** Reeded

Date	Mintage	F	VF	XF	Unc	BU
2002	16,000,000	—	—	0.50	1.20	1.60
2002 Proof	3,250	Value: 8.00				

KM# 287 50 CENTS
5.0000 g., Bronze Plated Steel, 22 mm. **Obv:** New national arms **Obv. Legend:** Aforika - Borwa **Rev:** Soccer player **Edge:** Reeded **Designer:** A. L. Sutherland

Date	Mintage	F	VF	XF	Unc	BU
2002	—	—	—	—	9.00	12.00

KM# 276 50 CENTS
5.0000 g., Bronze Plated Steel, 22 mm. **Obv:** New national arms **Obv. Legend:** Afrika - Borwa **Obv. Designer:** A.L. Sutherland **Rev:** Cricket player diving towards the wicket **Rev. Designer:** A. L. Sutherland **Edge:** Reeded

Date	Mintage	F	VF	XF	Unc	BU
2003	11,749	—	—	—	9.00	12.00

KM# 329 50 CENTS
5.0000 g., Bronze Plated Steel, 22 mm. **Obv:** New national arms **Obv. Legend:** Aforika Borwa **Rev:** Cricket player diving towards the wicket **Edge:** Reeded **Designer:** A. L. Sutherland

Date	Mintage	F	VF	XF	Unc	BU
2003	—	—	—	—	9.00	12.00
2003 Proof	—	Value: 15.00				

KM# 330 50 CENTS
5.0000 g., Bronze Plated Steel, 22 mm. **Obv:** New national arms **Obv. Legend:** Afrika - Borwa **Obv. Designer:** A. L. Sutherland **Rev:** Strelitzia plant, value **Rev. Designer:** Linda Lotriet **Edge:** Reeded

Date	Mintage	F	VF	XF	Unc	BU
2003	—	—	—	0.50	1.60	1.20
2003 Proof	2,909	Value: 8.00				

KM# 331 50 CENTS
5.0000 g., Bronze Plated Steel, 22 mm. **Obv:** New national arms **Obv. Legend:** Suid Afrika **Obv. Designer:** A. L. Sutherland **Rev:** Strelitzia plant, value **Rev. Designer:** Linda Lotriet **Edge:** Reeded

Date	Mintage	F	VF	XF	Unc	BU
2004	—	—	—	0.50	1.20	1.60
2004 Proof	1,935	Value: 8.00				

KM# 294 50 CENTS
5.0000 g., Bronze Plated Steel, 22 mm. **Obv:** New national arms **Obv. Legend:** uMzantsi Afrika **Obv. Designer:** A. L. Sutherland **Rev:** Strelitzia plant, value **Rev. Designer:** Linda Lotriet **Edge:** Reeded **Shape:** Round

Date	Mintage	F	VF	XF	Unc	BU
2005	—	—	—	0.50	1.20	1.60
2005 Proof	—	Value: 8.00				

KM# 489 50 CENTS
5.0000 g., Bronze Plated Steel, 22 mm. **Obv:** National arms **Obv. Legend:** uMzantsi Afrika **Rev:** Strelitzia plant and value

Date	Mintage	F	VF	XF	Unc	BU
2006	—	—	—	—	1.20	1.60
2006 Proof	—	Value: 8.00				

KM# 493 50 CENTS
5.0000 g., Brass Plated Steel, 22 mm. **Obv:** National arms **Obv. Legend:** iSewula Afrika **Rev:** Strelitzia plant and value

Date	Mintage	F	VF	XF	Unc	BU
2007	—	—	—	—	1.20	1.60
2007 Proof	—	Value: 8.00				

KM# 500 50 CENTS
5.0000 g., Bronze Plated Steel, 22 mm. **Obv:** National arms **Obv. Legend:** Afurika Tshipembe **Rev:** Strelitzia plant and value

Date	Mintage	F	VF	XF	Unc	BU
2008	—	—	—	—	1.20	1.60
2008 Proof	—	Value: 8.00				

KM# 343 50 CENTS
5.0000 g., Bronze Plated Steel, 21.97 mm. **Obv:** National arms **Obv. Legend:** iSewula Afrika **Rev:** Strelitzia plant at lower left, value at upper right **Edge:** Reeded

Date	Mintage	F	VF	XF	Unc	BU
2008	—	—	—	0.50	1.20	1.60
2008 Proof	—	Value: 8.00				

KM# 227 RAND
4.0000 g., Nickel Plated Copper, 20 mm. **Obv:** New national arms **Obv. Legend:** SUID-AFRIKA **Obv. Designer:** A.L.

Sutherland **Rev:** Springbok, value **Rev. Designer:** Linda Lotriet **Edge:** Segmented reeding

Date	Mintage	F	VF	XF	Unc	BU
2001	—	—	—	0.60	1.50	2.00
2001 Proof	3,678	Value: 10.00				

KM# 272 RAND
4.0000 g., Nickel Plated Copper, 20 mm. **Obv:** New national arms **Obv. Legend:** Suid-Afrika Afrika Borwa **Obv. Designer:** A. L. Sutherland **Rev:** Springbok, value **Rev. Designer:** Linda Lotriet **Edge:** Segmented reeding

Date	Mintage	F	VF	XF	Unc	BU
2002	—	—	—	0.60	1.50	2.00
2002 Proof	3,250	Value: 10.00				

KM# 275 RAND
4.0000 g., Nickel Plated Copper, 20 mm. **Subject:** Johannesburg World Summit on Sustainable Development **Obv:** New national arms **Obv. Legend:** Suid-Afrika - Afrika Borwa **Obv. Designer:** A.L. Sutherland **Rev:** World globe and logo **Rev. Designer:** M. J. Scheepers **Edge:** Segmented reeding

Date	Mintage	F	VF	XF	Unc	BU
2002	—	—	—	—	12.00	18.00

KM# 332 RAND
4.0000 g., Nickel Plated Copper, 20 mm. **Obv:** New national arms **Obv. Legend:** uMzantsi Afrika Suid-Afrika **Obv. Designer:** A. L. sutherland **Rev:** Springbok, value **Rev. Designer:** Linda Lotriet **Edge:** Segmented reeding

Date	Mintage	F	VF	XF	Unc	BU
2003	—	—	—	0.60	1.50	2.00
2003 Proof	2,909	Value: 10.00				

KM# 333 RAND
4.0000 g., Nickel Plated Copper, 20 mm. **Obv:** New national arms **Obv. Legend:** iNingizimu Afrika - uMzantsi Afrika **Obv. Designer:** A. L. Sutherland **Rev:** Springbok, value **Rev. Designer:** Linda Lotriet **Edge:** Segmented reeding

Date	Mintage	F	VF	XF	Unc	BU
2004	—	—	—	0.60	1.50	2.00
2004 Proof	1,935	Value: 10.00				

KM# 295 RAND
4.0000 g., Nickel Plated Copper, 20 mm. **Obv:** new national arms **Obv. Legend:** iSewula Afrika - iNingizimu Afrika **Obv. Designer:** A. L. Sutherland **Rev:** Springbok, value **Rev. Designer:** Linda Lotriet **Edge:** Segmented reeding **Shape:** Round

Date	Mintage	F	VF	XF	Unc	BU
2005	—	—	—	0.60	1.50	2.00
2005 Proof	—	Value: 10.00				

KM# 490 RAND
4.0000 g., Nickel Plated Copper, 20 mm. **Obv:** National arms **Obv. Legend:** Afurika Tshipembe - iSewula Afrika **Rev:** Springbok and value

Date	Mintage	F	VF	XF	Unc	BU
2006	—	—	—	—	1.50	2.00
2006 Proof	—	Value: 10.00				

KM# 494 RAND
4.0000 g., Nickel Plated Copper, 20 mm. **Obv:** National arms **Obv. Legend:** Ningizimu Afrika - Afurika Tshipembe **Rev:** Springbok and value

Date	Mintage	F	VF	XF	Unc	BU
2007	—	—	—	—	1.50	2.00
2007 Proof	—	Value: 10.00				

KM# 344 RAND
3.9300 g., Nickel Plated Copper, 19.94 mm. **Obv:** Natinal arms **Obv. Legend:** Ningizimu Afrika - Afurika Tshipemba **Rev:** Springbok leaping right **Edge:** segmented reeding

Date	Mintage	F	VF	XF	Unc	BU
2007	—	—	—	0.60	1.50	2.00
2007 Proof	—	Value: 10.00				

KM# 501 RAND
4.0000 g., Nickel Plated Copper, 20 mm. **Obv:** National arms **Obv. Legend:** Afrika-Dzonga - Ningizimu Afrika **Rev:** Springbok and value

Date	Mintage	F	VF	XF	Unc	BU
2008	—	—	—	—	2.00	2.75
2008 Proof	—	Value: 12.00				

KM# 228 2 RAND
5.5000 g., Nickel Plated Copper, 23 mm. **Obv:** New national arms **Obv. Legend:** UMZANSTI AFRIKA **Rev:** Greater Kudu, value **Edge:** Segmented reeding **Designer:** A. L. Sutherland

Date	Mintage	F	VF	XF	Unc	BU
2001	3,600,000	—	—	0.80	2.00	3.00
2001 Proof	3,678	Value: 12.00				

KM# 273 2 RAND
5.5000 g., Nickel Plated Copper, 23 mm. **Obv:** New national arms **Obv. Legend:** iNingizimu Afrika - uMzantsi Afrika **Rev:** Greater Kudu, value **Edge:** Segmented reeding **Designer:** A.L. Sutherland

Date	Mintage	F	VF	XF	Unc	BU
2002	12,000,000	—	—	0.80	2.00	3.50
2002 Proof	3,250	Value: 12.00				

KM# 335 2 RAND
5.5000 g., Nickel Plated Copper, 23 mm. **Obv:** New national arms **Obv. Legend:** iNingizimu Afrika - iSewula Afrika **Rev:** Greater Kudu, value **Edge:** Segmented reeding **Designer:** A. L. Sutherland

Date	Mintage	F	VF	XF	Unc	BU
2003	5,000,000	—	—	0.80	2.00	3.50
2003 Proof	2,909	Value: 12.00				

KM# 336 2 RAND
5.5000 g., Nickel Plated Copper, 23 mm. **Obv:** New national arms **Obv. Legend:** SOUTH AFRICA **Rev:** Greater Kudu, value **Edge:** Segmented reeding **Designer:** A. L. Sutherland

Date	Mintage	F	VF	XF	Unc	BU
2004	—	—	—	0.80	2.00	3.50
2004 Proof	1,935	Value: 12.00				

KM# 334 2 RAND
5.5000 g., Nickel Plated Copper, 23 mm. **Subject:** 10 Years of Freedom - 1994-2004 **Obv:** New national arms **Obv. Legend:** Afurika Tshipembe - iSewula Afrika **Obv. Designer:** A. L. Sutherland **Rev:** Value, flag logo, people **Rev. Designer:** M. J. Scheepers **Edge:** Segmented reeding **Note:** 5,885 issued in souvenir card.

Date	Mintage	F	VF	XF	Unc	BU
2004	—	—	—	0.80	2.00	2.75

KM# 296 2 RAND
5.5000 g., Nickel Plated Copper, 23 mm. **Obv:** New national arms **Obv. Legend:** Ningizimu Afrika - Afurika Tshipembe **Rev:** Greater Kudu, value **Edge:** Segmented reeding **Designer:** A. L. Sutherland

Date	Mintage	F	VF	XF	Unc	BU
2005	—	—	—	0.80	2.00	2.75
2005 Proof	—	Value: 12.00				

KM# 491 2 RAND
5.5000 g., Nickel Plated Copper, 23 mm. **Obv:** National arms **Obv. Legend:** Afrika-Dzonga - Ningizimo Afrika **Rev:** Greater kudu and value

Date	Mintage	F	VF	XF	Unc	BU
2006	—	—	—	—	2.00	2.75
2006 Proof	—	Value: 12.00				

KM# 495 2 RAND
5.5000 g., Nickel Plated Copper, 23 mm. **Obv:** National arms **Obv. Legend:** South Africa - Afrika Dzonga **Rev:** Greater kudu and value

Date	Mintage	F	VF	XF	Unc	BU
2007	—	—	—	—	2.00	2.75
2007 Proof	—	Value: 12.00				

KM# 345 2 RAND
5.4700 g., Nickel Plated Copper, 22.98 mm. **Obv:** National arms **Obv. Legend:** Afrika-Dzonga - South China **Rev:** Kudu at center left, value at right **Edge:** Segmented reeding

Date	Mintage	F	VF	XF	Unc	BU
2007	—	—	—	0.80	2.00	2.75
2007 Proof	—	Value: 12.00				

KM# 229 5 RAND
7.0000 g., Nickel Plated Copper, 26 mm. **Obv:** New national arms **Obv. Legend:** ININGIZIMU AFRIKA **Rev:** Wildebeest, value **Edge:** Segmented reeding **Designer:** A.L. Sutherland

Date	Mintage	F	VF	XF	Unc	BU
2001	2,000,000	—	—	1.20	4.50	6.00
2001 CW	779	—	—	—	67.50	90.00
2001 Proof	3,678	Value: 15.00				

KM# 274 5 RAND
7.0000 g., Nickel Plated Copper, 26 mm. **Obv:** New national arms **Obv. Legend:** Afurika Tshipembe - Isewula Afrika **Rev:** Wildebeest, value **Edge:** Segmented reeding **Designer:** A.L. Sutherland

Date	Mintage	F	VF	XF	Unc	BU
2002	—	—	—	1.20	4.50	6.00
2002 CW	106	—	—	—	—	150
2002 Proof	3,250	Value: 15.00				

KM# 337 5 RAND
7.0000 g., Nickel Plated Copper, 26 mm. **Obv:** New national arms **Obv. Legend:** Afurika Tshipembe - Ningizimu Afrika **Rev:** Wildebeest, value **Edge:** Segmented reeding **Designer:** A. L. Sutherland

Date	Mintage	F	VF	XF	Unc	BU
2003	—	—	—	1.20	4.50	6.00
2003 Proof	2,909	Value: 15.00				

KM# 281 5 RAND
9.5000 g., Bi-Metallic Brass center in Copper-Nickel ring, 26 mm. **Obv:** New national arms **Obv. Legend:** Afrika-Dzonga - Ningizimu Afrika **Rev:** Wildebeest, value **Edge:** Security type with lettering **Edge Lettering:** "SARB R5" repeated ten times

Date	Mintage	F	VF	XF	Unc	BU
2004	—	—	—	1.20	5.00	6.50
2004 CW	3,243	—	—	—	—	22.50
2004 Proof	1,935	Value: 15.00				

KM# 297 5 RAND
9.5000 g., Bi-Metallic Brass center in Copper-Nickel ring, 26 mm. **Obv:** New national arms **Obv. Legend:** Afrika Dzonga - South Africa **Rev:** Wildebeest, value **Edge:** Security type with lettering **Edge Lettering:** "SARB R5" repeated ten times **Designer:** A. L. Sutherland

Date	Mintage	F	VF	XF	Unc	BU
2005	—	—	—	1.20	3.75	5.00
2005 CW	997	—	—	—	—	50.00
2005 Proof	—	Value: 15.00				

KM# 492 5 RAND
5.5000 g., Nickel Plated Copper, 26 mm. **Obv:** National arms **Obv. Legend:** Aforika Borwa - South Africa **Rev:** Wildebeest and value

Date	Mintage	F	VF	XF	Unc	BU
2006	—	—	—	—	4.50	6.00
2006 Proof	—	Value: 12.00				

KM# 496 5 RAND
7.0000 g., Nickel Plated Copper, 26 mm. **Obv:** National arms **Obv. Legend:** Aforika-Borwa - Afrika Borwa **Rev:** Wildebeest and value

Date	Mintage	F	VF	XF	Unc	BU
2007	—	—	—	—	4.50	6.00
2007 Proof	—	Value: 15.00				

KM# 346 5 RAND
9.4400 g., Bi-Metallic Bronze center in Copper-Nickel ring, 26 mm. **Obv:** National arms **Obv. Legend:** Aforika Borwa - Afrika Borwa **Rev:** Wildebeest rearing left **Edge:** Security type and lettered **Edge Lettering:** "SARB R5" repeated ten times **Designer:** A. L. Sutherland

Date	Mintage	F	VF	XF	Unc	BU
2007	—	—	—	1.20	3.00	4.00
2007 CW	—	—	—	—	—	22.50
2007 Proof	—	Value: 15.00				

GOLD BULLION COINAGE

KM# 105 1/10 KRUGERRAND
3.3930 g., 0.9170 Gold .1000 AGW 0.1000 oz. AGW, 16.50 mm. **Obv:** Bust of Paul Kruger left **Rev:** Springbok walking right divides date **Edge:** Reeded, 180 serrations for uncirculated, 220 serrations for

Date	Mintage	F	VF	XF	Unc	BU
2001	17,936	—	—	—	BV+15%	—
2001 Proof	4,058	Value: 125				
2002	12,890	—	—	—	BV+15%	—
2002 Proof	3,110	Value: 125				
2003	15,893	—	—	—	BV+15%	—
2003 Proof	1,893	Value: 125				
2004	—	—	—	—	BV+15%	—
2004 Proof	3,811	Value: 125				
2005	—	—	—	—	BV+15%	—
2005 Proof	—	Value: 125				
2006	—	—	—	—	BV+15%	—
2006 Proof	—	Value: 125				

Date	Mintage	F	VF	XF	Unc	BU
2007	—	—	—	—	BV+15%	—
2007 Proof	4,400	Value: 125				
2008	—	—	—	—	BV+15%	—
2008 Proof	4,800	Value: 125				
2009	—	—	—	—	BV+15%	—
2009 Proof	6,000	Value: 125				

KM# 106 1/4 KRUGERRAND
8.4820 g., 0.9170 Gold 0.2501 oz. AGW, 22 mm. **Obv:** Bust of Paul Kruger left **Obv. Legend:** SUID — AFRIKA • SOUTH AFRICA **Rev:** Springbok bounding right divides date **Rev. Designer:** Coert L. Steynberg **Edge:** Reeded, 180 serrations for uncirculated, 220 serrations

Date	Mintage	F	VF	XF	Unc	BU
2001	10,607	—	—	—	BV+10%	—
2001 Proof	3,841	Value: 320				
2002	10,558	—	—	—	BV+10%	—
2002 Proof	2,442	Value: 320				
2003	11,468	—	—	—	BV+10%	—
2003 Proof	2,450	Value: 320				
2004	—	—	—	—	BV+10%	—
2004 Proof	4,570	Value: 320				
2005	—	—	—	—	BV+10%	—
2005 Proof	—	Value: 320				
2006	—	—	—	—	BV+10%	—
2006 Proof	—	Value: 320				
2007	—	—	—	—	BV+10%	—
2007 Proof	4,400	Value: 320				
2008	—	—	—	—	BV+10%	—
2008 Proof	4,800	Value: 320				
2009	—	—	—	—	BV+10%	—
2009 Proof	6,000	Value: 320				

KM# 107 1/2 KRUGERRAND
16.9650 g., 0.9170 Gold 0.5001 oz. AGW, 27 mm. **Obv:** Bust of Paul Kruger left **Obv. Legend:** SUID - AFRIKA - SOUTH AFRICA **Rev:** Springbok walking right divides date **Rev. Designer:** Coert L. Steynberg **Edge:** Reeded, 180 serrations for uncirculated, 220 serrations for

Date	Mintage	F	VF	XF	Unc	BU
2001	6,429	—	—	—	BV+8%	—
2001 Proof	3,696	Value: 625				
2002	—	—	—	—	BV+8%	—
2002 Proof	2,295	Value: 625				
2003	11,588	—	—	—	BV+8%	—
2003 Proof	1,285	Value: 625				
2004	—	—	—	—	BV+8%	—
2004 Proof	3,288	Value: 625				
2005	—	—	—	—	BV+8%	—
2005 Proof	—	Value: 625				
2006	—	—	—	—	BV+8%	—
2006 Proof	—	Value: 625				
2007	—	—	—	—	BV+8%	—
2007 Proof	3,400	Value: 625				
2008	—	—	—	—	BV+8%	—
2008 Proof	3,300	Value: 625				
2009	—	—	—	—	BV+8%	—
2009 Proof	2,500	Value: 625				

KM# 73 KRUGERRAND
33.9300 g., 0.9170 Gold 1.0003 oz. AGW, 32.7 mm. **Obv:** Bust of Paul Kruger left **Obv. Legend:** SUID — AFRIKA • SOUTH AFRICA **Rev:** Springbok walking right divides date **Rev. Designer:** Coert L. Steynberg **Edge:** Reeded, 180 serrations for uncirculated, 220 serrations for

Date	Mintage	F	VF	XF	Unc	BU
2001	5,889	—	—	—	—	BV+5%
2001 Proof	5,563	Value: 1,250				
2002	16,469	—	—	—	—	BV+5%

Date	Mintage	F	VF	XF	Unc	BU
2002 Proof	3,531	Value: 1,250				
2003	47,789	—	—	—	—	BV+5%
2003 Proof	2,136	Value: 1,250				
2004	71,269	—	—	—	—	BV+5%
2004 Proof	3,492	Value: 1,250				
2004 W/MM Proof	500	Value: 1,250				
2005	—	—	—	—	—	BV+5%
2005 Proof	—	Value: 1,250				
2006	—	—	—	—	—	BV+5%
2006 Proof	—	Value: 1,250				
2007	—	—	—	—	—	BV+5%
2007 Proof	3,400	Value: 1,250				
2008	—	—	—	—	—	BV+5%
2008 Proof	3,300	Value: 1,250				
2009	—	—	—	—	—	BV+5%
2009 Proof	2,500	Value: 1,250				

SILVER BULLION NATURA COINAGE

KM# 242 2-1/2 CENTS
1.4140 g., 0.9250 Silver 0.0420 oz. ASW, 16.3 mm.
Obv: Crowned arms **Rev:** Dolphin **Edge:** Reeded

Date	Mintage	F	VF	XF	Unc	BU
2001 Proof	—	Value: 27.50				

KM# 480 2-1/2 CENTS
1.1410 g., 0.9250 Silver 0.0339 oz. ASW, 16.3 mm. **Obv:** Flower
Obv. Designer: A. L. Sutherland **Rev:** Vasco de Gama's ship
"Sao Gabriel" **Rev. Designer:** L. Guerra and M. J. Scheepers

Date	Mintage	F	VF	XF	Unc	BU
2009 Proof	3,500	Value: 15.00				

KM# 243 5 CENTS
8.4560 g., 0.9250 Silver 0.2515 oz. ASW, 26.7 mm.
Series: Wildlife - Power **Obv:** Water buffalo's head **Obv. Designer:** A. L. Sutherland **Rev:** Two water buffalo heads within
circle below value **Rev. Designer:** C Moses **Edge:** Reeded

Date	Mintage	F	VF	XF	Unc	BU
2001 Proof	1,853	Value: 40.00				

KM# 351 5 CENTS
8.4560 g., 0.9250 Silver 0.2515 oz. ASW, 26.7 mm.
Series: Wildlife - Strength **Obv:** Elephant walking, facing
Obv. Designer: A. L. Sutherland **Rev:** Elephant 3/4 left bathing
Rev. Designer: C. Moses **Edge:** Reeded

Date	Mintage	F	VF	XF	Unc	BU
2002 Proof	2,425	Value: 40.00				

KM# 355 5 CENTS
8.4560 g., 0.9250 Silver 0.2515 oz. ASW, 26.7 mm.
Series: Wildlife - Survivor **Obv:** New national arms
Obv. Designer: A. L. Sutherland **Rev:** 2 White Rhinoceros
drinking at stream **Rev. Designer:** M. J. Scheepers
Edge: Reeded

Date	Mintage	F	VF	XF	Unc	BU
2003 Proof	1,870	Value: 40.00				

KM# 359 5 CENTS
8.4560 g., 0.9250 Silver 0.2515 oz. ASW, 26.7 mm.
Series: Wildlife - The Legend **Obv:** New national arms
Obv. Designer: A. L. Sutherland **Rev:** Head of Leopard right
drinking **Rev. Designer:** C. Moses **Edge:** Reeded

Date	Mintage	F	VF	XF	Unc	BU
2004 Proof	—	Value: 40.00				

KM# 320 5 CENTS
8.4560 g., 0.9250 Silver 0.2515 oz. ASW, 27.12 mm.
Series: Wildlife - African Wild Dog **Obv:** New national arms
Obv. Designer: A. L. Sutherland **Rev:** Painted Dog's head facing
slightly left **Rev. Designer:** C. Moses **Edge:** Reeded

Date	Mintage	F	VF	XF	Unc	BU
2005 Proof	1,500	Value: 40.00				

KM# 316 5 CENTS
8.4560 g., 0.9250 Silver 0.2515 oz. ASW, 27 mm.
Series: Wildlife - Black-backed Jackal **Obv:** New national arms
Obv. Designer: A. L. Sutherland **Rev:** Black-backed jackal
drinking **Rev. Designer:** C. Moses **Edge:** Reeded

Date	Mintage	F	VF	XF	Unc	BU
2006 Proof	1,500	Value: 40.00				

KM# 363 5 CENTS
8.4560 g., 0.9250 Silver 0.2515 oz. ASW, 26.7 mm.
Series: Wildlife - Kgalagadi Transfrontier Peace Park **Obv:** New
national arms **Obv. Designer:** A. L. Sutherland **Rev:** Local desert
melons, value **Rev. Designer:** C Moses **Edge:** Reeded

Date	Mintage	F	VF	XF	Unc	BU
2007 Proof	—	Value: 40.00				

KM# 482 5 CENTS
8.4060 g., 0.9250 Silver 0.2500 oz. ASW, 27 mm.
Subject: Maloti Drakensberg Transfrontier Project **Obv:** Arms
Obv. Designer: A. L. Sutherland **Rev:** Spiral Aloe Tree (aloe
polyphylla) **Rev. Designer:** L. Guerra and C. Moses

Date	Mintage	F	VF	XF	Unc	BU
2009 Proof	3,700	Value: 25.00				

KM# 244 10 CENTS
16.8630 g., 0.9250 Silver 0.5015 oz. ASW, 32.7 mm. **Series:**
Wildlife - Power **Obv:** Water buffalo's head **Obv. Designer:** A.
L. Sutherland **Rev:** Two water buffalo bulls fighting
Rev. Designer: M. J. Scheepers **Edge:** Reeded

Date	Mintage	F	VF	XF	Unc	BU
2001 Proof	1,989	Value: 65.00				

KM# 352 10 CENTS
16.8630 g., 0.9250 Silver 0.5015 oz. ASW, 38.3 mm.
Series: Wildlife - Strength **Obv:** Elephant walking, facing
Obv. Designer: A. L. Sutherland **Rev:** 2 elephant heads facing
each other **Rev. Designer:** M. J. Scheepers **Edge:** Reeded

Date	Mintage	F	VF	XF	Unc	BU
2002 Proof	2,395	Value: 65.00				

KM# 356 10 CENTS
16.8630 g., 0.9250 Silver 0.5015 oz. ASW, 32.7 mm.
Series: Wildlife - Survivor **Obv:** New national arms
Obv. Designer: A. L. Sutherland **Rev:** 2 Black Rhinoceros
standing, facing **Rev. Designer:** A. Minnie **Edge:** Reeded

Date	Mintage	F	VF	XF	Unc	BU
2003 Proof	1,815	Value: 65.00				

KM# 360 10 CENTS
16.8630 g., 0.9250 Silver 0.5015 oz. ASW, 32.7 mm. **Series:**
Wildlife - The Legend **Obv:** New national arms **Obv. Designer:**
A. L. Sutherland **Rev:** Leopard and impala above two leopard
cubs playing **Rev. Designer:** C. Moses **Edge:** Reeded

Date	Mintage	F	VF	XF	Unc	BU
2004 Proof	—	Value: 65.00				

KM# 321 10 CENTS
16.8630 g., 0.9250 Silver 0.5015 oz. ASW, 32.82 mm.
Series: Wildlife - African Wild Dog **Obv:** New national arms
Obv. Designer: A. L. Sutherland **Rev:** Two Painted Dogs walking
right **Rev. Designer:** C. Moses **Edge:** Reeded

Date	Mintage	F	VF	XF	Unc	BU
2005 Proof	1,500	Value: 65.00				

KM# 317 10 CENTS
16.8630 g., 0.9250 Silver 0.5015 oz. ASW, 32.7 mm.
Series: Wildlife - Black-backed Jackel **Obv:** New national arms
Obv. Designer: A. L. Sutherland **Rev:** Black-backed jackal
chasing birds **Rev. Designer:** L. Guerra **Edge:** Reeded

Date	Mintage	F	VF	XF	Unc	BU
2006 Proof	1,500	Value: 65.00				

KM# 364 10 CENTS
16.8630 g., 0.9250 Silver 0.5015 oz. ASW, 32.7 mm.
Series: Wildlife - Kgaladadi Transfrontier Peace Park **Obv:** New
national arms **Obv. Designer:** A. L. Sutherland **Rev:** Local tribe,
value **Rev. Designer:** L. Guerra **Edge:** Reeded

Date	Mintage	F	VF	XF	Unc	BU
2007 Proof	—	Value: 65.00				

KM# 483 10 CENTS
16.8130 g., 0.9250 Silver 0.5000 oz. ASW, 32.7 mm.
Subject: Maloti Drakensberg Transfrontier Project **Obv:** Arms
Obv. Designer: A. L. Sutherland **Rev:** Native Basotho riding pony
Rev. Designer: L. Guerra and A. Minnie

Date	Mintage	F	VF	XF	Unc	BU
2009 Proof	3,700	Value: 45.00				

KM# 245 20 CENTS
33.7260 g., 0.9250 Silver 1.0030 oz. ASW, 38.3 mm.
Series: Wildlife - Power **Obv:** Water buffalo's head
Obv. Designer: A. L. Sutherland **Rev:** Two water buffalo heads
facing **Rev. Designer:** P. Botes **Edge:** Reeded

Date	Mintage	F	VF	XF	Unc	BU
2001 Proof	1,902	Value: 85.00				

KM# 353 20 CENTS
33.7260 g., 0.9250 Silver 1.0030 oz. ASW, 38.3 mm.
Series: Wildlife - Strength **Obv:** Elephant walking, facing
Obv. Designer: A. L. Sutherland **Rev:** Family of four elephants
Rev. Designer: C. Moses **Edge:** Reeded

Date	Mintage	F	VF	XF	Unc	BU
2002 Proof	2,435	Value: 85.00				

KM# 357 20 CENTS
33.7260 g., Silver, 38.3 mm. **Series:** Wildlife - Survivor
Obv: New national arms **Obv. Designer:** A. L. Sutherland
Rev: White Rhinoceros mother with an offspring **Rev. Designer:**
C. Moses **Edge:** Reeded

Date	Mintage	F	VF	XF	Unc	BU
2003 Proof	1,930	Value: 85.00				

KM# 361 20 CENTS
33.7260 g., 0.9250 Silver 1.0030 oz. ASW, 38.3 mm.
Series: Wildlife - The legend **Obv:** New national arms **Obv.
Designer:** A. L. Sutherland **Rev:** Leopard looking left, cub on
branch behind her **Rev. Designer:** A. Minnie **Edge:** Reeded

Date	Mintage	F	VF	XF	Unc	BU
2004 Proof	—	Value: 85.00				

KM# 322 20 CENTS
33.7500 g., 0.9250 Silver 1.0037 oz. ASW, 38.67 mm.
Series: Wildlife - African Wild Dog **Obv:** New National arms
Obv. Designer: A. L. Sutherland **Rev:** Three Painted Dogs
Rev. Designer: M. J. Scheepers **Edge:** Reeded

Date	Mintage	F	VF	XF	Unc	BU
2005 Proof	1,500	Value: 85.00				

KM# 318 20 CENTS
33.7260 g., 0.9250 Silver 1.0030 oz. ASW, 38.7 mm.
Series: Wildlife - Black-backed Jackal **Obv:** National arms
Obv. Designer: A. L. Sutherland **Rev:** Two Black-backed jackals
Rev. Designer: C. Moses **Edge:** Reeded

Date	Mintage	F	VF	XF	Unc	BU
2006 Proof	1,500	Value: 85.00				

KM# 365 20 CENTS
33.7260 g., 0.9250 Silver 1.0030 oz. ASW, 38.3 mm.
Series: Wildlife - Kgalagadi Transfrontier Peace Park **Obv:** New
national arms **Obv. Designer:** A. L. Sutherland **Rev:** Lion's head
3/4 right at left, meerkat standing with offspring at right, value
Rev. Designer: A. Minnie **Edge:** Reeded

Date	Mintage	F	VF	XF	Unc	BU
2007 Proof	—	Value: 85.00				

KM# 460 20 CENTS
33.7250 g., 0.9990 Silver 1.0832 oz. ASW, 38.7 mm.
Subject: Richtersveld Transfrontier Park **Obv:** Arms
Obv. Designer: A. J. Sutherland **Rev:** Two shy Kipspringer
(Oreotragus oreotragos) **Rev. Designer:** L. Guerra and A. Minnie

Date	Mintage	F	VF	XF	Unc	BU
2008 Proof	2,200	Value: 30.00				

KM# 484 20 CENTS
33.6200 g., 0.9250 Silver 0.9998 oz. ASW, 38.72 mm.
Subject: Maloti Drakensberg Transfrontier Project **Obv:** Arms
Obv. Designer: A. L. Sutherland **Rev:** Cape griffon vulture
Rev. Designer: L. Guerra and M. J. Scheepers

Date	Mintage	F	VF	XF	Unc	BU
2009 Proof	3,700	Value: 75.00				

KM# 246 50 CENTS
76.4020 g., 0.9250 Silver 2.2721 oz. ASW, 50 mm.
Series: Wildlife - Power **Obv:** Water buffalo's head
Obv. Designer: A. L. Sutherland **Rev:** Water buffalo head, value
Rev. Designer: A. Minnie **Edge:** Reeded

Date	Mintage	F	VF	XF	Unc	BU
2001 Proof	1,866	Value: 110				

KM# 354 50 CENTS
76.4020 g., Silver, 50 mm. **Series:** Wildlife - Strength
Obv: Elephant walking, facing **Obv. Designer:** A. L. Sutherland
Rev: Elephant right with head raised **Rev. Designer:** P. Botes
Edge: Reeded

Date	Mintage	F	VF	XF	Unc	BU
2002 Proof	2,318	Value: 110				

KM# 358 50 CENTS
76.4020 g., 0.9250 Silver 2.2721 oz. ASW, 50 mm.
Series: Wildlife - Survivor **Obv:** New national arms
Obv. Designer: A. L. Sutherland **Rev:** White Rhinoceros' head
3/4 right, value **Rev. Designer:** J. Steyn **Edge:** Reeded

Date	Mintage	F	VF	XF	Unc	BU
2003 Proof	1,918	Value: 110				

KM# 362 50 CENTS
76.4620 g., 0.9250 Silver 2.2738 oz. ASW, 50 mm. **Series:**
Wildlife - The Legend **Obv:** New national arms **Obv. Designer:**
A. L. Sutherland **Rev:** Leopard facing snarling, two leopards at
lower left **Rev. Designer:** M. J. Scheepers **Edge:** Reeded

Date	Mintage	F	VF	XF	Unc	BU
2004 Proof	—	Value: 110				

KM# 323 50 CENTS
76.8600 g., 0.9250 Silver 2.2857 oz. ASW, 50.48 mm.
Series: Wildlife - African Wild Dog **Obv:** New national arms
Obv. Designer: A. L. Sutherland **Rev:** Two painted Dog's heads
facing **Rev. Designer:** L. Guerra **Edge:** Reeded

Date	Mintage	F	VF	XF	Unc	BU
2005 Proof	1,500	Value: 110				

KM# 319 50 CENTS
76.2520 g., 0.9250 Silver 2.2676 oz. ASW, 50 mm.
Series: Wildlife - Black-backed Jackal **Obv:** New national arms
Obv. Designer: A. L. Sutherland **Rev:** Two black-backed jackals
fighting over a carcass **Rev. Designer:** M. J. Scheepers
Edge: Reeded

Date	Mintage	F	VF	XF	Unc	BU
2006 Proof	1,500	Value: 110				

KM# 366 50 CENTS
76.4020 g., 0.9250 Silver 2.2721 oz. ASW, 50 mm.
Series: Wildlife - Kgalagadi Transfrontier Peace Park **Obv:** New
national arms **Obv. Designer:** A. L. Sutherland **Rev:** Antelope
running right **Rev. Designer:** M. J. Scheepers **Edge:** Reeded

Date	Mintage	F	VF	XF	Unc	BU
2007 Proof	—	Value: 110				

KM# 461 50 CENTS
76.2520 g., 0.9250 Silver 2.2676 oz. ASW, 50 mm.
Subject: Richtersveld Transfrontier Park **Obv:** Arms
Obv. Designer: A. J. Sutherland **Rev:** Giant aloe pillansii tree
Rev. Designer: L. Guerra and M. J. Scheepers

Date	Mintage	F	VF	XF	Unc	BU
2008 Proof	2,200	Value: 60.00				

KM# 485 50 CENTS
76.2520 g., 0.9250 Silver 2.2676 oz. ASW, 50 mm.
Subject: Maloti Drakensberg Transfrontier Project **Obv:** Arms
Obv. Designer: A. L. Sutherland **Rev:** Amphitheatre and Trukela
River **Rev. Designer:** L. Guerra and M. J. Scheepers

Date	Mintage	F	VF	XF	Unc	BU
2009 Proof	3,700	Value: 100				

KM# 248 2 RAND
33.6260 g., 0.9250 Silver 100000 oz. ASW, 38.7 mm. **Obv:** New
national arms **Obv. Designer:** A. L. Sutherland **Rev:** Dolphins
Rev. Designer: N. van Niekerk **Edge:** Reeded

Date	Mintage	F	VF	XF	Unc	BU
2001 Proof	2,987	Value: 65.00				

KM# 280 2 RAND
33.6260 g., 0.9250 Silver 100000 oz. ASW, 38.7 mm. **Obv:** New
national arms **Obv. Designer:** A. L. Sutherland **Rev:** Southern
Right Whale **Rev. Designer:** N van Niekerk **Edge:** Reeded

Date	Mintage	F	VF	XF	Unc	BU
2002 Proof	1,808	Value: 70.00				

KM# 286 2 RAND
33.6260 g., 0.9250 Silver 100000 oz. ASW, 38.7 mm. **Obv:** New
national arms **Obv. Designer:** A. L. Sutherland **Rev:** Martial and
Bateleur Eagles **Rev. Designer:** C. Moses **Edge:** Reeded

Date	Mintage	F	VF	XF	Unc	BU
2003 Proof	2,166	Value: 75.00				

KM# 284 2 RAND
33.6260 g., 0.9250 Silver 100000 oz. ASW, 38.7 mm. **Obv:** New
national arms **Obv. Designer:** A. L. Sutherland **Rev:** Verreaux's
Eagle Owl face and value **Rev. Designer:** A. Minnie
Edge: Reeded

Date	Mintage	F	VF	XF	Unc	BU
2004	—		—	—	50.00	55.00
2004 Proof	1,752	Value: 65.00				

KM# 372 2 RAND
33.6260 g., 0.9250 Silver 100000 oz. ASW, 38.7 mm. **Obv:** New
national arms **Obv. Designer:** A. L. Sutherland **Rev:** Three
vultures **Rev. Designer:** C. Moses **Edge:** Reeded

Date	Mintage	F	VF	XF	Unc	BU
2005 Proof	—	Value: 60.00				

KM# 374 2 RAND
33.6260 g., 0.9250 Silver 100000 oz. ASW, 38.7 mm. **Series:**
Bird of Prey **Obv:** New national arms **Obv. Designer:** A. L.
Sutherland **Rev:** Two Secretary birds **Rev. Designer:** C. Moses
Edge: Reeded

Date	Mintage	F	VF	XF	Unc	BU
2006 Proof	—	Value: 65.00				

KM# 481 2 RAND
33.6260 g., 0.9250 Silver 100000 oz. ASW, 38.7 mm.
Obv: Arms and country name **Obv. Designer:** A. L. Sutherland
Rev: Jan van Riebeeck's ship "Drommedaries" **Rev. Designer:**
L. Guerra

Date	Mintage	F	VF	XF	Unc	BU
2009 Proof	3,500	Value: 45.00				

SILVER BULLION PROTEA COINAGE

KM# 282 2-1/2 CENTS
1.4140 g., 0.9250 Silver 0.0420 oz. ASW, 16.3 mm. **Obv:** Protea
flower **Rev:** Southern Right Whale **Edge:** Plain

Date	Mintage	F	VF	XF	Unc	BU
2002 Proof	3,000	Value: 27.50				

KM# 285 2-1/2 CENTS
1.4140 g., 0.9250 Silver 0.0420 oz. ASW, 16.3 mm. **Obv:** Protea
flower **Rev:** Martial and Bateleur Eagles **Edge:** Plain

Date	Mintage	F	VF	XF	Unc	BU
2003 Proof	—	Value: 25.00				

KM# 283 2-1/2 CENTS
1.4140 g., 0.9250 Silver 0.0420 oz. ASW, 16.3 mm.
Series: Birds of Prey **Obv:** Protea flower **Rev:** Pearl Spotted
Owlet **Edge:** Plain

Date	Mintage	F	VF	XF	Unc	BU
2004 Proof	2,000	Value: 25.00				

KM# 348 2-1/2 CENTS
1.4140 g., 0.9250 Silver 0.0420 oz. ASW, 16.3 mm. **Obv:** Protea
flower **Obv. Legend:** SOUTH AFRICA **Rev:** Vulture alighting
Edge: Plain

Date	Mintage	F	VF	XF	Unc	BU
2005 Proof	—	Value: 25.00				

KM# 349 2-1/2 CENTS
1.4140 g., 0.9250 Silver 0.0420 oz. ASW, 16.3 mm. **Obv:** Protea
flower **Obv. Legend:** SOUTH AFRICA **Rev:** Head of Secretary
bird **Edge:** Plain

Date	Mintage	F	VF	XF	Unc	BU
2006 Proof	—	Value: 25.00				

KM# 350 2-1/2 CENTS
1.4140 g., 0.9250 Silver 0.0420 oz. ASW, 16.3 mm. **Subject:**
International Polar Year **Obv:** Protea flower **Obv. Legend:**
SOUTH AFRICA **Rev:** Globe displaying South Pole **Edge:** Plain

Date	Mintage	F	VF	XF	Unc	BU
2007 Proof	—	Value: 25.00				

KM# 231 RAND
15.0000 g., 0.9250 Silver 0.4461 oz. ASW, 32.7 mm.
Subject: Tourism **Obv:** Protea flower **Rev:** Steam locomotive
and flower **Edge:** Reeded

Date	Mintage	F	VF	XF	Unc	BU
2001	2,400	—	—	—	30.00	35.00
2001 Proof	1,784	Value: 45.00				

KM# 277 RAND
15.0000 g., 0.9250 Silver 0.4461 oz. ASW, 32.7 mm.
Subject: Soccer **Obv:** Protea flower **Obv. Designer:** A.L.
Sutherland **Rev:** Goalkeeper in action **Edge:** Reeded

Date	Mintage	F	VF	XF	Unc	BU
2002	1,777	—	—	—	35.00	40.00
2002 Proof	1,250	Value: 50.00				

KM# 367 RAND
15.0000 g., 0.9250 Silver 0.4461 oz. ASW **Subject:** World
Summit - Johannesburg **Obv:** Protea flower **Obv. Designer:** A.
L. Sutherland **Rev:** Globe **Edge:** Reeded

Date	Mintage	F	VF	XF	Unc	BU
2002	1,531	—	—	—	55.00	60.00
2002 Proof	1,413	Value: 70.00				

KM# 298 RAND
15.0500 g., 0.9250 Silver 0.4476 oz. ASW, 32.7 mm.
Obv: Protea flower **Obv. Designer:** A. L. Sutherland **Rev:** Cricket
player **Edge:** Reeded

Date	Mintage	F	VF	XF	Unc	BU
2003	1,697	—	—	—	40.00	45.00
2003 Proof	1,250	Value: 55.00				

KM# 288 RAND
15.0000 g., 0.9250 Silver 0.4461 oz. ASW, 32.7 mm.
Subject: 10th Anniversary of South African Democracy
Obv: Protea flower **Rev:** Flora and fawna **Edge:** Reeded

Date	Mintage	F	VF	XF	Unc	BU
2004	3,427	—	—	—	35.00	40.00
2004 Proof	2,930	Value: 50.00				

KM# 368 RAND
15.0000 g., 0.9250 Silver 0.4461 oz. ASW, 32.7 mm.
Series: Nobel Peace Prize Winners **Obv:** Protea flower
Obv. Designer: A. L. Sutherland **Rev:** Bust of Chief A. J. Luthuli
facing at center, Luthuli seated at desj left at lower right
Edge: Reeded

Date	Mintage	F	VF	XF	Unc	BU
2005	—	—	—	—	50.00	55.00
2005 Proof	—	Value: 65.00				

KM# 369 RAND
15.0000 g., 0.9250 Silver 0.4461 oz. ASW, 32.7 mm.
Series: Nobel Peace prize Winners **Obv:** Protea flower
Obv. Designer: A. J. Sutherland **Rev:** 1/3 length figure of
Archbishop Desmond Mpilo Tutu facing at right **Edge:** Reeded

Date	Mintage	F	VF	XF	Unc	BU
2006	—	—	—	—	60.00	65.00
2006	—	Value: 75.00				

KM# 370 RAND
15.0000 g., Silver, 32.7 mm. **Series:** Nobel Peace Prize Winners
Obv: Protea flower **Obv. Designer:** A. J. Sutherland **Rev:** Bust
of De Klerk facing **Edge:** Reeded

Date	Mintage	F	VF	XF	Unc	BU
2007	—	—	—	—	55.00	60.00
2007 Proof	—	Value: 70.00				

KM# 371 RAND
15.0000 g., 0.9250 Silver 0.4461 oz. ASW, 32.7 mm.
Series: Nobel Peace Prize Winners **Obv:** Protea flower
Obv. Designer: A. J. Sutherland **Rev:** Bust of Mandela facing
Edge: Reeded

Date	Mintage	F	VF	XF	Unc	BU
2007	—	—	—	65.00	75.00	
2007 Proof	—	Value: 95.00				

KM# 451 RAND
15.5500 g., 0.9250 Silver 0.4624 oz. ASW, 32.7 mm.
Obv: Protea flower **Obv. Designer:** A. L. Sutherland **Rev:** Ghandi
portrait **Rev. Designer:** M. J. Scheepers and N. van Niekerk

Date	Mintage	F	VF	XF	Unc	BU
2008	—	—	—	—	—	20.00
2008 Proof	11,000	Value: 25.00				

KM# 475 RAND
15.5500 g., 0.9250 Silver 0.4624 oz. ASW, 32.7 mm.
Obv: Protea flower **Obv. Designer:** A. L. Sutherland
Rev: Portraits of C. J. Langenhoven and N. L. de Villiers with
musical score **Rev. Designer:** A. Minnie and M. J. Scheepers

Date	Mintage	F	VF	XF	Unc	BU
2009	—	—	—	—	—	15.00
2009 Proof	11,000	Value: 25.00				

SILVER BULLION CULTURE COINAGE

KM# 456 2-1/2 CENTS
1.1400 g., 0.9250 Silver 0.0339 oz. ASW, 16.3 mm. **Obv:** Flower
Obv. Designer: A. J. Sutherland **Rev:** Map of Antartica
Rev. Designer: L. Guerra and M. J. Scheepers

Date	Mintage	F	VF	XF	Unc	BU
2008 Proof	3,000	Value: 15.00				

KM# 458 5 CENTS
8.4060 g., 0.9250 Silver 0.2500 oz. ASW, 27 mm.
Subject: Richtersveld Transfrontier Park **Obv:** Arms
Obv. Designer: A. L. Sutherland **Rev:** Orbea Namaquensis
suculant flower **Rev. Designer:** L. Guerra and C. Moses

Date	Mintage	F	VF	XF	Unc	BU
2008 Proof	2,200	Value: 15.00				

KM# 459 10 CENTS
16.8130 g., 0.9250 Silver 0.5000 oz. ASW, 32.7 mm.
Subject: Richtersveld Transfrontier Park **Obv:** Arms
Obv. Designer: A. J. Sutherland **Rev:** Local Nama native and
livestock **Rev. Designer:** L. Guerra and A. Minnie

Date	Mintage	F	VF	XF	Unc	BU
2008 Proof	2,200	Value: 20.00				

KM# 373 2 RAND
33.6260 g., 0.9250 Silver 100000 oz. ASW, 38.7 mm.
Subject: 2006 FIFA World Cup Soccer - Germany **Obv:** New
national arms **Obv. Designer:** A. L. Sutherland **Rev:** Soccer ball
above globe **Rev. Designer:** M. Scheepers **Edge:** Reeded

Date	Mintage	F	VF	XF	Unc	BU
2005 Proof	—	Value: 60.00				

KM# 435 2 RAND
33.6300 g., 0.9250 Silver 1.0000 oz. ASW, 38.7 mm.
Subject: 2010 World Cup

Date	Mintage	F	VF	XF	Unc	BU
2006	—	—	—	—	—	35.00

KM# 375 2 RAND
33.6260 g., 0.9250 Silver 100000 oz. ASW, 38.7 mm.
Subject: FIFA World Cup Soccer - Germany **Obv:** New national
arms **Obv. Designer:** A. L. Sutherland **Rev:** FIFA logo at center
Rev. Designer: M. J. Scheepers **Edge:** Reeded

Date	Mintage	F	VF	XF	Unc	BU
2006 Proof	—	Value: 60.00				

KM# 436 2 RAND
33.6300 g., 0.9250 Silver 1.0000 oz. ASW, 38.7 mm.
Subject: 2010 World Cup

Date	Mintage	F	VF	XF	Unc	BU
2007	—	—	—	—	—	35.00

KM# 376 2 RAND
33.6260 g., 0.9250 Silver 100000 oz. ASW, 38.7 mm.
Subject: International Polar Year **Obv:** New national arms
Obv. Designer: A. L. Sutherland **Rev:** Logo above globe
Rev. Designer: A. Minnie **Edge:** Reeded

Date	Mintage	F	VF	XF	Unc	BU
2007 Proof	—	Value: 50.00				

KM# 377 2 RAND
33.6260 g., 0.9250 Silver 100000 oz. ASW, 38.7 mm.
Subject: 2010 FIFA World Cup Soccer - South Africa **Obv:** New
national arms **Obv. Designer:** A. L. Sutherland **Rev:** Tower at
left, animal heads at top. animal at right, soccer ball ar bottom
Rev. Designer: M. J. Scheepers **Edge:** Reeded

Date	Mintage	F	VF	XF	Unc	BU
2007 Proof	—	Value: 50.00				

KM# 437 2 RAND
33.6260 g., 0.9250 Silver 100000 oz. ASW, 38.7 mm.
Subject: 2010 World Cup

Date	Mintage	F	VF	XF	Unc	BU
2008 Proof	—	Value: 45.00				

KM# 457 2 RAND
33.6200 g., 0.9250 Silver 0.9998 oz. ASW, 38.7 mm. **Obv:** Arms
Obv. Designer: A. L. Sutherland **Rev:** Polar ship "SA Sgulhas"
Rev. Designer: L. Guerra

Date	Mintage	F	VF	XF	Unc	BU
2008 Proof	3,000	Value: 50.00				

GOLD BULLION NATURA COINAGE

KM# 389 2 RAND
7.7770 g., 0.9999 Gold 0.2500 oz. AGW, 22 mm. **Series:** World
Heritage Site **Subject:** Mapungubwe **Obv:** New national arms
Obv. Designer: A. L. Sutherland **Rev:** Rhinoceros standing right
Rev. Designer: M. J. Scheepers **Edge:** Reeded

Date	Mintage	F	VF	XF	Unc	BU
2005 Proof	—	Value: 320				

KM# 455 2 RAND
7.7700 g., 0.9999 Gold 0.2496 oz. AGW, 22 mm. **Subject:**
Vredefort Dome **Obv:** Arms **Obv. Designer:** A. J. Sutherland
Rev: Meteorite **Rev. Designer:** K. Pillay and M. J. Scheepers

Date	Mintage	F	VF	XF	Unc	BU
2008 Proof	2,000	Value: 325				

KM# 410 10 RAND
3.1107 g., 0.9999 Gold 0.1000 oz. AGW, 16.5 mm.
Series: Natura **Obv:** Cheetah's head **Obv. Designer:** A. L.
Sutherland **Rev:** Cheetah drinking water **Rev. Designer:** M. J.
Scheepers **Edge:** Reeded

Date	Mintage	F	VF	XF	Unc	BU
2002 Proof	3,156	Value: 150				

KM# 414 10 RAND
3.1107 g., 0.9999 Gold 0.1000 oz. AGW, 16.5 mm.
Series: Natura **Obv:** Male and female lion's heads
Obv. Designer: A. L. Sutherland **Rev:** Two lioness drinking water
Rev. Designer: C. Moses **Edge:** Reeded

Date	Mintage	F	VF	XF	Unc	BU
2003 Proof	4,233	Value: 150				

KM# 418 10 RAND
3.1107 g., 0.9999 Gold 0.1000 oz. AGW, 16.5 mm.
Series: Natura **Obv:** Caracal's head and shoulders
Obv. Designer: Aldrid Minnie **Rev:** Caracal drinking water
Rev. Designer: C. Moses **Edge:** Reeded

Date	Mintage	F	VF	XF	Unc	BU
2004 Proof	1,809	Value: 150				

KM# 422 10 RAND
3.1107 g., 0.9999 Gold 0.1000 oz. AGW, 16.5 mm.
Series: Natura **Obv:** Hippopotamus 1/2 way in water
Rev: Hippopotamus deeply in water **Edge:** Reeded
Designer: Aldrid Minnie

Date	Mintage	F	VF	XF	Unc	BU
2005 Proof	—	Value: 150				

KM# 426 10 RAND

3.1107 g., 0.9999 Gold 0.1000 oz. AGW, 16.5 mm.
Series: Natura **Obv:** Giraffe's head and neck
Obv. Designer: M. J. Scheepers **Rev:** Giraffe drinking water
Rev. Designer: C. Moses **Edge:** Reeded

Date	Mintage	F	VF	XF	Unc	BU
2006 Proof	—	Value: 150				

KM# 430 10 RAND

3.1107 g., 0.9999 Gold 0.1000 oz. AGW, 16.5 mm.
Series: Natura **Obv:** Forepart of Eland left **Rev:** Eland drinking water right **Edge:** Reeded **Designer:** Aldrid Minnie

Date	Mintage	F	VF	XF	Unc	BU
2007 Proof	—	Value: 150				

KM# 447 10 RAND

3.1100 g., 0.9990 Gold 0.0999 oz. AGW, 16.5 mm. **Obv:** Large elephant head and elephant family below **Rev:** One elephant eating, three elephants below **Designer:** C. Moses and N. van Niekerk

Date	Mintage	F	VF	XF	Unc	BU
2008 Proof	3,300	Value: 145				

KM# 471 10 RAND

3.1100 g., 0.9990 Gold 0.0999 oz. AGW, 16.5 mm. **Obv:** White rhino, silouette and forepart **Obv. Designer:** N. van Niekerk and M. J. Scheepers **Rev:** Two rhino foreparts facing left within large silouette **Rev. Designer:** N. van Niekerk and A. Minnie

Date	Mintage	F	VF	XF	Unc	BU
2009 Proof	2,500	Value: 145				

KM# 411 20 RAND

7.7770 g., 0.9999 Gold 0.2500 oz. AGW, 22 mm. **Series:** Natura **Obv:** Cheetah's head **Obv. Designer:** A. L. Sutherland **Rev:** Cheetah family resting **Rev. Designer:** Aldrid Minnie **Edge:** Reeded

Date	Mintage	F	VF	XF	Unc	BU
2002 Proof	2,548	Value: 320				

KM# 415 20 RAND

7.7770 g., 0.9999 Gold 0.2500 oz. AGW, 22 mm. **Series:** Natura **Obv:** Male and female lion's heads **Obv. Designer:** A. L. Sutherland **Rev:** Lion family resting **Rev. Designer:** M. J. Scheepers **Edge:** Reeded

Date	Mintage	F	VF	XF	Unc	BU
2003 Proof	2,799	Value: 320				

KM# 419 20 RAND

7.7770 g., 0.9999 Gold 0.2500 oz. AGW, 22 mm. **Series:** Natura **Obv:** Caracal's head and shoulders **Obv. Designer:** Aldrid Minnie **Rev:** Caracal with cub standing right **Rev. Designer:** M. J. Scheepers **Edge:** Reeded

Date	Mintage	F	VF	XF	Unc	BU
2004 Proof	1,407	Value: 320				

KM# 423 20 RAND

7.7770 g., 0.9999 Gold 0.2500 oz. AGW, 22 mm. **Series:** Natura **Obv:** Hippopotamus 1/2 way in water **Obv. Designer:** Aldrid Minnie **Rev:** Mother and baby Hippopotamus grazing **Edge:** Reeded

Date	Mintage	F	VF	XF	Unc	BU
2005 Proof	—	Value: 320				

KM# 427 20 RAND

7.7770 g., 0.9999 Gold 0.2500 oz. AGW, 22 mm. **Series:** Natura **Obv:** Giraffe's head and neck **Obv. Designer:** M. J. Scheepers **Rev:** Mother and baby giraffes grazing **Rev. Designer:** C. Moses **Edge:** Reeded

Date	Mintage	F	VF	XF	Unc	BU
2006 Proof	—	Value: 320				

KM# 431 20 RAND

7.7770 g., 0.9999 Gold 0.2500 oz. AGW, 22 mm. **Series:** Natura **Obv:** Forepart of Eland left **Rev:** Mother Eland and calf grazing **Edge:** Reeded **Designer:** Aldrid Minnie

Date	Mintage	F	VF	XF	Unc	BU
2007 Proof	—	Value: 320				

KM# 448 20 RAND

7.7770 g., 0.9990 Gold 0.2498 oz. AGW, 22 mm. **Obv:** Large elephant head and elephant family below **Obv. Designer:** C. Moses and N. van Niekerk **Rev:** Two elephants fighting, three elephants below **Rev. Designer:** M. J. Scheepers and N. van Niekerk

Date	Mintage	F	VF	XF	Unc	BU
2008 Proof	3,300	Value: 320				

KM# 472 20 RAND

7.7770 g., 0.9990 Gold 0.2498 oz. AGW, 22 mm. **Obv:** White rhino silouette and forepart **Obv. Designer:** N. van Niekerk and M. J. Scheepers **Rev:** Two rhinos walking forward within silouette **Rev. Designer:** N. van Niekerk and C. Moses

Date	Mintage	F	VF	XF	Unc	BU
2009 Proof	2,500	Value: 320				

KM# 412 50 RAND

15.5530 g., 0.9999 Gold 0.5000 oz. AGW, 27 mm.
Series: Natura **Obv:** Cheetah's head **Obv. Designer:** A. L. Sutherland **Rev:** Cheetah attacking Impala **Rev. Designer:** Johan Steyn **Edge:** Reeded

Date	Mintage	F	VF	XF	Unc	BU
2002 Proof	2,295	Value: 700				

KM# 416 50 RAND

15.5530 g., 0.9999 Gold 0.5000 oz. AGW, 27 mm.
Series: Natura **Obv:** Male and female lion's heads
Obv. Designer: A. L. Sutherland **Rev:** Female and male lions playing **Rev. Designer:** Aldrid Minnie **Edge:** Reeded

Date	Mintage	F	VF	XF	Unc	BU
2003 Proof	2,600	Value: 700				

KM# 420 50 RAND

15.5530 g., 0.9999 Gold 0.5000 oz. AGW, 27 mm.
Series: Natura **Obv:** Caracal's head and shoulders **Rev:** Caracal eating prey **Edge:** Reeded **Designer:** Aldrid Minnie

Date	Mintage	F	VF	XF	Unc	BU
2004 Proof	1,327	Value: 750				

KM# 424 50 RAND

15.5530 g., 0.9999 Gold 0.5000 oz. AGW, 27 mm.
Series: Natura **Obv:** Hippopotamus 1/2 way in water
Obv. Designer: Aldrid Minnie **Rev:** Hippopotamus submergered in water with head raised above, mouth wide open
Rev. Designer: M. J. Scheepers **Edge:** Reeded

Date	Mintage	F	VF	XF	Unc	BU
2005 Proof	—	Value: 650				

KM# 428 50 RAND

15.5530 g., 0.9999 Gold 0.5000 oz. AGW, 27 mm.
Series: Natura **Obv:** Giraffe's head and neck
Obv. Designer: M. J. Scheepers **Rev:** Giraffe family walking left
Rev. Designer: Aldrid Minnie **Edge:** Reeded

Date	Mintage	F	VF	XF	Unc	BU
2006 Proof	—	Value: 650				

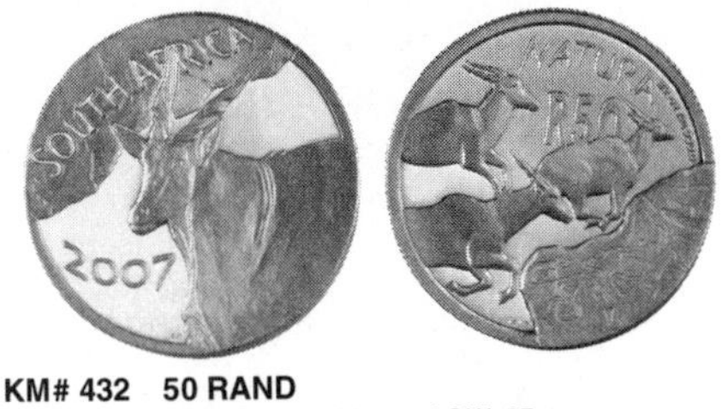

KM# 432 50 RAND

15.5530 g., 0.9999 Gold 0.5000 oz. AGW, 27 mm.
Series: Natura **Obv:** Forepart of eland left **Obv. Designer:** Aldrid Minnie **Rev:** Three eland running right **Rev. Designer:** M. J. Scheepers **Edge:** Reeded

Date	Mintage	F	VF	XF	Unc	BU
2007 Proof	—	Value: 700				

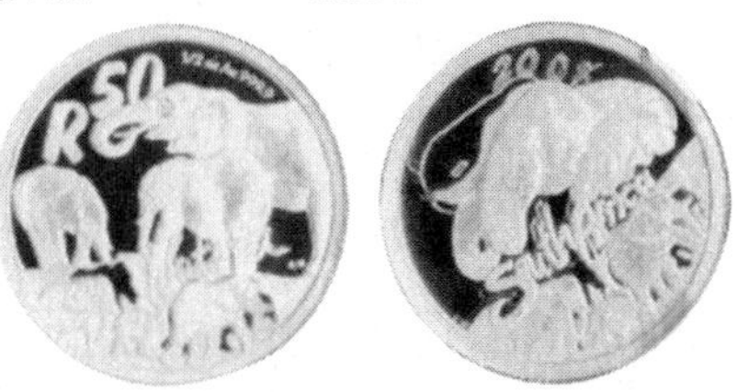

KM# 449 50 RAND

15.5530 g., 0.9990 Gold 0.4995 oz. AGW, 27 mm. **Obv:** Large elephant and elephant family below **Obv. Designer:** C. Moses and N. van Niekerk **Rev:** Three elephants, one trumpeting, three elephants below **Rev. Designer:** A. Minnie and N. van Niekerk

Date	Mintage	F	VF	XF	Unc	BU
2008 Proof	4,800	Value: 700				

KM# 473 50 RAND

15.5500 g., 0.9990 Gold 0.4994 oz. AGW, 27 mm. **Obv:** White rhino silouette and forpart **Obv. Designer:** N. van Niekerk and M. J. Scheepers **Rev:** Two rhinos facing off within large silouette **Rev. Designer:** N. van Niekerk and C. Moses

Date	Mintage	F	VF	XF	Unc	BU
2009 Proof	4,000	Value: 675				

KM# 413 100 RAND

31.1070 g., 0.9999 Gold 100000 oz. AGW, 32.69 mm.
Series: Natura **Obv:** Cheetah's head **Obv. Designer:** A. L. Sutherland **Rev:** Cheetah posing **Rev. Designer:** P. Botes **Edge:** Reeded

Date	Mintage	F	VF	XF	Unc	BU
2002 Proof	2,550	Value: 1,250				
2002 RSA logo Proof	496	Value: 1,600				

KM# 417 100 RAND

31.1070 g., 0.9999 Gold 100000 oz. AGW, 32.69 mm.
Series: Natura **Obv:** Male and female lion's heads
Obv. Designer: A. L. Sutherland **Rev:** Snarling male and female lion's heads **Rev. Designer:** P. Botes **Edge:** Reeded **Note:** L P RSA - LION PARK RSA.

Date	Mintage	F	VF	XF	Unc	BU
2003 Proof	2,758	Value: 1,250				
2003 L P RSA Proof	498	Value: 1,600				

KM# 421 100 RAND

31.1070 g., 0.9999 Gold 100000 oz. AGW, 32.69 mm.
Series: Natura **Obv:** Caracal's head and shoulders
Obv. Designer: Aldrid Minnie **Rev:** Caracal crouching on branch left **Rev. Designer:** M. J. Scheepers **Edge:** Reeded **Note:** C/C - CARACAL / CARACAL

Date	Mintage	F	VF	XF	Unc	BU
2004 Proof	1,405	Value: 1,250				
2004 C/C Proof	500	Value: 1,600				

KM# 425 100 RAND

31.1070 g., 0.9999 Gold 100000 oz. AGW, 32.69 mm.
Series: Natura **Obv:** Hippopotamus 1/2 way in water
Obv. Designer: Aldrid Minnie **Rev:** Two hippopotamus submered in water, heads raised, mouths open faced in combat **Rev. Designer:** M. J. Scheepers **Edge:** Reeded **Note:** MAPU - MAPUNGUBWE.

Date	Mintage	F	VF	XF	Unc	BU
2005 Proof	—	Value: 1,250				
2005 MAPU Proof	—	Value: 1,500				

KM# 429 100 RAND

31.1070 g., 0.9999 Gold 100000 oz. AGW, 32.69 mm. **Series:** Natura **Obv:** Giraffe's head and neck **Rev:** Giraffe's head an neck eating tree leaves **Edge:** Reeded **Designer:** M. J. Scheepers **Note:** lpp/EWT - lion's paw print / EWT.

Date	Mintage	F	VF	XF	Unc	BU
2006 Proof	—	Value: 1,250				
2006 lpp/EWT Proof	—	Value: 1,500				

KM# 433 100 RAND

31.1070 g., 0.9999 Gold 100000 oz. AGW, 32.7 mm.
Series: Natura **Obv:** Forepart of eland left **Obv. Designer:** Aldrid Minnie **Rev:** Eland grazing left **Rev. Designer:** C. Moses **Edge:** Reeded

Date	Mintage	F	VF	XF	Unc	BU
2007 Proof	—	Value: 1,250				
2007 Proof	—	Value: 1,500				

KM# 450 100 RAND

31.1070 g., 0.9990 Gold 0.9991 oz. AGW, 32.69 mm.
Obv: Large elephant head and elephant family below
Obv. Designer: C. Moses and N. van Niekerk **Rev:** Large elephant facing, three elephants below **Rev. Designer:** A. Minnie and N. van Niekerk

Date	Mintage	F	VF	XF	Unc	BU
2008 Proof	4,800	Value: 1,250				

KM# 474 100 RAND
31.1070 g., 0.9990 Gold 0.9991 oz. AGW **Obv:** White rhino silouette and forepart **Obv. Designer:** N. van Niekerk and M. J. Scheepers **Rev:** Rhino standing facing within large silouette **Rev. Designer:** N. van Niekerk and A. Minnie **Shape:** 32.7

Date	Mintage	F	VF	XF	Unc	BU
2009 Proof	4,000	Value: 1,250				

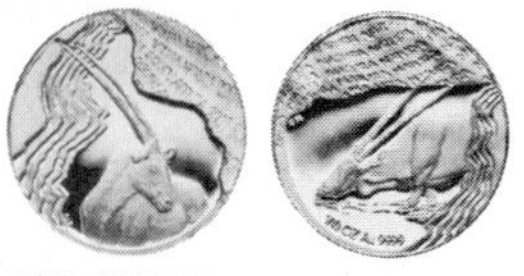

KM# 264 1/10 OUNCE
3.1107 g., 0.9999 Gold 0.1000 oz. AGW, 16.5 mm.
Series: Natura **Obv:** Gemsbok's upper body **Obv. Designer:** A. L. Sutherland **Rev:** Gemsbok drinking **Rev. Designer:** C. Moses **Edge:** Reeded

Date	Mintage	F	VF	XF	Unc	BU
2001 Proof	3,498	Value: 145				

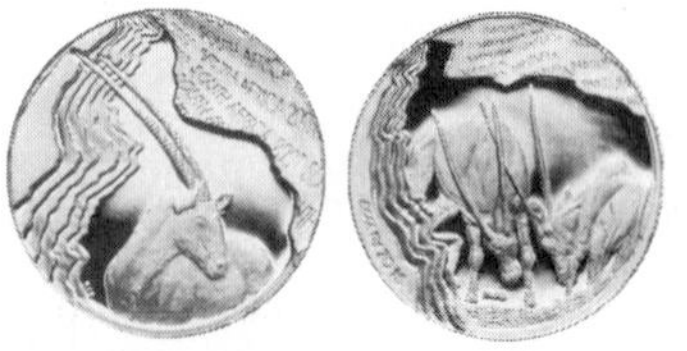

KM# 265 1/4 OUNCE
7.7770 g., 0.9999 Gold 0.2500 oz. AGW, 22 mm. **Series:** Natura **Obv:** Gemsbok's upper body **Obv. Designer:** A. L. Sutherland **Rev:** Two Gemsbok bulls facing off **Rev. Designer:** M. J. Scheepers **Edge:** Reeded

Date	Mintage	F	VF	XF	Unc	BU
2001 Proof	2,904	Value: 320				

KM# 266 1/2 OUNCE
15.5530 g., 0.9999 Gold 0.5000 oz. AGW, 27 mm.
Series: Natura **Obv:** Gemsbok's upper body **Obv. Designer:** A. L. Sutherland **Rev:** Gemsbok family grazing **Rev. Designer:** P. Botes **Edge:** Reeded

Date	Mintage	F	VF	XF	Unc	BU
2001 Proof	2,754	Value: 650				

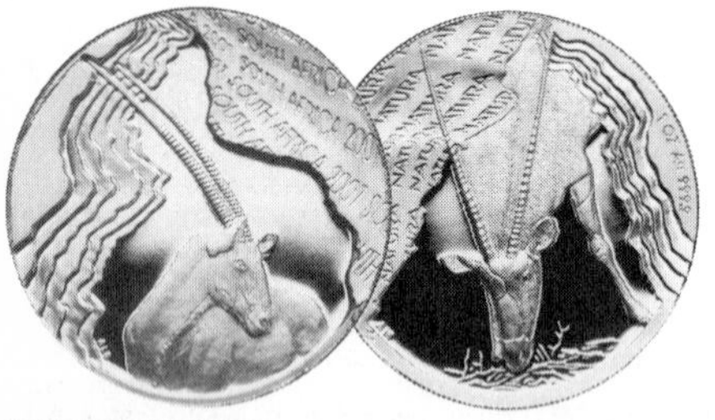

KM# 267 OUNCE
31.1070 g., 0.9999 Gold 100000 oz. AGW, 32.69 mm.
Series: Natura **Obv:** Gemsbok's upper body **Obv. Designer:** A. L. Sutherland **Rev:** Gemsbok grazing **Rev. Designer:** Aldrid Minnie **Edge:** Reeded **Note:** ghCW - Gemsbok's head CW

Date	Mintage	F	VF	XF	Unc	BU
2001 Proof	3,104	Value: 1,250				
2001 Proof	491	Value: 1,600				

GOLD BULLION CULTURE COINAGE

KM# 247 RAND
3.1103 g., 0.9999 Gold 0.1000 oz. AGW, 16.5 mm.
Series: Cultural **Obv:** New national arms **Obv. Legend:** UMZANTSI AFRIKA - SOUTH AFRICA **Obv. Designer:** A.L. Sutherland **Rev:** Seated Sotho figure with headdress **Rev. Designer:** Johan Steyn **Edge:** Reeded

Date	Mintage	F	VF	XF	Unc	BU
2001 Proof	236	Value: 275				

KM# 378 RAND
3.1103 g., 0.9999 Gold 0.1000 oz. AGW, 16.5 mm.
Series: Cultural **Obv:** New national arms **Obv. Legend:** UMZANTSI AFRIKA - SOUTH AFRICA **Obv. Designer:** A. L. Sutherland **Rev:** Three Xhosa tribe members **Rev. Designer:** P. Botes **Edge:** Reeded

Date	Mintage	F	VF	XF	Unc	BU
2001 Proof	—	Value: 675				

KM# 379 RAND
3.1103 g., 0.9999 Gold 0.1000 oz. AGW, 16.5 mm.
Series: Cultural **Subject:** Tswana Nation **Obv:** New national arms **Obv. Legend:** Aforika Borwa - South Africa **Obv. Designer:** A. L. Sutherland **Rev:** Four tribe people standing **Rev. Designer:** C. Moses **Edge:** Reeded

Date	Mintage	F	VF	XF	Unc	BU
2002 Proof	300	Value: 350				

KM# 380 RAND
3.1103 g., 0.9999 Gold 0.1000 oz. AGW, 16.5 mm.
Series: Cultural **Obv:** New national arms **Obv. Legend:** Afrika-Dzonga - South Africa **Obv. Designer:** A. L. Sutherland **Rev:** Tsonga tribe dancer and drummer **Rev. Designer:** A. Minnie **Edge:** Reeded

Date	Mintage	F	VF	XF	Unc	BU
2003 Proof	348	Value: 350				

KM# 381 RAND
3.1103 g., 0.9999 Gold 0.1000 oz. AGW, 16.5 mm.
Series: Cultural **Obv:** New national arms **Obv. Legend:** Afurika Tshipembe - South Africa **Obv. Designer:** A. L. Sutherland **Rev:** Six Venda tribe members crossing bridge **Rev. Designer:** M. J. Scheepers **Edge:** Reeded

Date	Mintage	F	VF	XF	Unc	BU
2004 Proof	380	Value: 350				

KM# 382 RAND
3.1103 g., 0.9999 Gold 0.1000 oz. AGW, 16.5 mm.
Series: Cultural **Obv:** New national arms **Obv. Legend:** iSewula Afrika - South Africa **Obv. Designer:** A. L. Sutherland **Rev:** Ndebele woman standing, native print in background **Rev. Designer:** A. Minnie **Edge:** Reeded

Date	Mintage	F	VF	XF	Unc	BU
2005 Proof	—	Value: 200				

KM# 383 RAND
3.1103 g., 0.9999 Gold 0.1000 oz. AGW, 16.5 mm.
Series: Cultural **Obv:** New national arms **Obv. Legend:** Ningizimu Afrika - South Africa **Obv. Designer:** A. L. Sutherland **Rev:** 1/2 length figure of Ema-Swati Chief left at right **Rev. Designer:** A. Minnie **Edge:** Reeded

Date	Mintage	F	VF	XF	Unc	BU
2006 Proof	1,000	Value: 200				

KM# 385 RAND
3.1103 g., 0.9999 Gold 0.1000 oz. AGW, 16.5 mm. **Subject:** 2010 FIFA World Cup Soccer - South Africa **Obv:** New national arms **Obv. Legend:** SOUTH AFRICA **Obv. Designer:** A. L. Sutherland **Rev:** Bird head at left facing animal at right, soccer ball at bottom **Rev. Designer:** A. Minnie **Edge:** Reeded

Date	Mintage	F	VF	XF	Unc	BU
2007 Proof	—	Value: 200				

KM# 384 RAND
3.1103 g., 0.9999 Gold 0.1000 oz. AGW, 16.5 mm. **Subject:** The Afrikaner Nation **Obv:** New national arms **Obv. Legend:** SOUTH AFRIKA **Obv. Designer:** A. L. Sutherland **Rev:** Ox drawn wagon up hillside **Rev. Designer:** A. Minnie **Edge:** Reeded

Date	Mintage	F	VF	XF	Unc	BU
2007 Proof	—	Value: 200				

KM# 454 RAND
3.1100 g., 0.9990 Gold 0.0999 oz. AGW, 16.5 mm. **Obv:** Arms **Obv. Designer:** A. J. Sutherland

Date	Mintage	F	VF	XF	Unc	BU
2008 Proof	1,000	Value: 125				

KM# 478 RAND
3.1100 g., 0.9990 Gold 0.0999 oz. AGW, 16.5 mm.
Subject: Northern Sotho (Bapedi) peoples **Obv:** Arms **Obv. Designer:** A. L. Sutherland **Rev:** Woman seated, cooking **Rev. Designer:** C. Moses and M. J. Scheepers

Date	Mintage	F	VF	XF	Unc	BU
2009 Proof	1,000	Value: 125				

KM# 249 2 RAND
7.7770 g., 0.9999 Gold 0.2500 oz. AGW, 22 mm. **Obv:** New national arms **Obv. Designer:** A.L. Sutherland **Rev:** Gondwana theoretical landmass and dinosaur **Rev. Designer:** M. J. Scheepers **Edge:** Reeded

Date	Mintage	F	VF	XF	Unc	BU
2001 Proof	558	Value: 400				

KM# 386 2 RAND
7.7770 g., 0.9999 Gold 0.2500 oz. AGW, 22 mm. **Series:** World Heritage Site **Subject:** Robben Island **Obv:** New national arms **Obv. Designer:** A. L. Sutherland **Rev:** Carved stone, island in background **Rev. Designer:** M. J. Scheepers **Edge:** Reeded

Date	Mintage	F	VF	XF	Unc	BU
2002 Proof	999	Value: 800				

KM# 387 2 RAND
7.7770 g., 0.9999 Gold 0.2500 oz. AGW, 22 mm. **Series:** World heritage Site **Subject:** Greater St. Lucia Wetland Park **Obv:** New national arms **Obv. Designer:** A. L. Sutherland **Rev:** Various birds **Rev. Designer:** M. J. Scheepers **Edge:** Reeded

Date	Mintage	F	VF	XF	Unc	BU
2003 Proof	637	Value: 400				

KM# 388 2 RAND
7.7770 g., 0.9999 Gold 0.2500 oz. AGW, 22 mm. **Series:** World Heritage Park **Subject:** "Ukhahlamba" Drakensberg Park **Obv:** New national arms **Obv. Designer:** A. L. Sutherland **Rev:** Early painting of animal and hunters **Rev. Designer:** M. J. Scheepers **Edge:** Reeded

Date	Mintage	F	VF	XF	Unc	BU
2004 Proof	750	Value: 375				

KM# 390 2 RAND
7.7770 g., 0.9999 Gold 0.2500 oz. AGW, 22 mm. **Subject:** 2006 FIFA World Cup Soccer - Germany **Obv:** New national arms **Obv. Designer:** A. L. Sutherland **Rev:** Soccer ball at center above partial globe within ornate border art **Rev. Designer:** M. J. Scheepers **Edge:** Reeded

Date	Mintage	F	VF	XF	Unc	BU
2005 Proof	—	Value: 375				

KM# 391 2 RAND
7.7770 g., 0.9999 Gold 0.2500 oz. AGW, 22 mm. **Series:** World Heritage Site **Subject:** Cradle of Mankind **Obv:** New national arms **Obv. Designer:** A. L. Sutherland **Rev:** Early man standing at upper left, ape's head at upper right, skull at lower left, value at lower right **Rev. Designer:** M. J. Scheepers **Edge:** Reeded

Date	Mintage	F	VF	XF	Unc	BU
2006 Proof	—	Value: 375				

KM# 392 2 RAND
7.7770 g., 0.9999 Gold 0.2500 oz. AGW, 22 mm. **Subject:** 2006 FIFA World Cup Soccer - Germany **Obv:** New national arms **Obv. Designer:** A. L. Sutherland **Rev:** Logo in ornate frame **Rev. Designer:** M. J. Scheepers **Edge:** Reeded

Date	Mintage	F	VF	XF	Unc	BU
2006 Proof	—	Value: 375				

KM# 393 2 RAND
7.7770 g., 0.9999 Gold 0.2500 oz. AGW, 22 mm. **Series:** World Heritage Site **Subject:** Cape Floral **Obv:** New national arms **Obv. Designer:** A. L. Sutherland **Rev:** Bird perched on branch at left, plant at center, land in distance **Rev. Designer:** M. J. Scheepers **Edge:** Reeded

Date	Mintage	F	VF	XF	Unc	BU
2007 Proof	—	Value: 375				

KM# 394 2 RAND
7.7770 g., 0.9999 Gold 0.2500 oz. AGW, 22 mm. **Subject:** 2010 FIFA World Cup Soccer - South Africa **Obv:** New national arms **Obv. Designer:** A. L. Sutherland **Rev:** Animal in ornate frame at left and right, small soccer ball at bottom below value **Rev. Designer:** M. J. Scheepers **Edge:** Reeded

Date	Mintage	F	VF	XF	Unc	BU
2007 Proof	—	Value: 375				

KM# 479 2 RAND
7.7700 g., 0.9990 Gold 0.2496 oz. AGW, 22 mm.
Subject: Richtersveld Cultural and Botonical Landscape **Obv:** Arms **Obv. Designer:** A. L. Sutherland **Rev:** Native "haru on" hut adn aloe pilansil tree **Rev. Designer:** J. Lloyd

Date	Mintage	F	VF	XF	Unc	BU
2009 Proof	2,000	Value: 325				

GOLD BULLION PROTEA COINAGE

KM# 395 5 RAND

3.1107 g., 0.9999 Gold 0.1000 oz. AGW, 16.5 mm.
Subject: 10th Anniversary Soccer "Bafana Bafana" **Obv:** Protea flower **Obv. Designer:** A. L. Sutherland **Rev:** Two players running right **Rev. Designer:** P. Botes **Edge:** Reeded

Date	Mintage	F	VF	XF	Unc	BU
2002 Proof	386	Value: 240				

KM# 397 5 RAND

3.1107 g., 0.9999 Gold 0.1000 oz. AGW, 16.5 mm.
Subject: World Summit on Sustainable Development
Obv: Protea flower **Obv. Designer:** A. L. Sutherland **Rev:** Globe featuring Africa **Rev. Inscription:** prosperity **Rev. Designer:** M. J. Scheepers **Edge:** Reeded

Date	Mintage	F	VF	XF	Unc	BU
2002 Proof	511	Value: 185				

KM# 278 5 RAND

3.1104 g., 0.9999 Gold 0.1000 oz. AGW, 16.5 mm. **Obv:** Protea flower **Rev:** Soccer player heading the ball **Edge:** Reeded

Date	Mintage	F	VF	XF	Unc	BU
2002 Proof	—	Value: 150				

KM# 399 5 RAND

3.1107 g., 0.9999 Gold 0.1000 oz. AGW, 16.5 mm.
Subject: Cricket World Cup **Obv:** Protea flower **Obv. Designer:** A. L. Sutherland **Rev:** Cricket ball striking stumps **Rev. Inscription:** Protea **Rev. Designer:** C. Moses **Edge:** Reeded

Date	Mintage	F	VF	XF	Unc	BU
2003 Proof	925	Value: 145				

KM# 289 5 RAND

3.1100 g., 0.9999 Gold 0.1000 oz. AGW, 16.5 mm.
Subject: 10th Anniversary of South African Democracy
Obv: Protea flower **Rev:** Inscription covered flag **Edge:** Reeded

Date	Mintage	F	VF	XF	Unc	BU
2004 Proof	1,000	Value: 150				

KM# 401 5 RAND

3.1107 g., 0.9999 Gold 0.1000 oz. AGW, 16.5 mm.
Subject: 10th Anniversay Democracy **Obv:** Protea flower
Obv. Designer: A. L. Sutherland **Rev:** Flag made of constitution **Rev. Designer:** M. J. Scheepers **Edge:** Reeded **Note:** 10YF - circular 10 YEARS FREEDOM

Date	Mintage	F	VF	XF	Unc	BU
2004 Proof	2,089	Value: 375				
2004 10YF Proof	492	Value: 600				

KM# 403 5 RAND

3.1107 g., 0.9999 Gold 0.1000 oz. AGW, 16.5 mm.
Subject: Nobel Prize Winners **Obv:** Protea flower
Obv. Designer: A. L. Sutherland **Rev:** Freedom Charter, Luthuli seated left at desk at lower right **Rev. Designer:** M. J. Scheepers **Edge:** Reeded **Note:** FR - FREEDOM

Date	Mintage	F	VF	XF	Unc	BU
2005 Proof	—	Value: 135				
2005 FR Proof	—	Value: 500				

KM# 405 5 RAND

3.1107 g., 0.9999 Gold 0.1000 oz. AGW, 16.5 mm.
Subject: Nobel Prize Winners **Obv:** Protea flower
Obv. Designer: A. L. Sutherland **Rev:** Cross, inscription
Rev. Designer: M. J. Scheepers **Edge:** Reeded

Date	Mintage	F	VF	XF	Unc	BU
2006 Proof	—	Value: 135				
2006 logo Proof	—	Value: 400				

KM# 407 5 RAND

3.1107 g., 0.9999 Gold 0.1000 oz. AGW, 16.5 mm. **Subject:** Nobel Prize winners **Obv:** Protea flower **Obv. Designer:** A. L. Sutherland **Rev:** Extract from de Klerk's acceptance speech **Rev. Designer:** M. J. Scheepers **Edge:** Reeded

Date	Mintage	F	VF	XF	Unc	BU
2007 Proof	—	Value: 150				
2007 dove Proof	—	Value: 400				

KM# 408 5 RAND

3.1107 g., 0.9999 Gold 0.1000 oz. AGW, 16.5 mm. **Subject:** Nobel Prize Winners **Obv:** Protea flower **Obv. Designer:** A. L. Sutherland **Rev:** Extract from Mandela's acceptance speech **Rev. Designer:** M. J. Scheepers **Edge:** Reeded

Date	Mintage	F	VF	XF	Unc	BU
2007 Proof	—	Value: 150				
2007 dove Proof	—	Value: 400				

KM# 452 5 RAND

3.1100 g., 0.9990 Gold 0.0999 oz. AGW, 16.5 mm. **Obv:** Protea flower **Obv. Designer:** A. J. Sutherland **Rev:** Ghandi figure at prayer **Rev. Designer:** C. Moses and N. van Niekerk

Date	Mintage	F	VF	XF	Unc	BU
2008 Proof	8,000	Value: 150				

KM# 476 5 RAND

3.1100 g., 0.9990 Gold 0.0999 oz. AGW, 16.5 mm. **Obv:** Protea flower **Obv. Designer:** A. L. Sutherland **Rev:** Portraits of C. J. Langenhoven and M. L. de Villiers with musical score **Rev. Designer:** A. Minnie and M. J. Scheepers

Date	Mintage	F	VF	XF	Unc	BU
2009 Proof	8,000	Value: 135				

KM# 396 25 RAND

31.1070 g., 0.9999 Gold 100000 oz. AGW, 32.69 mm.
Subject: 10th Anniversary Soccer "Bafana Bafana" **Obv:** Protea flower **Obv. Designer:** A. L. Sutherland **Rev:** Two players running left **Rev. Designer:** Aldrid Minnie **Edge:** Reeded

Date	Mintage	F	VF	XF	Unc	BU
2002 Proof	137	Value: 1,275				
2002 flag/CW Proof	84	Value: 2,250				

KM# 398 25 RAND

31.1070 g., 0.9999 Gold 100000 oz. AGW, 32.69 mm.
Subject: World Summit on Sustainable Development
Obv: Protea flower **Obv. Designer:** A. L. Sutherland **Rev:** Globe featuring Africa **Rev. Designer:** M. J. Scheepers **Edge:** Reeded

Date	Mintage	F	VF	XF	Unc	BU
2002 Proof	421	Value: 1,250				

KM# 279 25 RAND

31.1035 g., 0.9999 Gold 0.9999 oz. AGW, 32.7 mm.
Obv: Protea flower **Rev:** Soccer player kicking ball
Edge: Reeded

Date	Mintage	F	VF	XF	Unc	BU
2002 Proof	—	Value: 1,275				

KM# 400 25 RAND

31.1070 g., 0.9999 Gold 100000 oz. AGW, 32.69 mm.
Subject: Cricket World Cup **Obv:** Protea flower **Obv. Designer:** A. L. Sutherland **Rev:** Batsman on one knee about to sweep the ball **Rev. Legend:** PROTEA **Rev. Designer:** P. Botes
Edge: Reeded

Date	Mintage	F	VF	XF	Unc	BU
2003 Proof	210	Value: 1,350				
2003 ball/RSA Proof	208	Value: 1,500				

KM# 290 25 RAND

31.1035 g., 0.9999 Gold 0.9999 oz. AGW, 32.7 mm.
Subject: 10th Anniversary of South African Democracy
Obv: Protea flower **Rev:** Two images of Nelson Mandela
Edge: Reeded

Date	Mintage	F	VF	XF	Unc	BU
2004 Proof	5,000	Value: 1,250				

KM# 402 25 RAND

31.1070 g., 0.9999 Gold 100000 oz. AGW, 32.69 mm.
Subject: 10th Anniversary Democracy **Obv:** Protea flower
Obv. Designer: A. L. Sutherland **Rev:** Two heads of Mandela, one left, one facing, Union building in background **Rev. Designer:** Natanya van Nirkirk **Edge:** Reeded **Note:** 10FP - 10/flag, people

Date	Mintage	F	VF	XF	Unc	BU
2004 Proof	6,000	Value: 3,000				
2004 10FP Proof	492	Value: 5,400				

KM# 404 25 RAND

31.1070 g., 0.9999 Gold 100000 oz. AGW, 32.69 mm.
Subject: Nobel Prize Winners **Obv:** Protea flower **Obv. Designer:** A. L. Sutherland **Rev:** Bust of Chief Albert Luthuli facing **Rev. Designer:** Natanya van Niekirk **Edge:** Reeded **Note:** FC - FREEDOM / CHARTER / 26 JUNE 1955

Date	Mintage	F	VF	XF	Unc	BU
2005 Proof	—	Value: 1,250				
2005 FC Proof	—	Value: 3,750				

KM# 406 25 RAND

31.1070 g., 0.9999 Gold 100000 oz. AGW, 32.69 mm.
Subject: Nobel Prize Winners **Obv:** Protea flower
Obv. Designer: A. L. Sutherland **Rev:** Cross, bust of Archbishop Desmond Tutu right **Rev. Designer:** Natanya van Niekirk
Edge: Reeded

Date	Mintage	F	VF	XF	Unc	BU
2006 Proof	—	Value: 1,250				
2006 logo Proof	—	Value: 2,600				

KM# 409 25 RAND

31.1070 g., 0.9999 Gold 100000 oz. AGW, 32.69 mm. **Subject:** Nobel Prize Winners **Obv:** Protea flower **Obv. Designer:** A. L. Sutherland **Rev:** Busts of Mandela, de Klerk right **Rev. Designer:** Natanya van Niekirk **Edge:** Reeded **Note:** d-P - dove Peace

Date	Mintage	F	VF	XF	Unc	BU
2007 Proof	—	Value: 1,450				
2007 d-P Proof	—	—	—	—	—	—

KM# 453 25 RAND

31.1070 g., 0.9990 Gold 0.9991 oz. AGW, 32.7 mm.
Obv: Protea flower **Obv. Designer:** A. J. Sutherland **Rev:** Ghandi profile at right **Rev. Designer:** N. van Niekerk

Date	Mintage	F	VF	XF	Unc	BU
2008 Proof	12,000	Value: 1,250				

KM# 477 25 RAND

31.1070 g., 0.9990 Gold 0.9991 oz. AGW, 32.7 mm.
Obv: Protea flower **Obv. Designer:** A. L. Sutherland
Rev: Portraits of C. J. Langenhoven and M. L. de Villiers and musical score **Rev. Designer:** A. Minnie and M. J. Scheepers

Date	Mintage	F	VF	XF	Unc	BU
2009 Proof	11,000	Value: 1,200				

KM# 262 1/10 PROTEA

3.1107 g., 0.9999 Gold 0.1000 oz. AGW, 16.5 mm.
Subject: Tourism **Obv:** Protea flower **Obv. Designer:** A. L. Sutherland **Rev:** Lion's head facing, partial shield **Rev. Inscription:** PROTEA **Rev. Designer:** P. Botes **Edge:** Reeded

Date	Mintage	F	VF	XF	Unc	BU
2001 Proof	1,076	Value: 145				

KM# 263 PROTEA

31.1070 g., 0.9999 Gold 100000 oz. AGW, 32.6 mm.
Subject: Tourism **Obv:** Protea flower **Obv. Designer:** A. L. Sutherland **Rev:** Child on sandy beach, Table Mountain in background, partial star at right **Rev. Inscription:** PROTEA
Rev. Designer: Aldrid Minnie **Edge:** Reeded

Date	Mintage	F	VF	XF	Unc	BU
2001 Proof	972	Value: 1,250				
2001 GRC(pp) Proof	196	Value: 1,600				

MINT SETS

KM#	Date	Mintage	Identification	Issue Price	Mkt Val
MS52	2006 (7)	—	KM#291-297	—	22.50
MS53	2006 (7)	—	KM#291-297, circulated coins	—	10.00
MS54	2006 (7)	—	KM#291-297, Baby	—	15.00
MS55	2006 (7)	—	KM#291-297, Wedding	—	15.00
MS1	1967 (7)	50,000	KM#65.1-70.1, 72.1	7.50	10.00
MS2	1967 (7)	50,000	KM#65.2-70.2, 72.2	7.50	10.00
MS3	1968 (7)	50,000	KM#71.1, 74.1-79.1	7.50	12.00
MS4	1968 (7)	50,000	KM#71.2, 74.2-79.2	7.50	12.00
MS5	1969 (7)	7,500	KM#65.1-70.1, 80.1	7.50	50.00
MS6	1969 (7)	7,500	KM#65.2-70.2, 80.2	7.50	50.00
MS7	1970 (8)	16,000	KM#81-88	7.50	12.00
MS8	1971 (8)	20,000	KM#81-88	7.50	8.00
MS9	1972 (8)	20,000	KM#81-88	7.50	8.00
MS10	1973 (8)	20,000	KM#81-88	7.50	8.00
MS11	1974 (8)	20,000	KM#81-87, 89	7.50	17.50
MS12	1975 (8)	20,000	KM#81-88	7.50	8.00
MS13	1976 (8)	20,000	KM#88, 90-96	5.65	8.00
MS14	1977 (8)	20,000	KM#81-87, 88a	—	8.00
MS15	1978 (8)	20,000	KM#81-87, 88a	—	8.00
MS16	1979 (8)	20,000	KM#97-104	—	25.00
MS17	1980 (7)	20,000	KM#82-87, 88a	—	8.00
MS18	1981 (7)	10,000	KM#82-87, 88a	—	10.00
MS19	1982 (7)	10,000	KM#109-115	—	25.00
MS20	1983 (7)	23,000	KM#82-87, 88a	—	8.00
MS21	1984 (7)	13,875	KM#82-87, 88a	—	10.00
MS22	1985 (7)	10,200	KM#82-87, 117	—	17.50
MS23	1986 (7)	9,100	KM#82-87, 88a	—	12.00

KM#	Date	Mintage	Identification	Issue Price	Mkt Val
MS24	1987 (7)	7,642	KM#82-87, 88a	—	12.00
MS25	1988 (7)	6,250	KM#82-87, 88a	—	25.00
MS26	1989 (7)	13,000	KM#82-87, 88a	—	15.00
MS27	1990 (8)	12,000	KM#132-137, 139, 148	—	30.00
MS28	1991 (8)	15,000	KM#132-139	—	30.00
MSA29	1992 (8)	15,000	KM#132-139	—	30.00
MS29	1993 (8)	11,000	KM#132-139	—	30.00
MS30	1994 (9)	6,786	KM#132-140	—	35.00
MS31	1995 (9)	8,477	KM#132-140 Plastic holder	—	35.00
MS32	1995 (9)	—	KM#132-140 Cardboard holder	—	30.00
MS33	1996 (9)	12,000	KM#158-166	12.50	15.00
MS34	1997 (9)	7,515	KM#159-166, 170	—	30.00
MS35	1998 (9)	—	KM#159-166, 170	—	30.00
MS36	1999 (9)	10,000	KM#159-166, 170	19.50	30.00
MS37	2000 (9)	—	KM#159-166, 170	—	30.00
MS39	2001 (9)	5,577	KM#221-229	—	60.00
MS38	2002 (7)	—	KM#268-274 plus 1- and 2- cent medals	30.00	32.50
MS40	2002 (7)	3,886	KM#268-274	—	52.50
MS41	2002 (7)	1,640	KM#268-274, circulated coins	—	10.00
MS42	2003 (7)	2,602	KM#324, 327, 330, 332, 335, 337, 347	—	45.00
MS43	2003 (7)	1,380	KM#324, 327, 330, 332, 335, 337, 347, circulted coins	—	10.00
MS44	2004 (7)	1,948	KM#281, 325, 326, 328, 331, 333, 336	—	37.50
MS45	2004 (7)	1,131	KM#281, 325, 325, 328, 331, 333, 336, circulated coins	—	10.00
MS46	2004 (7)	325	KM#281, 325, 326, 328, 331, 333, 336, Baby	—	22.50
MS47	2004 (7)	23	KM#281, 325, 326, 328, 331, 333, 336, Wedding	—	22.50
MS48	2005 (7)	—	KM#291-297	—	30.00
MS49	2005 (7)	—	KM#291-297, circulated coins	—	10.00
MS50	2005 (7)	—	KM#291-297, Baby	—	23.00
MS51	2005 (7)	—	KM#291-297, Wedding	—	22.50
MS56	2007 (7)	—	KM#340-346	—	22.50
MS57	2007 (7)	—	KM#340-346, circulated coins	—	10.00
MS58	2007 (7)	—	KM#340-346, baby	—	15.00
MS59	2007 (7)	—	KM#340-346, wedding	—	15.00

PIEFORT PROOF SETS (PPS)

KM#	Date	Mintage	Identification	Issue Price	Mkt Val
PS242	2007 (4)	—	KM#430-433, leatherette	—	1,950

PROOF SETS

KM#	Date	Mintage	Identification	Issue Price	Mkt Val
PS185	2006 (7)	—	KM#291-297	—	65.00
PS186	2006 (7)	—	KM#291-297, baby	—	65.00
PS187	2006 (7)	—	KM#291-297, wedding	—	65.00
PS1	1923 (10)	655	KM#12.1-17.1, 18, 19.1, 20-21	—	4,900
PS2	1923 (8)	747	KM#12.1-17.1, 18, 19.1	—	1,000
PS3	1926 (6)	3	KM#12.2, 14-2-17.2, 19.2	—	33,500
PS5	1930 (8)	—	KM#12.2 (dated 1928), 13.2-17.2, 18, 19.2	—	15,000
PS4	1930 (8)	14	KM#12.2-17.2, 18, 19.2	—	8,000
PS6	1931 (8)	62	KM#12.3-17.3, 19.3, 22	—	10,500
PS7	1932 (8)	12	KM#12.3-17.3, 19.3, 22	—	10,250
PS8	1933 (8)	20	KM#12.3-17.3, 19.3, 22	—	13,000
PS9	1934 (8)	24	KM#12.3-17.3, 19.3, 22	—	11,750
PS10	1935 (8)	20	KM#12.3-17.3, 19.3, 22	—	11,000
PS11	1936 (8)	40	KM#12.3-17.3, 19.3, 22	—	6,000
PS12	1937 (8)	116	KM#23-30	—	800
PS13	1938 (8)	44	KM#23-30	—	1,525
PS14	1939 (8)	30	KM#23-30	—	10,250
PS15	1943 (8)	104	KM#23-30	—	750
PS16	1944 (8)	150	KM#23-30	—	650
PS17	1945 (8)	150	KM#23-30	—	650
PS18	1946 (8)	150	KM#23-30	—	700
PS19	1947 (8)	2,600	KM#23-31	—	300
PS20	1948 (9)	1,120	KM#32.1, 33, 34.1-40.1	—	325
PS21	1949 (9)	800	KM#32.1, 33, 34.1-40.1	—	500
PS22	1950 (9)	500	KM#32.1, 33, 34.1-40.1	—	525
PS23	1951 (9)	2,000	KM#32.2, 33, 34.2-40.2	—	80.00
PS24	1952 (11)	12,000	KM#32.2, 33, 34.2-39.2, 41-43	—	400
PS25	1952 (9)	3,500	KM#32.2, 33, 34.2-39.2, 41	—	45.00
PS26	1953 (11)	3,000	KM#44-54	29.40	400
PS28	1953 (2)	1,000	KM#53-54	25.20	350
PS27	1953 (9)	2,000	KM#44-52	4.35	50.00
PS29	1954 (11)	875	KM#44-54	29.40	435
PS31	1954 (2)	350	KM#53-54	25.20	350
PS30	1954 (9)	2,275	KM#44-52	4.35	80.00
PS32	1955 (11)	600	KM#44-54	29.40	400
PS34	1955 (2)	300	KM#53-54	25.20	350
PS33	1955 (9)	2,250	KM#44-52	4.35	55.00
PS35	1956 (11)	350	KM#44-54	29.40	525
PS37	1956 (2)	158	KM#53-54	25.20	450
PS36	1956 (9)	1,350	KM#44-52	4.35	65.00
PS38	1957 (11)	380	KM#44-54	29.40	500
PS40	1957 (2)	180	KM#53-54	25.20	415
PS39	1957 (9)	750	KM#44-52	4.35	75.00
PS41	1958 (11)	360	KM#44-54	29.40	530

KM#	Date	Mintage	Identification	Issue Price	Mkt Val
PS43	1958 (2)	155	KM#53-54	25.20	435
PS42	1958 (9)	625	KM#44-52	4.35	95.00
PS44	1959 (11)	390	KM#44-54	29.40	600
PS45	1959 (9)	560	KM#44-52	4.35	225
PS46	1959 (2)	240	KM#53-54	25.20	400
PS47	1960 (11)	1,500	KM#44-51, 53-55	29.40	300
PS48	1960 (9)	1,860	KM#44-51, 55	4.35	20.00
PS49	1960 (2)	450	KM#53-54	25.20	275
PS50	1961 (9)	3,139	KM#56-64	—	200
PS51	1961 (7)	4,391	KM#56-62	—	20.00
PS52	1961 (2)	793	KM#63-64 BV + 20%	—	—
PS53	1962 (9)	1,544	KM#56-64	—	210
PS54	1962 (7)	2,300	KM#56-62	—	15.00
PS55	1962 (2)	800	KM#63-64 BV+20%	—	—
PS56	1963 (9)	1,500	KM#56-64	—	200
PS57	1963 (7)	2,525	KM#56-62	—	12.00
PS58	1963 (2)	1,008	KM#63-64 BV+20%	—	—
PS59	1964 (9)	3,000	KM#56-64	—	190
PS60	1964 (7)	13,000	KM#56-62	—	10.00
PS61	1964 (2)	1,000	KM#63-64 BV+20%	—	—
PS63	1965 (9)	85	KM#63-64, 65.1-66.2, 67.1, 68.2, 69.1, 70.2, 71.2 V.I.P.	—	1,200
PS62	1965 (9)	5,099	KM#63-64, 65.1, 66.2, 67.1, 68.2, 69.1, 70.2, 71.1	23.50	185
PS64	1965 (7)	19,889	KM#65.1, 66.2, 67.1, 68.2, 69.1, 70.2, 71.1	5.00	12.00
PS65	1965 (2)	925	KM#63-64 BV+20%	18.15	—
PS66	1966 (9)	10,000	KM#63-64, 65.2, 66.1, 67.2, 68.1, 69.2, 70.1, 71.2	24.10	185
PS67	1966 (7)	15,000	KM#65.2, 66.1, 67.2, 68.1, 69.2, 70.1, 71.2	5.00	8.00
PS68	1966 (2)	1,000	KM#63-64 BV+20%	18.15	—
PS69	1967 (9)	10,000	KM#63-64, 65.2, 66.1, 67.2, 68.1, 69.2, 70.1, 72.2	24.10	185
PS70	1967 (7)	15,000	KM#65.2, 66.1, 67.2, 68.1, 69.2, 70.1, 72.2	5.00	8.00
PS71	1967 (2)	1,000	KM#63-64 BV+20%	18.15	—
PS72	1968 (9)	10,000	KM#63-64, 71.1, 74.1, 75.2, 76.1, 77.2, 78.1, 79.2	35.00	185
PS73	1968 (7)	15,000	KM#71.1, 74.1, 75.2, 76.1, 77.2, 78.1, 79.2	16.00	8.00
PS74	1968 (2)	1,000	KM#63-64 BV+20%	28.00	—
PS75	1969 (9)	7,000	KM#63-64, 65.2, 66.1, 67.2, 68.1, 69.2, 70.1, 80.2	34.85	185
PS76	1969 (7)	5,000	KM#65.2, 66.1, 67.2, 68.1, 69.2, 70.1, 80.2	13.95	8.00
PS77	1969 (2)	1,000	KM#63-64 BV+20%	27.85	—
PS78	1970 (10)	6,000	KM#63-64, 81-88	35.05	185
PS79	1970 (8)	4,000	KM#81-88	14.00	9.00
PS80	1970 (2)	1,000	KM#63-64 BV+20%	28.05	—
PS81	1971 (10)	7,000	KM#63-64, 81-88	35.00	185
PS82	1971 (8)	5,000	KM#81-88	14.00	9.00
PS83	1971 (2)	650	KM#63-64 BV+20%	28.00	—
PS84	1972 (10)	6,000	KM#63-64, 81-88	32.80	185
PS85	1972 (8)	4,000	KM#81-88	13.10	9.00
PS86	1972 (2)	1,500	KM#63-64 BV+20%	26.25	—
PS87	1973 (10)	6,850	KM#63-64, 81-88	32.00	185
PS88	1973 (8)	4,000	KM#81-88	12.80	9.00
PS89	1973 (2)	6,088	KM#63-64 BV+20%	25.60	—
PS90	1974 (10)	11,000	KM#63-64, 81-87, 89	52.50	185
PS91	1974 (8)	4,000	KM#81-87, 89	15.00	9.00
PS92	1974 (2)	5,600	KM#63-64 BV+20%	45.00	—
PS93	1975 (10)	12,500	KM#63-64, 81-87, 88	116	185
PS94	1975 (8)	5,500	KM#81-88	14.55	9.00
PS95	1975 (2)	7,000	KM#63-64 BV+20%	102	—
PS96	1976 (10)	14,000	KM#63-64, 88, 90-96	92.00	185
PS97	1976 (8)	7,000	KM#88, 90-96	11.50	9.00
PS98	1976 (2)	8,000	KM#63-64 BV+20%	80.50	—
PS100	1977 (8)	7,000	KM#81-88	11.50	12.00
PS99	1977 (10)	12,000	KM#63-64, 81-88	92.00	185
PS101	1977 (2)	8,000	KM#63-64 BV+20%	80.50	—
PS102	1978 (10)	10,000	KM#63-64, 81-88	—	185
PS103	1978 (8)	7,000	KM#81-88	—	12.00
PS104	1978 (2)	9,000	KM#63-64 BV+20%	—	—
PS106	1979 (8)	5,000	KM#88, 97-103	—	22.00
PS105	1979 (10)	10,000	KM#63-64, 97-103, 104a	—	185
PS107	1979 (2)	10,000	KM#63-64 BV+20%	—	—
PS108	1980 (10)	10,000	KM#63-64, 81-88	—	185
PS109	1980 (8)	5,000	KM#81-88	—	22.00
PS110	1980 (2)	8,000	kM#63-64 BV+20%	—	—
PS111	1980 (2)	8,000	KM#63-64	—	—
PS112	1980 (3)	60	KM#105-107	—	9,000
PS113	1981 (10)	6,000	KM#63-64, 81-88	—	185
PS114	1981 (8)	4,900	KM#81-88	—	22.00
PS115	1981 (2)	6,238	KM#63-64 BV+20%	—	—
PS116	1982 (10)	7,100	KM#63-64, 108-115	—	190
PS117	1982 (8)	4,900	KM#88, 108-114	—	22.00
PS118	1982 (2)	6,930	KM#63-64 BV+20%	—	—
PS119	1983 (10)	7,300	KM#63-64, 81-88	—	185
PS120	1983 (8)	6,835	KM#81-88	—	22.00
PS121	1983 (2)	7,300	KM#63-64 BV+20%	—	—
PS122	1984 (8)	11,250	KM#82-88, 88a	—	15.00
PS123	1985 (8)	9,859	KM#82-87, 116, 117	—	25.00
PS125	1986 (2)	428	KM#73, 121 Plus large gold plated Silver #1	—	1,400
PS126	1986 (2)	750	KM#121, 131	—	700
PS127	1986 (3)	500	KM#119, 121, 131	—	725
PS124	1986 (8)	7,000	KM#82-87, 88a, 119	—	25.00

KM#	Date	Mintage	Identification	Issue Price	Mkt Val
PS129	1987 (4)	750	KM#73, 105-107	—	1,050
PS130	1987 GRC (4)	1,121	KM#73, 105-107	—	2,900
PS128	1987 (8)	6,781	KM#82-88, 88a	—	25.00
PS132	1988 (4)	806	KM#73, 105-107	—	1,050
PS133	1988 GRC (4)	835	KM#73, 105-107	—	2,900
PS135	1988 (3)	600	KM#124, 127, 130	—	2,750
PS131	1988 (8)	7,250	KM#82-88, 88a	—	50.00
PS134	1988 (3)	3,388	KM#122, 125, 128	—	70.00
PS136	1989 (8)	9,571	KM#82-88, 88a	—	50.00
PS137	1989 (4)	—	KM#73, 105-107	—	1,050
PS138	1989 GRC (4)	318	KM#73, 105-107	—	5,500
PS139	1990 (8)	10,000	KM#132-137, 139, 148	—	70.00
PS140	1990 (4)	—	KM#73, 105-107	—	1,050
PS141	1990 GRC (4)	1,066	KM#73, 105-107	—	2,775
PS142	1991 (8)	12,000	KM#132-139	—	70.00
PSA14 3	1991 GRC (4)	426	KM#73, 105-107	—	2,775
PS143	1992 (8)	10,000	KM#132-139	—	50.00
PS144	1993 (8)	—	KM#132-139	—	50.00
PS146	1994 (4)	166	KM#189-192 Wood case	—	1,200
PS147	1994 (4)	1,750	KM#189-192 Velvet case	—	1,175
PS148	1994 (3)	420	KM#167, 187-188	—	750
PS145	1994 (9)	5,804	KM#132-140	—	60.00
PS152	1995 (4)	89	KM#195-198 Wood case	—	1,200
PS153	1995 (4)	926	KM#195-198 Velvet case	—	1,175
PS154	1995 (3)	210	KM#152, 193-194	—	755
PS150	1995 (4)	750	KM#73, 105-107	—	1,400
PS151	1995	—	KM#73, 105-107 Wooden box	—	1,425
PS149	1995 (9)	5,816	KM#132-140	—	65.00
PS156	1996 (4)	368	KM#201-204, Wood case	—	1,200
PS157	1996 (4)	1,677	KM#201-204 Velvet case	—	1,175
PS158	1996 (3)	346	KM#169, 199-200	—	760
PS155	1996 (9)	4,827	KM#158-166	30.00	36.00
PS160	1997 (4)	500	KM#207-210 Wood case	—	1,200
PS161	1997 (4)	1,015	KM#207-210 Velvet case	—	1,175
PS162	1997 (3)	144	KM#181, 205-206	—	780
PS159	1997 (4)	500	KM#73, 105-107	—	1,100
PS163	1997 (4)	30	KM#73, 105-107, 30 Year Wine set with privy marks	—	2,550
PS164	1997 (9)	3,596	KM#159-166, 170	—	40.00
PS165	1998 (9)	—	KM#159-166, 170	—	40.00
PS166	1998 (4)	—	KM#213-216 Wood case	—	1,200
PS167	1998 (4)	—	KM#213-216 Velvet case	—	1,175
PS168	1998 (3)	—	KM#177, 211-212	—	780
PS169	1999 (9)	6,000	KM#159-166, 170	39.50	40.00
PS220	1999 (4)	509	KM#252.1, 253-255, prestige	—	1,325
PS221	1999 (4)	1,046	KM#252.1, 253-255, leatherette	—	1,950
PS222	1999 (4)	537	KM#252.1, 253-255, special	—	2,250
PS191	2000 (4)	236	KM#234-237, wood case	—	325
PS192	2000 (4)	1,140	KM#234-237, velvet lined case	—	300
PS195	2002 (3)	81	KM#234, 243, 351 (mixed dates)	—	90.00
PS196	2002 (3)	95	KM#235, 244, 352 (mixed dates)	—	135
PS197	2002 (3)	81	KM#236, 245, 353 (mixed dates)	—	180
PS198	2002 (3)	92	KM#237, 246, 354 (mixed dates)	—	240
PS201	2003 (4)	59	KM#234, 243, 351, 355 (mixed dates)	—	120
PS202	2003 (4)	47	KM#235, 244, 352, 356 (mixed dates)	—	47.00
PS203	2003 (4)	75	KM#236, 245, 353, 357 (mixed dates)	—	240
PS204	2003 (4)	62	KM#237, 246, 354, 358 (mixed dates)	—	360
PS207	2004 (5)	132	KM#234, 243, 351, 355, 359 (mixed dates)	—	150
PS208	2004 (5)	133	KM#235, 244, 352, 356, 360 (mixed dates)	—	225
PS209	2004 (5)	181	KM#236, 245, 353, 357, 361 (mixed dates)	—	300
PS210	2004 (5)	158	KM#237, 246, 354, 358, 362 (mixed dates)	—	450
PS223	2000 (4)	483	KM#258-261, prestige	—	2,350
PS224	2000 (4)	334	KM#258-261, leatherette	—	2,000
PS193	2001 (4)	411	KM#243-246, wooden case	—	375
PS194	2001 (4)	746	KM#243-246, velvet (med case)	—	270
PS225	2001 (4)	691	KM#264-267	—	2,250
PS226	2001 (4)	985	KM#264-267, leatherette	—	1,950
PS227	2001 (4)	310	KM#264-267, special export	—	1,950
PS172	2001 (9)	3,678	KM#221-229	—	75.00
PS173	2001 (9)	—	KM#221-229 wedding	—	75.00
PS174	2002 (7)	—	KM#268-274	—	75.00
PS175	2002 (7)	330	KM#268-274, baby	—	75.00
PS199	2002 (4)	411	KM#351-354, wooden case	—	375
PS200	2002 (4)	746	KM#351-354, velvet lined case	—	240
PS228	2002 (4)	698	KM#410-413, prestige	—	2,250
PS229	2002 (4)	529	KM#410-413, leatherette	—	1,950

KM#	Date	Mintage	Identification	Issue Price	Mkt Val
PS230	2002 (4)	682	KM#410-413, special	—	1,950
PS170	2002 (7)	—	KM#268-274 plus 1- and 2-cent medals	40.00	42.50
PS205	2003 (4)	532	KM#355-358, wooden case	—	375
PS206	2003 (4)	1,029	KM#355-358, velvet lined case	—	240
PS231	2003 (4)	698	KM#414-417, prestige	—	2,250
PS232	2003 (4)	908	KM#414-417, leatherette	—	1,950
PS233	2003 (4)	722	KM#414-417, anniversary	—	2,250
PS176	2003 (7)	2,356	KM#324, 327, 330, 332, 335, 337, 347	—	65.00
PS177	2003 (7)	500	KM#324, 327, 330, 332, 335, 337, 347, baby	—	65.00
PS178	2003 (7)	53	KM#324, 327, 330, 332, 335, 337, 347, wedding	—	65.00
PS211	2004 (4)	645	KM#359-362, wooden case	—	375
PS212	2004 (4)	454	KM#359-362, velvet lined case	—	240
PS213	2004 (4)	299	KM#359-362, plus 1/4 oz. medal	—	300
PS234	2004 (4)	700	KM#418-421, prestige	—	2,250
PS235	2004 (4)	440	KM#418-421, leatherette	—	1,950
PS236	2004 (4)	125	KM#418-421, special export with silver African Continent	—	—
PS179	2004 (7)	1,935	KM#281, 325, 326, 328, 331, 333, 336	—	65.00
PS180	2004 (7)	326	KM#281, 325, 326, 328, 331, 333, 336, baby	—	65.00
PS181	2004 (7)	23	KM#281, 325, 326, 328, 331, 333, 336, wedding	—	65.00
PS171	2005 (4)	1,500	KM#320-323	—	200
PS214	2005 (4)	—	KM#320-323, wooden case	—	300
PS215	2005 (4)	—	KM#320-323, velvet lined case	—	225
PS237	2005 (4)	—	KM#422-425, prestige	—	2,100
PS238	2005 (4)	—	KM#422-425, leatherette	—	1,950
PS182	2005 (7)	—	KM#291-297	—	65.00
PS183	2005 (7)	—	KM#291-297, baby	—	65.00
PS184	2005 (7)	—	KM#291-297, wedding	—	65.00
PS216	2006 (4)	—	KM#316-319, wooden case	—	265
PS217	2006 (4)	—	KM#316-319, velvet lined case	—	225
PS239	2006 (4)	—	KM#426-429, prestige	—	2,100
PS240	2006 (4)	—	KM#426-429, leatherette	—	1,950
PS218	2007 (2)	—	KM#363-364, wooden case	—	150
PS219	2007 (2)	—	KM#363-364	—	90.00
PS241	2007 (4)	—	KM#430-433, prestige	—	2,100
PS188	2007 (7)	—	KM#340-346	—	65.00
PS189	2007 (7)	—	KM#340-346, baby	—	65.00
PS190	2007 (7)	—	KM#340-346, wedding	—	65.00

SPECIMEN SETS (SS)

KM#	Date	Mintage	Identification	Issue Price	Mkt Val
SS1	1994 (9)	5,508	KM#132-140	—	25.00
SS2	1995 (9)	4,956	KM#132-140	—	25.00
SS3	1996 (9)	5,766	KM#158-166	19.50	25.00
SS4	1997 (9)	4,236	KM#159-166, 170	—	25.00
SS5	1998 (9)	—	KM#159-166, 170	—	25.00
SS6	1999 (9)	—	KM#159-166, 170	—	25.00

S. GEORGIA & THE S. SANDWICH IS.

South Georgia and the South Sandwich Islands are a dependency of the Falkland Islands, and located about 800 miles east of them. South Georgia is 1,450 sq. mi. (1,770 sq. km.), and the South Sandwich Islands are 120 sq. mi. (311 sq. km.) Fishing and Antarctic research are the main industries. The islands were claimed for Great Britain in 1775 by Captain James Cook.

RULER
British since 1775

BRITISH OVERSEAS TERRITORY

STANDARD COINAGE

KM# 7   2 POUNDS
28.2800 g., Copper-Nickel, 38.6 mm.   **Subject:** Sir Ernest H. Shackleton **Obv:** Crowned bust right **Obv. Designer:** Ian Rank-Broadley **Rev:** Bust facing and ship "Endurance" **Edge:** Reeded

Date	Mintage	F	VF	XF	Unc	BU
2001	—	—	—	—	10.00	12.00

KM# 7a   2 POUNDS
28.2800 g., 0.9250 Silver 0.8410 oz. ASW. **Obv:** Crowned bust right **Rev:** Bust facing and ship "Endurance"

Date	Mintage	F	VF	XF	Unc	BU
2001 Proof	Est. 10,000	Value: 50.00				

KM# 9   2 POUNDS
Copper-Nickel   **Subject:** Sir Joseph Banks **Obv:** Crowned bust right **Obv. Designer:** Ian Rank-Broadley **Rev:** Cameo and ship

Date	Mintage	F	VF	XF	Unc	BU
2001	—	—	—	—	10.00	12.00

KM# 9a   2 POUNDS
28.2800 g., 0.9250 Silver 0.8410 oz. ASW. **Obv:** Crowned bust right **Rev:** Ship and cameo

Date	Mintage	F	VF	XF	Unc	BU
2001 Proof	Est. 10,000	Value: 50.00				

KM# 11   2 POUNDS
28.2800 g., Copper-Nickel, 38.6 mm.   **Subject:** Queen Elizabeth II's Golden Jubilee **Obv:** Crowned bust right **Obv. Designer:** Ian Rank-Broadley **Rev:** Young crowned bust right **Edge:** Reeded

Date	Mintage	F	VF	XF	Unc	BU
2002	—	—	—	—	10.00	12.00

KM# 11a   2 POUNDS
28.2800 g., 0.9250 Gold Clad Silver 0.8410 oz., 38.6 mm. **Subject:** Queen Elizabeth II's Golden Jubilee **Obv:** Crowned bust right **Rev:** Young crowned bust right **Edge:** Reeded

Date	Mintage	F	VF	XF	Unc	BU
2002 Proof	10,000	Value: 50.00				

KM# 13   2 POUNDS
28.2800 g., Copper-Nickel, 38.6 mm.   **Subject:** Queen Elizabeth II's Golden Jubilee **Obv:** Crowned bust right **Obv. Designer:** Ian Rank-Broadley **Rev:** Small crown above shield flanked by flower sprigs **Edge:** Reeded

Date	Mintage	F	VF	XF	Unc	BU
2002	—	—	—	—	10.00	12.00

KM# 13a   2 POUNDS
28.2800 g., 0.9250 Gold Clad Silver 0.8410 oz., 38.6 mm. **Subject:** Queen Elizabeth II's Golden Jubilee **Obv:** Crowned bust right **Rev:** Small crown above shield flanked by flower sprigs **Edge:** Reeded

Date	Mintage	F	VF	XF	Unc	BU
2002 Proof	10,000	Value: 50.00				

KM# 15   2 POUNDS
28.2800 g., Copper-Nickel, 38.6 mm.   **Subject:** Diana, Princess of Wales - The Work Continues **Obv:** Crowned bust right **Obv. Designer:** Ian Rank-Broadley **Rev:** Head 1/4 left **Edge:** Reeded

Date	Mintage	F	VF	XF	Unc	BU
2002	—	—	—	—	10.00	12.00

KM# 17   2 POUNDS
28.2800 g., Copper-Nickel, 38.6 mm.   **Subject:** Prince William's 21st Birthday **Obv:** Crowned bust right **Obv. Designer:** Ian Rank-Broadley **Rev:** Arms of Prince William of Wales **Edge:** Reeded

Date	Mintage	F	VF	XF	Unc	BU
2003PM	—	—	—	—	10.00	12.00

KM# 17a   2 POUNDS
28.2800 g., 0.9250 Silver 0.8410 oz. ASW, 38.6 mm. **Subject:** Prince William's 21st Birthday **Obv:** Crowned bust right **Rev:** Arms of Prince William of Wales **Edge:** Reeded

Date	Mintage	F	VF	XF	Unc	BU
2003PM Proof	—	Value: 50.00				

KM# 18   2 POUNDS
28.2800 g., Copper-Nickel, 38.6 mm.   **Obv:** Crowned bust right **Rev:** Capt. Cook, ship and map **Edge:** Reeded

Date	Mintage	F	VF	XF	Unc	BU
2003PM	—	—	—	—	10.00	12.00

KM# 18a   2 POUNDS
28.2800 g., 0.9250 Silver 0.8410 oz. ASW, 38.6 mm. **Obv:** Crowned bust right **Rev:** Capt. Cook, ship and map **Edge:** Reeded

Date	Mintage	F	VF	XF	Unc	BU
2003PM Proof	—	Value: 47.50				

KM# 20   2 POUNDS
28.2800 g., Copper-Nickel, 38.6 mm.   **Obv:** Crowned bust right **Obv. Designer:** Ian Rank-Broadley **Rev:** Sir Ernest Shackleton and icebound ship **Edge:** Reeded

Date	Mintage	F	VF	XF	Unc	BU
2004	—	—	—	—	15.00	16.50

KM# 20a   2 POUNDS
28.2800 g., 0.9250 Silver 0.8410 oz. ASW, 38.6 mm.
Obv: Crowned bust right **Rev:** Sir Ernest Shackleton and icebound ship **Edge:** Reeded

Date	Mintage	F	VF	XF	Unc	BU
2004 Proof	10,000				Value: 50.00	

KM# 21   2 POUNDS
28.2800 g., Copper-Nickel, 38.6 mm.   **Subject:** Centennial of Grytviken **Obv:** Crowned bust right **Obv. Designer:** Ian Rank-Broadley **Rev:** Portrait above ship in harbor **Edge:** Reeded

Date	Mintage	F	VF	XF	Unc	BU
2004	—	—	—	—	15.00	16.50

KM# 21a   2 POUNDS
28.2800 g., 0.9250 Silver 0.8410 oz. ASW, 38.6 mm.
Subject: Centennial of Grytviken **Obv:** Crowned bust right **Rev:** Portrait above ship in harbor **Edge:** Reeded

Date	Mintage	F	VF	XF	Unc	BU
2004 Proof	—				Value: 50.00	

KM# 25   2 POUNDS
Copper-Nickel   **Subject:** Marriage of Charles to Parker Bowles **Rev:** Arms of Prince of Wales

Date	Mintage	F	VF	XF	Unc	BU
2005	—	—	—	—	8.50	10.00

KM# 22   2 POUNDS
28.3700 g., Copper-Nickel, 38.5 mm.   **Obv:** Elizabeth II **Rev:** Rockhopper Penguin and chick **Edge:** Reeded

Date	Mintage	F	VF	XF	Unc	BU
2006	—	—	—	—	12.00	14.00

KM# 23   2 POUNDS
28.3700 g., Copper-Nickel, 38.5 mm.   **Obv:** Elizabeth II **Rev:** Elephant Seal and cub **Edge:** Reeded

Date	Mintage	F	VF	XF	Unc	BU
2006	—	—	—	—	10.00	12.00

KM# 24   2 POUNDS
28.3700 g., Copper-Nickel, 38.5 mm.   **Obv:** Elizabeth II **Rev:** Humpback Whale and calf **Edge:** Reeded

Date	Mintage	F	VF	XF	Unc	BU
2006	—	—	—	—	8.50	10.00

KM# 26   2 POUNDS
Copper-Nickel   **Subject:** Queen Elizabeth's II 80th Birthday **Rev:** Queen on horseback taking part in Trouping of the Color ceremony

Date	Mintage	F	VF	XF	Unc	BU
2006	—	—	—	—	8.50	10.00

KM# 26a   2 POUNDS
28.2800 g., 0.9167 Silver 0.8334 oz. ASW   **Subject:** Queen Elizabeth's II 80th Birthday **Rev:** Queen on horseback taking part in Trouping of the Color ceremony

Date	Mintage	F	VF	XF	Unc	BU
2006 Proof	25,000				Value: 75.00	

KM# 27   2 POUNDS
Copper-Nickel, 38.5 mm.   **Rev:** Pair of Grey-headed Albatros

Date	Mintage	F	VF	XF	Unc	BU
2006	—	—	—	—	8.50	10.00

KM# 28   2 POUNDS
Copper-Nickel   **Subject:** Queen Elizabeth's II 80th Birthday **Rev:** 1953 Royal family

Date	Mintage	F	VF	XF	Unc	BU
2006	—	—	—	—	8.50	10.00

KM# 28a   2 POUNDS
28.2800 g., 0.9167 Silver 0.8334 oz. ASW   **Subject:** Queen Elizabeth's II 80th Birthday **Rev:** 1953 Royal family

Date	Mintage	F	VF	XF	Unc	BU
2006 Proof	25,000				Value: 75.00	

KM# 29   2 POUNDS
Copper-Nickel   **Subject:** Queen Elizabeth's II 80th Birthday **Rev:** Wedding of Queen Elizabeth II and Prince Philip

Date	Mintage	F	VF	XF	Unc	BU
2006	—	—	—	—	8.50	10.00

KM# 29a   2 POUNDS
28.2800 g., 0.9167 Silver 0.8334 oz. ASW   **Subject:** Queen Elizabeth's 80th Birthday **Rev:** Wedding of Queen Elizabeth II and Prince Philip

Date	Mintage	F	VF	XF	Unc	BU
2006 Proof	25,000				Value: 75.00	

KM# 30   2 POUNDS
Copper-Nickel   **Subject:** Queen Elizabeth's II 80th Birthday **Rev:** Queen in Robes of Garter

Date	Mintage	F	VF	XF	Unc	BU
2006	—	—	—	—	8.50	10.00

KM# 30a   2 POUNDS
28.2800 g., 0.9167 Silver 0.8334 oz. ASW   **Subject:** Queen Elizabeth's II 80th Birthday **Rev:** Queen in Robes of Garter

Date	Mintage	F	VF	XF	Unc	BU
2006 Proof	25,000				Value: 75.00	

KM# 31   2 POUNDS
Copper-Nickel   **Rev:** Queen Elizabeth II 1926 (1953 portrait)

Date	Mintage	F	VF	XF	Unc	BU
2007	—	—	—	—	8.50	10.00

KM# 32   2 POUNDS
Copper-Nickel   **Subject:** 25th Anniversary of Liberation **Rev:** Warship and helicopters

Date	Mintage	F	VF	XF	Unc	BU
2007	—	—	—	—	8.50	10.00

KM# 33   2 POUNDS
Copper-Nickel   **Rev:** Trans Artic Expedition

Date	Mintage	F	VF	XF	Unc	BU
2007	—	—	—	—	8.50	10.00

KM# 34   2 POUNDS
Copper-Nickel   **Subject:** International Polar Year **Rev:** Shackelton Expedition

Date	Mintage	F	VF	XF	Unc	BU
2007	—	—	—	—	8.50	10.00

KM# 35   2 POUNDS
Copper-Nickel   **Rev:** Ernest Shacketon

Date	Mintage	F	VF	XF	Unc	BU
2007	—	—	—	—	8.50	10.00

KM# 36   2 POUNDS
Copper-Nickel   **Rev:** James Cook

Date	Mintage	F	VF	XF	Unc	BU
2007	—	—	—	—	8.50	10.00

KM# 37   2 POUNDS
28.2800 g., Copper-Nickel, 38.60 mm.   **Ruler:** Elizabeth II **Subject:** Diamond Wedding Anniversary **Obv:** Conjoined busts with Prince Philip right **Obv. Legend:** SOUTH GEORGIA & SOUTH SANDWICH ISLANDS **Rev:** Bust of Princess Elizabeth facing **Rev. Legend:** Diamond Wedding of H.M. Queen Elizabeth II & H.R.H. Prince Philip **Rev. Inscription:** THE BRIDE **Edge:** Reeded

Date	Mintage	F	VF	XF	Unc	BU
2007	—	—	—	—	15.00	16.50

KM# 37a   2 POUNDS
28.2800 g., 0.9167 Silver ASW 0.8335 0.8334 oz. ASW, 38.60 mm.   **Ruler:** Elizabeth II **Subject:** Diamond Wedding Anniversary **Obv:** Conjoined busts with Prince Philip right **Obv. Legend:** SOUTH GEORGIA & SOUTH SANDWICH ISLANDS **Rev:** Bust of Princess Elizabeth facing **Rev. Legend:** Diamond Wedding of H.M. Queen Elizabeth II & H.R.H. Prince Philip **Rev. Inscription:** THE BRIDE **Edge:** Reeded

Date	Mintage	F	VF	XF	Unc	BU
2007 Proof	25,000				Value: 75.00	

KM# 38   2 POUNDS
28.2800 g., Copper-Nickel, 38.60 mm.   **Ruler:** Elizabeth II **Subject:** Diamond Wedding Anniversary **Obv:** Conjoined busts with Prince Philip right **Obv. Legend:** SOUTH GEORGIA & SOUTH SANDWICH ISLANDS **Rev:** Bust of the bridegroom facing **Rev. Legend:** Diamond Wedding of H.M. Queen Elizabeth II & H.R.H. Prince Philip **Rev. Inscription:** THE BRIDEGROOM **Edge:** Reeded

Date	Mintage	F	VF	XF	Unc	BU
2007	—	—	—	—	15.00	16.50

KM# 38a   2 POUNDS
28.2800 g., 0.9167 Silver ASW 0.8335 0.8334 oz. ASW, 38.60 mm.   **Ruler:** Elizabeth II **Subject:** Diamond Wedding Anniversary **Obv:** Conjoined busts with Prince Philip right **Obv. Legend:** SOUTH GEORGIA & SOUTH SANDWICH ISLANDS **Rev:** Bust of the bridegroom facing **Rev. Legend:** Diamond Wedding of H.M. Queen Elizabeth II & H.R.H. Prince Philip **Rev. Inscription:** THE BRIDEGROOM **Edge:** Reeded

Date	Mintage	F	VF	XF	Unc	BU
2007 Proof	25,000				Value: 75.00	

KM# 39   2 POUNDS
28.2800 g., Copper-Nickel, 38.60 mm.   **Ruler:** Elizabeth II **Subject:** Diamond Wedding Anniversary **Obv:** Conjoined busts with Prince Philip right **Obv. Legend:** SOUTH GEORGIA & SOUTH SANDWICH ISLANDS **Rev:** 1/2 length figures of royal engaged couple looking at each other **Rev. Legend:** Diamond Wedding of H.M. Queen Elizabeth II & H.R.H. Prince Philip **Rev. Inscription:** ROYAL ENGAGEMENT • JULY • 10 • 1947 **Edge:** Reeded

Date	Mintage	F	VF	XF	Unc	BU
2007	—	—	—	—	15.00	16.50

KM# 39a   2 POUNDS
28.2800 g., 0.9167 Silver ASW 0.8335 0.8334 oz. ASW, 38.60 mm.   **Ruler:** Elizabeth II **Subject:** Diamond Wedding Anniversary **Obv:** Conjoined busts with Prince Philip right **Obv. Legend:** SOUTH GEORGIA & SOUTH SANDWICH ISLANDS **Rev:** 1/2 length figures of royal engaged couple looking at each other **Rev. Legend:** Diamond Wedding of H.M. Queen Elizabeth II & H.R.H. Prince Philip **Rev. Inscription:** ROYAL ENGAGEMENT • JULY • 10 • 1947 **Edge:** Reeded

Date	Mintage	F	VF	XF	Unc	BU
2007 Proof	25,000				Value: 75.00	

KM# 40   2 POUNDS
28.2800 g., Copper-Nickel, 38.60 mm.   **Ruler:** Elizabeth II **Subject:** Diamond Wedding Anniversary **Obv:** Conjoined busts with Prince Philip right **Obv. Legend:** SOUTH GEORGIA & SOUTH SANDWICH ISLANDS **Rev:** Marriage license, jubilant crowd scene **Rev. Legend:** Diamond Wedding of H.M. Queen Elizabeth II & H.R.H. Prince Philip **Rev. Inscription:** THE MARRIAGE LICENSE **Edge:** Reeded

Date	Mintage	F	VF	XF	Unc	BU
2007	—	—	—	—	15.00	16.50

KM# 40a   2 POUNDS
28.2800 g., 0.9167 Silver ASW 0.8335 0.8334 oz. ASW, 38.60 mm.   **Ruler:** Elizabeth II **Subject:** Diamond Wedding Anniversary **Obv:** Conjoined busts with Prince Philip right **Obv. Legend:** SOUTH GEORGIA & SOUTH SANDWICH ISLANDS **Rev:** Marriage license, jubilant crowd scene **Rev. Legend:** Diamond Wedding of H.M. Queen Elizabeth II & H.R.H. Prince Philip **Rev. Inscription:** THE MARRIAGE LICENSE **Edge:** Reeded

Date	Mintage	F	VF	XF	Unc	BU
2007 Proof	25,000				Value: 75.00	

KM# 19   10 POUNDS
155.5100 g., 0.9990 Silver 4.9946 oz. ASW, 65 mm.
Obv: Crowned bust right **Obv. Designer:** Ian Rank-Broadley **Rev:** Capt. Cook, ship and map **Edge:** Reeded

Date	Mintage	F	VF	XF	Unc	BU
2003PM Proof	2,003				Value: 175	

KM# 8   20 POUNDS
6.2200 g., 0.9999 Gold 0.1999 oz. AGW, 22 mm.   **Obv:** Crowned bust right **Obv. Designer:** Ian Rank-Broadley **Rev:** Sir Ernest H. Shackleton and ship **Edge:** Reeded

Date	Mintage	F	VF	XF	Unc	BU
2001 Proof	Est. 2,000				Value: 250	

KM# 10   20 POUNDS
6.2200 g., 0.9999 Gold 0.1999 oz. AGW   **Obv:** Crowned bust right **Obv. Designer:** Ian Rank-Broadley **Rev:** Sir Joseph Banks cameo and ship

Date	Mintage	F	VF	XF	Unc	BU
2001 Proof	Est. 2,000				Value: 250	

KM# 16   20 POUNDS
6.2200 g., 0.9999 Gold 0.1999 oz. AGW, 22 mm.   **Subject:** Princess Diana **Obv:** Crowned bust right **Obv. Designer:** Ian Rank-Broadley **Rev:** Diana's portrait **Edge:** reeded

Date	Mintage	F	VF	XF	Unc	BU
2002PM Proof	—				Value: 250	

KM# 12   20 POUNDS
6.2200 g., 0.9990 Gold 0.1998 oz. AGW, 22 mm.   **Subject:** Queen Elizabeth II's Golden Jubilee **Obv:** Crowned bust right **Obv. Designer:** Ian Rank-Broadley **Rev:** Young crowned bust right **Edge:** Reeded

Date	Mintage	F	VF	XF	Unc	BU
2002 Proof	2,002				Value: 250	

KM# 14   20 POUNDS
6.2200 g., 0.9990 Gold 0.1998 oz. AGW, 22 mm.   **Subject:** Queen Elizabeth II's Golden Jubilee **Obv:** Crowned bust right **Obv. Designer:** Ian Rank-Broadley **Rev:** National arms **Edge:** Reeded

Date	Mintage	F	VF	XF	Unc	BU
2002 Proof	2,002				Value: 250	

SPAIN

North Atlantic Ocean
FRANCE
Navarre
PORTUGAL
Aragon
Catalonia
Barcelona
Castilla y Leon
Valencia
BALEARIC ISLANDS
Mediterranean Sea
MOROCCO

The Spanish State, forming the greater part of the Iberian Peninsula of southwest Europe, has an area of 195,988 sq. mi. (504,714 sq. km.) and a population of 39.4 million including the Balearic and the Canary Islands. Capital: Madrid. The economy is based on agriculture, industry and tourism. Machinery, fruit, vegetables and chemicals are exported.

RULER
Juan Carlos I, 1975-

MINT MARK
(M) - Crowned "M" – Madrid

KINGDOM
DECIMAL COINAGE
100 Centimos = 1 Peseta

KM# 832 PESETA
Aluminum, 14 mm. **Ruler:** Juan Carlos I **Obv:** Vertical line divides head left from value **Rev:** Crowned shield flanked by pillars with banner **Edge:** Plain

Date	Mintage	F	VF	XF	Unc	BU
2001	—	—	—	0.10	0.30	0.50

KM# 833 5 PESETAS
3.0500 g., Aluminum-Bronze, 18 mm. **Ruler:** Juan Carlos I **Obv:** Stylized design and date **Rev:** Value above stylized sailboats **Edge:** Plain

Date	Mintage	F	VF	XF	Unc	BU
2001	—	—	—	0.10	0.25	0.35

KM# 1013 25 PESETAS
4.2000 g., Nickel-Brass, 19.5 mm. **Ruler:** Juan Carlos I **Subject:** Navarra **Obv:** Center hole divides bust left and vertical letters **Rev:** Crowned above center hole, order collar at right, value at left **Edge:** Plain

Date	Mintage	F	VF	XF	Unc	BU
2001	—	—	—	—	2.00	2.50

KM# 1016 100 PESETAS
9.8000 g., Aluminum-Bronze, 24.4 mm. **Ruler:** Juan Carlos I **Subject:** 132nd Ann. of the Peseta **Obv:** Head left **Rev:** Seated allegorical figure from an old coin design **Edge:** Ornamented

Date	Mintage	F	VF	XF	Unc	BU
2001	—	—	—	—	2.25	2.75

KM# 924 500 PESETAS
11.9000 g., Copper-Aluminum-Nickel **Ruler:** Juan Carlos I **Obv:** Conjoined heads of Juan Carlos and Sofia left **Rev:** Crowned shield flanked by pillars with banner, vertical value at right

Date	Mintage	F	VF	XF	Unc	BU
2001	—	—	—	—	12.00	15.00

KM# 1131 500 PESETAS
6.7300 g., Silver, 26.96 mm. **Ruler:** Juan Carlos I **Obv:** Minting equipment **Obv. Legend:** ESPAÑA **Rev:** Copy of Charles II silver Reales coin **Rev. Legend:** CASA DE LA MONEDA DE SEGOVIA **Edge:** Reeded **Note:** Aqueduct and crowned M mintmarks appear on obverse

Date	Mintage	F	VF	XF	Unc	BU
2001 Proof	—	Value: 20.00				

KM# 1017 2000 PESETAS
18.0000 g., 0.9250 Silver 0.5353 oz. ASW, 32.9 mm. **Ruler:** Juan Carlos I **Subject:** 132nd Anniversary of the Peseta **Obv:** Conjoined heads left **Rev:** Seated allegorical design from the 1869 Spanish coin series **Edge:** Plain

Date	Mintage	F	VF	XF	Unc	BU
2001	—	—	—	—	25.00	30.00

KM# 1038 2000 PESETAS
27.0000 g., 0.9250 Silver 0.8029 oz. ASW, 40 mm. **Ruler:** Juan Carlos I **Subject:** Segovia Mint's 500th Anniversary **Obv:** Hammer coining scene within beaded circle **Rev:** Segovia Mint 8 reales coin design of 1588 **Edge:** Reeded

Date	Mintage	F	VF	XF	Unc	BU
2001 Proof	15,000	Value: 55.00				

EURO COINAGE
European Union Issues

KM# 1040 EURO CENT
2.3000 g., Copper Plated Steel, 16.3 mm. **Ruler:** Juan Carlos I **Obv:** Cathedral of Santiago de Compostela **Obv. Designer:** Garcilano Rollan **Rev:** Value and globe **Rev. Designer:** Luc Luycx **Edge:** Plain

Date	Mintage	F	VF	XF	Unc	BU
2001(M)	130,900,000	—	—	—	0.25	0.30
2002(M)	141,100,000	—	—	—	0.25	0.30
2002(M) Proof	35,000	Value: 10.00				
2003(M)	670,500,000	—	—	—	0.25	0.30
2003(M) Proof	20,000	Value: 10.00				
2004(M)	206,700,000	—	—	—	0.25	0.30
2005(M)	444,200,000	—	—	—	0.25	0.30
2005(M) Proof	3,000	Value: 10.00				
2006(M)	383,900,000	—	—	—	0.25	0.35
2007(M)	—	—	—	—	0.25	0.35
2007(M) Proof	5,000	Value: 10.00				
2008(M)	—	—	—	—	0.25	0.35
2008(M) Proof	5,000	Value: 10.00				
2009(M)	—	—	—	—	0.25	0.35
2009(M) Proof	5,000	Value: 10.00				
2010(M)	—	—	—	—	0.25	0.35
2010(M) Proof	—	Value: 10.00				

KM# 1041 2 EURO CENT
3.0300 g., Copper Plated Steel, 18.7 mm. **Ruler:** Juan Carlos I **Obv:** Cathedral of Santiago de Compostela **Obv. Designer:** Garcilano Rollan **Rev:** Value and globe **Rev. Designer:** Luc Luycx **Edge:** Grooved

Date	Mintage	F	VF	XF	Unc	BU
2001(M)	463,100,000	—	—	—	0.25	0.30
2002(M)	4,100,000	—	—	—	1.25	1.50
2002(M) Proof	35,000	Value: 10.00				
2003(M)	31,600,000	—	—	—	1.00	1.25
2003(M) Proof	20,000	Value: 10.00				
2004(M)	206,700,000	—	—	—	0.25	0.30
2005(M)	275,100,000	—	—	—	0.25	0.30
2005(M) Proof	3,000	Value: 10.00				
2006(M)	262,200,000	—	—	—	0.25	0.30
2007(M)	—	—	—	—	0.25	0.30
2007(M) Proof	5,000	Value: 10.00				
2008(M)	—	—	—	—	0.25	0.30
2008(M) Proof	5,000	Value: 10.00				
2009(M)	—	—	—	—	0.25	0.30
2009(M) Proof	5,000	Value: 10.00				
2010(M)	—	—	—	—	0.25	0.30
2010(M) Proof	—	Value: 10.00				

KM# 1042 5 EURO CENT
3.9200 g., Copper Plated Steel, 21.25 mm. **Ruler:** Juan Carlos I **Obv:** Cathedral of Santiago de Compostela **Obv. Designer:** Garcilano Rollan **Rev:** Value and globe **Rev. Designer:** Luc Luycx **Edge:** Plain

Date	Mintage	F	VF	XF	Unc	BU
2001(M)	216,100,000	—	—	—	0.50	0.60
2002(M)	8,300,000	—	—	—	1.00	1.50
2002(M) Proof	35,000	Value: 10.00				
2003(M)	327,600,000	—	—	—	0.50	0.60
2004(M)	258,700,000	—	—	—	0.40	0.50
2005(M)	411,400,000	—	—	—	0.40	0.50
2005(M) Proof	3,000	Value: 10.00				
2006(M)	142,800,000	—	—	—	0.40	0.50
2007(M)	—	—	—	—	0.40	0.50
2007(M) Proof	5,000	Value: 10.00				
2008(M)	—	—	—	—	0.40	0.50
2009(M)	—	—	—	—	0.40	0.50
2010(M)	—	—	—	—	0.40	0.50

KM# 1043 10 EURO CENT
4.0700 g., Brass, 19.7 mm. **Ruler:** Juan Carlos I **Obv:** Head of Cervantes with ruffed collar 1/4 left within star border **Rev:** Value and map **Edge:** Reeded

Date	Mintage	F	VF	XF	Unc	BU
2001(M)	160,100,000	—	—	—	0.60	0.75
2002(M)	113,100,000	—	—	—	0.60	0.75
2002(M) Proof	35,000	Value: 10.00				
2003(M)	292,500,000	—	—	—	0.75	0.90
2003(M) Proof	20,000	Value: 10.00				
2004(M)	121,900,000	—	—	—	0.40	0.50
2005(M)	321,300,000	—	—	—	0.40	0.50
2005(M) Proof	3,000	Value: 10.00				
2006(M)	91,800,000	—	—	—	0.40	0.50

KM# 1070 10 EURO CENT
4.1000 g., Brass, 19.7 mm. **Ruler:** Juan Carlos I **Obv:** Cervantes **Rev:** Relief map of Western Europe, stars, lines and value **Edge:** Reeded

Date	Mintage	F	VF	XF	Unc	BU
2007(M)	—	—	—	—	0.75	1.00
2007(M) Proof	5,000	Value: 12.00				
2008(M)	—	—	—	—	0.75	1.00
2008(M) Proof	5,000	Value: 12.00				

Date	Mintage	F	VF	XF	Unc	BU
2009(M)	—	—	—	—	0.75	1.00
2009(M) Proof	5,000	Value: 12.00				
2010(M)	—	—	—	—	0.75	1.00
2010(M) Proof	—	Value: 12.00				

KM# 1044 20 EURO CENT

5.6200 g., Brass, 22.2 mm. **Ruler:** Juan Carlos I **Obv:** Head of Cervantes with ruffed collar 1/4 left within star border **Obv. Designer:** Begoña Castellanos **Rev:** Value and map **Rev. Designer:** Luc Luycx **Edge:** Notched

Date	Mintage	F	VF	XF	Unc	BU
2001(M)	146,600,000	—	—	—	1.00	1.25
2002(M)	91,500,000	—	—	—	0.60	0.75
2002(M) Proof	35,000	Value: 12.00				
2003(M)	4,100,000	—	—	—	1.25	1.50
2003(M) Proof	20,000	Value: 12.00				
2004(M)	3,900,000	—	—	—	0.60	0.75
2005(M)	4,000,000	—	—	—	0.60	0.75
2005(M) Proof	3,000	Value: 12.00				
2006(M)	102,000,000	—	—	—	0.60	0.75

KM# 1071 20 EURO CENT

5.7300 g., Brass, 22.3 mm. **Ruler:** Juan Carlos I **Obv:** Cervantes **Obv. Designer:** Begoña Castellanos **Rev:** Relief map of Western Europe, stars, lines and value **Rev. Designer:** Luc Luycx **Edge:** Notched

Date	Mintage	F	VF	XF	Unc	BU
2007(M)	—	—	—	—	1.00	1.25
2007(M) Proof	5,000	Value: 12.00				
2008(M)	—	—	—	—	1.00	1.25
2009(M)	—	—	—	—	1.00	1.25
2009(M) Proof	5,000	Value: 12.00				
2010(M)	—	—	—	—	1.00	1.25
2010(M) Proof	—	—	—	—	—	—
2010(M) Proof	5,000	Value: 12.00				

KM# 1045 50 EURO CENT

7.8100 g., Brass, 24.2 mm. **Ruler:** Juan Carlos I **Obv:** Head of Cervantes with ruffed collar 1/4 left within star border **Obv. Designer:** Begoña Castellanos **Rev:** Value and map **Rev. Designer:** Luc Luycx **Edge:** Reeded

Date	Mintage	F	VF	XF	Unc	BU
2001(M)	351,100,000	—	—	—	1.00	1.25
2002(M)	9,800,000	—	—	—	3.00	3.50
2002(M) Proof	35,000	Value: 12.00				
2003(M)	6,000,000	—	—	—	3.00	3.50
2003(M) Proof	20,000	Value: 12.00				
2004(M)	4,400,000	—	—	—	1.50	2.00
2005(M)	3,900,000	—	—	—	1.25	1.50
2005(M) Proof	3,000	Value: 12.00				
2006(M)	4,000,000	—	—	—	1.25	1.50

KM# 1072 50 EURO CENT

7.8500 g., Brass, 24.2 mm. **Ruler:** Juan Carlos I **Obv:** Cervantes **Obv. Designer:** Begoña Castellanos **Rev:** Relief map of Western Europe, stars, lines and value **Rev. Designer:** Luc Luycx **Edge:** Reeded

Date	Mintage	F	VF	XF	Unc	BU
2007(M)	—	—	—	—	1.25	1.50
2007(M) Proof	5,000	Value: 12.00				
2008(M)	—	—	—	—	1.25	1.50
2008(M) Proof	5,000	Value: 12.00				
2009(M)	—	—	—	—	1.25	1.50
2009(M) Proof	5,000	Value: 12.00				
2010(M)	—	—	—	—	1.25	1.50
2010(M) Proof	—	—	—	—	—	—

KM# 1046 EURO

7.5000 g., Bi-Metallic Copper-Nickel center in Brass ring, 23.2 mm. **Ruler:** Juan Carlos I **Obv:** Head 1/4 left within circle and star border **Obv. Designer:** Luiz Jose Diaz **Rev:** Value and map within circle **Rev. Designer:** Luc Luycx **Edge:** Reeded and plain sections

Date	Mintage	F	VF	XF	Unc	BU
2001(M)	259,100,000	—	—	—	3.00	4.00
2002(M)	335,600,000	—	—	—	2.00	2.50
2002(M) Proof	23,000	Value: 15.00				
2003(M)	297,400,000	—	—	—	2.00	2.50
2003(M) Proof	20,000	Value: 15.00				
2004(M)	9,870,000	—	—	—	2.00	2.50
2005(M)	77,800,000	—	—	—	2.00	2.50
2005(M) Proof	3,000	Value: 15.00				
2006(M)	101,600,000	—	—	—	2.00	2.50

KM# 1073 EURO

7.4000 g., Bi-Metallic Copper-Nickel center in Brass ring, 23.2 mm. **Ruler:** Juan Carlos I **Obv:** King's portrait **Obv. Designer:** Luiz Jose Diaz **Rev:** Relief map of Western Europe, stars, lines and value **Rev. Designer:** Luc Luycx **Edge:** Reeded and plain sections

Date	Mintage	F	VF	XF	Unc	BU
2007(M)	—	—	—	—	3.00	3.50
2007(M) Proof	5,000	Value: 15.00				
2008(M)	—	—	—	—	3.00	3.50
2008(M) Proof	5,000	Value: 15.00				
2009(M)	—	—	—	—	3.00	3.50
2009(M) Proof	5,000	Value: 15.00				
2010(M)	—	—	—	—	3.00	3.50
2010(M) Proof	—	—	—	—	—	—

KM# 1047 2 EURO

8.5200 g., Bi-Metallic Brass center in Copper-Nickel ring, 25.7 mm. **Ruler:** Juan Carlos I **Obv:** Head 1/4 left within circle and star border **Obv. Designer:** Luis Jose Diaz **Rev:** Value and map within circle **Rev. Designer:** Luc Luycx **Edge:** Reeded **Edge Lettering:** 2's and stars

Date	Mintage	F	VF	XF	Unc	BU
2001(M)	140,200,000	—	—	—	4.50	5.00
2002(M)	164,000,000	—	—	—	3.50	4.00
2002(M) Proof	35,000	Value: 20.00				
2003(M)	44,500,000	—	—	—	4.50	5.00
2003(M) Proof	20,000	Value: 20.00				
2004(M)	4,100,000	—	—	—	4.50	5.00
2005(M)	4,000,000	—	—	—	4.50	5.00
2005(M) Proof	3,000	Value: 20.00				
2006(M)	4,000,000	—	—	—	4.50	5.00

KM# 1063 2 EURO

8.5200 g., Bi-Metallic Brass center in Copper-Nickel ring, 25.7 mm. **Ruler:** Juan Carlos I **Obv:** Stylized half length figure of Don Quiote holding spear within circle and star border **Rev:** Value and map within circle **Edge:** Reeding over stars and 2's **Note:** Mint mark: Crowned M.

Date	Mintage	F	VF	XF	Unc	BU
2005	8,000,000	—	—	—	5.00	6.00

KM# 1074 2 EURO

8.5000 g., Bi-Metallic Brass center in Copper-Nickel ring, 25.8 mm. **Ruler:** Juan Carlos I **Obv:** King's portrait **Obv. Designer:** Luis Jose Diaz **Rev:** Relief map of Western Europe, stars, lines and value **Rev. Designer:** Luc Luycx **Edge:** Reeded **Edge Lettering:** 2's and stars

Date	Mintage	F	VF	XF	Unc	BU
2007(M)	—	—	—	—	4.75	5.00
2007(M) Proof	5,000	Value: 20.00				
2008(M)	—	—	—	—	4.75	5.00
2008(M) Proof	5,000	Value: 20.00				
2009(M)	—	—	—	—	4.75	5.00
2009(M) Proof	5,000	Value: 20.00				
2010(M)	—	—	—	—	4.75	5.00
2010(M) Proof	—	Value: 20.00				

KM# 1130 2 EURO

8.5300 g., Bi-Metallic Brass center in Copper-Nickel ring, 25.70 mm. **Ruler:** Juan Carlos I **Subject:** 50th Anniversary Treaty of Rome **Obv:** Open treaty book **Obv. Legend:** ESPAÑA **Rev:** Large value at left, modified outline of Europe at right **Edge:** Reeded with 2's and stars

Date	Mintage	F	VF	XF	Unc	BU
2007	—	—	—	—	7.00	9.00

KM# 1142 2 EURO

8.5300 g., Bi-Metallic Brass center in Copper-Nickel ring **Ruler:** Juan Carlos I **Subject:** European Monetary unit, 10th Anniversary **Obv:** Stick figure and large E symbol **Rev:** Large value at left, modified map of Europe at right

Date	Mintage	F	VF	XF	Unc	BU
2009 small stars	—	—	—	—	5.00	6.00
2009 large stars	—	—	—	—	6.00	9.00
2009 Proof	—	Value: 10.00				

KM# 1048 10 EURO

27.0000 g., 0.9250 Silver 0.8029 oz. ASW, 40 mm. **Ruler:** Juan Carlos I **Subject:** Spanish Presidency of the European Union **Obv:** Head left **Rev:** Map of Europe **Edge:** Reeded

Date	Mintage	F	VF	XF	Unc	BU
2002 Proof	30,000	Value: 50.00				

KM# 1078 10 EURO

27.0000 g., Silver **Ruler:** Juan Carlos I **Subject:** XIX Winter Olympics - Salt Lake City **Obv:** Head left **Obv. Legend:** JUAN CARLOS I REY DE ESPAÑA **Rev:** Cross country skier right, stylized snowflake at right **Rev. Legend:** JUEGOS OLIMPICOS DE - INVERNO 2002

Date	Mintage	F	VF	XF	Unc	BU
2002(M) Proof	—	Value: 60.00				

KM# 1079 10 EURO

27.0000 g., Silver **Ruler:** Juan Carlos I **Subject:** XVII Football World Games 2002 - South Korea and Japan **Obv. Legend:** MUNDIAL DE FUTBOL/2002 - ESPANA **Rev:** Football against net

Date	Mintage	F	VF	XF	Unc	BU
2002(M) Proof	25,000	Value: 60.00				

KM# 1080 10 EURO

27.0000 g., Silver **Ruler:** Juan Carlos I **Subject:** XVII Football World Games 2002 - South Korea and Japan **Obv. Legend:** MUNDIAL DE FUTBOL/2002 - ESPANA **Rev:** Glove

Date	Mintage	F	VF	XF	Unc	BU
2002(M) Proof	25,000	Value: 60.00				

KM# 1087 10 EURO

27.0000 g., 0.9250 Silver 0.8029 oz. ASW **Ruler:** Juan Carlos I **Subject:** 100th Anniversary birth of Luis Cernuda **Obv:** Head left

Date	Mintage	F	VF	XF	Unc	BU
2002(M) Proof	25,000	Value: 60.00				

KM# 1088 10 EURO

27.0000 g., 0.9250 Silver 0.8029 oz. ASW **Ruler:** Juan Carlos I **Subject:** 100th Anniversary - Birth of Rafael Alberti **Obv:** Head left **Obv. Legend:** JUAN CARLOS I REY DE ESPANA **Rev:** Bust of Alberti facing 3/4 right

Date	Mintage	F	VF	XF	Unc	BU
2002(M) Proof	25,000	Value: 60.00				

KM# 1082 10 EURO
27.0000 g., 0.9250 Silver 0.8029 oz. ASW, 40.0 mm.
Ruler: Juan Carlos I **Subject:** 150th Anniversary Birth of Antoni
Gaudi **Obv:** Bust of Gaudi at right facing **Obv. Legend:** Año
Internacional **Rev:** Casa Milà

Date	Mintage	F	VF	XF	Unc	BU
2002(M) Proof	25,000	Value: 55.00				

KM# 1083 10 EURO
27.0000 g., 0.9250 Silver 0.8029 oz. ASW, 40.0 mm.
Ruler: Juan Carlos I **Subject:** 150th Anniversary Birth of Antoni
Gaudi **Obv:** Bust of Gaudi at right facing **Obv. Legend:** Año
Internacional **Rev:** El Capricho

Date	Mintage	F	VF	XF	Unc	BU
2002(M) Proof	25,000	Value: 55.00				

KM# 1084 10 EURO
27.0000 g., 0.9250 Silver 0.8029 oz. ASW, 40.0 mm.
Ruler: Juan Carlos I **Subject:** 150th Anniversary - Birth of Antoni
Gaudi **Obv:** Bust of Gaudi at right facing **Obv. Legend:** Año
Internacional **Rev:** Parque Güell

Date	Mintage	F	VF	XF	Unc	BU
2002(M) Proof	25,000	Value: 55.00				

KM# 1089 10 EURO
27.0000 g., 0.9250 Silver 0.8029 oz. ASW **Ruler:** Juan Carlos I
Series: Ibero-America V - ships **Obv:** Crowned arms in center
circle, 10 participating country arms in outer circle **Obv. Legend:**
JUAN CARLOS I REY DE ESPNA **Rev:** Galleon of the Spanish
Armada **Rev. Legend:** ENCUENTRO DE DOS MUNDOS
Note: Issued in 2003.

Date	Mintage	F	VF	XF	Unc	BU
2002(M) Proof	12,000	Value: 135				

KM# 1050 10 EURO
27.0000 g., 0.9250 Silver 0.8029 oz. ASW, 40 mm.
Ruler: Juan Carlos I **Subject:** Annexation of Minorca
Obv: Conjoined heads left **Rev:** Uniformed equestrians shaking
hands flanked by ships **Edge:** Reeded **Note:** Mint mark: Crowned
M.

Date	Mintage	F	VF	XF	Unc	BU
2002 Proof	30,000	Value: 50.00				

KM# 1076 10 EURO
27.0000 g., 0.9250 Silver 0.8029 oz. ASW **Ruler:** Juan Carlos I
Subject: FIFA World Cup **Obv:** Kings head left **Rev:** Goalie
jumping for ball by net **Edge:** Reeded **Note:** Issued in 2004.

Date	Mintage	F	VF	XF	Unc	BU
2003(M) Proof	50,000	Value: 55.00				

KM# 1090 10 EURO
27.0000 g., 0.9250 Silver 0.8029 oz. ASW **Ruler:** Juan Carlos I
Obv: Conjoined heads left **Obv. Legend:** JUAN CARLOS I Y
SOFIA **Rev:** Ediface of Parliament building in Madrid
Rev. Legend: CONSTITUCION ESPANOLA

Date	Mintage	F	VF	XF	Unc	BU
2003(M) Proof	30,000	Value: 60.00				

KM# 1092 10 EURO
27.0000 g., 0.9250 Silver 0.8029 oz. ASW, 40.0 mm.
Ruler: Juan Carlos I **Subject:** !st Anniversary of Euro
Obv: Conjoined heads left **Obv. Legend:** PREMIER
ANIVERSARIO EURO ? JUAN CARLOS I Y SOFIA **Rev:** Europa
riding steer left

Date	Mintage	F	VF	XF	Unc	BU
2003(M) Proof	50,000	Value: 60.00				

KM# 1094 10 EURO
27.0000 g., 0.9250 Silver 0.8029 oz. ASW **Ruler:** Juan Carlos I
Subject: World swimming championship games - Barcelona
2003 **Obv:** Head left **Obv. Legend:** JUAN CARLOS I REY DE
ESPANA **Rev:** Swimmer doing the crawl right **Rev. Legend:** X
FINA CAMPEONATOS DEL MUNDO DENATACION

Date	Mintage	F	VF	XF	Unc	BU
2003(M) Proof	30,000	Value: 60.00				

KM# 1052 10 EURO
27.0000 g., 0.9250 Silver 0.8029 oz. ASW, 40 mm.
Ruler: Juan Carlos I **Obv:** Head left **Rev:** Bust facing flanked by
ship and value **Edge:** Reeded

Date	Mintage	F	VF	XF	Unc	BU
2003 Proof	50,000	Value: 50.00				

KM# 1053 10 EURO
27.0000 g., 0.9250 Silver 0.8029 oz. ASW, 40 mm.
Ruler: Juan Carlos I **Obv:** Juan Carlos I **Rev:** Miguel Lopez de
Legazpi **Edge:** Reeded

Date	Mintage	F	VF	XF	Unc	BU
2003 Proof	25,000	Value: 50.00				

KM# 1054 10 EURO
27.0000 g., 0.9250 Silver 0.8029 oz. ASW, 40 mm.
Ruler: Juan Carlos I **Obv:** Head facing **Rev:** Seated female
figure and Swan **Edge:** Reeded

Date	Mintage	F	VF	XF	Unc	BU
2003 Proof	25,000	Value: 50.00				

KM# 1055 10 EURO
27.0000 g., 0.9250 Silver 0.8029 oz. ASW, 40 mm.
Ruler: Juan Carlos I **Obv:** Head facing **Rev:** Dali's painting "El
gran masturbador" of 1929 **Edge:** Reeded

Date	Mintage	F	VF	XF	Unc	BU
2004 Proof	25,000	Value: 50.00				

KM# 1056 10 EURO
27.0000 g., 0.9250 Silver 0.8029 oz. ASW, 40 mm.
Ruler: Juan Carlos I **Obv:** Head facing **Rev:** Dali's self portrait
with bacon strip **Edge:** Reeded

Date	Mintage	F	VF	XF	Unc	BU
2004 Proof	25,000	Value: 50.00				

KM# 1059 10 EURO
27.0000 g., 0.9250 Silver 0.8029 oz. ASW, 40 mm.
Ruler: Juan Carlos I **Obv:** Conjoined heads left **Rev:** Bust of St.
James facing **Edge:** Reeded

Date	Mintage	F	VF	XF	Unc	BU
2004 Proof	20,000	Value: 50.00				

KM# 1060 10 EURO
27.0000 g., 0.9250 Silver 0.8029 oz. ASW, 40 mm.
Ruler: Juan Carlos I **Obv:** Conjoined heads left within beaded
circle **Rev:** Bust 1/4 left within beaded circle (1451-1504)
Edge: Reeded

Date	Mintage	F	VF	XF	Unc	BU
2004 Proof	20,000	Value: 50.00				

KM# 1099 10 EURO
27.0000 g., 0.9250 Silver 0.8029 oz. ASW **Ruler:** Juan Carlos I
Subject: Expansion of the European Union **Obv:** Head left
Obv. Legend: JUAN CARLOS I Y SOFIA **Rev:** Outlined map of
European Union

Date	Mintage	F	VF	XF	Unc	BU
2004(M) Proof	50,000	Value: 75.00				

KM# 1101 10 EURO
27.0000 g., 0.9250 Silver 0.8029 oz. ASW **Ruler:** Juan Carlos I
Subject: XXVIII Summer Olympics - Athens 2004 **Obv:**
Conjoined heads left **Obv. Legend:** JUAN CARLOS I Y SOFIA
Rev: Broad jumper, outlined world map in background
Rev. Legend: JUEGOS OLIMICOS

Date	Mintage	F	VF	XF	Unc	BU
2004(M) Proof	30,000	Value: 60.00				

KM# 1102 10 EURO
27.0000 g., 0.9250 Silver 0.8029 oz. ASW **Ruler:** Juan Carlos I
Subject: XVIII World Football games - Germany 2006 **Obv:** Head
left **Obv. Legend:** JUAN CARLOS I REY DE ESPANA
Rev: Goalie deflecting ball at net

Date	Mintage	F	VF	XF	Unc	BU
2004(M) Proof	50,000	Value: 60.00				

KM# 1097 10 EURO
27.0000 g., 0.9250 Silver 0.8029 oz. ASW, 40.0 mm. **Ruler:**
Juan Carlos I **Subject:** Wedding of Prince Philip and Letizia Ortiz
Rocasolano **Obv:** Conjoined heads left **Obv. Legend:** JUAN
CARLOS I T SOFÍA **Rev:** Busts of wedding couple facing 3/4 right,
crowned shield below **Rev. Legend:** FELIPE Y LETIZIA - 22.V.2004

Date	Mintage	F	VF	XF	Unc	BU
2004(M) Proof	100,000	Value: 55.00				

KM# 1104 10 EURO
27.0000 g., 0.9250 Silver 0.8029 oz. ASW, 40.0 mm.
Ruler: Juan Carlos I **Obv:** Quixote seated reading a large book
Obv. Legend: ESPAÑA - IV CENTENARIO DE LA PRIMERA
EDICIÓN DE " EL QUIJOTE" **Rev:** Quixote being knocked off his
horse by windmill blade **Rev. Legend:** LA AVENTURA - DE LOS
- MOLINOS DE VIENTO

Date	Mintage	F	VF	XF	Unc	BU
2005(M) Proof	18,000	Value: 65.00				

KM# 1105 10 EURO
27.0000 g., 0.9250 Silver 0.8029 oz. ASW, 40.0 mm.
Ruler: Juan Carlos I **Obv:** Quixote esated reading a large book **Obv. Legend:** ESPAÑA - IV CENTENARIO DE LA PREMERA EDICIÓN DE LA "EL QUIJOTE" **Rev:** Quixote thrusting his sword into an animal skin wine sack **Rev. Legend:** CON UNOS CUEROS DE VINO - BATALLA

Date	Mintage	F	VF	XF	Unc	BU
2005(M) Proof	18,000	Value: 65.00				

KM# 1106 10 EURO
27.0000 g., 0.9250 Silver 0.8029 oz. ASW, 40.0 mm.
Ruler: Juan Carlos I **Obv:** Quixote seated reading a large book **Obv. Legend:** ESPAÑA - IV CENTENARIO DE LA PRIMERA EDICIÓN DE "EL QUIJOTE" **Rev:** Boy mounting a hobby horse with Quixote on it **Rev. Legend:** LA VENIDA DE CLAVAILEÑO CON...DILATADA AVENTURA

Date	Mintage	F	VF	XF	Unc	BU
2005(M) Proof	18,000	Value: 65.00				

KM# 1110 10 EURO
27.0000 g., 0.9250 Silver 0.8029 oz. ASW, 40.0 mm.
Ruler: Juan Carlos I **Rev:** Crowned shield at left, head of Prince Philip at right **Rev. Legend:** XXV ANIVERSARIO - PREMIOS PRÍNCIPE DE ASTURIAS

Date	Mintage	F	VF	XF	Unc	BU
2005(M) Proof	35,000	Value: 60.00				

KM# 1109 10 EURO
27.0000 g., 0.9250 Silver 0.8029 oz. ASW **Ruler:** Juan Carlos I **Series:** Ibero-America VI - Architecture **Obv:** Crowned arms in center circle, 10 participating country arms in outer circle **Obv. Legend:** JUAN CARLOS I REY DE ESPAÑA **Rev:** General Archives building of West Indies in Seville **Rev. Legend:** ENCUENTRO DE DOS MUNDOS

Date	Mintage	F	VF	XF	Unc	BU
2005(M) Proof	12,000	Value: 90.00				

KM# 1064 10 EURO
27.0000 g., 0.9250 Silver 0.8029 oz. ASW, 40 mm.
Ruler: Juan Carlos I **Subject:** 2006 Winter Olympics **Obv:** Juan Carlos **Rev:** Skier **Edge:** Reeded

Date	Mintage	F	VF	XF	Unc	BU
2005 Proof	25,000	Value: 45.00				

KM# 1065 10 EURO
27.0000 g., 0.9250 Silver 0.8029 oz. ASW, 40 mm.
Ruler: Juan Carlos I **Subject:** European Peace and Freedom **Obv:** Juan Carlos **Rev:** European map on clasped hands **Edge:** Reeded

Date	Mintage	F	VF	XF	Unc	BU
2005 Proof	40,000	Value: 40.00				

KM# 1114 10 EURO
26.8000 g., 0.9250 Silver 0.7970 oz. ASW, 39.98 mm.
Ruler: Juan Carlos I **Subject:** 500th Anniversary Death of Columbus **Obv:** Bust of Columbus facing at right, astrolabe at lower left **Obv. Legend:** ESPAÑA **Rev:** Sailing ship "Santa Maria" **Rev. Legend:** CRISTOBAL COLON **Edge:** Reeded

Date	Mintage	F	VF	XF	Unc	BU
2006(M) Proof	12,000	Value: 65.00				

KM# 1119 10 EURO
27.0000 g., 0.9250 Silver 0.8029 oz. ASW, 40.0 mm.
Ruler: Juan Carlos I **Subject:** 20th Anniversay of Spain and Portugal membership in European Union **Obv:** Juan Carlos I **Rev:** Outlined map of Europe, bridge below **Rev. Legend:** ADHESIÓN A LAS COMUNIDADES EUROPEAS **Rev. Inscription:** ESPAÑA - PORTUGAL

Date	Mintage	F	VF	XF	Unc	BU
2006(M) Proof	12,000	Value: 60.00				

KM# 1122 10 EURO
27.0000 g., 0.9250 Silver 0.8029 oz. ASW, 40.0 mm.
Ruler: Juan Carlos I **Obv:** Head left **Obv. Legend:** JUAN CARLOS I REY DE ESPAÑA **Rev:** Charles I (V) standing facing 3/4 right in front of portal **Rev. Legend:** CAROLVS IMPERATOR

Date	Mintage	F	VF	XF	Unc	BU
2006(M) Proof	35,000	Value: 65.00				

KM# 1115 10 EURO
18.0000 g., 0.9250 Silver 0.5353 oz. ASW, 39.98 mm.
Ruler: Juan Carlos I **Subject:** 500th Anniversary - Death of Columbus **Obv:** Bust of Colombus facing at left, astrolabe at lower right **Obv. Legend:** ESPAÑA **Rev:** Sailing ship "Pinta" **Rev. Legend:** CRISTOBAL COLON **Edge:** Reeded

Date	Mintage	F	VF	XF	Unc	BU
2006(M) Proof	12,000	Value: 65.00				

KM# 1116 10 EURO
26.8000 g., 0.9250 Silver 0.7970 oz. ASW, 39.98 mm.
Ruler: Juan Carlos I **Subject:** 500th Anniversary - Death of Columbus **Obv:** Bust of Columbus facing at right, astrolabe at lower left **Obv. Legend:** ESPAÑA **Rev:** Sailing ship "Niña" **Rev. Legend:** CRISTOBAL COLON **Edge:** Reeded

Date	Mintage	F	VF	XF	Unc	BU
2006(M) Proof	12,000	Value: 65.00				

KM# 1124 10 EURO
27.0000 g., 0.9250 Silver 0.8029 oz. ASW, 40 mm.
Ruler: Juan Carlos I **Rev:** Two ornate portals **Rev. Legend:** V ANIVERSARIO DEL EURO

Date	Mintage	F	VF	XF	Unc	BU
2007 Proof	12,000	Value: 65.00				

KM# 1125 10 EURO
27.0000 g., 0.9250 Silver 0.8029 oz. ASW, 40 mm.
Ruler: Juan Carlos I **Rev:** Stone arch bridge **Rev. Legend:** V ANIVERSARIO DEL EURO

Date	Mintage	F	VF	XF	Unc	BU
2007 Proof	12,000	Value: 65.00				

KM# 1126 10 EURO
27.0000 g., 0.9250 Silver 0.8029 oz. ASW, 40 mm.
Ruler: Juan Carlos I **Rev:** Stone archway **Rev. Legend:** V ANIVERSARIO DEL EURO

Date	Mintage	F	VF	XF	Unc	BU
2007 Proof	12,000	Value: 65.00				

KM# 1132 10 EURO
27.0000 g., 0.9250 Silver 0.8029 oz. ASW, 40 mm.
Ruler: Juan Carlos I **Obv:** Conjoined heads left **Obv. Legend:** JUAN CARLOS I Y SOFÍA - AÑO DE ESPAÑA EN CHINA **Rev:** Early silver "Pillar" reales coin with Chinese characters to left and right of pillars **Rev. Legend:** VTRAQUE VNVM

Date	Mintage	F	VF	XF	Unc	BU
2007 Proof	20,000	Value: 60.00				

KM# 1134 10 EURO
27.0000 g., 0.9250 Silver 0.8029 oz. ASW, 40 mm.
Ruler: Juan Carlos I **Obv:** Head left **Obv. Legend:** JUAN CARLOS I REY DE ESPAÑA **Rev:** Basketball player shooting basket **Rev. Legend:** EUROBASKET 2007

Date	Mintage	F	VF	XF	Unc	BU
2007 Proof	12,000	Value: 65.00				

KM# 1141 10 EURO
27.0000 g., 0.9250 Silver 0.8029 oz. ASW, 40 mm.
Ruler: Juan Carlos I **Subject:** Zaragoza Expo 2008

Date	Mintage	F	VF	XF	Unc	BU
2007 Proof	—	Value: 60.00				

KM# 1135 10 EURO
27.0000 g., 0.9250 Silver 0.8029 oz. ASW, 40 mm.
Ruler: Juan Carlos I **Subject:** Treaty of Rome, 50th Anniversary **Obv:** Head left **Rev:** Map of Western Europe

Date	Mintage	F	VF	XF	Unc	BU
2007 Proof	15,000	Value: 60.00				

KM# 1137 10 EURO
27.0000 g., 0.9250 Silver 0.8029 oz. ASW, 40 mm.
Ruler: Juan Carlos I **Subject:** El Cid 700th Anniversary **Obv:** Female standing before arches **Rev:** Monk writing

Date	Mintage	F	VF	XF	Unc	BU
2007 Proof	12,000	Value: 65.00				

KM# 1140 10 EURO
27.0000 g., 0.9250 Silver 0.8029 oz. ASW, 40 mm.
Ruler: Juan Carlos I **Subject:** International Polar Year

Date	Mintage	F	VF	XF	Unc	BU
2007 Proof	—	Value: 60.00				

KM# 1143 10 EURO
0.2700 g., 0.9250 Silver 0.8029 oz. ASW, 32.94 mm.
Ruler: Juan Carlos I **Obv:** Head left **Rev:** Soccer player, ball and net

Date	Mintage	F	VF	XF	Unc	BU
2009 Proof	—	Value: 30.00				

KM# 1049 12 EURO
18.0000 g., 0.9250 Silver 0.5353 oz. ASW, 33 mm.
Ruler: Juan Carlos I **Subject:** Spanish European Union Presidency **Obv:** Conjoined heads left **Rev:** Distorted star design **Edge:** Reeded

Date	Mintage	F	VF	XF	Unc	BU
2002	1,500,000	—	—	—	20.00	22.50
2002 Special select	25,000	—	—	—	—	30.00
2002 Proof	50,000	Value: 50.00				

KM# 1051 12 EURO
18.0000 g., 0.9250 Silver 0.5353 oz. ASW, 33 mm.
Ruler: Juan Carlos I **Subject:** 25th Anniversary of Constitution **Obv:** Conjoined heads left **Rev:** National arms above denomination **Edge:** Plain

Date	Mintage	F	VF	XF	Unc	BU
2003	1,469,000	—	—	—	25.00	27.50

KM# 1069 12 EURO
Silver **Ruler:** Juan Carlos I **Obv:** Juan Carlos and Sofia **Rev:** Felipe and Letizia

Date	Mintage	F	VF	XF	Unc	BU
2004M	—	—	—	—	25.00	27.50

KM# 1095 12 EURO
18.0000 g., 0.9250 Silver 0.5353 oz. ASW, 32.93 mm.
Ruler: Juan Carlos I **Subject:** 500th Anniversary - Death of Isabel **Obv:** Conjoined heads left **Obv. Legend:** JUAN CARLOS I Y SOFIA **Rev:** Bust of Isabella I left **Rev. Legend:** ISABEL I DE CASTILLA / 1481-1504 **Edge:** Plain

Date	Mintage	F	VF	XF	Unc	BU
2004(M)	1,500,000	—	—	—	25.00	27.50

KM# 1096 12 EURO
18.0000 g., 0.9250 Silver 0.5353 oz. ASW, 32.94 mm.
Ruler: Juan Carlos I **Subject:** Wedding of Prince Philip and Letizia Ortiz Rocasolano **Obv:** Conjoined heads left **Obv. Legend:** JUAN CARLOS I Y SOFIA **Rev:** Busts of wedding couple facing 3/4 right **Rev. Legend:** FELIPE Y LETIZIA - 22.V.2004 **Edge:** Plain

Date	Mintage	F	VF	XF	Unc	BU
2004(M)	4,000,000	—	—	—	22.50	25.00

KM# 1067 12 EURO
18.0000 g., 0.9250 Silver 0.5353 oz. ASW, 33 mm.
Ruler: Juan Carlos I **Subject:** Don Quixote **Obv:** Conjoined heads left **Rev:** Man seated on books **Edge:** Reeded

Date	Mintage	F	VF	XF	Unc	BU
2005	4,000,000	—	—	—	22.50	25.00

KM# 1113 12 EURO
18.0000 g., 0.9250 Silver 0.5353 oz. ASW, 32.95 mm.
Ruler: Juan Carlos I **Subject:** 500th Anniversary - Death of Columbus **Obv:** Conjoined heads left **Obv. Legend:** JUAN CARLOS I Y SOFIA **Rev:** Bust of Columbus facing 3/4 right, latitude and longitude lines with three small sailing ships in background **Edge:** Plain

Date	Mintage	F	VF	XF	Unc	BU
2006(M)	4,000,000	—	—	—	22.50	25.00

KM# 1129 12 EURO
18.0000 g., 0.9250 Silver 0.5353 oz. ASW, 32 mm.
Ruler: Juan Carlos I **Rev:** Hand with pen **Rev. Legend:** 50 ANIVERSARIO • TRATADO DE ROMA **Rev. Inscription:** EUROPA

Date	Mintage	F	VF	XF	Unc	BU
2007 Proof	25,000	Value: 30.00				

KM# 1133 20 EURO
1.2400 g., 0.9990 Gold 0.0398 oz. AGW, 13.92 mm.
Ruler: Juan Carlos I **Obv:** National arms **Obv. Legend:** JUAN CARLOS I REY DE ESPAÑA - AÑO DE ESPAÑA EN CHINA **Rev:** Early silver "Pillar" reales coin with Chinese chopmarks

Date	Mintage	F	VF	XF	Unc	BU
2007 Proof	15,000	Value: 65.00				

KM# 1085 50 EURO
168.7500 g., 0.9250 Silver 5.0183 oz. ASW, 73 mm.
Ruler: Juan Carlos I **Subject:** 150th Anniversary - Birth of Antoni Gaudi **Obv:** Bust of Gaudi at right facing **Obv. Legend:** Año Internacional **Rev:** Sagrada Familia

Date	Mintage	F	VF	XF	Unc	BU
2002(M) Proof	8,000	Value: 200				

KM# 1093 50 EURO
168.7500 g., 0.9250 Silver 5.0183 oz. ASW, 73 mm.
Ruler: Juan Carlos I **Subject:** 1st Anniversary of Euro **Obv:** Conjoined heads left **Obv. Legend:** PREMIER ANIVERSARIO EURO • JUAN CARLOS I Y SOFÍA **Rev:** National arms at center surrounded by various items of achitecture

Date	Mintage	F	VF	XF	Unc	BU
2003 Proof	20,000	Value: 550				

KM# 1057 50 EURO
168.7500 g., 0.9250 Silver with removeable gold plated silver insert 5.0183 oz. ASW, 73 mm. **Ruler:** Juan Carlos I **Obv:** Dali's "Dream State" painting **Rev:** Dali's "Rhinocerotic Disintegration..." painting **Edge:** Reeded **Note:** Illustration reduced.

Date	Mintage	F	VF	XF	Unc	BU
2004 Proof	12,000	Value: 175				

KM# 1061 50 EURO
168.7300 g., 0.9250 Silver 5.0177 oz. ASW, 73 mm.
Ruler: Juan Carlos I **Obv:** Crowned bust left(1451-1504) and castle within beaded circle **Rev:** Surrender of Grenada scene within beaded circle **Edge:** Reeded **Note:** Illustration reduced.

Date	Mintage	F	VF	XF	Unc	BU
2004 Proof	8,000	Value: 180				

KM# 1107 50 EURO
168.7500 g., 0.9250 Silver 5.0183 oz. ASW, 73 mm.
Ruler: Juan Carlos I **Obv:** 1/2 length figure of Miguel de Cervantes Saavedra facing writing in manuscript with quill pen **Obv. Legend:** ESPAÑA - IV CENTENARIO DE LA PRIMERA EDICIÓn DE "EL QUIJOTE" **Rev:** Quixote

Date	Mintage	F	VF	XF	Unc	BU
2005(M) Proof	12,000	Value: 225				

KM# 1117 50 EURO
168.2500 g., 0.9250 Silver 5.0035 oz. ASW, 73.95 mm.
Ruler: Juan Carlos I **Subject:** 500th Anniversary - Death of Columbus **Obv:** Landing party at Guanahani **Obv. Legend:** ESPAÑA **Rev:** Columbus standing facing 3/4 left with right arm outstretched standing on outline of the northern part of South America **Rev. Legend:** CRISTOBAL COLON **Edge:** Plain **Note:** Illustration reduced.

Date	Mintage	F	VF	XF	Unc	BU
2006(M) Proof	6,000	Value: 225				

KM# 1127 50 EURO
168.7500 g., 0.9250 Silver 5.0183 oz. ASW, 73 mm.
Ruler: Juan Carlos I **Rev:** Euro seated on resting bull left **Rev. Legend:** V ANIVERSARIO DEL EURO

Date	Mintage	F	VF	XF	Unc	BU
2007 Proof	6,000	Value: 220				

KM# 1138 50 EURO
168.7500 g., 0.9250 Silver 5.0183 oz. ASW, 73 mm. **Ruler:** Juan Carlos I **Subject:** El Cid 700th Anniversary **Obv:** Statue of Rodrigo Diaz de Vivar in Burgas **Rev:** Two seated trumpeters

Date	Mintage	F	VF	XF	Unc	BU
2007 Proof	6,000	Value: 200				

KM# 1077 100 EURO
6.7500 g., 0.9990 Gold 0.2168 oz. AGW **Ruler:** Juan Carlos I **Obv:** Head left **Obv. Legend:** JUAN CARLOS I REY DE ESPANA **Rev:** Player running right kicking ball **Rev. Legend:** ALEMANIA 2006 at bottom **Note:** Issued in 2004.

Date	Mintage	F	VF	XF	Unc	BU
2003(M) Proof	25,000	Value: 375				

KM# 1103 100 EURO
6.7500 g., 0.9990 Gold 0.2168 oz. AGW **Ruler:** Juan Carlos I **Subject:** XVIII World Football Games - Germany 2006 **Obv:** Head left **Obv. Legend:** JUAN CARLOS I REY DE ESPANA **Rev:** Goalie deflecting ball at net **Rev. Inscription:** COPA MUNDIAL DE LA FIFA

Date	Mintage	F	VF	XF	Unc	BU
2004(M) Proof	25,000	Value: 350				

KM# 1081 200 EURO
13.5000 g., 0.9990 Gold 0.4336 oz. AGW **Ruler:** Juan Carlos I **Subject:** XVII Football World Games 2002 - South Korea and Japan **Obv. Legend:** MUNDIAL DE FUTBOL/2002 - ESPANA **Rev:** Ball hitting net

Date	Mintage	F	VF	XF	Unc	BU
2002(M) Proof	4,000	Value: 600				

KM# 1091 200 EURO
13.5000 g., 0.9990 Gold 0.4336 oz. AGW **Ruler:** Juan Carlos I **Obv:** Conjoined heads left **Obv. Legend:** JUAN CARLOS I Y SOFIA **Rev:** Ediface of Parliament Building in Madrid **Rev. Legend:** CONSTITUCION ESPANOLA

Date	Mintage	F	VF	XF	Unc	BU
2003(M) Proof	4,000	Value: 575				

KM# 1075 200 EURO
13.5000 g., 0.9990 Gold 0.4336 oz. AGW, 30 mm. **Ruler:** Juan Carlos I **Subject:** Birth of the Euro **Obv:** Spanish King and Queen left **Rev:** Mythological Europa riding on the back of a bull

Date	Mintage	F	VF	XF	Unc	BU
2003 Proof	20,000	Value: 525				

KM# 1062 200 EURO
13.5000 g., 0.9990 Gold 0.4336 oz. AGW, 30 mm.
Ruler: Juan Carlos I **Obv:** Seated crowned figures on shield flanked by date and value **Rev:** Crowned busts facing each other on coin design **Edge:** Reeded

Date	Mintage	F	VF	XF	Unc	BU
2004 Proof	5,000	Value: 550				

KM# 1100 200 EURO
13.5000 g., 0.9990 Gold 0.4336 oz. AGW **Ruler:** Juan Carlos I **Subject:** Expansion of the European Union **Obv:** Head left **Obv. Legend:** JUAN CARLOS I Y SOFIA **Rev:** Outlined map of the European Union

Date	Mintage	F	VF	XF	Unc	BU
2004(M) Proof	5,000	Value: 600				

KM# 1098 200 EURO
13.5000 g., 0.9990 Gold 0.4336 oz. AGW, 30 mm.
Ruler: Juan Carlos I **Subject:** Wedding of Prince Philip and Letizia Ortiz Rocasolano **Obv:** Conjoined heads left **Obv. Legend:** JUAN CARLOS I Y SOFIA **Rev:** Busts of wedding couple facing 3/4 right at center left, crowned shield at right **Rev. Legend:** FELIPE Y LETIZIA - 22.V.2004

Date	Mintage	F	VF	XF	Unc	BU
2004(M) Proof	30,000	Value: 550				

KM# 1111 200 EURO
13.5000 g., 0.9990 Gold 0.4336 oz. AGW, 30 mm.
Ruler: Juan Carlos I **Rev:** Crowned shield at left, head of Prince Philip left at right **Rev. Legend:** XXV ANIVERSAIO - PREMIOS PRÍNCIPE DE ASTURIAS

Date	Mintage	F	VF	XF	Unc	BU
2005(M) Proof	3,500	Value: 650				

KM# 1066 200 EURO
13.5000 g., 0.9990 Gold 0.4336 oz. AGW, 30 mm.
Ruler: Juan Carlos I **Subject:** European Peace and Freedom **Obv:** Juan Carlos **Rev:** European map on clasped hands **Edge:** Reeded

Date	Mintage	F	VF	XF	Unc	BU
2005 Proof	4,000	Value: 650				

KM# 1123 200 EURO
13.5000 g., 0.9990 Gold 0.4336 oz. AGW, 30 mm.
Ruler: Juan Carlos I **Obv:** Head left **Obv. Legend:** JUAN CARLOS I REY DE ESPAÑA **Rev:** Charles I (V) standing facing 3/4 right in front of portal **Rev. Legend:** CAROLVS IMPERATOR

Date	Mintage	F	VF	XF	Unc	BU
2006(M) Proof	5,000	Value: 600				

KM# 1136 200 EURO
13.5000 g., 0.9990 Gold 0.4336 oz. AGW, 30 mm.
Ruler: Juan Carlos I **Subject:** Treaty of Rome, 50th Anniversary **Obv:** Head left **Rev:** Map of Western Europe

Date	Mintage	F	VF	XF	Unc	BU
2007 Proof	3,500	Value: 600				

KM# 1139 200 EURO
13.5000 g., 0.9990 Gold 0.4336 oz. AGW, 30 mm.
Ruler: Juan Carlos I **Subject:** El Cid, 700th Anniversary **Obv:** Rodrigo Diaz de Vivar bust facing **Rev:** Knight on horseback within rectangle

Date	Mintage	F	VF	XF	Unc	BU
2007 Proof	3,500	Value: 550				

KM# 1112 300 EURO
Bi-Metallic .554 AGW Gold center in .343 ASW Silver ring, 40 mm.
Ruler: Juan Carlos I **Subject:** XVIII World Championship Football Games - Germany 2006 **Obv:** Football player facing kicking ball **Obv. Legend:** ESPAÑA **Rev:** Football player kicking ball into net at foreground **Rev. Legend:** COPA MUNDIAL DE LA FIFA - ALEMANIA **Shape:** 12-sided

Date	Mintage	F	VF	XF	Unc	BU
2005(M) Proof	2,006	Value: 900				

KM# 1121 300 EURO
Bi-Metallic Gold center in silver ring, 40 mm.
Ruler: Juan Carlos I **Rev:** Basketball player facing tossing ball **Rev. Legend:** CAMPEONES DEL MUNDO - JAPÓn 2006 **Shape:** 12-sided

Date	Mintage	F	VF	XF	Unc	BU
2006(M) Proof	2,000	Value: 900				

KM# 1086 400 EURO
27.0000 g., 0.9990 Gold 0.8672 oz. AGW, 38 mm.
Ruler: Juan Carlos I **Subject:** 150th Anniversary - Birth of Antoni Gaudi **Obv:** Bust of Gaudi at right facing **Obv. Legend:** Año Internacional **Rev:** Casa Batlló

Date	Mintage	F	VF	XF	Unc	BU
2002(M) Proof	3,000	Value: 1,150				

KM# 1058 400 EURO
27.0000 g., 0.9990 Gold 0.8672 oz. AGW, 38 mm.
Ruler: Juan Carlos I **Obv:** Bust facing **Rev:** Dali's painting "Girl at the Window" **Edge:** Reeded

Date	Mintage	F	VF	XF	Unc	BU
2004 Proof	5,000	Value: 1,100				

KM# 1108 400 EURO
27.0000 g., 0.9990 Gold 0.8672 oz. AGW, 38 mm.
Ruler: Juan Carlos I **Obv:** Quixote seated reading a large book **Obv. Legend:** ESPAÑA - IV CENTENARIO DE LA PRIMERA EDICIÓN DE "EL QUIJOTE" **Rev:** Quixote on horseback 3/4 right followed by his friend on a burro **Rev. Legend:** DON QUIJOTE DE LA MANCHA SANCHO PANZA

Date	Mintage	F	VF	XF	Unc	BU
2005(M) Proof	3,000	Value: 1,200				

KM# 1118 400 EURO
27.0000 g., 0.9990 Gold 0.8672 oz. AGW **Ruler:** Juan Carlos I **Subject:** 500th Anniversary - Death of Columbus **Obv:** Columbus **Rev:** Audience with Ferdinand and Isabella

Date	Mintage	F	VF	XF	Unc	BU
2006(M) Proof	3,000	Value: 1,200				

KM# 1128 400 EURO
27.0000 g., 0.9990 Gold 0.8672 oz. AGW, 38 mm.
Ruler: Juan Carlos I **Rev:** Large ring of stars around globe **Rev. Legend:** V ANIVERSARIO DEL EURO

Date	Mintage	F	VF	XF	Unc	BU
2007 Proof	3,000	Value: 1,200				

MINT SETS

KM#	Date	Mintage	Identification	Issue Price	Mkt Val
MS27	2000-01 (8)	49,426	KM#832-833, 924, 991-992 (both dated 2000), 1012-1013, 1016	15.50	20.00
MS28	2002 (8)	99,301	KM#1040-1047	—	15.00
MS29	2003 (8)	149	KM#1040-1047	—	15.00
MS30	2004 (8)	43,000	KM#1040-1047	—	70.00
MS31	2005 (8)	49,923	KM#1040-1047	—	30.00
MS32	2006 (8)	49,996	KM#1040-1047	—	12.50
MS33	2007 (8)	—	KM#1040-1042, 1070-1074	—	30.00

PROOF SETS

KM#	Date	Mintage	Identification	Issue Price	Mkt Val
PS34	2002 (9)	35,000	KM#1040-1047, 1049	125	150
PS35	2003 (3)	—	KM#1186, 1187, 1188	—	320
PS36	2007 (2)	—	KM#1132-1133	—	65.00

SRI (SHRI) LANKA

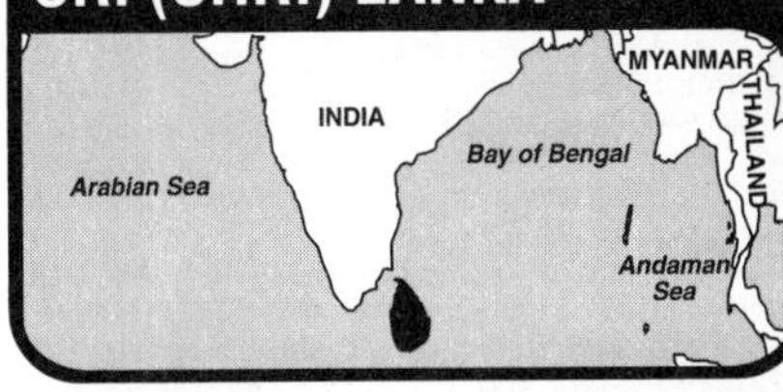

The Democratic Socialist Republic of Sri Lanka (formerly Ceylon) situated in the Indian Ocean 18 miles (29 km.) southeast of India, has an area of 25,332 sq. mi. (65,610 sq. km.) and a population of *16.9 million. Capital: Colombo. The economy is chiefly agricultural. Tea, coconut products and rubber are exported.

Sri Lanka is a member of the Commonwealth of Nations. The president is Chief of State. The prime minister is Head of Government. The present leaders of the country have reverted the country name back to Sri Lanka.

DEMOCRATIC SOCIALIST REPUBLIC

DECIMAL COINAGE

100 Cents = 1 Rupee

KM# 141a 25 CENTS
Nickel Clad Steel **Obv:** National arms **Rev:** Value **Edge:** Reeded

Date	Mintage	F	VF	XF	Unc	BU
2001	10,000,000	—	—	0.10	0.25	0.45
2002	10,000,000	—	—	0.10	0.25	0.45

KM# 141.2b   25 CENTS
Copper Plated Steel, 16 mm. **Obv:** Denomination **Rev:** National arms

Date	Mintage	F	VF	XF	Unc	BU
2005	—	—	—	0.10	0.25	0.45
2006	—	—	—	0.10	0.25	0.45

KM# 141b   25 CENTS
1.7000 g., Copper Plated Steel, 15.94 mm. **Obv:** National arms **Rev:** Value **Edge:** Plain

Date	Mintage	F	VF	XF	Unc	BU
2005	—	—	—	0.10	0.25	0.45
2006	—	—	—	0.10	0.25	0.45

KM# 135.2a   50 CENTS
Nickel Plated Steel, 21.5 mm. **Obv:** National arms **Rev:** Value **Edge:** Reeded

Date	Mintage	F	VF	XF	Unc	BU
2001	30,000,000	—	0.10	0.25	0.65	1.00
2002	10,000,000	—	0.10	0.25	0.65	1.00
2004	—	—	0.10	0.25	0.65	1.00

KM# 135.2b   50 CENTS
2.4900 g., Copper Plated Steel, 17.92 mm. **Obv:** National arms **Rev:** Value **Edge:** Reeded

Date	Mintage	F	VF	XF	Unc	BU
2005	—	—	—	0.25	0.60	1.00
2006	—	—	—	0.25	0.60	1.00

KM# 166   RUPEE
7.1300 g., Copper-Nickel, 25.4 mm. **Subject:** Air Force's 50th Anniversary **Obv:** Badge of the Sri Lanka Air Force **Rev:** Two jets above propeller plane within circle **Edge:** Reeded

Date	Mintage	F	VF	XF	Unc	BU
2001 Proof	2,000	Value: 100				

KM# 136a   RUPEE
Nickel Clad Steel **Obv:** National arms **Rev:** Value **Edge:** Reeded

Date	Mintage	F	VF	XF	Unc	BU
2002	50,000,000	—	0.25	0.50	1.00	1.50

KM# 136.2   RUPEE
Copper-Nickel **Obv:** Inscriptions below designs within wreath **Rev:** National arms **Edge:** Reeded

Date	Mintage	F	VF	XF	Unc	BU
2004	—	—	0.25	0.50	1.00	1.50

KM# 177   RUPEE
Nickel Clad Steel

Date	Mintage	F	VF	XF	Unc	BU
2004	—	—	—	—	1.00	1.50

KM# 136.3   RUPEE
3.6200 g., Brass Plated Steel, 20 mm. **Obv:** National emblem **Rev:** Value and date **Edge:** Segmented reeding

Date	Mintage	F	VF	XF	Unc	BU
2005	—	—	—	—	0.75	1.00
2006	—	—	—	—	0.75	1.00

KM# 136b   RUPEE
3.6700 g., Brass Plated Steel, 19.91 mm. **Obv:** National arms **Rev:** Value **Edge:** Segmented reeding

Date	Mintage	F	VF	XF	Unc	BU
2005	—	—	—	0.35	0.85	1.25
2006	—	—	—	0.35	0.85	1.25

KM# 147   2 RUPEES
8.2500 g., Copper-Nickel, 28.5 mm. **Obv:** National arms **Rev:** Value

Date	Mintage	F	VF	XF	Unc	BU
2001	10,000,000	—	0.30	0.60	1.35	1.75
2002	40,000,000	—	0.30	0.60	1.35	1.75
2004	—	—	0.30	0.60	1.35	1.75

KM# 167   2 RUPEES
8.2500 g., Copper-Nickel, 28.5 mm. **Subject:** Colombo Plan's 50th Anniversary **Obv:** Value within inscription above date **Rev:** Gear wheel **Edge:** Reeded

Date	Mintage	F	VF	XF	Unc	BU
2001	10,000,000	—	—	—	2.00	3.00

KM# 147a   2 RUPEES
7.0800 g., Nickel Clad Steel, 28.5 mm. **Obv:** National arms **Rev:** Value **Edge:** Reeded

Date	Mintage	F	VF	XF	Unc	BU
2005	—	—	—	0.45	1.10	1.50
2006	—	—	—	0.45	1.10	1.50

KM# 175   2 RUPEES
8.2500 g., Copper-Nickel, 28.5 mm. **Subject:** 50th Anniversary of the Employees Provident Fund

Date	Mintage	F	VF	XF	Unc	BU
2008	—	—	—	—	2.00	3.00

KM# 178   2 RUPEES
7.0000 g., Nickel Plated Steel, 28.4 mm. **Subject:** Employees Provident Fund, 50th Anniversary **Obv:** Large 2 **Rev:** Open hands with image of tea pluckers, garment workers and office worker

Date	Mintage	F	VF	XF	Unc	BU
2008	—	—	—	—	1.35	1.75

KM# 148.2   5 RUPEES
9.5000 g., Aluminum-Bronze, 23.4 mm. **Obv:** National arms **Rev:** Value **Edge:** Lettered **Edge Lettering:** CBSL - Central Bank of Sri Lanka

Date	Mintage	F	VF	XF	Unc	BU
2002	30,000,000	—	0.35	0.65	2.00	2.75
2004	—	—	0.35	0.65	2.00	2.75

KM# 168   5 RUPEES
9.5200 g., Aluminum-Bronze, 23.4 mm. **Subject:** 250th Annniversary of the "Upasampada" Rite **Obv:** Value **Rev:** 1/2-length figure facing divides dates

Date	Mintage	F	VF	XF	Unc	BU
2003	—	—	—	—	3.00	4.50

KM# 169   5 RUPEES
9.5200 g., Aluminum-Bronze, 23.4 mm. **Subject:** 250th Anniversary - Upasampada **Obv:** Value **Rev:** Bust facing standing behind shield **Edge:** Reeded and lettered

Date	Mintage	F	VF	XF	Unc	BU
2003	—	—	—	—	3.00	4.50

KM# 148.2a   5 RUPEES
Bronze Plated Steel, 23.4 mm. **Obv:** National arms **Rev:** Value **Edge:** Reeded

Date	Mintage	F	VF	XF	Unc	BU
2005	—	—	—	0.65	2.00	2.75
2006	—	—	—	0.65	2.00	2.75

KM# 148a   5 RUPEES
7.6700 g., Brass Plated Steel, 23.49 mm. **Obv:** National arms **Rev:** Value **Edge:** Reeded and Lettered **Edge Lettering:** CBSL repeated in various languages

Date	Mintage	F	VF	XF	Unc	BU
2005	—	—	—	0.75	1.85	2.50
2006	—	—	—	0.75	1.85	2.50

KM# 170   5 RUPEES
7.6500 g., Brass Plated Steel, 23.5 mm. **Subject:** 2550th Anniversary of Buddha **Obv:** Value **Rev:** "Buddha Jayanthi", wheel above mountain **Edge:** Reeded and lettered

Date	Mintage	F	VF	XF	Unc	BU
2006	—	—	—	—	3.00	4.00

KM# 173   5 RUPEES
7.6500 g., Brass Plated Steel, 23.5 mm. **Subject:** Cricket World Cup

Date	Mintage	F	VF	XF	Unc	BU
2007	—	—	—	—	3.00	4.00

KM# 180   200 RUPEES
11.9000 g., 0.9250 Silver 0.3539 oz. ASW, 28.4 mm. **Subject:** Customs Service, 200th Anniversary **Obv:** Proposed new Customs Building **Rev:** Customs Logo

Date	Mintage	F	VF	XF	Unc	BU
2009 Proof	3,000	Value: 30.00				

KM# 174   1000 RUPEES
Nickel **Subject:** Cricket World Cup

Date	Mintage	F	VF	XF	Unc	BU
2007	—	—	—	—	10.00	12.00

KM# 179   1000 RUPEES
Nickel Plated Steel, 28.5 mm. **Subject:** Employees Provident Fund, 50th Anniversary **Obv:** Large 1000 **Rev:** Open hands with image of tea pluckers, garment workers and office worker

Date	Mintage	F	VF	XF	Unc	BU
2008 Proof	1,200	Value: 125				

KM# 176   1000 RUPEES
Nickel **Subject:** 50th Anniversary of the Employees Provident Fund

Date	Mintage	F	VF	XF	Unc	BU
2008 Proof	1,200	Value: 125				

KM# 171   1500 RUPEES
Silver **Subject:** 2550 Anniversary of Buddha

Date	Mintage	F	VF	XF	Unc	BU
2006 Proof	—	Value: 50.00				

KM# 172   2000 RUPEE
Silver **Subject:** 2550 Anniversary of Buddha

Date	Mintage	F	VF	XF	Unc	BU
2006 Proof	—	Value: 75.00				

SUDAN

The Democratic Republic of the Sudan, located in northeast Africa on the Red Sea between Egypt and Ethiopia, has an area of 967,500 sq. mi. (2,505,810 sq. km.) and a population of *24.5 million. Capital: Khartoum. Agriculture and livestock raising are the chief occupations. Cotton, gum arabic and peanuts are exported.

REPUBLIC
REFORM COINAGE

100 Qurush (Piastres) = 1 Dinar

10 Pounds = 1 Dinar

KM# 119   5 DINARS
3.3500 g., Brass, 19 mm. **Obv:** Value **Rev:** Central Bank building

Date	Mintage	F	VF	XF	Unc	BU
AH1424-2003	—	—	0.75	1.50	3.00	5.00

KM# 120.1 10 DINARS
4.6800 g., Brass, 22 mm. **Rev:** Central Bank building, "a" above "n" at the left end of the Arabic inscription, 64 border beads

Date	Mintage	F	VF	XF	Unc	BU
AH1424-2003	—	—	1.00	2.00	3.50	6.00

KM# 120.2 10 DINARS
4.5600 g., Brass, 22 mm. **Obv:** Value **Rev:** Larger Central Bank building, "a" to right of "n" at the left end of the Arabic inscription, 72 border beads

Date	Mintage	F	VF	XF	Unc	BU
AH1424-2003	—	—	1.00	2.00	3.50	6.00

KM# 121 50 DINARS
Copper-Nickel, 24 mm. **Rev:** Central Bank building

Date	Mintage	F	VF	XF	Unc	BU
AH1423-2002	—	—	2.00	3.50	6.00	9.00

REFORM COINAGE
100 Piastres = 1 Pound

KM# 126 PIASTRE (Ghirsh)
2.2500 g., Aluminum-Bronze, 16 mm. **Obv:** Clay pot **Obv. Legend:** CENTRAL BANK OF SUDAN **Rev:** Value

Date	Mintage	F	VF	XF	Unc	BU
2006	—	—	—	0.90	2.25	3.00

KM# 125 5 PIASTRES
2.9200 g., Brass, 18.32 mm. **Obv:** National arms **Rev:** Large value **Edge:** Reeded

Date	Mintage	F	VF	XF	Unc	BU
2006	—	—	—	1.20	3.00	4.00

KM# 122 10 PIASTRES
3.4200 g., Nickel, 20 mm. **Obv:** Pyramid **Obv. Legend:** CENTRAL BANK OF SUDAN **Rev:** Large value **Edge:** Reeded

Date	Mintage	F	VF	XF	Unc	BU
2006	—	—	—	1.25	3.00	4.00

KM# 124 20 PIASTRES
5.0200 g., Bi-Metallic Copper-Nickel center in Brass ring., 22.19 mm. **Obv:** Ankole Bull in right profile **Obv. Legend:** CENTRAL BANK OF SUDAN **Rev:** large value **Edge:** Reeded

Date	Mintage	F	VF	XF	Unc	BU
2006	—	—	—	1.20	3.00	4.00

KM# 123 50 PIASTRES
5.8600 g., Bi-Metallic Brass center in Copper-Nickel ring, 24.27 mm. **Obv:** Dove in flight **Obv. Legend:** CENTRAL BANK OF SUDAN **Rev:** Value **Edge:** Reeded

Date	Mintage	F	VF	XF	Unc	BU
2006	—	—	—	0.90	2.25	3.00

SURINAME

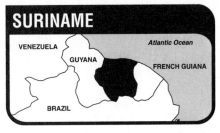

The Republic of Suriname also known as Dutch Guiana, located on the north central coast of South America between Guyana and French Guiana has an area of 63,037 sq. mi. (163,270 sq. km.) and a population of *433,000. Capital: Paramaribo. The country is rich in minerals and forests, and self-sufficient in rice, the staple food crop. The mining, processing and exporting of bauxite is the principal economic activity.

Lieutenants of Amerigo Vespucci sighted the Guiana coast in 1499. Spanish explorers of the 16th century, disappointed at finding no gold, departed leaving the area to be settled by the British in 1652. The colony prospered and the Netherlands acquired it in 1667 in exchange for the Dutch rights in Nieuw Nederland (state of New York). During the European wars of the 18th and 19th centuries, which were fought in part in the new world, Suriname was occupied by the British from 1781-1784 and 1796-1814. Suriname became an autonomous part of the Kingdom of the Netherlands on Dec. 15, 1954. Full independence was achieved on Nov. 25, 1975. In 1980, a coup installed a military government, which has since been dissolved.

MINT MARKS
(u) - Utrecht (privy marks only)

MONETARY SYSTEM
After January, 2004
1 Dollar = 100 Cents

REPUBLIC
MODERN COINAGE

KM# 11b CENT
2.5000 g., Copper Plated Steel, 18 mm. **Obv:** Arms with supporters within wreath **Rev:** Value divides date within circle **Edge:** Plain

Date	Mintage	F	VF	XF	Unc	BU
2004(u)	4,000	—	—	—	1.00	1.50
Note: In sets only						
2005(u)	1,500	—	—	—	1.00	1.50
Note: In sets only						
2006(u)	1,500	—	—	—	1.00	1.50
Note: In sets only						
2007(u)	1,000	—	—	—	1.00	1.50
Note: In sets only						
2008(u)	—	—	—	—	1.00	1.50

KM# 12.1b 5 CENTS
3.0000 g., Copper Plated Steel, 18 mm. **Obv:** Arms with supporters within circle **Rev:** Value divides date within circle **Edge:** Plain **Shape:** Square

Date	Mintage	F	VF	XF	Unc	BU
2004(u)	4,000	—	—	—	1.00	1.50
Note: In sets only						
2005(u)	1,500	—	—	—	1.00	1.50
Note: In sets only						
2006(u)	1,500	—	—	—	1.00	1.50
Note: In sets only						
2007(u)	1,000	—	—	—	1.00	1.50
Note: In sets only						
2008(u)	—	—	—	—	1.00	1.50

KM# 13a 10 CENTS
2.0000 g., Nickel Plated Steel, 16 mm. **Obv:** Arms with supporters within wreath **Rev:** Value and date within circle **Edge:** Reeded

Date	Mintage	F	VF	XF	Unc	BU
2004(u)	4,000	—	—	—	1.00	2.50
Note: In sets only						
2005(u)	1,500	—	—	—	1.00	2.50
Note: In sets only						

Date	Mintage	F	VF	XF	Unc	BU
2006(u)	1,500	—	—	—	1.00	2.50
Note: In sets only						
2007(u)	1,000	—	—	—	1.00	2.50
Note: In sets only						
2008(u)	—	—	—	—	1.00	2.50

KM# 14a 25 CENTS
3.5000 g., Nickel Plated Steel, 20 mm. **Obv:** Arms with supporters within wreath **Rev:** Value and date within circle **Edge:** Reeded

Date	Mintage	F	VF	XF	Unc	BU
2004(u)	4,000	—	—	—	2.00	4.00
Note: In sets only						
2005(u)	1,500	—	—	—	2.00	4.00
Note: In sets only						
2006(u)	1,500	—	—	—	2.00	4.00
Note: In sets only						
2007(u)	1,000	—	—	—	2.00	4.00
Note: In sets only						
2008(u)	—	—	—	—	2.00	4.00

KM# 23 100 CENTS
Copper-Nickel, 23 mm. **Obv:** Arms with supporters within wreath **Rev:** Value and date within circle **Edge:** Reeded

Date	Mintage	F	VF	XF	Unc	BU
2004(u)	4,000	—	—	—	4.00	7.00
Note: In sets only						
2005(u)	1,500	—	—	—	4.00	7.00
Note: In sets only						
2006(u)	1,500	—	—	—	4.00	7.00
Note: In sets only						
2007(u)	1,000	—	—	—	4.00	7.00
Note: In sets only						
2008(u)	—	—	—	—	4.00	7.00

KM# 24 250 CENTS
9.5700 g., Copper-Nickel, 28 mm. **Obv:** Arms with supporters within wreath **Rev:** Value and date within circle

Date	Mintage	F	VF	XF	Unc	BU
2004(u)	4,000	—	—	—	6.00	10.00
Note: In sets only						
2005(u)	1,500	—	—	—	6.00	10.00
Note: In sets only						
2006(u)	1,500	—	—	—	6.00	10.00
Note: In sets only						
2007(u)	1,000	—	—	—	6.00	10.00
Note: In sets only						
2008(u)	—	—	—	—	6.00	10.00

KM# 64 400 DOLLARS
Gold **Subject:** 30 Years of Independence

Date	Mintage	F	VF	XF	Unc	BU
2005 Proof	1,000	Value: 500				

MINT SETS

KM# Date	Mintage	Identification	Issue Price	Mkt Val
MS1 2004 (6)	4,000	KM#11b, 12.1b, 13a, 14a, 23, 24	25.00	27.50
MS2 2005 (6)	1,500	KM#11b, 12.1b, 13a-14a, 23-24	25.00	27.50
MS3 2006 (6)	1,500	KM#11b, 12.1b, 13a-14a, 23-24	25.00	27.50
MS4 2007 (6)	1,000	KM#11b, 12.1b, 13a-14a, 23-24	27.00	27.50
MS5 2008 (6)	—	KM#11b, 12.1b, 13a-14a, 23-24	27.00	27.50

SWAZILAND

The Kingdom of Swaziland, located in southeastern Africa, has an area of 6,704 sq. mi. (17,360 sq. km.) and a population of *756,000. Capital: Mbabane (administrative); Lobamba (legislative). The diversified economy includes mining, agriculture, and light industry. Asbestos, iron ore, wood pulp, and sugar are exported.

The Kingdom is a member of the Commonwealth of Nations. King Mswati III is Head of State. The prime minister is Head of Government.

RULER
King Mswati III, 1986-

MONETARY SYSTEM
100 Cents = 1 Luhlanga
25 Luhlanga = 1 Lilangeni
(plural - Emalangeni)

KINGDOM
DECIMAL COINAGE

KM# 48   5 CENTS
2.1000 g., Copper-Nickel, 18.5 mm.   **Ruler:** King Msawati III
Obv: Bust 3/4 right **Rev:** Arum lily and value **Rev. Designer:**
Michael Rizzello **Edge:** Plain **Shape:** Scalloped

Date	Mintage	F	VF	XF	Unc	BU
2001	—	—	—	—	0.20	0.50	0.75
2002	—	—	—	—	0.20	0.50	0.75
2003	—	—	—	—	0.20	0.50	0.75
2005	—	—	—	—	0.20	0.50	0.75
2006	—	—	—	—	0.20	0.50	0.75
2007	—	—	—	—	0.20	0.50	0.75

KM# 49   10 CENTS
3.6000 g., Copper-Nickel, 22 mm.   **Ruler:** King Msawati III
Obv: Bust 3/4 right **Rev:** Sugar cane and value **Rev. Designer:**
Michael Rizzello **Edge:** Plain **Shape:** Scalloped

Date	Mintage	F	VF	XF	Unc	BU
2001	—	—	—	0.30	0.75	1.00
2002	—	—	—	0.30	0.75	1.00
2005	—	—	—	0.30	0.75	1.00
2006	—	—	—	0.30	0.75	1.00

KM# 50.2   20 CENTS
5.5200 g., Copper-Nickel, 25.2 mm.   **Ruler:** King Msawati III
Obv: Small bust 3/4 right **Rev:** Elephant head, value **Rev.**
Designer: Michael Rizzello **Edge:** Plain **Shape:** Scalloped

Date	Mintage	F	VF	XF	Unc	BU
2001	—	—	—	0.35	0.90	1.25
2002	—	—	—	0.35	0.90	1.25
2003	—	—	—	0.35	0.90	1.25

KM# 52   50 CENTS
8.9000 g., Copper-Nickel, 29.45 mm.   **Ruler:** King Msawati III
Obv: Head 1/4 right **Rev:** Arms with supporters
Rev. Designer: Michael Rizzello

Date	Mintage	F	VF	XF	Unc	BU
2001	—	—	—	—	3.75	4.50
2003	—	—	—	—	3.75	4.50

KM# 45   LILANGENI
9.5000 g., Brass, 22.5 mm.   **Ruler:** King Msawati III **Obv:** Head
1/4 right **Rev:** Bust facing

Date	Mintage	F	VF	XF	Unc	BU
2002	—	—	—	1.50	2.75	3.50
2003	—	—	—	1.50	2.75	3.50

KM# 46   2 EMALANGENI
5.0000 g., Brass   **Ruler:** King Msawati III **Obv:** Head 1/4 right
Rev: Lilies and value

Date	Mintage	F	VF	XF	Unc	BU
2003 sm. bust	—	—	—	—	3.75	4.25

KM# 47   5 EMALANGENI
7.6000 g., Brass   **Ruler:** King Msawati III **Obv:** Head 1/4 right
Rev: Arms with supporters above value that divides date

Date	Mintage	F	VF	XF	Unc	BU
2003 sm. bust	—	—	—	—	6.00	7.00

SWEDEN

The Kingdom of Sweden, a limited constitutional monarchy
located in northern Europe between Norway and Finland, has an
area of 173,732 sq. mi. (449,960 sq. km.) and a population of *8.5
million. Capital: Stockholm. Mining, lumbering and a specialized
machine industry dominate the economy. Machinery, paper, iron
and steel, motor vehicles and wood pulp are exported.

RULER
Carl XVI Gustaf, 1973-

MINT OFFICIALS' INITIALS

Letter	Date	Name
B	1992-2005	Stefan Ingves
D	1986-2005	Bengt Dennis
SI	2006-	Stefan Ingves

MONETARY SYSTEM
100 Ore = 1 Krona

KINGDOM
REFORM COINAGE

KM# 878   50 ORE
3.7000 g., Bronze, 18.7 mm.   **Ruler:** Carl XVI Gustaf **Obv:** Value
Rev: Three crowns and date **Edge:** Reeded

Date	Mintage	F	VF	XF	Unc	BU
2001 B	30,120,532	—	—	0.10	0.15	0.25
2002 B	—	—	—	0.10	0.15	0.25
2003 H	—	—	—	0.10	0.15	0.25
2004 H	25,958,649	—	—	0.10	0.15	0.25
2005 H	—	—	—	0.10	0.15	0.25
2006 SI	—	—	—	0.10	0.15	0.25
2007 SI	—	—	—	0.10	0.15	0.25

KM# 894   KRONA
6.9800 g., Copper-Nickel, 24.9 mm.   **Ruler:** Carl XVI Gustaf
Obv: Head left **Rev:** Crown and value **Edge:** Reeded

Date	Mintage	F	VF	XF	Unc	BU
2001 B	23,905,454	—	—	—	0.65	1.00
2002 B	—	—	—	—	0.65	1.00
2003 H	—	—	—	—	0.65	1.00
2004 H	42,060,252	—	—	—	0.65	1.00
2005 H	—	—	—	—	0.65	1.00
2007 B	—	—	—	—	0.65	1.00

KM# 916   KRONA
6.9800 g., Copper-Nickel, 24.9 mm.   **Ruler:** Carl XVI Gustaf
Subject: Seperation from Finland, 200 Anniversary **Obv:** Head
left **Obv. Designer:** Ernest Nordin **Rev:** Horizontal sea waves
Rev. Designer: Anne Winblad Jakubowski

Date	Mintage	F	VF	XF	Unc	BU
2009	—	—	—	—	0.65	1.00

KM# 853a   5 KRONOR
9.6000 g., Copper-Nickel Clad Nickel, 28.5 mm.   **Ruler:** Carl XVI
Gustaf **Obv:** Crowned monogram **Rev:** Value

Date	Mintage	F	VF	XF	Unc	BU
2001 B	6,001,481	—	—	—	1.00	1.25
2002 B	—	—	—	—	1.00	1.25
2003 H	—	—	—	—	1.00	1.25
2004 H	6,732,730	—	—	—	1.00	1.25
2005 H	—	—	—	—	1.00	1.25

KM# 895   10 KRONOR
6.5700 g., Copper-Aluminum-Zinc, 20.4 mm.   **Ruler:** Carl XVI
Gustaf **Obv:** Head left **Rev:** Three crowns and value
Edge: Reeded and plain sections

Date	Mintage	F	VF	XF	Unc	BU
2001 B	4,171,757	—	—	—	1.75	2.00
2002 B	—	—	—	—	1.75	2.00
2003 H	—	—	—	—	1.75	2.00
2004 H	9,045,581	—	—	—	1.75	2.00
2005 H	—	—	—	—	1.75	2.00
2006 SI	—	—	—	—	1.75	2.00

KM# 910   50 KRONOR
22.0000 g., Brass, 36 mm.   **Ruler:** Carl XVI Gustaf **Subject:** 95th
Anniversary of the birth of Astrid Lindgren **Obv:** Playful young
girl **Rev:** Astrid Lindgren **Edge:** Plain

Date	Mintage	F	VF	XF	Unc	BU
ND (2002)	100,000	—	—	—	8.00	10.00

KM# 915   50 KRONOR
22.0000 g., Brass, 36 mm.   **Ruler:** Carl XVI Gustaf
Subject: 150th Anniversary of Sweden's first postage stamp
Obv: Winged letter flying over landscape **Rev:** Sweden's first
postage stamp design **Edge:** Plain **Designer:** Annie Wildblad
Jakubowski

Date	Mintage	F	VF	XF	Unc	BU
ND (2005)	100,000	—	—	—	8.00	10.00

KM# 896   200 KRONOR
27.2500 g., 0.9250 Silver 0.8104 oz. ASW, 36 mm.
Ruler: Carl XVI Gustaf **Subject:** 25th Wedding Anniversary
Obv: Conjoined busts left **Rev:** Crowned arms with supporters
Edge: Plain **Designer:** Philip Nathan

Date	Mintage	F	VF	XF	Unc	BU
ND (2001)	50,000	—	—	—	35.00	45.00

KM# 908   200 KRONOR
27.0000 g., 0.9250 Silver 0.8029 oz. ASW, 36 mm.
Ruler: Carl XVI Gustaf **Subject:** 750th Anniversary of Stockholm
Obv: City seal with three towers and gate **Rev:** Three towers of
city hall **Edge:** Plain **Designer:** Bo Thoréu

Date	Mintage	F	VF	XF	Unc	BU
ND (2002) Proof	25,000	Value: 35.00				

KM# 902 200 KRONOR

Silver **Ruler:** Carl XVI Gustaf **Subject:** 30th Anniversary of Reign **Designer:** Ernest Nordin

Date	Mintage	F	VF	XF	Unc	BU
2003	—	—	—	—	35.00	45.00

KM# 904 200 KRONOR

27.0300 g., 0.9250 Silver 0.8038 oz. ASW, 36 mm. **Ruler:** Carl XVI Gustaf **Subject:** 700th Anniversary, St. Birgitta **Obv:** Cross in circle above value **Rev:** St. Birgitta **Edge:** Plain **Designer:** Ernest Nordin

Date	Mintage	F	VF	XF	Unc	BU
ND (2003)	60,000	—	—	—	35.00	45.00

KM# 911 200 KRONOR

27.0000 g., 0.9250 Silver 0.8029 oz. ASW, 36 mm. **Ruler:** Carl XVI Gustaf **Subject:** Royal Palace in Stockholm 250th Anniversary **Obv:** Two antique keys over map **Rev:** Royal Palace in Stockholm **Edge:** Plain **Designer:** Annie Windblad Jakubowski

Date	Mintage	F	VF	XF	Unc	BU
ND (2004) Proof	35,000	Value: 35.00				

KM# 913 200 KRONOR

27.0000 g., 0.9250 Silver 0.8029 oz. ASW, 36 mm. **Ruler:** Carl XVI Gustaf **Obv:** Stylized flames **Rev:** Dag Hammarskjöld **Edge:** Plain **Designer:** Ernst Nordin

Date	Mintage	F	VF	XF	Unc	BU
ND (2005) Proof	35,000	Value: 35.00				

KM# 906 200 KRONOR

27.0300 g., 0.9250 Silver 0.8038 oz. ASW, 36 mm. **Ruler:** Carl XVI Gustaf **Subject:** Centennial of the end of the Union between Norway and Sweden **Obv:** Split disc **Rev:** Flag on pole and two clouds **Designer:** Annie Windblad Jakubowski

Date	Mintage	F	VF	XF	Unc	BU
2005	35,000	—	—	—	35.00	45.00

KM# 909 2000 KRONOR

12.0000 g., 0.9000 Gold 0.3472 oz. AGW, 26 mm. **Ruler:** Carl XVI Gustaf **Subject:** 750th Anniversary of Stockholm **Obv:** City seal with three towers and gate **Rev:** Three towers of city hall **Edge:** Plain **Designer:** Bo Thoréu

Date	Mintage	F	VF	XF	Unc	BU
ND (2002) Proof	5,000	Value: 425				

KM# 903 2000 KRONOR

12.0000 g., 0.9990 Gold 0.3854 oz. AGW **Ruler:** Carl XVI Gustaf **Subject:** 30th Anniversary of Reign **Designer:** Ernst Nordin

Date	Mintage	F	VF	XF	Unc	BU
2003	—	—	—	—	450	475

KM# 905 2000 KRONOR

12.0000 g., 0.9000 Gold 0.3472 oz. AGW, 26 mm. **Ruler:** Carl XVI Gustaf **Subject:** St. Birgitta's 700th Anniversary of birth **Obv:** Gothic letter B above value **Rev:** St. Birgitta **Edge:** Plain **Designer:** Ernst Nordin

Date	Mintage	F	VF	XF	Unc	BU
ND (2003)	8,000	—	—	—	425	450

KM# 912 2000 KRONOR

12.0000 g., 0.9000 Gold Royal Palace in Stockholm 250th Anniversary 0.3472 oz. AGW, 26 mm. **Ruler:** Carl XVI Gustaf **Subject:** Royal Palace in Stockholm **Obv:** Two antique keys over map **Edge:** Plain **Designer:** Annie Windblad Jakubowski

Date	Mintage	F	VF	XF	Unc	BU
ND (2004) Proof	5,243	Value: 445				

KM# 914 2000 KRONOR

12.0000 g., 0.9000 Gold 0.3472 oz. AGW, 26 mm. **Ruler:** Carl XVI Gustaf **Obv:** Stylized flames **Rev:** Dag Hammarskjold **Edge:** Plain **Designer:** Ernst Nordin

Date	Mintage	F	VF	XF	Unc	BU
ND (2005) Proof	5,000	Value: 445				

KM# 907 2000 KRONOR

12.0000 g., 0.9000 Gold 0.3472 oz. AGW, 26 mm. **Ruler:** Carl XVI Gustaf **Subject:** Centennial of the end of the Union between Norway and Sweden **Obv:** Split disc **Rev:** Flag pole dividing two clouds **Designer:** Annie Windblad Jakubowski

Date	Mintage	F	VF	XF	Unc	BU
2005	5,000	—	—	—	425	450

MINT SETS

KM#	Date	Mintage	Identification	Issue Price	Mkt Val
MS107	2002 (4)	—	KM#853a, 878, 894, 895 plus medal	—	10.00

SWITZERLAND

The Swiss Confederation, located in central Europe north of Italy and south of Germany, has an area of 15,941 sq. mi. (41,290 sq. km.) and a population of *6.6 million. Capital: Bern. The economy centers about a well-developed manufacturing industry. Machinery, chemicals, watches and clocks, and textiles are exported.

The Swiss Constitutions of 1848 and 1874 established a union modeled upon that of the United States.

MINT MARK

B – Bern

CONFEDERATION

Confoederatio Helvetica

MONETARY SYSTEM

100 Rappen (Centimes) = 1 Franc

DECIMAL COINAGE

KM# 46 RAPPEN

1.5000 g., Bronze, 16 mm. **Obv:** Cross **Rev:** Value and oat sprig **Edge:** Plain **Designer:** Josef Tannheimer

Date	Mintage	F	VF	XF	Unc	BU
2001B	1,522,000	—	—	—	0.50	1.00
2001B Proof	6,000	Value: 2.00				
2002B	2,024,000	—	—	—	0.50	1.00
2002B Proof	5,500	Value: 2.00				
2003B	1,522,000	—	—	—	0.50	1.00
2003B Proof	5,500	Value: 2.00				
2004B	1,526,000	—	—	—	0.50	1.00
2004B Proof	5,000	Value: 2.00				
2005B	1,524,000	—	—	—	0.50	1.00
2005B Proof	4,500	Value: 2.00				
2006B	26,000	—	—	—	—	135

Note: In sets only, circulation strikes not released

Date	Mintage	F	VF	XF	Unc	BU
2006B Proof	4,000	Value: 2.00				

KM# 26c 5 RAPPEN

1.8000 g., Aluminum-Brass, 17.15 mm. **Obv:** Crowned head right **Obv. Designer:** Karl Schwenzer **Rev:** Value within wreath **Rev. Designer:** Karl Friedrich Voigt **Edge:** Plain

Date	Mintage	F	VF	XF	Unc	BU
2001B	5,022,000	—	—	—	0.50	1.00
2001B Proof	6,000	Value: 2.00				
2002B	12,024,000	—	—	—	0.50	1.00
2002B Proof	6,000	Value: 2.00				
2003B	10,022,000	—	—	—	0.50	1.00
2003B Proof	5,500	Value: 2.00				
2004B	10,026,000	—	—	—	0.50	1.00
2004B Proof	5,000	Value: 2.00				
2005B	13,024,000	—	—	—	0.50	1.00
2005B Proof	4,500	Value: 2.00				
2006B	12,026,000	—	—	—	0.50	1.00
2006B Proof	4,000	Value: 2.00				
2007B	13,024,000	—	—	—	0.50	1.00
2007B Proof	4,000	Value: 2.00				
2008B	40,015,000	—	—	—	0.50	1.00
2008B Proof	4,000	Value: 2.00				
2009B	45,015,000	—	—	—	0.50	1.00
2009B Proof	4,000	Value: 2.00				

KM# 27 10 RAPPEN

3.0000 g., Copper-Nickel, 19.15 mm. **Obv:** Crowned head right **Obv. Legend:** CONFOEDERATIO HELVETICA **Obv. Designer:** Karl Schwenzer **Rev:** Value within wreath **Rev. Designer:** Karl Friedrich Voigt **Edge:** Plain

Date	Mintage	F	VF	XF	Unc	BU
2001B	7,022,000	—	—	—	0.50	1.00
2001B Proof	6,000	Value: 2.00				
2002B	15,024,000	—	—	—	0.50	1.00
2002B Proof	6,000	Value: 2.00				
2003B	12,022,000	—	—	—	0.50	1.00
2003B Proof	5,500	Value: 2.00				
2004B	5,026,000	—	—	—	0.50	1.00
2004B Proof	5,000	Value: 2.00				
2005B	7,024,000	—	—	—	0.50	1.00
2005B Proof	4,500	Value: 2.00				
2006B	2,026,000	—	—	—	0.50	1.00
2006B Proof	4,000	Value: 2.00				
2007B	18,024,000	—	—	—	0.50	1.00
2007B Proof	4,000	Value: 2.00				
2008B	35,015,000	—	—	—	0.50	1.00
2008B Proof	4,000	Value: 2.00				
2009B	35,015,000	—	—	—	0.50	1.00
2009B Proof	4,000	Value: 2.00				

KM# 29a 20 RAPPEN

4.0000 g., Copper-Nickel, 21.05 mm. **Obv:** Crowned head right **Obv. Designer:** Karl Schwenzer **Rev:** Value within wreath **Rev. Designer:** Karl Friedrich Voigt **Edge:** Plain

Date	Mintage	F	VF	XF	Unc	BU
2001B	7,022,000	—	—	—	1.00	2.00
2001B Proof	6,000	Value: 3.00				
2002B	12,024,000	—	—	—	1.00	2.00
2002B Proof	6,000	Value: 3.00				
2003B	10,022,000	—	—	—	1.00	2.00
2003B Proof	5,500	Value: 3.00				
2004B	10,026,000	—	—	—	1.00	2.00
2004B Proof	5,000	Value: 3.00				
2005B	6,024,000	—	—	—	1.00	2.00
2005B Proof	4,500	Value: 3.00				
2006B	5,026,000	—	—	—	1.00	2.00
2006B Proof	4,000	Value: 3.00				
2007B	22,024,000	—	—	—	1.00	2.00
2007B Proof	4,000	Value: 3.00				
2008B	41,015,000	—	—	—	1.00	2.00
2008B Proof	4,000	Value: 3.00				
2009B	32,015,000	—	—	—	1.00	2.00
2009 Proof	4,000	Value: 3.00				

KM# 23a.3 1/2 FRANC

2.2000 g., Copper-Nickel, 18.2 mm. **Obv:** 23 Stars around figure **Rev:** Value within wreath **Edge:** Reeded **Designer:** A. Bovy

Date	Mintage	F	VF	XF	Unc	BU
2001B	6,022,000	—	—	—	2.50	3.50
2001B Proof	6,000	Value: 5.00				
2002B	2,024,000	—	—	—	2.50	3.50
2002B Proof	6,000	Value: 5.00				
2003B	2,022,000	—	—	—	2.50	3.50
2003B Proof	5,500	Value: 5.00				
2004B	2,026,000	—	—	—	2.50	3.50
2004B Proof	5,000	Value: 5.00				
2005B	1,024,000	—	—	—	2.50	3.50
2005B Proof	4,500	Value: 5.00				
2006B	2,025,000	—	—	—	2.50	3.50
2006B Proof	4,500	Value: 5.00				
2007B	18,024,000	—	—	—	2.00	3.00
2007B Proof	4,000	Value: 5.00				
2008B	25,015,000	—	—	—	2.00	3.00
2008B Proof	4,000	Value: 5.00				
2009B	27,015,000	—	—	—	2.00	3.00
2009B Proof	4,000	Value: 5.00				

KM# 24a.3 FRANC

4.4000 g., Copper-Nickel, 23.2 mm. **Obv:** 23 Stars around figure **Rev:** Value and date within wreath **Edge:** Reeded **Designer:** A. Bovy

Date	Mintage	F	VF	XF	Unc	BU
2001B	3,022,000	—	—	—	3.00	5.00
2001B Proof	6,000	Value: 7.00				
2002B	1,024,000	—	—	—	3.00	5.00
2002B Proof	6,000	Value: 7.00				
2003B	2,022,000	—	—	—	3.00	5.00
2003B Proof	5,500	Value: 7.00				
2004B	2,026,000	—	—	—	3.00	5.00
2004B Proof	5,000	Value: 7.00				
2005B	1,024,000	—	—	—	3.00	5.00
2005B Proof	4,500	Value: 7.00				
2006B	2,026,000	—	—	—	3.00	5.00
2006B Proof	4,000	Value: 7.00				
2007B	3,024,000	—	—	—	3.00	5.00
2007B Proof	4,000	Value: 7.00				
2008B	7,015,000	—	—	—	3.00	5.00
2008B Proof	4,000	Value: 7.00				
2009B	11,015,000	—	—	—	3.00	5.00
2009B Proof	4,000	Value: 7.00				

KM# 21a.3   2 FRANCS
8.8000 g., Copper-Nickel, 27.4 mm. **Obv:** 23 Stars around figure
Rev: Value within wreath **Edge:** Reeded **Designer:** A. Bovy

Date	Mintage	F	VF	XF	Unc	BU
2001B	4,022,000	—	—	—	4.00	7.00
2001B Proof	6,000	Value: 10.00				
2002B	1,024,000	—	—	—	4.50	7.50
2002B Proof	6,000	Value: 10.00				
2003B	1,022,000	—	—	2.50	4.50	7.50
2003B Proof	5,500	Value: 10.00				
2004B	1,026,000	—	—	2.50	4.50	7.50
2004B Proof	5,000	Value: 10.00				
2005B	2,024,000	—	—	—	4.50	7.50
2005B Proof	4,500	Value: 10.00				
2006B	7,026,000	—	—	—	4.50	7.50
2006B Proof	4,000	Value: 10.00				
2007B	16,024,000	—	—	—	4.50	7.50
2007B Proof	4,000	Value: 10.00				
2008B	6,015,000	—	—	—	4.50	7.50
2008B Proof	4,000	Value: 10.00				
2009B	8,015,000	—	—	—	4.50	7.50
2009B Proof	4,000	Value: 10.00				

KM# 40a.4   5 FRANCS
13.2000 g., Copper-Nickel, 31.45 mm. **Obv:** William Tell right
Rev: Shield flanked by sprigs **Edge:** DOMINUS PROVIDEBIT
and 13 stars raised **Designer:** Paul Burkhard

Date	Mintage	F	VF	XF	Unc	BU
2001B	1,022,000	—	—	—	7.00	10.00
2001B Proof	6,000	Value: 15.00				
2002B	1,024,000	—	—	—	7.00	10.00
2002B Proof	6,000	Value: 15.00				
2003B	1,022,000	—	—	—	7.00	10.00
2003B Proof	5,500	Value: 15.00				
2004B	526,000	—	—	—	7.50	11.00
2004B Proof	5,000	Value: 15.00				
2005B	524,000	—	—	—	7.50	11.00
2005B Proof	4,500	Value: 15.00				
2006B	526,000	—	—	—	7.50	11.00
2006B Proof	4,000	Value: 15.00				
2007B	524,000	—	—	—	7.50	11.00
2007B Proof	4,000	Value: 15.00				
2008B	515,000	—	—	—	7.50	11.00
Note: Not yet released for circulation						
2008B Proof	4,000	Value: 15.00				
2009B	2,015,000	—	—	—	7.50	11.00
2009B Proof	4,000	Value: 15.00				

COMMEMORATIVE COINAGE

KM# 92   5 FRANCS
15.0000 g., Bi-Metallic Brass center in Copper-Nickel ring,
32.85 mm. **Subject:** Zurcher Sechselauten **Obv:** Value within
circle **Rev:** Burning strawman within circle **Edge:** Reeded
Edge Lettering: DOMINUS PROVIDEBIT (13 stars)
Designer: John Grüniger

Date	Mintage	F	VF	XF	Unc	BU
2001B	170,000	—	—	—	8.00	12.00
2001B Proof	20,000	Value: 24.00				

KM# 98   5 FRANCS
15.0000 g., Bi-Metallic Brass center in Copper-Nickel ring,
32.85 mm. **Subject:** Escalade 1602-2002 **Obv:** Value within
circle **Rev:** Swirling ladders design within circle **Edge:** Reeded
Edge Lettering: DOMINUS PROVIDEBIT (13 stars)
Designer: P.A. Zuber

Date	Mintage	F	VF	XF	Unc	BU
2002B Proof	15,000	Value: 24.00				
2002B	130,000	—	—	—	8.00	12.00

KM# 103   5 FRANCS
15.0000 g., Bi-Metallic Brass center in Copper-Nickel ring,
32.85 mm. **Subject:** Chalandamarz **Obv:** Value within circular
inscription and designed wreath **Rev:** Boys shaking bells within
3/4 designed wreath **Edge:** Reeded **Edge Lettering:** DOMINUS
PROVIDEBIT (13 stars) **Designer:** Gian Vonzun

Date	Mintage	F	VF	XF	Unc	BU
2003B	96,000	—	—	—	8.00	12.00
2003B Proof	13,500	Value: 24.00				

KM# 107   10 FRANCS
15.0000 g., Bi-Metallic Copper-Nickel center in Aluminum-
Bronze ring, 32.85 mm. **Obv:** Value **Rev:** Matterhorn Mountain
Edge: Segmented reeding **Designer:** Stephan Bundi

Date	Mintage	F	VF	XF	Unc	BU
2004B	94,976	—	—	—	—	20.00
2004B Proof	12,168	Value: 42.00				

KM# 111   10 FRANCS
15.0000 g., Bi-Metallic Copper-Nickel center in Aluminum-
Bronze ring, 32.85 mm. **Obv:** Value **Rev:** Jungfrau mountain
Edge: Segmented reeding **Designer:** Stephan Bundi

Date	Mintage	F	VF	XF	Unc	BU
2005B	77,791	—	—	—	—	17.00
2005B Proof	10,495	Value: 40.00				

KM# 114   10 FRANCS
15.0000 g., Bi-Metallic Copper-Nickel center in Aluminum-
Bronze ring, 32.85 mm. **Obv:** Value **Rev:** Piz Bernina mountain
Edge: Segmented reeding **Designer:** Stephan Bundi

Date	Mintage	F	VF	XF	Unc	BU
2006B	66,000	—	—	—	—	16.00
2006B Proof	9,000	Value: 40.00				

KM# 118   10 FRANCS
15.0000 g., Bi-Metallic Copper-Nickel center in Aluminum-
Bronze ring, 32.85 mm. **Subject:** Swiss National Park
Obv: Value **Rev:** Ibex **Edge:** Segmented reeding

Date	Mintage	F	VF	XF	Unc	BU
2007B	Est. 96,000	—	—	—	—	16.00
2007B Proof	Est. 12,000	Value: 40.00				
2009						

KM# 126   10 FRANCS
15.0000 g., Bi-Metallic Copper-Nickel center in Aluminum-
Bronze ring, 32.85 mm. **Obv:** Small national arms **Obv. Legend:**
CONFEDERATIO - HELVETICA **Rev:** Golden Eagle alighting
Rev. Legend: PARK NATIONAL SUISSE **Rev. Designer:**
Niklaus Heeb **Edge:** Segmented reeding

Date	Mintage	F	VF	XF	Unc	BU
2008B	Est. 95,000	—	—	—	—	16.00
2008B Proof	Est. 12,000	Value: 40.00				

KM# 130   10 FRANCS
15.0000 g., Bi-Metallic Copper-nickel center in brass ring,
32.85 mm. **Subject:** Swiss National Park **Obv:** Value **Rev:** Red
deer **Rev. Designer:** Niklaus Heeb

Date	Mintage	F	VF	XF	Unc	BU
2009B	Est. 95,000	—	—	—	—	16.00
2009B Proof	Est. 12,000	Value: 40.00				

KM# 134   10 FRANCS
15.0000 g., Bi-Metallic Copper-nickel center in brass ring
Subject: Swiss National Park **Obv:** Value **Rev:** Marmot

Date	Mintage	F	VF	XF	Unc	BU
2010B Proof	12,000	Value: 30.00				
2010B	95,000	—	—	—	—	16.00

KM# 93   20 FRANCS
20.0000 g., 0.9250 Silver 0.5948 oz. ASW, 32.8 mm.
Subject: Mustair Cloister **Obv:** Church floor plan **Rev:** Cloister
of Müstair **Edge Lettering:** DOMINUS PROVIDEBIT and 13 stars
Designer: Hans-Peter von Ah

Date	Mintage	F	VF	XF	Unc	BU
2001B	50,076	—	—	—	25.00	30.00
2001B Proof	15,000	Value: 45.00				

KM# 94   20 FRANCS
20.0000 g., 0.8350 Silver 0.5369 oz. ASW, 32.8 mm.
Subject: Johanna Spyri **Obv:** Value within handwritten
background **Rev:** Bust facing **Edge Lettering:** DOMINUS
PROVIDEBIT (13 stars) **Designer:** Silvia Goeschke

Date	Mintage	F	VF	XF	Unc	BU
2001B	60,364	—	—	—	25.00	30.00
2001B Proof	15,000	Value: 50.00				

KM# 99   20 FRANCS
20.0000 g., 0.8350 Silver 0.5369 oz. ASW, 32.8 mm. **Obv:** St.
Gall and bear cub **Rev:** St. Gall Cloister **Edge Lettering:**
DOMINUS PROVIDEBIT (13 stars) **Designer:** Hans-Peter von
Ah

Date	Mintage	F	VF	XF	Unc	BU
2002B	35,895	—	—	—	25.00	30.00
2002B Proof	6,250	Value: 50.00				

KM# 100   20 FRANCS
20.0000 g., 0.8350 Silver 0.5369 oz. ASW, 32.8 mm.
Subject: REGA **Obv:** Value, inscription and raised cross above rotating propeller **Rev:** Rescue helicopter in flight
Edge Lettering: DOMINUS PROVIDEBIT (13 stars)
Designer: Raphael Schenker

Date	Mintage	F	VF	XF	Unc	BU
2002B	37,314	—	—	—	25.00	30.00
2002B Proof	6,453	Value: 50.00				

KM# 101   20 FRANCS
20.0000 g., 0.8350 Silver 0.5369 oz. ASW, 32.8 mm.
Subject: Expo '02 **Obv:** Value and date within circle **Rev:** Child at water's edge within beaded circle **Edge Lettering:** DOMINUS PROVIDEBIT (13 stars) **Designer:** Hervé Graumann

Date	Mintage	F	VF	XF	Unc	BU
2002B	51,899	—	—	—	25.00	30.00
2002B Proof	7,691	Value: 50.00				

KM# 104   20 FRANCS
19.9700 g., 0.8350 Silver 0.5361 oz. ASW, 32.8 mm.
Subject: St. Moritz Ski Championships **Obv:** Value in snow storm **Rev:** Skier in snow storm **Edge Lettering:** DOMINUS PROVIDEBIT (13 stars) **Designer:** Claude Kuhn

Date	Mintage	F	VF	XF	Unc	BU
2003B	39,411	—	—	—	25.00	30.00
2003B Proof	6,471	Value: 50.00				

KM# 106   20 FRANCS
20.0000 g., 0.8350 Silver 0.5369 oz. ASW, 32.8 mm.
Subject: Bern, Old Town **Obv:** Stylized clock tower and buildings **Rev:** Stylized aerial view of Berner Altstadt **Edge Lettering:** DOMINUS PROVIDEBIT **Designer:** Franz Fedier

Date	Mintage	F	VF	XF	Unc	BU
2003B	38,644	—	—	—	25.00	30.00
2003B Proof	5,909	Value: 60.00				

KM# 108   20 FRANCS
20.0000 g., 0.8350 Silver 0.5369 oz. ASW, 32.8 mm.
Obv: Value **Rev:** The Three Castles of Bellinzona **Edge Lettering:** DOMINUS PROVIDEBIT **Designer:** Marco Prati

Date	Mintage	F	VF	XF	Unc	BU
2004B	29,697	—	—	—	25.00	30.00
2004B Proof	5,190	Value: 50.00				

KM# 109   20 FRANCS
20.0000 g., 0.8350 Silver 0.5369 oz. ASW, 32.8 mm.
Obv: Value **Rev:** Chillon Castle and reflection **Edge Lettering:** DOMINUS PROVIDEBIT **Designer:** Jean-Benoît Lévy

Date	Mintage	F	VF	XF	Unc	BU
2004B	35,133	—	—	—	22.00	28.00
2004B Proof	5,670	Value: 50.00				

KM# 121   20 FRANCS
20.0000 g., 0.8350 Silver 0.5369 oz. ASW, 32.8 mm.
Subject: FIFA Centennial **Obv:** Soccer ball with value at left **Rev:** Flower in center of cross

Date	Mintage	F	VF	XF	Unc	BU
2004B Proof only	14,041	Value: 110				

KM# 122   20 FRANCS
20.0000 g., 0.8350 Silver 0.5369 oz. ASW, 32.8 mm.
Subject: Chapel Bridge Lucerne **Obv:** Value **Rev:** View of Chapel Bridge **Edge Lettering:** DOMINUS PROVIDEBIT

Date	Mintage	F	VF	XF	Unc	BU
2005B	44,359	—	—	—	25.00	30.00
2005B Proof	5,998	Value: 50.00				

KM# 112   20 FRANCS
20.0000 g., 0.8350 Silver 0.5369 oz. ASW, 32.8 mm.
Subject: Geneva Motor Show **Obv:** Value **Rev:** Partial view of prototype car **Edge Lettering:** DOMINUS PROVIDEBIT
Designer: Roger Pfund

Date	Mintage	F	VF	XF	Unc	BU
2005B	65,000	—	—	—	25.00	30.00
2005B Proof	8,000	Value: 50.00				

KM# 115   20 FRANCS
20.0000 g., 0.8350 Silver 0.5369 oz. ASW, 32.8 mm.
Obv: Value **Rev:** 1906 Post Bus **Edge Lettering:** DOMINUS PROVIDEBIT **Designer:** Raphael Schenker

Date	Mintage	F	VF	XF	Unc	BU
2006B	40,000	—	—	—	25.00	30.00
2006B Proof	6,000	Value: 55.00				

KM# 117   20 FRANCS
20.0000 g., 0.8350 Silver 0.5369 oz. ASW, 32.8 mm.
Obv: Value and legend **Rev:** Swiss Parliament Building
Edge Lettering: DOMINUS PROVIDEBIT (13 stars)
Designer: Benjamin Pfäffli

Date	Mintage	F	VF	XF	Unc	BU
2006B	35,000	—	—	—	25.00	30.00
2006B Proof	6,000	Value: 55.00				

KM# 119   20 FRANCS
20.0000 g., 0.8350 Silver 0.5369 oz. ASW, 32.8 mm.
Subject: National Bank Centennial **Obv:** Value **Rev:** Partial face of Arthur Honegger (Composer) **Edge Lettering:** DOMINUS PROVIDEBIT

Date	Mintage	F	VF	XF	Unc	BU
2007B	Est. 50,000	—	—	—	25.00	30.00
2007B Proof	Est. 12,000	Value: 65.00				

KM# 124   20 FRANCS
20.0000 g., 0.8350 Silver 0.5369 oz. ASW, 32.8 mm. **Series:** Famous buildings **Subject:** Munot castle of Schaffhausen **Obv. Legend:** CONFEDERATIO - HELVETICA **Rev:** Two views of castle **Rev. Legend:** MUNOT **Designer:** Hansveli Holzer

Date	Mintage	F	VF	XF	Unc	BU
2007B	50,000	—	—	—	30.00	25.00
2007B Proof	7,000	Value: 55.00				

KM# 127   20 FRANCS
20.0000 g., 0.8350 Silver 0.5369 oz. ASW, 32.8 mm.
Subject: 100th Anniversary Hockey **Obv:** Small national arms **Obv. Legend:** CONFEDERATIO - HELVETICA **Rev:** Two players, one about to swing at puck **Rev. Legend:** ICE HOCKEY 1908-2008 **Rev. Designer:** Roland Hirter

Date	Mintage	F	VF	XF	Unc	BU
2008B	Est. 50,000	—	—	—	30.00	25.00
2008B Proof	Est. 7,000	Value: 65.00				

KM# 128 20 FRANCS
20.0000 g., 0.8350 Silver 0.5369 oz. ASW, 32.8 mm.
Subject: Vitznau-Rigi Cog Railway **Obv:** Value **Rev:** Modern
locomotive descending, early locomotive ascending (inverted)
Rev. Designer: Benno Zehnder

Date	Mintage	F	VF	XF	Unc	BU
2008B	50,000	—	—	—	25.00	30.00
2008B Proof	7,000	Value: 65.00				

KM# 131 20 FRANCS
20.0000 g., 0.8350 Silver 0.5369 oz. ASW, 33 mm.
Subject: Swiss Museum of Transport **Obv:** Value **Rev:** Spiral of
transport vehicles **Rev. Designer:** Werner Meier

Date	Mintage	F	VF	XF	Unc	BU
2009	50,000	—	—	—	25.00	30.00
2009 Proof	7,000	Value: 65.00				

KM# 132 20 FRANCS
20.0000 g., 0.8350 Silver 0.5369 oz. ASW, 33mm mm. **Subject:**
Brienz-Rothorn Railway **Obv:** Value **Designer:** Bruno K. Zehnder

Date	Mintage	F	VF	XF	Unc	BU
2009	50,000	—	—	—	25.00	30.00
2009 Proof	7,000	Value: 65.00				

KM# 135 20 FRANCS
20.0000 g., 0.8350 Silver 0.5369 oz. ASW, 32.8 mm.
Subject: 100 Years Bernina Railway

Date	Mintage	F	VF	XF	Unc	BU
2010B	—	—	—	—	—	20.00
2010B Proof	—	Value: 50.00				

KM# 136 20 FRANCS
20.0000 g., 3835.0000 Silver 2465.8 oz. ASW **Subject:** 100
Anniversary Death of Henry Dunant (Red Cross founder)
Rev. Designer: Pierre-Alain Zuber

Date	Mintage	F	VF	XF	Unc	BU
2010B	—	—	—	—	—	20.00
2010B Proof	—	Value: 50.00				

KM# 95 50 FRANCS
11.2900 g., 0.9000 Gold 0.3267 oz. AGW, 25.1 mm.
Obv: Landscape and value **Rev:** Heidi and goat running
Edge: Lettered **Edge Lettering:** DOMINUS PROVIDEBIT (13
stars) **Designer:** Albrecht Schnider

Date	Mintage	F	VF	XF	Unc	BU
2001B Proof	3,967	Value: 550				

KM# 102 50 FRANCS
11.2900 g., 0.9000 Gold 0.3267 oz. AGW, 25.1 mm.
Subject: Expo '02 **Obv:** Value **Rev:** Aerial view of 3 lakes
landscape **Edge:** Lettered **Edge Lettering:** DOMINUS
PROVIDEBIT (13 stars) **Designer:** Max Matter

Date	Mintage	F	VF	XF	Unc	BU
2002B Proof	4,856	Value: 450				

KM# 105 50 FRANCS
11.2900 g., 0.9000 Gold 0.3267 oz. AGW, 25.1 mm. **Obv:** Skier
and value **Rev:** St. Moritz city view **Edge Lettering:** DOMINUS
PROVIDEBIT (13 stars) **Designer:** Andreas His

Date	Mintage	F	VF	XF	Unc	BU
2003B Proof	4,000	Value: 450				

KM# 110 50 FRANCS
11.2900 g., 0.9000 Gold 0.3267 oz. AGW, 25.1 mm. **Obv:** Value
Rev: Matterhorn Mountain **Edge Lettering:** DOMINUS
PROVIDEBIT (13 stars) **Designer:** Stephan Bundi

Date	Mintage	F	VF	XF	Unc	BU
2004B Proof	7,000	Value: 600				

KM# 123 50 FRANCS
11.2900 g., 0.9000 Gold 0.3267 oz. AGW, 25.1 mm. **Subject:**
FIFA Centennial **Obv:** FIFA depicting Wilhelm Tell **Rev:** Soccer
ball on left value on right **Designer:** Joaquin Jimenez

Date	Mintage	F	VF	XF	Unc	BU
2004B Proof	10,000	Value: 625				

KM# 113 50 FRANCS
11.2900 g., 0.9000 Gold 0.3267 oz. AGW, 25.1 mm. **Subject:**
Geneva Motor Show **Obv:** Value **Rev:** Partial view of an antique
car **Edge Lettering:** DOMINUS PROVIDEBIT **Designer:** Roger
Pfund

Date	Mintage	F	VF	XF	Unc	BU
2005B Proof	6,000	Value: 475				

KM# 116 50 FRANCS
11.2900 g., 0.9000 Gold 0.3267 oz. AGW, 25.1 mm. **Obv:** Value
Rev: Swiss Guardsman **Edge Lettering:** DOMINUS
PROVIDEBIT **Designer:** Rudolf Mirer

Date	Mintage	F	VF	XF	Unc	BU
2006B Proof	6,000	Value: 600				

KM# 120 50 FRANCS
11.2900 g., 0.9000 Gold 0.3267 oz. AGW, 25.1 mm.
Subject: National Bank Centennial **Obv:** Value **Obv. Legend:**
CONFEDERATIO - HELVETICA **Rev:** "Lumberjack" from
painting by Ferdinand Hodler **Rev. Inscription:** SNB BNS +
Edge Lettering: DOMINUS PROVIDEBIT

Date	Mintage	F	VF	XF	Unc	BU
2007B Proof	6,000	Value: 475				

KM# 129 50 FRANCS
11.2900 g., 0.9000 Gold 0.3267 oz. AGW, 25 mm. **Subject:**
International Year of Planet Earth **Obv:** Value **Rev:** Dancing child
with 3 globes above head, in hands and standing on one globe
Rev. Inscription: DE LA PLANETE TERRE ANNEE
INTERNATIONALE **Designer:** Claude Sandoz

Date	Mintage	F	VF	XF	Unc	BU
2008B Proof	6,000	Value: 550				

KM# 133 50 FRANCS
11.2900 g., 0.9000 Gold 0.3267 oz. AGW, 25 mm. **Subject:** Pro
Patria, 100th Anniversary **Obv:** Value **Rev. Designer:** Hans Erni

Date	Mintage	F	VF	XF	Unc	BU
2009 Proof	6,000	Value: 550				

KM# 137 50 FRANCS
11.2900 g., 0.9000 Gold 0.3267 oz. AGW, 25.1 mm.
Subject: 100th Anniversary Death of Alber Anker (Painter)

Date	Mintage	F	VF	XF	Unc	BU
2010B Proof	—	Value: 400				

COMMEMORATIVE COINAGE
Shooting Festival

The listings which follow have traditionally been catego-
rized in many catalogs as Swiss Shooting Thalers. Techni-
cally, all are medallic issues rather than coins, excepting
the Solothurn issue of 1855. According to the Swiss Federal
Finance Department, the issue was legally equal to the
then current-silver 5 Francs issue to which it was identical
in design, aside from bearing an edge inscription which

read, EIDGEN FREISCHIESSEN SOLOTHURN (National
Shooting Fest Solothurn).

For the silver issues of 1855-1885, the presence of the denomination was only intended to indicate these coins were
of the same weight and fineness as prescribed for legal tender coins.

Beginning with the issues of 1934, denominations and sizes
were no longer the same as regular Swiss legal tender issues. These coins all have legends indicating that they
could only be redeemed during and at the shooting fest of
issue.

Exceptional quality BU examples for 1934 and 1939 will
command a premium over the prices listed.

X# S61 50 FRANCS
25.0000 g., 0.9000 Silver 0.7234 oz. ASW **Subject:** Uri Festival
Obv: Head laureate left within star border **Rev:** Train and tunnel
Note: Prev. KM#S61.

Date	Mintage	F	VF	XF	Unc	BU
2001 Proof	1,500	Value: 100				

X# S63 50 FRANCS
25.0000 g., 0.9000 Silver 0.7234 oz. ASW **Subject:** Zurich
Festival **Obv:** Small wreath above shield flanked by sprigs within
beaded border **Rev:** Standing figure walking left with lion within
beaded circle **Note:** Prev. KM#S63.

Date	Mintage	F	VF	XF	Unc	BU
2002 Proof	1,500	Value: 165				

X# S65 50 FRANCS
25.0000 g., 0.9990 Silver 0.8029 oz. ASW **Subject:** Basel
Festival **Note:** Prev. KM#S65.

Date	Mintage	F	VF	XF	Unc	BU
2003 Proof	1,500	Value: 100				

X# S67 50 FRANCS
25.0000 g., 0.9000 Silver 0.7234 oz. ASW **Subject:** Fribourg
Festival **Note:** Prev. KM#S67.

Date	Mintage	F	VF	XF	Unc	BU
2004 Proof	1,500	Value: 100				

X# S69 50 FRANCS
25.0000 g., 0.9000 Silver 0.7234 oz. ASW **Subject:** Brusio Festival **Note:** Prev. KM#S69.

Date	Mintage	F	VF	XF	Unc	BU
2005	1,500	Value: 100				

X# S71 50 FRANCS
25.0000 g., 0.9000 Silver 0.7234 oz. ASW **Subject:** Solothurn Festival **Note:** Prev. KM#S71.

Date	Mintage	F	VF	XF	Unc	BU
2006	2,000	Value: 100				

X# S73 50 FRANCS
25.0000 g., 0.9000 Silver 0.7234 oz. ASW **Subject:** Luzern Festival **Note:** Prev. KM#S73.

Date	Mintage	F	VF	XF	Unc	BU
2007	2,000	Value: 100				

X# S75 50 FRANCS
25.0000 g., 0.9000 Silver 0.7234 oz. ASW **Subject:** Geneva Festival

Date	Mintage	F	VF	XF	Unc	BU
2008	1,500	Value: 100				

X# S77 50 FRANCS
25.0000 g., 0.9000 Silver 0.7234 oz. ASW **Subject:** Obwalden Festival

Date	Mintage	F	VF	XF	Unc	BU
2009	1,500	Value: 100				

X# S79 50 FRANCS
25.0000 g., 0.9000 Silver 0.7234 oz. ASW, 37 mm. **Subject:** Aarau Festival

Date	Mintage	F	VF	XF	Unc	BU
2010HF Proof		Value: 75.00				

X# S62 500 FRANCS
0.9990 Gold **Issuer:** Uri Festival **Obv:** Head laureate left within star border **Rev:** Locomotive and tunnel **Note:** Prev. KM#S62.

Date	Mintage	F	VF	XF	Unc	BU
2001 Proof	150	Value: 1,500				

X# S64 500 FRANCS
13.0000 g., 0.9990 Gold 0.4175 oz. AGW **Subject:** Zurich Sechselauten **Note:** Prev. KM#S64.

Date	Mintage	F	VF	XF	Unc	BU
2002 Proof	150	Value: 1,950				

X# S66 500 FRANCS
13.0000 g., 0.9990 Gold 0.4175 oz. AGW **Issuer:** Basel Festival **Note:** Prev. KM#S66.

Date	Mintage	F	VF	XF	Unc	BU
2003 Proof	150	Value: 1,600				

X# S68 500 FRANCS
15.5000 g., 0.9990 Gold 0.4978 oz. AGW **Subject:** Fribourg Festival **Note:** Prev. KM#S68.

Date	Mintage	F	VF	XF	Unc	BU
2004 Proof	150	Value: 1,200				

X# S70 500 FRANCS
15.5000 g., 0.9990 Gold 0.4978 oz. AGW **Subject:** Brusio Festival **Note:** Prev. KM#S70.

Date	Mintage	F	VF	XF	Unc	BU
2005 Proof	150	Value: 1,375				

X# S72 500 FRANCS
25.6000 g., 0.5850 Gold 0.4815 oz. AGW **Subject:** Solothurn Festival **Note:** Prev. KM#S72.

Date	Mintage	F	VF	XF	Unc	BU
2006 Proof	200	Value: 1,000				

X# S74 500 FRANCS
25.6000 g., 0.5850 Gold 0.4815 oz. AGW **Subject:** Luzern Festival **Note:** Prev. KM#S74.

Date	Mintage	F	VF	XF	Unc	BU
2007	200	Value: 1,000				

X# S76 500 FRANCS
25.6000 g., 0.5850 Gold 0.4815 oz. AGW **Subject:** Geneva Festival

Date	Mintage	F	VF	XF	Unc	BU
2008 Proof	150	Value: 1,000				

X# S78 500 FRANCS
19.5900 g., 0.9999 Gold 0.6297 oz. AGW **Subject:** Obwalden Festival

Date	Mintage	F	VF	XF	Unc	BU
2009 Proof	175	Value: 1,000				

ESSAIS

KM#	Date	Mintage	Identification	Mkt Val
E13	2001	—	20 Francs. Silver. KM#93	285
E14	2002	700	5 Francs. Bi-Metallic. KM#98 Escalade	185
E15	2003	700	5 Francs. Bi-Metallic. KM#103 Chalandamarz	195
E16	2004	700	10 Francs. Bi-Metallic. KM#107.	285
E19	2005	500	20 Francs. Silver. 20.0000 g. 33 mm. Motor Show. KM#112.	285
E20	2006	500	20 Francs. Silver. 20.0000 g. 33 mm. Parliament Building. KM#117.	285
E21	2007	500	20 Francs. Silver. 20.0000 g. 33 mm. KM#119. Munot	250
E23	2008	700	10 Francs. Bi-Metallic. KM#118 Golden Eagle	225
E24	2009	500	20 Francs. Silver. 33mm KM#132 Brienz-Rothorn Railway	275
E22	2009B	—	20 Francs. 0.8350 Silver. 20.0000 g. 33 mm. Value.	—

PIEFORTS

KM#	Date	Mintage	Identification	Mkt Val
	2003	500	5 Europ. Silver. X#Pn10a.	65.00

MINT SETS

KM#	Date	Mintage	Identification	Issue Price	Mkt Val
MS35	2001 (9)	21,532	KM#21a.3, 23a.3, 24a.3, 26c, 27, 29a, 40a.4, 46, 92 Zurich Sechselauten	—	35.00
MS36	2002 (9)	17,920	KM#21a.3, 23a.3, 24a.3, 26c, 27, 29a, 40a.4, 46, 98 Escalade	—	40.00
MS37	2002 (9)	2,000	KM#21a.3, 23a.3, 24a.3, 26c, 27, 29a, 40a.4, 46, 98 Includes a medal and different cover (intended as a birth year set for 2002 from the mint)	—	220
MS38	2003 (9)	17,200	KM#21a.3, 23a.3, 24a.3, 26c, 27, 29a, 40a.4, 46, 103 Chalandamarz	—	35.00
MS39	2004 (9)	16,000	KM#21a.3, 23a.3, 24a.3, 26c, 27, 29a, 40a.4, 46, 107 Matterhorn	—	80.00
MS40	2005 (9)	16,000	KM#21a.3, 23a.3, 24a.3, 26c, 27, 29a, 40a.4, 46, 111 Jung Frau	—	45.00
MS41	2006 (9)	16,000	KM#21a.3, 23a.3, 24a.3, 26c, 27, 29a, 40a.4, 46, 114 Piz Berhina	—	225
MS42	2007 (8)	16,000	KM#21a.3, 23a.3, 24a.3, 26c, 27, 29a, 40a.4, 118 (IBEX)	—	40.00
MS43	2008 (8)	15,000	KM#21a.3, 23a.3, 24a.3, 26c, 27, 29a, 40a.4, 126 Golden Eagle	—	40.00
MS44	2009 (8)	15,000	KM#21a.3, 23a.3, 24a.3, 26c, 27, 29a, 40a4, 118 (Red Deer)	—	40.00

PROOF SETS

KM#	Date	Mintage	Identification	Issue Price	Mkt Val
PS30	2001 (9)	5,184	KM#21a.3, 23a.3, 24a.3, 26c, 27, 29a, 40a.4, 46, 92 Zurich Sechselauten	—	75.00
PS31	2002 (9)	4,518	KM#21a.3, 23a.3, 24a.3, 26c, 27, 29a, 40a.4, 46, 98 Escalade	—	80.00
PS32	2003 (9)	4,520	KM#21a.3, 23a.3, 24a.3, 26c, 27, 29a, 40a.4, 46, 103 Chatandamarz	—	80.00
PS33	2004 (9)	4,168	KM#21a.3, 23a.3, 24a.3, 26c, 27, 29a, 40a.4, 46, 107 Matterhorn	68.00	115
PS34	2005 (9)	4,497	KM#21a.3, 23a.3, 24a.3, 26c, 27, 29a, 40a.4, 46, 111 Jung Frau	68.00	80.00
PS35	2006 (9)	4,000	KM#21a.3, 23a.3, 24a.3, 26c, 27, 29a, 40a.4, 46, 114 Piz Berhina	68.00	300
PS36	2007 (7)	4,000	KM#21a.3, 23a.3, 24a.3, 26c, 27, 29a, 40a.4, plus National Park	68.00	85.00
PS37	2008 (7)	4,000	KM#21a.3, 23a.3, 24a.3, 26c, 27, 29a, 40a.4, plus Golden Eagle	72.00	100
PS38	2009 (7)	4,000	KM#21a.3, 23a.3, 24a.3, 26c, 27, 29a, 40a.4, plus Red Deer	75.00	100

SYRIA

The Syrian Arab Republic, located in the Near East at the eastern end of the Mediterranean Sea, has an area of 71,498 sq. mi. (185,180 sq. km.) and a population of *12 million. Capital: Greater Damascus. Agriculture and animal breeding are the chief industries. Cotton, crude oil and livestock are exported.

TITLES

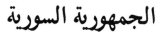

al-Jumhuriya(t) al-Suriya(t)

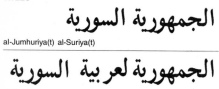

al-Jumhuriya(t) al-Arabiya(t) as-Suriya(t)

SYRIAN ARAB REPUBLIC

STANDARD COINAGE

KM# 129   5 POUNDS
7.5300 g., Nickel Clad Steel, 24.5 mm. **Obv:** National arms within design and beaded border **Rev:** Old fort and latent image above value within design and beaded border **Edge:** Reeded and lettered **Edge Lettering:** CENTRAL BANK 5 SYP

Date	Mintage	F	VF	XF	Unc	BU
AH1424-2003	—	—	—	—	1.25	1.75

KM# 130   10 POUNDS
9.5300 g., Copper-Nickel-Zinc, 27.4 mm. **Obv:** National arms within beaded border **Rev:** Ancient ruins with latent image within beaded border **Edge Lettering:** 10 SYRIAN POUNDS

Date	Mintage	F	VF	XF	Unc	BU
AH1424-2003	—	—	—	—	2.50	3.50

KM# 131   25 POUNDS
8.4000 g., Bi-Metallic Copper-Nickel center in Nickel-Brass ring, 25 mm. **Obv:** National arms within beaded border **Rev:** Building and latent image within beaded border **Edge Lettering:** CENTRAL BANK OF SYRIA 25

Date	Mintage	F	VF	XF	Unc	BU
AH1424-2003	—	—	—	1.50	3.75	5.00

TAJIKISTAN

The Republic of Tajikistan (Tadjiquistan), was formed from those regions of Bukhara and Turkestan where the population consisted mainly of Tajiks. It is bordered in the north and west by Uzbekistan and Kyrgyzstan, in the east by China and in the south by Afghanistan. It has an area of 55,240 sq. miles (143,100 sq. km.) and a population of 5.95 million. It includes 2 provinces of Khudzand and Khatlon together with the Gorno-Badakhshan Autonomous Region with a population of 5,092,603. Capital: Dushanbe. Tajikistan was admitted as a constituent republic of the Soviet Union on Dec. 5, 1929. In August 1990 the Tajik Supreme Soviet adopted a declaration of republican sovereignty, and in Dec. 1991 the republic became a member of the CIS.

After demonstrations and fighting, the Communist government was replaced by a Revolutionary Coalition Council on May 7, 1992. Following further demonstrations President Nabiev was ousted on Sept. 7, 1992. Civil war broke out, and the government resigned on Nov. 10, 1992. On Nov. 30, 1992 it was announced that a CIS peacekeeping force would be sent to Tajikistan. A state of emergency was imposed in Jan. 1993. A ceasefire was signed in 1996 and a peace agreement signed in June 1997.

MONETARY SYSTEM
100 Drams = 1 Somoni

REPUBLIC

DECIMAL COINAGE

KM# 2.1   5 DRAMS
2.0500 g., Brass Clad Steel, 16.5 mm. **Obv:** Crown within 1/2 star border **Rev:** Small value within design **Edge:** Plain

Date	Mintage	F	VF	XF	Unc	BU
2001(sp)	—	—	—	—	0.50	0.75
2001(sp) Proof	—	Value: 2.50				

KM# 2.2   5 DRAMS
2.0500 g., Brass Clad Steel, 16.5 mm. **Obv:** Crown with 1/2 star border **Rev:** Large value within design

Date	Mintage	F	VF	XF	Unc	BU
2006(sp)	—	—	—	—	0.75	1.25

KM# 3.1   10 DRAMS
2.4700 g., Brass Clad Steel, 17.5 mm. **Obv:** Crown within 1/2 star border **Rev:** Small value within design **Edge:** Plain

Date	Mintage	F	VF	XF	Unc	BU
2001(sp)	—	—	—	—	0.75	1.00
2001(sp) Proof	—	Value: 3.00				

KM# 3.2   10 DRAMS
2.4700 g., Brass Clad Steel, 17.5 mm. **Obv:** Crown within 1/2 star border **Rev:** Large value within design

Date	Mintage	F	VF	XF	Unc	BU
2006(sp)	—	—	—	—	1.00	1.50

KM# 4.1   20 DRAMS
2.7300 g., Brass Clad Steel, 18.5 mm. **Obv:** Crown within 1/2 star border **Rev:** Small value within design **Edge:** Plain

Date	Mintage	F	VF	XF	Unc	BU
2001(sp)	—	—	—	—	1.00	1.25
2001(sp) Proof	—	Value: 3.75				

KM# 4.2   20 DRAMS
2.7300 g., Brass Clad Steel, 18.5 mm. **Obv:** Crown within 1/2 star border **Rev:** Large value within design

Date	Mintage	F	VF	XF	Unc	BU
2006(sp)	2	—	—	—	1.50	2.00

KM# 5.1   25 DRAMS
2.8000 g., Brass, 19.1 mm. **Obv:** Crown within 1/2 star border **Rev:** Small value within design **Edge:** Plain

Date	Mintage	F	VF	XF	Unc	BU
2001(sp)	—	—	—	—	1.50	1.75
2001(sp) Proof	—	Value: 5.00				

KM# 5.2   25 DRAMS
2.8000 g., Brass, 19.1 mm. **Obv:** Crown within 1/2 star border **Rev:** Large value within design

Date	Mintage	F	VF	XF	Unc	BU
2006(sp)	—	—	—	—	1.75	2.50

KM# 6.1   50 DRAMS
3.5500 g., Brass, 21 mm. **Obv:** Crown within 1/2 star border **Rev:** Value within design **Edge:** Plain

Date	Mintage	F	VF	XF	Unc	BU
2001(sp)	—	—	—	—	2.00	3.00
2001(sp) Proof	—	Value: 7.00				

KM# 6.2   50 DRAMS
3.5500 g., Brass, 21 mm. **Obv:** Crown within 1/2 star border **Rev:** Large value within design

Date	Mintage	F	VF	XF	Unc	BU
2006(sp)	—	—	—	—	2.00	3.00

KM# 7   SOMONI
5.1500 g., Copper-Nickel-Zinc, 23.9 mm. **Obv:** King's bust 1/2 right **Rev:** Value **Edge:** Reeded and plain sections

Date	Mintage	F	VF	XF	Unc	BU
2001(sp)	—	—	—	—	3.50	5.00
2001(sp) Proof	—	Value: 12.00				

KM# 12   SOMONI
5.2100 g., Copper-Nickel-Zinc, 24 mm. **Subject:** Year of Aryan Civilization **Obv:** National arms above value **Rev:** Ancient archer in war chariot **Edge:** Segmented reeding

Date	Mintage	F	VF	XF	Unc	BU
2006(sp)	100,000	—	—	—	3.50	5.00

KM# 13   SOMONI
5.2100 g., Copper-Nickel-Zinc, 24 mm. **Subject:** Year of Aryan Civilization **Obv:** National arms above value **Rev:** Two busts left **Edge:** Segmented reeding

Date	Mintage	F	VF	XF	Unc	BU
2006(sp)	100,000	—	—	—	3.50	5.00

KM# 12a   SOMONI
20.0000 g., 0.9250 Silver 0.5948 oz. ASW, 24 mm. **Subject:** Year of Aryan Civilization **Obv:** National arms above value **Rev:** Ancient archer in war chariot **Edge:** Segmented reeding

Date	Mintage	F	VF	XF	Unc	BU
2006(sp) Proof	1,500	Value: 50.00				

KM# 13a   SOMONI
20.0000 g., 0.9250 Silver 0.5948 oz. ASW, 24 mm. **Subject:** Year of Aryan Civilization **Obv:** National arms above value **Rev:** Two busts left **Edge:** Segmented reeding

Date	Mintage	F	VF	XF	Unc	BU
2006 Proof	1,500	Value: 50.00				

KM# 16   SOMONI
5.2400 g., Copper-Nickel-Zinc, 23.95 mm. **Subject:** 800th Anniversary Birth of Jaloliddini Rumi **Obv:** Small arms above value in cartouche **Rev:** 1/2 length figure facing **Edge:** Segmented reeding

Date	Mintage	F	VF	XF	Unc	BU
2007	—	—	—	—	3.50	5.00

KM# 8   3 SOMONI
6.3200 g., Copper-Nickel-Zinc, 25.5 mm.   **Obv:** National arms
Rev: Crown above value within design **Edge:** Lettered

Date	Mintage	F	VF	XF	Unc	BU
2001(sp)	—	—	—	—	5.00	7.00
2001(sp) Proof	—	Value: 18.00				

KM# 10   3 SOMONI
6.3000 g., Bi-Metallic Copper-Nickel center in Brass ring,
25.5 mm.   **Subject:** 80th Year - Dushanbe City **Obv:** Value below
arms within circle **Rev:** Statue in arch within circle

Date	Mintage	F	VF	XF	Unc	BU
2004(sp)	—	—	—	—	6.50	9.00

KM# 10a   3 SOMONI
6.9800 g., 0.9250 Silver 0.2076 oz. ASW, 25.5 mm.
Subject: 80th Anniversary of Republic **Obv:** Value below arms
within circle **Rev:** Statue in arch within circle

Date	Mintage	F	VF	XF	Unc	BU
2004 Proof	1,000	Value: 55.00				

KM# 14   3 SOMONI
6.3000 g., Bi-Metallic Copper-Nickel center in Brass ring,
25.5 mm.   **Subject:** 2700th Anniversary of Kulyab **Obv:** National
arms above value **Rev:** Kulyab city arms **Edge:** Lettered

Date	Mintage	F	VF	XF	Unc	BU
2006(sp)	100,000	—	—	—	6.00	7.50

KM# 14a   3 SOMONI
6.9800 g., 0.9250 Silver 0.2076 oz. ASW, 25.5 mm.
Subject: 2700th Anniversary of Kulyab **Obv:** National arms
above value **Rev:** Kulyab city arms

Date	Mintage	F	VF	XF	Unc	BU
2006(sp)	—	Value: 50.00				

KM# 9   5 SOMONI
7.1000 g., Copper-Nickel-Zinc, 26.4 mm.   **Obv:** Turbaned head
right **Rev:** Crown above value within design **Edge:** Reeded and
plain sections with a star

Date	Mintage	F	VF	XF	Unc	BU
2001(sp) Proof	—	Value: 25.00				
2001(sp)	—	—	—	—	7.50	9.00

KM# 11   5 SOMONI
6.9400 g., Bi-Metallic Copper-Nickel center in Brass ring,
26.5 mm.   **Subject:** 10th Anniversary - Constitution **Obv:** Arms
above value within circle **Rev:** Flag and book within circle
Edge: Lettered

Date	Mintage	F	VF	XF	Unc	BU
2004(sp)	—	—	—	—	7.50	10.00

KM# 11a   5 SOMONI
8.5500 g., 0.9250 Silver 0.2543 oz. ASW, 26.5 mm.
Subject: 10th Anniversary - Constitution **Obv:** Arms above value
within circle **Rev:** Flag and book within circle

Date	Mintage	F	VF	XF	Unc	BU
2004 Proof	2,000	Value: 50.00				

KM# 15   5 SOMONI
7.0000 g., Bi-Metallic Copper-Nickel center in Brass ring,
26.5 mm.   **Subject:** 15th Anniversary of Independence
Obv: National arms above value **Rev:** Government building
Edge: Lettered

Date	Mintage	F	VF	XF	Unc	BU
2006(sp)	100,000	—	—	—	7.50	10.00

KM# 17   5 SOMONI
7.0000 g., Bi-Metallic Copper-Nickel center in Brass ring,
26.5 mm.   **Subject:** 1150th Anniversary founding of Persian
(Tajik) literature by Abuabdullo Rudaki **Obv:** National arms above
value **Rev:** Bust of Rudaki left, scroll, feather pen

Date	Mintage	F	VF	XF	Unc	BU
2008	—	—	—	—	7.50	10.00

MINT SETS

KM#	Date	Mintage Identification	Issue Price	Mkt Val
MS1	2001 (8)	— KM#2.1-6.1, 7-9	—	30.00

PROOF SETS

KM#	Date	Mintage Identification	Issue Price	Mkt Val
PS1	2001 (8)	— KM#2.1-6.1, 7-9	—	80.00

TANZANIA

The United Republic of Tanzania, located on the east coast
of Africa between Kenya and Mozambique, consists of Tang-
anyika and the islands of Zanzibar and Pemba. It has an area of
364,900 sq. mi. (945,090 sq. km.) and a population of *25.2 million. Capital: Dar es Salaam (Haven of Peace). The chief exports
are cotton, coffee, diamonds, sisal, cloves, petroleum products,
and cashew nuts.

Tanzania is a member of the Commonwealth of Nations. The
President is Chief of State.

NOTE: For earlier coinage see East Africa.

REPUBLIC
STANDARD COINAGE
100 Senti = 1 Shilingi

KM# 56   500 SHILLINGS
31.4600 g., 0.9250 Silver 0.9356 oz. ASW, 38.6 mm.   **Obv:** Arms
with supporters above value **Rev:** African dhow **Edge:** Reeded

Date	Mintage	F	VF	XF	Unc	BU
2001 Proof	—	Value: 35.00				

THAILAND

The Kingdom of Thailand (formerly Siam), a constitutional
monarchy located in the center of mainland Southeast Asia
between Burma and Laos, has an area of 198,457 sq. mi.
(514,000 sq. km.) and a population of *55.5 million. Capital:
Bangkok. The economy is based on agriculture and mining. Rubber, rice, teakwood, tin and tungsten are exported.

RULER
Rama IX (Phra Maha Bhumibol Adulyadej), 1946-

KINGDOM OF THAILAND
DECIMAL COINAGE
25 Satang = 1 Salung; 100 Satang = 1 Baht

Y# 187   25 SATANG = 1/4 BAHT
1.9000 g., Aluminum-Bronze, 15.93 mm.   **Ruler:** Bhumipol
Adulyadej (Rama IX) **Obv:** Head left **Rev:** Steepled building
Edge: Reeded

Date	Mintage	F	VF	XF	Unc	BU
BE2545 (2002)	—	—	—	—	0.10	0.15
BE2545 (2003)	—	—	—	—	0.10	0.15
BE2547 (2004)	—	—	—	—	0.10	0.15
BE2548 (2005)	—	—	—	—	0.10	0.15
BE2549 (2006)	—	—	—	—	0.10	0.15
BE2550 (2007)	—	—	—	—	0.10	0.15

KM# 441   25 SATANG = 1/4 BAHT
Copper Plated Steel, 15.93 mm.   **Ruler:** Bhumipol Adulyadej
(Rama IX) **Obv:** King's portrait

Date	Mintage	F	VF	XF	Unc	BU
BE2551 (2008)	—	—	—	—	0.10	0.15
BE2552 (2009)						

Y# 203   50 SATANG = 1/2 BAHT
2.4000 g., Brass, 18 mm. **Ruler:** Bhumipol Adulyadej (Rama IX)
Obv: Head left **Rev:** Steepled building divides value

Date	Mintage	F	VF	XF	Unc	BU
BE2544 (2001)	—	—	—	—	0.10	0.15
BE2545 (2002)	—	—	—	—	0.10	0.15
BE2547 (2004)	—	—	—	—	0.10	0.15
BE2548 (2005)	—	—	—	—	0.10	0.15
BE2549 (2006)	—	—	—	—	0.10	0.15
BE2550 (2007)	—	—	—	—	0.10	0.15

KM# 442   50 SATANG = 1/2 BAHT
Copper Plated Steel   **Ruler:** Bhumipol Adulyadej (Rama IX)
Obv: King's portrait

Date	Mintage	F	VF	XF	Unc	BU
BE2551 (2008)	—	—	—	—	0.10	0.15

Y# 183   BAHT
3.4500 g., Copper-Nickel, 20 mm. **Ruler:** Bhumipol Adulyadej
(Rama IX) **Obv:** Head left **Rev:** Palace **Edge:** Reeded
Note: Varieties exist.

Date	Mintage	F	VF	XF	Unc	BU
BE2544 (2001)	—	—	—	—	0.10	0.15
BE2545 (2002)	—	—	—	—	0.10	0.15
BE2546 (2003)	—	—	—	—	0.10	0.15
BE2547 (2004)	—	—	—	—	0.10	0.15
BE2548 (2005)	—	—	—	—	0.10	0.15
BE2549 (2006)	—	—	—	—	0.10	0.15
BE2550 (2007)	—	—	—	—	0.10	0.15
BE2551 (2008)	—	—	—	—	0.10	0.15

KM# 443   BAHT
Nickel Plated Steel, 20 mm. **Ruler:** Bhumipol Adulyadej
(Rama IX) **Obv:** King's portrait

Date	Mintage	F	VF	XF	Unc	BU
BE2548 (2009)	—	—	—	—	0.10	0.15

KM# 444   2 BAHT
Nickel Plated Steel   **Ruler:** Bhumipol Adulyadej (Rama IX)
Shape: 22

Date	Mintage	F	VF	XF	Unc	BU
BE2548 (2005)	—	—	—	—	0.15	0.20
BE2549 (2006)	—	—	—	—	—	—

KM# 445   2 BAHT
Aluminum-Bronze, 22 mm. **Ruler:** Bhumipol Adulyadej
(Rama IX) **Obv:** King's portrait

Date	Mintage	F	VF	XF	Unc	BU
BE2551 (2008)	—	—	—	—	0.15	0.20
BE2552 (2009)	—	—	—	—	—	—

Y# 219   5 BAHT
7.4600 g., Copper-Nickel Clad Copper, 24 mm.
Ruler: Bhumipol Adulyadej (Rama IX) **Obv:** Head left
Rev: Penjahwat **Edge:** Coarse reeding

Date	Mintage	F	VF	XF	Unc	BU
BE2544 (2001)	—	—	—	—	0.50	0.75
BE2545 (2002)	—	—	—	—	0.50	0.75
BE2547 (2004)	—	—	—	—	0.50	0.75
BE2548 (2005)	—	—	—	—	0.50	0.75
BE2549 (2006)	—	—	—	—	0.50	0.75
BE2550 (2007)	—	—	—	—	0.50	0.75
BE2551 (2008)	—	—	—	—	0.50	0.75

KM# 446   5 BAHT
Copper-Nickel Clad Copper, 24 mm. **Ruler:** Bhumipol
Adulyadej (Rama IX) **Obv:** King's portrait **Rev:** Temple top does
not break legend

Date	Mintage	F	VF	XF	Unc	BU
BE2551 (2008)	—	—	—	—	0.50	0.75
BE2552 (2009)	—	—	—	—	—	—

Y# 373   10 BAHT
8.5000 g., Bi-Metallic Brass center in Copper-Nickel ring, 26 mm.
Ruler: Bhumipol Adulyadej (Rama IX) **Subject:** Department of
Lands Centennial February 17 2444-2544 **Obv:** Conjoined busts
facing divides circle **Rev:** Department seal within circle
Edge: Alternating reeded and plain

Date	Mintage	F	VF	XF	Unc	BU
BE2545 (2001)	—	—	—	—	2.50	3.00

Y# 227   10 BAHT
8.5400 g., Bi-Metallic Brass center in Copper-Nickel ring, 26 mm.
Ruler: Bhumipol Adulyadej (Rama IX) **Obv:** Head left within
circle **Rev:** Temple of the Dawn within circle **Edge:** Segmented
reeding **Note:** Varieties exist.

Date	Mintage	F	VF	XF	Unc	BU
BE2544 (2001)	—	—	—	—	3.00	3.50
BE2545 (2002)	—	—	—	—	3.00	3.50
BE2546 (2003)	—	—	—	—	3.00	3.50
BE2547 (2004)	—	—	—	—	3.00	3.50
BE2548 (2005)	—	—	—	—	3.00	3.50
BE2549 (2006)	—	—	—	—	3.00	3.50
BE2550 (2007)	—	—	—	—	3.00	3.50
BE2551 (2008)	—	—	—	—	3.00	3.50

Y# 387   10 BAHT
8.5500 g., Bi-Metallic Brass center in Copper-Nickel ring, 26 mm.
Ruler: Bhumipol Adulyadej (Rama IX) **Subject:** King's 75th
Birthday December 5 **Obv:** Head left **Rev:** Royal crown in radiant
oval **Edge:** Alternating reeded and plain

Date	Mintage	F	VF	XF	Unc	BU
BE2545 (2002)	—	—	—	—	2.00	2.75

Y# 381   10 BAHT
8.5500 g., Bi-Metallic Brass center in Copper-Nickel ring, 26 mm.
Ruler: Bhumipol Adulyadej (Rama IX) **Subject:** Centennial of
Irrigation Department June 13 **Obv:** Conjoined busts facing
divides circle **Rev:** Department logo **Edge:** Alternating reeded
and plain

Date	Mintage	F	VF	XF	Unc	BU
BE2545 (2002)	—	—	—	—	2.00	2.75

Y# 382   10 BAHT
8.5500 g., Bi-Metallic Brass center in Copper-Nickel ring, 26 mm.
Ruler: Bhumipol Adulyadej (Rama IX) **Subject:** Department of
Internal Trade 60th Anniversary May 5 **Obv:** Head left
Rev: Department logo **Edge:** Alternating reeded and plain

Date	Mintage	F	VF	XF	Unc	BU
BE2545 (2002)	—	—	—	—	2.00	2.75

Y# 383   10 BAHT
8.5500 g., Bi-Metallic Brass center in Copper-Nickel ring, 26 mm.
Ruler: Bhumipol Adulyadej (Rama IX) **Subject:** State Highway
Department 90th Anniversary April 1 **Obv:** Conjoined busts facing
divides circle **Rev:** Department logo **Edge:** Alternating reeded
and plain

Date	Mintage	F	VF	XF	Unc	BU
BE2545 (2002)	—	—	—	—	2.00	2.75

Y# 384   10 BAHT
8.5500 g., Bi-Metallic Brass center in Copper-Nickel ring, 26 mm.
Ruler: Bhumipol Adulyadej (Rama IX) **Subject:** Vajira Hospital
90th Anniversary January 2 **Obv:** Conjoined busts facing
circle **Rev:** Hospital logo **Edge:** Alternating reeded and plain

Date	Mintage	F	VF	XF	Unc	BU
BE2545 (2002)	—	—	—	—	2.00	2.75

Y# 385   10 BAHT
8.5500 g., Bi-Metallic Brass center in Copper-Nickel ring, 26 mm.
Ruler: Bhumipol Adulyadej (Rama IX) **Subject:** 20th World
Scouting Jamboree **Obv:** Rama IX wearing a scouting uniform
Rev: Jamboree log **Edge:** Alternating reeded and plain

Date	Mintage	F	VF	XF	Unc	BU
BE2546 (2003)	—	—	—	—	2.00	2.75

Y# 405   10 BAHT
8.5400 g., Bi-Metallic Brass center in Copper-Nickel ring, 26 mm.
Ruler: Bhumipol Adulyadej (Rama IX) **Subject:** "CITES COP"
Obv: Bust 3/4 left within circle **Rev:** "CITES" logo
Edge: Segmented reeding

Date	Mintage	F	VF	XF	Unc	BU
ND (2003)	—	—	—	—	2.00	2.75

Y# 400   10 BAHT
8.5500 g., Bi-Metallic Brass center in Copper-Nickel ring, 26 mm.
Ruler: Bhumipol Adulyadej (Rama IX) **Obv:** Head left
Rev: APEC logo **Edge:** Segmented reeding

Date	Mintage	F	VF	XF	Unc	BU
BE2546-2003	—	—	—	—	2.25	3.00

Y# 409   10 BAHT
8.5000 g., Bi-Metallic Brass center in Copper-Nickel ring,
25.95 mm. **Ruler:** Bhumipol Adulyadej (Rama IX)
Subject: 150th Anniversary of King Rama V **Obv:** Bust of Rama
V left **Rev:** Royal crown **Edge:** Segmented reeding

Date	Mintage	F	VF	XF	Unc	BU
BE2546 (2003)	—	—	—	—	1.80	2.40

Y# 391   10 BAHT
8.5000 g., Bi-Metallic Brass center in Copper-Nickel ring, 26 mm.
Ruler: Bhumipol Adulyadej (Rama IX) **Subject:** Inspector
General's Department Centennial May 6 **Obv:** Head left within
circle **Rev:** Department seal within circle and design
Edge: Alternating reeded and plain

Date	Mintage	F	VF	XF	Unc	BU
BE2546 (2003)	—	—	—	—	1.75	2.50

Y# 392 10 BAHT
8.5000 g., Bi-Metallic Brass center in Copper-Nickel ring, 26 mm.
Ruler: Bhumipol Adulyadej (Rama IX) **Subject:** 80th Birthday of
Princess May 6 **Obv:** Bust 1/4 right **Rev:** Crowned emblem and
value **Edge:** Alternating reeded and plain **Note:** This is the king's
sister.

Date	Mintage	F	VF	XF	Unc	BU
BE2546(2003)	—	—	—	—	1.75	2.50

Y# 396 10 BAHT
8.5500 g., Bi-Metallic Brass center in Copper-Nickel ring, 26 mm.
Ruler: Bhumipol Adulyadej (Rama IX) **Subject:** 90th
Anniversary of the Government Savings Bank April 1
Obv: Uniformed bust facing within circle **Rev:** Bank emblem
Edge: Alternating reeded and plain

Date	Mintage	F	VF	XF	Unc	BU
BE2546(2003)	—	—	—	—	2.00	2.75

Y# 411 10 BAHT
8.5000 g., Bi-Metallic Brass center in Copper-Nickel, 25.95 mm.
Ruler: Bhumipol Adulyadej (Rama IX) **Subject:** 70th
Anniversary Royal Scholar Board **Obv:** 1/2 length civilian busts
of 2 kings facing **Rev:** Royal Scholar Board seal
Edge: Segmented reeding

Date	Mintage	F	VF	XF	Unc	BU
BE2547(2004)	—	—	—	—	1.80	2.40

Y# 412 10 BAHT
8.5000 g., Bi-Metallic Brass center in Copper-Nickel ring,
25.95 mm. **Ruler:** Bhumipol Adulyadej (Rama IX)
Subject: Queen's 70th Birthday **Obv:** Bust of queen facing 3/4
left **Rev:** Royal seal **Edge:** Segmented reeding

Date	Mintage	F	VF	XF	Unc	BU
BE2547(2004)	—	—	—	—	1.80	2.40

Y# 413 10 BAHT
8.5000 g., Bi-Metallic Brass center in Copper-Nickel ring,
25.95 mm. **Ruler:** Bhumipol Adulyadej (Rama IX)
Subject: World IUCN Conservation Congress **Obv:** Civilian bust
3/4 right **Rev:** IUCN logo **Edge:** Segmented reeding

Date	Mintage	F	VF	XF	Unc	BU
BE2547(2004)	—	—	—	—	1.80	2.40

Y# 414 10 BAHT
8.5000 g., Bi-Metallic Brass center in Copper-Nickel ring,
25.95 mm. **Ruler:** Bhumipol Adulyadej (Rama IX) **Subject:** Anti
Drug Campaign **Obv:** Civilian bust left **Rev:** Tear drop shaped
logo **Edge:** Segmented reeding

Date	Mintage	F	VF	XF	Unc	BU
BE2547(2004)	—	—	—	—	1.80	2.40

Y# 415 10 BAHT
8.5000 g., Bi-Metallic Brass center in Copper-Nickel ring,
25.95 mm. **Ruler:** Bhumipol Adulyadej (Rama IX)
Subject: Bicentennial of King Rama IV **Obv:** Bust of Rama IV
3/4 right **Rev:** Royal seal **Edge:** Segmented reeding

Date	Mintage	F	VF	XF	Unc	BU
BE2547(2004)	—	—	—	—	1.80	2.40

Y# 410 10 BAHT
8.4500 g., Bi-Metallic Brass center in Copper-Nickel ring,
25.9 mm. **Obv:** Civilian bust 3/4 left **Rev:** Thammasat University
seal **Edge:** Segmented reeding **Note:** 70th Anniversary of
Thammasat University

Date	Mintage	F	VF	XF	Unc	BU
BE2547 (2004)	—	—	—	—	1.80	2.40

Y# 416 10 BAHT
8.5000 g., Bi-Metallic Brass center in Copper-Nickel ring,
25.95 mm. **Ruler:** Bhumipol Adulyadej (Rama IX)
Subject: 100th Anniversary of Army Transportation Corp
Obv: 2 king's military busts left **Rev:** Steering wheel, badge at
center **Edge:** Segmented reeding

Date	Mintage	F	VF	XF	Unc	BU
BE2548(2005)	—	—	—	—	1.80	2.40

Y# 402 10 BAHT
8.4400 g., Bi-Metallic Brass center in Copper-Nickel ring, 26 mm.
Ruler: Bhumipol Adulyadej (Rama IX) **Obv:** Bust 1/4 left within
circle **Rev:** Treasury Department seal within circle
Edge: Segmented reeding

Date	Mintage	F	VF	XF	Unc	BU
BE2548(2005)	—	—	—	—	2.50	3.25

Y# 418 10 BAHT
8.5000 g., Bi-Metallic Brass center in Copper-Nickel ring,
25.95 mm. **Ruler:** Bhumipol Adulyadej (Rama IX) **Subject:** 25th
Asia-Pacific Scout Jamboree **Obv:** Rama IX in scout uniform 3/4
left **Rev:** Logo **Edge:** Segmented reeding

Date	Mintage	F	VF	XF	Unc	BU
BE2548(2005)	—	—	—	—	1.80	2.40

Y# 424 10 BAHT
8.4300 g., Bi-Metallic Brass center in Copper-Nickel ring,
25.98 mm. **Ruler:** Bhumipol Adulyadej (Rama IX) **Subject:**
150th Birthday of Prince Jaturon Ratsamee **Obv:** Bust of Prince
facing 3/4 right **Rev:** Radiant badge **Edge:** Segmented reeding

Date	Mintage	F	VF	XF	Unc	BU
BE2549(2006)	—	—	—	—	2.50	3.25

Y# 417 10 BAHT
8.5000 g., Bi-Metallic Brass center in Copper-Nickel ring, 26 mm.
Ruler: Bhumipol Adulyadej (Rama IX) **Subject:** Prince Royal
Cradle Ceremony **Obv:** Prince's baby head 3/4 left **Rev:** 4-line
inscription **Edge:** Segmented reeding

Date	Mintage	F	VF	XF	Unc	BU
BE2549(2006)	—	—	—	—	1.80	2.40

Y# 406 10 BAHT
8.4400 g., Bi-Metallic Brass center in Copper-Nickel ring, 26 mm.
Ruler: Bhumipol Adulyadej (Rama IX) **Subject:** 60th
Anniversary of Reign **Obv:** Bust 1/4 left within circle **Rev:** Royal
Crown on display **Edge:** Segmented reeding

Date	Mintage	F	VF	XF	Unc	BU
BE2549 (2006)	—	—	—	—	2.50	3.25

Y# 428 10 BAHT
8.5000 g., Bi-Metallic Brass center in Copper-Nickel ring,
25.95 mm. **Ruler:** Bhumipol Adulyadej (Rama IX) **Subject:**
72nd Anniversary Secretariat of the Cabinet **Obv:** Military bust
3/4 right **Rev:** Royal Cabinet seal **Edge:** Segmented reeding

Date	Mintage	F	VF	XF	Unc	BU
BE2549(2006)	—	—	—	—	1.80	2.40

Y# 429 10 BAHT
8.5000 g., Bi-Metallic Brass center in Copper-Nickel ring.,
26 mm. **Ruler:** Bhumipol Adulyadej (Rama IX) **Subject:**
Princess Petcharat 80th birthday **Obv:** Bust of Princess facing
Rev: Royal seal of Princess **Edge:** Segmented reeding

Date	Mintage	F	VF	XF	Unc	BU
BE2549(2006)	—	—	—	—	1.80	2.40

Y# 430 10 BAHT
8.5000 g., Bi-Metallic Brass center in Copper-Nickel ring, 26 mm.
Ruler: Bhumipol Adulyadej (Rama IX) **Subject:** 130th
Anniversary Budget Inspection Department **Obv:** Conjoined
kings' busts left **Rev:** Ornate scale **Edge:** Segmented reeding

Date	Mintage	F	VF	XF	Unc	BU
BE2549(2006)	—	—	—	—	1.80	2.40

Y# 431   10 BAHT
8.5000 g., Bi-Metallic Brass center in Copper-Nickel ring, 25.95 mm. **Ruler:** Bhumipol Adulyadej (Rama IX)**Subject:** 60th Anniversary of reign **Obv:** Bust 3/4 right **Rev:** Royal throne **Edge:** Segmented reeding

Date	Mintage	F	VF	XF	Unc	BU
BE2549(2006)	—	—	—	—	1.80	2.40

Y# 432   10 BAHT
8.5000 g., Bi-Metallic Brass center in Copper-Nickel ring, 25.95 mm. **Ruler:** Bhumipol Adulyadej (Rama IX) **Subject:** Centenary of Military Council **Obv:** Conjoined kings' busts left **Rev:** Military scale emblem **Edge:** Segmented reeding

Date	Mintage	F	VF	XF	Unc	BU
BE2549(2006)	—	—	—	—	1.80	2.40

Y# 425   10 BAHT
8.4300 g., Bi-Metallic Brass center in Copper-Nickel ring, 25.98 mm. **Ruler:** Bhumipol Adulyadej (Rama IX) **Subject:** Centenary of Royal Mounted Army **Obv:** Conjoined kings' busts left **Rev:** Royal crown above emblem **Edge:** Segmented reeding

Date	Mintage	F	VF	XF	Unc	BU
BE2550(2007)	—	—	—	—	1.50	2.00

Y# 426   10 BAHT
8.4300 g., Bi-Metallic Brass center in Copper-Nickel ring, 25.98 mm. **Ruler:** Bhumipol Adulyadej (Rama IX) **Subject:** Centenary of 1st Thai Commercial Bank **Obv:** Conjoined kings' busts left **Rev:** Garuda Bird **Edge:** Segmented reeding

Date	Mintage	F	VF	XF	Unc	BU
BE2550(2007)	—	—	—	—	1.50	2.00

Y# 433   10 BAHT
8.5000 g., Bi-Metallic Brass center in Copper-Nickel ring, 25.95 mm. **Ruler:** Bhumipol Adulyadej (Rama IX) **Subject:** Queen's WHO Food Safety Award **Obv:** Queen's bust 3/4 right **Rev:** WHO emblem at upper left of inscription in sprays **Edge:** Segmented reeding

Date	Mintage	F	VF	XF	Unc	BU
BE2550(2007)	—	—	—	—	1.50	2.00

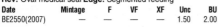

Y# 434   10 BAHT
8.5000 g., Bi-Metallic Brass center in Copper-Nickel ring, 25.95 mm. **Ruler:** Bhumipol Adulyadej (Rama IX)**Subject:** 50th Anniversary Thai Medical Technique **Obv:** Robed bust 3/4 right **Rev:** Oval medical seal **Edge:** Segmented reeding

Date	Mintage	F	VF	XF	Unc	BU
BE2550(2007)	—	—	—	—	1.50	2.00

Y# 435   10 BAHT
8.5000 g., Bi-Metallic Brass center in Copper-Nickel ring, 25.95 mm. **Ruler:** Bhumipol Adulyadej (Rama IX) **Subject:** UNIVERSIADE - World University Games **Obv:** Civilian bust 3/4 right **Rev:** Games logo **Edge:** Segmented reeding

Date	Mintage	F	VF	XF	Unc	BU
BE2550(2007)	—	—	—	—	1.50	2.00

Y# 436   10 BAHT
8.5000 g., Bi-Metallic Brass center in Copper-Nickel ring, 25..95 mm. **Ruler:** Bhumipol Adulyadej (Rama IX) **Subject:** Queen's 75th birthday **Obv:** Bust of Queen wearing tiara 3/4 left **Rev:** Queen's Royal seal **Edge:** Segmented reeding

Date	Mintage	F	VF	XF	Unc	BU
BE2550(2007)	—	—	—	—	1.50	2.00

Y# 437   10 BAHT
8.5000 g., Bi-Metallic Brass center in Copper-Nickel ring, 26 mm. **Ruler:** Bhumipol Adulyadej (Rama IX) **Subject:** IASAJ Conference - Bangkok **Obv:** Civilian bust 3/4 left **Rev:** Oval seal with scale above conference logo **Edge:** Segmented reeding

Date	Mintage	F	VF	XF	Unc	BU
BE2550(2007)	—	—	—	—	1.50	2.00

Y# 438   10 BAHT
8.5000 g., Bi-Metallic Brass center in Copper-Nickel ring, 26 mm. **Ruler:** Bhumipol Adulyadej (Rama IX) **Subject:** King's 80th birthday **Obv:** Royal bust 3/4 left **Rev:** Royal seal **Edge:** Segmented reeding

Date	Mintage	F	VF	XF	Unc	BU
BE2550(2007)	—	—	—	—	1.50	2.00

Y# 439   10 BAHT
8.5000 g., Bi-Metallic Brass center in Copper-Nickel ring, 26 mm. **Ruler:** Bhumipol Adulyadej (Rama IX) **Subject:** 24th SEA Games **Obv:** Civilian bust 3/4 left **Rev:** Games logo above inscription **Edge:** Segmented reeding

Date	Mintage	F	VF	XF	Unc	BU
BE2550(2007)	—	—	—	—	1.50	2.00

Y# 440   10 BAHT
8.5000 g., Bi-Metallic Brass center in Copper-Nickel ring, 25.95 mm. **Ruler:** Bhumipol Adulyadej (Rama IX) **Subject:** 120th Anniversary Siriraj Hospital **Obv:** Conjoined kings' busts right **Rev:** Royal hospital's seal **Edge:** Segmented reeding

Date	Mintage	F	VF	XF	Unc	BU
BE2550(2007)	—	—	—	—	1.50	2.00

Y# 374   20 BAHT
15.1000 g., Copper-Nickel, 32 mm. **Ruler:** Bhumipol Adulyadej (Rama IX) **Subject:** Chulalongkorn University 84th Anniversary March 26 **Obv:** Three conjoined busts right **Rev:** University emblem divides value **Edge:** Reeded

Date	Mintage	F	VF	XF	Unc	BU
BE2544(2001)	—	—	—	—	3.50	5.00
BE2544(2001) Proof	—	Value: 17.50				

Y# 375   20 BAHT
15.1000 g., Copper-Nickel **Ruler:** Bhumipol Adulyadej (Rama IX) **Subject:** Civil Service Comission 72nd Anniversary April 1 **Obv:** Conjoined busts left **Rev:** Civil service emblem divides value **Edge:** Reeded

Date	Mintage	F	VF	XF	Unc	BU
BE2544(2001)	—	—	—	—	3.50	5.00
BE2544(2001) Proof	—	Value: 17.50				

Y# 393   20 BAHT
5.0000 g., Copper-Nickel, 32 mm. **Ruler:** Bhumipol Adulyadej (Rama IX) **Subject:** 80th Birthday of Princess May 6 (King's sister) **Obv:** Bust 1/4 right **Rev:** Crowned emblem and value **Edge:** Reeded

Date	Mintage	F	VF	XF	Unc	BU
BE2546(2003)	—	—	—	—	3.50	5.00
BE2546(2003) Proof	—	Value: 17.50				

Y# 419   20 BAHT
Copper-Nickel, 31.9 mm. **Ruler:** Bhumipol Adulyadej (Rama IX) **Subject:** 50th Anniversary of Audit Department of Cooperatives

Date	Mintage	F	VF	XF	Unc	BU
BE2545(2002)	—	—	—	—	3.50	5.00

Y# 386   20 BAHT
15.0000 g., Copper-Nickel, 32 mm. **Ruler:** Bhumipol Adulyadej (Rama IX) **Subject:** Centennial of Thai Banknotes 2445-2545 **Obv:** Conjoined busts left **Rev:** Coat of arms in center of seal **Edge:** Reeded

Date	Mintage	F	VF	XF	Unc	BU
BE2545(2002)	—	—	—	—	3.50	5.00
BE2545(2002) Proof	—	Value: 17.50				

Y# 388   20 BAHT
15.0000 g., Copper-Nickel, 32 mm. **Ruler:** Bhumipol Adulyadej (Rama IX) **Subject:** King's 75th Birthday December 5 **Obv:** Head left **Rev:** Royal crown in radiant oval **Edge:** Reeded

Date	Mintage	F	VF	XF	Unc	BU
BE2545(2002)	—	—	—	—	3.50	5.00
BE2545(2002) Proof	—	Value: 17.50				

Y# 397   20 BAHT
15.0000 g., Copper-Nickel, 32 mm. **Ruler:** Bhumipol Adulyadej (Rama IX) **Subject:** Centennial of the National Police April 19 **Obv:** Conjoined busts left **Rev:** National Police emblem above banner **Edge:** Reeded

Date	Mintage	F	VF	XF	Unc	BU
BE2545(2002)	—	—	—	—	3.50	5.00

Y# 398   20 BAHT
15.0000 g., Copper-Nickel, 32 mm. **Ruler:** Bhumipol Adulyadej (Rama IX) **Subject:** 50th Birthday of the Crown Prince July 28 **Obv:** Bust facing **Rev:** Crowned monogram **Edge:** Reeded

Date	Mintage	F	VF	XF	Unc	BU
BE2545(2002)	—	—	—	—	3.50	5.00
BE2545(2002) Proof	—	Value: 40.00				

Y# 420   20 BAHT
Copper-Nickel, 31.9 mm. **Ruler:** Bhumipol Adulyadej (Rama IX) **Subject:** 150th Anniversary Rama V

Date	Mintage	F	VF	XF	Unc	BU
BE2546(2003)	—	—	—	—	3.50	5.00

Y# 421   20 BAHT
Copper-Nickel, 31.9 mm. **Ruler:** Bhumipol Adulyadej (Rama IX) **Obv:** King Rama IV

Date	Mintage	F	VF	XF	Unc	BU
BE2547(2004)	—	—	—	—	3.50	5.00

Y# 422   20 BAHT
Copper-Nickel, 31.9 mm. **Ruler:** Bhumipol Adulyadej (Rama IX) **Subject:** 72nd Anniversary of Queen's Birthday

Date	Mintage	F	VF	XF	Unc	BU
BE2547(2004)	—	—	—	—	3.50	5.00

Y# 423   20 BAHT
Copper-Nickel, 31.9 mm. **Ruler:** Bhumipol Adulyadej (Rama IX) **Subject:** 50th Birthday of Princess Sirinahorn

Date	Mintage	F	VF	XF	Unc	BU
BE2548(2005)	—	—	—	—	4.00	6.00

Y# 403   20 BAHT
15.0200 g., Copper-Nickel, 32 mm. **Ruler:** Bhumipol Adulyadej (Rama IX) **Obv:** Bust 1/4 left **Rev:** Treasury Department seal **Edge:** Reeded

Date	Mintage	F	VF	XF	Unc	BU
BE2548(2005)	—	—	—	—	4.00	6.00

Y# 407   20 BAHT
15.0200 g., Copper-Nickel, 32 mm. **Ruler:** Bhumipol Adulyadej (Rama IX) **Subject:** 60th Anniversary of Reign **Obv:** Head left **Rev:** Royal Crown on display **Edge:** Reeded

Date	Mintage	F	VF	XF	Unc	BU
BE2549(2006)	—	—	—	—	4.00	6.00
BE2549(2006) Proof	—	Value: 18.50				

Y# 404   50 BAHT
21.0000 g., Copper-Nickel, 36 mm. **Ruler:** Bhumipol Adulyadej (Rama IX) **Subject:** Air Force 50th Anniversary May 7 **Obv:** Uniformed bust facing **Rev:** Crowned wings within 3/4 wreath **Edge:** Reeded

Date	Mintage	F	VF	XF	Unc	BU
BE2546(2003)	—	—	—	—	12.50	15.00

Y# 389   600 BAHT
22.1500 g., 0.9250 Silver 0.6587 oz. ASW, 35 mm. **Ruler:** Bhumipol Adulyadej (Rama IX) **Subject:** King's 75th Birthday **Obv:** King's portrait **Rev:** Royal crown in radiant oval **Edge:** Reeded

Date	Mintage	F	VF	XF	Unc	BU
BE2545(2002)	—	—	—	—	30.00	35.00
BE2545(2002) Proof	—	Value: 55.00				

Y# 394   600 BAHT
22.1500 g., 0.9250 Silver 0.6587 oz. ASW, 35 mm. **Ruler:** Bhumipol Adulyadej (Rama IX) **Subject:** 80th Birthday of Princess **Obv:** Bust half right **Rev:** Crowned emblem and value **Edge:** Reeded

Date	Mintage	F	VF	XF	Unc	BU
BE2546(2003)	—	—	—	—	35.00	40.00
BE2546(2003) Proof	—	Value: 75.00				

Y# 401   600 BAHT
22.1500 g., 0.9250 Silver 0.6587 oz. ASW, 35 mm. **Ruler:** Bhumipol Adulyadej (Rama IX) **Subject:** Queen's Birthday **Obv:** Crowned monogram **Rev:** Crowned bust of Queen 3/4 right **Edge:** Reeded

Date	Mintage	F	VF	XF	Unc	BU
BE2547(2004) Proof	—	Value: 85.00				

Y# 427   600 BAHT
22.1500 g., 0.9250 Silver 0.6587 oz. ASW, 34.90 mm. **Ruler:** Bhumipol Adulyadej (Rama IX) **Subject:** Princess Maha Chakri Sirindhom's 50th Birthday **Obv:** National arms in oval **Rev:** Bust of Princess 3/4 right **Edge:** Reeded

Date	Mintage	F	VF	XF	Unc	BU
BE2548(2005) Proof	15,000	Value: 80.00				

Y# 408   600 BAHT
22.1500 g., 0.9250 Silver 0.6587 oz. ASW, 35 mm. **Ruler:** Bhumipol Adulyadej (Rama IX) **Subject:** 60th Anniversary of Reign **Obv:** Rama IX **Rev:** Royal Crown on display **Edge:** Reeded

Date	Mintage	F	VF	XF	Unc	BU
BE2549(2006)	—	—	—	—	35.00	40.00
BE2549(2006) Proof	—	Value: 75.00				

Y# 390   7500 BAHT
15.0000 g., 0.9000 Gold 0.4340 oz. AGW, 26 mm. **Ruler:** Bhumipol Adulyadej (Rama IX) **Subject:** King's 75th Birthday **Obv:** King's portrait **Rev:** Royal crown in radiant oval **Edge:** Reeded

Date	Mintage	F	VF	XF	Unc	BU
BE2545(2002) Proof	—	Value: 600				
BE2545(2002)	—	—	—	—	500	525

Y# 395   9000 BAHT
15.0000 g., 0.9000 Gold 0.4340 oz. AGW, 26 mm. **Ruler:** Bhumipol Adulyadej (Rama IX) **Subject:** 80th Birthday of Princess **Obv:** Bust half right **Rev:** Crowned emblem and value **Edge:** Reeded

Date	Mintage	F	VF	XF	Unc	BU
BE2546(2003)	—	—	—	—	500	525
BE2546(2003) Proof	—	Value: 700				

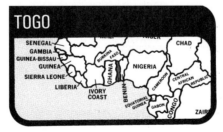

TOGO

The Republic of Togo (formerly part of German Togoland), situated on the Gulf of Guinea in West Africa between Ghana and Dahomey, has an area of 21,622 sq. mi. (56,790 sq. km.) and a population of *3.4 million. Capital: Lome. Agriculture and herding, the production of dyewoods, and the mining of phosphates and iron ore are the chief industries. Copra, phosphates and coffee are exported.

MINT MARK
(a) - Paris, privy marks only

MONETARY SYSTEM
100 Centimes = 1 Franc

REPUBLIC
STANDARD COINAGE
100 Centimes = 1 Franc

KM# 51   100 FRANCS
26.0000 g., Copper-Nickel, 38.6 mm. **Rev:** Blue bird, prism technology

Date	Mintage	F	VF	XF	Unc	BU
2010 Prooflike	2,500	—	—	—	—	20.00

KM# 52   100 FRANCS
26.0000 g., Copper-Nickel, 38.6 mm. **Rev:** Green bird, prism technology

Date	Mintage	F	VF	XF	Unc	BU
2010 Prooflike	2,500	—	—	—	—	20.00

KM# 53   100 FRANCS
26.0000 g., Copper-Nickel, 38.6 mm. **Rev:** Yellow bird, prism technology

Date	Mintage	F	VF	XF	Unc	BU
2010 Prooflike	2,500	—	—	—	—	20.00

KM# 43   250 FRANCS
5.0000 g., 0.9990 Silver 0.1606 oz. ASW **Subject:** German President Horst Kohler **Obv:** National arms **Obv. Legend:** REPUBLIQUE TOGOLAISE **Rev:** Gilt figure

Date	Mintage	F	VF	XF	Unc	BU
2004 Proof	—	Value: 15.00				

KM# 29   500 FRANCS
7.0500 g., 0.9990 Silver 0.2264 oz. ASW, 30 mm. **Obv:** National arms above value **Rev:** Multicolor big cat **Edge:** Plain

Date	Mintage	F	VF	XF	Unc	BU
2001 Proof	—	Value: 35.00				

KM# 41   500 FRANCS
10.0000 g., 0.9990 Silver 0.3212 oz. ASW **Subject:** XVIII World Football Championship - Germany 2006 **Obv:** National arms **Obv. Legend:** REPUBLIQUE TOGOLAISE **Rev:** Two players, map of Germany in background

Date	Mintage	F	VF	XF	Unc	BU
2001 Proof	—	Value: 22.50				

KM# 47   500 FRANCS
14.9700 g., 0.9250 Silver 0.4452 oz. ASW, 30 mm. **Obv:** Arms with supporters **Rev:** Full figures of Johann Wolfgang von Goethe and Friedrich von Schiller on pedestal facing

Date	Mintage	F	VF	XF	Unc	BU
2004 Proof	—	Value: 22.50				

KM# 44   500 FRANCS
7.0000 g., 0.9990 Silver 0.2248 oz. ASW **Subject:** German Chancellor Helmut Schmidt **Obv:** National arms **Obv. Legend:** REPUBLIQUE TOGOLAISE **Rev:** Gilt figue

Date	Mintage	F	VF	XF	Unc	BU
ND(2004) Proof	—	Value: 22.50				

KM# 17   1000 FRANCS
14.9500 g., 0.9990 Silver 0.4802 oz. ASW, 35 mm.
Obv: National arms **Obv. Legend:** REPUBLIQUE TOGOLAISE
Rev: German sailing ship **Rev. Legend:** Adler von Lübeck
Edge: Plain

Date	Mintage	F	VF	XF	Unc	BU
2001 Proof	—	Value: 50.00				

KM# 35   1000 FRANCS
14.7000 g., 0.9990 Silver 0.4721 oz. ASW, 36 mm.
Subject: World Cup Soccer - Bern 1954 **Obv:** National arms
Rev: Bust facing and tower **Edge:** Plain

Date	Mintage	F	VF	XF	Unc	BU
2001 Proof	—	Value: 40.00				

KM# 36   1000 FRANCS
19.9100 g., 0.9990 Silver 0.6395 oz. ASW, 38.1 mm.
Subject: World Cup Soccer - France 1938 **Obv:** National arms
Rev: Eiffel Tower behind soccer player kicking ball **Edge:** Reeded

Date	Mintage	F	VF	XF	Unc	BU
2001 Proof	—	Value: 40.00				

KM# 40   1000 FRANCS
14.9700 g., Silver, 35 mm.   **Obv:** National arms
Obv. Legend: REPUBLIQUE TOGOLAISE **Rev:** Imperial
German sailing ship **Rev. Legend:** "PREUSSEN" **Edge:** Plain

Date	Mintage	F	VF	XF	Unc	BU
2001 Proof	—	Value: 40.00				

KM# 37   1000 FRANCS
19.9700 g., 0.9990 Silver 0.6414 oz. ASW, 40 mm.
Subject: World Cup Soccer - USA 1994 **Obv:** National arms
Obv. Legend: REPUBLIQUE TOGOLAISE **Rev:** Soccer player
kicking ball **Rev. Legend:** COUPE MONDIALE DE FOOTBALL
Edge: Reeded

Date	Mintage	F	VF	XF	Unc	BU
2002 Proof	—	Value: 40.00				

KM# 34   1000 FRANCS
30.9200 g., 0.9931 oz. ASW, 39 mm.   **Obv:** Bust
with headdress left within circle **Rev:** Gold plated baboon within
circle **Edge:** Reeded **Note:** Date in Chinese numerals.

Date	Mintage	F	VF	XF	Unc	BU
2004 Proof	—	Value: 45.00				

KM# 39   1000 FRANCS
62.2400 g., 0.9999 Silver 2.0008 oz. ASW, 50 mm.   **Subject:** Year
of the Monkey **Obv:** Gold plated world globe **Rev:** Gold plated center
with radiant holographic monkey within circle **Edge:** Reeded and
lettered sections **Edge Lettering:** PAN ASIA BANK TAIWAN in
English and Chinese **Note:** Date in Chinese numerals.

Date	Mintage	F	VF	XF	Unc	BU
2004 Proof	—	Value: 90.00				

KM# 38   1000 FRANCS
30.7300 g., 0.9990 Silver 0.9870 oz. ASW, 39 mm.
Subject: Year of the Monkey **Obv:** Head with headdress 1/4 right
within circle **Rev:** Gold plated baboon within circle **Edge:** Reeded
Note: Note: Date in Chinese numerals.

Date	Mintage	F	VF	XF	Unc	BU
2004 Proof	—	Value: 45.00				

KM# 24   1000 FRANCS
31.1035 g., 0.9990 Silver 0.9990 oz. ASW, 40 mm.   **Obv:**
National arms **Obv. Legend:** REPUBLIQUE TOGOLAISE **Rev:**
Incuse rendering of statue of Princess Kyninska of Sparta
horseback left **Rev. Legend:** SPORTS - ANTIQUES **Edge:** Plain

Date	Mintage	F	VF	XF	Unc	BU
2004	2,500	—	—	—	—	55.00

KM# 25   1000 FRANCS
31.1035 g., 0.9990 Silver 0.9990 oz. ASW, 40 mm.   **Obv:** National
arms **Obv. Legend:** REPUBLIQUE TOGOLAISE **Rev:** Relief
rendering of statue of Princess Kyninska of Sparta horseback right
Rev. Legend: SPORTS - ANTIQUES **Edge:** Plain

Date	Mintage	F	VF	XF	Unc	BU
2004	2,500	—	—	—	—	55.00

KM# 26   1000 FRANCS
1.2440 g., 0.9999 Gold 0.0400 oz. AGW, 13.92 mm.
Obv: National arms **Obv. Legend:** REPUBLIQUE TOGOLAISE
Rev: Convex statue of Nike **Edge:** Plain

Date	Mintage	F	VF	XF	Unc	BU
2004 Proof	5,000	Value: 65.00				

KM# 27   1000 FRANCS
1.2440 g., 0.9999 Gold 0.0400 oz. AGW, 13.92 mm.
Obv: National arms **Obv. Legend:** REPUBLIQUE TOGOLAISE
Rev: Concave statue of Nike **Edge:** Plain

Date	Mintage	F	VF	XF	Unc	BU
2004 Proof	5,000	Value: 65.00				

KM# 45   1000 FRANCS
Silver   **Subject:** 170th Anniversary German Railroad, Nürnberg
- Fürth **Obv:** National arms **Obv. Legend:** REPUBLIQUE
TOGOLAISE **Rev:** Early steam locomotive "Adler"

Date	Mintage	F	VF	XF	Unc	BU
2005 Proof	—	Value: 50.00				

KM# 46   1000 FRANCS
1.2400 g., 0.9999 Gold 0.0399 oz. AGW **Subject:** 250th
Anniversary Birth of Wolfgang Amadeus Mozart **Obv:** National
arms **Obv. Legend:** REPUBLIQUE TOGOLAISE

Date	Mintage	F	VF	XF	Unc	BU
2006 Proof	—	Value: 75.00				

KM# 48   1000 FRANCS
25.0000 g., 0.9250 Silver 0.7435 oz. ASW, 38.6 mm.   **Rev:** Blue
bird, prism technology

Date	Mintage	F	VF	XF	Unc	BU
2010 Proof	2,500	Value: 50.00				

KM# 50   1000 FRANCS
25.0000 g., 0.9250 Silver 0.7435 oz. ASW, 38.6 mm.
Rev: Yellow bird, prism technology

Date	Mintage	F	VF	XF	Unc	BU
2010 Proof	2,500	Value: 50.00				

KM# 49   1000 FRANCS
25.0000 g., 0.9250 Silver 0.7435 oz. ASW, 38.6 mm.
Rev: Green bird, prism technology

Date	Mintage	F	VF	XF	Unc	BU
2010 Proof	2,500	Value: 50.00				

KM# 42   2000 FRANCS
62.2000 g., 0.9990 Silver 1.9977 oz. ASW **Series:** Lunar
Subject: Year of the Monkey **Obv:** World map **Obv. Legend:**
REPUBLIQUE TOGOLAISE **Rev:** Monkey

Date	Mintage	F	VF	XF	Unc	BU
2004 Proof	—	Value: 125				

ESSAIS

KM#	Date	Mintage	Identification	Mkt Val
E17	ND(2003)	2	150000 Cfa Francs-100 Africa. Bi-Metallic. President and map. Elephant head on map.	250

TOKELAU ISLANDS

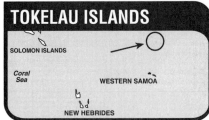

Tokelau or Union Islands, a New Zealand Territory located in the South Pacific 2,100 miles (3,379 km.) northeast of New Zealand and 300 miles (483 km.) north of Samoa, has an area of 4 sq. mi. (10 sq. km.) and a population of *2,000. Geographically, the group consists of four atolls - Atafu, Nukunono, Fakaofo and Swains – but the last belongs to American Samoa (and the United States claims the other three). The people are of Polynesian origin; Samoan is the official language. The New Zealand Minister for Foreign Affairs governs the islands; councils of family elders handle local government at the village level. The chief settlement is Fenuafala, on Fakaofo. It is connected by wireless technology with the offices of the New Zealand Administrative Center, located at Apia, Samoa. Subsistence farming and the production of copra for export are the main occupations. Revenue is also derived from the sale of postage stamps and, since 1978, coins.

Tokelau Islands issued its first coin in 1978, a "$1 Tahi Tala," Tokelauan for "One Dollar."

RULER
British

MINT MARK
PM - Pobjoy

NEW ZEALAND TERRITORY
STANDARD COINAGE

KM# 30   5 TALA
31.1000 g., 0.9990 Silver with Mother-of-Pearl inlay 0.9988 oz. ASW, 40 mm. **Series:** Save the Whales **Obv:** Crowned head right **Obv. Legend:** TOKELAU **Obv. Designer:** Raphael Maklouf **Rev:** Fin Whale on mother of pearl insert **Edge:** Plain

Date	Mintage	F	VF	XF	Unc	BU
2002 Proof	2,000	Value: 85.00				

KM# 32   5 TALA
31.1000 g., 0.9990 Silver 0.9988 oz. ASW, 40 mm.
Ruler: Elizabeth II **Obv:** Elizabeth II **Rev:** Capt. Smith and ship General Jackson **Edge:** Reeded

Date	Mintage	F	VF	XF	Unc	BU
2003 Proof	—	Value: 35.00				

KM# 33   5 TALA
28.6500 g., Silver, 38.60 mm. **Ruler:** Elizabeth II **Obv:** Crowned head right **Obv. Legend:** TOKELAU **Rev:** Sailing ship **Rev. Legend:** CUTTY SARK 1869 **Edge:** Reeded

Date	Mintage	F	VF	XF	Unc	BU
2005 Proof	—	Value: 45.00				

KM# 46   10 TALA
1.2400 g., 0.9990 Gold 0.0398 oz. AGW, 13.92 mm. **Ruler:** Elizabeth II **Obv:** Crowned head right **Obv. Legend:** TOKELAU **Rev:** Two whales **Rev. Legend:** ENDANGERED WILDLIFE **Edge:** Reeded

Date	Mintage	F	VF	XF	Unc	BU
2003 Proof	—	Value: 70.00				

TONGA

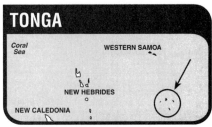

The Kingdom of Tonga (or Friendly Islands) is an archipelago situated in the southern Pacific Ocean south of Western Samoa and east of Fiji comprised of 150 islands. Tonga has an area of 270 sq. mi. (748 sq. km.) and a population of *100,000. Capital: Nuku'alofa. Primarily agricultural, the kingdom exports bananas and copra.

The monarchy is a member of the Commonwealth of Nations. King Siosa Tupou V is Head of State and Government.

RULER
King Taufa'ahau IV, 1965-2006
King Siosa Tupou V, 2006-

KINGDOM
DECIMAL COINAGE

100 Senti = 1 Pa'anga; 100 Pa'anga = 1 Hau

KM# 66a   SENITI
Copper Plated Steel, 17.5 mm. **Ruler:** King Taufa'ahau Tupou IV **Series:** World Food Day **Obv:** Ear of corn **Obv. Legend:** TONGA **Rev:** Vanilla plant **Rev. Legend:** FAKALAHI ME'AKAI **Edge:** Plain

Date	Mintage	F	VF	XF	Unc	BU
2002	—	—	—	0.10	0.35	0.75
2003	—	—	—	0.10	0.35	0.75
2004	—	—	—	0.10	0.35	0.75

KM# 66   SENITI
1.8000 g., Bronze, 16.51 mm. **Ruler:** King Taufa'ahau Tupou IV **Series:** World Food Day **Obv:** Ear of corn **Rev:** Vanilla plant **Edge:** Plain

Date	Mintage	F	VF	XF	Unc	BU
2005	—	—	—	0.10	0.35	0.75

KM# 67a   2 SENITI
Copper Plated Steel, 21 mm. **Ruler:** King Taufa'ahau Tupou IV **Series:** World Food Day **Obv:** Taro plants **Obv. Legend:** TONGA **Rev:** Paper doll cutouts form design in center circle of sprays **Rev. Legend:** PLANNED FAMILIES • FOOD FOR ALL

Date	Mintage	F	VF	XF	Unc	BU
2002	—	—	—	0.15	0.65	1.25
2003	—	—	—	0.15	0.65	1.25
2004	—	—	—	0.15	0.65	1.25

KM# 68a   5 SENITI
2.7900 g., Nickel Plated Steel, 19.39 mm. **Ruler:** King Taufa'ahau Tupou IV **Series:** World Food Day **Obv:** Hen with chicks **Obv. Legend:** TONGA **Rev:** Coconuts **Rev. Legend:** FAKALAHI ME'AKAI **Edge:** Reeded

Date	Mintage	F	VF	XF	Unc	BU
2002	—	—	—	0.25	0.75	1.35
2003	—	—	—	0.25	0.75	1.35
2004	—	—	—	0.25	0.75	1.35
2005	—	—	—	0.25	0.75	1.35

KM# 68   5 SENITI
2.8000 g., Copper-Nickel, 19.5 mm. **Ruler:** King Taufa'ahau Tupou IV **Series:** World Food Day **Obv:** Hen with chicks **Rev:** Coconuts above sprig **Edge:** Reeded

Date	Mintage	F	VF	XF	Unc	BU
2005	—	—	0.10	0.25	0.75	1.25

KM# 69a   10 SENITI
Nickel Plated Steel, 23.5 mm. **Ruler:** King Taufa'ahau Tupou IV **Series:** World Food Day **Obv:** Uniformed bust facing **Obv. Legend:** F • A • O - TONGA **Rev:** Banana tree **Rev. Legend:** FAKALAHI ME'AKAI

Date	Mintage	F	VF	XF	Unc	BU
2002	—	—	—	0.30	1.00	1.75
2003	—	—	—	0.30	1.00	1.75
2004	—	—	—	0.30	1.00	1.75

KM# 70   20 SENITI
11.3000 g., Copper-Nickel, 28.5 mm. **Ruler:** King Taufa'ahau Tupou IV **Series:** World Food Day - FAO **Obv:** Uniformed bust facing **Obv. Legend:** TONGA **Rev:** Yams **Rev. Legend:** FAKALAHI ME'AKAI **Edge:** Reeded

Date	Mintage	F	VF	XF	Unc	BU
2002	—	—	0.25	0.50	1.25	2.00
2003	—	—	0.25	0.50	1.25	2.00
2004	—	—	0.25	0.50	1.25	2.00

KM# 71   50 SENITI
14.6000 g., Copper-Nickel, 32.5 mm. **Ruler:** King Taufa'ahau Tupou IV **Series:** World Food Day **Obv:** Uniformed bust facing **Obv. Legend:** TONGA **Rev:** Tomato plants **Rev. Legend:** FAKALAHI ME'AKAI **Edge:** Plain **Shape:** 12-sided

Date	Mintage	F	VF	XF	Unc	BU
2002	—	—	0.45	0.75	1.50	2.50
2003	—	—	0.45	0.75	1.50	2.50
2004	—	—	0.45	0.75	1.50	2.50

KM# 178   PA'ANGA
31.1000 g., 0.9990 Silver with Mother-of-Pearl inlay 0.9988 oz. ASW, 40 mm. **Ruler:** King Taufa'ahau Tupou IV **Series:** Save the Whales **Obv:** Crown within wreath above national arms within circle **Obv. Legend:** KINGDOM OF TONGA **Rev:** Right Whale on mother of pearl insert **Edge:** Plain

Date	Mintage	F	VF	XF	Unc	BU
2002 Proof	2,000	Value: 85.00				

KM# 179   2 PA'ANGA
Silver **Ruler:** King Taufa'ahau Tupou IV **Subject:** King's 85th Birthday **Obv:** National arms

Date	Mintage	F	VF	XF	Unc	BU
2003 Proof	—	Value: 100				

TRANSNISTRIA

The Pridnestrovskaia Moldavskaia Respublica was formed in 1990, even before the separation of Moldavia from Russia. It has an area of 11,544 sq. mi. (29,900 sq. km.) and a population of 555,000. Capital: Tiraspol.

Transnistria (or Transdniestra) has a president, parliament, army and police forces, but as yet it is lacking international recognition.

MOLDAVIAN REPUBLIC

STANDARD COINAGE

1 Rublei = 100 Kopeek

KM# 50 5 KOPEEK

0.7000 g., Aluminum, 17.9 mm. **Obv:** Modified national arms **Obv. Legend:** ПРИДНЕСТРОВСКАЯ МОЛДАВСКАЯ РЕСПУБЛИКА **Rev:** Value flanked by wheat stalks. **Edge:** Plain **Note:** Prev. KM#2, 16.

Date	Mintage	F	VF	XF	Unc	BU
2005	—	—	—	0.20	0.50	0.65

KM# 51 10 KOPEEK

1.0000 g., Aluminum, 20 mm. **Obv:** Modified national arms **Obv. Legend:** ПРИДНЕСТРОВСКАЯ МОЛДАВСКАЯ РЕСПУБЛИКА **Rev:** Value flanked by wheat stalks **Edge:** Plain **Note:** Prev. KM#3, 17.

Date	Mintage	F	VF	XF	Unc	BU
2005	—	—	—	0.25	0.65	0.90

KM# 5 25 KOPEEK

2.1500 g., Aluminum-Bronze, 16.88 mm. **Obv:** National arms **Rev:** Value within sprays **Edge:** Plain

Date	Mintage	F	VF	XF	Unc	BU
2002	—	—	0.15	0.35	0.90	1.20

KM# 52 25 KOPEEK

Aluminum-Bronze, 16.9 mm. **Obv:** Modified national arms **Obv. Legend:** ПРИДНЕСТРОВСКАЯ МОЛДАВСКАЯ РЕСПУБЛИКА **Rev:** Value within sprays **Edge:** Plain **Note:** Prev. KM#18.

Date	Mintage	F	VF	XF	Unc	BU
2005	—	—	0.15	0.35	0.90	1.20

KM# 52a 25 KOPEEK

2.1000 g., Bronze Plated Steel, 16.9 mm. **Obv:** Modified national arms **Obv. Legend:** ПРИДНЕСТРОВСКАЯ МОЛДАВСКАЯ РЕСПУБЛИКА **Rev:** Value within sprays **Edge:** Plain **Note:** Prev. KM#5a; 18a.

Date	Mintage	F	VF	XF	Unc	BU
2005	—	—	0.15	0.35	0.90	1.20

KM# 53 50 KOPEEK

2.7800 g., Aluminum-Bronze, 18.9 mm. **Obv:** Modified national arms **Obv. Legend:** ПРИДНЕСТРОВСКАЯ МОЛДАВСКАЯ РЕСПУБЛИКА **Rev:** Value within sprays **Edge:** Plain **Note:** Prev. KM#4a; 19.

Date	Mintage	F	VF	XF	Unc	BU
2005	—	—	0.15	0.45	1.10	1.50

KM# 53a 50 KOPEEK

Bronze Plated Steel, 18.9 mm. **Obv. Legend:** ПРИДНЕСТРОВСКАЯ МОЛДАВСКАЯ РЕСПУБЛИКА **Edge:** Plain **Note:** Prev. KM#19a.

Date	Mintage	F	VF	XF	Unc	BU
2005	—	—	0.15	0.45	1.10	1.50

KM# 14 RUBLE

14.1400 g., 0.9250 Silver 0.4205 oz. ASW, 32 mm. **Obv:** National Arms **Rev:** Cathedral in Tyraspol

Date	Mintage	F	VF	XF	Unc	BU
2001 Proof	1,000	Value: 80.00				

KM# 55 RUBLE

14.1400 g., 0.9250 Silver 0.4205 oz. ASW, 32 mm. **Obv:** National Arms **Rev:** Building with dome

Date	Mintage	F	VF	XF	Unc	BU
2005 Proof	500	Value: 125				

KM# 77 RUBLE

14.1400 g., 0.9250 Silver 0.4205 oz. ASW, 32 mm. **Obv:** National Arms **Rev:** Moth and caterpillar

Date	Mintage	F	VF	XF	Unc	BU
2006 Proof	1,000	Value: 145				

KM# 79 RUBLE

14.1400 g., 0.9250 Silver 0.4205 oz. ASW, 32 mm. **Obv:** Olympics - Turin **Rev:** Slalom

Date	Mintage	F	VF	XF	Unc	BU
2006 Proof	500	Value: 150				

KM# 95 3 RUBLYA

8.0000 g., 0.9000 Gold 0.2315 oz. AGW, 21 mm. **Obv:** National Arms **Rev:** Shield **Rev. Legend:** РЫБНИЦА

Date	Mintage	F	VF	XF	Unc	BU
2007 Proof	100	Value: 550				

KM# 97 3 RUBLYA

8.0000 g., 0.9000 Gold 0.2315 oz. AGW, 21 mm. **Obv:** National Arms **Rev:** Shield **Rev. Legend:** ТИРАСПОЛЬ

Date	Mintage	F	VF	XF	Unc	BU
2007 Proof	100	Value: 550				

KM# 110 3 RUBLYA

14.1400 g., 0.9250 Silver 0.4205 oz. ASW, 32 mm. **Obv:** National Arms **Rev:** Aquarius within zodiac emblems

Date	Mintage	F	VF	XF	Unc	BU
2007 Proof	100	Value: 550				

KM# 100 5 RUBLES

33.8500 g., 0.9250 Silver 1.0066 oz. ASW, 39 mm. **Obv:** National Arms **Rev:** Wooley mammoth

Date	Mintage	F	VF	XF	Unc	BU
2007 Proof	500	Value: 200				

KM# 101 5 RUBLES

33.8500 g., 0.9250 Silver 1.0066 oz. ASW, 39 mm. **Obv:** National Arms **Rev:** Moose

Date	Mintage	F	VF	XF	Unc	BU
2007 Proof	500	Value: 200				

KM# 112 10 RUBLEI

14.1400 g., 0.9250 Silver 0.4205 oz. ASW, 32 mm. **Obv:** National Arms **Rev:** Aquarius within circle of zodiac symbols

Date	Mintage	F	VF	XF	Unc	BU
2007 Proof	500	Value: 100				

KM# 102 10 RUBLEI

14.1400 g., 0.9250 Silver 0.4205 oz. ASW, 32 mm. **Obv:** National Arms **Rev:** Multicolor sprinter

Date	Mintage	F	VF	XF	Unc	BU
2007 Proof	500	Value: 100				

KM# 103 10 RUBLEI

14.1400 g., 0.9250 Silver 0.4205 oz. ASW, 32 mm. **Obv:** National Arms **Rev:** Multicolor female gymnast

Date	Mintage	F	VF	XF	Unc	BU
2007 Proof	500	Value: 100				

KM# 104 10 RUBLEI

14.1400 g., 0.9250 Silver 0.4205 oz. ASW, 32 mm. **Obv:** National Arms **Rev:** Multicolor runner, sports designs

Date	Mintage	F	VF	XF	Unc	BU
2007 Proof	500	Value: 100				

KM# 105 10 RUBLEI

0.9250 Silver, 32 mm. **Obv:** National Arms **Rev:** Multicolor javlin thrower

Date	Mintage	F	VF	XF	Unc	BU
2007 Proof	500	Value: 100				

KM# 106 10 RUBLEI

0.9250 Silver, 32 mm. **Obv:** National Arms **Rev:** Multicolor runner breaking tape at finish line

Date	Mintage	F	VF	XF	Unc	BU
2007 Proof	500	Value: 100				

KM# 107 10 RUBLEI

14.1400 g., 0.9250 Silver 0.4205 oz. ASW, 32 mm. **Obv:** National Arms **Rev:** Multicolor soccer player

Date	Mintage	F	VF	XF	Unc	BU
2007 Proof	500	Value: 100				

KM# 111 10 RUBLEI

14.1400 g., 0.9250 Silver 0.4205 oz. ASW, 32 mm. **Obv:** National Arms **Rev:** Constellation ophiuchus (man grasping serpant)

Date	Mintage	F	VF	XF	Unc	BU
2007 Proof	500	Value: 100				

KM# 125 10 RUBLEI

14.1400 g., 0.9250 Silver 0.4205 oz. ASW, 32 mm. **Obv:** National Arms **Rev:** Sturgeon fish

Date	Mintage	F	VF	XF	Unc	BU
2008 Proof	500	Value: 150				

KM# 126 10 RUBLEI

14.1400 g., 0.9250 Silver 0.4205 oz. ASW, 32 mm. **Obv:** National Arms **Rev:** Owl

Date	Mintage	F	VF	XF	Unc	BU
2008 Proof	500	Value: 165				

KM# 127 10 RUBLEI

14.1400 g., 0.9250 Silver 0.4205 oz. ASW, 32 mm. **Obv:** National Arms **Rev:** Flower

Date	Mintage	F	VF	XF	Unc	BU
2008 Proof	500	Value: 185				

KM# 128 10 RUBLEI

14.1400 g., 0.9250 Silver 0.4205 oz. ASW, 32 mm. **Obv:** National Arms **Rev:** Otter

Date	Mintage	F	VF	XF	Unc	BU
2008 Proof	500	Value: 190				

KM# 54 15 RUBLEI

156.4000 g., 0.9990 Gold 5.0231 oz. AGW, 50 mm. **Obv:** National Arms **Rev:** Building with dome

Date	Mintage	F	VF	XF	Unc	BU
2005 Proof, Rare	15	—	—	—	—	—

KM# 75 15 RUBLEI

156.4000 g., 0.9990 Gold 5.0231 oz. AGW, 15 mm. **Obv:** National Arms **Rev:** Building with tower

Date	Mintage	F	VF	XF	Unc	BU
2006 Proof, Rare	15	—	—	—	—	—

KM# 17 100 RUBLEI

14.1400 g., 0.9250 Silver 0.4205 oz. ASW, 32 mm. **Obv:** National Arms **Rev:** Cathedral 1844

Date	Mintage	F	VF	XF	Unc	BU
2001 Proof	1,000	Value: 100				

KM# 10 100 RUBLEI

14.1400 g., 0.9250 Silver 0.4205 oz. ASW, 32 mm. **Obv:** National Arms **Rev:** D. Zielinskieg, chemist

Date	Mintage	F	VF	XF	Unc	BU
2001 Proof	1,000	Value: 65.00				

KM# 11 100 RUBLEI

14.1400 g., 0.9250 Silver 0.4205 oz. ASW, 32 mm. **Obv:** National Arms **Rev:** S. Berg, fish

Date	Mintage	F	VF	XF	Unc	BU
2001 Proof	1,000	Value: 65.00				

KM# 12 100 RUBLEI

14.1400 g., 0.9250 Silver 0.4205 oz. ASW, 32 mm. **Obv:** National Arms **Rev:** N.F. Skilfosowskieg, portrait at right

Date	Mintage	F	VF	XF	Unc	BU
2001 Proof	1,000	Value: 65.00				

KM# 13 100 RUBLEI

14.1400 g., 0.9250 Silver 0.4205 oz. ASW, 32 mm. **Obv:** National Arms **Rev:** M.F. Larionowa, bust, painter

Date	Mintage	F	VF	XF	Unc	BU
2001 Proof	1,000	Value: 65.00				

KM# 15 100 RUBLEI

14.1400 g., 0.9250 Silver 0.4205 oz. ASW, 32 mm. **Obv:** National Arms **Rev:** Cathedral XVII

Date	Mintage	F	VF	XF	Unc	BU
2001 Proof	1,000	Value: 100				

KM# 16 100 RUBLEI

14.1400 g., 0.9250 Silver 0.4205 oz. ASW, 32 mm. **Obv:** National Arms **Rev:** Cathedral 1800

Date	Mintage	F	VF	XF	Unc	BU
2001 Proof	1,000	Value: 100				

KM# 18 100 RUBLEI

14.1400 g., 0.9250 Silver 0.4205 oz. ASW, 32 mm. **Obv:** National Arms **Rev:** Cathedral 1825

Date	Mintage	F	VF	XF	Unc	BU
2001 Proof	1,000	Value: 100				

KM# 19 100 RUBLEI

14.1400 g., 0.9250 Silver 0.4205 oz. ASW, 32 mm. **Obv:** National Arms **Rev:** Cathedral 1776

Date	Mintage	F	VF	XF	Unc	BU
2001 Proof	1,000	Value: 100				

KM# 20 100 RUBLEI

14.1400 g., 0.9250 Silver 0.4205 oz. ASW, 32 mm. **Obv:** National Arms **Rev:** Cathedral XIX

Date	Mintage	F	VF	XF	Unc	BU
2001 Proof	1,000	Value: 100				

KM# 21 100 RUBLEI

14.1400 g., 0.9250 Silver 0.4205 oz. ASW, 32 mm. **Obv:** National Arms **Rev:** Cathedral 1784

Date	Mintage	F	VF	XF	Unc	BU
2001 Proof	1,000	Value: 100				

KM# 22 100 RUBLEI

14.1400 g., 0.9250 Silver 0.4205 oz. ASW, 32 mm. **Obv:** National Arms **Rev:** Cathedral 1854

Date	Mintage	F	VF	XF	Unc	BU
2001 Proof	1,000	Value: 100				

KM# 37 100 RUBLEI

14.0400 g., 0.9250 Silver 0.4175 oz. ASW, 32 mm. **Subject:** 10th Anniversary - Trans-Dniester Republican Bank **Obv:** National arms **Rev:** Colorized monogram within 3/4 wreath with "1992" at top **Edge:** Plain **Note:** Prev. KM#10.

Date	Mintage	F	VF	XF	Unc	BU
2002 Proof	500	Value: 90.00				

KM# 35   100 RUBLEI
14.1600 g., 0.9250 Billon 0.4211 oz., 32 mm.   **Subject:** City of Tiraspol **Obv:** National arms **Rev:** Statue and buildings **Edge:** Plain **Note:** Prev. KM#7.

Date	Mintage	F	VF	XF	Unc	BU
2002 Proof	—			Value: 80.00		

KM# 36   100 RUBLEI
14.1600 g., 0.9250 Silver 0.4211 oz. ASW, 32 mm. **Subject:** City of Tiraspol **Obv:** National arms **Rev:** Cameo above fortress **Edge:** Plain **Note:** Prev. KM#8.

Date	Mintage	F	VF	XF	Unc	BU
2002 Proof	—			Value: 80.00		

KM# 38   100 RUBLEI
14.1600 g., 0.9250 Silver 0.4211 oz. ASW, 32 mm.   **Subject:** K. K. Gedroets **Obv:** National arms **Rev:** Bust facing flanked by sprigs, beaker and book **Edge:** Plain **Note:** Prev. KM#9.

Date	Mintage	F	VF	XF	Unc	BU
2002 Proof	500			Value: 80.00		

KM# 40   100 RUBLEI
14.1400 g., 0.9250 Silver 0.4205 oz. ASW, 32 mm.
Obv: National Arms **Rev:** Shield **Rev. Legend:** ТИРАСЛОЛЬ

Date	Mintage	F	VF	XF	Unc	BU
2002 Proof	500			Value: 100		

KM# 41   100 RUBLEI
14.1400 g., 0.9250 Silver 0.4205 oz. ASW, 32 mm.
Obv: National Arms **Rev:** Shield **Rev. Legend:** ГРНГОРКОПОЛЛ

Date	Mintage	F	VF	XF	Unc	BU
2002 Proof	500			Value: 100		

KM# 45   100 RUBLEI
14.1400 g., 0.9250 Silver 0.4205 oz. ASW, 32 mm.
Obv: National Army **Rev:** Soccer Player

Date	Mintage	F	VF	XF	Unc	BU
2003 Proof	500			Value: 100		

KM# 43   100 RUBLEI
14.1400 g., 0.9250 Silver 0.4205 oz. ASW, 32 mm.
Obv: National arms **Rev:** Hoopoe (Upupa Epops) bird on branch **Edge:** Plain **Note:** Prev. KM#11.

Date	Mintage	F	VF	XF	Unc	BU
2003 Proof	500			Value: 95.00		

KM# 42   100 RUBLEI
14.1400 g., 0.9250 Silver 0.4205 oz. ASW, 32 mm.
Obv: National arms **Rev:** Shield flanked by sprigs **Edge:** Plain **Note:** Prev. KM#12.

Date	Mintage	F	VF	XF	Unc	BU
2003 Proof	500			Value: 75.00		

KM# 48   100 RUBLEI
14.1400 g., 0.9250 Silver 0.4205 oz. ASW, 32 mm.
Subject: 80th Anniversary of Nationhood **Obv:** National arms **Rev:** Map and multicolor flag **Edge:** Plain **Note:** Prev. KM#13.

Date	Mintage	F	VF	XF	Unc	BU
2004 Proof	500			Value: 225		

KM# 44   100 RUBLEI
14.1400 g., 0.9250 Silver 0.4205 oz. ASW, 32 mm.
Obv: National arms **Rev:** Doe and fawn flanked by trees **Edge:** Plain **Note:** Prev. KM#14.

Date	Mintage	F	VF	XF	Unc	BU
2004 Proof	1,000			Value: 225		

KM# 46   100 RUBLEI
14.1400 g., 0.9250 Silver 0.4205 oz. ASW, 32 mm.
Obv: National arms **Rev:** A.G. Rubinstein and music score

Date	Mintage	F	VF	XF	Unc	BU
2004 Proof	1,000			Value: 100		

KM# 47   100 RUBLEI
14.1400 g., 0.9250 Silver 0.4205 oz. ASW, 32 mm.
Obv: National arms **Rev:** JS Grousul

Date	Mintage	F	VF	XF	Unc	BU
2004 Proof	1,000			Value: 100		

KM# 60   100 RUBLEI
14.1400 g., 0.9250 Silver 0.4205 oz. ASW, 32 mm.
Obv: National arms **Rev:** Eurasian Griffin bird on rock **Edge:** Plain **Note:** Prev. KM#15.

Date	Mintage	F	VF	XF	Unc	BU
2005 Proof	1,000			Value: 125		

KM# 56   100 RUBLEI
14.1400 g., 0.9250 Silver 0.4205 oz. ASW, 32 mm.
Obv: National Arms **Rev:** Building with tower

Date	Mintage	F	VF	XF	Unc	BU
2005 Proof	500			Value: 110		

KM# 57   100 RUBLEI
14.1400 g., 0.9250 Silver 0.4205 oz. ASW, 32 mm.
Obv: National Arms **Rev:** Zodiac - Capricorn

Date	Mintage	F	VF	XF	Unc	BU
2005 Proof	1,000			Value: 90.00		

KM# 58   100 RUBLEI
14.1400 g., 0.9250 Silver 0.4205 oz. ASW, 32 mm.
Obv: National Arms **Rev:** Statue and long building

Date	Mintage	F	VF	XF	Unc	BU
2005 Proof	500			Value: 110		

KM# 59   100 RUBLEI
14.1400 g., 0.9250 Silver 0.4205 oz. ASW, 32 mm.
Obv: National Arms **Rev:** Flag as book

Date	Mintage	F	VF	XF	Unc	BU
2005 Proof	500			Value: 180		

KM# 61   100 RUBLEI
14.1400 g., 0.9250 Silver 0.4205 oz. ASW, 32 mm.
Obv: National Arms **Rev:** PP Werszygora

Date	Mintage	F	VF	XF	Unc	BU
2005 Proof	500			Value: 110		

KM# 62   100 RUBLEI
14.1400 g., 0.9250 Silver 0.4205 oz. ASW, 32 mm.
Obv: National Arms **Rev:** Zodiac - Aquarius

Date	Mintage	F	VF	XF	Unc	BU
2005 Proof	500			Value: 90.00		

KM# 63   100 RUBLEI
14.1400 g., 0.9250 Silver 0.4205 oz. ASW, 32 mm.
Obv: National Arms **Rev:** Zodiac - Pisces

Date	Mintage	F	VF	XF	Unc	BU
2005 Proof	500			Value: 90.00		

KM# 64   100 RUBLEI
14.1400 g., 0.9250 Silver 0.4205 oz. ASW, 32 mm.
Obv: National Arms **Rev:** Zodiac - Aries

Date	Mintage	F	VF	XF	Unc	BU
2005 Proof	500			Value: 90.00		

KM# 65   100 RUBLEI
14.1400 g., 0.9250 Silver 0.4205 oz. ASW, 32 mm.
Obv: National Arms **Rev:** Zodiac - Taurus

Date	Mintage	F	VF	XF	Unc	BU
2005 Proof	500			Value: 90.00		

KM# 66   100 RUBLEI
14.1400 g., 0.9250 Silver 0.4205 oz. ASW, 32 mm.
Obv: National Arms **Rev:** Zodiac - Gemini

Date	Mintage	F	VF	XF	Unc	BU
2005 Proof	500			Value: 90.00		

KM# 67   100 RUBLEI
14.1400 g., 0.9250 Silver 0.4205 oz. ASW, 32 mm.
Obv: National Arms **Rev:** Zodiac - Cancer

Date	Mintage	F	VF	XF	Unc	BU
2005 Proof	500			Value: 90.00		

KM# 68   100 RUBLEI
14.1400 g., 0.9250 Silver 0.4205 oz. ASW, 32 mm.
Obv: National Arms **Rev:** Zodiac - Leo

Date	Mintage	F	VF	XF	Unc	BU
2005 Proof	500			Value: 90.00		

KM# 69   100 RUBLEI
14.1400 g., 0.9250 Silver 0.4205 oz. ASW, 32 mm.
Obv: National Arms **Rev:** Zodiac - Virgo

Date	Mintage	F	VF	XF	Unc	BU
2005 Proof	500			Value: 90.00		

KM# 70   100 RUBLEI
14.1400 g., 0.9250 Silver 0.4205 oz. ASW, 32 mm.
Obv: National Arms **Rev:** Zodiac - Libra

Date	Mintage	F	VF	XF	Unc	BU
2005 Proof	500			Value: 90.00		

KM# 71   100 RUBLEI
14.1400 g., 0.9250 Silver 0.4205 oz. ASW, 32 mm.
Obv: National Arms **Rev:** Zodiac - Scorpio

Date	Mintage	F	VF	XF	Unc	BU
2005 Proof	500			Value: 90.00		

KM# 72   100 RUBLEI
14.1400 g., 0.9250 Silver 0.4205 oz. ASW, 32 mm.
Obv: National Arms **Rev:** Zodiac - Sagittarius

Date	Mintage	F	VF	XF	Unc	BU
2005 Proof	500			Value: 90.00		

KM# 76   100 RUBLEI
0.9250 Silver, 32 mm. **Obv:** National Arms **Rev:** Lunar Year of the (fire) Dog

Date	Mintage	F	VF	XF	Unc	BU
2006 Proof	1,000			Value: 60.00		

KM# 78   100 RUBLEI
14.1400 g., 0.9250 Silver 0.4205 oz. ASW, 32 mm.
Obv: National Arms **Rev:** Stag Beetle

Date	Mintage	F	VF	XF	Unc	BU
2006 Proof	500			Value: 285		

KM# 80   100 RUBLEI
14.1400 g., 0.9250 Silver 0.4205 oz. ASW, 32 mm.
Obv: National Arms **Rev:** Biathlon

Date	Mintage	F	VF	XF	Unc	BU
2006 Proof	300			Value: 300		

KM# 81   100 RUBLEI
14.1400 g., 0.9250 Silver 0.4205 oz. ASW, 32 mm.
Subject: Turin Olympics **Obv:** National Arms **Rev:** Ski Jump

Date	Mintage	F	VF	XF	Unc	BU
2006 Proof	200			Value: 325		

KM# 82   100 RUBLEI
14.1400 g., 0.9250 Silver 0.4205 oz. ASW, 32 mm.
Obv: National Arms **Rev:** Town View - Tyraspol

Date	Mintage	F	VF	XF	Unc	BU
2006 Proof	500			Value: 160		

KM# 83   100 RUBLEI
14.1400 g., 0.9250 Silver 0.4205 oz. ASW, 32 mm.
Obv: National Arms **Rev:** Town view Bendery

Date	Mintage	F	VF	XF	Unc	BU
2006 Proof	500			Value: 130		

KM# 84   100 RUBLEI
14.1400 g., 0.9250 Silver 0.4205 oz. ASW, 32 mm.
Obv: Naational Arms **Rev:** Man in forest legend

Date	Mintage	F	VF	XF	Unc	BU
2006 Proof	1,000			Value: 80.00		

KM# 85   100 RUBLEI
14.1400 g., 0.9250 Silver 0.4205 oz. ASW, 32 mm.
Obv: National Arms **Rev:** Legend - Fisherman in rowboat

Date	Mintage	F	VF	XF	Unc	BU
2006 Proof	1,000			Value: 80.00		

KM# 86 100 RUBLEI

14.1400 g., 0.9250 Silver 0.4205 oz. ASW, 32 mm. **Obv:** National Arms **Rev:** Legend dragon slayer

Date	Mintage	F	VF	XF	Unc	BU
2006 Proof	1,000	Value: 80.00				

KM# 87 100 RUBLEI

14.1400 g., 0.9250 Silver 0.4205 oz. ASW **Obv:** National Arms **Rev:** Kossak

Date	Mintage	F	VF	XF	Unc	BU
2006 Proof	500	—	—	—	—	—

KM# 88 100 RUBLEI

14.1400 g., 0.9250 Silver 0.4205 oz. ASW, 32 mm. **Obv:** National Arms **Rev:** General Bursak

Date	Mintage	F	VF	XF	Unc	BU
2006 Proof	500	Value: 80.00				

KM# 89 100 RUBLEI

14.1400 g., 0.9250 Silver 0.4205 oz. ASW **Obv:** National Arms **Rev:** Multicolor baseball player hitting ball **Shape:** 32

Date	Mintage	F	VF	XF	Unc	BU
2006 Proof	500	—	—	—	—	—

KM# 90 100 RUBLEI

14.1400 g., 0.9250 Silver 0.4205 oz. ASW, 32 mm. **Obv:** National Arms **Rev:** Cathedral of the Arch Angel Michael

Date	Mintage	F	VF	XF	Unc	BU
2006 Proof	500	Value: 100				

KM# 91 100 RUBLEI

14.1400 g., 0.9250 Silver 0.4205 oz. ASW, 32 mm. **Obv:** National Arms **Rev:** Sidor Bialy bust at right

Date	Mintage	F	VF	XF	Unc	BU
2006 Proof	300	Value: 175				

KM# 92 100 RUBLEI

14.1400 g., 0.9250 Silver 0.4205 oz. ASW, 32 mm. **Obv:** National Arms **Rev:** Seal impression, partially plated

Date	Mintage	F	VF	XF	Unc	BU
2006 Proof	300	—	—	—	—	—

KM# 120 100 RUBLEI

14.1400 g., 0.9250 Silver 0.4205 oz. ASW, 32 mm. **Obv:** National Arms **Rev:** General Potiomkin

Date	Mintage	F	VF	XF	Unc	BU
2007 Proof	300	Value: 160				

KM# 96 100 RUBLEI

14.1400 g., 0.9250 Silver 0.4205 oz. ASW, 32 mm. **Obv:** National Arms **Rev:** Shield **Rev. Legend:** РЫЪЦИUA

Date	Mintage	F	VF	XF	Unc	BU
2007 Proof	500	Value: 100				

KM# 113 100 RUBLEI

14.1400 g., 0.9250 Silver 0.4205 oz. ASW, 32 mm. **Obv:** National Arms **Rev:** Lunar year of the pig

Date	Mintage	F	VF	XF	Unc	BU
2007 Proof	300	Value: 160				

KM# 114 100 RUBLEI

14.1400 g., 0.9250 Silver 0.4205 oz. ASW, 32 mm. **Obv:** National Arms **Rev:** Castle view, 4 towers

Date	Mintage	F	VF	XF	Unc	BU
2007 Proof	500	Value: 110				

KM# 115 100 RUBLEI

14.1400 g., 0.9250 Silver 0.4205 oz. ASW, 32 mm. **Obv:** National Arms **Rev:** Castle view central tower and gate

Date	Mintage	F	VF	XF	Unc	BU
2007 Proof	500	Value: 110				

KM# 116 100 RUBLEI

14.1400 g., 0.9250 Silver 0.4205 oz. ASW, 32 mm. **Obv:** National Arms **Rev:** Zachary Czerega Kulis, ship at left

Date	Mintage	F	VF	XF	Unc	BU
2007 Proof	300	Value: 175				

KM# 117 100 RUBLEI

14.1400 g., 0.9250 Silver 0.4205 oz. ASW, 32 mm. **Obv:** National Arms **Rev:** Anton Goloway

Date	Mintage	F	VF	XF	Unc	BU
2007 Proof	300	Value: 135				

KM# 118 100 RUBLEI

14.1400 g., 0.9250 Silver 0.4205 oz. ASW, 32 mm. **Obv:** National Arms **Rev:** Alexander Kuszer

Date	Mintage	F	VF	XF	Unc	BU
2007 Proof	500	Value: 125				

KM# 119 100 RUBLEI

14.1400 g., 0.9250 Silver 0.4205 oz. ASW, 32 mm. **Obv:** National Arms **Rev:** Field Marshal - Rumiancew-Zadunajski

Date	Mintage	F	VF	XF	Unc	BU
2007 Proof	300	Value: 160				

KM# 121 100 RUBLEI

14.1400 g., 0.9250 Silver 0.4205 oz. ASW, 32 mm. **Obv:** National Arms **Rev:** General Panin

Date	Mintage	F	VF	XF	Unc	BU
2007 Proof	300	Value: 175				

KM# 25 1000 RUBLEI

8.0000 g., 0.9000 Gold 0.2315 oz. AGW, 21 mm. **Obv:** National Arms **Rev:** 1800 Cathedral of God's Assension

Date	Mintage	F	VF	XF	Unc	BU
2001 Proof	50	Value: 650				

KM# 23 1000 RUBLEI

8.0000 g., 0.9000 Gold 0.2315 oz. AGW, 21 mm. **Obv:** National Arms **Rev:** Church of the Blessed Virgins

Date	Mintage	F	VF	XF	Unc	BU
2001 Proof	50	Value: 650				

KM# 24 1000 RUBLEI

Gold, 21 mm. **Obv:** National Arms **Rev:** Orthodox Church of the Virgin's Assumption

Date	Mintage	F	VF	XF	Unc	BU
2001 Proof	50	Value: 650				

KM# 26 1000 RUBLEI

8.0000 g., 0.9000 Gold 0.2315 oz. AGW, 21 mm. **Obv:** National Arms **Rev:** Cathedral of the Birth of Christ

Date	Mintage	F	VF	XF	Unc	BU
2001 Proof	50	Value: 650				

KM# 27 1000 RUBLEI

8.0000 g., 0.9000 Gold 0.2315 oz. AGW, 21 mm. **Rev:** Cathedral of the Transfigeration

Date	Mintage	F	VF	XF	Unc	BU
2001 Proof	50	Value: 650				

KM# 28 1000 RUBLEI

8.0000 g., 0.9000 Gold 0.2315 oz. AGW, 21 mm. **Obv:** National Arms **Rev:** Church of the Blessed Virgin's Birth

Date	Mintage	F	VF	XF	Unc	BU
2001 Proof	50	Value: 650				

KM# 29 1000 RUBLEI

8.0000 g., 0.9000 Gold 0.2315 oz. AGW, 21 mm. **Obv:** National Arms **Rev:** Church of the Transfiguration

Date	Mintage	F	VF	XF	Unc	BU
2001 Proof	50	Value: 650				

KM# 30 1000 RUBLEI

8.0000 g., 0.9000 Gold 0.2315 oz. AGW, 21 mm. **Obv:** National Arms **Rev:** Church of the Lifegiving Trinity

Date	Mintage	F	VF	XF	Unc	BU
2001 Proof	50	Value: 650				

KM# 31 1000 RUBLEI

8.0000 g., 0.9000 Gold 0.2315 oz. AGW, 21 mm. **Obv:** National Arms **Rev:** Orthodox Church to the Serbian Paraskeva (1854)

Date	Mintage	F	VF	XF	Unc	BU
2001 Proof	50	Value: 650				

KM# 32 1000 RUBLEI

8.0000 g., 0.9000 Gold 0.2315 oz. AGW, 21 mm. **Obv:** National Arms **Rev:** Church of Michael the Arch Angel in Stoiesti

Date	Mintage	F	VF	XF	Unc	BU
2001 Proof	50	Value: 650				

TRINIDAD & TOBAGO

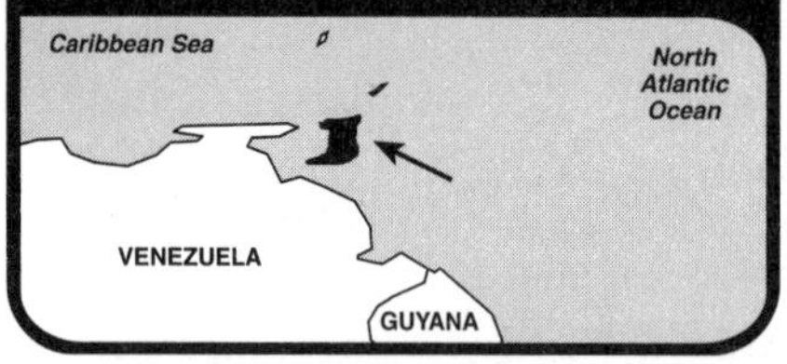

The Republic of Trinidad and Tobago is situated 7 miles (11 km.) off the coast of Venezuela, has an area of 1,981 sq. mi. (5,130 sq. km.) and a population of *1.2 million. Capital: Port-of-Spain. The island of Trinidad contains the world's largest natural asphalt bog. Birds of Paradise live on little Tobago, the only place outside of their native New Guinea where they can be found in a wild state. Petroleum and petroleum products are the mainstay of the economy. Petroleum products, crude oil and sugar are exported.

Trinidad and Tobago is a member of the Commonwealth of Nations. The President is Chief of State. The Prime Minister is Head of Government.

MONETARY SYSTEM

100 Cents = 1 Dollar

REPUBLIC

STANDARD COINAGE

KM# 29 CENT

1.9500 g., Bronze, 17.76 mm. **Obv:** National arms **Rev:** Hummingbird and value **Edge:** Plain

Date	Mintage	F	VF	XF	Unc	BU
2001	—	—	—	0.10	0.30	0.40
2002	—	—	—	0.10	0.30	0.40
2003	—	—	—	0.10	0.30	0.40
2005	—	—	—	0.10	0.30	0.40
2006	—	—	—	0.10	0.30	0.40
2007FM	—	—	—	0.10	0.30	0.40

KM# 30 5 CENTS

3.3100 g., Bronze, 21.2 mm. **Obv:** National arms **Rev:** Bird of paradise and value **Rev. Designer:** Norman Nemeth **Edge:** Plain

Date	Mintage	F	VF	XF	Unc	BU
2001	—	—	—	0.15	0.45	0.60
2002	—	—	—	0.15	0.45	0.60
2003	—	—	—	0.15	0.45	0.60
2004	—	—	—	0.15	0.45	0.60
2005	—	—	—	0.15	0.45	0.60
2006	—	—	—	0.15	0.45	0.60
2007	—	—	—	0.15	0.45	0.60

KM# 31 10 CENTS

1.4000 g., Copper-Nickel, 16.2 mm. **Obv:** National arms **Rev:** Hibiscus and value **Edge:** Reeded

Date	Mintage	F	VF	XF	Unc	BU
2001	—	—	—	0.25	0.60	0.80
2002	—	—	—	0.25	0.60	0.80
2003	—	—	—	0.25	0.60	0.80
2004	—	—	—	0.25	0.60	0.80
2005	—	—	—	0.25	0.60	0.80
2006	—	—	—	0.25	0.60	0.80

KM# 32 25 CENTS

3.6000 g., Copper-Nickel, 20 mm. **Obv:** National arms **Rev:** Chaconia and value **Edge:** Reeded

Date	Mintage	F	VF	XF	Unc	BU
2001	—	—	—	0.30	0.75	1.00
2002	—	—	—	0.30	0.75	1.00
2003	—	—	—	0.30	0.75	1.00
2004	—	—	—	0.30	0.75	1.00
2005	—	—	—	0.30	0.75	1.00
2006	—	—	—	0.30	0.75	1.00
2007	—	—	—	0.30	0.75	1.00

KM# 33 50 CENTS

7.0000 g., Copper-Nickel, 26 mm. **Obv:** National arms **Rev:** Kettle drums and value **Edge:** Reeded

Date	Mintage	F	VF	XF	Unc	BU
2003	—	—	—	1.00	2.00	4.00

KM# 65 50 CENTS

Copper-Nickel, 26 mm.

Date	Mintage	F	VF	XF	Unc	BU
2003	—	—	—	—	2.00	4.00

KM# 63 10 DOLLARS

Copper-Nickel **Subject:** FIFA - XVIII World Football Championship - Soca Warriors - Germany 2006 **Obv:** Native hands playing steel drum, gilt **Rev:** Logo

Date	Mintage	F	VF	XF	Unc	BU
2006	—	—	—	5.00	12.00	35.00

KM# 64 100 DOLLARS

28.2800 g., 0.9250 Silver 0.8410 oz. ASW **Subject:** FIFA - XVIII World Football Championship - Soca Warriors - Germany 2006 **Obv:** Native hands playing steel drum, gilt **Rev:** Logo

Date	Mintage	F	VF	XF	Unc	BU
2006 Proof	—	Value: 70.00				

TRISTAN DA CUNHA

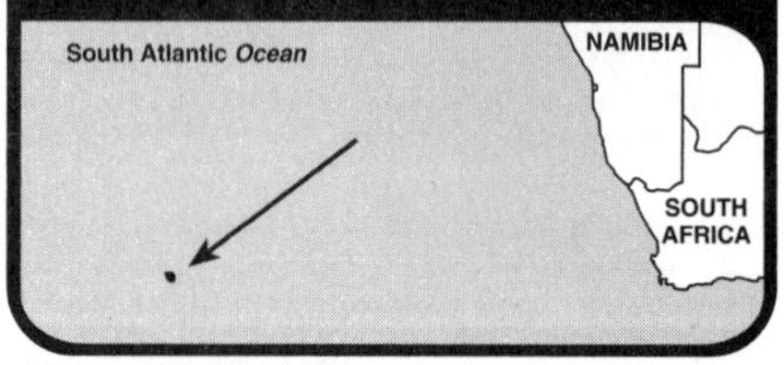

Tristan da Cunha is the principal island and group name of a small cluster of volcanic islands located in the South Atlantic midway between the Cape of Good Hope and South America, and 1,500 miles (2,414 km.) south-southwest of the British colony of St. Helena. The other islands are inaccessible, Gough, and the three Nightingale Islands. The group, which comprises a dependency of St. Helena, has a total area of 40 sq. mi. (104 sq. km.) and a population of less than 300. There is a village of 60 houses called Edinburgh. Potatoes are the staple subsistence crop.

MONETARY SYSTEM

100 Pence = 1 Pound

ST. HELENA DEPENDENCY
STANDARD COINAGE

KM# 27 1/2 PENNY
3.8300 g., Copper, 16.91 mm. **Ruler:** Elizabeth II **Obv:** Head with tiara right **Rev:** Snipe Eel **Edge:** Plain

Date	Mintage	F	VF	XF	Unc	BU
2008	—	—	—	—	0.75	1.00

KM# 28 PENNY
4.6300 g., Copper, 18.66 mm. **Ruler:** Elizabeth II **Obv:** Head with tiara right **Rev:** Lobster **Edge:** Plain

Date	Mintage	F	VF	XF	Unc	BU
2008	—	—	—	—	1.20	1.60

KM# 29 2 PENCE
6.6000 g., Copper, 22.02 mm. **Ruler:** Elizabeth II **Obv:** Head with tiara right **Rev:** Violet Seasnail **Edge:** Plain

Date	Mintage	F	VF	XF	Unc	BU
2008	—	—	—	—	1.50	2.00

KM# 30 5 PENCE
3.7400 g., Copper-Nickel, 16.90 mm. **Ruler:** Elizabeth II **Obv:** Head with tiara right **Rev:** Sea Turtle **Edge:** Plain

Date	Mintage	F	VF	XF	Unc	BU
2008	—	—	—	—	1.80	2.40

KM# 31 10 PENCE
6.4900 g., Copper-Nickel, 22.03 mm. **Ruler:** Elizabeth II **Obv:** Head with tiara right **Rev:** Crab **Edge:** Plain

Date	Mintage	F	VF	XF	Unc	BU
2008	—	—	—	—	2.25	3.00

KM# 32 20 PENCE
6.1000 g., Aluminum-Bronze, 22.02 mm. **Ruler:** Elizabeth II **Obv:** Head with tiara right **Rev:** Orcha - Killer Whale **Edge:** Plain

Date	Mintage	F	VF	XF	Unc	BU
2008	—	—	—	—	3.00	4.00

KM# 33 25 PENCE
Bi-Metallic Aluminum-Bronze center in Copper-Nickel ring., 25.76 mm. **Obv:** Head with tiara right **Rev:** 2 Bottlenose Dolphins **Edge:** Plain

Date	Mintage	F	VF	XF	Unc	BU
2008	—	—	—	—	6.00	8.00

KM# 12 50 PENCE
29.1000 g., Copper-Nickel, 38.6 mm. **Subject:** Queen Elizabeth's 75th Birthday **Obv:** Crowned bust right **Obv. Designer:** Raphael Maklouf **Rev:** Crowned bust facing **Edge:** Reeded

Date	Mintage	F	VF	XF	Unc	BU
2001	—	—	—	—	7.00	8.00

KM# 13 50 PENCE
29.6000 g., Copper-Nickel, 38.7 mm. **Subject:** Centennial of Queen Victoria's Death **Obv:** Crowned bust right **Obv. Designer:** Raphael Maklouf **Rev:** Crown and veil on half-length figure of Queen Victoria facing left within oval circle **Edge:** Reeded

Date	Mintage	F	VF	XF	Unc	BU
2001	—	—	—	—	8.00	10.00

KM# 12a 50 PENCE
28.2800 g., 0.9250 Silver 0.8410 oz. ASW, 38.6 mm. **Subject:** Queen's 75th Birthday **Obv:** Crowned bust right **Rev:** Crowned bust facing **Edge:** Reeded

Date	Mintage	F	VF	XF	Unc	BU
2001 Proof	10,000	Value: 25.00				

KM# 12b 50 PENCE
47.5400 g., 0.9166 Gold 1.4009 oz. AGW, 38.6 mm. **Obv:** Crowned bust right **Rev:** Crowned bust facing

Date	Mintage	F	VF	XF	Unc	BU
2001 Proof	75	Value: 1,750				

KM# 13a 50 PENCE
28.2800 g., 0.9250 Silver 0.8410 oz. ASW, 38.6 mm. **Subject:** Centennial of Queen Victoria's Death **Obv:** Crowned bust right **Rev:** Crown and veil on half-length figure of Queen Victoria facing left within oval circle **Edge:** Reeded

Date	Mintage	F	VF	XF	Unc	BU
2001 Proof	10,000	Value: 35.00				

KM# 13b 50 PENCE
47.5400 g., 0.9166 Gold 1.4009 oz. AGW, 38.6 mm. **Subject:** Centennial of Queen Victoria's Death **Obv:** Crowned bust right **Rev:** Crown and veil on half-length figure of Queen Victoria facing left within oval circle **Edge:** Reeded

Date	Mintage	F	VF	XF	Unc	BU
2001 Proof	100	Value: 1,750				

KM# 14a CROWN
24.1200 g., 0.9250 Silver 0.7173 oz. ASW, 38.5 mm. **Obv:** Crowned bust right **Rev:** Pope John Paul II **Edge:** Reeded

Date	Mintage	F	VF	XF	Unc	BU
2005 Proof	—	Value: 45.00				

KM# 14 CROWN
Copper-Nickel, 38.5 mm. **Obv:** Crowned bust right **Rev:** Pope John Paul II **Edge:** Reeded

Date	Mintage	F	VF	XF	Unc	BU
2005	—	—	—	—	8.50	12.00

KM# 15 CROWN
25.0000 g., Copper-Nickel, 38.83 mm. **Ruler:** Elizabeth II **Series:** Privateering ships of the South Atlantic **Obv:** Crowned bust right **Obv. Legend:** ELIZABETH II — TRISTAN DA CUNHA **Rev:** Sailing ship "Tybalt" **Edge:** Reeded

Date	Mintage	F	VF	XF	Unc	BU
2006	—	—	—	—	8.50	12.00

KM# 16 CROWN
25.0000 g., Copper-Nickel, 38.83 mm. **Ruler:** Elizabeth II **Series:** Privateering ships of the South Atlantic **Obv:** Crowned bust right **Obv. Legend:** ELIZABETH II — TRISTAN DA CUNHA **Rev:** Sailing ship "Syren" **Edge:** Reeded

Date	Mintage	F	VF	XF	Unc	BU
2006	—	—	—	—	8.50	12.00

KM# 17 CROWN
25.0000 g., Copper-Nickel, 38.83 mm. **Ruler:** Elizabeth II **Series:** Privateering ships of the South Atlantic **Obv:** Crowned bust right **Obv. Legend:** ELIZABETH II — TRISTAN DA CUNHA **Rev:** Sailing ship "Pride of Baltimore" **Edge:** Reeded

Date	Mintage	F	VF	XF	Unc	BU
2006	—	—	—	—	8.50	12.00

KM# 18 CROWN
25.0000 g., Copper-Nickel, 38.83 mm. **Ruler:** Elizabeth II **Series:** Privateering ships of the South Atlantic **Obv:** Crowned bust right **Obv. Legend:** ELIZABETH II — TRISTAN DA CUNHA **Rev:** Sailing ship "Hornet" **Edge:** Reeded

Date	Mintage	F	VF	XF	Unc	BU
2006	—	—	—	—	8.50	12.00

KM# 19 CROWN
25.0000 g., Copper-Nickel, 38.83 mm. **Ruler:** Elizabeth II **Series:** Privateering ships of the South Atlantic **Obv:** Crowned bust right **Obv. Legend:** ELIZABETH II — TRISTAN DA CUNHA **Rev:** Sailing ship "Griffin" **Edge:** Reeded

Date	Mintage	F	VF	XF	Unc	BU
2006	—	—	—	—	8.50	12.00

KM# 20 CROWN
25.0000 g., Copper-Nickel, 38.83 mm. **Ruler:** Elizabeth II **Series:** Privateering ships of the South Atlantic **Obv:** Crowned bust right **Obv. Legend:** ELIZABETH II — TRISTAN DA CUNHA **Rev:** Sailing ship "Enterprise" **Edge:** Reeded

Date	Mintage	F	VF	XF	Unc	BU
2006	—	—	—	—	8.50	12.00

KM# 21 CROWN
25.0000 g., Copper-Nickel, 38.83 mm. **Ruler:** Elizabeth II **Series:** Privateering ships of the South Atlantic **Obv:** Crowned bust right **Obv. Legend:** ELIZABETH II — TRISTAN DA CUNHA **Rev:** Sailing ship "Columbus" **Edge:** Reeded

Date	Mintage	F	VF	XF	Unc	BU
2006	—	—	—	—	8.50	12.00

KM# 22 CROWN
25.0000 g., Copper-Nickel, 38.8 mm. **Ruler:** Elizabeth II **Series:** Privateering ships of the South Atlantic **Obv:** Crowned bust right **Obv. Legend:** ELIZABETH II — TRISTAN DA CUNHA **Rev:** Sailing ship "Chasseur" **Edge:** Reeded

Date	Mintage	F	VF	XF	Unc	BU
2006	—	—	—	—	8.50	12.00

KM# 23 CROWN
25.0000 g., Copper-Nickel, 38.8 mm. **Ruler:** Elizabeth II **Series:** Privateering ships of the South Atlantic **Obv:** Crowned bust right **Obv. Legend:** ELIZABETH II — TRISTAN DA CUNHA **Rev:** Sailing ship "Cabot" **Edge:** Reeded

Date	Mintage	F	VF	XF	Unc	BU
2006	—	—	—	—	8.50	12.00

KM# 24 CROWN
25.0000 g., Copper-Nickel, 38.8 mm. **Ruler:** Elizabeth II **Series:** Privateering ships of the South Atlantic **Obv:** Crowned bust right **Obv. Legend:** ELIZABETH II — TRISTAN DA CUNHA **Rev:** Sailing ship "Black Prince" **Edge:** Reeded

Date	Mintage	F	VF	XF	Unc	BU
2006	—	—	—	—	8.50	12.00

KM# 25 CROWN
25.0000 g., Copper-Nickel, 38.8 mm. **Ruler:** Elizabeth II **Series:** Privateering ships of the South Atlantic **Obv:** Crowned bust right **Obv. Legend:** ELIZABETH II — TRISTAN DA CUNHA **Rev:** Sailing ship "Argus" **Edge:** Reeded

Date	Mintage	F	VF	XF	Unc	BU
2006	—	—	—	—	8.50	12.00

KM# 26 CROWN
25.0000 g., Copper-Nickel, 38.8 mm. **Ruler:** Elizabeth II **Series:** Privateering ships of the South Atlantic **Obv:** Crowned bust right **Obv. Legend:** ELIZABETH II — TRISTAN DA CUNHA **Rev:** Sailing ship "True Blooded Yankee" **Edge:** Reeded

Date	Mintage	F	VF	XF	Unc	BU
2006	—	—	—	—	8.50	12.00

KM# 34 CROWN
Copper-Nickel, 38 mm. **Ruler:** Elizabeth II **Obv:** Head with tiara right **Rev:** 2 whales

Date	Mintage	F	VF	XF	Unc	BU
2008	—	—	—	—	6.00	8.00

KM# 35 CROWN
Copper-Nickel, 38.75 mm. **Ruler:** Elizabeth II **Rev:** HNS Victory

Date	Mintage	F	VF	XF	Unc	BU
2008	—	—	—	—	—	15.00

KM# 36 CROWN
25.1800 g., Copper-Nickel **Ruler:** Elizabeth II **Obv:** HMS Belfast

Date	Mintage	F	VF	XF	Unc	BU
2008	—	—	—	—	—	15.00

KM# 37 CROWN
25.1800 g., Copper-Nickel, 38.75 mm. **Ruler:** Elizabeth II **Obv:** HMS Sceptre

Date	Mintage	F	VF	XF	Unc	BU
2008	—	—	—	—	—	15.00

KM# 38 CROWN
25.1800 g., Copper-Nickel, 38.75 mm. **Ruler:** Elizabeth II **Obv:** HMS Beagle

Date	Mintage	F	VF	XF	Unc	BU
2008	—	—	—	—	—	15.00

KM# 39 CROWN
28.1500 g., Copper-Nickel, 38.75 mm. **Ruler:** Elizabeth II **Obv:** HMS Dreadnought

Date	Mintage	F	VF	XF	Unc	BU
2008	—	—	—	—	—	15.00

PIEFORTS

KM#	Date	Mintage	Identification	Mkt Val
P1	2001	500	50 Pence. 0.9250 Silver. 56.5400 g. 38.6 mm.	100
P2	2001	500	50 Pence. 0.9250 Silver. 56.5600 g. 38.6 mm. Reeded edge. Proof KM-13a.	100

TUNISIA

The Republic of Tunisia, located on the northern coast of Africa between Algeria and Libya, has an area of 63,170sq. mi. (163,610 sq. km.) and a population of *7.9 million. Capital: Tunis. Agriculture is the backbone of the economy. Crude oil, phosphates, olive oil, and wine are exported.

TITLES

المملكة التونسية

al-Mamlaka al-Tunisiya

الجمهورية التونسية

al-Jumhuriya al-Tunisiya

al-Amala al-Tunisiya
 (Tunisian Protectorate)

REPUBLIC

DECIMAL COINAGE
1000 Millim = 1 Dinar

KM# 348 5 MILLIM
1.4900 g., Aluminum, 24 mm. **Obv:** Oak tree and dates **Rev:** Value within sprigs

Date	Mintage	F	VF	XF	Unc	BU
AH1425-2004	—	—	—	—	0.50	—
AH1426-2005	—	—	—	—	0.50	—

KM# 306 10 MILLIM
3.5000 g., Brass, 19 mm. **Obv:** Inscription and dates within inner circle of design **Rev:** Value in center of design **Edge:** Reeded

Date	Mintage	F	VF	XF	Unc	BU
AH1425-2004	—	—	0.15	0.25	0.50	—
AH1426-2005	—	—	0.15	0.25	0.50	—

KM# 307 20 MILLIM
4.5000 g., Brass, 22 mm. **Obv:** Inscription and dates within center circle of design **Rev:** Value within center of design

Date	Mintage	F	VF	XF	Unc	BU
AH1425-2004	—	—	0.30	0.50	0.80	—
AH1426-2005	—	—	0.30	0.50	0.80	—
AH1428-2007	—	—	0.30	0.50	0.80	—

KM# 308 50 MILLIM
6.0000 g., Brass, 25 mm. **Obv:** Inscription and dates within center circle of design **Rev:** Value in center of design

Date	Mintage	F	VF	XF	Unc	BU
AH1425-2004	—	—	0.65	0.85	1.25	—
AH1426-2005	—	—	0.65	0.85	1.25	—
AH1428-2007	—	—	0.65	0.85	1.25	—

KM# 309 100 MILLIM
7.5000 g., Brass, 27 mm. **Obv:** Inscription and dates within center circle of design **Rev:** Value in center of design

Date	Mintage	F	VF	XF	Unc	BU
AH1425-2004	—	—	1.25	1.50	2.00	—
AH1426-2005	—	—	1.25	1.50	2.00	—
AH1429-2008	—	—	1.25	1.50	2.00	—

KM# 346 1/2 DINAR
Copper-Nickel **Obv:** Shield within circle **Rev:** 2 hands with fruit and wheat sprig **Note:** Rim width varieties exist.

Date	Mintage	F	VF	XF	Unc	BU
AH1426-2005	—	—	1.00	2.50	4.50	—
AH1428-2007	—	—	1.00	2.50	4.50	—

KM# 347 DINAR
10.1000 g., Copper-Nickel, 28 mm. **Series:** F.A.O. **Obv:** Shield within circle **Rev:** Female half figure right

Date	Mintage	F	VF	XF	Unc	BU
AH1428-2007	—	—	2.00	4.00	7.50	—

KM# 330 5 DINARS
9.4060 g., 0.9000 Gold 0.2722 oz. AGW **Subject:** Anniversary of 7 Nov 1987 **Obv:** Shield **Rev:** Upstretched hand, flag **Note:** Arabic legends vary by year.

Date	Mintage	F	VF	XF	Unc	BU
2001-1421	40	—	—	—	500	550

KM# 329 5 DINARS
9.4060 g., 0.9000 Gold 0.2722 oz. AGW **Subject:** Anniversary of 7 Nov 1987 **Obv:** Shield **Rev:** Upstretched hand, flag **Note:** French legends vary by year.

Date	Mintage	F	VF	XF	Unc	BU
2001-1422	40	—	—	—	500	550

KM# 435 5 DINARS
9.4800 g., 0.9000 Gold 0.2743 oz. AGW, 22 mm. **Subject:** 7 November 1987, 15th Anniversary **Obv:** Shield **Rev:** Stylized dove **Note:** Arabic legends

Date	Mintage	F	VF	XF	Unc	BU
AH1423-2002 Proof	40	Value: 450				

KM# 436 5 DINARS
9.4800 g., 0.9000 Gold 0.2743 oz. AGW, 22 mm. **Subject:** 7 November 1987, 15th Anniversary **Obv:** Shield **Rev:** Stylized dove **Note:** French legends

Date	Mintage	F	VF	XF	Unc	BU
AH1423-2002 Proof	40	Value: 450				

KM# 443 5 DINARS
Bi-Metallic Silver center in Gold ring, 29 mm. **Subject:** 2nd Anniversary of Death **Obv:** Shield **Rev:** Head left

Date	Mintage	F	VF	XF	Unc	BU
AH1423-2002 Proof	750	Value: 275				

KM# 444 5 DINARS
Bi-Metallic Copper-Nickel center in Copper ring, 29 mm. **Obv:** Shield **Rev:** Head left

Date	Mintage	F	VF	XF	Unc	BU
AH1423-2002	20,275,000	—	—	—	8.00	10.00

KM# 350 5 DINARS
10.0000 g., Bi-Metallic Copper-Nickel center in Brass ring, 29 mm. **Obv:** National arms **Rev:** Former President Habib Bourguiba **Edge:** Six reeded and six plain sections **Shape:** 12-sided

Date	Mintage	F	VF	XF	Unc	BU
2002-1423	—	—	—	—	6.50	8.00

KM# 350a 5 DINARS
Bi-Metallic .925 Silver center in .900 gold ring, 29 mm. **Obv:** National arms **Rev:** Former President Habib Bourguiba **Edge:** 6 reeded and 6 plain sections **Shape:** 12-sided

Date	Mintage	F	VF	XF	Unc	BU
2002-1423 Proof	—	—	—	—	—	—

KM# 445 5 DINARS
9.4800 g., 0.9000 Gold 0.2743 oz. AGW, 22 mm. **Subject:** 7 November 1987, 16th Anniversary **Obv:** Shield **Rev:** Hand with UN logo **Note:** Arabic legends

Date	Mintage	F	VF	XF	Unc	BU
AH1424-2003 Proof	40	Value: 450				

KM# 446 5 DINARS
9.4800 g., 0.9000 Gold 0.2743 oz. AGW, 22 mm. **Subject:** 7 November 1987, 16th Anniversary **Obv:** Shield **Rev:** Hand with UN logo **Note:** French legend

Date	Mintage	F	VF	XF	Unc	BU
AH1424-2003 Proof	40	Value: 450				

KM# 456 5 DINARS
9.4000 g., 0.9000 Gold 0.2720 oz. AGW, 22 mm. **Subject:** 7 November 1987, 17th Anniversary - Elections **Obv:** Shield **Rev:** Star and crescent adn stylized flame **Note:** French legend

Date	Mintage	F	VF	XF	Unc	BU
AH1425-2004 Proof	40	Value: 450				

KM# 455 5 DINARS
9.4000 g., 0.9000 Gold 0.2720 oz. AGW, 22 mm. **Subject:** 7 November 1987, 17th Anniversary - Elections **Obv:** Shield **Rev:** Star and crescent and stylized flame **Note:** Arabic legend

Date	Mintage	F	VF	XF	Unc	BU
AH1425-2004 Proof	40	Value: 450				

KM# 465 5 DINARS
9.4000 g., 0.9000 Gold 0.2720 oz. AGW, 22 mm. **Subject:** 7 November 1987, 18th Anniversary **Obv:** Shield **Rev:** Globe in stylized ship **Note:** Arabic legend

Date	Mintage	F	VF	XF	Unc	BU
AH1426-2005 Proof	40	Value: 450				

KM# 466 5 DINARS
9.4000 g., 0.9000 Gold 0.2720 oz. AGW, 22 mm. **Subject:** 7 November 1987, 18th Anniversary **Obv:** Shield **Rev:** Globe in stylized ship **Note:** French legend

Date	Mintage	F	VF	XF	Unc	BU
AH1426-2005 Prook	40	Value: 450				

KM# 479 5 DINARS
9.4000 g., 0.9000 Gold 0.2720 oz. AGW, 22 mm. **Subject:** 7 November 1987, 19th Anniversary **Obv:** Shield **Rev:** Dove and atom **Note:** French legend

Date	Mintage	F	VF	XF	Unc	BU
AH1427-2006 Proof	40	Value: 450				

KM# 472 5 DINARS
24.0000 g., 0.9000 Silver 0.6944 oz. ASW, 35 mm. **Subject:** 50th Anniversary **Obv:** Shield **Rev:** Logo **Note:** Arabic legend

Date	Mintage	F	VF	XF	Unc	BU
AH1427-2006 Proof	900	Value: 50.00				

KM# 478 5 DINARS
9.4000 g., 0.9000 Gold 0.2720 oz. AGW, 22 mm. **Subject:** 7 November 1987, 19th Anniversary **Obv:** Shield **Rev:** Dove and atom **Note:** Arabic legends

Date	Mintage	F	VF	XF	Unc	BU
AH1427-2006 Proof	40	Value: 450				

KM# 473 5 DINARS
24.0000 g., 0.9000 Silver 0.6944 oz. ASW, 35 mm. **Subject:** 50th Anniversary **Obv:** Shield **Rev:** Logo **Note:** French legends

Date	Mintage	F	VF	XF	Unc	BU
AH1427-2006 Proof	100	Value: 60.00				

KM# 491 5 DINARS
9.4000 g., 0.9000 Gold 0.2720 oz. AGW, 22 mm. **Subject:** 7 November 1987, 20th Anniversary **Obv:** Head of Zine el Abidine Ben Ali right **Rev:** Two profiles, keyboard, Satelite receiver **Note:** French legends

Date	Mintage	F	VF	XF	Unc	BU
AH1428-2007 Proof	40	Value: 450				

KM# 486 5 DINARS
24.0000 g., 0.9000 Silver 0.6944 oz. ASW, 35 mm. **Subject:** 50th Anniversary **Obv:** Shield **Rev:** Ship, scales of Justice **Note:** Arabic legend

Date	Mintage	F	VF	XF	Unc	BU
AH1428-2007	900	Value: 50.00				

KM# 490 5 DINARS
9.4000 g., 0.9000 Gold 0.2720 oz. AGW, 22 mm. **Subject:** 7 November 1987, 20th Anniversary **Obv:** Head of Zine el Abidine Ben Ali right **Rev:** Two profiles, keyboard, satelite receiver **Note:** Arabic legend

Date	Mintage	F	VF	XF	Unc	BU
AH1428-2007 Proof	43	Value: 450				

KM# 487 5 DINARS
24.0000 g., 0.9000 Silver 0.6944 oz. ASW, 35 mm. **Subject:** 50th Anniversary **Obv:** Shield **Rev:** Ship, scales of Justice **Note:** French legend

Date	Mintage	F	VF	XF	Unc	BU
AH1428-2007 Proof	100	Value: 60.00				

KM# 378 10 DINARS
38.0000 g., 0.9000 Silver 1.0995 oz. ASW **Subject:** 14th Anniversary 7 Nov and 19th Mediterranean Games **Edge:** Reeded

Date	Mintage	F	VF	XF	Unc	BU
AH1422-2001	—	—	—	—	250	—

KM# 341 10 DINARS
18.7700 g., 0.9000 Gold 0.5431 oz. AGW **Subject:** Anniversary - 7 Nov 1987 **Obv:** Shield **Rev:** Upstretched hand, flag **Note:** Arabic legends vary by year.

Date	Mintage	F	VF	XF	Unc	BU
2001-1422	40	—	—	—	800	850

KM# 430 10 DINARS
38.0000 g., 0.9000 Silver 1.0995 oz. ASW, 40 mm. **Subject:** 7 November 1987, 14th Anniversary **Obv:** Shield **Rev:** Open door **Note:** French legend

Date	Mintage	F	VF	XF	Unc	BU
AH1422-2001 Proof	400	Value: 65.00				

KM# 340 10 DINARS
18.7700 g., 0.9000 Gold 0.5431 oz. AGW **Subject:** Anniversary - 7 Nov 1987 **Obv:** Shield **Rev:** Upstretched hand, flag **Note:** French legends vary by year.

Date	Mintage	F	VF	XF	Unc	BU
2001-1422	40	—	—	—	800	850

KM# 438 10 DINARS
18.8000 g., 0.9000 Gold 0.5440 oz. AGW, 28 mm. **Subject:** 7 November 1987, 15th Anniversary **Obv:** Shield **Rev:** Stylized dove **Note:** French legends

Date	Mintage	F	VF	XF	Unc	BU
AH1423-2002 Proof	40	Value: 750				

KM# 379 10 DINARS
38.0000 g., 0.9000 Silver 1.0995 oz. ASW **Subject:** 15th Anniversary 7 Nov 1987 **Obv:** National arms **Edge:** Reeded

Date	Mintage	F	VF	XF	Unc	BU
AH1423-2002	—	—	—	—	250	—

KM# 433 10 DINARS
38.0000 g., 0.9000 Silver 1.0995 oz. ASW, 40 mm. **Subject:** 7 November 1987, 15th Anniversary **Obv:** Shield **Rev:** Stylized dove **Note:** Arabic legends

Date	Mintage	F	VF	XF	Unc	BU
AH1423-2002 Proof	490	Value: 65.00				

KM# 437 10 DINARS
18.8000 g., 0.9000 Gold 0.5440 oz. AGW, 28 mm. **Subject:** 7 November 1987, 15th Anniversary **Obv:** Shield **Rev:** Stylized dove **Note:** Arabic legends

Date	Mintage	F	VF	XF	Unc	BU
AH1423-2002 Proof	40	Value: 750				

KM# 380 10 DINARS
38.0000 g., 0.9000 Silver 1.0995 oz. ASW **Subject:** 16th Anniversary 7 Nov 1987 plus International Solidarity Fund **Obv:** National arms **Rev:** Large 16 with hands holding globe within the 6, banner which says International Solidarity Fund **Edge:** Reeded

Date	Mintage	F	VF	XF	Unc	BU
AH1424-2003	—	—	—	—	200	—
AH1424-2003 Proof	—	Value: 250				

KM# 452 10 DINARS
38.0000 g., 0.9000 Silver 1.0995 oz. ASW, 40 mm. **Subject:** 7 November 1987, 16th Anniversary **Obv:** Shield **Rev:** Large 16 and globe

Date	Mintage	F	VF	XF	Unc	BU
AH1423-2003	24	Value: 85.00				
Proof						

KM# 447 10 DINARS
18.1800 g., 0.9000 Gold 0.5260 oz. AGW, 28 mm. **Subject:** 7 November 1987, 16th Anniversary **Obv:** Shield **Rev:** Hand with UN logo **Note:** Arabic legend

Date	Mintage	F	VF	XF	Unc	BU
AH1424-2003	40	Value: 700				
Proof						

KM# 448 10 DINARS
18.1800 g., 0.9000 Gold 0.5260 oz. AGW, 28 mm. **Subject:** 7 November 1987, 16th Anniversary **Obv:** Shield **Rev:** Hand with UN logo **Note:** French legends

Date	Mintage	F	VF	XF	Unc	BU
AH1424-2003	40	Value: 700				
Proof						

KM# 454 10 DINARS
38.0000 g., 0.9000 Silver 1.0995 oz. ASW, 40 mm. **Subject:** 7 November 1987, 17th Anniversary - Elections **Obv:** Shield **Rev:** Star and crescent and stylized flame **Note:** French legends

Date	Mintage	F	VF	XF	Unc	BU
AH1425-2004	24	Value: 85.00				
Proof						

KM# 458 10 DINARS
18.8000 g., 0.9000 Gold 0.5440 oz. AGW, 28 mm. **Subject:** 7 November 1987, 17th Anniversary - Elections **Obv:** Shield **Rev:** Star and crescent adn stylized flame **Note:** French legend

Date	Mintage	F	VF	XF	Unc	BU
AH1425-2004	40	Value: 750				
Proof						

KM# 457 10 DINARS
18.8000 g., 0.9000 Gold 0.5440 oz. AGW, 28 mm. **Subject:** 7 November 1987, 17th Anniversary - Elections **Obv:** Shield **Rev:** Star and crescent and stylized flame **Note:** Arabic legend

Date	Mintage	F	VF	XF	Unc	BU
AH1425-2004	40	Value: 750				
Proof						

KM# 381 10 DINARS
38.0000 g., 0.9000 Silver 1.0995 oz. ASW **Subject:** 17th Anniversary of 7 Nov 1987 plus Elections of President and Parliament **Obv:** National arms **Edge:** Reeded

Date	Mintage	F	VF	XF	Unc	BU
AH1425-2004	—	—	—	—	250	—

KM# 453 10 DINARS
38.0000 g., 0.9000 Silver 1.0995 oz. ASW, 40 mm. **Subject:** 7 November 1987, 17th Anniversary - Elections **Obv:** Shield **Rev:** Star and crescent and stylized flame **Note:** Arabic legends

Date	Mintage	F	VF	XF	Unc	BU
AH1425-2004	375	Value: 65.00				
Proof						

KM# 467 10 DINARS
18.8000 g., 0.9000 Gold 0.5440 oz. AGW **Subject:** 7 November 1987, 18th Anniversary **Obv:** Shield **Rev:** Globe in stylized ship **Shape:** 28 **Note:** Arabic legends

Date	Mintage	F	VF	XF	Unc	BU
AH1426-2005	40	Value: 750				
Proof						

KM# 382 10 DINARS
38.0000 g., 0.9000 Silver 1.0995 oz. ASW **Subject:** 18th Anniversary of 7 Nov 1987 and Conference on Information in Tunis 2005 **Edge:** Reeded

Date	Mintage	F	VF	XF	Unc	BU
AH1426-2005	—	—	—	—	250	—

KM# 464 10 DINARS
38.0000 g., 0.9000 Silver 1.0995 oz. ASW, 40 mm. **Subject:** 7 November 1987, 18th Anniversary **Obv:** Shield **Rev:** Globe in stylized ship **Note:** Arabic legend

Date	Mintage	F	VF	XF	Unc	BU
AH1426-2005	431	Value: 65.00				
Proof						

KM# 468 10 DINARS
18.8000 g., 0.9000 Gold 0.5440 oz. AGW, 28 mm. **Subject:** 7 November 1987, 18th Anniversary **Obv:** Shield **Rev:** Globe in stylized ship **Note:** French legend

Date	Mintage	F	VF	XF	Unc	BU
AH1426-2005	40	Value: 750				
Proof						

KM# 463 10 DINARS
38.0000 g., 0.9000 Silver 1.0995 oz. ASW, 40 mm. **Subject:** 7 November 1987, 18th Anniversary **Obv:** Shield **Rev:** Globe in styliuzed ship **Note:** French legends

Date	Mintage	F	VF	XF	Unc	BU
AH1426-2005	50	Value: 75.00				
Proof						

KM# 475 10 DINARS
18.8000 g., 0.9000 Gold 0.5440 oz. AGW, 28 mm. **Subject:** 50th Anniversary **Obv:** Shield **Rev:** Logo **Note:** French legends

Date	Mintage	F	VF	XF	Unc	BU
AH1427-2006	200	Value: 725				
Proof						

KM# 477 10 DINARS
38.0000 g., 0.9000 Silver 1.0995 oz. ASW, 40 mm. **Subject:** 7 November 1987, 19th Anniversary **Obv:** Shield **Rev:** Dove and atom **Note:** French legend

Date	Mintage	F	VF	XF	Unc	BU
AH1427-2006	30	Value: 85.00				
Profo						

KM# 481 10 DINARS
18.8000 g., 0.9000 Gold 0.5440 oz. AGW, 28 mm. **Subject:** 7 November 1987, 19th Anniversary **Obv:** Shield **Rev:** Dove and atom **Note:** French legend

Date	Mintage	F	VF	XF	Unc	BU
AH1427-2006	40	Value: 750				
Proof						

KM# 476 10 DINARS
38.0000 g., 0.9000 Silver 1.0995 oz. ASW, 40 mm. **Subject:** 7 November 1987, 19th Anniversary **Obv:** Shield **Rev:** Dove and atom **Note:** Arabic legend

Date	Mintage	F	VF	XF	Unc	BU
AH1427-2006	300	Value: 65.00				
Proof						

KM# 480 10 DINARS
18.8000 g., 0.9000 Gold 0.5440 oz. AGW, 28 mm. **Subject:** 7 November 1987, 19th Anniversary **Obv:** Shield **Rev:** Dove and atom **Note:** Arabic legend

Date	Mintage	F	VF	XF	Unc	BU
AH1427-2006	40	Value: 750				
Proof						

KM# 383 10 DINARS
38.0000 g., 0.9000 Silver 1.0995 oz. ASW **Subject:** 50th Anniversary of Independence (12.3.1956) **Obv:** National arms **Rev:** Stylized bird, "50", crescent moon with stars

Date	Mintage	F	VF	XF	Unc	BU
AH1427-2006	—	—	—	—	250	—

KM# 383a   10 DINARS
19.0000 g., 0.9000 Gold 0.5498 oz. AGW   **Subject:** 50th
Anniversary of Independence

Date	Mintage	F	VF	XF	Unc	BU
AH1427-2006	600	Value: 725				
Proof						

KM# 474   10 DINARS
18.8000 g., 0.9000 Gold 0.5440 oz. AGW, 28 mm.   **Subject:**
50th Anniversary **Obv:** Shield **Rev:** Logo **Note:** Arabic legends

Date	Mintage	F	VF	XF	Unc	BU
AH1427-2006	1,800	Value: 700				
Proof						

KM# 488   10 DINARS
18.8000 g., 0.9000 Gold 0.5440 oz. AGW, 28 mm.
Subject: 50th Anniversary **Obv:** Shield **Rev:** Ship, scales of
Justice **Note:** Arabic legend

Date	Mintage	F	VF	XF	Unc	BU
AH1428-2007	450	Value: 725				
Proof						

KM# 492   10 DINARS
18.8000 g., 0.9000 Gold 0.5440 oz. AGW, 28 mm.   **Subject:** 7
November 1987, 20th Anniversary **Obv:** Heas of Zine El abidine
Ben Ali right **Rev:** Two profiles, keyboard, satelite receiver
Note: Arabic legend

Date	Mintage	F	VF	XF	Unc	BU
AH1428-2007	42	Value: 750				
Proof						

KM# 489   10 DINARS
18.8000 g., 0.9000 Gold 0.5440 oz. AGW, 28 mm.
Subject: 50th Anniversary **Obv:** Shield **Rev:** Ship, scales of
Justice **Note:** French legend

Date	Mintage	F	VF	XF	Unc	BU
AH1428-2007	50	Value: 750				
Proof						

KM# 493   10 DINARS
18.8000 g., 0.9000 Gold 0.5440 oz. AGW, 28 mm.   **Subject:** 7
November 1987, 20th Anniversary **Obv:** Head of Zine El Abidine
Ben Ali right **Rev:** Two profiles, keyboard, satelite receiver
Note: French legends

Date	Mintage	F	VF	XF	Unc	BU
AH1428-2007	40	Value: 750				
Proof						

KM# 396   50 DINARS
21.0000 g., 0.9000 Gold 0.6076 oz. AGW, 34 mm.
Subject: 14th Anniversary 7 Nov 1987 and 19th Mediterranean
Games **Edge:** Reeded **Note:** Arabic legends.

Date	Mintage	F	VF	XF	Unc	BU
AH1422-2001	—	Value: 1,000				
Proof						

KM# 431   50 DINARS
21.0000 g., 0.9000 Gold 0.6076 oz. AGW, 34 mm.   **Subject:** 7
November 1987, 14th Anniversary **Obv:** Shield **Rev:** Open door
Note: French legends

Date	Mintage	F	VF	XF	Unc	BU
AH1422-2001	150	Value: 850				
Proof						

KM# 397   50 DINARS
21.0000 g., 0.9000 Gold 0.6076 oz. AGW, 34 mm.
Subject: 15th Anniversary of 7 Nov 1987 **Edge:** Reeded

Date	Mintage	F	VF	XF	Unc	BU
AH1423-2002	—	Value: 1,000				
Proof						

KM# 440   50 DINARS
21.0000 g., 0.9000 Gold 0.6076 oz. AGW, 21 mm.   **Subject:** 7
November 1987, 15th Anniversary **Obv:** Shileld **Rev:** Stylized
dove

Date	Mintage	F	VF	XF	Unc	BU
AH1423-2002	80	Value: 875				
Proof						

KM# 439   50 DINARS
21.0000 g., 0.9000 Gold 0.6076 oz. AGW, 34 mm.   **Subject:** 7
November 1987, 15th Anniversary **Obv:** Shield **Rev:** Stylized
dove **Note:** Arabic legend

Date	Mintage	F	VF	XF	Unc	BU
AH1423-2002	580	Value: 825				
Proof						

KM# 450   50 DINARS
21.0000 g., 0.9000 Gold 0.6076 oz. AGW, 34 mm.   **Subject:** 7
November 1987, 16th Anniversary **Obv:** Shield **Rev:** Hand with
UN logo **Note:** French legends

Date	Mintage	F	VF	XF	Unc	BU
AH1424-2003	55	Value: 875				
Proof						

KM# 449   50 DINARS
21.0000 g., 0.9000 Gold 0.6076 oz. AGW, 34 mm.   **Subject:** 7
November 1987, 16th Anniversary **Obv:** Shield **Rev:** Hand with
UN logo **Note:** Arabic legends

Date	Mintage	F	VF	XF	Unc	BU
AH1424-2003	545	Value: 825				
Proof						

KM# 459   50 DINARS
21.0000 g., 0.9000 Gold 0.6076 oz. AGW, 34 mm.   **Subject:** 7
November 1987, 17th Anniversary - Elections **Obv:** Shield
Rev: Star and crescent and stylized flame **Note:** Arabic legend

Date	Mintage	F	VF	XF	Unc	BU
AH1425-2004	379	Value: 850				
Proof						

KM# 398   50 DINARS
21.0000 g., 0.9000 Gold 0.6076 oz. AGW, 34 mm.
Subject: 17th Anniversary of 7 Nov 1987 plus Elections of
President and Parliament **Edge:** Reeded

Date	Mintage	F	VF	XF	Unc	BU
AH1425-2004	—	Value: 1,000				
Proof						

KM# 460   50 DINARS
21.0000 g., 0.9000 Gold 0.6076 oz. AGW, 34 mm.   **Subject:** 7
November 1987, 17th Anniversary - Elections **Obv:** Shield
Rev: Star and crescent and stylized flame **Note:** French legend

Date	Mintage	F	VF	XF	Unc	BU
AH1425-2004	28	Value: 900				
Proof						

KM# 470   50 DINARS
21.0000 g., 0.9000 Gold 0.6076 oz. AGW, 34 mm.   **Subject:** 7
November 1987, 18th Anniversary **Obv:** Shield **Rev:** Globe and
stylized ship **Note:** French legend

Date	Mintage	F	VF	XF	Unc	BU
AH1426-2005	45	Value: 900				
Proof						

KM# 482   50 DINARS
21.0000 g., 0.9000 Gold 0.6076 oz. AGW, 34 mm.   **Subject:** 7
November 1987, 19th Anniversary **Obv:** Shield **Rev:** Dove and
atom **Note:** Arabic legend

Date	Mintage	F	VF	XF	Unc	BU
AH1427-2006	183	Value: 850				
Proof						

KM# 483   50 DINARS
21.0000 g., 0.9000 Gold 0.6076 oz. AGW, 34 mm.   **Subject:** 7
November 1987, 19th Anniversary **Obv:** Shield **Rev:** Dove and
atom **Note:** French legends

Date	Mintage	F	VF	XF	Unc	BU
AH1427-2006	23	Value: 900				
Proof						

KM# 432 100 DINARS
38.0000 g., 0.9000 Gold 1.0995 oz. AGW, 43 mm. **Subject:** 7 November 1987, 14th Anniversary **Obv:** Shield **Rev:** Open door **Note:** Arabic legend

Date	Mintage	F	VF	XF	Unc	BU
AH1422-2001	375	Value: 1,400				
Proof						

KM# 412 100 DINARS
38.0000 g., 0.9000 Gold 1.0995 oz. AGW, 40 mm. **Subject:** 14th Anniversary of 7 Nov 1987 and 19th Mediterranean Games **Obv:** National arms **Rev:** Olympic rings divide 2 portals **Edge:** Reeded

Date	Mintage	F	VF	XF	Unc	BU
AH1422-2001	—	Value: 1,600				
Proof						

KM# 441 100 DINARS
38.0000 g., 0.9000 Gold 1.0995 oz. AGW, 43 mm. **Subject:** 7 November 1987, 15th Anniversary **Obv:** Shield **Rev:** Stylized dove **Note:** Arabic legends

Date	Mintage	F	VF	XF	Unc	BU
AH1423-2002	380	Value: 1,400				
Proof						

KM# 442 100 DINARS
38.0000 g., 0.9000 Gold 1.0995 oz. AGW, 43 mm. **Subject:** 7 November 1987, 15th Anniversary **Obv:** Sheild **Rev:** Stylized dove **Note:** French legend

Date	Mintage	F	VF	XF	Unc	BU
AH1423-2002	110	Value: 1,450				
Proof						

KM# 352 100 DINARS
38.0000 g., 0.9000 Gold 1.0995 oz. AGW, 40 mm. **Subject:** United Nations **Obv:** National arms above value **Rev:** UN logo on stylized hand **Edge:** Reeded

Date	Mintage	F	VF	XF	Unc	BU
AH1424-2003	—	Value: 1,600				
Proof						

KM# 451 100 DINARS
38.0000 g., 0.9000 Gold 1.0995 oz. AGW, 43 mm. **Subject:** 7 November 1987, 16th Anniversary **Obv:** Shield **Rev:** Hand with UN logo **Note:** French text

Date	Mintage	F	VF	XF	Unc	BU
AH1424-2003	53	Value: 1,500				
Proof						

KM# 462 100 DINARS
38.0000 g., 0.9000 Gold 1.0995 oz. AGW, 43 mm. **Subject:** 7 November 1987, 17th Anniversary - Elections **Obv:** Shield **Rev:** Star and crescent and stylized flame **Note:** French legends

Date	Mintage	F	VF	XF	Unc	BU
AH1425-2004	44	Value: 1,500				
Proof						

KM# 461 100 DINARS
38.0000 g., 0.9000 Gold 1.0995 oz. AGW, 43 mm. **Subject:** 7 November 1987, 17th Anniversary - Elections **Obv:** Shield **Rev:** Star and crescent and stylized flame **Note:** Arabic legend

Date	Mintage	F	VF	XF	Unc	BU
AH1425-2004	385	Value: 1,400				
Proof						

KM# 469 100 DINARS
21.0000 g., 0.9000 Gold 0.6076 oz. AGW, 34 mm. **Subject:** 7 November 1987, 18th Anniversary **Obv:** Shield **Rev:** Globe in stylized ship **Note:** Arabic legend

Date	Mintage	F	VF	XF	Unc	BU
AH1426-2005	390	Value: 850				
Proof						

KM# 413 100 DINARS
38.0000 g., 0.9000 Gold 1.0995 oz. AGW **Subject:** 18th Anniversary of 7 Nov 1987 and Conference on Information in Tunis 2005 **Edge:** Reeded

Date	Mintage	F	VF	XF	Unc	BU
AH1426-2005	—	Value: 1,600				
Proof						

KM# 471 100 DINARS
38.0000 g., 0.9000 Gold 1.0995 oz. AGW, 43 mm. **Subject:** 7 November 1987, 18th Anniversary **Obv:** Shield **Rev:** Globe in stylized ship **Note:** French legends

Date	Mintage	F	VF	XF	Unc	BU
AH1426-2005	45	Value: 1,500				
Proof						

KM# 485 100 DINARS
38.0000 g., 0.9000 Gold 1.0995 oz. AGW, 43 mm. **Subject:** 7 November 1987, 19th Anniversary **Obv:** Shield **Rev:** Dove and atom **Note:** French legend

Date	Mintage	F	VF	XF	Unc	BU
AH1427-2006	23	Value: 1,600				
Proof						

KM# 484 100 DINARS
38.0000 g., 0.9000 Gold 1.0995 oz. AGW, 43 mm. **Subject:** 7 November 1987, 19th Anniversary **Obv:** Shield **Rev:** Dove and atom **Note:** Arabic legend

Date	Mintage	F	VF	XF	Unc	BU
AH1427-2006	212	Value: 1,400				
Proof						

TURKEY

The Republic of Turkey, a parliamentary democracy of the Near East located partially in Europe and partially in Asia between the Black and the Mediterranean Seas, has an area of 301,382 sq. mi. (780,580 sq. km.) and a population of *55.4 million. Capital: Ankara. Turkey exports cotton, hazelnuts, and tobacco, and enjoys a virtual monopoly in meerschaum.

RULER
Republic, AH1341/AD1923-

Mint mark
"d" for darphane (meaning mint) is used on coins for overseas market.

REPUBLIC

DECIMAL COINAGE
Western numerals and Latin alphabet

40 Para = 1 Kurus; 100 Kurus = 1 Lira

KM# 1104 25000 LIRA (25 Bin Lira)
2.7000 g., Copper-Zinc, 17 mm. **Obv:** Head left **Rev:** Value **Edge:** Plain

Date	Mintage	F	VF	XF	Unc	BU
2001	—	—	—	—	2.00	—
2002	—	—	—	—	2.00	—
2003	—	—	—	—	2.00	—

KM# 1105 50000 LIRA (50 Bin Lira)
3.2000 g., Copper-Nickel-Zinc, 17.75 mm. **Obv:** Head left within circle **Rev:** Value **Edge:** Plain

Date	Mintage	F	VF	XF	Unc	BU
2001	—	—	—	—	0.50	—
2002	—	—	—	—	0.50	—
2003	—	—	—	—	0.50	—
2004	—	—	—	—	0.50	—

KM# 1106 100000 LIRA (100 Bin Lira)
4.6000 g., Copper-Nickel-Zinc, 21 mm. **Obv:** Head with hat right within circle **Rev:** Value **Edge:** Plain

Date	Mintage	F	VF	XF	Unc	BU
2001	—	—	—	—	0.75	1.25
2002	—	—	—	—	0.75	1.25
2003	—	—	—	—	0.75	1.25
2004	—	—	—	—	0.75	1.25

KM# 1137 250000 LIRA
6.4200 g., Copper-Nickel-Zinc, 23.4 mm. **Obv:** Bust facing within circle **Rev:** Value **Edge Lettering:** "T.C." six times dividing reeded sections

Date	Mintage	F	VF	XF	Unc	BU
2002	—	—	—	—	1.00	1.50
2003	—	—	—	—	1.00	1.50
2004	—	—	—	—	1.00	1.50

KM# 1161 500000 LIRA
4.6000 g., Copper-Nickel, 21 mm. **Obv:** Value and date within sprigs **Rev:** One sheep **Edge:** Plain

Date	Mintage	F	VF	XF	Unc	BU
2002	—	—	—	—	2.00	3.00

KM# 1162 750000 LIRA
6.4000 g., Copper-Nickel, 23.5 mm. **Obv:** Value and date within sprigs **Rev:** Angora Ram **Edge:** Plain

Date	Mintage	F	VF	XF	Unc	BU
2002	—	—	—	—	3.00	4.00

KM# 1163 1000000 LIRA
12.0000 g., Copper-Nickel, 31.9 mm. **Obv:** Value and date within sprigs **Rev:** Turbaned bust 1/4 left divides dates **Edge:** Reeded

Date	Mintage	F	VF	XF	Unc	BU
2002	—	—	—	—	5.00	6.00

KM# 1170 1000000 LIRA
31.4200 g., 0.9250 Silver 0.9344 oz. ASW, 38.6 mm. **Subject:** Mevlana Celaleddin-I Rumi **Obv:** Value and date in wreath **Rev:** Turbaned bust **Edge:** Reeded

Date	Mintage	F	VF	XF	Unc	BU
2002 Proof	—	Value: 30.00				

KM# 1139.1 1000000 LIRA
11.8700 g., Bi-Metallic Brass center in Copper-Nickel ring, 32.1 mm. **Subject:** Foundation of the Mint **Obv:** Building and value within circle **Rev:** Legend and date inscription **Edge:** Plain **Note:** This coin type is produced by a machine outside the money museum at the Istanbul Mint. Visitors pay 1 mio lira, press a button and strike a coin with the actual date of their visit. Many other dates exist in unknown and unregistered quantities. Only Turkish months are on struck coins.

Date	Mintage	F	VF	XF	Unc	BU
Mayis 2002	—	—	—	—	5.00	6.00
Haziran 2002	—	—	—	—	5.00	6.00

Date	Mintage	F	VF	XF	Unc	BU
Temmuz 2002	—	—	—	—	5.00	6.00
Agostos 2002	—	—	—	—	5.00	6.00
Eylul 2002	—	—	—	—	5.00	6.00
Ekim 2002	—	—	—	—	5.00	6.00
Kasim 2002	—	—	—	—	5.00	6.00
Aralik 2002	—	—	—	—	5.00	6.00

KM# 1139.2 1000000 LIRA
Bi-Metallic Brass center in Copper-Nickel ring, 32.1 mm. **Subject:** Foundation of the Mint **Obv:** Building and value within circle **Rev:** Legend and date inscription **Edge:** Plain **Note:** This coin type is produced by a machine outside the money museum at the Istanbul Mint. Visitors pay 1 mio lira, press a button and strike a coin with the actual date of their visit. Many other dates exist in unknown and unregistered quantities. The months are listed in both Turkish and English on struck coins.

Date	Mintage	F	VF	XF	Unc	BU
Ocak/January 2003	—	—	—	—	5.00	6.00
Subat/February 2003	—	—	—	—	5.00	6.00
Mart/March 2003	—	—	—	—	5.00	6.00
Nisan/April 2003	—	—	—	—	5.00	6.00
Mayis/May 2003	—	—	—	—	5.00	6.00
Haziran/June 2003	—	—	—	—	5.00	6.00
Temmuz/July 2003	—	—	—	—	5.00	6.00
Agostos/August 2003	—	—	—	—	5.00	6.00
Eylul/September 2003	—	—	—	—	5.00	6.00
Ekim/October 2003	—	—	—	—	5.00	6.00
Kasim/November 2003	—	—	—	—	5.00	6.00
Aralik/December 2003	—	—	—	—	5.00	6.00

KM# 1107 3000000 LIRA
31.4700 g., 0.9250 Silver 0.9359 oz. ASW, 38.6 mm. **Series:** Olympics **Obv:** Value and date within wreath **Rev:** Long jumper and logo **Edge:** Reeded

Date	Mintage	F	VF	XF	Unc	BU
2002 Proof	—	Value: 32.50				

KM# 1110 5000000 LIRA
67.0000 g., Bronze, 50 mm. **Subject:** Children's Day **Obv:** Legend and inscription **Rev:** Dancing children **Edge:** Plain

Date	Mintage	F	VF	XF	Unc	BU
2001 Matte	1,583	—	—	—	25.00	

KM# 1142 7500000 LIRA
31.2500 g., 0.9250 Silver 0.9293 oz. ASW, 38.5 mm. **Subject:** Cahit Arf, Turkish mathematician (1910-1997) **Obv:** Mathematical formula within circle **Rev:** 1/2-length figure facing **Edge:** Reeded

Date	Mintage	F	VF	XF	Unc	BU
2001 Proof	—	Value: 35.00				

KM# 1143 7500000 LIRA
31.2500 g., 0.9250 Silver 0.9293 oz. ASW, 38.5 mm. **Obv:** Ornamented circle design **Rev:** 1/2-length bust facing **Edge:** Reeded

Date	Mintage	F	VF	XF	Unc	BU
2001 Proof	—	Value: 35.00				

KM# 1144 7500000 LIRA
31.2500 g., 0.9250 Silver 0.9293 oz. ASW, 38.5 mm. **Subject:** Koca Yusuf Baspehlivan **Obv:** Two figures wrestling **Rev:** Portrait on circular background **Edge:** Reeded

Date	Mintage	F	VF	XF	Unc	BU
2001 Proof	—	Value: 32.50				

KM# 1120 7500000 LIRA
15.4000 g., 0.9250 Silver 0.4580 oz. ASW **Subject:** Bird Series - Saz Horozu **Obv:** Value and date within sprigs **Rev:** Purple swamphen on ground **Edge:** Plain **Shape:** 4-sided **Note:** 28.1 x 28.1mm

Date	Mintage	F	VF	XF	Unc	BU
2001 Proof	—	Value: 27.50				

KM# 1121 7500000 LIRA
15.4000 g., 0.9250 Silver 0.4580 oz. ASW **Subject:** Bird Series - Toy **Obv:** Value and date within sprigs **Rev:** Greater Bustard on ground **Edge:** Plain **Shape:** 4-sided **Note:** 28.1 x 28.1mm

Date	Mintage	F	VF	XF	Unc	BU
2001 Proof	—	Value: 27.50				

KM# 1122 7500000 LIRA
15.4000 g., 0.9250 Silver 0.4580 oz. ASW **Subject:** Bird Series - Yaz Ordegi **Obv:** Value and date within sprigs **Rev:** White-headed Duck on ground **Edge:** Plain **Shape:** 4-sided **Note:** 28.1 x 28.1mm

Date	Mintage	F	VF	XF	Unc	BU
2001 Proof	—	Value: 27.50				

KM# 1123 7500000 LIRA
15.4000 g., 0.9250 Silver 0.4580 oz. ASW **Subject:** Bird Series - Dikkuyruk **Obv:** Value and date within sprigs **Rev:** Marbled teal on water **Edge:** Plain **Shape:** 4-sided **Note:** 28.1 x 28.1mm

Date	Mintage	F	VF	XF	Unc	BU
2001 Proof	—	Value: 27.50				

KM# 1124 7500000 LIRA
15.4000 g., 0.9250 Silver 0.4580 oz. ASW **Subject:** Bird Series - Yesil Arikusu **Obv:** Value and date within sprigs **Rev:** Bee-eater on branch **Edge:** Plain **Shape:** 4-sided **Note:** 28.1 x 28.1mm

Date	Mintage	F	VF	XF	Unc	BU
2001 Proof	—	Value: 27.50				

KM# 1125 7500000 LIRA
15.4000 g., 0.9250 Silver 0.4580 oz. ASW **Subject:** Bird Series - Kucuk Karabatak **Obv:** Value and date within sprigs **Rev:** Three pygmy cormorants **Edge:** Plain **Shape:** 4-sided **Note:** 28.1 x 28.1mm

Date	Mintage	F	VF	XF	Unc	BU
2001 Proof	—	Value: 27.50				

KM# 1126 7500000 LIRA
15.4000 g., 0.9250 Silver 0.4580 oz. ASW **Subject:** Bird Series - Kizil Akbaba **Obv:** Value and date within sprigs **Rev:** Eurasian griffon **Edge:** Plain **Shape:** 4-sided **Note:** 28.1 x 28.1mm

Date	Mintage	F	VF	XF	Unc	BU
2001 Proof	—	Value: 27.50				

KM# 1127 7500000 LIRA
15.4000 g., 0.9250 Silver 0.4580 oz. ASW **Subject:** Bird Series - Sah Kartal **Obv:** Value and date within sprigs **Rev:** Eagles **Edge:** Plain **Shape:** 4-sided **Note:** 28.1 x 28.1mm

Date	Mintage	F	VF	XF	Unc	BU
2001 Proof	—	Value: 27.50				

KM# 1128 7500000 LIRA
15.4000 g., 0.9250 Silver 0.4580 oz. ASW **Subject:** Bird Series - Ala Sigireik **Obv:** Value and date within sprigs **Rev:** Rosy starling on ground **Edge:** Plain **Shape:** 4-sided **Note:** 28.1 x 28.1mm

Date	Mintage	F	VF	XF	Unc	BU
2001 Proof	—	Value: 25.00				

KM# 1129 7500000 LIRA
15.4000 g., 0.9250 Silver 0.4580 oz. ASW **Subject:** Bird Series - Izmir Yalicapkini **Obv:** Value and date within sprigs **Rev:** White-throated kingfisher on stump **Edge:** Plain **Shape:** 4-sided **Note:** 28.1 x 28.1mm

Date	Mintage	F	VF	XF	Unc	BU
2001 Proof	—	Value: 25.00				

KM# 1130 7500000 LIRA
15.4000 g., 0.9250 Silver 0.4580 oz. ASW **Subject:** Bird Series - Turac **Obv:** Value and date within sprigs **Rev:** Black francolin birds on the ground **Edge:** Plain **Shape:** 4-sided **Note:** 28.1 x 28.1mm

Date	Mintage	F	VF	XF	Unc	BU
2001 Proof	—	Value: 25.00				

KM# 1131 7500000 LIRA
15.4000 g., 0.9250 Silver 0.4580 oz. ASW **Subject:** Bird Series - Kelaynak **Obv:** Value and date within sprigs **Rev:** Two Bald Ibis birds on ground **Edge:** Plain **Shape:** 4-sided **Note:** 28.1 x 28.1mm

Date	Mintage	F	VF	XF	Unc	BU
2001 Proof	—	Value: 25.00				

KM# 1132 7500000 LIRA
15.4000 g., 0.9250 Silver 0.4580 oz. ASW **Subject:** Bird Series - Sakalli Akbaba **Obv:** Value and date within sprigs **Rev:** Bearded vulture **Edge:** Plain **Shape:** 4-sided **Note:** 28.1 x 28.1mm

Date	Mintage	F	VF	XF	Unc	BU
2001 Proof	—	Value: 25.00				

KM# 1133 7500000 LIRA
15.4000 g., 0.9250 Silver 0.4580 oz. ASW **Subject:** Bird Series - Tepeli Pelikan **Obv:** Value and date within sprigs **Rev:** Dalmatian pelican on rock **Edge:** Plain **Shape:** Square **Note:** 28.1 x 28.1mm

Date	Mintage	F	VF	XF	Unc	BU
2001 Proof	—	Value: 22.50				

KM# 1134 7500000 LIRA
15.4000 g., 0.9250 Silver 0.4580 oz. ASW **Subject:** Bird Series - Ishakkusu **Obv:** Value and date within sprigs **Rev:** European scops owl on branch **Edge:** Plain **Shape:** Square **Note:** 28.1 x 28.1mm

Date	Mintage	F	VF	XF	Unc	BU
2001 Proof	—	Value: 22.50				

KM# 1117 7500000 LIRA
31.4700 g., 0.9250 Silver 0.9359 oz. ASW **Subject:** Iznik Tabak **Obv:** Two peacocks within circle **Rev:** Iznik Tabak (Nicean pottery) 1570; Circle of flowers at center

Date	Mintage	F	VF	XF	Unc	BU
2001 Proof	1,349	Value: 40.00				

KM# 1135 7500000 LIRA
31.0300 g., 0.9250 Silver 0.9228 oz. ASW, 38.5 mm. **Subject:** Mevlana Celaleddin-i Rumi **Obv:** Dancer within circle **Rev:** Turbaned bust 3/4 right above dates **Edge:** Reeded

Date	Mintage	F	VF	XF	Unc	BU
2001 Proof	—	Value: 35.00				

KM# 1145 7500000 LIRA
15.6100 g., 0.9250 Silver 0.4642 oz. ASW, 27.9 x 38.6 mm. **Series:** Flowers **Obv:** Value and date within sprigs **Rev:** Paeonia turcica **Edge:** Reeded **Shape:** Oval

Date	Mintage	F	VF	XF	Unc	BU
2002 Proof	—	Value: 17.50				

KM# 1146 7500000 LIRA
15.6100 g., 0.9250 Silver 0.4642 oz. ASW, 27.9 x 38.6 mm. **Series:** Flowers **Obv:** Value and date within sprigs **Rev:** Orchis anatolica **Edge:** Reeded **Shape:** Oval

Date	Mintage	F	VF	XF	Unc	BU
2002 Proof	—	Value: 17.50				

KM# 1147 7500000 LIRA
15.6100 g., 0.9250 Silver 0.4642 oz. ASW, 27.9 x 38.6 mm. **Series:** Flowers **Obv:** Value and date within sprigs **Rev:** Iris pamphylica **Edge:** Reeded **Shape:** Oval

Date	Mintage	F	VF	XF	Unc	BU
2002 Proof	—	Value: 17.50				

KM# 1148   7500000 LIRA
15.6100 g., 0.9250 Silver 0.4642 oz. ASW, 27.9 x 38.6 mm.
Series: Flowers **Obv:** Value and date within sprigs
Rev: Gladiolus anatolicus **Edge:** Reeded **Shape:** Oval

Date	Mintage	F	VF	XF	Unc	BU
2002 Proof	—	Value: 17.50				

KM# 1152   7500000 LIRA
15.6100 g., 0.9250 Silver 0.4642 oz. ASW, 27.9 x 38.6 mm.
Series: Flowers **Obv:** Value and date within sprigs
Rev: Tchihatchewia isatidea **Edge:** Reeded **Shape:** Oval

Date	Mintage	F	VF	XF	Unc	BU
2002 Proof	—	Value: 17.50				

KM# 1156   7500000 LIRA
15.6100 g., 0.9250 Silver 0.4642 oz. ASW, 27.9 x 38.6 mm.
Obv: Value and date within sprigs **Rev:** Stenbergia candida
Edge: Reeded **Shape:** Oval

Date	Mintage	F	VF	XF	Unc	BU
2002 Proof	—	Value: 17.50				

KM# 1149   7500000 LIRA
15.6100 g., 0.9250 Silver 0.4642 oz. ASW, 27.9 x 38.6 mm.
Series: Flowers **Obv:** Value and date within sprigs **Rev:** Crocus
sativus **Edge:** Reeded **Shape:** Oval

Date	Mintage	F	VF	XF	Unc	BU
2002 Proof	—	Value: 17.50				

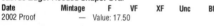

KM# 1153   7500000 LIRA
15.6100 g., 0.9250 Silver 0.4642 oz. ASW, 27.9 x 38.6 mm.
Series: Flowers **Obv:** Value and date within sprigs **Rev:** Linum
anatolicum **Edge:** Reeded **Shape:** Oval

Date	Mintage	F	VF	XF	Unc	BU
2002 Proof	—	Value: 17.50				

KM# 1157   7500000 LIRA
15.6100 g., 0.9250 Silver 0.4642 oz. ASW, 27.9 x 38.6 mm.
Series: Flowers **Obv:** Value and date within sprigs **Rev:** Arum
maculatum **Edge:** Reeded **Shape:** Oval

Date	Mintage	F	VF	XF	Unc	BU
2002 Proof	—	Value: 17.50				

KM# 1150   7500000 LIRA
15.6100 g., 0.9250 Silver 0.4642 oz. ASW, 27.9 x 38.6 mm.
Series: Flowers **Obv:** Value and date within sprigs
Rev: Campanula betulifolia **Edge:** Reeded **Shape:** Oval

Date	Mintage	F	VF	XF	Unc	BU
2002 Proof	—	Value: 17.50				

KM# 1154   7500000 LIRA
15.6100 g., 0.9250 Silver 0.4642 oz. ASW, 27.9 x 38.6 mm.
Series: Flowers **Obv:** Value and date within sprigs
Rev: Cyclamen trochopteranthum **Edge:** Reeded **Shape:** Oval

Date	Mintage	F	VF	XF	Unc	BU
2002 Proof	—	Value: 17.50				

KM# 1118   10000000 LIRA
31.4700 g., 0.9250 Silver 0.9359 oz. ASW, 38.6 mm. **Subject:**
Divrigi Ulu Camii **Obv:** Artwork within circle **Rev:** Ornate door at
the Divrigi ulu Camii (Divrigi Great Mosque) built 1228 in Sivas
Province **Edge:** Reeded

Date	Mintage	F	VF	XF	Unc	BU
2001 Matte	15,000	—	—	—	30.00	—

KM# 1151   7500000 LIRA
15.6100 g., 0.9250 Silver 0.4642 oz. ASW, 27.9 x 38.6 mm.
Series: Flowers **Obv:** Value and date within sprigs
Rev: Centaurea tchihatcheffii **Edge:** Reeded **Shape:** Oval

Date	Mintage	F	VF	XF	Unc	BU
2002 Proof	—	Value: 17.50				

KM# 1155   7500000 LIRA
15.6100 g., 0.9250 Silver 0.4642 oz. ASW, 27.9 x 38.6 mm.
Series: Flowers **Obv:** Value and date within sprigs **Rev:** Tulipa
orphanidea **Edge:** Reeded **Shape:** Oval

Date	Mintage	F	VF	XF	Unc	BU
2002 Proof	—	Value: 17.50				

KM# 1159   10000000 LIRA
31.4200 g., 0.9250 Silver 0.9344 oz. ASW, 38.6 mm.
Subject: Bogazici'nde Yalilar **Obv:** Value and date within sprigs
Rev: Waterfront buildings **Edge:** Reeded

Date	Mintage	F	VF	XF	Unc	BU
2001 Proof	—	Value: 40.00				

KM# 1160   10000000 LIRA
31.4200 g., 0.9250 Silver 0.9344 oz. ASW, 38.6 mm.
Obv: Turkish mint symbol within circle **Rev:** Mosque within surrounding buildings **Edge:** Reeded

Date	Mintage	F	VF	XF	Unc	BU
2002 Proof	—	Value: 45.00				

KM# 1140   10000000 LIRA
31.4600 g., 0.9250 Silver 0.9356 oz. ASW, 38.6 mm.
Subject: 75th Anniversary of TRT (Türkiye Radyo Televizyon) **Obv:** Large mint mark and design within circle **Rev:** Radio microphone **Edge:** Reeded

Date	Mintage	F	VF	XF	Unc	BU
2002 Proof	—	Value: 45.00				

REFORM DECIMAL COINAGE
2005
100,000 Old Lira = 1 New Lira

KM# 1239   KURUS
Copper Plated Steel **Obv:** Head of Ataturk left **Rev:** Plant and value

Date	Mintage	F	VF	XF	Unc	BU
2009	—	—	—	—	0.30	0.50

KM# 1164   NEW KURUS
2.7200 g., Aluminum-Bronze, 17 mm. **Obv:** Head of Atatürk left within circle **Rev:** Value **Edge:** Plain

Date	Mintage	F	VF	XF	Unc	BU
2005	148,419,560	—	—	—	0.15	0.20
2006	9,002,010	—	—	—	0.15	0.20
2007	5,357,000	—	—	—	0.15	0.20
2008	—	—	—	—	0.15	0.20

KM# 1240   5 KURUS
Brass **Obv:** Head of Ataturk left **Rev:** Value and traditional embroidery pattern

Date	Mintage	F	VF	XF	Unc	BU
2009	—	—	—	—	0.30	0.50

KM# 1165   5 NEW KURUS
2.9500 g., Copper-Nickel-Zinc, 17.1 mm. **Obv:** Head of Atatürk left within circle **Rev:** Value **Edge:** Plain

Date	Mintage	F	VF	XF	Unc	BU
2005	203,339,160	—	—	0.10	0.25	0.35
2006	202,253,310	—	—	0.10	0.25	0.35
2007	122,090,000	—	—	0.10	0.25	0.35

KM# 1241   10 KURUS
Brass **Obv:** Head of Ataturk left **Rev:** Value

Date	Mintage	F	VF	XF	Unc	BU
2009	—	—	—	—	0.30	0.50

KM# 1166   10 NEW KURUS
3.8300 g., Copper-Nickel-Zinc, 19.4 mm. **Obv:** Head of Atatük with hat right within circle **Rev:** Value **Edge:** Plain

Date	Mintage	F	VF	XF	Unc	BU
2005	261,538,050	—	—	0.20	0.45	0.60
2006	196,717,510	—	—	0.20	0.45	0.60
2007	134,104,000	—	—	0.20	0.45	0.60

KM# 1242   25 KURUS
Copper-Nickel **Obv:** Head of Ataturk left **Rev:** Value

Date	Mintage	F	VF	XF	Unc	BU
2009	—	—	—	—	0.50	0.75

KM# 1167   25 NEW KURUS
5.3000 g., Copper-Nickel-Zinc, 21.5 mm. **Obv:** Bust of Atatürk facing within circle **Rev:** Value **Edge:** Reeded

Date	Mintage	F	VF	XF	Unc	BU
2005	173,705,760	—	—	0.25	0.60	0.80
2006	67,803,010	—	—	0.30	0.75	1.00
2007	33,463,500	—	—	0.25	0.60	0.80

KM# 1243   50 KURUS
Bi-Metallic Brass center in Copper-Nickel ring **Obv:** Head of Ataturk left **Rev:** Value above suspension bridge

Date	Mintage	F	VF	XF	Unc	BU
2009	—	—	—	—	0.75	1.00

KM# 1168   50 NEW KURUS
7.0000 g., Bi-Metallic Copper-Nickel center in Nickel-Brass ring, 23.8 mm. **Obv:** Head of Atatürk right within circle **Rev:** Value within circle **Edge:** Reeded

Date	Mintage	F	VF	XF	Unc	BU
2005	203,749,569	—	—	0.60	1.50	2.00
2006	45,089,010	—	—	0.60	1.50	2.00
2007	21,946,500	—	—	—	1.20	1.60

KM# 1244   LIRA
Bi-Metallic Copper-Nickel center in Brass ring **Obv:** Head of Ataturk left **Rev:** Value

Date	Mintage	F	VF	XF	Unc	BU
2009	—	—	—	—	3.00	5.00

KM# 1169   NEW LIRA
8.5000 g., Bi-Metallic Nickel-Bronze center in Copper-Nickel-Zinc ring, 26 mm. **Obv:** Bust of Atatürk 3/4 left within circle **Rev:** Value within circle **Edge:** Segmented reeding

Date	Mintage	F	VF	XF	Unc	BU
2005	305,235,560	—	—	—	2.25	3.00
2006	69,247,010	—	—	—	2.25	3.00
2007	56,498,200	—	—	—	2.25	3.00
2008	—	—	—	—	2.25	3.00

KM# 1171   5 NEW LIRA
12.0000 g., Bi-Metallic Brass center in Copper-Nickel ring, 32 mm. **Subject:** 23rd Universiade in red holder **Obv:** Stylized bird within circle **Rev:** Logo within circle **Designer:** Nesrin Ek

Date	Mintage	F	VF	XF	Unc	BU
ND (2005)	2,957	—	—	—	12.50	14.50

KM# 1172   5 NEW LIRA
12.0000 g., Bi-Metallic Copper-Nickel center in Brass ring, 32 mm. **Subject:** 23rd Universiade in blue holder **Obv:** Stylized bird within circle **Rev:** Logo within circle **Designer:** Nesrin Ek

Date	Mintage	F	VF	XF	Unc	BU
ND (2005)	2,900	—	—	—	12.50	14.50

KM# 1195   15 NEW LIRA
1.2400 g., 0.9990 Gold 0.0398 oz. AGW, 13.92 mm. **Subject:** Nemrud **Obv:** Value within wreath **Rev:** Two large statue heads **Designer:** Nesrin Ek **Note:** Dated 2003 but released in 2005

Date	Mintage	F	VF	XF	Unc	BU
2003	1,820	Value: 65.00				

KM# 1193   15 NEW LIRA
15.5500 g., 0.9250 Silver 0.4624 oz. ASW, 32 mm. **Obv:** Bird **Rev:** Logo **Designer:** Nesrin Ek

Date	Mintage	F	VF	XF	Unc	BU
2005 Proof	1,237	Value: 25.00				

KM# 1203   15 NEW LIRA
31.4700 g., 0.9250 Silver 0.9359 oz. ASW, 38.6 mm. **Subject:** Scouting in Turkey, 100th Anniversary **Obv:** Scout emblem, multicolor **Rev:** Flag, Scouts saluting, camp scene

Date	Mintage	F	VF	XF	Unc	BU
2007 Proof	1,414	Value: 40.00				

KM# 1180.1   20 NEW LIRA
23.5000 g., 0.9250 Silver 0.6988 oz. ASW, 38.6 mm. **Obv:** Value within sprigs and circle **Rev:** Angora Cat with plain eyes **Edge:** Reeded

Date	Mintage	F	VF	XF	Unc	BU
2005 Proof	5,000	Value: 60.00				

KM# 1180.2   20 NEW LIRA
23.5000 g., 0.9250 Silver 0.6988 oz. ASW, 38.6 mm. **Obv:** Value within sprigs and circle **Rev:** Cat with mismatched colored eyes **Edge:** Reeded

Date	Mintage	F	VF	XF	Unc	BU
2005 Proof	—	Value: 65.00				

KM# 1173   20 NEW LIRA
31.3600 g., 0.9250 Silver 0.9326 oz. ASW, 38.6 mm. **Obv:** Value within sprigs and circle **Rev:** Aegean Carpet **Edge:** Reeded

Date	Mintage	F	VF	XF	Unc	BU
2005 Proof	1,195	Value: 45.00				

KM# 1174   20 NEW LIRA
31.4300 g., 0.9250 Silver 0.9347 oz. ASW, 38.6 mm. **Obv:** Value within sprigs and circle **Rev:** Mostar Bridge **Rev. Designer:** Nesrin Ek **Edge:** Reeded

Date	Mintage	F	VF	XF	Unc	BU
2005 Proof	1,592	Value: 50.00				

KM# 1175   20 NEW LIRA
23.4500 g., 0.9250 Silver 0.6974 oz. ASW, 38.6 mm.
Obv: Value within sprigs and circle **Rev:** Angora Goat
Rev. Designer: Nesrin Ek **Edge:** Reeded

Date	Mintage	F	VF	XF	Unc	BU
2005 Proof	898	Value: 60.00				

KM# 1176   20 NEW LIRA
23.4600 g., 0.9250 Silver 0.6977 oz. ASW, 38.6 mm.
Obv: Value within sprigs and circle **Rev:** Long-eared Desert
Hedgehog **Rev. Designer:** Nesrin Ek **Edge:** Reeded

Date	Mintage	F	VF	XF	Unc	BU
2005 Proof	744	Value: 60.00				

KM# 1177   20 NEW LIRA
23.4100 g., 0.9250 Silver 0.6962 oz. ASW, 38.6 mm.
Obv: Value within sprigs and circle **Rev:** Anatolian Mouflon **Rev.
Designer:** Nesrin Ek **Edge:** Reeded

Date	Mintage	F	VF	XF	Unc	BU
2005 Proof	779	Value: 60.00				

KM# 1178   20 NEW LIRA
23.4300 g., 0.9250 Silver 0.6968 oz. ASW, 38.6 mm.
Obv: Value within sprigs and circle **Rev:** Striped Hyena
Rev. Designer: Nesrin Ek **Edge:** Reeded

Date	Mintage	F	VF	XF	Unc	BU
2005 Proof	778	Value: 60.00				

KM# 1179   20 NEW LIRA
23.4300 g., 0.9250 Silver 0.6968 oz. ASW, 38.6 mm.
Obv: Value within sprigs and circle **Rev:** Hazel Dormouse
Rev. Designer: Nesrin Ek **Edge:** Reeded

Date	Mintage	F	VF	XF	Unc	BU
2005 Proof	744	Value: 60.00				

KM# 1181   20 NEW LIRA
23.3700 g., 0.9990 Silver 0.7506 oz. ASW, 38.6 mm.
Obv: Value within sprigs and circle **Rev:** Anatolian Leopard
Rev. Designer: Nesrin Ek **Edge:** Reeded

Date	Mintage	F	VF	XF	Unc	BU
2005 Proof	855	Value: 60.00				

KM# 1182   20 NEW LIRA
23.2500 g., 0.9250 Silver 0.6914 oz. ASW, 38.6 mm.
Obv: Value within sprigs and circle **Rev:** Turkish Kangal Dog
Rev. Designer: Nesrin Ek **Edge:** Reeded

Date	Mintage	F	VF	XF	Unc	BU
2005 Proof	1,128	Value: 60.00				

KM# 1183   20 NEW LIRA
23.4600 g., 0.9250 Silver 0.6977 oz. ASW, 38.6 mm.
Obv: Value within sprigs and circle **Rev:** Five-toed Jerboa
Rev. Designer: Nesrin Ek **Edge:** Reeded

Date	Mintage	F	VF	XF	Unc	BU
2005 Proof	746	Value: 60.00				

KM# 1184   20 NEW LIRA
23.2600 g., 0.9250 Silver 0.6917 oz. ASW, 38.6 mm.
Obv: Value within sprigs and circle **Rev:** Brown Bear
Rev. Designer: Nesrin Ek **Edge:** Reeded

Date	Mintage	F	VF	XF	Unc	BU
2005 Proof	802	Value: 60.00				

KM# 1185   20 NEW LIRA
23.5300 g., 0.9250 Silver 0.6997 oz. ASW, 38.6 mm.
Obv: Value within sprigs and circle **Rev:** Desert Monitor
Rev. Designer: Hakk Baha Cavu G L **Edge:** Reeded

Date	Mintage	F	VF	XF	Unc	BU
2005 Proof	753	Value: 60.00				

KM# 1188   20 NEW LIRA
31.4700 g., 0.9250 Silver 0.9359 oz. ASW, 38.6 mm.
Subject: Edirne Selimiye Mosque **Obv:** Value within wreath
Rev: Mosque **Rev. Designer:** Nalan Yerl Bucak

Date	Mintage	F	VF	XF	Unc	BU
2005 Proof	1,660	Value: 45.00				

KM# 1189   20 NEW LIRA
31.4700 g., 0.9250 Silver 0.9359 oz. ASW, 38.6 mm.
Obv: Crescent and star **Obv. Designer:** Suat Ozyuonum
Rev: Large 85 above building **Rev. Designer:** Suat Ozyuonom

Date	Mintage	F	VF	XF	Unc	BU
2005 Proof	1,216	Value: 45.00				

KM# 1190   20 NEW LIRA
31.4700 g., 0.9250 Silver 0.9359 oz. ASW, 38.6 mm.
Subject: Galatasaray Spor **Obv:** 100 above team mascot
Rev: GS monogram

Date	Mintage	F	VF	XF	Unc	BU
2005 Proof	2,828	Value: 45.00				

KM# 1194   20 NEW LIRA
31.4700 g., 0.9250 Silver 0.9359 oz. ASW, 38.6 mm.
Subject: Belt Maglova Cultural Heritage site **Obv:** Value within
wreath **Rev:** Aqueduct

Date	Mintage	F	VF	XF	Unc	BU
2005 Proof	1,250	Value: 45.00				

KM# 1191   20 NEW LIRA
31.4700 g., 0.9250 Silver 0.9359 oz. ASW, 38.6 mm.
Subject: Galatasaray Spor **Obv:** 100 above team mascot
Rev: GS monogram, colored

Date	Mintage	F	VF	XF	Unc	BU
2005 Proof	1,250	Value: 45.00				

KM# 1196   25 NEW LIRA
31.4700 g., 0.9250 Silver 0.9359 oz. ASW, 38.6 mm.
Subject: 800 year of Medical Education in Turkey **Obv:** Two
snakes **Rev:** Figure **Designer:** Nesrin Ek

Date	Mintage	F	VF	XF	Unc	BU
2006 Proof	1,650	Value: 45.00				

KM# 1198   25 NEW LIRA
31.4700 g., 0.9250 Silver 0.9359 oz. ASW, 38.6 mm.
Subject: Nevruz of Hatira **Obv:** Flower and rays **Rev:** Statue
holding flames **Designer:** Betul U Urlu

Date	Mintage	F	VF	XF	Unc	BU
2006 Proof	1,300	Value: 45.00				

KM# 1199   25 NEW LIRA
31.4700 g., 0.9250 Silver 0.9359 oz. ASW, 38.6 mm.
Subject: Hattat Hamid Aytac **Obv:** Design **Rev:** Bust facing
Designer: Nesrin Ek

Date	Mintage	F	VF	XF	Unc	BU
2006 Proof	1,301	Value: 40.00				

KM# 1200   25 NEW LIRA
31.4700 g., 0.9250 Silver 0.9359 oz. ASW, 38.6 mm.
Subject: T.C. Devlet Demiryollari, 150th Anniversary **Obv:** 150
above laural **Rev:** Building

Date	Mintage	F	VF	XF	Unc	BU
2006 Proof	1,950	Value: 40.00				

KM# 1201   25 NEW LIRA
31.4700 g., 0.9250 Silver 0.9359 oz. ASW, 38.6 mm.
Subject: Mehmet Ersoy Akif, 70th Anniversary of death
Obv: Scroll **Rev:** Linear portrait facing **Designer:** Nesrin Ek

Date	Mintage	F	VF	XF	Unc	BU
2006 Antiqued	1,500	—	—	—	40.00	—

KM# 1211   25 NEW LIRA
15.5500 g., 0.9250 Silver 0.4624 oz. ASW, 38.6x28 mm.
Obv: Legend **Rev:** Zodiac - Pisces **Rev. Designer:** Nesrin EK
Shape: Oval

Date	Mintage	F	VF	XF	Unc	BU
2008 Proof	—	Value: 40.00				

KM# 1212   25 NEW LIRA
15.5500 g., 0.9250 Silver 0.4624 oz. ASW, 38.6x28 mm.
Obv: Text **Rev:** Zodiac - Aquarius **Shape:** Oval

Date	Mintage	F	VF	XF	Unc	BU
2008 Proof	—	Value: 40.00				

KM# 1213   25 NEW LIRA
15.5500 g., 0.9250 Silver 0.4624 oz. ASW, 38.6x28 mm.
Obv: Text **Rev:** Zodiac - Capricorn **Rev. Designer:** Nesrin EK
Shape: Oval

Date	Mintage	F	VF	XF	Unc	BU
2008 Proof	—	Value: 40.00				

KM# 1214   25 NEW LIRA
15.5500 g., 0.9250 Silver 0.4624 oz. ASW, 38.6x28 mm.
Obv: Text **Rev:** Zodiac - Sagitarius **Shape:** Oval

Date	Mintage	F	VF	XF	Unc	BU
2008 Proof	—	Value: 40.00				

KM# 1215   25 NEW LIRA
15.5500 g., 0.9250 Silver 0.4624 oz. ASW, 38.6x28 mm. **Obv:**
Text **Rev:** Zodiac - Libra **Rev. Designer:** Nesrin Ek **Shape:** Oval

Date	Mintage	F	VF	XF	Unc	BU
2008 Proof	—	Value: 40.00				

KM# 1216   25 NEW LIRA
15.5500 g., 0.9250 Silver 0.4624 oz. ASW, 38.6x28 mm. **Obv:**
Text **Rev:** Zodiac - figure **Rev. Designer:** Nesrin Ek **Shape:** Oval

Date	Mintage	F	VF	XF	Unc	BU
2008 Proof	—	Value: 40.00				

KM# 1217   25 NEW LIRA
15.5500 g., 0.9250 Silver 0.4624 oz. ASW, 38.6x28 mm.
Obv: Text **Rev:** Zodiac - Leo **Rev. Designer:** Nesrin Ek
Shape: Oval

Date	Mintage	F	VF	XF	Unc	BU
2008 Proof	—	Value: 40.00				

KM# 1218   25 NEW LIRA
15.5500 g., 0.9250 Silver 0.4624 oz. ASW, 38.6x28 mm.
Obv: Text **Rev:** Zodiac - Virgo **Rev. Designer:** Nesrin Ek
Shape: Oval

Date	Mintage	F	VF	XF	Unc	BU
2008 Proof	—	Value: 40.00				

KM# 1219 25 NEW LIRA
15.5500 g., 0.9250 Silver 0.4624 oz. ASW, 38.6x28 mm. **Obv:** Text **Rev:** Zodiac - Gemni **Rev. Designer:** Nesrin EK **Shape:** Oval

Date	Mintage	F	VF	XF	Unc	BU
2008 Proof	—	Value: 40.00				

KM# 1220 25 NEW LIRA
15.5500 g., 0.9250 Silver 0.4624 oz. ASW, 38.6x28 mm. **Obv:** Text **Rev:** Zodiac - Tarus **Rev. Designer:** Nesrin Ek **Shape:** Oval

Date	Mintage	F	VF	XF	Unc	BU
2008 Proof	—	Value: 40.00				

KM# 1192 30 NEW LIRA
31.4700 g., 0.9250 Silver 0.9359 oz. ASW, 38.6 mm. **Subject:** Galatasaray Spor **Obv:** 100 above team mascot **Rev:** GS monogram colored and selective gold plating

Date	Mintage	F	VF	XF	Unc	BU
2005 Proof	1,106	Value: 45.00				

KM# 1197 30 NEW LIRA
23.3300 g., 0.9250 Silver partially gold plated 0.6938 oz. ASW, 38.61 mm. **Subject:** Solar Eclipse **Obv:** Turkey map with route of the eclipse **Rev:** Sun, gilt **Designer:** Nesrin Ek

Date	Mintage	F	VF	XF	Unc	BU
2006 Proof	2,475	Value: 50.00				

KM# 1204 30 NEW LIRA
31.4700 g., 0.9250 Silver 0.9359 oz. ASW, 38.6 mm. **Subject:** Bank of Sarfanbolu **Obv:** Building **Rev:** Landscape **Designer:** Nesrin Ek

Date	Mintage	F	VF	XF	Unc	BU
2007 Proof	1,312	Value: 40.00				

KM# 1205 30 NEW LIRA
31.4700 g., 0.9250 Silver 0.9359 oz. ASW, 38.6 mm. **Obv:** Crescent and star at center of four objects **Rev:** Knoted fabric pattern **Designer:** Ayse Sirin

Date	Mintage	F	VF	XF	Unc	BU
2007 Proof	1,210	Value: 40.00				

KM# 1206 30 NEW LIRA
31.4700 g., 0.9250 Silver 0.9359 oz. ASW, 38.6 mm. **Obv:** Crescent and star within four objects **Rev:** Twirling Dirvishes **Designer:** Leman Tin

Date	Mintage	F	VF	XF	Unc	BU
2007 Proof	1,224	Value: 40.00				

KM# 1207 30 NEW LIRA
31.4700 g., 0.9250 Silver 0.9359 oz. ASW, 38.6 mm. **Obv:** Crescent and star within four designs **Rev:** Twirling Dirvish and town facades around **Designer:** Sessile Beatris Kalayciyan

Date	Mintage	F	VF	XF	Unc	BU
2007 Proof	1,179	Value: 40.00				

KM# 1208 30 NEW LIRA
31.4700 g., 0.9250 Silver 0.9359 oz. ASW, 38.6 mm. **Obv:** Mosque **Rev:** Entranceway arch **Designer:** Nalan Yerl Bucak

Date	Mintage	F	VF	XF	Unc	BU
2007 Proof	1,222	Value: 40.00				

KM# 1222 30 NEW LIRA
10.0000 g., 0.9250 Silver 0.2974 oz. ASW, 22 mm. **Obv:** Seal within border **Rev:** Large seal rendering

Date	Mintage	F	VF	XF	Unc	BU
2008 Proof	—	Value: 20.00				

KM# 1210 35 NEW LIRA
23.2300 g., 0.9250 Silver 0.6908 oz. ASW, 38.6 mm. **Subject:** Antikabir, 70th Anniversary **Obv:** Value within wreath **Rev:** Antikabir building **Designer:** Tenkin Gulbasar

Date	Mintage	F	VF	XF	Unc	BU
2008 Proof	3,000	Value: 40.00				

KM# 1232 35 NEW LIRA
23.3300 g., 0.9250 Silver 0.6938 oz. ASW, 38.6 mm. **Obv:** Value within wreath **Rev:** Bust at left

Date	Mintage	F	VF	XF	Unc	BU
2008 Proof	—	Value: 40.00				

KM# 1233 35 NEW LIRA
23.3300 g., 0.9250 Silver 0.6938 oz. ASW, 38.6 mm. **Obv:** Classical design **Rev:** Mahmud of Kashgar at right

Date	Mintage	F	VF	XF	Unc	BU
2008 Proof	—	Value: 40.00				

KM# 1238 35 NEW LIRA
23.3300 g., 0.9250 Silver 0.6938 oz. ASW, 38.6 mm. **Obv:** Value within wreath **Rev:** Sultan on horseback **Designer:** Nesrin Ek

Date	Mintage	F	VF	XF	Unc	BU
2008 Proof	—	Value: 40.00				

KM# 1202 40 NEW LIRA
31.4700 g., 0.9250 Silver 0.9359 oz. ASW, 38.6 mm. **Subject:** Troy **Obv:** Linear design **Rev:** Stylized Trojan Horse **Designer:** Nalan Yerl Bucak

Date	Mintage	F	VF	XF	Unc	BU
2007 Proof	1,500	Value: 40.00				

KM# 1224 40 NEW LIRA
31.4700 g., 0.9990 Silver 1.0107 oz. ASW, 38.6 mm. **Obv:** Historic map **Rev:** Kyrgistan bilding

Date	Mintage	F	VF	XF	Unc	BU
2008 Antiqued	—	—	—	—	40.00	—

KM# 1225 40 NEW LIRA
31.4700 g., 0.9250 Silver 0.9359 oz. ASW, 38.6 mm. **Obv:** Village scene **Rev:** Large classical figure **Designer:** Nesrin Ek

Date	Mintage	F	VF	XF	Unc	BU
2008 Proof	—	Value: 40.00				

KM# 1227 40 NEW LIRA
31.4700 g., 0.9250 Silver 0.9359 oz. ASW, 38.6 mm. **Obv:** Building **Rev:** Seated figure

Date	Mintage	F	VF	XF	Unc	BU
2008 Proof	—	Value: 40.00				

KM# 1228 40 NEW LIRA
31.4700 g., 0.9250 Silver 0.9359 oz. ASW, 38.6 mm. **Obv:** Classical intricate design **Rev:** Mosque

Date	Mintage	F	VF	XF	Unc	BU
2008 Proof	—	Value: 40.00				

KM# 1229 40 NEW LIRA
31.4700 g., 0.9250 Silver 0.9359 oz. ASW, 38.6 mm. **Obv:** Head left above school building **Rev:** Monogram at center **Designer:** Nesrin Ek

Date	Mintage	F	VF	XF	Unc	BU
2008 Proof	—	Value: 40.00				

KM# 1230 40 NEW LIRA
31.4700 g., 0.9250 Silver 0.9359 oz. ASW, 38.6 mm. **Obv:** Large tower and acqueduct **Rev:** Classical scene **Designer:** Tekin Gulbasar

Date	Mintage	F	VF	XF	Unc	BU
2008 Proof	—	Value: 40.00				

KM# 1231 40 NEW LIRA
31.4700 g., 0.9250 Silver 0.9359 oz. ASW, 38.6 mm. **Obv:** Tourtise, seal and lighthouse in distance **Rev:** Lighthouse

Date	Mintage	F	VF	XF	Unc	BU
2008 Proof	—	Value: 40.00				

KM# 1234 40 NEW LIRA
23.3300 g., 0.9250 Silver 0.6938 oz. ASW, 38.6 mm. **Subject:** Vefs Sports Club, 100th Anniversary **Obv:** Club seal multicolor **Rev:** Large 100 and logo

Date	Mintage	F	VF	XF	Unc	BU
2008 Proof	—	Value: 40.00				

KM# 1235 40 NEW LIRA
31.4700 g., 0.9250 Silver 0.9359 oz. ASW, 38.6 mm. **Obv:** Ancient craft items **Rev:** Cave paintings

Date	Mintage	F	VF	XF	Unc	BU
2008 Proof	—	Value: 40.00				

KM# 1236 40 NEW LIRA
31.4700 g., 0.9250 Silver 0.9359 oz. ASW, 38.6 mm. **Obv:** Ancient map **Rev:** Uzbekistan mosque **Designer:** Tekin Gulbasar

Date	Mintage	F	VF	XF	Unc	BU
2008 Antiqued	—	—	—	—	40.00	—

KM# 1237 40 NEW LIRA
31.4700 g., 0.9250 Silver 0.9359 oz. ASW **Obv:** Tower **Rev:** Tower **Shape:** 38.6 **Designer:** Tekin Gulbasar

Date	Mintage	F	VF	XF	Unc	BU
2008 Proof	—	Value: 40.00				

KM# 1256 50 LIRA
36.0800 g., 0.9250 Silver 1.0730 oz. ASW, 38.6 mm. **Obv:** Eastern Hemisphere logo **Rev:** Small seedling within colored water droplet, dried earth background **Rev. Designer:** Mustafa Akinci

Date	Mintage	F	VF	XF	Unc	BU
2009 Antiqued	—	—	—	—	40.00	—

KM# 1209 60 NEW LIRA
1.5000 g., 0.9160 Gold 0.0442 oz. AGW, 13.95 mm. **Obv:** Text **Rev:** Ancient pottery **Designer:** Nesrin Ek

Date	Mintage	F	VF	XF	Unc	BU
2007 Proof	1,925	Value: 70.00				

KM# 1223 100 NEW LIRA
7.2160 g., 0.9160 Gold 0.2125 oz. AGW, 22 mm. **Obv:** Seal within border **Rev:** Large seal

Date	Mintage	F	VF	XF	Unc	BU
2008 Proof	—	Value: 350				

KM# 1226 100 NEW LIRA
7.2160 g., 0.9160 Gold 0.2125 oz. AGW, 22 mm. **Obv:** Village scene **Obv. Designer:** Nes rin Ek **Rev:** Large classical figure **Rev. Designer:** Nesrin Ek

Date	Mintage	F	VF	XF	Unc	BU
2008 Proof	—	Value: 350				

REFORM DECIMAL COINAGE

2009

KM# 1249 LIRA
6.4000 g., Copper-Nickel, 23.5 mm. **Obv:** Lammergeier standing on rock **Rev:** Two eagles **Designer:** Nesrin Ek

Date	Mintage	F	VF	XF	Unc	BU
2009	120,000	—	—	—	4.50	6.00

KM# 1263 LIRA
8.3000 g., Bi-Metallic Copper-Nickel center in Brass ring, 26.15 mm. **Obv:** Value within wreath **Rev:** Elephant and calf **Rev. Designer:** Nalan Yerl Bucak

Date	Mintage	F	VF	XF	Unc	BU
2009	5,000	—	—	—	5.00	7.50

KM# 1264 LIRA
8.3000 g., Bi-Metallic Copper-Nickel center in Brass ring, 26.15 mm. **Obv:** Value within wreath **Rev:** Sea tourtise **Rev. Designer:** Nalan Yerl Bucak

Date	Mintage	F	VF	XF	Unc	BU
2009	5,000	—	—	—	5.00	7.50

KM# 1250 10 LIRA
23.3300 g., Bronze, 38.6 mm. **Obv:** Scroll and inkwell **Rev:** Child's story **Edge:** Reeded **Designer:** Tekin Gulbasar

Date	Mintage	F	VF	XF	Unc	BU
2009 Antiqued	—	—	—	—	15.00	—

KM# 1258 20 LIRA
27.5000 g., Copper-Nickel, 38.6 mm. **Subject:** Year 1430 **Obv:** Inscription within rose wreath **Rev:** Interior of the Grand Mosque in Mecca **Designer:** Nesrin Ek

Date	Mintage	F	VF	XF	Unc	BU
2009 Antiqued	—	—	—	—	40.00	—

KM# 1221 25 NEW LIRA
15.5500 g., 0.9250 Silver 0.4624 oz. ASW, 38.6x28 mm. **Obv:** Text **Rev:** Zodiac sign **Rev. Designer:** Nesrin Ek **Shape:** Oval

Date	Mintage	F	VF	XF	Unc	BU
2008 Proof	—	Value: 40.00				

KM# 1255 50 LIRA
36.0800 g., 0.9250 Silver 1.0730 oz. ASW, 38.6 mm. **Subject:** Sunlight **Obv:** Eastern Hemisphere logo **Rev:** Eastern Hemisphere in Sun

Date	Mintage	F	VF	XF	Unc	BU
2008 Proof	—	Value: 40.00				

KM# 1247 50 LIRA
36.0000 g., 0.9250 Silver 1.0706 oz. ASW, 38.6 mm. **Obv:** Value within wreath **Rev:** Samsun 90th Anniversary

Date	Mintage	F	VF	XF	Unc	BU
2009 Proof	—	Value: 40.00				

KM# 1252 50 LIRA
36.0800 g., 0.9250 Silver 1.0730 oz. ASW, 38.6 mm. **Subject:** Frederic Chopin, 200th Anniversary **Obv:** Piano and map of Europe **Rev:** Chopin's bust at left, piano at right, score in background **Designer:** Nalan Yerl Bucak

Date	Mintage	F	VF	XF	Unc	BU
2009	—	Value: 40.00				

KM# 1253 50 LIRA
36.0800 g., 0.9250 Silver 1.0730 oz. ASW, 38.6 mm. **Subject:** IMF Meeting, Istanbul **Obv:** Istanbul Skyline **Rev:** World Bank Group logo, multicolor **Designer:** Nesrin Ek

Date	Mintage	F	VF	XF	Unc	BU
2009 Proof	—	Value: 40.00				

KM# 1254 50 LIRA
36.0800 g., 0.9250 Silver 1.0730 oz. ASW, 38.6 mm. **Subject:** Water, source of life **Obv:** Eastern Hemisphere logo **Rev:** Clock hands, small amount of water, cracked and dried earth in rest of area

Date	Mintage	F	VF	XF	Unc	BU
2009 Proof	—	Value: 40.00				

KM# 1257 50 LIRA
36.0800 g., 0.9250 Silver 1.0730 oz. ASW, 38.6 mm. **Obv:** Eastern Hemisphere logo **Rev:** Female face with hair forming waves and vine

Date	Mintage	F	VF	XF	Unc	BU
2009 Proof	—	Value: 40.00				

KM# 1259 50 LIRA
36.0000 g., 0.9250 Silver 1.0706 oz. ASW, 38.6 mm. **Subject:** Year 1430 **Obv:** Inscription within rose wreath **Rev:** Interior courtyard of Grand Mosque in Mecca **Designer:** Nesrin Ek

Date	Mintage	F	VF	XF	Unc	BU
2009 Proof	—	Value: 40.00				

KM# 1261 50 LIRA
36.0000 g., 0.9250 Silver 1.0706 oz. ASW, 38.6 mm. **Subject:** 150th Anniversary **Obv:** Shield and text **Rev:** Building facade **Designer:** Nesrin Ek

Date	Mintage	F	VF	XF	Unc	BU
2009 Proof	—	Value: 40.00				

KM# 1262 50 LIRA
36.0000 g., 0.9250 Silver 1.0706 oz. ASW, 38.6 mm. **Subject:** Chalabi clerks **Obv:** Symbol **Rev:** Classical figure seated

Date	Mintage	F	VF	XF	Unc	BU
2009 Proof	—	Value: 40.00				

KM# 1245 50 NEW LIRA
36.0800 g., 0.9250 Silver 1.0730 oz. ASW, 38.6 mm. **Obv:** US and Turkish flags **Rev:** Barak Obama portrait facing **Designer:** Nesrin Ek

Date	Mintage	F	VF	XF	Unc	BU
2009 Proof	—	Value: 40.00				

KM# 1251 60 NEW LIRA
36.0800 g., 0.9250 Silver 1.0730 oz. ASW, 38.6 mm. **Obv:** Scroll and inkwell **Obv. Designer:** Tekin Gulbasar **Rev:** Children's story character **Rev. Designer:** Yekin Gulbasar

Date	Mintage	F	VF	XF	Unc	BU
2009 Proof	—	Value: 40.00				

KM# 1248 100 LIRA
1.5000 g., 0.9160 Gold 0.0442 oz. AGW, 13.95 mm. **Obv:** Classical orniament **Rev:** Hittite artifacts

Date	Mintage	F	VF	XF	Unc	BU
2009 Proof	—	Value: 75.00				

KM# 1246 200 LIRA
36.0800 g., 0.9160 Gold 1.0625 oz. AGW, 38.6 mm. **Obv:** US and Turkish flags **Rev:** Barak Obama portrait facing **Designer:** Nesrin Ek

Date	Mintage	F	VF	XF	Unc	BU
2009 Proof	—	Value: 1,375				

KM# 1260 200 LIRA
36.0000 g., 0.9160 Gold 1.0602 oz. AGW, 38.6 mm. **Obv:** Inscription within rose wreath **Rev:** Central courtyard of the Grand Mosque in Mecca **Designer:** Nesrin Ek

Date	Mintage	F	VF	XF	Unc	BU
2009 Proof	—	Value: 1,375				

GOLD BULLION COINAGE

Since 1943, the Turkish government has issued regular and deluxe gold coins in five denominations corresponding to the old traditional 25, 50, 100, 250, and 500 Kurus of the Ottoman period. The regular coins are all dated 1923, plus the year of the republic (e.g. 1923/40 = 1963), de Luxe coins bear actual AD dates. For a few years, 1944-1950, the bust of Ismet Inonu replaced that of Kemal Atatürk.

KM# 851   25 KURUSH
1.8041 g., 0.9170 Gold 0.0532 oz. AGW **Obv:** Head of Atatürk left **Rev:** Legend and date within wreath

Date	Mintage	F	VF	XF	Unc	BU
1923/78	—	—	—	BV	65.00	75.00
1923/79	—	—	—	BV	65.00	75.00
1923/70	—	—	—	BV	65.00	75.00
1923/71	—	—	—	BV	65.00	75.00
1923/72	—	—	—	BV	65.00	75.00
1923/73	—	—	—	BV	65.00	75.00
1923/74	—	—	—	BV	65.00	75.00
1923/75	—	—	—	BV	65.00	75.00
1923/76	—	—	—	BV	65.00	75.00
1923/77	—	—	—	BV	65.00	75.00

KM# 870   25 KURUSH
1.7540 g., 0.9170 Gold 0.0517 oz. AGW **Series:** Monnaie de Luxe **Obv:** Head of Atatürk left **Rev:** Country name and date in ornate monogram within circle of stars, floral border surrounds

Date	Mintage	F	VF	XF	Unc	BU
2001	—	—	—	BV	60.00	80.00
2002	—	—	—	BV	60.00	80.00
2003	—	—	—	BV	60.00	80.00
2004	—	—	—	BV	60.00	80.00
2005	—	—	—	BV	60.00	80.00
2006	—	—	—	BV	60.00	80.00
2007	—	—	—	BV	60.00	80.00
2008	—	—	—	BV	60.00	80.00
2009	—	—	—	BV	60.00	80.00
2010	—	—	—	BV	60.00	80.00

KM# 853   50 KURUSH
3.6083 g., 0.9170 Gold 0.1064 oz. AGW **Obv:** Head of Atatürk left **Rev:** Legend and date within wreath

Date	Mintage	F	VF	XF	Unc	BU
1923/78	—	—	—	BV	120	130
1923/79	—	—	—	BV	120	130
1923/80	—	—	—	BV	120	130
1923/81	—	—	—	BV	120	130
1923/82	—	—	—	BV	120	130
1923/83	—	—	—	BV	120	130
1923/84	—	—	—	BV	120	130
1923/85	—	—	—	BV	120	130
1923/86	—	—	—	BV	120	130
1923/87	—	—	—	BV	120	130

KM# 871   50 KURUSH
3.5080 g., 0.9170 Gold 0.1034 oz. AGW **Series:** Monnaie de Luxe **Obv:** Head of Kemal Atatürk left within circle of stars, wreath surrounds **Rev:** Country name and date in ornate monogram within circle of stars, floral border surrounds

Date	Mintage	F	VF	XF	Unc	BU
2001	—	—	—	BV	120	130
2002	—	—	—	BV	120	130
2003	—	—	—	BV	120	130
2004	—	—	—	BV	120	130
2005	—	—	—	BV	120	130
2006	—	—	—	BV	120	130
2007	—	—	—	BV	120	130
2008	—	—	—	BV	120	130
2009	—	—	—	BV	120	130
2010	—	—	—	BV	120	130

KM# 855   100 KURUSH
7.2160 g., 0.9170 Gold 0.2127 oz. AGW **Obv:** Head of Atatürk left **Rev:** Legend and date within wreath

Date	Mintage	F	VF	XF	Unc	BU
1923/78	—	—	—	BV	245	260
1923/79	—	—	—	BV	245	260
1923/80	—	—	—	BV	245	260
1923/81	—	—	—	BV	245	260
1923/82	—	—	—	BV	245	260
1923/83	—	—	—	BV	245	260
1923/84	—	—	—	BV	245	260
1923/85	—	—	—	BV	245	260
1923/86	—	—	—	BV	245	260
1923/87	—	—	—	BV	245	260

KM# 857   250 KURUSH
18.0400 g., 0.9170 Gold 0.5318 oz. AGW **Obv:** Head of Atatürk left **Rev:** Legend and date within wreath

Date	Mintage	F	VF	XF	Unc	BU
1923/78	—	—	—	BV	650	—
1923/79	—	—	—	BV	650	—
1923/80	—	—	—	BV	650	—
1923/81	—	—	—	BV	650	—
1923/82	—	—	—	BV	650	—
1923/83	—	—	—	BV	650	—
1923/84	—	—	—	BV	650	—
1923/85	—	—	—	BV	650	—
1923/86	—	—	—	BV	650	—
1923/87	—	—	—	BV	650	—

KM# 873   250 KURUSH
17.5400 g., 0.9170 Gold 0.5171 oz. AGW **Series:** Monnaie de Luxe **Obv:** Head of Atatürk left within circle of stars, wreath surrounds **Rev:** Country name and date in ornate monogram within circle of stars, floral border surrounds

Date	Mintage	F	VF	XF	Unc	BU
2001	—	—	—	BV	600	625
2002	—	—	—	BV	600	625
2003	—	—	—	BV	600	625
2004	—	—	—	BV	600	625
2005	—	—	—	BV	600	625
2006	—	—	—	BV	600	625
2007	—	—	—	BV	600	625
2008	—	—	—	BV	600	625
2009	—	—	—	BV	600	625
2010	—	—	—	BV	600	625

Date	Mintage	F	VF	XF	Unc	BU
1923/80	—	—	—	BV	245	260
1923/81	—	—	—	BV	245	260
1923/82	—	—	—	BV	245	260
1923/83	—	—	—	BV	245	260
1923/84	—	—	—	BV	245	260
1923/85	—	—	—	BV	245	260
1923/86	—	—	—	BV	245	260
1923/87	—	—	—	BV	245	260

KM# 872   100 KURUSH
7.0160 g., 0.9170 Gold 0.2068 oz. AGW **Series:** Monnaie de Luxe **Obv:** Head of Atatürk left within circle of stars, wreath surrounds **Rev:** Country name and date in ornate monogram within circle of stars, floral border surrounds

Date	Mintage	F	VF	XF	Unc	BU
2001	—	—	—	—	BV	240
2002	—	—	—	—	BV	240
2003	—	—	—	—	BV	240
2004	—	—	—	—	BV	240
2005	—	—	—	—	BV	240
2006	—	—	—	—	BV	240
2007	—	—	—	—	BV	240
2008	—	—	—	—	BV	240
2009	—	—	—	—	BV	240
2010	—	—	—	—	BV	240

KM# 859   500 KURUSH
36.0800 g., 0.9170 Gold 1.0637 oz. AGW **Obv:** Head of Atatürk left **Rev:** Legend and date within wreath

Date	Mintage	F	VF	XF	Unc	BU
1923/78	—	—	—	BV	1,250	1,300
1923/79	—	—	—	BV	1,250	1,300
1923/80	—	—	—	BV	1,250	1,300
1923/81	—	—	—	BV	1,250	1,300
1923/82	—	—	—	BV	1,250	1,300
1923/83	—	—	—	BV	1,250	1,300
1923/84	—	—	—	BV	1,250	1,300
1923/85	—	—	—	BV	1,250	1,300
1923/86	—	—	—	BV	1,250	1,300
1923/87	—	—	—	BV	1,250	1,300

KM# 874   500 KURUSH
35.0800 g., 0.9170 Gold 1.0342 oz. AGW **Series:** Monnaie de Luxe **Obv:** Head of Atatürk left within circle of stars, wreath surrounds **Rev:** Country name and date in ornate monogram within circle of stars, floral border surrounds

Date	Mintage	F	VF	XF	Unc	BU
2001	—	—	—	BV	1,200	1,250
2002	—	—	—	BV	1,200	1,250
2003	—	—	—	BV	1,200	1,250
2004	—	—	—	BV	1,200	1,250
2005	—	—	—	BV	1,200	1,250
2006	—	—	—	BV	1,200	1,250
2007	—	—	—	BV	1,200	1,250
2008	—	—	—	BV	1,200	1,250
2009	—	—	—	BV	1,200	1,250
2010	—	—	—	BV	1,200	1,250

TURKMENISTAN

The Turkmenistan Republic (formerly the Turkmen Soviet Socialist Republic) covers the territory of the Trans-Caspian Region of Turkestan, the Charjiui Vilayet of Bukhara and the part of Khiva located on the right bank of the Oxus. Bordered on the north by the Autonomous Kara-Kalpak Republic (a constituent of Uzbekistan), by Iran and Afghanistan on the south, by the Usbek Republic on the east and the Caspian Sea on the west. It has an area of 186,400 sq. mi. (488,100 sq. km.) and a population of 3.5 million. Capital: Ashkhabad (formerly Poltoratsk). Main occupation is agricultural products including cotton and maize. It is rich in minerals, oil, coal, sulphur and salt and is also famous for its carpets, Turkoman horses and Karakui sheep.

The Turkomans arrived in Trancaspia as nomadic Seluk Turks in the 11th century. It often became subjected to one of the neighboring states. Late in the 19th century the Czarist Russians invaded with their first victory at Kyzyl Arvat in 1877, arriving in Ashkhabad in 1882 resulting in submission of the Turkmen tribes. By March 18,1884 the Transcaspian province of Russian Turkestan was formed. During WW I the Czarist government tried to conscript the Turkmen; this led to a revolt in Oct. 1916 under the

leadership of Aziz Chapykov. In 1918 the Turks captured Baku from the Red army and the British sent a contingent to Merv to prevent a German-Turkish offensive toward Afghanistan and India. In mid-1919 a Bureau of Turkestan Moslem Communist Organization was formed in Moscow hoping to develop one large republic including all surrounding Turkic areas within a Soviet federation. A Turkestan Autonomous Soviet Socialist Republic was formed and plans to partition Turkestan into five republics according to the principle of nationalities was quickly implemented by Joseph Stalin. On Oct. 27, 1924 Turkmenistan became a Soviet Socialist Republic and was accepted as a member of the U.S.S.R. on Jan. 29, 1925. The Bureau of T.M.C.O. was disbanded in 1934. In Aug. 1990 the Turkmen Supreme Soviet adopted a declaration of sovereignty followed by a declaration of independence in Oct. 1991 joining the Commonwealth of Independent States in Dec. A new constitution was adopted in 1992 providing for an executive presidency.

REPUBLIC

STANDARD COINAGE

100 Tenge = 1 Manat

KM# 25   500 MANAT
28.2800 g., 0.9250 Silver 0.8410 oz. ASW, 38.5 mm.
Subject: 10th Anniversary of Independence **Obv:** Head of President Saparmyrat Nyyazow left within circle **Rev:** Monument divides dates within circle **Edge:** Reeded

Date	Mintage	F	VF	XF	Unc	BU
ND(2001) Proof	5,000	Value: 60.00				

KM# 41   500 MANAT
28.2800 g., 0.9250 Silver 0.8410 oz. ASW **Subject:** President's 61st Birthday **Obv:** National Flag

Date	Mintage	F	VF	XF	Unc	BU
2001	2,000	—	—	—	—	55.00

KM# 42   500 MANAT
28.2800 g., 0.9250 Silver 0.8410 oz. ASW **Subject:** President's 61st Birthday **Rev:** State arms

Date	Mintage	F	VF	XF	Unc	BU
2001	2,000	—	—	—	—	55.00

KM# 43   500 MANAT
28.2800 g., 0.9250 Silver 0.8410 oz. ASW **Subject:** Historical leaders **Rev:** Artogrul Grazy Turkmen (1191-1281)

Date	Mintage	F	VF	XF	Unc	BU
2001	100	—	—	—	—	55.00

KM# 44   500 MANAT
28.2800 g., 0.9250 Silver 0.8410 oz. ASW **Subject:** Historical leaders **Rev:** Oguz Khan Turkmen

Date	Mintage	F	VF	XF	Unc	BU
2001	1,000	—	—	—	—	55.00

KM# 45   500 MANAT
28.2800 g., 0.9250 Silver 0.8410 oz. ASW **Subject:** Historical leaders **Rev:** Gara Yusup Beg Turkmen

Date	Mintage	F	VF	XF	Unc	BU
2001	1,000	—	—	—	—	55.00

KM# 46   500 MANAT
28.2800 g., 0.9250 Silver 0.8410 oz. ASW **Subject:** Historical leaders **Rev:** Keymir Kor Turkmen

Date	Mintage	F	VF	XF	Unc	BU
2001	—	—	—	—	—	65.00

KM# 47   500 MANAT
28.2800 g., 0.9250 Silver 0.8410 oz. ASW **Subject:** Historical leaders **Rev:** Uzun Khasan Beg Turkmen

Date	Mintage	F	VF	XF	Unc	BU
2001	1,000	—	—	—	—	55.00

KM# 48   500 MANAT
28.2800 g., 0.9250 Silver 0.8410 oz. ASW **Subject:** Historical leaders **Rev:** Gorogly Beg Turkmen

Date	Mintage	F	VF	XF	Unc	BU
2001	1,000	—	—	—	—	55.00

KM# 49   500 MANAT
28.2800 g., 0.9250 Silver 0.8410 oz. ASW **Subject:** Historical leader **Rev:** Gorkut Ata Turkmen

Date	Mintage	F	VF	XF	Unc	BU
2001	—	—	—	—	—	55.00

KM# 50   500 MANAT
28.2800 g., 0.9250 Silver 0.8410 oz. ASW **Subject:** Historical leaders **Rev:** Muhammet Togrul Beg Turkmen

Date	Mintage	F	VF	XF	Unc	BU
2001	1,000	—	—	—	—	55.00

KM# 51   500 MANAT
Silver **Subject:** Historical leaders **Rev:** Muhammet Bayram Khan Turkmen

Date	Mintage	F	VF	XF	Unc	BU
2001	1,000	—	—	—	—	55.00

KM# 52   500 MANAT
28.2800 g., 0.9250 Silver 0.8410 oz. ASW **Subject:** Historical leaders **Rev:** Soltan Sawjar Turkmen

Date	Mintage	F	VF	XF	Unc	BU
2001	1,000	—	—	—	—	55.00

KM# 53   500 MANAT
28.2800 g., 0.9250 Silver 0.8410 oz. ASW, 46 mm.
Subject: Historical writers **Obv:** State emblem **Rev:** Bust and Laurel branch **Rev. Legend:** Seyitnazar Seydi (1760-1830)

Date	Mintage	F	VF	XF	Unc	BU
2003	—	—	—	—	—	65.00

KM# 54   500 MANAT
28.2800 g., 0.9250 Silver 0.8410 oz. ASW **Subject:** Historical authors **Obv:** State emblem **Rev:** Bust and Laurel branch **Rev. Legend:** Mammetweli Kemine (1770-1840)

Date	Mintage	F	VF	XF	Unc	BU
2003	—	—	—	—	—	65.00

KM# 55   500 MANAT
28.2800 g., 0.5000 Silver 0.4546 oz. ASW, 46 mm.
Subject: State emblem **Rev:** Bust and Laurel branch **Rev. Legend:** Mollanepes (1810-1862)

Date	Mintage	F	VF	XF	Unc	BU
2003	—	—	—	—	—	50.00

KM# 56   500 MANAT
28.2800 g., 0.9250 Silver 0.8410 oz. ASW, 46 mm.
Subject: Historical authors **Obv:** State emblem **Rev:** Bust and Laurel branch **Rev. Legend:** Annagylyc Mataji (1824-1882)

Date	Mintage	F	VF	XF	Unc	BU
2003	—	—	—	—	—	65.00

KM# 62   500 MANAT
28.2800 g., 0.9250 Silver 0.8410 oz. ASW **Obv:** Bust left **Rev:** Wheat ears as rays

Date	Mintage	F	VF	XF	Unc	BU
2004	—	—	—	—	—	65.00

KM# 64   500 MANAT
28.2800 g., 0.9250 Silver 0.8410 oz. ASW **Obv:** Bust left **Rev:** Wheat ears forming rays

Date	Mintage	F	VF	XF	Unc	BU
2004	1,000	—	—	—	—	55.00

KM# 66   500 MANAT
28.2800 g., 0.9250 Silver 0.8410 oz. ASW **Subject:** 60th Anniversary of WWII **Obv:** State emblem **Rev:** Soldier standing, rays behind

Date	Mintage	F	VF	XF	Unc	BU
2005	1,000	—	—	—	—	65.00

KM# 68   500 MANAT
28.2800 g., 0.9250 Silver 0.8410 oz. ASW, 75 mm.
Subject: President Nijazov, 60th Birthday **Obv:** State emblem **Rev:** Head left above tree design

Date	Mintage	F	VF	XF	Unc	BU
2005	—	—	—	—	—	65.00

KM# 40   1000 MANAT
7.9800 g., 0.9160 Gold 0.2350 oz. AGW, 28.28 mm.
Obv: President Nyyazow **Rev:** Monument

Date	Mintage	F	VF	XF	Unc	BU
2001	1,000	—	—	—	—	1,800

KM# 57   1000 MANAT
47.6400 g., 0.9160 Gold 1.4029 oz. AGW, 46 mm.
Subject: Historical authors **Obv:** State emblem **Rev:** Bust and Laurel branch **Rev. Legend:** Seyitnazar Seydi (1760-1830)

Date	Mintage	F	VF	XF	Unc	BU
2003	—	—	—	—	—	2,000

KM# 58   1000 MANAT
47.6400 g., 0.9160 Gold 1.4029 oz. AGW, 46 mm.
Subject: Historical authors **Obv:** State arms **Rev:** Bust and Laurel branch **Rev. Legend:** Mammetweli Kemine

Date	Mintage	F	VF	XF	Unc	BU
2003	—	—	—	—	—	2,000

KM# 59   1000 MANAT
47.6400 g., 0.9250 Gold 1.4167 oz. AGW, 46 mm.
Subject: Historical authors **Obv:** State emblem **Rev:** Bust and Laurel branch **Rev. Legend:** Mollanepes (1810-1862)

Date	Mintage	F	VF	XF	Unc	BU
2003	—	—	—	—	—	2,000

KM# 60   1000 MANAT
47.6400 g., 0.9160 Gold 1.4029 oz. AGW, 46 mm.
Subject: Historical authors **Obv:** State emblem **Rev:** Bust and Laurel branch **Rev. Legend:** Annagylyc Mataji (1824-1882)

Date	Mintage	F	VF	XF	Unc	BU
2003	—	—	—	—	—	2,000

KM# 61   1000 MANAT
28.2800 g., 0.9250 Silver 0.8410 oz. ASW **Subject:** 10th Anniversary of Reform

Date	Mintage	F	VF	XF	Unc	BU
2003	—	—	—	—	—	85.00

KM# 63   1000 MANAT
7.9800 g., 0.9160 Gold 0.2350 oz. AGW **Subject:** 100th Anniversary **Obv:** Bust left **Rev:** Wheat ears forming rays above

Date	Mintage	F	VF	XF	Unc	BU
2004	—	—	—	—	—	1,450

KM# 65   1000 MANAT
7.9800 g., 0.9160 Gold 0.2350 oz. AGW **Obv:** Bust left **Rev:** Wheat ears forming rays

Date	Mintage	F	VF	XF	Unc	BU
2004	250	—	—	—	—	1,250

KM# 67   1000 MANAT
47.5400 g., 0.9160 Gold 1.4000 oz. AGW **Subject:** 60th Anniversary of WWII **Obv:** Stae arms **Rev:** Soldier standing, rays behind

Date	Mintage	F	VF	XF	Unc	BU
2005	—	—	—	—	—	2,000

KM# 69   1000 MANAT
155.5000 g., 0.9990 Gold 4.9942 oz. AGW, 75 mm.
Subject: President Nijazov Goth **Obv:** State emblem **Rev:** Head left above tree

Date	Mintage	F	VF	XF	Unc	BU
2005	—	—	—	—	—	7,000

KM# 70   1000 MANAT
28.2800 g., 0.9250 Silver 0.8410 oz. ASW **Subject:** Writings of President Nijazov

Date	Mintage	F	VF	XF	Unc	BU
2006	—	—	—	—	—	85.00

KM# 71   1000 MANAT
28.2800 g., 0.9250 Silver 0.8410 oz. ASW **Subject:** Writings of President Nijazov

Date	Mintage	F	VF	XF	Unc	BU
2006	—	—	—	—	—	85.00

KM# 72   1000 MANAT
28.2800 g., 0.9250 Silver 0.8410 oz. ASW **Subject:** Writings of President Nijazov

Date	Mintage	F	VF	XF	Unc	BU
2006	—	—	—	—	—	85.00

KM# 73   1000 MANAT
28.2800 g., 0.9250 Silver 0.8410 oz. ASW **Subject:** Writings of President Nijazov

Date	Mintage	F	VF	XF	Unc	BU
2006	—	—	—	—	—	85.00

KM# 74   1000 MANAT
28.2800 g., 0.9250 Silver 0.8410 oz. ASW **Subject:** Writings of President Nijazov

Date	Mintage	F	VF	XF	Unc	BU
2006	—	—	—	—	—	85.00

KM# 75   1000 MANAT
28.2800 g., 0.9250 Silver 1.8410 oz. AGW **Subject:** Writings of President Nijazov

Date	Mintage	F	VF	XF	Unc	BU
2006	—	—	—	—	—	85.00

REFORM COINAGE

January 1, 2009 - 5000 Old Manat = 1 New Manat
100 Tenge = 1 Manat

KM# 95   TENGE
Nickel Plated Steel, 16 mm. **Obv:** Spire over country map **Rev:** Denomination and date

Date	Mintage	F	VF	XF	Unc	BU
2009	—	—	—	—	0.50	0.75

KM# 96   2 TENGE
Nickel Plated Steel, 18 mm. **Obv:** Spire over country map **Rev:** Denomination and date

Date	Mintage	F	VF	XF	Unc	BU
2009	—	—	—	—	0.75	1.00

KM# 97   5 TENGE
Nickel Plated Steel, 20 mm. **Obv:** Spire over country map **Rev:** Denomination and date

Date	Mintage	F	VF	XF	Unc	BU
2009	—	—	—	—	1.00	1.25

KM# 98   10 TENGE
Brass, 22 mm. **Obv:** Spire over country map **Rev:** Denomination and date

Date	Mintage	F	VF	XF	Unc	BU
2009	—	—	—	—	1.50	1.75

KM# 99 20 TENGE
Brass, 23 mm. **Obv:** Spire over country map **Rev:** Denomination and date

Date	Mintage	F	VF	XF	Unc	BU
2009	—	—	—	—	2.50	3.00

KM# 100 50 TENGE
Brass, 26 mm. **Obv:** Spire over country map **Rev:** Denomination and date

Date	Mintage	F	VF	XF	Unc	BU
2009	—	—	—	—	3.00	3.50

TURKS & CAICOS ISLANDS

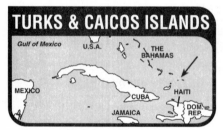

The Colony of the Turks and Caicos Islands, a British colony situated in the West Indies at the eastern end of the Bahama Islands, has an area of 166 sq. mi. (430 sq.km.) and a population of *10,000. Capital: Cockburn Town, on Grand Turk. The principal industry of the colony is the production of salt, which is gathered by raking. Salt, crayfish, and conch shells are exported.

RULER
British

MONETARY SYSTEM
1 Crown = 1 Dollar U.S.A.

BRITISH COLONY
STANDARD COINAGE

KM# 233 5 CROWNS
26.4300 g., Copper-Nickel, 39.2 mm. **Ruler:** Elizabeth II **Subject:** Royal Navy Submarines **Obv:** Head with tiara right **Obv. Designer:** Ian Rank-Broadley **Rev:** Old and modern submarines **Edge:** Reeded

Date	Mintage	F	VF	XF	Unc	BU
2001	—	—	—	6.00	10.00	12.00

KM# 236 20 CROWNS
31.2000 g., 0.9990 Silver 1.0021 oz. ASW, 38.9 mm. **Obv:** Crowned head right **Obv. Designer:** Ian Rank-Broadley **Rev:** Bust right facing divides dates **Edge:** Reeded

Date	Mintage	F	VF	XF	Unc	BU
2001 Proof	—	Value: 40.00				

KM# 245 20 CROWNS
31.1600 g., 0.9990 Silver 1.0008 oz. ASW, 39 mm. **Obv:** Crowned head right **Rev:** Richard II (1377-1399) **Edge:** Reeded

Date	Mintage	F	VF	XF	Unc	BU
2002 Proof	—	Value: 40.00				

KM# 246 20 CROWNS
Hafnium, 38.6 mm. **Ruler:** Elizabeth II **Subject:** H.M. Queen Elizabeth, The Queen Mother **Obv:** Crowned head right **Rev:** Crowned bust right within circle **Edge:** Reeded

Date	Mintage	F	VF	XF	Unc	BU
2002 Proof	—	Value: 125				

TUVALU

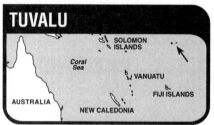

Tuvalu (formerly the Ellice or Lagoon Islands of the Gilbert and Ellice Islands), located in the South Pacific north of the Fiji Islands, has an area of 10 sq. mi. (26 sq.km.) and a population of *9,000. Capital: Funafuti. The independent state includes the islands of Nanumanga, Nanumea, Nui, Niutao, Viatupa, Funafuti, Nukufetau, Nukulailai and Nurakita. The latter four islands were claimed by the United States until relinquished by the Feb. 7, 1979, Treaty of Friendship signed by the United States and Tuvalu. The principal industries are copra production and phosphate mining.

Tuvalu is a member of the Commonwealth of Nations. Elizabeth II is Head of State as Queen of Tuvalu.

RULER
British, until 1978

MONETARY SYSTEM
100 Cents = 1 Dollar

CONSTITUTIONAL MONARCHY WITHIN THE COMMONWEALTH
STANDARD COINAGE

KM# 40 DOLLAR
20.0000 g., Brass, 38.7 mm. **Ruler:** Elizabeth II **Subject:** Dinosaurs **Obv:** Crowned head right **Obv. Designer:** Raphael Maklouf **Rev:** Giganotosaurus **Edge:** Reeded **Note:** See KM#49.

Date	Mintage	F	VF	XF	Unc	BU
2002	50,000	—	—	—	18.00	22.00

KM# 41 DOLLAR
20.0000 g., Brass, 38.7 mm. **Ruler:** Elizabeth II **Subject:** Dinosaurs **Obv:** Crowned head right **Rev:** Dromaeosaurus **Edge:** Reeded **Note:** See KM#50.

Date	Mintage	F	VF	XF	Unc	BU
2002	50,000	—	—	—	18.00	22.00

KM# 43 DOLLAR
20.0000 g., Brass, 38.7 mm. **Ruler:** Elizabeth II **Subject:** Dinosaurs **Obv:** Crowned head right **Rev:** Stegosaurus **Edge:** Reeded **Note:** See KM#51.

Date	Mintage	F	VF	XF	Unc	BU
2002	50,000	—	—	—	18.00	22.00

KM# 42 DOLLAR
20.0000 g., Brass, 38.7 mm. **Ruler:** Elizabeth II **Subject:** Dinosaurs **Obv:** Crowned head right **Rev:** Seismosaurus **Edge:** Reeded **Note:** See KM#52.

Date	Mintage	F	VF	XF	Unc	BU
2002	50,000	—	—	—	18.00	22.00

KM# 53 DOLLAR
Silver **Ruler:** Elizabeth II **Obv:** Crowned head right **Rev:** 1955 Mercedes Benz 300 SL Gullwing

Date	Mintage	F	VF	XF	Unc	BU
2006 Proof	—	Value: 45.00				

KM# 54 DOLLAR
Silver **Ruler:** Elizabeth II **Obv:** Crowned head right **Rev:** 1963 Jaguar E-Type colorized

Date	Mintage	F	VF	XF	Unc	BU
2006 Proof	—	Value: 45.00				

KM# 55 DOLLAR
Silver **Ruler:** Elizabeth II **Obv:** Crowned head right **Rev:** 1969 Datsun 240Z

Date	Mintage	F	VF	XF	Unc	BU
2006 Proof	—	Value: 65.00				

KM# 58 DOLLAR
31.3100 g., 0.9990 Silver enameled 1.0056 oz. ASW, 40.51 mm. **Ruler:** Elizabeth II **Subject:** 400th Anniversary of First European Sighting of Australia **Obv:** Crowned bust right **Obv. Legend:** QUEEN ELIZABETH II **Rev:** Bust of Captain James Cook at left, his ship; "H.M.S. Endeavor" within ship's wheel **Rev. Inscription:** 1770 DISCOVERY - EASTERN AUSTRALIA **Edge:** Reeded

Date	Mintage	F	VF	XF	Unc	BU
2006 Proof	—	Value: 60.00				

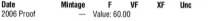

KM# 59 DOLLAR
31.3100 g., 0.9990 Silver enameled 1.0056 oz. ASW, 40.51 mm. **Ruler:** Elizabeth II **Subject:** 400th Anniversary of First European Sighting of Australia **Obv:** Crowned bust right **Obv. Legend:** QUEEN ELIZABETH II **Rev:** Bust of Abel Jansoon Tasman at left, his Dutch ship within ship's wheel **Rev. Legend:** 1642 DISCOVERY OF VAN DIEMAN'S LAND **Edge:** Reeded

Date	Mintage	F	VF	XF	Unc	BU
2006 Proof	—	Value: 65.00				

KM# 60 DOLLAR

Silver enameled, 40.51 mm. **Ruler:** Elizabeth II **Subject:** 400th Anniversary of First European Sighting of Australia **Obv:** Crowned bust right **Obv. Legend:** QUEEN ELIZABETH II **Rev:** Bust of William Dampier at right, his ship within ship's wheel **Rev. Legend:** 1688 BRITISH DISCOVERY OF AUSTRALIA **Edge:** Reeded

Date	Mintage	F	VF	XF	Unc	BU
2006 Proof	—	Value: 65.00				

KM# 61 DOLLAR

31.3100 g., 0.9990 Silver enameled 1.0056 oz. ASW, 40.51 mm. **Ruler:** Elizabeth II **Subject:** 400th Anniversary of First European Sighting of Australia **Obv:** Crowned bust right **Obv. Legend:** QUEEN ELIZABETH II **Rev:** Dutch ship"Duyfken" within ship's wheel **Rev. Legend:** 1606 FIRST EUROPEAN DISCOVERY AUSTRALIA **Edge:** Reeded

Date	Mintage	F	VF	XF	Unc	BU
2006 Proof	—	Value: 65.00				

KM# 68 DOLLAR

31.1030 g., 0.9990 Silver 0.9989 oz. ASW, 40 mm. **Ruler:** Elizabeth II **Obv:** Crowned bust right **Obv. Legend:** QUEEN ELIZABETH II - TUVALU **Rev:** Red-back Spider, multicolor

Date	Mintage	F	VF	XF	Unc	BU
2006 Proof	5,000	Value: 250				

KM# 62 DOLLAR

31.1035 g., 0.9990 Silver 0.9990 oz. ASW, 40.51 mm. **Ruler:** Elizabeth II **Obv:** Crowned bust right **Obv. Legend:** ELIZABETH II **Rev:** Multicolor Great White Shark **Edge:** Reeded

Date	Mintage	F	VF	XF	Unc	BU
2007 Proof	5,000	Value: 115				

KM# 63 DOLLAR

0.9990 Silver, 40 mm. **Ruler:** Elizabeth II **Series:** Fighting Ships of WW II **Obv:** Crowned bust right **Obv. Legend:** QUEEN ELIZABETH II - TUVALU **Obv. Designer:** Raphael Maklouf **Rev:** USSR Sevastopol, multicolor water

Date	Mintage	F	VF	XF	Unc	BU
2007 Proof	1,500	Value: 75.00				

KM# 64 DOLLAR

0.9990 Silver, 40 mm. **Ruler:** Elizabeth II **Series:** Fighting Ships of WW II **Obv:** Crowned bust right **Obv. Legend:** QUEEN ELIZABETH II - TUVALU **Obv. Designer:** Raphael Maklouf **Rev:** HMS Hood, multicolor water and smoke

Date	Mintage	F	VF	XF	Unc	BU
2007 Proof	1,500	Value: 75.00				

KM# 65 DOLLAR

0.9990 Silver, 40 mm. **Ruler:** Elizabeth II **Series:** Fighting Ships of WW II **Obv:** Crowned bust right **Obv. Legend:** QUEEN ELIZABETH II - TUVALU **Obv. Designer:** Raphael Maklouf **Rev:** Bismarck, multicolor water and gun flashes

Date	Mintage	F	VF	XF	Unc	BU
2007 Proof	1,500	Value: 75.00				

KM# 66 DOLLAR

0.9990 Silver, 40 mm. **Ruler:** Elizabeth II **Series:** Fighting Ships of WW II **Obv. Legend:** QUEEN ELIZABETH II - TUVALU **Obv. Designer:** Raphael Maklouf **Rev:** IJN Yamato, multicolor water and rising sun

Date	Mintage	F	VF	XF	Unc	BU
2007 Proof	1,500	Value: 75.00				

KM# 67 DOLLAR

0.9990 Silver, 40 mm. **Ruler:** Elizabeth II **Series:** Fighting Ships of WW II **Obv:** Crowned bust right **Obv. Legend:** QUEEN ELIZABETH II - TUVALU **Obv. Designer:** Raphael Maklouf **Rev:** USS Missouri

Date	Mintage	F	VF	XF	Unc	BU
2007 Proof	1,500	Value: 75.00				

KM# 86 DOLLAR

31.1050 g., 0.9990 Silver 0.9990 oz. ASW **Ruler:** Elizabeth II **Rev:** Great White Shark

Date	Mintage	F	VF	XF	Unc	BU
2007 Proof	—	Value: 75.00				

KM# 75 DOLLAR

31.1030 g., 0.9990 Silver 0.9989 oz. ASW, 40.6 mm. **Obv:** Head right **Rev:** Multicolor Lahlan Macquarie

Date	Mintage	F	VF	XF	Unc	BU
2008 Proof	1,808	Value: 90.00				

KM# 71 DOLLAR

31.1030 g., 0.9990 Silver 0.9989 oz. ASW, 40.6 mm. **Ruler:** Elizabeth II **Subject:** Early Governors of Australia **Obv:** Head right **Rev:** Multicolor Arthur Phillip **Edge:** Reeded

Date	Mintage	F	VF	XF	Unc	BU
2008 Proof	1,808	Value: 90.00				

KM# 72 DOLLAR

31.1030 g., 0.9990 Silver 0.9989 oz. ASW, 40.6 mm. **Ruler:** Elizabeth II **Subject:** Early Governors of Australia **Obv:** Head right **Rev:** Multicolor John Hunter **Edge:** Reeded

Date	Mintage	F	VF	XF	Unc	BU
2008 Proof	1,808	Value: 90.00				

KM# 73 DOLLAR

31.1030 g., 0.9990 Silver 0.9989 oz. ASW, 40.6 mm. **Ruler:** Elizabeth II **Subject:** Early Governors of Australia **Obv:** Head right **Rev:** Multicolor Philip G. King

Date	Mintage	F	VF	XF	Unc	BU
2008 Proof	1,808	Value: 90.00				

KM# 74 DOLLAR

31.1030 g., 0.9990 Silver 0.9989 oz. ASW, 40.6 mm. **Ruler:** Elizabeth II **Subject:** Early Governors of Australia **Obv:** Head right **Rev:** Multicolor William Bligh **Edge:** Reeded

Date	Mintage	F	VF	XF	Unc	BU
2008 Proof	1,808	Value: 90.00				

KM# 76 DOLLAR

37.1080 g., 0.9990 Silver 1.1918 oz. ASW, 40.6 mm. **Ruler:** Elizabeth II **Obv:** Multicolor Australian Lesser Blue-ringed Octopus **Edge:** Reeded

Date	Mintage	F	VF	XF	Unc	BU
2008 Proof	5,000	Value: 200				

KM# 81 DOLLAR

31.1050 g., 0.9990 Silver 0.9990 oz. ASW **Ruler:** Elizabeth II **Subject:** Motorcycles **Rev:** Indian Chief

Date	Mintage	F	VF	XF	Unc	BU
2008 Proff	—	Value: 75.00				

KM# 82 DOLLAR

31.1050 g., 0.9990 Silver 0.9990 oz. ASW **Ruler:** Elizabeth II **Subject:** Motorcycles **Rev:** BMW R12

Date	Mintage	F	VF	XF	Unc	BU
2008 Proof	—	Value: 75.00				

KM# 83 DOLLAR

31.1050 g., 0.9990 Silver 0.9990 oz. ASW **Ruler:** Elizabeth II **Subject:** Motorcycles **Rev:** BSA Gold Star DBD34

Date	Mintage	F	VF	XF	Unc	BU
2008 Proof	—	Value: 75.00				

KM# 84   DOLLAR
31.1050 g., 0.9990 Silver 0.9990 oz. ASW **Ruler:** Elizabeth II
Subject: Motorcycles **Rev:** Norton - Commando 750

Date	Mintage	F	VF	XF	Unc	BU
2008 Proof	—	Value: 75.00				

KM# 85   DOLLAR
31.1050 g., 0.9990 Silver 0.9990 oz. ASW **Ruler:** Elizabeth II
Subject: Motorcycles **Rev:** Honda CB760

Date	Mintage	F	VF	XF	Unc	BU
2008 Proof	—	Value: 75.00				

KM# 80   DOLLAR
31.1050 g., 0.9990 Silver 0.9990 oz. ASW **Ruler:** Elizabeth II
Subject: Barbie, 50th Anniversary **Rev:** Barbie doll and drawing

Date	Mintage	F	VF	XF	Unc	BU
2009 Proof	20,000	Value: 65.00				

KM# 87   DOLLAR
31.1050 g., 0.9990 Silver 0.9990 oz. ASW **Ruler:** Elizabeth II
Rev: Saltwater Crocodile

Date	Mintage	F	VF	XF	Unc	BU
2009 Proof	—	Value: 125				

KM# 88   DOLLAR
31.1050 g., 0.9990 Silver 0.9990 oz. ASW **Ruler:** Elizabeth II
Subject: Battle of Hastings **Rev:** Battle scene in multicolor

Date	Mintage	F	VF	XF	Unc	BU
2009 Proof	—	Value: 75.00				

KM# 89   DOLLAR
31.1050 g., 0.9990 Silver 0.9990 oz. ASW **Ruler:** Elizabeth II
Subject: Battle of Cannae, 216 BC **Rev:** Battlefield scene,
multicolor

Date	Mintage	F	VF	XF	Unc	BU
2009 Proof	—	Value: 75.00				

KM# 90   DOLLAR
31.1050 g., 0.9990 Silver 0.9990 oz. ASW **Ruler:** Elizabeth II
Subject: Battle of Gettysburg **Rev:** Battlefield scene, multicolor

Date	Mintage	F	VF	XF	Unc	BU
2009 Proof	—	Value: 75.00				

KM# 91   DOLLAR
31.1050 g., 0.9990 Silver 0.9990 oz. ASW **Ruler:** Elizabeth II
Subject: Battle of Balaklava, 1854 **Rev:** Battle scene, multicolor

Date	Mintage	F	VF	XF	Unc	BU
2009 Proof	—	Value: 75.00				

KM# 92   DOLLAR
31.1050 g., 0.9990 Silver 0.9990 oz. ASW **Ruler:** Elizabeth II
Subject: Poltava, Peter the Great's 300th Anniversary
Rev: Statue of Peter on horseback, multicolor battle scene

Date	Mintage	F	VF	XF	Unc	BU
2009 Proof	—	Value: 75.00				

KM# 94   DOLLAR
31.1050 g., 0.9990 Silver 0.9990 oz. ASW, 40.6 mm.
Ruler: Elizabeth II **Subject:** Transformers **Rev:** Optimus Prime,
multicolor

Date	Mintage	F	VF	XF	Unc	BU
2009 Proof	5,000	Value: 75.00				

KM# 95   DOLLAR
31.1050 g., 0.9990 Silver 0.9990 oz. ASW, 40.6 mm. **Ruler:**
Elizabeth II **Subject:** Transformers **Rev:** Megatron, multicolor

Date	Mintage	F	VF	XF	Unc	BU
2009 Proof	5,000	Value: 75.00				

KM# 96   DOLLAR
31.1050 g., 0.9990 Silver 0.9990 oz. ASW, 40.6 mm.
Ruler: Elizabeth II **Subject:** Fall of the Berlin Wall, 20th
Anniversary **Rev:** Brandenburg gate, multicolor

Date	Mintage	F	VF	XF	Unc	BU
2009 Proof	5,000	Value: 60.00				

KM# 97   DOLLAR
31.1050 g., 0.9990 Silver 0.9990 oz. ASW, 40.6 mm.
Ruler: Elizabeth II **Subject:** Golden Age of Piracy - Black Bart
Obv: Head right **Obv. Designer:** Ian Rank-Broadley **Rev:** Black
Bart at left, multicolor treasure items at right

Date	Mintage	F	VF	XF	Unc	BU
2009 Proof	1,500	Value: 80.00				

KM# 98   DOLLAR
31.1050 g., 0.9990 Silver 0.9990 oz. ASW, 40.6 mm.
Ruler: Elizabeth II **Subject:** Golden Age of Piracy - Black Beard
Obv: Head right **Obv. Designer:** Ian Rank-Broadley **Rev:** Black
Beard at left, multicolor treasure chest at right

Date	Mintage	F	VF	XF	Unc	BU
2009 Proof	1,500	Value: 80.00				

KM# 99   DOLLAR
31.1050 g., 0.9990 Silver 0.9990 oz. ASW, 40.6 mm.
Ruler: Elizabeth II **Subject:** Golden Age of Piracy - William Kidd
Obv: Head right **Obv. Designer:** Ian Rank-Broadley **Rev:** William
Kidd at left, multicolor pistol and treasure map at right

Date	Mintage	F	VF	XF	Unc	BU
2009 Proof	1,500	Value: 80.00				

KM# 100   DOLLAR
31.1050 g., 0.9990 Silver 0.9990 oz. ASW, 40.6 mm.
Ruler: Elizabeth II **Subject:** Golden Age of Piracy - Henry
Morgan **Obv:** Head right **Obv. Designer:** Ian Rank-Broadley
Rev: Henry Morgan at left, multicolor kegs at right

Date	Mintage	F	VF	XF	Unc	BU
2009 Proof	1,500	Value: 80.00				

KM# 101   DOLLAR
31.1050 g., 0.9990 Silver 0.9990 oz. ASW, 40.6 mm.
Ruler: Elizabeth II **Subject:** Golden Age of Piracy - Calico Jack
Obv: Head right **Obv. Designer:** Ian Rank-Broadley **Rev:** Calico
jack at left, multicolor pirate flag at right

Date	Mintage	F	VF	XF	Unc	BU
2009 Proof	1,500	Value: 80.00				

KM# 102   DOLLAR
31.1050 g., 0.9990 Silver 0.9990 oz. ASW, 40.6 mm.
Ruler: Elizabeth II **Subject:** Nikolai Gogol, 200th Anniversary of
Birth **Obv:** Head right **Obv. Designer:** Raphael Maklouf
Rev: Bust at left, multicolor

Date	Mintage	F	VF	XF	Unc	BU
2009 Proof	6,000	Value: 60.00				

KM# 93   DOLLAR
62.2100 g., 0.9990 Silver 1.9980 oz. ASW **Ruler:** Elizabeth II
Subject: Battle of Marathon **Rev:** Pheidippides' run

Date	Mintage	F	VF	XF	Unc	BU
2010 Proof	5,000	Value: 85.00				

KM# 103   DOLLAR
31.1050 g., 0.9990 Silver 0.9990 oz. ASW, 40.6 mm.
Ruler: Elizabeth II **Subject:** Anton Chekhov, 150th Anniversary
of Birth **Obv:** Head right **Obv. Designer:** Raphael Maklouf
Rev: Chekhov multicolor portrait at left, comedy adn tradidy
masks at right

Date	Mintage	F	VF	XF	Unc	BU
2010 Proof	6,000	Value: 60.00				

KM# 104   DOLLAR
31.1050 g., 0.9990 Silver 0.9990 oz. ASW, 40 mm.
Ruler: Elizabeth II **Subject:** Great River Journies - The Rhine
Obv: Head right **Obv. Designer:** Raphael Maklouf **Rev:** Tour
boat, color castle in background

Date	Mintage	F	VF	XF	Unc	BU
2010 Proof	1,500	Value: 90.00				

KM# 105   DOLLAR
31.1050 g., 0.9990 Silver 0.9990 oz. ASW, 40 mm.
Ruler: Elizabeth II **Subject:** Great River Journies - Volga
Obv: Head right **Obv. Designer:** Raphael Maklouf **Rev:** Tour
boat and color river front view

Date	Mintage	F	VF	XF	Unc	BU
2010 Proof	1,500	Value: 90.00				

KM# 106   DOLLAR
31.1050 g., 0.9990 Silver 0.9990 oz. ASW, 40 mm.
Ruler: Elizabeth II **Subject:** Great River Journies - Yangtzee
Obv: Head right **Obv. Designer:** Raphael Maklouf **Rev:** Sail boat
and color river gorge

Date	Mintage	F	VF	XF	Unc	BU
2010 Proof	1,500	Value: 90.00				

KM# 107   DOLLAR
31.1050 g., 0.9990 Silver 0.9990 oz. ASW, 40 mm.
Ruler: Elizabeth II **Subject:** Great River Journies - Mississippi
Obv: Head right **Obv. Designer:** Raphael Maklouf **Rev:** Delta
Queen and multicolor New Orleans skyline

Date	Mintage	F	VF	XF	Unc	BU
2010 Proof	1,500	Value: 90.00				

KM# 108   DOLLAR
31.1050 g., 0.9990 Silver 0.9990 oz. ASW, 40 mm.
Ruler: Elizabeth II **Subject:** Great River Journies - The Nile
Obv: Head right **Obv. Designer:** Raphael Maklouf **Rev:** Dohw,
classical sculpture, multicolor sandscape

Date	Mintage	F	VF	XF	Unc	BU
2010 Proof	1,500	Value: 90.00				

KM# 109   DOLLAR
31.1050 g., 0.9990 Silver 0.9990 oz. ASW, 40 mm.
Ruler: Elizabeth II **Subject:** Ned kelly - Outlaw **Obv:** Head right
Obv. Designer: Raphael Maklouf **Rev:** Ned kelly multicolor -
Reward Poster

Date	Mintage	F	VF	XF	Unc	BU
2010 Proof	1,880	Value: 90.00				

KM# 110   DOLLAR
31.1050 g., 0.9990 Silver 0.9990 oz. ASW, 40 mm.
Ruler: Elizabeth II **Subject:** Ned Kelly - Armour **Obv:** Head right
Obv. Designer: Raphael Maklouf **Rev:** Ned Kelley's helmet in
multicolor

Date	Mintage	F	VF	XF	Unc	BU
2010 Proof	1,880	Value: 90.00				

KM# 111   DOLLAR
31.1050 g., 0.9990 Silver 0.9990 oz. ASW, 40 mm.
Ruler: Elizabeth II **Subject:** Ned Kelly - Siege **Obv:** Head right
Obv. Designer: Raphael Maklouf **Rev:** Ned Kelly in shoutout,
multicolor

Date	Mintage	F	VF	XF	Unc	BU
2010 Proof	1,880	Value: 90.00				

KM# 112   DOLLAR
31.1050 g., 0.9990 Silver 0.9990 oz. ASW, 40 mm.
Ruler: Elizabeth II **Subject:** Ned Kelly - Gallows **Obv:** Head right
Obv. Designer: Raphael Maklouf **Rev:** Ned Kelly standing at the
gallows, multicolor

Date	Mintage	F	VF	XF	Unc	BU
2010 Proof	1,880	Value: 90.00				

KM# 113   DOLLAR
25.0000 g., 0.9250 Silver 0.7435 oz. ASW **Ruler:** Elizabeth II
Rev: Sea horse facing left, swarovski crystal chip eye
Shape: 38.61

Date	Mintage	F	VF	XF	Unc	BU
2010 Proof	2,500	Value: 50.00				

KM# 114   DOLLAR
0.5000 g., 0.9990 Gold 0.0161 oz. AGW, 11 mm.
Ruler: Elizabeth II **Rev:** Sea horse facing right

Date	Mintage	F	VF	XF	Unc	BU
2010 Proof	15,000	Value: 50.00				

KM# 115   DOLLAR
25.0000 g., 0.9250 Silver 0.7435 oz. ASW, 38.6 mm.
Ruler: Elizabeth II **Subject:** Marine Life **Rev:** Hawksbill sea
turtle, multicolor

Date	Mintage	F	VF	XF	Unc	BU
2010 Proof	2,500	Value: 50.00				

KM# 116   DOLLAR
1.2400 g., 0.9990 Gold 0.0398 oz. AGW, 13.92 mm.
Ruler: Elizabeth II **Rev:** Los Reyes sailing ship

Date	Mintage	F	VF	XF	Unc	BU
2010 Proof	15,000	Value: 75.00				

KM# 49   5 DOLLARS
62.5000 g., 0.9990 Silver 2.0073 oz. ASW, 49.9 mm.
Ruler: Elizabeth II **Subject:** Dinosaurs **Obv:** Crowned head right
Rev: Giganotosaurus **Edge:** Reeded

Date	Mintage	F	VF	XF	Unc	BU
2002 Proof	1,000	Value: 90.00				

KM# 50 5 DOLLARS
62.5000 g., 0.9990 Silver 2.0073 oz. ASW, 49.9 mm.
Ruler: Elizabeth II **Subject:** Dinosaurs **Obv:** Crowned head right
Rev: Dromaeosaurus **Edge:** Reeded

Date	Mintage	F	VF	XF	Unc	BU
2002 Proof	1,000	Value: 90.00				

KM# 51 5 DOLLARS
62.5000 g., 0.9990 Silver 2.0073 oz. ASW, 49.9 mm.
Ruler: Elizabeth II **Subject:** Dinosaurs **Obv:** Crowned head right
Rev: Stegosaurus **Edge:** Reeded

Date	Mintage	F	VF	XF	Unc	BU
2002 Proof	1,000	Value: 90.00				

KM# 52 5 DOLLARS
62.5000 g., 0.9990 Silver 2.0073 oz. ASW, 49.9 mm.
Ruler: Elizabeth II **Subject:** Dinosaurs **Obv:** Crowned head right
Rev: Seismosaurus **Edge:** Reeded

Date	Mintage	F	VF	XF	Unc	BU
2002 Proof	1,000	Value: 90.00				

KM# 69 100 DOLLARS
Gold **Ruler:** Elizabeth II **Obv:** Crowned head right **Rev:** Red
1963 Corvette Sting Ray

Date	Mintage	F	VF	XF	Unc	BU
2006 Proof	250	Value: 1,450				

UGANDA

The Republic of Uganda, a former British protectorate located astride the equator in east-central Africa, has an area of 91,134 sq. mi. (236,040 sq. km.) and a population of *17 million. Capital: Kampala. Agriculture, including livestock, is the basis of the economy; there is some mining of copper, tin, gold and lead. Coffee, cotton, and tea are exported.

Uganda is a member of the Commonwealth of Nations. The president is Chief of State and Head of Government.

For earlier coinage refer to East Africa.

MONETARY SYSTEM
100 Cents = 1 Shilling

REPUBLIC
STANDARD COINAGE

KM# 66 50 SHILLINGS
Nickel Plated Steel **Obv:** National arms **Rev:** Antelope head facing **Rev. Designer:** Stan Witten

Date	Mintage	F	VF	XF	Unc	BU
2003	—	—	—	—	1.00	1.25

KM# 67 100 SHILLINGS
7.0000 g., Copper-Nickel, 26.9 mm. **Obv:** National arms
Rev: African bull **Rev. Designer:** Stan Witten **Edge:** Reeded

Date	Mintage	F	VF	XF	Unc	BU
2003	—	—	—	—	1.50	1.75

KM# 129 100 SHILLINGS
3.5400 g., Stainless Steel, 23.98 mm. **Series:** Zodiac
Obv: National arms **Rev:** Monkey with elf-like ears **Edge:** Plain

Date	Mintage	F	VF	XF	Unc	BU
2004	—	—	—	—	1.50	2.50

KM# 135 100 SHILLINGS
3.5400 g., Steel, 23.98 mm. **Series:** Zodiac **Obv:** National arms
Rev: Ox **Edge:** Plain

Date	Mintage	F	VF	XF	Unc	BU
2004	—	—	—	—	1.50	2.50

KM# 136 100 SHILLINGS
3.5400 g., Steel, 23.98 mm. **Series:** Zodiac **Obv:** National arms
Rev: Goat **Edge:** Plain

Date	Mintage	F	VF	XF	Unc	BU
2004	—	—	—	—	1.50	2.50

KM# 137 100 SHILLINGS
3.5400 g., Steel, 23.98 mm. **Series:** Zodiac **Obv:** National arms
Rev: Horse **Edge:** Plain

Date	Mintage	F	VF	XF	Unc	BU
2004	—	—	—	—	1.50	2.50

KM# 138 100 SHILLINGS
3.5400 g., Steel, 23.98 mm. **Series:** Zodiac **Obv:** National arms
Rev: Dragon **Edge:** Plain

Date	Mintage	F	VF	XF	Unc	BU
2004	—	—	—	—	1.50	2.50

KM# 139 100 SHILLINGS
3.5400 g., Steel, 23.98 mm. **Series:** Zodiac **Obv:** National arms
Rev: Dog **Edge:** Plain

Date	Mintage	F	VF	XF	Unc	BU
2004	—	—	—	—	1.50	2.50

KM# 140 100 SHILLINGS
3.5400 g., Steel, 23.98 mm. **Series:** Zodiac **Obv:** National arms
Rev: Tiger **Edge:** Plain

Date	Mintage	F	VF	XF	Unc	BU
2004	—	—	—	—	1.50	2.50

KM# 141 100 SHILLINGS
3.5400 g., Steel, 23.98 mm. **Series:** Zodiac **Obv:** National arms
Rev: Snake **Edge:** Plain

Date	Mintage	F	VF	XF	Unc	BU
2004	—	—	—	—	1.50	2.50

KM# 142 100 SHILLINGS
3.5400 g., Steel, 23.98 mm. **Series:** Zodiac **Obv:** National arms
Rev: Rooster **Edge:** Plain

Date	Mintage	F	VF	XF	Unc	BU
2004	—	—	—	—	1.50	2.50

KM# 143 100 SHILLINGS
3.5400 g., Steel, 23.98 mm. **Series:** Zodiac **Obv:** National arms
Rev: Rabbit **Edge:** Plain

Date	Mintage	F	VF	XF	Unc	BU
2004	—	—	—	—	1.50	2.50

KM# 144 100 SHILLINGS
3.5400 g., Steel, 23.98 mm. **Series:** Zodiac **Obv:** National arms
Rev: Rat **Edge:** Plain

Date	Mintage	F	VF	XF	Unc	BU
2004	—	—	—	—	1.50	2.50

KM# 145 100 SHILLINGS
3.5400 g., Steel, 23.98 mm. **Series:** Zodiac **Obv:** National arms
Rev: Pig **Edge:** Plain

Date	Mintage	F	VF	XF	Unc	BU
2004	—	—	—	—	1.50	2.50

KM# 130 100 SHILLINGS
Steel, 23 mm. **Rev:** Type I of five different monkeys

Date	Mintage	F	VF	XF	Unc	BU
2004	—	—	—	—	1.75	2.75

KM# 131 100 SHILLINGS
Steel, 23 mm. **Rev:** Type II of five different monkeys

Date	Mintage	F	VF	XF	Unc	BU
2004	—	—	—	—	1.75	2.75

KM# 132 100 SHILLINGS
Steel, 23 mm. **Rev:** Type III of five different monkeys

Date	Mintage	F	VF	XF	Unc	BU
2004	—	—	—	—	1.75	2.75

KM# 133 100 SHILLINGS
Steel, 23 mm. **Rev:** Type IV of five different monkys

Date	Mintage	F	VF	XF	Unc	BU
2004	—	—	—	—	1.50	2.75

KM# 134 100 SHILLINGS
Steel, 23 mm. **Rev:** Type V of five different monkeys

Date	Mintage	F	VF	XF	Unc	BU
2004	—	—	—	—	1.75	2.75

KM# 188 100 SHILLINGS
3.5300 g., Nickel Plated Steel, 24 mm. **Series:** Zodiac
Obv: National arms **Obv. Legend:** BANK OF UGANDA
Rev: Head of a rat **Rev. Legend:** BANK OF UGANDA
Edge: Plain

Date	Mintage	F	VF	XF	Unc	BU
2004	—	—	—	—	1.75	2.75

KM# 189 100 SHILLINGS
3.5300 g., Nickel Plated Steel, 24 mm. **Series:** Zodiac
Obv: National arms **Obv. Legend:** BANK OF UGANDA **Rev:** Head of an ox **Rev. Legend:** BANK OF UGANDA **Edge:** Plain

Date	Mintage	F	VF	XF	Unc	BU
2004	—	—	—	—	1.75	2.75

KM# 190 100 SHILLINGS
3.5300 g., Nickel Plated Steel, 24 mm. **Series:** Zodiac
Obv: National arms **Obv. Legend:** BANK OF UGANDA **Rev:** Head of a tiger **Rev. Legend:** BANK OF UGANDA **Edge:** Plain

Date	Mintage	F	VF	XF	Unc	BU
2004	—	—	—	—	1.75	2.75

KM# 191 100 SHILLINGS
3.5300 g., Nickel Plated Steel, 24 mm. **Series:** Zodiac
Obv: National arms **Obv. Legend:** BANK OF UGANDA **Rev:** Head of a rabbit **Rev. Legend:** BANK OF UGANDA **Edge:** Plain

Date	Mintage	F	VF	XF	Unc	BU
2004	—	—	—	—	1.75	2.75

KM# 192 100 SHILLINGS
3.5300 g., Nickel Plated Steel, 24 mm. **Series:** Zodiac
Obv: National arms **Obv. Legend:** BANK OF UGANDA
Rev: Head of a dragon **Rev. Legend:** BANK OF UGANDA
Edge: Plain

Date	Mintage	F	VF	XF	Unc	BU
2004	—	—	—	—	1.75	2.75

KM# 193 100 SHILLINGS
3.5300 g., Nickel Plated Steel, 24 mm. **Series:** Zodiac
Obv: National arms **Obv. Legend:** BANK OF UGANDA
Rev: Head and hood of Cobra snake **Rev. Legend:** BANK OF UGANDA **Edge:** Plain

Date	Mintage	F	VF	XF	Unc	BU
2004	—	—	—	—	1.75	2.75

KM# 194 100 SHILLINGS
3.5300 g., Nickel Plated Steel, 24 mm. **Series:** Zodiac
Obv: National arms **Obv. Legend:** BANK OF UGANDA
Rev: Head of a horse **Rev. Legend:** BANK OF UGANDA
Edge: Plain

Date	Mintage	F	VF	XF	Unc	BU
2004	—	—	—	—	1.75	2.75

KM# 195 100 SHILLINGS
3.5300 g., Nickel Plated Steel, 24 mm. **Series:** Zodiac
Obv: National arms **Obv. Legend:** BANK OF UGANDA
Rev: Head of a goat **Rev. Legend:** BANK OF UGANDA
Edge: Plain

Date	Mintage	F	VF	XF	Unc	BU
2004	—	—	—	—	1.75	2.75

KM# 196 100 SHILLINGS
3.5300 g., Nickel Plated Steel, 24 mm. **Series:** Zodiac
Obv: National arms **Obv. Legend:** BANK OF UGANDA
Rev: Head of a monkey **Rev. Legend:** BANK OF UGANDA
Edge: Plain

Date	Mintage	F	VF	XF	Unc	BU
2004	—	—	—	—	1.75	2.75

KM# 197 100 SHILLINGS
3.5300 g., Nickel Plated Steel, 24 mm. **Series:** Zodiac **Obv:** National arms **Obv. Legend:** BANK OF UGANDA **Rev:** Forepart of a rooster **Rev. Legend:** BANK OF UGANDA **Edge:** Plain

Date	Mintage	F	VF	XF	Unc	BU
2004	—	—	—	—	1.75	2.75

KM# 198 100 SHILLINGS
3.5300 g., Nickel Plated Steel, 24 mm. **Series:** Zodiac **Obv:** National arms **Obv. Legend:** BANK OF UGANDA **Rev:** Head of a dog **Rev. Legend:** BANK OF UGANDA **Edge:** Plain

Date	Mintage	F	VF	XF	Unc	BU
2004	—	—	—	—	1.75	2.75

KM# 199 100 SHILLINGS
3.5300 g., Nickel Plated Steel, 24 mm. **Series:** Zodiac **Obv:** National arms **Obv. Legend:** BANK OF UGANDA **Rev:** Head of a pig **Rev. Legend:** BANK OF UGANDA **Edge:** Plain

Date	Mintage	F	VF	XF	Unc	BU
2004	—	—	—	—	1.75	2.75

KM# 200 100 SHILLINGS
Copper-Nickel **Subject:** Year of the Monkey **Obv. Legend:** BANK OF UGANDA **Rev:** Monkey swingging right

Date	Mintage	F	VF	XF	Unc	BU
2004	—	—	—	—	2.00	3.00

KM# 201 100 SHILLINGS
Copper-Nickel **Subject:** Year of the Monkey **Obv. Legend:** BANK OF UGANDA

Date	Mintage	F	VF	XF	Unc	BU
2004	—	—	—	—	2.00	3.00

KM# 202 100 SHILLINGS
Copper-Nickel **Subject:** Year of the Monkey **Obv. Legend:** BANK OF UGANDA **Rev:** Monkey right on all fours

Date	Mintage	F	VF	XF	Unc	BU
2004	—	—	—	—	2.00	3.00

KM# 203 100 SHILLINGS
Copper-Nickel **Subject:** Year of the Monkey **Obv. Legend:** BANK OF UGANDA **Rev:** Monkey seated left

Date	Mintage	F	VF	XF	Unc	BU
2004	—	—	—	—	2.00	3.00

KM# 204 100 SHILLINGS
Copper-Nickel **Subject:** Year of the Monkey **Obv. Legend:** BANK OF UGANDA **Rev:** Monkeys seated right, looking left over his shoulder

Date	Mintage	F	VF	XF	Unc	BU
2004	—	—	—	—	2.00	3.00

KM# 68 200 SHILLINGS
8.0500 g., Copper-Nickel, 24.9 mm. **Obv:** National arms **Rev:** Cichlid fish above value and date **Rev. Designer:** Stan Witten **Edge:** Plain

Date	Mintage	F	VF	XF	Unc	BU
2003	—	—	—	—	2.00	2.50

KM# 69 500 SHILLINGS
9.0000 g., Aluminum-Brass, 23.5 mm. **Obv:** National arms **Rev:** East African crowned crane head left **Rev. Designer:** Stan Witten **Edge:** Reeded

Date	Mintage	F	VF	XF	Unc	BU
2003	—	—	—	—	3.50	4.50

KM# 77 1000 SHILLINGS
19.8400 g., Copper-Nickel, 38.6 mm. **Subject:** Colourful Big Five of Africa **Obv:** Arms with supporters **Rev:** Multicolor rhinocerous within stamp design in front of outlined African map **Edge:** Reeded

Date	Mintage	F	VF	XF	Unc	BU
2001 Proof	—	Value: 22.50				

KM# 78 1000 SHILLINGS
19.8400 g., Copper-Nickel, 38.6 mm. **Subject:** Colourful Big Five of Africa **Obv:** Arms with supporters **Rev:** Multicolor lion within stamp design in front of outlined African map **Edge:** Reeded

Date	Mintage	F	VF	XF	Unc	BU
2001 Proof	—	Value: 22.50				

KM# 79 1000 SHILLINGS
19.8400 g., Copper-Nickel, 38.6 mm. **Subject:** Coulourful Big Five of Africa **Obv:** Arms with supporters **Rev:** Multicolor water buffalo within stamp design in front of outlined African map **Edge:** Reeded

Date	Mintage	F	VF	XF	Unc	BU
2001 Proof	—	Value: 22.50				

KM# 80 1000 SHILLINGS
19.8400 g., Copper-Nickel, 38.6 mm. **Subject:** Colourful Big Five of Africa **Obv:** Arms with supporters **Rev:** Multicolor leopard within stamp design in front of outlined map **Edge:** Reeded

Date	Mintage	F	VF	XF	Unc	BU
2001 Proof	—	Value: 22.50				

KM# 81 1000 SHILLINGS
19.8400 g., Copper-Nickel, 38.6 mm. **Subject:** Colourful Big Five of Africa **Obv:** Arms with supporters **Rev:** Multicolor elephant within stamp design in front of outlined map **Edge:** Reeded

Date	Mintage	F	VF	XF	Unc	BU
2001 Proof	—	Value: 22.50				

KM# 173 1000 SHILLINGS
Silver **Subject:** XVII World Football Championship Games - Korea and Japan **Obv. Legend:** BANK OF UGANDA **Rev:** Football - gilt

Date	Mintage	F	VF	XF	Unc	BU
2001 Proof	—	Value: 25.00				

KM# 82 1000 SHILLINGS
24.8300 g., 0.9990 Silver 0.7975 oz. ASW, 38.6 mm. **Subject:** World of Football **Obv:** Arms with supporters **Rev:** Soccer ball globe **Edge:** Reeded

Date	Mintage	F	VF	XF	Unc	BU
2002 Proof	—	Value: 25.00				

KM# 83 1000 SHILLINGS
24.8300 g., 0.9990 Silver 0.7975 oz. ASW, 38.6 mm. **Subject:** World of Football **Obv:** Arms with supporters **Rev:** Soccer ball in net **Edge:** Reeded

Date	Mintage	F	VF	XF	Unc	BU
2002 Proof	—	Value: 17.50				

KM# 84 1000 SHILLINGS
24.8300 g., 0.9990 Silver 0.7975 oz. ASW, 38.6 mm. **Subject:** World of Football **Obv:** Arms with supporters **Rev:** Goalie catching ball, red kicker insert at right **Edge:** Reeded

Date	Mintage	F	VF	XF	Unc	BU
2002 Proof	—	Value: 27.50				

KM# 85 1000 SHILLINGS
24.8300 g., 0.9990 Silver 0.7975 oz. ASW, 38.6 mm. **Subject:** World of Football **Obv:** Arms with supporters **Rev:** Two players going after the ball, red runner insert at left **Edge:** Reeded

Date	Mintage	F	VF	XF	Unc	BU
2002 Proof	—	Value: 27.50				

KM# 86 1000 SHILLINGS
24.8300 g., 0.9990 Silver 0.7975 oz. ASW, 38.6 mm. **Subject:** World of Football **Obv:** Arms with supporters **Rev:** Player kicking ball, blue kicker insert at right **Edge:** Reeded

Date	Mintage	F	VF	XF	Unc	BU
2002 Proof	—	Value: 27.50				

KM# 101 1000 SHILLINGS
29.4400 g., Silver Plated Bronze (Specific gravity 8.8675), 38.5 mm. **Series:** Gorillas of Africa **Obv:** National arms **Rev:** Seated gorilla **Edge:** Reeded

Date	Mintage	F	VF	XF	Unc	BU
2002 Proof	—	Value: 12.50				
2003 Proof	—	Value: 12.00				

KM# 102 1000 SHILLINGS
29.4400 g., Silver Plated Bronze (Specific gravity 8.8675), 38.5 mm. **Series:** Gorillas of Africa **Obv:** National arms **Rev:** Gorilla eating **Edge:** Reeded

Date	Mintage	F	VF	XF	Unc	BU
2002 Proof	—	Value: 12.50				
2003 Proof	—	Value: 10.00				

KM# 103 1000 SHILLINGS
29.4400 g., Silver Plated Bronze (Specific gravity 8.8675), 38.5 mm. **Series:** Gorillas of Africa **Obv:** National arms **Rev:** Gorilla on all fours **Edge:** Reeded

Date	Mintage	F	VF	XF	Unc	BU
2002 Proof	—	Value: 12.50				
2003 Proof	—	Value: 10.00				

KM# 104 1000 SHILLINGS
29.4400 g., Silver Plated Bronze (Specific gravity 8.8675), 38.5 mm. **Series:** Gorillas of Africa **Obv:** National arms **Rev:** Gorilla female with infant **Edge:** Reeded

Date	Mintage	F	VF	XF	Unc	BU
2002 Proof	—	Value: 12.50				
2003 Proof	—	Value: 10.00				

KM# 106 1000 SHILLINGS
29.1600 g., Silver Plated Bronze (Specific gravity 8.8096), 38.6 mm. **Subject:** Marine Life **Obv:** Arms with supporters **Rev:** Multicolor sea horses **Edge:** Reeded

Date	Mintage	F	VF	XF	Unc	BU
2002 Proof	—	Value: 22.00				

KM# 107 1000 SHILLINGS
29.1600 g., Silver Plated Bronze (Specific gravity 8.8096), 38.6 mm. **Subject:** Marine Life **Obv:** Arms with supporters **Rev:** Multicolor Hammerhead sharks **Edge:** Reeded

Date	Mintage	F	VF	XF	Unc	BU
2002 Proof	—	Value: 22.00				

KM# 108 1000 SHILLINGS
29.1600 g., Silver Plated Bronze (Specific gravity 8.8096), 38.6 mm. **Subject:** Marine Life **Obv:** Arms with supporters **Rev:** Multicolor Stingray **Edge:** Reeded

Date	Mintage	F	VF	XF	Unc	BU
2002 Proof	—	Value: 22.00				

KM# 109 1000 SHILLINGS
29.1600 g., Silver Plated Bronze (Specific gravity 8.8096), 38.6 mm. **Subject:** Marine Life **Obv:** Arms with supporters **Rev:** Multicolor Seal **Edge:** Reeded

Date	Mintage	F	VF	XF	Unc	BU
2002 Proof	—	Value: 22.00				

KM# 110 1000 SHILLINGS
29.1600 g., Silver Plated Bronze (Specific gravity 8.8096), 38.6 mm. **Subject:** Marine Life **Obv:** Arms with supporters **Rev:** Multicolor sea turtle **Edge:** Reeded

Date	Mintage	F	VF	XF	Unc	BU
2002 Proof	—	Value: 22.00				

KM# 111 1000 SHILLINGS
29.1600 g., Silver Plated Bronze (Specific gravity 8.8096), 38.6 mm. **Subject:** Marine Life **Obv:** Arms with supporters **Rev:** Multicolor dolphins **Edge:** Reeded

Date	Mintage	F	VF	XF	Unc	BU
2002 Proof	—	Value: 22.00				

KM# 112 1000 SHILLINGS
29.1600 g., Silver Plated Bronze (Specific gravity 8.8096), 38.6 mm. **Subject:** Marine Life **Obv:** Arms with supporters **Rev:** Multicolor octopus **Edge:** Reeded

Date	Mintage	F	VF	XF	Unc	BU
2002 Proof	—	Value: 22.00				

KM# 113 1000 SHILLINGS
29.1600 g., Silver Plated Bronze (Specific gravity 8.8096), 38.6 mm. **Subject:** Marine Life **Obv:** Arms with supporters **Rev:** Multicolor red fish **Edge:** Reeded

Date	Mintage	F	VF	XF	Unc	BU
2002 Proof	—	Value: 22.00				

KM# 114 1000 SHILLINGS
29.1600 g., Silver Plated Bronze (Specific gravity 8.8096), 38.6 mm. **Subject:** Marine Life **Obv:** Arms with supporters **Rev:** Multicolor black fish with white dots **Edge:** Reeded

Date	Mintage	F	VF	XF	Unc	BU
2002 Proof	—	Value: 22.00				

KM# 115 1000 SHILLINGS
29.1600 g., Silver Plated Bronze (Specific gravity 8.8096), 38.6 mm. **Subject:** Marine Life **Obv:** Arms with supporters **Rev:** Multicolor yellow and black striped fish **Edge:** Reeded

Date	Mintage	F	VF	XF	Unc	BU
2002 Proof	—	Value: 22.00				

KM# 240 1000 SHILLINGS
Silver **Obv:** Arms **Rev:** Pope John Paul II bust facing

Date	Mintage	F	VF	XF	Unc	BU
2003 Proof	—	Value: 75.00				

KM# 105 1000 SHILLINGS
29.2000 g., Silver Plated Bronze (Specific gravity 9.0123), 38.6 mm. **Subject:** Pope John Paul II **Obv:** Arms with supporters **Rev:** Pope saying mass, design of Zambian 1000 Kwacha KM-160 **Edge:** Reeded **Note:** Muling error

Date	Mintage	F	VF	XF	Unc	BU
2003 Proof	—	Value: 300				

KM# 216 1000 SHILLINGS
Bronze **Subject:** Christmas **Obv. Legend:** BANK OF UGANDA **Rev:** Peace on Earth

Date	Mintage	F	VF	XF	Unc	BU
2004	500	—	—	—	—	40.00

KM# 75 2000 SHILLINGS
49.9000 g., 0.9990 Silver 1.6027 oz. ASW, 50 mm. **Subject:** Illusion: "Spirit of the Mountain" **Obv:** Crowned head right divides date above arms with supporters **Rev:** Landscape and tree that looks like a male portrait **Edge:** Reeded

Date	Mintage	F	VF	XF	Unc	BU
2001 Proof	—	Value: 50.00				

KM# 121 2000 SHILLINGS
25.0000 g., 0.9250 Silver 0.7435 oz. ASW, 38.6 mm. **Subject:** Queen Elizabeth's 75th Birthday **Obv:** Arms with supporters above crowned head right **Rev:** Queen accepting flowers from children **Edge:** Reeded

Date	Mintage	F	VF	XF	Unc	BU
2001 Proof	2,000	Value: 35.00				

KM# 100 2000 SHILLINGS
31.4000 g., 0.9990 Silver 1.0085 oz. ASW, 38.8 mm. **Obv:** Crowned head right divides date above arms with supporters **Rev:** Bust of Henry M. Stanley facing **Edge:** Reeded

Date	Mintage	F	VF	XF	Unc	BU
2002	—	—	—	—	28.00	35.00

KM# 177 2000 SHILLINGS
15.5500 g., 0.9990 Silver 0.4994 oz. ASW **Series:** Famous Places in China **Subject:** Mount Huangshan - Anhwei **Obv:** Two dragons **Obv. Legend:** BANK OF UGANDA

Date	Mintage	F	VF	XF	Unc	BU
2003 Proof	3,000	Value: 35.00				

KM# 178 2000 SHILLINGS
15.5500 g., 0.9990 Silver 0.4994 oz. ASW **Series:** Famous Places in China **Subject:** Zhangjiajie - Hunan **Obv:** Two dragons **Obv. Legend:** BANK OF UGANDA

Date	Mintage	F	VF	XF	Unc	BU
2003 Proof	3,000	Value: 35.00				

KM# 179 2000 SHILLINGS
15.5500 g., 0.9990 Silver 0.4994 oz. ASW **Series:** Famous Places in China **Subject:** Stone Forest - Yunnan **Obv:** Two dragons **Obv. Legend:** BANK OF UGANDA

Date	Mintage	F	VF	XF	Unc	BU
2003 Proof	3,000	Value: 35.00				

KM# 180 2000 SHILLINGS
15.5500 g., 0.9990 Silver 0.4994 oz. ASW **Series:** Famous Places in China **Subject:** Potala Palace - Lhasa, Tibet **Obv:** Two dragons **Obv. Legend:** BANK OF UGANDA

Date	Mintage	F	VF	XF	Unc	BU
2003 Proof	3,000	Value: 35.00				

KM# 181 2000 SHILLINGS
15.5500 g., 0.9990 Silver 0.4994 oz. ASW **Series:** Famous Places in China **Subject:** Yangtse River Gorges **Obv:** Two dragons **Obv. Legend:** BANK OF UGANDA

Date	Mintage	F	VF	XF	Unc	BU
2003 Proof	3,000	Value: 35.00				

KM# 182 2000 SHILLINGS
31.1000 g., 0.9990 Silver 0.9988 oz. ASW **Series:** Chinese symbolism **Subject:** Harmony **Obv. Legend:** BANK OF UGANDA **Rev:** Dragon and phoenix

Date	Mintage	F	VF	XF	Unc	BU
2003 Proof	3,000	Value: 60.00				

KM# 183 2000 SHILLINGS
31.1000 g., 0.9990 Silver 0.9988 oz. ASW **Series:** Chinese symbolism **Subject:** Happiness **Obv. Legend:** BANK OF UGANDA **Rev:** Unicorn

Date	Mintage	F	VF	XF	Unc	BU
2003 Proof	3,000	Value: 60.00				

KM# 184 2000 SHILLINGS
31.1000 g., 0.9990 Silver 0.9988 oz. ASW **Series:** Chinese symbolism **Subject:** Health and long life **Obv. Legend:** BANK OF UGANDA **Rev:** Two cranes

Date	Mintage	F	VF	XF	Unc	BU
2003 Proof	3,000	Value: 60.00				

KM# 185 2000 SHILLINGS
31.1000 g., 0.9990 Silver 0.9988 oz. ASW **Series:** Chinese symbolism **Subject:** Success **Obv. Legend:** BANK OF UGANDA **Rev:** Carp

Date	Mintage	F	VF	XF	Unc	BU
2003 Proof	3,000	Value: 60.00				

KM# 186 2000 SHILLINGS
31.1000 g., 0.9990 Silver 0.9988 oz. ASW **Series:** Chinese symbolism **Subject:** Wealth **Obv. Legend:** BANK OF UGANDA **Rev:** Toad

Date	Mintage	F	VF	XF	Unc	BU
2003 Proof	3,000	Value: 60.00				

KM# 175 2000 SHILLINGS
15.5500 g., 0.9990 Silver 0.4994 oz. ASW **Series:** Famous Places in China **Subject:** Yugan Garden - Shanghai **Obv:** Two dragons **Obv. Legend:** BANK OF UGANDA

Date	Mintage	F	VF	XF	Unc	BU
2003 Proof	3,000	Value: 35.00				

KM# 176 2000 SHILLINGS
15.5500 g., 0.9990 Silver 0.4994 oz. ASW **Series:** Famous Places in China **Subject:** Tiger Hill Pagoda - Jiangsu **Obv:** Two dragons **Obv. Legend:** BANK OF UGANDA

Date	Mintage	F	VF	XF	Unc	BU
2003 Proof	3,000	Value: 35.00				

KM# 187 2000 SHILLINGS
4.0000 g., 0.9999 Gold 0.1286 oz. AGW **Series:** Guanyin **Subject:** Fulun **Obv:** Lotus blossom **Obv. Legend:** BANK OF UGANDA

Date	Mintage	F	VF	XF	Unc	BU
2003 Proof	—	Value: 200				

KM# 205   2000 SHILLINGS
Silver   Subject: XXVIII Summer Olympics - Athens 2004
Obv. Legend: BANK OF UGANDA   Rev: Sprinter

Date	Mintage	F	VF	XF	Unc	BU
2003 Proof	500	Value: 60.00				

KM# 210   2000 SHILLINGS
31.1000 g., 0.9990 Silver 0.9988 oz. ASW   Series: Chinese symbolic floral New Year paintings   Subject: Happiness
Obv. Legend: BANK OF UGANDA   Rev: Multicolor

Date	Mintage	F	VF	XF	Unc	BU
2004 Proof	2,000	Value: 60.00				

KM# 211   2000 SHILLINGS
31.1000 g., 0.9990 Silver 0.9988 oz. ASW   Series: Chinese Dieties   Subject: Happiness   Obv. Legend: BANK OF UGANDA   Rev: Fú - multicolor

Date	Mintage	F	VF	XF	Unc	BU
2004 Proof	2,000	Value: 60.00				

KM# 212   2000 SHILLINGS
31.1000 g., 0.9990 Silver 0.9988 oz. ASW   Series: Chinese Dieties   Subject: Prosperity   Obv. Legend: BANK OF UGANDA   Rev: Lù - multicolor

Date	Mintage	F	VF	XF	Unc	BU
2004 Proof	2,000	Value: 60.00				

KM# 213   2000 SHILLINGS
31.1000 g., 0.9990 Silver 0.9988 oz. ASW   Series: Chinese Dieties   Subject: Health and Long Life   Obv. Legend: BANK OF UGANDA   Rev: Shòu - multicolor

Date	Mintage	F	VF	XF	Unc	BU
2004 Proof	2,000	Value: 60.00				

KM# 206   2000 SHILLINGS
31.1000 g., 0.9990 Silver 0.9988 oz. ASW   Series: Chinese symbolic floral New Year paintings   Obv. Legend: BANK OF UGANDA   Rev: Carp and Lotus blossom - multicolor

Date	Mintage	F	VF	XF	Unc	BU
2004 Proof	2,000	Value: 60.00				

KM# 207   2000 SHILLINGS
31.1000 g., 0.9990 Silver 0.9988 oz. ASW   Series: Chinese symbolic floral New Year paintings   Obv. Legend: BANK OF UGANDA   Rev: Deer - multicolor

Date	Mintage	F	VF	XF	Unc	BU
2004 Proof	2,000	Value: 60.00				

KM# 208   2000 SHILLINGS
31.1000 g., 0.9990 Silver 0.9988 oz. ASW   Series: Chinese symbolic floral New Year paintings   Subject: Abundance   Obv. Legend: BANK OF UGANDA   Rev: Fruit - multicolor

Date	Mintage	F	VF	XF	Unc	BU
2004 Proof	2,000	Value: 60.00				

KM# 209   2000 SHILLINGS
31.1000 g., 0.9990 Silver 0.9988 oz. ASW   Series: Chinese symbolic floral New Year paintings   Subject: Peace and prosperity   Obv. Legend: BANK OF UGANDA   Rev: Multicolor

Date	Mintage	F	VF	XF	Unc	BU
2004 Proof	2,000	Value: 60.00				

KM# 221   2000 SHILLINGS
Silver Plated Bronze   Series: XIX World Football Championship - South Africa 2010   Obv: National arms   Obv. Legend: BANK OF UGANDA   Rev: Player about to kick

Date	Mintage	F	VF	XF	Unc	BU
2005 Proof	10,000	Value: 15.00				

KM# 222   2000 SHILLINGS
Silver Plated Bronze   Series: XIX World Football Championship - South Afrika 2010   Obv: National arms   Obv. Legend: BANK OF UGANDA   Rev: Ball in net

Date	Mintage	F	VF	XF	Unc	BU
2005 Proof	10,000	Value: 15.00				

KM# 223   2000 SHILLINGS
Silver Plated Bronze   Series: XIX World Football Championship - South Afrika 2010   Obv: National arms   Obv. Legend: BANK OF UGANDA   Rev: Player, map of Afrika

Date	Mintage	F	VF	XF	Unc	BU
2005 Proof	10,000	Value: 15.00				

KM# 224   2000 SHILLINGS
Silver Plated Bronze   Series: XIX World Football Championship - South Afrika 2010   Obv: National arms   Obv. Legend: BANK OF UGANDA   Rev: Goalkeeper with ball

Date	Mintage	F	VF	XF	Unc	BU
2005 Proof	10,000	Value: 15.00				

KM# 225   2000 SHILLINGS
Silver Plated Bronze   Series: XIX World Football Championship - South Afrika 2010   Obv: National arms   Obv. Legend: BANK OF UGANDA   Rev: Player and ball

Date	Mintage	F	VF	XF	Unc	BU
2005 Proof	10,000	Value: 15.00				

KM# 217   2000 SHILLINGS
31.1000 g., 0.9990 Silver 0.9988 oz. ASW   Obv: Lotus blossom   Obv. Legend: BANK OF UGANDA   Rev: Guanyin - multicolor

Date	Mintage	F	VF	XF	Unc	BU
2005 Proof	2,000	Value: 75.00				

KM# 226   2000 SHILLINGS
40.0000 g., Bronze Gilt   Series: Zodiac   Subject: Year of the Dog   Obv: Two dragons   Obv. Legend: BANK OF UGANDA   Rev: Three dogs - multicolor

Date	Mintage	F	VF	XF	Unc	BU
2006 Proof	—	Value: 45.00				

KM# 227   2000 SHILLINGS
40.0000 g., Bronze Gilt   Series: Zodiac   Subject: Year of the Dog   Obv: Archaic Chinese characters   Obv. Legend: BANK OF UGANDA   Rev: Two dogs - multicolor

Date	Mintage	F	VF	XF	Unc	BU
2006 Proof	—	Value: 45.00				

KM# 227a   2000 SHILLINGS
31.1000 g., 0.9990 Silver 0.9988 oz. ASW   Series: Zodiac   Subject: Year of the Dog   Obv: Archaic Chinese characters   Obv. Legend: BANK OF UGANDA   Rev: Two dogs - multicolor

Date	Mintage	F	VF	XF	Unc	BU
2006 Proof	3,000	Value: 75.00				

KM# 234   2000 SHILLINGS
31.1000 g., 0.9990 Silver 0.9988 oz. ASW   Series: Zodiac   Subject: Year of the Dog   Obv. Legend: BANK OF UGANDA   Rev: Tibet Terrier with pup surrounded by 10 symbols

Date	Mintage	F	VF	XF	Unc	BU
2006 Proof	—	Value: 75.00				

KM# 237   2000 SHILLINGS
31.1000 g., 0.9990 Silver 0.9988 oz. ASW   Series: Zodiac   Subject: Year of the Dog   Obv: National arms   Obv. Legend: BANK OF UGANDA   Rev: Chow-chow as watchdog, gold bars, bat and flower

Date	Mintage	F	VF	XF	Unc	BU
2006 Proof	—	Value: 60.00				

KM# 172   5000 SHILLINGS
4.0000 g., 0.9999 Gold 0.1286 oz. AGW   Series: Guanyin   Subject: Chilian   Obv: Lotus blossom   Obv. Legend: BANK OF UGANDA

Date	Mintage	F	VF	XF	Unc	BU
2001 Proof	—	Value: 200				

KM# 87   5000 SHILLINGS
33.7300 g., 0.8500 Silver 0.9217 oz. ASW, 38.65 mm.
Subject: "The Big Five"   Obv: Arms with supporters
Rev: Rhinoceros   Edge: Reeded

Date	Mintage	F	VF	XF	Unc	BU
2002 Proof	—	Value: 65.00				

KM# 88   5000 SHILLINGS
33.7300 g., 0.8500 Silver 0.9217 oz. ASW, 38.65 mm.
Subject: "The Big Five"   Obv: Arms with supporters   Rev: Lion   Edge: Reeded

Date	Mintage	F	VF	XF	Unc	BU
2002 Proof	—	Value: 65.00				

KM# 89   5000 SHILLINGS
33.7300 g., 0.8500 Silver 0.9217 oz. ASW, 38.65 mm.
Subject: "The Big Five"   Obv: Arms with supporters   Rev: Cape Buffalo   Edge: Reeded

Date	Mintage	F	VF	XF	Unc	BU
2002 Proof	—	Value: 50.00				

KM# 90   5000 SHILLINGS
33.7300 g., 0.8500 Silver 0.9217 oz. ASW, 38.65 mm.
Subject: "The Big Five"   Obv: Arms with supporters   Rev: Leopard   Edge: Reeded

Date	Mintage	F	VF	XF	Unc	BU
2002 Proof	—	Value: 65.00				

KM# 91   5000 SHILLINGS
33.7300 g., 0.8500 Silver 0.9217 oz. ASW, 38.65 mm.
Subject: "The Big Five"   Obv: Arms with supporters
Rev: Elephant   Edge: Reeded

Date	Mintage	F	VF	XF	Unc	BU
2002 Proof	—	Value: 65.00				

KM# 96   5000 SHILLINGS
31.1035 g., 0.9990 Silver 0.9990 oz. ASW, 40.6 mm.   Subject: Matthew Flinders   Obv: Arms with supporters below crowned head right dividing date   Rev: Multicolor bust half left at right with ship and harbor scene at left   Edge: Plain   Shape: Continent of Australia

Date	Mintage	F	VF	XF	Unc	BU
2002 Proof	2,500	Value: 50.00				

KM# 97   5000 SHILLINGS
31.1035 g., 0.9990 Silver 0.9990 oz. ASW, 40.6 mm.
Subject: Matthew Flinders - H. M. S. Investigator   Obv: Crowned head right divides   date above arms with supporters   Rev: Multicolor cameo at upper right of ship   Edge: Plain   Shape: Continent of Australia

Date	Mintage	F	VF	XF	Unc	BU
2002 Proof	2,500	Value: 50.00				

KM# 98   5000 SHILLINGS
31.1035 g., 0.9990 Silver 0.9990 oz. ASW, 40.6 mm.
Subject: Matthew Flinders - Meeting at Encounter Bay   Obv: Crowned head right divides   date above arms with supporters   Rev: Date and inscription divides multicolor busts facing   Edge: Plain   Shape: Continent of Australia

Date	Mintage	F	VF	XF	Unc	BU
2002 Proof	2,500	Value: 50.00				

KM# 99 5000 SHILLINGS
31.1035 g., 0.9990 Silver 0.9990 oz. ASW, 40.6 mm.
Subject: Matthew Flinders - First Circumnavigation of Terra Australia - 1802 **Rev:** Multicolor bust right on Australian map showing his route around Australia **Edge:** Plain **Shape:** Continent of Australia

Date	Mintage	F	VF	XF	Unc	BU
2002 Proof	2,500	Value: 50.00				

KM# 174 5000 SHILLINGS
4.0000 g., 0.9999 Gold 0.1286 oz. AGW **Series:** Guanyin **Subject:** Fuyu **Obv:** Lotus blossom **Obv. Legend:** BANK OF UGANDA

Date	Mintage	F	VF	XF	Unc	BU
2002 Proof	—	Value: 200				

KM# 214 5000 SHILLINGS
4.0000 g., 0.9999 Gold 0.1286 oz. AGW **Series:** Guanyin **Subject:** Shile **Obv:** Lotus blossom **Obv. Legend:** BANK OF UGANDA

Date	Mintage	F	VF	XF	Unc	BU
2004 Proof	—	Value: 200				

KM# 220 5000 SHILLINGS
4.0000 g., 0.9999 Gold 0.1286 oz. AGW **Series:** Guanyin **Subject:** Songjing **Obv:** Lotus blossom **Obv. Legend:** BANK OF UGANDA

Date	Mintage	F	VF	XF	Unc	BU
2005 Proof	—	Value: 200				

KM# 235 6000 SHILLINGS
3.1100 g., 0.9999 Gold 0.1000 oz. AGW **Series:** Zodiac **Subject:** Year of the Dog **Obv. Legend:** BANK OF UGANDA **Rev:** Tibet Terrier with pup surrounded by 10 symbols

Date	Mintage	F	VF	XF	Unc	BU
2006 Proof	—	Value: 150				

KM# 228 6000 SHILLINGS
4.0000 g., 0.9999 Gold 0.1286 oz. AGW **Series:** Zodiac **Subject:** Year of the Dog **Obv:** Archaic Chinese characters **Obv. Legend:** BANK OF UGANDA **Rev:** Yorkshire Terrier and "Fú" - Happiness

Date	Mintage	F	VF	XF	Unc	BU
2006 Proof	14,000	Value: 225				

KM# 229 6000 SHILLINGS
4.0000 g., 0.9999 Gold 0.1286 oz. AGW **Series:** Zodiac **Subject:** Year of the Dog **Obv:** Archaic Chinese characters **Obv. Legend:** BANK OF UGANDA **Rev:** Yorkshire Terrier and "Lù" - Prosperity

Date	Mintage	F	VF	XF	Unc	BU
2006 Proof	14,000	Value: 225				

KM# 230 6000 SHILLINGS
4.0000 g., 0.9999 Gold 0.1286 oz. AGW **Series:** Zodiac **Subject:** Year of the Dog **Obv:** Archaic Chinese characters **Obv. Legend:** BANK OF UGANDA **Rev:** Yorkshire Terrier and "Shòu" - Health and Long Life

Date	Mintage	F	VF	XF	Unc	BU
2006 Proof	14,000	Value: 225				

KM# 238 6000 SHILLINGS
3.1100 g., 0.9999 Gold 0.1000 oz. AGW **Series:** Zodiac **Subject:** Year of the Dog **Obv:** National arms **Obv. Legend:** BANK OF UGANDA **Rev:** Chow-chow as watchdog, gold bars, bat and flower

Date	Mintage	F	VF	XF	Unc	BU
2006 Proof	—	Value: 150				

KM# 231 8000 SHILLINGS
8.0000 g., 0.9999 Gold 0.2572 oz. AGW **Series:** Zodiac **Subject:** Year of the Dog **Obv:** Archaic Chinese characters **Obv. Legend:** BANK OF UGANDA **Rev:** Yorkshire Terrier and "Fú" - Happiness

Date	Mintage	F	VF	XF	Unc	BU
2006 Proof	1,000	Value: 375				

KM# 232 8000 SHILLINGS
8.0000 g., 0.9999 Gold 0.2572 oz. AGW **Series:** Zodiac **Subject:** Year of the Dog **Obv:** Archaic Chinese characters **Obv. Legend:** BANK OF UGANDA **Rev:** Yorkshire Terrier and "Lù" - Prosperity

Date	Mintage	F	VF	XF	Unc	BU
2006 Proof	1,000	Value: 375				

KM# 215 10000 SHILLINGS
10.0000 g., 0.9999 Gold 0.3215 oz. AGW **Obv:** Lotus blossom **Obv. Legend:** BANK OF UGANDA **Rev:** Buddha

Date	Mintage	F	VF	XF	Unc	BU
2004 Proof	3,000	Value: 450				

KM# 76 12000 SHILLINGS
6.2207 g., 0.9999 Gold 0.2000 oz. AGW, 22 mm.
Subject: Illusion: "Spirit of the Mountain" **Obv:** Crowned head right divides date above arms with supporters **Rev:** Landscape and tree that looks like a male portrait **Edge:** Reeded

Date	Mintage	F	VF	XF	Unc	BU
2001 Proof	—	Value: 275				

KM# 236 20000 SHILLINGS
15.5500 g., 0.9999 Gold 0.4999 oz. AGW **Series:** Zodiac **Subject:** Year of the Dog **Obv. Legend:** BANK OF UGANDA **Rev:** Tibet Terrier with pup surrounded by 10 symbols

Date	Mintage	F	VF	XF	Unc	BU
2006 Proof	—	Value: 675				

KM# 239 20000 SHILLINGS
15.5500 g., 0.9999 Gold 0.4999 oz. AGW **Series:** Year of the Dog **Obv:** National arms **Obv. Legend:** BANK OF UGANDA **Rev:** Chow-chow as watchdog, gold bars, bat and flower

Date	Mintage	F	VF	XF	Unc	BU
2006 Proof	—	Value: 675				

UKRAINE

Ukraine (formerly the Ukrainian Soviet Socialist Republic) is bordered by Russia to the east, Russia and Belarus to the north, Poland, Slovakia and Hungary to the west, Romania and Moldova to the southwest and in the south by the Black Sea and the Sea of Azov. It has an area of 233,088 sq. mi. (603,700 sq. km.) and a population of 51.9 million. Capital: Kyiv (Kiev). Coal, grain, vegetables and heavy industrial machinery are major exports.

Ukraine is a charter member of the United Nations and has inherited the third largest nuclear arsenal in the world.

MONETARY SYSTEM
(1) Kopiyka
(2) Kopiyky КОПИКН
(5 and up) Kopiyok КОПІІОК
100 Kopiyok = 1 Hrynia ГРИВЕНЬ

REPUBLIC
REFORM COINAGE

KM# 6 KOPIYKA
1.5300 g., Stainless Steel, 15.96 mm. **Obv:** National arms **Rev:** Value within wreath **Edge:** Plain

Date	Mintage	F	VF	XF	Unc	BU
2001	—	—	—	0.35	0.75	—
2002	—	—	—	0.35	0.75	—
2003	—	—	—	0.35	0.75	—
2004	—	—	—	0.35	0.75	—
2005	—	—	—	0.35	0.75	—
2006	—	—	—	0.35	0.75	—
2007	—	—	—	0.35	0.75	—
2008	—	—	—	0.35	0.75	—
2008 Prooflike	5,000	—	—	—	—	1.50
2009	—	—	—	—	0.50	—

KM# 4b 2 KOPIYKY
1.8000 g., Stainless Steel, 17.3 mm. **Obv:** National arms **Rev:** Value in wreath **Edge:** Plain

Date	Mintage	F	VF	XF	Unc	BU
2001	—	—	0.20	0.50	1.00	—
2002	—	—	0.20	0.50	1.00	—
2003	Est. 5,000	—	—	—	—	300
2004	—	—	0.20	0.50	1.00	—
2005	—	—	0.20	0.50	1.00	—
2006	—	—	—	0.50	1.00	—
2007	—	—	—	0.50	1.00	—
2008	—	—	—	0.50	1.00	—
2008 Proof-like	5,000	—	—	—	—	2.00
2009	—	—	—	0.50	1.00	—

KM# 7 5 KOPIYOK
4.3000 g., Stainless Steel, 23.91 mm. **Obv:** National arms **Rev:** Value within wreath **Edge:** Reeded

Date	Mintage	F	VF	XF	Unc	BU
2001 In sets only	10,000	—	—	—	—	10.00
2003	—	—	—	0.50	1.00	—
2004	—	—	—	0.50	1.00	—
2005	—	—	—	0.50	1.00	—
2006	—	—	—	0.50	1.00	—
2007	—	—	—	0.50	1.00	—
2008	—	—	—	0.50	1.00	—

Date	Mintage	F	VF	XF	Unc	BU
2008 Proof-like	5,000	—	—	—	—	2.50
2009	—	—	—	0.50	1.00	—

KM# 1.1b 10 KOPIYOK
1.7000 g., Aluminum-Bronze, 16.24 mm. **Obv:** National arms **Rev:** Value within wreath

Date	Mintage	F	VF	XF	Unc	BU
2001 In sets only	10,000	—	—	—	—	7.50
2002	—	—	0.60	1.25	2.50	—
2003	—	—	0.50	1.00	2.25	—
2004	—	—	0.50	1.00	2.25	—
2005	—	—	—	1.00	2.25	—
2006	—	—	—	1.00	2.25	—
2007	—	—	—	1.00	2.25	—
2008	—	—	—	1.00	2.25	—
2008 Proof-like	5,000	—	—	—	—	5.00
2009	—	—	—	1.00	2.00	—

KM# 2.1b 25 KOPIYOK
2.9000 g., Aluminum-Bronze, 20.8 mm.

Date	Mintage	F	VF	XF	Unc	BU
2001	—	—	0.80	3.00	6.00	—
2003	Est. 5,000	—	—	—	—	300
2006	—	—	0.80	2.00	4.00	—
2007	—	—	0.80	2.00	4.00	—
2008	—	—	—	2.00	4.00	—
2008 Prooflike	5,000	—	—	—	—	8.00
2009	—	—	—	2.00	2.50	—

KM# 3.3b 50 KOPIYOK
4.2000 g., Aluminum-Bronze, 23 mm.

Date	Mintage	F	VF	XF	Unc	BU
2001 In sets only	—	—	—	—	10.00	—
2003	Est. 5,000	—	—	—	—	300
2006	—	—	1.00	2.00	4.00	—
2007	—	—	1.00	2.00	4.00	—
2008	—	—	—	2.00	4.00	—
2008 Prooflike, in sets only	5,000	—	—	—	8.00	—

KM# 8b HRYVNIA
6.9000 g., Aluminum-Bronze, 26 mm. **Obv:** National arms **Rev:** Value, sprigs design **Edge:** Lettered

Date	Mintage	F	VF	XF	Unc	BU
2001	—	—	—	2.50	4.50	—

KM# 8b.1 HRYVNIA
7.1000 g., Aluminum-Bronze, 26 mm.

Date	Mintage	F	VF	XF	Unc	BU
2002	—	—	—	3.50	6.50	—
2003	—	—	—	2.50	4.50	—

KM# 208 HRYVNIA
6.8000 g., Aluminum-Bronze, 26 mm. **Subject:** 60th Anniversary - Victory over the Nazis **Obv:** National arms above value **Rev:** Uniform lapel with Soviet military medals group **Edge:** Lettered **Edge Lettering:** Date and denomination

Date	Mintage	F	VF	XF	Unc	BU
2004	5,000,000	—	—	—	5.00	—

KM# 209 HRYVNIA
6.7400 g., Aluminum-Bronze, 26 mm. **Obv:** National arms above value **Rev:** Half length figure of Volodymyr the Great facing holding church model building and staff **Edge:** Lettered **Edge Lettering:** Date and denomination

Date	Mintage	F	VF	XF	Unc	BU
2004	10,000,000	—	—	—	4.00	—
2005	—	—	—	—	3.00	—
2006	—	—	—	—	3.00	—
2008 Prooflike, in sets only	5,000	—	—	—	—	12.50

KM# 228 HRYVNIA
6.8000 g., Aluminum-Bronze, 26 mm. **Subject:** WW II Victory 60th Anniversary **Obv:** Value **Rev:** Soldiers in a "V" of search lights **Edge:** Reeded

Date	Mintage	F	VF	XF	Unc	BU
2005	5,000,000	—	—	—	5.00	—

KM# 106 2 HRYVNI
12.8000 g., Copper-Nickel-Zinc, 31 mm. **Series:** Olympics - Salt Lake City, 2002 **Obv:** National arms, value and designs **Rev:** Stylized ice dancing couple **Edge:** Reeded

Date	Mintage	F	VF	XF	Unc	BU
2001	30,000	—	—	—	14.00	—

KM# 133 2 HRYVNI
12.8000 g., Copper-Nickel-Zinc, 31 mm. **Subject:** Kindness to Children **Obv:** National arms above value flanked by sprigs and doves **Rev:** Two children frolicking under fountain of knowledge **Edge:** Reeded

Date	Mintage	F	VF	XF	Unc	BU
2001	100,000	—	—	—	9.00	—

KM# 134 2 HRYVNI
12.8000 g., Copper-Nickel-Zinc, 31 mm. **Subject:** 5th Anniversary of Constitution **Obv:** National arms above value flanked by sprigs **Rev:** Building above book flanked by sprigs **Edge:** Reeded

Date	Mintage	F	VF	XF	Unc	BU
2001	30,000	—	—	—	20.00	—

KM# 111 2 HRYVNI
12.8000 g., Copper-Nickel-Zinc, 31 mm. **Series:** Flora and Fauna **Obv:** National arms and date divides wreath, value within **Rev:** Lynx and offspring **Edge:** Reeded

Date	Mintage	F	VF	XF	Unc	BU
2001	30,000	—	—	—	50.00	—

KM# 136 2 HRYVNI
12.8000 g., Copper-Nickel-Zinc, 31 mm. **Subject:** Mykolaiv Zoo **Obv:** Man running alongside large cat **Rev:** Twelve animals **Edge:** Reeded

Date	Mintage	F	VF	XF	Unc	BU
2001	30,000	—	—	—	30.00	—

KM# 137 2 HRYVNI
12.8000 g., Copper-Nickel-Zinc, 31 mm. **Subject:** Mykhailo Ostrohradskiy (Mathematician) **Obv:** National arms divides date and value divided by wavy line graph **Rev:** Head 1/4 left **Edge:** Reeded

Date	Mintage	F	VF	XF	Unc	BU
2001	30,000	—	—	—	12.00	—

KM# 138 2 HRYVNI
12.8000 g., Copper-Nickel-Zinc, 31 mm. **Subject:** Larix Polonica **Obv:** Value within wreath **Rev:** Pine branch with cone **Edge:** Reeded

Date	Mintage	F	VF	XF	Unc	BU
2001	30,000	—	—	—	40.00	—

KM# 139 2 HRYVNI
12.8000 g., Copper-Nickel-Zinc, 31 mm. **Subject:** Volodymyr Dal **Obv:** Books **Rev:** Head right **Edge:** Reeded

Date	Mintage	F	VF	XF	Unc	BU
2001	30,000	—	—	—	12.00	—

KM# 147 2 HRYVNI
12.8000 g., Copper-Nickel-Zinc, 31 mm. **Series:** Olympics - Salt lake City, 2002 **Obv:** National arms and value on ice design **Rev:** Stylized hockey player **Edge:** Reeded

Date	Mintage	F	VF	XF	Unc	BU
2001	30,000	—	—	—	14.00	—

KM# 149 2 HRYVNI
12.8000 g., Copper-Nickel-Zinc, 31 mm. **Subject:** Mykhailo Drahomanov (Historian, Politician, etc.) **Obv:** National arms and value **Rev:** Bust right **Edge:** Reeded

Date	Mintage	F	VF	XF	Unc	BU
2001	30,000	—	—	—	12.00	—

KM# 150 2 HRYVNI
12.8000 g., Copper-Nickel-Zinc, 31 mm. **Series:** Olympics - Salt lake City, 2002 **Obv:** National arms and value on ice design **Rev:** Speed skater **Edge:** Reeded

Date	Mintage	F	VF	XF	Unc	BU
2002	30,000	—	—	—	12.50	—

KM# 155 2 HRYVNI
12.8000 g., Copper-Nickel-Zinc, 31 mm. **Series:** Flora and Fauna **Obv:** National arms and date divides wreath, value within **Rev:** Eurasian Eagle Owl **Edge:** Reeded

Date	Mintage	F	VF	XF	Unc	BU
2002	30,000	—	—	—	60.00	—

KM# 156 2 HRYVNI
12.8000 g., Copper-Nickel-Zinc, 31 mm. **Subject:** Olympics - Athens, 2004 **Obv:** Two ancient figures above value **Rev:** Swimmer **Edge:** Reeded

Date	Mintage	F	VF	XF	Unc	BU
2002 Prooflike	30,000	—	—	—	12.50	—

KM# 166 2 HRYVNI
12.8000 g., Copper-Nickel-Zinc, 31 mm. **Subject:** Leonid Glibov, writer (1827-1893) **Obv:** National arms and value within scroll and wreath **Rev:** 1/2-length bust right **Edge:** Reeded

Date	Mintage	F	VF	XF	Unc	BU
2002	30,000	—	—	—	12.00	—

KM# 154 2 HRYVNI
12.8000 g., Copper-Nickel-Zinc, 31 mm. **Subject:** Mykola Lysenko (composer) **Obv:** Musical score and value **Rev:** Head 1/4 right **Edge:** Reeded

Date	Mintage	F	VF	XF	Unc	BU
2002	30,000	—	—	—	12.00	—

KM# 167 2 HRYVNI
12.8000 g., Copper-Nickel-Zinc, 31 mm. **Series:** Flora and Fauna **Obv:** National arms and date divides wreath, value within **Rev:** European Bison **Edge:** Reeded

Date	Mintage	F	VF	XF	Unc	BU
2003	50,000	—	—	—	20.00	—

KM# 168 2 HRYVNI
12.8000 g., Copper-Nickel-Zinc, 31 mm. **Obv:** National arms and date divides wreath, value within **Rev:** Long-snouted Sea Horse **Edge:** Reeded

Date	Mintage	F	VF	XF	Unc	BU
2003	50,000	—	—	—	20.00	—

KM# 169 2 HRYVNI
12.8000 g., Copper-Nickel-Zinc, 31 mm. **Subject:** Volodymyr Vernadskyi (academic) **Obv:** National arms, value and world globe **Rev:** Head on hand looking down **Edge:** Reeded

Date	Mintage	F	VF	XF	Unc	BU
2003	30,000	—	—	—	12.00	—

KM# 170 2 HRYVNI
12.8000 g., Copper-Nickel-Zinc, 31 mm. **Subject:** Volodymyr Korolenko (writer) **Obv:** National arms above book and value **Rev:** Bearded head 1/4 right above dates **Edge:** Reeded

Date	Mintage	F	VF	XF	Unc	BU
2003	30,000	—	—	—	12.00	—

KM# 171 2 HRYVNI
12.8000 g., Copper-Nickel-Zinc, 31 mm. **Subject:** Viacheslav Chornovil (politician) **Obv:** Arms with supporters within beaded circle **Rev:** Head 1/4 left **Edge:** Reeded

Date	Mintage	F	VF	XF	Unc	BU
2003	30,000	—	—	—	14.00	—

KM# 178 2 HRYVNI
1.2400 g., 0.9999 Gold 0.0399 oz. AGW, 13.92 mm. **Obv:** National arms flanked by dates within beaded circle **Rev:** Spotted Salamander divides beaded circle **Edge:** Plain

Date	Mintage	F	VF	XF	Unc	BU
2003	10,000	—	—	—	—	220

KM# 179 2 HRYVNI
12.8000 g., Copper-Nickel-Zinc, 31 mm. **Subject:** Singer Boris Gmyrya **Obv:** Value, arms ,date and musical symbol **Rev:** Head 1/4 left and dates **Edge:** Reeded

Date	Mintage	F	VF	XF	Unc	BU
2003	30,000	—	—	—	12.00	—

KM# 180 2 HRYVNI
12.8000 g., Copper-Nickel-Zinc, 31 mm. **Subject:** 70th Anniversary National Aviation University **Obv:** World globe behind national arms, value and date **Rev:** Wright Brothers biplane **Edge:** Reeded

Date	Mintage	F	VF	XF	Unc	BU
2003	30,000	—	—	—	15.00	—

KM# 181 2 HRYVNI
12.8000 g., Copper-Nickel-Zinc, 31 mm. **Subject:** Ostap Veresay (musician) **Obv:** Musical stringed instrument and ornamental design **Rev:** Bust facing playing stringed instrument **Edge:** Reeded

Date	Mintage	F	VF	XF	Unc	BU
2003	30,000	—	—	—	12.50	—

KM# 182 2 HRYVNI
12.8000 g., Copper-Nickel-Zinc, 31 mm. **Subject:** Olympics **Obv:** Two ancient women with seedlings **Rev:** Boxer **Edge:** Reeded

Date	Mintage	F	VF	XF	Unc	BU
2003	30,000	—	—	—	15.00	—

KM# 183 2 HRYVNI
12.8000 g., Copper-Nickel-Zinc, 31 mm. **Subject:** Vasyl Sukhomlynski (teacher) **Obv:** Children, books, value and national arms **Rev:** Head 1/4 right **Edge:** Reeded

Date	Mintage	F	VF	XF	Unc	BU
2003	30,000	—	—	—	12.00	—

KM# 184 2 HRYVNI
12.8000 g., Copper-Nickel-Zinc, 31 mm. **Subject:** Andriy Malyshko (poet) **Obv:** Ornamental shawl, national arms and value **Rev:** Head 1/4 right flanked by radiant sun and tree **Edge:** Reeded

Date	Mintage	F	VF	XF	Unc	BU
2003	30,000	—	—	—	12.00	—

KM# 201 2 HRYVNI
12.8000 g., Copper-Nickel-Zinc, 31 mm. **Subject:** Azov Dolphin **Obv:** National arms and date divides wreath, value within **Rev:** Harbor Porpoises **Edge:** Reeded

Date	Mintage	F	VF	XF	Unc	BU
2004	30,000	—	—	—	30.00	—

KM# 203 2 HRYVNI
12.8000 g., Copper-Nickel-Zinc, 31 mm. **Subject:** Serhiy Lyfar (ballet artist) **Obv:** Stylized dancer **Rev:** Head right **Edge:** Reeded

Date	Mintage	F	VF	XF	Unc	BU
2004	30,000	—	—	—	12.00	—

KM# 210 2 HRYVNI
12.8000 g., Copper-Nickel-Zinc, 31 mm. **Subject:** 170 Years of the Kyiv National University **Obv:** National arms in center above value dividing scientific items **Rev:** University building main entrance **Edge:** Reeded

Date	Mintage	F	VF	XF	Unc	BU
2004	50,000	—	—	—	10.00	—

KM# 211 2 HRYVNI
12.8000 g., Copper-Nickel-Zinc, 31 mm. **Subject:** Oleksander Dovzhenko (movie producer, writer) **Obv:** Boy standing in small boat **Rev:** Head facing **Edge:** Reeded

Date	Mintage	F	VF	XF	Unc	BU
2004	30,000	—	—	—	11.00	—

KM# 212 2 HRYVNI
12.8000 g., Copper-Nickel-Zinc, 31 mm. **Subject:** Mykola Bazhan (poet, translator) **Obv:** Winged pens and value **Rev:** Head 1/4 left **Edge:** Reeded

Date	Mintage	F	VF	XF	Unc	BU
2004	30,000	—	—	—	11.00	—

KM# 213 2 HRYVNI
12.8000 g., Copper-Nickel-Zinc, 31 mm. **Subject:** Mykhailo Kotsubynsky (writer) **Obv:** Two reclining figures **Rev:** Head 1/4 right **Edge:** Reeded

Date	Mintage	F	VF	XF	Unc	BU
2004	30,000	—	—	—	11.00	—

KM# 202 2 HRYVNI
12.8000 g., Copper-Nickel-Zinc, 31 mm. **Subject:** Football World Cup - 2006 **Obv:** Soccer ball in net **Rev:** Two soccer players **Edge:** Reeded

Date	Mintage	F	VF	XF	Unc	BU
2004	50,000	—	—	—	12.00	—

KM# 214   2 HRYVNI
12.8000 g., Copper-Nickel-Zinc, 31 mm.   **Subject:** Maria Zankovetska (actress) **Obv:** National arms, value and drawn curtain **Rev:** Hooded head 1/4 left **Edge:** Reeded

Date	Mintage	F	VF	XF	Unc	BU
2004	30,000	—	—	—	11.00	—

KM# 215   2 HRYVNI
12.8000 g., Copper-Nickel-Zinc, 31 mm.   **Subject:** Mykhailo Maksymovych (historian, archaeologist) **Obv:** National arms above building and value **Rev:** Bust left **Edge:** Reeded

Date	Mintage	F	VF	XF	Unc	BU
2004	30,000	—	—	—	11.00	—

KM# 216   2 HRYVNI
12.8000 g., Copper-Nickel-Zinc, 31 mm.   **Subject:** Mykhailo Deregus (painter) **Obv:** National arms and value on artists palette **Rev:** Head right **Edge:** Reeded

Date	Mintage	F	VF	XF	Unc	BU
2004	30,000	—	—	—	11.00	—

KM# 217   2 HRYVNI
12.8000 g., Copper-Nickel-Zinc, 31 mm.   **Subject:** Nuclear Power Engineering of Ukraine **Obv:** National arms and value in atomic design **Rev:** Nuclear reactor **Edge:** Reeded

Date	Mintage	F	VF	XF	Unc	BU
2004	30,000	—	—	—	15.00	—

KM# 227   2 HRYVNI
1.2400 g., 0.9999 Gold 0.0399 oz. AGW, 13.92 mm.
Obv: National arms divides dates within beaded circle
Rev: Flying White Stork divides beaded circle **Edge:** Plain

Date	Mintage	F	VF	XF	Unc	BU
2004	10,000	—	—	—	—	220

KM# 330   2 HRYVNI
12.8000 g., Copper-Nickel-Zinc, 31 mm.   **Subject:** 200th Anniversary of Kharkiv University **Obv:** National arms and atom **Rev:** University building and reflection **Edge:** Reeded

Date	Mintage	F	VF	XF	Unc	BU
2004	50,000	—	—	—	10.00	—

KM# 331   2 HRYVNI
12.8000 g., Copper-Nickel-Zinc, 31 mm.   **Subject:** Ukraine National Academy of Law named after Yaroslav the Wise **Obv:** National arms above National Academy of Law arms and date **Rev:** Building **Edge:** Reeded

Date	Mintage	F	VF	XF	Unc	BU
2004	30,000	—	—	—	17.00	—

KM# 332   2 HRYVNI
12.8000 g., Copper-Nickel-Zinc, 31 mm.   **Subject:** Yuri Fedkovych (poet, writer) **Obv:** National arms, value and man on horse **Rev:** Bust 1/4 right and dates **Edge:** Reeded

Date	Mintage	F	VF	XF	Unc	BU
2004	30,000	—	—	—	11.00	—

KM# 346   2 HRYVNI
12.8000 g., Copper-Nickel-Zinc, 31 mm.   **Subject:** Boris Liatoshynsky (composer) **Obv:** Musical G Clef symbol and value below national arms **Rev:** Head 1/4 left **Edge:** Reeded

Date	Mintage	F	VF	XF	Unc	BU
2005	20,000	—	—	—	12.50	—

KM# 347   2 HRYVNI
12.8000 g., Copper-Nickel-Zinc, 31 mm.   **Subject:** Volodymyr Filatov (surgeon) **Obv:** Light passing through the lens of an eye **Rev:** Head with cap facing **Edge:** Reeded

Date	Mintage	F	VF	XF	Unc	BU
2005	20,000	—	—	—	12.50	—

KM# 348   2 HRYVNI
12.8000 g., Copper-Nickel-Zinc, 31 mm.   **Obv:** Books between stylized horsemen **Rev:** Ulas Samchuk **Edge:** Reeded

Date	Mintage	F	VF	XF	Unc	BU
2005	20,000	—	—	—	12.50	—

KM# 349   2 HRYVNI
12.8000 g., Copper-Nickel-Zinc, 31 mm.   **Subject:** Pavlo Virsky (ballet artist) **Obv:** National arms in flower circle **Rev:** Bust right **Edge:** Reeded

Date	Mintage	F	VF	XF	Unc	BU
2005	20,000	—	—	—	12.50	—

KM# 350   2 HRYVNI
12.8000 g., Copper-Nickel-Zinc, 31 mm.   **Obv:** Roses and grapes **Rev:** Poet Maksym Rylsky **Edge:** Reeded

Date	Mintage	F	VF	XF	Unc	BU
2005	20,000	—	—	—	12.50	—

KM# 351   2 HRYVNI
1.2400 g., 0.9999 Gold 0.0399 oz. AGW, 13.9 mm.
Obv: National arms within beaded circle **Rev:** Scythian horseman depicted on golden plaque **Edge:** Plain

Date	Mintage	F	VF	XF	Unc	BU
2005	15,000	—	—	—	200	—

KM# 352   2 HRYVNI
12.8000 g., Copper-Nickel-Zinc, 31 mm.   **Subject:** Serhiy Vsekhsviatsky (astronomer) **Obv:** "Solar Wind" depiction **Rev:** Head right **Edge:** Reeded

Date	Mintage	F	VF	XF	Unc	BU
2005	20,000	—	—	—	12.50	—

KM# 353   2 HRYVNI
12.8000 g., Copper-Nickel-Zinc, 31 mm.   **Subject:** 50 Years of Kyivmiskbud **Obv:** National arms **Rev:** Buildings **Edge:** Reeded

Date	Mintage	F	VF	XF	Unc	BU
2005	20,000	—	—	—	12.50	—

KM# 354   2 HRYVNI
12.8000 g., Copper-Nickel-Zinc, 31 mm.   **Subject:** 75 Years of Zhukovsky Aerospace University in Kharkiv **Obv:** Building divides book outline **Rev:** Airplane, computer monitor and books **Edge:** Reeded

Date	Mintage	F	VF	XF	Unc	BU
2005	30,000	—	—	—	12.50	—

KM# 356 2 HRYVNI
12.8000 g., Copper-Nickel-Zinc, 31 mm. **Subject:** Oleksander Korniychuk (writer, playright) **Obv:** Theatrical masks and feather **Rev:** Bust 1/4 right **Edge:** Reeded

Date	Mintage	F	VF	XF	Unc	BU
2005	20,000	—	—	—	12.00	—

KM# 357 2 HRYVNI
12.8000 g., Copper-Nickel-Zinc, 31 mm. **Obv:** National arms and date divides wreath, value within **Rev:** Sandy Mole Rat **Edge:** Reeded

Date	Mintage	F	VF	XF	Unc	BU
2005	60,000	—	—	—	10.00	—

KM# 359 2 HRYVNI
12.8000 g., Copper-Nickel-Zinc, 31 mm. **Obv:** National arms **Rev:** Tairov Wine Institute building and cameo **Edge:** Reeded

Date	Mintage	F	VF	XF	Unc	BU
2005	20,000	—	—	—	20.00	—

KM# 360 2 HRYVNI
12.8000 g., Copper-Nickel-Zinc, 31 mm. **Subject:** 300 Years to David Guramishvili (poet) **Obv:** Georgian and Ukrainian style ornamentation **Rev:** Head right **Edge:** Reeded

Date	Mintage	F	VF	XF	Unc	BU
2005	30,000	—	—	—	10.00	—

KM# 361 2 HRYVNI
12.8000 g., Copper-Nickel-Zinc, 31 mm. **Subject:** Dmytro Yavornytsky (historian, archaeologist, writer) **Obv:** National arms **Rev:** Bust 3/4 right **Edge:** Reeded

Date	Mintage	F	VF	XF	Unc	BU
2005	30,000	—	—	—	10.00	—

KM# 375 2 HRYVNI
12.8000 g., Copper-Nickel-Zinc, 31 mm. **Subject:** Oleksiy Alchevsky (banker) **Obv:** Steam train, factory, National arms and value **Rev:** Head with beard 1/4 right **Edge:** Reeded

Date	Mintage	F	VF	XF	Unc	BU
2005	20,000	—	—	—	17.50	—

KM# 376 2 HRYVNI
12.8000 g., Copper-Nickel-Zinc, 31 mm. **Subject:** Illia Mechnikov (biologist, Nobel prize laureate) **Obv:** Amoeba and National arms **Rev:** Bust with beard facing **Edge:** Reeded

Date	Mintage	F	VF	XF	Unc	BU
2005	20,000	—	—	—	20.00	—

KM# 377 2 HRYVNI
12.8000 g., Copper-Nickel-Zinc, 31 mm. **Subject:** Vsevolod Holubovych (politician) **Obv:** National arms **Rev:** Head 1/4 left **Edge:** Reeded

Date	Mintage	F	VF	XF	Unc	BU
2005	20,000	—	—	—	12.50	—

KM# 378 2 HRYVNI
12.8000 g., Copper-Nickel-Zinc, 31 mm. **Subject:** Volodymyr Vynnychenko (writer, politician) **Obv:** National arms **Rev:** Head facing **Edge:** Reeded

Date	Mintage	F	VF	XF	Unc	BU
2005	20,000	—	—	—	13.00	—

KM# 383 2 HRYVNI
12.8000 g., Copper-Nickel-Zinc, 31 mm. **Subject:** Kyiv National University of Economics **Obv:** National arms, value and graph **Rev:** University building **Edge:** Reeded

Date	Mintage	F	VF	XF	Unc	BU
2006	60,000	—	—	—	9.00	—

KM# 384 2 HRYVNI
12.8000 g., Copper-Nickel-Zinc, 31 mm. **Subject:** Viacheslav Prokopovych (historian, publist) **Obv:** National arms **Rev:** Bust facing **Edge:** Reeded

Date	Mintage	F	VF	XF	Unc	BU
2006	30,000	—	—	—	9.00	—

KM# 385 2 HRYVNI
12.8000 g., Copper-Nickel-Zinc, 31 mm. **Subject:** Heorhii Narbut (artist) **Obv:** Peasant couple **Rev:** Silhouette of standing figure on one leg facing right **Edge:** Reeded

Date	Mintage	F	VF	XF	Unc	BU
2006	30,000	—	—	—	10.00	—

KM# 386 2 HRYVNI
12.8000 g., Copper-Nickel-Zinc, 31 mm. **Subject:** Oleh Antonov (aircraft engineer) **Obv:** Large jet plane **Rev:** Bust 1/4 right **Edge:** Reeded

Date	Mintage	F	VF	XF	Unc	BU
2006	45,000	—	—	—	12.50	—

KM# 391 2 HRYVNI
12.8000 g., Copper-Nickel-Zinc, 31 mm. **Obv:** National arms above value in wreath **Rev:** Bush Katydid Grasshopper **Edge:** Reeded

Date	Mintage	F	VF	XF	Unc	BU
2006	60,000	—	—	—	15.00	—

KM# 398 2 HRYVNI
12.8000 g., Copper-Nickel-Zinc, 31 mm. **Subject:** Mykhailo Hrushevskyi **Obv:** National arms and value **Edge:** Reeded

Date	Mintage	F	VF	XF	Unc	BU
2006	45,000	—	—	—	10.00	—

KM# 408 2 HRYVNI
1.2400 g., 0.9999 Gold 0.0399 oz. AGW, 13.92 mm. **Subject:** Hedgehog **Obv:** National arms **Edge:** Plain

Date	Mintage	F	VF	XF	Unc	BU
2006	10,000	—	—	—	110	—

KM# 399 2 HRYVNI
12.8000 g., Copper-Nickel-Zinc, 31 mm. **Subject:** Serhii Ostapenko **Obv:** National arms **Edge:** Reeded

Date	Mintage	F	VF	XF	Unc	BU
2006	30,000	—	—	—	10.00	—

KM# 401   2 HRYVNI
12.8000 g., Copper-Nickel-Zinc, 31 mm. **Subject:** Economic
University of Kharkiv

Date	Mintage	F	VF	XF	Unc	BU
2006	30,000	—	—	—	12.00	—

KM# 393   2 HRYVNI
12.8000 g., Copper-Nickel-Zinc, 31 mm. **Subject:** Mykola
Strazhesko **Obv:** National arms and value **Edge:** Reeded

Date	Mintage	F	VF	XF	Unc	BU
2006	45,000	—	—	—	9.00	—

KM# 394   2 HRYVNI
12.8000 g., Copper-Nickel-Zinc, 31 mm. **Subject:** Volodymyr
Chekhivsky **Obv:** National arms and value **Edge:** Reeded

Date	Mintage	F	VF	XF	Unc	BU
2006	30,000	—	—	—	12.00	—

KM# 395   2 HRYVNI
12.8000 g., Copper-Nickel-Zinc, 31 mm. **Subject:** Mykola
Vasylenko **Obv:** National arms and value **Edge:** Reeded

Date	Mintage	F	VF	XF	Unc	BU
2006	30,000	—	—	—	12.00	—

KM# 396   2 HRYVNI
12.8000 g., Copper-Nickel-Zinc, 31 mm. **Subject:** Ivan Franko
Obv: National arms and value **Edge:** Reeded

Date	Mintage	F	VF	XF	Unc	BU
2006	45,000	—	—	—	12.00	—

KM# 397   2 HRYVNI
12.8000 g., Copper-Nickel-Zinc, 31 mm. **Subject:** Dmytro
Lutsenko **Obv:** National arms and value **Edge:** Reeded

Date	Mintage	F	VF	XF	Unc	BU
2006	30,000	—	—	—	10.00	—

KM# 400   2 HRYVNI
12.8000 g., Copper-Nickel-Zinc, 31 mm. **Subject:** Mykhailo
Lysenko **Obv:** National arms and value **Edge:** Reeded

Date	Mintage	F	VF	XF	Unc	BU
2006	35,000	—	—	—	10.00	—

KM# 403   2 HRYVNI
1.2400 g., 0.9999 Gold 0.0399 oz. AGW, 13.92 mm.
Subject: Ram **Obv:** National arms **Edge:** Plain

Date	Mintage	F	VF	XF	Unc	BU
2006	10,000	—	—	—	100	—

KM# 404   2 HRYVNI
1.2400 g., 0.9999 Gold 0.0399 oz. AGW, 13.92 mm.
Subject: Bull **Obv:** National arms **Edge:** Plain

Date	Mintage	F	VF	XF	Unc	BU
2006	10,000	—	—	—	100	—

KM# 406   2 HRYVNI
1.2400 g., 0.9999 Gold 0.0399 oz. AGW, 13.92 mm.
Subject: The Twins **Obv:** National arms **Edge:** Plain

Date	Mintage	F	VF	XF	Unc	BU
2006	10,000	—	—	—	100	—

KM# 428   2 HRYVNI
12.8000 g., Copper-Nickel-Zinc, 31 mm. **Subject:** Serhii
Koroljov **Obv:** National arms **Edge:** Reeded

Date	Mintage	F	VF	XF	Unc	BU
2007	35,000	—	—	—	15.00	—

KM# 429   2 HRYVNI
12.8000 g., Copper-Nickel-Zinc, 31 mm. **Subject:** Les Kurbas
Obv: National arms **Edge:** Reeded

Date	Mintage	F	VF	XF	Unc	BU
2007	35,000	—	—	—	12.00	—

KM# 430   2 HRYVNI
12.8000 g., Copper-Nickel-Zinc, 31 mm. **Subject:** Olexander
Liapunov **Obv:** Small national arms above geometrical depiction
of celestial mechanics grafics **Rev:** Large bust facing
Edge: Reeded

Date	Mintage	F	VF	XF	Unc	BU
2007	35,000	—	—	—	11.00	—

KM# 431   2 HRYVNI
1.2400 g., 0.9999 Gold 0.0399 oz. AGW, 13.92 mm.
Subject: Steppe Marmot **Obv:** National arms **Edge:** Plain

Date	Mintage	F	VF	XF	Unc	BU
2007	10,000	—	—	—	110	—

KM# 440   2 HRYVNI
12.8000 g., Copper-Nickel-Zinc, 31 mm. **Subject:** Ivan Ohienko
Obv: Cross **Rev:** Head and hands clasped at prayer
Edge: Reeded

Date	Mintage	F	VF	XF	Unc	BU
2007	35,000	—	—	—	—	10.00

KM# 441   2 HRYVNI
12.8000 g., Copper-Nickel-Zinc, 31 mm. **Subject:** Oleh Olzhych
Obv: Chestnut leaf and stone path **Rev:** Bust facing
Edge: Reeded

Date	Mintage	F	VF	XF	Unc	BU
2007	35,000	—	—	—	—	10.00

KM# 442   2 HRYVNI
12.8000 g., Copper-Nickel-Zinc, 31 mm. **Subject:** Donetsk
Region 75th Anniversary **Obv:** Miner's lamp illuminating industrial
plants **Rev:** Flag and 75 **Edge:** Reeded

Date	Mintage	F	VF	XF	Unc	BU
2007	35,000	—	—	—	—	20.00

KM# 443   2 HRYVNI
12.8000 g., Copper-Nickel-Zinc, 31 mm. **Subject:** Olena Teliha
Obv: Scorched cherry blossom **Rev:** Bust facing **Edge:** Reeded

Date	Mintage	F	VF	XF	Unc	BU
2007	35,000	—	—	—	—	10.00

KM# 444   2 HRYVNI
12.8000 g., Copper-Nickel-Zinc, 31 mm. **Subject:** Orienteering
Obv: Compass, star and benchmarks **Rev:** Runner
Edge: Reeded

Date	Mintage	F	VF	XF	Unc	BU
2007	35,000	—	—	—	—	12.00

KM# 445   2 HRYVNI
12.8000 g., Copper-Nickel-Zinc, 31 mm. **Subject:** Ivan Bahrianji
Obv: Book edge **Rev:** Bust facing, book edge **Edge:** Reeded

Date	Mintage	F	VF	XF	Unc	BU
2007	35,000	—	—	—	—	11.00

KM# 446 2 HRYVNI
12.8000 g., Copper-Nickel-Zinc, 31 mm. **Subject:** Perro Hryhorenko **Obv:** Sprout squeezing brick wall **Rev:** Head right **Edge:** Reeded

Date	Mintage	F	VF	XF	Unc	BU
2007	35,000	—	—	—	—	10.00

KM# 447 2 HRYVNI
12.8000 g., Copper-Nickel-Zinc, 31 mm. **Subject:** 90th Anniversary of 1st Government **Obv:** Parts of early 20th century banknots and industrial elements **Rev:** Volodymyr Vynnychenko and ornamentation **Edge:** Reeded

Date	Mintage	F	VF	XF	Unc	BU
2007	35,000	—	—	—	—	11.00

KM# 448 2 HRYVNI
1.2400 g., 0.9990 Gold 0.0398 oz. AGW, 13.9 mm. **Subject:** Capricorn **Obv:** Elements of earth, air, water and fire **Rev:** Zodiac sign

Date	Mintage	F	VF	XF	Unc	BU
2007	10,000	—	—	—	—	100

KM# 450 2 HRYVNI
1.2400 g., 0.9990 Gold 0.0398 oz. AGW, 13.9 mm. **Subject:** Pisces **Obv:** Elements of earth, air, water and fire **Rev:** Zopdiac sign, two fish

Date	Mintage	F	VF	XF	Unc	BU
2007	10,000	—	—	—	—	100

KM# 449 2 HRYVNI
1.2400 g., 0.9990 Gold 0.0398 oz. AGW, 13.9 mm. **Subject:** Aquarius **Obv:** Elements of earth, air, water and fire **Rev:** Zodiac sign, man pouring water

Date	Mintage	F	VF	XF	Unc	BU
2007	10,000	—	—	—	—	100

KM# 451 2 HRYVNI
1.2400 g., 0.9990 Gold 0.0398 oz. AGW, 13.9 mm. **Subject:** Scorpion **Obv:** Elements of earth, air, water and fire **Rev:** Zodiac sign

Date	Mintage	F	VF	XF	Unc	BU
2007	10,000	—	—	—	—	100

KM# 452 2 HRYVNI
1.2400 g., 0.9990 Gold 0.0398 oz. AGW, 13.9 mm. **Subject:** Sagitarius **Obv:** Elements of earth, air, water & fire **Rev:** Zodiac sign, archer

Date	Mintage	F	VF	XF	Unc	BU
2007	10,000	—	—	—	—	100

KM# 433 2 HRYVNI
12.8000 g., Copper-Nickel-Zinc, 31 mm. **Obv:** Small national arms at top, value in sprays with bird at left, butterfly at right **Rev:** Cinereous Vulture perched on nest with chick **Rev. Legend:** AEGYPIUS MONACHUS - ГРИФ ЧОРНИЙ **Edge:** Reeded

Date	Mintage	F	VF	XF	Unc	BU
2008	45,000	—	—	—	—	11.00

KM# 475 2 HRYVNI
12.8000 g., Copper-Nickel-Zinc, 31 mm. **Subject:** Vasyl Stus, Poet **Edge:** Reeded

Date	Mintage	F	VF	XF	Unc	BU
2008	35,000	—	—	—	—	10.00

KM# 476 2 HRYVNI
12.8000 g., Copper-Nickel-Zinc, 31 mm. **Subject:** Leo Landau **Edge:** Reeded

Date	Mintage	F	VF	XF	Unc	BU
2008	35,000	—	—	—	—	10.00

KM# 477 2 HRYVNI
12.8000 g., Copper-Nickel-Zinc, 31 mm. **Subject:** Sydir Holubovych **Edge:** Reeded

Date	Mintage	F	VF	XF	Unc	BU
2008	35,000	—	—	—	—	10.00

KM# 478 2 HRYVNI
12.8000 g., Copper-Nickel-Zinc, 31 mm. **Subject:** Kyiv Zoo, 100th Anniversary **Edge:** Reeded

Date	Mintage	F	VF	XF	Unc	BU
2008	50,000	—	—	—	—	11.00

KM# 479 2 HRYVNI
12.8000 g., Copper-Nickel-Zinc, 31 mm. **Subject:** Yevhen Petrushevych **Edge:** Reeded

Date	Mintage	F	VF	XF	Unc	BU
2008	35,000	—	—	—	—	10.00

KM# 481 2 HRYVNI
12.8000 g., Copper-Nickel, 31 mm. **Subject:** Heorhii Voronyi

Date	Mintage	F	VF	XF	Unc	BU
2008	35,000	—	—	—	—	—

KM# 482 2 HRYVNI
1.2400 g., 0.9990 Gold 0.0398 oz. AGW, 13.9 mm. **Subject:** Skythian Gold (Goddess Api)

Date	Mintage	F	VF	XF	Unc	BU
2008	10,000	—	—	—	—	100

KM# 483 2 HRYVNI
1.2400 g., 0.9990 Gold 0.0398 oz. AGW, 13.9 mm. **Subject:** Cancer

Date	Mintage	F	VF	XF	Unc	BU
2008	10,000	—	—	—	—	100

KM# 484 2 HRYVNI
1.2400 g., 0.9990 Gold 0.0398 oz. AGW, 13.9 mm. **Subject:** Virgo

Date	Mintage	F	VF	XF	Unc	BU
2008	10,000	—	—	—	—	100

KM# 485 2 HRYVNI
1.2400 g., 0.9990 Gold 0.0398 oz. AGW **Subject:** Virgo

Date	Mintage	F	VF	XF	Unc	BU
2008	10,000	—	—	—	—	100

KM# 486 2 HRYVNI
1.2400 g., 0.9990 Gold 0.0398 oz. AGW, 13.9 mm. **Subject:** Libra

Date	Mintage	F	VF	XF	Unc	BU
2008	—	—	—	—	—	100

KM# 487 2 HRYVNI
12.8000 g., Copper-Nickel-Zinc, 31 mm. **Subject:** Nataliia Vzhvii **Edge:** Reeded

Date	Mintage	F	VF	XF	Unc	BU
2008	35,000	—	—	—	—	10.00

KM# 488 2 HRYVNI
12.8000 g., Copper-Nickel-Zinc, 31 mm. **Subject:** Hryhorii Kvitka - Osnovianenko **Edge:** Reeded

Date	Mintage	F	VF	XF	Unc	BU
2008	35,000	—	—	—	—	10.00

KM# 489 2 HRYVNI
12.8000 g., Copper-Nickel-Silver-Zinc, 31 mm. **Subject:** Western Ukraine People's Repbulic, 90th Anniversary **Edge:** Reeded

Date	Mintage	F	VF	XF	Unc	BU
2008	35,000	—	—	—	—	10.00

KM# 490 2 HRYVNI
12.8000 g., Copper-Nickel-Zinc, 31 mm. **Subject:** Vasyl Symonenko **Edge:** Reeded

Date	Mintage	F	VF	XF	Unc	BU
2008	35,000	—	—	—	—	10.00

KM# 533 2 HRYVNI
12.8000 g., Copper-Nickel, 31.0 mm. **Subject:** Pavlo Chubynskyi **Obv:** Folk music instruments. **Obv. Legend:** НАЦІОНАЛЬНИЙ БАНК УКРА?НИ - 2/ ГРИВНІ **Rev:** Chubynskyi portrait. **Rev. Legend:** ПАВЛО ЧУБИНСЬКИЙ - 1839-1884

Date	Mintage	F	VF	XF	Unc	BU
2009	35,000	—	—	—	—	5.00

KM# 534 2 HRYVNI
12.8000 g., Copper-Nickel, 31.0 mm. **Subject:** Andrii Kivytskyi **Obv:** State Emblem. **Obv. Legend:** НАЦІОНАЛЬНИЙ БАНК УКРА?НИ - ДВІ ГРИВНІ **Rev:** Livytskyi portrait. **Rev. Legend:** АНДРІЙ ЛІВИЦЬКИЙ - 1879/1954 - ПРЕЗИДЕНТ УНР В ЕКЗИЛІ

Date	Mintage	F	VF	XF	Unc	BU
2009	35,000	—	—	—	—	3.00

KM# 535 2 HRYVNI
1.2400 g., 0.9990 Gold 0.0398 oz. AGW, 13.92 mm. **Subject:** Turtle **Obv:** National Emblem. **Obv. Legend:** НАЦІОНАЛЬНИЙ БАНК УКРА?НИ - 2 ГРИВНІ **Rev:** Turtle. **Rev. Legend:** ЧЕРЕПАХА - TESTUDINES

Date	Mintage	F	VF	XF	Unc	BU
2009 Proof	10,000	Value: 60.00				

KM# 536 2 HRYVNI
12.8000 g., Copper-Nickel, 31.0 mm. **Subject:** Borys Martos **Obv:** Coat of Arms. **Obv. Legend:** НАЦІОНАЛЬНИЙ БАНК УКРА?НИ - ДВІ ГРИВНІ **Rev:** Martos portrait. **Rev. Legend:** БОРИС МАРТОС

Date	Mintage	F	VF	XF	Unc	BU
2009	35,000	—	—	—	—	5.00

KM# 537 2 HRYVNI
12.8000 g., Copper-Nickel, 31.0 mm. **Subject:** Symon Petliura **Obv:** Military men, wreath, woman's profile. **Obv. Legend:** НАЦІОНАЛЬНИЙ БАНК УКРА?НИ - 2 ГРИВНІ **Rev:** Petliura portrait. **Rev. Legend:** СИМОН ПЕТЛЮРА

Date	Mintage	F	VF	XF	Unc	BU
2009	35,000	—	—	—	—	5.00

KM# 538 2 HRYVNI
12.8000 g., Copper-Nickel, 31. mm. **Subject:** Igor Sikorskyi **Obv:** Airplane. **Obv. Legend:** НАЦІОНАЛЬНИЙ БАНК УКРА?НИ - 2 ГРИВНІ **Rev:** Sikorskyi portrait, Da Vinci drawing. **Rev. Legend:** ІГОР СІКОРСЬКИЙ

Date	Mintage	F	VF	XF	Unc	BU
2009	35,000	—	—	—	—	5.00

KM# 539 2 HRYVNI
Copper-Nickel **Subject:** Mykola Bogolijubov

Date	Mintage	F	VF	XF	Unc	BU
2009	35,000	Value: 5.00				

KM# 540 2 HRYVNI
12.8000 g., Copper-Nickel-Zinc, 31.0 mm. **Subject:** Volodymyr Ivasiuk **Obv:** Flower of Chervona Ruta, electrical musical instruments **Obv. Legend:** НАЦІОНАЛЬНИЙ БАНК УКРА?НИ - 2/ГРИВНІ/2009 **Rev:** Ivasiuk portrait. **Rev. Legend:** ВОЛОДИМИР ІВАСЮК **Edge:** Reeded

Date	Mintage	F	VF	XF	Unc	BU
2009	35,000	—	—	—	—	5.00

KM# 541 2 HRYVNI
12.8000 g., Copper-Nickel, 31.0 mm. **Subject:** Bohdan-Igor Antonych **Obv:** Figurative interpretation of Antonych's poetry. **Obv. Legend:** НАЦІОНАЛЬНИЙ БАНК УКРА?НИ - 2/ГРИВНІ **Rev:** Antonych portrait. **Rev. Legend:** БОГДАН-ІГОР АНТОНИЧ

Date	Mintage	F	VF	XF	Unc	BU
2009	35,000	—	—	—	—	5.00

KM# 542 2 HRYVNI
12.8000 g., Copper-Nickel, 31.0 mm. **Subject:** Kost Levytskyi **Obv:** State Coat of Arms, issue year. **Obv. Legend:** НАЦІОНАЛЬНИЙ БАНК УКРАЇНИ - ДВІ ГРИВНІ **Rev:** Levytskyi bust. **Rev. Legend:** КОСТЬ ЛЕВИЦЬКИЙ

Date	Mintage	F	VF	XF	Unc	BU
2009	35,000	—	—	—	—	5.00

KM# 551 2 HRYVNI
12.8000 g., Copper-Nickel, 31.0 mm. **Subject:** 70th Anniversary, Carpathian Ukraine **Obv:** Carpets. **Obv. Legend:** НАЦІОНАЛЬНИЙ БАНК УКРАЇНИ **Rev:** Transcarpathian holding flag. **Rev. Legend:** 70/РОКІВ - ПРОГОЛОШЕННЯ КАРПАТСЬКОЇ УКРАЇНИ

Date	Mintage	F	VF	XF	Unc	BU
2009	35,000	—	—	—	—	5.00

KM# 107 5 HRYVEN
9.4000 g., Bi-Metallic Brass center in Copper-Nickel ring, 28 mm. **Subject:** New Millennium **Obv:** Spiral design within circle **Rev:** Mother and child within circle **Edge:** Segmented reeding

Date	Mintage	F	VF	XF	Unc	BU
2001	50,000	—	—	—	30.00	—

KM# 112 5 HRYVEN
16.5400 g., Copper-Nickel-Zinc, 35 mm. **Subject:** Ostrozhska Academy **Obv:** Value, old writing and printing artifacts **Rev:** Seated figures, partial building and crowned arms with supporters **Edge:** Reeded

Date	Mintage	F	VF	XF	Unc	BU
2001	30,000	—	—	—	25.00	—

KM# 129 5 HRYVEN
16.5400 g., Copper-Nickel-Zinc, 35 mm. **Subject:** 10th Anniversary - National Bank **Obv:** National arms between two arches **Rev:** Large building central entrance **Edge:** Reeded

Date	Mintage	F	VF	XF	Unc	BU
2001	50,000	—	—	—	15.00	—

KM# 132 5 HRYVEN
16.5400 g., Copper-Nickel-Zinc, 35 mm. **Subject:** 10th Anniversary - National Independence **Obv:** Arms with supporters within beaded circle **Rev:** Building on map within beaded circle **Edge:** Reeded

Date	Mintage	F	VF	XF	Unc	BU
2001	100,000	—	—	—	12.50	—

KM# 135   5 HRYVEN
16.5400 g., Copper-Nickel-Zinc, 35 mm. **Subject:** 1100th
Anniversary - Poltava **Obv:** National arms above value flanked
by flower sprigs **Rev:** Buildings above shield **Edge:** Reeded

Date	Mintage	F	VF	XF	Unc	BU
2001	50,000	—	—	—	15.00	—

KM# 140   5 HRYVEN
9.4000 g., Bi-Metallic Brass center in Copper-Nickel ring, 28 mm.
Subject: 10th Anniversary of Military forces **Obv:** Crossed
maces, arms and date within wreath and circle **Rev:** Circle in
center of cross within wreath and circle **Edge:** Reeded and plain
sections

Date	Mintage	F	VF	XF	Unc	BU
2001	30,000	—	—	—	100	—

KM# 148   5 HRYVEN
16.5400 g., Copper-Nickel-Zinc, 35 mm. **Subject:** 400 Years of
Krolevets **Obv:** National arms above gateway and value **Rev:**
Krolivets city arms flanked by designs **Edge:** Reeded

Date	Mintage	F	VF	XF	Unc	BU
2001	30,000	—	—	—	25.00	—

KM# 151   5 HRYVEN
16.5400 g., Copper-Nickel-Zinc, 35 mm. **Subject:** City of Khotyn
Obv: Value within arch above military fittings **Rev:** Castle below
crowned shield **Edge:** Reeded

Date	Mintage	F	VF	XF	Unc	BU
2002	30,000	—	—	—	40.00	—

KM# 152   5 HRYVEN
16.5400 g., Copper-Nickel-Zinc, 35 mm. **Obv:** Sun and flying
geese divides beaded circle **Rev:** "AN-225 Mrija" cargo jet divide
beaded circle **Edge:** Reeded

Date	Mintage	F	VF	XF	Unc	BU
2002	30,000	—	—	—	75.00	—

KM# 158   5 HRYVEN
9.4300 g., Bi-Metallic Brass center in Copper-Nickel ring, 28 mm.
Subject: 70th Anniversary of Dnipro Hydroelectric Power Station
Obv: Turbine within circle **Rev:** Large dam within circle
Edge: Reeded and plain sections

Date	Mintage	F	VF	XF	Unc	BU
2002	30,000	—	—	—	40.00	—

KM# 159   5 HRYVEN
16.5400 g., Copper-Nickel-Zinc, 35 mm. **Obv:** Arms with
supporters within beaded circle **Rev:** Battle scene around Batig
in 1652 divides beaded circle **Edge:** Reeded

Date	Mintage	F	VF	XF	Unc	BU
2002	30,000	—	—	—	25.00	—

KM# 163   5 HRYVEN
16.5400 g., Copper-Nickel-Zinc, 35 mm. **Subject:** Christmas
Obv: National arms in star above value flanked by designed
sprigs **Rev:** Christmas pageant scene **Edge:** Reeded

Date	Mintage	F	VF	XF	Unc	BU
ND(2002)	30,000	—	—	—	95.00	—

KM# 157   5 HRYVEN
16.5400 g., Copper-Nickel, 35 mm. **Subject:** 1100th
Anniversary - City of Romny **Obv:** Sprigs divide national arms
and value **Rev:** City view **Edge:** Reeded

Date	Mintage	F	VF	XF	Unc	BU
2002	30,000	—	—	—	25.00	—

KM# 200   5 HRYVEN
9.4000 g., Bi-Metallic Brass center in Copper-Nickel ring, 28 mm.
Obv: Bandura strings over ornamental design **Rev:** Bandura
divides circle and wreath **Edge:** Segmented reeding

Date	Mintage	F	VF	XF	Unc	BU
2003	30,000	—	—	—	20.00	—

KM# 172   5 HRYVEN
16.5400 g., Copper-Nickel-Zinc, 35 mm. **Subject:** Easter
Obv: Circle of Easter eggs, national arms in center above value
Rev: Religious celebration **Edge:** Reeded

Date	Mintage	F	VF	XF	Unc	BU
2003	50,000	—	—	—	35.00	—

KM# 173   5 HRYVEN
16.5400 g., Copper-Nickel-Zinc, 35 mm. **Subject:** Antonov AN-
2 Biplane **Obv:** National arms sun face and flying geese divide
beaded circle **Rev:** World's largest biplane divides beaded circle
Edge: Reeded

Date	Mintage	F	VF	XF	Unc	BU
2003	50,000	—	—	—	20.00	—

KM# 185   5 HRYVEN
9.4000 g., Bi-Metallic Brass center in Copper-Nickel ring, 28 mm.
Subject: 150th Anniversary of the Central Ukrainian Archives
Obv: Value, signature and seal **Rev:** Hourglass divides books
and circle **Edge:** Segmented reeding

Date	Mintage	F	VF	XF	Unc	BU
2003	30,000	—	—	—	12.50	—

KM# 186   5 HRYVEN
16.5400 g., Copper-Nickel-Zinc, 35 mm. **Subject:** 2500th
Anniversary of the City of Yevpatoria **Obv:** National arms, date
and value with partial sun background **Rev:** Ancient amphora
and modern city view **Edge:** Reeded

Date	Mintage	F	VF	XF	Unc	BU
2003	30,000	—	—	—	19.00	—

KM# 187   5 HRYVEN
16.5400 g., Copper-Nickel-Zinc, 35 mm. **Subject:** 60th
Anniversary - Liberation of Kiev **Obv:** Eternal flame monument
Rev: Battle scene and map of the offense **Edge:** Reeded

Date	Mintage	F	VF	XF	Unc	BU
2003	30,000	—	—	—	15.00	—

KM# 204   5 HRYVEN
16.5400 g., Copper-Nickel-Zinc, 35 mm. **Subject:** 50th
Anniversary - Pivdenne Space Design Office **Obv:** Satellite
orbiting Earth **Rev:** Satellite above moonscape **Edge:** Reeded

Date	Mintage	F	VF	XF	Unc	BU
2004	30,000	—	—	—	15.00	—

KM# 205   5 HRYVEN
16.5400 g., Copper-Nickel-Zinc, 35 mm. **Subject:** 2500
Anniversary City of Balaklava **Obv:** National arms between two
ancient ships **Rev:** Harbor view above pillar **Edge:** Reeded

Date	Mintage	F	VF	XF	Unc	BU
2004	30,000	—	—	—	17.00	—

KM# 218 5 HRYVEN
16.9400 g., 0.9250 Silver 0.5038 oz. ASW, 33 mm.
Obv: National arms, value and atom **Rev:** Kharkov University building **Edge:** Reeded

Date	Mintage	F	VF	XF	Unc	BU
2004 Proof	7,000	Value: 40.00				

KM# 219 5 HRYVEN
16.9400 g., 0.9250 Silver 0.5038 oz. ASW, 33 mm.
Obv: National arms above value dividing scientific items
Rev: Kiev University building main entrance **Edge:** Reeded

Date	Mintage	F	VF	XF	Unc	BU
2004 Proof	7,000	Value: 40.00				

KM# 220 5 HRYVEN
9.4300 g., Bi-Metallic BRASS center in COPPER-NICKEL ring, 28 mm. **Subject:** 50 Years of Ukraine's Membership in UNESCO **Obv:** National arms in center of sprigs and circle **Rev:** Building within sprigs and circle **Edge:** Segmented reeding

Date	Mintage	F	VF	XF	Unc	BU
2004	50,000	—	—	—	15.00	—

KM# 221 5 HRYVEN
16.5400 g., Copper-Nickel-Zinc, 35 mm. **Subject:** Ice Breaker "Captain Belousov" **Obv:** National arms on ship's wheel and anchor **Rev:** Ice breaker ship **Edge:** Reeded

Date	Mintage	F	VF	XF	Unc	BU
2004	30,000	—	—	—	13.00	—

KM# 222 5 HRYVEN
16.5400 g., Copper-Nickel-Zinc, 35 mm. **Subject:** Whit Sunday **Obv:** National arms in flower wreath above value flanked by sprigs **Rev:** Four dancing women and child **Edge:** Reeded

Date	Mintage	F	VF	XF	Unc	BU
2004	50,000	—	—	—	15.00	—

KM# 333 5 HRYVEN
9.4000 g., Bi-Metallic Brass center in Copper-Nickel ring, 28 mm.
Obv: Horizontal lines across flowery design **Rev:** Cossack-style lyre within circle and wreath **Edge:** Segmented reeding

Date	Mintage	F	VF	XF	Unc	BU
2004	30,000	—	—	—	15.00	—

KM# 334 5 HRYVEN
16.5400 g., Copper-Nickel-Zinc, 35 mm. **Subject:** 250th Anniversary of Kirovohrad **Obv:** National arms above crossed cannons and value **Rev:** Arms with supporters above city view **Edge:** Reeded

Date	Mintage	F	VF	XF	Unc	BU
2004	30,000	—	—	—	15.50	—

KM# 335 5 HRYVEN
16.5400 g., Copper-Nickel-Zinc, 35 mm. **Subject:** 350 Years to Kharkiv **Obv:** Assumption Cathedral, value and national arms **Rev:** Kharkiv State Industrial Building complex **Edge:** Reeded

Date	Mintage	F	VF	XF	Unc	BU
2004	30,000	—	—	—	22.50	—

KM# 336 5 HRYVEN
9.4000 g., Bi-Metallic Brass center in Copper-Nickel ring, 28 mm.
Subject: 50th Anniversary of Crimean Union With Ukraine
Obv: National arms on wheat sheaf on map **Rev:** Crowned lion on shield flanked by pillars within rope wreath **Edge:** Segmented reeding

Date	Mintage	F	VF	XF	Unc	BU
2004	30,000	—	—	—	15.00	—

KM# 337 5 HRYVEN
16.5400 g., Copper-Nickel-Zinc, 35 mm. **Obv:** National arms on sun, flying geese divide beaded circle **Rev:** AN-140 Airliner divides beaded circle **Edge:** Reeded

Date	Mintage	F	VF	XF	Unc	BU
2004	50,000	—	—	—	12.50	—

KM# 362 5 HRYVEN
16.5400 g., Copper-Nickel-Zinc, 35 mm. **Obv:** National arms on sun with flying geese divide beaded circle **Rev:** AN-124 jet divides beaded circle **Edge:** Reeded

Date	Mintage	F	VF	XF	Unc	BU
2005	60,000	—	—	—	12.50	—

KM# 364 5 HRYVEN
16.5400 g., Copper-Nickel-Zinc, 35 mm. **Subject:** City of Korosten 1300th Anniversary **Obv:** National arms **Rev:** Ancient earring below modern building and bridge **Edge:** Reeded

Date	Mintage	F	VF	XF	Unc	BU
2005	30,000	—	—	—	13.00	—

KM# 365 5 HRYVEN
16.5400 g., Copper-Nickel-Zinc, 35 mm. **Subject:** City of Sumy 350th Anniversary **Obv:** National arms **Rev:** City view behind city arms **Edge:** Reeded

Date	Mintage	F	VF	XF	Unc	BU
2005	30,000	—	—	—	13.00	—

KM# 366 5 HRYVEN
16.5400 g., Copper-Nickel-Zinc, 35 mm. **Subject:** The Protection of the Virgin **Obv:** National arms on Cossack regalia **Rev:** Wedding scene **Edge:** Reeded

Date	Mintage	F	VF	XF	Unc	BU
2005	45,000	—	—	—	15.00	—

KM# 368 5 HRYVEN
16.5400 g., Copper-Nickel-Zinc, 35 mm. **Subject:** Sorochynsky Fair **Obv:** Busts facing each other flanked by sprigs **Rev:** Farmer with family in ox cart **Edge:** Reeded

Date	Mintage	F	VF	XF	Unc	BU
2005	60,000	—	—	—	14.00	—

KM# 379 5 HRYVEN
16.5400 g., Copper-Nickel-Zinc, 35 mm. **Subject:** 500th Anniversary - Kalmiuska Palanqua Cossack Settlement **Obv:** Cossack in ornamental frame and national arms **Rev:** Soldiers **Edge:** Reeded

Date	Mintage	F	VF	XF	Unc	BU
2005	30,000	—	—	—	15.00	—

KM# 380   5 HRYVEN

16.5400 g., Copper-Nickel-Zinc, 35 mm.   **Subject:** Sviatohirsky Assumption Monastery **Obv:** Madonna and child flanked by angels **Rev:** Hillside monastery **Edge:** Reeded

Date	Mintage	F	VF	XF	Unc	BU
2005	45,000	—	—	—	15.00	—

KM# 387   5 HRYVEN

16.5400 g., Copper-Nickel-Zinc, 35 mm.   **Subject:** Vernadsky Antarctic Station **Obv:** Flag and buildings **Rev:** Antarctica map within compass face **Edge:** Reeded

Date	Mintage	F	VF	XF	Unc	BU
2006	60,000	—	—	—	12.50	—

KM# 388   5 HRYVEN

16.9300 g., 0.9250 Silver 0.5035 oz. ASW, 33 mm.
Subject: Year of the Dog **Obv:** Value on textile art **Rev:** Stylized dog **Edge:** Reeded

Date	Mintage	F	VF	XF	Unc	BU
2006 Proof	12,000	Value: 150				

KM# 389   5 HRYVEN

16.9300 g., 0.9250 Silver 0.5035 oz. ASW, 33 mm.
Subject: Zodiac - Ram **Obv:** Sun face **Rev:** Ram **Edge:** Reeded

Date	Mintage	F	VF	XF	Unc	BU
2006 Proof	10,000	Value: 75.00				

KM# 390   5 HRYVEN

16.9300 g., 0.9250 Silver 0.5035 oz. ASW, 33 mm.   **Subject:** Kyiv National University of Economics **Obv:** National arms, graph above value **Rev:** University building within circle **Edge:** Reeded

Date	Mintage	F	VF	XF	Unc	BU
2006 Proof	5,000	Value: 45.00				

KM# 402   5 HRYVEN

9.4200 g., Bi-Metallic Brass center in Copper-Nickel ring, 28 mm.
Obv: Symbolic sound of music **Rev:** Tsimbal stringed musical instrument **Edge:** Segmented reeding

Date	Mintage	F	VF	XF	Unc	BU
2006	100,000	—	—	—	—	10.00

KM# 409   5 HRYVEN

16.5400 g., Copper-Nickel-Zinc, 35 mm.   **Subject:** 10 Years of the Constitution of Ukraine **Obv:** National arms **Edge:** Reeded

Date	Mintage	F	VF	XF	Unc	BU
2006	30,000	—	—	—	20.00	—

KM# 411   5 HRYVEN

16.5400 g., Copper-Nickel-Zinc, 35 mm.   **Subject:** 15 Years of Ukraine Independence **Obv:** National arms **Edge:** Reeded

Date	Mintage	F	VF	XF	Unc	BU
2006	75,000	—	—	—	10.00	—

KM# 413   5 HRYVEN

16.5400 g., Copper-Nickel-Zinc, 35 mm.   **Subject:** 10 Years to the Currency Reform in Ukraine **Obv:** National arms **Edge:** Reeded

Date	Mintage	F	VF	XF	Unc	BU
2006	45,000	—	—	—	15.00	—

KM# 405   5 HRYVEN

16.8200 g., 0.9250 Silver 0.5002 oz. ASW, 33 mm.
Subject: Bull **Obv:** National arms

Date	Mintage	F	VF	XF	Unc	BU
2006 Proof	10,000	Value: 75.00				

KM# 415   5 HRYVEN

16.5400 g., Copper-Nickel-Zinc, 35 mm.   **Subject:** 750 Years of the City of L'viv **Obv:** National arms **Edge:** Reeded

Date	Mintage	F	VF	XF	Unc	BU
2006	60,000	—	—	—	15.00	—

KM# 416   5 HRYVEN

16.8200 g., 0.9250 Silver 0.5002 oz. ASW, 33 mm.
Subject: Mykhailo Hrushevskyi **Obv:** National arms

Date	Mintage	F	VF	XF	Unc	BU
2006 Proof	5,000	Value: 50.00				

KM# 417   5 HRYVEN

16.8200 g., 0.9250 Silver 0.5002 oz. ASW, 33 mm.
Subject: Dmytro Lutsenko **Obv:** National arms

Date	Mintage	F	VF	XF	Unc	BU
2006 Proof	3,000	Value: 75.00				

KM# 418   5 HRYVEN

16.8200 g., 0.9250 Silver 0.5002 oz. ASW, 33 mm.
Subject: Ivan Franko **Obv:** National arms

Date	Mintage	F	VF	XF	Unc	BU
2006 Proof	5,000	Value: 50.00				

KM# 407   5 HRYVEN

16.8200 g., 0.9250 Silver 0.5002 oz. ASW, 33 mm.
Subject: Gemini **Obv:** National arms

Date	Mintage	F	VF	XF	Unc	BU
2006 Proof	10,000	Value: 80.00				

KM# 420   5 HRYVEN

16.5400 g., Copper-Nickel-Zinc, 35 mm.   **Subject:** Epiphany **Obv:** National arms **Edge:** Reeded

Date	Mintage	F	VF	XF	Unc	BU
2006	75,000	—	—	—	15.00	—

KM# 422   5 HRYVEN

16.5400 g., Copper-Nickel-Zinc, 35 mm.   **Subject:** Saint Kyryl Church **Obv:** National arms

Date	Mintage	F	VF	XF	Unc	BU
2006	45,000	—	—	—	15.00	—

KM# 432   5 HRYVEN

16.5400 g., Copper-Nickel-Zinc, 35 mm.   **Subject:** 100th Anniversary of "Motor Sich" **Obv:** Small national arms above falcon in flight with two globes in background **Rev:** Jet engine **Edge:** Reeded

Date	Mintage	F	VF	XF	Unc	BU
2007	45,000	—	—	—	15.00	—

KM# 419   5 HRYVEN

16.8200 g., 0.9250 Silver 0.5002 oz. ASW, 33 mm.   **Subject:** Year of the Pig **Obv:** National arms **Edge:** Reeded

Date	Mintage	F	VF	XF	Unc	BU
2007 Proof	15,000	Value: 80.00				

KM# 453   5 HRYVEN

9.4000 g., Bi-Metallic Brass center in copper-nickel ring, 28 mm.
Subject: Pure water is the source of life **Obv:** Drop of water in pond **Rev:** Man taking drink at waterfall

Date	Mintage	F	VF	XF	Unc	BU
2007	50,000	—	—	—	—	10.00

KM# 455   5 HRYVEN

9.4000 g., Bi-Metallic Brass center in copper-nickel ring, 28 mm.
Subject: Organization Safety and Cooperation, 16th Annual Meeting **Obv:** State emblem and ornamentation **Rev:** Parliamentary Assemby Building in Kyiv

Date	Mintage	F	VF	XF	Unc	BU
2007	35,000	—	—	—	—	12.50

KM# 456   5 HRYVEN

16.5000 g., Copper-Nickel-Zinc, 35 mm.   **Subject:** Odesa National Opera and Ballet, 120th Anniversary **Obv:** Ballet scene in oval **Rev:** Opera house in Odesa **Edge:** Reeded

Date	Mintage	F	VF	XF	Unc	BU
2007	35,000	—	—	—	—	11.00

KM# 457 5 HRYVEN
16.5000 g., Copper-Nickel-Zinc, 35 mm. **Subject:** Chernihiv, 1100th Anniversary **Obv:** Sword hilts and slate fragment **Rev:** Town view and open book **Edge:** Reeded

Date	Mintage	F	VF	XF	Unc	BU
2007	45,000	—	—	—	—	12.00

KM# 458 5 HRYVEN
9.4000 g., Bi-Metallic Brass center in copper-nickel ring, 28 mm. **Subject:** Buhai **Obv:** Sound waves as a baroque ornament **Rev:** Drum like musical instrument

Date	Mintage	F	VF	XF	Unc	BU
2007	50,000	—	—	—	—	12.00

KM# 459 5 HRYVEN
16.5400 g., Copper-Nickel-Zinc, 35 mm. **Subject:** The Famine, Genocide of the Ukranian People **Obv:** Girl standing on fallow ground **Rev:** Stork within cross, candles in background **Edge:** Reeded

Date	Mintage	F	VF	XF	Unc	BU
2007	75,000	—	—	—	—	10.00

KM# 460 5 HRYVEN
16.5400 g., Copper-Nickel-Zinc, 35 mm. **Subject:** Crimean Resorts, 200th Anniversary **Obv:** Seaside Resort **Rev:** Felix De Searr and well **Edge:** Reeded

Date	Mintage	F	VF	XF	Unc	BU
2007	35,000	—	—	—	—	10.00

KM# 461 5 HRYVEN
15.5500 g., 0.9250 Silver 0.4624 oz. ASW, 33 mm. **Subject:** Capricorn **Obv:** Sun and seasons **Rev:** Zodiac sign

Date	Mintage	F	VF	XF	Unc	BU
2007 Proof	15,000	Value: 40.00				

KM# 462 5 HRYVEN
16.8200 g., 0.9250 Silver 0.5002 oz. ASW, 33 mm. **Subject:** Aquarius **Obv:** Sun and seasons **Rev:** Zodiac sign, man pouring water

Date	Mintage	F	VF	XF	Unc	BU
2007 Proof	15,000	Value: 40.00				

KM# 463 5 HRYVEN
16.8200 g., 0.9250 Silver 0.5002 oz. ASW, 33 mm. **Subject:** Pisces **Obv:** Sun and seasons **Rev:** Zodiac sign, two fish

Date	Mintage	F	VF	XF	Unc	BU
2007 Proof	15,000	Value: 40.00				

KM# 464 5 HRYVEN
16.8200 g., 0.9250 Silver 0.5002 oz. ASW, 33 mm. **Subject:** Scorpion **Obv:** Sun and seasons **Rev:** Zodiac sign, scorpion **Edge:** Reeded

Date	Mintage	F	VF	XF	Unc	BU
2007 Proof	15,000	Value: 40.00				

KM# 465 5 HRYVEN
16.8200 g., 0.9250 Silver 0.5002 oz. ASW, 33 mm. **Subject:** Sagittarius **Obv:** Sun and seasons **Rev:** Zodiac sign, archer

Date	Mintage	F	VF	XF	Unc	BU
2007 Proof	15,000	Value: 30.00				

KM# 531 5 HRYVEN
16.5400 g., Copper-Nickel, 35.0 mm. **Subject:** 1100th Anniversary of Perejaslav-Khmelnytskyi **Obv:** Parchment. **Obv. Legend:** НАЦІОНАЛЬНИЈ БАНК УКРА?НИ - 5 ГРИВЕНЬ / 2007 **Rev:** Old Rus cathedral, old Rus and Cossacks. **Rev. Legend:** ПЕРЕЯСЛАВ-ХМЕЛЬНИЦЬКИЈ - 1100

Date	Mintage	F	VF	XF	Unc	BU
2007	45,000	—	—	—	—	7.50

KM# 511 5 HRYVEN
16.5400 g., Copper-Nickel-Zinc, 35 mm. **Subject:** Rivne, 725th Anniversary **Edge:** Reeded

Date	Mintage	F	VF	XF	Unc	BU
2008	45,000	—	—	—	—	10.00

KM# 500 5 HRYVEN
16.5000 g., Copper-Nickel, 35 mm. **Subject:** The Annunciation

Date	Mintage	F	VF	XF	Unc	BU
2008	45,000	—	—	—	—	7.50

KM# 501 5 HRYVEN
16.5000 g., Copper-Nickel-Zinc, 35 mm. **Subject:** Chernivtsi, 600th Anniversary **Edge:** Reeded

Date	Mintage	F	VF	XF	Unc	BU
2008 45000	—	—	—	—	—	10.00

KM# 502 5 HRYVEN
16.5000 g., Copper-Nickel-Zinc, 35 mm. **Subject:** Sniatyn, 850th Anniversary **Edge:** Reeded

Date	Mintage	F	VF	XF	Unc	BU
2008	45,000	—	—	—	—	10.00

KM# 503 5 HRYVEN
16.8200 g., 0.9250 Silver 0.5002 oz. ASW, 33 mm. **Subject:** Year of the rat **Edge:** Reeded

Date	Mintage	F	VF	XF	Unc	BU
2008 Proof	15,000	Value: 80.00				

KM# 504 5 HRYVEN
16.8200 g., 0.9250 Silver 0.5002 oz. ASW, 33 mm. **Subject:** Cancer **Edge:** Reeded

Date	Mintage	F	VF	XF	Unc	BU
2008	15,000	Value: 45.00				

KM# 505 5 HRYVEN
16.8200 g., 0.9250 Silver 0.5002 oz. ASW, 33 mm. **Subject:** Roman Shukheugch **Edge:** Reeded

Date	Mintage	F	VF	XF	Unc	BU
2008	3,000	—	—	—	—	175

KM# 506 5 HRYVEN
16.8200 g., 0.9250 Silver 0.5002 oz. ASW, 33 mm. **Subject:** Leo **Edge:** Reeded

Date	Mintage	F	VF	XF	Unc	BU
2008	15,000	Value: 45.00				

KM# 507 5 HRYVEN
16.8200 g., 0.9250 Silver 0.5002 oz. ASW, 33 mm. **Subject:** Virgo **Edge:** Reeded

Date	Mintage	F	VF	XF	Unc	BU
2008	15,000	Value: 45.00				

KM# 508 5 HRYVEN
16.8200 g., 0.9250 Silver 0.5002 oz. ASW, 33 mm. **Subject:** Libra **Edge:** Reeded

Date	Mintage	F	VF	XF	Unc	BU
2008	15,000	Value: 45.00				

KM# 509 5 HRYVEN
16.5400 g., Copper-Nickel-Zinc, 35 mm. **Subject:** State Arboretum "Trostianet-s", 175th Anniversary **Edge:** Reeded

Date	Mintage	F	VF	XF	Unc	BU
2008	45,000	—	—	—	—	12.00

KM# 510 5 HRYVEN
16.5400 g., Copper-Nickel-Zinc **Subject:** Kievan Rus **Edge:** Reeded

Date	Mintage	F	VF	XF	Unc	BU
2008	45,000	—	—	—	—	12.00

KM# 512 5 HRYVEN
16.5400 g., Copper-Nickel-Zinc, 35 mm. **Subject:** Bohuslav, 975th Anniversary **Edge:** Reeded

Date	Mintage	F	VF	XF	Unc	BU
2008	45,000	—	—	—	—	12.00

KM# 513 5 HRYVEN
9.4000 g., Bi-Metallic Brass center in copper-nickel ring, 28 mm. **Subject:** Taras Shevchenko "Prosvita Society" 140th Anniversary

Date	Mintage	F	VF	XF	Unc	BU
2008	45,000	—	—	—	—	12.00

KM# 514 5 HRYVEN
16.8200 g., 0.9250 Silver 0.5002 oz. ASW, 33 mm. **Subject:** Mariya Prymachenko

Date	Mintage	F	VF	XF	Unc	BU
2008 Proof	5,000	Value: 40.00				

KM# 530 5 HRYVEN
16.8200 g., 0.9250 Silver 0.5002 oz. ASW, 33 mm. **Subject:** Year of the Bull **Edge:** Reeded

Date	Mintage	F	VF	XF	Unc	BU
2009 Proof	15,000	Value: 50.00				

KM# 543 5 HRYVEN
15.5500 g., 0.9990 Silver 0.4994 oz. ASW, 33.0 mm. **Subject:** Nikolai Gogol **Obv:** Compositions of two main subjects of Gogol's work. **Obv. Legend:** НАЦІОНАЛЬНИЈ БАНК УКРАІНИ - 5 ГРИВЕНЬ/2009 **Rev:** Portrait of Nikolai. **Rev. Legend:** МИКОЛА ГОГОЛЬ

Date	Mintage	F	VF	XF	Unc	BU
2009 Proof	5,000	Value: 35.00				

KM# 544 5 HRYVEN
15.5500 g., 0.9990 Silver 0.4994 oz. ASW, 33.0 mm. **Subject:** Sholem Aleichem **Obv:** Conventionalized composition, book sheets, Aleichem's personal signet. **Obv. Legend:** НАЦІОНАЛЬНИЈ БАНК УКРАІНИ - 5 ГРИВЕНЬ/2009 **Rev:** Aleichem bust. **Rev. Legend:** МИР ВАМ - ШОЛОМ-АЛЕЈХЕМ - РАБИНОВИЧ ШОЛОМ

Date	Mintage	F	VF	XF	Unc	BU
2009 Proof	5,000	Value: 35.00				

KM# 545 5 HRYVEN
16.5400 g., Copper-Nickel, 35.0 mm. **Subject:** Simferopol, 225th Anniversary **Obv:** Railway station. **Obv. Legend:** НАЦІОНАЛЬНИЈ БАНК УКРА?НИ - 5 ГРИВЕНЬ 2009 **Rev:** City Coat of Arms, two architectural monuments. **Rev. Legend:** 225/РОКІВ - СІМФЕРОПОЛЬ

Date	Mintage	F	VF	XF	Unc	BU
2009	45,000	—	—	—	—	8.00

KM# 546 5 HRYVEN
15.5500 g., 0.9990 Silver 0.4994 oz. ASW, 33 mm. **Subject:** Ivan Kotljarevskyi **Obv:** State Coat of Arms, boat, column and helmet. **Obv. Legend:** НАЦІОНАЛЬНИЈ БАНК УКРАІНИ - ГІЯТЬ ГРИВЕНЬ **Rev:** Kotliarevskyi bust. **Rev. Legend:** ...ПОКИ СОНЦЕ З НЕБА СЯЕ, ТЕБЕ НЕ ЗАБУДУТЬ! - ІВАН КОТЛЯРЕВСЬКИЈ

Date	Mintage	F	VF	XF	Unc	BU
2009 Proof	5,000	Value: 35.00				

KM# 547 5 HRYVEN
16.5400 g., Copper-Nickel, 35.0 mm. **Subject:** Mykolaiv, 220th Anniversary **Obv:** Sea gull, Varvarivskyi Bridge, ship, anchor. **Obv. Legend:** НАЦІОНАЛЬНИЈ БАНК УКРА?НИ - П'ЯТЬ ГРИВЕНЬ **Rev:** Frigate, Architectural monuments of Mykolaiv. **Rev. Legend:** МИКОЛА?В - РІК ЗАСНУВАННЯ/1789

Date	Mintage	F	VF	XF	Unc	BU
2009	35,000	—	—	—	—	8.00

KM# 548 5 HRYVEN
9.4000 g., Copper-Nickel, 28.0 mm. **Subject:** Council of Europe, 60th Anniversary **Obv:** Stars, map of Europe. **Obv. Legend:** НАЦІОНАЛЬНИЈ БАНК УКРА?НИ - П'ЯТЬ ГРИВЕНЬ **Rev:** Council of Europe logo, stars. **Rev. Legend:** COUNCIL OF EUROPE, CONSEIL DE EUROPE, РАДА ?ВРОПИ

Date	Mintage	F	VF	XF	Unc	BU
2009	45,000	—	—	—	—	8.00

KM# 549 5 HRYVEN
15.5500 g., 0.9990 Silver 0.4994 oz. ASW, 33.0 mm. **Subject:** Livi National Medical University, 225th Anniversary **Obv:** Initial lines of the Hippocratic Oath in Latin. **Obv. Legend:** НАЦІОНАЛЬНИЈ БАНК УКРАІНИ - 5/ГРИВНЬ **Rev:** University building. **Rev. Legend:** 225/РОКІВ - ІМЕНІ/ДАНИЛА/ГАЛИЦЬКОГО - ЛЬВІВСЬКИЈ НАЦІОНАЛЬНИЈ МЕДИЧНИЈ УНІВЕРСИТЕТ

Date	Mintage	F	VF	XF	Unc	BU
2009 Proof	7,000	Value: 35.00				

KM# 550 5 HRYVEN
Copper-Nickel **Subject:** National Shevchenko Museum

Date	Mintage	F	VF	XF	Unc	BU
2009	30,000	—	—	—	—	8.00

KM# 553 5 HRYVEN
Copper-Nickel **Subject:** Pysanka - Easter Egg Painting

Date	Mintage	F	VF	XF	Unc	BU
2009	50,000	—	—	—	—	8.00

KM# 555 5 HRYVEN
16.5000 g., Copper-Nickel, 35.0 mm. **Subject:** Bokorash **Obv:** Two birds, Carpathian landscape, trees, cottages, logs. **Obv. Legend:** НАЦІОНАЛЬНИЈ БАНК УКРА?НИ - 5/ГРИВЕНЬ/2009 **Rev:** Bokorash directing raft. **Rev. Legend:** БОКОРАШ

Date	Mintage	F	VF	XF	Unc	BU
2009	45,000	—	—	—	—	8.00

KM# 557 5 HRYVEN
16.5400 g., Copper-Nickel, 35.0 mm. **Subject:** International Year of Astronomy **Obv:** Urania, planets, stars, solar system. **Obv. Legend:** НАЦІОНАЛЬНИЈ БАНК УКРА?НИ - 5 ГРИВЕНЬ **Rev:** Yurii Drohobych, International Year of Astronomy logo, Astronomy artifacts. **Rev. Legend:** МІЖНАРОДНИЈ/РІК/АСТРОНОМІ?

Date	Mintage	F	VF	XF	Unc	BU
2009	45,000	—	—	—	—	8.00

KM# 515 10 HRYVNI
33.6220 g., 0.9250 Silver 0.9999 oz. ASW, 38.6 mm. **Subject:** The Annunciation **Edge:** Reeded

Date	Mintage	F	VF	XF	Unc	BU
2008 Proof	8,000	Value: 75.00				

KM# 113 10 HRYVEN
33.6220 g., 0.9250 Silver 0.9999 oz. ASW, 38.61 mm. **Subject:** Ivan Mazepa (Cossack leader) **Obv:** Arms with supporters within beaded circle **Rev:** Half figure divides beaded circle flanked by palace and oval shield **Edge:** Reeded

Date	Mintage	F	VF	XF	Unc	BU
2001 Proof	5,000	Value: 200				

KM# 114   10 HRYVEN
33.6220 g., 0.9250 Silver 0.9999 oz. ASW, 38.61 mm.
Subject: Yaroslav the Wise (Cossack leader) **Obv:** Value within
grape wreath **Rev:** Mosaic head facing, half length figure facing
holding scroll and dome building **Edge:** Reeded

Date	Mintage	F	VF	XF	Unc	BU
2001 Proof	3,000	Value: 1,300				

KM# 115   10 HRYVEN
33.6220 g., 0.9250 Silver 0.9999 oz. ASW, 38.61 mm. **Series:**
Ukranian Flora and Fauna **Obv:** National arms and date divides
wreath, value within **Rev:** Lynx with offspring **Edge:** Reeded

Date	Mintage	F	VF	XF	Unc	BU
2001 Proof	3,000	Value: 475				

KM# 130   10 HRYVEN
33.6220 g., 0.9250 Silver 0.9999 oz. ASW, 38.61 mm. **Subject:**
10th Anniversary - National Bank **Obv:** National arms and value
between arches **Rev:** Large building entrance **Edge:** Reeded

Date	Mintage	F	VF	XF	Unc	BU
2001 Proof	3,000	Value: 250				

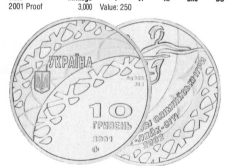

KM# 131   10 HRYVEN
33.6220 g., 0.9250 Silver 0.9999 oz. ASW, 38.61 mm.
Series: Olympics **Obv:** National arms and value on ice
Rev: Stylized ice dancing couple **Edge:** Reeded

Date	Mintage	F	VF	XF	Unc	BU
2001 Proof	15,000	Value: 60.00				

KM# 141   10 HRYVEN
33.6220 g., 0.9250 Silver 0.9999 oz. ASW, 38.61 mm. **Subject:**
Flora and Fauna **Obv:** National arm and date divides wreath,
value within **Rev:** Pine branch with cone **Edge:** Reeded

Date	Mintage	F	VF	XF	Unc	BU
2001 Proof	3,000	Value: 350				

KM# 142   10 HRYVEN
33.6220 g., 0.9250 Silver 0.9999 oz. ASW, 38.61 mm.
Subject: Khan Palace in Bakhchisarai **Obv:** Value in arch
Rev: Courtyard view **Edge:** Reeded

Date	Mintage	F	VF	XF	Unc	BU
2001 Proof	3,000	Value: 400				

KM# 143   10 HRYVEN
4.3110 g., 0.9000 Gold 0.1247 oz. AGW, 16 mm. **Subject:** 10
Years Independence **Obv:** National arms **Rev:** Parliament
building on map **Edge:** Plain

Date	Mintage	F	VF	XF	Unc	BU
2001 Proof	3,000	Value: 1,100				

KM# 165   10 HRYVEN
33.6220 g., 0.9250 Silver 0.9999 oz. ASW, 38.61 mm.
Subject: Olympics **Obv:** National arms and value on ice
Rev: Stylized hockey player **Edge:** Reeded

Date	Mintage	F	VF	XF	Unc	BU
2001 Proof	15,000	Value: 60.00				

KM# 229   10 HRYVEN
33.6220 g., 0.9250 Silver 0.9999 oz. ASW, 38.61 mm.
Obv: National arms and date divides wreath, value within
Rev: Eurasian Eagle Owl on branch **Edge:** Reeded

Date	Mintage	F	VF	XF	Unc	BU
2002 Proof	3,000	Value: 650				

KM# 145   10 HRYVEN
33.6220 g., 0.9250 Silver 0.9999 oz. ASW, 38.61 mm. **Subject:**
Ivan Sirko **Obv:** Arms with supporters within beaded circle **Rev:**
Cossack battle scene divides beaded circle **Edge:** Reeded

Date	Mintage	F	VF	XF	Unc	BU
2002 Proof	3,000	Value: 350				

KM# 146   10 HRYVEN
33.6220 g., 0.9250 Silver 0.9999 oz. ASW, 38.61 mm.
Obv: National arms and value on ice **Rev:** Stylized speed skater
Edge: Reeded

Date	Mintage	F	VF	XF	Unc	BU
2002 Proof	3,000	Value: 150				

KM# 160   10 HRYVEN
33.9500 g., 0.9250 Silver 1.0096 oz. ASW, 38.61 mm.
Obv: Value encircled by angels flanked by stars **Rev:** Steepled
church and tower **Edge:** Reeded

Date	Mintage	F	VF	XF	Unc	BU
2002 Proof	3,000	Value: 375				

KM# 161   10 HRYVEN
33.6220 g., 0.9250 Silver 0.9999 oz. ASW, 38.61 mm.
Subject: Grand Prince Vladimir Monomakh **Obv:** Value within
jewelry design **Rev:** Bust holding book flanked by buildings and
St. George **Edge:** Reeded

Date	Mintage	F	VF	XF	Unc	BU
2002 Proof	3,000	Value: 550				

KM# 162   10 HRYVEN
33.6220 g., 0.9250 Silver 0.9999 oz. ASW, 38.61 mm.
Subject: Prince Svyatoslav **Obv:** Value in ornate design
Rev: Armored half length figure facing **Edge:** Reeded

Date	Mintage	F	VF	XF	Unc	BU
2002 Proof	3,000	Value: 550				

KM# 164   10 HRYVEN
33.6220 g., 0.9250 Silver 0.9999 oz. ASW, 38.61 mm.
Subject: Christmas **Obv:** National arms within star above value
Rev: Christmas pageant scene **Edge:** Reeded

Date	Mintage	F	VF	XF	Unc	BU
ND(2002) Proof	3,000	Value: 600				

KM# 176 10 HRYVEN
33.6220 g., 0.9250 Silver 0.9999 oz. ASW, 38.61 mm.
Subject: Olympics **Obv:** Two ancient women with seedlings
Rev: Swimmer **Edge:** Reeded

Date	Mintage	F	VF	XF	Unc	BU
2002 Proof	15,000	Value: 60.00				

KM# 177 10 HRYVEN
33.6220 g., 0.9250 Silver 0.9999 oz. ASW, 38.61 mm.
Subject: Hetman Pylyp Orlik 1672-1742 **Obv:** Arms with
supporters within beaded circle **Rev:** Standing figure facing
holding scroll flanked by other standing figures **Edge:** Reeded

Date	Mintage	F	VF	XF	Unc	BU
2002 Proof	3,000	Value: 350				

KM# 198 10 HRYVEN
33.6220 g., 0.9250 Silver 0.9999 oz. ASW, 38.61 mm.
Obv: National arms and date divides wreath, value within
Rev: European bison **Edge:** Reeded

Date	Mintage	F	VF	XF	Unc	BU
2003 Proof	2,000	Value: 600				

KM# 189 10 HRYVEN
33.6220 g., 0.9250 Silver 0.9999 oz. ASW, 38.61 mm.
Subject: Olympics **Obv:** Two ancient women with seedlings
Rev: Boxer **Edge:** Reeded

Date	Mintage	F	VF	XF	Unc	BU
2003 Proof	15,000	Value: 60.00				

KM# 190 10 HRYVEN
33.6220 g., 0.9250 Silver 0.9999 oz. ASW, 38.61 mm.
Obv: Fancy art work and sculpture **Rev:** Livadia Palace view
Edge: Reeded

Date	Mintage	F	VF	XF	Unc	BU
2003 Proof	3,000	Value: 300				

KM# 191 10 HRYVEN
33.6220 g., 0.9250 Silver 0.9999 oz. ASW, 38.61 mm. **Obv:**
National arms on sun, flying geese divides beaded circle **Rev:**
Antonov AN-2 biplane divides beaded circle **Edge:** Reeded

Date	Mintage	F	VF	XF	Unc	BU
2003 Proof	3,000	Value: 320				

KM# 192 10 HRYVEN
33.6220 g., 0.9250 Silver 0.9999 oz. ASW, 38.61 mm.
Obv: Easter eggs around arms above value **Rev:** Easter
celebration **Edge:** Reeded

Date	Mintage	F	VF	XF	Unc	BU
2003 Proof	3,000	Value: 500				

KM# 193 10 HRYVEN
33.6220 g., 0.9250 Silver 0.9999 oz. ASW, 38.61 mm.
Obv: Angels, national arms and value **Rev:** The protection of the
Virgin Mary over the Pochayiv Monastery **Edge:** Reeded

Date	Mintage	F	VF	XF	Unc	BU
2003 Proof	Est. 8,000	Value: 150				

KM# 194 10 HRYVEN
33.6220 g., 0.9250 Silver 0.9999 oz. ASW, 38.61 mm.
Obv: National arms and date divide wreath, value within
Rev: Long-snouted seahorse **Edge:** Reeded

Date	Mintage	F	VF	XF	Unc	BU
2003 Proof	2,000	Value: 750				

KM# 195 10 HRYVEN
33.6220 g., 0.9250 Silver 0.9999 oz. ASW, 38.61 mm.
Subject: Kyrylo Rozumovskyi (Cossack leader) **Obv:** Arms with
supporters within beaded circle **Rev:** Half length figure 1/4 left
within beaded circle **Edge:** Reeded

Date	Mintage	F	VF	XF	Unc	BU
2003 Proof	3,000	Value: 350				

KM# 196 10 HRYVEN
33.6220 g., 0.9250 Silver 0.9999 oz. ASW, 38.61 mm.
Subject: Pavlo Polubotok (Cossack leader) **Obv:** Arms with
supporters within beaded circle **Rev:** Half length figure within
beaded circle **Edge:** Reeded

Date	Mintage	F	VF	XF	Unc	BU
2003 Proof	3,000	Value: 375				

KM# 197 10 HRYVEN
33.6220 g., 0.9250 Silver 0.9999 oz. ASW, 38.61 mm.
Obv: Map, national arms and value **Rev:** Genoese Fortress in
Sudak **Edge:** Reeded

Date	Mintage	F	VF	XF	Unc	BU
2003 Proof	3,000	Value: 300				

KM# 206 10 HRYVEN
33.9100 g., 0.9250 Silver 1.0084 oz. ASW, 38.61 mm. **Subject:**
Azov Dolphin **Obv:** National arms and date divides wreath, value
within **Rev:** Harbor Porpoises **Edge:** Reeded

Date	Mintage	F	VF	XF	Unc	BU
2004 Proof	8,000	Value: 120				

KM# 207 10 HRYVEN
33.9100 g., 0.9250 Silver 1.0084 oz. ASW, 38.61 mm.
Subject: Football World Cup - 2006 **Obv:** Soccer ball in net
Rev: Two soccer players **Edge:** Reeded

Date	Mintage	F	VF	XF	Unc	BU
2004 Proof	50,000	Value: 140				

KM# 223 10 HRYVEN
33.9100 g., 0.9250 Silver 1.0084 oz. ASW, 38.61 mm. **Obv:**
National arms on sun, flying geese and value divides beaded
circle **Rev:** AH-140 Airliner divides beaded circle **Edge:** Reeded

Date	Mintage	F	VF	XF	Unc	BU
2004 Proof	10,000	Value: 150				

KM# 224 10 HRYVEN
33.9100 g., 0.9250 Silver 1.0084 oz. ASW, 38.61 mm. **Subject:**
Ice Breaker "Captain Belousov" **Obv:** National arms on ship's
wheel and anchor **Rev:** Ice breaker ship **Edge:** Reeded

Date	Mintage	F	VF	XF	Unc	BU
2004 Proof	10,000			Value: 60.00		

KM# 225 10 HRYVEN
33.6220 g., 0.9250 Silver 0.9999 oz. ASW, 38.61 mm.
Subject: Whit Sunday **Obv:** National arms within wreath above
value flanked by sprigs **Rev:** Four women folk dancers and child
Edge: Reeded

Date	Mintage	F	VF	XF	Unc	BU
2004 Proof	10,000			Value: 250		

KM# 339 10 HRYVEN
33.6220 g., 0.9250 Silver 0.9999 oz. ASW, 38.61 mm.
Subject: Ostrozhsky Family **Obv:** Our Lady of Duben and Elias
Icon **Rev:** Three cameos above crowned shield **Edge:** Reeded

Date	Mintage	F	VF	XF	Unc	BU
2004 Proof	3,000			Value: 270		

KM# 340 10 HRYVEN
33.6220 g., 0.9250 Silver 0.9999 oz. ASW, 38.61 mm.
Subject: St. Yura Cathedral **Obv:** Statue of St. George on horse
killing dragon **Rev:** Cathedral **Edge:** Reeded

Date	Mintage	F	VF	XF	Unc	BU
ND (2004) Proof	8,000			Value: 80.00		

KM# 342 10 HRYVEN
33.6220 g., 0.9250 Silver 0.9999 oz. ASW, 38.61 mm. **Subject:**
Defense of Sevastopol 1854-56 **Obv:** National arms and value
above fortifications map **Rev:** Cannon and ships **Edge:** Reeded

Date	Mintage	F	VF	XF	Unc	BU
2004 Proof	10,000			Value: 90.00		

KM# 343 10 HRYVEN
33.6220 g., 0.9250 Silver 0.9999 oz. ASW, 38.61 mm.
Subject: Perejaslav Cossack Rada of 1654 **Obv:** National arms
above value **Rev:** Standing figures facing **Edge:** Reeded

Date	Mintage	F	VF	XF	Unc	BU
2004 Proof	8,000			Value: 125		

KM# 358 10 HRYVEN
33.6220 g., 0.9250 Silver 0.9999 oz. ASW, 38.61 mm. **Subject:**
Spalax Arenarius Reshetnik **Obv:** National arms and date divides
wreath, value within **Rev:** Sandy mole rat **Edge:** Reeded

Date	Mintage	F	VF	XF	Unc	BU
2005 Proof	8,000			Value: 100		

KM# 367 10 HRYVEN
33.6220 g., 0.9250 Silver 0.9999 oz. ASW, 38.61 mm.
Subject: The Protection of the Virgin **Obv:** National arms on
Cossack regalia **Rev:** Wedding scene **Edge:** Reeded

Date	Mintage	F	VF	XF	Unc	BU
2005 Proof	8,000			Value: 140		

KM# 370 10 HRYVEN
33.6220 g., 0.9250 Silver 0.9999 oz. ASW, 38.61 mm. **Subject:**
60 Years UN Membership **Obv:** National arms, value and olive
branch **Rev:** UN logo above partial globe **Edge:** Reeded

Date	Mintage	F	VF	XF	Unc	BU
2005 Proof	5,000			Value: 55.00		

KM# 371 10 HRYVEN
33.6220 g., 0.9250 Silver 0.9999 oz. ASW, 38.61 mm. **Subject:**
National Anthem **Obv:** Musical score, national arms,
value and date **Rev:** Coiled legend around holographic flower
Edge: Reeded

Date	Mintage	F	VF	XF	Unc	BU
2005 Proof	3,000			Value: 200		

KM# 372 10 HRYVEN
33.6220 g., 0.9250 Silver 0.9999 oz. ASW, 38.61 mm.
Subject: 100 Years of Olha Kobylianska Music and Drama
Theatre in Chernivtsi **Obv:** Statue **Rev:** Theater **Edge:** Reeded

Date	Mintage	F	VF	XF	Unc	BU
2005 Proof	5,000			Value: 75.00		

KM# 373 10 HRYVEN
33.6220 g., 0.9250 Silver 0.9999 oz. ASW, 38.61 mm. **Subject:**
Sviatohirsky Lavra Monastery **Obv:** Madonna and child flanked
by angels **Rev:** Monastery on river bank **Edge:** Reeded

Date	Mintage	F	VF	XF	Unc	BU
2005 Proof	8,000			Value: 100		

KM# 381 10 HRYVEN
33.8600 g., 0.9250 Silver 1.0069 oz. ASW, 38.61 mm.
Subject: Baturyn Hetman Capital City **Obv:** National arms within
sun rays, value flanked by standing figures **Rev:** Four cameos
and banner above city view **Edge:** Reeded

Date	Mintage	F	VF	XF	Unc	BU
2005 Proof	5,000			Value: 100		

KM# 382 10 HRYVEN
33.8600 g., 0.9250 Silver 1.0069 oz. ASW, 38.61 mm.
Subject: Symyrenko Family **Obv:** Country name below national
arms within sprigs **Rev:** Family tree **Edge:** Reeded

Date	Mintage	F	VF	XF	Unc	BU
2005 Proof	5,000			Value: 55.00		

KM# 392   10 HRYVEN
33.6220 g., 0.9250 Silver 0.9999 oz. ASW, 38.61 mm.
Obv: National arms above value in wreath **Rev:** Grasshopper
Edge: Reeded

Date	Mintage	F	VF	XF	Unc	BU
2006 Proof	8,000	Value: 120				

KM# 424   10 HRYVEN
33.6221 g., 0.9250 Silver 0.9999 oz. ASW, 38.61 mm.
Subject: Chyhyryn **Obv:** National arms

Date	Mintage	F	VF	XF	Unc	BU
2006 Proof	5,000	Value: 110				

KM# 425   10 HRYVEN
33.6220 g., 0.9250 Silver 0.9999 oz. ASW, 38.61 mm.
Subject: 10 Years of the Clearing House **Obv:** National arms

Date	Mintage	F	VF	XF	Unc	BU
2006 Proof	5,000	Value: 65.00				

KM# 410   10 HRYVEN
33.6220 g., 0.9250 Silver 0.9999 oz. ASW, 38.61 mm. **Subject:**
10 Years of the Constitution of Ukraine **Obv:** National arms

Date	Mintage	F	VF	XF	Unc	BU
2006 Proof	5,000	Value: 80.00				

KM# 421   10 HRYVEN
33.6200 g., 0.9250 Silver 0.9998 oz. ASW, 38.61 mm.
Subject: Epiphany **Obv:** National arms **Edge:** Reeded

Date	Mintage	F	VF	XF	Unc	BU
2006 Proof	10,000	Value: 110				

KM# 423   10 HRYVEN
33.6220 g., 0.9250 Silver 0.9999 oz. ASW, 38.61 mm.
Subject: Saint Kyryl Church **Obv:** National arms **Edge:** Reeded

Date	Mintage	F	VF	XF	Unc	BU
2006 Proof	8,000	Value: 95.00				

KM# 427   10 HRYVEN
33.6220 g., 0.9250 Silver 0.9999 oz. ASW, 38.61 mm.
Subject: Twentieth Winter Olympic Games of 2006
Obv: National arms

Date	Mintage	F	VF	XF	Unc	BU
2006 Proof	5,000	Value: 60.00				

KM# 466   10 HRYVEN
33.6220 g., 0.9250 Silver 0.9999 oz. ASW, 38.6 mm.
Subject: Odessa National Opera and Ballet, 120th Anniversary
Obv: Interior view from stage **Rev:** Opera house in Odessa
Edge: Reeded

Date	Mintage	F	VF	XF	Unc	BU
2007 Proof	5,000	Value: 60.00				

KM# 467   10 HRYVEN
33.6220 g., 0.9250 Silver 0.9999 oz. ASW, 38.61 mm.
Subject: Ivan Bohun **Edge:** Reeded

Date	Mintage	F	VF	XF	Unc	BU
2007 Proof	5,000	Value: 90.00				

KM# 516   10 HRYVEN
33.6220 g., 0.9250 Silver 0.9999 oz. ASW, 38.61 mm.
Subject: Black Griffin **Edge:** Reeded

Date	Mintage	F	VF	XF	Unc	BU
2008 Proof	7,000	Value: 85.00				

KM# 517   10 HRYVEN
33.6220 g., Silver, 38.61 mm. **Subject:** Sevastopol, 225th
Anniversary **Edge:** Reeded

Date	Mintage	F	VF	XF	Unc	BU
2008 Proof	5,000	Value: 100				

KM# 518   10 HRYVEN
33.6220 g., 0.9250 Silver 0.9999 oz. ASW, 38.61 mm.
Subject: Swallow's Nest **Edge:** Reeded

Date	Mintage	F	VF	XF	Unc	BU
2008 Proof	5,000	Value: 90.00				

KM# 519   10 HRYVEN
33.6220 g., 0.9250 Silver 0.9999 oz. ASW, 38.61 mm.
Subject: Tereschenko Family **Edge:** Reeded

Date	Mintage	F	VF	XF	Unc	BU
2008 Proof	7,000	Value: 60.00				

KM# 520   10 HRYVEN
33622.0000 g., 0.9250 Silver 999.85 oz. ASW, 38.61 mm.
Subject: Ukranian Swedish Alliances XVII-XVIII Century

Date	Mintage	F	VF	XF	Unc	BU
2008 Proof	5,000	Value: 75.00				

KM# 521   10 HRYVEN
33.6220 g., 0.9250 Silver 0.9999 oz. ASW, 38.61 mm.
Subject: Hlukhiv

Date	Mintage	F	VF	XF	Unc	BU
2008 Proof	7,000	Value: 65.00				

KM# 522   10 HRYVEN
33.6220 g., 0.9250 Silver 0.9999 oz. ASW, 38.61 mm.
Subject: UNESCO World Heritage Site - LVIV

Date	Mintage	F	VF	XF	Unc	BU
2008 Proof	5,000	Value: 90.00				

KM# 523   10 HRYVEN
33.6220 g., 0.9250 Silver 0.9999 oz. ASW, 38.61 mm.
Subject: Cathedral in Buky Village

Date	Mintage	F	VF	XF	Unc	BU
2008 Proof	5,000	Value: 85.00				

KM# 532   10 HRYVEN
31.1050 g., 0.9990 Silver 0.9990 oz. ASW, 38.61 mm. **Subject:**
Annunciation **Obv:** Conventionalized setting of the Gospel, lilies.
Obv. Legend: НАЦІОНАЛЬНИЈ БАНК УКРАЇНИ - 10 ГРИВЕНЬ
Rev: Annunciation scene. **Rev. Legend:** БЛАГОВІЩЕННЯ

Date	Mintage	F	VF	XF	Unc	BU
2008 Proof	8,000	Value: 55.00				

KM# 556   10 HRYVEN
31.1050 g., 0.9990 Silver 0.9990 oz. ASW, 38.61 mm.
Subject: Bokorash **Obv:** Two birds, Carpathian landscape, trees, cottages, logs. **Obv. Legend:** НАЦІОНАЛЬНИЙ БАНК УКРАЇНИ - 10/ГРИВЕНЬ/2009 **Rev:** Bokorash directing raft.
Rev. Legend: БОКОРАШ

Date	Mintage	F	VF	XF	Unc	BU
2009 Proof	10,000	Value: 50.00				

KM# 559   10 HRYVEN
31.1050 g., 0.9990 Silver 0.9990 oz. ASW, 38.61 mm.
Subject: Surb Khach Monastery **Obv:** Cross-stone.
Obv. Legend: НАЦІОНАЛЬНИЙ БАНК УКРАЇНИ - ДЕСЯТЬ ГРИВЕНЬ **Rev:** Monastery buildings. **Rev. Legend:** СТАРИЙ КРИМ - ВІРМЕНСЬКИЙ МОНАСТИР XIV СТ. - СУРБ ХАЧ

Date	Mintage	F	VF	XF	Unc	BU
2009	10,000	Value: 45.00				

KM# 560   10 HRYVEN
31.1050 g., 0.9990 Silver 0.9990 oz. ASW, 38.61 mm. **Subject:** Konotop Battle, 350th Anniversary **Obv:** Hetman Insignia, Cossack arms, bandura. **Obv. Legend:** НАЦІОНАЛЬНИЙ БАНК УКРАЇНИ - 10/ГРИВНЬ **Rev:** Ivan Vyhovskyi, Cossacks, Konotop fortifications, banners. **Rev. Legend:** ПЕРЕМОГА В КОНОТОПСЬКІЙ БИТВІ - 350 РОКІВ

Date	Mintage	F	VF	XF	Unc	BU
2009 Proof	8,000	Value: 55.00				

KM# 561   10 HRYVEN
31.1050 g., 0.9990 Silver 0.9990 oz. ASW **Subject:** Church of the Holy Spirit in Rogatyn

Date	Mintage	F	VF	XF	Unc	BU
2009 Proof	10,000	Value: 50.00				

KM# 562   10 HRYVEN
31.1050 g., 0.9990 Silver 0.9990 oz. ASW **Subject:** Halahan Family

Date	Mintage	F	VF	XF	Unc	BU
2009 Proof	7,000	Value: 60.00				

KM# 563   10 HRYVEN
31.1050 g., 0.9990 Silver 0.9990 oz. ASW, 38.61 mm.
Subject: Kiev Academy of Operatta Theater, 75th Anniversary **Obv:** Dancers, light beams. **Obv. Legend:** НАЦІОНАЛЬНИЙ БАНК УКРАЇНИ - 10/ГРИВНЬ/2009 **Rev:** Theater building, operetta character silhouettes. **Rev. Legend:** КИЇВСЬКИЙ АКАДЕМІЧНИЙ ТЕАТР ОПЕРЕТИ - 75/РОКІВ

Date	Mintage	F	VF	XF	Unc	BU
2009 Proof	5,000	Value: 65.00				

KM# 144   20 HRYVEN
67.2400 g., 0.9250 Silver 1.9996 oz. ASW, 50 mm. **Subject:** 10 Years Independence **Obv:** National arms **Rev:** Parliament building on map within beaded circle **Edge:** Segmented reeding

Date	Mintage	F	VF	XF	Unc	BU
2001 Proof	1,000	Value: 4,000				

KM# 174   20 HRYVEN
14.7000 g., Bi-Metallic .916 Gold center in .925 silver ring, 31 mm. **Subject:** "Kyiv Rus" Culture **Obv:** Old arms of Ukraine, Prince and a cathedral model in his hand and princess **Rev:** Old Rus earring **Edge:** Reeded and plain sections

Date	Mintage	F	VF	XF	Unc	BU
2001 Proof	2,000	Value: 1,000				

KM# 175   20 HRYVEN
14.7000 g., Bi-Metallic .916 Gold center in .925 Silver ring, 31 mm. **Subject:** Scythian Culture **Obv:** Warrior with a bowl in his hand and to the right, a Queen of Scythia **Rev:** Stylized horse flanked by pagasists **Edge:** Reeded and plain sections

Date	Mintage	F	VF	XF	Unc	BU
2001 Proof	2,000	Value: 1,200				

KM# 153   20 HRYVEN
67.2400 g., 0.9250 Silver 1.9996 oz. ASW, 50 mm.
Obv: National arms on sun and flying geese divides beaded circle **Rev:** "AN-225 Mrija" cargo jet divides beaded circle **Edge:** Reeded and plain sections

Date	Mintage	F	VF	XF	Unc	BU
2002 Proof	2,002	Value: 1,000				

KM# 188   20 HRYVEN
67.2400 g., 0.9250 Silver 1.9996 oz. ASW, 50 mm. **Subject:** 60th Anniversary - Liberation of Kiev **Obv:** Eternal flame monument **Rev:** Map and battle scene **Edge:** Segmented reeding

Date	Mintage	F	VF	XF	Unc	BU
2003 Proof	2,000	Value: 350				

KM# 226   20 HRYVEN
67.2440 g., 0.9250 Silver 1.9997 oz. ASW, 50 mm.
Subject: "Our Souls Do Not Die" **Obv:** National arms above value **Rev:** Bust of Taras Shevchenko facing flanked by standing figures **Edge:** Segmented reeding

Date	Mintage	F	VF	XF	Unc	BU
2004 Proof	4,000	Value: 250				

KM# 344   20 HRYVEN
67.2440 g., 0.9250 Silver 1.9997 oz. ASW, 50 mm.
Subject: 2006 Olympic Games **Obv:** Woman holding flame and branch **Rev:** Six athletes around flame within square design
Edge: Segmented reeding

Date	Mintage	F	VF	XF	Unc	BU
2004 Proof	5,000	Value: 100,000				

KM# 363   20 HRYVEN
67.2440 g., 0.9250 Silver 1.9997 oz. ASW, 50 mm.
Obv: National arms on sun with flying geese divides beaded circle **Rev:** AN-124 jet plane divides beaded circle **Edge:** Segmented reeding

Date	Mintage	F	VF	XF	Unc	BU
2005 Proof	5,000	Value: 150				

KM# 369   20 HRYVEN
67.2440 g., 0.9250 Silver 1.9997 oz. ASW, 50 mm.
Subject: Sorochynsky Fair **Obv:** Busts facing each other flanked by flower sprigs **Rev:** Farmer leading family in ox cart
Edge: Segmented reeding

Date	Mintage	F	VF	XF	Unc	BU
2005 Proof	5,000	Value: 200				

KM# 374   20 HRYVEN
67.2440 g., 0.9250 Silver 1.9997 oz. ASW, 50 mm.
Subject: 60th Anniversary of Victory in WWII **Obv:** Flying cranes divides value, date and national arms **Rev:** V-shaped searchlight beams filled with soldiers, order of the Patriotic War at bottom left **Edge:** Segmented reeding

Date	Mintage	F	VF	XF	Unc	BU
2005 Proof	5,000	Value: 100				

KM# 412   20 HRYVEN
67.2500 g., 0.9250 Silver 1.9999 oz. ASW, 50 mm. **Subject:** 15 Years of Ukraine Independency **Obv:** National arms

Date	Mintage	F	VF	XF	Unc	BU
2006 Proof	7,000	Value: 150				

KM# 468   20 HRYVEN
14.2300 g., Bi-Metallic Center in silver ring, 31 mm.
Subject: Pure water is source of life **Obv:** Drop of water in pond
Rev: Man taking drink from waterfall

Date	Mintage	F	VF	XF	Unc	BU
2007 Proof	5,000	Value: 480				

KM# 469   20 HRYVEN
67.2500 g., 0.9250 Silver 1.9999 oz. ASW, 50 mm.
Subject: Chumaky's Way **Obv:** Hologram wheel at center of fiery
spiral **Rev:** Merchant's carts under night sky

Date	Mintage	F	VF	XF	Unc	BU
2007 Proof	5,000	Value: 330				

KM# 470   20 HRYVEN
67.2500 g., 0.9250 Silver 1.9999 oz. ASW, 50 mm.
Subject: The Famine, Genocide of the Ukranina People
Obv: Girl standing on fallow ground, small green plant at left
Rev: Swan at center of cross, candles in background

Date	Mintage	F	VF	XF	Unc	BU
2007 Antique finish	10,000	—	—	—	100	—

KM# 524   20 HRYVEN
67.2500 g., 0.9250 Silver 1.9999 oz. ASW, 50 mm.
Subject: Kyiv, 1000th Anniversary of minting

Date	Mintage	F	VF	XF	Unc	BU
2008 Proof	5,000	Value: 150				

KM# 552   20 HRYVEN
62.2100 g., 0.9990 Silver 1.9980 oz. ASW, 50.0 mm.
Subject: 70th Anniversary Carpathian Ukraine **Obv:** Carpets.
Obv. Legend: НАЦІОНАЛЬНИЈ БАНК УКРАЇНИ - 20/ГРИВНЬ
Rev. Transcarpathian holding flag. **Rev. Legend:** 70/РОКІВ -
ПРОГОЛОШЕННЯ КАРПАТСЬКОЇ УКРАЇНИ

Date	Mintage	F	VF	XF	Unc	BU
2009 Proof	3,000	Value: 85.00				

KM# 554   20 HRYVEN
62.2100 g., 0.9990 Silver 1.9980 oz. ASW **Subject:** Pysanka -
Easter Egg painting

Date	Mintage	F	VF	XF	Unc	BU
2009 Proof	8,000	Value: 80.00				

KM# 426   50 HRYVEN
17.6300 g., 0.9000 Gold 0.5101 oz. AGW, 25 mm.
Subject: Nestor - The Chronicler **Obv:** National arms

Date	Mintage	F	VF	XF	Unc	BU
2006 Proof	5,000	Value: 1,000				

KM# 525   50 HRYVEN
17.6300 g., 0.9000 Gold 0.5101 oz. AGW, 25 mm.
Subject: Swallow's Nest Castle

Date	Mintage	F	VF	XF	Unc	BU
2008 Proof	4,000	Value: 1,000				

KM# 526   50 HRYVEN
500.0000 g., 0.9999 Silver 16.073 oz. ASW **Subject:** Visit of
Ecumenical Patriarch Bartholomew I

Date	Mintage	F	VF	XF	Unc	BU
2008 Proof	1,000	Value: 2,200				

KM# 564   50 HRYVEN
500.0000 g., 0.9990 Silver 16.058 oz. ASW **Subject:** Gogol's
Evenings on a farm

Date	Mintage	F	VF	XF	Unc	BU
2009 Proof	1,500	Value: 2,000				

KM# 199   100 HRYVEN
31.1000 g., 0.9000 Gold 0.8999 oz. AGW, 32 mm.
Subject: Ancient Scythian Culture **Obv:** National arms above
ornamental design and value within rope wreath **Rev:** Ancient
craftsmen and jewelry **Edge:** Reeded

Date	Mintage	F	VF	XF	Unc	BU
2003 Proof	1,500	Value: 7,500				

KM# 345   100 HRYVEN
34.5594 g., 0.9000 Gold 100000 oz. AGW, 32 mm.
Subject: The Golden Gate **Obv:** National arms above value
between two stylized cranes **Rev:** Riders approaching castle gate
Edge: Segmented reeding

Date	Mintage	F	VF	XF	Unc	BU
2004 Proof	2,000	Value: 5,000				

KM# 414   100 HRYVEN
1000.0000 g., 0.9990 Silver 32.117 oz. ASW, 100 mm.
Subject: 10 Years to the Currency Reform in Ukraine
Obv: National arms **Note:** Illustration reduced.

Date	Mintage	Good	VG	F	VF	XF
2006 Proof	1,501	Value: 6,500				

KM# 471   100 HRYVEN
31.1000 g., 0.9000 Gold 0.8999 oz. AGW, 32 mm. **Subject:** The
Ostroh Bible **Obv:** Part of illumination on page **Rev:** Ivan Fedorov
and Kostiantyn of Ostroth holding open bible

Date	Mintage	F	VF	XF	Unc	BU
2007 Proof	4,000	Value: 2,000				

KM# 527   100 HRYVEN
1000.0000 g., 0.9990 Silver 32.117 oz. ASW **Subject:** Kievan
Rus

Date	Mintage	F	VF	XF	Unc	BU
2008 Proof	800	Value: 4,500				

KM# 558   100 HRYVEN
1000.0000 g., 0.9990 Silver 32.117 oz. ASW, 100.0 mm.
Subject: International Year of Astronomy **Obv:** Solar System,
armillary sphere, stars. **Obv. Legend:** НАЦІОНАЛЬНИЈ БАНК
УКРАЇНИ-100/ГРИВНЬ **Rev:** Galileo, stars, telescope, galaxies,
observatory, Saturn (as the letter O). **Rev. Legend:**
МІЖНАРОДНИЈ РІК АСТРОНОМІІ

Date	Mintage	F	VF	XF	Unc	BU
2009 Proof	700	Value: 4,000				

KM# 565   100 HRYVEN
31.1050 g., 0.9990 Gold 0.9990 oz. AGW **Subject:** Hersones
Tavrijsky

Date	Mintage	F	VF	XF	Unc	BU
2009 Proof	3,000	Value: 2,250				

MINT SETS

KM#	Date	Mintage	Identification	Issue Price	Mkt Val
MS2	2001 (8)	5,000	KM#1.1b, 2.1b, 3.3b, 4b, 6, 7, 8b, 129	—	60.00
MS3	2006 (8)	5,000	KM#1.1b, 2.1b, 3.3b, 4b, 6, 7, 8b, 411	—	25.00
MS4	2008 (7)	5,000	KM#1.1b, 2.1b, 3.3b, 4b, 6, 7, 209, prooflike	—	40.00

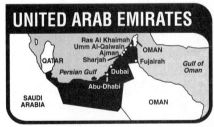

The seven United Arab Emirates (formerly known as the Trucial Sheikhdoms or States), located along the southern shore of
the Persian Gulf, are comprised of the Sheikhdoms of Abu Dhabi,
Dubai, al-Sharjah, Ajman, Umm al Qaiwain, Ras al-Khaimah and
al-Fujairah. They have a combined area of about 32,000 sq. mi.
(83,600 sq. km.) and a population of *2.1 million. Capital: Abu
Zaby (Abu Dhabi). Since the oil strikes of 1958-60, the economy
has centered about petroleum.

TITLES

الامارات العربية المتحدة

al-Imara(t) al-Arabiya(t) al-Muttahida(t)

UNITED EMIRATES
STANDARD COINAGE

KM# 2.2   5 FILS
Bronze **Series:** F.A.O. **Obv:** Value **Rev:** Fish above dates
Rev. Designer: Geoffrey Colley **Note:** Reduced size.

Date	Mintage	F	VF	XF	Unc	BU
AH1422-2001	—	—	0.10	0.15	0.30	1.00

KM# 3.2   10 FILS

Bronze, 19 mm. **Obv:** Value **Rev:** Arab dhow above dates
Rev. Designer: Geoffrey Colley **Note:** Reduced size.

Date	Mintage	F	VF	XF	Unc	BU
AH1422-2001 (2001)	—		0.20	0.35	0.80	1.20
AH1425-2005 (2005)			0.20	0.35	0.80	1.20

KM# 4   25 FILS

3.5000 g., Copper-Nickel, 20 mm. **Obv:** Value **Rev:** Gazelle
above dates **Rev. Designer:** Geoffrey Colley

Date	Mintage	F	VF	XF	Unc	BU
AH1425-2005	—		0.20	0.40	0.75	1.00

KM# 16   50 FILS

4.3000 g., Copper-Nickel, 21 mm. **Obv:** Value **Rev:** Oil derricks
above dates **Rev. Designer:** Geoffrey Colley **Shape:** 7-sided
Note: Reduced size.

Date	Mintage	F	VF	XF	Unc	BU
AH1425-2005	—		0.25	0.45	1.35	1.85

KM# 49   DIRHAM

6.4000 g., Copper-Nickel, 24 mm. **Subject:** 25th Anniversary -
Armed Forces Unification **Obv:** Value **Rev:** Heraldic eagle within
rope wreath **Edge:** Reeded

Date	Mintage	F	VF	XF	Unc	BU
ND(2001) (2001)	250,000	—	—	—	3.50	5.00

KM# 51   DIRHAM

6.3300 g., Copper-Nickel, 24 mm. **Subject:** 50 Years of Formal
Education **Obv:** Value **Rev:** Symbolic design **Edge:** Reeded

Date	Mintage	F	VF	XF	Unc	BU
ND (2003)	—	—	—	—	3.50	5.00

KM# 52   DIRHAM

6.4000 g., Copper-Nickel, 24 mm. **Subject:** Abu Dhabi National
Bank 35th Anniversary **Obv:** Value **Rev:** Bank building tower
divide dates within circle **Edge:** Reeded

Date	Mintage	F	VF	XF	Unc	BU
ND (2003)	—	—	—	—	3.50	4.00

KM# 54   DIRHAM

6.4000 g., Copper-Nickel, 24 mm. **Subject:** 40th Anniversary
of Crude Oil Exports **Obv:** Value **Rev:** "ADCO" logo
Edge: Reeded

Date	Mintage	F	VF	XF	Unc	BU
ND (2003)	—	—	—	—	3.50	5.00

KM# 73   DIRHAM

6.4000 g., Copper-Nickel, 23.93 mm. **Subject:** WBG & IMF
meeting in Dubai 2003 **Obv:** Denomination **Rev:** Mosaic arc
Edge: Reeded

Date	Mintage	F	VF	XF	Unc	BU
2003	250,000	—	—	—	4.00	5.00

KM# 74   DIRHAM

6.4000 g., Copper-Nickel, 24 mm. **Subject:** First Gulf Bank 25th
Anniversary **Obv:** Value **Rev:** Bank logo **Edge:** Reeded

Date	Mintage	F	VF	XF	Unc	BU
ND(2004)	—	—	—	—	4.00	5.00

KM# 6.2   DIRHAM

6.4000 g., Copper-Nickel, 24 mm. **Obv:** Value **Rev:** Jug above
dates **Rev. Designer:** Geoffrey Colley **Edge:** Reeded
Note: Reduced size.

Date	Mintage	F	VF	XF	Unc	BU
AH1425-2005	—		0.35	0.65	1.85	2.25
AH1428-2007	—		0.35	0.65	1.85	2.25

KM# 96   DIRHAM

6.4000 g., Copper-Nickel, 24 mm. **Subject:** U.A.E. Boy Scouts,
50th Anniversary **Obv:** Value at center **Rev:** Scout Fleur-de-lis

Date	Mintage	F	VF	XF	Unc	BU
ND(2007)	—	—	—	—	3.50	5.00

KM# 84   DIRHAM

6.4000 g., Copper-Nickel, 24 mm. **Subject:** 10th Anniversary
of the Hamdan Bin Rashed Award for Distinguished Academic
Performance **Obv:** Large value **Rev:** 10 below pen with tip
touching star **Edge:** Reeded

Date	Mintage	F	VF	XF	Unc	BU
ND(2007)	—	—	—	—	4.00	5.00

KM# 77   DIRHAM

6.3300 g., Copper-Nickel, 24 mm. **Obv:** Value **Rev:** Zakum
Development Co. logo **Edge:** Reeded

Date	Mintage	F	VF	XF	Unc	BU
ND(2007)	—	—	—	—	3.50	5.00

KM# 76   DIRHAM

6.4000 g., Copper-Nickel, 24 mm. **Subject:** Sharjah
International Airport, 75th Anniversary **Obv:** Value **Obv. Legend:**
UNITED ARAB EMIRATES **Rev:** Three birds in flight under arc
Edge: Reeded

Date	Mintage	F	VF	XF	Unc	BU
ND(2007)	—	—	—	—	3.00	4.00

KM# 78   DIRHAM

6.4000 g., Copper-Nickel, 24 mm. **Obv:** Value **Obv. Legend:**
UNITED ARAB EMIRATES **Rev:** Large "50" with Police badge
in "0" **Rev. Legend:** DUABI POLICE GOLDEN JUBILEE
Edge: Reeded

Date	Mintage	F	VF	XF	Unc	BU
ND(2007)	—	—	—	—	3.50	5.00

KM# 79   DIRHAM

6.4300 g., Copper-Nickel, 24.03 mm. **Obv:** Value **Obv. Legend:**
UNITED ARAB EMIRATES **Rev:** Large "30" and logo
Rev. Legend: 30TH ANNIVERSARY OF THE 1ST LNG
SHIPMENT **Rev. Inscription:** ADGAS **Edge:** Reeded

Date	Mintage	F	VF	XF	Unc	BU
ND(2007)	—	—	—	—	3.50	5.00

KM# 85   DIRHAM

6.4000 g., Copper-Nickel **Subject:** National Bank of Abu Dhabi,
40th Anniversary **Obv:** Large value **Obv. Legend:** UNITED
ARAB EMIRATES **Rev:** Large stylized "40" **Edge:** Reeded

Date	Mintage	F	VF	XF	Unc	BU
ND(2008)	—	—	—	—	3.00	4.00

KM# 47   50 DIRHAMS

40.2200 g., 0.9250 Silver 1.1961 oz. ASW, 40 mm.
Subject: 25th Anniversary - Women's Union (1975-2000)
Obv: Bust of President H. H. Sheikh Zayed bin Sultan Al Nahyan
7/8 right **Rev:** Stylized gazelle **Edge:** Reeded

Date	Mintage	F	VF	XF	Unc	BU
ND(2001) Proof	5,000	Value: 75.00				

KM# 59   50 DIRHAMS

40.0000 g., 0.9250 Silver 1.1895 oz. ASW, 40 mm.
Subject: 25th Anniversary - Arab Bank of Investment and
Foreign Trade **Edge:** Reeded

Date	Mintage	F	VF	XF	Unc	BU
ND(2001) Proof	2,000	Value: 95.00				

KM# 60   50 DIRHAMS

40.0000 g., 0.9250 Silver 1.1895 oz. ASW, 40 mm.
Subject: 25th Anniversary - Armed Forces Unification
Edge: Reeded

Date	Mintage	F	VF	XF	Unc	BU
ND(2001) Proof	10,000	Value: 70.00				

KM# 61   50 DIRHAMS

40.0000 g., 0.9250 Silver 1.1895 oz. ASW, 40 mm.
Subject: 30th Anniversary - Al-Ain National Museum
Edge: Reeded

Date	Mintage	F	VF	XF	Unc	BU
ND(2002) Proof	5,000	Value: 80.00				

KM# 62   50 DIRHAMS

40.0000 g., 0.9250 Silver 1.1895 oz. ASW, 40 mm.
Subject: 25th Anniversary - University of the U.A.E. **Obv:** Bust
of President H. H. Sheikh Zayed bin Sultan Al Nahyan 7/8 right
Rev: Inscriptions **Edge:** Reeded

Date	Mintage	F	VF	XF	Unc	BU
ND(2002) Proof	5,000	Value: 80.00				

KM# 63   50 DIRHAMS

40.0000 g., 0.9250 Silver 1.1895 oz. ASW, 40 mm.
Subject: Etisalat - Emirates Telecommunications, 25th
Anniversary **Obv:** Value **Rev:** Stylized 25 **Edge:** Reeded

Date	Mintage	F	VF	XF	Unc	BU
ND(2002) Proof	5,000	Value: 80.00				

KM# 64   50 DIRHAMS

40.0000 g., 0.9250 Silver 1.1895 oz. ASW, 40 mm.
Subject: Sheikh Hamdan bin Rashid al Maktoum Award for
Medical Sciences **Obv:** Value **Rev:** Sheikh Hamdan bin Rashid
al Maktoum bust 3/4 left **Edge:** Reeded

Date	Mintage	F	VF	XF	Unc	BU
ND(2002) Proof	2,000	Value: 95.00				

KM# 65   50 DIRHAMS

40.0000 g., 0.9250 Silver 1.1895 oz. ASW, 40 mm. **Subject:** Al
Ahmadia School, 90th Anniversary **Obv:** Sheikh Rashid bin
Saaed al Maktoum 3/4 left **Rev:** School building **Edge:** Reeded

Date	Mintage	F	VF	XF	Unc	BU
ND(2002) Proof	5,000	Value: 80.00				

KM# 67   50 DIRHAMS

40.0000 g., 0.9250 Silver 1.1895 oz. ASW, 40 mm.
Subject: Administrative Development Institute, 20th Anniversary
Obv: Sheikh Zayed bin Sultan al Nahyan bust 3/4 right
Rev: Eagle **Edge:** Reeded

Date	Mintage	F	VF	XF	Unc	BU
ND(2002) Proof	2,000	Value: 95.00				

KM# 68   50 DIRHAMS

40.0000 g., 0.9250 Silver 1.1895 oz. ASW, 40 mm.
Subject: U.A.E. Central Bank, 30th Anniversary **Obv:** Sheikh
Zayed bin Sultan al Nahyan bust 3/4 right **Rev:** Sheikh Maktoum
bin Rashid al Maktoum bust 3/4 right **Edge:** Reeded

Date	Mintage	F	VF	XF	Unc	BU
ND(2003) Proof	5,000	Value: 80.00				

KM# 69   50 DIRHAMS

40.0000 g., 0.9250 Silver 1.1895 oz. ASW, 40 mm.
Subject: 58th Annual Meeting of the World Bank Group and the Int'l Money Fund **Obv:** Colored dots **Edge:** Reeded

Date	Mintage	F	VF	XF	Unc	BU
ND(2003) Proof	10,000	Value: 70.00				

KM# 50   50 DIRHAMS

40.0000 g., 0.9250 Silver 1.1895 oz. ASW, 40 mm. **Obv:** Value
Rev: FIFA 2003 World Youth Soccer Championship
Edge: Reeded

Date	Mintage	F	VF	XF	Unc	BU
ND(2003) Proof	—	Value: 80.00				

KM# 66   50 DIRHAMS

40.0000 g., 0.9250 Silver 1.1895 oz. ASW, 40 mm.
Subject: Ministry of Finance and Industry ISO Certification
Obv: Value **Rev:** Eagle at center **Edge:** Reeded

Date	Mintage	F	VF	XF	Unc	BU
ND(2003) Proof	3,000	Value: 90.00				

KM# 70   50 DIRHAMS

40.0000 g., 0.9250 Silver 1.1895 oz. ASW, 40 mm. **Subject:** 40th Anniversary - First Oil Export from Abu Dhabi Onshore Oil Fields (ADCO) **Obv:** Bust of President H. H. Sheikh Zayed bin Sultan Al Nayhan 3/4 right **Rev:** Logo **Edge:** Reeded

Date	Mintage	F	VF	XF	Unc	BU
ND(2004) Proof	—	Value: 300				

KM# 71   50 DIRHAMS

40.0000 g., 0.9250 Silver 1.1895 oz. ASW, 40 mm.
Subject: 25th Anniversary - Sharjah City for Humanitarian Services (SCHS) **Edge:** Reeded

Date	Mintage	F	VF	XF	Unc	BU
ND(2005) Proof	—	Value: 80.00				

KM# 87   50 DIRHAMS

40.0000 g., 0.9250 Silver 1.1895 oz. ASW, 40 mm.
Subject: Mother of the Nation - Seikha Fatima Bint Mubarak

Date	Mintage	F	VF	XF	Unc	BU
2005 Proof	—	Value: 80.00				

KM# 82   50 DIRHAMS

40.0000 g., Silver, 40 mm. **Subject:** 25th Anniversary Emirates Banks Association **Obv:** Value **Obv. Legend:** UNITED ARAB EMIRATES **Rev:** Logo **Edge:** Reeded

Date	Mintage	F	VF	XF	Unc	BU
ND(2007) Proof	—	Value: 85.00				

KM# 95   50 DIRHAMS

40.0000 g., 0.9250 Silver 1.1895 oz. ASW, 40 mm.
Subject: Hamdan Bin Rashed Award for Distinguished Academic Performance **Obv:** Denomination, legend above **Rev:** Pen with tip touching star, legend above **Edge:** Reeded **Note:** Issued 10th Anniversary of the Award

Date	Mintage	F	VF	XF	Unc	BU
ND(2008) Proof	—	Value: 600				

KM# 80   100 DIRHAMS

60.0000 g., 0.9250 Silver 1.7843 oz. ASW, 50 mm. **Obv:** Sheikh Zayed bin Sultan **Rev:** Sheikh Zayed Mosque

Date	Mintage	F	VF	XF	Unc	BU
2004 Proof	—	Value: 90.00				

UNITED STATES OF AMERICA

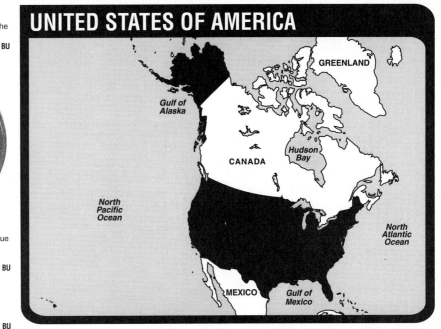

The United States of America as politically organized, under the Articles of Confederation consisted of the 13 original British-American colonies; New Hampshire, Massachusetts, Rhode Island, Connecticut, New York, New Jersey, Pennsylvania, Delaware, Virginia, North Carolina, South Carolina, Georgia and Maryland. Clustered along the eastern seaboard of North America between the forests of Maine and the marshes of Georgia. Under the Article of Confederation, the United States had no national capital: Philadelphia, where the "United States in Congress Assembled", was the "seat of government". The population during this political phase of America's history (1781-1789) was about 3 million, most of whom lived on self-sufficient family farms. Fishing, lumbering and the production of grains for export were major economic endeavors. Rapid strides were also being made in industry and manufacturing by 1775, the (then) colonies were accounting for one-seventh of the world's production of raw iron.

On the basis of the voyage of John Cabot to the North American mainland in 1497, England claimed the entire continent. The first permanent English settlement was established at Jamestown, Virginia, in 1607. France and Spain also claimed extensive territory in North America. At the end of the French and Indian Wars (1763), England acquired all of the territory east of the Mississippi River, including East and West Florida. From 1776 to 1781, the States were governed by the Continental Congress. From 1781 to 1789, they were organized under the Articles of Confederation, during which period the individual States had the right to issue money. Independence from Great Britain was attained with the American Revolution in 1776. The Constitution organized and governs the present United States. It was ratified on Nov. 21, 1788.

MINT MARKS

C – Charlotte, N.C., 1838-61
CC – Carson City, NV, 1870-93
D – Dahlonega, GA, 1838-61
D – Denver, CO, 1906-present
O – New Orleans, LA, 1838-1909
P – Philadelphia, PA, 1793-present
S – San Francisco, CA, 1854-present
W – West Point, NY, 1984-present

MONETARY SYSTEM

Trime = 3 Cents
Nickel = 5 Cents
Dime = 10 Cents
Quarter = 25 Cents
Half Dollar = 50 Cents
Dollar = 100 Cents
Quarter Eagle = $2.50 Gold
Stella = $4.00 Gold
Half Eagle = $5.00 Gold
Eagle = $10.00 Gold
Double Eagle = $20.00 Gold

BULLION COINS

Silver Eagle = $1.00
Gold 1/10 Ounce = $5.00
Gold ¼ Ounce = $10.00
Gold ½ Ounce = $25.00
Gold Ounce = $50.00
Platinum 1/10 Ounce = $10.00
Platinum ¼ Ounce = $25.00
Platinum ½ Ounce = $50.00
Platinum Ounce = $100.00

CIRCULATION COINAGE

CENT
Lincoln Cent
Lincoln Memorial reverse

KM# 201b • Copper Plated Zinc, 19 mm. • **Notes:** MS60 prices are for brown coins and MS65 prices are for coins that are at least 90% original red.

Date	Mintage	XF-40	MS-65	Prf-65
2001	4,959,600,000	—	4.00	—
2001D	5,374,990,000	—	4.00	—
2001S	3,099,096	—	—	4.00
2002	3,260,800,000	—	4.00	—
2002S	3,157,739	—	—	4.00
2002D	4,028,055,000	—	4.00	—
2003	3,300,000,000	—	3.50	—
2003D	3,548,000,000	—	3.50	—
2003S	3,116,590	—	—	4.00
2004	3,379,600,000	—	3.50	—
2004D	3,456,400,000	—	3.50	—
2004S	2,992,069	—	—	4.00
2005	3,935,600,000	—	3.50	—
2005D	3,764,450,000	—	3.50	—
2005S	3,273,000	—	—	4.00
2006	4,290,000,000	—	2.00	—
2006D	3,944,000,000	—	2.50	—
2006S	2,923,105	—	—	4.00
2007	—	—	1.50	—
2007D	—	—	1.50	—
2007S	—	—	—	4.00
2008	—	—	1.50	—
2008D	—	—	1.50	—
2008S	—	—	—	4.00

Lincoln Bicentennial
Log cabin reverse

KM# 441 • 2.5000 g., Copper Plated Zinc, 19 mm. •
Rev. Designer: Richard Masters and Jim Licaretz

Date	Mintage	XF-40	MS-65	Prf-65
2009P	284,400,000	—	1.50	—
2009D	350,400,000	—	1.50	—
2009S	—	—	—	4.00

Lincoln seated on log reverse

KM# 442 • 2.5000 g., Copper Plated Zinc, 19 mm. •
Rev. Designer: Charles Vickers

Date	Mintage	XF-40	MS-65	Prf-65
2009P	376,000,000	—	1.50	—
2009D	363,600,000	—	1.50	—
2009S	—	—	—	4.00

Lincoln standing before Illinois Statehouse reverse

KM# 443 • 2.5000 g., Copper Plated Zinc, 19 mm. •
Rev. Designer: Joel Ishowitz and Don Everhart

Date	Mintage	XF-40	MS-65	Prf-65
2009P	316,000,000	—	1.50	—
2009D	336,000,000	—	1.50	—
2009S	—	—	—	4.00

Capitol Building reverse

KM# 444 • 2.5000 g., Copper Plated Zinc •
Rev. Designer: Susan Gamble and Joseph Menna

Date	Mintage	XF-40	MS-65	Prf-65
2009P	129,600,000	—	1.50	—
2009D	198,000,000	—	1.50	—
2009S	—	—	—	4.00

Lincoln bust right obverse   Shield reverse

KM# 469 • Copper Plated Zinc • **Obv. Designer:** Victor D. Brenner

Date	Mintage	XF-40	MS-65	Prf-65
2010P	—	—	—	—
2010D	—	—	—	—
2010S	—	—	—	—

5 CENTS

Jefferson Nickel

Pre-war design resumed reverse

KM# A192 • 5.0000 g., Copper-Nickel, 21.2 mm. •
Designer: Felix Schlag **Edge Desc:** Plain

Date	Mintage	XF-40	MS-60	MS-65	Prf-65
2001P	675,704,000	—	.25	.50	—
2001D	627,680,000	—	.25	.50	—
2001S	3,099,096	—	—	—	2.00
2002P	539,280,000	—	.25	.50	—
2002D	691,200,000	—	.25	.50	—
2002S	3,157,739	—	—	—	2.00
2003P	441,840,000	—	.25	.50	—
2003D	383,040,000	—	.25	.50	—
2003S	3,116,590	—	—	—	2.00

Jefferson - Westward Expansion - Lewis & Clark Bicentennial

Jefferson era peace medal design: two clasped hands, pipe and hatchet reverse

KM# 360 • 5.0000 g., Copper-Nickel, 21.2 mm. • **Obv. Designer:** Felix Schlag **Rev. Designer:** Norman E. Nemeth

Date	Mintage	MS-65	Prf-65
2004P	361,440,000	1.00	—
2004D	372,000,000	1.00	—
2004S	—	—	13.00

Lewis and Clark's Keelboat reverse

KM# 361 • 5.0000 g., Copper-Nickel, 21.2 mm. •
Obv. Designer: Felix Schlag **Rev. Designer:** Al Maletsky

Date	Mintage	MS-65	Prf-65
2004P	366,720,000	1.00	—
2004D	344,880,000	1.00	—
2004S	—	—	13.00

Thomas Jefferson large profile right obverse   American Bison right reverse

KM# 368 • 5.0000 g., Copper-Nickel, 21.2 mm. •
Obv. Designer: Joe Fitzgerald and Don Everhart II
Rev. Designer: Jamie Franki and Norman E. Nemeth

Date	Mintage	MS-65	Prf-65
2005P	448,320,000	1.00	—
2005D	487,680,000	1.00	—
2005S	—	—	7.50

Jefferson, large profile obverse Pacific coastline reverse

KM# 369 • 5.0000 g., Copper-Nickel, 21.2 mm. •
Obv. Designer: Joe Fitzgerald and Don Everhart
Rev. Designer: Joe Fitzgerald and Donna Weaver

Date	Mintage	MS-65	Prf-65
2005P	394,080,000	1.00	—
2005D	411,120,000	1.00	—
2005S	—	—	6.50

Jefferson large facing portrait - Enhanced Monticello Reverse

KM# 381 • 5.0000 g., Copper-Nickel, 21.2 mm. •
Obv. Designer: Jamie N. Franki and Donna Weaver
Rev. Designer: Felix Schlag and John Mercanti

Date	Mintage	MS-65	Prf-65
2006P	693,120,000	1.00	—
2006D	809,280,000	1.00	—
2006S	—	—	4.00
2007P	—	1.00	—
2007D	—	1.00	—
2007S	—	—	4.00
2008P	—	1.00	—
2008D	—	1.00	—
2008S	—	—	4.00
2009P	—	1.00	—
2009D	—	1.00	—
2009S	—	—	4.00

DIME

Roosevelt Dime

KM# 195a • 2.2700 g., Copper-Nickel Clad Copper, 17.9 mm. • **Designer:** John R. Sinnock **Notes:** The 1979-S and 1981-S Type II proofs have clearer mint marks than the Type I proofs of those years. On the 1982 no-mint-mark variety, the mint mark was inadvertently left off.

Date	Mintage	MS-65	Prf-65
2001P	1,369,590,000	1.00	—
2001D	1,412,800,000	1.00	—
2001S	2,249,496	—	1.00
2002P	1,187,500,000	1.00	—
2002D	1,379,500,000	1.00	—
2002S	2,268,913	—	2.00
2003P	1,085,500,000	1.00	—
2003D	986,500,000	1.00	—
2003S	2,076,165	—	2.00
2004P	1,328,000,000	1.00	—
2004D	1,159,500,000	1.00	—
2004S	1,804,396	—	4.75
2005P	1,412,000,000	1.00	—

Date	Mintage	MS-65	Prf-65
2005D	1,423,500,000	1.00	—
2005S	—	—	2.25
2006P	1,381,000,000	1.00	—
2006D	1,447,000,000	1.00	—
2006S	—	—	2.25
2007P	—	1.00	—
2007D	—	1.00	—
2007S	—	—	2.25
2008P	—	1.00	—
2008D	—	1.00	—
2008S	—	—	2.25
2009P	—	1.00	—
2009D	—	1.00	—
2009S	—	—	2.25

KM# 195b • 2.5000 g., 0.9000 Silver, 0.0723 oz. ASW, 17.9 mm. • **Designer:** John R. Sinnock

Date	Mintage	Prf-65
2001S	849,600	5.00
2002S	888,826	5.00
2003S	1,090,425	4.00
2004S	—	4.50
2005S	—	3.50
2006S	—	3.50
2007S	—	3.50
2008S	—	3.50
2009S	—	3.50

QUARTER

50 State Quarters

Kentucky

KM# 322 • 5.6700 g., Copper-Nickel Clad Copper •

Date	Mintage	MS-63	MS-65	Prf-65
2001P	353,000,000	1.20	7.00	—
2001D	370,564,000	1.00	8.00	—
2001S	3,094,140	—	—	11.00

KM# 322a • 6.2500 g., 0.9000 Silver, 0.1808 oz. ASW •

Date	Mintage	MS-63	MS-65	Prf-65
2001S	889,697	—	—	21.00

New York

KM# 318 • 5.6700 g., Copper-Nickel Clad Copper •

Date	Mintage	MS-63	MS-65	Prf-65
2001P	655,400,000	1.00	8.50	—
2001D	619,640,000	1.00	8.50	—
2001S	3,094,140	—	—	11.00

KM# 318a • 6.2500 g., 0.9000 Silver, 0.1808 oz. ASW •

Date	Mintage	MS-63	MS-65	Prf-65
2001S	889,697	—	—	24.00

North Carolina

KM# 319 • 5.6700 g., Copper-Nickel Clad Copper •

Date	Mintage	MS-63	MS-65	Prf-65
2001P	627,600,000	1.00	7.50	—
2001D	427,876,000	1.00	8.50	—
2001S	3,094,140	—	—	11.00

KM# 319a • 6.2500 g., 0.9000 Silver, 0.1808 oz. ASW •

Date	Mintage	MS-63	MS-65	Prf-65
2001S	889,697	—	—	22.00

Rhode Island

KM# 320 • 5.6700 g., **Copper-Nickel Clad Copper** •

Date	Mintage	MS-63	MS-65	Prf-65
2001P	423,000,000	1.00	6.50	—
2001D	447,100,000	1.00	8.00	—
2001S	3,094,140	—	—	11.00

KM# 320a • 6.2500 g., 0.9000 **Silver**, 0.1808 oz. ASW •

Date	Mintage	MS-63	MS-65	Prf-65
2001S	889,697	—	—	19.00

Mississippi

KM# 335 • 5.6700 g., **Copper-Nickel Clad Copper** •

Date	Mintage	MS-63	MS-65	Prf-65
2002P	290,000,000	1.00	5.00	—
2002D	289,600,000	1.00	6.00	—
2002S	3,084,245	—	—	4.00

KM# 335a • 6.2500 g., 0.9000 **Silver**, 0.1808 oz. ASW •

Date	Mintage	MS-63	MS-65	Prf-65
2002S	892,229	—	—	9.00

Arkansas

KM# 347 • 5.6700 g., **Copper-Nickel Clad Copper** •

Date	Mintage	MS-63	MS-65	Prf-65
2003P	228,000,000	1.00	7.00	—
2003D	229,800,000	1.00	7.00	—
2003S	3,408,516	—	—	3.50

KM# 347a • 6.2500 g., 0.9000 **Silver**, 0.1808 oz. ASW •

Date	Mintage	MS-63	MS-65	Prf-65
2003S	1,257,555	—	—	5.25

Vermont

KM# 321 • 5.6700 g., **Copper-Nickel Clad Copper** •

Date	Mintage	MS-63	MS-65	Prf-65
2001P	423,400,000	1.20	7.00	—
2001D	459,404,000	1.00	7.00	—
2001S	3,094,140	—	—	11.00

KM# 321a • 6.2500 g., 0.9000 **Silver**, 0.1808 oz. ASW •

Date	Mintage	MS-63	MS-65	Prf-65
2001S	889,697	—	—	19.00

Ohio

KM# 332 • 5.6700 g., **Copper-Nickel Clad Copper** •

Date	Mintage	MS-63	MS-65	Prf-65
2002P	217,200,000	1.00	6.50	—
2002D	414,832,000	1.00	7.00	—
2002S	3,084,245	—	—	4.00

KM# 332a • 6.2500 g., 0.9000 **Silver**, 0.1808 oz. ASW •

Date	Mintage	MS-63	MS-65	Prf-65
2002S	892,229	—	—	9.00

Illinois

KM# 343 • 5.6700 g., **Copper-Nickel Clad Copper** •

Date	Mintage	MS-63	MS-65	Prf-65
2003P	225,800,000	1.10	7.00	—
2003D	237,400,000	1.10	6.00	—
2003S	3,408,516	—	—	3.50

KM# 343a • 6.2500 g., 0.9000 **Silver**, 0.1808 oz. ASW •

Date	Mintage	MS-63	MS-65	Prf-65
2003S	1,257,555	—	—	5.25

Indiana

KM# 334 • 5.6700 g., **Copper-Nickel Clad Copper** •

Date	Mintage	MS-63	MS-65	Prf-65
2002P	362,600,000	1.00	6.00	—
2002D	327,200,000	1.00	6.50	—
2002S	3,084,245	—	—	4.00

KM# 334a • 6.2500 g., 0.9000 **Silver**, 0.1808 oz. ASW •

Date	Mintage	MS-63	MS-65	Prf-65
2002S	892,229	—	—	9.00

Tennessee

KM# 331 • 5.6700 g., **Copper-Nickel Clad Copper** •

Date	Mintage	MS-63	MS-65	Prf-65
2002P	361,600,000	1.40	6.50	—
2002D	286,468,000	1.40	7.00	—
2002S	3,084,245	—	—	4.00

KM# 331a • 6.2500 g., 0.9000 **Silver**, 0.1808 oz. ASW •

Date	Mintage	MS-63	MS-65	Prf-65
2002S	892,229	—	—	9.00

Maine

KM# 345 • 5.6700 g., **Copper-Nickel Clad Copper** •

Date	Mintage	MS-63	MS-65	Prf-65
2003P	217,400,000	1.00	6.50	—
2003D	213,400,000	1.00	8.00	—
2003S	3,408,516	—	—	3.50

KM# 345a • 6.2500 g., 0.9000 **Silver**, 0.1808 oz. ASW •

Date	Mintage	MS-63	MS-65	Prf-65
2003S	1,257,555	—	—	5.25

Louisiana

KM# 333 • 5.6700 g., **Copper-Nickel Clad Copper** •

Date	Mintage	MS-63	MS-65	Prf-65
2002P	362,000,000	1.00	6.50	—
2002D	402,204,000	1.00	7.00	—
2002S	3,084,245	—	—	4.00

KM# 333a • 6.2500 g., 0.9000 **Silver**, 0.1808 oz. ASW •

Date	Mintage	MS-63	MS-65	Prf-65
2002S	892,229	—	—	9.00

Alabama

KM# 344 • 5.6700 g., **Copper-Nickel Clad Copper** •

Date	Mintage	MS-63	MS-65	Prf-65
2003P	225,000,000	1.00	7.00	—
2003D	232,400,000	1.00	7.00	—
2003S	3,408,516	—	—	3.50

KM# 344a • 6.2500 g., 0.9000 **Silver**, 0.1808 oz. ASW •

Date	Mintage	MS-63	MS-65	Prf-65
2003S	1,257,555	—	—	5.25

Missouri

KM# 346 • **Copper-Nickel Clad Copper** •

Date	Mintage	MS-63	MS-65	Prf-65
2003P	225,000,000	1.00	7.00	—
2003D	228,200,000	1.00	7.00	—
2003S	3,408,516	—	—	3.50

KM# 346a • 6.2500 g., 0.9000 **Silver**, 0.1808 oz. ASW •

Date	Mintage	MS-63	MS-65	Prf-65
2003S	1,257,555	—	—	5.25

Florida

KM# 356 • 5.6700 g., **Copper-Nickel Clad Copper** •

Date	Mintage	MS-63	MS-65	Prf-65
2004P	240,200,000	.75	6.50	—
2004D	241,600,000	.75	7.00	—
2004S	2,740,684	—	—	5.00

KM# 356a • 6.2500 g., 0.9000 **Silver**, 0.1808 oz. ASW •

Date	Mintage	MS-63	MS-65	Prf-65
2004S	1,775,370	—	—	6.00

Iowa

KM# 358 • 5.6700 g., **Copper-Nickel Clad Copper** •

Date	Mintage	MS-63	MS-65	Prf-65
2004P	213,800,000	.75	6.50	—
2004D	251,800,000	.75	7.00	—
2004S	2,740,684	—	—	5.00

KM# 358a • 6.2500 g., 0.9000 **Silver**, 0.1808 oz. ASW •

Date	Mintage	MS-63	MS-65	Prf-65
2004S	—	—	—	6.00

Michigan

KM# 355 • 5.6700 g., **Copper-Nickel Clad Copper** •

Date	Mintage	MS-63	MS-65	Prf-65
2004P	233,800,000	.75	6.50	—
2004D	225,800,000	.75	6.50	—
2004S	2,740,684	—	—	5.00

KM# 355a • 6.2500 g., 0.9000 **Silver**, 0.1808 oz. ASW •

Date	Mintage	MS-63	MS-65	Prf-65
2004S	1,775,370	—	—	6.00

Texas

KM# 357 • 5.6700 g., **Copper-Nickel Clad Copper** •

Date	Mintage	MS-63	MS-65	Prf-65
2004P	278,800,000	.75	7.00	—
2004D	263,000,000	.75	7.00	—
2004S	2,740,684	—	—	5.00

KM# 357a • 6.2500 g., 0.9000 **Silver**, 0.1808 oz. ASW •

Date	Mintage	MS-63	MS-65	Prf-65
2004S	1,775,370	—	—	6.00

Wisconsin

KM# 359 • 5.6700 g., **Copper-Nickel Clad Copper** •

Date	Mintage	MS-63	MS-65	Prf-65
2004P	226,400,000	1.00	8.00	—
2004D	226,800,000	1.00	10.00	—

Date	Mintage	MS-63	MS-65	Prf-65
2004D Extra Leaf Low	Est. 9,000	300	600	—
2004D Extra Leaf High	Est. 3,000	400	900	—
2004S				5.00

KM# 359a • 6.2500 g., 0.9000 **Silver**, 0.1808 oz. ASW •

Date	Mintage	MS-63	MS-65	Prf-65
2004S	1,775,370	—	—	6.00

California

KM# 370 • 5.6700 g., **Copper-Nickel Clad Copper** •

Date	Mintage	MS-63	MS-65	Prf-65
2005P	257,200,000	.75	5.00	—
2005P Satin Finish	Inc. above	3.50	6.00	—
2005D	263,200,000	.75	5.00	—
2005D Satin Finish	Inc. above	3.50	6.00	—
2005S	3,262,960	—	—	3.00

KM# 370a • 6.2500 g., 0.9000 **Silver**, 0.1808 oz. ASW •

Date	Mintage	MS-63	MS-65	Prf-65
2005S	1,679,600	—	—	5.50

Kansas

KM# 373 • 5.6700 g., **Copper-Nickel Clad Copper** •

Date	Mintage	MS-63	MS-65	Prf-65
2005P	263,400,000	.75	5.00	—
2005P Satin Finish	Inc. above	3.50	6.00	—
2005D	300,000,000	.75	5.00	—
2005D Satin Finish	Inc. above	3.50	6.00	—
2005S	3,262,960	—	—	3.00

KM# 373a • 6.2500 g., 0.9000 **Silver**, 0.1808 oz. ASW •

Date	Mintage	MS-63	MS-65	Prf-65
2005S	1,679,600	—	—	5.50

Minnesota

KM# 371 • 5.6700 g., **Copper-Nickel Clad Copper** •

Date	Mintage	MS-63	MS-65	Prf-65
2005P	226,400,000	.75	5.00	—
2005P Satin Finish	Inc. above	3.50	6.00	—
2005D	226,800,000	.75	5.00	—
2005D Satin Finish	Inc. above	3.50	6.00	—
2005S	3,262,960	—	—	3.00

KM# 371a • 6.2500 g., 0.9000 **Silver**, 0.1808 oz. ASW •

Date	Mintage	MS-63	MS-65	Prf-65
2005S	1,679,600	—	—	5.50

Oregon

KM# 372 • 5.6700 g., **Copper-Nickel Clad Copper** •

Date	Mintage	MS-63	MS-65	Prf-65
2005P	316,200,000	.75	5.00	—
2005P Satin Finish	Inc. above	3.50	6.00	—
2005D	404,000,000	.75	5.00	—
2005D Satin Finish	Inc. above	3.50	6.00	—
2005S	3,262,960	—	—	3.00

KM# 372a • 6.2500 g., 0.9000 **Silver**, 0.1808 oz. ASW •

Date	Mintage	MS-63	MS-65	Prf-65
2005S	1,679,600	—	—	5.50

West Virginia

KM# 374 • 5.6700 g., **Copper-Nickel Clad Copper** •

Date	Mintage	MS-63	MS-65	Prf-65
2005P	365,400,000	.75	5.00	—
2005P Satin Finish	Inc. above	3.50	6.00	—
2005D	356,200,000	.75	5.00	—
2005D Satin Finish	Inc. above	3.50	6.00	—
2005S	3,262,960	—	—	3.00

KM# 374a • 6.2500 g., 0.9000 **Silver**, 0.1808 oz. ASW •

Date	Mintage	MS-63	MS-65	Prf-65
2005S	1,679,600	—	—	5.50

Colorado

KM# 384 • 5.7100 g., **Copper-Nickel Clad Copper**, 24.2 mm. •

Date	Mintage	MS-63	MS-65	Prf-65
2006P	274,800,000	.75	5.00	—
2006P Satin Finish	Inc. above	3.00	5.00	—
2006D	294,200,000	.75	5.00	—
2006D Satin Finish	Inc. above	3.00	5.00	—
2006S	2,862,078	—	—	5.00

KM# 384a • 6.2500 g., 0.9000 **Silver**, 0.1808 oz. ASW •

Date	Mintage	MS-63	MS-65	Prf-65
2006S	1,571,839	—	—	5.75

Nebraska

KM# 383 • 5.6700 g., **Copper-Nickel Clad Copper** •

Date	Mintage	MS-63	MS-65	Prf-65
2006P	318,000,000	.75	6.00	—
2006P Satin Finish	Inc. above	3.00	6.00	—
2006D	273,000,000	.75	6.00	—
2006D Satin Finish	Inc. above	3.00	5.00	—
2006S	2,862,078	—	—	5.00

KM# 383a • 6.2500 g., 0.9000 **Silver**, 0.1808 oz. ASW •

Date	Mintage	MS-63	MS-65	Prf-65
2006S	1,571,839	—	—	5.75

Nevada

KM# 382 • 5.6700 g., **Copper-Nickel Clad Copper** •

Date	Mintage	MS-63	MS-65	Prf-65
2006P	277,000,000	.75	6.00	—
2006P Satin Finish	Inc. above	3.00	5.00	—
2006D	312,800,000	.75	6.00	—
2006D Satin Finish	Inc. above	3.00	5.00	—
2006S	2,862,078	—	—	5.00

KM# 382a • 6.2500 g., 0.9000 **Silver**, 0.1808 oz. ASW •

Date	Mintage	MS-63	MS-65	Prf-65
2006S	1,571,839	—	—	5.75

North Dakota

KM# 385 • 5.7200 g., **Copper-Nickel Clad Copper**, 24.2 mm. •

Date	Mintage	MS-63	MS-65	Prf-65
2006P	305,800,000	.75	5.00	—
2006P Satin Finish	Inc. above	3.00	5.00	—
2006D	359,000,000	.75	5.00	—
2006D Satin Finish	Inc. above	3.00	5.00	—
2006S	2,862,078	—	—	5.00

KM# 385a • 6.2500 g., 0.9000 **Silver**, 0.1808 oz. ASW •

Date	Mintage	MS-63	MS-65	Prf-65
2006S	1,571,839	—	—	5.75

South Dakota

KM# 386 • 5.6500 g., **Copper-Nickel Clad Copper**, 24.3 mm. •

Date	Mintage	MS-63	MS-65	Prf-65
2006P	245,000,000	.75	5.00	—
2006P Satin Finish	Inc. above	3.00	5.00	—
2006D	265,800,000	.75	5.00	—
2006D Satin Finish	Inc. above	3.00	5.00	—
2006S	2,862,078	—	—	5.00

KM# 386a • 6.2500 g., 0.9000 **Silver**, 0.1808 oz. ASW •

Date	Mintage	MS-63	MS-65	Prf-65
2006S	1,571,839	—	—	5.75

Idaho

KM# 398 • 5.6700 g., **Copper-Nickel Clad Copper** •

Date	Mintage	MS-63	MS-65	Prf-65
2007P	294,600,000	.75	8.00	—
2007D	286,800,000	.75	8.00	—
2007S	2,374,778	—	—	4.00

KM# 398a • 6.2500 g., 0.9000 **Silver**, 0.1808 oz. ASW •

Date	Mintage	MS-63	MS-65	Prf-65
2007S	1,299,878	—	—	6.50

Montana

KM# 396 • 5.6700 g., **Copper-Nickel Clad Copper** •

Date	Mintage	MS-63	MS-65	Prf-65
2007P	257,000,000	.75	8.00	—
2007D	256,240,000	.75	5.00	—
2007S	2,374,778	—	—	4.00

KM# 396a • 6.2500 g., 0.9000 **Silver**, 0.1808 oz. ASW •

Date	Mintage	MS-63	MS-65	Prf-65
2007S	1,299,878	—	—	6.50

Utah

KM# 400 • **Copper-Nickel Clad Copper** •

Date	Mintage	MS-63	MS-65	Prf-65
2007P	255,000,000	.75	8.00	—
2007D	253,200,000	.75	8.00	—
2007S	2,374,778	—	—	4.00

KM# 400a • 6.2500 g., 0.9000 **Silver**, 0.1808 oz. ASW •

Date	Mintage	MS-63	MS-65	Prf-65
2007S	1,299,878	—	—	6.50

Washington

KM# 397 • 5.6700 g., **Copper-Nickel Clad Copper** •

Date	Mintage	MS-63	MS-65	Prf-65
2007P	265,200,000	.75	8.00	—
2007D	280,000,000	.75	8.00	—
2007S	2,374,778	—	—	4.00

KM# 397a • 6.2500 g., 0.9000 **Silver**, 0.1808 oz. ASW •

Date	Mintage	MS-63	MS-65	Prf-65
2007S	1,299,878	—	—	6.50

Wyoming

KM# 399 • 5.6700 g., **Copper-Nickel Clad Copper** •

Date	Mintage	MS-63	MS-65	Prf-65
2007P	243,600,000	.75	8.00	—
2007D	320,800,000	.75	8.00	—
2007S	2,374,778	—	—	4.00

KM# 399a • 6.2500 g., 0.9000 **Silver**, 0.1808 oz. ASW •

Date	Mintage	MS-63	MS-65	Prf-65
2007S	1,299,878	—	—	6.50

Alaska

KM# 424 • 5.6700 g., **Copper-Nickel Clad Copper** •

Date	Mintage	MS-63	MS-65	Prf-65
2008P	251,800,000	.75	8.00	—
2008D	254,000,000	.75	8.00	—
2008S	2,100,000	—	—	4.00

KM# 424a • 6.2500 g., 0.9000 **Silver**, 0.1808 oz. ASW •

Date	Mintage	MS-63	MS-65	Prf-65
2008S	1,200,000	—	—	6.50

Arizona

KM# 423 • 5.6700 g., **Copper-Nickel Clad Copper** •

Date	Mintage	MS-63	MS-65	Prf-65
2008P	244,600,000	.75	8.00	—
2008D	265,000,000	.75	8.00	—
2008S	2,100,000	—	—	4.00

KM# 423a • 6.2500 g., 0.9000 **Silver**, 0.1808 oz. ASW •

Date	Mintage	MS-63	MS-65	Prf-65
2008S	1,200,000	—	—	6.50

Hawaii

KM# 425 • 5.6700 g., **Copper-Nickel Clad Copper** •

Date	Mintage	MS-63	MS-65	Prf-65
2008P	254,000,000	.75	8.00	—
2008D	263,600,000	.75	8.00	—
2008S	2,100,000	—	—	4.50

KM# 425a • 6.2500 g., 0.9000 **Silver**, 0.1808 oz. ASW •

Date	Mintage	MS-63	MS-65	Prf-65
2008S	1,200,000	—	—	6.50

New Mexico

KM# 422 • 5.6700 g., **Copper-Nickel Clad Copper** •

Date	Mintage	MS-63	MS-65	Prf-65
2008P	244,200,000	.75	8.00	—
2008D	244,400,000	.75	8.00	—
2008S	2,100,000	—	—	4.00

KM# 422a • 6.2500 g., 0.9000 **Silver**, 0.1808 oz. ASW •

Date	Mintage	MS-63	MS-65	Prf-65
2008S	1,200,000	—	—	6.50

Oklahoma

KM# 421 • 5.6700 g., **Copper-Nickel Clad Copper** •

Date	Mintage	MS-63	MS-65	Prf-65
2008P	222,000,000	.75	8.00	—
2008D	194,600,000	.75	8.00	—
2008S	2,100,000	—	—	4.00

KM# 421a • 6.2500 g., 0.9000 **Silver**, 0.1808 oz. ASW •

Date	Mintage	MS-63	MS-65	Prf-65
2008S	1,200,000	—	—	6.50

DC and Territories

American Samoa

KM# 448 • 5.6700 g., **Copper-Nickel Clad Copper**, 24 mm. •

Date	Mintage	MS-63	MS-65	Prf-65
2009P	42,600,000	.75	8.00	—
2009D	39,600,000	.75	8.00	—
2009S	—	—	—	4.00

KM# 448a • 6.2500 g., 0.9000 **Silver**, 0.1808 oz. ASW, 24 mm. •

Date	Mintage	MS-63	MS-65	Prf-65
2009S	—	—	—	6.50

District of Columbia

KM# 445 • 5.6700 g., Copper-Nickel Clad Copper, 24 mm. •

Date	Mintage	MS-63	MS-65	Prf-65
2009P	83,600,000	.75	8.00	—
2009D	88,800,000	.75	8.00	—
2009S	—	—	—	4.00

KM# 445a • 6.2500 g., 0.9000 Silver, 0.1808 oz. ASW, 24 mm. •

Date	Mintage	MS-63	MS-65	Prf-65
2009S	—	—	—	6.50

Guam

KM# 447 • 5.6700 g., Copper-Nickel Clad Copper, 24 mm. •

Date	Mintage	MS-63	MS-65	Prf-65
2009P	45,000,000	.75	8.00	—
2009D	42,600,000	.75	8.00	—
2009S	—	—	—	4.00

KM# 447a • 6.2500 g., 0.9000 Silver, 0.1808 oz. ASW, 24 mm. •

Date	Mintage	MS-63	MS-65	Prf-65
2009S	—	—	—	6.50

Northern Mariana Islands

KM# 466 • 5.6700 g., Copper-Nickel Clad Copper •

Date	Mintage	MS-63	MS-65	Prf-65
2009P	35,200,000	.75	8.00	—
2009D	37,600,000	.75	8.00	—
2009S	—	—	—	4.00

KM# 466a • 6.2500 g., 0.9000 Silver, 0.1808 oz. ASW •

Date	Mintage	MS-63	MS-65	Prf-65
2009S	—	—	—	6.50

Puerto Rico

KM# 446 • 5.6700 g., Copper-Nickel Clad Copper, 24 mm. •

Date	Mintage	MS-63	MS-65	Prf-65
2009P	53,200,000	.75	8.00	—
2009D	86,000,000	.75	8.00	—
2009S	—	—	—	4.00

KM# 446a • 6.2500 g., 0.9000 Silver, 0.1808 oz. ASW, 24 mm. •

Date	Mintage	MS-63	MS-65	Prf-65
2009S	—	—	—	6.50

US Virgin Islands

KM# 449 • 0.6250 oz., 0.9000 Copper-Nickel Clad Copper, 0.0181 oz., 24 mm. •

Date	Mintage	MS-63	MS-65	Prf-65
2009P	41,000,000	.75	8.00	—
2009D	41,000,000	.75	8.00	—
2009S	—	—	—	4.00

KM# 449a • 6.2500 g., 0.9000 Silver, 0.1808 oz. ASW, 24 mm. •

Date	Mintage	MS-63	MS-65	Prf-65
2009S	—	—	—	6.50

National Parks and Historic Sites

Grand Canyon

KM# 472 • Copper-Nickel Clad Copper •

Date	Mintage	MS-63	MS-65	Prf-65
2010P	—	—	—	—
2010D	—	—	—	—
2010S	—	—	—	—

Hot Springs, Ark.

KM# 468 • Copper-Nickel Clad Copper •

Date	Mintage	MS-63	MS-65	Prf-65
2010P	—	—	—	—
2010D	—	—	—	—
2010S	—	—	—	—

Mount Hood

KM# 473 • Copper-Nickel Clad Copper •

Date	Mintage	MS-63	MS-65	Prf-65
2010P	—	—	—	—
2010D	—	—	—	—
2010S	—	—	—	—

Yellowstone

KM# 470 • Copper-Nickel Clad Copper •

Date	Mintage	MS-63	MS-65	Prf-65
2010P	—	—	—	—
2010D	—	—	—	—
2010S	—	—	—	—

Yosemite

KM# 471 • Copper-Nickel Clad Copper •

Date	Mintage	MS-63	MS-65	Prf-65
2010P	—	—	—	—
2010D	—	—	—	—
2010S	—	—	—	—

HALF DOLLAR
Kennedy Half Dollar

Regular design resumed reverse

KM# A202b • 11.1000 g., Copper-Nickel Clad Copper, 30.4 mm. • Edge Desc: Reeded Notes: KM#202b design and composition resumed. The 1979-S and 1981-S Type II proofs have clearer mint marks than the Type I proofs of those years.

Date	Mintage	MS-65	Prf-65
2001P	21,200,000	9.00	—
2001D	19,504,000	9.00	—
2001S	2,235,000	—	8.00
2002P	3,100,000	10.00	—
2002D	2,500,000	10.00	—
2002S	2,268,913	—	8.00
2003P	2,500,000	14.00	—
2003D	2,500,000	14.00	—
2003S	2,076,165	—	6.00
2004P	2,900,000	7.00	—
2004D	2,900,000	7.00	—
2004S	1,789,488	—	13.00
2005P	3,800,000	9.00	—
2005P Satin finish	1,160,000	8.00	—
2005D	3,500,000	9.00	—
2005D Satin finish	1,160,000	10.00	—
2005S	2,275,000	—	7.00
2006P	2,400,000	12.00	—
2006P Satin finish	847,361	12.00	—
2006D	2,000,000	20.00	—
2006D Satin finish	847,361	14.00	—
2006S	1,934,965	—	10.00
2007P	—	7.00	—
2007P Satin finish	—	8.00	—
2007D	—	7.00	—
2007D Satin finish	—	8.00	—
2007S	—	—	10.00
2008P	—	7.00	—
2008P Satin finish	—	8.50	—
2008D	—	7.00	—
2008D Satin finish	—	8.50	—
2008S	—	—	12.00
2009P	—	7.00	—
2009P Satin finish	—	8.50	—
2009D	—	7.00	—
2009D Satin finish	—	8.50	—
2009S	—	—	6.00

KM# A202c • 12.5000 g., 0.9000 Silver, 0.3617 oz. ASW, 30.6 mm. • Designer: Gilroy Roberts

Date	Mintage	Prf-65
2001S	849,600	20.00
2002S	888,816	14.00
2003S	1,040,425	15.00
2004S	1,175,935	14.00
2005S	1,069,679	10.00
2006S	988,140	11.00
2007S	1,384,797	12.00
2008S	620,684	12.00
2009S	—	20.00

DOLLAR
Sacagawea Dollar

Sacagawea bust right, with baby on back obverse   Eagle in flight left reverse

KM# 310 • 8.0700 g., Copper-Zinc-Manganese-Nickel Clad Copper, 26.4 mm. •

Date	Mintage	MS-63	Prf-65
2001P	62,468,000	2.00	—
2001D	70,939,500	2.00	—
2001S	3,190,000	—	100.00
2002P	3,865,610	2.00	—
2002D	3,732,000	2.00	—
2002S	3,210,000	—	28.50
2003P	3,080,000	3.00	—
2003D	3,080,000	3.00	—
2003S	3,300,000	—	20.00
2004P	2,660,000	2.50	—
2004D	2,660,000	2.50	—
2004S	2,965,000	—	22.50
2005P	2,520,000	2.50	—
2005D	2,520,000	2.50	—
2005S	3,273,000	—	22.50
2006P	4,900,000	2.50	—
2006D	2,800,000	5.00	—
2006S	3,028,828	—	22.50
2007P	3,640,000	2.50	—
2007D	3,920,000	2.50	—
2007S	2,563,563	—	22.50
2008P	9,800,000	2.50	—
2008D	14,840,000	2.50	—
2008S	—	—	22.50

Native American female planting corn, beans and squash reverse

KM# 467 • Copper-Zinc-Manganese-Nickel Clad Copper •

Date	Mintage	MS-63	Prf-65
2009P	37380000	—	—
2009D	33880000	—	—
2009S	—	—	22.50

Hiawatha belt and bundle of five arrows reverse

KM# 474 • 8.0700 g., Copper-Zinc-Manganese-Nickel Clad Copper, 26.4 mm. •

Date	Mintage	XF-40	MS-65	Prf-65
2010P	—	—	—	—
2010D	—	—	—	—
2010S	—	—	—	—

Presidents
George Washington

KM# 401 • 8.0700 g., Copper-Zinc-Manganese-Nickel Clad Copper, 26.4 mm. • Edge Lettering: IN GOD WE TRUST date, mint mark E PLURIBUS UNUM Notes: Date and mint mark incuse on edge.

Date	Mintage	MS-63	MS-65	Prf-65
2007P	176,680,000	2.00	5.00	—
(2007) Plain edge error	Inc. above	75.00	—	—
2007D	163,680,000	2.00	5.00	—
2007S	3,883,103	—	—	8.00

John Adams

KM# 402 • 8.0700 g., **Copper-Zinc-Manganese-Nickel Clad Copper**, 26.4 mm. • **Edge Lettering:**IN GOD WE TRUST date, mint mark E PLURIBUS UNUM **Notes:** Date and mint mark incuse on edge.

Date	Mintage	MS-63	MS-65	Prf-65
2007P	112,420,000	2.00	5.00	—
2007P Double edge lettering	Inc. above	250	—	—
2007D	112,140,000	2.00	5.00	—
2007S	3,877,409	—	—	8.00

Thomas Jefferson

KM# 403 • 8.0700 g., **Copper-Zinc-Manganese-Nickel Clad Copper**, 26.4 mm. • **Edge Lettering:**IN GOD WE TRUST date, mint mark E PLURIBUS UNUM **Notes:** Date and mint mark incuse on edge.

Date	Mintage	MS-63	MS-65	Prf-65
2007P	100,800,000	2.00	5.00	—
2007D	102,810,000	2.00	5.00	—
2007S	3,877,573	—	—	8.00

James Madison

KM# 404 • 8.0700 g., **Copper-Zinc-Manganese-Nickel Clad Copper**, 26.4 mm. • **Edge Lettering:**IN GOD WE TRUST date, mint mark E PLURIBUS UNUM **Notes:** Date and mint mark incuse on edge.

Date	Mintage	MS-63	MS-65	Prf-65
2007P	84,560,000	2.00	5.00	—
2007D	87,780,000	2.00	5.00	—
2007S	3,876,829	—	—	8.00

James Monroe

KM# 426 • 8.0700 g., **Copper-Zinc-Manganese-Nickel Clad Copper**, Date and mint mark incuse on edge., 26.4 mm. • **Edge Lettering:**IN GOD WE TRUST date, mint mark E PLURIBUS UNUM

Date	Mintage	MS-63	MS-65	Prf-65
2008P	64,260,000	2.00	5.00	—
2008D	60,230,000	2.00	5.00	—
2008S	3,000,000	—	—	8.00

John Quincy Adams

KM# 427 • 8.0700 g., **Copper-Zinc-Manganese-Nickel Clad Copper**, 26.4 mm. • **Edge Lettering:**IN GOD WE TRUST date, mint mark E PLURIBUS UNUM **Notes:** Date and mint mark incuse on edge.

Date	Mintage	MS-63	MS-65	Prf-65
2008P	57,540,000	2.00	5.00	—
2008D	57,720,000	2.00	5.00	—
2008S	3,000,000	—	—	8.00

Andrew Jackson

KM# 428 • 8.0700 g., **Copper-Zinc-Manganese-Nickel Clad Copper**, 26.4 mm. • **Edge Lettering:**IN GOD WE TRUST date, mint mark E PLURIBUS UNUM **Notes:** Date and mint mark incuse on edge.

Date	Mintage	MS-63	MS-65	Prf-65
2008P	61,180,000	2.00	5.00	—
2008D	61,070,000	2.00	5.00	—
2008S	3,000,000	—	—	8.00

Martin van Buren

KM# 429 • 8.0700 g., **Copper-Zinc-Manganese-Nickel Clad Copper**, 26.4 mm. • **Edge Lettering:**IN GOD WE TRUST date, mint mark E PLURIBUS UNUM **Notes:** Date and mint mark incuse on edge.

Date	Mintage	MS-63	MS-65	Prf-65
2008P	51,520,000	2.00	5.00	—
2008D	50,960,000	2.00	5.00	—
2008S	3,000,000	—	—	8.00

William Henry Harrison

KM# 450 • 8.0700 g., **Copper-Zinc-Manganese-Nickel Clad Copper**, 26.4 mm. • **Edge Lettering:**IN GOD WE TRUST date, mint mark E PLURIBUS UNUM **Notes:** Date and mint mark on edge

Date	Mintage	MS-63	MS-65	Prf-65
2009P	43,260,000	2.00	5.00	—
2009D	55,160,000	2.00	5.00	—
2009S	—	—	—	8.00

John Tyler

KM# 451 • 8.0700 g., **Copper-Zinc-Manganese-Nickel Clad Copper**, 26.4 mm. •

Date	Mintage	MS-63	MS-65	Prf-65
2009P	43,540,000	2.00	5.00	—
2009D	43,540,000	2.00	5.00	—
2009S	—	—	—	8.00

James K. Polk

KM# 452 • 8.0700 g., **Copper-Zinc-Manganese-Nickel Clad Copper**, 26.4 mm. •

Date	Mintage	MS-63	MS-65	Prf-65
2009P	46,620,000	2.00	5.00	—
2009D	41,720,000	2.00	5.00	—
2009S	—	—	—	8.00

Zachary Taylor

KM# 453 • 8.0700 g., **Copper-Zinc-Manganese-Nickel Clad Copper**, 26.4 mm. •

Date	Mintage	MS-63	MS-65	Prf-65
2009P	41,580,000	2.00	5.00	—
2009D	36,680,000	2.00	5.00	—
2009S	—	—	—	8.00

Millard Filmore

KM# 475 • 8.0700 g., **Copper-Zinc-Manganese-Nickel Clad Copper** •

Date	Mintage	MS-63	MS-65	Prf-65
2010P	—	—	—	—
2010D	—	—	—	—
2010S	—	—	—	—

Franklin Pierce

KM# 476 • 8.0700 g., **Copper-Zinc-Manganese-Nickel Clad Copper** •

Date	Mintage	MS-63	MS-65	Prf-65
2010P	—	—	—	—
2010D	—	—	—	—
2010S	—	—	—	—

James Buchanan

KM# 477 • 8.0700 g., **Copper-Zinc-Manganese-Nickel Clad Copper** •

Date	Mintage	MS-63	MS-65	Prf-65
2010P	—	—	—	—
2010D	—	—	—	—
2010S	—	—	—	—

Abraham Lincoln

KM# 478 • 8.0700 g., **Copper-Zinc-Manganese-Nickel Clad Copper** •

Date	Mintage	MS-63	MS-65	Prf-65
2010P	—	—	—	—
2010D	—	—	—	—
2010S	—	—	—	—

$20 (DOUBLE EAGLE)

KM# 464 0.9990 Gold 0 oz. AGW. 27 mm. **Obverse:** Liberty holding torch, walking forward **Reverse:** Eagle in flight left, sunrise in background **Designer:** Augustus Saint-Gaudens **Notes:** Ultra high relief

Date	Mintage	MS-65	Prf-65
2009	115,178	—	1,275

COMMEMORATIVE COINAGE
2001-PRESENT

All commemorative silver dollar coins of 1982-present have the following specifications: diameter — 38.1 millimeters; weight — 26.7300 grams; composition — 0.9000 silver, 0.7736 ounces actual silver weight. All commemorative $5 coins of 1982-present have the following specificiations: diameter — 21.6 millimeters; weight — 8.3590 grams; composition: 0.9000 gold, 0.242 ounces actual gold weight.

Note: In 1982, after a hiatus of nearly 20 years, coinage of commemorative half dollars resumed. Those designated with a 'W' were struck at the West Point Mint. Some issues were struck in copper-nickel. Those struck in silver have the same size, weight and composition as the prior commemorative half-dollar series.

HALF DOLLAR

U. S. CAPITOL VISITOR CENTER. KM# 323 Copper-Nickel Clad Copper 11.3400 g. **Obverse:** Capitol sillouete, 1800 structure in detail **Reverse:** Legend within circle of stars **Obv. Designer:** Dean McMullen **Rev. Designer:** Alex Shagin and Marcel Jovine

Date	Mintage	MS-65	Prf-65
2001P	99,157	13.50	—
2001P	77,962	—	15.50

FIRST FLIGHT CENTENNIAL. KM# 348 Copper-Nickel Clad Copper 11.3400 g. **Obverse:** Wright Monument at Kitty Hawk **Reverse:** Wright Flyer in flight **Obv. Designer:** John Mercanti **Rev. Designer:** Donna Weaver

Date	Mintage	MS-65	Prf-65
2003P	57,726	15.00	—
2003P	109,710	—	16.00

AMERICAN BALD EAGLE. KM# 438 Copper-Nickel Clad Copper 0 oz. 30.6 mm. 11.3400 g. **Obverse:** Two eaglets in nest with egg **Reverse:** Eagle Challenger facing right, American Flag in background

Date	Mintage	MS-65	Prf-65
2008P	120,000	10.00	—
2008P	175,000	—	15.00

DOLLAR

CAPITOL VISITOR CENTER. KM# 324 Obv. Designer: Marika Somogyi **Rev. Designer:** John Mercanti **Obverse:** Original and current Capital facades **Reverse:** Eagle with shield and ribbon

Date	Mintage	MS-65	Prf-65
2001P	35,400	30.00	—
2001P	143,793	—	39.00

NATIVE AMERICAN - BISON. KM# 325 Designer: James E. Fraser. **Obverse:** Native American bust right **Reverse:** Bison standing left

Date	Mintage	MS-65	Prf-65
2001D	227,100	175	—
2001P	272,869	—	180

2002 WINTER OLYMPICS - SALT LAKE CITY. KM# 336 Obv. Designer: John Mercanti **Rev. Designer:** Donna Weaver **Obverse:** Salt Lake City Olympic logo **Reverse:** Stylized skyline with mountains in background

Date	Mintage	MS-65	Prf-65
2002P	40,257	30.00	—
2002P	166,864	—	38.00

U.S. MILITARY ACADEMY AT WEST POINT - BICENTENNIAL. KM# 338 Obv. Designer: T. James Ferrell **Rev. Designer:** John Mercanti **Obverse:** Cadet Review flagbearers, Academy buildings in background **Reverse:** Academy emblems - Corinthian helmet and sword

Date	Mintage	MS-65	Prf-65
2002W	103,201	18.50	—
2002W	288,293	—	18.50

FIRST FLIGHT CENTENNIAL. KM# 349 Obv. Designer: T. James Ferrell **Rev. Designer:** Norman E. Nemeth **Obverse:** Orville and Wilbur Wright busts left **Reverse:** Wright Flyer over dunes

Date	Mintage	MS-65	Prf-65
2003P	53,761	33.50	—
2003P	193,086	—	28.50

LEWIS AND CLARK CORPS OF DISCOVERY BICENTENNIAL. KM# 363 Obverse: Lewis and Clark standing **Reverse:** Jefferson era clasped hands peace medal

Date	Mintage	MS-65	Prf-65
2004P	90,323	31.00	—
2004P	288,492	—	27.50

THOMAS A. EDISON - ELECTRIC LIGHT 125TH ANNIVERSARY. KM# 362 Obv. Designer: Donna Weaver **Rev. Designer:** John Mercanti **Obverse:** Edison half-length figure facing holding light bulb **Reverse:** Light bulb and rays

Date	Mintage	MS-65	Prf-65
2004P	68,031	34.00	—
2004P	213,409	—	34.50

JOHN MARSHALL, 250TH BIRTH ANNIVERSARY. KM# 375 Obv. Designer: John Mercanti **Rev. Designer:** Donna Weaver **Obverse:** Marshall bust left **Reverse:** Marshall era Supreme Court Chamber

Date	Mintage	MS-65	Prf-65
2005P	67,096	32.00	—
2005P	196,753	—	35.00

U.S. MARINE CORPS, 230TH ANNIVERSARY. KM# 376 Obverse: Flag Raising at Mt. Suribachi on Iwo Jima **Reverse:** Marine Corps emblem

Date	Mintage	MS-65	Prf-65
2005P	49,671	37.00	—
2005P	548,810	—	39.00

BENJAMIN FRANKLIN, 300TH BIRTH ANNIVERSARY. KM#387 Obv. Designer: Norman E. Nemeth **Obverse:** Youthful Franklin flying kite **Reverse:** Revolutionary era "JOIN, or DIE" snake cartoon illustration

Date	Mintage	MS-65	Prf-65
2006P	61,856	32.00	—
2006P	137,808	—	45.00

Date	Mintage	MS-65	Prf-65
2007W	47,050	—	345

BENJAMIN FRANKLIN, 300TH BIRTH ANNIVERSARY.
KM# 388 Obverse: Bust 3/4 right, signature in oval below
Reverse: Continental Dollar of 1776 in center

Date	Mintage	MS-65	Prf-65
2006P	64,014	33.00	—
2006P	137,808	—	44.00

SAN FRANCISCO MINT MUSEUM. KM# 394 Obv. Designer:
Sherl J. Winter **Obverse:** 3/4 view of building **Reverse:** Reverse
of 1880s Morgan silver dollar

Date	Mintage	MS-65	Prf-65
2006S	65,609	41.00	—
2006S	255,700	—	42.00

CENTRAL HIGH SCHOOL DESEGREGATION. KM# 418
Rev. Designer: Don Everhart II **Obverse:** Children's feet walking
left with adult feet in military boots **Reverse:** Little Rock's Central
High School

Date	Mintage	MS-65	Prf-65
2007P	66,093	50.00	—
2007P	124,618	—	50.00

JAMESTOWN - 400TH ANNIVERSARY. KM# 405
Obv. Designer: Donna Weaver **Rev. Designer:** Don Everhart II
Obverse: Two settlers and Native American **Reverse:** Three
ships

Date	Mintage	MS-65	Prf-65
2007P	79,801	36.50	—
2007P	258,802	—	35.00

AMERICAN BALD EAGLE. KM# 439 Obverse: Eagle with
flight, mountain in background at right **Reverse:** Great Seal of the
United States

Date	Mintage	MS-65	Prf-65
2008P	110,073	39.50	—
2008P	243,558	—	38.50

LINCOLN BICENTENNIAL. KM# 454 Obv. Designer: Justin
Kunz and Don Everhart II **Rev. Designer:** Phebe Hemphill
Obverse: 3/4 portrait facing right **Reverse:** Part of Gettysburg
Address within wreath

Date	Mintage	MS-65	Prf-65
2009P	125,000	41.00	—
2009P	375,000	—	38.50

LOUIS BRAILLE BIRTH BICENTENNIAL. KM# 455 Obv.
Designer: Joel Iskowitz and Phebe Hemphill **Rev. Designer:**
Susan Gamble and Joseph Menna **Obverse:** Louis Braille bust
facing **Reverse:** School child reading book in Braille, BRL in
Braille code above

Date	Mintage	MS-65	Prf-65
2009P	82,639	32.50	—
2009P	135,235	—	42.50

$5 (HALF EAGLE)

CAPITOL VISITOR CENTER. KM# 326 Designer: Elizabeth
Jones. **Obverse:** Column at right **Reverse:** First Capital building

Date	Mintage	MS-65	Prf-65
2001W	6,761	1,750	—
2001W	27,652	—	420

2002 WINTER OLYMPICS. KM# 337 Designer: Donna Weaver.
Obverse: Salt Lake City Olympics logo **Reverse:** Stylized
cauldron

Date	Mintage	MS-65	Prf-65
2002W	10,585	440	—
2002W	32,877	—	365

SAN FRANCISCO MINT MUSEUM. KM# 395 Obverse: Front
entrance façade **Reverse:** Eagle as on 1860's $5. Gold

Date	Mintage	MS-65	Prf-65
2006S	16,230	285	—
2006S	41,517	—	295

JAMESTOWN - 400TH ANNIVERSARY. KM# 406
Obverse: Settler and Native American **Reverse:** Jamestown
Memorial Church ruins

Date	Mintage	MS-65	Prf-65
2007W	18,843	345	—

AMERICAN BALD EAGLE. KM# 440 Obverse: Two eagles on
branch **Reverse:** Eagle with shield

Date	Mintage	MS-65	Prf-65
2008W	13,467	285	—
2008W	59,269	—	300

$10 (EAGLE)

FIRST FLIGHT CENTENNIAL. KM# 350 0.9000 Gold 0.4837
oz. AGW. 16.7180 g. **Obverse:** Orvile and Wilbur Wright busts
facing **Reverse:** Wright flyer and eagle **Designer:** Donna
Weaver

Date	Mintage	MS-65	Prf-65
2003P	10,129	650	—
2003P	21,846	—	650
2003P	21,846	—	650

AMERICAN EAGLE BULLION COINS

SILVER DOLLAR

KM# 273 0.9993 **SILVER** 0.9993 oz. ASW. 40.6mm. 31.1050
g. **Obv. Designer:** Adolph A. Weinman
Rev. Designer: John Mercanti

Date	Mintage	Unc	Prf.
2001	9,001,711	20.50	—
2001W	746,398	—	55.00
2002	10,539,026	20.50	—
2002W	647,342	—	55.00
2003	8,495,008	20.50	—
2003W	747,831	—	55.00
2004	8,882,754	20.50	—
2004W	801,602	—	55.00
2005	8,891,025	20.50	—
2005W	816,663	—	55.00
2006	10,676,522	22.80	—
2006W	1,093,600	—	55.00
2006P Reverse Proof	—	—	175
2006W Burnished Unc.	468,000	75.00	—
2006 20th Aniv. 3 pc. set	—	—	320
2007	9,028,036	20.80	—
2007W	821,759	—	55.00
2007W Burnished Unc.	690,891	20.00	—
2008	20,583,000	20.50	—
2008W Reverse of '07	—	410	—
2008	—	—	79.00
2008W Burnished Unc.	—	30.50	—
2009	—	20.50	—
2010	—	22.00	—

GOLD $5

KM# 216 0.9167 **GOLD** 0.1000 oz. AGW. 16.5mm. 3.3930 g. **Obv. Designer:** Augustus Saint-Gaudens **Rev. Designer:** Miley Busiek

Date	Mintage	Unc	Prf.
2001	269,147	141	—
2001W	37,530	—	185
2002	230,027	141	—
2002W	40,864	—	185
2003	245,029	141	—
2003W	40,027	—	185
2004	250,016	141	—
2004W	35,131	—	185
2005	300,043	141	—
2005W	49,265	—	185
2006	285,006	141	—
2006W	47,277	—	185
2006W Burnished Unc.	20,643	140	—
2007	190,010	141	—
2007W	58,553	—	200
2007W Burnished Unc.	22,501	135	—
2008	305,000	151	—
2008W	—	—	200
2008W	—	215	—
2009	27,000	145	—

GOLD $10

KM# 217 0.9167 **GOLD** 0.2500 oz. AGW. 22mm. 8.4830 g. **Obv. Designer:** Augustus Saint-Gaudens **Rev. Designer:** Miley Busiek

Date	Mintage	Unc	Prf.
2001	71,280	321	—
2001W	25,613	—	433
2002	62,027	321	—
2002W	29,242	—	433
2003	74,029	321	—
2003W	30,292	—	433
2004	72,014	321	—
2004W	28,839	—	433
2005	72,015	321	—
2005W	37,207	—	433
2006	60,004	321	—
2006W	36,127	—	433
2006W Burnished Unc.	15,188	335	—
2007	34,004	321	—
2007W	46,189	—	448
2007W Burnished Unc.	12,786	420	—
2008	—	321	—
2008W	28,000	—	448
2008W Burnished Unc.	—	950	—
2009	27,500	321	—

GOLD $25

KM# 218 0.9167 **GOLD** 0.5000 oz. AGW. 27mm. 16.9660 g. **Obv. Designer:** Augustus Saint-Gaudens **Rev. Designer:** Miley Busiek

Date	Mintage	Unc	Prf.
2001	48,047	750	—
2001W	23,240	—	885
2002	70,027	620	—
2002W	26,646	—	885
2003	79,029	620	—
2003W	28,270	—	885
2004	98,040	620	—
2004W	27,330	—	885
2005	80,023	620	—
2005W	34,311	—	885
2006	66,004	623	—

Date	Mintage	Unc	Prf.
2006W	34,322	—	885
2006W Burnished Unc.	15,164	900	—
2007	47,002	623	—
2007W	44,025	—	885
2007W Burnished Unc.	11,458	845	—
2008	61,000	623	—
2008W	27,800	—	885
2008W Burnished Unc.	—	1,650	—
2009	55,000	623	—

GOLD $50

KM# 219 0.9167 **GOLD** 100000 oz. AGW. 32.7mm. 33.9310 g. **Obv. Designer:** Augustus Saint-Gaudens **Rev. Designer:** Miley Busiek

Date	Mintage	Unc	Prf.
2001	143,605	1,184	—
2001W	24,555	—	1,710
2002	222,029	1,184	—
2002W	27,499	—	1,710
2003	416,032	1,184	—
2003W	28,344	—	1,710
2004	417,149	1,184	—
2004W	28,215	—	1,710
2005	356,555	1,184	—
2005W	35,246	—	1,710
2006	237,510	1,184	—
2006W	47,000	—	1,710
2006W Reverse Proof	10,000	—	2,200
2006W Burnished Unc.	45,912	1,125	—
2007	140,016	1,196	—
2007W	51,810	—	1,710
2007W Burnished Unc.	18,609	1,125	—
2008	710,000	1,184	—
2008W	29,000	—	1,710
2008W Burnished Unc.	—	1,550	—
2009	122,000	1,184	—
2010	—	—	—

PLATINUM $10

KM# 327 0.9995 **PLATINUM** 0.0999 oz. 17mm. 3.1100 g. **Obv. Designer:** John Mercanti

Date	Mintage	Unc	Prf.
2001W	12,174	—	250

KM# 283 0.9995 **PLATINUM** 0.0999 oz. 17mm. 3.1100 g. **Obv. Designer:** John Mercanti **Rev. Designer:** Thomas D. Rogers Sr

Date	Mintage	Unc	Prf.
2001	52,017	209	—
2002	23,005	209	—
2003	22,007	209	—
2004	15,010	209	—
2005	14,013	209	—
2006	11,001	209	—
2006W Burnished Unc.	—	425	—
2007	13,003	280	—
2007W Burnished Unc.	—	210	—
2008	17,000	206	—
2008 Burnished Unc.	—	210	—
2009	—	180	—

KM# 339 0.9995 **PLATINUM** 0.0999 oz. 17mm. 3.1100 g. **Obv. Designer:** John Mercanti

Date	Mintage	Unc	Prf.
2002W	12,365	—	250

KM# 351 0.9995 **PLATINUM** 0.0999 oz. 17mm. 3.1100 g. **Obv. Designer:** John Mercanti **Rev. Designer:** Al Maletsky

Date	Mintage	Unc	Prf.
2003W	9,534	—	255

KM# 364 0.9995 **PLATINUM** 0.0999 oz. 17mm. 3.1100 g. **Obv. Designer:** John Mercanti

Date	Mintage	Unc	Prf.
2004W	7,161	—	595

KM# 377 0.9995 **PLATINUM** 0.0999 oz. 17mm. 3.1100 g. **Obv. Designer:** John Mercanti **Rev. Designer:** Donna Weaver

Date	Mintage	Unc	Prf.
2005W	8,104	—	218

KM# 389 0.9995 **PLATINUM** 0.0999 oz. 17mm. 3.1100 g. **Obv. Designer:** John Mercanti

Date	Mintage	Unc	Prf.
2006W	10,205	—	190

KM# 414 0.9995 **PLATINUM** 0.0999 oz. 17mm. 3.1100 g. **Obv. Designer:** John Mercanti

Date	Mintage	Unc	Prf.
2007W	8,176	—	250

KM# 434 0.9995 **PLATINUM** 0.0999 oz. 17mm. 3.1100 g. **Obv. Designer:** John Mercanti

Date	Mintage	Unc	Prf.
2008W	8,176	—	405

KM# 460 0.9995 **PLATINUM** 0.0999 oz. 17mm. 3.1100 g. **Obv. Designer:** John Mercanti

Date	Mintage	Unc	Prf.
2009W	5,600	—	245

KM# 485 0.9990 **PLATINUM** 0.0999 oz. 3.1100 g. **Obv. Designer:** John Mercanti

Date	Mintage	Unc	Prf.
2010W	—	—	—

PLATINUM $25

KM# 328 0.9995 **PLATINUM** 0.2502 oz. 22mm. 7.7857 g. **Obv. Designer:** John Mercanti

Date	Mintage	Unc	Prf.
2001W	8,847	—	500

KM# 284 0.9995 **PLATINUM** 0.2502 oz. 22mm. 7.7857 g. **Obv. Designer:** John Mercanti **Rev. Designer:** Thomas D. Rogers Sr

Date	Mintage	Unc	Prf.
2001	21,815	490	—
2002	27,405	490	—
2003	25,207	490	—
2004	18,010	490	—
2005	12,013	490	—
2006	12,001	490	—

Date	Mintage	Unc	Prf.
2006W Burnished Unc.	—	585	—
2007	8,402	490	—
2007W Burnished Unc.	—	495	—
2008	22,800	665	—
2008 Burnished Unc.	—	490	—
2009	—	490	—

KM# 340   0.9995 **PLATINUM** 0.2502 oz. 22mm. 7.7857 g.
Obv. Designer: John Mercanti

Date	Mintage	Unc	Prf.
2002W	9,282	—	500

KM# 352   0.9995 **PLATINUM** 0.2502 oz. 22mm. 7.7857 g.
Obv. Designer: John Mercanti **Rev. Designer:** Al Maletsky

Date	Mintage	Unc	Prf.
2003W	7,044	—	500

KM# 365   0.9995 **PLATINUM** 0.2502 oz. 22mm. 7.7857 g.
Obv. Designer: John Mercanti

Date	Mintage	Unc	Prf.
2004W	5,193	—	1,150

KM# 378   0.9995 **PLATINUM** 0.2502 oz. 22mm. 7.7857 g.
Obv. Designer: John Mercanti
Rev. Designer: Donna Weaver

Date	Mintage	Unc	Prf.
2005W	6,592	—	525

KM# 390   0.9995 **PLATINUM** 0.2502 oz. 22mm. 7.7857 g.
Obv. Designer: John Mercanti

Date	Mintage	Unc	Prf.
2006W	7,813	—	445

KM# 415   0.9995 **PLATINUM** 0.2502 oz. 22mm. 7.7857 g.
Obv. Designer: John Mercanti

Date	Mintage	Unc	Prf.
2007W	6,017	—	440

KM# 435   0.9995 **PLATINUM** 0.2502 oz. 22mm. 7.7857 g.
Obv. Designer: John Mercanti

Date	Mintage	Unc	Prf.
2008W	6,017	—	690

KM# 461   0.9995 **PLATINUM** 0.2502 oz. 22mm. 7.7857 g.
Obv. Designer: John Mercanti

Date	Mintage	Unc	Prf.
2009W	3,800	—	600

KM# 486   0.9990 **PLATINUM** 0.2501 oz. 7.7857 g.
Obv. Designer: John Mercanti

Date	Mintage	Unc	Prf.
2010W	—	—	—

PLATINUM $50

KM# 329   0.9995 **PLATINUM** 0.4997 oz. 27mm. 15.5520 g.
Obv. Designer: John Mercanti

Date	Mintage	Unc	Prf.
2001W	8,254	—	999

KM# 285   0.9995 **PLATINUM** 0.4997 oz. 27mm. 15.5520 g.
Obv. Designer: John Mercanti **Rev. Designer:** Thomas D.
Rogers Sr

Date	Mintage	Unc	Prf.
2001	12,815	996	—
2002	24,005	996	—
2003	17,409	996	—
2004	13,236	996	—
2005	9,013	996	—
2006	9,602	996	—
2006W Burnished Unc.	—	1,012	—
2007	7,001	996	—
2007W Burnished Unc.	—	1,012	—
2008	14,000	996	—
2008W Burnished Unc.	—	1,200	—
2009	—	996	—

KM# 341   0.9995 **PLATINUM** 0.4997 oz. 27mm. 15.5520 g.
Obv. Designer: John Mercanti

Date	Mintage	Unc	Prf.
2002W	8,772	—	999

KM# 353   0.9995 **PLATINUM** 0.4997 oz. 27mm. 15.5520 g.
Obv. Designer: John Mercanti **Rev. Designer:** Al Maletsky

Date	Mintage	Unc	Prf.
2003W	7,131	—	999

KM# 366   0.9995 **PLATINUM** 0.4997 oz. 27mm. 15.5520 g.
Obv. Designer: John Mercanti

Date	Mintage	Unc	Prf.
2004W	5,063	—	1,700

KM# 379   0.9995 **PLATINUM** 0.4997 oz. 27mm. 15.5520 g.
Obv. Designer: John Mercanti **Rev. Designer:** Donna Weaver

Date	Mintage	Unc	Prf.
2005W	5,942	—	980

KM# 391   0.9995 **PLATINUM** 0.4997 oz. 27mm. 15.5520 g.
Obv. Designer: John Mercanti

Date	Mintage	Unc	Prf.
2006W	7,649	—	865

KM# 416   0.9995 **PLATINUM** 0.4997 oz. 27mm. 15.5520 g.
Obv. Designer: John Mercanti

Date	Mintage	Unc	Prf.
2007W	22,873	—	875
2007W Reverse Proof	16,937		950

KM# 436   0.9995 **PLATINUM** 0.4997 oz. 27mm. 15.5520 g.
Obv. Designer: John Mercanti

Date	Mintage	Unc	Prf.
2008W	22,873	—	1,185

KM# 462   0.9995 **PLATINUM** 0.4997 oz. 27mm. 15.5520 g.
Obv. Designer: John Mercanti

Date	Mintage	Unc	Prf.
2009	3,600	—	—

KM# 487   0.9990 **PLATINUM** 0.4995 oz. 15.5520 g.   **Obv.**
Designer: John Mercanti

Date	Mintage	Unc	Prf.
2010W	—	—	—

PLATINUM $100

KM# 330   0.9995 **PLATINUM** 0.9995 oz. 33mm. 31.1050 g.
Obv. Designer: John Mercanti

Date	Mintage	Unc	Prf.
2001W	8,969	—	1,998

KM# 286   0.9995 **PLATINUM** 0.9995 oz. 33mm. 31.1050 g.
Obv. Designer: John Mercanti   **Rev. Designer:** Thomas D.
Rogers Sr

Date	Mintage	Unc	Prf.
2001	14,070	1,916	—
2002	11,502	1,916	—
2003	8,007	1,916	—
2004	7,009	1,916	—
2005	6,310	1,916	—
2006	6,000	1,916	—
2006W Burnished Unc.	—	1,913	—
2007	7,202	1,916	—
2007W Burnished Unc.	—	1,913	—
2008	21,800	1,916	—
2008W Burnished Unc.	—	1,913	—
2009	—	1,680	—

KM# 342   0.9995 **PLATINUM** 0.9995 oz. 33mm. 31.1050 g.
Obv. Designer: John Mercanti

Date	Mintage	Unc	Prf.
2002W	9,834	—	1,998

KM# 354   0.9995 **PLATINUM** 0.9995 oz. 33mm. 31.1050 g.
Obv. Designer: John Mercanti **Rev. Designer:** Al Maletsky

Date	Mintage	Unc	Prf.
2003W	8,246	—	2,017

KM#367   0.9995 **PLATINUM** 0.9995 oz. 33mm. 31.1050 g.
Obv. Designer: John Mercanti **Rev. Designer:** Donna Weaver

Date	Mintage	Unc	Prf.
2004W	6,007	—	2,150

KM#380   0.9995 **PLATINUM** 0.9995 oz. 33mm. 31.1050 g.
Obv. Designer: John Mercanti **Rev. Designer:** Donna Weaver

Date	Mintage	Unc	Prf.
2005W	6,602	—	2,017

KM#392   0.9995 **PLATINUM** 0.9995 oz. 33mm. 31.1050 g.
Obv. Designer: John Mercanti

Date	Mintage	Unc	Prf.
2006W	9,152	—	1,998

KM#417   0.9995 **PLATINUM** 0.9995 oz. 33mm. 31.1050 g.
Obv. Designer: John Mercanti

Date	Mintage	Unc	Prf.
2007W	8,363	—	1,998

KM#437   0.9995 **PLATINUM** 0.9995 oz. 33mm. 31.1050 g.
Obv. Designer: John Mercanti

Date	Mintage	Unc	Prf.
2008W	8,363	—	2,250

KM#463   0.9995 **PLATINUM** 0.9994 oz. 33mm. 31.1020 g.
Obv. Designer: John Mercanti

Date	Mintage	Unc	Prf.
2009W	4,900	—	—

KM# 488   0.9990 **PLATINUM** 0.9990 oz. 31.1050 g.
Obv. Designer: John Mercanti

Date	Mintage	Unc	Prf.
2010W	—	—	—

MINT SETS

Date	Sets Sold	Issue Price	Value
2001	1,066,900	14.95	15.85
2002	1,139,388	14.95	21.00
2003	1,002,555	14.95	16.75
2004	844,484	16.95	29.00
2005	—	16.95	9.75
2006	—	16.95	14.00
2007	—	—	24.50
2008	—	—	59.00

MODERN COMMEMORATIVE COIN SETS

Capitol Visitor Center

Date	Price
2001 3 coin set: proof half, silver dollar, gold $5; KM323, 324, 326.	475

American Buffalo

Date	Price
2001 2 coin set: 90% silver unc. & proof $1.; KM325.	335
2001 coin & currency set 90% unc. dollar & replicas of 1899 $5 silver cert.; KM325.	180

Winter Olympics - Salt Lake City

Date	Price
2002 2 coin set: proof 90% silver dollar KM336 & $5.00 Gold KM337.	413
2002 4 coin set: 90% silver unc. & proof $1, KM336 & unc. & proof gold $5, KM337.	837

First Flight Centennial

Date	Price
2003 3 coin set: proof gold ten dollar KM350, proof silver dollar KM349 & proof clad half dollar KM348.	683

Lewis and Clark Bicentennial

Date	Price
2004 Coin and pouch set.	100.00
2004 coin and currency set: Uncirculated silver dollar, two 2005 nickels, replica 1901 $10 Bison note, silver plated peace medal, three stamps & two booklets.	85.00
2004 Westward Journey Nickel series coin and medal set: Proof Sacagawea dollar, two 2005 proof nickels and silver plated peace medal.	35.00

Thomas Alva Edison

Date	Price
2004 Uncirculated silver dollar and light bulb.	60.00

U.S. Marine Corps.

Date	Price
2005 American Legacy: Proof Marine Corps dollar, Proof John Marshall dollar and 10 piece proof set.	180
2005 Uncirculated silver dollar and stamp set.	80.00

Chief Justice John Marshall

Date	Price
2005 Coin and Chronicles set: Uncirculated silver dollar, booklet and BEP intaglio portrait.	60.00
2005 American Legacy: Proof Marine Corps dollar, Proof John Marshall dollar and 10 piece proof set.	180

Benjamin Franklin Tercentennary

Date	Price
2006 Coin and Chronicles set: Uncirculated "Scientist" silver dollar, four stamps, Poor Richards Almanac and intaglio print.	65.00

PROOF SETS

Date	Sets Sold	Issue Price	Value
2001S 10 piece	2,249,498	19.95	63.50
2001S 5 quarter set	774,800	13.95	39.50
2001S Silver	849,600	31.95	105
2002S 10 piece	2,319,766	19.95	24.50
2002S 5 quarter set	764,419	13.95	16.50
2002S Silver	892,229	31.95	72.00
2003 X#207, 208, 209.2	—	44.00	28.75
2003S 10 piece	2,175,684	16.75	16.75
2003S 5 quarter set	1,225,507	13.95	9.75
2003S Silver	1,142,858	31.95	30.50
2004S 11 piece	1,804,396	22.95	28.00
2004S 5 quarter set	987,960	23.95	19.25
2004S Silver 11 piece	1,187,673	37.95	25.00
2004S Silver 5 quarter set	594,137	—	19.25
2005S American Legacy	—	—	88.00
2005S 11 piece	—	22.95	12.50
2005S 5 quarter set	—	15.95	8.75
2005S Silver 11 piece	—	37.95	30.50
2005S Silver 5 quarter set	—	23.95	16.00
2005S American Legacy	—	—	98.00
2006S 10 piece clad	—	22.95	28.50
2006S 5 quarter set	—	15.95	19.00
2006S Silver 10 piece	—	37.95	31.00
2006S Silver 5 quarter set	—	23.95	19.25
2007S 5 quarter set	—	13.95	15.25
2007S Silver 5 quarter set	—	22.95	19.75
2007S 14 piece clad	—	—	38.50
2007S Silver 14 piece	—	—	51.00
2007S Presidential $ set	—	—	20.00
2007S American Legacy	—	—	210
2008 14 pieces clad	—	—	92.00
2008S Silver 14 piece	—	—	68.50
2008S Presidential $ set	—	—	22.50
2008S 5 quarter set	—	22.95	48.50
2008S Silver 5 quarter set	—	—	24.50
2008S American Legacy	—	—	145

UNCIRCULATED ROLLS

Listings are for rolls containing uncirculated coins. Large date and small date varieties for 1960 and 1970 apply to the one cent coins.

Date	Cents	Nickels	Dimes	Halves
2001P	3.75	4.75	7.75	16.50
2001D	2.00	6.50	7.25	16.00
2002P	2.00	4.00	7.25	20.00
2002D	3.25	4.10	7.25	20.00
2003P	3.35	7.50	7.00	22.50
2003D	2.00	3.50	7.00	19.50
2004P Peace Medal Nickel	1.75	6.75	7.00	30.00
2004D Peace Medal Nickel	2.50	7.00	7.00	30.00
2004P Keelboat Nickel	—	4.00	—	—
2004D Keelboat Nickel	—	3.50	—	—
2005P Bison Nickel	1.75	3.25	7.00	21.00
2005D Bison Nickel	2.75	3.25	7.00	21.00
2005P Ocean in view Nickel	—	3.25	—	—
2005D Ocean in view Nickel	—	3.25	—	—
2006P	2.75	3.25	8.50	29.00
2006D	1.75	3.25	8.50	29.00
2007P	1.75	3.50	8.00	21.00
2007D	1.75	3.50	7.75	21.00
2008P	1.75	3.75	8.00	24.50
2008D	1.75	3.75	7.50	25.50
2009P Log Cabin	2.00	23.00	13.50	18.50
2009D Log Cabin	2.15	13.50	13.50	18.50
2009P Log Splitter	1.75	—	—	—
2009D Log Splitter	1.75	—	—	—
2009P Professional	1.75	—	—	—
2009D Professional	1.75	—	—	—
2009P President	2.00	—	—	—
2009D President	2.00	—	—	—
2009 DC	18.00	15.50	—	—
2009 Puerto Rico	15.00	15.50	—	—
2009 Guam	15.00	16.50	—	—
2009 American Samoa	15.00	15.00	—	—
2009 Virgin Islands	15.00	15.00	—	—

URUGUAY

The Oriental Republic of Uruguay (so called because of its location on the east bank of the Uruguay River) is situated on the Atlantic coast of South America between Argentina and Brazil. This South American country has an area of 68,536 sq. mi. (176,220 sq. km.) and a population of *3 million. Capital: Montevideo. Uruguay's chief economic asset is the rich, rolling grassy plains. Meat, wool, hides and skins are exported.

MINT MARKS
(ba) – Buenos Aires
(br) – Acunaciones Espanolas S.A., Barcelona
(k) – Kremnica (Slovakia)
(m) - Madrid
Mo, (mo) and Mx - Mexico City
(p) – thunderbolt: Poissy, France
(rcm) – Royal Canadian Mint
(rj) – Rio de Janeiro
(sa) – Pretoria, South Africa
So, (so) – Santiago (Small o above S); (except 2007 2 Pesos Uruguayos)

REPUBLIC

REFORM COINAGE

March 1993

1,000 Nuevos Pesos = 1 Uruguayan Peso; 100 Centesimos = 1 Uruguayan Peso (UYP)

KM# 106   50 CENTESIMOS
3.0000 g., Stainless Steel, 21 mm. **Obv:** Bust of Artigas right
Obv. Legend: REPUBLICA ORIENTAL DEL URUGUAY
Rev: Value, date and sprig **Edge:** Plain **Note:** Coin rotation.

Date	Mintage	F	VF	XF	Unc	BU
2002	10,000,000	—	—	0.35	0.75	1.00
2005	15,000,000	—	—	0.35	0.75	1.00
2008	35,000,000	—	—	0.35	0.75	1.00

KM# 103.2   UN PESO URUGUAYO
3.5000 g., Aluminum-Bronze, 20 mm. **Obv:** Bust of Artigas right
Obv. Legend: REPUBLICA ORIENTAL DEL URUGUAY
Rev: Value and date **Edge:** Plain **Note:** Medal rotation; left point of bust shoulder points at "P" in Republic.

Date	Mintage	F	VF	XF	Unc	BU
2005So	40,000,000	—	—	—	0.50	0.75
2007So	25,000,000	—	—	—	0.50	0.75

KM# 104.2 2 PESOS URUGUAYOS
4.5000 g., Aluminum-Bronze, 23 mm. **Obv:** Bust of Artigas right
Obv. Legend: REPUBLICA ORIENTAL DEL URUGUAY
Rev: Value and date **Edge:** Plain **Note:** Medal rotation. Left point of bust shoulder points at "P" in "Republic".

Date	Mintage	F	VF	XF	Unc	BU
2007So	25,000,000	—	—	0.75	1.50	2.00

Note: Minted at Paris with the So mintmark.

2008So		—	—	0.75	1.50	2.00

KM# 120.1 5 PESOS URUGUAYOS
6.3000 g., Aluminum-Bronze, 26 mm. **Obv:** Bust of Antigas right
Obv. Legend: REPUBLICA ORIENTAL DEL URUGUAY
Rev: Value **Edge:** Plain **Note:** Left point of bust shoulder points at "U" in "Republic".

Date	Mintage	F	VF	XF	Unc	BU
2003	15,150,000	—	—	—	2.50	3.00

KM# 120.2 5 PESOS URUGUAYOS
6.3000 g., Aluminum-Bronze, 26 mm. **Obv:** Bust of Antigas right
Obv. Legend: REPUBLICA ORIENTAL DEL URUGUAY •
Rev: Value, date **Note:** Left point of bust shoulder points at "P" in "Republic".

Date	Mintage	F	VF	XF	Unc	BU
2005So	30,000,000	—	—	—	2.50	3.00
2008So	20,000,000	—	—	—	2.50	3.00

KM# 121 10 PESOS URUGUAYOS
10.4000 g., Bi-Metallic Aluminum-Bronze center in Stainless Steel ring, 28 mm. **Obv:** Artigas head right within circle
Rev: Value above signature within circle **Edge:** Plain

Date	Mintage	F	VF	XF	Unc	BU
2000 (rcm)	40,000,000	—	—	—	3.50	5.00

Note: 5-pointed star to each side of date, issued 2006

KM# 134 10 PESOS URUGUAYOS
Bi-Metallic **Obv:** Oval arms **Rev:** Lion walking left, runrise in background

Date	Mintage	F	VF	XF	Unc	BU
2008		—	—	—	7.50	10.00

KM# 133 500 PESOS URUGAUAYOS
12.5000 g., 0.9000 Silver 0.3617 oz. ASW, 33 mm.
Subject: Salto, 250th Anniversary **Obv:** Uruguay map with City of Salto location **Rev:** Emblem of the Department of Salto

Date	Mintage	F	VF	XF	Unc	BU
2006(u) Proof	10,000	Value: 20.00				

KM# 122 1000 PESOS URUGUAYOS
27.0000 g., 0.9250 Silver 0.8029 oz. ASW, 40 mm.
Subject: XVIII World Championship Football - Germany 2006
Obv: National arms **Obv. Legend:** REPUBLICA ORIENTAL DEL URUGUAY **Rev:** Soccer player and value **Edge:** Reeded

Date	Mintage	F	VF	XF	Unc	BU
2003 Proof	—	Value: 40.00				

KM# 128 1000 PESOS URUGUAYOS
27.0000 g., 0.9000 Silver 0.7812 oz. ASW **Subject:** 2006 World Cup **Obv:** Arms **Rev:** Soccer player

Date	Mintage	F	VF	XF	Unc	BU
2003 Proof	—	Value: 50.00				

KM# 123 1000 PESOS URUGUAYOS
27.0000 g., 0.9250 Silver 0.8029 oz. ASW, 40 mm.
Subject: XVIII World Championship Football - Germany 2006
Obv: National arms above date **Obv. Legend:** REPUBLICA ORIENTAL DEL URUGUAY **Rev:** Stylized soccer player and value **Edge:** Reeded

Date	Mintage	F	VF	XF	Unc	BU
2004 Proof	—	Value: 40.00				

KM# 125 1000 PESOS URUGUAYOS
27.0000 g., 0.9250 Silver 0.8029 oz. ASW, 40 mm.
Subject: 100th Anniversary FIFA - 1930 Championship
Obv: Football before net **Obv. Legend:** REPUBLICA ORIENTAL DEL URUGUAY **Rev:** Sun of national flag **Edge:** Reeded

Date	Mintage	F	VF	XF	Unc	BU
2004 Proof	—	Value: 37.50				

KM# 124 1000 PESOS URUGUAYOS
27.0000 g., 0.9250 Silver 0.8029 oz. ASW, 40 mm.
Subject: XVIII World Championship Football - Germany 2006
Obv: National arms above date **Obv. Legend:** REPUBLICA ORIENTAL DEL URUGUAY **Rev:** FIFA trophy **Edge:** Reeded

Date	Mintage	F	VF	XF	Unc	BU
2005 Proof	—	Value: 40.00				

KM# 126 5000 PESOS URUGUAYOS
6.7500 g., 0.9250 Gold 0.2007 oz. AGW, 23 mm. **Subject:** 100th Anniversary FIFA - 1930 Championship **Obv:** Football
Obv. Legend: REPUBLICA ORIENTAL DEL URUGUAY
Rev: Tower of Homage in Montevideo **Edge:** Reeded

Date	Mintage	F	VF	XF	Unc	BU
2004 Proof	—	Value: 350				

KM# 127 5000 PESOS URUGUAYOS
6.7500 g., 0.9250 Gold 0.2007 oz. AGW, 23 mm. **Subject:** XVIII World Championship Football - Germany 2006 **Obv:** National arms **Obv. Legend:** REPUBLICA ORIENTAL DEL URUGUAY **Rev:** Stylized player and value **Edge:** Reeded

Date	Mintage	F	VF	XF	Unc	BU
2004 Proof	—	Value: 500				

UZBEKISTAN

The Republic of Uzbekistan (formerly the Uzbek S.S.R.), is bordered on the north by Kazakhstan, to the east by Kirghizia and Tajikistan, on the south by Afghanistan and on the west by Turkmenistan. The republic is comprised of the regions of Andizhan, Bukhara, Dzhizak, Ferghana, Kashkadar, Khorezm (Khiva), Namangan, Navoi, Samarkand, Surkhan-Darya, Syr-Darya, Tashkent and the Karakalpak Autonomous Republic. It has an area of 172,741 sq. mi. (447,400 sq. km.) and a population of 20.3 million. Capital: Tashkent. Crude oil, natural gas, coal, copper, and gold deposits make up the chief resources, while intensive farming, based on artificial irrigation, provides an abundance of cotton.

MONETARY SYSTEM
100 Tiyin = 1 Som

REPUBLIC

STANDARD COINAGE

KM# 13 5 SOM
3.3500 g., Brass Plated Steel, 21.2 mm. **Obv:** National arms
Rev: Value and map **Edge:** Plain

Date	Mintage	F	VF	XF	Unc	BU
2001	—	—	—	—	1.35	1.75

Note: 2 reverse map varieties known

KM# 14 10 SOM
2.7100 g., Nickel Clad Steel, 19.75 mm. **Obv:** National arms
Rev: Value and map **Edge:** Plain

Date	Mintage	F	VF	XF	Unc	BU
2001	—	—	—	—	2.00	2.50

Note: 2 reverse map varieties exist

KM# 15 50 SOM
8.0000 g., Nickel Clad Steel, 26.2 mm. **Obv:** National arms
Rev: Value and map **Edge:** Segmented reeding

Date	Mintage	F	VF	XF	Unc	BU
2001	—	—	—	1.20	3.00	4.00

KM# 16 50 SOM
7.9000 g., Nickel Clad Steel, 26.3 mm. **Subject:** 2700th Anniversary of Shahrisabz Town **Obv:** National arms **Rev:** Statue and ruins above value **Edge:** Segmented reeding

Date	Mintage	F	VF	XF	Unc	BU
2002	—	—	—	1.00	2.50	3.50

KM# 20 100 SOM
31.1000 g., 0.9990 Silver 0.9988 oz. ASW **Obv:** National arms
Obv. Legend: O'ZBEKISTON MARKAZIY BANKI **Rev:** Amir-Timur Museum

Date	Mintage	F	VF	XF	Unc	BU
2001 Proof	1,000	Value: 225				

KM# 21 100 SOM
31.1000 g., 0.9990 Silver 0.9988 oz. ASW **Obv:** National Arms
Obv. Legend: O'BEKISTON MARKAZY BANKI **Rev:** Toskent town hall

Date	Mintage	F	VF	XF	Unc	BU
2001 Proof	1,000	Value: 225				

KM# 22 100 SOM
31.1000 g., 0.9990 Silver 0.9988 oz. ASW **Obv:** National arms
Obv. Legend: O'ZBEKISTON MARKAZIY BANKI **Rev:** World

Date	Mintage	F	VF	XF	Unc	BU
2001 Proof	1,000	Value: 225				

KM# 18 100 SOM
Bronze **Subject:** 500th Anniversary Death of 'Aliser Navoi
Obv: National arms **Obv. Legend:** O'ZBEKISTON MARKAZIY BANKI **Rev:** 'Aliser Navoi

Date	Mintage	F	VF	XF	Unc	BU
2001	—	—	—	—	15.00	18.00

KM# 19 100 SOM
31.1000 g., 0.9990 Silver 0.9988 oz. ASW **Obv:** National arms
Obv. Legend: O'ZBEKISTON MARKAZIY BANKI
Rev: Parliament building in Toskent

Date	Mintage	F	VF	XF	Unc	BU
2001 Proof	1,000	Value: 225				

KM# 23 100 SOM
31.1000 g., 0.9990 Silver 0.9988 oz. ASW **Obv:** National arms
Obv. Legend: O'ZBEKISTON MARKAZIY BANKI **Rev:** Football player

Date	Mintage	F	VF	XF	Unc	BU
2001 Proof	1,000	Value: 225				

KM# 24 100 SOM
31.1000 g., 0.9990 Silver 0.9988 oz. ASW **Obv:** National arms
Obv. Legend: O'BEKISTON MARKAZIY BANKI **Rev:** Track runner

Date	Mintage	F	VF	XF	Unc	BU
2001 Proof	1,000	Value: 225				

KM# 25 100 SOM
31.1000 g., 0.9990 Silver 0.9988 oz. ASW **Obv:** National arms
Obv. Legend: O'ZBEKISTON MARKAZIY BANKI **Rev:** Judo expert

Date	Mintage	F	VF	XF	Unc	BU
2001 Proof	1,000	Value: 225				

KM# 26 100 SOM
31.1000 g., 0.9990 Silver 0.9988 oz. ASW **Obv:** National arms
Obv. Legend: O'ZBEKISTON MARKAZIY BANKI **Rev:** Tennis player

Date	Mintage	F	VF	XF	Unc	BU
2001 Proof	1,000	Value: 225				

KM# 27 100 SOM
31.1000 g., 0.9990 Silver 0.9988 oz. ASW **Obv:** National arms
Obv. Legend: O'ZBEKISTON MARKAZIY BANKI **Rev:** Lenk monument in Timur

Date	Mintage	F	VF	XF	Unc	BU
2001 Proof	1,000	Value: 225				

KM# 28 100 SOM
31.1000 g., 0.9990 Silver 0.9988 oz. ASW **Obv:** National arms
Obv. Legend: O'ZBEKISTON MARKAZIY BANKI **Rev:** Aliser Navoi monument

Date	Mintage	F	VF	XF	Unc	BU
2001 Proof	1,000	Value: 225				

KM# 29 100 SOM
31.1000 g., 0.9990 Silver 0.9988 oz. ASW **Obv:** National arms
Obv. Legend: O'ZBEKISTON MARKAZIY BANKI **Rev:** Registan in Samarkand

Date	Mintage	F	VF	XF	Unc	BU
2001 Proof	1,000	Value: 225				

KM# 30 100 SOM
31.1000 g., 0.9990 Silver 0.9988 oz. ASW **Obv:** National arms
Obv. Legend: O'BEKISTON MARKAZIY BANKI **Rev:** Bell tower in Toskent

Date	Mintage	F	VF	XF	Unc	BU
2001 Proof	1,000	Value: 225				

KM# 17 100 SOM
7.9200 g., Nickel Plated Steel, 26.95 mm. **Subject:** 10th Annniversary State Currency **Obv:** National arms **Obv. Legend:** O'ZBEKISTON MARKAZIV BANKI **Rev:** Sun rays over outlined map and value **Rev. Legend:** O'BEKISTON MILLIY VALYUTASIGA **Edge:** Lettered

Date	Mintage	F	VF	XF	Unc	BU
2004	—	—	—	—	12.50	15.00

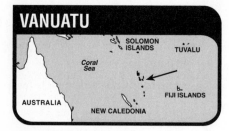

VANUATU

The Republic of Vanuatu, formerly New Hebrides Condominium, a group of islands located in the South Pacific 500 miles (800 km.) west of Fiji, were under the joint sovereignty of Great Britain and France. The islands have an area of 5,700 sq. mi. (14,760 sq. km.) and a population of 165,000, mainly Melanesians of mixed blood. Capital: Port-Vila. The volcanic and coral islands, while malarial land subject to frequent earthquakes, are extremely fertile, and produce copra, coffee, tropical fruits and timber for export.

The New Hebrides were discovered by Portuguese navigator Pedro de Quiros (sailing under orders by the King of Spain) in 1606, visited by French explorer Bougainville in 1768, and named by British navigator Capt. James Cook in 1774. Ships of all nations converged on the islands to trade for sandalwood, prompting France and Britain to relinquish their individual claims and declare the islands a neutral zone in 1878. The New Hebrides were placed under the control of a mixed Anglo-French commission of naval officers during the native uprisings of 1887, and established as a condominium under the joint sovereignty of France and Great Britain in 1906.

Vanuatu became an independent republic within the Commonwealth in July 1980. A president is Head of State and the Prime Minister is Head of Government.

MONETARY SYSTEM
Vatu to Present

REPUBLIC
STANDARD COINAGE

KM# 45 10 VATU
Copper-Nickel silver plated **Obv:** Arms **Rev:** Multicolor butterfly (Papilio Toboroi)

Date	Mintage	F	VF	XF	Unc	BU
2006	2,500	—	—	—	—	30.00

KM# 50 10 VATU
Copper-Nickel silver plated **Obv:** Arms **Rev:** Multicolor butterfly (Delias Sagessa)

Date	Mintage	F	VF	XF	Unc	BU
2006	2,500	—	—	—	—	30.00

KM# 46 10 VATU
Copper-Nickel silver plated **Obv:** Arms **Rev:** Multicolor butterfly (Taenaris Catops)

Date	Mintage	F	VF	XF	Unc	BU
2006	2,500	—	—	—	—	30.00

KM# 47 10 VATU
Copper-Nickel silver plated **Obv:** Arms **Rev:** Multicolor Butterfly (Ornithoptera Priamus Urvillianus)

Date	Mintage	F	VF	XF	Unc	BU
2006	2,500	—	—	—	—	30.00

KM# 48 10 VATU
Copper-Nickel silver plated **Obv:** Arms **Rev:** Multicolor butterfly (Ornithoptera Paradisea)

Date	Mintage	F	VF	XF	Unc	BU
2006	2,500	—	—	—	—	30.00

KM# 49 10 VATU
Copper-Nickel silver plated **Obv:** Arms **Rev:** Multicolor butterfly (Cethosia Cydippe)

Date	Mintage	F	VF	XF	Unc	BU
2006	2,500	—	—	—	—	30.00

KM# 38 50 VATU
28.3200 g., Silver, 38.6 mm. **Obv:** National arms **Obv. Legend:** RIPABLIK / VANUATU **Rev:** Early sailing ship center - left, stylized compass at right **Rev. Legend:** HISTORY OF SEAFARING / PEDRO FERNANDEZ DE QUIRÓS **Edge:** Reeded

Date	Mintage	F	VF	XF	Unc	BU
2005 Proof	—	Value: 45.00				

KM# 41 50 VATU
25.0000 g., 0.9000 Silver 0.7234 oz. ASW **Series:** Protection of Marine Life **Obv:** National arms **Rev:** Tiger Shark - multicolor

Date	Mintage	F	VF	XF	Unc	BU
2005 Proof	—	Value: 75.00				

KM# 42 50 VATU
25.0000 g., 0.9000 Silver 0.7234 oz. ASW **Series:** Protection of Marine Life **Obv:** National arms **Rev:** Sea Turtle - multicolor

Date	Mintage	F	VF	XF	Unc	BU
2006 Proof	—	Value: 75.00				

KM# 43 50 VATU
25.0000 g., 0.9000 Silver 0.7234 oz. ASW **Series:** Protection of Marine Life **Obv:** National arms **Rev:** Sea Horse - multicolor

Date	Mintage	F	VF	XF	Unc	BU
2006 Proof	—	Value: 75.00				

VATICAN CITY

The State of the Vatican City, a papal state on the right bank of the Tiber River within the boundaries of Rome, has an area of 0.17 sq. mi. (0.44 sq. km.) and a population of *775. Capital: Vatican City.

Today the Pope exercises supreme legislative, executive and judicial power within the Vatican City, and the State of the Vatican City is recognized by many nations as an independent sovereign state under the temporal jurisdiction of the Pope, even to the extent of ambassadorial exchange. The Pope is of course, the head of the Roman Catholic Church.

PONTIFFS
John Paul II, 1978-2005
  Sede Vacante, April 2 - 19, 2005
Benedict XVI, 2005-

MINT MARK
R – Rome

MONETARY SYSTEM
100 Centesimi = 1 Lira (thru 2002)
100 Euro Cent = 1 Euro

DATING
Most Vatican coins indicate the regnal year of the pope preceded by the word *Anno* (or an abbreviation), even if the *anno domini* date is omitted.

CITY STATE
DECIMAL COINAGE
100 Centesimi = 1 Lira

KM# 331 10 LIRE
1.6000 g., Aluminum, 23.2 mm. **Ruler:** John Paul II **Obv:** Bust left **Rev:** Papal arms **Edge:** Plain **Designer:** Laura Cretella

Date	Mintage	F	VF	XF	Unc	BU
2001/XXIII	—	—	0.50	1.00	3.00	—

KM# 332 20 LIRE
3.5700 g., Brass, 21.2 mm. **Ruler:** John Paul II **Obv:** Bust left **Rev:** Papal arms **Edge:** Plain **Designer:** Laura Cretella

Date	Mintage	F	VF	XF	Unc	BU
2001/XXIII	—	—	0.50	1.00	3.00	—

KM# 333 50 LIRE
4.5000 g., Copper-Nickel, 19.2 mm. **Ruler:** John Paul II **Obv:** Pius XII bust left **Rev:** Papal arms **Edge:** Plain **Designer:** Laura Cretella

Date	Mintage	F	VF	XF	Unc	BU
2001/XXIII	—	—	0.50	1.00	3.00	—

KM# 334 100 LIRE
4.5000 g., Copper-Nickel, 22 mm. **Ruler:** John Paul II **Obv:** Bust left **Rev:** Papal arms within circle **Edge:** Reeded and plain sections **Designer:** Laura Cretella

Date	Mintage	F	VF	XF	Unc	BU
2001/XXIII	—	—	0.50	1.00	3.00	—

KM# 335 200 LIRE
5.0000 g., Brass, 22 mm. **Ruler:** John Paul II **Obv:** Bust right **Rev:** Papal arms within circle **Edge:** Reeded **Designer:** Laura Cretella

Date	Mintage	F	VF	XF	Unc	BU
2001/XXIII	—	—	0.50	1.00	3.00	—

KM# 336 500 LIRE
6.7700 g., Bi-Metallic Aluminum-Bronze center in Stainless steel ring, 25.7 mm. **Ruler:** John Paul II **Obv:** Head left **Rev:** Papal arms within circle **Edge:** Reeded and plain sections **Designer:** Laura Cretella

Date	Mintage	F	VF	XF	Unc	BU
2001/XXIII	—	—	—	3.50	7.00	—

KM# 338 1000 LIRE
14.6000 g., 0.8350 Silver 0.3919 oz. ASW, 31.4 mm. **Ruler:** John Paul II **Subject:** Peace **Obv:** Stylized dove in front of globe **Rev:** Crowned shield **Edge Lettering:** +++ TOTVSTVVS +++ MMI

Date	Mintage	F	VF	XF	Unc	BU
2001/XXIII	—	—	—	20.00	35.00	—

KM# 337 1000 LIRE
8.8500 g., Copper-Nickel, 26.9 mm. **Ruler:** John Paul II **Obv:** Bust right **Rev:** Crowned shield **Edge:** Reeded and plain sections **Designer:** Laura Cretella

Date	Mintage	F	VF	XF	Unc	BU
2001/XIV	—	—	—	5.50	9.00	—

KM# 339 2000 LIRE
16.0000 g., 0.8350 Silver 0.4295 oz. ASW, 31.4 mm. **Ruler:** John Paul II **Subject:** Dialog for Peace **Obv:** Bust right holding croizer **Rev:** Dove above crowd **Edge:** Reeded **Designer:** Floriano Bodini

Date	Mintage	F	VF	XF	Unc	BU
2001/XXIII	16,000	—	—	25.00	40.00	—
2001/XXIII Proof	8,000	Value: 45.00				

KM# 340 5000 LIRE
18.0000 g., 0.8350 Silver 0.4832 oz. ASW, 32 mm.
Ruler: John Paul II **Subject:** Easter **Obv:** Kneeling Pope praying
Rev: Standing figure flanked by clouds below dove
Edge: Reeded and plain sections **Designer:** Floriano Bodini

Date	Mintage	F	VF	XF	Unc	BU
2001	—	—	—	30.00	45.00	—
2001/XXIII Proof	16,000	Value: 35.00				

KM# 390 50000 LIRE
7.5000 g., 0.9170 Gold 0.2211 oz. AGW, 23 mm.
Ruler: John Paul II **Subject:** Religeous symbols **Obv:** Bust right
Rev: Cross

Date	Mintage	F	VF	XF	Unc	BU
2001R	—	—	—	—	550	—
2001//XXIIIR Proof	6,000	Value: 550				

KM# 391 100000 LIRE
15.0000 g., 0.9170 Gold 0.4422 oz. AGW, 28.00 mm.
Ruler: John Paul II **Subject:** Religious symbols **Obv:** Bust right
Rev: Chi rho with Alpha and Omega letters

Date	Mintage	F	VF	XF	Unc	BU
2001R	—	—	—	—	800	—
2001//XXIIIR Proof	6,000	Value: 800				

EURO COINAGE
John Paul II

KM# 341 EURO CENT
2.2700 g., Copper Plated Steel, 16.2 mm. **Ruler:** John Paul II
Obv: Bust 1/4 left **Obv. Designer:** Guido Veroi **Rev:** Value and
globe **Rev. Designer:** Luc Luycx **Edge:** Plain

Date	Mintage	F	VF	XF	Unc	BU
2002R	80,000	—	—	—	115	—
2002R Proof	9,000	Value: 175				
2003R In sets only	65,000	—	—	—	55.00	—
2003R Proof	13,000	Value: 145				
2004R In sets only	65,000	—	—	—	25.00	—
2004R Proof	13,000	Value: 145				
2005R In sets only	85,000	—	—	—	25.00	—
2005R Proof	16,000	Value: 140				

KM# 342 2 EURO CENT
3.0300 g., Copper Plated Steel, 18.7 mm. **Ruler:** John Paul II
Obv: Bust 1/4 left **Obv. Designer:** Guido Veroi **Rev:** Value and
globe **Edge:** Grooved

Date	Mintage	F	VF	XF	Unc	BU
2002R	80,000	—	—	—	115	—
2002R Proof	9,000	Value: 175				
2003R In sets only	65,000	—	—	—	55.00	—
2003R Proof	13,000	Value: 145				
2004R In sets only	65,000	—	—	—	25.00	—
2004R Proof	13,000	Value: 145				
2005R In sets only	85,000	—	—	—	25.00	—
2005R Proof	16,000	Value: 140				

KM# 343 5 EURO CENT
3.8600 g., Copper Plated Steel, 21.2 mm. **Ruler:** John Paul II
Obv: Bust 1/4 left **Obv. Designer:** Guido Veroi **Rev:** Value and
globe **Edge:** Plain

Date	Mintage	F	VF	XF	Unc	BU
2002R	80,000	—	—	—	115	—
2002R Proof	9,000	Value: 175				

Date	Mintage	F	VF	XF	Unc	BU
2003R In sets only	65,000	—	—	—	55.00	—
2003R Proof	13,000	Value: 145				
2004R In sets only	65,000	—	—	—	28.00	—
2004R Proof	13,000	Value: 145				
2005R In sets only	85,000	—	—	—	28.00	—
2005R Proof	16,000	Value: 140				

KM# 344 10 EURO CENT
4.0700 g., Brass, 19.7 mm. **Ruler:** John Paul II **Obv:** Bust 1/4
left **Obv. Designer:** Guido Veroi **Rev. Designer:** Luc Luycx
Edge: Reeded

Date	Mintage	F	VF	XF	Unc	BU
2002R	80,000	—	—	—	115	—
2002R Proof	9,000	Value: 175				
2003R In sets only	65,000	—	—	—	55.00	—
2003R Proof	13,000	Value: 145				
2004R In sets only	65,000	—	—	—	35.00	—
2004R Proof	13,000	Value: 145				
2005R In sets only	85,000	—	—	—	35.00	—
2005R Proof	16,000	Value: 140				

KM# 345 20 EURO CENT
5.7300 g., Brass, 22.1 mm. **Ruler:** John Paul II **Obv:** Bust 1/4
left **Obv. Designer:** Guido Veroi **Rev:** Map and value
Rev. Designer: Luc Luycx **Edge:** Notched

Date	Mintage	F	VF	XF	Unc	BU
2002R	80,000	—	—	—	115	—
2002R Proof	9,000	Value: 175				
2003R In sets only	65,000	—	—	—	55.00	—
2003R Proof	13,000	Value: 145				
2004R In sets only	65,000	—	—	—	38.00	—
2004R Proof	13,000	Value: 145				
2005R In sets only	85,000	—	—	—	38.00	—
2005R Proof	16,000	Value: 140				

KM# 346 50 EURO CENT
7.8100 g., Brass, 24.2 mm. **Ruler:** John Paul II **Obv:** Bust 1/4
left **Obv. Designer:** Guido Veroi **Rev:** Map and value
Rev. Designer: Luc Luycx **Edge:** Reeded

Date	Mintage	F	VF	XF	Unc	BU
2002R	80,000	—	—	—	115	—
2002R Proof	9,000	Value: 175				
2003R In sets only	65,000	—	—	—	55.00	—
2003R Proof	13,000	Value: 145				
2004R In sets only	65,000	—	—	—	42.00	—
2004R Proof	13,000	Value: 145				
2005R In sets only	85,000	—	—	—	42.00	—
2005R Proof	16,000	Value: 140				

KM# 347 EURO
7.5000 g., Bi-Metallic Copper-Nickel center in Brass ring,
23.2 mm. **Ruler:** John Paul II **Obv:** Bust 1/4 left **Obv. Designer:**
Guido Veroi **Rev:** Value and map **Rev. Designer:** Luc Luycx
Edge: Reeded and plain sections

Date	Mintage	F	VF	XF	Unc	BU
2002R	80,000	—	—	—	100	—
2002R Proof	9,000	Value: 185				
2003R In sets only	65,000	—	—	—	75.00	—
2003R Proof	13,000	Value: 145				
2004R In sets only	65,000	—	—	—	60.00	—
2004R Proof	13,000	Value: 145				
2005R In sets only	85,000	—	—	—	60.00	—
2005R Proof	16,000	Value: 140				

KM# 348 2 EURO
8.5200 g., Bi-Metallic Brass center in Copper-Nickel ring,
25.7 mm. **Ruler:** John Paul II **Obv:** Bust 1/4 left **Obv. Designer:**
Guido Veroi **Rev:** Value and map **Rev. Designer:** Luc Luycx
Edge: Reeded **Edge Lettering:** 2's and stars

Date	Mintage	F	VF	XF	Unc	BU
2002R	80,000	—	—	—	165	—
2002R Proof	9,000	Value: 215				
2003R In sets only	65,000	—	—	—	100	—
2003R Proof	13,000	Value: 185				
2004R In sets only	65,000	—	—	—	80.00	—
2004R Proof	13,000	Value: 185				
2005R In sets only	85,000	—	—	—	80.00	—
2005R Proof	16,000	Value: 180				

KM# 358 2 EURO
8.5000 g., Bi-Metallic Brass center in Copper-Nickel ring,
25.75 mm. **Ruler:** John Paul II **Subject:** 75th Anniversary of the
Founding of the Vatican City State **Obv:** St. Peter's Square within
city walls, dates 1929-2004 **Rev:** Value and map **Edge:** Reeding
over 2's and stars **Designer:** Luciana de Simoni

Date	Mintage	F	VF	XF	Unc	BU
2004R	85,000	—	—	—	25.00	—

KM# 349 5 EURO
18.0000 g., 0.8350 Silver 0.4832 oz. ASW, 32 mm.
Ruler: John Paul II **Subject:** 24th Anniversary of Reign
Obv: Bust 1/4 left **Rev:** Allegorical female and bridge
Edge: Lettered **Edge Lettering:** +++ TOTUS TUUS +++ MMII

Date	Mintage	F	VF	XF	Unc	BU
2002R Proof	10,000	Value: 125				

KM# 354 5 EURO
18.0000 g., 0.9250 Silver 0.5353 oz. ASW, 34 mm. **Ruler:**
John Paul II **Subject:** Year of the Rosary **Obv:** Pope praying the
rosary **Rev:** "Our Lady of Pompei" presenting rosaries to Saints
Dominic and Catherine **Edge:** Reeded **Designer:** Roberto Mauri

Date	Mintage	F	VF	XF	Unc	BU
2003R Proof	10,000	—	—	—	65.00	—

KM# 359 5 EURO
18.0000 g., 0.9250 Silver 0.5353 oz. ASW, 32 mm.
Ruler: John Paul II **Subject:** 150th Anniversary of the
Proclamation of the Dogma of the Immaculate Conception
Obv: Virgin Mary **Rev:** Two Papal coat of arms **Edge:** Reeded
and plain sections **Designer:** Claudia Momoni

Date	Mintage	F	VF	XF	Unc	BU
2004R	13,000	—	—	—	60.00	—

KM# 350 10 EURO
22.0000 g., 0.8350 Silver 0.5906 oz. ASW, 34 mm.
Ruler: John Paul II **Subject:** 24th Anniversary of Reign
Obv: Pope holding crucifix **Rev:** Risen Christ (Message of peace)
Edge: Reeded **Designer:** Floriano Bodini

Date	Mintage	F	VF	XF	Unc	BU
2002R Proof	10,000	Value: 80.00				

KM# 355 10 EURO
22.0000 g., 0.9250 Silver 0.6542 oz. ASW, 34 mm.
Ruler: John Paul II **Subject:** 25th Anniversary of Reign
Obv: Pope praying **Rev:** St. Peter receiving the keys of Earth
and Heaven **Edge:** Reeded **Designer:** Amalia Mistichelli

Date	Mintage	F	VF	XF	Unc	BU
2003R Proof	10,000	Value: 80.00				

KM# 360 10 EURO
22.0000 g., 0.9250 Silver 0.6542 oz. ASW, 34 mm.
Ruler: John Paul II **Obv:** Pope praying for peace **Rev:** Tree of
Life rooted in virtues **Edge:** Reeded and plain sections
Designer: Maria Carmela Colaneri

Date	Mintage	F	VF	XF	Unc	BU
2004R	13,000	—	—	—	90.00	—

KM# 361 20 EURO
6.0000 g., 0.9170 Gold 0.1769 oz. AGW **Ruler:** John Paul II **Subject:** Roots of Faith **Rev:** Noah's Ark **Designer:** Floriano Bodini

Date	Mintage	F	VF	XF	Unc	BU
2002	2,800	Value: 1,200				

KM# 351 20 EURO
6.0000 g., 0.9166 Gold 0.1768 oz. AGW, 21 mm. **Ruler:** John Paul II **Rev:** Moses being found in floating basket **Edge:** Reeded **Designer:** Floriano Bodini

Date	Mintage	F	VF	XF	Unc	BU
2003R Proof	2,800	Value: 1,300				

KM# 363 20 EURO
6.0000 g., 0.9170 Gold 0.1769 oz. AGW, 21 mm. **Ruler:** John Paul II **Rev:** David slaying Goliath **Designer:** Floriano Bodini

Date	Mintage	F	VF	XF	Unc	BU
2004/XXVIIR Proof	3,050	Value: 1,200				

KM# 362 50 EURO
15.0000 g., 0.9170 Gold 0.4422 oz. AGW **Ruler:** John Paul II **Subject:** Roots of Faith **Rev:** Sacrifice of Abraham **Designer:** Floriano Bodini

Date	Mintage	F	VF	XF	Unc	BU
2002 Proof	2,800	Value: 2,200				

KM# 352 50 EURO
15.0000 g., 0.9166 Gold 0.4420 oz. AGW, 28 mm. **Ruler:** John Paul II **Rev:** Moses receiving the Ten Commandments **Edge:** Reeded **Designer:** Floriano Bodini

Date	Mintage	F	VF	XF	Unc	BU
2003R Proof	2,800	Value: 2,200				

KM# 364 50 EURO
15.0000 g., 0.9170 Gold 0.4422 oz. AGW **Ruler:** John Paul II **Rev:** Judgement of Solomon **Designer:** Floriano Bodini

Date	Mintage	F	VF	XF	Unc	BU
2004/XXVIIR Proof	3,050	Value: 2,200				

Sede Vacante

KM# 365 EURO CENT
2.2700 g., Copper Plated Steel **Ruler:** Sede Vacante **Obv:** Arms of Cardinal Eduardo Martinez Somalo **Obv. Designer:** Daniela Longo **Rev:** Value and globe **Rev. Designer:** Luc Luycx

Date	Mintage	F	VF	XF	Unc	BU
MMV (2005)R In sets only	60,000	—	—	—	—	45.00

KM# 366 2 EURO CENT
3.0300 g., Copper Plated Steel **Ruler:** Sede Vacante **Obv:** Arms of Cardinal Eduardo Martinez Somalo **Obv. Designer:** Daniela Longo **Rev:** Value and globe **Rev. Designer:** Luc Luycx

Date	Mintage	F	VF	XF	Unc	BU
MMV (2005)R In sets only	60,000	—	—	—	—	42.00

KM# 367 5 EURO CENT
3.8600 g., Copper Plated Steel **Ruler:** Sede Vacante **Obv:** Arms of Cardinal Eduardo Martinez Somalo **Obv. Designer:** Daniela Longo **Rev:** Value and globe **Rev. Designer:** Luc Luycx

Date	Mintage	F	VF	XF	Unc	BU
MMV (2005)R In sets only	60,000	—	—	—	—	45.00

KM# 368 10 EURO CENT
4.0700 g., Brass **Ruler:** Sede Vacante **Obv:** Arms of Cardinal Eduardo Martinez Somalo **Obv. Designer:** Daniela Longo **Rev:** Map and value **Rev. Designer:** Luc Luycx

Date	Mintage	F	VF	XF	Unc	BU
MMV (2005)R In sets only	60,000	—	—	—	—	48.00

KM# 369 20 EURO CENT
Brass **Ruler:** Sede Vacante **Obv:** Arms of Cardinal Eduardo Martinez Somalo **Obv. Designer:** Daniela Longo **Rev:** Map and value **Rev. Designer:** Luc Luycx

Date	Mintage	F	VF	XF	Unc	BU
MMV (2005)R In sets only	60,000	—	—	—	—	50.00

KM# 370 50 EURO CENT
7.8100 g., Brass **Ruler:** Sede Vacante **Obv:** Arms of Cardinal Eduardo Martinez Somalo **Obv. Designer:** Daniela Longo **Rev:** Map and value **Rev. Designer:** Luc Luycx

Date	Mintage	F	VF	XF	Unc	BU
MMV (2005)R In sets only	60,000	—	—	—	—	55.00

KM# 371 EURO
7.5000 g., Bi-Metallic Copper-Nickel center in brass ring **Ruler:** Sede Vacante **Obv:** Arms of Cardinal Eduardo Martinez Somalo **Obv. Designer:** Daniela Longo **Rev:** Value and map **Rev. Designer:** Luc Luycx

Date	Mintage	F	VF	XF	Unc	BU
MMV (2005)R In sets only	60,000	—	—	—	—	70.00

KM# 372 2 EURO
8.5200 g., Bi-Metallic Brass center in Copper-Nickel ring **Ruler:** Sede Vacante **Obv:** Arms of Cardinal Eduardo Martinez Somalo **Obv. Designer:** Daniela Longo **Rev:** Map and value **Rev. Designer:** Luc Luycx

Date	Mintage	F	VF	XF	Unc	BU
MMV (2005)R In sets only	60,000	—	—	—	—	75.00

KM# 373 5 EURO
18.0000 g., 0.9250 Silver 0.5353 oz. ASW, 32 mm. **Ruler:** Sede Vacante **Obv:** Dove within square **Rev:** Arms of Cardinal Jorge Arturo Medina Estevez **Edge:** Reeded **Designer:** Daniela Longo

Date	Mintage	F	VF	XF	Unc	BU
MMV (2005)R Proof	13,440	Value: 200				

Benedict XVI

KM# 375 EURO CENT
2.2900 g., Copper Plated Steel, 16.24 mm. **Ruler:** Benedict XVI **Obv:** Pope's bust facing 3/4 right **Obv. Legend:** CITTA' DEL VATICANO **Rev:** Value and globe **Edge:** Plain

Date	Mintage	F	VF	XF	Unc	BU
2006R In sets only	85,000	—	—	—	—	12.00
2006R Proof	16,000	Value: 18.00				
2007R In sets only	85,000	—	—	—	—	12.00
2007R Proof	16,000	Value: 18.00				
MMVIII (2008)R In sets only	85,000	—	—	—	—	12.00
MMVIII (2008)R Proof	16,000	Value: 18.00				
2009R In sets only	85,000	—	—	—	—	12.00
2009R Proof	16,000	Value: 18.00				
2010R In sets only	91,400	—	—	—	—	12.00
2010R Proof	15,000	Value: 18.00				

KM# 376 2 EURO CENT
3.0300 g., Copper Plated Steel, 18.73 mm. **Ruler:** Benedict XVI **Obv:** Pope's bust facing 3/4 right **Obv. Legend:** CITTA' DEL VATICANO **Rev:** Value and globe **Edge:** Plain

Date	Mintage	F	VF	XF	Unc	BU
2006R In sets only	85,000	—	—	—	—	15.00
2006R Proof	16,000	Value: 20.00				
2007R In sets only	85,000	—	—	—	—	15.00
2007R Proof	16,000	Value: 20.00				
MDVIII (2008)R In sets only	85,000	—	—	—	—	15.00
MDVIII (2008)R Proof	16,000	Value: 20.00				
2009R In sets only	85,000	—	—	—	—	15.00
2009R Proof	16,000	Value: 20.00				
2010R In sets only	91,400	—	—	—	—	15.00
2010R Proof	15,000	Value: 20.00				

KM# 377 5 EURO CENT
3.9600 g., Copper Plated Steel, 21.21 mm. **Ruler:** Benedict XVI **Obv:** Pope's bust facing 3/4 right **Obv. Legend:** CITTA' DEL VATICANO **Rev:** Value and globe **Edge:** Plain

Date	Mintage	F	VF	XF	Unc	BU
2006R In sets only	85,000	—	—	—	—	16.50
2006R Proof	16,000	Value: 22.50				
2007R In sets only	85,000	—	—	—	—	16.50
2007R Proof	16,000	Value: 22.50				
MDVIII (2008)R In sets only	85,000	—	—	—	—	16.50
MDVIII (2008)R Proof	16,000	Value: 22.50				
2009R In sets only	85,000	—	—	—	—	16.50
2009R Proof	16,000	Value: 22.50				
2010R In sets only	91,400	—	—	—	—	16.50
2010R Proof	15,000	Value: 22.50				

KM# 378 10 EURO CENT
4.0800 g., Brass, 19.73 mm. **Ruler:** Benedict XVI **Obv:** Pope's bust facing 3/4 right **Obv. Legend:** CITTA' DEL VATICANO **Rev:** Map and value **Edge:** Coarse reeding

Date	Mintage	F	VF	XF	Unc	BU
2006R In sets only	85,000	—	—	—	—	17.50
2006R Proof	16,000	Value: 25.00				
2007R In sets only	85,000	—	—	—	—	17.50
2007R Proof	16,000	Value: 25.00				

KM# 385 10 EURO CENT
4.0700 g., Brass **Ruler:** Benedict XVI **Obv. Designer:** Daniela Longo **Rev:** Relief map of Western Europe, stars, lines and value **Rev. Designer:** Luc Luycx

Date	Mintage	F	VF	XF	Unc	BU
MMVIII (2008)R In sets only	85,000	—	—	—	—	17.50
MMVIII (2008)R Proof	16,000	Value: 25.00				
2009R In sets only	85,000	—	—	—	—	17.50
2009R Proof	16,000	Value: 25.00				
2010R In sets only	91,400	—	—	—	—	17.50
2010R Proof	15,000	Value: 25.00				

KM# 379 20 EURO CENT
5.7200 g., Brass, 22.23 mm. **Ruler:** Benedict XVI **Obv:** Pope's bust facing 3/4 right **Obv. Legend:** CITTA' DEL VATICANO **Rev:** Map and value **Edge:** Plain with seven indents

Date	Mintage	F	VF	XF	Unc	BU
2006R In sets only	85,000	—	—	—	—	18.00
2006R Proof	16,000	Value: 28.00				
2007R In sets only	85,000	—	—	—	—	18.00
2007R Proof	16,000	Value: 28.00				

KM# 386 20 EURO CENT
Brass **Ruler:** Benedict XVI **Obv. Designer:** Daniela Longo **Rev:** Relief map of Western Europe, stars, lines and value **Rev. Designer:** Luc Luycx

Date	Mintage	F	VF	XF	Unc	BU
MMVIII (2008)R In sets only	85,000	—	—	—	—	18.00
MMVIII (2008)R Proof	16,000	Value: 28.00				
2009R In sets only	85,000	—	—	—	—	18.00
2009R Proof	16,000	Value: 28.00				
2010R In sets only	91,400	—	—	—	—	18.00
2010R Proof	15,000	Value: 28.00				

KM# 380 50 EURO CENT
7.8200 g., Brass, 24.23 mm. **Ruler:** Benedict XVI **Obv:** Pope's bust facing 3/4 right **Obv. Legend:** CITTA' DEL VATICANO **Rev:** Map and value **Edge:** Coarse reeding

Date	Mintage	F	VF	XF	Unc	BU
2006R In sets only	85,000	—	—	—	—	22.50
2006R Proof	16,000	Value: 35.00				
2007R In sets only	85,000	—	—	—	—	22.50
2007R Proof	16,000	Value: 35.00				

KM# 387 50 EURO CENT
7.8100 g., Brass **Ruler:** Benedict XVI **Rev:** Relief map of Western Europe, stars, lines and value **Rev. Designer:** Luc Luycx

Date	Mintage	F	VF	XF	Unc	BU
MMVIII (2008)R In sets only	85,000	—	—	—	—	32.50
MMVIII (2008)R Proof	16,000	Value: 40.00				
2009R In sets only	—	—	—	—	—	32.50
2009R Proof	—	Value: 40.00				
2010R In sets only	—	—	—	—	—	32.50
2010R Proof	—	Value: 40.00				

KM# 381 EURO
7.4700 g., Bi-Metallic Copper-Nickel center in brass ring., 23.23 mm. **Ruler:** Benedict XVI **Obv:** Pope's bust facing 3/4 right **Obv. Legend:** CITTA' - DEL VATICANO **Rev:** Value and map **Edge:** Segmented smooth and reeded

Date	Mintage	F	VF	XF	Unc	BU
2006R In sets only	85,000	—	—	—	—	25.00
2006R Proof	16,000	Value: 40.00				
2007R In sets only	85,000	—	—	—	—	25.00
2007R Proof	16,000	Value: 40.00				

KM# 388 EURO
7.5000 g., Bi-Metallic Copper-Nickel center in Brass ring **Ruler:** Benedict XVI **Rev:** Relief map of Western Europe, stars, lines and value **Rev. Designer:** Luc Luycx

Date	Mintage	F	VF	XF	Unc	BU
MMVIII (2008)R In sets only	85,000	—	—	—	—	25.00
MMVIII (2008)R Proof	16,000	Value: 40.00				
2009R In sets only	85,000	—	—	—	—	25.00
2009R Proof	16,000	Value: 40.00				
2010R In sets only	91,400	—	—	—	—	25.00
2010R Proof	15,000	Value: 40.00				

KM# 374 2 EURO
8.5200 g., Bi-Metallic Brass center in Copper-Nickel ring, 25.7 mm. **Ruler:** Benedict XVI **Subject:** World Youth Day **Obv:** Cologne Cathedral **Rev:** Value and Euro map

Date	Mintage	F	VF	XF	Unc	BU
2005R	—	—	—	—	90.00	—

KM# 382 2 EURO
8.5200 g., Bi-Metallic Brass center in Copper-Nickel ring., 25.69 mm. **Ruler:** Benedict XVI **Obv:** Pope's bust facing 3/4 right **Obv. Legend:** CITTA' - DEL VATICANO **Rev:** Value and map **Edge:** Reeded with stars and alternating 2's

Date	Mintage	F	VF	XF	Unc	BU
2006R In sets only	85,000	—	—	—	—	28.00
2006R Proof	16,000	Value: 50.00				
2007R In sets only	85,000	—	—	—	—	28.00
2007R Proof	16,000	Value: 50.00				

KM# 394 2 EURO
8.5200 g., Bi-Metallic Brass center in copper-nickel ring, 25.7 mm. **Ruler:** Benedict XVI **Subject:** Swiss guards, 500th Anniversary **Obv:** Swiss guard taking oath on flag **Rev:** Map and value

Date	Mintage	F	VF	XF	Unc	BU
ND (2006)R	100,000	—	—	—	80.00	—

KM# 399 2 EURO
8.5200 g., Bi-Metallic Brass center in copper-nickel ring, 25.7 mm. **Ruler:** Benedict XVI **Subject:** Pope Benedict's 80th Birthday **Obv:** Bust left **Rev:** Map and value

Date	Mintage	F	VF	XF	Unc	BU
2007R	100,000	—	—	—	50.00	—

KM# 389 2 EURO
8.5200 g., Bi-Metallic Brass center in Copper-Nickel ring, 25.7 mm. **Ruler:** Benedict XVI **Rev:** Relief map of Western Europe, stars, lines and value **Rev. Designer:** Luc Luycx

Date	Mintage	F	VF	XF	Unc	BU
MMVIII (2008)R In sets only	85,000	—	—	—	—	28.00
MMVIII (2008)R Proof	16,000	Value: 50.00				
2009R In sets only	85,000	—	—	—	—	28.00
2009R Proof	16,000	Value: 50.00				
2010R In sets only	91,400	—	—	—	—	28.00
2010R Proof	15,000	Value: 50.00				

KM# 404 2 EURO
8.5200 g., Bi-Metallic Brass center in copper-nickel ring, 25.7 mm. **Ruler:** Benedict XVI **Obv:** St. Paul being blinded on reary horse **Rev:** Map and value

Date	Mintage	F	VF	XF	Unc	BU
ND (2008)R	106,084	—	—	—	25.00	—

KM# 410 2 EURO
8.5200 g., Bi-Metallic Brass center in copper-nickel ring, 25.7 mm. **Ruler:** Benedict XVI **Subject:** International Year of Astronomy **Rev:** Map and value

Date	Mintage	F	VF	XF	Unc	BU
2009R	100,000	—	—	—	25.00	—

KM# 420 2 EURO
8.5200 g., Bi-Metallic **Ruler:** Benedict XVI **Subject:** Year of the Priest

Date	Mintage	F	VF	XF	Unc	BU
2010R	—	—	—	—	20.00	25.00

KM# 383 5 EURO
18.0000 g., 0.9250 Silver 0.5353 oz. ASW **Ruler:** Benedict XVI **Subject:** Life reborn **Obv:** Bust left **Rev:** Children playing among branches of an olive tree

Date	Mintage	F	VF	XF	Unc	BU
2005R Proof	13,000	Value: 100				

KM# 395 5 EURO
18.0000 g., 0.9250 Silver 0.5353 oz. ASW, 32 mm. **Ruler:** Benedict XVI **Subject:** World Day of Peace **Obv:** Half-length figure Benedict right in vestments with coizer **Rev:** St. Benedict of Nursia seated

Date	Mintage	F	VF	XF	Unc	BU
MMVI (2006)R Proof	14,160	Value: 90.00				

KM# 400 5 EURO
22.0000 g., 0.9250 Silver 0.6542 oz. ASW, 34 mm. **Ruler:** Benedict XVI **Subject:** World Day of Peace **Obv:** 1/2 length figure kneeling in prayer **Rev:** Standing St. Francis of Assissi, rays in background

Date	Mintage	F	VF	XF	Unc	BU
MMVII (2007)R Proof	13,693	Value: 55.00				

KM# 406 5 EURO
18.0000 g., 0.9250 Silver 0.5353 oz. ASW, 32 mm. **Ruler:** Benedict XVI **Subject:** World Youth Day - Sydney **Obv:** Pope right, blessing **Rev:** Sydney Harbor sites

Date	Mintage	F	VF	XF	Unc	BU
MMVIII (2008)R Proof	9,600	Value: 60.00				

KM# 415 5 EURO
18.0000 g., 0.9250 Silver 0.5353 oz. ASW, 32 mm. **Ruler:** Benedict XVI **Subject:** World day of Peace **Obv:** Bust right in prayer **Rev:** Candle, family

Date	Mintage	F	VF	XF	Unc	BU
2009R Proof	9,600	Value: 60.00				

KM# 421 5 EURO
18.0000 g., 0.9250 Silver 0.5353 oz. ASW, 32 mm. **Ruler:** Benedict XVI **Subject:** Migrants and Refugees

Date	Mintage	F	VF	XF	Unc	BU
2010R Proof	—	Value: 75.00				

KM# 384 10 EURO
22.0000 g., 0.9250 Silver 0.6542 oz. ASW **Ruler:** Benedict XVI **Subject:** Disciples of Emanaus **Obv:** Bust left **Rev:** Three men seated at table

Date	Mintage	F	VF	XF	Unc	BU
2006R Proof	13,000	Value: 215				

KM# 396 10 EURO
22.0000 g., 0.9250 Silver 0.6542 oz. ASW, 34 mm. **Ruler:** Benedict XVI **Subject:** St. Peter's Collonade, 350th Anniversary **Obv:** Collonade & Pope Benedict **Rev:** Collonade Schematics

Date	Mintage	F	VF	XF	Unc	BU
AN II MMVI (2006)R Proof	14,160	Value: 90.00				

KM# 401 10 EURO
22.0000 g., 0.9250 Silver 0.6542 oz. ASW, 34 mm. **Ruler:** Benedict XVI **Subject:** World Mission Day **Obv:** Bust right in ermine cape **Rev:** Blessed Mother Theresa of Calcutta and child

Date	Mintage	F	VF	XF	Unc	BU
AN III MVII (2007)R Proof	13,694	Value: 80.00				

KM# 407 10 EURO
22.0000 g., 0.9250 Silver 0.6542 oz. ASW, 34 mm. **Ruler:** Benedict XVI **Subject:** World Day of Peace **Obv:** Pope seated on chair in full robes and miter **Rev:** The Holy Family - Jesus, Mary, Joseph

Date	Mintage	F	VF	XF	Unc	BU
A VI MMVIII (2008)R Proof	9,602	Value: 95.00				

KM# 417 10 EURO
22.0000 g., 0.9250 Silver 0.6542 oz. ASW, 22 mm. **Ruler:** Benedict XVI **Subject:** Lateran Treaty, 80th Anniversary **Obv:** Bust right **Rev:** Rolled treaty with seal

Date	Mintage	F	VF	XF	Unc	BU
2009R Proof	9,602	Value: 95.00				

KM# 422 10 EURO
22.0000 g., 0.9250 Silver 0.6542 oz. ASW, 34 mm. **Ruler:** Benedict XVI **Subject:** 43rd World day of Peace

Date	Mintage	F	VF	XF	Unc	BU
2010R Proof	—	Value: 80.00				

KM# 392 20 EURO
6.0000 g., 0.9160 Gold 0.1767 oz. AGW, 21 mm. **Ruler:** Benedict XVI **Subject:** Christian Initiation - Baptism **Obv:** Pope seated **Rev:** Fountain

Date	Mintage	F	VF	XF	Unc	BU
AN I MMV (2005)R Proof	3,046	Value: 600				

KM# 397 20 EURO
6.0000 g., 0.9160 Gold 0.1767 oz. AGW, 21 mm. **Ruler:** Benedict XVI **Subject:** Christian Initiation - Confirmation **Obv:** Bust right **Rev:** Bishop confirming three

Date	Mintage	F	VF	XF	Unc	BU
AN II MMVI (2006)R Proof	3,326	Value: 600				

KM# 402 20 EURO
6.0000 g., 0.9160 Gold 0.1767 oz. AGW, 21 mm. **Ruler:** Benedict XVI **Subject:** Christain Initiation - Eucharist **Obv:** Bust left in ermine cape **Rev:** Basket of fish and bread

Date	Mintage	F	VF	XF	Unc	BU
AN III (2007)R Proof	3,426	Value: 600				

KM# 408 20 EURO
6.0000 g., 0.9170 Gold 0.1769 oz. AGW, 21 mm. **Ruler:** Benedict XVI **Subject:** Vatican sculpture **Obv:** Pope right in mitre **Rev:** Torso of Belvedere

Date	Mintage	F	VF	XF	Unc	BU
AN IV MMVIII (2008)R Proof	2,930	Value: 500				

KM# 416 20 EURO
6.0000 g., 0.9170 Gold 0.1769 oz. AGW, 21 mm. **Ruler:** Benedict XVI **Subject:** Masterworks in the Vatican Collection **Rev:** Christ and the Lamb

Date	Mintage	F	VF	XF	Unc	BU
2009R Proof	2,934	Value: 550				

KM# 423 20 EURO
6.0000 g., 0.9170 Gold 0.1769 oz. AGW **Ruler:** Benedict XVI **Subject:** Vatican Sculpture - Apollo Belvedere

Date	Mintage	F	VF	XF	Unc	BU
2010R Proof	—	Value: 550				

KM# 393 50 EURO
15.0000 g., 0.9160 Gold 0.4417 oz. AGW, 28 mm. **Ruler:** Benedict XVI **Subject:** Christian Initiation - Baptism **Obv:** Pope seated **Rev:** John baptising Christ

Date	Mintage	F	VF	XF	Unc	BU
AN I MMV (2005)R Proof	3,044	Value: 1,500				

KM# 398 50 EURO
15.0000 g., 0.9160 Gold 0.4417 oz. AGW, 28 mm. **Ruler:** Benedict XVI **Subject:** Christian Initiation - Confirmation **Obv:** Bust right **Rev:** Tongues of fire decending on Apostles

Date	Mintage	F	VF	XF	Unc	BU
AN II MMVI (2006)R Proof	3,324	Value: 1,500				

KM# 403 50 EURO
15.0000 g., 0.9160 Gold 0.4417 oz. AGW, 28 mm. **Ruler:** Benedict XVI **Subject:** Christian Initiation - Eucharist **Obv:** Bust left in ermine cape **Rev:** Scene of the Last Supper

Date	Mintage	F	VF	XF	Unc	BU
ANIII MMVII (2007)R Proof	—	Value: 1,500				

KM# 409 50 EURO
15.0000 g., 0.9170 Gold 0.4422 oz. AGW, 28 mm. **Ruler:** Benedict XVI **Subject:** Vatican sculpture **Obv:** Pope right in mitre **Rev:** The Pieta

Date	Mintage	F	VF	XF	Unc	BU
AN IV MMVIII (2008)R Proof	—	Value: 1,000				

KM# 418 50 EURO
15.0000 g., 0.9170 Gold 0.4422 oz. AGW **Ruler:** Benedict XVI **Subject:** Masterworks in the Vatican Collection **Rev:** Hercules statue group **Edge:** 28

Date	Mintage	F	VF	XF	Unc	BU
2009R Proof	2,930	Value: 1,200				

KM# 424 50 EURO
15.0000 g., 0.9170 Gold 0.4422 oz. AGW, 28 mm. **Ruler:** Benedict XVI **Subject:** Vatican Sculpture - Augustus of Prima

Date	Mintage	F	VF	XF	Unc	BU
2010R Proof	—	Value: 1,200				

KM# 405 100 EURO
30.0000 g., 0.9170 Gold 0.8844 oz. AGW, 30 mm. **Ruler:** Benedict XVI **Obv:** Bust left **Rev:** The Creator from the Sistine Chapel ceiling

Date	Mintage	F	VF	XF	Unc	BU
AN IV MMVIII (2008)R Proof	960	Value: 1,600				

KM# 419 100 EURO
30.0000 g., 0.9170 Gold 0.8844 oz. AGW, 30 mm. **Ruler:** Benedict XVI **Subject:** Sistine Chapel - Banishment from Eden

Date	Mintage	F	VF	XF	Unc	BU
2009R Proof	—	Value: 1,600				

KM# 425 100 EURO
30.0000 g., 0.9170 Gold 0.8844 oz. AGW, 30 mm. **Ruler:** Benedict XVI **Subject:** Sistine Chapel - Last Judgement

Date	Mintage	F	VF	XF	Unc	BU
2010R Proof	—	Value: 1,400				

MINT SETS

KM#	Date	Mintage	Identification	Issue Price	Mkt Val
MS107	2001 (8)	26,000	KM#331-338	21.25	200
MS108	2002 (8)	65,000	KM#341-348	12.00	975
MS109	2003 (8)	65,000	KM#341-348	15.00	500
MS110	2004 (8)	85,000	KM#341-348	16.50	335
MS111	2005 (8)	85,000	KM#341-348.	32.50	335
MS112	MMV (2005)(8)	60,000	KM#365-372 Sede Vacante	—	435
MS113	2006 (8)	—	KM#375-382	—	210
MS114	2007 (8)	—	KM#375-382	—	230
MS115	2008 (8)	85,000	KM#375-377, 385-389	45.00	150
MS116	2009 (8)	91,400	KM#375-377, 385-389	30.00	150
MS117	2010 (8)	—	KM#375-377, 385-389	30.00	150

PROOF SETS

KM#	Date	Mintage	Identification	Issue Price	Mkt Val
PS13	2001 (2)	—	KM#390, 391	—	1,350
PS15	2002 (8)	9,000	KM#341-348	75.00	1,450
PS16	2003 (8)	13,000	KM#341-348	78.00	1,200
PS17	2004 (8)	13,000	KM#341-348	—	1,200
PS18	2005 (8)	16,000	KM#341-348 plus silver medal	150	1,175
PS19	2006 (8)	16,000	KM#375-382 plus silver medal	—	375
PS20	2007 (8)	16,000	KM#375-382 plus silver medal	—	315
PS21	2008 (8)	16,000	KM#375-377, 385-389 plus silver medal	195	240
PS22	2009 (8)	15,000	KM#375-377, 385-389 plus silver medal	195	240
PS23	2010 (8)	—	KM#375-377, 385-389 plus silver medal	195	240

VENEZUELA

Caribbean Sea
North Atlantic Ocean
GUYANA
SURINAME
FRENCH GUIANA
COLOMBIA
BRAZIL

The Bolivarian Republic of Venezuela ("Little Venice"), located on the northern coast of South America between Colombia and Guyana, has an area of 352,145 sq. mi.(912,050 sq. km.) and a population of 20 million. Capital: Caracas. Petroleum and mining provide a significant portion of Venezuela's exports. Coffee, grown on 60,000 plantations, is the chief crop. Metalurgy, refining, oil, iron and steel production are the main employment industries.

GOVERNMENT
Republic, 1823-2000
Republic Bolivarian, 2000-

MINT MARKS
Maracay

REPUBLIC
Bolivariana
REFORM COINAGE
1896; 100 Centimos = 1 Bolivar

Y# 80   10 BOLIVARES
2.3300 g., Nickel Clad Steel, 17 mm. **Obv:** National arms left of denomination **Obv. Legend:** REPÚBLICA BOLIVARIANA DE VENEZUELA **Rev:** Head of Bolívar left in 7-sided outline **Rev. Legend:** BOLÍVAR - LIBERTADOR **Rev. Designer:** Albert Barre **Edge:** Reeded

Date	Mintage	F	VF	XF	Unc	BU
2001	—	—	—	—	0.25	0.50
2002	—	—	—	—	0.25	0.50

Y# 80a   10 BOLIVARES
1.7390 g., Aluminum-Zinc, 16.92 mm. **Obv:** Nat. arms and value **Obv. Legend:** REPÚBLICA BOLIVARIANA DE VENEZUELA **Rev:** Head of Bolívar left in 7-sided outline **Rev. Legend:** BOLÍVAR - LIBERTADOR **Rev. Designer:** Albert Barre **Edge:** Reeded

Date	Mintage	F	VF	XF	Unc	BU
2001	—	—	—	0.15	0.45	0.60
2002	—	—	—	0.15	0.45	0.60
2004	—	—	—	0.15	0.45	0.60

Y# 81   20 BOLIVARES
4.3200 g., Nickel Clad Steel, 20 mm. **Obv:** National arms left of denom. **Obv. Legend:** REPÚBLICA BOLIVARIANA DE VENEZUELA **Rev:** Head of Bolivar left in 7-sided outline **Rev. Legend:** BOLÍVAR - LIBERTADOR **Rev. Designer:** Albert Barre **Edge:** Plain

Date	Mintage	F	VF	XF	Unc	BU
2001	—	—	—	—	0.25	0.50
2002	—	—	—	—	0.25	0.50

Y# 81a.1   20 BOLIVARES
3.2650 g., Aluminum-Zinc, 20 mm. **Obv:** National arms and value with wavy based "2" **Obv. Legend:** REPÚBLICA BOLIVARIANA DE VENEZUELA **Rev:** Head of Bolívar left in 7-sided outline **Rev. Legend:** BOLÍVAR - LIBERTADOR **Rev. Designer:** Albert Barre **Edge:** Plain

Date	Mintage	F	VF	XF	Unc	BU
2001	—	—	—	—	0.65	1.00

Y# 81a.2   20 BOLIVARES
3.2400 g., Aluminum-Zinc, 20 mm. **Obv:** National arms and value with flat based "2" **Obv. Legend:** REPÚBLICA BOLIVARIANA DE VENEZUELA **Rev:** Head of Bolívar left in 7-sided outline **Rev. Legend:** BOLÍVAR - LIBERTADOR **Rev. Designer:** Albert Barre **Edge:** Plain

Date	Mintage	F	VF	XF	Unc	BU
2002	—	—	—	0.25	0.60	0.80
2004	—	—	—	0.25	0.60	0.80

Y# 82   50 BOLIVARES
6.5800 g., Nickel Clad Steel, 23 mm. **Obv:** National arms left of denomination **Obv. Legend:** REPÚBLICA BOLIVARIANA DE VENEZUELA **Rev:** Head of Bolivar left in 7-sided outline **Rev. Legend:** BOLÍVAR - LIBERTADOR **Rev. Designer:** Albert Barre **Edge:** Reeded

Date	Mintage	F	VF	XF	Unc	BU
2001	—	—	—	0.30	0.75	1.00
2004	—	—	—	0.30	0.75	1.00

Y# 83   100 BOLIVARES
6.8200 g., Nickel Clad Steel, 25 mm. **Obv:** National arms and value **Obv. Legend:** REPÚBUBLICA BOLIVARIANA DE VENEZUELA **Rev:** Head of Bolívar left in 7-sided ouline **Rev. Legend:** BOLÍVAR - LIBERTADO **Rev. Designer:** Albert Barre **Edge:** Plain

Date	Mintage	F	VF	XF	Unc	BU
2001	—	—	—	0.45	1.10	1.50
2002	—	—	—	0.45	1.10	1.50
2004	—	—	—	0.45	1.10	1.50

Y# 94   500 BOLIVARES
8.5000 g., Nickel Plated Steel, 28.4 mm. **Obv:** National arms and denomination **Obv. Legend:** REPÚBLICA BOLIVARIANA DE VENEZUELA **Rev:** Head of Bolívar left in 7-sided outline **Rev. Legend:** BOLÍVAR - LIBERTADOR **Rev. Designer:** Albert Barre **Edge:** Segmented reeding

Date	Mintage	F	VF	XF	Unc	BU
2004	—	—	—	0.60	1.50	2.00

Y# 85   1000 BOLIVARES
8.3500 g., Bi-Metallic Copper-Nickel center in Brass ring, 24 mm. **Obv:** National arms and value in center **Obv. Legend:** REPÚBLICA BOLIVARIANA DE VENEZUELA **Rev:** Head of Bolívar left **Rev. Legend:** BOLÍVAR - LIBERTADOR **Rev. Designer:** Albert Barre **Edge:** Lettered **Edge Lettering:** "BCV 1000" four times

Date	Mintage	F	VF	XF	Unc	BU
2005	9,000,000	—	—	0.90	2.25	3.00

REFORM COINAGE
2007-
1000 Bolivares = 1 Bolivar Fuerte

Y# 87   CENTIMO
1.3600 g., Copper Plated Steel, 14.9 mm. **Obv:** National arms **Obv. Legend:** REPÚBLICA BOLIVARIANA DE VENEZUELA **Rev:** Eight stars at left, large value at right **Edge:** Reeded

Date	Mintage	F	VF	XF	Unc	BU
2007	—	—	—	—	0.25	0.35

Y# 88   5 CENTIMOS
2.0300 g., Copper Plated Steel, 16.9 mm. **Obv:** National arms **Obv. Legend:** REPÚBLICA BOLIVARIANA DE VENEZUELA **Rev:** Eight stars at left, large value at right **Edge:** Plain

Date	Mintage	F	VF	XF	Unc	BU
2007	—	—	—	—	0.50	0.75

Y# 89   10 CENTIMOS
2.6200 g., Nickel Plated Steel, 18 mm. **Obv:** National arms **Obv. Legend:** REPÚBLICA BOLIVARIANA DE VENEZUELA **Rev:** Eight stars at left, large value at right **Edge:** Reeded

Date	Mintage	F	VF	XF	Unc	BU
2007	—	—	—	—	0.75	1.00

Y# 90   12-1/2 CENTIMOS
3.9300 g., Nickel Plated Steel, 23 mm. **Obv:** National arms **Obv. Legend:** REPÚBLICA BOLIVARIANA DE VENEZUELA **Rev:** Large value, eight stars below in sprays **Edge:** Plain

Date	Mintage	F	VF	XF	Unc	BU
2007	—	—	—	—	1.50	1.75

Y# 91   25 CENTIMOS
3.8600 g., Nickel Plated Steel, 20 mm. **Obv:** National arms **Obv. Legend:** REPÚBLICA BOLIVARIANA DE VENEZUELA **Rev:** Eight stars at left, large value at center right **Edge:** Plain

Date	Mintage	F	VF	XF	Unc	BU
2007	—	—	—	—	2.00	2.50

Y# 92   50 CENTIMOS
4.3000 g., Nickel Plated Steel, 21.9 mm. **Obv:** National arms **Obv. Legend:** REPÚBLICA BOLIVARIANA DE VENEZUELA **Rev:** Eight stars at left, large value at center right **Edge:** Segmented reeding

Date	Mintage	F	VF	XF	Unc	BU
2007	—	—	—	—	3.00	3.50

Y# 93 BOLIVAR
8.0400 g., Bi-Metallic Nickel center in Aluminum-Bronze ring, 24 mm. **Obv:** Eight stars at left of national arms, large value at right **Obv. Legend:** REPÚBLICA BOLIVARIANA DE VENEZUELA **Rev:** Head of Bolívar left **Rev. Designer:** Albert Barre **Edge:** Lettered **Edge Lettering:** "BCV 1" repeated

Date	Mintage	F	VF	XF	Unc	BU
2007	—	—	—	—	5.00	6.00

VIET NAM

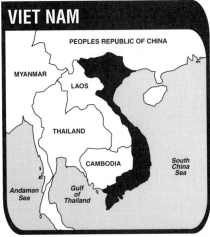

The Socialist Republic of Viet Nam, located in Southeast Asia west of the South China Sea, has an area of 127,300 sq. mi. (329,560 sq. km.) and a population of *66.8 million. Capital: Hanoi. Agricultural products, coal, and mineral ores are exported.

The activities of Communists in South Viet Nam led to the second Indochina war which came to a brief halt in 1973 (when a cease-fire was arranged and U.S. forces withdrew), but it didn't end until April 30, 1975 when South Viet Nam surrendered unconditionally. The two Viet Nams were reunited as the Socialist Republic of Viet Nam on July 2, 1976.

NOTE: For earlier coinage refer to French Indo-China or Tonkin.

SOCIALIST REPUBLIC
STANDARD COINAGE

KM# 71 200 DONG
3.1000 g., Nickel Clad Steel, 20.75 mm. **Obv:** National emblem **Rev:** Denomination

Date	Mintage	F	VF	XF	Unc	BU
2003	125,000,000	0.15	0.20	0.35	0.75	0.50

KM# 74 500 DONG
4.5000 g., Nickel Clad Steel, 21.86 mm. **Obv:** National emblem **Rev:** Denomination **Edge:** Segmented reeding

Date	Mintage	F	VF	XF	Unc	BU
2003	175,000,000	0.15	0.25	0.50	0.75	1.00

KM# 72 1000 DONG
3.7000 g., Brass Plated Steel, 19.75 mm. **Obv:** National emblem **Rev:** Bat De Pagoda in Hanoi **Edge:** Reeded

Date	Mintage	F	VF	XF	Unc	BU
2003	250,000,000	0.20	0.35	0.60	0.80	1.50

KM# 75 2000 DONG
5.0000 g., Brass Plated Steel, 23.92 mm. **Obv:** National emblem **Rev:** Highland Stilt House in Tay Nguyen above value **Edge:** Segmented reeding

Date	Mintage	F	VF	XF	Unc	BU
2003	—	—	—	—	2.25	2.75

KM# 64 5000 DONG
1.2441 g., 0.9999 Gold 0.0400 oz. AGW, 13.92 mm. **Subject:** Year of the Snake **Obv:** State emblem **Rev:** Sea snake **Edge:** Reeded

Date	Mintage	F	VF	XF	Unc	BU
2001	—	—	—	—	60.00	75.00

KM# 67 5000 DONG
1.2441 g., 0.9999 Gold 0.0400 oz. AGW, 13.9 mm. **Subject:** Year of the Horse **Obv:** State emblem **Rev:** Horse **Edge:** Reeded

Date	Mintage	F	VF	XF	Unc	BU
2002	28,000	—	—	—	50.00	65.00

KM# 73 5000 DONG
7.6000 g., Brass, 25 mm. **Obv:** National emblem **Rev:** Chua Mot Cot Pagoda in Hanoi

Date	Mintage	F	VF	XF	Unc	BU
2003	500,000,000	0.50	0.75	1.00	1.25	2.50

KM# 57 10000 DONG
20.0000 g., 0.9250 Silver 0.5948 oz. ASW, 38.7 mm. **Subject:** Year of the Snake **Obv:** State emblem above value **Obv. Legend:** "CONG HOA XA HOI CHU NGHIA VIET NAM" **Rev:** Sea snake **Rev. Legend:** "...VIET NAM" **Edge:** Reeded

Date	Mintage	F	VF	XF	Unc	BU
2001(S) Proof	3,500	Value: 50.00				

KM# 58 10000 DONG
20.0000 g., 0.9250 Silver 0.5948 oz. ASW **Subject:** Year of the Snake **Obv:** State emblem above value **Obv. Legend:** "CONG HOA XA HOI CHU NGHIA VIET NAM" **Rev:** Bamboo viper **Rev. Legend:** "...VIET NAM"

Date	Mintage	F	VF	XF	Unc	BU
2001(S) Proof	3,500	Value: 50.00				

KM# 59 10000 DONG
20.0000 g., 0.9250 Silver 0.5948 oz. ASW **Subject:** Year of the Snake **Obv:** State emblem above value **Obv. Legend:** "CONG HOA XA HOI CHU NGHIA VIET NAM" **Rev:** Multicolor holographic, cobra in center **Rev. Legend:** "...VIET NAM"

Date	Mintage	F	VF	XF	Unc	BU
2001(S) Proof	3,500	Value: 40.00				

KM# 61 10000 DONG
20.0000 g., 0.9990 Silver 0.6423 oz. ASW, 38.7 mm. **Subject:** Year of the Horse **Obv:** State emblem **Rev:** Horse with octagonal latent image **Edge:** Reeded

Date	Mintage	F	VF	XF	Unc	BU
2001 Proof	3,800	Value: 40.00				

Note: In proof set only

KM# 62 10000 DONG
20.0000 g., 0.9990 Silver 0.6423 oz. ASW, 38.7 mm. **Subject:** Year of the Horse **Obv:** State emblem **Rev:** Horse with multicolor accouterments **Edge:** Reeded

Date	Mintage	F	VF	XF	Unc	BU
2001 Proof	3,800	Value: 40.00				

Note: In proof set only

KM# 63 10000 DONG
20.0000 g., 0.9990 Silver 0.6423 oz. ASW, 38.7 mm. **Subject:** Year of the Horse **Obv:** State emblem **Rev:** Multicolor holographic horse in center **Edge:** Reeded

Date	Mintage	F	VF	XF	Unc	BU
2001 Proof	3,800	Value: 37.50				

Note: In proof set only

KM# 76 10000 DONG
20.0000 g., 0.9990 Silver 0.6423 oz. ASW, 38.7 mm. **Obv:** State emblem **Rev:** Multicolored Grey-shanked Douc Langur monkey **Edge:** Reeded

Date	Mintage	F	VF	XF	Unc	BU
2004 Proof	6,200	Value: 40.00				

KM# 65 20000 DONG
7.7759 g., 0.9999 Gold 0.2500 oz. AGW, 22 mm. **Subject:** Year of the Snake **Obv:** State emblem **Rev:** Sea snake **Edge:** Reeded

Date	Mintage	F	VF	XF	Unc	BU
2001(S) Proof	—	Value: 350				

Note: Issued in a replica Faberge egg

KM# 68 20000 DONG
7.7759 g., 0.9999 Gold 0.2500 oz. AGW, 22 mm. **Subject:** Year of the Horse **Obv:** State emblem **Rev:** Horse **Edge:** Reeded

Date	Mintage	F	VF	XF	Unc	BU
2002 Proof	1,800	Value: 350				

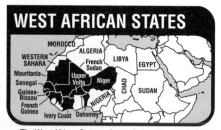

KM# 66 50000 DONG
15.5518 g., 0.9999 Gold 0.4999 oz. AGW, 27 mm. **Subject:** Year of the Snake **Obv:** State emblem **Rev:** Multicolor holographic King Cobra **Edge:** Reeded

Date	Mintage	F	VF	XF	Unc	BU
2001(S) Proof	3,200	Value: 675				

KM# 69 50000 DONG
15.5518 g., 0.9999 Gold 0.4999 oz. AGW, 27 mm. **Subject:** Year of the Horse **Obv:** State emblem **Rev:** Multicolor holographic horse **Edge:** Reeded

Date	Mintage	F	VF	XF	Unc	BU
2002 Proof	3,800	Value: 650				

PROOF SETS

KM#	Date	Mintage	Identification	Issue Price	Mkt Val
PS4	2001(S) (3)	3,500	KM#57-59	120	140
PS5	2001(S) (2)	—	KM#59, 66	—	715
PS6	2001(S) (2)	—	KM#65-66	—	1,025
PS7	2002 (3)	3,800	KM#61-63	—	120

WEST AFRICAN STATES

The West African States, a former federation of eight French colonial territories on the northwest coast of Africa, has an area of 1,831,079 sq. mi. (4,742,495 sq. km.) and a population of about 17 million. Capital: Dakar. The constituent territories were Mauritania, Senegal, Dahomey, French Sudan, Ivory Coast, Upper Volta, Niger and French Guinea.

The members of the federation were overseas territories within the French Union until Sept. of 1958 when all but French Guinea approved the constitution of the Fifth French Republic, thereby electing to become autonomous members of the new French Community. French Guinea voted to become the fully independent Republic of Guinea. The other seven attained independence in 1960. The French West Africa territories were provided with a common currency, a practice which was continued as the monetary union of the West African States which provides a common currency for the autonomous republics of Dahomey (now Benin), Senegal, Upper Volta (now Burkina Faso), Ivory Coast, Mali, Togo, Niger, and Guinea-Bissau.

For earlier coinage refer to Togo, and French West Africa.

MINT MARK
(a)- Paris, privy marks only

MONETARY SYSTEM
100 Centimes = 1 Franc

FEDERATION

STANDARD COINAGE

KM# 8 FRANC
1.6000 g., Steel **Obv:** Taku - Ashanti gold weight **Rev:** Value and date **Designer:** R. Joly

Date	Mintage	F	VF	XF	Unc	BU
2001(a)	—	—	—	0.10	0.35	0.60
2002(a)	—	—	—	0.10	0.35	0.60

KM# 2a 5 FRANCS
3.0000 g., Aluminum-Nickel-Bronze, 20 mm. **Obv:** Taku - Ashanti gold weight divides value **Rev:** Gazelle head facing

Date	Mintage	F	VF	XF	Unc	BU
2001(a)	—	—	0.10	0.20	0.40	0.60
2002(a)	—	—	0.10	0.20	0.40	0.60
2003(a)	—	—	0.10	0.20	0.40	0.60
2004(a)	—	—	0.10	0.20	0.40	0.60
2005(a)	—	—	0.10	0.20	0.40	0.60
2006(a)	—	—	0.10	0.20	0.40	0.60

KM# 10 10 FRANCS
4.0400 g., Brass, 23.4 mm. **Series:** F.A.O. **Obv:** Taku - Ashanti gold weight divides value **Rev:** People getting water **Designer:** R. Joly

Date	Mintage	F	VF	XF	Unc	BU
2002(a)	—	—	0.25	0.50	1.25	1.50
2003(a)	—	—	0.25	0.50	1.25	1.50
2004(a)	—	—	0.25	0.50	1.00	1.50
2005(a)	—	—	0.25	0.50	1.00	1.50
2006(a)	—	—	0.25	0.50	1.00	1.50

KM# 9 25 FRANCS
7.9500 g., Aluminum-Bronze, 27 mm. **Series:** F.A.O. **Obv:** Taku - Ashanti gold weight divides value **Rev:** Figure filling tube

Date	Mintage	F	VF	XF	Unc	BU
2001(a)	—	—	0.25	0.75	1.75	2.00
2002(a)	—	—	0.25	0.75	1.75	2.00
2003(a)	—	—	0.25	0.75	1.75	2.00
2004(a)	—	—	0.25	0.75	1.50	2.00
2005(a)	—	—	0.25	0.75	1.50	2.00

KM# 6 50 FRANCS
5.0900 g., Copper-Nickel, 22 mm. **Series:** F.A.O. **Obv:** Taku - Ashanti gold weight **Rev:** Value within mixed beans, grains and nuts **Designer:** R. Joly

Date	Mintage	F	VF	XF	Unc	BU
2001(a)	—	—	0.35	0.50	1.25	1.50
2002(a)	—	—	0.35	0.50	1.25	1.50
2003(a)	—	—	0.35	0.50	1.25	1.50
2004(a)	—	—	0.35	0.50	1.25	1.50
2005(a)	—	—	0.35	0.50	1.25	1.50

KM# 4 100 FRANCS
7.0700 g., Nickel, 26 mm. **Obv:** Taku - Ashanti gold weight **Rev:** Value within flowers **Designer:** R. Joly

Date	Mintage	F	VF	XF	Unc	BU
2001(a)	—	—	0.60	0.85	2.25	2.75
2002(a)	—	—	0.60	0.85	2.25	2.75
2003(a)	—	—	0.60	0.85	2.25	2.75
2004(a)	—	—	0.60	0.75	2.00	2.75
2005(a)	—	—	0.60	0.75	2.00	2.75

KM# 14 200 FRANCS
6.9000 g., Bi-Metallic Brass center in Copper-Nickel ring, 24.4 mm. **Obv:** Taku - Ashanti gold weight **Rev:** Agricultural produce and value **Edge:** Segmented reeding **Designer:** Raymond Joly

Date	Mintage	F	VF	XF	Unc	BU
2003	—	—	1.00	1.60	4.00	6.00
2004(a)	—	—	1.00	1.60	4.00	6.00
2005(a)	—	—	1.00	1.60	4.00	6.00

KM# 15 500 FRANCS
10.6000 g., Bi-Metallic Copper-Nickel center in Brass ring, 27.9 mm. **Obv:** Taku - Ashanti gold weight **Rev:** Agricultural produce and value **Edge:** Segmented reeding **Designer:** Raymond Joly

Date	Mintage	F	VF	XF	Unc	BU
2003	—	—	2.25	4.00	10.00	14.00
2004(a)	—	—	2.25	4.00	10.00	12.00
2005(a)	—	—	2.25	4.00	10.00	12.00

KM# 16 1000 FRANCS
22.2000 g., 0.9000 Silver 0.6423 oz. ASW **Obv:** Taku - Ashanti gold weight **Rev:** Agricultural produce above sprays surrounded by names of member countries

Date	Mintage	F	VF	XF	Unc	BU
2002(a) Proof	500	Value: 100				

KM# 17 1000 FRANCS
22.2000 g., 0.9000 Silver 0.6423 oz. ASW **Subject:** FIFA World Championship Football - Germany 2006 **Obv:** Player kicking ball, tree in background **Obv. Legend:** COUPE DU MONDE DE LA FIFA - ALLEMAGNE **Rev:** Agricultural produce above sprays surrounded by names of member countries

Date	Mintage	F	VF	XF	Unc	BU
2004(a) Proof	50,000	Value: 75.00				

YEMEN REPUBLIC

The Republic of Yemen, formerly Yemen Arab Republic and Peoples Democratic Republic of Yemen, is located on the southern coast of the Arabian Peninsula. It has an area of 205,020 sq. mi. (531,000 sq. km.) and a population of 12 million. Capital: San'a. The port of Aden is the main commercial center and the area's most valuable natural resource. Recent oil and gas finds and a developing petroleum industry have improved their economic prospects. Agriculture and local handicrafts are the main industries. Cotton, fish, coffee, rock salt and hides are exported.

On May 22, 1990, the Yemen Arab Republic (North Yemen) and Peoples Democratic Republic of Yemen (South Yemen) merged into a unified Republic of Yemen. Disagreements between the two former governments simmered until civil war erupted in 1994, with the northern forces of the old Yemen Arab Republic eventually prevailing.

TITLES

المملكة المتوكلية اليمنية

al-Mamlaka(t) al-Mutawakkiliya(t) al-Yamaniya(t)

REPUBLIC
MILLED COINAGE

KM# 26 5 RIYALS
4.5000 g., Stainless Steel, 22.9 mm. **Obv:** Denomination within circle **Rev:** Building **Shape:** 21-sided

Date	Mintage	F	VF	XF	Unc	BU
AH1421-2001	—	—	—	—	1.75	2.25
AH1425-2004	—	—	—	—	1.75	2.25

KM# 27 10 RIYALS
6.0500 g., Stainless Steel, 26 mm. **Obv:** Denomination within circle **Rev:** Bridge at Shaharah

Date	Mintage	F	VF	XF	Unc	BU
AH1424-2003	—	—	—	—	2.75	3.50

KM# 29 20 RIALS
7.1000 g., Bi-Metallic Brass plated Steel center in Stainless Steel ring, 29.85 mm. **Obv:** Value within circle **Rev:** Tree within circle **Edge:** Reeded

Date	Mintage	F	VF	XF	Unc	BU
AH1425-2004	—	—	—	—	4.00	5.00

KM# 29a 20 RIALS
Stainless Steel, 29.85 mm. **Obv:** Value within circle **Rev:** Tree within circle **Edge:** Reeded

Date	Mintage	F	VF	XF	Unc	BU
AH1427-2006	—	—	—	—	4.00	5.00

KM# 30 500 RIALS
21.2500 g., Copper-Nickel-Zinc, 35.2 mm. **Subject:** City of San'a **Obv:** Value **Rev:** City gate below artwork **Edge:** Reeded

Date	Mintage	F	VF	XF	Unc	BU
AH1425-2004	—	—	—	—	50.00	60.00

KM# 32 500 RIALS
13.0000 g., Copper-Nickel gilt, 30 mm. **Subject:** City of San'a as Arab Cultural Capital **Note:** Pin added to reverse

Date	Mintage	F	VF	XF	Unc	BU
2004	—	—	—	—	—	50.00

KM# 31 1000 RIALS
73.3000 g., Pewter Antique silver finish, 60.3 mm. **Subject:** City of San'a **Obv:** Value **Rev:** City gate below artwork **Edge:** Plain **Note:** Illustration reduced.

Date	Mintage	F	VF	XF	Unc	BU
AH1425-2004	—	—	—	—	70.00	80.00

YUGOSLAVIA

The Federal Republic of Yugoslavia, formerly the Socialist Federal Republic of Yugoslavia, a Balkan country located on the east shore of the Adriatic Sea, has an area of 39,450 sq. mi. (102,173 sq. km.) and a population of 10.5 million. Capital: Belgrade. The chief industries are agriculture, mining, manufacturing and tourism. Machinery, nonferrous metals, meat and fabrics are exported.

The name Yugoslavia appears on the coinage in letters of the Cyrillic alphabet alone until formation of the Federated Peoples Republic of Yugoslavia in 1953, after which both the Cyrillic and Latin alphabets are employed. From 1965, the coin denomination appears in the 4 different languages of the federated republics in letters of both the Cyrillic and Latin alphabets.

MONETARY SYSTEM
100 Para = 1 Dinar

FEDERAL REPUBLIC
STANDARD COINAGE

KM# 180 DINAR
4.4000 g., Copper-Zinc-Nickel, 20 mm. **Obv:** National arms within circle **Rev:** Building **Edge:** Reeded

Date	Mintage	F	VF	XF	Unc	BU
2002	60,780,000	—	—	—	0.25	0.45

KM# 181 2 DINARA
5.2000 g., Copper-Nickel-Zinc, 21.9 mm. **Obv:** National arms within circle **Rev:** Church **Edge:** Reeded

Date	Mintage	F	VF	XF	Unc	BU
2002	71,053,000	—	—	—	0.30	0.50

KM# 182 5 DINARA
6.3000 g., Copper-Nickel-Zinc, 24 mm. **Obv:** National arms **Rev:** Domed building, denomination and date at left **Edge:** Reeded

Date	Mintage	F	VF	XF	Unc	BU
2002	30,966,000	—	—	—	1.25	1.50

ZAMBIA

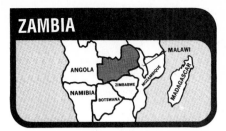

The Republic of Zambia (formerly Northern Rhodesia), a landlocked country in south-central Africa, has an area of 290,586 sq. mi. (752,610 sq. km.) and a population of*7.9 million. Capital: Lusaka. The economy of Zambia is based principally on copper, of which Zambia is the world's third largest producer. Copper, zinc, lead, cobalt and tobacco are exported. Zambia is a member of the Commonwealth of Nations. The President is the Head of State and the Head of Government.

REPUBLIC
DECIMAL COINAGE
100 Ngwee = 1 Kwacha

KM# 156 500 KWACHA
15.0000 g., 0.9990 Silver 0.4818 oz. ASW, 34.2 mm. **Subject:** Football World Champion - 1954 Germany **Obv:** Crowned head right within circle above arms with supporters and value **Rev:** Soccer game scene in front of Berlin Wall **Edge:** Plain

Date	Mintage	F	VF	XF	Unc	BU
2001 Proof	—	Value: 35.00				

KM# 174 500 KWACHA
15.0000 g., 0.9990 Silver 0.4818 oz. ASW, 34.2 mm. **Subject:** 1972 Munich Olympics **Obv:** Crowned head right above arms with supporters **Rev:** Torch runner in stadium **Edge:** Reeded

Date	Mintage	F	VF	XF	Unc	BU
2002 Proof	—	Value: 25.00				

KM# 87 1000 KWACHA
28.9100 g., Copper-Nickel, 38 mm. **Series:** Patrons of the Ocean **Obv:** Arms with supporters above crowned head right within circle **Rev:** Loggerhead sea turtle **Edge:** Reeded

Date	Mintage	F	VF	XF	Unc	BU
2001 Proof	—	Value: 17.00				

KM# 88   1000 KWACHA
28.9100 g., Copper-Nickel   **Series:** Patrons of the Ocean
Obv: Arms with supporters above crowned head right within circle
Rev: Coelacanth

Date	Mintage	F	VF	XF	Unc	BU
2001 Proof	—		Value: 17.00			

KM# 89   1000 KWACHA
28.9100 g., Copper-Nickel   **Series:** Patrons of the Ocean
Obv: Arms with supporters above crowned head right within circle
Rev: Sea horse and fish

Date	Mintage	F	VF	XF	Unc	BU
2001 Proof	—		Value: 17.00			

KM# 90   1000 KWACHA
28.9100 g., Copper-Nickel   **Series:** Patrons of the Ocean
Obv: Arms with supporters above crowned head right within circle
Rev: Two dolphins

Date	Mintage	F	VF	XF	Unc	BU
2001 Proof	—		Value: 17.00			

KM# 181   1000 KWACHA
20.0300 g., Silver   **Subject:** 75th Birthday Queen Elizabeth II
Obv: Crowned head of Elizabeth II in circle, national arms below
Obv. Legend: BANK OF ZAMBIA **Rev:** Bust of Elizabeth II facing
wearing tiara **Edge:** Reeded

Date	Mintage	F	VF	XF	Unc	BU
2001 Proof	—		Value: 20.00			

KM# 74   1000 KWACHA
29.0000 g., Copper-Nickel, 40 mm.   **Obv:** Crowned head right
above arms with supporters divides date **Rev:** Dated calendar
within circular design **Shape:** 7-sided

Date	Mintage	F	VF	XF	Unc	BU
2002 Proof-like	—	—	—	—	—	12.50
2003 Proof-like	—	—	—	—	—	12.50
2004 Proof-like	—	—	—	—	—	12.50

KM# 159   1000 KWACHA
31.2200 g., 0.9990 Silver 1.0027 oz. ASW, 38.6 mm.
Obv: Crowned head right divides date above arms with
supporters **Rev:** Bust 1/4 left **Edge:** Reeded

Date	Mintage	F	VF	XF	Unc	BU
2002	—	—	—	—	37.50	40.00

KM# 167   1000 KWACHA
25.0000 g., Copper-Nickel, 38.6 mm.   **Subject:** 50th Anniversary
of Elizabeth II's Coronation **Obv:** Crowned head right above arms
with supporters **Rev:** Crown on pillow above crossed scepters
Edge: Reeded

Date	Mintage	F	VF	XF	Unc	BU
ND(2003)	—	—	—	—	8.50	10.00

KM# 169   1000 KWACHA
25.0000 g., Copper-Nickel, 38.6 mm.   **Obv:** Crowned head right
above arms with supporters **Rev:** Prince William on jet ski
Edge: Reeded

Date	Mintage	F	VF	XF	Unc	BU
2003	—	—	—	—	8.50	10.00

KM# 171   1000 KWACHA
25.0000 g., Copper-Nickel, 38.6 mm.   **Obv:** Crowned head right
above arms with supporters **Rev:** Crowned bust facing
Edge: Reeded

Date	Mintage	F	VF	XF	Unc	BU
ND(2003)	—	—	—	—	8.50	10.00

KM# 172   1000 KWACHA
25.0000 g., 0.9250 Silver 0.7435 oz. ASW, 38.6 mm.
Obv: Crowned head right above arms with supporters
Rev: Crowned bust facing **Edge:** Reeded

Date	Mintage	F	VF	XF	Unc	BU
ND(2003) Proof	5,000		Value: 45.00			

KM# 183   1000 KWACHA
7.7700 g., 0.9990 Silver 0.2496 oz. ASW, 26 mm.   **Rev:** Elephant
pair

Date	Mintage	F	VF	XF	Unc	BU
2003 Proof	2,000		Value: 15.00			

KM# 160   1000 KWACHA
29.3000 g., Silver Plated Bronze (Specific gravity 9.099),
38.6 mm.   **Subject:** Pope John Paul II **Obv:** National arms
Rev: Pope saying mass **Edge:** Reeded **Note:** Specific gravity
9.099

Date	Mintage	F	VF	XF	Unc	BU
2003 Proof	—		Value: 20.00			

KM# 118   2000 KWACHA
31.1035 g., 0.9990 Silver 0.9990 oz. ASW, 38.6 mm.
Subject: Centennial of the Anglo-Japanese Alliance **Obv:** Queen
Elizabeth **Rev:** Fantasy Japanese coin design **Edge:** Reeded

Date	Mintage	F	VF	XF	Unc	BU
2002	500	—	—	—	75.00	80.00

KM# 184   2000 KWACHA
15.1500 g., 0.9990 Silver 0.4866 oz. ASW   **Rev:** Elephant pair

Date	Mintage	F	VF	XF	Unc	BU
2003 Proof	2,000		Value: 15.00			

KM# 166   4000 KWACHA
25.0000 g., 0.9250 Silver 0.7435 oz. ASW, 38.6 mm.   **Subject:**
Queen Elizabeth's 75th Birthday **Obv:** Crowned head right above
arms with supporters **Rev:** Bust with hat facing **Edge:** Reeded

Date	Mintage	F	VF	XF	Unc	BU
2001 Proof	2,000		Value: 35.00			

KM# 85   4000 KWACHA
25.1000 g., 0.9250 Silver 0.7464 oz. ASW, 37.9 mm.
Series: Wildlife Protection **Obv:** Crowned head right below arms
Rev: Lion head hologram **Edge:** Reeded **Note:** Lighter weight
and smaller diameter than official specifications

Date	Mintage	F	VF	XF	Unc	BU
2001 Proof	—		Value: 60.00			

KM# 110 4000 KWACHA
20.0000 g., 0.9990 Silver 0.6423 oz. ASW, 37.9 mm.
Series: Patrons of the Ocean **Obv:** Crowned head right within circle below arms with supporters **Rev:** Loggerhead sea turtle **Edge:** Reeded

Date	Mintage	F	VF	XF	Unc	BU
2001 Proof	—				Value: 25.00	

KM# 111 4000 KWACHA
20.0000 g., 0.9990 Silver 0.6423 oz. ASW **Series:** Patrons of the Ocean **Obv:** Crowned head right divides date below arms with supporters **Rev:** Coelacanth fish

Date	Mintage	F	VF	XF	Unc	BU
2001 Proof	—				Value: 30.00	

KM# 112 4000 KWACHA
20.0000 g., 0.9990 Silver 0.6423 oz. ASW **Series:** Patrons of the Ocean **Obv:** Crowned head right divides date below arms with supporters **Rev:** Sea horse and fish

Date	Mintage	F	VF	XF	Unc	BU
2001 Proof	—				Value: 28.00	

KM# 113 4000 KWACHA
20.0000 g., 0.9990 Silver 0.6423 oz. ASW **Series:** Patrons of the Ocean **Obv:** Crowned head right divides date below arms with supporters **Rev:** Two dolphins

Date	Mintage	F	VF	XF	Unc	BU
2001 Proof	—				Value: 30.00	

KM# 114 4000 KWACHA
50.0000 g., 0.9990 Silver 1.6059 oz. ASW **Subject:** Illusion **Obv:** Arms with supporters below crowned head right **Rev:** Cat within window **Edge:** Plain **Note:** 50x50mm

Date	Mintage	F	VF	XF	Unc	BU
2001 Proof	5,000				Value: 75.00	

KM# 175 4000 KWACHA
23.0000 g., 0.9990 Silver 0.7387 oz. ASW, 40 mm. **Obv:** Head with tiara right divides date above arms **Rev:** Dated calendar **Shape:** Seven-sided

Date	Mintage	F	VF	XF	Unc	BU
2002 Prooflike	—				—	45.00
2003 Prooflike	15,000				—	45.00
2004 Prooflike	5,000				—	45.00

KM# 168 4000 KWACHA
25.0000 g., 0.9250 Silver 0.7435 oz. ASW, 38.6 mm. **Subject:** 50th Anniversary of Elizabeth II's Coronation **Obv:** Crowned head right above arms with supporters **Rev:** Crown on pillow above crossed scepters **Edge:** Reeded

Date	Mintage	F	VF	XF	Unc	BU
ND(2003) Proof	5,000				Value: 45.00	

KM# 170 4000 KWACHA
25.0000 g., 0.9250 Silver 0.7435 oz. ASW, 38.6 mm. **Obv:** Crowned head right above arms with supporters **Rev:** Prince William on jet ski **Edge:** Reeded

Date	Mintage	F	VF	XF	Unc	BU
2003 Proof	5,000				Value: 45.00	

KM# 117 5000 KWACHA
31.3000 g., 0.9990 Silver 1.0053 oz. ASW, 38.6 mm. **Subject:** African Wildlife **Obv:** Arms with supporters **Rev:** Elephant mother and calf grazing on grass **Edge:** Reeded

Date	Mintage	F	VF	XF	Unc	BU
2001 Matte	—	—	—	—	35.00	—
2001 Proof	—				Value: 45.00	

KM# 143 5000 KWACHA
28.8600 g., 0.9990 Silver 0.9269 oz. ASW, 38.5 mm. **Subject:** African Wildlife **Obv:** Arms with supporters **Rev:** Elephant **Edge:** Reeded

Date	Mintage	F	VF	XF	Unc	BU
2002 Matte	—	—	—	—	35.00	—
2002 Proof	—				Value: 45.00	

KM# 142 5000 KWACHA
28.6400 g., 0.9990 Silver 0.9198 oz. ASW, 38.5 mm. **Subject:** African Wildlife **Obv:** Queen Elizabeth's portrait above national arms and denomination **Rev:** Adult and juvenile elephants **Edge:** Reeded

Date	Mintage	F	VF	XF	Unc	BU
2002 Matte	—	—	—	—	35.00	—
2002 Proof	—				Value: 45.00	

KM# 165 5000 KWACHA
31.1000 g., 0.9990 Silver 0.9988 oz. ASW, 38.5 mm. **Obv:** Crowned bust right divides date **Rev:** Two African elephants **Edge:** Reeded

Date	Mintage	F	VF	XF	Unc	BU
2003 Matte	—	—	—	—	32.50	—
2003 Proof	—				Value: 40.00	

KM# 185 5000 KWACHA
31.1050 g., 0.9990 Silver 0.9990 oz. ASW **Rev:** Elephant pair

Date	Mintage	F	VF	XF	Unc	BU
2003 Proof	2,000				Value: 45.00	

KM# 186 5000 KWACHA
31.1050 g., 0.9990 Silver 0.9990 oz. ASW **Obv:** Head right **Rev:** Multicolor elephant pair

Date	Mintage	F	VF	XF	Unc	BU
2003 Proof	—				Value: 30.00	

KM# 187 5000 KWACHA
31.1050 g., 0.9990 Silver partially gilt 0.9990 oz. ASW, 40 mm. **Rev:** Elephant pair, partially gilt

Date	Mintage	F	VF	XF	Unc	BU
2003 Proof	—				Value: 40.00	

KM# 188 10000 KWACHA
62.2100 g., 0.9990 Silver 1.9980 oz. ASW, 50 mm. **Rev:** Two elephants

Date	Mintage	F	VF	XF	Unc	BU
2003 Proof	2,000				Value: 120	

KM# 94 40000 KWACHA
31.1035 g., 0.9999 Gold 0.9999 oz. AGW, 37.9 mm. **Series:** Wildlife Protection **Obv:** Arms with supporters above crowned head right **Rev:** Holographic lion head **Edge:** Reeded

Date	Mintage	F	VF	XF	Unc	BU
2001 Proof	—				Value: 1,250	

KM# 153.1 40000 KWACHA
47.5400 g., 0.9166 Gold 1.4009 oz. AGW, 39 mm. **Subject:** Queen Victoria **Obv:** Crowned head right within ornate frame divides date above arms with supporters **Rev:** Crowned veiled bust of Queen Victoria left **Edge:** Reeded

Date	Mintage	F	VF	XF	Unc	BU
2001 Proof	1					

Note: Medallic die alignment

KM# 153.2 40000 KWACHA
47.5400 g., 0.9166 Gold 1.4009 oz. AGW, 39 mm.
Subject: Queen Victoria **Obv:** Crowned head right within ornate frame divides date above arms with supporters **Rev:** Crowned veiled bust of Queen Victoria left **Edge:** Reeded

Date	Mintage	F	VF	XF	Unc	BU
2001 Matte	1	—	—	—	—	—

Note: Coin die alignment

KM# 154.1 40000 KWACHA
47.5400 g., 0.9166 Gold 1.4009 oz. AGW, 39 mm.
Subject: Edward VII **Obv:** Crowned head right within ornate frame divides date above arms with supporters **Rev:** Crowned bust of King Edward VII right **Edge:** Reeded

Date	Mintage	F	VF	XF	Unc	BU
2001 Proof	1	—	—	—	—	—

Note: Medallic die alignment

KM# 154.2 40000 KWACHA
47.5400 g., 0.9166 Gold 1.4009 oz. AGW, 39 mm.
Subject: Edward VII **Obv:** Crowned head right within ornate frame divides date above arms with supporters **Rev:** Crowned bust of King Edward VII right **Edge:** Reeded

Date	Mintage	F	VF	XF	Unc	BU
2001 Matte	1	—	—	—	—	—

Note: Coin die alignment

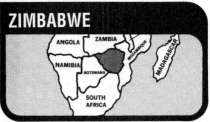

ZIMBABWE

The Republic of Zimbabwe (formerly the Republic of Rhodesia or Southern Rhodesia), located in the east-central part of southern Africa, has an area of 150,804 sq. mi. (390,580 sq. km.) and a population of *10.1 million. Capital: Harare (formerly Salisbury). The economy is based on agriculture and mining. Tobacco, sugar, asbestos, copper, chrome, ore and coal are exported.

On April 18, 1980 pursuant to an act of the British Parliament, the colony of Southern Rhodesia became independent as the Republic of Zimbabwe, a member of the Commonwealth of Nations, until recently suspended.

MONETARY SYSTEM
100 Cents = 1 Dollar

MINT
Harare

REPUBLIC
DECIMAL COINAGE

KM# 3a 10 CENTS
Nickel Plated Steel, 20 mm. **Obv:** National emblem **Rev:** Baobab tree, value **Edge:** Plain **Mint:** Harare **Designer:** Jeff Huntly

Date	Mintage	F	VF	XF	Unc	BU
2001	—	—	0.15	0.30	0.75	1.00
2002	—	—	0.15	0.30	0.75	1.00
2003	—	—	0.15	0.30	0.75	1.00

KM# 4a 20 CENTS
Nickel Plated Steel, 23 mm. **Obv:** National emblem **Rev:** Birchenough Bridge over the Sabi River, value below **Edge:** Plain **Mint:** Harare **Designer:** Jeff Huntly

Date	Mintage	F	VF	XF	Unc	BU
2001	—	—	0.20	0.40	1.25	1.50
2002	—	—	0.20	0.40	1.25	1.50
2003	—	—	0.20	0.40	1.25	1.50

KM# 5a 50 CENTS
Nickel Plated Steel, 26 mm. **Obv:** National emblem **Rev:** Radiant sun rising, symbolic of independence, value **Edge:** Plain **Mint:** Harare **Designer:** Jeff Huntly

Date	Mintage	F	VF	XF	Unc	BU
2001	—	—	0.40	1.00	1.75	2.00
2002	—	—	0.40	1.00	1.75	2.00
2003	—	—	0.40	1.00	1.75	2.00

KM# 6a DOLLAR
Nickel Plated Steel, 29 mm. **Obv:** National emblem **Rev:** Zimbabwe ruins amongst trees, value **Edge:** Reeded **Mint:** Harare **Designer:** Jeff Huntly

Date	Mintage	F	VF	XF	Unc	BU
2001	—	—	1.00	1.50	2.50	3.00
2002	—	—	1.00	1.50	2.50	3.00
2003	—	—	1.00	1.50	2.50	3.00

KM# 12a 2 DOLLARS
Brass Plated Steel, 24.5 mm. **Obv:** National emblem **Rev:** Pangolin below value **Edge:** Reeded **Mint:** Harare

Date	Mintage	F	VF	XF	Unc	BU
2001	—	—	1.25	2.25	4.00	5.00
2002	—	—	1.25	2.25	4.00	5.00
2003	—	—	1.25	2.25	4.00	5.00

KM# 13 5 DOLLARS
9.0500 g., Bi-Metallic Nickel-plated-Steel center in Brass ring, 27.4 mm. **Obv:** National emblem **Rev:** Rhinoceros standing right **Edge:** Reeded **Mint:** Harare

Date	Mintage	F	VF	XF	Unc	BU
2001	—	—	—	—	5.00	6.00
2002	—	—	—	—	5.00	6.00
2003	—	—	—	—	5.00	6.00

KM# 14 10 DOLLARS
5.2000 g., Nickel Plated Steel, 21.5 mm. **Obv:** National emblem **Rev:** Water buffalo **Edge:** Reeded **Mint:** Harare

Date	Mintage	F	VF	XF	Unc	BU
2003	—	—	—	1.50	2.50	3.50

KM# 15 25 DOLLARS
7.3300 g., Nickel Plated Steel, 24.5 mm. **Obv:** National emblem **Rev:** Military monument **Edge:** Segmented reeding **Mint:** Harare

Date	Mintage	F	VF	XF	Unc	BU
2003	—	—	—	1.75	3.00	4.00